WATERLOO PUBLIC LIBRARY
3 3420 00634 507 9

P9-DGV-916

Rex rogat Abbatem / Mathildim supplicat atq;
49

Emperor Henry IV, before Hugh of Cluny, asking Matilda to intercede on his behalf.

NEW CATHOLIC ENCYCLOPEDIA

NEW CATHOLIC ENCYCLOPEDIA

SECOND EDITION

9

Mab–Mor

Detroit • New York • San Diego • San Francisco • Cleveland • New Haven, Conn. • Waterville, Maine • London • Munich

in association with
THE CATHOLIC UNIVERSITY OF AMERICA • WASHINGTON, D.C.

The New Catholic Encyclopedia, Second Edition

Project Editors
Thomas Carson, Joann Cerrito

Editorial
Erin Bealmear, Jim Craddock, Stephen Cusack, Miranda Ferrara, Kristin Hart, Melissa Hill, Margaret Mazurkiewicz, Carol Schwartz, Christine Tomassini, Michael J. Tyrkus

Permissions
Edna Hedblad, Shalice Shah-Caldwell

Imaging and Multimedia
Randy Bassett, Dean Dauphinais, Robert Duncan, Leitha Etheridge-Sims, Mary K. Grimes, Lezlie Light, Dan Newell, David G. Oblender, Christine O'Bryan, Luke Rademacher, Pamela Reed

Product Design
Michelle DiMercurio

Data Capture
Civie Green

Manufacturing
Rhonda Williams

Indexing
Victoria Agee, Victoria Baker, Lynne Maday, Do Mi Stauber, Amy Suchowski

For more information, contact
The Gale Group, Inc.
27500 Drake Rd.
Farmington Hills, MI 48331-3535
Or you can visit our Internet site at
http://www.gale.com

LIBRARY OF CONGRESS CATALOGING-IN-PUBLICATION DATA

New Catholic encyclopedia.—2nd ed.
p. cm.
Includes bibliographical references and indexes.
ISBN 0-7876-4004-2
1. Catholic Church—Encyclopedias. I. Catholic University of America.
BX841 .N44 2002
282' .03—dc21
2002000924

ISBN: 0-7876-4004-2 (set)
0-7876-4005-0 (v. 1)
0-7876-4006-9 (v. 2)
0-7876-4007-7 (v. 3)
0-7876-4008-5 (v. 4)
0-7876-4009-3 (v. 5)
0-7876-4010-7 (v. 6)
0-7876-4011-5 (v. 7)
0-7876-4012-3 (v. 8)
0-7876-4013-1 (v. 9)
0-7876-4014-x (v. 10)
0-7876-4015-8 (v. 11)
0-7876-4016-6 (v. 12)
0-7876-4017-4 (v. 13)
0-7876-4018-2 (v. 14)
0-7876-4019-0 (v. 15)

Printed in the United States of America
10 9 8 7 6 5 4 3 2 1

For The Catholic University of America Press

Foreword

This revised edition of the *New Catholic Encyclopedia* represents a third generation in the evolution of the text that traces its lineage back to the *Catholic Encyclopedia* published from 1907 to 1912. In 1967, sixty years after the first volume of the original set appeared, The Catholic University of America and the McGraw-Hill Book Company joined together in organizing a small army of editors and scholars to produce the *New Catholic Encyclopedia.* Although planning for the *NCE* had begun before the Second Vatican Council and most of the 17,000 entries were written before Council ended, Vatican II enhanced the encyclopedia's value and importance. The research and the scholarship that went into the articles witnessed to the continuity and richness of the Catholic Tradition given fresh expression by Council. In order to keep the *NCE* current, supplementary volumes were published in 1972, 1978, 1988, and 1995. Now, at the beginning of the third millennium, The Catholic University of America is proud to join with The Gale Group in presenting a new edition of the *New Catholic Encyclopedia.* It updates and incorporates the many articles from the 1967 edition and its supplements that have stood the test of time and adds hundreds of new entries.

As the president of The Catholic University of America, I cannot but be pleased at the reception the *NCE* has received. It has come to be recognized as an authoritative reference work in the field of religious studies and is praised for its comprehensive coverage of the Church's history and institutions. Although Canon Law no longer requires encyclopedias and reference works of this kind to receive an *imprimatur* before publication, I am confident that this new edition, like the original, reports accurate information about Catholic beliefs and practices. The editorial staff and their consultants were careful to present official Church teachings in a straightforward manner, and in areas where there are legitimate disputes over fact and differences in interpretation of events, they made every effort to insure a fair and balanced presentation of the issues.

The way for this revised edition was prepared by the publication, in 2000, of a Jubilee volume of the *NCE,* heralding the beginning of the new millennium. In my foreword to that volume I quoted Pope John Paul II's encyclical on Faith and Human Reason in which he wrote that history is "the arena where we see what God does for humanity." The *New Catholic Encyclopedia* describes that arena. It reports events, people, and ideas—"the things we know best and can verify most easily, the things of our everyday life, apart from which we cannot understand ourselves" (*Fides et ratio,* 12).

Finally, I want to express appreciation on my own behalf and on the behalf of the readers of these volumes to everyone who helped make this revision a reality. We are all indebted to The Gale Group and the staff of The Catholic University of America Press for their dedication and the alacrity with which they produced it.

Very Reverend David M. O'Connell, C.M., J.C.D.
President
The Catholic University of America

Preface to the Revised Edition

When first published in 1967 the *New Catholic Encyclopedia* was greeted with enthusiasm by librarians, researchers, and general readers interested in Catholicism. In the United States the *NCE* has been recognized as the standard reference work on matters of special interest to Catholics. In an effort to keep the encyclopedia current, supplementary volumes were published in 1972, 1978, 1988, and 1995. However, it became increasingly apparent that further supplements would not be adequate to this task. The publishers subsequently decided to undertake a thorough revision of the *NCE,* beginning with the publication of a Jubilee volume at the start of the new millennium.

Like the biblical scribe who brings from his storeroom of knowledge both the new and the old, this revised edition of the *New Catholic Encyclopedia* incorporates material from the 15-volume original edition and the supplement volumes. Entries that have withstood the test of time have been edited, and some have been amended to include the latest information and research. Hundreds of new entries have been added. For all practical purposes, it is an entirely new edition intended to serve as a comprehensive and authoritative work of reference reporting on the movements and interests that have shaped Christianity in general and Catholicism in particular over two millennia.

SCOPE

The title reflects its outlook and breadth. It is the *New Catholic Encyclopedia,* not merely a new encyclopedia of Catholicism. In addition to providing information on the doctrine, organization, and history of Christianity over the centuries, it includes information about persons, institutions, cultural phenomena, religions, philosophies, and social movements that have affected the Catholic Church from within and without. Accordingly, the *NCE* attends to the history and particular traditions of the Eastern Churches and the Churches of the Protestant Reformation, and other ecclesial communities. Christianity cannot be understood without exploring its roots in ancient Israel and Judaism, nor can the history of the medieval and modern Church be understood apart from its relationship with Islam. Interfaith dialogue requires an appreciation of Buddhism and other world religions, as well as some knowledge of the history of religion in general.

On the assumption that most readers and researchers who use the *NCE* are individuals interested in Catholicism in general and the Church in North America in particular, its editorial content gives priority to the Western Church, while not neglecting the churches in the East; to Roman Catholicism, acknowledging much common history with Protestantism; and to Catholicism in the United States, recognizing that it represents only a small part of the universal Church.

Scripture, Theology, Patrology, Liturgy. The many and varied articles dealing with Sacred Scripture and specific books of the Bible reflect contemporary biblical scholarship and its concerns. The *NCE* highlights official church teachings as expressed by the Church's magisterium. It reports developments in theology, explains issues and introduces ecclesiastical writers from the early Church Fathers to present-day theologians whose works exercise major influence on the development of Christian thought. The *NCE* traces the evolution of the Church's worship with special emphasis on rites and rituals consequent to the liturgical reforms and renewal initiated by the Second Vatican Council.

Church History. From its inception Christianity has been shaped by historical circumstances and itself has become a historical force. The *NCE* presents the Church's history from a number of points of view against the background of general political and cultural history. The revised edition reports in some detail the Church's missionary activity as it grew from a small community in Jerusalem to the worldwide phenomenon it is today. Some entries, such as those dealing with the Middle Ages, the Reformation, and the Enlightenment, focus on major time-periods and movements that cut across geographical boundaries. Other articles describe the history and structure of the Church in specific areas, countries, and regions. There are separate entries for many dioceses and monasteries which by reason of antiquity, size, or influence are of special importance in ecclesiastical history, as there are for religious orders and congregations. The *NCE* rounds out its comprehensive history of the Church with articles on religious movements and biographies of individuals.

Canon and Civil Law. The Church inherited and has safeguarded the precious legacy of ancient Rome, described by Virgil, "to rule people under law, [and] to establish the way of peace." The *NCE* deals with issues of ecclesiastical jurisprudence and outlines the development of legislation governing communal practices and individual obligations, taking care to incorporate and reference the 1983 *Code of Canon Law* throughout and, where appropriate, the *Code of Canons for the Eastern Churches.* It deals with issues of Church-State relations and with civil law as it impacts on the Church and Church's teaching regarding human rights and freedoms.

Philosophy. The Catholic tradition from its earliest years has investigated the relationship between faith and reason. The *NCE* considers at some length the many and varied schools of ancient, medieval, and modern philosophy with emphasis, when appropriate, on their relationship to theological positions. It pays particular attention to the scholastic tradition, particularly Thomism, which is prominent in Catholic intellectual history. Articles on many major and lesser philosophers contribute to a comprehensive survey of philosophy from pre-Christian times to the present.

Biography and Hagiography. The *NCE,* making an exception for the reigning pope, leaves to other reference works biographical information about living persons. This revised edition presents biographical sketches of hundreds of men and women, Christian and non-Christian, saints and sinners, because of their significance for the Church. They include: Old and New Testament figures; the Fathers of the Church and ecclesiastical writers; pagan and Christian emperors; medieval and modern kings; heads of state and other political figures; heretics and champions of orthodoxy; major and minor figures in the Reformation and Counter Reformation; popes, bishops, and priests; founders and members of religious orders and congregations; lay men and lay women; scholars, authors, composers, and artists. The *NCE* includes biographies of most saints whose feasts were once celebrated or are currently celebrated by the universal church. The revised edition relies on Butler's *Lives of the Saints* and similar reference works to give accounts of many saints, but the *NCE* also provides biographical information about recently canonized and beatified individuals who are, for one reason or another, of special interest to the English-speaking world.

Social Sciences. Social sciences came into their own in the twentieth century. Many articles in the *NCE* rely on data drawn from anthropology, economics, psychology and sociology for a better understanding of religious structures and behaviors. Papal encyclicals and pastoral letters of episcopal conferences are the source of principles and norms for Christian attitudes and practice in the field of social action and legislation. The *NCE* draws attention to the Church's organized activities in pursuit of peace and justice, social welfare and human rights. The growth of the role of the laity in the work of the Church also receives thorough coverage.

ARRANGEMENT OF ENTRIES

The articles in the *NCE* are arranged alphabetically by the first substantive word using the word-by-word method of alphabetization; thus "New Zealand" precedes "Newman, John Henry," and "Old Testament Literature" precedes "Oldcastle, Sir John." Monarchs, patriarchs, popes, and others who share a Christian name and are differentiated by a title and numerical designation are alphabetized by their title and then arranged numerically. Thus, entries for Byzantine emperors Leo I through IV precede those for popes of the same name, while "Henry VIII, King of England" precedes "Henry IV, King of France."

Maps, Charts, and Illustrations. The *New Catholic Encyclopedia* contains nearly 3,000 illustrations, including photographs, maps, and tables. Entries focusing on the Church in specific countries contain a map of the country as well as easy-to-read tables giving statistical data and, where helpful, lists of archdioceses and dioceses. Entries on the Church in U.S. states also contain tables listing archdioceses and dioceses where appropriate. The numerous photographs appearing in the *New Catholic Encyclopedia* help to illustrate the history of the Church, its role in modern societies, and the many magnificent works of art it has inspired.

SPECIAL FEATURES

Subject Overview Articles. For the convenience and guidance of the reader, the *New Catholic Encyclopedia* contains several brief articles outlining the scope of major fields: "Theology, Articles on," "Liturgy, Articles on," "Jesus Christ, Articles on," etc.

Cross-References. The cross-reference system in the *NCE* serves to direct the reader to related material in other articles. The appearance of a name or term in small capital letters in text indicates that there is an article of that title elsewhere in the encyclopedia. In some cases, the name of the related article has been inserted at the appropriate point as a *see* reference: (*see* THOMAS AQUINAS, ST.). When a further aspect of the subject is treated under another title, a *see also* reference is placed at the end of the article. In addition to this extensive cross-reference system, the comprehensive index in volume 15 will greatly increase the reader's ability to access the wealth of information contained in the encyclopedia.

Abbreviations List. Following common practice, books and versions of the Bible as well as other standard works by selected authors have been abbreviated throughout the text. A guide to these abbreviations follows this preface.

The Editors

Abbreviations

The system of abbreviations used for the works of Plato, Aristotle, St. Augustine, and St. Thomas Aquinas is as follows: Plato is cited by book and Stephanus number only, e.g., Phaedo 79B; Rep. 480A. Aristotle is cited by book and Bekker number only, e.g., Anal. post. 72b 8–12; Anim. 430a 18. St. Augustine is cited as in the Thesaurus Linguae Latinae, e.g., C. acad. 3.20.45; Conf. 13.38.53, with capitalization of the first word of the title. St. Thomas is cited as in scholarly journals, but using Arabic numerals. In addition, the following abbreviations have been used throughout the encyclopedia for biblical books and versions of the Bible.

Books

Acts	Acts of the Apostles
Am	Amos
Bar	Baruch
1–2 Chr	1 and 2 Chronicles (1 and 2 Paralipomenon in Septuagint and Vulgate)
Col	Colossians
1–2 Cor	1 and 2 Corinthians
Dn	Daniel
Dt	Deuteronomy
Eccl	Ecclesiastes
Eph	Ephesians
Est	Esther
Ex	Exodus
Ez	Ezekiel
Ezr	Ezra (Esdras B in Septuagint; 1 Esdras in Vulgate)
Gal	Galatians
Gn	Genesis
Hb	Habakkuk
Heb	Hebrews
Hg	Haggai
Hos	Hosea
Is	Isaiah
Jas	James
Jb	Job
Jdt	Judith
Jer	Jeremiah
Jgs	Judges
Jl	Joel
Jn	John
1–3 Jn	1, 2, and 3 John
Jon	Jonah
Jos	Joshua
Jude	Jude
1–2 Kgs	1 and 2 Kings (3 and 4 Kings in Septuagint and Vulgate)
Lam	Lamentations
Lk	Luke
Lv	Leviticus
Mal	Malachi (Malachias in Vulgate)
1–2 Mc	1 and 2 Maccabees
Mi	Micah
Mk	Mark
Mt	Matthew
Na	Nahum
Neh	Nehemiah (2 Esdras in Septuagint and Vulgate)
Nm	Numbers
Ob	Obadiah
Phil	Philippians
Phlm	Philemon
Prv	Proverbs
Ps	Psalms
1–2 Pt	1 and 2 Peter
Rom	Romans
Ru	Ruth
Rv	Revelation (Apocalypse in Vulgate)
Sg	Song of Songs
Sir	Sirach (Wisdom of Ben Sira; Ecclesiasticus in Septuagint and Vulgate)
1–2 Sm	1 and 2 Samuel (1 and 2 Kings in Septuagint and Vulgate)
Tb	Tobit
1–2 Thes	1 and 2 Thessalonians
Ti	Titus
1–2 Tm	1 and 2 Timothy
Wis	Wisdom
Zec	Zechariah
Zep	Zephaniah

Versions

Apoc	Apocrypha
ARV	American Standard Revised Version
ARVm	American Standard Revised Version, margin
AT	American Translation
AV	Authorized Version (King James)
CCD	Confraternity of Christian Doctrine
DV	Douay-Challoner Version

ERV	English Revised Version
ERVm	English Revised Version, margin
EV	English Version(s) of the Bible
JB	Jerusalem Bible
LXX	Septuagint
MT	Masoretic Text
NAB	New American Bible
NEB	New English Bible
NIV	New International Version
NJB	New Jerusalem Bible
NRSV	New Revised Standard Version
NT	New Testament
OT	Old Testament
RSV	Revised Standard Version
RV	Revised Version
RVm	Revised Version, margin
Syr	Syriac
Vulg	Vulgate

M

MABILLON, JEAN

Seventeenth century French Maurist; b. Saint-Pierremont (Ardennes), Nov. 23, 1632; d. Saint-Germain-des-Prés, Dec. 27, 1707. He studied at Reims before becoming a Benedictine monk (1654), was ordained at Corbie (1660), and collaborated with Jean Luc d' Achéry at Saint-Germain-des-Prés in the edition of the works of St. BERNARD OF CLAIRVAUX, *Sancti Bernardi opera omnia* (Paris 1667). Following his master's plan, he collected the documents pertaining to the lives of the saints of the Benedictine Order, which, with T. Ruinart, he published in nine volumes in the *Acta Sanctorum ordinis sancti Benedicti* (Paris 1668–1701). These lives of the Benedictine saints in chronological order (500–1100) served as a commentary for his *Annales ordinis sancti Benedicti,* which were continued after his death by R. Massuet and É. Martène (1703–39). Mabillon also organized voyages of investigation in search of manuscripts in Champagne, Lorraine, and Flanders (1672); Bourgogne (1682); Germany and Switzerland (1683); and Italy (1685). He described their results in *Itinerarium Burgundicum, Itinerarium Germanicum* (1685) and the more famous *Musaeum Italicum* (2 v. Paris 1687–89). The discovery of a Lectionary at Luxeuil was the origin of his study on the Gallican liturgy, *Liturgia gallicana* (3 v. Paris 1675). He wrote a *Traité des études monastiques* (1691) and a monograph, devoted mainly to the study of relics, on the cult of unknown saints (1698). When the authenticity of the Merovingian charters of the monastery of Saint-Germain was questioned by the Bollandist D. Papebroch (1675), Mabillon studied the question for six years and published his famous *De re diplomatica libri sex* (Paris 1681), an exposition of the principles of documentary criticism that laid the foundation for a scientific approach to this discipline. The work was attacked by B. Germon (1703), and Mabillon supplied a supplement by way of a definitive answer (*see* DIPLOMATICS, ECCLESIASTICAL). The treatise on monastic studies was his response to the rigorism of A. J. de RANCÉ demonstrating the value of scholarly work for monks. Mabillon also supported the claim of John GERSON for authorship of the *Imitation of Christ.* He displayed true monastic equanimity in all his undertakings and courageously opened a path for the conscientious and realistic study of church history. He was made a member of the Royal Academy of Inscriptions and considered one of the most learned men of his age.

Bibliography: H. LECLERCQ, *Dictionnaire d'archéologie chrétienne et de liturgie*, ed. F. CABROL, H. LECLERCQ and H. I. MARROU, 15 v. (Paris 1907–53) 10.1:427–724; *Mabillon,* 2 v. (Paris 1953–57). G. HEER, *Johannes Mabillon und die Schweizer Benediktiner* (St. Gallen 1938); *Lexikon für Theologie und Kirche*, ed. J. HOFER and K. RAHNER, 10 v. (2d, new ed. Freiburg 1957–65) 6:1254–55. M. D. KNOWLES, *The Journal of Ecclesiastical History*, 10 (1959) 153–173. A. PRATESI, *Enciclopedia cattolica*, ed. P. PASCHINI et al., 12 v. (Rome 1949–54) 7:1737–38. J. BERGKAMP, *Dom Jean Mabillon* (Washington 1928).

[P. ROCHE]

MACARIUS MAGNES

Oriental bishop and apologist, flourished early 5th century. He is author of a dialogue in five books called the *Apocriticus,* or Response, to the pagans. Macarius is identified by PHOTIUS as an opponent of JOHN CHRYSOSTOM at the Synod of the OAK in 403 (biblical codex, 59), and he is said to have condemned Heraclides of Ephesus, one of the bishops whom John Chrysostom had consecrated. Nothing is known of his origin or career. His apology represents a fictitious five day dispute with a pagan philosopher; it proves of considerable value for preserving verbatim texts of what seems to be a later redaction of the 3rd century work *Against the Christians* (15 books) by the philosopher Porphyry. Only half of the *Apocriticus* has been preserved (2.7–4.30). It was used in the 9th century iconoclast controversy and is cited at some length by the 16th century Jesuit F. Torres (Turrianus). Its interest centers on the type of objection brought against Christianity in early times: the criticism of Old and New Testament texts, and attacks against the doctrines of the

Incarnation, Redemption, and the monarchy of God. L. DUCHESNE thought the pagan philosopher quoted was the Neoplatonist Hierocles of Bithynia; but A. von Harnack and later scholars agree that it must be Porphyry. One fragment of a homily on Gn 3.21 by Macarius has also been preserved; other fragments attributed to him are spurious.

Bibliography: J. QUASTEN, *Patrology*, 3 v. (Westminster 1950—) 3:486–488. B. ALTANER, *Patrology*, tr. H. GRAEF, from 5th German ed. (New York 1960) 388. G. BARDY, *Dictionnaire de thélologie catholique*, ed. A. VACANT et al., 15 v. (Paris 1903–50) 9.2:1456–59. L. DUCHESNE, *De Macario Magnete* (Paris 1877). T. W. CRAFER, *Journal of Theological Studies*, 15 (1913–14) 360–395, 481–512; tr., *The Apocriticus of Macarius Magnes* (Society for Promoting Christian Knowledge 1919). A. B. HULSEN, *Porphyry's Work Against the Christians* (New Haven 1934).

[F. X. MURPHY]

MACARIUS OF ALEXANDRIA, ST.

Ascetic monk and priest; d. *c.* 394. He was called *politicus* to distinguish him from his contemporary MACARIUS THE EGYPTIAN, called the Great. Macarius settled in the desert of Cellia at age 40. PALLADIUS met him several times and stated that he was a priest and led an exemplary life (*Hist. Lausiaca* 18). He was endowed with the gifts of healing and expelling demons and was responsible for the training in severe asceticism of monks in the desert of Nitria. None of the literary works attributed to him is authentic. His life is recorded in the *Historia monachorum* (ch. 30), and he is named in the *anaphora* of the Coptic Mass.

Feast: Jan. 2 (West); Jan. 19 (Greek Church).

Bibliography: É. AMANN, *Dictionnaire de théologie catholique* (Paris 1903–50) 9.2:1440–41. B. ALTANER, *Patrology* (New York 1960) 305–306. J. QUASTEN, *Patrology* (Westminster MD 1950) 3:168–169.

[P. ROCHE]

MACARIUS OF JERUSALEM, ST.

Bishop from *c.* 312; d. Jerusalem, *c.* 334. Both EUSEBIUS OF CAESAREA and Macarius attended the Council of NICAEA I, whose seventh canon dealt with the jurisdictional relationship between Caesarea and JERUSALEM, and that condemned ARIUS. Macarius, a stanch Nicaean, differed with his metropolitan, Eusebius, on the Arian question. When Arius was banished from Alexandria, he found hospitality with Eusebius and stigmatized Macarius as a ''heretical ignoramus'' (Epiphanius, *Panar.* 69.6.4). Macarius partly directed the erection of the architectural complex on the recently rediscovered sacred sites of Jerusalem that, in addition to churches in Bethlehem and on Mt. Olivet, CONSTANTINE I commissioned *c.* 326 (Eusebius, *Vita Const.* 3.25–43). Later Macarius consecrated Maximus, an upholder of Nicaea I, to the See of Diospolis (Lydda), 25 miles from Jerusalem, but he subsequently kept Maximus as his coadjutor and successor (Sozomen, *Hist. eccl.* 2.20) in acquiescence to the desire of the Jerusalem flock. Later tradition ascribed to Macarius a part in the identification of the true CROSS (Rufinus, *Hist. eccl.* 10.7.8).

Feast: March 10.

Bibliography: M. LE QUIEN, *Oriens Christianus,* 3 v. (Paris 1740; repr. Graz 1958) 3:154–155. L. H. VINCENT and F. M. ABEL, *Jérusalem nouvelle,* 2 v. (Paris 1922) 201–208, 539, 903–904. *Martyrologium Romanum,* ed. H. DELEHAYE (Brussels 1940); v.68 of *Acta Sanctorum* 92. *Bibliotheca hagiographica Graeca,* ed. F. HALKIN, 3 v. (Brussels 1957) 1:3002.

[A. A. STEPHENSON]

MACARIUS OF PELECETE, ST.

Byzantine monk and defender of the cult of images; b. Constantinople, *c.* 750; d. ''Aphrysia'' (unknown island), *c.* 829. Orphaned at an early age, Macarius was educated by his uncle. He entered the monastery of Pelecete in Bithynia and succeeded St. HILARION as hegumen, or abbot. His reputation as a saint and wonder-worker earned him the title of Thaumaturgus, and he was ordained a priest by the patriarch of Constantinople, Tarasius (784–806). In the iconoclastic controversy, he resisted the policy of Emperor LEO V the Armenian, and was imprisoned and tortured. Liberated by Michael II (820–829), he returned to Pelecete but did not take over the direction of the monastery. Although the emperor flattered and menaced him to force him to accept ICONOCLASM, he steadfastly refused, and was finally exiled to the island where he died, a septuagenarian. His vita was written by his successor, Sabas.

Feast: April 1.

Bibliography: *Acta Sanctorum* April 1:31. J. VAN DEN GHEYN, ed., *Analecta Bollandiana* 16 (1897) 140–163. C. VAN DE VORST, *ibid.* 32 (1913) 270–273. H. G. BECK, *Kirche und theologische Literatur im byzantinischen Reich* (Munich 1959) 210, 558.

[F. CHIOVARO]

MACARIUS SCOTTUS, BL.

Benedictine abbot; b. Ireland or Scotland; d. Germany, 1153. A BENEDICTINE at the Abbey of Regensburg, he was called in 1139 by Bishop Embrico of Würzburg to become the first abbot of the monastery of Sankt Jakob. He journeyed to Rome in 1146 to obtain relics for his community. He was esteemed as a holy man even during his lifetime, and in 1615 his body was exhumed and transferred to the choir of the abbey church. Following this, many miraculous cures were alleged, and in 1818 his relics were moved into the Marienkapelle in Würzburg. From 1731 to the time of World War II, a Macarius brotherhood existed in Würzburg. A summary of his life was written by J. TRITHEMIUS, abbot of Sankt Jakob in the early 16th century.

Feast: Jan. 23 or Dec. 19.

Bibliography: I. GROPP *Collectio novissima scriptorum et rerum Wirceburgensium . . .* , 2 v. (Frankfurt 1741–44) 1:808–812; summary of his life according to J. TRITHEMIUS, 2:123–127. W. HUNT, *The Dictionary of National Biography from the Earliest Times to 1900,* 63 v. (London 1885–1900; repr. with corrections, 21 v., 1908–09, 1921–22, 1938; suppl. 1901–) 12:400. A. M. ZIMMERMANN, *Kalendarium Benedictinum: Die Heiligen und Seligen des Benediktinerorderns und seiner Zweige,* 4 v. (Metten 1933–38) 1:122–124. A. WENDEHORST, *Lexikon für Theologie und Kirche,* ed. J. HOFER and K. RAHNER, 10 v. (2d, new ed. Freiburg 1957–65) 6:1255–56.

[C. R. BYERLY]

MACARIUS THE EGYPTIAN, ST.

Hermit renowned for his miracles and spiritual counsel; b. Upper Egypt, *c.* 300; d. Scete, *c.* 389. He is erroneously considered the author of a collection of spiritual homilies. Macarius, called the Elder or the Great, is known as one of the DESERT FATHERS described in the *History of the Monks of Egypt* (ch. 28) ascribed to RUFINUS OF AQUILEIA and in the *Lausiac History* (ch. 17) of PALLADIUS. He is mentioned also by Socrates (*Hist. eccl.* 4.23) and Sozomen (*Hist. eccl.* 3.14; 6.20). Macarius joined a scattered settlement of hermits in Scete (*c.* 330), west of the Nile Delta, and became famous for his spiritual maturity and his power over demons. He was ordained *c.* 340, presumably to celebrate the divine mysteries on Sundays for the hermits to whom he appears to have given spiritual conferences. He met St. ANTHONY OF EGYPT at least once, and his sayings are recorded in the *APOPHTHEGMATA PATRUM* of the Desert Fathers, although the eight letters and two prayers there cited are not authentic. Under Emperor Valens, Macarius was one of the hermits who was banished by Bp. Lucius of Alexandria to an island in the Nile (*c.* 374) for his determined anti-Arianism. He was soon allowed to return to the desert and resumed the solitary life until his death.

Neither Rufinus nor Palladius mentions any literary activity of Macarius, although a full volume of writings in Migne's *Patrologia Graeca* (34) bears his name. Macarius had little, if any, formal education; when Sozomen praised his ''divine knowledge and philosophy,'' he referred to his proficiency in the way of detachment and contemplation. While circles of monks in the north Egyptian desert apparently cultivated the Christian gnosis and could be plausibly suspected of ORIGENISM (*c.* 400), Palladius represents Macarius as being of the old school in the tradition of Anthony, whose ''book was nature'' (Socrates, *Hist. eccl.* 4.23). The monastic ideal proposed in the spiritual homilies is more relevant to the tightly organized communities PACHOMIUS developed to the south of Nitria *c.* 320. É. Amann noted Stoic and other non-Christian influences in the 50 homilies that have been almost doubled by recent discoveries. It also appears that doctrines connected with the 18 Messalian propositions condemned at the Council of EPHESUS (431) have a considerable representation in these homilies. This would relate them to Mesopotamia or Constantinople. However, W. Jaeger has denied this, arguing that the great letter, which serves as preface to the collection and whose doctrinal homogeneity with the homilies has been questioned, is not Messalian. In fact, the second section of this letter is a compilation culled from GREGORY OF NYSSA's *De Instituto Christiano*. Apparently the homilies were gradually purged of the grosser errors of Messalianism by later editors; they contain much pure and lofty teaching.

Feast: Jan. 15; Jan. 19 (Greek Menaea).

Bibliography: A. J. MASON, tr., *Fifty Spiritual Homilies of St. Macarius the Egyptian* (Society for Promoting Christian Knowledge; 1921). G. L. MARRIOTT, ed., *Macarii Anecdota* (Cambridge, Mass. 1918). É. AMANN, *Dictionnaire de théologie catholique,* ed. A. VACANT et al., 15 v. (Paris 1903–50; Tables générales 1951–) 9.2:1452–55. G. GRAF, *Geschichte der christlichen arabischen Literatur,* 5 v. (Vatican City 1944–53); *Studi e Testi*, 118, 133, 146, 147, 172, 1:389–395. H. DÖRRIES, *Symeon von Mesopotamien* [*Texte und Untersuchungen zur Geschichte der altchristlichen Literatur*, 55.1; 1941]. W. JAEGER, *Two Rediscovered Works of Ancient Christian Literature* (Leiden 1954), 145–230. L. VILLECOURT, *Revue de l'Orient chrétien* 22 (1921) 29–56; *Muséon* 35 (1922) 203–212. J. QUASTEN, *Patrology,* 3 v. (Westminster, Md. 1950–) 3:161–168. H. C. GRAEF, *Lexikon für Theologie und Kirche,* ed. J. HOFER and K. RAHNER, 10 v. (2d, new ed. Frieburg 1957–65) 6:1309–10. G. QUISPEL, *Makarius, das Thomasevangelium und das Lied von der Perle* (Leiden 1967). R. STAATS, *Gregor von Nyssa und die Messalianer; die Frage der Priorität zweier altkirchlicher Schriften* (Berlin 1968). *Finnisch-Deutsche Theologentagung* (Goslar, Germany 1980), *Makarios- Symposium über das Böse*, ed. W. STROTHMANN (Wiesbaden 1983). *Bibelauslegung und Gruppenidentität*, ed. H.-O. KVIST (Åbo 1992). *Grundbegriffe christlicher Ästhetik*, ed. K. FITSCHEN and R. STAATS (Wiesbaden 1997).

[A. A. STEPHENSON]

MACAU, THE CATHOLIC CHURCH IN

Capital: Macau.
Size: 6 sq. miles.
Population: 445,594 in 2000.
Languages: Portuguese, Chinese.
Religions: Almost all of the Chinese (comprising some 93% of the total population) practice a mixture of Buddhism, Taoism and Confucianism. About 5% of the total population are Roman Catholics, comprising virtually the entire Portuguese and mixed Portuguese-Asian population, the Filipinos and a small Chinese community. There are also small communities of Southern Baptists, Anglicans and Muslims.
Archdiocese: Macau

Macau (Aomen in Chinese) is a special administrative region of CHINA located some 40 miles west of HONG KONG, comprising: (1) a small peninsula projecting from the mainland Chinese province of Guangdong (Kwantung) on the western side of the Pearl River estuary, and (2) the two small islands of Taipa and Coloane. The region was settled in the 1550s by Portuguese merchants involved in the trade with Japan and China. Portugal administered the area as an overseas territory until December 20, 1999, when it reverted to Chinese sovereignty, becoming a Special Administrative Region of the People's Republic of China.

The Church in Colonial Macau. With the arrival of the Portuguese, missionaries used Macau as an important haven of rest after a long voyage from Europe and as a strategic base for the evangelization of Japan and China. Franciscans, Dominicans, Augustinians, and above all, Jesuits transformed the small fishing village on the peninsula into a religious stronghold that received the extraordinary name the City of the Name of God. The Jesuit Visitor to the East, Alessandro VALIGNANO, did much of his organization of the Jesuit Far Eastern missions in Macau. It was from Macau that in 1583 he dispatched Michele Ruggieri and Matteo RICCI to China, reversing what had until then been a missionary failure. In 1576, Pope GREGORY XIII detached Macau from Malacca and made it a diocese with jurisdiction over Japan, China, the Moluccas, and other territories. This immense jurisdiction was reduced by the erection of the short-lived diocese of Funai, Japan, in 1588, and the two Chinese dioceses of Beijing (Peking) and Nanjing (Nanking) in 1690.

From the beginning Macau was under the Portuguese padroado. Government intervention in religious affairs frequently caused friction between the Holy See and Portugal and between the bishops and municipal officials in Macau. The papal legate Charles-Thomas Maillard de Tournon died in Macau in 1710 a virtual prisoner after his important but unsuccessful mission to the emperor of China to settle the CHINESE RITES CONTROVERSY. In 1594, Valignano founded St. Paul's College. The Jesuits ran it for nearly two centuries as a school for missionaries and as a unique center of cultural and scientific exchange on Chinese and Japanese culture on the one hand and Europe on the other. It closed in 1762 when the Jesuit order was disbanded and their members expelled from Macau. In 1835, the magnificent church that the Jesuits had built next to the college burned to the ground. St. Paul Church, also known in Chinese as Da Sanba, was never restored. Its famous facade still stands and has become a symbol for Macau. In the course of the 19th century the size of the diocese of Macau continued to shrink as new vicariates apostolic were established in mainland China.

The Arrival of Protestant Missionaries. Robert Morrison was the first Protestant missionary to arrive in Macau in 1807. His translation of the Bible into Chinese in 1819 was of paramount significance in promoting Christianity in China. From the beginning, Catholic authorities opposed the influx of Protestant newcomers and even today the Protestant community of Macau remains small. The Southern Baptists arrived in 1910. At the beginning of 2001 they ran seven small parishes and a medical clinic called Hope Clinic.

The Catholic Church in Present-Day Macau. In 1990, after more than four hundred years of appointing bishops from Portugal and its territories, the Holy See chose a Chinese priest from Macau, Domingos Lam Katseung (Lin Jianjun), for the position. Bishop Lam, in April 2001, ordained Jose Lai Hangseng, the pastor of the cathedral, as his bishop coadjutor. As of the year 2000, the number of Catholics since 1990 has remained steady, oscillating between 21,000 and 19,000 members (approximately 5 percent of the total population).

Since the handover, the new administration has respected the freedom of religious belief for all the residents of Macau. It has permitted the Catholic Church to continue operating seven parishes and 34 schools unhindered. The Church's influence on education is very significant with half of the school children in Macau studying in the 34 Catholic schools. During Portuguese rule, the Portuguese government financed the Catholic clergy and its schools. Today, the priests' salaries come from the coffers of the diocese, and schools are largely relying on school fees and limited government subsidies. Through its social services, the Church also operates four homes, a hostel and a day center for the aged as well as a small hospice. Caritas Macau maintains a home for the handicapped, a halfway house for ex-prisoners and a center for the homeless.

O Clarim, the diocesan weekly newspaper, founded in 1949, is the oldest newspaper still in circulation in Macau. In 1977, recognizing the power of the media in its missionary work, the diocese of Macau established the Centro Diocesano dos Meios de Communicação Social. It coordinates work on radio and television and produces audio-visual material for educational purposes. Some of the best films shown in Macau are screened in the three cinemas of its Cineteatro. The center also runs a library and a bookstore.

Bibliography: T. B. DA SILVA and W. RADASEWSKY, *Macau* (Berlin 1992). C. R. BOXER, *The Portuguese Seaborne Empire 1415–1825* (London 1969). C. M. B. CHENG, *Macau: A Cultural Janus* (Hong Kong 1999). R.D. CREMER, ed. *Macau: City of Commerce and Culture* (Hong Kong 1991). L.G. GOMES, *Efemêridas da história de Macau* (Lisbon 1954). *Pursuing the Dream: Jesuits in Macao* (Macau 1990). R. MALEK, ed., *Macau: Herkunft ist Zukunft* (Sank Augustin, Germany 2000). *Papers of the International Conference on Macao at the Eve of the Handover. Held by the Centre of Asian Studies at The University of Hong Kong, October 29–30, 1999.* M. TEIXEIRA, *Macau e sua diocese no ano dos centenarios de fundaçao e restauraçao,* 3 vols. (Macau 1940–1963). *Macau.* Special 92: *The Catholic Church at the Gates of China.* (1992). *Tripod* special issue: ''Macau in Transition.'' vol. XIX, no. 114, November-December 1999.

[J.-P. WIEST]

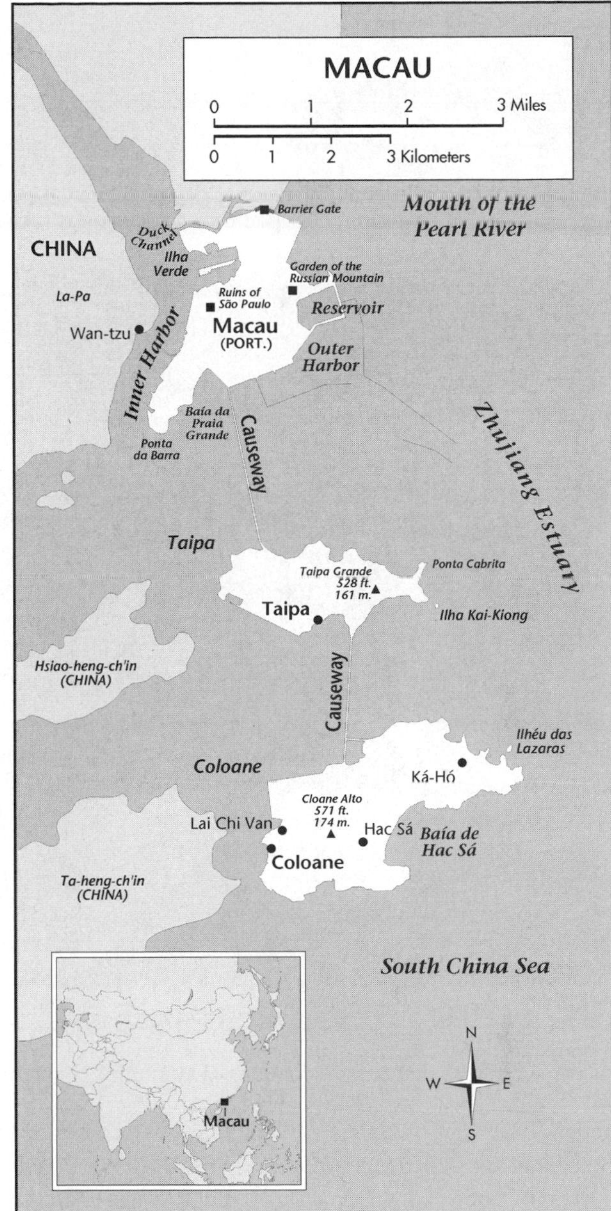

MACCABEES, BOOKS OF

The two books of the Maccabees deal substantially with the same theme: the history of how the Jews, under the inspirational leadership of the Maccabean (Hasmonaean) family, managed to prevail over their Syrian oppressors (the Seleucid Dynasty) and the ''Hellenizing party'' in Palestine in the second century B.C. (*see* MACCABEES, HISTORY OF). The two books are not two parts of a history, such as 1 and 2 Samuel, but are independent compositions partially covering the same period. They fall under the deuterocanonical division of the Catholic Biblical canon, and are to be distinguished from the apocryphal works known as 3 and 4 Maccabees. [*See* APOCRYPHA, 1. APOCRYPHA OF THE OLD TESTAMENT.]

First Maccabees

The first book embraces events from 175 to 134 B.C. It is divided into four parts: a prelude, followed by three sections treating the activity of three Maccabeans—Judas, Jonathan, and Simon, respectively.

Contents. Part 1 (ch. 1–2) provides a prelude to the history of the Maccabean revolt. The account moves quickly from the advent of Hellenism in the Near East under Alexander the Great to the rise of Antiochus IV Epiphanes in 175 B.C. and the initiation of his program of Hellenization of Judea and consequent religious persecution of the Jews. The prelude concludes with a description of the outbreak of the Jewish rebellion, under the priest Mathathias and his five sons, the Maccabees.

Part 2 (3.1–9.22) presents the military exploits of Judas Maccabee: his victories over Apollonius and Seron in Samaria and at Bethoron, over Nicanor and Gorgias at Emmaus, and over Lysias at Bethsura. Following the account of Judas's recapture and rededication of the Temple, the author describes the death of Antiochus IV, the inconclusive battles of Judas against the Syrian army

The facade of St. Paul's Cathedral in Macau, 1960. The remainder of the building caught fire after a typhoon in 1835. (©Paul Almasy/CORBIS)

under Lysias and Antiochus V Eupator at Bethsura and Bethzacharam, the death of Lysias and Antiochus V, and the rise of a new King, Demetrius I, to the throne of Syria. This section concludes with the account of Judas's victory over Nicanor in 160 B.C., and of his defeat and death in battle against Bacchides at Laisa (Elasa) shortly afterwards.

Part 3 (9.23–12.54) describes the diplomatic and military victories of Jonathan Maccabee (160–143 B.C.): his negotiation of a truce with Bacchides, whereby he preserved the battered remnants of Judas's guerrilla army from disintegration; and his later alliance with a new pretender to the throne of Syria, Alexander Balas, who named Jonathan high priest, military leader, and civil governor of Judea. Part 3 concludes with Jonathan's initial support of Demetrius II, his switch to the side of Tryphon and Antiochus VI, and finally his own betrayal and capture by Tryphon at Ptolemais in 143 B.C.

Part 4 (13.1–16.17) deals with the exploits of Simon, the last of the Maccabean brothers (143–134 B.C.): his support of Demetrius II against Tryphon, for which he received almost complete political independence; his initial support of Antiochus VII (successor of Demetrius II), followed by their quarrel; and the defeat of Antiochus's army by Simon's sons, Judas and John. Part 4 concludes with the treacherous assassination of Simon and his two sons, Judas and Mathathias, by Ptolemy near Jericho in 134 B.C. A short subscript relates the escape of Simon's son, John Hyrcanus, who established himself as successor to his father.

Author. Nothing certain is known concerning the identity of the author. His knowledge of Palestinian geography, however, plus his intimate acquaintance with the politics of the period, the military campaigns, the court intrigues, and the Maccabean chieftains, indicate that he was a contemporary of the events about which he has written. His failure to speak of the future life (a doctrine popular among the Pharisees), as well as his tolerant attitude concerning the observance of the Sabbath, suggest that he belonged to Sadducean rather than Pharisaic circles (*see* SADDUCEES; PHARISEES). His work reflects a notable patriotism and a genuine admiration for the Maccabean family.

Language. Although the book was certainly written in Hebrew, and its Hebrew text was still known to Origen and Jerome, only its Greek translation has survived. The Vulgate retains the Old Latin version unrevised, made from a Greek MS much older than our extant Greek MSS and consequently of great value.

Sources. The author includes in his history a number of letters and documents (dispersed among ch. 5 through 15). Although some critics have considered these entries literary creations, most modern scholars defend their authenticity. A few critics consider ch. 13.31–16.24 a later addition, on the grounds that Josephus, who follows the first part of the book step by step, does not utilize these last chapters; this view is no longer seriously considered. At most, it can be said that the book was completed by other inspired writers who added the subscript (16.18–24) and perhaps added or modified a few other passages. Finally, 1 Mc 9.22 would seem to indicate that the author drew from a ''Life of Judas.'' The reference in 16.23–24 may be to some annals in which official acts of the high priests were recorded.

Date. The book was written after the death of Simon Maccabeus in 134 B.C., and if the subscript (16.23–24) belongs to the original MS, then it probably was written after the death of John Hyrcanus in 104 B.C. Since the author speaks kindly of the Romans, it is likely that he wrote before 63 B.C., when Pompey the Great conquered Jerusalem and outraged Jewish feelings by entering the Holy of Holies. The book must have been completed, therefore, sometime between 104 and 63 B.C.

Literary and Historical Value. The graphic descriptions of events, the exactitude of the topographical and chronological details, the ease with which the author's presentation of his facts fits the contemporaneous history of the Near East, and the honesty of the author in relating the defeats as well as the victories of his heroes, testify convincingly to the historical value of the composition.

The author, nonetheless, was a man of his times. He is not entirely unbiased, nor is he perfectly objective. Since he writes to glorify the Maccabees as ''those men by whom salvation was brought to Israel'' (5.62), his viewpoint is that of one who writes history, but the history of a propagandist. After the manner of the ancient historians, he has no scruples about exaggerating the size of the armies sent against the Maccabees, in order to enhance their victories. Although he records the defeats as well as the victories of the Maccabees, he does not hesitate to play up the victories and play down the defeats. The Maccabean revolt appears in his eyes as a world-shaking event, of importance to Rome and Sparta, and as the pivotal point of Seleucid politics. Despite such imperfections, common to most historians before the modern age of strictly objective history, there is no reason to doubt the substantial historicity of the book.

Illumination in the Book of Maccabees 1 from the ''Great Bible of Demeter Neksei-Lipocz.''

Religious Value. The absence of the name of God from the book has led many who refuse to acknowledge its inspired character to consider it a purely secular work devoid of religious value. (There are some passages in the Vulgate in which the words ''God'' and ''Lord'' appear, but these are missing in the Greek.) Although the author does not use the name of God (probably out of the scrupulous reverence for the name of God so common in late post-Exilic times), he does use numerous paraphrases for God, e.g., ''Heaven'' (3.18–19; 4.10, 40; 9.46; 12.15; 16.3), and the personal pronoun ''He'' (2.61; 3.22; 16.3). His heroes pray before they go into battle (3.46–54; 4.10–11; 7.37–38; 9.49; 11.71; 12.11), and the author speaks about God as the savior of Israel (2.61; 3.19; 4.30;

12.15; 16.3). Despite the author's emphasis on the human rather than the divine element in history, there is no doubt that he is deeply penetrated with the truth that it is God who is guiding the history and deciding the fate of His chosen people. He wishes to impress his readers with the virtues of the heroes of the Maccabean resistance—love of God and nation, fidelity to law, and determination to serve God at any cost rather than man. In its implicit invitation to its readers to emulate the religious zeal and generosity of the Maccabees lies the lasting appeal of the book.

Second Maccabees

The second book is not a sequel to 1 Maccabees; it partially covers the same history (176–160 B.C.). Prefixed to the book are two ''festive'' letters (1.1–10a and 1.10b–2.19), sent from the Jews in Jerusalem to the Jews in Egypt. Many scholars believe that they were placed there after the composition of the book by some inspired editor because they contain information about the troubles in Palestine during the Maccabean period. The book proper begins with a short foreword, followed by two sections, each ending with an account of the death of a persecutor of the Jews and the institution of a feast.

Contents. Part 1 (2.20–33) is a preface explaining the sources used by the author; namely, the five-volume work of Jason of Cyrene, and the principles that guided him in making his epitome.

Part 2 (3.1–10.9) covers the period from 176 to 164 B.C. The author describes the struggles for the office of high priest (ch. 3–5), the desecration of the Temple, the persecution of the Jews who refused to give up their faith (ch. 6–7), the outbreak of the Jewish rebellion under Judas Maccabee, and the winning back and rededication of the desecrated Temple (8.1–10.9).

Part 3 (10.10–15.40) concentrates on the successful military campaigns of Judas Maccabee in the time of Antiochus V and Demetrius I, concluding with Judas's conquest of Nicanor in 160 B.C. and the institution of a new feast, popularly referred to as ''the Day of Nicanor.''

Author and Language. Nothing is known about Jason, the author of the original five books condensed in 2 Maccabees, except that he was a Jew from Cyrene in North Africa. Less is known about the anonymous author who abridged the books of Jason to form our present 2 Maccabees. Both authors wrote in Greek, but since the main task of the epitomist was to make a choice of episodes from the longer work of Jason, there is no way of determining how much of the Greek style belongs to Jason and how much to his abridger.

Sources. Many authors judge that Jason's main sources were oral. It is likely that he also used documents from the chronicles of the Seleucid Kings. He includes several letters (cf. 9.18–20; 11.15–17; 11.27–29; 11.34–36) that probably came from the Maccabean archives.

Date. The last event recorded in 2 Maccabees is the death of Nicanor, which took place on March 28, 160 B.C. Since no mention is made of Judas's death, which took place shortly afterwards, it has been suggested that Jason's history was completed in the early part of the year 160 B.C. However, events subsequent to Nicanor's death may have seemed to the writer to be of little value for the purpose of his story. If the letter attached to the composition (1.1–10a) was sent with 2 Maccabees to the Jews in Egypt at the time of the book's first publication, the year 124 B.C., or shortly before, may be established as the date of completion, since this letter is explicitly dated. Many, however, judge that the book was completed sometime after 1 Maccabees.

Literary Form and Historical Value. This book belongs to that category of historical writing popular in the Hellenistic world known as ''pathetic history.'' It is a type of literature that uses every means to appeal to the imagination and the emotions of the reader: colorful descriptions, rhetorical appeals, exaggerated numbers, prodigious miracles involving celestial manifestations, and a preference in general for the edifying and dramatic in place of a straightforward detailing of events. In a way similar to that of the author of Chronicles, the author idealizes his story, arranges chronology to suit his purpose, and concentrates on certain aspects of the general picture to the relative exclusion of others. The substantial historicity of the events recorded can be vouched for safely on the basis of a comparison with 1 Maccabees and with extra-Biblical sources that treat the same period.

Purpose. The general purpose of the author was to edify and instruct his Egyptian compatriots. This he accomplished by extolling Onias III, Eleazar, the seven martyr brothers and their mother, and Judas Maccabee, and by excoriating such enemies of the Jews as Heliodorus, Antiochus IV, the two wicked high priests Jason and Menelaus, Nicanor, and pagans in general.

There are indications that the author also had a specific purpose in mind. From beginning to end he shows a persistent interest in the Temple, the priesthood, and the Temple feasts. Since a rival temple to the Temple of Jerusalem had been erected at Leontopolis in Egypt under Onias IV, it seems not unlikely that the author of 2 Maccabees wished to wean the Egyptian Jews away from the temple of Leontopolis and to secure their allegiance to the one legitimate Temple in Jerusalem. This consideration leads one to suspect a late date for the composition.

Religious Value. Unlike 1 Maccabees, 2 Maccabees not only frequently uses the name of God, but the author visualizes God always close at hand, anxious to answer the prayers of His chosen ones. Throughout the book, the activity and intervention of God in the affairs of His people are constantly highlighted. The author stresses the doctrines of resurrection from the dead (7.9 11; 14.46), the intercession of the saints (15.11–16), and the ability of the living to assist the dead by their prayers and sacrifices (12.39–46). (*See* PURGATORY.) Faith, hope, and sincere love of God pervade the whole book.

Bibliography: A. LEFÈVRE, *Dictionnaire de la Bible* suppl., ed. L. PIRROT, et al. (Paris 1928–) 5:597–612. F. M. ABEL and J. STARCKY, *Les Livres des Maccabées* (*Bible de Jérusalem* (Paris 1948–54) 12; 1962). J. C. DANCY, *A Commentary on I Maccabees* (Oxford 1954). H. FISCHEL, ed., *The First Book of Maccabees* (New York 1948). R. H. CHARLES et al., eds., *The Apocrypha and Pseudepigrapha of the Old Testament in English,* 2 v. (Oxford 1913) v.1. F. GRZYGLEWICZ, ''Paradoxes of the First Book of Maccabees,'' *Scripture* 4 (1950) 197–205. H. W. ETTELSON, ''The Integrity of I Maccabees,'' *Transactions of the Connecticut Academy of Arts and Science* 27 (1925) 249–384. E. BICKERMANN, *The Maccabees,* tr. M. HADAS (New York 1947).

[P. F. ELLIS]

MACCABEES, HISTORY OF THE

The name ''Maccabee'' is generally given to John, Simon, Judas, Eleazar, and Jonathan—the five sons of Mathathias, a Jewish priest of the line of Joarib who died in the year 166 B.C. (1 Mc 2). The name is derived properly from that of the third son, Judas Maccabee. The Greek form, Μακκαβαῖος, probably goes back to the Aramaic word *maqqābai,* the meaning of which is uncertain. The name is generally explained as derived ultimately from the Hebrew word *maqqebet* meaning hammer. Hence, ''Judas, the hammer (or hammerer),'' because of the hammerlike blows he inflicted on the Syrian oppressors of Israel in the early years of the Maccabean wars. Some scholars, however, maintain that the name is a shortened form of the Hebrew maqqab-yāhû (from *nāqab,* ''to mark, to designate''), meaning ''the one designated by Yahweh.'' The name, which was applied first to Judas, then to his brothers, was subsequently used to designate all their kinsmen and adherents, and ultimately given to all the champions of religion during the Greek period.

According to Josephus, Simeon, the grandfather of Mathathias, was called ''the son of Hasmonaeus.'' The family is thus more correctly designated by the name of Hasmonaeans.

This article will treat the remote and proximate background of the Maccabean wars and give an account of the three Maccabean brothers, Judas, Jonathan, and Simon.

Judas Maccabees on medieval manuscript page.

Historical Background

The Maccabees liberated Judea from oppression by the Syrian kings, restored religious freedom, and regained political independence for the Jewish people. To be adequately appreciated these achievements must be seen against the background of the times.

The Hellenization of Palestine. After the return from the Babylonian exile in 538 B.C., Judea was subject for four centuries to the great powers that ruled the Near East: Persia, Alexander the Great, the Ptolemaic kings of Egypt, and finally the Seleucid kings of Syria beginning *c.* 200 B.C. With the exception of the Seleucid King ANTIOCHUS IV EPIPHANES (175–164 B.C.) and his successors, none of Judea's pagan overlords interfered seriously with the practice of the Jewish religion; their policy had been that of subjection and tribute in temporal affairs, freedom in spiritual affairs. Antiochus IV, however, attempted to unify his domains, and especially Palestine, by imposing upon all his subjects the practice of Hellenistic religion. This included the worship of Zeus and other gods of the

Greek pantheon, as well as the king himself as the visible manifestation of Zeus (the name "Epiphanes" meaning "the god manifest").

In its civil and cultural aspects Hellenism was nothing new to the Jews. Hellenization of Palestine had been in progress under both Ptolemaic and Seleucid kings since the era of Alexander. By the time of Antiochus IV, however, serious tensions had come to exist among the Jews between the liberal factions, enthusiastic about Hellenistic culture, and the conservative factions, suspicious of Hellenistic culture and antagonistic to Hellenistic religion. Between 175 and 174 B.C. Jason (the brother of the legitimate high priest Onias III), a leader of the pro-Hellenist faction among the Jews, offered Antiochus IV, in return for the office of high priest, a large sum of money and a promise of cooperation with his policy of Hellenization of Judea. Having been recognized as high priest by Antiochus IV, Jason immediately initiated an active policy of Hellenization. He established a gymnasium in Jerusalem and encouraged Greek sports and fashions (1 Mc 1.13–15; 2 Mc 4.10–15). Three years later a rival, Menelaus, managed to outbid Jason for the office of high priest and began to sell the Temple vessels. When the legitimate high priest Onias III protested, Menelaus had him assassinated (2 Mc 4.23–36). In 169 B.C., with the connivance of Menelaus, Antiochus IV pillaged the Temple. When it became apparent that the religious Jews would not submit voluntarily to Hellenization, Antiochus IV decided to use force. A Syrian army under Apollonius looted and partially destroyed Jerusalem. A Syrian garrison was installed in 167 B.C. in a newly built citadel called the Akra, located on the hill west of the Temple. Antiochus IV then began a systematic persecution of the Jews aimed at destroying the Jewish faith and substituting Hellenistic religion in its place. Regular sacrifices in the Temple were suspended; Jews were no longer permitted to observe the Sabbath and the traditional feasts; it became a crime to possess a copy of the Law or to circumcise Jewish children. Pagan altars were set up throughout the land, and Jews who refused to sacrifice swine's flesh upon these altars were liable to death. In December 167 B.C., the cult of Olympian Zeus was instituted in the Temple, an altar to Zeus was erected, and Jews were compelled to take part in the pagan feasts. A systematic religious persecution of the Jews was in full progress (1 Mc 1.43–67; 2 Mc 6.1–11).

The Outbreak of the Maccabean Wars. Israelite response to Antiochus's program of enforced Hellenization and the suppression of the Jewish faith was threefold. Those enthusiastic about Hellenism apostatized. Some through fear of torture and death unwillingly complied and forsook the faith of their fathers. Others, however, defied the persecutors and either died for their faith or went into hiding (2 Mc 6.8–11).

Meanwhile, in the hill towns and in the desert resistance smoldered, awaiting only a spark to ignite active rebellion. In the little town of Modin, in the foothills northwest of Jerusalem, sometime in late 167 B.C. the spark was struck. The King's officers came to Modin and urged the old priest Mathathias and his five sons to be the first to offer sacrifice on the pagan altar. Mathathias refused vehemently, but while he was still speaking, another Jew approached the altar to sacrifice and abjure his faith. Inflamed with righteous anger, Mathathias slew the man on the spot; turned and killed the King's men; tore down the pagan altar; and then fled to the hills with his sons, where they were joined by the HASIDAEANS and others who refused to accept Hellenization. In a short time the nucleus of a guerrilla army had taken form. Shortly afterward, having confided the leadership of the resistance to his third son, Judas Maccabee (1 Mc 1.66), Mathathias died.

The Maccabean Brothers

Of the five sons of Mathathias, Eleazar and John played only minor roles in the Maccabean wars. Eleazar, called "Abaron," was killed in battle at Bethzacharam (Bethzacharia) in 163 B.C., crushed to death beneath an elephant that he had attempted to kill, believing that it was carrying the Syrian King Antiochus V (1 Mc 6.43–46). John, called "Gaddis," was killed by raiders from Medaba in Transjordan shortly after the death of Judas in 160 B.C. (1 Mc 9.35–42). Judas, Jonathan, and Simon played major roles in the Maccabean wars. They will be treated at length.

Judas Maccabee (166–160 B.C.). When Judas took over the leadership of the Jewish resistance in 166 B.C., there was no army; there were no supplies, no weapons, and no plans. When he died in battle six years later, his name was a byword throughout the Near East. He had formed a close-knit, hard-hitting guerrilla army, armed them with the weapons of defeated Syrian troops, repulsed a series of Syrian armies sent against him, won back Jerusalem and the Temple, and re-established the daily sacrifices. He had set the stage for the eventual return of religious and political freedom to Judea.

A man of contagious courage, invincible confidence, and extraordinary ability, Judas infected his troops with his own indomitable faith and won battle after battle against almost insuperable odds. His fortress was the hills; his strategy, guerrilla tactics—the unsuspected slashing attack followed by a swift retreat and disappearance into the hills.

Judas's first victory was over Apollonius, sent by Antiochus IV from Samaria to subdue the rebellion (1 Mc 3.10–12). A short time later he reduced and scattered a second Syrian force under Seron at the pass of Bethhoron (1 Mc 3.13–24). Neither defeat was a disaster for the Syrians, but the effect of the victories on the morale of Judas's guerrilla army was dramatic. When Lysias, the regent of Antiochus IV, sent an army into Judea in the following year (165 B.C.) under Nicanor and Gorgias, Judas met the enemy near Emmaus and was victorious again (1 Mc 3.38–4.25). Lysias then took charge himself and approached Judea from the south. The battle took place near Bethsura, and again Judas was able to secure a victory (2 Mc 11.1–2). Lysias was forced for a time to recognize Jewish interests in order to give himself to his duties as regent. An account of the diplomatic negotiations between Judas and Lysias, as well as those between Judas and Rome at that time, is preserved in the 11th chapter of 2 Maccabees.

When Antiochus IV died in the autumn of 164 B.C., Lysias seized the government in the name of Antiochus V, the nine-year-old son of Antiochus IV. On December 14 of that same year, Judas purified and rededicated the Temple at Jerusalem. In the following summer, he was able to extend his influence in Palestine by rescuing faithful Jews in Galilee and Galaad, and by punishing pro-Hellenistic Jews throughout the land (1 Mc 5).

In the autumn of 163 B.C. Judas besieged the Syrian citadel in Jerusalem, intending to rid Judea of all Syrian influence. Forced into action by Judas's actions, Lysias and the young King came from Antioch with a large army and besieged Judas's base of operations at Bethsura, forcing Judas to quit the siege of the citadel. When Judas came south to assist the garrison at Bethsura, his army met the Syrians at Bethzacharam, but was forced back to Jerusalem, where refuge was taken in the fortress of the Temple. When Bethsura fell, Lysias's army besieged the Temple fortress. Fortunately for Judas, Lysias was forced to make peace when news arrived that Philip, the rival regent who had been designated by Antiochus IV on his deathbed, was advancing toward Antioch. Lysias successfully disposed of Philip's threat, but was later executed, along with Antiochus V, by Demetrius I Soter (161–150 B.C.), nephew of Antiochus IV (1 Mc 6.17–7.50).

In the meantime, the Hellenistic faction in Jerusalem persuaded Demetrius I to recognize Alcimus, a Hellenistic Jew, as high priest and to send an army against Judas. Demetrius sent Nicanor, and in the ensuing battle near Adarsa (Adasa), Judas had his last victory. Shortly afterward, a Syrian army under Bacchides defeated Judas's army at Laisa (Elasa), and Judas died on the field of battle (1 Mc 9.1–22).

Jonathan Maccabee (160–143 B.C.). The youngest of the Maccabees, Jonathan, also called "Apphus," took command after the death of Judas and wisely withdrew to the desert with the remnants of the shattered Jewish army. With Judea once more under Syrian control, Bacchides returned to Antioch, leaving to the triumphant Hellenistic Jews the task of patrolling the country and keeping the peace. After some time Bacchides returned to Judea to annihilate Jonathan's guerrilla army. Having failed in his first attempts, he made a truce with Jonathan. Quarrels with the Hellenistic Jews and internal difficulties in the Seleucid state may have prompted him to negotiate (1 Mc 9.23–73).

Unhindered by the Syrians from 157 to 152 B.C., Jonathan increased his army and his influence. When Alexander Balas, a pretender to the throne of Syria, contended with Demetrius I for Jonathan's support, Jonathan wisely supported Alexander, who named him high priest, dubbed him "friend of the king," and made him both military and civic governor of Judea.

When Demetrius II in 145 B.C. succeeded with the help of Ptolemy IV of Egypt in deposing Alexander, he at first accepted the friendship of Jonathan. Later, however, Demetrius II broke his promise to Jonathan to remove the Syrian troops from the Akra in Jerusalem, and Jonathan went to the side of Tryphon, who was regent to a new pretender to the throne, Antiochus VI, son of Alexander Balas. However, when Jonathan built a high wall between the Syrian-occupied Akra and the rest of Jerusalem, Tryphon became distrustful. He invited Jonathan to a parley, took him prisoner, and later executed him in the land east of the Jordan at a place called Bascama whose location is now unknown (1 Mc 11–12;13.23).

Simon Maccabee (143–134 B.C.). The last of the Maccabees, Simon (also called "Thasi") rallied the Jewish army after the capture of Jonathan and succeeded in preventing Tryphon's army from assisting the Syrian garrison in Jerusalem. Later, when Tryphon executed Antiochus VI and declared himself king of Syria, Simon went over to the side of Demetrius II, who gave him, in return for his support, almost complete political freedom along with the abolition of all tribute past and future. Simon himself was acknowledged as "the high priest, the great captain, and Prince of the Jews" (1 Mc 13.42). It is from Simon, therefore, that the Hasmonaean dynasty arose, for his less scrupulous sons took the name of king and ruled an independent Judea for the better part of a century (1 Mc 13–14).

In the meantime, Demetrius II had been captured by the Parthians, and when his brother Antiochus VII requested Simon's aid in destroying Tryphon, Simon complied with alacrity. Not long after, however, the two allies quarreled. Antiochus VII sent his general, Cendebeus, to attack Judea. In a battle at Cedron, south of Jamnia, the Jewish army under the leadership of Simon's sons, Judas and John, routed the army of Cendebeus, and Judea was at peace once more. Simon enjoyed the peace for only a few years. In 134 B.C., while at a banquet in the fortress of Doch near Jericho, he was treacherously assassinated along with his sons Judas and Mathathias, by his son-in-law Ptolemy. His remaining son, John Hyrcanus, succeeded him and carried on the Hasmonaean dynasty (1 Mc 15–16).

See Also: HASMONAEANS; MACCABEES, BOOK OF.

Bibliography: JOSEPHUS, *Antiquities* (*Loeb Classical Library* [London-New York-Cambridge, Mass. 1912–]) Bks. 12–13. J. BRIGHT, *A History of Israel* (Philadelphia 1959) 407–412. G. RICCIOTTI, *The History of Israel,* tr. C. DELLA PENTA and R. T. A. MURPHY, 2 v. (2d ed. Milwaukee 1958) 236–279. F. M. ABEL, *Histoire de la Palestine depuis la conquête d'Alexandre jusqu'à; l'invasion Arabe,* 2 v. (Paris 1952) 1:108–206. M. NOTH, *The History of Israel,* tr. and rev. P. R. ACKROYD (2d ed. New York 1960). E. BICKERMANN, *The Maccabees,* tr. M. HADAS (New York 1947). H. A. FISCHEL, ed., *First Book of Maccabees* (New York 1948). W. R. FARMER, *Maccabees, Zealots and Josephus* (New York 1956). A. BEVAN, ''The Origin of the Name Maccabee,'' *Journal of Theological Studies* 30 (1929) 191–193.

[P. F. ELLIS]

MACDONALD, ALEXANDER

Highland Scottish patriot, Gaelic poet, and lexicographer (Gaelic name, Alasdair mac Mhaighstir Alasdair); b. Dalilea, Argyllshire, 1700?; d. Sandaig, Invernesshire, 1770? He was the son of Alexander MacDonald, nonjuring minister of Ardnamurchan, Scotland. The younger MacDonald is known to have been employed (1729–45) by the Protestant SOCIETY FOR PROMOTING CHRISTIAN KNOWLEDGE and to have served in his native district as catechist and schoolmaster. The aims of this society were so wholly at variance with the sentiments of MacDonald's chief, Allan MacDonald of Clanranald, and his Catholic fellow-clansmen, that one can only conclude that Alexander worked for it because of some personal quarrel.

Around 1730 he was asked to prepare for the society a Gaelic-English vocabulary in an effort to introduce English more widely into the Highlands. After revision by the Presbytery of Mull, this work, *A Galick and English Vocabulary,* the first Scottish-Gaelic vocabulary to be separately printed, was published at Edinburgh (1741). MacDonald's increasing absences from his school and his alleged composition of ''Galick songs, stuffed with obscene language'' caused his dismissal from the society on July 4, 1745.

Prince Charles landed (July 25, 1745) at Loch nan Uamh not far from Ardnamurchan. About this time MacDonald is said to have been received into the Catholic Church. He served throughout the Rising of 1745 as an officer in the Jacobite army [*see* JACOBITES (ENGLISH)]. There is strong internal evidence that he was the ''Highland Officer'' who wrote the ''Journall and Memoirs of P. C.'s Expedition into Scotland, etc. 1745–6.'' If so, he was one of the first persons to greet the Prince, whose Gaelic tutor he became, and he received the first commission given by the Prince in Scotland. After the Battle of Culloden (April 16, 1746) he became, in effect, an outlaw.

After the Act of Indemnity (1747), MacDonald was appointed Baillie of the Island of Canna by Clanranald. He visited Bishop Forbes in Edinburgh (1747, 1748), and in April of 1751 brought him an account of the Hanoverian atrocities on the islands of Eigg and Canna. His book of Gaelic poems, *Ais-Eiridh na Sean Chánoin Albannaich* (The Resurrection of the Ancient Scottish Language), published at Edinburgh probably during this visit in 1751, was reportedly destroyed by official order because of its vehement Jacobite sentiments; only one copy of a 1764 reprint is known to exist.

MacDonald's Gaelic verse is distinguished by the vigor and breadth of its vocabulary, its depth of outlook, and the passion with which it expresses the Highlanders' attachment to the Jacobite cause. MacDonald had great if uneven talent for descriptive poetry; he merits a high place in the literature of abuse, though his ribald verses are sometimes obscene. His *Ais-Eiridh,* the first book of original verse in Scottish Gaelic, has influenced the style and vocabulary of Scottish Gaelic poets even to the present. He left poems in manuscripts, since included in nine later editions, the latest in 1924.

Bibliography: A. MACDONALD, *Poems,* tr. A. and A. MACDONALD (Inverness 1924). J. REID, *Bibliotheca Scoto-Celtica* (Glasgow 1832). J. L. CAMPBELL, ''Some Notes on the Poems of A. MacDonald,'' *Scottish Gaelic Studies,* 4 (1934) 18–23; ''Some Words from the Vocabulary of A. MacDonald,'' *ibidem,* 6 (1949) 27–42; ''The Royal Irish Academy Text of *Birlinn Chlann Raghnaill,*'' *ibidem,* 9 (1961) 39–79; ''A. MacDonald: Portrait of a Traditionalist,'' *Scots Magazine,* 24 (1935) 61–76; tr. and ed., *Highland Songs of the Forty-Five* (Edinburgh 1933).

[J. L. CAMPBELL]

MACDONELL, ALEXANDER

Missionary, bishop; b. Invernesshire County, Scotland, July 17, 1762; d. Dumfries, Scotland, Jan. 14, 1840. After early education at Strathglass, he attended a little seminary at Scalan in the Braes of Glenlivat, the Scot's

College in Paris (1778), and the Scot's College of Valladolid, Spain, where he was ordained (1787). He returned to Scotland as a missionary in Badenoch. In 1792 he embarked upon a plan to improve the plight of his Highlanders by securing employment for them in Glasgow. He organized (1794) the Glengarry Fencibles, a Roman Catholic Highland regiment that saw service on the island of Guernsey (1795–98) and in Ireland (1798–1802). Macdonell's appointment as chaplain to the regiment made him the first Catholic chaplain in the British army since the Reformation. When his regiment was disbanded (1802), he successfully negotiated with the British government (1803) to secure grants of land in Upper Canada for as many of the men as desired them. He sailed from Ayr, Scotland, Sept. 5, 1804, and on his arrival was appointed to the Glengarry district by the bishop of Quebec. In 1807 he was appointed vicar-general of Upper Canada. He organized and acted as chaplain to the Second Glengarry Regiment, which served in the War of 1812. Between 1815 and 1826 he fought with the government authorities in Britain to obtain assistance for the Catholic Church in Upper Canada, particularly in the fields of education and support of the clergy.

In a papal brief of Jan. 12, 1819, never executed, he was appointed bishop of Rhosina and vicar apostolic. A new brief in February 1820 preconized him bishop of Rhosina without any specific territory; he was consecrated Dec. 31, 1820, at Quebec. Macdonell was named first bishop of Kingston, Ontario, on the erection of that see, Feb. 26, 1826. He took formal possession of the cathedral April 26, 1829. In 1831 he was appointed a member of the Legislative Council of Upper Canada. On May 29, 1839, he embarked from Kingston for Europe to seek aid for a new college, to promote British immigration to Canada, and to seek a division of his diocese. His remains were interred at St. Mary's Church, Edinburgh, Scotland, and later (1861) reinterred in Kingston. Alexandria, Glengarry County, Upper Canada is named in his honor. His *Reminiscences* were published posthumously (Toronto 1888).

Bibliography: H. J. SOMERS, *The Life and Times of the Hon. and Rt. Rev. Alexander Macdonell* (Washington 1931). J. A. MACDONELL, *A Sketch of the Life of the Hon. and Rt. Rev. Alexander Macdonell* (Alexandria, Ont. 1890); *Sketches Illustrating the Early Settlement and History of Glengarry* (Montreal 1893).

[J. T. FLYNN]

MACEACHEN, EVAN

Scottish Gaelic scholar and translator; b. Arisaig, Scotland, 1769; d. Tombae, Scotland, Sept. 9, 1849. Ordained in 1798 at Scots College, Valladolid, Spain, he was sent to the seminary of Lismore, Scotland in 1806 as a professor. In 1814 he was appointed to the mission of Aigeas in Strathglass, and was transferred in 1818 to Braemar in Aberdeenshire, Scotland. Nearly all the devotional literature extant in Scottish Gaelic before 1850 came from MacEachen's pen. He translated *The Abridgement of Christian Doctrine* (1815), Lorenzo Scupoli's *Spiritual Combat* (1835); Thomas à Kempis's *The Imitation of Christ* (1836), of which an earlier Gaelic translation had been published in 1785 by Robert Menzies; the *Declaration of the British Catholic Bishops* (1838); the *New Testament* (published in 1875 after revision by C. C. Grant); and Bishop Challoner's *Meditations* (still in manuscript). There is reason to believe that MacEachen was the original editor of the Scottish Gaelic prayer book *Iùl a' Chrìosdaidh,* which first appeared in 1834 (8th ed. 1963). He also published (1832) a treatise (in English) on arithmetic and a Gaelic-English dictionary, based on his native dialect of Arisaig, in 1842.

From 1814 MacEachen lived and worked in the eastern district of Scotland, though the great majority of Gaelic-speaking Catholics (about 13,000 as against 3,000) were in the western district. Bitter criticism by certain western-district clergymen of MacEachen's Gaelic orthography and style led Bishop Scott of the western district to insist that MacEachen's writings be revised by two of the bishop's clergy before publication, a step that MacEachen resented. Some of MacEachen's usages show a reaction against the influence of literary Irish and Argyllshire Gaelic in favor of his Invernessshire dialect.

Bibliography: D. MACLEAN, *Typographia Scoto-Gadelica* (Edinburgh 1915). *The Dictionary of National Biography From the Earliest Times to 1900*, 63 v. (London 1885–1900) 12:513.

[J. L. CAMPBELL]

MACEDO COSTA, ANTÔNIO DE

Brazilian bishop and active opponent of regalism; b. Maragogipe, Bahia, Aug. 7, 1830; d. Barbacena, Minas Gerais, March 21, 1891. He was educated in Maragogipe and Salvador, finished his seminary training at Saint-Sulpice in Paris, and was ordained on Dec. 19, 1857. He received the degree of doctor of Canon Law in Rome on June 28, 1859, and entered teaching when he returned to Brazil the same year. Dom Antônio was nominated to fill the vacant See of Pará, and was consecrated in Petrópolis on April 21, 1861, and took formal possession of his see in August.

Dom Antônio is remembered for his memorials directed to the imperial government condemning the interference of the state in the spiritual jurisdiction of the

Brazilian church. He involved himself early in the controversy over FREEMASONRY's infiltration of the religious brotherhoods. Such action brought about his arrest on April 28, 1874. He was tried and sentenced on July 28, 1874. During his imprisonment, Dom Antônio continued his fight against Freemasonry and carried on his episcopal ministry: on Oct. 22, 1874, he issued a pastoral giving the reasons behind the Religious Question and on Jan. 6, 1875, he ordained two candidates for the priesthood. Dom Antônio was amnestied with Dom Vital GONÇALVES DE OLIVEIRA on Sept. 17, 1875, and visited Pius XI in February of 1877.

Some historians maintain that Pedro II granted this amnesty because he and his ministers recognized in the actions of these prelates, signs of a growing independent ecclesiastical leadership that threatened regalism. To quash such a movement the Religious Question had to be quickly and effectively settled. When Dom Antônio returned to his remote diocese of Pará, he had a much less advantageous platform from which to carry on his battle against imperial regalism; nevertheless, he did protest, and apparently won the intense dislike of Dom Pedro II.

After the fall of the empire on Nov. 15, 1889, it was Dom Antônio and not the archbishop of Bahia, the primate of Brazil, who wrote the *Pastoral colectiva,* March 19, 1890, enunciating the Church's acceptance of the republic and explaining its relation to the Church. When the bishops of Brazil convened in Sãao Paulo on July 16, 1890, Dom Antônio presided. He had been transferred to the primatial see of Bahia on June 26, 1890. In September of 1890, despite his failing health, Dom Antônio went to Rome to apprise the pope of conditions in the Brazilian church. He returned in early November because he wanted to be in Rio de Janeiro when the Constituent Assembly convened later that month. Responsibility for shaping the political events weighed heavily on Dom Antônio. It was one of his sorrows that his involvement in government affairs prevented his going to his new See of Bahia. He never took official possession of his archdiocese even though he assumed the presidency of the Brazilian hierarchy.

Government statements at the time of Dom Antônio's death as well as general newspaper comment reveal the high regard in which he was held in his own country. He made a positive contribution to ecclesiastical vigor and to the prestige of the Church at the advent of the republic.

Bibliography: F. GUERRA, *A questãao religiosa do segundo império brasileiro* (Rio de Janeiro 1952). F. DE OLÍVOLA, *Um grande brasileiro* (Recife 1936).

[M. C. THORNTON]

MACEDONIA, THE CATHOLIC CHURCH IN

The Former Yugoslav Republic of Macedonia, located in the Balkan Peninsula, is bordered on the north by SERBIA, on the east by BULGARIA, on the south by GREECE and on the west by ALBANIA. A plateau, the region also features heavily forested mountains and enjoys a moderate climate. Three large lakes and the Vardar River provide water to this landlocked region. Natural resources include chromium lead, iron, ore, zinc, tungsten and nickel, while cereals, rice, tobacco and livestock are among Macedonia's agricultural products.

In 1913, following the Balkan War, the Balkans were divided between Greece (Greek Macedonia) and Serbia. The Serbian portion, known as South Serbia until 1947, became a constituent of the Yugoslav Republic under its new name, Macedonia. The region declared its independence in 1991, although conflicts with Greece over its flag, certain Hellenic symbols and the potential for confusion with Greek Macedonia to the south delayed full recognition and membership in the European Community until 1995. Most Macedonians worked as migrant laborers in the economically advanced nations of Germany and Switzerland.

Early History. In 379 the Roman Empire divided Illyricum into east and west. Eastern Illyricum, which includes modern Macedonia, was ruled by the Eastern Roman Empire, where Greek Byzantine culture predominated. It belonged ecclesiastically to the Rome Patriarchate until 732, when Emperor Leo III made it subject to the CONSTANTINOPLE Patriarchate. Slavs settled in the region during the 7th and 8th centuries and avoided assimilation with Greek culture. The region would be independent under Czar Samuel (980–1014), but otherwise was almost continually subject to Byzantine, Serbian or Turkish overlords. The centuries of domination by the Ottoman Turks in particular left Macedonian culture unrefined, and the Macedonian people uneducated and lacking a strong sense of ethnic identity. Even in the 20th century Bulgaria claimed Macedonian Slavs were actually Bulgars, while Greece countered that the inhabitants of Aegean Macedonia were ethnic Greeks who happened to speak a Slavic language.

Macedonia received Christianity from its Byzantine neighbors during the 8th and 9th centuries. The disciples of Saints Cyril and Methodius were mostly Macedonians. After they were banished from Great Moravia they returned to their homeland and promoted the Slavonic liturgy and culture. One of them, St. Clement of Ohrid (d. 916), was consecrated in 893 as the first Slav bishop. After the destruction of the first Bulgarian Empire in 971 the Bulgarian patriarch sought refuge in independent Macedonia and fixed his residence in Ohrid, Czar Samuel's capital. The Byzantine Emperor Basil II Bulgaroktonos defeated Macedonia in 1018 and annexed it to Byzantium, but in 1019 he decreed that Ohrid should remain an autocephalous major archiepiscopate with jurisdiction over the dioceses in the western part of the Balkan peninsula. This status lasted until 1767, when the Turks suppressed and subjected Ohrid to Constantinople. Not until 1958 did the Macedonian Orthodox Church regain autonomous status within the Serbian Patriarchate. In 1859 a movement toward union with the Catholic Church began in Macedonia and soon enrolled about 50,000 people. This led the Holy See in 1883 to erect a vicariate apostolic in Thessalonike.

By the 19th century Bulgars, Serbs and Greeks entered the region, creating an ethnic mix. After Bulgaria's defeat in the Second Balkan War, an anti-Bulgarian campaign began in the region causing Bulgarian schools and churches to close and thousands of Macedonians to flee to Bulgaria. Yugoslavia, which came into being on Dec. 1, 1918, as the Kingdom of the Serbs, Croats and Slovenes, included Serbia, Macedonia, Croatia, Slovenia, Dalmatia, Montenegro and Voivodina. Between the world wars Macedonian terrorist groups, supported by Bulgaria, fought the Serb-controlled Yugoslav government. While Yugoslavia refused to recognize a Macedonian nation, many Macedonians accepted that country's control. During World War II Bulgaria occupied Macedonia, but their occupation proved little better. After the war communists seized power and in 1946 established the Federal People's Republic of Yugoslavia, let by Josip Broz Tito. Macedonia was the poorest nation in the new federation.

Under Yugoslav Domination. While Yugoslavia promulgated a constitution (Nov. 30, 1946) that guaranteed religious liberty, it concurrently demonstrated its opposition to all religions by openly persecuting them. Leaders from Catholic and Muslim congregations were imprisoned on charges of treason, Catholic and other religious schools were closed, Church property was confiscated and religious associations were suppressed. Fortunately such persecution diminished after the late 1940s as Tito attempted to court favor with Western powers, although they did not cease altogether until the 1980s.

In Macedonia's case, the government's fight against religious faith took a different course, due to Yugoslavia's desire to develop Macedonian nationalism. Several years after taking power, the government recognized Macedonian nationhood by making the region a separate republic with its own parliament. Through this action Yugoslavia countered claims by Greece and Bulgaria that "Macedonian" was merely a territorial signifier. The government continued to encourage the development of a uniquely Macedonian consciousness through use of the Macedonian language (the first standardized Macedonian grammar was published in 1948). Federal support for Macedonian cultural institutions included funding a university in Skopje.

Capital: Skopje.
Size: 9,928 sq. miles.
Population: 2,041,460 in 2000.
Languages: Macedonian, Serbo-Croat.
Religions: 60,420 Catholics (3%), 613,050 Muslims (30%), 1,367,990 Macedonian Orthodox (67%).
Diocese: Skopje-Prijren, suffragan to Vrhbosna (Sarajevo), in Bosnia-Herzegovina.

The Macedonian Orthodox Church. While the Orthodox community at first refused to recognize an independent Macedonian Orthodox Church, in 1958 the Serbian Orthodox hierarchy recognized the Macedonian dioceses by consecrating a Macedonian bishop. The activities of Macedonian Orthodox remained under the authority of the Serbian Orthodox Church until 1967, when the church was proclaimed independent. After that point, the Serbian Orthodox Church discontinued further relations. Aware that a self-governing Macedonian church would enhance the sense of Macedonian ethnicity and nationhood they were attempting to develop, the Yugoslav political authorities in Belgrade awarded the Macedonian Orthodox Church favored status. Without recognition from the Serbian hierarchy, however, the Macedonian church remained isolated from the international Orthodox community. By the late 20th century it had six dioceses in Yugoslavia and two abroad, 225 parishes, 102 monasteries, about 250 priests and about 15 monks, and one school of theology.

Into the 21st Century. In 1990 a democratic party won elections in Macedonia, and the nation gained independence on Sept. 17, 1991, under a new constitution. President Kiro Gligorov was injured in an assassination attempt in 1995, after winning his second election. As violence against ethnic Albanians accelerated in neighboring Kosovo, the Kiro government feared that the significant Albanian population in Macedonia would demand that the country take action. After U.N troops stepped in, a newer threat emerged: the stress of tending for thousands of Kosovar refugees that was falling on a Macedonian economy weakened by a three-year trade blockade by Greece. Fortunately, nations such as Great Britain, Saudi Arabia, Israel and Iran ultimately stepped in to help. In 1999 Boris Trajkovski was elected presi-

dent, his primary task was to boost the region's still-sagging economy and deal with a pending border dispute with Serbia.

As a Latin-rite church in an Eastern Orthodox region, Macedonia's Roman Catholic Church continued to be a minority faith, although the Macedonian Church did not have official status under the constitution. By 2000 Catholics in Macedonia lived primarily in or near Skopje; they had 30 parishes tended by 58 secular and two religious priests, while 120 sisters administered educational and medical assistance. Macedonian Catholics shared their diocese with Catholics in Kosovo, and provided much needed assistance in efforts to care for Albanian refugees during Serbian efforts to ethnically cleanse the area of Muslim influences in the late 1990s. During the air strikes by NATO, the region's Catholics aided British troops and international aid agencies in tending to the thousands of Kosovars' forced over the Serbian border into Macedonia. The government encouraged relations between the nation's three major faiths by hosting ecumenical functions on a regular basis.

Bibliography: *Monumenta spectantia historiam Slavorum meridionalium* (Zagreb 1868–), 46 v. to 1951. M. SPINKA, *A History of Christianity in the Balkans* (Chicago, IL 1933). R. RISTELHUEBER, *Histoire des peoples balkaniques* (Paris 1950). P. D. OSTROVÍC, *The Truth about Yugoslavia* (New York 1952). W. MARKERT, *Jugoslawien* (Cologne 1954). F. DVORNIK, *The Slavs: Their Early History and Civilization* (Boston 1956); *The Slavs in European History and Civilization* (New Brunswick, NJ 1962). K. S. LATOURETTE, *Christianity in a Revolutionary Age: A History of Christianity in the Nineteenth and Twentieth Centuries,* 5 v. (New York 1958–62) v.1, 2, 4. B. KONESKI, *Toward the Macedonian Renaissance,* tr. I. KOVILOSKA (Skopje 1961). S. P. RAMET, *Nihil Obstat: Religion, Politics, and Social Change in East-Central Europe and Russia* (Durham, NC 1998). *J. MATL, Lexikon für Theologie und Kirche*, eds., J. HOFER and K. RAHNER, 10 v. (2d, new ed. Freiburg 1957–65) 5:1191–94. B. SPULER and H. KOCH, *Die Religion in Geschichte und Gegenwart*, 7 v. (3d ed. Tübingen 1957–65) 3:1054–60. *Bilan du Monde* 2:914–928. *Annuario Pontificio* has annual data on all dioceses and apostolic administrations.

[P. SHELTON]

MACEDONIUS, ST.

Anchorite renowned throughout Syria, Phoenicia, and Cilicia; d. near Antioch, *c.* 430. THEODORET (*Hist. relig.* 13) furnishes information about Macedonius, who was called *Critophages* because for 40 years, refusing bread, he lived on barley moistened with water. For the first 45 years of his desert life (360–430 according to L. de Tillemont) Macedonius disdained a tent or hut and lived in a cave which the crowds, flocking to see him, often forced him to change. He worked many miracles with water and the sign of the cross, and Theodoret, whose mother had been childless for the first 13 years of her marriage, attributed his own birth to the hermit's prayers. Macedonius was persuaded by Patriarch Flavian of Antioch to accept priestly ordination (after 381), and his counsels of moderation profited the Antiochenes in their peril from the riots over the imperial statutes in 387 (*see* JOHN CHRYSOSTOM).

Feast: Jan. 24.

Bibliography: THEODORET OF CYR, *Historia religiosa, Patrolofia Graeca*, ed. J. P. MIGNE (Paris 1857–66) 82:1399. *Acta Sanctorum* Jan. 3:207–212. S. C. TILLEMONT, *Mémoires pour servir à l'histoire ecclésiastique des six premiers siècles* (Paris 1693–1712) 10:533; 12:487, 681. C. HOLE, *A Dictionary of Christian Biography*, ed. W. SMITH and H. WACE (London 1877–87) 3:778. A. BUTLER, *The Lives of the Saints*, ed. H. THURSTON and D. ATTWATER (New York 1956) 1:161.

[A. A. STEPHENSON]

MACELWANE, JAMES BERNARD

Educator, geophysicist, and founder of the Jesuit Seismological Association; b. Port Clinton, Ohio, Sept.

28, 1883; d. St. Louis, Missouri, Feb. 15, 1956. The son of Alexander and Catherine (Carr) Macelwane, he entered the Society of Jesus in 1903 and was ordained in 1918. After receiving his doctorate in physics, with a dissertation in seismology under Elmer E. Hall, at the University of California, Berkeley, in 1923, he was appointed assistant professor of geology at Berkeley, where he helped to organize a chain of seismograph stations in California. He was named professor of geophysics and director of the new department of geophysics at St. Louis University in 1925. Macelwane published his first paper, ''Physics of the Seismograph,'' in 1911. He was interested in the physical state of the core of the earth and studied microseisms and their relation to the earth's surface and to regional atmospheric conditions and explored geophysical methods of prospecting for oil. He published 133 technical papers and two books besides contributing chapters to several other books. During World War II he was a member of the research and development board of the Department of Defense and was appointed a member of the board of the National Science Foundation in 1954. At the time of his death he was serving his third year as president of the American Geophysical Union and was chairman of the United States Technical Panel on Seismology and Gravity for the International Geophysical Year. He was a member of the National Academy of Sciences.

Bibliography: P. BYERLY and W. V. STAUDER, ''James B. Macelwane, S.J.,'' *Biographical Memoirs, National Academy of Sciences*, 31 (1958) 254–281.

[P. H. YANCEY]

MACEVILLY, JOHN

Archbishop and exegete; b. Louisburgh, County Mayo, Ireland, April 15, 1818; d. Tuam, Ireland, Nov. 26, 1902. He was educated at St. Jarlath's College, Tuam, and at Maynooth, and was ordained in 1842. Appointed professor of Sacred Scripture at St. Jarlath's in 1844, he was its president from 1852 to 1857. He was elected bishop of Galway in 1857, appointed apostolic administrator of Kilmacduagh and Kilfenora in 1866, and attended the Vatican Council I (1869–70). H was made coadjutor of Tuam in 1877, and he became archbishop in 1881, a post he held till his death. In spite of his many episcopal cares, he found time to engage in serious Scripture studies and has the honor of being the first English-writing Catholic commentator on all the New Testament Books (except Revelation). His works, formerly in wide use in the English-speaking world, are now largely outmoded.

Bibliography: J. J. TWOMEY, *Lexikon für Theologie und Kirche*, ed. J. HOFER and K. RAHNER, 10 v. (2d, new ed. Freiburg 1957–65) 6:1256–57. J. HEALY, *Maynooth College: Its Centenary History* (New York 1895) 622–624.

[K. O'SULLIVAN]

MACHALE, JOHN

Archbishop of TUAM and Irish patriot; b. Tubbernavine, County Mayo, March 6, 1791; d. Tuam, County Galway, Nov. 4, 1881. He was the son of Patrick MacHale, a tenant farmer and innkeeper of Tirawley, County Mayo, and Mary (Mulchiarian) MacHale. His native tongue was Gaelic and his primary education was at the local hedge school. The uprising of 1798 in Ireland, particularly the execution of Andrew Conroy, the priest who had baptized him, fired young MacHale's patriotism. After studying at the preparatory school in Castlebar (1803–07), he was granted a scholarship at St. Patrick's College, MAYNOOTH, the national seminary. MacHale excelled in theology and languages and lectured in theology while still a subdeacon. He was ordained in 1814 and then taught theology at Maynooth as an assistant and later as a professor (1814–25).

In 1820 he began a series of letters that appeared in various newspapers. Under the pseudonym ''Hieropolis'' he articulated the discontent of many Irish Catholics concerning the established Church of Ireland and the system of vestry taxes and tithes paid by Catholics to support its clergy and church edifices. MacHale appealed for Catholic EMANCIPATION and the repeal of the political union of Great Britain and Ireland. This series of letters attracted the notice of Daniel O'CONNELL; soon MacHale became one of his most prominent allies. In 1825 MacHale became coadjutor bishop of Killala, but he continued to participate in the agitation for emancipation. He was instrumental in breaking the stranglehold of a Tory family, the Brownes, on the political life of County Mayo (1826). MacHale was constantly involved in controversies over the Protestant Bible societies and proselytism among the tenant farmers. In 1830 he wrote open letters to Charles Grey, the prime minister, seeking famine relief and describing the hardships inflicted by the decline of the linen trade and by the exorbitant rents paid by Irish tenant farmers. He also joined a delegation to impress upon the prime minister the urgency of conditions in western Ireland.

MacHale began the construction of a cathedral in Ballina (1827), but in 1831 poor health compelled him to reside in Rome, where he won the friendship and confidence of Pope Gregory XVI. He became bishop of Killala (May 1834), but in July he was transferred to the Archdiocese of Tuam, despite strong governmental opposition because of his fiery nationalism. His vigorous denunciations of London's neglect and maladministration of Ireland and his enthusiastic advocacy of Irish culture and the use of the Irish language gave some credibility to beliefs that he was anti-English. The English Catholic Lords Clifford and Shrewsbury engaged in a bitter newspaper controversy with him over the fairness of his criticisms (1835). Although MacHale disagreed with O'Connell on many points, he approved the latter's agitation for repeal of the Act of Union of 1801 and for the establishment of an Irish parliament in Dublin. However, MacHale disapproved of the violent methods of Young Ireland. During the terrible famine of 1847 he was indefatigable in seeking relief for his starving flock by appealing abroad for assistance and by urging the government to more effective measures. His episcopal residence became a center for distributing food. This experience strengthened his interest in the tenants right movement and in the Irish Land League as means of alleviating the situation.

MacHale's persistent opposition to any system of education that mixed Catholic with Protestant children and that excluded the teaching of religion led to the rejection by the Irish hierarchy of the plans for national schools and queen's colleges as advocated by the governments of Robert Peel and John Russell (1847–50). Within his own archdiocese, MacHale laid the foundation for a Catholic school system by utilizing the Irish Christian Brothers, Third Order Regulars of St. Francis, and Sisters of Mercy. MacHale's views prevailed in Rome, although they did not have the assent of all the Irish bishops. At the Synod of Thurles (1850) MacHale joined forces with Paul CULLEN, Archbishop of Armagh (later of Dublin), to win a majority of one vote in favor of rejecting the government's educational system and forbidding Catholic attendance and cooperation. In 1869 the Irish hierarchy formally condemned the system of mixed education, and Pius IX ratified their decision. MacHale also approved the projected Catholic University in Dublin, but his opposition to the selection of John Henry NEWMAN as first rector and to Newman's management was in good part responsible for the failure of the plan.

After 1854 MacHale's influence on the Irish hierarchy and in Rome declined as Cullen's grew. The archbishop of Tuam was considered too independent and too immoderate. In his declining years, he withdrew completely from political controversy. At VATICAN COUNCIL I he was among the minority of bishops who considered a solemn definition of papal primacy and infallibility inopportune, but he accepted the conciliar decisions without difficulty.

Among the Irish-speaking people of Connaught, MacHale was cherished for his kindness, charity, and zeal for their spiritual and material welfare. His practice each Sunday was to preach in Gaelic, and he used this language regularly in addressing his flock. He published poems, textbooks, catechisms, prayerbooks, and devotional works in Gaelic; but his most significant publications were his translations of the Pentateuch (1861) and Homer's *Iliad* (1841–71). The archbishop was austere, energetic, and industrious. Not until 1879, when he was 88 years old, did he receive a coadjutor to aid him in administering the see. At the age of 90 he preached regularly at Sunday Mass.

Bibliography: U. J. BOURKE, *The Life and Times of the Most Rev. John MacHale* (Baltimore 1882). O. J. BURKE, *The History of the Catholic Archbishops of Tuam* (Dublin 1882). B. O'REILLY, *John MacHale, Archbishop of Tuam,* 2 v. (New York 1890). E. A. D'ALTON, *History of the Archdiocese of Tuam,* 2 v. (Dublin 1928). N. COSTELLO, *John MacHale, Archbishop of Tuam* (Dublin 1939), lists MacHale's pubs. in the Irish lang. J. F. BRODERICK, ''The Holy See and the Irish Movement for the Repeal of the Union with England,'' *Analecta Gregoriana* 55 (1951). N. MOORE, *The Dictionary of National Biography from the Earliest Times to 1900,* 63 v. (London 1885–1900) 12:550–552.

[P. K. EGAN]

MACHAUT, GUILLAUME DE

14th-century poet and *ars nova* composer (also Machault, Machauld, Machaud); b. Machault, France, *c.* 1300; d. Reims, *c.* 1377. Sometime secretary to John of Luxembourg (king of Bohemia) and later a canon of Reims cathedral, he achieved renown for his secular lais, ballades, rondeaux, and chansons, for the remarkable structure of his motets, of which six are of undoubted liturgical intent, and for the masterly design of his *Messe de Notre Dame*. The motets, because of their use of isorhythmic tenors and resulting long-held notes (*see* MOTET), sometimes recall earlier techniques such as organum. In rhythmic subtlety and harmonic interest they are forward-looking. In the *Mass,* he unified the *Kyrie, Sanctus, Agnus Dei,* and *Ite missa est* by skillful use of isorhythm; the *Gloria* and *Credo* were set in a direct and declamatory style, thus providing contrast in texture and the necessary freedom demanded by longer texts. His poetry was influenced by Ovid, St. BEDE, and other Latin poets, and in its turn became a source for Chaucer and other writers. In style it is a step away from the generalized romanticism of the trouvères in the direction of the more personal idiom of Villon, with a certain preoccupation with form that marks the decline of medieval poetry and the beginnings of a new French school.

Bibliography: G. MACHAUT, *Musikalische Werke,* ed. F. LUDWIG, 4 v. (Leipzig 1926–54); *Opera,* ed. G. DE VAN (*Corpus mensurabilis musicae* 2; 1949–); *Oeuvres,* ed. E. HOEPFFNER (Paris 1908–21). A. MACHABEY, *G. de Machaut,* 2 v. (Paris 1955). S.

LEVARIE, *Guillaume de Machaut* (New York 1954). S. J. WILLIAMS, *The Music of Guillaume de Machaut* (Doctoral diss. unpub. Yale U. 1952). G. REANEY, ''Ars Nova in France,'' *New Oxford History of Music*, ed. J. A. WESTRUP, 11 v. (New York 1957–) 3: 1–30. L. SCHRADE, ed., *Polyphonic Music of the 14th Century,* 4 v. (Monaco 1956–58), v.2–3, with comment. G. REESE, *Music in the Middle Ages* (New York 1940) 347–359. W. A. NITZE and E. P. DARGAN, *A History of French Literature* (3d ed. New York 1938). L. M. EARP, *Guillaume de Machaut: A Guide to Research* (New York, 1995). *Machaut's World: Science and Art in the Fourteenth Century*, conference proceedings (New York 1978). W. CALIN, *A Poet at the Fountain: Essays on the Narrative Verse of Guillaume de Machaut* (Lexington, Ky. 1974). D. LEECH-WILKINSON, *Machaut's Mass: An Introduction* (Oxford 1990). Y. PLUMLEY, ''Guillaume de Machaut 700 Years On,'' *Early Music,* vol. 28, no. 3 (2000) 487. D. LEECH-WILKINSON, '''Le Voir Dit' and 'La Messe de Nostre Dame': Aspects of Genre and Style in the Late Works of Machaut,'' *Plainsong and Medieval Music* 2, no. 1 (1993) 43.

[D. STEVENS]

MACHEBEUF, JOSEPH PROJECTUS

Bishop and missionary; b. Riom, France, Aug. 11, 1812; d. Denver, Colorado, July 10, 1889. He was educated by the Brothers of the Christian Schools. After pursuing classical studies at the College of Riom, he entered the Grand Seminary of Montferrand; he was ordained on Dec. 21, 1836. He arrived in the United States on Aug. 21, 1839, with John Baptiste Lamy. After serving in the Ohio missions, where he was known as a church builder and temperance advocate, he became pastor of Lower Sandusky in 1841. In 1851 he went to Santa Fe, North Mexico to serve under Lamy, the first vicar-general of the territory and later its bishop and archbishop. Between adventurous missionary journeys, which took him into Mexico and Arizona, Machebeuf acted as pastor at Albuquerque and Santa Fe, where he helped to restore discipline to the native clergy. In 1860 he was sent by Lamy to Denver to care for the mining population of the new community. He soon established churches and became a familiar figure in every boom town in the territory. On Aug. 16, 1868, Machebeuf became the first vicar apostolic of Colorado, a jurisdiction that then included Utah and Wyoming territories.

The vicariate of Colorado was made a diocese on Aug. 16, 1887, with Denver as the see city and Machebeuf as the first bishop. In a diocese that embraced the entire state of Colorado, he established churches at Central City (1863), Trinidad (1865), Golden (1863), Walsenburg (1869), and Colorado Springs (1876). He invited the first teaching and charitable orders to Colorado and established the Catholic educational system in the state. In 1873, he founded St. Joseph's Hospital, the first permanent hospital in Denver. He was responsible for the establishment, in 1888, of Colorado's first Catholic college for men, the College of the Sacred Heart (later Regis College, Denver). The state's first Catholic charitable institutions, St. Vincent's Orphanage and the Good Shepherd's Home, were built in his time. By 1889 there were 102 churches and chapels, 16 parish schools, nine academies, one orphanage, one protective home, one college for men, and 40,000 Catholics in his diocese.

Bibliography: Archives, Archdiocese of Denver. W. J. HOWLETT, *Life of the Rt. Reverend Joseph P. Machebeuf, D.D.* (Pueblo, Colo. 1908).

[W. H. JONES]

MACHIAVELLI, NICCOLÒ

Political theorist and historian; b, Florence, Italy, May 3, 1469; d. there, June 2, 1527. The Machiavelli family belonged to the old rural nobility, which, on taking up residence in the city, gave the Commune numerous magistrates, priors, and gonfaloniers. Despite Machiavelli's distinguished lineage, Niccolò's own father counted among the poorest members of the family. He was an attorney, forbidden to practice law in the city of FLORENCE, because he had been for a time imprisoned as a debtor. His father eked out a living in genteel poverty on the city's outskirts, administering the few lands that he had and furtively practicing the law. These straightened circumstances affected Niccolò Machiavelli's early years. Although he was educated, he was never trained as a humanist, nor could he read or speak Greek, one of the chief signs of social and educational distinction in late fifteenth-century Florence.

Life. Niccolò's life may be divided into three periods: the first, the time of study and preparation that ended in 1494 when he entered public office of the Republic; the second (1494–1512), a period of political activity; the third, from 1512 to his death. In the last period he devoted himself to intense literary activity, apart from the last two years of his life, when he was again occupied with affairs of state.

First Two Periods. No reliable information is available for his first period. His works contain very little autobiographical data, and his letters do not refer to the years of his youth. From 1494 he emerges as an official of the Republic of Florence. In 1498, Niccolò Machiavelli was made head of Florence's second chancery, an important office for one who was then only 29 years old. The town's second chancery was concerned with foreign policy, military organization and in part with internal affairs (e.g. police matters). Machiavelli made more than 30 diplomatic missions while serving in this capacity. His associations with the first chancery were also important:

it was headed by the learned humanist Marcello Virgilio Adriana, who perhaps exercised some influence on Machiavelli's cultural formation.

In the midst of political events and intrigues, Machiavelli reflected on them and derived inspiration for his future thought. He was constant in his devotion to experience as an effective teacher and in his daily observation of men and things, a habit he was still to retain even at San Casciano after his political disgrace. All this is clear from a letter to his friend Francesco Vettori (Dec. 10, 1513): "Then I betake myself to the street and go to the inns. I talk with those who pass, asking them for news about their localities. I hear various things and I note the different tastes and diverse thoughts of men" (*Letter* 137).

Some of the embassies exercised a decisive influence on Machiavelli's mind, such as the two (June and October 1502) to Cesare Borgia (Il Valentino), the astute and unscrupulous prince in whom the young secretary saw the type of statesman needed in a divided Italy overrun by foreigners, or the two missions to the Court of Rome (1503, 1506), which gave him an opportunity to study the temporal government of the Church. When entrusted with a mission to Pisa, that rebellious city within the Tuscan state, he conceived the plan of establishing a citizen militia that would replace Florence's untrustworthy mercenary troops. He began to enroll soldiers throughout the territory of Florence, and in 1506 he obtained the establishment of a special magistracy, the Nove di Milizia, and became its secretary. In 1509, in the final phase of the siege of Pisa, Machiavelli himself employed the first detachments of his *ordinanza,* or new militia. During these years Machiavelli also appears to have been involved with the artist Leonardo da Vinci in an ill-fated plan to divert Tuscany's Arno River away from the restive city of Pisa.

New matter for observation and meditation was offered to Machiavelli by his missions outside of Italy to Louis XII of France (1500, 1504, 1510) and to the Emperor Maximilian I in the Tyrol (1507). For this intense activity as a functionary, diplomat, and penetrating observer, there is copious documentation extant in the form of official correspondence and of reports.

Third Period. When the Republic of Soderini fell in 1512 and the Medici reentered Florence with the aid of the forces of the Holy League, Machiavelli, the devoted functionary and republican at heart, was put aside. He was exiled in the territory of the state and condemned to forced leisure at San Casciano, precisely in the country (the "four houses") of Sant'Andrea in Perussina. For his life in this period there is extant correspondence with his friend Francesco Vittori, the Florentine orator close to Pope LEO X (DE' MEDICI). It is especially important for an understanding of the origins and value of Machiavelli's major works and for his judgments on the particular events of the time. He was born for political action—or so at least he believed—and did not resign himself to the role of an idle spectator, even if his writings are owed to this period of political inactivity. He entertained the false hope that his friend could influence the pope so that he might be recalled to Florence and enter the service of the Medici. But his republican past stood in the way. There was nothing left for him to do except to unbosom his angry despair to Vettori, play practical jokes with his friends in the shop of Donato Del Corno, or find consolation in good dinners—although his means were limited. Machiavelli himself describes his day in detail in the letter to Vettori cited above.

In 1520 came the first sign of benevolence from the Medici. Cardinal Giulio (the future Pope CLEMENT VII) requested Machiavelli to write a history of Florence, but he was not given any position of even modest importance before 1525, when, at the request of Clement VII and Medicean Florence, he was entrusted with two missions to his friend Francesco Guicciardini, lieutenant general of the papal army in the war against the Spaniards. After the pope had decided to strengthen the defenses of Florence, Machiavelli was asked to work out a plan for the fortifications and was appointed chancellor of the five procurators for the walls. This was a modest post, in which he experimented again with his citizen militia (*ordinanza*), entrusted to the command of Giovanni dalle Bande Nere.

Events, however, took a rapid and disastrous turn. The German mercenaries (*lanzichenecchi*), under the command of the Lutheran Georg Frundsberg, invaded and sacked Rome. Clement VII shut himself up in the Castel Sant' Angelo; Florence rebelled against the Medici, and they were forced to leave. Machiavelli, who had come to intimate terms with them, found himself again put aside. He did not survive long following this second embarrassment. His son wrote to Nelli that "he confessed his sins to Friar Matteo, who stayed with him until his death" ("lasciossi confessare le sue peccata da un frate Matteo"). His remains lie in S. Croce in Florence near those of Galileo, Alfieri, and Foscolo. His monument bears the inscription "tanto nomini nullum par elogium"; it was erected only in 1787 on the initiative of the Englishman Lord Cooper.

Works. The first significant work was *Descrizione del modo tenuto dal Duca Valentino nell' ammazzarre Vitellozzo Vitelli, Oliverotto da Fermo, il signor Paolo e il duca di Gavina Orsini* (written perhaps 1509). It describes with cold and penetrating observation the massacre at Senigallia that was skillfully prepared and carried out with deliberate ferocity by Cesare BORGIA. As Norsa has noted [*Machiavelli* (Milan 1948) 47], this short piece exhibits one of Machiavelli's characteristic procedures: "his tendency to transform reality by interpreting and evaluating it according to the principles of his political doctrine. History has value in so far as it furnishes experimental confirmation of these principles." His most famous work, *Il Principe,* a brief treatise in 26 chapters, was composed between the second half of 1513 and the first days of 1514. The author delineates with artistic power the figure of the prince, resolved without any scruple whatever to attain his end, i.e., to rescue Italy from ruin and even to unify the peninsula politically. *The Prince* is completed by the *Discorsi sulla prima Deca di Tito Livio,* in three books. Begun in this period and continued to the end of 1517, it is a free political commentary on certain passages of Livy and of other ancient historians, an unsystematic but effective exposition of the political thought of its author. The fundamental importance that Machiavelli attached to the army in relation to the government of the state is revealed, especially by the systematic exposition and the very careful form in which he presents his ideas, in the treatise *L'arte della guerra,* written between 1516 and 1520. The *Vita di Castruccio Castracani* (1520) is a kind of historical novel, representing as an ideal warrior prince a *condottiere* of Lucca. But Machiavelli wrote genuine historical works. His *Istorie florentine,* composed between 1520 and 1525 in eight books, covers the city's history from its beginning to the death of Lorenzo the Magnificent (1492). Even here Machiavelli applies his political doctrines to historical facts in such a way that the latter serve to demonstrate the former.

In these works he already reveals himself also as a powerful and original writer, taking a high place among the great prose artists of the Italian tongue. His artistic propensities and qualities are more prominent in works more explicitly literary. *Il Decennale primo* and *Il Decennale secondo* (incomplete) are chronicles in *terza rima* dealing with Florentine events from 1494 to 1504 and from 1504 to 1509. These and other verse compositions, e.g., *I Canti Carnascialeschi,* give him no claim to be called a poet. His *I Capitoli morali* have little interest as compared with his incomplete *L'Asino d'Oro,* written between 1516 and 1517. His authorship of *Il Discorso o dialogo intorno alla nostra lingua* is dubious. The *Favola del demonio che prese moglie,* better known as *Novella di Belfagor Arcidiavolo,* is a mordant satire on women, but a reworking of a traditional story. His *La mandragola,* the masterpiece of Cinquecento comedy, was first played at Florence, perhaps in 1520, and often elsewhere, with great success, and continues to live. His other comedy, *La Clizia,* is an imitation, being a verse translation of Terence's *Andria;* its influence was marked. Except for *L'arte della guerra* and *Mandragola,* all his works were published posthumously; during his lifetime the principal works circulated in MSS among friends.

Thought. In 1531 and 1532 the printers Baldi at Rome and Giusti at Florence published *Il Principe* and the *I Discorsi* respectively, the two basic texts containing the political thought of Machiavelli, "the first theorist on the interests of the state," as Meinecke calls him, and the founder of modern political science. Machiavelli establishes this science in its own autonomous domain, free from all moral implications and religious influence. His method relies upon historical and empirical observation of political events, either those he is familiar with from contemporary Europe or stories drawn from the works of the ancients. From these events he attempts to derive universal scientific observations about politics. He thus reduces politics to a series of technical problems, to the essential theory of power that is obedient to certain perennial laws that either ensures failure or success in the exercise of power. This is the originality of Machiavelli's concept of politics. Even if it has its limits by what it excludes (all moral and religious implication) and what it includes, politics is regarded as the body of practical rules and immutable laws to be applied coldly to obtain or preserve power, for affirming one's own will to power and for achieving success, and all this "technically" and "scientifically."

Corruption of Nature. Human nature has always been and is, immutably, corrupt and turned toward evil, Machiavelli affirms, in accordance with a Christian tradition of original sin. Man is ruthless in seeking what he regards as useful to him, but is never satisfied. He abandons himself blindly to the most insane passions, to the lust for riches, pleasures, power, and success. He follows the blind determinism of his natural instinct (and this permits us to make use of "the experience of the ancients" for understanding modern affairs and for providing for the present and, in some measure, even for the future), which is turned not only to cupidity, but also to meanness, cowardice, duplicity, etc. Christianity has not redeemed humanity; on the contrary, it has promoted man's decline by its glorification of humble and contemplative men: "And if our religion demands that you have fortitude in you, it means that you should be able to suffer bravely rather than to do anything bravely. This manner of life, therefore, seems to have made the world weak and to have given it only as a prey to wicked men. . ." (*Discorsi* 2.2).

On the one hand, the remedy lies in the few good men—exceptions to the rule of human wickedness—who think of the common good and not of themselves alone; on the other, it lies in the state, understood as a power of dominion and coercion. This power should be employed in such a way that the ruler takes no thought about the means he uses to enforce order. Machiavelli understands order as a superior end that justifies the use of political power. In this way of thinking, religion is only an instrument of rule, a means to an end. It is not privileged among all means at a prince's disposal, but only one means on the level of all the others.

Fortune and virtù. Thus the effective prince imposes his will over the human passions so that he can curb and govern them. Machiavelli defines ''fortune'' as all that is unforeseeable and irrational, all that is chaotic and contingent in human experience. By contrast those things that fall within the sphere of human action—whatever is knowable, foreseeable and controllable—is what he identifies as *virtù. Virtù,* he also defines as vigor and physical health, heroic fortitude of spirit, astuteness and ability, the capability of foreseeing events and of controlling them through one's will. These allow the prince to establish order in chaos and in evil. Fortune ''shows its power where there is no ordered *virtù* to resist it and it turns its force where it knows that no embankments or barriers have been made to hold it'' (*Principe* ch. 25).

Decline of States. But order is always partial and temporal; as soon as the master loosens his grip, the chaos of the passions reassumes its sovereignty. The iron and ruthless will of the statesman can restrain, control, and build an order by fear and force, but it cannot educate and redeem corrupt humanity. States, created by the *virtù* of a few men and by the purpose of *virtù* itself, are a temporal triumph of superior wills over the chaos of the unbridled mass. However, because of the irreparable corruption of man, states are destined to decline and decay. Hence the necessity for other dominating wills to put the blind forces of fortune back into their proper channels—and to this end any and every means is legitimate—and thus bring them under the laws of order. The study of the means best adapted to achieve this purpose is precisely what constitutes ''technical politics,'' or the totality of the maxims that the statesman ought to follow and that, basically for Machiavelli, are suggested by the practice of his age and of all ages. It would be better if men were good, but this is not possible. Therefore, ''men are so far removed in how they live from how they ought to live, that he who abandons what is done for what ought to be done will soon learn to bring about his own ruin rather than his preservation. Accordingly, a man who wishes to make a profession of goodness in all respects, invites his own ruin since he is among so many who are not good'' (*Principe* ch. 15).

It has been said that to understand fully the Machiavellian principle that every means is legitimate to secure order, it is necessary to keep in mind the Italy of Machiavelli's time, with its attendant strains caused by political disunity and foreign invasion. It must also be remembered that Machiavelli wrote *The Prince* in part to rehabilitate his fortunes with the MEDICI following the collapse of Florence's republic. Scholars have long debated whether *Il principe* represents an ironic document, one in which Machiavelli subsumed his republicanism to curry favor with the Medici. Whatever the source of the ideas in Machiavelli's *Principe*—whether they derived from his deep concern about the course of Italian politics or from his exile from the center of power in Florence—the ideas of that work have long been seen as one of the most troubling products of early-modern European political theory. When they are viewed from one direction, Machiavelli helped to establish the modern science of political theory, a science that emphasized observed political behavior and eventually natural law. Yet seen from another, his works gave birth to a tradition of Machiavellianism in which the ends of political order and stability were to be justified with any and all means.

Bibliography: Works. A complete critical ed. and a comprehensive systematic bibliog. do not exist. *Opere,* ed. P. FANFANI et al., 6 v. (Florence 1875–77), contains the *Legazioni* and other official correspondence; *Lettere familiari,* ed. E. ALVISI (Florence 1883); ed. G. LESCA (Florence 1929); ed. F. GAETA (Milan 1961); *Tutte le opere storiche e letteraria,* ed. G. MAZZONI and M. CASELLA (Florence 1928); *Opere,* ed. A. PANELLA, 2 v. (Milan 1939); *Tutte le opere,* ed. F. FLORA and C. CORDIE (Milan 1949–); *Opere,* ed. M. BONFANTINI (Milan 1954); *Istorie florentine,* ed. P. CARLI, 2 v. (Florence 1927); *Dell' arte della guerra,* ed. P. PIERI (Rome 1937); *Il Principe,* ed. L. A. BURD (Oxford 1891), with full commentary; ed. M. CASELLA (Rome 1929); ed. F. CHABOD (Turin 1924; new ed. L. FIRPO 1961); *Discorses,* ed. and tr. L. J. WALKER, 2 v. (London 1950), with English tr. and full, accurate commentary. Literature. A. NORSA, *Il principio della forza nel pensiero di Niccolò Machiavelli* (Milan 1936), a bibliog. of 2,113 items. L. RUSSO, *Machiavelli* (4th ed. Bari 1957). A. H. GILBERT, *Machiavelli's Prince and Its Forerunners* (Durham, NC 1938). H. BUTTERFIELD, *The Statecraft of Machiavelli* (New York 1956). A. RENAUDET, *Machiavel* (new ed. Paris 1955). U. SPIRITO, *Machiavelli e Guicciardini* (2d ed. Rome 1945). G. SASSO, *Niccolò Machiavelli: Storia del suo pensiero politico* (Naples 1958). J. NAMER, *Machiavel* (Paris 1961). F. GILBERT, *Machiavelli and Guicciardini* (Princeton 1965). J. H. HEXTER, ''The Loom of Language and the Fabric of Imperatives: The Case of *Il Principe* and *Utopia,*'' *American Historical Review* 69.4 (1964) 945–968. P. GODMAN, *From Poliziano to Machiavelli* (Princeton 1998). J. HEXTER, *The Vision of Politics on the Eve of the Reformation* (New York 1973). J. NAJEMY, *Between Friends: Discourses of Power in the Machiavelli-Vettori Letters of 1513–1515* (Princeton 1993). J. G. A. POCOCK, *The Machiavellian Movement* (Princeton 1975). R. RIDOLFI, *Vita di Niccoli Machiavelli* (Florence 1969). Q. SKINNER, *Machiavelli* (New York 1981).

[M. F. SCIACCA]

MACKILLOP, MARY HELEN, BL.

Known in religion as Mary of the Cross, born Maria Ellen MacKillop, educator, foundress of the Josephite Sisters; b. Jan. 15, 1842, Fitzroy (near Melbourne), Australia; d. Aug. 8, 1909, Sydney, New South Wales.

The daughter of Highland Scottish immigrants, she was working as a governess when in 1861 she met Father Julian Tenison Woods, a missionary from England and one of the chief architects of Australia's Catholic education system. He inspired her to dedicate her life to teaching the children of the bush. In 1865, Mary and two younger sisters began teaching in an abandoned stable at Penola, South Australia.

Moving to Adelaide, Mary MacKillop and Father Woods founded the Institute of the Sisters of St. Joseph of the Sacred Heart. Together with her companions Mary pronounced the vows of religion Aug. 15, 1866, and took the name of Mother Mary of the Cross. Her efforts to adapt the new community to a colonial environment encountered a decade of lay and clerical misunderstanding and opposition. In 1871, the bishop of Adelaide excommunicated her and disbanded the sisterhood. A Jewish person gave the homeless nuns a house rent free, until their restoration in 1872.

In 1874, Mother Mary traveled to Rome and submitted her rule to Pope Pius IX. Rome's eventual decision was a compromise but the foundress won her principal point of central government for the sisters throughout the Australian colonies. She established 160 Josephite houses and 117 schools attended by more than 12,000 children. When she died after a long illness, her congregation numbered about 1,000.

Her tomb is in a vault donated by a Presbyterian woman in front of Our Lady's Altar in the Mount Street Josephite Chapel, North Sydney. At her beatification by John Paul II Jan. 19, 1995, at Randwick Racecourse in Sydney, she became the first Australian beata. Patron of Australia.

Feast: Aug. 7.

Bibliography: M. MACKILLOP, *Julian Tension Woods, A Life* (Blackburn, Vic., 1997). Australian Catholic Truth Society, *Mother Mary of the Cross: Her Personality, Her Spirit* (Melbourne 1973). C. DUNNE, *Mary MacKillop: No Plaster Saint* (Sydney 1994). P. GARDINER, *Mary MacKillop: An Extraordinary Australian* (Newtown, N.S.W. 1993). A. HENDERSON, *Mary MacKillop's Sisters: A Life Unveiled* (Sydney 1997). D. LYNE, *Mary MacKillop, Spirituality and Charisma* (Sydney 1983). W. MODYSTACK, *Mary MacKillop: A Woman Before Her Time* (New York 1982). F. O'BRIEN, *Called to Love* (Homebush, NSW 1993). L. O'BRIEN, *Mary MacKillop Unveiled* (N. Blackburn, Vic. 1994). L. STAUB-STAUDE, *The Anatomy of A Saint* (Naracoorte, S. Aust. 1993). O. THORPE, *Mary MacKillop,* (3d ed. Sydney 1994).

[J. G. MURTAGH/EDS.]

Bl. Mary Helen MacKillop. (Catholic News Service)

MACLOVIUS, ST.

Bishop also known as Machutus and Malo; b. Gwent, in southern Wales; d. near Saintes, France, *c.* 640. Educated in the monastery of Llancarfan, Maclovius became a monk there despite his parents' resistance. After ordination he wandered from Britain to Brittany, where he established several monasteries, among them Aleth (Saint-Malo), and reportedly visited COLUMBAN at LUXEUIL. Legend also connects him with the fabulous voyages of St. BRENDAN. Bili, a deacon of Aleth and author of two of the several extant medieval lives of Maclovius, relates that he was consecrated bishop by an archbishop of Tours. Toward the end of his life he lived as a hermit near Saintes.

Feast: Nov. 15.

Bibliography: *Bibliotheca hagiographica latina antiquae et mediae aetatis,* 2 v. (Brussels 1898–1901; suppl. 1911) 2:5116–24. *Deux vies inédites de S. Malo,* ed. F. PLAINE and A. DE LA BORDERIE (Rennes 1884). L. DUCHESNE, ''La Vie de Saint Malo: Étude critique,'' *Revue Celtique* 11 (1890) 1–22. F. DUINE, *Memento des sources hagiographiques de l'histoire de Bretagne* (Rennes 1918). H. LECLERCQ, *Dictionnaire d'archéologie chrétienne et de liturgie,* ed. F. CABROL, H. LECLERCQ, and H. I. MARROU, 15 v. (Paris 1907–53) 10.1:1293–1318. A. M. ZIMMERMANN, *Kalendarium Benedictinum: Die Heiligen und Seligen des Benediktinerorderns und seiner Zweige,* 4 v. (Metten 1933–38) 3:310–311. BILI (9th cent.), *The Old English Life of Machutus,* ed. D. YERKES (Toronto 1984); with Fr. tr. G. LE DUC (Rennes 1979).

[R. T. MEYER]

MACMAHON, EVER

Irish bishop and national leader; b. district of Farney, County Monaghan, 1600; executed Sept. 17, 1650, Enniskillen, County Fermanagh. Son of Loughlin MacMahon, he was a scion of the ruling family of the Gaelic territory of Oriel. He studied at the Irish College at Douai, and at the Pastoral College in Louvain where he obtained his D.D. degree and was appointed superior. In 1633 he returned to Ireland as vicar apostolic of his native Clogher. On the Continent he had engaged in plots to secure aid for an Irish uprising, and later was active in enlisting troops in Ireland for Owen Roe O'Neill's regiment of the Spanish army in Flanders. After his appointment to the See of Down and Connor in 1641, he was involved in insurrection and was one of Ulster's representatives on the Supreme Council of the Confederation of Kilkenny and counselor of Owen Roe O'Neill. He opposed the Ormond Peace of 1646, since he rejected any settlement with Charles I's representative that did not provide religious freedom and the restoration of confiscated Catholic property. On O'Neill's death he was in 1650 chosen to lead the Ulster army, and was defeated at Scariffhollis on June 21 of that year. Wounded and captured in a skirmish with Cromwellian troops, he was executed and his head was impaled outside Enniskillen Castle.

Bibliography: J. T. GILBERT, ed., *Contemporary History of Affairs in Ireland from 1641 to 1652* (Dublin 1879–80). P. F. MORAN, *Spicilegium Ossoriense* (Dublin 1874–84). S. P. Ó MÓRDHA "Ever MacMahon," *Studies* 40 (1951) 323–333; 41 (1952) 91–98. *Commentarius Rinuccinianus,* ed. J. KAVANAGH, 6 v. (Dublin 1932–49).

[S. P. Ó MÓRDHA]

MACNUTT, FRANCIS AUGUSTUS

Papal courtier, author; b. Richmond, Ind., February 15, 1863; d. Bressanone, Italy, December 30, 1927. He was the son of Joseph and Laetitia Jane (Scott) MacNutt, well-to-do Episcopalians. MacNutt attended Philips Academy, Exeter, N.H. (1878–80), and Harvard University Law School (1880–81), spending also many months in foreign travel and the study of languages. He was received into the Catholic Church in Rome on March 22, 1883, and first began ecclesiastical training as an associate of the "Priests of Expiation," an abortive religious society projected by Rev. Kenelm Vaughan of England. While a student (1887–89) of the Pontifical Academy of Noble Ecclesiastics, Rome, he concluded that he was not called to the priesthood and secured appointments as first secretary of the U.S. legations at Constantinople (1890–92) and Madrid (1892–93). In 1898 he married Margaret van Cortlandt Ogden of New York and took up residence in Rome. Leo XIII, who in 1895 had made MacNutt an honorary papal chamberlain "of cape and sword," assigned him to active service in the papal court. He was the first American to hold such a post. In 1904 Pius X named him onc of four ranking chamberlains. However, since he had become the object of a defamatory campaign in certain lay circles, MacNutt decided to resign his Vatican post in 1905. He succeeded in vindicating his good name, but declined invitations to reassume his court functions. Settling in Schloss Ratzötz, his Tyrolese home near Bressanone, he spent the rest of his life in social activities and writing. Of his seven books, the most important were: *Letters of Cortes* (1908); *De orbe novo, The Eight Decades d'Anghera* (1912); and *Bartholomew de las Casas* (1909). His posthumously published memoirs, *A Papal Chamberlain* (1936), are the recollections of a U.S. expatriate who found himself at home in the courtly society of a bygone era.

[R. F. MCNAMARA]

MACPHERSON, JOHN

Pioneer of Catholic periodical literature in Scotland; b. Tomintoul, Banffshire, August 29, 1801; d. Dundee, July 16, 1871. He was born of crofter parents in one of the continuously Catholic districts of Scotland. He studied for the priesthood at Aquhorties College, Aberdeenshire, the seminary of the Lowland Vicariate of Scotland, and at Paris, where he was ordained in 1827. Returning to Scotland that year, he was appointed a professor at Aquhorties. On the College's small handpress he produced (1828) the first issue of *The Catholic Directory for the Clergy and Laity in Scotland.* Macpherson was not, of course, the first to use the printing press on behalf of the Church in Scotland: throughout the 16th, 17th, and 18th centuries there had been a small, but steady and interesting, production of polemical works. Macpherson, however, produced the first periodical devoted to the service of the Church.

During its first three years, this 40-page publication provided the liturgical calendar for Mass and the Divine Office. In 1831, it grew to 84 pages, printed by John Johnstone of Edinburgh, and in addition to the liturgical calendar, provided information about Catholic churches and clergy in Scotland. From letters in the Scottish Catholic archives it is evident that in the mid-19th century, the *Directory* was being used in such faraway places as Tasmania and the West Indies.

Macpherson served the Church in Scotland in many capacities: he built St. Andrew's church in Dundee, where he was pastor from 1832 to 1847; he was president of St. Mary's College, Blairs, from 1847 to 1858; from 1858, when he received the honorary degree of Doctor of Divinity from Pope Pius IX, until his death, he was vicar-general to two bishops. He continued until the last year of his life to edit the *Directory,* which is the only publication dealing with the Catholic Church in Scotland that has appeared uninterruptedly since 1828. Its rich historical, biographical, and statistical material makes it an indispensable source for the study of the Catholic Church in modern Scotland.

[D. MCROBERTS]

MACRINA, SS.

Macrina the Elder; d. Neocaesarea, *c.* 340. Grandmother of BASIL and his holy siblings, and disciple of GREGORY THAUMATURGUS, Macrina was a Christian witness and exile during DIOCLETIAN's persecution. She had a great influence on the early education of her grandson Basil.

Feast: Jan. 14.

Macrina the Younger, granddaughter of Macrina, the Elder, superior of one of the earliest communities of women ascetics; b. Neocaesarea, Cappadocia, *c.* 330; d. by the river Iris in Pontus, December of 379 or 380. Macrina was the eldest daughter of SS. Basil and Emmelia, and sister of SS. Basil the Great, GREGORY OF NYSSA, and Peter of Sebastea (d. *c.* 391). She had a great influence in this remarkable family, chiefly with her brothers Basil and Peter, both of whom she persuaded to a religious vocation. She rejected a proposed marriage and simultaneously with Basil chose the ascetic life, becoming locally renowned as a nun and spiritual directress. Returning from a synod of Antioch (379), Gregory of Nyssa visited her and wrote her life at the request of the monk Olympus. An unusual number of manuscripts of this biography coming from the environs of Pontus suggest a strong local cult after 379, which spread through the East in the Greek, Egyptian, Syrian, and Arab Churches. She is mentioned or elaborately described in numerous calendars and menologies. Her cult in the West is late since the life was not translated into Latin until the 16th century.

Gregory's *Life of Macrina* is a remarkable piece of early hagiography that provides information on contemporary monastic and liturgical life and furnishes biographical details concerning her brothers. Gregory's *Macrinia,* or dialogue ''On the Soul and Resurrection,'' purports to be a record of deathbed conversation. She is the principal interlocutor and is described as ''the Teacher.'' While the theological views are undoubtedly Gregory's, it is revealing that he can represent her with verisimilitude as so learned.

Feast: July 19.

Bibliography: GREGORY OF NYSSA, ''Vita S. Macrinae,'' ed. V. W. CALLAHAN, in *Gregorii Nysseni Opera,* ed. W. JAEGER (Leiden 1960–) 8.1:347–414; *The Life of St. Macrina,* tr. and ed. W. K. L. CLARKE (London 1916); *Vie de sainte Macrine*, Fr. tr. P. MARAVAL (Paris 1971). J. QUASTEN, *Patrology,* 3 v. (Westminister, MD 1950–) 3:261. *Acta Sanctorum* July 4:589–604. J. DANIÉLOU, ''La Résurrection des corps chez Grégoire de Nysse,'' *Vigiliae christianae* 7 (1953) 154–170. F. J. DÖLGER, ''Das Anhängekreuzchen der hl. Makrina,'' *Antike und Christentum* 3 (1932) 81–116. R. ALBRECHT, *Das Leben der heiligen Makrina auf dem Hintergrund der Thekla-Traditionen* (Göttingen 1986). J. PELIKAN, *Christianity and Classical Culture: The Metamorphosis of Natural Theology in the Christian Encounter with Hellenism* (New Haven 1993). F. DÍAZ, *La hermandad más santa y fina: Basilio el Magno y Macrina*, ed. M. DEL MAR VENEGAS (Madrid 1994).

[D. MEEHAN]

MACROBIUS

Ambrosius Theodosius, Latin writer, born toward the end of the 4th century, probably in Africa. It is unlikely that he was a Christian, since his works are entirely pagan. All his theology derives from cult of the sun. His treatise comparing Greek and Latin verbs, dedicated to SYMMACHUS, is known by excerpts in the works of a certain John, perhaps Scotus Erigena. His commentary in two books on Cicero's *Dream of Scipio* is an encyclopedia written for his son Eustachius. In it he shows little respect for Aristotle and defends Platonism, which was for him a religion gleaned probably from Porphyry. The work, which was long popular as a source for data on many topics, accepts the Stoic division of moral, physical, and rational philosophy. Macrobius's most important work, the *Saturnalia* (seven books), was written to impart antiquarian lore to his son. It imitates the literary device of Plato's *Banquet* and is eclectic in its philosophical outlook. There are lacunae in the work. Along with Calcidius and Martianus Capella, the Saturnalia and the Commentary on the Dream of Scipio were used as source books in the Middle Ages and early Renaissance. They were known to Bernard of Tours and to Bede. Macrobius borrows frequently from other encyclopedists, especially from Aulus Gellius and Plutarch, often without acknowledgment. The subject matter and presentation illustrate pagan culture at the beginning of the 5th century. The style is simple, the exposition of Neoplatonic themes oversimplified. The exaggerated praise of Vergil as an orator and a philosopher was responsible for many of the interpretations of Vergil throughout the Middle Ages and early Renaissance.

Bibliography: Macrobius. *Opera,* ed. J. WILLIS, 2 v. (Leipzig 1963); *Commentary on the Dream of Scipio,* tr. W. STAHL (New York 1952); *Saturnalia,* tr. H. BORNECQUE and F. RICHARD, 2 v. (Paris 1937–38). H. KEIL, ed. *Grammatici Latini,* 7 v. (Leipzig 1857–80) v.5. P. COURCELLE, *Les Lettres grecques en Occident, de Macrobe à Cassiodore* (new ed. Paris 1948). W. STAHL, *Isis* 50 (1959) 95–124, F. EYSSENHARDT, ed., *Macrobius* (Leipzig 1893).

[J. R. O'DONNELL]

MACRORY, JOSEPH

Cardinal, Scripture scholar; b. Ballygawley, Tyrone County, Ireland, March 19,1861; d. Armagh, Ireland, October 13, 1945. After his education at Armagh and Maynooth, he was ordained in 1885. He was the first president of Dungannon Academy (1886–87), professor of moral theology and Sacred Scripture at Olton Seminary, England (1887–89), professor of Oriental languages at Maynooth (1889–1905), professor of NT exegesis at Maynooth (1905–15), and vice president of that college (1912–15). He was appointed bishop of Down and Connor in 1915, consecrated archbishop of Armagh in 1928, and raised to the cardinalate in 1929. One of the founders of the *Irish Theological Quarterly* (1906—), he served for a time as its coeditor. Besides his many articles for periodicals, he published commentaries on St. John's Gospel (1897) and the Epistles to the Corinthians (1915). These practical works went through several editions.

Bibliography: J. J. TWOMEY, *Lexikon für Theologie und Kirche* 2 6:1262. J. J. MURPHY, *The People's Primate* (Dublin 1945) 10.

[K. O'SULLIVAN]

MADAGASCAR, THE CATHOLIC CHURCH IN

The fourth largest island in the world (excluding Australia), the Republic of Madagascar is located in the Indian Ocean, 260 miles east of MOZAMBIQUE in Africa. The terrain alternates between plateaus and mountains, rising to the volcanic Ankaratra range near the island's center, thence to the highest point, the Tsaratanana Massif, in the north. Many streams cross the forested inland terrain, while Madagascar's coastline is dotted by numerous small islands. Natural resources include graphite, mica, chromite, salt and bauxite, while agricultural products consist of rice, sweet potatoes, tobacco, coffee, sugar and cloves. The climate, which is tropical near the eastern coast, is characterized by cyclones and heavy rains.

Formerly known as the Malagasy Republic, Madagascar was formed by federated kingdoms and remained under Portuguese domination until the 17th century, when it was formed into a native empire. During the 19th century, English and French interests battled for the region. Three years after the succession of the last native monarch, Queen Rànavàlona III, in 1883, French forces laid claim to certain coastal areas, establishing a protectorate in 1890 and annexing the island and its dependencies as a colony in 1896. Madagascar became an autonomous member of the French Community in 1958 and an independent republic in 1960.

Capital: Antananarivo.
Size: 226,657 sq. miles.
Population: 15,506,470 in 2000.
Languages: Malagasy, French.
Religions: 4,460,000 Catholics (29%), 1,250,490 Muslims (8%), 5,960,500 Protestants (38%), 3,835,480 follow indigenous beliefs.

History. Detached from Africa as a result of continental drift, the island of Madagascar was originally inhabited by Indo-Melanesian and Malay peoples, while Bantu, Arab, Indian and Chinese immigrated to the island between the 10th and 14th centuries. Madagascar was discovered by Portuguese Captain Diego Dias in 1500 and was named by Marco Polo after the island kingdom of Mogadisho he described but never visited. From 1500 until mid-18th century Catholic missionaries, especially the Vincentians from 1648, made futile attempts at evangelization, their efforts disrupted due to pirate activity along the coast. Bishop Henri de Solages, the prefect apostolic, labored for a few years with little success until his death in 1832. Despite continued hostility from the monarch of the region's most populous and powerful tribe, the Hova, who was influenced by English Protestants, the Jesuits arrived in 1845 and penetrated to the capital city of Antananarive. In 1850 the Jesuits were entrusted with the Prefecture Apostolic of Madagascar, which became a vicariate apostolic in 1885, after the region had been proclaimed a French colony.

During her reign, Queen Rànavàlona I actively persecuted Catholics and other Christians, expelling foreign missionaries and putting many Catholics to death. Her own death in 1861 brought the Protestant King Rànavàlona II to power and finally permitted open evangelization throughout the island. In 1885 and 1895 wars between native tribes and French troops interrupted the mission, but otherwise evangelization progressed without interruption, missionaries often attempting to assimilate facets of native religions into the Catholic faith to make it more understandable. In 1896, a year before the monarchy of Rànavàlona II was abolished, the southern part of

Archdioceses	Suffragans
Antananarivo	Ambatondrazaka, Antsirabé, Miarinarivo, Tsiroanomandidy
Antsiranana	Ambanja, Fenoarivo Atsinanana, Mahajanga, Port-Bergé, Toamasina
Fianarantsoa	Ambositra, Farafangana, Ihosy, Mananjary, Morombe, Morondava, Tôlagnaro, Toliara.

the island was detached and confided to the Vincentians as the Vicariate of Southern Madagascar. The Vicariate of Northern Madagascar, created in 1898, was given to the Holy Ghost Fathers. Other religious active in the region included Trinitarians, La Salette Missionaries, Montfort Fathers, Capuchins, Holy Family Fathers and Assumptionists.

By 1900 there were nearly 100,000 Catholics living on the island. After World War I and the reorganization of the island's political administration, more vicariates were created and entrusted to various religious orders. The first nine Malagasy priests were ordained in 1925, and the first native bishop was consecrated in 1936. A rebellion that broke out in 1947 in response to Madagascar's entry into the French Union had little effect on the missions, and agitation for independence likewise did little to stir up anti-Catholic sentiments. The hierarchy was established in 1955, with Antananarive as the sole metropolitan see. A reorganization in 1958 divided the island into three ecclesiastical provinces, with the capital city entrusted to the Jesuits. After the region gained political independence from France on June 26, 1960, and became the Malagasy Republic, a special apostolic delegation was created for Madagascar and the islands of Réunion and Mauritius. The region was renamed Madagascar in 1975.

Evangelization on the island continued to be successful throughout the 20th century, and men and women found their vocation in the Church in increasing numbers. During the second half of the 20th century, the island was beset by economic problems that resulted in several changes in governments and a decaying infrastructure. In the 1980s and 1990s the Church added its voice to those advocating that President Didier Ratsiraka focus his attention on social programs. Although Ratsiraka abolished one-party rule in 1990 and established free elections two years later, the political climate continued to be volatile; a period of rioting resulted in the abolishment of the country's national assembly and a new constitution in August of 1992 that protected freedom of religion. In

February of 1997 Ratsiraka resumed the presidency, promising to continue efforts to stabilize Madagascar's sagging economy. In April of 2000 Ratsiraka responded to a call by Church leaders and released 3,000 Madagascar prisoners—many of them minors or men and women over age 65—as a response to Pope John Paul II's plea that the plight of prisoners be considered during Jubilee 2000. The country's bishops praised the president's effort as a ''significant gesture of reconciliation for the Holy Year.''

By 2000 there were 379 secular and 581 religious priests, 392 brothers and 3,363 sisters on Madagascar, a preponderance of whom were native Malagasy. The Catholic schools located throughout the island included 2,209 Primary and 316 secondary schools, while religious also administered orphanages and other humanitarian concerns. The Benedictines and the Cisterians each had a monastery. In addition to a strong Catholic press, the lay movement Catholic Action remained involved in its grass-roots humanitarian efforts. The influence of the Church was most marked in the southern part of the island, and it continued to wield political influence due to its strong humanitarian presence and its status as one of Madagascar's largest landowners. The Protestant population on Madagascar consisted of members of the Church of Jesus Christ, located in Fianarantsoa North.

Bibliography: H. DESCHAMPS, *Histoire de Madagascar* (Paris 1960). K. S. LATOURETTE, *A History of the Expansion of Christianity,* 7 v. (New York 1937–45) v.5. *Le missioni cattoliche: Storia, geographia, statistica* (Rome 1950) 196–202. A. BOUDOU, *Les Jésuites à Madagascar au XIXe siècle,* 2 v. (Paris 1943). *Bilan du Monde,* 2:574–58 I. *Annuario Pontificio* has statistics on all dioceses.

[J. BOUCHAUD/EDS.]

MADAURA, MARTYRS OF

Martyrs of Madaura is a title given to four African martyrs grouped together in the letter written *c.* 390 by Maximus of Madaura to St. AUGUSTINE, in which Maximus complained that Miggin is preferred by Christians to Jupiter; Sanam, to the four goddesses; and the archimartyr Namphano, to all the immortal gods. A fourth, Lucitas, is said to enjoy no less cult. In reply to this letter, Augustine stated that the names are Punic indeed, but that pagans also admit this type of name. He contents himself with dwelling on the name of Namphano, which he explains means a person whose coming brings good luck. Had these four persons been known as Donatist or Circumcellion martyrs, as some have claimed, Augustine certainly would have pointed this out to the pagan Maximus, who had criticized the Christians in his letter. That he did not do so indicates that the four martyrs were venerated by the Catholic Church in Africa, even though the Donatists may have accepted them, according to their custom of retaining what the Catholics had practiced before the outbreak of the Donatist schism.

The title archimartyr, given by Maximus to the slave Namphano, may mean that he was the protomartyr of Africa or Numidia. More probably it proves that he enjoyed a great veneration. The names of both Namphano and Miggin are frequent in African inscriptions; those of Sanam and Lucitas less so. The name Martyrs of Madaura comes from the Roman MARTYROLOGY, where Baronius placed them for July 4. In the MARTYROLOGY OF ST. JEROME, on June 15 the name of Miggin is cited along with Saianus and Iovianus. By the error of a copyist, this entry is found, in garbled form, also on May 16 in the same work, which refers to Namphano on December 18. Their existence and early veneration seem assured, though the year of their martyrdom, usually placed in 180, cannot be substantiated.

Bibliography: A. GOLDBACHER, ed., *Epistulae S. Augustini 16–17* [*Corpus scriptorum ecclesiasticorum latinorum* 34.1; Vienna 1895] 37–44; *Acta Sanctorum* July 2:6. *Martyrologium Hieronymianum,* ed. H. DELEHAYE (*ibid.* Nov.2:2; 1931) 257, 320, 652. P. MONCEAUX, *Histoire littéraire de l'Afrique chrétienne,* 7 v. (repr. Brussels 1963) 1:42–43. W. H. C. FREND, *The Donatist Church* (London 1952). J. ZEILLER, in A. FLICHE and V. MARTIN, eds., *Histoire de l'église depuis les origines jusqu'à nos jours* (Paris 1935–) 1:318. J. H. BAXTER, ''The Martyrs of Madaura, A.D. 180'' *Journal of Theological Studies* (1923–24) 21–37. J. QUASTEN, *Patrology,* 3 v. (Westminster, Md., 1950–53) 1:178–179, confuses these martyrs with the martyrs Scillitani.

[J. J. GAVIGAN]

MADELEVA, MARY, SISTER

Poet and educator; b. Mary Evaline Wolff, Cumberland, Wisconsin, May 24, 1887; d. Boston, Massachusetts, July 25, 1964. She attended public elementary and high schools in Cumberland (1893–1904) and spent one year at the University of Wisconsin, before entering St. Mary's College, Notre Dame, Indiana, in1906. She received her A.B. in 1909, a year after joining the Congregation of the Holy Cross. After a period of teaching at St. Mary's, she took her M.A. (University of Notre Dame, 1918) and taught at Sacred Heart Academy, Ogden, Utah, until she went to the University of California at Berkeley (1922–25). There she was awarded a Ph.D. in English. She was president of St. Mary-of-the-Wasatch (Salt Lake City, Utah) from 1926 to 1933, spent a year at Oxford University, England, and in travel in Europe and the Holy Land (1933–34), and was appointed president of St. Mary's College (1934), holding that post until 1961.

Sister Madeleva was the first of the U.S. nun-poets to achieve national and international fame. Her 12 volumes of verse, for all their modernity, reveal her wide knowledge of medieval culture and manifest, in their deliberately colloquial diction, a kinship with the religious poems of John Donne, one of her favorite authors. Her interest in the Middle Ages led to studies on Chaucer, the *Pearl,* Julian of Norwich, and Hilda of Whitby. Her prose works appeared in some 36 publications and covered a wide variety of topics—the familiar essay, poetic composition, 19th century poetry, and many authors.

Sister Madeleva's influence on education was stimulating and widespread, through membership in educational associations, lecturing, and writing. Her vision was evident in the establishment at St. Mary's of the first graduate program in sacred doctrine for women and the interdepartmental major in Christian culture; she helped begin the SISTER FORMATION MOVEMENT. Her published works include *Chaucer's Nuns and Other Essays* (1925), *Pearl: A Study in Spiritual Dryness* (1925), *A Lost Language and Other Essays* (1951), *My First Seventy Years* (1959), *The Four Last Things: Collected Poems* (1959), and *Conversations with Cassandra* (1961). The whole of Sister Madeleva's work and notes are currently kept at both St. Mary's College Archives and at the Holy Cross Sisters Provincial Archives in Notre Dame, Indiana.

Bibliography: K KENNELLY, "Wolff, Sister Madeleva (Mary Evaline)," *Notable American Women: Modern Period,* A–Z (Cambridge 1980). M. E. KLEIN, *Sister M. Madeleva Wolff, C.S.C., Saint Mary's College, Notre Dame, Indiana: A Study in Presidential Leadership 1934–1961* (Ph.D. diss., Kent State University, 1983).

[M. J. RAUH]

Sister Mary Madeleva.

MADRUZZO

The Madruzzo is an illustrious family of Trent, whose recorded history can be traced to 1155. Of note are the four bishops who occupied the See of Trent from 1539 to 1658 without interruption.

Cristoforo; b. Trent, July 5, 1512; d. Tivoli, July 5, 1578. After studies at Padua and Bologna he began his rapid rise in the hierarchy, becoming a canon of Trent (1529), Salzburg (1536), Brixen (1537), and then prince bishop of Trent (1539). In 1542 he was ordained a priest and consecrated a bishop, and in the next year, named administrator to the See of Brixen and created a cardinal by Paul III. He resigned the See of Trent in 1567 to become in turn cardinal bishop of Sabina, Palestrina, and Porto. A man of ability and conviction, though no thorough theologian, Cristoforo was entrusted with several diplomatic missions, including his appointment as governor of Milan by Philip II of Spain (1556) and the legation of the Marches by Pius IV (1561). His friendship with Emperor Charles V and the Emperor's younger brother and successor, Ferdinand, suited his role as mediator between the Hapsburgs and the Curia. His most notable achievement centered on the first convocation of the Council of Trent (1545–47), where as bishop he was responsible for the details that would assure its tranquil progress. In the Council he insisted with success that Church reform be discussed in each session together with the theological debates, being hopeful that such measures would win the Protestants. He strongly opposed the Council's transfer to Bologna. His friendship with cardinals Jacopo SADOLETO, Giovanni MORONE, Reginald POLE, and Ercole Gonzaga place him justly among the forces of Catholic reform, although his own career is marred by pluralism. He governed his diocese well and wrote a constitution of reform for his clergy.

Lodovico; b. Trent, 1532; d. Rome, April 2, 1600. Following ecclesiastical studies at Louvain and Paris, he became ambassador to France and, in 1561, was created a cardinal. Nephew of Cristoforo, he succeeded to the See of Trent at his uncle's resignation in 1567. As prince bishop, he participated in the third session of the Council of Trent (1562–63), where he joined the party advocating the chalice for the Bohemians, and the obligation of residency for bishops. He proved his diplomatic skill as papal legate to the imperial court (1581), the Diet of Augsburg (1582), and the Diet of Regensburg (1594).

Carlo Gaudenzio; b. Issogne in the valley of Aosta, 1562; d. Rome, Aug. 4, 1629. The course of his education brought him to Munich, Ingolstadt, and ultimately, to Pavia where he received his laureate in theology in 1595, He was named titular bishop of Smyrna, then coadjutor

Cardinal Cristoforo Madruzzo, painting by Titian.

at Trent to his uncle Lodovico, whom he succeeded (1600). He was created a cardinal in 1604. During his episcopate he erected a seminary, and became an ardent opponent of trials for WITCHCRAFT. As legate to the Diet of Regensburg (1613), he spoke against the confessional policy toward Protestants that had been advocated by the powerful Cardinal Melchior KLESL.

Carlo Emanuele; b. Trent, 1599; d. there, Dec. 15, 1658. His studies at Monaco, Ingolstadt, and Perugia were followed with his appointment (age 21) as coadjutor to his uncle Carlo Gaudenzio at Trent. He succeeded to the see in 1629. In order to prevent the extinction of the Madruzzo line, he made long and futile efforts to secure the legitimatization of his children by his mistress, Claudia Particella. This scandal marred his episcopate and gave the occasion for elaborate legends.

Bibliography: A. GALANTE, *La corrispondenza del cardinale Cristoforo Madruzzo* (Innsbruck 1911). Jedia Trent v. 1, 2. T. GAR, *Cenni biografici di 4 vescovi di Trento* (Trent 1857). A. POSCH, *Lexikon für Theologie und Kirche*, ed. J. HOFER and K. RAHNER, 10v. (2d, new ed. Freiburg 1957–65) 6:1265–67. M. MORSELETTO, A. MERCATI and A. PELZER, *Dizionario ecclesiastico* (Turin 1954–58) 2:771, K. D. SCHIMDT, *Die Religion in Geschichte und Gegeuwart* (Tübingen 1957–65) 5:575. G. GEROLA. *Enciclopedia Italiana di scienzi, littere ed arti* 21:854–855, bibliog.

[E. D. MCSHANE]

MAES, BONIFACE

Franciscan spiritual writer; b. Ghent, East Flanders, 1627; d. there, October 3, 1706. Maes entered the Recollect province of St. Joseph in 1647. From 1653 to 1665 he was lector of philosophy and theology; he then became guardian at Iperen (*c.* 1665–77); provincial of the Flemish province (1677–90), commissary general of the provinces of Belgium, Germany, France, and Ireland (1690–96), and then definitor general.

His writings include eight works on the spiritual life (1668–80), two on the practice of Franciscan poverty (1675), and a *Vocabularium psalterii* (1705). One of his principal ascetical treatises is *Mystieke Theologie ofte verborghen Godtsgheleertheyt* (Ghent 1668), which had at least 20 editions—nine in Flemish (the last ed. H. Mahieu, 1921); six in Latin (1st ed. Ghent 1669); three in French (Cologne 1677; Ghent 1687; Paris 1927); one in German (Innsbruck 1704); and one in English [*Mystical Theology or Spiritual Life,* tr. B. Whelan (New York 1928)]. This work excels in succinctness of style as well as in simplicity and clarity of thought. It does not treat of mystical theology in the strict sense, but contains maxims and practical rules to bring Christians by ordinary ways to contemplation and moral perfection. Its three parts consider the notion of mystical theology, the active life with its three exercises, and the contemplative life with its preparation, its three exercises, and its five effects. It treats also of the trials, austerities, and perils of contemplatives. In conformity with Franciscan spirituality, the humanity of Christ and especially the Passion occupy a central place, with emphasis on the affective element. Its principal sources are the Franciscans HENRY OF HERP and Alfonso of Madrid.

Another of his ascetical treatises is *Consolatorium piorum* (Ghent 1672), which asserts that every Christian, and especially every religious, is obliged under mortal sin to be perfect. However, Maes distinguished two degrees of perfection: the observance of the Commandments, and a perfection that consists in the continual progress in moral perfection. He taught that every Christian is obliged only to the first degree.

The importance of Maes does not lie in the originality or depth of his thought, but rather in the didactic qualities of his writings and in their charitable and even cheerful spirit.

Bibliography: S. DIRKS, *Histoire litteraire et bibliographique des Fréres Mineurs* (Antwerp 1885) 337–344. P. NAESSEN, *Franciscaansch Vlaanderen* (Mechelen 1895) 275–278. J. B. POUKENS, "De *Mystieke Theologie* van P. Bon. Maes," *Ons geestelijk erf* 2 (1928) 413–419. H. BRINK, *Theologisch Woordenboek,* v.2 (Roermond 1957) 3053.

[A. EMMEN]

MAES, CAMILLUS PAUL

Bishop; b. Courtrai, Belgium, March 13, 1846; d. Covington, Ky., May 11,1915. His parents, John Baptist and Justine (Ghyoot) Maes, had him educated at St. Amandus College in Courtrai, the seminaries in Roulers and Bruges, and the American College in Louvain. He was ordained for the Diocese of Detroit, Mich., December 19, 1868, at Mechlin, Belgium. His appointments in Michigan included pastorates at St. Peter Church in Mount Clemens (1869–71), St. Mary Church in Monroe (1871–73), and St. John the Baptist Church in Monroe (1873–80), as well as chancellorship of the Diocese of Detroit (1880–85). He was consecrated third bishop of Covington, Ky., January 25, 1885, at the Covington cathedral. During his episcopate, Maes conducted an extensive building program and erected in Covington the Cathedral of the Assumption. He labored for conversions in the Appalachian Mountain area of his diocese, issued numerous pastoral letters, and founded two diocesan papers, the *New Cathedral Chimes* and the *Christian Year*. For many years he served as secretary (1900–15) of the board of trustees of The Catholic University of America, Washington, D.C., which he had helped to establish, and as president (1897–1915) of the board of bishops for the American College at Louvain, Belgium.

In the 1890s, Maes opposed the leasing of Catholic schools to state authorities. He resisted proponents of the state's right of compulsory education, although in the related controversy over Cahenslyism (*see* CAHENSLY, PETER PAUL) he aligned himself with the Americanizers. He was among the first to advocate publication of *The Catholic Encyclopedia and the Catholic Historical Review,* and to encourage the organization of the United States Catholic Historical Society. Among his personal literary achievements was a biography of the early Kentucky missionary Rev. Charles Nerinckx. Maes was a member (1905–15) of the board of governors of the Catholic Church Extension Society and honorary president (1908–15) of the Belgian and Holland section of the society. He was the organizer of a national Eucharistic movement and became the first president (1893–1915) and protector (1894–1915) of the Priests' Eucharistic League; he was also founder and editor (1895–1903) of the league's journal, *Emmanuel;* and president of the first five Eucharistic Congresses in the U.S. Although seriously considered for promotion to rectorships at The Catholic University of America and at the American College of Louvain, as well as to the archbishoprics of Milwaukee, Wis., New Orleans, La., and Cincinnati, Ohio, Maes remained bishop of Covington until his death.

Bibliography: P. E. RYAN, *History of the Diocese of Covington, Kentucky* (Covington 1954).

[E. J. BAUMANN]

MAFFEI

Noble Italian family with two branches: that of Verona-Rome and that of Volterra. The Verona-Rome branch was especially distinguished by its scholars.

Verona-Rome Branch. Three members of the Verona-Rome Maffei were important in the Canon Regulars of the LATERAN. *Paolo,* b. Verona; d. Venice, 1480, was superior in Padua and Venice and general of the order in 1425. *Timoteo,* b. *c.* 1400; d. Rome, 1470, was prior in Fiesole, general three times, and bishop of Ragusa. He traveled to many cities on preaching tours, was a most effective speaker, and taught others how to preach. His sermons exerted a wide influence on the laity of his day. *Celso,* b. Verona, *c.* 1425; d. Verona, 1508, nephew of Timoteo, was general of his order eight times. Besides writing, he collected manuscripts and books for monasteries.

In the 16th century there were three very able Maffei in Rome. *Bernardino,* b. Bergamo, 1514; d. Rome, 1553, one of the most learned men of his day, had charge of the education of the younger Cardinal Alessandro FARNESE, whose grandfather, Pope PAUL III, appointed Bernardino bishop of Massa Marittima in 1547 and then of Chieti, creating him cardinal in 1549. Held in great esteem by the new pope, JULIUS III, Cardinal Maffei served as a member of two reforming commissions and as legate to Parma. When he died, his brother *Marcantonio,* b. Rome?, 1521; d. Rome?, 1583, succeeded him as bishop of Chieti and became its archbishop in 1566. Pope PIUS IV selected him to restore the churches of Rome. His ability was recognized also by Pope PIUS V, who put him in charge of the datary, which he administered well. The pope also appointed him a member of two commissions: one, to examine the quality and character of prospective bishops and abbots; another, to prepare written defenses against Lutheran teachings. He was created a cardinal in 1570. *Giampietro,* b. Bergamo, *c.* 1535; d. Tivoli, 1603, taught in Genoa, was secretary for the Republic of Genoa (1563–64), and then became a Jesuit. He lived in Portugal (1572–81), preparing a history of Jesuit missions in India (Florence 1588). His biography of IGNATIUS OF LOYOLA was published in 1585. Pope CLEMENT VIII valued these writings so much that he gave Giampietro rooms in the Vatican. His collected works were later published (Bergamo 1747).

Francesco Scipione, b. Verona, 1675; d. Verona, 1755, was a versatile author and scholar, most of his early writings being poems and plays. He visited contemporary poets in Milan, Genoa, and Rome (1698–99). His play *Merope,* first presented in 1713 and later translated into several languages, was an important production in the history of Italian tragedy. His comedies, however, were not successful. He then turned to history and other subjects. His four-volume *Verona illustrata* (Verona 1731–32) included information about his family, especially those members who were writers. In 1733 he went to France, where he stayed for more than three years, visiting England, Holland, Germany, and Austria before returning home in 1736. The theological discussions he heard in Paris led him to write about the early Church. In his travels he studied Roman remains, a subject that had interested him as early as 1711, when he arranged some ancient sculptures in Turin. He wrote a work on antiquities in France and another on ancient amphitheaters and founded the Museo Lapidario Maffeiano in Verona. His defense of taking interest on loans, his history of journals, and his analysis of the decline of the Venetian Republic are other examples of the wide range of his intellectual curiosity. His discovery and study of early medieval MSS in Verona led him to be one of the first to realize the essential unity of Latin writing and to recognize majuscule, minuscule, and cursive script (*see* PALEOGRAPHY, LATIN). His collected works were published in 21 volumes (Venice 1790). Honored at home and abroad, he was a member of academies in Berlin, Paris, and London and received a degree from Oxford.

Volterra Branch. The Volterra branch of the Maffei family included the scholar *Raffaele,* b. Volterra, 1451; d. Rome, 1522. Having spent some of his early years in Rome while his father taught at the university there, Raffaele returned to Volterra, where he wrote on the history of Rome and translated the *Odyssey,* the *Koran,* and the works of Xenophon into Latin. *Paolo Alessandro,* b. Volterra, 1653; d. Rome, 1716, published a biography of Pope Pius V in 1712.

Bibliography: F. VESPASIANO DA BISTICCI, *Vite di uomini illustri del secolo XV,* ed. P. D'ANCONA and E. AESCHLIMANN (Milan 1951) 152–153. Moroni 41:229–232. Pastor 17:82, 129, 168, 220. F. S. MAFFEI, *Opere drammatiche e poesie varie,* ed. A. AVENA (Bari 1928); *Epistolario, 1700–1755,* ed. C. GARIBOTTO, 2 v. (Milan 1955). G. SILVESTRI, *Un europeo del settecento, Scipione Maffei* (Treviso 1954). G. GASPERONI, *Scipione Maffei e Verona settecentesca* (Verona 1955). F. L. CROSS *The Oxford Dictionary of the Christian Church* (London 1957) 842. L. FIORE et al., *Enciclopedia cattolica* 7:1811–13. A. POSCH, *Lexikon für Theologie und Kirche,* ed. J. HOFER and K. RAHNER (Freiburg 1957–65) 6:1267–69.

[M. L. SHAY]

MAGALLANES JARA, CRISTÓBAL (CHRISTOPHER), ST.

Martyr, priest; b. July 30, 1869, La Sementera Ranch, Totatiche, Jalisco, Archdiocese of Guadalajara, Mexico; d. May 25, 1927, Colotitlán near Durango, Jalisco, Diocese of Zacatecas. Cristóbal was raised in a humble family and worked in the fields until he entered Guadalajara's seminary (1888). Following his ordination in Santa Teresa's, Guadalajara (Sept. 17, 1899), he was chaplain and assistant director of a school in Guadalajara. He was also parochial priest in his hometown for seventeen years before his death. In that capacity he organized catechetical centers and schools on the outlying ranches, constructed an irrigation system, founded an orphanage, and established garden plots to help the poor. He also evangelized the native Huicholes and propagated the Rosary. When the government closed Guadalajara's seminary, he founded one in his parish to ensure the formation of future priests. En route to celebrate Mass on a farm (May 21, 1927), he was caught in a gun battle between Cristeros and the troops of President Calles commanded by General Goñi. He was arrested, taken to the municipal prison at Totatiches, and later transferred to Colotitlán. He died with St. Agustín CALOCA. Magallanes was both beatified (Nov. 22, 1992) and canonized (May 21, 2000) by Pope John Paul II. [*see* GUADALAJARA (MEXICO), MARTYRS OF, SS.].

Feast: May 25 (Mexico).

Bibliography: J. CARDOSO, *Los mártires mexicanos* (Mexico City 1953). J. DÍAZ ESTRELLA, *El movimiento cristero: sociedad y conflicto en los Altos de Jalisco* (México, D.F. 1979). V. GARCÍA JUÁREZ, *Los cristeros* (Fresnillo, Zac. 1990).

[K. I. RABENSTEIN]

MAGDALEN ALBRICI, BL.

Augustinian; b. Como, Italy, end of 14th century; d. Brunate (near Como), May 13 or 15, 1465. When orphaned by the death of her parents, the nobly born and piously reared Magdalen entered the Convent of St. Andrew at Brunate. Admired for her many virtues, she was soon elected abbess there. Besides effecting the incorporation of the convent into the Augustinian Reform Congregation of Lombardy (*see* AUGUSTINIAN NUNS), she promoted holiness among her nuns in many special ways, notably by encouraging frequent reception of Communion. Distinguished by her great charity, humility, and trust in God, she reputedly obtained miracles for others and at times foretold the future. She was beatified on Dec. 10, 1907.

Feast: May 13, 15, or 21.

Bibliography: *Acta Sanctorum* May 3:252–261. G. B. MELLONI, *Vita della beata Maddalena Albrici, nobile comasca dell'Ordine di S. Agostino* (Bologna 1764). A. M. CONFALONIERI, *La beata Maddelena Albrici, badessa del convento di S. Andrea in Brunate* (Como 1938). W. HÜMPFNER, *Lexikon für Theologie und Kirche,* ed. J. HOFER and K. RAHNER, 10 v. (2d, new ed. Freiburg 1957–65) 6:1263. C. JUST, ibid. 1269–70.

[J. E. BRESNAHAN]

MAGDALENS

Called also Penitents or White Ladies (they wore white), a religious order of women, some of them converted public sinners, founded to reform or protect women and girls. Although St. DOMINIC had organized a short-lived cloistered community of penitent women at Toulouse in 1215, the Order of Magdalens proper was founded at Metz by Rudolf of Worms and confirmed by Gregory IX in 1227. After 1232 most houses changed from the original Cistercian rule to a Dominican form of the rule of St. AUGUSTINE. A male branch following the original Dominican constitutions was attached to the Magdalens for direction and government: each house had a prior, three priests, and laymen, as well as a prioress. There were provincial priors, and a general prior for the entire order (Rudolf was the first, until 1235).

The order spread quickly in Germany (Worms, 1224; Strasbourg, 1225; Mühlhausen and Würzburg, 1227; Speyer, 1228; Mainz, Cologne, Goslar, 1229), France, Italy, Spain, and Portugal, with more than 40 convents in Germany in the 13th century. It was placed under the direction of the DOMINICANS in 1286, was incorporated by them in 1287, and in 1291 again became independent. After 1370, however, it declined: the male branch and General Chapter had little meaning; unity was lacking and noble women without vocation were accepted in great number. Many houses passed to the Dominicans and FRANCISCANS. Most convents were lost at the Reformation. A few Magdalen public health institutes still exist: at Lauban (founded 1320) and Studenz. There is also a convent in Seyboldsdorf (Bavaria).

Small communities of Magdalens, once connected with the Order and with the same purpose, developed independently. A foundation of Magdalens at Marseilles, with the approval of Nicholas III, became a religious congregation under the rule of St. Augustine (*c.* 1272). The so-called Magdalens of the Rue Saint-Denis were founded early in the 17th century. Similar communities were founded at Naples (1324), Paris (1592), Rome (1520), and Seville (1550). A community called the Madelonnettes, which had the same purpose, was founded in 1618 by the Capuchin Athanase Molé; it is no longer in existence. This group was permitted to take religious vows by FRANCIS DE SALES, who placed it successively under various women's congregations. It was raised to monastic status by Urban VIII and augmented by branches at Rouen and Bordeaux. It contained three congregations: Magdalens proper with solemn vows; Sisters of St. Martha with simple vows; and Sisters of St. Lazarus, who had once been public sinners confined against their will.

Bibliography: P. HÉLYOT, *Dictionnaire des ordres religieux,* 4 v. (Paris 1847–59). A. SIMON, *L'Ordre des Penitents de Ste. M.-Madeleine en Allemagne* (Fribourg 1918). Heimbucher 1: 646–648. G. GIERATHS, *Lexikon für Theologie und Kirche*, J. HOFER and K. RAHNER, eds. (Freiburg 1957–65) 6:1270–71.

[A. CONDIT]

MAGI

Magi is the plural form of a little–used singular, magus (from Old Persian *magu*), that designates a member of an ancient Near Eastern priestly caste.

According to the ancient Greek historian Herodotus (*Histories* I), the Magi were originally a Median tribe. Herodotus described their peculiar customs, that they neither buried nor burnt their dead, but exposed them to the birds, that they practiced consanguineous marriage and were specialists in oneiromancy, i.e. divination through dreams, astrology, and magic—this last art taking its name from them. They forbade the killing of certain animals, but made the killing of certain others obligatory. Their view of the world was dualistic.

When the Persians displaced the Medes, DARIUS the Great (521–486 B.C.), put to death several Magi who challenged his power, an event commemorated by an annual feast called ''The Killing of the Magi.'' Nonetheless, their political influence grew steadily until they obtained a religious monopoly, for Herodotus reports it was not permitted to offer a sacrifice without the assistance of a Magus.

Zoroaster, engraving from a bas relief at Persepolis. (The Gamma Liaison Network)

The Magi and Zoroastrianism. That the Magi were specialists in magic and astrology, according to the Greeks, is hardly characteristic of Zoroastrianism. The relationship between the Magi and the reform which found expression in ZOROASTER's *Gāthās* is problematic. Probably by the time of Artaxerxes I (465–425 B.C.), but certainly under Seleucus I (306–280 B.C.), the fusion was complete between the religion of the Achaemenids and that of Zoroaster. The Magi, as they enjoyed a religious monopoly, called themselves the disciples of Zoroaster. Thus, many Greek sources call Zoroaster a Magus, as did Xanthus (5th century B.C.) and Dinon (4th century B.C.) who were cited by Hermippus (3rd–2nd centuries B.C.).

The Magusaioi. The word is a Semitic and Greek adaptation of the Iranian term magus, and it designates the ''Hellenized Magi'' to whom a vast lore of pseudoscience, written in Greek, was attributed. In the dialogue *Alcibiades,* ascribed to Plato, two kinds of magic are distinguished: popular magic, which was tantamount to sorcery, and the authentic, or Persian magic, which was a form of religion. Although the philosophers maintained the distinction, it was lost to the general public, and the Magi in Hellenistic and Roman times were commonly considered as astrologers and sorcerers.

The Old Testament book of Daniel ascribes to *magoi*, in the Bablyonian kingdom of Nebuchadnezzar, occult powers, such as divination and dream interpretation (Dan 1.20, 2.2, 4.4, 5.7). In the New Testament the term μάγος, outside of the Gospel of Matthew, has a perjorative connotation, with reference to SIMON MAGUS in Acts 8.9–24 and Bar–Jesus in Acts 13.6–12. The Magi (μάγοι) in Mt 2.1–12, however, represent wise pagans who do homage to Jesus as Messiah.

Popular Traditions. Traditions about the Magi concern their social rank, their number, their names, and their place of origin.

Rank of the Magi. Popular tradition, by *c.* 500 A.D., knew the Magi as kings, although no historical evidence justifies this belief. Nor did any Father of the Church hold the opinion that the Magi were kings. In the liturgy of the Feast of EPIPHANY the Magi are associated with Psalms 71(72).10: ''The kings of Tharsis and the Isles shall offer gifts,'' a Psalm to which Matthew alludes in 2.7–12. From such an association it was an easy, if uncertain, step to confer kingship upon the wise men.

Number and Names of Magi. In the West, at least, the ''three kings'' has become so common a synonym for the Magi that few people are aware that in Matthew's Infancy Narrative no mention is made of their number. The idea that the Magi were three in number seems to have grown from the number of gifts (gold, frankincense, and myrrh) offered to the infant Christ. In the East, however, the number of the Magi is set at 12. In art they are depicted as two, three, four, or even eight.

Regarding the names of the wise men, again, popular tradition embellishes where the evangelist is silent. In Western tradition the names Gaspar, Melchior, and Balthasar appear only in the 8th century. In Syrian tradition such names as Larvandad, Harmisdas, and Gushnasaph occur, while the Armenians refer to Kagba, Badalima, etc.

Place of Origin. Matthew's narrative states only that the Magi were from the East, which could mean Mesopotamia or Persia, though the gifts seem to indicate South Arabia (Is 60.6; Ps 72.15). Along these lines Maximus speculates Babylon; Clement and Cyril of Alexandria, Persia; Justin and Tertullian, Arabia. Bede thought that the three represented the continents of Europe, Asia, and Africa. The Magi are sometimes considered descendants of the three sons of Noah. As offspring of the families of Sem, Ham, and Japheth, they would represent the major families of humanity. Although it can only be a later elaboration, this interpretation suggests the call of all people to Christ.

Relics of the Magi. The cathedral of Cologne possesses and venerates the relics of ''the holy three kings.''

The relics were brought to Cologne from Milan in the 12th century, but little is known about them before that date.

Magi in the Gospel. In the Christian tradition, the theological significance of the Magi's visit is more important than its historical significance. The visit of the Magi is the first of two episodes in Matthew 2. The evangelist fashioned the chapter by drawing from two Old Testament stories. The visit of the Magi is modeled after Numbers 22–24 while the second episode (Mt 2.13–23) draws upon the Exodus story, as told in the Old Testament (Ex 1–4) and supplemented by midrashic expansions of the kind recounted by the Jewish historians Josephus and Philo. The Exodus motifs, in the latter, draw a parallel between Moses and Jesus.

The use of Numbers 22–24 in the episode concerning the Magi, prepares the stage for the Exodus to follow. In Numbers 22–24, the wicked king Balak of Moab seeks to destroy the Israelites under Moses just as the wicked king Herod sets into motion, in vv.1–12, a plot to destroy Jesus, which will be carried out explicitly in due time (vv.13, 18). In Numbers, a seer, Balaam, called a magus by midrashic lore, and coming "from the east," delivers favorable oracles, predicting prosperity for Israel and a strong, royal leader, thus thwarting the malicious designs of the wicked king. Similarly, the Magi in the Gospel come from the East (Mt 2.1) and, in virtue of visionary gifts, recognize and pay homage to Jesus as Messiah (vv.2, 11), thus auguring well for the defeat, in the next episode, of King Herod's plot. Numbers 24.17, concerning a star that will come forth from Jacob, was a well-known messianic text in Judaism; it furnishes the star in the Magi episode (Mt 2.2, 9, 10).

Matthew weaves scripture citations into the episode. Verse 6 blends Micah 5.1 and 2 Samuel 5.2 to articulate a Davidic messianic theme, for the Messiah was to be born in Bethlehem. Although the Magi are not so well schooled in Jewish scriptures as the Jewish king and rulers would be, they, by contrast to the rulers, are able to recognize the fulfilment of Jewish scripture: that Jesus is King of the Jews, Messiah. Their homage to him (v.11) alludes to Psalms 72.10–11 and Isaiah 60.6, which features foreigners bearing gold and frankincense in homage to Israel's anointed ruler. This allusion demonstrates that the Magi are representative of the world outside of Israel, the Gentiles to whom the kingdom is given once Israel refuses the Messiah (Mt 21.42–43).

Bibliography: M. M. BOURKE, "The Literary Genus of Matthew 1–2," *The Catholic Biblical Quarterly* (Washington 1939–) 22 (1960) 160–175. J. E. BRUNS, "The Magi Episode in Matthew 2," *ibid.*, 23 (1961) 51–54. E. J. HOUDOUS, "The Gospel of the Epiphany," *ibid.*, 6 (1944) 69–84. D. DAUBE, "The Earliest Structure of the Gospels," *New Testament Studies* (Cambridge, Eng.–Washington 1954–) 5 (1958–59) 174–187. R. LEANEY, "The Birth Narratives in St. Luke and St. Matthew," *ibid.*, 8 (1961–62) 158–166. A. M. DENIS, "L'Adoration des Mages vue par S. Matthieu," *Nouvelle revue théologique* (Tournai–Louvain–Paris 1869–) 82 (1960) 32–39. S. M. IGLESIAS, "El género literario del Evangelio de la Infancia en San Mateo," *Estudios biblicos* (Madrid 1941–) 17 (1958) 243–273. P. A. KING, "Matthew and Epiphany," *Worship*, 36 (1961–62) 89–95. G. MESSINA, "Ecce *Magi* ab Oriente venerunt," *Verbum Domini* (Rome 1921–) 14 (1934) 7–19. H. J. RICHARDS, "The Three Kings," Scripture 8 (1956) 23–28. D. SQUILLACI, "I Magi," *Palestra del clero,* 39 (1960) 16–20. R. E. BROWN, *The Birth of the Messiah*, rev. ed. (New York 1999). The Pontifical Biblical Commission, *The Interpretation of the Bible in the Church* (Vatican City 1993).

[J. DUCHESNE–GUILLEMIN/E. J. JOYCE/M. STEVENSON]

"Adoration of the Magi," whale bone relief carving, English or northern French, c. 1120–1130. (Victoria & Albert Museum, Crown Copyright/Art Resource, NY)

MAGIC

On the basis of its appearance and manifestations the phenomenon of magic (from Greek μαγία, WITCHCRAFT)

"Adoration of the Magi," tempera painting on panel by Bartolo di Fredi.

falls primarily in the realm of human thought and action. The man concerned with magic wishes to overcome the threatening powers of nature and to enlist the help of the good or favorable forces. Above all he wants to be master over earthly life by being able, apparently, to banish uncertainty and to meet the unforeseen. Magic accordingly appears in a causal connection (cause-effect relation) with practical daily life as a special manner of "dominating" it.

Since the powers and forces in question are beyond visible control and its efficacy, it is necessary for the causal sequence to have its own special character. Hence, its beginning extends to the whole scale of possible symbols, from concrete manipulation in things magical, to rites and knowledge, insofar as the cause producing the effect is seen in them.

Both the idea of magical causal connection and the symbolism of its domination signify an implicit assumption of a transcendent dimension of invisible reality, an assumption based immediately on intellectual and religious conviction. Accordingly, magic may be understood very broadly as an actualization of transcendence, in the sense that transcendence is drawn into causal-empirical existence and that the latter is carried over into the former. Magic, therefore, is nondifferentiating and leveling delivery of the invisible, spiritual, and hidden into the power of the dominant pragmatism and automatism of everyday life, or the attempt to control without distinction or difference the transcendent reality in the interests and purposes of a visibly pragmatic conduct and fulfillment of life. In this sense, it is "a kind of mechancial compulsion of power" (E. S. Brightman). If one wishes to give a precise definition of the phenomenon from the ideological point of view, magic ideology is present when it is believed that life can be ordered or controlled by the help of certain manipulations, incantations, prayerlike practices, amulets, and rites, or through special knowledge.

Magic is not restricted to specific levels of culture or to specific peoples, but exists as a possibility in all cultures and among all peoples, although in different ways. For this reason, it is absurd to see magic as a preliminary stage leading to religion (J. G. Frazer) or as the source of religion (E. DURKHEIM). However, the boundaries between magic and religion are often fluid in concrete instances.

Magic and Religion. They have a certain connection, and in a given case it is often difficult to determine whether an action or attitude is magical or religious. The explanation is this: on the one hand, there is transcendent reality that is more or less identical with that of religious experience and is implicitly assumed as a postulate for giving actuality to magical actions; on the other hand, even the religious man, in accordance with his nature and existence, needs tangible or concrete signs (cult, rites, symbols, prayers, knowledge) in order to establish himself in actual relation with God and the Divine.

In the first case, it depends essentially on the determination and understanding of the spiritual-dynamic dimension whether the attitude or action based upon it is to be spoken of as magical or religious. The highest being may be worshiped, for example, as the "greatest magician." The vital energy coming from him, as in a sense the *megbe* of the Bambuti Pygmies, the *wakanda* of the Sioux, or the *manitu* of the Algonquins, may be experienced and employed in such a way that—as among the Algonquins—the highest being is identified with the name of the power itself. In such a case, the structural difference that is essential for religion (God is the holy one, who is free in His giving and taking and cannot be compelled or forced) is thought of concomitantly in some way and enters, accordingly, more or less as a religio-mythical element into the magical action. The situation is different if, as in the instance of the *mana* of the Melanesians, the power is regarded as independent—a phenomenon that is found especially in disintegrating cultures. This power, or control, like that over an extremely fine material, can be possessed and used, provided that one knows the proper techniques. The procedure built upon it is entirely under the control of man's "knowledge" and "capability," of human machinations, and is *ipso facto* magical.

In the second case, it is the given attitude of man at a given time that determines whether there is religion or magic. Thus, the wearing of an amulet or the veneration of any object whatever (for example, a relic) can be a symbol for a religious idea or attitude, but it can also become an effective magical means of protection, or, if the "power" in the object is thought of as vital and real in itself, a form of fetishism. Among the Semang-Negrito, a blood sacrifice silences a violent storm, but only if the angry divinity is reconciled. Their neighbors, the Senoi, on the other hand, believe that the storm dragon is put to flight by the pouring out of a blood mixture in six places. In the first instance the rite reveals a symbolism that expresses a definite religious conviction, while in the second it becomes a necessarily effective cause. However, the Semang also, in the given situation, may think very much as the Senoi do.

Official and Private Magic. It is a characteristic feature of magic everywhere that it is employed not only to produce tangible results through automatically effective rites, but also to order and determine every last detail in the life of the individual.

Official Magic. Insofar as it is concerned with things that affect either the community as a whole or only the individual, a distinction can be made between official and private magic. Official magic is present—and in this case the boundaries between religion and magic are quite fluid—when public affairs are conducted in accordance with a magically effective ritual. This happens when, e.g., in a region of South Africa, public ceremonies are held in time of drought and those present give effectiveness to their wishes by means of imitative magic (in this instance by the sprinkling of water) or when public fertility ceremonies of a magic character are performed to guarantee better crops.

Such ceremonies are conducted by the community and also by an official priesthood or a professional magician (a medicine man). The latter can be called to his office by spirits or dreams without shamanism proper necessarily being already present or without shamanism being identical with magic. The one qualified to serve in this capacity is usually trained according to rules so that he can carry out his function publicly. Institutions of this kind are found where certain callings have a special significance for the community (e.g., smiths) or where the community has a primarily religious organization. It is natural in the case of the sacred kingship, actually founded on a religious basis, that the king himself is thought of in terms of magic. The king or chief is endowed with power and is responsible for the weal or woe of his subjects. He, or persons designated by him, fulfills this responsibility in the community by magically effective practices and rites. Not only actions of an institutional nature, but also those that through general use are regarded as more or less public and with which every one is naturally concerned, may be designated as official magic. The individual examples are legion. It is enough to think merely of the actions of hunters or planters, which each individual can perform or with which he must be concerned, within the framework of traditional usage.

Private Magic. In contrast to public magic there is private magic, which is employed in a secret manner by individuals (magicians) or groups, whether for exclusive personal use or to harm others (witchcraft). In extreme cases and in contrast to the white magic described above, one also finds black magic, which can be fittingly designated by the Bantu word *bulozi.* The term signifies the employment of magical knowledge completely separated from any connection with religion for the purpose of harming others by destroying their magico-divine vitality, and it is regarded as the worst of sins in the Bantu area. *Bulozi* therefore is no longer like magic, in a kind of neutrality outside religion, but is brought into religion as its contradiction (sin).

Anyone can practice private magic. Since, however, secret knowledge is assumed, special traditions (schools or families) arise in connection with it. Very often parapsychological factors may also play a role in it; or, insofar as there is question of *bulozi,* even something like the "compact with the devil" is found.

Kinds and Forms of Magic. The universal diffusion of magic exhibits basic ways in which magic intent is active. On the basis of the degree and clarity of the symbolism employed in magic and its manner of operation, the following successive stages can be worked out. Symbolism as such must always be present, since there is always a question of a transcendent form of reality. The boundaries between types are again very fluid.

Object Magic. This is based on the idea that the part serves for the whole and operates of itself and immediately by means of power-laden objects (human bones, hair, and nails, but also stones, tools, fetishes, etc.). If a man possesses anything at all belonging to another—in Australia even a footprint suffices—he has the other in his power. Object magic is employed especially in *bulozi.*

Contagious Magic. Magical effect is attained by the touching of power-laden objects. The immediate command over the power itself gives way to an indirect mastery. Magic objects can be stones, animals, plants, etc. Mythical ideas are often present in the background, and these create a magic interest respecting individual objects. Such transfers of power can also take place from man to man, an idea that is not without importance for the phenomenon of cannibalism. As distinguished from object magic, contagious magic is closer to symbolism. Thus the power of the lion is concealed in the lion's tooth worn as an amulet, or the strength of bast is concealed in rings made of this material (in Papua). The power, which in the last analysis possesses a certain independence and unavailability of its own, is not only received, but by means of contact for the purpose, can also be employed, for example, to carry offerings placed upon a stone to one's ancestors (as among the Corumba in West Africa).

Sympathetic Magic. Magical causal sequence is thought of here in its parallel relation to the sympathetic capacity of man. When once the sympathetic analogue is established, the desired effect is attained or the *conditio sine qua non* is fulfilled, without which the effect cannot take place. The analogue itself ranges from the picture-like setting (J. G. Frazer's ''magic by similarity'') to the imageless, but sense-fixed magic word of expression (*see* CURSE; BLESSING). When the hunter strikes the animal drawn in the sand, he effects the presumption of a successful hunt. Likewise is the belief that a man can kill another by looking down on the water—as is done among the Ovambo (S.W. Africa)—until he sees the image of his enemy; he then spits at it and curses it. Conversely, one obtains the presence of the divine or of the divinity when in the possession of a pertinent image or picture. In ancient Egypt, *usebtis* (little figurines) were buried with the dead. By means of magic formulas, which were written for the dead, the *usebtis* could be summoned to work in their place. The use of curse figurines or ''dolls'' is also common. They represent human beings upon whom the magic work is to take effect (tight and intricate tying of the ''doll,'' strangulation; and pricking of the ''doll,'' death). Here too belongs every kind of fear in respect to pictures.

Gnosiological Magic. In this kind of magic one no longer attains his results primarily by the performance of object-related or of sympathetico-analogous actions. Rather it is in the intellectual sphere, in the knowledge of the magical constellations connected with the universe and of the actions harmonized with them, that he sees the sound and appropriate establishment of existence guaranteed. It is also possible to speak under this head of negative, or passive, magic. Here belongs the setting of an action at the right time (e.g., at the waxing or waning of the moon), and likewise the discovery of in what manner the favor and blessing of the gods can be obtained (*see* DIVINATION; ASTROLOGY). Worship, which is religious in origin, and religious (ascetico-mystical) conduct, under the influence of automatism and the object itself of the given rite, slip thereby imperceptibly into the magical, as for example in the use of the meaningless repetitions and heaping up of prayers in the belief that this makes prayers themselves more efficacious.

This phenomenon is to be noted especially in the syncretistic combining and mutual acceptances of different religions. Thus, in Hellenistic-Roman syncretism, as well as in that of the Far East, existence is ruled and ordered in a certain measure by one's knowing to what god he must turn (*deus certus*) and what appertains in particular to each god. Cicero speaks appropriately of the *iustitia adversus deos.* The sacred in the strict sense sinks, in the syncretistic process and under the influence of magic, into a state of impersonal anonymity and loses much of its transcendent character.

Magic and Science. The gnosiological form of magic, which ranges in time from the teachings and practices of the ancient BRAHMANS to modern THEOSOPHY, has not been without influence on the development of science. The magical attitude or outlook not only shaped those presuppositions that were the foundation for the elaboration and use of logical thinking and that exhibited the inherent possibility of employment for the domination of nature; but also, running parallel with the development of quasi-magical knowledge (the invention and use of writing, the use of numbers and measuring methods in the observation of the stars), it helped to make possible the external crystallization of knowledge as knowledge. Naturally, the further progress of knowledge by the recognition of causal-empirical relations signifies at the same time the discovery of the laws of science. However, a belief in gnosiological magic can only be vanquished by knowledge if that knowledge is combined with a positive faith.

See Also: HOROSCOPES; SUPERSTITION; ALCHEMY; SHAMAN AND MEDICINE MAN.

Bibliography: G. LANCZKOWSKI et al., *Lexikon für Theologie und Kirche*, ed. J. HOFER and K. RAHNER (Freiberg 1957–65) 6:1274–80. A. BERTHOLET and C. M. EDSMAN, *Die Religion in Geschichte und Gegenwart* (Tübingen 1957–65) 4:595–601. R. R. MARETT et al., J. HASTINGS, ed. *Encyclopedia of Religion and Ethics* (Edinburgh 1908–27) 8:245–321, a systematic world survey. H. WEBSTER, *Magic: A Sociological Study* (Stanford 1947). W. GOODE, ''Magic and Religion: A Continum,'' *Ethnos* 14 (1949) 172–182. C. H. RATSCHOW, *Magie und Religion* (2d ed. Gütersloh 1955). B. MALINOWSKI, *Magic, Science and Religion* (New York 1955). G. B. VETTER, *Magic and Religion* (New York 1958). R. ALLIER, *Magie et Religion* (Paris 1935). A. E. JENSEN, *Myth and Cult among Primitive Peoples,* tr. M. T. CHOLDIN and W. WEISSLEDER (Chicago 1963). G. VAN DER LEEUW, *Religion in Essence and Manifestation,* tr. J. E. TURNER (London 1938). L. THORNDIKE, *A History of Magic and Experimental Science* (New York 1923–58). M. ELIADE, *Patterns in*

Comparative Religion, tr. R. SHEED (New York 1958), Index s.v. "Magic, Magico-religious powers."

[W. DUPRÉ]

MAGIC (IN THE BIBLE)

The common Hebrew verb meaning to practice magic or sorcery is *kiššēp* (Ex 7.11, 22.17; Dt 18.10; 2 Chr 33.6; Dn 2.2; Mal 3.5). That magic was practiced in Israel is clear from the denunciation of it in the Bible. Seemingly there were many varieties of magicians (Lv 19.26; Dt 18.10; 1 Sm 15.23, 28.3; 2 Kgs 17.17, 21.6). There are also references to the practice of magic in Is 3.2; Mi 3.11; Jer 27.9 and 29.8; Ez 13.6, 9; 22.28; and Zec 10.2.

Magic played a much less important role in Israel than elsewhere. Yet the many prohibitions of the use of magic by law and the zealous struggle of the Prophets against it show that it had quite a hold on the people (Ez 13.18–21; Mi 5.11; Mal 3.5). Saul at one time banished the "mediums and wizards" but later sought their help (1 Sm 28.3–7). From Is 3.2–3 it is evident that diviners and magicians were influential on the people of Judah. King Manasseh availed himself publicly of the service of the magicians (2 Chr 33.6). Jeremiah (27.9) warns the people against putting any trust in "diviners, soothsayers and sorcerers." Magic as such was alien to Yahwism; the Israelites were too profoundly aware of God as creator and of their own insignificance and total dependence on Him. In Dt 18.10 mention is made of eight different varieties of magic, all of which were forbidden by Yahweh (Dt 18.14).

The New Testament writers held the same views on magic. SIMON MAGUS, a raw neophyte (Acts 8.9–24), and Elymas (Bar–Jesus), a Jewish magician, pretended to foretell the future (Acts 13.6–12), and reference is made to the legendary magicians of Pharaoh, Jannes, and Mambres, who tried to counteract the marvels worked by Moses (2 Tm 3.8). These are the only magicians mentioned in the New Testament. St. Paul berates Elymas, calling him an "enemy of all justice, full of deceit and villainy" (Acts 13.10), and places the sorcerer with the immoral, the licentious, and the idolatrous (Gal 5.19–21); St. John puts him with liars and murderers (Rv 9.21, 18.23, 21.8, 22.15).

Bibliography: A. LEFÈVRE, *Dictionnaire de la Bible,* suppl. ed. L. PIROT et al., (Paris 1928–) 5:732–739. *Encyclopedic Dictionary of the Bible,* tr. and adap. by L. HARTMAN (New York 1963) from A. VAN DEN BORN, *Bijbels Woordenboek,* 1417–18. H. GROSS and J. SINT, *Lexikon für Theologie und Kirche*[2], ed. J. HOFER and K. RAHNER, 10 v. (Freiburg 1957–65) 6:1277–78.

[M. J. HUNT]

MAGISTRI COMACINI

Magistri Comacini is a term applied in the early Middle Ages to the master architects who supervised the construction of medieval cathedrals. It first appears *c.* 643 in a charter [L. A. Muratori, *Rerum italicarum scriptores, 500–1500,* cont. by G. Carducci and V. Fiorini (Città di Castello 1900–) 1.2:25; *Monumenta Germaniae Historica: Leges* (Berlin 1826–) 4:33] of the Lombard King Rotharius, and later in a document (*ibid.* 4:176) of King Liutprand to a group of builders (741). The term is derived probably from Comacina, an island in Lake Como; the area was known for the skill of its architects during this period. It is unlikely that the *magistri comacini* can be linked with the organized *collegia* of builders under the Roman Empire, who are said to have taken refuge on the island during the barbarian invasions. By the 9th century, the terms *magister marmorarius* and *magister casarius* also describe those in the building trades.

Although the north Italian style had great impact on Romanesque architecture, it was not the only source of inspiration or craftsmanship; the *magistri comacini* appear elsewhere throughout medieval Europe. They often were granted charters and were organized along the lines of a corporation or guild, but their history is obscure, perhaps due to a secrecy that excluded outsiders. A few monks served as architects, such as the Benedictine Winidharius at SANKT GALLEN *c.* 835 [*Monumenta Germaniae Historica: Poetae* (Berlin 1826–) 1:89–90], but most master builders were laymen; mastership seems to have passed from father to son. The masters moved from place to place and developed an international style in their work. Their artistic canons tended to break with classical and Byzantine traditions. Some, however, spent years on a large edifice, and several generations of a family might work on the construction of one cathedral complex. Miniatures in the codex of the *Relatio translationis sancti Geminiani* in Modena offer a view of the masters' duties in the reconstruction of the cathedral there (1099–1106); the master builder, Lanfranc, was a figure of authority and dignity, supervising diverse assistants, artisans, and laborers.

The Lombard *magistri,* who were fond of signing their work, are better known than others. The highly organized Italian lodges of architects and masons continued in existence to early modern times and played an important part in the development and spread of Baroque architecture in Italy and south Germany. With the decline of European cathedral building (16th–17th century) many lodges began to initiate nonmasons into their secret ritual and organization in order to maintain their membership and treasury; it is with these groups that modern FREEMASONRY claims affinity.

See Also: CHURCH ARCHITECTURE.

Bibliography: G. MERZARIO, *I maestri Comacìni, storia artistica di mille duecento anni 600–1800,* 2 v. (Milan 1893). G. T. RIVOIRA, *Le origini della architectura lombarda,* 2 v. (Rome 1901) 1:127–131. W. RAVENSCROFT, *The Comacines, Their Predecessors and Successors* (London 1910). A. K. PORTER, *Lombard Architecture,* 4 v. (New Haven 1915–17) 1:8–20. A. M. ZENDRALLI, *I magistri Grigioni* (Poschiavo 1958). C. CORDIÉ "I Maestri commacini (*impresari construttori e non comensi*)," *Annali di Scuola normale superiore di Pisa,* 2d ser., 31 (1962) 151–172. L. E. BAXTER, *The Cathedral Builders, the Story of a Great Masonic Guild* (New York 1899).

[B. J. COMASKEY]

MAGLIONE, LUIGI

Cardinal, papal secretary of state; b. Casoria (Napoli), Italy, March 2, 1877; d. there, Aug. 22, 1944. After ordination (1901) he received doctorates in theology (1902) and Canon Law (1904) and studied at the papal diplomatic academy (1905–07). From 1907 until 1918 he worked in the section dealing with extraordinary affairs in the papal secretariate of state and taught diplomatic history at the papal diplomatic academy. He was sent as provisory papal representative to Bern, Switzerland (February 28, 1918), and also as representative for ecclesiastical matters at the League of Nations. After the resumption of diplomatic relations between the Holy See and Switzerland (August 1, 1920), Maglione occupied the nunciature there and was named titular archbishop of Caesarea. He was appointed nuncio to Paris (May 24, 1926) and remained there during a period of controversy concerning the ACTION FRANÇAISE. His successor Valerio Valeri was appointed June 3, 1936. After becoming cardinal (Dec. 3, 1935), Maglione was named prefect of the Congregation of the Council in 1938. From March 10, 1939, until his death, he was secretary of state. In 1939, in pursuit of Pius XII's attempt to keep peace, he sought to arrange a conference with England, France, Germany, Poland, and Italy in order to compose the differences between Germany and Poland, and between France and Italy. Maglione warned Joachim von Ribbentrop, the German foreign minister, that England and France would not abandon Poland in the event of an attack. When Ribbentrop visited the Vatican (March 1940), the cardinal handed him a memorandum containing seven points listing actions inimical to the Church in Poland and in other areas under German control. As a statesman Maglione was highly esteemed for his realistic judgments in ecclesiastical and political matters. Pius XII valued his assistance in the settlement of problems that beset the Holy See continually from the outset of World War II.

Bibliography: *L'Osservatore romano* (Aug. 23, 1944), necrology. W. SANDFUCHS, ed., *Die Aussenminister der Päpste* (Munich 1962) 124–130 by K. WÜSTENBERG.

[R. LEIBER]

MAGLORIUS, ST.

Bishop and abbot also known as Magloire and Maelor; b. Britain (probably Wales), sixth century; d. Island of Sark (English Channel), *c.* 595. His predominately legendary vita (from the tenth century) claims that Maglorius was a pupil of ILLTUD in the monastery of Llantwit Major in Glamorgan and a companion of Samson of Dol. He supposedly accompanied the latter to Brittany, where he succeeded him as abbot and bishop of Dol. It is further alleged that he spent the last years of his life as abbot of the monastery that Lascon, the chieftain of the island of Sark, gave him in gratitude for a miraculous cure. Legend ascribes many posthumous miracles to Maglorius. His relics were translated (*c.* 850) from Sark to the Abbey of Lehon near Dinan and subsequently (*c.* 963) to Paris to the former Abbey of St. Magloire. Maglorius is specially venerated as a Breton saint, but his cult spread into Italy. He is pictured as a pilgrim or as a monk being crowned by an angel.

Feast: Oct. 24.

Bibliography: *Bibliotheca hagiographica latina antiquae et mediae aetatis,* 2 v. (Brussels 1898–1901; suppl. 1911) 5139–47. *Acta Sanctorum* Oct. 10:772–793. A. DE LA BORDERIE, *Les Miracles de Saint Magloire* (Rennes 1891). *The Book of Saints* (4th ed. New York 1947). J. L. BAUDOT and L. CHAUSSIN, *Vies des saints et des bienheureux selon l'ordre du calendrier avec l'historique des fêtes,* ed. by the Benedictines of Paris, 12 v. (Paris 1935–56) 10:823–825. A. BUTLER, *The Lives of the Saints,* rev. ed. H. THURSTON and D. ATTWATER, 4 v. (New York 1956) 4:192–193. G. LUCCHESI, *Il culto di s. Maglorio a Faenza* (Faenza 1957). L. RÉAU, *Iconographie de l'art chrétien,* 6 v. (Paris 1955–59) 3.2:860–861. D. ATTWATER, *A Dictionary of Saints* (new ed. New York 1958). M. BATESON, *The Dictionary of National Biography from the Earliest Times to 1900,* 63 v. (London 1885–1900; repr. with corrections, 21 v., 1908–09, 1921–22, 1938; suppl. 1901–) 12:767–768. F. DUINE, *Memento des sources hagiographiques de l'histoire de Bretagne* (Rennes 1918).

[M. CSÁKY]

MAGNA CARTA

In May 1215 King JOHN put his seal to the articles of peace that his rebellious barons presented to him. A few days later a formal charter based on these articles was granted to the people of England by the King. The charter was known as the Great Charter because of its size; in its final form it represents the influence, not the actual composition, of STEPHEN LANGTON, Archbishop of Canterbury. The charter has always been recognized as one of the great documents of English history. It stands at the head of the Statutes of the Realm, it was repeatedly reissued by later medieval kings, and in the 17th century was an inspiration to those who opposed the personal rule of Charles I. Its origin is popularly supposed to lie in the shortcomings of King John, but there is more to the charter than that.

John is not the medieval ruler with the most savory of reputations. He inherited a remarkable collection of countries, stretching from the Spanish border to the German marches, with England at the heart of this "empire." Within a few years he had lost all his northern French possessions. He had then taxed the English to an unheard of extent to mount a counteroffensive, which duly met with disaster at Bouvines (1214); the campaign emptied his treasury but did not restore his overseas possessions. The result was a baronial rebellion that the King could stave off only at the price of the concessions embodied in the Magna Carta. It is true that John was treacherous, unstable, greedy, and unlucky, but it is doubtful if a better man could have met with greater success. In spite of his reputation with his contemporaries, he was within limits an able ruler, conscientious, hardworking, and surprisingly just where his own interests were not concerned. Unfortunately for him the ties between his English and Norman subjects were now growing looser while the King of France, PHILIP II AUGUSTUS, was pressing relentlessly on John's French possessions. More and more the English exchequer had to pay for expensive campaigns that did no more than preserve the *status quo.* John used comparatively new and very efficient methods of taxation, which, unlike most royal taxes at that time, lay heavily on the rich as well as on the poor. Consequently he was blamed for problems he did not create and which no one could have solved.

King John "Lackland" (seated), after signing the Magna Carta. (©Bettmann/CORBIS)

The charter was not merely a demand for redress of grievances. There had been many previous baronial revolts that represented little more than gangs of disaffected nobles seeking remedies for individual grievances. However, in 1215 for the first time the opposition united as a party with the common program of demanding general and responsible reforms.

The problem they had to face was how to preserve the manifest good which efficient government under the last three kings had brought to the English, while restraining the increasing power of that government within reasonable limits. The barons in 1215 were quite frank in stating that it was the tyranny of HENRY II, as well as that of John, that they were opposing. They were equally clear that they did not wish to destroy the elaborate structure of law and courts and the powerful, if crude, civil service these kings had built up. However it was intolerable to find Henry II using his servants, not to put down injustice, but to hound his archbishop out of the the kingdom; or that John used the legal weapon of distraint for debt to drive one of his magnates into penniless exile while starving his wife and son to death. The King's excuse in this case had been the enormity of his debt; but everyone knew that the real reason was that the magnate, William de Briouse, and his family knew too much about the death of Prince Arthur, who had been captured by John.

The charter reflects these concerns. It contains many particular grievances and even some attempt to turn the clock back in a most undesirable way. For the most part, however, the Angevin legal reforms were accepted and their scope even extended. The royal right to tax at will was heavily circumscribed. The heart of the charter however, was an attempt to put the King under the law. His power of arbitrary distraint was abolished. In future the king could imprison nobody without a judgment according to the law of the land in a case decided by the defendant's social equals. The barons, it is true, failed to establish any workable machinery for enforcing the charter, but even so, despite the fact that within a few weeks of its sealing war had broken out again, the King took care to observe its rules, as did his successor Henry III. The barons had only begun the building of the characteristic English constitution; but they had shown once and for all that tyranny could be checked if the will to check it were there.

Bibliography: W. S. MCKECHNIE, *Magna Carta* (2d ed. Glasgow 1914). H. E. MALDEN, ed., *Magna Carta Commemoration Essays* (London 1917). F. M. POWICKE, *Stephen Langton* (Oxford 1928). V. H. GALBRAITH, *Studies in the Public Records* (New York

1948). S. PAINTER, *The Reign of King John* (Baltimore 1949). J. E. A. JOLLIFFE, *Angevin Kingship* (London 1955). J. C. HOLT, *The Northerners: A Study in the Reign of King John* (Oxford 1961); *King John* (London 1963). J. C. HOLT, *Magna Carta*, 2nd ed. (Cambridge, England 1992). A.E.D. HOWARD, *Magna Carta: Text and Commentary* (Charlottesville 1998).

[E. JOHN/EDS.]

MAGNANIMITY

A moral virtue, classified as a potential part of the virtue of fortitude, that perfects a person by inclining him reasonably to perform excellent works of virtue that are worthy of great honor. The proper object of the virtue of magnanimity is great works of virtue, but secondarily and indirectly, magnanimity moderates the pleasure taken in present honor and the desire of future honors, because these are necessarily associated with the accomplishment of great works.

Other virtues also incline a person to seek and to achieve difficult and excellent works. It is the precise function of the virtue of magnanimity to moderate and control an individual's inclination to shy from works of this kind because of the difficulty involved in them.

Magnanimity involves a general inclination to nobility of spirit because it inclines a man to direct his efforts at great and outstanding deeds. The magnanimous man is a superior type of person. He is never overcome by envy or covetousness, nor is he embarrassed or humiliated when others do great things. He is open and frank; he is primarily concerned about virtue and noble works, and is untroubled by the petty things that disturb others. He is neither overjoyed by the praise of others, nor saddened by criticism. He is a man intent upon following the precept of Christ: ''You, therefore, are to be perfect, even as your heavenly Father is perfect'' (Mt 5.48). The truly magnanimous man is more intent upon the excellence at which he aims than on the honors which may come to him from men on its account. As to honor itself, he values most that which he hopes to receive from God.

It may seem that magnanimity is opposed to Christian humility, for the seeking of honor appears to be incompatible with humility. Actually, these virtues complement one another. ''There is in man something great which he possesses through the goodness of God, and something defective which comes to him through the weakness of nature. Accordingly, magnanimity makes a man deem himself worthy of great things because of the gifts he has from God. . . . On the other hand, humility makes a man think little of himself in consideration of his own deficiency'' (ST. THOMAS AQUINAS, *Summa theologiae* 2a2ae,129.3 ad 4).

There are four vices opposed to the virtue of magnanimity—three by excess: presumption, ambition, and vainglory; one by defect: pusillanimity. Presumption inclines a person to attempt actions or projects that are beyond his strength and ability. (This is different from the vice of presumption that is opposed to the theological virtue of hope). Presumption is the result of a culpably erroneous judgment a person may have of his ability or virtue, or of an erroneous judgment of the works that are worthy of honor, causing a person to seek honor in the wrong kind of works. Presumption always implies an unreasonable reliance on one's own powers. AMBITION impels a person to seek honors that are not due to his state or to his merit. VAINGLORY is a vice by which a person seeks fame and popularity without sufficient reason, or without directing them to their true goal, i.e. the glory of God and the good of neighbor. PUSILLANIMITY, which is opposed to magnanimity by defect, is a vice by which a person tends unreasonably and erroneously to think his abilities insufficient to justify attempting difficult works. Magnanimity is a virtue that must be possessed by all Christians if they would strive for the greatest work of all, the perfection of the Christian life. It is expressed in the words ''I can do all things in him who strengthens me'' (Phil 4.13).

Bibliography: THOMAS AQUINAS, *Summa theologiae* 2a2ae, 129–133. A. THOUVENIN, *Dictionnaire de théologie*, ed. A. VACANT et al. (Paris 1903–) 9.2:1550–53. J. PIEPER, *Fortitude and Temperance*, tr. D. F. COOGAN (New York 1954). F. L. B. CUNNINGHAM, ed., *The Christian Life* (Dubuque 1959). F. ROBERTI et al., comps., *Dictionary of Moral Theology*, ed. P. PALAZZINI et al. (Westminster, Md. 1962).

[R. DOHERTY]

MAGNERICUS OF TRIER, ST.

Archbishop; b. early sixth century; d. 596. He was from childhood a protégé of St. NICETIUS, whom he succeeded in the See of TRIER before 570. Like his young friend at Poitiers, Venantius FORTUNATUS, he had a deep devotion to St. Martin of Tours, to whom he dedicated several churches and an abbey (in which Magnericus is buried). Through his pilgrimages to Tours he came to know Bp. GREGORY OF TOURS. Magnericus died of a fever at an advanced age. Eberwin, abbot of St. Martin of Tours at Trier, included the verses Fortunatus had written to Magnericus in his copious *Vita s. Magnerici*. His disciples included GÉRY OF CAMBRAI.

Feast: July 25.

Bibliography: *Acta Sanctorum* July 6:168–192). *Bibliotheca hagiographica latina antiquae et mediae aetatis* 2:5149–50. E. EWIG, *Trier im Merowingerreich* (Trier 1954). A. BUTLER, *The Lives of the Saints* (New York 1956) 3:188–189.

[W. A. JURGENS]

MAGNI, VALERIANO

Capuchin priest, diplomat, and missioner; b. Prague, Bohemia, October 15, 1586; d. Salzburg, Austria, July 29, 1661. Valeriano, although of the noble family of Magni of Milan, entered the Capuchin Order in 1602. He spent his first years as lector. In 1627, as diplomat, he was commissioned by Emperor Ferdinand to implement the Edict of Restitution. Pope Urban VIII appointed him missionary apostolic to Bohemia in 1629. As the pope's delegate he attended the Diet of Ratisbon (1630). As missionary, Valeriano reestablished the Church in Saxony and Hesse (1652). Between 1635 and 1661, he was often a controversial figure. However, history testifies to his orthodox Catholic spirit. He wrote penetrating and progressive philosophical writings, together with apologetical-theological works, but Valeriano the philosopher and theologian was overshadowed by Valeriano the diplomat and missionary.

Bibliography: *Lexicon Capuccinum* (Rome 1951) 1776–77. C. PULVERMACHER, ''Missionary, Scholar, Diplomat: Valerian the Great,'' *Round Table of Franciscan Research* 23 (1958) 56–65. FATHER CUTHBERT, *The Capuchins,* 2 v. (London 1928). I. DA MILANO, *Enciclopedia cattolica* 7:1844–45.

[L. MILLER]

MAGNIEN, ALPHONSE

Educator; b. Bleymard, Mende, France, June 9, 1837; d. Baltimore, Md., December 21, 1902. After early classical studies at the minor seminary of Chirac, he did his philosophical and theological studies at the Sulpician diocesan seminary of Orléans (1857–62), the diocese to which he had become affiliated after an appeal for clerical recruits by Msgr. F. A. P. Dupanloup. For two years after ordination in June 1862, he taught at the minor seminary of La-Chapelle-Saint-Mesmin. Magnien then began his Sulpician work, first as a teacher of science at Nantes (1864–65) and then, after his novitiate at Issy near Paris, as professor of theology and Scripture at Rodez (1866–69). In the fall of 1869, he went to St. Mary's Seminary, Baltimore, Md., where he taught philosophy and then liturgy, dogma, and Scripture. Although Magnien became the sixth superior of St. Mary's Seminary in 1878, he continued his teaching until 1886. After that he had to confine his efforts solely to the administration of the seminary, where his position made him also superior (not provincial) of all the Sulpicians in the U.S.

During his administration, St. Mary's grew in size and in prestige as the oldest and largest major seminary in the country; a new wing was added to the building; its six-year course of studies was thoroughly revised; St. Austin's College for the graduate training of Sulpician novices was established at The Catholic University of America, Washington, D.C.; the Sulpician fathers assumed the disciplinary and spiritual direction of the young priest students at the University; and the direction of major seminaries in the Archdioceses of New York, Boston, and San Francisco was turned over to the society. Meanwhile, the Abbé Magnien, as he came to be called, was appointed by Cardinal James Gibbons of Baltimore to his archdiocesan council (1879) and made director of the Society for the Propagation of the Faith (1896). For almost 25 years Magnien was the confidant and advisor of the cardinal, and was intimately involved in national and international ecclesiastical affairs. When his health began to fail in the summer of 1897, Magnien went to France, where he underwent a serious operation. After he returned to Baltimore in May 1898, it soon became evident that his strength was failing; he resigned his office in the summer of 1902 and died a few months later.

Bibliography: *Bulletin Trimestriel des Anciens Elèves de S. Sulpice* (Paris 1903) 160–169. P. J. DONAHUE et al., *Very Rev. A. L. Magnien: A Memorial* (Baltimore 1903). J. T. ELLIS, *The Life of James Cardinal Gibbons,* 2 v. (Milwaukee 1952). M. F. FOLEY, ''Very Rev. Alphonse L. Magnien,'' *Catholic World* 76 (March 1903) 814–822. C. G. HERBERMANN, *The Sulpicians in the United States* (New York 1916). *Memorial Volume of the Centenary of St. Mary's Seminary* (Baltimore 1891).

[C. M. CUYLER]

MAGNIFICAT (CANTICLE OF MARY)

Mary's song of thanksgiving and praise for the mighty act that God had wrought in her and for the salvation that has been given to Israel (Lk 1.46–55) is called the Magnificat after the first word of its Latin text. The canticle, which was sung by the Blessed Virgin Mary when greeted by her cousin Elizabeth as the mother of Our Lord (Lk 1.46–55), comprises three parts. In 1.46 to 1.50 Mary, the eschatological personification of her people, sings praise to God her Savior; in 1.51 to 1.53 she recalls what God has done for Israel, and in 1.54 to 1.55 she sings of the divine plan foretold in Abraham and perfected in herself. In Mary a new beginning has been made as well as a fulfillment.

The Magnificat is used in the Eastern liturgies on certain days in the morning Office, while in the Western Church it has been, from a very early date, the canticle of VESPERS (Evening Prayer) in the Catholic, Anglican and Lutheran traditions. In solemn Vespers in the Catholic tradition, the ceremonies accompanying its singing in choir, such as incensation of the altar (as at the beginning of solemn Mass), are impressive. By reason of its daily use in medieval times a number of antiphons have been associated with the Magnificat, among them the notable O ANTIPHONS of the week preceding CHRISTMAS.

Bibliography: R. C. TANNEHILL, ''Magnificat as Poem,'' *Journal of Biblical Literature* 93 (1974) 263–275. F. FLECKENSTEIN, ''Marienverehrung in der Musik,'' in *Handbuch der Marienkunde* (Regensburg 1984) 622–663. R. E. BROWN, ''The Annunciation to Mary, the Visitation, and the Magnificat (Luke 1:26–56),'' *Worship* 62 (1988) 249–259. R. F. TAFT, *The Liturgy of the Hours in East and West: The Origins of the Divine Office and Its Meaning for Today*, 2d rev. ed. (Collegeville, Minn. 1993). G. GUIVER, *Company of Voices: Daily Prayer and the People of God* (New York 1988). P. F. BRADSHAW, *Daily Prayer in the Early Church: A Study of the Origin and Early Development of the Divine Office* (London 1981).

[M. E. MCIVER/L. J. WAGNER/EDS.]

MAGNIFICENCE

A moral virtue annexed to the virtue of fortitude that disposes a person to moderate his love for money in such a way that he is reasonably inclined to incur heavy expenses in order to carry out great projects. The virtue of magnanimity inclines a man to carry out great works of virtue; magnificence is concerned with external works—great buildings, celebrations, endowments, great social works, etc. These projects are the proximate matter of the virtue of magnificence; the remote matter is the money that is involved. Because the attraction for money is so strong, there is a special difficulty when a man must expend a large amount of money on some project; it requires a special disposition of soul to dispose a person to perform such a work easily and connaturally.

Because it is a virtue that is concerned with great sums of money, it is especially the virtue of the rich and of those in charge of large and important enterprises. The ordinary person can exercise only relative magnificence. He does not expend large sums of money, but there are times when he must spend money in sums large in proportion to his means. When the ordinary family celebrates a wedding or buys a new home, the expenditure involves a relatively large outlay. Every Christian, no matter how poor he may be, ought to develop a readiness of soul to expend relatively large sums of money when circumstances require it. It requires the same disposition of soul for a person of small means to contribute $25 to the construction of the new parish school as it requires for a richer person to contribute $2,500. Even externally, there is something magnificent about the widow contributing her mite to the temple, a magnificence somehow lacking in a million-dollar grant from a foundation.

Opposed to magnificence at one extreme is the vice of stinginess or meanness; at the other extreme is the vice of prodigality or wastefulness. Stinginess is particularly distasteful; it is the vice of those who are unreasonably attached to their money and spend it so sparingly that their projects cannot be carried out in a manner commensurate with their importance. It is the vice of those who would build a smaller, less magnificent church or cut down the guest list for their daughter's wedding merely in order to save money that they really do not need. The prodigal or wasteful person disregards the due proportion between the task and the amount he spends. He either has such a disregard for wealth or is so desirous of praise that he scatters money foolishly. He celebrates his daughter's wedding with unreasonable extravagance, and gives a casual beggar a needlessly large gift. Stinginess and prodigality are, in themselves, venial sins, but they may become grave by reason of circumstances, especially by reason of sinful motives.

There are no divine precepts concerning magnificence because it is a virtue that pertains to excellence, but we find that Mary Magdalene was eulogized by Our Lord after she had anointed him with a costly ointment: ''Amen I say to you, wherever in the whole world this gospel is preached, this also that she has done shall be told in memory of her'' (Mk 14.9).

Bibliography: THOMAS AQUINAS, *Summa theologiae* 2a2ae, 134–135. F. L. B. CUNNINGHAM, ed., *The Christian Life* (Dubuque 1959). F. ROBERTI et al., comps., *Dictionary of Moral Theology*, ed. P. PALAZZINI et al., tr. H. J. YANNONE et al., from 2d Ital. ed. (Westminster, Md. 1962).

[R. DOHERTY]

MAGNOBOD OF ANGERS, ST.

Bishop, b. *c.* 574; d. after 635. According to his biographer MARBOD, archdeacon of ANGERS and later bishop of Rennes, Magnobod was the son of a prominent family in the region of Angers. His aptitude for studies and his love of prayer attracted the attention of the local bishop, LICINIUS, who ordained him to the priesthood and later placed him in charge of the monastery situated in Challones-Sur-Loire (*Répertoire topobibliographique des abbayes et prieurés* 1:675). About the year 610 Magnobod was consecrated bishop of Angers, and he proved himself to be a competent and holy shepherd of his flock. He took part in synods at Paris in 614, and at Clichy in 627 (*Monumenta Germaniae Historica: Concilia* 1:191, 201; *Sacrorum Conciliorum nova et amplissima collectio* 10:594). Magnobod wrote the life of St. Maurilius (d. 453), one of his early predecessors in the See of Angers (*Monumenta Germaniae Historica: Auctores antiquissimi* 4.2:82–101), and is said to have built a large church in honor of St. Saturninus (third century), in which he was later buried. In the region of Segré, Magnobod is invoked as the patron of livestock. There are those who see the foundation for this cult in a popular play on words among the peasants, for the French for Magnobod is Mainbeuf, and thus the last syllable in the saint's name, *-beuf,* rhymes easily with *bœuf,* ox, bullock, beef.

Feast: Oct. 16.

Bibliography: *Gallia Christiana* (Paris 1856–65) 14:550, 598. *Acta Sanctorum* Oct. 7.2:928–950. L. RÉAU, *Iconographie de l'art chrétien,* 6 v. (Paris 1955–59) 3.2:863. J. CAMBELL, *Lexikon für Theologie und Kirche,* ed. J. HOFER and K. RAHNER, 10 v. (2d, new ed. Freiburg 1957–65) 6:1286. *Bibliotheca hagiographica latina antiquae et mediae aetatis,* 2 v. (Brussels 1898–1901; suppl. 1911) 5151–53. J. L. BAUDOT and L. CHAUSSIN, *Vies des saints et des bienheureux selon l'ordre du calendrier avec l'historique des fêtes,* ed. by the Benedictines of Paris, 12 v. (Paris 1935–56) 10:498–500.

[H. DRESSLER]

MAGNUS, JOHANNES AND OLAUS

Johannes, Swedish archbishop and historian; b. Linköping, Sweden, March 19, 1488; d. Rome, March 22, 1544. Olaus, historian and geographer; b. Linköping, Oct. 1490; d. Rome, Aug. 1, 1557. Sweden became Lutheran during their lifetime.

They were sons of a burgher of Linköping and were educated at the cathedral school of Västerås and at European universities. In 1523 Adrian VI sent Johannes, his former student at Louvain, to Sweden as papal legate to investigate the accusations of Gustavus Vasa, the newly elected king, that Abp. Trolle of Uppsala was treasonably supporting the Danish king's claims to the Swedish throne. In 1524 Clement VII refused the request of the canons of Uppsala to depose Trolle and to make Johannes archbishop, but Johannes was made administrator of the archdiocese. By 1526 Vasa began to support Lutheranism openly, partly because the pope supported Trolle. Johannes resisted the religious changes. He was arrested for treason, but he was released eventually and allowed to leave Sweden. He and Olaus, who had been away from Sweden since 1534 on missions for the king, lived in Danzig until they moved to Rome (1541). Johannes was consecrated archbishop of Uppsala in 1533 but never resided in his see. When he died (1544), Olaus was named archbishop of Uppsala. Olaus distinguished himself at the Council of Trent.

Both men were renowned scholars. Johannes wrote a history of Scandinavian kings, edited and published by Olaus (Rome 1554), and a history of the metropolitan See of Uppsala (Rome 1557) with a biography of him by Olaus. Olaus published a *Carta marina* (Venice 1539), a work remarkable for its description of the physical features of Northern Europe. It furnishes much information on the type of geographic data available in the 16th century. Olaus published a companion volume (Rome 1555) on the topography, natural history, ethnography, and the economic and political conditions of the Scandinavian world, of which there is an abridged English translation (Antwerp 1658) and an Italian translation (Turin 1958).

Bibliography. E. LYNAM, *The Carta Marina of Olaus Magnus* (Jenkintown, Pa. 1949). H. JÄGERSTADT, *Lexikon für Theologie und Kirche*, ed. J. HOFER and K. RAHNER, 10 v. (2d, new ed. Freiburg 1957–65) 6:1287.

[E. RENNER]

MAGNUS OF FÜSSEN, ST.

Apostle of the Algäu; b. *c.* 699; d. Füssen, Germany, Sept. 6, 772. A legend-clouded vita confuses him in part with St. Magnoald (or Magnus, d. 666), student of St. GALL. Magnus was called from SANKT GALLEN by Bp. Wichpert of Augsburg to Christianize the region of the Algäu. About 746 he established a cell at Füssen on a site that later became the monastery of Sankt Mang. With the support of King PEPIN he converted the heathen, cleared lands for cultivation and settlement, and opened the region to iron mining. Buried at Füssen, he was recognized as a saint between 838 and 847 and became the patron of Füssen and Kempten. Under the name of St. Mang he is a popular folk saint, especially in southern Germany, Tirol, and Switzerland, where his aid is invoked against snakes, vermin, and mice. A chalice, stole, maniple, and staff, which he is said to have used, are still preserved.

Feast: Sept. 6.

Bibliography: *Acta Sanctorum,* including the vita, Sept. 2:700–781, second part, 745–756, contains historic core. F. ZOEPFL, *Das Bistum Augsburg und seine Bischiöfe im Mittelalter* (Munich 1956), *passim.* A. BIGELMAIR, *Lebensbilder aus dem bayerischen Schwaben,* ed. G. VON PÖLNITZ, v. 2 (Munich 1953) 1–46. *Festschrift zum 1200 jährigen jubiläum des heiligen Magnus* (Füssen 1950). M. COENS, "La Vie de S. Magne de Füssen par Otloh de Saint-Emmeran," *Analecta Bollandiana* 81 (1963) 159–227.

[D. ANDREINI]

MAGUIRE, CHARLES BONAVENTURE

Missionary; b. Dungannon, County Tyrone, Ireland, December 16, 1768; d. Pittsburgh, Pa., July 17, 1833. Maguire, a priest of the Order of Friars Minor, studied at the Catholic University, Louvain, Belgium, and taught theology at the College of St. Isidore, Rome. For eight years he ministered to the Germans in the Netherlands, narrowly escaping death at the hands of French Revolutionists and Napoleon's troops. In 1817 he arrived in the U.S. as a missionary apostolic with faculties from Cardinal Lorenzo Litta, Prefect of the Congregation de Propaganda Fide. These faculties were endorsed by Ambrose Maréchal, Archbishop of Baltimore, whereupon the missionary was sent to Ebensburg in western PENNSYLVANIA. He was soon appointed to succeed the German Capuchin, Rev. Peter Helbron, as pastor of Sportsman's Hall. In 1820 Maguire's name was recommended by the hierarchy of Ireland as a suitable candidate for a bishopric in the U.S, but he was instead chosen to replace Rev. William F. X. O'Brien as pastor of St. Patrick's Church, Pittsburgh. Under Maguire's guidance the Catholic population of Pittsburgh increased in the 1820s to about 4,000 and baptisms for the decade numbered 1,214. With the influx of German Catholic immigrants into the area, Maguire decided on a second church for the Catholics of Pittsburgh. He bought property at the corner of Fifth Avenue and Grant Street and on June 29, 1829, he laid the cornerstone of what the newspapers called ''the cathedral.'' He did not live to see the completion of the church. The church, dedicated under the patronage of St. Paul the Apostle on May 4, 1834, became the cathedral of the newly erected Diocese of PITTSBURGH on August 11, 1843. Maguire's zeal won the admiration of the Catholics and non-Catholics of Pittsburgh, as his learning won him a professorship at the academy that became the University of Pittsburgh. In 1825, he published a representative apologetic: *A Defense of the Divinity of Jesus Christ and of the Mystery of the Real Presence.*

Bibliography: A. A. LAMBING, *A History of the Catholic Church in the Diocese of Pittsburgh and Allegheny* (New York 1880).

[D. F. SWEENEY]

MAGUIRE, JOHN WILLIAM ROCHFORT

Educator, labor arbitrator; b. County Roscommon, Ireland, Aug. 11, 1883; d. Miami, Florida, Feb. 11, 1940. His parents, William Thomas and Caroline (Geoffcott) Maguire, sent him to All Hallows School near Lyme Regis, England. He emigrated to Canada, entered the United States, and found employment as a reporter for the Spokane *Spokesman Review.* His most notable work as a journalist was his coverage of the trial of William Dudley Haywood (1869–1928), founder of the Industrial Workers of the World (IWW). Maguire entered Western Theological Seminary in Chicago as a candidate for the Protestant Episcopal Diocese of Chicago; but he was not satisfied with the branch theory of the church expounded by his professors. He was introduced (1908) to Peter J. MULDOON, Auxiliary Bishop of Chicago. It was on Muldoon's advice that he made a retreat at the Passionist Monastery in Chicago, where he was received into the Catholic Church.

Maguire was advised to study philosophy at St. Viator College, Bourbonnais, Illinois, where he came into contact with the Clerics of St. Viator, the religious community that he eventually joined. In 1914 he was sent to The Catholic University of America, Washington, D.C., and on Dec. 18, 1914, he became the first priest to be ordained by Bp. Thomas J. Shahan, Rector of the University. Upon receiving his master's degree in 1915, he returned to St. Viator College, where for over 20 years he taught economics and sociology. Maguire, an advocate of social reform, became closely associated with such organizations as the Social Reform party and the Illinois State Federation of Labor. During World War I he served as a U.S. Army chaplain.

After his return from Europe in 1918, he gave conspicuous public support to the Bishops' Program of Social Reconstruction. During his later years he was a frequent arbitrator of strikes. In 1934 he was appointed arbitrator of the long and bitter strike of the Kohler Company in Wisconsin, and in 1939 he succeeded in settling a labor dispute between five American Federation of Labor unions and the Warner Construction Company. He was known as one of labor's best friends.

Bibliography: Archives, Clerics of St. Viator. L. V. RYAN,''John Maguire, Seeker after Justice,'' *Social Order* 6 (May 1956) 217–221.

[J. T. ELLIS]

MAHAYANA

Literally, ''Great Vehicle,'' the name adopted by a series of movements in Buddhism between the first centuries B.C. and A.D. that came together to form a new synthesis of BUDDHISM. The movements involved represented revolutions in practice, morality, and philosophy.

In both the liturgical and moral arenas, these movements reacted against earlier ways of thinking about what it meant to be a buddha and to engage in religious practice. Earlier, it was thought that one's religious practice benefitted only oneself beyond teaching others methods of cultivation, there was no way for others to receive the direct results of one's own practice, any more than one could practice a musical instrument so that another might be able to play. They questioned the view that the enlightened one, or buddha, simply vanished from the phenomenal world upon the achievement of final nirvana, passing beyond the realm of conditioned existence in such a way that was completely ungraspable by the conventional mind.

The Mahayana movement developed a comprehensive teaching of compassion that denied both of these premises. They believed that one could express the intention to "transfer the merit" of one's religious practice so that others could indeed enjoy its fruits, and that not to do so showed a miserly spirit. In addition, they reasoned that a buddha, having perfected the virtue of compassion, would surely not simply abandon suffering beings, but would remain in the world and continue offering help and salvation. Thus, early Mahayana texts such as the *Lotus Sutra* began teaching that buddhas exist in great numbers, and that their lifespan is immeasurable. If they seem to die, it is an illusion deployed in order to spur followers on to greater efforts, but not ultimately real.

This led to the adoption of the "bodhisattva ideal" as the model for the average practitioner. The BODHISATTVA came to be seen as the one who expressly rejected nirvana as long as other beings remained caught in the cycle of suffering. Instead, the bodhisattva would continue refining and perfecting his practice virtually forever, and would dedicate the merit of his practices to the direct benefit of other beings.

Concomitant with the rise of Mahayana Buddhism was the growth of Buddhist devotional cults. As buddhas and bodhisattvas came to be seen more as direct agents of salvation by their practice of merit-transfer, individuals began devoting themselves to one particular buddha or bodhisattva, calling upon them for assistance both with immediate problems and dangers, and with the larger issue of escape from the world of suffering. The most popular bodhisattva in this regard was Avalokiteshvara, who protected devotees from danger, and the most popular buddha was Amitabha, who dwelt in the "Pure Land" to the west, a place to which he would bring devotees upon their death and in which they would have ideal conditions for practice.

Philosophically, Mahayanists raised objections to the "dharma" theories of the earlier philosophical texts known generically as "Abhidharma." One of the core teachings of Buddhism from the start was the radical impermanence and insubstantiality of things, and one way of accounting for this state was to posit "dharmas," which functioned much like "atoms" in ancient Greek thought. That is to say, they were infinitesimal building blocks of reality. Eternal and permanent in themselves, they combined and recombined with each other to form the phenomena of the world, thus accounting for the arising and decay of things.

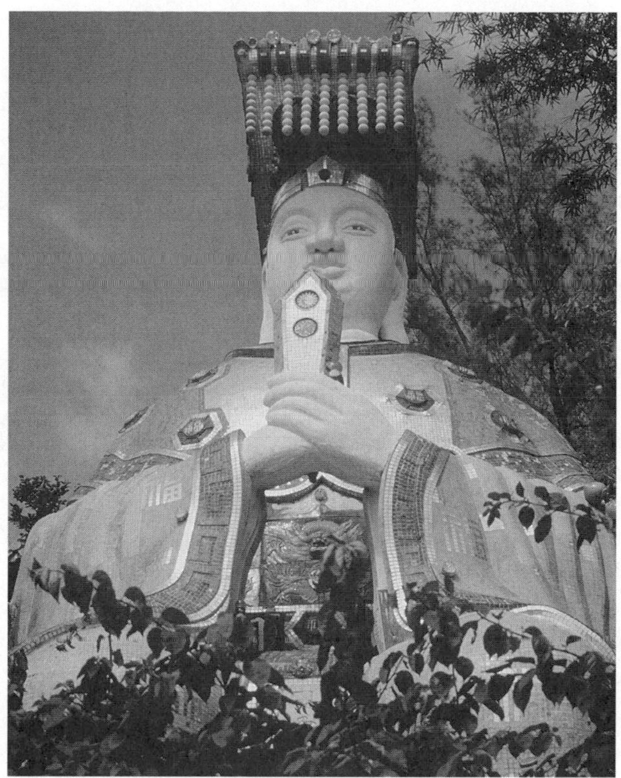

Buddha, Tin Hau Shrine. (©Buddy Mays/CORBIS)

However, many philosophers such as Nāgārjuna (2nd century A.D.) objected to even this degree of permanence, and critiqued these theories for not being radical enough. Following his lead, Mahayana came to accept "emptiness" as the ultimate state of things, meaning that they were "empty" of any kind of permanent or independent existence. Thus, all schools of Mahayana came to accept the idea that all phenomena whatsoever are radically impermanent and insubstantial, and exist only by virtue of their dependence upon causal conditions and relations with other phenomena.

In its earliest stages, the movement that grew from the convergence of all these trends called itself the "bodhisattvayana," or vehicle of the bodhisattva. However, later on the term "Mahayana," or "greater vehicle" came into popular use. This term, opposed to "Hinayana" or "lesser vehicle," was intended to depict a form of religious practice that was greater both in the goal toward which it directed individuals and the means of conveyance by which it took them to that goal. Its greater compassion and keener philosophical insights, it claimed, would enable it to carry many to the "farther shore" of liberation, while the small compassion and wisdom of their opponents would carry only the single individual.

This form of Buddhism came to predominate in Northern India, Central Asia, Tibet, China, Korea, Japan, and parts of Vietnam, and is currently the dominant form of Buddhism in North and South America and Europe.

See Also: BUDDHISM; HINAYANA.

Bibliography: B.L. SUZUKI, *Mahayana Buddhism* (London-Boston 1981) P. WILLIAMS, *Mahayana Buddhism: the doctrinal foundations* (London- New York 1989).

[C. B. JONES]

MAHDĪ, AL-

Al-Mahdī is a Muslim title. In Arabic the term al-mahdī (passive verbal adjective from hadā, to guide) means literally "the guided one," technically "the divinely guided one." The verb hadā with its multiderivatives, especially meaningful to desert people, is used frequently in the QUR'ĀN, where God is called *al-Hādī* ("the guiding one": 22:53; 25:33). The form mahdī, however, does not occur there.

Less than 25 years after the death of the Prophet, civil wars broke out, the Muslim community was irreparably split into two, and a dark period of perplexities and uncertainties, theological and political, set in. Among the masses of both groups— SUNNITES and SHĪ'ITE—the idea that a restorer, a renovator (*mujaddid*), would come took root. The hope became personified in a future deliverer. The Sunnites, however, did not go far beyond that. Certain theologians among them included even 'Īsa (Jesus) among the awaited restorers. When the term Mahdī was used by them, it carried no eschatological connotation. The suppressed minority, however, the Shī'ites, developed the theory that a descendant of 'ALĪ and Fāṭimah would appear in due course, fill the ungodly world with righteousness and justice, and rule for a short millennium, which would be followed by the ending of the world and final judgment. Clearly this is a reflex of Judeo–Christian messianic belief. In Shī'ite theology the creed became central. To give it sanction, a tradition was ascribed to the Prophet foretelling the advent of a descendant of his at the end of time.

The theory lent itself to imposture. Pretenders appeared from time to time. Finally the bulk of the Shiī'ites, known as the Twelvers, fixed on a son of the 11th IMĀM, Ḥasan al-'Askarī, who died in 874—as the Mahdī. Not much is known about al–Mahdī other than his name Muḥammad and that he was short-lived. He disappeared mysteriously in or about 878 in a cellar at al-Ḥillah, according to some, or in a mosque at Sāmarrā, according to others. But all of the Twelvers agree that he is "the expected one"; hence, his surname al-Muntaẓar. As such he will reappear as the infallible guide and absolute ruler. Then 'Īsa will descend and slay the false prophet (*al-dajjāl*, antichrist). One tradition makes 'Īsa himself al-Mahdī.

In ISLAM, where the admixture of religion and politics is inextricable, Mahdism has through the ages been exploited by ambitious conquerors. Noteworthy among these was 'Ubaydullāh al-Mahdī (909–934), founder of the Fāṭimid caliphate in North Africa. The last was Muḥammad al-Mahdī of Sudan, who from 1883 to 1885 warred against Egyptian misgovernment in his country. It should also be remembered that Mahdī was used as a proper name with no eschatological connotation, one example of this use being the name of the third 'Abbāsid caliph al-Mahdī (775–785).

Bibliography: *Shorter Encyclopedia of Islam*, ed. H. A. R. GIBB and J. H. KRAMERS (Leiden 1953) 310–313. IBN KHALDŪN, *The Muqaddimah*, tr. F. ROSENTHAL, 3 V. (New York 1958) 1: 407–408; 2:156–157, 184–186.

[P. K. HITTI]

MAHLER, GUSTAV

Late romanticist conductor and composer; b. Kalischt, Bohemia (Austria), July 7, 1860; d. Vienna, May 18, 1911. His musical gifts became apparent when he was very young. Between four and six years he was already able to sing more than 200 folk songs, and he loved to listen to military marches—these two influences were to play an elemental role in his work. In 1875 he was accepted as a pupil at the Vienna conservatory, where he won prizes in piano and composition. His rise as a conductor began after graduation, and culminated in his appointment as director of the Vienna Court Opera. His ten years there (1897–1907) mark an artistic peak in that organization's history. Intrigues and ill health, however, drove him from Vienna. In the U.S. he conducted the Metropolitan Opera (1907–09) and the New York Philharmonic (1909–11). In April 1911 he returned to Vienna mortally ill; he died the following month. Mahler excelled as song writer and symphonist, in the expansive post-Brucknerian style. In his nine massive symphonies, the unfinished Tenth, and *The Song of the Earth,* he exhausted the instrumental and vocal resources of post-Wagnerian romanticism and cleared a way for the modern idiom. In his use of texts and of "progressive tonality" his influence on Arnold Schoenberg (1874–1951) was especially strong.

Mahler's conversion to Catholicism in 1897 stirred considerable speculation, some of it to the effect that this was merely a "Catholicism of convenience." He no doubt realized that his Jewish origin was an obstacle to his gaining directorship of the Vienna Court Opera, but he could not have made this decision without an inner attraction to Catholicism. He considered writing a Mass, but confessed that he would never be able to set the Credo as he could not bring himself to such an affirmation of faith. Later, speaking of his Eighth Symphony (which uses *Veni, Creator Spiritus* and the closing scene of Goethe's *Faust* as texts), he proclaimed, ''This is my Mass!'' Opinions have differed as to whether his work benefited by the conflict between his heritage and his adopted religion. His own attitude was characteristic: ''I am a musician. That covers everything.''

Bibliography: B. WALTER, *Gustav Mahler,* tr. L. W. LINDT (New York 1958). D. MITCHELL, *Gustav Mahler: The Early Years* (London 1958). H. F. REDLICH, *Bruckner and Mahler* (2d ed. New York 1963); *Die Musik in Geschichte und Gegenwart,* ed. F. BLUME (Kassel-Basel 1949–) 8:1489–1500. D. NEWLIN, *Bruckner, Mahler, Schoenberg* (New York 1947); ''Alienation and Gustav Mahler,'' *Reconstructionist,* 25 (1959) 7:21–25. T. REIK, *The Haunting Melody: Psychoanalytic Experiences in Life and Music* (New York 1953). P. H. LÁNG, *Music in Western Civilization* (New York 1941). D. COOKE, ''The Facts Concerning Mahler's Tenth Symphony,'' *Chord and Discord* 2/10 (1963) 3–27. C. FLOROS, ''Prinzipien des Liedschaffens von Gustav Mahler,'' *Österreichische Musik Zeitschrift* 45 (1990) 7–14. E. E. GARCIA, ''A New Look at Gustav Mahler's Fateful Encounter with Sigmund Freud,'' *Journal of the Conductors' Guild* 12 (1991) 16–30. S. A. GOTTLIEB, ''Gustav Mahler's *Rückert Lieder* and the Art of Error in Interpretation,'' *Journal of the Conductors' League* 14 (1993) 107–115. S. E. HEFLING, ''*Das Lied von der Erde:* Mahler's Symphony for Voices and Orchestra—or Piano,'' *Journal of Musicology* 10 (1992) 293–341. S. OECHSLE, ''Strukturen der Katastrophe: Das Finale der VI. Symphonie Mahlers und die Endzeit der Gattung,'' *Die Musikforschung* 50 (1997) 162–182. A. P. SIMCO, ''The Timpani Parts to Mahler's Symphony No. 2, *Resurrection,*'' *Percussive Notes: The Journal of the Percussive Arts Society* 37/3 (1999) 46–54. S. WILENS, ''Zum werkbegriff Gustav Mahlers und der Entstehungsgeschichte der Fünften Symphonie,'' *Studien zur Musikwissenschaft* 43 (1994) 273–295. J. L. ZYCHOWICZ, ''Toward an *Ausgabe letzter Hand:* The Publication and Revision of Mahler's Fourth Symphony,'' *Journal of Musicology* 13 (1995) 260–276.

[D. NEWLIN]

Gustav Mahler.

MAḤZOR

Jewish term (Heb. *maḥăzôr,* cycle) designating originally the calendar encircling the lunar year and enumerating the appropriate prayers for all the days of the year. Gradually more and more synagogal poems, called piyyuṭim, were added. Eventually these became all-important, and the original calendar motif faded into obscurity; thus the maḥzor became the prayerbook for feasts only, while a separate prayerbook, called a siddur, came into use for Sabbaths and weekdays.

The evolution of the maḥzor prayer structure may be regarded as a wheel whose hub was the recitation of the Shema (derived from Dt 6.4–9; 11.13–21; Nm 15.37–41)—the essence of Jewish worship—fortified, on the one hand, by the benedictions and prayers preceding and following the Shema and the prayers and 18 benedictions forming the Amidah (literally, the ''standing'') formulated by the so-called men of the Great Assembly (from the 6th century B.C. to the 1st Christian century) and enhanced, on the other hand, by lyrical Psalms that had been taken over from the ritual of the Jerusalem Temple. The spokes emanating from the wheel were the specific services designated for the various parts of the day: Shaḥarit (morning), Musaph (addition), Minḥah (afternoon), Arvit (evening), and (for the Day of Atonement only) Neilah (closing). The outer rim of the wheel, the variable factor, consisted of layer after layer of hymns, litanies, poems, selections from oral law, meditations, and piyyuṭim that were gradually added to the ''cycle of prayers'' as it rolled through century after century, country after country, through eras of glory and tragedy. This material varied greatly in accordance with the custom and rite of the particular locale in which it developed (at least 60 different texts have been counted), each certainly influenced by its chronological niche in history. Two general roads were traveled. One originated in the Jewish community of Babylonia in the period of the important academies of the Geonim (*see* GAON) and wound down through the Arabic-Spanish civilizations. This became known as the Sephardic version of the maḥzor. The second stemmed from the Holy Land and came down through the Roman-German areas, branching off into Germany, France, and England on the West and Poland, Russia, Austria, Hungary, Bohemia, and Moravia on the East (with the Elbe River being the dividing boundary). This became known as the Ashkenazic maḥzor.

At the apex of the golden age of Spain, much of the Hebrew liturgy was enhanced by such poets as Solomon ibn Gabirol (AVICEBRON), Judah Ben Samuel Ha-Levi, and Moses ben Jacob Ibn Ezra; their elegant verse, in the style of the Arabic poets, is still part of the maḥzor. Less polished but more poignant is much of the East European piyyuṭim—penitential prayers and epics of tragic community experiences calling for divine forgiveness and blessing. Among the composers were the famed Gershom Ben Judah, Rabbi Meir of Rothenburg (*c.* 1220–93), and RASHI. Many of the earlier prayers for Rosh ha-Shana (New Year's Day) had been composed by Rabbi AKIBA BEN JOSEPH; in the 3d century in Babylonia, Rav (early 3d century) and Samuel (*c.* 177–257) contributed voluminously to the High Holiday prayers.

The earliest-known maḥzor is the *Maḥzor Yannai.* Yannai (*c.* A.D. 550), one of the early paytanim (composers of piyyuṭim;), was the first to use the name acrostic and rhyme. Eleazar Kallir (7th century) found a warmer reception to his piyyuṭim;, for, in contrast with the legalistic material used by Yannai, he used legends and homilies suited for prayers. One of the oldest preserved maḥzorim is the *Seder Ray Amram,* prepared by Rav Amram bar Sheshna, Gaon of the Sura academy, at the request of Spanish Jewry about A.D. 870. The maḥzor of Gaon SA'ADIA BEN JOSEPH was compiled in the 10th century. The famous *Maḥzor Vitry* (11th century) combined elements of both Ashkenazic and Sephardic. In Venice and Constantinople the *Maḥzor Romaniya* (known also as *Grigos*) was edited (1573–76) by Elijah ben Benjamin ha-Levi. After the invention of the printing press, the texts began to be more stabilized. Gradually, translations into the spoken language of the various countries were made, starting from the Judeo-German translation in 1571 by Abigdor ben Moses. In 1852 Elhanan Durlocher made a French translation, and the earliest English translation was by A. Alexander in 1787. A Russian translation was made by Rabbi S. Hurwitz in 1880.

During the Middle Ages new influences, such as the CABALA movement, were reflected in the maḥzor. The modern era added readings and petitions, as in the Yizkor memorial service; prayers for heads of state; and prayers connected with the rebirth of the State of Israel. New prayerbooks have been produced by the newer movements of Reform, Conservative, and Reconstructionist belief of JUDAISM. Across the span of the centuries, the prayers of the maḥzor have formed a network of "bridges leading from the heart to God."

Bibliography: I. BROYDÉ, *Jewish Encyclopedia* 8:262–264. I. ELBOGEN, *Universal Jewish Encyclopedia* 8:619–621. T. H. GASTER, *Festivals of the Jewish Year* (New York 1953). S. GREENBERG, *The Jewish Prayerbook: Its Ideals and Values* (United Synagogue of America; New York 1957). A. Z. IDELSOHN, *Jewish Liturgy and Its Development* (New York 1932) ch. 7. E. MUNK, *The World of Prayer,* tr. H. BIBERFELD and L. OSCHRY (New York 1954). I. ABRAMSON, *A Companion to the Authorized Daily Prayerbook* (London 1922). H. KIEVAL, The High Holy Days (New York 1959–). J. ROSENTHAL, "Toldot ha-maḥzor," in *Sefer ha-shanah l'yehude Amerikah* (New York 1947). Isaac ben Jacob, *Otsar ha-sefarim: Maḥzor* (Vilna 1880).

[E. SUBAR]

MAI, ANGELO

Cardinal and paleographer; b. Schilpario, Italy, March 7, 1782; d. Castelgandolfo, September 9, 1854. He became a Jesuit in 1799 and taught at Naples from 1804 until the anti-Jesuit policy of Joseph Napoleon forced him to Rome and then to Orvieto, where he was ordained in 1808. As scriptor of the Ambrosian Library in Milan in 1813, he discovered numerous texts of lost works of Cicero, Fronto, Homer, Plautus, and others. In visits to other European libraries he discovered more lost works. He left the Jesuits in 1819 to become the first Vatican librarian and in 1838 was made a cardinal. In all, he discovered 359 lost texts of ancient pagan and Christian authors, for the most part published in his four collections: the *Scriptorum veterum nova collectio* (10 v., 1825–38); *Classici auctores* (10 v., 1828–38); *Spicilegium Romanum* (10 v., 1839–44); and the *Nova patrum bibliotheca* (8 v., 1852–57). He arranged and catalogued MSS of the Vatican Library. Unfortunately, owing to imperfect methods of restoring palimpsest texts, some MSS were damaged in his work.

Bibliography: A. MAI, *Epistolario,* ed. G. GERVASONI (Florence 1954). G. POLETTO, *Del cardinale Angelo Mai* (Siena 1886). H. LECLERCQ, *Dictionnaire d'archéologie chrétienne et de liturgie* 10.1:1196–1202. S. TIMPANARO, "Angelo Mai," *Atene e Rome* NS 1 (1956) 3–34. V. VIETTI, A. MERCATI and A. PELZER *Dizionario ecclesiastico* 2:781–782.

[F. X. MURPHY]

MAIER, ANNELIESE

Historian of science, b. Tübingen, Nov. 17, 1905; d. Rome, Dec. 2, 1971. Born of Lutheran parents, she was the daughter of Anna Sigwart and Heinrich Maier, a distinguished philosopher. After early studies in Tübingen,

Göttingen, and Heidelberg, she studied philosophy, physics, and the history of art at the Universities of Zurich and Berlin, where she presented her doctoral thesis *Kants Qualitätskategorien.* In 1936 she went to Italy to work on the letters of Leibniz preserved in the Vatican Library. In 1938 she published her first major work, *Die Mechanisierung des Weltbildes im 17. Jahrundert,* which was reedited in 1968. Under the influence of Auguste Pelzer she turned her attention to medieval science, publishing her first efforts in 1939 concerning intensive quantities.

During World War II she lived in Rome, thanks to the generosity of Cardinal Angelo Mercati, and made it her home. In 1945 she became a collaborator of the Vatican Library, publishing her catalogue of Latin Borghese MSS in 1952 and MSS Vat. lat. 2118–92 in 1961. In 1954 she became research professor of the Max-Planck-Gesellschaff with full title and subsidy. Between 1943 and 1958 she published five major volumes on the history of medieval science under the general title of *Studien zur Naturphilosophie der Spätscholastik.* Becoming a Catholic in 1943, she was baptized by Placido M. Niccolini, bishop of Assisi. Maier was deeply devoted to the Barnabite Fathers in Rome. At the time of her death she was working on a project, approved by John XXIII, to publish with Giuseppe de Luca documents concerning the beatific vision controversy involving John XXII.

Bibliography: *Studien:* 1. *Die Vorläufer Galileis im 14. Jahrundert* (1949; 2d ed. 1966). 2. *Zwei Grundprobleme der scholastichen Naturphilosophie* (1951; 3d ed. 1968). 3. *An der Grenze von Scholastik und Naturwissenschaft* (1943; 2d ed. 1952). 4. *Metaphysiche Hinter-gründe der spätscholastichen Naturphilasophie* (1955). 5. *Zwischen Philosophie und Mechanik* (1958). *Ausgehendes Mittelalter,* 2 v. (1964–67). Works about Maier, M. CLAGETT, *Speculum* 48 (1973) 626–627. E. GRANT, *Archives intern. d'hist. des sciences.* J. BIGNAMI ODIER, *Rivista di Storia della Chiesa in Italia* (1972) 245–248. S. V. ROVIGHI, *Rivista di Filosopia Neo-Scholastica,* (1972) 353–354.

[J. A. WEISHEIPL]

MAILLA, JOSEPH ANNE MARIE MOYRIA DE

Missionary, historian, and cartographer; b. Maillat (Ain), France, December 16, 1669; d. Beijing, China, June 28, 1748. The young noble entered the Society of Jesus on September 12, 1686, and departed France for China in 1701. After arrival at Macau in 1703, he took up residence in Canton, where he acquired marked proficiency in the language. His religious writings were mainly Chinese translations of the Sunday Gospels, lives of the saints, prayers for Communion, devotions to the Sacred Heart, and the SPIRITUAL EXERCISES of Ignatius Loyola. When Emperor Khang-hi commissioned the Jesuits to make a cartographical survey of China, Mailla was selected with two other Jesuits to map the provinces of Henan, Jiangsu, Zhejiang, Fujian, and Taiwan. For this he received the rank of mandarin. Later he learned the Manchurian language and translated the annals of the empire into French. The completed manuscript was sent to France in 1737, but was not published until Abbé Grosier incorporated it into a *Histoire générale de la China . . .* (13 v. Paris 1777–85). Mailla also wrote the early history of Formosa, translated into English in 1774, and an account of the persecution of Christians in China that was published in the *Lettres édifiantes.* Having been in imperial favor, Mailla was honored with a state funeral at his death.

Bibliography: C. SOMMERVOGEL, *Bibliothèque de la Compagnie de Jésus* 5:330–334; 9:629; 12:564. *Lettres édifiantes,* ed. C. LE GOBIEN and J. B. DU HALDE, 34 v. (Paris 1707–73) 2.19:327—. R. STREIT and J. DINDINGER *Biblioteca missionum*7:503. L. PFISTER, *Notices biographique et bibliographique sur les Jésuites de l'ancienne mission de Chine, 1552-1773* (Shanghai 1932-34).

[J. V. MENTAG]

MAIMBOURG, LOUIS

Church historian, controversialist, and preacher; b. Nancy, France, January 10, 1610; d. Paris, August 13, 1686. He was admitted to the Jesuit novitiate, May 20, 1626, completed his theological courses at Rome, and then taught humanities at Rouen for six years. Maimbourg developed a skill for polemics and was known for his preaching and writings against Jansenists and Protestants. He criticized Antoine Arnauld, and under the pseudonym François Romain, he wrote a reply to the circular letter written on April 25, 1668, by Bps. Nicolas Pavillon of Alet, François Caulet of Pamiers, Henri Arnauld of Angers, and Nicolas Buzenval of Beauvais, in which they explained their refusal to sign Alexander VII's formulary, *Regiminis apostolici* (February 15, 1665). Seeking common ground for discussion and possible agreement with Protestants, he wrote: *La Méthode pacifique pour remaner sans dispute les protestants à la vraie foi sur le point de l'eucharistie . . .* (Paris 1670); *Traité de la vraie Église . . .* (Paris 1671); and *Traité de la vraie parole de Dieu . . .* (Paris 1671). Maimbourg's reputation rests principally upon his historical works, some of which because of their sympathy for Gallican Liberties were placed on the Index. These include: *Historie du grand schisme d'occident . . .* (Paris 1678; condemned May 23, 1680); *Histoire de la décadence de l'empire depuis Charlemagne . . .* (Paris 1679; condemned May 23, 1680); *Traité historique de l'etablissement et des prérogatives de l'Église de Rome et de ses évêques* (Paris 1685; condemned June 4, 1685); *His-*

toire du pontificat de St. Gregoire le Grand (2 v. Paris 1686; condemned February 26, 1687). His *Histoire du luthéranisme* (Paris 1680) was similarly censured by a decree of December 12, 1680, for its treatment of indulgences. On Feb. 10, 1682, he left the Jesuits at the order of Innocent XI. Louis XIV granted him a pension of 3,000 livres and a lodging in the Abbey of Saint-Victor at Paris. At the time of his death from apoplexy he was working on a history of Anglican orders. Among Maimbourg's works that escaped proscription by the Index are: *Histoire de l'arianisme* . . . (2 v. Paris 1673); *Histoire de l'hérésie des iconoclastes* . . . (3 v. Paris 1674); *Histoire des croisades pour la déliverance de la Terre Sainte* (2 v. Paris 1675); *Histoire du schisme des Grecs* (2 v. Paris 1677); *Histoire du calvinisme* (2 v. Paris 1682); and a book of his sermons, *Sermons pour le carême* . . . (2 v. Paris 1672).

Bibliography: H. REUSCH, *Der Index der verbotenen Bücher,* 2 v. (Bonn 1885) 2:583–586. C. SOMMERVOGEL, *Bibliothèque de la Compagnie de Jésus* 5:343–356. J. CARREYRE, *Dictionnaire de la Théologie Catholique* 9.2:1656–61, bibliog. and description of Maimbourg's major works. F. STEGMÜLLER, *Lexikon für Theologie und Kirche* 2 6:1298. H. LIEBING, *Die Religion in Geschichte und Gegenwart* 3 4:610–611.

[E. D. MCSHANE]

MAIMONIDES (MOSES BEN MAIMON)

Medieval Jewish scholar; b. Córdoba, Spain, March 30, 1135; d. Fosṭāṭ, Egypt, Dec. 13, 1204. In Jewish circles often called ''the second Moses'' or ''the RaMBaM'' (an acrostic composed of the initial letters of the title Rabbi and his name), Moses Maimonides was known to the Islamic world as Abū 'Imrān Mūsā ibn Maimūn ibn 'Ubayd-Allāh and to medieval Latin theologians as Rabbi Moyses (Aegyptius).

Life. He was born on the Preparation Day of Passover. Maimonides's first instruction was at the hands of his father, Rabbi Maimon ben Joseph, a mathematician, astronomer, and author of Talmudic commentaries, a study on the ritual, and notes on the Pentateuch. To a thorough formation in rabbinics, Moses was able to add the wealth of Greco-Arabian learning accessible in Islamic Spain and North Africa. With the fall of Córdoba in 1148 to the Almohades, Muslim zealots from Morocco, both Judaism and Christianity were proscribed, and the Maimon family entered upon 12 years of wandering through Spain before attempting to settle at Fez in Morocco. But persecution raged in Morocco as well as in Spain, and the family escaped only through the good offices of a friendly Muslim poet and theologian, whose name is given as Abū-'l-'Arab ibn Ma'īšah. On April 18, 1165, they left Fez for Palestine. Landing at Acre, they made the pilgrimage to Jerusalem and Hebron but, disappointed by the unhappy state of Judaism in the Holy Land, finally established themselves at Fosṭāṭ in Egypt, an ancient settlement ''two Sabbath-day-journeys'' south of Cairo. There Maimon ben Joseph died in 1166, and David, a younger brother of Moses, who had been supporting the family by trading in jewels, was drowned in the course of a voyage to the Indies. With him were lost the family resources, and funds entrusted to him by other merchants. Prostrated for a time by this disaster, Moses recovered to undertake the practice of medicine and rose to become personal physician of A-Qāḍī al-Fāḍil, Vizier of Saladin. Al-Qifṭī has recorded that Maimonides declined the offer of a comparable post with ''the King of the Franks at Ascalon,'' Richard I of England. More than 20 years after he had rescued the Maimon family at Fez, Abū'l-'Arab ibn Ma'īšah encountered Moses in Egypt living openly as a Jew and there denounced him as having lapsed from Islam. This has suggested that the Maimons had passed as Muslims while residing at Fez. But the charge was dismissed, and Maimonides was granted the office of *nāgîd,* chief of all the Jewish communities in Egypt. Maimonides was active both as a physician and as *nāgîd* until his last illness. Jews and Muslims alike observed three days of public mourning at Fosṭāṭ; a funeral service and a general fast were kept at Jerusalem; and the body of the great rabbi was entombed at Tiberias in Galilee.

Works. Maimonides's writings include an Arabic *Treatise on Logic,* said to have been published when the author was but 16 (1151), and translated into Hebrew by Moses IBN TIBBON (*c.* 1240–83). In 1158 he produced a treatise in Hebrew on the Jewish Calendar. A ''Letter on Apostasy,'' written in Arabic and addressed to the persecuted Jews of Morocco, the authenticity of which is not uncontested, belongs to the year 1160. In 1168 after a decade of labor, he published his *Sirāj* (Enlightenment), an Arabic commentary on the MISHNAH that may be the earliest application of scientific method to the interpretation of that collection. In 1172 Maimonides answered a plea for counsel from the suffering Jews of Yemen with his ''Letter to the South.'' His personal ''deuteronomy,'' the *Mishneh Torah* (Repetition of the Law), later known as ''The Strong Hand,'' an echo of Dt 34.12, appearing in 1180, was intended to introduce systematic order into the centuries-old accumulation of the laws and commentaries of Judaism. Written in Hebrew, this took the form of a vast codification of Jewish legislation, both Biblical and rabbinical. A ''Book of Precepts,'' published in Arabic at an undetermined date, deals with the traditional 613 precepts of the Mosaic Law. Maimonides's major influence outside Judaism has been exercised through his *Guide of the Perplexed.* Published in Arabic in 1190, the *Guide* appeared with the author's approval in the Hebrew version of Samuel ibn Tibbon on Nov. 30, 1204, and under the title *Môrēh Nebûkîm.* The Latin version of the *Guide, Dux dubiorum, Dux neutrorum,* known to 13th-century Christian theologians, seems to have been produced before 1240; it stems from a Hebrew translation by Judah Al-Ḥarīzī. In 1520 a printing of the medieval Latin version, with revisions characteristic of Renaissance editions, was published in Paris by Augustinus Justinianus, and a Latin translation of the ibn Tibbon version was published as *Dux perplexorum* by John Buxtorf the Younger at Basel in 1629. It was in the Buxtorf edition that the *Guide* was known to Leibniz, whereas Spinoza possessed the Hebrew version of ibn Tibbon. Maimonides responded to accusations that he had denied the resurrection of the body with a treatise on the subject in 1191. Unlike the immortality of the soul, for which rational demonstrations are possible, he explained, this doctrine is held exclusively on faith. A request from the Jews of Marseilles was the occasion of his *Letter on Astrology* in 1194, in which he totally rejected the pseudo-scientific subordination of human affairs to celestial phenomena. To these may be added collections of his *Responsa* and *Letters.* A treatise on the unity of God, ascribed to him, is of uncertain authenticity. Maimonides's practice as a physician is reflected in a series of medical treatises that includes his translation into Hebrew of the Canon of AVICENNA and his annotated extracts from GALEN.

Doctrine. Persuaded that faith has nothing to fear from a circumspect application of reason to Scripture, Maimonides acknowledged the value of a preparation in the quadrivium and in logic for the believer who must contend with the metaphysical questions broached by the *mutakallimūn,* Muslim devotees of the rational discussion of faith called KALĀM (discourse). Although few in number, erudite believers deserve guidance, for the confrontation of science and Scripture can beget grave perplexity; hence his *Guide of the Perplexed* (see the introduction to the English translation by S. Pines, p. lvii; and 2.23, *ibid.,* pp. 321–322). Biblical terms must be understood correctly, and the arguments that seem to militate against the Mosaic Law must be classified as apodictic, merely probable, or fallacious if they are to be solved (*ibid.* 2.16, p. 293). In his *Treatise on Logic,* Maimonides had taken into account not only the books usually assigned to the *Organon* of ARISTOTLE, but also the *Rhetoric* with its probable reasonings and the *Poetics* with its discussion of fiction and imitation. The purpose of the *Guide* is to illumine Scripture (*ibid.,* introductory essay by Leo Strauss, p. xiv; 2.2 pp. 253–254); the first part recalls Maimonides's youthful interest in precise ter-

Maimonides (Moses Ben Maimon). (©Bettmann/CORBIS)

minology, while the second and third parts elaborate the Talmudic themes of ''Creation'' and the ''Divine Chariot.'' The *Guide* stated, in 26 propositions, the main theses from which philosophers proved the existence of God, and Maimonides rejected only the one that asserts the eternity of the world. The point in Aristotle, he claimed, is held as merely probable, whereas, according to his commentators, the Philosopher had demonstrated the proposition. On the other hand, the *mutakallimūn* tried to demonstrate temporal creation. Maimonides thought both commentators and *mutakallimūn* wrong (*ibid.* 2 Introd., pp. 235–241). Should reason demand it, the scriptural passages on temporal creation could be explained figuratively (*ibid.* 2.25 pp. 327–328), but the philosophical objections to the eternity of the world are stronger than those urged against the doctrine of creation as ''held by our Father Abraham and our Teacher Moses'' (*ibid.* 2.22 p. 320); hence the Bible account prevails (*ibid.* 2.23 p. 322). Since we cannot demonstrate that the world is not eternal, philosophical integrity demands that we give such proofs of God's existence as would be valid even if it were; Aristotelian demonstrations meet this challenge (*ibid.* 2.1 pp. 245–246) and, what is more, support the Biblical teaching that God is One: His essence and existence are identical (*ibid.* 1.57 p. 132). God has no essential attributes, and because He has nothing in common with creatures, human language is radically inadequate to express Him (*ibid.* 1.50–53 pp. 111–123). Even in Scripture, terms predicated of God are but metaphors (*ibid.* 1.26 pp. 56–57). The true attributes of God are negative ones (*ibid.* 1.58 pp. 134–135), but those based on His many actions are permissible since they do not compromise the divine unity (*ibid.* 1.54 pp. 123–128).

The eternity of the world apart, Aristotle is reliable on what transpires under the sphere of the moon (*ibid.* 2.22 pp. 319–320), but later thinkers have improved upon his teaching concerning what is above. These have shown that there are nine intelligences to animate the nine spheres and a tenth, the agent intellect, which reduces to act our individual possible intellects (*ibid.* 2.4 pp. 257–258). These intelligences are philosophical analogues of Scripture's angels (*ibid.* 2.6 pp. 261–262). Nor were the philosophers wrong to say that Providence does not extend to every individual, for Providence has regard for a man in direct proportion to his merits (*ibid.* 3.18 pp. 475–476) and departs from those who occupy themselves with creatures (*ibid.* 3.51 pp. 624–626). Prophecy, itself susceptible of many grades and most fully realized in Moses, is the height of human knowledge (*ibid.* 2.37–48 pp. 373–412). Intellectual perfection bespeaks moral perfection (*ibid.* 1.34 pp. 75–78), and the possession of intellectual qualities assures a man of immortality (*ibid.* 3.54 p. 635). Knowledge through union with the agent intellect is identified with the eternal life promised by faith: the souls of the pious will not die (*ibid.* 2.27 p. 333).

Familiar from his youth with persecution, Maimonides counseled patience and even flight in his ''Letter to the South,'' addressed to the Jews of Yemen, and warned them at the same time against a fatuous messianism. If the ''Letter on Apostasy'' is indeed his, it may reflect the straits of his own family at Fez, where some Jews had made an external profession of faith in Islam but continued to practice Judaism in secret. Against the condemnation by a rigorous rabbi of this dissembling, the second letter likens the Law to a rope let down from heaven to earth: to grasp it firmly with both hands offers the best hope, but to hold on with the tips of the fingers is better than to let go altogether (*Cahiers juifs,* 8–12).

Influence. Maimonides's theological and exegetical works soon counted as classics in Egypt, Arabia, Palestine, Spain, and France; but the author's alleged pretension to supremacy in the rabbinate, his freedom in interpreting venerated texts, and his policy of omitting his authorities, all invited attack. To the distress of those who deplored dogmatism, Maimonides had formulated in his ''Enlightenment'' 13 articles of faith as the minimum that would guarantee every Israelite a part in the world to come. The disciple to whom the *Guide* was addressed expressed his disappointment with Maimonides's reconciliation of faith and learning, while readers who found the resurrection of the body in neither the ''Repetition of the Law'' nor in the *Guide* did not miss the echoes of Averroës and Aristotle when the Rambam dealt with the immortality of the soul. Judah al-Fakhar of Toledo and Moses ben Naḥmān declined his leadership. By about 1230, the anti-Maimonists Solomon ben Abraham, David ben Saul, and Jonas ben Abraham led an assault in the name of the letter of the Mosaic Law against the Maimonists of Lunel, Béziers, and Narbonne. LEVI BEN GERSON (1288–1344) and Ḥasdāi Crescas (1340–1410) were to subject Maimonides to severe critiques, and Cabbalists managed to mark his tomb as that of ''an excommunicate and heretic'' (Levy, 233–235). The sympathetic use of the *Guide* by Christian theologians makes it tempting to exaggerate his influence on St. Albert the Great, St. Thomas Aquinas, and John Duns Scotus; but it remains true that in the Christian universities no other master of Judaism was so much esteemed as Rabbi Moses. Despite all controversies, the Rambam has inspired the popular saying: ''From Moses to Moses, there has been no one like Moses.''

Bibliography: Texts and translations. *Le Guide des égarés,* tr. and ed. S. MUNK, 3 v. (Paris 1856–66; reprint 1960), contains Arabic text and Fr. tr.; *Dalālat al-ḥā'irīn,* ed. I. JOEL (Jerusalem 1930–31); *Guide of the Perplexed,* tr. with introd. and nn. S. PINES, introd. essay L. STRAUSS (Chicago 1963), the best tr.; *Guide for the Perplexed,* tr. M. FRIEDLÄNDER, 3 v. (London 1881, abr. 1904; repr. Gloucester, Mass. 1962), older rendering; *The Code of Maimonides* (*Mishneh Torah*) (Yale Judaica Ser.; New Haven 1949-), to date Bks. 3–14, ann. Eng. trs.; *Treatise on Logic,* ed. and tr. I. EFROS (New York 1938), contains orig. Arabic text and three Hebrew trs. I. EFROS, ''Maimonides' *Treatise on Logic:* The New Arabic Text,'' *Jewish Quarterly Review* 53 (1963) 269–273. R. LERNER and M. MAHDI, eds., *Medieval Political Philosophy; A Sourcebook* (Glencoe, Ill. 1963), contains *Letter on Astrology* and further references. C. P. FARRAR and A. P. EVANS, *Bibliography of English Translations from Medieval Sources* (New York 1946) 2790–2807. Literature. A. HESCHEL, *Maimonides: Eine Biographie* (Berlin 1935). L. G. LEVY, *Maïmonide* (Paris 1932). I. MÜNZ, *Maimonides: The Story of His Life and Genius,* tr. H. T. SCHNITTKIND (Boston 1935). ''Maïmonide, sa vie, son oeuvre, son influence,'' *Cahiers juifs* 16–17 (1935). A. COHEN, *The Teachings of Maimonides* (London 1927). J. GUTTMANN, *Das Verhältniss des Thomas von Aquino zum Judenthum und zur jüdischen Litteratur* (Göttingen 1891).

[E. A. SYNAN]

MAINE, CATHOLIC CHURCH IN

Maine is unique among New England states in that it alone can trace its Catholic roots back to the era of the earliest European colonization. It was in 1604 that the French established a settlement on an island near the mouth of the St. Croix River. This settlement, Holy Cross, was the first European colony in New England.

Though primarily a business venture headed by the Calvinist Pierre du Guast, Sieur de Monts, and Samuel Champlain, it included a Catholic chaplain, Nicholas Aubry. The colony failed to endure the first harsh winter, but its fate was no deterrent to further exploration. In 1613 the Jesuits Peter Biard and Enemond Masse accompanied a colonizing venture of Pierre La Saussaye bound for the Penobscot River (which they had earlier visited in 1611, offering Mass in the vicinity of present-day Bangor), but dense fog forced the ship to land sooner than planned. At Fernald Point near Southwest Harbor on Mount Desert Island they planted their colony of St. Sauveur. They were welcomed by the indigenous people, and prospects for the young colony seemed good, but within two months it had been destroyed by the Englishman Samuel Argall, Admiral of Virginia, who had been given instructions to frustrate French attempts to colonize the Penobscot region.

The territory known as Acadia would be exchanged nine times by the French and English in subsequent decades. The history of the settlement at the town on Penobscot Bay, now known as Castine, is typical of this instability. The Plymouth Pilgrims had a trading post there by 1629. In 1632 the area reverted to French control, and the Capuchin Franciscans arrived in 1635, establishing the mission of Our Lady of Hope at the site the French called Pentagoet. The cornerstone of a substantial church was laid in 1648, but its existence was fragile. The English would regain control of the territory from 1654 to 1667 and the mission collapsed, though the French were once more in charge from 1667 to 1703. Franciscans returned during these years when the post was in the hands of John Vincent d'Abbadie, Baron of Saint-Castin. The baron encouraged pastoral work among the natives, and it was by his patronage that a chapel dedicated to St. Ann was erected for their use on an island in the Penobscot river (''Indian Island''), the first of a succession of chapels at a mission that endures to this day.

More enterprising work among the indigenous peoples was carried out by Fr. Gabriel Druillettes, S.J., sent to work among the natives of the Kennebec region in 1646. He established a mission to the Abenakis near present-day Augusta, and lived among them till 1647. Following a diplomatic mission to the English at Plymouth and Boston in 1650, he again carried out missionary work with the tribes along the Kennebec in the winters of 1651 and 1652, establishing the village of Norridgewock as his headquarters.

Druillettes work was continued after a lapse of a few decades by his intrepid brother-Jesuit Sebastian RÂLE, who arrived in Norridgewock in 1694. Proficient in native dialects, he worked tirelessly among the Abenakis, catechizing, adjudicating disputes, caring for the sick, and teaching music, all amidst the ongoing political tensions between the English and the French. Norridgewock village was destroyed in a raid by the Massachusetts colony in 1705; another attack followed in 1722 during which the village was again destroyed. Finally, in 1724, an assault was launched during which Râle himself was murdered, and his scalp sent with 26 others back to Boston. Many of the surviving Abenakis fled north towards Canada.

The next century, with its ongoing political tensions and reversals, saw little activity by Catholics. Most of the state had been included in the ecclesiastical jurisdiction of the Diocese of Boston when it was erected in 1808.

Maine Becomes a State. In 1820 the State of Maine was admitted to the Union. At this time there were three centers of Catholic life in the state, which would serve as the building blocks of the Church in Maine: the surviving native peoples, grouped at Indian Island and Pleasant Point (near Eastport); a group of Acadians at Madawaska by the St. John River; and Irish immigrants living near Damariscotta and Whitefield. It was thanks to the intervention of some prominent citizens of the latter group that the new state constitution contained no anti-Catholic restrictions, unlike those of MASSACHUSETTS (from which the state was carved) and New Hampshire.

By the 1800s only 750 native peoples remained in Maine. Members of the Penobscot tribe were restricted to Indian Island, while Passamaquody lived near Pleasant Point. Three exiled priests from revolutionary France worked among these tribes from 1792 to 1818. One of the three, Jean CHEVERUS, visited both tribes in 1797 and 1798. He was replaced by James ROMAGNÉ, who built a church at Pleasant Point, and labored among the natives till 1818. A learned, pious, affable man, he introduced farming to his flock, and translated a prayer book into the native dialect.

By 1820 there were about 108 Catholic families living near Damariscotta and Whitefield. Fr. (later Bishop of Boston, 1808–23) Cheverus first visited the community in 1798, and returned almost every summer from Boston until 1818, using it as a base from which to search the surrounding countryside for isolated Catholics. James Kavanagh and Matthew Cottrill, who had arrived in Newcastle as young Irish immigrants in the early 1790s, and had prospered as merchants and shipbuilders, were the leaders of this prosperous district, which boasted its own church, St. Patrick's. This edifice, built in the year 1808, is the oldest extent Catholic church in New England. Kavanagh's son Edward, though preparing for ordination in 1813, turned his attention to his father's failing businesses, later distinguishing himself as a state legislator, congressman (1831–35), and governor (1843), the first Catholic in New England to hold these latter offices.

Meanwhile, in the far north of Maine, 20 Acadian families, displaced from St. John, New Brunswick, by American Loyalists, had settled near the St. John and Madawaska Rivers. Between 1790 and 1794 they were joined by Acadians from Nova Scotia, and about this time asked the Bishop of Quebec for a priest and church. An influx of new arrivals swelled their numbers to 2,000 by 1831. Most of the Madawaskans were deeply religious Catholics, and could boast of a resident priest after 1808. In 1842 the boundary between the United States and Canada was fixed at the St. John River, leaving the Madawaskans divided. Forty days after the treaty was signed, Rome assigned the care of the Catholics in the region to the Diocese of Fredericton, New Brunswick, including St. Bruno's parish on the southern (U.S.) side of the river, which had been established in 1838. In 1860 the Catholics of Maine Madawaska were given over to the care of the Diocese of St. John, New Brunswick. Not until 1870 and the First Vatican Council was Bishop Bacon of the Diocese of PORTLAND given the spiritual care of the Catholics of northern Maine (though the state had been providing education there since 1843).

Maine's earliest Catholic churches were built where the immigrant Irish settled. Fr. Dennis Ryan, ordained by Bishop Cheverus in 1817 (the first ordination in New England), spent 25 years pastoring, first at Damariscotta and later at Whitefield (where he built a brick church in 1838). He ministered to Catholics from the Kennebec to the Penobscot, including the towns of Bath, Augusta, and Bangor. Already in 1836 there were 1,000 Irish in the latter town, drawn by jobs in the lumber industry. St. Michael's church there was dedicated in 1839. In Augusta, Ryan made do with a converted Unitarian church purchased in 1836, which served till St. Mary's was built in 1847.

Another intrepid Maine pastor was Fr. Charles Ffrench. His assignment was to care for the large numbers of Irish emigrating into Maine, and settling along the seacoast. He based his ministry first in Eastport—the immigrant's gateway from New Brunswick—where St. Joseph's was dedicated in 1835. It was from the flock in Eastport that John E. BARRY, the Portland diocese's first native vocation, would hail. Ffrench later moved the focus of his pastoral activity to Portland, where St. Dominic's church had been dedicated in 1833. The Catholic population of Maine's largest city was growing, bolstered by a large number of converts including Josue Young, the future bishop of Erie, Pennsylvania.

Growth and Trials. Despite the growing Catholic population, not all communities were as fortunate as Bangor, Eastport, or Portland. There was a Catholic presence in Belfast from 1827, but there would be no permanent church until 1894 (a rented hall was used until 1851, and then again from 1870 to 1885). A lack of priests and resources meant that congregations were slow to grow, and loss of faith was common.

The growing numbers of Irish immigrants, and the squalid conditions of the urban slums in which many were forced to live, moved Bishop Benedict FENWICK of Boston to propose and promote a Catholic immigrant colony in northern Maine. In 1834 the bishop purchased 11,358 acres in northern Maine, and by 1840 about 65 families had taken up residence there. Though Benedicta (as it was named) boasted a church, sawmill, and orphanage, and was soon a thriving farming town, it never developed sufficiently to support the college and seminary that Fenwick had envisioned.

In 1848 Bishop Fenwick's successor in Boston, John Fitzpatrick, obtained two Jesuits from the Maryland province for work in Maine. Fr. John Bapst, a 35-year-old exiled Swiss, was the first to arrive and the last of his brethren to leave in 1859. Bapst worked for two years at Indian Island north of Bangor. Divisions among the tribe, however, led to his being transferred to Eastport in 1851. By 1852, he had promoted the construction of three new churches (at Oldtown, Waterville, and Ellsworth), and was regularly visiting 33 stations on his mission circuit. In Ellsworth his pastoral work resulted in a number of prominent converts (including a young lady, Mary Agnes Tincker, who would become a prominent novelist of the Victorian age), but also stirred up the ire of local Nativists. Incensed by his vocal support for the rights of Catholic children to withdraw from public schools that promoted the King James Bible, and egged on by Bapst's obvious "foreigness" and success as an evangelist, a local mob assaulted, robbed, tarred, and feathered the Jesuit on a visit to Ellsworth in October of 1854. Public sentiment in Bangor and Portland was outraged, and prominent citizens offered him a gold watch to replace one which had been stolen from him, and a purse of $500 to aid him in his work (nonetheless, not all were repentant—the Catholic Church in Ellsworth was burned in 1856).

Bangor and Eastport were now the centers of the Jesuits' mission. Bangor was growing rapidly (Catholics alone numbered 6,000), and in 1856 a new church, St. John's, was dedicated. Though the site chosen for the church was deliberately inconspicuous (given the recent wave of anti-Catholicism), the building itself was in the grandest Gothic style, and was acclaimed one of the most beautiful churches in New England. Ironically, the very success of the Jesuits in Bangor and down east Maine led to the first bishop of Portland's desire to reclaim St. John's as a diocesan parish. Fr. Bapst and his fellow Jesuits departed the diocese in 1859, and would not return for almost a century. They had, however, overseen the construction of seven churches: Waterville, Oldtown, Ellsworth, Winterport, Rockland, Trescott, and Bangor. Churches in Machias and Calais, though started prior to their ministry in Maine, were completed during their watch.

A Diocese for Maine. The Diocese of PORTLAND was established on July 29, 1853 (the same day as Brooklyn and Burlington, Vermont), encompassing the states of Maine and NEW HAMPSHIRE. The first candidate named to fill the see, Henry Coskery of Baltimore, declined the appointment, and so there was delay before David William BACON's (1813–74) name was announced. A priest of the New York archdiocese, he was an energetic pastor and builder in his native Brooklyn before being appointed to Maine. He was consecrated at St. Patrick's Cathedral in New York on April 22, 1855, and installed at St. Dominic's in Portland on May 31. As there were only six priests working in Maine, the bishop's first task was to find clergy; nine new arrivals from Europe and America would swell the rolls by year's end. Bacon was a talented administrator, and worked to remedy a number of deficiencies. Land was purchased in Portland for a cathedral in 1856, and a small chapel constructed. Tragically, work begun on the main structure in 1866 was destroyed in the great fire that struck the city on July 4 of that year. Spurred on by Bacon, funds for construction were sought once more, and work was resumed in 1868. When dedicated on September 9, 1869, the Cathedral of the Immaculate Conception was declared one of the finest in the country.

No parochial schools greeted Bacon upon his arrival in the diocese, but by the year of his death they numbered 20, in addition to six private academies. The bishop was aided in his work by the Sisters of Notre Dame, who came to Portland to run St. Aloysius school in 1864. Mother M. Xavier Warde and four SISTERS OF MERCY arrived in Manchester, New Hampshire, in 1858, and soon opened three houses in Maine, at Bangor (1865), Whitefield (1871) and Portland (1873—replacing the Notre Dame Sisters).

After almost 20 years of vigorous labor, the bishop died on November 5, 1874, while in transit to Rome for his *ad limina* visit, his life ended by a painful bladder ailment that had plagued him throughout his tenure in Portland.

New Arrivals in Maine. On February 12, 1875, James A. HEALY, pastor of St. James Church in Boston, the largest parish in New England, was appointed to the see of Portland. A native of Georgia, Healy and his brothers had been sent north to attend Holy Cross by their father, who realized that their status as sons of a mulatto slave mother was an insurmountable obstacle to their advancement. The Healy sons prospered: James and Sherwood studying for the diocesan priesthood, Patrick joining the Jesuits. Healy's 25 years as bishop of Portland were years of growth: in population, churches, priests, schools and religious. Besides a heavy indebtedness of $110,000, another challenge to the diocese during Healy's tenure was the massive influx of French-Canadians who arrived during the last quarter of the 19th century. Facing continual economic distress in Quebec, tens of thousands of these deeply religious migrants came to New England in search of work, bringing with them their strong attachment to "la foi, la langue, et les moeurs" (faith, language and customs). A few towns in Maine were completely transformed; Biddeford, for example, was 80 percent French-Canadian by the 1880s. Healy was zealous in his efforts to obtain compatriot clergy and religious to serve the newcomers. Ten new communities of religious women entered the diocese at Healy's invitation, as well as the Dominican and Marist priests and Brothers, all of them French-speaking. Lewiston was an outstanding Franco-American center, where the Dominican priests staffed the parish, Marist Brothers taught the boys, Daughters of Sion instructed the girls, and Sisters of Charity ran the orphanage and hospital. Healy's undertakings did not blind him to the contentious nature of some of the new arrivals, who he found to be quite forceful in their demands.

The year 1884 saw the state of New Hampshire removed from the territory of the Diocese of Portland and formed into the Diocese of Manchester. It was the same year that the Sisters of Mercy in Maine achieved their independence, with Sr. Mary Teresa Pickersgill as superior. Two years later the Marist Fathers opened St. Mary's College in Van Buren, the first Catholic college in Maine, enrolling a large number of French-Canadians among its students.

Healy celebrated his 70th birthday in 1900, his silver jubilee as bishop of Portland. Sadly, his labors for the church in Maine had sapped his strength, and he died on August 5, after feeling unwell for a few days. The *Boston Pilot* eulogized him as "humble, considerate [and] generous." He left behind 86 churches, 76 diocesan priests, and a Catholic population of approximately 96,400.

Healy was followed in the see of Portland by a rising star, William O'CONNELL, rector of the North American College in Rome, and a native of Lowell, Massachusetts (born 1859). His appointment did not come till 1901, as deliberations at the Vatican were complicated when Franco-American priests and laity wrote opposing the terna of names forwarded by the consultors and advocating the nomination of a French-speaker. O'Connell was installed on July 4, and brought a flamboyant touch to the diocese (he employed an Italian valet and coachman). As bishop he was highly visible, and used public appearances to enhance the self-esteem of Maine Catholics. He was lionized by the Protestant community and Portland society; chosen to deliver a public oration on the death of President McKinley, he was accepted for membership in the exclusive Cumberland Club. Insisting on an intensely personal management style, he scrutinized parish reports, exercising minute oversight of liturgy and devotions. In 1903 he issued a pastoral on the new wave of immigrants arriving from Eastern Europe and Italy, asking that they be made welcome by the Church in Maine.

An avid traveler (e.g. the winter of 1904 to 1905 was spent in Rome), O'Connell was away on a diplomatic mission to Japan on behalf of the Vatican when word arrived that he had been appointed as coadjutor to Archbishop Williams in Boston. He bid farewell to the Portland diocese on September 9, 1906 and became archbishop of Boston on August 30, 1907, and was made a cardinal in 1911.

Love of the Past and Work for the Future. Rome lost no time in appointing a new bishop for the diocese of Portland. Louis Walsh (1858–1924) was a priest from Boston, known for his work at the Seminary of St. John and as an administrator of the archdiocesan schools. A dignified, scholarly, affable man, he was a builder for the future who had a love of Maine's rich history. He restored a monument Bishop Fenwick had erected for Fr. Râle, celebrated the centenary of St. Patrick's church in Damariscotta in 1908, and honored the 300th anniversary of the Mt. Desert mission with commemorations in 1913 (August 6 in Bar Harbor, October 12 in Portland). He founded the Maine Catholic Historical Society in 1908, and promoted the *Maine Catholic Historical Magazine* (1913–28).

During Walsh's 18-year tenure, 36 new parishes were founded (four in Portland, three in Lewiston). To deal with the vast number of immigrants, the bishop encouraged pastors to schedule visits of compatriot priests at least a few times a year to assist the foreign-born among their flocks. Such consideration did not prevent him from stirring up dissension in Biddeford over his reorganization of a French parish and measures to curb the activities of ethnic societies.

Walsh was no stranger to political action. He watched the state legislature closely, always a vocal advocate for state aid to what he referred to as his ''Catholic Public Schools.'' His efforts to obtain a portion of the ''State Public Fund'' for schools, however, were rejected in 1915. The bishop was also a prominent figure on the national stage, serving as chairman of the Press and Publicity Department of the National Catholic Welfare Conference (NCWC), successfully working to reverse that organization's suppression by the Holy See in 1922. The energy devoted to that cause, and his energetic defense of the Church against the attacks of the Ku Klux Klan in 1922 and 1923 led to the bishop's increasing exhaustion. Walsh died on May 12, 1924, four days after suffering a cerebral hemorrhage.

Connecticut Natives for Maine. Maine's fifth and sixth bishops were both natives of Waterbury, Connecticut, and boyhood friends, attending Crosby High School and Holy Cross College. John Gregory Murray (born 1877), ordained after studies in Louvain, was a brilliant administrator of the diocese of Hartford, and served as its chancellor and auxiliary bishop. On October 11, 1925 he was installed as Bishop of Portland. A friendly and informal man, he continued Walsh's tradition of involvement on the national stage, serving on administrative committees of the NCWC. In Maine he faced a growing number of Catholics in a state whose population growth was modest overall. In 1930, 60 percent of Maine residents lived in rural areas, yet the number of non-Catholic churches was declining rapidly outside the cities. The bishop worried about his flock's vulnerability to the rising tide of indifferentism, and spoke out against mixed marriages and birth control.

The number of vacationers in Maine was increasing, however, and these visitors ''from away'' brought not only a financial windfall for struggling parishes but also edified natives by their faith and devotion. Thirty new parishes were established by Murray, the number of churches rose from 168 to 183, and the number of priests from 172 to 216. Sadly, St. Mary's College in Van Buren closed its doors in 1927, but a Catholic collegiate presence was maintained by St. Joseph's College (for women), opened in Maine in 1915 by the Sisters of Mercy (by century's end it would become co-ed and move to a suburban site in Standish). Catholics in the diocese were kept informed on Church news more effectively after the appearance of the *Church World*, a diocesan paper that debuted in July of 1930.

Murray responded aggressively to the dislocation occasioned by the Great Depression by committing the diocese to the needs of the poor. He borrowed heavily to maintain the Church's charitable foundations, and ordered that relief committees be established in every parish to oversee fundraising for the assistance of the homeless, destitute and unemployed. His work in Maine was brought to an abrupt conclusion in November of

1931 when he was transferred to the Archdiocese of ST. PAUL, Minnesota. He was hailed by all as a man of compassion who had worked to ease religious prejudice.

His friend Joseph McCarthy (born in 1876) was consecrated on August 24 of 1932, the first such ceremony to be carried on radio. A kind and courteous man, he had served both as a seminary teacher and administrator, as well as a parish priest (with many French Canadians in his congregations). His primary task upon becoming bishop was to deal with a diocesan debt, which had mushroomed during the Depression to dangerous levels, totaling nearly $5 million. He devised a funding plan, approved by Rome in 1935, which authorized a bond issue and scheduled annual payments on the debt. Though construction was curtailed, 12 new churches were built by 1948, and a Catholic hospital erected in Portland in 1940. Even with the restricted finances, the diocese was able to respond to ruinous fires in Ellsworth and Auburn in 1933 with state-wide collections.

The bishop was heartened by the arrival in the diocese of two contemplative communities of nuns, the Adorers of the Precious Blood in Portland, and the Sisters of the BLESSED SACRAMENT in Waterville. The Jesuits returned to the diocese after an absence of 83 years to staff Cheverus High in Portland in 1942, and a group of exiled Lithuanian Franciscans were welcomed in 1944, ultimately settling on a beautiful property in Kennebunkport. McCarthy's declining health necessitated the appointment of an auxiliary, Daniel Feeney (a Portland native), on June 22, 1946, the first native-son to be elevated to the episcopacy. In July of 1948 Feeney was given administrative control of the diocese, and appointed coadjutor in 1952. Bishop McCarthy died in the fall of 1955, the centenary of Bishop Bacon's consecration.

The Second Vatican Council and Beyond. Bishop Feeney labored to eradicate the Diocese's indebtedness, and sought to implement the pastoral provisions of the Second Vatican Council. His successor, Peter Gerety, though bishop for only five years (1969–74), was responsible for a progressive interpretation of the conciliar decrees that reshaped the diocese before his departure for the see of Newark, New Jersey. Bishop Gerety was succeeded by the second native-son, Edward O'Leary (1974–88), who, assisted by his auxiliary Amedee Proulx (1975–93) sought to guide the church in Maine through an era of declining numbers of clergy and religious. Bishop Joseph Gerry, the former abbot of the Benedictine community of St. Anselm's in Manchester, New Hampshire, the third Maine native to shepherd the Portland diocese has, since 1988, sought to revitalize and renew his flock of some 140 parishes through a varied and active ministry, aided by auxiliary bishop Michael Cote, appointed in 1995, and about 150 active priests and around 400 women religious. This task has had to take account of a shrinking population in Maine's northern and eastern counties, and growing suburban communities in the central and southern counties. At the beginning of the new millennium, Catholics comprise some 18 percent of the total state population.

The Catholic Church in Maine has a rich heritage and has been a vibrant force for evangelization amidst ever-present challenges. Besides those mentioned above, other Maine Catholic notables include Donald Pelotte, S.S.S., bishop of Gallup, New Mexico (the first native American to be ordained a bishop), and politicians such as Emery San Souci, elected governor of Rhode Island in 1920 (the first Franco-American to be elected a governor in New England), Joseph Brennan (governor of Maine, 1979–87), and Margaret Chase Smith (the first woman to serve in both houses of the U.S. Congress).

Bibliography: D. LIPTAK, R.S.M., ''French-Canadians Plead for Survivance,'' in *Immigrants and Their Church* (New York 1989), 160–170. R. H. LORD, J. E. SEXTON, and E. T. HARRINGTON, *The History of the Archdiocese of Boston in the Various Stages of Its Development,* 3 v. (New York 1944). W. L. LUCEY, S.J., *The Catholic Church in Maine* (Francestown, N.H. 1957).

[J. C. LINCK]

MAINE DE BIRAN

French philosopher who defended the importance of inward experience as a source of knowledge; b. Marie-François-Pierre Gonthier de Biran, Bergerac, southern France, Nov. 29, 1766; d. Paris, July 20, 1824. After attending the College of Périguex, he moved between the two poles of public and private life, occupying important public offices during and after the French Revolution, while pursuing in solitude his mathematical, psychological, and philosophical researches. In 1813 he became a member of the famous ''Committee of Five,'' which tried to curb Napoleon's international ambitions, and under the first Restoration he was in charge of the liaison between the king and the National Assembly on financial matters.

Teaching. In 1802 Biran's essay ''The Influence of Habit on Thought'' won first prize in a contest sponsored by the Institute of France, then dominated by the ''ideologists,'' who reduced all experience to the outward data of sight, touch, and the like. In 1805 he was elected to the institute mainly on the strength of his essay ''The Analysis of Thought.'' In the course of his association with such ideologists in the institute as A. L. C. Destutt de Tracy and P. J. G. Cabanis, he gradually clarified and deepened his own doctrines. Because of the originality of his opposition to the ideologists, and despite the personal

Maine De Biran.

and philosophical friction this opposition created, he came to be acknowledged by many French philosophers as their leader and teacher.

His thought went through stages. When he was close to the ideologists (1800–03), he viewed outward sensations as basic to most knowledge. Then, developing his own philosophy (*c.* 1805), he taught that (1) all experience has an inwardly felt, volitional, and kinesthetic component (when man sees, he moves his eyeballs, keeps his eyelids apart, etc.); (2) the self is felt by man to be primarily this inward experience of willingly moving the body; (3) man's belief in effective causation (as against the mere compresence or succession of disparate external objects) is a result of this inward experience of causing his body to move; and (4) in experiencing this voluntary bodily movement (*effort voulu*) through his inward sense (*sens intime*), man acquires his belief in freedom, since such movement is frequently unhindered by external objects and is even independent of those objects. This development influenced, among others, V. COUSIN, J. LACHELIER, and J. Ravaisson in the nineteenth century, and M. BLONDEL and H. BERGSON in the twentieth century. On the basis of these four doctrines, Maine de Biran has been described as the father of French EXISTENTIALISM.

In his last years (1819–24), Biran wrote a great deal about *la croyance*—faith in God who is spiritual, like the self revealed in inward experience, but who, unlike this self, is not temporal but eternal, not individual but universal. This last rather mystical stage has not had much influence because of its ambiguities; for instance, it is difficult to know whether he thought he was presenting a proof of God's existence or taking that existence as an article of faith. This is an undeveloped part of his philosophy.

Appreciation. More generally speaking, the philosophy of Biran is anthropocentric. His *Journals*, which he kept scrupulously, are as substantial a part of his lifework as his formal essays, and this is so because the basis of his philosophy was the experience of voluntarily moving his own frequently frail and always changing body. More important to him than impersonal, external objects (stressed by J. LOCKE, É. B. CONDILLAC, D. HUME, and the *philosophes* in general) was his own intimately felt awareness of willing and his experience of bodily resistance to that willing. This inwardly felt give-and-take convinced Biran that R. Descartes' dualism was an arbitrary separation of two entities deeply and intimately involved with each other. Only by starting from abstract words such as ''mind'' and ''body,'' and defining these terms as negations of each other, did Descartes create his dualism. Biran found as a matter of experience that mind and body are intimately related with each other and, in emphasizing experience, he opposed his own kind of empiricism to the rationalism of Descartes. There was little of the system builder in Biran and much of the introspective psychologist; he was not so much trying to prove elaborate metaphysical conclusions as he was trying to clarify and personalize the basic terminology of psychology and philosophy. To sensationalism, materialism, and rationalism Biran opposed the descriptions and analyses of his own experience. It is a mistake to think of him primarily as a spiritualistic metaphysician; he was an empirical philosopher, at least in his rich middle period.

See Also: ENLIGHTENMENT, PHILOSOPHY OF.

Bibliography: Works. *Journal,* ed. H. GOUHIER, 2 v. (Neuchâtel 1954–55); *Oeuvres,* ed. P. TISSERAND and H. GOUHIER, 14 v. (Paris 1920–49). Literature. A. HUXLEY, *Themes and Variations* (New York 1950), a good intro. to the journals. P. P. HALLIE, *Maine de Biran: Reformer of Empiricism, 1766–1824* (Cambridge, Mass. 1959). H. GOUHIER, *Les Conversions de Maine de Biran* (Paris 1947). G. LE ROY, *L'Expérience de l'effort et de la grâce chez Maine de Biran* (Paris 1937).

[P. P. HALLIE]

MAISTRE, JOSEPH MARIE DE

Philosophical writer, proponent of TRADITIONALISM, who influenced the antirevolutionary movement in

France; b. Chambéry, Savoy, April 1, 1754; d. Turin, Italy, February 26, 1821. Austerity and unquestioning obedience were demanded both in his noble family and in his schooling with the Jesuits. He made the early acquaintance of the *philosophes* whom he, like LOUIS DE BONALD, combated all his life. After studying law at Turin, he entered the magistracy of Savoy in 1774, rose in the civil service, and in 1788 became a member of the Senate, of which his father was president. When the French revolutionary army occupied and annexed Savoy in 1792, he fled to Lausanne. There he wrote first his *Lettres d'un royaliste savoisien* (1793), published anonymously, to warn his countrymen that the horrors of the revolution would produce no lasting benefits. The wealth of ideas he gained in exile inspired him to produce ''a work which would be read with avidity,'' the *Considérations sur la France* (1796), which established his reputation as an enthusiastic defender both of the divine mission of France and of the principle of authority. On the restoration of Charles Emmanuel IV in 1799, Maistre became regent of the Sardinian kingdom. In 1802 Victor Emmanuel I appointed him ambassador at St. Petersburg, and there, for 14 years, his profound learning and frank judgment enabled him to exercise considerable influence on Czar Alexander and the leading Russian nobility. Although he published only a single treatise during this time, it was in Russia that he wrote most of his notable works.

In his *Essai sur le principe générateur des constitutions politiques* (1814), he elaborated his theory of the divine origin of constitutions. His masterpiece, *Du pape* (1819), contained his doctrine of papal supremacy and became the charter of ULTRAMONTANISM. He translated and expanded Plutarch in *Sur les délais de la justice divine* (1816) and wrote *De l'Église gallicane dans son rapport avec les Souverains Pontifes* (1821), and the posthumously published *Soirées de St. Pétersbourg* (1821) and *L'Examen de la philosophie de Bacon* (1836). The unfinished *Soirées* exemplified the versatility of his intellectual and religious interests through 11 ''conversations'' on virtue and vice and the divine management of the world, conducted between a young and impetuous French officer, a serious and stubborn Russian senator, and a Sardinian count, Maistre himself. The last years at St. Petersburg were not agreeable because of the Czar's suspicion of Maistre's religious activities. He returned to Turin in 1817 to serve as regent of the kingdom, a position that allowed him some leisure to attend to the publication of his works, the task in which death overtook him.

The idea of a superintending Providence is the dominant theme in Maistre's interpretation of history. In his view, religious truth was not to be discovered in individuals but in tradition, which God revealed steadily throughout the development of history. BOSSUET had pictured Providence as erasing empires and writing the gospel in the hearts of the gentiles or the monogram of Christ on Constantine's banners. Maistre placed more emphasis on a divine equation; he held that the great amount of wrong done in the world required a proportionate quantity of punishment to satisfy the justice of a stern Judge. For example, having found ''the most striking feature'' of the French Revolution to be ''the sweeping force that curbs all obstacles, the revolution guiding men more than being guided by them'' (*Considérations*), he saw the Reign of Terror as God's way of chastising the assault against SOVEREIGNTY in the execution of Louis XVI. In promoting the doctrines of the *philosophes* and independence of God, France had abused its influence and demoralized Europe; therefore, ''one must not be surprised that she be brought back by terrible means'' (*ibid.*). The mysterious power of redemption by suffering and war—called ''divine'' in the *Soirées*—was Maistre's law of expiation: good results from evil.

He defended papal INFALLIBILITY ardently, especially in *Du pape,* declaring that ''no sovereign pontiff has ever made a mistake in speaking on matters of faith.'' Moreover, the papacy better than any other sovereignty could serve as arbiter in settling the mutual differences of nations, because the popes had always promoted progress in European civilization.

Maistre's clear, forceful style proclaimed obedience as the highest political virtue, in order to restore the power of God, the pope, and the monarch. His influence on 19th-century philosophy and history was unquestionably important.

Bibliography: *Oeuvres complètes* (Lyons 1884–86). L. ARNOULD, *La Providence et le bonheur d'après Bossuet et Joseph de Maistre* (Paris 1917). F. BAYLE, *Les Idèes politiques de J. de M.* (Paris 1945). A. CAPONIGRI, *Some Aspects of the Philosophy of J. de M.* (Chicago 1945). G. COGORDAN, *J. de M.* (Paris 1894; 2d ed. 1922). J. LACROIX, *Vocation personnelle et tradition nationale* (Paris 1942). J. LIVELY, *Works of J. de M.* (New York 1965).

[L. DU S. C. MERCIER]

MAJELLA, GERARD, ST.

Redemptorist lay brother and mystic; b. Muro Lucano (Potenza), Italy, April 6, 1726; d. Caposele (Avellino), Oct. 16, 1755. Left fatherless at an early age, he was apprenticed to a tailor, Martin Pannuto, and endured the persecution of a journeyman who did not understand his gifts of grace and ascetical practices. Later as a servant of the irascible bishop of Lacedonga, he bore with patience three years of misery. After he was refused admission to the Capuchins because of his youth, he lived for a while as a hermit, and then applied for entrance into the Redemptorists. Paul Cafaro rejected him at first because of his frail health but gave way to his persistence, sending him to the novitiate at Deliceto in 1749 with the written message, "I send you a useless laybrother." At Deliceto as porter, sacristan, and tailor, he startled all with his zeal and ability. After his profession (July 16, 1752), the phenomena of his mystical life commenced. He had powers of bilocation, could discern spirits, and control the forces of nature. His many miracles and conversions earned him the title of wonder-worker. At one time he was accused of immorality by a young woman, Neria Caggiano, and his forbearance and trust until his innocence was established further tested his sanctity. He died of consumption when he was 29, at the day and hour he had foretold. He was beatified by LEO XIII, Jan. 29, 1893, and canonized by St. PIUS X, Dec. 11, 1904.

Feast: Oct. 16.

Bibliography: A. M. TANNOJA, *The Lives of the Companions of St. Alphonsus Liguori,* tr. London Oratory (London 1849) 241–453. J. CARR, *To Heaven through a Window, St. Gerald Majella* (New York 1949). N. FERRANTE, *Storia meravigliosa di San Gerardo Majella* (Rome 1955). J. H. M. EVERS, *Historisch repertorium met betrekking tot Wittem als bedevaartsoord* (Heerlen 1986). *San Gerardo tra spiritualità e storia,* ed. G. DE ROSA (Materdomini, Italy 1993). A. BUTLER, *The Lives of the Saints,* rev. ed. H. THURSTON and D. ATTWATER, 4 v. (New York 1956) 4:131–134. D. DE FELIPE, *San Gerardo Mayela* (Madrid 1954).

[M. J. CURLEY]

MAJOLUS OF CLUNY, ST.

Fourth abbot of Cluny; b. Valensolle or Avignon, France, *c.* 906–15; d. Souvigny, May 11, 994. Majolus (or Mayeul) studied at Lyons and became archdeacon of Mâcon. He refused the bishopric of Besançon and was instead admitted to CLUNY as a BENEDICTINE monk. There Abbot Aymard made him *apocrisiarius* and librarian and appointed him coadjutor abbot in 954 when Aymard himself went blind. Majolus held that post until Aymard's death in 965, when he succeeded him as abbot of Cluny. Under Majolus's rule the CLUNIAC REFORM spread widely. He reformed monasteries in the Kingdom of Burgundy, in Italy (at Pavia, Ravenna, and Rome), and in France (Saint-Maur-des-Fossés and Saint-Bénigne-de-Dijon, to which he sent WILLIAM OF SAINT-BÉNIGNE). In 974 Emperor OTTO II offered Majolus the papal tiara, which he refused. In 991 Majolus appointed ODILO his coadjutor abbot at Cluny so that he could devote the rest of his life to prayer. He died at the Abbey of SOUVIGNY, while traveling to Paris to reform SAINT-DENIS at the request of Hugh Capet; he was canonized by popular acclaim.

Feast: May 11.

Bibliography: Two lives, one by the monk Syrus, the other by Odilo, *Acta Sanctorum* May 2:653–698. *Recueil des chartes de l'abbaye de Cluny,* comp. A. BERNARD and ed. A. BRUEL, 6 v. (Paris 1876–1903). E. SACKUR, *Die Cluniacenser,* 2 v. (Halle 1892–94) 1:205–256. L. M. SMITH, *The Early History of the Monastery of Cluny* (Oxford 1920) 100–143. P. SCHMITZ, *Histoire de l'Ordre de Saint-Benoît,* 7 v. (Maredsous, Bel. 1942–56) v.1, 2, *passim.* S. HILPISCH, *Lexikon für Theologie und Kirche,* ed. J. HOFER and K. RAHNER, 10 v. (2d, new ed. Freiburg 1957–65) 6:1307. D. IOGNA-PRAT, *Agni immaculati: recherches sur les sources hagiographiques relatives à Saint Maieul de Cluny* (Paris 1988).

[B. HAMILTON]

MAJOR, GEORG (MAIER)

Lutheran theologian; b. Nuremberg, April 25, 1502; d. Wittenberg, Nov. 28, 1574. He studied under Martin LUTHER and Philipp MELANCHTHON. After eight years as rector in Magdeburg (1529–37), he served as court preacher in Wittenberg till 1545, when he became a professor of theology there. In 1546 he took part in the Conference of Regensberg, where he was befriended by Martin BUCER. After brief intervals in Magdeburg as a refugee from the Schmalkaldic War and in Merseburg for church affairs, he was back in Wittenberg in 1547. In 1548 his support of Melanchthon's concessions involved him in the Interim controversy which became more heated when he ceased opposing Maurice of Saxony and favored state measures against anti-Interimists (*see* INTERIMS). For his Interimism he received a princely favor of the superintendency at Eisleben (1552). Because the Gnesiolutherans opposed any conciliatory interpretations of pure Lutheranism, Major was compelled to make a public defense of himself, and this led to his having to flee to Wittenberg the same year. There he remained as a foremost leader of PHILIPPISM, and also as dean of the theological faculty from 1558 till his death.

Bibliography: *Opera,* 3 v. (Wittenberg 1569–70), incomplete. O. RITSCHL, *Dogmengeschichte des Protestantismus,* 4 v. (Leipzig 1908–27) v. 2. R. BRING, *Das Verhältnis von Glauben und Werken in der lutheranischen Theologie* (Munich 1955). H. W. GENSICHEN, *Damnamus: Die Verwerfung von Irrlehre bei Luther und im Luthertum des 16. Jahrhunderts* (Berlin 1955). R. BÄUMER, *Lexikon für Theologie und Kirche,* ed. J. HOFER and K. RAHNER, 10 v. (2d, new ed. Freiburg 1957–65) 6:1307–08. F. LAU, *Die Religion in Geschichte und Gegenwart,* 7 v. (3rd ed. Tübingen 1957–65) 4:617.

[Q. BREEN]

MAJORISTIC CONTROVERSY

Named after Georg MAJOR, pertained to most of the 16th-century disputations between the exponents of Philipp MELANCHTHON's conciliatory interpretations of the theology of Martin LUTHER, and the Gneisolutherans, who resisted any modifications of the original or pure Lutheranism (*see* PHILIPPISM; GNESIOLUTHERANISM). The debates ranged over the acceptance by Lutherans of certain Catholic religious practices as indifferent matters (Adiaphorism), the nature of the Real Presence in the Lord's Supper (*see* CRYPTO-CALVINISM), and chiefly the role of good works in the process of justification (Solafideism). The original setting of the controversy was supplied by the Interim conferences, in which some *rapprochement* was sought with Catholics (*see* INTERIMS). While Major held that good works have no merit in justification as such, still they are necessary because they are divinely commanded and are evidence of faith. He was attacked by Nickolaus von AMSDORF in 1551 and by other Gnesiolutherans, notably Matthias FLACIUS ILLYRICUS and Nikolaus Gallus (1516–70). By 1553 it was agreed that Major had not erred in doctrine, but in expression only, and that among themselves Lutherans might not insist upon the words ''by faith alone,'' although they would when among Catholics, as in the Interim conferences, to avoid misunderstanding.

For bibliography, *see* MAJOR, GEORG.

[Q. BREEN]

MAKEMIE, FRANCIS

Presbyterian minister, missionary, and businessman, a leader of the PRESBYTERIANS in the American Middle Colonies; b. Ramelton, County Donegal, Ireland, 1653; d. 1708. He was trained at Glasgow, Scotland, and ordained (1682) for service in America. From correspondence with Increase MATHER, the Boston, Puritan leader, who helped English Presbyterians unite with Congregationalists after the breakdown of English state Presbyterianism, Makemie derived some of the concepts that formed American Presbyterianism. He was sent to Maryland (1683) by the Presbytery of Laggan, Ireland, and resided in Accomac County, VA, and Rehoboth, MD (1691, 1698– 1708). He disputed with the Quaker, George Keith, advocating a reformed ecclesiology. Beginning in 1698, Makemie organized Presbyterian congregations in Maryland, recruited clergy in England, and took the lead in founding the Presbytery of Philadelphia (1706), the parent body of American Presbyterianism. He was its first moderator (chairman). In a famous incident, Makemie was arrested by Lord Cornbury, Governor of New York, and imprisoned six to eight weeks on a charge of being a ''strolling preacher.'' Makemie claimed the protection of the English Act of Toleration of 1689 and the validity of his previous license to preach, issued in the Barbados, British West Indies. His victory disgraced Cornbury, who was recalled, to the advantage of religious liberty in the colonies.

Bibliography: L. J. TRINTERUD, *The Forming of An American Tradition* (Philadelphia 1949). *Journal of the Presbyterian Historical Society* (Philadelphia 1901–) v.4, 15, 18. Some materials are deposited in the Presbyterian Historical Society, Philadelphia, Pennsylvania.

[F. A. SMITH]

MALACHI, BOOK OF

The last of the 12 MINOR PROPHETS. The Prophet's name Malachi, as it appears in the Hebrew Bible (*mal'ākî*), meaning ''my messenger,'' was borrowed from Mal 3.1; an editor inserted it at the beginning of the book when the three chapters of Malachi were separated from Zechariah. The original title, therefore, seems to have been simply ''an oracle'' or ''a burden'' (Heb. *maśśā'*), conformable to Zech 9.1 and 12.1. The Greek Septuagint leaves the Prophet anonymous, reading *mal'ākô* in Mal 1.1, which it translates as a common word, not a proper name, ''through the hand of his messenger [or angel].'' The Vulgate calls the author *Malachis* (Heb. *mal'āk-yāh*, messenger of Yahweh).

Author. The Prophet, however, is not lost in complete anonymity, for we can assess his personality from the spontaneous reactions and considered judgments in the book. A staunchly patriotic Jew, he assailed the practice of mixed marriages, especially when these involved the divorce of ''the wife of your youth'' (Mal 2.14), in order that the Jewish man could be joined to a young foreign girl. This act was ''an abominable thing . . . [for it] profaned the temple'' (2.11). Not only did it endanger Judaism with idolatrous practices, but it also struck at the strong religious spirit of the home. Malachi's loyalty to his religion kept him well acquainted with its ancient traditions, and he frequently alludes to Deuteronomy and Ezekiel.

Malachi was no literary artist like Isaiah or even like the less gifted Zechariah. His vocabulary remained very limited and his style colorless, without appeal to the imagination. As a result, however, he did speak simply, clearly, and forcefully. The most notable literary characteristic about Malachi's prophecy is its catechetical style of question and answer. A lead-off statement is generally questioned or challenged by the listeners, thereby providing Malachi with a good opening for a blunt reply.

Date. The Prophet exercised his ministry after 515 B.C., because the Temple had been rebuilt (Mal 1.10; 3.1, 10; Ezr 6.15), but sometime before the religious reforms instituted in Jerusalem by Ezra and Nehemiah toward the

Francis Makemie.

end of the 5th century B.C. What Malachi condemned these two leaders energetically and successfully removed: mixed marriages and unworthy liturgy. (*See* HAGGAI, BOOK OF; ZECHARIAH, BOOK OF, for further details about postexilic Judaism.) For this reason Malachi's ministry is usually placed around the middle of the 5th century B.C.

Contents. This prophecy is best remembered for its announcement of a liturgical sacrifice in which all men of every nationality would participate (Mal 1. 10–11). In this passage Malachi could not have been thinking of contemporary pagan sacrifices, for he remained adamantly loyal to the Levitical priests, despite their many shortcomings (2.4–7; 3.4). Malachi, in fact, did not advance beyond earlier prophecies that had expected a great day when all men of every country would share in the messianic blessings (Gn 12.1–3; Is 41.20) and even take an active part in the new and perfect liturgy (Is 2.2–5; 66.18–3; Zec 8.23).

The other important aspect of his messianic hopes is his preoccupation with ''the great and terrible day'' of the Lord (ch. 3). It will dawn at the Temple of Jerusalem, where the Lord will be wondrously present among His people (3.1–2), completely burning away all uncleanness (3.3, 19) and granting the fulfillment of all promises(3.20). Either the original editor of the prophet's words or a later redactor added a note (3.22–24) that ''the great and terrible day'' would be inaugurated by the return of Elijah (2 Kgs 2.11–12).

The book consists principally of six oracles: (1) God's special love for Israel (1.2–5); (2) the sins of the priests (1.6–2.9); (3) against divorce and mixed marriages (2.10–16); (4) Yahweh, God of justice (2.17–3.5); (5) ritual offenses (3.6–12); and (6) triumph of the just (3.13–21). Sometime after the oracles were collected, perhaps at the time when they were cut off from the oracles in Zechariah ch. 9–14 to form the 12th book of the Minor Prophets, someone added a superscription (1.1) and two appendices (3.22–24). Note that 3.19–24 of the Hebrew text and Confraternity of Christian Doctrine Version are considered ch. 4 in the Septuagint, the Vulgate, the Douay, the Authorized, and the Revised Standard Version. The last lines, found in most translations, are absent from the Hebrew; they reflect the Jewish practice of repeating verse 23a, lest the scroll of the Minor Prophets should end on the word ''doom'' in verse 24a.

Bibliography: L. H. BROCKINGTON, *Peake's Commentary on the Bible,* ed. M. BLACK and H. H. ROWLEY (London 1962) 573–575.

T. CHARY, *Les Prophètes et te culte á partir de l'Exil* (Tournai 1955) 160–189. A. GELIN, *Aggée, Zacharie, Malachie* (*Bible de Jérusalem*; 3d ed. 1960). T. H. ROBINSON and F. HORST, *Die zwölf Kleinen Propheten* (*Handbuch zum Alten Testament* 14; 2d ed. 1954) 261–275, with complete bibliog. C. LATTEY, *The Book of Malachy* (Westminster Version; New York 1934). E. F. SUTCLIFFE, *Catholic Commentary on Holy Scripture,* ed. B. ORCHARD et al. (London–New York 1957) 555–558.

[C. STUHLMUELLER]

MALACHY, ST.

Archbishop of Armagh; b. Armagh, Ireland, *c.* 1094; d. Clairvaux, France, Nov. 2, 1148. Born Máel Máedoc Úa Morgair (Servant of St. M' Áedóc, descendant of Morgar), he had at least one brother, Gilla Críst, bishop of Clogher (d. 1138). His father appears to have been Mugrón, chief professor at Armagh, who died (1102) at the monastery of Mungret near Limerick. Malachy received his early education at an unnamed hamlet near Armagh, later studying in ARMAGH, then ruled by the reforming Bp. (St.) Cellach Úa Sínaig. There, a formative influence on his spiritual life was an austere anchorite, probably one of the CULDEES, called Ímar Úa Áedacáin. Malachy was ordained in 1119.

Reform. When appointed vicar in Armagh during the absence of Cellach in 1120, Malachy began his career as a reformer. On Cellach's return (*c.* 1122), he retired to the monastery of LISMORE to learn the Benedictine way of life from Máel Ísu Úa Ainmire, formerly archbishop of Cashel. Shortly afterward Malachy was recalled to reinvigorate decayed monastic observance in BANGOR, County Down, and was appointed bishop of Down (probably in 1123) and of Connor (1124). But powerful opposition forced him to leave (*c.* 1127), and he became abbot of Iveragh, County Kerry. In 1132, Máel Ísu of Lismore and the papal legate Gilla Epscuip prevailed upon Malachy to return to Armagh as bishop. Once there Malachy came immediately into conflict with hereditary customs by which Muirchertach Úa Sínaig had already been installed as *Comarba Pátric* (lay abbot) in Armagh. Malachy succeeded in establishing himself there only in 1137, when he immediately resigned and returned to Down as bishop, living a monastic life at Bangor. He was regarded as the leading Irish ecclesiastical figure of his day and was responsible for introducing the Roman liturgy into Ireland. He went to Rome to request the PALLIUM for Armagh and for Cashel from INNOCENT II. The pope refused to grant them until requested by a general council of Irish bishops, clergy, and nobles, but he appointed Malachy papal legate. Malachy returned to Ireland, where he called at CLAIRVAUX and Arrouaise in Flanders, leaving some of his monks in each place to learn the Cistercian and Arroasian rules, with a view to establishing these orders in Ireland. MELLIFONT, the first Irish Cistercian abbey, was founded in 1142. In 1148 a synod was held at Inis Phátric (County Dublin) that again requested the pallia and appointed Malachy as its agent. Malachy departed for Rome but died on the way, surrounded by St. BERNARD and his monks. He was canonized by CLEMENT III on July 6, 1199. Bernard vouched for his exalted sanctity, characterized by a love of poverty, which he called his spouse.

Prophecy of St. Malachy. A ''prophecy'' attributed to Malachy designates the 111 successors of Pope CELESTINE II (elected 1143) not by name but by short epithet. The prophecy first appeared in the *Lignum vitae* (ed. A. Wion, Venice 1595). For the period from 1143 to 1590, when GREGORY XIV was elected, the epithets were obviously derived from the popes' family or baptismal names, native places, or cardinalatial titles. After 1590 the epithets become very vague. The prophecy is a 16th-century forgery.

Feast: Nov. 3.

Bibliography: BERNARD OF CLAIRVAUX, *Vita Patrologia Latina*, ed. J. P. MIGNE, 217 v., indexes 4 v. (Paris 1878–90) 187:1073–1118; Eng. tr.. *The Life and Death of Saint Malachy, the Irishman*, tr. R. T. MEYER (Kalamazoo, Mich. 1978). H. J. LAWLOR, ed. and tr., *St. Bernard's . . . Life of St. Malachy . . .* (New York 1920). J. F. KENNEY, *The Sources for the Early History of Ireland* (New York 1929) 1:764–765, for Bernard's writings to and about Malachy. A. J. LUDDY, *Life of St. Malachy* (Dublin 1930, repr. Felinfach 1994). J. O'BOYLE, *Life of St. Malachy* (Belfast 1931); cf. *Analecta Bollandiana* 51 (1933) 179–180, 318–324. E. VACANDARD, ''La prophetie de Malachie . . . ,'' *Revue apologetique* 33 (1922) 657–671. P. J. DUNNING, ''The Arroasian Order in Medieval Ireland,'' *Irish Historical Studies* 4 (1945) 297–315. A. GWYNN, ''St. Malachy of Armagh,'' *The Irish Ecclesiastical Record* 70 (1948) 961–978; 71 (1949) 134–148; ''Armagh and Louth in the Twelfth Century,'' *Seanchas Ardmhacha* 1 (1954) 1–11. J. LECLERCQ, ''Documents of the Cult of St. Malachy,'' *ibid.* 3 (1959) 318–332. G. MURPHY, ''St. Malachy of Armagh,'' *Month* 18 (1957) 219–231. L. PASTOR, *The History of the Popes from the Close of the Middle Ages*, 40 v. (London-St. Louis 1938–61): v.1, 6th ed.; v.2, 7th ed.; v.3–6, 5th ed.; v.7–8, 11–12, 3d ed.; v.9–10, 4th ed.; v.13–40, from 1st German ed. *Geschichte der Päpste seit dem Ausgang des Mittelalters*, 16 v. in 21 (Freiburg 1885–1933; repr. 1955–) 22:349.

[C. MCGRATH]

MALAGRIDA, GABRIEL

Missionary and preacher; b. Menaggio, Italy, Dec. 5, 1689; d. Lisbon, Sept. 21, 1761. He made his first studies in Como and Milan and joined the Society of Jesus in Genoa, Oct. 23, 1711. After having taught humanities in Nizza, Bastia, and Vercelli, he was sent to Portugal. In 1721 he left Lisbon for the missions of northern BRAZIL. Malagrida was a teacher of theology and humanities, spiritual counselor in the colleges of the society, missionary among the native people, popular preacher in towns and villages from Bahia to Pará, and the founder of convents, seminaries, and retreat houses. He was a zealous apostle, though somewhat theatrical and very credulous, and he soon acquired the fame of a saint. In 1750 he went to Portugal to discuss with John V the affairs of the missions in Pará; he returned to Maranhão in 1751 as royal councilor for the Portuguese overseas possessions, entrusted with royal powers to conduct missions. Three years later he was again in Portugal, this time as confessor of Queen Mariana of Austria and spiritual guide of many noble men and women. When the earthquake of 1775 almost destroyed Lisbon, Malagrida wrote a book called *Juizo da verdadeira causa do Terremoto* (Lisbon 1756), which attributed the earthquake to God's punishment. This attracted the wrath of the powerful minister Pombal, more interested in the rebuilding of the city than in prayers and idle laments. Malagrida was exiled to Setúbal, where he continued to gather people together for Spiritual Exercises. In 1758 Malagrida was unjustly accused of having instigated an attempt on the life of Joseph I. He was put in jail, where he became quite insane. Nevertheless, the Marquis of Pombal, who disliked Malagrida because he had opposed his policy in regard to the missions, denounced the missionary to the Inquisition. Condemned as a heretic, Malagrida died at the stake in 1761, in one of the saddest episodes of the Portuguese Inquisition. The basis for his condemnation was taken from two books he had written after he was no longer mentally responsible: *Life of St. Ann, Mother of Mary* and *Kingdom of the Antichrist.* Many of Malagrida's letters are extant, and there is a vast bibliography on his trial by the Inquisition.

Bibliography: S. LEITE, *História de Companhia de Jesús no Brasil,* 10 v. (Lisbon 1938–50).

[T. BEAL]

MALASPINA, GERMANICO

Papal nuncio and promoter of Tridentine reform; b. place and date unknown; d. San Severo, Italy, 1604. He showed diplomatic skill as nuncio for Gregory XIII at Graz (1582), at the imperial Diet of Augsburg (1582), and at Cologne (1583). During his nunciature at Prague, where Emperor Rudolf II (reign 1576–1612) usually resided, Malaspina, together with Giovanni Francesco Bonhomini, nuncio at Cologne, worked with energy to move the timorous emperor toward a plan of effective reform. They achieved success at Breslau, Paderborn, and Münster, and were aided by the Jesuits. In June 1592, Clement VIII entrusted Malaspina with the difficult nunciature of Poland. There he brought peace between King Sigismund III (reign 1587–1632) and his chancellor, Jan Zamojki (1587–1605), winning the confidence of both. At the death (Nov. 17, 1592) of Sigismund III's father, John III of Sweden, Sigismund became the claimant for the throne of Sweden. Malaspina accompanied him to Uppsala, witnessed the crowning (Feb. 19, 1593), but saw his hopes for a Catholic restoration in Sweden destroyed by strong religious opposition and the ambitions of Sigismund's uncle Charles, Protestant Duke of Södermanland, who in July 1599 assumed power. Malaspina was instrumental in the negotiations for the return of the Ruthenian Church to the See of Rome (1595) and the restoration of peace in Transylvania after the abdication of King SIGISMUND BÁTHORY (1599). From 1599 until his death he remained in his Diocese of San Severo.

Bibliography: L. PASTOR *The History of the Popes from the Close of the Middle Ages* 23:282, 308–309; 24:87–95, 97–101, 117–122. R. SPIRITO, *Dizionario ecclesiastico* 2:790. A. POSCH, *Lexikon für Theologie und Kirche* 2 6:1324, bibliog.

[E. D. MCSHANE]

MALATESTA

A family of Rimini, Italy, considered by the historian Jacob Burckhardt to be a representative RENAISSANCE ruling house. Descended from the counts of Carpegna, their line can be traced from 1150 on. In Rimini, where they had been granted citizenship in recognition of their support against Cesena, the Malatesta gained such power that *Giovanni* Malatesta became *podestà* in 1237. He was succeeded in 1247 by his long-lived son *Malatesta da Verucchio,* who ruled until 1312 and was leader of the GUELFS in the Romagna. Malatesta was succeeded by *Malatestina* (1312–17), the eldest of four sons. The second son, *Giovanni* (d. 1304), married the beautiful Francesca de Pollenta, daughter of Guido, seigneur of Ravenna. Giovanni surprised his handsome brother *Paolo,* who had seduced Francesca, and killed them both, a tragedy immortalized by Dante (*Inferno* 5.73–142). The deformed *Pandolfo* (d. *c.* 1326) succeeded his brother in office. In the following decades the Malatesta conquered Cesena, Pesaro, Fano, Fossombrone, Cervia, and other territories, but were caught in an uncomfortable position between Venice on one side and the expanding STATES OF THE CHURCH on the other. The family divided into three lines, and produced some of the leading condottieri and patrons of the arts and letters in Renaissance Italy. Cardinal ALBORNOZ forced *Pandolfo II* (d. 1373) of the main line to submit to papal dominance, but Pandolfo retained the Malatesta territories as a vicar of the Apostolic See. *Carlo* (d. 1429) was an ardent supporter of the popes, representing Gregory XII at the Council of CONSTANCE. His brother *Pandolfo III* left three sons, *Galeotto Roberto* (d. 1432), *Sigismondo di Pandolfo* (d. 1468), and *Domenico di Pandolfo,* known as *Novello* (d. 1465). Of these three, Bl. Galeotto (feast, Oct. 10), a pious and gentle person, married Margarita d' ESTE. Sigismondo was a notorious, but typical, Renaissance prince: well educated, an amateur poet, philosopher, and patron of the arts, a skeptical and immoral man, yet the builder of the beautiful Renaissance style cathedral of S. Francesco in Rimini. This powerful and tyrannous ruler, capable of cruelty and frivolity, took advantage of Pope Eugene IV's preoccupation with CONCILIARISM to expand his territories. In 1460 he attacked the States of the Church and was excommunicated, burned in effigy in Rome, and defeated after a two-year struggle by Pope PIUS II. He fought for and against the Venetians, for and against the Aragonese, for and against the Sienese, and against the Turks. The third brother, *Domenico,* is perhaps best remembered for the famous library, the Malatestiana, that he founded in Cesena; it still contains a priceless collection of manuscripts and incunabula. An illegitimate son of Sigismondo named *Roberto* (d. 1482) murdered Sigismondo's widow, Isotta, and their son, *Salustio,* and succeeded to the inheritance. He served as field marshal for Pope SIXTUS IV in his war against Naples. His son, *Pandolfo IV* (d. 1523), was defeated by Caesar BORGIA in 1500, and in 1503 sold the Malatesta rights in Rimini to Venice.

Bibliography: L. TONONI, *Storia civile e sacra di Rimini,* 5 v. (Rimini 1860–82). C. É. YRIARTE, *Un Condottiere au XV e siècle* (Paris 1882). E. HUTTON, *Sigismondo Pandolfo Malatesta* (New York 1906). L. BIGNAMI, *Splendori ed ombre alla corte di Malatesta di Rimini* (Milan 1942). R. WEISS, *Il primo secolo dell'Umanesimo* (Rome 1949) 67–102. P. ZAMA, *I Malatesti* (Faenza 1956).

[L. W. SPITZ]

MALAWI, THE CATHOLIC CHURCH IN

Malawi is a landlocked, largely agricultural country located in southeast Africa. It is bordered by on the north and east by TANZANIA, on the southeast and southwest by MOZAMBIQUE and on the west by ZAMBIA. Predominately plateau, the terrain rises from rolling plains to low mountains with the region's sub-tropical climate characterized by a winter rainy season and a dry summer. Natural resources include limestone and deposits of uranium, coal and bauxite, although these minerals remained unexploited at the end of the 20th century. Agricultural products, which served as the basis for the Malawian economy, consisted of tobacco, sugar cane, cotton, tea and cassava.

Capital: Lilongwe.
Size: 46,055 sq. miles.
Population: 10,385,849 (est.) in 2000.
Languages: English, Chichewa, Tumbuku; tribal languages are spoken in various regions.
Religions: 2,285,750 Catholics (22%), 2,077,180 Muslims (20%), 5,712,150 Protestants (55%), 310,769 follow indigenous beliefs.
Archdiocese: Blantyre, with suffragans Dedza, Lilongwe, Zomba, Mzuzu, Chikwawa, and Mangochi.

Formerly known as Nyasaland, the region became a British protectorate in 1891 and was part of the Federation of Rhodesia and Nyasaland from 1954 to 1963. In 1964 it became the independent state of Malawi within the Commonwealth. Following three decades of dictatorial rule, the nation held its first multi-party elections in 1994. The average life expectancy of a Malawian was estimated at 37.5 years in 2000.

Early History. Jesuit missionaries from Mozambique penetrated the area around Lake Nyasa in the late 16th and early 17th centuries. In 1861, two years after British explorer David Livingstone reached Lake Nyasa, Anglican missionaries entered the area. The White Fathers began evangelizing Malawi in 1889, but tribal wars, disputes between the British and the Portuguese, and disease compelled them to leave after a year. The Vicariate Apostolic of Nyasa, erected in 1897 with jurisdiction over part of modern Zambia, was entrusted to the White Fathers. The Montfort Fathers founded a mission in the south (1901) that became the Prefecture Apostolic of Shire in 1903 (vicariate in 1952, then Archdiocese of Blantyre in 1959). The hierarchy was established in 1959, with Blantyre as the metropolitan see for the country.

The Church as a Vehicle for Change. By the late 20th century the Church had grown in Malawi, in part due to the availability of a translation of the Bible in the two main local languages, Chichewa and Tumbuka, which was completed in 1971. Other factors included the achievement of political independence, the Church's emerging role as a leader in the push for a democratic society and the influence of the Second Vatican Council in shaping Church life and pastoral activities in Malawi during the first decades of independence.

On July 6, 1964 Malawi achieved independence from Great Britain. Hastings Kamuzu Banda, who was elected president in 1966, extended his term of office to a life-presidency in 1971 amid charges of corruption. While professing the desire for a partnership with the Church, Banda acted to restrict the role of the Church in public life by suppressing all forms of public dissent. Although Malawian bishops issued annual Lenten pastoral

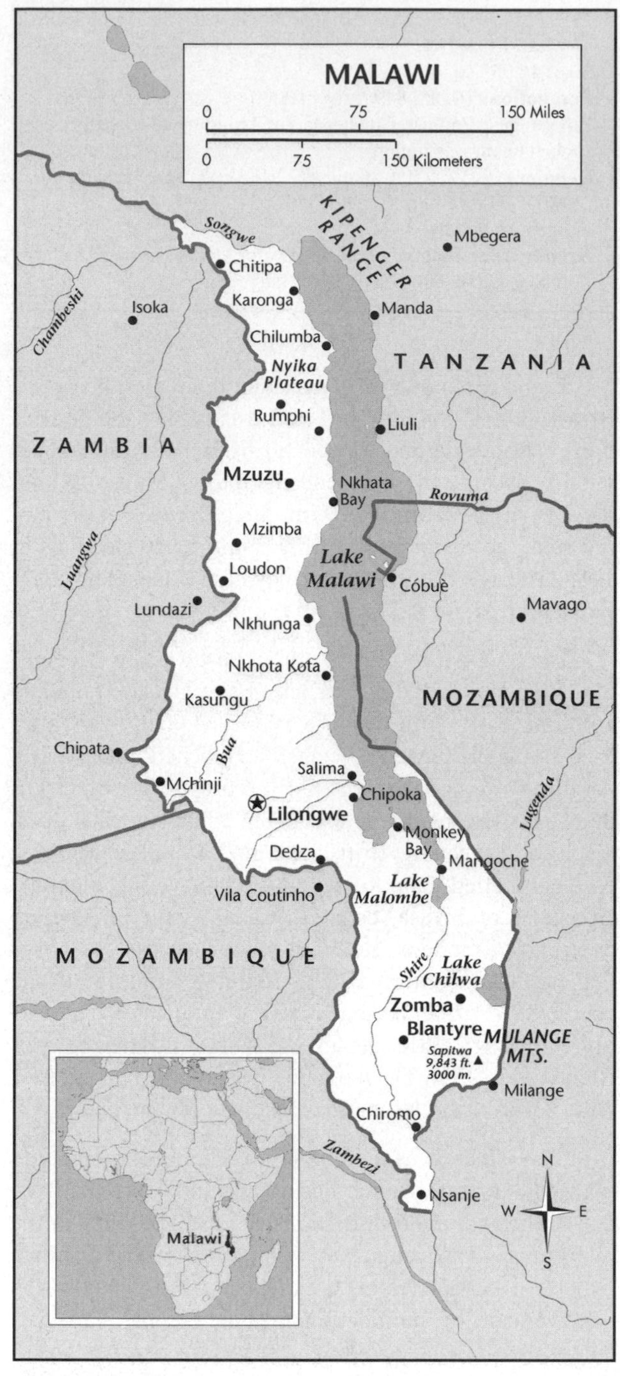

letters, they avoided publicly discussing serious moral and social issues for fear of imprisonment. Similarly, priests focused their attention away from government issues during sermons. The growing tension reached a peak in 1982, when Archbishop James Chiona was harassed for his outspokenness.

A few years later, in May of 1989 Pope John Paul II visited Malawi and encouraged Church leaders to take an active role in righting the wrongs perpetrated by the Malawi government. In 1992 the bishops issued the pastoral letter *Living Our Faith,* condemning the extensive human rights abuses of the Banda dictatorship. The letter served as a catalyst for political change: while government action was taken against the bishops, it prompted such public defiance as student marches and strikes, while Malawians of all faiths showed solidarity by attending overcrowded Catholic masses. The bishops were soon joined by Protestant leaders, and in 1992, an ecumenical public affairs committee was organized to campaign for democratic reforms.

As a result, Western relief agencies suspended much-needed aid to Malawi, forcing the government to address reform issues. In an attempt to improve relations with the Church, Banda met Archbishop Chiona in December of 1993, and elections were scheduled for the following spring. In March of 1994 Malawian bishops published a pre-election pastoral letter, *Building Our Future,* and distributed over 30,000 copies throughout the country. The bishops adopted a nonpartisan approach by encouraging citizens to vote responsibly and stressing the need to accept the election results. On May 17, 1994 the first multiparty election was held amid charges of fraud and Banda's government was unseated. A new constitution went into effect, guaranteeing freedom of religion.

In addition to speaking out on a national level, beginning in the 1970s the Church was active on the grassroots level through small Christian communities. These groups, which met to pray, study the scriptures and examine ways to help their local community, were viewed by the government as potentially subversive and were banned. A decade later they began to reappear and by the 1990s were flourishing. Among the challenges to such groups were the social consequences to the spread of AIDS in the region; government estimates showed 30 percent of the population infected with HIV by 2000, leaving thousands of children homeless.

Into the 21st Century. By 2000 Malawi had 162 parishes tended by 270 diocesan and 160 religious priests. Religious included over 90 brothers and 710 sisters, who operated the nation's 1,110 primary and 58 secondary Catholic schools. The Church was estimated to staff over half of all health care facilities in Malawi, among them 19 mission hospitals and seven orphanages. Every diocese had at least one minor seminary, and the Inter-Congregational Seminary at Balaka provided philosophy studies for Malawians wanting to join a particular order. Retreats for young people gained in popularity and each diocese had a full-time youth chaplain. In 1994 a Chichewa edition of the Liturgy of the Hours was published. A weekly Catholic newspaper and a monthly Catholic magazine were published in the country.

In 1994 newly elected Muslim President Bakili Muluzi publicly acknowledged the leading role of the Church in the fight for democracy. Pope John Paul II's directive to identify areas of injustice continued to bear fruit as Church leaders monitored the country's human rights situation. By 2000 Muluzi' efforts to promote Islam within the public schools was suspended after criticism from Church leaders, although tensions between Christians and Malawi's Islamic minority were increasingly visible elsewhere.

Bibliography: AFRICA WATCH, *Where Silence Rules: The Suppression of Dissent in Malawi* (London 1990). AMNESTY INTERNATIONAL, *Malawi: Preserving the One-Party State* (London 1993). T. CULLEN, *Malawi: A Turning Point* (Cambridge 1994). J. LWANDA, *Kamuzu Banda of Malawi* (Glasgow 1993). B. PACHAI, *The History of the Nation* (London 1973). P. SHORT, *Banda* (London 1974). T. D. WILLIAMS, *Malawi: The Politics of Despair* (London 1978). *Bilan du Monde,* 2:735–744. *Annuario Pontificio* has annual data on all dioceses. For additional bibliography, *see* AFRICA.

[J. F. O'DONOHUE/T. CULLEN/EDS.]

Capital: Kuala Lumpur.
Size: 128,727 sq. miles.
Population: 22,229,040; the population is highly diversified. About 58% are ethnic Malays and other indigenous tribal groups, 26% are ethnic Chinese, 7% ethnic Indians. There are small minorities of Eurasians, Arabs, Filipinos and transient aliens.
Languages: Bahasa Melayu (official), English, Chinese dialects, Tamil, Telugu, Malayalam, Panjabi, Thai; in East Malaysia several indigenous languages are spoken, most commonly Iban and Kadazan.
Religions: Islam is the official religion of Malaysia. Ethnic Malays are Muslim by law, as the Federal Constitution defines a "Malay" as one who professes the Islamic religion and practices the Malay culture. Most Chinese practice a syncretic mix of the Chinese religions of Taoism, Confucianism and Buddhism, while most Indians are adherents of Hinduism, Jainism or Sikhism. Christians are exclusively non-Malays and comprise about 8% of the population. Approximately half of the Christian population is Catholic.
Metropolitan Sees: Kuala Lumpur, with suffragans Melaka-Johor and Penang; and Kuching with suffragans Keningau, Kota Kinabalu, Miri, and Sibu.

MALAYSIA, THE CATHOLIC CHURCH IN

Background. Located above the Equator in Southeast Asia, Malaysia comprises two distinct regions separated by a 400-mile span across the South China Sea. West Malaysia is located on the Malaya peninsula extending southward from Thailand, and East Malaysia, which comprises the two states of Sabah and Sarawak, lies in the northern region of the island of Borneo.

The earliest Malay kingdom was the Buddhist kingdom of Langkasuka in the northern region of the Malay peninsula during the 4th to the 6th centuries A.D. Between 682 and 692, the Buddhist Srivijaya empire from Palembang conquered the Malay peninsula to control maritime traffic across the Straits of Malacca. From the 13th century onward, the Siamese-Buddhist Ayudhia Empire and the Javanese-Hindu Majapahit Empire claimed competing suzerainty over the Malay peninsula as the Srivijaya empire crumbled. These empires bequeathed a lasting socio-religious legacy, significant traces of which are still present in the language, customs and court ceremonies of the Malay-Muslim community. The Islamization of the Malay community began from the 13th century onward. Indian-Muslim Gujerati missionary-traders carried out much of the Islamic missionary work, promoting a Sufi form of Islam that blended orthodox Islamic teachings with existing animistic, Hindu and Buddhist elements. Islam was firmly entrenched when a Hindu prince of the port kingdom of Melaka, Parameswara, embraced Islam in 1414 and adopted the name Megat Iskandar Shah. In 1445, Muzaffar Shah assumed the title of sultan and decreed Islam as the official religion of the Melakan empire. Under the patronage of successive sultans, Islam spread throughout the Malay peninsula.

The early years of the 16th century saw successive flotillas of warships bringing the European colonial powers and Christian missionaries: the Portuguese in 1511, the Dutch in 1641 and the British in 1786. In 1511, Alfonso d'Albuquerque captured Melaka for Portugal. Portugal lost control of Melaka to the Dutch in 1641. In 1786 English influence was extended to the Malay peninsula when Sir Francis Light claimed Pulau Pinang for the British. The British took control of Singapore in 1819, Melaka in 1824 and Perak, Selangor, Negeri Sembilan and Pahang in the 1870s and 1880s. With the transfer of the four northern states of Kedah, Kelantan, Perlis and Terengganu from Siamese suzerainty to England in 1909 as well as Johor's acceptance of a British adviser in 1914, the entire Malay peninsula came under British control.

Sabah and Sarawak, the two northern states of Borneo island, were part of the ancient Brunei sultanate that controlled the entire island of Borneo until the 19th century. Sabah came into existence as a commercial venture when Claude Lee Moses, the American consul to Brunei, secured a 10-year lease for a vast tract of land from the Sultan of Brunei in 1865. After changing hands several times, the British North Borneo Company acquired the land in 1880 and named it British North Borneo. In 1946, British North Borneo was turned over to the British government. Sarawak was given by the Sultan of Brunei to

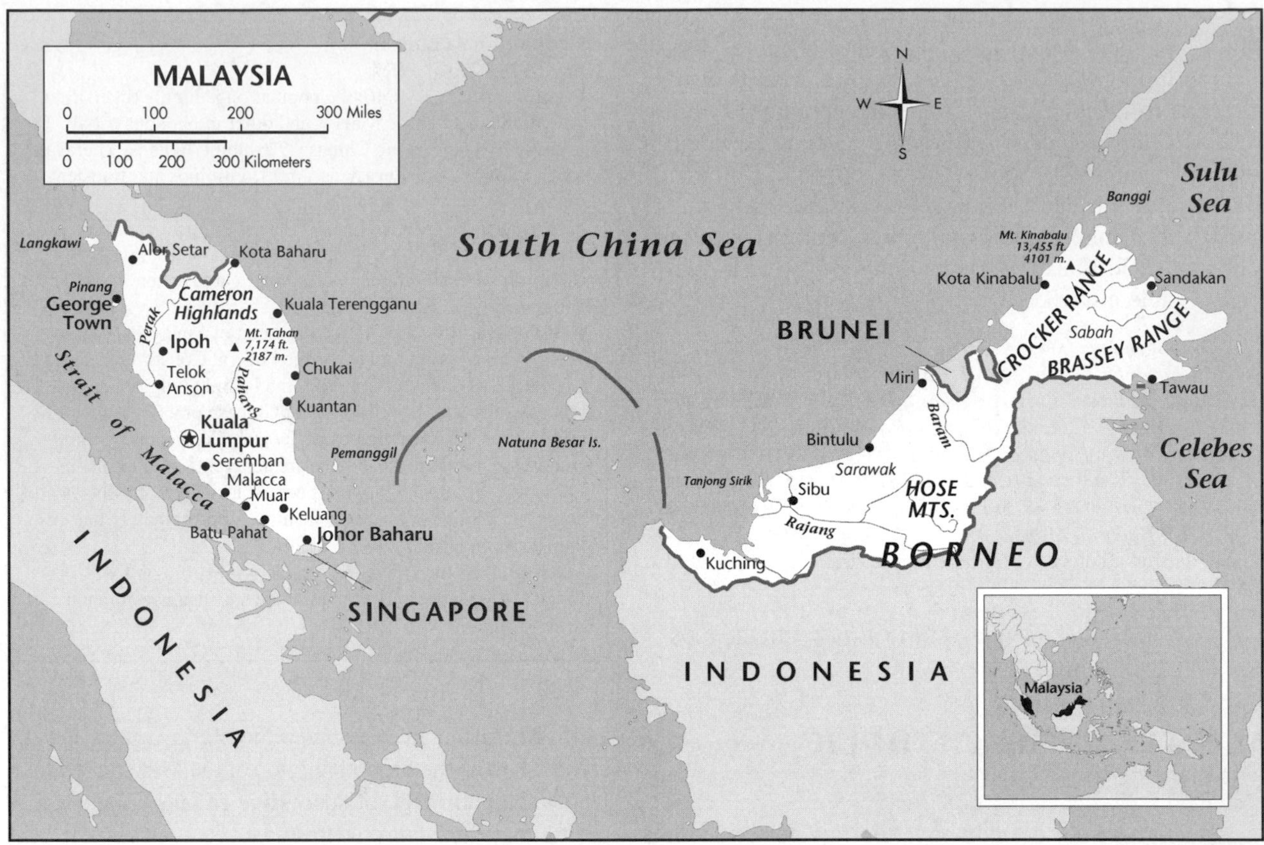

the English adventurist, Sir James Brooke in 1844 as a reward for pacifying the marauding pirates who plundered costal settlements. Brooke made himself the ''White Rajah'' and founded a dynasty that lasted three generations. Sarawak remained the private fiefdom of the Brooke family until 1946, when Sir Charles Vyner Brooke, the last ''White Rajah'' abdicated and surrendered the state to the British Crown.

Modern-day Malaysia is a federation of 13 states (Johor, Kedah, Kelantan, Melaka, Negeri Sembilan, Pahang, Perak, Perlis, Pulau Pinang, Terengganu, Selangor, Sabah and Sarawak) that was formed on September 16, 1963, following a United Nations supervised referendum that was bitterly contested by Indonesia. Originally a member of the federation, Singapore seceded in 1965 over racial and political differences.

Portuguese Missionary Activities. The coming of Christianity to the Malay archipelago is conventionally dated to the Portuguese conquest of 1511. Along with Alfonso D'Albuquerque and his fleet came eight Catholic chaplains under the flagship of the Military Crusading Order of Christ. Full-scale missionary activities began with the arrival of the Jesuit missionary St. Francis XAVIER to Melaka. Not only did he emphasize preaching and Christian instruction, he also built the first school during his five visits to Melaka from 1545 until his death in 1552. Converts to Christianity also came from among the resident Chinese, some local Muslims and many Indian Hindu merchants. The diocese of Melaka, which encompassed the whole of the Malay peninsula, was formally constituted and made a suffragan see of the *Padroado* Archdiocese of Goa by Pope Paul IV in the papal bull *Pro excellenti preeminentia* dated Feb. 4, 1557. When the Dutch captured Melaka from the Portuguese in 1641, they destroyed most of the churches and chapels, killed or deported most Portuguese, and enacted anti-Catholic laws. Through it all, the Catholic community survived as a result of the clandestine activities of the Catholic clergy and lay movements, including the Confraternity of the Holy Rosary. The Portuguese bishops of Melaka resided in exile either in Timor or Flores, and barely exercised their apostolic ministry in the face of a Dutch blockade of all Portuguese missionaries. In 1818, the diocese of Melaka was dissolved and its territories were placed under the direct rule of the *Padroado* Metropolitan of Goa.

French Missionary Activities. The arrival in Melaka and Kedah of two MEP missionaries expelled from the Vicariate Apostolic of Siam in 1780 marked a revival of Catholic missionary activity in the region. The

MEP missionaries quickly established themselves, working tirelessly to evangelize the local populate, thereby filling the void left by the Portuguese. The prolific activities of the MEP missionaries did not sit well with the *Padroado* Metropolitan of Goa, who claimed jurisdiction over the defunct *Padroado* diocese of Melaka and strongly opposed the MEP Vicar Apostolic of Siam's claim of jurisdiction pursuant to a decree of Pope LEO XII in 1827. Pope GREGORY XVI intervened in 1838, removing the Malay peninsula and Singapore from the jurisdiction of the *Padroado* Metropolitan of Goa and placing them under the Vicar Apostolic of Ava and Pegu pursuant to the papal bull *Multa praeclare* of 1838. Subsequently, the region was made an independent vicarate apostolic pursuant to the papal bull *Universi dominici gregis* dated Sept. 10, 1831. Nevertheless the Portuguese refused to surrender their existing missions in Melaka and Singapore. This impasse was finally resolved by a concordat signed between Pope Leo XIII and the Portuguese Crown on June 23, 1886, whereby the Portuguese missions in Melaka and Singapore were transferred to the jurisdiction of the *Padroado* Metropolitan of Macao. On Aug. 10, 1888, Pope Leo XIII re-established the Diocese of Melaka as a suffragan see of the Pondicherry Archdiocese and under the direct control of Propaganda Fide. The Malay Peninsula and Singapore came under the jurisdiction of Propaganda Fide, except the existing Portuguese missions in Melaka and Singapore, which remained under the Padroado Metropolitan of Macau.

Borneo Missions. While there are reports of brief Portuguese and Spanish missionary visits in the late 16th century, it was not until the late 17th century that Theatine missionaries were commissioned to spearhead the mission to Borneo. The Borneo mission was made a vicariate apostolic in 1692. Missionary activities received a new impetus when Don Carlos Cuarteron, the Prefect of northern Borneo, arrived in Borneo in 1857 with two Milan Foreign Missionaries and worked there for more than twenty years. Upon his withdrawal, the Mill Hill Missionaries, who arrived in Borneo in 1881, were given charge of northern Borneo. After World War II, the Catholic Mission in East Malaysia grew rapidly, with mass conversions of the indigenous people. In the aftermath of the war, the general dislocation of society undermined some of the animistic customs and ancestral traditions of these indigenous people. In addition, the suppression of head-hunting required new patterns of leadership to take over its function as a stabilizing force in longhouse life. This stabilizing force was supplied by education and a new system of religious beliefs which the missionaries were able to provide. By the 1960s, Christianity became the largest religious denomination in East Malaysia.

Renewal of Church Life. In the wake of VATICAN COUNCIL II, the Catholic Church in Malaysia has enthusiastically embraced the use of vernacular languages at Mass. However, the introduction of local cultural elements into the Church's liturgical life has been limited. BASIC CHRISTIAN COMMUNITIES (BCCs) have mushroomed as a way of circumventing governmental restrictions on the construction of new churches. Lay catechists play a major role in pastoral and missionary work, especially among rural and indigenous and tribal communities. In 1975, the Catholic Church in Peninsula Malaysia organized a month-long renewal convention for its clergy. The convention's recommendations include the development of indigenous models of church life, greater laity-clergy-religious cooperation, better clerical and lay formation, efforts at youth outreach, dialogue with adherents of other religions, and engagement in integral human development. These recommendations were affirmed at the Peninsula Malaysia Pastoral Conventions of 1986 and 1996.

Challenges. Although the federal constitution designates Islam as the official religion of Malaysia, it also guarantees freedom of religion for all, albeit with an express prohibition against the propagation of non-Muslim religions among the Muslims. Apostasy from the Islamic religion is a criminal offense under various state legislation. As a result, Christian missionary activity is effectively restricted to non-Muslim Malaysians. In addition, from the 1970s onwards the government refused to issue or renew entry permits for foreign Christian missionaries. Mission schools were nationalized in the name of integration. Permits for building new churches became almost impossible to obtain. Since the 1980s, the circulation of Malay language translations of the Bible has been restricted to Christians. Anti-Christian sentiments were greatest in Sabah from the mid-1960s to the mid-1970s. Sabah's chief minister, Tun Mustapha Harun, suspended civil liberties and initiated a systematic campaign of forced Islamization. He expelled all foreign missionaries and most of the clergy, and even prohibited the Vicar Apostolic, Bishop Peter Chung, a Malaysian citizen, from residing in his see. A group of dedicated lay Catholic leaders filled the leadership void by forming the Persatuan Agama Katolik Sabah, or PAX, a ''parliament'' comprising lay representatives and the remnant of the local clergy who escaped expulsion. PAX was formed from the statewide federation of parish councils and took over effective leadership of the Catholic Church in Sabah. With the laity stepping forward to assume pastoral and leadership roles, Tun Mustapha's plan to destroy the Catholic Church by expelling its clergy and forbidding its bishop to reside in the state failed miserably. A unique situation developed in 1976 when Pope PAUL VI erected the diocese of Kota Kinabalu by the decree *Quoniam Deo Favente*. In recognition of its efforts during the darkest days of persecution, PAX was incorporated into the diocesan leadership structure, thereby creating a unique phenomenon of a diocese that is administered jointly by a bishop and a diocesan parliamentary assembly of lay and clerical leaders.

Ecumenical Collaboration. In the face of the continuing efforts of the Malaysian government to restrict the rights of Christians to practice and propagate their faith, representatives of the Catholic Church in Malaysia, the Council of Churches of Malaysia (CCM) representing the mainline Protestant Churches, and the National Evangelical Christian Fellowship (NECF) representing the Evangelical, Brethren and Pentecostal churches met on Feb. 6, 1985 and voted unanimously for the establishment of the Christian Federation of Malaysia (CFM). CFM came into existence on Jan.14, 1986 with the Catholic Church, CCM and NECF as equal partners, and with leadership positions rotated among representatives from these three organizations. CFM seeks to promote Christian unity, foster mutual collaboration among the various Christian churches, defend the rights and interests of the Christian community as a whole and present a united voice for the Christian community. The CFM is also an active member of the Malaysian Consultative Council of Buddhism, Christianity, Hinduism and Sikhism (MCCBCHS), which was formed in 1983 to promote understanding and cooperation among different religions, study and resolve problems affecting all interreligious relationships, and make representations regarding religious matters. The MCCBCHS has become an organized channel for dialogue between the non-Muslims and the Malaysian government on religious freedom and Islamization.

Bibliography: M. CHEW, *The Journey of the Catholic Church in Malaysia* (Kuala Lumpur 2000). F. G. LEE, *The Catholic Church in Malaya* (Singapore 1963). K. P. GOH, ed., *The Malaysian Church in the 90s* (Kuala Lumpur 1992). R. HUNT et al., eds., *Christianity in Malaysia* (Petaling Jaya 1992). J. ROONEY, *Khabar Gembira: A History of the Catholic Church in East Malaysia and Brunei, 1880–1976* (London, 1981). M. TEIXEIRA, *The Portuguese Mission in Malacca and Singapore* (Lisbon 1961–63). K. WILLIAMS, *The Church in West Malaysia and Singapore* (Leuven 1976).

[E. CHIA/J. TAN]

MALDERUS, JOHN

Bishop and theologian; b. Leuw-Saint-Pierre, near Brussels, Aug. 14, 1563; d. Antwerp, July 26, 1633. John Malderus, also called Malder or Van Malderen, studied humanities at Brussels, learned philosophy at Douai, and received his theological training at Louvain, where he was the student of Leonard LESSIUS. In 1596 he was the first to hold the chair at Louvain endowed by Philip II for explaining the text of St. Thomas Aquinas. He became director of the seminary of Louvain in 1598 and was appointed rector of the university in 1604. Malderus was consecrated bishop of Antwerp in 1611, and his episcopacy was marked by unusual pastoral zeal. He labored energetically to provide adequate instruction for the laity and to prevent the encroachments of Calvinism. For this purpose he prepared in 1613 a catechism in the vernacular, carefully supervised the training of priests, and wrote many letters of pastoral direction. Among his theological writings were notable commentaries on the *Summa theologiae* of Thomas Aquinas: *De virtutibus theologicis et justitia et religione, commentaria ad 2am2ae D. Thomae* (Antwerp 1616); *In 1am2ae commentaria de fine et beatitudine hominis, de actibus humanis, de virtutibus, vitiis et peccatis, de legibus, de gratia, de justificatione et meritis* (1623); and *Commentaria de S. Trinitate, creatione in genere et de angelis ad 1 am partem D. Thomae* (1634).

Bibliography: *Biographie nationale de Belgique* 13:223–226. A. PASTURE, *La Restauration religieuse aux Pays-Bas catholiques sous les archiducs Albert et Isabelle, 1596–1633* (Louvain 1925). H. HURTER, *Nomenclator literarius theologiae catholicae* 3:882. E. VANSTEENBERGHE, *Dictionnaire de thèologie catholique* 9.2:1766–72.

[J. C. WILLKE]

MALDONADO LUCERO, PEDRO (PETER) DE JESÚS, ST.

Martyr, priest; b. June 15, 1892, Sacramento, Chihuahua, Mexico; d. Feb. 11, 1937, Chihuahua. At seventeen he entered the archdiocesan seminary at Chihuahua. When political upheaval interrupted his schooling (1914), he studied music. Following his ordination (1918) in El Paso, Texas, he dedicated himself to catechizing children, and promoting all–night vigils and Marian associations at S. Isabel, Chihuahua. In 1934, Pedro was imprisoned, mistreated, and exiled to El Paso, but he soon returned. A group of drunk soldiers apprehended him after Ash Wednesday liturgy, beat him and shot him. He died later from the injuries he sustained. Fr. Maldonado was both beatified (Nov. 22, 1992) and canonized (May 21, 2000) with Cristobal MAGALLANES [*see* GUADALAJARA (MEXICO), MARTYRS OF, SS.] by Pope John Paul II.

Feast: May 25 (Mexico).

Bibliography: J. CARDOSO, *Los mártires mexicanos* (Mexico City 1953). J. H. CONTRERAS OROZCO, *El mártir de Chihuahua: persecución y levantamientos de católicos: Vida y martirio del P. Pedro Maldonado* (Chihuahua, Chih., Mexico 1992).

[K. I. RABENSTEIN]

MALDONATUS, JOHANNES

Spanish exegete and theologian, also known as Juán de Maldonado; b. Casas de la Reina, Estremadura, 1534; d. Rome, Jan. 5, 1583. After his studies at Salamanca (1547–58) and Rome (1558–62), he became a Jesuit (1562) and was ordained (1563). After having taught philosophy at the Roman College (1563) and at Paris (1564–65), he was professor of theology at Paris for nine years (1565–74). For the first five of these years he lectured in the traditional way by commenting on the *Sentences* of PETER LOMBARD, but in 1570 he initiated his own, original theological course. His teaching was interrupted in 1574 by the accusation of the Sorbonne professors that he denied the doctrine of the Immaculate Conception. Although defended by the Archbishop of Paris, Pierre de Gondi, by the papal nuncio, and by the Holy See, he withdrew to Bourges and there composed his celebrated commentaries, highly prized until modern times, on the four Gospels. Having served for a period (1578–80) as visitor of the Society of Jesus in France, he was called to Rome in 1581 by Gregory XIII to work on the critical edition of the Septuagint. Here he also collaborated on the Jesuit RATIO STUDIORUM. His more important works are the *Comment. in IV Evangelia* (2 v. Pont-à-Mousson 1596–97, and many later editions), *Traité des anges et demons* (Paris 1606), *Comment. in Prophetas quatuor* (Lyons 1609), and the *Miscellanea de Maldonado* (lectures given at Paris) ed. R. Galdos (Madrid 1947).

Bibliography: J. I. TELLECHEA, *Lexikon für Theologie und Kirche* 6:1326, esp. bibliog. C. SOMMERVOGEL, *Bibliothèque de la Compagnie de Jésus* 5:403–412; 9:631.

[J. I. TELLECHEA IDÍGORAS]

MÂLE, ÉMILE

Art historian who raised the study of medieval iconography from an antiquarian interest to a scholarly discipline; b. Commentry, France, June 2, 1862; d. Château-de-Chaalis, Oct. 6, 1954. Early medieval writers such as ISIDORE OF SEVILLE, BEDE, and RABANUS MAURUS were used by Mâle to identify and interpret religious imagery and to assign symbolic or theological meanings accurately. *Religious Art in France of the Thirteenth Century* was the title of his dissertation (1899) and first published book (1902). This study won him immediate acclaim and a post at the Sorbonne as professor of medieval art. He published similar studies for the end of the Middle Ages (1908), the 12th century (1922), and the three centuries following the Council of Trent (1932). The last book dealt with the diffusion and continuity of Christian themes in the art of Italy, Spain, and Flanders, in addition to France. In 1924 Mâle left the Sorbonne to become director of the French Archeological Institute in the Palazzo Farnese, Rome, a post he held until his retirement in 1937.

Nicolas Malebranche, lithograph.

He expanded the comprehensive design of his earlier publications with volumes on *The Early Churches of Rome* (tr. D. Buxton, Chicago 1960) and *La Fin du paganisme en Gaule, et les plus anciennes basiliques chrétiennes* (Paris 1950). He was a member of the French Academy, a Grand Officer of the Legion of Honor, and a director of the scholarly journal *Monuments et memoires.*

Bibliography: M. AUBERT, in *Monuments et memoires* 48.2 (Paris 1956) 1–7.

[P. GOULD]

MALEBRANCHE, NICOLAS

French philosopher and priest of the Oratory; b. Paris, Aug. 5, 1638; d. there, Oct. 13, 1715. A son of King Louis XIII's secretary, Malebranche studied philosophy at the Collége de la Marche and theology at the Sorbonne. He entered the ORATORIANS in 1660 and was ordained in 1664. Except for a few vacations in the country, he lived and died at the motherhouse in Paris. His philosophical search for, and defense of, truth culminated in religious meditation. As a scientist, he made detailed observations of insects, was well versed in mathematics, and presented the first analysis of colors in terms of frequencies of vibration at his election to the Académie des Sciences in 1699.

Works and Polemics. Disgusted with scholasticism, Malebranche renewed his interest in philosophy upon reading R. Descartes's *Traité de l'homme* in 1664. The editors of this work accentuated the spiritualist counterpart of its mechanistic physiology and certain affinities with the thought of St. Augustine. Malebranche's first work, *De la Recherche de la Vérité* (Paris 1674–75, 6th ed. 1712), espoused Cartesian dualism, stressing the opposition between thought and bodily extension. Sensible qualities, for Malebranche, are only a modification of the soul, a warning of what is or is not suitable for the conservation of life. Like other Cartesians, he explained the correspondence between sensations and bodily changes, as well as the soul-body union in general, in terms of the regularity of the laws of occasional causes, and held that God alone exercises true efficacy (*see* MIND-BODY PROBLEM). Malebranche was to extend this solution to all relations between creatures. Although continuing the Cartesian criticism of scholastic physics and of human errors as originating in the senses, the imagination, and the passions, he parted company with Descartes by basing his rational argumentation on certain facts of faith and by rejecting the Cartesian doctrine of innate ideas. In Malebranche's view, the soul is directly linked to universal Reason and sees the essence of bodies in God.

Abbé Simon Foucher (1644–96), in his *Critique de la recherche de la vérité* (Paris 1675), disputed this mixture of reason and faith and, through his hasty interpretations, led Malebranche to clarify his differences with Descartes over eternal truths as uncreated and over ideas as essences and not as modes of human thought. Dom Robert Desgabets (1620–78) intervened but defended Malebranche clumsily in his *Critique de la critique de la recherche. . .* (Paris 1675). Malebranche himself replied in volume two of the *Recherche* (1675, 2d ed. 1676). After the *Conversations chrétiennes* (Paris 1677), the third edition of the *Recherche* adds a volume of *Eclaircissements* that contains, among other things, an explanation of ''intelligible extension.'' Between 1680 and 1682 Malebranche engaged in a polemic with the Jesuit Le Valois (pseudonym, Louis de La Ville) on reconciling Cartesian physics with the doctrine of Tran-substantiation.

Malebranche's *Traité de la Nature et de la Grâce* (Amsterdam 1680; placed on the Index in 1690) evoked marked reservations from BOSSUET, FÉNELON, and especially ARNAULD; the better to undermine it, Arnauld first attacked the theory of knowledge (*Traité des vraies et fausses idées,* Cologne 1683), then the entire system. The writings of the two rivals multiplied; Malebranche later reedited his answers to Arnauld in *Recueil de toutes les réponses. . . à M. Arnauld* (4 v. Paris 1709). The principal points of the dispute are pointed out in the *Méditations chrétiennes* (Cologne 1683), the *Traité de morale* (Cologne 1684), the *Entretiens sur la métaphysique et la religion* (Rotterdam 1688), which is Malebranche's principal work, and the *Entretiens sur la mort* (Paris 1696).

In 1686 Malebranche engaged in a brief polemic with Bernard le Bovier de Fontenelle (1657–1757) over occasionalism and, in 1692, 1700, and 1712 successively, reworked his laws of impact in response to the criticisms of G. W. LEIBNIZ. Criticized also by P. S. REGIS in the latter's *Système de la philosophie. . .* (Paris 1690), Malebranche replied with his *Réponse* (1693), which dealt with the perception of distance, the beatific vision, and the intrinsic goodness of pleasure. Called upon to endorse QUIETISM by Dom François LAMY, he opposed it in his *Traité de l'amour de Dieu (Lyons 1697)*, and again in three *Lettres* and a *Réponse générale* to Lamy in 1699 and 1700. His *Entretien d'un philosophe chrétien et d'un philosophe chinois* (Paris 1707) reveals some of his dealings with the Jesuits; in 1712 he dealt with them again in a review of Fénelon's *Traité de l'existence de Dieu.* but in both cases avoided polemics. Despite his distaste for argumentation, he replied to the *Traité de l'action de Dieu sur les créatures* of L. F. Boursier (1679–1749) in his *Réflexions sur la prémotion physique* (Paris 1715).

Though often fierce in controversy, Malebranche showed mildness and spiritual elevation in his works of piety, which were always nourished by philosophical reflection. Among these his *Petites méditations pour se disposer à l'humilité et à la pénitence* (Paris 1677) is noteworthy.

Teaching. Malebranche's occasionalism finds divine action everywhere, but this is not the ''perpetual miracle'' for which Leibniz reproved him. Malebranche distinguishes the true miracle, which depends on the particular will of God, from the general laws of occasional causes, which, for him as for other Cartesians, explain the communication of mechanical motion to bodies and the union between soul and body. To these laws of occasional causes Malebranche added the laws that regulate, through the intermediary of the attention, the mind's access to ideas in God, and, on the supernatural level, those that give to the angels control over bodies and to Christ omnipotence for the distribution of graces to souls and bodies. In conformity with the Christocentrism of Pierre de BÉRULLE, the Second Person of the Trinity, as the Eternal Word and as Christ Incarnate, is at the very heart of Malebranchism.

As Universal Reason, Christ illumines man's mind by giving it, on the occasion of the ''natural prayer'' of attention, the intellectual intuition of essences. It is here that one can see how Malebranche's AUGUSTINIANISM converges with CARTESIANISM, which reduces all modalities of bodies to extension. The absence of interaction between souls and real bodies and the absolute freedom of God with respect to creation makes the existence of bodies both indemonstrable and inaccessible. But faith makes clear that God really has created such bodies; and occasionalism establishes the correlation between the vision in God of their essences, where they appear as determinations of intelligible extension, and the sensations that concretely diversify extension and correspond to cerebral modifications.

Because Malebranche places intelligible extension in God, he has been compared with B. SPINOZA; yet he sharply criticized Spinoza and insisted on a difference between intelligible extension, the spiritual archetype of corporeity, and materially created extension. The first ideally comprises the infinity of geometrical figures; only the second is actually divided and changing. Therefore, man sees the essence of God only ''as participable by corporeal creatures,'' that is, according to an order of determined perfections but without understanding how these perfections are reconciled with God's transcendent unity; vision in God is not vision of God. Malebranche, however, has been accused of ontologism (A. Fonck, *Dictionnaire de théologie catholique* 11.1:1046). Certainly he grants to the human mind the vision of the infinite or indeterminate being as a condition of all determinate thought. But Malebranche rejects the basic error of ontologism, viz, the confusion between man's knowledge in the present life and the beatific vision. He insists that no one can see God without first having died.

Again, on earth man does not see the essences of souls. Malebranche limits the Cartesian *cogito* to the unquestionable awareness of the existence of spirit, while denying that spirit is more clearly known than body. Man, in his view, experiences his own attributes in a confused way and will contemplate his archetype only in the future life; the vision of God, however, will then prevent him from being absorbed by his own perfections. He holds that immortality is sufficiently founded on spirituality and is confirmed by revelation.

As the Incarnate Christ, Jesus unites in Himself both corporeal and spiritual substance and makes creation infinitely priceless. Original sin, foreseen by God, enriches the plan of the Incarnation—which in itself is independent of the Redemption, following the Scotist tradition. Malebranche holds that evil is positive; contrary to St. Augustine, he refuses to explain disorder as a simple dissonance contributing to universal harmony. A man of his time, he excludes from salvation pagans, heretics, and children who have died unbaptized, and is shocked by the great numbers of the damned. An almighty and infinitely good God can save all men and wills to save them (against Jansenism), but He must in His wisdom reconcile the perfection of the work with the simplicity of the means available. Just as physical evils (monsters, cataclysms, etc.) are the consequence of the simplicity of mechanical laws, so inequalities in the distribution of grace are traceable to the cause that best glorifies God, viz, the desires of the soul of Christ, subject as it is to the succession of human thoughts. Bossuet and Fénelon protested against this limitation of the soul of Christ, and Arnauld saw in it an intimation of the Nestorian heresy. Yet through it, Malebranche sought to avoid the opposed errors of Jansenism and Pelagianism. As he viewed the matter, original sin did not destroy nature, and every man who discovers his true Good has access to the graces of light. But through sin the soul is subject to concupiscence and, without the grace of reparation, is incapable of always preferring the good. Malebranche, like St. Augustine, considers this grace as a ''prevenient delectation'' that opposes itself to the attraction of concupiscence and reestablishes man's freedom. Its proper use follows on the distribution of grace by Christ, and neither commands this giving of grace (contrary to Pelagianism) nor follows from it necessarily (contrary to Jansenism). For human freedom, which conditions man's access to clear ideas through the agency of his attentiveness, permits man to follow or not to follow the divine impulse that draws him toward the Good. God gives man the impulse always to go farther, to the infinite, but sin stops man at false particular goods. The love of God includes beatitude (contrary to quietism), and the queen of virtues, charity, includes the love of God and that of neighbor. The resulting morality is ''Christian,'' as is all of Malebranche's philosophy. It is also rational, however, and is founded on the intellectual vision of the order of perfections. Malebranche applied its principles to defend the dignity of all human beings and the rights of conscience, and concerned himself with concrete efforts in the fields of social relations and of pedagogy.

Influence. Through the breadth of his synthesis and the richness of his psychological and moral analyses, Malebranche attracted many readers. There have been numerous reeditions and translations of his major works, both in his lifetime and after his death. His philosophy was developed by his disciples to the end of the 18th century, principally in France by the Oratorian Bernard LAMY and the Benedictine François Lamy, both contemporaries of Malebranche, and later by the Jesuit Yves Marie André (1675–1764) and, in the second half of the

18th century, by Charles Hercules of Keranflech; in England, by John Norris (1657–1711); and in Italy, by the Franciscan Michelangelo Fardella (1650–1718) and, at the end of the 18th century, by Cardinal H. S. Gerdil (1718–1802). Malebranchism appeared, at that time, as the best bulwark of SPIRITUALISM against unbelief.

See Also: OCCASIONALISM; ONTOLOGISM.

Bibliography: Works and translations. *Oeuvres complètes,* gen. ed. A. ROBINET, 20 v. (Paris 1958–66) v.1–3, ed. G. RODIS-LEWIS; v.5, ed. G. DREYFUS; v.17.1–2, ed. P. COSTABEL; *Treatise concerning the Search after Truth. Treatise of Nature and Grace. . . Defense against Accusations of Mr. De La Ville,* tr. T. TAYLOR, 2 v. (Oxford 1694), 2d ed. with *Discourse upon Light and Colours* (1700); *Search after Truth,* tr. R. SAULT, 2 v. (London 1694–95); *Christian Conferences* (London 1695); *Treatise of Morality,* tr. J. SHIPTON (London 1699); *Dialogues in Metaphysics and on Religion,* tr. M. GINSBERG (London 1923), pref. by G. D. HICKS, exposition of M.'s epistemology and metaphysics by Ginsberg. Studies. A. DEL NOCE, ''Bibliografia malebranchiana,'' *Malebranche nel terzo centenario della nascita* spec. suppl. of *Revista de filosofia neo-scolastica* 30 (1938) 361–380. G. SEBBA, *N. Malebranche: A Preliminary Bibliography* (Athens, Geo., 1958). A. ROBINET, *Documents biographiques et bibliographiques,* v.20 of MALEBRANCHE, *Oeuvres complètes, op. cit.* Copleston v.4. J. MOREAU, *Enciclopedia filosofica,* 4 v. (Venice-Rome 1957) 3:272–277. J. WEHRLÉ, *Dictionnaire de théologie catholique*, ed. A. VACANT et al., 15 v. (Paris 1903–50) 9.2:1774–1804. G. RODIS-LEWIS, *Nicolas Malebranche* (Paris 1963). R. W. CHURCH, *A Study in the Philosophy of M.* (London 1931). B. K. ROME, *The Philosophy of M.: A Study in His Integration of Faith, Reason and Experimental Observation* (Chicago 1963). V. DELBOS, *Étude de la philosophie de M.* (Paris 1924). H. GOUHIER, *La Vocation de M.* (Paris 1926); *La Philosophie de M. et son expérience religieuse* (2d ed. Paris 1948). M. GUEROULT, *Malebranche*, 2 v. in 3 (Paris 1955–59) v.1 *La Vision de Dieu;* v.2 *Les Cinq abîmes de la Providence.* Y. DE MONTCHEUIL, *M. et le quiétisme* (Paris 1946). G. DREYFUS, *La Volonté selon M.* (Paris 1958). A. ROBINET, *Systéme et existence dans l'oeuvre de M.* (Paris 1965). L. VERGA, *La filosofia morale di M.* (Milan 1964).

[G. RODIS-LEWIS]

MALI, THE CATHOLIC CHURCH IN

One of the world's poorest nations, the Republic of Mali is a tropical, landlocked country in west Africa. Located south of ALGERIA, it is bound on the east by Niger, on the south by BURKINA FASO and the IVORY COAST, on the southwest by GUINEA, on the west by SENEGAL and on the northwest by MAURITANIA. Known as the French Sudan until 1958, Mali joined with Senegal and as the Federation of Mali, gained increasing political autonomy until it was granted political independence by French Prime Minister Charles de Gaulle in 1960. A flat, semiarid region, Mali suffers from desertification by the encroachment of the Western Sahara to its north. To the south it is crossed by the Upper Niger, allowing for the seasonal cultivation of rice, millet, cotton and peanuts along the river. Mali's population consists mostly of Bambara, Fulani, Snufo, Soninke, Tuareg and other tribes, although Berbers and a European minority are also represented. Cotton, account's for most of the nation's agricultural exports, while government efforts to attract international mining operations to the region bode well for its future as a major gold exporter.

Capital: Bamako.
Size: 465,040 sq. miles.
Population: 10,685,948 in 2000.
Languages: French; Bambara, Fulani, and local dialects are spoken in various regions.
Religions: 125,800 Catholics (1.2%), 9,617,353 Muslims (90%), 192,350 Protestants (1.8%), 750,445 adherents to indigenous pagan beliefs.
Archdiocese: Bamako, with suffragans Kayes (created 1963), Mopti (1964), San (1964), Ségou (1962), and Sikasso (1963).

History. Islam entered the area in the 11th century, and an empire was established by conqueror Sundjata Keita 200 years later, made rich through its control of the gold trade across the Sahara. From the 15th through the 18th century Mali fell under Moroccan rule, and then was ruled by native tribes. While Christianity appeared during the 19th century, brought by French colonists who renamed the region French Sudan *c.* 1899, it made slow progress. In 1868 the Prefecture Apostolic of the Sahara and Sudan was erected, with Cardinal Charles LAVIGERIE, Archbishop of Algiers, as superior and apostolic delegate. The first two groups of White Fathers to enter the region were massacred by local tribes as they traveled the Sahara (1876, 1881); a later group successfully entered Mali from Senegal and established missions at Ségou and Tombouctou in 1895. The White Sisters arrived in 1898 and established hospitals at Kati and Ségou. From 1904 to 1920 Mali was joined with other French territories to form the colony of Upper Senegal-Niger.

Until 1921 the growth of the mission in Mali was hampered by the hostility of French colonial officials, epidemics of yellow fever and the mobilization of missionaries during World War I. The mission began to develop with the creation of the Vicariate Apostolic of Bamako in 1921, whose limits were practically the same as those of Mali. Following World War II the region was reorganized as the French overseas territory of the Sudan. The Church established a hierarchy there in 1955, with Bamako as its archdiocese and metropolitan see. Despite native Malian's increasingly vocal movement for independence from French rule, the region agreed to join the other five nations comprising French West Africa in 1958 and accept the political status of a republic within the French Community. On Sept. 22, 1960 the Sudanese Republic

and Senegal achieved political independence as the Mali Federation; when Senegal withdrew less than a year later, the region was renamed Mali. The first Malian bishop, Luc Sangaré, became archbishop of Mali in 1962.

Mali's first independent government was socialist in its leanings, and it was overthrown by a military coup led by Lieutenant Moussa Traoré in 1968. This military dictatorship lasted for the next 23 years, although Traoré held mock elections beginning in 1972. In 1991 Touré was arrested, and Mali held its first democratic, multiparty elections in 1992. President Alpha Oumar Konare held the position of president through 2000

The 28 parishes established in the region in 1964 had grown to 42 parishes by 2000, reflecting the work of Church evangelicalism. In addition to 71 secular and 83 religious priests, 22 brothers and 206 sisters tended the region. During the second half of the 20th century the Church worked to promote the role of women within this predominately Sunni Muslim nation, freeing them from their traditional cloistered life. In 1998 President Konare traveled to the Vatican for a respectful audience with Pope John Paul II, a reflection of Konare's willingness to promote cooperation among his people's diverse faiths. As Mali entered the 21st century, tribal warfare in Mali's northern region, the nation's heavy reliance on foreign aid and the social and economic devastation caused by desertification and drought were the problems most directly confronting this nation. In 2000 the average life expectancy of a Malian was only 47 years, a situation that troubled the Church hierarchy. Through his personal charity, distributed by Core Unum, the Pope continued in his efforts to combat the effects of the spread of the

Sahara, donating $5.5 million to Mali and other nations in the Sahel region in 1999 alone.

Bibliography: *Bilan du Monde,* 2:587– 590. *Annuario Pontificio* has annual data for all dioceses. For additional bibliography, *see* AFRICA.

[J. DE BENOIST/EDS.]

MALINES CONSERVATIONS

A series of five unofficial talks between Roman Catholics and Anglicans at Malines (Mechelen), Belgium. The first took place Dec. 6–8, 1921, and the last Oct.11–12, 1926. The chief Anglican representatives were Charles Lindley Wood, second Viscount HALIFAX; Dr. Armitage Robinson; Rev. Dr. B. J. Kidd; Rev. W. H. Frere; and Rev. Dr. Charles GORE. The Catholics were represented by Cardinal MERCIER, Cardinal Joseph van Roey, the abbés Fernand Portal and Hippolyte Hemmer, and Msgr. Pierre BATIFFOL. The moving spirits were Halifax and Portal, who were encouraged by a declaration of the sixth Lambeth Conference that the Anglican bishops were prepared, in return for the recognition of their ministry, to accept "from the authorities of other churches a form of commission or recognition." Halifax approached Mercier, who agreed to a series of talks. The proceedings were clouded by the hesitancy of Dr. Randall DAVIDSON, Abp. of Canterbury, and the hostile attitude of the English Catholic hierarchy. Initially Pius XI was not opposed to the Malines meetings, although he made it clear that they were confidential and that the Catholic representatives had no other function than to discuss the differences dividing the two churches.

In the first discussion it was clear that both churches had much in common. The most difficult point to reconcile concerned ecclesiastical jurisdiction. Both groups readily admitted that bishops held office by divine right (*jure divino*), but the Anglicans feared Roman centralization. The most notable advance during the conversations was made by Mercier who in the fourth session presented a memoir entitled "The English Church United Not Absorbed," which suggested that the archbishop of Canterbury be established as patriarch with broad powers, that Latin Canon Law not be imposed in England, that the English Church have its own liturgy, and that all the historic sees of the English Church be maintained and the recent Catholic ones suppressed. Between the fourth and fifth conversations the irenical atmosphere darkened; Cardinal BOURNE expressed displeasure because English Catholics had been so little consulted. More significant were the deaths of both Mercier and Portal in 1926. Cardinal van Roey, whose ecumenical interests were far less intense than Mercier's, presided over the anticlimactic fifth conversation. All those present agreed that conditions were distinctly unfavorable for further talks. Rome's attitude had cooled partly as a result of the negative attitude of Cardinals Bourne and GASQUET. The encyclical *MORTALIUM ANIMOS* (1928) did not explictly mention the Malines Conversations; but it placed restrictions on Catholic participation in such matters. With the progress of the ECUMENICAL MOVEMENT, particularly since the pontificate of JOHN XXIII, Rome has relaxed such restrictions.

Bibliography: J. DE BIVORT DE LA SAUDÉE, *Anglicans et catholiques*, 2 v. (Paris 1949). C. L. WOOD, SECOND VISCOUNT HALIFAX, ed., *The Conversations at Malines* (London 1930). W. H. FRERE, *Recollections of Malines* (London 1935). H. M. HEMMER, *Fernand Portal (1855–1926) Apostle of Unity,* tr. A. T. MACMILLAN (New York 1961).

[S. J. MILLER]

MALLINCKRODT, PAULINE VON, BL.

Foundress of the Sisters of CHRISTIAN CHARITY, also known as Marie Bernadine Sophia Pauline Mallinckrodt; b. June 3, 1817, Minden, Westphalia, Germany; d. April 30, 1881, Paderborn (near Münster), Germany.

Her mother was a devout Catholic; her father, a high-ranking civil servant, was a Protestant of tolerant views. Her brother, Hermann, became a Catholic leader in public life. In Aachen, where she spent her earlier years, Pauline frequented the circle of the poet Louise Hensel (1798–1876), who became a Catholic in 1818. When she was 18, she declined to marry a well-to-do Protestant. In Paderborn, where she lived from 1839, Pauline dedicated herself to works of charity, founded an association of women to help the impoverished sick in 1839, and in 1840 established a day nursery. In 1842, Pauline opened a school for blind children. She persuaded St. Madeleine Sophie BARAT to have her institute take charge of this school, but the Prussian government would not grant admittance to the French religious congregation.

As a result Pauline founded her own congregation Aug. 21, 1849, and served as its first superior general. During her lifetime the institute extended its apostolate to include teaching in elementary and secondary schools. When the Kulturkampf caused the closing of 17 houses in Germany, Pauline moved the motherhouse to Mont-Saint-Guibert near Brussels, Belgium, and also began to establish houses abroad. She visited the U.S. in 1873 shortly after the first group of her sisters arrived in New Orleans, and again in 1879 after journeying to her foundation in Chile. She traveled also to England, where houses were started. By the time of her death from pneumonia in 1881, the Sisters of Christian Charity had 492 members in 45 houses.

Mother Pauline is buried in the motherhouse in Paderborn. The decree introducing her cause for beatification was issued in 1958, which ended with her beatification by Pope John Paul II, April 14, 1985.

Feast: April 30.

Bibliography: P. VON MALLINCKRODT, *Kurzer Lebensabriß unserer teuren Würdigen Mutter und Stifterin Pauline v. Mallinckrodt, von ihr selbst verfaßt* (Paderborn 1889). T. BARKEY, *Damit ihr Leben gelingen kann* (Paderborn 1984). A. BUNGERT, *Pauline v. Mallinckrodt*, (Würzburg 1980). K. BURTON, *Whom Love Impels: The Life of Mother Pauline von Mallinckrodt, Foundress of the Sisters of Christian Charity* (New York 1952). J. J. DEGENHARDT, *Dienstbereit in der Liebe Christi* (Paderborn 1985). BR. ERNEST, *A Happy Heart: A Story of Mother Pauline von Mallinckrodt* (Notre Dame, Ind. 1956). C. FRENKE, *Pauline v. Mallinckrodt in ihrer Zeit* (Paderborn 1984). A. HÜFFER, *Pauline von Mallinckrodt* 2d. ed. (Münster 1902). *The Life of Mother Pauline von Mallinckrodt, Foundress of the Sisters of Christian Charity* (New York 1917). A. METTE, *Die Liebe zählt nicht—nur die Liebe zählt* (Paderborn 1985). *L'Osservatore Romano,* English edition, no. 19 (1985): 6–8. K. SANDER-WIETFELD, *Pauline von Mallinckrodt: Ein Lebensbild nach ihrer Briefen und Aufzeichnungen* (Paderborn 1985). A. SCHMITTDIEL, *Pauline von Mallinckrodt* (Paderborn 1949). SISTERS OF CHRISTIAN CHARITY (U.S.), *Enriching Many* (Mendham, N.J. 1942). D. WEDMORE, *The Woman Who Couldn't Be Stopped* (Mendham, N.J. 1986).

[N. BACKMUND]

MALMÉDY, ABBEY OF

Former Benedictine monastery in the Diocese of LIÈGE in the Province of Liège, Belgium (Latin *Malmundariense*). The abbey was founded on the banks of the Ambleve near the forest of the Ardennes *c.* 650 by Sigebert III of Austrasia, at the instance of St. Remaclus of Aquitaine (d. 672), former monk of LUXEUIL and former abbot of SOLIGNAC. The church was dedicated to SS. Peter and Paul, Our Lady, and St. John the Baptist. At a site near Malmédy, Remaclus simultaneously created the sister abbey of STAVELOT. This double MONASTERY, embracing a territory 12 miles in circumference, first followed the Columban-Benedictine Rule. A single abbot generally ruled both monasteries, but in the course of centuries the primacy was disputed between the two communities. In 862 LOTHAIR II began to distribute the considerable goods of the double abbey and to name lay abbots. St. Odilo, monk of GORZE and then abbot of Stavelot-Malmédy (938–954) introduced the monastic reform, and Emperor OTTO I granted the monks freedom to elect their abbot. Abbot Werinfrid (954–980) obtained from Bp. Notker of Liège a charter that promoted the supremacy of Stavelot over Malmédy.

When Malmédy was restored and reconstituted, the Council of Ingelheim in 980 imposed on both monasteries a single abbot who was chosen by the monks of Stavelot. From 1020 to 1048, POPPO, first auxiliary to Richard of Saint-Vanne (d. 1046), ruled the double abbey and distinguished himself by his reforming activity in Belgium and Germany. The monastery entered a period of intense artistic and literary activity during the 11th century. In the following century, Abbot WIBALD maintained discipline, continued the abbey's literary activity, and put its finances on a solid footing, serving at the same time as an imperial administrator. Wibald was abbot also of MONTE CASSINO (1137) and CORVEY (1146); he died on mission to the Byzantine Emperor Manuel I Comnenus, leaving an important correspondence. In the 15th century, the monastery declined at a rapid pace. Under Henry of Mérode (d. 1460) there were only eight monks at Stavelot and nine at Malmédy. In the 16th century the abbey was administered by princes of the House of BAVARIA and in the 17th century by the Fürstenberg family. Both monasteries were sacked during the wars between the empire and France in 1689. Abbot Nicholas Massin (1731–37) worked at restoring discipline; and in 1784 under Jacques de Hulin, the abbey church of Malmédy, which still stands today, was consecrated. During the FRENCH REVOLUTION the monks were expelled, and on Oct. 1, 1795, France annexed the principalities of Liège and Stavelot-Malmédy. The monastery buildings today house a school and a law court.

Bibliography: L. H. COTTINEAU, *Répertoire topobibliographique des abbayes et prieurés*, 2 v. (Mâcon 1935–39) 2:1719–20. J. MABILLON, *Annales ordinis s. Benedicti . . . ,* 6 v. (Lucca 1739–45), v. 1–5, tables. *Gallia Christiana*, v. 1–13 (Paris 1715–85) 3:724. U. BERLIÈRE, *Monasticon belge,* 2 v. (Bruges 1890–1955) 2:84ff. N. PIETKIN, ''Vieux Malmédy,'' *Terre Wallonne* 2 (1920) 407–421. H. LECLERCQ, *Dictionnaire d'archéologie chrétienne et de liturgie*, ed. F. CABROL, H. LECLERCQ, and H. I. MARROU, 15 v. (Paris 1907–53) 15.2:1669–73. A. DELVAUX DE FENFFE, *Les Abbés et princes-abbés des abbayes de Malmédy du XIIe au XVIIe siècle* (Tongres 1935).

[J. DAOUST]

MALMESBURY, ABBEY OF

Malmesbury Abbey, located on a hilltop at the southern edge of the Cotswolds, had its origins in a monastery built in the late seventh century. An Irish monk, Maidulph, arrived in England around the year 642 and established a hermitage and school there near the river Bladon. He chose a very strategic location for his school; in the sixteenth century, the antiquarian John Leland wrote ''The toun of Malmesbyri standith on the very toppe of a greate slay rok, and ys wonderfully defended by nature.'' Several years after Maidulph established his school, a young monk named ALDHELM, who was a relative of King Ine of Wessex, came to study with him. Ald-

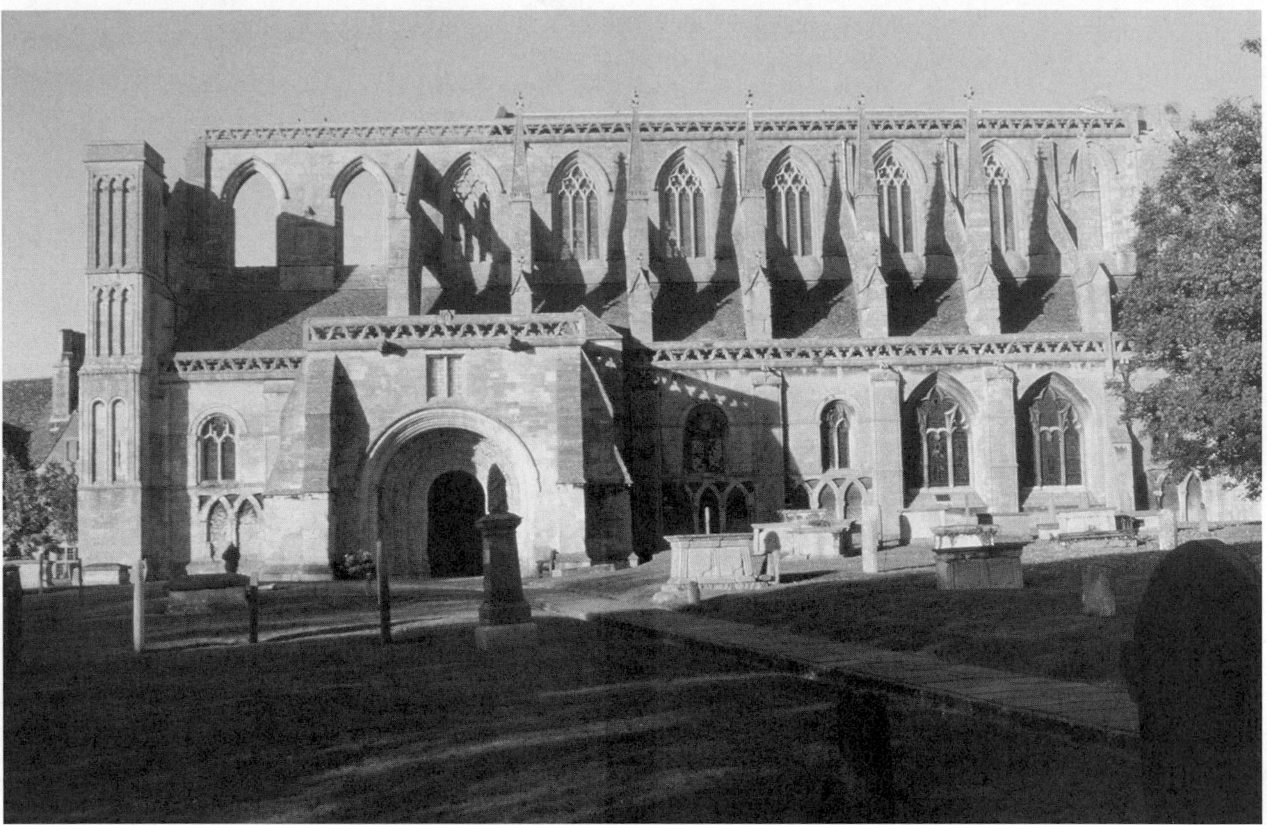

Malmesbury Abbey. (©Philippa Lewis; Edifice/CORBIS)

helm also studied at Canterbury under St. Adrian the African, and later in Rome. William of Malmesbury, who in the twelfth century chronicled the Abbey's history, wrote that after Aldhelm returned to England, he received a land grant at ''Meildulfesburh'' (Malmesbury) from Leutherius, bishop of the West Saxons, in 672. In the document, Bishop Leutherius praised Aldhelm for his education and devotion to the church, and he gave him land ''for the purpose of leading a life according to strict rule.'' Aldhelm returned to the site of his old school, and there founded a flourishing Benedictine monastery. As Aldhelm was much revered by his contemporaries, the site soon became a popular center of pilgrimage.

Malmesbury claims to be the oldest borough in England, having allegedly received a charter in 880 from King Alfred (r. 871–899). Half a century later, Alfred's grandson, King Athelstan (r. 925–939) used Malmesbury as a base of operations from which to fight the Danes that had encroached upon southern England. He contributed many religious relics and other gifts to the abbey, further enhancing its appeal to pilgrims and scholars. After Athelstan died at Gloucester, his body was brought to Malmesbury for burial; legend has it that he was buried under the High Altar.

In 1010, an extraordinary event happened at Malmesbury. Eilmer, a young monk, fastened wings to his arms and feet, and flew from the top of the abbey tower. According to WILLIAM OF MALMESBURY, who most likely had heard the story as a youth, Eilmer flew about 600 feet before he panicked, lost altitude and landed rather suddenly, breaking both legs. He was undeterred, however, and was planning his second flight, this time with a tail to provide him with more stability, when his abbot declared there were to be no further attempts at flight.

Malmesbury's most famous occupant was the historian William of Malmesbury, (*c.* 1095–1143) author of *De Gestis Regem Anglorum* (Deeds of the Kings of the English), which chronicled England's history from the arrival of the Saxons to 1120; *De Gestis Pontificium Anglorum* (Deeds of the Archbishops and Bishops of the English), which recorded the ecclesiastical history of England from the arrival of the missionary St. Augustine of Canterbury to 1125; and the *Historia Novella* (Recent History), which recounted King Stephen's reign. A student of the Scriptures, hagiography, theology, the classics, and civil and cannon law, William represents a ''golden age'' for Malmesbury Abbey. He was perhaps the most popular English historian of his time; son of one Norman and one English parent, he was educated at Malmesbury under Abbot Godfrey (ruled 1087–91?), and later he became a monk there. As a child he had helped Abbot Godfrey in the library and apparently learned to love such work. William collected many historical and legal documents, and while he might have been Abbot of Malmesbury, he apparently preferred the the library, holding the office of librarian. He is considered the finest and most accurate historian of his generation; certainly he was one of the most prolific. Among his other works were the *Life of St. Wulfstan of Worcester, On the Antiquity of the Church of Glastonbury*, and the *Life of St. Dunstan*, among many other saint's lives.

The present building was begun shortly after William's death and consecrated in 1180. This Romanesque church was renowned for its remarkable sculptured friezes of biblical history and of the apostles in the South Porch. It was expanded over the next few centuries, and eventually had one of the tallest spires in England. This spire, along with the east end choir, lady chapels and several other areas of the abbey, were destroyed in a great storm of 1470; they were not replaced for lack of money. In 1539, HENRY VIII dissolved the monastery and sold the land and buildings to William Stumpe, a wealthy clothier. Stumpe used the monastery as a textile manufacturing site for two years, and then he decided to donate it back to the people of Malmesbury. On August 20, 1541, Malmesbury became a parish church.

Over the ensuing centuries, the abbey began to decay, until it was finally being used to store hay and keep animals. In the early twentieth century, however, major renovations were begun on the abbey. The local landowners and manor houses contributed greatly toward the upkeep of the abbey, as they were, according to the Curator of Malmesbury, the only ones with the money to do so. In 1928, the floor, which was said to have had a surface like a ploughed field, was taken down six inches to its original level; the choir stalls were then introduced, the long pews removed, and King Athelstan's tomb moved to a more convenient position. That same year, the building was re-consecrated and a Bishop of Malmesbury was appointed. Today, while Malmesbury is still referred to as an abbey historically, it does not function as such.

Bibliography: D. DUMVILLE, *Wessex and England from Alfred to Edgar* (Woodbridge 1992). J. MORRIS, ed. *Domesday Book: Wiltshire* (Chichester 1977). R. THOMSON, *William of Malmesbury* (Woodbridge 1986). R. THOMSON and M. WINTERBOTTOM, ed. *William of Malmesbury: Gesta Regum Anglorum* (Oxford 1999).

[L. A. LEHTOLA]

MALONE, SYLVESTER

Parish priest, social reformer; b. Trim, County Meath, Ireland, May 8, 1821; d. Williamsburg, N.Y., Dec. 29, 1899. His parents, Laurence and Marcella (Martin) Malone, sent him for his early education to an academy run by the Protestant Carroll brothers. He later said that this offered him an early breadth of viewpoint. In 1838 Rev. Andrew Byrne of New York induced him to study for the priesthood. He started his theological studies at St. Joseph's Seminary, New York, and he was ordained on Aug. 15, 1844, for that diocese, which included the states of New York and New Jersey. In September of 1844 he was assigned to a parish in Williamsburg (later part of Brooklyn, N.Y.), a village of 5,000 that included 500 Catholics. He reported 37 years later that 25 parishes had been erected within his original parish of SS. Peter and Paul. As pastor he constructed a Gothic church, the first designed by Patrick C. Keely, leading architect of the time; zealously cared for immigrants; and increased his flock to 5,000 within a decade. In 1866 he was Bp. John Loughlin's theologian at the Second Plenary Council of Baltimore.

Malone attracted wide attention by his public positions. He was an abolitionist and a Republican. When he received word of the surrender of Fort Sumter to the Confederates, he ran up an American flag at the foot of the cross on his church steeple. He later recalled that no parishioners protested, despite the crosscurrents of opinion in the area. After the Civil War, he toured the South and, when he returned, spoke on behalf of the rights of African Americans. Although he visited and admired Cardinal Henry Manning, he became a strong supporter of the Irish Land League. Malone adopted liberal views on a variety of civic subjects, and these were widely publicized in the New York press. He was himself, as he wrote to Leo XIII in defense of Dr. Edward MCGLYNN, "the advocate of temperance and of every good cause that works for the public good." As a defender of the public schools, he was supported by Hamilton Fish and Abp. John Ireland for a Catholic vacancy on the New York Board of Regents. Because the bishops of the state had supported Bp. Bernard MCQUAID, some interpreted his election in 1894 as a victory for the anti-Catholic faction. When he died, he was still pastor of the parish that he had founded.

Bibliography: J. K. SHARP, *History of the Diocese of Brooklyn, 1853–1953*, 2 v. (New York 1954).

[F. E. FITZPATRICK]

MALTA, THE CATHOLIC CHURCH IN

Capital: Valletta.
Size: 95 sq. miles.
Population: 391,670 in 2000.
Languages: English, Maltese (a Semitic language).
Religions: 382,870 Catholics (98%), 2,500 Muslims (.6%), 379,370 Protestants (1.2%), 1,000 Jews (.2%).
Archdiocese: On the main island of Malta, with suffragan on the island of Gozo (created 1864).

The Republic of Malta is located 58 miles south of Sicily, in the central Mediterranean. The Maltese islands comprise Malta, Gozo (26 square miles), Comino (1 square mile) and a number of uninhabited rocky islets. Low, rocky plains characterize the region, which contains deposits of limestone, with cliffs edging the sea. With its Mediterranean climate, the region produces a variety of crops, including vegetables, grapes, wheat, barley, citrus and cut flowers, although the lack of fresh water continues to be problematic.

Allotted to Constantinople in A.D. 533, the islands fell to Saracens in the late 9th century, and with the Norman conquest in 1090 became a dependency of SICILY. In 1530 CHARLES V gave the region to the KNIGHTS OF MALTA, an equestrian order who were for the most part French. Under the Knights, Malta served as a Christian bulwark against the OTTOMAN TURKS. Napoleon expelled the Knights in 1798 but, with the failure of his expedition to Egypt, could not hold Malta itself. A British protectorate from 1800 to 1964, Malta flourished but suffered heavily from Italian and German bombing in World War II. Independent in the British Commonwealth after 1964, Malta became an independent republic in 1974 and by 2000 was debating a decision to join the European Union. The capital of Malta, Valletta, is named after Jean de LA VALETTE, who led Malta's heroic defense against a siege of the Turks in 1565. By the late 20th century, Malta was the most densely populated country in Europe; more than half the population was under 40 years of age.

History. With large prehistoric monuments, Malta was held by Phoenicians from the 16th to 10th centuries B.C., and perhaps also by Greeks, before it came under the sway of CARTHAGE *c.* 480 B.C.. The region was conquered by Rome 200 years later and named Melita. In A.D. 60, after being shipwrecked, St. Paul stayed on Malta for three months and founded the region's first Christian community under Publius. Several early Christian catacombs and a few Christian inscriptions in Latin and Greek survive. Maltese Bishop Julianus (Lucianus) sided with Pope Vigilius in the THREE CHAPTERS Schism (553), bringing Malta to the Byzantine Church which controlled the region for the next 300 years; Lucillus was deposed by Pope Gregory the Great (598) and was succeeded by Trajanus, formerly the abbot of a monastery in Syracuse. In 870 the Ottoman Turks invaded the region. Manas (868–874) was imprisoned in Palermo, and no further bishops appear, for freedom of religion was restricted and church buildings were neglected.

Following the Norman conquest of the region in the 11th century, Malta was linked with Sicily and fell under a series of rulers: Hohenstaufen from 1194, Angevins from 1266, Aragon from 1283, Castile from 1412 and the Hapsburg empire from 1516. In 1090 Roger I of Sicily initiated a Christian revival in the islands. The cathedral and its chapter became famous, and from Walter (1090), Malta's bishop list is nearly complete. At first immediately subject to the Holy See, the diocese became suffragan to Palermo in 1154. Maurus Calì (1393–1408) was a prominent jurist. Five mendicant orders founded houses in the 14th and 15th centuries, and two convents of Benedictine nuns were established.

The 1530 cession of Malta to the Knights and the 1575 apostolic visitation by Pietro Duzina opened a new era in the island's ecclesiastical, political and cultural history. Friction between the bishops and the Knights concerning jurisdiction, together with the spread of heresy and superstition, led to the establishment of the Inquisition (1574–1798). The reforms of TRENT, under resident bishops brought about general religious improvement. Baldassare Cagliares (1615–33) convoked three synods and performed five visitations. Priests were well trained in religious novitiates at the seminary (from 1617), and the Jesuit college (1592), which became the university (1769). Parishes and religious foundations increased in number. In 1797 Pius VI added the titular archbishopric of Rhodes to Malta but kept Malta suffragan to Palermo. In 1797 Czar Paul I of Russia asserted his protection of the Knights, of whom he was elected grand master in 1798. Napoleon, who promised to safeguard Malta's Catholicism, sanctioned the expulsion of foreign clerics and the closing of several monasteries, transferred marriages to the civil authorities, prohibited appeals to the pope and despoiled the churches of their riches. The angry Maltese, under Canon Francis X Caruana (who became bishop in 1831) and aided by British and Portuguese fleets, forced the surrender of the French in 1800.

In 1814 Malta formally came under the protection of British commissioners and governors, who maintained peaceful and amicable relations with the Church but occasionally encroached on its rights. When the king of Naples and the British disputed the right to appoint the bishop of Malta in 1829, Gregory XVI removed the see from the jurisdiction of Palermo and again made it imme-

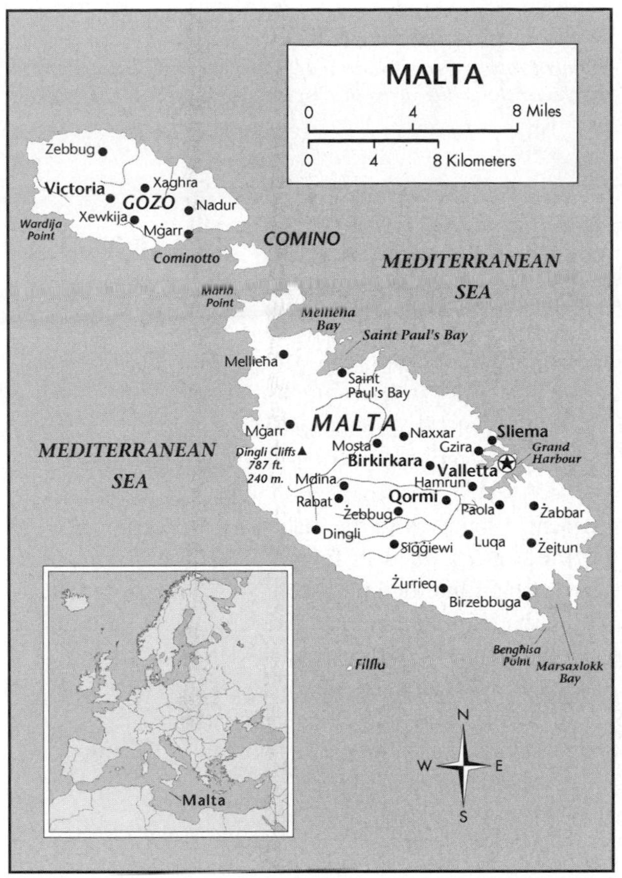

diately subject to the Holy See. The British sanctioned laws contrary to Canon Law, which was observed in Malta. The rights of sanctuary and clerical immunity, except for bishops, were abolished; ecclesiastical jurisdiction was restricted to purely spiritual matters, and a law controlling MORTMAIN was introduced. A political-religious clash in 1928 followed the appointment of Lord Strickland to office. Negotiations between the British and the Holy See failed, and the constitution was suspended (1930–32) and revoked (1933–36). A new constitution (1939–46) was followed by self-government in 1947. In 1944 the hierarchy was established. A political crisis in 1958 caused the revocation of the constitution a year later and the issuance of a new constitution in 1961. Malta became independent on Sept. 14, 1964.

Following independence, the new government adopted a more secular policy, which was reflected by the constitution promulgated on Dec. 13, 1974, when it became a republic. Under this constitution, Roman Catholicism was still declared the state religion, divorce continued to be banned and Catholic instruction in all schools was compulsory. While conflicts arose between the Church and the government over the funding of Catholic schools and the ownership of Church property, a 1985 commission was established that resolved many of these conflicts. While the state continued to subsidize Church schools, it did so through a foundation with contributions from both the state and the Church. Under the 1991 Ecclesiastical Entitles Act, the Church transferred ownership rights of its non-pastoral property to this foundation. By 2000 there were 80 parishes tended by 491 diocesan and 451 religious priests. Other religious included approximately 90 brothers and 1,310 sisters, who aided in the Church's educational programs. Estimates showed that in 2000, 65 percent of Maltese Catholics attended mass on a regular basis. In 1998 the Knights of Malta celebrated their 900th anniversary, which event was honored by the Vatican through a gift of fort St. Angelo, where Maltese hero La Valette repulsed a Turkish siege in 1565. The Order, founded in the 12th century to protect pilgrims traveling to the Holy Land, had 11,500 members worldwide and engaged in humanitarian efforts that included operating hospitals in the Middle East. Pope John Paul II visited the region for the second time in May of 2001, during a pilgrimage in the footsteps of St. Paul.

Bibliography: A. BONNICI, *Church and State in Malta: 1800–50* (La Vallette 1958); *Ecclesiastical History of Malta* (Malta 1966). A. A. FERRIS, *Storia ecclesiastica di Malta* (Malta 1877). P. DE BONO, *Sommario della storia della legislazione a Malta* (Malta 1897). W. HARDMAN, *History of Malta: 1798–1815* (London 1909). A. V. LAFERLA, *The Story of Man in Malta* (Malta 1935); *British Malta,* 2 v. (Malta 1938–47). H. LECLERCQ, *Dictionnaire d'archéologie chrétienne et de liturgie,* eds., F. CABROL, H. LECLERCQ and H. I. MARROU, 15 v. (Paris 1907–53) 10.1:1318–42. *Bilan du Monde* 2:590–593. *Annuario Pontificio.*

[A. BONNICI/EDS.]

MALTHUS, THOMAS ROBERT

English economist; b. near Guildford, Surrey, England, Feb. 14, 1776; d. Bath, England, Dec. 29, 1834. Malthus was an Anglican clergyman but devoted much attention to economics. In 1805 he became professor of history and political economy at the East India Company's college in Haileybury. Although best known for his theory of population, Malthus also contributed to other topics in economics, especially the theory of market gluts.

Malthus's *Essay on Population* (1st ed. 1798) was primarily an answer to the ''Utopian'' writings of William Godwin, who argued that poverty and misery were the result of social institutions and could be cured by the elimination of private property, inheritance, and social classes. In rebuttal, Malthus argued that there is a ''natural tendency'' for population to increase at a geometric rate. Food production, however, would grow less rapidly, being governed by the law of diminishing returns. The result would be increasing misery, pestilence, and war, which would increase the death rate to match the birth rate and hold population stable. Although without optimism, later editions of the *Essay* discussed the possibility that ''preventive checks'' on birth rate could lessen the need for the previously mentioned ''positive checks'' on the population. Among the preventive checks discussed were moral restraint and postponement of marriage. Contraception, as advocated by later neo-Malthusians, was not mentioned by Malthus and would probably have been opposed by him.

In his theory of market gluts Malthus emphasized effective demand and the necessity to keep purchasing power sufficiently high in order to purchase the output that can be produced. J. M. Keynes gives Malthus credit for being the major forerunner of the ideas he put forth in his *General Theory of Employment, Interest and Money* (London 1936). Malthus has been both praised and condemned, especially for his population theory, but there is little doubt of his significant contributions to the understanding of the economic process.

Bibliography: T. R. MALTHUS, *An Essay on the Principle of Population* (London 1798); *Principles of Political Economy* (London 1820). J. M. KEYNES, *Essays in Biography* (New York 1933). J. BONAR, *Malthus and His Work* (London 1885).

[J. P. MCKENNA]

MALVENDA, TOMÁS

Dominican theologian, historian, and exegete; b. Játiva, Spain, May 1566; d. Valencia, May 7, 1628. While still a young professor of sacred sciences, Malvenda so impressed C. BARONIUS with his critique (published in 1600) of that scholar's *Annales Ecclesiastici* that he was invited in the following year to Rome, where he assisted in emendations on this work and on Baronius's recension of the Roman Martyrology. At Rome Malvenda was the principal reviser of the Dominican Breviary, Martyrology, and Missal; and here he annotated Brasichelli's *Librorum prohibitorum index expurgatorius,* edited M. de La Bigne's *Biblotheca SS. Patrum,* gathered material for his *Annales O.P.* (published in 1627 without his approval), and wrote *De Antichristo libri XI* (1604) and *De paradiso voluptatis* (1605). After returning to Spain in 1608, when he was made provincial of the Aragon Dominican province, he undertook a literal Latin translation of the Hebrew OT, with commentary, which reached Ez 16.16 at the time of his death. It was later published as *Commentaria in S. Scripturam, una cum nova de verbo in verbum ex hebraeo translatione . . .* (5 v. Lyons 1650).

See Also: MARTYROLOGIES.

Bibliography: J.QUÉTIF and J. ÉCHARD, *Scriptores Ordinis Praedicatorum* (New York 1959) 2.1:454–457. *Monumenta Ordinis Fratrum Praedicatorum Historica* 11:62, 77, 84. H. HURTER, *Nomenclator literarius theologiae catholicae* 13 3:763–767.

[L. F. HARTMAN]

MALVERN, ABBEY OF

Former BENEDICTINE monastery dedicated to the Blessed Virgin, in the county and Diocese of WORCESTER, England. St. WULFSTAN, bishop of Worcester, inspired its foundation *c.* 1085 under Prior Aldwin. It became *c.* 1090 a dependency of WESTMINSTER ABBEY under the BENEDICTINE RULE and was known as Great Malvern priory. This connection with Westminster led to frequent disputes with the bishop of Worcester, until in 1283 Edward I ruled in favor of the priory's independence. Much fine building there was directed by Henry VII's architect, Sir Reginald Bray. Windows were filled with beautiful glass, some panels depicting the priory's history. In 1540, despite Bishop LATIMER's pleading, the priory was suppressed and pensions granted to the prior and ten monks. The church was bought by the townsmen for use as their parish church.

Bibliography: W. DUGDALE, *Monasticon Anglicanum* (London 1655–73); best ed. by J. CALEY et al., 6 v. (1817–30) 3:440–454. *The Victoria History of the County of Worcester,* ed. J. W. B. WILLIS-BUND et al., 4 v. (Westminster, Eng. 1901–24) v. 2.

[F. R. JOHNSTON]

MAMERTUS OF VIENNE, ST.

Bishop of Vienne, France, *c.* 461–475. Nothing certain is known of his early life or family except that he was the brother of CLAUDIANUS MAMERTUS. He was rebuked by Pope HILARY for appointing a bishop to Die, a suffragan diocese of ARLES; he was condemned by a synod at Arles, and apparently submitted. In his own diocese he promoted the cult of St. FERREOLUS. Mamertus is best known for organizing ROGATION processions, or Minor Litanies, the prayers of the people in time of calamity. It is not known whether his Rogations were held before or after Ascension Day, but it is certain that they were continued by his successors and prescribed for all Gaul by the Council of Orléans in 511. He is buried in the church of St. Peter at Vienne.

Feast: May 11.

Bibliography: P. JAFFÉ, *Regesta pontificum romanorum ab condita ecclesia ad annum post Christum natum 1198,* ed. F. KALTENBRUNNER, 2 v. (2d ed. Leipzig 1881–88; repr. Graz 1956) 1:76. L. DUCHESNE, *Fastes épiscopaux de l'ancienne Gaule,* 3 v. (2d ed.

Paris 1970–15) 1:205. *Acta Sanctorum* May 2:628–631. SIDONIUS APOLLINARIS, *Epistulae,* bk. 4, ch. 11; bk. 5, ch. 1 in *Monumenta Germaniae Historica: Auctores antiquissimi* (Berlin 1826–) v.8. HILARY, *Monumenta Germaniae Historica: Epistulae* (Berlin 1826–) 3:28–32. GREGORY OF TOURS, *De passione et virtutibus sancti Iuliani martyris,* ch. 2 in *Monumenta Germaniae Historica: Scriptores rerum Merovingicarum* (Berlin 1826–) 1:565. AVITUS, "Homilia de rogationibus," *Patrologia Latina,* ed. J. P. MIGNE, 271 v., indexes 4 v. (Paris 1878–90) 59:289–294. H. G. J. BECK, *The Pastoral Care of Souls in South-East France during the Sixth Century* (*Analecta Gregoriana* 51; 1950) 104–108, 290.

[M. C. MCCARTHY]

MAMMON

New Testament term for wealth, derived through the late-Latin *mammona* from the Greek μαμωνᾶς, a transliteration of the Aramaic *māmônā',* "emphatic state," corresponding to the late-Hebrew *māmôn,* "financial gain, riches," probably a contraction of hypothetical *ma'ămōn,* "thing entrusted, deposit, security." The Hebrew word māmôn occurs in the Old Testament only in Sir 31.8 ("gain"), but it is found in the Dead Sea Scrolls, the TALMUD, and modern Hebrew. In the New Testament the term occurs in Mt 6.24; Lk 16.9, 11, 13. In Lk 16.9–13 it serves as a catchword to connect three sayings of Jesus. Verse 9 serves to explain the preceding parable: the disciples too, are to exercise cleverness, but in their case, by giving in charity to the poor their wealth (called "wicked" because acquired so often unjustly) in order to provide an eternal home for themselves. In verses 10 through 12 earthly goods are called "a very little thing,""wicked mammon," and "what belongs to another." Those who rightly use them will be entrusted with heavenly goods, which, by way of contrast, are called "much," "true," and "what is your own." A different aspect is expressed in Lk 16.13 and Mt 6.24: riches are here personified and contrasted with God. This personification, however, is purely literary; there actually never was a pagan god or demon called "Mammon," as is sometimes wrongly supposed.

Bibliography: E. HAUCK, G. KITTEL, *Theologisches Wörterbuch zum Neuen Testament* (Stuttgart 1935) 4:390–392. J. SCHMID, *Das Evangelium nach Lukas* (4th ed. Regensburg 1960).

[C. BERNAS]

MAN, ARTICLES ON

In the *Encyclopedia,* "man" is frequently used in a non-gender-specific way, most typically when man is considered as a theological or philosophical entity. The principal article is MAN (1. In the Bible; 2. In Philosophy; 3. In Theology). For the science that examines the Christian understanding of man, see ANTHROPOLOGY, THEOLOGICAL and CHRISTIAN ANTHROPOLOGY. For articles that deal specifically with women, see WOMAN; WOMEN IN THE BIBLE; WOMEN AND PAPAL TEACHING.

Throughout the *Encyclopedia* man is considered from a variety of perspectives. For the origin of man see, e.g., CREATION; SOUL, HUMAN, ORIGIN OF. There are several articles that deal with human nature and its supernatural fulfillment, e.g., MAN, NATURAL END OF; SUPERNATURAL; GRACE AND NATURE; PURE NATURE, STATE OF; DESTINY, SUPERNATURAL; SUPERNATURAL EXISTENTIAL; DESIRE TO SEE GOD, NATURAL; ELEVATION OF MAN. In the area of moral theology the principal articles are MORAL THEOLOGY and MORAL THEOLOGY, HISTORY OF; see also NATURAL LAW. There are in addition general articles on social justice (SOCIAL THOUGHT, CATHOLIC; SOCIAL THOUGHT, PAPAL), sexual morality (SEX; SEX [IN THE BIBLE]), and medical ethics (MEDICAL ETHICS), as well as individual articles on various virtues, vices, and ethical issues (e.g., JUSTICE; LYING; HUMAN GENOME). Spirituality is understood in the *Encyclopedia* as part of anthropology. The general article is SPIRITUALITY, CHRISTIAN; there are also articles on various approaches of spirituality (e.g., CARMELITE SPIRITUALITY; SPIRITUALITY, RHENISH; LAY SPIRITUALITY) and terms and concepts important in the history of Christian spirituality (e.g., ECSTASY; RAPTURE; HOLY SPIRIT, GIFTS OF).

[G. F. LANAVE]

MAN

Man here is an inclusive term taken to mean the human being or humankind in general. This article treats of man (1) in the Bible, (2) in philosophy, and (3) in theology.

IN THE BIBLE

The Bible views man existentially, not essentially. In the Bible there is no dichotomy of body and soul. The man is the "I" who receives, feels, thinks, and loves. Thus, such concepts as soul [*see* SOUL (IN THE BIBLE)], spirit [*see* SPIRIT (IN THE BIBLE)], heart [*see* HEART (IN THE BIBLE)], flesh are all designations of the "I" under different aspects. The Bible teaches that man is the highest creature and the center of the visible universe. In the Old Testament, until late, man's destination is SHEOL (*see* AFTERLIFE, 2). In the New Testament man's end is eternal happiness or sorrow.

The Old Testament concept of man may be considered under two headings: that of Gn ch. 1–3, and the idea as found in the rest of the Old Testament. In Gn 1.1–2.4a

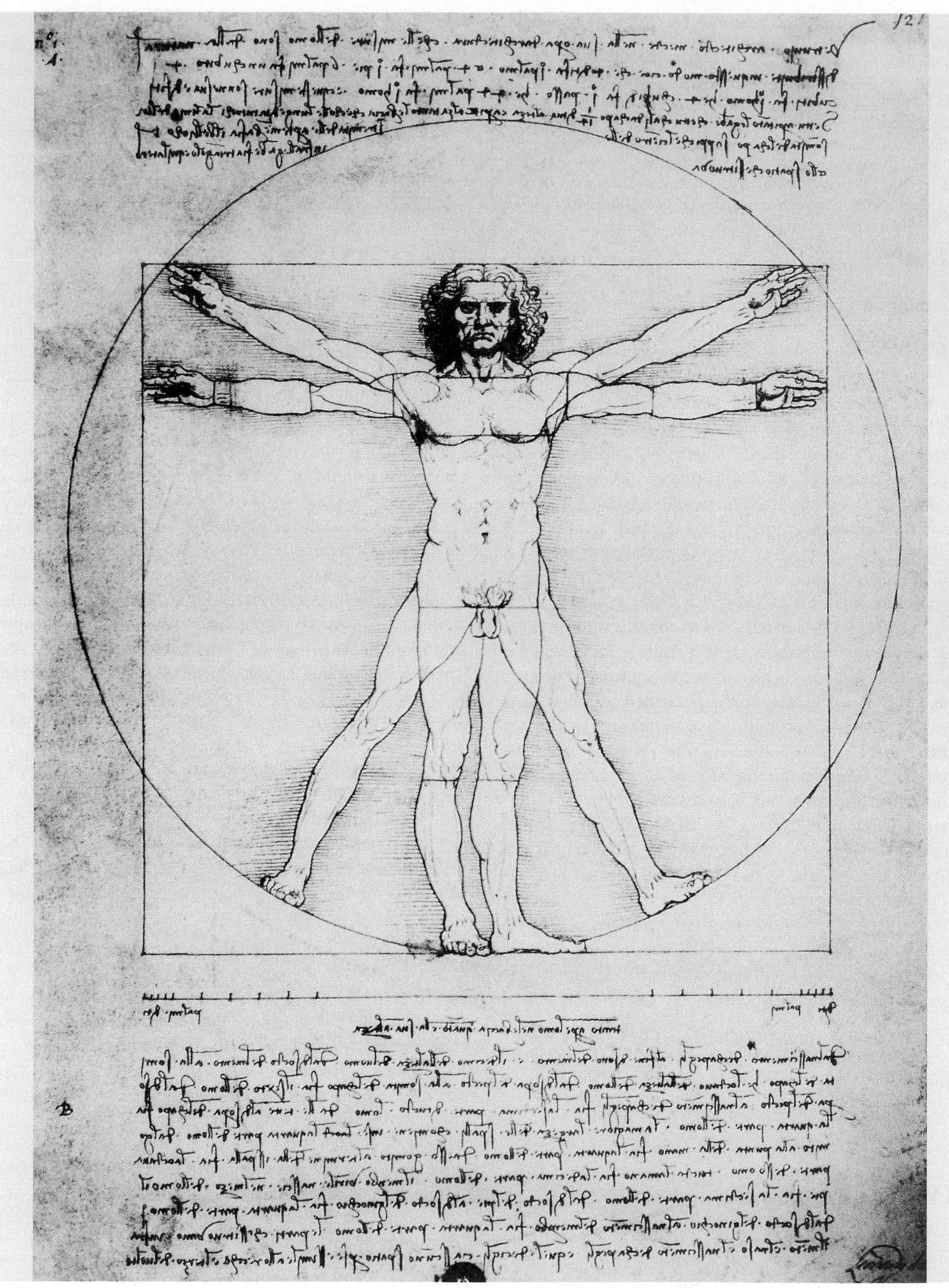

"Vitruvian Man," drawing by Leonardo da Vinci. (©Bettmann/CORBIS)

man is the epitome of creation. He comes at the end of creation. Introduced by God's deliberation—''let us make'' (Gn 1.26)—man names the animals, a manifestation of his mastery. Man alone is made to the IMAGE OF GOD (Gn 1.26–27). In the anthropomorphic account of Gn 2.4b–3.24, man is the center of creation around whom all other creatures revolve. All things are made for man. Raised to friendship with God [*see* GRACE (IN THE BIBLE)], man disobeyed and was punished. Thus, Genesis ch. 1–3 teaches man's excellence, friendship with God, his fall, and the divine promise of help.

The rest of the Old Testament considers man's destiny, his maker, and his holiness in the sight of God. Both good and bad are destined for Sheol, a place where all go after death. The notion of an afterlife of happiness or punishment is not found in revelation until *c.* 160 B.C. in the books of Wisdom, Daniel, and Maccabees. Reward in the Old Testament came in the form of God's blessings here on earth; the divine blessing guaranteed a long life, prosperity, property, and progeny. Responsibility was corporate as well as individual [*see* RESPONSIBILITY (IN THE BIBLE)].

Man's maker was ultimately God. The conception of man was considered a marvelous event [see Jb 10.8–12; Ps 118(119).73]. The conservation of man depended on Almighty God.

After the Fall, man was inwardly renewed and spiritually transformed by the grace of God and faith [Gn 15.6; Ps 23(24).3–4]: ''Be holy, for I, the Lord, your God, am holy'' (Lv 19.2; 11.44; 20.26). He is a jealous God who demands holiness of His people (Jos 24.19) and punishes those who violate His holiness (1 Sm 6.20; 2 Sm 6.6–12). In messianic times, according to Deutero-Isaiah, man's spiritual renewal would be mediated by the Servant of the Lord (Is 41.14; 43.3, 14; 47.4; *see* SUFFERING SERVANT, SONGS OF). God's people were obliged to be holy because they were closely bound to Him by the covenant. This collective holiness (Lv 20.26; Dt 7.6; 26.19; Is 63.18; Jer 2.3) presupposed individual holiness, for the pious are called holy by reason of the holiness of their personal lives [Ps 15 (16).3; 33 (34).10; Is 4.3; 6.13; Dt 7.18, 27]. [*See* FAITH, 1; HOLINESS (IN THE BIBLE); HOLINESS, LAW OF.]

In the New Testament many of the terms and expressions regarding man were borrowed from the Old Testament. However, such concepts as immortality, a deeper and wider revelation about the supernatural life, and heaven [*see* HEAVEN (IN THE BIBLE)] and hell [*see* HELL (IN THE BIBLE)] were more developed in the New Testament.

Paul moreover distinguishes the ''old man'' and the ''new man,'' the ''outer man'' and the ''inner man,'' and lastly the ''first Adam'' and the ''last Adam.'' According to St. Paul, the old man was fallen human nature; the new man was a new creation that was effected by Baptism. By this Sacrament man was gifted with the Holy Spirit and was already risen with Christ. In sum, the old man—that is, fallen human nature—was recreated into Christ (Rom 6.6; Eph 4.22; Col 3.9). Again, according to St. Paul, the outer man designates man's tendency to sin; the inner man his tendency to virtue. There is a struggle between the outer man and the inner man, that is, between the two tendencies in man. The struggle, when victorious, will complete the new creation so that a person will live in holiness and justice toward God (2 Cor 4.16; Rom 7.22; Eph 3.16). Paul uses the terms ''first Adam'' and ''last Adam.'' The first Adam was earthly and actually sinful; the second Adam is the heavenly Christ and sinless. The first Adam brought sin into the world. The second or last Adam reverses what the first Adam had done and achieves justification and glorification for those who accept Him (1 Cor 15.45, 47; Rom 5.12, 18; 8.1–39).

Thus, man in the Bible is the total existing being. With the fullness of Christ's revelation, man knows his final dwelling is not Sheol but heaven or hell. Raised after the first man's fall, he is aided against the tendency to sin by God's grace. His struggle is not without assurance of victory since he is risen (1 Cor ch. 15) with ''The Man, Jesus Christ'' (1 Tm 2.5).

Bibliography: *Encyclopedic Dictionary of the Bible*, tr. and adap. by L. HARTMAN (New York 1963), from A. VAN DEN BORN, *Bijbels Woordenboek* 1426–29. J. SCHMID, *Lexikon für Theologie und Kirche*, ed. J. HOFER and K. RAHNER, 10 v. (2d, new ed. Freiburg 1957–65) 7:284–287. A. S. KAPELRUD and N. A. DAHL, *Die Religion in Geschichte und Gegenwart*, 7 v. (3d ed. Tübingen 1957–65) 4:861–867. W. EICHRODT, *Man in the Old Testament*, tr. K. and R. GREGOR SMITH (Chicago 1951); *Theology of the Old Testament*, tr. J. A. BAKER (Philadelphia 1961–). R. BULTMANN, *Theology of the New Testament*, tr. K. GROBEL, 2 v. (New York 1951–55) 1:190–259. M. BAILY, ''Biblical Man and Some Formulae of Christian Teaching,'' *The Irish Theological Quarterly* 27 (1960) 173–200. E. HILL, *Being Human: A Biblical Perspective* (London 1984). U. SCHNELLE, *The Human Condition: Anthropology in the Teachings of Jesus, Paul, and John*, tr. O. C. DEAN, JR. (Minneapolis 1996).

[W. E. LYNCH]

IN PHILOSOPHY

The term *man* seems to be derived from a Sanskrit root meaning to think. Should this etymology be correct, it gives an indication that thought was early considered a distinctive characteristic of man. For the Greek ἄνθρωπος no convincing etymological explanation is given. Some consider it to signify ''the one that looks up (i.e., to the gods) from below''; if so, this would express both a distinction and a certain kinship between man and God. The etymology of the Latin *homo* is more certain: it is de-

"Judgement of Adam and Eve," engraving by William Blake. (©Burstein Collection/CORBIS)

rived from *humus* meaning earth or soil. The meaning seems to be either genetic, that man had his origin from the earth or was made out of earth; or more general, that man by his very nature is akin to earth. The same etymological connection and derivation is found in the Hebrew: *Adam-adama.* [*See* ADAM]

From such indications one learns that on the one hand man has an essential relation to earth, that he belongs to the earthly sphere below, and on the other that he is a thinking being, and so has contact with the gods, although he is different from them. This shows that man is something of a paradox—he is bound to earth by his nature, and yet transcends earth by his mind. This kind of dualism, more explicitly expressed as that between mind and body or between soul and body, constitutes one of the most difficult and constant problems in a philosophical understanding of man. (*See* SOUL-BODY RELATIONSHIP.)

Similarly, reflection about himself shows man that he has something in common with other realities: he is a body, a living being, an animal, akin to the transcendent world of divinity—in a word, he is a microcosm, containing all things within himself. On the other hand, he is aware of his unique nature and searches for proper characteristics that distinguish himself from other beings. Such reflection gives further indication of a duality in man's nature.

Early Greek Thought. The Greek conception of man is derived from two distinct sources: one, mythology, explains man's origin, nature, and condition as the result of the activity of the gods; the other, cosmology (partly dependent upon mythology and partly opposed to it, but becoming increasingly independent), offers a profane, realistic, and rational consideration of man. This awakening philosophical reflection was focused on the phenomenal world and thus studied man in the context of a philosophy of nature.

Although somewhat opposed, both the religious-mythological and the rational-naturalistic approaches led to a cosmic conception of man. In this context various *anthropina* or human characteristics, later useful for an accurate determination of man's nature, were developed in a half-mythological, half-philosophical way. Protagoras (5th century B.C.) stressed how animals are well equipped to defend themselves against enemies, are protected from cold by their furs, and have food available for them, whereas man lacks all these natural advantages. Instead he possesses wisdom, and this enables him to provide, by art and industry, what nature had not provided (see Plato, *Prot.* 321). Similar considerations are to be found, for example, in Diogenes of Appolonia (5th century B.C.). This author describes man as privileged by the gods, both in bodily equipment and in mental capacity. His upright position is superior to that of other animals, his vision is freed and broadened, his hands enable him to make tools and useful or beautiful objects, and his mouth and tongue are so disposed as to give the capacity for speech. More important still are the endowments of his mind: man has received a soul and is able to know the gods, to find remedies against illness, to acquire new knowledge, and to build human society. All of this makes man, although an earthly being, akin to the gods.

Aristotelian View. These ideas greatly influenced the further elaboration of a philosophical notion of man, particularly by Aristotle. Applying his hylomorphic and teleological conceptions to these and other data, Aristotle regarded man as the supreme being on earth, primarily spirit and capable of intellectual knowledge, but with a bodily constitution adapted to, and informed by, the spiritual soul in a type of matter-form composition (*see* MATTER AND FORM). Since FORM (here the human soul) is the dominant and determining factor from which every disposition and activity of matter flows, all features stressed by his predecessors, including those of the body, became so many manifestations of the spiritual nature of man.

Although he continued the cosmological tradition, regarding the study of man as part of the *Physics,* Aristotle stressed man's spiritual nature as transcending material conditions. He even considered the Nous as immaterial, as belonging to a nonbodily or spiritual realm, as coming from without, and as not mixed with the body. If such notions do not seem to fit into his hylomorphic doctrine, it should be noted that Aristotle not only discusses man in natural philosophy, but also treats of him in his *Ethics* and *Politics;* in the latter works, he develops more spiritual conceptions, defining man, for example, as ζῷον πολιτικόν. Difficulties of interpretation notwithstanding, one finds in Aristotle's works a highly technical, complex, and well-balanced conception of man that has had an immense influence on Western philosophy. The Stoa continued this Aristotelian line of development, stressing the logos as the most important element in man; their classical definition of the human being was ζῷον λογικόν.

Platonic Conceptions. The view of man offered by Plato, while not ignoring bodily aspects, had insisted more on man's spiritual nature and had tended to depreciate his body. This explains why the Platonic view appealed more than that of Aristotle to thinkers with a spiritualist orientation, particularly among the early Christians. In an oversimplified, almost Manichean way, the body was often considered as the enemy of the spiritual soul, and sexual pleasure in its human form—praised by Diogenes of Apollonia as one of man's privileges—

began to be viewed as contrary to human dignity. St. GREGORY OF NYSSA, for example, taught that man originally had neither body nor sex and that both are due to sin. In St. Augustine and his school one finds similar exaggerations, overemphasizing the spirit and usually underestimating the role of the body in human nature.

Thomistic Synthesis. With the development of scholastic philosophy and the reintroduction of Aristotle in the West, a more classical view of man gradually reasserted itself. This conception found its most adequate expression in the doctrine of St. Thomas Aquinas. Guided by the light of Christian revelation, Aquinas worked out a synthetic conception of man that was fundamentally Aristotelian, but also assimilated spiritualist notions that had not been completely integrated into the original Aristotelian position.

Substantial Unity. The body is an essential part of man, and has a positive value. Yet the body exists, not in its own right, but by virtue of the spiritual soul, which is a form in the most real sense and the unique substantial form of the body. This implies a type of DUALISM in the ontological structure of man that at the same time does not destroy his substantial unity. Since the body is only human through the soul, and the soul in turn determines the body, the body-soul union is not a mere juxtaposition of parts but rather the unity of a complex being. Notwithstanding its ontological function as a substantial form that is essentially related to the body, the human soul transcends the material world by its spirituality, and has in itself the adequate reason for its own existence. In this way the absolute primacy of spirit in man is safeguarded, without neglecting the essential role of the body. Such ontological transcendence of the human soul explains its immortality, notwithstanding its essential union with a mortal body. Again, despite a bodily conditioned earthly existence, man is called to an eternal destiny; and this is not only a tenet of Christian faith, but a property of human nature itself. (*See* SOUL, HUMAN; IMMORTALITY.)

Mind and Spirit. Since man's mind is capable of universal, unlimited knowledge, his perfection cannot be limited to earthly experiences. His mind has a capacity for the infinite. This kinship with divine reality, already stressed in Greek mythological conceptions of man, here becomes part of a philosophy of man. In this way it also becomes evident how man belongs both to the material and to the spiritual world. Sharing in materiality through his body and in spirituality through his mind, he is, in a way, the meeting place of both: the *horizon et confinium spiritualis et corporalis naturae,* the meeting point of time and eternity (*C. gent.* 2.68). Thus man, by that which is most noble in him, is essentially related to a world of spiritual values, which also includes God.

Free Will. The very fact of existing in a concrete, materially conditioned situation, and of discovering in and through this an unlimited degree of being and value (*ens et bonum*), is itself the ontological foundation of human freedom. Because man encounters different realities and situations not only as biological correlates, as is the case with animals, but under the transcendental notion of BEING, these do not appeal to him merely as limited biological values that stimulate determined reactions. And just as they appear to man's INTELLECT under the transcendental notion of being, to be delimited only on the horizon of being, so they appeal to man's WILL under the transcendental aspect of GOOD, on a universal horizon where their limited goodness becomes apparent. For this reason their appeal is always a limited one. While there is sufficient reason for desiring them, since they present man with a certain goodness, at the same time there is sufficient reason not to desire them, because the good they represent is itself limited. Thus man, by his very nature, is free—situated as it were at the intersection of material limitation and determination and of spiritual illimitability and transcendental openness. He is not compelled to act by any particular object that appeals to him. Dominating, as it were, every single appeal by his transcendental openness to good in the broadest possible sense, he has every particular appeal under his control. In other words, he is capable of autodetermination; he is free. (*See* FREE WILL; FREEDOM.)

Ethics and Morality. Human freedom opens up the entire realm of ETHICS or MORALITY, and this not by the mere introduction of a CATEGORICAL IMPERATIVE, but by man's very nature as capable of active self-determination toward what he recognizes as good and suitable. When this is seen not only through philosophical reflection but also in the light of divine revelation, morality becomes more than an anonymous obligation; it is God's personal appeal to man's personal decision.

Nature and Supernature. Precisely because of this connatural openness to the transcendental, man is capable of knowledge and values beyond the limits of his natural possibilities, all the way to the supreme Transcendental, God Himself. This is not to be understood in the sense that man by his own capacities can actually attain God as He is in Himself. Yet, while lacking the active capacity to reach God in His intimate nature, man has the possibility of intimacy with God, provided that God Himself actively communicates Himself to man. Here is the link between man's natural and supernatural perfection. Thus, literally speaking, man by his own nature has the promise of a superhuman destiny. Seen in this light, the supernatural end of man that is revealed by Christian faith is not something inhuman, but appears as the highest achievement of human nature. In the Thomistic synthesis man is not only an *animal rationale;* he is also *capax divinitatis,* conceived and designed by the Creator to enter into personal contact with Him and to share in His own intimate life. Thus, what the Greek thinkers obscurely hinted at as man's kinship to the gods here becomes a profound philosophical synthesis that is open to theological development.

The Thomistic conception of man is thus philosophically complete and balanced, and at the same time agrees with the tenets of Catholic faith, thereby providing a framework for an understanding of the interplay between the natural and supernatural elements in man. To have explained this conception at length, however, need not imply that with St. Thomas thought about man came to a standstill, or that the following ages had nothing valuable to say about him.

Modern Thought. With R. DESCARTES, man's unity was replaced by a dualistic conception that sharply distinguished the *res extensa* from the *res cogitans.* In a way this stressed the spiritual nature of man; it also prepared the way for the *homo noumenon* of Kant, and, in general, for idealist conceptions that describe man as a manifestation of Absolute Spirit. Proposed at a time of limited religious and theological influence on philosophical thought, this led to a very high appreciation of human dignity. It also led, however, to an overemphasis of man's autonomy, resulting in the dangerous exaltation of Nietzsche's superman. In fact, the newly found autonomy appeared to be a burden too heavy for man to bear. One might consider the existentialist despair—describing man as "being unto death" (Heidegger) or stressing his absurdity, "man is a useless passion" (Sartre)—as a logical consequence of this overevaluation of man's autonomy, the breakdown of an illusion that was impossible to maintain. In this rather negative way, EXISTENTIALISM has contributed to a renewed and more realistic view of man, replacing an unreal rationalistic and idealistic, and ultimately inhuman, conception with the body-conditioned concept of an "incarnate spirit."

Paralleling this spiritualist Cartesian heritage there was also a mechanistic and materialistic heritage that was taken up by those interested in modern science and its development. This led, through the *"hommemachine"* concept of J. O. de La Mettrie, to L. Feuerbach's "*Der Mensch ist was er isst* (man is what he eats)." Marxist MATERIALISM is, in a way, the ultimate consequence of this materialistic conception, for here man is regarded as nothing but the highest form of organized matter. Scientific studies, especially the theory of human EVOLUTION, seemed at first to support a purely biological conception of man, explaining him in terms of his animal origin. More accurate study and analysis, however, have shown that an evolutionistic interpretation of man's origin does not explain away man's spirituality, but on the contrary, poses the problem of man's spiritual nature in a new and more urgent way. Some evolutionistic thinkers, such as P. TEILHARD DE CHARDIN, find in evolutionism a new and outstanding testimony of man's unique spiritual nature and destiny, thus making him the ultimate goal and achievement of the cosmos.

Karol Wojtyła. In the 1950s and 1960s, Father Karol Wojtyła (later Pope JOHN PAUL II) wrote several books dealing with the nature of man from the perspective of a personalist philosophy. Archbishop Wojtyła was influential in the writing of Vatican II's *Gaudium et spes,* which speaks at length of the person in the modern world. Many of his papal writings (e.g., the encyclicals *REDEMPTOR HOMINIS, VERITATIS SPLENDOR,* and *LABOREM EXERCENS*) reflect this same personalistic view.

In his philosophical writings Wojtyła argued that it is neither reason alone nor experience but the whole person who deliberates, selects, decides, and performs a moral action. It is with the integrity of the whole person in mind, therefore, that in his *Lublin Lectures* the young professor undertook a tour through the history of philosophy, gathering up the factors that enter into the constitution of the person who acts. He gathered these metaphysical factors first from Plato, who highlighted the Good as the supreme value in which the person is called to participate. While Aristotle retained the finality of the good, he also inscribed it in the rational nature of the individual. Moreover, Aristotle provided an account of how one becomes good, moving from the potentiality to the good to its actualization through action. Augustine drew upon Plato, but recognized the highest good as personal, so that Platonic participation is transformed into Augustinian love. The significance of Thomas Aquinas for Wojtyła is that he rooted the foregoing dynamic structure in the deepest source of actuality: in existential act (*esse*), so that what is good and true is so by virtue of its actual existence. Wojtyła continued his tour, spending considerable time in a critical study of Hume and Bentham; but the positive elements of his analysis are drawn from the metaphysical philosophers already mentioned. In sum, it is not the will or the consciousness, but the person, constituted in the unity of his being, who is the *suppositum,* the concrete, existing agent of moral action.

Having assembled his metaphysics of the person as the underlying foundation of ethical action, Wojtyła turned to phenomenology in order to analyze the action from within the agent. Because the horizon of understanding in metaphysics, and consequently its vocabulary, is comprehensive, embracing everything insofar as each is a member of the community of being, the intimate and interior experience of action itself does not fall within the principal concern of metaphysics. PHENOMENOLOGY, on the other hand, in its adaptation to the experience of values by Scheler, provides a method by which reflection can articulate ethical action precisely as experienced from within the action itself.

In Wojtyła's view, human action is a dramatic affair in which the fulfillment or non-fulfillment of the human person is at stake. Since action is a positive fulfillment of the person, his analysis implies the possibility that we may fail in the task of integration and transcendence with the consequent diminution of our personhood. Fortunately, we are not called upon to act in isolation. As persons we are open to intersubjective, interpersonal relations. What is more, our very fulfillment as persons is to be realized in "acting together with others," who are not simply members of this or that organization, but whose well-being is inscribed in our motivation (solidarity). Each is our neighbor, and in acting together with others, we realize our own personhood as participants in the community of persons. In sum, the interplay of metaphysics and phenomenology in Wojtyła's thought has resulted in grounding the person objectively in the community of beings, while at the same time permitting him to enter into the lived experience of the person as an existential subjectivity.

See Also: MAN, NATURAL END OF; PSYCHOLOGY

Bibliography: M. J. ADLER, ed. *The Great Ideas: A Syntopicon of Great Books of the Western World*, 2 v. (Chicago 1952); v.2, 3 of *Great Books of the Western World* 2:1–41. J. E. ROYCE, *Man and His Nature* (New York 1961). G. P. KLUBERTANZ, *The Philosophy of Human Nature* (New York 1953). R. E. BRENNAN, *The Image of His Maker* (Milwaukee 1948). M. J. ADLER, *What Man Has Made of Man* (New York 1937). K. L. SCHMITZ, *At the Center of the Human Drama, The Philosophical Anthropology of Karol Wojtyła/Pope John Paul II* (Washington, D.C. 1993).

[N. A. LUYTEN/K. L. SCHMITZ/EDS.]

IN THEOLOGY

In a sense, all revelation and, consequently, all theology is a theology of man (2 Tm 3.16). But here the term theology of man is used in a restricted sense: the supernatural understanding of man's nature and destiny found in revelation and systematized in theology. The theology of man does not exclude man's natural knowledge of himself, but (1) throws new light upon his nature and (2) gives him knowledge of new realities and of a destiny he could not otherwise know. Moreover, implicit in a theology of man is a SUPERNATURAL view of all visible creation and of temporal existence. The created universe can only be fully and rightly understood in the light of divine revelation (*see* MATTER, THEOLOGY OF).

Man before the Fall. Man, in the whole of his being, was created—his soul by immediate (first) creation; his body in a manner that has not been precisely revealed, i.e., the possibility of evolution is not excluded. In addition, man received supernatural gifts of GRACE and virtue that made him a partaker of the nature of God (2 Pt 1.4) and other prerogatives and powers transcending ordinary human nature (*see* ORIGINAL JUSTICE).

Potentiality of Man. Despite the diversity of elements in man, he was a unity, an ensouled body, an incarnated spirit; he was a divinized unity of body and spirit. Equally important, man, although the pinnacle of visible creation, was, in all elements of his nature, eminently perfectible. He was not created in a fully developed state. Instead, there were almost unlimited potentialities left for him to exploit and bring to reality. God sketched in man the lineaments of a divine image, the most perfect visible image He made. Then He left to man himself the task of evoking by his life and work the potentialities inherent in himself to be the most expressive possible reproduction of his Creator's infinite perfection.

Furthermore, because man was a horizon between matter and spirit, time and eternity, material creation and God, he was, under God, lord and builder of creation. Because he was partly material, he could act on matter. Because he was a divinized, spiritual being, he could understand both creation and God's divine plan. As a result, he was capable of discerning those potentialities in creation that depended on his initiative and bringing them to reality. He could see God, as He was then expressed in the cosmos, and sense the further revelations that were implicit in the virtualities of what God has made.

This is not to say that man always knows the full implications of his work upon nature. He works within the dual context of his own nature and of the possibilities in the materials he uses. His purpose may be primarily concerned with his own needs: seeking food, shelter, or the fulfillment of any of his needs. But so long as he works within the designed capacities of nature, his efforts will result in the mutual development of himself and of nature. (Sinful action will be considered later.)

Elevation. Moreover, his entire nature was elevated by grace and the virtues to a divine level. Consequently, he was able to know divine realities, including God's plan for man himself and the whole of visible creation, and to direct his activities in accordance with that plan. His purpose was not completely achieved within creation. His destiny was eternal and divine. He was intended to possess God beatifically throughout eternity precisely to the degree that he developed the potentialities of his existential nature. Man had no natural end. His end was divine.

To this extent philosophy, that is, human reason, is radically incapable of understanding man or his destiny.

The philosopher's view of man is crucially incomplete and, thus, most open to error. Man has no merely temporal, intramundane purpose or meaning. There is no merely human, natural scale according to which his actions can be evaluated. Neither before nor after the Fall nor consequent upon the Redemption is there any situation in which man is the proper object of consideration for the philosopher alone. The purely natural man of the philosopher never existed. Nor is the end that the philosopher assigns to man existentially meaningful. Man and his destiny are totally supernatural. Man will either be with God eternally or, by his own catastrophic choice, cut off from God eternally. And every human action will contribute to man's beatification or to his exclusion from God.

Potentiality of Cosmos. The cosmos was, as the term implies, a unified, organized, purposive system. Each kind of being in the cosmos was an expression of God; it taught man something about God. And the total cosmos was simultaneously a further expression of God (St. Thomas, *Comp. theol.* 102). But the cosmos, including man, was radically perfectible at the outset. This does not mean that God made a defective cosmos, but rather that He produced a world rich in potentialities. These potentialities were to be realized partly by the internal dynamisms of the cosmos and partly by man's rational action. And, as the cosmos achieved its own possibilities, it would at each step be a more expressive reproduction of God.

More important still, unfolding the potentialities of the cosmos was not only one of man's chief temporal duties but was also a primary instrumentality of his own development. Man's work upon nature—growing crops, caring for animals, developing resources of the mineral kingdom—was never a unilateral action. Provided he worked in ways consonant with his own and creation's natures, his work perfected not only material creation, but himself as well. Man was to grow by helping nature grow.

Thus, both the dynamisms of nature and man's work were ordained constantly to make creation a more perfect reproduction of God's perfections. Working in personal communion with God, man was to be the instrument of God's creative power, continuing His work upon creation, thus preparing himself for eternal beatitude. This total perfective system had as its mediate objective the perfection of man. [*See* GLORY OF GOD (END OF CREATION).] Creation was intended in various ways to contribute to man's development and to his ultimate beatification through eternal union with God. This truth was strikingly put by Henri BERGSON: "The universe is a machine for making gods" [*The Two Sources of Morality and Religion* (2d ed. New York 1954) 317].

Toward the Pleroma. Knowing God by faith and seeing Him revealed in creation, man was able to grow in likeness to God both by contemplating God and by all his operations upon the world in which he lived.

But men were not intended to work in isolation. United together by sharing a common nature and destiny and above all by participation in the one life of God, men were to be One Man, a Mystical Body. In charity aiding each other to grow and in the process corporately building Man by their endlessly varied evocations of the species' possibilities, men were to carry out God's creative will. Making Man in the plenitude of his divinized human nature is willed by God as the chief created good of the universe. This was to have been the pleroma, the fulfillment, toward which all of its purposiveness was directed.

Man, then, is unique within the cosmos. He alone of all kinds of beings is the object of God's personal solicitude both for his own sake and for the sake of his species. "Now a rational creature exists under divine providence as a being governed and provided for in himself, and not simply for the sake of his species, as is the case with other corruptible creatures" (St. Thomas, *C. gent.* 3.113.1).

Adam. This was man's work in time. In addition, ADAM, the first man, had a unique responsibility. By his decision he was to determine what man was to be. Adam was created more than man, as a human being to whom had been given by God's free gift preternatural and supernatural prerogatives. Adam was to determine in perpetuity whether his descendants were to begin existence with the full complement of nature and its supplementary gifts (with which it would be possible to attain their eternal destiny) or with denuded and deprived nature. If he fulfilled his personal injunction of fidelity to God's ordinance, his descendants would come into existence possessing nature and grace. But if he failed to fulfill his personal role as head of the human race, those gifts added to human nature that were either necessary or useful for attaining a supernatural destiny would be lost. Adam's original sin would radically change the model according to which all men were to be fashioned.

The Fall. Adam's sin forfeited the supernatural endowments of human nature not only for himself but for all his descendants, since he was the primeval man from whom and according to whom others were to be formed. St. Paul says: ". . . through one man sin entered into the world and through sin death, and thus death has passed into all men because all have sinned [in Adam]" (Rom 5.12). Moreover, the order that had existed in the cosmos, both within man and in creation as a whole, was shattered. Neither man nor creation through him could attain the eternal destiny ordained by God. Yet the destiny remained: "[Man] is born in a fallen *state,* while all the time retaining his place in the supernatural *order*'' (Mouroux 136). This does not mean that all development was frustrated. But it does mean that the purposive development that should ultimately have flowered in the pleroma was absolutely frustrate (*see* ORIGINAL SIN).

Personal sin can be defined as a word, deed, or desire contrary to the eternal law of God. From the restricted point of view of a theology of man, it is an act that fails, by man's willful decision, to contribute to the pleroma. While it is obvious that it is not under this precise formality that men sin, since not all have cognizance of this effect of sin, this is its concrete effect with respect to man's supernatural temporal responsibility.

Incarnational Redemption. The Son of God became man to restore God's plan by redeeming mankind by His passion and death.

In a sense one can say that God's purpose was accomplished by the INCARNATION itself, even if one prescinds from its redemptive effects. This is not the place to discuss the Incarnation. Yet one can note that the HYPOSTATIC UNION of Christ's sacred humanity with the Person of the Son of God effected results in creation infinitely transcending the gifts given by God when He made the cosmos. Even more, Christ equally transcends the perfection that would have been achieved if there had been no Fall and mankind had attained the fullest conceivable fruition. This is the meaning of the liturgy's exultant cry: ''*O felix culpa.* O happy fault, that merited a Redeemer so holy and so great!'' (Holy Saturday, *Exultet*).

The God-Man, Christ Jesus, is Himself the pleroma.''For in him dwells all the fullness of the Godhead bodily'' (Col 2.9). For it has pleased God the Father that in him all his fullness should dwell'' (Col 1.19). Man was created as an image of God. His work in time was to perfect that image with the help of grace by all his actions. This was the work of the first man, of each man, of all men corporately. In this work man failed. Yet in Christ at the Incarnation man had become par excellence ''the image of the invisible God'' (Col 1.15). ''And the Word was made flesh, and dwelt among us. And we saw his glory—glory as of the only-begotten of the Father—full of grace and of truth'' (Jn 1.14; cf. 14.8–11).

Son of God and fullness of man, Christ is endowed with a plenitude of dignity and perfection so immeasurably surpassing the worth of all other creatures that His sacred humanity is adorable with the latria due to God alone.

> He who is the Son of God and is God incarnate was born of the Virgin. He is not merely a man bearing God, but is God made flesh. He is anointed not by action, as a prophet, but by the presence of the anointing Person, so that He who anointed has become man, and that which was anointed has become God, not by any change of nature but by a union of hypostasis. [St. John Damascene, *On Orthodox Faith* 4.14; *Patrologica Graeca*, ed. J. P. Migne 94:1160–61]

Although Christ more than achieved the pleroma by the Incarnation, He did not intend to remain alone. He did two further things that made participation in Him and His work accessible to other men.

First, He offered superabundant satisfaction for the sins of all mankind. ''But when the fullness of time came, God sent his Son . . . that he might redeem those who were under the Law, that we might receive the adoption of sons'' (Gal 4.4–5; *see* SATISFACTION OF CHRIST).

Second, and for our purpose more important, He became a unique archetype, a life-giving spirit, according to which and into whom redeemed man is reborn by a second genesis [echoing both the rebirth of Jn 3.5 and the primordial Genesis; *see* REBIRTH (IN THE BIBLE)]. He is, as St. Paul insists, the second Adam, new head of divinized man (1 Cor 15.44–49; Rom 5.12–21). Those who are united in Christ, the second Adam, while remaining discrete human beings, possess one common divine life, lived initially and shared with them by the Head of the MYSTICAL BODY. In the supernatural order all who possess grace constitute one living organism.

Redeemed Man. Those who died in the first Adam have access to grace and life through the second Adam. But man must receive life voluntarily, as it was voluntarily lost. There must be an aversion from sin and self and a conversion to Christ and God, if life is to be received. This is the sense of Acts: ''Therefore to the Gentiles also God has given repentance unto life'' (11.18). In the grace of that repentance unto life, man is to ''Strip off the old man with his deeds and put on the new, one that is being renewed unto perfect knowledge 'according to the image of his Creator''' (Col 3.9–10).

Two considerations about ''repentance unto life'' are important here. (1) Even at the outset of the Christian life, man's own actions are significant. God *gives* repentance unto life, but man must repent; he must freely die to his old life and freely rise with and in Christ. (2) Man is to live a new divinized life that has dimensions in both time and eternity. The Christian is to live a life one sees demonstrated in the two great principles of action: ''without me you can do nothing'' (Jn 15.5); and ''I can do all things in him who strengthens me'' (Phil 4.13; *see* CONVERSION AND GRACE, CONTROVERSIES ON).

The newborn Christian is like an infant (1 Pt 2.2), undeveloped but rich in inestimable potential. He is to grow.

The various faculties of the supernatural life are to be developed, and this development is the principal purpose of time and activity.

Ideally, every moment of life and every action is developmental; actually, many will be wasted through negligence or malice. The Christian effort for perfection could be described as a constant attempt to minimize the number of wasted or harmful actions and to maximize the number and quality of those that develop man. Thus, the only theoretical limit to human development for the Christian is the injunction, ''You therefore are to be perfect, even as your heavenly Father is perfect'' (Mt 5.48).

Redeeming the Cosmos. The Redemption inaugurated a regime the same in essentials as that before the Fall. Salvation is once more accessible to man in Christ. But there are differences. The most obvious is that the preternatural gifts are not restored. More significant, ultimately, is the fact that the order of the cosmos is not reinstated. This is to be slowly and painfully reconstituted by man's effort. Man must make his personal contribution to his own justification; so he must work out the Redemption of the cosmos. St. Paul's testimony on this is profoundly obscure, but it makes plain that man, somehow, is to achieve the Redemption of material creation that fell with man's sin.

> For the eager longing of creation awaits the revelation of the sons of God. For creation was made subject to vanity—not by its own will but by reason of him who made it subject—in hope, because creation itself also will be delivered from its slavery to corruption into the freedom of the glory of the sons of God. [Rom 8.19–21]

The precise meaning of the passage is obscure, but clearly it affirms the solidarity of man and creation. By man's sin the cosmos was disrupted and rendered frustrate of its destiny. By redeemed man it can be restored. Man can progressively reconstitute the cosmos, i.e., an ordered, purposive system, by using material creation in accord with its nature and his, once he has himself been redeemed—or he can further subject creation to vanity by misusing it.

The noblest examples of the right use of creation are found in the liturgical uses: water in Baptism, wine and bread in the Eucharist; oil, wax, linen, incense. By such uses matter receives a great dignity and becomes both sanctified and sanctifying. But the redemptive and incarnational principle is not restricted to sacred uses. Everything that a Christian does can be redemptive: ''Whatever you do, work at it from the heart as for the Lord and not for men'' (Col 3.23).

Life in Christ. The Christian's work, then, is to prolong Christ's redemptive work. Having risen with Christ, he is to ''mind the things that are above, not the things that are on earth'' (Col 3.2). Yet he is not to flee from the world of men and work. The passage just quoted is followed by a lengthy exhortation to live daily life holily, including the advice to slaves quoted earlier:''Whatever you do, work at it from the heart as for the Lord.''

Clearly, then, no human action is irrelevant to the work of Redemption and SALVATION, whether performed by Christian or pagan. Christian works can actively build the KINGDOM OF GOD; those of pagans can be steps toward justification. Justified man is thus seen as an intensely dynamic being, informed and divinized by grace. Good actions not only perfect him but dignify and sanctify matter on which he works. This is the fundamental insight regarding man and creation. Man exists in an imperfect, fallen—but redeemable and perfectible—system, a system that is dynamic and purposive, whose order and perfection are to be as perfect a replica of God as man, guided by the wisdom and grace of Christ, can make it. And in building the cosmos, he builds himself—and Man.

Christ is the pleroma. But He is a pleroma, paradoxically, that can grow. It grows by the extension of divine life to men, by their incorporation into and growth in Christ. And among the means by which men grow in life, grace, and fullness, not least is the work they do in time and upon the cosmos.

Teaching of the Church. The Church's solemn teaching concerning the composition of man is not extensive. It has defined that souls are not of the substance of God, did not preexist their bodies (H. Denzinger, *Enchiridion symbolorum*, ed. A. Schönmetzer 455–456), do not result from transformation of sensitive souls, and are not generated (*Enchiridion symbolorum* 3220; *see* TRADUCIANISM). Each man has a unique, created soul, which is the form of the body (*Enchiridion symbolorum* 1440). The soul is created by God from nothing (*Enchiridion symbolorum* 685).

See Also: MAN, ARTICLES ON; CHURCH, ARTICLES ON; DESTINY, SUPERNATURAL; ELEVATION OF MAN; GRACE AND NATURE; RECAPITULATION IN CHRIST; SECULARISM; SUPERNATURAL ORDER; TEMPORAL VALUES, THEOLOGY OF

Bibliography: P. OVERHAGE et al., *Lexikon für Theologie*, ed. J. HOFER and K. RAHNER, 10 v. (2d, new ed. Freiburg 1957–65) 7:278–294. *Dictionnaire de théologie catholique: Tables générales*, ed. A. VACANT et al. (Paris 1951– 2:2100–06. P. HERMAND et al., *Catholicisme* 5:853–886. T. AQUINAS, *Summa theologiae* 1a, 75–88. J. MOUROUX, *The Meaning of Man,* tr. A. H. G. DOWNES (New York 1948). R. GUARDINI, *Freedom, Grace, and Destiny,* tr. J. MURRAY (New York 1961). J. FICHTNER, *Theological Anthropology* (Notre Dame, Indiana 1963). G. THILS, *Théologie des réalités terrestres,* 2 v. (Bruges 1946–49). L. J. LEBRET, *Human Ascent,* tr.

R. and M. FAULHABER (Chicago 1955). E. SUHARD, *Growth or Decline?*, tr. J. A. CORBETT (South Bend, Indiana 1948). *Social Order* 3 (May-June 1953) 193–288, on Christian humanism. E. I. WATKIN, *The Bow in the Clouds* (New York 1932). F. D. WILHELMSEN, *The Metaphysics of Love* (New York 1962). H. DE LUBAC, *A Brief Catechesis on Nature and Grace* (San Francisco 1984). W. PANNENBERG, *Anthropology in a Theological Perspective*, tr. M. J. O'CONNELL (Philadelphia 1985). POPE JOHN PAUL II, *The Theology of the Body According to John Paul II. Human Love in the Divine Plan* (Boston 1997).

[F. J. CORLEY]

MAN, NATURAL END OF

End here means purpose or objective, not extinction or last state; thus END of man means the general objective of human action or the final purpose of life. Catholics believe that besides the natural reality God has given human beings through creation, He has offered them the further gift of a share of His own life. God gives this special gift within the soul by GRACE. God is not only the source but also the end of the life of grace; its consummation is the soul's enjoyment of God's goodness in union with Him in heavenly beatitude, the BEATIFIC VISION. Hence, the end that Catholic faith indicates is above human NATURE. The achievement of this end transcends every ability naturally inherent in man, and the entire life of grace is SUPERNATURAL.

Because the end of Christian life is supernatural, Catholic thinkers have wondered about the natural end of man. The problem is important for two reasons: (1) If God had created man without giving him grace, would there have been any end for human life proportionate to man's abilities? (2) Since grace does not abridge what belongs to the natural reality of man, is there an end implicitly required by human nature that might help even Christians to direct their lives?

This article presents a historical introduction to the problem, a summary of the state of the question among contemporary Catholic thinkers, and some suggestions for its resolution.

HISTORICAL INTRODUCTION

Because the history of this problem is so extensive, only a few of the most important positions can be outlined in detail. Major consideration is therefore given to the thought of Aristotle, St. Augustine, and St. Thomas Aquinas, after which follows a summary treatment of the thought of modern philosophers on this subject.

Aristotle. ARISTOTLE begins his study of the end of man by observing that every activity implies a definite objective, since every effort presupposes a good at which it aims. Different spheres of activity have different ends, but each is unified and guided by its final objective. The basic question of ETHICS, then, concerns the single, final objective of the inclusive sphere of action called ''human life as a whole.''

Everyone agrees that the end of man is HAPPINESS—living or doing well—but people differ on what constitutes happiness. Some people think it is bodily PLEASURE, or such external goods as wealth and status, or good character. Aristotle maintains that happiness must be examined precisely as the end of action. So considered, whatever true happiness is, it must be the ultimate objective, sought always for itself and never for anything else. Moreover, in order to organize all of life, happiness must be complete in itself, requiring no addition to be an adequate principle of organization. Hence, Aristotle rejects the popular ideas of happiness, for they indicate only what belongs to the lower part of man (bodily pleasure), or what is only a means (external goods), or what is not desirable apart from action (character).

Platonic Solution. Although Aristotle follows PLATO up to this point, he rejects Plato's answer to the main question. To eliminate RELATIVISM, Plato posited as ultimate end a pure form of goodness—the Good itself—independent of everything else. But an ideal goodness that is not a good something seemed to Aristotle unintelligible. Moreover, if there were a Good itself, either it would remain irrelevant to the peculiar good for man, or it would conflict with the differences among goods appropriate to man and to other things.

Still, Aristotle agreed with Plato that happiness must not be defined subjectively by the desires one happens to have; that approach would lead to relativism. Aristotle's solution is to define happiness objectively by what fulfills the capacities from which human action arises. He concludes that man's true happiness lies in his distinctive action, the use of reason, which best realizes specifically human capacities.

Reason, Virtue, and Contemplation. Many use reason without becoming happy because they do not use it fully. For maximum use, reason must be cultivated until it reaches habitual excellence. The Greek word for habitual excellence is translated as VIRTUE, and so we find Aristotle concluding that the happiness that is man's end consists in continuous activity of the soul according to its highest virtue.

For Aristotle, the highest excellence of reason is philosophical WISDOM, and so he considers the philosophical life best. The truest human happiness is in the CONTEMPLATION of the truths the philosopher can know about the highest realities. Such a life is godlike, since it belongs to man only because he has intelligence like that of immaterial beings. But it is not supernatural in the theological sense, for it belongs to the higher part of man himself and is attained by his own efforts.

Prudence and Active Life. All human feelings, actions, and social life should be organized as a preparation and foundation for the philosophical life. But in organizing the rest of life, reason also functions in a properly human way; in this practical capacity, reason has a special excellence distinct from philosophic wisdom. This virtue, practical wisdom or PRUDENCE, is best exemplified in the great lawgivers and founders of cities. The practical life of affairs, then, also is a fulfillment of man's proper capacities, and it constitutes happiness secondarily.

The goods people mistakenly think are the end of man are not altogether excluded by Aristotle. Good fortune and external goods take a subordinate place. Friendship is important to happiness, but true friendship is a shared virtuous life. Moreoever, the truly happy life is the most pleasant, for pleasure is merely the conscious aspect of the perfect functioning of any capacity. Since happiness is the perfect use of man's highest capacity, it includes the deepest and most human pleasure.

For Aristotle, then, man's end is not a quality or a state, and it is not found in any good above man himself. Rather, happiness is in life itself, in the fulfillment of human capacities, chiefly in philosophical contemplation, for there man's best capacity is used to its fullest extent, not for any practical result beyond itself but simply for its own sake.

St. Augustine. AUGUSTINE did not ask whether man has a natural end or whether God could have created man without offering him grace. Augustine did not deny a natural end; he simply did not consider the possibility. Nevertheless, he is of interest because he presented the Christian doctrine on heaven in contrast with the philosophers' teachings on happiness and the end of man.

In his youth Augustine read in Cicero's *Hortensius,* which is the earliest, most Platonist version of Aristotle's ethics. The ideal of happiness in philosophical contemplation inflamed Augustine's heart, and he set out in quest of wisdom. But for many years he lived in error and immorality. Nothing ended his inner conflict and frustration until he received the grace of conversion to Christ.

From the vantage point of faith, Augustine reflects that all along he has sought Christianity, and he sees heavenly beatitude, the hope of Christians, as the only fully satisfying end of his previously fruitless quest. Thus from personal experience Augustine knows that only God can satisfy man's yearning for happiness, and this psychological discovery dominates his thinking about the end of man. Man's heart is made for God and shall not rest except in Him.

Pagan Neoplatonism. Augustine ridicules the pagan philosophers who placed happiness in natural goods or in virtue, and who valued the social life of man in this world. The present life is full of miseries; true happiness will be found only in the peace of eternal life with God. Thus Augustine contrasts this life to the next as false happiness is contrasted to heavenly beatitude.

One sees better why Augustine took this step in noting that he greatly respected one pagan philosophy—NEOPLATONISM. Itself indebted to Christianity as well as to GREEK PHILOSOPHY, GNOSTICISM, and perhaps also to Indian thought, to which it is similar, Neoplatonism teaches a natural mysticism. The basic notions are that man's mind comes from the divine by emanation, a kind of necessary creation, and that in this life the mind is unnaturally restrained (*see* EMANATIONISM). The practical conclusion follows: man should free himself from the world by an ascent to philosophical wisdom, and eventually he can redissolve into his divine source.

Augustine corrected Neoplatonism by insisting that God creates freely, that in heaven man is united to God by knowing Him rather than by dissolving into Him, and that man's return to God depends upon divine grace through Christ rather than upon a human effort of philosophical ascent. Augustine found Neoplatonism, so corrected, a useful framework for exploring Christian faith in a way that would satisfy his own experience and ideas.

End as Final State. Aristotle defined happiness in terms of the end of action and identified this end with the highest perfection of man himself. Augustine, on the other hand, defined happiness as the fulfillment of man's fundamental desire and identified this fulfillment with heavenly beatitude, in which man's mind attains the perfect goodness of God by knowing Him just as He is. Although the two approaches are quite different, they are not directly opposed. Indeed, Augustine was not concerned primarily with the end in relation to action, but with perfect happiness in the attainment of the supreme good. He does not use ''end'' precisely in Aristotle's sense—an objective of action sought as a fulfillment of the agent. Rather, Augustine thinks of the end as the absolute limit and the final state. Thus he contrasts the ''end of good,'' heavenly beatitude, with the ''end of evil,'' eternal separation from God; in both cases ''end'' means supreme instance, and the two absolute limits are final states. Aristotle would not speak of an ''end of evil,'' because no one acts for the sake of evil.

Effect on Boethius. BOETHIUS, a Christian philosopher who followed Augustine, also determined the end of man by examining man's desire for happiness. Man wants happiness and he does not find it in any particular good. Only complete happiness (beatitude), a state perfected by the conjunction of all goods, leaves nothing to be desired. Nowhere but in God, whose perfect goodness is the source of every created and partial good, are all goods present together. Hence man's desire for happiness cannot be satisfied unless he shares in the beatitude of God.

St. Thomas Aquinas. THOMAS AQUINAS used Aristotle's doctrine to bring the theological theory of the end of man to a new stage of development. The resulting teaching is complex; several points in it are disputed among scholars. Three points must be noted: (1) Aquinas teaches that there is a twofold end or beatitude of man. One is proportioned to his natural abilities; the other is supernatural and becomes proportionate to man only if he is given divine grace (*De ver.* 14.2, 10; 27.2; *In 2 sent.* 41.1.1; *Summa theologiae* 1a, 62.1; la2ae, 62.1–2). (2) He presents only one end, heavenly beatitude, as the absolutely ultimate goal of human life (*C. gent.* 3.1–63). (3) Beatitude means the perfect and stable attainment of a perfect good; it is a happiness that leaves nothing to be desired. Only the supernatural end is perfect beatitude. The natural end is an imperfect beatitude, a happiness that is somewhat like perfect beatitude but lacks the perfection required for it (*Summa theologiae* 1a2ae, 3). To understand these points and the disputes that have arisen, it is necessary to notice how Thomas transformed Aristotle's notion of end and his theory of man.

Notion of End. The transcendent aspect of end that Aristotle excluded by rejecting Plato's ideal goodness is restored by Thomas. He identifies perfect goodness with the reality of God, and he explains that God directs creatures to Himself by creating them as an expression of His own goodness, i.e., of Himself. Thus the ultimate end of all creatures is God. Creatures lacking intelligence attain divine goodness merely by reflecting it in their own perfection; intelligent creatures may attain it more directly by knowing God and loving Him (*C. gent.* 3.17–25; *In 2 sent.* 1.2.1–2). The end of every creature's action thus has two aspects. On the one hand, it is a perfection within the creature itself. On the other hand, it is the transcendent perfection of God.

Man and the Good. Aristotle held that man is complete in his own reality and that human desire is limited to human good. Thomas teaches that man's will is not oriented primarily toward himself but toward the good in general. Even by nature, man should not seek his perfection because it is his, but because it is good and a reflection of divine goodness (*De ver.* 22.1–5). Because God is the end of all creation, He should be loved above all things, and but for original sin, man would so love Him naturally (*Summa theologiae* 1a, 60.5; *In 3 sent.* 29.3). Man necessarily desires happiness, which he understands generally as the good that would satisfy his will. In fact, man's will is indefinitely open toward good and is naturally oriented toward God. But men do not necessarily recognize and accept this fact (*Summa theologiae* 1a, 82.1–2). Moreover, the greatest perfection man can receive, heavenly beatitude, would fulfill and surpass his capacities in a way he can neither suspect nor wish for without faith and grace. Man's desire for happiness thus has two aspects as well. On the one hand, it implicitly refers to the perfect goodness of God. On the other hand, it refers to man's capacity for perfection, which may be considered either according to the limits of attainment established by man's natural powers or according to what man can receive from God and achieve with supernatural aid (*In 3 sent.* 27.2.2).

Issues of Interpretation. The following five issues arise in the interpretation of Thomas's teaching:

1. Does Thomas consider Aristotle's doctrine an adequate account of the natural end of man? Thomas never describes the natural end of man in detail; rather, he constantly refers his readers for details to Aristotle or, more vaguely, to "the philosophers." In commenting on Aristotle's *Nicomachean Ethics,* Thomas seems to accept the teaching as correct within its limitations (*In 1 eth.* 9). At the same time, in his own works Thomas so transformed Aristotle's notions of end and of will that most Thomists have not considered Aristotle's teaching to be an adequate account of the natural end of man.

2. Does Thomas restrict the natural end to the present life? His references to Aristotle, whose treatment deals with this world exclusively, and his use of the contrast between earthly and heavenly beatitude suggest that he does. On the other hand, Thomas knows that some philosophers have put the end of man after death (*In 4 sent.* 49.1.1.4). He teaches that the separated soul naturally can attain a certain perfection (*De anim.* 17–20). And he holds that the souls of unbaptized infants enjoy goods proportionate to natural abilities, although they do not attain heavenly beatitude (*In 2 sent.* 33.2.2; *De malo* 5.3).

3. What is the meaning of Thomas's teaching that man "naturally" desires perfect happiness in a knowledge of God that in fact can be achieved only in supernatural beatitude? Thomas argues from natural desire that the beatific vision is not impossible and that the hope of Christians is not mistaken and perverse (*C. gent.* 3.50–57; *Comp. theol.* 1.104; *Summa theologiae* la, 12.1; la2ae, 3.8). But he also teaches constantly that without

grace man can neither know nor desire heavenly beatitude (*Summa theologiae* 1a2ae, 114.2; *De ver.* 14.2). How could a natural end be a true objective of human action if the desire of nature itself goes beyond all that man can achieve by his own abilities? In what sense does man ''naturally'' desire that which is in fact his supernatural end? These questions have been debated from the time of Thomas's first commentators to the present day.

4. If man were created without grace, could he ever be truly happy? The explanation of the meaning of beatitude—the attainment of perfect goodness (God) by a perfect and permanent act—and the presentation of the supernatural end alone as absolutely ultimate suggest a negative answer (*Summa theologiae* 1a2ae, 1–3). But Thomas explicitly considers the possibility that God could have created man without grace (*De malo* 4.1 ad 14; *Quodl.* 1.4.3). His teaching that man necessarily seeks happiness in something he knows and accepts as an ultimate end (*In 4 sent.* 49.1.3.3) suggests that a man created without grace could achieve a true happiness that would be an imperfect likeness of beatitude. The account of the state of unbaptized infants—they exist without pain and frustration despite original sin—indicates the minimum of which human nature is capable.

5. Given grace, does man have a natural last end as well as a supernatural one? The negative answer is indicated because man cannot have two ultimate ends. But Thomas's derivation of a complete doctrine on natural virtues and natural law from a consideration of goods proportionate to human nature (*Summa theologiae* la2ae, 61, 94) suggests that man's natural end is not removed by grace; therefore, the natural end must take a subordinate place within Christian life. This conclusion agrees also with Thomas's general teaching that grace presupposes and complements nature but does not abridge it.

Aquinas's teaching has given rise to many controversies because it is inherently complex and because the synthesis he presents is not wholly complete and explicit. The works of other great schoolmen have hardly been examined by scholars in relation to this problem. All the positions now current among Catholic thinkers plausibly claim some support from Thomas Aquinas.

Modern philosophy. A few early modern philosophers continued to treat the problem of the end of man according to its classic formulation. SPINOZA is one example; his position is somewhat like that of Neoplatonism. Generally the old concept of end is unknown, and happiness is equated with the subjective feeling of satisfaction.

The main British thinkers from LOCKE and HUME through those holding utilitarianism (Bentham and Mill) to RUSSELL and other recent empiricists have assumed that pleasure or the lessening of psychic tension is the sole effective motive of human action. Their chief problem in moral science is to show how selfishness can be limited by social restraint. Many other philosophers, following KANT, renounce happiness as a principle of ethics precisely because they consider it merely subjective. For the guidance of an end they substitute moral law derived from some source independent of good and desire, e.g., from reason in Kant, from freedom itself in Sartre. Such theories recognize that man seeks ends, but they consider these ends to be in themselves morally indifferent.

It must be noted that evolutionary theories of human life do not necessarily exclude an end, although the doctrine of end implicit in such a theory can be uncovered only by interpretation. Every evolutionary theory of man assumes that development implies progress, and although evolutionists consider the possibilities of progress unlimited, the principle that measures progress serves in fact as an end, i.e., a guiding principle that gives human life a purpose.

HEGEL and his followers teach an evolutionary PANTHEISM that views the whole of things as a process developing toward an absolute reality. The end of man is simply his place in the system. In the last analysis, man takes his place willy-nilly, since human freedom is ultimately unreal.

Dialectical MATERIALISM derived from Hegel, but by discarding the Absolute it radically transformed man's relationship to reality. Like American PRAGMATISM (which adopted evolution from natural science but also owed much to Hegel), dialectical materialism teaches in effect that the end of man is within man himself and consists in the realization of the possibilities of human nature. This view is similar to Aristotle's position, but the contemplative ideal is omitted in favor of rationally guided activity and work, mankind's social solidarity is emphasized, and human capacities are believed to enlarge as evolution progresses.

During the past century, work in psychology and the social sciences more and more obviously has needed a conception of the end of man as a standard for human health and well-being and as a guide for social reform and intercultural communication. Much recent psychology uses a concept of the mature, integrated, and effective personality—again an end somewhat like Aristotle's—and many social scientists assume that values such as health, technological efficiency, and political freedom are standards for human welfare. Contemporary philosophers have hardly noticed this aspect of psychology and social science, and have contributed little to it. Catholic moralists also, on the whole, have been unfortunately isolated from these developments in the sciences of man.

CONTEMPORARY CATHOLIC POSITIONS

The state of the question concerning the natural end of man among Catholic thinkers can be indicated by summaries of five positions representative of the present spectrum of views.

Farrell and Adler's view. Walter FARRELL and Mortimer Adler, collaborating in a series of articles entitled "The Theory of Democracy," showed the superiority of democratic government on the ground that it best subserves the natural end of man. In so doing, they had to discuss this end. That there is a natural end, they argue from the naturalness of the state, of social virtues, and of natural law. They criticize those who identify the natural end with the social good, identifying it instead with the perfection of individual lives to which the good of society is merely a means.

Farrell and Adler consider the natural end only in respect to the happiness of this life. This happiness they consider to be a true conjunction of all the goods man naturally desires by active desire. They solve the Thomistic problem of natural desire by holding that Thomas's arguments refer to a passive desire. Happiness applies analogously to heavenly beatitude and to the natural end; natural happiness is true happiness proportionate to human abilities. The natural end is subordinate to supernatural beatitude but is not a means to it. The natural end is absolutely ultimate in its own order.

These authors explain the nature of happiness very much as did Aristotle. However, they reject interpretations of Aristotle that equate philosophical contemplation with happiness. Philosophical activity is only the best among many goods that constitute the perfect human life. Moreover, they deny that the good life is a stable act; instead, they consider it a constant process. Hence, they reject a distinction between contemplative and active in the life connatural to man. Moreover, although admitting that the attainment of God is man's supernatural beatitude, they deny that God is the good attained (the objective aspect) in man's natural end.

Ramirez's traditional position. Beginning in the 16th century, Catholic theologians, faced with heresies that confused nature and grace, tended to sharpen the distinction between the two principles and to insist on the completeness of nature in its own order. This development included extensive use by post-Reformation theologians of the notion of a logically possible state of pure nature. To make this notion consistent and complete, the doctrine of the natural end of man, already present in Thomas, was greatly developed.

Although details vary in different authors, the teaching still most generally found in manuals of Catholic moral theology and philosophy is that there is a natural end of man that gives true happiness proportionate to human abilities. This end would naturally be attained by a natural knowledge and love of God after death. In this teaching, the natural end approximates the supernatural end as closely as possible, for the natural end objectively consists in God. Moreover, its attainment is referred to the next life, often rather as a reward than as a result of man's life on earth.

Santiago Ramirez gives a careful and complete theological statement of this position. Even according to nature, God is the objective good that man should seek as his end. The attainment of God is effected by an act of speculative knowledge that is man's highest perfection. The essential difference between heavenly beatitude and the natural end is the kind of knowledge by which God is attained—in heavenly beatitude by an intuitive vision that surpasses man's natural abilities, in the natural end by natural knowledge through creatures.

From a theological standpoint, Ramirez carefully distinguishes the conditions under which the natural end of man could give perfect happiness. He maintains that if human nature is considered in itself rather than in comparison with the order of grace, under ideal conditions (integral nature) the natural end of man would give a perfect natural happiness. This perfect happiness would be attained fully, however, not in the present life but in an undisturbed knowledge of God after death.

Maritain's thesis. Although in his earlier writings Jacques MARITAIN sometimes seemed to hold that the only natural end of man is the temporal COMMON GOOD that is the objective of political action, in his *Neuf Leçons* he treats the problem more carefully. He concludes first that God, as absolute and complete goodness, is the objective aspect of the end both of man and of the whole of creation. But in the natural order the goodness of God is reached only imperfectly and mediately, since the natural happiness of man is not found in sharing with God in His own life, but in man's fulfillment through action. Natural knowledge of God is only one aspect of this humanly perfective end.

The good that man can attain naturally does not constitute beatitude, because imperfect beatitude is not really beatitude at all. Natural happiness is imperfect, never finished, and always capable of increase. Hence the natural end of man is somewhat indeterminate; it would involve an endless progress even after death in the perfection of intelligence.

Man naturally desires to know what God is, but this desire is merely the thrust of human curiosity seeking to know the causes of things as fully as possible. This natural desire is not a desire for supernatural beatitude. Since natural happiness is never perfect in any case, the satisfaction of this particular natural desire, which is only one among many, is not necessary for the natural end of man.

Only the believer recognizes that man's natural desires are transformed by grace into the Christian's hope for perfect happiness in the beatific vision of God. But a philosopher may investigate religious teachings as a supplement to the other available sources of information. From Christianity he can learn that man in fact is called to perfect and supernatural beatitude. Thus the natural, indeterminate end has been replaced, but it is virtually contained in the supernatural end, for heavenly beatitude is the determinate attainment of perfect good. Hence Maritain rejects the parallelism between the natural and supernatural ends suggested by the common view of which Ramirez is representative.

Buckley's proposal. Joseph Buckley's *Man's Last End* is the only book in English devoted exclusively to the problem of the natural end of man. His position is like Maritain's in its denial of a definite end of man in the natural order analogous to heavenly beatitude in the supernatural order. Buckley sharply distinguishes the metaphysical view of ends, in which God is seen as the creator directing all things to the expression of His own goodness, and the moral or psychological view of ends, in which man directs his own action toward a good. Man's end, considered psychologically, is not the divine goodness itself, except supernaturally; naturally, man's will is ordered to the aspect of goodness in all things. God is included in the object of the will only as the primary and causal source of the entire realm of goods.

Buckley concludes that according to nature there is no concrete and determinate last end for man. If there were such an end, it would have to be a supreme good capable of fulfilling all desires and organizing the whole of life. But no single good, not even God as we naturally conceive Him, can meet these requirements. Thus, the ultimate natural end of man is his indeterminate fulfillment in the indefinite realm of the whole of goods. Man naturally acts for ends that are concrete and determinate goods, but no such end is a last end, for none of these goods is adequate to the indefinite capacity of the will for whatever is good, and hence none of them can constitute perfect happiness or the fulfillment of all desires. Happiness considered indeterminately remains the only natural ultimate end of man from the psychological point of view.

Buckley is at pains to emphasize that although his view of the natural end reveals how fitting the supernatural perfection of man by divine grace is, this elevation is not necessary. God could have created man without calling him to a life of grace, but in that case human life would lack the definiteness of direction and pervasive unity of purpose that only a concrete and determinate end can give. Buckley assumes that moral standards are established apart from the consideration of the ultimate end.

De Lubac's position. Unlike Buckley, who developed his position within the framework of Thomistic philosophy, Henri de LUBAC considers the problem of the end of man from an Augustinian viewpoint and offers his *Surnaturel: Études historiques* as a contribution to the history of theology. De Lubac tries to show that in man, an intelligent and free being created in the image of God, openness to God transcends the restrictive limits of determinate nature. De Lubac emphasizes the freedom with which God offers grace and the freedom with which man accepts it. He thinks that passages in St. Thomas that seem to teach a natural end of man really only assert that there are some goods accessible to man in this life, not that there is or could be an ultimate end of man other than heavenly beatitude. De Lubac goes so far as to reject the entire notion of a possible purely natural order. His conclusion is that it is entirely impossible that there be a natural ultimate end of man.

Although De Lubac did not deny that heavenly beatitude is above man's nature and his own abilities of attainment, his position was widely regarded by theologians as a threat to the gratuity of the supernatural. His critics offered many arguments to show that De Lubac's position is incompatible with the teaching of faith that the life of grace is in no way required by or necessary to human nature. Much of this debate was quieted by the appearance in 1950 of the encyclical *HUMANI GENERIS* in which certain unnamed theologians were criticized: "Others destroy the gratuitous character of the supernatural order by suggesting that it would be impossible for God to create rational beings without ordaining them for the beatific vision and calling them to it" [*Acta Apostolicae Sedis* 42 (1950) 570].

TOWARD A SOLUTION

The present disagreement among Catholic thinkers concerning the natural end of man indicates that there is not yet a completely satisfactory resolution of this problem. However, Catholic theologians and philosophers who have studied the problem do generally agree that there is a natural end of man. All agree that the supernatural end, concerning which faith teaches, either replaces or subordinates the natural end. The present trend of thought is away from the position that had become common since the 16th century, toward a view that accentuates the lack of parallelism between the natural and the supernatural ends.

Natural Desire and Happiness. No one approaching the problem of the natural end within the Christian tradition can avoid being influenced by St. Augustine. Thus Catholic thinkers have tended to focus upon happiness and man's desires rather than upon human action and the principles of its moral quality. Generally they have tried to determine what in fact would give man the greatest happiness of which his nature would be capable if he were not called to the supernatural life of grace. This emphasis has significant consequences. If attention is focused upon the restless heart and the real possibility of absolutely perfect happiness, the comparative imperfection of any natural end is clarified, but its positive character remains obscure.

Of course, even Aristotle considered happiness the ultimate end of man, and Aristotle did not identify this end with supernatural beatitude. This fact should be a reminder that an examination of the meaning of happiness is necessary if the problem of the end of man is to be formulated as an inquiry into what constitutes true happiness.

The universality of the human desire for happiness shows that man naturally and necessarily seeks *something* as an ultimate end in the enjoyment of which his will might rest. But the variety of goods that different men in fact accept as their ultimate ends proves that the human will is not determined to any definite good, even the highest. From this point of view, Buckley's analysis of the natural end appears to be correct. Perhaps, however, a different formulation of the problem of the natural end of man would lead to a more positive result.

Nature and moral obligation. From a psychological point of view, what each man seeks as a concrete last end is determined by himself; but from an ethical point of view, what last end every man should seek is predetermined by the nature of man and by his inescapable place in reality. This consideration suggests the following formulation that avoids the difficult notions of happiness and natural desire: Consider man strictly according to the requirements and possibilities of his nature. To what end *ought* he to direct his entire life? What good *should* man seek for its own sake, while rightly treating all other goods either as its constituent elements or as mere means to it?

Because Catholic philosophers generally accept Aristotle's thesis that choice is only of means, never of ends as such, some object to this formulation of the problem. But Aristotle lacked a clear notion of will and had only a limited understanding of freedom of choice. Moreover, one need not suppose that the last end is directly an object of choice, but only that man either chooses to consider and act for the good he should accept as his last end, or that he chooses to ignore the end to which he is obliged in favor of some other good that he prefers. A basic commitment to the morally required end is the first and most fundamental means for attaining it. Obligation with respect to the end need not be explained by any ulterior principle, for the last end is itself a first principle, the source of all obligations and primarily of the obligation to accept its own primacy.

Infinite and finite good. In attempting to describe the morally required natural last end, the first task is to determine whether the perfect goodness of God belongs to the objective aspect of man's natural end. As previously mentioned, there is disagreement among Catholic thinkers on this point. Some confusion seems to arise from a tacit assumption, most obvious in De Lubac, that if God is the end of man even according to nature, man's natural relationship to God would be the personal association that only grace can open to man.

But the orientation to God that belongs to man according to mere nature is other than the Christian's relationship to his Lord, Redeemer, and Sanctifier. Even by nature, man should not love any finite good as if it were the perfect goodness of God, or commit himself to any particular good as if his will could rest content in the enjoyment of it alone. Human reason can discern the limitations of finite goods, and man is obligated by nature to act according to reason. It seems to follow that finite goods belonging to man's natural end may rightly be sought only so far as they are participations in the perfect goodness of God, although no act within man's natural ability can attain God as He is in Himself, since intimate sharing in divine life depends upon divine grace.

Specific perfective goods. However, even if it is agreed that finite goods directly attainable by man belong to his morally required natural last end only so far as they are participations in the perfect goodness of God, it still must be determined exactly what goods accessible to human abilities coalesce to form the organizing principle of a good human life. Aristotle thought that the highest perfection of man is some action desirable only for itself and perfect by itself alone. However, human actions receive value from the goods attained in and by them, and no single natural mode of human action has the perfection that Aristotle required of the end. The fact that human nature can be elevated by grace indicates that man is less closed upon himself than Aristotle believed.

Hence, it seems that Farrell, Adler, and Maritain are correct in holding that all goods truly perfective of man have a place in his natural end. Most noble among these is the truth man can know about God and about his own place in reality, but most fundamental is man's physical and psychological health. Health truly perfects man; it deserves cultivation and demands respect, even when no further perfection happens to be accessible. Truth, health, and other perfective goods underlie the fundamental precepts of NATURAL LAW, for as constituents in the natural end, such goods first require that man act and first guide human action.

As already noted, especially in Maritain and Buckley, the present trend among Catholic thinkers is to admit a certain indeterminacy in the natural end. The ensemble of perfective goods has this characteristic, both because none of them is perfectly attained in any single act and because among them there is a twofold priority: that of nobility centering upon truth, and that of necessity centering upon health. Moreover, since each of these accessible goods must sometimes be subordinated to others and since none of them is self-sufficient, the dispositions of upright character, by which man avoids subservience to any particular good and maintains his openness toward God, are themselves desirable for their own sake. Thus the natural end of man includes complete moral virtue, a good in principle accessible to man's natural abilities, although fallen man cannot attain it without healing grace. To determine the precise relationship within the ensemble of perfective goods between substantive goods, such as truth and health, and the peculiar good of moral virtue remains one of the most difficult tasks in the investigation of man's natural end.

See Also: END; FINAL CAUSALITY; FINALITY, PRINCIPLE OF; GOOD; COMMON GOOD; NATURAL LAW; DESIRE TO SEE GOD, NATURAL; BEATIFIC VISION; WILL; NATURE; GRACE, ARTICLES ON.

Bibliography: ARISTOTLE, *L'Éthique à Nicomaque,* tr. R. A. GAUTHIER and J. Y. JOLIF, 2 v. (Louvain 1958–59). L. ROBIN, *La Morale antique* (2d ed. rev. and corr. Paris 1947). G. DE BROGLIE, *De fine ultimo humanae vitae: Tractatus theologicus, pars prior, positiva* (Paris 1948). J. ROHMER, *La Finalité morale chez les théologiens de saint Augustin à Duns Scot* (Paris 1939). V. CAUCHY, *Désir naturel et béatitude chez saint Thomas* (Montreal, Canada 1958). W. R. O'CONNOR, *The Eternal Quest* (New York 1947). A. R. MOTTE, ''Désir naturel et béatitude surnaturelle,'' *Bulletin Thomiste* 3 (1930–33) 651–676; ''La Possibilité de la vision béatifique,'' *ibid.* 4 (1934–36) 573–590. M. J. ADLER and W. FARRELL, ''The Theory of Democracy,'' *Thomist* 4 (1942) 121–181. THOMAS AQUINAS, *De hominis beatitudine tractatus theologicus ad primam secundae Summae theologicae,* ed. J. M. RAMIREZ, 3 v. (Madrid 1942–47). V. CATHREIN, ''De naturali hominis beatitudine,'' *Gregorianum* 11 (1930) 398–409. J. MARITAIN, *Neuf Leçons sur les notions premières de la philosophie morale* (Paris 1951) 89–117. J. BUCKLEY, *Man's Last End* (St. Louis, Mo. 1949). H. DE LUBAC, *Surnaturel: Études historiques* (Paris 1946); ''Duplex hominis beatitudo,'' *Recherches de science religieuse* 35 (1948) 290–299. P. J. DONNELLY, ''Discussions on the Supernatural Order,'' *Theological Studies* 9 (1948) 213–249; ''A Recent Critique of P. de Lubac's 'Surnaturel,''' *ibid.* 554–560. T. DEMAN, ''Surnaturel,'' *Bulletin Thomiste* 7 (1943–46) 461–472. P. M. DE CONTENSON, ''Surnaturel,'' *ibid.* 8.2 (1947–53) 794–804.

[G. G. GRISEZ]

MANASSES I OF REIMS

Archbishop, patron of letters; b. Champagne, France, *c.* 1040; d. between 1081 and 1100. This archbishop cannot be traced with certainty before his election in 1070 or after May 1081. It is established that Manasses was a well-educated noble, had a taste for Latin verse, possessed some knowledge of Canon Law, and was eager to continue the reputation of the cathedral school of Reims. That he was bellicose, avaricious, narrow-minded, and unreliable can be proved also. It was his defiance of the GREGORIAN REFORM and his refusal to appear in council to answer charges of uncanonical conduct that led to his deposition (1077) and excommunication (1080). Last mentioned by BENZO OF ALBA, he is remembered as the patron of FULCOIUS OF BEAUVAIS.

Bibliography: J. R. WILLIAMS, ''Archbishop Manasses I of Rheims and Pope Gregory VII,'' *American Historical Review* 54 (1948–49) 804–824. A. BECKER, *Lexikon für Theologie und Kirche,* 10 v. (2d, new ed. Freiburg 1957–65) 6:1342.

[S. WILLIAMS]

MANCE, JEANNE

First Catholic lay nurse in North America and first director of the Hôtel-Dieu, Montreal, Canada; b. Langres, Picardy, France, 1606; d. Montreal, June 18, 1673. She was 35 when she joined the first Montreal colonists, and she was present at the Mass celebrated by the Jesuit B. Vimont on May 17, 1642, during the founding ceremonies of the city. The initial plan for Montreal included the establishment of a hospital; Jeanne was its first administrator under conditions that constantly demanded heroic acts. In 1658 she made her second trip to France and brought back from La Flèche the hospital nuns of St. Joseph to staff the Hôtel-Dieu. The reputation for sanctity that she enjoyed during her lifetime continued to grow after her death. In 1909 a monument to her memory was erected in front of Hôtel-Dieu. In 1942 at a congress in Montreal, the Catholic nurses of the U.S. and Canada asked that her cause be introduced at Rome; the process of diocesan inquiry was subsequently initiated.

Bibliography: ABBÉ FAILLON, *Vie de Mlle. Mance et histoire de l'Hôtel-Dieu de Villemarie,* 2 v. (Tours 1854). J. K. FORAN, *Jeanne Mance, or the ''Angel of the Colony,'' Foundress of the Hôtel-Dieu Hospital, Montréal, Pioneer Nurse of North America* (Montreal 1931). M. MONDOUX, *L'Hôtel-Dieu: Premier hôpital de Montréal* (Montreal 1942). M. C. DAVELUY, *Jeanne Mance* (2d ed Montreal 1962).

[L. POULIOT]

MANDAEAN RELIGION

The syncretistic, Gnostic religion of the pagan baptist sect of Mandaeans who survive in small numbers in southern Iraq and Iran. They were first brought to the attention of the West by 16th- and 17th-century merchants and missionaries and erroneously called Christians of St. John because of their veneration for John the Baptist. Scientific study of Mandaeism began in the 19th century with the travels and writings of H. Petermann and the grammar of Mandaean, a dialect of East Aramaic, by T. Nöldeke (1875). The works of W. Brandt and M. Lidzbarski and, more recently, the many manuscripts obtained and published by Lady E. S. Drower, furnish copious documentation for Mandaeism but do not fully solve its problems.

The name Mandaean means ''gnostic,'' from the Aramaic *maddā'<mandā'* ''knowledge.'' Other names used are Ṣabaeans, ''baptizers,'' and Naṣoraeans, probably ''observers'' (of the code and cult). The name observers is more properly reserved for the priests who are fully initiated into the esoteric doctrine. The sect won toleration from the conquering Muslims as a ''people of the book'' because they possessed their own literature, which may have been set down or at least first collected for that purpose in the 7th and 8th centuries A.D. Their principal works include the *Ginza* (Treasure) or *Book of Adam,* the *Book of John,* the *Canonical Prayerbook,* and many esoteric works of varying antiquity. Generally, these are not unified compositions but loose collections of cultic and other materials, many of them traditional and very ancient.

Mandaean ritual life is more important than its mythological framework and may indeed be more primitive. The two principal rites are the *maṣbūtā* or baptism, a frequently repeated ritual washing in ''living'' (i.e., running) water, and the *masiqtā,* a ceremony for the dead which includes a sacred meal. The teaching combines elements of Jewish, Iranian, Babylonian, Gnostic, and Christian origin into a nonphilosophical synthesis with an underlying dualism contrasting light and darkness, the world of spirits (*Uthras*) and the earth, the supreme being Great Life or Lord and the evil Holy Spirit, the human soul and the body. Salvation is possible by an ascent of the soul to the world of light, which is to be achieved by knowledge, ethical living, and practice of the cult. The savior figure is called *Hibil-Ziwa* (Abel-radiance). The strict moral code of Mandaeism is of Jewish origin.

The antiquity and provenance of the Mandaeans are disputed. Extrinsic evidences make it reasonably certain that the sect existed in the 4th or 5th century A.D. and some scholars are reluctant to go any further. T. Säve-Söderbergh [*Studies in the Coptic-Manichean Psalmbook* (Uppsala 1949)] has argued that the 3d-century Manichean *Psalms of Thomas* depend on Mandaean hymns, which are therefore older. Other arguments based on the peculiar Mandaean script, certain elements of cultic practice, etc., would place Mandaeism in the earliest Christian or even pre-Christian times. It was once thought to have originated in Mesopotamia or Iran, where it certainly flourished at an early date, but most authorities now think it had Palestinian or Syrian origin. For the sect's migration to the East under persecution, a date around A.D. 38 has recently been proposed [R. Macuch, ''Alter und Heimat des Mandäismus nach neuerschlossenen Quellen,'' *Theologische Literaturzeitung* 82 (1957) 401–408]. The Mandaeans probably developed from a heretical Jewish baptist sect under Gnostic influence. Mandaean influence upon the NT is improbable, though remote parallelism is to be expected from their common Palestinian background.

See Also: GNOSTICISM; ARAMAIC; MANICHAEISM.

Bibliography: Texts and translations. M. LIDZBARSKI, *Ginza: Der Schatz oder das Grosse Buch der Mandäer* (Göttingen 1925); *Das Johannesbuch der Mandäer,* 2 v. (Giessen 1915). E. S. DROWER, *The Canonical Prayerbook of the Mandaeans* (Leiden 1959); *Diwan Abatur or Progress through the Purgatories* (*Studi e Testi* 151; 1950); *The Haran Gawaita and the Baptism of Hibil-Ziwa* (*Studi e Testi* 176; 1953); *The Thousand and Twelve Questions* (Berlin 1960). Bibliographies. S. A. PALLIS, *Essay on Mandaean Bibliography 1560–1930* (London 1933). S. SCHULZ, ''Die Bedeutung neuer Gnosisfunde für die neutestamentliche Wissenschaft,'' *Theologische Rundschau* 26 (1960) 301–329. Studies. W. BRANDT, *Die Mandäer, ihre Religion und ihre Geschichte* (Amsterdam 1915). J. SCHMID, *Lexikon für Theologie und Kirche,* ed. J. HOFER and K. RAHNER (Freiburg 1957–65) 6:1343–47. C. COLPE, *Die Religion in Geschichte und Gegenwart* (Tübingen 1957–65) 4:709–712. E. S. DROWER, *The Mandaeans of Iraq and Iran* (Oxford 1937; reprint 1962); *The Secret Adam* (Oxford 1960). K. RUDOLPH, *Die Mandäer,* 2 v. (Göttingen 1960–61) v. 1 *Prolegomena: Das Mandäerproblem,* v. 2 *Der Kult.* E. S. DROWER and R. MACUCH, *A Mandaic Dictionary* (Oxford 1963).

[G. W. MACRAE]

MANDATUM, ACADEMIC

According to Canon 812 of the 1983 Code of CANON LAW, those who teach theological disciplines in Catholic institutions of higher learning must have a *mandatum* from the competent ecclesiastical authority. *The Application of Ex Corde Ecclesiae for the United States,* approved by the bishops of the United States in 1999 and granted *recognitio* by the Holy See in 2000, defines the *mandatum* as ''fundamentally an acknowledgment by Church authority that a Catholic professor of a theological discipline is a teacher within the full communion of the Catholic Church.'' It ''recognizes the professor's commitment and responsibility to teach authentic Catholic doctrine and to refrain from putting forth as Catholic teaching anything contrary to the Church's magisterium.'' Guidelines for granting the *mandatum,* approved by the bishops in 2001, define the theological disciplines as Sacred Scripture, DOGMATIC THEOLOGY, MORAL THEOLOGY, Pastoral Theology, Canon Law, LITURGY, and Church History. The competent ecclesiastical authority for granting the *mandatum* is the bishop of the diocese in which the Catholic university or college is located. The bishop may also grant it through a delegate.

[J. STRYNKOWSKI]

MANDIČ, LEOPOLD BOGDAN, ST.

Baptized Bogdan (Adeodato in Italian); also known as Leopold da Castelnovo (Castronovo); Capuchin priest; b. May 12, 1866, Castelnuovo of Càttaro (Herceg Novi, Kotor Bay in Croatian), southern Dalmatia, Bosnia-Hercegovina; d. July 30, 1942, Padua, Venetia, Italy. Bogdan was the 11th of 12 children in a noble but poor family headed by Peter Mandič, who owned a fishing fleet, and Carlotta Zarevič, daughter of Countess Elena Bujovič. Bogdan began his seminary studies at Udine, Venetia, Italy Nov. 16, 1882, with the desire to work for the unification of Orthodox and Catholic Christians in foreign lands, but his Capuchin superiors knew that his frail health could not withstand the hardships. He received the habit and took the name Leopold at Bassano del Grappa, Vicenza in 1884. After pronouncing his vows in 1885, Leopold studied for the priesthood at Padua, where he made his solemn profession in 1888, and Venice, where he was ordained in 1890. Following assignments in various friaries, in 1906 he was transferred to Padua, where he remained for the rest of his life, except for one year's incarceration during World War I because he would not renounce his Croat nationality. In Padua, he was known for his cheerfulness, modesty, care for the sick, and his patient compassion in the confessional, where he heard confessions extended hours every day, and his penances and prayer ''for the full reunification of the separated Oriental and Latin Churches'' (canonization homily). Leopold was beatified by Pope Paul VI May 2, 1976, and canonized by Pope John Paul II Oct. 16, 1983.

Feast: May 12 (Capuchins).

Bibliography: L. MANDIČ, *Spisi Svetoga Leopolda Bogdana Mandiča*, ed. O. H. BORAK (Zagreb 1992). *Acta Apostolicae Sedis* 68 (1976) 548–550; 76 (1984) 937–944. *L'Osservatore Romano* Eng. ed. 1976, n. 20, 6–7; 1983, n. 43, 1, 3. T. CATTAROSSI, *Leopoldo Mandič: valori umani nell'azione pastorale* (Rome 1980). L. GUTWENGER, *Pater Leopold Mandič, der Heilige zwischen Ost und West: ein charismatischer Beichtvater* (Stein am Rhein 1983). F. DA RIESE PIO X, *Beato Leopoldo Mandič da Castelnovo: servì i peccatori per l'unità della Chiesa* (Rome 1976). U. SUMAN, *C'era una volta padre Leopoldo: la bontà di un santo in 50 racconti* (Padua 1993).

[K. I. RABENSTEIN]

MANDONNET, PIERRE

French Dominican historian and medievalist who zealously promoted the history of the DOMINICANS, THOMISM, and ARISTOTELIANISM in the 13th century; b. Beaumont (Puy-de-Dôme), Feb. 26, 1858; d. at the Saulchoir, Jan. 4, 1936. Mandonnet entered the Dominicans in 1882, was ordained in 1887, and from 1891 to 1918 was professor of church history at the University of Fribourg, Switzerland. He withdrew to Paris in 1919 and to the Saulchoir in 1927.

His *Siger de Brabant et l'averroïsme latin au XIII e siècle* (2 v., 2d ed. Louvain 1908–11) marked an era in the study of doctrinal history. Among other notable works are *Le Décret d'Innocent XI contre le probabilisme* (Paris 1903) and *Dante le théologien* (2d ed. Paris 1935). He established a solid foundation for Thomistic studies with *Des Écrits Authentiques de saint Thomas d'Aquin* (2d ed. Fribourg 1910); *Bibliographie Thomiste*, written in collaboration with J. Destrez (Paris 1921); and the periodical *Bulletin thomiste*, which he also established, together with *Société, Bibliothèque*, and *Institut historique d'études thomistes*. In collaboration with Father Coconnier, in 1893 he founded the *Revue thomiste* at Fribourg, where in 1925 he published a series of studies on the life of St. Thomas. In addition to his numerous books, articles, and historical notes on Dominican history, including *Les Dominicains et la découverte de l'Amérique* (Paris 1893) and the posthumous collection compiled by M. H. Vicaire, *S. Dominique, l'idée, l'homme et l'oeuvre* (2 v. Paris 1938, Eng. *St. Dominic and His Work* tr. M. B. Larkin, Milwaukee 1944), are his studies on the Order of Penance, especially *Les Règles et le gouvernement de l'ordo de Poenitentia au XIII e siècle* (Paris 1902).

Bibliography: *Année Dominicaine* 72 (1936) 41–48. ''In Memoriam,'' *Analecta Sacri Ordinis Praedicatorum* 22 (1935–36) 370–374. *Nova et Vetera* 13 (1938) 158–168. G. GIERATHS, *Lexikon für Theologie und Kirche* 2 6:1348. *Mélanges Mandonnet*, 2 v. (*Bibliothèque Thomiste*; Le Saulchoir 1930) 13, 14; 1:7–17.

[M. H. VICAIRE]

MANEGOLD OF LAUTENBACH

Canon regular; teacher and polemical writer on the papal side in the INVESTITURE STRUGGLE; b. Lautenbach

(Alsace), *c.* 1030; d. Marbach, soon after 1103. At first he was a wandering master in France. He entered the monastery of Lautenbach shortly before 1084, although he had previously been married. He became known as the prefect of the schools in Alsace. Against the Emperor HENRY IV he wrote *Manegoldi ad Gebhardum liber* (ed. K. Francke, *Monumenta Germaniae Historica: Libelli de lite* 1:308–340), a violent polemical treatise defending a contractual theory of kingship. His *Opusculum contra Wolfelmum Coloniensem* (*Patrologia Latina* 155:147–176) warns Christians against the dangers of the study of pagan poets and philosophers. In 1086, he fled from his opponents to the monastery of Raitenbuch (Bavaria); he became dean there, and later, prior of the monastery of MARBACH in Alsace. After attending the synod of Tours (1096) with Pope URBAN II, he was imprisoned by the imperialist party in 1098. Among his numerous writings were commentaries on Scripture, Plato, and Ovid.

Bibliography: F. STEGMÜLLER, *Repertorium biblicum medii aevi* (Madrid 1949–61) v.3. M. T. STEAD, ''Manegold of Lautenbach,'' *English Historical Review* 29 (1914) 1–15. M. MANITIUS, *Geschichte der lateinischen Literatur des Mittelalters* 3:25–28, 175–180. F. CHÂTILLON, ''Recherches critiques sur les différents personnages nommés Manegold,'' *Revue du moyen -âge latin* 9 (1953) 153–170. T. GREGORY, *Platonismo medievale* (Rome 1958). J. GROSS, ''Die Erbsündenlehre Manegolds von Lautenbach nach seinem Psalmen-Kommentar,'' *Zeitschrift für Kirchengeschicte* 71 (1960) 252–261.

[F. COURTNEY]

MANETTI, TERESA MARIA DELLA CROCE, BL.

Baptized Teresa Adelaida Cesina, also known as Teresa di Firenze (Teresa of Florence), foundress of the Third Order Carmelite Sisters of Saint Teresa (Congregazione delle Carmelitane di S. Teresa); b. March 2, 1846, San Martino a Campi Bisenzio (near Florence), Tuscany, Italy; d. there, April 23, 1910. Daughter of Salvatore Manetti and Rosa Bigali, Teresa sought to alleviate the difficulties of others. In 1872, she retired with a few friends to the countryside, where they could pray, work together, and provide a Christian education to local children. Their formal religious community, founded July 15, 1874 with the arrival of other young women, combined the contemplative Carmelite spirituality of prayer and Eucharistic Adoration with apostolic work in parishes, schools, and mission fields. On July 16, 1876, Teresa was admitted to the Third Order of Discalced Carmelites and changed her name to Teresa della Croce. In 1877, the sisters opened their home to orphans. The first twenty-seven sisters were veiled in the Discalced Carmelite habit, July 12, 1888. In 1902, her special desire to have perpetual adoration was granted. Before her death, Teresa saw the institute receive approbation by Pope Saint Pius X (Feb. 27, 1904) and the first sisters leave to establish missions in Lebanon (1904) and Palestine (1907). The woman of fervent devotion and ''angelic innocence'' died at age sixty-four. Her writings were approved Nov. 27, 1937, and the beatification process opened in Rome in 1944. She was declared venerable in 1975 and a decree issued on the approval of a miracle in Nov. 1985. Pope John Paul II beatified her at Florence, Italy, Oct. 19, 1986.

Feast: April 23 (Carmelites).

Bibliography: *Acta Apostolicae Sedis* (1986) 1144. *L'Osservatore Romano,* Eng. Ed. 39 (1986) 9.

[K. I. RABENSTEIN]

MANHARTER

Known also as Hagleitnerianer or as Michaelsbrüder, members of a small, short-lived schismatical sect in the Austrian Tirol. The Tirolean uprising of 1809 found religious expression in the refusal of the peasants, particularly in the Brixenthal, to accept the ecclesiastical changes introduced by the Bavarians or to receive the ministrations of priests who had taken the oath of allegiance to Napoleon despite his excommunication by Pius VII. Taking its name from a farm called *Untermanhart* that belonged to one of its key figures, Sebastian Manzl, the group found a powerful advocate in a local priest, Kaspar Hagleitner (1779–1836). Its members refused to attend local churches and held services of their own; they even traveled long distances to receive the Sacraments from Hagleitner. When the area was restored to Austrian rule in 1816 and placed under the jurisdiction of the See of Salzburg, the sect continued to exist, because it protested also against innovations and mitigations in Austrian Church discipline. Manzl led a deputation to Rome in 1825 to seek reconciliation, which was achieved in 1826 through the efforts of Archbishop Gruber of Salzburg. But a small group at Inntal refused to submit and persisted in its sectarianism. Not until the end of the 19th century did the Manharter disappear.

Bibliography: A. FLIR, *Die Manharter* (Innsbruck 1852). W. SCHATZ, *Lexikon für Theologie und Kirche*, J. HOFER and K. RAHNER, eds. (Freiburg 1957–65) 6:1350–51.

[W. B. SLOTTMAN]

MANICHAEISM

Once considered a Christian heresy, Manichaeism is now regarded as a complex dualistic religion essentially

Painting fragment believed to depict Mani and followers, 8th or 9th century, Turfan region of China.

gnostic in character. Its founder, Mānī, Manes, Μάνης, Μανιχαίος, Manichaeus, was born in the year 527 of the Babylonian astronomers, and the year 4 of Artaban V, last of the Arsacids, probably April 14, A.D. 216. His father, Patek (Πατήκιος, Fātak, Futtak), who came apparently from Hamadan, the ancient Ecbatana in Media, descended from the Haskanyas, a dynasty of the Arsacids, a Parthian stock. His mother, Mēis, Utākhim, Taashit, Karossa, or Maryam (the name best attested by the Arabic, Syriac, and Greek traditions) came from the family of the Kamsarakan, likewise a dynasty of the Arsacids. Mānī, of Armenian race and of aristocratic lineage, became a Babylonian through his place of birth. There are two traditions regarding its locality. The first and better tradition insists on Mardīnū, in the district of Nahr Kūthā in Northern Babylonia, a city situated on the canal that connects the Euphrates and the Tigris, south of Al-Madain (Ctesiphon-Seleucia) and Daīr-Qunna. The second tradition, represented by Theodore Bar Khonai (8th century A.D.), holds for Abrūmya near Gaukhai, in the center of Mesene in Southern Babylonia.

The father of Mānī, a religious man, had left his country as an *émigré* very probably after the decisive victory of the Sassanids over the Arsacids. He became a member of a baptist sect in Babylonia, the Mughtasilas. This sect, which abstained from meat, held views hostile to wine and marriage, and was, perhaps, related to the Mandaeans, made a definite impression on the young Mānī.

He owed his faith to a double revelation. According to the Arabic and Coptic traditions, in 539 and 551 of the Seleucid Era (A.D. 228–229 and 240–241), Mānī, at the ages of 12 and 24, respectively, received from the angel at-Taum, the messenger of the King of the Paradise of Lights, his mission as preacher of a gnosis, a definitive and ultimate divine revelation. At the age of 24 the preacher left Babylonia, the crossroads of the religions of

East and West. He reached India by boat just at the end of the reign of the Persian King Ardashīr, when his son, Shāpūr I, conquered the banks of the Indus.

India, the farthest point of Mānī's first missionary journey, influenced the subsequent development of his thought. He returned by boat to Persia, from Persia he went to Mesene, then to Asōrestān (classical Babylonia), and thence to Media and Parthia. He sojourned also for some time at Karka at the head of the Persian Gulf.

After this great missionary tour, Mānī, now well known as a young religious reformer, was summoned to court by Shāpūr I, successor of Ardashīr in 553 of the Seleucid Era (A.D. 241–242). In the same year Shāpūr declared war on Rome, against the Emperor Gordian III. Probably he saw in Mānī a man who, thanks to his power of synthesis and his talent as a religious leader, would be capable of serving his political designs toward the Roman Empire, and he took Mānī into his entourage. This circumstance marks the first expansion of Manichaeism in the West, and perhaps also the definitive synthesis of the Manichaean gnosis through the addition of the Christian element, after the missionary travels in Babylon and India.

Manichaean missionaries subsequently infiltrated the Roman Empire, especially Egypt, but they were harried and persecuted as enemies of the Roman people. Mānī continued his religious activity during 30 years, enjoying the protection of Shāpūr. This protection, combined with Mānī's unusual personality, explains the great expansion of the movement. In April 273, Hormisdas succeeded his father and likewise protected the prophet; from April 274, to July 277, Bahrām I, his brother, ruled the Persian Empire. Under Bahrām the leaders of Mazdaism assumed control, accused Mānī of heresy, and convinced the King of his guilt. The King ordered Mānī's arraignment. He was thrown into prison at Gundēshāpūr (Belāpāt), in Susiana, and, worn out, he died 26 days later, at the end of March 276 or 277. His head was exposed above the gate of the city. Later his disciples buried his remains at Ctesiphon.

Mānī had attained his 60th year. As the founder of a revealed religion, a book religion, a missionary religion, and as the prophet of Babylon, he attracted a large number of apostles and disciples who subsequently traversed the world, preached in the languages of Asia, Africa, and Europe, and made Manichaeism a universal religion, of which a few living vestiges remain in the 20th century.

Missionary Routes of the Religion of Light

''I have come from the land of Babel to make my cry heard throughout the whole world'' (*Frag. Turf.* M4).

The Routes in Central and Eastern Asia. The sojourn of Mānī in India is attested by all the traditions. Archeological traces of the existence of his religion are found near the ancient Bāmiyan, on the confines of Bactriana, Persia, and India. Numerous influences on the religions of Tibet were noted by missionaries in the 18th century. At the beginning of the 20th century some thousands of fragments of Manichaean literature, found at Turfan in western China, furnished information on the spread of the religion in Asia. In 621 a Manichaean temple was erected at Singanfu in China. The king of the Uighurs, a Turkish people of Central Asia, in 762 accepted the Religion of Light as the official religion of his state. He became a proselyte and influenced some Chinese princes, so that in 768, an imperial edict gave the Manichaeans authorization to erect temples in China. When the Khirghiz came down from Siberia, and in 840 destroyed the kingdom of the Uighurs, the Manichaean missionaries took advantage of the situation, pushed into Siberia, and established themselves in the valley of the Yenisei River. The *via Serica* was the main route of their penetration from Persia into China. Under the pressure of the peoples of the North, the Uighurs fell back upon the Chinese Empire, bringing with them so many apostles of Manichaeism that an imperial edict of 843 made Manichaeism a forbidden religion. This was a signal for an emigration to the South, where, in the province of Fukien, traces of Manichaeism were discovered in the 17th century.

In Central Asia the Mongols of Genghis Khan definitely ruined the sect in the 13th century. However, it maintained itself in Manchuria until an edict of 1646 completely suppressed it. Recent discoveries, supplementing the ancient traditions, attest the presence of Mānī in India. He himself or one of his disciples sojourned in Christian communities of Malabar *c.* 270. Thus Babylon, for more than a 1,000 years, covered Asia with an unceasing flow of missionaries.

Routes to the West. Although driven from Babylonia by persecutors, the Manichaeans returned, as to their home port, in each period of calm. From Babylon their missionaries set out also for the West, where Mānī had made his first tour during the Persian Wars (242–243). In any case, the route from Mesopotamia to the West can be clearly traced through the anti-Manichaean Christian and pagan polemics written to stem the spread of the doctrine of Mānī. Syria, which had been prepared by the gnosis of Bardesanes, was a fertile ground for Manichaeism, but the treatises of ''Mānī, apostle of Jesus Christ,'' written in or translated into Syriac, met a formidable adversary in St. EPHREM (d. 373). In his struggle against the heresy, Ephrem himself composed popular polemic songs or hymns. The existence of a flourishing

Manichaean community at Edessa in the 5th century bears witness to the persistence of this teaching. The *Acta Archelai* [GCS] constituted in 325 a first anti-Manichaean *summa* by Manichaeism's Christian opponents. This work and its MS tradition show that in the period of Constantine, 50 years after the death of its founder, Manichaeism had spread widely in the Roman Empire. TITUS, Bishop of Bostra (d. 371), read the ''Mysteries of Mani'' and wrote a refutation of it for the Christians of the Decapolis [*Patrologia Graeca* 18:1069–1264; R. P. Casey, *Harvard Theological Review* 21 (1928) 97–111]. To combat the Manichaeans, Titus found it necessary also to compose a Christian commentary on the Gospel [*Homilies on Luke,* ed. J. Sickenberger (Leipzig 1901) *Texte und Untersuchungen zur Gerschicte der altchristlichen Literatur* 21].

In 390 at Antioch, JOHN CHRYSOSTOM fulminated in his powerful eloquence against Mānī (''Homilies on Matthew,'' *Patrologia Graeca* 58:975–1058). About 348 CYRIL OF JERUSALEM instructed catechumens who had renounced Manichaeism (*Catech.* 6, *Patrologia Graeca* 33:331–1180). In 376 EPIPHANIUS, Bishop of Salamis in Cyprus, devoted the largest section in his book against heresies to the Manichaeans [GCS].

Manichaeism entered Egypt very early. Already in 297, following a revolt against Rome in which the Manichaeans participated, a harsh edict of Diocletian had ordered the annihilation of the sect. The Manichaeans came from Mesopotamia by sea, disembarked on the shores of the Red Sea, and followed the route of merchants engaged in transporting goods from Asia. The center from which they spread was probably Hypsela, south of Assiut in the Thebaid. From Upper Egypt they went down the Nile to engage in their apostolate in the Mediterranean lands. At the end of the 3d century a bishop of Alexandria published a pastoral letter against them, which coincided in time with the edict of Diocletian [C. H. Roberts, *Catal. Gk. and Lat. Papyri* 3 (Manchester 1938) no. 469]. The 3,000 Manichaean leaves found in 1930 at Medīnēt-Mādi [C. Schmit and H. J. Polotzky, *Mani-Fund* (Berlin 1931)] prove that Diocletian's edict did not stop the new religion. About 339 SERAPION, Bishop of Thmuis, wrote a refutation of Manichaeism [ed. R. P. Casey (Cambridge 1931)]. In the same years a pagan, Alexander of Lycopolis, having given up Manichaeism, refuted it on the basis of reason [ed. A. Brinkmann, (Leipzig 1895)]. Like Serapion, Didymus of Alexandria, about the end of the 4th century, found it necessary to write a commentary on those sacred texts the Manichaeans were citing in support of their position (*Patrologia Graeca* 39:1085–1110).

From Egypt Manichaeism passed to Africa Proconsularis, and from 373 to 383 AUGUSTINE was a Manichaean hearer. MONTANISM had prepared the way for the new religion, and Africa, furthermore, was receptive to teachings from Asia. Following his conversion to Christianity, Augustine fought for some 15 years to save the Bible from Manichaean interpretation (J. Ries, RevÉtAug 231–243). After being driven from Africa, the Manichaeans went to Spain, where in 434 VINCENT OF LERINS attacked them in his *Commonitorium* (*Patrologia Latina* 50:637–686). A formula of abjuration (*Patrologia Latina* 65:23–28) from Lyons shows that Manichaeism was regarded as a danger to Christians in 526. In this period St. CAESARIUS OF ARLES denounced the *immundissimi Manichaei* to his flock.

Meanwhile, Rome and Italy were infected, and imperial edicts were issued against the sect by Valentinian I in 372 (*Codex Theodosianus* 16.5.3) and Theodosius I in 382 (*ibid.* 16.5.9). Theodosius II (408–450), Anastasius I (491–518), Justin I (518–527), and Justinian (in 529) attacked the Manichaeans without mercy. From 440 on the Manichaeans, in fleeing from the Vandals, surged back into Italy. The letter of Pope LEO I in 444, *ad episcopos per Italiam,* indicates that there were Manichaean infiltrations of the Catholic clergy. In the same year the Pope had the error condemned by a Roman synod. An inscription at Salonae in Dalmatia gives proof of the presence of Manichaean communities in the Balkans from the 4th century.

Secondary Routes. A later neo-Manichaean current came from Asia, perhaps from Armenia, where Bishop Eznik of Kolb opposed Mānī *c.* 441. The various new dualistic teachings called Paulicianism, Bogomilism, or Catharism were attacked as Manichaean doctrines by Christian polemical writers of Byzantium and the West from the 6th to the 15th century. Many doctrinal analogies and practices seemed to connect them with Manichaeism. These dualistic systems penetrated deeply into every social milieu of western Asia, the Balkans, Italy, and France. Their history is known in detail, but their direct connection with the doctrine of Mānī is far from established.

Here again the writings of Christian opponents make it possible to follow the expansion of the sects. The decree of Justinian (529) occasioned the dissemination of a Manichaean tract that led to a reply and refutation by ZACHARIAS THE RHETOR (d. 553), Bishop of Mytilene [ed. A. Demetrakopoulos, *Bibl. Ecc.* (Leipzig 1866) 1:1–18]. In the 9th century an important body of Byzantine literature attacked the dualistic heresy and reused certain documents of the 4th and 5th centuries. Peter Higumenos [*Epitome,* ed. J. C. L. Gieseler, in *Appendix ad Petri Siculi historiam* (Göttingen 1849)], George the Monk (*Patrologia Graeca* 110:883–891), Peter of Sicily

(*History, Patrologia Graeca* 104:1305–50), and Photius (*Patrologia Graeca* 102: 15–264) strove to uproot the evil, while the Byzantine Church refined and imposed formulas of abjuration [G. Ficker, ZKirchgesch (1906) 27:443–464].

In this period of Paulicianism at Byzantium, another neo-Manichaean movement was spreading in Bulgaria, namely, Bogomilism. Michael Psellos [1018–78 (*Patrologia Graeca* 122:818–876)] and Euthymius of Zigabenos [early 12th century (*Patrologia Graeca* 130:305–325)] wrote against it. But the heresy had a stubborn life and flourished in the Second Bulgarian Empire during the 13th century. The treatises of Cosmas the Presbyter [10th century, ed. H. C. Puech and A. Vaillant (Paris 1945)] and of John of TORQUEMADA [1388–1468 (ed. N. Lopez Martinez and V. Proaño Gil, Burgos 1958)] indicate that contemporaries were convinced that they were dealing with a form of Manichaeism. The history of the manuscript of the *Acta Archelai* is significant in this regard, and the Manichaean routes can be traced through this history alone. A Latin translation of the original text circulated in Rome and Africa *c.* 400. New copies existed in Italy in the 6th century, in the period of the condemnations by Gelasius I and Gregory the Great. From the 9th century copies of the MSS of the *Acta Archelai* were numerous in France—a sign that they were utilized against the ALBIGENSES and the CATHARI [L. Traube, *Sitzungsberichte der Akademie der Wissenshaften zu München*, (1903) 533–539.

The doctrine preached by Mānī is not dead. The Swiss Rudolf STEINER (1861–1925), founder of ANTHROPOSOPHY, attracted numerous disciples. Thus, having adopted Manichaean and Catharian teachings, they wish to unite again in an esoteric way with the prophet of Babylon who, according to them, is the true continuator of the message of Jesus.

The Elements of Manichaean Doctrine

These elements can best be analyzed and summarized under the respective headings given below.

Revealed Dualistic Gnosis. Like all forms of gnosis, Manichaeism has a dualistic conception of the structure of the world. It emphasizes this concept to the extreme, admitting from the very beginning of everything a radical duality and opposition, Light-Darkness, Good-Evil. The origin of the material world, of evil, of sin, is found in this duality of the two uncreated principles, the central point in Manichaeism's doctrine. There was a first time, the *initium,* the time of the total separation of the two kingdoms, Light-Darkness. Following a struggle of Darkness against Light, a cosmogonic movement resulted in the mingling of the two substances. This is the *medium* or middle time, the present universe. Through the ambassadors of Light who have succeeded one another since Adam, the third time, *finis,* is being prepared, the eschatological age in which will take place anew the separation that existed in the beginning. These ambassadors are called Seth, Abraham, Sem, Enos, Nikotheos, Henoch, perfect men. Light's great ambassadors of the revelation of the kingdom of Light are Buddha, ZOROASTER, Jesus, and the final seal of all revelation, Mānī. The definitive revelation came to Mānī through the angel, at-Taum. All Manichaean texts exhibit a multitude of marvelous details as a kind of halo around the personality of the founder.

Totalitarian Gnosis. As a revealed religion and a dualistic system in its explanation of the beginning of the universe, Manichaeism proposes a tripartite conception of the world's history. Thus, totalitarian gnosis embraces all human knowledge—theology, theogony, cosmology, astronomy, geology, botany, anthropology, history, soteriology, and eschatology. The structure of the system is markedly intellectual and postulates knowledge and understanding as the first condition of salvation for its followers. Gnosis is a message destined for men, destined to make a redeeming church. It was necessary, therefore, to give it a popular aspect and make it acceptable to simple minds. It is in this popularizing that Mānī's personal work is so amazing; it gave his teaching the power to win the masses.

Living Gnosis. Mānī, endowed with the ability to make a religious synthesis and with a fertile imagination, worked out a series of cosmogonic and soteriological myths capable of arousing the enthusiasm of the West as well as of the East. He had the art of adapting these myths to the religious conceptions of the various peoples. There are two basic types of Manichaean myths. (1) The first describes a struggle between two trees, one of Good, the other of Evil. Titus of Bostra and Severus of Antioch especially have noted this presentation of the myth, and it is frequent also in the Coptic texts of the Fayum. This form, moreover, is mingled with the second. (2) The Manichaean cosmogony is presented, too, under the form of an epic in which the creation of the world is the result of a battle in three phases between the powers of Good and Evil, the celestial spirits and the infernal powers. This is the myth of the two kingdoms, each governed by a head, the Father of Greatness and the Prince of Darkness, respectively.

These two types resume the Biblical history from the creation of Adam and Eve, which is regarded as an element at the beginning of the second historical time. Each myth presents basic information intelligible to all, the antithesis Good-Evil, Light-Darkness. In brief: a very simple cosmic experience served as the foundation for a religious structure at once cosmogonic and soteriological.

Perfect Gnosis. Manichaean dogmatics is concerned with the explanation of these myths directed to a practical end: an attitude of knowledge, a grasp of the mysteries, a perfect gnosis (τέλεια γνῶσις)—at once knowledge, acceptance, and moral conformity. Since humanity is living in the second historical time, the cosmogony of current development is already in part a soteriology, a process of salvation, and of liberation of Light, the prisoner of Darkness in Creation.

Manichaean ethic or morality is based on this dogmatic foundation. It too is a soteriology, but oriented entirely toward eschatology, to the liberation of light. Eschatology governs all moral life and gives the Manichaeans, in a perspective of hope, the strength to endure the difficulties and persecutions inherent in the missionary life imposed on the elect.

Duality, present everywhere in the visible world, dictates the moral attitude to be adopted in effecting a necessary division in daily realities. Light resides in knowledge, revelation, spirit, soul, heaven, the heights, repose, endurance—in all that is characterized by the Good. Darkness is ignorance, matter, body, depth, unrest—briefly, Evil. The Manichaean learns to understand and adopt these antitheses, and he proceeds to salvation, to the kingdom of Light, which will be totally free after the final destruction of the cosmos by an eschatological fire.

Practical and Missionary Gnosis. Creation continues to take place. It is indispensable that salvation be accomplished even in the very process of creation. In other words, the cosmogonic myth and the soteriological myth compenetrate each other on this dualistic background. The whole cosmos is engaged in a struggle. Cosmic mechanisms, history, human life, religious message—all are found in the microcosm that is constituted by each man and that has to assume a twofold attitude. (1) Negative morality, abstention. This morality is dictated by the acute knowledge and consciousness of evil, of sin residing in matter as in its substance. This morality is a form of asceticism rather than an ethic: withdrawal, separation, abstinence from meat, wine, and sexual contacts; renunciation of property and work, frequent repose, war, hunting, business, and agriculture. The elect must live this ascetic life to the highest degree. (2) Positive morality. Manichaeism goes further. It wishes to give a consciousness of evil that impels to positive liberation and urges the need of redemption, the liberating action of the particles of Light. Every Manichaean is charged with this message of salvation. He must make known around him the method and the means of salvation. This method has its repercussions in all the details of daily life, even down to the menu of the disciple, who must distinguish luminous foods (melons, fruits) from dark foods (wine, meat). Manichaean gnosis makes its devotees carriers of revelation, conscious of their role in a dualistic world that is to be saved by them. The refusal to accept truth—Manichaean dualism—is one of the greatest of human faults, it is the refusal of salvation and means certain damnation.

From all this it is easy to understand both the enthusiasm of the Manichaean church and its violent clash with other religions and, especially, with civil authority charged with the organization and regulation of social life.

The Principal Elements in the Manichaean Myth. The fundamental mythical element in the struggle of the two kingdoms, *Primus Homo,* Primal Man, is an emanation of the Father of Greatness, king of the Paradise of Light. Through the Great Spirit, the Sophia of the Father and Mother of the Living, the Father orders Primal Man to engage in battle against Darkness in its attack on the kingdom of Light. The Primal Man is clothed in an armor of five luminous elements: Light, Wind, Fire, Water, and Air. These five elements constitute his soul, his life. The struggle ends in the defeat of Primal Man. He is knocked senseless and lies unconscious in the midst of Darkness, which takes away his armor and swallows his soul, the five luminous elements. By this soul Darkness gives birth to matter, ὕλη. On coming to himself Primal Man cries out and calls for help. When his cry is repeated seven times, it is heard in the kingdom of Light. This is the first cry of salvation that every Manichaean must repeat to the end of the second time. Through this cry salvation begins. The Father of Greatness, through the Mother of the Living, causes the emanation of a second luminous power and sends it forth, the Living spirit armed with his five sons. He reaches the frontier of the kingdom of Darkness and shouts out an appeal to Primal Man, who is a prisoner there.

The dark matter is poisoned and put to sleep by the five luminous elements taken from Primal Man, who hears the cry of the Living Spirit and replies. The cry and response, these two divine hypostases, meet and form the prototype of Manichaean salvation: message and acceptance. The Living Spirit, with the help of the Mother of the Living, gives his right hand to Primal Man and leads him back into the Paradise of Light. The savior is saved; he suffered, and he had need of salvation.

The Primal Man left his soul, namely, the five luminous elements, a prisoner of Darkness. These elements, too, must be freed and brought back to the Paradise of Light. This is again the work of the Living Spirit, who is charged with punishing the Archons of Darkness, with building a prison for them, and with liberating the particles of Light.

The Living Spirit seizes Light from Darkness; he thus creates the sun and the moon in order to make them two conveyors of Light. Then he tears off the skins of the Archons to spread out the ten firmaments. From their bones he makes the mountains, and from their flesh and excrement he makes the earth. The universe is arranged in eight regions and is the result of a mingling of Light and Darkness. As long as all the luminous souls are not liberated, it is necessary to mount guard in the universe. The Living Spirit gives this guard duty to his five sons: Splenditenens holds the firmaments; the King of Honor is charged with collecting again the particles of Light; Adamas, armed with sword and shield, holds back Darkness; the King of Glory keeps the vault of the sky turning; and Atlas, the Giant, bears on his shoulders the eight regions of the world. The Living Spirit creates also three giant wheels charged with effecting the ascent of the liberated particles of Light.

The Third Messenger. This myth describes the temptation of the Archons. The problem is how to liberate the luminous particles in this universe. The Father of Greatness sends a third emanation, the principal personage in which is called the Third Messenger, *Tertius Legatus,* the father of the 12 Virgins of Light (the 12 signs of the Zodiac). The Third Messenger puts in motion the three liberating wheels of Light and creates a luminous column (the milky way), which is to conduct the particles of Light to the Moon. The Moon will pour them into the Sun (lunar phenomena). During the work of putting the celestial machinery into operation, the bodies of the Virgins of Light appear to the Archons, who are both male and female. These, aroused by their concupiscence, let fall upon the earth their semen and abortions, respectively. Vegetation, trees, and fruits are the products of the demoniac semen of the male Archons. The abortions of the female Archons develop, become demons, devour the fruits, copulate, and give birth to the animals.

The Myth of Adam and Eve. The Prince of Darkness and the leaders of the Archons, always under the influence of their concupiscence for the Virgins of Light, try to collect all the light particles seized from their kingdom. The image of the Third Messenger has impressed them and will serve as a model for creating a living couple, male and female. Saklas and Nebroel, the chief pair of Archons, devour the demons filled with Light. They create a pair of dark origin but made to the image of the *Tertius Legatus.* This pair is Adam and Eve, and their first-born, Seth, will be the Father of the Human Race. Procreation, then, is of demoniac origin and has as its purpose the enslavement of the luminous particles. These myths of the temptation of the Archons and the creation of Adam and Eve are the basis for all the accusations of eroticism and immorality cast at the sect.

The Third Messenger has put in operation the liberating machine, salvation, while the struggle between Light and Darkness continues. Adam has already received a message from the Kingdom of Light. The prophets will follow and announce the mysteries of the universe and of redemption. After the three great messengers, Zoroaster, Buddha, and Jesus, will come Mānī, charged with the last message, with the definitive teaching on origins and eschatology, and with the organization of the Church of Light. This world will last only for a time. Some day the five bearers, sons of the Living Spirit, will receive a signal from the Kingdom of Light, and they will let the universe fall. It will be destroyed in an infernal crash and will be consumed by a fire lasting for 1,468 years, after which all the luminous particles will have rejoined the Paradise of Light. This is the final stage in the Manichaean eschatology.

The Manichaean Church

The church Mānī founded has two aspects under which it can be considered, both stemming from the nature of its message.

A Missionary Church. The appeal of Primal Man, the reply to this appeal, the emanation of liberating powers of Light, and the necessity of continuing this liberation in this created world were the principles upon which Mānī founded his church. The need to transmit the message made it a missionary church, the heir of the prophets, especially Zoroaster, Buddha, and Jesus, and the announcer of the Paraclete and of the final seal of revelation, Mānī. Mānī completed the earlier messages before teaching the origins and the end, and he organized his church, which was charged with making the message known. His disciples were to go through the world proclaiming the revealed mysteries and establishing and maintaining everywhere the state of redemption and of liberation.

A Religion of the Word. The call to salvation occupied an important place in the life of the Manichaean. Teaching was given first in the assembly of the community of the brethren, where an exposition of the mysteries of the world and salvation was presented, interspersed with liturgical chants that are filled also with doctrinal content. The *Kephalaia* and euchology of Medīnēt Mādi shed a new light on these assemblies, which were very calm, pious, and mystical. The popular and animated theology and liturgy, inspired perhaps by the method of Bardesanes, must have made a deep impression upon the elect and the auditors during these assemblies, which were the real center of the missionary life of the sect. These assemblies were the whole secret of the expansion of Manichaeism, for the eschatological hope, renewed by each liturgical meeting, rendered members capable of enduring indifference, hostility, and even persecutions.

An Organized Church. It was a fully organized church with two categories of members, the elect (*electi, fideles,* the perfect) and the auditors.

The Elect. These were the liberators of Light. They lived the whole doctrine, traveled, and preached. Three principles of abstinence marked their lives: the *signaculum oris,* watch over the senses, avoidance of blaspheming, and abstinence from meat and wine; the *signaculum manus,* watch over actions, abstention from work and from destruction of plants and animals; *signaculum sinus,* abstinence from all sexual contact. The elect took a ritual meal every day. This meal was necessary for the liberation of the light particles contained in their food. It was taken in an atmosphere of prayers and chants after the auditors had brought the elect fruits and melons gathered by their hands. Some scholars have considered this meal the eucharist of the sect. Fasts were frequent; every Sunday and Monday and during the whole month that preceded the Manichaean Easter, the great annual feast of the throne of the Master, the *Bēma,* the high point of the Manichaean liturgy. This feast, a commemoration of the death, the *staurōsis,* of Mānī, by the magnificence of its liturgical pomp and by the consciousness of the invisible but real presence of the Master upon his throne, placed at the top of five steps, gave unquestionably a new ''paschal stimulus'' to the Manichaean Church. The elect members led a priestly life, with all nature and all the auditors in their service. They awaited death as liberation in the certitude that they were going immediately to join the Paradise of Light.

The Auditors, or Catechumens. They represented a lesser perfection and were much more numerous. One of their functions consisted in participating in the liberation of the Light by procuring for the elect the necessary foods for their daily ritual meal. The moral code for them was less strict. They had to fast one day a week, on Sunday, and to abstain from procreation. Marriage was tolerated, concubinage was permitted, but the procreation of children was to be avoided. This life, unlike that of the elect, was not free from sins. It did not prepare the auditor for immediate entrance into the Kingdom of Light. After his death, he entered into transmigration (Greek, μεταγγισμός; Syriac, *taš pīkā*), a method of purification and means of liberation for the souls of auditors. By passing through a series of revolutions—metempsychosis in the true sense of the word—and by reincarnation in the luminous bodies of fruits, especially melons, and finally in the body of an elect, the souls of auditors were gradually liberated. The rapidity of this liberation was directly related to their usefulness in the service of the Manichaean community. Men who refused to accept this dualistic system were reincarnated in the souls of beasts and ended finally in hell. For them no salvation was possible.

This church also had a hierarchy, although the texts give little information about it. A supreme head, the successor of Mānī, 12 *magistri,* and 72 bishops governed the whole church. Manichaean priests were in charge of the local communities.

A Religion of the Book. Mānī reproached the founders of religion for not having written their doctrine themselves. He wished to avoid this omission in the case of his own church, which was charged with transmitting the last revelation. He himself was its sole author or transmitter. To be such, he invented an alphabet, a Western Aramaic script very close to the Syriac of Edessa, the literary and religious language of the Sassanid Empire and of the eastern provinces of the Roman Empire. He translated his works himself, or had them translated, into the languages of the peoples evangelized. According to the best established tradition, he wrote seven works.

The *Shāpūraqān* was written in Middle Persian for King Shāpūr. Some fragments of this treatise on cosmogony and eschatology have been found at Turfan in Chinese Turkestan. All his other writings were probably composed in Syriac. The *Gospel of Life,* a doctrinal exposition in 22 chapters corresponding to the letters of the Syriac alphabet, was composed probably against the *Diatessaron* of Tatian, which enjoyed a wide dissemination in Babylonia. Some fragments of this work are found in the Turfan texts. The *Treasure of Life,* a treatise on anthropology and psychology, is known through some fragments preserved in the *De fide contra Manichaeos* of Augustine (*Patrologia Latina* 42:1143–44). A book entitled *Pragmateia* has not yet been found, and the same is true of the famous *Book of Mysteries,* which was written especially against the teachings of Bardesanes and seems to have been widely known in the Christian East. The Manichaean mythology is described in the *Book of the Giants,* of which a fair number of fragments were found at Turfan. There is also the precious corpus of the *Letters of Mani.* A collection of these in a Coptic version was discovered at Medīnēt Mādi and deposited in the Berlin Museum, but was carried off by the Soviets at the end of World War II. It seems definitely lost. Al-Bīrūnī (973–1048) read these seven books of Mānī, which in his time were difficult to find.

The discoveries of the 20th century at Turfan and in the Fayum have cast a new light on the literary importance of the disciples of Mānī. The production and the ornamentation of the religious books were very noble activities in the Religion of Light.

Historiography of Manichaeism

The investigation of Manichaeism since the Renaissance can be divided into three main periods. It is only in the 20th century, however, that, owing in part to new discoveries, Manichaeism has become properly understood and evaluated not as a Christian heresy but as a complex gnostic religion.

Manichaeism, a Christian Heresy (16th to 18th Centuries). During the whole medieval period there was a tendency to apply the term Manichaean to every heretic. The various dualistic doctrines, from Mānī to the Cathari and the Albigenses, seemed to be branches of the same tree. Following the publication of Luther's teachings on sin and free will, Catholic opponents spoke of a *Manichaeus redivivus.* This led some Protestant historians to investigate the life and work of the reformer of Babylon in order to clear the Reform of such accusations. Protestant controversy thus gave birth to the study of Manichaeism.

During two centuries apologetic works, historical researches, and Catholic and Protestant polemical books followed and refuted one another. Thus the 17th century became the first important period in the publication of sources and in the knowledge of Manichaeism, and more precisely of its so-called Western sources. To the work of anti-Manichaean writers already known (Augustine, Pope Leo the Great, and Fabius Marius Victorinus) were now added important texts: the *Acta Archelai,* works of Cyril of Jerusalem, Epiphanius of Salamis, Alexander of Lycopolis, Serapion of Tmuis, Titus of Bostra, Didymus of Alexandria, Zacharias of Mytilene, John Damascene, Photius, and Peter of Sicily; and some formulas of abjuration against Manichaeism. This copious documentation, coming from the great Christian adversaries of Mānī, permitted the development of a conception of the prophet's work in the perspective of Christian heresiology. Mānī, regarded as a Christian heretic, was repudiated by the Protestants, but in the eyes of Catholics he remained one of the founders of Luther's thought. From the end of the 17th century, however, investigation turned to other sources, especially Arabic and Syriac, which were independent of the struggle against Manichaeism.

In 1734 Isaac de Beausobre, a Calvinist historian, modified completely the Protestant concept of Manichaeism during the two previous centuries. He did his best to show that the teachings of Mānī were not the absurd collection of doctrines refuted by Western opponents, but constituted indeed, in the Church of Christ, a brilliant attempt at liberation, and that Mānī was a harbinger of the reform of Luther. His severe criticism of the Western authorities, his emphasis on the Oriental sources that were all but unknown, and his study on the use of the Apocrypha by the Manichaeans were all new elements that helped the subsequent research of the 18th century to disengage gradually the religion of Mānī from the simple cadre of Christian heresiology.

Manichaeism, a Great Oriental Religion (19th Century). In 1831 F. C. BAUR took a decisive step. He introduced Manichaean studies into the history of Oriental religions by presenting Mānī as the founder of a new faith. Baur gave full value to the known sources, Western as well as Oriental. Through these he got back to the origins of the dualism of the Babylonian prophet: Oriental forms of paganism, nature religions, and some traces of idolatry purified by contact with Parsiism, but especially the religion of India. According to Baur, Mānī took the essentials of his thought from Buddhism and later added some superficial elements from Christianity, especially his myth of a cosmological Jesus.

The research of Baur and his school was followed by the second important stage in the publication of sources shedding light on Manichaeism. The discovery of the Arab historians, and especially of the two great encyclopedias of the literature and religious ideas of the Orient, brought Manichaean studies into the sphere of Oriental studies. The two Arab authors who dominated this period of research were Sharastānī (A.D. 1086–1152) with his religious encyclopedia, *Kital al-Milal wan-Nih'al,* and the historian an-Nadīm, whose *Fihrist* (A.D. 987) gives a long account of the religion of Mānī based on the prophet's books themselves. These two authors worked on original documents and were free from all polemics. According to them, Marcion and Bardesanes were among the spiritual masters of Mānī. The study of these documents led G. Flügel to propose a new hypothesis: Manichaeism was an Asiatic religion that had its origins in the teaching of Zoroaster and in the Sabaism of the Mughtasilas. Mānī seized upon these religious currents and turned them into Biblical channels.

Toward the end of the 19th century Assyriology furnished new orientations. K. Kessler claimed that the Manichaean synthesis contained a current going back to the ancient Babylonian religion. Mānī had wished to give the Iranian peoples a more perfect teaching than that of the Sassanid priests. He went back, therefore, to the source itself of Zoroaster's thought, the Chaldeo-Babylonian beliefs. His thought developed in a framework that was very close to Zoroastrianism. In his final synthesis of a new universal religion, Mānī adopted the moral teaching of Buddhism and some elements from

Christian vocabulary. To all this, it was necessary to add an indispensable popular element, namely, a cult. The religion of Mithra was at hand for this purpose. Manichaeism presents itself, accordingly, as a gnosis born at Babylon, the cradle of all the Asiatic *gnoseis.* A. HARNACK and W. BOUSSET adopted this hypothesis of Kessler.

The Great Discoveries of the 20th Century. The scientific expeditions of Grünwedel, Huth, A. von Le Coq, Sir Aurel Stein, É. Chavannes, and P. Pelliot, at the beginning of the 20th century, brought from the oasis of Turfan in Chinese Turkestan numerous Manichaean writings that were employed by Oriental communities in the 8th century A.D. The texts, written in Arsacid and Sassanid Pahlevi, in Sogdian, in Uighur, and in Chinese, shed full light on the beliefs and cult of the Manichaeans in Asia, which had spread from the center in the kingdom of the Uighurs (A.D. 762–840). The manuscripts of Turfan furnish examples of the Manichaean form of writing, which was derived from a Palmyrian alphabet.

The essential texts from Central Asia have been published. The most important documents are: (1) the *Khuastuanift* (ed. A. von Le Coq), a formulary of confession giving the list of sins against the ten commandments of the Manichaeans and the ceremonies of their confession; (2) a dogmatic treatise in Chinese found at Tuen-Huang (ed. É. Chavannes and P. Pelliot), which is a kind of collection of extracts taken from the various works of Mānī and intended for the instruction of the community; (3) liturgical texts, among them several collections of hymns. F. C. Burkitt, E. Waldschmidt, and W. Lentz have demonstrated the marked Christian influence on these Asiatic Manichaean texts.

In 1930 Egypt made an important contribution through the discovery (made at Medīnēt Mādi, in the Fayum) of a Manichaean library containing about 3,000 leaves in Coptic and dating from the period of St. Augustine. These texts, written on papyrus and bound into codices, have cast a new light on the ''Religion of the Book'' and on the respect that the sect gave to its sacred texts. The texts were divided between London (Chester Beatty) and Berlin (Carl Schmidt).

These Coptic texts are the most precious sources to date for the knowledge of Manichaeism. The *Kephalaia,* or *capitula,* a collection of the utterances of the Master, are presented under the form of discussions between Mānī and his disciples, and they date probably from the first generation. A collection of homilies on the *Gospel of Life* and an important collection of hymns furnish information on the apostolic life and life of prayer of the Manichaean communities in Egypt. A historical work and a collection of the founder's letters were, unfortunately, in the Berlin group of texts.

The publication of these various texts employed by flourishing Manichaean communities in Asia and Africa, and a comparative study of the patristic and Arabic sources published in the 17th and 18th centuries, have made possible a more exact knowledge of the Religion of Light. The new documents of the 20th century complete and often confirm the data of the earlier sources. They have moved the study of Manichaeism into a new and decisive phase, and from this stage it will help to clarify the history of gnostic movements in the early Christian centuries.

Bibliography: G. BARDY, *Dictionnaire de théologie catholique* 9 (1927) 1841–95. H. J. POLOTSKY, *Paulys Realenzyklopädie der Klassischen Altertumswissenschaft,* ed. G. WISSOWA et al. (Stuttgart 1893–) Suppl. 6 (1935) 240–272. C. H. BEESON, *Die grieschischen Schriftsteller der ersten drei Jahrhunderte* (Leipzig 1905). A. A. MOON, *The De Natura Boni of St. Augustine* (Catholic University of America, Patristic Studies 88; Washington 1955) esp. xiv–xvi, 8–41. F. C. BURKITT, *The Religion of the Manichees* (Cambridge, Eng. 1925). A. V. WILLIAMS JACKSON, *Researches in Manichaeism* (New York 1932). H. C. PUECH, *Le Manichéisme* (Paris 1949). G. WIDENGREN, *Mani und der Manichäismus* (Stuttgart 1961). P. ALFARIC, *Les Écritures manichéennes,* 2 v. (Paris 1918–19). J. RIES, ''Introduction aux études manichéennes,'' *Ephemerides theologicae Lovanienses* 33 (1957) 453–482; 35 (1959) 362–409, with bibliography. C. SPANGENBERG, *Historia Manichaeorum* (Ursel 1578). I. DE BEAUSOBRE, *Histoire de Manichée,* 2 v. (Amsterdam 1734–39). F. C. BAUR, *Das manichäische Religionssystem* (Göttingen 1831; reprint 1928). G. FLÜGEL, *Mani* (Leipzig 1862). K. KESSLER, *Mani* (Berlin 1889). H. J. POLOTSKY and A. BÖHLIG, *Kephalaia* I (Stuttgart 1940). A. BÖHLIG, *Probleme des manichäischen Lehrvortrages* (Munich 1953). T. SÄVE-SÖDERBERGH, *Studies in the Coptic Manichaean Psalmbook* (Uppsala 1949). M. BUSSAGH and L. HAMBIS, ''Manichaean Art,'' *Encyclopedia of World Art* (New York 1959–) 9:433–443, plates 281–287.

[J. RIES]

MANIFESTATION OF CONSCIENCE

Manifestation of Conscience is the revelation of intimate and personal matters made to another in order that the revealer might be guided more efficaciously by his director in the spiritual life. Intimate and personal matters alluded to would include such phenomena as good intentions, secret acts of virtue, special lights and graces, and also sins, faults, imperfections, weaknesses, propensities to evil, and special repugnances and attractions.

History. References to extrasacramental revelation of intimate matters are found as early as A.D. 300 in the *Rules and Precepts* of St. ANTHONY the Great of Egypt, and in the writings of St. BASIL the Great, St. JEROME, and JOHN CASSIAN, all of whom wrote in the late 4th or early 5th centuries.

St. Benedict, the patriarch of western monasticism, makes several references to the manifestation in his Rule.

He incorporates the manifestation of conscience into his monastic legislation as an implicit instrument of spiritual advancement. The significance of his testimony is primarily an extension of the area embraced by the manifestation to include not only imperfections and propensities to evil, but also all tendencies and aspirations to a more perfect observance.

Throughout the first 1,000 years of the Church's history the sole purpose of the manifestation of conscience was the spiritual advancement of the individual. There is no explicit awareness of any social benefits that the manifestation might effect or even occasion.

St. BONAVENTURE (1221–74) compares the provincial and local superiors of religious orders to Aaron and his sons, remarking that they ought to know the internal dispositions of each of their subjects. This intimate knowledge may be utilized by the superiors to apportion the burdens of religious observance according to the varying capacities of their subjects.

It is under the aegis of the Society of Jesus that the manifestation of conscience has come to its full term. For by adopting this now familiar yet still rather generic implement, and by effecting a number of adjustments, St. IGNATIUS (1491–1556) and the first legislators of the Society transformed the manifestation into a rigidly controlled yet rewarding apparatus of the spiritual life.

Within the framework of the legal system of the Society the manifestation of conscience underwent several modifications. These changes were not concerned with the nature or internal structure of the practice. They dealt with certain extrinsic features: the relation of the manifestation to the social order in the community; the obligation and frequency of the manifestation; and the numeric extension of qualified recipients.

Canonical History. The role of canon law in the development of the manifestation has been largely a negative one. Its relation to the subject at hand can be described under two historical divisions of unequal duration.

Throughout the first 18 centuries, the pope had limited his activity to the approbation of particular religious laws prescribing the manifestation. The attitude of the Church may be summarized as abstention from direct legislation on the matter—an extended silence, as it were, interrupted by a single isolated reference. This occurs in the constitution *Cum ad regularem,* issued by Clement VIII, March 19, 1603. Although this document does not use the phrase "manifestation of conscience," it prescribes that a daily opening of the interior movements of the heart and a manifestation of temptations be made by novices to their masters. Practically speaking, therefore, over the first 1,800 years of Church history the manifestation was prescribed by particular religious law and by ascetical writers.

The second historical phase of the manifestation's legal development begins with the mid-19th century. At this time the increasing interest of the Church in the manifestation finds expression successively in the regulation, de-emphasis, and ultimate abrogation of the obligatory or elicited manifestation.

The direction of souls is an exacting art, necessitating great prudence as well as an appreciable knowledge of theology and of human nature. It becomes an especially sensitive matter when the manifestation of conscience is involved, and all the more so when the recipient of confidential information is also a superior in the external forum. It is not difficult to envision misuses, such as violations of liberty of conscience and infringement upon the jurisdiction of the confessor.

By a gradual positive process proper law had, in the course of the centuries, altered the manifestation from an optional ascetical aid to a legally imposed practice. But by a corresponding negative process on the part of the Holy See, from 1850 to 1917, the manifestation reverted to its free and spontaneous character.

A number of particular replies from the Congregation of Bishops and Regulars demand that all references to the obligatory or elicited manifestation be expunged from the constitutions of lay institutes sent to it for approval. The second phase of legal development is represented by the decree *Quemadmodum* of 1890, which, being much broader in purpose, abrogated the obligatory or elicted manifestation in all lay religious communities.

Code of Canon Law. The most comprehensive legislation on the manifestation of conscience is found in canon 630 §5 of the *Code of Canon Law.* This canon proscribes the obligatory or elicited manifestation of conscience in all religious institutes, clerical as well as lay.

The text of the fifth paragraph of canon 630 reads: "With trust members are to approach superiors, to whom they can freely and on their own initiative open their minds. Superiors, however, are forbidden to induce members in any way to make a manifestation of conscience to them." It should be clear that the Church does not intend to interdict the manifestation of conscience as such. The code condemns the manifestation in its solicited and obligatory form, but allows it as an aid to spiritual progress in its free and spontaneous form.

Bibliography: J. CREUSEN, *Religious Men and Women in Church Law* (Milwaukee 1958) 99–104. G. NICHOLAS, *The Spiritual Prefect in Clerical Religious Houses of Study* (Catholic University of American Canon Law Studies 216; Washington 1945). J. F.

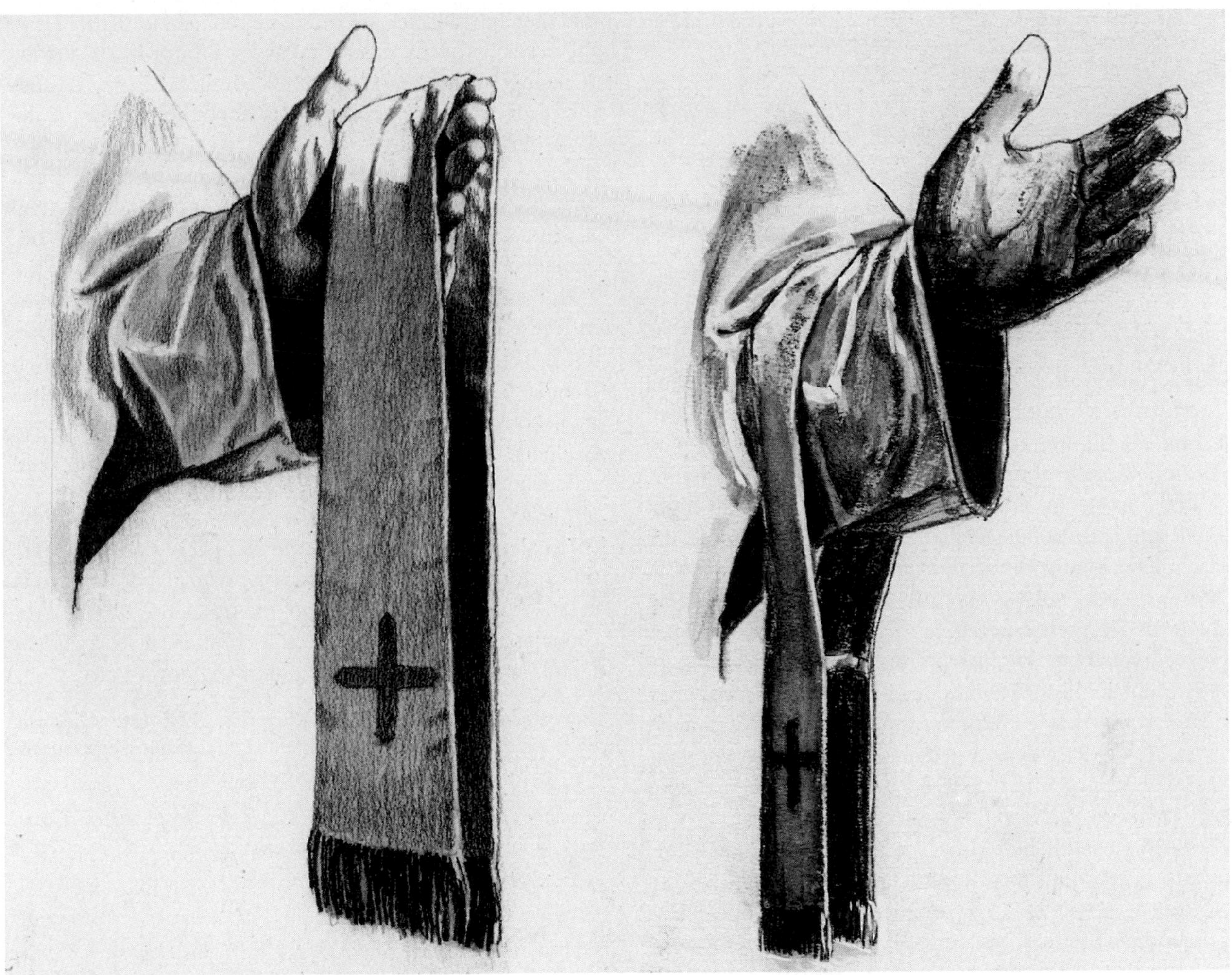

The maniple held in left hand, and worn on left forearm.

LOVER, *The Master of Novices* (Catholic University of America Canon Law Studies 254; Washington 1947). F. N. KORTH, *The Evolution of "Manifestation of Conscience" in Religious Rules, III–XVI Centuries* (Rome 1949). F. HUYSMANS, *La Manifestation de conscience en religion d'après le canon 530* (Louvain 1953). D. DEE, *The Manifestation of Conscience* (Catholic University of America Canon Law Studies 410; Washington 1960).

[D. DEE/EDS.]

MANIPLE

The maniple was originally a cloth used by Roman high society to dry moisture from the hands and face during oppressive summer heat and to wipe the mouth after eating. Servants used it to assure the cleanliness of vessels used at meals. It was carried in the hand or tied to the left arm when not needed. In time it became also a mark of social etiquette. The use of the maniple at meals offers some explanation as to why it is worn by the priest only when he is fulfilling some function directly connected with the Eucharistic meal. It is noteworthy that the celebrant is asked to leave off the maniple on Good Friday when the Communion rite is followed without the usual receiving and offering of gifts. However, monasteries have known the practice in centuries past of having all the monks wear it in choir on great feasts simply to look dressed up for the solemnity. No longer made from absorbent materials, the maniple was cut from richer fabric and had become a mere ornament having only ceremonial significance. In the passage of time, the meaning of the maniple has been lost. By a notice published in *Notitiae* 30 (1967), the use of the maniple at Mass was declared no longer necessary.

Bibliography: H. NORRIS, *Church Vestments* (London 1948). E. A. ROULIN, *Vestments and Vesture*, tr. J. MCCANN (Westminster, MD 1950). J. BRAUN, *Die liturgische Gewandung im Occident und Orient* (Freiburg, 1907). J. MAYO, *A History of Ecclesiastical Dress* (London : B.T. Batsford, 1984) D. HINES, *Dressing for Worship: A Fresh Look at What Christians Wear in Church* (Cambridge 1996).

D. PHILIPPART, ed., *Clothed in Glory: Vesting the Church* (Chicago 1997).

[M. MCCANCE]

MANKIDIYAN, MARIAM THRESIA CHIRAMEL, BL.

Baptized Thresia Mankidiyan (or Mankudian), virgin, mystic, founder of the Congregation of the Sisters of the Holy Family; b. April 26, 1876, Trichur, Puthenchira, Kerala, India; d. June 8, 1926, Kuzhikattusery. When Thresia was 12, her once-wealthy mother (Thanda) died leaving her with a father (Thoma) and elder brother who were alcoholics, along with three other siblings. Even as a child Thresia fasted four times weekly, kept all-night vigils, and, at age ten, consecrated her life to God, the poor, sick, lonely, and orphaned. Beginning in 1909, Thresia experienced many mystical phenomena. She joined the Carmelite tertiaries in 1910. Three years later she received long-awaited permission from her bishop, Apostolic Vicar Mar John Menachery, to enter consecrated community life with three friends, who also dedicated themselves to prayer and penance. They defied convention by venturing into the streets unaccompanied to serve those in need. The Congregation of the Holy Family was canonically established May 14, 1914 with Mariam Thresia as superior and the Rule of the Holy Family Sisters of Bordeaux. In 1915, she founded a girls school in Puthenchira. At the time of her death 11 years later, the congregation had 55 sisters in three convents running four schools, a study home, and an orphanage. By 2000, the congregation had grown to more than 1,500 members serving the poor in Germany, Ghana, India, and Italy. Thresia, considered the forerunner of Mother Teresa of Calcutta, was beatified by John Paul II, April 9, 2000.

Feast: June 6.

Bibliography: K. C. CHACKO, *Mother Mariam Thresia* (Trichur 1992). Mother Mariam Thresia Committee, *Gharhika sabhayute pravācika* (Trichur, Kerala, India 1989).

[K. I. RABENSTEIN]

MANN, HORACE KINDER

Priest, educator, and historian of the medieval papacy; b. London, England, Sept. 27, 1859; d. Edinburgh, Scotland, Aug. 1, 1928. After being educated at St. Cuthbert's College, Ushaw, Durham, England, he was ordained in 1886. For the next year he taught at St. Cuthbert's Grammar School, Newcastle-upon-Tyne, where he became prefect of discipline from 1887 to 1890, and then headmaster, an office he retained until 1917. On the occasion of his sacerdotal silver jubilee in 1911, Pius X bestowed on him the honorary pontifical degree of doctor of divinity. In 1917 he was appointed rector of the Collegia Beda in Rome and received from Benedict XV the rank of domestic prelate. He remained at the Beda until his sudden death while on vacation. Mann devoted his intellectual activity to the medieval papacy and became the outstanding English historian in this field in the 20th century. His major work is the *Lives of the Popes in the (Early) Middle Ages* (18 v. in 19, London 1902–32), treating the popes from Gregory I through Benedict XI; the last four volumes were issued posthumously. Although still valuable, the *Lives* has been largely superseded by later research. Mann wrote also an independent biography of *Nicholas Breakspear (Hadrian IV) A.D. 1154–1159* (London 1914), *Tombs and Portraits of the Popes of the Middle Ages* (London 1929), articles for the *Catholic Encyclopedia,* and numerous essays and reviews. He held memberships in the Accademia d'Arcadia, the Royal Historical Society of Spain, and the R. Società Romana di Storia Patria.

Bibliography: *Tablet* 152 (London 1928) 186. *Who Was Who, 1916–1928* (London 1929) 698. *The Catholic Encyclopedia and Its Makers* (New York 1917) 111–112.

[R. H. SCHMANDT]

MANNA

Manna is food provided for the Israelites in the desert by God in reply to one of their chronic murmurings (Ex 16.4–36; Nm 11.6–9; Dt 8.3). This ''bread from heaven'' appeared first in the second month after the Exodus as fine flakes on the ground. It was ''like coriander seed, but white, and it tasted like wafers made with honey'' (Ex 16.31). Ground into flour, it made palatable loaves, and it helped sustain the people for 40 years.

The manna of the Exodus was certainly providential and may even have been miraculous with reference to the times at which and the quantity in which it was supplied. Basically, however, it is a natural product, widely found in the Near East to this day. It is produced by excretion by two scale insects (*Trabutina mannipara Ehrenberg* and *Najacoccus serpentinus Green*) and is similar to the honeydew of many types of plant lice; it falls to the ground as drops and there hardens into the grains described in the Bible.

That a deeply religious significance was seen in the providential supply of manna is already evident in the accounts in Exodus and Numbers and becomes more apparent in Dt 8.3, in the midrash in Wis 16.20–29, and in the

Moses ordering the Jews to gather manna. (©Bettmann/CORBIS)

New Testament. In 1 Cor 10.1–6 the manna is termed ''spiritual food'' and is referred to Christ, together with water from the rock. St. Paul concludes: ''Now all these things happened to them as a type . . .'' (v. 11); then, in v. 15 he turns his attention to the Eucharist (*see* TYPE AND ANTITYPE). In Jn 6.32, 48 Jesus contrasts the manna with the ''true bread from heaven'' given by His Father. He leads his audience from physical bread (the loaves multiplied for them) to divine teaching, and finally, to the Sacrament of His flesh (6.51–56). Part of the background of this miracle was the rabbinic belief that the manna would reappear in the messianic era.

Bibliography: *Encyclopedic Dictionary of the Bible,* tr. and adap. by L. HARTMAN (New York 1963), from A. VAN DEN BORN, *Bijbels Woordenboek* 1434–36. J. SCHILDENBERGER, *Lexikon für Theologie und Kirche*[2], ed. J. HOFER and K. RAHNER, 10 v. (Freiburg, 1957–65) 6:1360–61. R. MEYER, G. KITTEL, *Theologisches Wörterbuch zum Neuen Testament* (Stuttgart 1935–) 4:466–470. F. S. BODENHEIMER, ''The Manna of Sinai,'' *The Biblical Archaeologist,* 10 (1947) 2–6. A. DE GUGLIELMO, ''What Was the Manna?'' *The Catholic Bible Quarterly* 2 (1940) 112–129.

[M. K. HOPKINS]

MANNA, PAOLO

Founder of the Pontifical Missionary Union of the Clergy, mission author, b. Avellino, Italy, 1872, d. 1952. He was a member of the Missionaries of SS. Peter and Paul who served in Burma between 1895 and 1907. Upon his return to Italy, he published several books over the next years to promote the missionary vocation and to encourage the cooperation of missionary clergy. The latter was achieved when, with the approval of the Congregation for the Propagation of Faith, Manna inaugurated the Missionary Union of the Clergy in 1916. By 1934, eighty-four percent of Italian clergy were members.

At the time Manna wrote *Operarii autem pauci* (*The Workers Are Few*, 1908), most of Catholic mission literature was written in German and Italian. Translations and adaptations of this book and *The Conversion of the Pagan World* (1921) provided English-speaking audiences with a popularized form of mission theology and practice and encouraged missionary vocations for clergy, women religious, and the laity. In the United States, the adaptations of Manna's two books were done by Father Joseph P. McGlinchey, the director of the Boston Archdiocesan Office of the Society for the Propagation of the Faith. McGlinchey was the successor in that office to James A. Walsh, co-founder of the Catholic Society of Foreign Missions (Maryknoll), who had decried the dearth of mission materials in English. Manna's works in Italian and, especially the English translations, alerted Catholics not formally engaged as missionaries, to the centrality of mission in the life of the Church.

Bibliography: P. MANNA and N. MAESTRINI, *Forward with Christ: Thoughts and Reflections on Vocations to the Foreign Missions* (Westminster, MD 1954); J. F. MCGLINCHEY, *Conversion of the Pagan World: A Treatise upon Catholic Foreign Missions.* adapted from P. MANNA (Boston 1921); J. F. MCGLINCHEY, *The Workers Are Few*, translation and adaptation of P. MANNA (Boston 1912); F. GERMANI, *P. Paolo Manna*, vol. 1, *Da Avellino alla Birmania, (1872–1907)* (Rome 1989), vol. 2, *L'Unione Missionaria del Clero e il. Seminario Meridionale per le Missione Estere (1907–1924)* (Rome 1990), vol. 3, *Superiore Generale (1924–34)* (1992), *Paolo Manna maestro di spiritualita missionarie* (Rome 1993).

[A. DRIES]

MANNING, HENRY EDWARD

Cardinal, archbishop of WESTMINSTER; b. Copped Hall, Totteridge, Hertfordshire, July 15, 1808; d. London, Jan. 14, 1892. He was descended from a family of merchant-bankers. His father, William Manning, was a member of Parliament, and married twice. Henry was the youngest son of William's second wife, Mary, daughter of Henry Leroy Hunter of Reading. At 14 the boy entered Harrow Public School and matriculated (1827) at Balliol College, Oxford. There he distinguished himself in the debating society and in studies, taking a first-class degree in classics (1830). In 1832 he was elected to a fellowship at Merton College and was ordained to the Anglican ministry. The following year he was presented to the rectory of Lavington-with-Graffham in Sussex and married Caroline, daughter of the Rev. J. Sargent of Lavington. His wife died, childless, in 1837.

Anglican Career. Manning's original destination was politics. Briefly in 1831 he worked in the colonial office, but attractions of an ecclesiastical career proved irresistible. Soon he established himself as one of the leading Anglican thinkers of his day. Before reaching the age of 33 he became archdeacon of Chichester. His reforming influence was quickly felt. Life in a country parish had removed him from direct contact with the OXFORD MOVEMENT, but he kept in touch with its leading protagonists. At the same time he kept developing a keen perception of contemporary social evils. In his pastoral "charges" he attacked the abuses of wealth, the poverty of the agricultural poor, the lack of educational provision for the new middle classes, the practice of reserved family pews in the Anglican Church. He warred relentlessly against RATIONALISM. Unceasingly he urged the clergy to personal sanctification. By 1848 a note of disillusionment had crept into the charge he delivered in defense of his creed upon Renn Hampden's appointment to the See of Hereford. This uneasiness spread until in 1851, as a direct result of the Gorham Judgment by the judicial committee of the privy council, he became a Catholic. The privy council had ordered the bishop of Exeter to appoint the Calvinist theologian George Gorham to the living of Brampford Speke despite the bishop's grave misgivings concerning Gorham's views on baptismal regeneration. This decision was palpable proof to Manning of the supremacy of the temporal over the spiritual in the Church of England.

Catholic Years. Manning was received into the Church (April 6, 1851) at the Jesuit Church, Farm Street, London. Within ten weeks Cardinal WISEMAN ordained him to the priesthood. In the autumn he proceeded to Rome, where he spent three years at the Accademia dei Nobili Ecclesiastici, which he entered at the wish of Pius IX.

Wiseman in 1856 appointed Manning diocesan inspector of schools. In this, his first important post after conversion, he began the long, successful career in education that is perhaps his most permanent claim to fame. This career enabled him to organize a network of elementary schools throughout the Archdiocese of Westminster and to make the first provision for university education for Catholics, besides special training courses, chiefly in science, for Catholics of the middle class. Honors and work went hand in hand. By 1854 Manning had received the degree of D.D. from the Pope and had succeeded Dr. R. Whitty as provost of the Metropolitan Chapter. At the instigation of Wiseman, he established (1851) in England the OBLATES OF ST. CHARLES. At the new church of St. Mary of the Angels, Bayswater, Manning was the first superior. Many "old Catholic" families manifested great jealousy of his rapid advancement. They also resented his endeavors to arouse Catholics from their long torpor. Despite these attacks, Manning always regarded his eight years as superior of the infant community as the happiest of his life. In1860 Pius IX made him a prothonotary apostolic and domestic prelate in recognition of his staunch defense of the papal temporal power, at that time seriously threatened.

One of Manning's heaviest crosses was imposed by the titular archbishop of Trebizond, Dr. Errington, whose attacks on the Oblates flowed from a desire to remove from the diocesan seminary those professors who had entered the new community. Manning defended his group with spirit at Rome. Complicating the dispute was the poor relationship between Wiseman and Errington, his coadjutor, who had led the Metropolitan Chapter in open revolt against the archbishop. Manning, as provost and adherent of Wiseman, necessarily became involved. The incident caused much unhappiness and led eventually to Pius IX's removal of Errington from the coadjutorship.

Archbishop of Westminster. Two months after the See of Westminster fell vacant through the death of Wiseman (February 1865), Pius IX appointed Manning his successor. The *London Times* greeted the news with contempt; but the Pope's choice proved admirable, for Manning became one of the outstanding occupants of the see, which he occupied for 27 years. His constant effort was to make the Church more social-conscious and to bring English Catholics into the full stream of national life. He made friends with all the public figures of his day, men as diverse as William BOOTH, John Burns, GLADSTONE, Archbishop CROKE, RUSKIN, W. G. WARD, and J. E. C. Bodley.

Social Work. Manning always claimed that to work for the good of the soul it was necessary also to work for amelioration of social ills. Many lived vicious lives, he held, because of evil social conditions. He considered education one of the best remedies. Much of his energy was devoted to promoting total abstinence, better education, improved labor relations, and social welfare in Ireland. His intervention in 1889 ended the Great Dock Strike. He rejoiced that he lived to welcome Leo XIII's social encyclicals *IMMORTALE DEI* and *RERUM NOVARUM.*

Relations with Newman. The great aim of Manning's life was his determination to ally the new scientific liberalism to the Church and thus to Christianize it. This brought him into conflict with NEWMAN, a conflict never fully resolved. Newman's refusal to have anything to do with London University or with the Metaphysical Society, his distrust of a scientific education, and his sympathy with the old privileged Catholic families alienated Manning. The lack of sympathy between the two men cannot simply be explained as a clash of personalities. It owed more to the deep and fundamental philosophical conflict that divided them.

Religious Orders. Manning's desire to enhance the status of the pastoral clergy, many of whom were of Irish extraction, led him into conflict with the religious orders and not least with the JESUITS, whom he described as "a mysterious permission of God for the chastisement of England." Yet the papal document *Romanos Pontifices* (1881), which regularized relations between the English bishops and religious, was largely due to Manning's influence.

Henry Edward Cardinal Manning. (Hulton-Deutsch Collection/ CORBIS)

Vatican Council I. Manning was one of the leading figures in VATICAN COUNCIL I. His activities in promoting the definition of papal primacy and infallibility have been criticized severely. His motivation was not personal ambition, but a conviction that a principle of authority was the only satisfactory antidote to the excesses of Continental nationalism, the attacks of French anticlericals, and the widespread decline in moral standards. He fought for his "principle of authority" with characteristic thoroughness, alienating many by his firmness. Later he defended the conciliar decisions against the attack by Gladstone.

In 1875 he was raised to the cardinalate. At the conclave in 1878 he supported from the start Cardinal Pecci, who emerged as Leo XIII.

Administrator, Preacher, Writer. Manning's administrative talents were of a very high order. As a society preacher he was always in demand. His writings were voluminous and sufficiently popular to be translated into several languages during his lifetime. *The Eternal Priesthood,* dealing with the rights and duties of the pastoral clergy, is still widely read.

Character. Manning has emerged from the pages of Lytton Strachey as a cold, ruthless schemer and an austere ascetic. His physical appearance was gaunt and emaciated, but the exterior was deceptive. Ruskin testified to his warmth of heart and to his qualities as a host in glowing terms.

Bibliography: J. E. C. BODLEY, *Cardinal Manning and other Essays* (London 1912). J. FITZSIMONS, ed., *Manning, Anglican and Catholic* (London 1951). A. W. HUTTON, *Cardinal Manning* (London 1892) contains complete list of Manning's publications. S. LESLIE, *Henry Edward Manning: His Life and Labours* (London 1921). V. A. MCCLELLAND, *Cardinal Manning: His Public Life and Influence, 1865–1892* (New York 1962). E. S. PURCELL, *Life of Cardinal Manning, Archbishop of Westminster,* 2 v. (4th ed. London 1896).

[V. A. MCCLELLAND]

MANNING, TIMOTHY

Cardinal, archbishop of Los Angeles; b. Nov. 14, 1909, Ballingeary, County Cork, Ireland; d. June 23, 1989, Los Angeles, California. One of four children of Cornelius and Margaret (Cronin) Manning. He studied at the local National School and under the Christian Brothers at nearby Cork. His preparation for the priesthood began in 1923 at Mungret College, a secondary school staffed by the Society of Jesus for the foreign missions. Attracted to California by an appeal on behalf of the Diocese of Los Angeles–San Diego, Manning left Ireland in October of 1928 for Menlo Park, where he joined the student body of Saint Patrick's Seminary. He was ordained to the priesthood by Bishop John J. Cantwell on June 16, 1934, in Saint Vibiana's Cathedral. The following year, Fr. Manning was sent to Rome for post-graduate studies at the Pontifical Gregorian University, where he received a doctorate in canon law in 1938. Upon his return to southern California, Manning was named secretary to Archbishop Cantwell, a post he occupied for eight years. On Aug. 17, 1946, he was appointed auxiliary of Los Angeles, with the titular see of Lesvi. With the appointment of Archbishop J. Francis A. McIntyre to Los Angeles in 1948, Manning was named chancellor, and on Nov. 29, 1955 he became vicar general for the archdiocese.

Upon realignment of ecclesial boundaries in central California, Bishop Manning was named to the newly erected Diocese of Fresno, Oct. 24, 1967. In 18 brief but intensely fruitful months, he created a diocesan housing commission, established four new parishes and five missions, approved the formation of a priest's senate, authorized a task force to marshal resources for inner city and minority groups, shared the bitter anguish of the Delano labor dispute, and visited each of the 80 parishes scattered through the 35,239 square mile jurisdiction. He was recalled to the scene of his earlier priestly labors on May 26, 1969, as coadjutor to Cardinal McIntyre, whom he succeeded on Jan. 21, 1970. He received the gallium, symbolic of the metropolitan office, on June 17, 1970. Paul VI named him a cardinal in 1973.

In addition to pursuing administrative and expansionary policies, Archbishop Manning energetically supported a host of ecumenical involvements and warmly endorsed the Cursillo movement. He personally chaired the commission for liturgy, established a spirituality house and erected an archival center. He made a solemn pilgrimage to Mexico City's National Shrine of Our Lady of Guadalupe where it all began for California, where he thanked the Hispanic people for their role in bedrocking the faith along the Pacific Slope. In his concern for and identification with the archdiocesan founded and sponsored Lay Mission Helpers, Manning visited missionaries in South Africa, Rhodesia, Ghana, Kenya, Malawi, and Uganda. Though the Catholics of Orange County were given their own diocese in 1976, Los Angeles continued to expand and, by 1984, was acknowledged as the largest ecclesial jurisdiction in the United States. In 1985, with the acceptance of his retirement by Pope John Paul II, Cardinal Manning turned the reins of leadership over to his successor, Archbishop Roger M. Mahony.

A popular speaker and writer, Bishop Manning published a chapter of his doctoral thesis dealing with *Clerical Education in Major Seminaries,* a 50-page treatise on *The Grey Ox* (a biography of Fray Junipero Serra) and the entry for the ''Archdiocese of Los Angeles'' in the *New Catholic Encyclopedia.* A number of his sermons and addresses appeared in various ecclesiastical journals over the years; his collected homilies, addresses, and talks appeared in two volumes, *Days of Change, Years of Challenge* and *Times of Tension, Moments of Grace.* In 1990, Manning's invocations, blessings, and dedications were published under the title *Hours of Consecration, Minutes of Prayer.*

Manning remained active in his retirement years. In addition to working a day each week in the archdiocesan archives and spending another visiting infirm priests and religious, he traveled widely and gave numerous retreats throughout the West. He died on June 23, 1989, of a cerebrovascular accident due to marantic endocarditis, and was buried at Calvary Cemetery in East Los Angeles.

Bibliography: F. J. WEBER, comp., *Days of Charge, Years of Challenge: The Homilies, Addresses and Talks of Timothy Cardinal Manning* (Los Angeles 1987); *Times of Tension, Moments of*

Grace: The Homilies, Addresses and Talks of Timothy Cardinal Manning (Los Angeles 1990); *Hours of Consecration, Minutes of Prayer: The Invocations, Blessings and Dedications of Timothy Cardinal Manning* (Los Angeles 1990); *Magnificat: The Life and Times of Timothy Cardinal Manning* (Mission Hills 1999).

[F. J. WEBER]

MANNIX, DANIEL

Archbishop; b. Charleville, County Cork, Ireland, March 4, 1864; d. Melbourne, Australia, Nov. 6, 1963. After studies at St. Patrick's College, Maynooth, he was ordained (1890). He was appointed junior professor of philosophy there (1891), professor of theology (1894), and president of the college (1903). During his term as president, until 1912, Maynooth acquired the status of a university college, a constituent of the newly created National University of Ireland, in whose senate Mannix sat as a member. Mannix became coadjutor archbishop of Melbourne in 1912 and archbishop in 1917. During World War I he was a controversial figure as Australia's spokesman for Irish independence and a leader of the successful opposition to conscription of Australians for overseas military service. At the height of the troubles in Ireland Mannix went to Rome (1920) for his *ad limina* visit by way of the U.S., where he was greeted by large crowds in cities across the country. He sailed from New York amid scenes of extraordinary enthusiasm, and proposed to visit Ireland next, but two British destroyers intercepted his vessel off the Irish coast. The archbishop was removed, landed at Penzance, England, and forbidden to speak at the main centers of Irish population in England. In Australia Mannix gained a reputation as a national ecclesiastical leader, far-sighted, zealous, creative, and inspiring. During his 46 years as archbishop he established 108 parishes, more than 150 grade schools, 17 high schools, and 14 specialized schools for technical, commercial and domestic arts training. He founded Newman College for men and St. Mary's Hall for women at the University of Melbourne as well as the provincial seminary of Corpus Christi College. He also promoted Catholic Action, the Catholic press, the liturgical movement, and the Catholic social movement. He is buried in St. Patrick's Cathedral, Melbourne which he saw completed in 1939.

Bibliography: F. MURPHY, *Daniel Mannix, Archbishop of Melbourne* (Melbourne 1948). R. SPEAIGHT, "Some Recollections of a Great Pastor," *Tablet* 217 (Nov. 16, 1963) 1233.

[J. G. MURTAGH]

Daniel J. Archbishop Mannix.

MANOGUE, PATRICK

Missionary, first bishop of Sacramento, Calif.; b. Desart, Kilkenny, Ireland, March 15, 1831; d. Sacramento, Feb. 27, 1895. One of seven orphaned children, all of whom became noted clergymen, he received his early education at Callan, Ireland. His eldest brother, Michael, preceded him to America in an effort to provide for the family. Manogue himself arrived in the U.S. in 1848. After living in Connecticut for two years, he left for Chicago, Ill., where he spent three years studying for the priesthood at the College of St. Mary of the Lake. By this time the entire family had settled in Connecticut and were in great need of money. Manogue felt that he could help them and further his own plans for the priesthood by going to California and the gold mines. There he worked for three years as a common laborer before saving enough money to go to Paris to continue his theological studies at the Seminary of Saint-Sulpice. After being ordained there by Cardinal François Morlot on Christmas Day 1861, Manogue returned from Europe (1862) to the Sierra Nevadas. Eugene O'Connell, Bishop of Grass Valley, requested Manogue to take the whole of northern Nevada for his parish. After touring his new parish he settled in Virginia City, where he lived with one of the old Irish families; he said Mass and conducted other services in a log cabin. By the middle of 1863 Manogue had collected

Patrick Manogue.

$12,000 and had erected a new church. He converted many native peoples, who could always be distinguished by their Irish names, and made long trips into the wilderness, sleeping on the floor of log cabins. He once traveled more than 150 miles to hear the confession of a condemned man, for whom he subsequently gained a pardon. His favorite method of teaching religion to wandering bands of native peoples was to gather them into the church and explain the significance of such things as the altar and tabernacle.

After 20 years of such ministry, Manogue was named (1870) vicar-general of the Diocese of Grass Valley. On Jan. 16, 1881, he was consecrated titular bishop of Ceramos and coadjutor of Grass Valley by Abp. Joseph Alemany in St. Mary's Cathedral, San Francisco, Calif. He succeeded Bishop O'Connell on March 17, 1884. That same year Leo XIII changed the diocesan boundaries to include ten additional counties and moved the episcopal see to Sacramento. Manogue's first work as bishop was to build the Cathedral of the Blessed Sacrament, designed in Italian Renaissance style by the architect Brian J. Clinch. With a seating capacity of 1,600, the cathedral was built in memory of those who had sustained the faith during the early years of the Church in California. Before his death the bishop became very active in public affairs, exerting considerable influence among the miners and mine owners.

Bibliography: H. L. WALSH, *Hallowed Were the Gold Dust Trails: The Story of the Pioneer Priests of Northern California* (Santa Clara 1946).

[J. L. MORRISON]

MANRÍQUEZ Y ZÁRATE, JOSÉ DE JESÚS

Mexican bishop and militant defender of the Church; b. León, Guanajuato, Nov. 7, 1884; d. Mexico City, June 28, 1951. He studied at the seminary of León and the South American College in Rome. Ordained on Oct. 28, 1907, he obtained his doctorate in theology, Canon Law, and philosophy, and returned to Mexico on June 19, 1909. He was vicar of the sacristy and prefect of the seminary of León (1909–11). As pastor of Guanajuato (1912–22), he founded nine parochial schools, a secondary school for boys and one for girls, the school of higher studies for men, the Ketteler Workers' Circle, and the League for Catholic Social Action (which supplied clothing for the poor, loan and saving facilities, medical service, and libraries). He was nominated first bishop of Huejutla on Dec. 11, 1922. After being consecrated on Feb. 4, 1923, he organized his diocese, evangelized 60,000 Indians, and multiplied schools and Catholic social works, showing intransigence toward the Revolution. A fearless defender of the Church, he challenged the actions of President Calles (March 10, 1926), who imprisoned him for one year and exiled him to the United States (April 24, 1927). There he was an apologist for Mexican Catholic armed defense and put an end to the revolutionary ''Arreglos'' (June 21, 1929), which, suppressing all Catholic counterrevolutionary resistance, consolidated the power of the revolutionary group. Bishop Manríquez y Zárate called them a ''shameful modus vivendi.'' This abrogation gave life to the crusade (1934), which was stimulated by the prelate, whom José Vasconcelos called ''the standard-bearer'' of the persecuted faith, *de facto* leader of the militant Church. Manríquez y Zárate had to resign his bishopric on July 6, 1939. Gravely ill, he was permitted to return to Mexico, March 8, 1944, after 17 years in exile. He regained his health and preached all over the country (1944–49). On Nov. 7, 1949, he was named vicar-general of the archbishopric of Mexico City, representing it in Rome (1950) at the declaration of the dogma of the Assumption. He made a pilgrimage to the Holy Land on his way back to Mexico City. When he died, thousands of Catholics venerated his body and attended the burial, at which they sang the hymn to Christ the King and waved the flag of the National League for

Defense of Liberty. In 1963 his remains were transferred to the national monument to Christ the King. He left 23 pastoral letters; the books *En la hora de suprema angustia, Jesucristo a través de las edades, Luchando contra la bestia,* and *El socialismo;* and a great many sermons, addresses, statements, articles, prefaces, and personal letters. He preached a strong, bold Catholicism as the only way of religious survival and insisted that it should be combined with a love of the traditions of Mexico.

[A. BARQUIN Y RUÍZ]

MANSI, GIOVANNI DOMENICO

Catholic theologian; b. Lucca, Italy, Feb. 16, 1692; d. Lucca, Sept. 27, 1769. With his entry in 1710 into the MARIAN FATHERS, Mansi began his career as a theologian. He taught moral theology for several years in Naples; then Abp. Fabio Colloredo recalled him to Lucca, where Mansi founded an academy for Church history and liturgy. In 1765 he was named archbishop of Lucca by CLEMENT XIII. The only one of Mansi's independent works of note is his *Tractatus de casibus et excommunicationibus episcopis reservatis* (Lucca 1724). Mansi's real importance lies in his work as an editor, publishing about 90 volumes during his lifetime. His famous collection of the acts of the councils down to 1440 was based substantially on the older collections of N. Coletti, Philippe LABBE, and G. Cossart. The older editions, especially the 12-volume *Acta Conciliorum* of Jean HARDOUIN (down to 1714), are better than Mansi's work; but despite its editorial shortcomings, the *Amplissima collectio,* which Mansi himself brought only up to volume 14, is the most useful source for conciliar history because of its exhaustiveness. The most important of the other authors brought out in new editions and commented on by Mansi are C. BARONIUS (with O. Raynald's continuation and A. Pagi's critique), PIUS II, and É. BALUZE. Mansi also translated into Latin A. CALMET's exegetical writings.

Bibliography: Works. *Sacrorum conciliorum nova et amplissima collectio,* 31 v. (Florence-Venice 1759–98); repr. and continued by L. PETIT and J. B. MARTIN, 53 v. in 60 (Paris 1901–27; repr. Graz 1960–61); microcard ed. from the Microcard Foundation (Washington 1961). Literature. H. QUENTIN, *Jean-Dominique Mansi et les grandes collections conciliaires* (Paris 1900). G. FRANCESCHINI, *Vita* in v. 19 of the *Amplissima collectio.* D. PACCHIUS, *Vita* in v.1 of J. A. FABRICIUS, *Bibliotheca latina,* 6 v. in 3 (Florence 1858–59). R. BÄUMER, *Lexikon für Theologie und Kirche* 2 6:1365. C. TESTORE, *Enciclopedia cattolica* 7:1979.

[H. RUMPLER]

MANTELLATE SISTERS

Also called Servants of Mary (OSM), they were founded in 1861 by Sisters M. Filomena Rossi and M. Giovanni Ferrari in Treppio, Italy. They chose as their model St. Juliana FALCONIERI, the traditional foundress of the several communities of Servite Sisters (*see* SERVANTS OF MARY). The motherhouse of the congregation, a pontifical institute, was transferred to Pistoia and later to Rome. The Mantellate Sisters are engaged in kindergartens, elementary and high schools, colleges, hospitals, orphanages, homes for the aged and for working girls, and catechetical and social work. In 1913 the first house in the U.S. was established in Chicago, Ill., but the American motherhouse and novitiate are in Blue Island, Ill. The original foundation is known as the Mantellate Sisters of Blue Island (Official Catholic Directory #3570), with its headquarters in Blue Island, Ill. There is a separate branch, the Mantellate Sisters of Plainfield (Official Catholic Directory #3572), which was established in 1977. It has its headquarters in Plainfield, Ill.

[M. F. DE MATO/EDS.]

MANTRA

A sacred formula believed to have a magic power. The term was used originally of the verses of the VEDAS, the sacred books of the Hindus, chanted at the time of sacrifice. However, certain verses were believed to have a special power, of which the most famous is the *Gāyatrī*, the invocation of the Sun-God, used on all the most solemn occasions. The most sacred word of all is the syllable *Om*, which is held to contain in itself all sounds and to symbolize the universe, so that by its repetition it is possible to realize one's identity with the Absolute. The theory of the *mantra*, developed in later times, is that the sacred word or sound makes present what it signifies. Thus, by repetition of a *mantra* under proper conditions it is possible to obtain all power. A *mantra* can absolve from sin, avert danger, secure success, and confer sanctity. In certain *mantras*, it is believed, all wisdom is contained.

See Also: HINDUISM.

[B. GRIFFITHS]

MANUEL II PALAEOLOGUS, BYZANTINE EMPEROR

Theologian; b. Constantinople, June 27, 1350; d. Constantinople, July 21, 1425. The second son of Emperor John V, he was named successively despot (*c.* 1355) and governor of Thessalonica in 1369. The following year he sailed to Venice to help his father in his financial difficulties. After the rebellion of his older brother, Andronicus IV, Manuel was given the title of emperor, Sept. 25, 1373. But from 1376 to 1379 he was imprisoned by Andronicus, who had usurped the throne. His escape in 1379 began a civil war that ended with a compromise in May 1381, by which Andronicus was again named heir to John V.

In the fall of 1382 Manuel sailed secretly to Thessalonica where he ruled as an all-but-independent emperor. After a four-year siege by the Turks (1383–87) the city surrendered and Manuel was forced into exile to Lemnos; but as Andronicus had died in 1386, Manuel was again recognized as heir to the throne. In 1390 he prevented John VII, Andronicus's son, from assuming control of the capital; but he was compelled to lead a Byzantine force in the service of the Ottoman Emir Bajezid in Asia Minor. On the death of John V on Feb. 16, 1391, Manuel became sole emperor. At first he followed a conciliatory policy, but *c.* 1394, events made him take a strong anti-Turkish position.

In hope of obtaining Western aid, he visited northern Italy, Paris, and London between December 1399 and June 1403. Although received with great honor, he returned with little more than promises. The defeat of the Turks at Ankara by Tamerlane in 1402 provided a respite, and Manuel used the time to strengthen Byzantine military positions, particularly in the Peloponnesus. In 1421 he suffered a stroke and retired from active government.

Along with his diplomatic and military activities, Manuel was genuinely interested in theology and literature and composed an impressive array of theological tracts including an Apology for Christianity in the form of 26 dialogues with an Islamic disputant (written 1392–96, probably while on a military campaign near Ankara). The first series controverted Islamic theology, and the second justified Christian faith and moral teaching. Manuel also wrote 156 chapters against the Syllogism of a Latin monk of Saint-Denis, Paris, and a dissertation on the Palamite Teaching addressed to Alexius Iagupes. He strongly encouraged the work of the Byzantine humanists, who played an important role in the beginnings of the Italian RENAISSANCE.

Bibliography: G. T. DENNIS, *The Reign of Manuel II Palaeologus in Thessalonica, 1382–1387* (*Orientalia Christiana Analecta* 159; 1960). G. OSTROGORSKY, *History of the Byzantine State* (New Brunswick, NJ 1957) 481–498. J. BARKER, *Manuel II Palaeologus (1391–1425)* (New Brunswick, N.J. 1965). H. G. BECK, *Kirche und theologische Literatur im byzantinische Reich* (Munich 1959) 747–749.

[G. T. DENNIS]

MANUEL II, PATRIARCH OF CONSTANTINOPLE

Reigned 1244–1254; d. 1254. Because of the Latin occupation of Constantinople (1204–61), Manuel resided at the temporary Byzantine capital in Nicaea. He worked in close collaboration with Emperor JOHN III DUCAS VATATZES, particularly in negotiations concerning possible union with the Roman Church. In 1247–48 he wrote to the Armenian King and the Catholicos regarding their relations with the Byzantine Church, and in July 1250 he composed a series of responses to canonical questions. About the same time he sent envoys to Pope INNOCENT IV to discuss ecclesiastical union in the summer of 1253, and renewed these negotiations. In 1253–54 he received solemn assurance, under pain of censure, from the regent MICHAEL VIII PALAEOLOGUS, that he would not intrigue against the Emperor of Nicaea, Theodore II Lascaris (1254–58); and early in 1254 he addressed a letter to the emperor instructing him on his duties. Manuel died in office that year, before November 3.

Bibliography: V. GRUMEL, *Les Regestes des actes du patriarchat de Constantinople* v.1.4. W. NORDEN, *Das Papsttum und Byzanz* (Berlin 1903) 368–378, 756–759, letter to Innocent IV.

[G. T. DENNIS]

MANUEL CALECAS

Byzantine theologian and rhetorician, opponent of HESYCHASM, and advocate of union with the West; b. Constantinople; d. Lesbos, 1410. There is evidence of his relationship to John Calecas, Patriarch of Constantinople (1334–47). What little is known of his life is gathered mainly from his letters. While still a layman, he conducted a school that did not flourish, partly because of his extreme gentleness. About 1390 he came under the influence of Demetrius CYDONES, who introduced him to Aristotelian philosophy. Later Calecas taught himself Latin in order to read Thomas Aquinas. Forced to leave Constantinople because of his opposition to Hesychasm, he traveled through Italy and the Orient, entering the DOMINICANS at Lesbos toward the end of his life. Latin SCHOLASTICISM (medieval) is very evident in his works, which include: *On Faith and the Principles of the Catholic Faith* (*Patrologia Graeca* 152:429–661), a systematic explanation of theology in nine books written at the request of friends, and containing the pseudo-Augustinian *Sermo de purgatorio* and sermons concerning the Holy Eucharist attributed to Aquinas; treatises *On the Substance and Operation of God* (PG 152:283–428), against Gregory PALAMAS; *Against the Errors of the Greeks* (PG 152:11–258); *Against Joseph BRYENNIOS* [G. Mercati,

Notizie . . . ed altri appunti (Vatican 1930) 454–473]; *Concerning the Procession of the Holy Spirit* (PG 144:864–958), formerly attributed to Cydones; and also Greek translations of Boethius's *De Trinitate,* Anselm of Canterbury's *Cur Deus homo,* a Christmas Mass of the Ambrosian rite, and a Mass of the Holy Spirit from the Roman Missal.

Bibliography: *Correspondance,* ed. R. J. LOENERTZ (*Studi et Testi* 152; 1950). R. J. LOENERTZ, ''Manuel Calécas: Sa vie et ses oeuvres,'' *Archivum Fratrum Praedicatorum* 17 (1947) 195–207. J. QUÉTIF and J. ÉCHARD, *Scriptores Ordinis Praedicatorum* 1.2: 718–720. K. KRUMBACHER *Geschichte der byzantinischen Literatur* 110–111. H. G. BECK, *Kirche und theologische Literatur im byzantinischen Reich* 740–741.

[M. C. HILFERTY]

MANUSCRIPT ILLUMINATION

The illustration of manuscript pages, in whole or in part, by miniature painting and drawing was a major technique of medieval Christian art. The greater proportion of the painting that survives from the Middle Ages is in the form of manuscript illumination, which frequently provides the only evidence of the style of painting of a particular place or time.

Charles II the Bald, illumination from miniature in psalter, c. 842–869.

EASTERN

Byzantine manuscript texts of the Bible were as richly illuminated as Byzantine church interiors that were decorated with painting and mosaics. From the 6th to the 10th century, artists adapted the techniques of Hellenistic artists who illustrated the Greek classics. The Gospel Book of Rabbula contains one of the first representations of the Crucifixion. Outstanding works of Byzantine manuscript illumination are the Vienna Genesis, the Paris Psalter, the Joshua Roll in the Vatican Library, and the sermons of St. Gregory of Nazianzus (Bibliothèque Nationale, Paris). The 46 miniatures of the last reflect the practices of contemporary fresco painters. In later Byzantine manuscripts the pictorial background of the Hellenistic manuscripts was replaced by gold. The 430 miniatures in the Menologium of Basil II were the work of eight painters. Many of them show resemblances to the larger icons. In the 11th and 12th centuries, miniature painting, after having earlier assumed an independent character, began to reflect a strong classicizing tendency, as in the sermons of St. John Chrysostom (Bibliothèque Nationale, Paris).

WESTERN

In western Europe the earliest examples of manuscript illumination are among the most brilliant and original. Three masterpieces of Anglo-Irish art of the 7th and 8th centuries are the Books of DURROW and KELLS (Trinity College, Dublin) and the *LINDISFARNE GOSPELS* (British Museum, London). The *Book of Durrow* was decorated *c.* 675; its ornamentation bears resemblance to Irish and Saxon work in metal of the mid-7th century. Its intricate interlace patterns, curvilinear designs, and animal ornament are characteristic of the books produced in the British monastic establishments of the period. The volume of the *Lindisfarne Gospels*, dating from the closing years of the 7th century, survives complete, in 258 folios. The beautiful decoration of the text is the work of the artist Eadfrith, the first known by name in the history of the British Isles. The *Book of Kells* is a vellum Gospel Book like the others. An authentic masterpiece of European art, it was illuminated in the last quarter of the 9th century. The style is derived from the *Book of Durrow* and the *Lindisfarne Gospels*, though a greater sophistication is demonstrated than in either of them. The pages are covered with fantastic ornament, intricately drawn and colored. A remarkable series of ornamented initials, all different, runs through the text. The decoration of the book was the collaborative work of not less than four artists. Though their virtuoso work varies in style, the color is uniformly rich.

Guillaume de Machaut (visited by angels), manuscript illumination. (©Bettmann/CORBIS)

Manuscripts are among the principal art works of the Carolingian period. The *Gospels of Godescalc*, done at Charlemagne's capital of Aachen (781–783; Bibliothèque Nationale, Paris), inaugurated the style perfected at Trèves under the Abbess Ada; the principal manuscript of the so-called Ada group is the *Gospels of Saint-Médard-de-Soissons* (Bibliothèque Nationale), which shows Eastern, particularly Syrian, influence. The Vivian Bible of the mid-9th century is a product of the school of Tours, whose manuscripts are notable for their script and narrative scenes. The *Utrecht Psalter* (University Library, Utrecht), written at Hautvillers near Reims about 832, is the most creative of all 9th-century manuscripts. The illustration consists of line drawings of extraordinary liveliness. No color is used, and the pictorial narrative has a cumulative epic quality. Also noteworthy are the *Sacramentary of Drogo* (855) in Paris and the *Codex Aureus* from Regensburg (870), now in Munich. Under the influence of Carolingian miniatures the school of Winchester in England produced drawings in the vivacious manner of the school of Reims but with more body to the total design of the page and with an exciting use of color and lush scrollwork in the frames around the picture.

The center of manuscript production during the Ottonian period in Germany was the island of Reichenau in Lake Constance, on the imperial route to Rome. Illuminated books from its scriptorium, executed in a new regal style, were sent to important towns of the empire such as Trier, Fulda, Bamberg, Regensburg, and Echternach. The outstanding surviving works are the *Codex Egberti* (980; Trier) and the *Evangeliary of Otto III* (Staatsbibliothek, Munich), the most lavishly decorated of the Reichenau manuscripts. The *Sacramentary of Henry II* (*c.* 1010; Staatsbibliothek) shows, like the others, a richness of color and use of gold suggestive of Byzantine influence. The *Codex Aureus* (*c.* 990; Landesbibliothek, Gotha) and the *Gospels of Speyer* (Escorial, Madrid) were commissioned at Echternach by emperors. The Munich Evangelistary illuminated in the early 11th century at Regensburg is one of the most complex manuscripts surviving from the Ottonian period.

The expansion of monasticism in the Romanesque period afforded additional opportunity for the copying of manuscripts and their adornment. Manuscript copies of the *Commentary of the Apocalypse* written by the Spanish monk Beatus of Liébana (*c.* 776) are noteworthy for their remarkable coloring. The manuscripts were copied for three centuries after the original composition of the text and had a wide influence on the work of schools of illumination throughout Europe. The earliest of the 24 manuscripts that survive dates from 926 (Pierpont Morgan Library, New York City). The illustrations are marked by a sure grasp of design elements and an intense feeling for color. The program of illumination for the *Beatus Apocalypse* influenced the imagery of later medieval art work.

In the high medieval period, the work of the Paris miniaturists rivaled the stained glass in the windows of Gothic cathedrals in richness of color. Illumination, being a more flexible medium, surpassed stained-glass work in freedom of handling of elements, subtlety of expression, and capacity for exploring, interpreting, and recording natural phenomena. In the 13th century, devotional books intended for personal use were handsomely decorated by the miniaturists. The accentuation of human traits in Gothic sculpture is evident in the style of manuscript illumination. In the margins of the manuscript pages artists were able to give full rein to their inventiveness. Gothic manuscript illumination culminated in the famous Psalter *Les Très riches heures du Duc de Berry* (Musée Condé, Chantilly), executed at the outset of the 15th century by the Flemish miniaturist Jacquemart de Hesdin. The illumination techniques of Jacquemart's Psalter constitute a summary of the stylistic elements of International Gothic. The great tradition ended with the minutely realistic work of the Limbourg brothers and Jean Fouquet, who was also a panel painter.

With the advent of printing in the 15th century and the perfection of new means of pictorial representation in the 16th century, the art of manuscript illumination declined and by the end of the 16th century ceased to exist as a vital mode of artistic expression.

For further discussion and additional illustrations, *see* ANGLO-SAXON ART; CAROLINGIAN ART.

Bibliography: J. A. HERBERT, *Illuminated Manuscripts* (London 1911). Dictionnaire d'archéologie chrétienne et de liturgie, ed. F. CABROL, H. LECLERQ, and H. I. MARROW (Paris 1907–53). 11.1:1225–1374. S. DE RICCI and W. J. WILSON, *Census of Medieval and Renaissance Manuscripts in the United States and Canada,* 3 v. (New York 1935–40). L. RÉAU, *La Miniature: Histoire de la peinture au Moyenâge* (Melun 1946). K. WEITZMANN, *Roll and Codex* (Princeton 1947). D. MINER, *Illuminated and Illustrated Books* (Baltimore 1949).

Illuminated page from the "Lindisfarne Gospels," c. 700.

[L. P. SIGER]

MANUTIUS

An Italian family that distinguished itself in early printing and publishing. Aldus Manutius (also known as Teobaldo Manucci; Aldo Manuzio); b. Bassiano, 1450; d. Venice, Feb. 6, 1515. He was a Venetian publisher, noted for well-edited versions of Greek and Latin classics, especially the five-volume folio edition of Aristotle (1495–98) and a total of 28 *editiones principes,* or first printed editions of MSS. His development of an italic type, designed by Francesco Griffo, made possible and popular small octavo volumes, often produced in editions of 1,000 copies. The Aldine *Hypernotomachia Poliphili* (1499), by Francesco Colonna, is considered the best example of a 15th-century printed illustrated book. Aldus's printer's mark, a dolphin entwined around an anchor, became identified with high-quality printing. The establishment at his home of an academy of scholars, such as ERASMUS and Marcus Musurus, helped make Venice a center of classical culture.

Paulus Manutius, Aldus's son; b. Venice, June 12, 1512; d. Rome, April 16, 1574. Following an interim during which Andreas Torresanus was in charge of Aldus's enterprises, Paulus continued the tradition, especially in the printing of Cicero's works. In 1561 he was invited to Rome by Pius IV to establish a press to publish the Church Fathers for apologetic use against the Protestant reformers. Under Pius V (1566–72), he published the *Canones et Decreta* of the Council of Trent and similar works.

Aldus the Second, son of Paulus; b. Venice, Feb. 13, 1547; d. Rome, Oct. 28, 1597. Under Clement VIII he was appointed director of the Vatican press in 1590. The history of the Manutius family as printers terminated with his death.

Bibliography: H. R. BROWN, *The Venetian Printing Press* (London 1891). A. A. RENOUARD, *A Bibliographical Sketch of the Aldine Press at Venice . . .* translated and abridged from *Annales de l'Imprimerie des Aldes,* ed. E. M. GOLDSMID (Edinburgh 1887). J. E. SANDYS, *A History of Classical Scholarship* (New York 1958) 2:98–101.

[E. P. WILLGING]

MANYANET Y VIVES, JOSÉ (JOSEPH), BL.

Priest, founder of the Congregation of the Sons of the Holy Family and the Institute of the Missionary Daughters of the Holy Family of Nazareth; b. Jan. 7, 1833, Tremp, Pallars Jussá, Catalonia, Spain; d. Dec. 17, 1901, San Andres de Palomar, Barcelona, Spain.

José Manyanet, the youngest of nine children born to farmers Antonio Manyanet and Bonaventura Vives, was baptized on the day of his birth. Following the death of his father in 1834, José informally became the ward of Father Valentín Lledós, who influenced his future vocation, as did his mother Bonaventura's piety. At age 12, he left home to begin his education in the Piarist school at Barbastro from 1845 to 1850. He continued his study of philosophy at the seminary of Lleida (1850–53) and theology at Seu d'Urgell (1853–59), where he was mentored by Bishop José Caixal and ordained as priest April 9, 1859.

From his ordination until 1865, Manyanet successfully served Bishop Caixal in several offices while engaging in pastoral ministry as confessor, spiritual director, preacher, catechist, and promoter of several associations. Because he had a heroic concern for the family, which he recognized was threatened by divorce and personal independence, he founded two institutions: *Hijos de la Sagrada Familia* (1864 in Tremp) and *Hijas de la Sagrada Familia* (1874 in Talarn). Manyanet and his first companions made their religious profession in Barcelona Feb. 2, 1870, and received pontifical approval June 22, 1901. The order operates schools for the Christian education of children and promotes devotion to the Holy Family in Argentina, Brazil, Colombia, Italy, Mexico, Spain, the United States (from 1920), and Venezuela. They also publish the periodical *Revista La Sagrada Familia.*

The founding of the female branch was more difficult. Bishop Caixal placed a new community of women founded by Ana María Janer in 1859 under the direction of Manyanet. The order was consumed by crisis until it was again recognized by Bishop José Morgades of Vich in 1892, under the direction of the co-foundress, Mother Encarnación Colomina. She gave the order its new name *Misioneras Hijas de la Sagrada Familia de Nazaret,* which was approved by the Vatican May 10, 1958.

In addition to writing the constitutions of both the orders he founded, Manyanet contributed several books: *Meditaciones: El espíritu de la Sagrada Familia* (Meditations: The Spirit of the Holy Family); *La Escuela de Nazaret* (The School of Nazareth); and *Preciosa joya de familia* (The Precious Jewel of Family). He also advocated for the liturgical celebration of the Feast of the Holy Family, which was instituted by Pope Leo XII in 1892. For many years before his death Father Manyanet secretly bore the stigmatization of Jesus.

His mortal remains are enshrined in a bronze urn in the Beato José Manyanet Chapel in the School of Jesus, Mary, and Joseph of Saint Andrew of Palomar (Barcelona). The ordinary informative process for his beatification began in 1931, and his cause was formally introduced by Pope Pius XII in 1951. Pope John Paul II declared Manyanet venerable July 12, 1982, and beatified him Nov. 25, 1984.

Bibliography: D. MORERA, *Among the Stars: The Life of Father Joseph Manyanet* (New York 1957). *Acta Apostolicae Sedis* 77 (1985) 935–39. *L'Osservatore Romano,* Eng. ed. 50 (1984): 2, 12.

[K. I. RABENSTEIN]

MARANATHA

Maranatha is an Aramaic expression used by St. Paul in 1 Cor 16.22 in its transliterated form μαρανα θα. It must have originated in the early Aramaic–speaking Church of Palestine. The DIDACHE (10.6) indicates that it was apparently a liturgical acclamation like the Hebrew expressions HOSANNA and AMEN. Perhaps it was also used frequently by the charismatics who had the gift of tongues.

Since the Apostle did not translate or explain maranatha for his Greek–speaking readers, he must have presumed that they understood its significance. Now, however, its exact meaning and usage is uncertain. All agree that it is composed of two Aramaic elements: *mārān(a)*, ''Our Lord'' [from *mār*, ''lord,'' and –*ān*(*a*), the suffix meaning ''our''], plus ('ă) *tā*', which, if read as *tā*', would be the imperative ''come!'' but which, if read as 'ă*tā*', would mean ''has come.''

If understood as an invocation, maranatha would be a prayer for the Parousia. Because of the liturgical context in which it occurs both in 1 Corinthians and in the Didache, this interpretation seems the more probable one and is confirmed by the closing words of the Revelation, ''Amen. Come, Lord Jesus!'' (Rv 22.20). Maranatha would then express both the Church's belief in the risen Jesus as the Lord (Phil 2.11) and its hope in His glorious coming at the last day, already anticipated and guaranteed by His presence in the Eucharist.

However, since maranatha occurs in 1 Cor 16.22 immediately after anathema (''If any man does not love the Lord, let him be anathema. Maranatha. The grace of the Lord Jesus be with you.''), some scholars prefer to regard the expression as part of the preceding curse formula, confirming the anathema by an appeal to the Lord who either has come or will come in judgment. This interpretation is already met with in the 4th century [AMBROSIASTER, *Patrologia Latina,* ed. J. P. Migne (Paris 1878–90) 17:276] and it seems to have led to the use of maranatha in formulas of excommunication or cursing. Thus, a 4th– or 5th–century inscription from Salamis threatens with ΑΝΑΘΕΜΑ ΜΑΡΑΝΑΘΑ anyone who dares to place another body in a certain tomb (A. Boeckh, *Corp. Inscr. Gr.* 4: 9303), and an excommunication formula of the Fourth Council of Toledo (A.D. 633) is *anathema maranatha,* which is explained as *perditio in adventu Domini* (perdition in the coming of the Lord). Nevertheless, this interpretation seems less probable than the one that understands the expression as a prayer for the Parousia.

Bibliography: C. F. D. MOULE, ''A Reconsideration of the Context of Maranatha,'' *New Testament Studies* 6 (1959–60) 307–310. S. SCHULZ, ''Maranatha und Kyrios Jesus,'' *Zeitschrift für die Neutestamentliche Wissenschaft und die Kunde der Älteren Kirche* 53 no. 3–4 (1962) 125–144. J. A. EMERTON, ''Maranatha and Ephphatha,'' *Journal of Theological Studies* 18 (1967) 427–431. M. BLACK, ''The Maranatha Invocation and Jude 14,15 (1 Enoch 1:9),'' in *Christ and Spirit in the New Testament: In Honour of Charles Francis Digby Moule,* S.S. SMALLEY, ed. (Cambridge, Eng. 1973) 189–196.

[R. KUGELMAN/EDS.]

MARAÑÓN, DAVID CARLOS, BL.

Martyr, lay brother of the Order of Poor Clerics Regular of the Mother of God of the Pious Schools (Piarists); b. Dec. 29, 1907, in Asartam, Spain; d. July 28, 1936. David was professed as a lay brother in 1932 and made his solemn profession in 1935. He was the cook and gardener for the community at Peralta. After refusing an offer of freedom in exchange for abandoning his religious habit, he was shot along with Manuel SEGURA LÓPEZ. He was beatified on Oct. 1, 1995 by Pope John Paul II together with 12 other Piarists (*see* PAMPLONA, DIONISIO AND COMPANIONS, BB.).

Feast: Sept. 22.

Bibliography: ''Decreto Super Martyrio,'' *Acta Apostolicae Sedis* (1995): 651–656. *La Documentation Catholique* 2125 (Nov. 5, 1995): 924.

[L. GENDERNALIK/EDS]

MARBACH, ABBEY OF

A former foundation of CANONS OF ST. AUGUSTINE near Colmar, in the Diocese of Bale, Department of Haut-Rhin, France. It was founded in 1089 by Burkhard of Geberschweier (d. 1120); its first dean was MANEGOLD OF LAUTENBACH (d. 1103). Papal approval came in 1096. The beautiful triple-naved church was consecrated Nov. 15, 1119. The Romanesque main portal with its two towers and two choir apses remained intact until 1830. Deans had assumed the title of abbot since granting of pontifical rights by Pope HONORIUS III *c.* 1216, and from 1463 they were called priors in accordance with the statutes. The abbey buildings were often destroyed during the Middle Ages by fire and pillage. Until 1462, Marbach was head of a congregation to which 13 monasteries belonged. It was attached to the WINDESHEIM congregation from 1462 to 1769. Marbach flourished under Prior Petrus Kroppenberg (1650–80). In addition to the canonry, there was from 1117 a women's convent that was moved in 1149 to Schwarzenthann but continued to be subject to the abbey. In 1786 Marbach became a convent; it was dissolved in 1790. Its buildings are used today as a sanatorium. The *Codex regulae* of Canon Sintram, written *c.* 1150, is famous for its numerous and valuable miniatures. The *Marbach Annals* are an important source for the history of the empire in the 12th and 13th centuries; they were compiled about 1210 in the Convent of Hohenburg (*see* MONT SAINTE-ODILE, CONVENT OF).

Bibliography: L. H. COTTINEAU, *Répertoire topobibliographique des abbayes et prieurés* (Mâcon 1935–39) 2:1735–36. J. CLAUSS, *Historischtopographisches Wörterbuch des Elsass* (Saverne 1895–1914) 636–637. A. M. BURG, *Lexikon für*

Theologie und Kirche, ed. J. HOFER and K. RAHNER (Freiburg 1957–65) 6:1371–72. F. A. GOEHLINGER, *Historie de l'abbaye de Marbach* (Colmar 1954).

[P. VOLK]

MARBECK, PILGRAM

Anabaptist leader and engineer; b. Rattenberg, Tyrol, *c.* 1495; d. Augsburg, 1556. He attended the Latin school at Rattenberg, became an engineer in the mines of the lower Inn Valley, and was a member of city council and a mine judge. He lost the last position because he refused to prosecute some ANABAPTISTS at the end of 1527. He joined the movement and fled to Strassburg (1528), where he built a complex water system and wood floating flumes in the valleys of Alsace and Baden, whereby Strassburg gained access to the wealth of the Black Forest. Because of his leadership in Anabaptist circles, he was soon under suspicion and pressure by Martin BUCER and the city council, which led to his imprisonment, a colloquium before the assembled city council, and his expulsion in January 1532. He traveled extensively and even returned to Strassburg before he found labor as a well engineer and Anabaptist leader and writer in Augsburg (1544–56). He was a prolific writer of books, pamphlets, and correspondence, and gained a leading position among the south German Anabaptists. He rejected Caspar Schwenckfeld's spiritualism and emphasized the significance of the visible church of Christ (*see* SCHWENCKFELDERS). With Hans Denck he stressed the consecrated, disciplined Christian life, but he was not as rigid as the Swiss Anabaptists. Only recently, through the discovery of new sources and writings by Marbeck, has his significance as Anabaptist leader become fully established.

Bibliography: W. KLASSEN, *The Hermeneutics of Pilgram Marbeck* (Doctoral diss. microfilm; Princeton 1960). J. J. KIWIET, *Pilgram Marbeck* (Kassel 1957), bibliog. H. TÜCHLE, *Lexikon für Theologie und Kirche* [2] 6:1372. H. FAST, *Die Religion in Geschichte und Gegenwart* [3] 4:733.

[C. KRAHN]

MARBOD OF RENNES

Bishop, teacher, poet; b. Angers, France, *c.* 1035; d. Angers, Sept. 11, 1123. After completing his studies at the CATHEDRAL SCHOOL of ANGERS under Rainald, a pupil of FULBERT OF CHARTRES, Marbod became a teacher in the school, and *c.* 1067, its master. He became also chancellor of the Diocese of Angers *c.* 1069. In 1096 Pope Urban II appointed Marbod Bishop of Rennes in Brittany. He resigned his bishopric at the age of 88, and died soon after in the Benedictine Abbey of Saint-Aubin.

A product of the educational revival of the 11th century as originally promoted by such men as SYLVESTER II and Fulbert, Marbod marks the transition to the Christian humanism of the 12th century. His skill as a Latin poet was especially admired, though he was outranked in this field by his younger admirer, HILDEBERT OF LAVARDIN. Marbod was fond of the leonine hexameter and he versified every kind of topic, though his poems became more serious with advancing years. He could write simple lyrics, such as *Upon a Beautiful Girl* and *To a Devout Virgin,* as well as long Biblical narratives in verse. He wrote poems on the lives and virtues of the saints and the Mother of Christ, such as *On St. Lawrence, On the Passion of St. Victor, To the Virgin,* and *On the Annunciation.* He composed poetic eulogies, such as those *To Queen Mathilda,* the wife of Henry I, and *To Countess Ermenegarde,* as well as metrical philosophical reflections *On Old Age, On Time, On Fate,* etc. One of his more extensive poems won him a place in the history of science, viz, *The Book of Stones* (or *Gems*), which describes the qualities and virtues (real and imaginary) of some 60 different stones. This very popular work was translated into several languages. Marbod composed also a treatise on versification entitled *De ornamentis verborum* (On Verbal Ornamentation).

Two lives of Marbod have been published, one in French by L. Ernault (Rennes 1890), the other in Latin by C. Ferry (Paris 1899). Marbod's works were edited by J. Mayeux (Rennes 1524) and A. Beaugendre (Paris 1708) and were reprinted in *Patrologia Latina* 171:1451–1780.

Bibliography: *Histoire littéraire de la France* 10:343–392. *Analecta hymnica* (Leipzig 1886-1922) 50:388–403. M. MANITIUS, *Geschichte der lateinischen Literatur des Mittelalters* 3:719–730. A. WILMART, ''Un nouveau poème de Marbode . . .'' *Revue Bénédictine* 51 (1939) 169–181, L. THORNDIKE, *A History of Magic and Experimental Science* (New York 1923-58) v.1. J. DE GHELLINCK, *L'Essor de la littérature latine au XIIe siècle* (Brussels-Paris 1946) 2:239–240. F. J. E. RABY, *A History of Christian-Latin Poetry from the Beginnings to the Close of the Middle Ages* (Oxford 1953) 273–277. F. J. E. RABY, *A History of Secular Latin Poetry in the Middle Ages* (Oxford 1957) 1:329–337.

[D. D. MCGARRY]

MARCA, PIERRE DE

Prelate, public servant, canonist, historian; b. Gan in Béarn, France, Jan. 24, 1594; d. Paris, Jun. 29, 1662. He was the son of Jacques de Marca, a merchant-noble, one of the leaders of the Catholic party in Béarn. Pierre studied letters at the Jesuit College of Auch and law at the University of Toulouse. He served as lawyer and councilor at Pau (1615); and when the council at Pau was converted to a parliament by Louis XIII in 1621, Pierre was appointed to preside. After the death of his wife, Marguerite de Forges, he entered the priesthood and was ordained April 2, 1642. He was consecrated bishop of Conserans on Dec. 20, 1648. Before his consecration Marca had been appointed intendant in Catalonia, in which position he continued for seven years, giving distinguished service to the Crown. On May 28, 1652, Cardinal Jules MAZARIN had him appointed to the archiepiscopal See of Toulouse. Rising rapidly in royal favor, he was made minister of state (1659) and nominated to succeed Cardinal Jean de RETZ as archbishop of Paris (1662). He never assumed the duties of that office, since he died on the same day he received the papal bull of appointment.

Next to his accomplishments as civil and ecclesiastical administrator are his writings in Canon Law and local history. His *Rélations des déliberations du clergé de France* (1661), against the Jansenists, demanded their adherence to the decrees of Innocent X and Alexander VII. As a historian he is credited with works of great erudition in his *Histoire de Béarn* and his *Marca Hispanica,* the latter a description of Catalonia.

Marca is important also for his attempt, at Richelieu's orders, to formulate a statement of Gallicanism that would reconcile the authority of the Roman pontiff with the full exercise of sovereign functions in the state. His treatise, *De concordantia sacerdotii et imperii* (1641), stated that the infallibility of the Church rests in the pope, but it can be exercised validly only *cum aliquo consensu ecclesiae* (with a certain consent of the Church); an ecclesiastical law must receive the consent of the nation that has to apply it; and the king has the right to censure the action of an ecclesiastic who violates canons and decrees confirmed by the royal power. The work did not meet with approval at Rome and was put on the Index. Marca then tried to extenuate his views in a subsequent publication, *Dissertatio de primatu Lugdunensi et aliis primatibus* (1644), which won him enough favor to be confirmed and consecrated as bishop in 1648.

Bibliography: The most noted editions of his writings are by É. BALUZE (Paris 1641, 1663), P. DE FAGET (Paris 1668, 1669), and V. P. DUBARAT (Pau 1894–1912). A prefatory life is found in the *Dissertationes de concordia,* ed. É. BALUZE (1663) and *Dissertationes posthumae,* ed. P. DE FAGET (1669). F. GAQUÈRE, *Pierre de Marca, 1594–1662* (Paris 1932). J. CARREYRE, in *Dictionnaire de théologie catholique,* ed. A. VACANT et al., 15 v. (Paris 1903–50; Tables générales 1951–) 9.2:1987–91, bibliog. R. METZ, in *Lexikon für Theologie und Kirche,* ed. J. HOFER and K. RAHNER, 10 v. (2d new ed. Freiburg 1957–65) 6:1375. H. HURTER, *Nomenclator literarius theologiae catholicae,* 5 v. in 6 (3rd edition Innsbruck 1903–13) 3:1179–84.

[J. W. BUSH]

Gabriel Marcel. (Archive Photos)

MARCEL, GABRIEL

Christian existentialist philosopher; b. Paris, Dec. 7, 1889; d. Paris, Oct. 8, 1973. Since his father was at one time French minister to Stockholm, Marcel benefitted from a multilingual milieu and from extensive foreign travel. He studied at the Sorbonne but did not complete his doctorate, and as a philosopher was unusual in not pursuing an academic career. He did some teaching, but for most of his life devoted himself to free-lance intellectual work as essayist, critic, editor, and lecturer. Marcel wrote that unpleasant aspects of his childhood, including the death of his mother when he was four, led him to take up idealistic philosophy in an attempt to transcend his situation. But experiences as a Red Cross worker in World War I, he wrote, shattered his idealism and turned him toward an existentialist approach.

Though he had little religious influence in his upbringing—his father being a Catholic-turned-agnostic and his stepmother a Protestant whose religion was primarily ethics—he began developing a deep interest in the religious dimension of experience. In 1929 he converted to Catholicism and later came to exert a considerable influence in Catholic intellectual circles.

Rejecting the atheistic existentialism of Camus and Sartre, he moved along lines closer to such theistic existentialists as KIERKEGAARD and BUBER. Although usually reckoned among existentialists, Marcel himself did not relish this designation. He was largely an underivative thinker; not only was the influence of the progenitor of existentialism, Kierkegaard, next to nil, but the direction of Marcel's thought was quite fully determined prior to that of other 20th-century existentialists such as HEIDEGGER, JASPERS, and SARTRE. He also rejected the systematic approach of academic philosophy and developed what he called ''concrete philosophy,'' contending that a philosopher must do his work as a participant in life rather than as an observer. The author of several plays, he found drama a congenial form in which to express his existentialist viewpoint. He was also a composer of music. It is symptomatic of the radically integral character of his thought that he ranked music as one of the most important influences on his philosophy. In 1933 he became involved in Moral Re-Armament and in 1958 edited a book of testimonies, *Fresh Hope for the World,* in which he and others expressed support for the movement.

Participation and Presence. The leitmotiv of Marcel's philosophy is the notion of PARTICIPATION; this slowly emerged as Marcel defined his thought in opposition both to Descartes and to the early influence of the German idealists. The aspiration toward system so prominent in the idealists was not acceptable to him, for a system would be available only for a thought that could view reality as a detached observer. However, the human self is not a spectator of reality, but a participant: for man, ''to be'' is to participate in being. Hence, too, there is no problem of breaking through to realism, for the Cartesian private ego is an abstraction: the concretely experienced SELF is ''founded'' by participation and can claim no precedence over other selves.

Human thought tends to withdraw from the immediacy of participation, to treat the presence there met as an object confronting an autonomous subject, or, as Marcel says, to transform being into having. Man even thinks of his body as something that he ''has,'' whereas the primordial experience of incarnation is better conveyed by his saying ''I *am* my body.'' An object, in Marcel's sense, is something that one can regard as external to himself. Here is the basis for Marcel's already classic distinction between a problem and a mystery. A problem is an inquiry into an object in this strict sense, typified by the scientific inquiry. But some data do not permit objectification of this type. The meaning of being, for instance, cannot be revealed objectively. For one cannot treat being as ''outside'' oneself: being includes the self that thinks it. The question of being is thus a mystery and not a problem. Again, all influences that crystallize man's habit of conceiving the real in an exclusively objectified way weaken his awareness of being. Thus the very virtues and successes of the present rationalist-technical civilization constitute a threat to the sense of mystery. For the more man treats reality in an objectified manner, the more he is tempted to regard himself, too, as an object, a set of functions that can be tabulated and manipulated. It is no accident that, in an age often succumbing to this temptation, human existence is emptied of depth and falls prey to anxiety and absurdity.

Human Communion. Marcel attempts in his''concrete philosophy'' and in his plays to recover by ''secondary reflection'' the presence that objectifying primary reflection has forsaken. In particular, he attempts to recover the special dimension of being revealed in human communion. That is why he concentrates on novel philosophical themes such as love, hope, and fidelity. For it is in these experiences that the ''thou'' is delivered to the perceiver; and the ''I-thou'' relation is a pivotal form of participation. The ''thou'' is not an ''it,'' a characterizable object about which one speaks, but a unique presence; and this makes possible a unique self-presence. The tenuous and fugitive nature of this communion, stressed also by M. Buber, is the prevailing theme in Marcel's plays: openness to the ''thou'' is the human access to the peace of being, but egoism and insincerity wall one up in his own self.

In awakening to the ontological plenitude of human communion, one awakens to the aura of the eternal and inexhaustible that pervades communion. It is among Marcel's deepest convictions that the transcendent dimension of human existence cannot be revealed to an impersonal thought; rather it is the intelligible epiphany of an authentic human existence. God is the Absolute ''Thou'' who lurks in the truncated experience of presence felt in human communion. To ''prove'' the existence of God is simply to raise to speculative recognition a truth already present to participation. Marcel speaks of a ''blinded intuition'' of the plenitude of being, but this intuition is not an object of vision. It is a presentiment or intimation: it is like the artist's creative idea that is revealed in the work itself. The intuition of transcendence must be read back out of the works it makes possible: chiefly this reading-back is accomplished in the ''I-thou'' experiences. Finally, the truth of transcendence is not something that is imposed upon a person ''automatically.'' Since, in the area of mystery, the presence affirmed cannot be externalized vis-à-vis the singular self, the affirmation of such a presence involves personal singularity—and hence personal freedom. The transcendent haunts human existence as an appeal, and one's recognition of its presence is at the same time a creative response.

Works. Marcel's main philosophical works are *Metaphysical Journal, The Mystery of Being* (2 v.), *Being* *and Having, Homo Viator,* and the essay ''On the Ontological Mystery.'' Among his plays are: *Un homme de dieu, Le chemin de Crête, Le dard,* and *La soif* (*Les coeurs avides*).

Bibliography: K. TROISFONTAINES, *De l'existence à l'être: La philosophie de Gabriel Marcel,* 2 v. (Namur 1953). K. T. GALLAGHER, *The Philosophy of Gabriel Marcel* (New York 1962). S. KEEN, *Gabriel Marcel* (Richmond, Va. 1967). G. MARCEL, *The Philosophy of Existence,* tr. M. HARARI (New York 1949). D. APPELBAUM, *Contact and Attention: The Anatomy of Gabriel Marcel's Metaphysical Method* ([Pittsburgh, Pa.] 1986, c1987). J. C. MCCOWN, *Availability: Gabriel Marcel and the Phenomenology of Human Openness* (Missoula, Mont. [1977]). C. PAX, *An Existential Approach to God: A Study of Gabriel Marcel* (The Hague 1972).

[T. EARLY/K. T. GALLAGHER/EDS.]

MARCELLA, ST.

Widow, ascetic; b. *c.* 325–335 of the noble Roman family of the Marcelli; d. late 410 or early 411. Her father died while she was young, and although she was left a childless widow after a marriage of only seven months, she declined an opportunity to remarry and instead consecrated herself to God. In her home on the Aventine, where she lived with her mother, Albina, she gathered together a number of noble Roman widows and virgins interested in pursuing the religious life. This group was given instruction by St. JEROME during his stay in Rome (382–385). A zealous student of scripture, Marcella directed a flow of philological and exegetical questions to Jerome, and his extant correspondence includes a number of letters addressed to her. Marcella took a vigorous interest in the dispute over ORIGENISM. During the plunder of Rome (410), she was beaten by soldiers of Alaric and died not long thereafter. Jerome left (*Ep.* 127) a touching account of her life.

Feast: Jan. 31.

Bibliography: I. HILBERG, *Sancti Eusebii Hieronymi epistulae* (*Corpus scriptorum ecclesiasticorum latinorum* 54–56; 1910–18), esp. nos. 23–29, 32, 34, 37, 38, 40–44, 46, 59, 127. F. CAVALLERA, *Saint Jérôme,* 2 v. (*Spicilegium sacrum Lovaniense* 1, 2; 1922), *passim.* S. LETSCH-BRUNNER, *Marcella: discipula et magistra* (Berlin 1998).

[T. C. LAWLER]

MARCELLINUS, POPE, ST.

Pontificate: June 30, 296 to Oct. 25, 304. The *Libe pontificalis* calls Marcellinus a Roman, the son of Projectus, and places his pontificate during the persecution of Diocletian. It repeats the story, circulated later by the Donatists (*see* DONATISM), that the pope, when apprehended and ordered to sacrifice to the gods, complied and handed over the sacred books to the persecuting authorities. Torn with remorse, the pope is said to have repented and sought martyrdom several days later. His body was buried by the priest Marcellus in the private cemetery of Priscilla on the Via Salaria.

The accusations of apostasy brought against Marcellinus and other Catholic bishops, including the future popes Miltiades, Marcellus, and Silvester, are acknowledged and rejected by St. Augustine (*Contra Litteram Petil.* 2.92.202; *De unico baptismo* 16; *Brev. coll.* 3.18) and repeated in the Acts (*c.* 500) of the alleged Council of Sinuessa, which lays great stress on the pope's repentance and martyrdom. Eusebius states that the pope ''was overcome by the persecution'' and locates his grave in the cemetery of Priscilla (*Ecclesiastical History.* 7.32); but Pope DAMASUS I ignored him when he composed the epitaphs of past Roman bishops, and neither the MARTYROLOGY OF ST. JEROME nor the Gelasian Sacramentary mentions Marcellinus.

The Eastern bishop Theodoret of Cyrus records that Marcellinus bore a distinguished role in the persecution (*Ecclesiastical History.* 1.2), however, scholars consider the Western evidence decisive and believe that somehow Marcellinus compromised himself during the persecution, although they also take his repentance seriously. The *Depositio episcoporum* names a ''Marcellinus,'' but it is evident from the dates given that Pope MARCELLUS I, not Marcellinus, was meant. A late fifth–century *passio* and the seventh–century ITINERARIA credit him with martyrdom and witness to the veneration of his tomb. While the *Annuario Pontificio* (2001) lists the dates of Marcellinus as June 30, 296, to Oct. 25, 304, historians hesitate to distinguish him from his successor Marcellus.

Feast: April 26.

Bibliography: A. STUIBER, *Lexikon für Theologie und Kirche,* ed. J. HOFER and K. RAHNER (Freiberg 1957–65) 7:1. É. AMANN, *Dictionnaire de théologie catholique,* ed. A. VACANT et al. (Paris 1903–50) 9.2:1999–2001. *Liber pontificalis,* ed. L. DUCHESNE (Paris 1886–92, 1958) 1: LXXIII–LXXV, 32–36, 72–73, 162–163. E. H. RÖTTGES, *Zeitschrift für katholische Theologie* (Vienna 1877–) 78 (1956) 385–420. E. FERGUSON, *Encyclopedia of Early Christianity* (New York 1997) 2:713. J. N. D. KELLY, *Oxford Dictionary of Popes* (New York 1986) 24–25.

[E. G. WELTIN]

MARCELLINUS, FLAVIUS

Fifth-century Roman tribune and notary, friend of St. Augustine; d. Carthage, *c.* 413. He was a correspondent of St. AUGUSTINE, having made his acquaintance during the conference of Carthage (411) between the Catholics and Donatists. Marcellinus presided and upheld the Catholic cause. On the charge, which was put forward by the Donatists, that he and his brother Apringius were implicated in the revolt of Heraclian, Marcellinus and his brother were arrested by Marinus, Count of Africa, who had them condemned and decapitated. Augustine visited him in prison and testified to his upright character. Subsequently Emperor Honorius exonerated his name and recognized his work in the interests of peace. Augustine praised Marcellinus highly in several letters and dedicated his *De civitate Dei* to him. Cardinal Baronius added his name to the Roman Martyrology.

Feast: Apr. 6.

Bibliography: OROSIUS, *Hist.* 7:42; 17. JEROME, *Adv. Pelag.* 3:19. AUGUSTINE, *Epist.* 128; 129; 133; 136; 143. W. ENSSLIN, *Paulys Realenzyklopädie der klassischen Altertumswissenschaft* 14.2 (1930) 1445–46. H. W. PHILLOT, *A Dictionary of Christian Biography* 3: 806–807. F. VAN DER MEER, *Augustine the Bishop,* tr. B. BATTERSHAW and G. R. LAMB (New York 1962).

[P. ROCHE]

MARCELLINUS AND PETER, SS.

Martyrs under Diocletian in Rome, 303. Marcellinus, a priest, and Peter, an exorcist, were, according to the MARTYROLOGY OF JEROME and itineraria of the seventh century, buried in the cemetery *ad duas lauros* on the Via Labicana. They are also commemorated in the Gelasian and Gregorian sacramentaries. Constantine had a basilica built in their honor over the crypt in which they were buried. The crypt, with a fresco of the martyrs from *c.* 400, was discovered in 1896. Pope DAMASUS I (366–384) composed a poetic epitaph for them that was apparently founded on the report of their executioner. This epitaph seems to be the source of a legendary *passio,* composed perhaps when Pope VIGILIUS (537–555), who introduced their names into the Canon of the Mass, restored their tomb. The legend states that the martyrs were beheaded after they had dug their graves in a woods, but their relics were miraculously discovered and brought to the crypt.

Feast: June 2.

Bibliography: EINHARD, *The History of the Translation of the Blessed Martyrs of Christ, Marcellinus and Peter*, tr. B. WENDELL (Cambridge 1926).

[E. G. RYAN]

MARCELLO, BENEDETTO

Baroque composer and satirical writer; b. Venice, Aug. 1, 1686; d. Brescia, July 24, 1739. Though a student of Gasparini and Lotti, he referred to himself as *nobile Veneto dilettante di contrappunto,* thus implying that he did not consider music his principal vocation, and in fact he was successful as a lawyer and state employee. Yet he made a considerable contribution to sacred music too. His compositions certainly belong to the *stile moderno* typical of Venice, but like many musicians of his time he wrote with equal skill in the *stile antico.* Marcello composed Masses, motets, and oratorios. His great work is the *Estro poetico-armonico, parafrasi sopra i primi 50 psalmi, poesia di Girolamo Giustiniani* (Venice 1724–26). Here he set the Psalms for from one to four voices with thorough bass, and at times with two violins and cello as obbligato instruments, using such concertato devices as question and answer and contrast of solo and choral singing, so that each Psalm became really a cantata. Very little of his music is available in modern transcription, but his pamphlet *Teatro alla moda* (*c.* 1720), a seriocomic satire on the state of the opera, has become a minor classic of stage literature.

Benedetto Marcello, painting by Pasquale Ruggiero. (©Archivo Iconografico, S.A./CORBIS)

Bibliography: F. GIEGLING, *Die Musik in Geschichte und Gegenwart,* ed. F. BLUME (Kassel-Basel 1949–) 8:1616–1619. F. GEHRING, *Grove's Dictionary of Music and Musicians,* ed. E. BLOM 9 v. (5th ed. London 1954) 5:563–564. O. STRUNK, ed., *Source Readings in Music History* (New York 1950) 518–531. M. F. BUKOFZER, *Music in the Baroque Era* (New York 1947) *Baker's Biographical Dictionary of Musicians,* ed. N. SLONIMSKY (5th, rev.

ed. New York 1958) 1025. D. J. GROUT, *A Short History of Opera*, 2 v. (2d, rev. and enl. ed. New York 1965) W. S. NEWMAN, ''The Keyboard Sonatas of Benedetto Marcello,'' *Acta Musicologia* 29 (1957) 28–41. R. G. PAULY, ''B. M.'s Satire on Early 18th Century Opera,'' *Musical Quarterly* 34 (1948) 222–233. E. SELFRIDGE-FIELD, *The Music of Benedetto and Alessandro Marcello: A Thematic Catalogue, with Commentary on the Composers, Repertory, and Sources* (Oxford 1990). C. S. FRUCHTMAN, *Checklist of Vocal Chamber Works by Benedetto Marcello* (Detroit 1967).

[T. CULLEY]

MARCELLUS, SS.

In addition to Pope MARCELLUS I and MARCELLUS AKIMETES, there are several other saints of that name, notably the following.

Marcellus of Chalon-sur-Saône, priest, martyr; d. *c.* 178. According to his legendary *passio* he was martyred under Marcus Aurelius. A cult and church in his honor are first mentioned by GREGORY OF TOURS [*In glor. martyr.* 52; *Hist. Franc.* 5.20 (27); 9.3.27]. His name appears subsequently in calendars, martyrologies, and sacramentaries.

Feast: Sept. 4.

Marcellus of Die, bishop; b. Avignon; d. Bareuil in Provence, 510. Following his consecration by St. MAMERTUS, bishop of Vienne, who had ignored the rights claimed by the metropolitan of Arles, he was imprisoned and exiled by Gundiok, the Arian king of the Burgundians. Later he was permitted to return to his see and became distinguished for his piety and pastoral zeal. His cult at Die began very early and was confirmed for the Diocese of Valence by Pope Pius IX.

Feast: April 9 (formerly Jan. 17).

Marcellus of Paris, bishop; fl. early fifth century. His vita, which depicts him as a zealous pastor of souls and a miracle worker, was composed, at the request of St. Germain of Paris (*see* GERMAIN, SS.), by Venantius FORTUNATUS who apparently relied on vague oral tradition.

Feast: Nov. 3 (formerly 1).

Marcellus the Centurion, martyr; d. Tingis (Tangier), 298. At a banquet held in honor of the emperor's birthday, he suddenly arose to protest against pagan practices and threw down his belt and arms, declaring that it was not right for a Christian, who serves Christ, to serve in the armies of the world. When he maintained the same position at his trial, he was condemned to death and beheaded. The fragments of the original acts are preserved in two later reworked versions that are extant.

Feast: Oct. 30.

Bibliography: Marcellus of Chalon-sur-Saône. *Acta Sanctae Sedis* (Sept. 2, 1868) 187–202. *Bibliotheca hagiographica latina antiquae et mediae aetatis*. (Brussels 1898–1901) 5245–47. H. LECLERCQ, *Dictionnaire d'archéologie chrétienne et de liturgie*. ed. F. CABROL, H. LECLERCQ and H. I. MARROU (Paris 1907–53) 9.2:2568–75. J. L. BAUDOT and L. CHAUSSIN, *Vies des saints et des bienheureux selon l'ordre du calendrier avec l'historique des fêtes*, ed. by the Benedictines of Paris (Paris 1935–56) 9:103–105. Marcellus, Bishop of Die. G. KIRNER, *Studi storici* 9 (Pisa 1900) 289–327. L. DUCHESNE, *Fastes épiscopaux de l'ancienne Gaule* (Paris 1907–15) 1:234. J. L. BAUDOT and L. CHAUSSIN, *Vies des saints et des bienheureux selon l'ordre du calendrier avec l'historique des fêtes*, ed. by the Benedictines of Paris (Paris 1935–56) 4:212–213. Marcellus, Bishop of Paris. *Acta Sanctae Sedis* (Nov. 1, 1887) 259–267. *Monumenta Germaniae Historica* (Berlin 1826–) division Auctores antiquissimi. 4.2:49–54. *Bibliotheca hagiographica latina antiquae et mediae aetatis* (Brussels 1898–1901) 5248–50. L. DUCHESNE, *Fastes épiscopaux de l'ancienne Gaule* (Paris 1907–15) 2:470. W. BÖHNE, *Dictionnaire d'archéologie chrétienne et de liturgie*, ed. F. CABROL, H. LECLERCQ and H. I. MARROU (Paris 1907–53) 13.2:1839. A. BUTLER, *The Lives of the Saints*, rev. ed. H. THURSTON and D. ATTWATER (New York 1956) 4:238. J. L. BAUDOT and L. CHAUSSIN, *Vies des saints et des bienheureux selon l'ordre du calendrier avec l'historique des fêtes*, ed. by the Benedictines of Paris (Paris 1935–56) 11:45–49. Marcellus the Centurion. H. DELEHAYE, ''Les Actes de S. Marcel le Centurion,'' *Analecta Bollandiana* 41 (1923) 257–278. B. DE GAIFFIER, ''L'Elogium dans la passion de S. Marcel le Centurion,'' *Archivum latinitatis medii aevi* 16 (1942) 127–136; ''S. Marcel de Tanger ou de Léon: Évolution d'une légende,'' *Analecta Bollandiana* 61 (1943) 116–139. G. LAZZATI, *Gli sviluppi della letteratura sui martiri nei primi quattro secoli* (Turin 1956) 141–146. A. BUTLER, *The Lives of the Saints*, rev. ed. H. THURSTON and D. ATTWATER (New York 1956) 4:220–221. J. L. BAUDOT and L. CHAUSSIN, *Vies des saints et des bienheureux selon l'ordre du calendrier avec l'historique des fêtes*, ed. by the Benedictines of Paris (Paris 1935–56) 10:990–993.

[M. R. P. MCGUIRE]

MARCELLUS I, POPE, ST.

Pontificate: 306? to January 16, 309?. Marcellus is not mentioned in the Church history of Eusebius, and it is possible that the similarity of his name with his predecessor's caused confusion. His ascension occurred two years after his predecessor's death. This delay resulted from the disorder caused by pagan persecution and by the civil war among Roman generals to become emperor. It seems that Marcellus governed the Christian community during the strife and was eventually chosen bishop. According to the *Liber pontificalis* Marcellus reorganized the Church of Rome into twenty-five parishes, founded a new cemetery, ordained twenty-five priests, and consecrated twenty-one bishops. According to the verse epitaph composed by Pope DAMASUS I, his authority was challenged by a faction under Heraclius when Marcellus imposed a penance on the *LAPSI* or apostates of the persecutions. Because of the public disorder resulting from this dissension, the Emperor Maxentius exiled Marcellus from the city as a disturber of the peace, and he died

Pope Marcellus I, fresco from 9th-century series of papal portraits, formerly at basilica of St. Paul, Rome.

shortly afterward. His body was returned to Rome for burial in the cemetery of Priscilla. A fifth-century *Passio Marcelli* and the *Liber pontificalis* contain the legend that Maxentius turned the title church (*titulus*) of Marcellus into a stable, and that the Pope died there as a result of his labors as a stable boy.

Feast: January 16.

Bibliography: *Liber pontificalis*, ed. L. DUCHESNE (Paris 1886–92, 1958) 1:LXXIII–LXXIV, LXXIX, CCXLIX, XCIX–C, 72–75, 164–166. *Acta Sanctorum* Jan. 2:3–14. A. FERRUA, ed., *Epigrammata Damasiana* (Rome 1942). E. H. RÖOTTGES, ''Marcellinus-Marcellus,'' *Zeitschrift für katholische Theologie* 78 (1956) 385–420. H. LECLERCQ, *Dictionnaire d'archéologie chrétienne et de liturgie*. ed. F. CABROL, H. LECLERCQ and H. I. MARROU (Paris 1907–53) 10.2:1753–60. G. SCHWAIGER, *Lexikon für Theologie und Kirche*, ed. J. HOFER and K. RAHNER (Freiberg 1957–65) 7:3. J. N. D. KELLY *Oxford Dictionary of Popes* (New York 1986), 25–26.

[E. G. WELTIN]

MARCELLUS II, POPE

Pontificate: April 9, 1555, to May 1, 1555; b. Marcello Cervini, Montepulciano, Tuscany, May 6, 1501. His father, Ricciardo, served as scriptor in the Apostolic Penitentiary in the reign of Innocent VIII and vice-treasurer of the Marches of Ancona under Alexander VI. Marcello studied humanities at Siena, and was called to Rome by Clement VII to continue the work of correcting the calendar, begun by Ricciardo. His interest in the New Learning brought him into familiarity with many of the humanists in the Curia, such as Lampridio, Tebaldeo, Lascari, and Bembo. He also gained the patronage of the powerful Cardinal Alessandro Farnese, who, upon his election as PAUL III in 1534, made Marcello tutor of his young nephew, Alessandro Farnese. When Paul III entrusted much of papal affairs, including foreign policy, to Alessandro, Marcello, as his private secretary, was brought into ecclesiastical politics. At the end of August 1539 he received the See of Nicastro in Calabria and in December, the cardinal's hat with the title of Santa Croce in Gerusalemme. The next year he was made administrator of the See of Reggio Emilia. In these offices he was active in promoting reform and took interest in his role of protector of the Servites and the Augustinian hermits, winning praise from the Augustinian general, Girolamo SERIPANDO. In 1540 he accompanied Alessandro as papal legate *a latere* on legations to Francis I, King of France, at Amiens and to the Emperor Charles V at Ghent, in an effort to interest these monarchs in a general council. The next year he was with Paul III in the meeting with Charles at Lucca, and in 1543 was appointed papal legate to the imperial court. On Feb. 6, 1545, in a general consistory he was chosen to share the presidency of the Council of TRENT with cardinals Giovanni Maria Ciocchi del Monte (afterward JULIUS III, 1550–55) and Reginald POLE. Until the prorogation of the council in1547, he opposed the emperor in favor of papal policy, thereby earning imperial disfavor. In 1548 he was appointed Vatican librarian and a member of the reform commission of Paul III. He became president of this commission under Julius III, until his outspoken criticism of the pope's NEPOTISM forced him to retire to his See of Gubbio, which he had administered since 1544. In the conclave that started on April 4, 1555, he was not considered a papal prospect because of the contravention of the emperor, but after four days he was elected, consecrated bishop, and crowned. As pope, he was one of the few in the modern period to keep his baptismal name. During his short reign of 22 days, he appointed Angelo Massarelli as secretary to the Council of Trent and entrusted him to gather all the reform documents drawn up by Julius III, his predecessor, seeking to have them quickly published. He attempted a posture of neutrality in politics, initiated police measures for peace in Rome, and befriended the Jesuits, who had frequently been his confessors.

Bibliography: G. B. MANNUCCI, *Il conclave di papa Marcello* (Siena 1921). H. JEDIN, *History of the Council of Trent*, tr. E. GRAF, (St. Louis 1957–60) v.1. L. PASTOR, *The History of the Popes from the Close of the Middle Ages* (London–St. Louis 1938–61) 14:1–55. H. LUTZ, *Lexikon für Theologie und Kirche,* ed. J. HOFER and K. RAHNER, 10 v. (2d, new ed. Freiburg 1957–65) 7:3–4. G. MOLLAT, *Dictionnaire de théologie catholique,* ed. A. VACANT et al., 15 v. (Paris 1903–50; Tables générales 1951–) 9.2:1992–93. W. HUDON, *Marcello Cervini and Ecclesiastical Government in Tridentine Italy* (De Kalb, Ill. 1992). E.G. GLEASON, ''Who Was the First

Counter-Reformation Pope?'' *Catholic Historical Review* (April 1995) 173–184.

[E. D. MCSHANE]

MARCELLUS AKIMETES, ST.

Abbot of the acoemetic monastery of Eirenaion on the Bosporus; d. *c.* 469. Marcellus, who had been born of rich parents, probably at Apamea, studied at Antioch and copied manuscripts at Ephesus before joining the Akoimeti monks (literally, the ''insomniacs'' or ''watchers,'' hence of perpetual ADORATION), who sang the Divine Office in relays day and night. Marcellus was one of the score of archimandrites who, undaunted by Emperor Theodosius II and Eutychian bishops, signed the condemnation of EUTYCHES at a synod at Constantinople in 448. Before the Council of CHALCEDON (451), he petitioned Emperor MARCIAN against Eutyches. Two letters to him from Theodoret of Cyr (*Epist.* 141, 142) congratulate him, apparently on his stand for orthodoxy in the troubles following the Robber Council of EPHESUS (449). At Chalcedon, during the session of October 17, he gave evidence against the Eutychian abbots.

Feast: Dec. 29.

Bibliography: J. D. MANSI, *Sacrorum Conciliorum nova et amplissima collectio.* (Florence–Venice 1757–98) 6:753; 7:61, 76. J. PARGOIRE, *Dictionnaire d'archéologie chrétienne et de liturgie.* (Paris 1907–53) 1.1:315–318; *Échos d'Orient* 2 (1898–99) 304–308, 365–372.

[A. A. STEPHENSON]

MARCELLUS OF ANCYRA

Bishop and controversial figure in the Trinitarian debate after Nicaea; b. *c.* 280; d. 374. As bishop of Ancyra he attended the council there in 314 and that of NICAEA in 325, where he strongly opposed ARIANISM. He published a major work against ASTERIUS the Sophist *c.* 330, in which he not only attacked both Eusebius of Nicomedia and Eusebius of Caesarea but also laid himself open to the accusation of SABELLIANISM. Consequently he became one of the main targets of the anti-Nicene party. EUSEBIUS OF CAESAREA attacked him in his *Contra Marcellum* and *De ecclesiastica theologia.* At a synod of Constantinople, Marcellus' book was condemned, and he was deposed and exiled. After the death of Constantine I in 337, when all exiled bishops were repatriated, Marcellus regained his see but was soon forced to leave again. He took his case to the West, where both a synod in Rome (340) and the Western assembly of SARDICA (343) declared his doctrine orthodox.

The Eastern Councils of Antioch (341) and Sardica (343), however, reaffirmed their condemnation in strong terms. The openly heretical doctrines of Photinus of Sirmium, a disciple of Marcellus, finally induced ATHANASIUS OF ALEXANDRIA and his Western allies to sever communion with Marcellus. Nothing is heard of him after 345, but many continued to write against him. EPIPHANIUS OF SALAMIS included him in his list of heretics (*Panarion* 72.1), as did the first canon of the Council of Constantinople I in 381.

Although Marcellus' treatise against Asterius is no longer extant, the numerous citations in Eusebius prove that his trinitarian doctrine was definitely unorthodox and closely related to a pre-Nicene type of dynamic MONARCHIANISM. While he admits the eternity of the Logos as such, he denies an eternal generation in God, holding that the Logos became Son at the Incarnation only. Similarly, at the consummation of the world, both the Son and the Spirit will reenter the Godhead, and there will be the absolute Monad again. Hence the affirmation against Marcellus in many creeds: ''. . . of Whose Kingdom there will be no end.''

According to St. Jerome (*De vir. ill.* 86) Marcellus wrote several other volumes against the Arians, but nothing remains of them, unless one agrees with F. Scheidweiler, who recently defended the Marcellan authorship of the pseudo-Athanasian treatises *Sermo maior de fide* and *Expositio fidei.* Also, a small treatise, *De sancta ecclesia,* formally attributed to Anthimus of Nicomedia, has been restored to Marcellus by M. Richard.

Bibliography: J. QUASTEN, *Patrology* 3:197–201, with bibliog. F. LOOFS, *Sitzungsberichte der Deutschen Akademie der Wissenschaften zu Berlin* 764–781. J. J. HERZOG and A. HAUCK, eds., *Realencyklopädie für protestantische Theologie* 12 (1903) 259–265. M. D. CHENU, *Dictionnaire de théologie catholique* 9.2:1993–98. J. M. FONDEVILLA, *Ideas trinitarias y cristologicas de Marcelo de Ancyra* (Madrid 1953); *Estudios Eclesiasticos* 27 (1953) 20–64. *Eusebius Werke,* ed. E. KLOSTERMANN, *Die greichischen christlichen Schriftsteller der ersten drei Jahrhunderte* 4 (1906) 183–215. F. SCHEIDWEILER, *Byzantinische Zeitschrift* 47 (1954) 333–357. M. RICHARD, *Mélange de science religieuse* 6 (1949) 5–28.

[V. C. DE CLERCQ]

MARCH MESA, NAZARÍA IGNACIA, BL.

In religion, Nazaría Ignacia of Santa Teresa of Jesús; foundress of the Missionary Crusaders of the Church (*Las Misioneras Cruzadas de la Iglesia*); b. Jan. 10, 1889, Madrid, Spain; d. July 6, 1943, Buenos Aires, Argentina. Nazaría was the fourth of the ten children of José March y Reus, a sailor and later businessman, and his wife Nazaría Mesa Ramos. She first sensed a call to religious life while she was preparing for her first communion (1898) and made a vow of perpetual virginity at age 11. Desiring to be a Jesuit missionary like Saint Francis XAVIER, she formed her young friends into a secret missionary society of the Sacred Heart; they prayed and offered sacrifices for the missions. Her family moved to Mexico due to economic reasons in 1906. En route, Nazaría became acquainted with two members of the *Hermanitas de los Ancianos Desamparados* (Little Sisters of the Abandoned Elderly) with whom she began her religious life (1908). In 1912, she went to Bolivia, where with the approval of the nuncio, the Bolivian Church hierarchy, and 40 centavos, she founded at Oruro the Missionary Crusaders. Nazaría was soon joined by others, elected superior general, and began to evangelize workers in cities, mines, and the countryside. Among other works she organized the first syndicate for female workers in Latin America, opened soup kitchens for the unemployed, and advocated for the advancement of women. Her foundation with houses in Argentina, Bolivia, Spain, and Uruguay, received definitive approval, June 9, 1947, four years after her death. Her mortal remains were enshrined in her community at Oruro in 1972. Nazaría, the patroness of Mexican barrios, was beatified by Pope John Paul II, Sept. 27, 1992.

Bibliography: A.-M. MAC AS LÓPEZ, *La fuerza del si: semblanza de M. Nazaria-Ignacia. . . .* (Sevilla 1992). *Acta Apostolicae Sedis* (1992): 919.

[K. I. RABENSTEIN]

MARCHANT, JACQUES

Pastoral theologian; b. Couvin, Namur, *c.* 1585; d. there, 1648. After his ordination he taught theology in the Abbeys of Floreffe and Lobbes and became pastor in his native village in 1616 and administrator of the Canton of Chimay in 1630. His writings in pastoral theology were highly esteemed, especially his *Hortus pastorum sacrae doctrinae* (3 v. Mons 1626–27), which adapted theology to the teaching of the catechism, to preaching, and to the confessional. He added a treatise on the Sacraments. Several other works of this type had numerous editions, and a 13-volume edition of his works was published in a French translation (ed. Vivès, Paris 1865–67).

Bibliography: *Biographie nationale de Belgique* 13:447–450. H. HURTER, *Nomenclator literarius theologiae catholicae* 3.1204.

[M. M. BARRY]

MARCHANT, PIERRE

Franciscan theologian; b. Couvin, Liège, 1585; d. Ghent, Nov. 11, 1661. He became a Franciscan in 1601 and taught for some years in the schools of his order. While still young he held a series of high offices in the order, becoming provincial, definitor general in 1625, and commissary general over the provinces of Germany, Belgium, Holland, England, and Ireland in 1639. The last office involved him in Irish politics during the era of the Kilkenny Confederation. Being deceived by false reports on the situation, he took sides with the Ormondists and supported Peter Walsh and those who opposed the nuncio, Giovanni Rinuccini. When called upon to justify this policy, he read his *Relatio veridica et sincera status Provinciae Hiberniae* to the 1661 general chapter at Rome. This book was condemned by the general chapter and ordered to be destroyed.

Marchant was a prolific writer. His principal work, *Tribunal sacramentale* (3 v. Ghent 1642), is a full treatise on moral theology for the use of confessors. Avoiding all disputed positions, he states the Church's teaching and draws his arguments from Sacred Scripture, the councils, the constant tradition of the Church, and the writings of the Doctors. The principles underlying his distinguished treatise on probabilism are in accord with the restrictions later imposed by the decrees of Alexander VII and Innocent XI.

His *Sanctificatio S. Joseph Sponsi Virginis in utero asserta* (Bruges 1630) involved him in a lively controversy with Claude d'Ausque of Tournai, and was placed on the Index in 1633. His other writings include *Baculus pastoralis sive Potestas episcoporum in regulares exemptos ab originibus suis explicata* (Bruges 1638), *Resolutiones notabiles variorum casuum et quaestionum a multis hactenus desideratae* (Antwerp 1655), and many treatises on Franciscan history and legislation that are of particular importance within the order.

Bibliography: L. WADDING, *Scriptores Ordinis Minorum* (Rome 1650). H. HURTER, *Nomenclator literarius theologiae catholicae* 3:1202–04. É. D'ALENÇON, *Dictionnaire de thèologie catholique* 9.2:2004–06. *Bulletin de l'Institut archéologique liègeois* 68 (1951) 59–62.

[F. C. LEHNER]

MARCHISIO, CLEMENTE, BL.

Priest, founder of the Institute of the Daughters of Saint Joseph; b. March 1, 1833, Racconigi, near Turin, Italy; d. Dec. 16, 1903, Rivalba, Piedmont, Italy.

Clemente was the eldest of the five children of a cobbler of modest means. His secondary education and study of philosophy was made possible with the financial help of Fr. Sacco. Following his ordination (Sept. 21, 1856), Marchisio continued his ministerial training for two years at a boarding school founded by St. Joseph CAFASSO. Although his first assignment was an easy one in a small town full of pious Christians, his second was a challenge. As pastor in the anti clerical Rivalba, his mettle was tested and proved strong. His strong sermons, unwaveringly proclaiming the truth, caused many to leave the Church and others to interrupt the Mass, but after ten years of persecution his example of Christian charity and virtue won souls.

Father Marchisio is known for his assiduous attention to duty, his devotion to the Holy Eucharist, and his concern for the poor. He gave away any of his possessions to help those in need, even his own bedding. Between 1871 and 1876, he established a home for children and a weaving mill to provide work for young girls.

Together with Rosalia Sismonda, who died just two hours before him, he found the Daughters of Saint Joseph to extend his care of the needy. He stressed to the sisters the necessity of prayer to support the congregation's apostolate. Later, wounded by the neglect of liturgical vestments and linens, he tasked the sisters with a new mission. The work of the Congregation now centers around the altar: making hosts and wine for the Eucharist, and preparing and maintaining linens for the liturgy.

Pope John Paul II beatified him on Sept. 30, 1984.

Feast: Sept. 20.

Bibliography: N. SARALE, *Teologia della semplicità: biografia di don Clemente Marchisio. . . .* (Rome 1975). *Acta Apostolicae Sedis* 77 (1985) 931–35. *L'Osservatore Romano,* Eng. ed. 44 (1984): 6–7.

[K. I. RABENSTEIN]

MARCIAN, BYZANTINE EMPEROR

Reigned 450 to 457; b. Thrace *c.* 392; d. Constantinople, Jan. 26, 457. Marcian, an aide-de-camp of the emperor-maker Aspar and a retired tribune, was 58 when THEODOSIUS II died leaving no heir. The Empress Pulcheria, elder sister of Theodosius, chose Marcian as her consort; he was proclaimed emperor (Aug. 26, 450) with the aid of the barbarian patrician, Aspar, and immediately informed VALENTINIAN III and Pope LEO I of his assumption of office. Having executed the eunuch Chrysaphius, who had exercised effective power since 443, Marcian and Pulcheria proceeded to reverse his politics in domestic, foreign, and religious affairs. The pope had confided in Pulcheria since 443; hence papal legates were well-received by Marcian. The body of the patriarch of Constantinople FLAVIAN, who had been maltreated after the Robber Council of EPHESUS (Aug. 449), was brought to Constantinople, and THEODORET OF CYR was recalled from exile.

In September 450 Leo had expressed a desire for a council. Unaware that with the change of emperors Leo had decided against holding a new council in the Orient, Marcian convoked an ecumenical council to meet at Nicaea in the fall. Despite misgivings, the pope acquiesced and sent his legates. Having decided to restrain Attila and the Huns by force instead of tribute, Marcian held the council at CHALCEDON where he could follow its actions at first hand, and in the sixth session (Oct. 25) he proclaimed the definition of the council, whereupon the assembly saluted him as a "new Constantine."

Marcian supported the disciplinary legislation of the council and in particular the so-called 28th canon, which gave the patriarch of Constantinople a primacy after that of the pope, as well as jurisdiction over the metropolitans in the civil dioceses of Thrace, Asia, and Pontus. This action was repudiated by Pope Leo, who delayed giving approbation to the council until Marcian informed him of the use the Eutychians were making of his hesitation (Feb. 15, 453). In a letter addressed to the bishops as if they were still assembled in council (March 21, 453), Leo confirmed its doctrinal decrees but condemned the 28th canon. When this letter was published by Anatolius, Patriarch of Constantinople, he left out the condemnation (cf. Leo, *Epist.* 127, Jan. 9, 454).

In Palestine Marcian repressed the rebellion started by the monk Theodosius, who had forced Bp. Juvenal of Jerusalem to flee. He requested Pope Leo to intervene with Eudocia, the estranged widow of Theodosius II, who had been in the Holy Land since 443 and was encouraging the anti-Chalcedonians. In Egypt he supported Proterius of Alexandria as successor of the deposed DIOSCORUS (d. Gangra, Sept. 4, 454). After the death of Pulcheria (July 453). Aspar suggested a tempering of the anti-Chalcedonian measures, since the enemies of Proterius had appealed to the imperial legate in Alexandria; upon the death of Marcian, Proterius was murdered by Monophysites. During the reign of Anastasius I (491–518) Marcian was still looked upon by the people as the ideal type of emperor.

Bibliography: E. STEIN, *Histoire du Bas-Empire* tr J. R. PALANQUE (Paris 1949–59) 1:311–315, 351–353. W. ENSSLIN, *Paulys Realenzyklopädie der klassischen Altertumswissenschaft* 14.2 (1930) 1514–29. F. HOFMANN, *Das Konzil von Chalkedon: Geschichte un Gegenwart* 2:15–24. R. HAACKE, *ibid.* 95–107. H. BACHT, *ibid.* 235–257. A. H. M. JONES, *The Later Roman Empire . . . ,* 4 v. (Oxford 1964).

[H. CHIRAT]

MARCIAN OF CYR, ST.

Monk and ascetic; b. Cyr, Syria, *c.* 300; d. in the desert of Chalcis, north Syria, *c.* 381–391. He was the son of patricians, but he preferred the life of a hermit, alone with God, praying and fasting. After some time he acquired as disciples Eusebius and Agapetus, who later initiated other monks to his spiritual and ascetic doctrine. Out of humility he refused to be ordained a priest and sought to hide his miraculous gifts. Before his death, friends built oratories to receive his relics, but he ordered his body concealed, and it was not discovered until 50 years after his death. THEODORET discusses Marcian in his *History of the Monks* 3 (*Patrologia Graeca*, ed. J. P. Migne 83:1324–40).

Feast: Nov. 2.

Bibliography: *Acta Sanctorum* Nov. 1:532–542. C. BARONIUS, *Annales ecclesiastici* 5:535. ''Le Synaxaire de Sirmond,'' *Analecta Bollandiana* 14 (1895) 420. J. L. BAUDOT and L. CHAUSSIN, *Vies des saints det des bienheureux selon l'ordre du calendrier avec l'historique des fêtes* (Paris 1935–56) 11:84–86. J. LEBON, *Le moine saint Marcien. Étude critique des sources*, ed. A. VAN ROEY (Leuven 1968).

[J. VAN PAASSEN]

MARCION

Christian Gnostic of the 2d century, founder of heretical Marcionite sect; d. *c.* 160. Marcion was probably the son of the bishop of Sinope, and *c.* 130, as a prosperous shipowner, left Pontus to spend some years in Asia Minor and Syria. It was there apparently that he encountered POLYCARP, and on asking ''Do you recognize me?'' was told ''I recognize you for the firstborn of Satan'' (Irenaeus, *Adv. haer.* 3.3.4); but this exchange may have taken place in 154 or 155 after Marcion's excommunication at Rome, where he certainly arrived in 139 or 140. At Rome Marcion was at first the disciple of the heretic Cerdo, but soon developed his own system and outshone his master. Summoned before the Roman *presbyterium* in July 144, Marcion steadfastly maintained that the Church had been mistaken in retaining the OT and in regarding Jesus as the Messiah foretold by the Prophets. He cited Luke (5.36–38 and 6.43) to show that Jesus's message was entirely new. Marcion was promptly excommunicated; he then gained many disciples among those who found the OT unconvincing or unattractive. He required baptism, celibacy, and a rigorous asceticism as the condition of salvation. From Rome the heresy spread rapidly throughout the empire. The dates and geographical locations of its orthodox opponents attest the extent and duration of its success. When Marcion died, his movement was powerful in Rome: ''invaluit sub [Pope] Aniceto'' (*c.* 154–166) says Irenaeus (*Adv. haer.* 3.4.3); and although *c.* 200 it was gradually checked, it still flourished in the East in the 5th century, especially in Syria, and groups of adherents survived down to the Middle Ages. Its influence (*c.* 200) among Latin-speaking Christians appears from the facts that it is still uncertain whether the first Latin translation of the NT was Marcionite or orthodox and that the genuineness of the ''Marcionite Prologues'' to ten of St. Paul's epistles found in the Codex Fuldensis and some 13 other ancient MSS of the Vulgate is increasingly accepted by scholars.

System. In his moral earnestness and special concern with the problem of evil, Marcion was impressed by Paul's denunciations of the Mosaic Law as the cause of sin and the principle of injustice. Concluding that the Law could not be the work of the Christian God, Marcion in his *Antitheses* (lost) repudiated the Demiurge or Creator God of the OT, who was not wicked, but who was the cause of the world and of evil. He considered this god as legal-minded, offering material rewards, capricious, violent, vindictive, a tyrant, and a petty-minded bungler, while the absolutely perfect God, the God of pure love and mercy, was visibly embodied in Jesus. Marcion characterized the former as ''just,'' ''the ruler of this aeon,'' ''predicable,'' and ''known'' through the creation and the OT. The latter he confessed to be the forgiving and saving God, as ''the Father of Jesus,'' ''good'' and ''unknown,'' ''the hidden or Stranger God,'' ''other,'' ''different,'' and ''new.'' He was unknown and new, because He was revealed only in Jesus; stranger and good because, despite John the Evangelist, He came not unto His own but, out of disinterested love, to save those who were strangers and for whom He had no reason to be concerned. Marcion's further description of Him as ''unperceivable'' and ''unpredictable'' supports H. A. Wolfson's suggestion based on Origen (*Cont. Celsum* 6.19) of a debt to such passages in Plato as *Phaedrus* 247C, with its contrast between Zeus's Olympus and ''that supercelestial place'' where dwells ''true Being, colourless, formless, impalpable, visible only to the intelligence, the soul's master, and the object of true knowledge.''

Able to see nothing in common between the God of the OT and the God of the NT, Marcion concluded that the Gospel must be dissociated from Judaism and Jewish apocalyptic eschatology. He repudiated the OT as devoid of any revelation of the Christian God. Yet the NT manifestly claims a certain continuity with the OT. Marcion found the answer in Paul's claim (Gal 1.1, 11–12; one Cor 11.23) to have received revelation not from man, but directly from the Lord. Paul alone, then, had correctly understood Jesus, though even his epistles had been interpolated. The earlier disciples had misunderstood Him, and their Gospels showed how their Jewish preconceptions had contaminated Jesus's message. However, the Gospel of Luke, who was the friend and companion of Paul, proved an exception. Moreover, his account of the Last Supper clearly derived from Paul's.

Since Marcion believed himself to be recovering authentic Christianity, he needed an *organon*. He framed a canon of Scripture that contained for its gospel an expurgated Luke and for its *Apostolikon* 10 Epistles of St. Paul. Hebrews and the Pastorals were excluded as manifestly non-Pauline. Luke's Infancy Narrative was among the discarded passages, for Marcion's soteriology was Docetic insofar as he thought that Christ had appeared suddenly, unannounced, and full-grown in the 15th year of Tiberius. Yet according to Tertullian (*Cont. Marcionem* 1.14), Marcion could say that "the better God chose to love, and for man's sake he laboured to descend. . . ." Moreover, quoting *Galatians* (3.13), Marcion interpreted the Redemption as a "buying free" in which the purchase price was Christ's blood, given not as an atonement, but for the cancellation of the Creator's legal claim to his property. It was thus that he interpreted Paul.

Reaction. The orthodox Christians, in reaction, established the true canon, and their apologists were not slow to appeal to tradition and to point to the arbitrary and implausible character of Marcion's procedure. The Alexandrine school developed the allegorical interpretation of the OT, and distinguished between the literal and the spiritual sense. The great body of Christians declared themselves in favor of life, for the goodness of the world, and the unity of the God of the creation and the redemption. IRENAEUS of Lyons developed his theory of a gradual revelation whereby God treated men as servants before He made them sons, and they first learned the duty of obedience before they could respond to love.

Bibliography: A. VON HARNACK, *Marcion* (2d ed. TU 45; 1924). G. BARDY, *Dictionnaire de la Bible* Suppl 5:862–877. F. L. CROSS, *The Early Christian Fathers* (London 1960) 64–65. H. JONAS, *The Gnostic Religion* (2d ed. Boston 1963) 137–146. H. A. WOLFSON, *The Philosophy of the Church Fathers,* v.1 (2d ed. Cambridge, Mass. 1956–) 571–573. J. H. CARPENTER, "The Bible in the Early Church," in *The Interpretation of the Bible,* ed. C. W. DUGMORE (London 1944). J. QUASTEN *Patrology*, v.1–3, *passim.*

[A. A. STEPHENSON]

MARCUS AURELIUS, ROMAN EMPEROR

Reigned A.D. 161 to March 17, 180; b. Rome, April 26, 121; d. Sirmium (Mitrovica) or Vindobona (Vienna). Marcus Aurelius Antoninus was originally named Marcus Annius Verus. He was the son of Annius Verus and Domitia Lucilla. His father, who was of Spanish descent and had been three times consul and prefect of Rome, died when Marcus was only three months old. Adopted by his paternal grandfather, he was enrolled among the equestrians by Hadrian at the age of six and made a Salian priest at eight. Of a serious and retiring temperament, Marcus was given the best education available. He studied literature and rhetoric under Herodes Atticus and Marcus Cornelius Fronto, but later abandoned these pursuits to take up philosophy under the Stoic Rusticus and law under Lucius Volusius Moecianus. In 138, shortly before his death, Hadrian adopted Antoninus Pius on the condition that he would in turn adopt Marcus Aurelius and Lucius Verus.

Marcus Aurelius, Roman Emperor, sculpted bust. (©Bettmann/ CORBIS)

Marcus was quaestor in 139 and consul for the first time in 140 and married the daughter of Antoninus Pius, Faustina the Younger, in 145, when he was consul for the second time. After living for years in the household of Antoninus, Marcus succeeded him as emperor on March 7, 161. He immediately asked the Senate to appoint Lucius Aurelius Verus as his colleague and gave him his daughter Lucilla in marriage. Verus, who proved to be an ineffective ruler, died early in 169, leaving Marcus as sole ruler of the Empire.

Marcus Aurelius was undoubtedly one of the best of the "good emperors." He tried valiantly to live up to

Plato's ideal of the philosopher-king (Julius Capitolinus, *Marcus Antoninus* 27.7), but his reign was marked by continued misfortunes: a pestilence that swept through the empire, revolts in Britain and Asia Minor, and frequent incursions of Germanic tribes in Pannonia and Noricum. It was while engaged in defending the frontiers in 172 that Marcus began his *Meditations.* Written in Greek, these reflections are a kind of philosophical diary in which Marcus gives a Stoic interpretation to the meaning of life and the practice of virtue. They reveal the nobility of his soul in the face of suffering, but also the shortcomings of STOICISM for a man of affairs.

Among Marcus's most important civil acts was a reform of the judiciary. As a natural conservative and official protector of the traditional religion, he looked with disfavor upon the introduction of superstitious practices (Modestinus, *Dig.* 48.19.30; Paulus, *Sent.* 5.21.2). He attributed the refusal of Christians to offer sacrifice to ''mere obstinacy'' (*Meditations* 11.3). Though no general persecution can be attributed to him, he seems to have done nothing during his reign to stop the popular uprisings against the Christians in various parts of the empire. When consulted by the governor of Lyons and Vienne on what to do with Roman citizens accused of Christianity, he replied that they should be executed if they did not recant (Eusebius, *Hist. eccl.* 5.1.47). Among those known to have suffered for the faith at this time may be numbered Sagaris of Laodicea; Thraseas of Eumenus; Publius, Bishop of Athens; and JUSTIN MARTYR and his companions.

The extent of the persecutions is indicated by the protests made in the apologies of Justin, Melito, Apollinaris, and ATHENAGORAS. Despite his many natural virtues, such a policy was consistent with Marcus's convictions, which placed the good of the state over that of individuals: ''What is not good for the swarm is not good for the bee'' (*Meditations* 6.54); ''The end of rational animals is to follow the reason and the law of the most ancient city and polity'' (*ibid.* 2.16). As M. J. Lagrange has observed, ''paganism laid her hand upon this man, naturally good, to make of him the minister of her works'' [RevBibl 10 (1913) 584].

Bibliography: H. VON ARNIM, *Paulys Realenzyklopädie der klassischen Altertumswissenschaft* (Stuttgart 1893–) 1.2:2279–2309. M. J. LAGRANGE in *Revue biblique* l0 (1913) 243–259, 394–420,568–587. H. D. SEDGWICK, *Marcus Aurelius* (New Haven 1921). ROBERTO PARIBENI, *Enciclopedia Italiana di scienzi, littere ed arti* (Rome 1929–39; suppl. 1938–) 22:256–259.

[M. J. COSTELLOE]

MARDUK

Marduk, chief god of the Babylonian pantheon from the 18th century on, is a relative a newcomer in the genealogy of the gods of ancient Mesopotamia (*see* MESOPOTAMIA, ANCIENT, 3). Originally Marduk (from Sumerian *amar-utu-ka,* ''calf of the sun'') was the god of the rising sun and spring vegetation and the local city god of Babylon. But with the establishment of the First Dynasty of Babylon *c.* 1830 B.C. by the AMORRITES and the development of Babylon into a capital of an empire under HAMMURABI, Marduk became the chief god of Mesopotamia. On the one hand, he was identified with En–lil of Nippur, the leading god of the ancient Sumerian pantheon, and as such was called BEL (from *ba'al,* ''lord''); on the other hand, he was identified with Asaru of the city of Eridu, who, as the son of En-ki, the lord of the abyss, was ''the lord of wisdom,'' i.e., of the knowledge of the magical properties of the life-giving waters of the abyss. Because of this double character, Marduk was represented Janus-like with two faces. The main temple of Marduk was the *É-sag-ila* (Sumerian, ''the house that raises high its head''), with its famous step tower (ziggurat; *see* TOWER OF BABEL), the *É-temen-an-ki* (Sumerian, ''house of the foundation of heaven and earth''). The temple's great eastern portal, the holy door, bricked up the whole year, was opened only on Marduk's principal feast, the Akitu feast on New Year's Day, the first day of Nisan, when in a solemn procession his image was carried through it (see the application to Yahweh in Ez 44.1–3). On this day, Marduk's wedding with his bride Sarpanitu (*Zēr-bānītu,* ''seed-creating'') was celebrated by bringing their two statues together and by sexual intercourse of the king, Marduk's representative on earth, with a priestess representing the goddess. This was to ensure the land's fertility for the coming year. The *ENUMA ELISH* creation epic was recited, thus pantomimically reenacting Marduk's enthronement as creator and king, and finally Marduk determined the fate of the gods and of men for the coming year. Toward the end of the Neo–Babylonian period (6th century B.C.), Marduk's son, the scribe god Nabu (Biblical NEBO), began to supplant his father in popularity. The only mention of Marduk by name is in the Old Testament (besides the proper names Merodach-Baladan; Mardochai is in Jer 50.2 in reference to Marduk's overthrow at the coming capture of Babylon; here the name of the god appears as Merodach (*m*[e]*rōdāk,* perhaps by taking the vowels of *m*[e]*bōrāk,* ''accursed''). In Jer 51.44, Is 46.1, and especially in Dn 14.1–22 and Baruch ch. 6, Marduk's helplessness as god of Babylon under the name of Bel is ridiculed.

Bibliography: M. JASTROW, *Die Religion Babyloniens und Assyriens,* 2 v. (Giessen 1905–12) 1:110–111, 493–495. B. MEISSNER, *Babylonien und Assyrien,* 2 v. (Heidelberg 1920–25) 2:15–17.

H. ZIMMERN, *Das babylonische Neujahrsfest* (Leipzig 1926). J. BOTTÉRO, *La Religion babylonienne* (Paris 1952) 40–41. F. M. T. DE LIAGRE BÖHL, *Die fünfzig Namen des Marduk* (Gröningen 1953) 282–312; *Lexikon für Theologie und Kirche*[2], ed. J. HOFER and K. RAHNER (Freiburg 1957–65); suppl. *Das Zweite Vatikanische Konzil: Dokumente und Kommentare,* ed. H. S. BRECHTER et al., pt. 1 (1966) 7:15–16. *Encyclopedic Dictionary of the Bible,* tr. and adap. by L. HARTMAN (New York 1963), from A. VAN DEN BORN, *Bijbels Woordenboek,* 1443–45.

[H. MUELLER]

MARÉCHAL, AMBROSE

Third archbishop of BALTIMORE, Md.; b. Ingres, near Orléans, France, Aug. 28, 1764; d. Baltimore, Jan. 29, 1828. After early classical studies at Orléans, he yielded to his parents' desires and chose the law as his profession. Shortly thereafter, however, he entered the priesthood, and began his theological studies at the diocesan seminary of Orléans. He joined the Sulpicians, and was ordained at Bordeaux in 1792. Then, accompanied by fellow Sulpicians Gabriel Richard and François Ciquard, he sailed for America and arrived at Baltimore on June 24, 1792. He first ministered to the Maryland Catholics in St. Mary's County (1792–93) and then went to Bohemia on the Eastern Shore of MARYLAND, where he served as pastor and administrator of the manor until 1799. He returned to St. Mary's Seminary, Baltimore, to teach theology (1799–1801), and then he taught philosophy at Georgetown College, Washington, D.C. (1801–02). In 1803 he was recalled to France because his superior general was discouraged with the Baltimore attempt and needed Sulpicians for the diocesan seminaries of France, where Napoleon's government had recently allowed them to return. Between 1803 and 1811 Maréchal taught in the diocesan seminaries of Saint-Flour, Lyons, Aix, and Marseilles. In 1811 the Sulpicians were again expelled from the French seminaries; Maréchal returned to the U.S. in 1812 as professor of theology in the Baltimore seminary; he later acted as temporary president of St. Mary's College (1815).

Although he had previously declined episcopal nomination to New York and Philadelphia, Maréchal was named coadjutor with right of succession to Abp. Leonard Neale of Baltimore (1817). However, the bulls did not arrive until November 10, more than five months after Neale's death. Hence on Dec. 14, 1817, Maréchal was consecrated archbishop of Baltimore by Bp. Jean Cheverus of Boston, Mass. The new archbishop immediately visited his extensive diocese, which included 100,000 Catholics in Maryland, Virginia, the Carolinas, Georgia, and the territory west of Georgia to the Mississippi. He restored order where both clerical and lay insurgents were causing trouble; and he advanced the work on the Baltimore cathedral, begun under Abp. John CARROLL in 1806, and dedicated it on May 31, 1821. During his *ad limina* visit to Rome later that year, he suggested to the Holy See that nominations for American bishoprics should come from the provincial bishops of the U.S., a policy still followed. He also succeeded in securing advice on the government of lay trustees and managed, temporarily, to quiet the problems of trusteeism. Finally, he persuaded Pius VII to raise his diocesan seminary of St. Mary to the rank of a pontifical university by letters dated April 18, 1822.

To secure the uniform development of the Church in the U.S. and plan for its future growth, Maréchal envisioned a provincial council, but ill health and eventually death intervened. After a journey to Canada in 1826 he was taken ill while confirming at Emmitsburg, Md.; he never recovered fully. His writings consist almost entirely of letters and documents, called ''scholarly in style,'' which may be found in T. A. Hughes's *History of the Society of Jesus in North America.*

Bibliography: R. H. CLARKE, *Lives of the Deceased Bishops of the Catholic Church in the U.S.,* 4 v. (New York 1887–89). C. G. HERBERMANN, *The Sulpicians in the United States* (New York 1916). T. A. HUGHES, *History of the Society of Jesus in North America: Colonial and Federal,* 3 v. in 4 (New York 1907–17). *Memorial Volume of the Centenary of St. Mary's Seminary of St. Sulpice* (Baltimore 1891). J. W. RUANE, *The Beginnings of the Society of St. Sulpice in the United States, 1791–1829* (Catholic University of America, *Studies in American Church History* 22; Washington 1935).

[C. M. CUYLER]

MARÉCHAL, JOSEPH

Belgian Jesuit philosopher; b. Charleroi, July 1, 1878; d. Louvain, Dec. 11, 1944. He entered the society in 1895, received a Ph.D. in biology from the University of Louvain in 1905, and was ordained in 1908. He taught biology, experimental psychology, and philosophy in the Jesuit house of studies, Louvain. Maréchal's main work is *Le Point de départ de la métaphysique,* essentially a vindication of Thomistic realism in five volumes—Maréchal called them *cahiers* (notebooks). The first three volumes were published together (Bruges-Paris 1922–23; 3d ed. Brussels-Paris 1944). The first two volumes try to show that some of the main inconsistencies of modern philosophy derive from a breakdown of the Thomistic synthesis under WILLIAM OF OCKHAM. The third is a remarkable reevaluation of I. KANT. Volume four was published posthumously (Brussels 1947). The famous fifth *cahier* is a study of THOMISM in the light of critical philosophy. Its leading idea is that, although Kant's objections are unanswerable if the human intellect is conceived as a static power, they can be overcome if that faculty is conceived dynamically, as St. THOMAS AQUINAS conceived it. Maréchal has influenced such philosophers as A. Marc, J. de Finance, G. Isaye, K. Rahner, J. B. Lotz, E. Coreth, and B. F. Lonergan.

Bibliography: Work in Eng. *Studies in the Psychology of the Mystics,* tr. A. THOROLD (pa. New York 1964). Studies. *Mélanges Joseph Maréchal,* 2 v. (Brussels 1950), biog. and bibliog. B. F. LONERGAN, ''Metaphysics as Horizon,'' Grey 44 (1963) 307–318. J. F. DONCEEL, *Philosophical Psychology* (2d ed. New York 1961) ch. 16; *Natural Theology* (New York 1962) pt. 1.

[J. F. DONCEEL]

MAREDSOUS, ABBEY OF

Benedictine abbey in the Diocese of Namur, Belgium, since 1920 part of the Belgian Benedictine Congregation, formerly part of the Congregation of Beuron. Founded in 1872 by monks from BEURON, with aid from the Desclée family, it became an abbey in 1878. The buildings are neo-Gothic. Abbots Placidus Wolter, later Archabbot of Beuron, and Hildebrand de Hemptinne (1890–1909), made primate of the Benedictines by Leo XIII (1893), were followed by Columba Marmion (1909), Célestin Golenvaux (1923), and Godefroid Dayez (1950). The abbey restored the Benedictine Congregation of Brazil (1895) and founded the abbeys of Mont César in Louvain (1899) and Glenstal in Ireland (1927) and the priory of Gihindamuyaga in RWANDA (1959). It publishes *Revue bénédictine* (1884–), the accompanying *Bulletin d'histoire bénédictine* (1897–), *Bulletin d'ancienne littérature chrétienne latine* (1921–), *Bible et vie chrétienne* (1953–), and *Lumière du Christ* (1960–). Patristic, liturgical, and monastic studies have been specially cultivated, notably by Germain MORIN, Ursmer BERLIÈRE, Donatien de Bruyne, Bernard CAPELLE, C. Charlier, Gerard VAN CALOEN, H. Duesberg, and Cyril Lambot. The abbey has a college of Greco-Latin humanities (1882) and an art school for gold work, ebony, and ceramics (1900).

Bibliography: L. H. COTTINEAU, *Répertoire topobibliographique des abbayes et prieurés,* 2 v. (Mâcon 1935–39) 2:1744. O. L. KAPSNER, *A Benedictine Bibliography: An Author-Subject Union List,* 2 v. (2d ed. Collegeville, Minn. 1962): v. 1, author part; v. 2, subject part, 2:228. D. MISONNE, *Lexikon für Theologie und Kirche,* ed. J. HOFER and K. RAHNER, 10 v. (2d, new ed. Freiburg 1957–65) 7:17. H. DE MOREAU, *Dom Hildebrand de Hemptinne* (Maredsous 1930).

[D. MISONNE]

MARELLO, GIUSEPPE (JOSEPH), BL.

Bishop of Asti, Piedmont, Italy, founder of the OBLATES OF SAINT JOSEPH; b. Dec. 26, 1844, Turin, Italy; d. May 30, 1895, of a cerebral hemorrhage in the bishop's residence at Savona, Italy. While still a child, Giuseppe (Joseph) moved from Turin to Santi Martino Alfieri with his father, Vincenzo, after the death of his mother, Anna Maria. He entered the minor seminary at age 12 and was ordained priest in 1868. While in the seminary he was miraculously cured of typhus by the Blessed Virgin. In his capacity as secretary to Bishop Carlo Savio of Asti for 13 years, Father Marello attended Vatican Council I from 1869 to 1870. During this time he also assumed responsibility for a retirement home, served as spiritual director, and taught catechism. He founded the Oblates of St. Joseph in 1878 to be ''hermits at home'' in order to be ''effective apostles away from home.'' Marello wanted his followers to be humble servants of the Church, ready to serve the bishops in whatever tasks were assigned them. The congregation was approved in 1909 by the Vatican after Marello's death. They opened their first mission in the United States in 1929. Following his episcopal consecration Feb. 17, 1889, Bishop Marello dedicated his work especially to youth and the abandoned. His remains were enshrined at Asti. He decisively opposed ''materialism, Masonry, and anti-clericalism, which prevailed at the time'' (decree of canonization, Dec. 18, 2000). Marello was beatified by John Paul II, Sept. 26, 1993, in the Campo del Palio at Asti, Italy. He was canonized on Nov. 25, 2001.

Bibliography: G. MARELLO, *Los escritos y las enseñanzas del bienaventurado José Marello,* ed. M. PASETTI (Santa Cruz, Calif. 1993). J. B. CORTONA, *Brief Memories of the Life of Joseph Marello, Bishop of Acqui, and of the Congregation He Founded . . .* (Santa Cruz, Calif. 1993). G. SISTO, *I, the Undersigned Poor Sinner: The Life of Blessed Joseph Marello* (Santa Cruz, Calif. 1993). L. M. TOSCHI, *Holiness in the Ordinary: Three Essays on the Spirituality of Blessed Joseph Marello* (Santa Cruz, Calif. 1993).

[K. I. RABENSTEIN]

MARENZIO, LUCA

Renaissance composer, renowned for his madrigals; b. Coccaglio (near Brescia), Italy, 1553; d. Rome, Aug. 22, 1599. As a boy he may have studied with Giovanni Contino at Brescia cathedral. While serving Cardinal Luigi d'Este in Rome (1579–86), he often visited the brilliant ESTE court in Ferrara. From 1591 to 1595 Cardinal Aldobrandini was his patron, and from 1596 to 1598 he was at the Polish court of Sigismund III. He was one of the rare Italian musicians of the period who never held a church appointment. His influence as a composer of matchless Italian madrigals is directly responsible for the flowering of the English madrigal school. Although his secular works are most numerous, his sacred music includes a Mass for 8 voices, two books of 4-voice motets (1588,1592), a book of 12-voice motets (1614), a book of *Sacri concenti* for 5 to 7 voices (1616), and a series of motets for church festivals. Reprints of his sacred works include: *Luca Marenzio: Motetten* (ed. H. Engel, 1926); motets in F. X. Haberl's *Repertorium Musicae Sacrae* (1886–1925); and other items in K. Proske's *Musica Divina* (1853–63).

Bibliography: *Sämtliche Werke,* ed. A. EINSTEIN (Leipzig 1929–). There are modern eds. of the motets by M. HALLER in *Repertorium Musicae Sacrae,* ed. F. X. HABERL (1886–1925) and H. ENGEL (Vienna 1926). H. ENGEL, *Luca Marenzio* (Florence 1956). A. EINSTEIN, *The Italian Madrigal,* tr. A. H. KRAPPE et al., 3 v. (Princeton N.J. 1949), v. 2. G. REESE, *Music in the Renaissance* (rev. ed. New York 1959). J. RAVELL and S. BROMAN, *Grove's Dictionary of Music and Musicians,* ed. E. BLOM, 9 v. (5th ed. London 1954) 5:574–576. N. SLONIMSKY, ed., *Baker's Biographical Dictionary of Musicians* (5th ed. New York 1958) 1028. O. CULLIN, ''Luca Marenzio: *Madrigaux à 5 voix, Livres 5 et 6,* Part 1,'' *Analyse Musicale,* 25 (1991) 53–64; ''Luca Marenzio: *Madrigaux à 5 voix, Livres 5 et 6,* Part 2,'' *Analyse Musicale,* 26 (1992) 65–71. R. FREEDMAN, ''Marenzio's *Madrigali a quattro, cinque et sei voci of 1588:* A Newly Revealed Madrigal Cycle and Its Intellectual Context,'' *Journal of Musicology,* 13 (1995) 318–354. S. LEDBETTER and R. JACKSON, ''Luca Marenzio,'' in *The New Grove Dictionary of Music and Musicians,* ed. S. SADIE, v. 11 (New York 1980) 667–674. B. JANZ, ''Die *Petrarca-Vertonungen* von Luca Marenzio'' (Ph.D. diss. Frankfurt am Main 1987). L. MACY, ''The Late Madrigals of Luca Marenzio'' (Ph.D. diss. University of North Carolina at Chapel Hill 1991). J. STEELE, ''Marenzio: From Mannerist to Expressionist,'' *Miscellanea Musicologica,* 11 (1980) 129–153.

[L. J. WAGNER]

MARESCOTTI, HYACINTHA, ST.

Virgin of the Third Order Regular of St. Francis; b. Vignanello, Papal States, 1585; d. Viterbo, Italy, Jan. 30 1640. Daughter of Count Marc Antonio di Mariscotti and Ottavia Orsini, Clare entered the convent of St. Bernardino in Viterbo and received the name Hyacintha. Taken ill after ten unhappy years, she was persuaded by a confessor to give up her well-furnished cell and follow a strict religious life. Devotion to the Passion, harsh penance, poverty, and humility flowered in mystical prayer and charity. She became mistress of novices. During a plague she founded two congregations, Oblates of Mary, to care for the sick and orphaned. She followed the common life even during a long exhausting illness. She left a small diary. Cardinal G. Mariscotti requested her beatification, and BENEDICT XIII, an Orsini, beatified her in 1726. PIUS VII canonized her in 1807. Her incorrupt body lay in the convent in Viterbo until the church was destroyed by aerial bombardment.

Feast: Jan. 30.

Bibliography: G. VENTIMIGLIA, *Vita di s. G. M.* (Rome 1695; 2d ed. 1907). C. R. HALLACK and P. F. ANSON, *These Made Peace,* ed. M. A. HABIG (Paterson, N.J. 1957). A. MERCATI and A. PELZER, *Dizionario ecclesiastico,* 3 v. (Turin 1954–58) 2:95–96.

[M. O'CALLAGHAN]

MARET, HENRI LOUIS CHARLES

French bishop, theologian; b. Meyrueis (Lozére), April 20, 1805; d. Paris, June 16, 1884. Studies at Saint-Sulpice Seminary, Paris, preceded his ordination (1830). After spending a short time in the circle of Hugues Félicité de LAMENNAIS, he became chaplain of St. Philippe du Roule in Paris (1832) and then professor (1841) and dean (1853) in the theology faculty at the Sorbonne. With OZANAM and LACORDAIRE he founded the journal *L'Ère nouvelle* (1848). When the government nominated him to the See of Vannes (1860), Pius IX refused to confirm the appointment because he was wary of Maret's GALLICANISM and his association with Catholic liberals. In 1861, however, Maret became titular bishop of Sura. During the Second Empire (1852–70) Maret, an acquaintance of NAPOLEON III, exercised considerable influence in the government's nominations to bishoprics. He continued his efforts to obtain outstanding professors for the Sorbonne theology faculty, whose degrees Rome did not recognize.

Maret was zealous and pious, well acquainted with contemporary intellectual movements, and an effective opponent of pantheism and atheism. He did not regard a breach between the Church and modern society inevitable and tried to deter Pius IX from publishing the SYLLABUS OF ERRORS. In a letter to the pope on the eve of its appearance, he argued that the separation of Church and State could be reconciled with the Church's traditions, rights, and doctrines. After VATICAN COUNCIL I was announced, he published his best-known work, *Du concile général et de la paix religieuse* (2 v. 1869), which opposed a definition of papal INFALLIBILITY and stressed the place of bishops in the Church's constitution and the vital importance of holding general councils at regular intervals. At the council he was a leading opponent of the definition of the papal prerogatives. He voted *non placet* in the definitive ballot (July 13) and absented himself from the solemn session (July 18) that promulgated the constitution *Pastor aeternus;* but he subscribed to the conciliar decisions the following month. At the insistence of Pius IX he retracted publicly everything in his book contrary to the above constitution (Aug. 15, 1871).

Bibliography: G. BAZIN, *Vie de Mgr. Mater* 3 v. (Paris 1891). C. BUTLER, *The Vatican Council,* 2 v. (New York 1930). É. AMANN, *Dictionnaire de théologie catholique* 9.2:2033–37. S. LÖSCH, *Döl-*

linger und Frankreich (Munich 1955) 209–229. R. THYSMAN, ''Le Gallicanisme de Mgr. M. et l'influence de Bossuet,'' *Revue d'histoire ecclésiastique* 52 (1957) 401–465. U. BETTI, *La costituzione dommatica ''Pastor aeternus'' del Concilio vaticano I* (Rome 1961).

[V. CONZEMIUS]

MARGARET, SS.

The name of several martyr saints in the early Church. An early *passio* of St. Margaret is intimately related to a series of legends that had Pelagia of Antioch as their heroine. Probably a martyr of Antioch under Diocletian, Margaret (Marina in the East) quickly became the subject of a cult that spread throughout Christendom in the Middle Ages. One of the voices heard by JOAN OF ARC was that of Margaret. As one of the 14 helper saints, Margaret is prayed to in difficult childbirth (feast, July 20).

St. Ambrose (*Patrologia Latina,* 16:241, 1093) and St. John Chrysostom (*Patrologia Graeca,* 50:579–585) knew of the historical Margaret, or Pelagia, a 15-year-old virgin of Antioch who preserved her chastity from violation by jumping off a building. Mistakenly identified with this Margaret of Antioch was an actress, also known as Margaret, or Pelagia, who left a dissolute life to become a Christian penitent. So many legends were based upon the account of the actress's conversion that the true story of Margaret of Antioch has been distorted beyond recognition.

Bibliography: St. Margaret. A. BUTLER, *The Lives of the Saints,* ed. H. THURSTON and D. ATTWATER, 4 v. (New York 1956) 3:152–153. H. DELEHAYE, *The Legends of the Saints,* tr. D. ATTWATER (New York 1962) 51, 56, 151. St. Margaret of Antioch. A. BUTLER, *The Lives of the Saints,* ed. H. THURSTON and D. ATTWATER, 4 v. (New York 1956) 2:510–511; 4:59–61. H. DELEHAYE, *The Legends of the Saints,* tr. D. ATTWATER (New York 1962) 152–153.

[E. DAY]

MARGARET COLONNA, BL.

Mystic; b. Rome, Italy, *c.* 1254–55; d. there, Dec. 30, 1280. She was the daughter of Odo Colonna and Margaret Orsini and first cousin to the future NICHOLAS III (*see* COLONNA). Left an orphan about the age of 11, she was placed under the guardianship of her oldest brother, Giovanni, who later became a Roman senator. On the advice of her brother Giacomo (d. 1318), she refused all marriage proposals and left Palestrina on March 6, 1273, for the castle of San Pietro. She took the habit and adopted the way of life of the POOR CLARES without actually entering into the order, and some pious young ladies soon joined her. Margaret, an intelligent and practical girl, led an exemplary life nursing the sick and giving generously of her resources to the poor. She was blessed with mystical visions, and after her death many miracles were observed at her grave. Her brother Giovanni reputedly wrote her biography, and Giacomo, after 1278 a cardinal, promoted her cause for canonization. On Sept. 24, 1285, the sisters who had joined her were transferred from the castle of San Pietro to the convent of San Silvestro in Rome, where they adopted the rule followed by the Clares of the Abbey of Longchamp near Paris. In 1875 they moved to the convent of S. Cecilia in Trastevere, Rome. Margaret's cult became widespread, but all proceedings for her canonization came to a standstill during the crisis of 1297–98 between the Colonna and BONIFACE VIII. In the 15th century her relics were venerated in San Silvestro, and in 1605 a silver reliquary bust was donated by Giovanna Pignatelli-Colonna. In 1847 an immemorial cult was approved, and the following year her feast was included in the Franciscan Breviary. The same Office has been used in the Diocese of Palestrina since 1883.

Feast: November 7 (formerly December 30).

Bibliography: G. COLONNA, *B. Margherita Colonna,* ed. L. OLIGER (Rome 1935). LEO OF CLARY, *Lives of the Saints and Blessed of the Three Orders of St. Francis,* v.4 (Taunton 1887) 70–73. *Vies des saintes et des bienheuruex* 12:798–799. F. BOCK, *Lexikon für Theologie und Kirche*, ed. J. HOFER and K. RAHNER, 10v. (Freiburg 1957–65) 3:10.

[J. CAMPBELL]

MARGARET OF CORTONA, ST.

Franciscan tertiary, penitent; b. Laviano, 1247(?); d. Cortona, Italy, Feb. 22, 1297. At the age of sixteen Margaret fled an unhappy family life to live for nine years as the mistress of a nobleman of Montepulciano. Upon his death, she returned to Cortona with her young son and put herself under the guidance of the Franciscans. Abandoning her son (who later became a Franciscan) to charity, she was allowed to join the Third Order of Penance of St. Francis in 1275. The major source for her life is the *Legenda de vita et miraculis beatae Margaritae de Cortona* written by her confessor, the friar Giunta of Bevegnati. It consists in ten chapters depicting the life and virtues of the saint, as well as one chapter dedicated to the miracles she performed while she was still alive and after her death. There is no doubt that the *Legenda* follows the typology of the classic hagiographical genre, which makes it difficult to sort out fact from fiction. It was meant to present Margaret as a ''new Mary Magdalene'' and provide a complete program of Christian living in particular for Franciscan lay women for whom she was set up as a model. She no doubt lived a harsh ascetical life and was gifted with exceptional mystical graces. She was also involved in peace-making activities and is credited with founding a hospital for the poor. Pope Benedict XIII canonized her on May 16, 1728. Her incorrupt body is venerated in her church at Cortona.

Feast: Feb. 22.

Bibliography: F. IOZELLI, ed., *Legenda de vita et miraculis beatae Margaritae de Cortona* (Grottaferrata 1997). T. RENNA, *St. Margaret of Cortona* intro. and trans. (St. Bonaventure, NY 2001). E. MENESTÒ, ''La mistica di Margherita da Cortono,'' in *Temi e problemi nella mistica feminile trecentesca* (Todi 1983), 183–206. R. RUSCONI, ''Margherita da Cortona, Peccatrice redenta e patrona citadina,'' in *Umbria sacra e civile* (Turino 1989), 89–104. J. CANNON and A. VAUCHEZ, *Margherita of Cortona and the Lorenzetti: Sienese Art and the Cult of a Holy Woman in Medieval Tuscany* (Philadelphia 2000).

[P. LACHANCE]

MARGARET OF HUNGARY, ST.

Dominican contemplative; b. 1242–43; d. Budapest, Jan. 18, 1270. She was a daughter of King Béla IV of Hungary and Mary Lascaris, and a sister of Bl. Jolenta and St. KINGA. At an early age Margaret took the habit at Veszprém, Hungary. In 1254 she made profession at the monastery of St. Mary of the Isle, built by her father near Budapest. After refusing offers of royal marriages three times, Margaret went through the solemn ceremony for the consecration of virgins. A true contemplative, endowed with mystical gifts, she spent an austere life in expiation for her people and manifested heroic charity, especially for the poor. Her cult began at her death and was approved in 1789. PIUS XII canonized her in 1943.

Feast: Jan. 26 (formerly 16).

Bibliography: Congregatio Sacrorum Rituum, *Extensionis seu concessionis officii et missae ad universam ecclesiam . . . B. Margaritae ab Hungaria* (Rome 1943), contains vita and depositions. *Acta Apostolicae Sedis* 36 (1944) 33–34. C. BÖLE, *Margherita d'Ungheria* (Rome 1938). M. CATHERINE, *Margaret: Princess of Hungary* (Oxford 1945). A. BUTLER, *The Lives of the Saints,* rev. ed. H. THURSTON and D. ATTWATER, 4 v. (New York 1956) 1:176–178. I. KIRÁLY, *Árpádházi Szent Margit és a sziget* (Budapest 1979). I. BELLUS and Z. SZABÓ, eds., *Árpád-házi Szent Margit legrégibb legendája és szentté avatási pere* (Budapest 1999), legends.

[C. MULLAY]

MARGARET OF LORRAINE, BL.

Widowed duchess of Alençon; b. Vaudemont in Lorraine, France, 1463; d. Argentan, Brittany, France, Nov. 2, 1521. Her parents, Ferri of Lorraine and Yolande of Anjou, having died when she was a child, Margaret was reared at the court of her grandfather, René of Anjou. In 1488 she married René, duke of Alençon, to whom she bore a son and two daughters. Widowed in 1492, she ruled the duchy with considerable skill during her son's minority. It was at this period that she came under the influence of St. FRANCIS OF PAOLA and began living a life of asceticism. When her responsibility to her children was discharged, she joined the Third Order of St. Francis, withdrew from court life, and devoted herself to the care of the poor in the neighborhood of Mortagne. Sometime after 1513 she founded at Argentan a convent whose inmates observed the Rule of St. Clare. In 1519 she entered this convent but refused to accept the office of abbess. She was buried in the convent at Argentan where her incorrupt body was venerated until profaned by the Jacobins in 1793. Her cult was confirmed by BENEDICT XV in 1921.

Feast: Nov. 6.

Bibliography: *Acta Apostolicae Sedis* 13 (1921) 231–233. R. GUÉRIN, *La Bienheureuse Marguerite de Lorraine, duchesse d'Alençon et religieuse clarisse* (Paris 1921); *Vie de l'aïeule d'Henri IV, 1463–1521. Bienheureuse Marguerite de Lorraine* (Paris 1953).

[C. J. LYNCH]

MARGARET OF METOLA, BL.

Virgin; b. Metola, Italy, 1287; d. Città di Castello, Italy, Apr. 13, 1320. She was of noble birth, but because of her deformities (she was dwarfed, blind, lame, and hunch-backed), her parents kept her hidden in a prison from the age of six to 16. She was then taken to a ''miraculous'' shrine in Città di Castello. As no miracle occurred, her parents abandoned her in that city. Her cheerfulness, based on her trust in God's love and goodness, was extraordinary. She became a Dominican tertiary and, despite her severe handicaps, devoted herself to tending the sick and the dying. Her solicitude for the prisoners in the city jail was remarkable. After her death more than 200 miracles testified to her heroic sanctity. She was beatified in 1609.

Feast: Apr. 13.

Bibliography: Bologna, Dominican Monastery, MS A. Paris, Bib. Nat. Ital. 2178. W. R. BONNIWELL, *Margaret of Castello* (Dublin 1955). M. C. LUNGAROTTI, *Le Legendae di Margherita da Città di Castello* (Spoleto 1994).

[W. R. BONNIWELL]

MARGARET OF ROSKILDE, ST.

Local Danish saint; d. Ølse, near Køge, Denmark, Oct. 25, 1176. She was of the great Sjaelland noble family of Skjalm the White and thus a relative of Abp. ABSALON OF LUND. Her husband Herlog strangled her and so hung her body as to simulate suicide. But when she was buried on the beach of Køge in unconsecrated ground, a miraculous light shone on her tomb and caused people to believe in her sanctity. After an investigation ordered by Absalon, Herlog confessed his crime. The archbishop had Margaret's body transferred to the Cistercian Abbey for nuns of Our Lady of Roskilde on July 19, 1177. Her cult remained purely local, limited to the Island of Sjaelland (Zealand), being especially popular at Køge, where a chapel was built in her honor. She was never officially canonized.

Feast: Oct. 25.

Bibliography: *Vitae sanctorum Danorum,* ed. M. C. GERTZ (new ed. Copenhagen 1908–12) 387–390. E. JØRGENSEN, *Helgendyrkelse i Danmark* (Copenhagen 1909).

[L. MUSSET]

MARGARET OF SAVOY, BL.

Widow, abbess and foundress; b. Pinerolo, Piedmont, 1390?; d. Alba, Italy, Nov. 23, 1464. Margaret, a member of the house of Savoy-Achaea, married Marquis Theodore II of Montferrat in 1403. At his death in 1418, she went to her estate in Alba where eventually she and her companions became Dominican tertiaries, taking simple vows and living in community. She founded the Monastery of St. Mary Magdalen 25 years later and made solemn vows as a nun of the Second Order of St. Dominic (*see* DOMINICANS). She ruled as abbess until her death. In 1566 Pope Pius V authorized her cult; Clement IX confirmed it in 1669. Her body is incorrupt. In art she is represented as either holding three arrows or receiving them from Christ. There is usually a deer in the background. The symbol of the arrows derives from her mystical experience; that of the deer, from the tradition that she kept a domesticated deer in her monastery.

Feast: Nov. 23.

Bibliography: F. G. ALLARIA, *Vita della beata Margherita di Savoia,* 2 v. (Alba, Italy 1877). S. SOLERO, A. MERCATI and A. PELZER, *Dizionario ecclesiastico,* 3 v. (Turin 1954–58) 2:826. A. BUTLER, *The Lives of the Saints*, rev. ed. H. THURSTON and D. ATTWATER (New York, 1956) 4:603–604. G. GIERATHS, *Lexikon für Theologie und Kirche*, ed. J. HOFER and K. RAHNER, 10 v. (2d, new ed. Freiburg 1957–65) 7:22.

[M. E. CASALANDRA]

MARGARET OF SCOTLAND, ST.

Queen; b. Reska, Hungary, 1046; d. Edinburgh, Scotland, Nov. 16, 1093. Margaret, the daughter of the Anglo-Saxon Prince Edward Atheling and Princess Agatha of Hungary, spent much of her youth at the court of her great-uncle EDWARD THE CONFESSOR. While attempting to return to Hungary in 1067 after the Battle of Hastings, she was shipwrecked off the Scottish coast, and in 1070 she married the Scottish King Malcolm III. She was the mother of St. DAVID I OF SCOTLAND. With the cooperation of Malcolm and the advice of LANFRANC, she initiated a series of ecclesiastical reforms that transformed the religious and cultural life of Celtic Scotland. A great benefactress, she founded Holy Trinity Abbey at DUNFERMLINE, restored IONA and other Celtic churches, and especially devoted herself to the care of the sick and the destitute. She was canonized by INNOCENT IV in 1249, and named patroness of Scotland in 1673. Her cult was widespread throughout medieval Scotland, where she is still venerated. Her body was translated from Dunfermline to a chapel in the Escorial in Madrid during the Reformation, but her head is with the Jesuits of Douai.

Feast: Nov. 16; June 19 (translation).

Bibliography: *The Gospel Book of Queen Margaret,* ed. W. FORBES-LEITH (Edinburgh 1896). *Acta Sanctorum* June 2:316–335. *Bibliotheca hagiographica latina antiquae et mediae aetatis* (Brussels 1898–1901) 2:5325–29. A. C. LAWRIE, ed., *Early Scottish Charters* (Glasgow 1905). J. R. BARNETT, *Margaret of Scotland* (London 1926). R. L. G. RITCHIE, *The Normans in Scotland* (Edinburgh 1954). G. W. S. BARROW, *Innes Review* 11 (1960) 22–38. K. NAGY, *St. Margaret of Scotland and Hungary* (Glasgow 1973). W. M. METCALFE, tr. *Lives of the Scottish Saints* (Felinfach 1990). N. G. TRANTER, *Margaret the Queen* (London 1979, repr. London 1993). A. J. WILSON, *St. Margaret, Queen of Scotland* (Edinburgh 1993).

[L. MACFARLANE]

MARGARET OF THE BLESSED SACRAMENT, VEN.

Discalced Carmelite nun and promotor of the devotion of the Divine Infancy (name in the world, Margarite Parigot); b. Beaune, France, 1619; d. Beaune, May 26, 1648. When she was 11 years old she received her first Holy Communion; she took the Discalced Carmelite habit in the convent of her native city on June 6, 1631, and was professed June 24, 1634, with the name of Margaret of the Blessed Sacrament. The wise and prudent direction of two Oratorians, Fathers Parisot (1637–43) and Blase Chaduc (1643–48), greatly aided her spiritual progress. She was the main apostle of devotion to the Infancy of Jesus that rapidly spread throughout France. She died a holy death; her cause for beatification was immediately introduced. The Congregation of Rites has decreed the heroicity of her virtues (Dec. 10, 1905), the first step toward eventual beatification, which is still under consideration.

Although she wrote nothing, her spiritual message soon had extraordinary success in the Church, especially in France, through the active and intelligent cooperation of her prioress, Mother Elizabeth of the Trinity (Quatreverbes), who gathered her spiritual experiences and confidences for publication (1631–40). This work has been the source of numerous biographies translated into the principal European languages.

Bibliography: D. AMELOTE, *La Vie de Soeur Marguerite du Saint Sacrement* (Paris 1654). ANTOINE-MARIE DE LA PRÉSENTATION, *La Vénérable servant de Dieu: Soeur Marguerite du S. Sacrement* (Bar-le-Duc 1929). J. AUVRAY, *L'Enfance de Jésus et sa famille, honorées en la vie du Soeur Marguerite du Saint Sacrement* (Paris 1654). P. FLICHE, *Année de l'Enfant Jésus, d'après les instructions de la Soeur Marguerite du Saint-Sacrement* (Paris 1866).

[O. RODRIGUEZ]

MARGIL, ANTONIO, VEN.

Franciscan missionary, promoter of missionary colleges in Spanish America; b. Valencia, Spain, Aug. 18, 1657; d. Mexico City, Aug. 6, 1726. Margil had been a Franciscan since 1673 and had been ordained (1682) when he arrived, with 22 other friars, in Veracruz, Mexico, on June 6, 1683. His name is linked inseparably with the development of the missionary college of the Propagation of the Faith. This institution, an autonomous community of friars dedicated to missionary work, was planned to meet the changed circumstances in 17th-century Mexico.

The natives, now dispersed from the pueblos where Christianization was carried on in the 16th century, required that the Church come to them, rather than that they come to the Church. This necessitated the development of highly mobile missionaries trained in new methods, and supported from outside the area where they worked. The missionary college was designed to meet this need. The first college, founded by Antonio Llinás in 1683, was Santa Cruz de Querétaro. Since its founder left Mexico in 1684 and never returned, Margil was responsible for the transformation of the college into an effective reality. He guided the college of Querétaro through its formative years and developed two other missionary colleges as well: Cristo Crucificado, Guatemala City, founded in June 1701, and Our Lady of Guadalupe, near Zacatecas, in July 1708.

In addition to his administrative work at these colleges, Margil worked out from them in the missions in

Antonio Margil preaching to Native Americans. (The Granger Collection Ltd.)

Mexico, Central America as far south as Cartago near Panama, and north to present-day Louisiana and Texas. He was an indefatigable missionary and a powerful preacher. At his death his reputation for sanctity was widespread. His remains, buried in the Franciscan church, were transferred to the Cathedral in 1861. The formal canonical investigation of his life was begun in 1771; Pope Gregory XVI issued the decree that his virtues were heroic in 1836.

Bibliography: E. E. RIOS, *Life of Fray Antonio Margil, O.F.M.*, tr. B. LEUTENEGGER (Washington 1959).

[B. LEUTENEGGER]

MARGOTTI, GIACOMO

Journalist; b. San Remo, May 11, 1823; d. Turin, May 6, 1887. He was ordained in 1846 at Turin, and began working two years later with the *Armonia della religione con la civiltà,* the first Catholic Italian newspaper (at first biweekly, then triweekly, and finally a daily after 1855). The paper had been founded through the efforts of Bishop Moreno of Ivrea and a group of Piedmontese Catholics that included Antonio Rosmini and Gustavo Benso, elder brother of Camillo Benso di CAVOUR. In those years, Margotti also published several short works against the liberal ministries. In September 1849, he joined the staff of *Armonia* as editor and substitute for Guglielmo Audisio, whom he succeeded that same year as publisher.

Under Margotti's direction, the paper became increasingly more polemical as it expressed the thinking of the ''intransigent'' Catholics; its editorial attitude was contrapuntal to the development of the anticlerical, antipapal, and anti-Catholic impetus of the Italian drive for independence. Margotti, a polished and brilliant writer, also continued the publication of shorter works and books in which he amplified the arguments made in the newspaper, especially in defense of the suppressed religious congregations and of bishops arrested or exiled from their sees. *Armonia* had the largest circulation in the Piedmont region, but it was also the paper most frequently seized by the police. On Jan. 27, 1856, Margotti was assaulted and injured; in the same year, he stood trial. In 1857, he was elected deputy to the Subalpine Parliament, but his election was predictably annulled by the government under hardly legal pretexts. In 1859 *Armonia* was under governmental suspension for several months. During the election of 1861, Margotti used the paper to urge Catholics to be ''neither elected, nor electors'' until free voting and elections were guaranteed, and until a Parliament was chosen that did not seek to take Rome from the pope.

Margotti left *Armonia* (1863) after feuding with its owners and founded *L'Unità cattolica* wherein he continued the most uncompromising policy toward the Italian state. From 1870 to 1898, Margotti issued his journal bordered in black to protest the occupation of Rome by Italian troops. *Armonia,* transferred in 1866 to Florence (then the capital of the Kingdom of Italy), ceased publication in 1870. *L'Unità cattolica,* which became the property of the Holy See and moved to Florence in 1893, ceased publication in 1929.

[E. LUCATELLO]

MARIA CRISTINA OF SAVOY, VEN.

Queen; b. Cagliari, Sardinia, Nov. 14, 1812; d. Naples, Jan. 31, 1836. She was the youngest of five children whose devout parents were Victor Emmanuel I (1759–1824), King of Sardinia (1802–21), and Maria Theresa (1773–1832), of the house of Hapsburg-Lorraine. From early years Maria displayed the kind, charitable, and pious traits that characterized all her life. Relinquishing her own wish to enter religion, she bowed to the will of her sovereign, Charles Albert, and married Ferdinand II, King of Naples. While fulfilling the obligations of her state in the Bourbon court, she continued unchanged her religious practices and exercised an exemplary influence on her husband and others about her. Neapolitans referred to her as a saint, even though they were unaware of the full extent of her good deeds. Stories circulated about her ill treatment by her husband, but these were the inventions of liberal political opponents of the ruler. She died in giving birth to her only child, who became Francis II, the last Bourbon king of Naples. The decree introducing her cause was issued in 1859, and the decree approving the heroic nature of her virtues, in 1937.

Bibliography: C. TESTORE, *Beati e venerabli di Casa Savoia* (Turin 1928). A. BRESCIANI, ''La Venerabile Maria Cristina di Savoia,'' *La civiltà cattolica* ser. 4, v.4 (1859) 129–144, 309–325, the first biog. pub.; rev. ed. E. ROSA (Rome 1936). B. CROCE, *Uomini e cose della vecchia Italia,* ser. 2 (2d ed. Bari 1943) 268–308, important essay. H. M. ACTON, *The Last Bourbons of Naples (1825–1861)* (London 1961). *Acta Apostolicae Sedis* 29 (1937) 349–352.

[M. L. SHAY]

MARIA LAACH, ABBEY OF

Benedictine foundation in the Rhineland, near Andernach, West Germany. Founded in 1093 by Count Palatine Henry II and his wife and settled with monks from St. Maximin in TRIER and later from AFFLIGEM, it had possessions on the Rhine and Moselle and in the Eifel. The Romanesque church (patrons, Our Lady and St. Nicholas), consecrated by Abp. Hillin of Trier (1156), is almost unchanged despite several restorations. The abbey flourished under the customary of CLUNY. After a late medieval decline, it joined the BURSFELD union (1474) in which it had a leading role after the Reformation. Prior Johannes Butzbach (d. 1516), influenced by Abbot J. Trithemius, was a prominent humanist author. The abbey was suppressed during the French Revolution and secularized (1797–1802), the state holding the church (1815–1924) and private individuals holding the property and the buildings (damaged by fire in 1855). Jesuits acquired Maria Laach (1862), establishing a *collegium maximum* and building a library (1864) and gatehouses (1869). They produced there *Philosophia Lacensis* (13 v. 1888–1919), *Collectio Lacensis* of councils (7 v. 1870–90), and *Stimmen aus Maria Laach* (1871–1915), since called *Stimmen der Zeit.* Expelled in the Kulturkampf, they kept an administrator at the abbey until they sold it to Benedictines of BEURON (1892), title and rights of the old abbey being restored in 1893. Willibrord Benzler (bishop of Metz in 1901), Fidelis von Stotzingen (to 1913), Ildefons HERWEGEN (d. 1946), and B. Ebel have served as abbots. Under Abbot Herwegen, the abbey became a center of the liturgical reform: Odo CASEL (d. 1948), Kunibert MOHLBERG (d. 1963); the collection *Ecclesia orans* (1918–); and a German missal (1929–). Besides liturgical studies have appeared studies in Benedictine history, hymnology, and art. Since 1948 scholarship has been concentrated in the Abbot Herwegen Institute for Liturgical and Monastic Research. Pius XI made the abbey church a minor basilica.

Bibliography: H. EMONDS, ed., *Enkainia. Gesammelte Arbeiten zum 800 jährigen Weihegedächtnis der Abteikirche Maria Laach am 24 August 1956* (Düsseldorf 1956). T. BOGLER, *Maria Laach: Vergangenheit und Gegenwart der Abtei am Laacher See* (4th ed. Munich 1961); *Benedikt und Ignatius: Gesammelte Aufsätze* (Maria Laach 1963). E. VON SEVERUS, *Lexikon für Theologie und Kirche*, ed. J. HOFER and K. RAHNER, 10 v. (2d, new ed. Freiburg 1957–65) 7:45–46.

[E. VON SEVERUS]

MARIA LAURENTIA LONGO, VEN.

Foundress of the Capuchinesses (*see* FRANCISCAN SISTERS); b. Barcelona, 1463; d. Naples, 1542. Her husband, the Catalan Juan Llonc, royal chancellor in Naples, died in 1507. As a widow, she was active in the Oratory of Divine Love of St. CAJETAN and founded (1521–22) a hospital for incurables in Naples. To the convent of nuns she instituted in 1535 she gave first the rule of St. CLARE OF ASSISI and then statutes inspired by those of the Capuchin monks: personal sanctification by work, poverty, and humility, and the service of one's neighbor with sacrifice and works of charity. Pope Paul III approved the order in December 1538. In 1576 a house was founded in Rome, and in 1599 (Ven.) Angela Serafina de Manresa founded the first convent outside Italy, in Barcelona. The process for Maria's beatification was introduced in 1892.

Bibliography: J. A. DE HARSBERG, *Die Maria Laurentia Longo, Stifterin der Kapuzinerinnen* (Munich 1903). F. S. DA BRUSCIANO, "M. L. L. e l'opera divino amore a Napoli," *Collectanea Franciscana* 23 (1953) 166–228, sources, literature. *Lexicon Capuccinum* (Rome 1951) 1049.

[J. PÉREZ DE URBEL]

MARIA-MÖDINGEN, CONVENT OF

Former house of Dominican nuns now occupied by Franciscan teaching sisters, near Dillingen, Bavaria, Germany. The convent was founded by Hartmann IV of Dilligen before 1239 and affiliated to the DOMINICANS in 1246. At first it was one of the most noted convents of southern Germany and the home of the mystic Margaret Ebner. Religious observance there, however, declined late in the 14th century. It was restored in 1468. The nuns

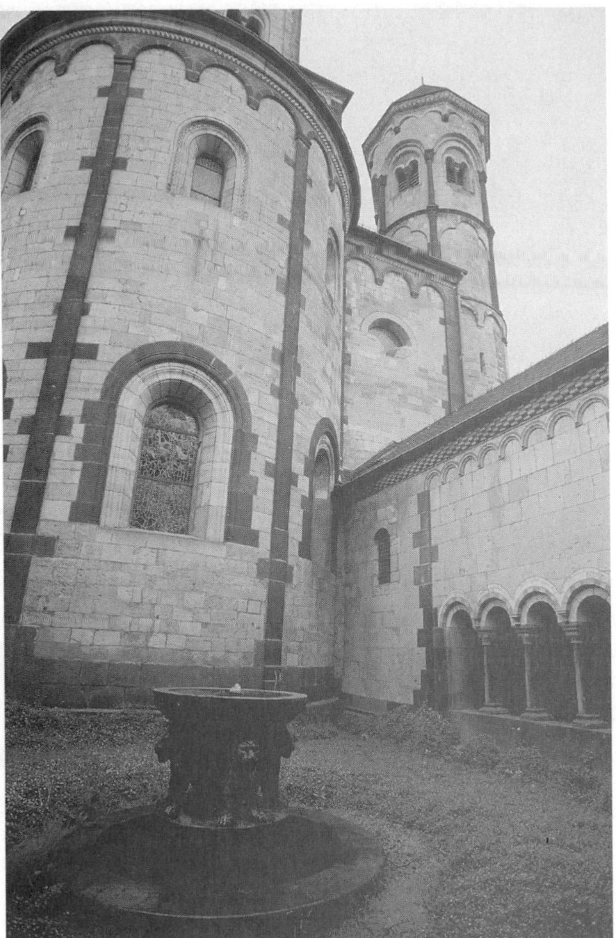

Abbey of Maria Laach. (©Vanni Archive/CORBIS)

resisted all attempts to protestantize them, but they were driven out when the monastery was confiscated in 1546. Duke Wolfgang Wilhelm of Pfalz-Neuburg, a Catholic, returned the monastery to the Dominicans; it was reconstituted by nuns from St. Catherine's in Augsburg in 1616. It was again suppressed in 1802. Since 1842 Franciscan teaching sisters have occupied the buildings. The present church, built from 1716 to 1718, enshrines the tomb of Margaret Ebner in a chapel built in 1755.

Bibliography: F. ZOEPFL, *Jahrbuch des historischen Vereins Dillingen . . .* (Dillingen 1960) 7–77; *Lexikon für Theologie und Kirche,* ed. J. HOFER and K. RAHNER, 10 v. (2d, new ed. Freiburg 1957–65) 7:47–48. J. SCHÖTTL, *Kloster M.-M.* (2d ed. Zurich 1961).

[J. A. DOSHNER]

MARIA THERESA OF AUSTRIA

Reigned Oct. 20, 1740, to Nov. 29, 1780; Empress, Queen of Hungary and Bohemia, Archduchess of Austria; b. Vienna, May 13, 1717; d. Vienna. She was mar-

"Maria Theresa, Empress of Austria," painting by Martin Mytens the Younger. (©Archivo Iconografico, S.A./CORBIS)

ried (1736) to Duke Francis Stephen of Lorraine-Tuscany (later Emperor Francis I 1745–65). The sudden death of her father, the Holy Roman Emperor Charles VI, forced the inexperienced heiress to assume the government of the Hapsburg domains, which had shortly before her accession been united by the Pragmatic Sanction. This document (1720) decreed that the Austrian Empire was indivisible, and that upon the failure of a male heir, it should devolve upon the eldest daughter of Charles VI. Within a few months, war broke out. During this war Frederick II of Prussia claimed the province of Silesia, and Charles Albert, Prince Elector of Bavaria, who did not recognize the Pragmatic Sanction, claimed other parts of the Hapsburg monarchy. The young queen soon familiarized herself with the heavy responsibilities of high office, took up the challenge to battle her enemies, and ended the struggle honorably, notwithstanding the loss of Silesia. Once peace was established (1748), she started to reorganize, with prudence and fortitude, her heterogeneous domains, which, in response to the demands of her time, she sought to transform into a centralized bureaucracy. In trying to raise financial means and to increase the capacity of the whole population to pay taxes, she met opposition from the Catholic Church. The Church would not and could not relinquish its constitutional position, dating from the Middle Ages, and the economic privileges attached thereto. The resulting disputes between the Catholic Austrian state and the Catholic Church, which had important consequences for both, cannot be understood without knowing the background of the preceding reign.

Church and State. While still a 12-year-old princess, Maria Theresa had received a false picture of the Church. Her teacher of history, the jurist Gottfried Spannagl, had represented the medieval struggle between Emperor and Pope as caused solely by the Pope's lust for power. A few days after her accession to the throne, Maria Theresa wrote to the Pope asking for his moral support. Her letter, however, had not been countersigned by the responsible minister, thereby giving the impression that the young ruler wanted to write a mere private letter; but from this procedure, the inference could also be drawn that the Austrian government intended to infringe upon papal sovereign rights, something that the Queen's ancestors had occasionally attempted. This unfortunate circumstance caused ill feeling and the belated recognition of Maria Theresa by the HOLY SEE. The election of Albert of Bavaria to the imperial inheritance, and the War of the Austrian Succession (1740–48) that followed, furthered the estrangement. Notwithstanding repeated protests from the court of Vienna, Pope Benedict XIV could not refuse to recognize this election, since it had met all legal requirements. Maria Theresa allowed herself to be influenced to such an extent by the enmity of her ministers against the papal court that she ordered the sequestration of all benefices on the Austrian territory of the Cardinal Secretary of State Ludovico Valenti, himself an Austrian. Added to this was the violation of papal neutrality by the warring parties, who invaded the Papal States and harrassed papal subjects, especially in Ferrara, Pesaro, Rimini, and Bologna.

All these factors caused new complaints and protests from the Roman Curia. Only years later did the Austrian governor of Milan, Count Beltrame Cristiani, who enjoyed the fullest confidence of the Empress, succeed in convincing her of the injustice of her action against the Pope and his secretary of state and in moving her to release the confiscated properties. Renewed protests by the Roman Curia were provoked by such other imperial ordinances as the enactment that the Lombard clergy could appeal to Rome only by imperial permission. The Republic of Venice was not slow to quote this article as a precedent in its concurrent conflict with Rome. Notwithstanding repeated requests from Benedict XIV, Maria Theresa steadfastly refused to repeal this ordinance; the most she did was to give it an interpretation that would pacify the Pope. At this time, Count Cristiani had entered into promising negotiations with the Holy See about the creation of a church fund for the increase of parishes; to this fund the great foundations and monasteries should contribute. When it appeared, however, that Maria Theresa intended to administer this fund through her civil servants, the Pope feared the disadvantages more than the advantages that would come of state control. The whole undertaking came to nought after the start of the Seven Years' War (1756–63).

The Origins of Josephinism. The tensions between Vienna and Rome were only the symptoms of a fundamental conflict between Church and State in Austria. At the same time, they show clearly the monarch's conception of sovereignty, which was cleverly exploited by Prince Wenzel Anton von Kaunitz, her chancellor. At his counsel the empress initiated the new ecclesiastical policy by ordering an investigation into the privilege Pope Nicholas V had granted Emperor Frederick III in 1451–52. This privilege concerned taxation of the Austrian clergy under certain conditions. The Minister of the Interior, Count Johann Chotek, an upright soldier, explained to her how this privilege had been exercised during all those years. He stressed that the supervision of a papal representative, provided for in the document and exercised subsequently, had in no way harmed the state so that the established practice could safely be continued. The Empress, however, corrected her minister, whom she soon changed in favor of his more adaptable brother, "that in this as in other privileges of my archducal house many rights have been sacrificed." She then ordered a research into all royal archives to discover relevant tax privileges granted by various popes and confirmed as late as 1523 by Adrian VI. But since all these documents presupposed on principle the assent of the Holy See, it was impossible to prove the right of the state to tax the clergy independently of the pope.

The Empress, however, regardless of precedent and without previous negotiations with the Holy See remained firm—and this is a decisive point for the judgment of her unjust and revolutionary action. After 1763, she had her court lawyers construct a new canon law. The teachers of this subject, the JESUITS, were replaced by lay professors. In 1767 she signed in effect the first decrees for the Austrian provinces in Italy. The first of these decrees restricted the freedom of communication of the Lombard clergy with the Roman Curia and appointed two political agents to watch over such movements. The second degree created the so-called Giunta Economale, which greatly interfered with episcopal jurisdiction. The third decree renewed the notorious laws against MORTMAIN, interpreting them so that the Church could no longer acquire any considerable real property without the consent of the state. The Cardinal Archbishop of Milan, Giuseppe Pozzobonelli, the leading churchman of Lombardy, thereupon protested and warned the Empress that she could not in conscience promote these laws. Maria Theresa, after hesitation, rejected this protest, and a year later approved the general principles underlying State-Church relations as laid down by Kaunitz and already in effect through the above-named decrees in Austrian Lombardy, which he administered. Again it was Kaunitz who made the Empress reject the representations of the Pope himself. Instead, the new State-Church system was soon formally extended over all Austrian dominions.

Suppression of the Jesuits. Among the numerous decrees and ordinances "in publico-ecclesiaticis" harmful to the Church that followed each other rapidly in the last decade of Maria Theresa's reign and that touched the religious orders in particular, must be counted the suppression of the Society of Jesus (1773). The attitude of the Empress in the *affaire célèbre* of the age was fateful for religion and government in Austria. The Bourbon courts had used powerful threats to force the Pope to suppress the JESUITS. But Clement XIV for a long time could point out that Maria Theresa, as *advocata ecclesiae,* took the opposite standpoint and had assured the menaced Society of her protection. The Bourbons then intimidated Maria Theresa by reminding her that, in view of her friendly attitude toward the Jesuits, her daughter, Maria Antonia (later Marie Antoinette) could not become queen of France. Thereupon the Empress broke the word she had given the Jesuits. She even wrote to Charles III, King of Spain, who had been the driving force behind the suppression of the Society, that she was glad to be able to oblige him in a matter so close to his heart. At the same time she put such pressure on the Pope, already hard pressed from all sides, that the Pope in the end abandoned to her all Jesuit assets. In the last years of her reign her physical powers failed and her life was darkened also by the conflict with her son and successor, JOSEPH II, of whose character and reign she had no great hopes.

Bibliography: F. MAASS, ed., *Der Josephinismus: Quellen zu seiner Geschichte in Österreich 1760–1850,* 5 v. (Fontes rerum Austriacarum II.71–75; Vienna 1951–61); "Maria Theresia und der Josephinismus." *Zeitschrift für katholische Theologie* 79 (1957) 201–213. H. VON ARNETH, *Geschichte Maria Theresias,* 10 v. (Vienna 1863–76). E. GUGLIA, *Maria Theresia, ihr Leben und ihre Regierung,* 2 v. (Munich 1917). P. REINHOLD, *Maria Theresia* (Wiesbaden 1958). G. P. GOOCH, *Maria Theresa and other Studies* (New York 1951). G. DORSCHEL, *Maria Theresias Staats- und Lebensanschauung* (Gotha 1908).

[F. MAASS]

MARIAN ANTIPHONS

A somewhat inexact term for several chants with texts about the Blessed Virgin, or addressed to her. They originated during the Middle Ages when feasts of the Virgin were provided, and when the custom arose of celebrating special offices honoring her, which also required special music. The chants were used in different ways in different places; they might be used as antiphons in the ordinary sense—to introduce and to follow the chanting of a psalm or canticle in the office (*see* LITURGY OF THE HOURS); alone as processional chants; or singly as a votive antiphon after one of the offices, particularly after Compline.

The four Marian antiphons remaining in use today are *ALMA REDEMPTORIS MATER, AVE REGINA CAELORUM, REGINA CAELI*, and *SALVE REGINA*. One of them is sung every day after Compline, according to the season. Other medieval Marian antiphons are *Ibo mihi ad montem myrrhae, Quam pulchra es et quam decora, Speciosa facta es, Sancta Maria succurre miseris,* and *0 gloriosa genetrix virgo*; all are found in the late 13th-century MS Cambridge University Library Mm. ii. 9, as reproduced in *Antiphonale Sarisburiense,* ed. W. H. Frere (1901–25); *Nesciens mater* and *Mater ora filium* (used at Lincoln, England, 1380); *Sancta Maria virgo* (used at Salisbury, 1395); and *Sub tuam protectionem, Haec est regina,* and *Tota pulchra es* (used at Senlis, France, late 14th century). J. DUNSTABLE (d. 1453) set the second, third, and fourth Cambridge texts for three voices, but did not quote their chant melodies.

Composers of the later Middle Ages and Renaissance frequently set the texts of Marian antiphons, occasionally quoting the melody in the process. *Nesciens mater* by Byttering (English, active *c.* 1420) involves the chant theme in all three of its voices in turn; *Sancta Maria virgo,* in an English source from the second half of the 14th century, is composed for three voices, the lower two sharing the *cantus firmus*. These settings were in rather simple style, but others were more elaborate, e.g., Lionel POWER's *Mater ora filium,* Plummer's *Tota pulchra es,* and Forest's *Tota pulchra es*—all from the early 15th century. Composers continued setting these antiphons polyphonically well into the 16th century. Perhaps the most remarkable of all Renaissance compositions in which Marian antiphons are quoted is a motet by GOMBERT (prefaced by the words ''Diversi diversa orant'') in which both words and melodies of seven Marian chants are enveloped in rich polyphony.

Bibliography: ''Les Auteurs présumés du *Salve Regina,*'' *La Tribune de Saint-Gervais* 18 (1912) 76. F. L. HARRISON, *Music in Medieval Britain* (New York 1958). G. REESE, *Music in the Middle Ages* (New York 1940). B. STÄBLEIN, ''Antiphon,'' *Die Musik in Geschchte und Gegenwart*, ed. F. BLUME (Kassel-Basel 1949–) 1:523–545. P. WAGNER, *Einführung in die gregorianischen Melodien*, 3 v. (Leizig); repr. (Hildesheim 1962). W. APEL, *Gregorian Chant* (Bloomington, Ind. 1958).

[R. STEINER]

MARIAN FATHERS

The Congregation of Marians of the Immaculate Conception of the Blessed Virgin Mary (MIC, Official Catholic Directory #0740), popularly called Marian Fathers, were founded in Poland in 1673 by Stanislaus of Jesus and Mary PAPCZYNSKI to honor the Immaculate Conception of the Virgin Mary, to teach the poor, and to pray for the souls in purgatory. The Marians first began as a diocesan community with simple vows. Within six years of their founding, King John III Sobieski granted permission to establish houses throughout his dominions. In 1699 Innocent XII gave the Marian Fathers the Rule of Ten Evangelical Virtues of Our Lady (approved by Alexander VI in 1501) and designated the community as an order with solemn vows. This rule was complemented by statutes composed by the founder. The distinctive religious garb of the Marians was a white habit with cincture and cape.

The Marians made foundations in Lithuania, Portugal, and Italy, but religious persecutions gradually forced them out of Rome in 1798, Portugal in 1834, and Poland and Lithuania in 1864. Most Marians were either exiled to Siberia or absorbed into the diocesan clergy by 1864. Those who remained were permitted to live in the monastery of Mariampole, Lithuania, but were forbidden to accept novices. In 1908 there remained in Mariampole the last surviving Marian, Vincent Senkowski-Senkus, superior general. However, the order was saved from extinction by two Lithuanian priests, professors of the Roman Catholic Ecclesiastical Academy in St. Petersburg, Russia, who appealed to the Holy See to be admitted secretly into the order. In order to facilitate restoration, Pius X approved the change from solemn to simple vows, and from the conspicuous white habit to the black cassock of a diocesan priest. On Aug. 29, 1909, by papal dispensation, George Matulaitis-Matulewicz made his religious profession without the required novitiate, and Rev. Francis Bucys was admitted into the novitiate. To rescue the reborn congregation from Russian persecution, the novitiate was transferred in 1911 from St. Petersburg to Fribourg, Switzerland. In 1910 a new constitution (revised in 1930) was approved by Pius X and supplanted the original rule. In 1930 Pius XI confirmed the former status of the Marians as exempt religious.

In 1913 the Marian Fathers first settled in Chicago, Ill., and from there spread to Wisconsin, Michigan, New York, Connecticut, Massachusetts, and Washington, D.C. Some of them minister in the Byzantine-Slavonic rite. In the spirit of their founder, they preach missions, teach, administer parishes, and publish newspapers, books, and periodicals.

The generalate is in Rome. There are two American provinces: St. Casimir (with its headquarters in Chicago,

IL) and St. Stanislaus Kostka (with its headquarters in Stockbridge, MA).

[M. RZESZUTEK/EDS.]

MARIAN FEASTS

Although Marian liturgical cult appeared at mid-5th century, it was slow in growth and gained momentum only at the end of the 7th.

History

Marian devotion originated very early; for prayers to Mary, such as the *Sub tuum* of Greek origin, were already known in Egypt in the 3rd century, and some paintings of her and the Child in the Roman catacombs date probably from the middle of the 2nd century. This devotion, however, was not at first accompanied by liturgical worship. When, at the end of the 4th century, the anniversary celebrations for martyrs and bishops began to multiply, there was still no feast of the Blessed Virgin. The reason for this was the fact of the ASSUMPTION. No church claimed possession of her tomb, and at that time veneration of the saints started only at their tombs.

Beginnings of Liturgical Cult. During the 4th century, however, veneration of Mary discreetly entered the liturgical year because of Christmas. This feast, introduced at Rome toward the middle of the 4th century, commemorates not only the Savior's birth but also the virginal maternity of Mary. This theme held an important place in the 13 Christmas sermons of St. AUGUSTINE, for example. Moreover, St. Augustine insisted on it because the perpetual virginity of Mary had been denied by Helvidius and Jovinian at the end of the 4th century. This apologetic concern, as well as the desire to present Mary as a model for consecrated virgins, led preachers in their Christmas sermons to accentuate Mary's role and the privilege of her virginity. In the latter part of the 5th century, i.e., after the Council of EPHESUS (431) had defined the divine maternity, a liturgical commemoration of the MOTHER OF GOD appeared in many places. Its date varied, but generally it was close to Christmas: December 18 in Spain; January 18 in Gaul; January 1, the octave of Christmas, in Rome. The Marian Mass at Rome was composed of the Introit *Vultum tuum,* the Epistle Sir 24.11–13, 15–20, the Gradual *Diffusa est,* the Gospel Mt 13.44–52, and the Communion *Simile est* (taken from the Gospel). The first Marian feast was therefore a feast of the divine maternity of Mary. And since, at that time, Christmas celebrated the manifestation of the Son of God, who came to save the world, more than the birth of the Child Jesus, the Marian feast honored Mary especially as the Mother of the Savior, as the one through whom salvation came to the human race.

The Ancient Feasts. Until the middle of the 7th century the West does not seem to have known any other Marian feast than this commemoration of the Mother of God. Sometime between the pontificate of Theodore I (642–649) and that of Sergius I (687–701), the feasts of the Assumption and the Nativity of the Blessed Virgin Mary were introduced. These feasts, of Oriental origin, were brought to Rome by those Christian communities that had been banished from the East by the Muslims.

Assumption of Mary (August 15). This feast comes from Jerusalem. In the Old Armenian Lectionary (early 5th century) modeled on the Jerusalem Lectionary for August 15, the title is ''Day of Mary, Mother of God.'' And the readings indicated there are: Is 7.10–15 (the Emmanuel prophecy), Gal 3.29–4.7 (which contains the phrase ''God sent His Son born of a woman''), and Lk 2.1–7 (the Nativity). Therefore, the first feast for August 15, undoubtedly instituted after the Council of Ephesus in 431, celebrated the divine maternity. At the beginning of the 6th century it was transformed into a feast of the *Dormitio.* Toward 600 a decree from the Emperor Maurice extended this feast to the whole Byzantine Empire. Shortly after 650 it was accepted at Rome, where it was generally called the feast of the Assumption. From Rome it spread in the West—not, however, without having to surmount certain obstacles, notably in Gaul, where Mary's eminent glory was readily admitted but also where the basis for the affirmation of her corporeal Assumption was not clearly seen. Following the definition of the dogma of the Assumption in 1950, the Mass on August 15 was given a new formulary that explicitly celebrates Mary's Assumption and the power of her intercession.

Nativity of Mary (September. 8). This feast, witnessed to in the East by Romanos Melodos toward 550, appeared at Rome shortly before the pontificate of Sergius I, but it spread somewhat slowly in the West. The date, September 8, is that of the dedication of a Marian church in Jerusalem. The object of the feast is the eternal predestination and the ''blessing'' of her who one day would become the Mother of the Son of God rather than Mary's birth itself.

Presentation of Mary (November 21). According to the *Proto-Gospel of James,* an apocrypha without value, Mary was supposed to have been led to the temple in Jerusalem at the age of 3 to be consecrated to the service of the Lord. Despite this purely legendary basis, the Feast of the Presentation has been celebrated in the Christian East since the 6th century in connection with the dedication of the church of St. Mary the New in Jerusalem. It was introduced in the West at a late date and rather hesitatingly; conceded to the Franciscans in 1371 by Gregory

XI, it became quite widespread in the 15th century. Although suppressed by Pius V, it was reestablished and extended to the whole Church by Sixtus V in 1585. The object of this feast, precious to Christian piety, is Mary herself as the true temple where God dwells rather than the legendary fact of the Presentation.

Modern Feasts. Whereas the ancient Marian feasts were of Oriental origin and commemorate the essential facts of Mary's life, the object of almost every feast instituted in the West since the 12th century is one of Mary's attributes or the commemoration of some marvelous intervention. The feasts arose and developed, in most cases, under the influence of the medieval religious orders or of private devotion.

Immaculate Conception. Since the 8th century the East has known a feast called ''the conception of Ann,'' celebrating the miracle, related by the Apocrypha, of Ann conceiving Mary after a long sterility. However, the feast did not long endure in the West. The Western feast of the IMMACULATE CONCEPTION appeared in England in the 12th century. It was promoted by some spiritual writers, such as the English monk Eadmer, but energetically opposed by others, such as SS. Bernard and Thomas Aquinas, who deemed such a privilege to be irreconcilable with the doctrine of universal redemption. It was only in 1476 that Sixtus IV introduced the feast at Rome; at the same time he ordered the composition of a new formulary for the Mass and Office. In 1708 Clement XI extended the feast to the whole Church. Finally, in 1863, nine years after the definition of the dogma, Pius IX promulgated the Office and Mass formulary for the feast, celebrated on December 8.

Queenship of Mary. This feast was instituted by Pius XII in 1954 ''so that all may more clearly recognize and more zealously venerate the kind and maternal rule of the Mother of God'' [*Ad Caeli Reginam, Acta Apostolicae Sedis* 46 (1954) 639]. This idea of Mary's royalty is already expressed in the Feast of the Assumption. Originally, this feast was celebrated on May 31. The 1969 reform of the liturgical calendar transferred the feast to August 22.

Visitation. Already in the 8th century the Roman liturgy commemorated the mystery of the VISITATION on Friday of the Advent Embertide. The feast, originally celebrated on July 2, celebrated by the Franciscans since 1263, was extended to the whole Church by Boniface IX in 1401. A revised Mass formulary was approved by Clement VIII in 1608. The 1969 revision of the liturgical calendar transferred the feast to May 31.

Immaculate Heart of Mary. Since the beginning of the 19th century, certain dioceses had celebrated a feast of the Most Pure Heart of Mary. After having consecrated the world to the IMMACULATE HEART OF MARY in 1942, Pius XII instituted the feast in 1944 and set its celebration on the octave of the Assumption. Originally celebrated on August 22, the 1969 reform of the Roman Calendar transferred the feast to the Saturday after Pentecost Sunday.

*Seven Sorrows of Mary.*Celebrated on September 15, this feast has been celebrated by the SERVITES since the 17th century. After his return from captivity in France, Pius VII extended it to the universal Church in 1814 in memory of the sufferings he had endured.

Our Lady of the Rosary. This feast was already celebrated on October 7 at the end of the 15th century by some confraternities of the Rosary. Its wide diffusion was due initially to the fact that Pius V ordered the feast to be solemnized in thanksgiving for victory over the Turks at LEPANTO (Oct. 7, 1571). It was extended to the universal Church by Clement XI (1716) after Prince Eugene's victory at Peterwardein.

The Revised Roman Calendar (1969)

In the revised Roman Calendar (1969) there are 13 Marian feasts included for universal observance. The Solemnity of Mary, Mother of God (January 1), restores the octave day of Christmas to its original character as a Marian celebration. Two other Marian feasts rank as solemnities: the Immaculate Conception (December 8) and the Assumption (August 15). The Birth of Mary (September 8) and the Visitation (May 31) now rank as feasts. The Queenship of Mary (August 22), Our Lady of Sorrows (September 15), Our Lady of the Rosary (October 7), and the Presentation of Mary (November 21) are celebrated as obligatory memorials. Four Marian feasts remain on the universal calendar as optional memorials: Immaculate Heart of Mary (Saturday after Pentecost), Our Lady of Mount CARMEL (July 16), Our Lady of LOURDES (February 11), Dedication of St. Mary Major (August 5).

In the past, popular piety celebrated the Feast of the Annunciation (March 25) and the Presentation (February 2) as Marian feasts. The revised Roman Calendar stresses these feasts as primarily celebrations of the Lord in which Mary as His Mother is intimately associated. The full titles of the two feasts indicate their non-Marian character: Annunciation of the Lord, Presentation of the Lord (formerly called the Purification of Mary).

The particular liturgical calendar for the United States includes one additional Marian feast: Our Lady of GUADALUPE (December 12). It ranks as an obligatory memorial. The Proper for this feast was approved by the National Conference of Catholic Bishops in November 1973.

According to the general norm of the Roman Calendar: "On Saturdays of the year when there is no obligatory memorial, an optional memorial of the Blessed Virgin Mary may be observed." The texts for the liturgical celebration of the Marian feasts witness to the general euchological enrichment brought about in the revision of the Roman Missal (1970). In addition to the Marian feasts already outlined, the Roman Missal includes seven other sets of Mass formulas as Commons of the Blessed Virgin Mary to be used for the Saturday celebrations and for votive Masses of the Blessed Virgin Mary.

Theology

To grasp adequately the meaning of the Marian feasts, one must avoid placing them all on the same level. They can be divided into three groups, which more or less correspond to the three chronological stages of the history of Mary's liturgical cult: the feast of the divine maternity, the feasts that commemorate the events of the Blessed Virgin's life, and those that celebrate one of Our Lady's attributes or interventions.

Solemnity of Mary, Mother of God. Since the 4th century, the Solemnity of Mary, Mother of God (January 1) has remained the greatest Marian feast. The Church venerates the one through whom the Savior was given to the whole world, thereby clarifying what is fundamental to Mary's role and the cause of all her privileges.

Feasts of the Blessed Virgin. This second group comprises those feasts whose objects are real or legendary events from Mary's life: her Nativity, her Presentation, and her Assumption. These feasts point up Mary's personal holiness rather than her role in the history of salvation; they strive to show the reflection of her exceptional vocation in her life and soul. With various nuances, they all proclaim Mary's beauty and sanctity.

Feasts of Our Lady. This last group is composed of those feasts that celebrate Mary especially as model, advocate, and protectress of the world. They venerate in Mary "Our Lady" more than her divine maternity or her virginity. It is quite significant that, at least in current usage, many of these feasts justly bear the name of "Feast of Our Lady of . . . ." The same is true of most of the local Marian feasts that celebrate Mary as patron or protectress of a particular place or community. The purpose of these feasts is only to distribute, according to local needs, the truth of faith that Mary is the one by whom the Savior is given to the human race—a truth that is expressed on the human level in the mystery of the Incarnation, celebrated at Christmas.

Bibliography: F. G. HOLWECK, *Calendarium liturgicum festorum Dei et Dei matris Mariae* (Philadelphia 1925). B. BOTTE, "La Première fête mariale de la liturgie romaine," *Ephemerides liturgicae* 47 (1933) 425–430. P. BRUYLANTS, "Les Origines du culte de la Sainte Vierge à Rome," *Questions liturgiques et paroissiales* (1938) 200–210, 270–281. A. RAES, "Aux origines de la fête de l'Assomption en Orient," *Orientalia Christiana periodica* 12 (1946) 262–274. B. CAPELLE et al., "Marie dans la liturgie," *Maria: Études sur la Sainte Vierge,* ed. H. DU MANOIR (Paris 1949–) 1:215–413. M. RIGHETTI, *Manuale di storia liturgica* (Milan 2d. ed. 1955) 2:265–303. E. FLICOTEAUX, *Mystères et fêtes de la Vierge Marie* (Paris 1956). A. CHAVASSE, *Le Sacramentaire gélasien* (Strasbourg 1958) 375–402. B. CAPELLE, "Les fêtes mariales," *L'Èglise en prière,* ed. A. G. MARTIMORT (Paris 1961) 747–765. J. PASCHER, *Das liturgische Jahr* (Munich 1963) 611–659. J. H. MILLER, *Fundamentals of the Liturgy* (Notre Dame, Ind. 1960) 419–423. E. BISHOP, *Liturgica historica* (Oxford 1918; repr. 1962) 238–259. C. BOUMAN, "The Immaculate Conception in the Liturgy," in *The Dogma of the Immaculate Conception: History and Significance,* ed. E. D. O'CONNOR (Notre Dame, Ind. 1958) 113–159. United States Catholic Conference, *Roman Calendar,* rev. by decree of Vatican Council II (Washington, D.C. 1970); *Lectionary for Mass,* the Roman Missal rev. by decree of Vatican Council II (Washington, D.C. 1969)—both published by authority of Pope Paul VI. *Missale Romanum,* Ex decreto Sacrosancti Oecumenici Concilii Vaticani II instauratum auctoritate Pauli PP. VI promulgatum (Typis Polyglottis Vaticanis 1970).

[P. ROUILLARD/T. KROSNICKI/EDS.]

MARIAN PRIESTS

Although the term strictly applies to priests beneficed during the reign of MARY (1553–58), it is usually applied to all holding ecclesiastical preferments during her reign, including those ordained under HENRY VIII and Edward VI. In law, Marian priests suffered less than seminary priests. The former came only under the law that inflicted penalties on all who maintained the spiritual jurisdiction of any foreign prelate, or that made it high treason to maintain the authority of the bishop of Rome or to refuse the Oath of Supremacy. Because of this, fewer Marian priests lost their lives for religion. Those who did so are Bl. Thomas Plumtree, rector of Stubton, Lincolnshire (d. Durham, 1570), Bl. James BELL (d. Lancaster, 1584), and Ven. Richard Williams (d. Tyburn, 1592). As late as 1596, there were 50 Marian priests still working on the English Mission, among them William Ely, who died in a Hereford jail in 1609. It has been reckoned that, in the early years of ELIZABETH I, about 2,000 priests were either deprived, ejected, or resigned their ecclesiastical offices for the sake of conscience.

Bibliography: H. GEE, *The Elizabethan Clergy and the Settlement of Religion, 1558–1564* (Oxford 1898). H. N. BIRT, *The Elizabethan Religious Settlement* (London 1907). *The First and Second Diaries of the English College, Douay* (*Publications of the Catholic Record Society* 1; London 1878). G. R. ELTON, ed., *The Tudor Constitution* (Cambridge, Eng. 1960).

[C. W. FIELDS]

MARIANA, JUAN DE

Spanish theologian and historian; b. Talavera, Spain, April 2, 1536; d. Toledo, Feb. 16, 1624. He entered the Jesuits in 1554; studied philology, theology, and history at ALCALÁ; taught theology in Rome (1561), Sicily (1564), and Paris (1569); and preached in Italy, France, and Flanders. In 1574 he returned to Toledo and devoted himself to writing. His history of Spain, first published in Latin in Toledo in 1592, was augmented, revised, and translated into Spanish by him in later editions. It is somewhat uncritical. His *Re rege et regis institutione* (Toledo 1599), written at the request of Philip II and dedicated to Philip III, did not attract much attention until the assassination of Henry IV of France in 1610. In the work Mariana held that power was conferred on monarchs and sanctioned by the people, who in the last analysis, as he saw it, had the right of tyrannicide. Kings, therefore, should be educated so that this extreme may be avoided. Henry's assassin, however, had never heard of Mariana. There was an outcry in France against Mariana and the Jesuits, and the Jesuit general threatened any approval of tyrannicide with severe penalties. In his *De monetae mutatione,* one of the *Tractatus VII theologici et historici* (Cologne 1609), Mariana attacked monetary debasement and openly accused Spanish fiscal officials of fraud. He was imprisoned in a Franciscan monastery for a year, where he is supposed to have composed a discourse on the ills of the Jesuits. Some scholars hold that this work is not entirely his; others hold that he had completed it in MS by 1605 and that it was confiscated by the government when he was imprisoned in 1610. It was published in Bordeaux in 1625, the year after Mariana's death, and was frequently used as a weapon against the Jesuits. Mariana was one of a group of Spanish Jesuits who, by splitting from the rest of the society in its early years, would almost have destroyed the society. He composed the *Scholia in Vetus et Novum Testamentum* (Madrid 1613). A monument was erected to him in Talavera in 1888.

Bibliography: A. ASTRAIN, *Historia de la compañia de Jesús,* 7 v. (Madrid 1902–25) v.3–4. J. LAURES, *The Political Economy of Juan de Mariana* (New York 1928). L. KOCH, *Jesuiten-Lexikon* 1163–65. C. TESTORE, *Enciclopedia cattolica* 8:146–147. A. MERCATI and A. PELZER, *Dizionario ecclesiastico* (Turin 1954-58) 2:849. D. MANSILLA, *Lexikon für Theologie und Kirche* 2 7:48–49.

[M. B. MARTIN]

MARIANIST SISTERS

Or Daughters of Mary, popular title for the Congregation of the Daughters of Mary Immaculate (*Filiae Mariae,* FMI, Official Catholic Directory #0870), a religious congregation founded in 1816 in Agen, France, by Guillaume CHAMINADE and Adèle de Trenquelléon (1798–1828). Like the MARIANISTS, this institute developed from the sodality of the Blessed Mother organized in 1800 by Chaminade. The Holy See gave final approval to the constitutions in 1888. The sisters engage chiefly in primary and secondary education; they also work as catechists, retreat directors, and youth ministers. In the U.S., the first house was established in 1949 in Somerset, Texas. The generalate is in Rome. The U.S. provincialate is in San Antonio, Texas.

[G. J. RUPPEL/EDS.]

MARIANISTS

(SM, Official Catholic Directory #0760); formally known as the Society of Mary (Societas Marie); founded in Bordeaux, France, in 1817 by William Joseph CHAMINADE (1761–1850), a priest who had initiated a distinctive sodality movement in post-revolutionary France (1800). He and Adéle Trenquelléon co-founded the Daughters of Mary (Marianist Sisters) in 1816. In 1817, after several sodalists had made private vows under Chaminade, seven of them professed vows on Sept. 5, 1818. Marianist schools were then opened in Bordeaux and Agen. The former, with its faculty of sodalists, enjoyed an excellent reputation while the latter was intended as a primary school for new children, but people of the better classes contrived to obtain certificates of indigence permitting their boys to enter the school. The French government recognized the work of the Marianists by subsidizing the school that opened at St. Remy, although it was not a state school. In 1834 a school was opened at Colmar. Two years later, the Brothers of Christian Doctrine merged with the Marianists, with the result that the College of Sant Hippolyte, and schools in Ribeauville and Ammschwir were opened in Alsace.

When Chaminade retired as superior general in 1848 the Marianists were conducting schools in France and Switzerland, and before his death (1850) they had spread to the United States. By 1963 there were more than 3,300 Marianists in ten provinces centered in France, Austria, Italy, Switzerland, Spain, and Japan. The European branch of the society maintains missions in Tunis, the Central African Republic, Congo Republic (French), Spanish Morocco, Togo, Argentina, and Chile, and schools in Belgium, Hungary, and Germany. The Americans serve missions in Peru, Kenya, Nigeria, Nyasaland, Lebanon, Korea, and supply religious to Canada, Japan, and various missions of European provinces. The apostolic mission of the Marianist is characterized by his total consecration to Mary, while the society is designed on an egalitarian spirit among priests, teaching brothers, and working brothers.

Symbolic of the spirit to dispel ANTICLERICALISM, the Marianists have never worn a religious habit, but rather the rule prescribed a simple black suit. The Marianists received papal approval on Aug. 11, 1865; but final approbation of the constitutions was finally granted by Leo XIII only on July 24, 1891. To the usual vows of poverty, chastity, and obedience, the Marianists add the vow of stability. As an outward sign of this fourth vow, which is consecration to Mary, they wear a gold ring on their right hand. Marianists, including priests, teaching and working brothers, are governed by a superior general, who with his council, appoints all superiors. The vast majority of the Marianists are teaching brothers.

The American Experience. The foundation period opened in July 1849. Francis X. WENINGER, S.J., an Austrian Jesuit familiar with the Marianist schools in Alsace, wrote to the superior general in Bordeaux on behalf of two pastors of German-speaking parishes in need of Marianists to staff the parish schools in Cincinnati. Leo Meyer, an Alsatian Marianist priest eager to be missioned to the United States, arrived in Cincinnati in July; the following December four brothers arrived to take charge of the parish schools and assist Meyer, who had purchased property in Dayton upon which was built St. Mary's Institute. With accommodations for postulants and novices, Nazareth, as the Marianist center in Dayton was called, was adjacent to St. Mary's (later University of Dayton) and housed a normal school. With the establishment of the U.S. province in 1855 Nazareth was the provincialate as well as the motherhouse where Marianists would make their annual retreat and receive their teaching assignments.

Bishop (after 1850, Archbishop) John B. Purcell of Cincinnati, who had witnessed ethnic rivalry between German- and Irish-Americans, promoted German national parishes such as Holy Trinity in 1834 and St. Mary's in the Over-the Rhine area of Cincinnati in 1840. During the 1850s the Marianists staffed these schools and taught catechism in German illustrative of the prevailing principle: the German language preserves the faith of the people.

The French-born bishop of Galveston, Jean-Marie Odin, made two visits to Bordeaux searching for Marianists to staff a school. In 1852 three brothers arrived in San Antonio, where they met Br. Edel from Cincinnati, to form a community that laid the foundation of St. Mary's College, today called St. Mary's University. Another French bishop, Amadeus Rappe of Cleveland, successfully sought brothers to teach at St. Patrick's, the school of the Irish parish. Rappe was a self-styled Americanizer who alienated both the German-American and Irish-American communities. The Marianists, who had made

Adèle de Trenquelléon.

a significant impact upon the school, remained at St. Patrick's for several years.

Expansion into Pittsburgh, New York, Baltimore, Chicago, and New Orleans occurred principally in response to Redemptorist pastors of German-speaking parishes. In 1880 the Marianists opened a school in Winnipeg, Manitoba, and as a result of a request from the community for missions in the Hawaiian Islands in 1882 the brothers opened schools in Honolulu, Wailuki (1883), and Hilo (1885). In 1884 the brothers responded to a call from a priest of the Archdiocese of San Francisco and opened a school in Stockton, California. The provincial associated with this national expansion was Fr. John N. Reinbolt; by the end of his 20-year administration in 1886 there were 40 Marianist houses with 350 brothers and priests.

Modernization and Professionalization. In 1897, at the request of the German-American pastor, the Marianists opened their first high school at SS. Peter and Paul parish, which represented their entrance into the St. Louis area where they established several high schools. The Marianists opened Spalding Academy in Peoria, Illinois, named after John Lancaster Spalding, the bishop who invited them into the diocese. Many of their parish schools evolved into high schools such as St. Michael's in Chicago.

With the growth of the society by more than 50 schools and over 500 members—from New York to California, Texas to Manitoba—a western province centered in St. Louis was established in 1908. The Hawaii and California houses remained the Cincinnati Province.

While provincials were priests, the provincial inspectors of schools, a position first created in 1869, were brothers. Brother John Waldron was inspector of the St. Louis province and a dominant presence in the early years of the National Catholic Education Association (NCEA). Inspectors were associated with the society's adaptation to the development of diocesan school systems, particularly its central Catholic high school movement. During this period the University of Dayton and St. Mary's College in San Antonio achieved modernization and professionalization. Illustrative of the significance of education in their provinces of the United States, American brothers have dominated the position of assistant superior general in charge of instruction from the late 19th through the 20th century. The MARIANIST SISTERS opened their first house in the United States in 1949; their continuous growth led to the establishment of a U.S. province in 1969.

In 1946 the general chapter elected its first American superior general, Sylvester P. Jurgens, former provincial of the western province. In 1948 he announced the creation of the Pacific province with houses in California and Hawaii. By this time there was a trend to focus almost entirely upon secondary education; the Pacific province was in the vanguard of that movement. Also during the early phase of modernization the sodality movement was revitalized in tandem with the renewed devotion to the founder, William Joseph Chaminade. Father William Feree, even before he became Provincial of the Cincinnati Province (1968–1993) was a dynamic leader in the sodality and the retrieval of the founder's charism. During the late 1940s the Marianist accepted their first African-American candidate and by 1960 there were a few Black Brothers of Mary. The continuous growth of the Marianists during 1950s led to the foundation of the New York Province in 1961, which included St. John's Boys' Home in Brooklyn, Chaminade High School in Mineola (Long Island), other high schools, and Colegio San Jose, Rio Padres, Puerto Rico. In 1961 there were about 1,500 Marianists in the North American provinces, which represented nearly a 100 percent growth in 25 years.

Vatican II and After. The period, 1960 to 1995, followed a pattern etched into the post-Vatican II trends of renewal and reform: the composition of a new constitution based upon the principles of collegiality, subsidiary, personal responsibility, and a scripturally based spirituality. Since the early 1990s brothers were allowed to be appointed provincials. Some of the missions that were founded between the 1930s and the 1950s in Latin America and Africa are flourishing today.

The general decline in traditional vocations has entailed removing brothers and priests from several schools in each of the provinces. However, the rise of Marianists' lay communities dedicated to a way of life infused with the Society's spirituality as a positive force on the horizon. Subsidiarity was severely tested in a conflict between the Marianists of the community of Chaminade High School in Mineola eager to maintain traditional structures in the school and community life (which they perceived as in accord with the best in Marianist life) and the New York Provincial Council with its commitment to reform or renewal in post-Vatican II and based upon contemporary anthropological and ecclesiological understandings of personal development, authority, and subsidiarity. The dispute, which originated in 1968, was resolved by the Vatican Congregation of Religious in 1976; Mineola became the independent Meribah Province with self-determination to pursue its own identity within Marianist traditions.

Lay Marianists, sisters, brothers, and priests form the Family of Mary in the 21st century. In 2001 the Cincinnati, New York, St. Louis and Pacific Provinces merged to form one Province. The Meribah Province, with two high schools and a retreat center, retains its separate status.

Bibliography: J. E. GARVIN, *Centenary Book of the Society of Mary* (Dayton, Ohio; 1917). C. J. KAUFFMAN, *Education and Transformation: Marianist Ministries in America since 1849* (New York 1994). E. PAULIN and J. A. BECKER. *New Ways: The History of the Brothers of Mary (Marianists) in Hawaii, 1883–1954* (Milwaukee 1959). J. W. SCHMITZ, *The Society of Mary in Texas* (San Antonio 1951). G. J. SCHNEPP, *Province of St. Louis 1908–1983, The First Seventy-Five Years* (St. Louis 1985).

[C. J. KAUFFMAN]

MARIANITES OF THE HOLY CROSS

A congregation of religious women (MSC, Official Catholic Directory #2410) founded in Le Mans, France, in 1841 by Basil Anthony MOREAU, who was also the founder of the Fathers of the Holy Cross and reorganizer of the Brothers of the Holy Cross. Mother Mary of the Seven Dolors Gascoin (d. 1900), the first superior, and her early companions received their training in religious life from the Good Shepherd nuns in Le Mans. At first Moreau intended his little community to be housekeepers in the seminaries and boarding schools staffed by the Holy Cross fathers and brothers, but the sisters' field of activity expanded to include teaching, nursing, caring for orphans and elderly people, and laboring in foreign missions. In 1869 Pius IX approved their constitutions.

Four Marianites began work in Indiana in 1843; others came to Canada in 1847, to Louisiana in 1848, and to New York in 1855. The sisters are engaged in education, healthcare, parish ministries, youth ministries, social work, and pastoral work. The U.S. headquarters is located in New Orleans, LA.

[M. L. DORSEY/EDS.]

MARIANNHILL MISSIONARIES, CONGREGATION OF

The Congregation of Mariannhill Missionaries (CMM, Official Catholic Directory #0750) traces its origin to Mariannhill Monastery, established in 1882 near Durban, South Africa, by a group of TRAPPIST monks headed by Father Franz PFANNER. It became an independent society in 1909.

The first foundation, dedicated to the Blessed Virgin Mary and St. Ann, combined their names into Mariannhill, and grew so rapidly that by 1885 it was raised to the status of an abbey with Pfanner as first abbot. Although the first missionary efforts were limited to the Zulu natives in the immediate area of Mariannhill, by 1899 there were 22 mission stations and 285 members of the congregation. The mission stations were centers of learning and civilization where the priests and brothers taught the natives to read and trained them in farming and other skills and trades. Colleges tò train native teachers were set up at Mariannhill and Mariazell. In much of their work, the missionaries were ably assisted by the Sisters of the Precious Blood, a community also founded by Pfanner.

The missionary work had been undertaken with the approval of the general chapter of the Trappists held at Sept-Fons, France, in 1879, but it became increasingly clear that the monastic and the missionary ways of life were incompatible. When the problem was referred to the Congregation of the Propagation of the Faith in Rome, it directed that a general chapter of the Mariannhill monks should be held to discuss their situation. This chapter, which met on May 11, 1908, under Bp. William Miller, vicar apostolic of the Transvaal, recommended that the 300 Mariannhill monks be banded into a new missionary society loosely tied to the Trappist Order. However, the Holy See decided that the Mariannhill Society should be entirely independent of the Trappist Order and a decree of separation was approved by Pius X on Feb. 2, 1909. The constitutions for the new Congregation of Mariannhill Missionaries, approved June 24, 1914, set up a modern religious congregation, to be governed by a superior general and his councilors. Because of World War I, the first general chapter was not held until 1920, when Adalbero Fleischer was elected as first superior general. The distinctive garb of the society then adopted consisted of a simple black cassock with a red cincture for priests, a black cincture for clerics, and a black belt for the brothers.

After the separation from the Trappist Order, the society expanded to the rest of the world. The first European seminaries were opened in Germany, Switzerland, and Austria. Subsequently establishments were made in the United States, England, Canada, and Spain. The Mariannhill fathers continued to work in South Africa, among the people of Natal and Southern Rhodesia. Mariannhill and Umtata in South Africa and Bulawayo in Southern Rhodesia were raised to the status of dioceses.

The Mariannhill fathers, always interested in furthering a native clergy and native religious life, established an indigenous religious order of priests and brothers and another order of sisters under Fleischer, their first superior general. The first native priest from Mariannhill was ordained in Rome in 1898.

In the United States, the Mariannist Missionaries are found in the Archdiocese of Detroit. The U.S. provincialate is in Dearborn Heights, MI. The generalate is in Rome.

Bibliography: B. HOFMANN, *The Founder of Mariannhill* (Detroit 1946). B. HUSS, *Mariannhill: Half a Century of African Mission Life* (Detroit 1935). F. SCHIMLEK, *Mariannhill: A Study in Bantu Life and Missionary Effort* (Mariannhill, Natal, South Africa 1953).

[T. MOCK/EDS.]

MARIANUS SCOTUS

The name of two Irish monks on the Continent. Marianus Scotus of Mainz, chronicler; b. Ireland,1028; d. Mainz, Germany, Dec. 22, 1082 or 1083. Marianus (in Irish Móel Brigte) entered the monastery of Mag Bile (Moville, Co. Down) when he was 24 years old. He left Ireland in 1056, during the abbacy of Tigernach Bairrcech, who apparently banished him for some trifling fault. He next appeared on the Continent, at the Irish monastery of St. Martin in Cologne. In 1058 he was in FULDA; in 1059, having been ordained priest at the Irish church of St. Kilian at Würzburg, he had himself walled up as an incluse. In 1069, however, he was moved to Mainz by order of the abbot of Fulda and the bishop of Mainz. There he continued as an incluse in the monastery of St. Martin until his death. He left behind him a chronicle, preserved in MS Vat. Pal. 830, which is, in part, apparently his own autograph. A work of great value for the history of the Irish in Germany in the 10th and 11th centuries, it is also of some importance in the history of ANNALS and chronicles and was used extensively by SIGEBERT OF GEMBLOUX and later writers.

Marianus Scotus of Regensburg, Bl., monastic founder, scribe; b. County Donegal, Ireland; d. Regensburg, Germany, April 24, 1088 (feast, Feb. 9). Marianus (in Irish Muirchertach Mac Robartaig) came from a learned family. In 1067 he set off on a pilgrimage to Rome with two companions, John and Candidus. Having spent some time at the monastery of Michelsberg at Bamberg, they proceeded to Regensburg (1072–73). There they were persuaded by an Irish incluse named Muircheriach to take up a permanent abode. Inspired perhaps by the example of Muirchertach, John chose to become an incluse at Göttweich in Lower Austria. The abbess of Obermünster gave Marianus the priory of Weih-Sankt-Peter, outside Regensburg, which he restored (*c.* 1076). His community increased, and he built another monastery. He spent his life copying the Scriptures and works of devotion, not only for monasteries but also, as an act of charity, for anyone in need. Of the many manuscripts he must have written, there is certain knowledge of only one that is extant. It is a copy of the Epistles of St. Paul according to the Vulgate text (MS Vienna 1247) that contains the spurious Epistle to the Laodiceans.

Bibliography: M. S. of Mainz. Stenzel, ''Über Marianus Scotus,'' *Archiv der Gesellschaft für ältere deutsche Geschichtskunde,* 5 (1824) 768–779. G. WAITZ, ''Hersfelder Annalen. 2. Annales Fuldenses, Lobienses, Monasterienses, Marianus Scotus,'' *ibid.,* 6 (1838) 670–675. J. F. KENNEY, *Sources for the Early History of Ireland* 605, 614–616, 786. L. GOUGAUD, *Christianity in Celtic Lands,* tr. M. JOYNT (London 1932) 172. O. DOERR, ''Das Institut der Inclusen in Süddeutschland,'' *Beiträge zur Geschichte des alten Mönchtums und des Benediktinerordens,* fasc. 18 (1934) 19, 27, 53, 57, 69, 107, 126, 135. M. S. of Regensburg. For his life, written by an Irish monk of Regensburg about a century after his death and the extant MS, see J. F. KENNEY, *Sources for the Early History of Ireland* 618–619. D. BINCHY, ''The Irish Benedictine Congregation in Medieval Germany,'' *Studies* 18 (1929) 198–199. L. GOUGAUD, *op. cit.* 180–182. M. DÖRR, *Lexikon für Theologie und Kirche* 2 7:52–53.

[C. MCGRATH]

MARIAVITES

A Polish religious sect with pronounced national characteristics. It was founded in 1906 in Warsaw, Poland, by Jan Kowalski, a diocesan priest, and Sister Maria Felicja Kozłowska (1862–1921) of the Third Order Franciscans. It developed out of the community of sisters founded by the latter in Plock in 1888 and the community of secular priests organized at her instigation by Kowalski in 1893. Both groups adopted the Franciscan Rule and aimed at a religious, moral, and social renewal of clergy and people. They stressed the veneration of the Eucharist and the Blessed Virgin Mary (*Mariae vitam imitantes*). Because of their mystical bent they were not approved by Rome. On Sept. 4, 1904, the Holy Office condemned the community of priests and on Dec. 5, 1906, excommunicated Kozłowska, Kowalski, and 40 priests. As minister general, Kowalski then organized a Mariavite union, which was given recognition as a ''religious sect'' by the ministry of the interior at St. Petersburg (Nov. 28, 1906). Negotiations with the members of the UTRECHT SCHISM culminated in the reception of the Mariavites into the OLD CATHOLICS (1909–24) at the Old Catholic Congress held in Vienna in 1909. Kowalski was consecrated bishop Oct. 5, 1909. The Polish Duma recognized the Mariavites as a Christian confession. After the death of Kozłowska, whom Kowalski described in 1922 as the ''bride of the Lamb and the espoused wife of Christ,'' the fanaticism of the Mariavites became more pronounced. This trait was revealed especially by ''mystic marriages'' between priests and nuns whose children would be conceived without original sin and would be destined to constitute the beginning of a new and sinless humanity. In 1935 Archbishop Kowalski was divested of his offices. A split developed among the Mariavites. A small group, which regarded the monastery of Felicjanów as its main center, continued to adhere to Kowalski. The latter was arrested by the Nazis and died in the concentration camp of Dachau. The great majority of the Mariavites placed themselves under the jurisdiction of Bp. Clemens Philipp Feldmann (1935–45). During World War II the Mariavites were suppressed by the National Socialists. Since 1957 their leader has been Bp. Michał Sitek.

In 1911 there were about 200,000 Mariavites, but by the end of World War II their number was reduced by half. In 1962 the main group comprised 25,000, including 25 priests and about 200 sisters. They were organized into three bishoprics with 41 parishes. The motherhouse of the sisters was located at Płock. The Felicjanów group numbered 5,000, distributed over 22 parishes.

Bibliography: K. ALGERMISSEN, *Lexikon für Theologie und Kirche,* J. HOFER and K. RAHNER, eds. (Freiburg 1957–65) 7:55. I. RHODE, *Die Religion in Geschichte und Gegenwart* 4:752–754; *Die Mariaviten: Gestalten und Wege der Kirche im Osten* (Ulm 1959). J. GRÜNDLER, *Lexikon der christlichen Kirchen und Sekten,* 2 v. (Vienna 1961) 2:867–869. C. P. FELDMANN, *Die altkatholische Kirche der Mariaviten* (2d ed. Płock 1940), *Mariavita* (Płock 1962), Jubilee issue. É. APPOLIS, ''Une Église des derniers temps: L'Église Mariavite,'' *Archives de sociologie des religions* 10 (1965) 51–67.

[B. STASIEWSKI]

MARIE DE L'INCARNATION, BL.

Discalced Carmelite nun and mystic, baptized Barbé Avrillot; b. Paris, France, Feb. 1, 1566; d. Pontoise,

France, April 18, 1618. At 16 she married the viscount of Villemor, Pierre Acarie. A mother of six children, three boys and three girls, Mme. Acarie, characterized as La Belle Acarie, was popular and respected in society at the French capital. However, her husband met with misfortune; his property was confiscated and he was exiled by the king for his part in La Ligue. Mme. Acarie bore this adversity with faith and courage, and dedicated herself to the education of their children. Deepening her spiritual life, she took an active part in various religious enterprises, especially the introduction of the Discalced Carmelite nuns into France (1604). Her three daughters entered the Reformed Carmel; upon the death of her husband, she herself took the habit of St. TERESA OF ÁVILA as a lay sister in the convent of Amiens, with the religious name of Marie of the Incarnation. Shortly afterward she was transferred to the new foundation of Pontoise, and died there with a reputation for holiness.

She wrote two small works: *Les Vrays exercises* (Paris, 1622) and *Oraison,* resembling the works of St. JOHN OF THE CROSS in tone; she inserted both into the *Constitutions of Pontoise.* Her influence in that period of French Catholicism, which H. BRÉMOND calls "L'invasion mystique" of the Teresian Reform in France, was enormous, because of her social position, her personality and spirituality, and her connections with the élite of French spirituality: St. FRANCIS DE SALES, Jean Duval, Cardinal PIERRE BÉRULLE, Brétigny, and others.

PIUS VI signed the decree of the heroicity of her virtues (Sept. 27, 1788), and she was beatified in 1794. Her cause has recently been resumed.

Feast: April 18 (Discalced Carmelites).

Bibliography: A. DUVAL, *La Vie admirable de Soeur Marie de l'Incarnation* (Paris 1621). BRUNO DE JÉSUS-MARIE, *La Belle Acarie, bienheureuse Marie de l'Incarnation* (Paris 1942). L. C. SHEPPARD, *Barbe Acarie, Wife and Mystic* (New York 1953). GABRIEL DE JESÚS, *La Beata María de la Encarnación* (Madrid 1923).

[O. RODRIGUEZ]

MARIE MARTIN DE L'INCARNATION, BL.

The first woman missionary to the New World; b. Tours, France, Oct. 28, 1599; d. Quebec, Canada, April 30, 1672. The daughter of middle-class parents Florent and Jeanne (Michelet) Guyard, Marie acceded to her father's wishes and in 1617 married Claude Martin, despite her own attraction to religious life. When her husband died less than three years later, she became housekeeper for her sister, Madame Paul Buisson. Shortly after, Marie received revelations concerning the Incarnation, the Sacred Heart, and the Blessed Trinity. Influenced by the unusual caliber of Marie's interior life, her spiritual director, Dom Raymond of St. Bernard, agreed to her desire for religious consecration. On Jan. 25, 1632, she entered the Ursuline monastery at Tours, leaving her 12-year-old son in the care of her sister. During her novitiate Marie wrote a full account of her spiritual life in obedience to her Jesuit director. Known as the *Relation of 1633,* this account, along with that written later from Canada as the *Relation of 1654,* provide the most important documents for a study of her mystical life.

In 1635 Marie received in a dream the first hint of her missionary vocation. Four years later she finally set sail, accompanied by two other Ursulines and Mme. Madeleine de la Peltrie (1603–71), their lay foundress and chief financial support. Arriving in Quebec on Aug. 1, 1639, the missionaries immediately opened their first school in the Lower City. Despite sickness, poverty, and persecution by native tribes, the school grew, and in 1642 the Ursulines moved to a larger monastery. In 1648, when Iroquois hostilities endangered Quebec, Marie was advised to return to Europe, but she and her nuns chose to remain in New France. Her letters to her son Claude, a Benedictine monk, were collected and published by him in 1681 [2d ed., 2 v. (Paris 1876), 3d ed. by Albert Jamet, 4 v. (Paris 1929–39)] and provide a valuable source for 17th-century Canadian history. She also composed catechisms in Huron and Algonquian and a dictionary of French and Algonquian. She was beatified on June 22, 1980.

Feast: April 30 (Canada).

Bibliography: *Écrits spirituels et historiques,* ed. A. JAMET, 4 v. (Paris 1929–39). *The Autobiography of Venerable Marie of the Incarnation,* tr. J. J. SULLIVAN (Chicago 1964). D. MAHONEY, *Marie of the Incarnation,* (Garden City, N.Y. 1964). D. DESLANDRES, "L'éducation des Amérindiennes d'après la correspondance de Marie Guyart de l'Incarnation," *Studies in Religion/Sciences religieuses* 16 no 1 (1987) 91–110. G. M. OURY, "Le recueil des Retraites des Ursulines de Québec," *Église et Théologie* 9 (1978) 271–289. A. BÉLANGER, "Une éducatrice d'hier pour aujourd'hui: Marie Guyart de l'Incarnation," *Société Canadienne d'Histoire de l'Église Catholique* v. 39 (Ottawa, 1973) 55–64.

[D. MAHONEY]

MARIENBERG, ABBEY OF

Benedictine abbey in the Tirol, Diocese of Bressanone, north central Italy. After being founded in 1090 near Schuls, Switzerland, by Eberhard and Ulrich of Tarasp, it moved to St. Stephen in the Upper Vintschgau (1146) and to its present location near Burgisio (1150), where it was settled from OTTOBEUREN. Never wealthy, the abbey had as *advocati* the barons of Matsch and (from

1421) Austria. From 1440 the abbots were mitered. The abbey was reduced to one monk in 1598, but Mathias Lang (1615–40) proved a second founder. In the suppression by Bavaria (1807) many precious art objects and properties were alienated and could not be recovered after the abbey's restoration by Emperor Francis I of Austria (1816). Marienberg joined the Benedictine congregations of Swabia (1834), Austria (1889), and Switzerland (1931). In 1960 the abbey had 31 monks, a college in Merano, and four incorporated parishes. The Romanesque church (made baroque) has 12th-century paintings in the crypt.

The former Cistercian Abbey of Marienberg in Burgenland, Austria, was founded by the Hungarian Ban Dominic of the Miskolc family and settled from HEILIGENKREUZ. Destroyed by Turks (1532), it was given to LILIENFELD (1680), which still maintains pastoral care there.

Bibliography: T. WIESER, ''Abt Matthias Lang von Marienberg,'' *Studien und Mitteilungen zur Geschichte des Benediktiner-Ordens und seiner Zweige,* 34 (1913) 315–342, 424–450, 700–722. J. WEINGARTNER, *Die Kunstdenkmäler Südtirols: Vintschgau* (Augsburg 1930; 2d ed. Innsbruck 1957). L. H. COTTINEAU, *Répertoire topobibliographique des abbayes et prieurés,* 2 v. (Mâcon 1935–39) 2:1750–51. S. PAMER, *Lexikon für Theologie und Kirche,* ed. J. HOFER and K. RAHNER, 10 v. (2d, new ed. Freiburg 1957–65) 7:57–58.

[N. BACKMUND]

Francisco Marín-Sola.

MARÍN-SOLA, FRANCISCO

Theologian; b. Carcar (Navarre), Spain, Nov. 22, 1873; d. Manila, Philippine Islands, June 5, 1932. He entered the Order of Preachers and received the habit at Toledo, Spain, in 1897. On completion of his philosophical and theological studies, he was assigned to the Philippines, ordained on Sept. 18, 1897, and posted to the parish in Amulung, Province of Cagayan. While there he was imprisoned during the revolution of 1898. He returned to Manila in 1900, joined the staff of the Colegio de San Juan de Letran, and won recognition for his articles in *Libertas.* After seven years, the ill effects of his imprisonment caused his superiors to send him to Spain to teach in the house of studies in Avila. In 1908 he was back in Manila and received a doctorate in theology at the University of Santo Tomás. He was then appointed to its faculty and to the moderatorship of *Libertas.* In 1910 he returned to Avila and again crossed the ocean to found the Dominican College in Rosaryville (Ponchatoula), La. He taught there and also at the University of Notre Dame (Indiana). In 1917 the University conferred on him an honorary doctor of laws degree. He returned to Europe in 1918, occupied the chair of theology at the Catholic University of Fribourg (Switzerland), and acted as the dean of its faculty of theology. Ill health forced his resignation in 1927. During the remaining years of his life he divided his time and labors between Spain and the Philippines.

Marín-Sola was a theologian of vitality and resourcefulness. His outstanding work is *L'Evolution homogéne du dogme catholique* (Fribourg 1924). In this work he expanded upon the idea of a Dominican confrere, A. GARDEIL, and in doing so restored the correct notion of another Dominican, Melchior CANO, on the subject of theological conclusions. While many theologians deny that there is a homogeneity between a revealed principle and a conclusion deduced from it, when that deduction has been made by reason in a strictly illative process, and hold that such a theological conclusion cannot represent an objective truth susceptible of being incorporated into dogma, Marín-Sola held that strictly illative theological reasoning can discover truths capable of being defined as dogmas of the faith. Two propositions with the same subject (God) differ or are identical in meaning, only by reason of their predicates. If therefore, their predicates are identical, so will be the meaning and likewise the doctrine. Marín-Sola is noted also for his concept of the role of instrumental causality in relation to the REVIVISCENCE of the Sacraments and for his notion of divine premotion. His Spanish brethren revere him as the classical personification of a Spanish Thomistic theologian.

Bibliography: T. TASCÓN; *Ciencia Tomista* 46 (1932) 132–135. M. J. CONGAR, *Bulletin Thomista* 3 (1930–33) 679–681. *Analecta Sacri Ordinis Praedicatorum* 20 (1931–32) 776–778. G. GIERATHS, in *Lexikon für Theologie und Kirche,* ed. J. HOFER and K. RAHNER, 10 v. (2d new ed. Freiburg 1957–65) 7:83.

[F. D. NEALY]

MARINUS, SS.

Marinus is the name of several saints mentioned in the MARTYROLOGIES.

Marinus of San Marino, patron of the Republic of San Marino, Italy; b. on an island near Dalmatia; d. San Marino, fourth century. According to a 10th-century legend, Marinus and Leo (Feast Day: Aug. 1) were Dalmatian Christians who were condemned to work on the walls of Rimini during the DIOCLETIAN persecution (*c.* 304), and used the opportunity to preach the Gospel successfully in that city. Later they became hermits—Marinus on Mt. Titano, and Leo at Montefeltro—and were raised to orders by St. Gaudentius of Rimini in 359.

Feast: Sept. 4 (Roman MARTYROLOGY); Sept. 3 (San Marino).

Marinus of Anazarbus, in Asia Minor; d. *c.* 305. He is said to have been decapitated in the Diocletian persecution.

Feast: Aug. 8.

Marinus of Caesarea, in Palestine; d. *c.* 262. Eusebius (*Hist. Eccl.* 7.15) mentions him as an officer in the Roman legion stationed at Caesarea who suffered martyrdom in the VALERIAN persecutions. He does not seem to be identified with the St. Marinus cited by the MARTYROLOGY OF JEROME for March 3.

Marinus of Rome; d. 283. The story of St. Marinus, connected with the son of a Roman senator and put to death in the Numerian persecution, is sheer legend.

Feast: Dec. 26 (Roman MARTYROLOGY).

Bibliography: A. GAROSCI, ''La formazione del mito di San Marino,'' *Rivista Storica Italiana* 71 (1959) 21–47. R. KNOPF and G. KRÜGER, *Ausgewählt Märtyrerakten* (3d ed. Tübingen 1929). J. L. BAUDOT and L. CHAUSSIN, *Vies des saints et des bienheureux selon l'ordre du calendrier avec l'historique des fêtes* (Paris 1935–56). 12:683–684. R. BURIGANA, *La leggenda ''Sancti Marini'': una storia religiosa tra Rimini e il monte Titano* (San Marino 1992), legends.

[J. VAN PAASSEN]

MARINUS I, POPE

Pontificate: Dec. 16, 892 to May 15, 884. Born at Gallese, near Rome, Marinus entered the service of the Roman Church at the age of 12. In that capacity he enjoyed a distinguished career. As a deacon he was one of three legates sent by Pope ADRIAN II to Constantinople to represent the papacy at the Fourth (Eighth Ecumenical) Council of CONSTANTINOPLE, 869–870. With Marinus playing a leading role in guiding the Council's proceedings, Partriarch PHOTIUS was deposed and IGNATIUS was confirmed as patriarch. Marinus subsequently became an archdeacon and treasurer (*arcarius*) of the Roman Church and then was made bishop of Caere in Etruria by Pope JOHN VIII.

Upon the assassination of John VIII, Marinus was quickly elected pope but did not receive imperial confirmation of his election until later. Since he was the first bishop from another see to be elevated to the bishopric of Rome, some viewed his election as uncanonical. Although the evidence is vague, perhaps his election was marked by bitter partisanship soon to disrupt order in the Papal State. Despite the fact that he had played a key role in deposing Photius at the Council of Constantinople in 869–870, Mariunus did nothing to challenge the decisions of a council held in Constantinople in 879–880 which had confirmed Photius' return as patriarch of Constantinople. Thereby he continued the conciliatory policy toward the Byzantine church that had been instituted by Pope John VIII as a means of reducing tension between Rome and Constantinople. In an attempt to quiet partisan rivalry in Rome, Marinus reversed John VIII's condemnation of the leaders of a faction that opposed John's policies; among those favored was FORMOSUS (later pope) whose excommunication was lifted and his office as bishop of Porto restored. In 883 Marinus met with Emperor Charles III, the Fat, seeking help against the aggressions of Italian princes, especially Guido (Guy), duke of Spoleto, but the emperor was able to do little to constrain Guido's growing threat to the Papal State beyond declaring him deposed from his office as duke and ordering him to surrender properties illegally seized; to enforce these decisions Charles was forced to seek the services of another Italian potentate. On occasion the Pope was in contact with important ecclesiastical officials in Francia who sought his help in resolving disputes. At the request of the Anglo-Saxon king, ALFRED THE GREAT, he granted exemption from taxes to the Schola Saxonum in Rome.

Bibliography: *Le Liber Pontificalis,* ed. L. DUCHESNE, 3 v., 2nd ed. (Paris 1955–1957), 2: 224. *Regesta Pontificum Romanorum ab condita ecclesia ad annum post Christum MCXCVIII,* ed. P. JAFFÉ, 2 v., 2nd ed. (Leipzig 1885–1888) 2:425–426. *Flodoard von Reims, Die Geschichte der Reimser Kirche,* Liber IV, ch. 1, ed. M. STRATMANN, *Monumenta Germaniae Historica, Scriptores* 36 (Hannover 1998) 363–364. L. DUCHESNE, *The Beginnings of the Temporal Sovereignty of the Popes, A.D. 754–1073,* tr. A. H. MATTHEW (London 1908) 1403–202. F. X. SEPPELT, *Geschichte des Papsttums. Eine Geschichte der Päpste von den Anfängen bis zum Tod Pius X,* v. 2: *Das Papsttums im Frühmittelalter. Geschichte des Päpste von Regierungsantritt Gregors des Grossen bis zum Mitte des ll. Jahrhundert* (Leipzig 1934) 321–323. É. AMANN, *L'époque carolingienne,* Histoire de l'Église depuis les origines jusqu'a nos jours, ed. A. FLICHE and V. MARTIN 6 (Paris 1947) 436–441. P. LLEWELLYN, *Rome in the Dark Ages* (London 1993) 286–315.

[W. GELLHAUS]

MARINUS II, POPE

Pontificate: Oct. 30, 942 to April or May 946. The cardinal priest Marinus was one of several popes designated by Alberic II, a member of the family of Theophylactus, who in 932 had seized control of Rome and the Papal State from his mother, Marozia, and her son, Pope JOHN XI, said by some to have been fathered by Pope SERGIUS III. Alberic II, ''glorious Prince and Senator of all the Romans,'' ruled the Papal State with an iron hand until his death in 954. Of Marinus II it was said by a contemporary chronicler that he did nothing except by order of Alberic II.

Despite his dictatorial actions, Alberic II did select a succession of popes whose activities were inspired by genuine religious motives. Marinus II was one of them. He devoted his brief pontificate to promoting discipline among the Roman clergy and monks, restoring churches, and helping the poor. He was especially concerned with protecting monasteries against depredations by bishops and nobles, thereby helping to provide the proper setting for monastic reforms, already under way at such places as Cluny, that would transform the Church by the end of the tenth century. His concerns for reform reached beyond Rome, as demonstrated by his appointment of Frederick, archbishop of Mainz, as papal vicar charged with rooting out the abuses of clergy and monks in France and Germany.

Bibliography: Sources: *Le Liber Pontificalis,* ed. L. DUCHESNE, 3 v., 2nd ed. (Paris 1955–1957) 2: 245. *Regesta Pontificum Romanorum ab condita ecclesia ad annum post Christum MCXCVIII,* ed. P. JAFFÉ, 2 v., 2nd ed. (Leipzig 1885–1888) 2: 458–459. *Papsturkunden,* ed. H. ZIMMERMANN, v. 1, *896–996,* 2nd ed. rev., Denkschriften, Österreichische Akademie der Wissenschaft, Philosophisch–Historische Klasse 174 (Vienna 1989) 172–191. **Literature.** A. FLICHE, in vol. 2, *L'Europe occidentale de 888 à 1125,* in *Histoire générale: Histoire du Moyen Age* (Paris 1941) 41–59, 110–131. É. AMANN and A. DUMAS, *L'Église au pouvoir des laïques (888–1037),* in vol. 7 of *Histoire de la Église depuis les origines jusqu'a nos jours,* ed. A. FLICHE and V. MARTIN (Paris 1948) 41. P. LLEWELLYN, *Rome in the Dark Ages* (London 1993) 286–315.

[R. E. SULLIVAN]

MARIOLOGY

Since the 17th century, Mariology has designated the part of dogmatic theology that concerns the Blessed Virgin Mary in her relation to God and to her fellow creatures under God.

Origin and History. Revelation provides the primary data. ''In the books of both the Old and New Testaments, the Sacred Scriptures tell us many glorious things about the Blessed Virgin. . . her virginal motherhood and unspotted holiness are expressly asserted'' [Pius XII, *Acta Apostolicae Sedis* 46 (1954) 678]. However, it is not ''possible to define adequately and to explain correctly the Blessed Virgin's great dignity and sublimity from the Sacred Scriptures alone . . . without taking into account Catholic tradition and the teaching authority of the Church'' (*ibid.*). Hence the importance of tracing the faith of the Church in the evidences of Christian tradition. Solemn pronouncements concerning Mary are few—only four doctrines are certainly dogmatically defined: divine motherhood, virginity, IMMACULATE CONCEPTION, ASSUMPTION.

Development in Early Christian Authors. Early writings concerning Marian theology are in reflections on the Scriptures. The Pauline comparison of Jesus Christ to ADAM (Rom 5.15) is amplified in the 2d-century description of Mary as the new EVE, bringing forth in obedience the Holy One, in contrast to the first Eve who brought forth disobedience and death (St. Justin, St. Irenaeus).

Evidence of the first three centuries reflects a clear conviction of Mary's virginity in conceiving Christ, *ante partum* (before childbirth), but does not yet show acceptance of Mary's virginity *in partu* (in childbirth), and *post partum* (after childbirth). Ambrose (d. 397) and Augustine (d. 430) defend Mary's virginity in and after the childbearing of Christ as well as in His conception (*see* VIRGIN BIRTH).

The holiness of Our Lady has an equally slow maturation in Christian consciousness. Some accuse her of fault; for example, of importunity at Cana (Irenaeus), of vainglory during her Son's public life (Chrysostom; cf. Mt 12.46), and even of doubt on Calvary (Origen). The patristic conviction of Mary's total freedom from personal sin is gradually strengthened; no serious question is raised about it after the definition of the divine maternity by the Council of EPHESUS (431; *Enchiridion symbolorum,* 251).

The delay in emergence of these Marian truths is explained in various ways. Christological and Trinitarian truths receive first attention. Possibilities of erroneous interpretation sometimes make the publication of a Marian truth inopportune. The Mediterranean pagan world knows of mother goddesses, and so Christianity cannot risk calling Mary MOTHER OF GOD prematurely. To hold Mary free of even the least personal sin seems to take away from Christ's unique holiness. Similarly, to state the virginal childbearing incautiously might play into the hands of Docetism, which denies a real body to Christ.

It is only in 649 that a Lateran council under Pope St. Martin I proclaims the perfect and perpetual virginity of Mary—before and after the birth of Jesus (*Enchiridion symbolorum,* 503). Historians of dogma disagree as to whether or not this council affirmed also the virginity *in partu,* although it is taught explicitly by Pope Paul IV (*Enchiridion symbolorum,* 1880). The Church has never specified the precise meaning of virginity *in partu,* but a common theological opinion is that it was a further miraculous sign of the divine origin of Christ.

Late Patristic, Early Medieval Times. By the 6th century the Assumption is being discussed, though there is need to distinguish between the exaggerations of the apocryphal *Transitus Mariae* (Passing of Mary) literature and authentic tradition. Other points of Marian doctrine are considered only in passing. Belief in the heavenly mediation of Mary underlies appeals to her intercession, as in the familiar prayer *Sub tuum praesidium confugimus* (We fly to thy patronage), traceable to at least a 4th-century Greek version. The title mediatrix appears in the 8th-century East with St. Andrew of Crete and St. Germanus of Constantinople; about the same time it comes to the West through Paul the Deacon's translation of ''The Life of Theophilus'' (although it might be said that recognition of the dates of the title's appearance varies).

An at least indirect spiritual maternity is found in early texts. Origen, for example, says that the Mother of Jesus can be called mother of those who are joined to Christ as John the beloved disciple was (Jn 19.26). St. Ambrose Autpert (d. 784) regards Mary as *mater gentium* (mother of the nations), *mater credentium* (mother of believers), and *mater electorum* (mother of the elect), whom she has generated in generating Christ.

As early as Epiphanius of Constantia (d. 403) Eve's title, mother of the living, is extended to Mary, but Mary's spiritual motherhood of the members of the MYSTICAL BODY appears clearly only in the 12th century, e.g., in Hermann of Tournai. A factor here is the mutual enrichment of Mariology and the theology about the Church. The maternal meaning that has always been part of the concept of the Church as new Eve is applied now also to Our Lady as new Eve. ''Like the Church of which she is the figure, Mary is mother of all those who are born again to life'' (Guerric of Igny, d. 1155; *Patrologia Latina,* 185:188).

Sculpture of the Virgin Mary, Tuscany, Italy. (©Gary Braasch/ CORBIS)

From the 12th century onward the meaning of Mary's compassion with Christ on Calvary becomes part of Mariology, e.g., in Rupert of Deutz, on ''Woman, behold your son.'' In harmony with belief in the Assumption a stronger consciousness develops also of Mary's power to intercede for men's SALVATION, e.g., in John the Geometer in the 10th century.

Systematic Mariology. Systematic Mariology has its beginnings in St. ANSELM (d. 1109), father of scholasticism. His axiom is famous: ''It was becoming that the Virgin should shine with a purity so great that nothing greater under God can be imagined. For to her God determined to give His only Son'' (*De conceptu virginali* 18; *Patrologia Latina,* 158:451). St. Anselm relates Mary's sanctity and virginity, her mediation and INTERCESSION to the divine maternity.

"Annunciation," painting by Andrea del Sarto, archangel Gabriel kneeling, facing the Virgin Mary, 16th century. (©Arte & Immagini sri/CORBIS)

St. BERNARD (d. 1153) preaches a sober, spiritual Marian theology in *De laudibus beatae virginis* (*Patrologia Latina,* 183:55–88), consisting of homilies on the Annunciation Gospel, *Missus est* (Lk 1.26). He compares Mary's mediation to an aqueduct bringing graces from Christ, the source. Never avant-garde in his Mariology, he does not call Mary spiritual mother; she is rather "Our Lady"—a powerful, yet tender queen of mercy. His opposition to the feast and doctrine of the conception of Mary sets a pattern followed by even the greatest scholastics (*Patrologia Latina,* 182:332–336).

Peter Lombard's *Sentences* devotes to Our Lady only a few questions by way of corollary to Christology. The commentaries of other schoolmen on the *Sentences* follow the lead of Lombard (d. 1160): St. Bonaventure's, St. Albert the Great's, St. Thomas Aquinas's. To appreciate the full Marian theology of the scholastics, their other writings need to be taken into account. The unknown author of the contemporary *Mariale super missus est,* once attributed to St. Albert, takes a step forward when he describes Mary in her compassion as "the associate of Christ, the helpmate similar to Him (Gn 2.21)."

St. Thomas shows deep insight into the divine maternity in the *Summa theologiae.* Starting from the revealed truth that Mary is Mother of Jesus, St. Thomas examines the holiness of Mary, her virginity, her dignity. His homiletic writings, on the Hail Mary, for example, introduce also Mary's mediation and queenship (*see* MARY, BLESSED VIRGIN, QUEENSHIP OF). He does not attempt a Mariological synthesis, and the necessity of Mary's Redemption inhibits him in the matter of the Immaculate Conception.

For centuries there is to be no significant advance in the overall approach to Mariology, although individual questions continue to be agitated. The prime example of these is the Immaculate Conception. DUNS SCOTUS intuits the theological solution of the main problem besetting what the Church will eventually proclaim a dogma—the preservative Redemption of Mary from ORIGINAL SIN.

J. Gerson (d. 1429) is a conspicuous exception in a mediocre period. In his sermons and in an explanation of the MAGNIFICAT there is a rich Mariology-Mary's mediation, her queenship, her role in the Eucharist. The sermons of St. Bernardine of Siena (d. 1444) offer a sound theology of the mediation and Assumption. He attributes to Mary jurisdiction over all graces without exception.

Reformation and Aftermath. In accord with their theology of the communion of saints, the early reformers deny a privileged intercession on Mary's part; in practice, they forbid the invocation of Mary as prejudicial to the unique mediation of Christ. The Council of Trent devotes only slight attention to Our Lady, stating it has no intention of including her under the universal law of original sin, mentioning her freedom from actual sin (some theologians consider Trent to define this, e.g., J. de Aldama, SJ), and defending veneration of her images.

In the post-Tridentine theologians a great period opens for Mariology—not only in Spain, where Protestantism is not a domestic threat, but also in Germany, where the defense of Marian doctrine and devotion is a pressing need. St. Peter Canisius (d. 1597) refutes the *Centuriators of Magdeburg* with a wide use of quotations from Scripture and the Fathers, in a pioneering work of documention, *De Maria virgine incomparabili.* Francisco Suárez, SJ (d. 1617), deserves the title father of scientific Mariology. Suárez's Roman lectures (1584–85), *Quaestiones,* are an approach toward a full and separate tract of Mariology, although he is less bold in his definitive Marian theology, *De mysteriis vitae Christi* (1592). Both works contain extensive considerations on Mary's HOLINESS. Suárez studies Mary's life as one of love of God, of GRACE demanded by the dignity of the divine maternity.

The 17th century is a high point in Marian theology. The relationship of Mary to the redemptive work of Christ is a prominent theme, e.g., in F. Q. Salazar, SJ (d. 1646), S. Saavedra, Mercedarian (d. 1643?), and D. Petau, SJ (d. 1652). In Cardinal Pierre de Bérulle, founder of the French school, the central notion of Mariology is the ''state of the Mother of God.'' Bérulle proposes a reverent admiration of the place of Mary in the mystery of the INCARNATION. St. John Eudes (d. 1680) writes of the doctrine underlying devotion to the Heart of Mary (*see* IMMACULATE HEART OF MARY). St. Louis Grignion de Montfort (d. 1716) develops the ideas of the French school in the direction of Mary's spiritual motherhood. In *The Love of Eternal Wisdom* Montfort mentions devotion to Mary as a preferred way to obtain Wisdom Incarnate, Jesus Christ. *True Devotion* elaborates this means.

By the end of the 17th century, however, the cold wind of JANSENISM is blowing strong. Jansenists are accused of minimizing devotion to Mary by denying her mediation and spiritual motherhood. A. Widenfeldt's controversial but often justly critical brochure, *Monita salutaria* (Ghent 1673; soon tr. into English as *Wholesome Advices from the Blessed Virgin to her Indiscreet Worshippers,* London 1687) provokes a storm in which the original work is often lost sight of. St. Alphonsus Liguori (d. 1787) advocates, especially in *The Glories of Mary,* the universal mediation of Mary, not only against Jansenism and Protestantism, but also in reply to the hesitations of L. A. Muratori.

1854 to 1962. The definition of the Immaculate Conception (1854) inspires a flowering of Marian studies, exemplified in Newman and Scheeben. Writing in defense of the Immaculate Conception, Newman cites the patristic sources on Mary as the new Eve (*Letter to Dr. Pusey*). His studies on the development of doctrine enrich Mariology as well, e.g., *On Consulting the Faithful in Matters of Doctrine,* 1859 (*see* DOCTRINE, DEVELOPMENT OF). Matthias Scheeben makes a place for Mariology in his *Dogmatik* (1873–82); C. Feckes (d. 1958) and E. Druwé, SJ (d. 1950), do much to make it known. The identifying feature of Scheeben's Marian theology is ''bridal motherhood''; this is Mary's ''personal character'' and the foundation of her privileges and mission. Worthy of mention at the turn of the century is J. B. Terrien, SJ, *Marie, la mère de Dieu et la mère des hommes,* 4 v. (Paris).

The main themes of the first half of the 20th century are the mediation of Mary and the Assumption. The first international Marian congress (Lyons 1900) holds a study, session on the role of Mary in the plan of salvation. At subsequent conventions, national and international, many papers on mediation are offered, e.g., by R. de la Broise, SJ, J. V. Bainvel, SJ, and E. Hugon, OP. Cardinal A. Lépicier, OSM, in 1901 and C. Van Crombrugghe in 1913 reflect the trend in their manuals of Mariology. The movement gains momentum when the Brussels Marian Congress (1921) takes Mary's mediation as its motif.

Cardinal Mercier forms an episcopal committee to study the definability of the mediation; pontifical commissions are appointed for this purpose in Belgium, Spain, and Italy. Around Mercier gathers a group of distinguished theologians, e.g., B. M. Merkelbach, OP (d. 1942), author of *Mariologia* (Paris 1939); J. Bittremieux (d. 1950), founder of the Flemish Mariological Society in 1931, author of *De mediatione universali B. Mariae Virginis quoad gratias* (Bruges 1926); J. Lebon (d. 1957), indefatigable protagonist of mediation in many writings.

After the definition of the Immaculate Conception, interest grows in a definition of the Assumption. With regard to both truths, however, the Church is moved to solemn definition more by the faith of the Christian people than by the state of theological study. In the intellectual doldrums of the mid-19th century the definition of the Immaculate Conception settles questions that once had Christian thinkers at loggerheads. In 1950, at a thriving time for Marian studies, the Church defines the Assumption, a doctrine that has not been the main focus of attention in Marian theology. Not surprisingly, the definition has called attention to differences between Catholics and other Christians, because the Assumption is a test case for intricate questions of Scripture and tradition and their relationship to each other and to the teaching authority of the Church.

The progress made in mariological studies during this period also owed much to the guidance of the popes. In addition to the definitions of the Immaculate Conception (*Ineffabilis Deus*) and Assumption (*MUNIFICENTISSIMUS DEUS*), many other Marian documents have emanated from the Holy See. Leo XIII is remembered for his encyclicals on the rosary and its doctrinal meaning (e.g., *Iucunda semper,* 1894); St. Pius X for *Ad diem illum* (1904), on the spiritual motherhood; Benedict XV for *Inter sodalicia* (1918), on Mary's compassion; Pius XI for *Lux veritatis* (1931), on the Ephesus anniversary. The acts of Pius XII contain an immense amount of material, e.g., the encyclicals *Fulgens corona* (1953), for the Marian year, and *Ad caeli reginam* (1954), on the queenship. Pius XII wrote of Our Lady's place in the general theology of Christ and the Church in his great doctrinal encyclicals: *MYSTICI CORPORIS* (1943), *MEDIATOR DEI* (1947), and *Haurietis aquas* (1956). In his Marian messages Pope John XXIII spoke frequently of the spiritual motherhood, e.g., to the eighth French National Marian Congress at Lisieux, *C'este bien volontiers,* July 6, 1961 [*Acta Apostolicae Sedis* 53 (1961) 504–506]; also in placing under Mary's patronage VATICAN COUNCIL II.

Vatican II and Beyond. The mystery of the Blessed Virgin Mary was further developed by Vatican Council II, meeting from 1962 to 1965. The Council mentioned Mary in many documents, initially in the Constitution on the Sacred Liturgy (No. 103), but particularly in the Dogmatic Constitution on the Church (ch. 8). It was most significant for the renewal of Mariology and of devotion to Mary that the Council Fathers voted, October 29, 1963, in favor of making the Marian schema a part of the document on the Church. The very title of the chapter, "The Blessed Virgin Mary, Mother of God, in the Mystery of Christ and the Church," placed her in close relationship with her Son (CHRISTOCENTRIC Mariology) and with his Mystical Body (ecclesiotypical Mariology). This is the proper setting in which to assess Mary's role in the work of Redemption. The true ecumenical importance of the Council's decision is derived not from minimizing her place in Catholic faith and piety, but from emphasizing a sharing-oriented Mariology instead of one that is privilege-centered.

Vatican II resulted in a shift in mariological studies, moving away from a privilege-centered to a sharing-oriented consideration of Mary, in association to Christ (Christocentric) and in relationship to the Church (ecclesiotypical). In contrast to the discussions in the early 20th century, the postconciliar period witnessed few studies on such themes as principles of Mariology or Marian mediation, but many positive investigations, especially into biblical and patristic sources. The Mary-Church relation attracted serious notice.

Ecumenical concern has affected theological exploration also; among the operative factors here was Vatican II's reference to the "hierarchy of truths" which "vary in their relationship to the foundation of the Christian faith" (Decree on Ecumenism, 11, 20). In 1967 the English Ecumenical Society of the Blessed Virgin Mary was founded, and along with regular meetings and publications (the pamphlet series, *Mother of Jesus*), it sponsored several international conferences. Its American branch was established in 1976 and has brought together Roman Catholic, Anglican, Orthodox and Protestant Christian scholars to explore the thorny differences for which the Virgin Mary often served as a symptom: the bonds between Scripture and tradition, and the Church's teaching authority; the legitimacy within the communion of saints of calling on the saints in prayer (invocation). A theologian in the Reformed tradition, Dr. J. A. Ross Mackenzie (Union Theological Seminary, Richmond, Virginia) received the president's patronal medal at Catholic University, Washington, DC, December 7, 1977. The medal, founded in 1974, recognizes promotion of study and veneration of Mary (previous recipients were Archbishop Fulton J. Sheen, Mother Mary Claudia, IHM, and Theodore Koehler, SM, curator of the Marian Library at the University of Dayton).

Postconciliar theological developments showed a two-fold orientation in Mariology: continuation of the directions of Vatican Council II; new areas, as explorations in the devotional life of the faithful. Study was spurred by important papal documents and joint pastorals by national episcopal conferences, as in the United States, the NCCB's *Behold Your Mother, Woman of Faith* (November 21, 1973), Switzerland (1973), Puerto Rico (1976), and Poland (1977).

Pope Paul VI's apostolic exhortation *Marialis cultus* (February 1, 1974), "for the right ordering and development of devotion to the Blessed Virgin Mary," showed Mary's place in the revised Western liturgy and included significant points on anthropology, on the Virgin Mary in respect to women's rights, and on human dignity.

In the ensuing decades after Vatican II, Mariological societies in various countries continued to function. In the United States, the Mariological Society of America met for the 25th time, January 1974. Its speakers and subjects showed an increasing ecumenical orientation, e.g., the virginal conception of Jesus was discussed at the 1973 St. Louis convention, with A. C. Piepkorn (Lutheran) and H. W. Richardson (Presbyterian) giving papers [*Marian*

Studies 24 (1973)]. National societies concerned with Marian theology continued to meet, for example, French (*Bulletin de la soliété française d'études mariales*), Spanish (*Estudios Marianos*), Canadian (French-speaking, occasional publication) and American (*Marian Studies*). The topics of the French society during this period illustrated postconciliar concerns: ''Mary's place in religious congregations of Marian Inspiration'' (1972); ''Mary and the Question of Women'' (1973 and 1974); and ''Representations of Mary in Popular Piety, Historically, Iconographically, and Psychologically'' (1976 and 1977). The Spanish society has reached its 40th volume of proceedings; recent themes have been: ''The Psychology of Mary'' (1972); ''Mary and the Mystery of the Church'' (1973); ''Marian Dogmas and the Interpretation of Dogma'' (1976).

Marian Library Studies (Dayton), the international *Marianum* (Rome) and *Ephemerides Mariologicae* (Madrid), and other periodicals, both scholarly and general, illustrate present centers of Mariological interest: popular piety; Scripture, especially the infancy narratives; catechetics; Mary and ecumenism; Mary as model of the Church, Mary and women, and Mary in popular devotion. The popular cult of the Virgin Mary has increasingly become a topic of investigation. Research interest has focused on the origins and significance of folk devotion in various cultures, both in the Old World (pilgrimage sites and shrines like Czestochowa and Lourdes, more visited than ever), and in the New World (Guadalupe, Argentina, and other countries). An associated theme is the place of Mary in the ''way of beauty,'' complementing the ''way of the intellect,'' as Pope Paul suggested to the Roman congress of May, 1975.

John Paul II and Redemptoris Mater. The papacy of John Paul II marked another important milestone in mariological studies, with the publication of the encyclical *REDEMPTORIS MATER* on March 25, 1987. *Redemptoris Mater* was a comprehensive scriptural, conciliar, and theological meditation on the Mother of God, directed to all Christians. The encyclical explained her subordinate mediatorial role, her role as model of mother and obedient expectant follower of the divine will. It cited the Marian piety as a common tradition binding Catholics and the Orthodox together.

Theological Aspects. Under the impetus of Vatican II the theology of Mary stresses the truth that her special graces and prerogatives are to be seen as primarily for the sake of her Son and his redeemed-redeeming Body, the Church. Divine Revelation about Mary makes the central mysteries of faith more intelligible and meaningful for Christian living.

The Christocentric and ecclesiotypical emphases of contemporary Mariology are mutually complementary and not in conflict. For Mary cannot be related to Christ without being intimately associated with the ecclesial Body that he received through his redemptive activity. At the same time, she is the archetype of the Church only because her unique relationship with Christ is the basis for the Church's share in his redeeming work (see Semmelroth 1963, esp. 80–88). Consequently, concentration upon the ecclesiotypical significance of Marian doctrine and devotion should not obscure their basic Christocentric character.

Theologians today are more inclined to include the Mary-Church analogy within the basic Marian idea or fundamental principle of Mariology. ''Her concrete motherhood with regard to Christ, the redeeming God-Man, freely accepted in faith—her fully committed divine motherhood—this is both the key to the full understanding of the Marian mystery and the basic Mariological principle, which is concretely identical with Mary's objectively and subjectively unique state of being redeemed'' (Schillebeeckx 106). Within one organic principle the two emphases are contained, i.e., both the Christocentric (Mary's ''fully committed divine motherhood''), and the ecclesiotypical (her ''objectively and subjectively unique state of being redeemed''). Her vocation to be the mother of the Word incarnate must be considered in close connection with the graces that reveal her calling to be the prototype of the Church.

Immaculate Conception. Accordingly, Mary's Immaculate Conception is God's special favor preparing her to accept freely the invitation to be the Reedeemer's mother and so to share in the redemption. Following St. Bernard, St. Thomas Aquinas taught that her consent was given ''in place of the whole human race'' (*Summa Theologiae* 3a, 30.1). Because she was so completely receptive to God's loving plan, the members of Christ's Body can receive the fruits of Christ's redeeming love into their own lives. Being the first fruit of her Son's Redemption, Mary is uniquely redeemed *objectively* (preservation from all sin through the grace of the Immaculate Conception). Responding to her vocation with total commitment, she is uniquely redeemed *subjectively.* Since she received the Savior into her own life of loving faith, Mary cooperated maternally in Christ's objective redemption of the human race. Indeed Christ alone is the Redeemer who reconciles the world to the Father in the Holy Spirit. Mary's ''fully committed divine motherhood,'' however, gives her free act of identifying with his objective redemption a redemptive meaning and value for all the members of the Church.

Divine Maternity. The truth that Mary's motherhood of Christ is both bridal and virginal has rich ecclesiotypical significance (see Semmelroth 1963, esp. 117–142).

Her vocal *fiat* of free consent at the annunciation and her silent *fiat* at the foot of the cross make Mary the spiritual bride of the Redeemer. In her compassion she received the fruits of her Son's sacrifice both for her own redemption and for that of the whole Church. Concomitantly, and as a result of this creative receptivity to grace, her bridal motherhood is also virginal. Her maternal fruitfulness cannot come from human power but from the breath of the Holy Spirit. Had she conceived Christ other than as a virgin, her bridal relationship with the *Logos* incarnate would have been obscured. Without her perpetual virginity, the revelation of her complete and continuous fidelity to Christ and his messianic mission would have been blurred. Mary then is the archetype of the Church as the Church is also the virginal bride of Christ. As the community of persons redeemed by him, the Church is called to be constantly faithful to his word. The Immaculate Conception is the perfect exemplar of a grace-filled Church. As the sacramental community called to mediate Redemption to the world, the Church also images the bridal motherhood of Mary. The Assumption makes her ''the sign of sure hope, and comfort for the pilgrim people of God'' (*Lumen gentium* 68—69). All the Marian dogmas, therefore, converge toward a theological and prayerful contemplation of Mary as the archetype of the Church.

As bridal and virginal mothers, both Mary and the Church are to be dynamically united together with the Holy Spirit. The sole source of their spiritual fecundity is the abiding presence and activity of the risen Lord's Spirit. A closer connection between Mariology and Pneumatology will contribute greatly to a balanced Christology, ecclesiology, and Christian anthropology. Much remains to be done in this regard, especially by theologians of the Western Church who have begun to study more seriously the magnificent heritage of the Eastern tradition on the Holy Spirit.

New Eve. A portion of the patristic patrimony common to East and West is the image of Mary as the New Eve. Its rediscovery, under the special inspiration of Cardinal Newman's Marian writings, has led to a renewed research into the witness of the Fathers who made use of this image in their teaching about Mary. After the Scriptures, it reflects the most ancient meditation upon Mary and is a very fertile source of the Mary-Church analogy and typology. The National Conference of Catholic Bishops (NCCB) in the pastoral on the Blessed Virgin Mary points out: ''Even more anciently, the Church was regarded as the 'New Eve.' The Church is the bride of Christ, formed from his side in the sleep of death on the cross, as the first Eve was formed by God from the side of the sleeping Adam'' (NCCB 41). From her earliest days the Church has seen herself symbolized in Mary and has come to understand her mysterious self more profoundly in light of Mary as archetype. Mary ''personifies'' all that the Church is and hopes to become.

The impact of an ecclesiotypical Mariology upon Marian devotion has been most salutary. Pope Paul VI in his apostolic exhortation for the right ordinary and development of devotion to the Blessed Virgin Mary, stated: ''She is worthy of imitation because she was the first and most perfect of Christ's disciples. All of this has a permanent and universal exemplary value'' (Paul VI 35). Mary, of course, is not an exemplar in the sense of being a stereotyped blueprint upon which contemporary Christians are to model their lives. Nevertheless, if Christians are to mature as members of Christ's living Body, the Church, they must prayerfully penetrate the perennial meaning of Mary-like faith, courage, concern, constancy, etc.

Still a stumbling block for many, especially members of other Christian Churches, is the concept of Mary's mediation and intercession. It seems to interfere with the unique mediatorship of Christ. Vatican II's Marian chapter clearly teaches: ''Mary's function as mother of men in no way obscures or diminishes this unique mediation of Christ, but rather shows its power'' (*Lumen gentium* 60). Reconceptualization of the mystery must remove from Mary's mediatory role any image of her being a go-between, as though the risen Lord were made remote. Such a misconception misses the basic meaning of the Incarnation and true grandeur of Mary, namely, that God the Son has chosen to become man in her and to be an abiding presence in human history in his risen humanity forever. Her spiritual motherhood primarily helps dispose believers to encounter the ever-present Christ more intimately in their daily Christian lives. Both by her example as archetype of the Church and by her intercessory ministry in glory, Mary enlightens and inspires her spiritual children to grow more docile to the direct action of her Son's spirit and to cooperate more generously with the special graces of God's redeeming love.

Bibliography: *Marian Studies* (1950–), annual proceedings of the Mariological Society of America. J. B. CAROL, *Fundamentals of Mariology* (New York 1956). P. F. PALMER, *Mary in the Documents of the Church* (Westminster, MD 1952). M. THURIAN, *Mary, Mother of All Christians* (New York 1964). G. PHILIPS et al., *De Mariologia et oecumenismo* (Rome 1962). O. SEMMELROTH, *Mary, Archetype of the Church,* tr. M. VON EROES and J. DEVLIN (New York 1963); National Conference of Catholic Bishops, *Behold Your Mother, Woman of Faith,* a pastoral letter on the Blessed Virgin Mary November 21, 1973 (Washington 1973). D. FLANAGAN, commentary on ch. 8 of *Lumen Gentium,* in *Vatican II: The Constitution on the Church,* ed. K. MCNAMARA (Chicago 1968). H. DU MANOIR DE JUAYE, ed., *Maria: Études sur la Sainte Vierge* 8 v. (Beauchesne, Paris 1949–71). R. LAURENTIN, *Court traité sur la Vierge Marie* (5th ed. Lethielleux, Paris 1968). J. C. DE SATGÉ, *Down to Earth: The New Protestant Vision of the Virgin Mary* (Wilmington, NC 1976). R. E. BROWN et al., eds., *Mary in the New Testament* (New

York, Philadelphia, Toronto 1978). E. R. CARROLL, *Understanding the Mother of Jesus* (Wilmington, DE 1978). L. DEISS, *Mary, Daughter of Sion* tr. B. T. BLAIR (Collegeville, MN 1972). D. FLANAGAN, *The Theology of Mary* (Hales Corners, WI 1978). F. M. JELLY, "Marian Dogmas within Vatican II's Hierarchy of Truths," *Marian Studies* 27 (1976) 17–40; G. F. KIRWIN, "Mary's Salvific Role Compared with That of the Church," *Marian Studies* 25 (1974) 29–43. T. A. KOEHLER, "Mary's Spiritual Maternity after the Second Vatican Council," *Marian Studies* 23 (1972) 39–68. J. A. R. MACKENZIE, "The Patristic Witness to the Virgin Mary as the New Eve," *Marian Studies* 29 (1978) 67–78. G. A. MALONEY, *Mary: The Womb of God* (Danville, NJ 1976). J. H. NEWMAN, *The New Eve* (Westminister, MD 1952). PAUL VI, *Marialis cultus*, apostolic exhortation, February 2, 1974, *Acta Apostolicae Sedis* (Rome 1974) 66 113–168; tr. *Devotion to the Blessed Virgin Mary* (USCC Publ. Office, Washington, DC 1974). E. SCHILLEBEECKX, *Mary, Mother of the Redemption*, tr. N. D. SMITH (New York 1964). A. SCHMEMANN, "Our Lady and the Holy Spirit," *Marian Studies* 23 (1972) 69–78. F.M. JELLY, *Madonna: Mary in the Catholic Tradition* (Huntington, IN 1986). Ibid., "The Theological Context of and Introduction to Chapter 8 of Lumen Gentium," *Marian Studies* 37 (1986) 43–73. *Mary: God's Yes to Man—John Paul's Encyclical "Redemptoris Mater."* Introduction by J. CARDINAL RATZINGER, commentary by H. URS VON BALTHASAR, San Francisco: Ignatius Press, 1988. F. M. JELLY, O.P. "Ecumenical Aspects of *Redemptoris Mater.*" *Marian Studies* 39 (1988): 115–129. J. PELIKAN, *Mary Through the Centuries: Her Place in the History of Culture* (New Haven, CT 1996)

[E. R. CARROLL/F.M. JELLY/EDS.]

MARION-BRÉSILLAC, MELCHIOR MARIE JOSEPH DE

Founder of the Society of the AFRICAN MISSIONS; b. Castelnaudary (Aude), France, Dec. 2, 1813; d. Freetown, Sierra Leone, June 28, 1859. Born of penurious, pious, and intelligent former aristocrats, and educated at home until his 18th year, de Brésillac was ordained (1838) and worked in a parish until 1841, when he joined the PARIS FOREIGN MISSION SOCIETY (MEP). As a missionary in India (1842–54) he was disliked by other missionaries because of his advocacy of an indigenous CLERGY and his opposition to caste. He became superior of the seminary at Pondicherry (1844) and provicar apostolic (1845) and vicar apostolic (1850) of Coimbatore. The continued resistance to his policies led him to resign (1854) and to leave the MEP. His report to Rome, however, served as the basis for later changes in missionary policies. Bishop de Brésillac was attracted to the mission field in AFRICA and founded his own congregation at Lyons (1856). He was appointed vicar apostolic of Sierra Leone (1858) and journeyed to Africa (1859). He went first to Dakar and then to Freetown, where he insisted on going ashore despite a yellow fever epidemic. He and his four companions died within six weeks. His body was returned to Lyons. De Brésillac's ideals of a native priesthood and the adaptation of culture became the mainstay of his religious institute.

Bibliography: M. LE GALLEN, *Vie de Mgr de Marion Brésillac* (Lyons 1910). L. LELOIR, *Marion de Brésillac* (Namur 1939). M. J. BANE, *Catholic Pioneers in West Africa* (Dublin 1956). J. BONFILS, *L'Oeuvre de Msgr. De Marion Brésilliac en faveur du clergé local dans les missions de l'Inde au XIXe siècle* (Lyons 1959).

[J. M. TODD]

MARIST BROTHERS

Officially known as Marist Brothers of the Schools (FMS, Official Catholic Directory #0770), also called the Little Brothers of Mary, a pontifical congregation of lay religious of men; it was founded Jan. 2, 1817, near Lyons, France, by St. Marcellin CHAMPAGNAT for the Christian education of French youth. Champagnat, ordained in 1816, was relieved of his parochial duties in 1824, to spend all his time in furthering and guiding the work of the brothers. At the time of his death (1840), there were 280 brothers teaching about 7,000 pupils in 48 schools in France. In 1851, the French government approved the congregation, and in 1863, it was officially recognized and approved by Pius IX.

Champagnat himself was one of the first members of the Society of Mary, or MARIST FATHERS, and he originally envisioned a single congregation of priests and brothers under one superior. This union never materialized, since the Holy See judged that the size and diversity of purpose of the two congregations would make such a union impractical. In the course of their history, the Marist Brothers have absorbed several other congregations of brothers: in 1842 the Brothers of Saint-Paul-Trois-Châteaux in France; in 1844 the Brothers of Christian Instruction of Viviers, France; in 1956 the Brothers of St. Peter Claver, a congregation composed entirely of native Nigerians; and in 1959 the Brothers of St. Francis Regis, in Canada and France.

In the United States, the Marist Brothers have operated schools since 1886, when Canada and the United States formed a single province. In 1911 the United States became an independent province, which was divided into two (Esopus and Poughkeepsie) in 1959. The brothers provide Christian education to students on the primary, secondary, college, and university levels. They maintain academic, vocational, technical, and agricultural schools. The congregation is governed from the motherhouse in Rome.

Bibliography: J. COSTE and G. LESSARD, *Origines Maristes, 1786–1836,* 4 v. (Rome 1960–61). M. COTÉ, *The Historical Growth and Development of the Marist Brothers in the United States* (Poughkeepsie, N.Y. 1961).

[L. A. VOEGTLE/EDS.]

MARIST FATHERS

The Society of Mary (SM, Official Catholic Directory #0780), whose members are known as Marists, is distinct from another congregation of the same title, the members of which are called Marianists, although both societies began in France at about the same time.

History. The founders of the Marists were Jean Claude Courveille and Jean Claude Marie COLIN. The idea of the society and its initial propagation are credited to Courveille. He was born at Usson-en-Forez in the Diocese of Le Puy on May 15, 1787 and became as a child very devoted to the Blessed Virgin Mary. In 1812 he felt convinced that Mary wanted to help the Church, in great need at that time, through a congregation especially dedicated to her and bearing her name, the Society of Mary. During his last year of theology at the major seminary of Lyons, he discussed this project with other seminarians there. In 1816 seven priests, on the day after ordination, and four seminarians consecrated themselves to Mary and pledged themselves to the founding of her society. Only four of these ever became Marists. Courveille himself remained for ten years the reputed leader and filled what might be called, in modern terms, the role of a public relations expert. He finally disappeared from Marist history in 1826, and he was eventually received by the Benedictines at the Abbey of SOLESMES, where he died in 1866.

Colin, one of the 11 who had promised to work for the foundation of the society, was also ordained in 1816. Overcoming the hesitancy and timidity that had characterized him during his seminary days, he became a truly apostolic man while assisting his brother who was pastor of Cerdon, a small village east of Lyons. During this time he was able to put into writing the basic ideas of the constitutions for the priests, sisters, and secular third order of the society. After having written twice to Rome, he received the initial approval on March 9, 1822, which was addressed to Courveille at Cerdon. In 1836, upon Colin's acceptance of the Oceania missions, the Society of Mary was given final approval by Rome. The first missionaries left for the South Seas that same year. During his generalate (1836–54), Colin sent 74 priests to Oceania and began new establishments in France, chief among which were residences for home missionaries and educational institutions.

During the administration of Julien Favre (1854–84), the society grew to 512 members and began its foundations in the United States. Under his successor, Antoine Martin (1885–1905), the congregation established itself in Spain, Italy, and Belgium. Martin also opened houses of formation outside of France.

At first Colin had tried to obtain approval for a single, four-branched society, composed of priests, brothers, religious sisters, and a third order. A series of refusals from Rome, however, forced him to surrender this idea of one multiple family. Colin's original concept has since developed in the form of four independent congregations: the Marist Fathers (aided by Marist lay brothers), the MARIST BROTHERS, the MARIST SISTERS, and the MARIST MISSIONARY SISTERS. The Marist Third Order, is also attached to the Marist Fathers. These are united by one common spirit and are appropriately designated today as the Marist Family.

Spirit and apostolate. The particular spirit that unites and characterizes the members of the society is the spirit of Mary. Through meditating upon her personality as presented in the Gospels and through a prayerful union with her now reigning with her Son, the Marists attempt to bring that spirit into their lives and works. Another point of reference for the development of this spirit is an intuition of their founder, according to which he was conscious of the obstacle to the religious life created by self-seeking and by an apostolate that is not oriented to the spreading of God's kingdom. These thoughts of the founder serve as guidelines to the society's tradition, as it tries to adapt itself to the ever new needs of the Church. The Marist constitutions recount the purpose of the congregation, the means to attain that goal, and a description of the spirit. The subsequent chapters describe the training of the religious, the works of the apostolate they engage in, the rules of government, and the virtues vital to the existence of the congregation.

The society engages in parish work, high school teaching, catechetics, youth ministries, retreats, spiritual direction, and chaplaincies. In the United States, where the society first arrived in 1863, there are three provinces: Boston (1924), Washington, D.C. (1924) and San Francisco (1962).

Bibliography: J. COSTE, *The Spirit of the Society,* tr. S. FAGAN (Rome 1963). J. COSTE and G. LESSARD, eds., *Origines maristes,* 4 v. (Rome 1960—). N. WEBER and J. L. WHITE, *The Marists: A History* (privately printed; Washington 1959).

[J. L. WHITE/EDS.]

MARIST MISSIONARY SISTERS

Also know as Missionary Sisters of the Society of Mary (SMSM, Official Catholic Directory #2420), was founded in 1845 at Saint-Brieuc, France, as the first society of women formed solely for the apostolate in foreign missions. The first missionaries departed for the South Sea Islands in 1845 and 1857. The sisters have maintained a significant presence in the Southwest Pacific, devoting their efforts to catechetical, medical, educational, and social service work. The generalate is in Rome, the U.S. provincialate in Waltham, Mass.

[M. A. KERBY/EDS.]

MARIST SISTERS

Popular name for the Sisters of the Congregation of Mary (SM, Official Catholic Directory #2430), a religious congregation founded in 1817 in Cerdon (Ain), France, by Jean Claude COLIN and Jeanne Marie Chavoin (Mother St. Joseph), who acted as superior general (1824–53). The Holy See approved the institute in 1884 and the revised constitutions in 1958. The sisters engage mainly in educational and catechetical work, pastoral ministry, counseling, youth ministry and social outreach. The sisters arrived in the United States in 1956, opening a school in Dearborn, Mich. The generalate is in Rome; the U.S. provincialate is in Abilene, TX.

Bibliography: L. DE ROUVRAY, *Origines et histoire des religieuses Maristes* (Paris 1951). E. LEONARD, *Enriching Many: Jeanne-Marie Chavoin* (London 1956).

[S. W. HOSIE/EDS.]

MARITAIN, JACQUES

French Catholic philosopher; b. Paris, Nov. 18, 1882; d. Toulouse, April 28, 1973. Maritain was one of the great Catholic thinkers of the 20th century, and a leading figure in the revival of Thomism within both Catholic philosophical tradition and the public sphere. He was the author of some 70 books, among them the widely read and influential *The Degrees of Knowledge, Integral Humanism, The Person and the Common Good, Man and the State, Creative Intuition in Art and Poetry, The Range of Reason, Approaches to God, Education at the Crossroads*, and *The Peasant of the Garonne*. Pope Paul VI, long a student of his work, presented his ''Message to the Men of Thought and of Science'' to Maritain at the close of Vatican II.

Life. Maritain was the son of Paul Maritain, a lawyer, and Geneviève Favre, daughter of Jules Favre (one of the founders of the Third French Republic). He was raised in a progressive Protestant environment, and received his education at the Lycée Henri IV (1898–99) and at the Sorbonne, where he prepared a *licence* in philosophy (1900–01) and in the natural sciences (1901–02). Initially interested in the philosophy of Spinoza, he soon fell under the spell of teachers convinced that science alone could provide the answers to all questions of the human condition.

Jacques Maritain, 1948. (AP/Wide World Photos)

At the Sorbonne, Maritain met a young Russian Jewish student, Raïssa Oumansoff (*see* MARITAIN, RAÏSSA OUMANSOFF), who was to share his life and his quest for truth. (Over 50 years later, in 1954, Jacques wrote: ''The aid and the inspiration of my beloved Raïssa have penetrated all my life and all my work. If there is something good in that which I have done, it is to her, after God, that I owe it.'') Jacques and Raïssa became engaged in 1902. Shortly thereafter, because the scientism of their teachers had left them with a profound sense of the meaninglessness of life, they went through a period of depression. At the urging of a friend, Charles Péguy, Jacques and Raïssa attended the lectures of Henri Bergson at the Collège de France (1903–04); Bergson's philosophy offered an alternative to scientific materialism and, for a time, Jacques was attracted by *bergsonisme*. In 1904 Jacques and Raïssa married and, through the influence of another friend, Léon Bloy, were received into the Catholic church on June 11, 1906. A few months later, in August, the Maritains moved to Heidelberg, where Jacques studied biology under Hans Driesch (1906–08).

In 1908, Jacques and Raïssa, together with Raïssa's sister Véra, returned to France. Véra was to live with the Maritains continuously until her death. Within a few months, at the suggestion of Raïssa, Jacques began to read some of the writings of St. Thomas Aquinas; Raïssa had, during a period of convalescence, herself been introduced to St. Thomas's works by Father Humbert Clérissac, a Dominican. Jacques described the effect of reading St. Thomas's *Summa Theologiae* as a ''luminous flood,'' and definitively abandoned *bergsonisme*.

In 1912, Maritain began teaching at the Lycée Stanislaus. In his early philosophical work (e.g., ''La science moderne et la raison,'' 1910, and *La philosophie bergsonienne*, 1913), he sought to defend Thomistic philosophy from its Bergsonian and secular opponents. He was soon named Assistant Professor at the Institut Catholique de Paris (attached to the Chair of the History of Modern Philosophy), became full Professor in 1921 and, in 1928, was appointed to the Chair of Logic and Cosmology, which he held until 1939.

Beginning in the mid-1920s, Maritain developed a strong interest in applying philosophy to social concerns. Initially attracted by the social movement *L'ACTION FRANÇAISE*, he left it when it was condemned by the Catholic Church. Maritain's ideas were especially influential in Latin America and, largely as a result of the character of his political philosophy, he came under attack from both the left and the right, in France and abroad. Lectures in Latin America in 1936 led to him being named as a corresponding member of the Brazilian Academy of Letters, but also to being the object of a campaign of vilification.

Beginning in December 1932, Maritain travelled annually to North America, often to teach in Toronto at the Institute (later, the Pontifical Institute) of Mediaeval Studies. Following his lectures in Toronto at the beginning of 1940, he moved to the United States and, by June, decided to stay. During the Second World War, he taught at Princeton (1941–42) and at Columbia University (1941–44). He was instrumental in the establishment of a French university in exile in New York—the École Libre des Hautes Études—and active in the war effort, recording broadcasts destined for occupied France.

In December 1944, Maritain was named French ambassador to the Vatican, and was involved in discussions that led to the drafting of the United Nations' Universal Declaration of Human Rights. Upon the completion of his appointment in 1948, Maritain returned to Princeton as professor emeritus where he lectured annually on topics in moral and political philosophy, though in the summers he frequently returned to France to give short courses in philosophy—notably at L'Eau vive. A few months following Véra's death, on January 1, 1960, Jacques and Raïssa returned to France. But Raïssa herself soon fell ill, and died on November 4, 1960. Jacques moved to Toulouse, to live with a religious order, the Little Brothers of Jesus. He had long loved the Little Brothers, who pursued an essentially contemplative life in the very midst of the world and ''at the core of the masses''; he had attended their Mass of foundation in the Basilica of Sacré-Coeur in 1933, and from the beginning had a great influence on their intellectual and spiritual formation. It was in this ''fraternity'' in Toulouse that Maritain wrote his celebrated and controversial book *The Peasant of the Garonne* on what he considered to be some of the confusions in the post-Vatican II world. He completed several other books— *God and the Permission of Evil, On the Grace and Humanity of Jesus*, and *On the Church of Christ: The Person of the Church and Her Personnel.* In 1970, he petitioned to join the order, and died in Toulouse on April 28, 1973. He is buried alongside Raïssa in Kolbsheim, Alsace, France.

Works and Thought. In his many books, articles, and lectures, Maritain developed and deepened the classical doctrines of Thomistic philosophy. He insisted that Catholic philosophers had to do more than merely repeat St. Thomas's views, and his own efforts to engage problems raised by contemporary philosophy and culture often presented St. Thomas's insights in a highly original way. While the most profound inspiration of many of Maritain's ideas was the work of St. Thomas, his epistemology and aesthetics show other influences as well, particularly that of St. JOHN OF THE CROSS. Maritain never swerved from his conviction that in St. Thomas's thought are to be found the principles of a realistic and existential metaphysics and the bases of a political and ethical philosophy that does justice to the dignity of human beings and their relationship with God.

Throughout his work, Maritain repeatedly called attention to there being in every aspect of modern culture—art, poetry, science, philosophy, and even in the spiritual life—a *prise de conscience*, a growth in self-awareness. He saw this striving for autonomy and a fuller identity as a characteristic feature of the modern age; at the same time, he deplored the loss of the sense of being and of love in modern life. Although Maritain consistently made trenchant criticisms of modern culture (e.g., in *Antimoderne*, 1922), he recognized and placed even greater emphasis on its positive contributions. The task ahead for Christian philosophers of the future, as he envisioned it, was to become aware of their mission, their resources, and their methodology, and the importance of restoring a philosophy of being and a social and political philosophy that is open to the evangelical message of love.

Moral, Social, Political Philosophy. In *Moral Philosophy*, Maritain turned to the great moral philosophers of the past and assessed the problems they considered fundamental in ethics. In his *Neuf leçons sur la philosophie morale* and his posthumously published *La loi natu-*

relle ou loi non-ecrite (lectures given, in 1949 and 1950 at L'Eau vive, and which, together, would have been the basis for the projected second volume of *Moral Philosophy*), Maritain provided a positive account of a moral theory, based on natural law, that is both truly philosophical and yet wholly consistent with the Christian tradition.

In *Integral Humanism,* Maritain provided a charter for a Christian social philosophy. Starting with the concrete situation of human beings before their destiny, Maritain envisaged a form of civilization that would be characterized by an integral HUMANISM, theocentric as opposed to anthropocentric, and that would strive toward the ideal of true community by showing respect for human dignity and human rights. In this and other works (*Freedom and the Modern World, Christianity and Democracy, The Rights of Man and the Natural Law*), Maritain called for a Christian humanism to achieve the goal of a New Christendom. In *Man and the State*, he redefined basic political concepts—e.g., body politic, state, the people, and sovereignty—and defended democratic principles and institutions for all nations. To show that certain basic rights are recognized by all, he pointed to the general agreement on those rights found in the 1948 United Nations Universal Declaration of Human Rights. Maritain recognized the rights of workers as well as those of the human and the civic person.

Throughout Maritain's ethics and social and political philosophy runs the leitmotiv of FREEDOM. By ''freedom'' he does not mean license, but the full development of the human person in accord with his or her nature—specifically, the achievement of moral and spiritual perfection which is a ''common good.'' In works such as *The Person and the Common Good*, Maritain importantly distinguishes between the human being as an individual and as a PERSON. Human beings are individuals so far as they are part of a material, social order, and have responsibilities to it. Yet, because they are part of a spiritual order, they are also persons. The person is a whole, has dignity, ''must be treated as an end,'' and has a transcendent destiny. Maritain's PERSONALISM is a *via media* between individualism and collectivism, and has been influential in the writings of Edith Stein (Blessed Teresa Benedicta) and Karol Wojtyła (Pope JOHN PAUL II).

Knowledge. Since the movement of humanity is, Maritain says, towards freedom, it is no surprise that the primary goal of education is the conquest of interior freedom (*Education at the Crossroads*). Such freedom is one of fulfillment and expansion and is analogous to that enjoyed by those united to God in the BEATIFIC VISION. For Maritain, the pursuit of the highest freedom and of the highest contemplation are but two aspects of the same quest (*Confession de foi*). This search after wisdom and freedom are the goals of his.

In *The Degrees of Knowledge* Maritain surveyed a wide range of issues in order to show the diversity and essential compatibility of the various areas of knowledge, from science and philosophy to religious faith and mysticism. He argued that there were different orders of knowledge and, within them, different degrees determined by the nature of the object to be known and the ''degree of abstraction'' involved. Yet all are organically related. Maritain called his own view ''critical realism,'' and maintained that, despite the differences among them, KANTIANISM, IDEALISM, PRAGMATISM, and POSITIVISM all reflected the influence of NOMINALISM—that universal notions are creations of the human mind and have no foundation in reality.

Throughout his writings on theoretical philosophy, and particularly in *A Preface to Metaphysics* and *Existence and the Existent*, there is an emphasis on the existential character of a realistic philosophy of being; in Maritain's view, knowledge as well as love is immersed in existence.

Like St. Thomas, Maritain held that there was no conflict between faith and true reason, that religious belief was open to rational discussion, and that the existence of God and certain fundamental religious beliefs could be philosophically demonstrated. There are many ways for human beings to approach God, Maritain says, but in *Approaches to God* he insisted on the importance of restating the five ways of St. Thomas for the modern mind and of discovering new approaches based on poetic and other concrete experiences. In addition to developing a 'sixth way,' Maritain argued that human beings also have a prephilosophical knowledge or intuition of God that, while rational, cannot be expressed in words.

Art and Poetry. In the areas of art and poetry, on which he reflected over his lifetime, Maritain's major work is undoubtedly *Creative Intuition in Art and Poetry*. Here, he sought to shed light on the ''mysterious nature of poetry'' and on the process of creativity with its sources in ''the spiritual unconscious.'' In this book, and in *Art and Scholasticism*, Maritain drew frequently on the artistic and poetic opinions of Raïssa, herself an artist and poet.

Influence. At the time of his death, Maritain was likely the best-known Catholic philosopher in the world. The breadth of his philosophical work, his influence on the social teachings of the Catholic Church, and his ardent defenses of human rights made him one of the central figures of his times.

Maritain's philosophy is marked by a deeply religious impulse and on occasion takes on a theological and even contemplative dimension. His calling, as Yves

Simon pointed out, is that of the Christian philosopher who examines philosophical issues without losing sight of their relation to faith and theology. Maritain was ''scarcely enchanted'' by the expression ''Christian philosophy,'' but accepted the notion as legitimate so far as it indicates a philosophy that exists in a climate of explicit faith. Nevertheless—and this is a point Maritain himself stressed in his later works—his own work is philosophical, not theological; it pursues philosophical ends by means of strictly philosophical methods. His work is intended to bear witness on behalf of the autonomy of philosophy and to investigate ''the mystery of created existence.'' At the same time, he says, philosophy cannot be isolated from concrete life and faith. It achieves its goals only when totally united to every source of light and experience in the human mind. Only a Christian philosophy that conceives and pursues such an ideal is capable of ''ransoming the time and of redeeming every human search after truth.''

Maritain's philosophical work has been translated into some twenty languages. Its popularity was due, in part, to it being written for a general, rather than an academic, audience. Some of Maritain's writings are polemical and, because his concern was often to address very specific issues of his time, they occasionally have a rather dated tone. In his own time, controversy swirled around the following topics in particular: the distinction between personality and individuality in relation to the common good (e.g., Charles de Koninck), the empiriological vs. ontological distinction within the first degree of abstraction (*see* PHILOSOPHY AND SCIENCE), the independence of moral philosophy from theology, and the notion of Christian philosophy itself (e.g., Étienne GILSON). Other topics to which Maritain made valuable contributions include authority and freedom in a pluralistic society, the nature and exercise of free will, the existential intuition of subjectivity, the intentional being of love, and the analogy of being and its perfections—which Maritain saw as a principle operating in the most diverse regions of reality and thought. He himself hoped that he made some contribution to a deeper understanding of the mystery of evil (*God and the Permission of Evil*).

Nevertheless, it is not easy to place Maritain's thought within the history of philosophy in the 20th century. Clearly, the impact of his work was strongest in those countries where Catholicism was influential. Although his political philosophy led him, at least in his time, to be considered a liberal and even a social democrat, he eschewed socialism and, in *The Peasant of the Garonne*, was an early critic of many of the religious reforms that followed the Second Vatican Council. He is therefore often considered by contemporary liberals as too conservative, and by many conservatives as too liberal. Again, though generally considered to be a Thomist, according to Gilson, Maritain's ''Thomism'' was really an EPISTEMOLOGY and, hence, not a real Thomism at all.

Since 1958, the Jacques Maritain Center has operated at the University of Notre Dame in the United States; the Cercle d'Études Jacques et Raïssa Maritain, in Kolbsheim, France, also holds an extensive collection of manuscripts, and has been active in producing both books and articles on Maritain's work and the *Oeuvres complètes de Jacques et Raïssa Maritain*, 15 vols. (Fribourg, Switzerland: Éditions universitaires, 1982-95). There are several academic journals devoted to Maritain's work, such as *Études maritainiennes/Maritain Studies*, the *Cahiers Jacques Maritain* (edited by the Cercle d'Études in Kolbsheim), and *Notes et documents* (in international and in Brasilian editions). In addition to the Institut International Jacques Maritain (Rome), there are currently some twenty national associations which meet regularly to discuss Maritain's work. The continuity of interest in Maritain's thought in the English-speaking world has led to the publication of a 20-volume set, in English, of *The Collected Works of Jacques Maritain* under auspices of the University of Notre Dame Press.

Bibliography: The most comprehensive list of books and articles on Maritain's philosophy and life is found in J.-L. ALLARD and P. GERMAIN, *Répertoire bibliographique sur la vie et l'oeuvre de Jacques et Raïssa Maritain* (Ottawa, 1994). *The Achievement of Jacques and Raïssa Maritain: A Bibliography, 1906–1961* (Garden City, N.Y. 1962), by D. and I. GALLAGHER, also lists approximately 1,600 items by and about the Maritains in many languages. An exhaustive list of the various editions of Maritain's writings and of their translations is being compiled in occasional supplementary volumes of the *Cahiers Jacques Maritain*. Principal Works. *Bergsonian Philosophy and Thomism*, tr. M. L. and J. G. ANDISON (New York 1955); *Art and Scholasticism and The Frontiers of Poetry*, tr. J. W. EVANS (New York 1962); *Distinguish to Unite, or The Degrees of Knowledge*, tr. G. B. PHELAN (New York 1959); *An Essay on Christian Philosophy*, tr. E. FLANNERY (New York 1955); *A Preface to Metaphysics: Seven Lectures on Being* (New York 1939); *Philosophy of Nature*, tr. I. C. BYRNE (New York 1951); *Integral Humanism: Temporal and Spiritual Problems of a New Christendom*, tr. J. W. EVANS (New York 1968); *Education at the Crossroads* (New Haven 1943); *Existence and the Existent*, tr. L. GALANTIÈRE and G. B. PHELAN (New York 1948); *The Person and the Common Good*, tr. J. J. FITZGERALD (New York 1947); *The Range of Reason* (New York 1952); *Man and the State* (Chicago 1951); *An Introduction to Basic Problems of Moral Philosophy* (Albany, N.Y. 1990); *Approaches to God*, tr. P. O'REILLY (New York 1954); *Creative Intuition in Art and Poetry* (New York 1953); *On the Philosophy of History* (New York 1957, London 1959); *Moral Philosophy: An Historical and Crtical Survey of the Great Systems*, tr. M. SUTHER et al. (New York 1964); *The Peasant of the Garonne*, tr. M. CUDDIHY and E. HUGHES (New York 1968); *Lectures on Natural Law*, tr. W. SWEET (Notre Dame 2002).

[D. A. GALLAGHER/J. W. EVANS/W. SWEET]

MARITAIN, RAÏSSA OUMANSOFF

Author; b. Rostov on the Don, Russia, Sept. 12, 1883; d. Paris, Nov. 4, 1960. To escape persecution of the Jews, the Oumansoff family left Russia for Paris, where Raïssa studied at the Sorbonne. She married Jacques Maritain in 1904, was converted to Catholicism in 1906 under the influence of LÉON BLOY, and with her husband played an important role in the French Catholic revival. Both in France and in the U.S. (since 1940) she shared Jacques Maritain's lifelong labor to make known to the 20th century the wisdom of St. THOMAS AQUINAS. Her works include four volumes of poetry; her memoirs, *We Have Been Friends Together* (New York 1942) and *Adventures in Grace* (New York 1945); several books with Jacques Maritain, notably *The Situation of Poetry* (New York 1955); and (posthumously) *Notes on the Lord's Prayer* (New York 1964) and *Journal de Raïssa* (Paris 1963).

Bibliography: D. A. and I. J. GALLAGHER, *The Achievement of Jacques and Raïssa Maritain: A Bibliography, 1906–1961* (Garden City, N.Y. 1962).

[I. J. GALLAGHER]

MARIUS MERCATOR

Fifth-century Latin polemicist; b. probably Africa; d. probably Thrace, after 431. Marius Mercator, known only through his writings and translations, was a friend of St. AUGUSTINE, to whom he sent, apparently from Rome, two anti-Pelagian tracts (now lost) in 418. He seems to have visited Constantinople and joined a Latin community of monks in Thrace. During the Nestorian troubles in 431 he composed another work against PELAGIUS and supplied his monks with several tracts and translations in reference to both Pelagianism and NESTORIANISM. His theological knowledge reflects that of St. CYRIL OF ALEXANDRIA and St. Augustine, and his contribution consisted in making Augustine's position known in the East while supplying the West with translations of Nestorius's sermons. His known writings are preserved in the so-called *Collectio Palatina* (ed. E. Schwartz, ActConOec 1.5:5–70), published by a Scythian monk after 533. They include the *Commonitorium super nomine Caelestii* (Greek version 429, Latin 431); *Commonitorium contra Pelagium, Caelestium et Julianum;* the translations of four anti-Pelagian sermons of Nestorius together with the latter's *Letter to Caelestius;* the *Refutatio symboli Theodori Mopsuestii;* the *Comparatio dogmatum Pauli Samosateni et Nestorii;* and translations of five sermons of Nestorius on the THEOTOKOS and of excerpts made by St. Cyril from the writings of Nestorius.

Bibliography: K. BAUS, *Lexikon für Theologie und Kirche* 2 7:89. W. ELTESTER, *Paulys Realenzyklopädie der Klassischen Altertumswissenschaft 14.2* (1930) 1831–35. É. AMANN, *Dictionnaire de théologie catholique* 9.2:2481–85. Altaner 534–535. A. LEPKA, ''L'Originalité des répliques de Marius Mercator à Julien d'Éclane,'' *Revue d'histoire ecclésiastique* 27 (1931) 572–579. S. PRETE, *Mario Mercatore* (Turin 1958).

[F. X. MURPHY]

MARIUS OF AVENCHES, ST.

Chronicler and bishop of Avenches from 574; b. Autun, 530–31; d. there, Dec. 31, 594. As bishop he transferred the episcopal see from Avenches to Lausanne, Switzerland. Marius's *Chronicle* of the years 455–581, a continuation of the work of PROSPER OF AQUITAINE, reported important contemporary events in Italy and the Orient and is especially valuable for its account of Burgundian affairs after 533–534, which it uniquely transmits. Books 2–4 of GREGORY OF TOURS's *Historia Francorum* show striking textual similarities with Marius's *Chronicle,* indicating their dependence on common sources (Burgundian annals). He was thoroughly Roman in his culture and, despite contemporary barbarian rule, was convinced that the Roman Empire, ''the fourth empire of Daniel,'' would continue till the end of time. He was buried at Lausanne, where the church first consecrated to St. Thyrsius was renamed for him. His cult was approved in 1605.

Feast: Dec. 31; Feb. 9 (Basel); Feb. 12 (Lausanne).

Bibliography: M. BOUQUET, *Recueil des historiens des Gaules et de la France (Rerum gallicarum et francicarum scriptores),* 24 v. (Paris 1738–1904) 2:12–19. *Patrologia Latina,* ed. J. P. MIGNE, 271 v., indexes 4 v. (Paris 1878–90) 82:21–25. *Monumenta Germaniae Historica: Auctores antiquissimi* (Berlin 1826–) 11:227–239. G. J. J. MONOD, *Études critiques sur les sources de l'histoire mérovingienne,* 2 v. (Paris 1872–85) 1:147–163. J. FAVROD, tr. *La Chronique de Marius d'Avenches* (Lausanne 1991). L. DUCHESNE, *Fastes épiscopaux de l'ancienne Gaule,* 3 v. (2d ed. Paris 1970–15). H. LECLERCQ, *Dictionnaire d'archéologie chrétienne et de liturgie,* ed. F. CABROL, H. LECLERCQ, and H. I. MARROU, 15 v. (Paris 1907–53) 10:2167–77. É. BROUETTE, *Lexikon für Theologie und Kirche,* ed. J. HOFER and K. RAHNER, 10 v. (2d, new ed. Freiburg 1957–65) (1966) 7:88.

[B. D. HILL]

MARIUS VICTORINUS

Roman rhetorician, whose conversion to Christianity influenced St. Augustine; b. Caius Marius Victorinus (the surname ''Afer'' seems to be a Renaissance addition) *c.* the end of the third century; d. after 363. He had published many works on grammar and rhetoric, as well as translations of Aristotle's tracts on logic and Neoplatonic books before his conversion (*c.* 354).

In his *Confessions* (bk. 8), Augustine gives a moving account of the intellectual evolution and conversion of

Victorinus, based on information he received from the priest Simplician. Between 357 and 363, in his old age, Victorinus composed several theological essays in refutation of ARIANISM. He opposed successively the Anomoean doctrine of Ursacius and Valens expressed in the symbol of Sirmium (357); the Homoiousian doctrine of Basil of Ancyra, expressed in a memoir published during the summer of 358 at Sirmium; and finally the Homoean doctrine of the Credo of Sirmium (May 22, 359) and Rimini (July–November 359).

Together with the traditional theological arguments against Arianism, Victorinus employed Neoplatonic notions probably taken from Porphyry to present a systematic explanation of the Trinity. The Father is identified with the first Neoplatonic hypostasis wherein, according to Porphyry, the One and Being is the first term of the triad Being-Life-Thought. The Son is identified with the second hypostasis, which, according to the Porphyrian schema, is constituted by the dyad Life-Thought. In this dyad, Life is identified with Christ, and Thought with the Holy Spirit. The Holy Spirit leads toward the Father, through a process of conversion, those souls to whom Christ has given life in a movement of emanation and procession.

The Holy Spirit is ''of the Father'' in the Son, although Victorinus does not have a real theory concerning His procession. The consubstantiality of the Father, Son, and Holy Spirit is assured in two ways; originally the Son and the Holy Spirit were identified with the Father in the same fashion as Life and Thought preexist in the state of potency in the core of Being. At the same time the three divine hypostases, Being, Life, and Thought, are mutually identified—the three are in the three, and are distinguished only by a predominance of particular aspects in the total Being.

This attempt at a systematic explanation of the Trinity had no influence on the history of theology. St. Augustine either was unaware of its existence or ignored it. However, there are traces of it in ALCUIN. In fact, Victorinus's synthesis oscillates between SUBORDINATIONISM (the Son is a second hypostasis inferior to the Father) and MODALISM (the Father, Son, and Holy Spirit are distinguished only by predominance).

Victorinus composed the first Latin commentaries on the Epistles of St. Paul: Galatians, Philippians, and Ephesians. In referring to Victorinus as ''an Augustine before Augustine,'' Harnack had in mind particularly his doctrine on predestination, which has received considerable attention in recent studies.

Bibliography: MARIUS VICTORINUS, *Traités théologiques sur la Trinité,* ed. P. HENRY, tr. P. HADOT, 2 v. (*Sources Chrétiennes* 68, 69; 1960). P. SÉJOURNÉ, *Dictionnaire de théologie catholique* 15.2:2887–2954. P. MONCEAUX, *Histoire littéraire de l'Afrique chrétienne,* 7 v. (Paris 1901–23) 3: 377–422. E. BENZ, *Marius Victorinus* (Stuttgart 1932). A. SOUTER, *The Earliest Latin Commentaries on the Epistles of St. Paul* (Oxford 1927). R. SCHMID, *Marius Victorinus Rhetor und seine Beziehungen zu Augustin* (Kiel 1895). P. HADOT, ''Marius Victorinus et Alcuin,'' *Archives d'histoire doctrinale et littéraire du moyen-âge* 29 (1954) 5–19; ''Les Hymnes de Victorinus.'' *ibid.,* 35 (1960) 7–16; ''L'Image de la Trinité dans l'éme,'' *Studia Patristica* 6 (*Texte und Untersuchungen zur Geschichte der altchristlichen Literatur* 81; 1962) 409–442. G. HUBER, *Das Sein und das Absolute* (Basel 1955).

[P. HADOT]

MARK, EVANGELIST, ST.

There is no reason to doubt that the Mark or John Mark mentioned in the NT is the same person to whom the tradition, following PAPIAS OF HIERAPOLIS, ascribed the authorship of the second Gospel (*see* MARK, GOSPEL ACCORDING TO). For knowledge of Mark, except for the statement of Papias, one is completely dependent on the NT. Mark was a member of the first Christian community in Jerusalem. His mother, Mary, owned a house in Jerusalem, which the Christians used as a place of prayer during Peter's imprisonment under Herod AGRIPPA I (Acts 12.12). When Paul and Barnabas returned from their visit to Jerusalem (11.30), they took Mark back with them to Antioch in Syria (12.25). Later they brought him along as their ὑπηρέτης (servant or assistant) on their first missionary journey from Antioch (13.5). However, after he had accompanied the Apostles through Cyprus, Mark chose to leave them rather than continue on to the mainland of Asia Minor (13.13). Luke offers no explanation for Mark's departure, but the fact that he returned to Jerusalem, not Antioch, suggests homesickness. He is mentioned later in Acts as again in Antioch and the subject of dispute between Paul and Barnabas as they made their preparations for a return journey to the churches they founded in Asia Minor; Barnabas, Mark's cousin (Col 4.10), was sympathetic to him, but Paul would not hear of his again accompanying them (Acts 15.36–38). The disagreement ended in the separation of Paul and Barnabas. Mark accompanied Barnabas by ship to Cyprus, while Paul took an overland route with another companion (15.39–40). Eventually, Mark redeemed himself in the eyes of Paul, and the Apostle became dependent upon him during one of his imprisonments (Col 4.10; Phlm 24). Writing to Timothy during his final Roman imprisonment, Paul asked for Mark's assistance (2 Tm 4.11). The reference in 1 Pt 5.13 to Mark as ''my son'' indicates that he was an associate also of St. Peter.

In Christian iconography medieval artistic representations of Mark as an EVANGELIST depict him with his Gospel and frequently, though not always, as having a

Scene from the legend of St. Mark, detail of the 13th-century mosaics in the vaults of S. Marco, Venice.

winged lion as a distinguishing feature. The image of the lion seems to be derived from Mark's description of John the Baptist as ''a voice crying in the desert'' (Mk 1.3), which artistic tradition came to compare to a roaring lion. The wings come from the application of Ezekiel's vision of the four winged ''living creatures'' to the four Evangelists. Following the datum of 1 Pt 5.13, artists sometimes associate Mark with St. Peter. Other representations of Mark follow the legends of his association with Alexandria. According to these legends he was bishop of Alexandria, cured a shoemaker there, and suffered martyrdom in the streets of the city.

Feast: April 25.

See Also: PAUL, APOSTLE, ST.

Bibliography: H. B. SWETE, ed., *The Gospel according to St. Mark* (London 1920) xiii–xxviii. V. TAYLOR, ed., *The Gospel according to St. Mark* (London 1952) 27–31. C. E. B. CRANFIELD, ed., *The Gospel according to Saint Mark* (Cambridge, Eng. 1959) 5–6. J. SCHMID, ed. and tr., *Das Evangelium nach Markus* (3d ed. Regensburg 1954) 6–7. J. BLINZLER, *Lexikon für Theologie und Kirche*, ed. J. HOFER and K. RAHNER (Freiburg 1957–65) 7:12–13.

[C. P. CEROKE]

MARK, GOSPEL ACCORDING TO

Background

Questions concerning the authorship, date, place of composition, audience, and purpose of Mark's Gospel continue to receive a variety of answers from contemporary scholars. The shortest of the three Synoptic Gospels (661 verses as compared to 1,068 in Mt and 1,149 in Lk), the Gospel of Mark was probably the first of the three to be written, and Matthew and Luke made use of it as a major source in composing their own Gospels.

Authorship. Although the Gospel is attributed to ''Mark,'' the author of the Gospel never explicitly identifies himself. The superscriptions or titles of the Four Gospels (''According to Matthew,'' ''According to Mark,'') come from the late 1st, or early 2d, century when it became necessary to distinguish one Gospel from another. Eusebius (263–339), however, preserves an important quotation from Papias, a 2d century bishop of Hieropolis in Asia Minor, that identifies Mark as the author of the Gospel and associates him with Peter. In this text, Papias relates a quotation from someone called the PRESBYTER.

> This, too, the presbyter used to say. ''Mark, who had been Peter's interpreter, wrote down careful-

Manuscript illumination of Saint Mark inspired from the ''Gospel Book of Ebbo'' (©Gianni Dagli Orti/CORBIS)

> ly, but not in order, all that he remembered of the Lord's sayings and doings. For he had not heard the Lord or been one of His followers, but later, as I said, one of Peter's. Peter used to adapt his teaching to the occasion, without making a systematic arrangement of the Lord's sayings, so that Mark was quite justified in writing down some things just as he remembered them. For he had one purpose only—to leave out nothing that he had heard, and to make no misstatement about it.'' *Ecclesiastical History* (3, 39, 15)

This text is difficult to interpret since it is not clear if the entire quotation is from the Presbyter. Part of this quotation may represent Papias's commentary on the Presbyter's words. If this is so, where does the quotation from the Presbyter end and the commentary of Papias begin? Moreover, the statement that Mark was Peter's interpreter (*hermeneutes Petrou*) can have a number of meanings ranging from translator to some kind of authorship. Nonetheless, this text stands at the origin of a constant tradition that relates the author of this Gospel to Peter and thus anchors the Gospel in the witness of an apostolic figure. For example, Justin Martyr speaks of Peter's memories (*en tois apomnemoneumasin autou; Dialogue with Trypho,* 106, 3), probably referring to Mark's Gospel. Irenaeus says that Mark, ''the disciple and interpreter of Peter'' (*ho mathetes kai hermeneutes*) wrote after the deaths of Peter and Paul (*Against Heresies,* 3.1.1). An ancient Latin prologue to the Gospel says that Mark was Peter's interpreter (*Iste interpres fuit Petri*) and that he wrote in the regions of Italy after the death of Peter. CLEMENT OF ALEXANDRIA, on the other hand, says that Mark, a companion of Peter, wrote during Peter's lifetime at the urging of the people of Rome where Peter preached (*Ecclesiastical History,* 6, 14, 6–7). Origen maintains that the Gospel of Mark was written by Mark as Peter instructed him (*Ecclesiastical History,* 6, 25, 5), and Jerome says that ''the interpreter of the Apostle Peter'' (*Interpres apostoli Petri*) was the first bishop of Alexandria (*Commentary on Matthew, Prooemium,* 6). Who, however, was this person called Mark?

The ACTS OF THE APOSTLES speaks of ''John Mark,'' the cousin of Barabbas (12.12,25; 13.5; 15.37–39) and several of the Pauline letters mention someone named ''Mark'' (Col 4.10, Phlm 24; 2 Tm 4.11). In 1 Pt 5.13, ''Peter'' speaks of Mark as his son (though some scholars question the Petrine authorship of this letter). Although there is no conclusive evidence that the person mentioned in these writings was the author of the second Gospel, early tradition identified this ''Mark'' or ''John Mark'' as the evangelist who composed the Gospel.

Place and Date. In light of the tradition noted above, most scholars argue that the Gospel was written in Rome. Others, however, maintain that it originated in Galilee, Syria, or Asia Minor. Although the exact date of the Gospel is disputed, there is general agreement that it belongs to the period of the Jewish revolt against Rome, A.D. 66–70. The point of contention is whether the Gospel was composed before or after A.D. 70, when the Romans entered Jerusalem and destroyed its temple. The answer to this problem, which cannot be resolved with certainty, depends upon the interpretation of Jesus' final discourse (Mark 13), in which He prophesies the temple's destruction (13.2, 14). While some believe that this chapter indicates that the temple was already destroyed at the time that the Gospel was composed, others do not. Thus it may more prudent to give the Gospel an approximate date of A.D. 70, acknowledging that it may have been written shortly before, or after, the Romans destroyed Jerusalem and its temple.

Audience. Most scholars believe that Mark wrote for a Gentile audience since the evangelist explains Jewish customs (7.3–4), and makes an important side comment that Jesus declared all foods clean (7.19). This comment, which comes from the evangelist and is omitted by Matthew, suggests that the audience of this Gospel did not observe the Jewish dietary prescriptions. Moreover, the fact that a Gentile, a Roman centurion, makes the most important confession of the Gospel (that Jesus was truly the Son of God; 15.39) may also suggest a Gentile audience.

Purpose. The purpose of the Gospel is to announce, in narrative form, the gospel of Jesus Christ: what God accomplished in the ministry, death, and resurrection of Jesus Christ (1.1). If the Gospel was written in Rome for a Gentile community, shortly before, or shortly after, the destruction of Jerusalem and its temple, it undoubtedly responded to the needs of the Christian community at Rome, which had already suffered persecution under Nero (64) and was bracing for yet another period of persecution because of the Jewish revolt against Rome. Thus, Mark may be writing to strengthen a fledgling community of Gentile Christians by reminding them that Jesus was a crucified Messiah who suffered persecution. Therefore, those who follow Him in the way of discipleship can expect no less.

Composition. The tradition that originates with Papias suggests that the evangelist received some of his material from Peter. The actual composition of the Gospel, however, was probably more complicated, and Mark undoubtedly had access to other sources of information, for example, traditions about Jesus' controversies with the religious leader (2.1–3.6; 11.27–12.37), parables (4.1–34); miracles (4.35–5.43); teachings on discipleship (9.33–10.31); sayings about the temple's destruction and Jesus' return at the end of the ages (13.1–37); and an early version of the Passion Narrative (14.1–15.47). Mark edited and arranged this material and his Petrine traditions into a coherent narrative of Jesus' ministry that culminated in His death and Resurrection. In doing so, Mark was the first to compose a gospel that, in the view of many scholars, represents a literary genre without an exact parallel in the ancient world.

The Ending of the Gospel. There are four endings to the Gospel of Mark. (1) In the oldest and best manuscripts (*Vaticanus* and *Sinaiticus*), the Gospel ends at 16.8, the story of the women at the empty tomb. (2) Some manuscripts expand this ending to include a brief report of the Risen Jesus sending His disciples to proclaim the gospel to the whole world. This is called the ''shorter ending.'' (3) Mark 16.9–20 represents the so-called longer ending of the Gospel. Found in the majority of manuscripts and accepted as inspired Scripture by the Council of Trent, it is absent from the two oldest Greek codices (*Vaticanus* and *Sinaiticus*). Moreover, Clement of Alexandria and Origen were not aware of this ending, and Eusebius and Jerome say that the passage was absent from almost all Greek copies of Mark known to them. (4) The Washington manuscript contains this longer ending with an expansion after v. 14, the so-called Freer logion, named after the gallery where the manuscript is kept in Washington, D.C. Overall, the best manuscript tradition concludes at 16.8 with the account of the empty tomb. While some have argued that the original ending of the Gospel was lost, others maintain that the evangelist purposely concluded his work at this point to emphasize the need for the disciples to return to Galilee, the starting point of Jesus' ministry, and make their own ''way'' to Jerusalem as He did.

Narrative

Structure. The Gospel of Mark is difficult to outline, and scholars structure it in various ways. Most would agree, however, that after a brief introduction (1.1–13), the Gospel falls into three parts. In the first (1.13–8.26), Mark describes the beginning of Jesus' ministry in Galilee. This ministry is characterized by Jesus' proclamation that the time of waiting is fulfilled, and the kingdom of God is at hand. Consequently, people must repent and believe in God's own good news that the kingdom is making its appearance in Jesus' ministry (1.14–15). After this initial announcement, Jesus calls His first disciples (1.16–20) and proclaims the kingdom by mighty deeds of casting out demons and healing the sick (1.21–45). Although the religious leaders oppose him (2.1–3.6), people throughout Galilee and beyond receive Jesus favorably (3.7–12).

Eventually Jesus summons ''the Twelve'' to be with Him (3.13–19) and sends them on mission to cast out demons, heal the sick, and preach repentance (6.7–13). Before sending them on mission, however, Jesus reveals the mystery of the kingdom of God to them (4.1–34) and manifests His power over nature, demons, sickness, and death (4.35–5.43).

After the disciples return from their missions, the question of Jesus' identity takes center stage. While some think that Jesus is ELIJAH or one of the prophets, Herod mistakenly believes that Jesus is JOHN THE BAPTIST returned to life. By feeding the crowds in the wilderness on two occasions (6.30–44; 8.1–10), Jesus shows that He is Israel's Shepherd and MESSIAH, and Peter eventually confesses that Jesus is the Messiah (8.27–30).

In the second part of the Gospel (8.27–10.52), Jesus explains that as the Messiah He must suffer, die, and rise from the dead. Thus, His fate is the fate of the Son of Man. The disciples, however, fail to comprehend this dimension of discipleship and its implication for following Jesus. Thus, after each of Jesus' passion predictions, there is a misunderstanding on their part about the meaning of discipleship, and Jesus must instruct them anew. The entire section is built on a pattern of prediction, misunderstanding, and teaching that is repeated three times: Cycle one (8.31; 8.32–33; 8.34–9.1); Cycle two (9.30–31; 9.32–34; 9.35–10.31); Cycle three (10.32–34; 10.35–41; 10.42–45).

The third part of the Gospel (11.1–16.8) describes Jesus' ministry in Jerusalem, which becomes the proximate occasion for His Passion and death. Jesus enters Jerusalem (11.1–11) and cleanses the temple (11.15–19), which leads the religious leaders to challenge His authority (11.27–33). After a series of controversies with the religious leaders (12.13–37), Jesus pronounces a final discourse in which He prophesies the destruction of the temple and His return at the close of the ages as the glorious SON OF MAN (13.1–37). Jesus' Jerusalem ministry, then, becomes the proximate occasion for the religious authorities to arrest and hand Him over to Pilate, who condemns Him to death as a messianic pretender, ''the King of the Jews.'' At Jesus' death, the curtain of the temple is torn from top to bottom (15.38), and a Roman centurion confesses that Jesus was truly the Son of God (15.39). The tearing of the temple's curtain indicates that the death of Jesus, the Messiah, is the perfect sacrifice that makes all other sacrifices irrelevant. The new temple will consist of those who believe in Jesus. The confession that Jesus was truly the Son of God indicates that Jesus' sonship cannot be understood apart from His shameful death upon the cross. The Gospel concludes with the angel instructing the women to tell the disciples that Jesus has gone ahead of them to Galilee (16.7). There the Risen Lord will gather His scattered flock as He promised (14.28).

The Plot. Read as a narrative, the Gospel is driven by a plot of conflict that operates on three levels. On the first, there is a conflict between the kingdom of God that Jesus' ministry inaugurates and the rule of Satan, which oppose God's kingship. By casting out demons, Jesus shows that God's rule is displacing that of Satan. On the second level, there is a conflict between Jesus and the religious leaders over the question of authority: who has the authority to speak in God's name: the religious leaders or Jesus? On the third level, there is a conflict between Jesus and His own disciples over the meaning of messiahship and discipleship. While Jesus speaks of a suffering Messiah and calls His disciples to selfless service, the disciples think in terms of a glorious Messiah and seek seats of honor at Jesus' right and left (10.35–40).

The question of Jesus' identity lies at the heart of the conflict between Jesus and the religious leaders, and Jesus and His disciples. Who is He? Throughout the Gospel the identity of Jesus (that He is the Messiah, the Son of God) is hidden from the characters of the story. Thus, even when Peter correctly confesses that Jesus is the Messiah, he does not know that Jesus is the Messiah who must suffer, die, and rise. It is only after Jesus has died that the centurion, a Gentile, correctly confesses that this Man was truly the Son of God (15.39).

This mystery of Jesus' identity is the Gospel's ''messianic secret.'' This expression, first introduced by W. Wrede (*The Messianic Secret,* 1901), properly refers to a literary motif whereby Jesus' identity is hidden from the characters of the narrative. Only after He dies and is raised from the dead is His identity fully disclosed. Thus the death of Jesus as the crucified Messiah plays a crucial role in this Gospel that proclaims a theology of the cross.

Theological Themes

Among the most important theological themes of the Markan Gospel are Jesus' proclamation of the kingdom of God; the mystery of Jesus' identity, which is expressed through three titles (Messiah, Son of God, Son of Man); and Jesus' teaching on the nature of discipleship.

The Kingdom of God. The central theme of the Gospel and of Jesus' teaching is the appearance of the kingdom of God, by which Jesus means God's rule over history and creation. Although the precise term does not occur with any frequency in the Old Testament, the concept of God as king over history and creation does, especially in the Psalms of Enthronement (Psalms 47, 93, 95–99) and 2 Isaiah, see Is 52.7. Within the Gospel, Jesus proclaims that the kingdom of God has made its appearance in His ministry. Thus, He summons people to repent and believe in this good news. In addition to preaching that the kingdom has arrived, Jesus effects the presence of the kingdom by His mighty deeds. These deeds of casting out demons, healing the sick, and raising the dead point to the in-breaking of God's kingdom and the destruction of Satan's rule. Although the kingdom has made its appearance in Jesus' ministry, Jesus is aware that it has not yet come in power. Therefore, in a series of parables (4.1–34), He explains the mystery of the kingdom to His disciples: namely, at the present time the kingdom is a hidden from those who do not believe, but when it is finally revealed (at Jesus' parousia as the Son of Man), its presence and power will be known to all, whether they believe or not. Although Jesus' Jerusalem ministry was the proximate occasion for His Passion and death, His claim to be the authoritative spokesman for the in-breaking kingdom of God was the ultimate reason for His death, inasmuch as this proclamation informs the whole of His ministry.

Messiah, Son of God, Son of Man. The Gospel of Mark begins by identifying Jesus as the Christ (Messiah), the Son of God. At Caesarea Philippi, Peter correctly confesses that Jesus is the Messiah (8.29), and at Jesus' trial the high priest asks Jesus if He is the Messiah, the Son of the Blessed One (14.61). Jesus' own understanding of His messiahship, however, was dramatically different from that of the high priest and Peter. Whereas the high priest thought in terms of a Davidic Messiah who would deliver Israel from its enemies and establish justice in Jerusalem (Psalms of Solomon 17, 18), and whereas Peter could not countenance that Jesus must suffer and die as the Messiah (8.32), Jesus referred to Himself as the Son of Man who must suffer and die before entering into His glory.

From the point of view of the evangelist, Jesus the Messiah is the Son of God because He enjoys a unique relationship to God shared by no one else. Although the title does not occur frequently, it does appear at strategic moments in the Gospel: the opening verse (1.1); Jesus' baptism (1.11); the transfiguration (9.7); and the centurion's confession (15.39). At Jesus' baptism, in a private theophany, God addresses Jesus as His beloved Son, in whom He is well pleased. At the transfiguration, God reveals to Peter, James, and John that Jesus is His beloved Son, and He instructs them to listen to Him. Finally, after Jesus' death, a Roman centurion becomes the first person within the Gospel narrative to confess that Jesus was the Son of God.

The key to understanding how the Gospel comprehends Jesus' identity as the Messiah, the Son of God, is found in a number of sayings in which Jesus refers to Himself as the Son of Man. This strange expression probably goes back to a similar expression in Daniel 7 that speaks metaphorically of ''one like a son of man'' who received power and kingship from God after a period of intense persecution (Dn 7.9–14). By referring to himself as the Son of Man, Jesus points to His destiny as the Messiah, the Son of God. As the one like a son of man in the Book of Daniel, Jesus will be vindicated by God despite His sufferings. Thus, the fate of the Messiah, the Son of God, is to be rejected, suffer, die, and rise (8.31; 9.9; 13.31; 10.33; 14.21,41) and return as God's eschatological agent at the end of the ages (8.38; 13.26; 14.62). While ''Son of God'' and ''Messiah'' are confessional titles that point to Jesus' *identity* (Jesus is the Messiah, the Son of God), ''Son of Man'' points to Jesus' *destiny* as the Messiah, the Son of God, who must suffer, die, and rise. This is what neither Peter nor the high priest understand.

The Path of Discipleship. Discipleship is a central theme of the Markan Gospel. After His initial proclamation of the Gospel, Jesus calls His first disciples (1.16–20). Gathering still other disciples, He chooses 12 to represent the 12 tribes of Israel. While the disciples show themselves to be generous in their response to Jesus (10.28), they misunderstand Him on a number of occasions (6.52; 8.14–21; 9.32). Moreover, they often manifest a desire for prominence and positions of authority (9.33–34; 10.35–41). Consequently, Jesus must teach them that greatness in the kingdom of God consists in service to the least important (9.35–37; 10.42–44). Jesus, the Son of Man, came not ''to be served but to serve and to give His life as a ransom for many'' (10.45). Here Christology and discipleship intersect, since true discipleship is patterned after the life of Jesus. Thus, authentic disciples know that Jesus, the Son of God, is the Messiah who must suffer, die, and rise.

In brief, the Gospel of Mark develops a theology of the cross that proclaims that no one can know Jesus and live as His disciple apart from embracing a path of service that leads to rejection, suffering, death, and resurrection. Such disciples will enter the KINGDOM OF GOD.

Bibliography: Commentaries. H. ANDERSON, *The Gospel of Mark* (Grand Rapids, Mich. 1981). J. GNILKA, *Das Evangelium nach Markus,* 2 v. (Zürich 1978, 1979). R. A. GUELICH, *Mark 1–8.26* (Dallas 1989). M. D. HOOKER, *The Gospel According to Mark* (Peabody, Mass. 1991). J. MARCUS, *Mark 1–8* (New York 1999). R. PESCH, *Das Markusevangelium,* 2 v. (Freiburg 1984). V. TAYLOR, *The Gospel According to Mark* (2d ed. New York 1966). L. WILLIAMSON, *Mark* (Atlanta 1983). Studies. P. J. ACHTEMEIER, *Mark* (Philadelphia 1986). E. BEST, *Mark the Gospel as Story* (Edinburgh 1983). M.-E. BOISMARD, *Jésus un homme de Nazareth: raconté par Marc L'évangeliste* (Paris 1996). A. Y. COLLINS, *The Beginnings of the Gospel: Probings of Mark in Context* (Minneapolis 1992). M. HENGEL, *Studies in the Gospel of Mark* (Philadelphia 1985). M. D. HOOKER, *The Message of Mark* (London 1983). D. JUEL, *Messiah and Temple: The Trial of Jesus in the Gospel of Mark* (Missoula, Mont. 1977). H. C. KEE, *Community of the New Age: Studies in Mark's Gospel* (Philadelphia 1977). J. D. KINGSBURY, *The Christology of Mark's Gospel* (Philadelphia 1983); *Conflict in Mark: Jesus, Authorities, Disciples* (Minneapolis 1989). J. MARCUS, *The Way of the Lord: Christological Exegesis of the Old Testament in the Gospel of Mark* (Louisville 1992). C. D. MARSHALL, *Faith as a Theme in Mark's Narrative* (Cambridge, Eng. 1989). R. MARTIN, *Mark—Evangelist and Theologian* (Grand Rapids, Mich. 1973). B. D. SCHILDGEN, *Power and Prejudice: The Reception of the Gospel of Mark* (Detroit 1999). W. R. TELFORD, *The Theology of the Gospel of Mark* (Cambridge, Eng. 1999). M. A. TOLBERT, *Sowing the Gospel: Mark's World in Literary-Historical Perspective* (Minneapolis 1989).

[F. J. MATERA]

MARK, POPE, ST.

Pontificate: Jan. 18 to Oct. 7, 336. Virtually nothing is known about Mark who is described by the *Liber pontificalis* as ''a Roman by birth, son of Priscus.'' According to the Liberian catalogue, he was consecrated on Jan. 18, 336. He died after a reign of less than ten months, and was buried, according to the *Depositio Episcoporum,* in the cemetery of Balbina on the Via Ardeatina (Oct. 7,

Pope St. Mark, effigy from 9th-century series of papal portraits, formerly at basilica of St. Paul, Rome.

336) in a basilica that he had probably built; its ruins survived until the seventeenth century. He may be the Mark mentioned in a letter of the Emperor CONSTANTINE to Pope MILTIADES in 313; if so, he was a longtime member of the Roman clergy before his election.

Mark founded the *Titulus Marci* (S. Marco), incorporated in the Palazzo Venezia during the Renaissance; S. Marco was at first named after him, and later placed under the patronage of the Evangelist. The *Liber pontificalis* states that this pope decreed that the bishop of Rome was to be consecrated by the bishop of OSTIA who was privileged to wear the PALLIUM. St. Augustine testifies (*c.* 400): ''The Roman pontiff is wont to be ordained by three bishops of whom the first is the bishop of Ostia'' (*Coll. c. Don.* 3.16); but ecclesiastical use of the pallium is attested only for the middle of the fifth century, as illustrated on the celebrated Ivory of Trier.

Feast: Oct. 7.

Bibliography: *Liber pontificalis*, ed. L. DUCHESNE (Paris 1886–92, 1958) 1:202–204; 3:81. H. LECLERCQ, *Dictionnaire d'archéologie chrétienne et de liturgie*, ed. F. CABROL, H. LECLERCQ and H. I. MARROU (Paris 1907–53) 13.1:1198–99. A. FERRUA, ''La basilica del papa Marco,'' *La civiltà cattolica* 99.3 (1948) 503–513, excavations. DAMASUS I, *Epigrammata Damasiana*, ed. A. FERRUA (Rome 1942). R. U. MONTINI, *Le tombe dei Papi* (Rome 1957). J. N. D. KELLY, *Oxford Dictonary of Popes* (New York 1986) 28–29. C. PIETRI, *Roma Christiana* (Rome 1976) 154–160.

[J. CHAPIN]

MARK OF ARETHUSA, ST.

Bishop; b. 250–270; d. Arethusa?, Lebanon, after 362. He is known only as a bishop active in the dispute over ARIANISM. Like many others, he shrank from the new term of CONSUBSTANTIALITY and so joined the Semi–Arians. He attended their synods and drafted the creed of SIRMIUM (351), approved at Rimini in 359. Under JULIAN THE APOSTATE he destroyed a beautiful pagan temple and was cruelly tortured by his fellow townsmen (362). His eulogy by St. GREGORY OF NAZIANZUS indicates that he died in orthodoxy. CLEMENT VIII approved his cult in 1598. He is mentioned in the Church histories of SOZOMEN (5.10) and THEODORET (3.3).

Feast: Mar. 29; Mar. 28 (Eastern Church).

Bibliography: *Patrologia Graeca* 35:616–634; 42:443, 451. *Acta Sanctorum* Mar. 3:771–775. C. BARONIUS, *Annales ecclesiastici* 5:83–84.

[J. VAN PAASSEN]

MARK OF THE NATIVITY

Carmelite of the Touraine Reform, whose secular name was Mark Genest and whose religious name in more complete form was Mark of the Nativity of the Blessed Virgin; b. Cuno near Saumur (southeast of Angers), Jan. 9, 1617; d. Feb. 23, 1696. After being educated by the Benedictines, then by the Jesuits at La Flèche, Mark entered the Carmelites in 1631 at Rennes, where earlier in the same century the TOURAINE REFORM had been inaugurated. He was influenced by the Carmelite Bernard of Saint-Magdalen and by the lay brother mystic JOHN OF SAINT-SAMSON of the same order. Taking prominent part in the reform, Mark completed and edited directories for novices (1650–51), which became the official manuals of the reform and influenced the *Directorium Carmelitanum vitae spiritualis* (Vatican 1940; Eng. tr. *The Carmelite Directory of the Spiritual Life,* Chicago 1951). Mark edited directories for external conduct (1677–79), wrote a manual for the Carmelite Third Order, served as confessor to the archbishop of Tours (Victor le Bouteiller), and at various times was novice master, prior, definitor, visitator, and provincial. He was also involved in a bitter dispute with the Jansenist Antoine Arnauld (d. 1694).

Bibliography: C. DE VILLIERS, *Bibliotheca carmelitana,* ed. G. WESSELS, 2 v. in 1 (Rome 1927) 2:312–330. *Méthode claire et facile pour bien faire l'oraison mentale et pour s'exercer avec fruit en la présence de Dieu,* rev. INNOCENT DE MARIE IMMACULÉE (Bruges 1962). K. HEALY, *Methods of Prayer in the Carmelite Reform of Touraine* (Rome 1956) 27–28, 30–38.

[K. J. EGAN]

MARK THE HERMIT

Ascetic, polemicist, and theological author; d. after 430. Nicephorus Callistus (*Hist. eccl.* 14) says Mark was a disciple of JOHN CHRYSOSTOM (d. 407) and a contemporary of NILUS OF ANCYRA (d. *c.* 430). He was abbot of a monastery in Ancyra, but later became an anchorite, probably in the Judean desert. Although Nicephorus speaks of 40 treatises, only nine were known to Photius (*Bibl. cod.* 200). A 10th treatise, the important *Contra Nestorianos,* was published by J. Cozza-Luzi. In this work Mark used Scripture and the baptismal CREED to refute the NESTORIANS. Mark's works show an ascetic preoccupation, but their importance was attributed to their polemic and dogmatic character. He combatted the Nestorians and Messalians. He energetically repudiated the identification of grace with mystical experience. He saw the role and efficacy of Baptism in the Christian life in relation to Adam's sin and its consequences; but he rejected any explanation or excuse for sins committed after Baptism because of the corruption of human nature, the devil's influence, or Adam's sin. For him Baptism both destroyed original sin in man and infused into the soul a power of the Holy Spirit by which, with the free cooperation of man's will, he can resist evil tendencies and live as God would have him live. Photius (*loc. cit.*) suspected Mark of Monophysitism; but his doctrine, particularly in the treatise *De Melchisedech,* is correctly based on the unity of person in the two natures of Christ.

Bibliography: *Patrologia Graeca* 65:893–1140. É. AMANN, *Dictionnaire de théologie catholique* 9.2:1964–68. M. JUGIE, *Dictionnaire de théologie catholique* 12.1:358–361. K. JÜSSEN, *Lexikon für Theologie und Kirche* 7:11. J. QUASTEN, *Patrology* 3:504–509. M. F. ARGLES, *Dictionary of Christian Biography* 3:826–827.

[P. W. HARKINS]

MARKS, MIRIAM

Executive Secretary of the National Office of the Confraternity of Christian Doctrine (CCD) in Washington, DC, 1935–1960; b. Tacoma, Washington, April 26, 1890; d. Apalachicola, July 18, 1961. The daughter of Charles and Anna Ryan Marks, she grew up in Apalachicola, Florida, and attended Florida College for Women. After a year of study at Columbia University in 1919, she supervised art for the public schools of Garland County, Arkansas (1920–23). Upon graduating from the National Catholic School of Social Service in Washington, DC in 1926, Marks began social work in Newark and Paterson, New Jersey. It was while working as an editor for St. Anthony's Guild in Paterson that she made the acquaintance of Father Edwin O'HARA, then working with the Rural Life Bureau of the National Catholic Rural Life Conference. When O'Hara became bishop of Great Falls, Montana, he asked Marks to organize the Confraternity of Christian Doctrine (CCD) in his diocese, and between 1931 and 1933 Marks developed CCD programs for three other dioceses. When the U.S. bishops established the National Office of the CCD in Washington, O'Hara, in his capacity of episcopal chairman, named Marks executive secretary, a position she held for 25 years. In that capacity Marks organized the Confraternity in 72 dioceses in the United States and Canada. She contributed essays to magazines, directed the CCD Office of Publications, and organized and spoke at various national conventions of the CCD. She taught at St. Mary's College, Notre Dame, Indiana in the summers of 1938, 1939, and 1943, and at the Catholic University of America in 1949 and 1950. She was awarded the Papal Medal Pro Ecclesia et Pontifice, in October of 1937. Marks retired in 1960 and died at her home in Apalachicola on July 18, 1961. A plaque in Memorial Hall at the Basilica of the National Shrine of the Immaculate Conception in Washington, DC, commemorates her work with the CCD.

Bibliography: CCD Files in the Archives of the Catholic University of America, Washington, DC; *The Confraternity Comes of Age: A Historical Symposium* (Paterson, NJ 1956).

[C. D. CLEMENT]

MARKS OF THE CHURCH

The problem of the scientific demonstration of the Catholic Church—or, concretely, the verification of the claims of the Catholic communion to be in total conformity with the intentions of Christ, founder of the Church—was raised, in principle, as soon as the schisms that the Apostle had announced appeared among the followers of Our Lord. Arguments and signs were proposed haphazardly according to circumstances. It was only in the 15th and 16th centuries, when Western Christianity was torn asunder, that the treatise *De ecclesia* was truly constituted and with it the three classical *viae* that should lead to Catholicism and that later received the names *via notarum, via historica, via empirica* [see C. Walter, *Tentamen historicum circa notas verae ecclesiae* (Würzburg 1792); G. Thils, *Les Notes de l'église dans l'apologétique catholique depuis la réforme* (Gembloux, Belgium 1937)].

Name, Number, Grouping. These marks were almost indiscriminately called *notae, argumenta, signa, proprietates, conditiones, caracteres, insignia, criteria, praerogativae* (Thils, 2–8). The names, however, became more precise in the course of the 16th and 17th centuries. Thus, when apologetics in two stages was introduced—*De vera religione* for unbelievers and then *De ecclesia* for separated Christians—the term sign was generally reserved for the first treatise, whereas for the *De ecclesia,* the term notes, or marks, was preferred. On the other hand, the term property was reserved, preferably, for essential qualities such as VISIBILITY, infallibility, and INDEFECTIBILITY.

The number of these marks has varied. The apologists of the 16th century proposed 2, 4, 7, 10, 15, and even 100. In this varying number four groups can be discerned: the scriptural group, composed of the marks mentioned in the inspired writings—indefectibility, infallibility, visibility, holiness, unity, and miracles; the Augustinian group, taken from an enumeration by St. Augustine—perfect wisdom, general accord in faith, miracles, pastoral succession, and even the name Catholic (*C. epist. fund.* 4; *Corpus scriptorum ecclesiasticorum latinorum* 25.1:196); the Lerinian group—namely, universality, antiquity, and universal accord—which was inspired by the *quod ubique, quod semper, quod ab omnibus* of Vincent of Lerins (*Commonit.* 2; *Enchiridion patristicum,* 2168); and, last, the creedal group, taken from the ninth article of the Creed of Constantinople—unity, holiness, catholicity, and apostolicity. Since the 17th century the marks have been stabilized in this group to form the four marks of the Church (Thils, 97–120).

Marks as Proof. The argument based on the marks can be summarized as follows. Christ endowed His Church with certain features that should permit it to be recognized among all Christian communions. But these characteristics are to be found in the Roman Catholic Church; therefore, it is the true Church. The major premise of this reasoning has never varied, although the manner—dogmatic or rational—of understanding it has at times caused some confusion. On the contrary, the minor premise has been presented by turns under three forms: (1) positive and absolute, when the polemicist affirms without restrictions that the Catholic Church, and it alone, possesses the characteristics or marks of the true Church; (2) negative and also absolute, when one limits himself to denying them to non-Roman communions; and (3) comparative, when, more circumspectly, the apologists declare that the marks are verified in the Catholic Church in a superior manner, that is, more perfectly than in other Christian communions.

Recognizing the type of argumentation used in the *via notarum* is of great importance to its understanding. One can emphasize the four marks—unity, holiness, catholicity, apostolicity—as an argument from Scripture or the Fathers, thus giving it a dogmatic value. One can also emphasize these same four marks for their intrinsic value, for the probative force they have either from their very nature or as evidencing a moral miracle; in this case, the argumentation belongs to the rational type. The preparation of a dogmatic argument differs considerably from the preparation of a rational argument, even when the matter of the argument is the same.

In the case here the following evolution is evident. In the 16th and 17th centuries, the argumentation of the polemicists belonged to the dogmatic type. In the 18th century, because of the rationalist spirit and of even unbelief in many spheres, the argumentation became rational. Catholic unity, it was said in the 18th century, *natura sua,* in itself, by its intrinsic value, is an argument for the true Church. At the end of the 19th century, after Vatican Council I and the constitution *Dei Filius* (''Quin etiam ecclesia per se ipsa, ob suam . . . magnum quoddam et perpetuum est motivum credibilitatis''—H. Denzinger, *Enchiridion symbolorum,* 3013), it was argued as follows: Catholic unity, as a moral miracle, shows where the true Church is. There are always the four marks, but the argumentation is different; it belongs to the rational type, to the *via empirica,* and no longer to the dogmatic, to the former *via notarum.* The material is the same; the marks, therefore, are not called into question, but the method and type of argumentation has changed.

Marks as Dynamic. In the second half of the 20th century the most important advance in understanding the marks of the Church was to emphasize the marks as those signs of the apostolic witness which, imperfectly realized as they are in any given moment of history, provide the Church with a starting place as it makes its way through time towards full eschatological realization in Christ. Thus, theologians put much stronger emphasis on the need to *become* more catholic (i. e., universal) rather than on the *de facto* universality of the Church measured by some numerical or statistical calculus. In that reading of catholicity, the emphasis is not on the present of universality of the Church but in its as yet unfilled task ''which speaks all tongues, which lovingly understands and accepts all tongues and thus overcomes the divisiveness of Babel'' (*Ad gentes,* n. 4). Likewise, in a similar fashion, the Church strives for that greater unity which Christ demands of the Church, just as it seeks to be ever more faithful to the apostolic witness on which is based while pursuing that holiness which will be fully realized only in the eschaton. Needless to say, the notion of unity pertains not only to the inner life of the Roman Catholic Church but to the wider communion of all Christian churches.

Marks as Realizable. The emphasis on the marks of the Church as realizable rather than as fully realized does not mean that the Church as it now exists is devoid of the characteristics of unity, holiness, catholicity, and apostolicity. The creedal affirmations in the liturgy both announce what the Church is and what it hopes to be. Recent ecclesiologists have focused on the marks in the local church where the Church is historically realized in the concrete. It is only in the lived experience of the worshiping community that the abstract notion of unity or holiness becomes experienced and valued. In that sense the marks of the Church exist in a dialectical fashion touching both the local and universal Church. It must be underscored, then, that the local church must, like the universal Church, be one, holy, catholic, and apostolic.

When in the creed we affirm our belief that the Church is one holy, catholic, and apostolic we are implicitly affirming three things: a belief that we hold about the nature of both the local worshipping community and the Great Church; an aspiration of what we would like the Church to be; and an act of faith that the spirit dwells within the Church and can make such an aspiration a reality.

See Also: UNITY OF FAITH; MIRACLE, MORAL; MIRACLE, MORAL (THE CHURCH); MIRACLES (THEOLOGY OF); CHURCH, ARTICLES ON.

Bibliography: *Dictionnaire de théologie catholique,* ed. A. VACANT et al., 15 v. (Paris 1903–50; Tables générales 1951–), Tables générales 1:113–14. A. KOLPING, *Lexikon für Theologie und Kirche*, ed. J. HOFER and K. RAHNER, 10 v. (Freiburg 1957–65); suppl., *Das Zweite Vatikanische Konzil: Dokumente und Kommentare,* ed. H. S. BRECHTER et al., pt. 1 (1966) 7:1044–48. J. C. FENTON, "The True Church and the Notes of the Church," *American Ecclesiastical Review* 114 (1946) 282–297. T. SPÁČIL, "Ist die Lehre von den Kennzeichen der Kirche zu ändern?" *Zeitschrift für katholische Theologie* 36 (1912) 715–741; "Zur Lehre von den Merkmalen der Kirche," *ibid.* 39 (1915) 231–255. L. BOFF, *Church, Charism, and Power* (New York 1985). A. DULLES, *The Catholicity of the Church* (Oxford 1985). Y. CONGAR, *I Believe in the Holy Spirit,* v. II (New York 1983). B. MARTHALER, *The Creed* (Mystic, Conn. 1987). J. MOLTMANN, *The Church in the Power of the Spirit* (San Francisco 1977).

[G. THILS/L. S. CUNNINGHAM]

MARLEY, MARIE HILDA, SISTER

Scottish teacher, educator, and leader in child guidance; b. Durham, England, Oct. 13, 1876; d. Glasgow, Scotland, Nov. 19, 1951. After attending school in Sheffield, Hilda Gertrude Marley studied at Our Lady's Training College for Teachers in Liverpool and at London University; she then entered the Congregation of the Sisters of Notre Dame of Namur. As Sister Marie Hilda, she was assigned to Notre Dame Convent of Teignmouth, South Devon, and later to Notre Dame Training College in Glasgow. While teaching she continued her studies and graduated in honors history from London University. She emphasized psychology in the training college curriculum, and prepared a textbook and established a laboratory for her psychology classes. In 1931 Sister Marie Hilda founded the Notre Dame Child Guidance Clinic in Glasgow and quickly became the chief pioneer of child guidance in Scotland. Upon retirement from teaching (1941), she lectured extensively throughout Europe. In 1947 she was awarded the cross *Pro Ecclesia et Pontifice* by Pope Pius XII. Her writings were few. She served as vice president of the Scottish Branch of the British Psychological Society, and was a fellow of the Educational Institute of Scotland and of the British Psychological Society. In 1951 Sister Marie Hilda was elected vice president of the International Congress of Catholic Psychotherapists.

Bibliography: H. MISIAK and V. M. STAUDT, *Catholics in Psychology* (New York 1954).

[V. S. SEXTON]

MARMION, JOSEPH COLUMBA, BL.

Abbot of Maredsous and spiritual writer; b. April 1, 1858, Dublin, Ireland; d. Jan. 30, 1923, MAREDSOUS, Belgium. Born of an Irish father and a French mother, Joseph studied at Belvedere College in Dublin and at Holy Cross seminary of Clonliffe. He was then sent to the Irish College in Rome and studied at the College of Propaganda Fide.

In the year following his ordination (June 16, 1881), he returned to Ireland, where he was assigned to the parish of Dundrum. Soon afterward he became professor of philosophy at Holy Cross seminary. In 1886, with the permission of Cardinal Edward MacCabe, he entered the Benedictine monastery at Maredsous in Belgium. In 1899 he became prior and then professor at Mont-Cesar in Louvain, and in 1909 was made abbot at Maredsous.

Marmion became recognized as a master of the spiritual life, and his reputation further increased after his death. His books have gone through numerous editions in ten languages and are considered classics on the spiritual life. His teaching was drawn essentially from the Gospels, the Epistles of St. Paul, and the Rule of St. Benedict. Emphasizing the doctrine of the adoption of the children of God, Marmion exalts the person of Christ, the center of the whole interior life.

Along with his writing, Marmion carried on an extensive apostolate. He occupied himself by giving fatherly guidance to a large Benedictine monastery; hearing confessions and preaching retreats especially to priests and religious in Belgium, England, and Ireland; and keeping up an enormous correspondence. He was the close friend and spiritual director of Cardinal D. S. MERCIER, Archbishop of Malines, who held the abbot in highest esteem.

His writings (in Eng. tr.) include: *Christ the Life of the Soul* (London 1925), *Christ in His Mysteries* (London 1925), *Christ the Ideal of the Monk* (London 1926), *Sponsa Verbi* (London 1939), *Union with God* (London 1949), *Words of Life on the Margin of the Missal* (London 1940), *Come to Christ, All You Who Labour* (London 1946), and *Christ the Ideal of the Priest* (London 1953).

Veneration of Dom Marmion began immediately after his death, and his reputation for sanctity gave rise to the opening of the process of his beatification in 1954. Pope John Paul II beatified Dom Marmion on Sept. 3, 2000. Two Benedictine monasteries have been placed under his patronage: Marmion Abbey in Aurora, IL, and Glenstall Abbey in Eire.

Feast: Oct. 3.

Bibliography: T. DELFORGE, *Columba Marmion: Servant of God*, tr. R. L. STEWART (London & St. Louis 1965). M. M. PHILIPON, *The Spiritual Doctrine of Dom Marmion,* tr. M. DILLON (Westminster, MD 1956). R. THIBAUT, *Abbot Columba Marmion,* tr. M. ST. THOMAS (St. Louis 1949). M. TIERNEY, *Dom Columba Marmion* (Blackrock, Co. Dublin 1994).

[J. C. WILLKE]

MARMOUTIER, ABBEY OF

Benedictine abbey founded at Tours by St. MARTIN, *c.* 372, near the grotto where St. Gatian celebrated Mass. In 853 Marmoutier (*Majus Monasterium*) was sacked by the Norse, and 116 monks were slain; 20 managed to escape and were sheltered by the canons of St. Martin, who rebuilt the abbey. In 986 it was transferred to St. MAJOLUS, abbot of Cluny, at the request of Eudes I, count of Blois, who himself became a monk of Marmoutier. The great church was dedicated by Urban II in 1096. At this time the abbey was placed under papal protection and prospered during the 11th century, when at one time it had 101 priories in its affiliation, ten of them in England. In 1105 Abbot William succeeded Hilgotus and quarreled with Archbishop Rudolph II of Tours over jurisdiction. William went to Rome and received from Paschal II the abbatial benediction refused by Rudolph. In 1253 St. Louis IX protected it against the attacks of the counts of Blois. During the religious wars it was pillaged by Calvinists. In 1637 RICHELIEU made it a commendatory abbey of the Benedictine Congregation of St. Maur. The French Revolution effected its destruction and suppression in 1792. At Marmoutier was kept the ampulla of miraculous oil said to have cured St. Martin and used by Nicolas de THOU, bishop of Chartres, in the anointing of King Henry IV (1553–1619) on Feb. 27, 1594.

Bibliography: L. H. COTTINEAU, *Répertoire topobibliographique des abbayes et prieurés,* 2 v. (Mâcon 1935–39) 2:1762–66. S. HILPISCH, *Lexikon für Theologie und Kirche,* ed. J. HOFER and K. RAHNER, 10 v. (2d, new ed. Freiburg 1957–65) suppl., *Das Zweite Vatikanische Konzil: Dokumente und Kommentare,* ed. H. S. BRECHTER et al., pt. 1 (1966) 7:100. *Gallia Christiana,* v. 1–13 (Paris 1715–85), v. 14–16 (Paris 1856–65) 14:192–236.

[E. D. MCSHANE]

MARO OF CYR, ST.

Syrian monk and spiritual father of the Maronites; b. near Apamea on the Orontes River, Syria, date unknown; d. there, before 423. He lived an ascetical life of penance and prayer on a mountaintop. His miraculous gifts and extraordinary spiritual knowledge attracted many disciples who became holy hermits, such as SS. James of Cyr, Limnaeus, Thalassius, and Zebinas (Theodoret, *History of the Monks, Patrologia Graeca* 82:1431, 1451, 1458). The whole development of monasticism at Cyr derives from Maro. Whatever position later Maronite authors held in the dispute over MONOTHELITISM, Maro, a friend of St. JOHN CHRYSOSTOM, had always supported orthodoxy (*Patrologia Graeca* 52:630). Possession of his relics was contested after his death. A church was built on his tomb, and the monastery of St. Maro, which became the center of the Maronites, was later founded there. Maro's cult was approved by BENEDICT XIV in 1753.

Feast: Feb. 14.

Bibliography: *Acta Sanctorum* Feb. 2:767–768. F. NAU, "Opuscules Maronites," *Revue de l'Orient chrétien* 4 (1899) 175–266, 318–353. H. LECLERCQ, *Dictionnaire d'archéologie chrétienne et de liturgie,* ed. F. CABROL, H. LECLERCQ, and H. I. MARROU, 15 v. (Paris 1907–53) 10.2:2188. P. DIB, *Dictionnaire de théologie catholique,* ed. A. VACANT et al., 15 v. (Paris 1903–50; Tables générales 1951–) 10.1:1–2. F. A. AL-BUSTĀNĪ, *Mār Mārūn* (s.l. 1965). P. NAAMAN, *Théodoret de Cyr le monastère de Saint Maroun* (Sin el-Fil, Lebanon 1971).

[J. VAN PAASSEN]

MARONITE CHURCH

The hermit Maron (Maroon) lived on a mountain in the region of Apamea (Aphamiah) the actual Qal'at Al-Modiq, capital of Syria Secunda. His biographer, Theodoret, bishop of Cyr (d. 458), says that he pursued a life of prayer and that he had consecrated a pagan temple as a church (*Religiosa Historia* 16, 21; *Patrologia Graeca* 82:1418–31). Later historians (see P. Dib, *Histoire . . .* 4) place his death in 410. The group of disciples who gathered around Maron during his lifetime and, after his death, around the monastery erected to his memory formed the nucleus of the Maronite Church.

Monastery of St. Maron. This was located on the banks of the Orontes in northern Syria and, according to

Abbey church, Marmoutier, Alsace, France. (©Leonard de Selva/CORBIS)

the Arabic historian Ma'soudi [*Livre de l'avertissement, et de la révision* (Kitāb at-Tanbīh Wal-Ischrāf), ed. M. J. de Goeje, in *Bibliotheca geographorum arabicorum,* v. 8 (Leiden 1894) 153], by the tenth century was of considerable size and wealth, a necessary stop on the imperial road from Antioch to Damascus.

During the early sixth century, the Maronite monks were foremost among the defenders of the doctrine of CHALCEDON, in defense of which 350 monks were slain and many monasteries burned by the MONOPHYSITES. (They are commemorated by the Maronite Church on July 31.) This is known by a memorandum sent to Pope Hormisdas by the monks of Syria Secunda and signed by Alexander, archimandrite of St. Maron (dated 517; J. D. Mansi, *Sacrorum Conciliorum nova et amplissima collectio,* 31 v. [Paris 1889–1927; repr. Graz 1960—] 8:425–429, 1023–30). The pope replied on Feb. 10, 518. Papal recognition of the Maronites is revealed in these documents, which also make it clear that the grand monastery of St. Maron was foremost among the monasteries of Syria Secunda and that together they formed a cohesive group.

The grand monastery was enlarged during the time of the Emperor Marcian (452) and under Justinian I. Until the mid-seventh century, the monastery of St. Maron was the stronghold of the Chalcedonians and the center of missionary activity in northern Syria. The preaching monks traveled about the villages, calling for a spiritual renewal and strengthening the faith of the people who often came to them for guidance. The attempted suppression of the Chalcedonians by civil and religious authorities served to strengthen the unity between the Maronite monks and their lay followers. This was further strengthened by the use of the Syriac language in the liturgy for this was the language of the people in the villages outside of the larger cities. On the eve of the formation of the Maronite patriarchate, the monachal way of life had shaped Maronite society. The heads of the monasteries

Maronite Monastery of Deir el Nourieh, Lebanon. (©Roger Wood/CORBIS)

were usually invested with the episcopal character, and the people of the surrounding area were under the direct jurisdiction of the monasteries. Over a period of time, the religious life of the people was shaped by monachal customs and traditions. This became an important and an enduring characteristic of the Maronite Church, and its canon law and church government still bear the marks of this influence. The jurisdiction and power of the Maronite patriarchs through the centuries have their origin and meaning in the power and jurisdiction given to the superior of St. Maron's Monastery. This monastic origin explains the influence, to the present day, of the patriarch in civil and religious matters, making him in fact an actual leader of his people who often acts as the representative of the whole Maronite ''nation.''

Constitution of the Maronite patriarchate and the monothelite controversy in Syria. Patriarch Anastasius II, the last Chalcedonian patriarch to reside in Antioch, was killed in 609. Titular patriarchs of Antioch were appointed by Constantinople until 702, but after that the see remained vacant until 742, when the caliph Hisham allowed the elected patriarch, Stephen III, to take possession (see C. Karalevski, *Dictionnaire d'histoire et de géographie ecclésiastiques,* [Paris 1912—] 3:563–703). During the vacancy, the Chalcedonian group was leaderless and the Maronite patriarchate was formed. Maronite monks had elected a bishop from their monastery before 745. See *La Chronique de Michel le Syrien ou le Grand (1166–1199)*, ed. J. B. Chabot (1899–1910) 2:511; this text lends solid proof to the Maronite tradition that the patriarchate had been established in the last years of the seventh century. [See Al-Douaihi, *Chronology of the Maronite Patriarch,* ed. Shartooni (Rashid, Beirut 1902); Le Quien, *Oriens Christianus,* v. 3; P. Chebli, *Biographie du Patriarche Étienne Douaihi* (Beirut 1913) 210]. Maronite sources place the election of the first Maronite patriarch, St. John Maron, in 685.

With the Antiochene see vacant, the Maronite monks realized the need for a leader and elected a bishop from their monastery to fill the vacant see. The election was certainly canonical; had it not been so, the Holy See would have condemned it as it did in the case of Macedonius, patriarch of Constantinople in 649 (J. D. Mansi, *Sacrorum Conciliorum nova et amplissima collectio,* 31 v. [Paris 1889–1927; repr. Graz 1960— 10:811). All available documents indicate that the Maronite patriarchs from the beginning held the title of ''Antioch'' (e.g., a document from the year 1141 in J. A. Assemani, *Bibliotheca Orientalis* 1:307).

Historically, the Maronites were the staunchest defenders of the Council of CHALCEDON, although in the eighth century they had never been informed officially of the condemnation of MONOTHELITISM at the Council of Constantinople in 680 (*see* Dib, Histoire . . . , 40). The annals of Eutyches (Sa'Id Ibn Batriq), Monophysite patriarch of Alexandria (933–940), contain many erroneous passages concerning the origin of the Maronites, including the actual dating of the life of St. Maron and the date of the Monothelite heresy itself. Unfortunately, Eutyches misled many later writers, such as William of Tyre, the standard authority on the Crusades (*Historia Rerum in Partibus Transmarinis Gestarum; Patrologia Latina,* 217 v. [Paris 1878–90] 201:855–856). William attributes Monothelitism to the Maronites and St. Maron and says that at the sight of the Crusaders they were divinely inspired to reject their ancient heresy and to enter the Catholic Church with their patriarch and bishops. Specifically citing Eutyches as his source, William merely repeats his errors (*ibid.*).

The position of the Maronites on the question of the two wills in Christ is best understood against the background of the circumstances in Syria at that time. On the eve of the Arab invasion, the Byzantine emperors were attempting to unify their subjects by offering a compromise acceptable to both Chalcedonians and Monophysites, founded in the duality of nature in Christ and the oneness of will. This doctrine was published in the *Ecthesis* (638) and displeased both parties. Some Chalcedonians had appealed to the pope, and although the pope had approved the project of the *Ecthesis,* the Ecumenical Council of Constantinople (680) condemned Pope Honorius and Patriarch Sergius and their Monothelite followers, without, however, any mention of the Maronites. The position of the Maronite party concerning the issue remained as it was prior to the council as the Maronites had not been informed of the council's actions. They learned of the council only through prisoners of war captured by the Arabs. The oldest Maronite documents prove that, in spite of a material Monothelitism, the Maronites believed that in Christ, ontologically speaking, there are two wills (see Dib, *Histoire* . . . , 30). When speaking of one will in Christ, they mean one practical will, which is equivalent to action in the terminology used by Bishop Thomas Kephartab [Ten Chapters, manuscript Syr. 203, fol. 21, v. 31, dated 1089; Metropolitan David, *Kitāb al-Hudā,* or *Book of Guidance,* 1059, ed. P. Fahed (Aleppo 1935) 44–48]. All of these texts stress the unity of action in Christ in that it is not possible to contemplate two opposing wills in Him. What was regarded as heresy was merely controversy over semantics.

The Maronites, under persecution by the caliphates of Damascus and Baghdad aided by the Maximites, began some time in the early eighth century to seek refuge from Muslim attacks in the inaccessible mountains of Lebanon, cut off from all contact with both old and new Rome.

Early middle ages. The juridical literature of the Maronite Church of the Middle Ages has been reduced to the compilation of the NOMOCANON known as *Kitāb al-Hudā* (Book of Guidance). The only copies available are written in Karshuni (Arabic written in Syriac characters). P. Fahed edited *Kitāb al-Hudā* at Aleppo in 1935, giving all the variant readings of the text in footnotes.

The Nomocanon is prefaced by a letter written by the priest monk Joseph, dated from 1058 to 1059, asking Metropolitan David to translate the canons into Arabic. The book is composed of two sections. The first 13 chapters treat doctrine, morality, and liturgy. Chapters 14 to 57 reproduce previous juridical sources.

The Maronites in Lebanon: First contact with Rome through the crusades. It is apparent from a study of the text of the Arab historian Mas'oudi (d. 956) that before the first half of the tenth century the bulk of the Maronites had left northern Syria. The first Maronite Church in the mountains of Lebanon was established around 749. Safeguarded by the mountains, they organized a feudal system of government under the combined leadership of clergy and nobility. The patriarch appears to have been the supreme head in religious and civil matters, aided by bishops who acted as his vicars.

When the crusaders journeyed along the Levantine coast en route to Jerusalem, the Maronites greeted them as natural allies and close relations grew from the first. The Maronites occupied the first place after the Franks [see Ristelhueber, *Les Traditions françaises au Liban* (Paris 1925) 58]. The CRUSADES made possible the first contact of the Maronites as an independent Church with the Holy See. The last communication had been the reply of Pope Hormisdas to the Maronite monks in 518; since then the Muslim tide had inundated all of Syria and half of Asia Minor, and the eleventh century had witnessed the Great Schism between East and West. The sixth-century persecution of the Maronites had faded from the memory of the West, and it considered the entire East as either heretic or dissident. The so-called return of the Maronites, which took place in Tripoli (1180–81) and was reported by William of Tyre (*op. cit., Patrologia Latina,* 217 v. [Paris 1878–90] 201:855–856), was apparently a profession of faith in recognition of the jurisdiction of Alexander III against an antipope. It seems highly unlikely that any church would, as a unit, leave the unity of the Catholic Church and return to it without any member remaining in heresy; it seems even stranger for the Maronites, after their cordial reception of the crusaders, to delay a century to make the so-called return, especially during a period when the Frankish Empire was divided from within and on the very eve of disaster.

Jeremias Al-Amshitti (1199–1230), who personally attended the Lateran Council (1215), was the first Maronite patriarch to visit Rome and take part in an ecumenical council. He returned to Lebanon in 1216 and received the bull *Quia Divinae Sapientiae*, signed by Innocent III, and the pallium. The Maronites began to strengthen their ties with the Holy See, remaining steadfast despite the persecutions suffered after the departure of the crusaders. The Latinizing of the Maronites began during this period.

Period of the crusades (1098–1291). There is a lack of documents concerning the juridical and ecclesiastical life of the Maronites in these times because members of the Maronite hierarchy, especially the patriarch, were the targets of persecution by the civil authorities. The patriarch lived in hiding. Many times he was discovered and jailed. Consequently the only documents that refer to the existence and activity of a few patriarchs of the eleventh and twelfth centuries are contained in notes found on the marginal spaces of certain manuscripts. The principal documents concerning the relations of the Maronites with the popes can be found in T. Anaissi's *Bullarium Maronitarum.* This edition is not critical, but it is the only one in existence. Other documents are found in Anaissi's *Collectio documentorum Maronitarum.* The first part of this collection relates to a period prior to the relations with the Holy See, and the second is made up of documents covering modern times until 1913. These are cataloged according to numerical order: the *Bullarium* bears Roman numerals, and the *Collectio,* Arabic numerals. This article will refer to these publications by abbreviations: AB to indicate the *Bullarium;* AC, the *Collectio.*

Pope Innocent III. Two bulls of Innocent III concerned the Maronites (AB 1–2). The first, dated April 18, 1213, convoked the forthcoming ecumenical council (1215). The second bull, dated January of 1216, was addressed to Patriarch (or Primate) Jeremias (Al-Amshitti), to the archbishops and bishops, men of note, clergy, and Maronite people. This bull enumerated a few points of doctrine and discipline that the Holy See wished to introduce into the Maronite Church: in the triple baptismal immersion, the Holy Trinity should be invoked only once; confirmation should be conferred only by the bishop, and Holy Chrism should be made of balm and oil; the faithful should go to confession once a year to their own priests and receive Holy Communion three times; there are two wills in Christ; chalices should not be made of glass or wood but only of gold, silver, or tin; and the churches should have bells.

In the Eastern Christian tradition, priests had had the power to confirm. Holy Chrism was made of various aromatic substances. In spite of the recommendation made to the Maronites to go to Confession and Communion once a year, it was not evident that this was not the practice among the Maronites. The notion of a proper pastor was not known in oriental canon law. Bells were not used in the East; instead the custom was to use a mallet on a wooden or iron board to announce the time of prayer.

The bull imposed on the Maronite bishops the use of the Latin vestments and enumerated the Maronite sees, two archbishoprics and three bishoprics. Jeremias Al-Amshitti (1199–1230) was granted the pallium, but with the stipulation that it was to be given to him by the Latin patriarch of Antioch. It extended the privilege of the canon (decreed by canon 15 of the Lateran Council, 1135) to the Maronites, but the patriarch was given the power of lifting the excommunication incurred by the violation of this privilege. It is noteworthy that the pope, while granting all these concessions, recognized the validity of customs and laws approved by the patriarch and his predecessors in the Church of Antioch. This bull, in spite of its expression of the benevolent attitude of the pope, constituted the first attempt at Latinization of Maronite canon law.

Pope Alexander IV. The same prescriptions of Innocent III were sent by Alexander IV (1254–64) in 1256 to Patriarch Simon (1245–77). In this bull the pope limited the power of the patriarch to absolve the censure incurred by violation of the privilege of the canon. Each case had to be referred to Rome (AB 3–4). These attempts at Latinization encountered partial success in the Maronite Church; however, it seems that the Maronite Church followed the practice of the Latin Church only in certain prescriptions. In making Holy Chrism it started to use only oil and balm; in the consecration of a bishop, the imposition of the miter was introduced. Certain ordinations were modeled after the Latin Pontifical. It is to be noted that none of these bulls of Innocent III and Alexander IV prescribed the use of the unleavened bread. Rather they expressed a general invitation to conform the liturgical usages of the Maronite Church to those of the Church of Rome.

Some of the Crusaders, after their defeat and the fall of their Syrian Empire, took refuge among the Maronites and were warmly welcomed by Patriarch Simon, who received a letter of thanks from Pope Alexander IV, addressing him as ''Maronite Patriarch of Antioch.'' Benedict XIV confirmed the title in 1744.

The Mamelukes tightened their watch on the Levantine coast after the departure of the crusaders in order to prevent a return; this rendered contact with the Holy See extremely difficult. Pontifical emissaries were sent to the Maronites during the fifteenth century, and under the government of the Moogaddameen they enjoyed a semi-independent political life.

Mamelukes (1291–1516). The Mamelukes were slaves of the Turks brought by the sultans of Egypt to be officers in their army. One of them succeeded in taking over the sultanate, becoming the first of a long line. The last Mameluke sultan was put to death by Salim I, the sultan of Constantinople, in 1517. The Mamelukes practiced a policy of devastation and destruction in order to impede the return of the crusaders. Thus the cities on the Lebanese coast were sacked and destroyed. The Maronites of this period lived in isolation and enjoyed an autonomous political life. This strengthened the judicial power of the patriarch and bishops over their subjects. *The Book of Guidance,* or *Kitāb al-Hudā,* became insufficient to guide them in their new role. The Maronites then adopted the *Collection of Canons* of the Coptic Ibn Al-'Assāl, whose second book treats the private law of Christians. A critical edition of this Nomocanon was published at Cairo, Egypt, in 1900 by Philouthaous 'Awad.

The relations of the Maronite patriarchate with the Holy See were interrupted because of the watching eye of the Mamelukes, who had occupied all the sea coast of Lebanon. During this period, the Maronites were grouped in the northern part of Lebanon in the regions of Batroom, Jobail, Ehden, and Besharree. Some of them had taken refuge on the islands of Rhodes and Cyprus, where their community was prosperous at the time of the Lusiganans (1192–1489).

In spite of the new prescriptions that Innocent III and Alexander IV introduced, and which the Maronites partially followed, it seems that the discipline and the liturgy of the Maronite Church kept its oriental physiognomy. It is probable that the Maronites at that time took back some of the oriental customs that they had somewhat abandoned at the time of the crusades. The danger of Latinization became less imminent because of the interruption of communication with Rome and the West.

Relations with the Holy See were reestablished during the reign of Patriarch John Al-Jaji (1404–45), who sent his profession of faith to Pope Eugene IV. The pope answered in general terms (AB 6). Another bull of Pope Eugene IV, dated Aug. 7, 1445 (AB 7), contained the following disciplinary prescription: the dough to make the Eucharistic bread should not be mixed with oil; the patriarch should replace Maronite liturgical and disciplinary custom with those of the Latin Church. It was after the Maronites abided by these prescriptions that the power was granted to Maronite bishops to excommunicate and absolve in the external forum, both clergy and faithful of the Maronite Church. This was the first time Rome asserted officially, although indirectly, the personal jurisdiction of the Maronite bishops. At the same time, the Maronite clergy were allowed to celebrate Mass in Latin churches and the Latin clergy to celebrate Mass in Maronite churches. Maronite clergy and laity were allowed to be buried from a Latin church. They were allowed to marry Latins, but the ceremony of marriage was to be held in the liturgical rite of the Latin Church.

Pope Paul II was the first pope to mention the title of Antioch used by the Maronite patriarch (*Patriarchae Maronitarum Antiochaeno nuncupato*). The bull is dated 1469 (AB 11). During the thirteenth century, the title of Antioch had been given only to the Latin patriarch; but when the crusaders left Syria, the title of patriarch of Antioch was given to a prelate who resided in Rome. During the sixteenth century, the general principle of unity of jurisdiction was abandoned; however, some popes addressed the Maronite patriarchs as patriarch of the Maronites; and others, for example, Pius IV, as patriarch or primate. Paul V, in his bull of 1608, was the first to address Joseph Al-Reezzee as *Patriarchae Maronitarum Antiocheni* (AB 55). In the four bulls addressed to his successor, John Makhloof, the same title was used, as it was in all other bulls that followed.

In August of 1515 Pope Leo X answered a letter from Patriarch Simon and told him that his profession of faith did not contain the FILIOQUE (the procession of the Holy Spirit from the Father and Son) and that the rule prescribed once to Patriarch Jeremias in the making of Holy Chrism was not observed. He indicated also that the Maronites should go once a year to confession and Communion. Pope Leo finally confirmed Simon in his dignity as patriarch of the Maronites and granted him the pallium.

Turkish domination. The period that followed was marked by the conquest of Syria and Cyprus by the Ottoman Turks under Salim I and by the rise to power in Lebanon of the Ma'nee family (1516–1697). It was marked religiously by the Catholic renewal of the Church through the Council of Trent and the introduction of its decisions into the Maronite canon law.

Modern times: 1515–1918. The Turks, under Sultan Salim I, in 1516 conquered all of Syria, Lebanon, and Egypt; in 1527 the patriarch, offering the aid of 50,000 troops, unsuccessfully asked Charles V, the Holy Roman Emperor, for aid in liberating the land [Rabbath, *Documents inédits pour servir à l'histoire du Christianisme en Orient,* v. 2 (Paris, Leipzig 1905–21) 616–623]. In 1562 Pius IV urged Patriarch Moses to follow the Roman Rite in the administration of the Sacraments and prescribed that the Maronite patriarchs should, thenceforth, after their elections, send with the letter of obedience a profession of faith (AC 32). In the last years of the sixteenth century, the Holy See sent three missions to the Maronites; at the suggestion of the papal legates, the Maronite patriarchs held three synods (1580, 1596, and 1598).

It was under the reigns of the three patriarchs of the Al-Reezzee family that the decrees of Trent were introduced into the Maronite Church through the successive missions sent by the pope to Lebanon. Michael Al-Reezzee was elected patriarch in 1567. Ten years later he sent emissaries to Rome to present his profession of faith (AC 42). Gregory XIII answered on Feb. 14, 1578 (AB 33), reminding the patriarch of the reforms that the popes wanted to introduce into the Maronite Church. It was the old request: the phrase ''who was crucified for us'' was to be suppressed from the Trisagion; Holy Chrism was to be made in the Latin style; conferring of Confirmation was to be reserved to the bishops; Holy Communion was not to be given to little children; and the Latin impediments to marriage of consanguinity and affinity were to be adopted.

Synods. John Baptist Eliano and John Bruno were pontifical legates to Lebanon when a synod was held at Qannoobeen from Aug. 15 to 18, 1580. The delegates had prepared a slightly modified text of the decrees. The first nine chapters treated dogma and the Sacraments; these were inspired principally by the Council of Florence with a few additional canons concerning the situation of the Maronites. The reform proposed by Gregory XIII was taken into consideration; but relative to the marriage impediments, only the complicated impediment of affinity was suppressed. Chapter 10 treated discipline and was inspired mainly by the Council of Trent. These decrees remained "dead letters" because it was practically impossible to change well-established customs among the Maronites.

Pope Gregory XIII in his brief *Humana Sic Ferunt* (1584) erected the Maronite College in Rome, under the Jesuit Fathers. This institution played an important role in the Maronite Church and in fostering oriental studies in the West. GABRIEL SIONITA (1577–1648), biblical scholar and linguist, ABRAHAM ECCHELLENSIS (d. 1644), and Joseph Simon ASSEMANI (1687–1768), famous orientalist and custodian of the Vatican Library, are among its most famous students.

In 1584 Gregory XIII erected a college for the Maronite students in Rome and gave its direction to the Jesuits (AB 43–45; AC 55). The next pontifical delegation sent to the Maronites was headed by Jerome Dandini, SJ, who was accompanied by Father Fabio Bruno. Both delegates brought with them 200 copies of the new Missal (strongly Latinized) edited in Rome in 1592. Not knowing the oriental languages, they used as interpreters some Maronite students of the Roman college. The first session was held from Sept. 22 to 28, 1596, and decreed 21 canons. In comparison with the legislation of 1580, this one was fragmentary and lacked systematization; conferring Confirmation was definitely reserved to the bishops and the use of the new Maronite Missal was imposed; Communion under both species was still allowed; and the use of the unleavened bread was imposed. There is no record that this synod was ever approved by Rome. After the death of Patriarch Michael, his nephew Joseph was elected on Nov. 13, 1596. The new patriarch promulgated six canons that encouraged the celibacy of the secular clergy. They decreed also that monasteries and convents be under separate administration.

Patriarch Joseph Al-Reezzee held a new synod at the village of Da'yat Moossa in 1598, which decreed 31 canons. The major part of these canons treated the Sacraments and repeated the prescriptions of 1580 and 1596. Another canon reduced the time of the three periods of fasting used in the East. The acts of this synod were not sent to Rome.

Clement VIII sent a letter to Patriarch Joseph, dated Aug. 17, 1599 (AB 52), in which he defined the extent of the Latin impediments of consanguinity, affinity, spiritual relationship, public propriety, and crime, and he asked the patriarch to introduce them into Maronite canon law, granting the patriarch broad faculties of dispensation. Patriarch Joseph tried in 1606 to impose the Gregorian calendar on the Maronite Church. He succeeded in Lebanon but failed in Cyprus. The other reforms were not accepted or enforced. These synods did not treat the organization of the hierarchy. As before, the bishops remained as delegates of the patriarch and not residential prelates.

After his election in 1644, Patriarch Joseph Al-Aqoori called a synod in Hrash. The canons of this synod were divided into 7 sections: Baptism, 6 canons; Confirmation, 6; marriage, 22; priesthood, 7; Extreme Unction, 3; inheritance, 3; and commandments of the Church, 6. The complicated way of computing the impediment of affinity was taken back along with the marriage impediments; the reduction of the three fasting seasons was maintained. There is no record of any other synods held in the seventeenth century.

The later half of the seventeenth century saw an era of religious toleration during which monasteries multiplied and many European missions were established. Under the reign of Patriarch Al-Douaihi, the Maronite Order of St. Anthony was established (1700; *see* ANTONINES), along with the Antonine Order of St. Isaias (1704).

From 1697 to 1841. A number of canonical collections were made in the early eighteenth century. Simon Awad, nephew of the patriarch James Awad, in collaboration with Joseph Assemanni, edited a collection in four parts: the number and authority of the patriarchs, their relationship with the Holy See and with the bishops, and the list of the patriarchs of the four great sees. Peter Toulawi, a Maronite priest, translated (*c.* 1720) the acts of the Council of Trent with its history and added to it the decisions of the two Maronite synods of 1596, underscoring their relationship with the Council of Trent. Abdulla Qarā'āli (1716–42) wrote a resume of civil law based on the ancient oriental canons, but it also contained some Muslim jurisprudence. This resume was divided into 31 chapters. Qarā'āli also wrote a manual of civil law in the form of questions and answers entitled Al-Fatawui or Pandectes. Both books were inspired by Ibn Al-'Assāl.

Synod of Mt. Lebanon. In July of 1734 Patriarch Joseph Al Khazen, with his bishops, requested the Holy See to send them an apostolic visitor in order to help them reform their Church. They suggested the name of Joseph Simon Assemani, who was prefect of the Vatican Library. Assemani was sent by the pope as his personal legate to call a synod of the Maronite hierarchy and to take part in it with the right to vote (AB 111–114).

Assemani prepared, in Latin, a wide project of canons to be adopted by the future synod. He had the Maronite priest Andrew Scandar translate it into Arabic (Vatican Manuscript Syr. 399, in Karshuni). It was the work of a scholar, containing learned dissertations inspired by Eastern and Western sources, for example, the Trent legislation and that of the 1720 Synod of Zamost.

Assemani also used the correspondence of popes and patriarchs and the acts of the 1596 Synod of Qannoobeen. Reference was made to the *Book of Guidance* and to the Nomocanon of the priest George.

The synod was opened at Ryfoon on Sept. 14, 1736; but because of dissensions, the patriarch left the assembly the following day. The synod then moved to Louaizee on September 30 of the same year and remained in session until October 2. Before the assembly adopted any canons, Assemani had to modify his project in many ways. The canons of this synod marked the ratification of liturgical and canonical Latinization that the Holy See had tried to introduce into the Maronite Church since the time of the crusades. The first part treated faith, feast days, and fasting; the reduction of the three seasons of fast was definitively approved; the compilation of collections of civil and canon law for use in the diocesan tribunals was decreed; and a decision was made to revise all liturgical books. The second part treated the Sacraments: most of the marriage legislation of the Latin canon law was accepted; the use of the unleavened bread was imposed; for the forms of Baptism, Confirmation, and Extreme Unction both Latin and oriental formulas were accepted, but for the form of absolution only the Latin formula was tolerated; finally, that part of the ritual of Al-Douaihi dealing with ordination was accepted. The third part dealt with the hierarchical organization: bishops became true hierarchs of eparchies; rights of the patriarch were made precise and limited; he was to be elected by bishops only and through secret ballot; election by acclamation was valid only when there was unanimity; he was answerable only to the pope; and the number of eparchies was limited to eight, with their limits drawn by mutual accord. The fourth part dealt with the churches, monasteries, convents, and schools: the obligation of keeping registers in the parishes was introduced; monasteries and convents had to be separated; and the constitutions of autonomous monasteries (which did not join the Lebanese congregation of the Antonines) were added to the acts of the synod. At the end of October of 1736, Assemani published an instruction containing a resume of the essential prescriptions of the synod concerning secular clergy, laymen, and churches.

On Sept. 1, 1741, Benedict XIV approved *in forma specifica* the Latin text of the decrees of the synod of 1736, after making some 15 minor corrections in it (AB 118–119). In another constitution dated Feb. 14, 1742, he approved the accord of the Maronite bishops concerning the eight Maronite eparchies (AB 120). Finally, on Oct. 15, 1742, the pope approved *in forma specifica* the declarations of the superiors of the Maronite congregations of St. Anthony, made in 1737, that their constitutions would be adjusted to the new legislation of the synod (AB 122). Because of the scarcity of copies of the synod proceedings and because of the opposition that it encountered in many fields, its decrees remained in practice unobserved.

Subsequent Synods. Patriarch Simon Awad and the Maronite bishops had made a very important decision on July 19, 1744: In civil matters the bishops had to use the two works on civil law by Qarā'āli. Benedict XIV, anxious to see the canons of the Synod of Mt. Lebanon applied, called this decision to the attention of Patriarch Simon. Simon called a synod from Nov. 28 to 30, 1755, which decreed 15 canons; the pontifical prescriptions of Benedict XIV were renewed and some new prescriptions were given, and the ritual of Al-Douaihi was to be observed, not the *Book of the Priestly Rites,* the work of Peter Moubarack, a Maronite Jesuit (d. 1742).

Another synod held by Tobias Al-Khazen at Beq'ata (Aug. 25 to 31, 1756) promulgated 18 canons. Patriarch Joseph Estephan held a synod at Ghosta (Sept. 16 to 21, 1768) attended by a Franciscan delegate of the Holy See to establish peace among the members of the Lebanese congregation. Among the important decisions of this synod was the decree requesting the patriarch to appoint two examiners before whom all candidates for the priesthood, secular and regular, would be examined. In the same synod, the separation between Lebanese and Aleppian congregations was decreed and later approved by Clement XIV on July 19, 1770 (AB 168).

A synod called by Bishop Michael Al-Khazen was held at Mayfooq (July 21 to 28, 1780) in the presence of the apostolic delegate. It promulgated 13 new canons, one of which was the condemnation of superstitious practices. The other canons referred to matters of discipline for the clergy and laymen. Patriarch Estephan held a synod in Ain-Shaqiq (Sept. 6 to 11, 1786), attended by few bishops and some of the Maronite nobility. The most important decision of this synod was to return to the old custom of having the bishops reside with the patriarch. On Dec. 15, 1787, Pius VI condemned this synod and asked Germanos Adam, Melkite bishop of Aleppo, to hold another synod in the name of the Holy See (AB 179). It was held at Bkerke from Dec. 3 to 18, 1790. Patriarch Estephan and his bishops attended it. Bishop Adam made them revoke the decisions of Ain-Shaqiq that were contrary to the decisions of the Synod of Mt. Lebanon. The synod reached a compromise decision concerning the juxtaposition of monasteries and convents. The Congregation of the Propagation of the Faith (AC 106) made a pronouncement about each one of the synod's disciplinary canons and ordered complete separation of religious houses for men and women.

On Nov. 1, 1816, Pius VII complained to the Maronite hierarchy about the abuses of the juxtaposition of religious houses for men and women, especially of autonomous monasteries unaffiliated with the Lebanese congregations (AB 188), and about bishops not residing in their eparchies despite the reinforcement of this obligation made in 1790. He ordered them to hold a synod in the presence of the apostolic delegate and to abolish these two abuses. The synod was held at Louaizee (April 14 to 15, 1818) and decreed 19 canons. The synod reserved certain convents to the nuns and ordered them to follow the rules decreed in 1736 for the autonomous convent of Hrash, with the exception of the rising at night for prayer. It assigned, for residence of the bishops, a monastery located in their eparchy. On March 25, 1819, Pius VII transmitted to the Maronite hierarchy a decree of the Congregation of the Propagation of Faith reproducing and making precise the decisions of this synod (AB 192–193).

In 1820 the Holy See edited an official Latin text of the Synod of Mt. Lebanon. In 1833 the Congregation of the Propagation of Faith declared that only the Latin edition of the Synod of Mt. Lebanon had force of law. It imposed in 1839 and 1840 a new edition of the Maronite ritual, which was a strongly Latinized edition, in major part inspired by that of Peter Moubarack.

From 1841 to 1955. At the request of the pope, Patriarch Paul Massad convoked a synod at Bekerke (April ll to 30, 1856), but the acts of this synod were never approved by the Holy See.

In 1891 Leo XIII, with Bishop Elias Hoyek (later patriarch), erected the new Maronite College in Rome; the original college had been suppressed by the armies of Napoleon in 1808. In 1895 the same bishop founded the Congregation of the Sisters of the Holy Family, a teaching order. In 1900 Bishop Joseph Nejm edited in Arabic a translation of the Synod of Mt. Lebanon, conforming to the Latin original. Father George Manaš published in Aleppo in 1925 *The Canon Law of the Maronites,* a comparison of the three editions of the Synod of Mt. Lebanon (1796, 1820, 1900). Elias Az-Zaynati published in Beirut in the following year *The Canon of the Lebanese Synod,* a systematic presentation of the canons of the synod similar to those of the Latin code.

The Maronite patriarch is held in great esteem and exercises great influence among Christians and non-Christians alike. His residence is at Bkerke during the winter and at Deeman during the summer.

Maronite church in the United States In the 1880s and 1890s, Maronite Catholics were already to be found throughout the United States. They had immigrated primarily from Lebanon but also from Syria and other parts of the Middle East. By the beginning of World War I, Maronite communities were to be found all over the United States, and there were at least 22 permanent Maronite parishes. Ten years later, the Maronite presence had grown to 37 churches and 46 priests.

Through the efforts of Maronite clergy and laity, and the assistance of the achbishop of Washington, Our Lady of Lebanon Maronite Seminary was established in Washington, D.C in 1961. In 1966 the Holy Father established the Maronite Apostolic Exarchate for the United States and appointed Bishop Francis Zayek as the exarch. The see city was Detroit, Michigan. In 1971 the exarchate was raised to the rank of diocese, and the see was transferred to Brooklyn, N.Y. in 1978. At the time of the exarchate's establishment, there were 43 Maronite parishes in the United States.

To solidify Maronite identity and to respond to the needs of the new generations of American Maronites, a vast program of liturgical reform and translations was inaugurated in the 1970s. This resulted in the publication in English of a Maronite Lectionary, Book of Anaphoras, several editions of the books of the Divine Liturgy, Ritual, Divine Office, and liturgical music. Catechetical texts for all twelve grades based on the Maronite tradition have been published.

On March 1, 1994, as a sign of the progress of the Maronite Church in the United States, the Holy Father established a second eparchy or diocese. The new Eparchy of Our Lady of Lebanon of Los Angeles incorporates all the territory west of the Ohio-Pennsylvania border. Bishop John Chedid, who had been auxiliary bishop since 1980, was named eparch of the new jurisdiction. The new eparchy comprises 24 parishes and 9 missions. The Eparchy of St. Maron of Brooklyn consists of 33 parishes and 5 missions. With the retirement of Archbishop Zayek, Stephen Hector Doueihi was appointed as the second bishop of the Eparchy of St. Maron.

Aside from second- and third-generation American Maronites, many Maronite parishes today have experienced a large influx of immigrants who have come to the United States and to other countries since the fighting began in Lebanon in 1975 and have chosen to remain. They are not only a significant presence, but have brought with them a new injection of contemporary Maronite and Lebanese culture.

Bibliography: P. DIB, *Histoire de l'Église maronite,* v. 1 (Beirut 1962). P. ABRAHAM, *The Maronites of Lebanon* (Wheeling, W.Va. 1931). G. DANDINI, *Missione apostolica al patriarca dei Maroniti del Monte Libano* (Cesena 1656). P. SFAIR, *La Messa siro-maronita* (Rome 1946); A. RABBATH, *Documents inédits pour servir à l'histoire du christianisme en Orient,* 2 v. (Leipzig 1905–21). T. ANAISSI, ed., *Bullarium Maronitarum* (Rome 1911); *Collectio documentorum Maronitarum* (Leghorn 1921). I. 'AOUWĀD, *Le Droit privé des Maronites au temps des émirs Chihab, 1697–1841*

(Paris 1938). J. A. ASSEMANI, *Codex liturgicus ecclesiae universae,* lib. 1–4, 8 v. in 13 (Rome 1749–66) v. 5, 7; *Bibliotheca iuris orientalis canonici et civilis,* 5 v. (Rome 1762–66). J. S. ASSEMANI *Bibliotheca orientalis,* 3 v. in 4. IBN AL-'ASSĀL, *Nomocanon: Kitāb al Quwānīn,* ed. M. GUIRGUIS (2d ed. Cairo 1927). A. QARĀ'ALI, *Muḫtaṣar as-Šarī'āt,* ed. P. MAS'AD (Beirut 1959), a resume of the law. C. DE CLERCQ, *Conciles des orientaux catholiques,* 2 v. (Paris 1949–52), 1:1575–1849. A. COUSSA, *Epitome praelectionum de iure ecclesiastico orientali,* 3 v. (Grottaferrata-Rome 1948–50; suppl. 1958) v. 1, 3. P. DIB, "Les Conciles de L'Église Maronite," *Revue des sciences religieuses* 4 (1924) 193–220, 421–439 and pub. sep. (Strasbourg 1926). F. GALTIER, *Le Mariage: Discipline orientale et occidentale* (Beirut 1950). P. MAS'AD, ed., *Le Concile Baladi of 1856* (Beirut 1959). P. FAHED, ed., *Kitāb al-Hudā* (Aleppo 1935), Maronite Nomocanon. G. MANAŠ, *At-Tuḫfa al-adabīya fī talāta magami' māraūnīya* (Juniya 1904), three Maronite synods; *Al-Haq al-qānuni 'indal-Mawarina* (Aleppo 1925), the canon law of the Maronites. S. ŠARTŪNĪ, "The Maronite Synods," *Al-Mashriq* 7 (1904), in Arabic. J. FÉGHALI, *Histoire du droit de l'Église Maronite,* v. 1 (Paris 1962). J. D. MANSI, *Sacrorum Conciliorum nova et amplissima collection,* 31 v. (Florence-Venice 1757–98) v. 2, 14, 25, 33, 35, 38.

[E. EL-HAYEK/S. BEGGIANI]

MARONITE LITURGY

The Maronite Church traces its origins to the fourth-century hermit, St. Maron, and the fifth-century Monastery of St. Maron, which was founded by his disciples. These Syriac-speaking monks and the laity who gravitated around them eventually succeeded in organizing an independent hierarchy. Located in a region that straddled both Antioch and Edessa, the MARONITE CHURCH was heir of both the liturgical practice of the church of Antioch and of the Semitic liturgical tradition that arose from Edessa and the region to the East.

The earliest extant manuscripts of the Maronite Missal highlight the *Anaphora of Third Peter* (also known by its Syriac name of *Sharar*), which shares a common root with the Chaldean *Anaphora of Addai and Mari*. The Maronites and CHALDEANS also share common Edessene elements in other prayers of the Divine Liturgy, in parts of the baptismal rite, and in the hymns of the divine office.

Living within the region of Antioch, the Maronites were also influenced by that tradition. With the establishment of the Maronite Patriarchate in Lebanon at the end of the seventh century, the Maronite Church adopted many Antiochene anaphoras and became a part of the Antiochene liturgical tradition. Besides the *Anaphora of Third Peter*, the Maronite Church employs the ancient Antiochene *Anaphora of the Twelve Apostles*, which became the foundation for the Byzantine *Anaphora of John Chrysostom*.

The first edition of the Maronite Missal was printed at Rome from 1592 to 1594. It contained some significant Latinizations. Instead of preserving the words of institution which differed in the various anaphoras, the words of institution of the Roman Missal were substituted in all the anaphoras of the Maronite Missal. The meaning of the *epiklesis* (invocation of the Holy Spirit) was changed. Rather than the celebrant invoking the Holy Spirit to transform the gifts into the body and blood of Christ, he prays that the effects of the Eucharist be applied to the faithful.

The most recent edition of the Missal was promulgated in 1992. It bears the title *The Book of Offering* (*Qorbono* in Syriac) *According to the Tradition of the Antiochene Syriac Maronite Church.* In this new edition all Latinizations and accretions have been removed. It contains six anaphoras. The traditional words of institution of the *Anaphora of the Twelve Apostles* have replaced those of the Roman rite in all the anaphoras. Also promulgated were a Book of Gospels and a Book of Epistles.

From its life in Lebanon over the centuries, the Maronite Church has also incorporated the poetry, prose, and music of the native culture and produced a rich legacy of festal rites, prayers, music, paraliturgical practices, and pious devotions. Alongside the simple, haunting melodies of Syriac chant are found the more polyphonic tones of Arabic music, and even a borrowing of European chants. The same may be said of religious art and architecture.

Bibliography: W. MACOMBER, "A Theory on the Origins of the Syrian, Maronite, and Chaldean Rites," *Orientalia Christiana Periodica* 39 (1973) 235–242. B. GEMAYEL, *Avant-Messe Maronite Orientalia Christiana Analecta.* v. 174 (Rome 1965). M. HAYEK, *Liturgie Maronite* (Paris 1964). S. BEGGIANI, *The Divine Liturgy of the Maronite Church* (New York 1998).

[S. BEGGIANI]

MAROZIA

An important figure in papal politics; fl. early tenth century. A member of the influential family of the CRESCENTII, she was the daughter of THEOPHYLACTUS, leader of the Roman nobility, and the elder THEODORA. If the reports of LIUTPRAND OF CREMONA (*Monumenta Germaniae Historica: Scriptores* 3:312) and the Liber pontificalis are accurate, she was the mistress of Pope SERGIUS III. She was married in turn to Alberic I, Marquess of Spoleto (*c.* 905); Guido, Marquis of Tuscany (925); and Hugh of Italy (932). This ambitious woman reached the zenith of her power over Rome and the papacy during the first three decades of the tenth century. She imprisoned Pope JOHN X in CASTEL SANT' ANGELO, where he died in 928 either by assassination (*Antapodosis* 3.45) or from other causes (*Annales Flodoardi* MGS 3.378). In 931 she

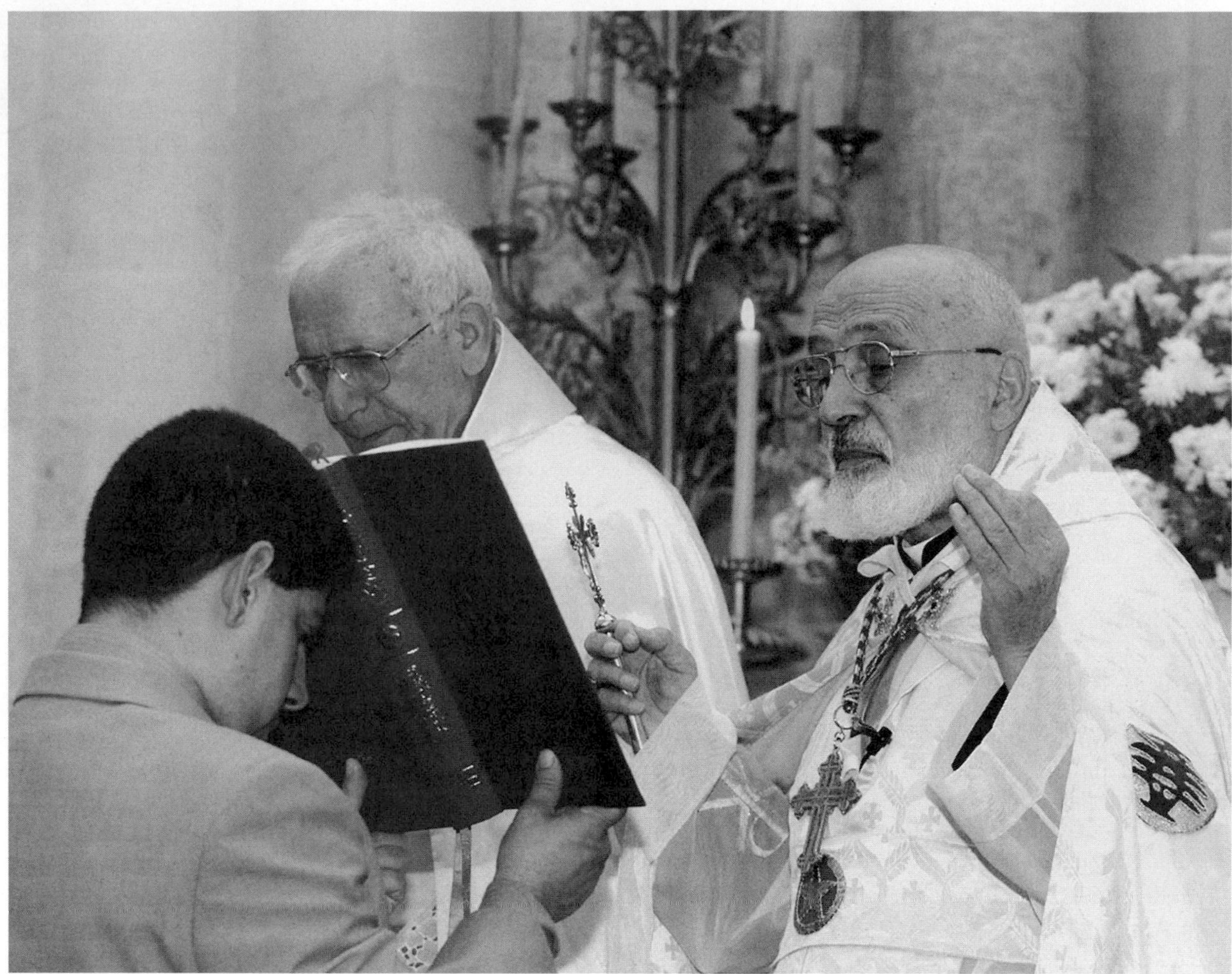

Lebanon's Maronite Christian Patriarch Nasrallah Sfeir (right) heads the Sunday Divine Liturgy at the Chapel of Bkerke in the mountains northeast of Beirut, November 26, 2000. (©APF/CORBIS)

had her son, probably by Sergius III (Duchesne, *Liber pontificalis* 2; 243), elected to the papacy as Pope JOHN XI. During an uprising of the Roman nobility (932) led by Alberic II, her son by her marriage to Alberic of Spoleto, she was captured and imprisoned in Castel Sant' Angelo. How she died is unknown.

Bibliography: L. BRÉHIER, *Dictionnaire d'histoire et de géographie ecclésiastiques* 1:1404–06. A. FLICHE, *L'Europe occidentale de 888 à 1125* (Histoire du moyen âge 2; Paris 1930) 54, 112, 113, 116, 120. A FLICHE and V. MARTIN, eds., *Histoire de l'église depuis les origines jusqu'à nos jours* 7:35–40. J. HALLER, *Der Papstitum* 2:201–202, 548–549. F. X. SEPPELT, *Geschichte der Päpste von dem Anfängen bis zur Mitte des 20.Jhr.* 2:354–356. *Cambridge Medieval History* 2d new ed., 3:151–154. P. VIARD, *Catholicisme* 6:480–482.

[H. DRESSLER]

MARQUETTE, JACQUES

Missionary and explorer; b. Laon, France, June 10, 1637; d. near Ludington, Mich., May 18–19, 1675. He entered the Jesuit novitiate at Nancy in 1654, studied philosophy and mathematics at the University of Pont-à-Mousson (1656–59, 1664–65), and taught at the Jesuit colleges of Reims (1659–61), Charleville (1661–63), and Langres (1663–64). Shortly after ordination at Toul, France, March 7, 1666, Marquette departed for the missions of New France, reaching Quebec on Sept. 20, 1666. The following month he set out for Trois Rivières to study Algonquian under Gabriel Druillettes, SJ. Three years later he assumed charge of the Holy Ghost mission at La Pointe, on the western end of Lake Superior, ministering to native peoples of numerous tribes—the Illinois, Pottawatamis, Foxes, Sioux, and others. When the Sioux routed his charges from La Pointe, Marquette founded a new mission for them at Michilimackinac (Mackinac), renamed by him Saint-Ignace. In 1673 he set out with Louis Jolliet on the expedition to explore the Mississippi River, during which they followed the shore of Lake Michigan to present-day De Pere, Wis., then ascended the Fox River, crossed overland to the Wisconsin, and at its mouth descended the Mississippi, which Marquette named River of the Conception (Rivière de la Conception), to the Arkansas River. The expedition furnished proof that the great river did not flow westward into the Gulf of California, but southward into the Gulf of Mexico. In accordance with the promise made to the Illinois native peoples on his first expedition, Marquette set out in November 1674 to found the mission of the Immaculate Conception, Ill., offering Mass there on Holy Thursday and Easter Sunday 1675. When serious illness befell him, he decided to return to Saint-Ignace, but died en route. A statue of Marquette by Trentanove is in the Hall of Fame of the Capitol, Washington, D.C.

See Also: STECK, FRANCIS BORGIA.

Bibliography: *Jesuit Relations,* ed. R. G. THWAITES, 73 v. (Cleveland 1896–1901). A. HAMY, *Au Mississippi: La Première exploration* (Paris 1903). C. DE ROCHEMONTEIX, *Les Jésuites et la Nouvelle-France au XVIIe siècle,* 3 v. (Paris 1895–96) v.3. J. DELANGLEZ, *Life and Voyages of Lords Jolliet* (Chicago 1948). "The Statue of Father Marquette in the National Capitol: Its Acceptance by the Senate," *Woodstock Letters* 25 (1896) 467–494. E. J. BURRUS "Father Jacques Marquette, S.J.: His Priesthood in the Light of the Jesuit Roman Archives," *Catholic Historical Review* 41 (1955) 257–271.

[E. J. BURRUS]

Jacques Marquette.

MARQUETTE LEAGUE

A mission society founded in New York City, May 1904, by Henry George Ganss, then chaplain (1890–1910) of the U.S. government Indian School at Carlisle, Pa. At the time of organization, it was decided that the league should be directed by a board of 25 members chosen from the councils of the St. Vincent de Paul Society. In the early 1960s, however, membership in a St. Vincent de Paul Society was no longer a requisite for membership in the board of directors, who were chosen from the general ranks of Catholic laity in the New York City and Brooklyn area. The purposes of the Marquette League were: to convert the indigenous people of the U.S. and to help preserve the faith among Catholic natives; to contribute to the support of native missions, mission schools, and chapels; to maintain trained catechists; and to improve the spiritual and physical condition of the Native American communities.

[M. MCDONNELL/EDS.]

MARRANOS

Opprobrious name given to those Jews (and, to a lesser degree, Muslims) of SPAIN and Portugal who, after being baptized under duress, practiced Judaism secretly while outwardly professing Catholicism. This crypto-Judaism was considered heretical by the Church, and the Inquisition was introduced to stamp it out. Three tragic centuries passed during which thousands died at the stake or were otherwise penanced before it disappeared. To the theologian, the Marranos posed the problem of the validity of so-called forced baptisms. The term Marrano came into popular use in the early 16th century, derived from the Spanish *marrano* (pig). The word does not appear in formal writings, in which the Marranos are called New Christians (*Nuevos Christianos*) or are simply referred to as converts (conversos).

Early History. A forerunner of Marranism is found in seventh-century Spain under the Visigoth kings, who presented the Jews with the alternative of Baptism or banishment. Many converted but Judaized secretly. The Councils of Toledo (third to 17th), A.D. 589 to 694, legislated that they must be forced to remain Christians. Again, during the First (1096–99) and Second (1147–49) CRUSADES many Jews were baptized under threat of death, but they later lapsed openly.

Marranism, however, as generally understood, dates from 1391 in Spain. During the 14th century the prosperity of Spain's highly integrated Jewry had become a source of scandal to the clergy and envy to the populace. The fanatical anti-Jewish preaching of Archdeacon Ferrand Martinez, whom neither king nor pope could silence, set off a wave of massacres in 1391, which swept over the Jewish communities of Spain. Faced with the option of death or Baptism, many Jews perished, but many more received Baptism. Estimates put the dead at 50,000 and the converts between 100,000 and 200,000. The number of the latter was further swelled by the impassioned preaching of St. VINCENT FERRER, who, passing from synagogue to synagogue with his followers, baptized about 35,000 Jews.

As things returned to normal, it became evident that not all the New Christians had broken with their former faith. Not all, of course, were insincere. Three categories are distinguishable: (1) the truly convinced, including many of Ferrer's converts; (2) lax Jews, who, having accepted Baptism from mere indifference, though insincere Catholics, could not be accused of Judaizing; (3) the Marranos properly speaking. Forced or frightened into the Church, but inwardly loyal to Judaism, the Marranos began to lead a double existence. Observing the externals of the Church and presenting their children for Baptism (which they ''washed off'' at home), they practiced Judaism whenever unobserved, abstaining from pork, observing Jewish holydays, circumcizing their children, etc. Throughout the 15th century, as evidences of their Judaizing multiplied, the pulpits rang out against them, and popular resentment rose. Why should these hypocrites, it was reasoned, enjoy high station unmolested, while professing Jews lived miserably because of their faith. Outbreaks, begun in 1449, culminated in the carnage of 1473–74, which fully matched the brutality that had occurred during 1391.

The Inquisition. It was now believed by many that one resort remained to restore order—the INQUISITION. The Church had always regarded Judaizers as heretics and hence subject to the discipline of the Church, and for several years the religious orders had been calling for the introduction of the Inquisition. It was formally established in 1478 by a bull of Sixtus IV under the auspices of Ferdinand and Isabella. The first AUTO-DA-FÉ (Act of Faith) was held in 1481 in Seville, where 12 Marranos were burned. Thus began the operations of the tribunal that for more than three centuries in all major Spanish cities condemned thousands of Marranos to confiscation, prison, penances, and burnings. In 1492, chiefly because of their ties with the Marranos, all Jews were expelled from Spain. About 100,000 of them crossed into Portugal, where, for a price, they were accepted. King Emanuel I (1495–1521), pressed by the Spanish monarchs to reexpel them but unwilling to forego the economic benefits they represented, literally drove them, along with their children, to the baptismal font.

Thus a new colony of Marranism was founded. The pattern set in Spain recurred: Marrano prosperity, popular resentment, massacres, and the introduction of the Inquisition. Proof of ''pure blood'' (*limpieza*) was required for admission to most professions in the Peninsula until the 18th century. Fugitives from the Iberian tribunals made their way to many European countries, to Turkey, North Africa, and the New World, thus forming a large Marrano DIASPORA. The Inquisition followed them to many of these places, even to the New World. At the end of the 19th century its task was complete: all Marranos had been exterminated or assimilated, with the surprising exception of numerous survivors discovered in northern Portugal in the 20th century.

Question of Marranos' Baptisms. The official policy of Judaism toward the Anusim (Heb. *'ănûsîm,* ''the forced'') was lenient. Since their conversions were considered unwilling, the *conversos* were looked upon as Jews. Renowned rabbis, such as Gershom Ben Judah (d. 1028) and RASHI (d. 1105), set the tradition of reinstating them without punishment or embarrassment. The attitude of the Church was not so simple. Pope Gregory I (590–604) had formulated the classical policy toward the Jews by prohibiting molestation of them or their worship and urging kindness and persuasion alone to convert them—a policy accepted in principle but not always observed in practice.

Baptisms elicited by force were always condemned; but when administered, they were deemed spontaneous and therefore valid and binding. For invalid ministration it was required that the recipient should have openly expressed opposition at the moment of reception, though at times this could mean instant death. The Councils of Toledo in the seventh century were rigorous in this respect. So also was Innocent III, who wrote in 1201: ''Whoever is led to Christianity by violence, by fear and torture . . . receives the imprint of Christianity and can be forced to observe the Christian faith'' (Potthast, *Bibliotheca historica medii aevi,* 1479). Not all popes were of this mind, however. Honorius I (625–638) apparently doubted the validity of such Baptisms and allowed Jews so converted to return to Judaism (*Patrologia Latina* 80:667–670). St. Thomas demonstrated the necessary role of intention and will in receiving Baptism (ST 3, 68.7) and concluded that ''since God does not force men to justification, it is clear that whoever approaches Baptism insincerely [*ficte*] does not receive its effects'' (ST 3, 69.9). Benedict XIV (1740–58) seems also to have been of this opinion, inasmuch as he considered Baptism received without sufficient understanding to be at least doubtfully valid (H. Denzinger, *Enchiridion symbolorum* 2558–62).

Contemporary theology takes a still dimmer view of Baptisms in which violence or ignorance is involved. More concerned with the subjective requirements of the Sacraments, it concedes a more decisive role to inner dispositions and free consent. In pastoral practice, converts from sects that have lost a clear notion of the supernatural must be rebaptized at least conditionally. The present Code of Canon Law requires for validity that the subject must be ''knowing and willing'' (*sciens et volens*). It is doubtful that the Baptisms of many Marranos would satisfy these standards.

Bibliography: C. ROTH, *A History of the Marranos* (New York 1959). F. BAER, *Die Juden im christlichen Spanien* (Berlin 1929). L. POLIAKOV, *Histoire de l'antisémitisme,* v. 2 *De Mahomet aux Marranes* (Paris 1961). B. BLUMENKRANZ, *Juifs et chrétiens dans le Monde Occidental* (Paris 1960) 97–158. H. ERHARTER, *Lexikon für Theologie und Kirche*, J. HOFER and K. RAHNER, eds. (Freiburg 1957–65) 7:106. E. H. FLANNERY, ''The Finaly Case,'' *The Bridge* 1 (New York 1955) 292–313.

[E. H. FLANNERY]

MARRIAGE ENCOUNTER

Marriage Encounter, both a program and a movement, is an opportunity for married couples to explore their lives in the presence of God. Although the term ''encounter'' signifies a confrontation or even a clash, Marriage Encounter (a literal translation of the Spanish *Encuentro Conjugal*) means ''to rediscover'' or ''to meet again.'' The program, which usually takes place on a weekend, helps couples to search for and rediscover their vision of love. With this program, God's presence is essential, because the gift of love given by the couple becomes fruitful only in God's presence through the discovery of the place of God within their lives. This belief, then, underlies Marriage Encounter's conviction of the sacredness of the covenant, the Sacrament, of marriage. Fr. Gabriel Calvo, the founder of Mariage Encounter, puts it this way: ''There is within each couple a divine energy of love. It has to be released by a deep sharing between husband and wife, through the communication of their feelings and of the whole of their lives together. It cannot be done in just one moment.''

The Marriage Encounter weekend provides the first moment for this release of the energy of love. During the weekend, the couples have the opportunity to search their own lives for their feelings, dreams, and desires. As they share, the Lord's presence enables the release of the energy of love. Also, as they share, they come to the discovery of God's vision for marriage, which, simply stated, is a call to become united with each other and with God.

Marriage Encounter has its origins in Spain in 1953 through the combined efforts of Fr. Calvo and several married couples (Mercedes and Jamie Ferrer; José and Marguerite Pick; Diego and Fina Bartimeo). The inspiration of the ''Marriage Teams of Pope Pius XII'' came from the weekly talks then being given by Pope Pius XII to newly married couples in Rome. Fr. Calvo and the couples would first read the pope's talk, along with several verses from Scripture. Then, after searching their own individual life's experience, each couple would meet to share their reflections. Afterwards, the couples would meet as a group and share these common reflections to deepen their commitment to marriage and the family. The papal talks and the reflections that flowed out of them eventually became the core topics for the presentations that are still given on Marriage Encounter weekends. The first *Encuentro Conjugal* was held in Barcelona in 1962. The program began in the U.S. in 1967, under the aegis of the Christian Family Movement. Marriage Encounter has also spread in Latin America, Europe, Africa, Oceania and Asia.

Within this initial group was also developed the method of communicating—a presentation based on the experience of life, a reflection on each individual's life experience, followed by a mutual sharing of this individual reflection. This is the method of dialogue as it is now practiced within Marriage Encounter, as well as such other offshoots as Family Encounter, *Retorno*, Priests' Encounter. The method is best summarized in another statement of Fr. Calvo: ''There is no unity without reconciliation. There is no reconciliation without communication. There is no communication without first encountering (discovering) oneself.''

Marriage Encounter has had a powerful impact on thousands of couples and enabled them to renew their commitment to marriage as a ministry. Because of Marriage Encounter, these same couples who in the past saw their lives more as confusion, now see their marriages as the means for grace and life for themselves and others. Inspired by this vision, they acquire a new understanding of the Gospel and its meaning for everyday life. Ultimately, however, the final goal of Marriage Encounter is much broader than the couples themselves. There is a natural outflow of love from the couple to family, relatives, friends and, finally, to the larger communities of Church and society. Through the gift of self, there occurs an inner conversion both in the individual and the couple. This conversion becomes the basis of understanding and acceptance, out of which flows the unity of love. Marriage

Encounter presents its method as a free sharing which can be accepted or rejected. Marriage Encounter helps a couple to explore their experience of life. As they share this individual experience, they begin a journey, a search toward unity with each other and with the wider community in order to build together the new creation promised by Jesus Christ. Together, couples and their families join in a new Exodus toward the promised land which will be built on the foundation of love they have rediscovered.

See Also: WORLDWIDE MARRIAGE ENCOUNTER.

[T. HILL/J. J. KAISING]

MARRIAGE LEGISLATION (CANON LAW)

The valid law of Matrimony found in the 1983 Code of CANON LAW, is significantly different from that of the 1917 Code. The inspiration for the change derives from the documents of Vatican Council II. *The Pastoral Constitution on the Church in the Modern World* (*Gaudium et spes*) which proclaimed marriage to be a covenant or *foedus*, ordered for the mutual help of the spouses and for the procreation and education of children. Other important documents, such as the *Decree on Ecumenism* (*Unitatis redintegratio*), which acknowledged the existence of Christian churches and ecclesiastical communities outside of the Catholic Church, the *Declaration on Religious Freedom* (*Dignitatis humanae*), which upheld the value of the individual conscience, and above all, the *Dogmatic Constitution on the Church* (*Lumen gentium*), which declared the universal call of the faithful to holiness, no matter what their state of life, each had its specific impact on the 1983 legislation on marriage. Each took a major step toward the integration of canonical traditions with the vision of the council. For detailed information about the 1983 law on marriage, a commentary should be consulted, but the spirit of the 1983 norms can be summed up in a few points.

Significant Changes. The law has been inserted into a broader theological context. Since the 12th century, canon law has used the model of Roman consensual contract to define marriage. Now the principal model is Yahweh's covenant (alliance) with his people, or Christ's union with his Church. The idea of ''religious covenant'' dominates the definition of marriage and provides an important hermeneutical principle for the interpretation of the new body of laws: their full and correct meaning can be grasped only if they are read and explained in their proper theological context. Although the Code continues to use the term ''contract,'' it no longer regards it as an adequate description of Christian marriage.

The doctrine of a hierarchy of ends has been abandoned. Previously, the law viewed procreation and education of children as the primary ends of marriage; mutual help and remedy of concupiscence were its secondary purpose. In practice, however, it gave much greater importance and support to the former than to the latter. The new code presents marriage as ordered to the same ends, but it does not grant priority to either of them, although interestingly, it does treat of mutual help first (c. 1055). This shift in the understanding of ends echoes throughout the marriage canons: the importance of a close union, *consortium*, between the spouses has been given new prominence in the legal order.

There is a new openness in the law towards the findings of empirical psychology. This is most obvious in the rule that those who lack the capacity, due to psychological causes, to fulfill their matrimonial obligations cannot contract validly, (cf. c. 1095n.3). While canon law is competent to define the obligations, it has no competence to discover the psychological causes of the inability to fulfill the obligations. For this it must turn to the science of medicine.

The law is animated by new ecumenical spirit. Mixed religion is no longer an impediment to marriage, hence no dispensation is required for a Catholic to marry a non-Catholic Christian, although a more easily obtainable permission is still necessary. The Catholic party alone should make the promise that the Children will be educated in the Catholic faith, but he or she is bound by such a promise ''as far as it can be done'' (*pro viribus*), that is, without doing violence to the conscience of the non-Catholic partner. Further, in the case of a ''mixed marriage'' the local ordinary can grant a dispensation from the canonical form, provided the marriage will be celebrated in some public form. The invalidating impediment of ''disparity of cult'' (marriage between a Catholic and a non-baptized person) remains, but once the necessary dispensation has been granted, analogous accommodations can be made regarding the baptism and education of the children and the celebration of the marriage.

The new law is simpler than the old, and the number of impediments have been reduced. There are no prohibiting impediments any more; 12 invalidating impediments remain, but the scope of several of them has been diminished. The dispensing power of the local ordinary has also been extended. The rules for the celebration of the marriage (e.g., place and time) are now much simpler; and it is easier to delegate a priest stranger to the parish or the diocese to receive the consent of the parties.

In general, the 1983 code represents a shift towards a more personalistic and less institutional approach to marriage. The old law was conceived with the goal of protecting the indissolubility of marriage even if that meant little attention would be paid to the personal disposition of the parties, such as their mistaken knowledge, their acting under duress, or their lack of maturity. The new law continues to uphold the permanency of marital commitment, but it goes a long way toward providing remedies in case of misguided or defective consent.

The complexity of the procedural norms in nullity cases have been reduced. Provided the diocesan tribunals take advantage of the new rules, the ''trials'' can be made more expeditious. The law allows the judges to give more weight to the depositions of the parties, and in exceptional circumstances it allows one (not three, as usual) judge to conduct the case and to decide it. It also permits the substitution of a ''review'' of the first sentence instead of a formal trial by an appellate court.

Remaining Uncertainties. On balance the 1983 code as a whole is a significant improvement over the 1917 code. Some notable problems, however, remain. Christian marriages are not distinguished with sufficient clarity from natural marriages. The result is that the unique character and effects of the sacramental covenant between the parties, and between God and the couple, remain obscured. This leads to some ambivalence, e.g., the code states that all marriages are indissoluble, yet it provides ways and means to dissolve any natural marriage ''for the sake of the faith''; methodologically it would have been better to speak of the indissolubility of the Christian covenant only.

The drafters of the new law did not find a solution for the case of the baptized unbelievers. According to sound theology, faith is necessary for the valid reception of a Sacrament. According to canon law, the reception of the Sacrament is necessary for the valid marriage of baptized persons, believers or not. This divergence between doctrine and law creates an absurd situation: the Church appears to be forcing the Sacrament on unbelievers.

The code displays an uneasy and precarious compromise between the principles of medieval metaphysical psychology and the findings of modern empirical psychiatry. Scholastic philosophy based on Aristotle's theories assumes a much sharper distinction between the ''faculties of the soul'' (that is, between the mind and the will) than the modern student of the human psyche accepts. Yet, the validity of a marriage must be determined, to a significant extent, by applying the ancient conceptions. The result is an uneven administration of justice.

There is still more centralization than necessary. For no apparent theological reason, most of the ordinary cases of the ''privilege of the faith'' cannot be handled by the diocesan bishop but must be submitted to the Holy See, which usually means expense and delay. The law offers no assurance of the speedy resolution of nullity cases, and the parties have no remedy in case of delays. The result is again an uneven administration of justice, depending on local circumstances. In general, the procedure still remains cumbersome, demanding an outlay in personnel, energy, and money that many churches, especially in developing countries, can ill afford.

Bibliography: J. P. BEAL et. al., eds. *The New Commentary on the Code of Canon Law* (New York 2000). T. MACKIN, *Marriage in the Catholic Church: Divorce and Remarriage* (New York 1984). R. MALONE and J. R. CONNERY, eds., *Contemporary Perspectives on Christian Marriage: Propositions and Papers from the International Theological Commission* (Chicago 1984). L. ORSY, *Marriage in Canon Law: Text and Comments, Reflections and Questions* (Wilmington, Del. 1986), B. A. SIEGLE, *Marriage According to the New Code of Canon Law* (New York 1986). L. WRENN, *Annulments* (4th rev. ed. Wash., D.C. 1983). I. GRAMUNT, J. HERVADA and L. WAUCK, *Canons and Commentaries on Marriage* (Collegeville 1987). L. WRENN, *The Invalid Marriage* (Washington, DC 1998). R. M. SABLE, ed. *Incapacity for Marriage: Jurisprudence and Interpretation* (Rome 1987).

[L. M. ORSY/EDS.]

MARROQUÍN, FRANCISCO

First bishop of Central America; b. probably in valley of Toranzo, Santander, Spain, 1477; d. Guatemala City, April 18, 1563. In November 1528, already ordained, he arrived in Mexico City with Bishop-elect ZUMÁRRAGA, who named him his first vicar-general. As such, Marroquín acted with great firmness at the time of the riot in the cathedral on Pentecost, May 16, 1529. The riot had been begun by the members of the royal court and their leader Nuño de Guzmán when Zumárraga had their cruelties against the native Mexicans publicly condemned. Marroquín excommunicated all of them. Because this action imperiled his life, Marroquín was sent by Zumárraga shortly thereafter to Central America as provost for Guatemala, Honduras, and El Salvador. His first task was to learn the languages of the indigenous people of his new jurisdiction. He welcomed Dominicans (1535) fleeing from Peru and brought Mercedarians (1537) from Mexico City and Franciscans (1540) from Spain. Marroquin personally taught the native languages to his priests and friars.

On April 7, 1537, Zumárraga consecrated him bishop of Guatemala: the first episcopal consecration in the New World. Using largely his own funds, Marroquín began the construction of churches and a cathedral, set up dowries for poor girls, and in 1553, a special school for Spanish orphan girls. In 1559 he tried to get royal permission to found a university. When this project failed, he founded the Colegio de Santo Tomás with the Dominicans. In his will he set aside generous sums for the future university. As bishop, Marroquín was protector of the indigenous people and to this task he devoted his best efforts. He often freed those unjustly enslaved and endowed them with lands to support themselves. He promoted the plan of the Dominicans to evangelize Tezulutlan through peaceful means. Marroquín, however, was far from an admirer of bishop Bartolomé de LAS CASAS and his impetuous methods and put his criticisms on record in a famous letter to the king, which the friends of Las Casas usually quietly ignore. In general, Marroquín tried to integrate the indigenous people in the spiritual, economic, and social life of the young colony.

Bibliography: F. A. DE FUENTES Y GUZMÁN, *Recordación florida: Discurso historial y demostración natural, material, militar y política del Reyno de Guatemala,* 3 v. (Guatemala 1932–33). L. LAMADRID, ''Bishop Marroquín-Zumárraga's Gift to Central America,'' *Americas* 5 (1948–49) 331–341.

[L. LAMADRID]

MARSEILLES

Marseilles is the chief seaport of France on the Mediterranean; capital of Bouches-du-Rhône department; and since 1948 seat of an archbishopric (*Massiliensis*) immediately subject to the Holy See.

City. Founded *c.* 600 B.C. by a Greek colony from Phocaea and taken by Julius Caesar in 49 B.C., it was a Gallo-Roman *civitas* occupied by Visigoths (480), Burgundians, and THEODORIC THE GREAT (507–537), and finally ceded to the Frankish kingdom. In 879 it was incorporated into the kingdom of Boso, later the kingdom of Arles. In feudal times it was divided among the seigneuries of the bishop, viscount, and Abbey of Saint-Victor. Louis of Anjou conquered it (1246), and Louis XI annexed it to the crown of France (1486). Rebuilding in the 17th century increased its area from 161 to 482 acres. Trade with the Levant made it rich, and in the 19th century it became an industrial city and France's main port.

Marseilles must have known Christianity early through its contact with the East, but its first bishop was not LAZARUS, risen from the dead in the Gospels, as 12th-century legends say (*see* AIX). A 2d-century inscription seems to be its oldest relic of Christianity. It probably had a bishop in the 3d century, but Oresius at the Council of Arles (314) is the first-known bishop. Marseilles had several famous priests and religious *c.* 400, including SALVIAN and John CASSIAN, who founded there *c.* 415 the oldest and most famous monastery in Gaul, SAINT-VICTOR, through which Eastern spirituality entered the West. The writer GENNADIUS died there *c.* 500.

Saracen raids and the establishment of a Saracen military colony on the coast of Provence ruined Marseilles. During the obscure period from the 6th to the 10th century, the bishops are said to have left the city for the Abbey of Saint-Victor; at least they administered the abbey's goods. Bishop and viscount divided the city *c.* 1069, and the walled episcopal part became a fortress. The Cathedral of Notre-Dame-la-Majeure, outside the walls from the 6th century (almost the only such instance known), was rebuilt *c.* 1150 in Romanesque within the bishop's quarter. In 1257 the bishop had to cede his seigneurial rights over the city to Charles of Anjou, but in 1275 he still regarded himself as a subject of the emperor.

As a military port, Marseilles was a center of galley slaves. St. VINCENT DE PAUL performed a mission of charity among them (1622) and contributed to a hospital founded for them (1643). The 19th century brought a profound change in the religious life of the city. Napoleon's fall was regarded as a blessing; his continental system had ruined trade. The city became legitimist, afire with a traditional and exuberant Catholicism. Caulkers and stevedores formed brotherhoods; there were penitents, and a mission in 1820 had great success. The episcopacies of the Mazenods (1823–37, 1837–61) were conservative, after the Old Regime. Then the population increased, and a new bourgeoisie, less faithful, arose; but the masses kept their faith, however little they practiced it (12 to 15 percent in 1953).

Archdiocese. From the 4th century Marseilles, the chief Greek colony in Provence, acted like a metropolitan. Its bishop created the Diocese of Nice, another Greek colony but not a Roman *civitas;* installed a bishop in Toulon; and then in the 5th century tried to do the same in two nearby villages, Cithariste and Garguier, dependent on the *civitas* of ARLES but cared for by Marseilles. Arles protested this invasion of its rights, and the papacy intervened. Marseilles had to yield, but these quarrels filled the whole episcopacy of Proculus (380–428), who at the Council of Turin (398) secured recognition of himself, for life, as a metropolitan (of *Narbonensis II*?). Pope Zosimus, however, withdrew the rights and finally forbade him to exercise his episcopal functions (417–418). But Proculus did as he wished and died (428) in the peaceful possession of his see. The incident shows Rome's wish to judge as a final court of appeal and to fix metropolitan boundaries according to civil provinces. Its metropolitanate ended, Marseilles had to content itself with being a suffragan of Arles. It was the only diocese in Gaul to be almost entirely urban.

Marseilles' bishops include: Honoratus I (*d.c.* 500), who wrote a vita of St. HILARY OF ARLES; the doubtful St. Cannas; St. Theodore (566–591), who was involved in the intrigues and quarrels of Frankish kings; William Sudre (1361–66), cardinal legate of Urban V; Philip Ca-

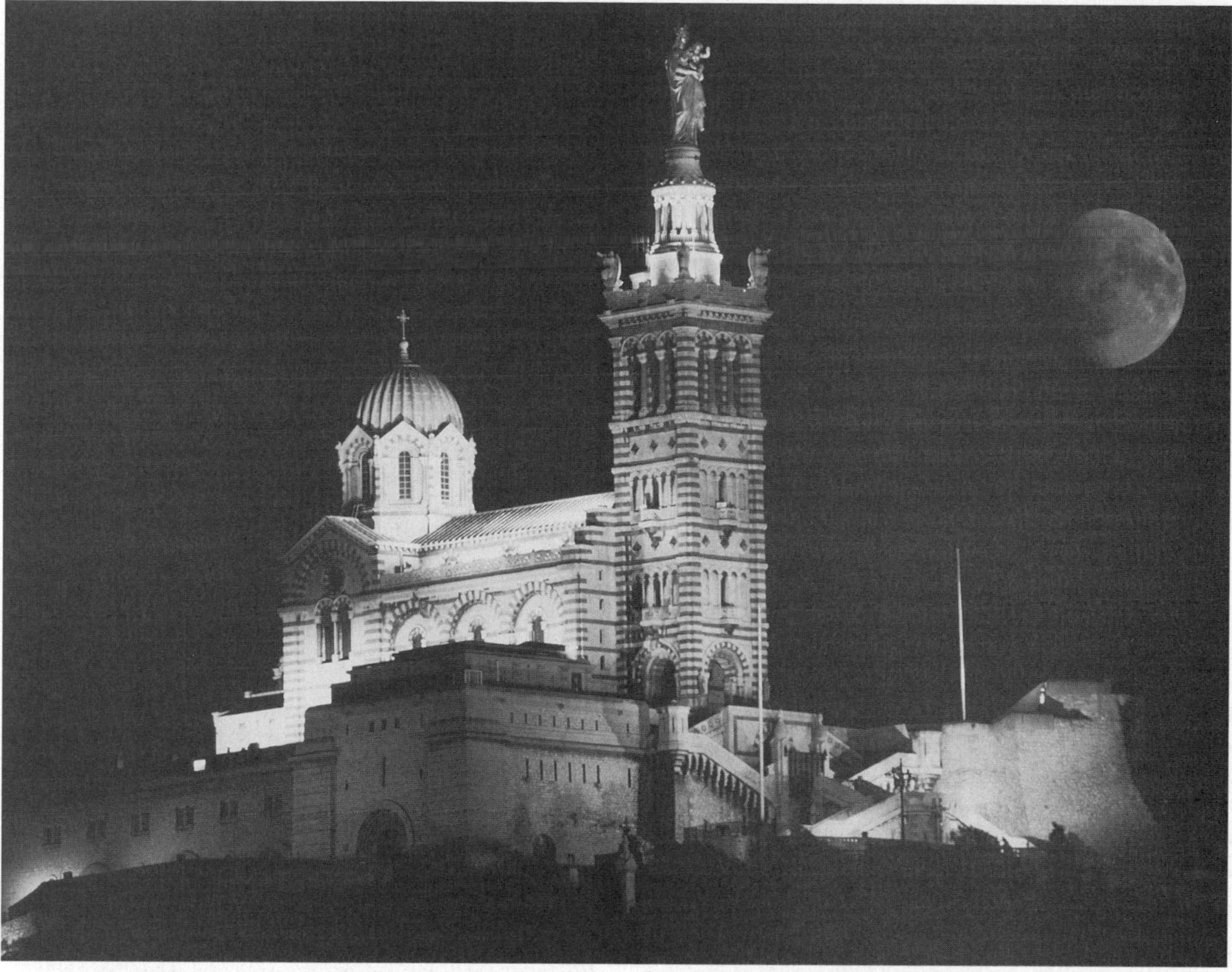

Notre-Dame de la Garde. (©Michael Freeman/CORBIS)

bassole (1366–68), who performed many missions for the popes of Avignon and was patriarch of Jerusalem, cardinal, *rector* of the county of Venaissin, and the friend and patron of PETRARCH; the Oratorian Jean-Baptiste Gault (1642–43), who in his four months in Marseilles made a lasting impression by his active and personal charity to galley slaves and by his care to restore the holiness of the priestly life; and Henri de BELSUNCE (1709–55), a converted Protestant and adversary of the Jansenists, whose heroic charity during the plague of 1720 and 1721 was marked by his consecration of the city to the Sacred Heart and who never left his diocese, of which he wrote a history. Suppressed as a suffragan of Arles by the CONCORDAT OF 1801, the see was restored in 1822 as a suffragan of Aix with its present borders (250 square miles).

Bernard, abbot of Saint-Victor (1065–79), was the legate of Gregory VII to the Diet of Forcheim (1077). St. ELZÉAR OF SABRAN (1286–1323) and his wife St. Delphine (1284–1360) were canonized by their nephew Urban V in 1369. Several modern programs for the education of youth prospered under the direction of priests [Fathers Allemand (1772–1836) and Caire]. Father Timon-David (1823–91) from 1847 to his death inspired the Work of Youth for the Working Class with the need for a deeply Christian life. The Work, which educated 15,000 children, had 17 affiliates during his lifetime.

Marseilles' monuments include Saint-Victor (11th century), the old cathedral (12th–15th century), and the new Byzantine style cathedral (1852–93). Its great shrine is the Romanesque Notre-Dame de la Garde (1214) on a hill overlooking the city. There are pilgrimages to Notre-Dame du Château, to Allauch, to Notre-Dame de Toussaint, and to Ste.-Marthe.

Bibliography: ALBANÈS and CHEVALIER, *Gallia christiana novi ssima: Marseilles* (Valence 1899). *Les Bouches-du-Rhône: Encyclopédie départementale,* 17 v. (Marseilles 1913–37). P. BROUTIN, *La Réforme pastorale en France au XVIIe siècle,* 2 v. (Tournai 1956). J. B. DUROSELLE, *Les Débuts du catholicisme social en*

France (1822–1870) (Paris 1951). J. LEFLON, *Eugène de Mazenod, Bishop of Marseilles, Founder of the Oblates of Mary Immaculate,* tr. F. D. FLANAGAN (New York 1961–), with recent bibliog. L. H. LABANDE, ''L'Église de Marseille et l'abbaye de Saint-Victor à l'époque Carolingienne,'' in *Mélanges F. Lot* (Paris 1925) 307–329. H. LECLERCQ, *Dictionnaire d'archéologie chrétienne et de liturgie,* ed. F. CABROL, H. LECLERCQ, and H. I. MARROU, 15 v. (Paris 1907–53) 10.2:2204–93; 8.2:2044–86. L. GROS, *La Pratique religieuse dans le Diocese de Marseille* (Marseilles 1954). O. ENGELS and L. VOEKL, *Lexikon für Theologie und Kirche*, ed. J. HOFER and K. RAHNER 10 v. (2d, new ed. Freiburg 1957–65); 7:107–108. *Annuario Pontificio* (1965) 265.

[E. JARRY]

MARSILIUS OF INGHEN

Scholastic philosopher and theologian; b. near Nijmegen, Holland, *c.* 1330; d. Heidelberg, Aug. 20, 1396. A disciple of JOHN BURIDAN, he taught arts at Paris with notable success and was twice elected rector (1367, 1371). In 1377 he represented the English nation of the university at Avignon. He was again in Avignon in 1378 and traveled to Italy. Studying theology at Paris, he became a master before 1382. When the University of Heidelberg was founded in 1385 by Urban VI, he was appointed its first rector and began lecturing in 1386. Through his efforts Heidelberg quickly became a center of nominalism and a cultural influence in Germany.

In logic he followed the *via moderna* of WILLIAM OF OCKHAM, denying the reality of UNIVERSALS and the traditional meaning of *suppositio simplex,* which he classified under material supposition. His nominalist revision of the *Summulae logicales* of Peter of Spain was published many times under the title of *Textus dialectices* (Vienna 1512, 1516, etc.) and used as a text in many German universities. He also commented on the *Prior Analytics* of Aristotle (Venice 1516).

In natural philosophy he followed Buridan rather than Ockham, teaching the new theory of IMPETUS to explain projectile motion and acceleration. He also adopted the graphic coordinate method of describing intension and remission of forms proposed by NICHOLAS ORESME. Because of the condemnation of Latin AVERROISM in 1277, he admitted the possibility of infinite magnitudes and of rectilinear movement of the universe as a whole. Accepting the proportions of velocities proposed by THOMAS BRADWARDINE, he combined the Mertonian *calculationes* with the new Parisian physics in his commentaries on Aristotle's *Physics* (Lyons 1518), *De generatione et corruptione* (Strasbourg 1501), and in his *Abbreviationes libri physicorum* (Venice 1521).

In his *Quaestiones supra quatuor libros sententiarum* (Strasbourg 1501) he was less skeptical than Ockham regarding the ability of reason to prove the existence of God, preferring the arguments of DUNS SCOTUS. However, since nothing can come from nothing, he insisted that philosophy cannot demonstrate the creation of the universe from nothing. Regarding free will, he followed Buridan in teaching a modified determinism, insisting that the will is not always free to choose. With ALBERT OF SAXONY, he promoted nominalism in German universities.

Bibliography: G. RITTER, *Studien zur Spätscholastik,* v.1 of *Marsilius von Inghen und die ockhamistische Schule in Deutschland* (Heidelberg 1921). J. HANSLMEIER, in *Lexikon für Theologie und Kirche,* ed. J. HOFER and K. RAHNER, 10 v. (2d new ed. Freiburg 1957–65); supplement, *Das Zweite Vatikanische Konzil: Dokumente und Kommentare,* ed. H. S. BRECHTER et al., part 1 (1966) 7:108. B. NARDI, *Enciclopedia filosofica,* 4 v. (Venice-Rome 1957) 3:330. A. C. CROMBIE, *Augustine to Galileo: The History of Science, A.D. 400–1650* (Cambridge, MA 1953). M. CLAGETT, *The Science of Mechanics in the Middle Ages* (Madison, WI 1959).

[A. MAURER]

MARSILIUS OF PADUA

Medieval political philosopher; b. Padua, Italy, probably between 1275 and 1280, the son of a Paduan notary.

Life. The details of his early life are obscure. It seems likely that he began his education at the University of Padua and subsequently studied medicine and philosophy at Paris. Certainly he was rector of the University of Paris in 1313, and he was teaching there in 1324 when he completed his one major work, a treatise called *Defensor pacis* (crit. ed. R. Scholz, Hanover 1932–33, and C. W. Previté-Orton, Cambridge, Eng. 1928; Eng. tr. A. Gewirch, New York 1956). This book was vehemently antipapal in tone, and when Marsilius's authorship of it became known he was forced to leave Paris. He took refuge at the court of the German king, Louis IV of Bavaria, who was engaged in a dispute with Pope JOHN XXII.

In 1327 Marsilius accompanied Louis on an expedition into Italy. The imperial forces occupied Rome early in 1328 and a series of assemblies of the Roman people was held (a procedure entirely in accordance with Marsilius's political theories). These assemblies acclaimed Louis as emperor, denounced the pope as a heretic, and approved the installation of an antipope. Marsilius himself was appointed vicar of Rome and vigorously persecuted the clergy who remained loyal to Pope John. Within a few months, however, the Roman mob turned against its new emperor and Louis was forced to leave Rome. Marsilius accompanied him back to Germany and spent the rest of his life at the imperial court. In 1342 he produced a brief treatise entitled *Defensor minor,* in the main a restatement of the conclusions of the earlier book. He died a few months after completing this work.

Teaching. Marsilius grew up at a time when the political role of the popes was a matter of intense controversy. During the 13th century the theory of a universal temporal dominion inhering in the papacy had come to be stated more and more explicitly by canonists, theologians, and popes. Some reaction against such a claim was natural and, perhaps, desirable. But with Marsilius the reaction was carried to a point where he advocated a radical secularism and denied to the pope any legitimate jurisdiction, even in ecclesiastical matters. The *Defensor pacis* was divided into three books. The first presented a philosophy of the state; the second, a theology of the church; and the third, a brief summary of conclusions.

In Book one Marsilius followed Aristotle in asserting that the state existed to enable men ''to live and live well.'' The only authority competent to enact law for the state, he maintained, was a *legislator humanus* composed of ''the whole body of citizens or the weightier part (*pars valentior*) thereof'' (1.12.3). This was because laws were made to promote civil justice and the common welfare, and the whole body of citizens was the best judge of the common utility of a law. Moreover, ''That law is better observed by every citizen which each one seems to have imposed upon himself . . .'' (1.12.6). Marsilius held that, for the preservation of peace, there had to be one single supreme ''governing part'' to enforce the law, and he insisted that it should be chosen by the whole community. Powers of government could be vested in one man or several and a people might even choose to install a line of hereditary monarchs, but, whatever the precise form adopted, legitimacy of government depended on popular consent. A ruler who persistently violated the laws established by the community was to be deposed and punished.

Book two is strikingly different in tone and in manner of argument. The author began by rebuking the papacy for its ''ardent desire for rulership'' (2.1.1), and, against the papal claims to temporal power, he quoted texts such as Jn 18.36, ''My kingdom is not of this world.'' According to Marsilius, Christ conferred on the Apostles only a power to administer Sacraments, not coercive jurisdiction of any kind. Marsilius would have liked to see the Church stripped of all its power, privileges, and property. His argument went even further, however, for he attacked root and branch the whole Petrine theory of papal primacy and indeed the whole conception of any divinely ordained hierarchical structure in the church. All the Apostles shared equally the same priestly power, he maintained, and Peter was given no jurisdiction over the rest. In any case, the bishops of Rome were not necessarily successors to any authority that might have inhered in Peter.

It remained true that there was a need for some regulation of ecclesiastical affairs. Marsilius argued, therefore, that the same *legislator humanus* (the whole community) that appointed the civil government should also control ecclesiastical appointments. All candidates for ordination as priests were to be selected by the community; so were the bishops. If a community wished to punish religious unorthodoxy, it was for the community to enact appropriate legislation and for the civil government to enforce it. If doubtful matters of faith had to be decided, the appropriate tribunal was a general council in which laity as well as clerics were represented. And, again, the summoning of such a council pertained to the *legislator* or an official to whom the legislator had delegated this authority (Marsilius had in mind the emperor). It was these views on the structure of the Church, not the preceding political argumentation, that John XXII condemned as heretical.

Critique. The significance of Marsilius's contribution to political theory has been sharply debated in modern times. He has been regarded as both a forerunner of modern democracy and a prophet of the modern totalitarian state. Some scholars argue that Marsilius rejected the whole preceding tradition of a rational natural law to substitute instead the theory that the will of a sovereign people was the sole source of law. Others point out that Marsilius did require law to conform to principles of justice and that he approvingly quoted Aristotle's dictum, ''Law is reason without desire'' (1.11.4). The view of Marsilius as a radical democrat cannot be sustained since he explicitly stated that the quality of persons as well as their numbers should be considered in determining the ''weightier part'' of a community. On the other hand, his insistence that rulers had to govern according to the law indicates that he was not intending to propound a theory of political absolutism. Marsilius's theory of the state was in fact firmly rooted in the earlier tradition of medieval constitutionalism. If it contains elements of thought that seem strikingly modern that is perhaps because the jurists and philosophers who preceded Marsilius had already begun to formulate the concepts of law and sovereignty that would be developed into the theory of the modern state. Marsilius certainly selected for emphasis just those ideas that would be most important in the future.

The very bitter antipapal polemics in Book two were of course far removed from the main stream of earlier medieval thought, though one can find anticipations of them among the Spiritual Franciscans and the legists of Philip the Fair. These views retained a considerable notoriety during the next two centuries. Several Catholic critics of Luther accused him of espousing the heresies of Marsilius, and the *Defensor pacis* was translated into English in 1536 to provide ideological support for the policies of Henry VIII.

Bibliography: C. K. BRAMPTON, ''Marsiglio of Padua: Life,'' *English Historical Review* 37 (1922) 501–515. R. W. and A. J. CARLYLE, *A History of Mediaeval Political Theory in the West,* 6 v. Edinburgh 1903–36; repr. New York 1953). A. GERWITH, *Marsilius of Padua: The Defender of the Peace,* 2 v. (New York 1951–56); ''John of Jandun and the *Defensor Pacis,*'' *Speculum* 23 (1948) 267–272. E. LEWIS, ''The 'Positivism' of Marsiglio of Padua,'' *ibid.* 38 (1963) 541–582.

[B. TIERNEY]

MARTÍ, MARIANO

Spanish bishop and educator; baptized Bafrim, Tarragona, Spain, Dec. 14, 1721; d. Caracas, 1792. The details of Martí's life are sketchy and hard to obtain. He was the son of a rural physician of Bafrim. He studied in the provincial seminary and took the doctorate in civil and Canon Law at the University of Cervera, no longer in existence. He was vicar-general of the archbishopric of Tarragona in 1761 when his name was suggested by the King of Spain for the See of Puerto Rico, left vacant on the death of Bp. Pedro Martínez de Oneca. As soon as the appointment was confirmed, Martí left for his diocese and he was consecrated on Jan. 17, 1762, in La Guaira, Venezuela, by Bp. Diego Antonio Díez Madroñero, to whose see Martí succeeded eight years later. In Puerto Rico he began his pastoral visits almost at once. On Nov. 26, 1763, he was in Arecibo and on Jan. 17, 1764, in Coamo and Río Piedras. The report of that visit, no longer available, contained important statistical data indicating that the island had 6,440 citizens and 46,197 residents. Martí gave special attention to the problem of education. By a decree of 1764, schools were established in Bayamó and Guaynabo and, according to Cuesta Mendoza, he was responsible for starting schools in 20 other towns on the island. The same year he began his visits to the overseas territories of the diocese: Trinidad, Margarita Island, and the vast expanse of eastern Venezuela, which later became part of the Diocese of Guiana. On Aug. 19, 1764, he arrived in Cumaná and on March 18, 1766, in Nueva Guayana or Angostura (now Ciudad Bolívar), Venezuela. In June he returned to Cumaná and then to Margarita where he survived an earthquake on Oct. 21, 1766. He stayed on the island until May 1767, possibly helping to repair the ravages of the disaster. Unfortunately the report of this visit has not been preserved. In poor health because of his arduous journeys, he renounced the episcopacy. The king would not accept the resignation, but instead ordered the Council of the Indies to find another diocese for Martí. On Dec. 9, 1768, he signed a confidential report on the clergy of Puerto Rico. The bishop of Caracas died on Feb. 3, 1769, and Martí was appointed in November to succeed him; he arrived in Caracas in June 1770 to take possession of the diocese. More is known of his work in Venezuela than of that in Puerto Rico. While he was bishop, part of the diocese was separated to form the bishopric of Mérida. During his 21 years in Caracas, Martí ordained 532 priests. His most memorable accomplishment was the pastoral visit that took from 1771 to 1784. A monument to his untiring zeal and spirit of sacrifice, the visit also supplied the most complete collection of geographical, demographical, statistical, and artistic data on Venezuela at that time. Martí's extant works are: the final *Relación;* the *Compendio;* manuscripts of two volumes of administrative suggestions and five volumes of inventories; and his ''personal'' or ''secret'' papers, which contain valuable confidential reports and references.

Bibliography: J. SURIA, *El eximo prelado doctor Mariano Martí, obispo de Caracas y Venezuela* (Caracas 1962). A. CUESTA, MENDOZA, *Historia de la educación en el Puerto Rico colonial,* 2 v. (Mexico 1946–48).

[L. G. CANEDO]

MARTIALL, JOHN (MARSHALL)

Controversialist; b. Daylesford, Worchestershire, 1534; d. Lille, France, April 3, 1597. He was educated at Winchester and at New College, Oxford, where he graduated as a bachelor of civil law in 1556. He left a teaching post at Winchester in 1560 and joined the group of English religious exiles studying at Louvain. He dedicated his *Treatise of the Cross* (Antwerp 1564) to Queen Elizabeth, who retained a crucifix in the royal chapel. Martiall wrote a reply to James Calfhill's attack on his work (Louvain 1566) and was corrector for the press of Thomas Harding's *Answer to Jewell's Challenge* (1566). He later received a bachelor of divinity degree at DOUAI (1568), and was one of the group of scholars WILLIAM ALLEN gathered there for the English College. But Martiall, always pressed for funds, returned to Louvain. His financial distress was relieved when Owen Lewis obtained for him a canonry in Lille. Because of civil disturbances in Flanders, however, he was not installed in the canonry till 1579. Little is known of his later life.

Bibliography: J. GILLOW *A Literary and Biographical History or Bibliographical Dictionary of the English Catholics from 1534 to the Present Time* 4:476–479. A. C. SOUTHERN, *Elizabethan Recusant Prose, 1559–1582* (London 1950).

[T. H. CLANCY]

MARTILLO MORÁN, NARCISA DE JESÚS, BL.

Lay mystic; b. 1832, at Daule (Nobol) near Guayaquil, Ecuador; d. Dec. 8, 1869, Lima, Peru. Narcisa's parents, Pedro Martillo Mosquera and Josefina Morán, were peasant farmers who died while Narcisa was very young. The middle child of nine, Narcisa moved to Guayaquil to find work as a seamstress to help support her siblings. For more than fifteen years, with a short break (*c.* 1865) in Cuenca, she dedicated her life to manual labor, prayer, teaching catechism, and caring for the neediest residents of the capital. In Cuenca, she was invited by the bishop to enter the Carmelites, but discerned that her vocation was in the world. In 1868, she travelled to Lima, Peru, where she lived as a lay woman in the Dominican convent. A pious woman, Narcisa did penances and was devoted to the Cross of Christ. Soon after her death pilgrims began praying at her tomb in Lima. Her cause for beatification was opened in 1889. In 1955, her body was translated to Guayaquil and now rests in her native town of Nobol under the altar of the Santuario de la Beata Narcisa de Jesús. During her beatification ceremony (Oct. 25, 1992), Pope John Paul II praised her as the glory of Ecuador.

Feast: Aug. 30.

Bibliography: *Acta Apostolicae Sedis* 21 (1992): 1017.

[K. I. RABENSTEIN]

MARTIN, GREGORY

Scripture scholar, best known for his Rheims-Douay Version of the Bible; b. Maxfield, Sussex, England, *c.* 1540; d. Reims, France, Oct. 28, 1582. One of the original scholars of St. John's College, Oxford (1557–69), Martin became an expert in Greek and Hebrew. Among his fellow students was Edmund CAMPION, whom he helped to bring into the Catholic Church. Martin then spent about a year (1569–70) in the household of Thomas Howard, fourth Duke of Norfolk, as tutor to his sons, one of whom later became Bl. Philip HOWARD. But always a stanch Catholic, Martin left this post when the Howard family began to be influenced by Protestantism. In 1570 he entered the college at DOUAI (Douay) that William ALLEN had founded (1559) for English Catholics. After his theology course there, he was ordained at Brussels (1573). Having taught at Douai for three years, he spent two years in Rome, assisting Allen in founding the English college (*Venerabile Collegio*) there. In July 1578, when Allen's college was removed from Douai to Reims, Martin moved to Reims, where for the next four years he taught Scripture, Greek, and Hebrew. During these years he produced, at Allen's request, an English translation of the whole Bible from the Latin Vulgate.

Although he received valuable assistance, mainly in the revision and the notes, from his Reims colleagues Thomas WORTHINGTON, Richard BRISTOW, John Reynolds, and Allen himself—all Oxford men—the bulk of the translation was a result of Martin's incredible industry. The pressure, however, was too much for him, and he died of consumption at the age of 42 as his NT was coming off the press at Reims. For lack of funds his OT, in two volumes, was not printed until 1609–10 at Douai. The statement on the title page of Martin's NT that this version was ''diligently conferred with the Greeke'' was no idle claim. Though made directly from the Latin, his translation shows the influence of the original Greek in several respects, notably in its correct use of the article. Despite its numerous Latinisms, caused partly by a desire for extreme fidelity to the Vulgate and partly by the current fashion in English literature, the Rheims-Douay Version often has original fine turns of expression, many of which were borrowed by the makers of the King James NT (1610); see J. G. Carleton, *The Part of Rheims in the Making of the English Bible* (Oxford 1902). As revised by R. CHALLONER (1749–50), Martin's Rheims-Douay Version was the only standard Bible used by English-speaking Catholics until the 20th century, when it was supplanted by new versions.

Bibliography: H. HURTER, *Nomenclator literarius theologiae catholicae* 3:278–280. E. VANSTEENBERGHE, *Dictionnaire de théologie catholique* 10.1:216–217. J. GILLOW, *A Literary and Biographical History or Bibliographical Dictionary of the English Catholics from 1534 to the Present Time* 4: 484–491. B. WARD, *Catholic Encyclopedia* 9: 727–728.

[L. F. HARTMAN]

MARTIN, KONRAD

Bishop, theologian; b. Geismar, Prussia, May 18, 1812; d. Mont-Saint-Guibert, Belgium, July 16, 1879. He studied at Munich under DÖLLINGER and afterward at Halle, Würzburg, and Münster. After ordination (1836) he became professor of moral and pastoral theology at the University of Bonn (1844) and wrote extensively on dogmatic and pastoral questions. As bishop of Paderborn from 1856, he was a leader in the Catholic revival in Germany, noted for his apostolic zeal and promotion of Christian unity. He founded a religious congregation of women, improved his diocesan government at a synod (1867), and advanced the education of his clergy. His concern for the Protestants within his diocese led him to publish *Ein bischöfliches Wort. . . über die Kontrover-*

spunkte (1864). It was written in a conciliatory spirit and won considerable attention, but also led to passionate controversy. *Wozu noch die Kirchenspaltung?* (1868) also caused much discussion by questioning Catholics and Protestants concerning the continued divisions within Christianity, but the outbreak of the KULTURKAMPF deprived it of its chances for success. Pius IX held Martin in high esteem and had him as a guest in the Quirinal in 1867 and again in 1869. At VATICAN COUNCIL I Martin was a prominent figure; as a member of the deputation on faith he had an important role in formulating the conciliar constitution on faith and the doctrine of papal infallibility, which he supported. During the Kulturkampf he was imprisoned (1874–75) and removed from office by the government. After his release he spent his remaining years in exile in Belgium. Several of his numerous works were translated into French, Dutch, Italian, Polish, and Hungarian.

Bibliography: W. LIESE, *Konrad Martin* (Paderborn 1937); "K. M.'s kirchliche Bedeutung," *Theologie und Glaube* 30:44–51. P. HADROSSEK, *Die Bedeutung des Systemgedankens für die Moraltheologie in Deutschland seit der Thomas-Renaissance* (Munich 1950) 107–115, *passim.* C. BUTLER, *The Vatican Council,* 2 v. (New York 1930). N. MIKO, "Publikation des Dogmas von der Unfehlbarkeit des Papstes durch das dt. Episkopat," *Römische Quartalschrift für Christliche Altertumskunde und für Kirchengeschichte* 58 (1963) 14–30.

[K. HONSELMANN]

MARTIN, MOTHER MARY

Founder of the MEDICAL MISSIONARIES OF MARY; b. Marie Helena Martin, in Dublin, Ireland, Apr. 25, 1892; d. Jan. 27, 1975, Drogheda, Ireland. During World War I, she trained as a Voluntary Aid Defense nurse and was posted to hospitals in Malta and in France, during which time she became inspired to continue her healing work after the war. It became her dream to found a religious congregation and do medical work as a missionary. Hearing of an opportunity to work in a mission in Calabar, South Nigeria, she trained in midwifery in Dublin and went to Africa for three years, primarily caring for women and maternity cases. Her commitment to the life of a religious healer deepened, but she had many years to wait until the Holy See decided to let religious do obstetrics and surgery. Martin and two companions received religious training from the Benedictines of Glenstal Abbey, County Limerick, in return for their housekeeping services at the abbey school. The abbey was founded in honor of Dom Columba Marmion who had always been a spiritual inspiration for her.

Permission for religious to practice medicine came in 1936 with the instruction *Constans ac sedula* of the Congregation for the Propagation of the Faith and in May of that year the Holy See gave its consent to the founding of a new congregation. Miss Martin and her two companions sailed for Calabar in early 1937, but soon after arrival she contracted malaria and nearly died. Her sickbed profession, Apr. 4, 1937, in Port Harcourt, marked the founding of the Medical Missionaries of Mary. Still severely ill, Sister Mary of the Incarnation, or Mother Mary, had to leave Africa under medical instructions, never to return. Her two companions remained behind in noviceship and worked to build the first mission.

At home and improved in health, Mother Mary's efforts were turned to getting support for her fledgling congregation. Her brother gave her a house called Rosemount in Dublin to be a house of studies for the new novices, and in December of 1938, the novitiate at Collon, County Louth, was canonically erected and five novices were received. The following December, a maternity hospital, Our Lady of Lourdes, was opened in Drogheda. The congregation, growing rapidly, needed a larger novitiate by 1940, and a new one was built in Drogheda, which also is the motherhouse. In 1942, the hospital received state recognition as a training school for sister-midwives, and today the International Missionary Training Hospital is in full operation.

Mother Mary continued as mother general until January of 1969 when she resigned. She was confined to bed for many of her last years and died at the motherhouse. Much of the growth and success of the Medical Missionaries of Mary throughout the world was due to the unflagging zeal of Mother Mary, who was able to excite the interest and cooperation of many supporters and vocations. Her community continues to expand, working on four continents with over 25 mission hospitals, many outpatient clinics and field stations.

[A. M. HUBBARD]

MARTIN, RAYMOND JOSEPH

Theologian; b. Neerpelt, Belgium, Sept. 27, 1878; d. Étiolles, France, Aug. 19, 1949. He entered the Dominican Order in 1896 and was ordained in 1902. He served as master of novices at La Sarte near Huy, Belgium, from 1906 until 1909, then as professor of theology at the Dominican theologate in Louvain until 1940. Specializing in medieval theology, he published an edition of the works of Robert of Melun, *Oeuvres de Robert de Melun* (3 v. Louvain 1932–41), and of Peter Comestor's work on the Sacraments, *Pierre Mangeur, De sacramentis* (Louvain 1937). In 1921, in collaboration with J. Lebon and J. de Ghellinck, he founded the well-known collection of patristic and theological studies, *Spicilegium sacrum Lovaniense.* In his work *La Controverse sur le péché; originel au debut du XIVe siècle* (Louvain 1930), Martin worked out a new opinion regarding the essence of original sin according to medieval theologians. He also wrote a few articles in defense of the Thomistic doctrine of the divine influence on human acts. With Martin the historical study of theology had its first representative among the Belgian Dominicans.

Bibliography: *Studia mediaevalia in honorem . . . R. J. Martin, O.P.* (Bruges 1948), see bibliog. of Martin's works, 27–37, two bio-bibliog. notices: L. VAN HELMOND, 7–8, and G. DE BRIE and S. BROUNTS, 9–25.

[J. COPPENS]

MARTIN, RICHARD, BL.

Gentleman, lay martyr; b. Shropshire, England; hanged at Tyburn (London), Aug. 30, 1588. Martin, who was educated at Broadgates Hall, Oxford, was condemned to execution for aiding a priest. For having paid sixpence for the supper of Bl. Fr. Robert MORTON, he died with BB. Fr. Richard LEIGH, Edward SHELLEY, Richard FLOWER, John Roche, and St. Margaret Ward. Richard Martin was beatified by Pius XI on Dec. 15, 1929.

Feast of the English Martyrs: May 4 (England).

See Also: ENGLAND, SCOTLAND, AND WALES, MARTYRS OF.

Bibliography: R. CHALLONER, *Memoirs of Missionary Priests,* ed. J. H. POLLEN (rev. ed. London 1924; repr. Farnborough 1969). J. H. POLLEN, *Acts of English Martyrs* (London 1891).

[K. I. RABENSTEIN]

MARTIN, VICTOR

French canonist and historian; b. Saint-Clément (Allier), May 23, 1886; d. there, Sept. 7, 1945. He was the youngest of seven children in a rural family. After studying in Moulins at the minor seminary (1899–1903) and major seminary (1903–06) and at the university seminary in Lyons (1906–10), he was ordained (1910) and then served as curate in Saint-Cosne d'Allier parish in the Diocese of Moulins (1910–14) and as chaplain in the church of Saint-Louis des Françis in Rome (1914–19). He gained the degrees of doctor in Canon Law (1914) and doctor of literature (*Docteur ès Lettres,* 1920). In 1919 he became a professor in the major seminary in Moulins. In 1921 he went to the University of Strasbourg as professor of Canon Law on the faculty of theology and acted as dean of this faculty (1923–45). In the latter capacity he reorganized the theology faculty when it was renewed after World War I and made numerous trips to Central Europe.

From 1928 to 1945 Martin was codirector of the 26-volume *Histoire de l'Église depuis les origines jusqu'à nos jours,* founded by Augustin FLICHE. He wrote the following books: *Le gallicanisme et la Réforme catholique. Essai historique sur l'introduction en France des décrets du concile de Trent, 1563–1615* (1919); *Le gallicanisme politique et le clergé de France* (1929); *Les origines du gallicanisme* (2 v. 1939); *Les negociations du nonce Silingardi . . . relatives à la publication du concile du Trent, 1599–1601* (1919), a collection of documents; *Les cardinaux et la Curie* (1930); and *Les Congrégations romaines* (1930). Martin's works on Gallicanism and its origins are regarded as the best on the subject.

Bibliography: A. FLICHE, ''Mgr. Victor Martin,'' *Revue d'histoire de l'Église de France* 32 (1946) 221–225.

[E. JARRY]

MARTIN I, POPE, ST.

Pontificate: July 5, 649 to June 17, 653 (when he was deported to Constantinople) or Sept. 16, 655 (when he died). He is venerated as a martyr.

Martin was born at Todi in Tuscany. After serving the Roman Church as lector and deacon, he was sent to Constantinople as *apocrisiarius* for Pope THEODORE. In that role he became aware of the efforts of the imperial court, including the patriarchs of Constantinople, to find a formula that would reconcile the opposing parties in the long-standing quarrel over the relationship between the divine and the human nature of Christ. On one side stood the those who accepted the decision of the Council of CHALCEDON (451) emphasizing the coexistence of the two natures; on the other were the adherents of MONOPHYSITISM who insisted on the preeminence of Christ's divine nature. At a time when Muslim forces were engulfing the Asian provinces of the Eastern Roman Empire, where the Monophysites predominated, the imperial government was desperate to find a dogmatic formula that would reconcile the Chalcedonian and the Monophysite positions and thus restore the religious unity of the Christian empire led by the emperor in Constantinople. The result was the promulgation in 638 of a decree called the *Ecthesis*, which established MONOTHELITISM as the official doctrine on the issue of the two natures of Christ. Since approval of the pope was crucial to the imperial quest for doctrinal unity, pressure was put on Rome to accept Monothelitism. Although Pope HONORIUS I (625–638) took a compromising stand, his successors refused to accept the imperial position; so also did Christians throughout Italy and Africa. Faced with prospect of the loss of the West over a theological issue, the imperial government issued the *Typos* in 648, forbidding further discussion of the Christological issue. The new order was sent to Pope Theodore for his approval, but he died before it arrived.

Upon his election as pope, Martin I disregarded traditional usage and was consecrated without seeking approval of the imperial government, an act that perhaps suggested his decision to defy the emperor. Convinced that the time was at hand to reinforce orthodoxy by an official, public action that would make Rome's position clear on the Christological dispute, the new pope summoned a Lateran synod which opened in October 649 with 105 bishops, mostly from Italy, in attendance. Also present was Maximus the Confessor, an accomplished theologian outspokenly opposed to Monothelitism and well qualified to assist the synod in defining orthodoxy. After five sessions during which the teachings of the fathers on Christ's divine and human natures were reviewed in detail, the synod issued a symbol of faith which confirmed the ruling of the Council of Chalcedon on Christ's nature, twenty canons condemning specific aspects of Monothelistism, and a judgment anathematizing the patriarchs of Constantinople—but not the emperors—responsible for promulgating the *Ecthesis* and the *Typos.* A letter was sent to the Emperor Constans II informing him of the decisions of the synod. Martin also circulated an encyclical summarizing the acts of the synod not only in the West but also in the East, where he sought to counter the disarray in ecclesiastical governance resulting from the Muslim conquests by designating apostolic vicars to act in the name of the pope in the cause of orthodoxy.

Even before the end of the Lateran synod Constans II moved to counter Martin's acts of independence. He ordered the exarch of Ravenna, Olympius, to arrest the pope and compel the acceptance of the *Typos* from all bishops and clerics, but only if the army in Rome agreed to such an action. Olympius found wide support for Martin's position, one indication among many that by the mid-sixth century imperial authority was waning in Italy, even in the army which was increasingly led and manned by native Italians whose interests were local. Olympius then contrived an assassination plot as a way of disposing of the pope, but that too failed, some believed because of divine intervention showing God's favor on the pope. Olympius then made peace with Martin and took his forces to Sicily, ostensibly to aid in the defense against Muslim attackers but more like to ally with the invaders as a step in seizing the imperial office; whatever plans he had ended shortly with his death. Freed for the moment from imperial threats, Martin devoted his energy to a far-flung correspondence attempting to defeat Monothelistism and to rally the Christian community around Rome.

But the pope's truce with the imperial government did not last long. In 653 Constans II ordered the new exarch, Theodore Calliopas, to arrest the pope and bring him to Constantinople for trial. Despite continued support from the Romans, Martin refused to resist the exarch for fear of violence. In June 653 he was taken prisoner and put aboard a ship for Constantinople. After a year-long trip during which he was treated brutally, the pope arrived in Constantinople in September 654. During that interval, the Romans elected a new pope, Eugenius I, an act that seemed to indicate the acceptance of Martin's deposition by the imperial government and a recognition of the emperor's willingness and ability to take action against those who defied his commands.

Upon his arrival in Constantinople Martin was publicly humiliated and imprisoned for three months. Although badly weakened from the treatment extended him during his long trip from Rome, he was eventually brought to trial as an usurper charged with treason stemming from his relationship with Olympius and for providing aid to the Muslim attackers of Sicily. Martin's efforts to introduce religious issues into the proceedings were rebuffed by the court. He was judged guilty, stripped of his insignia of office, and sentenced to death. On the plea of the patriarch, the death sentence was commuted to exile. Martin was sent to Cherson in the Crimea, where after more suffering he died on Sept. 16, 655. His colleague in defending orthodoxy against Monothelitism, Maximus the Confessor, suffered a like fate soon after. While Martin's career provided dramatic evidence of the extent to which the papacy was under imperial control at mid-sixth century, it also demonstrated the decisive role of the papacy in the definition of doctrine and thus on the unity of the Christian community, an issue crucial to the well-being of the imperial government. And it brought to light signs of the decline of imperial influence in the West in a context which gave the bishop of Rome a significant place as a rallying point in defying imperial control.

Feast: Nov. 12 (Western Church); April 13 (Greek Church).

Bibliography: *Le Liber Pontificalis* ed. L. DUCHESNE, 3 v., 2nd ed. (Paris 1955–1957) 1: 336–340, Eng. tr. in *The Book of Pontiffs (Liber Pontificalis). The Ancient Biographies of the First Ninety Roman Pontiffs to A.D. 715,* tr. with intro. by R. DAVIS, Translated Texts for Historians 5 (Liverpool 1989), 68–71. P. PEETERS, ''Une vie grecque du Pape S. Martin I,'' *Analecta Bollandiana* 51:299–346. *Regesta Pontificum Romanorum ab condita ecclesia ad annum post Christum MCXCVIII,* ed. P. JAFFÉ, 2 v., 2nd ed. (Leipzig 1885–1888) 1: 230–234. *Sancti Martini Pontificis Romani Epistolae,* Migne, Patrologia Latina 87 (Rome 1863) cols. 111–204; 89 (Rome 1879) cols. 591–604. *Concilium Lateranense a 649 celebratum*, ed.R. RIEDINGER, Acta conciliorum oecumenicorum, Series secunda, v. 1 (Berlin 1984). **Literature.** C. J. HEFELE, *Histoire des conciles d''après les documents originaux,* tr. H. LECLERCQ, v. 3, part 1 (Paris 1905) 434–461. W. M. PEITZ, ''Martin I und Maximus Confessor,''*Historisches Jahrbuch* 38: 213–238, 429–548. É. AMANN, ''Martin I,[er] (Saint),'' in *Dictionnaire de théologie catholique* 10/1 (Paris 1928) cols. 185–194. E. CASPAR, ''Die Lateransynod von 649,''*Zeitschrift für Kirchengeschichte* 51: 75–137; *Geschichte des Papsttums von den Anfängen bis zur Höhe der Weltherrschaft,* v. 2: *Das Papsttum unter byzantinisches Herrschaft* (Tübingen 1933) 553–574. F. X. SEPPELT, *Geschichte des Papsttums. Eine Geschichte der Päpste von den Anfängen bis zum Tod Pius X,* v. 2: *Das Papsttums im Frühmittelalter. Geschichte des Päpste von Regierungsantritt Gregors des Grossen bis zum Mitte des ll. Jahrhundert* (Leipzig 1934) 59–65. O. BERTOLINI, *Roma di fronte a Bisanzio e ai Langobardi,* Storia di Roma 9 (Bologna 1941) 337–350. L. BRÉHIER and R. AIGRAIN, *Grégoire le Grand, les États barbares et la conquête arabe (590–757),* Histoire de l'Église depuis les origines jusqu'a nos jours, ed. A. FLICHE and V. MARTIN, 5 (Paris 1947) 165–179, 402. J. HALLER, *Die Grundlagen.* V. 1 of *Das Papsttum: Idee und Wirklichkeit,* (Basel 1951) 305–327. P. LEMERLE, ''Les répercussions de le crise de l'empire au VIIe sur les pays d'Occident,'' and O. BERTOLINI, ''Reflessi politici delle contorversie religiose en Bisanzio nelle vicende del sec. VII in Italia,'' both in *Caratteri del secolo VII in Occidente,* 2 v., Settimane di studio del Centro italiano di studi sull'alto medieovo 5 (1958) 2: 713–731; 733–789, 791–810. J. RICHARDS, *The Popes and the Papacy in the Early Middle Ages, 476–752* (London, Boston, and Henley 1979) 181–200. T. F. X. NOBLE, *The Republic of St. Peter. The Birth of the Papal State, 680–825* (Philadelphia 1984) 1–14. P. CONTE, *Il Sinodo Lateranense dell'ottobre 649: la nuova edizione degli atti a cura de Rudolf Riedinger: rassenga critica di fonti dei secoli VII-XII,* Collezione Teologica 3 (Vatican City 1989). *Martino I papa (649–653) e il suo tempo. Atti del XXVIII Convegno storico internazionale, Todi, 13–16 ottobre 1991* (Spoleto 1992). P. LLEWELLYN, *Rome in the Dark Ages* (London 1993) 141–172, especially 150–156. S. COSETINO, ''Dissidenzia religiosa e insubordinazione militare nell'Italia bizantina: Martino I papa (649–653) e il suo tempo,'' *Rivista di storia della Chiesa de Italia* 48: 496–512. B. NEIL, ''The *Lives* of Pope Martin I and Maximus the Confessor: Some Reconsiderations of Dating and Provenance,'' *Byzantion* 68: 91–109.

[R. E. SULLIVAN]

MARTIN IV, POPE

Pontificate: Feb. 22, 1281 to Mar. 29, 1285; b. Simon de Brion, or Brie, near Angers; d. Orvieto. In 1260 he became chancellor of LOUIS IX. As cardinal (1261) he was papal legate in France under Urban IV, Clement IV, and Gregory X and supported the advancement of Louis's brother, Charles of Anjou, to the Sicilian throne. It was to Charles that he owed his election to the papal throne at Viterbo (1281) and his coronation at Orvieto, where he resided since he was not allowed to enter Rome. Martin in turn reinforced Charles's position in Italy by making him Roman senator and endorsing his Eastern projects. In 1281 he excommunicated the Emperor MICHAEL VIII PALEOLOGUS, thereby ruining any chance for the reunion of the Eastern and Western Churches before 1437. The anti–French rebellion in Sicily, the Sicilian Vespers (1282), forced Charles to abandon the hoped–for conquest of Constantinople in favor of the reconquest of Sicily. The Sicilians tried to place their League of Free Communes under papal suzerainty but later called in King Peter III of Aragon, who had long plotted to invade the island. Pope Martin reciprocated by excommunicating the Sicilians, declaring their new King deposed, and organizing a crusade gainst Peter under Philip III of France. Sicily and Aragon successfully resisted, but the papacy long remained committed to the reconquest of Sicily. Martin was deeply interested in the work of the FRANCISCANS, granting them the right of preaching and hearing confessions in the bull *Ad fructus uberes* (1281) and relaxing their rules on poverty in the *Exultantes* (1283).

Bibliography: MARTIN IV, *Les Registres de Martin IV,* 3 pts. (Paris 1901–35). H. K. MANN, *The Lives of the Popes in the Early Middle Ages from 590 to 1304* (London 1902–32) v. 16. J. HALLER, *Das Papsttum* (Stuttgart 1950–53) v. 5. J. R. STRAYER, ''The Crusade against Aragon,'' *Speculum* 28 (1953) 102–113. H. WIERUSZOWSKI, ''Politische Verschwörungen . . . König Peters von Aragon . . . ,'' *Quellen und Forschungen aus italienischen Archiven und Bibliotheken* 37 (1957) 136–191. D. J. GEANAKOPLOS, *Emperor Michael Palaeologus and the West, 1258–1282* (Cambridge, MA 1959). E. BOSHOF and F. R. ERKENS, *Rudolf von Hapsburg (1373–1291). Eine Königsherrschaft zwischen Tradition und Wandel* (Cologne 1993). E. BIGGI, ''Un intervento inedito di Martino IV tra frati minori e clero di Piacenza nel 1282,'' *Archivum Franciscanum Historicum* (1997) 349–53. O. CARTELLIERI, *Peter von Aragon und die Sizilianische Vesper* (1977). P.-V. CLAVERIE, ''L'ordre du Temple au coeur d'une crise politique majeure: La 'Querela Cypri' des années 1279–1285,'' *Le Moyen Âge* (1998) 495–507. A. FRANCHI, *I Vespri Siciliani e le relazioni tra Rome e Bisanzio. Studio critico sulle fonti* (Assisi 1997). R. KAY, ''Martin IV and the Fugitive Bishop of Bayeux,'' in *Councils and Clerical Culture in the Medieval West* (1997). K.B. MCFARLANE, *England in the Fifteenth Century* (London 1981). E. PÁSZTOR, ''Per la storia dell'amministrazione dello Stato Pontificio sotto Martino IV,'' in *Onus Apostolicae Sedis. Curia romana e cardinalato nei secoli XI–XV* (Rome 1999) 265–76. A. PAPADAKIS, *Crisis in Byzantium: The Filioque Controversy of the Patriarchate of Gregory II of Cyprus (1283–1289)* (New York 1982). J. N. D. KELLY, *Oxford Dictionary of Popes* (New York 1986) 202.

[H. WIERUSZOWSKI]

MARTIN V, POPE

Pontificate: Nov. 11, 1417 to Feb. 20, 1431; b. Oddo COLONNA in Genazzano, Italy, 1368; d. Rome. The only pope from this old Roman family, Martin was elected at the Council of CONSTANCE after a long discussion on electoral procedure and a very brief conclave, in which 22 cardinals and 30 deputies from the five nations participating in the council voted. He soon won general recognition, except in Aragon, where a minor schism (antipopes

"Tomb Effigy of Pope Martin V," bronze sculpture by Simone di Giovanni Ghini, located in the Basilica of St. John Lateran, Rome. (Alinari-Art Reference/Art Resource, NY)

BENEDICT XIII and Clement VIII) lasted until 1429. Emperor SIGISMUND attempted to detain the pope in Germany; the French offered him AVIGNON as a residence. But the council ended on April 22, 1418, and the pope left for Rome on May 16. However, he had to wait more than a year in Florence before he could finally enter Rome on Sept. 28, 1420. His return was of crucial importance for the future of the PAPACY and of the STATES OF THE CHURCH.

The pope energetically addressed himself to restoring the prestige of the papacy, which had suffered grievously during the WESTERN SCHISM. He initiated an extensive correspondence with all European sovereigns and sent numerous embassies on peace missions, especially to England and France, which were involved in the Hundred Years' War. He devoted special attention to the campaign against the HUSSITES. The Roman CURIA was reorganized in accord with the decrees of Constance, the curial officials of both Rome and Avignon were united, and a model administration built up. When the five-year concordats made at Constance expired, Martin returned to the old policy of papal reservations as far as the ecclesiastical policy of the individual states allowed. In the protracted and stubborn negotiations with Aragon, Martin made great concessions to the king; the Concordat of Genazzano (1426) with FRANCE contained provisions favorable to the Curia; Martin failed to get the hated regulations on the award of benefices in England revoked (*see* PRAEMUNIRE, STATUTE OF; PROVISORS, STATUTE OF). Yet the net result of these negotiations proved tolerable in practice. Of greater importance for the history of the papacy was Martin's restoration of papal power and hegemony in the Papal States—a restoration he pursued with the greatest energy and with all the means at his disposal. First of all, the dangerous *condottiere* Braccio di Montone was blocked and then overcome at the battle of Aquila by a great array of papal troops. Next, the pope successfully countered the attempt of King Alfonso V of Aragon to take Naples. He put down by force of arms the revolt in Bologna in 1429. To secure his power the pope maintained strong troop concentrations, and a large portion of papal revenues went to paying these troops.

In Rome the VATICAN and Lateran basilicas were again restored and the streets widened. Rome and Constantinople were in constant contact, the Greek embassy at the Council of Constance having already held forth prospects of reunion and of a council in Constantinople. But the negotiations foundered on the political situation and on the emperor's demand that every controversial question be exhaustively examined at such a council. In exact accord with the decree *Frequens,* the pope convoked a council in Pavia in 1423, moved it to Siena, and then dissolved it because of poor attendance and its tendency to adopt radical decrees. Likewise in accord with *Frequens,* he announced a council in BASEL for 1431 and named Cardinal CESARINI presiding officer. Though Martin had been a strong supporter of the Council of PISA (1409) and its CONCILIARISM, and though as pope he devoted himself to the program outlined at Constance, especially to the reform of the Church, he wisely and successfully opposed any overly strict limitation of papal power.

Bibliography: *Acta Concilii Constanciensis,* ed. H. FINKE, 4 v. (Münster 1896–1928) v. 4. *Repertorium Germanicum* (Berlin 1916) v. 4 *Martin V., 1417–1431,* ed. K. A. FINK (Berlin 1943–58). K. A. FINK, "Die politische Korrespondenz Martins V. nach den Brevenregistern," *Quellen und Forschungen aus italienischen Archiven und Bibliotheken* 26 (1935–36) 172–244; "Martin V. und Bologna, 1428–1429," *ibid.* 23 (1931–32) 182–217; "Die Sendung des Kardinals von Pisa nach Aragon im Jahre 1418," *Römische Quartalschrift für christliche Altertumskunde und für Kirchengeschichte* 41 (1933) 45–59; *Martin V. und Aragon* (Berlin 1938); "Papsttum und Kirchenreform nach dem grossen Schisma," *Theologische Quartalschrift* 126 (1946) 110–122; "Zur

Beurteilung des grossen abendländischen Schismas,'' *Zeitschrift für Kirchengeschichte* 73 (1962) 335–343; ''Die Wahl Martins V.,'' in *Das Konzil von Konstanz,* ed. A. FRANZEN and W. MÜLLER (Freiburg 1964) 138–151. J. HALLER, ''England und Rom unter Martin V.,'' *Quellen und Forschungen aus italienischen Archiven und Bibliotheken* 8 (1905) 249–304. R. LOENERTZ, ''Les Dominicains byzantins . . . et les négociations pour l'union . . . 1415 à 1430,'' *Archivum Fratrum Praedicatorum* 9 (1939) 5–61. P. PARTNER, *The Papal State under Martin V* (London 1958). W. J. KOUDELKA, ''Eine neue Quelle zur Generalsynode von Siena 1423–1424,'' *Zeitschrift für Kirchengeschichte* 74 (1963) 244–264. P. DE VOOGHT, ''Le Conciliarisme aux conciles de Constance et de Bâle,'' in *Le Concile et les conciles* (Chevetogne 1960) 143–181, but see *Irénikon* 36 (1963) 61–75; ''Le Concile oecuménique de Constance et le conciliarisme,'' *Istina* 9 (1963) 57–86. R. BÄUMER, ''Das Verbot der Konzilsappellation Martins V. in Konstanz,'' in *Das Konzil von Konstanz, op. cit.* 187–213. V. LAURENT, ''Les Préliminaires du concile de Florence. Les Neuf articles du pape Martin V et la réponse inédite du patriarche de Constantinople Joseph II (Octobre 1422),'' *Revue des études byzantines* 20 (1962) 5–60. J. N. D. KELLY, *Oxford Dictionary of Popes* (New York 1986) 239–241.

[K. A. FINK/L. SCHMUGGE]

MARTIN OF BRAGA, ST.

Distinguished missionary archbishop and writer; b. Pannonia, *c.* 515; d. Braga (ancient Bracara), *c.* 579. After a long pilgrimage to Palestine, where he learned Greek, Martin acquired good training in theology and entered the monastic life. He decided to go to the extreme West, to Gallaecia (modern Galicia and northern Portugal). In 550, he founded and was first abbot of a monastery at Dumio, not far from Bracara, the capital of the Suevian kings. In 557, he was elected first bishop of Dumio. He presided over the second synod of Bracara in 572, and, at the death of the metropolitan Lucretius, he became archbishop of that city. His life ambition, the conversion of the Suevian kings and people from Arianism to Catholicism, was crowned with success, and the poet Venantius FORTUNATUS could hail him justly as ''the apostle of Gallaecia.''

In spite of his active life as a zealous pastor, his extant writings reflect a remarkable breadth of knowledge and a high level of culture for his age. His *Aegyptiorum Patrum sententiae,* dealing with the lives of the Desert Fathers, is a translation from the Greek made for the edification of his monks. His *Formula vitae honestae,* addressed to King Miro, contains a series of precepts and expositions connected with the four cardinal virtues. It is based in large part, apparently, on the lost *De officiis* of Seneca. His *De ira,* as the title indicates, is likewise based on Seneca. On the other hand, his *Pro repellenda iactantia, De superbia,* and, especially, *Exhortatio humilitatis,* owe much to John CASSIAN's monastic *Instituta* as well as to Seneca.

His pastoral instruction, *De correctione rusticorum,* written deliberately in a plainer and more familiar Latin style, is of special interest because it furnishes so much information on the old Roman superstitions and practices that still persisted in Spain. For its content, he drew material from sermons of St. CAESARIUS OF ARLES dealing with the same theme. The canonical collection called the *Capitula Martini* contains some elements at least that belong to him. He also wrote a work on Baptism, *Epistola ad Bonifacium episcopum de trina mersione.* Finally, he tried his hand at metrical composition. Of the few verses extant, the most interesting are the six which he composed for his own epitaph. Collections of his sermons and letters are lost.

Feast: March 20.

Bibliography: *Opera omnia,* ed. C. W. BARLOW (Papers and Monographs of the American Academy in Rome 12; New Haven 1950). O. BARDENHEWER, *Geschichte der altkirchlichen Literatur* (Freiburg 1913–32) 5:379–388. É. AMANN, *Dictionnaire de théologie catholique*. ed. A. VACANT et al., (Paris 1903–50) 10.1:203–207. J. MADOZ, ''Martín de Braga,'' *Estudios Eclesiásticos* 25 (1951) 219–242. C. P. CASPARI, *Martin von Bracaras Schrifs De correctione rusticorum* (Christiania 1883), still important for its introduction. S. MCKENNA, *Paganism and Pagan Survivals in Spain Up to the Fall of the Visigothic Kingdom* (Washington 1938). H. HASELBACH, *Sénèque des IIII vertus: la Formula honestae vitae de Martin de Braga (pseudo-Sénèque),* tr. J. COURTECUISSE (Bern 1975), critical ed.

[M. R. P. MCGUIRE]

MARTIN OF LEÓN, ST.

Ascetic and theologian; b. near León, Spain, *c.* 1125; d. León, Jan. 12, 1203. Martin's biography, attributed to Lucas of Túy, says that Martin spent his childhood in a monastery but then went on a long pilgrimage before returning to León. In 1185 he began a series of 58 sermons for his fellow CANONS REGULAR OF ST. AUGUSTINE, in which, at times, he argued vehemently against Jews and heretics. The many Biblical quotations in Martin's writings have caused them to be called a *Concordia* of the Bible. He relies heavily on ISIDORE OF SEVILLE, AUGUSTINE, GREGORY I THE GREAT, and CASSIODORUS, while his doctrine on the Trinity is copied from PETER LOMBARD. He quotes no Arabic authors. His cult, authorized in 1632, was later suppressed and Martin has fallen into obscurity.

Feast: Feb. 11(?).

Bibliography: *Patrologia Latina,* ed. J. P. MIGNE, 271 v., indexes 4 v. (Paris 1878–90) 208–209. J. DE GHELLINCK, *L'Essor de la littéature latine au XIIe siècle,* 2 v. (Brussels-Paris 1946) 1:224–225. A. VIÑAYO GONZÁLEZ, *San Martín de León y su apologética anti judía* (Madrid 1948). BP. LUCAS OF TÚY, *Santo*

Martino de León: vida y obras narradas por el Tudense, tr. A. VIÑAYO (León, Spain 1984).

[E. P. COLBERT]

MARTIN OF TOURS, ST.

Monk and bishop of Tours (371 to 397), patron of France; b. Sabaria (Szombathely, Hungary), *c.* 316; d. Candes, Nov. 8, 397. The assertion of Sulpicius Severus [*Dialogues* 1 (2).7] that he was a septuagenarian when he visited Emperor Maximus at Trier (*c.* 385), taken with that of Gregory of Tours (*Historia Francorum* 1.36), who dates his birth in the 11th year of the Emperor Constantine (counting from July 306), suggests that he was born *c.* 316–317, though scholars differ in the matter of Martinian chronology. Martin's pagan parents reared him in Pavia, Italy, and he became a catechumen; at 15 he took the military oath and at 18 (*c.* 334–335) received Baptism (Sulpicius Severus, *Vita* 2.3). While one interpretation limits Martin's soldierly career to 5 years, the *Vita* supports the view that it was JULIAN THE APOSTATE (Caesar, 355–360) who gave him his discharge at Worms in 356.

HILARY OF POITIERS (*c.* 350–367) ordained Martin an exorcist following his discharge (*Vita* 5). Hilary's exile (356–360) by Arian Emperor CONSTANTIUS II (353–361) paralleled Martin's visit to his parents and his activity against ARIANISM in the Illyrian province, after which he embraced the monastic life, first at Milan and later on the island of Gallinaria (*Vita* 5.6).

Upon Hilary's restoration to his see, Martin returned to France, where at Ligugé, 8 kilometers south of Poitiers, he established *c.* 360–361 what may have been the first French monastery (*Vita* 7). Thence, drawn by a ruse to TOURS, he was consecrated bishop, probably on July 4, 371 (*Vita* 9; *Historia Francorum* 1.48; 2.14; 10.31). For a time the new bishop resided at his cathedral, until with 80 disciples he reassumed a monastic way of life at Marmoutier outside Tours (*Vita* 10) and established rural parishes (*Historia Francorum* 10.31). Occasionally consulted by Emperor Maximus (383–388) at Trier [*Dialogues* 1 (2).5, 6], Martin received a pledge from him that PRISCILLIAN, following his appeal from the synod of Bordeaux (384), would not be executed. Priscillian, however, was put to death (fall 386), and Martin broke communion with Bishop Ithacius and the Spanish bishops until he received a promise that measures against the Priscillianists would be dropped. Martin joined Ithacius at the consecration of Bishop Felix of Trier (*c.* 386–387), though afterward he reproached himself for weakness [*Dialogues* 2 (3).11–13]. He died on a pastoral visitation at Candes; three days later, a vast crowd of mourners attended the burial at Tours (*Historia Francorum* 1.48; 2.14; Sulpicius Severus, *Epistles* 3). His successor, Bishop Brice (397–*c.* 444), erected a small chapel that was replaced during the pontificate of Perpetuus (461–491) by a more pretentious edifice (*Historia Francorum* 10.31). Relics were dispersed three times—in the 9th century, in 1562, and in 1793—before the rediscovery of the saint's tomb on Dec. 14, 1860. The *confessio* formerly attributed to him is not considered authentic.

Feast: Nov. 11.

Bibliography: *Clavis Patrum latinorum,* ed. E. DEKKERS 1748a. *Bibliotheca hagiographica latina antiquae et mediae aetatis* 5610–66. SULPICIUS SEVERUS, *Vita s. Martini,* ed. C. HALM (*Corpus scriptorum ecclesiasticorum latinorum* 1; 1866). GREGORY OF TOURS, *Historia Francorum,* 1:36–38, 43 (*Monumenta Germaniae Historica: Scriptores rerum Merovingicarum* 1.1; 1884). E. C. BABUT, *Saint Martin de Tours* (Paris 1913). H. DELEHAYE, ''Saint Martin et Sulpice Sévère,'' *Analecta Bollandiana* 38 (1920) 5–136. É. GRIFFE, *La Gaule chrétienne à l'époque romaine* (Paris 1947) 1:199–220; ''La chronologie des années de jeunesse de s. Martin,'' *Bulletin de littérature ecclésiastique* 62 (1961) 114–118. *L'Année Martinienne à Tours, Revue d'histoire de l'Église de France* 47 (1961), memorial issue. J. FONTAINE, ''Chronologie,'' *S. Martin et son temps* (*Studia anselmiana* 46; 1961) 189–236.

[H. G. J. BECK]

MARTIN OF TROPPAU

Dominican in Prague, papal chaplain and apostolic penitentiary; b. probably Troppau (Silesia, then part of the kingdom of Bohemia), after 1200; d. Bologna, after June 22, 1278. Although the surname ''Polonus'' has another explanation besides his nationality, he was probably of Slavic origin. In any case, he was consecrated archbishop of Gnesen by Nicolas III on June 22, 1278, but died on the way to his see. Widely traveled, he was highly esteemed as a preacher (*Sermones de tempore et de sanctis*) and canonist (*Tabula decreti*); he revised and improved the format of the Italian catalogs of emperors and popes in his *Chronicon summorum pontificum imperatorumque* (ed. *Monumenta Germaniae Historica: Scriptores* 22:377–475) and thereby achieved an extraordinary reputation as a historian during the late Middle Ages. As a practical workbook for canonists and as an aid for preachers, Martin compiled a *summa* of historical material (cf. *Flores temporum* by a Franciscan of apparently the same name) until 1288, in which critical research and scholarship were singularly lacking. This work had been suggested by CLEMENT IV and reflected the point of view of the MENDICANT ORDERS. Fables, e.g., the story of the popess JOAN and popular legends, e.g., the establishment of the electoral college by Otto III, have survived as a result of this literary work and served as a source for later uncritical historiography. The chronicle saw numerous recensions and translations. Martin's name became a byword for unknown chroniclers.

St. Martin of Tours on horseback, giving half his cloak to the homeless poor. (Kean Collection/Archive Photos)

Bibliography: A. POTTHAST, *Regesta pontificum romanorum inde ab a. 1198 ad a. 1304* 2:1726, n. 21340. W. WATTENBACH., *Deutschlands Geschichtsquellen im Mittelalter bis zur Mitte des 13.Jhr.* 2:466–472. O. LORENZ, *Deutschlands Geschichtsquellen im Mittelalter,* 2 v. (Berlin 1886–87) 1:3–12. P. DAVID, *Les Sources de l'histoire de Pologne à l'époque des Piasts* (963–1386) (Paris 1934) 243–244. B. SCHMEIDLER, *Die deutsche Literatur des Mittelalters* 3:282–289. H. GRUNDMANN, "Geschichtsschreibung im Mittelalter," *Deutsche Philologie im Aufriss,* v.3 (2d ed. Berlin 1962) 2238–39, 2278. B. STASIEWSKI, *Lexikon für Theologie und Kirche* 2 7:119.

[H. WOLFRAM]

MARTINA, ST.

Virgin martyr. Her vita is an adaptation of the legend of St. Tatiana, according to which she was the orphaned daughter of a former consul, a deaconess, and a virgin martyr under Alexander Severus (222–235), tortured and beheaded for her faith. Her cult goes back to the seventh century in Rome, where she had an oratory near the Mamertine prison (*Patrologia Latina* 75:237). A church in her honor, built in the secretarium of the Roman senate by HONORIUS I (625–638) and enlarged by ADRIAN I (772–795), was reconstructed under URBAN VIII when her relics were discovered there in 1634. She is mentioned in the Roman *Capitularia evangeliorum* (mid–eighth century), in the martyrologies of St. Jerome, ADO, and USUARD, and in the Roman MARTYROLOGY.

Feast: Jan. 30 (formerly Jan. 1).

Bibliography: *Acta Sanctorum.* Jan. 1:11–19. J. W. LEGG, ed., *The Second Recension of the Quignon Breviary,* 2 v. (London 1908–12). M. ARMELLINI, *Le Chiese di Roma,* ed. C. CECCHELLI, 2 v. (Rome 1942). "Des publications hagiographiques," *Analecta Bollandiana* 23 (1904) 344.

[J. VAN PAASSEN]

MARTINDALE, CYRIL CHARLES

Jesuit scholar, writer, and preacher; b. London, May 25, 1879; d. March 18, 1963. The son of Sir Arthur Martindale, a civil servant who spent most of his active life in India and Ceylon, Cyril was educated at Harrow School. He was received into the Catholic Church by the Jesuit fathers at Bournemouth and soon afterward entered the English Jesuit novitiate. After philosophical studies at St. Mary's Hall, Stonyhurst, he matriculated at Pope's Hall (afterward Campion Hall), Oxford, in 1901 and had a distinguished academic career, receiving first-class honors in *literae humaniores* and numerous prizes and scholarships in classics and theology. He taught at Stonyhurst College and at Manresa House before returning to Oxford. He was ordained in August of 1911.

Despite his great scholarship, Martindale spent little time in formal teaching. At Oxford during World War I, he did much to help the wounded Australian soldiers in the hospital there, and so began an apostolate that reached the ends of the earth and every class of people. He was uniquely equipped to stimulate the awakening apostolic spirit of English Catholics, and in many fields he was prophetic in his understanding of the religious needs of his times. Thus, his work with university students (he was a tireless supporter of PAX ROMANA, for which he did much to establish) encouraged the intellectual development of Catholic life throughout the world.

He was an enthusiastic and informed pioneer of the liturgical revival, especially through his books on the Mass. His position on the Permanent Committee of the International Eucharistic Congresses took him to Australia, Africa, and South America and brought him close to the realities of missionary work. Deeply rooted in the Greco-Roman culture of the West, he saw very clearly that the future must bring great changes. The APOSTLESHIP OF THE SEA was established largely through his efforts. He was a preacher and speaker of unique appeal, lacking of rhetoric, but with a personal sympathy that later made him the most popular of broadcasters. An army of converts, from dukes to dustmen, bear witness to his patience as a teacher. He was never surprised by human folly, and he was never so much at home as in the East End of London, where he did an immense amount of work in clubs and settlements to manifest the Church's concern for the poor.

During World War II, he was in Denmark at the time of its invasion and was held captive until the end of the war. After his release he returned to England and, despite recurring illness, kept up a large correspondence and showed a lively interest in the new manifestations of Catholic life he had done so much to stimulate. Although he wrote some books and articles that were scholarly, his greater achievement was as a popularizer, in the best sense of the term; and his numerous lives of saints, books of travel, biographies, and spiritual writings, despite a discursive style, were always rooted in an exact intellectual discipline. He responded best to a subject that compelled compassion: Lourdes has found no truer interpreter, and St. Benedict Joseph Labre no more faithful friend.

Bibliography: T. D. ROBERTS et al., "C. C. Martindale: A Symposium," *Month* 30 (1963) 69–90. I. EVANS, "C. C. Martindale, S.J. 1879–1963," *America* (6 Apr. 1963) 466–467.

[I. EVANS]

MARTINEAU, JAMES

English Unitarian divine; b. Norwich, April 21, 1805; d. London, Jan. 11, 1900. Martineau, the brother of Harriet Martineau the writer, was of Huguenot descent. In 1822 he was converted from Presbyterianism to Unitarianism and entered Manchester College in York. After serving as minister in Dublin and Liverpool, he became in 1840 professor of philosophy and of political economy at Manchester New College. He became principal in 1869, by which time the college had moved to London. During these years he continued his pastoral activities. At the Little Portland Street chapel in London, his preaching aroused wide interest. Martineau was a prolific writer. Among his better-known books are *Rationale of Christian Enquiry* (1836), *Ideal Substitutes for God* (1879), *Types of Ethical Theology* (2 v. 1885), *A Study of Religion* (1888), and *The Seat of Authority in Religion* (1890). His philosophy was rationalistically theistic, but he excluded divine foreknowledge of contingencies in order to preserve human free will. Along with his natural religion, he combined a mystic spirituality that resulted from his poetic temperament rather than from his philosophy. His political views were unusual among Nonconformists because he opposed free education, favored the South in the American Civil War, and supported the continued establishment of the Church of England, hoping that it would evolve into a truly national Church.

Bibliography: J. DRUMMOND and C. B. UPTON, *The Life and Letters of James Martineau,* 2 v. (London 1902). A. H. CRAUFURD, *Recollections of James Martineau* (Edinburgh 1903). F. L. CROSS, *The Oxford Dictionary of the Christian Church* (London 1957) 865–866.

[W. HANNAH]

MARTÍNEZ, JUAN DE PRADO

Moral theologian; b. Valladolid, first quarter of the 17th century; d. Segovia, Feb. 25, 1668. He studied theology at Alcalá, where he later was a professor. He was a man of vivacious spirit and a prolific writer; in 1662 he was elected provincial of the province of Spain. While he was provincial, his devotion to study led him to foster a love for study in the students. His work on the Immaculate Conception, *Notitia veridica doctrinae ordinis praedicatorum de praeservatione Deiparae Immaculatae Virginis Mariae a peccato originali,* attempted to show that diverse pontifical decisions left the position of St. Thomas intact. It was suppressed by the Spanish Inquisition, and brought Martinez into difficulty with Philip IV.

Bibliography: J. QUÉTIF and J. ÉCHARD, *Scriptores Ordinis Praedicatorum* 2.2:624–625. É. AMANN, *Dictionnaire de théologie catholique* 10.1:218–219.

[R. J. POWERS]

MARTÍNEZ, LUIS MARÍA

Archbishop of Mexico, author, preacher, and peacemaker; b. Molinos de Caballero, Tlalpajahua, Michoacán, June 9, 1881; d. Mexico City, Feb. 8, 1956. Before he was quite ten years old, Martínez entered the seminary in Morelia where he performed brilliantly, winning prizes in Latin, philosophy, theology, and law. While he was a subdeacon, he became prefect of the Instituto del Sagrado Corazón, and in 1903, vice rector. In 1904 he returned to the seminary as prefect of discipline, and was ordained that fall. Much of Martínez' life was associated with this seminary; he was made vice rector in 1905 and rector in 1919, the same year he became a canon of the cathedral. Dominating the institution for more than a generation, his spirit and his learning exerted a major influence on many priests.

In 1922 Martínez was appointed apostolic administrator of Chilapa and the next year made titular bishop of Anemurio and auxiliary to the archbishop of Morelia. Having been consecrated Sept. 30, 1923, he was designated vicar general (1925), at the height of the religious persecution that forced Abp. Ruiz y Flores into exile. Martínez was in charge of the Church until the archbishop returned in 1929. During this time he skillfully negotiated with the government and saved many churches in Michoacán from being seized for nonreligious purposes. He was named coadjutor with the right of succession in Morelia in 1934, but Feb. 20, 1937, he was nominated as archbishop of Mexico; he took possession of his see in April. In Mexico City his diplomatic skill, simplicity, and compassion helped to bring about better relations between Church and State, bringing an end to active persecution, and even gaining the friendship of President Miguel Alemán. Under such improved circumstances he was able to build the new seminary and to continue the work of restoring the cathedral, a project for which he enlisted the active support of the laity.

Martínez was a renowned preacher and writer. Among his published works are *El espíritu santo, Simientes divinas, A propósito de un viaje, Santa María de Guadalupe, Jesus,* and *La pureza en el ciclo litúrgico.* He was a member of the Academia Mexicana de la Lengua. Its director, Alejandro Quijano, receiving him into membership for his literary work, his preaching, and his teaching, described his prose as beautiful and elegant, imbued with his love of God, his extraordinary sensitivity, and that most rare of virtues, a universal sympathy. Martínez was a friend of letters generally and a patron of many publications. He traveled widely and was highly esteemed both outside and within Mexico. A politician in the best sense of the word, he transformed an embattled, restricted Mexican Catholicism into a living part of the community, ready for action and change.

[J. GUISA Y AZEVEDO]

MARTÍNEZ COMPAÑÓN Y BUJANDA, BALTASAR JAIME

Bishop of Trujillo, Peru, and archbishop of Bogotá, Colombia; b. Cabredo, Navarre, Spain, Jan. 10, 1737; d. Bogotá, Aug. 17, 1797. He was ordained in 1761. In 1767 he went to Peru after being appointed canon of the cathedral of Lima. He was rector of the seminary and secretary of the provincial council of Lima of 1772. He was consecrated bishop of Trujillo in Lima on March 25, 1779. Taking over his see on May 13 of that same year, he governed it for ten years with such great talent and zeal that he became one of the outstanding bishops of Latin America. He spent five years, almost uninterruptedly, inspecting his vast diocese with excellent results, not only from the religious standpoint, but scientifically and culturally as well. Well ahead of his time, he raised the two basic problems of modern Peru, universal public education and the means of development, and stated the bases for realistic solutions. He also gave to the parish priests rules for the education of the people in faith and morals, as well as in manners and hygiene. At the same time he improved clerical training, reorganizing the major seminary and erecting three more seminaries, which becamc centers of enlightened pastoral ideas. He restored and erected numerous elementary schools and founded three centers for vocational and literary training for young indigenous children. He founded some 20 new villages and moved others to better locations. He built bridges and roads, opened sewage systems, promoted agriculture, and concerned himself with the improvement of mining conditions. He also increased the number of missions among indigenous people. He built 27 churches and restored 30 others, including his own cathedral.

A document that demonstrates his pastoral concern, his humanism, and his knowledge is the *Historia natural, civil y moral de Trujillo por mapas, planos y estampas con sus memorias para ella,* an interesting description of his diocese written between 1780 and 1785. He used material obtained at his request by the parish priests and other persons and also material collected during his pastoral visits. Of his work only the graphic part is known. Nine volumes include approximately 1,400 sketches on a great variety of subjects from folklore to natural sciences. It is of great value to history and ethnography. In 1788 he was transferred to the See of Bogotá. As archbishop there he continued to show his concern for raising public moral and educational standards.

Bibliography: J. M. PÉREZ AYALA, *Baltasar Jaime Martínez Compañón y Bujanda: prelado español de Colombia y el Perú* (Bogotá 1955). R. VARGAS UGARTE, *Historia de la iglesia en el Perú,* v.4 (Lima 1961).

[E. T. BARTRA]

MARTÍNEZ DE ALDUNATE, JOSÉ ANTONIO

Chilean prelate and scholar; b. Santiago, 1730?; d. there, April 8, 1811. A member of an aristocratic Chilean family, Martínez de Aldunate studied at the Convictorio of San Francisco Javier under the direction of the Jesuits. He received the master's degree in philosophy and the doctorate in theology. Subsequently, he received the doctorate in Canon and civil law from the University of San Felipe in 1755. That same year he was designated fiscal for the bishopric of Santiago; he was ordained in 1756. He served for many years as a professor at the University of San Felipe and became rector. He held most ecclesiastical positions in the diocese at one time or another, becoming dean in 1797. On a number of occasions he served as vicar-general. In 1804 he was made bishop of the Peruvian Diocese of Guamanga, where he served until 1809 when the Spanish regency proposed him for the bishopric of Santiago de Chile. On Sept. 18, 1810, the *cabildo abierto,* the first Creole government, had named him vice president of the junta on which all institutions of the area were represented. However, by the time hc arrived in Santiago in November 1810 he was already mentally ill and could not serve.

Bibliography: L. F. PRIETO DEL RÍO, *Diccionario biográfico del clero secular de Chile* (Santiago 1922).

[M. GONGORA]

MARTINI, GIOVANNI BATTISTA

Influential music authority and church-music composer; b. Bologna, April 24, 1706; d. there, Oct. 4, 1784. After musical studies, first with his father and later with Predieri, Riccieri, G. A. Perti, and F. A. Pistocchi, he became a Franciscan at Lugo di Romagna (1722) and was ordained the next year (hence his familiar title, Padre Martini). An avid student of music history and theory, he amassed a large music library and produced numerous scholarly works, among them the three-volume *Storia della musica* (Bologna 1757–81) and the two-volume *Saggio fondamentale pratico di contrappunto* (1774–75), which had a decisive influence on current teaching of counterpoint. He had close professional relations with musicians and scholars all over Europe, and as a teacher he attracted a whole generation of musicians, among whom were J. G. Naumann (composer of the ''Dresden Amen''), GRÉTRY, GLUCK, JOMMELLI, J. C. BACH, and MOZART. Church music and oratorios shared his creative activity with operas and instrumental music. His knowledge of Renaissance polyphony enabled him to employ the *stile antico* in strict *A CAPPELLA* polyphony, thus laying the foundation for the 19th-century church-music reform (*see* CAECILIAN MOVEMENT). At the same time he employed *stile moderno* in orchestrally accompanied sacred music characterized by the *galant* manner of the time. His own contrapuntal skill is evident in numerous canonic compositions. The breadth of his scholarly efforts, his discernment, and his clear presentation of the historical and artistic problems of his time are revealed clearly in his musical and historical studies (which, like his music, are largely unpublished). He had the same kind of appreciation for J. S. BACH as he had for PALESTRINA, the same understanding of the requirements of liturgical music as for those of opera and instrumental music. He was a leading figure in the Accademia dei Filarmonici in Bologna and the Accademia dei Arcadi in Rome.

Bibliography: G. B. MARTINI, *Carteggio,* ed. F. PARISINI (Bologna 1888); *Musikerbriefe* (Leipzig 1886) v. 1. L. BUSI, *Il Padre G. B. Martini* (Bologna 1891). A. PAUCHARD, *Ein italienischer Musiktheoretiker* (Lugano 1941). L. F. TAGLIAVINI, *Die Musik in Geschichte und Gegenwart,* ed. F. BLUME (Kassel-Basel 1949–) 8:1719–24. O. URSPRUNG, *Die katholische Kirchenmusik* (Potsdam 1931). P. H. LÁNG, *Music in Western Civilization* (New York 1941). N. SLONIMSKY, ed., *Baker's Biographical Dictionary of Musicians* (5th ed. New York 1958) 1037. I. CAVALLINI, ''L'idée d'histoire et d'harmonie du Padre Martini et d'autres penseurs de son temps,'' *International Review of the Aesthetics and Sociology of Music,* 21 (1990) 141–159. F. GONIN, ''Mozart et le Padre Martini: histoire d'une légende?,'' *Revue de Musicologie* 85 (1999) 277–295. N. LUCARELLI, ''Sulla condizione sociale di un musicista del settecento: Vincenzo Carmanini e un raccomandazione di Padre Martini,'' *Esercizi: Musica e Spettacolo,* 12 (1993) 69–86. A. POMPILIO, ed., *Padre Martini: Musica e Cultura nel settecento europeo* (Florence 1987). A. SCHNOEBELEN, ed., *Padre Martini's Collection of Letters in the Civico Museo Bibliografico Musicale in Bologna: An Annotated Index* (Hillsboro, N.Y. 1979). M. VANSCHEEUWIJCK, ''Mozart en Padre Martini (Bologna 1770),'' *Musica Antiqua* 8 (1991) 63–67.

[K. G. FELLERER]

Giovanni Battista Martini. (©Archivo Iconografico, S.A./ CORBIS)

MARTINI, MARTINO

Jesuit missionary, sinologist, and author, a central figure in the CHINESE RITES CONTROVERSY; b. Trent, 1614; d. Hangchow, China, June 6, 1661. Martini entered the Society of Jesus, Oct. 7, 1632, and after studies at the Roman College, he embarked for the Orient (March 23, 1640). From 1643 he exercised the apostolate in Chekiang Province during the upheaval caused by the Ming overthrow. Commissioned as procurator to Rome, he first stopped at Amsterdam and Antwerp to publish his two best-known works, *Novus atlas sinensis* (based largely on Chinese geographies) and *De bello tartarico in Sinis historia,* on the then current Manchu invasion. At Rome (fall 1654), besides pressing for the overland route to China and education of Chinese youth, he successfully defended the Jesuit position on the Rites, under fire since Propaganda's adverse *responsa* of 1645. Without waiting for Alexander VII's favorable decision of March 23, 1656, Martini sailed from Genoa in January with ten mission recruits, but their ship was captured by corsairs in a bloody battle in which the procurator played a heroic part. Back finally in his Hangchow center (June 11, 1659), he began construction of China's most imposing church, but within two years he succumbed to a lingering illness. His piety, learning and aristocratic stature (he was known by the sobriquet ''Admiral'') won him the esteem of the mandarin class and the common people alike. When 17 years after burial the watersoaked coffin was disinterred, the body and its robes were found perfectly preserved.

Bibliography: L. PFISTER, *Notices biographiques et bibliographiques sur les Jésuites de l'ancienne mission de Chine 1552-1773* 1:256–262, with an analysis of Martini's Chinese and foreign compositions that completes C. SOMMERVOGEL, *Bibliothèque de la Compagnie de Jésus* 5: 646–650.

[F. A. ROULEAU]

MARTINUZZI, GYÖRGY (JURAJ UTJEŠENOVIĆ)

Cardinal, Transylvanian statesman (popularly "Friar George"); b. Kamičic, Croatia, 1482; d. Alvinc, Transylvania, Dec. 17, 1551. Though he was the son of a Croatian father (Utiešenović), he preferred to use the name of his Venetian mother. After a brief military career he joined the Paulite Order and later became the close adviser of King JOHN I ZÁPOLYA (1526–40) of Hungary. In 1534 he was appointed bishop of Nagyvárad and negotiated the Treaty of Nagyvárad (1538), in which King John agreed to Hapsburg succession after his death and thus to the unification of Hungary under Ferdinand I. But the dying John repudiated the agreement and made Friar George swear allegiance to his newborn son John Sigismund. Martinuzzi, as governor of Transylvania, attempted to maintain the infant's position with the support of Sultan Suleiman I. After the capture of Buda (1541) by the Turks, Martinuzzi returned to the original plan of unification of Hungary under the Hapsburgs in order to resist Turkish expansion. After lengthy negotiations the new treaty was ratified in 1551, and Martinuzzi was rewarded with the archbishopric of Esztergom (Gran) and the cardinal's hat. Meanwhile, to forestall the expected attack of the Sultan, he maintained friendly relations with the Turks. Such secret contacts raised the suspicions of Ferdinand's military commander, Castaldo, who, with the connivance of Ferdinand himself, arranged the Cardinal's assassination in the castle of Alvinc.

Bibliography: M. HORVÁTH, *Frater György, élete* (Budapest 1868). O. M. UTIEŠENOVIĆ, *Lebensgeschichte des Cardinals Utiešenović genannt Martinusius* (Vienna 1881). K. JUHÁSZ, "Kardinal Georg Utjesenovich (T1551) und das Bistum Tschanad," *Historisches Jahrbuch der Görres-Gesellschaft* 80 (1961) 252–264.

[L. J. LEKAI]

MARTY, MARTIN

Bishop, missionary; b. Schwyz, Switzerland, Jan. 12, 1834; d. St. Cloud, Minn., Sept. 19, 1896. He was the son of a shoemaker and church sexton, Jacob Alois Marty, who had him educated at the Jesuit college of Klösterli at Hofmatt, at St. Michael's College, Fribourg, and at the Benedictine College of Einsiedeln. Marty was professed as a Benedictine monk at Einsiedeln on May 20, 1855, and ordained on Sept. 14, 1856. Before volunteering for the American missions, Marty taught at his abbey, Einsiedeln (1856–60). In the United States he served as prior of the St. Meinrad foundation in Indiana and became its first mitred abbot in 1871. After directing his abbey from missions in the Dakota Territory for three years, he was appointed vicar apostolic of Dakota by Leo XIII on Aug. 12, 1879. His episcopal consecration took place at Ferdinand, Ind., on Feb. 1, 1880. Marty at once attempted to secure laborers for his vicariate. Temporary help came with the arrival of the Sisters of the Holy Cross for hospital work in the Black Hills and of Benedictines for mission work at Standing Rock, the Sioux agency in Dakota. The staff at Standing Rock became permanent in 1880 with the arrival of additional Benedictine sisters and priests. Other workers in the vicariate included the foundations of Presentation sisters at Aberdeen and Benedictine sisters at Sturgis; Jesuit fathers and Franciscan sisters at the Rosebud and Pine Ridge Indian reservations; and Sisters of Charity (Gray Nuns) at Fort Totten. By 1884 the vicariate had 13 parochial schools and 82 churches served by 45 priests.

After the division of Dakota Territory into states, Marty was assigned as bishop to the new Diocese of Sioux Falls, S.D. (Nov. 15, 1889). He convened diocesan synods in 1892 and 1893, cooperated with other western bishops in securing Catholic immigrants, and served on the board of trustees of The Catholic University of America, Washington, D.C., and on the Federal Board of Indian Affairs (1893). Marty had a great interest in the Sioux tribe, which had been placed under the care of his abbey in 1876. He established strong missions for the Sioux on their reservations. Tribe members were encouraged to participate in liturgical chants and to take part in discussions in parish societies and the annual Indian congresses that he originated. Although transferred to the See of St. Cloud on Jan. 21, 1895, he retained jurisdiction over the Dakota tribes. He published a revision of Augustine Ravoux's Sioux ritual (1890), as well as a biography of Bp. John Martin Hennie of Milwaukee, Wis. (1888).

Bibliography: M. C. DURATSCHEK, *Beginnings of Catholicism in South Dakota* (Washington 1943). A. KLEBER, *History of St. Meinrad Archabbey, 1854–1954* (St. Meinrad, Ind. 1954). R. F. KAROLEVITZ, *With Faith, Hope and Tenacity: The First One Hundred Years of the Catholic Diocese of Sioux Falls, 1889–1989* (Mission Hills, S.D. 1989).

[M. C. DURATSCHEK]

MARTYR

A person who has given or exposed his life in testimony to the truth or relevance of the Christian faith. The word comes from the Greek μάρτυς (witness); and the theological concept is made precise by St. AUGUSTINE; *Martyrem non facit poena, sed causa* (It is the reason why, not the suffering that constitutes the martyr: *Epist.* 89.2). But it was only with the development of Christian teaching in the postapostolic Church that the words μάρτυς, μαρτυρεῖν, μαρτύριον took on this specific significance. According to Judaism, martyrdom was considered a work of individual piety and resistance to evil, perfecting the victim and serving as edification for the chosen people. In the Acts of the Pagan Martyrs and the Soliloquies of Epictetus, the stoic meaning of the term was rather that of the function of the philosopher who not only teaches by words, but confirms the truth of his message by deeds, particularly by showing indifference to the movements of passion, worldly experience, and even death.

In the Bible. Never in the OT and only rarely in the NT does the term extend beyond its basic, often juridical, meaning of witness, to embrace what later centuries have commonly understood by the word "martyr." Yet such an extension was inevitable because of the fierce opposition to the Christian witness from the beginning, and it is clearly reflected in the NT.

Thus, in Acts 22.20 St. Paul acknowledges his complicity in the first Christian martyrdom "when the blood of Stephen, thy witness [τοῦ μάρτυρός σου] was shed." In Rv 2.13 Christ reminds the Church at Pergamum of "Antipas, my faithful witness [ὁ μάρτυς μου ὁ πιστός μου] who was slain among you." In Rv 11.3 reference is made to the two witnesses of Christ (τοῖς δυσὶν μάρτυσίν μου) slain by the beast from the abyss; and in Rv 17.6, the woman Babylon is described as "drunk with the blood of the saints and with the blood of the martyrs [τῶν μαρτύρων] of Jesus."

Finally, two passages, Rv 1.5 and 3.14, identify Christ Himself as "the faithful witness [ὁ μάρτυς ὁ πιστός]." That here also the meaning may include the technical one of martyr is confirmed by (1) the parallel expression noted above in Rv 2.13; (2) the title "firstborn of the dead" that follows immediately in 1.5; and (3) the popular designation by the early Church of Christ Himself as "the first martyr."

In the Early Church. The postapostolic Epistle of CLEMENT I (*c.* 96) the verb μαρτυρείν (to witness) is used to describe the endurance of SS. Peter and Paul in their sufferings. "Peter who because of unrighteous jealousy suffered . . . and having given his testimony [μαρτυρίσας] went to the glorious place" (5.4); and "Paul showed the way to the prize of endurance. . . . He taught righteousness to the whole world, and gave testimony [μαρτυρίσας] before the rulers . . . and passed

Jean de Brébeuf and Gabriel Lalemant being martyred by the Iroquois in Canada, 1649.

from the world to the holy place" (5.5, 7). The reference in both these instances stresses the endurance of the Apostles almost in a stoic sense of the word; it stresses their indifference to suffering as the result of their faith rather than as a sign of its truth.

With IGNATIUS OF ANTIOCH (*c.* 116) the Christian sense of giving testimony to the belief in Christ as God by shedding one's blood appears; but Ignatius used the words μιμητής (imitator: *Phil.* 7.2; *Rom.* 6.3) and μαθητης (disciple: *Rom.* 5.3; *Mag.* 9.1) rather than μάρτυς; for according to his thinking the martyr was one who perfectly imitated Christ in his suffering and death. Ignatius further insisted on the bodily suffering of the martyr as an antidote to docetist (*see* DOCETISM) teaching that denied that Christ had a real body. He employed the term παθήματα or sufferings of the witnesses to Christ as proof that Christ "was clothed in flesh" (*Smyr.* 5.1–2).

In the account of the martyrdom of Polycarp (*c.* 165 or 170) the words "martyr" and "martyrdom" took on

"Torture of St. Hippolyte," by Dieric Bouts the Elder, c. 1470, St. Salvator Cathedral, Bruges, Belgium. (©Francis G. Mayer/ CORBIS)

the full significance of witnessing belief that the life and death of Christ was that of the Son of God: and they were so employed subsequently in the passions and legends of the martyrs. However, the martyrdom of James recorded by HEGESIPPUS (*c.* 170) seems to have ignored this meaning (Eusebius, *Hist. eccl.* 2.23.4–18). The Letter of the Churches of Lyons and Vienne (*ibid.* 5.1–4) explicitly used the term μάρτυς to describe the shedding of blood in persecution as a witness to Christ. The use of the word "martyr" for confessors who had not shed their blood was protested (*ibid.* 5.2.2–4); and Tertullian (*De cor.* 2), Hippolytus of Rome (*Comm. in Dan.* 2.36.6), and Cyprian of Carthage (*Epist.* 5.2; *De laps.* 3–4) likewise applied to living witnesses only the word "confessors" (ὁμόλογοι).

The Shepherd of HERMAS stated that those who "suffered for the name [of the Son of God] are glorious; all their sins have been taken away" (*Sim.* 9.28.3); and he further spoke of only those sitting on the right hand of God who had suffered stripes, imprisonments, crucifixions, and wild beasts for the sake of His name (*Vis.* 3.2.1). In the *Epistle to DIOGNETUS* the author insisted that the superhuman courage of the martyrs and the greatness of their sacrifice could be explained only as a manifestation of the power of God, acting in and through them (7.7–9). The author further warned of the contrast between a death that is the guarantee of eternal life in martyrdom and real death of eternal fire (10.7). The Christian assurance of the presence of God with the martyr was echoed in the *passio* of SS. Perpetua and Felicity, as well as in JUSTIN MARTYR (*Dial. Tryph.* 110.4), Tertullian (*Apol.* 50.13), and Lactantius (*Div. inst.* 5.13.11). But this fortitude was considered a scandalous carelessness by the pagans, as Marcus Aurelius (*Med.* 13.31) and Justin Martyr (2 *Apol.* 12.1) testify.

Although Cyprian spoke of the treasures that the Church enjoyed in its martyrs (*Epist.* 10.5), the cult of martyrs had a comparatively late and slow development. The earlier Christians had merely attempted to bestow on them a fitting burial in a pagan or private cemetery. The first martyr whose bones received known veneration with a yearly commemoration was POLYCARP of Smyrna (d. *c.* 155 or 165). The record of his martyrdom describes the gathering of his bones after the body was burned and their emplacement in a fitting depository and speaks of "celebrating the birthday of his martyrdom" (*Mart. Poly.* 18.1–3). JULIAN THE APOSTATE compared the veneration of martyrs with the cult of pagan gods and heroes (*c.* 360), but Jerome (*Cont. Vigil.* 4–5), Augustine (*Civ.* 22.10), Theodoret of Cyr (*Graec. aff. cur.* 8.34), and CYRIL OF ALEXANDRIA (*C. Jul.* 10) repudiated the comparison and clarified the specifically Christian concept in relation to a defense of the Christian faith and the value of Christian virtues, such as chastity.

Tertullian had considered martyrdom the *secunda intinctio* or second baptism (*De paenit.* 13) since it removed all sin and assured the martyr of his eternal crown. In this Tertullian echoed the Shepherd of Hermas. Clement of Alexandria (*Strom.* 4.9.75) said the martyr was assured of an immediate entrance into glory since Christ was present with the martyr in his suffering. For Origen, martyrdom was a proof of Christianity, not only because the Christian showed himself capable of dying for his faith but because the Christian defiance of death was a testimony of the victory already achieved over the evil powers and an assertion of the resurrection that would render him immune to suffering (*C. Celsum* 1.24; 2.47; *Comm. in Jn.* 6.54). Thus the martyr's life was the fulfillment of the Christian striving for perfection. For Clement of Alexandria (*Strom.* 4.7.43) likewise, both the preparation for martyrdom and the martyrdom of the passions were equivalent to the actual shedding of one's blood; and Origen acknowledged that there were many Christians who suffered a daily martyrdom of conscience by willingly carrying their cross behind the Savior (*Hom. in Num.* 10.2). Cyprian stated that if someone were unwillingly prevented from achieving martyrdom, he would receive the crown for which he had prepared (*Ad. Fortun.* 13) and admitted that "peace also has its crown" (*De zelo* 16). METHODIUS of Olympus maintained that the virgin who had preserved her chastity with patience was worthy of the same honor as a martyr (*Conviv.* 7.3.156);

Soliders capture Joan of Arc, manuscript illumination.

and DIONYSIUS of Alexandria believed that one who had given his life tending the sick during a pestilence should be considered a martyr (Eusebius, *Hist. eccl.* 7.22.7).

The notion of a white martyrdom was common among the desert fathers as the *APOPHTHEGMATA PATRUM* attest. Rufinus of Aquileia with his translation of the Rules of Basil of Caesarea (*Praef. in hom. Bas.*), Jerome (*Epist.* 108.31), Augustine (*Serm. de mart.*), and Caesarius of Arles (*Serm.* 41.) popularized the idea in the West, and GREGORY I (*Dial.* 3.26; *Hom. in Evang.* 2.36.7) handed it on to the Middle Ages. The Irish monks spoke of a white martyrdom "in giving up what one loved for the love of God"; and of a green martyrdom that consisted in suppressing the passions and doing penance ceaselessly.

In dealing with abuses that surrounded the cult of the martyrs on pilgrimages and the celebration of banquets at the martyrs' tombs, Augustine changed the emphasis on the sufferings and tortures suffered by the martyrs to a reconsideration of the martyr. He considered him to be one who professed his faith in Christ by the perfection of his virtues and the living of a life in full conformity with the spiritual teachings of the Church. Despite the wonders and extravagances attributed to the martyrs in the *Glories of the Martyrs* by Gregory of Tours, and even in the *Dialogues* of Gregory I, the latter insisted essentially on the life of the Christian as a spiritual martyrdom.

The Number of Martyrs. Since at least the 17th century, efforts have been made to modify the extravagant notion of an almost unlimited number of martyrs in the early Church. H. Dodwell published a tract *De paucitate martyrum* (Oxford 1648) in which he greatly reduced the estimate of early martyrs; but T. Ruinart, in his *Acta primorum martyrum* (Paris 1689), while selective in his research, held to the tradition of an immense number. In recent times L. Hertling estimated the number as close to 100,000, while H. Grégoire believed it closer to 10,000.

Tacitus had spoken of an *ingens multitudo* in the 1st century (*Annal.* 15.44.4); and it is certain that large numbers were put to death especially under Decius and Diocletian, as well as by the Persians. Reliable statistics are simply not available.

Bibliography: J. S. CONSIDINE, ''The Two Witnesses: Rv 11: 3–13,''*The Catholic Biblical Quarterly* 8 (1946) 377–392. I. FRANSEN, ''Jésus, le témoin fidèle,'' *Bible et vie chrétienne* 16 (1956) 66–79. A. P. FRUTAZ and J. BECKMANN, *Lexikon für Theologie und Kirche,* ed. J. HOFER and K. RAHNER (Freiburg 1957–65); 7: 127–133. H. LECLERCQ, *Dictionnaire d'archéologie chrétienne et de liturgie,* ed. F. CABROL, H. LECLERQ, and H. I. MARROU, 15 v. (Paris 1907–53) 10.2:2359–2512. E. PETERSON, *Zeuge der Wahrheit* (Leipzig 1937). H. DELEHAYE, *Origines des cultes des martyrs* (2d ed. Paris 1933); *Analecta Bollandiana* 39 (1921) 20–49. P. PEETERS, *ibid.* 50–64. M. VILLER, *Aszese und Mystik in der Väterzeit,* rev. and tr. K. RAHNER (Freiburg 1939) 29–40, 256, 308–315. G. JOUASSARD, *Recherches de science religieuse* 39 (1951) 362–367. E. E. MALONE, *The Monk and the Martyr* (Washington 1950). T. KLAUSER, *Christlicher Märtyrerkult* (Cologne 1960). N. BROX, *Zeuge und Märtyrer* (Munich 1961). A. J. VERMEULEN, *The Semantic Development of Gloria in Early Christian Latin* (Nijmegen 1956) 53–96. H. MUSURILLO, *Traditio* 12 (1956) 55–67, asceticism. A. RUSH, *Theological Studies* 23 (1962) 569–589, Gregory I. H. GRÉGOIRE et al., *Bulletin de la Classe des Lettres de l'Académie Royale de Belgique* 38 (1952) 37–60, 62–70, number of martyrs.

[F. X. MURPHY/W. F. DICHARRY]

MARTYRDOM, THEOLOGY OF

From μαρτύριον (testimony, proof), the condition of being a MARTYR, of enduring suffering or having undergone death for a cause, and, in theology and in this article, of having been put to death as a witness to Christ. Classically, three conditions were required: (1) that physical life has been laid down and real death undergone; (2) that death has been inflicted in hatred of Christian life and truth; and (3) that death has been voluntarily accepted in defense of these. Hence, on the first count those who ardently desire to die for Christ, or who accept or choose a life of suffering for His sake, are not technically martyrs; nor, on the second count, those who die from disease or in consequence of the accepted risks attendant on the way of life they have chosen for Christ, or from devotion to the cause of scientific research, or for their country, or, however exalted their motives, for error or by suicide; nor, on the third count, those who have not reached the age of reason or who are slain without making a choice. Such is the general teaching of theologians, although the final point is not beyond question if it is taken to mean that there must be a conscious act of deliberate choice. Cajetan, characteristically, allows that a man might be martyred in his sleep, and for the same underlying reason he holds that unbaptized babies can be saved in the faith of their parents; thus also is explained why the Church enrolls the Holy Innocents among the martyrs without crediting them with a miraculous precocity, and by common teaching that the blood that is shed takes the place of the water that flows in Baptism.

The second condition calls for some comment. Many of the martyrs in the calendar have been killed *in odium fidei,* that is, in direct witness to the truths of faith, but others, such as SS. JOHN THE BAPTIST and Maria GORETTI, have offered their lives in defense of Christian virtue, and some, such as St. THOMAS OF CANTERBURY and JOHN OF NEPOMUC (long popularly credited with martyrdom), for the sake of Church order and discipline. What is required is that the cause is the living truth of Christ. How transcendent this is, and consequently how wide are the fields in which martyrdom can be found, will vary according to the reading of theologians on the interpenetration of grace and nature. Some will tend to reserve it to orthodox confessional formularies, and of course liturgical celebration and the process of canonization will observe this restriction, while others, taking to heart the Ambrosian saying that all truth whatever it is and whoever utters it is from the Holy Spirit, will be quicker to recognize all heroic witness to the extremity of death as Christian martyrdom. Those who die for infidelity, or heresy, or schism, are in a special case. It may be doubted whether error as such ever evokes heroism: what happens is that men such as HUSS and CRANMER at the end die with dignity, not for such an abstraction, but in a concrete situation of mixed causes where they are prepared to affirm a value with their lives. The personal respect and admiration they deserve cannot amount to public and official recognition within the system of the Church's worship; and the same, it seems, should be said about non-Catholic missionaries who have been killed for preaching the gospel.

The rule of thumb for the martyr was stipulated by St. Augustine: martyrdom derives, not from the punishment inflicted, but the reasons for the punishment *(non poena sed causa).* Although such a rule seems straightforward, it is not always so in actual practice. Thomas Aquinas, for example, points out that John the Baptist was a martyr because he denounced adultery; hence he was a martyr for the sake of the ''truth of faith'' (*Summa Theologiae,* IIa IIae, q.124 art. 5). Pope Paul VI extended this further in beatifying Maximilian KOLBE (1971) as a ''martyr of charity.'' Kolbe witnessed in the ultimate gesture of love or charity. In that sense, he died for the ''defense of the faith'' as Aquinas described it. In the canonizations of Kolbe (1982) and Edith STEIN (1998), Pope John Paul II manifested an even more nuanced view of martyrdom. Martyrdom may be a public witness even unto the death for the truth of the Gospel, even when the explicit reason for the martyr's death is not a refusal to apostasize by denying the faith. Neither the sacrifice of a life for the sake of another (Kolbe) nor the death of one out of racial hatred (Stein) is what makes them martyrs. The reason(s) why the pope sees them as martyrs is that their lives stood in direct and dramatic counterpoint to forces of evil and untruth.

Martyrdom is treated by moral theologians as the chief act of the virtue of FORTITUDE. The inclusion of such an ultimate and final confession of love for Christ under the heading of a moral virtue can be partly explained for methodological reasons. Yet its heroism is elicited from man's emotional organism, and it is there that the pain and terror is mastered by the commanding virtues of religion, faith, and above all, charity. It is the constant teaching of the Church that such an intensity of love is expressed as to justify the sinner, baptized or unbaptized, and bring to him the forgiveness of all his sins, removing all guilt and stain, pardoning all debt of temporal punishment, and adorning him with a special crown, or aureole. He who prays for a martyr does him an injury, said Innocent III.

Bibliography: THOMAS AQUINAS, *Summa Theologiae* 2a2ae, 124. R. HEDDE, *Dictionnaire de théologie catholique,* ed. A. VACANT et al. (Paris 1903–50) 10.1:220–254. B. H. MERKELBACH, *Summa theologiae moralis* (8th ed. Paris 1949) 2:859–862.

[T. GILBY/L. S. CUNNINGHAM]

Three martyr saints, detail of 8th-century fresco in the chapel of San Quirco of the church of Santa Maria Antiqua, Rome.

MARTYRIUM

The edifice honoring the grave or memorial (*memoria*) of a martyr or witness for Christ. In the early Church the term came into usage with the cult of the martyrs, but was also applied to places where witness had been given by biblical happenings or by Christ himself in His birth, death, Resurrection, and Ascension. Primarily, however, martyrium signified the monument in a grave or cemetery in which a martyr was interred and where his cult was commemorated.

Proud of their martyrs, the primitive Christians strove to provide them with decent burial and the honors accorded the dead that were a feature of life in the ancient world. While the pagans attempted to conceal the fact of death by commemorating the *dies natalis,* or birthday of the deceased, the Christians quickly changed the meaning of *dies natalis* from earthly birth of the deceased to the day of entrance into eternal life.

By the middle of the 3rd century there is evidence of a formal veneration of the martyrs that accompanied the development of Christian worship. Prayers originally said for the martyrs came to be directed to the martyrs for their intercession. Likewise the gathering in the cemetery or at the grave site that was accompanied by a liturgical celebration soon dictated the need for a memorial in the form of a room as in the catacombs or a separate building. The graffiti acclamations honoring SS. Peter and Paul in the Memoria Apostolorum on the Via Appia are the earliest indications of the special martyr cult and of a *triclia,* or hall-like room, in which ceremonies were performed. The site is an originally pagan cemetery used by Christians, but the origin of the cult cannot be traced with certainty to either an original burial of the Apostles or a possible stay in a house there during their lifetime.

There is question whether the 2d-century monument over the grave of St. Peter in the VATICAN and the mausoleums and graves of martyrs in Salona and North Africa were originally considered martyria, although they became such in the Constantinian age when churches were built over them.

It is with Constantine and St. Helena that the tradition of erecting a monument over the remains of a martyr truly begins. In Rome basilicas were built over or close to the graves of the martyrs MARCELLINUS and Peter, LAWRENCE, and AGNES, which were originally hidden in the catacombs; and on the Vatican and on the Via Ostiense the graves of St. PETER and St. PAUL were likewise so honored. These martyria apparently had no fixed altars and were not used originally for Sunday worship. They were places for begging the intercession of the martyr, and early were used for burial by the imperial family desiring to rest *ad sanctos,* close to the saints.

The basilicas built as martyria in Palestine to commemorate Christ's birth, Crucifixion, and Ascension were likewise not originally intended for community acts of worship but quickly became places of pilgrimage where the Eucharist was celebrated. At Constantinople, the Church of the 12 Apostles, built by either Constantine I or Constantine II, was enriched with the remains of relics of the Apostle St. Andrew and SS. Luke and Timothy. Further impulse was given to the on-site cult of the martyrs by Pope DAMASUS I (366–384), who composed verses in honor of the martyrs found in the catacombs.

In Milan basilicas were constructed for the remains of SS. Nazarius and Celsus and SS. GERVASE and PROTASE, which were transferred with solemn rites to their new martyria. The same was done for St. Babylas at Antioch. A rich martyrium was erected at Alexandria for St. Menas, and another at Chalcedon for St. Euphemia at the end of the 4th century; later a basilica in honor of St. John the Evangelist in Ephesus. That the function of witness to Christ was still an important feature of a martyrium is indicated by the fact that the first certain imposition of an altar over the martyr site is met with in the Miracle of the Loaves Church at Genesareth.

In the 5th and 6th centuries the spread of the cult of martyrs led to the reconstruction of older churches and the building of new basilicas as martyria; thus St. PAULINUS OF NOLA rebuilt the church honoring St. Felix, and at Marusina near Salona a martyrium was built behind the altar over the mausoleum of the original church. This practice led to the attaching of chapels for the relics or remains of saints to older churches. Reliquary chapels were common in North Syria after the 5th century and gradually the custom spread of enclosing parts of the remains of martyrs and saints in mausoleums or beneath the altars of churches in ROME, Constantinople, and RAVENNA and led to the search for martyr graves as is indicated at Padua, Corinth, and CYPRUS. The architecture of the martyrium seems originally to have imitated the ancient sepulcher architecture, particularly that of the Heroiën, but there was no set style as the various types of basilicas throughout the Christian Empire attest.

See Also: RELIQUARIES.

Bibliography: T. KLAUSER, *Vom Heroon zur Märtyrerbasilika* (Bonn 1942). A. GRABAR, *Martyrium* 3 v. (Paris 1943–46), F. W, DEICHMANN and A. TSCHIRA, "Das Mausoleum der Kaiserin Helena . . . , "*Jahrbuch des Deutschen Archäologischen Instituts* 72 (1957) 44–110. J. JEREMIAS, *Heiligengräber in Jesu Umwelt* (Göttingen 1958). R. KRAUTHEIMER, "Mensa, coemeterium, martyrium," *Cahiers archéologiques* 11 (1960) 15–40. H. M. COLVIN, *Architecture and the After-life* (New Haven 1991).

[F. X. MURPHY]

MARTYROLOGIES

Lists of martyrs in the order of their feasts. The oldest catalogs of saints were also calendars that indicated the feasts of interest to particular churches. In Christian antiquity, each church had its own calendar that indicated what martyr or saint was to be commemorated in what church according to that specific local church's custom. A martyrology lists the names of a number of martyrs and saints whose anniversaries are reckoned on the same day, borrowing from among the more prominent ones of neighboring churches. One of the most ancient, which became the basis for the later Roman sanctoral, was that of the CHRONOGRAPHER of 354. This document was an almanac written and illustrated by Furius Dionysius Filocalus. It was compiled in 336 and completed down to 354. It contains, along with other listings, a *Deposition episcoporum* and a *Depositio martyrum*—lists of the anniversaries, as well as the dates and places of burial, of the bishops and of martyrs honored each year at Rome, the first martyr-pope of which is St. Callistus in 222 and the last martyrs of which suffered in the persecution under Diocletian at Rome that ended during 305. Still extant likewise are the calendars of the Churches of Tours (5th century), Carthage and Carmona (6th century), and Oxyrhynchus.

The martyrologies evolved through a combination of several such lists of martyrs to include the saints of the Church universal. The menology and SYNAXARY of the Oriental Churches correspond to the Latin martyrologies that were read during the canonical hours, specifically Prime, since the 8th century. While some orders preserved the reading of the martyrology at extraliturgical times, the suppression of the office of Prime by Vatican II mostly resulted in the disuse of the martyrology.

Historical Development. The oldest extant martyrology is the Syriac Breviary or Calendar of Antioch compiled between 362 and 381 with the title: "The names of our masters, the Martyrs and Victors, with the dates on which they received their crowns." The Greek text is lost, but a synopsis in Syriac dating from 411 has been preserved. To the names of martyrs anterior to the epoch of Diocletian it adds those of the great persecution, during which there were thousands of martyrs in the East, down to 313; those of the Licinian persecution in 320 and 361 to 363. To the martyrs of the eastern Mediterranean basin it added the Orientals of Armenia and Mesopotamia. In particular, mention is made of Stephen (December 26); John and James (December 27); Peter and Paul (December 28); Epiphany (January 6); Polycarp (February 23); Perpetua, Saturninus, and 10 other confessors (March 7); a memorial of all the confessors (Friday after Easter); the Machabees (August 1); Sixtus, bishop of Rome (August 8); and Ignatius of Antioch (October 17).

In the middle of the 5th century (*c.* 431) another martyrology appeared in northern Italy whose preface claimed falsely that it was the work of St. JEROME, thus known as the Hieronymian Martyrology. This martyrology, given a critical edition by H. Delehaye in 1931, is a basic document for hagiographical studies. The oldest manuscripts of the work go back to the 8th century and depend upon a single Gallican recension that was made in Auxerre between 592 and 600 (according to L. Duchesne) or at Luxeuil between 627 and 628 (B. Krusch). By the eliminating of later additions, it becomes comparatively easy to reconstruct the original text, which was compiled from three principal sources: the work of the Chronographer of 354 continued to 420, the Syriac Breviary, and an African calendar, as well as several other as yet unresolved sources. To give an air of authenticity to the work, the author added an apocryphal exchange of letters between Bps. Chromatius of Aquileia, Heliodorus of Altinum, and St. Jerome. Like the calendars, the martyrologies ordinarily mention only the martyr or saint's name, date of commemoration, and the place of martyrdom or cult. Sometimes, however, a brief notice is supplied concerning the circumstances of martyrdom.

A new development in the formation of martyrologies occurred in the 8th and 9th centuries with the compilation of ''historical'' martyrologies, which added two elements to the information furnished by the martyrology of St. Jerome: a brief account of the saint's life and a large number of names taken from Eusebius's *Ecclesiastical History,* the Scriptures, legends, and the writings of the Fathers. Thus they filled in the empty dates left in the earlier martyrologies. The Venerable BEDE (d. 735) was the first to compose such a martyrology, using his competence and knowledge as an historian. The historical martyrologies also added more detailed accounts of the martyr. Bede's work was continued at Lyons, first by an anonymous cleric who compiled a new martyrology (*c.* 800) by adding numerous notices to those of Bede (J. Dubois, *Edition pratique des martyrologes de Bède, de l'anonyme lyonnais et de Florus* [Paris 1978]) and later by the deacon FLORUS OF LYONS who completed the former's work (*c.* 850). Until then all went well. The number of notices was augmented from one redaction to another, and it was done conscientiously. But *c.* 865 a falsifier, ADO OF VIENNE, published a ''Small Roman Martyrology,'' which he claimed was an ancient papal martyrology that he had discovered in Italy (see J. Dubois, *Le Martyrologe d'Adon,* CNRS [Paris 1984]). As a matter of fact, he had manufactured it by unscrupulously changing the dates in the earlier martyrologies. Thus he fixed the date for Ignatius of Antioch on February 1 and that for St. Basil on June 14. In 875 USUARD of Saint-Germain, by reducing certain sections of the martyrology of Ado, and augmenting others, while retaining a substantial part, composed the martyrology that bears his name. This was long in use among the Benedictines of Rome and is still employed by the Cistercians. Practically speaking, it is the direct ancestor of the Roman Martyrology.

Roman Martyrology. The official record of saints and martyrs recognized by the Roman Church was officially published by Pope Gregory XIII in 1584. Having reformed the calendar of the Church with the bull *Inter gravissimas* (Feb. 14, 1582), Gregory formed a commission (7–10 members) under Cardinal Sirleto (d. 1585) with the future cardinal BARONIUS as leading light, to bring out a thoroughly revised edition of the Martyrology of Usuard then in use in Rome. A provisionary edition was printed in 1582 covering the period from October 15 to December 31. One dealing with the annual cycle of saints and martyrs was published (1583) without a letter of papal approbation. This edition had at base the Martyrology of Usuard, with additions from those of St. Cyriacus (MS F85 bibl. Vallicelliana), Bede, Florus, and Ado, and from the Greek menologies translated into Latin by Cardinal Sirleto, the Dialogues of St. GREGORY I, and calendars of individual churches, particularly those in Italy. After emendations this text was published as official for the universal Church by Pope Gregory XIII on Jan. 14, 1584, with the bull *Emendatio.* In 1586 it was republished under Sixtus V with the notes and treatise on the Roman Martyrology by Baronius, who had been encouraged by Sirleto to publish the *fontes* and documentation in anticipation of critical reaction. Though far from the standards required by modern hagiography, this edition was a first attempt at achieving historical accuracy. It was frequently revised, particularly in 1630 under URBAN VIII, and reorganized also under CLEMENT X in 1681 and BENEDICT XIV in 1748. Benedict studied many of the problems personally in view of his precisions on the beatification and canonization of saints. The edition of 1913 is a revision of that of Benedict XIV. Between 1913 and 1956 several further editions were published; that in 1924, known as the *editio prima post typicam,* contains many changes based on attempts at complete reform. It was, however, strongly criticized by Dom H. Quentin (*Analecta Bollandiana* 42 [1924] 387–406). Since then, other editions merely added new feasts and newly canonized saints. A thorough revision has been underway since 1984. John Paul II stimulated renewed interest in compiling local martyrologies in his apostolic letter *Tertio millenio adveniente.* Noting that the Church of the second millennium had once again become a church of the martyrs, the pope urged that, ''As far as possible, their witness should not be lost to the Church . . . The local Churches should do everything possible to ensure that the memory of those who have suffered martyrdom should be safeguarded'' (no. 37).

Bibliography: R. AIGRAIN, *L'Hagiographie* (Paris 1953). B. DE GAIFFIER, ''De l'usage et de la lecture du martyrologe: témoignages antérieur au XIe siècle,'' *Analecta Bollandiana* 79 (1961) 42–47. H. DELEHAYE, ed., *Commentarius perpetuus in martyrologium hieronymianum,* (*Acta Sanctorum* Nov. 2:2; 1931) ix–xxiii. J. DUBOIS, ''Introduction à la revision du Martyrologe romain,'' *Notitiae* 21 (1985) 90–100; ''Les martyrologes du moyen âge latin,'' *Typologie des sources du moyen âge occidental* 26 (Brepols 1978). H. QUENTIN, *Les Martyrologes historiques du moyen âge* (Paris 1908). H. A. SCHMIDT, *Introductio in liturgiam occidentalem* (Rome 1960).

[J. LE BRUN/EDS.]

MARTYROLOGY, ROMAN

Roman martyrology is the record of the saints and martyrs recognized by the Roman Church and used in the liturgy. It was officially published by Pope Gregory XIII in 1584. Having reformed the calendar of the Church with the bull *Inter gravissimas* (Feb. 14, 1582), Gregory formed a commission (7–10 members) under Cardinal Sirleto (d. 1585) with the future cardinal BARONIUS as leading light, to bring out a thoroughly revised edition of the Martyrology of Usuard then in use in Rome. A provisionary edition was printed in 1582 covering the period from October 15 to December 31. One dealing with the annual cycle of saints and martyrs was published (1583) without a letter of papal approbation. This editon had as its base the Martyrology of Usuard, with additions from those of St. Cyriacus (MS F85 bibl. Vallicelliana), Bede, Florus, and Ado, and from the Greek menologies translated into Latin by Cardinal Sirleto, the Dialogues of St. GREGORY I, and calendars of individual churches, particularly those in Italy. After emendations this text was published as official for the universal Church by Pope Gregory XIII on Jan. 14, 1584, with the bull *Emendatio.* In 1586 it was republished under Sixtus V with the notes and treatise on the Roman Martyrology by Baronius, who had been encouraged by Sirleto to publish the *fontes* and documentation in anticipation of critical reaction. Though far from the standards required by modern hagiography, this edition was a first attempt at achieving historical accuracy. It was frequently revised, particularly in 1630 under URBAN VIII, who reorganized also under CLEMENT X in 1681 and BENEDICT XIV in 1748. Benedict studied many of the problems personally in view of his precisions on the beatification and canonization of saints. The so-called *Editio Typica* of 1913 is a revision of that of Benedict XIV. Between 1913 and 1956 several further editions were published, and that published in 1924 contained many changes based on attempts at complete reform. It was, however, strongly criticized by Dom H. Quentin [*Analecta Bollandiana,* 42 (1924) 387–406] and more recent editions have merely added new feasts and newly canonized saints. A thoroughly reworked edition was published by the Congregation for Divine Worship and the Discipline of the Sacraments in October 2001.

Bibliography: H. LÄMMER, *De Martyrologio Romano* (Ratisbon 1878). R. AIGRAIN, *L'Hagiographie* (Paris 1953) 91–99.

[J. LE BRUN/EDS.]

MARTYROLOGY OF ST. JEROME

The martyrology of St. Jerome is a calendar recording of the feast days of saints in the early Roman, African, and Oriental Churches, whose authorship was falsely attributed to St. Jerome. The original source of its notations is a general martyrology, probably of Nicomedian origin, closely related to the earliest Syrian maryrology. During the early 5th century, the Greek text of this Eastern martyrology was translated into Latin by an unknown northern Italian cleric, and combined with several Western church calendars. The name of St. Jerome was employed to give the work value, and it was supplied with two spurious letters by way of a preface; the first supposedly from CHROMATIUS OF AQUILEIA and Heliodorus of Altinum, who asked Jerome to send them a list of feasts contained in the *Feriale* of Eusebius; the second, Jerome's response stating that he had shortened the list because of the plethora of names in the original, which cited between 500 and 800 saints for each day.

Besides the Oriental martyrology, L. Duchesne indicates two other principal sources found in the martyrology: the *CHRONOGRAPHER OF 354*, which furnishes the data under the rubric *Romae*, and an African martyrology of the 4th century with the names under the rubric *In Africa*.

The original Latin version of the martyrology was prepared for use in the daily liturgy as a supplement to the DIPTYCHS; but whether it was actually used as such is not known. In the 6th century the Martyrology of St. Jerome served as a book of edification in monasteries (Cassiodorus, *De inst. divin. lect.* 32) and was cited by GREGORY I in 598 (*Epist.* 1.8, 29). In the 7th century it disappeared from the Church of Italy; between 592 and 600, according to Duchesne; and before 627, according to J. Kirsch. Meanwhile, it was brought to Arles, and from there it spread to the rest of Gaul. This Gallican recension is the source of all the extant manuscripts, a fact that is verified not only by the mention of the local French saints, but also by the appearance of certain feasts of Christ, Our Lady, and the Apostles proper to the Gallic church such as the *depositio beatae Mariae* on January 18.

Many mistakes in the manuscripts were caused by the carelessness of copyists or by the juxtaposition of documents, as when saints or groups of saints are repeated two, three, or even as many as ten times. Long and difficult study regarding the source and provinience of the martyrology yielded few results until the principal key was found with the discovery by F. Wright of the Syrian Martyrology.

The Martyrology of St. Jerome begins with December 25 and gives, in calendar form, the names of saints commemorated each day, with a notation regarding the city where their cult or grave is located. Information is also supplied concerning the translation of RELICS, the consecration of bishops, and the dedication of churches.

Bibliography: Editions. J. B. DE ROSSI and L. DUCHESNE, eds., *Acta Sanctorum,* Nov. 2.1 (1894), new ed. H. QUENTIN, *Acta Sanctorum,* Nov. 2.2 (1931), with comment. by H. DELEHAYE. J. B. DE ROSSI and L. DUCHESNE, "Les Sources du Martyrologe hiéronymien," *Mélanges d'archéologie et d'histoire* 5 (1885) 115–160. J. P. KIRSCH, *Der staatsrömische christliche Festkalender im Altertum: Textkritisch Untersuchungen zu den römischen "Depositiones" und dem Martyrologium Hieronymianum* (Münster 1924). W. H. FRERE, *Studies in Early Roman Liturgy,* 3 v. (Oxford 1930–35) v.1 *The Kalendar. Dictionnaire d'archéologie chrétienne et de liturgie,* ed. F. CABROL, H. LECLERCQ and H. I. MARROU, 15 v. (Paris 1907–53) 10.2:2523–2619. R. AIGRAIN, *L'Hagiographie* (Paris 1953). B. DE GAIFFIER, *Analecta Bollandiana* 79 (1961) 40–59. B. ALTANER, *Patrology,* tr. H. GRAEF from 5th German ed. (New York 1960) 247–248. R. STIEGER, *Lexikon für Theologie und Kirche*, ed. J. HOFER and K. RAHNER, 10 v. (2d, new ed. Freiburg 1957–65) 7:138–140.

[R. BRYAN]

MARULIĆ, MARKO

Croatian humanist, poet, moralist, and "father of Croatian literature"; b. Split, Aug. 18, 1450; d. there, Jan. 6, 1524. He was the son of a lawyer who belonged to the nobility, and he studied classical languages and literature, poetry, rhetoric, and philosophy at Padua, Italy. Equipped with this wide culture, Marulić returned to Split and dedicated his life to study and literature. He was also proficient in painting and sculpture. At 60 he withdrew to a Franciscan monastery on the nearby island of Solta, but, disillusioned at the religious life he encountered there, he returned after two years to Split, where he continued to live an ascetical life. His reputation rests primarily on his Latin didactic-moral works, which were widely diffused, being translated into Italian, French, Spanish, Portuguese, German, and Czech; numerous editions of the works appeared up to the 19th century.

The most important of these works are *De institutione bene vivendi per exempla sanctorum* (1506), a treatise that St. Francis XAVIER carried on all his journeys; *Evangelistarium* (1506); *Quinquaginta parabolae* (1510); *De humilitate et gloria Christi* (1519); and *Dialogus de laudibus Herculis* (1524). His *Sermo de ultimo Christi judicio* remains in MS. In all these, inspired by the doctrine of St. Bernard and St. Bonaventure, he inculcated a practical Christian morality based on the Gospels and the examples of the saints. He wrote the *Carmen de doctrina Jesu Christi pendentis in cruce* in Latin verse, and his major Latin poetic work, the remarkable epic *Davideidos libri XIV,* is in Vergilian style. His archeological and historical studies led to the translation of a medieval Croatian chronicle under the title *Regum Dalmatiae et Croatiae gesta* and to a polemic piece, *In eos qui beatum Hieronymum Italum esse contendunt.* Both of these were published in *De Regno Dalmatiae et Croatiae* (1666) by the historian J. Lucius, who also included Marulić's *Inscriptiones Salonitanae antiquae* in his *Inscriptiones Dalmatiae* (1673). Marulić's *In epigrammata priscorum commentarius* is extant in MS.

Marulić's vernacular poetry marks the coming of age of Croatian literature. His most important work in this genre, *Istorija svete udovice Judit u versih hrvacki složena* (The History of the Holy Widow Judith), was written in 1501, published in 1521. It is an epic in six cantos, in whose classical structure lyrical Petrarchian elements and strains from popular Croatian poetry mingle. Marulić sought by the example of Judith to strengthen his people in their conflict with the Turks. The same impulse to save Christianity from the Turks inspired *Tuženje grada Hjeruzolima,* a summons to the Christian nations to organize a crusade; *Molitva suprotiva Turkom* (Prayer against the Turks); and the Latin *Epistola . . . ad Adrianum VI . . . de calamitatibus . . . et exhortatio ad communem omnium Christianorum unionem et pacem* (1522).

Marulić's moralistic and didactic bent is evident in other vernacular poems, e.g., the epic *Istorija od Suzane* (History of Susanna), *Urehe duhovne* (Spiritual Adornment), and *Dobri nauci* (Good Teaching). Writing for his nun sister and her convent companions, Marulić adopted at times a humorous-satiric tone, as in *Poklad i Korizma* (Carnival and Lent), *Spovid koludric od sedam smrtnih grihov* (Nuns' Confessions and the Seven Capital Sins), and *Anka Satira.* Finally, he wrote some dramatic pieces on the life of Christ and the saints, and translated *De Imitatione Christi,* the *Disticha moralia Catonis* and some selections from St. Bernard and St. Bonaventure.

As a poet, Marulić was not distinguished for profound inspiration or creative imagination, but he was kindly, cultured, deeply patriotic, endowed with a fine sensitivity to the demands and challenges of life and with an extraordinary, rich idiom. In him are epitomized all the elements that characterized subsequent Croatian literature: the strains of popular poetry, a Christian spirit, classical culture, and the consciousness of the Turkish threat.

Bibliography: Complete vernacular works, *Pjesme,* v.1 (1869) of *Stari pisci hrvatski,* 29 v. (Zagreb 1869); Latin works, *Zbornik u proslavu petstogodišnjice rodenja Marka Marulića,* ed. J. BADALIĆ and N. MAJNARIĆ (Zagreb 1950), contains complete bibliog. M. KOMBOL, *Poviest hrvatske književnosti do narodnog preporoda* (Zagreb 1945). F. TROGRANČIĆ, *Storia della letteratura croata* (Rome 1953).

[P. TIJAN]

MARUTHAS OF MARTYROPOLIS

Fifth-century Persian bishop of Martyropolis (modern Maipherqat); d. before 420. Maruthas took part in the Synods of Constantinople (381) and Side (382), and the Synod of the Oak in 403; he served as imperial ambassador to the Persian court in 399–400 and 409–410. During the latter sojourn he helped reorganize the Church in Persia at the Synod of Seleucia-Ctesiphon and collected the Acts of the Persian martyrs put to death by King Shapur II (d. 379). His *Tractatus de haeresibus* and *Homilia in Dominicam novam* have been preserved; but there is question as to whether Maruthas was actually the author of the *Hypomnemata of Oriental Martyrs.*

Bibliography: *Tractatus de haeresibus,* ed. I. RAHMANI, (Studia Syriaca 4; 1909) 98–103, 76–80; *Homilia,* ed. M. KMOSKO in *Oriens Christianus* 3 (1903) 384–415; *Acts of the Martyrs,* ed. R. MARCUS in *Harvard Theological Review* 25 (1932) 47–71. E. HAMMERSCHMIDT, *Lexikon für Theologie und Kirche* 2 7:140. G. TISSERANT, *Dictionnaire de théologie catholique* 10.1:142–149. J. M. VOSTÉ, *Orientalia Christiana periodica* 12 (1946) 201–205. *Patrologica syriaca* 43, 48–51.

[F. X. MURPHY]

MARUTHAS OF TAGRIT

First maphrian or archmetropolitan of the Persian Monophysite church (629); b. Surzaq, near Balad in modern Iraq, *c.* 565; d. Tagrit (Taghrith), in modern Iraq, May 2, 649. He was a monk and teacher in the monastery of Mar Mattai near Nineveh in 605. Patriarch Athanasius I Gammàlā consecrated him bishop of Tagrit, the only Monophysite community among the Nestorians of Sassanid Persia, when the Persians began to bring back Monophysites from Byzantine lands. He influenced the Syriac Jacobite liturgy and extended his jurisdiction over 12 suffragan sees to Azerbaijan, Herat, and Segestan. Of his writings an anaphora and fragments of homilies have been preserved. His biography was written by his successor, Denhā (*see* MONOPHYSITISM).

Bibliography: E. HAMMERSCHMIDT, *Lexikon für Theologie und Kirche* 2 7:140. O. RÜHLE, *Die Religion in Geschichte und Gegenwart* 3d ed., 4:785. DENHĀ, *Histoire de Marouta,* ed. and tr. F. NAU (*Patrologia orientalis* 3; 1909) 52–96. M. KMOSKO, "Homilia in *Dominicam novam,*" *Oriens Christianus* 3d ed., (1903) 384–415. E. RENAUDOT, *Liturgiarum Orientalium collectio,* 2 v. (2d ed. Frankfurt a.M. 1847) 2:260–268. A. BAUMSTARK, *Geschichte der syrischen Literatur* (Bonn 1922) 245. *Patrologia syriaca* ed. R. GRAFFIN 163–164.

[F. X. MURPHY]

MARX, KARL

German political philosopher; b. Treves, Prussia, May 5, 1818; d. London, March 14, 1883. He was the second of seven children of Hirschel (changed to Heinrich after conversion from Judaism to Protestantism in 1824) and Henrietta Marx; the male forebears of both his parents had been rabbis in Germany and Holland for many generations. As the first son of a well-to-do, small-town lawyer, Marx had the advantage of an intellectual background that was considerably broadened by access to the library of, and frequent conversations with, the cultivated Baron von Westphalen, to whose daughter, Jenny, he was betrothed in 1836 and married in 1843. This marriage took place shortly before his flight to Paris to avoid Prussian authorities who disapproved of his inflammatory writings as editor of *Rheinische Zeitung* (1842), an organ of Young Hegelians opposed to any kind of authoritarianism. The same unorthodoxy had prevented Marx from following his chosen academic career after receiving his doctorate in philosophy from the University of Berlin in 1841.

Collaboration with Engels. Although he was already recognized as a contributor to revolutionary causes, Marx's social philosophy did not reach fruition until 1844, when he renewed his acquaintanus with Friedrich ENGELS (1820–95) in Paris. Their collaboration was destined to father Marxism, a curious combination of dialectical materialism and revolutionary socialism that, adherents claim, has changed the world and that even opponents credit with influencing investigation and thought in related social sciences. It was as expatriates in Paris that Marx and Engels were invited by the newly formed Communist League—the forerunner of the First International (1865–71), a small worker-education group dominated by German intellectuals—to compose a convention resolution that could be used to propagandize and incite the working classes to improve their conditions during the then current period of political and economic unrest on the Continent. Thus, the *Communist Manifesto* was born in 1848, labeled ''communist'' to dissociate its authors from such utopian socialists as Saint-Simon, Fourier, and Owens.

During the next 20 years in London, Marx devoted himself exclusively to research and writing. He was supported in his poverty by charity, particularly that of Engels, who helped manage his own family's textile mill in Manchester while assisting Marx in his campaign to overthrow capitalism. Working at the British Museum library from dawn to dusk, Marx augmented his German philosophical background [I. KANT (1724–1804), G. W. F. HEGEL (1770–1831), Ludwig Feuerbach (1804–72)] with English political economy [Adam SMITH (1723–90), David Ricardo (1772–1823), and James MILL (1773–1836)] and made a systematic search through the classics, literature, and history for facts and ideas to support the three main tenets of Marxism: (1) that economic events shape history (economic interpretation of history); (2) that the class struggle underlies these economic events; and (3) that communism will conclude the struggle (proletarian revolution). *See* MATERIALISM, DIALECTICAL AND HISTORICAL.

Marx did not live to see his creed promulgated throughout the world; much less did he benefit financially from it. His family of six children suffered constant deprivation, which ultimately contributed to the death of all but three girls, who married late and unhappily: Jenny (Mrs. Charles Longuet), Laura (Mrs. Paul Lafargue), and Eleanor (Mrs. Edward Aveling). After the break-up of the First International Workingmen's party in 1872, Marx's failing health prevented him from any further active part in the movement, but he continued his studies in such widely divergent areas as American agriculture, Russian stock exchange, geology, and higher mathematics, as well as arranging manuscripts and the second volume of *Das Kapital* (the first volume had been published in 1867). After his wife's death in 1881, he steadily lost ground until his own end came in London, caused by various complications (liver disorder, bronchial catarrh, asthma, overexertion, heartbreak, and neuroticism have all been mentioned).

Major Contributions. Of Marx's theory of social classes, the late Joseph A. Schumpeter (1883–1950) said, ''If we get from Marx an ideologically warped definition of classes and class antagonisms, and if in consequence we get an unsatisfactory description of political mechanisms, we nevertheless get something very much worth having, namely, a perfectly adequate idea of the importance of the class phenomenon. If in this field there existed anything like unbiased research, Marx's suggestions would have led long ago to a satisfactory theory of it'' (*History of Economic Analysis,* 440). Of his interpretation of history, ''for which neither Hegelianism or materialism is necessary or sufficient,'' Schumpeter also said, ''If we reduce it to a working hypothesis and if we carefully formulate it, discarding all philosophical ambitions that are suggested by the phrases Historical Materialism or Historical Determinism, we behold a powerful analytic achievement'' (*ibid.*).

Marx is also considered the patriarch of the Institutional School of Economics that in the United States merged the human and social elements of economics with its purely scientific tools, especially in its application to the labor market. Marx would not have approved this association (he ridiculed utopian and so-called Fabian Socialists for a somewhat similar attempt), because institutionalism gave social reform a respectability and an impulse that made the proletarian revolution not only unnecessary but totally undesirable, even to the workingmen it was meant to free. And this is Marx's final unwitting legacy: stimulated by his exhaustive description and analysis of the birth, growth, and prospective inevitable demise of capitalism, a whole new team of economic, political, and social doctors took over the case, made a new diagnosis, devised new remedies, and proposed new injections to stimulate its growth, so that today a vigorous capitalism looks forward to a brighter future for all classes of society than at any time in the past.

Among Marx's published works are *The Holy Family,* [with Engels (1843)], *The German Ideology* [with Engels (1845)], *The Poverty of Philosophy* (1847), *Communist Manifesto* [with Engels (1848)], *Critique of Political Economy* (1859), *Capital,* v. 1 (1867), and *Capital,* v. 2 and 3 [with Engels, ed. (1885–95)]. As editor of *Rheinische Zeitung* (1842), contributor to the *German Yearbook* (1844), editor of *Neue Rheinische Revue* (1850), contributor to the *New York Tribune* (1852), and writer of innumerable pamphlets in support of socialist and communist causes throughout Europe, as well as a prolific correspondent with most of the social reformists throughout Europe [Engels, P. J. Proudhon (1809–65), Ferdinand Lassalle (1825–64), M. A. Bakunin (1814–76)], Marx left a tangible legacy of his thought and activity. Ardent followers [K. Kautsky (1854–1938), N. Lenin (1870–1924), H. Laski (1893–1950)] as well as vehement critics [Eugene Bohm-Bawerk (1851–1914), B. Croce (1866–1952), Tugen-Baranowsky] have swelled the literature on Marxism beyond enumeration. A few selective samples must suffice.

Bibliography: M. BEER, *The Life and Teaching of Karl Marx,* tr. T. C. PARTINGTON and H. J. STENNING (New York 1929). M. M. BOBER, *Karl Marx's Interpretation of History* (2d ed. Cambridge,

Mass. 1948). S. HOOK, *From Hegel to Marx* (New York 1936; repr. pa. Ann Arbor 1962). O. RÜHLE, *Karl Marx, His Life and Work,* tr. E. and C. PAUL (New York 1943). F. MEHRING, *Karl Marx: The Story of His Life,* tr. E. FITZGERALD, ed. R. and H. NORDEN (New York 1935). E. WILSON, *To the Finland Station* (New York 1940). J. A. SCHUMPETER, *History of Economic Analysis,* ed. E. B. SCHUMPETER (New York 1954).

[G. W. GRUENBERG]

MARY, BLESSED VIRGIN, ARTICLES ON

The *Encyclopedia* contains articles devoted to the Blessed Virgin Mary from a variety of perspectives: scriptural, theological, and devotional. Many of the articles blend these aspects, treating, for example, the scriptural background and theological meaning of a Marian dogma, or a scriptural event concerning Mary and the liturgical feast that celebrates it. The principal article on Mary in Scripture is MARY, BLESSED VIRGIN, I (IN THE BIBLE); see also ALMA; PROTO-EVANGELIUM; NATIVITY OF MARY; ANNUNCIATION. In theology, the principal article is MARY, BLESSED VIRGIN, II (IN THEOLOGY), a five-part article that discusses the holiness of Mary, her knowledge, her spiritual maternity, her relationship to the Church, and her mediation of grace. Related articles in theology include MOTHER OF GOD; VIRGIN BIRTH; IMMACULATE CONCEPTION; ASSUMPTION OF MARY; THEOTOKOS; MARY, BLESSED VIRGIN, QUEENSHIP OF; DORMITION OF THE VIRGIN; MARY IN PROTESTANT-CATHOLIC DIALOGUE. For the history and methodology of the theology of Mary, see MARIOLOGY (see also MOTHER OF GOD). Mary has been the subject of several papal encyclicals: see *MUNIFICENTISSIMUS DEUS; REDEMPTORIS MATER.* For her cult, see MARY, BLESSED VIRGIN, DEVOTION TO and MARIAN FEASTS; see also LOURDES; FATIMA; IMMACULATE HEART OF MARY; GUADALUPE, OUR LADY OF; LA VANG, OUR LADY OF; OUR LADY OF THE SNOW; MIRACULOUS MEDAL; SORROWS OF MARY. There are articles on ROSARY and HAIL MARY, and an article on Mary in art (MARY, BLESSED VIRGIN, ICONOGRAPHY OF).

[G. F. LANAVE]

MARY, BLESSED VIRGIN, I (IN THE BIBLE)

Biblical data on the Blessed Virgin Mary, the Mother of Jesus, is naturally found primarily in the New Testament (NT). But also certain passages of the Old Testament (OT) as interpreted by inspired writers in the NT concern her. By way of conclusion this article sums up the historical data on Mary and the inferences that can be drawn from it.

In the New Testament. The references to Mary in the NT are divided here into those that are merely allusions to her and those that speak directly of her and present theological reflections on her.

Allusions to the Mother of Jesus. In Gal 4.4. St. Paul alludes to Mary when he says that ''God sent his Son, born of a woman.'' Other indirect references to her are found in the Synoptic Gospels, which are treated here primarily as they are given in Mark, the earliest of the Synoptic Gospels.

Galatians 4.4. When St. Paul established the churches in Galatia, he did not impose circumcision and the resulting observances of the OT Law upon his converts. Judaeo-Christian missioners, perhaps from Jerusalem itself, who later visited these communities, urged them to adopt the OT Law. According to them St. Paul's proclamation of the gospel was incomplete as long as it failed to incorporate the religious culture of the OT into the lives of Christians (cf. Acts 15.5). The burden of Paul's exposition in his Epistle to the GALATIANS in defense of his teaching is that the redemptive death and Resurrection of Christ unveiled the true meaning of the OT: in OT times the Israelites were justified, i.e., remade to live in accordance with the will of God, by the merciful action of God received through their faith in His word of salvation to them and not by their endeavor to observe the OT Law (Gal 2.16). With this understanding of the significance of Christ, which Paul insists is Apostolic teaching rather than doctrine personal to himself (Gal 2.1–10), he did not instruct the Galatians in OT observances.

Paul's exposition of the meaning of the OT in Gal 2.15–3.18 naturally raised the question of the purpose of the Law: if the Law did not justify, what value did it have? He replied that one purpose of the Law was to keep man more conscious of his sinfulness than of his justice (Gal 3.19). The function of the Law was to stress man's inability to justify himself by its observance (Gal 3.22; see Rom 3.10–28). In this sense it was a preparation for man's clear understanding revealed in Christ, that the sanctifying power of God alone was the source of man's justice. Christ not only introduced the justifying power of God into history in a new way, i.e., through faith in His redemptive death and Resurrection, but at the same time liberated man from a source of anguish—his violation of the Law he agreed to observe as the presumptive condition of his salvation (Gal 2.15–16). One function of Christ's mission was to remove the burden of violations of the Law from the conscience of man (see Acts 15.10) by enabling him to center his faith in the justifying power of Christ, through whom he receives the strength and inspiration to live a life in the justice that he knows in his heart befits his human dignity (see Rom 7.13–25).

In this context concerning the liberative effect of Christ's death and Resurrection, Paul focuses attention on the reality of the human existence of Christ, Son of God, so that the Galatians might better understand why he did not instruct them in OT observances. In Gal 4.4 Paul traces Christ's redemptive mission to an eternal decree of God concerning the Son that became effective in history (''But when the fullness of time came'') in the birth of His Son (''God sent his Son, born of a woman''). To effect the liberation of man from sin, the Son identified Himself fully with humanity through His birth of a human mother (see Heb 4.15). Further, He was ''born under the Law,'' i.e., He identified Himself with the chosen people, Israel under the Covenant Law, so that the liberation from sin might include the Law itself: ''. . . That he might redeem those who were under the Law'' (Gal 4.5).

Since in Gal 4.4 Paul wished to emphasize the reality of Christ's humanity, he did not refer to the mother of Jesus by her proper name, ''Mary,'' nor did he use ''woman'' as a religious title. He designated her as ''woman'' to make clear that Christ, despite His divinity, possessed full humanity because He was born like all men from a human mother from whom His humanity derived. Paul's allusion to the reality of Mary's maternity of Christ presupposes some knowledge about her both on the part of Paul as well as the Galatians. But the allusion is so restricted that it is not possible to determine the extent of this knowledge or its nature. Nothing more need be assumed to account for Paul's reference to Mary in this passage than the knowledge that Christ accepted her as His mother in the ordinary sense. The words of Gal 4.4 are valuable as a reflection of the mind of the first Christian generation that Mary is the mother of Christ, Son of God, in the commonly accepted sense of motherhood, i.e., she conceived Christ and gave Him birth. Paul presented Mary's maternity as a fact of Christian faith without raising the further issue of the virginal conception of Christ, recorded by Luke and Matthew. Even if Paul was aware of the virginal conception, it would not have served his purpose to mention it in this passage. He was concerned only with the fact of Mary's maternity as the deliberate will of God that provided the Son of God with the same humanity He died to save and with the very subjection to the Law from which He freed men.

Mark 3.20–21 and 3.31–35. According to Mk 3.20–21, a group of people determined to exercise a certain control over Christ's conduct of His mission, for they concluded from information they had received that He was ''beside Himself,'' i.e., acting imprudently, or perhaps strangely. This group is designated by Mark as οἱ παρ' αὐτοῦ, literally, ''those with him.'' The phrase is commonly taken to mean the relatives of Jesus, but it can also mean friends or neighbors. (On this phrase and the relationship between it and ''his mother and brethren'' in Mk 3.31, see the commentaries on the Gospel of Mark.) While it seems more probable that the group is composed chiefly of the relatives of Jesus (see Jn 7.5 for the incredulous attitude of His relatives toward Him), it is doubtful that the mother of Jesus is included in it. The second evangelist is particularly concerned to indicate the attitude of various groups of people toward Jesus (e.g., Mk 1.22; 2.16; 3.6, 22). In Mk 3.20–21 he indicates a reaction of the relatives that is hostile toward Him, perhaps out of fear that His actions will lead to family embarrassment. But this reference to the attitude of the relatives of Jesus does not warrant ascribing the same sentiments to His mother, whom Mark does not here specifically mention and who may be presumed to have rendered her own judgment on the question of her Son's conduct.

Modern scholarship of the Gospels has questioned whether the visit of Jesus' ''mother and brethren'' in Mk 3.31–35 (parallel passages in Mt 12.46–50; Lk 8.19–21) was the historical outcome of the efforts of the relatives to control His ministry. From the literary standpoint it is clear that Mark connects the two events (''they went forth'' in Mk 3.21; the mother and brethren ''come'' in Mk 3.31). The specific mention of the presence of the mother of Jesus made in Mk 3.31 lends support to the older view assuming the events to be historically connected. Although it is true that according to Jewish family custom Jesus was no longer under the rule of His mother, neither was He subject to His other relatives. If, as the Catholic tradition holds (see on ''the brethren of Jesus' below), He was Mary's only child, it is comprehensible why the relatives might have enlisted her presence, the more readily to secure access to Him in view of His constant preoccupation with crowds (Mk 3.20). The announcement conveyed to Jesus in Mk 3.32 concerning the arrival of His mother as well as His brethren has an authentic historical ring when viewed in the entire context.

These observations allow the inference that Mary permitted herself to be pressed into service by the relatives so that they might have their confrontation with Jesus; but they do not allow the further inference that she thereby shared their sentiments concerning His conduct of the ministry. The evangelist provides no data from which a conclusion can be drawn concerning her own state of mind on the issue raised by the relatives. He affords only a basis for the judgment that in a matter of family concern Mary made the contribution for which the family asked.

Mark concludes his account of the visit, not by recording the meeting between Jesus and the relatives, but by citing His comment in the context of the hostility of the relatives. Jesus takes occasion of the announcement of the arrival of His mother and brethren to observe that His mother and brethren are those who ''do the will of God'' (Mk 3.35) like the audience before Him listening to His teaching (Mk 3.34). In Mark's context this saying of Jesus constitutes a telling response to His relatives who are disturbed at His acceptance of the crowds (Mk 3.20–21): His own relatives are unwilling to accept His teaching as prophetic (Mk 6.4). Not only do they feel free to instruct Him; they also refuse to be instructed by Him. Were they to accept His teaching themselves, they would discover a bond between Him and themselves of greater significance than ties of blood. (For the ultimate acceptance of Jesus and His teaching by His relatives, see Acts 1.14.)

This incident revealing Jesus' experience of rejection by His relatives may owe its recall to the persecution Judaeo-Christians underwent at the hands of their Jewish brethren (Acts 4.1–2; 5.17–18), in which Paul himself eventually played a leading role before his conversion (Acts 8.3; 22.4). The Gospel of Matthew (Mt 12.46–50) places the visit of Jesus' mother and brethren in close connection with the parables on the kingdom of God (Mk 13.1–52) in order to associate the rejection of Christians and the Christian message with the mystery of the kingdom of God. (On Lk 8.19–21, see below.)

Mark 6.1–4. In Mk 6.1–4 (parallel in Mt 13.54–57) the people of Nazareth refuse to accept Jesus and His message (see Lk 4.16–30). Apparently, they are insulted that His preaching and miracles were not presented first to themselves. In their opinion their familiarity with His family circle entitled them to this consideration. According to the parallel passage in Mt 13.55, they know Him as ''the carpenter's son.'' These were probably the original words in the early oral catechesis from which the Synoptic Gospels are derived. The best manuscripts in Mk 6.3 have: ''The carpenter, the son of Mary.'' But this does not accord with the Jewish custom of describing a man as the son of his father rather than of his mother, a practice well illustrated in the title given Jesus in Jn 6.42. A third reading, in a few manuscripts, ''the son of the carpenter and of Mary,'' is probably the result of a conflation of the other two variant readings. The title, ''the carpenter's son,'' implies no knowledge among the Nazarenes of Jesus' virginal conception, as is to be expected.

The family circle of Jesus is further described in Mk 6.3 as composed of His ''brothers'' and ''sisters,'' four of the brothers being explicitly named. The Greek words ἀδελφοί and ἀδελφαί that are used to designate the relationship between Jesus and these relatives have the meaning of full blood brother and sister in the Greek-speaking world of the evangelist's time and would naturally be taken by his Greek reader in this sense. Toward the end of the 4th century (*c.* 380) Helvidius, in a work now lost, pressed this fact in order to attribute to Mary other children besides Jesus so as to make her a model for mothers of larger families. St. Jerome, motivated by the Church's traditional faith in Mary's perpetual virginity, wrote a tract against Helvidius (A.D. 383) in which he developed an explanation of the Gospel usage of ἀδελφοί and ἀδελφαί for the relatives of Jesus that is still in vogue among Catholic scholars. In the Septuagint (LXX) ἀδελφόί is used in the sense of ''kinsman.'' In Gn 13.8; 14.14, 16 Abraham's nephew LOT is called his ''brother''; the same term is applied to Jacob's nephew Laban in Gn 29.15. In 1 Chr 23.22 the sons of Cis (Kish) are called the ''brothers'' of Eleazar's daughters, though they were their cousins. This usage of ἀδελφός in LXX derives from the fact that Hebrew is deficient in terminology for blood relationships (as is also Aramaic, the language behind the Greek of the Gospels). Both Hebrew and Aramaic were forced to use *āḥîm,* ''brothers,'' in the sense of ''kinsmen'' to supply for the deficiency. The translators who produced LXX transferred this broader meaning of Semitic *āḥîm* to ἀδελφοί and thus established a usage that the evangelists could follow.

It is important to note the point of St. Jerome's argument. He did not contend that the only possible linguistic meaning for ''brothers'' and ''sisters,'' used of Jesus' relatives in the Gospels, is ''cousins.'' To establish the relatives as cousins of Jesus he worked from other, complicated evidence in the Gospels that indicated that the James and Joseph of Mk 6.3 were children of a Mary who was a different person from the mother of Jesus (cf. Mt 13.55; 27.56, Mk 15.40). The validity of this argument depends on the assumption (probably correct) that the James and Joseph of Mk 6.3 are the same persons who are mentioned in Mk 15.40. On this supposition the mother of James and Joseph who is called Mary in Mk 15.40 was a relative of the mother of Jesus. Jerome considered her a sister of Jesus' mother and concluded that James and Joseph were His cousins. This conclusion, although reasonably probable, is less certain than the central point of Jerome's argument against Helvidius. Helvidius assumed that ἀδελφοί and ἀδελφαί in the Gospels, when used of blood relationships, had no other possible sense than full blood brother and full blood sister. Jerome's argument does not deny that such would be the normal usage of these terms in the Greek-speaking world, but he adduces evidence to show that the evangelists wrote within a linguistic tradition that enabled them to use the terms in a broader sense. There is, then, no necessary incompatibility between the Church's doctrine of Mary's perpetual virginity, in vogue long before Helvidius's time, and the Gospel usage of ''brothers'' and ''sisters'' for the relatives of Jesus.

The texts here under consideration, as well as Mk 3.31 and its parallels, reflect the view of Mary as the natural mother of Jesus that prevailed during His public ministry. Even those on familiar terms with the family circle of Jesus were unaware of the virginal conception. Since they regarded Jesus as the son of Mary and Joseph in the fully natural sense, they could not possibly have attached any particular religious significance to the fact that Jesus was the only child of Mary and Joseph. All the texts so far considered, including perhaps Gal 4.4, mirror a historical milieu that made no religious reflection on the person of the mother of Jesus.

Theological Reflections on the Mother of Jesus. When Mary is spoken of in the NT its inspired writers often convey a deeper theological meaning by their words than may be seen by the average modern reader. Such passages, which are treated here, are (1) Mt 1.18–25; 2.11, 13–14, 20–21; (2) Lk 1.26–38; 1.39–56; 2.1–7; 2.16, 19; 2.33–35; 2.41–51; (3) Lk 8.19–21; 11.27–28; (4) Rv ch. 12; (5) Jn 2.1–12; 19.25–27.

Matthew 1.18–25; 2.11, 13–14, 20–21. The theological conceptions that govern the thought of Matthew's INFANCY GOSPEL are expressed in his genealogy of Jesus (Mt 1.2–16). The genealogy invokes the messianic hope of Israel in recalling the divine promises to the patriarchs (Mt 1.2) and to David (Mt 1.6). It acknowledges Israel's sinfulness by pointing to David's murder of Uriah (Mt 1.6) and the disaster of the Babylonian captivity (Mt 1.11). It emphasizes the presence of God in Israel as continuously sustaining the faith and hope of the people (the sense of ἐγέννησεν, ''begot,'' constantly repeated throughout the genealogy).

It is in this context of God's continuous and beneficent presence in Israel that the events in Mt 1.18–2.23 are set. The evangelist's main purpose in these chapters is to declare that the saving action of God, begun in Abraham and carried forward throughout Israel's history, continues in Christ for the benefit of Israel and the world. Jesus is declared the Savior of His people (Mt 1.21); the King of the Jews (Mt 2.1); the Son of David (Mt 1.1), i.e., descended from the Davidic line in accordance with Nathan's prophecy (2 Sm 7.12–13); and the Son of Abraham (Mt 1.1), i.e., the one through whom the divine promise that all the nations are to be blessed in Abraham is fulfilled (Gn 12.3; Gal 3.8–9).

Matthew's concept of Jesus as the bearer in history of the messianic saving action of God clarifies the meaning of the evangelist when he sets out to explain the ''origin'' of Christ (Mt 1.18): he aims to show how God's presence in Israel produced the person of Christ. The salvific action of God (1) caused a virginal conception of Jesus in Mary, the fiancée of Joseph (Mt 1.18); (2) it resolved Joseph's perplexity over this event by directing him to marry her so as to give the Child legal status as a descendant of David (Mt 1.20); and (3) it provided the Child and His mother with necessary protection (Mt 2.11, 13–14, 20–21). As conceived by Matthew, the action of God involved a divine choice of the person of Joseph, since his role as legal father of the child had specific purposes.

The evangelist adds his own comment upon the events by citing Is 7.14 as here receiving its ''fulfillment,'' i.e., as revealing the continuity of God's saving action in history. In the virginal conception of Jesus, God acted in accordance with what He had planned all along, as faith perceives when it reads Is 7.14 in the light of Mary's virginal maternity and the meaning of her child as the bearer of salvation to the world ('''Emmanuel,' which is interpreted 'God with us'''). This position of Matthew that Is 7.14 already stated (so far as God is concerned) the virginal conception of Jesus that occurred in Mary implies a divine choice of her person to be the virgin mother of the Savior. The evangelist reenforces this point by stating that Joseph ''did not know her'' until the birth of the child; that is to say, Joseph recognized that Mary was divinely chosen to be Virgin Mother of the Child, and fully respected the divine will that she remain a virgin.

It is universally recognized that Matthew's famous ''until'' (''he did not know her until she brought forth a son''; Mt 1.25) is not a term of chronological intent: it neither affirms nor denies marital intercourse after the child's birth. The Evangelist is not looking forward in time through the history of the marriage between Joseph and Mary, but rather backward to his own citation of Is 7.14. He stresses this prophecy as being operative especially for the religious understanding of Joseph and Mary. This fact is important for the interpretation of the story of the Magi (Mt 2.1–12). The Magi learn that the messianic king of the Jews has been born, and they worship Him. [*See* MAGI (IN THE BIBLE).] But Matthew's readers are better informed than the Magi. The readers know that the king is EMMANUEL; in Him is found the salvific presence of God (2 Cor 5.19). They know also, as the Magi do not know, that the mother of the Child is the virgin mother of God's salvific plan. Matthew's Christian readers can perceive, not merely a continuity between the virginal conception of Christ and Is 7.14, but also a continuity in history: in God's design the virgin mother whom He destined to appear in Israel gave birth to the Savior in whom the Gentiles are to believe. God's plan is to bridge the gap between Jew and Gentile; this Israelite mother of divine choice becomes associated through her child with the Gentile world.

Joseph's further role in Mt 2.13–14, 20–21 is to care for the Child in whom the Gentiles are to believe and for the virgin mother whose maternity is ultimately to make their faith possible. These considerations indicate that in Matthew ch. 1–2 Mary's maternity is related to the Gentile world through faith in Christ, and it is not oriented to the question of the personal family of herself and Joseph. In the theological thought of Matthew, her maternal role is fully accounted for in her virginal maternity of Christ and its significance for the Gentile world. For the first evangelist Mary is the virgin mother of the Emmanuel whose salvific presence, once He is conceived, remains in the world forever (Mt 28.20).

Luke 1.26–38; 1.39–56; 2.1–7; 2.16, 19; 2.33–35; 2.41–51. The Lucan Infancy Gospel (Luke ch. 1–2) is a conscious product of literary artistry that offers a series of religious reflections on John the Baptist and Jesus, and on Zechariah, Elizabeth, and Mary. Considered as a whole, Luke's Infancy narrative is made up of two diptychs. The first diptych parallels the annunciation of John to Zechariah (Lk 1.5–25) with the ANNUNCIATION of Jesus to Mary (Lk 1.26–38). The second diptych parallels the birth of John (Lk 1.57–58) with the birth of Jesus (Lk 2.1–20). In addition to this broad scheme of parallelism, there is comparison and contrast of scene and detail throughout Luke ch. 1–2. The more detailed use of parallelism is evident in the Annunciations; it is less evident but clearly detectable elsewhere (e.g., in the contrast between Mary in Lk 1.39–46 and Zechariah in Lk 1.20–23). The purpose of the parallelisms in ch. 1–2 is to show adroitly the superior dignity in the order of the divine gifts of Jesus over John, and of Mary over Zechariah and Elizabeth.

In certain portions of ch. 1–2 the literary style draws heavily upon words, expressions, and figures of the OT, not by direct citation of them but by an interweaving of the OT elements into the Lucan narrative. In this way the author alludes to past prophecies, personages, and momentous events of the sacred history of Israel in order to bestow life, warmth, and relevance upon the events and people he describes. Beneath the surface of his Annunciation narratives, and the MAGNIFICAT especially, lie unusually rich undercurrents of theological thought.

All the personages and events of Luke ch. 1–2 derive their importance and meaning from Jesus. He is Son of the Most High, the Davidic messianic King (Lk 1.32–33; cf. 2 Sm 7.13–14), miraculously conceived by the power of God (Lk 1.35); He is Savior, Christ, and Lord (Lk 2.11), the very bearer of salvation (Lk 2.30), the light of the Gentiles and the glory of Israel (Lk 2.32). John's greatness consists in the fact that he was appointed by God to prepare the way for Him (Lk 1.15a). To fulfill this task John was consecrated to the Lord from birth [an idea conveyed by a combination of OT allusions taken from 1 Sm 1.11 (see especially the LXX); Jgs 13.2–5, 7] and endowed with the spirit and power of Elijah (Lk 1.17; cf. Mal 3.23). He is the last and the greatest of the OT Prophets because it was his function to prepare Israel for the immediate appearance of Jesus through his baptism for the remission of sins (Lk 1.76–77).

In the thought of the Lucan narrative, the mother of Jesus likewise derives her dignity from Jesus. The evangelist introduces her as a παρθένος (virgin) and the fiancée of Joseph (Lk 1.27). His judgment concerning her virginity is based not on historical data but on the more certain terrain of the action of God making choice of her, much in the line of thought of Mt 1.23 (see above). According to Luke, she is κεχαριτωμένη (highly favored, traditionally rendered as full of grace), the favored object of the divine choice, because of the person of Jesus she is about to conceive and bear (Lk 1.28). This title, ascribed by Luke to the angel Gabriel, is bracketed by χαῖρε (hail, greetings; literally ''rejoice'') and ὁ κύριος μετὰ σοῦ [the Lord (is) with you]. The entire ''greeting,'' as Luke terms it (Lk 1.29), is not to be interpreted conventionally, for the evangelist describes Mary as pondering it, attempting to penetrate its meaning (Lk 1.29).

A growing number of NT scholars concede that the greeting is a subtle allusion to a set of OT prophecies that invite Israel, under the figure of a woman, the ''daughter Sion,'' to rejoice at the prospect of the action of God bringing about the promised salvation of the people (Jl 2.21–27; Za 9.9–10; Zep 3.14–17). Luke's χαῖρε parallels the χαῖρε (rejoice) of Zep 3.14 (LXX). His κεχαριτωμένη parallels the OT figure, the ''virgin daughter Sion'' (Is 37.22), ''virgin Israel'' (Jer 31.4), an abstract personification of God's favored people Israel, directed in these prophecies to rejoice at the fulfillment of their messianic hope. The expression, ''The Lord [is] with you,'' as used in the OT (Gn 26.24; 28.15; 46.4; Ex 3.12; Jgs 6.12, 16), expresses the idea of God's salvific presence, here to inaugurate the messianic era by allusion to Zep 3.15b: ''The King of Israel, the Lord, is in your midst.'' After his notation on the necessity of reflection concerning the greeting, Luke introduces a parallel of contrast: ''Fear not, Mary'' (Lk 1.30), to parallel ''Fear not, Sion'' (Zep 3.16); ''you have found grace with God'' (Lk 1.30), to contrast with, ''you have no further misfortune to fear'' (Zep 3.15b). As the Prophet Zephaniah invites Israel to rejoice over the presence of God within it to save it from all its misfortunes (Zep 3.14–17), so the angel invites Mary to rejoice because she is favored with the presence of God who saves her from all its misfortunes. Whereas the prophecy of Zephaniah refers globally to Israel, or more exactly to the faithful Remnant of

Israel, under the figure of a woman, the angelic greeting concretizes the prophecy in Mary: she receives in her person the fulfillment of the messianic hope of her people.

The angel explains that Mary is to receive the fulfillment by conceiving and bearing a son whom she is to name Jesus (''Yahweh is salvation''; Lk 1.31). The Evangelist employs conventional language to allude to women favored by God with sons (Sarah: Gn 21.2; Samson's mother: Jgs 13.3; Anna: 1 Sm 1.19; the young woman of Is 7.14; see also the terms used in regard to Elizabeth: Lk 1.24, 57). After the Child is described as the Davidic Messiah, Mary presents her famous question, ''How shall this happen, since I do not know man?'' (Lk 1.34). Since Mary is fiancée to Joseph, since there is no historical background sustaining the possibility that she and Joseph would have entered a virginal marriage of their own accord, and since there is no evidence in the Biblical texts that, they were divinely enlightened to make such a decision at the time of their bethrothal, it is necessary to conclude that the thought in Lk 1.34 does not refer to a ''vow'' of virginity Mary would have already made.

The interpretation of Mary's question has not achieved a consensus among NT scholars. It is clear that Luke intends it to contrast with Zechariah's question (Lk 1.18). He requests evidence to verify the truth of Gabriel's prophecy concerning Elizabeth's child. Mary, however, does not challenge Gabriel's prophecy that she will be mother of the messianic King. Her question reflects upon the angel's announcement that it is out of the divine favor toward herself (Lk 1.30) that she will be mother of this King (Lk 1.31–33). She inquires how she is to understand the divine favor toward herself in this messianic maternity (''How shall this be''), for she is not married, and unlike women of the past favored with children she has no evidence that she is barren (''since I do not know man'').

The angel replies that the divine favor is to be shown her through a virginal conception of the child by the divine presence residing within her (Lk 1.35a). This divine action will be comparable to the cloud, the symbol of the divine presence, that settled down on the Meeting Tent housing the ark [Ex 40.35; to describe a special divine presence the Lucan text uses the verb ἐπισκιάζω, overshadow, the same word employed by LXX to translate the Hebrew verb *šākan* (to settle down, to abide) in Ex 40.35, where Yahweh's residence in the sanctuary is explained].

In consequence of God's action within her the Child to be born will be holy with the holiness of Yahweh, and the special divine presence within Him will come to be recognized (Lk 1.35b). Since the divine favor shown Mary, and through her to the Child, is concealed by the virginal conception, the angel gives her a sign, i.e., a pledge, that God's favor will be manifested in His own time. The sign is Elizabeth's pregnancy (Lk 1.36). Whether it is the case of the barren woman, Elizabeth, or the case of Mary, the virgin, God shows His favor when and as He chooses: ''because nothing shall be impossible with God'' (Lk 1.37).

Mary accepts the angelic message in its entirety, expressing her confidence in the virginal conception as an action of God, in the mystery of the divine presence in the Child, and in the pledge of God that the divine favor toward her and her Child will be manifested: ''Be it done to me according to your word'' (Lk 1.38). The Lucan scene ends on the note that in the chosen woman, Mary, the divine presence resides as it resided in a similar manner in the midst of Israel in the sanctuary.

Luke's scene of Mary's VISITATION (Lk 1.39–45, 56) utilizes 2 Sm 6.1–11, 15 to draw out the theological implications of the divine presence in child and mother that the Annunciation narrative has prophesied. Mary, carrying the Child in her womb, is compared to the ark of the covenant, the site of the permanent presence of Yahweh among His people. As the ark was brought to Jerusalem in David's time, so the mother of Jesus departs in the direction of the Holy City to visit Elizabeth (Lk 1.39; cf. 2 Sm 6.2). As Israel honored the presence of Yahweh in the ark during its trip toward Jerusalem, so Elizabeth recognizes at Mary's greeting that the mother of Jesus carries in herself the divine presence. But unlike David's (2 Sm 6.9), her reaction to the presence of the Lord is one of joyful awe, not reverential fear (Lk 1.43); for Mary carries the presence of God that sanctifies (Lk 1.41) in contrast to the terrible presence that dealt Uzzah a mortal blow (2 Sm 6.7). As the ark stayed in the house of Obededom for 3 months (2 Sm 6.11), so Mary remains with Elizabeth for about three months (Lk 1.56).

Despite her exalted role as bearer of the divine presence, the ark of the new covenant, Mary is characterized by Luke in the MAGNIFICAT (Lk 1.46–58) as the perfect representative of the *'ănāwîm* (lowly, humble, poor), the spiritual community of the poor, the remnant, whom God was to prepare to receive His expected salvation (cf. Zep 3.12). God has taken into consideration Mary's ταπείνωσις (humiliation, humble station, lowliness; Lk 1.48), both material and spiritual, and has looked favorably upon her longing for deliverance from this condition, as He promised to Abraham (Lk 1.55). Following the OT tradition of ascribing canticles to the person honored by them, Luke attributes the Magnificat to Mary. Essentially, it is a series of religious reflections invoking various OT ideas that concern the mystery of God's salvific plan come to term in Mary, through whose maternity of Jesus the generations to follow (the new Israel; Lk 1.50) will receive the blessings of the messianic era. All generations, recognizing the divine favor bestowed upon them through her, i.e., through her maternal role in the creation of the new Israel, will call her blessed (Lk 1.48).

The second chapter of Luke shifts its orientation somewhat away from consideration of the mother of Jesus to focus upon the mystery of salvation to occur through her Child, Jesus. However, the reader is invited to reflect upon this mystery through the eyes of the mother. The Child's birth occurs in simple and lowly surroundings that reflect the condition of the parents as classic examples of the *'ănāwîm* (Lk 2.6–7). The Lucan text makes discrete reference to Mi 5.1–5, with which it associates the birth of the Child at Bethlehem. It makes a second allusion by the use of φάτνη (crib, manger) to Is 1.3–4 (see especially the LXX, where the same Greek word is used) to give meaning to the circumstances surrounding the birth as forecasting the rejection of Jesus.

True to His pledge, God overcomes the poverty and isolation of the birth by the angelic revelation to the shepherds (Lk 2.8–15). Mary ponders the divine message to these *'ănāwîm* attempting to fathom its meaning as well as the circumstances of the birth (Lk 2.19; cf. Dn 7.28; Gn 37.11). In accordance with the Magnificat she remains among the 'ănāwîm. It is in this capacity that she presents the Child to the Lord in the Temple and makes the offering of the poor, two turtledoves (Lk 2.22–24). Again God acts to manifest the significance of the Child as Savior both of the Gentiles and of Israel, fulfilling a pledge to Simeon (Lk 2.32). When the parents marvel at the ingenuity of the divine plan, Simeon foretells the rejection of the Child (Lk 2:33–34) and addresses himself to the mother: "And thy own soul a sword shall pierce, that the thoughts of many hearts may be revealed" (Lk 2.35). This prophecy has not been convincingly interpreted. It appears to allude to Ez 14.17, where the sword is the sign of division that the action of God produces in Israel to separate the faithful remnant from the rest of the people. In the Lucan theology Mary is addressed as a member of the *'ănāwîm.* The probable meaning of the prophecy is that she, together with her Child (Lk 2.34), will be separated from her people. She is here envisioned by Luke in her representative capacity, already indicated in the Magnificat, as mother of the new Israel. Since Luke does not place Mary at the cross (cf. Lk 23.49 with Jn 19.25), it is improbable that he sees the prophecy as a direct reference to her compassion. He does associate her, however, with the primitive Christian community in Jerusalem (Acts 1.14).

Luke concludes his Infancy narrative with a cryptic allusion to the death and Resurrection of Jesus ("after three days"; Lk 2.46) in his account of the parents' discovery of Him in the Temple. Joseph and Mary are counted among the *'ănāwîm* (who properly belong in the Temple, according to OT thought). The mother is left in a state of reflection on all the events of the childhood of Jesus, prayerful and awaiting expectantly the deliverance of Israel through her Son (Lk 2.51).

Luke 8.19–21; 11.27–28. The first of these passages has parallels in Mk 3.31–35; Mt 12.46–50 (see above). From the Lucan designation of Mary as the perfect representative of the *'ănāwîm* it is evident that in both these passages the Evangelist intends to allude to the mother of Jesus as the perfect hearer of the word of God. In the Lucan theology she is the model of all Christians, who must respond to the word of God, and in this sense is already the figure or type of the Church.

The theological portrait of Mary in the Gospel of Luke as a whole exhibits a sweep of thought that takes the Christian reader from the lofty pinnacle of the symbolic ark of the new covenant in whose person the Son of God was conceived and resided, down to the humble station of the *'ănāwîm* and finally leaves her as an invitation to all Christians to allow the word of God to fructify in themselves through an obedient faith as it fructified in the woman chosen to be the mother of Jesus. Since for Luke the divine favor shown Mary and her child is at first concealed and only gradually manifested, it appears quite incompatible with his theology that Mary would have other children by Joseph. To be the virgin mother of Jesus, the messianic King in whom the divine presence resides, is her personal, religious mission. Luke does not propose her virginity as a moral ideal, but as a determination of the divine will, a mystery of faith requiring that she hear the word of God and keep it.

Revelation ch. 12. The image of the woman in ch. 12 of Revelation is a symbol of the people of God, Israel of the OT and the new Israel of the NT (see Gal 6.10). In a highly subtle and complex manner the author of Revelation ch. 12 transforms the OT comparisons of Israel to a woman from metaphor to symbol. The OT Prophets compare Israel to a faithless bride (Jer ch. 2; Ez ch. 16), to a mother (Hos 2.4; Is 66.7), to a woman in labor (Jer 6.24; 13.27; Is 37.36). Selecting the woman image itself, ch. 12 of Revelation draws further upon the imagery of the OT Prophets to produce an original symbol that is remarkable for its ambivalence. New Testament scholars are in virtual agreement that the woman symbol of Rv. 12.1 stands for the people of God of both Testaments; but on the development of the symbol in the remainder of the chapter opinions diverge considerably. (*See* WOMAN CLOTHED WITH THE SUN.)

The allusion to the Israel of the OT in the symbol of the woman is evident from the unmistakable relationship between Rv 12.2 and Is 26.17. The thought and language of the two passages coincide. In Is 26.17 the Prophet likens Israel's suffering under divine chastisement to a woman in labor who is writhing and crying out. Like the metaphorical woman of this passage in Isaiah, the symbolic woman of Rv 12.2 is with child, cries out, and writhes. But in Isaiah the pregnancy, like the woman, is metaphorical: the whole figure of the Isaian woman is meant to depict the incapacity of Israel to save itself from its sufferings (Is 27.18). God Himself must intervene if Israel is to be saved (Is 27.20–22). The symbol of the woman in Rv 12.2 pertains to the Israel of the OT yearning for salvation but unable of itself to fulfill this yearning.

The inclusion of the Christian Church under the symbol of the woman appears clearly from Rv 12.5, 13–18, when these passages are understood in the context of the entire Book of Revelation. In Rv 12.5 the woman bears a son who is described in terms that unmistakably designate Him as the Christ of Christian faith. Once born, the Child is taken up to God's throne, a plain reference to the Resurrection and Ascension of Christ. But the woman is separated from Him by the threat of a dragon. She escapes the dragon through the protection of God, who prepares a place for her on earth (Rv 12.6, 14). Frustrated in his attempt to destroy the woman, the dragon awaits reinforcements before launching himself against the rest of the woman's offspring (Rv 12.17). In the context of the Book of Revelation, the woman who flees the dragon and is protected from harm by God can only be the Christian Church, for it is the Church at once divinely protected and persecuted that is the main theme of Revelation.

The ambivalent meaning of the woman symbol in the broad sweep of Rv ch. 12, symbolizing both Israel and the Christian Church, is clear also from the imagery of Rv 12.1. There, at the opening of the chapter, the woman is described as clothed with the sun, having the moon at her feet, and crowned with 12 stars. The imagery of sun and moon is taken from Is 60.1–2, 19–20, where the Israel of the future is envisioned, under the figure of a mother, as illuminating the entire world. Placed in heaven, i.e., immediately below God's throne, she reflects the light of God Himself. She is, as it were a new luminary for the earth, comparable to the sun and moon (cf. Gn 1.14–15). This imagery of the woman illuminating the world combines the people of God of the OT and the people of God of the NT into a unity: the promise made to the Israel of the OT in Is ch. 60 finds its fulfillment in the Church of the NT. The crown of 12 stars probably refers to the 12 tribes of Israel, who are sealed in Rv 12.4–8, and to the 12 Apostles, whose names are inscribed on the foundation stones of the New Jerusalem in Rv 21.14. This interpretation corresponds perfectly to the ambivalence of the woman symbol.

The interpretation of the woman symbol meets with its greatest difficulty in the passage of thought from Rv 12.2, the portrait of the woman in labor, to Rv 12.4–5, the portrait of the woman bearing the child. Because of the utilization of Is 26.17 to describe the labor of the woman in Rv 12.2, it is necessary to conclude that the labor here is fruitless: the portrait reflects the Isaian contention that Israel cannot save itself from its sufferings, but must await the act of God (Is 26.20–22). In Rv 12.4–5, however, the woman, who is no longer specified as being in labor but instead is confronted by the dragon, is fruitful and bears the child. Since Rv 12.5 designates the child as Christ and as immediately seized to be brought to God's throne, it is legitimate to conclude that behind this allusion to the Resurrection and Ascension of Christ lies the Johannine concept of the ὕψωσις ''lifting up'' (Jn 3.14; 12.32), i.e., the Passion-death and Resurrection-Ascension of Jesus. This allusion to the historical Jesus is on the high plane of the theology of the Johannine Gospel: the reference is to the historical Christ who is glorified by the Father (Jn 12.28; 13.31–32). In the Johannine theology Christ always possesses this glory. It is gradually revealed at the determination of the Father (Jn 2.11; 8.54). The woman of Rv 12.5 gives birth to the Christ who is glorified by the Father because He possessed this glory, i.e., His self-revealing divine power, before creation (Jn17.5), and lived among men to manifest it (Jn 1.14), especially through His Resurrection and Ascension (Rv 12.5b). In Rv 12.5 an extremely complex set of ideas in the realm of Johannine theology is propounded: (1) by an act of God the OT Israel (the woman of Rv 12.5) received in herself the fulfillment of her longing for deliverance (Is 26.20); (2) the OT Israel (the woman of Rv 12.5) gave birth to the messianic King (Ps 2.7), whose proper dwelling is at the throne of God, where He now resides (Rv 12.5b); (3) but since Christ always possessed the divine glory He now enjoys, it must be recalled that it was through the Virgin Mary (the woman of Rv 12.5) that He first ''became flesh and tabernacled among us'' (Jn 1.14) for the purpose of manifesting this glory (''and we saw his glory''; Jn 1.14). (The Johannine ἐσκήνωσεν, ''tabernacled,'' has the same overtone of the divine presence as the ''overshadow'' of Lk 1.35.)

Through its complex symbolism Revelation ch. 12 combines into a single picture the mystery of God's salvific plan now operating through the Christian Church whose historical dependency on Israel lies in Christ, born of the Virgin Mary.

John 2.1–12; 19.25–27. The mother of Jesus appears in the Fourth Gospel in roles unequaled for their prominence in the synoptic accounts of the public ministry of Jesus. At CANA she takes an active role in Jesus' changing of water into wine at a marriage feast. On Calvary she is present beneath the cross, where she is instructed by her own dying Son to receive the beloved disciple as her son.

Attempts to interpret the Cana narrative (Jn 2.1–12) simply on the historical level have failed to account for all the data of the passage. Jesus' reply to Mary, "What wouldst thou have me do, woman? My hour has not yet come" (Jn 2.4), lacks coherence with Mary's confident instruction to the waiters, "Do whatever he tells you" (Jn 2.5). The expression τί ἐμοὶ καὶ σοί (literally, "What to me and to thee") is invariably used in both the OT and the NT to imply a certain rejection (Jgs 11.12; Jos 22.24; 2 Sm 16.10; 19.22; 1 Kgs 17.18; 2 Kgs 3.13; 2 Chr 35.21; Mt 8.29; Mk 1.24; 5.7; Lk 4.34; 8.28). The hour of Jesus in John is a technical term for His glorification through His Passion (Jn 7.30; 8.20; 12.23, 27;13.1; 17.1). Even if "hour" is read as part of a question ("Has my hour not yet come?") as some of the Fathers have understood it, an allusion to the Passion cannot be excluded from the text.

The impossibility of satisfactorily interpreting the Cana narrative on the assumption that it is solely the historical record of an objective event has forced exegetes to study the OT background to the account. It is obvious that an OT background saturates the Evangelist's thought in his Prologue (Jn 1.1–18), which alludes to Gn 1.1 and to the concept of the LOGOS in certain Psalms and in the Book of Wisdom. But the OT background is even more evident in Jn 1.19–51: the messianic expectancy (v. 19, 41), the citation of Is 40.3 in v. 23, and the allusions to Is 53.7 in v. 29 and v. 36, to the Law and the Prophets in v. 45, to the Davidic Messiah (2 Samuel ch. 7) in v. 49, and to Dn 7.13 ("Son of Man") and Gn 28.12 in v. 51. The Cana narrative alludes to the OT water of ritual purification in Jn 2.6, and Mary's statement to the waiters closely parallels Gn 41.55. Moreover, in Jn 1.19–51 titles are important to clarify the religious significance of personages: the Baptist is not Messiah, Elijah, or the Prophet, but "a herald's voice in the desert"; Jesus is Lamb of God, the Chosen One, teacher, Christ, Son of God, King of Israel, Son of Man; Simon is Rock; Nathanael is "a genuine Israelite." The use of titles is a procedure followed also in the case of Mary in the Cana narrative. The Evangelist avoids the use of her proper name, designating her instead as "the mother of Jesus" (four times, including Jn 2.12) and "woman" (once). The title, "the mother of Jesus" is to be understood according to the thought of Jn 1.14: the logos became flesh and "tabernacled" in her in order to manifest His glory.

Since the reply of Jesus to Mary in Jn 2.4 must be interpreted on a theological rather than a historical level, the title γυνή (woman) cannot be taken simply for the respectful term of address it represented in the Greek world of the Evangelist's time. Except for the possible correlation with "Son of Man" in Jn 1.51 no direct indication of the religious sense of "woman" is provided in the first two chapters of John. It is necessary to judge the sense of the title on the basis of the Cana narrative as a whole.

The narrative concerns the manifestation of the glory of Christ (Jn 2.11). The transformation of the ritual water of purification into wine is symbolic of the messianic benefits coming through Christ (for wine as one of the symbols of the messianic benefits, see Am 9.4; Is 25.6; Jer 31.12; Jl 4.18). The miracle is a prophetic action fulfilling Jesus' prophecy that Nathanael would see evidence that the messianic benefits promised to the Patriarchs are fulfilled in Him (Jn 1.51; Gn 28.12). The setting of the miracle is a γάμος (wedding banquet), a Christian term portraying the joys of the messianic kingdom (Mt 22.2; 25.10; Lk 12.36). Mary's declaration, "They have no wine" (Jn 2.3), petitions, or at least hints, that Jesus should bestow the benefits of the kingdom on Israel. Although He replies that the time for such action has not yet arrived, He responds by the performance of the miracle. The ambiguity between Jesus' reply and His action suggests that the term "woman" shares in this equivocation.

The only sound explanation presenting itself for this peculiar usage of "woman" in Jn 2.4 is the varied senses in which the same term is utilized in the Johannine theology of Revelation ch. 12. The reply of Jesus views Mary's petition eschatologically, i.e., in the light of His future action inaugurating the kingdom with finality through His death on the cross. In this final sense He cannot now act; Mary is "woman" in accordance with Is 26.17, the figure of the metaphorically pregnant woman, yearning for the kingdom but unable to bring it about. However, in Christ's ministry the kingdom has really arrived (Mk 1.15). Thus He can respond to her request with a prophetic miracle indicating the future advent in Himself; from this standpoint Mary is the future mother-Israel of Is 60.4, i.e., the figure of the future people of God. Through her participation in the miracle at Cana she is beginning to experience the joy of the gathering of the new people of God (Is 60.5) in the kingdom that Christ will finally establish. The title "woman" in the Cana narrative makes of Mary's person the figure of the people of God: first of the old Israel yearning for salvation through Christ, yet completely dependent on the action of God through Him; and secondly of the new Israel to come into existence through His Passion and Resurrection.

The Johannine scene of Mary at the cross (Jn 19.25–27) completes his gospel theology of the mother of Jesus as ''woman.'' That the Cana and Calvary narratives involving the mother of Jesus are intended to be mutually explanatory is clear from several considerations: the theological sense of the word ''hour'' in Jn 2.4, meaning the glorification of Jesus through His Passion: the absence of the proper name in favor of the titles ''the mother of Jesus'' and ''woman'' in both passages, and the phrase ''the third day'' in Jn 2.1, probably in itself an allusion orienting the Cana narrative to the Calvary scene (cf. Mt 16.21; Lk 9.22).

On Calvary Jesus addresses His mother from the cross, before He declares the Scriptures fulfilled (Jn 19.28), to inform her that she has a son in the beloved disciple. The promise of Cana here comes to term: the transition from the old to the new Israel, prefigured in Mary at Cana, is completed. The messianic fulfillment she yearned for in her declaration, ''They have no wine,'' is the gift to her of her Son: the gift is the new people of God, typified in the beloved disciple. The yearning of Israel for messianic salvation, so often spoken of by the Prophets under the imagery of the woman in labor, is concretized on Calvary in the historical mother of Jesus. Just as she is the woman chosen by God to be the tabernacle of the Logos become flesh so that He might manifest His saving power among men, so she depicts in her person the faith, the expectancy, the suffering, and the final mysterious destiny of the Christian Church.

IN THE OLD TESTAMENT

When the OT is interpreted from the standpoint of its literal historical meaning, i.e., the sense intended by the inspired human author for his OT audience, a Marian meaning is not discoverable in it. Such is true also of the Christological sense. Neither Christ nor Mary can be discovered in the books of the OT by the method of critical, historical exegesis of their literal sense.

Relation of OT Prophecy to NT Messianism. Messianic prophecy both in origin and in fulfillment is an event dependent upon the will of God; God prophesies, and God fulfills the prophecy according to His own free determination and wisdom. The messianism of the NT derives from the prophetic proclamation of the Twelve concerning Jesus of Nazareth: God raised Him from the dead so that the world might be saved from its sins through faith in Him (Acts 2.14–36). The entire NT is a prophetic elaboration of this fundamental prophecy. The messianism of the NT is a divinely instituted fulfillment of that of the OT, just as OT messianism is in itself of divine institution. The sense of the NT is that it possesses an essential bond with the OT as the divinely caused fulfillment of the messianic expectancy of the old Israel. Under the prophetic light of Christ, the Apostles, and the Church the NT endeavors to provide its own prophetic messianism with intelligibility, depth, and color by understanding itself, not as the logical outcome of the expectancy of the old Israel, that is, a result deducible by reason from OT texts, but rather as the divinely determined outcome of this expectancy.

To interpret the OT the authors of the NT begin with their own prophetic messianism; understanding the OT in this light, they show the unity and wisdom of the divine plan of salvation that courses through both Testaments. The NT quest into the OT has as its main objective the illumination of Christ, but of Christ as head of the Church; its quest is principally, if not exclusively, Christological and ecclesiological. In principle, the NT quest into the OT is not a Marian search, for the apostolic kerygma proclaims Christ alone to be the cause and source of salvation.

Mary in NT Messianism. The NT conceives of the mother of Jesus as a theologically significant discovery within the compass of its own prophetic messianism: the fact of this discovery is reflected in the Infancy narratives of Matthew and Luke, in ch. 12 of Revelation, and in the Fourth Gospel. The theological significance the NT Church attached to the discovery is that the mother of Jesus is relevant to its new messianism: her messianic maternity serves to flesh out the Church's CHRISTOLOGY and its ECCLESIOLOGY.

The discovery of Mary's messianic maternity, i.e., the fact that she became the mother of Jesus by the open manifestation of the divine mind and will in her virginal conception, led NT thought to search into the OT to forge a stronger bond between its Christological messianism and the messianic expectancy characteristic of the OT.

The bond is forged with theological care, subtlety, and delicacy. It does not consist in a series of affirmations that in the mother of Jesus God chose a salvific companion for Christ. It does consist in the affirmation that the divine plan of salvation included God's choice of a virgin in Israel whom He willed to make meaningful for the comprehension of His Christ and His Church.

The NT quest into the meaningfulness of the mother of Jesus for Christ and the Church relies, as for Christology itself, upon the prophetic grasp of the OT. This prophetic grasp is little, if at all concerned, with drawing a direct correlation between the mother of Jesus and the material content of OT messianic prophecy. The NT authors favor an allusive use of OT messianic texts and symbols to suggest the religious significance of the mother of Jesus against the broad background of OT messianism. The only passage directly applied to the mother of Jesus in the NT (Mt 1.22–23) is Is 7.14. But the Isaian text is not employed here to affirm the truth of the virginal conception by appeal to OT prophecy. It is used to point up the religious significance of the virginal conception in the plan of God: in this way He chose to inaugurate His presence in Christ, which remains permanent in the world (Mt 28.20).

Especially remarkable in the NT is that its quest into the OT to illuminate its Christological messianism does not cite Gn 3.15 directly of Christ and His mother. In Rv 12.9 the NT prefers to use Gn 3.15 to express its conception of the earthly existence of the Church in its struggle against satanic power. However, there is a delicate association of the serpent with the woman who gives birth to the messianic King in Rv 12.5, and therefore a complex Marian allusion to Gn 3.15 (*See Also Is 27.1*).

The NT preference for utilizing the woman images of the OT to present its conception of the mother of Jesus is the most striking aspect of its theological reflection upon her person and role. It is only through a deeper understanding of the NT's prophetic use of the OT imagery that a more exact appreciation of the Bible's view of Mary's place and function in the divine plan of salvation is attainable.

LIFE OF MARY ACCORDING TO THE GOSPELS

The sparseness of historical detail concerning the mother of Jesus is due to the theologically disciplined writing peculiar to Sacred Scripture: the interest of the inspired writers lies in the salvific action of God in history. Endeavoring to keep the divine activity in history foremost, they content themselves with only that data necessary to provide the minimal historical setting that renders the work of God comprehensible to their readers.

Historical Data. The main piece of historical data offered in the Gospels concerning Mary is the fact that she and Joseph were betrothed at the time of the Annunciation (Mt 1.18; Lk 1.27). Otherwise she is simply located at various places, always in connection with her Son: at Nazareth for the child's conception (Lk 1.26); in the hill country of Judea (near Jerusalem) for Elizabeth's recognition of her unique maternity (Lk 1.39); at Bethlehem for the Child's birth (Lk 2.4, 7; Mt 2.1); at Jerusalem for her own purification in the Temple and the offering of the Child to Yahweh (Lk 2.22); at Nazareth for the Child's rearing (Lk 2.51; Mt 2.23); at Jerusalem for the discovery of Jesus speaking with the teachers in the Temple (Lk 2.42, 46); at Cana for a wedding (Jn 2.1); end finally at Jerusalem when Jesus is crucified (Jn 19.25), where Luke places her at the origin of the Church (Acts 1.8). The datum of Mt 2.13 that Mary spent some time in Egypt is difficult to interpret and need not be pressed historically.

The Biblical texts offer no information on the proximity of Mary's virginal conception of Jesus and her impending marriage to Joseph. It is legitimate to presume that the Annunciation occurred shortly before the wedding date, and that the wedding took place at its predetermined time so that the shadow of scandal (quite likely in Galilee) over the conception of the Child would have been excluded. It is unnecessary to suppose from Mt 1.18–20 that Mary suffered from Joseph's suspicion of her adultery. The text of Matthew is better comprehended as a reflection on the fact that Joseph accepted the Child's paternity as the divine will in his own regard since in the actual circumstances he could not exercise his legal right of divorce without casting the suspicion of adultery upon her, and thus also injuring the Child. Luke's Annunciation narrative appears rather to exclude Mary from the Davidic line. If she were of Levitical descent, a possibility raised by her relationship to Elizabeth, the Evangelists have attached no importance to it; nor have they attempted to derive religious significance from her name. Her life seems to have been spent in the quiet and obscurity of Nazareth (Mk 1.9), where she acquired no other reputation than that of being the mother of Jesus.

Historical Inferences. The most important historical inferences to be drawn from the Gospel data about Mary's life are the religious implications of the Lucan Annunciation scene. According to the Lucan theology, her understanding of herself and of her future underwent profound alteration due to the virginal conception of the messianic King. She was required thereafter to live in the obscurity of faith, awaiting the realization of the angelic prophecies concerning her Son. In the thought of Mt 1.18–25 Joseph agreed to share this religious life of faith with her. That their married life would have pursued the normal course of preparing for other children besides Jesus seems excluded by the Lucan theology. This theology demands of Mary that she await the time for the manifestation of her choice by God as the Virgin Mother of His Son, the divine Messiah.

Bibliography: P. F. CEUPPENS, *De Mariologia Biblica* (Rome 1951). P. GAECHTER, *Maria im Erdenleben* (Innsbruck 1953). A. KASSING, *Das Verhältnis von Kirche und Maria* (Düsseldorf 1958). R. LAURENTIN, *Structure et théologie de Luc I–II* (*Études Biblique*; 1957). B. J. LE FROIS, *The Woman Clothed with the Sun* (Rome 1954). G. MIEGGE, *The Virgin Mary,* tr. W. SMITH (Philadelphia 1955). M. THURIAN, *Mary, Mother of All Christians* (New York 1964). G. F. WOOD, *The Form and Composition of the Lucan Annunciation Narratives* (Doctoral dissertation, Catholic University of America, microfilm; Ann Arbor 1963). M. M. BOURKE, ''The Literary Genus of Matthew 1–2,'' *The Catholic Biblical Quarterly* 22 (Washington 1960) 160–175. R. J. DILLON, ''Wisdom Tradition and Sacrament Retrospect in the Cana Account,'' *ibid.* 24 (1962) 268–296. S. LYONNET, *Le Récit de l'Annonciation et la maternité divine de la Sainte Vierge* (Rome 1956). *Marian Studies,* v.11 (Paterson, NJ 1960), v.12 (1961). B. F. MEYER, ''But Mary Kept All These Things,'' *The Catholic Biblical Quarterly* 26 (Washington 1964) 31–49. J. A. FITZMYER, ''The Virginal Conception of Jesus in the New Testament,'' *Theological Studies* 34 (1973) 541–75. J.

"The Virgin of the Cherries," painting by Titian, c. 1516–1518. (©CORBIS)

MCHUGH, *The Mother of Jesus in the New Testament* (Garden City 1975). J. M. REESE, "The Historical Image of Mary in the New Testament," *Marian Studies* 28 (1977) 27–44. J. LAMBRECHT, "The Relatives of Jesus in Mark," *Novum Testamentum* 16 (1974) 241–58. R. F. COLLINS, "Mary in the Fourth Gospel: A Decade of Johannine Studies," *Louvain Studies* 3 (1970) 99–142 R. E. BROWN, *The Birth of the Messiah. A Commentary on the Infancy Narratives of Matthew and Luke* (Garden City 1993). R. E. BROWN, "Roles of Women in the Fourth Gospel," *Theological Studies* 36 (1975) 688–99. R. E. BROWN et al. *Mary in the New Testament: A Collaborative Assessment by Protestant and Roman Catholic Scholars* (Philadelphia 1978).

[C. P. CEROKE/EDS.]

MARY, BLESSED VIRGIN, II (IN THEOLOGY)

In this encyclopedia, the theology of Mary and its methodology is more generally treated under the heading MARIOLOGY. Throughout this encyclopedia, there are specific entries dealing with Mary under her various titles or gifts: see ASSUMPTION OF MARY; DORMITION OF THE VIRGIN; IMMACULATE CONCEPTION; IMMACULATE HEART OF MARY; MOTHER OF GOD; MARY, BLESSED VIRGIN, QUEENSHIP OF; THEOTOKOS. For ecumenical developments in Marian theology, see MARY IN CATHOLIC-PROTESTANT DIALOGUE. The historical developments of Marian theology is dealt with under MARIOLOGY. This entry discusses the specific theological questions about Mary as traditionally presented in the the Roman Catholic theological tradition over the centuries under the following subheadings: (1) Holiness of Mary; (2) Knowledge of Mary; (3) Mary and the Church; (4) Mediatrix of all Graces; and (5) Spiritual Maternity.

PART 1: HOLINESS OF MARY

Supernatural holiness involves beyond a special union with God through sanctifying grace the identification of one's will with the will of God, evidenced through

14th-Century Spanish Devotional Image of the Virgin and Child Enthroned, polychromed and gilded wooden sculpture. (©CORBIS)

the practice of virtue and the exclusion of sin. In the case of the Mother of the Savior, the degree of supernatural holiness bestowed upon her and achieved through her meritorious life was most extraordinary and can be properly demonstrated through a consideration of her peculiar offices and privileges. Mary's freedom from sin, her fullness of grace, her virtues and gifts, and her final confirmation in grace at the end of her life were special factors of her sanctity, and each of these realities, considered in order below, contributed and gave testimony in its own way to the holiness of the Mother of God.

Freedom from Sin. Both the Scriptures and the teaching Church clearly indicate that the Blessed Virgin Mary, immaculately conceived, received the gift of sanctifying grace and other special gifts in an unparalleled manner. The Archangel Gabriel's words, ''Hail, full of grace'' (Lk 1.28), represent a unique salutation. They imply that Mary was adorned with an abundance of heavenly gifts from the treasury of the divinity, to a degree beyond that of all the angelic spirits and all the saints. In fact, official Catholic teaching holds that God's grace was bestowed on Our Lady ''in such a wonderful manner that she would always be free from absolutely every stain of sin, and that, all beautiful and perfect, she might display such fullness of innocence and holiness that under God none greater would be known . . .'' (Pius IX, *Ineffabilis Deus;* Denz 2800).

Mary's Immaculate Conception, therefore, was a unique and particular privilege. To be immaculately conceived, or to be ever without sin, is to possess grace; just as to be conceived without grace is to begin life in the state of sin. Catholic doctrine teaches, consequently, that Mary's predestination as the worthy mother of God postulates a fitting preparation in her soul and that from the very first moment of her existence she was filled with grace.

This positive aspect of holiness, measured in terms of her possession of grace, stands in contradistinction to what is termed Mary's perfect sinlessness, the negative aspect of her sanctity. In the case of Our Lady, this perfect sinlessness implies more than merely the absence of sin; it implies also a complete indefectibility in the moral order, or the actual inability to sin.

Mary's sinlessness, therefore, is properly described as absolute, and this as the consequence of several factors. Her freedom from the assaults of CONCUPISCENCE alone would not have been sufficient to ensure it, for the angels, free from the weaknesses of a fallen Adam were still able to revolt against God. Two other special factors constituted Mary perfectly impeccable. The first was her constant awareness of God, living always in His presence, and the second was her reception of special and extraordinary graces. These particular graces represented the most important factor, for they enabled Mary to maintain a perfect harmony in her mind, will, affections, and appetitive powers, and to recognize always, where error plagues lesser mortals, that true good and happiness are found only in union with God's will.

Such sinlessness in Our Lady, however, does not mean that Mary was intrinsically impeccable, but rather that the grace of her Immaculate Conception and her divine motherhood made sin utterly impossible in her life. She was free, as a consequence of her predestination, not only from all personal sin and from every voluntary imperfection but also from every involuntary moral fault and from even the first movements of concupiscence.

The fact and propriety of Mary's complete sinlessness, recognized in the Church long before other Marian mysteries were explored, can be established also through the theological axiom that the nearer one approaches to a principle of truth or life the more deeply one partakes of its effects. Hence, Mary's unique proximity to God and the possession of grace made her immune to any kind of personal sin. Her maternal relationship with her divine Son was more than a mere physiological relationship and even more than an office endowed with special graces. It was, in fact, a supernatural, sanctifying union, implying a highly intimate affinity and relationship with the Most Holy Trinity. It is evident, therefore, that Mary's relationship to the hypostatic order demanded that God, out of what was due Himself, bestow the grace of IMPECCABILITY upon His Mother.

Fullness of Grace. This fact of Mary's complete sinlessness implies conversely what is termed the fullness of grace. The teaching Church, therefore, in referring traditionally to Our Lady as full of grace, has never felt justified in attributing to Mary anything less than a supremacy of holiness. Whatever in providence has been given in any degree to individual saints must have been given to Mary in plenitude. If the first parents received an exceptional amount of grace from the moment of their creation, Mary must have possessed a far greater degree of sanctity from the time of her conception.

Even before papal authority confirmed their teaching, ecclesiastical writers and Doctors of the Church were unanimous in holding that from her very creation Mary possessed a greater degree of sanctity than any angel or other merely human being. Many theologians have not hesitated to claim for Mary a sanctity surpassing, even from the beginning, the combined holiness of all angels and other men, excluding, of course, that of her divine Son.

Traditionally, therefore, the Church has always attributed to Mary any grace that has been granted to a lesser saint, either in its own form or in some more eminent and fitting manner. Certain graces, of course, could not be directly bestowed on Mary. The priesthood, for an instance, was not appropriate for Our Lady as a woman, but the divine maternity brought her the local, not simply the sacramental, presence of Christ's body; and physical martyrdom, not providentially in God's plan for His Mother, was superseded by her participation in a singular manner in the Passion of her divine Son.

Our Lady's fullness of grace, however, preeminent as it was, was not comparable to the plenitude of grace in Christ. Our Savior is the source of grace; moreover, by reason of the hypostatic union, the plenitude of grace was complete in Our Lord from His conception. In Mary's case, grace was susceptible to growth. As Our Lady dealt with Christ, witnessed the events in the work of Redemption, and experienced one by one the episodes in her life linking her with the work of the Savior, her capacity for

Our Lady of Guadalupe is depicted on tiles in the garden of Mission San Gabriel in southern California, founded in 1771. (©Richard Cummins/CORBIS)

grace increased. In reference to the Blessed Mother, therefore, one speaks of the fullness of grace in a relative, not absolute, sense. No matter how extraordinary the graces granted her were, there would always remain an infinite distance between her greatest perfection and the ineffable HOLINESS OF GOD. No creature can possibly possess absolute perfection, and even though Our Lady fulfilled perfectly the will of God in every instance, her grace was perfect only in proportion to that degree to which God destined her.

Therefore, even though properly described by the Archangel Gabriel before the Incarnation as full of grace, Our Lady was destined to advance in grace according to God's providential designs. This she did more abundantly and perfectly than any other pure creature, and, inasmuch as grace begets grace, in her this sanctifying quality was multiplied throughout her life in geometric proportions.

Neither from Sacred Scripture nor from the teaching of the Church can it be proved, however, that Our Lady's meriting an increase in grace began from the very instant of her conception, though many theologians advance reasons indicating that such was the case. Certainly she advanced in grace with the attainment of the use of reason, whenever, prematurely or normally in God's arrangements, that occurred, and she especially advanced in grace at the time of the INCARNATION. From that moment on an ineffable relationship existed between the incarnate Word and His Mother, and whereas Mary gave Christ His humanity, Our Lord gave His Mother a constantly increasing participation in His divinity.

Besides Mary's unique degree of habitual grace as a permanent mode of being, she surpassed all other creatures, too, in the reception of actual graces. God granted her all the graces of intellect and will necessary to perform each action in her life with the greatest possible perfection.

Virtues and Gifts. Beyond sanctifying grace and its increase, beyond her actual graces, Our Lady received also the infused theological and moral VIRTUES, and the gifts of the Holy Spirit. The infused virtues enabled her to perform supernaturally meritorious acts, and the gifts aided her in perfecting her acts in complete accord with the inspirations of the Holy Spirit. The cooperation of the human will with divine grace in seeking that which is good results in progress and growth in the virtues. If they are properly developed they constitute holiness, not so much because of the quality of the exterior act as because of the perfection of the inner dispositions. In the case of our blessed Mother, her inner dispositions were of such special excellence that her power to live a supernatural life surpassed that of all the saints even at the end of their lives. The least of Mary's interior acts were animated by the purest motives and dispositions of love and realized with a perfection of charity beyond that of the most heroic efforts of even the greatest of God's other servants. No one denies, therefore, that the Blessed Virgin Mary practiced virtue in a most exemplary manner. The Scriptures give testimony to as much. Note her stalwart faith (Lk 1.45), her profound humility (Lk 1.38–55), and her prompt obedience (Lk 2.5, 22). Because of her freedom from sin she did not exercise such virtues as continence and penance, but this is not to deny that she possessed the habit of these virtues.

Both from the limited but pointed details of Sacred Scripture and from theological reasoning Mary is seen first of all as the perfect exemplar of the theological virtues. Her faith, strong, certain, and prompt in its assent, was enlightened by the gifts of wisdom, understanding, and knowledge. Extraordinary at the time of the ANNUNCIATION, it increased at CANA and throughout the public life of Our Lord until it reached its perfection on Mount Calvary. The point should be made, moreover, that Mary possessed the virtue of faith in the highest degree experienced by any soul on earth, for Our Lord, possessing the beatific vision from the very moment of His conception, never needed faith or hope. He already possessed what these virtues lead to—vision and possession.

Beyond this deep faith, since Mary firmly believed in the promises of the infallible Almighty, she awaited the fulfillment of these promises concerning herself and the human race with a perfect trust and confidence, displaying the greatest hope of the eternal possession of God. Despite the trials and forebodings in the life of Christ and the seeming contradictions in what had been promised, her hope never faltered. In fact, it was later in life evidenced in its preeminent perfection by its relation to that of the Apostles, who, after the Ascension of Our Lord were sustained by Mary's hope in the early and difficult days of the announcing of the gospel message.

If Mary's faith was singularly ardent and her hope so firm and sure, these virtues were perfected only in keeping with her love of God, her extraordinary charity. Mary, being intimately united with the Blessed Trinity, corresponded most perfectly with God's love for her. No human disorder or imperfection ever impeded her growth in the love of the Almighty. Especially at the moment of her cooperation in the mystery of the Redemption and all that it implied, a perfect example of heroic charity was evidenced. At the time of the Incarnation, Mary not only offered an extraordinary sacrifice for men, she offered that which was dearer than her own life, the life of her Son. Her charity was, in fact, of such abundance that her sacrifice lasted not only for a few moments at the Incarnation and on Calvary but throughout the whole of Christ's life.

It must be noted, too, that since the infused moral virtues exist in a soul in the state of grace with a perfection in proportion to its possession of charity, Mary possessed also the virtues of prudence, justice, fortitude, and temperance in an extraordinary degree. The full hierarchy of virtues along with her special intellectual endowments, constitute Mary, then, the model of both the contemplative and the active life. Her devotion to the Word incarnate, her charity, and her observance of the Law make her the exemplar of the Christian life.

In Catholic theological writings, a discussion is also sometimes found concerning Mary's reception of the Sacraments. Since the Sacraments were instituted as a chief means of growth in grace for the Christian, the graces gained by Our Lady would be immense since she was prepared to receive the Sacraments with ideal dispositions. Of course, not all the Sacraments were necessary in the case of Our Lady; some she could not even validly receive. The Holy Eucharist, however, for the time after its institution must have been for Mary the source of great consolation and increase in grace. The enormous graces that can be procured by an ordinarily devout soul from a single reception of the Eucharist bring one to understand what the Sacrament must have brought by way of an increase in grace to the absolutely perfect communicant, the Blessed Mother.

There are also special graces granted to certain individuals in particular situations not for the sanctification of the individual himself but for the sanctification of others. These are called by theologians, *gratiae gratis datae.* It would not have been necessary that Mary possess all such graces herself, because her duties in providence did not require them. However, it is likely that most of them were granted her, for it was fitting that she as queen of the Apostles, possess in an eminent degree these various charisms.

Consummated Fullness. Mary's special gifts and the marvels that grace and Divine Providence produced in her soul led Our Lady to an ultimate perfection in the supernatural life that is called her final perfection, or consummated fullness of grace. At the end of Our Lady's life, consequent upon the fulfilling of her sacred offices and fruition of her special privileges, her cooperation and growth in grace led to a culmination anticipating her heavenly glory. Although the final plenitude of grace in Mary was of an ineffable degree, it must never be, as indicated earlier, conceived as infinite. The possibilities of the state of grace itself were not exhausted in Mary, nor were all the possible effects of grace realized in her life. Of necessity, grace in Mary remained a created, accidental entity and consequently a finite reality. Hence, the plenitude of grace in Our Lady was limited in comparison with that of Christ, although it was still, in comparison with that of any other creature, inexpressibly superior.

For ordinary Christians, there are two general factors in supernatural growth. The one is fidelity to duties of state involving the Commandments and the practice of the virtues, the other is the reception of the Sacraments. These are the common ways of sanctification. In the case of our blessed Lady, however, there existed a third factor, her divine maternity and the offices and privileges consequent upon it. Since she was called to this special relationship with God, there followed for her the bestowal of extraordinary graces for extraordinary sanctification. These graces, like any others, became more and more numerous as Mary corresponded with them in greater charity and fidelity. Her perfect correspondence with grace, especially at the moment of the Incarnation and again on Calvary, produced in Mary's soul an increase, and plenitude, of grace that exceeds human description.

Hence, in an attempt to describe the holiness of Mary, the words of St. John Chrysostom in the Roman Breviary have become classical. "A great miracle . . . indeed was the blessed ever-virgin Mary. What greater or brighter has ever been found or will ever be found? . . . What is holier than she? Neither Prophets nor Apostles . . . neither seraphim nor cherubim . . . nor any created being, visible or invisible . . ." (Lesson 5, Common of the Feasts of the Blessed Virgin Mary).

Bibliography: E. DUBLANCHY, *Dictionnaire de théologie catholique,* ed. A. VACANT et al. (Paris 1903–50) 9.2:2413–30. I. A. ALDAMA, *Sacrae theologiae summa,* ed. Fathers of the Society of Jesus (3d ed. Madrid 1958) 2:335–367, 128–130. J. B. CAROL, *Fundamentals of Mariology* (New York 1956). C. FRIETHOFF, *A Complete Mariology,* tr. Religious of the Retreat of the Sacred Heart (Westminster, MD 1958). R. GARRIGOU-LAGRANGE, *The Mother of the Saviour and Our Interior Life,* tr. B. J. KELLY (St. Louis 1957). W. G. MOST, *Mary in Our Life* (3d ed. New York 1959). E. N. NEUBERT, *Mary in Doctrine* (Milwaukee 1954). L. J. SUENENS, *Mary the Mother of God,* tr. A. BRENNEL (New York 1959). S. BONANO, "Mary's Immunity from Actual Sin," Carol Mariol 1:395–410. F. P. CALKINS, "Mary's Fulness of Grace," *ibid.* 2:297–312. W. J. MCDONALD, "Holy Mary," *American Ecclesiastical Review* 140 (1959) 289–292. P. G. RHODES, "Our Lady's Endowments," in *Our Blessed Lady,* ed. C. LATTEY (London 1934). G. F. VAN ACKEREN, "Does the Divine Maternity Formally Sanctify Mary's Soul?" *Marian Studies* 6 (St. Louis 1955) 63–101.

[J. F. MURPHY/EDS.]

PT. 2: KNOWLEDGE OF MARY

The mystery of Mary, as any mystery of faith, is beyond the comprehension of the human mind in this life [*see* MYSTERY (IN THEOLOGY)]. This impenetrability becomes apparent when one tries to probe the nature and extent of Mary's knowledge. One finds that some conclusions concerning her knowledge are certain. With regard to others one can attain only probability, while a third group of assertions can be classified only as possible. They will be considered in that order.

Certain Conclusions. Since the time of her Assumption, Mary enjoys the beatific vision. She does not know all that can be known, for such knowledge would demand the infinite intelligence found only in God. The intensity and extent of Mary's vision, however, is second only to that possessed by the humanity of her Son. The degree of intensity of this vision is proportionate to the degree of sanctifying grace possessed at the end of earthly life. Since her grace surpassed that of any other blessed creature, her vision is superior to that of any other blessed. Further, she surpassed the other blessed in her knowledge of creatures, particularly in her knowledge of her fellow men. Those enjoying the beatific vision see in it the events in the lives of those who in some way pertain to them. Since all are related to Mary, the spiritual mother of men, Mary's knowledge of man is absolutely universal.

While on earth Mary exercised her natural powers of reason. Although there are limits to her naturally acquired knowledge, one is sure that she was never in ignorance. Here one must distinguish carefully between nescience (a lack of unnecessary knowledge) and ignorance (a deficiency in obligatory knowledge). Ignorance could never be in Mary because it results from original sin, from which she was preserved. She did not know such things as the structures of the atom, the nature of disease, or the full implications of philosophy and mathematics, since such knowledge was not necessary for her office of Mother and Mediatrix.

Probable Conclusions. Probability involves more than mere possibility. It is a mental commitment to one of two contrary propositions in which the mind is still aware of the possibility of error. About Mary's knowledge the following conclusions are probable.

On numerous occasions Mary received divine illumination through the infusion of concepts, charismatic gifts, and the operation of the cognitive gifts of the Holy Spirit. The reason is that these gifts were necessary for her exalted office.

At the time of the Annunciation she was illumined so that she had a knowledge of the divinty of her Son. Some have argued against this by pointing out, quite correctly, that Luke's account of the angel's visit to Mary contains no clear assertion of the divinity of Christ. Further they appeal to the text of Luke dealing with the finding of the boy Jesus in the Temple. "'Did you not know that I must be about my Father's business?' And they did not understand the word that he spoke to them" (Lk 2.49–50). This text does not necessarily indicate a lack of knowledge about His divinity, but rather a failure to see the full implications of His providential mission. Further, although it is true that Luke's account of the Annunciation does not clearly state the divinity of Jesus, nevertheless it did contain an assertion of His office as Messiah and the fact of His miraculous conception. The Scriptures do not disprove that Mary learned of His divinity at the time of His conception. Furthermore, if as St. Thomas contends (*Summa theologiae* 3a, 30.1) and as Pope Plus XII confirms in the encyclical *Mystici corporis* (epilogue), Mary represented the whole of humanity, giving her consent to a spiritual marriage between the Son of God and human nature, then she needed some knowledge of the divinity of her Son. Such knowledge could have come from a divinely enlightened understanding of certain Old Testament texts. Much of the difficulty here arises from a failure to distinguish between clear and distinct knowledge as opposed to hazy and confused knowledge. The latter, although lacking precision, is certain in the mind of its possessor.

Possible Conclusions. Some conclusions about Mary's knowledge must be listed as merely possible. Of these some have good reasons militating against their actuality, while others have good reasons neither against nor for their actuality. When dealing with the latter, one must recall the limitations of the human when faced with mystery. Although one can recognize them only as possibilities, it may well be that *de facto* Mary did possess such knowledge.

It is possible that Mary could have had the beatific vision in this life as a permanent possession. Endowed with an intellect, capable of being raised to this vision, Mary could have received this privilege. Yet tradition has always asserted that she was a wayfarer, who during her earthly life merited increases of grace, which would not be possible if she permanently possessed the beatific vision.

It is possible that on certain occasions Our Lady was granted temporarily the BEATIFIC VISION. Formerly many theologians thought this to be probable, arguing that since this gift was granted to Moses and St. Paul (Ex 33.19; 2 Cor 12.2–4), then by reason of Mary's preeminence she must have received the same gift. However, modern Scripture scholarship has established that these passages do not imply anything more than mystical experience such as that granted to St. Teresa of Avila. Although one cannot offer good reasons for asserting the probability, there are no strong reasons for denying it.

It is possible that Mary had as a permanent possession infused concepts. However, there are convincing reasons neither for asserting nor for denying the conclusion.

At the time of the VISITATION, Mary spoke of her lowliness and her exalted blessedness. Theologians must keep both in mind when dealing with her privileges. They must never fear to assert what her preeminent office demands, and yet they must temper their enthusiasm by the realization of the limitations of the human mind when faced with the supernatural.

Bibliography: E. DUBLANCHY, *Dictionnaire de théologie catholique,* ed. A. VACANT et al. (Paris 1903–50) 9.2:2409–13. F. J. CONNELL, "Our Lady's Knowledge," J. B. CAROL, ed., *Mariology* 2:313–324. With regard to Mary's knowledge at the time of the Annunciation, see bibliog. in Connell, 320.

[P. J. MAHONEY/EDS.]

PART 3: MARY AND THE CHURCH

In the modern development of Mariology, considerable interest focuses on the relationship between Mary and the Church. Such relationship was perceived even in the early centuries of the Christian era. The Fathers pointed out that, as the Virgin Mary is the mother of Christ, so also the Church is virginal mother of men. Their reflections were deeply influenced by their perception of the likeness that both Our Lady and the Church have with Eve, mother of all the living. However, the parallelism between Mary and the Church was not a major theme in the patristic period. The same may be said of the Middle Ages. Some medieval authors presented the Blessed Virgin as the image and type of the Church, its most eminent member, and its loving mother; some had nothing to say on the subject. After Albert the Great, the idea was neglected. The present age has returned to the inquiry because of a conviction that the analogy between Mary and the Church, far from being a secondary theme situated on the surface of Catholic teaching, is necessary for understanding the dogma of the Redemption.

The meaning of the terms used in the comparison is clear. Mary is the Blessed Virgin, mother of Jesus Christ. The Church is the Catholic Church, the community of the baptized that was founded by Jesus, the society that is known as the Mystical Body of Christ. To carry out the comparison, one must set the Blessed Virgin apart from the rest of the Church. That is, the Church is regarded, not as a totality composed of Mary and all other Christians but only as that part of the Church which is made up of the latter. More exactly, the comparison is between two parts of the same whole, Mary on one side, and all the rest of the members on the other.

Maternity of Mary and the Church. In the supernatural order, the Mother of Christ is also the mother of the Church and therefore of all the members of the Mystical Body. Mary's basic relationship to the Church is maternal. This truth is taught by St. Pius X (see above). By the very fact that the Blessed Virgin is the mother of Christ the head, she is the mother of the whole Body.

The Church, too, is the mother of men, for from her they receive supernatural life and education. The Church is the mother of men mainly by the administration of the Sacraments. Mary is the mother of men because grace, which is conferred by the Sacraments, is deposited in the treasury of the Church through her cooperation in Christ's redemptive sacrifice. When one compares Mary's spiritual motherhood with that of the Church, he perceives that the former is the nobler and is the source of the latter. But these two mothers do not have separate families or give birth to different children. They have the same sons and daughters whom they cherish with a common love. Mary brings forth the whole Body of Christ, the Church, which is also the mother of Christ's members.

The New Eve. The theme of the new Eve is developed by the Fathers in their reflections on the notion of recapitulation, which is prominent in St. Irenaeus. God's plan had been clear from the outset; a man and a woman, Adam and Eve, were to transmit the supernatural life of grace to all mankind. Restoration of the plan that was compromised by sin was to be made by another man and another woman. The man is Jesus Christ, the new Adam. A woman had to have a place in the restoration; from an early period, the Fathers of the Church recognized this woman. The new Eve is Mary and the Church.

Evil and death have been introduced into the world by the disobedience of the first Eve. The second Eve is the Church, formed from the side of the second Adam sleeping in death on the cross, as the first Eve had been formed from the side of the sleeping Adam. But the new Eve as a definite person who repaired by her obedience what the first Eve had devastated by her disobedience is Mary. Thus both Mary and the Church are celebrated in tradition as the new Eve, mother of all who live the new life brought by Christ. As Eve contributed to the ruin of men, Mary and the Church contribute to their Redemption.

Later ages made a further application. If Mary is mother of all the living, she is associated with her Son in His redemptive work. The consent that she freely gave at the Annunciation to be the mother of Christ was enlivened anew at the Crucifixion. By cooperating in the redeeming sacrifice, she is the new Eve in the most perfect sense, source of men's life, mother of the Body as she is mother of the head.

Virginity of Mary and the Church. From ancient times, Mary, mother and virgin, has been likened to the Church, which is also mother and virgin. This comparison involves great differences. Mary is the mother of Christ; the Church is the mother of Christians who are "other Christs." Mary is literally a virgin; the Church is virginal because it has never adulterated the faith but has always been true to Christ. Maternity and virginity are literal for Mary, but analogous and metaphorical for the Church.

In Judeo-Christian writings, a virgin is a person or a community that is dedicated to God and remains faithful to Him. In the Old Testament union with God consecrates virginity and at the same time makes it maternally fruitful, as long as Israel does not abandon its divine bridegroom for false gods. Virginity is fidelity; heresy and apostasy are adultery. Union with God hallows virginity by enriching it with fecundity; its fruit is imperishable life.

As applied to the Church, virginity is linked with the purity of faith. The very maternity of the Church is virginal because, loyal in faith and undefiled by heresy, it brings forth God's children by the activity of the Holy Spirit.

When the Biblical notion of virginity refers to persons, it implies bodily integrity, especially as a sign of spiritual fidelity and complete consecration to God. Mary, virgin of virgins, is the ideal of all virginity. She conceived and bore her Son with unimpaired virginity by the action of the Holy Spirit. Her spiritual maternity, too, is wholly virginal; like Christ, the members of His Body, which is the Church, are born of Mary as children of God solely by the Holy Spirit's power.

The virginity of the Church aids one to understand the virginity of Our Lady. The Church is not only one flesh, but one spirit, with Christ (1 Cor 6.17). Though real, the union is spiritual and mystical. Similarly, Mary's virginity is not only the absence of carnal association with any man, but is her spiritual and mystical union with God. By the perfection of its virginity, therefore, the Church draws very close to the virginal Mother of God.

Holiness of Mary and the Church. As the virginity of the Church helps one to understand Mary's virginity, so Mary's holiness assists one to grasp the HOLINESS OF THE CHURCH. The sanctity of both is caused by the same grace of God. The main difference lies in the receptivity of Mary and the Church. No refusal or reluctance ever marred Mary's acceptance of God's advances; but the Church is a collectivity of men and women who never hold their souls completely open to God's generosity.

All men are called to holiness in the Church. The Church is holy because it has received from God the means of holiness, faith and the Sacraments, which produce holiness in the members. However, although the Church is entirely holy, its members are subject to defects and sins that hamper the diffusion of its holiness.

Comparison between Mary's holiness and the holiness of the Church brings out Mary's superiority. She was redeemed by way of preservation, and her Immaculate Conception involved her freedom from concupiscence. But the Church is formed of members who all, with the exception of Mary, contract original sin. Consequently, although they are purified from all guilt by Baptism, they are burdened with the weight of concupiscence, which slows down the growth of grace.

The Blessed Virgin's progress in sanctity was constant and rapid. Her whole life and all her actions were unfailingly directed toward God. She mounted from holiness to holiness, always full of grace because each grace increased her capacity for further grace that promptly filled her soul to repletion. The Church also grows in grace, aspiring to the full stature of Christ (Eph 4.13). But the Church is an assembly of sinners, who must unceasingly repent and be converted anew; its progress is menaced by the members' sluggish response to grace.

Sanctity flowers into glory and resurrection, the final triumph. On earth, the Church plods along in the order of terrestrial holiness, with all its setbacks; in heaven, it has not yet attained resurrection, the ultimate radiation of holiness. But Mary is now in glory; prior to the Church, she was taken up to heaven, body and soul. Yet her Assumption, coming at the climax of her last fullness of grace, prefigures and anticipates the assumption of the Church. Thus the Blessed Virgin, who excels the Church by her Immaculate Conception and by her progress in sanctity, also precedes it by her resurrection.

Coredemptive Mission of Mary and the Church. Mary's maternal relation to Christ's Person has occupied the attention of theologians for centuries; recently their efforts concentrate on her relation to her Son's work. They seek a clearer insight into the part assigned by God to the Blessed Virgin and to the Church in the economy of salvation.

As representative and personification of the Church, Mary collaborated with Christ in the three great steps of the mystery of Redemption: the Incarnation, the cross, and the Resurrection. Both Mary and the Church have a redemptive mission; but Mary's was exercised on an essentially higher level than that of the Church.

God's Son became man that the Redemption might be a human as well as a divine achievement. But from the beginning He required the consent of the human race and the donation of its flesh and blood. Mary, acting in the name of all mankind, gave that consent and donation.

During the first phase of her salvific activity, Mary preceded the Church. In response to God's proposal she replied: "Behold the handmaid of the Lord." St. Thomas Aquinas says that her consent was given in the name of the whole human race (*Summa theologiae* 3a, 30.1), and this insight has been consecrated by the teaching authority of the Church: "In the name of the entire human race, she gave her consent for a spiritual marriage between the Son of God and human nature" (Pius XII, *Mystici corporis* 108).

The activity exercised by the Blessed Virgin at the time of the conception and birth of Christ was carried on all during her life and reached its culmination on Calvary. In His supreme hour of sacrifice, the Redeemer drew His mother into His suffering to associate her with His redeeming act. He received her dedication, love, and merits, and integrated her agony into His own Passion in order to offer them to the Father for the salvation of mankind.

Mary's suffering endowed her maternity over men with a new dimension. Her first childbearing, by which she became the mother of God, was without pain; her second childbearing, by which she became fully the mother of sinners, was painful in the extreme. While Jesus was offering Himself in sacrifice for men's Redemption, His mother offered her Son for the same purpose and, thus cooperating in men's birth to supernatural life, became in a heightened sense the mother of the Church.

The Mother's contribution to the work of Redemption far surpasses that of the Church. Not only did she precede the Church during Christ's mortal life, but she was integrated into the very Passion that procured men's reconciliation with God. She who was one with her Son at the Incarnation was one with Him at the moment of Redemption. The activity of the Church is exercised on the lower plane of application of the merits and atonement of Calvary.

A second phase of Mary's salvific mission extended from Pentecost to the Assumption. During this period she lived in the Church as its first and most important member, and by her intercession and merits collaborated in applying the Redemption. She had preceded the Church but was now in the Church, without official voice in its councils. Her hand did not hold the keys of the kingdom, but her prayers sustained the Apostle's hands that held them. She conferred no Sacraments, but their power derives from the sacrifice of the cross, in which she had her part.

During the final phase of her mediatory activity, from her Assumption to the end of the world, Mary again goes before the Church, assists it with supernatural aid, and awaits its triumph. The mystery of Christ's Resurrection and Ascension is the culmination of the mystery of Redemption. The Church is implicated in the mystery, and has inaugurated its own resurrection in its head. Mary has already risen; the resurrection of the collective Church at the end of time is personified in her, whose Assumption is the prelude of the future bodily victory of the rest of men.

Mary's coredemptive activity, obviously, has no gap to cover up in her Son's redemptive work. All she has, she received from Christ. What she received was power to act with the Redeemer for mankind's salvation. She stands next to the Redeemer, as coredemptress subordinate to Him, and she can act only in dependence on Him. But dependence does not exclude productivity. Mary's redemptive office is wholly derived from Christ, for it is the cooperation of a subordinate associate, which supposes His activity; yet she truly acts with Him.

Vatican II and Beyond. Vatican Council II's Marian doctrine in the Dogmatic Constitution on the Church (*Lumen gentium* ch. 8) was most significant for the renewal of Mariology. The Council Fathers voted, Oct. 29, 1963, in favor of making the Marian schema a part of the document on the Church. The very title of the chapter, ''The Blessed Virgin Mary, Mother of God, in the Mystery of Christ and the Church,'' placed her in close relationship with her Son (Christocentric Mariology) and with his Mystical Body (ecclesiotypical Mariology). This is the proper setting in which to assess Mary's role in the work of Redemption. The true ecumenical importance of the Council's decision is derived not from minimizing her place in Catholic faith and piety, but from emphasizing a sharing-oriented Mariology instead of one that is privilege-centered.

Under the impetus of Vatican II the theology of Mary stresses the truth that her special graces and prerogatives are to be seen as primarily for the sake of her Son and his redeemed-redeeming Body, the Church. Divine Revelation about Mary makes the central mysteries of faith more intelligible and meaningful for Christian living.

The Christocentric and ecclesiotypical emphases of contemporary Mariology are mutually complementary and not in conflict. For Mary cannot be related to Christ without being intimately associated with the ecclesial Body that he received through his redemptive activity. At the same time, she is the archetype of the Church only because her unique relationship with Christ is the basis for the Church's share in his redeeming work (see O. Semmelroth, *Mary, Archetype of the Church* 1963, esp. 80–88). Consequently, concentration upon the ecclesiotypical significance of Marian doctrine and devotion should not obscure their basic Christocentric character.

Theologians today are more inclined to include the Mary-Church analogy within the basic Marian idea or fundamental principle of Mariology. ''Her concrete motherhood with regard to Christ, the redeeming God-man, freely accepted in faith—her fully committed divine motherhood—this is both the key to the full understanding of the Marian mystery and the basic Mariological principle, which is concretely identical with Mary's objectively and subjectively unique state of being redeemed'' (E. Schillebeeckx, *Mary, Mother of the Redemption* 106). Within one organic principle the two emphases are contained, i.e., both the Christocentric (Mary's ''fully committed divine motherhood''), and the ecclesiotypical (her ''objectively and subjectively unique state of being redeemed''). Her vocation to be the mother of the Word incarnate must be considered in close connection with the graces that reveal her calling to be the prototype of the Church.

Divine Maternity. The truth that Mary's motherhood of Christ is both bridal and virginal has rich ecclesiotypical significance (see O. Semmelroth, *Mary, Archetype of the Church* 1963, esp. 117–142). Her vocal *fiat* of free consent at the annunciation and her silent *fiat* at the foot of the cross make Mary the spiritual bride of the Redeemer. In her compassion she received the fruits of her Son's sacrifice both for her own redemption and for that of the whole Church. Concomitantly, and as a result of this creative receptivity to grace, her bridal motherhood is also virginal. Her maternal fruitfulness cannot come from human power but from the breath of the Holy Spirit. Had she conceived Christ other than as a virgin, her bridal relationship with the *Logos* incarnate would have been obscured. Without her perpetual virginity, the revelation of her complete and continuous fidelity to Christ and his messianic mission would have been blurred. Mary then is the archetype of the Church as the Church is also the virginal bride of Christ. As the community of persons redeemed by him, the Church is called to be constantly faithful to his word. The Immaculate Conception is the perfect exemplar of a grace-filled Church. As the sacramental community called to mediate Redemption to the world, the Church also images the bridal motherhood of Mary. The Assumption makes her ''the sign of sure hope, and comfort for the pilgrim people of God'' (*Lumen gentium* 68–69). All the Marian dogmas, therefore, converge toward a theological and prayerful contemplation of Mary as the archetype of the Church.

As bridal and virginal mothers, both Mary and the Church are to be dynamically united together with the Holy Spirit. The sole source of their spiritual fecundity is the abiding presence and activity of the risen Lord's Spirit. A closer connection between Mariology and Pneumatology will contribute greatly to a balanced Christology, ecclesiology, and Christian anthropology. Much remains to be done in this regard, especially by theologians of the Western Church who have begun to study more seriously the magnificent heritage of the Eastern tradition on the Holy Spirit.

New Eve. A portion of the patristic patrimony common to East and West is the image of Mary as the New Eve. Its rediscovery, under the special inspiration of Cardinal Newman's Marian writings, has led to a renewed research into the witness of the Fathers who made use of this image in their teaching about Mary. After the Scriptures, it reflects the most ancient meditation upon Mary and is a very fertile source of the Mary-Church analogy and typology. The National Conference of Catholic Bishops (NCCB) in the pastoral on the Blessed Virgin Mary points out: ''Even more anciently, the Church was regarded as the 'New Eve.' The Church is the bride of Christ, formed from his side in the sleep of death on the cross, as the first Eve was formed by God from the side of the sleeping Adam'' (NCCB 41). From her earliest days the Church has seen herself symbolized in Mary and has come to understand her mysterious self more profoundly in light of Mary as archetype. Mary ''personifies'' all that the Church is and hopes to become.

The impact of an ecclesiotypical Mariology upon Marian devotion has been most salutary. Pope Paul VI in his apostolic exhortation for the right ordinary and development of devotion to the Blessed Virgin Mary, stated: ''She is worthy of imitation because she was the first and most perfect of Christ's disciples. All of this has a permanent and universal exemplary value'' (Paul VI 35). Mary, of course, is not an exemplar in the sense of being a stereotyped blueprint upon which contemporary Christians are to model their lives. Nevertheless, if Christians are to mature as members of Christ's living Body, the Church, they must prayerfully penetrate the perennial meaning of Mary-like faith, courage, concern, constancy, etc.

Bibliography: F. L. B. CUNNINGHAM, ''The Relationship between Mary and the Church in Medieval Thought,'' *Marian Studies* 9 (1958) 52–78. B. J. LE FROIS, ''The Mary-Church Relationship in the Apocalypse,'' *ibid.* 79–106. J. F. SWEENEY, ''Theological Considerations on the Mary-Church Analogy,'' *ibid.* 31–51. C. O. VOLLERT, ''The Mary-Church Analogy in Its Relationship to the Fundamental Principle of Mariology,'' *ibid.* 107–128; ''Mary and the Church,'' J. B. CAROL, ed., *Mariology* 2:550–595; *A Theology of Mary* (New York 1965), esp. 113–155. Q. QUESNELL, ''Mary is the Church,'' *Thought* 36 (1961) 25–39. G. F. KIRWIN, ''Mary's Salvific Role Compared with That of the Church,'' *Marian Studies* 25 (1974) 29–43. T. A. KOEHLER, ''Mary's Spiritual Maternity after the Second Vatican Council,'' *Marian Studies* 23 (1972) 39–68. J. A. R. MACKENZIE, ''The Patristic Witness to the Virgin Mary as the New Eve,'' *Marian Studies* 29 (1978) 67–78. G. A. MALONEY, *Mary: The Womb of God* (Danville, NJ 1976). J. H. NEWMAN, *The New Eve* (Westminister, MD 1952). PAUL VI, *Marialis cultus*, apostolic exhortation, Feb. 2, 1974, *Acta Apostolicae Sedis* 66 (1974) 113–168; tr. *Devotion to the Blessed Virgin Mary* (USCC Publ. Office, Washington, DC 1974). E. SCHILLEBEECKX, *Mary, Mother of the Redemption*, tr. N. D. SMITH (New York 1964). A. SCHMEMANN, ''Our Lady and the Holy Spirit,'' *Marian Studies* 23 (1972) 69–78. O. SEMMELROTH, *Mary, Archetype of the Church*, tr. M. VON EROES and J. DEVLIN (New York 1963); ''Dogmatic Constitution on the Church, Chapter 8,'' Vorgrimler, 1:285–296 (New York 1967).

[C. O. VOLLERT/F. M. JELLY/EDS.]

PART 4: MEDIATRIX OF ALL GRACES

By Mary's mediation Catholics designate, in general, that functional prerogative that embodies Our Lady's unique share in the soteriological mission of her Son. The belief of the faithful in this Marian role has found expression in Christian literature in a variety of ways from time immemorial. The genesis of the title Mediatrix itself, as applied to the Mother of God, is rather obscure. Perhaps the earliest sure witnesses are St. Andrew of Crete (d. 740), St. Germanus of Constantinople (d. 733), and St. Tarasius (d. *c.* 807). From the East the title was introduced into the literature of the West around the 9th century through a translation by Paul the Deacon of the *Life of Theophilus,* in which the term is used. From the 12th century on, it is applied to Our Lady with ever-increasing frequency until it becomes generally accepted in the 17th century.

Generally speaking, a mediator is one who interposes his good services between two physical or moral persons in order to facilitate an exchange of favors (e.g., an alliance). In most cases, the mission of a mediator is to bring about a reconciliation between parties at variance. In Catholic theology the title Mediatrix is applied to Our Lady for three reasons. First, because, owing to her divine motherhood and plenitude of grace, she occupies a middle position in the hierarchy of beings between the Creator and His creatures. This is known technically as her ontological mediation. Second, because during her earthly career she contributed considerably, through specific holy acts, to the reconciliation between God and man brought about by the Savior. Third, because through her powerful intercession in heaven she obtains for her spiritual children all the graces that God deigns to bestow on them. The last two phases constitute Mary's moral mediation. It should be borne in mind, however, that the mere use of the term Mediatrix need not always convey the above threefold meaning. In the more ancient writers that expression is restricted sometimes to the first, sometimes to the third phase of Mary's mediatorial office. The exact meaning in each case must be determined by the context and parallel passages.

Theologians are always careful to emphasize that Mary's mediation differs substantially from that of her Son. The latter is primary, self-sufficient, and absolutely necessary for men's salvation; the former is secondary, wholly dependent on Christ's, and only hypothetically necessary. However, Mary's mediation differs also, and indeed essentially, from that of other creatures (e.g., the angels, the saints, the priests of the New Testament). The latter avails only in particular cases and for particular graces; it is exercised dependently on Mary's will, and exclusively in the sphere of the actual application of graces. The former is universal, dependent on Christ only, and has a definite bearing on the acquisition (meriting) of graces, as well as on their application.

The actual exercise of Our Lady's mediatorial function may now be considered. The two phases of her moral mediation are treated in two separate sections.

Our Lady's Coredemption. As indicated, the first aspect of Mary's moral mediation refers to her active and formal share in the redemptive work brought about by Our Lord while still on earth. To express this complex activity in one single word, Catholic theology has coined the Latin term Coredemptrix. This title first appears in Catholic literature toward the end of the 14th century (e.g., in an *orationale* of St. Peter's in Salzburg). It was used quite frequently during the 17th, 18th, and 19th centuries. Since the Holy See itself has made use of it in its documents [*Acta Sanctae Sedis* 41 (1908) 409; *Acta Apostolicae Sedis* 5 (1913) 364; 6 (1914) 108], its legitimacy is no longer questioned by Catholics.

Meanings Attached to the Term. Apart from the question of the term's appropriateness, theologians are divided as to the nature and extent of the doctrine conveyed by that title. Their views may be summarized as follows.

A first group claims that Our Lady, by knowingly and willingly making possible the coming of the Savior into the world, cooperated only remotely in the objective Redemption. (By objective Redemption is meant the initial reconciliation of God and man as accomplished through the sacrifice of Calvary.) She has, besides, a direct share in the subjective Redemption, i.e., the dispensation of graces through which the objective Redemption is actually applied to individuals. The theologians of this group concede that Our Lady suffered and merited much for men's salvation during her life, but they contend that these sufferings and merits contributed not to bring about the Redemption itself but only to make it applicable to men. Such is the opinion of H. Lennerz, W. Goossens, G. D. Smith, and several others.

A second view, called the receptivity theory, has been advanced by a group of German theologians among whom H. M. Köster and O. Semmelroth are the most prominent. According to them, Christ alone redeemed the human race. Mary, however, may be said to have cooperated in the objective Redemption in the sense that at the foot of the cross she accepted the effects or the fruits of her Son's redemptive act and made them available to the members of the Mystical Body, whom she officially represented on Calvary. This theory has appealed to some outside of Germany (e.g., C. Dillenschneider) as a plausible explanation of the relationship between Mary and the Church.

A third group, representing the vast majority of theologians, considers the above explanations insufficient and unsatisfactory. According to them, Our Lady is to be styled Coredemptrix because she cooperated directly and immediately in the redemptive process itself (i.e., the objective Redemption) and not merely in the application of its effects to individual souls. In this third view Christ and Mary constitute one single principle of salvation for the whole human race in such a way that the restoration of mankind to the friendship of God as consummated on Calvary was the result of their joint causality. This joint causality does not place Our Lady on the same level with the Savior. In the orbit of primary, independent, and self-sufficient causality Christ remains utterly alone: men's only Redeemer. Mary's merits and satisfactions contributed to bring about objective Redemption only after the manner of a secondary cause, and as deriving their redemptive value wholly from the infinite merits and satisfactions of her Son.

In justification of the opinion just summarized, a few further clarifications are in order. The first truth to bear in mind is that, since Our Lady herself was redeemed by Christ, she could cooperate in the objective Redemption only after its effects had been applied to her. How could she cooperate to bring about something that had already produced its effects and that, therefore, must have been regarded by God as having been already accomplished? This becomes possible by distinguishing two logical stages (*signa rationis,* as the schoolmen say) in Christ's Redemption. First, He redeems Mary alone with a preservative Redemption; then, together with her, in a subsequent logical stage (*in signo posteriori rationis*), He redeems the rest of mankind with a liberative Redemption. Obviously, there is no chronological before and after in this process; merely a twofold acceptance of the Redemption on the part of the eternal Father, with a logical priority in favor of Mary.

Again, Our Lady's merits and satisfactions cannot be regarded as having enhanced the value of the infinite merits and satisfactions of her Son. Nevertheless, they were accepted by God as constituting a new title for the granting of pardon to the human race. Nothing prevents God from decreeing to cancel men's debt in view of a twofold title, each of them operative in its own sphere. On the contrary, this divine disposition seems most fitting in the light of the Church's teaching, which considers Our Lady as the Savior's intimate partner and as man's official representative in God's redemptive alliance with mankind.

Does it follow from the above that Our Lady's cooperation was an essential element of the Redemption? Here a distinction is in order. Mary's share may be said to have been essential in the sense that, without it, the Redemption would not have been what God decreed it to be. But it was not essential if by that is meant that Christ's merits and satisfactions were, by themselves, insufficient to redeem men. Something analogous happens when the Christian cooperates with divine grace in order to perform some meritorious action. That cooperation is essential only insofar as it meets a divine requisite.

Of course, in order to establish that Mary's coredemption, as championed by the majority of theologians, is a true Catholic doctrine resulting from divine revelation, it is not sufficient to show that it is theologically possible and even fitting. Two further questions remain to be answered. Is it also attested to in the sources of revelation, i.e., Sacred Scripture and divine tradition? Is it accepted by the magisterium, or teaching authority of the Church, as pertaining to the deposit of revelation?

Papal Teaching. Recent popes, beginning with Leo XIII in his rosary encyclical *Jucunda semper* (1894), have expressed their views on this question with ever-increasing forcefulness. The classical passage in this connection is from Benedict XV's apostolic letter *Inter sodalicia* (1918), wherein he states: ''To such an extent did [Mary] suffer and almost die with her suffering and dying Son, and to such an extent did she surrender her maternal rights over her Son for man's salvation, and immolated Him—insofar as she could—in order to appease the justice of God, that we may rightly say that she redeemed the human race together with Christ'' [*Acta Apostolicae Sedis* 10 (1918) 182]. In a radio broadcast by Pius XI (April 28, 1935) one finds the following words addressed to Our Lady: ''O Mother of love and mercy, who, when thy dearest Son was consummating the Redemption of the human race on the altar of the Cross, didst stand by Him, suffering with Him as a *Coredemptrix* . . . , preserve in us, we beseech thee, and increase day by day the precious fruit of His Redemption and of thy compassion'' (*L'Osservatore Romano,* April 29–30, 1935). In his encyclical *Haurietis aquas* (May 15, 1956) Pius XII affirms unequivocally that ''in bringing about the work of human Redemption, the Most Blessed Virgin Mary was, by the will of God, so indissolubly associated with Christ, that our salvation proceeded from the love and sufferings of Jesus Christ intimately joined with the love and sorrows of His Mother'' [*Acta Apostolicae Sedis* 48 (1956) 352]. The doctrine was briefly summarized by Vatican II as follows: ''In the work of the Savior, she [Mary] cooperated in an altogether singular way, by her obedience, faith, hope, and burning love, to restore supernatural life to souls'' (*Constitution on the Church* 8.61).

Sacred Scripture. Interpreted in the light of papal pronouncement, Sacred Scripture itself lends weight to the doctrine under discussion. The words addressed by almighty God to the devil in the Garden of Eden, ''I will put enmity between you and the woman, between your seed and her seed'' (Gn 3.15), are generally cited by Catholic theologians as a pertinent biblical argument. They see in the singular struggle between Christ and Satan, as related in the text, a prophetic announcement of the Savior's redemptive work. Since ''the woman'' spoken of is the mother of Christ in a true biblical sense, as Pius IX and Pius XII interpret it, and since her struggle with Satan is identical with her Son's, as Pius IX states, it follows that the prophecy foreshadows also Our Lady's coredemptive mission.

Another relevant passage is the Annunciation pericope. By her generous *fiat* to the angel's proposal (Lk 1.38), Our Lady willingly and knowingly made possible the redemptive Incarnation of the divine Word, and thus may be said to have formally participated in the soteriological mystery that was then being inaugurated. An insight into the concrete manner in which she was to share in that mystery is furnished by Simeon's prophecy: "And thy own soul a sword shall pierce" (Lk 2.35). This allusion to Mary's compassion found its dramatic fulfillment as she stood by the cross of her dying Son, sharing His bitter agony for the salvation of mankind. It was at this juncture that the Savior, pointing to St. John, addressed Our Lady saying: "Woman, behold thy son" (Jn 19.27). Recent popes, particularly Leo XIII in his encyclical *Adiutricem populi* (1895), have seen in the beloved disciple a representative of all the redeemed, and they have for this reason interpreted Christ's words to Our Lady as a proclamation of her spiritual motherhood of men. Since the regeneration of mankind to the life of grace was brought about by Christ precisely by means of His redemptive act, theologians reason that Mary's direct share in the former is inconceivable without her direct cooperation in the latter.

Tradition. If biblical passages in support of the coredemption are relatively meager, the data yielded by Catholic tradition, as a whole, are copious indeed. As in the case of so many other doctrinal theses, this one also had rather modest beginnings, but gradually attained its full development through an ever-increasing awareness of its implications. Chronologically, the first germ of the doctrine may be traced to the striking antithetical parallelism between Mary and Eve, so frequently described by ancient writers, specifically St. Irenaeus of Lyons (d. *c.* 202). Contrasting the episode of the Fall with the scene of the Annunciation, they pointed out that, just as the first woman, through her disobedience, had shared Adam's responsibility in the original prevarication, so likewise Mary, through her voluntary surrender to God's designs, was instrumental in bringing about men's supernatural rehabilitation in Christ. It is scarcely likely, however, that these early writers intended to attribute to Mary an immediate cooperation in the objective Redemption. They seem to have had in mind exclusively her conscious role in bringing the Savior into the world. At the end of the 10th century in the East, and the first half of the 12th in the West, the strictly soteriological character of Mary's cooperation begins to receive explicit notice, due particularly to the intervention of John the Geometer and Arnold of Chartres (d. 1156), respectively. The latter's remarkable teaching on this point actually became a *locus classicus* in the Marian literature of subsequent centuries. By the beginning of the 18th century virtually every aspect of Mary's coredemption (merit, satisfaction, ransom, sacrifice) had been studied at some length, and the doctrine accepted quite generally in its present formulation. The Jesuits Ferdinand Q. de Salazar and Maximilian Reichenberger, the Franciscans Roderick de Portillo and Charles del Moral, the Augustinian Bartholomew de los Rios, and the Dominican Lazarus Dassier are only a few of those deserving of mention for their notable contribution in this connection. From that time on, particularly in the decades of mid-20th century, the theory of Mary's coredemption in the strict sense has won so many adherents that it is rightly regarded as the opinion of the vast majority of theologians. After centuries of careful analysis and theological reflection, the complex doctrine, which had such modest beginnings in Christian antiquity, seems at last to have entered its final phase of scientific systematization. Indeed, in the judgment of some, the doctrine has attained sufficient maturity even to be solemnly sanctioned by the ecclesiastical magisterium. The first to voice these sentiments in an official petition to Pope Pius XII (Nov. 26, 1951) was the Cuban hierarchy, headed by Cardinal Manuel Arteaga y Betancourt, archbishop of Havana.

Controverted Points. While awaiting the official pronouncement of the Church, the theologians who champion the theory of a strict coredemption are divided among themselves concerning some secondary aspects of this doctrine. Thus, for example, a growing number of Mariologists hold (correctly, it seems) that Our Lady's soteriological merit was not merely based on fittingness (i.e., *de congruo*), as the majority still believe, but rather based on simple justice (*de condigno ex mera condignitate*). This latter is not to be confused with Christ's merit, which alone was condign in strict justice (*de condigno ex rigore justitiae*). The former involves a certain equality between the meritorious work performed and its reward, while the latter supposes, besides, an equality between the person giving the reward and the person meriting it.

Another phase of the coredemption that has given rise to prolonged discussion is the nature of Mary's share in the sacrifice of the cross *qua sacrifice.* Was her offering of the Victim on Calvary a sacrificial action in the proper sense? Some authors, such as H. Seiler, G. Petazzi, E. Sauras, and M. Llamera, claim that it was. Others, following N. García Garcés, G. M. Roschini, and C. Friethoff, believe that it was a sacrificial action only in a broad sense. The Holy See, by repeatedly cautioning against the use of the controversial title Virgin-Priest given by some to Our Lady, would seem to favor the latter view.

A third point of discrepancy concerns the exact relationship between the soteriological actions of Our Lady and those performed by the Savior Himself. Precisely in what sense did Mary cooperate immediately with her Son to bring about the Redemption? Some theologians, such as B. Merkelbach, H. Seiler, and P. Sträter, explain it in the sense that Our Lady's will directly determined (i.e., had some influence on) the will of her Son to perform His redemptive actions. Others, such as D. Bertetto, R. Gagnebet, and M. J. Nicolas, contend that Our Lady's cooperation was redemptive, not because it directly influenced or determined the soteriological actions of Christ, but rather because the actions of Christ conferred a redemptive value on her merits and satisfactions thus enabling them to concur (in a subordinate though direct manner) in bringing about the self-same effect, namely, men's reconciliation with God in its initial phase (*in actu primo*). This second position seems better to safeguard the unencroachable rights of the unique Redeemer, without in the least compromising the reality of Mary's immediate cooperation in His redemptive work.

Dispensation of Graces through Mary. The second phase of Our Lady's moral mediation concerns her share in the actual distribution of graces, that is to say, in the enduring process of applying to individual persons the supernatural merits acquired by Christ (and secondarily by herself) through the redemptive work. This is what theologians designate technically as Mary's cooperation in the subjective Redemption.

Meaning. Briefly stated, the meaning of this Marian prerogative is that all favors granted by God to all men are granted in view of and because of Our Lady's actual intervention. This causality of hers, which is totally subordinate to that of Christ in the same process, is universal as far as its beneficiaries are concerned, and likewise from the point of view of its object. That means that Mary's mediatorial intervention affects every member of the human race with the sole exception of Christ and herself. To those living before the objective Redemption was accomplished, including Adam and Eve, God made graces available in view of Mary's future merits, which were eternally present to Him. To those living after the objective Redemption was accomplished, graces are granted through Mary's secondary efficient causality. Her mediation is likewise universal in that it involves the granting of every single grace without exception: sanctifying grace, the infused virtues, the gifts of the Holy Spirit, all actual graces, and even favors of the natural order insofar as they are related to the supernatural order. Our Lady does not, of course, produce the sanctifying grace given to men through the Sacraments. She does, however, intervene in its infusion in a twofold manner: (1) remotely, inasmuch as that grace was merited by her (together with Christ) as coredemptrix; (2) proximately, inasmuch as the very desire to receive the Sacraments, and the proper dispositions to do so worthily are made possible only through actual graces obtained through Mary's intercession.

Concerning the precise nature of this causality there is a difference of opinion among theologians. Some, such as Cardinal Lépicier, E. Hugon, G. M. Roschini, and R. Garrigou-Lagrange, designate it as physical-instrumental. The majority, however, believe that it is a moral causality by way of intercession. The arguments in favor of a physical-instrumental causality are based mostly on the traditional references to Mary as the channel, aqueduct, almoner, and treasurer of grace. But the proponents of moral causality point out that since these are obviously metaphors, they can hardly constitute sufficient grounds for the theory in question. The manner, then, in which Our Lady discharges her office as dispensatrix of all graces is specifically her intercession. She intercedes for men either expressly, by actually asking God to bestow a certain grace on a certain person, or interpretatively, by presenting to God her previous merits in men's behalf. While it is highly commendable that one implore Our Lady's intercession in his prayers, it is not necessary that he do so. The graces he obtains from God are granted through her intercession whether she is invoked or not. As spiritual mother of men, Our Lady in Heaven is well aware of their spiritual needs and ardently desires to help them. Being the mother of God, the queen of all creation, and the coredemptrix of mankind, her appeal on men's behalf is most efficacious and always produces the intended results.

Position of the Magisterium. That Our Lady intervenes in the distribution of all heavenly favors to all men emerges quite clearly from the teaching authority of the Church as represented especially by the popes of the past two centuries. Thus Benedict XIV, in the bull *Gloriosae Dominae* (1748), likens Mary to "a heavenly stream through which the flow of all graces and favors reach the soul of every wretched mortal" [*Opera omnia,* v. 16 (Prato 1846) 428]. Among the frequent allusions made by Leo XIII to this doctrine, the passage in the encyclical *Octobri mense* (1891) is particularly trenchant. After recalling that God had not wished to become incarnate in Mary's womb without first obtaining her consent, the Pope adds: "It may be affirmed with no less truth and precision that, by the will of God, absolutely no part of that immense treasure of every grace which the Lord amassed . . . is bestowed on us except through Mary" [*Acta Sanctorum Sedis* 24 (1891) 195–196]. St. Pius X in his encyclical *Ad diem illum* (1904), Benedict XV in his *Inter sodalicia* (1918), and Pius XII in his *Superiore anno* (1940) and *Doctor mellifluus* (1953) explicitly corroborate the traditional theme: it is the will of God that one obtain every grace through Mary.

Liturgy. The liturgical books of the Church, always a reliable index of Catholic belief, faithfully echo the familiar strain found in papal documents. Thus the official prayer books of the Byzantines, Copts, Syrians, Armenians, and Chaldeans abound in references to Mary's role as dispensatrix of all graces. As to the Latin liturgy, its most notable witness is embodied in the Office and Mass of Mary Mediatrix of All Graces. The text was composed by J. Lebon of the University of Louvain at the suggestion of Cardinal Mercier, archbishop of Malines, and approved by Benedict XV in 1921. The privilege to celebrate this feast on May 31 of each year was originally granted to the dioceses of Belgium, but it was soon extended to numerous other dioceses and religious orders throughout the world. When in 1954 Pius XII ordered the universal observance of Mary's queenship on May 31, the feast of Mary's mediation was discontinued by some and transferred by others.

Scripture. What the popes and the liturgy proclaim in express terms, Sacred Scripture teaches by implication. It has been indicated above how the prophecy known as the Protoevangelium (Gn 3.15) already foreshadows the intimate association of Our Lady with her Son in the entire process of man's supernatural rehabilitation. Since the actual application of graces to the members of the Mystical Body is but the specific way in which they, as individuals, benefit from the redemptive work of the Savior, it seems logical to infer that Our Lady should have a share in it. In other words, if Our Lady, as coredemptrix, earned or acquired these graces with and under Christ, it is highly fitting that she should have a part in their actual dispensation to men. The unity of the divine plan would seem to demand it.

Another biblical passage bearing on the subject is Our Lord's testament from the cross (Jn 19.26–27), in which, according to the documents of recent popes, the Savior proclaimed His mother as mother of the entire human race. This motherhood of Mary implies a communication of grace (spiritual life) to her spiritual children, not only at the initial phase of regeneration on Calvary, but also in the subsequent process of conservation and development of that supernatural organism in the soul of her children.

Tradition. From the point of view of tradition the doctrine under discussion has undergone a gradual development very reminiscent of other Marian theses. In the early period, representing the germinal stage, the doctrine was taught only implicitly by the numerous Fathers and ecclesiastical writers who portrayed Our Lady as the second Eve, the mother of all the living in the supernatural plane, the associate of Christ as savior of mankind. Appropriate references may be found, for example, in St. Irenaeus (d.*c.* 202), St. Epiphanius (d. 403), St. Jerome (d. 420), St. Augustine (d. 430), and St. Modestus of Jerusalem (d. 634). The 8th century yields the explicit testimony of St. Germanus of Constantinople (d. 733), who assures one that "there is no one to whom the gift of grace is given except through Mary." It was, however, through the influence of St. Bernard of Clairvaux (d. 1153) that this doctrine became widely accepted during the Middle Ages. His statement that "God has willed that we should have nothing that did not pass through the hands of Mary" became a familiar apothegm in the Marian literature of subsequent centuries. The Franciscan St. Bernardine of Siena (d. 1444), who shares with St. Bernard the title doctor of Mary's mediation, summarizes the teaching of his age in these words: "I do not hesitate to say that she [Mary] has received a certain jurisdiction over all graces. . . . They are administered through her hands to whom she pleases, when she pleases, as she pleases, and as much as she pleases." During the 17th and 18th centuries the doctrine was not only generally accepted, but also the object of extensive treatment within the province of both dogmatic theology and devotional literature. The leading champion of the Catholic thesis during that period was St. Alphonsus Liguori (d. 1787), whose classic treatise *Glories of Mary* contains a vigorous refutation of the objections raised by L. Muratori (d. 1750). In more recent times those who have contributed most to the clarification of Mary's role as mediatrix are the Spanish Jesuit J. M. Bover (d. 1954) and J. Bittremieux of the University of Louvain (d. 1950). Despite a few scattered adversaries, the traditional doctrine is generally regarded as definable by the Church. Shortly after World War I, and on the initiative of Cardinal Mercier, numerous petitions began to be addressed to the Holy See urging the definition of the doctrine as an article of faith. These requests have multiplied in more recent years. For example, the already mentioned petition of the Cuban hierarchy (1951) urged Pius XII to define both Our Lady's coredemption and her actual intervention in the distribution of absolutely every grace.

Bibliography: E. DUBLANCHY,*Dictionnaire de théologie catholique,* ed. A. VACANT et al. (Paris 1903–50). J. MICHL et al., *Lexikon für Theologie und Kirche*, ed. J. HOFER and K. RAHNER (Freiburg 1957–65) 7:25–32. K. RAHNER, "Mariologie," ibid. 84–87. G. BARAÚNA, *De natura Corredemptionis marianae in theologia hodierna (1921–1958) disquisitio expositivocritica* (Rome 1960). J. B. CAROL, *De Coredemptione B. V. Mariae disquisitio positiva* (Vatican City 1950); "Our Lady's Co-redemption," J. B. CAROL, ed., *Mariology* 2:373–425. J. A. ROBICHAUD, "Mary, Dispensatrix of All Graces," *ibid.* 426–460. H. M. KÖSTER, *Die Magd des Herrn* 2d ed. (Limburg 1954). H. LENNERZ, *De Beata Virgine* (Rome 1957) 157–289. G. D. SMITH, *Mary's Part in Our Redemption*, rev. ed. (New York 1954). W. G. MOST, "Mary, the Coredemptrix," *The Marian Era* 1 (1960) 8–11, 121.

[J. B. CAROL/EDS.]

PT. 5: SPIRITUAL MATERNITY OF MARY

Of all the titles given to Mary by the faithful there is none more common than the one used to indicate her spiritual maternity—Mother; yet paradoxically there is perhaps no other prerogative of the Blessed Virgin that is less understood.

Two reasons may be advanced in explanation. There is, first of all, the nature of the terminology. When one calls Mary his mother in the supernatural order he is making use of analogy, a comparison between the divine and human levels. A failure to develop the full force of the comparison results in the deficient idea that Mary is spiritual mother of men simply because of the love she has for them or because of her adoption of mankind at the foot of the cross. Second, there is the neglect of an essential element of every maternity—a relationship with a person of the opposite sex. In the spiritual maternity this simply means the failure to associate Mary with Christ in the divine plan to give men spiritual life. Both of the above dangers have been avoided by the papal magisterium.

Reality of the Spiritual Maternity. Since Feb. 27, 1477, when Sixtus IV in his apostolic constitution *Cum praecelsa* became the first pope to allude to the spiritual motherhood of Mary [J. D. Mansi, *Sacrorum Conciliorum nova et amplissima collectio* 32.373; crit. ed. C. Sericoli, *Immaculata B.M. Virginis conceptio juxta Xysti IV constitutiones* (Rome 1945) 153], the doctrine has been taught with ever-increasing emphasis. It can safely be asserted that this doctrine, having been taught clearly and repeatedly by the ordinary and universal magisterium since Sixtus IV's time, is certainly definable as a doctrine of faith. [See the extensive articles by W. Sebastian, ''Mary's Spiritual Maternity,'' J. B. Carol, ed., *Mariology* 2:325–376, esp. 352; G. W. Shea, ''The Teaching of the Magisterium on Mary's Spiritual Maternity,'' *Marian Studies* 3 (1952) 35–110]. It is important, therefore, to ascertain the meaning given to the spiritual maternity in the explanations of the papal magisterium. There are three possible significations: (1) metaphorical—Mary acts in men's regard as a mother acts toward her children; she prays for them, she obtains grace for them, etc.; (2) adoptive—Christ willed that Mary adopt men as her children and that she possess the rights and fulfill all the duties of a mother toward men; and (3) real—Mary in some way transmits spiritual life to men by a kind of generation in the spiritual order and is, therefore, truly, the mother of men.

In the present state of research it cannot be affirmed with certitude that the sovereign pontiffs from Sixtus IV to Pius IX went beyond the metaphorical signification. While it is true that Leo XIII and his successors speak most often about Mary's action in men's regard and their filial attitude toward her, yet for them these complementary attitudes are based on a most stable reality. At least twice, in his encyclicals *Quamquam pluries* (August 1889) and *Adiutricem populi* (September 1895), Leo XIII affirms that Mary ''has brought us forth to life'' [Leonis XIII P.M., *Acta* (Rome 1881–1905) 9:175; 15:300].

Although it cannot be denied that Leo XIII went beyond the simple metaphorical sense, some are inclined to think that he stopped at the juridical notion of an adoptive motherhood. It is true that this pope placed great stress on Christ's donation of His mother as the spiritual mother of all mankind [see *Quamquam pluries, ibid.* 9:175; *Octobri mense, ibid.* 11:341; *Magnae Dei matris, ibid.* 12:221; *Jucunda semper, ibid.* 14:305; and *Amantissimae voluntatis, ibid.* 15:138]. Nevertheless, it must not be imagined that adoptive sonship necessarily excludes the idea of real filiation, for supernatural adoption surpasses a merely human adoption in one essential way: it really makes the person upon whom it is conferred a true son, for along with it comes a true participation in the nature and life of the Person adopting. In other words, if Mary cooperates with her Son in meriting the divine life of grace for mankind, she is really the spiritual mother of men.

Leo XIII's successor, St. Pius X, is explicit on the reality of Mary's spiritual motherhood. For him the foundation is men's incorporation in Christ and the role of Mary in the Incarnation.

> Is not Mary the mother of Christ? She is therefore also our mother. It must be stated as a principle that Jesus, the Word made flesh, is at the same time the savior of the human race. Now, inasmuch as He is God-Man, He has a body like other men; inasmuch as He is redeemer of our race, He has a spiritual body, or, as it is called, a Mystical Body, which is none other than the society of Christians bound to Him by faith. . . . But the Virgin did not conceive the Son of God only in order that, receiving from her His human nature, He might become man, but also in order that, by means of this nature received from her, He might become the savior of mankind. . . . And thus, in the Virgin's chaste womb itself, where Jesus took to Himself mortal flesh, He joined to Himself a spiritual Body formed of all those who were to believe in Him; and it can be said that, bearing Jesus in her womb, Mary bore there also all those whose life was included in that of the Savior. And so all of us, united to Christ, are, as the Apostle says ''members of his body, made from his flesh and from his bones'' (Eph 5.30); we ought to consider ourselves as having come forth from the womb of the Virgin, from which we once issued as a Body attached to its head.

> That is why we are called, in a truly spiritual and entirely mystical sense, the children of Mary, and why she, on her part, is the mother of the members of Jesus Christ that we ourselves are. [*Ad diem illum; Le encicliche mariane,* ed. A. Tondini (Rome 1950) 310–312]

The emphasis here is on Mary's free consent to the Incarnation, the first source of divine life in the present economy of salvation. This idea is taken up with one accord by St. Pius X's successors [see Benedict XV, *Cum sanctissima Virgo, Acta Apostolicae Sedis* 9 (1917) 324; *Cum annus,* ibid. 11 (1919) 38; Pius XI, *Lux veritatis,* ibid. 23 (1931) 493; Pius XII, *Mystici corporis,* ibid. 35 (1943) 247; *Mediator Dei,* ibid. 39 (1947) 521]. However, neither St. Pius X nor any of his successors rests his case for the spiritual maternity on her part in the Incarnation. All stress Mary's role at the foot of the cross, by which she participated directly with Christ in the act of Redemption through which the divine life of grace was won for all men. They see it as the logical consequence of her union with Christ from the moment of the Incarnation. Pius XI and Pius XII, it would seem, solve definitively the problem of an adoptive motherhood depending upon Christ's words from the cross, ''Woman, behold thy Son. . . . Behold thy mother'' (Jn 19.27), for they see in these words of the dying Redeemer not a creation but a ''proclamation'' and ''ratification'' of a spiritual motherhood begun at the Annunciation [Pius XI, allocution of Nov. 30, 1933, to the pilgrims of Vicenza, *Osservatore Romano,* Dec. 1, 1933; Pius XII, allocution of July 17, 1954, *Acta Apostolicae Sedis* 46 (1954) 491].

Association of Mary with Christ. The magisterium in the use of sources, Scripture and tradition, associates Christ and Mary in the doctrine of the spiritual maternity.

Scripture. Four major texts are commonly adduced. The first of these is the Proto-Evangelium (Gn 3.15): ''I will put enmity between you and the woman, between your seed and her seed; he shall crush your head, and you shall lie in wait for his heel.'' If, as an increasing number of modern writers affirm (and their opinion seems to be supported by both Pius IX's *Ineffabilis Deus* and Pius XII's *Munificentissimus Deus*), the prophecy is to be understood of Mary alone, then one may certainly use it as an argument to prove Mary's spiritual maternity, for the text then prophesies that Mary with her divine Son is to crush Satan's head. It is known that this takes place on Calvary at the objective Redemption, which marks the rebirth of mankind to the spiritual life. Therefore Mary by her share in this work can truly be called men's spiritual mother.

Second, there is the Annunciation pericope (Lk 1.26–38). The references cited above from St. Pius X, Benedict XV, Pius XI, and Pius XII are ample evidence of the importance attached to this passage by the magisterium. Pius XII can well speak for all:

> But when the little maid of Nazareth uttered her *fiat* to the message of the Angel . . . she became not only the Mother of God in the physical order of nature, but also in the supernatural order of grace she became the Mother of all, who through the Holy Spirit would be made one under the Headship of her divine Son. The Mother of the Head would be the Mother of the members. [*Acta Apostolicae Sedis* 39 (1947) 268; the English is the pope's own, his address to the Marian Congress at Ottawa, Canada]

Third, there is Christ's testament (Jn 19.26–27): ''When Jesus, therefore, saw his mother and the disciple standing by, whom he loved, he said to his mother, 'Woman, behold thy Son.' Then he said to the disciple, 'Behold thy mother.' And from that hour the disciple took her into his home.'' This passage has been so frequently used by the sovereign pontiffs as a strictly biblical support of the spiritual maternity that it seems impossible to maintain that Christ's words refer to Mary's spiritual motherhood only by accommodation [see W. Sebastian, 357; J. B. Carol, *Fundamentals of Mariology* (New York 1956) 51].

The final text of those commonly adduced concerns the vision of the woman clothed with the sun (Rv 12). Although St. Pius X in his encyclical *Ad diem illum* (Feb. 2, 1904) explicitly stated that ''no one is ignorant of the fact that this woman signified the Blessed Virgin'' and then made a direct application to Mary's spiritual maternity, still one cannot claim for this interpretation the support of the universal magisterium, for none of his successors has repeated this meaning.

Tradition. From the time of St. Justin and St. Irenaeus in the 2d century it has been traditional to use the Eve-Mary comparison to illustrate Mary's part in the Redemption of mankind. The popes of the last 100 years have frequently used the term new Eve or its equivalent (associate of Christ, coredemptrix, cooperatrix) to elucidate Mary's role in the lifegiving Redemption. The epilogue of Pius XII's encyclical *Mystici corporis* is a summary of the teaching on the spiritual maternity as well as a compendium of the Church's Mariological doctrine:

> ''. . . in the name of the whole human race'' she gave her consent for a ''spiritual marriage between the Son of God and human nature'' (St. Thomas Aquinas, *Summa Theologiae* 3a, 30.1). Within her virginal womb, Christ our Lord already bore the exalted title of head of the Church; in a marvelous birth she brought Him forth as

> source of all supernatural life. . . . Free from all sin, original and personal, always most intimately united with her Son, as another Eve she offered Him on Golgotha to the eternal Father for all the children of Adam, sin-stained by his fall, and her mother's rights and mother's love were included in the holocaust. Thus she, who corporally was the mother of our head, through the added title of pain and glory became spiritually the mother of all His members. . . . and she continued to show for the Mystical Body of Christ . . . the same mother's care and ardent love with which she clasped the infant Jesus to her warm and nourishing breast. [Pius XII, *Mystici corporis* 108]

Bibliography: E. DUBLANCHY, *Dictionnaire de théologie catholique,* ed. A. VACANT et al. (Paris 1903–50) 9.2:2405–09. F. J. KENNEY, *Mary's Spiritual Maternity According to Modern Writers* (Catholic University of America Studies in Sacred Theology, 2d ser., 93; 1957). *Marian Studies* (1950–), Annual Proceedings of the Mariological Society of America 3 (1952). E. N. NEUBERT, ''The Spiritual Maternity,'' *Mary in Doctrine* (Milwaukee 1954) 45–71. D. J. UNGER, ''The Meaning of John 19:26–27 in the Light of Papal Documents,'' *Marianum* 21 (1959) 186–221.

[W. J. COLE/EDS.]

MARY, BLESSED VIRGIN, DEVOTION TO

In popular usage, ''devotion to Mary'' is synonymous with the ''cult of Mary.'' Technically, however, ''cult'' in reference to Mary means the external recognition of her excellence and of the superior way she is joined to God; and ''devotion'' adds the notion of an interior readiness for cult. This article uses the words ''devotion'' and ''cult'' interchangeably.

Devotion to Mary ''proceeds from true faith, by which we are led to recognize the excellence of the MOTHER OF GOD, and by which we are moved to filial love toward our mother and to imitation of her virtues''[*Lumen gentium* 67; *Acta Apostolicae Sedis* 57 (1965) 66]. It comprises ''the duties of redeemed mankind toward the Mother of God, who is mother of Christ and mother of men'' (*ibid.* 59). Three elements enter into devotion to Mary: (1) veneration, or the reverent recognition of the dignity of the holy Virgin Mother of God; (2) invocation, or the calling upon our Lady for her motherly and queenly intercession; and (3) imitation, which may take such forms also as dedication and consecration. In addition to devotion in a generic sense, there are devotions to Mary, i.e., particular practices of piety, both liturgical (feasts, litanies) and nonliturgical (the rosary, the scapular, and private prayers)—the ''various forms of piety approved by the Church'' (*Lumen gentium* 66).

The singular cult of Mary is based on her special role in God's plan: by grace she is Mother of God-made-man. Associated in the mysteries of Christ's earthly life, she remains by her presence with the glorified Christ ''inseparably joined to the saving work of her Son'' [*De sacra liturgia* 103; *Acta Apostolicae Sedis* 56 (1964) 125].

Yet devotion to Mary differs essentially from the cult of adoration (''worship'' in American usage) offered to God alone, such as is given to Christ and to the Father and the Holy Spirit. The cult of the Blessed Virgin is called *hyperdulia* to distinguish it both from *latria* (adoration) and *dulia* (veneration of the other saints).

The cult of Mary is the response of the Christian people to the role of the Blessed Virgin Mary in the mystery of Christ and His Church, the reaction of ''redeemed mankind toward the Mother of God, who is mother of Christ and mother of men, particularly of the faithful'' [*Lumen gentium; Acta Apostolicae Sedis* 57 (1965) 59].

Scripture. The first evidence of response to the dignity of the Mother of Jesus is found in the NT, as part of the pattern of salvation history. Mary is involved in the mysteries of the Savior's life. The Gospels proclaim Mary blessed in her maternity—the Nativity narratives and indirectly Gal 4.4. Elizabeth hails Mary as ''Mother of my Lord'' (Lk 1.43) meaning ''queen-mother of the Messiah-king,'' likely the oldest Christian greeting of praise to the Mother of Jesus. The Johannine accounts of Cana and Calvary show her role as type of the believing Church, as do also, obliquely, the ''difficult sayings'' of the public life on keeping God's word (Mk 3.35; Lk 11.28; note the use made of these texts in *Lumen gentium* 61).

Early Church. Homage to Mary's holiness progressed further in the 2nd century with the conviction of her role as ''new Eve'' associated with Christ the ''new Adam'' (SS. Justin, Irenaeus). The art of the catacombs and the early apocrypha also bear witness to the increasing veneration of the Mother of Jesus; and as early as the 2nd century ''born of the Holy Spirit and the Virgin Mary'' was used in baptismal creeds. A Eucharistic anaphora in the Apostolic Tradition (traditionally attributed to Hippolytus of Rome) mentioned Mary. A manuscript fragment in Greek from the 4th century asks the ''Mother of God'' for protection—an ancient form of our ''We fly to thy patronage, oh holy Mother of God'' (Latin: *Sub tuum praesidium confugimus*), which influenced in turn the medieval *Memorare* (''Remember, oh most gracious Virgin Mary, that never was it known that anyone who fled to your protection . . .'').

St. Epiphanius (d. 403), who calls Mary ''mother of the living,'' mentioned an obscure sect, the Collyridians, that gave divine honors to the Virgin. Developing a line of thought hinted at in Origen (d. 253) a century before,

"Our Lady of Grace and the Grand Masters of the Military Order of Montesa." (©Gianni Dagli Orti/CORBIS)

Our Lady of Guadalupe Chapel, shrine where Juan Diego claimed visions of Virgin Mary in 1531, Guadalupe Hidalgo, Mexico. (Archive Photos)

St. Athanasius (d. 373) proposed the Virgin Mary as an example to dedicated virgins. St. Ambrose (d. 397) devoted a series of writings to Mary, model of Christian virginity.

From the dogmatic definition of the divine motherhood [(THEOTOKOS) at Ephesus (431)], the cult of Mary took on assurance and extension. Sixtus III (432–440) rebuilt St. Mary Major in Rome to commemorate the Ephesus event. Churches were dedicated to Our Lady as early as the 4th century. Severian of Gabala (d. after 408) called the praise of Mary a daily custom—she was called on before the apostles and martyrs. St. Nilus (d. 430) said the praise of Mary was found in every land and every language. Leaden seals have come down from the 5th and 6th centuries with the inscription *servus Mariae*—servant (or slave) of Mary.

Early Liturgical Cult. The first evidences of a liturgical cult are from the East and show the same Christocentric orientation as EPHESUS. The oldest feast was a ''remembrance of Mary,'' corresponding to the *dies natalis* (birthday into heaven) of the martyrs. This primitive *memoria Mariae* celebrated the return to God of the Virgin Mother of the Savior, who is the new Eve. It was probably kept as early as the 5th century, and was part of the Christmas liturgy, perhaps on December 26 at first, then on January 1 (as *natale S. Mariae*). The ANNUNCIATION was recalled in Advent, as is still done on the Advent Wednesday Ember day, but by the mid-6th century was celebrated on March 25. Emperor Maurice (d. 602) made universal in his territory the feast on August 15 of the ''falling-asleep of the Mother of the Lord'' (DORMITION, κοίμησις), the later ASSUMPTION feast. The NATIVITY OF MARY (Sept. 8) dates from the late 6th century. In the 7th century Oriental monks introduced these feasts to the West; all four were kept in Rome under the Greek-born Pope Sergius I (d. 701). Other feast days followed: the PRESENTATION OF MARY (8th century in the East, 1372 in the West); the ''conception of St. Anne'' (8th century in the East, eventually developing into the IMMACULATE CONCEPTION in the Christian West).

In the Roman liturgy Our Lady has had a place in the first prayer of remembrance (*communicantes*) before the consecration since the 6th century. This has been called the highest expression of the official Marian devotion of the Church, and is used to good effect in both the introduction and the conclusion to the Marian final chapter of the dogmatic constitution on the Church, *Lumen gentium* [*Acta Apostolicae Sedis* 57 (1965) 58–67].

8th to 15th century. Distinguishing marks of Marian devotion from the 1st through the 7th century were reverent admiration of Mary's holiness as Mother of God (Theotokos). In the next period there was greater concentration on Mary's present role as heavenly queen, spiritual mother, and all-powerful intercessor. Her ''suppliant omnipotence'' became the dominant object of attention. The Eastern homilists, SS. Sophronius (d. 638), Germanus of Constantinople (d. 733), defender of icons, and Andrew of Crete (d. 740) extolled Mary's power of intercession as they praised her assumption. In Carolingian times Alcuin (d. 804) promoted Saturday as Mary's day. Ambrose Autpert (d. 784) developed the theology of the spiritual motherhood. During the decadence after the Carolingian renaissance, religious life survived around the great abbeys. Marian prayers and sermons survive from Cluny (e.g., Odo of Cluny, d. 942) and Reichenau (a late 10th-century translation from the Greek of nine sermons on the Dormition).

The Marian devotion of the High Middle Ages accorded with general devotion to the saints; it was based on a sense of community between the Church on earth and the Church triumphant, with growing emphasis on the humanity of Jesus, e.g., the holy name of Jesus, the passion, the Real Presence in the Eucharist (*see* SACRED HUMANITY, DEVOTION TO THE). By this time the West was showing increasing independence of the East, the more so after the break-off of intercommunion between Orthodoxy and Rome in the mid-11th century.

There is a rich 11th-century Marian literature: sermons, prayers (as the *SALVE REGINA*), liturgical Offices (LITTLE OFFICE OF THE BVM) and Masses (especially for Saturday), and public proclamations of being ''servants or slaves of Mary'' (as by Odilo of Cluny, d. 1049, and also by Bl. Marinus, brother of St. Peter Damian). St. Peter Damian (d. 1072) wrote of Our Lady helping the poor souls in purgatory; by the 15th century this took the form in popular piety of the sabbatine privilege of the SCAPULAR.

The 12th century showed two doctrinal trends, strongly influencing devotion: (1) attention to Mary's compassion on Calvary and the interpretation of the Savior's words, ''Woman, behold your son'' (Jn 19.26) as signifying Mary's spiritual motherhood of Christ's brethren typified in the beloved disciple; (2) under the influence of the doctrine of the Assumption, emphasis on Mary's present assistance to all Christian people. St. Bernard (d. 1153) was noted for the Marian piety of his homilies, yet he remained bound to tradition; he called Mary not mother, but Our Lady, and he opposed the feast of the ''conception of holy Mary'' as an innovation.

In the 13th century doctrine and piety were intimately interwoven in the praise of Mary. Along with the great cathedrals of Marian dedication, Marian devotion was manifest in the lives of SS. Francis (d. 1226) and Dominic (d. 1221) and in the theological masterworks of SS. Bonaventure (d. 1274), Albert the Great (d. 1280), Thomas Aquinas (d. 1274), and of Duns Scotus (d. 1308). The familiar prayer, the HAIL MARY, combining the scriptural greetings (Lk 1.28, 42) of the first part to the petition of the second part, attained its current form only in the 15th century, but variants were in use from the 12th century and the Ave's were repeated to form the Psalter of Mary or the rosary. At this same time, independent litanies of Our Lady developed out of lists of Marian titles in the form of a litany—one of which has been preserved in the LITANY OF LORETO.

15th Century. The invention of printing in the 15th century put at the service of Marian devotion means of rapid diffusion, for example, the many editions of the Marian sermons, at once tender and terrible, of St. Bernardine of Siena (d. 1444); and early xylography helped spread the confraternities of the rosary.

The artistic representation of the ''mantle Virgin'' was characteristic of the devotional outlook of the 15th century. Under her protecting mantle, Mary, Mother of Mercy, kept in her care all peoples, nobles and humble folk alike. This picture was rejected by the Reformation, and disappeared in the Renaissance. Pope Sixtus IV gave the feast of the ''conception of Mary'' limited approval and the favor of indulgences (1477). In the late 14th century the Presentation of Mary (Nov. 21) and the Visitation (July 2, since 1969 transferred to May 31) were introduced in the West. In Christian spirituality meditation on the life of Mary, as on the life of Jesus, was a prominent note. The ideal was a deeper, richer interior life, well-expressed by J. Gerson (d. 1429) in his counsels for a truly Christian attitude to Mary.

The Reformation. Marian devotion became an object of attack for the Reformers not directly, but in inevitable connection with positions on doctrine and cult regarded by them as essential and evangelical. Neither Luther nor Calvin rejected totally the veneration of Mary, but they limited it to imitation of the humble, obedient, Virgin Mother of the Gospels (even as type of the believing Church). The Reformers and early Reformation confessions uniformly rejected calling upon the saints for assistance; such invocation (especially by the titles, queen of heaven and spiritual mother) was regarded as derogatory to the unique mediatorship of Christ, even as blasphemous to God, the one source of grace. The cult of the saints, especially of the Virgin Mary, has remained a point of division between Roman Catholicism and Protestantism, reflecting a differing understanding of the traditional and creedal COMMUNION OF SAINTS.

Trent defended the cult of Our Lady and the other saints—invocation as well as admiration and imitation, for the blessed who reign with Christ can intercede for men on earth. Both Catholic and Protestant positions hardened in the subsequent struggles of the Reformation and Counter Reformation, and the cult of Mary, like the doctrine of the Real Presence, became a favorite subject for controversy. St. Peter Canisius (d. 1597) replied to the Protestant positions in a long work, *De Maria virgine incomparabili,* which proved a veritable arsenal for Catholic apologists. Iconographically, the triumph of Mary—the Immaculate crushing the serpent's head—often represented victory over Protestantism.

The internal development of devotion continued within the Church. The Sodality of Our Lady was founded under Jesuit guidance in 1563; many Marian sodalities and associations developed from this prototype. High points of sodality history include the ''golden bull'' of Pope Benedict XIV (*Gloriosae Dominae,* 1748) and the bicentenary commemorative constitution of Pius XII (*Bis saeculari,* 1948).

17th and 18th Centuries. The 17th-century flowering of Marian studies, especially in Spain and France, had a corresponding development in devotion. Practices of the ''slavery of Mary'' grew up, variously rooted in the queenship and in imitation of the child Jesus in his dependence on Mary. The ''sanguinary vow'' was a pledge to defend to the death the Immaculate Conception, when it was still being debated within the Church. Some of these customs were carried to excess and aroused protest, even condemnation, e.g., certain forms of the ''slavery of Mary,'' complete with chains. A. Widenfeldt lashed out against foolish practices in his storm-provoking *Monita salutaria* (1672).

In the French school of spirituality founded by Cardinal de BÉRULLE, the cult of Mary was intimately joined to the mystery of the Word-made-flesh. J. J. OLIER developed the role of Mary in the interior life, especially of seminarians for the priesthood. St. John Eudes preached the Immaculate Heart of Mary. From the mystical life came the remarkable testimony of the laywoman Marie Petyt (d. 1677) and her director Michael of St. Augustine Ballaert, OCarm (d. 1684).

This period possessed the sense both of God's majesty (extending to Mary, as so close to God) and of the need for total commitment as is manifest in the practice of consecration to Mary, which is really to Jesus Christ through Mary. The most famous form of consecration is the ''holy slavery of Mary'' of St. Louis GRIGNION DE MONTFORT (d. 1716) even though it did not become generally known until the finding in 1842 of the book since called *True Devotion.* Popular exaggerations of Mary's intercessory role led to strong reactions, such as that of L. A. MURATORI. St. ALPHONSUS LIGUORI defended Marian devotion with solid arguments, especially in the widely spread *Glories of Mary* (1750).

19th Century. In the aftermath of the Enlightenment and the French Revolution the newly founded religious congregations and the restored older orders showed a special concern for Mary's role in the apostolate. Apostolic zeal was recognized as an authentic note of Marian dedication (cf. *Lumen gentium* 65). This was especially true of the missionary orders, founded in such numbers in this period, e.g., Marists, Oblates of Mary Immaculate, Claretians, and Scheut Fathers. Lay efforts were also made, such as that of G. J. CHAMINADE (d. 1850), who worked with lay sodalists some years before he founded the Society of Mary (Marianists). The apostolic pattern has continued in the 20th century with the Legion of Mary (from 1921), reactivated sodalities, etc., and is manifest also in the strong Marian devotion of the new secular institutes.

Another factor in the Marian devotion of the 19th century was the shrines of Lourdes (1858), LaSalette (1846), both in France, Knock (1879) in Ireland, and elsewhere (in the 20th century, e.g., Fatima, 1917), all of which continue to attract pilgrims. The Church has approved these practices particularly because of the good fruits of prayer and penance and the frequenting of the Sacraments by the pilgrims. Many other claims of private revelations, however, have been rejected by the Church and public devotions at such sites forbidden, e.g., Heroldsbach in Germany, Necedah in Wisconsin, and Bayside, New York. There was a general warning on these matters by Cardinal Ottaviani of the Holy Office in 1951 (*Osservatore Romano,* Feb. 4, 1951).

20th Century. Devotion to Mary in the 20th century was stimulated by many factors. Continuing the practice of Pius IX (who defined the Immaculate Conception) and Leo XIII (who issued encylical letters on the devotion of the rosary), St. Pius X wrote on the spiritual motherhood [''Mary is our sure way to Christ,'' *Ad diem illum, Acta Sanctae Sedis* 36 (1903-04) 451]. Benedict XV addressed incessant appeals to the Queen of Peace during World War I. Pius XI commemorated the Ephesus anniversary (*Lux veritatis,* 1931) and related Our Lady to the jubilee of the Redemption (1933–34). Pius XII showed his great interest in Marian doctrine and cult by the following acts: the definition of the Assumption (1950); the consecration of the world to the Immaculate Heart of Mary (1942), which was further explained in the encyclical on the Sacred Heart (*Haurietis aquas,* 1956); the inclusion in the encyclical on the Mystical Body, *MYSTICI CORPORIS*, of its Marian epilogue (1943); the proclamation of the Marian Year (1945), and its memorialization by the new feast of the queenship of Mary (May 31, transferred in 1969 to August 22); and the proclamation of the Lourdes centennial (1958). Particularly important for devotion were the directives of *Mediator Dei,* his encyclical on the sacred liturgy (1947): the liturgy was declared to be the norm of Marian cult, though other approved forms of piety were also encouraged. Devotion to Mary is an indication of our firm hope of salvation; indeed ''according to the opinion of the Saints it is a sign of predestination'' [*Mediator Dei; Acta Apostolicae Sedis* 39 (1947) 584–585].

Features distinctive of the 20th-century devotion to Mary included Marian congresses, local, national, international; and great pilgrimages to many Marian shrines, even through times of political unrest and wars.

The renewal of Biblical and patristic studies has focused attention on the Mary-Church analogy, especially after World War II. This has affected Marian devotion, as was obvious from the orientation of Vatican Council II as this appeared in the *Dogmatic Constitution on the Church,* in the decree on ecumenism, *Unitatis redintegratio* [*Acta Apostolicae Sedis* 57 (1965) 101, 104–105], and in the constitution on the liturgy [*Acta Apostolicae Sedis* 56 (1964) 125]. Vatican II reassessed Marian devotion in the light of scriptural, pastoral, and ecumenical perspectives. The role of Mary in the liturgy was proposed as the norm of devotion to Mary in chapter 8 of *Lumen gentium,* the dogmatic constitution on the Church from Vatican Council II. Traditional practices of devotion to Mary, e.g., the rosary, scapular, novenas and pilgrimages underwent searching examination and restatement in terms of current needs of Christian life—stronger emphasis on their integral relationship with the Scriptures, the Sacraments, and the Church itself.

In addition to Vatican II, Pius XII called for correct balance in MARIOLOGY and Marian devotion, in *Inter complures*, the message to the international Mariological and Marian Congress of Rome [*Acta Apostolicae Sedis* 46 (1954) 679], and also in *Ad caeli reginam,* the encyclical on the queenship of Mary [*Acta Apostolicae Sedis* 46 (1954) 637]. Pope John XXIII sounded the same note. In a discourse to the clergy of Rome, he warned of "particular practices or devotions, which may be excessive in their veneration of Jesus and our mother —who will not be offended by these words of Ours" [*Acta Apostolicae Sedis* 52 (1960) 969]. He cautioned the French National Marian Congress (Lisieux, July 9, 1961) to "look rather to the most traditional Marian devotion, as it has been handed down to us from the beginning in the prayers of successive generations in East and West" [*Acta Apostolicae Sedis* 53 (1961) 506]. Pope Paul VI also urged a sound, biblically and pastorally oriented devotion to Mary that is faithful to tradition [*Nous sommes heureux, Osservatore Romano* (Sept. 13, 1963), English translation from *The Pope Speaks* 9 (1964) 164–167] declaring that "It is in the history of salvation, in the Gospel, that you will find Mary. . . ." See also the encyclical *Ecclesiam suam* (Aug. 6, 1964), *Acta Apostolicae Sedis* 56 (1964) 635; and the commentary on "Mother of the Church," the allocution *La ceremonia dell'offerta* of Feb. 2, 1965, *Osservatore Romano* (Feb. 3, 1965). In his 1974 apostolic exhortation, *Marialis cultus*, Paul VI encouraged the development of a devotion to Mary that was biblical, liturgical, ecumenical and anthropological, as well as integrated into the mysteries of the Trinity, Christ, and the Church. The U.S. Catholic Bishops' letter *Behold Your Mother: Woman of Faith* (1973) also called for creativity on the part of the American peoples and their pastors in shaping a devotion to Mary suitable to this age. While there was a downtrend in devotion to Mary in the ensuing decades after Vatican II, such devotion remains strong and vibrant wherever the figure of Mary is intrinsically linked to national, ethnic, communal or cultural identity, e.g., Mexico (Our Lady of GUADALUPE), Poland (the Black Madonna of CZESTOCHOWA), Ireland (Our Lady of Knock), England (Our Lady of Walsingham), Portugal (Our Lady of FATIMA), France (Our Lady of LOURDES), continent of Africa (Our Lady of Africa), Vietnam (Our Lady of LA VANG) and India (Our Lady of Vellankani).

Bibliography: H. GRAEF, *Mary: A History of Doctrine and Devotion,* v.1 *From the Beginning to the Eve of the Reformation* (New York 1963), v.2 *From the Reformation to the Present Day* (London 1965). L. BOUYER, *Devotion to Mary in the Church* (Marian Library repr. No. 63; Dayton, Ohio 1959). B. CAPELLE, "La Liturgie mariale en Occident," *Maria: Études sur la Sainte Vierge,* ed. H. DU MANOIR (Paris 1949–) 1:215–245. A. DAVID, "La Dévotion à la Sainte Vierge," *ibid.* 5:689–720. I. CECCHETTI, "Sub tuum praesidium," *American Ecclesiastical Review* 140 (1959) 1–5. J. F. MURPHY et al., *Carol Mariol* v. 3. E. NEUBERT, *La Dévotion à Marie* (Le Puy 1942). W. TAPPOLET, ed., *Das Marienlob der Reformatoren* (Tübingen 1962). J. LECLERCQ, "Grandeur et misère de la dévotion mariale au moyen âge," *Maison-Dieu* 38 (1954) 122–135. L. BOUYER, "Le Culte de Marie dans la liturgie Byzantine," *ibid.* 79–94. *Maria im Kult* (*Mariologische Studien* 3; Essen 1965). National Conference of Catholic Bishops, *Behold Your Mother Woman of Faith,* a pastoral letter on the Blessed Virgin Mary Nov. 21, 1973 (Washington 1973). D. FLANAGAN, commentary on ch. 8 of *Lumen Gentium,* in *Vatican II: The Constitution on the Church,* ed. K. MCNAMARA (Chicago 1968). H. DU MANOIR DE JUAYE, ed., *Maria: Études sur la Sainte Vierge* 8 v. (Beauchesne, Paris 1949–71). R. LAURENTIN, *Court traité sur la Vierge Marie* (5th ed. Lethielleux, Paris 1968). E. R. CARROLL, *Understanding the Mother of Jesus* (Wilmington, DE 1978). L. DEISS, *Mary, Daughter of Sion* tr. B. T. BLAIR (Collegeville, MN 1972). D. FLANAGAN, *The Theology of Mary* (Hales Corners, WI 1978). PAUL VI, *Marialis cultus*, apostolic exhortation, 2 Feb. 1974, *Acta Apostolicae Sedis* 66 (1974) 113–168; tr. *Devotion to the Blessed Virgin Mary* (USCC Publ. Office, Washington, DC 1974). F. M. JELLY, *Madonna: Mary in the Catholic Tradition* (Huntington, IN 1986). "The Theological Context of and Introduction to Chapter 8 of *Lumen Gentium*," *Marian Studies* 37 (1986) 43-73. R. HARRIS, *Lourdes: Body and Spirit in the Secular Age* (New York 1999)

[E. R. CARROLL/EDS.]

MARY, BLESSED VIRGIN, ICONOGRAPHY OF

Marian iconography is an element of Christian art that has been of great importance, from the 3d century to the present day, in all Orthodox and Catholic countries. It is not, as has often been thought, a special development of the Gothic period of the Middle Ages. Actually, it has deep roots in early Christian thought and art and a continuous history through the centuries. It embraces single representations and liturgical Marian art; narrative cycles of her life, death, and glorification; portrayals of her miracles and apparitions; and symbolic Marian themes. For a guide to pertinent material *see* MARY, BLESSED VIRGIN, ARTICLES ON.

Single Images and Liturgical Marian Art

The oldest portrayal is thought to be that of a mother and child from the CATACOMB of Priscilla (3d century), perhaps connected with the prophecy of Isaiah (Is 7.14). The theme of the mother seated with her child on her lap occurs again in the Cappella della Velata in the same catacomb, of a somewhat later date, and in the 4th century,

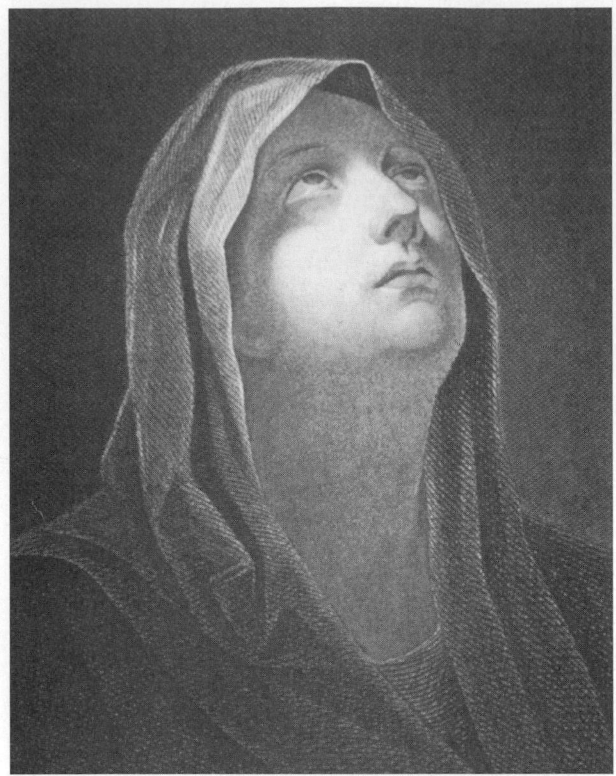

Mary, mother of Jesus Christ. (Archive Photos)

in the Cemeterium Majus, full-face, more hieratic and with a chrisom. Mary appeared also as praying on the bottom of gilt glasses. The 5th-century portrayals of Mary become more regal in the wake of the Council of EPHESUS (431), which initiated the veneration of the THEOTOKOS. A mosaic in St. Mary Major in Rome, inspired by Sixtus III and since lost, showed the Virgin enthroned with the Child. The clothing is stereotyped; the Virgin wears an oriental maphorion and red slippers (586, Gospel Book of Rabbula Laurentian Library, Florence). The solemn full-face pose of Mary in the *Adoration of the Magi* in S. Apollinare Nuovo, Ravenna, foreshadows the style of portrayal on the ivory diptychs. The type appears early in apses, surrounded by angels (Parenzo).

Eastern Types. From this point many modes developed, the most ancient in Byzantium being those of the liturgical icons, thought to be connected with relics such as portraits of Mary from life and articles of her clothing.

The Virgin Odigitria. The *Odigitria* or Our Lady Guide of Wayfarers was reputed to be St. Luke's portrait of the Virgin brought from Jerusalem to the Odigôn monastery in Constantinople. It represents a standing Madonna with the Child in the act of blessing held on her left arm; her right arm is either touching the Christ Child or raised (Gospel Book of Rabbula; early 7th-century icon of the Pantheon, Rome). There is another version of the Madonna seated, in the diptych of Etschmiadzin. The Madonna often has an angel on either side of her. The *Odigitria,* which is the most frequently encountered type, is enthroned in the apses or votive panels of churches (Hagia Sophia, Constantinople); she is standing in the mosaics of Kiti, Cyprus; later she is depicted without the angels at Torcello. This Madonna is found on icons, ivories, and larger reliefs.

The Virgin Blacherniotissa. The *Blacherniotissa,* preserved in the Blachernae monastery (founded by Pulcheria in the 5th century in honor of the Blessed Virgin) shows the Virgin in an attitude of prayer, alone or with a medallion of the Child on her breast. The ORANS or Praying Madonna, an ancient and widespread type, may be found in some apses (St. Sophia, Kiev). The Orans with medallion occurs full-length (12th-century icon from Kiev; Tretiakov Gallery, Moscow) or half-length. Another type is the *Nikopeia,* Our Lady of Victory. The *Kyriotissa* is standing and holds in front of her breast the Child, who is sometimes in a medallion.

The Virgin Chalcopratia. The Blachernae monastery was reputed to house the maphorion of Our Lady, while the Chalcopratia monastery was supposed to be in possession of her cincture, whence the type of the Virgin *Hagioritissa* or *Chalcopratia,* an intercessory Madonna, portrayed in three-quarter profile and with hands upraised, as in a Deësis, where Mary is at the right and John the Baptist at the left of Christ. The Deësis may be represented in apses and in tombs.

Other Greek and Russian Types. The Nursing Madonna or *Galaktotrophousa* appears very early in Egypt and is an adaptation of Isis nursing Horus. The *Eleousa* is a Virgin of Tenderness (9th-century ivory, Syrian or Egyptian; Walters Art Gallery, Baltimore), the *Glykophilousa* depicts the Child kissing the Mother. The latter types are predominantly folkloric in nature; although they are sometimes discovered in churches, they are found more often in the minor arts.

All the aforementioned types of the Virgin, alone or with the Child, are encountered on Byzantine seals. The Virgin with Child appears in the symbolic theme of the *Zôodochos Pigi* (Source of Life) in the illustration of the AKATHISTOS. The portrayals of Mary that illustrate her principal feasts drawn from the cycle of her life and death can also be classed with liturgical Marian art.

Russian art adopted to a large extent the Byzantine motifs. The *Blacherniotissa* becomes in Russian the *Znamenie,* i.e., Sign; the Virgin of Tenderness becomes the *Umileniye.* A large number of other Russian types were derived from Byzantine originals, especially that of

Madonna holding the Christ Child, detail of mosaic in the Istanbul Hagia Sophia. (©Charles and Josette Lenars/CORBIS)

"Mountain Sanctuary: Mother Mary of the Church," painting by A. Poz. (©Elio Ciol/CORBIS)

the *Pokrov* or Protection of the Mantle of Our Lady, from a Greek type, the *Episkepsis,* which is closely allied to the *Blacherniotissa.*

Western Types. Western iconography of the Virgin borrowed heavily from Byzantium. However, the picture of her as crowned like an empress, or *Maria Regina* (S. Maria Antica), originating in the 6th century, was a Western conception (*see* MARY, BLESSED VIRGIN, QUEENSHIP OF). The *Regina* appears in an attitude of prayer in the mosaic of the Oratory of John VII (early 8th century, now in Florence). The motif of the crowned Madonna reappears during the Middle Ages in Romanesque and Gothic art. But the Virgin in Majesty, *Majestas Mariae,* derived from the *Odigitria,* occurs enthroned in the apses of Roman churches, in Romanesque statuary, and on the tympanums of cathedrals. The Italians adopted the Byzantine modes of portrayal, initially retaining the Eastern manner of treatment, then picturing the Blessed Virgin according to the Renaissance canons of idealized beauty. Gothic art has given us a multitude of graceful examples of the Madonna standing with the Child. It is typical of the representations of Mary in the West that they have personified the ideal woman down to the present-day ("Mother and Child" by Henry Moore). The Italian Madonnas are so numerous that the name has passed into other languages as well.

Western artists have created a number of types of the Virgin that are often linked with a particular place or group such as a sanctuary, shrine, or association. Mary has been symbolically assimilated to the Church, *Ecclesia,* and the Woman of the Apocalypse. Some motifs have taken their inspiration from the events of her life. The Immaculate Conception, developed especially in the 17th century by Spanish artists, the Virgin of Expectation or Our Lady of Good Hope, the Virgin of the Ears of Corn, the *Vierges ouvrantes,* recalling Mary before the Birth of Christ, the Sorrowful Virgin, and especially the Virgin of the *Pietà,* inspired by the Passion. The Black Madonna is a folk creation. A frequent depiction is that of the Mother and Child shown with donors (*see* CHURCH, SYMBOLS OF; IMMACULATE CONCEPTION; PIETÀ).

Sources of the Life of Mary

The sources for the life of Mary are the Gospels and the apocryphal accounts of her life and of the childhood of Christ. The basic text for the childhood of Mary is the *Book of the Nativity of Mary* or *Protoevangelium of James,* as it was called by Guillaume Postel who brought back a manuscript of this book from Constantinople to the West in the 16th century and saw in it a prelude to the Gospels. The oldest manuscript (early 4th century) is complete from its title Γέννησις Μαρίας to the colophon naming as author James of Jerusalem (the "brother" of Christ), whence the name *Book of James.* The manuscripts have various title pages but always include a mention of the nativity of Mary. The account covers the time from the events preceding her birth to the Massacre of the Innocents. The texts present original material up to the Annunciation, then duplicate the narrative of the canonical Gospels. There are numerous versions of early date in the Christian East, in Syriac, Armenian, Georgian, Coptic, Ethiopic, Arabic, and Old Slavonic. Divergent amplifications such as are found in the Syriac and Armenian versions may, by their original features, have exerted an influence on iconography.

In the West there are two main Latin revisions, the Gospel of the Pseudo-Matthew and the Gospel of the Nativity of Mary. The former, which seems no earlier than the 7th or 8th century, amplifies the *Protoevangelium* and shows a propensity for the miraculous and the didactic, focusing on the life of Mary in the Temple. It is supplemented in some manuscripts by an account of the Childhood of Christ, inspired chiefly by the Pseudo-Thomas. The *Gospel of the Nativity of Mary,* apparently the work of Paschasius Radbert (9th century), is an adaptation of the Pseudo-Matthew, which eliminates the shocking or obscure passages; it ends with the first Dream of Joseph. Both texts were wrongly held to be translations by St. Jerome from the Hebrew. The Gospel of the Nativity of Mary became widely disseminated, especially from the 13th century on, when it was incorporated into the *Golden Legend* (*see* JAMES OF VORAGINE, BL.) and other pseudo-historical works. But the Pseudo-Matthew was the principal source for the narrative representations and for literary works such as the medieval French and English mystery plays (*see* DRAMA, MEDIEVAL).

The accounts of the Death of Mary, or *Transitus Mariae,* likewise go back to a very ancient tradition that was diffused throughout the entire Christian world. The *Transitus,* like the *De Nativitate* and other accounts of the Childhood of Christ, is mentioned in the *Decretum gelasianum* (6th century). The source of the Latin Pseudo-Melito goes back at least to the 5th century. The Greek account of Pseudo-John the Theologian is the best known because of its use in the liturgy. The homiletical writers preferred other texts, notably that used by John of Thessalonica (early 7th century), because these are clearer in their description of the Assumption. The most widely disseminated Latin versions are the Pseudo-Melito, which was incorporated into the Golden Legend and some of the mystery plays, and the account of the Pseudo-Joseph of Arimathea. The narrative in the *Codex Augiensis* 229 (early 9th century) is closest to the original tradition. The different texts contain variants that are of great importance for the iconography of Mary. The story of the *Transitus* was translated into all the languages listed above. In the West there are, apart from the Latin texts, Irish versions of the Childhood and Death of Mary.

Some texts, especially the Syriac ones, group the accounts of the childhood and of the death into a complete Life of Mary that is partly independent of the Gospel narratives. This procedure engendered whole cycles of the Life of Our Lady. In the West, the apocryphal legends were written off, in principle, by the Council of Trent. But although they have no foundation in historical fact, the apocrypha are orthodox in character, for they aim at mitigating the silence of the Gospels on the Mother of God. The accounts of her childhood were intended to buttress the dogma of her virginity. They exercised a profound influence on religious beliefs and writings, which in turn gave rise to a series of liturgical feasts and to innumerable figural representations throughout the course of Christian art. The liturgy played a considerable role in the development of Marian art through the transmission of its texts, for the majority of the Greek and Latin manuscripts we know are liturgical in origin, and by the introduction of scenes and cycles into the liturgical books and into churches. Many churches are dedicated to the ANNUNCIATION, the NATIVITY, the PRESENTATION in the Temple, and the DORMITION or ASSUMPTION of Mary. For apocrypha of the New Testament, *see* BIBLE, III (CANON), 5.

Historical Note. The narrative depictions of the Childhood of Mary preceded the institution of exactly defined liturgical feasts, within the general framework of veneration, in the East and in the West. We find them as early as the 6th century (the Annunciation to Anne is displayed by an ivory of Leningrad, and a cycle is depicted in column A on a ciborium at St. Mark's, Venice). Traces of narrative scenes in S. Maria Antiqua and S. Sabbas in Rome (8th century) and archaicized Cappadocian frescoes (9th or 10th century) prove the existence of a preiconoclastic cycle. The frescoes in S. Maria de Gradellis, Rome (late 9th century), belong to well-developed cycles of the Life and Death of Mary according to the Latin versions. In the absence of illustrated manuscripts, these early cycles are attested by the *Homilies of James of Kokkinobaphos* (early 12th century), based on the *Protoevangelium,* and by the *Wernherlied von der Magd* (early 13th century; Staatsbibliotek, Berlin), inspired by Pseudo-Matthew. The icon of Pisa called the *Madonna of San Martino* exemplifies the medieval Italian tradition. In the West, there is often a quite marked divergence between Italian and Northern iconography. Relatively few themes survived in the West after the condemnation of the apocryphal accounts by the Council of Trent, but they have been represented continuously. In the East, the tradition became impoverished after the Turkish conquest.

Iconography

Some iconographic motifs are common to all of Christian art, whereas others are peculiar either to the Byzantine or to the Western tradition. The principal sources for scenes before the Annunciation are the *Protoevangelium,* the Pseudo-Matthew, and the Gospel of the Nativity of Mary.

The Life of Anne and Joachim. The Munificence of Joachim, showing the youthful Joachim distributing alms, appears for the first time in the *Wernherlied von der Magd.* The scene is represented on the icon of Pisa and in 14th-century Lombard works. In the later French and Flemish pictures, Anne is added to broaden the theme to that of the Charity of Anne and Joachim. The Marriage of Anne and Joachim is rare, the earliest example being in the *Wernherlied;* it appears to have been unknown in Italy. The scene is modeled on the Marriage of Mary and Joseph and shows Anne and Joachim pressing each other's right hand before the priest. Both the charity and the marital themes were introduced into Flemish works of the late 15th and early 16th centuries, devoted to the life of St. Anne. There is no trace of either subject in the Byzantine tradition.

The Rejected Offerings of Joachim usually introduce the cycle. Although the texts rarely mention Anne, she figures in Byzantine images and in many Western pictures outside Italy. In Byzantine pictures closely linked with the texts (*Homilies of James;* frescoes of Mistra), other bearers of offerings also are shown. But the refined subject was reduced to three protagonists from the 12th century on in churches. The Italians show Joachim's eviction from the Temple rather than his offering (G. D. Tiepolo, 18th century; Morgan Library, New York). There have always been background figures in these pictures and by the end of the Middle Ages they had infiltrated all the Western compositions. Less commonly found themes related to the Rejected Offerings include the Consultation of the Twelve Tribes by Joachim and the Return of Joachim to his home, a subject derived from Eastern accounts and sometimes depicted in the West (Chartres Cathedral).

The Byzantine Annunciation to Anne includes the Threnody in the garden, near the tree where a bird is feeding its young, and the Annunciation of the angel. The Threnody itself is seldom represented. The ancient Annunciation pictures show Anne seated, but beginning with the 1lth century she is shown standing before her house where her servant is sometimes shown waiting; nearby is the tree with the birds above and below is the fountain where the angel appears. Anne's stance is like that of Mary at her Annunciation in post-Byzantine compositions; in later Russian art, as a result of Western influence, she sometimes is shown kneeling. The Western iconography of the Annunciation to Anne is quite varied. Anne is generally kneeling but only rarely under the tree with the birds. Though she may be seated, as in Byzantine art or standing before the angel, the kneeling position is the most customary. The scene is not very personalized because of its assimilation to various types of the Annunciation to Mary. The rare scene of the maid reproaching Anne for her barrenness precedes the Annunciation in some ancient cycles.

The Annunciation to Joachim comprises the Threnody and the Annunciation, combined in the pictures at Daphni but also on occasion figured separately in the same composition. Joachim is shown seated, lamenting among his shepherds, then standing to listen to the words of the angel. Joachim is traditionally seated in a rustic hut, often against a background of mountains. Later he is sometimes shown kneeling like Anne. Other scenes, such as the Departure for the Desert, the Conversation with the Shepherds, and the Return of Joachim to his Home, are encountered in only a few well-developed cycles. The Pseudo-Matthew is the source of the Sacrifice and the Dream of Joachim, which were taken up by Giotto. The Annunciation itself is frequently depicted. The 13th century was to adopt widely the synthesized Byzantine type showing Joachim seated on the mountain with his shepherds and flock. There is considerable variety in landscape and human figures. The Annunciation to Joachim may be combined with that to Anne. These events have been the basis of the most picturesque compositions having to do with the Childhood of the Blessed Virgin.

In Byzantine art, the Meeting of Anne and Joachim, or the Conception, is symbolized by the kiss of the spouses who meet before Anne's house. In the West, the scene occurs before the Golden Gate of Jerusalem and, especially in Italian art, in the presence of Anne's attendants and Joachim's shepherds (Taddeo Gaddi, 14th century; Baroncelli Chapel, S. Croce, Florence). Although the tender kiss of the Byzantine artists is depicted by Giotto and others, the embrace is often portrayed as reserved and even distant.

In the cycles, the Conception is symbolized by the Meeting down to the 16th century. Beginning with the 14th century, in liturgical and devotional books or volumes of piety, certain features allude more overtly to the Immaculate Conception, e.g., Mary crowned by a halo in Anne's womb. The symbolic theme of the Immaculata with her attributes, descending to earth on a cloud and a crescent moon, was created at the end of the 15th century. Two centuries later the painter MURILLO produced the most famous examples. In the detailed Byzantine cycles, the scene of the Meeting is sometimes preceded by Anne and the Messengers, who announce her husband's return, and followed by the Accepted Offerings or the Conversation of Anne and Joachim in their House. With the exception of the Accepted Offerings, these scenes appear also in the detailed Western cycles.

From the Birth of the Virgin to Her Marriage. The Nativity of Mary is the motif from the Childhood of Mary most frequently encountered in art. Since the texts recite the event without going into detail and since the parents of Mary were held to be rich, the Byzantine artists adopted the birth motif of antiquity, as found on the sarcophagi of children or in the illustrations of the lives of heroes and demigods. The mother is lying or sitting, sometimes assisted by a maidservant; the women bear gifts; and the child is being bathed. The ceremonial surrounding the birth of the porphyrogenite princes is reflected in the luxuriousness of the Daphni composition, the presence of the phylarchs and the child's cradle in the miniature of the *Homilies of James,* and the depiction of the gift table in the mosaic of Kariye Djami. The bathing motif comes to be rivaled by that of the cradle in the 12th century. In the art of Macedonia, the realistic motif of a young spinner rocking the child's cradle with her foot replaced that of the midwife of the bathing. The presentation of the baby to Anne, which is derived from early Christian art, occurs in the East in a fresco of Kizil Çukur, Cappadocia. The three or four women bearing gifts are shown presenting dishes and a fan; Joachim is often introduced into compositions after the 14th century.

In the West, the ancient depictions have not been preserved, and the miniatures of the 11th and 12th centuries are more symbolic than narrative. From the 12th century on, however, the bathing motif is found and tends more and more to supplant that of the cradle. The presentation of the baby to the mother, which seems to be a primitive illustration of the Pseudo-Matthew, is employed in the *Wernherlied.* In Italy, where the bathing motif persists, Giotto combined it with the presentation. Owing to the development of picturesque features and of the laws of perspective, it became the chief motif of later compositions. The component elements were borrowed from Byzantine art and were treated in either a symbolic or a realistic manner.

The early childhood of Mary, in Byzantine tradition, comprises three events: the First Steps, the Caresses, and the Blessing by the Priests. The first is an ancient but infrequently encountered theme. Anne, seated, holds the hands of the infant Mary who is walking toward her, followed by a maidservant. The Caresses, a motif showing Eastern influence, is quite widespread in the art of the Paleologi. Anne and Joachim, seated on a bench, are playing with the child; one or two serving maids are often pictured also in this touching scene that is found mostly in Macedonian painting. The Blessing by the Priests takes place on the occasion of the banquet offered by Joachim for the first birthday of Mary. In the detailed cycles, priests and laity are represented; the refined motif is reduced to Anne or Joachim, or both, carrying the child who is being blessed by three priests disposed behind a table spread with a banquet. The table sometimes has the appearance of an altar. In the West, there is an unusual depiction of the First Steps on an embroidered English orphrey (14th century; Victoria and Albert Museum, London) and in a Catalan fresco (15th century; Barcelona Museum). The Blessing by the Priests is introduced into some cycles as a first Presentation in the Temple, closely paralleling that of Christ.

Anne and the Child Mary are represented together in single pictures, modeled on those of the Virgin and Christ Child. In Byzantine art, Anne holds Mary on her arm, caressing her or nursing her. These pictures are not part of the narrative cycles, although they may accompany them. The motif of Anne carrying the Child Mary occurs quite early in Rome (S. Maria Antiqua); in the 13th century it appears on the north portal of Chartres and on Byzantine-influenced icons in Italy. The typically Western theme of Anne teaching Mary to read is widespread from the 14th century in England and France, both in the cycles and in single representations in miniatures and on small statuary. It also served as inspiration for artists, such as Rubens (*c.* 1625; Antwerp Museum) and Delacroix (*The Reading Lesson,* 1842). The addition of Jesus to the group produced the St. Anne Trinity, a very widely represented subject at the end of the Middle Ages and during the Renaissance (Leonardo da Vinci; Louvre, Paris). From there, artists went on to depict the Progeny of St. Anne in a family portrait, grouping Anne, Joachim, the Virgin, Mary Cleophas, Mary Salome (following the legend of Anne's *Trinubium*), and their children.

The Presentation in the Temple is a major theme of the childhood of the Blessed Virgin, especially in Byzantium, because of the importance of the liturgical feast. Numerous episodes are added in the developed cycles: Anne and Joachim Talking of Mary, the Preparations for the Presentation, the Train accompanying Mary, the Presentation and Greeting by the High Priest, the Placing of Mary in the Holy of Holies, Mary Fed by the Angel, the Visions of Zacharias, and the Visit of Anne and Joachim to their Daughter. Some of these scenes were introduced into the church decoration, but the prevailing composition is the synthesized one created for the Eastern menologium. Near the entrance to the building, the group of young girls carry candles; in the center, Anne and Joachim introduce the Virgin Child to the High Priest who receives her eagerly; in the choir, the Virgin is seated on the steps and receives the bread from the angel. The iconography is remarkably homogeneous with the exception of the mode of representation peculiar to Macedonia and Serbia, where the young girls are grouped in the center.

In the West, this scene is encountered only in the cycles but it is always present there, even in the most limited ones. The nourishment by the angel is generally not shown. Except in a few Byzantine-influenced pictures in Italy, the train is not shown; but the future companions of Mary in the Temple are depicted in Italy. Although the High Priest, who is accoutered as a bishop or a Jewish priest, is always shown in Italian art, he is often omitted in Western European pictures. The number of steps Mary is climbing varies from three to 15, and she is shown as a child or a young adolescent with long hair, not as the little adult of Byzantine art. Mary sometimes turns back toward her parents, contrary to the statements of the textual sources; in Flemish works, she is sometimes assisted by a small angel. Italian artists discovered in this motif a pretext for theatrical compositions far removed from the Byzantine spirit (Titian, 1538; Accademia, Venice).

The Life of Mary in the Temple is narrated at length in the Latin accounts with a didactic aim in view. The scenes include her work of weaving in the Temple, her encounters with angels, and her miracles. She is shown with companions and not as the unique child of destiny in Byzantine art. All these events are illustrated in the *Wernherlied,* and some of them in 14th-century works (ivory casket in the Paul Dupuy Museum, Toulouse). As late as the 17th century, Guido Reni shows Mary sewing in the Temple with her companions (Hermitage, Leningrad), whereas Zurbarán depicts her alone, abandoning her embroidery for prayer.

The Marriage of Mary and Joseph is represented in Byzantine art in an arrangement similar to that of the Presentation. The young Virgin is committed to Joseph, both of them submissive to the will of God, by the High Priest Zacharias. The revealing miracle is indicated by the presence of the dove or of the flowering rod, inspired by Aaron's Rod. The suitors are present at this scene, which is found only in the cycles. It is often preceded by the Prayer of Zacharias, who is generally prostrated before the altar on which have been placed the staffs of the suitors. The episode gave rise to numerous illustrations in the *Homilies of James* and to the Peribleptos of Mistra: the Meditation of Zacharias and the Council of the Priests, the Oracle, the Choice of Joseph who tries to decline, the Warning of the Priest, and finally the Entrusting of Mary to the Keeping of Joseph. Allied subjects, proper to the Latin textual tradition, are found also in the *Wernherlied.* They are encountered elsewhere only very rarely; the Prayer of Zacharias by Giotto is an exception.

The Marriage scene, on the contrary, is found very frequently in the West, where artists adopted a secular schema for the Marriage scene: the joining of the right hands (*dextrarum junctio*) in the Northern composition; the ring put on the finger in Italy; and the two partners standing on either side of the priest, who is seen full-face. The oldest depictions are linked with the Nativity of Christ (4th-century sarcophagus of Puy), and even the 11th-century miniatures are little influenced by the apocrypha. Soon Anne and Joachim are introduced (14th century, Sano di Pietro; Vatican Museum); so, a little later, are the suitors who in Italian art are shown breaking their staffs in anger. This scene gave rise to very elaborate compositions, especially in Italian art (Raphael, *Il Sposalizio*; Brera, Milan).

The episodes following the nuptials are illustrated in Byzantine art by the Farewell of Mary to the Priest, Joseph Leading Mary Away, the Lodging of Mary in Joseph's House, and Joseph's Exhortations before his Departure. Only a few of these exceptional scenes appear in church paintings. In Western illustrations Mary is tended by five of her companions in Joseph's house, where Byzantine art shows the four sons of Joseph. Mary's return to her parents' home after the ceremony, based on the *Gospel of the Nativity of Mary,* where it is a case of betrothal rather than marriage, is represented in several pictures in the Sienese tradition.

The Purple or the Distribution of the Skeins intended for the weaving of the veil of the temple is the final purely apocryphal episode of the life of Our Lady. Eastern examples show Mary, followed by a group of virgins, receiving from the hands of the priests the purple and the scarlet. In the West, the illustration of the event occurs in the *Wernherlied.* Some temple messengers are entering the house where Mary is waiting in the company of the five virgins. When the purple is alloted to her, the girls ironically call her ''Queen of Virgins,'' but an angel appears and terrifies them so that they beg Mary to pardon them. The subject is rare in both Eastern and Western art. Mary spinning the purple has sometimes been confused with Mary weaving in the Temple, a theme that is encountered frequently in art of the West.

From the Annunciation to the Death and Glorification. The Annunciation is the first event of the life of Mary that is related in the canonical Gospels (Lk 1.26–38); it opens the cycle of the Childhood of Christ (*see* ANNUNCIATION). This subject is extremely widespread, occurring both in cycles and independent representations, since it marks the inception of the processus of the Incarnation and recalls a very important feast. The apocryphal sources admit a dual Annunciation. Mary, who has gone to draw water, turns around surprised at the voice of an angel visibly present; then Mary, terrified, returns to her house and sets to work spinning the purple, at which point the angel appears to her. The two iconographic types, both going back to early Christian art, occur together in the apocryphal cycles (frescoes in St. Sophia, Kiev). The Annunciation in the house, with Mary spinning the purple, figures in the great feasts of the Byzantine Church. Mary is seated in the ancient images; later she is shown seated or standing. In the *Homilies of James,* the episode is narrated in detail from Gabriel's commission by the Court of Heaven to the recipient's joy in acceptance.

In Western art, the two Annunciations figure in the *Wernherlied* but this is a rare exception. The motif of the purple is more frequently encountered; that of the Holy Spirit in the form of a dove is still more frequent. Mary is often surprised at prayer or pious reading in a great variety of stances and settings. The angel and Mary are both standing in the Pisa icon, both kneeling in the fresco by Giotto; the angel kneels before Mary in the picture by Simone Martini; all the possible combinations are found painted by Fra Angelico. The Flemish painters show the scene in a room, but sometimes also in a garden, a palace, or a church. The Incarnation also may be recalled together with the Annunciation, by a scene of solemn veneration in the Akathist Hymn, or in the West, by the Plunging of Jesus into the womb of Mary. After the Council of Trent the renderings of the Annunciation lost some of their intimacy; the angel appeared above on a cloud.

The Visitation includes Mary Going over the Hills to Visit Elizabeth, the Meeting between them, and the Return to Nazareth and Justification of the Virgin. The two women are shown greeting each other from a distance, or embracing. Elizabeth is sometimes represented kneeling before the Virgin (15th century, D. Ghirlandaio; S. Maria Novella, Florence). The subject was especially popular in the 15th and 16th centuries (*see* VISITATION OF MARY).

The Reproaches of Joseph follow upon his return and discovery of Mary's condition. In Byzantine art, this is represented by a conversation between Joseph, staff in hand, and Mary. In the *Wernherlied,* Joseph speaks to the companions of Mary who protest that she is innocent. The Dream of Joseph (Mt 1.20–24), which occurs as early as the 4th century (sarcophagus of Puy), is surprisingly undifferentiated in Byzantium and the West. Joseph is asleep on his bed when the angel appears to him; Mary is sometimes represented symbolically in the scene. Some Western works show Joseph later kneeling before Mary to beg her pardon for his doubts.

The Ordeal by Water is portrayed at length in the *Homilies of James* and the *Wernherlied.* The Ordeal is frequently encountered in early Christian ivories where Mary alone, according to the ordeal reserved for adulteresses, drinks from the goblet of foul water handed to her by the priest; in the Byzantine apocryphal cycles, Mary and Joseph are both subjected to the ordeal. There is scarcely any trace of the theme in the West.

The Journey to Bethlehem (Lk 2.4) is an ancient motif going back to the primitive Church; in time it comes to be used less frequently, being too akin to the Flight into Egypt. On the throne of Maximian in Ravenna, an obviously pregnant Mary is seated on a donkey being led by an angel; Mary is supported by Joseph. In an apocryphal context, one of the sons of Joseph leads the animal. Mary's vision of a people in the depths of despair and of a people whose sorrow has been turned to joy is depicted in the *Wernherlied.*

The Census (Lk 2.1–5) provides the reason for the journey to Bethlehem, but in the apocrypha the Nativity occurs before the arrival in Bethlehem. Though the Census motif is represented only in a canonical context, the sons of Joseph may be introduced into the scene, as at Kariye Djami. The governor Cyrinus is present as those arriving are being registered by a scribe.

The Nativity of Christ is one of the most ancient themes from the New Testament (4th-century sarcophagi), and so is the Adoration of the Magi (catacombs; St. Mary Major, Rome), both having been represented in mosaics in the church of the Nativity, Bethlehem (4th century). The Virgin, sitting, or more often reclining, on a mattress, Joseph sitting, and Jesus in the cradle, or, after the 6th century, bathed by midwives, were later joined by shepherds and Magi offering presents in a synthesized composition. The scene was depicted in all the Byzantine churches, since the Nativity of Christ is one of the great feasts in the Eastern Church. In ancient cycles (Coptic frescoes at Bawît), but primarily in mid-Byzantine manuscripts and Paleologan painting, the scene may be shown in a narrative context, which includes various features, both canonical and apocryphal, concerning the Magi and the Massacre of the Innocents, as at Kariye Djami. From the 14th century on, the Adoration of the Child became the most favored representation in the West. The Virgin kneels before the Child, and frequently there are adoring angels present, hovering above the scene or, like the Virgin, also kneeling (*c.* 1475, Antonio Rossellino, marble relief; Monte Oliveto, Naples). The Adoration of the Shepherds (Lk 2.15–21) appeared in European art at the end of the 15th century (Giorgioni; National Gallery of Art, Washington). The Adoration of the Magi was represented in sumptuous proportion during the Renaissance (15th century, Botticelli; National Gallery, Washington). (*See* JESUS CHRIST, ICONOGRAPHY OF; NATIVITY OF CHRIST.)

The Presentation of Christ in the Temple, or Purification of the Virgin (Lk 2.22–38), includes Mary presenting the Infant to the priest Symeon, Joseph bearing two doves, and the prophetess Anna. The theme is widespread in Byzantine art. In the West, the artists frequently showed the act of the Circumcision with the Infant struggling in His mother's arms (Mantegna; Uffizi, Florence).

The Blessed Virgin appears again in the Return from Egypt (Mt 2.19–23), where the Holy Family is shown approaching the walls of Nazareth, Joseph carrying the Child on his shoulders. She appears also in the Arrival of the Holy Family in Jerusalem (Lk 2.41–42) for the celebration of the Passover when Jesus is 12 years old, and in the episodes of Jesus among the Doctors of the Temple (Lk 2.43–49). These subjects are well depicted in the mosaics of Kariye Dajmi. The Return from Egypt is sometimes portrayed in the West. The Apprenticeship of Jesus is recalled in a few pictures of a rather late date, where Mary sometimes is shown. She is absent from the episodes of the Sojourn in the Wilderness and the Public Life of Christ, except for the Wedding Feast in Cana. She appears again in the cycle of the Passion (Crucifixion, Deposition, Entombment, and Ascension). In the Pentecost scene, where the New Testament only hints at her presence (Acts 1.13–14; 2.1–39), she occupies a place of honor in the midst of the Apostles. The episodes of the Dormition are again inspired by apocryphal accounts. [*See* CRUCIFIXION (IN ART); PENTECOST, ICONOGRAPHY OF; PASSION OF CHRIST; ASCENSION OF JESUS CHRIST; DORMITION OF THE VIRGIN.]

The Annunciation *ante mortem,* recounted at the beginning of various pericopes dealing with the Dormition, is made by Gabriel, or more often by Michael the Psychopompos, who extends a palm branch to the Virgin while she is at prayer. The earliest monument preserved, a fresco in S. Maria de Gradellis, reveals a rare tradition in which Christ Himself appears to his aged Mother who is stretched out on her bed. In Byzantine art, Mary is standing in prayer at Golgotha. After the announcement of her impending destiny, she sometimes distributes her clothing to the women attending her. In the West, where the subject appears in the 12th century (York Psalter), Mary is usually kneeling in her room.

The Arrival of the Apostles is ordinarily found in the large-scale compositions of the Dormition in Byzantine art (10th century and after; Tokalikilise II, Cappadocia) under the Paleologi. The disciples are positioned on clouds singly, in small groups, or in files of six, and are generally conducted by angels. This scene is rarely encountered in the West. An unusual picture in S. Maria de Gradellis shows three of the disciples being carried off from the site of their missionary activity. The Farewell of the Virgin to the Apostles is the subject of a remarkable composition in the Brontochion of Mistra. Mary is seated fully dressed on her bed and in a solemn posture, holding the palm branch in her right hand and surrounded by the praying Apostles. Mary's conversation with the Apostles may be rendered in a more intimate manner as at Cračanica. In the York Psalter she gives John the palm branch, a special symbol and prerogative of the Blessed Virgin at the hour of her death. The Communion of Mary, which has no textual basis, begins to appear in the 16th and 17th centuries in the West as an image of piety promoted by the Counter Reformation (Alonso Carlo; Palazzo Bianco, Genoa).

The Death of Our Lady or the Dormition constitutes a major theme in Byzantine iconography, figuring in all churches among the cycle of the Great Feasts, and also depicted on various artifacts. On 10th-century ivories, Mary is reclining on her bed, surrounded by the Apostles, with Peter censing her; Christ stands behind her, holding aloft in his arms her soul in the form of a doll swaddled in white. One or two angels are descending from heaven to receive her. On the Brummer Gallery ivory an angel descends at the left and then reascends on the right with the soul, while the three women attending Mary appear among the Apostles. The synthesized compositions of a later date show not only the Apostles arriving on clouds but also the orders of angels. Sometimes there appears the episode of the Jew Jephonias who was desirous of carrying off the body of Mary; his hands, cut off by the angels, are still gripping the bed.

The 12th century saw the addition of the three hierarchs Dionysius the Areopagite, Hierotheus, and Timothy (following a commentary of Andrew of Crete). John Damascene and Cosmas the Poet, who significantly contributed to Marian literature, sometimes flank the composition. The Romanesque (tympanum of Senlis) and 14th-century (Duccio, *Maestá*; Siena) compositions owe much to Byzantium. The Byzantine influence continues to prevail in Italy in the 15th century, but the composition becomes more animated. In art of the northern Renaissance, Mary is shown lying or sitting on her bed surrounded by the Apostles and holding a candle. The scene is rendered intimately as the death of a pious bourgeois woman (*c.* 1480, painting by Hugo van der Goes; Bruges Museum). Christ and the angels, sometimes shown in the upper part of the picture, cease to appear.

The Funeral of the Blessed Virgin shows the Apostles carrying the body on a litter. It is here that the episode of Jephonias is inserted; in a Jean Fouquet miniature (*c.* 1450; Musée Condé, Chantilly), the Jews have been blinded by the angels. In the Interment the Apostles lower the body into a sarcophagus, with Peter in his traditional place supporting the head.

The Resurrection of the Virgin scarcely occurs in the Byzantine tradition, but the scene of the disciples finding the tomb empty on the third day inspired 12th- and 13th-century Western artists. The Blessed Virgin rises from the tomb aided by angels, who sometimes carry her in a shroud; occasionally she is assisted by Christ Himself. The Assumption of the Virgin is not often treated in Byzantine art; but the motif of the girdle thrown to Thomas to convince his doubting nature of the authenticity of the event is less rare than has been thought (St. Clement; Ohrid, Yugoslavia). In the West, the *Assumptio animae,* perhaps depicted on a fabric in Sens (8th century), derives from the Byzantine conception of the taking up of the soul of the Virgin to heaven. The true theme is the

Assumptio corporis, showing Mary rising to heaven on a cloud borne by angels. The scene occurs with outstanding frequency in Italian art (15th century, Masolino; Naples Museum). Mary rising by her own power indicates a borrowing from the Ascension (1643, Philippe de Champaigne; Marseilles Museum).

The Coronation, a theme more symbolical than narrative, seems to have evolved in the 12th-century Paris circle of Suger. In the oldest pictures the Blessed Virgin sits crowned at the side of Christ who is blessing her; later representations show her being crowned by Christ and sometimes by God the Father; the 15th century originated the presence of the Trinity at the Coronation. The earlier works show Mary seated, while later ones depict her kneeling. The Assumption and the Coronation may be combined in a single composition showing the Virgin being crowned upon her arrival in heaven (17th-century engraving by J. Callot).

Miracles and Apparitions of the Virgin. The miracles of the Virgin are derived from quite varied and often local sources. They are all posthumous, except for those attributed to Mary by a limited Latin tradition and supposed to have occurred during her stay in the Temple. There are collections in Latin and the vernaculars from the end of the 11th century in the West. In France, for example, there is the 14th-century illuminated manuscript of Gauthier de Coincy's *Miracles Notre-Dame* (Bibliothèque Nationale, Paris); in Ethiopia, the *Book of the Miracles of Mary*. The most famous miracles are, in France, the Miracle of Theophilus, which appears in the stained-glass windows of the great Gothic cathedrals; and, in Italy, the Madonna with the Club or *Madonna del Soccorso* (1506, Giovanni da Monte Rubrano; Montpellier Museum).

The miracles are often linked with local apparitions, the most important of which include: Our Lady of the Snows in Rome; the Holy House of Loretto; the Virgin of the Pillar in Saragossa, Spain (*c.* 1654, Poussin; Louvre); the Lactation of St. Bernard; the Holy Candle of Arras; and apparition as the Immaculate to Bernadette SOUBIROUS at Lourdes. The iconography of the miracles has been influenced by the visions of such mystics as St. BRIDGET OF SWEDEN.

Symbolic Representations. These are based on prefigurations drawn from the prophetic passages of the Old Testament. Initially they were literary motifs used by the homiletical writers; certain of these motifs became concretized by an image: the Burning Bush, the Rod of Aaron, Gideon's Fleece, the Closed Gate of the vision of Ezekiel. Typological motifs also were furnished in the Stone sealing up the Lions' Den of Daniel, the Revolving Stone in the Dream of Nebuchadrezzar explained by Daniel, and the Three Young Men in the Fiery Furnace. The Song of Solomon inspired the Enclosed Garden and the Sealed Fountain. The Virgin does not appear in person in these scenes, though she may be suggested in a medallion, as an apparition, notably in the Burning Bush.

The Byzantine art of the Paleologan renewal assigned a very important place to the symbolic cycles in the churches. The tradition of typological representations is perhaps more widespread in the West, particularly in the *Speculum historiale,* except in Italy where the subjects never really took root. Other symbolic portrayals show Mary assimilated to the Woman of the Apocalypse, in the West, or to the Bed of Solomon, in Byzantium.

Bibliography: Sources. For bibliography on apocrypha of the New Testament, *see* BIBLE, III (CANON), 5. Liturgical Marian Art. A. MUÑOZ, *Iconografia della Madonna* (Florence 1905). N. P. KONDAKOV, *Ikonografiia bogomateri,* 2 v. (St. Petersburg 1914–15). V. N. LAZAREV, ''Studies in the Iconography of the Virgin,'' *Art Bulletin* 20 (1938) 26–65. M. TRENS, *Maria: Iconografia de la Virgen en el arte español* (Madrid 1946). M. VLOBERG, *La Vierge et L'Enfant dans l'art française,* 2 v. (2d ed. Grenoble 1934, repr. 1954). L. RÉAU, *Iconographie de l'art chrétien,* 6 v. (Paris 1955–59) 2.2:70–128. C. BERTELLI, *Enciclopedia dell'arte antica* (1961) 2:839–51. V. I. ANTONOVA and N. E. MNEVA, *Katalog drevnerusskoj živopisi, I.XI-načalo XVI v* (Moscow 1963). Narrative cycles. O. SINDING, *Mariä Tod und Himmelfahrt* (Christiana 1903). C. STORNAJOLO, *Miniature delle Omilie di Giacomo Monaco* (Rome 1910). G. MILLET, *Recherches sur l'iconographie de l'Évangile aux XIV*[e], *XV* [e] *et XVI*[e] *siècles* (Paris 1916). H. DEGERING, *Des Priesters Wernher drei Lieder von der Magd* (Berlin 1925). H. A. OMONT, *Miniatures des Homélies sur la Vierge du moine Jacques* (Paris 1927). S. ROSSI, *L'Assunzione di Maria nella storia dell'arte cristiana* (Naples 1940). J. DUHR, ''La Dormition de Marie dans l'art chrétien,'' *Nouvelle revue théologique* (February 1950) 134–57. V. BENNET and R. WINCH, *The Assumption of Our Lady and Catholic Theology* (London 1950). *Iconographie de l'art chrétien* 2.2:155–94, 597–626. J. LAFONTAINE-DOSOGNE, *Peintures médiévales dans le temple dit de la Fortune Virile à Rome* (Brussels 1959); *Iconographie de l'Enfance de la Vierge dans l'Empire byzantin et en Occident,* 2 v. (Brussels 1964–65). P. UNDERWOOD, *The Art of the Kariye Djami,* 3 v. (New York 1966–). Miracles and apparitions. G. DE COINCY, *Les Miracles de la Sainte Vierge,* ed. M. POQUET (Paris 1857). E. A. W. BUDGE, *The Miracles of the Blessed Virgin Mary and the Life of Hannâ* (London 1900). E. LEVI, ''I Miracoli della Vergine nell' arte del medio evo,'' *Bollettino d'arte* 12 (1918) 1–25. A. C. FRYER, ''Theophilus, the Penitent, as Represented in Art,'' *Archaeological Journal* (1935). E. CERULLI, *Il libro etiopico dei Miracoli di Maria* (Rome 1943). L. RINIERI, *La Verità sulla Santa Casa di Loreto* (Turin 1950). *Iconographie de l'art chrétien* 2.2:626–35. Symbolic themes. E. MÂLE, ''L'Art symbolique à la fin du moyen âge,'' *Revue de l'art ancien et modern* 28 (1905) 81–96, 195–209, 435–45. J. LUTZ and P. PERDRIZET, *Speculum humanae salvationis,* 2 v. (Leipzig 1907–09). *Iconographie de l'art chrétien* 2.2:85–87. S. DER NERSESSIAN, ''Le Lit de Salomon,'' *Zbornik Radova Vizantološkog Instituta* 8 (1963) 77–82.

[J. LAFONTAINE-DOSOGNE]

"Christ and the Blessed Virgin," detail of the 12th-century mosaic in the apse of the Basilica of Santa Maria in Trastevere, Rome.

MARY, BLESSED VIRGIN, QUEENSHIP OF

Christian piety knows few titles for the Virgin Mary older than queen, and such equivalents as empress, lady, and *notre dame.* "The mother of my Lord" in Elizabeth's greeting to Mary (Lk 1.43) is an Old Testament phrase for the queen-mother (*g^{e}bîrâ,* e.g., 2 Kgs 10.13). In the Gospel it reflects the faith of the early Church that Jesus is the royal MESSIAH.

"Queen" is applied to Mary both in the wide sense because of her excellence, her holiness, and in the strict sense, for her real dominion in Christ's kingdom of GRACE. Mary is queen both in the sense that she excels all other saints and in the sense that she shares in a subordinate and analogous way Christ's rule.

Our Lady's titles to queenship are principally two: (1) divine motherhood (*see* MOTHER OF GOD); (2) "right of conquest." Christ is king both as Son of God made man and as Redeemer. He had a native right to be king from the INCARNATION, but He won His crown also by the conquest of Calvary. Mary is queen because she is Mother of Christ and also because by God's will she played a unique part in the Savior's work of Redemption (Pius XII).

In extent, Mary's queenship is as vast as that of her Son and God, nothing is excluded from her dominion. ". . . like her Son before her, she conquered death and was raised body and soul to the glory of heaven, where as queen she sits in splendor at the right hand of her Son, the immortal king of the ages" [Pius XII, *Munificentissimus Deus; Acta Apostolicae Sedis* 42 (1950) 768–769]. As "sovereign suppliant" she shares forever in the distribution of graces that flow from her Son's sacrifice.

Mary's power as queen has always been described in terms of mercy. In a perfect society the powers of government are legislative, judiciary, and executive. Theologians differ in their application of the threefold power to the queenship of Mary. All agree that Mary's queenly power is at least in the legislative category, that is, that the inner law of the kingdom of Christ is grace, and that she is the royal dispenser of grace. About her share in the executive and judiciary aspects there is no agreed opinion, except that punishment (coercive falls under executive) is not part of Mary's role. The voice of Christian tradition is that Mary rules with a mother's love.

The fact, titles, extent, and maternal character of Mary's queenship are all stated in documents of the Church, especially in Pius XII's *Ad caeli reginam* [*Acta Apostolicae Sedis* 46 (1954) 625–640]. The precise nature of the queenship is still discussed by theologians. Two approaches predominate. In the 1930s L. de Gruyter and C. Friethoff, OP, likened Mary's queenship to the kingship of Christ, because of her association in His redemptive work. M. J. Nicolas, OP, C. Dillenschneider, CSSR, and others reacted by emphasizing the intercessory nature of Mary's royal role, appealing to the feminine character of all queenship. Just as the consort of the king in an earthly monarchy can wield immense power, not by her presence in the council chamber, but by her influence over the heart of the king, so Our Lady has a comparable influence over her Son, and intercedes for the needs of all her spiritual children and subjects. The solution to the question of the nature of the queenship lies between the extremes of both views. The analogy of the queen's place in a monarchy is not enough, for the queenship of Mary has no earthly counterpart, no more than has her Son's kingdom. At the same time she must not appear as a royal figure on the same plane as Christ the Redeemer-King.

Our Lady's queenship has much in common with other Marian beliefs. The same person, the Virgin Mary, is associated with Christ the Mediator, with Christ head of His MYSTICAL BODY, and with Christ the King. Yet the doctrine that Mary is queen emphasizes the extent of her involvement in Christ's kingdom in a manner different from her other doctrinal titles of spiritual mother and mediatrix.

Pius XII affirmed strongly the queenship of Mary, inserting in the calendar for May 31 a new feast of Mary Queen, in place of Mary, Mediatrix of All Graces. The 1969 reform of the liturgical calendar transferred the feast to August 22. The new liturgical feast of the queenship could be regarded as a sequel to the definition of the ASSUMPTION, and as an implicit affirmation of Marian mediation. Pius XII consecrated thee world to the IMMACULATE HEART OF MARY, Mother and Queen, Oct. 31, 1942, as a public recognition of her queenship, just as consecration to the Sacred Heart of Jesus openly acknowledges the kingship of Christ. The consecration formula was as follows: ''As the Church and the entire human race were consecrated to the Sacred Heart of Jesus . . . so we in like manner consecrate ourselves forever also to you and your Immaculate Heart, our mother and queen of the world, that your love and patronage may hasten the triumph of the kingdom of God'' [*Acta Apostolicae Sedis* 34 (1942) 318–319].

Bibliography: *Souveraineté de Marie* (Compte rendu du congrès marial Boulogne-sur-Mer; Paris 1938). A. LUIS, *La realeza de Maria* (Madrid 1942). *Marian Studies,* v. 4 (1953). *Estudios Marianos,* v. 17 (1956). *La Royauté de l'Immaculée* (Ottawa 1957), esp. E. LAMIRANDE, ''Bibliographie sur la royauté universelle de Marie,'' 223–232. *Mariae potestas regalis in Ecclesiam,* v. 5 of *Maria et Ecclesia* (*Lourdes Congress Proceedings of 1958*; Rome 1959). S. G. MATHEWS, ed., *Queen of the Universe* (St. Meinrad, Ind. 1957), an anthology on the Assumption and queenship of Mary.

[E. R. CARROLL/EDS.]

MARY (IN CATHOLIC-PROTESTANT DIALOGUE)

Since Vatican II, Catholic and Protestant theologians have engaged in an historic series of irenic dialogues, conferences, and joint writings that have addressed differences in doctrine and devotion over Mary, the mother of Jesus, the mother of God, that have divided the churches since the Reformation. The turning point was the council's Dogmatic Constitution on the Church which in its lengthy, concluding chapter eight firmly integrated teaching about Mary with truth about Christ (he alone is Mediator and Savior) and the church (of which she is preeminent member and for which she is model of faith and charity), and warned of excesses in preaching and piety. Paul VI's letter calling for sound renewal of Marian devotion (*Marialis Cultus* 1973) also contributed to an open, sober atmosphere where long-standing disagreements could be addressed.

Basic to this dialogue is the testimony of Scripture, which provides significant common ground for understanding Mary's theological importance. The volume *Mary in the New Testament* (1978), produced by a team of Catholic and Lutheran scholars, broke through ignorance on this score, delineating wide areas of agreement about biblical material while identifying other areas where later ecclesial traditions diverged. Inviting participation by interested persons from different churches, Catholic international Mariological congresses in Saragossa, Spain (1979), Malta (1983), and Kevelaer, Germany (1987) produced noteworthy statements of agreement regarding Mary's role in the incarnation and salvation history. The English-speaking Ecumenical Society of the

Blessed Virgin Mary, founded in 1967, promotes study and devotion in an inter-church setting; its published papers reflect growing rapprochement.

As the twentieth century ended, two high-profile dialogues on Mary made exceptional contributions. From 1983 to 1990 the U.S. Lutheran-Catholic Dialogue discussed the person and role of Mary in the context of Christ, who is the one mediator, and the whole communion of saints. The published study (Anderson 1992) contains a common statement of convergences and divergences explained by historical background and buttressed by 15 supporting papers. In France the interconfessional body of 40 theologians known as the Groups des Dombes issued a two-part study (1999) based on biblical, historical, and systematic theological analysis. While each of these dialogues took place in the venue of particular nations, the incisive character of their final documents has had international impact.

The substance of agreement about Mary in ecumenical dialogue finds the Catholic and Protestant traditions together at the very center of Christian faith as expressed in Scripture and creed. As the woman whose ''yes'' to God's invitation brought about the birth of the Messiah ''for us and for our salvation,'' her story has significance for both Christ and the church. Her historic pregnancy is a bulwark of his genuine humanity against all DOCETISM; the title *THEOTOKOS* affirmed at the Council of EPHESUS signals that the one she bore is indeed the Son of God. At the same time her own life, fraught with difficulties, was a ''journey of faith'' from Nazareth to Bethlehem to Jerusalem. In this she is a type and outstanding model of the church as it seeks to follow Christ on the path of discipleship. This is more than example, however. LUTHER's insight that Mary embodied God's unmerited grace signals the fundamental relationship of faith in which every believer stands. Thus reference to Mary is not merely ornamental but serves to solidify profession of faith in the incarnation and to guide active living according to the gospel.

Serious differences remain, rooted in differing Catholic and Protestant historical experiences, sensibilities, and spiritualities. Of these, four stand out. One is the Catholic interpretation that Mary cooperated with grace and thereby with God's plan of salvation. This contradicts Protestant understanding of the relation between divine grace and human freedom in which the human will is totally dependent on God's initiative and can do nothing on its own merit apart from Christ. Another issue is the perpetual virginity of Mary, insisted upon by Catholic teaching but not clearly attested in Scripture and not considered essential by Protestants for appreciating Mary's holiness. Even more thorny is the issue of the two Marian dogmas defined by popes in the past two centuries: the IMMACULATE CONCEPTION (1854) and the ASSUMPTION (1950). Not only are the grounds in Scripture for these beliefs highly debatable, and not only do they appear to Protestant eyes to place Mary on a level with Christ, but they issued forth by infallible papal decree. Thus they are inseparably united with the question of authority in the church, which in these two instances Protestants judge to have bound consciences without legitimate warrant.

A final issue, perhaps the most nettlesome because connected with popular piety, is the practice of invocation, or calling upon Mary in her mediating role as an intercessor. To the Protestant mind, this is nothing short of religiously dangerous for in addition to not being commanded in Scripture it tends to displace the heart's trust from Christ to Mary, and thus substitute her for the One who alone is mediator. To the Catholic mind, however, Mary and all the saints form a community with us in Christ; pilgrimages, shrines, the rosary, the ''Hail Mary,'' and myriad artistic representations are concrete ways of expressing solidarity together in intercession before God (*see* MARY, BLESSED VIRGIN, DEVOTION TO).

The question now emerges of whether any of these obstacles needs to be finally church dividing. Dialogue groups note the need for a process of conversion—Catholics from uncritical engagement in excessive Marian expressions, Protestants from unwarranted silence and atrophied devotion toward Mary's role in Scripture and creed, and both toward respectful acceptance of legitimate differences. The process of dialogue itself seems to indicate that not uniformity but ecumenical conversion toward the Spirit-inspired insights of each other will overcome the effects of centuries of divisive opposition over teaching and devotional practice regarding Mary.

Bibliography: G. ANDERSON et al., eds., *The One Mediator, the Saints, and Mary: Lutherans and Catholics in Dialogue VIII* (Minneapolis, 1992). R. BROWN et al., eds., *Mary in the New Testament: A Collaborative Assessment by Protestant and Roman Catholic Scholars* (New York, Philadelphia 1978). GROUPE DES DOMBES, *Marie dans le dessein de Dieu et la communion des saints* (Paris 1999). J. MACQUARRIE, *Mary for All Christians* (Grand Rapids, Mich. 1990). H. KÜNG and J. MOLTMANN, eds., *Mary in the Churches* (New York 1983). T. O'MEARA, *Mary in Protestant and Catholic Theology* (New York 1966). J. PELIKAN et al., *Mary: Images of the Mother of Jesus in Jewish and Christian Perspective* (Philadelphia 1986). A. STACPOOLE, ed., *Mary's Place in Christian Dialogue* (Wilton, Conn. 1982). G. TAVARD, *The Thousand Faces of the Virgin Mary* (Collegeville, Minn. 1996). S. ZIMDARS-SCHWARTZ, *Encountering Mary: From LaSalette to Medjugorje* (Princeton 1991).

[E. A. JOHNSON]

MARY DE CERVELLÓN, ST.

Mercedarian foundress; b. Barcelona, Spain, Dec. 1, 1230; d. Barcelona, Sept. 19, 1290. Born of the noble family of Cervelló, Mary was educated at home and directed by Bernardo de Corbera, the first Mercedarian priest. After making a vow of chastity at 18, she began to wear the Mercedarian habit at home. After her parents died she established the second order of MERCEDARIANS, devoted to an active apostolate toward the sick and the poor. She reputedly enjoyed gifts of counsel and prophecy, and foretold the outcome of battles and her own death. She had thaumaturgic powers, especially toward seamen in danger who called her *Sor María del Socos* (Sra. Mary of Help) and frequently claimed they saw her (at the time in deep ecstasy in her convent) walking on the waters or hovering over their stricken ships. Her body, buried in the Mercedarian church in Barcelona, was found to be incorrupt and was exposed for public veneration in 1904 and 1939. Her cultus was confirmed in 1692. She is depicted in art holding an oar or a ship.

Feast: Sept. 19.

Bibliography: *Acta Sanctorum* Sept. 7:152–171. *Enciclopedia del la Religión Católica*, ed. R. D. FERRERES et al. (Barcelona 1950–56) 5:108–109. V. VIETTI, A. MERCATI and A. PELZER, *Dizionario ecclesiastico* (Turin 1954–58) 2:838.

[C. M. AHERNE]

"The Repentant St. Mary Magdalene," surrounded by eight scenes from her life, 13th-century Tuscan painting.

MARY IMMACULATE, SISTERS SERVANTS OF

(SSMI, Official Catholic Directory #3610); a congregation in the UKRAINIAN CATHOLIC CHURCH (EASTERN CATHOLIC), founded in Western Ukraine on Aug. 15 1892, under the guidance of Rev. Jeremias Lomnitskyj, a member of the Basilian Fathers (Byzantine), and Rev. Cyril Seletskyj, a diocesan priest who provided the first house for the sisters in Zhuzhel. Nine sisters started their novitiate in that house under the spiritual direction of the Basilian fathers. In 1893 the novitiate was transferred to the town of Krystynopil. The metropolitan of Lvov, Cardinal Silvester Sembratovych, approved the first sketch of the constitutions on May 5, 1892. Later the constitutions were enlarged and approved in 1907 by the metropolitan of Lvov, Andrew Sheptyckyj. In Rome the Congregation for the Oriental Church granted initial approval in 1932, and final approbation was given by Pius XII in 1956. The first superior general of the congregation (Veronica Gargil) was elected at the general chapter held in Lvov in 1934. The sisters established their first foundation in the United States in Stamford, Conn., in 1938. The general motherhouse was later located at Rome. The U.S. regional headquarters is in Sloatsburg, NY.

The purposes of the congregation are to educate children and youth; nurse and care for the sick and aged in hospitals and homes for the aged; care for orphans and the homeless; do pastoral ministry and social work.

[M. M. WOJNAR/EDS.]

MARY MAGDALENE, ST.

A holy woman who ministered to Jesus and His disciples during His public ministry (Lk 8.2–3) and who, according to Jn 20.1–2, 11–18 (see also Mk 16.9–11), was the first person to see the empty tomb and the resurrected Christ. She has been identified, without adequate justification, with the repentant woman of Lk 7.36–50 and with Mary of Bethany (Jn ch. 11).

Life and Character. Mary was a native of Magdala, a prosperous and somewhat infamous fishing village on

St. Mary Magdalene. (Archive Photos)

the western shore of the Sea of Galilee, four miles north of Tiberias. Sometime after she had been freed by Jesus from a demoniac possession by seven devils—an expression that probably describes a violent and chronic nervous disorder, rather than a sinful state—she and other women gave of their own wealth and service to provide for the material needs of Jesus' apostolic company (Lk 8.2–3). In the Passion narratives of the Synoptic Gospels Mary was a witness to Jesus' Crucifixion and burial (Mt 27.55 56, 61; Mk 15.40, 47; Lk 23.49–56; 24.10); in John's account of the Passion she stood near the cross with Jesus' mother and the Beloved Disciple (Jn 19.25–26). When she came, with other women, to anoint Jesus' corpse on Easter morning, she received the Resurrection proclamation from angels and the commission to transmit it to the APOSTLES (Mk 16.1–8 and parallels). Finally, she actually saw the risen Lord, who personally told her to report His Resurrection to His brothers (Mt 28.9–10; Jn 20.16–18). God thus exalted her kind service for the apostolic college to the highest ministry, the proclaiming of Jesus' victory over death to the Apostles and, through them, to the world.

Mary's character appears in the Gospels as that of a practical woman, anxious to serve Jesus and His Apostles. Since, along with her companions, she was prevented from completing Jesus' burial anointing because of the SABBATH (Mk 15.42; Jn 19.42), she returned to the tomb, as soon as permissible, to perform this service (Mk 16.1). Immediately on finding the empty tomb, thinking that Jesus' corpse had been stolen, she reported the fact to the Eleven (Jn 20.2). Later, when she saw Jesus, she was still searching for a corpse to be anointed (Jn 20.14–15). Only after Jesus pronounced her name, probably in a familiar way, did she "turn" from looking for a dead body to see and recognize the living "Rabboni," the Master who could no longer be "detained" on earth by her material and emotional service, but who must now be served by her proclamation to the Apostles that He had ascended to His God and Father and theirs (Jn 20.16–18).

These are not the actions of a contemplative and impractical person like Mary of Bethany who, because of her mystical grasp of the life-through-death mystery of Christ, had already anointed Jesus for His burial a week before He died (Jn 12.1–8), nor those of a penitent woman who on one occasion had gratefully shown so much affection to Jesus when He forgave her all her sins (Lk 7.36–50). They are the actions of a practical, material-minded woman, not given to mystical reverie, who would be an unshakable witness to the Resurrection and who reported it in a most matter-of-fact way, "I have seen the Lord, and these things he said to me" (Jn 20.18).

False Identification with Other Women. One can understand why a commentator could have inadvertently identified Luke's sinful woman of ch. 7 with Mary of Bethany, as, in fact, Tertullian did (*De pudicitia,* 11.2), for each were said to have anointed Jesus' feet and wiped them dry with her hair, while He was reclining at a banquet (Lk 7.38, 46; Jn 12.3). A more careful commentator such as Origen clearly distinguished between the two anointings and the different women involved (*In Mattheaum,* series 77). It is more difficult to understand how the repentant sinner, and therefore Mary of Bethany, following Tertullian, was identified with Mary Magdalene by Gregory the Great (*Hom.* 25.1.10), since St. Luke introduces Mary by name immediately after finishing the story of the penitent woman, whose name he either does not know or wishes not to reveal. Following Gregory, the Latin Church, generally but not universally, has continued to identify the three women and honors them and their different virtues under the title of St. Mary Magdalene on July 22. Following Origen, the Greek churches honor them, more appropriately, as separate and distinct saints. The late legend that Mary Magdalene, combining the virtues of repentant sinner, contemplative, and practical servant who was the primary witness of the Resurrection, was miraculously transported to southern France in an oarless boat deserves no credence.

Most modern Scripture scholars agree with Origen's opinion that the anointings in Luke and John (see also Mt 26.6–13; Mk 14.3–9) were distinct happenings, despite their partial and mutual assimilation (the anointing of the feet in Luke and John in contrast to that of the head in Matthew and Mark) by oral transmission. Further, they hold that the anointings described in John, Matthew, and Mark were the same occurrence, although there is an apparent chronological inexactness in Mark and Matthew (cf. Mt 26.2 and Mk 14.1 with Jn 12.1). The anointings were made in different places, Luke's in Galilee, John's in Judea; were performed by different women, a repentant, notorious sinner in Luke, an old and very close friend of Jesus in John; and had different purposes, the expression of a loving, tearful gratitude to Jesus for His having forgiven the sinner in view of her great faith, in Luke, the solemn and tearless honoring of Jesus for Lazarus' resurrection and the preparing of His body for burial, in John. Mary of Bethany was certainly not Luke's penitent, therefore, although she may have heard of her poignant gratitude and been prompted to imitate it.

The reasons for not identifying Mary of Magdala with Mary of Bethany are clear also, especially in John's Gospel. There the two Marys are patently distinguished one from the other and given markedly different roles to play in the inexorable movement toward the Johannine concept of Jesus' glorification, which included both His Passion and His Resurrection. Mary of Bethany apparently had a mystical premonition of His death and its victorious value; the Magdalene could only weep because of His stolen corpse, and the duties still to be done for it, until, through His voice calling her name, she was convinced by her senses, as was Thomas (Jn 20.24–27), that He had conquered death.

Iconography. Because the Latin Church fused the characteristics of the nameless penitent with the other two women and because the story of her conversion is so appealing and beautiful, most of the Christian art depicting Mary Magdalene portrays her as a penitent weeping at Jesus' feet. However, there are ancient examples of Resurrection scenes on ampullae, stone coffins, and various other materials, in which Mary can be clearly distinguished as the first witness of the RESURRECTION. She was often depicted carrying a vase and with her hair flowing freely. From the medieval period many of her images were inspired by the numerous popular legends that spread from southern France to all of Europe.

Feast: July 22.

Bibliography: V. SAXER, *Le Culte de Marie Magdeleine en Occident des origenes à fin du moyen âge,* 2 v. (Paris 1959). P. KETTER, *The Magdalene Question,* tr. H. C. KOEHLER (Milwaukee 1935). K. KÜNSTLE, *Ikonographie der christlichen Kunst* (Freiburg 1926–28) 2:426–433. L. RÉAU, *Iconographie de l'art chrétien,* 6 v. (Paris 1955–59) 2.2:556–559; 3.2:846–859. *Anchor Bible Dictionary* 4 (New York 1992) 579–581. C. M. GRASSI and J. A. GRASSI, *Mary Magdalene and the Women in Jesus' Life* (Kansas City 1986).

[J. E. FALLON]

MARY OF EGYPT, ST.

Penitent and ascetic; b. probably 344; d. *c.* 421. An early account of Mary of Egypt is in CYRIL OF SCYTHOPOLIS's *Life of Cyriacus* (ed. E. Schwartz, *Texte und Untersuchungen zur Geschichte der altchristlichen Literatur* 49.2:233.4–234.19). It was developed in legendary fashion by later Byzantine hagiographers using details from JEROME's *Life of Paul the Hermit,* and was falsely attributed to SOPHRONIUS of Jerusalem (634–638). A similar story was told by John Moschus (*Pratum Spirituale*); and JOHN DAMASCENE quoted the developed Life of St. Mary of Egypt, apparently regarding it as authentic.

Mary led an evil life in Alexandria for seventeen years after the age of twelve; then she accompanied a pilgrimage to Palestine for further adventure. In Jerusalem, on the Feast of the Exaltation of the Cross, she joined the crowd converging on the church in which the sacred relic was being venerated; but she was repelled by some secret force when she attempted to enter the church. In the courtyard of the church, near a statue of the Blessed Virgin Mary, she promised to repent her evil ways if allowed to enter the church. Her prayer was granted, and she kissed the relic of the cross; she was moved to seek a solitude beyond the Jordan, where she did penance for her sins. After some 47 years Zosimus, a priest and monk, met her there; she called him by his name and asked him to meet her at the Jordan on Holy Thursday evening with the Holy Eucharist. Zosimus did so and was met by Mary, who walked upon the waters to his side of the river. She received Communion and asked that he come within the following year to the spot where he had first met her. There he found her corpse and beside it, written in the sand, a request for burial with the explanation that she had died the evening he gave her Holy Communion.

Feast: April 2 (Roman Martyrology); April 1 (Greek Church).

Bibliography: J. GAMMACK, *Dictionary of Christian Biography* (London 1877–87) 3:830. F. L. CROSS, *Oxford Dictionary of the Christian Church* 868. *Acta sanctorum* Apr 1:68–90. *Bibliographica hagiographica latina* (Brussels 1898–1901) 5415–21. *Bibliotheca hagiographica orientalis* (Brussels 1910) 683–687. H. LECLERCQ, *Dictionnaire d'archéologie chrétienne et de liturgie* (Paris 1907–53) 10.2:2128–36. *Kirche und theologische Literatur im byzantinischen Reich* (Munich 1959) 435. A. B. BUJILA, ed., *La Vie de sainte Marie l'Égyptienne* (Ann Arbor, Mich. 1949). A. BUTLER, *The Lives of the Saints* (New York 1956) 2:14–16. M. S. DE CRUZ-SÁENZ, *The life of Saint Mary of Egypt: An Edition and Study of the Medieval French and Spanish Verse Redactions* (Barcelona 1979). S. BRUSAMOLINO ISELLA, ed., *La leggenda di santa Maria egiziaca* (Milan 1992). *The Legend of Mary of Egypt in Medieval Insular Hagiography*, ed. E. POPPE and B. ROSS (Blackrock, Co. Dublin 1996).

[E. D. CARTER]

MARY OF OIGNIES, BL.

Mystic; b. Nivelles, Brabant, 1177; d. Oignies, June 23, 1213. Married at 14, she persuaded her husband to distribute their possessions, to practice continence, and to assist her in nursing lepers in their house. Her mystical life, conversation, and miracles attracted so much attention that, with the consent of her husband, she moved to Oignies, where she could live under the direction of the Augustinian canons. James de Vitry, later cardinal, was her director and considered her his spiritual mother. Since he is a reliable witness of sober judgment, his account of her unusual gifts (which perhaps would now be called psychic) and of her miracles is not unworthy of credit. Mary is important with other mystics among the BEGUINES in anticipating the change in Catholic devotion, which is usually associated with the FRANCISCANS, in particular the development of devotion to the Passion of Christ and to the Holy Eucharist.

Feast: June 23.

Bibliography: JACQUES DE VITRY, *Vita, Acta Sanctorum* June 5:547–572. A. BUTLER, *The Lives of the Saints,* rev. ed. H. THURS-

St. Mary of Egypt. (Archive Photos)

TON and D. ATTWATER, 4 v. (New York 1956) 2:623–626. J. L. BAUDOT and L. CHAUSSIN, *Vies des saints et des bienheureux selon l'ordre du calendrier avec l'historique des fêtes,* ed. by the Benedictines of Paris, 12 v. (Paris 1935–56) 6:384–386. *Bibliotheca hagiographica latina antiquae et mediae aetatis,* 2 v. (Brussels 1898–1901; suppl. 1911) 2:5516–17. I. GEYER, *Maria von Oignies: eine hochmittelalterliche Mystikerin zwischen Ketzerei und Rechtgläubigkeit* (Frankfurt am Main 1992).

[M. J. BARRY]

MARY OF ST. JOSEPH SALAZAR

Associate of St. TERESA OF AVILA and writer; b. Toledo, 1548; d. Cuerva, Oct. 19, 1603. She came of a noble family linked with the ducal house of Medinacelli. As a child she entered the service of Doña Luisa de la Cuerda in Toledo where, at the age of 14, she met Teresa. Attracted to the Teresian enterprise by Teresa herself, Mary took the habit (May 6, 1570) and made her profession at Malagon (June 10, 1571). Teresa took her to her new foundation of Beas (1565), then to Seville (1565–66). The many extant letters of St. Teresa to Mary testify to the great affection and love that the mother foundress had for her. After the death of St. Teresa, Mary made the foundation of the Lisbon house (1588), where she soon became very popular. In 1603 she was sent to the new foundation of Talavera and Cuerva. Her writings remained unpublished until 1913, when they were published at Burgos in a single volume. They are unpretentious and of no great importance from a spiritual point of view. However, they do possess considerable historical value because of what she has to say about St. Teresa, especially in the declaration she made in the process of beatification.

Bibliography: SILVERIO DE SANTA TERESA, *Historia del Carmen Descalzo en España, Portugal y América,* 15 v. (Burgos 1935–49) 8:436–454. A short introduction to her writings by Silverio de Santa Teresa contained in MARÍA DE SAN JOSÉ, *Libro de Recreaciones, Ramillete de Mirra, Avisos, Máximas y Poesías* (Burgos 1913).

[O. RODRIGUEZ]

MARY REPARATRIX, SOCIETY OF

The Society of Mary Reparatrix (SMR) is a religious community of women with papal approbation in the spirituality of St. IGNATIUS OF LOYOLA. The sisters engage in contemplative prayer, catechetics, retreats and spiritual direction, pastoral ministries, social outreach, and making altar breads.

The foundress of the congregation was Baroness Emilie d'Hooghvorst (1818–78), daughter of Count d'Oultremont of Liège, Belgium, later (1840) Belgian minister to the Holy See. At 19 years of age Emilie was married to Baron Victor d'Hooghvorst. She bore four children before her husband's early death ten years later. Two of her children subsequently joined Mother Mary of Jesus (Emilie's name in religion) in establishing her community. Under the spiritual direction of the Jesuits, particularly that of Paul Ginhac (1824–95), the Society of Mary Reparatrix was canonically established in Strasbourg, Alsace-Lorraine, in May of 1857. The congregation later made foundations throughout Europe and in the Americas. The generalate is in Rome; the U.S. provincialate is in Riverview, Michigan.

[M. LAVIN/EDS.]

MARY STUART, QUEEN OF SCOTS

Queen Consort of France, Queen of Scotland; b. Linlithgow Castle, Scotland, Dec. 7, 1542; d. Fotheringay Castle, England, Feb. 8, 1587. As the daughter of James V of Scotland and Mary Guise, she became queen when six days old, and at ten months (September 1542) was crowned by Cardinal Beaton. During her minority Scotland faced frequent invasions from HENRY VIII, who deployed a policy known as the ''Rough Wooing,'' to try to secure Mary as bride for his son Edward VI. To safeguard Scotland's traditional alliance with France, her Guise uncles arranged her betrothal to the Dauphin Francis and in 1548 she was brought to France for her own safety. Here she became admired for her linguistic abilities and charm. In 1559, one year after her marriage, she became Queen Consort of France and also laid claim to the crowns of England and Ireland on the grounds of the illegitimacy of her cousin Elizabeth. Elizabeth's reply was quick and decisive. Soon after her accession in the same year, she sent armed aid to Scotland's Protestants who soon overturned the Catholic policies of Mary's mother, Mary of Guise. In December 1560 Mary was widowed, and despite the troubles in Scotland, she remained in France trying to find a suitable husband. In August 1561, she finally returned to face a country badly divided by religious strife. Although Mary was a nominal Catholic, she initially proclaimed her intention not to interfere with the religious status quo in the country. She promulgated an edict of toleration that led to violent diatribes from John KNOX and Scotland's growing Protestant faction on the one side and from Scottish Catholics on the other. In 1562, the lives of two of her Catholic advisors, her chaplain and the Jesuit Nicholas de Gouda, a papal observer and advisor sent to Mary by Pius IV, were threatened. As a result of the confused religious and political situation in these early years of her reign, Mary relied on her half-brother, James, Earl of Moray, and her secretary, William Maitland, to administer her government. The Protestant policies both pursued angered Scotland's Catholics.

Marriage to Lord Darnley. In 1565, Mary married Henry Stewart, Lord Darnley, following a long search for a suitable spouse. Darnley proved a poor choice. Politically inept and a drunkard, his status as a nominal Catholic irritated Moray, Maitland, and Scotland's Protestant nobles. Their union did produce an heir (the future James VI of Scotland and I of England) but otherwise proved disastrous and was marked by numerous intrigues. Darnley's weak and quarrelsome nature made many enemies and the murder of Mary's devoted secretary, Rizzio, alienated her as well. During the years that Mary was married to Darnley her policies first favored Catholics and then Protestants. Finally, the Queen came under the influence of James Hepburn, Earl of Bothwell, who saw the removal of Darnley as his path to power. Mary persuaded Darnley, recovering from severe illness, to go with her to Kirk-o-Field, near Edinburgh, to rest in a rented house, while she, under Bothwell's escort, moved on to Holyrood Palace. In the early morning of Feb. 10, 1567, the house was blown up and Darnley killed. Although her opponents implicated Mary and accused her officially of murdering her husband, 20th-century scholarship has cast doubt on her guilt. The evidence is too contradictory for a definitive judgment.

Coercion by Bothwell. Bothwell was charged after a superficial inquiry and the Queen now came under his influence. In order to secure his marriage to Mary he obtained a divorce from the Protestant Kirk Courts, apparently with the collusion of his wife, Lady Jane Gordon. On May 15, 1567, Bothwell married Mary in a Protestant ceremony, but his triumph was short-lived. The couple quarreled and Scotland's Protestant lords, Bothwell's former allies, rose in armed revolt. In June they defeated Mary's forces at Carberry Hill and she surrendered on condition of being treated as a sovereign. Bothwell escaped, later fleeing to Denmark where he was imprisoned and died insane. In the meantime, Mary, too, escaped her captors, raised an army, and was defeated in May 1568. She signed an abdication that named Moray regent.

Imprisonment in England. Having fled to England, she refused to vindicate herself of complicity in Darnley's murder except before Elizabeth in person. Elizabeth commanded that she was to be treated with respect but, to prevent her becoming the rallying point of English Catholics in the north, she was to be kept under close guard. She was imprisoned for 19 years. Cecil's immediate plan was to put her on trial, producing at York and Westminster the so-called Casket Letters, alleged to have been written to Bothwell by Mary and which blatantly incriminate her both in the Darnley murder and in sexual subjection to Bothwell. The authenticity of the letters was then (as now still) hotly contested, and an open verdict returned, which was generally accepted as one of not guilty (January 1569). In the wake of this acquittal, Mary considered plans for another marriage, with Thomas Howard, Duke of Norfolk. In November and December 1569 Northern English Catholics rose in support of Mary, but the revolt quickly collapsed. The following February Pope St. PIUS V hoped to encourage rebellion by excommunicating Elizabeth, but this show of support came too late and ultimately had the reverse effect. Norfolk, implicated in the schemes of Ridolfi, an Italian banker, to finance a Spanish invasion, was executed in June 1572. Parliament petitioned for Mary's head, but Elizabeth prudently declined, while ordering a close guard on her cousin, whose liberty would always prove a threat to the throne. For the next 14 years, Mary was implicated in a number of ill-conceived plans for revolt and she was moved from place to place in conditions of increasing harshness. In January 1586, a plot to set her free and as-

Mary Stuart, Queen of Scots.

sassinate Elizabeth was uncovered. The chief conspirators, Anthony Babington, Mary's former page and John Ballard, a priest, were executed, and Mary's complicity in the scheme was revealed to Walsingham.

Trial and Execution. Mary was moved to Fotheringay Castle and put on trial on Oct. 14–15, 1586. She was condemned, and Elizabeth eventually signed the warrant of execution. That document referred to her as "Mary Stuart, commonly called Queen of Scotland," her royal status denied in the warrant of execution that beheaded her on Feb. 8, 1587. Before her death she reputedly praised God for the privilege of dying for the "honour of his name and of his Church, Catholic, Apostolic and Roman." Mary Stuart may have long been accepted in some quarters as a martyr for the Catholic cause, but recent historical scholarship has been less charitable in that regard. Scholars have questioned the depth of Mary's religious commitment, and they have treated her as a tragic figure, who lacked political competence and judgment.

Bibliography: Mary Stuart remains, in a phrase attributed to Elizabeth, "the Daughter of Debate," so that historical judgment on her is vast, continuous, and still not definitive. A. BELLESHEIM, *History of the Catholic Church of Scotland,* tr. D. O. HUNTER-BLAIR 4 v. (Edinburgh 1887–90) v.3. S. S. MACNALTY, *Mary, Queen of Scots* (New York 1961). G. R. TURNER, *Mary Stuart: Forgotten Forgeries* (London 1933), all four translations of the Casket Letters in parallel columns; also the Simonds and Conference Letters; notes and comments on the opinion of various authors concerning Mary. T.F. HENDERSON, *Mary, Queen of Scots,* 2 v. (New York 1905), best complete scholarly biography. A. M. MACKENZIE, *The Scotland of Queen Mary and the Religious Wars, 1513–1638* (London 1936). T. F. HENDERSON, *Dictionary of National Biography* (London 1885–1900; repr. with corrections, 21 v., 1908–09, 1921–22, 1938; suppl. 1901–) 12:1258–75. J. H. POLLEN, *The Catholic Encyclopedia,* ed. C. G. HERBERMANN et al., 16 v. (New York 1907–14; suppl. 1922) 9:764–766. G. DONALDSON, *All the Queen's Men* (London 1983). A. FRASER, *Mary Queen of Scots* (London 1969). M. LYNCH, *Mary Stewart. Queen in Three Kingdoms* (Oxford 1988). J. WORMALD, *Mary Queen of Scots: A Study in Failure* (London 1988).

[G. ALBION/P. SOERGEL]

MARY TUDOR, QUEEN OF ENGLAND

Reigned, July 6, 1553, to Nov. 17, 1558; b. Feb. 18, 1516; d. Nov. 17, 1558. She was the only surviving child of HENRY VIII and CATHERINE OF ARAGON. Henry had hoped for a son who would perpetuate the fledgling Tudor dynasty. Although disappointed, he was sanguine. "We are both young," he told the Venetian ambassador, Giustinian. "If it is a daughter this time, by the grace of God the sons will follow."

Early Years. Henry, 25, and Catherine, 31, took the greatest interest and delight in their infant daughter. Both sovereigns were devout Catholics. The king was an enthusiastic sportsman, generous, affable, much concerned about theological questions, dedicated to peace, and universally beloved by his subjects. The queen was well educated and practiced an uncompromising austerity that was remarkable for a Renaissance sovereign. She fasted regularly and was accustomed to having religious books read to her. Henry and Catherine selected as Mary's first governess a widow of considerable discretion, Margaret POLE, Countess of Salisbury. Until she was 12, Mary's health and education were a constant concern of her parents. She received an excellent musical training and spoke French, Latin, Italian, and Spanish with great fluency. She was well versed in the writings of St. Ambrose and St. Augustine. When Henry expressed his desire to have his marriage to Catherine annulled so that he might marry Anne Boleyn, Mary opposed him.

"During the protracted proceedings of the marriage controversy, both Mary and her mother faced their adversities with dignity." Early in the following year, 1533, Abp. Thomas CRANMER, who had succeeded Cardinal Thomas WOLSEY, pronounced Henry's marriage invalid, making Mary technically illegitimate. With the early arrival of Anne Boleyn's child, the future Queen ELIZABETH I, Mary was no longer recognized as princess of Wales and the identity badges worn by her lackeys on their coats were removed. In the years between the divorce and the execution of Anne Boleyn, Mary's life was unpleasant. She was estranged from her father, because of her support of Catherine's cause. While her father did send his physician to attend her when she was ill, Henry refused to allow Catherine to visit Mary. When Catherine died in 1536, court officials finally were able to secure Mary's signature to a document in which she renounced the pope's "pretended authority" and acknowledged that her mother's marriage had been unlawful. Before signing the document though, Mary made a secret prostration that she acted only under compulsion.

Once again restored to her father's good graces, Mary passed the days pleasantly at court with her books, embroidery, and music. This period of peaceful obscurity ended abruptly with her father's death in 1547. Her sickly half-brother, Edward, son of Henry VIII and Jane Seymour, inherited the kingship at 11, but the real power was exercised by Jane's brother, Edward Seymour, the Protestant Duke of Somerset. The old order was changing inexorably. Frequent attempts were made to force Mary, next in line to the throne, to conform to the new innovations in religion. She refused. Edward VI sent a special commission to insist upon compliance. Mary promised obedience in all things except the novel religious services. The new bishop of London, Nicholas RIDLEY, offered to preach before her. She declined to listen to him or to read any books she regarded as heretical.

Queen Mary I. In 1553 Edward became seriously ill and the ambitious John Dudley, duke of Northumberland, who had gained an ascendancy over the council, persuaded the dying boy to set aside Mary's right to the throne, because it would mean a Catholic restoration, and to name as his successor Lady Jane Grey, a descendant of Henry VIII's sister Mary. Lady Jane became the bride of Northumberland's fourth son, Guilford Dudley, and Northumberland exerted heavy pressure on many prominent men to join the treasonable conspiracy. When Edward died, Lady Jane was proclaimed queen. Nine days later, Mary, having rallied a considerable force, marched on London. The vast majority of the English people decided in her favor and Northumberland's plot collapsed. Lady Jane Grey and her husband were confined to the Tower and later executed. Northumberland was beheaded but other traitors retained their freedom or were allowed to go into retirement. Mary's leniency was partly responsible for Sir Thomas Wyatt's rebellion, early in 1554, in opposition to the proposed marriage of Mary and PHILIP II of Spain. Queen Mary was 38, small, plain and shortsighted. Yet she organized the defense of London and the uprising was put down with little bloodshed. Only about 100 of the ordinary rebels were executed.

Mary Tudor believed that she was predestined and preserved by God for the throne in order that she might be His instrument for the reestablishment of Catholicism. Her principal adviser in religious matters, Cardinal Reginald POLE, declared that it was not enough that she honor God; she must compel her subjects to do likewise and punish the disobedient in virtue of the authority she had received from God. The papal legate expressed the dominant philosophy of the 16th century regarding nonconformity in religion: heresy and schism must be overcome—by peaceful means if possible, by force as a last resort.

Early in her brief reign, Mary was confronted by an indifferent laity, a nobility gorged with abbey lands, a vacillating hierarchy, and a nondescript but intransigent Protestant minority. She proceeded cautiously. It is significant, for example, that the arrival of Cardinal Pole in London was delayed for an entire year after Mary came to power because a violent anti-Catholic reaction was feared.

First of all, the religious legislation of Edward's reign had to be voided. This was followed by the parliamentary repeal of the antipapal legislation of Henry VIII. Finally, papal supremacy was grudgingly acknowledged in England only on condition that confiscated ecclesiastical property in private hands would not be restored to the Church. In a great variety of ways the queen sought to revitalize and strengthen Catholicism in her realm. She called for an active missionary apostolate to acquaint the people with the true nature of the Catholic religion. She secured the return of many English friars who, to avoid earlier persecutions, had been exiles in Flanders. She rebuilt and reestablished hospitals, churches, and monasteries. She subsidized ecclesiastics who had been deprived of their revenues. She sought to allay religious antagonisms, hoping that the passage of time and a policy of leniency, rather than severe punishment, would mitigate the rage of some ardent nonconformists. Her efforts, while aiding the Church, further antagonized the hard core of Protestant resistance. Accordingly, an obsequious Parliament revived the old laws against heresy.

Mary Tudor, Queen of England.

Religious innovations had brought nothing but grief to Mary Tudor in the reigns of her father and half-brother. Heresy, in her single-minded outlook, was an evil thing. In the following year a Catholic episcopal synod was convened to re-establish the Roman Church in England and a Protestant plot was unearthed. The number of executions rose to 90. In 1557, 70 were put to death, and in the final eleven months of Mary's reign in 1558, another 40 perished.

The specter of Mary's persecutions of Protestants survived long after her reign. John Foxe (1517–1587) was the first in a long line of Protestants martyrologists to celebrate the lives and deaths of the Marian matyrs in his *Acts and Monuments of These Latter and Perilous Times* (1570). His work, like many of this genre, called upon nationalist sentiments to denigrate Mary's attempt to re-establish Catholicism and praised the Elizabethan religious settlement. In truth, it must be admitted that Mary's relgious policies did re-invigorate Catholic beliefs in England and sustained the Church's tradition into the reign of Elizabeth I. In addition, the Marian period was marked by a number of positive social and economic developments. Mary tried to reverse the course of inflation and to revalue the country's debased currency. She made strides in dealing with England's deficits, its poverty, and its trade problems. Many of these successes have been credited, not to Mary, but to her half-sister Elizabeth, proof that her record as queen will likely continue to be overshadowed by the persecution she unleashed.

Bibliography: H. F. M. PRESCOTT, *Mary Tudor* (rev. ed. New York 1953). E. H. HARBISON, *Rival Ambassadors at the Court of Queen Mary* (Princeton 1940). P. HUGHES, *The Reformation in England,* 3 v. in 1 (5th, rev. ed. New York 1963) v. 2. B. WHITE, *Mary Tudor* (New York 1935). J. M. STONE, *The History of Mary I: Queen of England* (New York 1901). W. SCHENK, *Reginald Pole, Cardinal of England* (New York 1950). G. R. ELTON, *England under the Tudors* (London 1955). H. C. WHITE, *Tudor Books of Saints and Martyrs* (Madison 1963). G. MATTINGLY, *Catherine of Aragon* (Boston 1941). J. D. MACKIE, *The Earlier Tudors* (Oxford 1952). G. L. M. J. CONSTANT, *The Reformation in England,* tr. R. E. SCANTLEBURY and E. I. WATKIN, 2 v. (New York 1934–42) v. 1. A. VERMEERSCH, *Tolerance,* tr. W. H. PAGE (New York 1913). J. GAIRDNER, *The English Church in the Sixteenth Century from the Accession of Henry VIII to the Death of Mary* (New York 1902). C. READ, *The Tudors* (New York 1936). J. A. MULLER, *Stephen Gardiner and the Tudor Reaction* (New York 1926). D. M. LOADES, *Mary Tudor* (New York 1989). D. M. LOADES, *The Reign of Mary Tudor. Politics, Government and Religion in England, 1553–1558* (New York 1979). R. TITTLER, *The Reign of Mary I* (New York 1991).

[J. J. O'CONNOR]

MARYKNOLL FATHERS AND BROTHERS

The Catholic Foreign Mission Society of America, popularly known as the Maryknoll Fathers and Brothers, is a community of secular priests and lay brothers dedicated to mission work outside the United States, and to education about the meaning and realities of mission. Founded in 1911 by two diocesan priests, James A. WALSH (1867–1936) of Boston and Thomas F. PRICE (1860–1919) of Raleigh, North Carolina, the society today serves in 30 countries. The headquarters and formation center of the society are at Maryknoll, New York, near Ossining, New York.

Organization, Objectives, and Formation. Canonically a society of Apostolic Life of Pontifical Right, the society comprises secular priests, lay brothers, and candidates. Members commit themselves to missionary work by lifetime oath. Rather than seeking members outside the United States, the society has historically promoted within the local churches the development of their own diocesan, religious and lay vocations, and the creation of their own missionary societies. The society describes its missionary activity as ''integral evangelization'' carried out ''through: presence and witness, human promotion and liberation, liturgical life, prayer and contemplation, inter-religious dialogue, and explicit proclamation and catechesis.'' (General Chapter, 1996). The formation and education of Maryknoll priest and brother candidates includes one year of spiritual discernment and study at Maryknoll, New York, followed by accredited theological and ministry studies. Ministry preparation includes a supervised two-year intern experience overseas in a Maryknoll mission.

Foundation. It was not until 1908 (decree *sapienti consilio* of Pope PIUS X) that the church in the United States ceased to be administered as a mission territory under the Congregation for the PROPAGATION OF THE FAITH. By that time there was a growing concern by many that, despite religious needs at home, U.S. Catholics should assume without delay an active role in the Church's worldwide missionary effort. It was noted that North American Protestants already had several thousand missioners in overseas fields with millions of dollars in support. Catholic missioners from the United States numbered fewer than 18.

One early manifestation of foreign mission interest was the establishment in the United States of the Society for the Propagation of the Faith in 1897. A mission fundraising organization based in France, it was well promoted in the archdiocese of Boston under its director Fr. James A. Walsh. In 1904 Walsh attended a meeting of the Catholic Missionary Union in Washington, D.C., where he addressed priests who were leaders in missionary work within the United States, sharing with them his conviction that promotion of foreign missions would also give stimulus to missionary activity at home. Among his hearers was Fr. Thomas F. Price of Raleigh, North Carolina, an itinerant missioner who was struggling to develop a missionary community of secular priests for service in his home state. Price soon began promoting the foreign mission cause in his national magazine *Truth.* In 1907 Walsh began publishing his own mission magazine, the *Field Afar,* which urged the establishment of a foreign mission seminary for secular priests of the United States. Among those who assisted in the production of the magazine was Mary J. Rogers, who would later become foundress of the Maryknoll Sisters.

In September 1910 Walsh and Price met again by chance at a Eucharistic Congress in Montreal. Price urged that they take immediate steps themselves to establish a missionary society and seminary. Walsh accepted the challenge. Price conferred with Cardinal James GIBBONS of Baltimore, who was then the dean of the U.S. hierarchy and with whom Price was personally acquainted. Gibbons was immediately favorable to the project and recommended Price to the apostolic delegate, Archbishop Diomede Falconio, who was also favorable and advised that the society and seminary be national, rather than dependent on a diocese. He asked Gibbons to address a formal proposal to the archbishops that could be acted on at their next annual meeting. Walsh and Price drafted a letter to the bishops, and Price personally canvassed several of the bishops for their support of the proposal.

At their meeting at CATHOLIC UNIVERSITY in Washington, D.C., the project was discussed and on April 27, 1911, the archbishops affirmed unanimously: ''We heartily approve the establishment of an American Seminary for the Foreign Missions as outlined in the letter sent by his Eminence Cardinal Gibbons.'' Walsh and Price were instructed ''to proceed to Rome without delay, for the purpose of securing all necessary authorization and direction from [the Congregation of] the Propaganda for the proposed work.'' The two were readily received at the Roman congregation. On June 29, the feast of Saints Peter and Paul, the cardinal prefect, Girolamo Gotti, formally communicated to them papal authorization for the founding of the Catholic Foreign Mission Society of America. The following day they were received by Pope Pius X who gave them and the society his apostolic blessing.

On their return to the United States, Walsh and Price accepted the invitation of Archbishop John FARLEY to establish the new institution in the archdiocese of New York. After several months in rented quarters in Hawthorne, they acquired a hilltop tract of 93 acres overlooking the Hudson River near Ossining, New York, 35 miles north of New York City. It would become the permanent location of the headquarters and formation facility of the society. Dedicating the site to the Virgin Mary Queen of Apostles, they named it ''Maryknoll,'' a name that would later be shared with the Maryknoll Sisters' Congregation, the Maryknoll Mission Association of the Faithful, and the Maryknoll Affiliates.

Farm buildings provided living facilities, classrooms, and offices for the *Field Afar,* which now became the official publication of the society. At Price's request Walsh accepted the role of superior, organizing the society and seminary, while Price, aided frequently by Brother Thomas McCann, traveled throughout the East and

A priest sits outside the Maryknoll School reading to a group of children, near Seoul, Korea. (©Horace Bristol/CORBIS)

Middle West making the new society known and seeking vocations and support. In addition to priesthood candidates, the early community included several young laymen who generously contributed their technical skills and would soon become brothers. A small community of dedicated laywomen, led by Rogers, provided voluntary secretarial and other support services.

First Overseas Missions. By 1918 the young society was able to establish its first overseas mission. Frs. James E. Walsh, Francis X. FORD, and Bernard F. Meyer, under the leadership of Fr. Price, were commissioned to Yangjiang (Yeungkong) in Guangdong (Kuangtung) province, south CHINA, a territory ceded to Maryknoll by the Paris Foreign Mission Society. Fr. Price died in 1919 and was succeeded as superior of the mission by Fr. James E. Walsh. Within a few years the area entrusted to Maryknoll, newly based in Jiangmen (Kongmoon), was expanded to include three neighboring territories of Wuzhou (Wuchow), Guilin (Kweilin),and Jiaying (Kaying). In 1927 Fr. James E. Walsh was ordained bishop of the Jiangmen vicariate; Ford became bishop of Jiaying in 1935. In 1925 the society accepted the extensive mission of Fushun, in Manchuria. The society also assumed responsibility for the territory of Pyongyang in northern KOREA (1922), and in 1934 would undertake work in the area of Kyoto in JAPAN. Limited work among Asian immigrants was likewise accepted in Seattle (1920), the Philippines and Hawaii (1927).

During this time the society expanded its facilities in the United States. Construction of the principal part of the major seminary was completed, and with the cooperation of major local dioceses, five preparatory seminary programs, were organized. From 1931 a separate year of spiritual formation for all candidates was introduced.

World War II. At the onset of Japan's attacks on China's coastal cities in 1937, two Maryknoll missioners in southern China were kidnapped but later released. In 1937 Fr. Gerard Donovan was kidnapped in Manchuria by a group seeking ransom money. When this was not forthcoming he was killed (1938). During the war, the policy of the society was that missioners should remain with their people despite the hazards. During 1940 to 1941 Bishop Walsh and his vicar general, Fr. James Drought, at the request of Japanese authorities and the acceptance of the U.S. State Department, provided an unofficial channel for contacts between the two governments in the interest of finding a means of avoiding war. After Japan's attack on the United States at Pearl Harbor in 1941, Maryknollers in Japan, Hong Kong, and the Philippines were promptly interned as enemy aliens. Some remained in prison camps until the end of the war; others were repatriated in exchange for Japanese prisoners. Monsignor Patrick Byrne, head of Maryknoll's mission in Kyoto, was held under house arrest throughout the war. Only missioners in unoccupied inland China were able to continue their work. Two priests died in captivity, another was murdered at the end of the war, presumably by bandits. In the United States, Maryknollers accompanied their West Coast Japanese parishoners in the isolated relocation camps where they were illegally interned.

During this period, Rome encouraged Maryknoll to consider opening missions in Latin America. The first (1942) was in the Vicariate of the Pando in the northern jungle of Bolivia, followed by missions in Chile, Peru, Ecuador, Guatemala, and Mexico (1943)—all areas marked by deep poverty and long lacking adequate pastoral ministry. By 1945 there were 105 Maryknoll priests and brothers working in Latin America.

Postwar Developments. *Japan and China.* After the war, Maryknoll was able to return to all its Asian missions except Manchuria and northern Korea, which were under the control of the U.S.S.R. In Japan Maryknoll work included substantial relief programs, and mass media advertisement of Christianity. Service in the diocese of Sapporo began in 1954. In China promising new beginnings were soon blocked by the progressive expulsion of all foreign Church personnel by the communist government, which consolidated its control in 1949. Ninety-eight Maryknoll priests and brothers were expelled. Bishop Francis X. Ford was placed on public trial and mistreated; broken in health he died in a Canton prison in 1952. Bishop James E. Walsh, then secretary of the Catholic Central Bureau in Shanghai, a national service of the Chinese bishops, was placed under restrictive surveillance (1951), and later sentenced to 20 years imprisonment. In 1970, on the eve of the visit to the People's Republic of China of U.S. president Nixon, he was released and expelled. Many of the expelled missioners found new work in Hong Kong and Taiwan.

Korea. In 1949 Monsignor Byrne was named apostolic delegate to Korea and ordained archbishop. He was in Seoul when northern troops invaded the capital in June 1950. Taken prisoner with his secretary, Fr. William Booth, he was brought to the northern border where he died of pneumonia during a forced winter march. After service in Seoul and Pusan, the society accepted care of the South Korean dioceses of Inchon and Cheung-Ju (1958).

Philippines. In the Philippines the society, after initial service in Manila and the diocese of Lipa, accepted the territory of Tagum, in Mindanao (1961). In Tanzania (then Tanganyika) east Africa, the society was assigned the new missions of Musoma (1946) and Shinyanga (1954); later the society would also work in Kenya.

In the United States, the postwar period was a time of intensified mission education and recruitment by the society. New films, books, and teaching materials were produced under the direction of Frs. John Considine and Albert Nevins, and aided by Maryknoll sisters. In 1945 Maryknoll Fr. James Keller launched the Christopher Movement. The society had enjoyed steady growth since its foundation, but the post war period was a time of unprecedented increase in candidates for most communities in the United States, including Maryknoll. New preparatory seminaries were constructed and facilities at Maryknoll, New York, were expanded.

Vatican II. In the light of major changes to the Church's understanding of mission that the Second Vatican Council introduced, at its 1966 General Chapter the Maryknoll Society sought to refocus its vision in light of the council's documents and spirit. The General Chapter emphasized the importance of prophetic public witness in the process of evangelization, of the role of laity in mission, of inculturation, interreligious dialogue, action on behalf of justice, and of the ecclesial appropriateness of collegial structures within the society and the Church. Maryknoll brothers were recognized as equal members. Renewal programs were offered to enable the membership to understand the theological and historical factors underlying the new directions. The society upgraded its language schools in Taiwan, Tanzania, the Philippines, and Latin America and opened them to missioners of other communities.

In 1966 the society opened its ranks to include diocesan and religious priests and brothers as limited term associates by contract. In 1972 first steps were taken to incorporate lay associates into the society's missionary activity; in 1995 the Maryknoll Mission Association of the Faithful, largely lay missioners, became a self-governing branch of the Maryknoll family.

In Latin America many Maryknollers, inspired by the Church's social teaching newly articulated by VATICAN COUNCIL II, the encyclical *Populorum progressio* (1967) of Pope PAUL VI and the documents issued by the Latin American bishops at their meeting at MEDELLIN, Colombia (1968), joined in solidarity with the local churches in denouncing injustices and protesting the deepening poverty of the majorities in many countries. Many welcomed the theologies of LIBERATION that, proceeding from a social option for the poor, engaged the Christian conscience in a critical assessment of the factors causing poverty and repression with a view to taking just action for change. Maryknoll's ORBIS BOOKS (1971) became the principal publisher in English of these theologies. Theology and practice from Latin America was soon shared in parts of Asia, especially in the Philippines and Korea. Maryknollers were anguished and challenged by the suffering endured in these years by their people and colleagues, most notably in Central America where defenders of human rights and others were murdered by military and paramilitary forces. Among the Maryknoll victims were Fr. William Woods (1976) and Sisters Maura Clark and Ita Ford (1980), along with Ursuline Sr. Dorothy Kazel and Cleveland diocesan lay missioner Jean Donovan.

New Commitments. Despite its declining numbers, the society has continued to undertake new mission work in the postconciliar period. The first mission entrusted entirely to Maryknoll brothers was opened in Western Samoa (1976); other new society missions included Venezuela (1965), San Salvador (1966), Brazil (1975), Indonesia (1973), Sudan and Bangladesh (1975), Nepal (1977), Yemen (1978–82), Costa Rica (1981), Honduras (1982), Egypt (1981), Palestine (1988), Thailand (1982), Cambodia (1990), Vietnam (1992), and Mozambique (1997). Some of these commitments were temporary; most have had a more specialized focus rather than involving overall care of a diocese or parish. Many were undertaken with the participation of Maryknoll lay associates. In the Middle East and Asia the work has taken the form of human services witnessing to Christian compassion and is marked by sensitivity to other religious traditions. In China, at the request of educational authorities, Maryknollers are assisting students to improve their communication skills in English. In eastern Russia the society is assisting in the rebuilding of devastated Church communities in an ecumenical spirit.

Maryknoll Affiliates. In 1991, in response to many expressions of interest in sharing in some manner in Maryknoll's mission charism in the context of daily living in the United States, the society and the Maryknoll Sisters jointly established a program of Maryknoll affiliates. Participants are mostly, but not exclusively, lay. Organized in local chapters that meet regularly, affiliates determine their own goals and activities reflecting ''global vision, spirituality, community and action.'' They are currently active in a variety of mission-related activities within and outside the United States.

Mission Education. From its center in the United States the society continues to make available mission education materials for all levels. The society's periodicals *Maryknoll* (continuation of the *Field Afar* since 1939) and *Revista Maryknoll* offer ongoing reporting on the missionary activity of Maryknollers and others around the world. The book division, under the imprint of Orbis Books, continues an unbroken tradition of publishing begun by the Maryknoll cofounders. In addition, the society conducts ongoing research on mission-related issues both historical and contemporary, and offers lectures, workshops, and study programs on these subjects. Discernment workshops and other formational services are offered to persons of other communities preparing for cross-cultural ministries.

Bibliography: A. DRIES, ''The Foreign Mission Impulse of the American Catholic Church, 1893–1925,'' *International Bulletin of Missionary Research* 15:2 (April 1991) 61–66; *The Missionary Movement in American Catholic History* (Maryknoll, N.Y. 1998). R. A. LANE, *The Early Days of Maryknoll* (New York 1951). A. J. NEVINS, *The Meaning of Maryknoll* (New York 1954). G. C. POWERS, *The Maryknoll Movement* (Maryknoll, N.Y. 1926). P. R. RIVIERA, '''Field Found!' Establishing the Maryknoll Mission Enterprise in the United States and China, 1918–1928,'' *Catholic Historical Review* 84 (July 1998) 477–517. J.-P. WIEST, *Maryknoll in China: A History, 1918–1955* (Armonk, N.Y. 1988; repr. Maryknoll, N.Y. 1997).

[W. D. MCCARTHY]

MARYKNOLL MISSION ASSOCIATION OF THE FAITHFUL

The Maryknoll Mission Association of the Faithful (M.M.A.F.) is a Catholic community of predominantly, but not exclusively, lay men and women, including families, who commit themselves by contract to participate in the global missionary ministry of the Church. The term of the contract is normally three and a half years and is renewable. Today members are engaged in mission in 14 countries. The headquarters of the Association is at Maryknoll, N.Y., near Ossining, N.Y., 35 miles north of New York City. The mission statement of the Association states:

> We are a Catholic community of lay, religious and ordained people, including families and children. We participate in the mission of Jesus, serving in cross-cultural ministries in order to create a more just world in solidarity with the poor.

Admission to the M.M.A.F. is open to U.S. citizens and permanent residents according to established norms. There is a four-month period of formation in the United States before language study and work overseas.

History The Association in its present organization was established in 1994, following a history extending from the beginnings of the MARYKNOLL FATHERS AND BROTHERS and the MARYKNOLL SISTERS. The first Maryknoll Brothers initially volunteered their services as laypersons, as did the laywomen who later became Maryknoll Sisters. Later some single men who were not seeking the priesthood or brotherhood but wished to contribute their skills in meeting the society's needs in the United States were accepted into the life of the community under the designation of oblates. In 1922 cofounder Fr. James A. WALSH made a challenging appeal for lay missioners:

> Surely there will be generous souls, in numbers proportionate to the grace of God, who may not feel called to devote their entire lives to a religious work, but who would gladly spend a certain time, say five years or more, in teaching on the missions . . . If non-Catholic laymen are willing to make such sacrifices, is it too much to expect of the Catholic? . . . It should be our business now to prepare an organization that will enable us to accept such volunteers and utilize their services . . . (*Field Afar*, April 1922, p. 100).

No steps were taken at that time. In 1930 a physician, Dr. Harry Blaber of Brooklyn, N.Y., became the first layman to serve overseas with Maryknoll, treating victims of Hansen's Disease in southern China. After marrying, his wife Constance White, a nurse, served with him. When they returned to the United States in 1937, Dr. Artemio Bagalawis, a Filipino, continued the Hansens work with Maryknoll. Over the decades several other laypersons from the United States served overseas with Maryknollers by individual arrangement.

The Second Vatican Council deepened the Church's theology of the laity and urged all to a wider participation in the Church's mission. At its 1972 General Chapter the Maryknoll Society authorized the experimental beginning of an organized program for Maryknoll lay missioners. In 1975, with the collaboration of the Maryknoll Sisters, the organization was formally established under the Archdiocese of New York, and in 1979 leadership was assumed in part by lay missioners. Within the flexibility offered by the 1983 Code of Canon Law, the M.M.A.F. has sought recognition by the Pontifical Council for the Laity as a public association of the faithful. The association has close cooperative relationships with the Maryknoll Fathers and Brothers and with the Maryknoll Sisters.

[W. D. MCCARTHY]

MARYKNOLL SISTERS

Also known as Maryknoll Missioners (MM), a religious congregation with papal approbation, whose official title is Maryknoll Sisters of St. Dominic (see *Official Catholic Directory* [2470]). They devote themselves to catechetical, educational, medical, and social work in non-Christian and Christian countries. This first American Catholic community for women devoted exclusively to foreign missions began in 1912 with a group of laywomen who volunteered to help Rev. James A. WALSH, leader of the new Catholic Foreign Mission Society of America (*see* MARYKNOLL FATHERS AND BROTHERS), with the publication activities of the society's monthly, the *Field Afar.* By 1920 they numbered about 30, and, aided by Walsh and Father (later archbishop) John T. McNicholas OP, the community received canonical recognition as "The Foreign Mission Sisters of St. Dominic." Sister Fidelia Delaney of the Dominican Sisters of Sinsinawa, Wis., was the first novice mistress. Mother Mary Joseph ROGERS, one of the original helpers for *Field Afar,* and foundress of the congregation became the first superior and mother general. Twenty-two made first vows in February of 1921. In June, six were assigned to South China to collaborate in the apostolic work of the Maryknoll priests. The Holy See extended papal recognition with a *decretum laudes* in 1954.

The Second World War and subsequent communist seizure of many Far Eastern areas interrupted or destroyed many of the congregation's most promising endeavors. Nonetheless, numbers increased and by 1965 the sisters were engaged in ministry in Africa, the Far East, Central and South America, the United States, and the islands of the Pacific. The Eucharist and the Liturgy of the Hours are the center of the sisters' prayer life. A firmly established contemplative branch is an integral part of the community. In a number of areas indigenous religious communities have been formed with the congregation's direction. From the very beginning, the Maryknoll sisters were also open to the membership of the Catholic women of all nationalities who were seeking to follow a call to cross-cultural mission.

The post-Vatican II years brought an emphasis to strong educational and professional preparation of the sisters as well as an end to rapid growth. To meet the *aggiornamento* mandated by Vatican II, the sisters formulated new criteria that reaffirmed their dedication to missionary activity, the ''preferential option for the poor,'' the promotion of women in all cultures, works devoted to peace with justice, a serious commitment to interreligious dialogue and ministries to persons with AIDS. The sisters strive toward more effective evangelization through an integrated witness of Christian presence of life, word, and ministry in service of and to the Gospel. For the congregation, then as now, ''Mission is a total way of life.''

Bibliography: C. KENNEDY, *To the Uttermost Parts of the Earth: The Spirit and Charism of Mary Josephine Rogers* (Maryknoll, N.Y. 1980). P. LERNOUX, *Hearts on Fire: The Story of the Maryknoll Sisters* (Maryknoll, N.Y. 1993). J. M. LYONS, *Maryknoll's First Lady: The Life of Mother Mary Joseph, Foundress of the Maryknoll Sisters* (Garden City, N.Y. 1967). M. J. ROGERS, *Discourses of Mother Mary Joseph Rogers, M.M., Foundress, Maryknoll Sisters*, compiled by SR. MARY COLEMAN and staff, 4 v. (Maryknoll, N.Y. 1982). J.-P. WIEST, *Maryknoll in China: A History, 1918–1955* (Armonk, N.Y. 1988).

[J. M. LYONS/C. KENNEDY]

MARYLAND, CATHOLIC CHURCH IN

One of the 13 original colonies and seventh to ratify the Constitution of the United States (April 28, 1788), Maryland is situated on the Atlantic seaboard, bounded on the north by Pennsylvania and Delaware, on the east by Delaware and the Atlantic Ocean, on the south by Virginia and West Virginia, and on the west by West Virginia. Annapolis is its capital, and Baltimore, Cumberland, and Hagerstown are the state's chief industrial centers. Fishing predominates in the Chesapeake Bay area, and farming and mineral processing are important in the state's economy. In recent decades many high technology and other service industry companies that conduct business with the federal government have set up operations in the state in order to be close to the nation's capital.

History. The founding of the palatinate and proprietary colony of Maryland (1634), named in honor of Henrietta Maria, queen of Charles I of England, was the work of the first Lord Baltimore, George Calvert, and of his son and heir, Cecil Calvert (*see* CALVERT).

Colonial Period. In the charter signed in 1632 by the second Lord Baltimore, the proprietor was granted broad and generous powers, with provision made also for a representative form of government through an assembly of all freemen. Despite opposition from the Virginia Company and the Puritans, the expedition, under Leonard Calvert as governor, sailed from Gravesend on the *Ark* and the *Dove* with 128 persons aboard, the usual oaths being administered. Approximately 72 others joined the expedition before the vessels sailed on Nov. 22, 1633, from Cowes on the Isle of Wight. Since the oath contained material objectionable to Catholics, it is likely that many if not most of those boarding at Cowes were Catholics. Two Jesuits, Andrew WHITE and John Altham, accompanied the expedition; White's *Relatio Itineris* constitutes a prime source for the early history of the colony, which was founded in March of 1634 at St. Mary's, between the Potomac River and Chesapeake Bay.

From the beginning Calvert insisted on religious tolerance and separation of Church and State; all Christians were welcomed to the colony, and Jews were tacitly admitted. Treaties were made with the Native Americans, and for some years relations with them remained friendly. A problem arose, however, when a large element in Virginia headed by William Claiborne, who had already established trading posts on Kent Island in Chesapeake Bay within Baltimore's jurisdiction, refused to recognize Maryland's authority. It took two expeditions (1635 and 1638) to reduce the island; but subsequently (1645), when Richard Ingle, posing as a champion of Parliament and the Protestant cause, attacked and terrorized Calvert's colonists, the governor fled for a time to Virginia. White and his Jesuit companions were seized, their property sequestered, and the priests sent in chains to England to stand trial.

After Leonard Calvert reconquered his colony, increasing numbers of Puritans from Virginia sought and obtained refuge in Maryland, settling mainly near Annapolis, then called Providence. The toleration act of 1649, entitled ''An Act Concerning Religion,'' was designed to protect Catholics and others from the rising Puritan hostility in the colony and in England. In fact, however, it was less liberal than Baltimore's previous religious policy (*see* TOLERATION ACTS OF 1639 AND 1649, MARYLAND). By 1651 the Puritan element was strong enough to overthrow the authority of Baltimore; and until 1657 the colony, beset by turmoil and invasion, was in the hands of parliamentarians and Puritans. Help came to Cecil Calvert when Oliver CROMWELL began to question the acts of his adherents in Maryland and in 1657 returned the palatinate to Baltimore. When Charles, the heir of Cecil Calvert, became governor in 1660, there were about 12,000 colonists in Maryland, a total that increased to 20,000 during the next 10 years. The tobacco economy became established in the whole Chesapeake area, and there were a few iron furnaces; but the main industry was agriculture.

The Old Saint Joseph's Church, built in 1782, stands in Queen Anne, Maryland. (©Lee Snider/CORBIS)

Under Charles, who became the proprietor in 1675 at the death of his father, the colony enjoyed an era of relative peace and prosperity until the REVOLUTION OF 1688 in England. Thereafter, the proprietary government in Maryland was overthrown, and it became a royal colony, with Sir Lionel Copley as first royal governor (1691). After his arrival in 1692, the assembly abolished the practice of religious toleration and established the Anglican Church, which lasted until the revolution. In 1702 a limited toleration was granted to Dissenters and Quakers. A test act was imposed against Catholics in 1692, and an act of 1704 forbade Catholics to practice their religion. In 1715 and in 1729 laws provided that the Catholic survivor of a marriage should have any children removed from his care for the purpose of Protestant upbringing. In 1718 a severe law forbade to Catholics the franchise and the holding of governmental posts. A law in 1756 provided, among other disabilities, that any property then held by priests should be taken from them; the law provided also for double taxation on all Catholics.

Revolutionary and Post-Revolutionary Years. Charles, Lord Baltimore, died on Feb. 20, 1715, at the age of 85. He was succeeded by his son, Benedict Leonard, who had renounced his faith in favor of Anglicanism. When Benedict died April 15, 1715, his son, Charles II, Lord Baltimore, became proprietor under the terms of the original charter, and Maryland ceased to be a royal colony and again became proprietary. The famous boundary dispute between the Lords Baltimore and the Penns involved prolonged litigation and was not settled until the two proprietors engaged Charles Mason and Jeremiah Dixon, who, between 1763 and 1767, determined the line, later named after them. In the stirring times between 1763 and 1775, Maryland played the usual colonial role, repudiating the Stamp Act and passing resolves denouncing taxation without representation and claiming that the Assembly alone could tax the province. The colony took

Exterior of Catholic Cathedral, Baltimore. (AP/Wide World Photos)

part also in the nonimportation agreement and in the formation of committees of correspondence. Annapolis had its own tea party in October 1774, with the burning of the *Peggy Stewart.* During the administration of the last proprietary governor, Sir Robert Eden (1768–76), the famous debate took place between Daniel Dulany and Charles CARROLL of Carrollton over the question of officers' fees. When Carroll, a Catholic, had the better of the argument, not only was the popular side greatly strengthened but sympathy was won for the Catholic cause.

In June 1774, at the convention at Annapolis, delegates were appointed to the Continental Congress, one of whom was Charles Carroll. On June 28, 1776, the Maryland delegation was empowered to vote for independence. The first state constitution was adopted in 1776; sec. 33 of the Bill of Rights stated that all persons professing the Christian religion were equally entitled to protection of law. In the war that followed, Maryland regiments fought from Bunker Hill to Yorktown; the ''Old Line State'' is a fitting description of the military services of the Maryland Line during the revolution. The clashing interests of Maryland and Virginia resulted in the Mount Vernon and Annapolis meetings, which in turn resulted in the great Philadelphia Constitutional Convention (May 1787). One of the signers of this document was a third prominent CARROLL, DANIEL. Maryland ratified this document, and Charles Carroll was elected senator from Maryland. In 1791 Maryland ceded to the U.S. government its present site, the District of Columbia. During the War of 1812, the attack on Ft. McHenry in Baltimore harbor inspired Frances Scott Key to write ''The Star Spangled Banner.'' Between 1815 and 1860 the state expanded as a commercial and maritime entity, attracting a large and steady stream of immigrants. In turn a strong nativist sentiment developed, and in 1854 the American party elected a mayor of Baltimore (*see* NATIVISM, AMERICAN).

The fateful presidential election of 1860 reflected clearly the divided sentiment of Maryland, a border state. With secession Maryland's position was difficult—growing industrial and commercial ties bound the state to the North and the Union; its large and wealthy tidewater was the home of slavery and agriculture. A Marylander, James Ryder Randall, living in New Orleans, gave the state its song, ''Maryland, My Maryland,'' a consequence of the bloody riots in Baltimore on April 19, 1861. The former slave, renowned abolitionist, and civil rights leader, Frederick Douglass, was born in Maryland.

"First Mass in Maryland," which occurred March 25, 1634, from 19th-century engraving. (©The Granger Collection)

Harriet Tubman, the intrepid free black woman, who led hundreds of slaves to freedom, was also a native of the state. In the state constitution drawn up in 1864 provisions were made to end slavery, for increased representation for Baltimore, and for a state system of education. Since the Civil War the growth of the state has paced that of the nation, although after World War II, the state's growth exceeded that of the country. The steel industry, ship building, and aircraft manufacturing contributed heavily to the growth and expansion of the Baltimore area. The expansion of the federal government in Washington during the second half of the 20th century has precipitated rapid population growth in the neighboring Maryland counties. Combined, the Baltimore-Washington corridor is one of the largest metropolitan areas in the country. Improved facilities in transportation and communication have done much to weld Maryland's population and scattered areas into one.

After the Revolution the total population of Maryland was about 319,700, of whom approximately 15,000 were Catholics. The Archdiocese of Washington, erected in 1939, includes in its boundaries five Maryland counties, along with the nation's capital. The Diocese of Wilmington, Delaware, erected in 1868, includes eight Maryland counties on the eastern shore of Chesapeake Bay. The bishops of these three dioceses comprise the Maryland Catholic Conference and together they have lobbied the state government on education and social justice issues. The projected population of the state of Maryland in 2000 was 5,314,450, and it was estimated that the Catholic percentage has remained at approximately 20 percent for some time.

Education. From the foundation of Maryland, the Jesuits have been in the forefront of Catholic education in Maryland. Bishop John Carroll's designs and hopes for a college for his diocese were realized when Georgetown opened in what is now part of the District of Columbia in 1791. Four Sulpicians, including F. C. Nagot, landed in Baltimore in July 1791, and on October 3, St. Mary's Seminary opened. The Sulpicians opened St. Mary's College in 1799 as a preparatory seminary. This institution closed in 1852 to be succeeded by Loyola College. Mt. St. Mary's Seminary and College was opened in 1808. For women, the Georgetown Visitation Academy opened in what is now the District of Columbia in 1799 and St. Joseph's College, St. Elizabeth Ann Seton's establishment, opened in 1808 at Emmitsburg. The Christian Brothers opened Rock Hill College, Ellicott City, in 1865. In the course of time additional educational institutions were opened by various congregations, including a college at Woodstock (1867) by the Jesuits for training their own members, Calvert Hall College (1845) and La Salle Institute in Cumberland by the Christian Brothers, and Mt. St. Joseph's College by the Xaverian Brothers. Prominent among the earlier girls' schools are the College of Notre Dame of Maryland (1873), conducted by the School Sisters of Notre Dame, and Mt. St. Agnes College (1867), conducted by the Sisters of Mercy. The state currently has three Catholic colleges: Mt. St. Mary's, Loyola, and Notre Dame of Maryland, which remains a college for women. These three colleges had a total enrollment of 11,428 students at the end of the millennium.

Bibliography: R. T. CONLEY, *The Truth in Charity: A History of the Archdiocese of Washington* (Signe 2001). T. W. SPALDING, *The Premier See: A History of the Archdiocese of Baltimore, 1789–1989* (Baltimore 1989). P. K. GUILDAY, *The Life and Times of John Carroll: Archbishop of Baltimore, 1735–1815,* 2 v. (New York 1927). A. M. MELVILLE, *John Carroll of Baltimore* (New York 1955). R. BRUGGER et al., *Maryland: A Middle Temperament, 1634–1980* (Baltimore 1996). R. WALSH and W. L. FOX, *Maryland: A History, 1632–1974* (Baltimore 1974).

[J. J. TIERNEY/R. T. CONLEY]

MARYMOUNT COLLEGES AND UNIVERSITIES

A number of institutions of higher education in the United States sponsored by the Religious of the SACRED

HEART OF MARY (R.S.H.M.) have their roots in the tradition established by Mother Marie Joseph BUTLER, the founder of Marymount College in Tarrytown, N.Y. Mindful of Father Gailhac's advice to study and adapt to all that is good in local customs, the R.S.H.M. in North America became deeply involved in that uniquely American institution, the parochial school system. Their involvement in higher education dates from the founding of Marymount College in 1907. Butler created a place of learning where women could grow and receive an education that would prepare them for leadership and influence in society. Marymount was the first women's college to establish a study abroad program. A pioneer in women's education, in 2000 Marymount entered into a process of consolidation with Fordham University to become Marymount College of Fordham University.

Marymount Manhattan College began in 1936 as the city campus of Marymount College Tarrytown. Located in New York City, it became a four-year branch in 1948. In 1961 Marymount Manhattan College was separately incorporated. As an urban, independent undergraduate liberal arts college, it offers strong programs in the arts and sciences for students of all ages, as well as preprofessional preparation.

In 1923, the Religious of the Sacred Heart of Mary expanded to Los Angeles. Ten years later Marymount College opened as a two-year institution which in 1948 was chartered by the State of California as a four-year institution. In 1960 it moved to the Palos Verdes Peninsula, and in 1968 Marymount College moved again, this time to the campus of Loyola University. Five years later, the two became a single institution, Loyola Marymount University. Marymount Palos Verdes, a two-year college, was established at the same time on its present site. In 1983, Marymount College Palos Verdes added a weekend college to its programs.

At the request of Peter Ireton, Bishop of Richmond, Marymount University in Arlington, Va., began as a two-year liberal arts college for women in 1950. In 1973 it became a four-year college. With the inauguration of its first graduate program in 1979, it admitted its first male students. In 1986 Marymount moved to university status and became fully co-educational. As an independent, comprehensive Catholic university, combining a liberal arts tradition with career preparation, Marymount University is marked by the heritage of the Religious of the Sacred Heart of Mary, by its proximity to the nation's capital, and by its creative and enterprising spirit.

Each of these five institutions has its own relationship to the Religious of the Sacred Heart of Mary. All R.S.H.M. colleges and universities continue to be marked by an emphasis on a liberal arts education; internationality and respect for all cultures; care and concern for the total growth of the person; attention to justice which respects the rights and responsibilities of all persons; spiritual and ethical formation; and a special commitment to the education of women. Throughout its nearly century-long involvement in American higher education, the Religious of the Sacred Heart of Mary have endeavored to collaborate with others in educating students in this heritage, forming them to take responsibility for their own lives and making a positive contribution to the society and culture of their times.

[M. MILLIGAN]

MASÍAS, JUAN, ST.

Dominican brother; b. Rivera, Plasencia, Estremadura, Spain, March 2, 1585; d. Lima, Sept. 26, 1645. Orphaned at an early age, Masías worked as a shepherd to help care for his brothers. He continued in this occupation, leading a life of prayer under the patronage of St. John the Evangelist, until he was 21, when he felt inspired to go to America. He sailed from Seville in the service of a merchant, but was abandoned in Cartagena because he was illiterate. From there he made his way to Lima, where he entered the service of Pedro Jiménez Menacho, who put him to work caring for his cattle and sheep in the foothills of San Cristóbal. Again in the solitude of the fields, he resumed his life of prayer.

Masías (Macías) was inspired to ask for admission as a brother to the Recoleta Dominicana de Santa María Magdalena, and he received the habit on Jan. 22, 1622, from the prior, Salvador Ramírez. From his entrance into the order until his death, he served as porter. Every day the poor would come to him to receive bread. The convent in Lima still preserves the basket that he used for this ministration. He spent his free time praying in a hidden place in the orchard, a place he called Gethsemane. Prayer, penance, and charity unified the life of Juan Masías. He was declared blessed by GREGORY XVI on Jan. 31, 1837, and canonized by Paul VI on Sept. 28, 1975.

Feast: Sept. 18.

Bibliography: J. CIPOLLETI, *Vida del Beato Fray Juan Masías* (Cuzco 1949). A. LOBATO, *Yo, fray Juan Masías, hermano de los pobres* (Caracas 1986). V. OSENDE, *Vida del Beato Juan Masías* (Lima 1918). M. F. WINDEATT, *Warrior in White: The Story of Blessed John Masias* (New York 1944).

[J. M. VARGAS]

MASS, DRY

The medieval *Missa sicca* was a quasi–liturgical custom patterned on the Mass. The first certain mention of it is found in the 9th–century pontifical of Prudentius (d. 861), Bishop of Troyes. It was also discussed by William Durand (d. 1296), Bishop of Mende. It consisted of the recitation of prayers and readings from the Mass of the day by a priest, sometimes fully vested, sometimes wearing only a stole, and with the omission of the Mass parts from Offertory to Communion inclusive. It seemed to have enjoyed some popularity in pre–Reformation France, both in monasteries, where priest–monks sometimes celebrated after the conventual Mass as a private devotion, and in parish churches, as an embellishment of, or even a substitute for, the Eucharistic Sacrifice. Instances of the latter usage were at weddings, funerals, a gathering of huntsmen for the chase, or voyaging at sea—occasions when a complete Mass service might have been deemed inconvenient or impossible.

At Milan, the Palm Sunday procession used to halt at various churches in the city for a service resembling a dry Mass. In fact, the blessing of palms on Palm Sunday in the Roman rite was given a place in such a *Missa sicca* until Pius XII promulgated his *Holy Week Ordo* in 1956. Because of the danger of extremes, the general practice was condemned by theologians and synods, and eventually died out.

Bibliography: G. DURANDI, *Rationale divinorum officiorum* (Lyons 1560) 4:1. P. BROWE, ''Messa senza consacrazione e communione,'' *Ephemerides liturgicae* 50 (1936) 124–132.

[M. DUCEY/EDS.]

MASSACHUSETTS, CATHOLIC CHURCH IN

Archdiocese/Diocese	Year Created
Archdiocese of Boston	1875
Diocese of Fall River	1904
Diocese of Springfield in Massachusetts	1870
Diocese of Worcester	1950

One of the 13 original colonies, located in northeastern United States, bounded on the north by Vermont and New Hampshire, on the east and south by the Atlantic Ocean, on the south by Rhode Island and Connecticut, and on the west by New York. Boston is the capital and principal metropolis of the Commonwealth, the state's official designation. Other large cities include Worcester, Springfield, and Cambridge. In 2001 the Catholic population of Massachusetts was 2,968,693, about 48 percent of the total. In addition to the Archdiocese of Boston (1808), there were three other dioceses: Springfield (1870), Fall River (1904), and Worcester (1950).

Early History. The area was first settled by English religious dissenters. The Pilgrims, or Separatists, under John Carver and William BRADFORD, founded a colony in Plymouth (1620). The Puritans, or Congregationalists, led by John Endicott and John Winthrop, and under a charter for the Massachusetts Bay Colony, settled in Salem (1628) and Boston (1630). Hundreds of colonists followed Winthrop during the 1630s, and by the end of the decade the Bay Colony had 25,000 settlers and was the largest English colony in North America. The Puritan leaders established a Bible commonwealth based on CALVINISM. Congregational Church polity was transferred to the political system, and self-government developed in the towns. ''No man shall be admitted to the freedom of this body,'' declared the General Court, ''but such as are members of the [Congregational] church.'' Those who did not subscribe to Congregationalism were permitted to reside in the Bay Colony, but were not allowed to take an active role in the governance of the colony. Roman Catholics, however, along with Quakers and Jews, were not permitted in the colony at all. The Bible commonwealth, as planned, did not survive the 17th century, and control of the Congregational churches was further weakened by the Charter of 1691, ruling that representatives of the general court were to be elected on the basis of property rather than religious affiliation. Nevertheless, the Puritans, with their zeal for religion, intense hostility to the Catholic religion and practices, concern for education, and strict moral attitudes, dominated New England. Massachusetts took the lead in the events that led to the War for Independence, and the Battles of Lexington and Bunker Hill in 1775 marked that war's beginning. Maine remained a district of Massachusetts until 1820, when it entered the union under the Missouri Compromise.

Early Catholicism. Catholics avoided Massachusetts during the colonial period; especially after laws passed in 1647 and 1700 forbade Catholic priests to reside in the colony under pain of imprisonment and execution. The approximately 1,200 exiled Acadians assigned (1755–56) to Massachusetts were scattered among the towns, where they were gradually assimilated or from which they eventually escaped. Thanks largely to an alliance and friendship with France during the War for Independence, Americans became more tolerant of Roman Catholics, and by the time independence was achieved, a small group of French and Irish residents organized a small congregation and began holding services. While the new Massachusetts Constitution of 1780 provided a bill of rights guaranteeing ''equal protection of the law'' to all religious denominations, it required that all state officials swear that they were not subject to the authority of any ''foreign prince, person, prelate, state, or poten-

St. Stephen's Catholic Church, Boston. The church was originally Congregationalist. (©Kevin Fleming/CORBIS)

tate.'' Since all Protestants still assumed that Catholics were subject to both pope and prelate, this clause automatically excluded them from holding public office in Massachusetts until 1821, when the test was finally removed.

The Diocese of Boston. Despite the continued existence of political limitations, the number of Catholics continued to increase in Massachusetts, and in 1808 the Diocese of Boston was established with Frenchman Jean Lefebvre de CHEVERUS as its first bishop. The first diocese encompassed all of New England, extending from Buzzards Bay and Nantucket Sound in the south to Maine and the Canadian border in the north. Twelve years later, there were an estimated 3,850 Catholics in New England, including several Native American settlements in northern Maine whose members had been converted earlier by the French and who now came under the jurisdiction of the Bishop of Boston. When Benedict Joseph FENWICK succeeded Cheverus as bishop of Boston in 1825, he found himself in charge of the smallest and weakest of the nine dioceses that existed in the United States at that time. In all New England there were only eight churches, and the larger part of the Catholic population was still restricted to the Boston area. As the result of repressive land policies in the British Isles after the Napoleonic wars, the number of Irish immigrants coming to the United States grew so rapidly that Fenwick had to build several new churches in the city.

The sudden rise in the number of Irish Catholics created considerable anxiety among native Bostonians, who feared the social and economic impact of unskilled workers and resented their religious beliefs. During the summer of 1825, roving gangs of vandals broke windows, damaged furniture, and actually destroyed several small houses in the Irish district. In 1834, a local mob burned down the Ursuline Convent in nearby Charlestown; and in 1837 groups of Yankees and Irish residents clashed in downtown Boston in what became known as the Broad Street Riot.

Roman Catholicism also began to spread to other parts of Massachusetts during this same period. By the mid-1820s, for example, a number of Irish immigrants were moving some 45 miles north of Boston in search of work at locations along the Merrimack River, where new textile factories were being constructed by Boston investors. Irish workers from Boston, along with French-speaking Catholic workmen from Canada, soon made up a sizeable portion of the work force in such towns as Lowell and Lawrence, digging the canals and constructing the buildings. Acquiring a site of land near the Western Canal, on July 3, 1831, Bishop Fenwick dedicated St. Patrick's Church as further evidence of Catholic expansion. Between 1828 and 1830 he supervised the dedication of churches in Newport and Pawtucket, Rhode Island, as well as in New Bedford, Massachusetts. To serve a group of Irish glasssworkers who had moved to Sandwich, Fenwick had a small frame church constructed in Boston and shipped by water to the Cape Cod town. On June 17, 1830, he dedicated Holy Trinity, the first Catholic church in Connecticut. And all the while, he continued to minister to Native American populations at Old Town and Eastport, Maine.

Failing health did not prevent Bishop Fenwick from traveling incessantly during the 1840s, administering the sacrament of Confirmation in Lowell; dedicating a new church in Fall River; up to Vermont for another new church; down to Providence, Rhode Island, and then to Bridgeport, Connecticut. In September 1842 he dedicated a new church in Quincy, Massachusetts, and the following month he was in Lowell to dedicate St. Peter's Church. In 1842, Fenwick purchased property in Worcester, Massachusetts, for the site of the college he had always dreamed of—the College of the Holy Cross—named after the original church in Boston.

The Famine Years. Even though the Boston diocese lost some ten thousand Catholics when Fenwick detached Connecticut and Rhode Island in 1844, there were still nearly seventy thousand left in the remaining four states that John Fitzpatrick took over when he succeeded Fenwick in 1846. Massachusetts alone contained over fifty thousand Catholics, with nearly thirty thousand in the capital city. "In Boston, we are sadly off for want of churches," complained the new bishop as he proceeded to add to the number of churches in the diocese. In August 1846 he dedicated St. Joseph's Church in Roxbury, and a short time later saw the completion of Holy Trinity Church for German immigrants in the South End. As the terrible aftereffects of the Great Famine brought additional Irish-Catholic immigrants to the shores of America during the late 1840s, Bishop Fitzpatrick was kept busy creating new parishes and dedicating new churches in other parts of Massachusetts. On the north shore, new pastors were sent in to take charge of expanding Catholic populations in Chelsea and Lynn; St. Mary's Church in Salem was made responsible for mission stations in Marblehead, Gloucester, and Ipswich. On the south shore, St. Mary's Church in West Quincy provided a focal point for people in Quincy, Braintree, Weymouth, and Milton, for residents of Randolph and Stoughton, for those in Hingham and Cohasset, and for communities as south as Plymouth. Because of the increase in textile manufacturing, Fall River showed an amazing growth, and in August 1840 the Church of St. John the Baptist was constructed to serve the estimated one thousand Catholics in that area. To the west of Boston, things went even more rapidly. Before 1840, there had not been a single church or chapel west of Worcester. By the time Fitzpatrick took office in 1846, however, there were brand new churches at Cabotville, Pittsfield, Northampton, and Springfield. The number of Catholics in the city of Worcester alone had risen to nearly two thousand, and in June of 1846 Fitzpatrick dedicated the Church of St. John the Evangelist. But it was the region along the Merrimack River that had the most dramatic increase in numbers. The expanding textile center was attracting many Irish immigrant workers, and by 1841 the Catholic population of Lowell was estimated to have reached four thousand, requiring Bishop Fenwick to add St. Peter's Church in 1842 to the original St. Patrick's Church he had constructed ten years earlier. The nearby textile city of Lawrence, too, experienced a population explosion, going from fewer than two hundred Catholics in 1845 to over six thousand by 1848. At this time, the jurisdiction of the bishop of Boston included not only the commonwealth of Massachusetts, but also the states of Vermont, New Hampshire, and Maine. Vermont was the most populous of the three, but its five thousand Catholics were widely dispersed, with few churches and only a handful of priests. Most parishes were concentrated in the extreme northwestern parts of the state near the town of Burlington, where Fenwick had dedicated St. Peter's Church in 1841. In New Hampshire, the small number of Catholics received little attention until the Amoskeag Manufacturing Company began its textile operations at Manchester in 1839. After that it became necessary for an itinerant priest to say Mass on a regular basis until the bishop of Boston could work out a more permanent arrangement. With well over forty-five thousand Catholics, Maine ranked second to Vermont in northern New England, and during the 1830s its growing population resulted in new churches at Dover, Portland, and Eastport. As a result of the sale of valuable timber land, the town of Bangor experienced a speculative boom that attracted about a thousand new Catholics for whom

St. Michael's Church was built in 1839. There were also small Catholic communities at Ellsworth, West Mathias, and Lubec, with a small church at Houlton meeting the needs of those who lived close to the Canadian border. In addition to Catholics of European lineage, Bishop Fitzpatrick was also responsible for the Penobscot and Passamaquoddy tribes in the northern regions.

The continued influx of foreigners into the United States during the late 1840s and 1850s and the success of Catholic prelates in gaining some measure of social and economic benefits for their parishioners convinced many native-born Americans that they had to stem the immigrant tide. In 1852, a number of nativist groups formed the American party—more popularly known as the Know-Nothing party—to prevent further immigration and to keep immigrant-Americans in a subservient position. Despite an amazing burst of power in Massachusetts and other northern states during 1854 and 1855, the emergence of the slavery issue caused the party to fail completely in its attempt to nominate a presidential candidate in 1856. The slavery controversy continued to provoke hostilities between the states of the North and the South, and in November 1860 the election of Republican candidate Abraham Lincoln led to the secession of southern states from the Union. On the morning of April 12, 1861, with the bombardment of Fort Sumter, a federal fort in Charleston Harbor, the Civil War began. With the outbreak of war, Irish Catholics rushed to join fight to preserve the Union. With the approval of Governor John A. Andrew, Catholic leaders in Boston were encouraged to form a separate regiment of Irish soldiers. Companies from Boston, joined by military units from Salem, Milford, Marlboro, and Stoughton, banded together to form the 9th Regiment, Massachusetts Voluntary Infantry. In response to the gallant efforts of the ''Fighting Ninth,'' Governor Andrew approved recruitment for a second all-Irish regiment—the 28th—that was sworn into service in December 1861 and became one of the five regiments that made up the Irish Brigade. The impressive patriotism displayed by Boston Catholics, the heroism of Irish troops on the battlefield, and the support they received from loyal Catholic citizens did much to create a higher level of tolerance throughout the state. Bishop John Fitzpatrick was awarded an honorary degree from Harvard college, Catholic clergymen were permitted to attend patients in public institutions, and Catholic school children were no longer forced to read the Protestant version of the Bible in the public schools.

Immigration and Diocesan Development. Once the Civil War was over, large-scale immigration resumed, and additional numbers of Catholic immigrants joined earlier arrivals in spreading across the state of Massachusetts. Following the death of Bishop Fitzpatrick in 1866, his friend Fr. John J. WILLIAMS took over as bishop and began making arrangements for an expanding diocese. As early as 1868, he asked Rome's permission to divide the diocese of Boston. He proposed to separate the five counties of western and central Massachusetts and form them into a new diocese with Springfield as its see city. In 1870, Pope Pius IX signed the bull creating the diocese of Springfield. Patrick Thomas O'Reilly (1870–92), a native of Ireland, was consecrated the first bishop of the new diocese and was succeeded by Thomas Beaven, a native of Springfield (1892–1920). At the time the diocese was created there were nearly 100,000 Catholics in the area; that number more than doubled by 1900.

At the same time Bishop Williams suggested another diocese that would encompass Rhode Island and three counties in southeastern Massachusetts. In 1872 Rome established the diocese of Providence, Rhode Island. It grew so fast that in 1904 the three Massachusetts counties were formed into the diocese of Fall River. In his brief tenure, William Stang, the first bishop of Fall River (1904–1907) wrote three pastoral letters, summoned a diocesan synod and, within two months of its publication, began implementing *Acerbo nimis*, Pope Pius X's instruction on catechesis.

Despite these geographic divisions, the diocese of Boston was still growing at such a remarkable rate that on February 12, 1875, Pope Pius IX approved the transformation of Boston from a diocese into an archdiocese, and Bishop John William was elevated to the rank of archbishop. The new ecclesiastical province included all the dioceses of New England.

As Catholics increased in numbers during the late 1870s and early 1880s they were beginning to move up from political positions at the local level to more significant places in city, state, and even national government. In 1881, for example, the city of Lawrence chose John Breen as its first Catholic mayor; the following year the city of Lowell elected John J. Donovan as mayor; in 1884 Boston chose Hugh O'Brien as the first Irish-born, Roman Catholic mayor of the city. In 1894, John F. Fitzgerald of Boston's North End was elected to the U.S. House of Representatives from the 9th congressional district and Joseph F. O'Connell of Dorchester went to Washington from the 10th congressional district. The impoverished conditions of the immigrants during the 1850s, followed by the disruptive years of the Civil War during the 1860s, had caused earlier prelates to go slow in the building of Catholics schools. Archbishop John Williams, however, undertook the creation of a parochial school system throughout the archdiocese, and in 1884 reported to the Third Baltimore Council that 35 of his parishes had parochial schools, with many more to follow. The two dominant teaching communities in the archdiocese of Boston were the Sisters of Notre Dame de Namur, who had arrived in Boston in 1848, and the Sisters of St. Joseph who arrived in 1873.

The New Immigrants. It was in the late 1880s and early 1890s that the character of immigrants to Massachusetts changed dramatically. During the early part of the 19th century, most immigrants to the United States had come from northern and western Europe. In the late 1880s, the bulk of people entering the country came from southern and eastern Europe. Fleeing high taxes, low wages, drought, famine, political oppression, and religious persecution, these new immigrants came to America seeking liberty and opportunity. In the decade between 1900 and 1910, over 150,000 Italians entered the Bay State, along with some 80,000 Poles and nearly 25,000 Lithuanians. Many newcomers were Roman Catholics who settled in various parts of Massachusetts and who posed challenges to a Church that was overwhelmingly Irish in its clerical personnel and its cultural institutions. Sensitive to the desires of these non-English-speaking groups to have their own churches, their own priests, sermons in their own languages, and observances of their own religious feast days, Archbishop Williams permitted them as much national expression as possible in their religious observances, while keeping their new churches and their congregations under his episcopal authority.

There had been a small but active German-speaking community in Boston before the Civil War, and in 1872 Archbishop Williams laid the cornerstone to a new Holy Trinity Church that enlarged the original church that had been constructed in 1844. The number of French-speaking immigrants had also expanded after the Civil War, when the numerous textile mills in the Merrimack Valley began hiring immigrants from Europe as well as from Canada. In 1868, Archbishop Williams recruited French-speaking Oblates of Mary Immaculate to staff the first French parish of St. Joseph (later changed to St. Jean Baptiste) in Lowell. To further accommodate Canadian immigrants, the archbishop brought the MARIST FATHERS to Haverhill in the 1870s. After later assuming responsibility for St. Anne's parish in Lawrence, in 1885 the Marists purchased a site in Boston's Back Bay for the construction of the Church of Notre Dame des Victoires, popularly known as ''the French Church.'' Archbishop Williams also responded to the arrival, between 1899 and 1910, of over 45,000 Portuguese immigrants. He brought in several Portuguese-speaking priests to serve their spiritual needs while they lived in Boston's North End, and later support Portuguese parishes in Cambridge and in Lowell. By the turn of the century, nearly ten thousand Polish immigrants had settled in the Greater Boston area, and in 1894 a Polish-speaking priest named Fr. John Chmielinski dedicated the church of Our Lady of Czestochowa in the Boston area, and also ministered to groups of Polish immigrants in Lowell and Salem. From 1893 to 1918, Archbishop Williams and his successor Archbishop William O'CONNELL sanctioned as many as 15 Polish parishes, despite occasional efforts by separatist Polish groups to establish independent national churches. During the same period, about one thousand Lithuanian immigrants settled in the South Boston peninsula, and were provided with a young Lithuanian priest who established St. Joseph's Church, but whose controversial nature led a number of parishioners to erect a church of their own (St. Peter's). Five other Lithuanian parishes were established in various parts of the archdiocese—in Brockton, Lawrence, Lowell, Cambridge, and Norwood—places where Lithuanian immigrants had gone in search of work. The largest of the new immigrant groups arriving in Massachusetts came from Italy. As early as 1886, the average number of Italian immigrants had already reached 222,000, with many of the newcomers settling in Boston. At first they congregated along the waterfront in the city's North End, where the Italian population grew from a thousand in 1880 to seven thousand in 1895. As their numbers grew, it became obvious that steps would have to be taken to meet their spiritual needs. In 1876, St. Leonard's Church was constructed in the North End, with Franciscans providing the services; later, the Church of the Sacred Heart was established and placed under the direction of the Missionaries of St. Charles. Both churches developed parochial grammar schools, and also provided social clubs and religious centers for the predominantly Italian neighborhood that featured yearly outdoor festivals honoring various patron saints.

The Twentieth Century. On Feb. 2, 1907 Bishop Stang of Fall River died; he was succeeded by the Most Rev. Daniel F. Feehan (1907–1934). Later that same year, after 41 years of service as fourth bishop and first archbishop of Boston, Archbishop Williams died (August 30) and was succeed by William Henry O'Connell, bishop of Portland, Maine. Both Feehan and O'Connell came on the scene at a time that the Church in Massachusetts was expanding rapidly. At the time of his accession, Archbishop O'Connell assumed responsibility for an archdiocese that covered about 2500 square miles, and served some 850,000 Catholics. The archdiocese contained almost two hundred parish churches, had nearly six thousand priests, and almost 1600 sisters of various religious orders. Fifty thousand students attended church-related schools, from the elementary grades to the college level, and some 70,000 cases a year were being handled by various hospitals and charitable agencies operated by the archdiocese. In addition to increasing the number of parishes in the city of Boston, a series of new churches went up in other parts of the state. From Winthrop and Revere, to Lynnfield, Danvers, and Newburyport, the spires of new churches marked the Catholic movement into north shore areas. The archdiocese was kept busy supplying priests and building churches for new immigrant families moving into the textile centers of Lowell and Lawrence, as well as into the neighboring communities of North Andover, Tewksbury, and Dracut. South of Boston, St. John's Church in Quincy was the basis of a network of other churches and mission stations, while new parishes went up in the nearby towns of Braintree, Weymouth, Milton, and Randolph. Along the seashore areas of Hull, Cohasset, amd Scituate, as well as Plymouth, Kingston, and Duxbury, a number of new churches were constructed, and several temporary missions were converted into parishes. With numerous industries in the Brockton area offering employment for unskilled European immigrants, several large churches went up in Brockton itself, as well as in such nearby towns as Whitman, Bridgewater, and Middleboro. During this same period, the number of non-English-speaking churches also increased. By the time Cardinal O'Connell died in 1944, there were 29 such churches. Many were in such French-Canadian communities as Lowell, Lawrence, Haverhill, Salem, and Beverley; others were in Italian and Polish communities. By 1945 there were a total of 15 Italian churches in the North End, in east Boston, and in such towns as Revere, Somerville, and Everett, as well as Waltham and Salem. The original six Polish churches had expanded to 15 by 1945. During the first 18 months of his episcopacy, O'Connell could point to 31 new parishes, 29 additional priests, nine more parochial schools, two more orphan asylums, and three new religious orders of nuns added to those already serving the archdiocese.

In 1944, Richard J. CUSHING succeeded Cardinal O'Connell as archbishop of Boston, and found the Church in Massachusetts growing at a rate of about 250,000 to 300,000 every five years, with the number of parishes increasing from 325 in 1944 to 396 in 1960. At the time Cushing became archbishop, there were 4,054 young women serving in 44 female religious orders; by 1960 the number had risen to 5,543, representing 63 orders. In 1944 there were 253 seminarians; by 1960 the figure had jumped to 418. The archdiocese had such a surplus of priests that Cardinal Cushing created a program that sent Boston priests to dioceses in parts of the country like Utah, Louisiana, Colorado, and Wyoming, where there were serious shortages of clergy.

The diocese of Springfield was experiencing similar growth. The Catholic population had more than doubled since the turn of century. In January 1950 Worcester county, the central section of Massachusetts, was detached from the diocese of Springfield to form a separate diocese. The first bishop of the new diocese of Worcester was John Joseph Wright, formerly an auxiliary bishop in Boston. When Bishop Wright was transferred to Pittsburgh at the beginning of 1959, Bishop Joseph Flanagan was transferred from Norwich, Connecticut to succeed him.

In 1969 the bishops established the Massachusetts Catholic Conference to serve as the official voice of the four Catholic dioceses in the Commonwealth. The MCC identifies pressing needs in areas of welfare, health, education, and civil rights, and represents the Church's position on social issues and matters of public policy to government agencies.

By the late 1960s and early 1970s changes were evident throughout the state that reflected many of the tensions in the Church and the nation during those disruptive years. Mass attendance declined; the number of parochial schools was substantially reduced; the number of incoming seminarians dropped off dramatically; there were fewer women entering religious orders, and more and more parish priests were retiring because of age. In part, many of these statistical changes resulted from demographic shifts in Massachusetts that saw older populations moving out of the cities into the suburbs, and the arrival of new immigrants from Latin American countries and many parts of Southeast Asia who settled in urban centers. Cardinal Bernard F. Law, who became archbishop of Boston in 1984, confronted these changes as did other bishops in the state, by closing older parishes in depopulated urban districts, and by creating new parishes in recently developed suburban areas. With the decline in the number of priests and religious, the dioceses expanded programs for the training of lay ministers. These developments presented serious challenges for the Church in Massachusetts at the start of the 21st century.

Catholic Institutions of Higher Learning. Founded 1843 as a liberal arts college for men by the Jesuits, Holy Cross College shares the distinction of being the oldest Catholic college in Massachusetts. Its first graduating class included James Augustine HEALY and his brother Hugh, both freed African-American slaves, while the second graduating class included their brother Patrick, the first African-American to be awarded a Ph.D. James Healy, who was the also valedictorian for the first graduating class, went on to become the first African-American to be named bishop when he was appointed Bishop of Portland, Maine in 1875. In addition to Holy Cross College, the Jesuits also administer BOSTON COLLEGE, established 1863. Other Catholic colleges in the state include Stonehill College in North Easton (sponsored by the Holy Cross Fathers), Emmanuel College in Boston (established 1919 by the Sisters of Notre Dame de Namur), Regis College in Weston (sponsored by the Sisters of St. Joseph), College of Our Lady of the Elms in Chicopee (sponsored by the Sisters of St. Joseph), Merrimack College in North Andover (established, 1947, by the Augustinians), Anna Maria College in Paxton (sponsored by the Sisters of St. Anne), Assumption College in Worcester (sponsored by the Augustinians of the Assumption).

Bibliography: R. H. LORD et al., *History of the Archdiocese of Boston,1604 to 1943,* 3 v. (New York 1944; Boston 1945), T. H. O'CONNOR, *Boston Catholics: A History of the Church and Its People* (Boston 1998). S. E. MORISON, *Builders of the Bay Colony* (Boston 1930); *The Intellectual Life of Colonial New England* (2d ed. New York 1956). A. J. RILEY, *Catholicism in New England to 1788* (Catholic University of America Studies in American Christian History 24; 1936). The best study of the impact of the Irish on Boston is O. HANDLIN, *Boston's Immigrants 1790–1880: A Study of Acculturation* (rev. ed. Cambridge, Mass. 1959). M. L. HANSEN, ''The Second Colonization of New England,'' *The Immigrant in American History,* ed. A. M. SCHLESINGER (Cambridge, Mass. 1940), corrects some false ideas about the immigrants. L. E. TRUESDELL, *The Canadian Born in the United States* (New Haven 1943), statistics for Fr. Canadians. R. H. LORD et al., *History of the Archdiocese of Boston,* 3 v. (New York 1944). M. X. SULLIVAN, *The History of Catholic Secondary Education in the Archdiocese of Boston* (Washington 1946). *General Laws* (*Annotated*) (St. Paul, Minn. 1958–59). *Massachusetts Digest* (*Annotated*) *1761 to Date* (Boston 1933—). J. J. MCCOY, *History of the Catholic Church in the Diocese of Springfield* (Boston 1900). J. G. DEEDY, JR, *The Church in Worcester, New England* (Worcester 1956). F. J. BRADLEY, *Brief History of the Diocese of Fall River* (New York 1931).

[T. H. O'CONNOR/W. L. LUCEY]

MASSAJA, GUGLIELMO

Cardinal, missionary; b. Piova (Asti), Italy, June 8, 1809; d. San Giorgio da Cremano (Napoli), Aug. 6, 1889. Massaja, whose baptismal name was Lorenzo, joined the Capuchins in 1826. After ordination he taught philosophy and theology (1836–46) and acted as confessor to the royal family of Piedmont. In 1846 he was consecrated bishop and was sent to southern Ethiopia as the first vicar apostolic of Galla, but he was unable to reach the territory of the Gallas until 1852. Meanwhile he labored along the coast of East Africa, in Egypt, and in the Sudan. Besides winning numerous converts and baptizing more than 36,000, he pioneered in medical missions, developed an indigenous clergy, and consecrated St. Giustino de JACOBIS as bishop. His knowledge of the country, gained in apostolic journeys, and his aid to travelers won him esteem in Europe. His zeal, charity, and many-sided activities endeared him to the Ethiopians. He was a friend and counselor of Negus (king) Menelik, but in 1879 Negus John, at the instigation of the dissident hierarch, imprisoned him and sent him into exile. In Italy he was deeply venerated by the people. Leo XIII, who created him cardinal (1884), ordered him to complete his memoirs during his final years at the friary in Frascati. The result of Massaja's literary labors was his chief work: *I miei trentacinque anni di missione nell'alta Etiopia* (12 v. Rome 1885–95). This massive account of his 35 years in Ethiopia is still regarded as a work of great value. Massaja also published grammars and other works in African tongues for the use of his missionaries. Among modern African missionaries he was one of the most successful. His cause for beatification has been introduced.

Bibliography: M. GUGLIELMO, *Memorie storiche del Vicariato Apostolico dei Galla, 1845–1880,* Vols. 1–6, A. ROSSO, ed. (Manoscritto autografo Vaticano, 1984). C. D. DA SESSANO, *Guglielmo Massaja O. F. M. Cap.: Vicario apostolico deo Galla. Cardinale di Santa Romana Chiesa. Saggio storico-critico secondo documenti inediti* (Rome 1998).

[T. MACVICAR]

MASSENET, JULES

Romanticist opera composer; b. Montaud, France, May 12, 1842 (baptized Jules Émile Frédéric); d. Paris, Aug. 13, 1912. He was a graduate of the Paris Conservatory, which he had entered at age nine; he won the Prix de Rome in 1863, and in 1878 was appointed professor of counterpoint and composition at the conservatory. Although he was most successful in opera, *Manon* (1884) being accounted his masterpiece, some of his best early compositions, e.g., *Eve* and *Marie-Magdeleine*, were oratorios with religious themes. *Marie-Magdeleine*, as converted to an opera in 1903, is a travesty on the Gospels. *Le Jongleur de Nôtre Dame* (1902), in contrast, has a moving libretto and tastefully handled religious episodes, but the absence of a female role and a general lack of austerity are probably the chief obstacles to its revival. All his other operas, notably *Hérodiade* and *Thaïs* (from which the popular ''Méditation religieuse'' of violin repertory is taken), are marked by an authentic lyricism and sense of theater, and marred by a lack of spiritual depth and a too-obvious desire to please the public. His work for the lyric theater influenced DEBUSSY and, even more strongly, PUCCINI.

Bibliography: J. E. F. MASSENET, *My Recollections*, tr. H. V. BARNETT (Boston 1919). H. T. FINCK, *Massenet and His Operas* (New York 1910). A. BRUNEAU, *Massenet* (Paris 1935). *Baker's Biographical Dictionary of Musicians*, ed. N. SLONIMSKY (5th, rev. ed. New York 1958) 1045–46. J.-C. BRANGER, ''*Mes souvenirs*: De nouvelles sources relatives aux Mémoires de Jules Massenet,'' *Revue de Musicologie* 83 (1997) 117–135. J. A. FELDMAN, ''*Manon*'' in *International Dictionary of Opera* 2 v. ed. C. S. LARUE (Detroit 1993) 798–799. J. W. HANSEN, ''Sibyl Sanderson's Influence on *Manon*,'' *The Opera Quarterly* 15/1 (1999) 38–48. C. HEADINGTON, ''*Werther*'' in *International Dictionary of Opera* 2 v., ed. C. S. LARUE, (Detroit 1993)1456–1457. D. IRVINE, *Massenet:*

A Chronicle of His Life and Times (Portland, Oregon 1994). S. WILLIER, ''*Le Roi de Lahore*'' *International Dictionary of Opera* 2 v., ed. C. S. LARUE (Detroit 1993)1127–1128.

[R. M. LONGYEAR]

Guglielmo Massaja.

MASSES

The literature of 20th–century psychology, sociology, and political science reflects a variety of conflicting and even contradictory uses of this term. The concept has assumed particular importance as a description of the ''prepolitical dispositions'' that render a people susceptible to the imposition of totalitarian rule. Psychologists attribute to the mass person such qualities as spatial and temporal rootlessness, affectivity, susceptibility to appeals to blind passion (especially of a negative nature), a lack of felt need for a ''personal privacy,'' a strong impulse to be ''like everyone else,'' and an aggressive assertion of rights without a sense of corresponding duties or responsibilities. Sociologists analyze the dominant characteristics of mass communication media, e.g., the predominance of large-scale organization, the depersonalization of human relationships, the decline of a socially unifying ''public philosophy,'' and the substitution of the irrational dynamism of a social myth exalting a class, a race, or the state.

Contemporary Meanings. Since the concept of the masses is so elusive, its meaning may be better clarified by a series of contrasts than by direct definition. (1) Mass vs. individual: the human person, conscious of his or her own uniqueness and personal worth, is self-directed and self-responsible; seeks to develop his or her own special endowments, to find his or her own life vocation, and to make his or her own contribution to the communities of which he or she is a member [*see* PERSON (IN PHILOSOPHY)]. The mass person lacks a sense of personal worth, is ''other directed,'' loses his or her identity in the mass, and seeks fulfillment and meaning for life through total immersion in the collectivity. (2) Mass vs. elite: to theorists of the elitist school (e.g., ORTEGA Y GASSET, Mosca, Pareto), the masses lack quality, culture, and dignity; they are alienated; they have no respect for traditions and do not recognize that the great achievements of civilization have been made possible by hard work and sacrifice on the part of the ''creative minority'' who have self-discipline and a sense of *noblesse oblige.* The mass person expects to enjoy all the benefits of civilization (and claims them as a right) though he or she lacks the self-discipline to make the sacrifices requisite to preserve them and the capacity and sense of responsibility to contribute to their advancement. Many elitists consider DEMOCRACY to be an unrealistic dream. (3) Mass vs. people: this contrast describes two distinct prepolitical dispositions in the members of a body politic. Pope Pius XII made use of it as the basis for his analysis of the preconditions for sound democracy in his Christmas message of 1944. The people, he said, ''lives and moves by its own life energy''; the masses are ''inert of themselves and can only be moved from the outside.'' The people is made up of persons, each ''conscious of his own responsibility and his own views''; the masses are ''an easy plaything in the hands of anyone who seeks to exploit their instincts and impressions.'' The state based on a people possesses a ''constantly self-renewing vigor'' because it encourages personal initiative and a sense of responsibility for the common good; the mass state utilizes the elementary power of the masses who have been ''reduced to the minimum status of a mere machine,'' and used to impose the whims of manipulators on the whole community. The masses are the ''capital enemy of true democracy and of its ideal of liberty and equality.'' For them, ''liberty becomes a tyrannous claim to give free rein to one's impulses and appetites,'' and ''equality degenerates to a

Jules Massenet. (©Bettmann/CORBIS)

mechanical level and becomes a colorless uniformity'' [*Acta Apostolicae Sedis* (Rome 1909) 37 (1945) 10–23].

Totalitarian Concepts. The theory and practice of totalitarianism give a critical role to the masses. To Marx, the proletarian person, alienated from capitalist society because of his or her lack of property, was destined to be the new revolutionary force. Lenin envisioned the Communist party as the ''vanguard of the proletariat,'' the elite of the ''toiling masses'' who would spearhead the revolution because they were enlightened and liberated through insight into the dialectical process of history.

The consolidation of power under a dictatorship depends in large part on the incorporation of the masses through the dynamism of social myth. The myth is the core of the secular religion of totalitarianism, the means of ''moral regeneration'' of the masses through their absolute commitment to the collective goal. Its value as an integrating force lies not in its truth or in its power to fulfill human needs, but rather in its power to stir the masses to a delirium of enthusiasm and hatred that keeps them always in readiness for action against the ''enemy'' designated by the leaders.

Although totalitarianism is the extreme of the mass society, many of the phenomena of mass psychology are to be found in the so–called free societies; for example, the manipulation of PUBLIC opinion by irresponsible PROPAGANDA, sensational journalism, and the encouragement of a climate of hatred and violence by extremist political groups. The ''latent masses'' can be made active through appropriate leadership and organization and an effective social myth.

Bibliography: PIUS XII, *Benignitas et humanitas* (Radio address, Dec. 24, 1944); *Acta Apostolicae Sedis* (Rome 1909) 37 (1945) 10–23; *Catholic Mind* (Eng.) 43 (Feb. 1945) 65–77. T. A. CORBETT, *People or Masses: A Comparative Study in Political Theory* (Washington 1950), contains 20 pages of bibliography. J. MONNEROT, *Sociology and Psychology of Communism,* tr. J. DEGRAS and R. REES (Boston 1960). H. BROCH, *Massenpsychologie* (Zurich 1959). P. REIWALD, *Vom Geist der Massen: Handbuch der Massenpsychologie* (Zurich 1946).

[T. A. CORBETT]

MASSES, VOTIVE

In addition to the liturgical cycle of Sundays and feasts, the Roman Missal and Lectionary of Paul VI (1969) provide prayers and readings for Masses to be offered in response to various pastoral situations. There are three kinds of such occasional Masses: Ritual Masses for the celebration of certain Sacraments, Masses for Various Needs and Occasions, and Votive Masses (GenInstrRomMissal 326–341). In the former *Missale Romanum* of Pius V (1570), as well as in most sacramentaries from the Roman tradition, the term *Missae votivae* referred to all three varieties of such occasional Masses. In the present Missal (Sacramentary), however, the term Votive Mass refers only to fifteen Masses which celebrate such objects of devotion as the Sacred Heart, the Holy Name, the Precious Blood, the Holy Spirit, the Virgin Mary, St. Joseph, and the Apostles. In addition, the new Missal contains forty-six Masses for Various Needs and Occasions, and a great variety of Ritual Masses.

The Votive Masses may be celebrated on the following days of the liturgical year: (1) on weekdays in ordinary time when there is either an optional memorial of a saint or no memorial; (2) on obligatory memorials of saints, on weekdays of Advent, of Christmastime and of the Easter Season, only in the case of genuine pastoral need; and (3) by permission of the bishop, when serious need or pastoral advantage dictates, on any day except the Sundays of Advent, Lent and the Easter Season, Ash Wednesday, and during Holy Week. These same directives also apply for Masses for Various Needs and Occasions.

The practice of Votive Masses grew during the Middle Ages after the genesis of the liturgical calendar. Christians who had a special devotion to Jesus, Mary, or a saint would ask priests to offer Masses of petition or thanksgiving in the spirit of that devotion. The faithful would also request Masses for special needs or situations that arose in their daily lives and in society. Ritual Masses also arose from the sacramental needs of the people.

Bibliography: J. D. CRICHTON, *Christian Celebration: The Mass* (London 1971). G. DIX, *The Shape of the Liturgy* (London 1945). J. JUNGMANN, *Mass of the Roman Rite* (New York 1951, 1955).

[J. T. KELLEY]

MASSILLON, JEAN BAPTISTE

Celebrated French preacher and bishop; b. Hyères (Provence), June 24, 1663; d. Beauregard, Sept. 10, 1742. The son of François Massillon, a notary, he pursued his secondary studies in Hyères and Marseilles in the colleges of the Oratorians, whose congregation he entered at Aix in 1681, despite parental opposition. Upon completion of his theological studies, he taught in the Oratorian colleges at Pézenas, Marseilles, and Montbrison (1684–88) and at Vienne (1689–95), where he was ordained in 1691.

Jean Baptiste Massillon. (©Bettmann/CORBIS)

His superiors recognized his talent for preaching and in 1693 commissioned him to deliver the funeral orations for Villeroy, archbishop of Lyons, and M. de Villars, archbishop of Vienne. After a brief stay at the Oratory of Lyons, he was named director of the Seminary of Saint-Magloire in Paris (1696). Massillon's reputation as a preacher grew steadily as a result of his *conférences* to the young clerics and his highly successful Lenten sermons in Montpellier (1698) and at the Oratory in Paris (1699). He was summoned the same year to preach the Advent at Versailles, and his fame as a preacher became solidly established by this signal honor. His Lenten sermons before Louis XIV in 1701 and 1704 were acclaimed by his predecessors, Bossuet and Bourdaloue, and by the king himself, who declared that though formerly well pleased with the preachers, he was now quite displeased with himself. Included in the Lent of 1704 was Massillon's masterpiece ''On the Fewness of the Elect.'' At the apogee of his success, Massillon fell victim to jealousy and suspicion; accused of Jansenism and of compromising relations with certain prominent families, he was never again summoned to Versailles during the lifetime of Louis XIV. Nevertheless, he continued to preach panegyrics, funeral orations, Lent and Advent discourses in important Paris churches, as well as the Advent of 1715 at the court of Stanislas, king of Lorraine. In 1709 he delivered the funeral oration of the Prince de Conti, in 1711 that of the Dauphin, and in 1715 that of Louis XIV, styled ''The Great.'' On that momentous occasion Massillon began thus: ''God alone is great, my brethren.'' Once more in court favor, Massillon was nominated by the regent in 1717 to the bishopric of Clermont (Auvergne) and was consecrated in the Tuileries chapel on Dec. 21, 1718. In the interim he preached before young Louis XV a Lenten course of 10 sermons, which, published under the title *Le Petit Carême,* became his most popular work. Upon his reception into the French Academy in February of 1719, Massillon was eulogized by Fleury, the king's preceptor. At the regent's request, Massillon was instrumental in securing Cardinal de NOAILLES'S compliance with the bull *Unigenitus* (1720) and was consequently the object of frequent attacks in the Jansenist publication *Les Nouvelles Ecclésiastiques.* Before devoting himself entirely to his see, he assisted at the coronation of Louis XV and preached the funeral oration of the regent's mother, the duchess of Orléans (1723).

A conscientious worker, Massillon ably administered his vast diocese with its 29 abbeys, 284 priories, and 758 parishes. In his efforts to promote ecclesiastical discipline and public morals, he made frequent pastoral visits in his diocese, devoted attention to the temporal as well as spiritual needs of all, and held annual synods and retreats of priests. No less pastor than preacher, he eloquently exhorted his clergy to mutual charity and devotion to the poor. His correspondence with the king's intendants and ministers attests to his efforts to defend his flock against ministerial injustice and to improve their material condition.

More a moralist than theologian, Massillon was greatly admired as a preacher by such *philosophes* as Voltaire and D'Alembert. Less sublime than Bossuet, less logical than Bourdaloue, he excelled in a certain harmonious elegance and subtle persuasiveness not entirely devoid of rhetorical affectation. Even those faults so readily discernible upon literary analysis seem to have been quite transformed by his oratorical art. Described as "the Racine of the pulpit," he was equally gifted in understanding the human heart and analyzing its passions, and he put all his energies into combating the increasing impiety and incredulity of the time. This zeal, in conjunction with his rigorous Oratorian training, explains the severity of some of his sermons. His detractors did not hesitate to point out certain passages in his sermons on "Confession" and on "Communion" and "On the Fewness of the Elect" in which there is doctrinal exaggeration. However, the ensemble of Massillon's life and thought proves him to have been militantly anti-Jansenist, though at times theologically inexact, rather through excess of zeal than through heretical belief.

Although known principally as an orator, Massillon the man and bishop demonstrated in his life and work the teachings he so eloquently and fearlessly propounded to prince and priest alike. During his lifetime only the funeral oration on the Prince de Conti was published (1709). He disavowed unauthorized collections published at Trévoux in 1705, 1706, and 1714. In 1745 his nephew, Joseph Massillon, himself an Oratorian, published a collection of 15 volumes in Paris. The most recent and best edition is that of Blampignon (4 v. Bar-le-Duc 1865–68, Paris 1886), comprising 10 Advent sermons, 41 Lenten sermons, eight on the mysteries, and four on the virtues; 10 panegyrics; six funeral orations; 16 ecclesiastical conferences; 20 synodal discourses; 26 charges; paraphrases of 30 psalms; some *pensées choisies;* and 50 miscellaneous letters or notes.

Bibliography: J. LE ROND D'ALEMBERT, *Éloge de Massillon* in his *Histoire des Membres de l'Académie Française* (Paris 1810) v. 1, 5. L. F. F. THEREMIN, *Demosthenes und Massillon* (Berlin 1845). A. BAYLE, *Massillon* (Paris 1867). E. A. BLAMPIGNON, *Massillon d'après des documents inédits* (Paris 1879); *L'Épiscopat de Massillon* (Paris 1884); *Supplément à la vie et à la correspondance de Massillon* (Paris 1892). B. ATTAIX, *Étude sur Massillon* (Toulouse 1882). M. DE VALOIS COHENDY, *Correspondance Mandements de Massillon* (Clermont 1883). L. PAUTHE, *Massillon* (Paris 1908). A. MOLIEN, *Dictionnaire de théologie catholique,* ed. A. VACANT et al., (Paris 1903–50) 10.1:258–265. A. CHÉREL, *Massillon* (Paris 1943). J. CHAMPOMIER, *Massillon* (Paris 1942).

[S. J. WASHINGTON]

MASSOULIÉ, ANTONIN

Dominican theologian who participated in the controversies on physical premotion and quietism; b. Toulouse, Oct. 28, 1632; d. Rome, Jan. 23, 1706. After his education in the humanities, he entered the Order April 21, 1647, and studied in the Dominican schools at Toulouse and Bordeaux. He earned his doctorate at Toulouse. He refused the episcopate but held office in the Order as provincial of Occitania (1679); prior of the Novitiate General in Paris (1684–87); visitator general of the priories in Alsace (1687); and socius to the master general until his death. During four pontificates Massoulié served as consultor to papal commissions investigating the questions of philosophical sin, QUIETISM, and CHINESE RITES. He was inquisitor general at Toulouse (1693), and a consultor of the Holy Office. He was called upon to examine the *Maximes des Saints* (1697) of Fénelon, upon which he passed an unfavorable judgment.

In his two-volume work, *Divus Thomas sui interpres de divina motione et libertate creata* (v.1) and *De divinis auxiliis* (v.2) Massoulié sought to prove that physical premotion was not the invention of BÁÑEZ but was true THOMISM, and to disprove the accusation that Thomism was Jansenistic. He wrote three treatises against quietism: *Traité de la véritable orasion* (1697), *Traité de l'amour le Dieu* (1703), and *Méditations de St. Thomas sur les trois voies* (1678). His unpublished manuscripts rest in the Casanatense Library, Rome, where he had been appointed the first professor of St. Thomas in 1701.

Bibliography: C. RAYSSON, *Vie du V. P. Antonin Massoulié Dominicain* (Paris 1717). A. TOURON, *Histoire des hommes Illustres de l'ordre de St. Dominique,* 6 v. (Paris 1743–49) 5:751–773. J. QUÉTIF and J. ÉCHARD, *Scriptores Ordinis Praedicatorum* 2.2:769–770, 827–829.

[J. J. HALADUS]

MASTER OF CEREMONIES

The person in charge of the direction of a liturgical function. The responsibility of the master of ceremonies is to instruct the ministers before liturgical functions and direct them during the functions. The origins of this role can be traced to the deacons whom early documents portray as quasi–masters of ceremonies. Though ceremonial directives had already become very explicit in the 7th-century *Ordo Romanus Primus,* the first mention of the title of master of ceremonies appears in the 17th–century CEREMONIAL OF BISHOPS.

[J. W. KAVANAGH/EDS.]

MASTRIUS, BARTHOLOMAEUS

Franciscan philosopher and theologian; b. Meldola (Forli), in the Papal States, December 1602; d. there, Jan. 3, 1673. After entering the Order of Friars Minor Conventual at an early age, he studied at Bologna and then at Naples, where he came under the influence of Joseph da Trapani, an eminent Scotist. He completed his studies at Rome and then taught at Cesena, Perugia, and Padua. He was provincial of Bologna from 1647 to 1650 and also held other high positions in the order. His earliest writing was done in collaboration with Bonaventure Bellutus and was aimed at providing a complete course in philosophy based upon Scotist principles. This work was earlier published in individual volumes but was eventually brought together in *Philosophiae ad mentem Scoti cursus integer* (5 v. Venice 1671). He then turned his attention to examining theology in the light of Scotist teaching and wrote *Disputationes theologicae in quator libros Sententiarum ad mentem Scoti* (4 v. Venice 1675) and *Theologia moralis ad mentem dd. Seraphici et Subtilis concinnata* (Venice 1671). His writings reveal a profound knowledge of scholastic philosophy and theology, especially that of Duns Scotus, and his argument is clear, precise, and critical. In controversies with other Scotists, including Matthew Ferchi and John Punch, he was severely sharp and direct. In the question of predestination and divine grace, he found in Scotism the basis of Trapani's theory of concomitant decrees, which he adopted.

Bibliography: B. CROWLEY, ''The Life and Works of B. Mastrius,'' *Franciscan Studies* 8 (1948) 97–152. É. LONGPRÉ, *Dictionnaire de théologie catholique* 10.1:281–282. H. HURTER, *Nomenclator literarius theologiae catholicae* 4: 20–21.

[J. C. WILLKE]

MASTURBATION

Masturbation is the act or practice of stimulating the external sexual organs by oneself. This article gives an explanation of the nature of masturbation, Scriptural background for the Church's teaching on masturbation, and other factors in the Church's moral evaluation of masturbation.

Masturbation, also called self-abuse, self-pollution, and onanism (see below), is the manipulation of the external sexual organs for the purpose of erotic self-stimulation to the point of climax or orgasm, by movements of the hand or other physical contacts, or by sexually stimulating pictures or imaginations (psychic masturbation), or by a combination of physical and psychic stimulation. When such stimulation takes place during sleep, it is called ''nocturnal pollution'' or ''nocturnal emission.'' The term ''mutual masturbation'' is used to refer to the stimulation of the external genitals of one person by another, and vice versa, in order to produce climax or orgasm, but without engaging in sexual intercourse with each other.

Sexual studies done by social scientists show that some experience of masturbation is extremely common among young males at and after the age of puberty, and fairly common among girls and women. Such studies rarely distinguish between voluntary and involuntary acts, which is important for the moral evaluation of a particular masturbatory act.

Biblical Passages. In the tradition of the Church's teaching on masturbation, moral principles were drawn primarily from the interpretation of two Scriptural passages. The first, Genesis 38:8–10, from which the term ''onanism'' is coined, narrates Onan's unwillingness to produce offspring in the name of his older brother, Er, with his sister-in-law, Tamar. Er had died without an heir, and so Onan, upon the order of his father, Judah, is to take on this duty on behalf of his brother. Onan knew the child would not be considered his, but rather, would be considered his brother's offspring, so although he would lie with Tamar, he would spill his seed on the ground to avoid producing an offspring for his brother. For this sin, the Lord puts Onan to death. Although onanism was traditionally used as a synonym for masturbation, Onan's act could be more properly described as ''withdrawal.'' Moreover, from the biblical author's point of view, Onan's sin was his refusal to fulfill the important responsibility involved in the levirate law (cf. Dt 25:5–10).

The second passage, 1 Cor 6:9–10, is a list of vices, or more specifically, ''unjust persons'' (ἄδικοι—*adikoi*) engaged in particular vices that prevent them from inheriting the Kingdom of God. Among the terms is the plural masculine, μαλάκοι (*malakoi*), of the adjective μαλάκος (*malakos*), which means ''soft (to the touch),'' ''delicate'' (cf. Mt 11:8; Lk 7:25). Paul uses this adjective as a substantive (noun), and thus it could be translated, rather literally, as ''the soft,'' perhaps meaning the weak-willed, or, with its connection to fine clothing in the Gospels, perhaps the economically pampered. It has long been thought, however, that the term refers to some sexual deviance from Paul's point of view, at least in part because of its placement among other sexually related terms. The first term listed is πόρνοι (*pornoi*), ''fornicators,'' or more generally, ''sexually immoral.'' Paul then lists ''idolators'' (εἰδωλολάτραι—*eidō lolatrai*), followed by the sexually improprietous ''adulterers'' (μοιξοίν—*moichoi*). The fourth term is the one under consideration, which is followed by the problematic ἀρσενοκοῖται (*arsenokoitai*), a compound word, ἄρσεν

+ κοίτη *arsēn*; male + *koitē*; bed), which has been translated ''sodomites'' and even ''practicing homosexuals.'' Both of these translations, however, are quite anachronistic, in that the former term gets it start from St. Augustine, *De Civitate Dei 16:30* (Loader, 136), and the latter reflects very recent understandings of sexual orientation and the moral distinction between the unchosen orientation of homosexuality and freely chosen sexual acts by homosexual persons (whatever Paul's precise concern, he does not perceive people as ''homosexually oriented,'' but rather, is dealing with acts and the blurring of sex roles; cf. Moxnes, esp. 213). Paul rounds off his list with less problematic terms, at least from the point of view of translation, though the precise act(s) meant by each term may be arguable: ''thieves'' (κλέπται—*kleptai*), ''greedy'' (πλεονέκται—*pleonektai*), ''drunkards'' (μέθυσοι—*methusoi*), ''revilers'' (λοίδοροι—*loidoroi*), and ''robbers'' (ἅρπαγες—*harpages*).

During the Patristic period and the medieval ages, some commentators thought the term μαλάκοι (*malakoi*) meant ''masturbators.'' This is the only time in his authentic letters that Paul uses both this term as well as the difficult ἀρσενοκοῖται (*arsenokoitai*), which ''Paul may have coined . . . since 1 Cor. 6:9 is the oldest literary indication of its use'' (Collins, *Ethics,* 89; for Paul, this neologism might refer to Lv. 18:22; 20:13; the word is picked up in I Tm 1:10, which probably depends on 1 Cor. 6:9). Current scholarship tends to translate the term μαλάκοι (*malakoi*) as ''catamite'' (a boy kept by a pederast), or ''boy/male prostitute,'' and ἀρσενοκοῖται (*arsenokoitai*) as ''sodomites,'' despite, as noted, its anachronistic character. Additionally, some propose that these terms may, for Paul, refer to those who engage in homoerotic acts, whether in a passive or active role, respectively. Later uses of the latter term, however, can be found in the midst of economic vices, which ''seems to suggest that a century or so after Paul first used the word it had the connotation of paying a man for sex. In the light of this, it may well be that *malakoi* and *arsenokoitai* denote the passive and active partners in sex for a price among males'' (Collins, *Ethics,* 90). In the end, one must admit that all modern translations are ''attempts to understand what Paul meant. It is usage that allows one to understand the meaning of a word. When a term is not used very much, it is very difficult, and sometimes impossible, to know what an author or a speaker intended to say by using a particular word'' (Collins, *Ethics,* 87).

Moral Evaluation. Although it is rather clear that the above two Scriptural passages have little to do with the moral issue of masturbation per se, in addition to principles gleaned from them and others, the application of human reason, most especially to the understanding of the nature of the human person and human sexuality, supports the Church's understanding of human sexuality in general and, specifically, its moral evaluation of masturbation. The *Catechism of the Catholic Church* (*CCC*) teaches that the sexual function is meant by God to be enjoyed in ''the total meaning of mutual self-giving'' (*CCC* 2352) in the marriage relationship of a man and woman for the purposes of begetting children and of mutual pleasure for the building up of the couple's unity. Therefore, any deliberate activation of the sexual function outside the proper state of marriage and the purposes noted is seriously inordinate and, if voluntary and knowing, sinful. Within marriage such self- or mutual stimulation is moral only when it serves in some way to prepare for or to complete a natural act of sexual intercourse.

Within the Church's teaching on human sexuality, masturbation is considered to be objectively disordered or intrinsically evil (*in se malum* or *intrinsece malum*); that is, no circumstances or intentions can render the action of masturbation ''morally good.'' The degree or seriousness of the moral culpability of a particular act of masturbation, however, can be judged only in the light of the degree of the moral actor's knowledge, freedom, and intentions; full moral guilt requires a fully deliberate choice of what the person fully realizes is seriously evil, which can then be evaluated as gravely, or mortally, sinful. If the act is performed with only partial realization or only partial choice of the will, the person is guilty of venial sin. If there is no free choice of the will, there is no guilt of sin at all, even if the person is aware of what he is doing. This is true even when a person foresees that sexual stimulation and even orgasm will result from some action that he or she is freely performing, provided that he or she does not intend the sexual stimulation but merely permits it, and has a sufficiently good reason for what he or she is doing (*see* DOUBLE EFFECT, PRINCIPLE OF). ''One must take into account the affective immaturity, force of acquired habit, conditions of anxiety or other psychological or social factors that lessen or even extenuate moral culpability'' (*CCC* 2352). It can also be noted that the sexual instinct is one of the human person's strongest instincts, and the pleasure connected with its activation is one of the keenest of sensual pleasures. For this reason, many normal persons may at times choose this form of self- or mutual gratification when other more natural forms are not available without difficulty or unwanted involvement, though such a deliberate choice is considered in Church teaching a grave matter.

Bibliography: J. C. FORD and G. KELLY, *Contemporary Moral Theology* (Westminster, Md. 1958) v. 1. H. NOLDIN, *Summa theologiae moralis,* ed. A. SCHMITT and G. HEINZEL (Innsbruck 1954) v. 1, *De principiis* (31st ed.) 329; *Complementum: De castitate,* ed. G. HEINZEL (35th ed. 1955) 29–41, 48–50. A. VERMEERSCH, *De castitate et de vitiis contraries: Tractatus doctrinalis et moralis* (2d ed. Rome 1921). L. WOUTERS, *Tractatus dogmatico moralis de* *virtute castitatis et de vitiis oppositis* (rev. ed. Bruges 1932). R. J. CLIFFORD and R. E. MURPHY, "Genesis," in *New Jerome Biblical Commentary,* ed. R. E. BROWN et al. (Englewood Cliffs, N.J. 1990) 8–43. R. COLLINS, *First Corinthians* (Sacra Pagina 7; Collegeville, Minn. 1999); *Sexual Ethics in the New Testament: Behavior and Belief* (Companions to the New Testament; New York 2000). JOHN PAUL II, *Veritatis Splendor* (Vatican City 1993), in *Origins* 23:18 (Oct. 14, 1993) 297–334. J. A. LOADER, *A Tale of Two Cities: Sodom and Gomorrah in the Old Testament, Early Jewish and Early Christian Traditions* (Contributions to Biblical Exegesis and Theology 1; Kampen 1990). H. MOXNES, "Honor, Shame, and the Outside World in Paul's Letter to the Romans," in *The Social World of Formative Christianity and Judaism. Essays in Tribute to Howard Clark Kee,* ed. J. NEUSNER et al. (Philadelphia 1988) 207–218. E. A. SPEISER, *Genesis. Introduction, Translation, and Notes* (Anchor Bible 1; Garden City, N.Y. 1964). B. VAWTER, *On Genesis. A New Reading* (Garden City, N.Y. 1977).

[J. J. FARRAHER/T. A. FRIEDRICHSEN]

MATER ET MAGISTRA

An ENCYCLICAL letter dealing with Christian teaching on modern social questions, addressed by John XXIII on May 15, 1961, to all members of the hierarchy, clergy, and laity of the entire Catholic world. Although not officially published until July of the same year, it was dated May 15, to commemorate the 70th anniversary of *RERUM NOVARUM*. It may be noted that the later and in some ways more famous encyclical *Pacem in terris* (April 11 1963) was addressed not only to Catholics but to "all men of good will."

The intent of the pope was made clear in the title of *Mater et Magistra*, "On Recent Developments of the Social Question in the Light of Christian Teaching." Like Leo XIII, John began by emphasizing that the Church is not only a teacher of what is right and wrong, but that she is also a mother who gives herself freely, especially for the "lowly and oppressed." The first section reviews the social conditions and the underlying false social philosophy that induced Leo to write his "complete synthesis of social principles," also referred to as a "compendium of Catholic social and economic teaching" and as the "*Magna Charta* of social and economic reconstruction." Special consideration is given to Leo's teaching on the social role of the Church, the dignity of the worker and his work, the social aspects of the institution of private property, the rights and obligations of governments to intervene in social questions, the right of workers to form their own associations, and the importance of human solidarity and Christian brotherhood. Pius XI's *QUADRAGESIMO ANNO* (April 15, 1931) and Pius XII's radio broadcast *La solennità* (June 1, 1941) are discussed for their clarification of Leo's thought and their own unique contributions to the growing body of Catholic social thought.

The second section of *Mater et Magistra* analyzes certain major areas of Leo's teaching, in particular, the principle of SUBSIDIARITY; the importance of cooperation as a basic social and economic principle; the increased dependence of the individual on social groups; the necessity of maximizing the freedom of individuals and the lesser social groups; the demands of the common good; factors determining just wages; reconciliation of modern industrial and technological progress with the needs of all segments of the population; and, finally, questions of private property and public ownership. In this section John first applied the teaching of his predecessors to modern problems and, second, evinced a very real awareness of the importance of the community as an entity and of the interdependence of all men and of all nations.

The third section is the most original part of the document. It explores the problems of predominantly agricultural economies, especially in depressed areas of the world; calls for more vigorous action by public authorities to promote the interest of farmers and farm workers in every possible way, and stresses that the problems of depressed areas are the responsibility of the whole community, of nations, and especially of wealthier nations. Where there is imbalance between population and natural resources, Christian principles demand that the more fortunate nations take action to correct the situation by such measures as emergency aid and scientific, technical, and financial assistance. The autonomy of the receiving nations should be regarded as sacred, and the giving nations should not use the aid they render to develop a new form of colonialism.

The fourth and final section recalls the importance of truth, justice, and love in rebuilding a sound social order. The importance of the Church's social teachings is stressed with the injunction that these principles must not only be taught in all schools, especially seminaries, but that they must be implemented particularly through a vigorous lay apostolate. Furthermore, Catholics are asked not to hesitate to cooperate with people of other faiths in the tremendous task of humanizing and Christianizing modern civilization.

Bibliography: Official Latin text in *Acta Apostolicae Sedis* 53 (1961) 401–64. English translation in D.J. O'BRIEN and T.A. SHANNON, eds., *Catholic Social Thought: The Documentary Heritage* (Maryknoll, NY, 1992) 84–128. J. N. MOODY and J.G. LAWLER, *The Challenge of Mater et Magistra* (New York, 1963). J.F. CRONIN, *Christianity and Social Progress: A Commentary on Mater et Magistra* (Baltimore, 1965). J. Y. CALVEZ, *The Social Thought of John XXIII: Mater Et Magistra* (Chicago, 1964). D. J. O'BRIEN, "A Century of Catholic Social Teaching: Contexts and Comments" in J. COLEMAN, *One Hundred Years of Catholic Social Thought* (Maryknoll, NY, 1991) 13–24.

[T. J. HARTE]

People worshiping the dollar, Thomas Nast cartoon. (©Bettmann/CORBIS)

MATERIALISM

A philosophical position that regards MATTER as the only reality. Materialism is principally opposed to SPIRITUALISM, which admits the reality of SPIRIT, and to IDEALISM, which reduces matter itself to an idea or other manifestation of mind. The various forms it has assumed throughout history may be described as classical materialism and as dialectical and historical materialism. The former, which flourished in antiquity and modern times, proposes that all changes are merely quantitative and that these suffice to explain thought and phenomena otherwise attributed to spirit; the latter, originated by K. MARX and F. ENGELS, places a dialectical process within matter and uses this to explain the evolution of thought and man's history. This article considers only classical materialism, treating it in its Greek and Roman period and in its modern development; the other forms are treated elsewhere (*see* MATERIALISM, DIALECTICAL AND HISTORICAL).

Greek and Roman Period

In classical antiquity materialism was foreshadowed in the teaching of the early Greek naturalists who attempted to explain the universal in terms of one or other material principle (*see* GREEK PHILOSOPHY). It received systematic expression in the work of the atomists Leucippus and Democritus, and was more fully developed by Epicurus, whose doctrine was given wide diffusion through the efforts of the Roman poet Lucretius.

Leucippus and Democritus. For these thinkers, the only thing that really exists is the plenum, although this is not a unity, being divided by the void into a plurality of principles of being. Motion and alteration take place in this void, through processes of rarefaction and condensation associated with variations in the size of empty space. These processes presuppose that two bodies cannot occupy the same space or undergo any type of compenetration.

Atoms. Although Leucippus called the plenum ''what is'' and the void ''what is not,'' he regarded the latter as being as real as the former and reckoned both as the causes of things. For him, atoms existing in empty space are the basic principles of the universe. These are infinite in number, invisible because of their smallness, endowed with extension and corporeality, and on this account called ''first bodies.'' Physically indivisible also, they are named from this property ἄτομα, meaning indivisibles. They are qualitatively similar in all respects, differing from each other only quantitatively and spatially. From such atoms, themselves ingenerable and uncorruptible, all others things are generated. The different characteristics of such bodies are traceable to the various sizes, shapes, positions, and arrangements of atoms within them. Their generation and corruption is nothing more than a combination and separation of atoms, and their growth and diminution similarly an addition and subtraction of atoms.

The appearances of things do not constitute truth, although truth can be discerned from appearances through a proper understanding of what is perceived. The qualities that appear in things are really qualities of the senses (πάθη τῆς αἰσθήσεως); the various shapes and arrangements of atoms so affect man's senses as to provoke a reaction from them. Thus DEMOCRITUS states: ''According to convention (νόμῳ) alone is there sweet, bitter, warm, cold, and color; in reality there are only atoms and empty space'' (H. Diels, *Die Fragmente der Vorsokratiker: Greichisch und Deutsch,* ed. W. Kranz [Berlin 1960–61] 9). The ultimate principles can be grasped only by the mind. Democritus here foreshadowed the distinction between primary and secondary qualities that was to be proposed with the beginnings of modern science.

For Democritus, atoms have properties that are independent of man's mode of conceiving them, viz, shape or form, size, heaviness, hardness, and perpetual motion. Size is immediately dependent upon shape, and heaviness upon size. Atoms are fitted with hooks, loops, and fasteners of various sorts; these make possible their entering into different types of lattice structures and combinations. (*See* ATOMISM.)

Origins. Little is known of early discussions regarding the initial movement of atoms and the circumstances of the world's origin. Since atoms are in eternal movement, Democritus assigned it no cause; in his view, what never has a beginning needs no cause. Empty space is not the cause of motion, but rather a presupposition or CONDITION for its possibility. Governed by the law that like seeks like, the lighter and finer atoms rose to constitute the rotating mass of the heavens, while the heavier and larger atoms gathered together at the center and formed the body of the earth. The stars were carried upward by a type of vortex motion and made to glow by their rapid rotation. Similar explanations were offered for other cosmic phenomena.

Like Leucippus before him, Democritus taught the necessity (ἀνάγκη) of all events. ''Nothing arises without a cause, but everything for a determined reason and from necessity'' (frg. 2). Thus CHANCE was banished from the universe. Necessity was conceived mechanically: pushes and pulls propel atoms to and fro in eternal motion. All other types of causality were neglected by these thinkers, so much so that Aristotle could reproach them for their laziness in investigating the origins of motion (*Meta.* 985b 18).

Spirit. Democritus did not deny the superiority of spirit; he recognized the soul's supremacy over the body, but thought that soul could be explained in terms of atoms. In Aristotle's account, Democritus allowed for soul and spirit without distinguishing between the two, regarding them as composed of atoms of fire that were spherical in shape, the finest and smoothest of the atoms (*Anim.* 405a 8–13, 406b 15–22). Since there was no qualitative difference between bodily atoms and soul atoms, the soul-body problem posed him no difficulty. Likewise, in his view, no clearly defined boundary separated the living from the nonliving. Man, whom he regarded as a microcosm, abounds in soul atoms that are spread all over his body; between any two bodily atoms there is always a soul atom. The soul is therefore material, the principle of motion in living bodies, and also the principle of perception and of thought. How unity is achieved between the bodily atoms interspersed with soul atoms, or how a peculiar combination of matter can produce the unity of consciousness and of the spiritual life, is left unexplained.

Epicurus and Lucretius. The Socratic philosophers reacted strongly against the doctrines of Leucippus and Democritus, but materialism soon found another supporter in EPICURUS, who developed the system in greater detail and strengthened its foundations. He maintained that nothing comes from nothing, for otherwise everything might come from everything. In his view, bodies alone exist and only the void is incorporeal. Like his predecessors, he distinguished between composed bodies and simple bodies or atoms, which are absolutely unchangeable. Since space is infinite, atoms must likewise be infinite in number. Epicurus ascribed motion to his atoms a constant motion ''downward,'' although he supplied no referent for this direction. Since, in his view, atoms deviate from their uniform motion, they collide and group themselves in various combinations, thus giving rise to the bodies of experience.

Epicurus conceived soul as a kind of vapor spread throughout man's body and associated with its heat. Bodies surrounding man continually give off minute particles that penetrate to his soul through sense organs and there excite mental images. With the dissolution of man's body, his soul is also dissolved.

Epicurean materialism received poetic expression and further development in the didactic poem *De rerum natura* of LUCRETIUS. Disturbed by thoughts on death and disquieted by religious faith in the gods and in a future punishment, Lucretius launched an impassioned battle against religion. Among the Epicureans the key problem had already arisen whether fear of death or fear of the gods was the greater evil. Lucretius dispensed with the gods but, in attempting to disprove the immortality of the soul, emphasized the reality of death more strongly than any other philosopher. He himself could not put his speculative ideals to practice. The poet within him fought against his restrictive materialism, and St. Jerome records that he put an end to his own life. His poem, however, still stands as the most appealing and cogent explanation of materialism in classical antiquity.

Modern Development

Christianity provided an effective barrier to the growth of materialism, and only with the humanist revival of the classics in the Renaissance did it again assert itself. It reached the peak of its development in the 18th and 19th centuries, after which it bequeathed its inheritance to Marxism and to the 20th-century development of dialectical materialism.

18th Century. The materialism of the 18th century was never completely disjoined from the materialism of antiquity, particularly that of Epicurus. DEISM sought only to have the universe rid of chaos and the world left alone, but the step from deism to materialism was short. John LOCKE took a skeptical position with respect to the spiritual soul, admitting the possibility that soul was merely matter. René DESCARTES extended his mechanistic explanation of nature to plants and animals, denying any type of soul in either and conceiving both as machines. It remained only for someone to apply this thought to man. J. O. de La Mettrie did this in his *Histoire naturelle de l'âme* (1745) and *L'Homme machine* (1748). His thesis that the substance of things is unknowable is similar to agnosticism, but his statement that man knows through the properties of matter and that these properties can explain the higher functions of the soul has broader implications. La Mettrie traced the difference between man and animals to differences in brain size and structure and, with complete lack of evidence, maintained that animals are capable of speech and of having a culture. His atheism was without a theoretical foundation since he regarded it as a condition of human existence.

In 1776 there appeared anonymously in Amsterdam a book entitled *Le Système de la nature.* Its author was the German Baron P. H. D. von HOLBACH, then living in Paris; his work was destined to become the bible of materialism. Here the basic thought of a radical materialism was systematized and extended over a wider range. For Holbach, the only thing that exists is matter in motion. La Mettrie had previously distinguished between motion and perception as different properties of matter, but now perception came to appear as a particular kind of motion.

The materialistic determinism of La Mettrie and Holbach seemingly did away with evil, guilt, and disorder. Freed of illusions, man could take his fate and his future into his own hand; he could forge his own happiness. With God and immortality, faith and the fear of a future life set aside, the way seemed open for the full development of man. Just how freely obligations and norms could be conceived on the basis of a naturalistic determinism had already occupied the thinking of Diderot, Voltaire, and Frederick the Great. Yet G. W. LEIBNIZ had shown that man, despite mechanical and mathematical explanations of phenomena, could give nature another meaning, while Shaftesbury, J. G. Herder, and Goethe had demonstrated that a mechanical conception of nature need not lead one to atheism.

19th Century. There are various reasons why materialism occupied such an important place in mid-19th-century Germany. For example, the extravagance of Hegel's idealism led his opponents to war against a spiritual metaphysics and even against Christianity. Hegel's a priori construction of nature likewise encouraged those with scientific mentalities to make exact inductive investigations. The younger generation thereupon relinquished the lecture hall of Hegel for the laboratories of the leading natural scientists. As they became more interested in the sensible and material world, their interest in atomistic and mechanistic explanations of nature led them to a mechanistic philosophy.

Science and Technology. The success of the natural sciences and the related rise of technology aided this movement. Already flourishing in France and England, the positivistic, utilitarian, and industrial revolution, with its great discoveries and improvements of living conditions, dulled interest in knowledge of man's inner nature and thereby banished from the universe the living, the besouled, and the spiritual. Contributing to such philosophical consequences were two misinterpreted discoveries of natural sciences: the law of the conservation of energy and the first synthesis of an organic chemical, urea, from inorganic matter.

Young natural scientists, particularly biologists and physicians, including Karl Vogt (1817–95), Jakob Moleschott (1822–93), and Ludwig Büchner (1824–99), were spokesmen for the materialist movement. Büchner's *Kraft und Stoff* (Frankfurt 1855) went through 20 editions and served as the handbook of German materialism. In it, he used his fundamental principle that every power is joined to some matter to exclude an other-worldly creator. He and his associates directed their battle against any special kind of vital force and against a substantial, spiritual, immortal soul. Denying the basic distinction between living and non-living, they treated the living entirely as a complex problem in mechanics.

German materialism in the 19th century was itself only a further development of the French. Popularized by Descartes and La Mettrie, the mechanistic theory of life had found wide diffusion. The machine generally hypnotized scientists: plants and animals, man himself, and the universe were regarded as machines. Physiologists were at work with phenomenological methods to explain mental processes. Vogt, following the French physician P. J. G. Cabanis (1757–1808), maintained that thought stands in the same relation to the brain as bile does to the liver and urine to the kidneys. Teleology was excluded from the universe; there was no dominion of spirit in and over nature. Belief in God was regarded by such thinkers as L. FEUERBACH as an illusion of man's mind.

Evolution. Advocating an evolutionary materialism and invoking Darwinist principles, D. F. STRAUSS and E. H. Haeckel thereupon assumed prominence in the materialist movement. Strauss, a follower of the Hegelian "left" (*see* HEGELIANISM AND NEO-HEGELIANISM) and already famous for his radical Bible criticism *Leben Jesu* (Tübingen 1835), passed in his more mature work, *Der alte und der neue Glaube* (Leipzig 1872), from Hegelian idealism to materialism. For him, as for Hegel, new developments in biology led to a reinterpretation of the whole of nature.

The universe, in Strauss's view, is one mass of matter moving in infinite space and in infinite time. There is nothing outside of it, under it, before it, or after it. It is an infinite summation of universes that contains, in an unending circle of generations and corruptions, an eternally similar source of life within itself, a phoenix that burns itself out only to give birth from its ashes to a new life, a being that can be identified only with God.

For Strauss, as for other materialists, there is no essential distinction between living and nonliving; life is only a particular, though complicated, type of mechanism. Darwin's principles—the survival of the fittest, natural selection, small mutations taking place over a long period of time—he used to explain how various species take their origin. In man the organic evolutionary process reaches its highest point on this planet. All soul activities and spiritual life are traced back to the motion of atoms. Man has not come forth from the hand of God, but has sprung upward from the depths of nature. His first state was not the higher state of Paradise, from which he could fall, but that of an animal from which he has always been rising. There is no longer room for a supernatural God, for a realm of spirit, for a distinction between soul and body.

Haeckel's thought is similar to this. In a series of writings he sought to build Darwinism into a philosophical position. From the time of his *Generelle Morphologie der Organismen* (Berlin 1866) the fundamental thought behind this position is discernible. Two years later he published *Natürliche Schöpfungsgeschichte,* which explained the development of the world from the nebular hypothesis all the way to the origin of the spiritual in man. The work went through ten editions and was translated into 12 languages. A summary presentation of his philosophy was contained in the popularly oriented *Die Welträtsel* (Bonn 1899), of which 300,000 copies were printed in Germany and which was translated into 15 languages, and *Die Lebenswunder* (Stuttgart 1904).

Haeckel's theory of substance, in summary, envisioned an unchangeable, infinite matter endowed with eternal, infinite power, developing itself in an infinite and unbounded space and time. The formation of earth is a part of the evolution of the universe; with the appearance of carbon on its surface, organic life begins. In addition to traditional arguments from paleontology and anatomical similarities, Haeckel made extensive use of ontogeny, the basic law of biogenetics, which states that the development of the individual is a miniature reproduction of the development of the species. Knowledge of the animal origins of the human race he regarded as firmly established. He explained the human soul as a natural phenomenon, a physical process brought about by chemical changes and subject to the laws of matter. The material basis for all psychical reality is a body, the psychoplasm; each cell has a soul, and this soul is the sum of the elasticities stored up in the protoplasm. All living souls develop from the soul of the cell and its functions. Haeckel denied any peculiar properties to the human soul and thus any essential distinction between man and animal; he saw in man's gradual and stepwise development from the lower vertebrates his greatest triumph over the rest of nature.

Influence and Critique. The materialist movement reached its peak at the end of the 19th century. At that time SCIENTISM and the rationalist mentality held sway over the minds of men; mechanistic determinism and evolutionism seemed then to supply all the answers that could be asked about the physical universe. With the turn of the 20th century, however, advances in physical science, particularly in relativity and quantum theory, shook confidence in the world picture of Newton and Laplace. Scientists themselves gradually drifted away from mechanism; soon even they were questioning their ability to know matter in all its complexity. In philosophy, phenomenology and existentialism came into prominence, and schools that emphasized the reality of life, spirit, and culture attracted new interest. With the exception of Communist-dominated areas, where dialectical and historical materialism was given official endorsement, materialism ceased to be developed as a systematic philosophy. Antispiritualist thinkers, particularly in English-speaking countries, turned instead to pragmatism, naturalism, LOGICAL POSITIVISM, and analytical philosophy in an attempt to voice anew their materialist prejudices.

The inadequacies of materialism as a philosophy readily manifest themselves to those who examine seriously the concept of matter. Of itself inert and resistive to change, matter is insufficient to explain even motion, let alone life, perception, thought, and the supernatural. Those who maintain that it alone exists or that it alone has explanatory value do so only by blinding themselves to the realities that are most obvious and most intelligible to the human spirit.

See Also: ATHEISM; DEISM; HUMANISM, SECULAR; RATIONALISM; ENCYCLOPEDISTS.

Bibliography: F. C. COPLESTON, *History of Philosophy* (Westminster, Md. 1946–1963) v. 1, 4–7. S. CARAMELLA, *Enciclopedia filosofica* (Venice-Rome 1957) 3:407–414. H. KUHN, *Lexikon für Theologie und Kirche*, ed. J. HOFER and K. RAHNER (Freiberg 1957–65) 7:161–163. H. BRAUN, *Die Religion in Geschichte und Gegenwart* (Tübingen 1957–65) 4:800–803. R. EISLER, *Wörterbuch der philosophischen Begriffe* (Berlin 1027–30) 2:77–80. F. A. LANGE, *History of Materialism,* tr. E. C. THOMAS, 3 v. in 1 (3d ed. London 1957), introd. B. RUSSELL. C. J. H. HAYES, *A Generation of Materialism, 1871–1900* (New York 1941). I. M. BOCHEŃSKI, *Contemporary European Philosophy,* tr. D. NICHOLL and K. ASCHEN-

BRENNER (Berkeley 1956). A. BANFI, *Storia del materialismo,* 2 v. (Milan 1952–53).

[H. MEYER]

MATERIALISM, DIALECTICAL AND HISTORICAL

Dialectical materialism and historical materialism are two components of the philosophy associated with Marxism-Leninism, the theory of communism. This theory, apart from its distinctive philosophy, embraces also political economy and scientific socialism. Political economy deals with the analysis of capitalist and socialist economic structures; its theoretical sections overlap those of historical materialism. Scientific socialism, though not fully developed within Marxism-Leninism, is supposed to deal with the realization of theory in practice. Philosophy itself is there defined as the science of the most general laws of nature, society, and human thought. Since it is divided into dialectical materialism and historical materialism, these constitute the main divisions of the present treatment.

Dialectical Materialism

Dialectical materialism is pleonastically defined as the science of the most general laws of nature, society, and human thought. Thus it is given the same definition as philosophy in general, although in actual practice it is concerned only with the formal components that enter also into historical materialism.

General Characteristics. Dialectical materialism, as the central component of Marxist-Leninist philosophy, is purported to be a complete philosophical system, containing all the disciplines necessary for an explanation of reality. Nothing is regarded as outside its purvey. Moreover, it is said to be scientific, and this in two senses. First, it is proposed as the only contemporary philosophical system capable of explaining the world in accord with the results of progress in modern science; secondly, it is scientific in the sense that it operates according to scientific rules and logical procedures. This philosophy is also said to be Marxist, again with two meanings. First, it is Marxist because it is supposedly the doctrine of Karl MARX as developed and passed on by Friedrich ENGELS and V. I. Lenin. Secondly, it is Marxist because it is revolutionary, providing the world outlook of the ''revolutionary Marxist party.'' It is the philosophy of the proletariat, permitting the victorious march toward communism.

Materialist Aspects. As a MATERIALISM, dialectical materialism derives from a long tradition and shares some of the characteristics of previous materialisms, especially those of the 18th and 19th centuries. First, it is a thorough-going RATIONALISM. All that is can be known and explained; what now is unexplained will remain so only temporarily. Secondly, it is a complete SCIENTISM; the natural sciences are proposed as the last word in human knowing, and all philosophical activity must be based on the certitude provided by science. Thirdly, it is antimetaphysical (in the traditional sense of the term metaphysics) and, by the same token, antiphilosophical.

Dialectical Aspects. To these fundamental characteristics that it shares with other materialisms, dialectical materialism adds the new note that it is a completely different materialism—a ''dialectical'' materialism. This overcomes the basic defect of previous materialisms, i.e., their mechanistic reduction of the higher forms of material reality to lower and simpler forms. Its dialectical character also attentuates the rigidity of the first three characteristics. Thus, dialectical materialism is rationalist, but talks of the ''dialectic of absolute and relative truth [knowledge]''; it is scientistic but insists that philosophy cannot be reduced to a mere ''science of sciences''; it is anti-metaphysical, yet it develops doctrines on being and other ontological categories.

Monist Determinism. Finally, there are two characteristics that, although they mark previous forms of materialism, are nevertheless distinctive in the form they take in dialectical materialism. The first is MONISM: dialectical materialism is purported to be a materialist monism, meaning that it recognizes one reality—matter. The second is determinism: the complete intelligibility of reality postulated by the rationalism of dialectical materialism is based on the affirmation ''for every effect, a cause.'' In turn, each of these basic principles has a dialectical interpretation that supplies its distinctive flavor; behind the materialist monism there is a ''dialectic of being and thought,'' and behind the determinism there is a ''dialectic of chance and necessity.''

Basic Doctrines. For dialectical materialism, philosophy begins with the ''basic question'' as to which is primary, being (matter) or thought (spirit): materialists give primacy to the first and idealists to the second. Accordingly, there are three main chapters to dialectical materialism's exposition of the content of philosophy, dealing respectively with matter, with dialectic, and with thought.

Matter. This is consistently defined in the epistemological terms first used by Lenin: ''Matter is the philosophical category for the designation of that objective reality which is given to man in his sensations, and which is copied, photographed, reflected in sensations, [while] existing independently of them'' (V. I. Lenin, *Works* 14.133, in Russian). All matter is in motion. Without motion, there is no matter; without matter, there is no motion. Space and time are existential forms of matter. Again, without space and time, there is no matter; without matter, there is no space and time. The unity of the world consists in its materiality.

Dialectic. The dialectic—the Hegelian element in dialectical materialism—has two different, albeit complementary, meanings. First, the distinct components of reality are all in mutual interconnection: reality forms an organic whole in which the identity of the components is fully recognizable only as a function of the whole. Secondly, this organicity is of a dynamic nature, and the dynamic rhythm is determined by the ''basic laws of the dialectic.'' For Engels, there were three such laws; for Lenin, sixteen (in the form of ''points''); for Stalin, four; for mid-20th-century Soviet philosophy, the three that follow.

First, the ''law of the unity and conflict of contraries'' designates the *causa efficiens* (and *materialis*) of the movement of matter. Matter moves because the ''real contradictions'' it contains are in a triadic conflict that leads from ''thesis vs. antithesis'' to ''synthesis''; this, in its turn, constitutes a new ''thesis'' for the continuation of the eternal process. Second, the ''law of the transition from quantitative changes to qualitative changes'' defines the nature of the movement of matter: the accumulation of a series of changes in quantity leads to a leap (*skačok*), the result of which is a qualitative change. Finally, the ''law of negation of negation'' explains the continuity of material reality throughout the process of change: in negating the ''antithesis'' (which is the negation of the ''thesis''), the ''synthesis'' preserves all that was ''positive'' in the other two, but does this on a (qualitatively) higher plane.

Thought. Thought, or consciousness (*soznanie*), is for dialectical materialism—again following Lenin—a reflection (*otraženie*) of material (objective) reality. Knowledge progresses through the attainment of ''relative'' truths to the possession of ''absolute'' truths. Absolute truth is an ideal limit, but there are some ''absolute truths'' already known to man, e.g., the basic laws of the dialectic. Truth is the correspondence of thought to reality; but it is also the process of the accumulation of relative truths. ''Practice,'' or practical transformatory activity, is the basis of knowledge and the criterion of truth. It is the basis of knowledge because only in work does man come into concrete contact with reality and with problems that cognitive activity must solve; it is the criterion of truth because only by verifying his ideas in practical activity can man see if they correspond to reality. Logic, the ''logical,'' is a summary of the essential points of the ''historical,'' which is reality in all its diversity. Thought (the ''subjective dialectic'') is, as a reflection of reality (the ''objective dialectic''), abstract: the opposition of subject and object can be overcome only by an ''ascent from abstract to concrete'' (*vosxoždenie ot abstraktnomu do konkretnogo*).

Origins and Development. Although elements of dialectical materialism can be traced to most of the previous materialisms, especially the scientific materialism of 19th-century Germany represented by Karl Vogt, Ludwig Büchner, Jakob Moleschott, et al., its real formation began with the ''Hegelian left,'' M. Stirner, D. F. Strauss, L. FEUERBACH, B. Bauer, and K. Marx (*see* HEGELIANISM AND NEO-HEGELIANISM). This radical reaction to Hegelian idealism stressed a philosophy of action and advocated a pure rationalism. Feuerbach's *Das Wesen des Christentums* (1841) explained away religion as the creation and worship by man of an ''alienation'' (God) that was merely his conception of the ideal man. Marx made this notion fundamental, and pushed the analysis of alienation down to its economic roots. For him, all alienations—religious, civic, political—are derived from a basic alienation that is economic, i.e., that of man from his work and its fruits: this is a ''dehumanization,'' because work is the prime property of man. Man is here conceived as the sum of his material needs and work as the means of satisfying them. But, it was Engels, not Marx, who—in his *Dialectics of Nature* (published posthumously 1925) and *Anti-Dühring* (1878)—began the development of dialectical materialism as such. Historically seen, dialectical materialism is a distillation made by Engels from Marx's historical materialism. Lenin, while giving a revolutionary twist to historical materialism, developed the epistemology of dialectical materialism in his *Materialism and Empirio-Criticism* (1909). Stalin's contribution to dialectical materialism (a chapter in the *History of the Communist Party* of 1938) is a popular presentation of the basic doctrines of Lenin.

Communist philosophy as promulgated by proponents in the Soviet Union falls into three periods: (1) from the death of Lenin (1924) to the decision of 1930; (2) from 1930 to 1947; and (3) from 1947 to the fall of the Soviet Union in 1989. The first period was marked by intense philosophical activity that culminated in the discussion between the ''Deborinites'' (followers of A. M. Deborin, a Hegelian) and the ''mechanicists,'' or fundamentalist materialists. This discussion was decided by Stalin in favor of an orthodox wing, led by M. B. Mitin. Stalin's intervention discouraged independent philosophical thought, and the second or ''quiet'' period was marked by the dominance of ''quotationism,'' where Soviet philosophers limited themselves to repeating what the ''classics'' (Marx, Engels, Lenin, and Stalin) had said. The third period was again one of intense activity.

It began with the 1947 discussion of G. F. Aleksandrov's *History of Western European Philosophy.* Although this book was condemned for its "neutrality," Stalin—through A. A. Ždanov—encouraged Soviet philosophers to develop fresh views and gave them permission to do so.

The final period was marked by several discussions of some importance. The discussion of logic in 1950–51 dealt with the nature of dialectical logic and its relation to formal logic; it was decided that the dialectical logic of the classics is a higher form of logic, of which formal logic represents only a special case. The discussion on psychology (1950) decreed a "re-Pavlovization" of Soviet psychology, but failed to resolve the basic problem of the relationship between matter and spirit. The 1957 discussion on practice as an epistemological category has led to a redefinition of practice as "sense-contact." A large-scale attempt to develop dialectical logic as a logic began in 1958.

The most significant event of this period was Stalin's intervention in 1950 on the question of language. A Soviet linguist, N. J. Marr, had proposed that a theory of proletarian language be developed because of the unique class position of the proletariat. As it has its own art and philosophy, so the proletariat must have its own linguistic superstructure corresponding to its base. Stalin rejected this proposal, maintaining that language was one of the instruments of production, that it was not a part of the superstructure and, therefore, was not class-bound. Soviet philosophers took advantage of this loosening of the dogmatic strictures and argued that since logic is a matter of language, it is not class-bound either; and, since natural science is, like language, directly bound up with production, it too is not subject to class considerations. Thus, there was a general widening in the freedom of movement of Soviet philosophers and a restriction on the party's right to intervene in purely philosophical questions.

Influence and Critique. For better or worse, the influence of dialectical materialism on the philosophical currents of the Western world is almost nonexistent. With the exception of notorious communists or fellow travelers—Roger Garaudy in France, Maurice Cornforth in England, John Sommerville in the United States—only a few Western philosophers pay any serious attention to dialectical materialism. On the one hand, this is understandable since most of the valuable elements in this doctrine have been borrowed and simplified from other philosophers, notably Hegel and Aristotle; on the other, it is regrettable since, through historical materialism, this doctrine had a strong (though indirect) influence on the world's intelligentsia.

Thorough criticisms of dialectical materialism in general and of specific doctrines in particular are to be found in the books of Wetter and Bocheński (see bibliog.). The first thing that strikes one about this doctrine is its naïveté: almost all its affirmations are pre-philosophical and commonsensical. Secondly, there is an obvious contradiction between the Hegelian dialectic and the basically realist epistemology. Again, the belligerent attitude of Soviet philosophers not only renders discussion unproductive; it also has a deleterious effect on the doctrine itself, since only the polemically useful parts are developed. Finally, there is a fundamental dishonesty in a philosophy that maintains rank nonsense in order to prove an extraphilosophical point, e.g., its tenacity in affirming the existence of real contradictions in order to eliminate God. Soviet philosophers did not realize that putting the source of movement within matter was no explanation; or that their fear of the introduction of God was unfounded, since the philosopher's concept of deity (prime mover, etc.) does not necessarily entail the personal God of Revelation.

Historical Materialism

Historical materialism is dialectical materialism as applicable or applied to society and history. It is the study of society and history in terms of the categories and laws of dialectical materialism. Like the latter, it is complete, scientific, and revolutionary. It is materialist insofar as it considers the production of material goods basic. It is dialectical because it is "historicist," i.e., history is conceived as the evolution of reality and humanity, and these, as explained above, form an organic whole. Finally, it conforms epistemologically to dialectical materialism, where thought is a reflection of being, since "social thought" (ideology) is defined as a reflection of "social being" (production).

Basic Doctrines. The basic elements of the Marxist-Leninist explanation of society and history are the forces of production (tools, raw materials, muscular power, etc.) and the relations of production (commercial relations like those between worker and employer, creditor and debtor, etc.). The relations of production form the "base" of society and determine the "superstructure" (political and legal doctrines, art, philosophy, and religion). Since the base is in constant evolution (all matter is in movement), and since the superstructure tends by nature to lag, there develops a tension expressing itself in the formation of classes that can be exhaustively divided into two main groups, the "progressive" and the "reactionary." These main classes are the "contradictories" in society and their conflict follows the basic laws of the dialectic.

History falls into five main periods, according to the dominant forces and relations of production and classes:

primitive, ancient, feudal, capitalist, and socialist. The tension between classes builds up (quantitative changes) to a ''revolutionary situation'': revolution is a leap in which a new qualitative situation comes to be wherein one class negates the other. The ideologies are reflections of the base, i.e., of the class-conditions of their exponents. Thus, bourgeois ideology (philosophy, art, etc.) serves the interests of the exploiters, while proletarian ideology (Marxism-Leninism) serves the interests of the proletarian masses; the latter are the best interests of all of humanity. The Communist party, which is the ''vanguard,'' ''conscience,'' and ''honor'' of the proletariat, therefore represents the best interests of all of humanity and is entitled to govern all domains. Mankind, finally, is moving toward a final state of paradise on earth, communism, and it is led to this goal by the proletariat, i.e., by the Communist party.

Origins and Development. Elements of historical materialism are to be found in the writings of Jean Jacques ROUSSEAU, SAINT-SIMON, Fourrier, et al., but its true founder was Karl Marx. Engels contributed little to its formulation. Lenin attenuated Marx's economic determinism with his revolutionary voluntarism; he affirmed that revolution did not have to wait for changes in the economic base, but could be effected by a disciplined party of professional revolutionaries. Stalin's only contribution of note was the interpretation of language mentioned above.

Influence and Critique. It is difficult to overestimate the influence that this doctrine had, especially on the nonphilosophical intelligentsia. For those who put a price on certainty in the explanation of social and historical events, historical materialism purported to offer a doctrine that is simple (two basic elements), clear (everything follows from the conflict of these two), inspiring (history has a glorious goal), and directive (one knows what to do to aid history). Add to this the fact that the whole doctrine is couched in seemingly simple terms, and it becomes easy to see why it was most popular among the substitutes for religion in the twentieth century.

Yet historical materialism was also an a priori schematism with a conceptual coherence almost completely lacking in the events it was supposed to explain. Secondly, its conceptual apparatus was much too rough: e.g., the notion of class, which is fundamental, was always left vague. Finally, it was based on several gratuitous assumptions, e.g., on the nature of man, the origin of society, and ''communism of the future,'' which were all unacceptable, the last shown to be false with the fall of the USSR in 1989.

Bibliography: G. A. WETTER, *Dialectical Materialism: A Historical and Systematic Survey of Philosophy in the Soviet Union,* tr. P. HEATH (New York 1959), ample bibliography. I. M. BOCHEŃSKI, *Der sowjetrussische dialektische Materialismus* (3d ed. Bern 1960), ample bibliography. For more analytic treatment of special questions, see the books in the series *Sovietica* (Institute of East-European Studies, University of Fribourg). Also ref. *Studies in Soviet Thought,* quarterly of the same institute. T. J. BLAKELEY, *Soviet Philosophy: A General Introduction to Contemporary Soviet Thought* (Dordrecht, Holland 1964).

[T. J. BLAKELEY]

MATHEMATICS, PHILOSOPHY OF

Philosophy of mathematics is a broad term including any theory on the nature of mathematics as a whole or on the nature of any part or aspect of mathematics. A specialized branch of learning, it deals with the following and related topics: the origin of mathematical knowledge and its relation to the real world; the nature and type of existence peculiar to mathematical entities; mathematics as viewed by mathematicians and by other scientists—and this either absolutely, or in terms of its relationship to other human and cultural values (hence the ''logic of'' or the ''psychology of'' mathematics). A thorough presentation of the philosophy of mathematics would, then, include a discussion of each of these aspects. The analysis here is restricted to a consideration of various theories on the nature of mathematics and a critical evaluation of these theories.

Various Theories

Since a philosophy of mathematics is based on a given mathematical content, this exposition is divided into three parts, roughly corresponding to the three major developments within mathematics itself: the classical, the transitional, and the contemporary.

Classical Period: c. 3000 B.C. to A.D. 1600. From the time of its origin among the Egyptians and of its development as a science by the Greeks (*c.* 600 B.C.) until the 16th century, the content of pure mathematics embraced arithmetic and basic number theory, along with geometry, the conic sections, and basic trigonometry. Music, astronomy, geography, mechanics, and hydrostatics constituted applied mathematics.

Greek Theories. It is currently held that the philosophy of mathematics originated with the same Greeks who have also been credited with being the founders of mathematics as a science. Among the Pre-Socratics, the PYTHAGOREANS proposed the first complete theory: the principles of mathematics, number and form, are the principles and the basic reality of all things. Each thing has its own mathematical number and form: justice is the number four (and therefore a square); time is seven; perfection is ten, etc. The Pythagoreans were largely responsible also for the division of mathematics into arithmetic (and music, as applied arithmetic) and geometry (and astronomy, as applied geometry).

PLATO modified this view, placing mathematics within the framework of knowledge in general: ordinary knowledge of material things (''opinion'') is unstable because the objects known are constantly changing; mathematics achieves more stable knowledge because its objects, numbers and forms, do not change; while the most perfect kind of knowledge (''dialectic'') is the contemplation of ideas or forms of which the sense, and even the mathematical words, are but a participation and imitation. Mathematical entities, then, differ from sense objects in being eternal and unchangeable; they differ from the forms in that there are many alike (many circles), while the form is in each case unique. The Pythagorean-Platonic view is adopted totally or with modifications by PLOTINUS, PROCLUS, NICHOLAS OF CUSA, COPERNICUS, KEPLER, GALILEO, and many others.

The Aristotelian view classifies mathematics as one of three speculative sciences (*see* SCIENCES, CLASSIFICATION OF). Mathematics arises by means of ABSTRACTION from sense data and deals with ''quantified substance'' as discrete (number), whence arise the arithmetical branches, or as continuous (form), whence arise the geometrical branches. Mathematics is but one way of fulfilling man's ability to know reality; it has a pedagogical and useful value, but it is not a knowledge necessary for, or leading to, an other-worldly contemplation. BOETHIUS, AVICENNA, AVERROËS, THOMAS AQUINAS, and many medieval scholars support this view with modifications, and the writings of Francis BACON, G. W. LEIBNIZ, Auguste COMTE, and many others, show its influence.

The skeptical view of mathematics is ably expressed by Sextus Empiricus (*c.* 250 A.D.) whose analysis of mathematical notions denies that they are clear, universal, and necessary, and proposes that they are inexact, empirical, and conventional (*see* SKEPTICISM). The British empiricists of the 16th and 17th centuries and some contemporaries adopt a similar interpretation.

Medieval Theory. The view of St. Thomas Aquinas is an instance of the medieval theory of mathematics. Essentially that of Aristotle, whose ideas he enriches with insights and refinements of earlier commentators and by his own metaphysical and terminological precision, Aquinas's theory considers mathematics, physics, and metaphysics as the three speculative (pure) sciences. In mathematics, one considers those aspects of things that depend not on their qualitative modifications but only on the fact that they are ''quantified,'' that is, subject to quantity—either the numerableness of things, or the shapes and forms in which quantity is, or might be, arranged.

In common with the other speculative sciences, mathematics is based upon what might be called preliminary knowledge and experience (now referred to as ''prereflective'' knowledge) of the quantitative aspects of things. This preliminary knowledge must include at least a vague understanding of the terms with which one expresses quantity (one, two; circle, square). After adding to this prereflective data an explicit understanding of logical procedure, one establishes axioms and postulates, defines mathematical objects (e.g., a square), and then proceeds to deduce the characteristics of those objects that are necessarily implied by the given definition (e.g., that a square is equiangular). The conclusions that are thereby reached are restricted only by the scope of man's imagination. Mathematics is the most exact and certain of the three speculative sciences and exercises a certain hegemony over the sciences of nature.

Greek and medieval thought was familiar with several sciences in which the propositions of pure mathematics are applied to other sciences. Aquinas names astronomy and optics as instances of applied geometry, and music, of applied arithmetic. They are called ''intermediate'' (*scientiae mediae*) because they employ the mathematical method of DEMONSTRATION (formally mathematical) on subject matter from sensible nature (materially physical).

The liberal arts for Thomas Aquinas are ordered to knowledge and involve some sort of making, working, or producing, as making a syllogism or a speech, composing melodies, and reckoning the course of the stars. Mathematics (arithmetic and music; geometry and astronomy) form the quadrivium (four-ways), while logic, grammar, and rhetoric form the trivium (three-ways) of the seven liberal arts—all of which formed part of the medieval scheme of education, especially aimed at learning philosophy. As a liberal art, mathematics designates the mind's capacity to make concepts symbolic of quantity as discrete (number-symbols) or as continuous (form-symbols).

Transitional Period: 1600 to 1850. During this period, geometry lost its dominance over arithmetic through the invention of analytic geometry. A second significant discovery, the infinitesimal calculus, opened the way for the mathematical study of change and motion. Arithmetic and algebra, trigonometry, and various other branches and aspects of both pure and applied mathematics were either developed or founded anew.

Unfortunately, the philosophy of mathematics was given less attention, and no new and original theories arose to match the new mathematics. The philosopher George BERKELEY, offered some sound criticism of the loose reasoning that accompanied the first invention of the calculus. But the main growth in the philosophy of mathematics consisted in the dream of a universal science and method that haunted such thinkers as F. BACON, R. DESCARTES, B. PASCAL, and especially G. W. Leibniz. At the close of this period, this dream was fulfilled through the formulation of symbolic logic.

Immanuel KANT is well known for his analysis of mathematics and of science, but apparently he was unaware of the basic changes that mathematics had undergone. He considered mathematics as a system of absolute conceptions (synthetic a priori judgments) constructed within and unified by the central and regulative intuitions of space and time. Other theories during this period generally followed the philosophical outlook of their proponents, as in RATIONALISM, EMPIRICISM, IDEALISM, and POSITIVISM.

Contemporary Period: 1850 to the Present. In contrast to its earlier status, mathematics in the contemporary period is characterized by two significant changes. First, the invention of symbolic logic and the refinement of the axiomatic method have endowed it with a richer symbolism and led to its presentation as a system of purely deductive structures based on primitive axioms and propositions. Secondly, the change of outlook on such subjects as algebra and geometry, the development of analysis, and the introduction of the infinite into mathematics through Cantor's theory of sets have greatly enlarged the content of contemporary mathematics. Of special importance today are three theories included under the title of ''foundations of mathematics.''

Logicism, originating principally with G. Boole, G. Frege, and G. Peano, holds mathematics to be a branch of logic; the identity of mathematics with logic was formally proposed in B. Russell and A. N. Whitehead's *Principia Mathematica.*

Formalism, deriving mainly from David Hilbert (who claims Euclid as forerunner), originally began as a refinement of axiomatic method (as in Euclid's *Elements*). It was further developed by Hilbert and his followers to ease the crises caused by the paradoxes of *Principia Mathematica,* and to demonstrate the consistency of classical mathematics challenged by Brouwer and his school. Hilbert formulated classical mathematics by means of ''meaningless'' symbols as formal axiomatic theory (especially in his and P. Bernays' *Grundlagen der Mathematik*); this ''meaningless'' formalization, in turn, acquires meaning by becoming an object of a mathematical study called ''proof-theory'' or metamathematics.

Intuitionism, advocated by L. E. J. Brouwer, as a general philosophy holds that man's primordial experience is mathematical, that mathematics is identical with the exact part of human thought, and that no science (not even philosophy or logic) exercises priority or hegemony over mathematics. As a philosophy of mathematics, it holds to the dependence of mathematics on intuition alone and requires constructibility in terms of the natural numbers as the sole method of mathematical proof. Certain parts of classical mathematics and the logical law of excluded middle are rejected. Language and symbols are instruments for communicating mathematical ideas, but are not to be considered mathematics.

Critical Evaluation

It has been traditional in philosophy to view pure mathematics as a science dealing with quantity as discrete (arithmetic) or as continuous (geometry), and to consider astronomy and music as branches of applied mathematics. But this view needs now to be greatly enlarged by a deeper appreciation of tradition, an understanding of the development of mathematics itself, and an integration of current views on the foundations of mathematics.

Foundations. Mathematics can still be considered a highly abstract science having both a pure, or speculative, and a practical, or applied, aspect. As the intuitionists have partly shown, however, there are two ways in which pure mathematics originates from sense data. (1) Before mind actually ''abstracts'' the notion of circle or number, it must have previously generalized from sense experience such basic notions as structure (quantitative form), correspondence, the notions of singularity (unity) and group (multitude), and of sequence and order—a group of notions that form the basic architecture of the mind's mathematical universe. (2) It is only into this potentially prepared mathematical world that mind can ''abstract'' and then ''localize'' such mathematical entities as group, aggregate, circle, or number.

Once the mind has been equipped with these basic laws and foundational entities, it is to the credit of logicism and formalism to have shown that one can ''mathematicize'' in three ways. (1) Aided by creative imagination and by renewed recourse to sense imagery, the mind can tend to purify and perfect the entities (e.g., figures and numbers), or to embellish and create new instances of them (as inventing new numbers, or constructing topology). (2) The mind can neglect the basic mathematical paradigms themselves—even to the extent of considering them formless and meaningless inhabitants of this universe—and concentrate on their arrangement, i.e., their relations of priority and posteriority or of simplicity and complexity. Once this has been done, one can reintroduce mathematical entities to see if they can be made conformable to this new structural arrangement. At this point, the formalist school is content if no contradiction can be shown, while the intuitionists require that each new mathematical entity must be ''shown'' or constructed. (3) Another way of manipulating mathematical entities, pointed up by the invention of the infinitesimal calculus, is to consider them as relatively moveable and changeable, and to determine their laws of generation and their mutual reducibility within the mathematical universe. It is here that the import of such mathematical ''actions'' as squaring and differentiating is made clear, and the possibility of the infinitely small and the infinitely large is seen to be consistent.

Further Integration. A yet further advance is made when mind compares the mathematical with, say, the logical or the metaphysical universes or with the universe of language; or, again, when mind considers the methodology it employs in mathematics as similar to, or as contrasted with, that of other sciences. These considerations form a large area of interest in contemporary philosophy of mathematics.

A final way of considering mathematical entities is that proper to applied mathematics. This is the ''projective'' technique of matching such entities with, or imposing mathematical structures upon, the world of experience. Tradition has not always been clear on the distinction between pure and applied mathematics, and was given to emphasizing the static and immobile aspect of mathematics and its closeness to sense experience. The fact of various geometries and algebras shows that in pure mathematics, at least, there is no unique geometry or algebra of the real world, and that in applied mathematics the operational or pragmatic definition of truth applies: whatever mathematical system works best for the problem at hand is true.

A clear notion of mathematical abstraction, however, enables one to hold that mathematics is still a science of reality. To say that mathematics studies ''quantity'' is a traditional but inexact shorthand for stating that it studies any ''ordering or structuring of the parts of quantified substance'' (since, even in tradition, no ''accident'' as ''quantity'' can be the subject of science). The speculative mathematical universe, then, is the world of the traditional ''intelligible'' (imaginable) matter within which the mind engages in any of the various types of mathematical activity outlined above.

See Also: QUANTITY; CONTINUUM; EXTENSION.

Bibliography: E. W. BETH, *Foundations of Mathematics* (Amsterdam 1959). W. C. and M. KNEALE, *The Development of Logic* (New York 1962) 379–688. G. T. KNEEBONE, *Mathematical Logic and the Foundations of Mathematics* (New York 1963). E. A. MAZIARZ, *Philosophy of Mathematics* (New York 1950). S. KÖRNER, *The Philosophy of Mathematics* (London 1960). B. R. RUSSELL, *Principles of Mathematics,* v.1 (New York 1938).

[E. A. MAZIARZ]

MATHER, INCREASE AND COTTON

Father and son, Puritan clergymen.

Increase, b. Dorchester, Mass., June 21, 1639; d. Boston, Mass., Aug. 23, 1723. He was the youngest son of Richard Mather, a prominent Puritan clergyman and Katherine (Holt) Mather. He attended Harvard (B.A. 1656), but spent most of his time in Ipswich and Boston studying under Rev. John Norton. Later he entered Trinity College, Dublin, Ireland (M.A. 1658). In 1661, after serving as chaplain to the soldiers on Guernsey, he returned to Boston and married Maria Cotton, daughter of John. Mather was a leader in Puritan circles, becoming pastor (1664) of the Second Church in Boston, a post he retained throughout his life. From 1685 to 1701 he was president of Harvard, but spent little time in Cambridge, preferring to devote his time to church affairs. In 1688 the colony sent him to England, where, after three years, he finally obtained a new charter. After 1692 his influence declined. His numerous writings include theological, historical, and biographical works. *Cases of Conscience Concerning Evil Spirits* (1693) appeared during the witchcraft hysteria and cautioned against the abuses of the witch trials.

Cotton, b. Boston, Feb. 12, 1663; d. there, Feb. 13, 1728. He graduated from Harvard (B.A. 1678, M.A. 1681) and was ordained (1685), serving at the Second Church during his father's absences and after his father's death. In 1718, with his father, he assisted at the ordination of a Baptist minister, and three years later he championed the unpopular cause of innoculation against smallpox. He was one of the founders of Yale and was the first native American to be a fellow of the Royal Society. His publications include *Magnalia Christi Americana* (1702), a collection of materials on the ecclesiastical history of New England; *Wonders of The Invisible World* (1693); and *Essays to Do Good* (1710).

[E. DELANEY]

MATHEW, THEOBALD

Known as the apostle of temperance; b. Thomaston, County Tipperary, Ireland, Oct. 10, 1790; d. Cobh, County Cork, Dec. 8, 1856. He was the fourth of the 12 children of James Mathew, of a distinguished Catholic family, and Anne Whyte. From childhood he had personal charm and a spirit of generosity. In 1807 he entered Maynooth College but left. In 1808 he was accepted by the Capuchins. Soon after ordination (1813) he was assigned to Cork. He became Cork's most beloved citizen. In 1822 he was made Capuchin provincial, an office he held for 29 years, when he resigned because of ill health. After continued urging, he became (1838) head of the Cork Total Abstinence Society. Within a short time he enrolled thousands of members. Although it was a time of political unrest, Mathew kept his mission nonpolitical and won support even of non-Catholics. He sought no honors and always tried to correct the popular notion that he had miraculous power. His remarkable preaching drew hundreds of thousands throughout Ireland. In 1842 to 1843 he went to Scotland and England, giving the pledge to more than 200,000. In spring 1848, after the famine years, his untiring zeal (nearly six million had joined the society) took its toll: he had a stroke. Recovering somewhat, Mathew came to America in 1849. Despite ill health, he visited 25 states and gave the pledge to 600,000. In December 1851 he returned to Cork, broken in health and saddened by the failure of many to keep the pledge. His continued patience in the face of suffering and disappointment manifested his personal sanctity. Although his apostolate failed, it became the inspiration of later and more successful movements.

Bibliography: J. F. MAGUIRE, *Father Mathew: A Biography* (New York 1864), basic source. P. ROGERS, *Father Theobald Mathew, Apostle of Temperance* (New York 1945), good refs. FATHER AUGUSTINE, *Catholic Encyclopedia* 10:47–48. J. O'MAHONEY in *The Irish Way,* ed. F. J. SHEED (New York 1932).

[P. J. KELLY]

MATHEWS, SHAILER

Baptist theologian; b. Portland, Maine, May 26, 1863; d. Chicago, Ill., Oct. 23, 1941. After studying at Colby College, Waterville, Maine, the Newton Theological Institution, Mass., and the University of Berlin, Germany, Mathews taught at Colby College for seven years. Later he joined the faculty of the divinity school at the University of Chicago (1894–1908) and served as dean of the school (1908–33). As one of the early and influential proponents of the SOCIAL GOSPEL, he attempted to apply the teachings of Christ to modern social and economic problems. He was a defender of the modernist point of view and sought to effect a cooperation between science and religion. For him, theology was functional, its purpose being to give a rational statement of Christian attitudes and hopes in a particular era. He maintained that theological thought can be meaningful only when it uses the social patterns of the times as a vehicle of expression. ''Religion,'' he held, ''will have to find a pattern which is as axiomatic for modern man of our day as the pattern of sovereignty was to the modern man of the sixteenth century'' (Jackson, 35–36). He was the author of numerous books, including *The Social Teachings of Jesus* (1897), *The Faith of Modernism* (1924), *Creative Christianity* (1935), and *The New Faith for Old: An Autobiography* (1936). From 1903 to 1911 he was editor of the *World Today,* and later was editor of the *Biblical World* (1913–20). He served for four years as president of the Federal Council of Churches (1912–16).

See Also: NATIONAL COUNCIL OF THE CHURCHES OF CHRIST IN THE U.S.A.

Bibliography: J. H. JACKSON, *Many But One* (New York 1964).

[E. DELANEY]

MATHIEU, FRANÇOIS DÉSIRÉ

Archbishop of Toulouse, cardinal, historian; b. Einville (Meurtheet-Moselle), France, May 27, 1839; d. London, Oct. 26, 1908. He studied at the minor seminary in Pontà-Mousson and at the major seminary in Nancy. Even before ordination (1863) he taught in the minor seminary. After becoming a doctor of literature (1878), he acted as chaplain (1879) in the boarding school in Nancy run by the Dominicans, and was named honorary canon (1883) and pastor of St. Martin's parish in Pontà-Mousson (1893). He succeeded Charles FREPPEL as bishop of Angers (Jan. 3, 1893). In his diocese he founded the Society of Priestly Vocations, reestablished the titles of archpriest and dean, and strove to assure the prosperity of the Catholic university. In 1896 he was transferred to the Archdiocese of Toulouse, taking possession of the see September 29. After being created cardinal (June 19, 1899), he was called to Rome, but he continued to administer his diocese until March 1900. In the Roman Curia he was a member of several congregations and was also charged with diplomatic missions. His publications included his doctrinal theses, *L'Ancien régime dans la province de Lorraine et Barrois* and *De Joannis abbatis Gorziensis vita* (1878). *Le Concordat de 1801* (1903) attracted much attention, as did an article by him in the *Revue des Deux Mondes* (1904) on ''Les derniers jours de Léon XIII et le conclave, par un témoin.'' He was elected to the French Academy (June 1906) and was received into membership (Feb. 7, 1907) by the Count of Haussonville. He died in London, where he had gone to participate in a Eucharistic congress. An original and distinguished personality, good-humored and simple, Mathieu put into effect the directives of Leo XIII, notably those concerning reconciliation between Catholics and the French Third Republic.

Bibliography: E. RENARD, "Un Cardinal de Curie: Le Cardinal Mathieu," *Le Correspondant* 285 (1921) 224–256; *Le Cardinal Mathieu* (Paris 1925).

[R. LIMOUZIN-LAMOTHE]

MATHIS, MICHAEL AMBROSE

Liturgist, promoter of missions; b. South Bend, Ind., Oct. 6, 1885; d. University of Notre Dame, South Bend, March 10, 1960. His parents, Jacob P., a carpenter, and Elizabeth (Thome), had immigrated to the United States in 1881 from the Saarland in Germany. He joined the Congregation of Holy Cross in 1901, took his B.Litt. at the University of Notre Dame in 1910, and was ordained in 1914. He studied architecture at the Catholic University of America for a year and then Holy Scripture, earning his S.T.D. in 1920. He was professor of Holy Scripture for seven years at Holy Cross College, Washington, D.C.

Unable to go to the foreign missions because of World War I, he was appointed U.S. procurator for the Holy Cross missions in 1915. He organized the first systematic financial support of these missions, founding in 1917 the Bengal (later Holy Cross) Foreign Mission Society. In 1919 he launched the *Bengalese,* a magazine that published the work and the needs of the Holy Cross Missions. Mindful too of the importance of properly trained missionaries, he built the Holy Cross Foreign Mission Seminary, Washington, D.C., in 1924 and became its first superior. One of the first missiologists in the United States, he was a recognized authority on India's Catholic missions. In 1930 he was elected president of the Catholic Anthropological Conference. In 1922 he collaborated with Dr. Paluel Flagg and others to form the Medical Mission Committee, which by 1924 became the permanent Catholic Medical Mission Board. Along with Dr. Anna Dengel, he also founded the MEDICAL MISSION SISTERS in 1925, the first community of women to combine the religious life and the practice of medicine. From 1933 to 1938 he devoted his time and energy completely to them as their chaplain and ecclesiastical superior. To him more than to any other influence the community owes the liturgical spirit that has characterized it.

Mathis, influenced by Pius PARSCH, came to be known for his contribution to the liturgical apostolate in the United States even more than for his mission work. In the summer of 1947 he started the liturgy program at the University of Notre Dame, leading to an M.A. in liturgy. It was the first graduate school of liturgy in North America. He brought over from Europe outstanding liturgiologists, many of whose courses were published under the general title, *Liturgical Studies.* In 1954 he organized, as an offshoot of a course on liturgical architecture, an annual seminar for architects and artists at Notre Dame. He was an active member of the Liturgical Conference and a member of its board of directors from 1948 to 1956.

He thus attained distinction in two fields and was a pioneer in each. He was blessed with a tenacity of will that caused him to persevere in spite of difficulties and with a personal warmth and charm that served him well when it came to enlisting the assistance of others in his apostolic works.

Bibliography: G. E. SCHIDEL, "Never Too Much. In Memoriam: Rev. Michael Ambrose Mathis, C.S.C.," *Yearbook of Liturgical Studies* 3 (1962) 3–34.

[G. E. SCHIDEL]

MATIGNON, FRANCIS ANTHONY

Missionary; b. Paris, France, Nov. 10, 1753; d. Boston, Mass., Sept. 19, 1818. He attended the Sorbonne to prepare for the priesthood, was ordained Sept. 19, 1778, and received a doctorate in theology in 1785. Joining the theological faculty of the College of Navarre in 1786, he remained there until the anticlericalism of the French Revolution closed the college in 1791. When Matignon refused to take the oath to support the civil constitution of the clergy, he was forced to leave France.

After a few months in England, he returned to Paris to prepare for a mission in the U.S. In August 1792 Bp. John Carroll of Baltimore, Md., assigned him to Boston, Mass., where he found the Catholics internally divided into French and Irish parties and externally suffering under the contempt of Protestants. Within a year he healed the schism, resolving all differences between French and Irish Catholics in Boston. His influence with Protestants was also notable; when he applied for American citizenship in 1795, his petition was endorsed by five Protestant ministers. In 1796, his friend, Father John CHEVERUS, joined him in Boston for the difficult mission area that covered all of New England.

Matignon, dissatisfied with renting space for church services, initiated plans for building the Church of the Holy Cross, whose architect was Charles Bulfinch. Funds were scarce and he traveled throughout the Diocese of Baltimore for assistance. He himself gave $1,000 for this purpose, and 140 Protestants contributed to the building fund. Construction began in 1799 and the church was dedicated four years later by Carroll. A small school was operated under Matignon's direction from 1804 to 1807. When Matignon refused to have his name sent to Rome, Cheverus was named first bishop of Boston in 1808. Until he died in 1818, Matignon remained the bishop's closest aide.

Bibliography: R. H. LORD et al., *History of the Archdiocese of Boston . . . 1604 to 1943,* 3 v. (Boston 1945).

[T. F. CASEY]

MATILDA, EMPRESS

Lived from 1102 to 1167. Matilda was born Feb. 7, 1102 to King Henry I of England and his wife, Edith Matilda. At eight years of age she was sent to Germany as the bride of the Holy Roman Emperor, HENRY V. As an adult, she helped her husband govern his Italian lands and acted as regent for him upon occasion in Italy and Lotharingia. When Henry V died of stomach cancer in 1125, Matilda returned to her father's court.

Matilda's only brother, William, had perished in the wreck of the White Ship in 1120, leaving Henry I without an obvious heir. The king was under pressure from his nobles to appoint William Clito, the son of his elder brother and bitter enemy Robert Curthose, as his heir. Therefore, at his Christmas court in 1126, Henry I named Matilda as his heir and required all the barons to swear a solemn oath to support her, an oath that was repeated twice more prior to the king's death in 1135. Seeking an ally in this struggle, Henry betrothed his daughter to Geoffrey Plantagenet, the son of Count Fulk of Anjou. The decision was greeted with consternation by the Anglo-Norman barons, since the Angevins had always been the enemies of the dukes of Normandy.

When Henry I died suddenly in 1135, Matilda and Geoffrey moved at once to secure their possessions in Normandy. Meanwhile, Matilda's cousin, Stephen of Blois, the son of Henry's sister, Adela, dashed at once to England, where he had himself crowned king on Dec. 22, 1135. By 1137 he had consolidated his power sufficiently to confront Matilda and Geoffrey on the Continent, but quarreling among the baronial leaders of his army soon forced him to return to England.

In 1139, Matilda appealed to the Second Lateran Council in Rome for recognition of her right to the English throne, but the Church declined to rule on her case and continued to acknowledge Stephen as king. Supported by her half-brother, Earl Robert of Gloucester, Matilda invaded England in 1139. During the next two years the combatants sparred indecisively, but on Feb. 2, 1141, Matilda's forces routed Stephen's army at Lincoln and took the king himself prisoner. The empress traveled to London to arrange her coronation, but a violent uprising of the citizens forced her to flee to Oxford in June. The sources are vague about the causes of the rebellion, accusing the empress of haughtiness and excessive pride, of demanding money from the Londoners and of failing to listen to the advice of her chief magnates. However, it is more likely that the rebellion was instigated by Stephen's wife, Matilda of Boulogne, who kept the royal cause alive while her husband was imprisoned.

While the Empress Matilda's forces besieged the city of Winchester, a royalist army led by the queen surprised the attackers and captured Robert of Gloucester. Matilda agreed to exchange King Stephen for her chief adviser and military commander, which returned the situation to what it had been before the battle of Lincoln. Afterwards, Matilda's fortunes declined rapidly. In December 1142 she was forced to escape from Oxford by having herself lowered from the castle tower by ropes, and to walk through the snow to Abingdon. She remained in England for six more years, but from that time forward, neither party succeeded in making any inroads into the territory of the other.

In the meantime, Geoffrey of Anjou had fared better, capturing the city of Rouen and becoming duke of Normandy in 1144. Matilda returned to the continent in 1148 and settled at Rouen, where she remained for the rest of her life. Her son, Henry, succeeded peacefully to the English throne in 1154 following Stephen's death. Matilda assisted her son in ruling Normandy for the rest of her life, frequently acting as regent when his duties took him to other parts of his vast empire. She died on Sept. 10, 1167 and was buried at the abbey of Bec.

Bibliography: M. CHIBNALL, *The Ecclesiastical History of Orderic Vitalis,* v. 6 (Oxford 1978); *The Empress Matilda: Queen Consort, Queen Mother and Lady of the English* (Oxford 1991). K. R. POTTER, *Gesta Stephani* (Oxford 1976). E. KING and K. R. POTTER, *William of Malmesbury: The Historia Novella* (Oxford 1998). E. KING, *The Anarchy of Stephen's Reign* (Oxford 1994).

[J. TRUAX]

MATILDA, QUEEN OF GERMANY, ST.

Queen of Germany; b. 895; d. Quedlinburg, March 14, 968. Matilda was the daughter of the Saxon Count Dietrich and the lady Reinhild of Danish royalty. She was reared at the Benedictine convent at Herford where her grandmother was abbess. After her marriage in 909 to Henry the Fowler (later King Henry I), she bore him five famous children: OTTO (I) THE GREAT; Gerberga, wife of Louis IV of France; Hedwig, mother of Hugh Capet; St. BRUNO OF COLOGNE; and Henry, duke of Bavaria. Upon her husband's death she at first opposed, but later supported, Otto's succession to the throne. Suffering much from the strife among her sons, she found support in works of piety and in the foundation of several monasteries, notably Nordhausen, and QUEDLINBURG, where she was buried.

Matilda of Tuscany, fresco painting.

Feast: March 14.

Bibliography: Two *Vitae, Monumenta Germaniae Historica Scriptores* (Berlin 1826—) 4:283–302; 10:575–582. A. POTTHAST, *Bibliotheca historica medii aevi* (Graz 1954) 2:1468–69. A. BUTLER, *The Lives of the Saints*. rev. ed. H. THURSTON and D. ATTWATER (New York 1956) 1:592–593. M. LINTZEL, ''Die Mathilden-Viten und das Wahrheitsproblem in der Ueberlieferung der Ottonenzeit,'' *Archiv für Kulturgeschichte* 38 (1956) 152–166.

[C. DAVIS]

MATILDA OF TUSCANY

Countess of Tuscany and faithful ally of the papacy in the INVESTITURE STRUGGLE; b. 1046; d. Bondeno, near Ferrara, Italy, July 24, 1115. From her father Boniface of Canossa (d. *c.* 1052) she inherited the marches of Tuscany and Lombardy-Emilia, which she ruled jointly with her mother BEATRICE OF TUSCANY from 1069 to 1076. In 1069 she married Godfrey the Hunchback, Duke of Lorraine, but by 1071 had separated from him. Of mystical temperament and with aspirations toward an ascetic life, she became the ardent disciple of GREGORY VII. At Canossa in 1077 she interceded with Gregory for HENRY IV and guaranteed the Emperor's pledges, but after Henry's breach of faith she dedicated herself completely to the papal cause. For two decades she was the mainstay of the reform party in Italy. In 1081 Henry deposed her from her margraviate and drove her forces from Tuscany. After the election of Pope URBAN II, she resumed open warfare against Henry. In 1089 she contracted a short-lived political marriage with the young Welf V of Bavaria. She supported Conrad of Germany in his rebellion against his father. By an act of 1079 or 1080, confirmed in 1102, she donated to the papacy her allodial lands on both sides of the Alps, reserving the usufruct of them during her lifetime (*see* STATES OF THE CHURCH). In 1111 she was reconciled with the Emperor Henry V and made him her heir, without prejudice to the prior donation and in the hope of ending the investiture struggle. This donation later gave rise to a prolonged controversy. In 1115 Matilda's body was buried in the Mantuan monastery of SAN BENEDETTO POLIRONE. Five centuries later Pope Urban VIII had her body transferred to St. Peter's in Rome, where it rests in the tomb designed by Bernini in 1635.

Bibliography: DONIZO, *Vita Mathildis,* ed. L. SIMEONI, *Muratori* RIS2 5.2 (1940). A. OVERMANN, *Gräfin Mathilde von Tuscien* (Innsbruck 1895). R. DAVIDSOHN, *Geschichte von Florenz,* 4 v. (Berlin 1896–1927) v.1. L. TONDELLI, *Matilde di Canossa* (2d ed. Rome 1926); *Studi gregoriani* 4:365–371; *Il millenario di Canossa* (Reggio Calabria 1951). N. GRIMALDI, *La contessa Matilde e la sua stirpe feudale* (Florence 1928). A. FERRUA, ''La donazione della contessa Matilde,'' *La civiltà cattolica* 94.1 (1943) 212–223. L. SIMEONI, ''Il contributo della contessa Matilde al Papata nella lotta per le investiture,'' *Studi gregoriani* 1:353–372.

[C. E. BOYD]

MATINS

The Latin word *matutinum* means ''the morning hours.'' The term was first used for the morning prayer of praise (subsequently called LAUDS). The night choir Office was not originally called Matins but Vigils, because its proper place was around midnight or in the first half of the night. In the Middle Ages, this night choir Office was called Matins as it was celebrated at the end of the night toward the hour of prayer at dawn, Lauds.

Prayer during the night was already recommended to Christians of the 3d century. According to Tertullian (d. after 220), a vigil was observed by the whole community on many occasions during the year, and lasted throughout the whole of Easter night (*Ad uxorem* 2.4; *Patrologia Latina*, ed. J. P. Migne, 1:1407). Later, monks held the vigil every night (John Cassian, d. *c.* 430; *De institutione coenobiorum* 3.2; *Patrologia Latina* 49:115), and Emperor Justinian I (527–565) ordered it for all clerics of his empire (*Corpus iuris civilis, Codex Iustinianus*, ed. P. Krueger, 1.3.1.42). Its recitation remains an obligation for the secular and regular clergy under the 1971 revision of the Liturgy of the Hours.

The vigil that the bishop or priest held with the community consisted in readings with related singing and prayer; here the readings were most important. Monks, on the other hand, placed greater value on the psalmody.

This is shown by the Rule of St. Benedict, since one could, according to it, shorten the readings rather than the psalmody (ch. 10). The form of the public vigil is preserved in the Roman EASTER VIGIL.

The form of the monastic vigil consisted first in the singing of Psalms; the readings and responsories then followed. St. Benedict was acquainted with this form of the vigil in the Roman basilicas, where, already in his time, monks celebrated the hours of prayer. He modified somewhat the form he found there for the benefit of his own monks, so that Roman and monastic Matins were distinguished from that time on.

Traditionally, Matins opened with an Invitatory or invitation to prayer that consisted of Psalm 94, which was sung with intermittent short refrains. After the Invitatory came the hymn of the day. As with all the other hours of the Office, Matins, when separated from Lauds, was concluded with a Collect. Medieval monastic Matins, however, concluded with the *Te Deum,* the Gospel of the day, and the hymn *Te decet laus.*

Nocturn. On greater feast days, the medieval Matins was divided into three nocturns, each having three Psalms and three readings. There is disagreement among scholars regarding the origin of this tripartite division into nocturns. J. A. Jungmann claimed that nothing in the sources proves that the three nocturns were originally three separate prayer services; this arrangement was simply a subsequent external division of a single nocturn (*Pastoral Liturgy* 118). A. Baumstark, on the other hand, maintained that this threefold division came from Syria, where there were three (originally two) independent hours of prayer (*Nocturna laus* 145–155).

Psalmody. In the medieval Matins, the Psalms were sung by antiphonal choirs: one-half of the choir answers the other. The Psalm was opened by a verse through which the tone was given, the antiphon; the same verse was also sung at the end. At Matins, Psalms 1 to 108 were progressively distributed through the week, i.e., those not used for other hours of the Office. On more solemn feasts (e.g., the feasts of the Apostles), those Psalms were chosen that were suitable for the day.

Readings. The readings were drawn from Scripture, the Fathers, and the lives of the saints. Holy Scripture was read daily according to a determined order. Since the cursus of readings was computed for one year, only a selection of texts was read. During Lent as well as on several other days only a patristic homily on the Gospel of the day was used. The feasts of the saints had, as a rule, a short description of their lives, and often a legend of the saint.

Responsory. The Responsory comprised a response, a verse, and the repetition of half the response. For the individual books on Scripture there exist ancient series of responsories that in the Middle Ages were called ''histories'' because together they often form ballads about the history of Israel.

Since for priests in the active ministry Matins were too long, Pius X (d. 1914) had already begun to shorten them (nine instead of the 18 or 12 Psalms). Pius XII (d. 1958) and John XXIII (d. 1963) went even further and reduced the number of readings for most feast days. For a long time, priests were allowed to anticipate Matins, i.e., to recite them the previous afternoon, since an hour of prayer during the night was hardly possible for them. In the 1971 Liturgy of the Hours, Matins is called the Office of Readings and may be recited at any time of the day by those not in choir. The complete revision of this hour has resulted in a longer and better selection of readings from scriptural and patristic sources, with a corresponding reduction in legendary materials for the lives of the saints.

Bibliography: A. BAUMSTARK, *Nocturna laus* (Münster 1957). J. PASCHER, *Das Stundengebet der römischen Kirche* (Munich 1954); *Das liturgische Jahr* (Munich 1963). J. A. JUNGMANN, *Pastoral Liturgy* (New York 1962).

[J. PASCHER/EDS.]

MATRIMONY, SACRAMENT OF

The human experience of matrimony is a saving mystery. Traditional Christianity understands this as a lifelong union of conjugal love between woman and man, and calls this experience sacramental, binding spouses not just to one another but also to God. This entry examines the following topics: (i) the biblical and historical tradition; (ii) the meaning of sacramentality in a new conceptual framework; and, (iii) its pastoral and liturgical aspects.

Mystery and Sacrament

The 2000 years of Christian tradition provide a basis for examining the theology of marriage in order to develop a truly Catholic meaning of its sacramentality. History offers two historical tradition-bound eras of Christian marriage, corresponding to the two millennia. They represent two different theological contexts for the sacramentality of marriage. In the first millennium, the institution of marriage remained, largely, a secular reality. It was considered a holy and sacred state but not subjected to canonical legislation or ecclesiastical intervention. Nevertheless, Christians understood the conjugal partnership from a universal, open-ended and inclusive perspective of the Christian mystery. From the

An engraving depicting Roman emperor Theodosius I (347–395) officiating at the wedding of his niece's Catholic marriage. (©Bettmann/CORBIS)

eleventh century onward, wedding celebrations were gradually incorporated into the Church's canonical regulation and liturgical rituals. And the scholastics of the twelfth century developed the concept of sacrament.

The First Millennium: A Saving Mystery. The paramount vision of the ancient tradition stems from the consideration of the economy of salvation. Jesus gives marriage its ultimate meaning. He clearly indicates his intention to restore matrimony to the ideal presented in Genesis and to vigorously reinstate the law of marital unity. "Whoever puts away his wife, except for immorality, and marries another, commits adultery; and he who marries a woman who has been put away commits adultery" (Mt 19.9; see also Mk 10.11; Lk 16.18). Both Peter (1 Pt 3.1–7) and Paul (Col 3.18–21; Ti 2.4–5) instruct the faithful in the requirements of married life for Christians. Christian marriage should be lived "in the Lord" (l Cor 7:39) and this consideration has moral, spiritual and ecclesial implications. The foundational source of the Christian inspiration and symbolism of marriage comes from biblical revelation. It begins in the economy of creation (Gn 2:23–24) and was enlightened by prophetic revelation. Marriage images God's covenant perfected by Christ's covenantal sacrifice, and proclaimed as a reality of grace in the same covenant between Christ and the Church (Eph 5:21–33). This Pauline text presents the Christ-Church relationship as a paradigm of the husband-wife partnership.

The patristic view takes inspiration from this biblical background, developing the spiritual roots of marriage from biblical sources, especially from the heart of the biblical covenant. The patristic terminology used—such as mystery, image and type—have a deeper, broader and analogical meaning of marriage as a revelatory and participatory sign of the nuptial self-giving of Christ for the Church. Very often the Church Fathers' writings on virginity provide opportunity to envisage marriage as a covenant partnership.

St. AUGUSTINE's approach to both marriage ethos and mystery brought about a new stage of development, which influenced decisively the centuries that followed. On one hand, marriage as an institution was good and was elevated by Christ. In this sense it was endowed with three objective goods: procreation, fidelity, and sacrament. On the other hand, the conjugal act, whose purpose was procreation only, was extrinsically evil by virtue of the malice of concupiscence. The concept of sacrament had the broad sense of ''mystery'' related to Christ. This sacramentality constituted the Christocentric foundation and source of all marriage values, including indissolubility, because ''the holiness of the sacrament is more valuable than the fertility of the womb'' (*De Bono coniungali* 18, 21). The development of conjugal spirituality and sacramentality was also influenced and enriched by the Fathers of the Christian East, such as St. Basil and St. John Chrysostom. Again, the sacramental conception is broad, because marriage is seen as a mysterious icon, inserted in the whole of salvation history, centered in Christ rooted in baptism, and sealed by the Eucharist.

The Church's concern is exclusively pastoral because ''Christians marry like everybody else'' (*Epistle to Diognetus* 5, 6). They followed the customary folk marriage celebrations, which were also regulated by local traditions and Roman legislation. The pastoral concern of the Church is attested from the beginning: ''It is fitting that men and women who want to marry get the approval of the bishop, so that their marriage is according to the Lord, not according to passion'' (*Letter to Polycarp* 5, 2).

An incipient liturgical rite is evidenced from the fourth century onward. It cannot be equated with a formal realization of an ecclesiastical marriage of later centuries. In general, the veiling of the bride with a special blessing by the priest could be considered the Christian nuptial blessing in Rome. Garlanding (*stephanoma*) came to be the central symbolic rite in the East. Here a richer nuptial liturgy was characterized by the theological depth of the sacramental mystery, exuberant symbolic celebration, and a pastoral realism rooted in the human values of marriage and biblical revelation. Nevertheless, across the ancient world wedding rituals took place in a multiplicity of regional cultures and a variety of local rites under civil jurisdiction. The most important reference is perhaps found in Tertullian, who presented the theological implications and the Christian character of the marital covenant between two baptized believers. This covenant partnership becomes sacramental in the broad sense by virtue of the faith actualized within the participation in a Eucharistic community:

> How shall we ever be able to adequately describe the happiness of that marriage which the Church founds, and the Eucharist confirms, upon which the prayer of thanksgiving sets a consent? For not even on earth do children marry properly without their fathers permission. (*Ad Uxorem* 2, c.8:6–9)

Some historians see here an indisputable reference to an existing liturgy of marriage integrated into the celebration of the Eucharist. On the contrary, this text is correctly understood only if it is interpreted within the context of an exhortation to shun any contact with marriage with a pagan. The right interpretation of the key words of this text of the Catholic period of Tertullian is crucial.

''The Sacrament of Matrimony,'' 14th-century sculpture by Andrea Pisano on the campanile of the Cathedral at Florence. (Alinari-Art Reference/Art Resource, NY)

The Second Millennium: The Catholic Sacrament. Changes in the theological understanding of marriage came about because of social and historical changes, and the development of new religious ideas over centuries. Whereas in the first millennium the emphasis was on *spiritual foundations,* now it moved to *juridical categories of contract and indissolubility.* In the beginning, marriage had been seen as secular but was related to the ecclesial community by virtue of Christian dignity. Later, marriage was seen as religious, made holy in a sacred place, and was related to civil society by virtue of a canonical form. A family-centered and civil celebration of marriage remained the norm in Latin Churches until the ninth century. From then until the council of Trent, there was a gradual transfer of the discipline of marriage and the regulations of its ceremonies to the authority of the Church.

The first compilation of Canon Law—the Gratian's Decree—appeared around 1140 while Hugh of St. Victor (1079–1141) made a major contribution to the sacramental definition of marriage. A contract-centered theology of matrimony emerged from the emphasis on *consent* or *copula* (consummation) as the essential elements for the validity of the sacrament. In the ensuing centuries, this approach led to the juridical essence of marriage as a sacrament. Changes also took place in the liturgical ritual. The essential element remained consent, but now there was a pre-nuptial investigation made by the priest. All of this led to the development of a canonical and ecclesiastical character of marriage.

The first official declaration of marriage as a sacrament was made in 1184 at the Council of Verona. This was followed by Thomas Aquinas' synthesis of the sacrament of matrimony that combined St. Augustine's values of marriage as its ends within a new conception of its full sacramental dignity. In matrimony, the principal effect is the permanent sacramental bond, and grace is given for the evocation of the living image of unity that is a mysterious reflection of the union between Christ and His Church (*Summa theologiae* Supplement, 34.2 ad 1, ad 2; 35.1; 42.3).

The Protestant Reformers emphasized the holiness of marriage from the point of view of the Christian vocation as well as the covenantal nature of God's plan for the couple, although the sacramental reality was denied. In response, the Council of Trent (1563) ratified the Augustinian conception of marriage (DS 1797–1812) and this position prevailed until modern times. Trent aimed to lay the social groundwork for the validity and indissolubility of the sacrament. In the process, the biblical, mystical, and relational inspiration of Christian marriage was overlooked. This approach remained the basis of theological and pastoral thinking until Vatican II (1963–1965), supplemented by papal encyclicals such as Pius XI's *Casti connubi*.

Vatican II. The Second Vatican Council, facing the challenges posed by modern cultures, viewed the whole question of marriage in a much broader way (especially in *Lumen Gentium* 11, 35,41; and *Gaudium et Spes* 12, 47–52, 61.) The Council Fathers defined marriage as a personal community, in which partners give and accept each other (covenant), and also as an intimate partnership of marital life and love (personalist perspective). They avoided the legal term ''contract'' in favor of the biblical and classical term ''covenant'': Marriage is ''rooted in the conjugal covenant of irrevocable personal consent''; it is a ''reflection of the loving covenant uniting Christ with his Church, and a participation in that covenant''; it is compared to the ''covenant of love and fidelity through which God in the past made himself present to his people'' (*Gaudium et spes* 48).

This line of thinking was reiterated in the Apostolic Exhortation, *Familiaris Consortio* of Pope John Paul II, 1980 (especially nos. 13 and 51), and in the 1983 Code of Canon law. Canon 105 states:

> The matrimonial covenant, by which a man and a woman establish between themselves a partnership of the whole of life, is by its nature ordained toward the good of the spouses and the procreation and education of offspring; this covenant between baptized persons has been raised by Christ the Lord to the dignity of a sacrament.

Thus, the communion of the faithful and permanent love of the spouses has gradually replaced the juridical mind-set of past generations.

Postconciliar Theological Understandings of Matrimony

Marriage, like other sacraments, is fundamentally symbolic in nature. The conjugal partnership is a life experience replete with complex meanings and levels of reality, and a symbolic expression of something deep and transcendent. As a sacrament, Christian marriage has a symbolic structure that conveys a deeper meaning of the human mystery, and offers the possibility of *self-transcendence*. Their end is *salvation* both as a hope and as a means to it. Love can only be expressed through symbols, whether it is love of God or love of a human person. Although the images, gestures, or words express so deep a reality, they are, in themselves, simple. Simple gestures such as a kiss, a handshake, gift giving, or uttering the phrase ''I love you'' express in a profound manner a deeper yet readily understood reality.

The pledge of the old Anglican wedding rite, ''with my body I thee worship,'' speaks profoundly of the central meaning of the analogy. Like worship, which etymologically means, ''ascribing worth to another being,'' marriage is a total validation of the other in the devotion and service, celebration and mystery of the relationship. Just as the experience of worship engages the whole person, so too marriage is the total gift of self to the other.

Postconciliar developments in the theology of matrimony have explored the rich complexity of marriage from various overlapping perspectives. These include: marriage as vocation, marriage as communion, marriage as covenant, marriage as sacrament, and marriage as partnership. Taken together, these theological perspectives embrace and express the sacramentality of marriage.

Marriage as Vocation. Marriage is a true vocation. Theologically, a vocation means a call or invitation given by God to the Christian life or to some particular service or state. ''The vocation to marriage is written in the very nature of man and woman as they came from the hand of the Creator'' (*Catechism of the Catholic Church*

1603). Theologically speaking, marriage is a divine call, which empowers the couple to set up an intimate community of persons able to love and serve. The Church has always seen marriage as a vocation and has emphasized, especially in more recent times, the ''universal call to holiness.'' All people are called to this holiness, not only those in the monastic or celibate states. Marriage is perhaps the vocation ''par excellence,'' for here the spouses are God's co-creators in the gift of new life.

It is the desire of the Church, in promoting a better understanding of marriage as an on-going process, or an initiation into a vocation, that the spouses come to see that God has initiated a great work in them. An understanding of what it means to be ''called'' by God and to live out that special ''calling'' will greatly assist the married couple in dealing with the challenges of married life. God's call always implies a bestowal of grace to meet the challenge of the call, and therefore God's assistance and grace is constantly available to the spouses.

Marriage as Communion. Marriage is God's creative reality raised to the dignity of a sacrament, established as a covenant of intimate communion of life and love, by which the spouses signify and share in the mystery of love and fidelity between Christ and the Church (*Rite of Marriage*, 1990, Introduction). Communion with another means a mutual sharing of the gift of self. In marriage this means a total sharing of joys, sorrows, pains, and successes in a complete gift of self to the other. Thus, the man and the woman who ''are no longer two but one'' (Mt 19:6) help and serve each other by their marriage partnership; they become conscious of their unity and experience it more deeply from day to day (*Gaudium et spes* 48).

Marriage as covenant. ''Covenant'' is the graced and intimate personal encounter between God and His people fulfilled in Christ. It is the cornerstone of Christian sacramentality. Marriage when it is lived as mutual self-giving and intimate sharing between a man and a woman exemplifies this biblical concept of covenant.

From earliest times, the Church has regarded marriage in this way (cf. Eph 5:32). Patristic theology drew insights from the biblical paradigm to describe marriage as the ''image and likeness'' of God's covenant with humanity. This understanding was reiterated at Vatican II: ''Just as God encountered his people with a covenant of love and fidelity, so our Savior, the spouse of the Church, now encounters Christian spouses through the sacrament of marriage'' (*Gaudium et spes* 48). The section on Marriage in the *Catechism of the Catholic Church* begins with the assertion: ''The matrimonial covenant, by which a man and a woman establish between themselves a partnership of the whole of life'' (*Catechism of the Catholic Church* 1601). And again, ''Christian marriage in its turn becomes an efficacious sign, the sacrament of the covenant of Christ and the Church. Since it signifies and communicates grace, marriage between baptized persons is a true sacrament of the New Covenant'' (*ibid.* 1617). The ultimate prototype of this is the marriage of Christ and his bride, the Church, in which he sacrifices everything for her, even his life. It is the couple's faith as expressed in their lives that renders them people of the covenant and consequently makes their union a sign and a Christian sacrament of the covenant.

Marriage as Sacrament. The idea of marriage as one of the seven SACRAMENTS of the Church was developed by the eleventh-century scholastic theologians and adopted officially by the medieval hierarchy in the following century. This understanding stemmed from the meaning of sacrament as *mystery*, proposed by the early Church Fathers, especially Augustine, who spoke about the three foods of marriage: offspring, faithfulness, and sacrament. Consequently, ''marriage as a sacrament'' can be said to have two different, but not separate, dimensions—1) human mystery and 2) saving reality.

Marriage is a human mystery. Faithful love is the very essence of the marital partnership and the heart of its meaning; this unconditional fidelity makes marriage a primary and universal symbol. In addition, all peoples, of all religions, acknowledge marriage as the original, universal sacramentality known to human life. Thus, the sacramental mystery of marriage is fully anchored in human reality; it is a *radically human sacrament*. The three specific elements of Christian marriage—*faith, baptism, and community*—stem from the Christ-Church spousal relationship. This is the ecclesial dimension of marriage and what makes a marriage truly Christian.

Marriage as Partnership. Marriage is a life-long journey during which the couple widens its field of love to embrace the children. In this way, a partnership community is built, and a closer and closer union among the members is established: ''The intimate partnership of life and love which constitutes the married state has been established by the creator'' (*Gaudium et Spes* 48). This perspective takes into account what happens in the total life experience of husband and wife, and finds here the real sacrament. Although the aspect of partnership has been included in the other understandings of marriage, such as ''communion,'' the conjugal partnership against the background of the sacramentality of all creation, i.e., from the perspective of a renewed Christian anthropology, psychology, and a historical consciousness that envisions marriage as a process. Pope John Paul II articulates the view of marriage as a process in the following terms: ''The gift of Jesus Christ is not exhausted in the actual celebration of the sacrament of marriage, but rather accompanies the married couple throughout their lives'' (*Familiaris Consortio* 56). Therefore, the marriage partnership is not a mutual accommodation, but a total, whole-hearted and life-long commitment of each spouse. This implies the larger, inclusive, and life-long journey of the *sacramental* life of marriage and family.

The Celebration of Marriage: A Grand Feast of Life and Love

The development of the new Order of Celebrating Marriage, promulgated in Rome on March 19, 1990, was the liturgical response to the postconciliar II theological, pastoral and cultural developments. This revised Roman rite was built upon the basic structure and themes of the earlier 1969 rite. The theological focus in both the 1969 and 1970 rites stemmed from the Christocentric and the historico-salvific view of marriage, perceiving the celebration of marriage as a total giving of mutual service, and a sacramental action, which integrates all the aspects of conjugal life and love.

The preparation for the celebration of the Sacrament of Marriage is of paramount importance. In recent years, the Church has laid much greater stress upon this aspect of the whole ritual process of marriage. Within a broad theological and catechetical view of the sacrament, three themes are prominent: 1) marriage is God's creative reality raised to a sacrament of dignity; 2) established as a *covenant* of intimate communion of life and love; 3) by which the spouses *signify and share* in the mystery of love and fidelity between Christ and the Church. Here, the idea of a sacred and life-long bond, originating in God and effected by the irrevocable consent of the spouses is stressed, together with the sacramental nature of this bond, rooted in baptism. This human bond makes an indissoluble covenant, which images God's creating and redeeming relationship with us, and raises it to the sacramental dignity and holiness. In contrast with the contractual overemphasis of the past view of marriage, this view emphasizes that the essence of Christian marriage is spiritual, not legal.

The created reality of marriage is presented not simply as a historical fact but in relation to the ''great mystery'' (Eph 5:32). The 1990 Roman rite affirms that a sacramental marriage signifies and shares in the sacrificial and transformative, healing and fruitful mystery of grace by which Christ encounters the spouses. ''Those who marry in Christ are empowered to celebrate effectively with faith in God's word the mystery of Christ and the Church, to live rightly, and to bear witness in the eyes of all'' (*Rite of Marriage 1990*, 11). The theological, pastoral and liturgical content of the introduction to the 1990 Roman rite of Marriage presents the best of the Western patristic tradition, articulating the foundational themes of marriage as vocation and partnership. It offers a vision of the vocation of the spouses, and points out that their celebration actualizes the presence of and the encounter with the total mystery of Christ. Symbols, words and prayers focus on this mystery of graced love and call for its integration into ''the intimate community life and love'' (*Rite of Marriage 1990*, 4).

Mutual consent and the nuptial blessing reveal the sacramental meaning of marriage and are the two principal moments on which the whole celebration of matrimony hinges. They express the two essential aspects of the reality of marriage: the anthropological root of love manifested by the consent of the couple, and the covenantal bond that seals the Christian character of the marriage.

In the actual liturgical celebration of matrimony, the entrance rite, which allows for different arrangements of the procession, sets the tone for a joyful and prayerful celebration. The liturgy of the word, an integral and essential part of the sacramental celebration actualizes the mystery of the Bridegroom Jesus in the presence of the couple. The homily focuses primarily on ''the mystery of Christian marriage, the dignity of wedded love, the grace of the sacrament, and the responsibilities of married people, keeping in mind the circumstances of this particular marriage'' (*Rite of Marriage 1990*, 57). The function of the priest in receiving the consent, one of the central moments of the entire rite, is more than that of a witness. He is a sign of the presence of Christ, and, by means of his blessing, he ratifies the sacramental action accomplished by God through the couple's covenant. The 1990 rite provides an alternative formula in terms that make present the history of salvation, and emphasizes the sacramental meaning of God's covenantal action.

The symbolic action in which the central meaning of marriage and Eucharist intersect is the couple's sharing in the Eucharist, the nuptial banquet of Christ's love. As Pope John Paul II explains:

> The Eucharistic liturgy is the proper way to celebrate marriage, since both realities are intimately connected. The Eucharist is the very source of Christian marriage . . . In this sacrifice of the new and Eternal Covenant Christian spouses encounter the source from which their own marriage covenant flows, is interiorly structured and continuously renewed. (*Familiaris consortio*, 57)

Bibliography: G. MARTINEZ, *Worship: Wedding to Marriage* (Oregon 1993), from which much of the content of this essay derives. S. PARENTI, ''The Christian Rite of Marriage in the East,'' in A. CHUPUNGCO, ed., *Handbook for Liturgical Studies*, v. 4, *Sacraments and Sacramentals* (Collegeville, MN 2000) 255–274. A. NOCENT, ''The Christian Rite of Marriage in the West,'' *ibid.*,

275–301. T. BUCKLEY, *What Binds Marriage? Roman Catholic Theology in Practice* (London 1997). M. LAWLER, *Marriage and Sacrament: A Theology of Christian Marriage* (Collegeville 1993). W. KASPER, *Theology of Marriage* (New York 1980). E. SCHILLEBEECKX, *Marriage: Human Reality and Saving Mystery* (New York 1965).

[G. MARTINEZ]

MATTER, PHILOSOPHY OF

That of which things are made, an intrinsic determinable PRINCIPLE whose opposite (and correlative) is FORM. As a type of substance, matter is opposed also to SPIRIT. The term is defined differently in the various philosophical traditions and, even as employed by scholastic philosophers, has acquired a wide range of meanings in logic, epistemology, psychology, and ethics. This article is concerned primarily with the concept of matter as used in natural philosophy and metaphysics, and sketches its historical development from the earliest times to the present.

Greek naturalists. Matter is, in a sense, the oldest of philosophical concepts. When man first began to speculate about the world in which he lived and his own place in it, he tended to use concrete terms and images from everyday experience. His language did not possess the wealth of general terms, such as being and relation, that would later become available. So he spoke in terms of simple myth, of gods (who were like men) and processes of making and molding. As time went on, the characteristically human drive to understand the world took the form of reducing the complexity of human experience to some sort of unity. To understand was to make one of the diverse and dispersed many. If the many could be seen in some way as instances of a one, it would then be sufficient to grasp the one. For example, if a person knows what a horse is, he knows something about all horses, and the multiplicity and diversity of the group has been reduced to unity.

When the entire physical universe, and not a single species, is approached in this spirit, it is not at first sight obvious where the one is to be found. The two simplest kinds of unity (in terms of ordinary experience) are the unity of a common origin (e.g., a craftsman-god who is responsible for the diversity and change of man's world) and that of a common stuff (a single stuff that can take on diverse and changing forms). Stress on the former was characteristic of many early religions; however, it rarely led to any sort of speculative clarification of the notions involved (god, making, etc.). The latter approach was adopted by some speculative-minded thinkers of Ionia in the 6th century B.C., who saw the universe as bound together in some sort of material unity. Thales said that it had originally come from water. This first suggestion was undoubtedly influenced by myths of religious origin; Thales did not (as far as is known) go on to claim that the world is constituted of water in different forms. Anaximander held that the universe came from an ''indeterminate'' (Gr. ἄπειρον) to which it ultimately returns: this indeterminate is both inexhaustible (to allow for unceasing change) and lacking in any intrinsic properties (so that it can take on all properties freely). Anaximenes was the first to suggest that the universe actually consists of a single stuff that takes on different forms. And this stuff was no other than the familiar air that (he thought) could condense into cloud, then water, then earth, then rock. HERACLITUS preferred to think of the primary stuff as fire, though he spoke in allegory and it is difficult to be sure of his meaning. (*See* GREEK PHILOSOPHY.)

Several points should be noted at this stage. There was as yet no word for matter; to say that these Ionians had begun to articulate the concept of matter means that they were positing a single stuff (usually under some familiar guise such as that of air) as the answer to the central problem of unity-in-diversity. They were explaining diversity and change in terms of an as-yet-unnamed general category of matter-stuff. Second, this stuff was still vague in character. It was sometimes described as divine, sometimes as living. The later contrast between matter and spirit had not yet appeared; their matter-stuff was much too nondescript to allow one to regard them as materialist in the later, much more precise, sense of that term.

Pythagoras to Democritus. A stuff would provide unity. But what could explain change? Why should there be change in the first place? The first answer to this was expressed in terms of contraries such as full and empty, love and strife: the tension between these somehow provided the spring of action. The Pythagoreans were the first to push this to the limit and to posit a contrary of matter-stuff itself, namely, VOID. This was a new philosophical category, one whose history would continue to be bound up with that of matter. The void surrounded the world and served to differentiate things from one another. (*See* PYTHAGORAS AND PYTHAGOREANS.)

PARMENIDES rejected the entire ''matter'' approach to explanation of the physical world. He preferred to seek cosmic unity at a much more abstract level, that of BEING, or ''what is.'' Being does not allow of differences of density or of quality, so that diversity and change are alike illusory or at least can be dismissed from serious speculative consideration. But this was much too sweeping a conclusion for Parmenides's successors, even though they were influenced by his ideal of an unchanging Being. EMPEDOCLES argued for four different types of basic stuff. They could combine in endless ways; but each remained forever the same stuff, and each was structurally simple and homogeneous. Thus, instead of a single matter-stuff, he was holding for four elements, as they later came to be called (*see* ELEMENT). ANAXAGORAS suggested a much more sophisticated view: the universe contains an infinity of elements, each element forever itself but all mixed together in ever-varying proportions. The familiar things man perceives consist of a mixture of the elements; even apparently simple substances, such as water, contain small traces (seeds) of other things that can come to be from them. DEMOCRITUS tried perhaps the most interesting variation of all. Being does not change in itself (Parmenides), and yet change does occur. If void be admitted (Pythagoras), it allows one to have a multiplicity of beings or atoms whose movements explain all the changes of everyday experience. These beings must be below the level of perception, since their motions must explain growth, change of color, etc. They are in themselves unchanging and homogeneous. The atoms are thus a special sort of matter-stuff; the void is described as ''rarefied'' and appears as a diminished sort of reality—a second kind of stuff, it seems. Diversity and change are explained in terms of these two somewhat different sorts of material.

Plato. Matter plays two quite central roles in the complex metaphysics of PLATO. His analysis of knowledge led him to assert the existence of a realm of Forms on whose stability and immutability science depends. The Forms are imaged in a defective and flickering fashion in a matrix of extendedness or multiplicity. This world of image is the world man perceives. Its intelligibility arises from its relation to Form; the limited character of this intelligibility is traceable to the defective and multiple character of the ''space-matter'' in which the images occur. What is striking here is that matter, formerly the principle of unity (and therefore of intelligibility) for the Ionians, has become the principle of multiplicity, and thus of nonintelligibility, for Plato. Diversity is not to be understood by a reduction to one or more underlying types of stuff. One facet of diversity, the sheer and indefinite multiplicity of the sensible instances of any Form, is a ''given,'' not something that can be further understood. The other facet, the multiplicity of the Forms themselves, is more mysterious: it is apparently constituted by relations of negation, in which the original unity of the One-Good (the sole locus of true intelligibility) is gradually dissipated.

But there must also be motion. And the principle of this is soul, seen at its purest in man, but working less obviously in all moving things, even those apparently inanimate. The regular motions of the universe, noted in the stars and seasons, the working of all things toward an ordered good, argue to the existence of a WORLD SOUL animating the matter of the universe, just as the soul of man animates his body. Here matter is contrasted with living soul, not with unchanging Form; it is the passive, the resistant, not the empty space on which instances of a Form can be endlessly projected. Matter in this sense actively opposes soul; it is the source of defect, of breakdown in finality. Clearly the two notions are not the same, though they must be closely related. There is an uneasy tension between Plato's two great dualisms, the dualism of Form and the space-matrix of becoming in the *Timaeus* and that of soul and body in the *Phaedo.* There are two doctrines of matter here; or to put this in another way, since Soul and Form are not identical, their contrast-principles are not the same either.

Aristotle. ARISTOTLE was the first to coin an explicit term for the general category of material in the domain of scientific explanation. He adapted the common terms for timber, the material on which the carpenter works, ὕλη, to his technical usage, although he frequently made use of other terms as well. Though his analysis sounds like that of the Ionians, it is in reality of a significantly different sort. He begins with an analysis of PREDICATION itself, of how man talks about the kinds of things there are in the world, and claims to distinguish on the basis of this analysis two levels of reference. There are things to which man refers by names, things that are not predicated of anything else. These are the ultimate subjects of all predication about the natural world—SUBSTANCE is their common English designation, although perhaps entity would be a better translation for Aristotle's term. There are, besides, those second-order things that are predicated of entities and do not stand on their own: attributes of any kind, whether ''essential'' (pertaining properly, and in all cases, to a particular type of entity) or ''accidental'' (not necessarily belonging to all instances of a particular type of entity)—both commonly designated by the term ACCIDENT.

Principles of Change. Now when this simple distinction is applied to the domain of CHANGE, an interesting thing happens. In any change, there must be a subject of predication; there obviously must be something that can be said to change. Furthermore, if one is to have a truly ''scientific'' analysis that will remain true in all instances, it will not do to choose attributes at random, and say, for instance, that the musical entity comes to be from the black entity. Only one way of describing this will be ''scientifically'' true, and that is to say that the musical entity comes to be from the nonmusical entity. This description holds good for *any* change terminating in the attainment of the attribute ''musical.'' Three conditions are thus necessary and sufficient for any ''scientific'' description of change: there must be a SUBJECT of the proposition describing the change; this subject must first lack a certain attribute, and then it must come to possess it. Thus, when a nonmusical man becomes musical, the subject of predication is the man. Aristotle calls the man the matter of this change, and the other two conditions he calls PRIVATION and FORM, respectively. The man may be called the ''matter-subject'' of the change, in order to emphasize the function of the analysis of predication in Aristotle's assertion.

Note what has happened here. It is not that Aristotle has made an empirical inspection of changes, and discovered that in all cases a substratum remains throughout the change. The apparent similarity with the Ionian analysis is misleading. His form and privation are contradictories, not contraries, and thus whereas it would have taken observation to support the Ionian claim that all change involves contraries (e.g., black and white), it is analytic to say that it involves contradictories (white and nonwhite). Aristotle's claim that all change involves a matter-subject, a form, and a privation is, in fact, irrefutable because analytic. An understanding of the concept of change, or more exactly of predication about change, shows this immediately.

But here a major difficulty arises for Aristotle. If the matter-subject above be identified with an entity, or a substance, it seems that entitative change or SUBSTANTIAL CHANGE is impossible. For in *any* change there must be a common matter-subject of which the privation can first be predicated, and then subsequently the form. This matter-subject is either an entity, or it is not. If it is, then the change is not entitative, or substantial, since the same entity, or substance, is present throughout the change. If it is not, what can the matter-subject be? There are only two possible kinds of referent: entity and attribute, and the matter-subject of a properly entitative, or substantial, change is obviously neither of these.

To put the quandary in a yet sharper way: If there is a truly entitative, or substantial, change, of what can the privation and form be predicated? Can there be a common subject of predication before and after? How can it be named if it is not an entity? And how can it be a subject of predication if it cannot be named? If an acorn becomes an oak (to take one of Aristotle's examples), is there any way of maintaining the matter-subject type of analysis, which requires one to be able to break down ''*A* becomes *B*'' into ''*X* is non-*Y* and later *X* is *Y*''? ''That which was acornlike now is oaklike''—but what does the ''that'' stand for here?

Primary Matter. It was from this quandary that Aristotle's distinctive (and at first sight paradoxical) doctrine of primary matter took its origin. He wished at all costs to maintain as a basic ''given'' of experience that entitative, or substantial, changes occur, that entities truly come to be and pass away. He was opposing the Parmenidean tradition in all its varied forms (Empedocles, Democritus, Anaxagoras) on this point. The coming-to-be and passing-away that man perceives is not simply a rearrangement of atoms or elements or seeds, themselves unchanging; for if this were the case, the passing unities they form would be merely incidental, and a true science of the middle-sized objects of human perception would be impossible. Aristotle, as biologist, was quite sure that a science of living things *was* possible, and this proved to him that biological entities are not simply accidental conformations of more fundamental unchanging entities lying below the level of perception. Experience shows that living things have a unitary τέλος, or goal; one cannot dissolve it into incidental relationships without challenging the validity of perception generally, which Aristotle was determined to safeguard at all costs.

This meant that he had also to oppose the entire Ionian approach to physics. If intelligibility were to be sought through a permanent ''stuff'' that survives all changes, it would once again imply that the entities of everyday experience are simply complex configurations of a single underlying entity such as air or water. The fundamental reality, unity, and intelligibility would lie at the level of the ''stuff,'' and once again no proper science of the complex entities of everyday experience would be possible. Yet on the other hand, the matter-form-privation analysis had been shown to be fundamental to predication about change. There must be a matter-subject of some sort in entitative changes, but it could not be a ''stuff'' in the Ionian sense, that is, a material entity with definite properties. Thus Aristotle posits an indefinite matter-subject, itself lacking in all properties, even quality and quantity. It is not an entity, and thus it is not a proper subject of predication, nor can it even be named, properly speaking. It provides a sort of limit to predication itself, even apart from analysis of change. If one carries predication to more and more fundamental levels, there must be an ultimate matter-subject of which the basic form of the entity can (in a special terminal sense) be predicated; otherwise there would be an infinite regress.

The doctrine of primary matter thus depends on an analysis of predication, and especially on the notion of entity or substance. It does not depend on detailed observation of actual entitative changes, and is thus what later thinkers would call a typically metaphysical doctrine. To say that ''primary matter exists'' is simply to say that the notions of predication and of entity put forward by Aristotle are valid and that entitative changes occur. To say that a particular entity is ''composed of primary matter and substantial form'' (a popular later way of putting Aristotle's thesis) is to say that it is capable of ceasing to be and that it can give rise to other entities. It does not imply that the form is imposed upon the matter as a shape is imposed upon bronze; though Aristotle uses the bronze analogy in his original analysis of change-in-general, it seems fundamental to his entire ontology that primary matter not be regarded as a sort of limit-case of a qualityless ''stuff.'' Such a substratum would not be a ''this,'' could not individuate, would still be quantified, and so would not satisfy two central criteria of Aristotle's primary matter.

Material Causality. There is a second context in which Aristotle introduces the notion of a ''material,'' and this is in his analysis of the different types of explanation of physical change. He claims that there are four and only four of these, and that for a complete explanation all four ought be given, so that they are complementary to one another. One can ''explain'' a change (i.e., make it more intelligible) by mentioning the material in which it occurs, the intrinsic form involved, the AGENT responsible for it, or the END toward which it is directed. This division raises many problems, and one of the most difficult is that posed by the ''material'' mode of explanation (material causality, as it is often called, though the English term CAUSALITY is more often restricted to the category of agency alone). In what way is a change ''explained'' by specifying its material? To explain a statue in terms of the bronze that went to its making seems to involve the form of the bronze principally. When a nonmusical man becomes musical, is the material cause the man; i.e., is the material cause identical with the matter-subject of predication about the change? If it is, then what is had is description, not explanation. It seems dubious whether one should regard the man as a *causal* principle of this change.

One alternative would be to take the material cause of a particular physical explanation to be the material elements that are assumed (without any further enquiry into their nature) in this explanation. It would thus be relative to the particular explanation given and correlative to the level of formal explanation chosen as most appropriate. Clearly, material cause comes much closer to ''stuff'' than matter-subject does, but even here in most changes (other than elemental or artistic ones) the ''material'' will be a complex structure; yet the emphasis will not be on the structure as such, but rather on its being the substratum for a further structure of a higher order.

Potency. In discussing change, Aristotle introduced another crucial metaphysical category that was, in his mind, closely linked with matter. This was POTENCY. Besides saying of something that it is *X* or non-*X*, there is a third choice that the dichotomies of his predecessors had tended to obscure: one could say that though it is non-*X*, it has the capacity to become *X*. Potency is something more than mere privation, though it is less than actuality, or ACT. To say that an acorn can become an oak is an important fact about the acorn, one that is not conveyed by saying simply that it is non-oak. Thus a complete analysis of change requires one to introduce potency.

Potency has a dual aspect: it involves both capacity to be acted upon and capacity to act upon another. In both instances, potency is oriented to change; in both instances the complete actuality is lacking, but part of what it takes to bring about the complete actuality is already there. Passive potency can be said to reside in the material cause of the change, in the sense that it is the ''material'' aspect of the entity that makes it capable of change in the first place, the aspect that makes it part of an order in which outside agencies intervene and the unexpected can happen. Matter is thus in this sense the source of CHANCE and defect, not that there is something within it that (as Plato had suggested) works actively against the agency of form, but rather that it simply renders the entity subject to unpredictable outside interference with its proper intrinsic finality.

Stoics. The Stoic philosophers of the generation after Aristotle were the nearest to being materialist, in the modern sense, of any ancient school. For them, fire is the primary element; life and reason are its highest manifestations. From it issues the more inert elements in an unending cycle of growth and catastrophe. All things are corporeal, i.e., extended and capable of being acted upon by other bodies: this is true of soul and even of the Divinity, which is somehow immanent in the life-tension of the universe itself. Even qualities must somehow be bodies, since only bodies can act. Yet the alleged Stoic MATERIALISM has to be taken cautiously: the Stoics conceded an existence of a nonbodily sort to the void and, interestingly, to propositions; and their fire-stuff is more reminiscent of vitalism than of materialism.

Plotinus to Augustine. The solution to the problem of the one-in-many proposed by PLOTINUS constituted a powerful rethinking of the Neoplatonist themes. The One is beyond Mind and even Being; it is the source of the multiplicity of the world of Form, which is the product of Mind. As the lower contemplates the higher, the movement of contemplation issues in a product; in this way, by a movement of emanation, all multiplicity comes forth from the Mind, faced by One. Below Mind there is a Soul, and over against Mind there is matter, which is the featureless principle not of multiplicity (since each individual entity has its own form, and thus *all* multiplicity is the result of emanation) but of negation, and ultimately of evil and opposition.

AUGUSTINE inherited this dualism, but the Christian doctrine of creation forced him to modify it. He could not admit emanation, nor could he allow a matter over against, and thus not existentially dependent upon, God. Formless matter is the first and lowest of God's creatures. It is the condition of time, the principle of mutability of all creatures, whether spiritual or bodily, since all of them can turn away from the unity of God to the dispersion of the self. This matter does not exist by itself before the first forms but is concreated with them and has a reality, even though ''next to nothing.'' Multiplicity comes from God rather than from matter, at least in the case of rational creatures, who in some sense individually preexist in the divine mind. Mutability leads to evil and suffering. In the Augustinian tradition of theology, matter was always to have this overtone: it would be something to be turned away from. But matter is only one aspect of the physical world; the intelligibility of the material creation is a sign for man of God's power and love.

Thomas Aquinas. In the medieval period, the Aristotelian doctrine of matter was deepened in several directions. Because of the problem of UNIVERSALS, the question of what constitutes the principle of INDIVIDUATION of physical beings became a vital one. Aristotle had had very little to say on this point; since individual entities are prior in being, he seems to have held that ''thisness'' is rooted in form. But in general, it seems clear that individuation must depend on the multiplicity made possible by matter. Yet primary matter itself is not a ''this''; and quantity must be conceded some role in individuation too. THOMAS AQUINAS gradually worked out a complex theory, in which quantity is the principle of multiplicity, and primary matter is what constitutes the individual existentially as part of the physical order and as a unique object of reference.

Matter and Limitations. To the Greek mind, lack of limit meant imperfection; primary matter was the ''unlimited,'' whereas form and perfection lay on the side of limit. Plotinus and Aquinas together reversed this: God's perfection lies in His infinity, so that it is the principle of limit that is now imperfect, lacking (*see* INFINITY; INFINITY OF GOD). Thus primary matter is now described as a source of limitation, and the limitation is of a sort that escapes formal intelligible expression. What makes the individual unique is also what makes it material. A further development in Aquinas's doctrine comes from his shifting the boundary between Creator and creature from the matter-form distinction to a new essence-existence distinction, and thus implicitly changing the notion of matter itself. What divides the mutable creature from the Creator, according to St. Thomas, is finite essence, not matter, as Augustine had held. Angels are no longer regarded as ''spiritual-material.'' They can change, but they cannot cease to be. Primary matter is what situates certain creatures in an order in which they can cease to be. It is in no way a stuff (a stuff could never be a principle of uniqueness); it is not an entity at all, but rather the aspect of certain entities that marks them off as corruptible.

What, then, of the notion of a matter-substrate that guarantees permanence throughout change and that serves as a material cause of the change? It seems clear that even in entitative, or substantial, changes there are *some* continuities, of quantity, of location, etc. When a dog dies, most of the chemical substructures appear to remain. How can one speak here of a featureless substratum? Two answers were given to this question in the 13th century. Aquinas argued that there can be only a single substantial form in any being and that if one such form is succeeded by another, no determination can be properly said to persevere in the substratum. For if one does, the substratum itself is a substance, and one does not have substantial change. But he conceded that various subsidiary forms could be ''virtually'' present, though subordinated to the principal form, and that these could somehow persevere. Others preferred to say that an organized and unified plurality of forms is ''actually'' present in the composite and that the subsidiary ones could therefore ''actually'' persevere in entitative change. (*See* FORMS, UNICITY AND PLURALITY OF.)

No matter which of these views one follows, it is clear that the substratum of entitative, or substantial, change cannot be regarded as altogether indeterminate, since even the ''virtual'' form is still a determination. When a dog dies, the substratum of the change must carry certain quantitative and qualitative factors; it is obvious that a dog cannot change into just anything and that this limitation of potency must somehow be borne by the matter-substrate. What Aquinas insists on is the Aristotelian dichotomy between entity (substance) and attribute (accident). The substrate of substantial change cannot be *fully* qualified by any attribute, or it would have to be itself an entity; no third ontological possibility, he claims, is open. The problem is again one of predication: Can any attribute (e.g., ''weighing 20 lbs.'') be predicated throughout the change from dog to corpse? Aquinas answers: strictly speaking, no; different substantial forms are involved, and the perseverance of the accidental form of weight is ''virtual,'' not actual.

Matter and Knowledge. One final medieval theme was that of matter as the barrier to knowledge. Some scattered clues in Aristotle were woven into an elaborate theory of ABSTRACTION. Physics became the study of ''sensible matter,'' abstracting only from individual differences but still conceived as mutable and qualitatively defined. Mathematics studies ''intelligible matter,'' when one abstracts from all but the quantitative aspects of physical beings. Materiality here connotes both uniqueness and mutability; the more material an object is, the less knowable, on both scores. The Thomistic doctrine of the "three degrees of abstraction" (physics, mathematics, metaphysics) has an unmistakable Platonic overtone, insofar as it is based on degrees of relative distance from matter. (*See* SCIENCES, CLASSIFICATION OF.)

Giles of Rome to Newton. The Aristotelian primary matter that was somehow "conserved" in change was not quantified. So how did the notion of a "quantity of matter" conserved through all change arise, the notion that was to give rise in a very complicated way to the concept of mass? The metaphor of *materia* (stuff) exercised a constant pressure in this direction. Discussions of rarefaction indicated that when bodies expanded and contracted, a factor (often called "quantity of matter") remained the same. GILES OF ROME argued that quantity of matter was the most plausible subject for the accidents that remained in the miracle of TRANSUBSTANTIATION. John Buridan suggested that the IMPETUS given a body by its moving cause is proportional to the "quantity of matter" it contains; here matter is not only conserved precisely in its quantity but it also becomes the source of resistance to change of state. This view of matter as working against impressed force was central to J. Kepler's first formulation of the notion of inertia; the Neoplatonic influence on him is clear. I. NEWTON drew together the threads. The concept of mass was the key to his entire dynamics: it is a measure of the response of a given body to impressed force, and is different from weight. Newton speaks of it as "quantity of matter," but nowhere defines what he means by "matter." He appears to have some intuitive "stuff" view in mind; in practice he defines mass in terms of volume and density, thus risking circularity. Matter in his *Principia* is simply "that of which mass is the quantity." In actual calculations in mechanics, the notion of mass suffices; matter need never be introduced explicitly. Thus does the notion of matter begin to vanish from natural science, as the latter becomes more and more operational.

Descartes to Bergson. But matter continued to be a central category for most metaphysicians. R. DESCARTES went further than Plato had and equated matter with EXTENSION, thus making it entirely subject to geometrical thought and reducing physics to geometry. For the rationalistic tradition that followed (N. MALEBRANCHE, B. SPINOZA, G. W. LEIBNIZ), the problem of matter was the problem of individuation: how could the individual be secured in a world of purely intelligible relations? In the materialist tradition, on the other hand (T. HOBBES, J. O. de la Mettrie, etc.), the stress was on matter as opposed to spirit. It was identified with extended body operating under purely mechanical laws, and the existence of spirit was denied. J. LOCKE presented matter as a featureless inert substrate of extension.

G. BERKELEY launched the phenomenalist attack on this approach to matter by arguing that all man knows is ideas. These are necessarily mind-dependent, so that there is no reason to postulate an independent substratum over against mind, one in which the qualities of perceived objects are supposed to inhere. I. KANT in turn criticized Berkeley's view, holding that there must be a principle of "appearance," i.e. matter, that furnishes the object for outer sense and that makes physics irreducible to mathematics. Matter is the barrier to the a priori; it is the source of that which cannot be anticipated. Thus, to assert the "materiality" of the world was, for Kant, a compact way of rejecting both RATIONALISM and PHENOMENALISM.

G. W. F. HEGEL opposed this view of matter as the ground of appearance and returned to the Plotinian theme of matter as negation, as the product of spirit positing body and exteriority by way of negation. The tension between the materialist and the Hegelian philosophies is sharpest in their notions of matter, and it is thus no wonder that the dialectical materialism of MARX was unable to provide a satisfactory treatment of the category of matter, and especially of its relation to mind (*see* MATERIALISM, DIALECTICAL AND HISTORICAL). Evolutionary philosophers have seen in matter both the repository of the manifold potentiality of the evolutionary process and a barrier to that process. H. BERGSON, for instance, builds a basic dualism between life and matter; the impetus of life carries the universe on, but it tends to be "congealed" by the drag of matter.

It will be noted that the notion of matter differs greatly from one to the other of these philosophers, but that in all cases it is one of the central defining concepts of their entire philosophy. It may be noted also that the themes they introduce are recapitulations, often at a more sophisticated level, of the basic matter-themes of Greek philosophy.

See Also: MATTER, THEOLOGY OF; MATTER AND FORM.

Bibliography: E. MCMULLIN, ed., *The Concept of Matter* (Notre Dame, Ind. 1963). M. JAMMER, *The Concepts of Mass in Classical and in Modern Physics* (Cambridge, Mass. 1961). R. EISLER, *Wörterbuch der philosophischen Begriffe,* (4th ed. Berlin 1927–30) 2:80–94. F. C. COPLESTON, *History of Philosophy*, v.1–7 (Westminster, Md.). G. DINAPOLI and V. MATHIEU, *Enciclopedia filosofica* 3:376–382. H. DOLCH and M. MOSER, *Lexikon für Theologie und Kirche,* 7:163–165. A. MICHEL, *Dictionnaire de théologie catholique*, ed. A. VACANT et al. (Paris 1903–50) 10:335–355.

[E. MCMULLIN]

MATTER, THEOLOGY OF

Matter is a key word in the language of the modern technological culture, for it is intimately associated with man's increasing scientific knowledge of the phenomenal universe. THEOLOGY, on the other hand, is discourse about God, supposing both revelation and the knowledge of faith. Yet what is denoted by the word matter in its modern usage comes within the orbit of revelation in the scriptural categories of heaven and earth (Gn 1.1) or things visible (Col 1.16) and within the orbit of theology in the metaphysical category of material being. This article deals first with the teaching of revelation and theology on matter and then with the theological questions arising from man's new scientific knowledge of matter.

Teaching of Revelation and Theology. Matter comes within all three articles of the Christian faith.

In the first article, concerning God the Creator, the Church, against DUALISM in the form of MANICHAEISM (H. Denzinger, *Enchiridion symbolorum*, ed. A. Schönmetzer (32d ed. Freiburg 1963) 1336) and of PRISCILLIANISM (*ibid.* 463), has defined its doctrinal statement of the teaching of revelation that God is the sole author of material being (*ibid.* 3002). In this same context the Church has further defined that matter is an integral part of God's one work *ad extra:* the supernaturally elevated NATURAL ORDER. Therefore matter has its role within the divine purpose of the cosmos, which is the manifestation of the glory of God [*ibid.; see* GLORY OF GOD (END OF CREATION)]. And so the Church rejects (*ibid.* 433) the Gnostic position taken up by Origenism that matter's place in God's work is incidental, relative to the fall of spiritual being, and will, with the final restoration of spiritual being, disappear (*see* ORIGEN AND ORIGENISM). Also included in the Church's understanding in faith of revelation's teaching concerning matter is the divinely instituted relation between matter and man. It is one dimension of man's being (Gn 2.7); it is the object of the divine imperative placed on man (Gn 2.16); it is the meaning given by God to secular history (Gn 1.28); and it is involved in man's situation within the salvation history (Gn 3.17; Rom 8.19–23; *see* MAN). The Church has defined certain points of its doctrine concerning the relation between matter and man (*Enchiridion symbolorum* 461–464; 3002).

Matter comes within the second article of the Christian faith, which is concerned with God the Redeemer. Against Docetism revelation proclaims the reality (1 Jn 4.2) and the primacy within God's work of the human nature with its material dimension of JESUS CHRIST [Col 1.19–20]. Revelation also teaches (Jn 16.11) that one of the effects of God's redemptive work in Christ is the liberation in principle of matter from the power of sin; not that the ontological goodness of matter is in any way lessened by man's sin; but that, as a consequence of man's sin, matter is a sphere in which the power of sin, hostility to God, is operative.

Finally matter comes within the third article of the Christian faith, concerning God the Sanctifier. That matter is included within the divine work of sanctification is testified by belief in the paradisiacal state of Adam (Gn 2.8), by the Resurrection of Jesus (Rom 1.4), and by the expectation of a new heaven and earth (Rev 21.1) at the end. Then God's Lordship (1 Cor 15.28), the meaning of the divine work *ad extra* in its unity as a work of creation, Redemption, and sanctification will stand fully disclosed.

To make intelligible what is known from revelation concerning matter, scholastic theology uses the metaphysical concept of potentiality (*see* POTENCY AND ACT). This concept, together with its correlative concept of actuality, is applied to created being; and the distinction between material and spiritual being is seen as that between potentiality of being and actuality of being. Within the unity of the cosmos, matter and SPIRIT are degrees of being, ordered participations of absolute Being, each in its own manner manifesting the perfection of absolute Being. The theological conception of matter as potentiality of being implies that the proper cause of matter is absolute Being; and so matter in its first production depends immediately on God (*Summa theologiae* 1a, 65.4). It also implies that matter, as part of the cosmos, has its proper end in God; therefore the final perfection of matter depends immediately on God (*Summa theologiae* 1a, 66.3). Lastly it implies that the passage of matter from its first production to its final perfection is dependent in the first place on God as author of nature and of grace (*Summa theologiae* 1a, 73.1 ad 1).The content of this theological conception of matter is drawn from the divine ECONOMY, the theology of the divine work *ad extra.* Because it establishes the limits containing further theological speculation on matter, this conception of matter worked out in scholastic theology retains its usefulness.

Theological Questions. That matter as made known by modern science raises theological questions is evident from the writings of John XXIII, P. Teilhard de Chardin, and Dietrich Bonhoeffer. It is not primarily a question of reconciling scientific theories, such as those purporting to explain the origin of the universe, with Christian belief (Mascall, 162) but of recognizing the authenticity of matter as a dimension of man, a dimension in which the salvation history is operative, and a dimension in which the Church, the instrument of God's Lordship, is called to work. With this recognition goes the need for a reappraisal of the traditional Christian attitude to matter and to temporal values. In the past this attitude has been influenced by an excessive dichotomy between matter and spirit. The recognition of matter also calls for a theological statement of Christian belief in categories that give an understanding of that belief in its existential reality (Scheffczyk, 151). And with this recognition of matter the need for a new understanding of the Church's catholicity is apparent. The theological conception of the Church's catholicity needs to be enlarged to include the depth of human existence revealed by scientific knowledge of the phenomenal universe.

See Also: MATTER; MATTER AND FORM; CREATION, ARTICLES ON; SOUL, HUMAN; TIME.

Bibliography: M. SCHMAUS, *Gott der Schöpfer* (his *Katholische Dogmatik* 2.1; 6th ed. Munich 1962). L. SCHEFFCZYK, *Schöpfung und Versehung* (Handbuch der Dogmengeschichte 2.2a; Freiburg 1963). E. L. MASCALL, *Christian Theology and Natural Science* (London 1956). P. OVERHAGE and K. RAHNER, *Das Problem der Hominisation* (Quaestiones Disputatae 12, 13; Frieburg 1961) 44–55.

[E. G. HARDWICK]

MATTER AND FORM

Within the context of an Aristotelian-Thomistic PHILOSOPHY OF NATURE, matter and form are considered as the primary essential principles of changeable being. Although MATTER and FORM both merit consideration in their own right, additional problems attend an understanding of the relationship between these two, together with their relationship to PRIVATION, when all three are considered under the formality of PRINCIPLE. This article exposes in detail the teaching of ARISTOTLE concerning these relationships, discusses applications of his doctrine in various areas of scholastic philosophy, and concludes with a brief evaluation of historical controversies bearing on this general subject.

Aristotelian Doctrine

Aristotle's proposal of matter and form, as elaborated in Book 1 of his *Physics*, was in reply to a question concerning the first essential principles of changeable reality that must be properly understood. Not itself a query about the structure of matter, or a Platonic question of distinguishing between the sensible and the intelligible, Aristotle's is a question concerning primary principle, not ELEMENT in the modern sense. His problem is the nature of the mobile, and only indirectly, though still importantly, the nature of the sensible (*see* MOTION). The issues he raised were at a general level and consequently led to general solutions. This accords with his conviction that the mind begins with vague and universal notions and increases its knowledge by making these notions distinct and more particular.

Dialectics and induction. In his DIALECTICS, searching for first principles at this universal level, Aristotle is concerned initially with the positions of the pre-Socratics (*see* GREEK PHILOSOPHY). Though rejecting their views in the explicit form in which he reports them, he finds that all previous thinkers about the principles of nature implicitly affirm that such principles are contraries. For the modern reader, these predecessors of Aristotle may be of only historical interest; in the spirit of the *Physics* it is Aristotelian to turn also to modern philosophers of nature like Whitehead and Bergson, and to modern scientists who have developed the quantum and relativity theories. Alfred North WHITEHEAD, in his concepts of creativity and eternal objects, and Henri BERGSON, in noting two divergent aspects of evolution, attest to the existence of a dualism in nature, while the quantum theory, with its wave-particle view of matter, and relativity, with its space-time continuum, may be considered as further intimations of duality in the material universe.

Contraries and a Subject. The second phase of the dialectical search for factors that, when tested by INDUCTION, become the first principles of a natural science, requires a knowledge of the logic of contrariety (*see* OPPOSITION). Contraries are opposites within the same category. Thus the green is a contrary of the red but not a contrary of the musical. There is no direct CHANGE from not being red to being a musician. Should a man while getting sunburned also be practicing music, two changes are involved; any one change is between opposites in the same immediate genus, i.e., between contraries.

Moreover, and here again induction is invoked, there must be a subject in which the contraries succeed one another, e.g., the fruit that previously lacked a red color and now possesses it, the man who was not a musician and now is, the animal once young but now full grown. According to this analysis, there are three principles of motion, viz, two contraries and a subject.

This same conclusion can be confirmed by an analysis of language. After considering three alternative ways of stating that a man becomes a musician, Aristotle concludes that the most satisfactory sentence is: ''The non-musical man becomes a musical man.'' Here there is a subject possessing one of the contraries at the beginning of the process, and the same subject possessing the other contrary at the end. To supply inductive evidence from reality that supports this linguistic conclusion, Aristotle introduces an ANALOGY between natural becoming and the making of a statue by human art. The marble—or subject—has, with respect to being a statue, a shapeless character before carving and a recognizable shape after the sculpture is done. This example has led to some misunderstanding, as though Aristotle were putting the carving of a statue into literal correspondence with a motion taking place in nature. In reality statue-making is here only a model taken, like language, from the homely world that man knows best. As a dialectical device, it is not meant to be applied literally to nature but only to suggest the inductions through which the principles of natural change can be truly grasped.

Form and Privation. In technical terminology, the positive principle present in a subject at the end of a change is called form. Although this word originally meant shape and is commonly taken only in this sense, it had acquired a wider meaning even for PLATO. For the Aristotelian it means the positive term (*terminus ad quem*) of any change, a new shape or size or color. The other term (*terminus a quo*) has been identified as a contrary of the form. As a first approximation this language is adequate. Yet sometimes, as in the coming-to-be of a dog, the form does not have a contrary. Unlike a new color that comes to be from a positive opposite in the same genus, a dog comes to be from what is non-dog. To describe such changes, the opposite of the form is called privation, and even where a form, like red, has a positive opposite or true contrary like green, the green is regarded as the privation of the red. In this new and more general language, therefore, all natural motion involves a subject, a form, and a privation.

As another refinement of concept, the subject and the form, entering as they do into the intrinsic constitution of the product of change, say, the red apple, are called essential (per se) principles. Privation, on the other hand, does not enter into the thing made, and is thus called an incidental (*per accidens*) principle of motion.

Accidental and substantial change. Having treated change in general, Aristotle next distinguished two types of change, accidental and substantial (*see* ACCIDENT; SUBSTANCE). In the first case, as in the wrinkling of paper, the reddening of the human skin, and the growth of a puppy into a dog, a thing changes only in a qualified way. But in the second case, as in the burning of paper or the death of a dog, a thing changes wholly into another thing. This kind of change, which Aristotle called change ''in an unqualified sense,'' came to be known in scholastic language as SUBSTANTIAL CHANGE. It is divided into two types: generation, the change from NONBEING to BEING; and corruption or destruction, the change from being to nonbeing (*see* GENERATION-CORRUPTION).

Modern Difficulties. In distinguishing the two basic types of change, Aristotle had to do little more than cite examples to make his case. In modern thought, knowledge of substantial change and of substance itself has been called into question by philosopher and scientist alike. A sample objection, for example, would explain what is apparently substantial change as a mechanical motion of atoms from one aggregate or compound to another. In this reductionism, substantial change is only local motion, an accidental change (*see* ATOMISM; MECHANISM). There is no intention here of minimizing or of oversimplifying such objections. Yet Aristotle had also to contend with similar arguments from ancient atomists like DEMOCRITUS, who viewed substantial change as reducible to local motion. How then can one justify his giving a highly controverted point such brief treatment in the *Physics?*

Aristotelian Reply. The answer depends upon the much neglected pedagogical principle set down by Aristotle in the first chapter of the *Physics.* He argued that reason, following its natural tendency, must first consider changeable things at a vague and general level; at this level, the difference between accidental change and substantial change is evident. Moreover, at this level things are most intelligible to man and attainable with greater certitude; thus the evident difference between substantial and accidental change can be manifested by a few examples. When ancient or modern atomism, both envisaging more distinct and particular levels of knowledge, object to the concept of substantial change, they can then be dismissed as irrelevant. Whatever truth such views reflect at more specific levels must be interpreted to meet the demands of prior, more generic, and more certain notions. At specific levels of natural knowledge, where certitude is hard to find, many inductive tests are normally necessary to establish a truth. This is not the case at the more universal level, where certitude is easier to attain. Thus could Aristotle treat in an apparently naive way what becomes an embattled issue when argued, as by many moderns, in areas where certitude is weak and where only doubt, difficulty, and controversy can be expected.

EXPERIENCE, at the level where man's knowledge of nature yields maximal intelligibility and certitude, therefore discloses the difference between substantial and accidental change. Since the accidental, like size or color, depends upon the substantial, such as being a dog or being water, the first principles of changeable reality must be matter, form, and privation in the substantial order. These first principles can now be more precisely identified in the following discussion.

Primary matter. Matter has been generally identified as the subject of change. As such it is a POTENCY or capacity. The subject of substantial change is called primary matter, while the subject of accidental change is known as secondary matter. Secondary matter, such as a dog undergoing the accidental change called growth, is potential with respect to its new size; yet it possesses an actuality of its own insofar as it is a dog. By analogy to the subject in such accidental changes, there must be a subject also in substantial change. Experience manifests an abiding material or substratum in such changes as the burning of coal or the death of a dog. Among the arguments reason can supply for the necessity of such a substratum is the generally accepted principle that nothing can come from nothing. This first subject in any physical thing is primary matter, and its reality is that of potency.

The evidence that primary matter has no actuality of its own but of its nature is potency for substantial being is found in the unity of the so-called composite of matter and form, say a dog. If primary matter, prior to its union with the form or ACT that makes a dog come to be, had an act or form of its own, its composition with the form of dog could yield no more than an extrinsic type of unity. The dog, or the so-called composite, would then be an accidental unity, not the intrinsic and substantial type of unit that experience reveals (*see* POTENCY AND ACT). Such an argument, while metaphysical in character, serves to explain the nature of the first subject attained by induction in the philosophy of nature.

Substantial form. Form, in general, is the END or term of matter. The term in accidental change is called accidental form; examples would be the color, size, or shape of a thing, or its place. In the substantial order, the form is called substantial form. Accidental form makes its matter to be qualified in this or that way. Substantial form makes its matter to be; it confers BEING in an unqualified way.

From another viewpoint, matter is that out of which a thing is made, like marble in the case of a statue; form, on the other hand, is what makes a thing to be what it is, for instance the shape in the case of the statue. Arguing analogously, primary matter is that out of which a physical thing is made, while substantial form is what makes it to be a dog, a cat, copper, water, or a tomato plant. One limitation of this way of speaking is that such words do not respect the reality of matter in determining the ESSENCE of a thing. Further, as in the case of assigning a purely potential character to primary matter, the discussion passes beyond the limits of natural philosophy into the area of metaphysics. For form as a principle making a thing to be what it is becomes synonymous with essence, and essence is the proper concern of the metaphysician.

Substantial form, however, has a more particular application in the philosophy of nature. The form of living physical things is called a SOUL. As such it is an animating principle in plants, animals, and men. In the subhuman world (to avoid special difficulties concerning the human soul), modern knowledge of embryology affords striking evidence of form as the end of matter. The matter is gradually prepared in the embryo for the form or soul that makes possible the independent or substantial existence of the offspring. A similar disposition of matter is required for forms in the mineral world. Natural form is, therefore, considered to be the end of matter.

This way of defining form is more appropriate to the philosophy of nature than the metaphysical definition identifying it with essence; for the natural philosopher, substantial form is part of the essence of a mobile being, the other part being primary matter.

Privation. Unlike matter and form, privation is not divided into substantial and accidental kinds; as nonbeing it cannot be divided into species. Privation is contrasted with form but associated with matter, primary or secondary. For matter in either case is never without privation. When it has one form, it lacks all others, and when it acquires a new form, it lacks the one it previously had. Viewed in this second context, privation represents some kind of lack or loss. Thus, it implictly refers to a subject competent to possess the form that is not present. That is why, when contrasted with form, privation is associated with the subject or matter; it is the absence of form in a suitable subject. Finally, privation is an accidental principle insofar as it neither enters intrinsically into the thing produced (perfect act) nor into the motion toward that product (imperfect act).

Plato did not distinguish between matter and privation, regarding matter itself as nonbeing. Aristotle claims to be the first to make the distinction, and by means of it to resolve what he considered to be the great problem bequeathed to Greek speculation by PARMENIDES. If being is and nonbeing is not, how can anything come to be? For from being, which is what is, nothing can come to be; it already is. And in regard to the other alternative, nothing can come to be from nonbeing. The solution to this problem, which according to Aristotle's report led Parmenides to deny BECOMING, requires the distinction between matter (being in potency) and privation (nonbeing). From being that is actual, nothing, it is true, can come to be; but from being in potency, namely, matter, something can come to be. Again, regarding the second alternative in Parmenides' argument, one must distinguish the essential from the incidental. From nonbeing as an essential principle entering into the composition of the product of change, nothing can come to be. But from nonbeing as an incidental principle extrinsic to the change in question, a thing can come to be. Thus, by a recognition of matter and privation in themselves and in their relation to each other, did Aristotle resolve perhaps the most profound problem raised by the Greeks in the philosophy of nature.

Appetite of matter. Aristotle also spoke of the appetite of matter, probably to counteract the view that form alone is good and that matter is evil. The thesis that matter is evil, appearing in modified form in Plato, existed in the Mediterranean world long before and far beyond the confines of classical Greece. Thus, to answer an objection against his position that natural science concerns a subject worth studying, Aristotle was forced to deepen his contrast between matter and privation, even though his pursuit took him, for dialectical purposes, into metaphysics. To summarize his position, appetite is ascribed to matter but denied to privation. This raises the questions: Why is it necessary to recognize appetite in the physical world, and why is such an apparently psychic term as appetite introduced?

The starting point in answering such questions is the ordered character of natural change. If ORDER cannot be reduced to CHANCE, it has to be explained by means of FINAL CAUSALITY. It is in this spirit that form in the philosophy of nature is called an end or term. If such language is justified, then there must be a tendency to a term or end in every natural change. But what is the seat of such a tendency? This cannot be form because form, as the term of change, is not present at the beginning to strive or tend. Nor can it be the previous form, here viewed as a privation of the new form that is the term of the change; for in any change there is a repugnance between the old form and the new one, not an attraction or tendency. The seat of the tendency must therefore be the matter. Such a tendency is called a natural appetite by analogy to the appetite most known to man, namely, the APPETITE or inclination that is the human will. In more univocal language, the appetite of matter, as St. Thomas Aquinas explains it, is the ordination of such matter toward the form that is the term of the particular natural change (*In 1 phys.* 15.10).

Dispositions of matter. Though indeterminate in its substantial character, the primary matter involved in any change does not take on in random fashion any of the potential infinity of forms it may bear. Carbon, when burned, does not become stone or water. The reason is the so-called ''dispositions of matter.'' In any generation of a new substance, these are first known as the effects of the old form. Second, although substantial change is instantaneous, it is induced by accidental changes, first local motion and then alteration, both of which are exemplified when a source of heat is applied to carbon to be burned. In the third place, as explained by JOHN OF ST. THOMAS (*Curs. Phil.* 2.3.1.7), who synthesized the references of St. Thomas to the dispositions of primary matter, the final DISPOSITION of matter, in generation, is the effect of the new form.

In natural processes, which are to be distinguished from those occurring by art or by chance, form has to be regarded again as the end of matter, and the form that matter is eventually to bear is the end of all the dispositions of its matter. In this sense, all previous dispositions are the result of the most advanced form achieved, and this is the final cause of what went before. These notions are relevant to the evidences for EVOLUTION, especially with the extension of the evolutionary idea to cosmogony. Form is the end of matter in any given change, and matter in turn has an appetite, gradually disposed, to possess the form. But as in the case of the appetite of matter, the probing of its dispositions must pertain to the metaphysics of substance.

Nominal definitions. In the last chapter of Book 1 of the *Physics,* Aristotle comes to a nominal DEFINITION of primary matter as studied in the philosophy of nature: ''the primary substratum of each thing, from which it comes to be without qualification, and which persists in the result'' (192a 31). The ''primary'' of this definition marks the definiendum off from secondary matter, and ''substratum'' distinguishes it from form; the last two clauses further distinguish it from privation. The more classic and metaphysical definition of primary matter, expressing its purely potential or indeterminate character in the kind of negative way by which this principle is known, reads: ''By matter I mean that which in itself is neither a particular thing nor a certain quantity nor assigned to any other of the categories by which being is determined'' (*Meta.* 1029a 19).

As explained by St. Thomas, ''form is the end of matter,'' and ''privation is the negation of form in a subject'' (*In 1 phys.* 15). Both of these nominal definitions, like the characterizations of primary matter above, summarize the long discussions that make up Book 1 of the *Physics.*

Creation and eduction. Substantial form and its privation, two opposites in the primary genus, substance, are the first principles of change. Everything in the physical world is derived from them, and they are underived in the physical world. Primary matter and its form are essential principles of change, while privation is an incidental principle. None of these principles comes about through natural change; if they did, all of them would be again involved as principles of such change and a vicious circle would result. To account for their origins, it is necessary to go to metaphysics and there to raise the question of CREATION.

Given a world already created and given a thing or things that are informed in some way, new natural form (the human soul excepted) is brought to be from matter by what St. Thomas called eduction (*De pot.* 3.9)—a term that has the modern connotation of emergence. Eduction or emergence, as illustrated by the kneading of clay, to bring forth, say, a spherical shape from the matter being molded, calls attention to the inadequacy of such expressions as ''the union'' of form and matter or ''the acquisition'' or ''taking on'' of form by matter. On the other hand, eduction itself, it should be stated, is not generation. If it were, it would involve matter, form, and privation again, and the vicious circle would once more be opened.

Nature and causality. It is explained in the second book of the *Physics* that NATURE is an intrinsic principle or source of motion. As further specifications of their roles, both primary matter and its form fulfill this definition of nature. Matter is the source from which physical things come to be, and as such is an intrinsic principle of change. Form, as terminating matter to give a physical thing an intrinsic and original character, is also entitled to be called nature.

Matter and form, in addition to being principles, are also causes; privation, however, not being a positive reality, can exert no positive influence on the production of a thing and is therefore not a cause. The material and formal causes, though both intrinsic to the effect, are distinct from it since the effect is neither matter nor form but the result of both. There is thus a sufficient difference between matter and the result, on the one hand, and the form and the result, on the other, to preserve the distinction necessary in a cause-effect relationship (*see* CAUSALITY).

Uses of Matter and Form

In their fundamental meanings, matter and form are properly studied in the philosophy of nature, the only branch of philosophy that considers all four types of cause. The metaphysician also studies form, but form here is already used in a different sense, as synonymous with essence or with the logician's SPECIES This extension of the term has been previously noted; historically it is no doubt earlier than Aristotle's usage, since it appears to be the meaning that Plato had in mind when he developed his notion of matter and form through the contrast of the intelligible and the sensible (*Tim.* 52). Like form, matter also has many meanings in parts of philosophy other than the philosophy of nature, and sometimes even in the philosophy of nature itself. Thus the breakdown of a whole into its parts is characterized by St. Thomas as a resolution toward matter (*In 2 phys.* 5.9). But whatever the many applications of matter and form in human science, they received their first scientific formulation, in Aristotle's sense, at the physical level where the problem is change, not at the metaphysical level where Plato made his distinctions between universals and singulars.

Human learning. Some of these applications in other areas of knowledge deserve listing, just to show the uses of matter and form throughout the range of human learning. One of the most crucial areas where matter and form are invoked is in the study of the human soul in its relation to the matter of man (*see* SOUL-BODY RELATIONSHIP). Following a lead in St. Thomas, LOGIC is divided into material and formal parts. Such special logical entities as definition and SYLLOGISM have each a matter and a form: matter is the content and form the arrangement. Literary works—and in general all artistic products—also have a matter and form; in this context there should be mentioned the 20th-century study of the Bible through FORM CRITICISM. In mathematics, there is intelligible matter, e.g., the divisible parts within a triangle, and form, e.g., the three-sided character of the triangle. Even 20th-century thinkers in mathematics and in logic used terms like formalism, which owes its remote origin to the long Western tradition concerning matter and form. A similar residue of this tradition can be found in modern biology, where it is conventional to speak of ''living forms.''

Metaphysics and ethics. The extended uses of matter and form in logic and in mathematics are analogous to their primary applications in the physical order. So, too, are the impositions of these terms in metaphysics, where form has already been mentioned as a synonym for essence. The recipient of this essence in the physical world is matter—not pure prime matter but matter with one of the modes of quantity. In another context, when relating universals to reality, the metaphysician argues that these are formally in the mind and materially in physical things. Here again, there is a use of matter and form. The metaphysician also uses the various levels of remotion of form from matter to differentiate the sciences; mathematical physics, for instance, is said to be formally mathematical and materially physical (*see* SCIENCES, CLASSIFICATION OF). As other illustrations of these principles, angels are said to be pure forms, and even the act of EXISTENCE is expressed by St. Thomas as ''formal in respect of everything found in a thing'' (*Summa theologiae* 1a, 8.1).

In ETHICS, human acts have matter and form; so do VIRTUE, law, family, society, and government. All these subjects, studied again through the use of matter and form, are considered by the theologian, who adds dimensions of his own to the analogous application of these principles. Thus the relation of the natural to the supernatural is often expressed by the analogy of the material as related to the formal. Within the supernatural order itself charity is called, for instance, the form of all the infused virtues, and all the SACRAMENTS are explicated in terms of matter and form.

Thus, not only in those studies that are available to reason alone but through the whole range of Christian intellectual life, matter and form are truly fundamental principles. The above list has merely provided a sampling of their scope.

Historical Controversies

Like all other claims of human reason, matter and form have been objects of controversy inside and outside the Christian tradition. At least in some of his language, Plato seems to have identified matter and space because both are in some sense receptacles (*Tim.* 52). With PLOTINUS there is something of a return to a pre-Aristotelian view that matter is privation or evil (*Enneads* 2.4; 3.6.7; 6.3.7). St. AUGUSTINE, though his views on this question are not always uniform, referred to the existence of the so-called SEMINAL REASONS (*Gen. ad litt.* 6.5.8)—a term of Stoic origin. This has prompted the conclusion that Augustine did not hold to the purely potential character of primary matter. Remnants of Augustine's thought on this point, even though their meanings are not always clear, appear at least as late as St. BONAVENTURE (*In 2 sent.* 7.2.2.1). However, any attempt to recite even the most important figures in the Middle Ages who expressed views on primary matter would have to enter the complicated question of the plurality of forms (*see* FORMS, UNICITY AND PLURALITY OF). Though some partisans in this controversy, including at times St. Albert the Great (*Summa de creaturis,* Borgnet, 34:323), expressed the view that primary matter is purely potential, this point was most emphatically and unequivocally defended by St. Thomas. After his time, new interpretations of primary matter appear in the writings of John Duns Scotus (*Op. Ox.* 2.12.1.10) and Francisco SUÁREZ (*Disp. Met.* 34.5.36, 42) whose views, though differing from each other, both seem to accord primary matter at least some measure of act.

After the decline of scholastic thought in the Renaissance, matter and form continue to appear in the works of the great original philosophers, including KANT and HEGEL, though in many cases there is little similarity, except in name, with older Greek principles of mobile being. In their explanations of the material world, including living things, post-Renaissance thinkers, scientists and philosophers alike, turned away from matter and form and to either mechanism or dynamism.

Mechanism and dynamism. The typical version of mechanism attempts to explain nature by means of quantity and local motion; with advances in modern science, the raw material in such a mechanical view can be identified not merely as quantity in general but as atoms, in the case of lifeless world, and cells, in the case of the living. Prominent mechanists in the modern world were R. Descartes, P. Gassendi, E. H. Haeckel, J. Loeb, H. von Helmholtz, E. Du Bois-Reymond, Lord Kelvin, and, in general, all who took Newtonian mechanics in physics, and the cell theory in biology, or a Darwinian type of evolutionism, to provide an authentic philosophy of nature. Mechanism tends to deny nature as an intrinsic principle and to affirm that the fundamental stuff of the world is inert.

By contrast, DYNAMISM lays stress on the active, energetic character of the basic constituents of our world. G. W. LEIBNIZ, for instance, held to the existence of the MONAD, which is an indivisible, inextended unit of process having perception. R. Boscovich held to the existence of points of force as the underlying physical realities. Other prominent dynamists were Kant, D. Palmieri, and W. Ostwald, who envisioned physical things as fundamentally energy. More recent proponents of dynamism have been Henri Bergson (*Creative Evolution* [New York 1911]) with his theory of the *élan vital* as an all-pervading reality, and Alfred North Whitehead (*Process and Reality* [New York 1929]), who reduced the universe to units of process called actual entities, themselves manifestations of a still more fundamental principle called creativity.

Though constructive criticism of the modern alternatives to matter and form cannot be undertaken here, it bears mention that, in their typical forms, mechanism tends to see only passivity in the physical world and dynamism, only activity. This suggests that judged merely in the light of alternative philosophies of nature the explanation of change through matter, or the potential, and form, or the actual, would appear as a combination of the positive insights of its rivals, without their extremisms.

Modern Thomism. After the revival of THOMISM in 1879, matter and form, as discussed in the scholastic tradition, were also revived (*see* SCHOLASTICISM). Most scholastics have accepted the two principles, though for varying reasons. While claiming to be Thomistic in inspiration, many books and articles written in the 20th century presented the philosophy of nature as an applied metaphysics, despite the fact that metaphysics leaves the material cause out of account. Matter and form were thus treated in a rationalistic and even Cartesian spirit. Typical of this was the mathematical approach to matter and form through the nature of the continuum, and as an answer to the question: What is bodily essence? This is far different from the type of question Aristotle raised in the *Physics.*

In a modern context, the establishment of primary matter and substantial form through the kind of evidence invoked by Aristotle, namely the fact of substantial change, had to face, on the one hand, philosophical arguments like Hume's to the effect that the reality of substance cannot be grasped by the human mind, and on the other, arguments invoking the success of modern science in reducing all change to mechanical principles. Such difficulties led scholastics like P. Descoqs to reduce the status of matter and form to that of a probable explanation (*Essai critique sur l'hylémorphisme* [Paris 1924]).

Hylosystemism. Other scholastics like A. Mitterer in Germany (*Das Ringen der alten Stoff-Form-Metaphysik mit der heutigen Stoff-Physik* [Innsbruck 1935]), and C. Bittle in the United States (*From Aether to Cosmos* [Milwaukee 1941]) proposed a theory of bodily essence called HYLOSYSTEMISM, a term designed to parallel a modern name for matter-form doctrine, namely, HYLOMORPHISM. While retaining a so-called hylomorphic view of organisms, hylosystemism alleged that the findings of the modern sciences do not require the traditional view of matter and form as principles of inorganic things. In resolving the world into its constituents, hylosystemism argued that inorganic reality can be reduced to atoms and that atoms themselves are broken down into still simpler parts, such as protons, and electrons. These subatomic parts were called hylons, and atoms themselves were regarded as systems of such hylons. Hence the term hylosystemism.

Hylons are considered to be material substances, but not bodies, since they do not tend to exist in an independent status. Similarly, the system peculiar to each type of atom is not regarded as a mechanical sum to be explained by the mere addition of its parts. In comparing hylosystemism to hylomorphism, a critic might note that the former is a theory of an integral WHOLE, while the latter is an account of a physical whole. Thus the two may not be rivals, since they are not genuine alternatives.

Other Views. More recent philosophers who would claim, like the hylosystemists, to stand within the Aristotelian tradition, have also been beset by modern philosophical arguments against the knowability of material substances and by the success of science in accounting for change without recourse to matter and form. Yet F. Renoirte (*Cosmology,* [New York, 1950]) argued that when all is said and done there is a duality of space and time; this he offered as evidence for the more fundamental dualism of matter and form, even though man cannot designate this or that thing as being a substantial unit, and as thus having a substantial form of its own that informs primary matter. A. Van Melsen (*The Philosophy of Nature* [2d ed. Pittsburgh 1954]) has similar reservations about the proof of matter and form through change, but he finds evidence for dualism in the existence of discrete individuals that are each bearers of a common specific type.

Detailed criticisms aside, it is necessary to point out that philosophers who invoke modern science to reject the evidence for matter and form based on substantial change all neglect the investigative approach to this problem urged by Aristotle and carefully explained by St. Thomas. Primary matter and substantial form are established at the vague and universal level of knowledge where the mind is most at home and most sure of itself. When knowledge becomes more distinct and detailed, as in modern science, it can clarify fundamental knowledge but never replace it, just as a knowledge of polygons makes more specific man's knowledge of figure without rejecting the generic notion of figure itself. On such grounds, in any synthetic explanation of nature, the findings of science must be adjusted to a well-examined philosophy of nature, and not vice versa. In evaluating hylosystemism and the views of Renoirte and Van Melsen, it must be urged that it is not good methodology in the philosophy of nature to overestimate science as a starting point.

Testimony from scientists. Many of the objections to matter and form, from mechanism to philosophies that try to establish a physical dualism by means other than the evidence of substantial change, eventually became as outmoded as the science on which the objections were based. As the 20th century wore on, the mechanism which, except for scattered opposition from dynamists, had dominated science, had to be discarded in the face of facts. Using these new and non-mechanical theories of science, American naturalism in the early 20th century tried to define a so-called nonreductionist materialism in which a non-mechanical matrix was seen as tending to spawn various levels of reality—inorganic matter of various complexities, life in its various grades, and finally mind—with higher levels irreducible to lower ones, but with only one kind of reality underlying it all. The net result was a species of materialistic dynamism. Dialectical MATERIALISM used the same scientific evidences for dynamism to reexamine its philosophy of nature and, among some authors, to draw close to the principles of matter and form (G. Wetter, *Dialectical Materialism* [New York 1959]).

From among modern scientists themselves, though no substitute for the older mechanism had emerged, as the second half of the 20th century got under way there were evidences that primary matter and its form were slowly moving back into prominence. Thus W. Heisenberg (*Physics and Philosophy* [New York 1958]) found that quantum physics, with its emphasis on the indeterminate, restored the Aristotelian notion of potency or matter. Organismal biology also gained ground, suggesting the existence of a whole-making principle. It was also shown that Whitehead, who kept in such close touch with science, used concepts that have affinity with Aristotle's. The synthesis of TEILHARD DE CHARDIN envisioned a fundamental matrix in development toward a term. This list could be enlarged, if only to suggest rhetorically the respectability of matter and form in the light of recent science and philosophy. For withal, the fundamental evidence for primary matter and substantial form must remain the universal level of human knowledge that, in the proper logical order for constructing a synthetic world view, precedes the detailed theorizing of modern thought.

See Also: PHILOSOPHY OF NATURE; PHILOSOPHY AND SCIENCE.

Bibliography: THOMAS AQUINAS, *Commentary on Aristotle's Physics* (New Haven, Conn. 1963); *An Introduction to the Philosophy of Nature,* comp. R. A. KOCOUREK (St. Paul, Minn. 1948). JOHN OF ST. THOMAS, *Cursus philosophicus Thomisticus,* ed. B. REISER, 3 v. (Turin 1938) 2.1:2–6. V. E. SMITH, *The General Science of Nature* (Milwaukee, Wis. 1958). J. A. J. PETERS, ''Matter and Form in Metaphysics,'' *New Scholasticism* 31 (1957) 447–483. W. KANE, ''The First Principles of Changeable Being,'' *Thomist* 8 (1945) 27–67. D. DUBARLE, ''L'Idée hylémorphiste d'Aristote,'' *Revue des sciences philosophiques et religieuses* 36 (1952) 205–230. M. DE MUNNYNCK, ''L'Hylémorphisme dans la pensée contemporaine,'' *Divus Thomas* 6 (1928) 154–176. J. C. LA DRIERE, ''Form and Style,'' *Dictionary of World Literature,* ed. J. T. SHIPLEY (Paterson, N.J. 1960); ''Literary Form and Form in the Other Arts,'' in International Federation of Modern Languages and Literatures, *Still- und Formprobleme in der Literatur,* ed. P. BOCKMANN (Heidelberg 1959) 28–37.

[V. E. SMITH]

MATTHEW, APOSTLE, ST.

Traditional author of the first Gospel. His name (Gr. Ματθαῖος or Μαθθαῖος) is from Aramaic *mattai,* a shortened form of the Hebrew *mattanyâ* or *mattatyâ* (gift of Yahweh). By deriving it from another root, some give it the meaning of ''the faithful.'' He is named seventh in the list of APOSTLES in Mk 3.18 and Lk 6.15; eighth in Mt 10.3 and Acts 1.13. In Mt 10.3 he is called a τελώνης, i.e., tax collector or PUBLICAN; this fits with his being called by Jesus from the τελώνιον (toll-house) in Mt 9.9. The calling of a tax collector is found also in Mk 2.13–14 and Lk 5.27–29, but there he is called Levi (to which Mark adds, ''the son of Alphaeus''). Because all three Synoptics relate the same event, we must conclude that they speak of the same person: Matthew-Levi. This identification has been challenged by some: Heracleon and perhaps Origen (in Clement of Alexandria, *Stromata* 4.9; *Patrologia Graecae* 8.1281; Origen, *Contra Celsum* 1.62; see *Patrologia Graecae* 14.835). The banquet presented in Mk 2.15–17 and Lk 5.29–32 as given by Levi is also in Mt 9.10–13, where Matthew, however, is not expressly mentioned.

Nothing is definitely known about his later ministry. The *Liber de ortu beatae Mariae et infantia Salvatoris* attributed to him is a 5th-century apocryphon [*see* BIBLE, III (CANON), 5]. Tradition relates that he had an early ministry in Judea and later went to Gentile lands, given variously as Ethiopia, Persia, and Parthia. He is revered as a martyr and is commemorated in the Latin Church on September 21, in the Eastern on November 16. In art he is represented with a spear in his hand (an allusion to his martyrdom); his symbol (as EVANGELIST) is a winged man. His relics are said to have been found at Salerno in 1080.

Saint Matthew, engraving by Philippe Chery.

See Also: MATTHEW, GOSPEL ACCORDING TO ST.

Bibliography: *Encyclopedic Dictionary of the Bible,* tr. and adap. by L. HARTMAN (New York 1963) from A. VAN DEN BORN, *Bijbels Woordenboek,* 1479–80. M. BONNET and R. A. LIPSIUS, eds., *Acta apostolorum apocrypha* (Leipzig 1898) 1.2. E. MANGENOT, *Dictionaire de la Bible,* ed. F. VIGOUROUX, 5 v. (Paris 1895–1912) 4.1:872–876. H. LECLERCQ, *Dictionnaire d'archéologie chrétienne et de liturgie,* ed. F. CABROL and H. I. MARROU, 15 v. (Paris 1907–53) 10.2:2682–83. F. HAASE, *Apostel und Evangelisten in den orientalischen Überlieferungen* (Münster 1922) 102–103; 272.

[J. A. LEFRANÇOIS]

MATTHEW, GOSPEL ACCORDING TO

Traditionally placed first in almost all the texts of the New Testament, the gospel according to Matthew has enjoyed widespread popularity because of its richness of detail, its deliberate catechetical intent, and its special preoccupation with Church order. The liturgies have shown a predilection for the Matthean version of the Lord's Prayer and catechetical texts for the Matthean version of the Beatitudes. It alone gives the epochal *Tu es Petrus* (Mt 16.17–19), and it would be otiose to underline the magnitude of this text in Christian history.

This article is in two parts. The first, reflecting the approach that was common through the middle of the 20th century, outlines the general plan of the Gospel and discusses it in relationship to the other synoptic Gospels. The second part draws on the scholarship of the latter half of the century that focused more on the historical situation of the Matthean community. It presents the composition as the evangelist's response to challenges facing a Christian community in transition, emphasizes the gospel as narrative and, highlights its view of salvation-history.

Plan and Structure. Based on the simplest analysis of its contents, the gospel, after an introduction (1.1–4.11) that reports the circumstances surrounding the birth of Jesus—the so-called Infancy Narrative—can be divided into three principal sections, each with several divisions and subdivisions: the first section describes Jesus' ministry in Galilee (4.12– 13.58); the second section is an account of his journeys (14.1– 20.34); and the third, tells of ministry in Jerusalem, his passion and death and resurrection (21.1– 28.20).

Modern biblical scholars seeking clues to the author's purpose and intent have undertaken more sophisticated analysis. Approaching the text from different starting points, three schools of thought have emerged as to how the author organized his material: one school argues that it follows a broad geographical-chronological outline that traces Jesus' story from Galilee to Jerusalem, from his birth to his death and resurrection; another school finds topical patterns that highlight and explain the evangelist's basic themes; and a third detects a conceptual structure used by the author to focus on the theme of salvation.

Although scholars have grown more and more critical of the so-called Pentateuchal theory advocated by Benjamin Bacon early in the 20th century, they acknowledge his insight in pointing up the literary formula that clearly marked the boundaries of the five major parts of Jesus' public ministry. Each part is composed of a narrative section followed by a discourse, and all are directed to the progressive unfolding of the central theme of the SYNOPTIC GOSPELS, the good news of the Kingdom: (1) the promulgation of the Kingdom: ch. 3–7; (2) the preaching of the Kingdom: ch. 8–10; (3) the mystery of the Kingdom and its lowliness and inwardness as opposed to the triumphal aspirations of nationalistic theology: 11.1–13.52; (4) its initial growth among a tiny remnant of believers who are the seed of the future Church (13.53–18.35); (5) the divide: rejection of the Jews and admission of the Gentiles (ch. 19–25).

The five discourses (ch. 5–7; ch. 10; 13.1–52; ch. 18; ch. 24–25) all end with a conventional summary that remains fairly consistent: ''And it came to pass when Jesus had finished these words. . .'' (7.28; 11.1; 13.53; 19.1; 26.1). The formula is Semitic, and it is given here in its Septuagint (LXX) dress (cf. Jos 4.11; 1 Sm 13.10; 1 Sm 24.17; etc.). In Matthew it has a definitive ring, and he scarcely ever uses it outside these contexts; a possible exception is 9.10. All five discourses have the Kingdom of Heaven for their theme, but each in turn shifts the focus and so changes the definition in a marked manner.

The first (ch. 5–7) of the five discourses, commonly called the SERMON on the Mount, constitutes in profane metaphor the Magna Carta of the Kingdom. It embodies *inter alia* the ideal of what the disciple should be, and it gives an excellent insight into Matthew's method of composition. For him a chosen theme is a magnet that attracts to itself sayings of Jesus, which one knows, from comparing Matthew *in loco* with the other Synoptics, must belong to different periods in the public life. Not infrequently in fact Matthew himself reproduces such sayings as doublets in what seem to be more satisfying contexts logically.

Thus the Our Father, which is given in Lk 11.2–4 in a very natural context, seems to be placed by Matthew at Mt 6.9–15 by attraction to his theme that at this point is prayer, fasting, and almsgiving. In a similar way the words of Christ on divorce (5.31–32) reoccur as a doublet with no essential change in 19.9 (Mk 10.11–12; Lk 16.18). Matthew places them in the prior setting solely because his theme is adultery at that point. This type of composition is thematic and suits his purpose, but it must of course be carefully born in mind in the overall exegesis of his Gospel. Another case of such thematic attraction seems to be verifiable in Mt 16.13–23, where the *Tu es Petrus* text seems to have been drawn from a different *Sitz im Leben* since it is logically difficult to fit it into the total Synoptic context at this point (Mk 8.27–33; Lk 9.18–22; Mt 16.13–23).

The second discourse (ch. 10) is addressed to the missionary preachers of the good news and includes both instructions and a warning about impending persecutions.

Matthew writing the Gospel. (©Bettmann/CORBIS)

The third (ch. 13) is on the lowly and hidden nature of the Kingdom and presents a clear rejection of nationalistic messianism. The fourth (ch. 18) is a discourse for the followers of Jesus. They are the little flock through whom the Kingdom will grow, and these Jesus instructs in the way of humility, charity, and mutual support. And from these in fact came the inspired impulse that spread the Kingdom after the dawn of the Resurrection. The fifth (ch. 24–25) enshrines the great apocalyptic tableau that is probably the most mysterious element in the New Testament, here and in the other Synoptics. A double chord runs through it, the rejection of the people of the Old Law and the election of the believers in Christ, Jew and Gentile, the new people of God. There is great emphasis here on the need for vigilance, and all is unrolled against the background of the impending doom of Jerusalem and the Last Judgment.

Matthew separates the discourses by inserting narrative sections. His intention, and it is fairly well sustained, is to use the narrative to anticipate the themes of the discourses. This plan is not fully realized in the case of the first discourse. Here he had to follow inevitably the common beginnings of the Synoptic tradition (John the Baptist, Baptism, and temptations), but even at that his selective hand is visible. He confines himself to the necessary minimum of the common tradition (3.1–4.11), and omitting further elements common to Mark and Luke, e.g., Jesus in the synagogue at Capharnaum and the healing of Peter's mother-in-law, he subtly introduces an audience for the imminent Sermon on the Mount—chosen disciples (4.18–22) and the multitudes drawn by the growing fame of Jesus as a wonder-worker (4.23–25).

The plan is quite clear in the narrative section (ch. 8–9) before the second discourse. Here 10 miracles are grouped together because miracles are signs of the Messiah and His age (4.23–25; 9.35; 11.3–6; 12.28). Thus in the whole missionary context of ch. 8–10 there are not only missionary instructions but also the signs performed by Jesus that His disciples in their turn will do also.

Likewise the narrative section of ch. 11–12 admirably prepares the way for the ensuing discourse in parables. The theme here is the lowliness of the Kingdom, a conception so alien to the majority of the Jews that Jesus elects to speak of it under the veil of parables. To prepare this Kingdom-in-parables notion, the evangelist presents certain events and sayings calculated to justify, as it were, in advance the reason for the use of such a veiled device of divine revelation. The proud who refuse to believe in Jesus are introduced (11.16–24; 12.1–14, 24–45); even John the Baptist seems to have doubts (11.2–6); but the humble of heart are those who receive the message and who become true followers of Christ (11.25–27; 12.23, 46–50).

The narrative section 13.53–17.27 introduces the theme of the fourth discourse less clearly than in the preceding cases. There is, however, in this section a general orientation toward the ecclesiastical subject matter of ch. 18. It contains, for instance, two episodes that are fundamental to the constitution of the future Church: the confession of Peter at Caesarea Philippi and the multiplication of the loaves with its Eucharistic symbolism. In addition, the role of Peter is strongly emphasized in this section: he walks on the waters (14.28–31), he receives the solemn promise of Jesus (16.17–19), and he is closely related to Jesus when the latter pays the Temple tax for both (17.24–27). In fact, one may say that the person of Peter throws a prophetic shadow on the subsequent discourse.

As much may be said regarding ch. 19–23. Here the choice of events intended to introduce the eschatological discourse are not very systematically related to it. Yet the orientation toward it is quite discernible. In view of the supreme crisis that it presents, Jesus is shown calling for the humility that is a condition for entry into the Kingdom (19.10–30; 20.20–28). That a decisive spiritual event is at hand is clearly indicated by the solemn entry into Jerusalem on Palm Sunday (21.1–11) and by the symbolic cleansing of the Temple (21.12–17). The tone of Jesus is decisive and unprecedented as He rejects official Judaism and its hypocrisy (23.1–36). And the most poignant moment is reached in the "Jerusalem, Jerusalem . . ." passage, 23.37–39. Only the Resurrection can answer this cry of a broken heart.

Sources and Synoptics. St. IRENAEUS attributed to Matthew the "composition of the Gospel" while "Peter and Paul were preaching and founding the Church in Rome" (*Adversus haereses* 3.1.1, quoted by Eusebius, *Ecclesiastical History* 5.8.2). ORIGEN (d. 254) in his commentary on Matthew says: "The Gospel according to Matthew . . . was the first to be composed . . . in the Hebrew language for believers from Judaism" (Eusebius, *Ecclesiastical History* 6.25.4). Eusebius himself gives evidence in the same strain (*ibid.* 3.24.6), and one may note that the little phrase "in the Hebrew language" remains a constant. Early tradition, based on the testimony of Papias of Hieraplis (c. 60–130), held that Matthew composed a Gospel in Aramaic in Palestine. Papias presumably got his information from John the Presbyter since that was the source of his information on Mark (*ibid.* 23.2). Modern critical analysis, however, changes this view considerably. It shows in fact that the present canonical Greek Matthew and Luke presuppose Greek Mark as a basis. Matthew would therefore have been substantially constructed from a union of Mark with the hypothetical source called Q. The latter, already briefly referred to above, would have been used also by Luke, and this would explain the striking resemblance and at times identity of Matthew and Luke in passages of which Mark shows no trace. Additional critical study has followed this lead but with further modifications.

Some Catholic scholars of the Synoptic problem are loathe to set aside the ancient tradition of Matthew's priority. They see in the Papias tradition a reference not to the canonical Matthew but to an original Matthew in the Aramaic language which is now lost. What follows summarizes P. Benoit's assessment of the situation as he presented it in his Introduction to the Gospel of Matthew in the 1961 *Bible of Jerusalem.*

Material Common to Matthew and Mark. There exist the closest resemblances in subject matter and form between these Gospels. Matthew includes almost all the narrative material of Mark and adds little to it if one excludes the Infancy narrative. He follows the order of Mark very closely. One may certainly admit with the advocates of FORM CRITICISM that the Synoptic Gospels are the result of the grouping together of originally isolated units (miracle stories, pronouncement stories, *novellen,* sayings and parables, etc.). But when one finds that the units once grouped have a more or less identical order as between two Gospels, this cannot be due to chance and the conclusion must be drawn that one depends on the other or that both are following a common but anterior source that had already arranged the original units in the present grouping. Must one choose between these alternatives, or somehow suggest a solution by combining them? An Aramaic original could explain the common order but could not explain the resemblances of language, in this case Greek. There are many indications that Greek Matthew depends on Greek Mark.

Dependence of Greek Matthew on Greek Mark. Where the same narrative is in question Matthew's style is spare and dry and concerned only with the doctrinal point at issue, whereas Mark is leisurely and colorful and abounds in touches of realistic detail. If one compares Mt 9.18–26 with Mk 5.21–43, it is more likely that Matthew has made a schematic abstract from the vivid narrative of Mark than the other way around. This could also be explained by suggesting that Mark had embellished a common source that Matthew retained in its original and direct simplicity. But that seems quite unlikely in view of the coherent spontaneity of Mark.

The Greek of Matthew is solid and workmanlike, if not elegant, while that of Mark is rough and not without solecisms. When two parallel texts are compared carefully the refining hand of Matthew is evident as he attempts to improve on the deficiencies of Mark's language. This certainly shows a dependence of Matthew on Mark.

More important, however, are the cases in which Matthew betrays his dependence by keeping inexplicable details in his text on occasions in which he has reworked a Marcan narrative. Thus when he speaks of cures that took place ''in the evening'' (8.16), he retains a detail that has no meaning in his context, whereas in Mark (1.32) it has meaning since it marks the end of the Sabbath (1.21). In Matthew there had been no reference to a Sabbath, whereas in Mark there had to be since he is showing that Jesus waited until evening ended the Sabbath so as not to violate it by performing miracles, or more likely because the people would have been indoors during the Sabbath. In the same way the dinner with the sinners and the discussion on fasting (Mt 9.10–17) do not fit into the context of the ten miracles where Matthew places them. At this point the reference to the vocation of Matthew (8.9) was the relevant issue for the Evangelist, but that is found elsewhere in Mark (Mk 2.14–22) specifically linked to the two episodes referred to above. Apparently Matthew could see no way, or did not choose, to detach them and thus leaves evidence of his dependence on Mark. These and other indications could be presented to show dependence, but do they prove total dependence? Benoit believes that the matter may be explored even further.

Matthew's Use of the Old Testament. All the New Testament writers are concerned with the fulfillment of the Old Testament in the person of Christ, but none as much as Matthew. He quotes the Old Testament directly at least 60 times (Mark 23 and Luke 25 times), not to mention covert allusions and echoes. Some 10 of these quotations he cites as personal reflections on the event at hand; the rest he places on the lips of others. His Old Testament text is normally the LXX. This whole procedure is somewhat disconcerting to a modern reader, especially when on one occasion he apparently invents an *ad hoc* citation: ''He shall be called a Nazarene'' (2.23b). This is not in the Old Testament, nor is Nazareth ever mentioned there. At times he conflates two disparate Old Testament texts, a procedure that appears wholly artificial to the modern reader. Thus in 27.9–10, when showing that Judas is fulfilling a prophecy of Jeremiah, Matthew achieves his purpose by conflating Jer 32.6–15 with Jer 18.2–3 and Za 11.12–13. This is not the way of Western logic, but Matthew was in good rabbinical standing in his methods. The Messiah (the Christ) promised in the Old Testament had come. To Matthew's mentality the whole Old Testament had pointed to this, and therefore it was conceived as so charged with the promise of the Messiah that every word of it somehow ministered to this promise. Any text in it would therefore have some intimation to convey of the future Christ and could be used as such. It may be added that the New Testament use of the Old Testament is generally rather sober when compared to some of the extraordinary elaborations of the rabbinical traditions of exegesis. A selection of Matthean Old Testament citations is appended here to illustrate his spirit and method.

In Mt 1.23, Is 7.14 is quoted according to the LXX: "'Behold, the virgin shall be with child, and shall bring forth a son; and they shall call his name Emmanuel'; which is, interpreted, 'God with us.'" The Hebrew has "young woman" and "she shall call."

In Mt 2.15, Hos 11.1 is quoted: "Out of Egypt I called my son." In the original the reference is to the Exodus of Israel from Egypt. Matthew reinterprets the passage messianically.

In Mt 4.15–16, Is 9.1–2 is quoted: "Land of Zabulon and land of Nephthalim, by the way of the sea, beyond the Jordan, Galilee of the Gentiles; the people who sat in darkness have seen a great light; and upon those who sat in the region and shadow of death, a light has arisen." Isaiah was thinking of the Mediterranean coast and in terms of the Assyrians. Matthew uses this text quite loosely as a reflection citation to provide a theological reason for Jesus' transfer from Nazareth to Capharnaum on the shore of the Sea of Galilee.

In Mt 11.10, Mal 3.1 is quoted in a somewhat changed form: "Behold, I send my messenger before thy face, who shall make ready thy way before thee." The words of Malachia ("Lo, I am sending my messenger to prepare the way before me") have been changed (as also in the LXX and in Mk 1.2) because of the influence of Ex 23.20 ("See, I am sending an angel before you, to guard you on the way and bring you to the place I have prepared") and are then reinterpreted to refer to John the Baptist. [In Mk 1.2 the adapted citation from Mal 3.1 is attributed to Isaiah because it is followed (Mk 1.3) by a quotation of Is 40.3.]

In Mt 21.5 the evangelist writes: "Now this was done that what was spoken through the prophet might be fulfilled, 'Tell the daughter of Sion: Behold thy king comes to thee, meek and seated upon an ass, and upon a colt, the foal of a beast of burden.'" This is a combination of Is 62.11 ("Say to daughter Sion, your savior comes") and Za 9.9 ("See, your king shall come to you; a just savior is he, meek, and riding on an ass, on a colt, the foal of an ass"). Matthew or his source misunderstood the parallelism of the Hebrew poetry and spoke of two animals; the ass and colt are to be regarded as one in the original.

Matthew ranges widely over the Old Testament. He loves above all Isaiah, "the prophet of the Gospel," but he makes other Prophets, the Law, and the Psalms as well tributary to his theology of Christ in the Old Testament.

Historical Situation. A resurgent interest in Matthew's Gospel on the part of Scripture scholars has yielded significant studies of Matthean theology (Kingsbury, Meier) and a few commentaries. As already noted, the view that the Gospel according to Matthew was written by one of the Twelve in Hebrew or Aramaic and is the oldest and most complete account of the life and teachings of Jesus is no longer held. Although the Gospel numbers Matthew as one of the Twelve and describes him as a tax-collector (9:9; 10:3), there is a consensus that the evangelist was most likely a second- or third-generation Christian-Jew, probably trained as a scribe in a school where several versions of the Scriptures were available (Stendahl). Modern scholars see an autobiographical reference in Matthew's esteem for the scribe who brings new things and old out of the treasure house of tradition (13:52). Matthew's Gospel can be dated about A.D. 85, about 15 years after the Jewish revolt against Roman rule. It seems to have been composed in a predominantly Jewish-Christian community, probably in Antioch or some other urban center in Syria or Palestine where the post-revolt reform movement, influenced by the Pharisees of Jamnia, affected the religious environment.

In applying the methods of redaction criticism to Matthew's Gospel, scholars have discovered that the evangelist's community was coping with confusion caused by a time of transition. Christians, dispersed from Jerusalem, established communities throughout Palestine (Acts 8:1–3a), and Paul's missionary activities had opened the movement to Gentiles. Key leaders had been put to death: James in Jerusalem (A.D. 60); Peter and Paul in Rome (A.D. 67–68). What had been a predominantly Christian-Jewish movement was becoming progressively more Gentile.

Within Judaism dramatic changes were taking place. Prior to the revolt against Rome which ended with the destruction of Jerusalem and the temple (A.D. 66–70), Christian-Jews had understood themselves as a sect within Judaism, living under the same large umbrella as the Sadducees, the Essenes, the Pharisees, and the Zealots. But after the revolt they found themselves in conflict with the Jewish reform movement strongly influenced by the Pharisees. The movement took steps to control the rising significance of Christian-Jews and caused them to be gradually excommunicated from local synagogues.

These events caused Matthew's community to examine their own actions and their identity as followers of Jesus. Could they continue as a sect within Judaism? Should they continue to focus their missionary efforts on their fellow Jews or shift more to the Gentiles? What attitude should they take toward the Jewish Law, as it was being reinterpreted by the Pharisees? How should this community deal with the tension and hostility—a result of their belief that Jesus was the promised Messiah—between themselves and the synagogue leaders? These questions caused the community disorientation, confusion, tension, and internal conflict, as they wondered how to understand themselves in the world of postwar Judaism.

Important internal issues also included: persecution from Jewish and non-Jewish sources, scandal caused by mutual betrayal, hatred between members, the divisive influence of false prophets, and widespread wickedness causing love to grow cold (24:1–14). In a word, Matthew's community faced the challenges of a threefold transition: from an image of themselves as a sect within Judaism to an image of themselves as an independent movement; from a strong Jewish community to an increasingly Gentile community; and from a movement that included leaders who saw and heard Jesus during His earthly life to a movement more dependent on stories about what Jesus did and on collections of His sayings.

Evangelist's Composition. In response to these tensions, Matthew composed what we know as his Gospel. Weaving earlier traditions together, he retold the story of Jesus, so that his community might know what it meant to be Christian in the changing world of postwar Judaism. He affirmed their roots within Judaism and presented Jesus as the Messiah promised in the Hebrew Scriptures (Mt 1–2). He constructed five discourses to show that Jesus was their authoritative teacher, their Rabbi, not the Pharisees at Jamnia (Mt 5–7; 10; 13; 18; 24–25).

Matthew challenged his community to let Jesus deepen their ''little faith,'' as they encountered the storms of transition (8:18–27; 14:22–33). He taught them to cope with internal dissension by avoiding scandal, by seeking the one sheep gone astray, and by reconciling and forgiving the brother or sister who had sinned against them (18:1–35). Matthew also directed their evangelical mission to both Jews and Gentiles (24:14; 28:16–20) and promised entrance into the kingdom of heaven to those who used their talents properly and remained awake and watching for the Messiah's expected return (24:37–25:30). As he retold the story of Jesus, Matthew highlighted these themes to show his community that they remained rooted in their Jewish heritage, to instruct them on how to deal with their present confusion, and to direct them toward their future life and mission.

Gospel as Narrative. Scholars have used composition and narrative criticism to interpret the Gospel of Matthew as a story about Jesus that begins with His roots in Abraham and David (1:1–18) and ends when He commissions to carry His message into all the world (28:16–20). The Infancy Narrative, the flight from Bethlehem in Judea to Egypt, and the return to Nazareth in Galilee recapitulate the story of Israel (Mt 1–2). Jesus' public life begins in the desert in Judea (3:1—4:11), continues in the towns and villages of Galilee (4:12–18:35) and on the journey to Jerusalem (19:1–20:34), and ends with the events in Jerusalem (21:1–28:15) and his return to Galilee (28:16–20).

The story scenes alternate sequentially with five collections of sayings, but the story as a whole remains a narrative that is structured more by the overall dramatic movement of plot and characters, than by the five distinct discourses. The story pivots on ''hinge'' scenes that echo what has gone before and announce what is to come: beginning the ministry in Galilee (4:12–25); return to Nazareth (13:52–58); Caesarea Philippi (16:13–28); blind men at Jericho (20:29–34); plot to kill Jesus (26:1–5).

Jesus is the central character in a network of relationships to his followers, to the suppliants who seek his help, to the hostile Jewish religious authorities, and to the larger Jewish crowds. The evangelist shapes these characters so that his community might see themselves in the followers, the Gentiles in the suppliants, the Jamnia Pharisees in Jesus' enemies, and their fellow Jews in the crowds.

Matthew's story begins with scenes from Jesus' infancy that tell the entire story in miniature (1–2). Next, John the Baptist and Jesus meet in the desert of Judea (3:1–4:11). With John in prison Jesus then reveals himself in Galilee as mighty in word and deed (4:12–9:34), and he empowers the 12 disciples to carry his power to the cities of Israel (9:35–10:42). Various reactions for and against Jesus are portrayed (11:1–12:50), and then Jesus teaches about the kingdom of heaven in parables (13:1–58).

Jesus then focuses on forming His disciples by strengthening their faith and increasing their understanding in episodes concerning bread (14:1–16:12) and by revealing the paradox of His suffering, death, and Resurrection on the journey to Jerusalem (16:13–20:34). In Jerusalem, Jesus takes possession of the temple, debates with His enemies, publicly denounces them, and instructs His disciples about the end of the age (21:1–25:46). Finally, He gathers with His followers at the supper, prays in the garden, moves through His passion, death, and Resurrection, and appears to His disciples in Galilee (26:1–28:20).

Salvation-History. In this story the evangelist presents a distinctive view of salvation-history. Apocalyptic signs at Jesus' death and Resurrection (27:51–54; 28:2–3) reveal a significant turning point in that history and Matthew has used his understanding of the post-resurrectional era to interpret Jesus' public ministry. (Compare Mt 14:32–33 with Mk 6:51–52; and Mt 16:15–23 with Mk 8:29–33.) In the beginning Jesus limited his mission, like that of John the Baptist and the 12 disciples, to Israel (10:5–6). But as crucified and risen, Jesus has come into all power over heaven and earth, and He sends His followers on a more universal mission, that is, to make disciples of both Jews and Gentiles until the end of the age. It is Matthew's purpose to explain how, in the mystery of God's plan of salvation, the kingdom proclaimed by Jesus is accepted more readily by the nations than by the Jews (8:10–12; 21:43).

Matthew's community looked back on both the death of Jesus and the destruction of Jerusalem as marking the end of one era and the beginning of another. As Christians looked forward, the evangelist challenged them to use the story of Jesus to interpret their experience, to pattern their lives on the relationship between Jesus and His disciples, to live according to Jesus' teachings and teach others to observe His commands, and to devote themselves to the task predicted by Jesus: ''And this gospel of the kingdom will be preached throughout the whole world, as a testimony to all nations; and then the end will come'' (24:14). The continued presence of Jesus promised to the end of time (28:20) is to be found in a community that is committed to His teaching and willing to live by His commandments.

Bibliography: Commentaries. M. J. LAGRANGE, *Évangile selon saint Matthieu* (3d ed. *Études biblique*; 1927). J. SCHMID, *Das Evangelium nach Matthäus* (2d ed. Regensburger N.T. 3; Regensburg 1952). P. BENOIT, *L'Évangile selon saint Matthieu* (3d ed. *Bible de Jérusalem*, 43 v. [Paris 1948–54]; 1961). E. LOHMEYER and W. SCHMAUCH, *Das Evangelium des Matthäus* (Meyers Kritischexegetischer Kommentar über das N.T.; Göttingen 1956). P. BONNARD, *L'Evangile selon Saint Matthieu* (Neuchatel, Switzerland 1963). E. SCHWEIZER, *The Good News According to Matthew* (Atlanta 1975). J. P. MEIER, *Matthew* (Wilmington, Del. 1980). D. A. HAGNER, *Matthew*, 2 v. *World Biblical Commentary* 33A, 33B (Dallas, 1993, 1995). D. J. HARRINGTON, *The Gospel of Matthew. Sacra Pagina* 1 (Collegeville, MN 1991). W. D. DAVIES and D. C. ALLISON, JR., *Matthew*, 3 v. (*The International Critical Commentary*; Edinburgh, 1988, 1991, 1997). U. LUZ, *Matthew 1–7. A Commentary* (Minneapolis 1989). *Matthew 8–20. Hermeneia* (Minneapolis 2001). Studies. K. STENDAHL, *The School of Matthew* (Copenhagen 1968). G. BORNKAMM, et al., *Tradition and Interpretation in Matthew* (Philadelphia 1954). W. D. DAVIES, *The Setting of the Sermon on the Mount* (Cambridge, England 1966). J. D. KINSBURY, *The Parables of Jesus in Matthew 13* (Richmond, VA 1969). M. J. SUGGS, *Wisdom, Christology and Law in Matthew's Gospel* (Cambridge, MA 1970). W. G. THOMPSON, *Matthew's Advice to a Divided Community* (Rome 1970). O. L. COPE, *Matthew: A Scribe Trained for the Kingdom of Heaven* (Washington 1976). J. P. MEIER, *Law and History in Matthew's Gospel* (Rome 1976). R. A. EDWARDS, *Matthew's Story of Jesus* (Philadelphia 1985). J. LAMBRECHT, *The Sermon on the Mount* (Wilmington, DE 1985). G. D. KILPATRICK, *The Origins of the Gospel according to St. Matthew* (Oxford 1946). B. C. BUTLER, *The Originality of St. Matthew* (Cambridge, England 1951). J. DUPONT, *Les Béatitudes* (new ed. Bruges 1958). W. TRILLING, *Das wahre Israel: Studien zur Theologie des Matthäusevangeliums* (3d ed. *Studien zum A. und N.T. 10*; Munich 1964). D. L. BALCH, *Social History of the Matthean Community: Cross-Disciplinary Approaches* (Minneapolis 1991). J. A. OVERMAN, *Matthew's Gospel and Formative Judaism: The Social World of Matthew's Community* (Minneapolis, 1990). D. SENIOR, *What Are They Saying About Matthew?* (New York/Mahwah 1996).

[J. QUINLAN/W. G. THOMPSON/EDS.]

MATTHEW OF ALBANO

Cardinal; b. in the country of Laon, France, perhaps 1085; d. Pisa, Italy, Dec. 25, 1135. He studied at Laon under the celebrated master ANSELM, then left to become a priest at Laon. The disordered life of the clergy determined him instead to enter the Cluniac priory of St. Martindes-Champs at Paris (1110), where he became prior seven years later. Matthew was one of the leading monastic reformers of the 12th century and was active both in France and in northern Italy. He was a friend of the abbot of Cluny, PETER THE VENERABLE, and defended him against the deposed Abbot Ponce before Pope HONORIUS II, who created Matthew cardinal bishop of Albano in 1125. Honorius's successor, INNOCENT II, sent Matthew as legate to France in 1127 and to Germany in 1128 to restore monastic discipline there. Following the Council of PISA in 1134, he was invited by BERNARD OF CLAIRVAUX to restore Milan to papal obedience and he died soon after returning to Pisa.

Bibliography: *Patrologia Latina* ed J. P. MIGNE, 189:913–936, vita; 173:1261–68, letters. *Histoire littéraire de la France* 13:51–55. U. BERLIÈRE, ''Le Cardinal Matthieu d'Albano, 1085–1135,'' *Revue Bénédictine* 18 (1901) 113–140, 280–303. C. J. VON HEFLE, *Histoire des conciles d'apres les documents originaux* 5.1:668–672. J. LECLERCQ, *Pierre le Vénérable* (Paris 1946).

[D. S. BUCZEK]

MATTHEW OF AQUASPARTA

Franciscan cardinal and theologian; b. Aquasparta (Umbria), *c.* 1238; d. Rome, Oct. 29, 1302. After completing his preparatory studies as a Franciscan, Matthew was sent to Paris to obtain the degree of Master of Theology. In 1268 he was already a *baccalarius biblicus,* and from 1270 to 1273 he commented on the *Sententiae* of PETER LOMBARD. By the end of August of 1273, he had received the title of Doctor of Theology and was teaching in Bologna, where he remained for a year or two. He then returned to Paris, and from 1277 to 1279 he was *magister regens* of the Franciscan studium.

In 1279 Matthew succeeded JOHN PECKHAM as lector of the Sacred Palace, holding this illustrious professorship until 1287 when, at the Chapter of Montpellier, he was elected minister general of the order. In this post Matthew distinguished himself as a peacemaker, settling disputes within the order and reinstating John of Parma and PETER JOHN OLIVI.

On May 16, 1288, Nicholas IV named him cardinal priest, but Matthew was obliged to continue ruling the order until the general chapter, held at Rieti in 1289. In 1291 he was promoted to cardinal bishop of Porto and of San Ruffino. He spent the remainder of his life in the service of the Holy See. He served Boniface VIII (1294–1303) with great fidelity and devotion and thus found himself embroiled in the political struggles of that pontificate. He was appointed pontifical legate to Lombardy, Romagna, and Tuscany, and was assigned to pacify the various contending factions. It is probable that he had a part in the preparation of the famous bull *Unam Sanctam,* which was published only 20 days after his death.

Although Matthew did not attend St. Bonaventure's lectures in Paris, he was a faithful disciple of the Seraphic Doctor. He was well versed in the works of Aristotle and Thomas Aquinas, but he remained faithful in all respects to the tradition of the Augustinian-Franciscan school. He criticized his adversaries with moderation and set forth his own views with admirable clarity. Yet Matthew had little influence on subsequent thinkers; his great commentary on the *Sententiae,* for example, was never copied—possibly because of the poor hand in which it was written.

Matthew's literary legacy is truly considerable. It has been described in detail by V. Doucet in *Matthaei ab Aquasparta Quaestiones disputatae de gratia, cum introductione critica* (*Bibliotheca Franciscana scholastica medii aevi* [Quaracchi-Florence 1903–] 11). His principal works are a voluminous commentary on the first, second, and part of the fourth books of the *Sententiae,* which is, with the exception of a few questions, still unpublished; many *Quaestiones disputatae,* almost all of which have been published at Quaracchi (*ibid.* 1, 2, 11, 17, 18); quodlibetal questions; two series of *Quaestiones de anima;* and various scriptural commentaries and sermons (Bibliotheca Franciscana Ascetica Medii Aevi 9–10).

Bibliography: *Matteo d'Aquasparta (collected essays)* (Spoleto, Italy 1993). J. DOWD, ''Matthew of Aquasparta's De Productione Rerum and its Relation to St. Thomas Aquinas and St. Bonaventure,'' *Franciscan Studies* 34 (1974), 34–75. Z. HAYES, *The General Doctrine of Creation in the Thirteenth Century, with Special Emphasis on Matthew of Aquasparta* (Munich 1964). P. MAZZARELLA, *La dottrina dell'anima e della conoscenza in Matteo d'Acquasparta* (Padua 1969). E. BROCCHIERI, *La legge naturale nel pensiero di Matteo d'Acquasparta* (Rovigo 1967), bibliography.

[G. GÁL]

MATTHEW OF CRACOW

Theologian and bishop of Worms; b. Cracow, Poland, *c.* 1330; d. Worms, Germany, March 5, 1410. He should not be confused with another Matthew, also from Cracow, who was active at the end of the 15th century as a university theologian and preacher. The earlier Matthew was the son of a city notary and was first educated at St. Mary's collegiate school, Cracow. He pursued further studies at Charles University of Prague, where he received a bachelor of arts in 1355, a bachelor of theology in 1381, and a doctor of theology in 1387. For a short time, he was professor of theology at Prague and a city preacher. In 1390 he became a canon in Leslau at the church of St. Idzi. In 1391 Matthew returned to his native city and in 1395 left again to become a professor of theology at the University of Heidelberg. He became rector of the University the following year, and confessor and councilor to Rupert, King of the Romans (d. 1410). In 1397, at the request of Władysław JAGIEŁŁO, he returned to Poland to reorganize the University of Cracow. In 1405 the emperor nominated him to the See of Worms; in 1408 Pope GREGORY XII created him cardinal, and in the same year he was appointed papal legate for Germany.

Matthew of Cracow left several important theological writings, some published, others still in MS; many of them are preserved in the Cracow University library, but copies are scattered in various European libraries. His most important work, *De squaloribus curiae romanae,* known also as *Moyses sanctus,* was submitted to Pope INNOCENT VII in 1404 and published in 1551. In it he advocated supremacy of the council over the pope (*see* CONCILIARISM, HISTORY OF). A treatise, *Ars moriendi,* xylographed in 1450, is ascribed to Matthew of Cracow, but its authorship is uncertain. Another work, the homiletic *Rationale operum divinorum,* exists in MS in the University of Cracow library. The other theological treatise, *Dialogus rationis et conscientiae,* was printed supposedly by Guttenberg in 1459 and has been translated into Czech and German.

Bibliography: G. KORBUT, *Polish Literature,* 4 v. (2d ed. Warsaw 1929–31) 1:22–24, in Polish. K. MORAWSKI, *A History of the Jagiellonian University,* 2 v. (Cracow 1900) 1:60–63, in Polish. É. AMANN, *Dictionnaire de théologie catholique* 10.1:389–392. B. STASIEWSKI, *Lexikon für Theologie und Kirche* 2 7:174–175.

[B. B. SZCZESNIAK]

MATTHEW PARIS

Monk, artist, and most important of the English chroniclers of the 13th century; b. *c.* 1199; d. 1259. He received the Benedictine habit in 1217, and was trained as a scribe and illuminator in his abbey of ST. ALBAN's. His first works were illustrated lives of saints (ALBAN, Edward, and later, Thomas and Edmund of Canterbury). He started to write history, in about 1236, by helping Roger of Wendover whom he later replaced. In 1246, he was sent to reform the Norwegian abbey of St. Benet Holm, when the abbot disappeared with the community seal. Matthew arranged for loans from Cahorsin moneylenders and introduced the customs of St. Alban's there, but returned soon afterwards a disappointed man. Thenceforth, he worked tirelessly at writing and rewriting his extensive histories: *Chronica majora, Historia Anglorum, Flores historiarum,* and *Abbreviatio chronicorum.* These survive in part or in whole in Matthew's own hand and are enlivened with marginal drawings of coats of arms or of the events he describes. His exceptionally full and well-informed narrative, based often on conversations with royalty and magnates who stayed at the abbey, is at times prejudiced and partial. His illustrated life of St. Alban represents the highest development of the saint's legend, and his drawings of an elephant, and of himself prostrate before the Madonna and Child, are justly famous. One of his lesser literary works, the chronicle of his own abbey, describing several of its monks, and the works of art in the church, is both revealing and successful. He lacked the discipline and patience necessary for a true scholar and historian, but he excelled at retelling contemporary gossip and events.

Bibliography: Works. *Chronica majora,* ed. H. R. LUARD, 7 v. (Rolls Series 57); *Historia Anglorum,* ed. F. MADDEN, 3 v. (Rolls Series 44). T. WALSINGHAM, *Gesta abbatum monasterii Sancti Albani,* ed. H. T. RILEY, 3 v. (Rolls Series 28) v.1. Literature. *Illustrations to the Life of St. Alban in Trinity College Dublin ms. E. i. 40,* reproduced by W. R. L. LOWE and E. F. JACOB (Oxford 1924). V. H. GALBRAITH, *Roger Wendover and Matthew Paris* (Glasgow 1944). R. VAUGHAN, *Matthew Paris* (Cambridge, Eng. 1958).

[H. FARMER]

MATTHEWS, MARY BERNARDINA, MOTHER

First prioress of the Carmelites in America; b. Charles County, Md., 1732; d. Port Tobacco, Md., June 12, 1800. Ann Matthews was born into an aristocratic, religious family; she applied for admission to the English-speaking Discalced Carmelites in Hoogstraeten, Belgium, in 1754. The next year, at the age of 23, she was professed and received the name Sister Bernardina Teresa Xavier of St. Joseph. She was esteemed for her sanctity and her gift of directing souls, and became mistress of novices and later, mother prioress, a position she held for 28 years. In 1782 the suppression of all religious orders in the Netherlands by Joseph II made a new foundation imperative. Mother Bernardina's brother, Rev. Ignatius Matthews, SJ, suggested that a branch of the Carmelite Order be established in Maryland to foster vocations in the U.S. Under the spiritual guidance of Rev. Charles Neale and with financial aid from M. de Villegas, the foundation was made, and Mother Bernardina was chosen as first prioress. In 1790 with two nieces, Sister Eleanora and Sister Aloysia, and Sister Clare Joseph Dickinson of the convent at Antwerp, Mother Bernardina arrived at Port Tobacco, Md., where she established her monastery. This marked not only the site of the first Carmelite monastery, but also the introduction of the first religious order to the U.S. The earlier foundations of the Ursulines in Louisiana were then outside U.S. territory.

Bibliography: C. W. CURRIER, *Carmel in America: A Centennial History of the Discalced Carmelites in the United States* (Baltimore 1890). Discalced Carmelites, Boston, *Carmel: Its History, Spirit, and Saints* (New York 1927).

[M. V. GEIGER]

MATTHEWS, WILLIAM

The first native American ordained in the U.S.; b. Port Tobacco, Md., Dec.16, 1770; d. Washington, D.C., April 30, 1854. He was descended from one of Maryland's earliest colonial families and was related on his mother's side to Abp. Leonard NEALE of Baltimore. As a youth he was sent to Liège, Belgium, to begin classical studies. Matthews taught briefly at Georgetown College, Washington, D.C.; in 1797 he entered St. Mary's Seminary, Baltimore, and was ordained (March 1800) by Bp. John Carroll. After missionary work in southern Maryland, he was named (1804) pastor of St. Patrick's Church, Washington.

During his long career Matthews ably combined the roles of priest, public-minded citizen, educator, and philanthropist. Although not a Jesuit, he was named vice president (1808) and president (1809) of Georgetown College. He was cofounder of Washington's first permanent public library (1811) and became its president (1821), a position he held for 13 years. During Matthews's presidency the library moved into permanent quarters and substantially increased its holdings. From 1813 to 1844 he served also as a trustee of Washington's public-school system. In 1821 the Washington Catholic Seminary (Gonzaga College) was established by the Jesuits on land adjacent to St. Patrick's and donated by Matthews. But the seminary project failed, and the school was reorganized for the instruction of young men who came from prominent families. Ever interested in the plight of the orphan, Matthews established St. Vincent's

Female Orphan Asylum ''to produce intellectually and emotionally mature young women who could occupy a place of dignity in the community'' (Durkin,109). He was a prime mover also in the foundation of Visitation Girls' School, to which he gave $10,000, and he bequeathed $3,000 to the establishment of St. Joseph's Orphan Home for Boys.

Because of his background, Matthews was acquainted with Washington's elite and knew personally A. Jackson, D. Webster, H. Clay, and R. B. Taney. In 1828 he was named administrator of the Diocese of Philadelphia, Pa., and it was thought that he would succeed Henry Conwell as bishop of the see. However, Matthews was reluctant to leave Washington, so he pleaded with Rome and was relieved of the Philadelphia assignment.

Bibliography: J. T. DURKIN, *William Matthews: Priest and Citizen* (New York 1963).

[J. Q. FELLER]

William Matthews, photograph by Matt Brady.

MATTHIAS, APOSTLE, ST.

The name Μαθθίας is an abbreviation of the Hebrew name for ''gift of YHWH.'' The only mention of Matthias in the New Testament occurs in Acts 1:23–26 where he and Barsabbas are selected as candidates for replacing Judas Iscariot among the Twelve. Later traditions about him, including the idea that he was among the group of 70 disciples sent out by Jesus in Lk 10:1, are all legendary.

Modern commentators on Acts have debated the significance of Acts 1:23–26 and whether or not the passage outlines what Luke considers the basic requirements of the apostolic office (i.e., someone who had been part of the group who followed Jesus from the time of his baptism to his Ascension). This opinion, however, fails to account for the fact that Luke, while largely restricting his use of the term ''apostle'' to the Twelve, does call Paul an apostle even though he scarcely fits the ''criteria'' outlined here (Lk 14:4, 14). Luke is attempting to demonstrate that the church carries on Jesus' mission to the people of Israel, symbolically represented by the number Twelve, as well as the mission to witness to his life, death, and resurrection ''to the ends of the earth'' (Acts 1:8; cf. 1:22). Acts 1:26 states that the Eleven ''gave lots'' (ἔδωκαν κλήρους) to the candidates, and ''the lot fell on Matthias''' (ἐπεσεν ὁ κλῆρος ἐπὶ Μαθθίαν). The manner in which the successor to Judas is selected in Acts 1:26 seems odd at first glance, but the use of lots to ascertain the divine will is common in the Old Testament (e.g., Lev 16:7–10, Josh 18:6, Prv 16:33). Some commentators are of the opinion that the Greek text of Acts 1:26 implies that the Eleven voted on the two candidates. This opinion has been rightly challenged by those who claim that the phrase ''they gave lots'' is a Semitic idiom, and does not convey the idea that the Eleven assigned a ''lot'' to Matthias. Moreover, the Old Testament use of lots seems to fit in well with this passage, especially in light of the plea for divine guidance in 1:24–25. In the end it is plain that Luke is emphasizing the divine origin of Matthias's selection.

Legends about Matthias's missionary career emerged in latter centuries through the influence of *The Traditions of Matthias* and *The Acts of Andrew and Matthias*. No copy of the former work exists, though we have descriptions of the work and some fragments from the early Christian writers. Clement of Alexandria states that the Gnostics were fond of this work (*Strom.* 7, 13, 82; 7, 17, 108), and the *Decretum Gelasianum* lists it as a heretical work. *The Acts of Andrew and Matthias* is preserved in several manuscripts, and tells the story of the adventures of Matthias among ''the cannibals.''

In iconography Matthias is portrayed either with a halberd or an ax, the instrument of his martyrdom.

Feast: Feb. 24.

Bibliography: W. A. BEARDSLEE, ''The Casting of Lots at Qumran and in the Book of Acts,'' *Novum Testamentum,* 4 (1960)

St. Matthias the Apostle, terracotta plaque by Andrea and Luca dell Robbia in the Pazzi Chapel, Church of Santa Croce, Florence.

245–252. J. A. FITZMYER, *The Acts of the Apostles*, in *Anchor Bible*, v. 31 (New York 1998). T. MARTIN, ''Matthias,'' *Allgemeine deutsche Biographie* (Leipzig 1875–1910) IV, 644).

[C. MCMAHON]

MATTIAS, MARIA DE, BL.

Foundress of the Sisters Adorers of the Most Precious Blood; b. Vallecorsa (Frosinone), Italy, Feb. 4, 1805; d. Rome, Aug. 20, 1866. Maria's parents, Giovanni and Ottavia (de Angelis) de Mattias, were poor but afforded the girl a good education. During a mission preached in Vallecorsa by St. Gaspare del BUFALO (1822), she was inspired to dedicate her life to prayer and good works. Under the guidance of Giovanni MERLINI, her spiritual director, Mattias organized a group of religious women with special devotion to the PRECIOUS BLOOD, dedicated to the education of youth. The congregation dates its origin from the opening of a school at Acuto on the invitation of the bishop of Anagni (March 4, 1834). Despite habitual poor health and misunderstanding within the community concerning the foundress's intention, Mattias established 63 houses. In part this success was due to the generosity of a Russian widow, Princess Zena Wolkonska. Mattias was beatified Oct. 1, 1950.

Feast: Oct. 1 (*See* PRECIOUS BLOOD SISTERS).

Bibliography: M. E. PIETROMARCHI, *La beata Maria de Mattias: Fondatrice dell'istituto delle Suore Adoratice del Preziosissimo Sangue* (Rome 1950). A. MYERSCOUGH, *Redemptive Encounter: The Precious Blood in the Spirituality of Maria de Mattias* (Washington 1963). M. A. MASTERSON, *Smiling Maria: Blessed Maria de Mattias* (Ruma, Ill. 1966). N. BUFALINI, *Valore sociale ed assistenziale dell'opera di Maria de Mattias* (L'Aquila 1971). J. L. BAUDOT and L. CHAUSSIN, *Vies des saints et des bienheureux selon l'ordre du calendrier avec l'historique des fêtes,* ed. by the Benedictines of Paris, 12 v. (Paris 1935–56); v. 13, suppl. and table générale (1959) 13:174–176. *Acta Sanctae Sedis* 42 (1950) 719–723.

[A. J. POLLACK]

MATULAITIS-MATULEWICZ, JURGIS, BL.

In Polish his name is Jerzy Matulewicz; superior general of the MARIAN FATHERS; b. April 13, 1871, Lugine, Lithuania; d. Jan. 24, 1927, Kaunas, Lithuania.

Matulaitis completed his philosophical and theological studies at Kielce and Warsaw seminaries and at the Catholic Academy in St. Petersburg, Russia, where he was ordained Nov. 25, 1898. He continued his studies at the University of Fribourg (Switzerland) to earn his doctorate in sacred theology ''praeclarissime'' (1902) for his dissertation *Doctrina russorum de iustitia originali*. After two years as professor of Latin and Canon Law at the Kielce seminary, he went to Warsaw, where he pioneered the Catholic movement for social betterment among the workers. In 1907 he was nominated to the faculty of the Catholic Academy of St. Petersburg as professor of Sociology and later of Dogmatic Theology.

In 1909, while still professor and vice rector of the Academy, with the permission of Pope St. Pius X, he undertook the clandestine reform of the Order of Marians of the Immaculate Conception (Marian Fathers), which had been founded in 1673 by Stanislaus PAPCZÝNSKI. It was suppressed in 1864 by the Russian Czarist Government, and reduced in 1909 to a single member. Dispensed from the required novitiate, Matulaitis secretly entered the order and adapted it to the needs of the Church in modern times. He composed new constitutions and instructions to govern and direct the life and activity of the congregation, which he served as superior general from 1911 until his death. In 1913 he visited the U.S. and established the first Marian house at Chicago.

In 1918 he was nominated by Pope Benedict XV to the vast and troubled Diocese of Vilnius, which he governed for seven years. In 1925 he was elevated to the rank of titular archbishop and named by Pius XI as apostolic visitator to Lithuania in order to establish an ecclesiastical province and to negotiate a concordat between the Lithuanian government and the Holy See. In addition to being responsible for the renewal of the Congregation of

Marian Fathers, he wrote constitutions for some seven other religious congregations. In Lithuania he founded the Congregation of Sisters of the Immaculate Conception, and in Byelorussia, the Congregation of Servants of the Sacred Heart. He died in 1927, and in 1934, his body was translated from Kaunas cathedral to the Marianist church of Marijampolér (where he had been baptized), now a national shrine. He was beatified by John Paul II June 28, 1987, the 600th anniversary of the ''baptism'' of Lithuania (Apostolic Letter, June 5, 1987).

Feast: Jan. 27 (Marianists); July 12 (Lithuania).

Bibliography: V. CUSUMANO, *Innamorato della Chiesa* (Milan 1962). T. GÓRSKI and Z. PROCZEK, *Rozmilowany w Kosciele: błogoslawiony arcybiskup Jerzy Matulewicz* (Warsaw 1987). A. KUCAS, *Archbishop George Matulaitis*, tr. and ed. S. C. GAUCIAS (Chicago 1981). C. A. MATULAITIS, *A Modern Apostle* (Chicago 1955). S. MATULIS, *Lexikon für Theologie und Kirche,* 2d. ed., 7:183. *L'Osservatore Romano,* Eng. ed., 27 (1987): 6–7.

[W. FOGARTY]

MATURIN, BASIL WILLIAM

Spiritual writer; b. Grangegorman, Dublin, Ireland, February 1847; d. at sea, May 7, 1915. His father, a Tractarian clergyman, was the vicar of Grangegorman. Basil studied at Trinity College, Dublin, and was ordained deacon in the Anglican Church in 1870. On becoming curate in Peterstowe, Herefordshire, England, he was ordained priest there. On Feb. 22, 1873, he entered the novitiate of the Society of St. John the Evangelist (COWLEY FATHERS) at Oxford. In 1876 he began a mission in Philadelphia, Pa., where he stayed for ten years at the Episcopal church of St. Clement, first as one of the assistant clergy, then as rector. In the U.S. and later in England he was much esteemed as a preacher, retreat master, and spiritual director. After long heart-searching, Maturin joined the Catholic Church on March 5, 1897. He studied for the priesthood at the Canadian College in Rome, was ordained in 1898, and then returned to London to do parish work and preaching. In 1905 he joined the newly formed Society of Westminister Diocesan Missionaries and took charge of the parish at Pimlico. In 1910 he tried his vocation as a Benedictine at DOWNSIDE, but proved too old. When he returned to London he was not attached to a parish, but had a confessional at St. James's Church, Spanish Place, and great numbers of penitents. In 1914 he became chaplain to the Catholic undergraduates at Oxford, but he did not serve long in this capacity, for in the following spring he was one of those who lost their lives in the sinking of the ''Lusitania.'' Maturin published several books of spirituality and sermons: *Self Knowledge and Self Discipline* (1905); *Laws of the Spiritual Life* (1907); *Practical Studies on the Parables of Our Lord* (1908); *Some Principles and Practices of the Spiritual Life* (reissued 1915); *Fruits of the Life of Prayer* (1916); and *Sermons and Sermon Notes,* edited by F. Wilfrid Ward (1916).

Bibliography: B. W. MATURIN, *The Price of Unity* (New York 1912). M. WARD, *Father Maturin* (New York 1920).

[E. FALLAUX]

MAUBUISSON, ABBEY OF

A former French abbey of CISTERCIAN NUNS, located in the Diocese of Versailles. Maubuisson Abbey was founded and richly endowed by Queen Blanche of Castile in 1236 and illustrates the finest style of French Gothic. The queen was buried there. The nuns came from the nobility, and its abbesses from the highest French aristocracy. Being near Paris, the abbey enjoyed royal patronage; King PHILIP IV (1285–1314) often used it as his residence. The convent was badly damaged during the Hundred Years' War. After 1543 the appointment of the abbesses by the kings of France for personal or dynastic reasons resulted in the rapid decline of morals, especially when King HENRY IV installed as abbess Angélique d'Estrées (1597–1618), the sister of his mistress. Subsequent reform under the influence of Angélique Arnauld (d. 1661), abbess of PORT-ROYAL, brought only temporary improvement. Maubuisson was suppressed in 1791 and looted. When it was sold to private owners, both the church and cloister were demolished. Only ruins survive.

Bibliography: U. CHEVALIER, *Répertoire des sources historiques du moyen-âge. Topobibliographie,* 2 v. (Paris 1894–1903) 2:1875–76. O. VERGE DU TAILLIS, *Chroniques de l'Abbaye Royale de Maubuisson* (Paris 1947). L. H. COTTINEAU, *Répertoire topobibliographique des abbayes et prieurés,* 2 v. (Mâcon 1935–39) 2:1790–91.

[L. J. LEKAI]

MAUNOIR, JULIEN, BL.

Breton missionary and author; b. Saint-Georges de Reintembault, Rennes, France, Oct. 1, 1606; d. Plèvin, Jan. 28, 1683. He entered the Society of Jesus at Paris in 1625 and taught at the college of Quimper, where he dedicated himself to the Bretons. Having been born in the French-speaking part of Brittany, he had no knowledge of Breton language; but within two months after a pilgrimage to the shrine of Ty-Mamm-Doue (the House of the Mother of God) he was preaching fluently in this Celtic tongue. In 1640, after ordination, he began his apostolate and for the next 42 years conducted more than 400 missions in all parts of the duchy, preaching mostly in Breton. He was called universally ''An Tad Mad'' (The Good Father). Maunoir was the organizer of the Breton missions. He based his program on the *Spiritual Exercises* of St. IGNATIUS OF LOYOLA, but added catechetical instructions, symbolical charts, didactic hymns, and dramatic presentations of the Savior's life. He was a pioneer of the closed retreat, and was responsible for building at Quimper one of the earliest retreat houses.

At Maunoir's missions, which lasted from four to five weeks, attendance of 10,000 was common. At the great missions the numbers reached 20,000 and 30,000, and the sermons and catecheses had to be given in the open fields. To serve these Pentecostal assemblies he organized assistants from the diocesan clergy; these assistants eventually numbered 1,000 and included five bishops. For a mission he would invite 20 or 30 priests who would preach, hear confessions, catechize, teach hymns, or prepare the grand procession. During the mission they lived in common under his direction. They recited the Office and meditated together and participated twice daily in conferences on mission methods, problems of moral theology, and projects of their own personal holiness. Such itinerant seminaries elevated the standards of the Breton clergy, many of whom lacked formal training. Maunoir published seven works, including ascetical books, collections of hymns, and a Breton-French dictionary and grammar. His hymns became part of the literature of the Breton people. He was beatified by PIUS XII, May 20, 1951.

Feast: July 2 (Jesuits).

Bibliography: A. BOSCHET, *Le Parfait missionaire* (Paris 1697). X. A. SÉJOURNÉ, *Histoire du vénérable serviteur de Dieu Julien Maunoir,* 2 v. (Paris 1885). L. KERBIRIOU, *Les Missions bretonnes* (Brest 1934). H. BRÉMOND, *Histoire litteraire du sentiment religieux en France,* 11 v. (Paris 1916–33) 5:82–117. *Acta Apostolicae Sedis* (1951) 225–226, 428–432, 437–440. M. P. HARNEY, *Good Father in Brittany, the Life of Bl. Julien Maunoir* (Boston 1964). J. N. TYLENDA, *Jesuits Saints & Martyrs* (Chicago 1998) 18–20.

[M. P. HARNEY]

MAURIAC, FRANÇOIS

Novelist, Nobel Prize winner; b. Bordeaux, Oct. 11, 1885; d. Sept. 1, 1970. Mauriac wrote two dozen works of fiction, and also achieved distinction as a political essayist, critic, biographer and writer of spiritual works. Mauriac was the youngest of five children in what can be termed a landed, prosperous, middle-class family. His father died when he was 18 months old and he was raised by his pious mother, who appears as Mme. Dezaymeries in the novel *Evil.* As a child, Mauriac was frail and shy, admittedly guilt ridden, unhappy, and introverted. Upon leaving secondary school in the region of his birth, Mauriac went to Paris (1906) to study paleography and medieval archeology. He left school to be a writer, however.

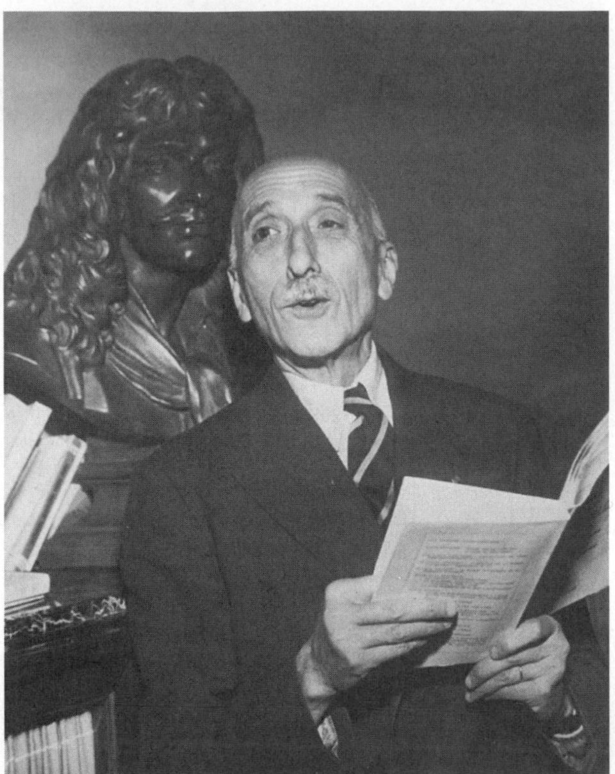

François Mauriac.

In November 1909 Mauriac privately published his first work, a collection of poems (*Les Mains jointes*), that gained favorable notice from influential critics. A second book of poetry followed two years later and then, in 1913, *L'enfant chargé de chaines (Young Man in Chains),* Mauriac's first novel, appeared. That same year he married. In 1914 he published *La robe prétexte (The Stuff of Youth)* but did little other writing until well after World War I, in which he served in a medical unit.

Prolific Years. Beginning in 1920, Mauriac published almost a novel a year for two decades (in all, he authored nearly 100 volumes). Among those which served to establish his reputation as a novelist were *La chair et le sang (Flesh and Blood)*; in 1922 *Le baiser au lepreux*, a story of a destructive yearning for love; in 1923, *Genetrix*, about the evil effects of possessive maternal love; in 1925, *Le desert de l'amour (The Desert of Love)*, wherein a father and son vie for the attentions of the same, unvirtuous, woman; in 1927, *Therese Desqueyroux (Therese)*, about a sinful woman who shares mankind's common guilt.

What may be Mauriac's masterpiece, *Le noeud de vipers (Vipers Tangle)*, came out in 1932. It is a story of impure human love wherein sinful creatures struggle to find grace. The next year he was elected to the French Academy at the relatively early age of 48. *La fin de la nuit* (1935) brings Therese Desqueyroux to the brink of salvation, and another major novel, *La pharisienne (A Woman of the Pharisees)*, was published in 1941 concerning a hypocritically religious woman and the evil effects she has on others.

In the 1930s Mauriac wrote some minor dramas and polemical works condemning totalitarianism in all forms. When France fell in World War II he wrote vigorously on behalf of the resistance movement, which he joined. He was a strong supporter of General Charles de Gaulle and wrote a biography of this friend (1964) beginning with ''The history of a man is the history of an age.'' *Men I Hold Great* (1951) includes biographical chapters on Pascal, Flaubert, Balzac, Graham Greene, and others.

Spiritual Writings and Major Themes. Mauriac's spiritual writings include *God and Mammon, The Eucharist, The Mystery of Holy Thursday* (the theme of which is Christ lives in individuals as a sacramental reality), and *St. Margaret of Cortona*, whose martyrdom distracted him from the World War II martyrdom of his nation. *What I Believe* (with a chapter on ''Purity,'' that illuminates much of his fiction), *Life of Jesus*, and *The Son of Man*, in which the author clearly proclaims a Christian hope, are other primarily religious volumes.

In November 1952 Mauriac earned the Nobel Prize for fiction. His major themes may be summarized as including the isolation of individuals, the abuse of maternal authority, the influence of childhood on adulthood (the individual past on the individual present), and the penetration of the human heart by God alone as well as the eternal conflict between good and evil within the soul.

Mauriac never recovered from a serious fall in April 1969 which led to his death. His last novel, *Un adolescent d'autrefois*, was published posthumously in the U.S. as *Maltaverne*. It is regarded as an autobiographical work and contains many of his important themes, proving that to the end Mauriac continued to be a brilliant psychologist of the anguished person who is led astray by temptations of the world and passions of the flesh.

Bibliography: A. M. CASPARY, *François Mauriac* (St. Louis 1968). N. CORMEAU, *L'art de François Mauriac* (Paris 1951). M. F. MALONEY, *François Mauriac: A Critical Study* (Denver 1958). E. PELL, *François Mauriac in Search of the Infinite* (New York 1947).

[H. J. CARGAS]

MAURICE, BYZANTINE EMPEROR

Reigned: Aug. 13, 582 to Nov. 22/23, 602; b. Arabissus, Cappadocia, 539; d. 602. His origins are obscure (Armenian by legend); he came to Constantinople as a notary and made a career as a military commander during the reign of Tiberius I, who appointed him Caesar and heir to the throne on Aug. 5, 582. After Tiberius' death, Maurice married Tiberius' daughter, Constantina.

At the time of his accession the empire was in trouble financially, and in order to deal with threats posed by foreign powers, Maurice took a number of unpopular measures to save money, for example, cutting the pay of the army in the East and Balkans. However, as he still pursued a lavish building policy and favored his own family with generous patronage, he became increasingly unpopular.

Concerned about imperial control of the provinces, he created the exarchates of Ravenna and Carthage (Africa). The exarchs were mainly military leaders and as they also had authority over most civil officials, their powers were almost unlimited. As Maurice struggled to control the Lombards who were encroaching on Italy, he needed a reorganisation of defense. His aggressive attitude to the Lombards brought him into conflict with Pope Gregory I, who preferred a policy of negotiation.

There was further disagreement between pope and emperor over theological matters, especially the use by the patriarch of Constantinople of the title ''oecumenical.'' In the East, Maurice continued Tiberius' tolerance of the Monophysites until 598, when his kinsman, Bishop Dometianus, unleashed a persecution in north Syria. The emperor dissolved the anti-Chalcedonian Ghassanid Arab client kingdom, while orthodox Christianity made great progress among the Arabs, particularly the Lakhmids, hitherto Persian allies. Roman Armenia was induced to elect a *catholicos* of its own and break with Persarmenia, from which Georgia also separated to join Constantinople. Maurice himself was very religious; he associated himself with popular cults, especially that of the Virgin, and he fixed the feast of the Dormition (Assumption) on August 15.

Maurice came to the throne during a war with Persia, but in 589 Persian King Hormizd IV was killed in an internal rebellion, and his heir, Chosroes II, sought protection and aid from Maurice, who restored him to his throne. In 591 a treaty was signed which gave Byzantium a larger share of Armenia, a valuable source of manpower, and cancelled Byzantium's contribution for the joint defense of the Caucasian pass. The Persian treaty allowed Maurice to deal with the Slavs and Avars who threatened the Danube frontier. After initial victories, however, there was dissatisfaction among the troops and when they were ordered to winter across the Danube, they proclaimed Phocas (a centurion) emperor and marched to the capital which the Blues handed over. Maurice and his sons were executed.

Bibliography: JOHN OF EPHESUS, *Ecclesiastical History*, Part III, ed. and tr. E.W. BROOKS (Louvain 1952); also tr. R. PAYNE SMITH as *The Third Part of the Ecclesiastical History of John of Ephesus* (Oxford 1860). Evagrius Books V and VI; *The Ecclesiastical History of Evagrius Scholasticus*, tr. M. WHITBY (Liverpool 2000), esp. 281ff. R. C. BLOCKLEY, *The History of Menander the Guardsman* (Liverpool 1985). M. WHITBY and L. M. WHITBY, *The History of Theophylact Simocatta* (Oxford 1986). C. FARKA, ''Räuberhorden in Thrakien. Eine unbeachtete Quelle zur Geschichte der Zeit des kaisers Maurikios,'' *Byzantinische Zeitschrift* 86/87 (1993/1994) 462–469. P. GOUBERT, *Byzance avant l'Islam*, 2 v. (Paris 1951–1965). J. F. HALDON, *Byzantium in the Seventh Century* (Cambridge 1990). M. J. HIGGINS, *The Persian War of the Emperor Maurice* (Washington 1939). D. M. OLSTER, *The Politics of Usurpation in the Seventh Century: Rhetoric and Revolution in Byzantium* (Amsterdam 1993). R. PARET, ''Dometianus de Mélitène et la politique religieuse de l'empereur Maurice,'' *Revue des études byzantines 15* (1957) 42–72. I. SHAHÎD, *Byzantium and the Arabs in the Sixth Century* (Washington 1995). L. M. WHITBY, ''Theophanes' Chronicle Source for the Reigns of Justin II, Tiberius and Maurice (A.D. 565–602),'' *Byzantion* 53 (1983) 312–345. M. WHITBY, *The Emperor Maurice and His Historian* (Oxford 1988). J. M. WORTLEY, ''The Legend of the Emperor Maurice,'' *Acts of the 15th International Congress of Byzantine Studies* (Athens 1976) IV.382–391.

[F. NICKS/M. J. HIGGINS]

MAURICE, FREDERICK DENISON

English theologian and Christian Socialist; b. Normanstown, near Lowestoft, April 29, 1805; d. Cambridge, April 1, 1872. Maurice's father was a Unitarian minister, but others in his family were Calvinists or Anglicans. He was baptized an Anglican (1831) and was ordained (1834). With Whitmore he was joint editor of the *Metropolitan Quarterly Magazine,* and edited the *London Literary Chronicle* before and after it was amalgamated with the *Athenaeum* (1830). In 1840 he was appointed professor of English literature and history at King's College, London, and in 1846 he combined this position with the chair of theology. He was dismissed from both positions in 1853, however, for his denial of the eternity of hell. From 1848 to 1854 he was associated with J. M. F. Ludlow and Charles Kingsley as a leader of the Christian Socialists, and acted as joint editor of their publication, *Politics for the People.* He drew up a scheme for a workingmen's college in London and became its first principal. From 1866 until his death he taught moral philosophy at Cambridge, and from 1871 he was also incumbent of St. Edward's church in Cambridge. His Christian Socialism was ahead of its time and was largely a failure, although his views later influenced Anglo-Catholics such as Charles GORE and the Lux Mundi school. The most important of his many writings are: *The Kingdom of Christ* (1838), *What is Revelation?* (1859), *The Claims of the Bible and of Science* (1863), and *Moral and Metaphysical Philosophy* (1871–72).

Bibliography: *The Life of Frederick Denison Maurice, Chiefly Told in His Letters,* ed. F. MAURICE, 2 v. (New York 1884). A. R. VIDLER, *The Theology of F. D. Maurice* (London 1948), issued in U.S. as *Witness to the Light* (New York 1948). F. M. G. HIGHAM, *Frederick Denison Maurice* (London 1947). F. L. CROSS, *Oxford Dictionary of the Christian Church* 877–878. W. M. DAVIES, *An Introduction to F. D. Maurice's Theology* (London 1964).

[W. HANNAH]

MAURICE OF CARNOËT, ST.

Cistercian abbot; b. Croixanvec, Brittany, *c.* 1114; d. Carnoët, Oct. 9, 1191. He entered the abbey of Langonnet (1143) and became its abbot in 1147. Respected for wisdom, he was often consulted by the duke of Brittany, who in 1171 charged him with founding the abbey of Carnoët of which he became abbot in 1176. The abbey was named St. Maurice after his death. He is renowned for his many miracles and is venerated as a saint in Brittany. His cause, introduced at Rome in 1221, was suspended because of technicalities and never resumed. His cultus was approved for the order in 1869 and for the certain dioceses in 1891 and 1893.

Feast: Oct. 5 (Dioceses of Quimper, Vannes, St. Brieuc); Oct. 13 (Cistercians).

Bibliography: *Vita I et miracula* (by a contemporary), ed. B. PLAINE, in *Studien und Mitteilungen aus dem Benediktiner–und Zisterzienserorden* 7.2 (1886) 380–393. *Vita II* (by William of Carnoët, *c.* 1320), ed. B. PLAINE, *ibid.* 7.3 (1886) 157–164. A. M. ZIMMERMANN, *Kalendarium Benedictinum: Die Heiligen und Seligen des Benediktinerorderns und seiner Zweige* (Metten 1933–38) 3:174. J. L. BAUDOT and L. CHAUSSIN, *Vies des saints et des bienheureux selon l'ordre du calendrier avec l'historique des fêtes* (Paris 1935–56) 10: 124–126.

[A. CONDIT]

MAURICE OF SULLY

Bishop of Paris, theologian, preacher, builder of the cathedral of Notre Dame; b. Sully, near Orléans, France, *c.* 1120; d. Saint-Victor, Paris, Sept. 11, 1196. Born of peasant parents, he was educated in the schools of Paris, where he was a student of ABELARD. By 1147 Maurice was canon and subdeacon of the cathedral chapter at Notre Dame. He became professor of theology at the University of PARIS and was famous as a preacher. PETER

LOMBARD, Bishop of Paris, died in July 1160, and Maurice succeeded him in October. Maurice, a practical administrator, quickly decided to replace the 300-year-old, small Carolingian cathedral church with one in the new Gothic style. He developed the financial resources of his wealthy diocese and collected funds for the project for three years before the ground was broken for Notre Dame in 1163. He built also the episcopal palace. Maurice worked hard to reform the clergy of his diocese. While bishop he retained an enthusiasm for study and preaching, and between 1168 and 1175 wrote his *Sermons on the Gospels* that became models for young priests. They form the oldest original prose in French and are a literary masterpiece. They were later translated into Latin and English. He wrote also a treatise on the Canon of the Mass. A close friend of Kings LOUIS VII and PHILIP II AUGUSTUS, he acted as a royal legate and a papal judge delegate. In 1196 Maurice retired to the monastery of SAINT-VICTOR where he died the same year. There is no critical edition of his works.

Bibliography: MAURICE OF SULLY, *Maurice of Sully and the Medieval Vernacular Homily,* ed. C. A. ROBSON (Oxford 1952). V. MORTEX, ''Maurice de Sully: Étude sur l'administration épiscopale pendant la seconde moitié du XIIe siècle,'' *Mem. Soc. Hist. de Paris* 16 (1889) 105–318. J. B. SCHNEYER, *Lexikon für Theologie und Kirche* 2 7:189.

[J. A. CORBETT]

MAURIN, ARISTIDE PETER

Cofounder of *The Catholic Worker;* b. Languedoc, southern France, May 9, 1877; d. New York City, May 15, 1949. Peter, the son of Jean Baptiste and Marie (Pages) Maurin, spent his early childhood working on the family farm. At the age of 14, he went to St. Privat's, a boarding school near Paris run by the Christian Brothers. On Oct. 1, 1893, he was received as a novice, and he took his first vows on Sept. 18, 1895. After interrupting his religious life when he was called to serve in the 142d Infantry regiment of Mende in 1898–99, Maurin left the Christian Brothers on Jan. 1, 1903. At the age of 32 he immigrated to western Canada to take up homesteading. When his partner was killed in a hunting accident, Maurin left the farm and took up unskilled jobs as a wandering worker. In 1925 he went to New York City. While studying history and giving French lessons at an art colony near Woodstock, N.Y., he began to write in a style named after his only book, the much reprinted *Easy Essays* (1936). His essays were characterized by phrased writing, succinct and easy to remember. In December 1932, he met Dorothy Day and urged her to start a paper devoted to carrying out his message. The first issue (2,500 copies) of *The Catholic Worker* was printed in May 1933. Maurin wrote every month for the paper, spoke at meetings around New York, and instructed members of the staff. Much of his life was devoted to traveling around the country lecturing to audiences in parks and universities. He was dedicated to making Catholics aware of their spiritual destiny, and he wanted people to do things for themselves, to take care of the poor and the needy, and to work on the land as an antidote for unemployment. He taught also the need for houses of hospitality and farming communes.

Bibliography: A. SHEEHAN, *Peter Maurin: Gay Believer* (Garden City, N.Y. 1959). R. COLE, ''On Moral Leadership: Dorothy Day and Peter Maurin in Tandem.'' *America* 178, no. 20 (1998) 5. P. G. COY, ed., *A Revolution of the Heart: Essays on the 'Catholic Worker'''* (Philadelphia 1988). D. DAY, *Loaves and Fishes* (London 1963). M. T. ARONICA, *Beyond Charismatic Leadership: The New York Catholic Worker Movement* (New Brunswick, N.J., 1987). M. PIEHL, *Breaking Bread: The 'Catholic Worker' and the Origin of Catholic Radicalism in America* (Philadelphia 1982).

[D. DAY]

MAURISTS

French Benedictine Congregation of St. Maur that flourished from 1621 to the time of the French Revolution (1792), and devoted itself to strict observance of the Benedictine Rule, education, preaching, and especially to ecclesiastical and historical scholarship. The Maurists, founded in 1621 as part of the reform movement initiated at the Benedictine Abbey of Saint-Vanne in Lorraine in 1589, established their superior general at SAINT-GERMAIN-DES-PRÉS in Paris. Their name goes back to the Benedictine Abbey founded as SAINT-MAUR-DES-FOSSÉS in 638.

Maurist Congregation. Most French Benedictine monasteries joined the Maurist Congregation—there were 178 by 1675. A superior general with two assistants presided over the congregation. Each of the six provinces had a visitor, and every cloister had a prior. A general chapter of 33 members, meeting every three years, held legislative and executive power and appointed men to all offices. The superior general could be elected for an indefinite number of three-year terms. Priors held office for six years and were assisted by a council of four *seniores.* Every province had a novitiate and a house of study. Monks could transfer from one monastery to another but only within the same province. There was a general procurator for the congregation in Rome from 1623 to 1733.

Piety and Scholarship. Under the guidance of Dom Gregory Tarisse (1630–48) a project was inaugurated for publishing the history and glories of the Benedictine Order; it was intended primarily to edify the monks themselves through the renewal of a discipline combining piety with scholarship. Tarisse's plan gave the first evidence that the Maurist school followed a uniform method. The Maurist ideal, pursued (1630–1725) by Abbots Tarisse, Audebert, Marsolles, and Ste-Marthe, fashioned many outstanding scholars: J. MABILLON, E. Martène, B. de MONTFAUCON, T. Blampin, J. Martianay, L. d' Achéry, R. Tassin, and C. Toustain—while others remained anonymous.

The Maurists produced such monumental publications as the *Gallia Christiana* (10 v., Paris 1715–65), *Acta SS. Ordinis S. Benedicti* (9 v., Paris 1668–1701; Venice 1733–40) *Annales Ordinis S. Benedicti* (6 v., Paris 1703–39; Lucca 1739–45), and the *Spicilegium veterum scriptorum et monumentorum ecclesiasticorum* (9 v., Paris 1724–33). The Maurist *Histoire littéraire de la France* (12 v., Paris 1733–68) is being continued by the École des Chartes. Many of their other publications were continued by learned societies during the 19th century. They likewise edited the works of Fathers of the Church, such as Basil, John Chrysostom, Ambrose, and Augustine (11 v.), most of which were incorporated into MIGNE's Latin and Greek patrologies. Much of their work remains in MS in the Bibliothèque Nationale in Paris.

In all, some 220 Benedictines working in close collaboration, though scattered in six monasteries, produced 710 scholarly works on asceticism (L. BÉNARD, C. Martin), the history of the Benedictine Order (D'Achéry, Mabillon, T. RUINART, Martène), patrology (J. Garnier, Mabillon, Montfaucon, Touttée), secular history (Bouquet, Vuisette), and the auxiliary sciences of diplomatics (Mabillon), chronology (Carpentier), numismatics, and paleography (Montfaucon).

Scholarly Precision. The essentially edifying and apologetic intent of their research did not interfere with their devotion to truth and scholarly precision. In the edition of ancient documents, particularly the theological writings of the Fathers, and in the deciphering of ancient monuments, they achieved success by a careful search for all available MSS, the scrupulous collation of variant readings, and an objective citation of traditions and testimonies. For each of their editions they provided informative introductions, notes, and indexes.

Despite their conviction that the publication of unadorned historical truth would help do away with the religious controversies of their age, they frequently had to enter disputes concerning the authenticity of their work. The famous Maurist edition of the works of St. Augustine, attacked by the Jesuits, had to be vindicated by papal intervention (letter of Clement XI, April 19, 1706, to Abbot Boistard).

The Maurist school of scholarship proved a turning point in the inauguration of modern philological and historical methods by attempting to achieve a complete accounting of all the materials available; a thorough study of documents using the auxiliary sciences of paleography, diplomatics, chronology, and archeology; and a meticulous citation of sources. Though in general they failed to attain a broad view of the historical process, their research and methods made possible the consideration of history on a world scale.

Aftermath. While some of the Maurists were afflicted with the rigorist ideas of the Jansenists, as a group they combated the propositions condemned by INNOCENT XI in 1679, and despite the inroads of GALLICANISM and a certain worldliness after 1750, they preserved a vigorous observance of the Benedictine Rule down to the French Revolution. On Sept. 2, 1792, the last superior general, Dom Antoine Chevreux, beatified in 1926, marched to the guillotine followed by 40 monks. The Congregation of St. Maur was formally dissolved by Pius VII in 1818.

Bibliography: E. MARTÈNE and F. FORTET, *Histoire de la congrégation de Saint-Maur,* ed. G. CHARVIN (Annales de la France Monastique 31–35, 42, 43, 46, 47; Ligugé 1928–1943). R. P. TASSIN, *Histoire littéraire de la congrégation de Saint-Maur* (Brussels 1770), with suppls. by U. ROBERT (Paris 1881) and H. WILHELM and U. BERLIÈRE (Paris 1908). J. DE GHELLINCK, *Patristique et Moyen Âge,* v.1–3 (Gembloux 1946) v.3. J. BAUDOT, *Dictionnaire de théologie catholique* 10.1:405–443. G. HEER, *Lexikon für Theologie und Kirche*, ed. J. HOFER and K. RAHNER, 10 v. (2d new ed. Freiburg 1957–65) 7:190–192. H. LECLERCQ, *Dictionnaire d'archéologie chrétienne et de liturgie*, ed. F. CARROLL, H. LECLERQ, and H. I. MARROU, 15 v. (Paris 1907–53). 10.1:427–724; *Mabillon,* 2 v. (Paris 1953–57).

[F. X. MURPHY]

MAURITANIA, THE CATHOLIC CHURCH IN

Located in northwest Africa, the Islamic Republic of Mauritania is bordered on the northwest by Western Sahara, on the east and southeast by Mali, on the southwest by Senegal and on the west by the North Atlantic Ocean. While much of the region's north is desert, in the south alluvial soil lines the border with Senegal. Plateaus in the north and central areas rise to mountains of 1,500 feet. Natural resources consist of iron ore and copper, while agricultural products from the south include millet, rice, and the raising of livestock. Several eastern oases allow for the cultivation of date palms.

A former territory of French West Africa, the region declared independence as the Islamic Republic of Mauritania in 1960. Its inhabitants, many of them nomadic farmers who were later forced into cities to work in the mining and manufacturing industries, were almost all Muslims. The average life expectancy for a Mauritanian was 48.7 years in 2000, and fewer than 38 percent were literate in French or Arabic.

The home of nomadic Berbers since the 1st century, the region was explored by the Portuguese in the 15th century, and trading outposts from many nations soon became established along the coast, leading to territorial disputes. Most of the country became part of the Prefecture Apostolic of Saint-Louis du Sénégal in Senegal, established in 1779. The Senegal treaty of 1817 gave the French official control of the region, although little colonization occurred as a result. Beginning in 1877 care of the region's Catholics was transferred from Senegal to the vicar apostolic of Senegambia. Within 25 years the region had become occupied and was made a part of French West Africa in 1904. Mauritania became a French colony in 1921 and following World War II was reclassified as an overseas territory of France.

By the 1950s, most of the region's Catholics were Europeans, while native Mauritanians remained Muslim. In 1955 the prefecture overseeing Mauritania was entrusted to the HOLY GHOST FATHERS. Seven sisters of the Congregation of St. Joseph of the Apparition served in Atar and Port Étienne. On Dec. 18, 1965 Mauritania became the jurisdiction of the new Diocese of Nouakchott, subject to the Archdiocese of Dakar, Senegal, under the Holy Ghost Fathers.

In 1958 Mauritania became an autonomous republic in the French community, and it gained its independence two years later, on Nov. 28, 1960. In 1963, after mineral deposits discovered in the region boosted the nation's economic outlook, Morocco claimed possession of Mauritania; these claims to territory were withdrawn in 1969. Further disputes occurred in 1976, after Spain withdrew from Western Sahara and both Morocco and Mauritania disputed ownership of the southernmost third of this region. In 1979, a year after its president was replaced by a military government, Mauritania relinquished all claims in favor of Morocco. In 1989 a border war began with Senegal that lasted until early 1992, its basis the continuing ethnic tensions between the black minority farming in the south and the native Arab-Berber population.

In July of 1991 multi-party politics and elections were reestablished, and a new constitution was passed, based on the Constitutional Charter of Feb. 9, 1985. Under this constitution, Muslim law (shari'a) became the basis for law and Islam was proclaimed the state religion. Despite the existence of multiple political parties, the government continued to be controlled by the ruling Democratic and Social Republican Party. Though a minority faith, Catholics remained free to practice their

Capital: Nouakchott.
Size: 397,955 sq. miles.
Population: 2,667,860 in 2000.
Languages: French, Arabic; tribal languages are spoken in various regions.
Religions: 5,300 Catholics (.2%), 2,654,760 Sunni Muslims (99.5%), 7,500 Protestants (.3%).
Diocese: Nouakchott, directly subject to the Holy See.

faith, although proselytization of Muslims was discouraged. Bibles were not printed or sold in Mauritania, although there was no law against possessing them. Instruction in the Islamic faith was required of all students in public schools, although exemptions were available to parents.

By 2000 Mauritania had six parishes tended by three secular and ten religious priests. Fewer than 40 sisters tended to the five Catholic kindergarten schools and other humanitarian concerns among the nation's small Catholic population, almost all of whom were foreign workers. While increasing fundamentalist sentiment among Muslims led to charges of discrimination in the late 1990s, Church leaders remained cautious about taking an aggressive stand against the nation's majority faith. In addition to a rise in foreign debt, the lack of fresh water due to drought and the encroachment of the Sahara continued to plague this region, prompting Pope John Paul II to contribute funds through his private charity, Cor Unum, and to request amnesty for debts. In 1999, at the urging of the Vatican, Great Britain announced plans to forgive Mauritania all monies owed it in debt service.

Bibliography: *Bilan du Monde* (Tournai 1964) 2:605–607. *Annuario Pontificio* has statistics on all diocese.

[J. BOUCHAUD/EDS.]

MAURITIUS, THE CATHOLIC CHURCH IN

A volcanic island in the Indian Ocean, the Republic of Mauritius is located in South Africa, 500 miles east of Madagascar. The main island is joined politically to the Agalega Islands, the Cardgados Carajos Shoals, and Rodriguez, the last located 350 miles to the east of Mauritius. Containing a central plateau falling from steep hills to flat coastal lava formations that have weathered into fertile plains, the region has agricultural crops that include tea, fruits and vegetables, and sugar cane. In addition to arable land, fish is another important resource. The region contains little or no mineral wealth.

Mauritius was discovered by the Portuguese in 1505 and was occupied by the Dutch from 1638 until 1710.

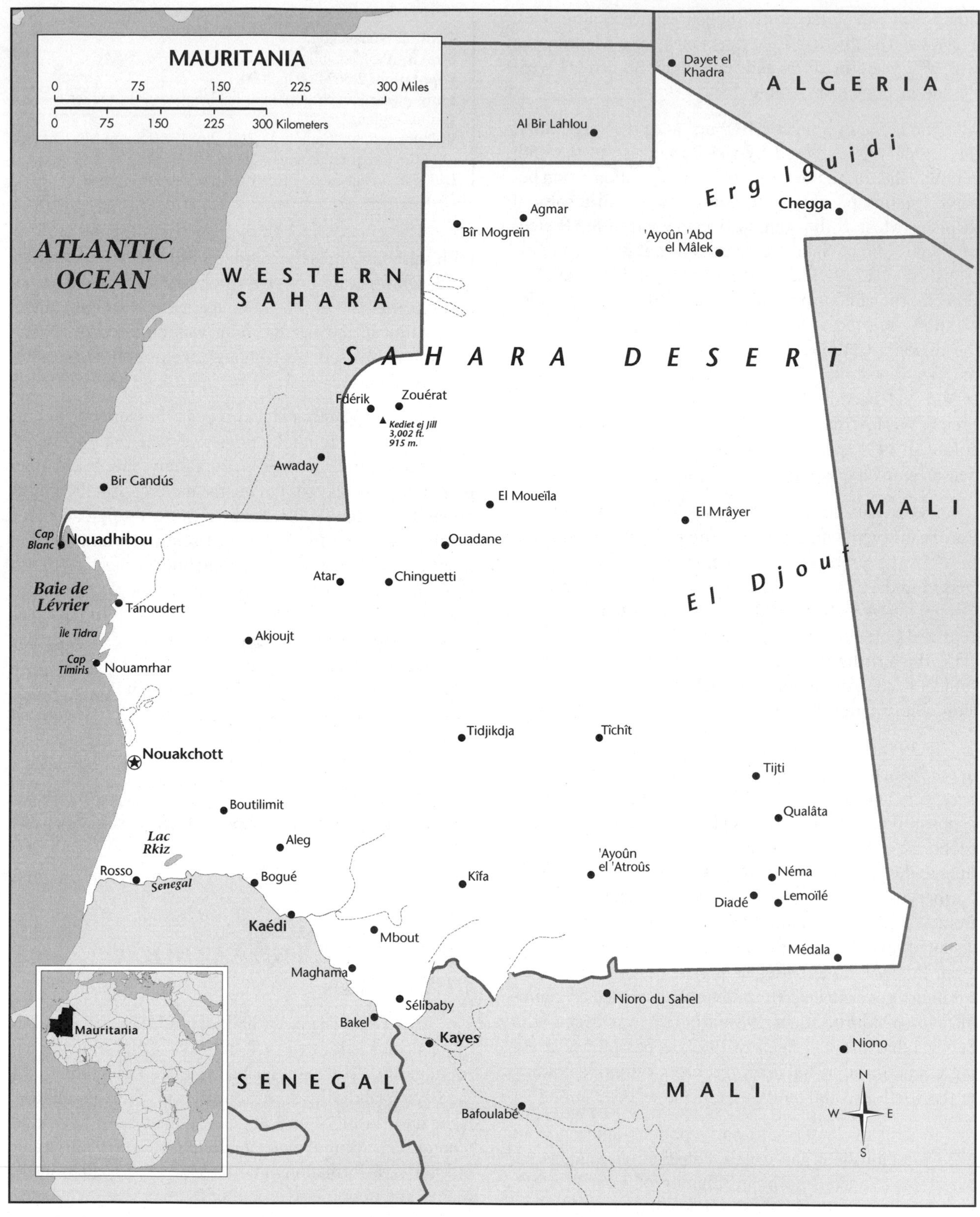

The French claimed the island in 1715, and it came under British control from 1810 until it gained independence as part of the Commonwealth of Nations in 1968. Since gaining political autonomy, the region has become increasingly industrialized, and by 2000 it had one of the highest per capita income levels in Africa.

After the region came under French control, VINCENTIANS evangelized the native tribes living in Mauritius from 1722 to 1819. At that point Port Louis became the center of an immense vicariate entrusted to the Benedictines that embraced Australia, South Africa, and Madagascar until 1837, and also the Seychelles Islands and Saint Helena until 1852. Bishop Collier, the third vicar apostolic, was eminent for his organizing ability. He was responsible for the arrival of Jacques Laval of the Holy Ghost Fathers, whose work among the enfranchised slaves gained him the title ''Peter Claver of modern times.'' Port Louis became a diocese in 1847, and almost all the vicars apostolic and bishops were Benedictines until 1916, when the diocese was confided to the HOLY GHOST FATHERS. Jesuit missionaries worked principally among the native tribes and after an increase in immigration from Asia and India, Chinese secular priests labored among their own compatriots. Pope John Paul II visited Mauritius in October of 1989.

By 2000 there were 49 parishes tended by 57 diocesan and 30 religious priests. Over 25 Christian Brothers and six communities totaling over 270 sisters—one community of native origin—directed the region's Catholic schools and tended to other social service needs. Under the 1968 constitution, the Church benefited financially from government subsidies in proportion to its members and like all other religions was accorded tax-free status. While Catholic life remained active, tensions between the Hindu majority and members of both the Church and Mauritius' Muslim population existed, resulting in rioting in February of 1999. An interreligious council was formed by the government later that year, in an effort to promote understanding among ethnic/religious groups. Many Chinese, while Buddhist, also practice the Catholic faith, a result of their attendance at the island's Catholic schools.

Bibliography: *Bilan du Monde* (Tournai 1964) 2:603–605. *Annuario Pontificio* has information on the diocese.

[J. BOUCHAUD/EDS.]

Capital: Port Louis.
Size: 788 sq. miles.
Population: 1,179,370 in 2000.
Languages: English, French Creole; Hindi, Urdu, Hadda, and Bojpoori are spoken in various regions.
Religions: 306,650 Catholics (26%), 194,600 Muslims (16.5%), 2,125 Protestants (2.3%), 613,275 Hindu (52%), 62,720 without religious affiliation.
Diocese: Port Louis, immediately subject to the Holy See.

MAURRAS, CHARLES

Writer, leader of ACTION FRANÇAISE; b. Martigues, near Marseilles, France, April 20, 1868; d. Saint-Symphorien, near Tours, Nov. 15, 1952. His father was a tax collector who died in 1874, and his mother a pious Catholic and ardent royalist, who sent him to Aix-en-Provence to receive a Catholic secondary education. Deafness, which afflicted him from the age of 14, forced him to abandon hope for a naval career and to pursue his studies privately. He became a literary critic, a well-regarded poet, and an esthete who greatly admired ancient classical civilization. For the masses and also for Jews he developed profound aversions. From early youth he was an avowed atheist. His fame rests mainly on his connection with Action Française, the nationalist and monarchist movement, which he founded and directed during its life-span, together with Léon DAUDET, and which he publicized with his prolific pen. His articles totaled several thousand, and for years included almost daily contributions to the newspaper *L'Action française.* He also published some 50 books on politics, philosophy and poetry.

Maurras was consistent and doctrinaire as a teacher, but did not systematically expose his ideas. His thought must be grasped in snatches throughout his writings. Basic to his outlook was an advocacy of nationalism and monarchy. He derived these notions from a study of the monarchy of the *ancien régime;* from Joseph de MAISTRE, Viscount de BONALD, and other counterrevolutionary doctrinaires; and even more from POSITIVISM and EVOLUTION. COMTE and DARWIN convinced him that man is a creature determined by his historical and biological background. Maurras claimed that the observation of phenomena permits political science to establish scientific laws, just as physics and chemistry do. On this basis Maurras derived as a law of French society that its prosperity depends on a return to the political and religious forms that assured this fortunate condition in the past. Darwin's theory on natural selection seemed to Maurras a condemnation of democratic egalitarianism. He concluded that society alone counts, not the individual; and so battle must be fought against the Reformation, the French Revolution, Romanticism, and other champions of individualism. Catholicism won his admiration as the religious form that formerly brought greatness to France; but the supernatural, specifically Christian elements in the Church did not attract him. His political views were based on physical and mechanical laws of social life and were elaborated without consideration for morality or religion. What he wanted to retain were the discipline inculcated by morality and religion and the hierarchical organization with the restraints it facilitates in human affairs. Maurras enjoyed a considerable following

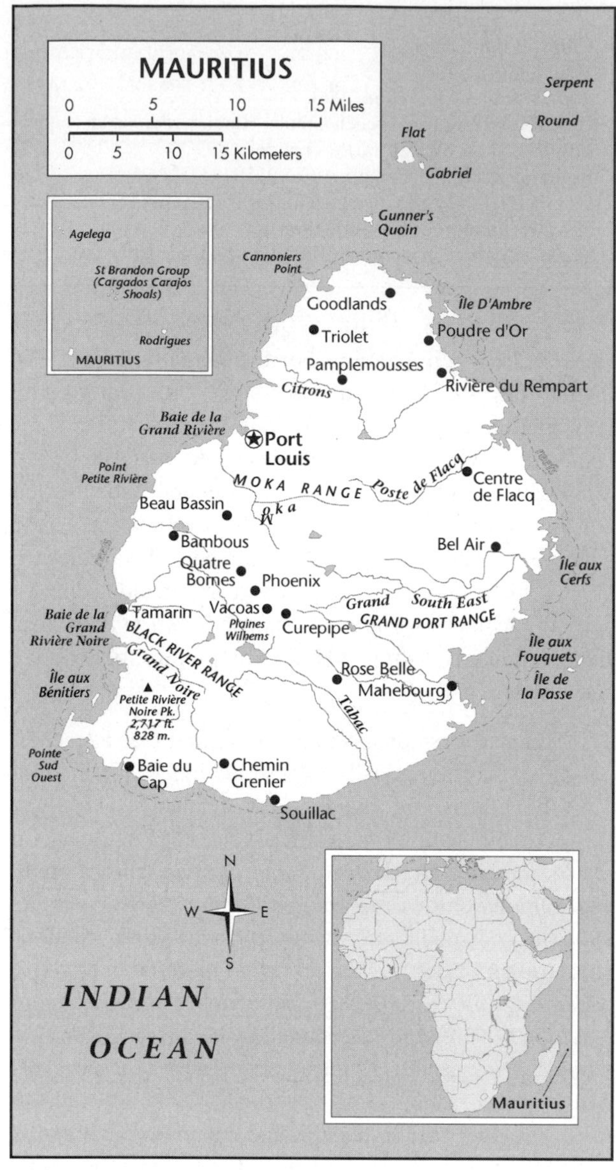

among the French Catholic laity and clergy; but Rome disapproved of his views and placed seven of his books on the Index (Dec. 29, 1926).

The violence of Maurras' pen earned him a prison sentence (1936–37) after a letter of his menaced members of the French national assembly with assassination. During World War II he supported the regime of Marshal Pétain. In 1945 he was sentenced to life imprisonment and civil degradation for collaborating with the enemy. This condemnation caused his expulsion from the French Academy, to which he had been elected in 1938; but it did not stop his writing. Ill health motivated his removal in the last year of his life to a hospital near Tours under close surveillance. Shortly before death he returned to the faith of his childhood.

Bibliography: H. TALVART and J. PLACE, *Bibliographie des auteurs modernes de langue française* (Paris 1928–) v.14. R. ROUQUETTE, "Charles Maurras et la papauté," *Études* 277 (1953) 392–405. E. BEAU DE LOMÉNIE, *Maurras et son système* (Paris 1953). M. MOURRE, *Charles Maurras* (Paris 1953). A. CORMIER, *La Vie intérieure de Charles Maurras* (Paris 1956). J. JUILLARD, "La Politique religieuse de C. M.," Esprit 26 (1958) 359–384. A. DANSETTE, *Religious Histry of Modern France*, 2 v. (New York 1961). M. CURTIS, *Three Against the Third Republic: Sorel, Barrès, and Maurras* (Princeton, N.J. 1959), with extensive bibliog. H. MASSIS, *Maurras et notre temps* (Paris 1960).

[A. DANSETTE]

MAURUS, SYLVESTER

Philosopher and theologian; b. Spoleto, Dec. 31, 1619; d. Rome, Jan. 13, 1687. Maurus came of a noble and respected family and was given a solid education in grammar, rhetoric, and philosophy at the Roman College. In 1636 he entered the Society of Jesus in Rome. Maurus became notably well versed in Greek and philosophy. After his ascetical and intellectual training, he taught philosophy at Macerata (1649), and, at the Roman College, philosophy (1652), theology (1658), and Scripture (1684). Maurus ranks among the leading teachers of scholasticism. Besides being a man of extraordinary intellectual talents and teaching ability, Maurus was very holy. Not only his pupils but the most illustrious personages of Rome went to discuss their problems with him. His great reputation and prudence merited for him the appointment as rector of the Roman College (1684–87).

Maurus's writings consist of two works in philosophy and two in theology, each of which takes up several volumes. The theological works are mostly compendiums written with great orderliness and clarity, but without any special originality. More famous are his philosophical works. His *Quaestionum philosophicarum libri quinque* (5 v. Rome 1658) discusses classical problems of philosophy, especially those pertaining to the philosophy of nature. These latter include some now-antiquated arguments in which Maurus attempts to refute the Copernican system. Maurus's greatest contribution, however, is his volumes of paraphrases and commentaries on all the works of Aristotle, *Aristotelis opera quae extant omnia brevi paraphrasi ac litterae perpetuo inhaerente explanatione illustrata* (6 v. Rome 1668). Whereas most of the earlier commentators had given detailed commentaries on one or other of the works of Aristotle, Maurus gave brief but pertinent commentaries on all of them. He had a gift for ferreting out the meaning of difficult passages and furnishing lucid comments on them. These commentaries are still of great help for an understanding of Aristotelian and scholastic philosophy. It has been claimed that Maurus makes Aristotle say much that he never did say, but perhaps ought to have said. Maurus's commentaries were considered valuable enough to be reprinted (1885) by Franz EHRLE as part of the series projected as an aid to the Leonine Revival of Thomism: the *Bibliotheca Theologiae et Philosophiae Scholasticae.*

Bibliography: É. AMANN, *Dictionnaire de théologie catholique* 10.1:447–448. L. MORATI, *Enciclopedia filosofica* 3:437–438. C. SOMMERVOGEL, *Bibliothèque de la Compagnie de Jésus* 5: 765–769.

[A. J. BENEDETTO]

MAURUS OF SUBIACO, ST.

Pupil and monk of St. Benedict; first half sixth century. He was the son of the Roman noble, Euthicius (Equitius) and is mentioned five times by GREGORY I THE GREAT in the second book of his *Dialogues,* which seems to be the only reliable source of information about Maurus. At Subiaco he was BENEDICT's trusted companion, though should be noted that Maurus's name does not appear in the Monte Cassino part of the *Dialogues.* He may have become Benedict's successor at Subiaco. The story of Maurus introducing the BENEDICTINES into France has no validity. Its basis, the *Vita sancti Mauri* (*Bibliotheca hagiographica latina antiquae et mediae aetatis* 5772–76), purportedly by the monk Faustus of Monte Cassino, is actually the work of the ninth-century Abbot Odo of Glanfeuil. The St. Maurus blessing of the sick with the particle of the true cross, accompanied by appropriate prayers, is still in use. On March 6, 1959, permission was granted for the use of a Benedictine medal instead of the particle of the cross.

Feast: Oct. 5 (formerly Jan. 15).

Bibliography: GREGORY I, *Gregorii Magni dialogi,* ed. U. MORICCA (Rome 1924). *Life and Miracles of St. Benedict: Book Two of the Dialogues,* tr. O. J. ZIMMERMANN and B. R. AVERY (Collegeville, Minn. 1949). H. LECLERCQ, *Dictionnaire d'archéologie chrétienne et de liturgie,* ed. F. CABROL, H. LECLERCQ, and H. I. MARROU, 15 v. (Paris 1907–53) 6.1:1283–1319. A. M. ZIMMERMANN, *Kalendarium Benedictinum: Die Heiligen und Seligen des Benediktinerorderns und seiner Zweige,* 4 v. (Metten 1933–38) 1:85–89. A. BUTLER, *The Lives of the Saints,* rev. ed. H. THURSTON and D. ATTWATER, 4 v. (New York 1956) 1:97. L. RÉAU, *Iconographie de l'art chrétien,* 6 v. (Paris 1955–59) 3.2: 932–934.

[V. GELLHAUS]

MAURY, JEAN SIFFREIN

Cardinal, orator, politico-ecclesiastical figure; b. Valréas in the Comtat-Venaissin, France, June 26, 1746; d. Rome, May 11, 1817. He was the son of a poor cobbler. He was ordained (1770) after studies in Avignon and Paris. Maury, vigorous in temperament and plebeian in manners, was noted for remarkable natural eloquence and restless ambition. In Paris from 1766 to 1791, he won renown as a preacher, delivering the Lenten sermons at Versailles before the king and court (1781). His often reprinted *Essai sur l'Éloquence de la Chaire* (1777) gained him fame as an author and membership in the French Academy (1785).

When the Estates-General met in 1789, he attended as elected deputy for the clergy of Péronne. He revealed himself a determined champion of the ''aristocrats'' and defended the cause of the privileged classes of nobles and clergy resolutely and passionately. Especially did he oppose the nationalization of ecclesiastical properties and the CIVIL CONSTITUTION OF THE CLERGY. With his sonorous voice, his witticisms, and skill in repartee, he did not fear to contest Mirabeau himself. When necessary, he addressed the public in the rostrum and in the streets.

Tempted occasionally to flee the Paris populace, he resisted courageously, being one of the last deputies of the Right to leave his post. Not until November 1791 did he join the *émigrés,* traveling to Belgium, Germany, and finally to Rome, where he was received as a hero. Pius VI showered on him marks of esteem, appointing him (1792) titular archbishop of Nicaea and nuncio extraordinary to Frankfurt, where he animated the zeal of Emperor Francis II for a crusade against the FRENCH REVOLUTION. In 1794 the pope made him bishop of Montefiascone in the States of the Church, and cardinal. King Louis XVIII also utilized him as his representative to the Holy See. Despite this accumulation of honors, he continued to be regarded by both adversaries and partisans as the *Abbé* Maury, the typical man of plebeian stock, reactionary by conviction, and indefectible as advocate of the union of throne and altar.

Maury returned to Rome after attending the conclave (1800) that elected Pius VII, but suffered from the minor role allotted him and from the prolongation of his exile. When he concluded that the Napoleonic Empire was solidly established and intended to act as protector of religion in the West, he arranged a return to Paris and offered his support to the regime. So clever was he as a courtier, even after the quarrel of NAPOLEON I with the pope, so determined was he to accept all roles that finally the emperor, who scarcely esteemed him, granted him provisorily the administration of the Archdiocese of Paris, which FESCH had turned down. At this point Pius VII sent to the Chapter of Paris a very severe reprobation of Maury and others who dared to promote the emperor's designs on the Church.

The fall of Napoleon definitely ruined Maury's career. He went to Rome, where he was imprisoned for six months and removed from control of his diocese. He passed his last few years in obscurity in the Roman monastery of San Silvestro.

Bibliography: J. S. MAURY, *Correspondance diplomatique et mémoires inédits du Cardinal Maury,* ed. A. RICARD (Paris 1891). A. G. BONET-MAURY, *Le Cardinal Maury d'après ses mémoires et sa correspondance inédits, 1746–1817* (Paris 1892). No satisfactory critical study exists.

[A. LATREILLE]

MAUSBACH, JOSEPH

Moral theologian and apologist; b. Wipperfeld, Feb. 7, 1861; d. Ahrweiler, Jan. 31, 1931. After being ordained in 1884, he labored in the pastoral ministry at Cologne until 1892, when he became professor of moral theology and apologetics at the University of Münster, a position he held for 40 years. Having both a profound knowledge especially of St. Augustine and St. Thomas and an acute sensitivity to modern problems, his teaching drew large numbers of students even from other departments. He advocated the admission of women students to the University, and he was influential in the Weimar National Assembly.

In the introduction to *Die katholische Moral* (Cologne 1901; New York 1914, under the title *Catholic Moral Teaching and Its Antagonists*) Mausbach indicated the principles and method that underlie all his work. These include: an examination of the attitudes of scientific Protestant theology toward Catholic morals; a reexamination of the fundamental ideas of Catholic morals, as established in the dogma and in the general consensus of the Church; a comparison of the Catholic and Protestant conceptions of the most important questions of morality; and an attempt to determine whether there were any points of friction or misunderstanding that a more thorough dialogue could eliminate.

Katholische Moraltheologie (3 v. Münster 1915–18) has appeared in successively revised and augmented editions. The 10th (ed. G. Ermecke, three v. Münster 1961) has been brought up to date by discussions of such contemporary problems as atomic warfare, capital punishment, advertising, automation, tax evasion, and new developments in natural-law theory. Other published works of Mausbach include: *Die Ethik des hl. Augustinus* (2 v. Fribourg 1909); *Naturrecht und Völkerrecht* (Frankfurt 1918); *Thomas von Aquin als Meister christlicher Sittenlehre* (Münster 1925); and *Dasein und Wesen Gottes* (2 v. Münster 1929–30).

Bibliography: P. MENOSSI, *Enciclopedia cattolica* 8:514. G. SCHREIBER, *Lexikon für Theologie und Kirche* 7:199–200. K. G. STECK, *Die Religion in Geschichte und Gegenwart* 4:813–814.

[M. S. CONLAN]

MAXFIELD, THOMAS, BL.

Priest and martyr; *vere* Macclesfield; b. Enville, Staffordshire, England, *c.* 1590; d. hanged, drawn, and quartered at Tyburn (London), July 1, 1616. Maxfield was the son of William Macclesfield and Ursula Roos, recusant Catholics who suffered persecution for their faith. Thomas studied at the English College of Douai (1602–10 and 1614) prior to his ordination (1614). He was captured in London within three months of landing in his homeland (1615) and imprisoned at the Gatehouse, Westminster. He unsuccessfully attempted to escape during the night of June 14, 1616, after which he was placed in stocks for 70 hours. While awaiting trial on June 26, he converted two hardened criminals. He was convicted and condemned the following day under 27 Eliz., c, 2. The Spanish ambassador intervened, seeking a pardon or reprieve. When that failed he supported the future martyr by solemnly exposing the Blessed Sacrament during the night before Thomas's execution and providing him with an honor guard en route to Tyburn, where they found the gallows decorated with flowers and the ground strewn with sweet herbs. The sentiment of the crowd of witnesses was such that the executioner delayed Thomas's disembowelment until he was senseless. Some of his relics were taken to Downside Abbey near Bath, England. He was beatified by Pius XI on Dec. 15, 1929.

Feast of the English Martyrs: May 4 (England).

See Also: ENGLAND, SCOTLAND, AND WALES, MARTYRS OF.

Bibliography: R. CHALLONER, *Memoirs of Missionary Priests,* ed. J. H. POLLEN (rev. ed. London 1924; repr. Farnborough 1969). J. H. POLLEN, *Acts of English Martyrs* (London 1891). The William Salt Archeological Society's Collections for a History of Staffordshire (London, 1882–1909), III, iii; V, ii, 207; new series, V, 128; XII, 248.

[K. I. RABENSTEIN]

MAXIMILIAN, SS.

The names of two martyrs of the early Church.

Maximilian (or *Mamilian*), martyr; b. 274; d. 295. The *passio* of this Maximilian is an authentic, unembroidered, and contemporary account. At Theveste in Numidia (modern Tebessa, Algeria), or near Carthage, during the consulship of Tuscus and Anulinus, Maximilian, the son of Victor, was brought before the proconsul Dion by the public prosecutor Pompeian and presented as suitable for military service. Maximilian refused to serve or to accept the leaden seal of the emperor; he declared himself a Christian and a soldier in the army of Christ, whom alone he served. For his refusal he was beheaded, as the *passio* states, at the age of 21 years, 3 months, and 18 days. His father was present as he greeted death with joy. The matron Pompeiana carried his body on a litter to Carthage and buried it close to that of St. CYPRIAN.

Feast: March 12.

Maximilian of Lorch, bishop, martyr; b. Cilli, Styria; d. there, *c.* 284. He was an apostle of Noricum, between Styria and Bavaria, where he was martyred; the particulars of his life are based on unreliable 13th-century *acta.* Born of a wealthy family of Cilli (modern Steiermark), Maximilian was given at age seven to a priest to be educated. As he grew older, he gave away his inheritance and traveled to Rome. SIXTUS II sent him to Noricum as a missionary; he established an episcopal see at Lorch, near Passau. Then he labored fruitfully for more than 20 years, surviving the persecutions of Valerian and Aurelian. Under Numerian, however, the prefect of Noricum started a persecution during which Maximilian was called upon to sacrifice to the gods. He refused and was beheaded outside the walls of Cilli.

Feast: Oct. 12; with St. Valentine on Oct. 29.

Bibliography: Maximilian, A. BUTLER, *The Lives of the Saints* 1:571–573. *Acta sanctorum* March 2: 103. H. DELEHAYE, *Les Passions des martyrs. . . .* (Brussels 1921) 104–110. *Gli Acta s. Maximiliani martyris*, tr. E. DI LORENZO (Naples 1975). P. ALLARD, *Histoire des persécutions,* 5 v. (3d ed. Paris 1903–09), v. 4. P. BROCK, *The Riddle of St. Maximilian of Tebessa* (Toronto 2000). P. SINISCALCO, *Massimiliano, un obiettore di coscienza del tardo Impero* (Turin 1974). Maximilian of Lorch. *Acta sanctorum* Oct. 6:23–58. A. BUTLER, *The Lives of the Saints* (New York 1956) 4:93. G. RATZINGER, *Forschungen zur bayrischen Geschichte* (Kempten 1898). J. ZEILLER, *Les Origines chrétiennes dans les provinces danubiennes* (Paris 1918).

[E. D. CARTER]

MAXIMOS III MAZLŪM

Catholic Melchite patriarch; b. Michael Mazlūm, Aleppo, Syria, November 1779; d. Alexandria, Egypt, Aug. 11, 1855. His ecclesiastical education was influenced by the Gallican ideas of his Catholic Melchite bishop, Germanos Adam. After his ordination in 1806, he acted as secretary of the Council of Karkafe. Elected metropolitan of Aleppo (1810), he took the name of Maximos. This election was contested by the Propaganda (1811); he was declared irregular (1813), but later (1815) made titular bishop of Myra. During his enforced residence in Rome, he obtained from the Austrian and French governments the protection of the persecuted Catholic Melchites in Syria and founded a Melchite church in Marseilles, France. Befriended by Gregory XVI, Maximos returned to Syria in 1831. On April 4, 1833, he was elected patriarch. Previous to the confirmation of this election by Rome (1836), he called the Council of *'Ain-Trāz* (1835), which became the only Melchite council approved *in forma generali* (1841). During his term of office he visited his entire patriarchate, preaching and founding churches. He is known especially for settling the dispute (1847) about the ecclesiastical headdress (*kalemavkion*) and for securing the complete autonomy of the Melchites under the civil leadership of their patriarch in the Ottoman Empire (1848). Gregory XVI granted him, on a personal basis, the title of patriarch of Antioch, Alexandria, and Jerusalem. In addition to his pastoral work, Maximos composed or translated into Arabic many works of theology, hagiography, and ascetics. Maximos's last years were less successful, when he met with opposition from Rome and some of his bishops. To many historians his life seems controversial, but to his people it was full of glorious accomplishments.

Bibliography: C. KARALEVSKIJ (CHARON), *Histoire des Patriarcats Melkites,* 3 v. in 2 (Rome 1909–10); *Dictionnaire d'histoire et de géographie ecclésiastique* 3:653–655. J. HAJJAR, *Un Lutteur infatigable: Le Patriarche Maximos III Mazloum* (Harissa 1958). G. GRAF, *Geschichte der christlichen arabischen Literatur* 5:107. E. HAMMERSCHMIDT, *Lexikon für Theologie und Kirche* 7:210–211.

[J. JADAA]

MAXIMOS IV SAYEGH

Greek Catholic patriarch, cardinal; b. Alep (Syria), April 10, 1878: d. Beirut, Nov. 5, 1967. Maximos studied first at the Episcopal College, then at the College de Terre Sainte des Pères Franciscains in his native town. In 1893, he entered into Seminaire Sainte-Anne de Jerusalem, directed by the White Fathers. There he completed his secondary education and philosophical and theological studies. After three years of professorship at the same seminary, he joined the young Society of Missionaries of St. Paul. He was ordained a priest on Sept. 17, 1905. In 1912, he became superior of the Missionary Society and kept this position until 1919. During this time he also directed *Al-Macarrat,* the magazine of the Greek Catholic patriarchate.

On Aug. 31, 1919, Maximos IV was consecrated metropolitan of Tyre, in Lebanon. The beginnings of his episcopacy were marked by political troubles, violence, and dangers of massacre. In 1921, he paid a long visit to the United States to organize the ministry for Greek Catholic emigrants from Syria and Lebanon. On Aug. 30, 1933 he was transferred to the See of Beirut, Lebanon. A new period of religious struggles then began. In 1936 he founded the Congregation of the Religious Missionaries of Our Lady of Perpetual Help. He played a major role in the nationalist movement that resulted in the recognition of the full independence of Lebanon in 1943.

At the death of Patriarch Cyrille IX, Maximos IV was elected patriarch of the Greek Catholic Church (Oct. 30, 1947). At least once a year he summoned all his episcopacy to a synod that lasted an entire week. Credit for the founding of a Community Parish Chest is given to Maximos IV, opening mutual diocesan aid designed to help financially deprived dioceses. His liturgical commission worked for 20 years revising and editing liturgical books. He opened his community to new religious institutes of the West. He gave particular attention to emigrants from his jurisdiction, obtaining for them the installations of Eastern hierarchies of their rite in Brazil and in the United States.

Ardent apostle of ecumenicism, he did not spare any effort to create in the Catholic church the psychological and theological atmosphere and indispensable discipline for the reconciliation of the churches, at the same time safeguarding the rights of the Eastern Catholic churches and defending the patriarchal prerogatives. In 1964 he visited Patriarch Athenagoras in Istanbul, and he established cordial relations with the churches of Constantinople, Canterbury, and Etchmiadzin. The Second Vatican Council, where he played a major role, was the supreme effort of his life. His books include, *Voice of the Church in the East,* published in 1962 and translated into several languages, and *The Greek Catholic Church at the Council* (1967), which contained the actions, notes, and reports of the patriarch and the prelates of his church at Vatican II.

In Feb. 1965 Pope Paul VI made Maximos IV a cardinal. His last days were clouded by the Israeli-Arab war of June 1967, and the seizure by the Syrian government of the Catholic schools.

Bibliography: MAXIMOS IV, *Voix de l'Eglise en Orient* (Bâle 1962) translated into several languages; *L'Eglise grecque melkite au Concile,* ed. D. AL-KALIMA (Beirut 1967). I. DICK, *Qu'est-ce que l'Orient chrétien?* (Tournai 1965). J. HAJJAR, *Les Chrétiens uniates du Proche-Orient* (Paris 1962). G. ZANANIRI, *Le christianisme oriental* (Paris 1966). E. INGLESSIS, *Maximos IV: L'Orient conteste l'Occident* (Paris 1969). N. EDELBY, *Les Eglises orientales catholiques* (Paris 1970) Coll. ''Unam Sanctam.''

[N. EDELBY]

MAXIMUS OF SARAGOSSA, ST.

Bishop; d. Saragossa?, *c.* 619. He is one of three chroniclers of the sixth century praised and used by ISIDORE OF SEVILLE (*Vir. ill.* 46), who notes that Maximus wrote other works both in prose and verse. Of his chronicle, which parallels those of VICTOR OF TUNNUNA and JOHN OF BICLARO, only 33 brief anonymous excerpts are extant. They seem to view Visigothic history (450–568) from Saragossa and constitute a marginal gloss to a MS of Victor's chronicle, which neglects Visigothic history. It is useless to speculate on which passages in Isidore's work derive from Maximus. The chronicle edited by Higuera in 1611 (*Patrologia Latina* 80:617–632) is a forgery. Maximus signed the acts of councils in Barcelona in 599, Toledo in 610, and Egara in 614.

Bibliography: *Monumenta Germaniae Historica: Auctores antiquissimi* 11:221–223. O. BARDENHEWER, *Geschichte der altkirchlichen Literatur* (Freiburg 1913–32) 5:398–399.

[E. P. COLBERT]

MAXIMUS OF TURIN, ST.

Bishop; place and date of birth unknown; d. *c.* 408–23. The only source for Maximus' life and work—apart from the evidence contained in his own extant sermons—is an early one, GENNADIUS's (d. *c.* 492–505) *De viris illustribus* 41. This brief notice lists 24 of Maximus's sermons by title, referring to others as ''many,'' and states that Maximus died in the reign of Honorius and Theodosius the Younger. However, Bp. Maximus of Turin signed the acts of the Council of Milan in 451 and those of the Council of Rome in 465. In the light of this evidence, BARONIUS identified the Maximus of Gennadius with the Maximus of the conciliar acts and maintained that Gennadius was in error about the date. The view of Baronius was widely accepted until the end of the nineteenth century, but since that time it has been rejected. It is now universally recognized that there were two bishops of Turin bearing the name of Maximus. Around the nucleus of the 24 sermons known by title, a large number of others came to be assigned to Maximus in the course of the MS tradition. B. Bruni was the first to attempt to separate the genuine from the false in his edition (Rome 1784; repr. in *Patrologia Latina* [Paris 1878–90] 57), but of the 240 sermons and treatises accepted as genuine, a large number, including 40 by the Arian bishop Maximinus, were wrongly assigned to Maximus of Turin.

A critical edition of Maximus by A. Mutzenbecher (1962) made it possible to evaluate Maximus and his work satisfactorily for the first time. On the basis of the converging evidence furnished by 16 carefully chosen criteria, the editor has included 119 sermons in his edition, but this number includes two belonging to St. JEROME, one belonging to BASIL (in Latin translation), five that must be regarded as dubious, and six that are labeled as spurious. Mutzenbecher's introduction covers the life and work of Maximus, the history of earlier editions, the

MS collections and their relations, and concordance tables indicating the listing and order of the sermons in the MS collections and the printed editions.

Maximus may be described as a zealous and effective pastor of souls. His Latin is clear and direct, if somewhat rhetorical in keeping with the taste of his age. His imagery is rich, vivid, and concrete. He shows a fondness for allegorical interpretation and for seeking Old Testament prototypes for all persons and events in the New Testament. His Lenten and paschal sermons are valuable for the history of contemporary ecclesiastical practice, and his repeated warnings against pagan superstitions and usages indicate that paganism was still very much alive in his area. *Sermon* 37 employs the story of Ulysses bound to the mast as a symbol of Christ bound to the cross, identifying the cross as the mast that has saved the human race.

Feast: June 25.

Bibliography: A. MUTZENBECHER, ed., *Maximi Episcopi Taurenensis Sermones* (*Corpus Christianorum. Series latina.* 23; Tournhout 1962), with bibliog. vi–xiii. B. ALTANER, *Patrology*, tr. H. GRAEF (New York 1960) 545–546. H. RAHNER, *Greek Myths and Christian Mystery,* tr. H. BATTERSHAW (New York 1963), esp. 382–383. C. DE FILIPPIS CAPPAI, *Massimo: vescovo di Torino e il suo tempo* (Turin 1995). M. MODEMANN, *Die Taufe in den Predigten des hl. Maximus v. Turin* (Frankfurt am Main 1995). A. MERKT, *Maximus I. von Turin* (Leiden 1997).

[M. R. P. MCGUIRE]

MAXIMUS THE CONFESSOR, ST.

A 7th-century Byzantine theologian and aescetical writer; b. Constantinople, *c.* 580; d. in exile, Lazica, on the Black Sea, Aug. 13, 662. Of a well-known family, Maximus received an excellent education, entered the civil service, and became secretary to Emperor HERACLIUS I. In 613 or 614 he retired to a monastery near Chrysopolis (Scutari) and later (625) to Cyzicus with his disciple, Anastasius. In flight before the Persian invasion of 626, he made his way to Crete and Cyprus and eventually to Africa (628–630); there he took part in a disputation over MONOTHELITISM with the expatriarch, Pyrrhus I, at Carthage (645). He visited Rome, where Pope MARTIN I invited him to participate in a synod of the Lateran (649) that condemned Monothelitism. In 653 he was arrested together with the pope by Emperor Constans II (641–668) and was brought to Constantinople and charged with treason. Condemned on this charge (655), he was exiled to Bizye in Thrace. In 662 he refused to accept an imperial edict that forbade further discussion of the Monothelite heresy and was condemned to have his tongue and right hand cut off. Together with his disciples, the *apocrisiarius* Anastasius and Anastasius the monk, he was finally exiled to Lazica, where he died.

Writings. Approximately 90 major writings make up the works of Maximus. In his earlier years Maximus wrote commentaries on the Scriptures. In 626 his *Quaestiones et dubia* appeared in the form of 79 questions and answers concerned with difficult passages in the Bible and with dogmatic questions. He later wrote an explanation of Psalm 59 and the Our Father and dealt with three scriptural problems in his *Quaestiones ad Theopemptum Scholasticum.* His *Quaestiones ad Thalassium* appeared between 630 and 633, addressed to a Libyan priest and monk, and contained some 65 answers to scriptural difficulties solved with the aid of patristic material, particularly the observations of GREGORY OF NAZIANZUS and PSEUDO-DIONYSIUS the Areopagite. He also produced two books entitled *Ambigua* (*c.* 630). The scholia to the works of Pseudo-Dionysius and of Gregory of Nazianzus are probably not authentic works of Maximus.

Under the title, *Opuscula theologica et polemica*, some 28 works are attributed to Maximus; they are devoted to refutations of MONOPHYSITISM and of the heresies of the Monergists and Monothelites, as well as to other dogmatic questions. His *opuscula* on the two natures in Christ were written between 626 and 634. Later, he dealt with speculative problems, including 12 possible types of union in Christ; a number of divergent definitions in Christology; and finally, in a work addressed to the priest Theodore, with the notions of quality, property, and difference in the HYPOSTATIC UNION.

He wrote a short tract against the arguments of the Monergists, then a long treatise addressed to the priest George, concerning the will in Christ. In his *Tome to Marinus*, written probably *c.* 640, he dealt with a number of citations of the Fathers that appeared to strengthen the position of Monergism, concentrating on the Patriarch ANASTASIUS I of Antioch, whose work against JOHN PHILOPONUS had favored the monergistic position. He likewise interpreted the letter of Pope HONORIUS I (625–638) to the Patriarch Sergius in an orthodox sense.

The best-known ascetico-moral works of Maximus are his dialogue *Liber asceticus*, 400 *Capita de caritate*, 200 *Capita theologica et oeconomica*, and the first 15 chapters of 500 *Diversa capita ad theologiam et oeconomiam spectantia* (the remainder of this last work is spurious). The most important liturgical work of the saint is his *Mystagogia*, a commentary on the mystical meaning of the liturgy that has been published many times and was translated into Turkish in 1799. Finally, over 100 of his letters have been edited; many of them are complete theological tracts.

Doctrine. The theological system of Maximus is a synthesis in which the principles of classical philosophy, particularly that of Aristotle, and the teachings of the Fathers, especially under the influence of PSEUDO-DIONYSIUS the Areopagite, are blended into an original exposition of Christian teaching. The center of this new system is Christ. In contradistinction to the teaching of Monophysitism and Monothelitism, he affirmed the existence of two complete and distinct natures—one human, the other divine—in the one Person of the Word.

As Christ is the center of all creation, the history of the universe until the coming of Christ is a preparation for God becoming man; and history after Christ is the story of man becoming divine in and through the Incarnation of the Word. By appearing in the midst of men, Jesus Christ revealed God, who is one by nature in the Trinity of Persons. Man, by his nature, tends toward God. Man's supernatural unification with Christ through baptism gives him the capability of freely realizing this tendency of his nature that urges him to unite with God by avoiding sin and practicing virtue. Thus, the spiritual life of the Christian grows not only morally but also ontologically. This natural disposition of man's nature to tend to God is something more than an intellectual act. It is the basis of an ecstatic experience born of love. This love (ἀγάπη) means the acceptance of the absolute supremacy of God and the interior rejection of the things of this world (ἀπάθεια). Also, it is the denial of one's own personal will (φιλαυτία) and the revelation of actual love for one's neighbor. The writings of Maximus are characterized by their Byzantine boldness in subtle speculation, Roman realism, and deep understanding of the nature of the Church.

In his spiritual counsel, Maximus is the successor of EVAGRIUS PONTICUS. He cultivated the three steps of *praxis*, or self-control through mortification, *theoria*, or contemplation of nature leading to God, and *theologia*, or the contemplation-union with divinity. But he dissociated this procedure from the cosmogony of ORIGEN.

Maximus maintained that the practice of virtue under the leadership of charity had to accompany the steps leading through contemplation (*theoria*) to perfection. He insisted on the practice of *sympathos* in dealing with worldly situations; and in the end he admitted two approaches to spiritual perfection: the practical, and the theoretical or contemplative. He insisted, however, that contemplation had to be informed by and achieved in charity. His mysticism preserved a humanistic element that was not always observed by his followers, but that gave a depth and balance to his spiritual teaching seldom equaled by his successors. He has been termed by H. G. Beck as, perhaps, the last independent theologian of the Byzantine Church.

Feast: Aug. 13.

Bibliography: *Patrologia Graeca*, ed. J. P. MIGNE (Paris 1857–66) 4:15–576; 19:1217–80, *computus*; v. 90–91. *Maximus Confessor: Weisheit*, ed. and tr. B. HERMANN (Würzburg 1941). *The Ascetic Life: The Four Centuries on Charity*, ed. and tr. P. SHERWOOD [*Ancient Christian Writers* 21, ed. J. QUASTEN et al. (Westminster MD, London 1955)]. P. SHERWOOD, *An Annotated Date List of the Works of St. Maximus the Confessor* [*Studia anselmiana* 30 (Rome 1952)]; *The Earlier Ambigua of St. Maximus the Confessor* (*ibid.* 36; 1955). H. G. BECK, *Kirche und theologische Literatur im byzantinischen Reich* (Munich 1959) 436–442. E. VON IVÁNKA, *Maximus der Bekenner* (Einsiedeln 1961). V. GRUMEL, *Dictionnaire de théologie catholique*, ed. A. VACANT et al. (Paris 1903–50) 10.1:448–459. O. BARDENHEWER, *Geschichte der altkirchlichen Literatur* (Freiburg 1913–32) 5:28–35. I. HAUSHERR, *Philautie* [*Orientalia Christiana periodica* 137 (Rome 1952)]. A. CERESA-GESTALDO, *Lexikon für Theologie und Kirche*, ed. J. HOFER and K. RAHNER (Freiburg 1957–65) 7:208–210. R. DEVREESSE, *Analecta Bollandiana* 46 (1928) 5–49; 73 (1955) 5–16. G. MAHIEU, *Travaux préparatoires à une édition critique des oeuvres de S. Maxime le Confesseur* (Diss. Louvain 1957). B. ALTANER, *Patrology*, tr. H. GRAEF (New York 1960) 629–633. W. VÖLKER, ''Der Einfluss des Pseudo-Dionysius Areopagita auf Maximus,'' *Universitas Festschrift . . . Albert Stohr*, v. 1 (Mainz 1960) 243–254; *Maximus Confessor als Meister des geistlichen Lebens* (Wiesbaden 1965). H. U. VON BALTHASAR, *Kosmische Liturgie* (Einsiedeln 1961). I. H. DALMAIS, *Revue d'ascétique et de mystique* 29 (Toulouse 1953) 123–159, Pater Noster. G. BARDY, *Revue biblique* 42 (Paris 1933) 332–339. A. CERESA-GESTALDO, *Orientalia Christiana periodica* 23 (Rome 1957) 145–158, *capita de caritate*. A. SINAITA, *The Life of our Holy Father, Maximus the Confessor*, tr. C. BIRCHALL (Boston 1982). L. THUNBERG, *Man and the Cosmos* (Crestwood, NY 1985); *Microcosm and Mediator* (Chicago 1995). M. L. GATTI PERER, *Massimo il confessore* (Milan 1987), bibliography. P. M. BLOWERS, *Exegesis and Spiritual Pedagogy in Maximus the Confessor* (Notre Dame, IN 1991). V. KARAYIANNIS, *Maxime le Confesseur: essence et énergies de Dieu* (Paris 1993). A. NICHOLS, *Byzantine gospel: Maximus the Confessor in Modern Scholarship* (Edinburgh 1993). J.-C. LARCHET, *La divinisation de l'homme selon saint Maxime le Confesseur* (Paris 1996); *Maxime le Confesseur, médiateur entre l'Orient et l'Occident* (Paris 1998). A. LOUTH, *Maximus the Confessor* (London 1996), incl. bibliography. J. P. WILLIAMS, *Denying Divinity: Apophasis in the Patristic Christian and Soto Zen Buddhist Traditions* (New York 2000).

[M. HERMANIUK]

MAXWELL, WINIFRED

Countess of Nithsdale, Catholic noblewoman famous for the rescue of her husband from the Tower of London after the Jacobite rising of 1715; b. *c.* 1678; d. Rome, 1749. Lady Nithsdale, daughter of William, first marquis of Powis, lived with her husband at the family seat of Terregles until his capture following the Battle of Preston. After leaving Scotland for England and pleading in vain with King George I to pardon her condemned husband, the intrepid countess smuggled female attire to him in the tower, and he succeeded in escaping on Feb. 23, 1716. She then hid her husband in London until he made his flight in safety to France. Returning to Scotland, Lady Nithsdale retrieved the family papers that she had hidden there. In these activities she had incurred great personal risk, and the wrathful George I declared she had "done him more mischief than any woman in Christendom." She joined Lord Nithsdale abroad and they traveled to Rome, where they ended their days in exile.

Bibliography: J. B. PAUL, ed., *The Scots Peerage* 9 v. (Edinburgh 1904–14) v. 6. *The Dictionary of National Biography from the Earliest Times to 1900* (London 1885–1900) 13:136. W. FRASER, *Book of Carlaverock* (Edinburgh 1873). M. SCOTT, *The Making of Abbotsford and Incidents in Scottish History* (London 1897).

[H. F. GRETSCH]

MAYA RELIGION

At the time of the Spanish conquest, Mayan civilization extended over much of present-day Guatemala, British Honduras, Honduras, El Salvador, and much of southern Mexico, including the Yucatan. Mayan religion consisted at first of a primitive personification of nature with little formal organization; later, it was fused with a complex philosophy built around the deification of heavenly bodies and the worship of time. In the postclassical period, the Mexicans introduced idolatry and placed a much greater emphasis on human sacrifice. The principal function of religion was to maintain and ensure life, health, and sustenance. The Mayans believed in the immortality of the soul and in an afterlife consisting of a heaven and a hell. Their religious philosophy was dualistic, focusing upon an eternal struggle between the powers of good and evil over the destiny of man. Mayan cosmology described the sky as consisting of 13 layers, the lowest layer being the earth. Beneath the earth were nine underworlds, in the lowest of which resided the death god. Each layer was ruled by its own god. The Mayans worshipped a complex of gods of whom Itzamna, son of the creator god Hunab Ku, was the head. Chacs, the gods of rain, were important deities and were regarded sometimes as a single god and sometimes as the four gods of the cardinal points. All the most important deities were connected with the growth of corn. The extensive priesthood was closely connected in power and goals with that of the nobility. The priestly hierarchy was assigned different duties. High priests were not only concerned with religious matters, but they also functioned as scholars, astronomers, mathematicians, and administrators. Other classes of priests included diviners, nacoms (executioners), and prophets. Religious ceremonies followed a regular yearly calendar and observances consisted of purification, divination, prayers, and sacrifice.

Sculpture of Chichen-Itza, a Mayan god. (©Bettmann/CORBIS)

Bibliography: S. G. MORLEY, *The Ancient Maya,* rev. G. W. BRAINARD (3d ed. Stanford 1958). J. E. S. THOMPSON, *The Rise and Fall of Maya Civilization* (Norman, OK 1956). D. R. REDFIELD, *The Folk Culture of Yucatan* (Chicago 1941). M. E. KAMPEN, The Religion of the Maya (Leiden 1981). T. R. ROBERTS, *Gods of the Maya, Aztecs, and Incas* (New York 1996). D. GILLETTE, *The Shaman's Secret: The Lost Resurrection Teachings of the Ancient Maya* (New York 1997). G. COOK, *Crosscurrents in Indigenous Spirituality: Interface of Maya, Catholic, and Protestant Worldviews* (Leiden 1997). L. SCHELE and P. MATHEWS, *The Code of Kings: The Language of Seven Sacred Maya Temples and Tombs* (New York 1998). S. MILBRATH, *Star Gods of the Maya* (Austin, TX 1999). R. BONEWITZ, *Timeless Wisdom of the Maya* (London 2000).

[J. RUBIN/EDS.]

MAYER, RUPERT, BL.

Priest of the Society of Jesus noted for his anti-Nazi activities; b. Stuttgart, Germany, Jan. 23, 1876; d. Munich, Germany, Nov. 1, 1945.

The son of Kolumban, a prosperous merchant, and Maria (Schäurer) Mayer, Rupert studied in the universities of Fribourg, Munich, and Tübingen before entering the seminary at Rottenburg. He was ordained a priest May 2, 1899, and the following year entered the Jesuits, making his novitiate in Lichtenstein and taking further theological studies at Valkenburg in the Netherlands. Mayer gained a reputation as a preacher of parish missions in Germany, Switzerland, and the Netherlands. During World War I he volunteered to be a chaplain, was wounded and lost his left leg.

In 1921 Mayer was appointed chaplain of the Men's Sodality, a position he held until his death. He cofounded and was spiritual director of the Sisters of the Holy Family, a community that works among the very poor. In 1925, he inaugurated the *Banhofsmission*, a ministry to travelers.

Mayer was one of the first to recognize the incompatibility of Nazism and Christianity. The Nazi rejection of the Old Testament and the Jewish element in Christianity seemed to him intolerable and absurd. He regarded Hitler as ''hysterical.'' These views made him an object of police attention after the Nazi accession to power in 1933. The Ministry of Justice gave him a warning because of his anti-Nazi position. In April 1936 Mayer was forbidden to preach throughout Germany and later arrested, but released on the condition that he should confine himself to the sacramental ministry and service of the poor. Although he accepted the condition under duress or ''obedience,'' on Nov. 3, 1939, Mayer was again arrested. Confined first to the concentration camp at Sachsenhausen, he spent the duration of the war in Ettal Abbey. On May 11, 1945, he returned to Munich, only days after World War II ended in Germany and began to preach again, but he died six months later at the age of 69. His tomb in the crypt of the Sodality Chapel on Neuhauserstrasse in Munich soon became a place of pilgrimage.

Pope John Paul II beatified Mayer on May 3, 1987, in the Olympic Stadium in Munich.

Feast: Nov. 3 (Jesuits).

Bibliography: A. KÖBLING, ed., *Father Rupert Mayer: A Modern Priest and Witness for Christ* (Munich 1950; 1975). O. GRITTSCHNEDER, ed., *Ich Predige Weiter: Pater Rupert Mayer und das Dritte Reich* (Rosenheim, Germany 1987). V. A. LAPOMARDA, *The Jesuits and the Third Reich* (n.p.). *L'Osservatore Romano*, Eng. ed., 22 (1987) 2, 3. J. N. TYLENDA, *Jesuit Saints And Martyrs* (Chicago 1998).

[P. HEBBLETHWAITE]

MAYFLOWER COMPACT

An agreement signed by the passengers of the Mayflower, while the ship lay at anchor in Provincetown harbor, Mass., on Nov. 11, 1620. Under the compact the settlers agreed to be ruled by the majority and to submit to the laws made by their government. Such an agreement became necessary when the Mayflower inadvertently landed at Cape Cod rather than Virginia, where the Pilgrim Fathers had a royal patent, and some members of the group refused to recognize the legal authority of their leaders, whose jurisdiction under the patent did not extend beyond the borders of Virginia. To ensure the proper ordering of the colony, the signers of the compact pledged to ''combine ourselves together in a civil body politic, for our better ordering and preservation and furtherance of the ends aforesaid; and by virtue thereof to enact, constitute, and frame such just and equal laws . . . as shall be thought most meet and convenient for the general good of the Colony, unto which we promise all due submission and obedience.'' The compact was not a constitution; nor was it a declaration of independence from the king. It was, rather, a social contract, important as an example of government by consent of the governed as well as of the remarkable capacity of the English people for self-government. These so-called Pilgrim Fathers were a group of Puritans, originally from the village of Scrooby, Nottinghamshire, England, who fled to Holland to preserve their religious purity. After a period of unhappy exile in Holland, they immigrated to America. They differed from other Puritans in that they had no wish to remain within the Church of England and broke with it entirely. The Mayflower Compact was the first of many such agreements by which groups of New Englanders established civil governments. These were actually extensions of the religious covenants by which members of each Congregational church mutually bound themselves in a fraternal religious association.

Bibliography: J. T. BLODGETT, ''The Political Theory of the Mayflower Compact,'' *Publications of the Colonial Society of Massachusetts* 12 (1911) 204–213. A. LORD, ''The Mayflower Compact,'' *Proceedings of the American Antiquarian Society,* NS 30 (1920) 278–294.

[E. DELANEY]

MAYNARD, THEODORE

Poet, critic, biographer, historian; b. Madras, India, Nov. 3, 1890; d. Port Washington, N.Y., Oct. 18, 1956; the son of Protestant missionaries Henry and Elizabeth (Teague) Maynard. His reading (particularly of G. K. Chesterton) led him into the Church in 1913, after which he spent seven months in a Dominican novitiate. On July 8, 1918, he married Sara Katherine Casey; they had seven children. While lecturing in the U.S. in 1920 he was offered a professorship at San Rafael College, California, although he had never taught and had no degree. The next 16 years were spent in remedying both deficiencies. He taught at San Rafael (1921–25); St. John's College, Brooklyn, and Manhattanville College of the Sacred Heart, N.Y. (1925–27); Fordham University, N.Y. (1927–29); Georgetown University, Washington, D.C. (1929–34); and Mount St. Mary's College, Emmitsburg, Md. (1934–36). He received the degrees of A.B. (Fordham), M.A. (Georgetown), and Ph.D. (Catholic University of America).

His *De Soto and the Conquistadores* (1930) led to a succession of biographies of figures chiefly in the Elizabethan era, among them *Queen Elizabeth* (1940) and

The Signing of the Mayflower Compact. (©Bettmann/CORBIS)

Thomas Cranmer (1956). Entering the field of hagiography, he produced popular lives of such saints as Francis Xavier (1936), Mother Cabrini (1945), Francis of Assisi (1948), and Ignatius Loyola (1956). He deemed his greatest prose achievement *The Story of American Catholicism* (1941), which led him to further studies in American Church history, such as the lives of Orestes Brownson (1943) and Junípero Serra (1954). After his first wife's death (1945), he married Kathleen Sheehan. In 1948 he became president of the Catholic Poetry Society of America. He had been serving as vice president of the Society since its founding some 12 years earlier.

Bibliography: T. MAYNARD, *The World I Saw* (Milwaukee 1938). J. A. O'BRIEN, *Road to Damascus* (Garden City 1949) 98–110.

[A. M. MELVILLE]

MAYNE, CUTHBERT, ST.

Protomartyr of the English College, Douai; b. Youlston, near Barnstaple, 1543 or 1544; d. Launceston, Nov. 30, 1577. His uncle, a schismatic priest, who held a rich benefice that he hoped to pass on to his nephew, sent him to Barnstaple Grammar School. At 17, Mayne was presented with the living at the parish of Huntshaw and was later ordained a minister of the new Anglican Church there. Five years later he went to Oxford where he took his arts degree at St. Alban's Hall (later incorporated into Merton College). At Oxford, Cuthbert fell under the influence of Edmund CAMPION and Gregory Martin. After they left, Cuthbert lingered on, torn between his duty to his uncle and the benefice and his wish to become a Catholic priest.

At last the matter was settled for him. Campion and Martin had sent several letters to Cuthbert urging him to join them at Douai. One letter fell into the hands of the bishop of London; he sent men to arrest Cuthbert, who, however, was away at the time. Having been warned by Thomas Ford, he decided to resign his chaplaincy and leave the country. This was toward the end of 1570 and nothing more is heard of him until he arrived at the English College, Douai, in 1573. On Feb. 7, 1575, he was ordained, and the following year he took his degree as a bachelor of theology. In April 1576, he returned to England with John Paine. He made his way to the house of Francis Tregian, Golden Manor in Cornwall, where he posed as a steward.

It was a short ministry. On June 8, 1577, Richard Grenville, Sheriff of Cornwall (the hero of Tennyson's *Revenge*), with nine or ten justices of peace and 100 armed men, arrived at Golden Manor. He arrested Cuthbert and almost the entire household. The whole party was brought to Truro to be questioned by Bishop Bradbridge, who closely examined Cuthbert's papers, but found nothing incriminating. From Truro, Cuthbert was taken to Launceston Castle and thrown into a foul dungeon. After three month's imprisonment, he was tried as a traitor before the Launceston Assizes on Sept. 16, 1577. This was a test case because Mayne was the first seminary priest to be caught. The prosecution had only circumstantial evidence that he was a priest and the jury returned from its first retirement puzzled and uncertain. However, after a threatening harangue from Grenville, it gave the verdict of guilty.

One of the judges, named Jeffreys, was not satisfied with the justice of the verdict and made a report to the Privy Council. The council submitted the matter to the whole bench of judges whose opinion was divided; whereupon the council ordered the execution to be carried out as "a terror to the Papists." Francis Tregian, then imprisoned in London, was offered his life and Cuthbert's also if he would join the Protestant Church but he replied that "he would not hazard his soul to hell to withhold his man's [Cuthbert's] from heaven."

On Nov. 30, 1577, Cuthbert was bound to a hurdle and drawn to the market square at Launceston. He was allowed to hang only for a minute and was then butchered alive. His skull is preserved at the Carmelite convent at Lanherne. There have been many reported miracles attributed to him. He was beatified by Leo XIII in 1886, and canonized by Paul VI in 1970.

Feast: Nov. 29.

Bibliography: T. COOPER, *The Dictionary of National Biography from the Earliest Times to 1900* 13:161–162. W. ALLEN, *A Briefe Historie of the Glorious Martyrdom of Twelve Reverend Priests* (Rheims 1582; reprint London 1908). R. CHALLONER, *Memoirs of Missionary Priests,* ed. J. H. POLLEN (rev. ed. London 1924). P. A. BOYAN and G. R. LAMB, *Francis Tregian* (New York 1955).

[G. FITZHERBERT]

MAYNOOTH, ST. PATRICK'S COLLEGE

During the 17th and 18th centuries, to counteract the penal laws that prohibited Catholic education, candidates for the Irish diocesan priesthood were educated in seminaries established in the Catholic countries of Europe. During the French Revolution, many of these seminaries were forced to close; access to the Continent became difficult. The Irish bishops petitioned the government to allow the endowment of seminaries in Ireland. An act of Parliament on June 5, 1795 (35 Geo. III, ch. 21) led to the opening of St. Patrick's College, Maynooth, in autumn 1795.

Early Development. Though the discussions between government and bishops had been concerned with the establishment of a seminary, the act of 1795 made general provision "for the better education of persons professing the Roman Catholic religion." In 1801, a lay college was set up in Maynooth operating as a private foundation. It was closed in 1817, however, not only because the government regarded with suspicion this juxtaposition of lay and clerical education, but also because the development of similar institutions elsewhere made it unnecessary. Maynooth then became what it until recently remained, a seminary to educate the majority of candidates for the Irish diocesan priesthood.

The act of 1795 provided a sum of £8,000 "towards establishing the said academy"; in some way which is not altogether clear the provision became an annual parliamentary grant of approximately this amount. This grant was of great help toward the large-scale building necessary in the early years of the college. However, it also gave an opportunity to the more hostile Protestants to voice their suspicions, both during the annual parliamentary debate and outside Parliament and to demand that the College be closely supervised. These annoyances were considerably lessened by Sir Robert Peel's legislation of 1845 (8 and 9 Vict. ch. 25), which provided £30,000 for buildings and increased the annual grant to £26,360, chargeable to the Consolidated Fund and therefore not subject to parliamentary debate.

Administration. Under the act of 1795, the College was governed by a board of trustees, responsible to Parliament and composed of government officials, Catholic laity, and representatives of the Catholic hierarchy. Under a further act of 1800 (40 Geo. III, ch. 85), however, the government officials ceased to be trustees.

After this the trustees, 17 in number, were all Catholics—11 bishops and six lay. The Irish Church Act of 1869 (32 and 33 Vict., ch. 42) freed the trustees from any further responsibility to Parliament. The lay trustees resigned; since then the board has been composed of four Irish archbishops and 13 bishops. While the college is legally vested in these 17 trustees, it is administered by the entire hierarchy. The immediate administration is in the hands of a president, vice president, and three directors of formation, together with spiritual directors and a vocational growth counsellor.

Finance. Under the act of 1869 mentioned above, the annual parliamentary grant was withdrawn. In its place the college received a capital sum of £369,040, equal to 14 years' purchase of the annual grant. While under the general provisions of the act this capital sum was fairly and in some respects generously calculated, the immediate result was to halve the income of the college. This capital sum remained the nucleus of college finances. The heavy inflation of the past century put it under considerable pressure. It has, however, been successfully rebuilt, though student fees now play a bigger part than they did in the past. An appeal for funds by the trustees in 1947 netted about £700,000, but most of this was absorbed by reconstruction and building repair. Further necessary conservation of extensive and ageing buildings has been made possible in more recent years by the establishment of the ''Friends of Maynooth.'' Friends in United States have been particularly generous.

Organization. Since 1906, Maynooth has been a Pontifical University, with faculties of theology, Canon Law, and philosophy. The college was also connected in various ways with the different attempts made in the later 19th century to secure an acceptable plan of university education for Catholics. Finally, under the Irish Universities Act of 1908 (8 Edw. VII, ch. 38) Maynooth became a recognized College of the National University of Ireland, and as such provided courses leading to degrees of the National University in philosophy, arts, Celtic studies, and science.

In 1966 the trustees declared their intention to develop Maynooth as ''an open centre of higher studies,'' with ''faculties and courses to meet the needs of priests, non-clerical religious, and the laity.'' At the time a government commission was evaluating the whole Irish university system. There was a tacit understanding among all parties that Maynooth had to expand to retain its university status, and that ''theology should be allowed to take its place in the university system.'' The Second Vatican Council stirred up much optimistic discussions, but nothing was accomplished until the Universities Act of 1997 established a civil university, the National University of Ireland at Maynooth (NUI Maynooth). St. Patrick's College remained autonomous as a seminary and pontifical university. The pontifical university offers baccalaureate, postgraduate and diploma programs in theology and canon law for seminarians, clergy, non-clerical religious and laity. Students also enroll in the relevant humanities courses at NUI Maynooth.

Postgraduate resident priest-students form the Dunboyne Establishment. This takes its name from John Butler, Bishop of Cork, who apostatized from the Church on succeeding to the title of Lord Dunboyne in 1786. He was reconciled on his deathbed in 1800; in his will he left lands that yielded an income of £1,000 per year to Maynooth. This revenue was used to finance post-ordination studies for selected students. Although the ''Dunboyne course'' carried no academic degree for nearly a century, it was justly regarded as the equivalent of a doctorate in theology. The Dunboyne Establishment now provides courses for all degrees that Maynooth is empowered to grant as a Pontifical University. Postgraduate priest-students in NUI Maynooth also reside in the Dunboyne Establishment. In the exceptional circumstances of World War II it had as many as 30 extern students (destined to serve in dioceses outside Ireland). Although it is seldom entirely without these externs, Dunboyne students normally graduate through the ordinary college courses.

Library and Publications. Library facilities are shared between St. Patrick's College and NUI Maynooth. The collection comprises over 400,000 volumes, including 60 *incunabula* and many rare works on Irish history. There are over 300 Gaelic manuscripts, notably the O'Curry, Murphy, and Renehan collections. The college archive also houses the archive of the Irish College at Salamanca, Spain, which closed in 1936.

The College publishes the following periodicals: *Irish Theological Quarterly*, *Furrow*, and *Archivium Hibernicum*, the annual journal of the Catholic Record Society of Ireland.

The Maynooth Union of Irish Priests meets annually in the College. The Catholic Truth Society of Ireland had its origin in a paper read before the Union in 1899, and the Catholic Record Society was similarly inaugurated in 1910. The College museum sprang from a paper read in 1931. In addition to valuable ecclesiastical material there is a collection of historical scientific instruments, assembled as a tribute to the distinguished priest-scientist Nicholas Callan, professor in the college from 1826 until his death in 1864. A paper read in 1955 by Most Rev. Dr. Philbin, then Bishop of Clonfert, led to the Maynooth Union Summer School.

Although Maynooth's primary purpose is the education of priests for Irish dioceses, it has consistently supplied priests to other English-speaking countries. Among its many contributions to mission outreach are the May-

Jules Cardinal Mazarin.

nooth Mission to China (St. Columban's Society), founded in 1916, and St. Patrick's Society for African Mission, founded in 1932.

Bibliography: *Calendarium Collegii S. Patritii,* annually since 1864. J. HEALY, *Maynooth College: Its Centenary History* (New York 1895). D. HOURIHANE, "College Buildings," *The Irish Ecclesiastical Record* series 5, 66 (1945) 238–43. D. MEEHAN, *Window on Maynooth* (Dublin 1949). P. J. CORISH, *Maynooth College 1795–1995* (Dublin 1995). *Eighth Report of the Commissioners of Irish Education, Roman Catholic College of Maynooth* (Dublin 1827). *Report of Her Majesty's Commissioners Appointed to Enquire into the Management and Government of the College of Maynooth* (Dublin 1855).

[P. J. CORISH]

MAZARIN, JULES

Cardinal, prime minister of France (1643–61) who continued the work of RICHELIEU and prepared for the reign of LOUIS XIV; b. Pescina, in the Abruzzi Apennines, July 14, 1602; d. Paris, March 9, 1661. His father, Pietro Mazzarini, came to Rome from Palermo and entered the service of the COLONNA family. Giulio (Jules) entered the Roman College at about seven years of age and after his studies accompanied Cardinal Colonna in Spain for three years. On his return he began his career in the army of the Papal States. In 1627, as a captain, he performed several diplomatic missions to states that had an interest in the succession of Mantua, and at this time he first visited France, where he met Richelieu (1630). He acquired fame in October 1630 by gaining a truce between Spanish and French troops ready to fight for the fortress of Casale. His work at the Treaty of Cherasco in 1631 allowed France to retain Pignerol.

Rise to Power. In 1632 he left the military for the clergy, became canon of the Lateran, auditor of the legate of Avignon (and later vice-legate), and was nuncio extraordinary in France (1634–36). He gained the trust of Richelieu, who asked Urban VIII to make him ordinary nuncio to Paris. When Urban refused, Richelieu had the king name Mazarin for the cardinal's hat reserved for France in the coming consistory. After three years Urban yielded, and Mazarin became a cardinal in the consistory of Dec. 16, 1641. He was then in France, and Richelieu wanted to send him to Rome to care for French interests, but Richelieu died, and LOUIS XIII appointed him to the royal council. When Louis died three months later, the regent, Anne of Austria, made Mazarin prime minister. France was then in the midst of a war against the empire and Spain. The victories of Rocroy, Fribourg, and Nordlingen enabled Mazarin, after difficult negotiations, to impose on the emperor the Treaties of WESTPHALIA, which gave France control of Alsace and bridgeheads on the Rhine and gave the German princes political and religious autonomy. But Spain continued the war, counting on the exhaustion of France and the discontent caused by taxation.

Opposition from the Fronde. Trouble did break out in the Fronde in 1648 and almost ruined Mazarin several times. When the Parlement of Paris protested against tax laws in 1648, the regent arrested a particularly violent councilor, Broussel. Barricades were then thrown up in Paris, and Mazarin had to yield, promising to suppress the *intendants* and *lettres de cachet.* In early January 1649 the court secretly left Paris, as Parlement and the archbishop coadjutor, Paul de Gondi, raised troops against the king, and Mazarin was declared a disturber of the peace. The king's army besieged Paris, but peace was restored only when Mazarin allied with the royal princes, Condé and the king's brother and brother-in-law. When they sought to impose their authority on the royal council, however, Mazarin allied with Parlement and had them arrested. A new Fronde then broke out. The provinces rebelled and the princes' troops confronted those of the king. Parlement finally turned against Mazarin, who had to seek safety in flight to the empire as a price had been placed on his head (1651). The Queen and her ministers continued to receive Mazarin's advice from abroad. The court again left Paris, and troops restored order in the provinces. Mazarin rejoined the court but left a second time to allow the king to enter Paris, Oct. 21, 1652. The die-hard *Frondeur* Cardinal de RETZ (Paul de Gondi, coadjutor of Paris) was arrested December 19 by order of the young king, and on February 3 Mazarin returned to the capital. Former *Frondeurs* submitted or went abroad, as did Condé, who went over to the service of Spain.

The Spanish War. Mazarin then had to finish the war against Spain. He gained an alliance with Cromwell, and Turenne's victory over Condé at the Dunes (June 14, 1657) hastened the end of the war. Mazarin persuaded the king to renounce his love for Maria Mancini, the cardinal's niece, in favor of a Spanish marriage to seal the peace. The Treaty of the Pyrenees, signed Nov. 7, 1659, gave France Artois and Roussillon, which Richelieu had already occupied. Louis XIV married the Infanta Maria Teresa, June 9, 1660. For all practical purposes, Austria had lost her preponderance in Europe to France, and the French nobility and parlements gave way to an absolute monarchy.

As the Italian minister of a Spanish regent, Mazarin brought to fruition the work of Richelieu. He was adaptable and better able to raise great hopes than to inspire fear. Aside from his trust in his own destiny, his great strength was that he could always rely on the support of the queen, who was so close to him that there were rumors of a secret marriage between them. This hypothesis had no basis of fact, nor did the attacks in pamphlets (Mazarinades) against the private life of the cardinal.

Relations with Rome. Mazarin, a cardinal deacon, never received Holy Orders. The king made him bishop of Metz, but he resigned the see before he was consecrated. His relations with Rome were not smooth. Innocent X was elected against his explicit instructions, and he could not conceal his irritation. He supported his former protectors, the two cardinals BARBERINI, against the pope. He was unwilling for Cardinal de Retz, who became archbishop of Paris while imprisoned at Vincennes, to govern his diocese. He criticized Innocent X and Alexander VII for sympathy with Spain and kept them out of negotiations for the Treaties of Westphalia and the Pyrenees. Nonetheless, in the Jansenist quarrel he presided over the assemblies of bishops that received the bull condemning the five propositions of the *AUGUSTINUS*, and he encouraged the Assembly of the Clergy of 1660 to require the clergy to sign its formula (*see* ASSEMBLIES OF FRENCH CLERGY). During his ministry the Council of Conscience was instituted to assure good episcopal appointments, and at one time VINCENT DE PAUL was called to it. Mazarin obtained the dissolution of the COMPAGNIE DU SAINT-SACREMENT, which vowed a secret fight against libertines and heretics. Protestants could but praise his rule, depending as it did on the Protestant princes of Germany and later on Cromwell.

The Bibliothèque Mazarin. Louis XIV, whose political education Mazarin supervised, let him govern until his death. The immense fortune he amassed and the precious collections he carefully accumulated were divided among his relatives. But the Bibliothèque Mazarin and the Bibliothèque Nationale still hold many valuable books that he acquired and then made available to scholars by bequeathing them to the Collège des Quatre Nations, which he had founded. It was in the Mazarin Library that the famed *Latin Bible of 42 Lines* was found. This folio of 1282 pages in two columns of 42 lines is known as the Mazarin Bible. Its printing, first ascribed to Johann Gutenberg (d. *c.* 1468), was more likely set by his partner Johann Fust and his son-in-law Peter Schöffer, who continued Gutenberg's printing establishment in Mainz

Bibliography: J. MAZARIN, *Lettres du cardinal Mazarin pendant son ministère*, ed. A. CHÉRUEL and G. D'AVENEL, 9 v. (Paris 1872–1906). For lack of a definitive study of Mazarin, one should consult general histories: A. CHÉRUEL, *Histoire de France pendant la minorité de Louis XIV,* 4 v. (Paris 1879–1880); *Histoire de France sous le ministère de Mazarin* (1651–1661), 3 v. (Paris 1882). G. DETHAN, ''Mazarin avant le ministère,'' *Revue historique* 227 (1962) 33–66. Paris, Bibliothèque Nationale, *Mazarin: Homme d'état et collectionneur* (Paris 1961). S. SKALWEITT, *Lexikon für Theologie und Kirche*, ed. J. HOFER and K. RAHNER (Freiburg 1957–65) 7:217.

[P. BLET]

MAZENOD, CHARLES JOSEPH EUGÈNE DE, ST.

Also known as Eugène de Mazenod, bishop, founder of the Oblates of Mary Immaculate; b. Aug. 1, 1782, Aix-en-Provence, France; d. May 21, 1861, Marseilles, France.

Mazenod was the son of the president of the Board of Excise in Provence, who belonged to the nobility of the robe. During the FRENCH REVOLUTION, he immigrated with his family in April 1791 to Nice, Turin, Venice, and Palermo without being able to undertake regular studies. He returned to France in 1802 and decided, after a grave personal religious crisis, to become a priest. During his three years at Saint Sulpice seminary, he was profoundly influenced by Msgr. Emery and participated in the Catholic resistance in favor of Pius VII and the black cardinals. Upon returning to Aix after ordination in 1811, the young priest devoted himself to ministering to the poor and to an association for youths.

In 1817, he became interested in popular missions. To promote them he founded a community that was the

St. Charles Joseph Eugène de Mazenod.

germ of the OBLATES OF MARY IMMACULATE. When his uncle, Fortuné de Mazenod, became bishop of Marseilles in 1823, he made Charles his vicar-general. Mazenod became a titular bishop in 1832 and succeeded his uncle as bishop in 1837. During these years Mazenod devoted himself to the restoration and reorganization of the diocese, while acting as superior general of his missionary institute, which received the approval of the Holy See in 1826.

Mazenod played a very active role also in the religious affairs of France and in 1856 became a senator of the Second Empire. In Marseilles he confronted difficult spiritual and material problems created by the changed economic and social situation in the city, whose population had doubled. The bishop established the structures used in the diocese for the next half-century and more. He created 22 parishes, rebuilt the cathedral, Notre-Dame de la Garde, and 25 other churches, increased clerical recruitment, and promoted religious congregations. The most celebrated of the societies inaugurated by him was Timon David for young workers.

Membership in the Oblates remained small until 1843 and then grew rapidly when Mazenod began to accept missions in Canada, U.S., Ceylon, and South Africa. In these lands the Oblate apostolate bore remarkable results.

Mazenod was an ardent ultramontane but displayed moderation in the controversies concerning the classics, the liturgy, Gallicanism, and liberalism. He supported Hugues Félicité de Lamennais in Rome to the end. On the other had, he was intransigent and resolute concerning educational freedom and the Roman Question.

Upon his death in 1861 he was buried in the cathedral of Marseilles. Mazenod's cause was introduced in Rome in 1936. He was beatified on Oct. 19, 1975, and canonized by John Paul II on Dec. 3, 1995. He is the patron of bishops, broken homes, dysfunctional families, evangelizers and missionaries, exiles, families in crisis, founders, those struggling with their vocations, and troubled marriages.

Feast: May 21 (Oblates of Mary Immaculate).

Bibliography: *Lettres aux correspondants d'Amérique* (Rome 1977). *Acta Apostolicae Sedis* 68 (1976) 241–243. *Beatificationis et canonizationis servi Dei Caroli Iosephi Eugenii de Mazenod* (Rome 1968). L. N. BOUTIN, *Le double charisme du bienheureux Joseph-Eugène de Mazenod* (Montréal 1978). R. ETCHEGARAY, *Petite vie de Eugène de Mazenod* (Paris 1995). A. HUBENIG, *Living in the Spirit's Fire* (Toronto 1995). J. LEFLON, *Eugène de Mazenod, évèque de Marseille, fondateur des missionaires oblats de Marie Immaculée*, 3 v. (Paris 1957–65), Eng. tr. F. D. FLANAGAN (Washington, D.C. 1994). S. C. LORIT, *La scelta dei poveri: vita di Eugenio de Mazenod* (Rome 1975). *L'Osservatore Romano,* Eng. ed., 44 (1975): 6–7; 49 (1995): 1–2. A. ROCHE, *Le Bienheureux Eugène de Mazenod: Évêque de Marseille, fondateur des missionnaires oblats de Marie-Immaculée* (Lyon 1975). G. SANTOLINI, *Evangelizzazione e missione* (Bologna 1984).

[J. LEFLON/EDS]

MAZZARELLA, MODESTINO, BL.

Baptized Domenico, known in religion as Modestino of Jesus and Mary, Franciscan Alcantarine priest; b. Sept. 5, 1802, Frattamaggiore, Naples, Italy; died July 24, 1854, Naples.

Domenico was the fourth child in a pious, working-class family headed by Nicolà Mazzarella, a cordmaker, and his wife Teresa Espósito, a weaver. In his youth Domenico showed such devotion as an altar boy and as patron of Our Lady of Good Counsel that Bishop Agostino Tommasi sponsored his seminary studies at Aversa (1820–21). After Tommasi's death (1821), Domenico continued his education at home.

In 1822, he joined the Franciscans at Grumo Nevano and received the habit and name Modestino at Piedimonte Matese in Caserta (Nov. 3, 1822). Following his novitiate at Santa Lucia del Monte, Naples, he was professed (Nov. 27, 1824), completed his studies at the convents of Grumo Nevano, Portici, and Santa Lucia, and was ordained priest at Aversa cathedral (Dec. 22, 1827). Thereafter he served in various roles within the order, including guardian of the friaries of Mirabella Eclano (Avellino) and Pignataro Maggiore (Caserta). In 1839, he was transferred to Santa Maria della Sanità in a populous Neopolitan slum, where he distinguished himself through his defense of life. He worked among the poor until his death from cholera, contracted while ministering to other victims of the epidemic.

A miracle attributed to Modestino's intercession was approved Dec. 23, 1993. Modestino was beatified by Pope John Paul II, Jan. 29, 1995.

Feast: July 24.

Bibliography: *Acta Apostolicae Sedis* (1995): 249.

[K. I. RABENSTEIN]

MAZZARELLO, MARIA DOMENICA, ST.

Cofoundress of the SALESIAN SISTERS; b. Marnese (Piedmont), Italy, May 9, 1837; d. Nizza Monferrato, May 14, 1881. Maria's parents, Giuseppe and Maddelena (Calcagno) Mazzarello, were farmers, and she worked in the fields and vineyards as a young girl. As a member of a local sodality, the Pious Union of Daughters of Mary Immaculate, she followed a regular rule of life and taught catechism. An attack of typhoid in 1860 caused her to give up heavy field labor and to work at dressmaking. Soon she was instructing girls in the trade. The sodality impressed St. John BOSCO during a visit to the village (1865). When his scheme for a boys' school at Marnese failed, he installed Mazzarello and her companions in the building. The Daughters of Our Lady Help of Christians, or Salesian Sisters, originated when Mazzarello, with ten companions, received the habit and pronounced first vows (Aug. 5, 1872). She was the first superior general of the congregation, whose rule was written by Bosco. The congregation's work was the education of poor girls, following the same methods and principles as the Salesian Fathers. In 1878 Mazzarello sent the first missionary sisters to Argentina. She moved in 1879 to the new motherhouse at Nizza Monferrato. By the time of her death the Salesian Sisters had opened more than 30 houses in Italy, France, and Latin America, and had 250 members. Mazzarello was beatified Nov. 20, 1938, and canonized June 24, 1951.

Feast: May 14.

Bibliography: H. L. HUGHES, *Maria Mazzarello: Life and Times* (London 1933). F. MACCONO, *Suor Maria Mazzarello prima superiora generale delle Figlie dei Marie Ausiliatrice* (4th ed. Turin 1960). A. DE LIMA, *A Santa Salesiana Maria Domingas Mazzarello* (Belo Horizonte 1971). L. CÀSTANO, *Madre Mazzarello: santa e confondatrice delle Figlie di Maria Ausiliatrice* (Turin 1981). P. LAPPIN, *Halfway to Heaven* (New Rochelle, N.Y. 1981). D. AGASSO, *St. Mary Mazzarello: The Spirit of Joy,* tr. L. PASSERO (Boston 1996). *Acta Apostolicae Sedis* 44 (1952) 553–565. A. BUTLER, *The Lives of the Saints,* rev. ed. H. THURSTON and D. ATTWATER, 4 v. (New York 1956) 2:313–314.

[T. P. JOYCE]

MAZZELLA, CAMILLO

Jesuit theologian, cardinal, noted for his contribution to the scholastic revival in the late 19th century; b. Vitulano, Italy, Feb. 10, 1833; d. Rome, March 26, 1900. He studied in the seminary of Benevento, which was directed by the Jesuits, and after his ordination in 1855 he entered the Society of Jesus (1857). At Lyons from 1860 to 1867, he completed his studies and was assigned to lecture in dogmatic theology for three years and in moral theology for two. He was in the U.S. from 1867 to 1878, lecturing on the same subjects at Georgetown University and Woodstock College. Leo XIII raised him to the chair of theology in the Gregorian University in 1878. He held this position for seven years, contributing significantly to the scholastic revival there. He was made a cardinal deacon in 1886, and the cardinal bishop of Palestrina in 1897. His later life was taken up with labors in the Roman Congregations of Studies and Rites, of both of which he was appointed prefect. He was known as an extremely creative theologian and an eminent representative of the neo-Thomistic movement. His period of publication dates from 1880 to his death; his works deal mainly with dogmatic theology, various questions concerning the reunion of the Greek Churches with Rome, and certain contemporary controversies involving Rosmini.

Bibliography: *La civiltà cattolica* 17.10 (1900) 91–95, obituary. L. KOCH, *Jesuiten-Lexikon: Die Gesellschaft Jesu einst und jetzt* (Paderborn 1934); photoduplicated with rev. and suppl., 2 v. (Louvain-Heverlee 1962) 2:1187.

[J. FLYNN]

MAZZOLINI, SYLVESTER

Dominican theologian (known also as Mazolini, Mozolini, or Prierias); b. Priero, Piedmont, 1460; d. Rome, 1523. He entered the Dominican Order in 1475 and manifested a brilliant grasp of the disciplines in his course of studies. He taught theology at Bologna, Pavia (by invitation of the senate of Venice), and was called by Julius II to Rome in 1511. On the advice of Cardinal Cajetan, Leo X named him master of the sacred palace in 1515, an office he held until his death. His voluminous writings include treatises on the planets, the power of the demons, history, homiletics, the works of St. Thomas Aquinas, and the primacy of the popes. Because of his position as master of the sacred palace, Mazzolini was the first theologian to write a forceful attack on the doctrine of Martin Luther. When Luther replied to Mazzolini's arguments, the latter published rejoinders, and a lively controversy thrived between them, especially on the question of papal supremacy, which Mazzolini saw as basic in the disagreement. His principal works are: *De juridica et irrefragabili veritate Romanae Ecclesiae Romanique Pontificis* (Rome 1520); *Epitoma responsionis ad Lutherum* (Perugia 1519); *Errata et argumenta M. Lutheri* (Rome 1520); *Summa summarum, quae Sylvestrina dicitur . . .* (Rome 1519); *Rosa aurea* (Bologna 1510), an explanation of the Gospels used during the liturgical year; and *In theoricas planetarum* (Venice 1513).

Bibliography: M. M. GORCE, *Dictionnaire de théologie catholique,* ed. A. VACANT et al. (Paris 1903–50) 10.1:474–477. J. QUÉTIF and J. ÉCHARD, *Scriptores Ordinis Praedicatorum* (New York 1959) 2.1:55–58. F. MICHALSKI, *De Sylvestri Prieratis . . . vita et scriptis* (Munster 1892). H. HURTER, *Nomenclator literarius theologiae catholicae* (Innsbruck 1903–13) 2:1344–47.

[F. C. LEHNER]

MAZZUCCONI, GIOVANNI BATTISTA, BL.

Missionary priest, martyr of the Pontifical Institute for Foreign Missions; b. March 1, 1826, Rancio di Lecco (near Milan), Italy; d. Sept. 7, 1855, Woodlark Bay, Papua New Guinea.

The ninth of the 12 children of Giacomo Mazzucconi and Anna Maria Scuri, Mazzucconi studied in the seminaries of Monza and Milan. In the summer of 1845, he and his friend Carlo Salerio met the prior of the Certosa of Pavia, who had been a missionary in India. This sparked an interest in the young men, who maintained correspondence with the priest. In the meantime Giovanni was ordained May 25, 1850, and the Pontifical Institute for Foreign Missions (PIME) was established with apostolic approval. Two months later in July 1850, Mazzucconi received an invitation from Msgr. Angelo Ramazzotti to become a charter member of the PIME, together with Father Salerio, three other clergymen (Timoleone Raimondi, Angelo Ambrosoli, and Paolo Reina), and two catechists (Giuseppe Corti and Luigi Tacchini).

They intended to go first to Oceania. Following a three-month journey, the missionaries arrived July 25, 1852, in Australia, where they studied the language and customs of New Guinea under the tutelage of a Marist for two months. Upon their arrival at Woodlark Island Oct. 28, 1852, the mission was divided into three groups with Mazzucconi, Reina, a catechist, and their Marist mentor continuing to Rook Island, where they worked for two years under difficult conditions. The missionaries attempted to gain the trust of the natives by helping and teaching them new agricultural methods.

After their attempts failed, Mazzuconi returned to Sydney January 1855, where he became seriously ill. Upon his recovery, he sailed Aug. 18, 1855, back to Woodlark not knowing that his companions had abandoned the mission stations at Woodlark and Rook. When his schooner ran aground on a coral reef, he was killed with an axe by one of the locals. Eight months later Father Raimondi led an expedition to find Mazzucconi and learned of his martyrdom.

Mazzucconi was beatified by Pope John Paul II, Feb. 19, 1984.

Feast: Sept. 10 (Archdiocese of Milan).

Bibliography: P. GHEDDO, *Mazzucconi di Woodlark: un martire per il nostro tempo* (Bologna 1983); *Missione i Oceania: Giovanni Mazzucconi, martire a Woodlark* (Turin 1984). N. MAESTRINI, *Mazzucconi of Woodlark: Biography of Blessed John Mazzucconi* (Detroit 1983). *Acta Apostolicae Sedis* (1984) 300. *L'Osservatore Romano,* Eng. ed. 12 (1984) 3–4.

[K. I. RABENSTEIN]

MAZZUCHELLI, SAMUEL

Dominican missionary and founder of the Sinsinawa Dominican Sisters; b. Milan, Italy, Nov. 4, 1806; d. Benton, Wis., Feb. 23, 1864. Mazzuchelli was the son of Louis Mazzuchelli, a Milanese banker, and Rachel (Merlini) Mazzuchelli. He was educated by the Somaschi Fathers at Lugano and entered the Dominican Order at St. Andrew's, Faenza, where he made his profession on Dec. 6, 1824. After study at S. Sabina and the Minerva in Rome, he was sent to the American missions in 1828. After being ordained in Cincinnati, Ohio, by Bp. Edward D. Fenwick, OP, on Sept. 5, 1830, he was assigned to Mackinac, Mich., where no priest had resided for 60 years.

Working among the scattered settlers of the Upper Peninsula of Michigan and northeastern Wisconsin, he built the first church in Wisconsin at Green Bay and established a school for Menominee children. Beginning in 1833, he visited the Winnebago near Portage, Wis., and compiled a prayer book for their use, perhaps the first publication in their dialect. When obliged to leave these missions, he settled in Galena, Ill., and Dubuque, Iowa; in 1835 he began churches in both villages. With the erection of the See of Dubuque in 1837 and the arrival of Bp. Matthias Loras in 1839, Mazzuchelli became vicar-general of the diocese. He built more than 20 churches and designed the old Market House in Galena. The courthouses in Galena; Ft. Madison, Iowa; and Dodgeville, Iowa; were his design, and he was responsible in part for the planning and design of the old state capitol in Iowa City, Iowa.

In 1843, after a serious illness, Mazzuchelli returned to Milan, where he published his *Memoirs.* In 1844, he became a missionary apostolic authorized to establish the Dominican Order on the banks of the upper Mississippi; the following year he founded a novitiate and built several small churches. He opened Sinsinawa Mound College for boys in southwestern Wisconsin, 1846. Three years later, when his collaborators failed him, he turned the foundation over to the Dominican Fathers of St. Joseph's Province. He continued, however, to direct a small community of Dominican Sisters that he had initiated at Sinsinawa in 1847 and that he transferred to Benton, Wis., in 1852. He resided as pastor at Benton from 1849 until he died while ministering to the sick during an epidemic.

Bibliography: R. CREPEAU, *Un Apôtre Dominicain aux États Unis: Le Père Samuel Charles Gaétan Mazzuchelli* (Paris 1932). S. MAZZUCHELLI, *The Memoirs of Father Samuel Mazzuchelli,* tr. M. ARMATO and M. FINNEGAN (Chicago 1967). M. N. MCGREAL, *Samuel Mazzuchelli O.P.: A Kaleidoscope of Scenes from His Life* (Sinsinawa, Wis. 1994).

[J. B. WALKER]

MCAULEY, CATHERINE ELIZABETH

Foundress of the Sisters of MERCY; b. Dublin, Ireland, Sept. 29, 1778; d. there, Nov. 10, 1841. After the death of her parents, Catherine was reared by Protestant foster parents, who left her a large legacy. Gradually she was attracted to helping the poor of Dublin. To this end she built a school for poor children and a residence for working women in Baggot Street, called the House of Mercy, which opened in 1827. Soon after this she added an employment agency and an orphanage as other young women came to help her. After deciding to form a religious congregation, she and two companions went to the Presentation Convent in Dublin to make their noviceship. They took simple vows (Dec. 12, 1831), and the Sisters of Mercy came into existence. When Mother McAuley applied to Rome for approval of her constitution, she stated that ''the principal purpose of this congregation is to educate poor little girls, to lodge and maintain poor young ladies who are in danger, that they may be provided for in a proper manner, and to visit the sick poor.'' In 1839 Mother McAuley established a house in London, the first one outside Ireland. Since then the Sisters of Mercy have grown to be the largest religious congregation ever founded in the English-speaking world.

Bibliography: M. B. DEGNAN, *Mercy Unto Thousands: Life of Mother Mary Catherine McAuley* (Westminster, MD 1957). M. E. EVANS, *The Spirit is Mercy* (Westminster, MD 1959). E. A. RYAN, ''The Sisters of Mercy: An Important Chapter in Church History,'' *Theological Studies* 18 (1957) 254–270.

[E. MCDERMOTT]

MCCAFFREY, JOHN HENRY

Educator; b. Emmitsburg, Maryland, Sept. 6, 1806; d. Emmitsburg, Sept. 26, 1881. He attended Mt. St. Mary's College and Seminary, Emmitsburg, and became a deacon in 1831, but deferred ordination to the priesthood for seven years. Meantime he taught at the college and served as its vice president from 1834 to 1837. In 1837 he entered St. Mary's Seminary, Baltimore, Maryland, and he was ordained to the priesthood on March 9, 1838. Upon returning to Mt. St. Mary's, he was immediately elected president and he served in this capacity until March 21, 1872, when he resigned because of ill health and was named president emeritus. He won notice for his pro-Southern views during the Civil War period. Under his administration, Mt. St. Mary's rose to a position of commanding importance in the Church in the United States. Twenty-six of its clergy were raised to the episcopate, including Cardinal John McCloskey and Archbishops John Hughes, John B. Purcell, Robert Seton, and Michael A. Corrigan. Preferring to train bishops, McCaffrey refused bishoprics for himself (Natchez, Savannah, Charleston). In 1871 archbishop John L. Spalding suggested that a Catholic university of America be established at ''the Mt. St. Mary's of John McCaffrey.'' McCaffrey was also active in the field of theology. Cardinal McCloskey and Archbishops Francis Patrick Kenrick and John L. Spalding chose him to act as their theologian at various Councils of Baltimore. Thirty-four years of pastoral service at the college church enabled him to develop his own Catechism, which was sent in 1865 to the bishops and priests of the country for critical comment. A revised version was proposed to the Second Plenary Council of Baltimore by Spalding, who recommended its adoption as the standard Catechism for the United States. The Baltimore Catechism that was later adopted closely followed the format, arrangement, and wording of McCaffrey's work (*see* BALTIMORE, COUNCILS OF).

Bibliography: Archives, Mt. St. Mary's College, Emmitsburg, Maryland. M. M. MELINE and E. F. X. MCSWEENEY, *The Story* *of the Mountain: Mt. St. Mary's College and Seminary,* 2 v. (Emmitsburg, Maryland 1911).

[G. D. MULCAHY]

MCCLOSKEY, JOHN

First United States cardinal, second archbishop of NEW YORK ARCHDIOCESE; b. Brooklyn, New York, March 10, 1810; d. New York City, Oct. 10, 1885. His parents, Patrick and Elizabeth (Harron) McCloskey, emigrated from Dungiven, County Derry, Ireland, in 1808 and settled in Brooklyn, New York, where his father became a clerk in the firm of H. B. Pierrepont and Company. John received his early education in a school for boys conducted by Mrs. Charlotte Milmoth, a retired English actress, and, after his parents moved to New York City (1817), in a Latin school kept by Thomas Brady. As a member of St. Peter's Church he was guided and influenced by the pastor, John POWER, and his assistant Peter Malou, SJ. Cornelius Heeney, a wealthy and philanthropic merchant, on the death of the boy's father (1820) became his guardian and arranged his entrance into Mt. St. Mary's College, Emmitsburg, Maryland, in September 1821. Here, profiting from direction by and association with John DUBOIS, Simon BRUTÉ, John HUGHES, and John PURCELL, all to become prominent members of the American hierarchy, he completed the college course. In 1827 he returned to Mt. St. Mary's as a seminarian and was ordained by Bishop Dubois of New York in old St. Patrick's Cathedral on Jan. 12, 1834, the first native of New York State to enter the diocesan priesthood. His assignment as professor of philosophy in the new seminary at Nyack, New York, ended as did the school, with the disastrous fire there in the late summer of 1834. In November McCloskey left New York to spend the next three years studying at the Gregorian University in Rome and traveling in Italy, Germany, Belgium, France, England, and Ireland.

Early Career. Upon return to New York in 1837, he was appointed rector of St. Joseph's Church where for nine months he encountered the hostility of pewholders and trustees, to whom Dubois had refused a pastor of their own choosing and who now withheld the pastor's salary. Finally, by mild persistence and gentle forbearance, traits characteristic of his whole career, McCloskey won the affection and loyalty of both congregation and trustees. In 1841 bishop John Hughes added to his responsibilities the post of first president of St. John's College (later Fordham University) which, after he had organized the college, he relinquished in the following year. On March 10, 1844, he was consecrated titular bishop of Axiere and coadjutor, with right of succession, to Hughes.

In a diocese that then comprised the whole of New York State and half of New Jersey, he assisted Hughes by making espiscopal visitations and settling trustee difficulties in numerous parishes. He was instrumental in the conversion of James Roosevelt BAYLEY (1842), later archbishop of Baltimore, and in 1844 he received into the Church Isaac HECKER, subsequently founder of the PAULISTS. When the New York diocese was reduced in size by the creation of the Sees of Albany and Buffalo, McCloskey was transferred and formally installed as first bishop of Albany on Sept. 19, 1847. During his 17-year pontificate, the diocese, including over two-thirds of the area of the state, experienced a threefold growth of churches and priests and a rise in the number of Catholic schools from two to 19. He overcame trustee problems, welcomed various religious communities into the diocese, constructed the Cathedral of the Immaculate Conception, and, in cooperation with Archbishop Hughes, prepared the way for the establishment of St. Joseph's Provincial Seminary in Troy. His attempt to prevent passage in the Albany legislature of Putnam's Bill of 1855, which was aimed at prohibiting Catholic bishops from passing on church property to their successors and thus forcing them to depend on the trustee system, was unsuccessful. The law, however, remained a dead letter and was repealed seven years later. Despite the popular anti-Catholic temper of the times, of which Putnam's Bill was a token, the bishop himself won the respect of such prominent state figures as Governor Horatio Seymour, Erastus Corning, Rufus King, and Thurlow Weed.

Archbishop and Cardinal. The metropolitan see of New York became vacant in January of 1864 with the death of Hughes. Although McCloskey had resigned all right of succession when he went to Albany, his name was first on the list of recommendations submitted by the bishops of the province to Rome. After an unsuccessful attempt to avert the honor, he was named archbishop of New York on May 6, 1864, and formally installed in old St. Patrick's Cathedral on August 21. His administration was singularly free of the controversies of his predecessor and of the problems of his successor Michael A. CORRIGAN. He resumed construction of the new cathedral, begun in 1858 but suspended during the Civil War. He made two trips to Europe to collect funds and furnishings for it and dedicated on May 25, 1879, what was then the largest Gothic structure in the United States. He rebuilt old St. Patrick's Cathedral after its destruction by fire in 1866. News of this disaster reached him just before he ascended the pulpit to preach the opening sermon at the Second Plenary Council of Baltimore, where he was the youngest archbishop.

In a pastoral letter of March 1866, he successfully admonished his people, the majority of whom were of

Irish descent, against participation in the Fenian movement, with its schemes of armed intervention in Ireland and in Canada. He welcomed numerous religious communities into the archdiocese, settled the longstanding difficulties Hughes had had with the Jesuits, and gave particular encouragement to the Sisters of Charity, to Hecker's new Paulist community, and to the pioneer Belgian priests and brothers who arrived in 1864 to conduct his provincial seminary in Troy. His patronage likewise enabled Dr. Levi Silliman IVES, a noted convert, to establish the New York Protectory and Father John DRUMGOOLE to set up his Mission of the Immaculate Virgin. At Vatican Council I (1869–70) he was a member of the commission on discipline and opposed a definition of papal infallibility as inopportune. However, at the final session on the subject, he voted in the affirmative.

He was named a cardinal by Pope Pius IX in the public consistory of March 15, 1875, and was invested in old St. Patrick's Cathedral the following April 27, receiving the red biretta from Archbishop Bayley of Baltimore. In September of the same year he visited Rome to take possession of his titular church, Santa Maria sopra Minerva. Three years later, although he arrived in Rome too late to attend the conclave that elected Leo XIII, he assisted at the coronation of the new pope and received formally from him the cardinal's hat in the consistory of March 28, 1878. The cardinalitial rank, which he bore in dignity, was acclaimed throughout the country in gratification that an American citizen had gained the highest honor of the Holy See.

In 1880 he welcomed to New York bishop Michael A. Corrigan of Newark, as coadjutor with right of succession. Thereafter age and declining health compelled McCloskey to withdraw gradually from the more taxing phases of the management of his large archdiocese. Although he convoked and presided over the fourth provincial council of New York in September 1883, the preparation of the agenda and the conduct of the business were largely the work of his coadjutor. His last public act was a successful appeal, again through his coadjutor, to President Chester Arthur and Secretary of State Frederick T. Frelinghuysen to protect the American College in Rome, as property of American citizens, from spoliation by the Italian government (1884). He spent the final year of his life in retirement and died at Mt. St. Vincent-on-Hudson. His body lies beneath the high altar in the new St. Patrick's Cathedral.

Bibliography: J. M. FARLEY, *The Life of John Cardinal McCloskey* (New York 1918). J. T. SMITH, *The Catholic Church in New York,* 2 v. (New York 1905) v.2.

[J. A. REYNOLDS]

MCCLOSKEY, WILLIAM GEORGE

Fifth bishop of LOUISVILLE, Kentucky, and first rector of the NORTH AMERICAN COLLEGE, Rome; b. Brooklyn, New York, Nov. 10, 1823; d. Louisville, Ky., Sept. 17, 1909. He was the fifth son of George and Ellen (Kenny) McCloskey; two of his brothers, John and George, also became priests. He was educated at Mt. St. Mary's College and Seminary, Emmitsburg, Maryland. After ordination on Oct. 6, 1852, he spent a year in parish work in New York and four years teaching at his alma mater; in 1859 he was appointed first rector of the newly established North American College at Rome. Although the nine years of his rectorate were successful in the academic and spiritual spheres, the financial administration of the college was rendered difficult by the circumstances of the American Civil War.

On March 3, 1868, McCloskey was named bishop of Louisville, and he was consecrated in the college chapel May 24, 1868. He assumed his episcopal duties on Oct. 11, 1868, and for more than 41 years directed the growth of the mother diocese of the Middle West. During that time the Catholic population of the diocese, comprising 23,000 square miles of central and western Kentucky, increased from 80,000 to more than 155,000; the number of priests grew from 84 to 201; almost 100 new churches were built; and religious and charitable institutions were greatly expanded.

McCloskey's independent and authoritarian disposition led to several unfortunate conflicts with some of his priests over canonical details of their pastorates, as well as to periods of friction with religious institutes. Despite this, he held no rancor toward his contestants and was a zealous shepherd, making frequent visitations of his diocese, directing collections for various appeals even from outside his diocese, and exhibiting a constant personal concern for the poor and for the needs of his priests, especially the aged and infirm.

McCloskey observed his twenty-fifth episcopal anniversary on May 23, 1893, and his sacerdotal golden jubilee in October 1902; he lived to become the dean and nestor of the American hierarchy. He was buried in the cemetery of the Sisters of Charity at Nazareth, Kentucky.

Bibliography: Archives, Archdiocese of Louisville, Kentucky. R. F. MCNAMARA, *The American College in Rome: 1855–1955* (Rochester 1956). J. B. CODE, *Dictionary of the American Hierarchy, 1789–1964* (2d ed. New York 1964).

[C. C. BOLDRICK]

MCCORMICK, RICHARD A.

Jesuit, moral theologian, writer; b. Oct. 3, 1922, Toledo, Ohio; d. Feb. 12, 2000, Clarkston, Mich., the son of Edward J. McCormick, a distinguished physician and sometime president of the American Medical Association, and Josephine Beck McCormick. McCormick entered the Society of Jesus in 1940; he then studied philosophy at the Jesuit seminary in West Baden Indiana. Beginning in 1947 he taught English and Greek at St. Ignatius High School, Cleveland, before returning to West Baden in 1950 to study theology. McCormick was ordained a priest in 1953. He attended the Pontifical Gregorian University in Rome (1955–57), where he earned a doctorate in moral theology. From 1957 to 1973, he taught moral theology at the Jesuit theologate, which during those years moved from West Baden to Chicago. In 1974, he was named the Rose F. Kennedy Professor of Christian Ethics at the Kennedy Institute of Ethics at Georgetown University, and in 1986 he became the John A. O'Brien Professor of Christian Ethics at the University of Notre Dame.

McCormick's numerous articles in theological and medical journals as well as in Catholic intellectual journals of opinion, especially the Jesuit magazine *America,* for which he once served as an associate editor, gained him an international reputation. McCormick's most important publications were the "Notes on Moral Theology" he published annually in *Theological Studies* (1965–84). These notes were subsequently collected in two volumes—*Notes on Moral Theology, 1965–80* (Washington 1981) and *Notes on Moral Theology 1981–84* (Lanham, Md. 1984). He authored *How Brave a New World? Dilemmas in Bioethics* (Garden City, N.Y. 1981) and *Health and Medicine in the Catholic Tradition* (New York, 1984). The volume he edited with Paul Ramsey, *Doing Evil to Achieve Good: Moral Choice in Conflict Situations* (Chicago 1978), brings together theologians from different churches and philosophers who discussed McCormick's theory of proportionalism. McCormick was co-editor with Charles E. Curran of eleven volumes in the series *Readings in Moral Theology* (Paulist Press). His last two books were collections of essays: *The Critical Calling: Moral Dilemmas Since Vatican II* (Washington, 1989) and *Corrective Vision: Explorations in Moral Theology* (Kansas City, Mo. 1994).

The time frame in which McCormick wrote witnessed a significant change toward a more academic understanding of the discipline itself. Prior to the 1960s, moral theology was associated with the seminary and the manuals of moral theology had as their purpose the training of confessors. The second VATICAN COUNCIL specifically called for a life-oriented moral theology that would reflect on the totality of the Christian life, including the vocation to perfection and holiness. Vatican II urged new methodological approaches that would give more prominence to the role of the Scriptures, seek to bridge the gulf between faith and daily life as well as the separation between the supernatural and the natural, recognize the importance of historicity, and engage in dialogue with other theological disciplines. The post-conciliar period was a time of great ferment in the theological disciplines. Pope PAUL VI's encyclical *HUMANAE VITAE* in 1968 reiterated the condemnation of artificial contraception for spouses and raised the two issues that dominated much of Catholic moral theology in succeeding decades, namely, the existence and grounding of absolute moral norms such as the condemnation of contraception, and practical questions of ecclesiology regarding the role and function of hierarchical teaching on moral matters and the proper response of Catholics. With his characteristic clarity and incisiveness, McCormick insisted on the [progresssive?] processive nature of the search for moral truth by all in the church and pointed out that the hierarchical church has a learning function as well as a teaching function. He firmly defended the possibility—and even the need—to dissent from some non-infallible church teaching. McCormick's early training and extensive knowledge of the manualist tradition continued to influence him, but over the years he modified his position on a number of significant issues. He himself listed ten areas in which his theological views changed: the nature of the church, the importance of lay witness, ecumenism and the search for moral truth, the role of dissent, the changeable and the unchangeable in the church, certainty and uncertainty, effective teaching in the church, the imperative of honesty, and the dynamic nature of faith.

In the course of his academic career, McCormick challenged and disagreed with the hierarchy's positions on specific points of sexual and marital ethics and some conflict situations, but he staunchly defended the very early beginning of the truly human life of the fetus and the condemnation of active euthanasia. In dealing with the question of absolute norms in moral theology, McCormick developed a theory of proportionalism by which he sought to establish a middle position between the traditional neoscholastic natural law approach, on the one hand, and a utilitarianism or consequentialism, on the other hand. The natural law with its theological acceptance of human sources of moral wisdom and knowledge and its philosophical emphasis on a realistic epistemology formed the basis for his understanding of moral theology. He proposed an understanding of natural law that involved a shift from classicism to historical consciousness with a greater emphasis on human experience, a move to the person and the subject away from the emphasis on the natural and the given, a development away from the teaching of the manuals that tended to identify the human and the moral with the physical structure of the act, and a change from the deontological or law model of the manuals of moral theology. While he recognized the need to incorporate both Scripture and systematic theology into moral theology, these two aspects are more implicit than explicit in his work.

McCormick served as a president of the CATHOLIC THEOLOGICAL SOCIETY OF AMERICA and was the recipient of its Cardinal Spellman Award as ''Outstanding Theologian of the Year'' in 1969. In addition to his service in many Catholic institutions and societies, he was the recipient of numerous honorary degrees. A member of the Ethics Advisory Board of the Department of Health, Education, and Welfare, he served on ethics committees of the American Hospital Association, the National Hospice Organization, and the American Fertility Society. In 1990, he was elected to membership in the prestigious American Academy of Arts and Sciences.

McCormick never fully recovered from the stroke he suffered in June of 1999, and he died at the Jesuit Healthcare Community at Colombiere Center in Clarkston, Mich. The funeral liturgy was celebrated at Gesù Jesuit Church in Toledo, Feb. 17, 2000, with burial in the Jesuit cemetery next door. His papers are at Loyola University of Chicago.

[C. E. CURRAN]

MCDEVITT, JOHN W.

Knights of Columbus executive and educator; b. Malden, Massachusetts, Dec. 27, 1906; d. New Haven, Connecticut, Dec. 6, 1994. John W. McDevitt was eleventh supreme knight of the KNIGHTS OF COLUMBUS, a position he held from February 1964 until he retired in January 1977. Having earned B.A. and M.A. degrees from Boston College, between 1942 and 1961 McDevitt taught, served as principal at Malden High School in Malden, and was superintendent of schools in Waltham, Massachusetts. During this period, he chaired the Massachusetts State Board of Education and served on various school boards. Long active in the Knights of Columbus in Massachusetts, he joined the Knights' headquarters staff in New Haven in 1961 as deputy supreme knight and was elected supreme knight six years later following the death of Luke E. Hart.

As head of the Catholic fraternal society in an era of rapid social and ecclesiastical change and frequent controversy, McDevitt encouraged the Knights to abandon admissions practices sometimes used for racial discrimination, place more emphasis on family life, and cultivate improved relations with the U.S. bishops and the Holy See, while continuing to uphold doctrinal and moral orthodoxy and cultural conservatism. Under his leadership, the Knights donated the land for the new audience hall to the Vatican, began a continuing program of funding the uplink costs of satellite telecasts for major papal ceremonies in Rome several times a year, and extended collaboration and support to such U.S. Church entities as the John La Farge Institute, the Center for Applied Research in the Apostolate, and the United States Catholic Conference's Task Force on Urban Problems. During McDevitt's tenure, membership in the Knights rose from approximately 1,150,000 to 1,250,000, and the organization's insurance program grew significantly. He was succeeded as supreme knight of the Knights of Columbus by Virgil C. Dechant.

Bibliography: C. J. KAUFFMAN, *Faith and Fraternalism: The History of the Knights of Columbus,* rev. ed. (New York 1992); ''John W. McDevitt,'' *Columbia* (May 1983).

[R. SHAW]

MCDONALD, BARNABAS EDWARD, BROTHER

Youth leader; b. Ogdensburg, NY, July 20, 1865; d. Santa Fe, NM, Apr. 22, 1929. Born Edward P. McDonald, he entered the Christian Brothers' schools in 1885. A vocational recruiter (1890–1901), he saw the plight of Catholic boys haphazardly placed by orphanages in rural families—some were exploited for cheap labor while more ran away to roam city streets. When asked by Abp. Michael A. Corrigan to study the problem, Brother Barnabas created a placing-out bureau and in 1902 founded St. Philip's Home for urban working boys. In establishing Lincoln Agricultural School, Lincolndale, NY, in 1909, he pioneered the use of the ''cottage system.'' He attended President Theodore Roosevelt's Child Welfare Conference of 1909. The same year, at Brother Barnabas's suggestion, the National Conference of Catholic Charities was organized. From 1919 to 1922 McDonald was director of Catholic Charities in Toronto, Canada, where he introduced Catholic Scouting. As executive secretary of the Boy Life Bureau of the Knights of Columbus, he founded the Columbian Squires and organized courses in the leadership of boys. At the University of Notre Dame in Indiana, he inaugurated a program for directors of boys' activities—an educational innovation copied by schools of social work in other universities. He was an energetic member of more than 40 organizations for youth and the recipient of numerous awards.

Bibliography: ANGELUS GABRIEL, *The Christian Brothers in the United States, 1848–1948* (New York 1948).

[B. R. WEITEKAMP]

MCDONNELL, THOMAS JOHN

Bishop, director of the Society for the Propagation of the Faith; b. New York City, Aug. 18, 1894; d. Huntington, West Virginia, Feb. 25, 1961. He was a graduate of St. Francis Xavier's High School and of Cathedral College in New York City, and completed his theological studies at St. Joseph's Seminary, Dunwoodie, Yonkers, New York. He was ordained Sept. 20, 1919. He served as curate in several New York City churches and in 1923 became secretary to bishop John J. Dunn, Director of the Society for the Propagation of the Faith in the Archdiocese of New York. In 1936 McDonnell was appointed national director of the society; he held this position until 1950 and firmly established the society throughout the United States. In 1947 he was consecrated auxiliary bishop of New York and titular bishop of Sela. He was appointed coadjutor bishop of Wheeling, West Virginia, with the right of succession, in 1951. In addition to the duties of his office, he served on the national board of the Society for the Propagation of the Faith; he also promoted the diocesan Serra Clubs, the diocesan Holy Name Societies, and the International Federation of Catholic Alumnae. McDonnell was appointed by the governor of West Virginia to various state commissions and was instrumental in having the state legislature enter the name of God in the preamble to the state constitution.

[J. J. SWINT]

MCELROY, JOHN

Chaplain, founder of Boston College; b. Enniskillen, County Fermanagh, Ireland, May 14, 1782; d. Frederick, MD, Sept. 12, 1877. After arriving in the United States on Aug. 25, 1803, McElroy worked as a clerk in the port of Georgetown, D.C. He entered the Society of Jesus as a lay brother on Oct. 10, 1806. At the urging of his superior he studied for the priesthood and was ordained on May 31, 1817. He was an instructor at Georgetown until 1822, when he was transferred to St. John's Church at Frederick, Maryland, where he served for over 23 years. In 1937 he built the new church of St. John there and constructed a boys' school, St. John's Institute (1829), an orphanage (1827), a convent (1825), a girls' free school, and a novitiate for the Society of Jesus. McElroy, responsible for ten parishes in the perimeter of Frederick, was the pioneer of parish missions. A noted preacher, he made many converts and conducted annual retreats of diocesan clergy. He was the personal friend of many bishops and in 1840 served as theologian to Bp. John B. Purcell of Cincinnati, Ohio, during the Fourth Provincial Council of Baltimore.

In 1846 McElroy was chosen, along with Rev. Anthony Rey, SJ, as chaplain to General Zachary Taylor's army at Matamoros, Mexico. He served for 11 months but felt that his mission as chaplain was a failure because the enterprise had been conceived as a political entity. General Taylor, however, had only the highest praise for the two Jesuits who had started a grammar school for the drummer boys and the children of local merchants. In October of 1847, McElroy was appointed pastor of St. Mary's Church in Boston's north end. With the rapid growth of Boston's Catholic population, he saw the need for a school of higher learning and secured property on Harrison Avenue. Boston College, Massachusetts, opened in 1863 and a collegiate church dedicated to the Immaculate Conception was erected. McElroy served as pastor from 1861 to 1863, but he spent his last years in the novitiate at Frederick.

Bibliography: Archives, Georgetown University.

[L. B. KINES]

MCFARLAND, FRANCIS PATRICK

Third bishop of Hartford, Connecticut; b. Franklin, Pennsylvania, April 16, 1819; d. Hartford, Oct. 2, 1874. After attending Mt. St. Mary's College, Emmitsburg, Maryland, he was ordained on May 18, 1845, by bishop John Hughes of New York in old St. Patrick's Cathedral there. He became an instructor at St. John's College, Fordham, New York, and then did pastoral work in Watertown (St. Patrick's) and Utica (St. John's), New York. In 1858, after declining the appointment as vicar apostolic of Florida (1857), he was named bishop of Hartford and consecrated on March 14 in SS. Peter and Paul Cathedral, Providence, Rhode Island (then part of the Hartford Diocese and the city of Episcopal residence). Despite poor health (because of which he sought permission to resign or to be given a coadjutor) and primitive traveling conditions, he visited parishes throughout the diocese and attended Vatican Council I (1869–70). Under the missionary conditions of his diocese he had to function primarily as a pioneer and consolidator; he was successful in obtaining the services of several religious communities expert in education and social service and was instrumental in securing the enactment of a useful state statute concerning the incorporation of Church property. When Providence was made an independent see (Feb. 16, 1872), McFarland returned the episcopal seat to Hartford. Almost immediately he set out to build a convent for the Sisters of Mercy; the convent chapel, dedicated on Nov. 29, 1873, less than a year before his death, became the procathedral for the diocese's approximately 120,000 Catholics.

Bibliography: R. H. LORD et al., *History of the Archdiocese of Boston in the Various Stages of Its Development, 1604–1943,* 3 v.

(New York 1944). J. H. O'DONNELL, *History of the Diocese of Hartford* (Boston 1900).

[D. Q. LIPTAK]

MCGIVNEY, MICHAEL JOSEPH

Founder of the Knights of Columbus; b. Waterbury, Conn., Aug. 12, 1852; d. Thomaston Conn., Aug. 14, 1890. He was the eldest of the six surviving children (13 in all) of Patrick and Mary (Lynch) McGivney, pioneer Catholic settlers in Connecticut. After early education in Waterbury, he attended St. Hyacinth College, Quebec, Canada; Our Lady of the Angels Seminary, Niagara Falls, N.Y.; St. Mary's Seminary, Montreal, Canada; and St. Mary's Seminary, Baltimore, Md., where he was ordained by Archbishop, later Cardinal James Gibbons on Dec. 22, 1877. While a curate at St. Mary's Church, New Haven, Conn., he conceived the idea of a mutual benefit society of Catholic laymen. The four pillars of the fraternal order are charity, unity, fraternity and patriotism and the name chosen by the first members, drawn from the working class and professional men of New Haven, was the ''Knights of Columbus.'' In the atmosphere of anti-Catholic sentiment prevalent in New England at the time, this title was significant for it claimed the discovery of the New World by Christopher Columbus as a Catholic event and expressed the conviction that the ideal of Catholic manhood among the children of immigrants, Catholic Knighthood, could be successfully integrated into American life. McGivney remained active in directing the growth of the fraternal order insofar as this was compatible with his primary mission as a parish priest. In 1884 he was appointed pastor of St. Thomas Church in Thomaston, Conn., where tuberculosis and pneumonia struck him down just two days after his 38th birthday. Always revered as a man of holiness and virtue, his grave in Waterbury soon became a place of annual pilgrimage. In 1982, to mark the centenary of the order, his body was transferred to a place of honor in St. Mary's Church, New Haven, where the organization, the Knights of Columbus, was founded. The formal cause for his canonization was begun in the archdiocese of Hartford, Conn. on Dec. 18, 1997 and was presented to the Congregation for the Causes of Saints in February of 2000.

Bibliography: C. J. KAUFFMAN, *Faith and Fraternalism: The History of the Knights of Columbus*, rev. ed. (New York 1992).

[C. F. MALONEY/G. O'DONNELL]

MCGLYNN, EDWARD

Social reformer who exerted considerable influence, particularly in New York City, between 1865 and 1900; b. New York City, Sept. 27, 1837; d. Newburgh, New York, Jan. 7, 1900. His Irish immigrant parents sent him to the public schools of New York until the age of 13, when he was sent by bishop John Hughes to the Urban College of the Propaganda in Rome. He received a doctorate in divinity, and was ordained there on March 24, 1860. On his return, he was assigned as an assistant to Thomas Farrell (1823–80), pastor of St. Joseph's Church, Waverly Place, New York City. Farrell, noted for his interest in social questions, became a counselor to McGlynn and a small group of priest friends. In 1866 McGlynn was appointed pastor of the large and important New York City parish of St. Stephen's, where the plight of his poverty-stricken parishioners moved him deeply. He was disturbed by the widespread unemployment, and began to study political economy. Eventually he accepted the doctrine of Henry George (1839–97) that the single tax was the universal and fundamental remedy for poverty.

McGlynn was active in George's campaign for mayor in 1886, and McGlynn's eloquence and influence among New York's Catholics and Non-Catholics were of inestimable advantage to George. However, on Sept. 29, 1886, McGlynn's ordinary, achbishop Michael CORRIGAN, forbade him to speak on behalf of George at a scheduled public meeting. When the priest replied that he could not prudently withdraw at such short notice but would refrain from any later meetings during the campaign, he was suspended by the archbishop for two weeks. In late November another temporary suspension was imposed on McGlynn, who refused to cease his public addresses on the single tax, and in January of 1887 he was removed from the pastorate of St. Stephen's. Two days later a cablegram from Cardinal Giovanni Simeoni, Prefect of Propaganda, commanded McGlynn to retract his land theory publicly and to come to Rome immediately. McGlynn's friend and canonical advocate, Dr. Richard BURTSELL, replied that his client would go on certain conditions. Failing to receive a reply from McGlynn, Leo XIII ordered him to come to Rome within 40 days under penalty of excommunication. Unaware that Dr. Burtsell's reply had never reached the pope, McGlynn, on the basis of health, refused to obey the order. He was excommunicated on July 4, 1887.

For the next five years while he was under censure, he defended the single tax doctrine at the Sunday afternoon meetings of the Anti-Poverty Society, which he helped found, and of which he was the first president. In December of 1892, upon the assurance of four professors of The Catholic University of America, Washington, D.C., that McGlynn's single tax views were not in conflict with Catholic teaching, archbishop (later Cardinal) Francesco Satolli, the papal ablegate in the United States, reinstated McGlynn in the ministry without retraction of his land views. In June of 1893 McGlynn visited Rome and was cordially received by the pope. Meanwhile, Cardinal James GIBBONS and his supporters had been exerting themselves to prevent the Holy See from passing the condemnation of George's works that Corrigan and his followers were equally intent on obtaining. In 1889 the Holy Office stated that George's land theory deserved to be condemned. This condemnation was received by Corrigan in 1893, but it was forbidden to make the decree public. In 1894 McGlynn was appointed pastor of St. Mary's in Newburgh; he continued without censure from his superiors to defend the single tax theory. Six years later his funeral, attended by all the Protestant ministers and the one Jewish rabbi in Newburgh, was termed the most impressive event of its character ever seen in the Hudson Valley.

Although McGlynn was a man of marked intellectual capacity, for the greater part of his mature years he was not a close student, and did not read widely. Although not the most eloquent or effective orator of his time, he was certainly, from 1865 to 1887, the one who was most in demand in Catholic circles. The land theory that brought him into conflict with his superiors continued to find only limited support. His conception of the parochial ministry, emphasizing the paramount importance of doing an apostolic rather than a pedagogic work, and his advocacy of public rather than parochial schools were likewise unconventional views for a Catholic clergyman of his time.

Bibliography: S. L. MALONE, *Dr. Edward McGlynn* (New York 1918). F. J. ZWIERLEIN, *Life and Letters of Bishop McQuaid,* 3 v. (Rochester 1925–27); *Letters of Archbishop Corrigan to Bishop McQuaid and Allied Documents* (Rochester 1946). S. BELL, *Rebel, Priest and Prophet: A Biography of Edward McGlynn* (New York 1937), partial to McGlynn and largely undocumented but with pertinent factual information. J. T. ELLIS, *The Life of James Cardinal Gibbons,* 2 v. (Milwaukee 1952) 1:547–594. C. A. BARKER, *Henry George* (New York 1955). *Burtsell Diaries (1865–1912),* Archives, Archdiocese of New York. J. A. RYAN, *Dictionary of American Biography*, ed. A. JOHNSON and D. MALONE, 20 v. (New York 1928–36) 12:53–54. B. MITCHELL, *Dictionary of American Biography*, ed. A. JOHNSON and D. MALONE, 20 v. (New York 1928–36) 7:215–216.

[E. H. SMITH]

MCGOWAN, RAYMOND AUGUSTINE

Expert in industrial relations, and second director of the Social Action Department of the National Catholic Welfare Conference (NCWC); b. Brookfield, Missouri, June 23, 1892; d. Kansas City, Missouri, Nov. 13, 1962. Son of Augustine and Margaret (Gannon) McGowan, Father McGowan was educated at St. Benedict's College, Atchison, Kansas; St. Bernard's Seminary, Rochester, New York; the North American College, Rome; and The Catholic University of America, Washington, D.C. Following ordination on Dec. 18, 1915, McGowan served as curate and pastor in Missouri and for a brief period as an Army chaplain in World War I. In 1919 he was assigned as a writer on social and economic matters to the National Catholic War Council, Washington, D.C., which in 1920 became the National Catholic Welfare Conference (NCWC). Shortly after he was appointed assistant director of the Social Action Department, NCWC, under Monsignor John A. Ryan, and became its director on Ryan's death in 1945. He remained in this office until his retirement in 1954.

Father McGowan was a man of unusual vision and initiative, and his perception of needed social reforms in the interest of social justice was far in advance of his time. He strove for a wider understanding of Catholic social principles and for their application to the problems of the American economy. He advocated the industry council idea in the early 1920s, well in advance of its endorsement by Pope Pius XI in *Quadragesimo anno.* To promote an effective system of labor, management, and government cooperation in American economic life he founded the Catholic Conference on Industrial Problems (CCIP) in the 1920s and subsequently organized conferences on industrial problems throughout the United States. His acceptance in 1923 of an invitation of Samuel Gompers, president of the American Federation of Labor, to meet with the executive committee of that body was the first of a long series of conferences that he held with representatives of labor organizations and employer associations in an effort to convince them of the necessity of mutual cooperation for the solution of their problems.

McGowan's assignment in 1933 to the Latin American Bureau of NCWC occasioned his extensive travel in the Latin American countries. His concern for the social, economic, and religious problems he encountered there gave impetus to his work for the improvement of inter-American relations. In 1943 President F. D. Roosevelt appointed him to an advisory committee to study changes in the organic law of Puerto Rico; and after his retirement as director of the Social Action Department, he served for several months as a consultant to governor Luis Muñoz Marín on the problems of longshoremen in Puerto Rico.

McGowan founded, in addition to the CCIP, the Catholic Association for International Peace (CAIP) and the American Catholic Social Action Confederation. He received the Quadragesimo Anno Award of the Association of Catholic Trade Unionists in 1951 and the Peace Award of CAIP in 1957. He was named a domestic prelate in 1952.

McGowan's publications include *Towards Social Justice, Europe and the United States, The Church and*

Social Reconstruction in Puerto Rico, and numerous articles for magazines and periodicals on the papal encyclicals, labor-management, and Latin American relations.

[A. MCPADDEN]

MCGRATH, JAMES

Missionary; b. Holy Cross, County Tipperary, Ireland, June 26, 1835; d. Albany, New York, Jan. 12, 1898. He took his perpetual vows as an Oblate of Mary Immaculate at Sickling-Hall, England, in 1855. After completing his philosophy and theology courses at Oblate seminaries in Galveston, Texas and in Ottawa, Ontario, Canada, he was ordained in 1859. For seven years he divided his time between teaching at the University of Ottawa and the parochial ministry at St. Edward's Church in Ottawa. In 1866, while resident at Holy Angels parish, Buffalo, New York, he began conducting parochial missions throughout the northeastern section of the United States and gained a reputation as a preacher. His missionary labors took him through the dioceses in New England, New York, Pennsylvania, Ohio and Illinois. When the growth of Oblate foundations warranted, he urged creation of a separate Oblate province in America free from Canadian domination, and he was named its first provincial in 1883. McGrath's administration embraced churches in Massachusetts, New York, Texas, and Mexico. After ten years as provincial, he was appointed pastor of Holy Angels Church, Buffalo. As a pastor McGrath was active as a church builder and an early advocate of parochial schools.

[J. H. KENNEDY]

MCGROARTY, JULIA, SISTER

Religious superior, foundress of Trinity College, Washington, DC; b. Inver, Donegal County, Ireland, Feb. 13, 1827; d. Peabody, MA, Nov. 12, 1901. Her parents, Neil and Catherine (Bonner) McGroarty, took Susan and the rest of their 10 children to Cincinnati, OH, in 1831. She was professed as Sister Julia of the Sisters of NOTRE DAME DE NAMUR on Aug. 3, 1848. An able teacher, she served at the Academy of Notre Dame, Roxbury, MA (1848–60), and in Philadelphia, where her school for African Americans (1877–82) attracted the support of St. Katherine Drexel. After the death of Sister Louise Van Der Schrieck in 1886, Sister Julia was appointed superior of all Notre Dame de Namur houses east of the Rocky Mountains and, after 1892, of the California province. Sister Julia founded some 14 convents in her jurisdiction and promoted academic progress in the schools conducted by her community. To this end she prepared a course of studies, introduced a system of general examinations, and arranged for systematic supervision. Her greatest achievement was the establishment of a college for women. The Catholic University of America, Washington, DC, annually refused many applications from women. In 1897, at the request of the authorities of The Catholic University and with the approval of the pope and Cardinal James Gibbons, she established Trinity College in Washington, DC. Although there was resistance by some Catholics, the act of incorporation and permission to grant degrees was signed on Aug. 20, 1897. Sister Julia lived to see the college begin its work on Nov. 7, 1900, and to watch over its first year of development.

Bibliography: H. L. NUGENT, *Sister Julia* (New York 1928).

[J. BLAND]

MCGUIRE, MARTIN R.P.

Language scholar, editor, educator; b. Whitinsville, Massachusetts, Dec. 30, 1897; d. Washington, D.C., March 15, 1969. He spent his youth on a farm, enrolled in the College of the Holy Cross, Worcester, Massachusetts, in 1916, and during World War I served in the U.S. Army, from which he was discharged as a second lieutenant. He graduated from Holy Cross in 1921 and for the next three years taught at Georgetown Preparatory School in Washington. He received a Ph.D. from The Catholic University of America in 1927 with the published dissertation *S. Ambrosii de Nabuthae: A Commentary with an Introduction and Translation.* In the same year he was appointed an instructor in the department of Greek and Latin and in 1946 was promoted to the rank of professor. In 1929 he married Florence Mattimore, and they subsequently adopted four boys and three girls.

From 1937 to 1947 he was dean of the Graduate School of Arts and Sciences, which he helped to save from dissolution during the war, and from 1949 to 1962 he was repeatedly elected head of the department of Greek and Latin, which was highly esteemed throughout the country. After World War II he was named a member of the President's Commission on Higher Education, the U.S. Advisory Commission on Educational Exchange, and the Fulbright Board of Foreign Scholarships. Besides discharging successfully his administrative and teaching duties, he devoted much time to research and writing. His principal publications are *An Introduction to Classical Scholarship: A Syllabus and Bibliographic Guide* (rev. ed. 1961), *Introduction to Medieval Latin Studies: A Syllabus and Bibliographic Guide* (1964), and *The Political and Cultural History of the Ancient World: A Syllabus with Suggested Readings* (1961). From 1946 on he was chairman of the executive committee of Mediaeval and Renaissance Latin Translations and Commentaries, and a member of the editorial board of *The Fathers of the Church: A New Translation.* Appointed senior editor of the *New Catholic Encyclopedia* in 1962, he was mainly responsible for planning and organizing the 15 volumes that appeared in 1967; he not only supervised the staff editors for the various areas but also wrote 114 articles and revised countless others.

Bibliography: R. TRISCO, ''In Memoriam: Martin R. P. McGuire,'' *Catholic Historical Review* 55 (July 1969) 153–158 (with photograph).

[R. TRISCO]

MCHUGH, ANTONIA, SISTER

College administrator and religious superior; b. Omaha, Nebraska, May 17, 1873; d. St. Paul, Minnesota, Oct. 11, 1944. As the daughter of Patrick and Rose (Welsh) McHugh, Sister Antonia spent her childhood on the Nebraska-Dakota frontier. Her elementary and secondary education in Winnipeg, Canada, and St. Paul, Minnesota, preceded her entering the Congregation of the Sisters of St. Joseph of Carondelet in St. Paul at the age of 18. She pursued baccalaureate and graduate studies in history at the University of Chicago, Illinois, supplementing them with European travel and courses at Columbia University, New York City, and the University of Minnesota.

With the encouragement of Abp. John Ireland and Mother Seraphine Ireland, she developed the College of St. Catherine in St. Paul, where she served as professor of history (1911–14), dean (1914–28), president (1928–37), and religious superior of the sisters (1931–37). She provided for the professional, cultural, and religious preparation of the teaching sisters at leading American and European universities, and she added lay professors to the faculty. By securing endowments, buildings, and equipment for the college, she obtained the approbation of the North Central Association, the National Education Association, and the American Association of Colleges and Universities. For St. Catherine's graduates, Sister Antonia secured eligibility in the American Association of University Women and foreign travel and study through International Institute Scholarships. In 1938 a chapter of Phi Beta Kappa was erected at the College of St. Catherine, which became the only U.S. Catholic women's college where this society was established. Our Lady of Victory Chapel, as well as Mendel Hall for the natural sciences and Fontbonne Hall for physical education, medical care, and athletic recreation, were built during her administration. Sister Antonia was honored by membership in the White House Conference on Child Health (1930), by the *Pro Ecclesia et Pontifice* medal (1931), and by an honorary degree from the University of Minnesota (1936).

Bibliography: H. A. HURLEY, *On Good Ground* (Minneapolis 1951).

[A. GLEASON]

MCINTYRE, JAMES FRANCIS ALOYSIUS

Archbishop of Los Angeles, cardinal; b. New York City, June 25, 1886; d. Los Angeles, July 16, 1979. The son of James and Mary (Pelley) McIntyre. After the death of his mother in 1896, James Francis Aloysius was reared by a cousin, Mrs. Robert F. Donley. He spent several years in the employ of H. L. Horton and Company, an investment house on the New York Stock Exchange; and meanwhile, took night courses at New York City College and Columbia. Following the death of his father in 1915, he entered the preparatory seminary for the Archdiocese of New York, and the next year enrolled in Saint Joseph's Seminary at Dunwoodie where he was ordained a priest by Patrick Cardinal Hayes on May 21, 1921.

Father McIntyre served as assistant to the pastor of Saint Gabriel's Church until September of 1923, when he was named vice chancellor and liaison officer between Cardinal Hayes and the curial staff. In 1934, he became chancellor and was designated a private chamberlain by Pope Pius XI. Two years later, on Nov. 12, 1936, he was promoted to the Domestic Prelacy. In 1939, Archbishop Francis J. Spellman appointed Monsignor McIntyre a member of the board of consultors for the archdiocese of New York.

On Nov. 16, 1940, Pope Pius XII appointed McIntyre to the titular see of Cyrene and auxiliary bishop of New York. He was consecrated by Archbishop Spellman in Saint Patrick's Cathedral on Jan. 9, 1941. Bishop McIntyre was made vicar general of the archdiocese on Jan. 17, 1945, and, 18 months later, on July 20, 1946, the Holy Father advanced the prelate to the titular see of Paltus as coadjutor archbishop of New York.

Archbishop. On Feb. 7, 1948, Archbishop McIntyre was transferred to Los Angeles as the eighth occupant of the jurisdiction originally established in 1840 under the title *Ambas Californias.* Shortly after his installation at Los Angeles, Archbishop McIntyre set about to reorganize the archdiocesan curia, to erect a new chancery, and to refurbish Saint Vibiana's Cathedral—all of which he deemed necessary for the efficient management of a jurisdiction encompassing an area of 9,508 square miles with a rapidly increasing Catholic population.

The new archbishop established secretariats and commissions for vocations, communications, archives, cemeteries and liturgy. He founded the Archbishop's Fund for Charity in 1951, to support otherwise unprovided-for welfare activities. In 1956, McIntyre formally sponsored the foundation of the Lay-Mission Helpers Association, the pioneer organization of its kind in the nation.

Among the prelate's most cherished works was the total revamping of the seminary program and his program for Catholic education. In addition to a new preparatory school in 1954, and expanded facilities at Saint John's Seminary in 1956, the archbishop built a college seminary. In the first 15 years of his tenure, Catholic schools were tripled from 141 to 347, an average of one a month. In addition to widening the scope and influence of the Confraternity of Christian Doctrine (CCD), McIntyre's influence was a compelling force in two favorable decisions by the electorate to repeal the burdensome state taxation of parochial schools.

Cardinal. Pope Pius XII elevated Archbishop McIntyre to the cardinalate on Jan. 12, 1953, assigned to the titular pastorate of Saint Anastasia in Rome. Growing out of the new position were additional duties such as his delegation as papal legate to the All-Nigerian Marian Congress at Lagos, on the West Coast of Africa, in December of 1954.

At the conclusion of the second archdiocesan synod, held on the Feast of Our Lady of Guadalupe, Dec. 12, 1960, Cardinal McIntyre was presented with the Golden Rose of Tepeyac by the canons of Mexico's National Shrine of Our Lady of Guadalupe in recognition of his zealous work among the Spanish-speaking inhabitants of California's southland.

In addition to serving a significant role in the central preparatory commission for Vatican Council II, the cardinal attended all the sessions of the council and was active in its deliberation. He made six oral interventions. In the first session, he raised the question of infants dying without baptism, a topic, he noted, that was not treated in any of the schemas. In later interventions he spoke in favor of the original schema on divine revelation, argued for the continued use of Latin, opposed changes in the Mass, and spoke against giving juridical status to episcopal conferences. Nonetheless, a national survey published by *America* in 1966, revealed that the archdiocese of Los Angeles was far ahead of other American jurisdictions in heeding the suggestions and spirit of Vatican Council II.

After his retirement in 1970, Cardinal McIntyre spent the final years of his life serving as a parish priest at Saint Basil's in midtown Los Angeles. His papers are in the Archival Center of the archdiocese of Los Angeles.

Bibliography: ''McIntyre, James Francis Aloysius,'' Archival Center, Archdiocese of Los Angeles. For an account of Cardinal McIntyre's interventions at Vatican II, see V. A. YZERMANS, *American Participation in the Second Vatican Council* (New York 1969).

[F. J. WEBER]

MCKENNA, CHARLES HYACINTH

Preacher; b. Fillalea, Co. Derry, Ireland, May 8, 1834; d. Jacksonville, Fla., Feb. 21, 1917. As the son of Francis and Anna (Gillespie-McDonald) McKenna, he came to the U.S. in 1851. At Lancaster, Pa., he continued his limited schooling for two years and then became a stonecutter. Support of his widowed mother delayed fulfillment of his priestly aspirations, but in 1859 he entered Sinsinawa Mound College, Wis., to complete his studies. He made profession in the Dominican Order at St. Joseph's Priory, Somerset, Ohio, April 20, 1863, and was ordained in Cincinnati on Oct. 13, 1867, by Abp. John B. Purcell. Except for a few years as novice master at St. Rose Priory, Springfield, Ky. (1868–70), and as prior and pastor in Louisville, Ky. (1878–81) and in Somerset (1889–91), McKenna was stationed at St. Vincent Ferrer's Church, New York City. There he devoted himself principally to the work of preaching. His lectures were well attended by the working class, and Cardinal James Gibbons considered him the best missionary preacher in the U.S. The Dominican Order conferred on him the rank of preacher general in 1881. McKenna wrote a number of pious manuals during his missionary years; representative titles are: *How to Make the Mission* (1873) and *The Angelic Guide* (1899). After 1900 he labored for the promotion of Catholic societies. He was the founder of St. Vincent Ferrer's Union and director-general of the confraternities of the Holy Name and of the Rosary. His efforts were responsible for mitigation of Vatican restrictions on the confraternities and for popularization of the Holy Name Society among American Catholic men. He was widely regarded as the Father of the Holy Name Society. In 1914 he retired to the Dominican House of Studies, Washington, D.C.

Bibliography: V. F. O'DANIEL, *Very Rev. Charles Hyacinth McKenna . . .* (New York 1917).

[J. L. MORRISON]

MCKENZIE, JOHN LAWRENCE

Scripture scholar, author, teacher, lecturer; b. Brazil, Indiana, Oct. 9, 1910; d. Claremont, California, March 2,

1991. The son of Harry and Myra McKenzie, John McKenzie entered the Society of Jesus after high school in 1928 and was ordained a priest in 1939. He received an M.A. in philosophy from Saint Louis University in 1934 and an S.T.L. from Saint Mary's College, Kansas, in 1940. His superiors wished him to earn an S.S.D. at the Pontifical Biblical Institute after his tertianship year, but, unable to go to Rome because of the war, he studied for an S.T.D. at Weston College, Weston, Massachusetts, 1941–42, learning Semitic languages on his own and preparing himself for biblical research through a rigorous and systematic study of the history, art, and literature of the ancient Near East.

McKenzie served as book review editor of *The Catholic Biblical Quarterly* 1953–54, was associate editor from 1955 to 1971, and was a member of the monograph series board from 1976 to 1984. He was president of the Catholic Biblical Association of America 1963–64, and in 1966 he became the first Roman Catholic scholar to be elected president of the Society of Biblical Literature.

He was in the forefront of American Catholic biblical scholarship once Pius XII's encyclical *Divino afflante Spiritu* (1943) allowed Catholics to apply the tools of language, history, archaeology, and literary criticism to the study of the Bible. McKenzie's first book, *The Two-Edged Sword: An Interpretation of the Old Testament* (1956), held up by Jesuit censors for more than three years, presented the fruits of recent scientific techniques in Old Testament research to the general Catholic reading public. Nine years later he published a companion volume on the New Testament, *The Power and the Wisdom: An Interpretation of the New Testament* (1965). In between, he produced singlehandedly his monumental 954-page *Dictionary of the Bible,* which for years remained a standard reference work of the field. Three more books appeared in 1966, including *Authority in the Church,* in which he argued that service of the people of God rather than approaches found in secular governments underlies Church authority. Others books followed, including *The Roman Catholic Church* (1969) and his last, *The Civilization of Christianity* (1986), in which he argued in light of wars of aggression and widespread moral degeneracy that Christian principles had never permeated Europe during the Middle Ages. In all, he wrote 15 books, 175 articles, and 250 reviews; he also composed countless audio tapes and study aids. McKenzie directed numerous Ignatian retreats, conducted institutes for religious women, taught weekly Bible classes to archdiocesan chancery officials in Chicago, and wrote extensively for newspapers and magazines.

McKenzie was a brilliant and world-renowned biblical scholar who considered it a duty to use his professional skills to bring the religious and spiritual values of the Bible to the ordinary believer. As a teacher he was a mine of information for serious students but unsympathetic to disinterested ones; as a much-sought after lecturer, he was witty, incisive, and trenchant, as well as sharp in his retorts; as an author he was a craftsman of superb prose: lucid, cogent, thought-provoking, and reflective. Through his popular writings, in which he was outspoken and a master of the memorable phrase, he frequently provoked controversy. In the late 1960s he opposed the war in Vietnam because he saw in Jesus' teaching a total repudiation of the use of arms and violence. He viewed current affairs in the light of radical biblical texts, and he felt that the Church had accommodated itself to a way of life that was a compromise between the world and the Gospel. He had a keen sense of the differences between the Church of the New Testament and the contemporary Church, which he perceived to be deficient especially in the areas of peace, poverty, and charity. He consequently encountered some opposition in the Church and in his own order, which he left in 1970, becoming incardinated in the diocese of Madison, Wisconsin. McKenzie's fundamental conviction was that the Gospel lives in the Church or it does not live anywhere.

Bibliography: See especially D. H. WIMMER and H. M. CULKIN, ''A Bibliography of the Books, Articles, and Reviews of John L. McKenzie,'' in J. W. FLANAGAN and A. W. ROBINSON, eds., *No Famine in the Land: Studies in Honor of John L. McKenzie* (Missoula MT 1975). Further works include: *Light on the Epistles: A Reader's Guide* (Notre Dame 1975); *Light on the Gospels: A Reader's Guide* (Notre Dame 1978); *The Old Testament without Illusions* (Chicago 1979); *The New Testament without Illusions* (Chicago 1980); *How Relevant is the Bible?* (Chicago 1981); *The Civilization of Christianity* (Chicago 1986).

[F. T. GIGNAC]

MCLAREN, AGNES

Physician and promoter of medical missions; b. Edinburgh, July 4, 1837; d. Antibes, southeastern France, April 17, 1913. Because the University of Edinburgh did not at the time grant medical degrees to women, she got her doctorate at the University of Montpellier in France and qualified for practice in the United Kingdom by passing the examinations at the Royal College of Physicians in Dublin. She became a Catholic Nov. 30, 1898, and was later received into the secular Third Order of St. Dominic. She became interested in medical mission work through her association with Dominic Wagner, a Mill Hill Father. In Rawalpindi, Pakistan, she founded a hospital to be run for women and by women exclusively. This was necessary because Muslim law prohibited women from being visited by men outside their own family. In order to obtain sufficient staff for the hospital, Dr. McLaren hoped to use a religious order. This was impossible because Canon Law forbade religious to practice medicine. Five times Dr. McLaren went to Rome to plead for a change of legislation. This was eventually obtained by a decree in 1936. Her ideals, however, were realized through Anna Dengel, an Austrian, who by the patronage of Dr. McLaren became a doctor and worked in the hospital at Rawalpindi. Anna Dengel later became foundress of the Medical Mission Sisters.

Bibliography: K. BURTON, *According to the Pattern: The Story of Dr. Agnes McLaren and the Society of Catholic Medical Missionaries* (New York 1946). *Fight for the Right,* motion picture 16 mm, sd., color, 60 min. (Medical Mission Sisters; Philadelphia 1958).

[J. MORRIS]

MCMAHON, THOMAS JOHN

Mission director; b. Tuxedo Park, N.Y., April 5, 1909; d. New York City, Dec. 6, 1956. His parents, James J. and Bridget (Brennan) McMahon, had him educated at Cathedral College, N.Y., and St. Joseph's Seminary, Dunwoodie, N.Y. He then enrolled at the North American College in Rome, where he was ordained for the New York Archdiocese on Dec. 5, 1933. After receiving a doctorate in sacred theology from the Gregorian University, Rome, in 1936, he was appointed to teach church history and patrology at Dunwoodie. On May 24, 1943, he became master of ceremonies to Abp. (later Cardinal) Francis Spellman and national secretary of the Catholic Near East Welfare Association (CNEWA), New York. He was made a papal chamberlain in 1945 and a domestic prelate in 1947.

On May 13, 1949, McMahon was named president of the Pontifical Mission for Palestine, erected by Pius XII to care for Palestinian Arab refugees of the Arab-Jewish war. He spent many months in the Middle East forming committees, directing the assignment of supplies, and opening schools and medical centers. He was praised for his work by Cardinal Eugene Tisserant, and he was made a Canon of the Holy Sepulchre, a Knight Grand Cross of the Order of the Holy Sepulchre, and a prothonotary apostolic. McMahon's health was badly affected by the rigors of Middle East life, and he resigned his missionary assignment in 1954 to become founder and first pastor of the Church of Our Savior in New York City.

McMahon served in 1948 as moderator of St. Paul's Guild, which was organized to help converts. He also directed the Morgan Fraternity, an association for alumni of Cathedral College and St. Joseph's Seminary who do not continue to ordination. As one of the organizers of the Fordham Conference on Eastern Rites, he wrote ''Islands of Christianity in the Rising Moslem Sea'' (*America,* March 4, 1944). In 1951 he published *Silver Threads,* a booklet describing CNEWA on its 25th anniversary.

[W. K. DUNN]

MCMASTER, JAMES ALPHONSUS

Editor; b. Duanesburg, N.Y., April 1, 1820; d. Brooklyn, N.Y., Dec. 29, 1886. The son of Gilbert MacMaster, a Presbyterian minister, and Jane (nee Brown), he graduated from Union College, Schenectady, N.Y., in two years (1839) and read law at Columbia College, N.Y., until studying for the Episcopal ministry at General Theological Seminary, New York City (1840–44). Professors and students alike were under surveillance because of ''Romanizing influences''—a phase of the ''American Oxford Movement.'' McMaster was outspoken against such repression and was forced to leave. Under the influence of the Redemptorist priest Gabriel Rumpler, he was converted to Catholicism (1845) and resolved to become a Redemptorist. With Clarence Augustus WALWORTH and Isaac Thomas HECKER he sailed to the novitiate at Saint-Trond, Belgium, visiting John Henry NEWMAN on the way.

Advised that he had no vocation, McMaster returned (1846) to New York City practically friendless and took up journalism. His association with the New York *Freeman's Journal and Catholic Register,* the official paper of Abp. John HUGHES edited by James Roosevelt BAYLEY, was a turning point in his life; in July 1848, he became sole owner and editor until his death. He married Gertrude Fetterman (1856) and had seven children, three of whom became nuns.

McMaster was a militant editor; he fought Protestantism and free thought as vigorously as he denounced the policies of Lincoln. His paper was called treasonable and seditious by the U.S. Postmaster General and withheld from the mails (August 24, 1861–April 19, 1862), and he was imprisoned at Ft. Lafayette (September 16–October 23, 1861). He criticized the handling of VATICAN COUNCIL I by the secular press. His ''Jus'' letters (1868–70), which urged full canonical rights for U.S. pastors, put him at odds with members of the hierarchy, notably Bishops Bernard MCQUAID, Peter Baltes, John L. SPALDING, and Amadeus Rappe.

Bibliography: McMaster Papers, Archives of the University of Notre Dame. C. A. WALWORTH, *Oxford Movement in America* (New York 1895). M. A. KWITCHEN, *James Alphonsus McMaster* (Washington 1949).

[M. A. KWITCHEN]

MCNABB, VINCENT

Dominican theologian, spiritual writer, and preacher; b. Portaferry, County Down, Ireland, July 8, 1868; d. London, June 17, 1943. He was baptized Joseph, one of 11 children of Joseph McNabb, sea captain, and Ann Shields. After early education at St. Malachy's, Belfast, and St. Cuthbert's, Newcastle-upon-Tyne, he entered the Dominican Order at Woodchester, Gloucestershire, and was given the name Vincent. He studied at Woodchester until his ordination in 1891 and then at Louvain (1891–94), where he took his lectorate in theology. After the completion of his studies he returned to England and taught in the Dominican studia at Woodchester and Hawkesyard until 1906. He was then assigned to parish work, first in London (1906–08) and then in Leicester (1908–14). This was followed by another period of teaching at Hawkesyard (1914–20), after which he returned to London, where he spent the remainder of his life occupied with preaching, lecturing, and writing.

Much of his writing and preaching was concerned with the social question, but he was also a popular retreat master and wrote a number of popular works on the spiritual life and some books on theological and scriptural subjects. In 1916 McNabb began a long association with Hilaire BELLOC, Eric GILL, and Hilary Pepler—and later with G. K. CHESTERTON—through which he came to see in DISTRIBUTISM, the land and craft movements, the solution to many contemporary social problems. In his last years he became less utopian and accepted some elements of industrial society. He was relentless in self-discipline and in his practice of poverty, going everywhere on foot if that were possible, and wearing his homespun habit; his open-air preaching made him a well known figure in London. His character remains enigmatic: he was a holy man and an eccentric, a zealot and a romantic, humble and pugnacious, loving and intolerant, sincere and histrionic; but always a pastoral priest, a lover of the poor, a conscientious religious, and a man of prayer.

His principal published works include: *Oxford Conferences on Prayer* (London 1903; reedited as *The Science of Prayer,* Ditchling 1936) and *Oxford Conferences on Faith* (London 1905), both of which were republished in one book as *Faith and Prayer* (London 1953); *From a Friar's Cell* (Oxford 1923); *The Church and the Land* (London 1926); *Thoughts Twice-Dyed* (London 1930); *The Craft of Prayer* (London 1935); *The Craft of Suffering* (London 1936); and *A Life of Jesus Christ our Lord* (London 1938).

Bibliography: *Blackfriars* 24 (Aug. 1943) 284–318, memorial number. E. A. SIDERMAN, *A Saint in Hyde Park* (Westminster, Md. 1950). F. VALENTINE, *Father Vincent McNabb, O.P.* (Westminster, Md. 1955).

[S. BULLOUGH]

MCNEIL, NEIL

Educator and missionary, archbishop; b. Hillsborough, Inverness County, Nova Scotia, Canada, November 23, 1851; d. Toronto, May 25, 1934. The eldest son of Malcolm McNeil and Ellen Meagher, he was educated at St. Francis Xavier University, Antigonish (1869–73), and the Propaganda College, Rome (1873–79), where he received his Ph.D. and D.D. After ordination in Rome April 12, 1879, he attended the University of Marseilles, France (1879–80). On his return to Canada he was appointed to the faculty of St. Francis Xavier University, Antigonish, where he served as rector from 1884 until 1891. In 1881 he founded and edited the *Aurora,* a weekly newspaper, and he later edited the *Casket.* In 1891 McNeil went to Cape Breton as parish priest of West Arichat and in 1893 was transferred to the parish of D'Escousse. On October 20, 1895, he was consecrated titular bishop of Nilopolis at Antigonish and named vicar apostolic of the West Coast of Newfoundland, which afterward was established as the Diocese of St. Georges (February 18, 1904). He became its first bishop. He was appointed archbishop of Vancouver, British Columbia (1910–12), and there concerned himself with development of the diocese and Catholic colonization. As archbishop of Toronto (1912–34) he dedicated himself to the development of the Extension Society and St. Augustine's Seminary. St. Michael's College and the Pontifical Institute of Mediaeval Studies there received valuable support from him, and he worked for more equitable distribution of taxes to Ontario's separate schools.

Bibliography: G. BOYLE, *Pioneer in Purple: . . . Archbishop Neil McNeil* (Montreal 1951).

[J. T. FLYNN]

MCNICHOLAS, JOHN TIMOTHY

Fourth archbishop of CINCINNATI, Ohio, archdiocese; b. Kiltimagh, County Mayo, Ireland, Dec. 15, 1877; d. Cincinnati, April 22, 1950. The youngest of the seven sons and one daughter of Patrick and Mary (Mullanny) McNicholas, Timothy (John was his name in religion) was brought to the U.S. in 1881 by his parents who settled in Chester, Pa. He received his early education at Immaculate Heart of Mary School, Chester, and at St. Joseph's Preparatory College, Philadelphia. At 17, he entered the Dominican Order at St. Rose's Priory, Springfield, Ky., and made simple profession of vows on October 10, 1895, followed by a solemn profession three years later. He completed his philosophical and theological studies at St. Joseph's House of Studies, Somerset, Ohio, where on October 10, 1901, he was ordained by Bp. Henry Moeller of Columbus, Ohio.

After ordination, McNicholas spent three years at the Minerva University in Rome where he received a doctorate in sacred theology. In 1904 he returned to St. Joseph's, Somerset, as master of novices. A year later when the Dominican House of Studies, Immaculate Conception College, was opened at The Catholic University of America, Washington, D.C., he was named regent of studies and professor of philosophy, theology, and Canon Law, a post he held until 1909. In that year he was appointed National Director of the Holy Name Society with headquarters in New York City, and first editor of the *Holy Name Journal.* While holding this position, he was pastor of St. Catherine of Siena Church and first prior of the convent attached to the parish. McNicholas was recalled to Rome in 1917 as socius (assistant) to the master general of the Dominicans. As socius he taught Canon Law and theology at the Angelicum University, was named a master of theology, and was awarded the honorary office of provincial of Lithuania. On July 18, 1918, Benedict XV named McNicholas bishop of Duluth, Minn.; he was consecrated at San Clemente church in Rome by Cardinal Tomaso Boggiani on September 8. Seven years later, in May 1925, McNicholas was named to the Diocese of Indianapolis, a see he never actually occupied, since on July 8, he was appointed to the Archdiocese of Cincinnati and installed there on August 12.

During his 25-year episcopate in Cincinnati, McNicholas established about 50 mission chapels, encouraged a convert program and the apostolate among the Negroes, championed the rights of labor and promoted lay retreats and the organization of Holy Name Societies. The number of schools was increased until the archdiocese became a model for Catholic education on the elementary, secondary, and college level. The Athenaeum of Ohio, incorporated by the state of Ohio in 1928, was organized for the control, direction, and supervision of all colleges, seminaries, academies, and institutions of higher learning in the archdiocese. A teachers' college was founded for training priests, sisters, and lay persons. Four Latin schools, wherein boys began the study of Latin in the seventh grade, were opened. An intensified program of higher education for the clergy resulted in 120 priests doing graduate studies. The Institutum Divi Thomae, a postgraduate school of theology, was opened in 1935.

On the national level, McNicholas was chairman of the pontifical commission for the sacred sciences of The Catholic University of America from 1934 until his death, and also a member of the board of trustees of the University. He served as the episcopal chairman of the department of education of the National Catholic Welfare Conference from 1930 to 1935 and again from 1942 to 1945, and was president general of the National Catholic Educational Association from 1946 to 1950. Other national offices of prominence held by McNicholas included the 10-year chairmanship (1933–43) of the episcopal committee on motion pictures that founded the National Legion of Decency; five terms (1945–50) as chairman of the administrative board of the NCWC; national chairman of the Catholic Students Mission Crusade; and 13 years' membership on the episcopal committee for the Confraternity of Christian Doctrine.

The annual statements issued in the name of the Catholic hierarchy of the U.S. for many years owed much of their form and forcefulness to McNicholas. In 1948, in endorsing the fundamental American principle of separation of Church and State, he declared: "We deny absolutely and without qualification that the Catholic Bishops of the United States are seeking a union of church and state by any endeavors whatsoever, either proximate or remote." A preacher of renown and a Church historian, McNicholas was also a national figure in the fields of apologetics and of social and racial justice. In his later writings, he excoriated the communism of Soviet Russia.

Bibliography: M. E. REARDON, *Mosaic of a Bishop* (Cincinnati 1957).

[M. E. REARDON]

MCPHERSON, AIMEE SEMPLE

American evangelist and founder of the International Church of the FOURSQUARE GOSPEL; b. Ingersoll, Ontario, Canada, Oct. 9, 1890; d. Oakland, CA, Sept. 27, 1944. As a girl of 17, Aimee Kennedy experienced a religious conversion at a revival conducted by Robert Semple. She later married Semple, and the couple worked as missionaries in Hong Kong until his death. Mrs. Semple returned to the United States in 1911 with her infant daughter and began her preaching career. She married Harold McPherson, a grocer in Florida, but the marriage did not last. "Sister" McPherson settled in Los Angeles, CA in 1918 and built a 5,300-seat auditorium called Angelus Temple. Her flamboyant preaching attracted thousands of followers and considerable newspaper publicity. She founded the International Church of the Foursquare Gospel in 1927 and established a radio station and a bible college to advocate her fundamentalist, adventist, and pentecostal theology. A third marriage in 1931 to a singer in her temple choir lasted four months. After her death, her son Rolf assumed leadership of the denomination.

Bibliography: W. G. MCLOUGHLIN, *Modern Revivalism* (New York 1959).

[W. J. WHALEN]

MCQUAID, BERNARD JOHN

Bishop, educator; b. New York, N.Y., December 15, 1823; d. Rochester, N.Y., January 18, 1909. His parents, Bernard and Mary (Maguire) McQuaid, were Irish immigrants. Orphaned of both by 1832, Bernard was confided to St. Patrick's Orphan Asylum in New York City, where Sister Elizabeth Boyle encouraged his priestly vocation. He attended Chambly College, near Montreal, Canada, and New York's diocesan seminary, then located at Fordham, New York City. Bp. John Hughes ordained him on January 16, 1848, in old St. Patrick's Cathedral, New York. Designated pastor of St. Vincent's Church, Madison, N.J., McQuaid built two churches within five years and planned a third. In keeping with Hughes's policy, he also started two parochial schools, and taught for six months at one, St. Vincent's, Madison, the first parochial school in New Jersey.

The Diocese of Newark was established in 1853, and James R. Bayley, chancellor of the New York Diocese, was appointed its first bishop. Bayley named McQuaid rector of St. Patrick's Cathedral in Newark where he organized the St. Vincent de Paul Society and set up a Young Men's Catholic Association with a large recreational center. During the Civil War he made a brief visit to Fredericksburg, Va., to minister to the wounded and dying soldiers. He founded Seton Hall College and Seminary (1856) and the Sisters of Charity of St. Elizabeth, Madison, N.J. (1859). Bayley appointed him vicar-general of the diocese and a theologian of the Second Plenary Council of Baltimore in 1866.

Bishop of Rochester. McQuaid was named first bishop of Rochester, N.Y., on March 3, 1868. He was consecrated in St. Patrick's Cathedral, New York, on July 12, 1868, and installed at St. Patrick's, Rochester, on July 17. He became deeply attached to his small diocese, declining subsequent offers of the bishopric of Newark, N.J., and archbishopric of Cincinnati, Ohio. He founded 69 parishes, enlarged orphanages, established the Home of Industry for dependent girls, the Excelsior Farm for dependent boys, the Young Men's Catholic Institute (recreational), and St. Ann's Home for the Aged. He secured admission of Catholic chaplains to the Western Home of Refuge, an institution for juvenile delinquents in Rochester. Through his influence, a state law was passed to provide paid chaplains at all state penal and welfare institutions. He took an active part in the Fourth Provincial Council of New York (1883), the Third Plenary Council of Baltimore (1884), and Vatican Council I (1869–70). At the last he voted against the definition of papal infallibility as inopportune and perhaps incapable of definition. After the definition he proclaimed his complete adherence from his own cathedral pulpit on Aug. 28, 1870.

Because of his positive views and tenacity of purpose, McQuaid became involved in several of the conflicts over policy that divided the American hierarchy of his day. He and his metropolitan, Abp. Michael A. CORRIGAN, of New York, held positions among the ''conservatives'' comparable to those of Abp. John IRELAND and Bp. John KEANE among the ''liberals.'' Both parties dissented from the extreme nationalistic ideas of some of the German-American clergy. But McQuaid, who had achieved rapport with his German diocesans, preferred gradualism to the accelerated Americanization of the ''liberals.'' He favored strict episcopal surveillance over secret societies, political or social, suspected of falling under the ban of Church law. When the U.S. archbishops took a more lenient stand regarding certain societies, McQuaid, blaming Ireland as their presumed leader, began to speak of current trends toward ''false liberalism.'' This charge was to reverberate widely during the controversy over what was called ''AMERICANISM.''

Interest in Education. McQuaid's support of Catholic education was his most significant contribution to the Church in the U.S. In his diocese he founded about 40 parochial schools and two high schools. To staff most of them he established the Rochester Sisters of St. Joseph. He instituted a preparatory seminary, St. Andrew's (1870), and a theological seminary, St. Bernard's (1893). He excluded from the Sacraments parents who sent their daughters to non-Catholic colleges; but at the time of his death he was projecting a Catholic college to be affiliated academically with Cornell University, Ithaca, N.Y. From 1871 on he also wrote and lectured on ''Christian Free Schools.''

McQuaid entered vigorously into controversies involving education. The issue was prominent in his contests with two New York priests, Louis A. LAMBERT and Edward MCGLYNN, and in his opposition to Ireland who tended, so McQuaid thought, to concede to the state too much authority over education. It formed the background of the New York State Regency affair in which Father Sylvester MALONE became regent instead of McQuaid. At the time he publicly denounced Ireland's ill-advised intervention in New York State politics, and merited for himself a rebuke from Rome. Fortunately, McQuaid and Ireland were reconciled in 1905, recalling that they had much in common. As a progressive conservative, McQuaid was an important moderating influence in the American Church of his generation.

Bibliography: H. J. BROWNE, ed., ''The Letters of Bishop McQuaid from the Vatican Council,'' *American Catholic Historical Review* 41 (1956). M. J. MURPHY, ''The Cornell Plan of Bishop J. McQuaid,'' *St. Meinrad Essays* 12 (1959) 76–87. F. J. ZWIERLEIN, *Life and Letters of Bishop McQuaid,* 3 v. (Rochester 1925–27); *Letters of Archbishop Corrigan to Bishop McQuaid and Allied Documents* (Rochester 1946).

[R. F. MCNAMARA]

MCQUAID, JOHN CHARLES

Educator, Archbishop of Dublin; b. Cootehill, County Cavan, Ireland, July 28, 1895; d. Dublin, Ireland, April 7, 1973; eldest son of Eugene McQuaid and Jennie Corry McQuaid. J. C. McQuaid came from a medical family: his father, paternal uncle, sister and half-brother were all doctors. Educated at St. Patrick's College, Cavan, the Holy Ghost school, Blackrock College, in Dublin, and the JESUIT school at Clongowes Wood, he entered the Holy Ghost novitiate at Kimmage Manor in 1913 and was professed in 1914. From the University College Dublin (UCD) he graduated in 1917 with first-class honors in classics. He continued his postgraduate studies at UCD with a master's degree and a teaching diploma, and subsequently he earned a doctorate in theology at the Gregorian University in Rome. Ordained in 1924, the theology in which McQuaid was trained was conservative—strongly neoscholastic and hostile to modernism and liberalism. His hatred of the French Revolution was expressed in several pastorals and speeches throughout his career. He also regarded Protestantism as a fundamental error from which Irish Catholics should be quarantined as much as possible.

Appointed dean of studies at Blackrock, he became a prominent figure in Catholic education and chaired the Catholic Headmasters' Association for several years. In 1931 he was appointed president of Blackrock, in which capacity he became acquainted with Eamon de Valera, the future Irish prime minister whose sons attended the school. In 1936 while drafting a new Irish constitution, de Valera consulted McQuaid, although he rejected McQuaid's draft ''One, True Church'' clause which stated, among other things, that the Catholic Church was the one true Church in Ireland. When McQuaid was appointed Archbishop of Dublin in 1940, the appointment of a priest from the regular clergy caused considerable surprise. Irish government archives reveal that de Valera, as was suspected at the time, pressed McQuaid's claims at the Vatican. However, it is doubtful whether the Vatican needed much persuasion; there was a dearth of potential episocopal talent and McQuaid had an outstanding reputation as a Catholic educationalist.

Once appointed, McQuaid proved to be one of the ablest administrators in the history of the Irish Church. In the first two years of his episcopate, McQuaid set up the Catholic Social Service Conference to alleviate the poverty and distress in Dublin which was aggravated by the war, and the Catholic Social Welfare Bureau to help the thousands of Irish emigrants going to Britain for war work. These two organizations filled a much-needed gap and continued to exist after the war. The expansion of Dublin city and its suburbs during McQuaid's episcopate required the building of new churches, schools, and hospitals. Meeting these demands also necessitated a considerable increase in the number of clergy, secular and regular, whose numbers more than doubled in the period from 1941 to 1972.

Given his previous career, the importance McQuaid assigned to education was not surprising. He was critical of the low priority accorded to education by successive governments and was particularly critical of the poor and pay conditions of teachers. His intervention in the primary teachers' strike in 1946 was poorly received by the government and marked the souring of his relationship with de Valera. During his episcopate the number of primary schools increased by a third while the number of secondary schools more than doubled but, as with social welfare, the government increasingly assumed a dominant role in education from the 1960s onwards. Almost immediately after his appointment in 1940, McQuaid took a hardline stand against the attendance of Catholic students at Trinity College Dublin. The ban lasted until 1970, when the increase in student numbers rendered it untenable; McQuaid acceded reluctantly.

McQuaid had a formidable list of achievements in health care, especially maternity and pediatric services, physical and mental handicap services, and the treatment of alcoholism. It was ironic, therefore, that the most controversial episode of his career occurred in this area—the Irish hierarchy's rejection in 1951 of a free mother-and-child health service. This led to the resignation of the health minister, Dr. Noel Browne, and was a watershed in Church-State relations in Ireland. With Irish tuberculosis and infant mortality statistics ranking among the highest in the world, the hierarchy, and particularly McQuaid, lost considerable support by lining up with the conservative medical establishment to resist efforts at socialized medicine.

From various pastorals that he issued at the time, it was clear that McQuaid did not see the need for the second VATICAN COUNCIL. As its deliberations proceeded, his unease grew, and he became increasingly preoccupied with the issue of episcopal power and independence that he believed were being threatened by the council. In the areas of liturgical reform, greater lay participation, and ecumenism, McQuaid was slow in implementing the Vatican II reforms. His views on ecumenism had always been lukewarm and had led to allegations that he was anti-Protestant. His personality and policies were criticized by a more assertive Dublin laity, but McQuaid, a shy, reserved man who increasingly felt the isolation of office, never responded to such comments. In 1968 the reaction to *Humanae Vitae* caused open rebellion in the Dublin diocese, the force of which caught McQuaid unaware. His last pastoral as archbishop in 1971 betrayed his anger and bemusement at the response to *Humanae Vitae* in Dublin.

At the age of 75, he submitted his resignation to the Vatican and it was accepted. His resignation was announced in January of 1972, when he was replaced by Dermot Ryan. McQuaid died the following year. His substantial archives were released by the Dublin Diocesan Archives in the late 1990s. In 1999 journalist John Cooney published a hostile biography of McQuaid, which made controversial allegations of sexual abuse against McQuaid. The allegations were based on tenuous evidence gathered by McQuaid's nemesis from the 1951 Mother and Child controversy, Dr. Noel Browne, who had died in 1997. No corroborating evidence was produced or has since emerged.

Bibliography: J. C. MCQUAID, *Wellsprings of the Faith* (Dublin 1956). R. BARRINGTON, *Health, Medicine and Politics in Ireland 1900–1970* (Dublin 1987). ROLAND BURKE-SAVAGE, "The Church in Dublin: 1940–1965," *Studies* 54 (1965) 297–346. J. COONEY, *John Charles McQuaid: Ruler of Catholic Ireland* (Dublin 1999). J. FEENEY, *John Charles McQuaid: The Man and the Mask* (Dublin 1974). D. KEOGH, "The Irish Constitutional Revolution: An Analysis of the Making of the Irish Constitution," *Administration* 35 (1987–88) 4–84. D. MCMAHON, "John Charles McQuaid, Archbishop of Dublin, 1940–1972," in *History of the Catholic Diocese of Dublin,* eds. J. KELLY and D. KEOGH (Dublin 2000) 349–380.

[D. MCMAHON]

MEAGHER, PAUL KEVIN

Dominican moral theologian and editor; b. Clarion, Pennsylvania, May 14, 1907; d. Washington, D.C., Jan. 2, 1977. Meagher's family moved to Portland, Oregon, from Pennsylvania. He joined the Holy Name Province of DOMINICANS at Ross, California in 1924. His novitate was spent in St. Rose Priory, Springfield, Kentucky; his philosophy course at River Forest, Illinois and Benicia, California; his theology at the Collegio Angelico (now the University of St. Thomas Aquinas) in Rome and at Blackfriars, Oxford, where he was ordained by Bp. Alban Goodier on May 30, 1931. At Blackfriars his mentor was Thomas GILBY, OP, and the two became life-long friends and collaborators. There also, Fr. Meagher and Fr. Gerald VANN, OP, became friends; in later years they coauthored *The Temptations of Christ* (London 1966; first published as *Stones Are Bread*, London 1957).

Fr. Meagher's teaching career was spent chiefly at St. Albert's College, Oakland, California, a house of studies of his province. He was professor of moral theology, *lector primarius* (1946), and, when it became a *studium generate* (1949), regent of studies. He received the highest Dominican degree in 1946, being made Master of Sacred Theology by Master General Emmanuel Suárez. During these teaching years Fr. Meagher was confessor and spiritual director to the Dominican students, preached retreats, and lectured in theology to many communities of women. He also taught at the Dominican College of San Rafael and assisted in establishing a graduate program in theology there in 1946.

Fr. Meagher left St. Albert's in 1961 to join Thomas Gilby at Blackfriars in launching the 60-volume English-Latin edition of *St. Thomas Aquinas, Summa theologiae* (completed in 1976). The following year, however, he took on the editorship of the area on moral theology for the *New Catholic Encyclopedia* at the request of Card. Patrick O'BOYLE and Rev. John P. WHALEN, managing editor. In 1967 he received the annual Cardinal Spellman award for excellence in theology. From 1966 to 1970 he conceived, planned, and was editor-in-chief of the dictionary program of Corpus Instrumentorum, Inc. This work, suspended for a period between 1970–73, led to the publication of the *Encyclopedic Dictionary of Religion* (3 v. 1979), on which he worked until the eve of his death in spite of ill-health. The period from 1970 to 77 was also one of great pastoral activity, in which he delighted, at St. Mary's Oneonta, New York (1970–73), then at St. Mark's, Hyattsville, Maryland (1973–77). His funeral was held at St. Mark's, and he was buried in St. Dominic's Cemetery, Benicia, California.

[P. KELLY]

MEASUREMENT

The process or technique of correlating numbers with things that are not patently numbered in the order of nature; also, the RELATION that arises from such a process. Measurement is usually affected by comparing observable phenomena with a suitable metric, although sometimes it is the result of a mathematical calculation based on data that are not directly accessible to experience. As employed in the physical sciences, the process of measurement is itself an interaction between a measuring instrument and the thing measured, and on this account is dependent for its objective validity on corrections (sometimes involving theoretical interpretations) to account for the perturbing effect of the instrument.

This article first presents a philosophical analysis of measurement in general, then considers specific problems associated with measurement in psychology, and concludes with a discussion of mathematical aspects of the measuring process.

MEASUREMENT IN GENERAL

Measurement, according to St. THOMAS AQUINAS, is the process by which the QUANTITY of a thing is made known (*In 1 sent.* 8.4.2 ad 3). It is applied directly to physical bodies (1) when their discrete quantity is ascertained, e.g., by counting the number of objects in a room, or (2) when their continuous quantity is measured, e.g., by using a scale to determine individual lengths. In current practice the term measurement is sometimes applied to counting, but is more usually reserved for determinations of dimensive or continuous quantity.

Quantitative Measurement. The elements involved in direct measurement can be explained in terms of the requirements for a quantitative measurement such as the determination of length. Such measurement first presupposes a unit; the unit may be one that occurs naturally, such as the foot, or it may be one fixed by convention. The choice of a conventional unit is not completely arbitrary, but is dictated by the unit's suitability as a minimum dimension into which lengths can be divided.

Secondly, the unit used must be homogeneous with the thing measured (*In 1 anal. post.* 36.11). For example, if length is to be determined, the unit must be a length. Similarly, the thing measured must be uniformly structured and continuous to permit the application of the same unit to each of its parts.

A third requirement is that the unit of measurement and the object being measured must be invariant throughout the measuring process (*Summa theologiae* 1a2ae, 91.3 ad 3; 97.1 ad 2). This ideal is never completely realized for any physical object, since all bodies continually undergo change. Because of such variation, as well as the infinite variety of contingent circumstances that accompany any measuring process, every measurement is at best an approximation. Yet a practical invariance is not only detectable, but is more or less guaranteed by the nature of both the object measured and the standard used. For example, a person's body temperature, although varying over a small range, is held constant by natural causes. Similarly, the unit of time is determined by the rotation of the earth and the gram by the weight of one cubic centimeter of water, both of which are maintained constant through the regularity of nature's operation.

A fourth requirement is that measurement involves a judgment of comparison between the object measured and the measuring unit (*Summa theologiae* 1a, 79.9 ad 4). Such a judgment is an intellectual operation, although it presupposes a physical process. The program associated with OPERATIONALISM to reduce every measurement to the manipulation of instruments alone thus disregards an essential feature of the measuring process. Instruments cannot measure. Ultimately they require mind, which, because of its reflexive character as a ''self-reading instrument,'' can effect the judgment of comparison and make the measurement.

These requirements for the direct measurement of quantity or of bodily extension are applicable to spatiotemporal measurements (*see* TIME). They can be applied also to other entities, such as certain types of quality, but not without some adaptations, as will now be explained.

Qualitative Measurement. Physical qualities, because present in quantified bodies and intimately associated with the quantity of such bodies, can themselves be said to be quantified. Their quantity can be measured in two different ways, giving rise to the two measurements that are usually associated with physical quality, viz, extensive and intensive quantification from the extension of the body in which they are present; thus there is a greater amount of heat in a large body than in a small body, assuming both to be at the same temperature (cf. *De virt. in comm.* 11 ad 10). They receive intensive quantification, on the other hand, from the degree of intensity of a particular quality in the body (*ibid.; Summa theologiae* 1a, 42.1 ad 1). If two bodies are at different temperatures, for example, there is a more intense heat in the body at the higher temperature, or it is the hotter, and this regardless of the size of either.

Measurement of the extensive aspect of physical qualities, being effectively the same as the measurement of length, area, and volume, has the same requirements as that for quantitative measurement. Measurement of the intensive aspect, on the other hand, is more difficult and requires slightly different techniques.

Two possibilities suggest themselves for the measurement of a quality's intensive aspect. The simplest is to arrange objects with a given quality in the order of increasing intensity, and then number them consecutively. For example, if bodies be arranged according to increasing hotness as discernible by touch, and these bodies be numbered, the higher number indicates the greater degree of heat. This is the closest one can come to a direct intensive measurement of quality. Such a measure offers difficulties, however, because of the subjectivity of sensation and the arbitrariness of assigning numbers depending on the number of objects that happen to be compared.

The other possibility is that of determining the intensity of a quality (1) from an effect, i.e., the change the quality produces in a body other than that in which it is subjected, or (2) from a cause, i.e., the agent that produces the quality's intensity in the subject.

Effect. If the quality is an active one, i.e., if it produces alterations in other bodies, it can be measured by the effect it produces in such bodies. This is usually done through special types of bodies known as instruments. Thus heat intensity is measured by a thermometer containing a substance that expands noticeably when contacting a hot object. Similarly, the intensity of sound is measured by vibrations produced in a microphone, and light intensity by electric current generated in a photocell. In each case, the intensity of an active quality in one subject is measured by the quantity of the effect it produces in a receiving subject, which is known on this account as the measuring instrument.

Active qualities, it may be noted, can sometimes be measured independently of external alterations of the type just mentioned. If they induce pronounced quantitative changes in the subject in which they are present, they can be measured directly through measurement of the subject body. In this way the temperature of mercury in an immersion thermometer is measured simply by reading the length of its own expansion. Similarly, the wavelength of sound in a resonating chamber of variable length is measured directly, using a standing wave technique to ascertain the length of the vibrating column. Such a method of concomitant variation, however, while of theoretical interest, is of limited applicability, since it is restricted to bodies that are quantitatively sensitive to the presence of the qualities being discussed.

Cause. If a quality is not particularly active, i.e., if it does not produce pronounced effects in itself or in another body, its intensity can alternatively be measured through some type of causality required to produce it in the subject body. In this way, one measures the intensity of light on a reflecting surface by the number of footcandles emitted by the source illuminating the surface. A variation on this technique is that of using an instrumental cause to measure some modality of the principal cause that actively produces the quality. An example would be using a prism or ruled grating selectively to refract and measure the wavelength of colored light incident on an opaque surface, and in this way indirectly to measure the ability of the surface to reflect light of a particular color.

All these methods are indirect ways of measuring qualitative intensity through a cause-effect relationship. All involve techniques whereby a precise quantity is assigned to the quality being measured, and on this account are considerably more accurate and objective than direct ordinal measures of qualitative intensities. As a consequence, these constitute the type of qualitative measurement most widely used in the physical sciences.

Accuracy. As employed in physical science, a measurement cannot be made to an infinite degree of accuracy. There are two reasons why this is so. The first is that all such measurements reduce to a measurement of continuous quantity, and the only way in which number can be assigned to such quantity is in terms of a conventional unit. For infinite accuracy, this unit would have to approach zero as a limiting case. Attaining the limit would itself involve a contradiction in terms, since a number cannot be assigned to a unit of zero, or nonexistent, magnitude. The second limitation arises from specifying the conditions that attend a particular measuring process. Since these involve details that are themselves infinitely variable, they can be only approximately specified. For all practical purposes, however, it is possible to specify the range of magnitudes between which a given measurement is accurate, depending upon the unit involved and the circumstances of measurement. Some Thomistic philosophers regard such accuracy as sufficient to permit a DEMONSTRATION with the CERTITUDE that is proper to physical science, although not with that proper to mathematics, while others see this as sufficient reason for questioning the strictly demonstrative character of any conclusion of modern science that is based upon a measuring process that has the above limitations.

Bibliography: W. A. WALLACE, "The Measurement and Definition of Sensible Qualities," *The New Scholasticism* 39 (1965) 1–25. M. HEATH, "Can Qualities Be Measured?" *Thomist* 18 (1955) 31–60. V. E. SMITH, "Toward a Philosophy of Physical Instruments," *ibid.* 10 (1947) 307–33. P. H. J. HOENEN, *Cosmologia* (5th ed. Rome 1956).

[W. A. WALLACE]

MEASUREMENT IN PSYCHOLOGY

In psychology, the term measurement means the assigning of numbers to quantitative variations in a distinguishable attribute of behavior, or of behaviorally related objects, with the expectation that something true or predictable may be derived from their relationship with other variables. The logic of measurement is concerned primarily with the construction of a scale or measuring device, and secondly with the application of that scale to a particular behavior or object, such as occurs in psychological testing.

Requirements for Measurement. Quantitative indexes of behavior, such as number of errors, perception time, and number of words recalled are often employed in laboratories of experimental psychology, but in a fairly simple way—e.g., as a convenience for the experimenter in distinguishing and recording various performances, where the only assumption involved is that the behaviors can be properly and meaningfully ranked. The numbers themselves refer to physical units and are not commonly scaled psychologically. Psychological scaling involves the following special features:

Isolation and Identification of a Dimension. What is measured is not an object, strictly speaking, but rather some property or dimension associated with an object, either directly, at the level of sensory observation, or indirectly, through the type of indicant specified by an operational definition. Such a property must first be qualitatively distinguished from other properties and seen as capable of quantification. Not all psychological properties are measurable, for measurability depends upon whether or not the property can be conceived in a quantitative way.

Human Significance. The numbers employed in a psychological scale must represent a value indicative of the experience or performance of the human subject, as opposed to a value inherent in the physical nature of the stimulus, situation, or condition evoking the behavior. Physics, for example, using the human subject as mediating observer, employs a physical system—e.g., a thermometer, based on a law relating liquid expansion to heat—to eliminate or reduce subjective variations within the sensing organism. The psychologist, however, is directly concerned with variations in sensation and with human performance; thus the numbers he uses must reflect, or be isomorphic with, variations in psychological meaningfulness. The basic law employed must include behavior as one of its terms.

Rule for Assigning Numbers. The derivation of a psychological scale involves perceiving or performing subjects on the one hand, and stimuli (physical objects, situations, words, tasks, or problems) on the other, and a search for some functional law relating the two. Systematic variations in the responses of the subjects, when quantified in terms of the human variation itself, become the key to establishing the function relating stimuli and responses and to assigning one, and only one, number to each object.

Usable Properties of Numbers. Not all arithmetical properties of numbers are usable in psychological scaling. The number four, for example, is greater than two (order); it is also greater by a definite amount (distance or interval); and it is counted off from zero (origin—in this case, an absolute zero) and contains two by addition or division (composition or extension). Corresponding to these distinguishable properties, scales are commonly identified as ordinal, interval, or ratio scales. The difficulty of establishing an absolute zero in psychological matters restricts the use of ratio scales, and such matters offer little opportunity for using the extensive or composite properties of numbers.

Examples of Psychological Scales. Commonly employed psychological scales include psychophysical scales, attitude scales, product and mental test scales, and multidimensional and other types of scaling procedures.

Psychophysical Scales. An instance of a psychophysical scale is the measurement of the loudness of a sound based on the Weber-Fechner law, which states that the intensity of a sensation increases as the logarithm of the stimulus. A unit difference between the logarithms of two physical sound pressures is divided into ten equal steps, called decibels. The zero is set at the point of the absolute threshold, the weakest sound that can be heard, and the scale extends to cover a range of about 140 decibels.

Attitude Scales. These are commonly derived from a large number of statements of opinion, favorable and unfavorable, about some commonly known subject such as communism or about a debatable social custom or institution. Agreement among a group of judges as to how favorable or unfavorable each opinion-statement may be is transformed into a scale value, using the law of comparative judgment. This law states that the psychological difference between items is a function of the relative frequency with which the difference is perceived. The zero is placed arbitrarily low.

Product and Mental Test Scales. Product scales, used for rating specimens of handwriting, soldering joints (in trade tests), art work, or other kinds of cultural product, are similarly based on the law of comparative judgment and have an arbitrary zero point. Mental test scales, such as those used in psychological testing, are based on a statistical analysis of the performance of a group of homogeneous subjects on each item.

Other Types. Multidimensional scaling is employed to discover the number of dimensions involved in a particular phenomenon and to rate each object on the various dimensions. An example of this type of scaling is the "semantic differential," which is used to measure the connotative meaning of common words. Other scales are used for the associative value of common words or of nonsense syllables, the frequency rating of associated responses to a standard word list, the frequency rating of words in common use, and ratings of abnormal or psychotic behavior in terms of basic trait content.

Role of Measurement in Psychology. Psychological measurement is based on empiriological properties that lend themselves readily to conceptual quantification and identification in terms of observed indicants. It thus serves to supplement logical definitions and to extend these into an area of finer objective discrimination. Among its other contributions, the following may be enumerated: (1) increased precision in identifying instances of the occurrence of a property; (2) better contexts of meaningfulness, to the extent that the assignment of numbers is based on behavioral laws; (3) evaluations of the influence of empirically established relationships on tentative definitions of objects or properties; and (4) more reliable inferences of causal relationships as these are discernible through the application of the principle of concomitant variation.

Bibliography: W. S. TOGERSON, *Theory and Methods of Scaling* (New York 1958). CONFERENCE ON THE HISTORY OF QUANTIFICATION IN THE SCIENCES, *Quantification of the Meaning of Measurement in the Natural and Social Sciences,* ed. H. WOOLF (Indianapolis 1961). C. W. CHURCHMAN and P. RATOOSH, eds., *Measurement: Definitions and Theories* (New York 1959).

[W. D. COMMINS]

MATHEMATICAL ASPECTS

From the viewpoint of the mathematician, measurement is the determination of the value of a measure function of a given attribute of an object. A measure function is a rule that correlates a set of attributes with a set of elements (usually numbers) of an algebra. For example, the measure function called ''length,'' which one may denote by *L,* is a rule or set of procedures that associates the set of attributes of ''extended objects'' with the set of real numbers for which addition and multiplication are already defined. The length of the edge of a table may be denoted by $L(t)$, in which case, for example, $L(t)$ = 3 feet 6 inches. The rule denoted by *L* is the set of procedures for measuring the length of the table, which results in the correlation ''length of table is 3'6".''

The element correlated with ''length of table,'' or more generally ''length of *x,*'' is not merely a real number; it is a dimension number, i.e., a number plus a dimension, as, for example, ''3 feet.'' The term ''feet'' refers to a unit of measurement previously established. ''To measure'' thus signifies that one knows a set of procedures and a unit of measurement (a dimension) such that, by applying the set of procedures, he can associate a unique number of units of measurement with a given measurable.

Requirements for Measure Functions. A minimal set of conditions imposed on a measure function are: (1) if $m(x_1)$ and $m(x_2)$ are measurements, then one and only one of $m(x_1)$ is equal to $m(x_2)$ or $m(x_1)$ is less than $m(x_2)$ or $m(x_1)$ is greater than $m(x_2)$ holds; (2) x_1 is equal to x_2 if and only if $m(x_1)$ is equal to $m(x_2)$, where x_1 and x_2 denote measurables, e.g., the length of this table and the length of that table; and (3) if $m(x_1)$ is less than $m(x_2)$ and $m(x_2)$ is less than $m(x_3)$, then $m(x_1)$ is less than $m(x_3)$. For a measure function using the set (or any subset of the set) of real numbers as dimension numbers, these conditions are easily satisfied.

In defining the measure function, one must also define the rule, i.e., the method of assigning a dimension number to each instance of the attribute. An illustration of this method can be seen in fixing the age of some person *P*. Evidently ''age of *P*'' is measured from the point ''birth of *P*.'' Moreover, to measure age one must define a dimension, i.e., a unit of measurement. In this case ''calendar year,'' in its ordinary meaning, can serve as the unit of measurement, which is also called the metric. One correlates the birth of *P* with a point on a given calendar year. The age of *P* at birth is defined as zero years, whereas the age of *P* at present is the number of calendar years from zero to the present date. This process defines a mapping of two points in the set of calendar years to two events in the life of *P,* and consequently defines the age of *P* as the ''distance'' between the two points in the set of calendar years.

Mapping. The problems associated with mapping may be seen in the following example. Suppose that one wishes to measure food preferences of a set of adults aged 20 to 30. He then must define a measure function that maps a set of foods into the set of elements of some algebra. The most obvious algebraic set to select is the set of nonnegative integers. The unit of measurement is the preferential attitude of an adult toward a food. The measure function $m(_p)$ is definable as follows: $m(_p)$ (F) = order of *F* in the ranking by person. So m $(_p)$ (cheese) = 3 means that a given individual ranks cheese third on his list.

There are difficulties involved in this procedure, however. For example, it is not clear how to define $m(_p)$ (F) = zero. The metric is neither precise nor unambiguous. The measure function gives different results at different times and for different persons. The fact that, for two individuals, the measure function for the same food gives different integers does not enable one to make any significant comparison between the two measures. Finally, the fact that the measure function for a given individual yields $m(_p)$ $(F_1) = a$ and $m(_p)$ $(F_2) = b$ does not provide any significant conclusion concerning the relation of the two preferences.

Whether or not a measure function can be defined for a particular attribute is an empirical problem. But when a measure function can be found that correlates the measurables with some algebra, particularly that of the real number system, the whole apparatus of mathematics becomes available for inferences. Assuming translation from mathematical equations to attributes, the mechanical derivation of mathematical consequences then suggests phenomena that may be related to the measurables.

In the empirical sciences, concrete models of the metric are often constructed, e.g., clocks, meters, and scales. Some concrete entity or objective phenomenon is then used to determine the number of units to be mapped to a particular appearance of the attribute being measured. Such an instrument can be considered to define the method of determining the measure.

Error in Measurement. There are two major sources of error in measurement: (1) the definition of the measure function, and (2) the construction and use of the measuring instrument. Since the use of the measuring instrument involves the recognition of the coincidence of ''points,'' the degree of accuracy with which the points can be seen to coincide influences the accuracy of the measurement. The size of the unit used also affects the accuracy. For example, a length measured by a measuring instrument graduated in inches is accurate only to within ½"; thus a length of 12" is really a length between 11½" and 12½". If the length is measured with an instrument graduated to ½", a length of 12" means a length between 11¾" and 12¼". Further errors arise if, unknown to the observer, the conditions under which the measurements are taken cause the measuring instrument to be altered, or the attribute measured to be affected.

Bibliography: C. G. HEMPEL, *Fundamentals of Concept Formation in Empirical Science* (Chicago 1952). H. MARGENAU, *The Nature of Physical Reality: A Philosophy of Modern Physics* (New York 1959). J. G. KEMENY, *A Philosopher Looks at Science* (Princeton 1959). S. S. STEVENS, ''On the Theory of Scales of Measurement,'' *Science* 103 (1946) 677–80.

[L. O. KATTSOFF]

MEAUX (MELSA), ABBEY OF

Former CISTERCIAN house, near Beverley, Yorkshire, England, Diocese of York, founded from FOUNTAINS in 1150 by William le Gros, earl of Albemarle. The first abbot, Adam, resigned in 1160 and dispersed the community because of lack of endowments. Under Philip, his successor, Meaux was impoverished by lawsuits, bad crops, and the ransom for King Richard; and the community dispersed once again. When the abbey refused King John's levy, his vengeance necessitated yet another dispersal in 1210. Monastic life resumed in 1211, but bad administration throughout the 13th century accumulated debts; these were, however, reduced from £4,000 to £400 by 1339. In 1349 the plague killed 40 out of 50 inmates; this calamity was followed by internal dissensions concerning abbacy. William of Scarborough, abbot from 1372 to 1396, enriched the fabric of the church; he was succeeded by Thomas Burton, a man of considerable ability, who represented the Yorkshire Cistercians at Vienna during the WESTERN SCHISM, taking the place of the abbot of CLAIRVAUX for the Cistercians of the Roman obedience. He resigned in 1399 and devoted the rest of his life to writing the history of the abbey, *Chronica de Melsa* (ed. E. Bond, *Rerum Britannicarum medii aevi scriptores,*). Meaux possessed a splendid library and a wonderful collection of relics, listed in the *Chronica.* The last abbot, Richard Stopes, and 24 monks surrendered the abbey on Dec. 11, 1539.

Bibliography: W. DUGDALE, *Monasticon Anglicanum* (London 1655–73); best ed. by J. CALEY et al., 6 v. (1817–30) 5:388-398. A. EARLE, *Essays upon the History of Meaux Abbey* (London 1906). W. PAGE, ed., *The Victoria History of the County of York,* 4 v. and index (London 1907-13). D. KNOWLES and R. N. HADCOCK, *Medieval Religious Houses: England and Wales* (New York 1953) 111. D. KNOWLES, *The Monastic Order in England, 943–1216* (2d ed. Cambridge, Eng. 1962) 349, 353-354, 368-369, 636.

[C. H. TALBOT]

MECCA

In Arabic Makka, city in southern Hijaz, about 70 miles from the coast of the Red Sea, the holy city of Islam and birthplace of MUḤAMMAD.

The city lies in a slight depression in the surrounding low hills. The region is oppressively hot, almost completely infertile, and devoid of rainfall, though infrequent winter storms of great violence with their concomitant torrents (*sayl,* pl. *suyûl*) present a serious threat to the lower parts of the city. The earliest history of Mecca is altogether obscure; no doubt its foundation is due to the presence of water (the sacred spring of Zamzam) and its position at the hub of a number of important trade routes joining Yemen and thereby Abyssinia and India in the south to Palestine, Syria, and Iraq in the north. According to tradition, a certain Quṣayy is said to have installed the tribe Quraysh as masters of the town over the Khuzâ'a. At the time of Muḥammad the city existed entirely on trade, although because of the presence of the Ka'aba (sacred Black Stone) it already formed an important religious center for the pagan Arabs. Under the reign of the UMAYYADS there was much building in the city, the great mosque (*al-masjid al-harām*) being completed under al-Walīd I, while a number of dikes were constructed in order to protect the Ka'aba from the danger of the *sayl.* During the period of the 'ABBĀSIDS (750-960) the city was ruled by governors appointed from Baghdad, but even from the time of al-Ma'mūn (813-833) the whole region around Mecca and Medina and *Tā'if* fell into near anarchy. It was subjected to the raids of the 'Alids [*see* 'ALĪ ('ALĪ IBN ABĪ ṬĀLIB)] some of whom managed to make themselves rulers of the holy city for brief periods. In 930 it was plundered by the Karmatians (*al-Qarāmiṭa*), who carried off the Black Stone, returning it finally in 950. With the rise of the Buyids in Baghdad (945) and the

Pilgrimage to Mecca, Saudi Arabia.

Fāṭimids in Egypt (969), the ʻAlids, taking on the title of *sharīf,* became the rulers of Mecca, with varying degrees of dependence upon Egypt. Under the rule of ʼAjlān (1346-75) the Sharīfs gave up the Zaydī creed (*see* SHĪʻTES) to follow the orthodox Shāfiʼī system thereafter. There was again a major political change with Sultan Selîm's conquest of Egypt (1517); the relative dependence of Mecca upon Constantinople and Egypt then varied with the relative strengths of the two. The city was taken by the WAHHĀBIS in 1803 but was freed by Muḥammad ʻAlī in 1813. In 1916 the last of the Sharīfs, Ḥusayn ibn ʻAlī, made himself ruler of the independent kingdom of the Hijaz but was forced to flee when the Wahhābi ʻAbd al-ʻAzīz ibn Saʼūd took the city in October 1924; he was there proclaimed king of Hijaz in 1926. In the following year the sultanate of the Nejd became the Kingdom of SAUDI ARABIA, with the ruler of the combined kingdoms residing at Riyadh.

[R. M. FRANK/EDS.]

MECHANISM

Mechanism attempts to explain the physical world by the movement of inert bodies that are pushed or pulled through direct or indirect physical contact with other bodies. Its proponents often hold that local motion is the only real motion, and that a body is maintained in such motion by its own inertia or impetus. Again, they frequently reduce physical bodies to purely quantitative principles, thereby giving mathematics primacy in physical science. Mechanists likewise deny purposes as explanatory principles, and sometimes deny the existence of inherent natural goals in bodies undergoing motion. Mechanism is often, but not necessarily, associated with the view that physical bodies are composed of atoms moving in a void (*see* ATOMISM). It also generally entails a denial of chance or contingency in nature; thus an apparent chance event is explained by the inability of man's finite mind to grasp all the relevant physical causes.

Mechanism is sometimes completely materialistic in orientation, though it need not be so (*see* MATERIALISM).

Since the meaning of the term mechanism has varied in the course of time, the details of its characteristics can best be noted in a survey of its historical development.

Greek and Medieval Origins. In ancient Greek philosophy, Democritus' theory of atoms moving in a void represents one form of mechanism. These atoms exert influence on each other only by physical contact and have no natural purposes. The Epicureans also espoused this rudimentary atomism of DEMOCRITUS, which reached the zenith of its development in the *De rerum natura* of the Roman poet, LUCRETIUS (*see* EPICUREANISM).

At the end of the 13th century, the Franciscan PETER JOHN OLIVI stressed an additional characteristic of mechanism. He defended a proposal made in the 6th century by JOHN PHILOPONUS, who maintained that a hurled projectile is given an IMPETUS that enables it to continue moving after it has lost contact with the original mover. This is an anticipation of the concept of inertia that plays an important role in later mechanism. Likewise Francis of Marchia and JOHN BURIDAN, in the 14th century, developed theories of impetus.

Other 14th-century philosophers, while not denying final causality in nature, nevertheless concentrated on approaches to nature which ignored finality. At Merton College in Oxford, THOMAS BRADWARDINE, who later became archbishop of Canterbury, studied relationships between distance, time, speed, and acceleration and expressed these in mathematical formulas that were basically algebraic. At Paris, NICHOLAS ORESME did similar work using graphing techniques that anticipated the development of modern analytic geometry. These kinematic studies, though not mechanistic in themselves, fostered mathematical, rational, and nonexperimental analyses of motion that were quite compatible with the mechanistic viewpoint.

Medieval mechanicians also considered forces acting on bodies and thus made beginnings in the science of dynamics that matched their work in kinematics. In his analysis of motive and resistive forces, Aristotle had stated that when a force was sufficient to put a body in motion, the velocity of the body was directly proportional to the force acting on it and indirectly proportional to the resistance of the medium through which it moved. In order to give intelligent meaning to Aristotle's proportionality, and also to explain why a small force cannot initiate motion, Bradwardine developed a logarithmic law of motion. This was not as accurate as later laws, but it did represent an improvement over earlier Aristotelian analyses.

In the 15th century NICHOLAS OF CUSA, although not a complete mechanist, invoked an impetus theory to explain the movements of the heavenly bodies. For him, God initiates all movement, but bodies afterward maintain themselves in motion. Cusanus was likewise sympathetic to atomism and the principle of the conservation of matter. The notion of impetus as a sustaining cause for local motion was accepted also by Leonardo da Vinci. In general, these late medieval philosophers advocated goals or purposes for moving bodies but did not concentrate upon them in their physics.

Scientific Revolution. In the early 17th century, Galileo GALILEI adopted and greatly promoted several ideas characteristic of mechanism. In his controversial work *Dialogue on the Two Chief Systems of the World* Galileo discussed sympathetically the Aristotelian doctrine of natural place as the normal goal of local motion. But in a later work, *Discourse on Two New Sciences,* he avoided discussions of purposes and concentrated on describing in mathematical terms how motions occur. His mechanism here consisted in denying the fruitfulness of studying purposes in physics rather than in denying that finality exists. Galileo also accepted the atomism of Democritus. He made colors, sounds, and other qualities subjective and stressed mathematics as the proper instrument for discovering physical natures.

In England at about the same time Francis BACON developed a system employing mechanistic features. He rejected the notion of Aristotle and of most medieval scholars that bodies have nonmathematical substantial forms and are the subjects of real qualities. While the Democritan idea of atoms moving in a void appealed to him, he regarded this as a hypothesis, and anything that was merely postulated and not immediately evident he looked upon with suspicion. Thus he differed from Galileo, who accepted atomism uncritically and favored a postulational approach in his science. Bacon believed in final causes or purposes in nature, but eliminated them from scientific considerations because he did not consider them useful for technological applications.

The writings of Johann KEPLER on the nature of the physical world were an unusual combination of science and mysticism. Pythagorean and Neoplatonic in his leanings, he nevertheless held some doctrines that are compatible with a mechanistic cosmology. Thus for him the real world is quantitative, and real qualities outside of man are reduced to the quantitative relations studied in mathematics.

Hobbes, Gassendi, and Descartes. Thomas HOBBES, a 17th-century Englishman, was clearly mechanistic in his views of the nature of the physical world. In his analysis of bodies he reduced all phenomena to matter in local motion. Hobbes was also much impressed with the power of quantitative analysis, and eliminated Aristotelian final causes or purposes for his science. While he did not deny that spiritual substances exist, he denied that philosophy could come to a knowledge of such substances. Therefore, for him, philosophy must be materialistic as well as mechanistic.

Furthermore, in Hobbes one sees mechanism linked to a general SKEPTICISM about man's ability to know the natures of things. The Greek atomists, Galileo, and Descartes, to the extent that they exhibited mechanistic elements in their work, believed that they were making statements about the natures of physical things. But Hobbes' skepticism caused him to associate mechanical conceptions with the appearances of things alone, and not with their true natures.

The impact of mechanistic thought in France in the early 17th century is reflected in the works of Pierre GASSENDI and René DESCARTES. Gassendi, a philosopher and mathematician, was an atomist. In fact he identified the Aristotelian notion of prime matter with the atoms of Democritus and Epicurus. He also accepted the ancient Greek notion that these atoms move in a void.

Descartes's view of the physical world is a classical statement of mechanism. For him final causality does not pertain to the study of cosmology. Descartes is also a good example of a mechanist who is not an atomist. Since he holds that extension is the essence of matter, wherever there is space there must be matter; therefore there is no void in which atoms can move. The entire cosmos is thus filled with rigid matter or with vortices of a very subtle matter. Causal influence is produced by the direct contact of bodies or by their indirect contact through some material medium.

Again, if extension is the essence of bodies, it follows that mathematics will be the science best suited to study their natures. In the thought of THOMAS AQUINAS and other scholastics, the substantial form is a principle of unity which makes the whole somehow greater than the aggregate of the parts. In the mechanistic world of Descartes, on the other hand, the universe resembles a mathematical whole which is merely the summation of its parts.

Boyle and Newton. In late 17th-century England, Robert Boyle continued the mechanist tradition. He affirmed that the qualities of bodies are derived from the size, shape, and local motion of their parts. Like other mechanists, he rejected the substantial forms of Aristotle and was hostile toward using the notion of natural end in physics. Yet his mechanistic views in cosmology never led him to doubt the reality or importance of spiritual entities.

At the same period, Sir Isaac Newton produced his great synthesis, which is usually associated with mechanistic philosophy. It does exhibit some key characteristics of mechanism, such as its aversion for final causality and its brilliant mathematical approach. But other aspects of Newton's thought, as expressed in *The Mathematical Principles of Natural Philosophy, The Opticks,* and his correspondence, reveal the presence of nonmechanical elements. While he accepts atomism and the notion of absolute space, for example, he also speaks of electric spirits. His famous three laws of motion are mechanistic in the sense that they invoke inertia, make no reference to finality, regard all motions as extrinsically determined, and explain causal interaction by making action mathematically equivalent to reaction. Yet Newton's universal law of gravitation, subsuming, as it does, celestial and terrestial phenomena under one law, is not mechanical in such a clear sense. It posits a mysterious force between bodies. These influence each others' motions even though they are not, and have never been, in contact. Though action through a void is not proposed, no physical substantial medium is posited. Cartesian mechanism is thus not in complete accord with the Newtonian variety (*see* MOTION).

Rise of Dynamism. G. LEIBNIZ strongly attacked Descartes's conception of the physical world. He claimed that both inorganic and organic bodies have within themselves unextended (and hence immaterial) substantial realities which he called monads (*see* MONAD). These simple unextended dynamic entities were centers of force and were inherently active in nature. Although Leibniz's cosmological system is sometimes referred to as DYNAMISM, it still incorporates some characteristics of mechanism. Whereas Descartes believed that the total quantity of motion in the universe was constant, Leibniz asserted the total amount of physical energy in the universe to be constant. Even God could not change this, and all motions of bodies were thus preestablished harmoniously by God. Leibniz also characterized the universe as a perfect clock that, once started, needs no adjusting. That Leibniz held this mechanical view of the universe is clear from his criticism of Newton's affirmation that God intermittently changes the courses of planets and comets, and thereby compensates for celestial irregularities.

Immanuel Kant was an 18th-century physicist turned philosopher. In his early writings, he was influenced not only by Leibniz's RATIONALISM, but also by the latter's proposal that force, as found in the monad, was more fundamental than space and time. Kant was influenced also by Ruggiero Boscovich, who, like Leibniz, rejected atoms and made points of force his fundamental cosmological entities. In his early work Kant had sought a compromise between the position of Leibniz, which made force more fundamental, and that of Descartes, which made extension and space more fundamental. Nevertheless, in his writings before the *Critique of Pure Reason,* the view of Leibniz seems to have predominated; for Kant, force, which may be both attractive and repulsive, leads to the notion of space by way of the notions of connection and order. Then, in his post-critical period, under the influence of David HUME, with his EMPIRICISM and skepticism, he denied the ability of the mind to know natures in the physical world. In this period, Kant reversed himself and attempted to work from a priori forms of space and time to the notions of order, connection, and force.

Undoubtedly, the views of Boscovich, Kant, and Leibniz conflict with the strict mechanism of Descartes. Yet they do not conflict with some tenets of mechanism such as those which would exclude final causality. Again, Kant never confused the study of pure mathematics with the study of the physical world. Even in his critical period, he saw mathematics as a set of deductions from clear definitions. Since philosophy of nature, as exemplified in Newtonian physics, derives its basic concepts from sense experience and these concepts are somewhat indistinct, definitions come at the end of the reasoning process in the philosophy of nature. For Kant, philosophy as a whole should follow the same procedure as physics.

Decline of Mechanism. Despite the sophisticated analyses of Leibniz, Boscovich, and Kant, atomistic versions of mechanism did not die in the 18th century. Several new attempts were made to explain gravitation atomistically. A vortex theory involving small particles was proposed by J. Bernoulli; according to this, bodies were pushed to earth by tiny pellets of a mysterious nature, in turn driven down by whirling motions in the heavens. It should be pointed out, however, that in the late 18th and early 19th centuries strong antimechanistic currents already existed in the form of philosophical ROMANTICISM and IDEALISM.

Within physics itself the central position of mechanics in physics was concurrently being challenged. New work in heat, light, electricity, and magnetism, as well as in the foundations of mathematics, challenged the ideas of strict mechanism. Hermann von Helmholtz maintained that the sum total of all forms of energy remains constant. This was in accord with mechanism in some ways, for it posited a closed nonevolutionary universe. Nevertheless, heat, light, and electrical energy now enjoyed equal status with mechanical energy. The second law of thermodynamics, formulated by Carnot and Kelvin, again departs from mechanism. In relating this law to mechanism it should be noted that it involves no presuppositions regarding the existence of atoms or of the void, and utilizes the concept of ''unavailable energy,'' which itself suggests a return to the occult qualities of the scholastics.

Field Concepts. In the areas of light and electricity, Young's diffraction experiments favored the wave theory of light over the more mechanistic corpuscular theory. This trend continued with the work of Michael Faraday. It culminated in the contribution of James Clerk Maxwell, who synthesized optical, electrical, and magnetic phenomena in his famous field theory, a theory that posited an ether and avoided the notions of atom and void. This theory also postulated the mysterious ability of bodies to influence each other when not in direct physical contact and when not connected by any obvious physical medium.

Additional difficulties for mechanistic philosophy developed from new studies on the foundations of mathematics. The work of Lobachevskiĭ, Riemann, and others introduced the concepts of non-Euclidean or curved geometries, and thereby questioned the objectivity of Euclidean straight-line geometry. This, in turn, affected the acceptance of Newtonian mechanics, since the law of inertia affirmed that the motion of a body tended to be in a straight line, just as the law of gravity affirmed that two bodies tend to approach each other in straight lines.

Positivism and Conventionalism. Scientists and philosophers toward the beginning of the 20th century undertook to draw philosophical implications from these new developments in science. Their thought led to a gradual acceptance of what is called positivist philosophy. Auguste COMTE, who earlier had introduced POSITIVISM, affirmed that our minds can only grasp phenomena or positive data. His basic idea was developed by three leading scientific minds, Ernst Mach, Pierre Duhem, and Henri Poincaré, all of whom reacted against classical mechanism. Mach criticized Newtonian mechanics on the grounds that its definitions of concepts such as force, mass, and acceleration were in fact circular, and that its laws were not objective representations of the physical world. Duhem and Poincaré thought along similar lines, although they concentrated more on the analysis of scientific methodology.

Relativity and Quantum Theory. The failure of the Michelson-Morley experiment (1887) to detect the notion of light relative to an ether or absolute space led Albert EINSTEIN to propose the thesis that the Newtonian concepts of absolute space, absolute rest, and absolute motion were meaningless in physics. In conformity with this view, in the theory of special relativity formulated in 1905, he postulated that the measured velocity of light would be constant and that the laws of physics would be the same in all systems of coordinates moving at constant velocity with respect to each other. Applying this to the laws of conservation of momentum and conservation of energy for collision problems, he deduced that the mass of a body varies with its velocity and that matter can be converted into energy. These notions have served to undermine the conception of matter in Newtonian mechanics and in philosophical mechanism. Again, while the notion of inherent finality or purpose in nature does not appear in the theory of special relativity, the concept of space-time geodesic associated with general relativity seems compatible with this type of teleology.

A second major reason for the downfall of strict mechanistic physics in the 20th century is found in quantum theory. Significant contributions to this microcosmic theory were made by Planck, Bohr, De Broglie, and Heisenberg in the first quarter of the century. Quantum theory, like relativity theory, discarded the idea of the void. De Broglie's work blurred the distinction between energy waves and corpuscles, and rejected the notion that subatomic particles have definite boundaries like billiard balls. Heisenberg's uncertainty principle, formulated in 1927, left room for chance and contingency in nature, as opposed to the determinism associated with the mechanism of Pierre Simon de Laplace. Again, there are intimations in recent theories that a whole atom is somehow more than the mechanical summation of its parts. Yet quantum theory seems to take no explicit account of purpose or finality in the processes of nature.

Out of relativity and quantum theory came a variation of positivism called OPERATIONALISM, which stresses that meaningful physical concepts can be derived only from measured activities of bodies. This fosters skepticism regarding the ability of the mind to reach the natures of things, and to this degree resembles the thought of Hobbes. Other streams of early 20th-century philosophy broke with mechanism in varying degrees— WHITEHEAD, BERGSON, the pragmatists, and the existentialists all stressed different points of departure (*see* EXISTENTIALISM).

Mechanism and Thomism. The most fundamental difference between mechanism and THOMISM is the former's denial of, and the latter's affirmation of, the existence of intrinsic purposes or goals for motions occurring in nature. Thomists and other scholastics assert the presence of finality in nature and use the manifestation of NATURAL LAW at the inorganic level as a foundation for its broader extension to the realms of organic and of human activity (*see* FINAL CAUSALITY). A mechanist philosophy does not encourage this type of reasoning.

Another basic difference is the attitude toward quantity and the notion of absolute space. Scholastic philosophers, following Aristotle, maintain that quantity is an accident of a physical body, and not its essence, as would be maintained by Cartesians. Therefore, while admitting the importance of mathematics and mathematical physics, they do not concede to these sciences complete autonomy from natural philosophy when using quantitative techniques to investigate the nature of the physical world (*see* PHILOSOPHY AND SCIENCE). Again, scholastics, such as Aquinas, deny the existence of a void or of absolute space, like that espoused by Newton, and in place of these notions apply the Aristotelian notion of natural PLACE to the analysis of local MOTION.

Scholastics likewise reject the atomistic concepts usually associated with mechanism. While affirming the existence of elementary particles, they do not regard these as indivisible subsisting entities, and maintain that a natural body is more than a mechanical aggregate of its parts. Thus they explain the organization and functioning of all bodies, including the inorganic, through an internal principle called the substantial form (*see* MATTER AND FORM; HYLOSYSTEMISM).

Finally, with regard to the strict determinism affirmed by classical mechanists, scholastic philosophers allow for a basic indeterminism in nature which permits the existence not only of CHANCE, but also of FREE WILL and miracles. Notwithstanding this, they still assert confidence in the ability of the human mind to attain truth and certitude through the habit of SCIENCE, and thus reject skepticism in favor of epistemological REALISM.

Bibliography: E. J. DYKSTERHUIS, *The Mechanization of The World Picture,* tr. C. DIKSHOOM (Oxford 1961). E. A. BURTT, *The Metaphysical Foundations of Modern Physical Science* (New York 1925). S. SAMBURSKY, *The Physical World of the Greeks,* tr. M. DAGUT (New York 1962). M. CLAGETT, *The Science of Mechanics in the Middle Ages* (Madison 1959). J. A. WEISHEIPL, *The Development of Physical Theory in the Middle Ages* (New York 1960). A. C. CROMBIE, *Medieval and Early Modern Science,* 2 v. (2d ed. rev. Garden City, N.Y. 1959). M. JAMMER, *Concepts of Force* (New York 1958). W. HEISENBERG, *Physics and Philosophy* (New York 1958). L. DE BROGLIE, *The Revolution in Physics* (New York 1953).

[J. F. O'BRIEN]

MECHANISM, BIOLOGICAL

Any application of the general principles of MECHANISM to the explanation of life and vital processes. The several varieties of biological mechanism that have appeared in the history of thought are first explained in this article and then subjected to philosophical analysis and critique.

Early Forms. Histories of biological mechanism commonly begin with the examination of Cartesian DUALISM. Both Aristotle and THOMAS AQUINAS, however, found themselves in opposition to a doctrine, similar to mechanism, elaborated as early as the 5th century B.C. This doctrine figures importantly in the objections raised by Simmias in Plato's *Phaedo*. Simmias, who had studied under a Pythagorean, Philolaus, argues in the *Phaedo* that life must be understood as flowing from a particular harmony of the body. This position may have arisen from a coalescence of the Pythagorean enthusiasm for explaining the whole of reality in terms of numerical proportions and of the Empedoclean thesis current in the Sicilian school of medicine, viz, that health consists in a balance of four basic qualities hot, cold, dry, and wet.

Aristotle and St. Thomas object to this position as if it were arguable on at least two levels, although they do not themselves explicitly distinguish these levels in their writings. The first sort of objection addresses itself to the inadequacy, for the explanation of vital phenomena, of certain special features of contemporary physics: vitality cannot be explained in terms of warmth, for fire tends to increase without limit; the explanation of nutrition and growth in terms of the tendency of the elements to move to their natural places ignores the unique function of roots and leaves in plants; the explanation of vital organization in terms of the ratio and spatial arrangement of physical elements accounts for special tissues or organs, but not for the organism as a whole.

The second sort of objection is more general, seeming to reject, principle, the possibility of any explanation of vital activity in terms of the concept of physical organization, regardless of the complication this concept might undergo with the advance of physical theories. For example, it is argued that the ''harmony,'' or organization, of a living body cannot explain its spontaneous initiation of its own movements (''nor can harmony move a body. . .'') and that any explanation in terms of structural or physically organizing principles ignores the fact that structure is inherently variable or modifiable without limit, whereas a thing is either living or it is not: ''Substance has no contrary, and does not admit a variation of degree'' (*C. gent.* 2.63– 64; cf. *In 1 anima.* 9, *In 2 anima.* 8; Aristotle, *anim.* 407b 30–409a 30, 416a 1–15).

Modern Types. The controversy between Aristotle and St. Thomas, on the one hand, and the mechanists of their day, on the other hand, may be clarified in terms of a modern distinction of mechanism into three types, characterized roughly by the adjectives physical, biological, and philosophical.

Physical Mechanism. The first type holds that biological laws may be explained by deriving them from a postulate set including the basic laws of physics and chemistry and a small number of additional, compatible postulates. This definition is both flexible and vague: obviously the laws regarded as basic in physics and chemistry do not remain the same in succeeding epochs. In the history of thought, science has moved from Empedocles's earth, air, fire, and water, to the solid, uncutable, and elastic atom of the 17th and 18th centuries, to the present, nearly organic model of the atom as an ordered array of electrically charged particles, capable of varying degrees of stability or reactivity. The words ''small'' and ''compatible'' appearing in the definition of this type of mechanism are left deliberately vague to reflect the informal character of the conditions of scientific advance. The standards of economy and consistency proper to a scientific theory are dependent on such a great variety of cultural and scientific factors that is inappropriate to attempt to specify them in a formal way.

A current variant of this type of mechanism, proposed by J. J. C. Smart (1963), holds that the complication of physical and chemical laws in biological systems inevitably involves reference to the idiosyncratic history of evolution on earth, i.e., to organisms that have the properties they do, not for any generally statable theoretical reason, but because they happened to evolve at a particular time under particular circumstances. In this view, biology is a form of technology or engineering rather than a science proper; its concern with the application of the laws of physics and chemistry is comparable to that of the electrical engineer, who is not properly concerned with the discovery of universal laws of nature. The key assumption of Smart's mechanism, viz, that the complicating postulates enabling the application of the laws of physics and chemistry to biological phenomena are inevitably of limited, contingent significance, is too recent to have been subjected to thorough debate.

Biological Mechanism. A second type of mechanism VITALISM. It rejects the introduction, into theoretical biology, of factors that either (1) fail to increase the simplicity and scope (fertility) of biological theory, (2) fail to increase the precision and facility with which biological theory may be empirically confirmed, or (3) are conceivable only by ''anthropomorphic empathy,'' in terms of such concepts as will, desire, and urge.

This type of mechanism is compatible with the recognition, e.g., in genetics or physiology, of system laws that elude reduction to laws governing physical and chemical processes. It may admit the unpredictable course of evolutionary history and the irreducibility of the principal of natural selection. Mendel's laws and the principles of crossing-over are also seen as eluding derivation from the theoretical principles of physics and chemistry.

Biological mechanism seems to involve the positive requirement that biological phenomena lend themselves to explanation in terms that have the same logical form as those of physics and chemistry. Yet neither the concepts nor the basic laws of biology and physics are required to be identical or even similar, so long as biology and physics have a similar theoretical structure.

This type of mechanism might be said to have as its primary aim, the preservation and clarification of an autonomous scientific method of inquiry into biological phenomena. So understood, it is not necessarily incompatible with philosophies of nature that recognize the independent validity of nonphilosophical investigation of vital processes, or that speculate about the human or metaphysical significance of such scientific inquiry.

Philosophical Mechanism. Whereas biological mechanism is primarily methodological, and hopefully neutral in substantive philosophical debate, the third type of mechanism is thoroughly philosophical, both in its inception and in its ultimate claims. It is primarily associated with R. DESCARTES, who may have been innocent of its more exaggerated aspects, but whose trenchant dicta do not always establish this innocence beyond question.

Descarte's mechanism shares all the strengths and weaknesses of his metaphysical system as a whole. Its foundations are the methodic DOUBT and the intuition of the existence of the thinking self. Its consequences are formulated as an absolute and exhaustive account of the nature of all reality below the level of human consciousness: inorganic objects, plants, animals, and thc human body itself. Thus understood, the foundation of Cartesian mechanism are not tentative and subject to the pragmatic tests of scope and precision; they are indubitable, primitive truths: man cannot doubt his own act of thought in doubting, but he can doubt the existence of any physical object whatsoever, including his own body. This difference marks mind and body as distinct concepts; and in the Cartesian system, reinforced with proofs that God is omnipotent and benevolent, separate conceivability is the surest mark of separate existence. Mind and body are distinct substances, totally distinct types of reality, each with its own laws and essential characteristics.

Biological mechanism excludes evidence gathered by means of ''anthropomorphic empathy'' from biology because of the practical difficulty in getting general agreement as to the meaning and consequences of such evidence. Philosophical mechanism, on the other hand, insists on the same exclusion because of a prior philosophical decision to regard consciousness and life as irreducibly distinct realms of reality.

Descartes also appears to have been committed to an excessively rigid version of physical mechanism, insisting that all the laws of biology and animal behavior are explicable in terms of a physics whose single primitive term was extension and whose dominant explanatory model was simple, mechanical clock work. It is a simple fact of history that Harvey's revolutionary success in explaining the circulation of the blood in terms of a mechanical system of a pump and vessels or tubes fitted with valves was not duplicated in efforts to explain ''animal heat'' and embryological development in terms of the same sort of clockwork. The explanation of these latter phenomena waited for the development of biochemical theories employing a more complex explanatory apparatus than that suggested by such concepts as pump, friction, momentum, and so on.

It may be argued that Cartesian mechanism leads to such a parochial form of physical mechanism because of its insistence on the privileged, clear and distinct status of its basic concepts, which consequently are made to seem beyond the need of the gradual process of reform and modification characteristic of scientific concepts as understood in biological mechanism and in more open forms of physical mechanism.

Analysis and Critique. The inadequacy of Decartes's rigid physical mechanism seems to follow upon the self-reforming, progressive nature of scientific method. To reply to this sort of inadequacy by the construction of a similarly inflexible form of vitalism is to share the fallacious belief that scientific concepts must be so clear and distinct that they are unchangeable, closed to modification in terms of expanding contexts and altered relations among themselves. Hans Driesch seems to have made this sort of error in reacting to the limits and indequacies of simple preformationist theories in embryology, T. H. Morgan opened a new field of biological research in the related and extremely productive area of genetics. Morgan explicitly advocated biological mechanism.

The foregoing discussion should clarify the issues involved in the two-level criticism of mechanism made by Aristotle and St. Thomas. At the first level, in objecting to explanations of vital activity in terms of the natural movement of fire or of some harmonic balance of the tendencies of physical elements to move to their natural places, they point out the inevitable shortcomings of any rigid form of physical mechanism that assumes that inorganic theories of the moment are totally adequate for the explanation of vital processes.

At the second level, careful research on a variety of related topics is still necessary to determine their evaluation of the more recent forms of mechanism as used in biological theory. The weight of evidence concerning their positions on the irreducible variety of man's methods of approaching truth seems to exclude the possibility of their opposition to all mechanistic explanations. In fact, the flexibility and pragmatic fertility of such explanations count against any attempt to reject their scientific acceptability. The only appropriate criterion by which they can be judged is their actual success or failure in the organization and clarification of biological research. On the other hand, philosophical mechanism suggests that all knowledge of life below the level of human consciousness is to be gained through a single method and explained in terms of a single set of univocal concepts. This form of mechanism is invalidated by the observation that such terms as substantial unity, vitality, and even homeostasis exhibit an analogical variety of uses, and by the continued use of a variety of techniques—molecular, cellular, organic, ecological, and ethological—for the accumulation of biological data.

See Also: LIFE; SOUL; MATTER AND FORM.

Bibliography: L. VON BERTALANFFY, *Problems of Life* (New York 1960), distinguishes types of mechanisms in a fashion similar to that presented here. R. SCHUBERT-SOLDERN, *Mechanism and Vitalism*, tr. C. E. ROBIN (Notre Dame, Indiana 1962), primarily a review of German literature, on this topic. E. NAGEL, *The Structure of Science* (New York 1961). M. BECKNER; *The Biological Way of Thought* (New York 1959). J. J. C. SMART, *Philosophy and Scientific Realism* (London 1963). G. J. GOODFIELD, *The Growth of Scientific Physiology* (London 1960). J. LOEB, *The Mechanistic Conception of Life* (Chicago 1912). B. FARRINGTON, *Greek Science* (rev. Baltimore 1961). J. MARITAIN *Distinguish to Unite, or The Degrees of Knowledge*, tr. G. B. PHELAN (New York 1959). T. H. MORGAN, ''Relation of Physics to Biology,'' Vassar College *Physics in its Relations: A Symposium* (Poughkeepsie, New York 1927). P. WEISS, ''From Cell to Molecule,'' *The Molecular Control of Cellular Activity*, ed. J. M. ALLEN (New York 1962). J. H. WOODGER, ''Biology and Physics,'' *British Journal for the Philosophy of Science* 11 (1960) 89–100.

[A. E. MANIER]

MECHITAR

Armenian Catholic priest, founder of the MECHITARISTS; b. Sivas (Sebaste), Asia Minor, Feb. 7, 1676; d. San Lazzaro (Venice), Italy, April 27, 1749. Baptized Peter Manug, Mechitar was educated at the schismatic Armenian monastery of Garmir-Vanq (Red Monastery), where he later (1691) received the religious habit from Bishop Ananya and took the name Mechitar (Mehitar; ''consoler''). A chance encounter with a Catholic missionary and an Armenian noble at Erzurum, Asia Minor, provided him with keen insights into Western culture and Catholicism. On a voyage to Syria he went to Aleppo, where he met Antoine Beauvillers, SJ, who received him into the Catholic Church and urged him to visit Rome. A sudden malady prevented this, and he returned to Sivas in 1695. Ordained a priest at Surp-Niššan (Holy Cross) monastery (1696), he received the title vartapet (doctor) in 1699. The church of St. George in Constantinople became the center of his apostolate to unite the Armenian Church with Rome, and in 1701 he founded the Order of St. Anthony for pastoral, educational, and scientific endeavors.

Mechitar's preaching and promotion of union with Rome aroused the hostility of Patriarch Ephraim and his successor, Avedek, and resulted in Mechitar's departure from Constantinople for Modone (Morea), in the territory then belonging to Venice, where he built a monastery and church. Rome approved his congregation (1711), but substituted St. Benedict's Rule for that of St. Anthony. The Turkish occupation of Modone (1715) forced Mechitar's withdrawal to Venice, where he was given the use of the island of San Lazzaro.

A great monastery with church and library was completed in 1740, and a printing press was established. Mechitar published approximately 20 works, dealing mainly with theology and philosophy. Notable among his writings are his commentary on the Gospel of St. Matthew (1737); his Armenian grammar, dictionary, and catechism; and an Armenian edition of the Bible (1733).

Bibliography: *Oriente Cattolico* (Vatican City 1962) 614–616.

[E. EL-HAYEK]

MECHITARISTS

The Benedictine Armenian Antonines, known also as Mechitarists, are members of an Armenian Catholic monastic congregation that follows the Benedictine Rule. They were founded in 1701 at Constantinople by MECHITAR. Father Stephen Melkonen, who was elected superior general in 1750, revised the constitutions. This move, although approved by the Congregation for the Propagation of the Faith in 1762, was opposed by a segment of the congregation. The failure of a general chapter (1772) to restore peace occasioned a division into two groups, one centered in Venice, Italy; the other in Vienna, Austria. Both groups work for a renaissance of the Armenian people through education and preaching and have a similar form of government, ruled by an abbot general and his assistants.

Ordo Mechitaristarum Venetiarum. The Mechitarists of Venice (OMechVen), whose revised constitutions were approved in 1928, transferred to that city from the Near East in 1715 and have as their specific aim the union of dissident Armenians with the Catholic Church. The generosity of two wealthy Armenian merchants enabled the congregation to found Raphael College at Venice (1836) and Samuel Moorat College at Padua (1834), later moved to Paris. Here Abp. Denis Affre permitted, under certain conditions, the matriculation of some Armenian dissidents. Closed by the Franco–Prussian War, the college in Paris was united to that of Venice and later reestablished at Sèvres, near Paris (1929).

The Armenian Academy at San Lazzaro was established in Rome through the efforts of Stephen Kövér Akontz, later abbot (1800–24) and titular archbishop of Siunia. Abbot Placide Sukias Somal (1824–46) collected some 3,000 manuscripts, thus contributing toward making San Lazzaro a center of Armenian scholarship. During his superiorship the great dictionary of the Armenian language was published (1836), and the scientific and literary periodical *Pazmaveb* was begun (1843). The congregation has schools at Istanbul, Turkey (1810); Aleppo, Syria (1936); Alexandria, Egypt (1936); and Buenos Aires, Argentina (1956); and a minor seminary at Bikfaya, Lebanon (1948). In 1965 there were four religious houses and 54 members engaged in the direction of two colleges and four schools as well as in the publication of the periodicals *Pazmaveb* and *Endanik,* and other Armenian classical, historical, and ecclesiastical works, at the publishing house on the island of San Lazzaro (Venice).

Ordo Mechitaristarum Vindobonensis. The Mechitarists of Vienna (OMechVd), whose constitutions were approved in 1885, are engaged especially in pastoral work for Armenians. After separating from the Mechitarists of Venice in 1772, they went to Trieste, where, under the protection of Empress Maria Theresa, they established a separate congregation. During the reign of their first abbot, Adeodatus Babighian (1803–25), they were forced to seek refuge in Vienna (1809), where St. Clement HOFBAUER was of great assistance. The congregation prospered under succeeding abbots, especially under Abbot Aristakes Azarian (1826–55), and undertook pastoral activity among the Armenians of the Austro–Hungarian Empire. At the motherhouse in Vienna there are a school, a theological college, a museum of natural history, a library, and a printing establishment that publishes books in many languages and the Armenian periodical *Handés Amsorya.* In 1965 the congregation had 32 members, who staffed parishes in Budapest, Hungary; Cambridge, Mass.; and Los Angeles, Calif.; and colleges in Istanbul, Turkey (1811); Heliopolis (Cairo), Egypt (1935); and Beirut, Lebanon (1937).

Bibliography: M. HEIMBUCHER, *Die Orden und Kongregationen der katholischen Kirche* 2 v. (3d ed. Paderborn 1932–34) 1:241–246. M. VAN DEN OUDENRIJN, *Lexikon für Theologie und Kirche,* ed. J. HOFER and K. RAHNER, 10 v. (2d, new ed. Freiburg 1957–65) 7:223–224. R. JANIN, *Dictionnaire de théologie catholique,* ed. A. VACANT et al., 15 v. (Paris 1903–50; Tables générales 1951) 10.1:497–502.

[E. EL-HAYEK]

MECHTILD OF HACKEBORN, ST.

Cistercian nun and mystic; b. Castle of Helfta, near Eisleben, Saxony, *c.* 1240; d. Helfta monastery, Nov. 19, 1298 (1299?). When Mechtild was seven years old, her parents brought her to visit her sister, Gertrude of Hackeborn, a nun of the monastery at Rodarsdorf, and at her request her parents permitted Mechtild to enter the cloister school. There her sister carefully supervised her education. Mechtild (or Matilda) was amiable and charming, highly gifted in mind and body, and possessed an excellent voice. In 1258 Gertrude, abbess since 1251, transferred her monastery to Helfta, and soon it became a center of learning, culture, and profound spirituality. Mechtild followed her and was appointed choirmistress and directress of the new cloister school. She became the spiritual mother of St. GERTRUDE THE GREAT, who, as a child of five in 1261, was entrusted to Mechtild's care.

Throughout her life, Mechtild received extraordinary graces. In 1292 she began to confide the secrets of her interior life to Gertrude the Great and another nun, and for seven years, without Mechtild's knowledge, her revelations were committed to writing. When she discovered this, she was at first deeply disturbed, but at last permitted Gertrude to edit what is now known as the *Liber specialis gratiae.*

The book is constructed upon the ecclesiastical year; it is liturgical, Trinitarian, and Christocentric, warmly affective and joyful, giving evidence of Mechtild's sound theological education. She urges the use of all the senses in the praise of God and stresses devotion to the Heart of Christ. Largely through the efforts of the Friars Preachers, who were in close contact with the nuns of Helfta, her book was widely read, especially in Italy. It has been suggested that she or Mechtild of Magdeburg may be the Matelda in Dante's *Purgatorio.* Iconography usually shows her with a book and a dove, holding a burning heart or healing a blind nun.

Feast: May 31.

Bibliography: *Revelationes Gertrudianae ac Mechtildianae,* ed. Benedictines of Solesmes (Paris 1877) 2:1–432. *Select Revelations of St. Mechtild,* tr. a secular priest (London 1872). *The Love of the Sacred Heart Illustrated by St. Mechtilde* (London 1922), ed. anon. *Les Belles prières de Ste. Mechtilde et Ste. Gertrude,* tr. D. A. CASTEL (Bruges 1926). *Mechtild von Hakeborn, Das Buch vom strömenden Lob,* ed. H. U. VON BALTHASAR (Einsiedeln 1955). *Mechtild van Hakeborn, Het boek der bijzondere genade,* ed. M. COSTANZA (Bruges 1958). Studies. I. MÜLLER, *Leben und Offenbarungen der hl. Mechtild* (Regensburg 1880). W. STAMMLER and K. LANGOSCH, eds. *Die deutsche Literatur des Mittelalters: Verfasserlexikon* (Berlin–Leipzig 1933–55) 3:321–323. W. PREGER, *Geschichte der deutschen Mystik im Mittelalter,* 3 v. (rev. ed. Aalen 1962). M. J. FINNEGAN, *The Women of Helfta: Scholars and Mystics* (Athens, Georgia 1991). M. HUBRATH, *Schreiben und Erinnern: zur* *''memoria'' im Liber Specialis Gratiae Mechthilds von Hakeborn* (Paderborn 1996).

[M. F. LAUGHLIN]

MECHTILD OF MAGDEBURG

Beguine mystic; b. Saxony, *c.* 1209; d. Helfta, between 1282 and 1294. Mechtild was apparently of noble or well-born parents. According to her own testimony, her first mystical experience occurred when, at the age of 12, she was greeted by the Holy Spirit. Desiring to live wholly for God, she became a Beguine at Magdeburg in 1230, and under the direction of the Dominicans led a life of intense prayer and austerity for 40 years. The hostility aroused by her extraordinary spiritual experiences and by her severe criticism of the clergy forced her, in 1270, to leave Magdeburg. Ailing and partially blind, she sought refuge in the Cistercian convent at Helfta, where she was warmly received by SS. MECHTILD OF HACKEBORN and GERTRUDE THE GREAT. She remained there, in the congenial atmosphere of holiness, until her death. Although regarded as a saint by her contemporaries, she has not been canonized.

Mechtild's writings, begun in 1250 and completed sometime after 1270, were collected by her friends and widely distributed under the title of *Das fliessende Licht der Gottheit,* from the words supposedly spoken to Mechtild by Christ saying that she was to be a witness to the ''light of my divinity flowing into all hearts that live without guile'' (*vliessende licht miner gotheit in allu die herzen die da lebent ane valscheit*). The original Low German text is lost, but a South German translation and a Latin translation from *c.* 1290 are extant.

Das fliessende Licht consists of somewhat disconnected compositions of varying length. There are spiritual poems about mystical experiences, love songs, and allegories, visions, moral reflections, and solid admonitions. Mechtild often borrows the language and imagery of the Song of Songs and frequently uses dialogue in the manner of the *minnesingers.* Her writings show that she was acquainted with the works of Bernard of Clairvaux, William of Saint-Thierry, the Victorines, David of Augsburg, Hildegard of Bingen, and Gregory the Great. While *Das fliessende Licht* lacks theological content, it does contain sound mystical doctrine and shows Mechtild's profound understanding of the mystery of Christ's love and mercy. Her poetry, which is interspersed throughout the book, reveals talent of a remarkably high order. Unfortunately, her poetic imagination obviously colors much of her writing, especially her descriptions of hell. It has been suggested that Dante was influenced by her, and that she is the Matelda referred to in *Purgatorio,* Cantos 27 to 33.

Medals from the secret archives of the Vatican. (©Vittoriano Rastelli/CORBIS)

Bibliography: Texts. G. MOREL, ed., *Das fliessende Licht der Gottheit* (Regensburg 1869). *Revelationes Gertrudianae ac Mechtildianae,* ed. Benedictines of Solesmes (Paris 1878) 2: 435–. *The Revelations of M. of Magdeburg (1210–1297) or, The Flowing Light of the Godhead,* tr. L. MENZIES (New York 1953). *Das fliessende Licht der Gottheit* (Einsiedeln 1955), introd. M. SCHMIDT, with study by H. U. VON BALTHASAR. Critical ed. in prep. by H. NEUMANN. Studies. W. PREGER, *Dante's Matelda* (Munich 1873); *Geschichte der deutschen Mystik im Mittelalter,* 3 v. (rev. ed. Aalen 1962). E. G. GARDNER, *Dante and the Mystics* (London 1913). J. ANCELET-HUSTACHE, *Mechtilde de Magdebourg: Étude de psychologie religieuse* (Paris 1926). W. STAMMLER and K. LANGOSCH, eds. *Die deutsche Literatur des Mittelalters: Verfasserlexikon* (Berlin-Leipzig 1933–55) 3:323–326. M. S. C. MOLENAAR, *Die Frau vom anderen Ufer* (Heidelberg 1946). M. SCHMIDT, *Lexikon für Theologie und Kirche,* ed. J. HOFER and K. RAHNER (Freiberg 1957–65) 7:225.

[M. F. LAUGHLIN]

MEDALS, RELIGIOUS

A religious medal is a piece of some solid substance generally but not necessarily metallic, in the form of a coin, adorned with some religious inscription or image, usually fitted to be worn suspended from the neck. Such devotional medals have been in use from the early Christian ages. St. Zeno (4th century) cited the wearing of medals as an example of the Church's practice of sanctifying pagan usages. He also referred to a custom of giving newly baptized Christians a medal to commemorate their baptism. A 5th-century life of St. Geneviève tells of St. Germain bestowing on her a medal marked with the sign of the cross, which was to be a memorial to her of her vow of virginity.

One medal bearing images of SS. Peter and Paul facing one another has been ascribed to the 2d century. Another, portraying a martyr, presumed to be St. Lawrence, on a grill, is assigned to the late 4th century. There are many others bearing religious images and dating from the 4th through the 8th century. Often coins of the late empire were stamped with the chrismon or with a figure of Christ, and it is thought that such pieces of money were converted to pious use as medals. The practice was widespread and was familiar at Rome and Constantinople, as well as in Africa.

There are no certain examples of religious medals from the early Middle Ages, but in the 12th century a custom grew of making medals, ''pilgrim signs,'' cast in lead to commemorate well-known shrines. This custom was known in Rome; in 1200 Innocent III granted the canons of St. Peter's a monopoly of casting pilgrim signs for distribution to those visiting the basilica. Also, there are references to pilgrim signs for Canterbury, England, Santiago de Compostela, Spain, the Holy Land, and Assisi, Italy.

A type of medal called a jetton appeared in the 13th century and was used until modern times. These medals bore either initials or a device by which the owner could be identified. They were used as a sort of ticket or calling card, and sometimes as money. Besides the mark of identification, the jetton usually bore a pious motto, such as: ''Love God and Praise Him''; ''O Lord, Our God''; or ''Hail Mary, Mother of God.'' The commonest motto used on the jetton was IHS, a way of writing the name Jesus. This jetton seems to have been connected with the devotion to the HOLY NAME.

Medals commemorating religious events, e.g., the preaching of Savonarola and papal jubilees, began to be popular in the 15th century. Religious medals as they are known today began to appear in the 16th century, and the blessing of medals came into use at this time. Pius V is credited with inaugurating the custom. In 1566 he blessed and indulgenced a medal bearing the image of Jesus and Mary. The usage spread rapidly. By the 17th century, every city in Europe had its own medals featuring Christ or His Mother, or a favorite saint or devotion. Surveys show types of medals beyond number. The events of Our Lord's life, the apparitions of Our Lady, the saints and blessed were commemorated in medals of some kind.

Religious medals used by Catholics are not to be regarded as magic charms and amulets. Such superstition has been severely condemned by the Church (H. DENZINGER, *Enchiridion symbolorum* 477, 581, 601, 1823). Catholic teaching attributes no intrinsic power to medals, blessed or not. The medal is a symbol that recalls to the believer his faith and his religious duties. Such a reminder moves him to acts of reverence to God or to Christ, immediately or mediately through the sacred person or event represented by the medal. It is not from the medal that the believer expects help or on which he puts reliance. The medal occasions acts of faith and hope in God whom it represents either directly or indirectly.

Bibliography: H. THURSTON, *The Catholic Encyclopedia*, ed. C. G. HERBERMANN et al., v. 10 (New York 1907–14) 111–115. H. LECLERCQ, *Dictionnaire d'archéologie chrétienne et de liturgie* (Paris 1907–53) 1.2:1822–33. S. DE ANGELIS, *De indulgentiis* (Vatican City 1950) 224, 226, 236, 266.

[P. F. MULHERN]

MÉDARD OF NOYON, ST.

Bishop; b. Salency (Picardy), France, early sixth century; d. *c.* 557. The son of a Frankish nobleman and a Gallo-Roman mother, Médard studied in Salency and Tournai. He succeeded Bp. Alomer of Vermand (*c.* 530). According to a highly suspect account by Bp. Radbod of Noyon (*c.* 1180), Médard moved the episcopal see to NOYON because of barbarian attacks and at the same time took over the Diocese of Tournai; the two sees were united until 1114. Médard accepted the monastic vows of Queen RADEGUNDA; his career was noteworthy for active missionary work. The Feast of the Roses, on which each year the most exemplary maiden of Salency received a crown of roses in church, is considered to be his invention. His cult was widespread in the Middle Ages and was rewarded with many miracles, especially in Soissons, where his relics are preserved. He is a patron of agriculture and horticulture, and is invoked in cases of toothache and migraine. Even today his feast is the occasion of prayers for good weather. He is represented with mouth open, laughing (*le ris de St. Médard*), teeth showing; a heart recalls his charitable activities.

Feast: June 8, Sept. 9, Oct. 1.

Bibliography: *Acta Sanctorum* June 2 (1863) 72–104. *Monumenta Germaniae Historica: Auctores antiquissimi* (Berlin 1826–) 4.1:44–48; 4.2:67–73, *Vita. Patrologia Latina,* ed. J. P. MIGNE, 271 v., indexes 4 v. (Paris 1878–90) 150:1499–1518. *Bibliotheca hagiographica latina antiquae et mediae aetatis,* 2 v. (Brussels 1898–1901; suppl. 1911) 5863–74. L. MAÎTRE, ''Le Culte de S. Médard,'' *Annales de Bretagne,* 15 (1900) 292–298. E. MÜLLER, ''Die Nithard-Interpolation und die Urkunden- und Legendenfälschungen im St. Medardus-Kloster bei Soissons,'' *Neues Archiv der Gesellschaft für ältere deutsche Geschichtskunde* 34 (1908) 681–722. *The Book of Saints* (4th rev. ed. New York 1947) 417. A. BAUDOUX, *Les Saints patrons de Noyon* (Compiègne 1951) 3. L. RÉAU, *Iconographie de l'art chrétien,* 6 v. (Paris 1955–59) 6:944–945. D. ATTWATER, *A Dictionary of Saints* (new ed. New

York 1958) 187. J. LECOMTE, *S. Médard, son tombeau, ses reliques* (Chauny 1959). A. BUTLER, *The Lives of the Saints,* rev. ed. H. THURSTON and D. ATTWATER, 4 v. (New York 1956) 2:502–503.

[M. CSÁKY]

MEDEIROS, HUMBERTO SOUSA

Fourth archbishop and seventh bishop of Boston, cardinal; b. Arrifes, Sao Miguel, in the Azores (Portugal), Oct. 6, 1915; d. Boston, Sept. 17, 1983. The eldest of four children, he attended elementary school in Arrifes and later worked in a wholesale store and law office until April 1931 when he emigrated to the U.S., joining his family in Fall River, Massachusetts.

Unable to speak English when he arrived, this future linguist worked as a sweeper and ''bob-watcher'' in the city's mills to help support the family in the depths of the Depression. In 1937 he was an honor graduate of Durfee High School, completing the course in only three years. Medeiros studied for the priesthood at The Catholic University of America, Washington, D.C., earning an M.A. (1942) and S.T.L. (1946) and was ordained there for the Fall River diocese on June 15, 1946.

Medeiros was assigned to various parishes until 1949, when he was asked to pursue doctoral studies in Washington and Rome. He was awarded an S.T.D. in 1951 from Rome's Gregorian University. From 1951 to 1966 he served as assistant chancellor, vice chancellor, and chancellor under the Most Rev. James L. Connolly, Bishop of Fall River. At the same time he was involved in parish work, especially among the city's growing Portuguese community, accepting the pastorate of St. Michael Parish in 1960. He was named a domestic prelate in 1958.

On April 14, 1966, Pope Paul VI named Msgr. Medeiros the second bishop of Brownsville, Texas. Ordained to the episcopacy on June 9, 1966, he soon earned a reputation for being close to his people, especially his large Mexican-American flock. He championed education, human and civil rights, and showed a particular pastoral care for migrant workers as they traveled in search of crops to be picked. While serving in Brownsville, *Critic* magazine named Medeiros one of the 12 leading U.S. bishops who held the ''most promise for the future of the Church in the U.S.''

When Pope Paul VI publicly accepted the resignation of Cardinal CUSHING in September 1970, he simultaneously announced that his successor as archbishop of the nation's second largest See would be the bishop of Brownsville. Within a month of Medeiros' installation on Oct. 7, 1970, in the Cathedral of the Holy Cross, the beloved Cardinal Cushing had died.

Archbishop. Both in temperament and style, he differed from his more flamboyant predecessor. But Medeiros soon earned respect and affection for his gentlemanly courtesy, even disposition, and obvious holiness. Inheriting an archdiocesan debt of approximately 42 million dollars, as well as the arduous task of implementing the directives which followed the Second Vatican Council, he restructured the archdiocese into three, and later four, regions each presided over by an auxiliary bishop. In turn, each region was subdivided into four smaller vicarates so as to better serve the archdiocese's two million people.

In August 1971, Medeiros issued a timely pastoral letter which gained international attention. In ''Man's Cities and God's Poor,'' his commitment to education, housing, racial and ethnic equality, as well as to alleviating the plight of the poor, was clearly articulated as his future pastoral agenda. Racial tensions and the subsequent solution of bussing to achieve integration in Boston's public schools placed an enormous strain on the Catholic community as well as its archbishop. He preached time and again on the sin of racism but would neither bless nor publicly oppose the specifics of the court-ordered bussing.

Cardinal. On Feb. 2, 1973, Pope Paul VI named Medeiros to the College of Cardinals, an honor which he maintained was more a compliment to the faithful of the archdiocese than to him personally. He received the ''red hat'' on March 5, 1973.

After the death of Pope Paul VI in August 1978, Medeiros participated in the elections of Pope John Paul I, ''The September Pope,'' and the first non-Italian pontiff in centuries, Pope John Paul II on Oct. 16, 1978. This same Holy Father, on his first pastoral visit to the Church in the U.S., visited Boston for two days, spending the night of Oct. 1, 1979, in the Cardinal's Brighton residence after having captured the hearts of millions during a spectacular Mass on Boston Common.

Medeiros' nearly 13 years as archbishop were marked by issues of unrest: racial tension, the legalization of abortion, human and civil rights, the decline in vocations, the consequent closing of parochial schools, as well as the elimination of a huge archdiocesan debt. He bore these difficulties with an equanimity and natural grace. Ever mindful of his humble origins, Medeiros embraced an attractive simplicity of style, a directness in speech, and a compassion for those whom society overlooked or discarded.

In the summer of 1983, it was obvious that Medeiros' health was declining. He underwent open-heart surgery at St. Elizabeth's Hospital, with apparent success. Unexpectedly, he died the next morning, Sept. 17, 1983. His death was followed by an immediate outpouring of grief and tribute, unprecedented for an archbishop of Boston. His obvious holiness, gentlemanly bearing, and unassuming presence made a deeper impression on the greater Boston community than had been evidenced during his years as archbishop. Only in death was his pastoral leadership adequately recognized and properly acknowledged.

Bibliography: ''Medieros, Humberto Sousa,'' Archdiocesan Archives of Boston.

[P. V. CONLEY]

MEDELLÍN DOCUMENTS

The Medellín Documents are the promulgated official results of Consejo Episcopal Latino-Americano (CELAM), the general assembly of bishops of all Latin America convened in Medellín, Colombia, in Aug.–Sept. 1968. The assembly was only the second such general episcopal conference ever held on the soil of Latin America, and the first since Vatican Council II. Often compared with Vatican Council II, Medellín in its impact was similarly crucial in shaping the modern discussions and contemporary agenda of the Latin American Church. The conference centered from the outset on the themes of revolution and class conflict. The working document for the CELAM meeting had been circulated to the bishops and made public two months before the assembly convened. This working draft is of considerable importance in itself and caused a furor that determined which issues the bishops must face to retain any credibility with the young, the militants, and the most vocal clergy. The working draft is a pale reflection of the kinds of radical agenda communicated to the preparatory committee by groups of Latin American priests and laity. The working document had been forwarded to Rome for a critique, and Rome had objected to its excessive concern with secular issues, but the document was circulated without incorporating Rome's objections. Pope Paul VI had already determined to attend the opening session of the conference in conjunction with his attendance at the Eucharistic Congress then being held in Bogotá. On three occasions the pope tried to dissuade the bishops from encouraging the militants who were interpreting the papal teaching set forth in *Populorum progressio* as condoning the resort to violence in resisting injustice. The pope's efforts were not completely successful.

The final documents of the conference incorporated the substance of the working draft in its descriptions of the tragic condition of the social order in most of Latin America; were unsparing in the condemnations of the imperialist powers and the violence of capitalism; agreed with papal emphases that the Church's main effort should be to appeal to the consciences of the ruling elites and that resort to violent resistance usually brings more suffering to the poor and may lead to newer forms of oppression. However, especially in the section on peace, the conference condemned the use of force by the ruling classes to repress opposition, characterized the current state of Latin America as a state of oppression and established violence, and seconded the teaching of *POPULORUM PROGRESSIO* that insurrection is legitimate in the face of evident and prolonged tyranny that attacks fundamental human rights and dangerously injures the common good. Various documents, including the report on pastoral planning for the different groups, cite favorably the social consciousness of revolutionary elites, in contrast to the insensitivity of traditionalist Catholics. The document on poverty calls for a new life-style for clergy and a new Church that will continue the painful process of turning from a position of support for the privileged minority to one of identity with the impoverished majority.

Bibliography: *The Church in the Present-Day Transformation of Latin America in the Light of the Council II Conclusions* (English tr. of the Medellín Documents, USCC Publ. Office, Washington, D.C. 1968). *Between Honesty and Hope*, tr. J. DRURY, Maryknoll Documentation Series (Maryknoll, N.Y. 1970) 171–277. A. GHEERBRANT, *The Rebel Church in Latin America* (London 1974). E. MUTCHLER, *The Church as a Political Factor in Latin America* (New York 1971), esp. 98–130.

[E. J. DILLON]

MEDES

One of the Iranian peoples who overran the plateau and settled in the area known to ancient sources as Media, corresponding to the modern area of Tehran, Hamadan, Isfahan, and southern Azerbaijan. The Medes are first mentioned as Matāi in the Assyrian inscriptions that recount the campaigns of Shalmaneser III in 836–835 B.C., although earlier notices record Iranian names from the area. Another term found in later Assyrian records is Umman-Manda, which sometimes includes the Medes as well as other peoples, but it may be a generic term for nomads or barbarians. The Assyrians made many expeditions to the land of the ''mighty Medes,'' primarily in search of horses for their cavalry. The Medes were famous for their horses, but there is mention also of castles or fortified towns of the Medes in Assyrian inscriptions.

It is impossible to reconstruct a history of the Medes before they captured NINEVEH, the Assyrian capital, in 612 B.C.; but one may assume that the Median tribes became united in a confederacy under a chief called Dayukku or Deioces in the second half of the 8th century B.C.

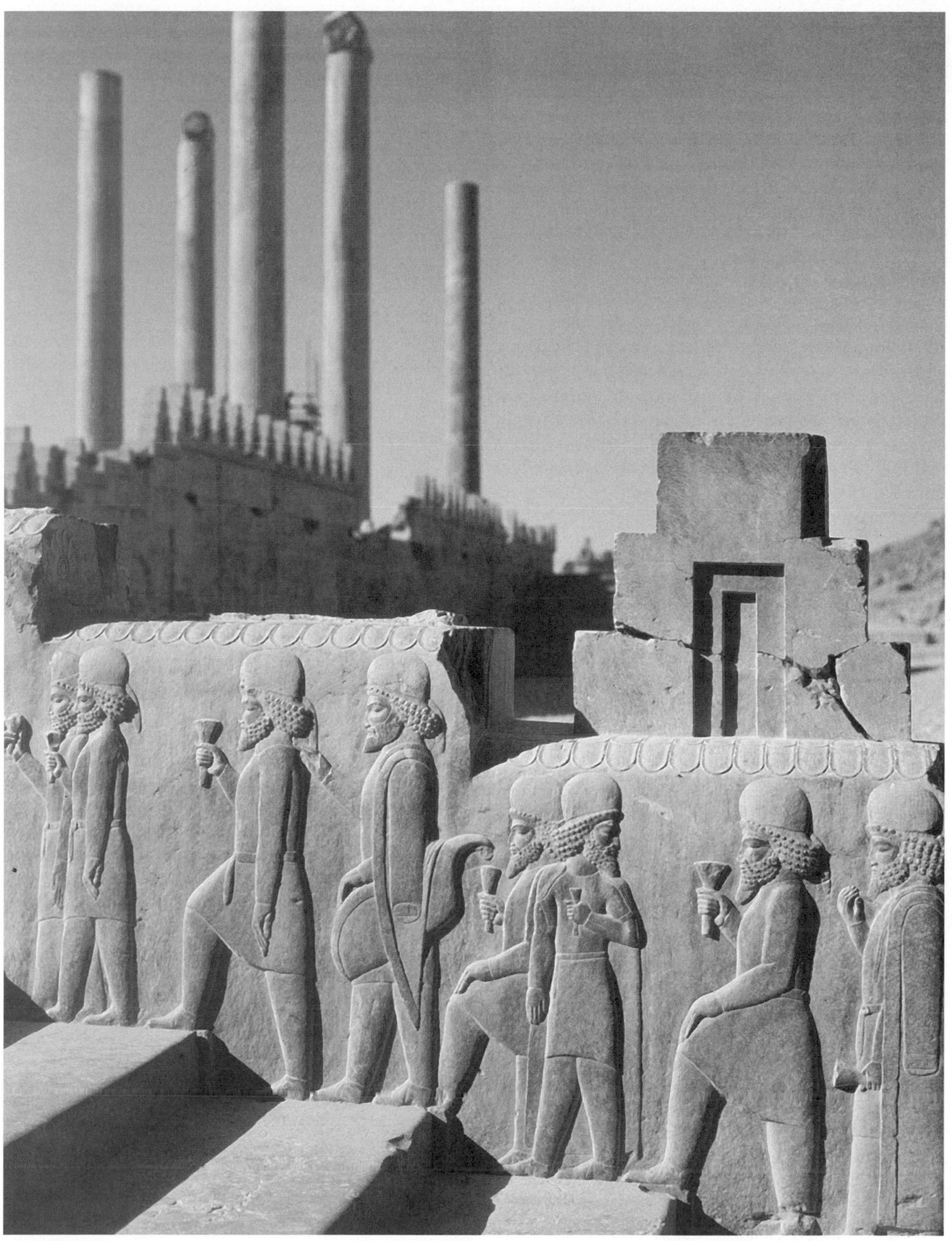

Tripylon stairway with Median dignitaries against the Apadana, Persepolis, Iran. (©Gianni Dagli Orti/CORBIS)

The center of his rule was probably the modern area of Hamadan, ancient Ecbatana. Herodotus (1.101) says the Medes were composed of six tribes, several of them probably non-Iranian in origin. In about 700 B.C. the Median state was disrupted by an invasion of Cimmerians from the north. These were followed by Scythians, who seem to have ruled over Media from *c.* 652 to 625 B.C. Another attempt to unite the Medes during the agitated 7th century by a chief Khshathrita (Akkadian Kashtaritu, Greek Phraortes) is reported in Assyrian annals, and this attempt bore fruit when his son Uvakhshtra or Cyaxares defeated the Scythians.

Cyaxares was the real founder of the empire of the Medes, and under him the Persians to the south and other Iranian tribes to the east were included in the empire. Herodotus (1.103) says he reorganized the army, and he probably reconstructed the state also. Cyaxares led the Median army against Assyria, and in 614 the city of ASSUR (Asshur) was captured. Then a pact was made with the new Babylonian King Nabopolasser (626–605), and the allies captured and destroyed Ninive in 612.

After the fall of Assyria, Cyaxares extended his kingdom into Anatolia. War with the Lydians ended in 585, after the battle of the ''eclipse of the sun,'' and the Halys River (modern Kizil Irmak) became the boundary between the Lydian and Median kingdoms.

The loose far-flung empire may have been organized into satrapies, but very little is known about the Medes, not only because of lack of sources, but also because of the absence of archeological excavations in Median territory. It is not known what writing the Medes employed in their empire, but Aramaic and Akkadian probably were two means of written communication. The religion of the Medes and the role of the Magoi or MAGI, one of the Median tribes, according to Herodotus, are both unclear.

The Median empire was overthrown by CYRUS, king of Persia, whose rise is told in several Greek sources as well as in the Akkadian ''Nabonidus Chronicle.'' The last ruler of Media, Astyages (Ishtumegu in Akkadian) *c.* 585–549 B.C., marched against his revolting vassal Cyrus in 549, but his army apparently revolted and gave Cyrus victory. The latter captured Ecbatana and carried off much booty. Cyrus founded the empire of the Achaemenids on the basis of the Median state. An unsuccessful revolt of the Medes at the beginning of the reign of DARIUS I is mentioned in his Behistun Inscription. The Medes continued to play an important role in the new empire, sometimes described as a dual monarchy of the Medes and the Persians. Although the name Media is found later in history, the people are not significant as a distinct entity. Some modern Kurds claim descent from the ancient Medes and begin a ''Kurdish era'' from the fall of Ninive.

See Also: PERSIA.

Bibliography: R. N. FRYE, *The Heritage of Persia* (London 1963) 69–81. Herodotus 1:95–130. I. M. DYAKONOV, *Istoriya Midii* (Moscow 1956). *Encyclopedic Dictionary of the Bible*, tr. and adap. by L. HARTMAN (New York 1963) 1492–94.

[R. N. FRYE]

MEDIATOR DEI

Encyclical letter on the sacred liturgy issued by Pius XII on Nov. 20, 1947. The immediate occasion of the writing of this significant document was probably the disturbed conditions in the Church in Germany during and immediately after World War II, but the real causes must be sought further back.

Spirit. Seen in its proper perspective, *Mediator Dei* is the crowning of the modern LITURGICAL MOVEMENT that began in the early years of the 20th century; by it the Holy See assumed the direction of the most significant movement in the Church in modern times and laid down the principles that must govern all future development. It was the first detailed official statement on the theology of the liturgy, and to be fully appreciated it must be seen in relation to the other great doctrinal encyclical of the same pontiff, *Mystici Corporis,* on the Mystical Body. Pius XII, having considered the nature of the Church, took the next natural step and considered the chief activity of the Church, the sacred liturgy. Moreover, *Mediator Dei* must be viewed in relation to all subsequent pronouncements of the Holy See on the nature and purpose of the liturgy, because, while it was the first official statement on the subject, it was by its nature only a beginning; it laid down principles but did not work out all their conclusions. In many ways it was a point of departure rather than a final goal.

Purpose. *Mediator Dei* cannot be adequately understood if it is regarded as a mere protest against the excesses of some promoters of the liturgical movement. Although it does condemn errors and aberrations that were attributed to some extremists, the letter gives condemnation a relatively small place. The document is a positive statement of the doctrine that lies at the basis of the liturgical celebration, and a careful study of the nature of the liturgy, of the principles that must animate the celebration of the liturgy, and of the results that this celebration will have upon the lives of those who participate in it.

It is not always noticed that the encyclical condemns indifference to the liturgy and sluggishness in living the liturgical life no less than it rebukes the immoderate and the extreme. Its whole aim is to impress upon all the necessity that Christians should live the liturgical life and be nourished and refreshed by the supernatural inspiration the liturgy provides.

Content. Given the extraordinary importance of this document, an outline of its contents may be of some help to the reader.

Introduction (1–12). Since through it the Church continues Christ's priestly mission of reconciling God and man, the liturgy deserves our best attention, an attitude beautifully exemplified in the initiative of the Order of St. Benedict and the liturgical movement. But the signs of wholesome revival of interest in the liturgy are accompanied by other signs of extremist tendencies on the one hand and indifference on the other.

Nature, Origin, and Development of the Liturgy (13–65). The liturgy is "the public worship of the whole Mystical Body, head and members," and while it is exterior worship, its chief element is interior. Instead of opposition between liturgy and personal piety, a union of the two should prevail. While the liturgy must evolve with society, both archeologism and novelty should be reproved, and regulation of the liturgy by the hierarchy is necessary.

Holy Eucharist (66–137). The Mass is the center of the Christian religion; in it Christ offers Himself and His members to the Father. Priest, victim, and ends of this sacrifice are the same as on Calvary. While the laity do not possess the priestly power to consecrate, their baptismal priesthood demands that they offer themselves in union with Christ through the ordained priest. Thus the whole Church offers the oblation. While certain erroneous tendencies are to be corrected, insistence must be laid on intelligent participation in the Mass on the part of the laity.

Divine Office (138–150). Since the Office is the prayer of the Mystical Body, greater participation in it by the laity is urged, especially by means of Sunday Vespers in the parish church.

Liturgical Year (151–170). The Church year is not a bare record of past events. In it Christ Himself is brought to us to relive His mysteries in His members and thus to transform them into Himself.

Practical Pastoral Suggestions (171–211). Pious exercises are of value as long as they are effective in making the liturgy loved and practiced more fervently. Concrete suggestions are provided for bishops, who are to promote the liturgical apostolate, since the most pressing duty of Christians is to live the liturgical life.

Bibliography: PIUS XII, "Mediator Dei," *Acta Apostolicae Sedis* 39 (1947) 521–595; Eng. tr. *On the Sacred Liturgy: Encyclical Letter "Mediator Dei,"* intro. and notes G. ELLARD (New York 1954). L. BEAUDUIN, "L'Encyclique 'Mediator Dei,'" *Maison-Dieu* 13 (1948) 7–25. E. FLICOTEAUX, "Notre sanctification par la liturgie," *La Vie Spirituelle* 79 (1948) 99–109. J. HILD, "L'Encyclique 'Mediator Dei' et le mouvement liturgique de Maria-Laach," *Maison-Dieu* 14 (1948) 15–29. A. THIRY, "L'Encyclique 'Mediator Dei' sur la liturgie," *Nouvelle Revue Theologique* 70 (1948) 113–136. *Les Aspects de la liturgie en fonction de l'encyclique 'Mediator'* (Cours et Conférences des Semaines Liturgiques 15; Louvain 1948). J. A. JUNGMANN, "Unsere liturgische Erneuerung im Lichte des Rundschreibens *Mediator Dei,*" *Geist und Lieben* 21 (1948) 249–259.

[W. J. O'SHEA]

MEDICAL ETHICS

Medical ethics can be defined as the systematic study of value problems that arise in the relationship between physicians and patients. This definition implies that the field of medical ethics should be clearly distinguished from medical jurisprudence or forensic medicine, on the one hand, and from medical etiquette or convention, on the other.

In the Western intellectual tradition the two major sources of literature on medical ethics have been the medical profession itself and various faith communities. Among the most important professional codes of medical ethics are the HIPPOCRATIC OATH (*c.* 400 B.C.), *Percival's Medical Ethics* (1803), and the Code of Medical Ethics of the American Medical Association (1847). More recent professional codes and statements include the Declaration of Geneva (1948), which is an updated version of the Hippocratic oath; the Nuremberg Code (1946–49); the World Medical Association's International Code of Medical Ethics (1949); and the Principles of Medical Ethics of the American Medical Association (1957). Individual physicians have also contributed to the literature of medical ethics, particularly during the 19th and 20th centuries, by writing numerous books and essays on the field in general or on specific ethical issues.

The Jewish and Christian faith communities have also devoted considerable attention to problems of medical ethics. Over the course of centuries, the Jewish tradition has developed a rather elaborate series of moral and legal rules pertaining to medical care, as the studies of I. Jakobovits and D. Feldman illustrate. Among Protestants, systematic interest in the field of medical ethics is a relatively recent phenomenon (see the books by J. Fletcher, H. L. Smith, and P. Ramsey), although the earlier ethical writing of Barth, Brunner, and Bonhoeffer included brief discussions of specific medical-ethical issues.

Within the Roman Catholic tradition, the field of medical ethics has been a major focus of attention for almost a century. Two of the pioneering works in Catholic medical ethics were Karl Capellmann's *Pastoral-Medizin* (1877) and Giuseppe Antonelli's *Medicina pastoralis* (1891). A major achievement of these two authors, both physicians, was their synthesis of contemporary medical knowledge and moral-theological discussion. Throughout their works there are repeated references to the standard textbooks of moral theology written by Alphonsus Liguori, Gury, and Lehmkuhl.

Twentieth-Century Catholic Analysis. During the 20th century Catholic analysis of medical-ethical issues was carried forward at two levels: in official Church statements and in the writings of scholars in the fields of pastoral medicine and moral theology. Early in the century, between 1902 and 1940, the Holy Office issued rulings on numerous medical-ethical questions, including birth control, sterilization, ectopic pregnancy, eugenics, and the disposal of corpses. During the 1940s and 1950s Pope PIUS XII took an intense personal interest in the field of medical ethics; indeed, he devoted major public addresses to the issues of artificial insemination, tissue transplantation, and medical research and experimentation. Official Church statements of the 1960s included the general guidelines concerning marriage enunciated by Vatican II and the specific discussion of the birth-control question by Pope PAUL VI in his encyclical *Humanae Vitae.* Finally, in 1970 and 1971 the Catholic bishops of Canada and the United States issued official statements on hospital ethics entitled, respectively, a *Medico-Moral Guide* and *Ethical and Religious Directives for Catholic Health Care Facilities.*

European and North American Catholic writers in the fields of pastoral medicine and moral theology have also contributed to the Church's reflection on issues in medical ethics. During the first half of the century such discussion was carried on in journal articles, scholarly monographs, surveys of pastoral medicine, and the relevant sections of moral theology textbooks. In addition there appeared, during the late 1940s and the 1950s, a substantial number of specialized medical ethics textbooks written by moral theologians (e.g., G. Kelly, T. J. O'Donnell, and C. J. McFadden).

In the last years of the 20th century there was a change in the texture of medical ethics, particularly from a Catholic viewpoint. The factors contributing to this change are many, complex, and not easily identifiable.

Forces of Change. Among the better recognized elements are: the responses of both medical science and the Church to a rapidly growing technology; the impact of value pluralism that marks contemporary society; concern for patients' rights against medical authoritarianism; and the developing revitalization of the faith dimension in secular life. Not to be overlooked in these changes is the influence of the insights of other faith communities.

Technological Advance. The rapid expansion of scientific knowledge especially in the area of electronics, computers, molecular biology, genetics, and immunology, and their respective applications to medicine, has resulted in problems that were not considered earlier in medical ethics. The proliferation of ethical issues has led to the emergence of the new field of bioethics (16:28). The presence of two apparently distinct disciplines dealing with overlapping areas of concern has resulted in some confusion about the names and areas of applicability. Thus such terms as ''medical ethics,'' ''medical-morals,'' ''bioethics,'' and ''biomedical ethics'' appear. The consequence is the tendency to use these terms almost interchangeably.

Value Pluralism. A survey of the writings in the field of medical ethics (or bioethics) reveals that two value-groups tend to predominate: one that seeks to incorporate a Christian viewpoint (or other religious viewpoints) and the other which espouses secular humanism. Frequently those fitting into the first category invoke the teachings of the Catholic Church, sometimes as overriding and decisive, in other instances simply as supportive. Those favoring a secular-humanistic approach do not necessarily deny religious values—even if their stance is ''negatively neutral''—but seem rather to be concerned about meeting the needs of the broader public, one characterized by a homogenization of values. For secular humanists man is the standard; their advocacy is of values that would be most acceptable to the majority of the concerned public. Yet, one can detect an increasing attention to ethical contributions from JUDAISM and ISLAM as well as from various Christian bodies.

Increased Concern for Patients' Rights. The issue of human rights, dramatically focused by post-World War II revelations, continues to generate increased attention and an urge to action. Rapidly escalating health costs have raised grave concern on the part of public and government alike that the health benefits of high medical technology are being outweighed by the cost of supporting sophisticated medicine. Questions are being asked about the wisdom of allowing technology to dominate the practice of medicine. Additional support for such questions and concerns is the collective impact of popular entertainment and educational forms—television and videotapes and films—which have begun to dramatize the dangers of a runaway technology. More and more, the public is turning to the Internet for information regarding medical matters. Some web sites offer ethical analyses on current medical issues. Many fear that medical technology is taking too dominant a role in medicine. Instead of the comforting presence of the nurse at the bedside, there is instead the cold watchful eye of the television camera and a variety of other monitors; between patient and physician complicated instrumentation intervenes. The patient fears that the clinical judgment of the physician will be replaced by impersonal responses of the computer. More frequently than before it is heard that physicians are praised for their technical skills but with reservations about their ''bedside manner.'' Scientific medicine is at times contrasted with humanistic medicine.

A few voices, such as those of Ivan Illich and Thomas Szasz, are raised to challenge what they perceive as a medical tyranny over health. They question whether modern medicine is truly effective in the treatment of disease. In the midst of medical advances the question is raised about the rights of the patients. Indeed, there has been a move toward codifications of a ''Patients' Bill of Rights.''

Taken together, these various factors have succeeded in alerting the public as well as the medical profession to the state of affairs in which the rights of the patient may have been very gradually and almost silently eroded. Questions, too, are raised about who makes the decision in a medical context. Toward clarification, distinctions are proposed between one set of decisions, *medical* decisions, which properly pertain to the physician, and *personal* decisions regarding life and health, which belong to the patient as a basic right. These controversies, however, have been viewed by some as ultimately constructive for both physician and patient because they promote a more precise definition of roles.

Increased Concern for the Faith Dimension. In concert with the elucidation of patients' rights and respect for the human person there has been growing articulation of the role of faith in daily life. Somewhat apart from both the medical and religious establishments there has been an increase in the popularity of faith healing—as one form of alternative medicine—which is largely associated with those involved in the charismatic renewal within the various faith communities. Such activity among believers is one indication of an increased awareness of the faith dimension in health and sickness.

Another indication of the same awareness has been the initiative taken by certain secular groups such as the American Association for the Advancement of Science to seek input from various religious faiths in connection with task forces dealing with such current issues as germline genetic intervention and stem-cell research. Within the Church, but not as part of the official structure, certain groups have endeavored to analyze the ethical and moral dimensions of various medical and scientific advances. For example, in the last quarter of the 20th century Catholic hospitals found themselves in the midst of painful and complex medical-moral problems for which there had been no adequate preparation. After consultation with medical and ecclesiastical representatives, the Catholic Hospital Association (which became the Catholic Health Association of the United States) founded the Pope JOHN XXIII Medical-Moral Research and Education Center (now known as the National Catholic Bioethics Center) for the purpose of studying the long-range medical-moral issues arising as a result of advances in science and medicine. Other groups were formed to meet a different set of problems: The Institute for Theological Encounter with Science and Technology, and the Human Life Center. Such existing organizations as the National Federation of Catholic Physicians Guilds (now officially known as the Catholic Medical Association) and the National Catholic Pharmacists Guild also responded to the newer ethical issues.

The official Church has itself acted vigorously to meet the developing ethical concerns by the establishment of a number of bishops' committees. Note, however, that U.S. bishops in 2001 underwent an internal restructuring so that what was functioning under two titles (NCCB and USCC) is now acting under one title, the U.S. Conference of Catholic Bishops (USCCB). Thus as part of the USCCB there were in 2001 bishops' committees on doctrine, human values, and pro-life activities. Although all of these committees, in one way or another, have a concern and interest in medical-moral issues, it is the committee on doctrine that has been given the special responsibility to deal with medical-moral issues. In addition to these committees, the Church's concern for the faith dimension in health and sickness is witnessed by its increased openness in testifying before congressional committees on issues it feels must be defended against legislation invasive of the basic rights of individuals. A major recent contribution of the bishops has been the issuance of a revised *Ethical and Religious Directives for Catholic Health Care Facilities* (4th edition, 2001).

Publications. Evidence of growth and vitality within the Church has been the increased number of periodicals that seek to deal with medical-moral issues from a Catholic perspective. Some deal exclusively with ethical issues in medicine, others are concerned with broader issues in health care. A representative list includes the *Linacre Quarterly, Health Progress, Medical-Moral Newsletter, Ethics & Medics,* and many others.

Important Current Topics. Clearly, at the start of the 21st century, the concerns of medical ethics go beyond what was traditionally its proper domain. Today writers on the topic of ethical issues in medicine do not consider themselves bound by the earlier parameters. The topics found under the heading of bioethics are now part and parcel of the publications of those who were once identified as medical ethicists. Of special concern today are such issues of distributive justice as the equitable allocation of scarce medical resources and the right to health care. In the increasingly complex society in which we live, issues of cooperation with objectively evil acts has become one of the major issues. A special concern for Catholic health institutions is the issue of cooperation when a variety of alliances are being considered between Catholic health care facilities and a non-Catholic institution. In a number of instances unresolved ethical issues have prevented the formation of an alliance.

The right to privacy has increasingly been challenged by computer data banks. The questions of genetic diagnosis and counseling are other topics. The question of personal freedom surfaces when the issue of behavioral control in its many forms is considered. The acute problems associated with recombinant DNA techniques in particular, and with genetic engineering in general, raise questions about the limits of human dominion over self and nature. In particular, cloning of human beings and the use of stem cells for research and therapy have become major issues.

Bibliography: T. PERCIVAL, *Percival's Medical Ethics* (Baltimore 1927). D. E. KONOLD, *A History of American Medical Ethics, 1847–1912* (Madison, Wis. 1962). K. CAPELLMANN, *Pastoral-Medizin* (Aachen 1877). G. ANTONELLI, *Medicina pastoralis* (Rome 1891). I. JAKOBOVITS, *Jewish Medical Ethics* (New York 1959). D. FELDMAN, *Birth Control in Jewish Law* (New York 1968). J. FLETCHER, *Morals and Medicine* (Princeton, N.J. 1954). H. L. SMITH, *Ethics and the New Medicine* (Nashville 1970). P. RAMSEY, *The Patient as Person* (New Haven, Conn. 1970). C. J. MCFADDEN, *Medical Ethics* (6th ed. Philadelphia 1967); *The Dignity of Life* (Huntington, Ind. 1976). G. KELLY, *Medico-Moral Problems* (St. Louis 1958). T. J. O'DONNELL, *Morals in Medicine* (2d ed. Westminster, Md. 1960); *Medicine and Christian Morality* (New York 1976). A. NIEDERMEYER, *Allgemeine Pastoralmedizin,* 2 v. (Vienna 1954–55). H. FLECKENSTEIN and M. VODOPIVEC, ''Pastoralmedizin,'' *Lexikon für Theologie und Kirche,* ed. J. HOFER and K. RAHNER, 10 v. (2d, new ed. Freiburg 1957–65) 8.161–162. C. E. CURRAN, *Contraception: Authority and Dissent* (New York 1969); ''Catholic Hospital Ethics,'' *Linacre Quarterly* 39 (1972) 246–268; *Politics, Medicine, and Christian Ethics* (Philadelphia 1973). R. A. MCCORMICK, ''Genetic Medicine: Notes on the Moral Literature,'' *Theological Studies* 33 (1972) 531–552. B. HÄRING, *Medical Ethics* (South Bend, Ind. 1972); *Ethics of Manipulation* (New York 1975). M. B. ETZIONY, ed., *The Physicians Creed* (Springfield, Ill. 1973). B. ASHLEY and K. O'ROURKE, *Health Care Ethics: A Theological Analysis,* 4th ed. (Washington, D.C. 1997). W. E. MAY, *Human Existence, Medicine and Ethics* (Chicago 1977). O. N. GRIESE, *Catholic Identity in Health Care: Principles and Practice* (St. Louis 1987). J. F. DEDEK, *Contemporary Medical Ethics* (New York 1975). P. CATALDO and A. S. MORACZEWSKI, eds., *Catholic Health Care Ethics: A Manual for Ethics Committees* (Boston 2001).

[L. WALTERS/A. S. MORACZEWSKI]

MEDICAL MISSION SISTERS

The Medical Mission Sisters (MMS) was founded in Washington, D.C., in 1925 as the Society of Catholic Medical Missionaries, the first group of religious women dedicated exclusively to the professional medical care of the sick in mission countries.

Early in the 20th century, missionary bishops realized the need for organized, dedicated, and professionally trained personnel to take care of the health of their people, particularly mothers and infants. Women physicians were needed since, in the medically less developed areas of the world, tradition frequently prevented women patients from having recourse to male doctors. Moreover, women doctors who were also religious would ensure dedication to the work and continuity of care.

With this end in view, Anna DENGEL, an experienced lay missionary doctor, founded the Society of Catholic Medical Missionaries. Because canon law then prohibited religious with public vows from the practice of medicine, the society was canonically erected as a pious union. In 1936 the Holy See, in the instruction *Constans ac Sedula,* approved the study and practice of medicine for missionary sisters with public vows. Subsequently, the Medical Mission Sisters became a religious congregation with simple vows. In 1959, John XXIII granted the *Decretum Laudis;* the congregation was erected as a society of pontifical rank.

Since the establishment in 1927 of the society's first hospital in Rawalpindi, North India (now Pakistan), the apostolate has been expanded to include hospitals, clinics, and other healthcare facilities in Asia, Africa, and Latin America. The generalate is in London, England. The North American headquarters is in Philadelphia, PA.

[M. G. DEMERS/EDS.]

MEDICAL MISSIONARIES OF MARY

The Medical Missionaries of Mary (MMM) was established at Anua, East Nigeria, Africa, on April 4, 1937. A visit to Nigeria in 1921 convinced Mary Martin, of Dublin, Ireland, that the great need of the missions was for trained medical missionaries. After Pius XI issued an instruction in 1936 granting permission to religious congregations to devote themselves to all branches of medicine, the Medical Missionaries of Mary came into existence. In January of 1938 Mother Mary, returning from Nigeria after a serious illness, established a house of studies at Booterstown, Dublin. The following year, she took over Our Lady of Lourdes Hospital, Drogheda, which served as the motherhouse of the congregation.

In the first 25 years of its existence, the community grew from three members to more than 400 doctors, nurses, medical technicians, secretaries, and teachers, many of whom worked in Africa. In 1950 the first American foundation was made in the Archdiocese of Boston. The motherhouse is in Blackrock, Ireland; the U.S. headquarters is in City Island, NY.

[J. J. GRANT/EDS.]

MEDICI

In adopting the Ordinances of Justice in 1293, the city of FLORENCE provided itself with a republican form of government that lasted at least formally for over two centuries. The outstanding political event of this period was the rise to power of the Medici family, which dominated political life in Florence throughout most of the 15th century. The Medici also ruled as grand dukes of Tuscany in an unbroken line from 1530 until 1737, when the duchy passed into the control of the House of Austria. The power of the family rested on its enormous wealth in the first phase of its prominence and upon personal family ties with ruling houses of Europe in the second.

Notable Members of the Family. Early in the 13th century individual Medici left their agrarian holdings at Cafaggiolo in the mountainous Mugello region north of Florence to make their way in the expanding commune. The name of *Bonagiunta* appears in an act of 1221. When the government of the priors was formed in 1282, the Medici were enrolled in the greater guilds as leading merchants. In 1291 *Ardingo* de' Medici served as a prior and in 1296, was elected gonfalonier, the highest office in the city. The family continued to grow in prestige during the subsequent century. *Salvestro* (1331–88) identified the family with popular causes by his role in the Ciompi revolt in 1378. *Giovanni di Bicci* (1360–1429), a shrewd and single-minded businessman, built up one of the greatest fortunes in Florence. He was absorbed in finances, was not politically ambitious, and failed to assume the role of advocate of the common people, but he nevertheless captured their sympathy by his liberality, constructing the church of S. Lorenzo, the Hospital of the Innocents, and the tomb of the antipope John XXIII, erected by Donatello and Michelozzo. The Albizzi oligarchy, which assumed power in 1382, was relatively permissive and allowed Giovanni to serve as prior repeatedly and as gonfalonier in 1421.

The break between the Albizzi and Medici developed under the rule of Rinaldo degli Albizzi and Giovanni's son *Cosimo* (1389–1464). Rinaldo undertook a popular war to subdue neighboring Lucca, failed to win, and on May 10, 1433 made an unsatisfactory peace. Civic sentiment swung in favor of Cosimo, who had been critical of Rinaldo's bungling. Rinaldo exiled Cosimo and his brother *Lorenzo* to Venice. On Sept. 1, 1434, a pro-Medici government took office and recalled Cosimo from exile. He then ruled the city by carefully controlling the public offices through a committee of ten electors, who appointed the members of the signory. Cosimo, in a rule of 30 years, allowed himself to be elected gonfalonier only three times, in 1435, 1439, and 1445, and for the rest of the time ruled indirectly. In directing the foreign policy of Florence, Cosimo's major aim was to achieve security and stability through the preservation of a balance of power and an emphasis on the common interests of the Italian city-states as opposed to the major powers of northern Europe. In order to prevent a Venetian hegemony to the north, he backed the SFORZAS of Milan with subsidies. In 1454 Venice and Milan signed the Peace of Lodi, which was accepted by Florence and Naples. The power configuration thenceforth rested on a combination of Milan, Florence, and Naples on one side, and Venice and the STATES OF THE CHURCH on the other.

Under Cosimo the family fortune expanded most rapidly. The Medici had one partnership in silk manufacturing and two in cloth manufacturing under a putting out or ''wholesale handicraft'' system. But the main source of their enormous wealth was their bank, one of the *banchi grossi* (great banks), which dealt in merchandise and exchange in all parts of the world. They combined foreign trade and dealing in bills of exchange, the trade being more significant than their banking operation as such. When Cosimo succeeded Giovanni in 1429 the house had branches in Venice and at the papal court. New branches were subsequently established in Pisa, Milan, Geneva (moved to Lyons in 1466), Avignon, Bruges, and London. The Medici bank was a decentralized combination of separate partnerships. Cosimo maintained a close vigil over the operation of all the branches, but his son *Piero* (1416–69) and grandson Lorenzo relaxed their grip on the managers. Lorenzo, preoccupied with politics, diplomacy, art, and letters, failed to give the business adequate attention and permitted disastrous loans to princes, so that under Lorenzo the Medici bank began a precipitous decline.

Cosimo's son Piero was in poor health and died five years after his father. He and his wife, Lucrezia Tornabuoni, a lady of great piety, had two sons, *Lorenzo il Magnifico* (1449–92) and *Giuliano* (1453–78). Lorenzo's good relations with Sixtus IV were strained when the pope's nephew Girolamo RIARIO sought to build a territorial holding for himself in central Italy. In 1473 the Riario kept Florence from acquiring Imola, and in 1478 he connived in the PAZZI revolt, which was triggered by the assassination of Giuliano during Mass in the cathedral on April 26. Lorenzo escaped to the vestry; he quickly

Cosimo de Medici.

quashed the conspiracy. The war with the pope and King Ferrante of Naples that followed went badly for Florence, which was threatened by Venice in the North. Lorenzo then ''risked his own life to restore peace to his country,'' as MACHIAVELLI put it later, by his dramatic journey to Naples to make a personal appeal to Ferrante for peace. Lorenzo's diplomacy was directed toward the same goal as Cosimo's had been, security and stability for the Italian city-states. As a great patron of the humanists and artists, he presided over the flowering of Renaissance culture in Florence, favoring the Neoplatonic philosophers, and writing sonnets, lyrics, eclogues, and other literary pieces in the vernacular.

Two years after Lorenzo's death his licentious son *Piero* (1471–1503) was driven out by the people when the French under Charles VIII invaded Italy. After the SAVONAROLA episode and republican interval, Piero's son *Lorenzo* (1492–1519) restored Medici rule. He was the father of CATHERINE DE MÉDICIS, who became queen of France. In 1527 the Medici were driven out again, but in 1530 *Alessandro,* Lorenzo's natural son, was made hereditary ruler of Florence by Emperor CHARLES V. In 1537 *Lorenzino* de' Medici (1514–47) murdered Alessandro. The able and utterly ruthless condottiere *Cosimo I* (1519–74), a great-great-grandson of Lorenzo, Cosimo the Elder's brother, with the help of imperial troops made himself ruler. In 1570 Pius V crowned him grand duke of Tuscany, a position that his descendants held until *Gian Gastone de' Medici's* death in 1737, when the Hapsburgs took possession of their territories. The family through the centuries contributed to the Church many high clergymen, notably Popes LEO X (GIOVANNI), CLEMENT VII (GIULIO), and LEO XI (ALESSANDRO OTTAVIANO).

Bibliography: G. A. BRUCKER, *Florentine Politics and Society, 1343–1378* (Princeton 1962), on Salvestro and early Medicis. F. SCHEVILL, *History of Florence* (New York 1936); *The Medici* (New York 1949). R. A. DE ROOVER, *The Medici Bank* (New York 1948). K. D. E. VERNON, *Cosimo de' Medici* (New York 1899). K. S. GUTKIND, *Cosimo de' Medici* (Oxford 1938). E. ARMSTRONG, *Lorenzo de' Medici* (New York 1896). E. L. S. HORSBURGH, *Lorenzo the Magnificent and Florence in her Golden Age* (London 1908). G. SPINI, *Cosimo I de' Medici e la indipendenza del principato mediceo* (Florence 1945). H. M. M. ACTON, *The Last Medici* (rev. ed. New York 1959). D. V. KENT, *The Rise of the Medici* (New York 1978). N. RUBINSTEIN, *The Government of Florence under the Medici (1434–1494)* (Oxford 1966).

[L. W. SPITZ]

MEDIEVAL ACADEMY OF AMERICA

Founded in 1925, the Medieval Academy of America was the first organization in the United States dedicated to medieval studies. Centered in Cambridge, Massachusetts, it is a constituent member of the American Council of Learned Societies. The Medieval Academy is the ''largest organization in the world devoted to medieval studies,'' attracting scholars from all over the world; in 2000 it had 4,160 members. The academy is more than a group of medieval historians, since it fosters teaching and research in ''medieval art, archaeology, history, law, literature, music, philosophy, religion, science, social and economic institutions, and all other aspects of the Middle Ages.'' It is open to anyone with an interest in the Middle Ages, which it defines as a period stretching from A.D. 500 to 1500. Although it concentrates on western Europe, the academy's interests also include Arabic, Byzantine, Hebrew, and Slavic studies

Interior of the New Sacristy of S. Lorenzo (also called the Medici Chapel) at Florence, designed by Michelangelo; against the right-hand wall is the tomb and monument of Lorenzo de Medici, sculpted by Michelangelo. (Alinari-Art Reference/Art Resource, NY)

The academy publishes *Speculum—A Journal of Medieval Studies,* which has the widest circulation of any journal in the field. Published four times a year, it includes annually over 1,000 pages of articles, book reviews, and short notices on newly published books. Three times a year, the *Medieval Academy News* appears, containing information on events, fellowships, prizes, and other opportunities for medievalists. Since 1928 the academy has been publishing books and monographs, having over 100 titles in print. To facilitate its book production, it has concluded a contract with the University of Toronto Press to co-publish Medieval Academy books. Together with the University of Toronto, it also reprints books that are useful for teaching but that are out of print and no longer generally available to the public. The book subvention program helps subsidize first books by academy members at other non-profit scholarly presses.

In the spring, the academy holds an annual meeting at various sites in the United States and Canada, where scholarly papers are read and a business meeting is conducted. It also conducts sessions at the annual medieval conferences in Kalamazoo, Michigan and Leeds (United Kingdom) as well as at the yearly meeting of the American Historical Society. In 2001 the academy began to sponsor an annual lecture at the International Medieval Congress at the University of Leeds.

The academy has also established a Committee on Centers and Regional Associations (CARA) that "serves as a forum for teachers, administrators, and organizers of centers, institutes, programs, and regional and other organizations devoted to medieval studies." Each summer it provides scholarships for four students to study Latin at the University of Notre Dame and the University of Toronto. CARA also offers a prize for dissertation research, as well as awards for excellence in teaching and outstanding service, which is defined as providing "leadership in developing, organizing promoting, and sponsoring medieval studies through the extensive administrative work that is so crucial to the health of medieval studies but that often goes unrecognized by the profession at large."

Each year the academy awards the Haskins medal "for a distinguished book in the field of medieval studies." It is named after Charles Homer Haskins, an outstanding medievalist and one of the founders of the academy. It also offers the John Nicholas Brown Prize. Named after another founder, it is given to a resident of North America who has written a "first book or monograph on a medieval subject judged by the selection committee to be of outstanding quality." Van Courtlandt Elliott, the executive secretary of the academy and editor of *Speculum* from 1965 to 1970, has given his name to a prize that is awarded annually for a first article in medieval studies that is judged to be outstanding. Travel grants and dissertation grants are also awarded.

[T. E. CARSON]

MEDIEVAL BOY MARTYRS

Beginning as early as 415 with an unnamed boy of Immestar, near Antioch, the deaths of many Christian children, especially around the time of the Passover, were attributed to Jews. Prominent Jews were accused of torturing a child in a fashion that mocked the Passion of Christ, then drained the blood for use in making the Paschal matzoth. When investigated, many of the deaths were accidental—regardless of whether a Jew was involved. Grieving relatives sought a reason for the death of a loved one and someone to blame.

Beginning with the death of (St.) WILLIAM OF NORWICH, there were six such cases in the 12th century, 15 in the 13th century, ten in the 14th century, 16 in the 15th century, 13 in the 16th century, eight in the 17th century, 15 in the 18th century, and 39 as late as the 19th century.

Nor was this phenomenon restricted to Western Europe. On March 21, 1690 (Holy Saturday), six-year-old Gavril Belostoksky was found murdered and drained of blood in Zverki, Belarus (now in Poland). Jews were accused of torturing the child and using his blood for the Passover matzoth. He was canonized in the 20th century by the Belarussian Orthodox Church, which celebrates Saint Gavril's feast on May 1. Although most of the victims were young boys, there are recorded cases such as the death (1623) of a girl in Ragusa, Dalmatia. Her body was found under the bed of a Christian woman, but the murder was attributed to Jews.

The cases of blood libel, which often resulted in pogroms or the death of the accused, became almost epidemic. The problem became so serious among German burghers that Emperor Frederick II undertook a formal inquiry of the charges, including a conference with Christian converts from Judaism. Thereafter he forbade such accusations under penalty of the law.

Most of the cults of these so-called boy martyrs have been suppressed; many were never recognized by the Church even locally. Among those included on various calendars were (in chronological order by death): St. WILLIAM OF NORWICH (d. 1144, Norwich, England); St. Harold of Gloucester (d. 1168 or 1160 to 1161, Gloucester, England); St. Richard of Pontoise (or of Paris; d. 1179, Pontoise, France; *passio* included in the *Acta Sanctorum* on March 25); Herbert of Huntingdon (d. 1180); St. Robert of Bury Saint Edmunds (d. 1181, Edmundsbury, England); St. Dominguito of Saragossa (or Dominic of Val; d. 1250; Saragossa, Aragon, Spain); Little St. HUGH OF LINCOLN (d. 1255, Lincoln, England); Blessed Werner of Oberwesel (or Wernher of Wesel; d. 1287, Oberwesel, Germany; feast formerly April 19); Rudolf of Berne (d. 1294); Conrad of Weissensee (d. 1303, Weissensee, Thuringia, Germany); Blessed Ludwig (Louis) von Bruck of Ravensburg (d. 1429, Ravensburg, Germany; feast formerly April 30); Blessed Andrew of Rinn (d. 1462, Rinn, near Innsbruck, Austria); St. SIMON (SIMEON) OF TRENT

(d. 1475, Trent, Italy); Blessed Lorenzino Sossio (d. 1485; Vicenza, near Padua, Italy; feast formerly April 15); and St. Cristoforo of Toledo (d. 1490, near Toledo, Spain).

Bibliography: M. D. ANDERSON, *A Saint at Stake* (London 1964). D. ATTWATER and C. R. JOHN, *Dictionary of Saints* (3d ed. New York 1995) 358. E. BAUMGARTEN, *Die Blutbeschuldigung gegen die Juden* (Vienna 1900). BENOÎT XIV, *Constitutio XLIV: Beatus Andreas, dans Bullarium romanum magnam sue ejusdem Continuatio* (Luxembourg 1758) t. xlx, 120–36. D. CHWOLSON, *Die Blutanklage und sonstige mittelalterliche Beschuldigungen der Juden: Eine historische Untersuchung nach den Quellen* (Frankfurt 1901); *Die päpstlichen Bullen über die Blutbeschuldigung* (Berlin 1893). CLEMENT XIV, *Die Päpstlichen bullen über die blutbeschuldigung* (Munich 1900). COMMISSION FOR RELIGIOUS RELATIONS WITH THE JEWS, *Notes on the Correct Way to Present the Jews and Judaism in Preaching and Catechesis in the Roman Catholic Church. L'Osservatore Romano* (July 1, 1985). *Consultation du cardinal Ganganelli (pape Clément XIV) sur l'accusation de meurtres rituels portée contre les Juifs, en italien, dans Revue des études juives*, t. XVIII, 201–02; en Français, dans H. –L. STRACK, *Le sang et le fausse accusalion du muertre rituel* (Paris, s. d.) 370–71. J. COULSON (ed.), *The Saints* (New York 1960) 229, 417. V. DAL, *Investigation of the Murder of Christian Babies by the Jews and the Use of Their Blood* (n.s. 1844). D. CHWOLSON, *Die Blutanklage und sonstige mittelalterliche Beschuldigungen der Juden* (Frankfurt 1901). J. DECKERT, *Vier Tiroler Kinder, Opfer des chassidischen Fanatismus* (Vienne 1893). A. DUNDES, ''The Ritual Murder or Blood Libel Legend: A Study of Anti-Semitic Victimization through Projective Inversion,'' in *The Blood Libel Legend: A Casebook in Anti-Semitic Folklore*, ed. A. DUNDES (Madison, Wisconsin 1991). R. ERB, ed., *Die Legende vom Ritualmord: zur Geschichte der Blutbeschuldigung gegen Juden* (Berlin 1993). L. GANGANELLI (Pope Clement XIV), *The Ritual Murder Libel and the Jews*, ed. C. ROTH (London 1935). W. KUNZEMANN, *Judenstein: Das Ende einer Legende* (Innsbruck 1995). G. LANGMUIR, ''Ritual Cannibalism,'' *Towards a Definition of Antisemitism* (Berkeley 1990). D. J. MILLER, *The Development of the 'Ritual Murder' Accusation in the Twelfth and Thirteenth Centuries and its Relationship to the Changing Attitudes of Christians towards Jews* (Cambridge 1991). R. I. MOORE, *The Formation of a Persecuting Society* (Oxford 1987). L. SHEPPARD, *The Saints Who Never Were* (Dayton, Ohio 1969), 115–23. M. STERN, ed., *Die päpstlichen Bullen über die Blutbeschuldigung* (Berlin 1893; Munich 1900), which includes papal bulls on the topic. H.-L. STRACK, *Das Blut im Glauen und Aberglauben der Menschenheit* (8th ed., Leipzig 1911); *Der Blutaberglaube in der Menschheit: Blutmorde und Blutritus* (Berlin 1892), tr. into English H. BLANCHAMP, *The Jew and Human Sacrifice (Human Blood and Jewish Ritual)* (London 1909).

[K. I. RABENSTEIN]

MEDIEVAL LATIN LITERATURE

The body of medieval Latin literature would be rather small if it were limited to literature in its narrower and more usual meaning of belles-lettres, i.e., writings distinguished by artistic form or emotional appeal. But the general histories of the subject treat of it as the total preserved Latin writings of the Middle Ages. It seems best to take this latter approach here, with due regard, however, for articles on medieval writings in particular fields and on individual authors. The matter thus becomes vast and unwieldy, much of it still being investigated, though the 20th century produced an imposing array of valuable studies on the period.

There is wide divergence of opinion as to the date that should be set for the beginning of the MIDDLE AGES, and there can be even less agreement as to when Latin writings should first be considered to have become medieval. In literature the patristic period superseded pagan writings as the latter declined. Edward K. Rand found a happy solution for the problem of beginnings by reaching back well into the patristic period for his *Founders of the Middle Ages* (1929). It is true that one cannot understand medieval thought without reference to earlier Christian writers, not only AMBROSE, AUGUSTINE, and JEROME, but also PRUDENTIUS, SULPICIUS SEVERUS, OROSIUS, LEO I, and GELASIUS I. They, however, are treated separately.

Jerome's *De viris illustribus,* a sort of dictionary of Christian biography, set the pattern for subsequent attempts to list and characterize the writings of succeeding generations: GENNADIUS OF MARSEILLES (late 5th century), ISIDORE OF SEVILLE, and ILDEFONSUS OF TOLEDO (7th century), SIGEBERT OF GEMBLOUX (late 11th century), Honorius Augustodunensis, and Anonymus Mellicensis (12th century), TRITHEMIUS (late 15th century), and Robert BELLARMINE (early 17th century). From the Latin Fathers the Middle Ages acquired a taste for scriptural ALLEGORY. Ambrose bequeathed the art of hymnody (*see* HYMNOLOGY); Jerome gave the Vulgate and his saints' lives; Augustine transmitted NEOPLATONISM, theology, catechetics, the art of autobiography, and a theology of history; John CASSIAN taught a psychological approach to the spiritual life; Sulpicius Severus became a model for HAGIOGRAPHY; Orosius, for history; Prudentius, for versification and the allegory of the virtues and vices; Leo the Great left his name on the art of letter writing and rhyming (*see* CURSUS); and Gelasius I laid down the fundamental teaching on CHURCH AND STATE. In secular learning, MACROBIUS and Servius initiated medieval scholars into the study of Vergil, and Martianus Capella disciplined them with his treatise on the seven LIBERAL ARTS.

Modern histories of medieval Latin literature, successors of the *De viris illustribus,* arbitrarily enough set the *terminus a quo* of this literature in the early 6th century. They conceive a first period extending to the CAROLINGIAN RENAISSANCE, a second, extending to the renaissance of the 12th century; a third, comprising the 12th century; and a fourth, covering the later Middle Ages.

From the 6th Century to the Carolingian Renaissance

The first authors usually treated are the more immediate founders, themselves trained in the educational system of the Ancient World, who, without being of the highest literary genius themselves, handed down the torch of learning in an age that threatened its extinction. With the coming of the LOMBARDS late in the 6th century, the secular schools went out of existence in Italy, just as previously, except for the vicinity of CARTHAGE, they had collapsed elsewhere.

Italy. Worthy to head the list of medieval Latin authors is BOETHIUS (d. 524), scion of a distinguished family, official in the Ostrogothic kingdom of THEODORIC THE GREAT, and prolific writer. It was through his translations of, and commentaries on, parts of the logical writings of ARISTOTLE and PORPHYRY that these philosophers were introduced to the Middle Ages. Many of his definitions and technical terms were taken up by medieval philosophy. His treatises on arithmetic and music, among others on the quadrivium, had great subsequent influence. Most famous of his writings is the *Consolation of Philosophy,* composed as he languished in prison before his execution. It is a highly literary creation of prose and verse in the form of the Menippean satire. The great variety of its verse afforded models to medieval versifiers, and the allegorical nature of the work appealed to medieval taste. It is so purely philosophical that doubts could be raised as to Boethius's Christianity. But he also left theological treatises of proven authenticity and Catholic content.

A contemporary of Boethius was ENNODIUS, Bishop of Pavia (d. 521). A rhetorician at heart, he wrote many works in prose and mediocre verse, most of them secular, some even pagan, in tone. His highly artificial style fails to cover the shallowness of his thought. A biography of EPIPHANIUS, his predecessor in the See of Pavia, is Ennodius's best work.

Somewhat younger than Boethius and longer-lived, CASSIODORUS (d. *c.* 583), son of a pretorian prefect, likewise served as an Ostrogothic official. He composed an extensive collection of letters and documents (*Variae*) that reflect the workings of Theodoric's government and that of his successors, though, with the names removed, the documents do not offer a direct aid to history. The style is involved and obscure. Parts of the *Variae* foreshadow the medieval formularies. Cassiodorus made a modest contribution to HISTORIOGRAPHY. A consular list represents the only useful part of a chronicle that he prepared. His history of the Goths is not extant, but extracts of it were reproduced by Jordanis in 551. Only fragments remain of a genealogical work, *Ordo generis Cassiodorum.* He himself was not proud of the *Historia ecclesiastica tripartita,* made up of excerpts from three Byzantine historians, THEODORET, SOZOMEN, and SOCRATES, which he selected and caused to be translated into Latin. His *De anima* reveals that he was not a profound philosopher. In 540 he withdrew to his family estate at Squillace in Calabria, where he founded the monastery of Vivarium. For the monks he wrote his two-part pedagogical *Institutiones divinarum et saecularium litterarum,* which was to have a profound effect on the history of monasticism. The first part offers a list of readings in Scripture, theology, and church history without, however, neglecting to make provision for those who would devote themselves to labor. On the highest manual level he placed the copying of manuscripts, thus ensuring the growth of monastic libraries. The second part of the *Institutiones* was a simple treatment of the liberal arts as a necessary preparation for the study of theology. His treatise on orthography, composed shortly before his death, consists of excerpts from various authors. It was Cassiodorus who gave the scholarly turn to Benedictinism.

The milieu for which Cassiodorus produced his program of study was set by the BENEDICTINE RULE. Written down about the 3d decade of the 6th century for the monks of MONTE CASSINO by Benedict of Nursia, this rule was to form the monastic life of Europe for centuries. Next to the Scriptures it was the most read book of the Middle Ages and became the object of many commentaries, even to the present day. Its text was written in Latin of the people so that it would be intelligible to simple men. But it was filled with solid spirituality, and a wise moderation gave it universal appeal.

Another official at the Ostrogothic court, later a subdeacon in Rome, the rhetorician ARATOR, left a poem of 2,326 hexameter lines based on the Acts of the Apostles. He read it to an audience in the church of St. Peter in Chains during four days in April and May 544. Though of lesser worth than the earlier poem of Sedulius on the Gospel narrative, it was highly prized in the Middle Ages.

At the end of the century appears the figure of Pope GREGORY I THE GREAT, who after a distinguished civil career became a Benedictine and promoted the cause of the order. As pope (590–604) he left a precious collection of 854 letters, which reveal his great activity. He had them arranged according to the years of his pontificate, and so they became the model for PAPAL REGISTERS. His letters have a personal and human character that makes them completely different from the rhetorical effusions of Cassiodorus's *Variae*, although Gregory too was educated in the schools and trained in civil administration. His commentary on the Book of Job, which he called *Libri morales,* was a learned work in the nature of a moral theology.

His moral homilies on Ezechiel and 40 homilies on texts of the Gospels were on a dignified popular level. The *Regula pastoralis* was destined to be of the utmost importance in the direction of future bishops. The *Dialogues* on saints and their miracles, in which Gregory reproduced much of the credulity of his sources, became one of the beloved books of the Middle Ages. Gregory and Augustine were the authors most used by medieval writers. Boniface VIII numbered Gregory among the four great Doctors of the Western Church.

There is some basis for connecting Gregory with liturgical development and GREGORIAN CHANT. The authorship of the so-called Leonine, Gelasian, and Gregorian sacramentaries bristles with problems, but they belong in the period under consideration. Their collects and prefaces are masterpieces of majestic thought and expression, their cadenced metrical *clausulae* gradually yielding to the accentual *cursus.* The concise dignity of the Roman liturgical formulae contrasts with the more exuberant Milanese, GALLICAN, and MOZARABIC RITES, and there were reciprocal influences. In connection with the liturgy came the further development of the hymn. The *TE DEUM LAUDAMUS*, of uncertain authorship, dates from early in this period, and the *Praeconium paschale* gradually assumed the set form of the EXSULTET (*IAM ANGELICA*).

The history of the individual popes from the time of Liberius (352–366) was recounted in the *LIBER PONTIFICALIS* by a succession of authors who gave a fuller and more exact account as time went on. It had considerable influence on the writing of religious history. The *LIBER DIURNUS ROMANORUM PONTIFICUM* was a formula book for papal documents. It was begun in the 7th century and, with subsequent additions, was much used for drafting documents in the papal chancery until the middle of the 9th century. After the 11th century it ceased to be used. In the middle of the 6th century, DIONYSIUS EXIGUUS, a Scythian, came to Rome and gave the Western Church a compilation of canons of Greek councils and a collection of papal letters. His work was fundamental for the development of Canon Law (*see* DIONYSIANA COLLECTIO). He likewise introduced the use of the Christian era into the calendar.

North Africa. Near the end of the 5th century, Dracontius, a gifted lay poet, wrote his verse in North Africa. In prison for offending his Vandal king, he composed his *Laudes Dei* in 2,327 hexameter lines. The work was reproduced in abbreviated and altered form in the 7th century by EUGENE II OF TOLEDO and was long known only in this text until the original was edited in 1791. Toward the end of the Vandal kingdom (534) an *Anthologia Latina,* or *Libri epigrammaton,* was compiled from a number of African poets. It proves the existence of a considerable group of classically trained teachers and poets. In 533 a law of Emperor JUSTINIAN I provided for teachers of grammar and rhetoric in Carthage, and classical education lasted there until the city fell at the end of the 7th century. Out of North Africa came Priscian, author of the *Institutio de arte grammatica* (before 526–527), the most comprehensive grammar handed down from the Roman world. He lived in Constantinople and Rome. Next to DONATUS, his grammar was the most used in the Middle Ages. Corippus, the author of a long and rather tedious epic on the Byzantine conquest of the Moors and of panegyrics on the emperors Justinian and Justin II, wrote between 549 and 567. He was a teacher by profession and a Christian. If the subject matter of his poetry was scarcely of epic quality, his exactness in regard to details of Berber life insures him a place as a worthwhile historical source.

The region around Carthage continued to produce theologians. FULGENTIUS OF RUSPE (467–532), writing in the spirit of Augustine, attacked ARIANISM and SEMIPELAGIANISM. Several others wrote in connection with the controversy of the THREE CHAPTERS. Among these was the biographer of Fulgentius, the deacon FERRANDUS (d. 546 or 547), who with Cresconius put together the *Breviatio canonum,* a collection of Greek and African conciliar canons. VICTOR, Bishop of Tunnuna (d. after 566), while in exile for defending the Three Chapters, wrote a general chronicle with emphasis on Africa. Much used in the Middle Ages was an introduction to Sacred Scripture by JUNILIUS AFRICANUS, a Byzantine lay official, who wrote in distinguished Latin. For content, Junilius had access to a manuscript by the Syrian Paul of Basra, who became metropolitan of Nisibis. Primasius, Bishop of Hadrumentum, wrote a commentary on Apocalypse, which was often to be found in medieval libraries.

Spain. After the invasions of the 5th century, letters in SPAIN revived very slowly in the 6th. Two bishops, Apringius of Pace and JUSTUS OF URGEL, wrote allegorical scriptural commentaries. The first writer of importance, St. MARTIN, Bishop of Braga (d. 580), a Pannonian by birth, put together an interesting account of existing superstitions and pagan practices in his *De correctione rusticorum.* Among his other works are moral writings, in which he relied heavily on SENECA, a collection of canons, a treatise on Baptism, and a translation from Greek of sayings of Egyptian Fathers. St. LEANDER, Archbishop of Seville (d. c. 600), older brother of St. Isidore, composed a rule for women religious and gave the opening address at the Third Council of TOLEDO (589), at which the Goths renounced their Arianism. St. Isidore of Seville (d. 636) deserves to be looked upon as one of the founders of the Middle Ages and has been called the last of the

Western Fathers of the Church. A prolific writer, he for the most part reproduced the *antiquorum monumenta,* bequeathing a vast encyclopedia to posterity. Chief among his works is the *Etymologiae,* or *Origines,* which embraces all fields of knowledge. His other writings are largely theological. The Fourth Council of Toledo (633), with its creed and 75 canons, seems to be to a great extent the work of Isidore. It should be noted that the series of national councils of Toledo forms an important element of the literature of Visigothic Spain. Isidore's chronicles, like the others of Visigothic Spain, are jejune, that of JOHN OF BICLARO being the best. Upon BRAULIO, Bishop of Saragossa (d. 651), disciple and friend of Isidore, devolved the task of arranging and editing the *Etymologiae.* Braulio left a collection of letters, written in stilted Latin, which throw much light on Spain in the middle of the 7th century. He also wrote a life of the saintly hermit AEMILIAN (S. Millán de la Cogolla).

For the most part the authors of Spain in this early period were bishops, who as theological writers surpassed their contemporaries in other parts of Europe. Tajo, who succeeded Braulio in the See of Saragossa (651–683), wrote *Libri sententiarum* based on Augustine and Gregory the Great. St. EUGENE, Metropolitan of Toledo (646–657), was a poet of considerable ability. St. ILDEFONSUS, his successor (657–667), famous in legend as well as history, wrote works on the perpetual virginity of the Blessed Virgin Mary and on Baptism. The former treatise is written *more synonymo,* in the bad taste and style in vogue in Spain and previously used by Isidore in one of his works. St. JULIAN OF TOLEDO, the keenest theologian to occupy that see (680–690), wrote on eschatology and in refutation of MONOTHELITISM. Besides, he was the author of a grammar and of a history of a war of King Wamba. In the western part of the peninsula, St. FRUCTUOSUS, Archbishop of Braga (656–665), previously active as abbot and bishop of Dumio, founded a number of religious houses for which he composed religious rules. These rules were followed in monasteries of Galicia and northern Portugal until the 11th century. His vita, an important hagiographical account, was written by an unidentified author. Later in the 7th century the cross-grained hermit VALERIO OF BIERZO left autobiographical works in a style full of devices that demonstrate his education in rhetoric. In the same century an unknown deacon, presumably of Mérida, wrote the *Lives of the Fathers of Mérida,* which, concerned with the preceding century, gives much information on social customs, religion, liturgy, and general history. It has the usual rhetorical conceits employed in early Spanish Latin, along with many departures from classical syntax.

It is of special interest to note that one of the Visigothic kings, Sisebut (612–620), left writings of his own: five letters, a poem of 61 hexameter verses on eclipses, and a life of St. DESIDERIUS OF VIENNE. Along with the canons of the councils, the texts of the *Leges Visigothorum* deserve consideration for their style and legal merit. The diffuse, poetic Mozarabic rite took form in the 7th century and thereafter suffered little change until its suppression in favor of the Roman rite in the late 11th century.

Gaul. By the 6th century the Roman schools of Gaul, once so flourishing, had ceased to exist. But St. AVITUS, Bishop of Vienne (490–518), continued to write under the influence of the schools, much as Sidonius had done, in a correct, artificial Latin style. He left letters, sermons, tracts against heresy, a poem in praise of virginity, and a very lengthy poem based on parts of Genesis and Exodus. Quite different from him, St. CAESARIUS, Bishop of Arles (503–543), preached moral sermons in lively popular language and wrote practical religious rules, one for monks, another for nuns.

Coming out of Italy, where he was born *c.* 530, FORTUNATUS brought with him into *Francia* a facility for Latin prose and poetry. Living by his wits, he wrote much trivial occasional verse, but his religious poetry is of profoundly Catholic inspiration. Two of his hymns, *VEXILLA REGIS PRODEUNT* and *PANGE LINGUA GLORIOSI*, have been immortalized in the liturgy of Passiontide. He wrote a number of saints' lives in prose, the best being that of his patroness, St. RADEGUNDA. A long vita of St. MARTIN OF TOURS in hexameter verse adds no new historical data. Fortunatus, who is given the cult of a saint, died as bishop of Poitiers toward the end of the century. F. J. E. Raby would regard him ''not as the last of the Romans, but as the first of the medieval poets.''

GREGORY OF TOURS (538–594), bishop and saint, most faithfully reflects the spirit of Merovingian Gaul in his writings. Gallo-Roman though he was, Gregory wrote in a Latin that, as he well realized, departed far from the classical norms. His diffuse *History of the Franks,* a chronicle, episodic and dramatic in treatment, is no masterpiece of historical writing, but it is incomparably richer than the other chronicles of his time. It reconstructs for posterity the beginnings of *Francia.* The narrative of Merovingian history was continued in the Chronicle of FREDEGARIUS, so called, a work by several authors who wrote in corrupt Latin. Only its last book offers independent material. After the middle of the 7th century the *Liber historiae Francorum* became a mediocre source for the end of the period. A short scientific treatise by Gregory of Tours, *De cursibus ecclesiasticis,* indicated the position of the constellations throughout the year with a view to establishing the time for the liturgical offices.

Gregory's numerous hagiographical writings reveal excessive credulity on his part, but he was conscientious about his sources and critical of quackery. His works set a pattern in hagiography, though the life of St. Martin by SULPICIUS SEVERUS had the greatest influence on early medieval biography. With their slight attention to personal characteristics, the vitae of this period belong to the heroic type. Some authors, such as Gregory of Tours and Gregory the Great, treat of holy persons in groups, as had been done earlier by Cassian and Rufinus. But scores of individual lives were written—more than 190 for the period between 613 and 751—most of them anonymously. The emphasis was on edification rather than history, and it was common practice to transfer episodes and miracles from one saint to another. Among the lives of greater historical value may be mentioned those of SS. GENEVIÈVE, AMANDUS, OUEN, ARNULF OF METZ, Vaast, and later of St. BONIFACE by Willibald of Mainz. The authenticity of some of these lives has been challenged, but criticism has vindicated it in a number of instances. Outside of the Frankish domain the vitae of St. COLUMBAN by JONAS OF BOBBIO; of St. SEVERIN of Noricum by Eugippius, Abbot of Lucullanum, near Naples; of St. PATRICK by Tirechan and Muirchu; of St. COLUMBA OF IONA by ADAMNAN; of St. BRIGID OF KILDARE by Cogitosus; and of St. CUTHBERT are outstanding.

Many legal texts have come down from the early medieval period. There were codes for the Roman subjects in the new Germanic kingdoms: the *Lex Romana Visigothorum*, the *Lex Romana Burgundionum*, the *Edictum Theodorici.* They represented largely an adaptation and simplification of the 5th-century Theodosian Code of Roman law. The 6th-century legal corpus of Justinian exerted little influence in the West until later in the Middle Ages. Collections of laws were likewise prepared for various Germanic peoples settled in Europe. Together these codifications are now called the *Leges barbarorum.* Much influenced by Roman law were the *Leges Visigothorum.* More Germanic in nature were, e.g., the *Lex Salica*, *Lex Ripuaria*, and the Lombard laws. Their Latinity was barbaric and mixed with Germanic words. The *diplomata* of the kings and especially private documents, of which there are many examples in the collections of *formulae,* were written in uncouth Latin strikingly paralleled by the crude form of Merovingian handwriting.

A shadowy, enigmatic figure probably of southern Gaul in the 7th century is the grammarian Virgilius Maro, whose *Epitomae* and eight letters are extant. His bizarre texts may have been intended as a parody on grammars. The whole setting of his writings seems to be a fabrication. Akin to this writing with similar grotesque vocabulary are the *Hisperica famina* and the rhythmical and rhymed exorcism, the Lorica, emanating, it seems, from southwestern Britain in the 7th century, as well as the iambic hymn *Altus Prosator,* of Irish origin, attributed to St. Columba.

Ireland. St. Patrick's *Confessio* and his letter addressed to the soldiers of Coroticus were written in vulgar Latin. But since Celtic, and not vulgar Latin, was the vernacular, it became necessary for Irish monks to study book Latin and so their language escaped the vulgar influence. Similarly, the missionaries appear to have brought the handwriting, traditionally known in PALEOGRAPHY as half-uncial, into Ireland, and from it developed the legible insular hand. There are few traces of the beginnings of Latin literature in Ireland. For the 6th century only a PENITENTIAL and a few hymns are extant. Further penitentials, tariffs of penances to be administered according to the gravity of sins, were subsequently brought by insular missionaries to the Continent. There the genre was taken up by Carolingian moralists. Though these texts show little originality or literary merit, they naturally had great moral and social effect.

St. Columban (d. 615), who toward the end of the 6th century crossed over to the Continent to spread monasticism, left several writings, notably his two rigorous religious rules and a number of letters. There has been controversy about the authenticity of a number of poems attributed to him. Some of the verses are in hexameter, and there is a long poem in adonics. Classical authors are cited, as well as Christian. A tradition of interest in the Latin classics is revealed in a 10th-century catalogue of the library of BOBBIO, where Columban finally settled down. Further evidence of the writing of poetry in Ireland is to be found in the collections of the *Liber hymnorum* and the *Antiphonary of Bangor.* The hymns are characterized by the use of alliteration, assonance, and rhyme and cannot be called either quantitative or rhythmical. The unique manuscript of the *Antiphonary* is of the late 7th century. In the 7th and 8th centuries, Irish scholars produced commentaries on the Bible, stressing the literal interpretation. Apparently these writings were not widely circulated. The anonymous treatise, *De duodecim abusivis saeculi,* commonly attributed to St. CYPRIAN but composed in Ireland in the middle of the 7th century, was much quoted in the Carolingian period. Among the types criticized in the treatise are the scholar without works, the contentious Christian, the unjust king, and the negligent bishop. Adamnan, Abbot of Iona (679–704), a native of Ireland, besides his vivid life of St. Columba, left an interesting account of a journey by Bishop Arculf to the Holy Land, *De locis sanctis,* which he secured from the lips of the pilgrim himself. Both his enlightened approach to history and his literary style mark Adamnan as an outstanding author of his period and attest the high level of Irish education.

Anglo-Saxon England. The history of the 5th-century German conquest of Britain and its results are narrated in the gloomy *De excidio et conquestu Britanniae.* At least part of it has been attributed to Gildas, a monk who crossed over from England to live in Brittany. The first part of the work, which treats of the Roman occupation of England, was not written until the 8th century; the part dealing with the conditions after the coming of the Anglo-Saxons may have been written in the late 6th century. The *Historia Brittonum,* a compilation attributed to Nennius (9th century), presents even greater critical difficulties.

An important figure in the field of letters appeared in the middle of the 7th century in the person of ALDHELM (d. 709). A native of Wessex, he became the pupil of Mailduib, Irish founder and abbot of MALMESBURY. He also studied in Kent under Archbishop THEODORE OF CANTERBURY and Abbot HADRIAN. Thus there was in his education a double influence, Irish and Roman. Both of these came to bear on the monasteries in England and passed with the missionaries and scholars, Anglo-Saxons and Scoti, to schools on the Continent. Aldhelm's writings show that he possessed a wide acquaintance with pagan and Christian authors. His prose strains toward the unusual in vocabulary and construction, so that it is difficult to understand. He wrote a letter glorying in the fact that this artificial style could be produced in Britain as well as in Ireland. On the other hand, his poems, even his versified riddles, while not of great inspiration, are metrically correct and quite intelligible. He became abbot of Malmesbury and, at the end of his life, bishop of Sherborne.

Far superior to Aldhelm in graces of character and literary skill was BEDE (673–735), saint and scholar, known affectionately in history as the Venerable Bede. Northumbrian by birth, Bede became a monk of WEARMOUTH and then of JARROW, where he taught and wrote for more than 40 years. He composed for his pupils works on spelling, figures of speech, metrics, the divisions of time, and, more learnedly, on chronology (*see* CHRONOLOGY, MEDIEVAL, 2). Commentaries on the Old and New Testaments form the greatest part of his writing. In them he draws heavily on his Latin predecessors and delights in allegorical interpretation, but he copies with discrimination and is not lacking in originality. He was able to use Greek in his research, but his Hebrew references are taken from Jerome. A number of Bede's homilies are used in the Roman Breviary. He wrote saints' lives in prose and in verse. Far the best known of his works is his *Ecclesiastical History of the English People,* on which knowledge of English history up to 731 largely depends. Less dramatic than Gregory of Tours, Bede attains a unity of presentation in his work that makes it deserve to be called a history.

Out of English Benedictinism too came Wynfrith (*c.* 675–754), renamed Boniface by Pope Gregory II as he sent him on the German mission. Boniface left many letters rich in information concerning his missionary lands. Early in life he wrote a grammar and a work on metrics, and he left some poems and versified riddles.

The Carolingian Renaissance

The Saracen conquest of Spain and the Danish invasions of Ireland and England stopped literary progress in those parts of Christendom. The next development was to take place in *Francia* and produce the Carolingian renaissance. In preparation for it came the replacement of the difficult, unlovely Merovingian handwriting by the pleasing, readable Caroline minuscule, which gradually was to become the handwriting of Europe. The renaissance got under way with CHARLEMAGNE's efforts, inspired by churchmen, to educate the clergy, not yet in philosophy and theology, but in the rudiments of the liberal arts. Teachers and writers came from England, Ireland, Spain, and Italy to start the movement. A literary flourishing of their labors followed in the reign of Charles II the Bald. This second phase of the renaissance brought out more Frankish scholars as compared with the numbers that came from other lands. The scholars played seriously at forming an academy about Charlemagne in which they assumed the names of ancient writers. A palace school was created to educate promising youths.

This renaissance deserves to be called so because it consisted to a great extent in a rebirth of ancient learning. There was much copying of classical and patristic texts in the monastic SCRIPTORIA and garnering of them into libraries. Latin grammar was thoroughly studied, especially Priscian, and a number of the prominent scholars taught grammar at some time in their lives and wrote on it. One of them, for example, was the deacon ALCUIN OF YORK (d. 804), who has been called Charlemagne's minister of education and, more broadly, minister of intellectual affairs. Martianus Capella, the favored guide concerning the seven liberal arts, became the object of many commentaries. Before and during the Carolingian period numerous Latin glossaries were prepared. These glossaries usually reveal acquaintance with ancient writers on the part of those who composed them, and they helped to enrich, often pedantically, the vocabulary of those who made use of them. Ancient authors were admired and avidly read. This enthusiastic study resulted in a fine mastery of Latin on the part of those who pursued it. Both in their poetry and prose, Carolingian writers tended to imitate the ancients. In many instances the imitation was slavish, but it served no few writers to present their own ideas with richness and elegance.

Historical Writing. The most familiar example of wholesome classical imitation is EINHARD's *Life of Charlemagne*. Frankish Einhard was a product of the palace school. For the vita he turned to SUETONIUS as a model of biography, taking over format, words, and ideas and appropriating them to Charlemagne. The form of his work profited greatly, while the facts doubtless suffered somewhat. His vita is better than other biographies of the time—the two histories of Louis I, the Pious, and Nithard's account of the sons of Louis. In hagiography efforts were made to put the crude Latinity of earlier lives into good style with no benefit to historical content. MARTYROLOGIES were written and rewritten. Wandalbert of PRÜM composed one in verse. In Carolingian times there were fewer saints than in the preceding period, but in many cases their lives were written down by contemporaries, and there were accounts of miracles and of the translation of relics. ANNALS AND CHRONICLES, though they multiplied, showed little development. Outstanding among them are the *Royal Annals. The History of the Lombards* by PAUL THE DEACON is not comparable to Bede's history. It does not include an account of the author's own times. But the period did produce a number of capable writers on government and on the relations of Church and State who in some cases wrote to offer solutions for current problems in the realm: ADALARD, Alcuin, RABANUS MAURUS, Kathvulf, SMARAGDUS OF SAINT-MIHIEL, JONAS OF ORLÉANS, AGOBARD OF LYONS, Sedulius Scotus, and HINCMAR OF REIMS.

Verse. Carolingian verse has been preserved in great quantity, as the stout volumes of the *Poetae Latini aevi Carolini* (still in progress) in the *Monumenta Germaniae historica* bear witness. The Carolingian poets went to school to their great ancient predecessors. Scholars in every field tried their hand at verse, so that the result was frequently little more than an exercise in Latin. But among the great mass of verse written in the period, there are poems of considerable inspiration. One important innovation was the greatly increased use of rhythmic verse. Many rhythmical poems of the time, generally in trochaic verse, with or without rhyme, have come down anonymously in a collection made at the monastery of St. Gall (*see* SANKT GALLEN). Among them there are alphabetical poems, an uninspired vogue of the period. Some of this abecedarian verse appears in connection with the plaintive instructions in prose composed (841–843) by Dhuoda (Dodana) for her son William, who with his younger brother had been taken from her by her husband, Bernard of Septimania, and who was at the court of Charles the Bald. Probably the best known of the accentual poems is the beautiful ''Hymn of Charity,'' coming, it seems, out of Italy and still used in the liturgy of Maundy Thursday. It must be noted, however, that metrical verse was more commonly employed until the 10th or 11th century.

Some of Alcuin's verses savor too much of the Latin class. Even his celebrated poem on the church of York is noted principally for its subject matter. But he could and did at times write graceful poetry. Paul the Deacon left behind only a little poetry, some of it of high quality. Spanish THEODULF, Bishop of Orléans, an outstanding poet, did not let the language of the past destroy his originality as he wrote his hexameters and elegiacs. The Church still uses part of his lovely pentameter hymn, *GLORIA LAUS*, on Palm Sunday. He had a gift for vivid description of nature and of people, as appears, for example, in his poem to Charlemagne describing the court and the courtiers. WALAFRID STRABO was another true poet, best remembered for his poem on the monastery garden of REICHENAU and his eschatological *Visio Wettini* with the themes eventually used by DANTE. The torch had been handed down to him by Rabanus Maurus, who in turn had Alcuin as his teacher. Rabanus too had written much verse, though not of high inspiration, unless the 9th-century *VENI CREATOR SPIRITUS*, sometimes attributed to him, is really his. Also of Rabanus's school was GOTTSCHALK OF ORBAIS, who put rhyme into his poems in classical meters and also wrote rhythmical verse. His verse, the first medieval lyrical poetry, bears the poignant touch of his own unhappy life. FLORUS, master of the cathedral school of Lyons, a deacon, wrote much religious poetry, but it can hardly be called great, and it is surpassed by his prose. Besides other verse, Milo, a monk of SAINT-AMAND, left an interesting didactic poem, *De sobrietate*.

Among a number of immigrant Irishmen who wrote verse, Sedulius Scotus about the middle of the 9th century was outstanding, comparing favorably with the best poets of the period. He wrote metrical verse with a light touch as he sought the patronage of bishops and princes. Other Irishmen who flocked to the Continent in the 9th century tried their hand at poetry: Donatus, Bishop of Fiesole; Colman, with his nostalgic verses on Ireland; and JOHN SCOTUS ERIGENA. Erigena, proficient in Greek, could not resist introducing Greek verses into his poems. This conceit was followed by a number of other versifiers who came under Irish influence in their training, e.g., HEIRIC OF AUXERRE, Emmerich of Elwangen, and Fredigard of SAINT-RIQUIER. Micon, deacon and monk of Saint-Riquier, was a better poet. A pupil of Heiric, HUCBALD OF SAINT-AMAND, wrote a humorous poem on baldness in which every word of 146 lines begins with the letter *c*. Bishop RADBOD OF UTRECHT left several poems, among them a charming one written about a swallow that nested beneath his eaves.

There were also attempts at epic poetry by Carolingian writers. Ermoldus Nigellus, who it seems was a secular cleric, wrote four books (*c.* 826) in honor of Louis the Pious and two panegyrics in honor of Louis's son Pepin. Though not great poetry, Ermoldus's works are a precious historical source. Later in the century the anonymous POETA SAXO wrote a dull epic on Charlemagne based entirely on chronicles and Einhard. At the end of the century, Abbo of Saint-Germain-des-Prés composed in three books a vigorous epic on the siege of Paris by the Norsemen. It is an eyewitness account. The third book is marred by a display of recondite words derived from glossaries after the manner of Aldhelm and many Celtic writers. Of somewhat the same genre as the epic were the versified lives of saints, which merely reproduced the facts of earlier prose lives. Some of them were of great length. Heiric, for example, wrote 3,400 lines on St. GERMAIN OF AUXERRE (not of Paris, as is sometimes stated).

Carolingian Humanists. Greatest humanist of all in the period was LUPUS, monk and eventually abbot of Ferriéres, who left a precious collection of 127 letters dealing mostly with literary and monastic affairs. Many letters of the period have come down to us, written by monks, bishops, kings, and popes, full of human interest. Those of Lupus show his passionate interest in securing manuscripts and improving texts of ancient authors for the library of his monastery. He was an expert scribe himself, and not a few of the manuscripts that he actually copied or annotated are extant. His Latin shows much influence of Cicero, though he suited the style of his letters to the addressees. Lupus also wrote on theological problems of the day, making skillful use of dialectics. Among his many pupils, Heiric in turn trained Hucbald and REMIGIUS OF AUXERRE. Heiric, who also studied under Irish masters at Laon, carried on the tradition of Lupus by putting together excerpts of ancient authors and commentaries on authors treated by him in his classes. With Remigius the humanist tradition passed into the 10th century. Teaching successively in Auxerre, Reims, and Paris, he wrote much: numerous commentaries on secular and Christian authors, on books of the Bible, and on treatises dealing with the seven liberal arts.

Theology and Scripture. Writings on theology and Biblical exegesis, of which there were many in the period, depended very much on patristic writers, Augustine and Gregory the Great especially, but also Hilary, Leo I, Jerome, Boethius, Cassiodorus, Isidore, and some Greek authors available in Latin translation. Even in the controversial literature that arose over heterodoxy, patristic texts were, in the main, used as arguments. A rather uninspired pedagogical form of dialogue with catechetical questions and answers was introduced, probably first by Alcuin, into some theological writings. At times it was enlivened by riddles.

Alcuin participated in the Adoptionist controversy (*see* ADOPTIONISM), writing to refute Felix of Urgel (d. 818) and ELIPANDUS OF TOLEDO, as did also PAULINUS OF AQUILEIA and Agobard of Lyons. But it appears now that Alcuin did not compose or edit the capitulary of Charlemagne on images, commonly called the *LIBRI CAROLINI*, which protested against the teaching of the Council of NICAEA II (787) on the worship of images. The acts of the council were known to the Latin world only in a very faulty translation. The council had been a reaction against ICONOCLASM, and the *Libri Carolini* repudiated certain exaggerations in its teachings, especially in the Latin translation of its proceedings. There has been much academic controversy about the authorship of the *Libri Carolini,* but it seems, in the light of recent study, that it must be attributed to Archbishop Theodulf of Orléans instead of to Alcuin.

CLAUDIUS, Bishop of Turin, a Spaniard by birth, after writing many Biblical commentaries, went far beyond the *Libri Carolini* in his *Liber apologeticus* and attacked all cult of the saints, worship of the Cross, pilgrimages to Rome, and the veneration of St. Peter. His work stirred up a storm of indignation. He was answered by the Irishman, DUNGAL, who cited against him praises of the saints from Christian poets, and by JONAS OF ORLÉANS, who quoted passages of Claudius's own *Apologeticus* against him. On the other hand, Agobard of Lyons wrote in the same vein as Claudius. Neither showed an influence of the classics on his style, but the writings of both reflect the strength of their own polemical personality. Agobard wrote against the use of ORDEALS, against superstitions, and against the Jews.

The *Libri Carolini* took up the controversy about the FILIOQUE, insisting that it be introduced into the Creed. A few years later Alcuin in his summa of dogmatic theology (*De fide sanctae et individuae Trinitatis*) gave detailed treatment to the doctrine involved in the Filioque. Among several writers who answered an appeal of Pope Nicholas I to refute PHOTIUS, Patriarch of Constantinople, RATRAMNUS, monk of Corbie, stands out with his powerful four books *Contra Graecorum opposita,* the first three of which deal with the Filioque.

Ratramnus was involved in a controversy with his abbot, PASCHASIUS RADBERTUS, concerning the Eucharist. The abbot had written *De corpore et sanguine Christi,* a presentation of the doctrine of transubstantiation. Ratramnus found fault with some points of this treatise, and as a result he himself has been accused of heterodoxy. The more common opinion at present holds that he was not heretical. Paschasius (d. 859) was perhaps the most learned theologian of the 9th century. He profited by the opportunity to use the rich library of his monastery to read deeply in classics and patristics. He is an important figure in the history of the cult of the Blessed Virgin Mary. Strangely enough, he attributed some of his own writings on her to St. Jerome; others are found among the homilies attributed to St. Ildefonse.

The greatest theological controversy of Carolingian times arose over the question of PREDESTINATION. Many of the important authors of the 9th century participated in it. Keen-witted and stubborn Gottschalk of Orbais, who had devoted much study to St. Augustine, started it. He was accused by his opponents of teaching absolute and complete predestination to eternal punishment. Rabanus Maurus and Hincmar wrote against him. He was condemned by synods and underwent severe punishment. Florus of Lyons dealt with Gottschalk's views in a rather ambiguous manner, whereas Archbishop Amolo of Lyons (d. 852) pointed out what he considered objectionable in Gottschalk's views and gently urged him to conform.

On the other hand, one of Gottschalk's former teachers, Ratramnus, as well as PRUDENTIUS OF TROYES and Lupus of Ferrières, wrote in his favor. John Scotus Erigena, at the request of Hincmar, prepared a treatise attacking Gottschalk. Erigena was the philosopher of his day, his mind nurtured on the teaching of PSEUDO-DIONYSIUS, whom he translated into Latin. His *Liber de predestinatione,* with its philosophical approach, was attacked by both sides of the controversy over Gottschalk, notably by Florus. Scotus's *De divisione naturae* was better received, though it met condemnation in the 13th century for its pantheistic tendency. Some of Gottschalk's own writings have been discovered in recent times, and modern research is inclined to rescue him from the charge of heterodoxy.

Commentaries on Scripture were produced in great numbers by Carolingian theologians, all of them depending on patristic writers and almost all emphasizing allegorical interpretation. As exceptions, Paschasius Radbertus criticized his authorities, and CHRISTIAN OF STABLO (STAVELOT) preferred historical interpretation. Late in the 8th century, Ambrosius Autpertus (d. 784) in Italy and BEATUS OF LIÉBANA in Spain compiled commentaries on the Apocalypse that had considerable influence. Rabanus Maurus and Claudius of Turin were the most prolific exegetes. Rabanus employed long excerpts from the Fathers and made his personal contribution by small additions and by blending his quotations into a coherent treatment. Teaching rather than original thinking characterized all that he did and earned him the title of pedagogue of his age. Claudius's many exegetical works were really scriptural glosses, the first of that genre in the Western Church, an imitation of the Greek *catenae.* Glosses were compiled from one or several early authors. They were much used by theological scholars as a ready source for citations. The most famous of them, the *Glossa ordinaria,* which cannot be attributed to Walafrid Strabo as such, was apparently started in the period. Much later it was developed by ANSELM OF LAON and was given its name by Stephen Lombard. In the 12th century, glosses ceased to be mere citations of ancient authors.

Liturgy. The reign of Pepin the Short had witnessed a great liturgical upheaval in *Francia,* with the replacing of the Gallican liturgy by the Roman. Bishops REMIGIUS OF ROUEN and CHRODEGANG OF METZ were especially active in this reform. In the next century AMALARIUS OF METZ and of Lyons wrote extensively on the liturgy. His exaggerated use of allegorical interpretation in explaining the liturgy and some careless expressions that lent themselves to suspicion of heresy caused a great outburst against him on the part of Agobard and Florus. Nevertheless he retained his popularity and was much used by subsequent liturgists. Besides criticizing Amalarius, Florus compiled a work on the liturgy from the Fathers, and Walafrid Strabo left a brief but solid treatise on the historical origins of liturgical ceremonies and institutions.

Law. In Canon Law, penitentials continued to be produced. The *FALSE DECRETALS* came out of the vicinity of Le Mans about the middle of the 9th century. About the same time, that other forgery, the *DONATION OF CONSTANTINE*, came into existence. Its authorship is still a mystery. Without valid proof it has been attributed to ANASTASIUS THE LIBRARIAN, cardinal priest of St. Marcellus, who, as an intermediary between the Greek and Latin world, among numerous other writings, translated the acts of the seventh and eighth councils (NICAEA II and CONSTANTINOPLE IV) into Latin. The most distinguished canonist of the century was Hincmar, for 40 years archbishop of Reims. Civil law witnessed a redaction of the *Leges barbarorum,* the production of the royal CAPITULARIES and efforts at codifying them, and the issuing of many royal *diplomata.*

Spain. Contemporary Spain showed little influence of the Carolingian renaissance, though it experienced its own revival of Latin letters. Invaded and conquered as it was, it could not fulfill the promise it had shown in literature during the Visigothic period. There were chronicles in the second half of the 8th century. One of them, the *Chronicle of 754,* written with some effort at style, has precious information on Spanish history during the Muslim invasions. Late in the next century two chronicles offer historical data on the Christian kingdom of the Asturias, the *Chronicle of Roda* (or *of Alfonso III*) and that of Albelda. The latter is found with an addition called the *Prophetic Chronicle*, which underwent a revision in the late 10th century. It talks of the Muslims and prophesies their overthrow in Spain.

A number of letters concerning disciplinary matters in the Church and doctrinal errors supply scattered details for the history of the late 8th century. The most important heresy was Adoptionism, championed by Elipandus of Toledo and Felix of Urgel, and condemned as has been indicated above. Elipandus, a master of invective, wrote many letters concerning his beliefs. Beatus of Liébana and Eterius of Osma wrote a learned apologetic treatise (785) against him and his teachings. Thereafter written documents become scarce for a time. The acts of the Council of Córdoba (839) afford information on the current state of the Church.

The most distinguished and prolific writers of Spain in the 9th century were the Córdobans, Albar and his friend EULOGIUS. Presumably a layman, Albar wrote freely of theological and ecclesiastical matters. He exchanged letters with five correspondents on religious questions, some of them his personal problems. One such exchange was with Bodo-Eleazar, a priest who had gone over to Judaism. Albar strove to prove to Bodo that Christ is the Messiah. Both correspondents indulged in harsh invective. Albar left some 500 lines of rather poor metrical verse, mostly hexameter, on nature and on the Bible, all of it deeply religious. He devoted some Asclepiadean verses to the martyr Eulogius. A small quantity of metrical verse by other contemporary writers in Spain has been preserved. Probably Albar is the author of the *Indiculus luminosus,* which chides compromising Christians, defends the ideals of the martyrs of Córdoba (850–859), and denounces Muḥammad as a precursor of Antichrist. The work concludes by deprecating the neglect of Latin and Latin studies in favor of Arabic learning on the part of Christian youth. A much more detailed account and defense of the Córdoban martyrs is to be found in the *Memoriale sanctorum,* the *Apologeticus martyrum,* and the *Documentum martyriale* of Eulogius. He himself died a martyr, and his life was written by Albar. They had studied together in the school of the learned Abbot Esperaindeo. Albar tells of a trip Eulogius made to monasteries around Pamplona, from which he brought back a number of classical and Christian writings. He praises Eulogius's virtue and zealous energy, as well as his learning, and pays ardent veneration to him as a saint in heaven. Probably Albar's final work was his *Confessio,* a long prayer of contrition. It has little in common with Augustine's *Confession* but is in the tradition especially of Isidore's *Synonyma* and several pseudo-Isidorian writings.

At a date not definitely known, but probably after the martyrdoms, a work on clerical discipline and dress was written by Leovigildus, presumably the otherwise well-known cleric of Córdoba of that name. In 864 Samson, abbot of the Basilica of St. Zoilus in Córdoba, wrote his *Apologeticus.* It treats of the Trinity and the Incarnation and gives an idea of the organization of the Church in Spain at the time. The most interesting part of the work is the attack on a bishop, Hostegesis, and a layman, Servandus, who were obsequious to the Muslim authorities and tyrannized over the Christians. Samson refutes their doctrinal errors and ridicules the bishop's bad Latin.

The 10th Century

The invasions of the Normans and Hungarians and the incursions of the Saracens in the Mediterranean regions discouraged the pursuit of letters in the 10th century. The organizational work of Charlemagne literally went to pieces. The period, not without reason, has been called an iron age, the DARK AGES, but even from the viewpoint of literature this should not be exaggerated. Remigius of Auxerre and Hucbald of St. Amand, as has been noted, passed on the torch of learning into the 10th century. Literary study was centered in the monasteries, among which that of St. Gall flourished in the period.

Sequence and Trope. NOTKER BALBULUS, a monk of St. Gall, lived only until 912, but he has a place in the early development of the SEQUENCE, or prose, a new departure in liturgical texts. There is much disagreement among authors about the actual origin of these texts, but Notker composed some of them and established the tendency to depart from the exact melody of the ALLELUIA and its prolongation, or *jubilus.* In France at the time the texts were made to follow the melody closely. At St. Gall assonance, rhyme, and rhythm gradually appeared in the Sequences, and with them a bold melodic development. From St. Gall this type of Sequence spread into Germany, where toward the middle of the 11th century, Wipo, chaplain to Emperors Conrad II and Henry III, composed the *VICTIMAE PASCHALI LAUDES*, the Easter Sequence, which marks a step toward the completely versified Sequences that was characteristic of the 12th century.

With St. Gall in the time of Notker is associated the composition of TROPES, i.e., texts interpolated into the Introit, Kyrie, Gloria, and other parts of the Mass. Probably originating in France, troping was more common there and in England and Italy than in Germany. Tropes, eventually rejected from the liturgy, were the beginnings of medieval drama (*see* DRAMA, MEDIEVAL).

Notker has more definite claim to literary greatness. He wrote occasional verse of superior quality, a life of St. GALL in mixed prose and verse, of which only fragments remain, and a martyrology. Best known of his works is, however, his *Gesta Karoli,* which laid the basis for the medieval legend of Charlemagne.

The Ottonian Renaissance. In the year Notker died, Otto, who in 936 became OTTO I of Germany, was born. The literary development in his reign and those of his two successors to the turn of the century is somewhat diffidently called a renaissance named after them (*see* OTTONIAN RENAISSANCE). It can be looked upon as a further flowering of the Carolingian renaissance. The Ottonian court by no means furnished a center of culture comparable to that of Charlemagne. But the steadying influence of the Ottos as rulers and the resumption of the imperial title established a milieu in which letters could thrive.

A number of rather ambitious epic and historical poems came out of German monasteries. An anonymous monk, perhaps of TEGERNSEE, using a Latin translation, put into leonine verse the old Greek romance *Historia Apollonii, regis Tyri.* He cast it into the form of a dialogue, or eclogue, and used many glossary terms and Greek words. The *Waltharius,* an epic of 1,456 hexameter lines with a setting in the time of the Hunnic invasions, is generally considered to have been written at St. Gall by EKKEHARD I (d. 973) and later revised by Ekkehard IV (d. 1060). It is maintained by some, however, that it was written in Aquitaine a century earlier. The epic is built on popular Germanic legends and is similar to the *Nibelungenlied.* It is a gory tale, but it has literary merit. Another, less successful, poem, the *Ecbasis captivi* in 1,229 hexameter lines with leonine rhyme, was composed in a monastery of Lorraine, apparently Saint-Evre of Toul. It is the oldest Germanic beast-epic, dating from *c.* 940, or, as recent scholarship proposes, from the next century. It is an allegory that tells a tale of monastic life, quite unintelligible now, under the guise of an animal story. Many classical and Christian poets were pillaged by the author.

At the convent of GANDERSHEIM in Saxony a nun, ROSWITHA (Hrotswitha), wrote six dramas in rhymed prose on Christian themes. She meant them to replace the reading of Terence, but he remained a favorite, and she survived in only one manuscript. Futile attempts have been made to prove her plays a forgery of the 15th century. Roswitha wrote a long poem in rather graceful rhyming hexameters, the *Gesta Othonis,* on Otto I, and another, the *Primordia coenobii Gandeshemensis,* which traces the history of her abbey down to 919. Her style is rather good and shows the influence of Vergil, Prudentius, and Sedulius. Saxony also produced WIDUKIND OF CORVEY (d. after 973), who wrote the history of Henry I and Otto I in prose, but with many poetic words and a patriotic approach that give his work qualities of an epic.

Between 915 and 924 an anonymous poet in northern Italy wrote four books of hexameters on the battle-filled history of Berengar I. He is not careful about chronology and leans heavily upon classical writers. The author, a schoolmaster, equipped his poem with glosses explaining difficult passages.

Along with historical poems the Ottonian period produced some histories. One of the most celebrated authors of the century was the Italian LIUTPRAND, cleric, courtier, ambassador, and, eventually, bishop of Cremona (961). He was successively at the courts of Hugh and Berengar in Italy, and of Otto I in Germany. His attempt at writing a universal history failed to deal with Europe west of Germany. It was called *Antapodosis* (Tit-for-Tat) because he praised his friends and excoriated his enemies, especially Berengar, with whom he had quarreled, and Emperor Nicephorus II Phocas, whom he despised. He wrote a history of Otto I during the years 960 to 964 and an account of one of his own embassies to Constantinople. His works are filled with anecdotes; his style is affected and interlarded with Greek, and verse of his own composition is introduced into his prose text. He writes with biting humor, and, though one cannot trust everything that he says, he is very interesting reading. A chronicle extending to 965 was written by Benedict, a monk of St. Andrew on the Soracte. In barbarous Latin he treats especially of the Lombards and of his own monastery. He is the first source for the legend of Charlemagne's expedition to the Holy Land. In better Latin the *Chronicon Salernitanum,* by a monk of St. Benedict of Salerno using archival material and oral tradition, gives the history of the Lombard dukedoms in southern Italy to 974.

In the north, in Lorraine, Abbot REGINO OF PRÜM (d. 915), besides works on music and Canon Law, wrote a chronicle from the birth of Christ to 906. It is curious that he did not know the Carolingian chronicles. The work becomes more original after 814 as he makes use of local annals, some sources no longer extant, and oral information. An anonymous writer extended the chronicle to 967, giving valuable information on the Saxon dynasty.

FLODOARD, a cleric of Reims (d. 966), distinguished himself as an historian. He wrote annals probably from the year 894, though the extant text begins with 919 and extends to 966. His great work is the *History of the Church of Reims* in four books, which as archivist of Reims he was well fitted to write. A poetical work by him on the triumphs of the saints of Palestine, Antioch, and Italy, in 19 books and many different verse forms, proves that he was no mean poet. He visited Rome to gather material on the saints of Italy. In both his prose and poetry he is singularly independent of classical influence. Richer (d. after 998), a monk of Saint-Remy in Reims, at the behest of Archbishop Gerbert, set out to write the history of Charles the Simple and Louis IV, but he carried it through to 995. It is a valuable source for the late Carolingians and the Capetian revolution. Richer's pretension to rhetoric and classical imitation, together with errors in chronology, make him inferior to Flodoard as a historian. The original manuscript of his work was found in 1883. The *Historia Francorum* (before 1004) of Aimon of Fleury is merely a rewriting in better Latin of earlier sources. It extends only to the middle of the 7th century.

Biography and hagiography were not neglected in the period. Notable were the accounts of the lives of the abbots of Cluny, two of whom, ODO (d. 942) and ODILO (d. 1049), wrote on spiritual matters in prose and in verse, though CLUNY produced no significant writer until PETER THE VENERABLE in the 12th century. It showed less enthusiasm for classical literature than did the great abbeys of the Carolingian period. Tenth-century abbots of several other monasteries received biographies. A number of good biographies of bishops were produced in the 10th and 11th centuries. In the valley of the Meuse, HERIGER, who became abbot of Lobbes (Laubach) in 995, under the influence of Notker, the great bishop of Liège, where the abbot had long been a teacher, wrote a history of the bishops of that see. It quotes ancient authors frequently and is better literature than history. First of the biographies in the time of the great Ottonian bishops was that of BRUNO, learned Archbishop of Cologne, brother of Otto I. It was written by Ruotger, a cleric, perhaps a monk, at the request of Folcmar, Bruno's successor (965–968). The author profited by Bruno's literary interests and rich library. He modeled his work after Sallust, as Widukind had done, and was influenced by Augustine and Sulpicius Severus. The life of ULRIC (d. 973), distinguished bishop of Augsburg, was written by Gerhard, provost of the cathedral chapter, his contemporary. There are biographies of the first bishop of Prague, the martyr St. ADALBERT, and of ADALBERO II, Bishop of Metz. Among the best biographies of the Middle Ages was that of Bishop BERNWARD OF HILDESHEIM (992–1022) by THANGMAR, his teacher, and later dean of his chapter, librarian, and notary. Completed by 1023, the vita treats not only of St. Bernward and his see, a great art center, but also affords much information on the history of the time. There were two attempts at a biography of Mathilda, mother of Otto I, a biography of King Robert II of France by Helgaud, monk of Fleury, two accounts of the martyred Duke WENCESLAUS OF BOHEMIA, and one of the writer on Canon Law, Bishop BURCHARD OF WORMS.

Gerbert, born in Auvergne and educated in the monastery of Aurillac, who became Pope Silvester II, is reputed to have been the most learned man of his age. In 967 he went into Spain to study mathematics and the natural sciences. Because of his scientific learning he was even thought to be a magician. His interest was especially the quadrivium, and he wrote on mathematics and on the use of the abacus. As scholasticus of the cathedral school of Reims (970–982) he had great influence on education. Gerbert was elected archbishop of Reims and named abbot of Bobbio and archbishop of Ravenna before he became pope (999–1003). Written in classical style, a sheaf of letters left by him throws light on his humanistic ideals and the history of the times. Another distinguished teacher, ABBO OF FLEURY (d. 1004), wrote works on logic and the calendar. ADSO, Abbot of Montier-en-Der and later of St. Benignus in Dijon (d. 992), a careful stylist, wrote *De Antichristo,* an eschatological work, for Gerberga, daughter of Henry the Fowler, as well as several saints' lives.

RATHERIUS, tempestuous ecclesiastic, born in Liège, bishop of Verona, which see he took up and laid down three times, spending most of his incumbency in prison, wielded an extremely facile pen. He used it, dipped in irony, to make charges against king, bishops, priests, and all classes of society and to urge his reforms. Thus he was a sort of mirror of his times. His chief work, in five books, he called *Praeloquia.* He likewise at times wrote introspectively, confessing with bitterness his own failings, always in a style that showed his command of the classics. He continued his cantankerous ways back in the region of the Meuse until he died (974).

A calmer spirit was Bishop ATTO OF VERCELLI (d. 961), who wrote against lay oppression of the Church in his *De pressuris ecclesiasticis* and preached against superstition. A work entitled *Polypticum,* attributed to him, discussed the disturbing political situation in Italy in the most obscure language, very unlike Atto's usual style. No one, however, seems to doubt its authenticity. In Rome earlier in the century EUGENIUS VULGARIUS wrote a defense in rhymed prose of Pope Formosus after his death. He also wrote *carmina figurata* of the worst kind, e.g., in the form of a pyramid and of a triangle, in praise of the Pope and the Emperor. In Naples, with somewhat less rhetoric, AUXILIUS wrote in defense of Formosus, as did also an anonymous writer (928). Archpriest Leo of Naples translated into Latin the Alexander romance (951–969), which enjoyed great vogue in the Middle Ages.

The 11th Century

Writers in the 11th century continued to be monastic. They produced writings intended for pedagogical use, much verse of various genres, chronicles and biographies, and some theological works, culminating in those of St. Anselm of Canterbury.

Writings on the Trivium. In St. Gall NOTKER LABEO translated into German a number of Latin authors used in the schools. Thus St. Gall became the cradle of German literature in the 11th century. Papias, an Italian cleric, in the middle of the century composed a lexicon and a simple grammar based on Priscian. Aimeric of Angoulême, also a cleric, in his *Ars lectoris* (1086), which treated the accentuation of words, cited verses from many authors, including some otherwise unknown verses of Luxorius. He attempted, with judgment somewhat less than unerring, to group ancient and medieval authors into classes according to their excellence. Conrad of Hirschau, in an early 12th-century dialogue, discussed and evaluated a number of authors. He insisted that the study of the Bible and theology were superior to the pursuit of profane learning.

Verse. Ekkehard IV of St. Gall composed a *Liber benedictionum* containing 60 hymns for the feasts of the liturgical year, written by students and revised by himself, and a number of formulas for blessing various objects. His *Casus sancti Galli* gives a glimpse into the monastery and its schools, though as history it is inaccurate.

The school of TEGERNSEE owed much to the teacher Froumund, who at the end of the 10th century succeeded in making good poetry out of themes for school exercises. In rather poor Latin, *Ruodlieb,* a romantic epic concerning the adventures of a German knight, was composed by a monk of Tegernsee *c.* 1050. The end of the poem is not extant, but the 2,400 verses in leonine hexameter that remain offer a mixture of Oriental wisdom, German saga, and history.

One of the fullest medieval autobiographers, OTHLO, Abbot of St. Emmeram in Regensburg (d. 1070), was trained in the monastic schools of Tegernsee and HERSFELD. His personality appears vividly in all his writings, and he gives precious information concerning his own education. Despite a vow to enter a monastery, he for some years remained a cleric in the world. In 1032 he entered St. Emmeram and soon became master of the school there. His first work, *De doctrina spirituali,* was a lengthy poem in 39 sections; the poet's introspective nature caused him to present an account of his temptations for the guidance of others. In the work he incidentally listed his writings and told of his calligraphic skill. In *De visionibus* he related visions of his own as well as some reported by other authors and by his contemporaries. Among Othloh's other writings are several hagiographical accounts of little historical value. All his writings, in a style pleasingly simple, were for the edification of others. Though he was versed in the classics himself and quoted from them in his *Proverbia,* he did not approve of their use in education. In theology, he felt, dialectics could be dangerous.

Somewhat earlier in the century Egbert of Liège had put together a collection of proverbs in some 2,000 verses of his *Fecunda ratis,* in which he drew from German tradition, the Bible, and patristic and pagan authors. At the same time WIPO, court chaplain to Conrad II, composed his *Proverbia,* with rhymes of two and three syllables, for Conrad's son Henry. Wipo carried over his love for proverbs into his history of Conrad II and Henry III, which is written in admirably correct Latin.

Intellectually highly gifted but physically maimed by paralysis, so that he could not move and could use his voice and fingers only with difficulty, Hermannus the Lame (*Contractus*), monk of REICHENAU, was called in contemporary annals the "marvel of his age." He wrote much on mathematics and astronomy. His chronicle of world history to 1054, the year of his death, is the earliest extant work of this kind written east of the Rhine. Its latter part is valuable for the history of southern Germany, Bohemia, and Hungary. Herman is the author of a long poem, *De contemptu mundi,* addressed to nuns; the versification, in a variety of meters, is correct. The text and music of several Sequences and a little treatise on music are by Herman, but the antiphons *ALMA REDEMPTORIS MATER* and *SALVE REGINA* cannot be attributed to him. The latter emanated from Le Puy in the 11th century, probably the work of Bishop Aimar. The *AVE MARIS STELLA* existed in the 9th century, and the *AVE REGINA COELORUM* and the *REGINA CAELI* are of the 12th century. The eclogue *Conflictus ovis et lini,* on the merits of the sheep and of flax, at one time attributed to Herman, is apparently the work of Winrich of Trier.

About the middle of the century Warnerius of Basel, perhaps of French origin, wrote two poems with smooth leonine rhyme: *Synodicus* and *Paraclitus.* The former is an imitation of the 9th-century *Eclogue of Theodulus,* a contest to demonstrate the superiority of the Old Testament over ancient mythology. Warnerius parallels persons and episodes of the Old Testament with some in the New Testament and in the history of the Church. The *Paraclitus* is a dialogue between a sinner and grace.

A shadowy figure of the middle Rhine region, a monk under the pseudonym Sextus Amaricius Piosistratus, composed his satirical *Sermones,* four books of verse in the form of dialogue and monologue. Writing in the reign of Henry III, in 1046 at the earliest, he castigated the vices of the time and presented the virtues as their cure. The *Sermones* are the first extant medieval satirical work of importance, though it has come down in only one manuscript.

Several historical poems in leonine hexameter were written by German ecclesiastics during the 11th century. Purchard of Reichenau in narrating the life of Abbot Witigowo described the coronation of Otto III in Rome. Abbot Gerard of Seeon wrote a historical poem in 54 hexameters on the church of Bamberg and its school, comparing it with ancient Athens. Bishop THIETMAR OF MERSEBURG interspersed his chronicle of the history of Saxony with dull leonine verses. The anonymous *Carmen de bello Saxonico* sings the praises of Henry IV in his victory over the Saxons from 1073 to 1075. Critics argue about its historical value.

In Italy, MONTE CASSINO, with its scriptorium and rich library, was a center of culture. There CONSTANTINE THE AFRICAN made translations of medical works from Arabic and Greek that were to be the fundamental texts in schools of medicine until the 15th century. Guaiferius and ALPHANUS were accomplished poets. The former wrote religious poetry for edification; the latter, more skilled, wrote odes in the lyrical measures of Horace, notably one on Monte Cassino and one dedicated to Archdeacon Hildebrand. LEO OF VERCELLI, *episcopus imperii,* wrote verse in praise of Gregory V and Otto III and an elegy on Otto. Rangerius, Bishop of Lucca, in a poem, *De anulo et baculo,* attacked lay investiture.

St. PETER DAMIAN (1007–72), unworldly ascetic called to be a cardinal and thrust into the fight against the evils of the age, was well schooled in the arts and gifted as a writer both in prose and verse. He was the author of much poetry, mostly metrical: majestic verses in trochaic tetrameter on judgment day and paradise, a rhythmical poem on the Song of Songs, and many hymns to Mary, the Apostles, martyrs, and other saints in a variety of meters. He was a skilled writer of epigrams. His rhymed prose could soar with poetical feeling. His prose works against simony and clerical incontinence played a significant role in the Gregorian reform. His many letters are of great value as historical sources. He was a master of the spiritual life, gentler in his asceticism and piety than many writers have made him out to be. Though he inveighed against pagan authors, he used them in his writing. He was especially fond of drawing some of his examples from the *PHYSIOLOGUS*.

In France the center of study was passing from the older monasteries to new schools, the cathedral school of CHARTRES and the monastery of BEC. But the significant poets began to flourish only at the turn of the century. With FULBERT, Bishop of Chartres (d. 1029), pupil of Gerbert, the reputation of the school of Chartres began. He wrote many religious poems in meter and rhythm, prose treatises, saints' lives, and sermons. He was versed in medicine, but his greatest fame was as a churchman. His pupil BERENGARIUS OF TOURS, whose writings on the Eucharist raised a storm of polemical works against him, was the author of a rhyming accentual poem in which he prayed for himself. The devious politician who in 977 became bishop of Laon, Adalbero, wrote satirical verse (1017) attacking monks and deploring the state of the kingdom in the reign of Robert the Pious. He knew the Roman satirists. Godfrey (d. 1095), scholasticus and chancellor of Reims, wrote letters in verse, patently school exercises, and a poem in honor of another poet, Odo of Orléans and Cambrai, which was cast in the form of a dream.

In the middle of the 11th century a collection of medieval lyrical verse made by an unknown German throws light on the development of such poetry. From the manuscript of Cambridge University in which it is found the collection is known as the Cambridge Songs. It contains a number of Sequences, profane as well as sacred, intended to be sung. A number of the poems show progress in the mastery of accentual verse in connection with romantic stories, love themes, and description of nature. One of the poems of the collection, in rhythmical dactylic tetrameter, *O admirabile Veneris idolum,* came out of Verona, probably in the 10th century. Its subject is perverted love, but it gives a key to the provenience of the beautiful poem in the same meter, *O ROMA NOBILIS, orbis et domina*, which sings of the Rome of virgins and martyrs, of SS. Peter and Paul. A lengthy love poem in elegiacs with leonine rhyme, found among other poems in a Psalter belonging to the cathedral of Ivrea, appears to be of the late 11th century. Its theme indicates that St. Peter Damian was not fighting imaginary evils in the Church.

Three gifted 11th-century poets lived well into the 12th century: MARBOD, Bishop of Rennes (d. 1123), Baudry of Bourgueil (d. 1130), and HILDEBERT OF LAVARDIN (d. 1133). Marbod, a product of the cathedral school of ANGERS and its master, wrote a poem on figures of words, illustrating them in his verse. His best-known work is a poem on the virtues of precious stones, *Liber lapidum.* He put Bible stories and saints' lives, as well as many of his letters, into verse. A poetical work of his old age, *Liber decem capitulorum,* shows him repenting of frivolous verse of his youth and lamenting the unbridled freedom and too secular training of the cathedral schools. He was overly fond of the leonine hexameter and little skilled in composing rhythmical verse.

Baudry, a gracious and clever writer, after study at Angers became a monk at Bourgueil, its abbot (1089), and archbishop of Dol (1107). His verse is, however, for the most part secular in spirit. Ovid was his master; and he was an ardent humanist, showing in his beautifully wrought metrical verse the secularizing effect of his education in a cathedral school. His prose writings and some of his verse are religious but without great depth of feeling. He carried on a wide correspondence.

Hildebert, more profound than Marbod and Baudry and a better churchman, may have been a pupil of Berengar of Tours. After serving successively as scholasticus, archdeacon, and bishop (1096) of Le Mans, he became archbishop of TOURS (1125). Though a distinguished humanist, he preferred to choose themes for his poetry from Scripture, liturgy, and hagiography. Two fine poems have Rome as their subject. Hildebert wrote in a variety of classical meters but likewise used rhythmical verse in masterly fashion. His many letters reveal him as an earnest prelate concerned with law and reform. They were used as models in the schools.

History. The writing of chronicles and history made progress in the 11th century, not in France with its feudal division, nor in Spain, but along the Rhine and in Germany. MARIANUS SCOTUS (d. *c.* 1082), a recluse who lived in several German monasteries, used various ancient and medieval sources in writing his world chronicle and made many corrections in chronology. He showed little interest in the history of his own times, but gave scattered data on kings, bishops, and his fellow Scoti. Thietmar, bishop of Merseburg, wrote a history of Saxony and adjacent Slavic regions up to 1018. The indication of his sources in the margin of his manuscript gives evidence of vast research. He strove to imitate ancient authors, and his style is somewhat affected. On the other hand, Lambert of Hersfeld (d. 1077) wrote his chronicle in a good style, dealing after 1046 with matters of which he had personal knowledge. A prolific writer, author of 15 treatises on the side of the papacy in the investiture struggle, in which he displays good judgment and considerable moderation, BERNOLD OF CONSTANCE (or of St. Blaise or Schaffhausen) composed a universal chronicle. Original from 1074 to his death in 1100, it is too much restricted to ecclesiastical matters and unimportant daily happenings. Bernold left a valuable work on the liturgy. The *History of the Bishops of Hamburg,* extending to 1075, in good, concise Latin, by Adam of Bremen is the best diocesan history of the period, with much information on northern Germany and the Scandinavian countries. Somewhat earlier several good monastic and diocesan histories were written: an account of the abbots of SAINT-TROND by Rudolph of that monastery; a history of the bishops of Tongres and LIÈGE by Anselm of Liège; and one concerning the bishops of CAMBRAI by an anonymous writer. In Italy the Abbey of Monte Cassino had its chroniclers. The Belgian monk SIGEBERT OF GEMBLOUX (1030–1112) was the greatest chronicler of his time. His world chronicle is independent from 1024 to 1111. Sigebert, who sided with the Emperor against the Pope in the struggle over investiture, was also the author of saints' lives and of a *De viris illustribus.*

In France Radulfus Glaber (d. *c.* 1050) wrote a life of St. WILLIAM, Abbot of St. Benignus in Dijon, and a rather poor history of his times, limited for the most part to Burgundy and France. Adhémar of Chabannes (d. 1034), preacher, poet, scribe, and historian, wrote a history of the abbots of St. Martial in Limoges, a letter defending the apostolicity of the Church of Limoges, and a chronicle that is especially useful for the history of Aquitaine. There were several chroniclers of the conquest of England by the Normans and of their history in Italy.

Toward the end of the period, from the pontificate of Gregory VII (1073–85) to that of Pascal II (1099–1118), Europe was deluged with polemical literature emanating from both sides in the struggle over lay investiture. Aside from letters, which were numerous, and canonical collections, there were more than 130 polemical works, most of them edited in the *Libelli de lite* of the *Monumenta Germaniae Historica.* They emanated especially from Germany and Italy but also from France, England, and Spain, and were written almost entirely by ecclesiastics, mostly monks, and only a few bishops. Of great value as historical sources, they also throw light on the literary culture in the various parts of Europe. Some were in verse; irony was much employed. Simony was frequently the topic of the papal defenders.

There were many biographies written in the period, usually of great churchmen. The life of Henry IV was an exception. Saints' lives were written largely in a stereotyped pattern with disregard for the facts of individual lives. Some apocryphal lives were written to satisfy vanity. Following an effort to put earlier biographies into good Latin there was a reversion of sentiment in favor of simplicity. But in both the 10th and 11th centuries there were no few saints' lives written that brought out the details and personal qualities of their heroes and thus have real historical value.

The chronicles of the First Crusade were written in the early 12th century, but their authors were really men of the 11th. These writings and those on the succeeding Crusades are of varied literary quality. They are available in good editions and modern translations and are among the better known texts of the Middle Ages.

Theological Writings. There was a decline in the production of theological literature after the Carolingian period. Toward the middle of the 11th century, however, theological controversy gave new impetus to the writing of theology. The controversy concerning the Eucharist and the struggle over lay investiture have been mentioned. Both were marked by a wider recourse to dialectic. Its use was deprecated by some authors, but it was on its way to triumph in the next century. Those who fought over investiture still preferred the citation of authorities, especially legal texts, St. Cyprian, and St. Augustine.

The influence of Augustine made itself strongly felt in 11th-century works on the spiritual life, some of which actually circulated under his name. Abbot John of Fécamp (1028–78), only recently recognized as the author of a number of spiritual writings, was one of the first to introduce affective devotion into his meditations. The prayer for each day of the week in the Preparation for Mass in the Missal, which was formerly attributed to St. Ambrose, has been vindicated for Abbot John. St. Peter Damian wrote similar prayers, as did St. Anselm.

Glory of the Benedictine Middle Ages, ANSELM, born in Aosta in northern Italy, successively abbot of Bec and archbishop of Canterbury, at the end of the 11th century (d. 1109) far outdistanced his age in power of thought and literary expression. He was taught at Bec by the Italian LANFRANC, himself no mean scholar and author, chief literary opponent of Berengar of Tours. Bent always on his principle of *fides quaerens intellectum,* Anselm meditated lovingly on the truth he studied, whether he wrote his philosophical and theological treatises or composed his prayers. His ontological argument for the existence of God, often repudiated, has charmed philosophers of all ages. His more than 400 letters deal with many problems of his time and often amount to treatises. The memory of Anselm's life and conversation is faithfully preserved in the biography by his companion and secretary EADMER, monk of Canterbury.

Abbot GUIBERT OF NOGENT (d. 1121), at the suggestion of Anselm, composed his *Moralia in Genesim* in imitation of the *Moralia* of Gregory the Great. Besides other exegetical works, Guibert wrote on relics, decrying veneration paid to relics that were not authenticated; on the Incarnation, against arguments of the Jews; in praise of the Blessed Virgin Mary; on virginity; and on the construction of sermons. He is best known for his *Gesta Dei per Francos,* a history of the First Crusade, and for his autobiography. He ornamented his prose writings with verses in diverse meters.

Bruno of Asti (*c.* 1040–1123), abbot of Monte Cassino, was a prolific author. His works include treatises on the Trinity and the Incarnation, liturgical and polemical writings, commentaries on Scripture, sermons, and letters, all composed in good Latin style.

Law. The period witnessed a renaissance of civil law brought about by the discovery, after centuries of neglect, of Justinian's *Digest,* which became the object of intensive study resulting in glosses. Bologna, with its famous master IRNERIUS, became the center for this study. The investiture struggle stirred up increased interest in Canon Law. Outstanding names among the canonists were BURCHARD OF WORMS, ANSELM OF LUCCA, BONIZO (BONITHO) OF SUTRI, and IVO OF CHARTRES.

The 12th-Century Renaissance

The impetus in Latin literature connected with what is known as the 12th-century renaissance had its beginnings in the last quarter of the 11th century and extended through the first quarter of the 13th. The renaissance developed in the milieu of the rising towns with their business and prosperity. Its intellectual aspects were centered in France, in the schools in and around Paris. Chartres, Laon, Reims, Tours, Anvers, and Poitiers, along with Tournai and Liège in Belgium, had schools that flourished more or less for a time, but Paris took and kept an undisputed ascendancy.

Schools and Scholars. The schools occupied themselves primarily with philosophy and theology. But their scholars in many cases did not limit their writings to those fields. After St. ANSELM, the outstanding figure to arise in the scholarly world was ABELARD (1079–1142), certainly one of the best known of medieval personalities. He had studied under ANSELM OF LAON (d. 1117), whom he later sought to discredit but who had made a contribution to the systematizing of theology and the organizing of scriptural glosses.

Brilliant, but combative, Abelard moved about France discussing dialectic and theology before large audiences. His teaching on the Trinity, faith, and grace brought condemnations upon him and antagonism from Bernard of Clairvaux. He wrote much on dialectic and used it in his theology, not limiting himself, as has been averred, to the problem of universals. Most of his works were concerned with theology and Scripture. His *Sic et non* brought together contradictory texts on theology culled from patristic writings. It was not, as was held by some, an evidence of skepticism on the part of Abelard but a challenge to his pupils to reconcile conflicting opinions. The introduction is a pioneer treatment on the theory of semantics. His disciples, to whom he was Master Peter, were numerous, and many of their writings have been identified as belonging to the school of Abelard. Other writings of Abelard belong more strictly to the field of literature: metrical and rhythmical hymns, sermons, his autobiographical *Historia calamitatum,* and letters. His correspondence includes the exchange of letters with HÉLOÏSE, the authenticity of which on both sides seems now to be established.

The first great name in the school of the Canons Regular of St. Augustine at the Abbey of Saint-Victor in Paris was HUGH OF SAINT-VICTOR (d. 1141). Attractive in character and versatile with his pen, he wrote theological treatises, commentaries on Scripture, a chronicle, and his widely circulated *Didascalion,* on education. He quoted Plato and Aristotle (as known through Latin translations), ancient Latin authors, grammarians, and poets, but most of all, St. Augustine. Medieval and modern writers have paid tribute to him, and his memory was flattered by the assignment to him of many works that are not actually his. Among other Victorine authors were ANDREW, who favored literal, historical interpretation of Scripture in his commentaries; RICHARD, distinguished for his mystical works; and Adam, whose Sequences mark the high point of that medieval genre.

The school of Chartres was a center of the cult of Platonic realism, but also, eventually, of the study of Aristotle. It was strongly devoted to humanism as against the rising tyranny of dialectic. BERNARD OF CHARTRES, a light of the school for 20 years or more after 1114, commanded great respect as a humanist, but his writings are not extant. His brother, THIERRY, strove to reconcile Platonic teachings and the Bible in his work on the six days of creation and left a valuable source for knowledge of the trivium and quadrivium in the 12th century in his *Heptateuchon.* BERNARD SILVESTRIS wrote in mixed verse and prose a work based on pagan authors concerning nature, *De mundi universitate.* CLARENBAUD (CLARENBALDUS) is considered to have written the best commentary on the *De Trinitate* of Boethius up to the time of St. Thomas Aquinas. WILLIAM OF CONCHES in his *De philosophia mundi* shows himself a Christian Platonist. The *Moralium dogma philosophorum,* best known of the writings attributed to him, is almost certainly the work of another author. It is a mélange of well-chosen texts from Scripture, the Fathers, and Roman philosophers. GILBERT DE LA PORÉE, professor and chancellor of Chartres, and from 1142 to 1154 bishop of Poitiers, had great scholarly influence, though he was not a prolific writer. Besides glosses on Scripture, he also composed a commentary on the *De Trinitate* of Boethius. His treatment of the Trinity and his use of dialectic in theology brought criticism from St. Bernard and others, though he escaped condemnation at the Council of Reims in 1148. His teachings were handed down in the collections of *auctoritates* of the Middle Ages, and he had followers identified as members of his school.

The Englishman JOHN OF SALISBURY began his studies at Chartres and ended his days (1180) as bishop there. In the meantime he had studied under many masters at Paris and had been secretary to Thomas Becket, whose biography he wrote. Though he never taught in the schools, he was one of the greatest humanists and authors of his century. His many letters are a rich source for history, as is his *Historia pontificalis,* though the last years of it (1153–62) are not extant. His best-known works present his political thought. The *Entheticus* is a long poem of philosophical and Christian counsel ending with a picture of the evils among churchmen and in the government of England. This latter part was developed in his *Policraticus sive de nugis et vestigiis curialium,* a brave attempt at a philosophy of government that fitted in well with the renaissance of canon and civil law of the century. His *Metalogicon* is a defense of logic in which he foretold the triumph of Aristotle in the schools. He was steeped in a knowledge of ancient authors, and his writings are permeated with classical quotations and allusions.

Akin to writers of Chartres because of his interest in nature though not of that school himself was another Englishman, ADELARD OF BATH, who appears to have lived until the middle of the 12th century. After travel, even into the Islamic East, he wrote and translated works on mathematics and astronomy. His *Quaestiones naturales,* in the form of a dialogue, tells of scientific matters he learned from the Arabs and of his own scientific observations. His *De eodem et diverso* states the case for philosophy and the liberal arts against the attractions of the world.

Monastic Authors. Away from the urban centers, monasteries continued to produce writers. The greatest personage of his age, St. BERNARD OF CLAIRVAUX (1090–1153), came from this milieu. Second founder and soul of the Cistercian movement, he brought about its phenomenal spread through western Christendom. His activities on behalf of the papacy, against heresy, and in the organizing of the Crusades add an important page to history. Mystic that he was, his writings all bear the mark of his contemplation. His sermons are an heirloom of the Christian world. They gave great impetus to the affective devotion that began to characterize piety in the Middle Ages. His letters, a record of his zeal, are a rich source for the history of the first half of the 12th century. He left 15 treatises, some of them dogmatic, some ascetical and mystical. The *De consideratione* was written as a guide to his protégé Pope Eugene III, and he wrote likewise on the duties of bishops and the reform of the clergy. His life of St. Malachy is a masterly piece of hagiography. Bernard's Latin style was unsurpassed in the Middle Ages, the prose of his sermons often attaining lyrical beauty. The Bible was the chief source of inspiration in his writing, and he drew much on the Fathers, whereas he almost never cited classical authors.

History was enriched by good biographies of St. Bernard, one of them, incomplete, by WILLIAM OF SAINT-THIERRY, his friend and adviser, well read in the classics and familiar with certain works of the Greek Fathers. He wrote brilliantly on faith, on monastic life, on contemplation, and on the dignity and nature of love as against Ovid's idea of love.

In England AELRED OF RIEVAULX (d. 1166) became a Cistercian and came to know Bernard. He was a gifted writer, reflecting the affective quality of his own spirituality in his *Speculum caritatis,* his *De Jesu puero duodenni,* and his *De spirituali amicitia.* The work on friendship was based on Cicero but sublimated. It was one of about a score of treatises on the subject written in the course of a century, along with about as many commentaries on the Song of Songs. Aelred wrote also history and saints' lives.

ISAAC OF STELLA, near Poitiers, was a Cistercian abbot who left exegetical works, a mystical explanation of the Canon of the Mass, and a *De anima.* Two other Cistercians, GUERRIC OF IGNY and ADAM OF PERSEIGNE, left collections of sermons composed in the manner of St. Bernard.

PETER THE VENERABLE (1090–1156), Abbot of Cluny, was second only to Bernard as a public figure in European ecclesiastical affairs. His collection of letters tells about the administering of the vast Cluniac congregation and gives interesting details concerning his relations with Bernard and Abelard. Some of the letters are theological in nature. His style is ordinarily very simple, but it rises to elegance on occasion. He had a translation of the Qur'ān made in Spain at considerable expense. Subsequently he wrote his work against the religion of Islam. Earlier he wrote works against the Petrobrusian heretics and against the Jews. His severity in these works was not in keeping with the general suavity of his character. He cared for the broken Abelard, who ended his days at Cluny. Under him the monastery possessed a remarkably fine collection of 500 manuscripts, 100 of them texts of the classics.

PETER OF CELLE (d. 1187) was another Cluniac monk and abbot who took active part in the affairs of the time. His collection of more than 225 letters shows that he was in correspondence with many important people, lay and ecclesiastic. His sermons and ascetical treatises are marred by an excessive use of allegory. He deplored the rising influence of Aristotelianism in the schools. HUGH OF AMIENS (d. 1164), Abbot of Reading and (1130) Archbishop of Rouen, wrote against heresy and simony and on Scripture.

In Germany the enigmatic figure who concealed his identity under the name Honorius Augustodunensis (not of Autun) wrote his voluminous works in the first half of the 12th century. Perhaps an Irishman, he calls himself *solitarius, scholasticus, presbyter.* In his continuation of the *De viris illustribus* he lists 22 works of his own—*non spernenda opuscula.* He wrote on Scripture, theology, catechetics, homiletics, liturgy, history, moral and politico-religious problems of his day, and natural science. In philosophy he was a Christian Platonist, in theology mainly Augustinian, but he preferred the dialectical method to citing authorities.

Firmly opposed to the use of dialectic, overly fond of allegory, RUPERT, ABBOT OF DEUTZ (d. 1130), wrote much in the various fields of theology and many poems in classical meters. He revealed a wide knowledge of ancient authors, whom he cited even in his theological works. In indignation he made a special trip into France to argue with Anselm of Laon and WILLIAM OF CHAMPEAUX against the use of dialectic. One of the most detailed apologetic treatises of the 12th century against Judaism came from his pen.

The most prolific writer of the century was the Bavarian GERHOH OF REICHERSBERG (d. 1169), a Canon Regular of St. Augustine. He was a man of great vehemence, irreproachable in his own character, except for his exaggerated severity, who incessantly attacked the evils of his time. His writings, many of which are still unedited, deal with the relations of Church and State, reform in the Church, and current theological controversies. Abelard, Gilbert de la Porée, and the school of Paris were attacked by him. He approved of St. Bernard. Though he shows a knowledge of the classics in his writings, he generally preferred to cite Christian authors.

Two German nuns made their mark in literature in the second half of the 12th century. St. HILDEGARD OF BINGEN (1179), who had only a very elementary education, dictated works on medicine and theology, knowledge of which she acquired in visions, and many letters. Her tomb was the scene of numerous miracles. HERRAD OF LANDSBERG (d. 1195), as abbess, had her *Hortus deliciarum* prepared for the instruction of her nuns. It consisted of extracts from Christian writers, ancient and medieval, on various religious subjects along with elaborate illustrations in color demonstrating truths of religion. The pictures imposed the garb and usages of the 12th century on scenes from Scripture. The original manuscript perished in the destruction of the library of Strassburg in 1870. Just what share the abbess had in the compilation of the book cannot be determined.

There were a number of writers among the followers of St. Norbert in his flourishing order of Prémontré. PHILIP OF HARVENGT (d. 1183) wrote learnedly on dogmatic and ascetical subjects and on the Bible with an effort at elegance in his style. Adam Scotus, Abbot of Dryburgh (d. c. 1210), wrote sermons in highly rhetorical style, which he preached to his religious, and works of ascetical and mystical nature. HERMAN OF SCHEDA, a convert from Judaism, wrote (1137) a good Latin account of his conversion.

The Augustinian Canon HUGH, Abbot of Fouilloy (near Corbie), wrote on the seven abuses of the cloister and against marriage. Among the Carthusians, two abbots general, GUIGO I (d. 1137) and GUIGO II (d. 1188), composed beautiful meditations, and the latter left other works of piety.

The strange figure of JOACHIM OF FIORE, founder of an order in Italy (1192), presents problems. He had a great reputation for sanctity in his lifetime, but his writings contained heresy and unfounded revelations concerning the future of the Church. As he was dying, however, he charged his brethren to submit his writings to the judgment of the Holy See. Some of his misguided followers adopted and further perverted his errors, causing great harm in the Church.

Paris and Theology. In the meantime, interest in theology continued to develop in Paris. Aside from the Victorines, WALTER OF MORTAGNE, opponent of Abelard, held forth in Paris, Reims, and Laon and wrote well on questions of philosophy and theology. ROBERT OF MELUN, of English birth, was associated with Peter Lombard in opposition to the teachings of Gilbert de la Porée. He wrote exegetical works and theological *sententiae.* From Italy PETER LOMBARD, to be known in the future as *Magister Sententiarum,* came to Paris, becoming its bishop in 1159. He wrote scriptural commentaries, but his fame is connected with his *Libri IV Sententiarum* (*Sentences*). Based heavily on an earlier anonymous *Summa Sententiarum,* it is a systematic presentation of theology with prudent conclusions, but it is colorless and impersonal. These latter qualities masked its intrinsic greatness but ensured its future fame, because it was admirably suited to the needs of the many theologians who, next to the Bible, the *sacra pagina,* used it as their textbook and wrote commentaries on it. Among the commentators were Thomas Aquinas and Bonaventure. The doctrine of the Lombard did not escape attacks. They came from John of Cornwall, and more bitterly from WALTER OF SAINT-VICTOR, Gerhoh of Reichersberg, and the heretical Joachim of Fiore, but the Fourth Lateran Council (1215) gave solemn approval to Peter's teaching. In Paris, PETER OF POITIERS (d. 1205), professor and chancellor of the school of Notre Dame of Paris for 38 years, was the Lombard's faithful disciple and expositor. Other followers were PETER CANTOR, who sprinkled his smooth Latin with references to the classics, and Cardinal ROBERT OF COURÇON. Subsequent great names in philosophy and theology at Paris up to the 1230s were Nicholas of Amiens; ALAN OF LILLE, who wrote poetry and a *De arte predicatoria,* as well as theology; SIMON OF TOURNAI; STEPHEN LANGTON; PRAEPOSITINUS OF CREMONA; WILLIAM OF AUXERRE, who began the extensive use of the new Aristotle; and PHILIP THE CHANCELLOR (not PHILIP OF GRÈVE, whose writings are unknown), distinguished preacher and poet, as well as metaphysician and psychologist, author of the *Summa de bono.*

Canon Law. What Paris was for theology, Bologna was for Canon Law. The great canonist of the 12th century is the monk GRATIAN, who somewhat as Abelard did for theology in his *Sic et non,* brought together (1139–41) Church law into his *Concordantia discordantium canonum.* Known also as the *Decretum Gratiani,* it contained, in addition to previous legislation, a commentary by Gratian himself, which, like Peter Lombard's *Sentences* for theology, became the textbook for canonists and the object of their commentaries. Among the commentators were three future popes, Alexander III, Gregory VIII, and Innocent III, as well as many other important ecclesiastical figures. The pursuit of Church law became more popular than the study of theology and was more lucrative. St. Dominic noted this as he directed his followers to the study of theology.

Letters in Britain. There had been a lull in the production of Latin writings in Britain for the long period of the Danish invasions. King ALFRED had kept the torch of knowledge burning through his interest in Latin and his translations into Old English. His biography attributed to Asser appears to be a later forgery, but the example he gave was an inspiration to writers, mostly bishops and abbots, of the 10th and 11th centuries, who kept patristic learning alive with their translations into the vernacular. The Norman invasions brought a renaissance of Latin in England, as has been seen, with scholars coming from abroad and Englishmen participating in the intellectual movement on the Continent.

A number of other 12th-century writers in Britain deserve mention. Eadmer (d. 1128?), monk of Christchurch in Canterbury, secretary and later biographer of St. Anselm, wrote, among other works on the Blessed Virgin, the first treatise in Latin on her Immaculate Conception. His *Historia novorum* is a valuable history of his time. The Welsh ecclesiastic GEOFFREY OF MONMOUTH (d. 1155?), in the guise of history, wrote down legends and stories of ancient Breton history, adding much of his own invention. His influence on English literature and that of all Europe has been enormous, whereas he did disservice to the cause of history. Gerald of Wales (GIRALDUS CAMBRENSIS, or de Barri; *c.* 1147–1223), son of a Norman father and Welsh mother, educated in Paris, became one of the most prolific writers of his time. An ambitious ecclesiastic, a servitor of the English king, vain and egotistical but learned and of vast experience, he reveals himself as he writes on Wales and its clergy, on the English conquest of Ireland and of Irish topography, on the right of the See of St. Davids as against Canterbury, and in criticism of the Church, especially its wealth, of religious orders, and of the Roman Curia. Some school exercises of his in verse also have been preserved. Gerald's compatriot and friend WALTER MAP (1140–1210) was rather like him in character and manner of living. Walter's *Nugae curialium,* a title borrowed from John of Salisbury, brings his invective to bear on a multiplicity of things in varying style.

Peter of Blois (1135–*c.* 1204), well traveled, secretary to Henry II of England, archdeacon of Bath, chancellor of Abp. Richard of Canterbury, left sermons, many letters written with a classical touch, and a number of religious treatises. ALEXANDER NECKHAM (1154–1217) left a *De nominibus utensilium,* an encyclopedia listing things used in daily life; a *De naturis rerum;* and a *De laudibus sapientiae divinae* (a versification of *De naturis*), which reveal knowledge of ancient authors.

Historians. The 12th century produced some universal chronicles, such as those of FLORENCE OF WORCESTER, Hugh of Flavigny, ROBERT OF TORIGNY, ORDERICUS VITALIS (*Historia ecclesiastica*), Gui of Bazoches, and OTTO OF FREISING, the last the most original historian of his century. The chronicling of the Crusades continued, and each country produced its chronicles, some of which have been mentioned. England stood out by its number of historians, the greatest of whom was the learned WILLIAM OF MALMESBURY. In Spain the *Historia Compostellana,* produced by several authors under the auspices of Abp. Diego Gelmirez, was a significant piece of biography and local history.

Latin Translations from Arabic and Greek. Spain was the center of many translations of Arabic work—philosophical, scientific, and pseudo-scientific. It was an indirect way of tapping Greek learning. Other centers of translation, especially of Greek texts, were northern Italy and Sicily. As a result of the labors of the translators, scholars of the 13th century had access to Greek and Arabic philosophy and science. Of a literary nature, though by no means elegantly written, were two translations from Oriental sources—the *Historia septem sapientum,* a tale that probably originated in India and came into Latin through Hebrew, and the *Disciplina clericalis,* a collection of Oriental maxims and stories presented in Latin by the Jewish convert to Christianity Peter Alfonsi.

Poetry. Versifiers multiplied in the 12th century, and among them there were many good poets. Rhythmical verse now prevailed and reached perfection. The gifted poets who wrote at the turn of the century have already been treated. Among many who made verse on ancient themes, Walter of Châtillon won fame for his *Alexandreis* (1182), a long epic on Alexander the Great. The *De bello Troiano* of Joseph of Exeter shows him to have been a consummate rhetorician, an emulator of Lucan. Geoffrey of Monmouth wrote a pseudo-historical epic on Merlin. Better source material was found by poets in the history of their own times. Henry of Pisa wrote of the conquest of Majorca (1114–15) from the Saracens by his fellow townsmen. William of Apulia in 1111 composed an epic on the deeds of Robert Guiscard and his successors. An anonymous poet of Bergamo was one of several to write (1162–66) of the deeds of Frederick Barbarossa. Godfrey of Viterbo and Peter of Eboli, both admirers of Emperor Henry VI, found their themes in imperial history. The CRUSADES stirred the imagination of many poets. Fulco and Gilo, both Frenchmen, wrote on the First Crusade. It is unfortunate that the epic of Joseph of Exeter on the crusading exploits of Richard I, the Lion-Hearted, is not extant except for fragments. Among the epics of the Crusades perhaps the best is that of the Florentine monk, bishop in the Latin East, who recounted the history of the Third Crusade in his *De recuperatione Ptolemaide.* Most of these epics were written in hexameters, but the bishop presented his in the accentual 13-syllable goliardic verse in rhyming stanzas. It is distinguished in both form and content. German poets wrote the lives of bishops and several epics on Frederick Barbarossa. The anonymous authors of the imperial accounts reveal their patriotism and no mean knowledge of classical poets.

Much satirical verse was composed attacking simony, the cupidity of chanceries and the Roman Curia, the morals of prelates and monks, and the evils of the time in general. Among the authors were Serlo of Bayeux, John of Salisbury, Nigel Wireker, Nivard of Ghent, PETER THE PAINTER of Saint-Omer, Henry of Settimello, and Philip the Chancellor. The *Architrenius* (Archmourner) of John of Hauteville (Auville) mixes allegory with sympathetic descriptions of the indigent students of Paris and satire on the gluttony of the rich, the ambition of courtiers, and the vices of clergy and people. Best known of such verse is the pious *De contemptu mundi* of BERNARD OF CLUNY, or Morlas. Composed in accentual dactylic hexameters with rhyme, it contains the lines from which *Jerusalem the Golden* was translated.

Comedy, which really amounted to versified tales with incidental dialogue, forerunners of the vernacular fabliaux, was composed in the 12th century in France and England. The *Amphitryo,* or *Geta,* was taken from Plautus by its author, Vitalis of Blois, who claimed the same source for his *Aulularia,* whereas it merely reproduced a work of the 4th century A.D. Other similar pieces were produced in France. English comedy was obviously modeled after the French.

Religious drama continued to develop out of the liturgy. In the 12th century it remained for the most part conservative and pious. But already there appeared the tendency to secularize it. Condemnations came from various sources, especially Pope Innocent III, which seem to have been directed at the FEAST OF FOOLS. The vernacular was beginning to displace Latin in the plays. The developing city life and the guilds were to take them over. In the 12th century the name of Hilary, a follower of Abelard, is connected with the authorship of plays on St. Nicholas, the raising of Lazarus, and the Prophets. Anonymous plays are contained in the collection *Carmina burana* of Benediktbeuern and in collections of Fleury and Klosterneuburg.

The broad term didactic may be used to characterize much of 12th-century verse. Proverbs, epigrams, and ancient fables were put into Latin verse, as were Biblical narratives and saints' lives. Much of the verse of Matthew of Vendôme was for the schools, e.g., his *Synonyma, Equivoca, Ars versificatoria,* and his art of writing versified letters, besides several poems that point a moral. Geoffrey of Vinsauf composed (*c.* 1210) his handbook on hexameter verse, *Poetria nova,* which amounts to a technical manual on the art of poetry. Eberhard of Bethune (d. *c.* 1212) was the author in part of a work in verse called *Graecismus.* He treated of Latin grammar, and sections on rhetorical ornaments were added by his pupils. The most important versified grammar of the Middle Ages was the *Doctrinale* (1199) of Alexander of Villa Dei. It was part of a vast encyclopedia that he was compiling. Another section of his research for the encyclopedia appeared as his versified *Ecclesiale.* It dealt with the ecclesiastical calendar and Canon Law. Alexander Neckham put much of his encyclopedia of popular science, *De naturis rerum,* into a composition in elegiac verse: *De laudibus divinae sapientiae.* The pedagogue John of Garland, who lived until *c.* 1258, wrote in prose and verse on grammar and rhetoric and some religious topics.

Some of the 12th-century philosophers used verse as a vehicle for their teaching. Bernard Silvestris of Tours and Chartres presented his allegorical treatment of cosmology, *De mundi universitate,* in mixed prose and verse. It is Neoplatonic rather than Christian in tone. GODFREY OF SAINT-VICTOR (d. *c.* 1194) composed his *Fons philosophiae* in goliardic verse. It treats of the liberal arts, ancient and contemporary philosophy, and theology. The *De mundi philosophia* of a certain Milo, perhaps Milo Crispinus of Bec, consists of two books of verse on cosmology, especially astronomy. Alan of Lille was the author of a long allegorical poem, entirely in hexameters, on the creation of the soul by God. It moves from philosophy to theology, has beautiful lines on the Blessed Virgin, and ascends with Faith to the court of the Trinity. Another work of his, the *De planctu naturae,* is a mixture of prose and verse in several different meters. It amounts to a deification of Nature, who is made to deplore unnatural vice. A few shorter poems of Alan show his skill in accentual verse.

Theology and ecclesiastical subjects were often treated in verse. Sometime after 1083 FULCOIUS OF BEAUVAIS composed versified letters, epigrams, epitaphs, saints' lives, and his long *De nuptiis Christi et Ecclesiae.* Some of his verse has only recently been edited. Richer of Metz wrote (*c.* 1135) a life of St. Martin of Tours in iambic and trochaic dimeters. The contents were based closely upon Sulpicius Severus. Between 1150 and 1160 Metellus, a monk of Tegernsee, composed a large number of odes in the manner of Horace on the life and miracles of St. Quirinus.

A monk of the monastery of St. Augustine in Canterbury, but a native of France, REGINALD, who was still alive in 1109, composed an epic of some 4,000 verses on St. Malchus, as well as verses on the saints buried or venerated in his monastery. He addressed three poems to St. Anselm during the saint's second exile. LAWRENCE, monk of Durham (d. 1154), versified narratives from Scripture along with hagiographical stories in his *Hypognosticon.* He wrote poems on the history of his monastery, not forgetting to include spiritual lessons. PETER RIGA, canon of Reims (d. *c.* 1209), composed his very long *Aurora,* mostly in distichs, on persons and things of the Old Testament. He collected his verse and added new poems, including some saints' lives, in his *Floridus aspectus.*

Lyric Poetry. The best known and most popularly appreciated genre among the 12th-century writings, and the part that deserves especially to be called literature in the strict sense, is the lyric verse. It is abundant and varied in theme and form. Some of it is secular, and some religious. Both meter and rhythm are employed in its composition. Both types of verse made increasing use of rhyme. The fact is worthy of note that in this century, just as skill in the use of many of the classical meters reached a high degree of proficiency, quantitative meter, depending on long and short syllables, should have yielded in popularity to rhythm, verse construction based on word accent. Accentual verse was not new in the 12th century, but it was then that it reached perfection and popularity.

It appears that accentual verse for the most part modeled itself on quantitative verse by substituting an accented syllable for the quantitative ictus and an unaccented syllable for one not having an ictus. This is most readily seen in iambic and trochaic verse. Sometimes accentual verse merely imitated the number of syllables of a metrical line or stanza, e.g., the sapphic strophe. The most interesting development in rhythmical poetry was the 13-syllable goliardic verse or line of the so-called wandering scholars. There existed no quantitative model for it in classical literature, but the form is found in the refrain of a hymn by Marius Victorinus (*c.* 350), in Mozarabic prayers, and in Middle High German. This verse has been described in various ways. Trochaic in nature, it divides into seven and six syllables with the accent on the antepenult (proparoxytone) at the end of the first part and on the penult (paroxytone) at the end of the second part. German scholars prefer to consider the first seven syllables as ascending to an accent (secondary) on the last, and the second six as falling, with the final syllable unaccented. English readers readily understand if the first part of the verse is considered to be seven-syllable trochaic dimeter catalectic, and the second, six-syllable trochaic. At times three goliardic rhyming lines were put together to form a strophe along with a fourth line in hexameter or pentameter taken from a classical or medieval author. The fourth line might rhyme with the others or not. The strophe has been called the goliardic strophe *cum auctoritate.* The goliardic line was used both for profane writings, serious as well as frivolous, and for religious subjects.

The Profane Lyric. In the 12th century, three authors stand out for their skill and productivity in the field of the secular lyric: Hugh of Orléans, known as Primas; the anonymous Archpoet; and WALTER OF CHÂTILLON. They all wrote satirical pieces as well as lyrics. Walter, the most versatile of the three, made contributions in the field of religious poetry in addition to his secular verse. Hugh Primas was truly a wandering scholar in France; he was small in stature, dissolute, cynical, malicious, and far from handsome. He wrote (mostly occasional verse on his woes and animosities) in both metrical and accentual verse and was a master of rhyme. He was admired by his contemporaries for his skill. Fifty poems have been identified as coming from him. The German Archpoet was of a gentler character, grateful to German bishops for patronage, though bitter toward those who refused it. He wrote accentual verse by preference. His best known piece is his *Confessio,* in goliardic verse, an unabashed avowal of his life as a roué, for which he declares his penitence.

Walter of Châtillon also wrote both metrical and accentual verse. His epic, the *Alexandreis,* has been mentioned above. He was a master of satire, for which he used the goliardic strophe *cum auctoritate* very adroitly, as well as the trochaic Sequence-measure. He wrote lyrically of spring and love, and his frank eroticism contrasts with poems of his that are devoutly religious. A number of poems, mostly in goliardic verse, have been identified as the product of the ''school of Walter of Châtillon.'' Serlo of Wilton, an English contemporary of Primas, the Archpoet, and Walter, wrote metrical verse of erotic character in his early life but underwent a conversion and as a Cistercian wrote religious poetry. Chancellor Philip of Paris (d. 1236) showed great skill in composing accentual verse, some of it religious, but the greater part of it satirical.

Collections of lyrical verse became common in the 13th century, and a number of manuscripts of these have been preserved. The most important such manuscript was found at the Abbey of BENEDIKTBEUERN and is now in Munich. The collection was given the name *Carmina Burana* by its first editor. Its content is chiefly profane: themes of wine, women, and song, parodies on Biblical subjects and the liturgy, satire on the clergy and especially on the Papal Curia. Other collections of poems of lesser scope than that of Benediktbeuern are contained in an Arundel manuscript of the British Museum; a *Vaticanus Latinus* manuscript; a manuscript that belonged to the monastery of Ripoll; and one belonging to the University of Basel. The form of this verse in many cases is highly refined as regards the use of meter, rhythm, and rhyme. The influence of the classics is strong. Some of the verse is by authors who can be identified, but most of it is anonymous. Obviously it was the product of the schools and of ecclesiastics; it was circulated and appreciated in all lands of the West because the scholarly and ecclesiastical groups were international and their language was Latin. English readers have access to many specimens of secular Latin lyric verse with penetrating comment in the two volumes of F. J. E. Raby, and to translations along with the Latin in the works of Helen Waddell.

Poetical Debates. With the secular lyric may be mentioned the poetical debates, of which there were many. They reached back to classical rhetoric, but the medieval themes were frequently of a popular nature. Thus, winter and summer were made to debate, as were wine and water, wine and beer. A contest between the violet and the rose was written in goliardic verse. The debate about love supposed to be carried on at a council of the nuns of Remiremont appears to be the product of the mordant humor of a cleric. A similar debate in a different setting is attributed to Henry of Avranches, author of many poems. The treatise *De amore* of Andreas Capellanus, the most ambitious work on courtly love, seems to be a piece of lumbering humor and not a true picture of a medieval aberration in morals.

The Religious Lyric. As was the case with the profane, the religious lyric reached perfection of form in rhythmical verse during the 12th century. But, whereas the secular poetry depended for its success on its form, its naughtiness, its sharp satire, and biting humor, the religious, in equally impeccable form, conveyed solid spiritual and theological thought. Most of the religious authors remained anonymous. The volumes of the *Analecta hymnica* and the *incipit*'s of hymns listed by Chevalier bear testimony to their industry.

Hymns, Sequences, tropes, and rhythmical Offices formed the main body of this literature. In the early part of the century Hildebert of Lavardin surpassed his contemporaries in the quality of his religious verse. His long poem in accentual iambics, *Lamentatio peccatricis animae,* is a forerunner of the *Dies irae*. His *Alpha et Omega* is sublime praise of the Trinity. Abelard somewhat later composed a collection of hymns for use in the liturgical year. Prepared at the request of Héloïse for her nuns, it suffers because it was produced at one time and not gradually, as inspiration came. ADAM OF SAINT-VICTOR, with about 45 Sequences attributed to him, was the outstanding master of that genre in his century. His preferred verse form was the regular Sequence strophe: two to four accentual trochaic lines of eight syllables followed by a trochaic line of seven syllables, together with the use of a two-syllable rhyme and a regular caesura occurring at the end of a word. The restraint imposed by the requirements of the liturgy prevented Adam from injecting personal emotion into his Sequences. The highest level of inspired verse in the century was reached in the *JESU, DULCIS MEMORIA*, a hymn of affective devotion that came out of the milieu of St. Bernard's followers. It is filled with the spirit of Bernard's devotion, but it is not of his own composition. Hymn writing was to continue, and some of the greatest masterpieces among hymns and Sequences were produced in the next century.

The liturgical form known as the rhythmical Office began to develop as early as the 9th century. The genre was in vogue for six centuries thereafter. These Offices consist of the canonical hours of the Divine Office, with the exception of the Psalms and Lessons, put into meter, rhythm, or rhyming prose. About 600 such Offices are known, mostly in honor of patronal saints. The century of their greatest development was the 13th, and the most renowned among their authors was JULIAN OF SPEYER, a German Franciscan who became a choirmaster in Paris. In use in all the countries of Europe, these Offices brought large numbers of ecclesiastics into contact with verse.

Ars Dictaminis. The 12th and 13th centuries suffered from a discipline imposed upon them as regards the art of composition. Manuals called *artes dictandi* were put together in great numbers. The verb *dictare* and its derivatives had been used since antiquity to designate the composing of a piece of writing. There was need for rules of literary composition, but the treatises of the *ars dictaminis* became conventionalized and served to put literary writing into a straitjacket. The predecessors of these treatises in early medieval times were the collections of *formulae* intended to aid in the preparation of documents and letters. Beginning with the end of the 11th century, the production of the *artes dictandi* continued through the next two centuries. Their purpose was largely to serve the need of chanceries in composing documents correctly and elegantly. The first such treatises were connected with Italy and the name of Alberic of Monte Cassino (d. 1108), though the extent of his work is not definitely established. Subsequently many others were composed in Italy, France, Germany, and England. They began to encompass all literary composition. Instead of adhering to good classical traditions they were inclined to insist too much on cadenced prose, the use of *cursus,* and tasteless rhetorical ornament. Under the influence of Cicero's *De inventione* and the *Rhetorica ad Herennium,* they imposed the rules of oratory on the writing of letters, so that spontaneity was sacrificed. Sermons were adversely affected because of the same techniques. A particularly ill-conceived trend was the attempt to moralize Ovid through allegorical interpretation. This movement, which came out of Orléans, was wisely repudiated by most contemporaries.

After the *artes dictandi,* Latin arts of poetry emerged in the course of the 12th century. Important names in their composition were Matthew of Vendôme, Geoffrey of Vinsauf, Gervaise of Merkley, Evrardus the German, Alexander of Villedieu, and John of Garland. The *arts poétiques* have been admirably studied by E. Faral. The treatises are inclined to devote themselves to the beginning and conclusion of poetical writings and to give scant attention to the rest. They lose themselves in detail and are too much concerned with mechanical points. Thus they treat of *amplificatio* in an uninspiring way, not as a means of presenting ideas more vividly, but simply as a means of lengthening, and *abbreviatio* is for them only a means of shortening. Figures of speech are treated extensively but chiefly under the influence of the *Rhetorica ad Herennium.* These *artes* are helpful to modern scholars inasmuch as they give an idea of the literary taste of their age.

From the 13th Century to the End of the Middle Ages

The surveys of Latin literature published down to 1965 do not extend into the later Middle Ages, and for that period one must pursue the study of it in monographs, encyclopedias, periodicals, and specialized works on philosophy, theology, and the history of science. By the 13th century, philosophy and theology had taken over the dominant position in the scholarly world, and interest in literary works in Latin declined. Vernacular literature was developing rapidly, appealing as it did to a wide public, whereas Latin writings, limited as they were to scholarly circles, became more and more bookish. Works in philosophy and theology became abundant and reached a great perfection in the technical use of Latin and effectiveness of presentation.

Religious Poetry. Some of the theological writers made contributions to religious poetry. In fact the best, or at least the most loved, hymns and Sequences came in this period. The Golden Sequence, the *VENI SANCTE SPIRITUS ET EMITTE COELITUS*, attributed to STEPHEN LANGTON (d. 1223) rather than to Pope Innocent III, probably came out of the late 12th century in the days when Langton was a student or master in Paris, though it could have been composed at Pontigny during the years he waited there to take over his See of Canterbury. It is used as the Sequence of Pentecost Sunday. St. THOMAS AQUINAS wrote the Sequence and hymns for the Feast of Corpus Christi. The Sequence *LAUDA SION SALVATOREM* presents the theology of the Eucharist with the utmost precision in perfect Sequence rhythm and rhyme, with the controlled lyrical emotion that befits the liturgy and Aquinas's own intellectual approach to the mysteries of faith. The *Tantum ergo* is part of his *PANGE LINGUA GLORIOSI CORPORIS MYSTERIUM*. Though the affective hymn *ADORO TE DEVOTE* is commonly attributed to him, there are reasons for considering it the work of another author. A. Wilmart, through a study of the manuscripts, has restored the text of this beautiful hymn to its original form.

Franciscan piety produced much verse charged with religious emotion. St. BONAVENTURE wrote verses on the Passion of Christ. JOHN PECKHAM, an English Franciscan who became archbishop of Canterbury, is the author of *Philomena* (Nightingale), one of the most appealing spiritual poems of the Middle Ages. Its theme is the Passion, and its form the rhythmical goliardic four-line strophe. Peckham wrote verses on the Blessed Virgin, as did the English canon JOHN OF HOVEDEN, his contemporary. The latter wrote also much verse on the Passion. His *Philomena* is filled with pathos, but it is less attractive than that of Peckham. About the middle of the 13th century a Cistercian abbot, Arnulf of Louvain, wrote a rhythmical poem, *De Passione Domini,* full of effective devotion, in honor of the wounds of Christ. The famous Sequence commemorating Mary's sorrow at the foot of the Cross, *STABAT MATER*, is attributed to the Italian Franciscan JACOPONE DA TODI (d. 1306). He wrote many *laude* in Italian for popular devotion, including the *Donna del Paradiso,* which is more replete with emotion than the *Stabat Mater,* but is of the same inspiration. Both in the vernaculars and in Latin, poems in imitation of the hours of the Divine Office were made to depict scenes of the Passion. St. CATHERINE OF BOLOGNA (d. 1463) composed a poem of 5,610 verses, all ending in *-is,* on the mysteries of the life of Christ and of Mary. The autobiography of her interior struggles composed by her in Italian was translated into Latin.

From the hands of the Franciscan biographer THOMAS OF CELANO (d. *c.* 1260) appears to have come the *DIES IRAE*, which eventually was introduced as the Sequence in Masses for the dead, though it was rather a sermon for the living. Both in form and content its inspiration goes back to Carolingian times and to the 12th century. Its theme, the Last Judgment, was frequently depicted on the tympanums of medieval cathedral portals. It is written in accentual trochaic dimeters in rhyming stropes of three lines. Magnificent musical accompaniments have been composed for it. A companion piece by an anonymous author is the *Mater Misericordiae,* a plea for Mary's help on Judgment Day.

Devotional Works in Prose. In connection with devotional poetry, prose works of similar inspiration should be considered. There were many of these on the life and suffering of Christ. St. BONAVENTURE presents material for meditation on phases of Christ's life in his *Lignum vitae*. DAVID OF AUGSBURG (d. 1272), a Franciscan, looked to Christ as the model of spiritual life in his writings. In his *De contemplatione* the Carthusian GUIGO DE PONTE (d. 1297) presented a method of meditating on the life of Christ. The *Speculum humanae salvationis,* written no earlier than 1309, an anonymous work in 42 chapters of 100 lines each in rhyming prose, consists of meditations on Christ's life. Of very great influence in stimulating affective devotion to Christ and His Passion were the *Meditationes in vita Christi*. They were written before 1330 and have been incorrectly attributed to St. Bonaventure.

Dominican authors as well as Franciscan wrote on the life of Christ. Some of them, such as Hugh of Strassburg (d. 1268), are speculative; but the *Horologium sapientiae* of Bl. Henry Suso (d. 1366), a dialogue between himself and the Incarnate Word, is affective and lyrical, if not emotional. Simone Fidati (d. 1348), an Italian belonging to the Hermits of St. Augustine, used the Gospels to draw lessons, topically and not chronologically arranged, from the life of Christ. He repudiated scholastic argumentation and the parading of citations from pagan authors.

Most of these works on Christ were used by LUDOLPH OF SAXONY (d. 1377), a Carthusian, as he skillfully compiled and composed his elaborate *Vita Christi,* the most detailed chronological account of Christ's life attempted up to that time. Its affective spirituality had great appeal, and the influence of Ludolph on later authors is marked. Adolph of Essen (d. 1439) reflects the *Vita Christi* in his *Meditations on the Life of Christ and His Mother;* as did HENRY OF HERP (d. 1477), in his *Theologia mystica;* Jerome of Mondsee, in his *De profectu religiosorum* (*c.* 1458); and John Monbaer (d. 1501), in his *Rosetum spirituale*. Beyond the medieval period, Ludolph was used by St. Ignatius of Loyola, Francis of Osuna, St. Teresa of Avila, St. Francis de Sales, and Suitbert Moeden (d. 1705).

Devotio Moderna and the German Mystics. The second half of the 14th century witnessed the rise of the DEVOTIO MODERNA. It was fruitful in writings from the time of its founder, Gerard GROOTE (d. 1384). The great masterpiece of the movement was the *De imitatione Christi,* which apparently took final form at the hands of THOMAS À KEMPIS, author of many spiritual treatises.

Out of Majorca came the zealous missionary and prolific author (more than 300 works) Raymond LULL (d. *c.* 1316). His chief mystical works are in Catalan. A number of his writings exist in both the vernacular and in Latin. His *Liber natalis pueri parvuli Jesu Christi* was presented to King Philip the Fair. In the form of a vision, it presents six maidens personifying virtues who praise the Divine Child and then ask Philip to further Lull's program for converting the Muslims and Jews to Christianity. Lull's *Ars generalis* presented a method for the work of conversion. His purely literary works are in Catalan.

A group of German mystics of the Dominican Order flourished in the 14th century. Meister ECKHART (d. *c.* 1327), founder of this movement, preached in German and left writings in both German and Latin. Impetuous and imprudent in his expression, he revealed a tinge of pantheism in his writings, which after his death brought about a condemnation of errors attributed to him. Recent years have seen a resurgence of interest in his writings. Johannes TAULER (d. 1361), to whom several sermons and works are attributed, continued to voice the teachings of mysticism in more orthodox language. HENRY SUSO, with affective writings in both Latin and German, was of this group. In the next century Johann NIDER, OP (d. 1438), wrote practical works on moral theology, on how to live a good life and prepare for death, and on aspects of the religious life. His *Formicarius* uses ants as an example of how to live virtuously.

Spiritual Writers in France and Italy. In France Peter d'Ailly (d. 1420) and John GERSON (d. 1429), outstanding figures in the scholarly world and in the conciliar movement, which they embraced in their efforts to settle the WESTERN SCHISM, both wrote extensively on theology—175 works are attributed to D'Ailly, and 400 to Gerson—especially mysticism. The most profound philosopher and theologian of his age, Cardinal NICHOLAS OF CUSA in the Diocese of Trier (d. 1464), who was active in the effort to bring about the reconciliation of the Greek Church with the Holy See, is especially celebrated for his teaching and his treatise *De docta ignorantia*.

In Italy, Bl. John DOMINICI (d. 1419) wrote works of spiritual guidance in Italian, and scriptural commentaries in Latin, as well as his apology for a Christian renaissance in *Lucula noctis*. He formed in the Dominican way of life the future archbishop of Florence, St. ANTONINUS (d. 1459), who, besides guiding religious life in the flourishing city of Florence, wrote his famous *Summa moralis* and his chronicle, the latter also with the purpose of teaching men how to live and hope and attain salvation. St. VINCENT FERRER, OP (d. 1419), native of Valencia, one of the greatest of medieval preachers, composed a *De vita spirituali* that was widely used as a manual. Four of his Latin sermons are the basis of his meditations on the life of Christ that were put into Spanish. His younger contemporary St. BERNARDINE OF SIENA (d. 1444), a Franciscan, emulated him in his vernacular sermons but was less effective in his Latin writings. Cardinal Juan de TORQUEMADA, OP (d. 1468), renowned for his *Summa de Ecclesia,* wrote meditations on the life of Christ in Latin and a defense of the visions of St. Bridget of Sweden. The fiery preacher SAVONAROLA (d. 1498) has about 90 works in Latin and Italian attributed to him—on the spiritual life, the love of Christ, and the Passion.

Historians. History continued to be written in Latin, but before the end of the Middle Ages the vernacular had taken over to a great extent. MATTHEW PARIS (D. 1279), Benedictine of St. Albans, is considered to be the greatest medieval historian of England, though numerous other Latin chronicles were written there. In France, Saint-Denis became the center of historiography for the kingdom. Beginning with Abbot SUGER on the reigns of Louis VI and VII, continuing with Rigord on Philip II, with the anonymous *Gesta* of Louis VIII and those of Louis IX and Philip III by William de Nangis, the chronicle reached almost to the 14th century in Latin. Then a French translation of chronicles was made that reached back to sources from the very beginning of *Francia,* and the *Grandes chroniques de France* continued to record French history in the vernacular. Latin was not, however, completely abandoned by French historians. Late in the 15th century it was used by Thomas Basin, Bishop of Lisieux, exiled by Louis XI, in his history of that king and his predecessor, Charles VII.

From a literary viewpoint the most interesting of medieval chronicles is that of the Franciscan SALIMBENE

(1221–c. 1289). His work, extending from 1167 to 1287, presents a history of the Franciscans and his own personal memoirs rather than universal history. It is full of digressions and anecdotes, with accounts of his wide travels and the many important personages he met. The Italian vernacular is visible in his style, beneath his Latin. Many other chronicles were written in Italy in the late Middle Ages.

Akin to history, and more or less serving its purpose, is historical and political verse. William the Breton was the author of a hexameter poem in 12 books, completed in 1224, on Philip Augustus of France. An unknown author, perhaps a Franciscan, wrote the *Song of Lewes,* a Latin poem written after the battle (1264). It shows considerable political wisdom on the author's part. A poem under the name of JOHN OF BRIDLINGTON deals with the history of Edward III of England. John GOWER (d. 1408) wrote Latin verse on Henry IV, and against Richard II and the Lollards. His *Vox clamantis* dealing with the causes of the peasant uprising in 1381 describes the conditions of society and decries the evils existing among all its classes. In Germany, Jordan of Paderborn wrote in hexameter verse an allegorical satire, *Pavo de natura saeculi* (1291), in which he defended the rights of the emperor and the pope. The various participants are pictured as birds and animals. Bishop Leopold of Bamberg (d. 1363) lamented in verse the passing of German power in Italy. In France a Latin poem in two books tells of the taking of Orléans by Joan of Arc.

In hagiography the period produced the *Legenda aurea,* stories of the saints arranged according to the sanctoral cycle of the liturgical year. The author, JAMES OF VORAGINE, OP, archbishop of Genoa (d. 1298), wrote for the edification of the people. CAESARIUS OF HEISTERBACH (d. 1245), a Cistercian, likewise wrote his *Dialogus miraculorum,* in 12 books, to edify. His life of St. Engelbert, Archbishop of Cologne (d. 1225), is one of the best hagiographical accounts by a medieval author. The numerous collections of *exempla* for the use of preachers, which often turn to hagiography for their material, are well represented by that of Cardinal JACQUES DE VITRY (d. 1240), Canon Regular of St. Augustine. His letters sent from the scene of the Fifth Crusade constitute a valuable historical source. Several biographies of saints came from the pen of the Belgian Dominican THOMAS OF CANTIMPRÉ, who died between 1263 and 1272. He made a study of bees, from which he drew lessons for Christian living, and composed an encyclopedia of natural science, *Opus de natura rerum.*

Epistolography. The art of writing letters in the later Middle Ages came under the influence of the *artes dictaminis,* and naturalness was sacrificed to mechanical phraseology. By the early 13th century chanceries had begun to preserve in registers copies of their letters and documents. Pope Innocent III, strong personality that he was, avoided the rigidity of *dictamen* in his own writings. Archbishop John Peckham of Canterbury composed his many letters according to its rules without seriously bad effect. The learned Franciscan scholar and gifted administrator ROBERT GROSSETESTE (d. 1253), Bishop of Lincoln, wrote his letters in good classical style.

Politico-Canonical Writings. Writings on government and Church-State relations became numerous in the period. The oldest of legal classics of England, the *Tractatus de legibus et consuetudinibus regni Angliae,* was composed by Rannulf de Glanville (d. 1190) or, perhaps, by his nephew, Bp. HUBERT WALTER. The greatest medieval work on law written in England was Henry de BRACTON'S (d. 1268) *De legibus et consuetudinibus Angliae libri quinque.* In France and Germany law books were being written in the vernacular. Even in the 15th century, Sir John Fortescue wrote in Latin on natural law and in praise of English law, though his greatest work is his *Governance of England.*

The additions to Canon Law were from time to time published in collections. Pope Gregory IX delegated to St. RAYMOND OF PEÑAFORT, OP, the task of putting together the laws enacted since the *Decretum Gratiani* had been completed. Promulgated as the Decretals of Gregory IX (1234), this collection gave rise to many commentaries. Pope BONIFACE VIII added a book of Decretals (1298), and Pope JOHN XXII published (1317) a collection made by Clement V.

The great authority of Innocent III in Christendom, his appeal to the indirect power of the papacy to justify his interference in matters of civil government, and his direct feudal suzerainty over vassal states (Aragon, Portugal, Sicily, and England) helped greatly to shape the theory of the numerous writers who championed the right of the papacy to the ''two swords,'' the spiritual and the material. As St. Bernard had taught long before, the sovereign pontiff was to use the former and hand the latter over to secular rulers to be used for the Church. Pope Innocent IV had formulated the theory more emphatically in his struggle with Emperor Frederick II, who claimed sovereignty over both Church and State and expressed his claims in the writings of his legist, Peter of Vinea. The distinguished canonists HOSTIENSIS and William DURANTI THE ELDER in the late 13th century wrote to advance proof for the temporal authority of the papacy. St. Thomas Aquinas was much more conservative than these canonists in his opinion of papal secular power. He adhered to the theory of Pope GELASIUS I and at most conceded an indirect power over secular government *ratione pec-*

cati. Ptolemy of Lucca, who continued the *De regimine principium* of Thomas, agreed with Hostiensis and Duranti. On the other hand, a number of canonists of the same period held rather closely to the teaching of St. Gelasius.

Writings on Church-State Controversies and the Conciliar Movement. In the controversy between BONIFACE VIII and PHILIP IV, the letters of Boniface are among the best known pieces of medieval writing. They claim nothing that had not been claimed before by the papacy, but after each letter Boniface had been obliged to retract his demands. The anonymous *Disputatio inter clerum et militem* emanating from Philip's camp repudiated all claims of the papacy to authority in secular affairs. Pamphleteers came to the defense of papal authority in temporal matters: Henry of Cremona, GILES OF ROME, JAMES OF VITERBO, and AUGUSTINE TRIUMPHUS. The last three were Augustinians. Somewhat later the Spanish Franciscan ALVARO PELAYO (d. 1349) wrote in the same vein.

On the side of the king the anticlerical Pierre Dubois, one of Philip's legists, is thought to have been the author of a *Deliberatio,* which accused Boniface of heresy and maintained that if the popes had ever possessed temporal authority over the kingdom of France they had lost it through prescription. Besides other polemical works of this nature, Dubois wrote an *abbreviatio* on how France could conquer Europe; tracts against the Templars; a *De pace et bello;* and a *De recuperatione terrae sanctae,* which dealt little with the Crusade but put together his ideas of reform. Also in the camp of the king, though more moderate, was the capable Dominican writer John of Paris (Quidort, who denied that the pope held the supreme temporal power and anticipated the conciliar theory by affirming that a council is greater than the pope. Outside of this controversy DANTE wrote his *De monarchia* to show the need of a universal monarchy and to defend the empire under Henry VI, which Dante looked upon as ideal, against encroachment by the Church. Dante also wrote his *De vulgari eloquentia* in Latin.

In the 14th century the controversy between Pope John XXII and Emperor Louis of Bavaria concerning the latter's election without papal approval gave rise to further antipapal writing. The nominalist philosopher WILLIAM OF OCKHAM (d. 1349), an English Franciscan, wrote to support the independence of the State in relation to the Church. He rejected papal absolutism even in spiritual matters and advocated the general council as a check upon papal authority. In the same feud against the Avignon papacy MARSILIUS OF PADUA (d. 1342), professor at Paris, wrote his *Defensor pacis,* which began with the accepted medieval idea that monarchical authority is delegated by the people, but in its second part places the Church under the control of the State. He denied the divine institution of the papacy and insisted that even the decisions of a general council needed to be ratified by the civil legislator. JOHN OF JANDUN (d. 1328) of the faculty of arts in the University of Paris, an Averroist, held views similar to those of Marsilius and collaborated with him.

The movement for a general council as a solution for the Western Schism occasioned much writing. Gerson and D'Ailly have been mentioned as favoring the movement, which they supported with their pens. Ockham, Marsilius and John of Paris had previously insisted on the holding of councils as a means of controlling the papacy. A number of canonists pleaded for a council to cope with the exceptional problems arising from the Schism. This was the attitude of CONRAD OF GELNHAUSEN and Henry Heinbuche of Langenstein in the early days of the Schism. Later on, the leading canonist of his generation, Francisco ZABARELLA, in his zeal for the conciliar theory, declared that the pope was only the first servant of the Church. From Spain came two staunch opponents of the conciliar movement who, after the Schism was ended, wrote vigorously in behalf of the papacy and against any further holding of councils at the time: Juan de Torquemada and Rodrigo Sánchez de Arávalo (d. 1470).

Scientific and Encyclopedic Writing. There were no few writers on natural science in the later Middle Ages, as the studies of Lynn Thorndike and George Sarton attest. It must suffice here to mention the Franciscan ROGER BACON and the Dominican ALBERT THE GREAT.

The best-known encyclopedist and compiler of the age was the Dominican VINCENT OF BEAUVAIS (d. 1264?). He wrote a treatise on the education of the young men of noble families (*De eruditione filiorum regalium*). His *Speculum maius* is a large work in three parts: *doctrinale, historiale,* and *naturale*. A *Speculum morale* that had been attributed to him is the work of another author. The *Speculum doctrinale* treats not only of theology but of all fields of learning. The *Speculum historiale* consists of passages taken from earlier historical accounts pieced together in chronological order down to *c.* 1264. The *Speculum naturale* takes excerpts concerning nature from previous authors, to secure which he had access to a good library. He himself made little contribution to scientific knowledge. There is a notable tendency on his part to make religious application of the lore he presents.

The demarcation between writers of the Middle Ages and of the Renaissance is necessarily vague. Some of the authors treated in this article lived after the Renaissance could be considered to have started, and they have been included here because they seem to be medieval in spirit.

See Also: ANNALS AND CHRONICLES; ARS PRAEDICANDI; CURSUS; HYMNOLOGY; LATIN (IN THE CHURCH); SPIRITUALITY, CHRISTIAN (HISTORY OF).

Bibliography: M. R. P. MCGUIRE, *Introduction to Mediaeval Latin Studies: A Syllabus and Bibliographical Guide* (Washington 1964). K. STRECKER, *Introduction to Medieval Latin,* ed. and tr. R. B. PALMER (2d ed. Berlin 1963). L. J. PAETOW, *A Guide to the Study of Medieval History* (rev. ed. New York 1931; repr. 1959), esp. pt. 3; to be supplemented by sec. J and K, ed. G. C. BOYCE, of *The Historical Association's Guide to Historical Literature* (New York 1961). M. HÉLIN, *A History of Medieval Latin Literature,* tr. J. C. SNOW (rev. ed. New York 1949). C. GROSS, *The Sources and Literature of English History from the Earliest Times to about 1485* (2d ed. New York 1915; repr. 1952). J. F. KENNEY, *The Sources for the Early History of Ireland:* v. 1, *Ecclesiastical* (New York 1929). A. E. MOLINIER et al., *Les Sources de l'histoire de France,* 6 v. (Paris 1901–06). W. WATTENBACH, *Deutschlands Geschichtsquellen im Mittelalter bis zur Mitte des 13. Jh.*, v. 1 (7th ed. Stuttgart-Berlin 1904), v. 2 (6th ed. Berlin 1894). W. WATTENBACH, *Deutschlands Geschichtsquellen im Mittelalter. Deutsche Kaiserzeit,* ed. R. HOLTZMANN, v. 1.1–4 (3rd ed. Tübingen 1948; repr. of 2d ed. 1938–43). W. WATTENBACH, *Deutschlands Geschichtsquellen im Mittelalter. Vorzeit und Karolinger,* Hefte 1–4, ed. W. LEVINSON and H. LÖWE (Weimar 1952–63). *Speculum: A Journal of Mediaeval Studies* (Cambridge, Mass. 1926–). *Histoire littéraire de la France* (Paris): v. 1–12, ed. Maurists (1733–68); v. 13–38, ed. Académie des Inscriptions et Belles-Lettres (1814–1941); v. 1–29 (repr. 1865–). M. MANITIUS, *Geschichte der lateinischen Literatur des Mittelalters* (Munich 1911–31). J. DE GHELLINCK, *L'Essor de la littérature latine au XIIe siècle,* 2 v. (Brussels-Paris 1946). J. DE GHELLINCK, *Littérature latine au moyen-âge,* 2 v. (Paris 1939): v. 1, *Depuis les origines jusqu'à la fin de la renaissance carolingienne*; v. 2, *De la renaissance carolingienne à saint Anselme; Bibliothèque catholique des sciences religieuses* 85–86. G. GRÖBER, *Übersicht über die lateinische Literatur von der Mitte des 6. Jahrhunderts bis zur Mitte des 14. Jahrhunderts* (Strassburg 1902; repr. Munich 1963, with table of contents and index of names) 2.1:97–432. *Patrologia Latina,* ed. J. P. MIGNE, 217 v., indexes 4 v. (Paris 1878–90). *Monumenta Germaniae Historica* (Berlin 1826–). *Rerum Britannicarum medii aevi scriptores,* 244 v. (London 1858–96; repr. New York 1964–), ordinarily called Rolls Series. *Acta Sanctorum* (Antwerp 1643–; Venice 1734–; Paris 1863–). *Analecta hymnica* (Leipzig 1886–1922). M. L. W. LAISTNER, *Thought and Letters in Western Europe, A.D. 500 to 900* (2d ed. New York 1957). E. K. RAND, *Founders of the Middle Ages* (2d ed. Cambridge, Mass. 1929). C. H. HASKINS, *The Renaissance of the 12th Century* (Cambridge, Mass. 1927; repr. 1933). E. R. CURTIUS, *European Literature and the Latin Middle Ages,* tr. W. R. TRASK (New York 1953). C. S. BALDWIN, *Medieval Rhetoric and Poetic (to 1400)* (New York 1928). E. FARAL, *Les Arts poétiques du XIIe et du XIIIe siècle* (Paris 1924). D. NORBERG, *Introduction à l'étude de la versification latine mediévale* (Stockholm 1958). F. J. E. RABY, *A History of Christian-Latin Poetry from the Beginnings to the Close of the Middle Ages* (2d ed. Oxford 1953). F. J. E. RABY, *A History of Secular Latin Poetry in the Middle Ages,* 2 v. (2d ed. Oxford 1957). F. J. E. RABY, ed., *Oxford Book of Medieval Latin Verse* (Oxford 1959). K. YOUNG, *The Drama of the Medieval Church,* 2 v. (Oxford 1933). H. J. WADDELL, *The Wandering Scholars* (6th ed. New York 1932; repr. Garden City, N.Y. 1955). A. HILKA and O. SCHUMANN, eds., *Carmina burana,* 2 v. (Heidelberg 1930–41). P. LEHMANN, *Die Parodie im Mittelalter* (Munich 1922); ed., *Parodistische Texte: Beispiele zur lateinischen Parodie im Mittelalter* (Munich 1923). É. H. GILSON, *History of Christian Philosophy in the Middle Ages* (New York 1955). J. W. THOMPSON and B. J. HOLM, *History of Historical Writing,* 2 v. (New York 1942). G. SARTON, *Introduction to the History of Science,* 3 v. in 5 (Baltimore 1927–48). L. THORNDIKE, *A History of Magic and Experimental Science,* 8 v. (New York 1923–58). R. W. and A. J. CARLYLE, *A History of Mediaeval Political Theory in the West,* 6 v. (Edinburgh 1903–36; repr. New York 1953). H. DELEHAYE, *The Legends of the Saints,* tr. D. ATTWATER (New York 1962). A. WILMART, *Auteurs spirituels et textes dévots du moyen âge latin* (Paris 1932). J. T. WELTER, *L'Exemplum dans la littérature religieuse et didactique du moyen âge* (Paris 1927).

[A. K. ZIEGLER]

MEDINA

A city (Arabic *al-Madīna*), originally named Yathrib, in the east-central Hejaz, some 210 miles north of MECCA; the residence of MUHAMMAD and his followers after the Hegira. The area around the city is extremely fertile and well watered and is known for its orchards of date palms, oranges, lemons, figs, etc. The original settlement was an unwalled agricultural community. Well before Islam, although at an uncertain date, the town came to be settled by three Jewish tribes, the Qaynūqā', Qurayza, and Nadīr, who possessed the city and cultivated its lands; it is probably they who first gave it the originally Aramaic name, al-Madīna, by which was meant ''the (chief or preeminent) city''; in the time of Mohammed it was called both Medina and Yathrib. Later, with the immigration of two Arab tribes, the 'Aws and Khazrağ, there ensued a continual and bloody struggle between the various factions, who finally negotiated to bring Mohammed to Medina from Mecca as an arbiter of the feuds. Following his death, it was up to the caliphate of Ali ('Alī), the capital of Islam. Later, particularly from the tenth century, its political importance declined until it became briefly the capital of the Kingdom of Hejaz under Husayn ibn 'Alī, from 1919 to 1924, after which it fell to the WAHHĀBIS under 'Abdal'azīz ibn Su'ūd. It has been, since the time of the Prophet, one of the chief religious centers of Islam; the MOSQUE over the tomb of the Prophet is one of the principal shrines of the Muslim world.

[R. M. FRANK]

MEDINA, BARTOLOMÉ DE

Dominican theologian; b. Medina de Rioseco, near Valladolid, 1527 or 1528; d. Salamanca, Jan. 29, 1580. He entered the Dominican Order at Salamanca. With Dominic Bañez, he was the pupil of Dominic Soto and Melchior Cano. Though well versed in Greek and Hebrew, Medina devoted his life almost entirely to teaching theology, at Alcalá and then at Salamanca, first in the chair of Durandus, and afterward as the principal professor. He was appointed, in 1576, to the *cathedra primaria* after a successful public debate against the learned Augustinian, John of Guevara. Medina's principal works are his commentaries on the *Summa theologiae* of St. Thomas Aquinas. Only the commentaries on the *prima pars* (Salamanca 1577) and the *tertia pars* to question 60 (Salamanca 1578) are published. He also wrote the *Breve instucción de comme se ha administrar el Sacramento de la Penitencia* (Salamanca 1580). Medina is usually called the father of PROBABILISM, but scholars are not agreed about his teaching on this question. Some hold that he only formulated probabilism when he wrote: ''An opinion is probable when we can follow it without censure and reproof. An opinion is not said to be probable because apparent reasons are adduced in its favor and many assert and defend it. If this were true, all errors would be probable. But an opinion is probable when wise men assert and confirm it with excellent proofs'' (*Comment. in ST,* 1a2ae, 19.6). Others say he proposed the principle but did not use it in practice. Quétif and Échard and also Billuart maintain that Medina's system differed greatly from later probabilism. Quétif and Échard admit that Medina opened the way for a flood of probabilist theory and said: ''St. Thomas is our master, others only insofar as they follow his teaching'' (*Scriptores Ordinis Praedicatorum* 2:257). Probabiliorists, when such were still to be found, were loath to admit that he proposed a new doctrine; probabilists do not wish to give him all the credit for introducing a new system of forming the conscience in doubtful cases.

Bibliography: J. QUÉTIF and J. ÉCHARD, *Scriptores Ordinis Praedicatorum* 2.1:256–257. M. M. GORCE, *Dictionnaire de théologie catholique*, ed. A. VACANT et al. (Paris 1903–50) 10.1:481–485. T. DEMAN, *ibid.* 13.1:463–470, esp. bibliog. 463.

[E. M. ROGERS]

MEDINA, JUAN

Moral theologian; b. Alcalá, 1490; d. probably there, 1546. Few facts are known about him except that he taught moral theology at the University of Alcalá from 1526 until his death. He won great renown as a teacher, drawing large crowds to his lectures. He published nothing himself, but after his death two of his works appeared that represent his moral teaching. (1) *De restitutione et contractibus tractatus sive codex, nempe de rerum dominio atque earum restitutione et de aliquibus contractibus, de usura, de cambiis, de censibus;* (2) *In titulum de poenitentia ejusque partibus commentarius, sc. de poenitentia cordis, de confessione, de satisfactione, de jejuniis, de eleemosyna* (2 v. Salamanca 1550; new eds. Ingolstadt 1581; Brixen 1589, 1606; Cologne 1607).

In addition to these works, two of Medina's manuscripts have been discovered in the Vatican archives (OTTOB 1044, fol. 162–231, 231v–261). These are a record of a course that he gave on the first book of the *Sentences* and a part of the second book. The text that he used was an exposition of the *Sentences* by Gabriel Biel (1425–95), the German nominalist whose commentary Martin Luther is said to have known by heart. The end of the 15th century had seen the introduction of nominalism into the Spanish and Portuguese universities from the University of Paris. The popularity of nominalist teachings in the Iberian schools led eventually to the establishment of a nominalist chair at Alcalá (as well as at Salamanca and Coimbra). Medina occupied this chair at Alcalá, as his exposition of Biel's commentary shows. This was a theological chair and the sophistical logic so highly acclaimed by the followers of Ockham was not allowed. But many of Medina's theses, following Biel, were in accord with Lutheran teaching, especially on justification and penance, and were later corrected by the Council of Trent.

Bibliography: V. HEYNCK, *Lexikon für Theologie und Kirche,* ed. J. HOFER and K. RAHNER, 10 v. (2d, new ed. Freiburg 1957–65) (1966) 7:233. É. AMMAN, *Dictionnaire de théologie catholique,* ed. A. VACANT et al., 15 v. (Paris 1903–50; Tables générales 1951–) 10.1:485–486. H. HURTER, *Nomenclator literarius theologiae catholicae,* 5 v. in 6 (3d ed. Innsbruck 1903–13); v. 1 (4th ed. 1926) 2:1559. M. M. C. DE WULF, *History of Mediaeval Philosophy,* tr. E. C. MESSENGER, 2 v. (3d ed. New York 1935–38) 2:289–290.

[P. F. MULHERN]

MEDITATION

Meditation comes from the Latin *meditatio*, meaning a thinking over, contemplating; exercise, practice, preparation. In modern usage it can refer to physical and psychological methods of calming oneself, reducing stress or sharpening mental awareness. From the Christian perspective, meditation generally refers to a type of prayerful reflection. Meditation is sometimes called mental prayer, although this can be misleading because meditation can be vocal and often uses the imagination, memory, will, and senses in addition to the mind. A great many different methods of meditation are recommended by different spiritual authors. The methods, however, are meant only as guides, the goal being growth in love of God and towards others.

In the early monastic tradition *meditatio* refers to a vocal activity. To meditate on a passage of Scripture was to repeat out loud a phrase over and over again until it was known by heart. For example, the sixth-century *Rule of Benedict* lists meditation as one of the works of the novices: they were responsible for memorizing the portions of Scripture needed for the monastic office (48.23, see also 8.3, 58.5). The recitation from memory was also called meditation and could be done while engaging in manual work or other activities and served as a stimulus for personal prayer. In these contexts, meditation is closely associated with *lectio divina*, the prayerful reading of Scripture. It's foundation can be found in psalms, ''Happy are those . . . whose delight is in the law of the Lord, and on this law they meditate day and night'' (Ps 1.1–2 see also 19.14, 77.6).

Contemplation. While earlier authors did not always make a distinction between meditation and contemplation, in the middle ages the two terms began to be separated, and contemplation was associated with the higher stages of mystical prayer. The Carthusian, Guigo II (1174–1180), writes of four stages of prayer in his *Ladder for Monks*: reading, meditation, prayer, and contemplation. Meditation refers here to thinking about what the text means and searching for hidden meanings for each word. This distinction is retained by many later authors, including the Carmelite mystics and Francis de Sales (1567–1622). Thus, Teresa of Avila (1518–1582) calls ''discursive meditation'' prayers in which one thinks systematically about religious material, Scripture, or the mysteries of faith. Such meditative prayer requires much human effort, graced by God. In contemplative prayer, however, human effort is less as God acts marvelously to transform the person. For Francis de Sales, meditation uses one's understanding, making various reflections in order to arouse the will to love of God and the things of God. In meditation the mind moves from point to point, examining the subject of reflection from various angles.

Ignatius of Loyola's *SPIRITUAL EXERCISES* outlines manifold methods of meditation, albeit without differentiating the term from contemplation. The famous text includes methods for examining one's conscience, saying the Our Father, and reflecting on imagined scenes from Christ's life and one's judgement before God. Ignatius suggests meditating on single words as long as one continues to find new meanings in them, as well as reciting the words of a prayer rhythmically with one's breathing. His imaginative meditations encourage the use of all the senses while putting oneself in a particular scene or setting. One is to consider what one would say and feel in such a situation, and what one might hear from others. Ignatius' meditations include preparatory prayers for the graces one desires, as well as concluding prayers and conversations with Christ or the saints.

Quest. *The Catechism of the Catholic Church* highlights the need for all Christians to engage in prayer, including vocal, meditative, and contemplative prayer. It making these distinctions the Catechism describes meditation as ''a quest'' in which ''the mind seeks to understand the way and how of the Christian life, in order to adhere and respond to what the Lord is asking.'' To assist in such meditation, one may use texts such as Scripture, seasonal liturgical texts, or other spiritual writings. Mental images may also be used, in particular recollections of events in the life of Christ. Meditation may be inspired by visual images such as icons or nature. Even the events in history can be used as a fruitful source of reflection, since history is ''the page on which the 'today' of God is written.'' Meditation intends on deepening faith, converting the heart, and strengthening the will to follow Christ. It should therefore include a movement toward discerning what it is that God wants one to do. In contrast to meditation, the Catechism describes vocal prayer as focusing on words, whether interior or vocal, and contemplation as focusing on a union with God, ''a silent love,'' in which the mind need not be as active.

Bibliography: *The Catechism of the Catholic Church* 2705–2708; J. LECLERCQ, ''Meditation as a Biblical Reading,'' *Worship* 33 (1958–59) 562–569; *The Love of Learning and the Desire for God* (New York 1961) 13–30. L. CUNNINGHAM and K. EGAN, *Christian Spirituality: Themes from the Tradition* (New York 1996) 84–104. CONGREGATIO PRO DOCTRINA FIDEI, *Letter to the Bishops of the Catholic Church on Some Aspects of Christian Meditation* (Washington, D.C. 1989). D. H. SHAPIRO JR. and R. N. WALSH, eds., *Meditation: Classic and Contemporary* (Hawthorne, NY 1984). K. KAISCH, *Finding God: A Handbook of Christian Meditation* (New York 1994). J. SUDBRACK, *Dictionnaire de Spiritualité* (Paris 1980) 10:906–934; *Meditation: Theorie und Praxis* (Wurtzbourg-Stuttgart 1971).

[K. YOHE]

MEDJUGORJE

A mountain town and pilgrimage center in the Diocese of Mostar in the Catholic Croatian region of Hercegovina, western central Yugoslavia. The name Medjugorje [Med-ju-gor-ee-ay] means ''between the hills.''

Beginning on June 24, 1981, six Croatian youths from the parish of St. James in Medjugorje reported receiving nearly daily apparitions of the Blessed Virgin Mary. The six visionaries, Vicka Ivankovic (b. July 3, 1964), Mirjana Dragicevic (b. March 18, 1965), Marija Pavlovic (b. April 1, 1965), Ivan Dragicevic (b. May 25, 1965), Ivanka Ivankovic (b. April 21, 1966), and Jakov Colo (b. June 3, 1971) reported to have seen the ''Gospa'' (Croatian for Madonna) in the form of a three-dimensional, external apparition, during which time the visionaries collectively entered an ecstatic state that medical and scientific researchers from Milan and the French University of Montpellier have described as 'removed from the spatio-temporal order.' The messages received from the Madonna are presented both as an authentic embodiment of Catholic doctrine and as a postconciliar formulation of the Marian messages transmitted at Lourdes and Fatima. The essence of the messages received for more than five years can be summarized into six foundational themes.

The Medjugorje message calls for a more resolute *faith* in the one God and in Jesus Christ as the one mediator to the Father, combined with faith in the apparitions themselves as a means of special graces and conversion. The call to *prayer* requests a greater generosity of Christian prayer that accentuates the daily recitation of the 15-decade Rosary, an invitation to daily Mass, the praying of Sacred Scripture, and a consecration of each person and family to the Sacred Heart of Jesus and the Immaculate Heart of Mary as a means of total abandonment to God. The Madonna requested a *strict* fast (bread and water) initially every Friday and later on Wednesdays as well, in reparation for sin and for the conversion of sinners. The call to *penance* comprises a general call to Christian self-denial offered for sinners. The message also asks for an interior *change of heart* to God made possible through greater faith, prayer, fasting, and penance. A monthly sacramental Confession is specified as a principal constituent of authentic conversion. The preeminent Medjugorje theme, the call to *peace*, requests an interior peace of Christ in the heart of every person, obtained by consistent faith, prayer, fasting, penance and conversion. Significant world chastisements because of humanity's refusal to convert, to take place within the lifetime of the visionaries, are also part of the Medjugorje message, but the acceptance of divine peace, in spite of upcoming external events, remains the heart of the reported Marian message.

The Church has made no official judgment regarding the Medjugorje apparitions. In July, 1986, 12 Italian bishops requested from Pope John Paul II pastoral directives for members of their diocese wanting to pilgrimage to the Marian site. The papal response recommended that pilgrims be allowed to go to Medjugorje, so that they may pray, fast, and convert.

Bibliography: R. FARICY and L. ROONEY, *Mary, Queen of Peace* (New York 1984). S. KRALJEVIC, *The Apparitions of Our Lady of Medjugorje* (Chicago 1984). R. LAURENTIN and L. RUPCIC, *Is the Virgin Mary Appearing in Medjugorje?* (Washington, D.C. 1984). M. MIRAVALLE, *The Message of Medjugorje: The Marian Message to the Modern World* (Lanham, Md. 1986). J. PELLETIER, *The Queen of Peace Visits Medjugorje* (Worcester, Mass. 1985).

[M. I. MIRAVALLE]

MEDRANO, MARIANO

Argentine prelate and philosopher; b. Buenos Aires, 1767; d. there, April 7, 1851. He entered the University of Chuquisaca in 1781 and received his doctorate in theology there. From 1793 to 1795 he taught philosophy in the Colegio de San Carlos, where he had among his students such outstanding personalities as Saturnino Segurola, Julián Navarro, José León Banegas, Martin Thompson, and Mariano Moreno. His unpublished lectures, still extant, show that the basis of his whole doctrine was scholastic, although it had eclectic and Cartesian ramifications. In La Plata he spread the ideas of Francisco SUÁREZ, the oracle of Argentine youth at the close of the 18th century, who had so much influence on the revolution. Medrano was pastor of the church of La Piedad and vicar-general of the Diocese of Buenos Aires in 1822; in that position he opposed the ecclesiastical reforms of Bernardino RIVADAVIA. In 1829 the government of Viamonte exercised the right of presentation, addressing a request to Gregory XVI for a bishop to be named in the diocese. Medrano was named apostolic vicar and consecrated titular bishop of Aulón. In 1832 he was named bishop of Buenos Aires by Gregory XVI. When the papal bulls to this effect were presented to Attorney General Pedro José Agrelo, he supported national patronage as the right of the respective governments. In order to resolve this involved question, the government in 1834 appointed a board of 39 jurists and theologians to consider 14 propositions presented to them on the state's right of presentation to ecclesiastical office, which seemed to have been ignored in the appointment of Bishop Medrano. After receiving the report, *Memorial ajustado,* the government accepted the appointment of Medrano. He remained in his bishopric during the Rosas administration and reestablished the ecclesiastical hierarchy.

Bibliography: A. TONDA, *Rivadavia y Medrano: Sus actuaciones en la reforma eclesiástica* (Santa Fé, Argentina 1952). J. C. ZURETTI, *Historia eclesiástica argentina* (Buenos Aires 1945).

[V. O. CUTOLO]

MEEHAN, CHARLES, BL.

Irish Franciscan priest and martyr; b. after 1639 (exact date and birthplace unknown); d. Ruthin, North Wales, Aug. 12, 1679. According to reliable contemporary sources, his surname was Mihan (modern Meehan), not Mahony as stated in a contemporary broadsheet. No details are available on his religious training and ordination. On Nov. 21, 1672, the Irish Franciscan provincial chapter approved him for hearing confessions of lay people. As a result of the edicts of banishment against bishops and regulars (1673–74), he fled to Flanders from

Ireland. Early in November 1674 he was sent to pursue studies at the Franciscan friary in Hammelburg, Bavaria, and thence to St. Isidore's College, Rome (summer 1676). While returning to Ireland in 1678 his ship was forced onto the Welsh coast. He was arrested at Denbigh and imprisoned. At his trial (1679), during the Titus Oates scare, he admitted his priesthood and was condemned to death. He was hanged, cut down alive, and brutally butchered. Meehan was beatified by Pope John Paul II on Nov. 22, 1987 with George Haydock and Companions.

Feast: Feb. 12; May 4 (Feast of the English Martyrs in England).

See Also: MARTYRS OF ENGLAND AND WALES.

Bibliography: J. M. CRONIN, ''The Other Irish Martyr of the Titus Oates Plot,'' *Blessed Oliver Plunket: Historial Studies* (Dublin 1937) 133–153. C. MOONEY, ''The Ven. Father Charles Meehan, d. 1679,'' *Franciscan College Annual* (Multyfarnham 1952) 91–93; ''Further Light on Father C. Meehan,'' *Collectanea Hibernica* 6–7 (1963–64) 225–230. C. GIBLIN, ed., *Liber Lovaniensis* (Dublin 1956) 131.

[B. MILLETT]

MEEHAN, THOMAS FRANCIS

Historiographer, chiefly of the Catholic Church in the U.S., editor; b. of Irish immigrant parents, Patrick J. and Mary Jane (Butler) Meehan, Brooklyn, N.Y., Sept. 19, 1854; d. New York City, July 7, 1942. He received his B.A. in 1873 and his M.A. in 1874 from the College of St. Francis Xavier, New York City. His father, who owned the *Irish American,* appointed Thomas its managing editor (1874–1904). He was also New York correspondent for several papers and was on the staff of the *New York Herald* (1894–96). He was assistant managing editor of the *Catholic Encyclopedia* (1906–08), contributing more than 100 articles to it. From 1909 to his death he was on the editorial staff of *America.* He also wrote for the *Encyclopedia Americana,* the *North American Review,* the *Catholic World,* the *Commonweal,* and other magazines and newspapers. As early as 1899 he had contributed articles to the *Records and Studies* published by the United States Catholic Historical Society and in 1905 became collaborator with Charles G. HERBERMANN, president and editor of the society, when the latter's sight began to fail. When Herbermann died in 1916, Meehan became editor and continued in this capacity until his death. He was editor of and contributor to *Catholic Builders of the Nation* (Boston 1925). Pius XI named him a knight of St. Gregory, May 17, 1931, and Fordham University, New York City, honored him with the LL.D. during its centenary year (1941).

[B. L. LEE]

MEEKNESS

A human characteristic that renders one mild of temper and slow to take offense. In modern English it also has a pejorative sense and applies to a man who is spiritless and tamely submissive.

In the Old Testament meekness was closely allied with the state of humility, lowliness, poverty, and affliction. The ancient Greeks brought it into a moral context in counting it better to suffer than to do wrong. The esteem attached to meekness is typical of New Testament morality. ''Blessed are the meek, for they shall possess the earth'' (Mt 5.4) is the most famous passage embodying this term, but the quality itself is included equivalently in the fruit of the spirit that St. Paul described as charity, joy, peace, patience, kindness, goodness, faith, modesty, and continency (Gal 5.22–23). Clearly the attitude that is recommended to the Christian is one of relative passivity in the face of aggravating invasion, or even one of active kindliness toward the covetous and domineering.

The Pauline reference in Galatians to the fruit of the Spirit, and the later association of the virtue of meekness with St. Benedict's steps of humility locate it more exactly in the organic process of Christian growth and development. In its fullness as a gift of the Spirit, there is a willing acceptance if not an element of positive relish in the reaction of those who possess it to the provoking behavior of others, as is exemplified in the martyrdom of the deacon Stephen. In more ordinary circumstances it shows itself in a lack of violence in dealing with one's enemies.

Scholastic theologians have narrowed this concept in making it a moral virtue, a potential part of temperance, that has as its effect the rational moderation of anger. However, their ideal embodiment of this character trait is still Jesus—''Now I myself Paul appeal to you by the meekness and gentleness of Christ'' (2 Cor 10.1). Failure in meekness by way of defect is commonly considered under the heading of anger. Excesses of meekness that usually come from extreme indolence, craven fear, or complete absence of even normal aggressiveness have been treated by Aquinas and St. Francis de Sales. Serious failures are conceivable only in such unusual circumstances that bad example would be gravely scandalous, or that failure to admonish with adequate impressiveness would lead those under one's charge to moral confusion.

Obviously the beatitude mentioned by Matthew as part of the Sermon on the Mount lists meekness as a value opposed to those values that normally prevail in society. From the simple evolutionary point of view, it might be thought that the meek would be eliminated by the process

Silo at Tel Megiddo, Israel. (©Richard T. Nowitz/CORBIS)

of natural selection. However, some degree of acceptance of this Christian ideal in Western society appears necessary to its survival. Nonetheless, it is certainly one of the traits of character that the average man finds confusing. But with the passing of the rugged frontier era and its appropriate code of morality, humility and meekness are again becoming more and more acceptable as qualities of a well-adjusted member of our society.

Bibliography: THOMAS AQUINAS, *Summa theologiae* 2a2ae, 157. D. BUZY, *Dictionnaire de spiritualité ascétique et mystique. Doctrine et histoire*, ed. M. VILLER et al. (Paris 1932–) 1:1298–1310. A. I. MENNESSIER, *ibid.* 3:1674–85. M. GAUCHERON, *Catholicisme* 3:1051–52. B. H. MERKELBACH, *Summa theologiae moralis*, 3 v. (8th ed. Paris 1949) 2:1033–36. D. M. PRÜMMER, *Manuale theologiae moralis*, ed. E. M. MÜNCH, 3 v. (12th ed. Freiburg-Barcelona 1955) 2:709.

[J. D. FEARON]

MEGIDDO

One of the most important Canaanite and Israelite fortress-cities of ancient Palestine. It is located in modern Israel, approximately 20 miles south-southeast of Haifa. The principal references to Megiddo in the OT, usually coupled with its lesser twin city Taanach, occur in Jos 12.21; 17.11; Jgs 1.27; 5.19; 1 Kgs 4.12;9.15; 2 Kgs 9.27; 23.29; 1 Chr 7.29; 2 Chr 35.22. Several features of Megiddo's location on a spur of the Mt. CARMEL ridge that thrusts into the southwestern edge of the Plain of Esdraelon account for its unique strategic value in antiquity. Control of Megiddo meant control of the best pass that cut northward from the coast through the Carmel range to the interior of Palestine and beyond. This was the main military and commercial route between Egypt and the Fertile Crescent. Megiddo also commanded the whole sweep of the fertile plain from east to north to west and therefore the traffic that traveled the busy trade route through this plain.

Because of the many battles that were fought at or near Megiddo in the distant past, the term Armageddon, which is probably the Hebrew for ''Mount of Megiddo'' and appears in the eschatological context of Rv 16.16, is commonly used as the symbol and the synonym for the battlefield where the final struggle between good and evil will take place.

[W. V. E. CASEY]

MEHEGAN, MARY XAVIER, MOTHER

Founder, New Jersey Sisters of Charity; b. Skibereen, Ireland, Feb. 19, 1825; d. Convent Station, New Jersey, June 24, 1915. Mehegan's parents, Patrick and Johanna (Miles) Mehegan, named her Catherine Josephine. In 1844 she and her sister Margaret left for the U.S. without the knowledge of their mother. In 1847 Mehegan became one of the first postulants received by the New York Sisters of Charity after their separation from the community in Emmitsburg, Maryland. As Sister Mary Xavier, she was one of the three sisters who opened St. Vincent's Hospital in New York.

In 1858 James Roosevelt Bayley, first bishop of Newark, N.J., and a nephew of Mother Elizabeth Seton, requested Sister Mary Xavier and Sister Mary Catherine Nevin to supervise five novices who had been trained for him by the Cincinnati Sisters of Charity. On this basis, the sisters' New Jersey community was formally inaugurated on Sept. 29, 1859. The motherhouse was located first at old St. Mary's, Newark, and then, after July 2, 1860, at Madison, New Jersey, where St. Elizabeth's school for girls was opened also.

During the Civil War, Mother Xavier worked with the sisters in hospitals in Newark and Trenton. After the war, her order increased in numbers; new land was purchased, and additional buildings were constructed. The missions of the order flourished, and new ones were opened in Massachusetts, New York, and Connecticut. In 1899 Mother Xavier founded, at Convent Station, the College of St. Elizabeth, the first college for women in New Jersey. In 1915, when she had served as superior for 57 years, her community numbered 1,200 sisters and maintained 94 missions, including schools, hospitals, orphanages, nurseries, and homes for the aged.

Bibliography: M. A. SHARKEY, *The New Jersey Sisters of Charity,* 3 v. (New York 1933). B. M. MCENIRY, *Woman of Decision: The Life of Mother Mary Xavier Mehegan* (New York 1953).

[B. M. MCENIRY]

MEHRERAU, ABBEY OF

Former Benedictine abbey on Lake Constance in Bregenz, west Austria; present seat of the Cistercian abbey *nullius* of WETTINGEN-MEHRERAU. The Benedictine Mehrerau had nothing to do with the foundation of St. COLUMBAN in Bregenz *c.* 610. Mehrerau was settled by monks from PETERSHAUSEN (1097), who had settled (1083) in Adelsbuch (Bregenzerwald). The Romanesque church recently excavated served as a burial place for the counts of Bregenz and Montfort and for many Benedictine abbots. Mehrerau colonized the region with clearances in the Bregenzerwald and model farms. In 1806 the abbey was suppressed, and the Vorarlberg baroque church and tower were torn down. The baroque convent buildings still stand. In 1854 Cistercians expelled from Wettingen (1841) restored Mehrerau. By canon and civil law Mehrerau is now a priory dependent on Wettingen, and at the same time the seat of the Abbey of Wettingen. The abbot of Wettingen, the only abbot *nullius* in Austria, is head of the Mehrerau Cistercian congregation. This includes seven monasteries of men, two of which are priories, and nine monasteries of women, of which two are priories.

The library has 90,000 volumes, 100 MSS and early printings, a collection of engravings, and 18,000 seals. Several altar paintings are late Gothic and Renaissance. Mehrerau has a humanities gymnasium and boarding school recognized by the state, an agricultural technical school, and a philosophical-theological school. Since 1889 the abbey has published the Cistercian chronicle. It directs the pilgrimage in Birnau and a sanatorium in Mehrerau. Cistercians from Mehrerau were the first to return to Germany (Marienstatt), to modern Yugoslavia (Stična), and to Switzerland (HAUTERIVE) after the secularizations of the 19th century.

Bibliography: A. ULMER, *Die Klöster und Ordensniederlassungen in Vorarlberg einst und jetzt* (Dornbirn 1926) 28–36, 116–131. B. BILGERI, *Zinsrodel des Klosters Mehrerau, 1290–1505* (Kempten 1940); "100 Jahre Zisterzienser in M.," *Mehrerauer Grüsse,* NS v. 1 (1954) 1–217. K. SPAHR, *Lexikon für Theologie und Kirche,* ed. J. HOFER and K. RAHNER, 10 v. (2d, new ed. Freiburg 1957–65) 7:240; *Mehrerau* (Bregenz 1964).

[C. SPAHR]

MEINHARD OF LIVONIA, ST.

Also known as Meinrad, Augustinian missionary, bishop; b. ca. 1130 in Germany; d. Aug. 14, 1196, Yxkill, Livonia (near Riga, Latvia). Meinhard entered religious life at the monastery of Segelberg, Germany. Following his profession as an Augustinian canon regular and ordination as a priest, he left the safety of his monastery to preach in pagan lands. He was consecrated the first bishop of Livonia (*c.* 1184) and fixed his see at Yxkill on the Düna. He brought monks from his former convent to form a community of canons regular at his castle. Christianity found firm footing in the region due to his efforts to form a native clergy and establish standards for their training. Originally he was buried at his castle in Livonia. The see was transferred to Riga (1201) following his death, and his relics translated later that century to Riga's cathedral. He was canonized by Pope John Paul II at Riga, Latvia, Sept. 8, 1993.

Feast: April 12.

Bibliography: S. KUCINSKIS, *Svetais Meinards: Ikskiles biskaps, 1186–1196: Latvijas apustulis* (Riga 1993).

[K. I. RABENSTEIN]

MEINRAD OF EINSIEDELN, ST.

Martyr; b. Sülichgau, near Württemberg, Germany, late eighth century; d. hermitage near Einsiedeln, Switzerland, Jan. 21, 861. He was educated at the Abbey REICHENAU, where he became a BENEDICTINE monk and priest. He was for a while headmaster of the school at Babinchowa on upper Lake Zurich, and then he spent seven years in a hermitage on the slopes of Mount Etzel. There he built a chapel that later became the site of the monastery of EINSIEDELN, and the same place witnessed his murder by two robbers to whom he had given hospitality. He was buried at Reichenau, and his remains were transferred to Einsiedeln in 1039. His symbol is two ravens, beloved pets of Meinrad and betrayers of his murderers.

Feast: Jan. 21.

Bibliography: *Acta Sanctorum* Jan. 2:381–385. O. RINGHOLZ, *Geschichte des fürstlichen Benediktinerstiftes U. L. F. von Einsiedeln* (New York 1904) 648–651; *Meinrads-Büchlein: Das Leben und die Verehrung des Märtyrers von Einsiedeln* (Einsiedeln 1905) 1–80. J. BRAUN, *Tracht und Attribute der Heiligen in der deutschen Kunst* (Stuttgart 1943) 536. L. HELBLING, *Das Blockbuch von Sankt Meinrad und seinen Mördern und vom Ursprung von Einsiedeln* (Einsiedeln 1961). I. LÜTHOLD-MINDER, *Das Leben des heiligen Meinrad* (Einsiedeln 1979). A. M. ZIMMERMANN, *Kalendarium Benedictinum: Die Heiligen und Seligen des Benediktinerorderns und seiner Zweige,* 4 v. (Metten 1933–38) 1:109–112.

[B. D. HILL]

MEINWERK OF PADERBORN, BL.

Bishop; d. Paderborn, June 5, 1036. Meinwerk, a scion of the aristocratic Saxon Immedinger family, was educated with the future Emperor HENRY II, who appointed him bishop of Paderborn in 1009 so that he might restore the impoverished see through his own immense wealth. Having been consecrated by WILLIGIS OF MAINZ, Meinwerk enriched his church and cajoled extensive donations from his friend the emperor. He administered his diocesan property meticulously and with a paternal pettiness that became legendary; he supervised his clergy and ecclesiastical foundations with equal care (*see* ABDINGHOF, ABBEY OF). He brought goldsmiths, architects, and Greek artisans to Paderborn; built energetically; refurbished his cathedral; and fortified the town. He stands in the front rank of the OTTONIAN RENAISSANCE figures. Although he campaigned occasionally, Meinwerk did not seem to be politically inclined.

Feast: June 5.

Bibliography: F. TENCKHOFF, ed. *Monumenta Germaniae Scriptores rerum Germanicarum* v.59 (1921). J. BAUERMANN, *Westfälische Lebensbilder* (Münster 1930) 1:18–21. E. N. JOHNSON, *The Secular Activities of the German Episcopate, 919–1024* (Lincoln, NE 1932). A. BUTLER, *The Lives of the Saints,* ed. H. THURSTON and D. ATTWATER, 4 v. (New York 1956) 2:482–483. K. HONSELMANN, *Lexikon für Theologie und Kirche,* ed. J. HOFER and K. RAHNER, 10 v. (2d, new ed. Freiburg 1957–65) 7:242–243. G. MIETKE, *Die Bautätigkeit Bischof Meinwerks von Paderborn und die frühchristliche und byzantinische Architektur* (Paderborn 1991).

[R. H. SCHMANDT]

MEISTERMANN, BARNABAS

Missionary, archeologist, and author of many books on the shrines of the Holy Land; b. Pfaffenheim, Alsace, March 27, 1850; d. Jerusalem, Sept. 29, 1923. Ordained in 1873, Meistermann became a Franciscan in 1875. From 1882 to 1887 he was stationed at the Basilica of St. Mary of the Angels, Assisi, as a confessor and as the director of the renovation of the Portiuncula. After a short stay in Rome, he left for China in 1887, where he was a missionary for six years. From 1893 until his death 30 years later, he labored in the Holy Land and devoted himself to the study of the history, topography, and archeology of Palestine and its sacred shrines. The fruits of his scientific research were published in several books and in articles contributed to the *Catholic Encyclopedia.* His *Nouveau guide de Terre Sainte* (Paris 1907, 3d ed. 1936), which was translated into several languages, is still of much value.

Bibliography: *Acta Ordinis Fratrum Minorum* 42 (1923) 287–288. B. CUNEO, ''Biblical Scholars in the Franciscan Order,'' *Franciscan Educational Conference* 7 (1925) 113–114.

[D. A. MCGUCKIN]

MELANCHTHON, PHILIP

Humanist, reformer with LUTHER, and educator: b. Bretten, Feb. 16, 1497; d. Wittenberg, April 19, 1560. His father was Georg Schwarzerd, an armorer; his mother was a niece of Johann REUCHLIN. He studied under Georg Simler in the Pforzheim Latin school; at Heidelberg (1509–18), where the new humanistic learning was still weak, but ecclesiastical reform after the fashion of Wimpfeling was well represented by Pallas Spangel; and from 1512 to 1518 at Tübingen, where he received an M.A. degree (1514) and where he became wholly devoted to humanism, as evidenced by a plan to publish an error-free edition of Aristotle. At Tübingen he was influenced by

Philip Melanchthon.

the writings of Rodolphus Agricola, and especially of ERASMUS. In 1518, he went to Wittenberg University where, with help from Reuchlin, he had been appointed to the chair of Greek. His inaugural address on curriculum reform won the hearty approval of Luther, who in turn won Melanchthon for his cause of reform. Thus he rejected Aristotle, helped in the Leipzig Disputation, and received a baccalaureate in theology. During the period 1523 to 1528 his earlier humanism reappeared, initially occasioned by the preaching of the Zwickau prophets. He sensed that ecclesiastical order, political stability, and culture were in danger. Therefore he began stressing the importance of divine law (by which he came to mean not only that law as the revealer of sin and the leader to Christ, but also the law of nature as the foundation of civil, social, and intellectual life). Melanchthon helped to design the system for primary education that Luther advocated and evangelical territorial rulers began to adopt in the second half of the 1520s, but his influence was most directly felt in the reform of the Lutheran universities' curriculum. These activities earned him the title ''Preceptor of Germany.'' Although Luther had longed for a curriculum free of the influence of Aristotle, it was through Melanchthon's influence that the Greek philosopher came to play an important role in the evangelical universities, particularly in the natural philosophical curriculum. Melanchthon was also instrumental in shaping the fledgling Church's relationship with Germany's princes. His spirit was irenic and was evidenced in his ecumenical concerns. To Luther's Schmalkaldic Articles (1536) Melanchthon added a statement that allowed papal primacy over bishops (*iure humano*); he sought a formula to bridge differences involving especially Bucer and Calvin concerning the Lord's Supper; against Matthias FLACIUS ILLYRICUS in the Interim controvery, he defended Catholic usages as adiaphora (indifferent usages). Melanchthon's affirmation of the necessity of good works (from obedience and as verification but not as cause of justification) involved him in the MAJORISTIC CONTROVERSY.

Melancthon remained loyal to Luther and his cause. His warm evangelical piety, clearly reflected in the AUGSBURG CONFESSION (1530), cannot be doubted. His book of theological commonplaces, *Loci communes* (1520–21), was the first effort to systematize the evangelical faith. Succeeding editions broadened the *Loci's* rational framework. Melanchthon's writings influenced much of the system–building of later Protestantism, which characterized both the strictly orthodox and their opponents.

See Also: HUMANISM; JUSTIFICATION; CRYPTO–CALVINISM; SYNERGISM; GNESIOLUTHERANISM; CONFESSIONS OF FAITH, PROTESTANT.

Bibliography: Writings. *Corpus reformatorum* (Halle 1834–52; Braunschweig 1852–96; Berlin 1900–06; Leipzig 1906–); *Supplementum Melanchthonianum: Dogmatische Schriften Philipp Melanchthons,* ed. O. CLEMEN (Leipzig 1910); *Melanchthons Werke in Auswahl . . . ,* ed. R. STUPPERICH et al. (Gütersloh 1961–); *Melanchthon: Selected Writings,* ed. E. E. FLACK and L. J. SATRE, tr. C. L. HILL (Minneapolis 1962); *The Loci Communes of Philip Melanchthon,* tr. C. L. HILL (Boston 1944). Literature. C. L. MANSCHRECK, *Melanchthon, the Quiet Reformer* (New York 1958). V. VAJTA, ed., *Luther and Melanchthon in the History and Theology of the Reformation* (Philadelphia 1961). R. STUPPERICH, *Der Unbekannte Melanchthon* (Stuttgart 1961). P. SCHWARZENAU, *Der Wandel im theologischen Ansatz bei Melanchthon . . .* (Gütersloh 1956). L. STERN et al., *Philipp Melanchthon: Humanist, Reformator, Praeceptor Germaniae* (Halle 1960). W. MAURER, *Die Religion in Geschichte und Gegenwart,* 7 v. (3d ed. Tübingen 1957–65) 4:834–841, bibliog. J. PAQUIER, *Dictionnaire de théologie catholique,* ed. A. VACANT, 15 v. (Paris 1903–50; Tables générales 1951–) 10.1:502–513. G. FRANK, *Die theologische philosophie Philipp Melanchthons 1497–1560* (Leipzig 1995). *idem,* ed., *Der Theologe Melanchthon* (Sigmaringen 1999). S. KUSUKAWA, *The Transformation of Natural Philosophy. The Case of Philip Melanchthon* (Cambridge 1995). *idem,* ed., *Philip Melanchthon: Orations on Philosophy and Education* (Cambridge, 1999). *K. Maag, ed., Melanchthon in Europe* (Grand Rapids, MI 1999). C. MAXCEY, *Bona opera. A Study in the Development of the Doctrine of Philipp Melanchthon* (Nieuwkoop 1980). H. SCHEIBLE, ''Melanchthon'' in *Theologische Realenzyklopädie,* (Berlin 1992), V. XXII, 371–410. *idem, Melanchthon und die Reformation* (Mainz 1996). G.

STRAUSS, *Luther's House of Learning* (Baltimore 1978). T. WENGERT, *Human Freedom, Christian Righteousness. Philipp Melanchthon's Exegetical Dispute with Erasmus of Rotterdam* (Oxford 1998).

[Q. BREEN/P. SOERGEL]

MELANIA THE ELDER

Heiress and ascetic; b. Rome, 342; d. Jerusalem, *c.* 409. Melania was born into the patrician family of Antonia, was related to PAULINAS OF NOLA (*Epistola* 29.5: *noster sanguis propinquat*), and at 16 married Valerius Maximus, prefect of Rome (361–363). She was widowed at 22 and apparently lost two of her children at the same time. Deciding on a life of strict asceticism, she confided her son Publicola to a tutor, disposed of much of her wealth, and departed for Egypt (372) where she aided the monks suffering in the Arian persecution. She visited Palestine and, with RUFINUS OF AQUILEIA (378) founded a double monastery in Jerusalem.

In 378 Publicola married the noble Albina Ceionia and had a daughter, MELANIA THE YOUNGER. After taking the part of Bishop JOHN OF JERUSALEM and Rufinus in the Origenistic quarrels with JEROME, Melania returned to Italy (400), visited Paulinus of Nola, and looked to the ascetical training of her granddaughter in Rome. She visited Sicily (404) and Hippo, where she met AUGUSTINE; she received the news of the death of Publicola (*c.* 405) with forbearance (Paulinus, *Epistolae.* 45.2–3) and died shortly after her return to Jerusalem.

Her life was written by PALLADIUS (*Hist. Laus.* 46, 54, 55), and she was eulogized by Paulinus (*Epistolae.* 28–29, 31, 45). Jerome's reference to Melania, *cuius nomen nigredinis (melania) testatur perfidiae tenebras* (''whose name means blackness and testifies to the darkness of her perfidy''; *Epistolae* 133.3), elicited caution among later hagiographers in admitting her sanctity; but Jerome was indulging his pique at her support for Rufinus in the Origenistic controversy (*see* ORIGEN AND ORIGENISM).

Feast: June 8.

See Also: MELANIA, THE YOUNGER, ST.

[F. X. MURPHY]

MELANIA THE YOUNGER, ST.

Granddaughter of MELANIA THE ELDER, heiress and ascetic; b. Rome, 383; d. Jerusalem, Dec. 31, 439. The daughter of Valerius Publicola and Albina Ceionia, and heiress to great wealth, Melania at 14 was forced to marry her cousin Valerius Pinian. After the early death of their two infants, she persuaded St. Pinian to live in married continence and to dispose of their wealth in favor of the poor. After the death of her father (*c.* 405) and despite the opposition of the Senate, fiscal agents, and her relatives, she converted her house on the Via Appia into a hostel for pilgrims and began the sale of her vast properties with the consent of the Emperor HONORIUS. With Pinian she visited PAULINUS OF NOLA (406) and, fleeing before the Gothic invasion from the north, settled in Sicily in the company of RUFINUS OF AQUILEIA. When he died (410), she and Pinian visited North Africa for seven years, met AUGUSTINE and ALIPIUS in Hippo, and encouraged the spread of ascetical movements. They settled in Jerusalem (417), made a pilgrimage among the Egyptian monks, and met CYRIL OF ALEXANDRIA. After returning to Jerusalem, Melania founded a convent for nuns on the Mt. of Olives (432) and a monastery nearby (436). Upon the death of Pinian (431), she increased her penitential activities, visited Constantinople (436) to convert her uncle Volusianus, and met the Empress Eudoxia Athenais, whom she later befriended in Jerusalem. Her life was written by the monk Gerontius.

Feast: Dec. 31.

Bibliography: GERONTIUS, *The Life of Melania, the Younger,* tr. E. A. CLARK (New York 1984). F. X. MURPHY, *Lexikon für Theologie und Kirche,* ed. J. HOFER and K. RAHNER, 10 v. (2d, new ed. Freiburg 1957–65) 7:249–250; *Traditio,* 5 (1947) 59–77. H. LECLERCQ, *Dictionnaire d'archéologie chrétienne et de liturgie,* ed. F. CABROL, H. LECLERCQ, and H. I. MARROU, 15 v. (Paris 1907–53) 11.1:209–230. D. GORCE, ed. and tr., *Vie de Sainte Mélanie* (*Sources Chrétiennes* 90; 1962). T. SPIDLÍK, *Melania la Giovane: la Benefattrice* (Milan 1996).

[F. X. MURPHY]

MELCHERS, PAULUS

German cardinal, archbishop; b. Münster in Westphalia, Jan. 6, 1813; d. Rome, Dec. 14, 1895. The Church-State conflict in Cologne (*see* COLOGNE, MIXED MARRIAGE DISPUTE IN) led him to abandon the legal profession and study for the priesthood. After ordination (1841), he became vicar-general of Münster (1852); bishop of Osnabrück (1857) as well as vicar apostolic for the northern missions, to which he devoted special pastoral care; and archbishop of COLOGNE (1866). At VATICAN COUNCIL I he was a leader in the minority group of bishops that considered a definition of papal primacy and infallibility inopportune, but he subscribed without hesitation to the conciliar decisions. His conscientious measures against the theology professors in his diocese who continued to oppose the definitions brought on him calumniations from the OLD CATHOLICS. During the early

Paulus Melchers.

years of the KULTURKAMPF, which he had sought vainly to avert, he was the prudent leader of the Prussian hierarchy, along with his friend Bp. Wilhelm von Ketteler. After spending several months in prison (1874), Melchers was forced to leave Germany (1875) and to administer his see from nearby Maastricht in the Netherlands. To facilitate a settlement, he resigned his see at Pope Leo XIII's request (1885) and became a cardinal (1885) in the Roman Curia, where his influence was slight. In 1892 he joined the Jesuits.

Bibliography: F. P. E. CRONENBERG, *Geschichte der Erzdiözese Köln* (Cologne 1882) 850–889. J. B. KISSLING, *Geschichte des Kulturkampfes im deutschen Reiche,* 3 v. (Freiburg 1911–16). A. CONSTABEL, *Die Vorgeschichte des Kulturkampfes* (Berlin 1956). J. METZLER, *Die Apostolischen Vikariate des Nordens* (Paderborn 1919) 192–196. E. C. BUTLER, *The Vatican Council, 1869–1870,* 2 v. (New York 1930). R. LILL, *Die ersten deutschen Bischofskonferenzen* (Freiburg 1964).

[R. LILL]

MELCHIZEDEK

Speculations surrounding this name in pre-Christian times have been found in a number of Dead Sea Scrolls fragments. In 1965, A. S. van der Woude published a fairly complete column of Hebrew text (11Q *Melchizedek* text from Qumran Cave 11) which, with a few small fragments, is what remains of a manuscript of the (?mid-) 1st century B.C. The text features a contest at the end of time between Melchizedek and Belial, thought of as leaders of opposing military camps, angelic forces each of which can claim a portion of mankind as their ''lot.'' The pattern is a familiar one. At Qumran, it is the conflict between the ''sons of light'' and the ''sons of darkness,'' each group with its own angelic princely leader; in Christian legend, that between Michael and Lucifer. Melchizedek, so understood, is no longer the mysterious human figure of Gn 14.18–20, alluded to again in Ps 110.4, upon whom the discussion of Christ's priesthood in Heb 5–7 is based.

Seemingly the oldest text that presents an angelic figure named Melchizedek is the ''Visions of Amram'' (the father of Moses). J. T. Milik (see bibliography) has published the pertinent passages; he dated the work to the 2d century B.C. or earlier. The extant Aramaic fragments tell of a dispute of two angelic beings, who between them have power over all mankind, as to which of them Amram must accept. Each of the two has three names; only one name is preserved directly, but that is Melchireshac, ''king of wickedness,'' the opposite of Melchizedek understood as ''king of justice.'' Other evidence makes it easy to equate the two with Belial and Michael, respectively. The Qumran sect, in its community rule (1QS *Serek Hayyahad [Rule of the Community, Manual of Discipline]*), in the ''War'' scroll (1QM *Milhâmâh [War Scroll]*), and in various liturgical blessings and curses only partially published (4Q280 ff., described by Milik), each year on the occasion of its ''renewal of the covenant'' at Pentecost formally execrated Belial and aligned themselves with his adversary. These texts are in Hebrew. A curse in 4Q280 names Melchireshac; and Milik restores the name Melchizedek in a broken line of the ''War'' scroll (at 1QM xiii, 10), though elsewhere in that composition the two leaders appear as Michael (1QM xvii, 5–8) and Belial (frequent).

The ''Visions of Amram,'' which was known to Origen, underlies a variety of later Jewish, Gnostic, and Christian presentations of Melchizedek as a superhuman figure. In a different direction, it became the prototype of the story reflected in Jude 9, with Michael and the devil disputing over the body of Moses. That these speculations were known to the author of the Epistle to the Hebrews can hardly be doubted. The latter, however, has carefully kept his portrayal of Melchizedek as a type of Christ within the framework provided by Gn 14 and Ps 110, and has not used the angelic figure Melchizedek as far as can be determined. From the known interest of the Qumran Essenes in a heavenly temple with an angelic liturgy (see Strugnell) scholars have inferred that the angel-

Melchizedek and Abel offering sacrifices, detail of a 6th-century mosaic in the church of S. Vitale, Ravenna.

ic warrior Melchizedek may also have been thought of as the high priest of the heavenly temple. Such a representation could have had a concealed influence on the development in Hebrews; but it remains unproved. The first text cited above (11Q Melch) is seen by Milik as forming part of a ''Commentary on the Book of the Periods,'' from about 120 B.C.; the beginning of this was badly published by J. M. Allegro (as 4Q 180–181). Dependent on earlier sources for both its angelology and its division of world history into periods, this work modified its borrowings in an effort to bring them into line with the canonical Old Testament, including Daniel, which it quotes. In the process, the figure of Melchizedek underwent a further transformation; and while Belial remains a fallen angel, the victorious Melchizedek is now a name applied to the Almighty himself, intervening on behalf of his people at the end of time. A human figure, the ''anointed of the spirit,'' serves as his herald.

See Also: QUMRAN COMMUNITY.

Bibliography: A. S. VAN DER WOUDE, ''Melchisedek als himmlische Erlösergestalt in den neugefundenen eschatologischen Midraschim aus Qumran Höhle XI,'' *Oudtestamentische Studiën* 14 (1965) 353–373, plates 1–2. M. DE JONGE and A. S. VAN DER WOUDE, ''11Q Melchizedeq and the New Testament,'' *New Testament Studies* 12 (1965–66) 301–326. J. A. FITZMEYER, ''Now This Melchizedek . . . (Heb 7,1),'' *The Catholic Biblical Quarterly* 25 (1963) 305–321; ''Further Light on Melchizedek from Qumran Cave 11,'' *Journal of Biblical Literature* 86 (1967) 25–41. J. STRUGNELL, ''The Angelic Liturgy at Qumran . . . ,'' *Vetus Testamentum* Supplement 7: Congress Volume (Oxford 1959, Leiden 1960) 318–345. J. T. MILIK, ''4Q Visions de ᶜAmram et une citation d'Origène,'' *Revue biblique* 79 (1972) 77–97, plates I–II; ''*Milkîṣedeq* et *Milkîreša* ᶜ dans les anciens écrits juifs et chrétiens,'' *Journal of Jewish Studies* 23 (1972) 95–144.

[P. W. SKEHAN]

MELÉNDEZ, JUAN DE

Dominican chronicler; b. Lima, Peru, date unknown; d. Lima, 1684. De Meléndez entered the Dominicans at the Convento del Rosario where he completed his studies. After teaching for some years, he was put in charge of studies in the convents of Cuzco and Lima. Later, he was vicar-general of the convents and doctrinas of the archbishopric of Lima and of the bishoprics of Cuzco, Arequipa, Huamanga, Panama, and Darien. In 1671 he was named procurator of the Peruvian Dominican province, and in connection with this position traveled to Madrid and Rome where he gathered material for and wrote his monumental work *Tesoros verdaderos de las Indias* (v.1, 2 Rome 1681, v.3 1682).

Although he took a great deal of material from other writers, the most valuable part of this chronicle is a detailed description of the city of Lima in the 17th century, including an inventory of corporations, churches, and convents. The last volume includes some lackluster biographical sketches of prominent Dominicans. The style is clear and concise, and shows a strong tendency toward Hispanism.

He was subsequently appointed regent of the Colegio de la Minerva in spite of the provision of its founder, Juan Solano, that the position be held by a religious from Spain. During his residence in Madrid and Rome he was commissioned by his province to promote the cause of the beatification and canonization of Fray Vicente Vernedo, of whom he published a biography in Lima in 1675, *La vida y virtudes del Venerable Padre Vicente Vernedo.* He published also a memorial to the king (1680), asking the royal influence to be exerted for the cause before the Holy See.

Bibliography: J. DE LA RIVA AGÜERO, *La historia en el Perú* (2d ed. Madrid 1952). D. ANGULO, *La orden de Santo Domingo en el Perú* (Lima 1910).

[J. M. VARGAS]

MELETIAN SCHISM

A schism of Antioch (360–418), which took its name from Meletius, a native of Melitene, bishop of Sebaste and then of Antioch (360–381), who died (May 381; feast, Feb. 12) while he was president of the Council of CONSTANTINOPLE I. In the anti-Nicene reaction after 330, the Catholic Bishop of Antioch, Eustathius, had been deposed and the see was occupied by Arian-minded bishops during the next two decades. The faithful were divided between a Eustathian minority following Paulinus and a majority who supported the doctrine of HOMOOUSIOS. When in 360 the homoean party took advantage of the political situation and occupied sees vacated in the persecution under JULIAN THE APOSTATE, ACACIUS OF CAESAREA had Meletius elected bishop of Antioch even though he was already bishop of Sebaste and in exile at Beroea in Syria. Meletius almost immediately rallied all the faithful, but under pressure the emperor exiled him and had him replaced by the Arian Euzoius.

Despite appearances, the Eustathians and Meletians were at variance, for the Eustathians recognized one God, one *ousia,* or *hypostasis,* in three persons; for this they were accused of SABELLIANISM by the Meletians, who believed in the Nicene doctrine of *ousia,* or substance, and three hypostases.

Before a synod of Alexandria could take a conciliatory position between the two expressions, LUCIFER OF CAGLIARI consecrated the Eustathian Paulinus as bishop of Antioch, and on his return from exile Meletius made the mistake of refusing communion with ATHANASIUS OF ALEXANDRIA, who in turn took the part of Paulinus (363). In spite of the synod that Meletius convened at Antioch to affirm the unity of substance (*ousia*) and the three hypostases, a schism ensued. Rome's attitude remained ambiguous despite the efforts of BASIL OF CAESAREA, who took the part of Meletius (see *Epist.* 92) and tried to win over the West. In 378 Rome communicated with both the bishops but delayed approval, awaiting the death of one of them. In synod at Antioch in 379, the Meletians manifested a conciliatory attitude. Nevertheless, upon the death of Meletius in 381, GREGORY OF NAZIANZUS, who preached the eulogy for Meletius, was not able to prevent the Meletian party from electing Flavian, who with Diodore of Tarsus had supported them during the exile of Meletius. AMBROSE OF MILAN expressed the discontent of the West, and Paulinus went to Rome in company with EPIPHANIUS OF SALAMIS and JEROME to protest the election of Flavian. Paulinus died in 388 but he had consecrated Evagrius before his death. Flavian succeeded in preventing the election of a successor to Evagrius and entered into communion with Alexandria. It was only in 398, when JOHN CHRYSOSTOM was patriarch of Constantinople, that Pope SIRICIUS finally recognized Flavian. The Eustathians ended the schism in 418, but the relics of Bishop Eustathius were returned to Antioch only in 482.

Bibliography: F. CAVALLERA, *Le Schisme d'Antioche* (Paris 1905). E. SCHWARTZ, "Zur Kirchengeschichte des vierten Jahrhunderts," *Zeitschrift für die neutestamentliche Wissenschaft und die Kunde der älteren Kirche* 34 (1935) 129–213. R. DEVREESSE, *Le Patriarcat d'Antioch* (Paris 1945). G. L. PRESTIGE, *St. Basil the Great and Apollinaris of Laodicea,* ed. H. CHADWICK (SPCK 1956). W. A. JURGENS, "A Letter of Meletius of Antioch," *Harvard Theological Review* 53 (1960) 251–260. M. RICHARD, "Saint Basile et la Mission du Diacre Sabinus," *Analecta Bollandiana* 67 (1949) 187–202.

[P. CANIVET]

MELFI, COUNCILS OF

Several significant church councils that met in this city of southern Italy.

In August 1059 NICHOLAS II and Hildebrand held a synod at Melfi in an effort to reform the Church in southern Italy, especially to enforce clerical CELIBACY. The occasion is famous because the pope recognized the title of the Norman conquerors of southern Italy, notably Robert Guiscard, who in return acknowledged himself a vassal of the papacy, promised annual payments, and pledged to defend the pope. This placed the Italian NORMANS on a legitimate basis; it renewed the papal claims on the region and gained Rome a powerful ally for the moment but also gave her a potential enemy for centuries to come.

ALEXANDER II held a council at Melfi in 1067, at which a Norman noble was excommunicated on complaint of the archbishop of Salerno.

The Truce of God (*see* PEACE OF GOD) was imposed on all the subjects of Roger I of Sicily in 1089 by a council at Melfi over which URBAN II presided; a series of canons also survives.

In 1100 PASCHAL II excommunicated the Beneventans in a synod at Melfi for not fulfilling their political obligations to the Holy See.

A series of statutes was enacted at Melfi in 1284 for the Church in the Norman kingdom.

Bibliography: C. J. VON HEFELE, *Histoire des conciles d'après les documents originaux* (Paris 1907–38) 4.2:1184–89 (1059), 1264–65 (1067); 5.1:344–345 (1089), 471 (1100); 6.1:293–294 (1284). P. F. KEHR, *Regesta Pontificum Romanorum. Italia Pontifica* (Berlin 1906–35) 8:11–16 (1059), 14, 351 (1067), 23–24 (1089), 27 (1100). P. F. KEHR, *Die Belehnungen der süditalienischen Normannenfürsten . . .* (Berlin 1934). S. KUTTNER and R. SOMERVILLE, *Pope Urban II: Collectio Britannica and the Council of Melfi* (Oxford 1996).

[R. KAY]

MELITO OF SARDES

Second-century apologist, theologian, and exegete; d. before 190. Information on his life is sparse and vague. Eusebius of Caesarea writes: "At that time Melito, Bishop of the Church of Sardes, and Apollinaris, Bishop of the Church of Hierapolis, shone in remarkable fashion: they addressed discourses to the Roman Emperor [Marcus Aurelius] . . . in defense of the faith" (*Hist. eccl.* 5.26.1). The letter (*c.* 190) of Polycrates of Ephesus speaks of "the eunuch [i.e., unmarried] Melito, who lived totally in the Holy Spirit and rests in Sardes in expectation of the visitation from the heavens" (*Hist. eccl.* 5.24.5). He was a Quartodeciman and *c.* 165 took part in a controversy over the date of Easter (*Hist. eccl.* 4.26.3).

A list of Melito's works is provided by Eusebius (*Hist. eccl.* 4.26.2): the *Apology, On Easter* (2 bks.), *On Christian Life and the Prophets, On the Church, On the Lord's Day, On the Faith of Man, On Creation, On the Obedience of the Senses to Faith, On the Soul and the Body, On Baptism, On Truth, On Faith and Christ's Birth, On Prophecy, On Hospitality, The Key, On the Devil, On the Apocalypse of John, On God Incarnate,* and six books of *Extracts from the Law and the Prophets.* This list does not coincide in all respects with the titles furnished by Jerome and Rufinus, or even with the titles of the fragments that have survived. Almost nothing of all this is extant other than some fragments and the homily(?) *On Easter,* edited in 1940 by Campbell Bonner and completed in 1960 by the publication of a new papyrus (Bodmer XIII) and by a Latin version.

The almost complete disappearance of the Melito corpus is not yet satisfactorily explained. Some have explained it by a suspicion of heresy, resting on certain formulas: "Insofar as He [Christ] engenders, He is Father; insofar as He is engendered, He is Son" (*Hom.* 9). "He [Christ] is . . . Son in the Father" (frag. 15). But most of these expressions can be interpreted in a satisfactory fashion, and it would seem that Melito's orthodoxy is not open to suspicion. His style too must be taken into account, for he is very fond of rhetorical devices: parallelism, antithesis, consonance, ecphrasis. In an age that no longer understands them, such turns of phrase can discredit an author; but it was not always thus, and the influence exercized by Melito was considerable. Regrettably, the present meager understanding of his thought makes it difficult to determine that influence with certainty. There is good reason to believe that Irenaeus was significantly influenced by Melito and is perhaps indebted to him for certain themes in his theological thought. Other authors he surely influenced were Tertullian, Clement of Alexandria, Origen, and the anonymous author of the paschal homily inspired by Hippolytus or by the *Adversus Judaeos* of Pseudo-Cyprian.

This would confirm the importance of Melito's theological thought, in which Christology plays a central role, inasmuch as his theology is organized around the problem of salvation: Christ, Son of God, "by Whom the Father has created everything" (*Hom.* 104), restores to man the salvation he has lost. He directs the history of the Old Testament and becomes present to humanity by His Incarnation; He frees man from sin and death by His Passion and introduces man to heaven by His Resurrection. The story of salvation is nothing but the story of the Word's presence to humanity from the beginning to the end. Melito's phraseology is precise enough to warrant the affirmation of an anonymous opponent of heresy: "Who does not know the books of Irenaeus, of Melito, and of others, where Christ is proclaimed God and man?'' (*Hist. eccl.* 5.28.5).

Melito holds an important place in the history of exegesis. He differentiated the problem of the meaning of Scripture and the problem of the meaning of history, distinguished clearly between figures and parables, interpreted remarkably well the relations between the Old and New Testaments with original insights, and gave the oldest list of Old Testament canonical writings (*Hist. eccl.* 4.26.14).

Bibliography: J. QUASTEN, ed. *Patrology,* 3 v. (Westminster, Md. 1950—) 1:242–248. J. BLANK, *Melito von Sardes, Vom Passa* (Freiburg 1963). M. TESTUZ, ed. and tr., *Papyrus Bodmer XIII* (Geneva 1960). O. PERLER, ''Recherches sur le *Peri Pascha* de M.,'' *Recherches de science religieuse* 51 (1963): 407–422. J. DANIÉLOU, ''Figure et événement chez M. de S.,'' *Neotestamentica et Patristica: Freundesgabe O. Cullmann* (*Novum Testamentum* suppl. 6; 1962) 282–292. R. CANTALAMESSA, ''M. de S.: Une christologie antignostique du IIe siècle,'' *Revue de sciences religieuses* 37 (1963): 1–26. G. RACLE, ''À propos du Christ-Père dans *L'Homélie pascale* de M. de S.,'' *Recherches de science religieuse* 50 (1962): 400–409. J. P. AUDET, ''L'hypothèse des Testimonia,'' *Revue biblique* 70 (1963): 381–406.

[G. RACLE]

MELK, ABBEY OF

Benedictine monastery on the Danube, 44 miles west of Vienna. After the Avars were destroyed, the area was given to the Bavarian abbey of Herrieden in 831, and in 976 the Babenbergs built their castle in Melk. A canonry was there *c.* 1000, and in 1014 the relics of the Irish martyr St. COLOMAN (d. 1012) were translated to Melk. In 1040 the abbey received a large fragment of the Holy CROSS. During the investiture struggle, Leopold II Babenberg brought Benedictines from LAMBACH to Melk (1089). The abbey flourished under Abbot Erchenfried (d. 1163), being famed for the Annals of Melk (1123–1564; *Monumenta Germaniae Historica: Scriptores*, 9:479–537), necrologies, the Melk hymn to the Virgin, the poet Heinrich, and the cloister school. St. LEOPOLD III gave the castle with a rich endowment to the Benedictines and in 1110 obtained from Rome an exemption for the abbey. A fire in 1297 destroyed the monastery and its library. In 1418, during the Council of Constance, Duke Albrecht V Hapsburg brought Austrian and German Benedictines from SUBIACO to Melk to reform monasteries in Austria, Bavaria, and Swabia. Reformers of this period at Melk were Abbot Nicholas Seyringer (d. 1425), Peter of Rosenheim (d. 1433), Martin of Senging, and Johann Schlitpacher (d. 1482). Melk did not form its own congregation or join those of KASTL or BURSFELD, and the reformed monasteries declined rapidly during the Reformation. A third period of growth began when Abbot Reiner of Landau (d. 1637) founded an Austrian Benedictine congregation, whose members included the canonist H. L. Engel; the historians A. Schramb (d. 1720), P. Hueber (d. 1725), B. and H. Pez; and the librarian M. Kropf (d. 1779). The abbey school was completely restored. Neither the Enlightenment (*c.* 1785) nor the increasing of the abbey's parish ministries (to 29) benefited Melk. The aesthetician M. Enk von der Burg (d. 1843) and the historian I. Keiblinger (d. 1869) were monks at Melk. In 1964 the abbey had 40 members, of whom 33 priests were engaged in parish work or in the direction of the liberal arts Gymnasium. The library had 75,000 volumes, 1,800 MSS, and 800 incunabula. The archives held 1,800 documents.

The small original castle, enlarged in the 15th century, was pulled down by Abbot B. Dietmayr (1700–39) for the baroque construction of Jakob Prandtauer (1660?–1726). Behind a massive gate flanked by two towers is the west façade, divided by pilasters and marked by a central and two lateral projections. The center story is made prominent, here as elsewhere, by greater height and broad window sills and lintels. The prelates' court (273 feet by 136.5 feet) is divided in the same way. The stuccoed main stairway leads to the Emperor's Walk (637 feet long). In the prelature are two table altars, one by Jörg Breu (*c.* 1502) and one by the school of A. Dürer (1526). The archives hold the gold cross of Melk (1362). To the west is the two-story Marble Hall, the walls divided by composite and Atlantean capitals. The balcony, with its wonderful view of the Danube valley, leads to the library, the counterpart of the Marble Hall. The paintings *Triumph of Reason* and *Glorification of Faith*, are by Paul Troger (1731). The architecture, the paintings, and the orange, gold, red-brown, and gray of the church walls combine in an impressive harmony. The nave is barrel-vaulted in three sections and has, on each side, three chapels with galleries. The walls of the church are divided by huge fluted pilasters and seem to hang from the rich and prominent ceiling cornices. The altars of St. Coloman and St. Benedict extend the transept but little beyond the nave. On the main altar, by A. Beduzzi, the patrons of the church, SS. Peter and Paul, take leave of each other before martyrdom. The paintings in the nave, *Sources of Grace*, *Three Divine Virtues*, and *Life of St. Benedict*, are by M. Rottmayr (1721). The saints in heaven are portrayed in the dome (208 feet high); the choir stalls are by P. Widerin (1736).

Bibliography: A. SCHRAMB, *Chronicon Mellicense* (Vienna 1702). C. LEONARDI and G. KOLLER, eds., *Sublacensium et Mellicensium consuetudines* (*Corpus consuetudinum monasteriorum*; Siegburg 1963). F. KLAUNER, *Die Kirche von Stift Melk* (Vienna 1946). G. DEHIO, *Die Kunstdenkmäler Österreichs* (Vienna 1962). E. KUM-

MER, *Lexikon für Theologie und Kirche*, ed. J. HOFER and K. RAHNER, 10 v. (2d, new ed. Freiburg 1957–65) 7:259–260.

[E. KUMMER]

MELKITE GREEK CATHOLIC CHURCH

The Melkite Church is one of the 22 autonomous Catholic churches (*ecclesiae sui juris*) with its own patriarch. Its origin goes back to the traditions of the Church of Antioch, today Antakia in Turkey. The term "Melkite" comprises a Syriac root with a Greek ending that means "kingly." *Mālkâ* is Syriac for king (Arabic *malik*). The word is used in all the Semitic languages for the Roman emperor, like the Greek *basileus*. By adding the Greek ending *-ites* we have the form *melkites*, a term equivalent to *basilikos*. It should be noted that the third radical of the Semitic root is *kaf*: there is no guttural. Therefore the correct form of the word is Melkite, rather than the latinized form "Melchite."

The term *Melkite* was originally used to refer to those Christians within the ancient Patriarchal Churches of Alexandria, Antioch, and Jerusalem who accepted the Christological Creed professed by the Byzantine emperor after the Council of Chalcedon in 451. Today, however, the term more often refers to Byzantine Catholics associated with those three patriarchal churches.

In the seventh century, the Byzantine empire was threatened by the Persians. Emperor Heraclius realized that he could not possibly withstand the Persians so long as he had factions feuding with each other within his empire, namely the Orthodox and the so-called Monophysites. As a compromise, he promoted the doctrine known as Monothelitism, a heresy that maintained that in Jesus Christ there was one divine energy and one will. This only served to create further division in the Antiochene Church that was already weakened by internal dissensions. In 637 Antioch fell to the Muslims as Islam was beginning its spread throughout the Middle East. Then in 969, Antioch was recovered by the Byzantines only to be conquered not too long afterwards by the Turks.

In 1098 the Crusaders came and took control of Antioch, replacing the Orthodox hierarchy with a Latin hierarchy. In 1154 the Byzantines reconquered Antioch, and the emperor restored the patriarch to his see. Hostility, however, made it virtually impossible for the patriarchs to reside in the city, so many of them governed from Constantinople. This situation caused the Melkite Church of Antioch to undergo heavy Byzantine influence. In time the ancient Syriac liturgical rite was replaced by the liturgical rite of Constantinople. By the end of the twelfth century, the adoption of the Byzantine liturgical rite became definitive, largely as a result of the influence of Patriarch Theodore IV (Balsamon) who headed the Church of Antioch from 1189 to 1195. When the Mameluks came to power in 1268, they recognized the Antiochian hierarchs but would not let them return to the city of Antioch. So the focus of the Antiochene patriarchate shifted from Antioch to Damascus. To this day Damascus in Syria remains the patriarchate center of the Melkite Church.

Abbey of Melk. (© Adam Woolfitt/CORBIS)

During the centuries of tumult in Antioch, there were several patriarchs who professed communion with the bishop of Rome despite the antagonism that had developed between the *Old Rome* and the *New Rome* (Constantinople). According to one estimate, between the twelfth and eighteenth centuries there were perhaps as many as 25 patriarchs of Antioch in communion with Rome. However, there was never a stable, enduring union between the Church of Antioch and the Church of Rome.

In the seventeenth and eighteenth centuries, the European powers, namely Great Britain and France, entered the scene of the Middle East. The French attained a strong diplomatic and economic influence in the region. It was this influence which eventually led to the formation of the Melkite Greek Catholic Church.

Latin missionaries began their activity in the Patriarchate of Antioch in the mid-seventeenth century. While there were some receptions into the Latin Church, the missionaries were primarily concerned with forming a pro-Catholic party within the patriarchate itself. By the early eighteenth century, the Antiochene Church was split by internal dissension, with the pro-Catholic party centered in Damascus and the anti-Catholic party in its rival city, Aleppo.

Patriarch Athanasius III (Dabbas), who died on Aug. 5, 1724, had designated a Cypriot monk named Sylvester as his successor. Sylvester had the support of the Aleppo party and the Patriarchs of Constantinople and Jerusalem. On Sept. 20, 1724, the Damascus party pre-empted the Aleppo faction by electing its pro-Catholic candidate as patriarch, who took the name Cyril VI (Tanas). A week later, the Patriarch of Constantinople responded by ordaining Sylvester as a rival patriarch. The Ottoman Sultan recognized Sylvester and expelled Cyril, who was exiled to Sidon, Lebanon. On Aug. 13, 1729, Pope Benedict XIII formally recognized Cyril's election as Patriarch of Antioch. The Catholic wing of the Antiochene Patriarchate became known as the Melkite Greek Catholic Church. In recognition of the growing diaspora of Melkite Catholics in Egypt and Palestine, Pope Gregory XVI bestowed the additional titles of Patriarch of Alexandria and Jerusalem on the the Melkite Catholic Patriarch *ad personam*.

Conditions improved for the fledging Melkite Church when the Ottoman Sultan extended civil guarantees to all Melkites on Oct. 31, 1837, and formally recognized Patriarch Maximos III (Mazloum) as the leader of the Melkite Greek Catholic Church, completely independent of any other ecclesiastical community in the Ottoman empire. This improved state of affairs resulted in the Melkite patriarchate's return to Damascus, Syria from Sidon, Lebanon, where it had been since 1724. This was followed by a period of expansion and growth, fueled by the popular perception of the Melkite Church as a focus of Arab resistance against the Turks.

The figure of Maximos III (Mazloum) towers over the Melkite Church of this period. His leadership gained his church respect and admiration; his educational reforms provided the Melkites with the most learned clergy of the Middle East. He also bequeathed to his church a sense of independence from the Roman Curia, vigorously resisting the Roman Curia's attempts to interfere in Melkite internal affairs. The Melkite Church owes him a great debt for setting a pattern which struck a balance between Eastern and Western traditions and separated the essentials from the accidental in both.

The 19th century witnessed much tension between the Melkite Church and the See of Rome. Many Melkites felt that their unique Byzantine identity, traditions and customs were being overwhelmed by the Latin tradition. This tension manifested itself publicly at the First Vatican Council (1868–70) when Melkite Patriarch Gregory II (Youssef) left Rome before the vote on the constitution *Pastor Aeternus*, which defined papal primacy and infallibility. Under intense pressure from Pope Pius IX, Gregory II reluctantly assented to the document on Feb. 8, 1872 only upon the addition of the qualifier, ". . . all rights and privileges of the patriarchs being respected."

The Melkite Church played a significant role at the Second Vatican Council (1962–65). The Melkite Patriarch Maximos IV (Sayegh) condemned the latinization of the Eastern Catholic Churches in forceful terms, and urged a greater receptivity to Eastern Christian traditions, especially in ecclesiology. The cause to which Maximos IV (Sayegh) devoted his life was the unity between Christians of the East and Christians of the West. For him, the celebration of Vatican II was the culmination of his life and patriarchal leadership.

Since the early 1990s, the Melkite Church and its orthodox counterpart, the Antiochene Orthodox Church have engaged in closer rapprochement. A bilateral commission was set up in 1995 to explore avenues of healing the 1724 schism. As relations improved, the Antiochene patriarch invited the Melkite Patriarch Maximos V (Hakim) to address a meeting of the Antiochene Synod in 1996. Since that date, the Melkite Synod has supported the idea of an eventual reintegration into the Orthodox Church of Antioch in the event of a reconciliation between the Orthodox and Catholic Churches.

The Melkite Church continues to witness great growth in the Middle East and the diaspora. The majority of her faithful live in Syria, Lebanon, Palestine, Israel, Jordan, Egypt and neighboring countries. Significant emigration has resulted in flourishing Melkite communities in the U.S., Europe and Australia. Besides the three Patriarchal Sees of Damascus, Cairo and Jerusalem, there are four eparchial sees in Syria: Aleppo, Hauran, Homs, and Lattakiah; seven in Lebanon: Baalbeck, Beirut, Marjeyoun, Sidon, Tripoli, Tyre, and Zahleh; and one respectively in Haifa, Palestine; in Sao Paulo, Brasil; in Newton, United States; in Montreal, Canada; in Sydney, Australia; in Mexico City, Mexico; and in Caracas, Venezuela. There are Melkite communities present in Iraq, Kwait, Italy, Belgium, Argentina, France, and Great Britain.

Bibliography: *Almanach de l'Eglise Grecque Melkite Catholique* (Beirut 1997). C. CHARON, *History of the Melkite Patriarchates*, 4 v. (Fairfax 1998–2000). S. DESCY, *The Melkite Church: An Historical and Ecclesiological Approach* (Boston 1993). I. DICK, *Les Melkites* (Turnhout 1994). MAXIMOS IV (SAYEGH), *The Melkite Greek Catholic Church at the Council: Interventions and Remarks of the Melkite Hierarchs at the Second Vatican Council* (French ed.

1967; English ed. Boston). E. SKAFF, *The Place of the Patriarchs of Antioch in Church Unity* (Boston 1994). E. ZOGHBY, *We Are All Schismatics* (Boston 1996).

[G. D. GALLARO]

MELLERAY, ABBEY OF

Trappist monastery in the diocese of Nantes, Brittany. It was founded in 1145 by CISTERCIANS from Pontron Abbey, Anjou. Melleray declined after it was granted *in commendam* (1544), and although the strict observance was later introduced, there were only three monks in 1768. After its suppression (1791), the property was purchased by TRAPPISTS of Lulworth, England (1817). By 1829 the community of 59 had increased to 192. They founded MOUNT MELLERAY in Ireland (1833), GETHESMANI ABBEY in the United States (1848), and a monastery in Algeria. Abbot Eugene Vachette (1875–1919) became vicar-general of LA TRAPPE and aided in uniting the three Trappist congregations into the order of Reformed Cistercians. John Baptist Ollitrault de Kéryvallen, his successor, became abbot-general in 1923. The community decreased between the world wars, but flourished later under Dom Columban Bissey.

Bibliography: A. GUILLOTIN DE CORSON, *Étude historique: L'Abbaye de Melleray avant la révolution* (Saint-Brieuc 1895). J. M. CANIVEZ, ed., *Statuta capitulorum generalium ordinis cisterciensis,* 8 v. (Louvain 1933–41) 8:329. L. H. COTTINEAU, *Répertoire topobibliographique des abbayes et prieurés,* 2 v. (Mâcon 1935–39) 2:1813. A. BERNARD, ''L'Abbaye de M. et les Trappistes,'' *Les Annales de Nantes,* 104 (1956). G. VENZAC, ''À M. au siècle dernier ou les romantiques à la Trappe,'' *Collectanea ordinis Cisterciensium Reformatorum* 21 (1959) 206–227, 336–356.

[C. Ó CONBHÚI]

MELLIFONT, ABBEY OF

CISTERCIAN monastery, County Louth, Diocese of Armagh, Ireland, founded in 1142 by SS. BERNARD OF CLAIRVAUX and MALACHY of Armagh. Its first abbot was Christian O Connairche. The *generatio Mellifontis* rose to 25 monasteries. After the Anglo-Norman invasion, regular observance declined. A complete breakdown of monastic discipline led to the visitation of Stephen de LEXINTON in 1228, which deprived Mellifont of her filiations until 1274. Discipline restored, the abbey flourished until the 15th century when it became relaxed, but abbots Roger Boley (*c.* 1471–1486) and John Troy (1486–1501) reformed the house. This community, however, which numbered 110 persons in 1228, comprised only 15 when the abbey was suppressed (1539). A line of titular abbots was maintained until 1718. Part of the old abbey lands (in Collon) was acquired by the TRAPPISTS of MOUNT MELLERAY ABBEY in 1938, and Mellifont was reborn, becoming an abbey in 1945. Remains of the original monastery include the chapterhouse, part of the cloister arcade, and a unique lavabo.

Ruins of the lavabo at Mellifont Abbey, County Meath, Ireland.

Bibliography: F. COGNASSO, ''Acta Cisterciensia,'' *Römische Quartalschrift für christliche Altertumskunde und für Kirchengeschichte* 26 (1912) 58*–80*, 114*–143*, 187*–206*. J. M. CANIVEZ, ed., *Statuta capitulorum generalium ordinis cisterciensis,* 8 v. (Louvain 1933–41) 8:329–330. B. GRIESSER, ''Registrum epistolarum Stephani de Lexinton,'' *Analecta Sacri Ordinis Cisterciensis* 2 (1946) 1–118. C. Ó CONBHÚI, *The Story of Mellifont* (Dublin 1958), including complete bibliog; *The Abbatial Succession at Mellifont, 1142–1539* (Dundalk 1963).

[C. Ó CONBHÚI]

MELLITUS OF CANTERBURY, ST.

Benedictine (?) monk, first bishop of London and third archbishop of Canterbury; d. April 24, 624. Possibly abbot of St. Andrew's monastery, Rome, he was sent by

Pope GREGORY I THE GREAT with the second group of missionaries to England (601). Having been consecrated bishop of the East Saxons by AUGUSTINE OF CANTERBURY in 604, he established his see in London, where ST. PAUL'S was built as his cathedral. He revisited Rome on church business and attended a council there on Feb. 27, 610. During the pagan reaction (*c.* 617) he was expelled from London and took refuge in Gaul. He returned a year later but was unable to resume his position among the East Saxons, who were to require reconversion a generation later. He succeeded Abp. LAWRENCE OF CANTERBURY after Feb. 2, 619, and as archbishop is reputed to have saved his see from destruction by averting a fire with prayer. He was buried in the church of SS. Peter and Paul, Canterbury.

Feast: April 24.

Bibliography: BEDE, *Historia ecclesiastica* 1.29–30; 2.3–7. A. W. HADDAN and W. STUBBS, eds., *Councils and Ecclesiastical Documents Relating to Great Britain and Ireland,* 3 v. in 4 (Oxford 1869–78) 3:61–71. W. BRIGHT, *Chapters of Early English Church History* (3d ed. Oxford 1897). W. STUBBS, *A Dictionary of Christian Biography,* ed. W. SMITH and H. WACE, 4 v. (London 1877–87) 3:900–901. F. M. STENTON, *Anglo-Saxon England* (2d ed. Oxford 1947) 109–113, 120.

[R. D. WARE]

MELROSE, ABBEY OF

Former Cistercian monastery in Melrose, Scotland. The first CISTERCIAN monastery in Scotland and the first daughterhouse of RIEVAULX, it was founded by King DAVID I in 1136 beside the river Tweed, a few miles distant from the Columban monastery founded *c.* 650 and memorable for its abbots, SS. AIDAN, Eata, Boisil, and CUTHBERT OF LINDISFARNE. The choice of the new site foreshadowed the royal policy of supplanting the Celtic church with the Roman, the creation of dioceses, the introduction of religious orders, and the adoption of the rite and liturgy of the Continental system. The earliest buildings, conforming to the simple, severe style enjoined by the Cistercian rule, were not completed until 1146, when the church was dedicated to the Virgin Mary. Melrose founded the Abbeys of NEWBATTLE, Kindloss, Holmcultram, Cupar, and BALMERINO. The abbey's situation on the Roman road from England to Tweeddale and central Scotland was advantageous in times of peace, but disastrous during the continuous wars that lasted from the reign of King Edward I to that of Queen Elizabeth. The abbey was pillaged by Edward II in 1322; from 1346 to 1389 it was in English hands, during which time the church was burned in 1385; in 1544 and 1545 the abbey was again sacked, this time by the troops of HENRY VIII, and by 1556 the buildings were in ruins; by 1570 much of the fabric had been cast down and plundered. In spite of the repeated raids, restoration and rebuilding went on; royal favor and generous benefaction facilitated repair and reconstruction. As it now stands, the abbey church belongs to the latter half of the 14th century and the first half of the 15th, a magnificent example of the late Decorated and early Perpendicular. Romanticized by Sir Walter Scott, it is perhaps not "the most splendid piece of later medieval architecture in Scotland," being somewhat cold, formal, and overelaborate—evidence of the extent to which the Cistercians had discarded the austere simplicity enjoined in their statutes. What remained of the church was, in 1618, adapted for use as a parish church and so continued until 1810. In 1919 the abbey was presented to the nation by the duke of Buccleuch and is now a national monument. The medieval abbots were granted the miter in 1391; many held high office in Church and state. The honorary title of abbot of Melrose seems to have been used only once, when it was bestowed upon the learned Juan CARAMUEL LOBKOWITZ (1606–82), later vicar general of the Cistercian Order in Great Britain.

Bibliography: *The Chronicle of Melrose,* ed. A. O. and M. O. ANDERSON (London 1936). *Liber Sancte Marie de Melros,* ed. C. INNES, 2 v. (Edinburgh 1837). J. MORTON, *The Monastic Annals of Teviotdale* (Edinburgh 1832). M. BARRETT, "Scottish Cistercian Houses," *Dublin Review* 130 (April 1902) 372–391. *Melrose Abbey,* published by H. M. Office of Works (London 1932), handiest guide to its architecture and history. D. E. EASSON, *Medieval Religious Houses: Scotland* (London 1957) 65.

[J. H. BAXTER]

MELUN, ARMAND DE

A major figure in the Catholic social movement of 19th-century France; b. Brametz (Aisne), Sept. 24, 1807; d. Paris, June 24, 1877. He belonged to the cadet branch of the De Melun family and remained faithful to the ideals of the Legitimists until 1830. The influence of Hugues Félicité de LAMENNAIS, Père LACORDAIRE, MONTALEMBERT, and Anne Sophie Swetchine directed his attention to the SOCIAL QUESTION. In 1838 he became one of the directors of the Amis de l'Enfance, the first of his innumerable activities in behalf of the indigent and the dispossessed. He carefully rejected the suggestion of Abp. Denis Auguste Affre that he enter orders, believing it important that his charitable work be that of a layman, especially in view of his high social status. Beginning in 1845 he published the important journal *Annales de la Charité,* which supported state responsibility to alleviate want as a general obligation rather than through individual charity. In 1847 he founded the Société d'Économie Charitable, which enlisted the support of the elite in

Abbey of Melrose. (©E.O. Hoppi/CORBIS)

France's public life and Catholic thought. In time the society participated significantly in the international congresses at Malines. Taking advantage of the social posture of NAPOLEON III, Melun played a major role in the formation of Catholic Sociétés de Sécours Mutuels in Paris and in the provinces. Throughout his long career he gave energy and a conservative center to the Catholic social movement before the Third Republic. His *Memoirs* were posthumously published in 1890.

Bibliography: L. BAUNARD, *Le Vicomte de Melun, d'après ses mémoires et sa correspondance* (Paris 1880). A. CHEVALIER, *Vie charitable du vicomte de Melun* (Tours 1895).

[E. T. GARGAN]

MELVILLE, ANDREW

Scottish Protestant divine; b. Baldovy, Aug. 1, 1545; d. Sedan, 1622. Melville was educated at Montrose grammar school and at the University of St. Andrews. In 1564 he left St. Andrews for Paris where he perfected his knowledge of Greek, studied Oriental languages, and attended the lectures of Peter Ramus, whose philosophical method and plan of teaching he afterward introduced into the universities of Scotland. Melville later studied law at Poitiers and, in the face of political troubles, sought refuge at Geneva where he was welcomed by Theodore BEZA (1569) and appointed to the chair of humanity in the academy of that city.

Upon returning to Scotland in 1574, Melville was appointed principal of Glasgow University, which had been largely reduced to ruin by the change of religion. There he expanded the scope of the university's teaching; the new chairs that he established were confirmed in 1577, in the *Nova Erectio,* the charter of James VI. He helped in the reconstitution of Aberdeen University in 1575 and, in 1580, he was appointed principal of St. Mary's College at St. Andrews. Melville was moderator of the General Assembly in 1582; and in the great issue of the day, the position of bishops in the Church of Scotland, he advocated a purely presbyterian system of Church government. The question became acute through the attempt of the court to force the acceptance of certain bishops on the reformed church. When summoned before the Privy Council in February 1584, Melville fled to England, but he returned after a few months and, in March of 1586, resumed his lectures at St. Andrews.

For the next 20 years he was the vigilant protagonist of the presbyterian system and the liberties of the Scottish Church. In 1606 Melville, with seven other clergy of the Scottish Church, was summoned to London in order "that his majesty (James VI and I) might treat with them of such things as would tend to settle the peace of the Church." Melville's overbearing assertion of the general assembly's independence of the Crown and his sarcastic Latin epigrams on the ritual of the royal chapel gave King James an excuse to commit Melville to the Tower where he was imprisoned for four years. He was released on condition that he accept a professional chair at the University of Sedan, where he taught for the last 11 years of his life.

Melville's intellectual gifts and his courage have never been in dispute, but like all autocrats, he identified his own will with the honor of Christ and His Church. His opposition to the Crown, however, grew into a legend and became the ideal that Scottish Presbyterians ever afterward admired. Melville is the true author of the presbyterian system of church government that has become an essential part of the established Church of Scotland.

Bibliography: A. M. MACKENZIE, *The Scotland of Queen Mary and the Religious Wars* (London 1936). T. MCCRIE, *Life of Andrew Melville,* 2 v. (2d ed. Edinburgh 1824). M. SCHMIDT, *Die Religion in Geschichte und Gegenwart* (Tübingen 1957–65) 4:847–848. A. GORDON, *The Dictionary of National Biography from the Earliest Times to 1900* (London 1885–1900) 13:230–237.

[D. MCROBERTS]

MELVILLE, ANNABELLE MCCONNELL

Biographer, professor; b. Minotola, New Jersey, Feb. 3, 1910; d. Taunton, Massachusetts, May 17, 1991. Melville received the A.B. and M.A. degrees from Albany State Teachers College, New York. Having been converted to Catholicism in 1936, she pursued doctoral studies at the Catholic University of America and wrote a dissertation under the direction of John Tracy Ellis. Two years after she was awarded the Ph.D. degree, her work was published under the title *Elizabeth Bayley Seton, 1774–1821* (New York 1951; reprinted 1960) and fostered devotion to the woman who was to be the first native-born American canonized a saint. Subsequently she published *John Carroll of Baltimore, Founder of the American Catholic Hierarchy* (New York 1955), *Jean Lefebvre de Cheverus, 1768–1836* (Milwaukee 1958); and *Louis William DuBourg, Bishop of Louisiana and the Floridas, Bishop of Montauban, and Archbishop of Besançon, 1766–1833* (2 vols.; Chicago 1986). Melville was also a member of the original editorial committee for the John Carroll Papers and co-author with Ellin M. Kelly of *Elizabeth Seton: Selected Writings* (New York 1987) in the series "Sources of American Spirituality." She won the John Gilmary Shea Prize of the American Catholic Historical Association for her biography of Carroll and the General L. Kemper Williams Prize of the Louisiana Historical Society for her biography of DuBourg. Her writings were distinguished by her reliance on manuscripts collected through extensive research in Europe as well as in the United States, for her keen analysis of the sources, and for her graceful style.

Melville was appointed to the faculty of Saint Joseph's College in Emmitsburg, Maryland, in 1947. From 1953 to 1975 she taught British and American history at Bridgewater State College, Massachusetts, and in 1963 she was given the title of Commonwealth Professor. After her retirement she was a visiting professor at the Catholic University of America. She established a fund for the publication of monographs in a series later named "Melville Studies in Church History."

Melville was recognized for her scholarship in several ways. After being elected second vice-president of the American Catholic Historical Association twice (1960 and 1985), she was the first woman to be elected first vice-president (1988) and to succeed to the presidency (1989, the bicentennial of the establishment of the American hierarchy). Known for her gracious charm, sparkling wit, and deep faith, she was widely respected, admired, and loved.

[R. TRISCO]

MEMORARE

A prayer beginning, "Remember, O most gracious Virgin Mary." Of unknown authorship, it has been attributed to St. Augustine, to St. John Chrysostom, and with more reason to St. Bernard or to Claude Bernard, "poor priest" of Paris. Passages in sermons of St. Bernard echo the theme (PL 183:428), but none comes close to the actual wording of the *Memorare*. The manuscript tradition can be traced only to the 15th century. It appears as a section of a longer prayer in the *Antidotarius animae* of Nicolas Salicetus (1489). J. Wellinger included it, possibly as a separate invocation, in his *Hortulus animae* (1503). Claude Bernard (1588–1641) did much to popularize the *Memorare,* teaching it in hospitals and prisons, working miracles of grace through Mary's intercession. Bishop Hefele [*Kirchenlexikon* (1882), ''Bernard, C.''] assumed that because of the similarity of names, St. Bernard's was substituted for Père Bernard's. The *Memorare* first appeared in the 12th edition of the *Raccolta* (Rome 1849).

Bibliography: H. THURSTON, ''Notes on Familiar Prayers: The *Memorare, ''Month* 132 (1918) 269–278; repr. in his *Familiar Prayers,* ed. P. GROSJEAN (Westminster, Md. 1953) 152–163, with refs. to earlier literature. A. BOUDINHON, ''Notes sur les prières les plus usitées,'' *Revue du clergé français* 100 (1919) 246–260, E. CAMPANA, *Maria nel culto cattolico,* 2 v. (Turin 1933) 1:801–807. G. S. SLOYAN, ''Marian Prayers,'' *Mariology*, ed. J. B. CAROL (Milwaukee 1954–61) 3: 80–81.

[M. I. J. ROUSSEAU]

MEMORY IN ANCIENT AND MEDIEVAL THOUGHT

In ancient and medieval thought, human memory was an object of consideration both as a phenomenon remarkable in itself and as an aid in education. The appreciation of it was expressed in discussion of the arts, of historical transmission, of education in the practice of rhetoric, and of psychology.

Role in Theory of Culture and the Arts. Memory was considered a basis of the poet's production, and as a measure of the public's capacity for adequate response to poetry. Mnemosyne, or Memory, was the daughter of Heaven and Earth, and as such was characterized as celestial permanence in transitory concreteness. She was mother of the nine Muses, daughters of Zeus, who were able to help men forget the sorrows of life (Hesiod, *Theog.* 53, 135). According to the rhapsodists, Memory preserved the hymns in which human experience was stored in school-trained minds and was thus the common mother of all the arts. She symbolized the individual and social traditions of ancient culture. Although Memory was thought to have had divine origin, she influenced terrestrial life. In the scientific discourse of Aristotle, memory was not personified; but reference was made to the fact that the plot of a tragedy, to be beautiful, must be limited in length and magnitude by the capacity of the hearer's memory (*Poet.* 1451a 5–6). In discussion of literary style the same law was applied to the length of the syntactical period (Aristotle, *Rhetoric* 3.9.3; Quintilian 9.4.125).

Role in Historical Continuity. The continuance of human personalities and institutions was owed to memory (μνήμη, *memoria*), a fact recognized throughout the OT and in historiography. Moreover, memory was dependent on oral tradition, written documents, and the repetition of actions. Oral tradition perpetuated events in the minds of men in such societies as that of the Druids (Caesar, *Gall.* 6.14.3). It is not a perfect instrument since the content transmitted is subject to change in the process (Thucydides 2.54.3). Preservation in writing, in that regard at least, was found more effectual, but it had the baneful educational effect of allowing the living memory to deteriorate (Plato, *Phaedrus* 275A; Caesar, *Gall.* 6.14.4). The periodical repetition of actions and of feasts in a community, as exemplified by the Eucharistic celebration and the honoring of saints' days, aided remembrance of history.

Education in Rhetoric. The student in ancient schools of rhetoric, after inventing, composing and wording his oration, memorized it before presenting it. Unlike natural memory, artificial memorization helped the mind to retain mnemonic material by an affective intensification of the mental images (Aristotle, *Anim.* 427b 19). The student was taught to distribute the mnemonic matter in a fixed order of points or headings (Gr. τόποι, Lat. *loci*) arranged in groups of five (*Rhet. Her.* 3.17.31) and taken, e.g., from geography (a landscape, a town) or architecture (peristyle, etc.). This conception of memory was based on an associative power in the soul (Aristotle, *Memor.* 452a 12). It influenced medieval mnemonics particularly among the Dominicans in the classrooms of Albert the Great and Thomas Aquinas, of Peter of Ravenna and Giordano Bruno. The system of points or headings was extended to many fields for the purpose of arranging vast complexes of thought. It is suggested in the five-part structure of literary and other works, such as the drama and the rosary.

Psychology. Memory figures in different systems as one of two or three psychological categories. As a faculty, it is opposed to an act of recollection by Plato (*Philebus* 34B), Aristotle (*Memor.* 453a 6), and Aquinas (*In lib. de memor.* 8.398). For Plato, cognition is a recollection of the forms seen by the soul in its preexistence (*Phaedo* 72E, *Meno* 81D; criticized by Arnobius, *Nat.* 2.24, and Augustine, *Trin.* 12.15). Even without the assumption of the preexistence of the soul, some innate notions actualized by recollection, not only of the soul generally but especially of the memory are acknowledged by Nemesius, who gives as example the existence of God (*De natura* 13), and by Augustine (*Conf.* 10.11). Memory extends to objects perceptible to sensation and to intelligible objects, both reproduced by memory-images (Aristotle, *Memor.* 450a; Aquinas, *In lib. de memor.* 2.320). Augustine, however, excludes memory-images of intelligible objects, these being, according to his doctrine, really present in the memory (*Conf.* 10.9).

Aristotle establishes a scale beginning with sensation and leading first to memory and then to experience, which is the basis of art and science (*Anal. post.* 100a; also Plutarch, *Moralia* 11, *De placitis* 4.11). Nemesius (*De natura* 13) localizes sensation, intellect, and memory in different parts of the brain. In Aristotle memory corresponds to past or absent, sensation to present, and hope to future objects (*Memor.* 449b, *Rhet.* 1.11.6–12; Aquinas, *In lib. de memor.* 1.309). Cicero subdivides the cardinal virtue of prudence into three parts by attributing memory to the past, intellect to the present, providence to the future (*Inv.* 2.53.160). Augustine (*Trin.* 14.11), Albert the Great (*De bono* 4.2), and Aquinas (ST 2a2ae, 48) share this Ciceronian scheme. Augustine extends the function of memory to self-consciousness and substitutes will or love for providence (*Anima* 4.7). He explains (*Trin.* 14.12) this psychological triad of memory, intellect, and will (love) as a symbol of the Trinity in the human soul, when the soul focuses these three functions on God. The three faculties are later discussed by Aquinas (*Summa theologiae* 1a, 79.6–7) and used in the famous prayer of St. Ignatius of Loyola, *Suscipe Domine.* By the medieval mystics, e.g., Bernard and the hymn *Jesu dulcis memoria,* memory is considered the ascetical means for obtaining the experience of Christ's mystical presence.

There are two classes of metaphor for memory. In one, memory is conceived as a wax tablet conserving impressions, which are interpreted as seals or letters (Plato, *Theaet.* 191C; Aristotle, *Memor.* 450a; Cicero, *Tusc.* 1.25.61). The conception of memory as a papyrus roll is analogous (Plutarch, *De placitis* 4.11). The metaphor of memory as space, on the other hand, appears under three forms. Memory is regarded as a storehouse of sensible perceptions and intelligible universals (Plato, *Philebus* 34A; Cicero, *Ac.* 2.10.30; Sextus Empiricus, *Adv. math.* 1.372; Aquinas, ST 1a, 79.7), as a landscape or room filled with the objects of memory distributed according to their places (Augustine, *Conf.* 10.8), or as a vessel (Cicero, *Tusc.* 1.25.61).

Etymologically, because of its connection with the root of the Greek verb μαίνεσθαι (to rage, to rave), memory can be extended to include the human disposition to give mimetic and cathartic representation, through mental images, of past but unmastered experiences.

Bibliography: S. EITREM, *Paulys Realenzyklopädie der klassischen Altertumswissenschaft,* ed. G. WISSOWA et al. (Stuttgart 1893–) 15.2:2257–58, 2265–69. E. WÜST, *ibid.* 15.2:2264–65. A. WALDE, *Lateinisches etymologisches Wörterbuch,* ed. J. HOFMANN, 3 v. (Heidelberg 1938–56) v.2. H. HAJDU, *Das mnemotechnische Schrifttum des Mittelalters* (Vienna 1936). F. A. YATES, ''The Ciceronian Art of Memory,'' *Medioevo e Rinascimento: Studi in onore di Bruno Nardi,* ed. UNIVERSATÀ DI ROMA, ISTITUTO DI FILOSOFIA, 2 v. (Florence 1955) v.2. D. L. CLARK, *Rhetoric in Greco-Roman Education* (New York 1957). H. LAUSBERG, *Handbuch der literarischen Rhetorik,* 2 v. (Munich 1960); *Der Hymnus ''Jesu dulcis memoria''* (Munich 1965). J. GUITTON, *Le Temps et l'éternité chez Plotin et saint Augustin* (3d ed. Paris 1959). P. ROSSI, *Clavis universalis: Arti mnemoniche e logica combinatoria da Lullo a Leibniz* (Milan 1960). G. KENNEDY, *The Art of Persuasion in Greece* (Princeton 1963). *Archiv für Begriffsgeschichte,* v.9, ed. E. ROTHACKER (Bonn 1964).

[H. LAUSBERG]

MENCIUS (MENGZI)

Philosopher, teacher, social thinker, and political theorist, venerated as the ''Second Sage'' of Rujiao (Confucianism) after CONFUCIUS (KONGFUZI); b. *c.* 372 B.C. in the state of Zou (Tsou) in modern-day Shandong province; d. *c.* 289 B.C. Mencius is the Latinized form of the Chinese Mengzi (Meng-tzu) or ''Master Meng.''

Mencius lived during the turbulent period of the Warring States (475–221 B.C.). An avid admirer of Confucius (Kongfuzi), he studied in the school founded by Confucius' grandson, Zisi (Tzu Ssu). In the treatise that bears his name, he elaborated upon the views of Confucius, defending them against scholars from rival schools. His unique contribution to the scholarly debate in particular, and Chinese philosophy in general, is his assertion on the goodness of the *benxing*, (''original human nature''). This assertion would not only undergird his entire philosophy and vision of life, but would eventually become the classical Confucian formulation on human nature (*renxing*). His proof was simple but elegant: he argued that the spontaneous and instinctive impulse of every person, however morally reprehensible, to save a child about to fall into a well is evidence of the presence of latent goodness inherent in that person, suggesting that the presence of goodness in human nature (Mencius 2A:6).

Correspondingly, Mencius insisted that selfish desires do not constitute the essence of benxing, explaining his position in the parable of ''Ox Mountain'' (Mencius 6A:8). In this parable, the Ox mountain is a metaphor for the totally evil person, devoid of any virtue. Just as it is natural for trees to grow on a mountain, so it is natural for incipient moral shoots to develop into moral virtues even in an evil person. Just as the constant felling of trees by axes and eating away of young shoots by cattle reduced the mountain to a hopeless barrenness, so the preoccupation with selfish thoughts and deeds destroys the incipient moral shoots in a person, precluding them from blossoming into virtues. Just as new shoots spring up if the mountain is left alone by woodcutters and livestock to rejuvenate, so too, new moral shoots spring up and blossom into virtues if given an opportunity to do in the evil person. And just as axes and livestock are not essential to the original nature of the mountain, so too, selfish desires do not constitute the benxing.

For Mencius, strictly speaking, a human is not a static sort of being, but a dynamic becoming striving toward sagehood. In his understanding, an infant is not born as an ''individual,'' but rather, born into a framework of familial and socio-cultural relations that would shape and nurture that infant's benxing. At birth, the *benxing,* comprises the four virtuous tendencies of commiseration, shame, deference, and preference that are incipient, underdeveloped, and fragile. With proper education and self-cultivation, these tendencies could mature and blossom into the four cardinal virtues of ''human-ness'' (*ren*), appropriateness (*yi*), propriety (*li*), and wisdom (*zhi*) in a fully developed human nature (*renxing*; see Mencius 2A:6). The self-cultivation of these four defining virtues is a lifelong process of deepening one's familial and social relationships to their fullest potential within the classic Five Relations of parent-child, ruler-minister, husband-wife, old-young, and friend-friend (Mencius 3A:4). What is meant here is a relational, rather than an essential understanding of personhood that understands the progressive maturing of human nature within an interlocking matrix of reciprocal relations that, over a lifetime, defines one's character.

Mencius recognized the possibility that everyone has the potential to become a sage (*shengren*). He reasoned that if everyone has the same innate orientation toward goodness at birth, and the sages represented the perfection of *renxing,* then with the right education and self-cultivation anybody could become a sage. Later philosophers would build upon this vision of sagehood as a realizable goal, the end point and highest fulfillment of learning and self-cultivation.

In the realm of statecraft, Mencius advocated the way of humane government over and against the way of a despot, arguing that if a ruler is righteous and humane, his subjects too will be righteous and humane (Mencius 4A:18). He asserted that a true king is a humane king (Mencius 2A:3) who looks after the material, emotional and moral-ethical well-being of his subjects (Mencius 1A:5). He advocated fair taxes, reduced punishments, proper use of natural resources, welfare assistance for the old and disadvantaged, and communal sharing of resources (see Mencius 1A:5, 1A:7, 3A:3). He reminded rulers that they do not gain the loyalty of their subjects by threats and force, but by virtuous example and leadership (Mencius 2A:3). To the delight of the commonfolk, but risking the wrath of rulers, he proclaimed that in a state, the people are the most important, the spirits of the land and grain are the next, the ruler is of the least importance'' (Mencius 7B:14). Mencius' vision of the goodness of original human nature (*benxing*) became the foundation upon which later generations of Chinese scholars and philosophers would articulate their philosophical views. His advocacy of humane government and condemnation of despots have endeared him to every generation of commonfolk of China and other East Asian nations.

See Also: CONFUCIANISM, CONFUCIUS

Bibliography: D. C. LAU, *Mencius* (New York 1970). J. LEGGE, tr. *The Works of Mencius* (New York 1970, reprint of 1895 ed.). W. T. CHAN, *A Source Book in Chinese Philosophy* (Princeton 1963). P. J. IVANHOE, *Ethics in the Confucian Tradition: The Thought of Mencius and Wang Yang-ming* (Atlanta 1990). L. H. YEARLEY, *Mencius and Aquinas: Theories of Virtue and Conceptions of Courage* (New York 1990). K. L. SHUN, ''Mencius on Jen-Hsing,'' *Philosophy East and West* 47:1–20. I. BLOOM, ''Human Nature and Biological Nature in Mencius,'' *Philosophy East and West* 47:21–32. B. I. SCHWARTZ, *The World of Thought in Ancient China* (Cambridge, Mass. 1985). A. C. GRAHAM, *Disputers of the Tao: Philosophical Argument in Ancient China* (Chicago 1989); ''The Background of the Mencian Theory of Human Nature,'' *Studies in Chinese Philosophy and Philosophical Nature* (Albany, N.Y. 1990) 7–66.

[J. Y. TAN]

MENDEL, GREGOR JOHANN

Augustinian priest and biologist; b. Hyncice, Moravia, July 22, 1822; d. Brünn (now Brno, Czech Republic), Jan. 6, 1884. The only son of a peasant farmer, Mendel attended local schools and the Philosophic Institute at Olomouc. In 1843, he entered the Augustinian Order at St. Thomas Monastery in Brünn and began his theological studies at the Brünn Theological College. He was ordained to the priesthood on Aug. 6, 1847.

The Augustinians had been established in Moravia since 1350, and St. Thomas Monastery was a center of creative interest in the sciences and culture. Its members included well-known philosophers, a musicologist, mathematicians, mineralogists, and botanists who were heavily engaged in scientific research and teaching. The library contained precious manuscripts and incunabula, as well as textbooks about problems in the natural sciences. The monastery also held a mineralogical collection, an experimental botanical garden, and a herbarium. It was in this atmosphere, Mendel later wrote, that his preference for the natural sciences developed.

After his ordination, Mendel was assigned to pastoral duties, but it soon became apparent that he was more suited to teaching. In 1849, he was assigned to a second-

Gregor Johann Mendel. (Archive Photos)

ary school in the city of Znaim, where he was well received by his students. However, when he took the qualifying state examination for teacher certification, he failed. Recognizing that Mendel was largely self-taught, one of his examiners recommended that he be sent for further studies in the natural sciences. The abbot agreed, and sent Mendel to the University of Vienna, where for two years (1851–1853) he attended lectures and seminars in the natural sciences and mathematics. It was there that he acquired the empirical, methodological, and scientific research skills that he was to apply to his later investigations. He returned to teaching in Brünn in 1854, but when two years later he again attempted the state certification examination, he became ill and withdrew. He did not pursue the examination further, but returned to Brünn in 1856 where he continued to teach part-time.

Mendel began his experiments after his return from Vienna. Using 34 different kinds of peas of the genus *Pisum* that had been tested for their genetic purity, he tried to determine whether it was possible to obtain new variants by crossbreeding. His research necessitated the use of thousands of experimental plants, and, by his own account, extended over eight years. Prior to Mendel, heredity was regarded as a ''blending'' process and the offspring essentially a ''dilution'' of the different parental characteristics. Mendel demonstrated that the appearance of different characters in heredity followed specific laws that could be determined by counting the diverse kinds of offspring produced from particular sets of crosses. He established two principles of heredity that are now known as the law of segregation and the law of independent assortment, thereby proving the existence of paired elementary units of heredity (factors) and establishing the statistical laws governing them. He was the first to understand the importance of statistical investigation and to apply a knowledge of mathematics to a biological problem.

Mendel's findings on plant hybridization were presented in two lectures before the Society for the Study of the Natural Sciences in Brünn in 1865. His paper, *Versuche uber Pflanzen-Hybriden* (''Experiments in Plant Hybridization''), was published in the society's *Proceedings* in 1866 and sent to 133 other associations of natural scientists and to the more important libraries in a number of different countries. His work, however, was largely ignored. In the spring of 1900, three botanists, Hugo de Vries (Holland), Karl Correns (Germany), and E. von Tschermak (Austria) reported independent verifications of Mendel's work, which amounted to a rediscovery of his first principle.

Mendel continued to conduct research in horticulture, apiculture, meteorology, and astronomy. He corresponded with Karl von Nageli who encouraged him to carry out his next series of experiments on various species of the genus *Hieracium* (hawkweed). Mendel was not able to replicate his findings because the hawkweed reproduces asexually from diploid tissue in the ovary (apomixis), producing clones of the parent. In 1869 he published a report that hinted that the results were different from those obtained for *Pisum*, but left the problem open for further research. The experiments caused such severe eyestrain and backaches that Mendel was obliged to interrupt his research for long periods of time.

On March 30, 1868, Mendel was elected abbot of St. Thomas Monastery. His new duties involved many civic responsibilities that took him away from his scientific work. Almost immediately he became involved in a confrontation with the government over the payment of past taxes. A new taxation law in 1874 increased the tax on the monasteries to cover the expenses of Church institutions. Mendel, alone among the monastery superiors, vigorously contested the tax and refused to recognize the validity of the law. He became isolated both in the monastery and in public life until his death. In his last years Mendel lived a solitary life. Just before his death he commented, ''My scientific labors have brought me a great deal of satisfaction, and I am convinced that before long the entire world will praise the result of these labors.''

His serene confidence, despite the lack of recognition his work received, was to be vindicated. Mendel is regarded as one of the great biologists of the nineteenth century and the inspiration for the science of genetics.

Bibliography: E. O. DODSON, ''Teilhard and Mendel: Contrasts and Parallels,'' *Teilhard Studies* 12 (Fall 1984). R. M. HENIG, *The Monk in the Garden* (Boston 2000). M. W. STRICKBERGER, *Genetics* (New York 1968).

[K. ELLIS]

MENDELSSOHN-BARTHOLDY, FELIX

Important composer in the romanticist style; b. Hamburg, Germany, Feb. 3, 1809; d. Leipzig, Nov. 4, 1847. Other given names were Jacob Ludwig, and he preferred the single surname Mendelssohn. Felix, a grandson of the Jewish philosopher Moses Mendelssohn, belonged to a wealthy, cultivated family, many of whose forebears had adopted Christianity in the generations before legal emancipation of German Jews in 1812. Yet his father, a deist, wrote Felix in 1829, ''There can no more be a Christian Mendelssohn than there can be a Jewish Confucius. If Mendelssohn is your name you are *ipso facto* a Jew''—sentiments to which the Nazis would later subscribe all too heartily in banning Mendelssohn's ''non-Aryan'' music. Felix, however, along with his brother Paul and devoted sisters Fanny and Rebecca, became thoroughly, if somewhat ambivalently, assimilated into the German Protestant culture of the romanticist era, although his Jewish background occasionally created problems that had traumatic repercussions on his personality (otherwise admirably balanced) and ultimate historical position. Nevertheless his musical genius, versatility, personal charm, and unflagging industry carried him through a series of triumphs as pianist, violinist, conductor, administrator, gentleman of letters, artist, linguist, and ''composer in royal service'' to the kings of Saxony and Prussia. On intimate terms with Goethe, student (in aesthetics) under Hegel, favorite of Queen Victoria (he made ten tours of England), friend of Chopin, the Schumanns, and countless others of high eminence, he remained essentially the loving son, husband, and father, the ethical man in search of eternal values.

The Octet (Opus 20) composed at 16 and the Overture to Shakespeare's *A Midsummer Night's Dream* at 17 reveal a Mozartean fluency and grace that were yet of his own time. They hold a permanent place in the repertory, along with the Violin Concerto (1844), the ''Hebrides'' Overture, and the ''Italian,'' ''Scotch,'' and ''Reformation'' symphonies, as major achievements of a composer who, soon after his untimely death at 39, lost general favor, but is now the subject of widespread reappraisal.

Felix Mendelssohn-Bartholdy.

Mendelssohn's consistent interest in religious music of the past (including Palestrina) inspired his celebrated performance at age 20, the first in modern times, of J. S. Bach's St. Matthew Passion (1829) and influenced numerous works of his own for both Protestant and Catholic liturgies. Among the latter are an early *Tu es Petrus* (1827), three motets for Trinità dei Monti in Rome (1830), and the important but neglected *Lauda Sion* (for the Eucharistic Congress at Liège, 1846). The oratorios *St. Paul* (1836) and *Elijah* (his masterpiece, 1846) have had notable influence on sacred choral style both in England and the U.S.

Bibliography: *Letters,* ed. G. SELDEN-GOTH (New York 1945), see esp. those from Rome. S. HENSEL, *Die Familie Mendelssohn, 1729–1847,* 3 v. (Berlin 1879), rev. F. A. HORST (Freiburg 1959), Eng. tr. C. KLINGMANN, 2 v. (New York 1882). P. RADCLIFFE, *Mendelssohn* (New York 1954). E. WERNER, *Die Musik in Geschichte und Gegenwart,* ed. F. BLUME (Kassel-Basel 1949–) 9:59–98; *Mendelssohn: A New Image of the Composer and His Age,* tr. D. NEWLIN (New York 1963), see also review by A. L. RINGER, *Musical Quarterly* (New York 1915–) 51 (1965) 419–425. P. M. YOUNG, *Grove's Dictionary of Music and Musicians,* ed. E. BLOM, 9 v. (5th ed. London 1954) 5:675–706. P. M. YOUNG, *The Choral Tradition* (New York 1962). P. H. LÁNG, *Music in Western Civilization* (New York 1941). L. BOTSTEIN, ''Mendelssohn, Werner, and the Jews: A Final Word,'' *Musical Quarterly* 83 (1999) 45–50. J. A. BOWEN, ''Mendelssohn, Berlioz, and Wagner as Conductors: The Origins of the Ideal of 'Fidelity to the Composer,''' *Performance Practice Review,* 6 (1993) 77–81. J. GARRATT, ''Mendelssohn's Babel: Romanticism and the Poetics of Translation,'' *Music and Letters* 8 (1999) 23–49. H. HOSHINO, ''Mendelssohns geistliche Vokalmusik,'' *Musik und Kirche* 69 (1999) 31–41. H. KOHLHASE, ''Studien zur Form in den Streichquartetten von Felix Mendelssohn Bartholdy,'' *Hamburger Jahrbuch für Musikwissenschaft* 2 (1977) 75–104. F. KRUMMACHER, ''Religiosität und Kunstcharakter Über Mendelssohns Oratorium *Paulus,*'' *Hamburger Jahrbuch für Musikwissenschaft* 8 (1985) 97–117. S. D. LINDERMAN, ''Mendelssohn and Moscheles: Two Composers, Two Pianos, Two Scores, One Concerto,'' *Musical Quarterly* 83 (1999) 51–74. M. P. STEINBERG, ''Mendelssohn's Music and German-Jewish Culture: An Intervention,'' *Musical Quarterly* 83 (1999) 31–44.

[F. J. BURKLEY]

MÉNDEZ, RAMÓN IGNACIO

Venezuelan archbishop and patriot, defender of the rights of the Church against the encroachments of the civil government; b. Barihas, Venezuela, 1775; d. Villeta, Colombia, August 1839. In the Royal Pontifical University of Caracas, he received the degrees of licentiate and doctor of philosophy in theology and in canon and civil law, and the title of lawyer. During several periods, he was a professor of both civil and canon law. In 1797 he was ordained and went to serve as parish priest in Barinas. In 1802 he was named vicar-general of the Diocese of Mérida, which he had occasion to govern several times. He taught canon law in the Collegiate Seminary of St. Bonaventure in Mérida; and, after being appointed rector in 1805, he obtained for the institution the right to confer graduate degrees in philosophy, theology, and Canon Law.

Among the patriots in Venezuela favoring independence from Spain in 1810 were many priests, including Méndez. He was named deputy to the Constituent Assembly in 1811 by the province of Barinas. As a signer of the Declaration of Independence, he was one of the founders of the nation. As he visited the towns in the llanos entrusted to his spiritual care, he also acted as a courier for Bolívar during the campaign of 1813. He was also a chaplain in the patriot armies, with Páez in 1816 and later with Bolívar in Guayana. He served as a deputy in the congresses of Angostura and of Cúcuta and in the congress in Bogotá from 1823 to 1826. Such activities did not interfere with his priestly duties. He was archdeacon of the cathedral of Caracas and *maestrescuela* in the cathedral of Bogotá. He was chosen archbishop of Caracas in 1823 with the full approval of Bolívar, who appreciated his talents, his patriotism, and his priestly character. He was consecrated on Feb. 18, 1828, and Caracas enthusiastically received its new archbishop whom it recognized also as a hero of the revolution.

The 1830 Venezuelan constitution denied certain rights and liberties of the Church, and Archbishop Méndez pointed out changes that would have to be made in it before he could swear to the constitution. Since his suggestions were not accepted, he refused to take the oath and was immediately expelled from the country. The bishops of Mérida and Guayana made common cause with him and they too were exiled. Within a year and a half, the exile was ended because ''the Chief Executive had agreed to a means by which we might be able to swear by the Constitution of the State without contradicting the duties of our holy office,'' according to the archbishop's explanation. Late in 1836 another political-religious conflict arose. The government, in an arbitrary use of the Law of Patronage—without an agreement with the Holy See—established budgetary allowances for the offices of the dean and archdeacon of the cathedral and presented the candidates for the positions. The archbishop considered those allowances unacceptable and refused to install the would-be dignitaries. Again the government expelled the archbishop. For almost three years he lived on the island of St. Thomas and later in Curaçao. Because of his ill health, he then traveled to Colombia, where he died upon arriving near Bogotá. In 1942 his remains were placed in the National Pantheon in Caracas among the heroes of the nation. His published writings include *Exposición sobre el patronato eclesiástico* (Caracas 1830), Observaciones sobre el proyecto de constitución (Caracas 1830), and *Reflexiones a sus diocesanos sobre varieo errores* (Caracas 1832, 1834).

Bibliography: H. GARCÍA CHUECOS, *Estudios de historia colonial Venezolana,* 2 v. (Caracas 1937–38). N. E. NAVARRO, *Anales eclesiásticos Venezolanos* (2d ed. Caracas 1951). M. WATTERS, *A History of the Church in Venezuela* (Chapel Hill 1933).

[P. P. BARNOLA]

MÉNDEZ MONTOYA, JESÚS, ST.

Martyr, priest; b. June 10, 1880, Tarímbaro, Michoacán, Archdiocese of Morelia, Mexico; d. Feb. 5, 1928, Morelia. Jesús completed his seminary studies in Michoacán and was ordained (1906). His ministry in various parishes centered on the confessional, the sick, lay groups, and the poor. He also taught music and formed a magnificent choir. At the time of his death, he was pastor of Valtierrilla, Guerrero, Archdiocese of Morelia. Having exhausted every legal recourse to counter the anti–religious laws of Calles, many took up arms. Federal soldiers entered Valtierrilla to suppress a small group of Cristeros. The soldiers found the house where Méndez was hiding; they took him to the town square and shot him repeatedly. Fr. Méndez was both beatified (Nov. 22, 1992) and canonized (May 21, 2000) with Cristobal MAGALLANES [*see* GUADALAJARA (MEXICO), MARTYRS OF, SS.] by Pope John Paul II.

Feast: May 25 (Mexico).

Bibliography: J. CARDOSO, *Los mártires mexicanos* (Mexico City 1953).

[K. I. RABENSTEIN]

MENDICANT ORDERS

So called from *mendicare,* to beg; orders of religious that, when founded, were committed by vow to the renunciation of all possessions, common as well as individual. Since the Council of Trent (Session 25, ch.3; *Conciliorum oecumenicorum decreta*, 753), however, most of the mendicant orders are permitted to hold goods in common; and there have also been papal concessions to the communal poverty of the Franciscan Conventuals. The Canon Law, of course, still recognizes the original status and privileges of the mendicants; e.g., those orders ''which are called Mendicant by institution and are such in fact'' have the right in law ''to quest,'' i.e., to gather alms, in any diocese in which they possess a house. Mendicants are subject only to their own religious superior (*Codex iuris canonici*, c. 621.1).

At its origins the mendicant movement grew out of the religious and economic conditions of the late 12th and early 13th centuries. For, as an urban economy gradually replaced that of FEUDALISM, the newly emerging townships or communes were soon in conflict with an entrenched clergy that, by way of defense, often resorted to punitive measures that on occasion deprived whole towns of the sacraments for long periods. Further, as a prosperous *bourgeoisie* developed, the poorer classes eagerly turned to those who, like John Valdes and his Poor Men of Lyons (*see* WALDENSES), were preaching that clerical affluence was a contradiction of the Gospel. About the same time as unlicensed preachers took the road to proclaim poverty, movements doctrinally more dangerous, such as those of the CATHARI and ALBIGENSES, were sweeping southern France and northern Italy. The various legates, crusades, and missionaries sent out in the name of the Church to bring these movements to heel made no lasting impression; but an answer in kind soon appeared in the Italian FRANCIS OF ASSISI, uniting poverty to obedience, and the Spaniard Dominic Guzman, allying learning and apostolic zeal.

After the Fourth LATERAN COUNCIL (1215) and its pastoral reforms, the Brethren (*Fratres:* hence *Friars*) of Dominic and Francis blossomed into orders of great influence, academically as well as pastorally. They were followed later by the CARMELITES (1245) and the AUGUSTINIANS (1256), together forming the four mendicant orders approved by the second Council of LYONS in 1274 (Session 23; *Conciliorum oecumenicorum decreta*, 302–303). To these the SERVITES were added some 150 years later; while in 1578 Gregory XIII recognized other orders as mendicants, e.g., the MINIMS, JESUATI, TRINITARIANS, and MERCEDARIANS.

From their beginning the mendicants have enjoyed a steady ecclesiastical popularity, marred now and then by an outburst such as that of Abp. RICHARD FITZRALPH of Armagh *c.* 1350, or by the celebrated action in France against the Friars in the second half of the 13th century. In 1253 the refusal of the DOMINICANS and FRANCISCANS to support a strike at the University of PARIS was the occasion of a spirited attack from the Faculty of Theology, led by WILLIAM OF SAINT-AMOUR. The Friars were ably defended by apologists such as THOMAS AQUINAS and BONAVENTURE; but a more radical campaign was opened by the bishops of France after Clement IV had renewed in 1267 the Friars' privilege of preaching, hearing confessions, and accepting burials, without having to seek the consent of diocesans. For if William of Saint-Amour simply saw the Friars as disruptive of a divinely arranged division of the ministers of the Church into seculars and monks, the bishops, on the other hand, felt that the papacy, by thus granting exemption to the mendicants, was in effect curtailing the jurisdiction of bishops over the pastoral care, if not tampering with the essential structure, of the Church. The problem was largely resolved in 1300 when Boniface VIII in the bull *Super cathedram* (*Corpus iuris canonici clementinae* 3.7.2; Friedberg 2.1162–64) limited the scope of the mendicants' privilege, ordering, for example, that licenses should be obtained from diocesans when Friars wished to preach or to hear confessions.

See Also: POVERTY CONTROVERSY; POVERTY MOVEMENT

Bibliography: C. H. LAWRENCE, *The Friars: The Impact of the Early Mendicant Movement on Western Society* (New York 1994). J. SARNOWSKY, ed., *Mendicants, Military Orders and Regionalism in Medieval Europe* (Brookfield 1999). J. ROHRKASTEN, ''The Origin and Early Development of the London Mendicant Houses,'' in *The Church in the Medieval Town* (Brookfield 1998) 76–99. J. MCINTYRE, ''Aquinas, Gratian, and the Mendicant Controversy,'' in *Proceedings of the Ninth International Congress of Medieval Canon Law* (Vatican City 1997) 1101–35. J. RAITT, B. MCGINN, and J. MEYENDORF, eds., *Christian Spirituality: High Middle Ages and Reformation* (New York 1987). C. T. MAIER, *Preaching the Crusades: Mendicant Friars and the Cross in the Thirteenth Century* (Cambridge 1994). E. DOYLE, ''A Bibliographical list by William Woodford, OFM: [with Excerpt from Defensorium Fratrum Menicantium],'' in *Franciscan Studies,* annual 8 (St. Bonaventure, N.Y. 1976) 93–106.

[L. E. BOYLE]

MENDIETA, GERÓNIMO DE

Franciscan missionary and author; b. Vitoria, Spain, 1525; d. Mexico, 1604. Mendieta took the Franciscan habit in Spain at an early age. In 1554 he arrived in Mexico where, with the exception of one trip to Spain, he devoted his long life to missionary labors among the native people. He also served as private secretary to several provincial superiors. One of the last flowerings of that brand of medieval Franciscan mysticism, whose two apexes were the image of the Apocalypse and the sanctification of "apostolic poverty," can be found in his *Historia eclesiástica indiana.* His temperamental inclination toward this tradition was intensified by the severe demographic crisis through which Mexico was then passing. Mendieta was a man of his times. His ideas, in themselves, were not novel. His talent for turning a phrase, however, made him more articulate in voicing those ideas, and his temperamental inclination for extremes impelled him to state his case in hyperboles. He was not alone, for example, in interpreting the age of discovery and colonization as an apocalyptical event. Yet nowhere can we find in the writings of other contemporaries a more systematic and more eloquent formulation of the proposition: the New World is the end of the world.

Mendieta's idealized conception of the native Mexican is rooted in the traditions of 13th-century Franciscan mysticism, yet his native also foreshadows the Noble Savage of the Enlightenment. His millennialism was, in reality, an other-worldly formulation of an ideal that received many secularized expressions in the 18th century and afterwards. Since America lacked the dead weight of tradition of Europe, the New World was the geographical theater where ideals of the Old World could be perfected by being applied.

Articulately resentful of Philip II's policy of favoring the secular clergy over the friars (which in his opinion contributed to the destruction of the "terrestrial paradise" that the Franciscans were beginning to organize among the native people) Mendieta was sharply critical of Philip II's reign. He was even more critical of the colonists' exploitation of native labor, which he ascribed to their unmitigated avarice. It was these attitudes that largely account for the *Historia eclesiástica*'s not being published until Joaquín García Icazbalceta did so in 1870.

See Also: TORQUEMADA, JUAN DE.

Bibliography: J. R. DE LARRIÑAGA, "Fr. Jerénimo de Mendieta, historiador de la Nueva España," *Archivo Ibero-Americano* 1 (1914) 290–300, 488–499; 2 (1914) 188–201, 387–404; 4 (1915) 341–373, J. L. PHELAN, *The Millennial Kingdom of the Franciscans in the New World: A Study of the Writings of Gerónimo de Mendieta (1525–1604)* (Berkeley 1956).

[J. L. PHELAN]

MENDOZA, PEDRO GONZÁLEZ DE

Cardinal archbishop of Toledo, statesman, and author; b. Guadalajara, May 3, 1428; d. Guadalajara, Jan. 11, 1495. Son of the Marquis of Santillana, he took his doctorate in law at the University of Salamanca (1452); he became bishop of Calahorra (Nov. 28, 1453) and Sigüenza (Oct. 30, 1467) and in 1473 cardinal and chancellor of Castile. After serving John II and Henry IV, he supported ISABELLA with his episcopal and family influence against her brother Henry IV and her niece Juana. His support in the Battle of Toro (1476) enabled her to secure the throne. She retained him as chancellor of Castile and cardinal deacon of Santa María in Dominica, and named him archbishop of Seville (May 9, 1474), cardinal priest of Santa Croce in Gerusalemme (July 6, 1478), and archbishop of Toledo (Nov. 13, 1482). Mendoza negotiated the constitutional aspects of Isabella's marriage with Ferdinand V of Aragon in 1474, supported them in the Conquest of Granada, and encouraged Columbus. He served as their chief adviser for so long that he was called "the third king of Spain." A typical Renaissance prelate, magnificent, luxurious, and morally lax, he patronized the new learning; translated Homer, Ovid, and Vergil into Spanish; and encouraged authors and scholars such as Gómez Manrique and PETER MARTYR D'ANGHIERA. He also wrote a catechism, organized the visitation of his dioceses, and founded (1484) the college of Santa Cruz at Valladolid for poor students. He left his fortune to the foundling hospital he had established in Toledo. He recommended XIMÉNEZ DE CISNEROS as his successor in Toledo.

Bibliography: A. MERINO ALVAREZ, *El cardenal Mendoza* (Barcelona 1942). F. LAYNA SERRANO, *Historia de Guadalajara y sus Mendozas en los siglos XV y XVI,* 4 v. (Madrid 1942–43) v. 2. T. DE AZCONA, *La elección y reforma del episcopado español en tiempo de los reyes católicos* (Madrid 1960).

[D. W. LOMAX]

MENÉNDEZ, JOSEFA, SISTER

Mystic and Religious of the Sacred Heart; b. Madrid, Feb. 4, 1890; d. Poitiers, Dec. 29, 1923. Sister Josefa, of humble parentage, made a promise of virginity on the day of her First Communion. At the School of Arts and Crafts in Madrid, she became a skilled needlewoman, and when her father became an invalid, she supported the family by dressmaking. Her attempts to become a Religious of the Sacred Heart, to which society she had long felt drawn, were thwarted several times; however, in 1910 she was accepted by Les Feuillants, a house of the society in Poitiers.

She led an obscure life there, working in the kitchen and linen room. Lack of knowledge of French made communication with others difficult, but she was a cheerful, deft, and untiring worker eager to help anyone. On July 16, 1922, she made her first vows and returned to her simple tasks. With the exception of a month spent at Marmoutiers and another short period in Rome, she spent the remaining 18 months of her life at Poitiers. After a short illness, she made her final profession on the day she was anointed.

Soon after Josefa's death, the depth of her inner life and the fact of her visionary communication with the Sacred Heart came to light. Diabolic temptations had alternated with frequent visits from the Sacred Heart, the Blessed Virgin, and St. Madeleine Sophie. She had been ordered to take notes and to submit them to her superiors. On her vow day in 1922, Christ had appeared to her ''divinely beautiful, His heart flooded with light.''

Her ''message'' was published posthumously, first partially [*Un appel à l'amour. Soeur Josefa Menéndez* (Toulouse 1938)], and then in its entirety [*Le message du Coeur de Jésus au monde et sa messagère soeur Josefa Menéndez* (Toulouse 1944)]. The burden of the message was that she should forget herself so that she might be the apostle of God's goodness and remind souls that the hour of justice had not yet approached and mercy might still prevail. Fidelity, sacrifice, suffering, and prayer are its keynotes.

Bibliography: J. MENÉNDEZ, *The Way of Divine Love* (rev. ed. Westminster, Md. 1957).

[J. VERBILLION]

MENESES, JUAN FRANCISCO

Chilean priest, politician, and educator; b. Santiago, 1785; d. there, 1860. He studied at San Felipe University and received the licentiate in canon and civil law in 1804. His strong character and unyielding defense of the royal prerogative won him office as attorney general and secretary to the last two Spanish governors. During the independence movement his attitude toward the patriots Ovalle and Rojas (1810) earned him the hostility of the Creoles. His loyalty to Spain during the independence movement brought him to power during the short period of the Spanish reconquest (1814–17). The victory of José San Martín at Chacabuco (1817) forced him to emigrate to Peru. His wife's early death so affected this fervent Catholic that he decided to embrace the religious life; he studied theology at Cuzco. In 1821 he was allowed to return to Chile, where he swore allegiance to the republican regime. After his ordination in 1822, his career was as brilliant in the Church as in politics. A preacher of great force and logic, he was pastor and vicar of Los Andes (1823) and dean of the cathedral. He was elected to Congress as deputy at large in 1823, and was successively reelected by Aconcagua. As a senator from 1830 to 1849, he was noted for his tireless work on commissions. He was one of the signers of the constitution in 1833. He held the ministries of interior, of foreign affairs, and of the treasury. Despite the liberal opposition that always remembered his royalist past, he held the high office of rector of the National Institute. The historian Amunátegui Solar has noted his contributions to pedagogy. He reformed the teaching of Latin, introduced scientific programs of study, reestablished the Forensic Academy, and maintained a very strict academic discipline. He became dean of the faculty of theology when the University of Chile was founded in 1842.

Bibliography: D. AMUNÁTEGUI SOLAR, *El Instituto Nacional* (Santiago de Chile 1891). L. F. PRIETO DEL RÍO, *Diccionario biográfico del clero secular de Chile* (Santiago de Chile 1922).

[E. PEREIRA SALAS]

MENGARINI, GREGORIO

Missionary, philologist; b. Rome, July 21, 1811; d. Santa Clara, Calif., Sept. 23, 1886. After entering the Jesuit novitiate on Oct. 28, 1828, he taught grammar in Italian Jesuit colleges for several years. Following his ordination in March 1840 he responded to Bp. Joseph Rosati's plea for priests to serve the Flathead people. In the company of the Rev. Pierre DE SMET and other missionaries, Mengarini journeyed to Fort Hall, Idaho, in 1841. From there Flathead guides took them to St. Mary's Mission, Montana. Difficulties with the Blackfeet forced St. Mary's to close in 1850, and Mengarini was transferred to the Oregon mission at St. Paul. Sent to California, he helped to found the College of Santa Clara; he remained at the college until his death, serving as an instructor of modern languages and filling various administrative posts. Mengarini maintained a continuing interest in the Flathead language after the publication in 1861 of his classic *Salish or Flathead Grammar; Grammatica linguae Salicae.* He compiled *A Dictionary of the Kalispel or Flathead Indian Language* (2 v. 1877–79) and furnished material on Salish dialects for John Wesley Powell's *Contributions to American Ethnology* (1877). Mengarini's reminiscences appeared in *Woodstock Letters* (1888).

[J. L. MORRISON]

MENNAS, PATRIARCH OF CONSTANTINOPLE

Patriarch of Constantinople 536 to 552; b. Alexandria, *c.* 500; d. Constantinople, August 552. Mennas first came into prominence as a priest and director of the xenodochium, or pilgrim hospice, of St. Samson in Constantinople. On the deposition of ANTHIMUS OF TREBIZOND, protégé of Theodora, he was selected and personally consecrated patriarch of Constantinople on March 13, 536, by Pope AGAPETUS, present in the Byzantine capital on a political mission.

The pope died there April 22, and on May 2 Mennas held a synod in which, with five Italian bishops present, he excommunicated Anthimus. In collaboration with the Roman deacon PELAGIUS (later pope) he urged JUSTINIAN I to condemn ORIGENISM, and early in 543 the emperor promulgated such an edict, which was signed by all the patriarchs, including the pope. When, by way of reprisal, Bishop THEODORE ASCIDAS persuaded Justinian to condemn the THREE CHAPTERS, Mennas signed the edict under protest, but encouraged his suffragans to sign. The papal *apocrisiarius* Stephen broke communion with the patriarch, and Pope VIGILIUS, summoned to Constantinople by the emperor, did likewise on his arrival on Jan. 25, 547. Five months later the pope and patriarch were reconciled (June 29, 547) when the pope acceded to the emperor and condemned the Three Chapters. Vigilius later addressed to Mennas a letter to this effect, the *Judicatum,* of April 11, 548. Upon the violent opposition of the Western bishops to the pope's action, Justinian was persuaded to allow Vigilius to abolish the *Judicatum,* which was returned to him by Mennas, whose name together with the pope's had been inscribed on the DIPTYCHS in January 550.

In the winter of 551, Vigilus escaped from imperial custody and took refuge in the Church of St. Euphemia in Chalcedon, having broken relations with the patriarch and the emperor over renewed agitation concerning the Three Chapters. In June of 552, Mennas and the episcopal entourage were sent by Justinian to make due apology to the pope, who then reentered communion with them on June 26. In August 552 Mennas died.

While he had been a determined opponent of both Nestorianism and MONOPHYSITISM, his position as patriarch under Justinian's rule had been most difficult, and he had yielded to the concept of caesaropapism in the Synod of 536, having stated: ''It is proper that no questions agitated in the Holy Church should be settled without the advice and command'' of the emperor.

Feast: Aug. 25, Latin; Aug. 27, Greek

Bibliography: *Acta conciliorum oecumenicorum* (Berlin 1914–) 3:181. O. VOLK, *Lexikon für Theologie und Kirche*, ed. J. HOFER and K. RAHNER (Freiburg 1957–65) 7:267. E. STEIN, *Histoire du Bas-Empire* tr. J. R. PALANQUE (Paris 1949–59) 383–385, 637–638, 642–645. H. G. BECK, *Kirche und theologische Literatur im byzantinischen Reich* (Munich 1959) 54, 63, 104, 379, 408, 430. W. M. SINCLAIR, *A Dictionary of Christian Biography*, ed. W. SMITH and H. WACE (London 1877–87) 3:902–903. *Acta Sanctorum* Aug. 5:164–171.

[D. MCGARRY]

MENNI FIGINI, BENEDETTO, ST.

Baptized Angelo Ercolino (Angel Hercules) Menni, priest of the Hospitallers of Saint John of God and founder of the Hospitaller Sisters of the Sacred Heart of Jesus; b. Milan, Italy, March 11, 1841; d. Dinan, northern France, April 24, 1914.

As one of the fifteen children of Luigi Menni and Luisa Figini, Angelo learned charity at home. He gave up his job as a bank clerk to serve the soldiers wounded in the Battle of Magenta. He joined the Brothers of St. John of God (1860) and was ordained priest in Rome (1866). In 1867, he was sent to Spain to revitalize the order following its suppression by anticlerical laws. Despite threats to his life and temporary expulsion, he founded a children's hospital in Barcelona (1867). His work over the next thirty-six years with the elderly, abandoned children, polio victims, and the mentally ill attracted many others with vocations, allowing him to open and staff twenty-two hospitals in Spain, Portugal, and Mexico, thus restoring the Hospitallers' work in Latin America.

In 1880, Menni founded the Hospitaller Sisters of the Sacred Heart of Jesus in Ciempozuelos (near Madrid, Spain) with María Josefa Recio and María Angustias Gimenez, who established a psychiatric hospital in Granada (1881). The female branch of the Hospitallers spread throughout Europe and to Africa, Asia, and Latin America. Menni later served as apostolic visitor (1909–11) and prior general (1911) before resigning due to ill health in 1912. His body rests in the motherhouse chapel of the Hospitaller Sisters in Madrid.

Menni was both beatified (June 23, 1985) and canonized (Nov. 21, 1999) by Pope John Paul II. In 2001 Menni was proposed as the universal patron of volunteers because he ''discovered his vocation precisely when he was engaged in volunteer work in Milan'' (John Paul II, canonization homily).

Feast: April 24.

Bibliography: *Acta Apostolicae Sedis* 78 (1986): 710–713. *L'Osservatore Romano,* English edition, no. 29 (1985): 6–7. M. SOROLDONI, *Santità alla sbarra: la vita contestata di Benedetto Menni* (Rome 1981). E. ZUÑEDA SALAZAR, *Benito Menni, testigo de la caridad* (Madrid 1985).

[K. I. RABENSTEIN]

Mennonite children, Cuauhtemoc, Mexico. (©Fulvio Roiter/CORBIS)

MENNONITE CHURCHES

Christian churches named after Menno Simons (*c.* 1496–1561), known first as ANABAPTISTS during the 16th century. After originating as a wing of the REFORMATION in Switzerland in 1525, the movement spread into various countries. Melchior HOFMANN transplanted Anabaptism via Emden (1530) into the Low Countries, where for a few decades it became the most outstanding Reformation effort. Most significant among the leaders of the North was Menno Simons, a Roman Catholic priest who joined the movement in 1536. Through his writings and preaching, he gathered the peaceful, persecuted believers who came mostly from the Sacramentarian movement. He traveled extensively in the Low Countries and the Cologne and Vistula River areas, and he found temporary shelter near Emden and a permanent home and printshop at Oldesloe near Hamburg. Among his closest coworkers were Dirk Philips and Leenaert Bouwens.

Basic Views. For the most part Mennonitism of the North and the South had a common basis of faith. It was a wing of the Reformation with a stronger emphasis on the use of the Bible and the spiritualization of the Sacraments and the worship practices of the Catholic Church. Characterized by voluntary church membership entered into by adults only through the act of Baptism upon confession of faith, it emphasized a personally dedicated and disciplined Christian life. From the beginning, the movement had a strong sense of mission, which suffered considerably during the many decades of persistent persecution, resulting in the withdrawal of the group into isolated areas of various countries, and often leading to stagnation of the spiritual and cultural life of this church of martyrs.

Spread and Development. Basic and unique views, severe persecution, and isolation resulted in the development of peculiar characteristics among some Mennonites. They became outstanding pioneers in agriculture in Switzerland, Alsace, South Germany, the Low Countries, the Vistula area, Poland, Russia, the American prairie states and Canadian provinces of North America, as well as Mexico and South America. In the Netherlands and northwest Germany, Mennonites also made significant contributions to the fishing, silk, and cotton industries and as business people. There, their traditional isolation from the culture of the country in which they lived was overcome during the 17th and 18th centuries. The Mennonites of the Netherlands were organized in a conference (*Algemeene Doopsgezinde Societeit*) in 1811. They are members of the WORLD COUNCIL OF CHURCHES.

The Mennonites of Germany are not so unified as the Dutch. The urban churches (Krefeld, Emden, Hamburg, Danzig, Berlin) differ from the rural congregations of West Prussia, the Palatinate, Hesse, and particularly of Baden and Bavaria. They all sponsor publications and mission and relief work. The *Vereinigung der deutschen Mennonitengemeinden* is a member of the World Council of Churches. The congregations of East Germany, Poland, and Galicia were wiped out during World War II. The refugees from these countries found new homes in West Germany, Canada, and Uruguay.

Invited by Catherine the Great, Mennonites from the Vistula area migrated to the Ukraine starting in 1788. From the Chortitza and the Molotschna settlements, they spread into other parts of European and Asiatic Russia, making a significant contribution to the development of the agriculture and industry of the country. The first migration of Mennonites from Russia, Poland, and Prussia to the United States and Canada took place between 1873 and 1882. A second and third migration to Canada, Paraguay, Brazil, and Uruguay followed between 1923 and 1930 and during and after World War II. The remaining Mennonites of the Ukraine were transplanted into the northern and eastern parts of Soviet Russia; many of them perished in concentration camps at the height of communist rule.

Emigration to America. Among the early settlers of New York were some Dutch Mennonites. Cornelis Pieter Plockhoy settled at Delaware with a group of Dutch Mennonites in 1664. Thirteen Quaker-Mennonite families from Krefeld, Germany, founded German-town near Philadelphia in 1683. It became the gateway for a Swiss and Palatinate immigration spreading into Pennsylvania, Virginia, Ontario, Ohio, Indiana, Illinois, Iowa, etc. Among the famous pioneers was the educator Christopher Dock.

Between 1873 and 1882 the first immigrants (18,000) from Russia, Poland, and Prussia settled in the prairie states and provinces between Kansas and Manitoba. They were instrumental in introducing the hard winter wheat. After World War I, some 21,000 Mennonites from Russia went to Canada, and some 4,000 to Brazil and Paraguay, where some Mennonites from Manitoba had previously settled in the Chaco. After World War II, approximately 14,000 went from Russia, Poland, and West Prussia, to Canada, Paraguay, and Uruguay. Within the United States and Canada, the Mennonites originally followed the move from the East to the West, and in the 20th century the move from the rural to the urban and industrial areas has continued.

Organizations. The Mennonite Churches of North America have their own colleges, Christian high schools, conference headquarters, publishing houses and papers. Mission work was started in 1880 among the Native Americans and later overseas. Originally, the language in worship and home was German or a German dialect. Now, English is used almost exclusively. The American religious revivals and other factors have influenced the Mennonites and caused the introduction of Sunday schools, higher education, mission work, and the abstinence movement. Originally scattered and divided into many religious and cultural groups, they now belong to a number of ecclesial affiliations, among which the largest is the Mennonite Church, itself a merger of the Mennonite Church and the General Conference Mennonite Church in 2001. The most conservative among the various Mennonite churches are the Old Order AMISH CHURCHES and the Old Order (Wisler) Mennonite Church. Most of the Mennonites of all countries are members of the Mennonite World Conference.

One principal characteristic that the Mennonite Christianss share with the Quakers, the Church of the Brethren, and some other groups, is their peace witness, which led them during the two world wars to accept alternative service, and to do relief work in war-stricken and underdeveloped countries. Immediately after World War I, this aid amounted to $2,500,000, and after World War II, to $12,640,000.

See Also: AMISH CHURCHES.

Bibliography: *The Mennonites: A Brief Guide to Information* (Newton, Kans.). *The Mennonite Encyclopedia,* ed. H. S. BENDER, C. KRAHN, et al., 4 v. (Scottdale, Pa. 1955–60). C. H. SMITH, *The Story of the Mennonites* (Newton, Kans. 1964). MENNO SIMONS, *Complete Writings,* tr. L. VERDUIN, ed. J. C. WENGER (Scottdale, Pa. 1956). D. L. GRATZ, *Bernese Anabaptists* (Scottdale, Pa. 1953). F. H. EPP, *Mennonite Exodus* (Altona, Can. 1962). J. D. UNRUH, *In the Name of Christ: A History of the Mennonite Central Committee and Its Service, 1920–1951* (Scottdale, Pa. 1952). F. S. MEAD, S. S. HILL and C. D. ATWOOD, eds., *Handbook of Denominations in the United States*, 11th ed (Nashville 2001).

[C. KRAHN/EDS.]

MENOCHIO, GIOVANNI STEFANO

17th-century theologian and exegete; b. Pavia, Italy, December 1575; d. Rome, Feb. 4, 1655. He entered the Society of Jesus in 1594, and after receiving the usual course of training, taught humanities, Sacred Scripture, and moral theology at Milan. He was superior successively at Cremona, Milan, and Genoa; then rector of the Roman College, provincial first of Milan and later of Rome, and finally Italian assistant to two Jesuit generals, Carafa and Piccolomini. His most notable work, *Brevis explicatio sensus literalis totius Sacrae Scripturae ex optimis quibusque auctoribus per epitomen collecta* (Cologne 1630), deservedly appeared in at least nine exegetical collections, most recently in *La Sainte Bible* of C. F. Drioux (Paris 1873). Other principal works of Menochio are *Hieropoliticum, sive Institutiones politicae e S. Scripturis depromptae* (Lyons 1625) and *Le suore di Giovanni Corona, tessute di varia erudizione sacra, morale e profana* (Rome 1646).

Bibliography: C. SOMMERVOGEL et al., *Bibliothèque de la Compagnie de Jésus* (Brussels-Paris 1890–1932) 5:948–955. H. HURTER, *Nomenclator literarius theologiae catholicae* (Innsbruck 1903–13) 3:1060–63.

[T. T. TAHENY]

MENORAH

Menorah is a Hebrew word that generally designates in the Bible the sacred candelabrum that was one of the chief appointments of the TENT OF MEETING and the Temple. The word (Heb. *m^e^nôrâ*) is used only once in the Old Testament (2 Kgs 4.10) to denote a lamp for profane use. The menorah as described in Ex 25.31 was a seven-branched lampstand made of pure hammered gold. It had a central shaft with three arms reaching out on each side. On each of the six branches, as well as on the middle column, there was a bowl for holding olive oil and a wick (Lv 24.2). These seven bowls were refilled and trimmed daily (Ex 27.21). Josephus states that three of the lights were kept burning during the daylight hours, and all seven were lighted at night. Later rabbinical commentators give a conflicting account, reporting that the lamp was lighted only at night.

Representations of the menorah as a symbol of Judaism were common, especially in the 1st century, on coins, on the walls of synagogues, and in Jewish catacombs in various parts of the Roman Empire. The seven-branched candlestick represented on the Arch of Titus in Rome is the most authentic and the earliest reproduction of the menorah known today; it depicts the candelabrum of the second Temple that was carried off by the soldiers of Titus in A.D. 70 at the end of the siege of Jerusalem.

Throughout the centuries the Jews have found the figure of the menorah rich in symbolic meaning. Josephus, for instance, interprets the seven lamps as the seven planets. Others have thought of it as portraying the tree of life. This is suggested by its arboreal shape and its bowls molded like almond flowers. At times it has been interpreted as symbolizing the creation of the universe in six days, the center light representing the Sabbath. Of greater interest and relevance is the judgment of E. R. Goodenough, who construes the portrayal of the menorah on Jewish tombs in the Greco-Roman period as being the mystic symbol of light and life. This is equivalently, he believes, the symbol for God manifest in the world, through whom the Jews hoped for immortality.

A direct development of the Temple menorah is the Hanukkah menorah used at the feast of Hanukkah or DEDICATION OF THE TEMPLE. This differs only slightly from the menorah of the Temple in that it consists of eight rather than seven lamps. At times a ninth lamp is added to serve as a pilot light and called the shammash (servant), since from it the other lamps are lighted. Legend connects the Hanukkah menorah with the ceremony of the rededication of the Temple by Judas Maccabee in 165 B.C. following its desecration by Antiochus Epiphanes three years earlier (1 Mc 4.37–39). It is alleged that, when the perpetual light of the Temple was to be relighted on the occasion of this rededication, it was found that there was oil enough for only one day; miraculously, however, the oil sufficed to sustain the light for eight days. In memory of this prodigy, the Hanukkah menorah is lighted, one lamp at a time on the eight successive days of the festival of Hanukkah.

Bibliography: PHILO, *Questions and Answers on Exodus* (*Loeb Classical Library,* Suppl. 2; 1953) 73–82; *De Vita Mosis,* (*ibid.* 1935) 2.105. Josephus, *Bell. Jud.* 5:217; *Antiquities* 3:144–146, 199. E. R. GOODENOUGH, *Jewish Symbols in the Greco-Roman Period,* 10 v. (*Bollinger Ser.* 37; New York 1953–) v.4. R. WISCHNITZER-BERNSTEIN, *Symbole und Gestalten der jüdischen Kunst* (Berlin 1935); *Universal Jewish Encyclopedia,* 10 v. (New York 1939–44) 7:487–490. *The Jewish Encyclopedia,* ed. J. SINGER, 13 v. (New York 1901–06) 8:493–495. B. HESSLER, *Lexikon für Theologie und Kirche,* ed. J. HOFER and K. RAHNER (Freiburg 1957–65) 6:991–992. K. GALLING, *Die Religion in Geschichte und Gegenwart,* 7 v. (Tübingen 1957–65) 4:332–333.

[J. C. TURRO]

MENTAL RESERVATION

A term used to describe an attempt to evade a perplexing moral situation by restricting the meaning of words used in an act of communicating. Not wanting to lie, a person may at the same time not want to tell the truth, because it would involve him or others in difficulty. If he accepts the traditional and still common teaching of Catholic moralists, he knows that he is bound by a negative precept never to lie in any circumstances, yet there is no positive precept binding him to tell the whole truth in all circumstances. Silence would often be the best solution, but in some cases silence itself would provide a damaging answer. An alternative to silence, suggested to extricate the beleaguered conscientious individual from his dilemma, is the device known as mental reservation.

Kinds of Mental Reservation. The term has been understood in two senses. In the strict sense it means giv-

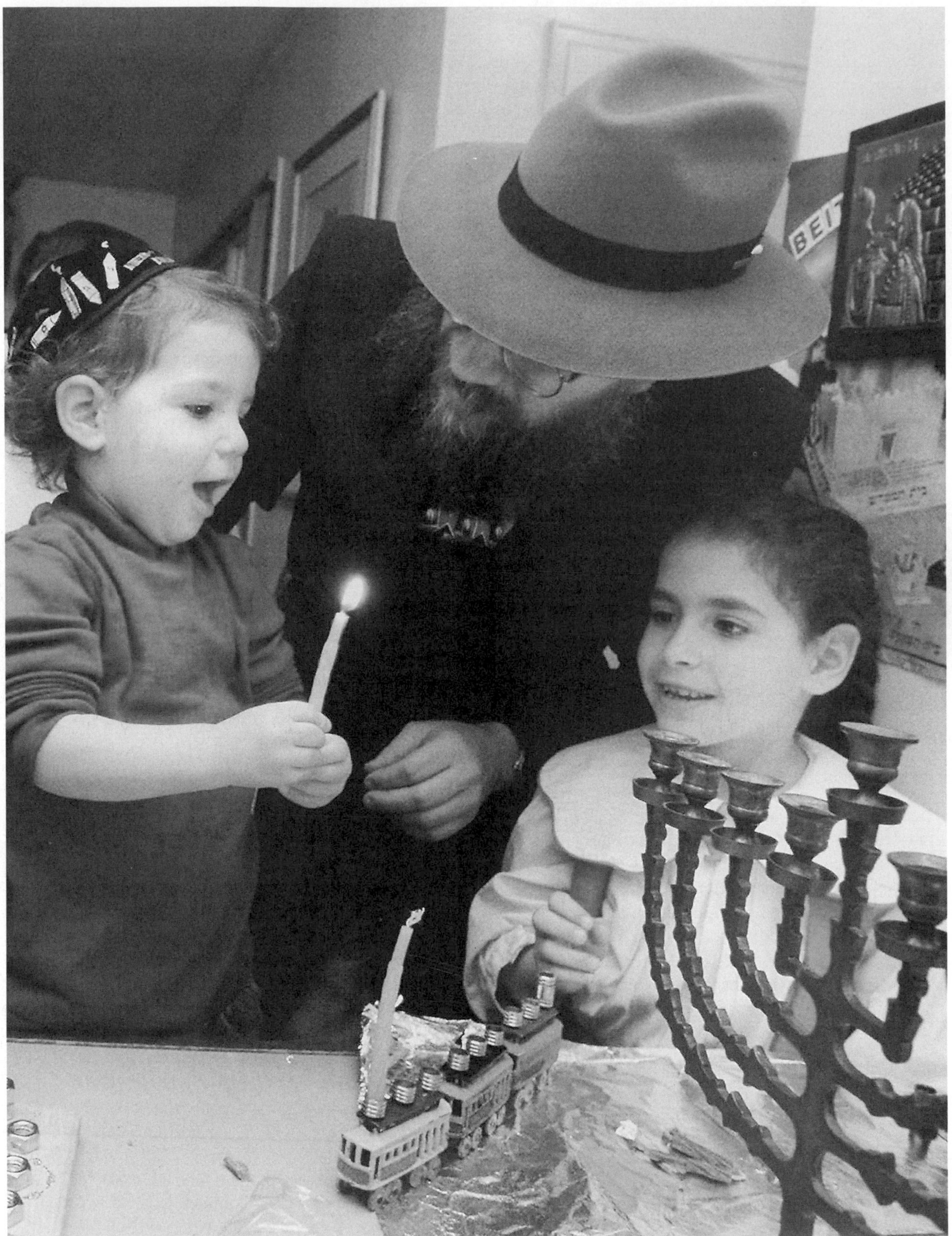

Young child prepares to place a lighted candle in a Hanukkah menorah. (AP/Wide World Photos)

ing utterance to only part of one's judgment while retaining in mind or whispering inaudibly another part necessary to make the statement objectively truthful. In the classical example, Titius privately said to a woman that he would take her for his wife, although he had no intention of marrying her. Later, when asked by a judge whether he had said he would take the woman for his wife, he replied that he had not, understanding that he had not spoken the words with the intention of marrying the woman.

In the broad sense, mental reservation is the use of equivocation or ambiguity to conceal the truth. What is said is not objectively untruthful, but it is phrased in such a way that it is possible, indeed even probable, that the true meaning of the words will escape the hearer, and that he will understand them in a sense in which they are not true.

History of the Problem. The need of protecting oneself against intrusive or unjust questioning so perplexed some of the early Fathers of the Church that in their solution of difficulties of this kind they seemed to tolerate lying. With St. Augustine, however, strong convictions were established on the subject of veracity. During the Middle Ages scholastic theologians accepted and expanded upon, but never deviated from, Augustine's definition of a lie and his teaching that to utter the opposite of what one holds to be true is intrinsically evil. In the 16th century this tradition began to weaken among some theologians. Martin ASPILCUETA (d. 1586) defended the licitness of mental reservation in the strict sense in his discussion of the classical example mentioned above. His near contemporary, Francisco de Toledo, and later theologians, such as Raynaud, Sánchez, Suárez, and Lessius, either espoused the doctrine of strict mental reservation or accorded it strong probability. Other theologians, such as Cajetan, Soto, Laymann, De Lugo, and Azor, along with most other Catholic moralists, repudiated it. With the condemnation by Innocent XI of one of the propositions of Tomas Sánchez (H. Denzinger, *Enchiridicu symbolorum* 2126), attempts to justify strict mental reservation came to an end, and thereafter it was considered permissible only if the meaning of the term was so broadened as to signify little more than ambiguity of speech.

Moral Evaluation. St. Thomas taught that to lie is one thing, and to keep the truth hidden is another; to affirm a restricted truth is not to deny a more extensive one (*Summa Theologiae* 2a2ae, 109.4). A man can affirm that he had coffee and toast for breakfast without denying that he had an egg, or he might affirm that he has a lesser amount of money in his pocket without denying that he also has a greater amount. So long as he has reasonable cause to conceal part of the truth, he does no wrong, provided, of course, that he is careful not to indicate that he has "only" so much to eat or that he has "only" so much money.

Similarly, a person could make a statement that has all the appearances of a reply to a question put to him, but which in fact is not, owing to some circumstance known to the speaker, which the hearer could know also but may not consider. If, for example, a wife, who has been unfaithful but after her lapse has received the Sacrament of Penance, is asked by her husband if she has committed adultery, she could truthfully reply: "I am free from sin." In any of these cases the speaker does not question the hearer's right to know a truth. He presents the truth as discoverable but not disclosed. He has made no false statement, but has allowed an admissible ambiguity, foreseeing a possible, or even probable, deception.

If deception follows from a broad mental reservation it is a by-product effect. Concealment of a truth legitimately hidden is the primary intention of the one who speaks evasively. Deception does not follow necessarily from the statement itself but from the circumstances of its utterance, especially from the dispositions of the hearer. By his own simplicity, ignorance, prejudices, or malice, a hearer may be deceived in listening to the evasive words of a broad mental reservation. The words themselves lack clarity and distinctness, which the hearer supplies for himself from his own assumptions. The words do not, however, distort the true, though vague, communication made by the speaker, and consequently they are not a lie.

Because deception of one's neighbor is an evil, one needs a just and proportionately grave cause to have recourse to evasive speech or writing. Simplicity in speech is to be regarded as obligatory under ordinary circumstances.

Moreover, in some circumstances the questioner may have a strict right to know the whole truth, and when such is the case, no type of mental reservation is allowable in answering a question. Consequently, mental reservation, even in the broad sense, is never tolerable when replying to questions of a superior in matters pertaining to his jurisdiction, or in formulating strict bilateral contracts, or in replying to a judge asking legitimate questions or to a confessor concerning something he needs to know for the proper administration of the Sacrament of Penance.

Bibliography: C. R. BILLUART, "Tractatus de religione et vitiis oppositis," 9.1–2, v.7 of *Summa Sancti Thomae,* 10 v. (new ed., Paris 1874–86). D. PRÜMMER, *Manuale theologiae moralis,* ed. E. M. MUNCH, 3 v. (10th ed. Barcelona 1945–46) 2:171–174. J. B.

BROSNAN, ''Mental Restriction and Equivocation,'' *The Irish Ecclesiastical Record* 16.2 461–470. A. VERMEERSCH, *Dictionnaire Apolgétique de la Foi Catholique* (Paris 1911–22) 4:958–982.

[D. HUGHES]

MERBOT, BL.

Martyr; d. Alberschwende near Bregenz, Austria, Mar. 23, 1120. He became a BENEDICTINE monk at the abbey of MEHRERAU, and then was named pastor when his monastery gained possession of the parish church at Alberschwende. According to legend he was a descendant of the count of Bregenz and the brother of Bl. Diedo of Andelsbuch and Bl. ILGA. Merbot was killed by settlers, and over his grave a chapel for pilgrims was erected, and subsequently restored in 1752.

Feast: Mar. 19; first Thursday of Lent (Bregenz).

Bibliography: *Acta Sanctorum,* Sept. 3:888–890. L. RAPP, *Topographischhistorische Beschreibung des Generalvikariates Voralberg,* 5 v. (Brixen and Dornbirn 1892–1924) 5:82, 131. J. TORSY, ed., *Lexikon der deutschen Heiligen, Seligen, Ehrwürdigen und Gottseligen* (Cologne 1959) 402. A. M. ZIMMERMANN, *Kalendarium Benedictinum: Die Heiligen und Seligen des Benediktinerorderns und seiner Zweige* 1:346–347.

[B. D. HILL]

MERCADO, TOMÁS DE

Dominican logician; b. Seville, date unknown; d. San Juan de Ulúa, Mexico, 1575. When he was very young, Mercado was taken to Mexico and received the Dominican habit in the Colegio de Santo Domingo of the province of Santiago in Mexico. There, after completing his studies, he was ordained on April 27, 1553. At the University of Mexico be excelled in theological studies under Fray Pedro de Pravia, an eminent master from Salamanca and the Colegio de Santo Tomas, Ávila. His superiors sent him to Spain, where at Salamanca he perfected his studies before being assigned to teach at the convent of Seville.

While there, he published his principal works, among them *Commentarii lucidissimi in textum Petri Hispani* (1571), a commentary on the principal dialectical work of Peter of Spain, *Summulae logicales.* Like Domingo de Soto, Mercado undertook the work to preserve the profound dialectical teaching of this illustrious 13th-century logician. Mercado's commentary is a precise, complete, original, and vigorous exposition of the genuine logical doctrine of Aristotle's *First Analytics* and constitutes one of the most important dialectical treatises of the post-Tridentine scholastic revival. Logic is raised to the science of sciences, a foundation for the other sciences. *In Dialecticam Aristotelis cum opusculo argumentorum* (1571) is an original, exact Latin translation from the Greek of Aristotle's *Logica major* divided into chapters and texts, each followed by a twofold commentary, one explaining the text itself in precise, well-chosen words, the other inquiring into the truth of the question. The reason for a new version was the corrupted state of current, literary, Ciceronian versions so dear to the Renaissance, into which had also crept various nondialectical questions such as the analogy of being, the identity or distinction of being, and the categories. Mercado's restoration of the purity of the original Greek is an eloquent testimony of the high level of studies in the newly founded schools of Mexico where he received all his classical training. *Suma de tratos y contratos, en seis libros* (1569) was written for the merchants of Seville and is principally an ethicotheological work of the times with only a few introductory questions of philosophical interest, for example, on natural law, which reflects the intellectualism of Thomas Aquinas, and on justice, which reflects the influence of Domingo de Soto.

Bibliography: O. ROBLES, ''Fray Tomás de Mercado,'' *Revista de filosofía* 9 (Madrid 1950) 541–559.

[O. ROBLES]

MERCATI, ANGELO

Prefect of Vatican Archives; b. Gaida, near Reggio-Emilia, Italy, June 10, 1870; d. Rome, March 10, 1955. Ordained in Rome in 1893 after his studies there, he taught dogma and Church history in his home diocese. From 1911 he was *scriptor* of the VATICAN LIBRARY, from 1918 *primo custode* of the VATICAN ARCHIVES, and in 1920 vice prefect. He served as prefect from 1925 until his death. Under his direction, extensive and important accessions were added to the archives, and their contents were analyzed in a series of inventories. The stacks were considerably expanded and the furnishings were modernized for the accommodation of numerous visitors and scholars. Mercati's activity as a writer began with his translation into Italian of German standard works, such as H. Grisar, *Rom beim Ausgang der antiken Welt;* G. Schnüer, *Entstehung des Kirchenstaates;* O. Bardenhewer, *Patrologie* v. 1–3; J. Wilpert, *Malereien der römischen Katakomben;* H. Denifle, *Luther und Luthertum;* and L. Pastor, *Geschichte der Päpste* v. 1–3. Mercati wrote many long treatises, miscellaneous essays, and shorter articles usually occasioned by the discovery of hitherto unknown documents. His kindness and generosity to users of the archives were notable. He is buried in S. Giorgio in Velabro, beside his brother, Giovanni MERCATI.

Bibliography: Works. Listed in *Miscellanea archivistica A.M.* (*Studi e Testi* 165; 1952) ix–xxvii, supplemented in nos. 178–186 of *Studi storici in memoria di Mons. A.M.* (Fontes Ambrosiani 30; Milan 1956), and further treated in A. MERCATI, ed., *I costituti di Niccolò Franco (1568–70) dinanzi l'inquisizione di Roma, esistenti nell'archivio segreto Vaticano* (*Studi e Testi* 178; 1955); *Raccolta di concordati su materie ecclesiastiche tra la Santa Sede e le autorità civili* (Rome 1919; repr. with suppl. in 2 v. 1954). His shorter works are collected as *Saggi di storia e letteratura* (Rome 1951–), v.1 only pub. to date. Literature. K. A. FINK, *Das Vatikanische Archiv* (2d ed. Rome 1951); *Historisches Jahrbuch der Görres-Gesellschaft* 75 (1956) 524–526. F. BOCK, *Archivalische Zeitschrift* 53 (1957) 138–152. M. MACCARRONE, *Rivista di storia della Chiesa in Italia* 9 (1955) 435–436. L. SANTIFALLER, *Lexikon für Theologie und Kirche* 2 7:304.

[K. A. FINK]

MERCATI, GIOVANNI

Cardinal, archivist, and librarian at the Vatican; b. Villa Gaida (Reggio Emilia), Italy, Dec. 17, 1866; d. Vatican City, Aug. 22, 1957. He was ordained in 1889; in 1893 he was called by Msgr. A. Ceriani to the Ambrosian Library in Milan. In 1898 Father Francis Ehrle, SJ, invited him to the Vatican Library as an expert on Greek MSS. On Oct. 23, 1919, he was appointed prefect of the Vatican Library, and on June 18, 1936, he became archivist and librarian of the Roman Catholic Church and was created cardinal deacon with the title of S. Giorgio in Velabro. Recognized as one of the most learned scholars of the times, he was equally skilled in Greek and Latin patristics, in the theology and literature of Byzantium, as well as in classical, medieval, and Renaissance literature. He is the author of more than 400 works in these various fields; among his more important contributions are the following: ''D'un palimpsesto Ambrosiano contenente i Salmi esapli . . . ,'' *Atti Acc. scienze Torino,* 31 (1895–96) 655–676; *Codices Vaticani graeci 1–329,* in collaboration with F. De' Cavalieri (Rome 1923); *Prolegomena de fatis bibliothecae monasterii S. Columbani Bobiensis et de codice ipso Vat. lat. 5757* (Vatican City 1934); *Note per la storia di alcune biblioteche romane nei secoli XVI–XIX, Studi e Testi,* 164 (Rome 1952); and four volumes of minor works, *Studi e Testi,* 76–79, in which all his articles before 1936 are collected. Cardinal Mercati exerted an influence on scholars throughout the world by his publications, scientific research, and competent advice; yet he was a living example of modesty and simplicity.

Bibliography: A. CAMPANA, *Nel Novantesimo Anno del Cardinale Mercati 1866–1956* (Vatican City 1956), with complete bibliog. of M.'s works. H. JEDIN, *Lexikon für Theologie und Kirche,* ed. J. HOFER and K. RAHNER, 10 v. (2d, new ed. Freiburg 1957–65) 7:303–304.

[S. PRETE]

MERCEDARIAN MISSIONARIES OF BERRIZ

(MMB) A religious community of women with papal approbation. It was founded in 1930 when a Spanish nun, Mother Margarita Maturana, formed the community from a cloistered monastery of the Order of Mercy in Berriz, Spain. Keeping its spiritual ties with the MERCEDARIANS, the congregation of Berriz applies the traditional Mercedarian vocation of the ransom of captives to the active tasks of evangelization and missionary outreach. The constitutions were approved in 1939. From Spain the institute spread to Italy, Mexico, Japan, Taiwan, Oceania, and the U.S. The sisters were invited to the Diocese of Kansas City, in 1946. In 1981, the revised constitutions were approved. The congregation maintains an active presence in Asia, where it has communities in China, Japan, the Philippines, Taiwan and Pacific Micronesia.

[P. CODY]

MERCEDARIANS

Popular name for the Order of Our Lady of Mercy (O.de.M., Official Catholic Directory #0970), derived from the Spanish word *merced* (mercy). Members have also been known as the Knights of St. Eulalia. Pope Piux XI bestowed the title by which the institute has since been known officially: Order of the Blessed Virgin Mary for the Ransom of Captives (*Ordo Beatae Mariae Virginis de Mercede Redemptionis Captivorum.*)

Foundation and Organization. St. PETER NOLASCO founded the order in 1218 for the ransom of Christian captives, in response to a request made by the Blessed Virgin Mary during an apparition (Aug. 1, 1218). In the presence of King James of Aragon and St. Raymond of Peñafort, Peter and 13 noblemen donned the religious habit and took the three religious vows in Barcelona cathedral. They added a fourth vow, to act as hostages if necessary to free from the Moors Christian captives whose faith was in danger. This fourth vow has since been adapted to changing historical circumstances. Originally the Mercedarians were one of the MILITARY ORDERS. The habit has always been white, a color selected to facilitate entrance into Muslim territories. The habit was adapted to the order's military character. Subsequently, it consisted of a scapular as long as the tunic; a white tunic fastened by a wide leather belt, from which hangs a chain reminiscent of the soldier's sword that was formerly worn; and a cape with a cowl. On the breast of the cape was a shield, granted by King James I, which bore four stripes on a field of gold, a Maltese cross, and a royal crown. The Mercedarians constitute a religious order, whose rule is that of St. Augustine. Pope Gregory IX approved the order Jan. 17, 1235. Members are priests, candidates for the priesthood, or brothers. A master general who resides in Rome governs the order. The U.S. headquarters is in Cleveland, OH.

History. Mercedarians have been responsible for the liberation of perhaps 70,000 prisoners, some 2,700 during the founder's lifetime. In 1318 Pope John XXII decreed that the master general must be a priest. Thereupon the lay knights left the order and joined the military order of Our Lady of Montesa, founded in 1319 by King James II to battle against the Moors. At that time, the Mercedarians changed from a military to a clerical order. It became a MENDICANT ORDER. From Spain, the Mercedarians spread to Africa, Italy, France, and Ireland. After the discovery of the New World, the Mercedarians engaged in missionary activities and contributed to the evangelization of the regions from the Rio Grande River southward to the tip of South America. During the 17th century, there were eight provinces and 265 monasteries in Latin America. As a result of a reform movement, Juan Bautista González founded in 1602 the discalced Mercedarians, who received Paul V's approval in 1606. The French Revolution and the liberal, anticlerical governments in 19th-century Spain nearly extinguished the order. Pedro Armengol Valenzuela, who became master general in 1880, revised the constitutions and guided the apostolate toward educational, charitable, and social works. His directives have been followed ever since.

Congregations of women who share the Mercedarian spirit and heritage include the second order of Mercedarians founded by St. MARY DE CERVELLÓ (1265); the Mercedarian Sisters of Charity (1878); the Mercedarian Missionaries of Berriz (1930); the Eucharistic Mercedarians in Mexico; the Missionary Mercedarians of Africa, founded by Cardinal LAVIGERIE and incorporated into the order by Armengol Valenzuela; and the Mercedarians of the Child Jesus and the Divine Master of Argentina. A Third Order exists that received an official rule of life in 1260; its members, imbued with the spirit of the first order, assist the latter in hospitals and prisons.

Bibliography: G. VÁZQUEZ, *Manual de historia de la Orden de N. Señora de la Merced* (Toledo 1931). F. D. GAZULLA GALVE, *La Orden de Nuestra Señora de la Merced* (Barcelona 1934). J. B. HERRADA ARMIJO, *El Voto de Redención en la Orden de la Merced* (Santiago de Chile 1951). M. HEIMBUCHER, *Die Orden und Kongregationen der Katholischen Kirche*, 2 v. (3d ed. Paderborn 1932–34) 1:571–576. *Enciclopedia de la Religión Católica,* ed. R. D. FERRERES, et al. (Barcelona 1950–56) 5:306–326. *Boletín de la Orden de la Merced* (Rome 1934—).

[A. MORALES/EDS.]

MERCERSBURG THEOLOGY

Designates the theological school of the German Reformed Church that set out to oppose the emotional revivalism of the mid-19th century by re-presenting the faith of the early reformers and by stressing doctrine, especially Christology, ecclesiology, and sacramental theology. It originated about 1836 with Profs. Frederick Rauch (1806–41), John Williamson NEVIN (1803–86), and Philip SCHAFF (1819–93), all faculty members of the German Reformed Seminary at Mercersburg, Pa. Convinced that popular revivalism was not in harmony with the HEIDELBERG CATECHISM, they undertook a positive and historical reexamination of earlier writings in order to recover the pre-Puritan faith of the reformers and to promote a historical appreciation of the Church's past. The result was a system grounded on the centrality of Christ and the Church.

The Mercersburg theologians taught that the Incarnate Word, Christ, is the primary truth of Christianity; in Him all men are regenerated and united as members of His body, a spiritual organism called the church. The Church, extending through all ages and destined to include all peoples, is ever the same, yet each age appreciates its fullness differently. From this they concluded that no doctrinal formula or organizational structure can be final, and the church must modify its teachings according to its progressive knowledge of Christian truth. While strongly upholding the general priesthood of the laity, these theologians also maintained that Christ, who is ever present in the Church, perpetuates His mediatorial mission through an order of men, all equal, who speak in His name, dispense His Sacraments, and rule His flock. The Sacraments (baptism and the Lord's Supper) are not mere signs, but ''real seals of God's covenant with man'' and channels of grace, made efficacious by faith. As a consequence of these teachings, the leaders at Mercersburg urged a liturgical restoration and openly attacked the then prevalent emotional revivalism. Constantly questioned and suspected, the Mercersburg professors were tried three times for heresy and acquitted. Because of disagreements with Nevin and Schaff, several congregations left the Reformed Church, but they had little influence beyond their own membership.

The Mercersburg theologians had hoped that their studies would eventually lead the Reformed Churches to union. Their own German Reformed Church united with the Evangelical Church in 1934, forming the EVANGELICAL AND REFORMED CHURCH; this Church, noted for its Christocentrism, experienced a liturgical revival. The Mercersburg influence helped to bridge the gap between the complete supernaturalism of the Calvinistic creeds and the religious liberalism of the early 20th century.

Bibliography: L. BINKLEY, *The Mercersburg Theology* (Lancaster, Pa. 1952).

[T. HORGAN]

MERCIER, DÉSIRÉ JOSEPH

Founder and first president of the Institut Supérieur de Philosophie at Louvain (Belgium), cardinal archbishop of Malines; b. Braine-l'Alleud (near Waterloo), Nov. 21, 1851; d. Brussels, Jan. 23, 1926. He was the son of Paul (1808–58), manufacturer and artist, and of A. M. Barbe Croquet (1815–82), sister of Msgr. Adrian Croquet (d. 1902), apostle of the Oregon native tribe. After his studies in the classics, philosophy, and theology at the seminary of Malines, Mercier was ordained (1874), obtained a licentiate in theology at Louvain (1877), and became professor of philosophy at Malines the same year. In 1882 he was commissioned to inaugurate the chair of Thomistic philosophy created at the University of Louvain at the request of Pope Leo XIII. Mercier endeavored to realize the program formulated in the 1879 encyclical *AETERNI PATRIS*: to restore the philosophy of St. Thomas Aquinas, harmonize it with the progress of modern science and thought, and extend its influence to the scientific and social disciplines. On the basis of his initial successes, he asked for, and received, the support of the pope for the creation of an Institut Supérieur de Philosophie that would provide a complete education in the various philosophical areas. When named president of this institute in 1889, Mercier gathered collaborators from among his first students and with their assistance formed an international group of enthusiastic and devoted disciples. The *Revue NéoScolastique,* founded in 1894, made the writings of the institute available throughout the scholarly world.

Philosophy. Mercier's views concerning philosophy differed greatly from those of most of his Catholic contemporaries. For him philosophy was a purely rational discipline distinct from theology; not only this, but it had to be free from every apologetical preoccupation. Furthermore, philosophy cannot be considered a finished work. It must be animated with the spirit of research found in other university disciplines. Without breaking with tradition, philosophy must address itself to men in their own times. It must stay in contact with the empirical sciences and gain support from them, while yet aspiring to explanations that transcend the order of observable data.

This view of philosophy explains why Mercier appealed to experience when treating the transcendental character of truth and goodness, finality, and other themes. It is also apparent in his view of psychology, Mercier's favorite discipline. Fighting the ''exaggerated spiritualism'' and the mechanism that flowed, according to him, from Cartesian dualism, Mercier appealed to biology, physiology, and neurology to show the substantial unity of man and to elaborate the hylomorphic explanation of this unity. In 1892 he installed at the institute one of the first laboratories of experimental psychology, under the direction of A. Thiéry (1868–1955). In the same way he encouraged D. Nys (1859–1927) to unite cosmology with physics and chemistry and S. Deploige (1868–1927) to link ethics with the social sciences.

Mercier recognized the critical problem as one of furnishing a CRITERION for truth and certitude. This criterion, he believed, must be furnished in and by reflection. Since the latter is characteristic of intelligence, the criterion must be the evidence arrived at in the domain of abstract ideas. Yet he made appeal to the principle of causality to explain that the content of these ideas comes from experience and to guarantee thereby the real character of the evidence. This ''illationism,'' later abandoned at Louvain because of the influence of L. Noël, had the merit of stimulating a fruitful controversy.

Episcopacy. On Feb. 7, 1906, Mercier was named archbishop of Malines. He administered this diocese of 2.5 million inhabitants with continual solicitude for every type of Catholic activity and deep concern for the spiritual development of his priests. As primate of Belgium he convoked a Catholic congress in 1909 to coordinate religious activity in the whole of Belgium. At the 1920 provincial council, he examined the rehabilitation necessary in the aftermath of the war. If at first he was actively engaged in the political life of the country—where a powerful Catholic party seemed to him the best guarantee of Church liberty and the surest defense against a de-Christianizing Marxism—his concern after the war centered more on national understanding and specifically religious action. Lacking somewhat in political adaptability, Mercier was led to identify *''la patrie''* unconditionally with a unitary Belgium. This deficiency, coupled with his native attachment to French culture, explains his lack of understanding in the face of Flemish grievances. During the war he was convinced that his duty was to build and sustain the morale of his countrymen, to protest against the excesses of the German troops, and to cry against the injustices of the occupying government. This attitude won for him enormous prestige in his own country and among the Allied nations, as witnessed by the enthusiastic welcome accorded him in the United States in 1919.

When created a cardinal in 1907, Mercier took a lively interest in problems of the universal Church. Resuming after the war the work undertaken by the Fribourg Union, he created the International Union of Social Studies and presided over its work; this led, among other things, to the publication in 1927 of a social code. He was preoccupied also with Church union, and he installed in Belgium the Institute of the Monks of Union (Chevetogne) to further reconciliation with the churches of the Orient. Most importantly perhaps, he presided over the Malines Conversations (1921–25); at the initiative of Lord Halifax, these studied the conditions for union between Catholics and Anglicans.

See Also: SCHOLASTICISM; NEOSCHOLASTICISM AND NEOTHOMISM.

Bibliography: Works. *Logique,* v. 1; *Métaphysique générale, ou Ontologie,* v. 2; *Psychologie,* v. 3; *Critériologie générale, ou théorie générale de la certitude,* v. 4, all 4 v. are in *Cours de philosophie* (Louvain 1892–99); *Les Origines de la psychologie contemporaine* (Louvain 1897); *Oeuvres pastorales,* 7 v. (Louvain 1911–29); *La Correspondance de S. É. le cardinal Mercier avec le gouvernement général allemand pendant l'occupation, 1914–1918,* ed. F. MAYENCE (Paris 1919). D. J. MERCIER et al., *Traité élémentaire de philosophie à l'usage des classes,* 2 v. (Louvain 1906). Literature. J. A. GADE, *The Life of Cardinal Mercier* (London 1935). J. J. HARNETT, ''Désiré Joseph Mercier and the Neoscholastic Revival,'' *The New Scholasticism* 18 (1944): 303–339. L. DE RAEYMAEKER, *Le Cardinal Mercier et l'Institut Supérieur de Philosophie de Louvain* (Louvain 1952). A. SIMON, *Le Cardinal Mercier* (Brussels 1960); *Position philosophique du cardinal Mercier: Esquisse psychologique* (Brussels 1962).

[A. L. WYLLEMAN]

MERCY

Compassionate sorrow at another's misfortune together with a will to alleviate it; it is genuine love in relation to an unhappy being. The encounter of love and misery gives birth to mercy, which is therefore one of the essential forms of charity, situated in the very heart of Christianity (St. Thomas Aquinas, *Summa Theologiae* 2a, 2ae 30).

Another's distress becomes one's own because the other is united and in a sense identified with oneself, or because his misfortune is of concern to one, for example, by reason of his recollection of something similar in the past, or fear of something like it in the future. This likeness between another's misfortune and one's own can be experienced on the level of pure sensibility and is then simply an emotion. On the other hand, the comparison can exist on a more spiritual level, and charity becomes merciful, assuming and controlling the emotion. Compassion in itself is not the virtue of mercy. For the virtue, a genuine effort to relieve the misfortune of others in all its forms is demanded. The particular form of misery with which mercy is most concerned is spiritual misery, the abandonment of God. Mercy then unites and makes more intense the love of human beings and the hatred of vice. In this sense, mercy is found in its most perfect expression in God, since mercy is the efficacious hatred of another's evil.

God wills that we practice mercy as the most excellent way of accomplishing the second Commandment ''like to the first.'' He expressly says so: ''I desire mercy and not sacrifice'' (Mt 9.13; cf. Hos 6.6). Mercy, to unite us with Him who is ''merciful and gracious'' (Ps 102.8; Ex 34.6) should tend to prompt imitation of Him. ''Be merciful, therefore, even as your heavenly Father is merciful'' (Lk 6.36). Mercy is intimately involved in our union with God Himself. ''With what measure you measure, it shall be measured out to you'' (Mt 7.2).

Christ is, in those who are His, the source of merciful love; He enlightens and inspires all forms of mercy. For example, almsdeeds take their inspiration from the Lord Jesus who, ''being rich . . . became poor for your sakes'' (2 Cor 8.9). The ''great sadness and continuous sorrow'' in the heart of St. Paul ''for the sake of my brethren . . . who are Israelites'' (Rom 9.2) is an extension of ''the love of God, which is in Christ Jesus, our Lord'' (Rom 8.39). Mercy like the Lord's springs from a care for the human condition involved in many misfortunes. ''Jesus saw a large crowd, and had compassion on them, because they were like sheep without a shepherd'' (Mk 6.34).

Mercy obtains pardon of sins in this life and the eternal possession of God in the life to come. ''Blessed are the merciful, for they shall obtain mercy'' (Mt 5.7).

See Also: CHARITY.

[J. M. PERRIN]

MERCY, BROTHERS OF

Officially known as the Brothers of Mercy of Montabaur (FMM, Official Catholic Directory #0810), dedicated to the care and nursing of those who are chronically ill. The congregation was founded in Germany in 1856 by Peter Loetschert (1820–86) and four others. In 1861 the motherhouse was established at Montabaur, Germany. The order grew steadily and spread to Holland, where by 1902 there were five houses. In Germany, their 23 establishments (1930) were later reduced to nine, as a consequence of war and Hitler's religious persecutions. The Brothers of Mercy opened their first U.S. house in Buffalo, N.Y., in 1924. The U.S. provincialate is in Clarence, N.Y., a Buffalo suburb.

[W. G. YOUNG/EDS.]

MERCY, FATHERS OF

This society, officially known as the Congregation of the Priests of Mercy (CPM, Official Catholic Directory #0820), was originally founded in Lyons, France, in 1808, by a zealous priest, Jean Baptist Rauzan. Rauzan brought together a small group of priests to form a missionary band, with the idea of counteracting the disastrous effects of the French Revolution on the faith of the people. For years, the little band of missionaries traveled up and down the country, preaching and administering the Sacraments. Rauzan, seeing the work that was accomplished, formed his priests into a community known as the Missionaries of France. In 1834 the community was approved by Pope Gregory XVI and became known as the Fathers of Mercy. The society came to the United States in 1839 at the request of Bp. John Hughes of New York. The Fathers of Mercy founded four parishes, two in New York and two in Brooklyn. In 1956 the society was reorganized by the Holy See. The four parishes in the United States were turned over to diocesan authorities, and the community took on a strictly mission character. As a result of the reorganization, the society assumed the status of a congregation, since the fathers, already under the vows of obedience and chastity, also took the vow of poverty. The U.S. headquarters is in South Union, KY.

[T. P. DOYLE/EDS.]

MERCY, WORKS OF

Works of mercy are acts that express MERCY and that could likewise be called the realizations of charity in its mode of mercy. Two specific works of mercy, almsgiving [*see* ALMS AND ALMSGIVING (IN THE CHURCH)] and fraternal CORRECTION, are explained elsewhere.

Christian Spirit of the Works of Mercy. The works of mercy warmly commended by the Law, the sages, and the prophets are at the heart of the Old Testament, e.g.,"Sharing your bread with the hungry, sheltering the oppressed and the homeless, clothing the naked when you see them, and not turning your back on your own" (Is 58.7). However, in the New Testament there is a profound development of the concept of mercy. Christ is now present in His people, and His people are not only those who are merciful, but those in misery and in need of mercy. In fact, the Incarnation itself is a work of mercy for human misery, both Jewish and pagan. "For God has shut up all in unbelief, that he may have mercy upon all" (Rom 11.32).

The Christian spirit brought first a new way of looking upon misfortune. Every kindness done "you did . . ." Our Lord said "for me" (Mt 25.40). Second, it

"Blessed Are the Merciful," lithograph by Ernst Barlach.

gave new scope to free generosity. No regulation can determine the extent or the opportunities for this duty of mercy, since faith has opened new horizons, as St. Paul pointed out to Philemon whom he wanted to persuade by love to free Onesimus: "May the sharing of thy faith be made evident in full knowledge of all the good that is in you, in Christ Jesus" (Phlm 1.6). Third, it involved a spirit of service. The Christian's mercy is really that of Christ; his own personal gain and the manifestation of superiority cannot be its motives. Instead, humble service will tend toward the development of the person in need in order to bring him to equality: "that at the present time your abundance may supply their want, and that their abundance may, in its turn, make up what you lack, thus establishing an equality" (2 Cor 8.14).

Corporal Works. The list is long established: to feed the hungry, to give drink to the thirsty, to clothe the naked, to shelter the homeless, to visit the sick, to ransom the captive, to bury the dead. All are found in the parable of the Judgment (Mt 25.34–40), except the last, to bury the dead, which was added out of the respect owed to the body as a "temple of the Holy Spirit" (1 Cor 3.16), and consideration of the sorrows caused by death. These seven are not to be considered as exclusive. Other real afflictions, such as those experienced by displaced persons who are without homes, or by prisoners, or alcoholics, or prostitutes, or others involved in evils that threaten human dignity, call for Christian mercy. Problems involved in getting aid to underdeveloped countries and the promotion of peace between men and races cannot be solved without the organized cooperation of many. Papal

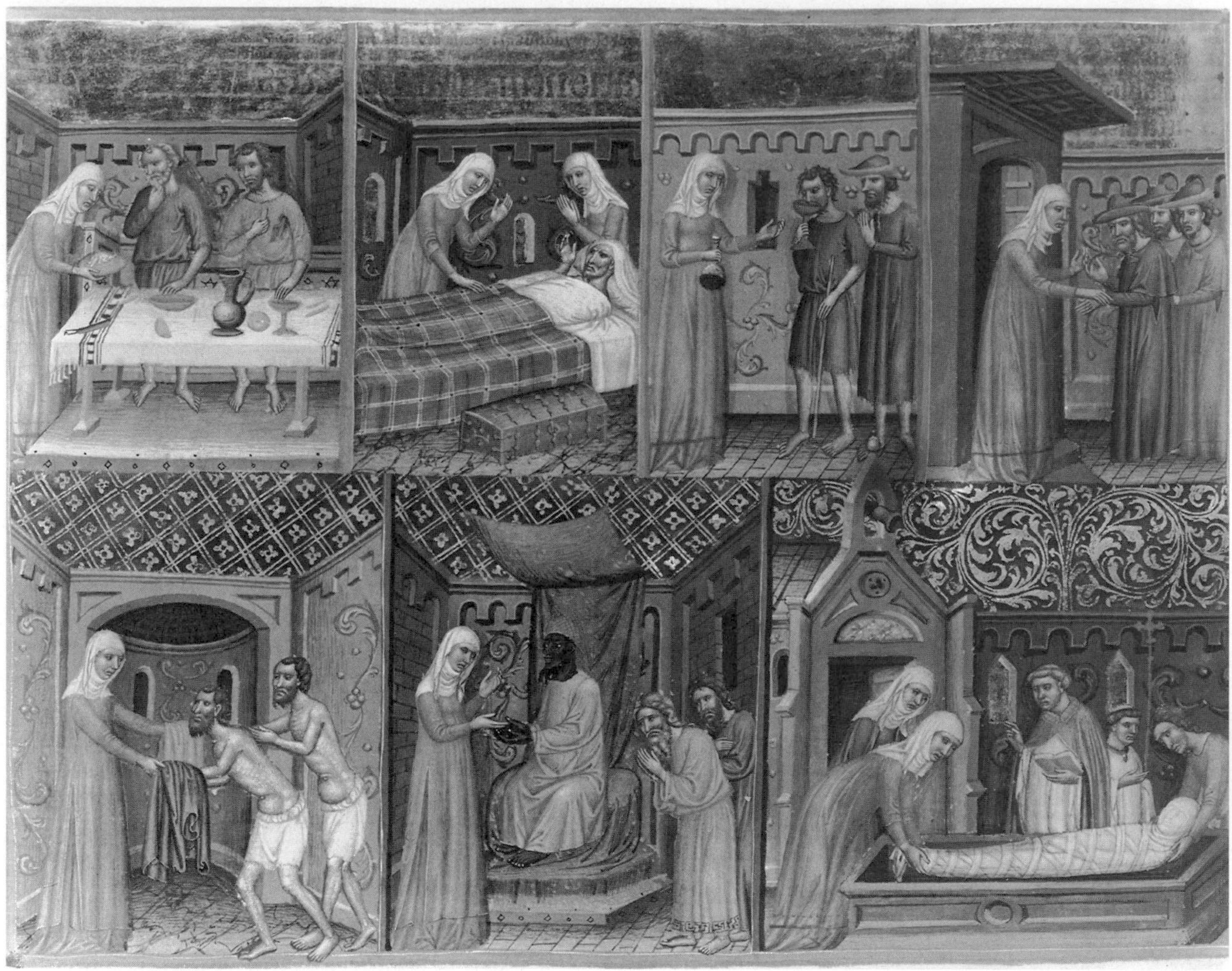

"The Seven Works of Mercy," illuminated manuscript painting in a Psalter by an artist of the Italian School, from the Bibliothèque Nationale, Paris (Biblio. Nat. MS Lat. 8846, fol. 156v.).

encyclicals have exhorted the faithful to effective participation in such works.

Spiritual Works. Seven are usually listed: to instruct the ignorant, to counsel the doubtful, to admonish sinners, to bear wrongs patiently, to forgive offenses, to comfort the afflicted, and to pray for the living and the dead. The instruction of the ignorant may be performed by an organization, although on occasion it may well be the work of an individual. But the other spiritual works remain in the realm of personal relationships, and on this account have a particular value. They make demands upon personal resources and hence are a more specific expression of charity toward another, and in this they tend to promote human unity. Their urgency comes from the threat of human depersonalization in contemporary civilization.

The works of mercy demand a spirit of service, the attention of love, and the sincerity of compassion. "I have given you an example . . ." the Lord said (Jn 13.15). The performance of these works was characteristic of Christ's life, who, as St. Peter expressed it, "went about doing good" (Acts 10.38).

The word of God is a challenge to every Christian: "I desired mercy, and not sacrifice" (Hos 6.6 DV); "God who is rich in mercy, by reason of his very great love wherewith he has loved us" (Eph 2.4) wants us to be united with Him and to come to know the joy of giving as He has given.

See Also: MERCY; CHARITY.

[J. M. PERRIN]

MERCY OF GOD

Biblical Basis. The Old Testament tells of God's love manifested in his mercy. This was first manifested in freeing his people from their slavery in Egypt. It is the merciful God who tells Moses that he has heard the cry of his enslaved people and that he will deliver them (Ex 3:7–17). However, God's mercy is manifested foremost in forgiving the infidelity of his people. ''The Lord, the Lord, a God merciful and gracious, slow to anger, and abounding in steadfast love and faithfulness, keeping steadfast love for thousands, forgiving the iniquity and transgression and sin'' (Ex 34:6–7). So important is this text for declaring God's mercy that it is repeated in various forms six times within the Old Testament (Ps 85/86:15, 102/103:8, 144/145:8; Jl 2:13; Neh 9:17; Jn 4:2). The Lord God is a merciful God (Dt 4:31, Ps 114/116:5), who will not turn away his face to those who return to him (2 Chr 30:9). Even though God sent his people into exile, he did not make an end of them or forsake them, ''for you are a gracious and merciful God'' (Neh 9:31). Similar examples and proclamations can be found throughout the Old Testament.

In the New Testament, the mercy of God finds its fulfillment in that the ''The Father of all mercies and the God of all comfort'' (2 Cor 1:3) so loved the world that he sent his Son into the world (Jn 3:16; 1 Jn 4:10). ''God, who is rich in mercy, out of the great love with which he loved us, even when we were dead through our trespasses, made us alive together with Christ'' (Eph 2:4). In so doing God remembered his mercy to Israel (Lk 1:54) ''to perform the mercy promised to our fathers . . . to give knowledge of salvation to his people in the forgiveness of their sin, through the tender mercy of our God'' (Lk 1:72 and 78). Even the Gentiles are now to ''glorify God for his mercies'' (Rom 15:9). Though Paul was the greatest of sinners he obtained the mercy of God so as to be the most extreme example and so hope of God's mercy to all (1 Tm 1:13–16). Thus everyone can now see ''how the Lord is compassionate and merciful'' (Jas 5:11), for ''by his great mercy we have been born anew to a living hope through the resurrection of Jesus Christ from the dead, and to an inheritance which is imperishable, undefiled, and unfading'' (1 Pt 1:3–4). Jesus is the everlasting great High Priest to whom we can draw near in confidence ''that we may receive mercy and find grace to help in time of need'' (Heb 4:16). Christians, therefore, are a chosen people, a royal priesthood, a holy nation and God very people because ''once you had not received mercy but now you have received mercy'' (1 Pt 2:10). God allowed all to become sinners precisely so ''that he may have mercy upon all'' (Rom 11:32). The New Testament thus accentuates the mercy of God manifested in the face of humankind's sin. It is the cross of Christ that displays most strikingly the mercy of God for through it the Father has granted forgiveness of sins and the divine transforming life of his Spirit. This mercy is exemplified in anticipation of the cross through Jesus' example and miracles. Jesus, in his mercy, has come to call sinners (Mt 9:13, 12:7). Those who desire to be healed cry out to Jesus to have mercy on them (Mt 9:27, 15:22, 17:15, 20:30–31; Mk 10:47–48; Lk 16:24,18:38–39), and he, in his mercy, attends to their need. Moreover, Jesus, through the parable of the Prodigal Son, illustrates the utter loving mercy of the Father (Lk 15:11–32). Like the Father then, Christians are called to love and forgive their enemies. Christian perfection consists in being ''merciful as your Father is merciful'' (Lk 6:36, Mt 5:48).

Christian Tradition. The Fathers of the Church continue the biblical theme of God manifesting his mercy through the redemption wrought in his incarnate Son and in the incorruptible life poured out in his Spirit. Irenaeus states: ''To exercise mercy is God's own function'' (*Demonstration on the Apostolic Preaching*, 60). Ambrose, in an astonishing statement, wrote that God did not rest from creating until he had made man, for now he could exercise his mercy, ''there now being someone whose sins he could forgive'' (*In Hex.*, 6.10). Augustine, in his *Confessions*, bears witness to the mercy of God throughout the whole of his life. So much was the mercy of God esteemed within the Church's tradition that Aquinas could ask whether mercy is the greatest virtue. He answers that ''mercy takes precedence of other virtues, for it belongs to mercy to be bountiful to others, and, what is more, to succor others in their wants, which pertains chiefly to one who stands above. Hence mercy is accounted as being proper to God: and therein his omnipotence is declared to be chiefly manifested'' (*Summa theologiae*, II–II.30.4). Mercy is God's greatest virtue because he gives not from any need of his own, but purely and freely from his own loving liberality and kindness (*Summa theologiae*, I.21.3, 4). For Aquinas, the chief manifestation of God's omnipotence is enacted through his omnipotent deeds of mercy, that is, in deeds that only he can perform. In his *Commentary on Ephesians* (2.2) Aquinas provides four examples of God's omnipotent deeds that display the richness of his mercy (Eph 2:4). First, the act of creation is itself an omnipotent deed of supreme mercy for in our non-existence, when we could not even cry out for mercy, God in his mercy brought us into existence. Second, God in his mercy made us in his own image and likeness so that we might enjoy his own beatitude. Third, he mercifully recreated us when we were corrupted by sin and death. Fourth, such a renewal was accomplished by the merciful Father sending his only Son. Pope John Paul II states that Jesus as the Incarnate Son ''is mercy'' in that he embodies in his own person the mercy of the Father (*Dives Misericordia*, 2). Likewise within the Christian tradition the mercy of God is found within the theology of and devotion to the Sacred Heart of Jesus.

The pierced heart of Jesus not only reveals the immense love and mercy of Jesus himself, but, through his open heart, we are also able to gaze into the merciful heart of the Trinity itself. Equally, more recently Bl. Faustina Kowalska (1905–38), because of her visions, promoted devotion to God's mercy through *The Chaplet of Divine Mercy* and *Novena of Divine Mercy.* Liturgically this has found expression in the Second Sunday after Easter being designated the Feast of Mercy.

For the relationship between God's mercy and his justice, *see* JUSTICE OF GOD.

Bibliography: Y. CONGAR, ''Mercy: God's Supreme Attribute,'' *The Revelation of God* (New York 1968) 49–62. B. DAVIES, *The Thought of Thomas Aquinas* (Oxford 1992). JOHN PAUL II, *Dives in Misericordia* (1980).

[T. G. WEINANDY]

MERICI, ANGELA, ST.

Foundress, b. Desenzano, Republic of Venice, probably on March 21, 1474; d. Brescia, Jan. 27, 1540. Except for some years when she lived with an uncle's family in Salo, Angela remained in Desenzano until she was about 40. Around 1506, she was favored with a vision in which she was told, ''Before your death, you will found a society of virgins at Brescia.'' She awaited a providential action that might lead her to Brescia, and in 1516 received such a sign in the invitation from the Patengoli family to live with them in order to console them because of the recent death of their two sons.

It was not until 1531 that she organized a small group of 12 girls to help her with the catechetical work she had already begun. By 1535 the group had increased to 28, and with characteristic simplicity Angela formed them (25 Nov. 1535) into the Company of St. Ursula by the simple inscription of their names in a book. Aware of the need for reform in both the Church and society, Angela thus founded the first religious order for the teaching of young girls. Her goal was the re-Christianization of family life and thus of society, through the solid Christian education of future wives and mothers. Each one in the Company was to continue living in her own home, exercising her apostolate among the members of her own family, her social acquaintances, and the children of her neighborhood. No formal vows were taken, but the primitive rule drawn up by Angela prescribed the practice of virginity, poverty, and obedience.

Thus, the original company was in reality a ''secular institute'' and it was only after St. Angela's death that the administrative organization was changed by St. Charles BORROMEO, bishop of Milan, in order to bring it into harmony with the decisions of the Council of TRENT. Later changes and adaptations have brought into being different forms of life for the members of the institute; both Angelines and Ursulines claim St. Angela as their foundress. The divergencies have resulted from fidelity to her counsel: ''. . . if according to times and needs you should be obliged to make fresh rules and change certain things, do it with prudence and good advice.''

Immediately after her death Angela was honored as a saint by the people of Brescia. The municipal council collected the necessary documents for beatification, but it was not until 1768 that the actual decree of beatification was approved by CLEMENT XIII. Angela was canonized on May 24, 1807, and in 1861 her cult was extended to the universal Church by PIUS IX.

Feast: Jan. 27 (formerly June 1).

Bibliography: *Angela Merici: vita della Chiesa e spiritualità nella prima metà del Cinquecento: convegno di studi storici*, ed. C. NARO, P. PRODI, et al. (Caltanisetta-Roma 1998). G. B. BARBIERI, *Lettera viva* (Brescia 1972). M. BENIGNI, *Angela Merici a Bergamo* (Villa di Serio, Bergamo 1994). M. BUSER, *Also in your midst: Reflections on the spirituality of St. Angela Merici* (Green Bay, Wis. 1990). G. GARIONI BERTOLOTTI, *S. Angela Merici, vergine bresciana, 1474–1540* (Brescia 1950, rep. Milan 1971). P. CARAMAN, *Saint Angela; the life of Angela Merici* (New York 1964). A. CONRAD, *Mit Klugheit, Mut und Zuversicht: Angela Merici und die Ursulinen* (Mainz 1994). M.-P. DESAING, *Angela Merici: Persönlichkeit und Auftrag* (Stein am Rhein 1976). T. LEDÓCHOWSKA, *Angèle Merici et la Compagnie de Ste-Ursule à la lumière des documents* (Rome 1968). F. M. SALVATORI, *Angela*, tr. M. DI MERCURIO of *Vita della Santa Madre Angela Merici* (Saint Martin, Ohio 1970). S. UNDSET, *Sant'Angela Merici* (Brescia 1965). P. M. WATERS, *The Ursuline achievement: A philosophy of education for women* (North Carlton, Vic., Australia 1994).

[M. A. GALLIN]

MÉRIDA

City of about 15,000 on the right bank of the Guadiana River, in Estremadura, southwest Spain. Founded by Augustus (25 B.C.), it became the capital of Roman Lusitania and one of the first dioceses and metropolitanates in Spain. The famous martyr, St. Eulalia (*c.* 304; feast, Dec. 10) is ascribed to Mérida (PRUDENTIUS, *Peristephanon* 3); she was joined in the Spanish liturgy *c.* 600 by St. Eulalia of Barcelona, usually regarded as a double of the martyr of Mérida. Eulalia, a voluntary martyr, is ascribed to Barcelona in the 1574 edition of EULOGIUS OF CÓRDOBA (*Memoriale sanctorum* 1.24), d. 859, who seems to have known Prudentius. Her cult spread through Spain, North Africa (a sermon by St. Augustine), Gaul, Germany, and Italy (Sant' Apollinare Nuovo in Ravenna).

Mérida, a center of PRISCILLIANISM, was the locale of a valuable Visigothic work, the *vitae* of the Fathers of

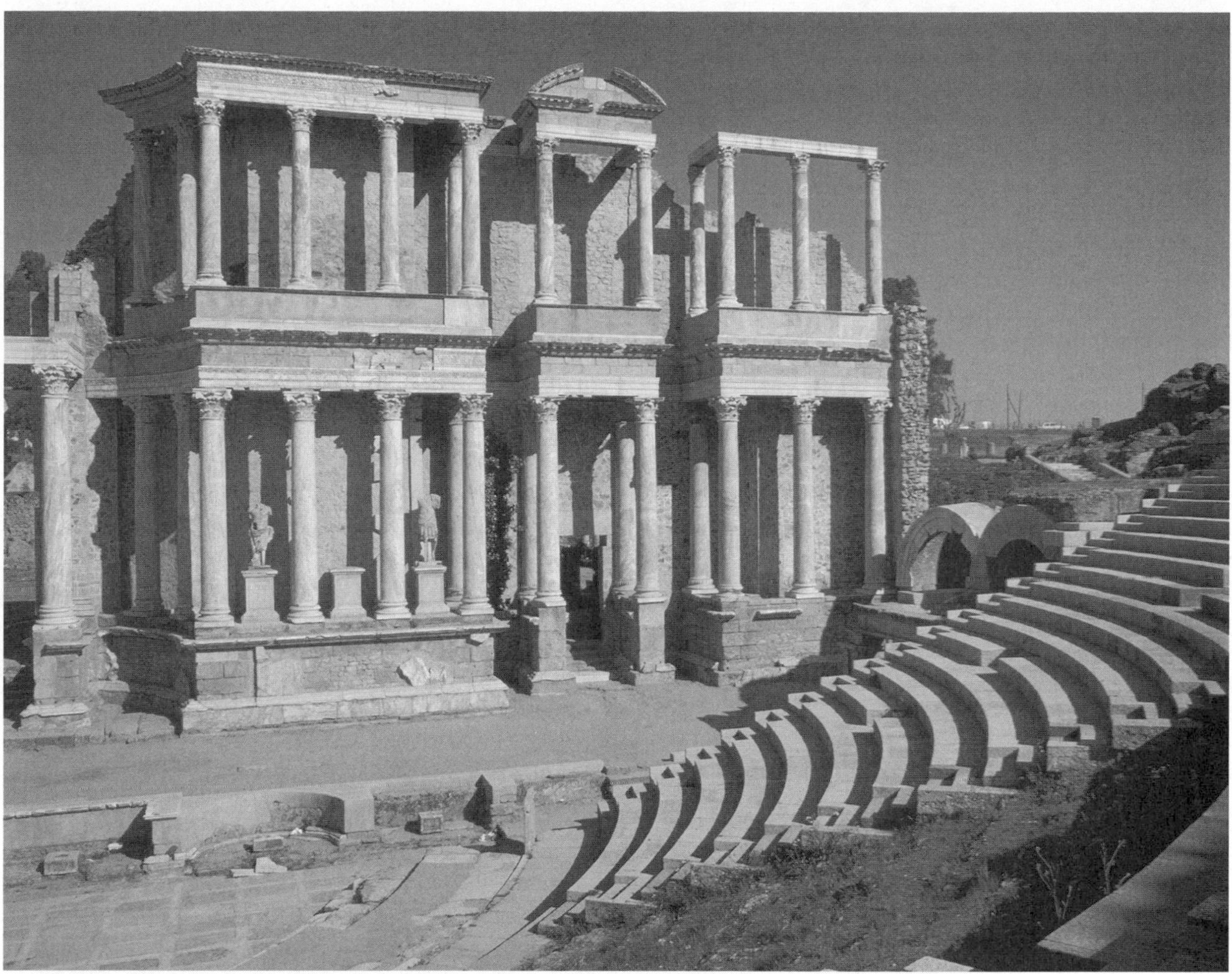

The cuneus and arcaded facade of a Roman building, Mérida, Plascencia. (©Adam Woolfitt/CORBIS)

Mérida (633–638), prized in León by Alfonso III in 906; Eulalia is mentioned 29 times in the vitae. The acts of a reform council held in Mérida (666) and the Arabic text of Mérida's contract of surrender to the Arabs (June 713) are extant. The city was the scene of almost constant rebellion against CÓRDOBA until 929. Louis I the Pious of France in 826 wrote to the magistrates and people of Mérida, encouraging them to continue resistance and promising them their full liberty of old, exemption from taxation, and the right to live under their own law if they would ally with him against Córdoba. In 828 Mahmud, a *mollitos* (offspring of a Christian-Muslim marriage), rebelled and fled with his followers to Christian Galicia. His sister, according to Arabic accounts, became a Christian, and her son became bishop of SANTIAGO DE COMPOSTELA. Ariulfus, metropolitan of Mérida, took part in ecclesiastical affairs of Betica (839–864).

When Badajoz was founded downstream with settlers from Mérida (868–875), the metropolitan also may have moved. Bishop Julius of Badajoz fled to Santiago, where he signed a document in 932. But Mérida appears as a metropolitanate with a varying number of suffragan sees in episcopal lists as late as the 13th century. The origin of these lists, which appear in several countries of Europe, is obscure; and it is not clear what period the lists would represent.

In 1120 the Metropolitanate of Mérida was transferred to Santiago. The city, after its reconquest (1228), was given to the KNIGHTS OF ST. JAMES (1232) until the 15th century. Settlers did not come, however, and Mérida was almost deserted from the 14th to the 16th century. Its many Roman ruins, still famous, survived in good state to the 18th century, when they suffered from neglect and abuse. Mérida is now part of the Diocese of Badajoz.

Bibliography: H. FLÓREZ et al., *España sagrada* (Madrid 1747–1957) 13:48–317. A. LAMBERT, *Dictionnaire d'histoire et de géographie ecclésiastiques*, ed. A. BAUDRILLART et al. (Paris

1912–) 6:96–117. A. FABREGA-GRAU, *ibid.* 15:1380–85. E. P. COLBERT, *The Martyrs of Córdoba, 850–859* (Washington 1962).

[E. P. COLBERT]

MÉRIDA, FATHERS OF

Five bishops—Paul, Fidelis, Masona, Innocent, Renovatus—of Mérida, from *c.* 550 to 633. An anonymous deacon of Mérida, arbitrarily named Paul in the 16th century, related edifying tales about the first three, with vague chronological indications. Paul, a physician from Greece, eventually became bishop. After many years, he recognized in a young man who came to Mérida with Greek merchants his nephew Fidelis, whom he trained for the sacred ministry and after many years chose as his successor. Fidelis was succeeded by Masona, a noble Goth who was called ''well-known'' by JOHN OF BICLARO in 573. Masons built and endowed many churches and monasteries, and established a hospital and a loan bank. He was exiled by the Arian King Leovegild (568–586) for three years, probably in 582 when Leovegild recaptured Mérida from his rebellious Catholic son HERMENEGILD. Masona and Leovegild's convert son and successor Recared (586–601) overcame uprisings of Arian bishops and nobles. Masona signed the acts of the Third Council of Toledo (589) and a Toledo synod (597) and, if a letter from St. ISIDORE to him is authentic, was still alive in 605 or 606. He was succeeded by Innocent, who signed a decree of King Gundemar (610–612) in 610, and by the learned and prudent Renovatus, who was bishop for many years. The next known bishop of Mérida, Stephen I, signed the acts of the Fourth Council of Toledo (633).

Bibliography: J. N. GARVIN, ed. and tr., *The Vitas sanctorum patrum Emeretensium* (Washington 1946).

[J. N. GARVIN]

MERIT

By the term ''merit,'' the Catholic theologian understands that ordination of a man's good act whereby this act is rendered worthy of receiving a reward. In the abstract, merit may be considered as that property of the act which renders it fit for reward; in the concrete, merit is to be defined as a man's title to the reward that the action deserves. Theologians divide the notion of merit into two classes, condign and congruent. The distinction stems from the different bases on which the title to a reward rests. Condign merit has a title arising from a concept of justice; congruent merit is based on the liberality of the one who gives a reward. The expression ''congruent merit'' appeared for the first time in the writings of Alan of Lille (d. 1203?); William of Auvergne (d. 1249) shortly thereafter taught that condign and congruent are the proper divisions of merit. Theological consideration of the doctrine of merit is restricted to supernatural merit, that is, merit that arises from an action performed with the assistance of divine GRACE.

The present article will summarize (1) the scriptural basis and (2) patristic testimony on which the Catholic doctrine rests, (3) the teaching of the medieval theologians, (4) the Tridentine formulation of the doctrine as found in the decree on justification, and (5) the theological synthesis of the doctrine of merit as it has been made by theologians since Trent.

Sacred Scripture. The positive theologian who carries out the task of investigating the revelation as it is found in the sources will look in vain for the word ''merit'' in Scripture, and he will find relatively rare instances of the use of this word by early ecclesiastical writers. A BIBLICAL THEOLOGY of merit can be formulated only from the ideas of merit. On the one hand, the reader of the Bible will note the gratuity of God's gifts to man, and on the other, he will see the promise of a reward that will be given for man's good works. These are the elements that served at a later date as the basis for that synthesis which the theologians call the doctrine of merit. It must be noted that these elements are not found together in the Scripture.

Old Testament. A history of the relations between God and Israel, the people whom He gratuitously chose for His own, is contained in the Old Testament. This history is in great measure a recital of the blessings that God bestowed upon this people as a reward for their fidelity to Him; it also makes clear that the punishments He imposed were occasioned by infidelity. What is most significant is that these rewards and punishments were in some way dependent upon the actions of Israel.

New Testament. The principal teaching of the New Testament is the doctrine that SALVATION has come for mankind through Jesus Christ. New Testament salvation is that which each man can share by accepting Christ's gratuitous invitation to His kingdom, the CHURCH. Salvation has a personal and a social dimension because salvation is for the individual man but it is accomplished in the Church.

In presenting the individual's role in attaining salvation, the Gospel writers make clear that Christ's kingdom is a free gift to men, but they also point out that in taking it from Israel of old, Christ intended to extend His kingdom to those who would yield the fruits of it. Numerous instances in the Gospel insist that a reward has been promised to man's works. For example, the Gospels attach the promise of a reward to love of enemies (Mt 5.46), almsgiving (Mt 6.1), forgiveness (Mt 6.15), fasting (Mt 6.18), faith (Lk 12.8), perseverance in face of persecution (Mt 13.18), and following Christ (Mt 11.29). This correlation between works and a reward is highlighted especially in the parable of the talents (Lk 19.11). There the gratuity of God's gifts and the notion that a reward is given for willingly using these gifts are placed side by side; and the parable suggests that God, in bestowing rewards, takes human efforts into account. It is valid to conclude that man's efforts to serve God have a value. The Gospel writers by their general reiteration that a man's work can deserve a reward thus provide the basic notion of the concept of merit.

In several Epistles St. Paul expresses the idea that God renders a reward for man's work and that the reason He does so is that He is just. The more significant of these passages are: ''God . . . will render to every man according to his works'' (Rom 2.6). ''For the rest, there is laid up for me a crown of justice, which the Lord, the just Judge, will give to me in that day'' (2 Tm 4.8). ''Now he who plants and he who waters are one, yet each will receive his own reward according to his labor'' (1 Cor 3.8). In each of these passages St. Paul indicates that the reward is given for the personal work of man. Objections have been raised against this position because of St. Paul's statement in Rom 6.22–23: ''the wages of sin is death, but the gift of God is life everlasting in Christ Jesus our Lord.'' The context of the passage indicates that just as the Romans have experienced the disorder arising from SIN, so now, since they have enrolled in the service of God, they will be able to realize the fruits of that service, life everlasting. The passage is not incompatible with the notion that life everlasting can be a reward as well as a gift.

Patristic Teaching. The writings of the Apostolic Fathers contain testimony to their belief that the works of the Christian are worthy of a reward. Yet this belief is not considered formally in any treatise on merit. In later patristic writings (Tertullian, *Apology* 1.28; Migne, *Patrologia Latina*, 1:435) one can find the term ''merit'' used in the precise sense in which it came to be used at a later date in theology. The concept of a reward given for man's work for which he has a title in some sort of justice can also be discerned throughout the patristic period (J. Rivière, *Dictionnaire de théologie catholique,* 10:612–661).

The classical writer on grace and its effects was St. AUGUSTINE. Much of his writing on grace was occasioned by Pelagianism, which was being successfully proposed during that period (*see* PELAGIUS AND PELAGIANISM). Augustine's viewpoint, therefore, stressed man's need for grace; his interest in merit was quite secondary. Since Pelagianism distorted man's capacities within the economy of salvation and unduly emphasized the value of his efforts, it is quite significant that Augustine did speak about man's works as being meritorious. Augustine always insisted that the first grace that a man receives is completely a gift (*see* FAITH, BEGINNING OF).

In support of this Augustine repeats with remarkable frequency St. Paul's question: ''Or what hast thou that thou hast not received?'' (1 Cor 4.7). He constantly reminded his readers and hearers that man is reborn not by his own efforts but by mercy, ''otherwise grace is no longer grace'' (Rom 11.6). Yet Augustine realized that when a man is justified, that is, when he has come to the position in which he can act from charity, then these works have a value, precisely because they are moved by charity. He stated very clearly that a man's works have a distinct value in the working out of salvation. Commenting on Phil 3.10, Augustine states that after death a man receives what his merits deserve and that when God then crowns a man's works, He is, in fact, crowning His own gifts (*Sermones* 170.10.10; *Patrologia Latina* 38:932).

The same two ideas are found also in Augustine's letter to Sixtus (*Epist.* 194.5.19; *Patrologia Latina* 33:880–1). In these instances Augustine is recognizing the reality of a reward attached to man's works and that the possibility of meriting is bestowed by God's gift. Augustine's repetition of the idea that the just Judge in crowning man's works, is crowning His own gifts is significant, because the expression not only insists that the works of man are rewarded but also shows that the fact that they can deserve a reward is due to God. By His Grace God has set up the economy within which meriting becomes possible. Since Augustine was a favored source for the reformers, his testimony regarding the existence of merit has a special value for those in the reformers' tradition.

Medieval Theologians. During the Middle Ages the theologians formulated a synthesis concerning merit. Peter Lombard was the first who treated of the doctrine at length; St. Bonaventure and Alexander of Hales, among others in the Franciscan tradition, did also. Although the varied schools agreed on the basic concept, that man's works, accomplished with divine assistance, are worthy of a reward, two medieval trends can be distinguished regarding the doctrine: the Thomist and the Scotist. St. Thomas taught that merit is a title based on justice. This title is rooted in the intrinsic JUSTIFICATION effected in a man by the coming of grace. If the justified man by a true exercise of secondary causality performs a good act, he deserves a reward. This is the economy that has been set up by God. According to Duns Scotus, justification gives to man's actions the motions of CHARITY by which these actions can become acceptable to God. Because these actions are accepted by God they are meritorious. It should be noted that the operation of charity is not the cause of God's accepting these works—but the movement of charity is the condition on which He accepts them. In keeping with his general approach, Duns Scotus attempted in his teaching on merit to emphasize the freedom of God's will.

Council of Trent. It was during the period of the rise of Protestantism that the doctrine of merit was definitively formulated at the Council of Trent (*see* TRENT, COUNCIL OF). This council did not set out to define the Catholic teaching on merit precisely, but the sixth session of the council (H. Denzinger, *Enchiridion symbolorum,* 1520–83) was devoted to the doctrine on justification, and the logic of the situation brought the Fathers of the council to consider merit.

Luther's Position. The doctrinal point from which Lutheran Protestantism started was Martin LUTHER's insistence that grace alone effected man's justification. When Luther was forced by the constant theological polemics of the period to define his position more exactly he came to link this assertion with the statement that grace can justify a man without effecting an intrinsic change in him. Thus, Lutheran justification became an extrinsic justification that is brought about by faith alone. It followed logically that Luther came to exclude the value of any works. Justification by grace alone already excludes value being attached to works done before justification; Luther's concept that faith alone is the source of continuing justification rendered all works after justification completely useless. In the face of this total rejection of man's works the council's examination of the value of man's work was unavoidable. Although the inner logic of Luther's concept of justification implied the total rejection of merit, there is surprising confusion among early Protestant divines about merit. Their opinions range from Philipp MELANCHTHON's refusal to reject the notion outright to John CALVIN's bitter attacks on those who use the term. This confusion was an added reason why Trent came to focus its attention on merit.

Ratisbon. The final reason why the members of the council were quite conscious of the doctrine of merit grew out of the ill-fated Conference of Ratisbon held in 1541. The conference was intended to make an attempt at religious unity. Cardinal Gasparo CONTARINI, the delegate of the pope to the conference, accepted a compromise that included an incomplete statement regarding the nature of justification and that deliberately omitted any reference to the concept of merit. This incident served to make some theologians conscious that the doctrine of justification must include teaching on the nature of merit.

Seripando and Laínez. The most significant section of the discussions on justification at Trent was directly concerned with the theory of double justice (*see* JUSTICE, DOUBLE). This theory was proposed by some theologians as the true doctrine of justification. In fact, it was a compromise position and one that destroyed the Catholic notion of justification. The principal proponent of this theory was Cardinal Girolamo SERIPANDO, and the theory was most effectively opposed by Diego Laínez, a Jesuit theologian. In a treatise that examined the whole question of justification, Laínez thoroughly criticized this theory of double justice and showed that in its ultimate dimensions it was incompatible with the traditional concept of merit. Thus, his speech contained an exposé of merit and included the following ideas: strict merit is based on a concept of justice; the source of the title to a reward arises from justice because meritorious actions come from the grace that truly transforms a man in justification; man's justification is intrinsic to him and makes him a new creature who becomes able to cooperate truly with divine assistance in performing meritorious acts.

Conciliar Doctrine. Chapter 16 of the Tridentine decree on justification deals specifically with merit, the fruit of justification. In the opening sentence of this chapter the Fathers of the council teach that merit is a valid concept that is based on the Scriptural teaching. They insist that the reward for the meritorious action is certain because God in His justice (*see* JUSTICE OF GOD) will not forget the promise He made to reward. Even though a man may sin after being justified and thereby lose his title to a reward, while he still lives there remains the possibility of the restoration of this title along with the grace he has lost by sin. The conciliar decree next states that merit must be proposed first as a grace, or a gift, and then as a reward given for good works. Herein the council implies two conditions for meriting: (1) God's willingness to accept man's works as worthy of a reward (implicit in the fact that God ordained the economy of meriting) and (2) the goodness of the meritorious act. The decree next specifies that the reward given will be truly a crown of justice. The man who is justified has all that he needs in order to be regarded as having fully satisfied the divine law and as having truly merited eternal life by his works.

The Fathers of the council explain that it is the activity of Christ on His members that supplies the basis for holding that the just man has all that he needs in order to be considered as having fully satisfied the divine law and truly merited eternal life. (It is interesting to note that the verb for merit employed here is *promereri,* by which theologians had ordinarily referred to condign merit.)

This influence of Christ is necessary and is such that it makes man's work pleasing and meritorious. Christ's influence precedes, accompanies, and follows the good act.

Many theologians after Trent believe that this description envisions the need for an actual grace to make an act meritorious, that there must be a special assistance given to a man to perform each meritorious act. The determination of the kind of special help was not detailed by the council. The Fathers describe the motivation that is to be found in the meriting subject by a general expression that they culled from Scripture. They are content to say that meritorious works must be those that are ''performed in God'' (Jn 3.21). Thus the council does not settle the question of the role of charity in the performing of meritorious acts.

The decree goes on to explain that meriting does not usurp the rights of God and does not excessively dignify man's actions. The Fathers insist that their understanding of justification makes clear the role of God, Christ, and man. When justice is given to a man it is truly in him and he can operate by it; this same justice is God's who has given it to men through Christ. This explanation shows that the Tridentine bishops conceive of merit as rooted in an intrinsic justification of which the meritorious act is the fruit. Although the justified man can merit, he must do so without overconfidence or a complete self-reliance, since he must recall that he merits only because God's goodness has so ordered things for him. In a note of warning the council teaches that man must look to final judgment with confidence in his merits since God will be faithful to His promise to reward; yet man must ever recall the severity of judgment and therefore not act presumptuously in living his life.

The last canon appended to the decree on justification also deals with merit. Here is found the Church's declaration that merit is a valid concept. The canon teaches that the meritorious action must be good, done through grace, and accomplished by a man who has been justified. Finally this canon states that a man can merit an increase of grace in this life, eternal life, the attaining of eternal life, and the increase of glory. The canon distinguishes between eternal life and the attaining of eternal life and thereby shows that a man's right to eternal life is always conditional while he is still alive. If he dies in the state of grace, however, man has an infallible right to come to eternal life. By mentioning the increase of glory as an object of merit, the canon implies the belief that there are degrees of heavenly beatitude. The degrees correspond to the degrees of merit attained in this life. Since glory is the full flowering of grace, it follows that where there is a greater degree of grace, there will be also a greater degree of glory.

After Trent. From the time of the Council of Trent, and in keeping with its teaching on merit, theologians have described the condignly meritorious act as a morally good act accomplished by a man in this life who is in the state of grace. This act is directed to God in some way. Since such an act must be moved somehow by love, theologians have discussed the influx of charity that would seem to be needed for a meritorious act. All agree that a more intense or a more perfect charity can achieve a greater reward. Since Trent deliberately avoided this question regarding the necessary influx of charity, however, the question has remained an open theological one.

Theologians have discussed also the question of how justice can be involved in meriting. Generally they hold to the Thomistic position that sees the presence of sanctifying grace as the foundation for the proportion existing between the meritorious act and the reward that man attains. Grace makes a man's acts proportionate to the reward, and thus it is the basis in justice for the concept of condign merit. The objects of merit have been studied in greater detail, and theologians generally have made explicit reference to the fact that a man cannot merit justification for himself, final perseverance, or repentance after a fall. Post-Tridentine theology has discussed also the question of the revival of merit after repentance for a fall. There is agreement that merit does revive but there are varying opinions regarding the degree of revival.

Moreover, theology recognizes congruent merit. This, too, is a title for reward but one that arises from the divine liberality. Since God's merciful providence has placed man in an order that looks to a SUPERNATURAL end and He has made the attaining of this end possible through the redemptive action of Christ, it is fitting that God's mercy should continue to operate in favor of the justified man who willingly serves God. Since the justified man is truly the adopted son of God, it is fitting that God's love continue to reward man's efforts to do good.

The justified man has an acquired intrinsic dignity, and God continues to act in a manner truly consonant with His nature when His liberality rewards the good acts of such a man. For this reason theologians hold that a man in grace can congruently merit special graces for himself. They also maintain that such a man can congruently merit a grace (even the grace of justification itself) for another man. This doctrine is basic to the understanding Catholics hold regarding the propriety of praying for another. Finally, a man who is in the state of sin cannot congruently merit the grace of repentance for himself—nor can he merit in behalf of another. The reason for maintaining this position is the fact that the loss of grace deprives a man of any basis for a title to God's liberality.

See Also: IMPUTATION OF JUSTICE AND MERIT; JUSTICE OF MEN; REVIVISCENCE OF MERIT; SALUTARY ACTS; SUPERNATURAL ORDER.

Bibliography: T. AQUINAS, *Summa theologiae* 1a2ae, 21.3–4; 114.1–10. P. DE LETTER, *De ratione meriti secundum sanctum Thomam* (Analecta Gregoriana 19; 1939). F. SUÁREZ, *In 1a2ae Summae theologiae S. Thomae, De gratia* 12:1–38 (Vivès ed. v. 10). J. RIVIÈRE, *Dictionnaire de théologie catholique,* ed. A. VACANT et al., 15 v. (Paris 1903–50) 10.1:574–785. H. QUILLIET, *Dictionnaire de théologie catholique,* ed. A. VACANT et al., 15 v. (Paris 1903–50) 3.1:1138–52. L. BILLOT, *De gratia Christi* (Rome 1954). ''Verdienst,'' *Lexikon für Theologie und Kirche,* ed. J. HOFER and K. RAHNER, 10 v. (2d, new ed. Freiburg 1957–65) v. 10. N. J. HEIN et al., *Die Religion in Geschichte und Gegenwart,* 7 v. (3d ed. Tübingen 1957–65) 6:1261–70. C. S. SULLIVAN, *Formulation of the Tridentine Doctrine on Merit* (Catholic University of America, Studies in Sacred Theology 2d ser. 116; Washington 1959). *Sacrae theologiae summa,* ed. FATHERS OF THE SOCIETY OF JESUS, PROFESSORS OF THE THEOLOGICAL FACULTIES IN SPAIN, 4 v. (4th ed. Madrid 1961) 3.3:329–352.

[C. S. SULLIVAN]

MERKELBACH, BENOÎT HENRI

Dominican moral theologian; b. Tongres, Belgium, Jan. 6, 1871; d. Louvain, July 25, 1942. He entered the diocesan seminary at Liège and was ordained in 1894. He continued his studies at the University of Louvain and received the licentiate in theology in 1898. He then acquired pastoral experience for seven years as a curate at Hasselt, after which he was recalled to Liège, where he taught dogmatic theology until he became a Dominican in 1917. He received the doctorate in theology at Liège in 1918 and then was assigned to teach moral and pastoral theology at the Dominican studium in Louvain. The master general called him to Rome in 1929 to teach at the Collegio Angelico, as it was then known, where he remained for seven years. In 1936 poor health forced him to return to Louvain, where he continued to teach until his death. Merkelbach wrote many articles for ecclesiastical journals on subjects in dogmatic, moral, and pastoral theology, as well as in sacred scripture. His best-known work, *Summa Theologiae Moralis,* was published in three volumes from 1931 to 1940. This work not only embodied Thomistic principles but also marked a departure from the casuistic method in moral theology and a return to that of St. Thomas. Merkelbach also had a deep interest in Mariology. He formed a pontifical commission, by order of the Holy See, to study the problem of the mediation of Mary in the economy of grace and produced many erudite studies in Marian doctrine. The most outstanding of these studies is *Mariologia: Tractatus de Beatissima Virgine Maria Matre Dei atque Deum inter et homines Mediatrice,* published in 1939.

Bibliography: G. M. VOSTÉ, *Analecta Sacri Ordinis Praedicatorum* 25 (1941–42) 258–262.

[C. LOZIER]

MERKS, THOMAS

Bishop of Carlisle; d. 1409. Merks joined the BENEDICTINE ORDER at WESTMINSTER ABBEY *c.* 1376, and he completed his doctoral studies in theology at the University of OXFORD by 1395. In 1397 he became bishop of CARLISLE by papal provision at the petition of Richard II. He was translated *in partes infidelium* by BONIFACE IX in 1399, was made rector of Todenham, Worcestershire, in 1404, and was granted papal indult on May 31, 1404, for ten years to let his rectory, Sturminster Marshall in Dorset, to farm while he was engaged in study at a university or in service of a prelate or resident at the Roman Curia. In 1404 Merks served as assistant bishop for one year in Winchester, and in 1406 he opened the convocation of Canterbury as the archbishop's commissary. At Lucca, in 1408, he sided against the pope, and he was present at the Council of PISA shortly before his death.

His royal service began when he attached himself to Richard II's Irish expedition in 1394, served the king on diplomatic missions, and was with him in Ireland again in 1399. In the assembly in Westminster Hall (Sept. 30, 1399) he pronounced a defense of Richard II against the general competence of the lords to judge the king, and he lodged a protest against their special iniquity in judging him in his absence. He was accused in a plot against the new King Henry IV (d. 1413) and was held in custody for a while, but he was eventually pardoned and released on bail. Merks was the author of a treatise *De moderno dictamine.*

Bibliography: A. STEEL, *Richard II* (Cambridge, Eng. 1941; repr. 1963). E. CURTIS, ed., *Richard II in Ireland,* 1394–95 (Oxford 1927). N. DENHOLM-YOUNG, ''The Cursus in England,'' *Oxford Essays in Medieval History, Presented to H. E. Salter,* ed. F. M. POWICKE (Oxford 1934) 68–103. A. B. EMDEN, *A Biographical Register of the University of Oxford to A. D. 1500* (Oxford 1957–59) 1263–64. J. TAIT, *The Dictionary of National Biography from the Earliest Times to 1900* (London 1885–1900) 13:282–285.

[V. MUDROCH]

MERLEAU-PONTY, MAURICE

French phenomenologist, professor of philosophy at the Collège de France; b. Rochefort-sur-mer (Charente-Maritime), March 14, 1908; d. Paris, May 3, 1961. Of Catholic origin, Merleau-Ponty was admitted to the École Normale Supérieure in 1926. After receiving his doctorate from the Sorbonne in 1945, he taught at the University of Lyons and the Sorbonne (1949–52) until his nomination to the Collège de France. Although not a philosophical theist, Merleau-Ponty requested and received a religious burial service, an indication that he remained open on the question of personal religious belief. Situated within the movement most accurately designated as existential PHENOMENOLOGY, Merleau-Ponty's thought manifests affinities with the work of J. P. Sartre, M. Heidegger, and G. Marcel (*see* EXISTENTIALISM). E. HUSSERL, especially of the late period, remains the principal philosophical influence; G. W. F. HEGEL was a significant but less dominant source. Committed to phenomenology as the philosophical method that would permit surpassing the subject-object, idealism-realism dichotomy of modern philosophy, Merleau-Ponty developed and transformed the phenomenology of Husserl into a more concrete and realistic philosophy. His major works consist of (1) detailed critical analyses of the sciences of man as well as of the classical modern rationalist philosophers and (2) an elucidation of the basic structures of human existence based upon man's immediate experience of the world, others, and himself. Later works develop his thought in the areas of aesthetics, political philosophy, and philosophy of history.

Bibliography: Works. *The Structure of Behavior,* tr. A. L. FISHER (Boston 1963); *The Phenomenology of Perception,* tr. C. SMITH (New York 1962); *Humanisme et terreur* (Paris 1947); *In Praise of Philosophy,* tr. J. WILD and J. M. EDIE (Evanston, Ill. 1963); *Les Aventures de la dialectique* (Paris 1955); Signs, tr. R. C. MCCLEARY (Evanston 1964); *Sense and Non-Sense,* tr. H. L. and P. A. DREYFUS (Evanston 1964); *The Primacy of Perception and Other Essays,* ed. J. M. EDIE (Evanston 1964). Literature. A. DE WAELHENS, *Une Philosophie de l'ambiguïté: L'Existentialisme de Maurice Merleau-Ponty* (Louvain 1951). A. DONDEYNE, *Contemporary European Thought and Christian Faith,* tr. E. MCMULLIN and J. BURNHEIM (Pittsburgh 1958). H. SPIECELBERG, *The Phenomenological Movement,* 2 v. (The Hague 1960).

[A. L. FISHER]

MERLINI, GIOVANNI

Moderator general of the Society of the Most PRECIOUS BLOOD; b. Spoleto, Italy, Aug. 28, 1795; d. Rome, Jan. 12, 1873. In 1820, two years after his ordination, he was received by St. Gaspare del BUFALO into the society, founded five years previously. As a preacher of missions Merlini gained so much renown that he was given charge of the more difficult ones. From 1847 until his death he served as the congregation's third moderator general. During his tenure of office, which coincided with a disturbed period in history, the institute expanded in the U.S., spread to Germany, and maintained itself well in Italy. At Merlini's suggestion, Pius IX extended (1849) to the universal Church the feast of the Most Precious Blood (July 1). Merlini was the spiritual director of Bl. Maria de MATTIAS from her youth and was her guide and ecclesiastical superior in the founding and direction of the Sisters Adorers of the Most Precious Blood. Among the many others who sought Merlini's spiritual counsel was Princess Adelaide Wolkonska, a convert and the mother of the Russian ambassador to Naples. Humility, meekness, and charity were prominent among Merlini's virtues. His remains rest in the society's church of S. Maria in Trivio, Rome. The decree introducing his cause for beatification was issued in 1927.

Bibliography: E. RIZZOLI, *Biografia del Servo di Dio Don Giovanni Merlini* (privately printed; 2d ed. Rome 1915). *Acta Apostolicae Sedis* 19 (1927), 143–146. J. N. MÜLLER, *Lexikon für Theologie und Kirche,* ed. J. HOFER and K. RAHNER, 10 v. (2d, new ed. Freiburg 1957–65) 7:310.

[A. J. POLLACK]

MERMILLOD, GASPARD

Swiss cardinal and pioneer in modern Catholic social movements; b. Carouge, Switzerland, Sept. 22, 1824; d. Rome, Feb. 23, 1892. After studies at the Jesuit college at Fribourg and ordination in 1847, Mermillod served as a curate in Geneva where he established two periodicals, *Les Annales Catholiques* and *L'Observateur Catholique* (1856–67). In 1857 he was appointed pastor of the city and vicar-general to the bishop of Lausanne for the canton of Geneva. He built the church of Notre Dame at Geneva between 1851 and 1859 with funds subscribed from all parts of Christendom. In 1864 he was consecrated titular bishop of Hebron and auxiliary bishop of Lausanne for the canton of Geneva. During his first seven years as bishop he was especially active in the cause of Catholic education, founding with Maria Salesia Chappuis the female Oblates of St. Francis of Sales at Troyes for the protection of poor working girls.

When the Holy See made him independent administrator of Geneva (1870), the radical government of the canton protested. A long and serious conflict ensued. Mermillod was at first forbidden to exercise any episcopal functions whatever and later was declared deposed even as a parish priest. When the bishop of Lausanne renounced unconditionally the title of Geneva and Mermillod was appointed vicar apostolic (1873), he was exiled from Switzerland. He repaired across Lake Geneva to Ferney in France, whence he governed his diocese as best he could. At the cessation of the religious conflict Leo XIII made the newly elected bishop of Lausanne bishop of Geneva as well, without, however, depriving Mermillod of his office. The government did not alter its tactics, and Mermillod was able to return to Switzerland only after he succeeded to the Diocese of Lausanne (1883). The conflict was by no means ended even then, for the canton of Geneva refused to recognize him as bishop, and normal relations were resumed only when he become a cardinal (1890).

Mermillod was one of the great preachers of modern times. In his far-sighted policy he founded, in 1885, the Union catholique d' études sociales et économiques (Union de Fribourg) that held international conferences on the social question and prepared the way for the encyclical *RERUM NOVARUM*. His *Lettres à un protestant sur l'autorité de l'Église et le schisme* (Paris 1859) made a great impression. Another important work was his *De la Vie surnaturelle dans les âmes* (Paris and Lyons 1865).

Bibliography: *Oeuvres,* ed. A. GROSPELLIER, 3 v. (Lyon 1893–94). J. T. DE BELLOC, *Le Cardinal Mermillod, sa vie, ses oeuvres et son apostolat* (Fribourg 1892). C. MASSARD, *L'Oeuvre sociale du card. Mermillod* (Louvain 1914).

[C. J. NUESSE]

MÉRODE, FRÉDÉRIC GHISLAIN DE

Archbishop, minister of war, and almoner of Pius IX; b. Brussels, March 20, 1820; d. Rome, July 10, 1874. Of noble birth, he studied classics at Namur, and military science at Brussels. After distinguishing himself for bravery as a soldier in Algiers (1844–45), he studied for the priesthood at the Roman College (1847–49). When Pius IX's prime minister Pellegrino ROSSI, was assassinated (Nov. 16, 1848), Mérode, with his usual impetuosity, doffed his cassock and hurried to the Quirinal with pistols at his hip to defend the beleaguered pope. When Pius IX returned from Gaeta (April 12, 1850), he learned of Mérode's loyalty and made him his chamberlain on active duty. An extraordinarily close friendship developed between the refined, handsome Italian pope and the gigantically tall, somewhat blustering Belgian soldier and priest. Pius IX took him on all his journeys through the STATES OF THE CHURCH. Mérode was the one who induced the pope to build an army, and to put Lamoricière in charge (*see* ZOUAVES, PAPAL). As war minister, Mérode was ever at odds with Cardinal ANTONELLI, the secretary of state, who preferred diplomacy to arms. The populace blamed Mérode for all the military reverses in the conflicts with the emerging Kingdom of Italy. Pressure became so strong that Pius IX reluctantly asked for his resignation (Oct. 6, 1865). Mérode then became papal almoner. He was consecrated titular archbishop of Melitene (June 22, 1866). Until 1870 he enlarged and modernized the streets of Rome and introduced agricultural reforms. Thereafter he devoted himself exclusively to charitable causes. His character was a mixture of romantic dreamer, ascetical monk, cavalier soldier, and outspoken counselor.

Bibliography: L. BESSON, *Frederick Francis Xavier de Mérode,* tr. LADY HERBERT (London 1887). T. J. LAMY, *Monseigneur de Mérode* (Brussels 1875). R. Aubert, ''Mgr. de Mérode, ministre de guerre sous Pie IX,'' *Revue générale Belge* 126 (May–June 1956) 1120–43, 1316–34; ''La Chute de Mgr. de Mérode,'' *Rivista di storia della Chiesa in Italia* 9 (1955) 331–392.

[W. H. PETERS]

MEROVINGIANS

A family of Frankish origin which established an extensive kingdom in Gaul during the late 5th and early 6th centuries over which the family ruled until 751. The Merovingian dynasty drew its name from Merovech, a semi-legendary chieftain of the Salian Franks during the period in the mid-5th century that witnessed the rise of that branch of the larger Frankish people to prominence in northern Gaul between the lower Rhine and the Somme rivers.

Clovis I. The real founder of the dynasty was CLOVIS (ruled 481 or 482–511), grandson of Merovech, whose succession as leader of the Salian Franks was by right of blood, giving to the heirs of Merovech a sacral position, which served them well in terms of retaining the allegiance of their subjects. But Clovis also owed much to the advantages his predecessors had gained as allies serving the Roman imperial government in its efforts to retain its hold over northern Gaul. Clovis made his mark chiefly as a successful warlord who won a series of victories over various rivals: over Syagrius, a general who was the last to claim to represent Roman imperial authority in northern Gaul; over the Alemanni, Germanic rivals of the Franks; over the VISIGOTHS, another Germanic people already established as rulers of southern Gaul and Spain; and over the chieftains of other Frankish tribes who were rivals of the Salians. These triumphs made Clovis the sole ruler over the kingdom of the Franks, which by his death in 511 embraced most of Gaul as well as an important foothold east of the Rhine and which was generally recognized as a major power in the western part of the old Roman Empire.

Clovis was more than a successful, albeit brutal warrior king. Although the extent of Frankish settlement in Gaul remains an open question, there seems little doubt that there were few Frankish settlers compared to the indigenous population and that the heaviest Frankish settlements were between the Seine and the Rhine. Their numerical inferiority made their rule of a vast realm inhabited by non-Franks difficult. Without ever abandoning the use of force as an instrument of power, Clovis took important steps to establish the effective institutional foundations that allowed his family to rule the Frankish kingdom for more than two centuries and to play an important role in shaping the future course of western European history. His conversion to orthodox Christianity, the religion of most of the people occupying the territory he conquered, was a decisive factor in making his regime acceptable. His decision meant that he repudiated ARIANISM, a version of Christianity adhered to by his rival Germanic kings but viewed as heretical by most of his Gallo-Roman subjects; his championing of orthodoxy was especially important in rallying the Gallic episcopacy to the support of his regime. In organizing the administration of his vastly enlarged kingdom Clovis left intact a wide array of Roman administrative structures and practices concerned with justice, taxation, and law enforcement. As a consequence, the establishment of the new ruling regime meant little change for much of the population of the kingdom of the Franks. From the beginning of his reign Clovis drew Gallo-Romans into service in his army and his political administration. He thereby provided a setting in which the assimilation of the conquering Franks and the conquered Gallo-Romans, especially the elite Gallo-Romans, rapidly took shape. The vast amount of land that his conquests put at his disposal allowed Clovis to reward his Frankish followers with grants of land that turned them into major landholders whose economic interests and lifestyles were increasingly similar to those of the indigenous aristocracy of Gaul. These measures marked a major step in making Clovis king of all who lived in Francia rather than being merely king of the Salian Franks.

Power Struggles after the Death of Clovis. After Clovis' death in 511, his kingdom was divided among his four sons, each being awarded a portion of the territory between the Rhine and Loire which constituted the heartland of kingdom of the Franks along with an important city in that territory as a capital (Paris, Soissons, Orleans, and Reims), and each was assigned a portion of Frankish holdings south of the Loire in Aquitaine. This division was dictated in part by Germanic custom which provided that each surviving male should receive a share of a father's patrimony while maintaining that that patrimony, that is, the kingdom, remained an entity belonging to the family. No less important in shaping the division were the concerns of Clovis' queen, Chlotilde, who was anxious to protect the interests of her three sons by Clovis against the ambitions of an older and more experienced son of Clovis by a concubine. This practice of dividing the kingdom among royal heirs became the source of endless intrigue and frequent bloody strife among members of the Merovingian family and their followers, who were trying to take advantage of their kinsmen to gain a larger share

Clovis, King of the Franks, leading his men into battle. (©Bettmann/CORBIS.)

of the kingdom of the Franks. The baneful effect of such civil strife was somewhat veiled during the reigns of Clovis' sons, the last of whom died in 561. It was muted by the continuation of Frankish expansion and the policy of assimilation begun by Clovis. Working together and separately, his sons solidified Frankish control in Aquitaine, added the realm of the Thuringians, the kingdom of Burgundy, Provence, and Rhaetia to the kingdom of the Franks. They also conducted raids into Spain, the land of the Saxons, and Italy that produced booty and tribute. By 561 the kingdom of the Franks under the Merovingians reached its greatest size and the zenith of its standing in the western part of the empire once ruled by the Romans.

In 561 the kingdom, briefly united under Clovis' last surviving son, Chlothar I, was again divided among his four sons. The next half-century witnessed a succession of savage struggles for power. The causes of these struggles were multiple: the ambitions of individual kings; the need of rival Merovingian family members to prove on the battlefield their suitability for kingship; the never-sated urge of members of the royal family to fill their coffers with booty to reward their followers; the unexpected death of kings, often at the hands of assassins, leaving a power vacuum that stoked the ambitions of royal relatives; muddied rights of succession brought about by serial marriages of the kings; the intrigues of aristocratic families seeking to win royal favor or to escape from rulers attempting to limit aristocratic privilege; and the ambitions of queens, especially widowed queens, to assure the well-being of their offspring. As the family rivalry and successive partitions of the kingdom unfolded, a division of the kingdom into three distinct entities began to take shape: Austrasia, in the northeast centered between the valleys of the Meuse and the Rhine rivers and including Alemannia and Thuringia east of the Rhine; Neustria, the northwestern region of the kingdom centered in the Seine valley and extending to the Loire on the south and the borders of Austrasia on the north and east; and Burgundy, located in the valleys of the Saôn and the Rhône rivers. Peripheral territories, such as Aquitaine, Provence, and Bavaria sought to elude Frankish control without ever being totally successful. Some of the most violent chapters in this phase of Merovingian history were stoked by a rivalry that pitted Brunhilde (d. 613), a Visigothic princess who was the wife, mother, and grandmother of a succession of kings ruling over Austrasia and for a time Burgundy, against Fredegund (d. 597), consort and mother of successive kings of Neustria. This violent chapter in Merovingian history finally ended with an uprising of the aristocracy of Austrasia which resulted in gruesome murder of Brunhilde in 613. That revolt was triggered in part by Brunhilde's effort to institute measures aimed at curbing the steady growth of aristocratic power at the expense of royal authority, a development that was a major consequence of a half-century of strife within the royal family.

With the elimination in 613 of Brunhilde and her grandsons as rulers of Austrasia and Burgundy, the entire Frankish kingdom was reunited under Chlothar II, a son of Fredegund, who had ruled in Neustria since 584, and his son, Dagobert I (629–638). During this quarter century of relative peace the Merovingian dynasty reached its apogee. Chlothar recognized that the local power of aristocratic families had expanded to the point where they played a decisive role in the governance of the kingdom and that their support was crucial to royal authority. He sought to regularize relationships between crown and nobles by issuing an edict in 614 that made important concessions to the nobles in terms of controlling appointments of local officials while clarifying the sphere of royal authority. Chlothar II and Dagobert I encouraged members of aristocratic families to come to the royal court, increasingly fixed at Paris, where they could be educated for royal office and earn rewards resulting from personal ties with the king. They could also make contacts with other aristocrats and fashion marriage alliances that would enhance family fortunes. The rulers increased their reliance on bishops and abbots as agents of royal power, a policy that involved royal control over appointments to those offices and grants of immunity, which freed church property from royal control. Their religious policy gave increasing weight to religious ideas as the ideological underpinning of monarchy that had earlier emphasized a warrior ethos.

The Rise of Aristocratic Families. Upon the death of Dagobert I in 639 the kingdom of the Franks was divided between his two sons; one ruled over Neustria and Burgundy, and the other reigned in Austrasia. Although men of some ability, they were unable to contain the seemingly irresistible advance of the local aristocratic families toward control of Gaul. The kings became ''do-nothing kings'' (*rois fainéants*), living dissolute lives and often dying young, sometimes as victims of assassins. Real power in the kingdom of the Franks was increasingly wielded by aristocratic factions, especially those led by one of the chief officials in each of the royal courts, the mayor of the palace. He utilized the wealth and prestige attached to that office to form extensive followings powerful enough to threaten royal power and rival aristocratic families. These factions and their leaders were not interested in ending Merovingian rule. Rather, they sought to control the royal office and its resources as a means of expanding and enriching their local bases of power. The violent rivalry among these factions finally culminated in 687, when an Austrasian faction, led by Pepin II of Herstal, won a decisive victory over a Neustrian force in a battle at Tertry. Pepin II counted among his ancestors a certain ARNULF (d. 643/647), a rich aristocrat who served many years in the Austrasian royal court and then became bishop of Metz, and Pepin I of Landen (d. 640), likewise a descendant of a powerful family who served the Austrasian king as mayor of the palace and used that office to increase his wealth and expand his circle of followers. These two men collaborated in bringing about the downfall of Queen Brunhilde in 613. The position of this dynasty, known variously as the Arnulfings or the Pippinids or eventually the CAROLINGIANS, was greatly strengthened by the marriage of Arnulf's son to Pepin I's daughter. Their son, Pepin II, was the victor at Tertry.

Decline of the Merovingians. Pepin II's victory at Tertry marked a turning point in the history of the Merovingian dynasty, setting it on a path toward its end. Pepin II assumed control of the office of mayor of the palace in Austrasia, Neustria, and Burgundy, thereby beginning a *de facto* reunification of the kingdom of the Franks. It was still theoretically ruled by Merovingian kings, but it was coming increasingly under Pepin's control. He was able to contain the resistance to his domination that still existed, and his cause was helped by the good will still enjoyed by the ''long-haired kings'' whom he claimed to serve. At his death in 714 the dominant position he had established was briefly threatened by efforts of aristocrats in Neustria to escape Austrasian authority, by the Frisians who allied with the Neustrians to remove the threat of Pippinid expansion, and by a quarrel within Pepin II's family over succession. The victor was his illegitimate son, Charles, later dubbed Martel (the Hammer), who until his death in 741 utilized his position as mayor of the palace, serving the Merovingian kings but also using them to overcome internal opposition. He reestablished control over Burgundians, Alemanni, Thuringians, and Aquitainians, all of whom had enjoyed some success in escaping Frankish control. He also won a victory over Muslim invaders of Gaul at a battle near Poitiers in 732 that led some to hail him as the savior of Christendom. Although CHARLES MARTEL left the Merovingian throne vacant after 737, his heirs as joint mayors of the palace, PEPIN III the Short and CARLOMAN, sought to fortify their position among the Frankish aristocracy by arranging the selection of a member of the Merovingian dynasty as king in 743. A few years later Pepin III, who became sole mayor of the palace after the retreat of Carloman to monastic life, turned to Pope STEPHEN II to ask whether or not it was right that he who had no power should enjoy the title of king. A response from the pope indicating that he who held power should be king emboldened Pepin in 751 to request and receive from his magnates election as king of the Franks. Once elected Pepin III deposed the last Merovingian, Childeric III.

The Significance of the Merovingian Dynasty. The Merovingian dynasty has not enjoyed a good reputation over the centuries; the period during which they ruled has repeatedly been described as the darkest of the Dark Ages. In part, they earned a bad name by their penchant for violence and treachery. In part, their reputation was blackened by Carolingian propagandists seeking to justify the usurpation of the Frankish crown by the dynasty that replaced the Merovingians. The dynasty had the misfortune to be center stage during an era when the territory and the population over which it ruled were suffering from the effects resulting from the transformation of the civilization of the Mediterranean world once ruled by the Romans. That tortured process witnessed long-term developments in western Europe that cast a shadow of failure over those involved: depopulation; the decline of urban life; the shrinking of trade; the onset of agricultural self-sufficiency; the fragmentation of political authority; the militarization of society; the depression of the lower classes of society into dependency; the barbarization of literary culture; the paganization of religious life; the vulgarization of manners.

When viewed from a perspective defined by this grim setting and when new evidence resulting from archeological investigations is taken into account, the history of the Merovingians does not seem quite so negative. Rather, the Merovingian epoch appears as a time of new beginnings which had major importance in relieving the stresses cause by the demise of Roman civilization and in shaping the future of Western Europe. As rulers the Merovingians created a political and social environment which promoted the assimilation of conquerors and conquered. That process resulted in the survival of vital elements of both pre-Merovingian Germanic and Roman cultures and the recombination of these survivals into political, legal, social, economic, and mental structures that provided the institutional framework for a new civilization based in northwestern Europe. Even in Merovingian times the vitality of the new structures was demonstrated by such things as slowly increasing population, land clearance, the renewal of cities as religious centers, the development of new trade routes linking northern Gaul, the British Isles, and Scandinavia, and the development of new technical skills, especially in metal-working. The Merovingian rulers pursued a policy that promoted the spread of a common form of Christianity as a unifying and stabilizing force in society. Their support of the episcopacy was crucial to the development of the internal organization of the Christian community and to the enhancement of that organization's capacity to enlarge its role in meeting the spiritual and material needs of the faithful, especially those living in an increasingly rural world. Their patronage of monasticism, especially that form introduced by the Irish monk, Columbanus, was crucial in expanding the role of that institution in converting pagans, defining new forms of piety, especially those appealing to the aristocracy increasingly rural in outlook, and encouraging the survival and renewal of Latin literary culture as an instrument for deepening the faith. When those facets of the history of the Merovingian dynasty are taken into account, it becomes obvious that the future history of Europe cannot be reconstructed without considering what happened during the two and a half centuries of Merovingian rule.

Bibliography: *Gregorii Episcopi Turonensis Historiarum Libri X*, ed. B. KRUSCH (Monumenta Germaniae Historica, Scriptores rerum Merowingicarum 1; Hannover 1937), English translation as *Gregory of Tours, History of the Franks,* trans, with intro. L. THORPE (Harmondsworth, Eng. 1974). *Chronicorum qui dicuntur Fredegarii Scholastici Liber IV cum continuationibus*, ed. B. KRUSCH (Monumenta Germaniae Historica, Scriptores rerum Merovingicarm 2; Hannover 1888) 1–214. *The Fourth Book of the Chronicle of Fredegar, with its Continuations*, trans. with intro. J. M. WALLACE-HADRILL (London 1960). *Liber historiae Francorum*, ed. B. KRUSCH, (Monumenta Germaniae Historica, Scriptores rerum Merovingicarm 2; Hannover 1888) 215–328, English translation as *Liber historiae Francorum*, trans. B. S. BACHRACH (Lawrence, Kans. 1973). *Capitularia Merowingica*, ed. A. BORETIUS (Monumenta Germanicae Historica, Leges, Sectio II: Capitularia regum Francorum 1; Hannover 1883) 1–23. *Concilia Galliae, A.511–A.695*, ed. C. DE CLERCQ (Corpus Christianorum, Series Latina 148A; Turnhout 1963). *Epistolae Merowingici et Karolini aevi*, vol. 1, ed. W. GUNDLACH and W. ARNDT (Monumenta Germaniae Historica, Epistolae 3; Berlin 1892) 110–213, 439–468. *Die Urkunden der Merowinger (Diplomata regum Francorum e stirpe Merovingia)*, ed. C. BRUHL, T. KÖLZER, M. HARTMANN, and A. STIELDORF (Monumenta Germaniae Historica, Diplomata; Hannover 2001). *Vita sanctorum generis regii*, ed. BRUNO KRUSCH, (Monumenta Germaniae Historica, Scriptores rerum Merowingicarum 2; Hannover 1888). *Passiones vitaeque sanctorum aevi merowingici et antiquiorum aliquot*, ed. B. KRUSCH and W. LEVISON (Scriptores rerum Merowingicarum 3–7; (Hannover 1896–1920; reprinted, 1984–1997). *Die Gesetze des Merowingerreiches 481–714*, vol. 1: *Pactus legis Salicae: Recensiones Merovingicae*, ed. K. A. ECKHARDT (Germanenrecht, Texte und Übersetzungen 1; Göttingen 1955). *Venantius Fortunatus, Personal and Political Peoms*, trans. with notes and intro. J. GEORGE (Translated Texts for Historians 23; Liverpool 1975).

[R. E. SULLIVAN]

MERRICK, MARY VIRGINIA

Social worker; b. Washington, D.C., Nov. 2, 1866; d. Washington, D.C., Jan. 10, 1955. Her father, Richard Merrick, a descendant of the Brents and Calverts of Maryland, was a lawyer, and her mother, Nannie McGuire, an Episcopalian convert. As a young girl, Mary Merrick was crippled; she spent the rest of her life confined to a bed and wheelchair. Cardinal James Gibbons gave permission, renewed by his successors, for Mass to be said for her wherever she might be. She was educated by a French governess, and translated two French books for children and wrote two other books, *Life of Christ* (1909) and *The Altar of God* (1920).

Her interest in the poor led to the founding in 1886 of the Christ Child Society, which provided clothing and gifts for children at Christmas. Later the society established a settlement house, a convalescent home, summer camps, a boys' club, and other services. From Washington, D.C., it spread to other cities where similar programs were developed. By 1955 there were 37 chapters and 12,000 members, with professional social workers directing many of the society's projects and volunteers giving extensive service. Until her death Merrick served as president of the society, enlisting the active cooperation of others interested in child welfare. She was awarded the Laetare medal (1915) by the University of Notre Dame, Ind., the Cosmopolitan Club medal (1933) for civic work, and the papal medal *Pro Ecclesia et Pontifice* (1937).

[D. A. MOHLER]

MERRY DEL VAL, RAFAEL

Cardinal, papal secretary of state (1903 to 1914); b. London, Oct. 10, 1865; d. Rome, Feb. 26, 1930. His father, a diplomat, was a Spanish marquis; his mother was English. After studies in England and Belgium, he entered the seminary at Ushaw, England, transferring (1885) to the Pontifical Scots College, Rome, and then, at the urging of Pope Leo XIII, to the Pontificia Accademia dei Nobili Ecclesiastici, where he was ordained (Dec. 30, 1888). Entering the papal diplomatic service, he was first named a chamberlain, and was then sent on missions to London, Berlin, and Vienna. Because of his competence and zeal for the conversion of England, he was asked to collaborate (1895–96) in the preparation of the apostolic letters *Amantissimae voluntatis* and *APOSTOLICAE CURAE*. He was also apostolic delegate to Canada (1897). From 1899 he presided over the Accademia dei Nobili Ecclesiastici. He became titular archbishop of Nicaea (1900). As secretary of the conclave (July 1903), he was commissioned to beg Cardinal Sarto not to refuse the papacy.

Pius X chose him pro-secretary of state immediately upon election, secretary of state (Oct. 18), and created him cardinal (Nov. 9). His distinction and lofty virtues attracted the pope, as did the diversity of his diplomatic and linguistic talents, which contrasted with and complemented Pius X's background. Thenceforth, he was the faithful executor of the decisions of Pius X, who was more self-willed than is sometimes realized. But Merry del Val remained to the end the pope's counselor. His personal rigidity and great influence with the pope made unlikely a lack of vigor in the conduct of the pontificate, especially in the affairs of the secretariate of state. Merry del Val has been reproached for his protest, addressed to Catholic governments, at the visit of the French President Loubet to the king of Italy in Rome (April 1904). Yet this note was no more vigorous than that in which Cardinal RAMPOLLA revealed (June 1903) to the Quai d'Orsay the grave implications of the ''offense'' given to the pope, despoiled of Rome and the states of the Church. Merry del Val's text was published in Paris (May 17) by the Socialist journal, *L'Humanité,* to which the prince of Monaco had mailed it. A violent campaign against the Roman note soon developed. Complaint was especially strong because the note had been sent to foreign chanceries and because this version contained a phrase (omitted from the text dispatched to Paris) judged unacceptable to France. As a result the French ambassador was recalled, and replaced for a short time by a chargé d'affaires. The secretary of state, however, actively supported the more conciliatory attitude of Pius X toward the Italian government. Despite the Irish problem, he maintained a good understanding with England. In 1914 he signed a concordat with Serbia. Merry del Val has been blamed for an extreme doctrinal rigorism, which led him to utilize Monsignor BENIGNI, head of Italian INTEGRALISM and founder of the SODALITIUM PIANUM. Yet the cardinal frequently strove to moderate Benigni, rousing the latter's open complaint.

Politically the influence of the secretary of state ended with the death of Pius X. Merry del Val also fulfilled diligently his duties of archpriest of Saint Peter's Basilica, secretary of the Holy Office, member of several Roman congregations, and papal legate to Assisi. He was buried, as he wished, in the grotto of St. Peter's Basilica at the foot of Pius X's tomb. At the request of the Spanish hierarchy, Pius XII authorized (Feb. 26, 1953) the opening of a process of information concerning his renown for sanctity.

Bibliography: R. MERRY DEL VAL, *Memories of Pope Pius X* (Westminster, Md. 1951). P. CENCI, *Il cardinale Raffaele Merry del Val* (Turin 1933), preface by E. PACELLI, later Pius XII. A. C. JEMOLO, *Church and State in Italy, 1850–1950,* tr. D. MOORE (Philadelphia 1961). F. A. M. FORBES, *Rafael, Cardinal Merry del Val* (London 1932). G. DAL-GAL, *Le Cardinal Merry del Val* (Paris 1955). C. LEDRÉ, "À propos de plusiers livres récents sur quelques aspects du gouvernement de Pie X," *Revue d'histoire de l'Église de France* 40 (1954) 249–267. H. MITCHELL, *Le Cardinal R. Merry del Val* (Paris 1956).

[C. LEDRÉ]

MERSCH, ÉMILE

Theologian; b. Marche, Belgium, July 30, 1890; d. Lenz, France, May 23, 1940. He entered the Society of Jesus in 1907. During his theological studies (1914–18) he began the long work that, with many other absorbing activities, was to occupy him until his premature death 23 years later: a synthesis of the doctrine of the MYSTICAL BODY OF CHRIST as the center of all the great Christian dogmas. As philosophy professor at Namur from 1920 to 1935, he assumed various intellectual and religious tasks at the college, at the diocesan seminary, and in the city itself. Among his philosophical works, *L'Obligation morale: Principe de liberté* (Louvain 1927) stands out. Mersch's religious influence was profound because of his human warmth and his ability to inspire others with his own ideals.

Before trying to construct the dogmatic synthesis of the doctrine of the Mystical Body, Mersch realized that a preliminary work based on scripture and patristic tradition was necessary. Lengthy research occupied all of his free time from 1920 to 1929, and he published in 1933 the two-volume *Le Corps mystique du Christ: Études de théologie historique* (Louvain). The book was an immediate success, not only among Catholics, but also in Protestant theological circles. This success necessitated a second (1936) and a third (1951) edition, and in 1938 the English translation, *The Whole Christ,* was published (Milwaukee).

Rafael Merry Del Val.

Mersch then returned to his initial plan, the theological synthesis of the doctrine of the Mystical Body. After his death three successive drafts were identified. While contributing many articles on this subject to various magazines (e.g., 24 articles in *Nouvelle Revue Théologique* from 1926 to 1940), he almost completed the third draft of his synthesis at Louvain (1935–40). He drew up a moral and ascetic synthesis parallel to the dogmatic synthesis: *Morale et corps mystique* appeared in 1937 [4th edition in 1951; English translation: *Morality and the Mystical Body* (New York 1939)].

In the beginning of May 1940, Mersch was forced by the events of war to leave Louvain for exile, having been given the task of looking out for the safety of several older fathers. He took with him the manuscript of the third draft of his dogmatic synthesis. His life ended in a series of acts of self-sacrifice. On May 23, 1940, in the presbytery of the French town of Lenz, in spite of the frequent bombardments, he offered to take relief to several wounded persons. In this act of charity he met death, a death probably preceded by a great sacrifice for him: uncertainty for two days about the fate of his manuscript, in which he had concentrated so much hope. His body was first buried in the cemetery of Lenz; after the war it was brought back to Namur.

The manuscript of the completed part of the third draft of his dogmatic synthesis was recovered. With the help of the two former drafts left by the author at Louvain and at Brussels, the work was reconstructed enough to remain the faithful expression of his whole thought. In July 1944, it appeared in two volumes under the title *Théologie du corps mystique* (Brussels) and is now in its 4th edition [English translation: *The Theology of the Mystical Body* (St. Louis 1951)].

Bibliography: J. LEVIE, ''Le Père Émile Mersch,'' in E. MERSCH, *Théologie du corps mystique,* 2 v. (Brussels 1944) 1:vii–xxxiii, with bibliography of Mersch's works. G. DEJAIFVE, '''La Théologie du corps mystique' du P. Ém. Mersch,'' *Nouvelle revue théologique* 67 (1945) 1016–24.

[J. LEVIE]

MERTEN, BLANDINA, BL.

Baptized Maria Magdalena, virgin of the Ursuline Sisters of Mount Calvary, Ahrweiler; b. July 10, 1883, Düppenweiler, Saarland, Germany; d. May 18, 1918, Trier, Rhineland Palatinate, Germany. Maria Magdalena was the ninth child of a peasant family. After she completed grammar school, a tutor helped her prepare (1898–99) for entrance to the teachers' college of Marienau bei Vallendar, where she studied from 1899 to 1902. After passing the licensing examination, she was a teacher in Oberthal, Saarland, then taught in Morscheid, Hunsrück (1903–07) and Großrosseln an der Saar (1907–08). A chance meeting with the Ursuline superior of Kalvarienberg, Ahrweiler, led to her entry into the order (April 22, 1908) and profession of temporary vows (Nov. 3, 1910). Thereafter she taught children in the order's schools at Saarbrücken and Trier. She professed her final vows in 1913 and contracted tuberculosis shortly thereafter. She endured her illness with resolute patience and remained committed to her teaching obligations until her death. On May 18, 1990, Sister Blandina's mortal remains were transferred to her new titular chapel, designed by Karl P. Böhr, in Trier's Saint Paulin cemetery. She was beatified by Pope John Paul II, Nov. 1, 1987.

Feast: May 18.

Bibliography: *L'Osservatore Romano,* Eng. ed. 47 (1987): 7–8. M. H. VISARIUS, *A Hidden Spouse of Our Lord: The Life of Sister Blandine Merten, Ursuline, Compiled from Recollections, Letters and Her Notes* (New York 1938).

[K. I. RABENSTEIN]

MERTON, THOMAS

Trappist monk, poet, and author; b. Jan. 31, 1915, Prades, France; d. Dec. 10, 1968, Bangkok, Thailand. The son of artists, his father, Owen Merton from New Zealand and his mother Ruth Jenkins Merton from America, Merton pursued his studies in Europe and America in literature, particularly in poetry, in which art he was first recognized and came to excel. Imbued with a strong social sense which led him simultaneously to espouse basic charity and to test an attraction to monasticism, he became a Catholic in 1938, and in 1941 entered the Trappist abbey of Our Lady of Gethsemani in Kentucky.

The publication of his autobiography, *The Seven Storey Mountain,* in 1948 brought him into international prominence. He began a series of writings on various spiritual subjects which was constantly to try his monastic vocation as they made him a famous celebrity. He was one of the first, and among the few in his time, to reemphasize the primary value of the contemplative life and to ground it in sound scholarship and social concern. Through his writings and example, he inspired and trained a generation of Christian contemplatives, not only in the Bernardian Cistercian tradition of strict monasticism with a watchful eye on the outside world, but also in the Carmelite tradition of St. John of the Cross. In his last years he lived out the same contradiction—a hermit yet one whose advice and friendship were sought by many great men, notably Jacques Maritain, a principal adviser of Pope Paul VI. As perhaps the most famous monk in the world at the time, and while investigating the ideologies and resources of Far Eastern spirituality, he died suddenly in Bangkok, at the first Pan-Asian Monastic Conference, an international congress on the future of monasticism, half a world away from the hermitage he had sought and found in Kentucky, and at the very height of his spiritual perception.

Merton's own works are numerous. Among the more significant are *Asian Journal* (New York 1972); *Conjectures of a Guilty Bystander* (Garden City 1968); *Faith and Violence* (South Bend 1968); *New Seeds of Contemplation* (New York 1972); *No Man Is an Island* (Garden City 1955); *Selected Poems* (Garden City 1967); *Seven Storey Mountain* (Garden City 1970); *The New Man* (New York 1981) and *The Climate of Monastic Prayer* (Kalamazoo, Mich. 1973).

Bibliography: J. FINLEY, *Merton's Palace of Nowhere: A Search for God through Awareness of the True Self* (Notre Dame, Ind. 1978). P. HART, ed. *The Message of Thomas Merton* (Kalamazoo, Mich. 1981). M. MOTT, *The Seven Mountains of Thomas Merton* (Boston 1984). M. B. PENNINGTON, *Thomas Merton Brother Monk: The Quest for True Freedom* (San Francisco 1987). W. H. SHANNON, *''Something of a Rebel'': Thomas Merton, His Life and Works: An Introduction* (Cincinnati, Ohio 1997). L. CUNNINGHAM,

Thomas Merton and the Monastic Vision (Grand Rapids, Mich. 1999). R. G. WALDRON, *Walking with Thomas Merton: Discovering His Poetry, Essays, and Journals* (New York 2001). For a convenient collection of extracts from Merton's principal writings, see *Thomas Merton: Essential Writings*, ed. C.M. BOCHEN (Maryknoll, N.Y. 2000)

[J. KRITZECK/EDS.]

MERULO, CLAUDIO

Renaissance organist and composer whose imaginative compositions initiated an independent literature for the organ; b. Correggio, Italy, April 8, 1533; d. Parma, May 4, 1604. His family name was Merlotti; he was known also as Claudio da Correggio. His career as organist began at the cathedral in Brescia in 1556. Thereafter he was second organist at St. Mark's, Venice (1557–66); first organist there (1566–82); and court organist at the Steccata (ducal) chapel in Parma (1584 on). He was an inspiring teacher, drawing students from all over Europe, and was also involved in organ building and, briefly, music publishing. Although he was a madrigalist of merit, his greater significance lies in his development of organ music. In particular by his use of alternating passages of technical virtuosity with passages of recitative quality or with quiet ricercar-like sections, he gave the toccata a more clearly defined character. His harmonies and passage work reveal much imagination and daring. In part 1 of *Il Transilvano* (1593), his pupil Girolamo Diruta (1550– ?) synthesizes current musical practice and especially Merulo's teachings regarding the aesthetic as well as the technical aspects of performance.

Bibliography: Modern eds. in several collections, e.g., L. TORCHI, ed., *L'arte musicale in Italia,* 7 v. (Milan 1897–1908) v. 1, 3; G. TAGLIAPIETRA, *Antologia di musica antica e moderna per pianoforte,* 18 v. in 14 (Milan 1931–32) v. 2; A. T. DAVISON and W. APEL, eds., *Historical Anthology of Music,* 2 v. (rev. ed. Cambridge, Mass. 1957) 1:168–170. A. CATELANI, *Memorie della vita e delle opere di Claudio Merulo* (Milan 1864; repr. 1931). A. EINSTEIN, *The Italian Madrigal,* tr. A. H. KRAPPE et al., 3 v. (Princeton N.J. 1949), *passim.* W. APEL, "The Early Development of the Organ Ricercar," *Musica Disciplina*, Yearbook of the History of Music, American Institute of Musicology, 3 (1949) 139–150. L. F. TAGLIAVINI, *Die Musik in Geschichte und Gegenwart,* ed. F. BLUME (Kassel-Basel 1949–) 9:139–143. J. R. STERNDALE BENNETT, *Grove's Dictionary of Music and Musicians,* ed. E. BLOM, 9 v. (5th ed. London 1954) 5:719–720. G. REESE, *Music in the Renaissance* (rev. ed. New York 1959). D. ARNOLD and T. W. BRIDGES, "Claudio Merulo," in *The New Grove Dictionary of Music and Musicians,* ed. S. SADIE, v. 12 (New York 1980) 193–194. R. A. EDWARDS, "Claudio Merulo: Servant of the State and Musical Entrepreneur in Later Sixteenth-Century Venice" (Ph.D. diss. Princeton University 1990). R. JUDD, *The Keyboard Works of Claudio Merulo: Organ Masses* (Neuhausen-Stuttgart 1991). D. KIEL, "The Madrigals of Claudio Merulo: An Edition of His 1566 and 1604 Books of Five-Voiced Madrigals with Commentary" (Ph.D. diss. North Texas State University 1979). D. M. RANDEL, ed., *The Harvard Biographical Dictionary of Music* (Cambridge, MA 1996) 581. M. C. TILTON, "The Influence of Psalm Tone and Mode on the Structure of the Phrygian Toccatas of Claudio Merulo," *Theoria: Historical Aspects of Music Theory,* 4 (1989) 106–122.

Thomas Merton.

[M. T. HYTREK]

MESCHLER, MORITZ

Jesuit spiritual writer; b. Brig (Switzerland), Sept. 16, 1830; d. Exaeten (Holland), Dec. 3, 1912. The religious training he received from his mother and a rigorous classical education under the Jesuits and Benedictines contributed to the formation of his robust and charming personality. He entered the Society of Jesus at the age of 20 and, after his ordination, filled various positions of trust: master of novices, provincial, assistant to the general, spiritual director, and writer. His spiritual doctrine, though rooted in revelation and developed according to solid theological principles, was the fruit of personal experience, keen observation and prolonged reflection during his years of religious life rather than the product of scientific research. His manner of presentation was clear, analytical, and systematic, yet graced with charm and richness of description. He conceived perfection as a height to be scaled—much like his native Alps—by heroic effort, with Christ as guide and source of strength, so that his doctrine revolved around two poles: the attractive force of Christ's humanity, and the need for earnest moral and intellectual effort. Though he predated the encyclicals *Mediator Dei* and *Mystici corporis* by 50 years, his spirituality was remarkably Christocentric and liturgically oriented. Among his best known works available in English are: *The Life of Jesus Christ* (Freiburg 1909) and *Three Fundamental Principles of the Spiritual Life* (2d ed. St. Louis, Mo. 1912).

Bibliography: N. SCHEID, *Pater Mortiz Meschler aus der Gesellschaft Jesu: Ein Lebensbild* (Freiburg 1925). L. KOCH, *Jesuiten-Lexikon: Die Gesellschaft Jesu einst und jetzt* (Paderborn 1934); photoduplicated with rev. and suppl., 2 v. (Louvain-Heverlee 1962) 1195–96.

[D. MARUCA]

MESHA INSCRIPTION

A 34–line inscription of King Mesha (Mesa) of Moab on a STELE of black basalt measuring 44 by 28 by 14 inches, discovered in 1868 at Dhībân (Old Testament, Dibon) in Transjordan, ancient Moab. While negotiations for its removal were going on, the local Bedouin, suspecting the value of the antiquity and hoping to command a higher price by selling each piece individually, smashed it into many pieces, but not before C. Clermont-Ganneau had secured a squeeze (facsimile impression) while it was still intact. Two large fragments and 18 small ones were recovered, and the missing portions were reconstructed from the squeeze; so that the inscription can be read in a fairly complete text. Since 1873 the stele has been in the Louvre.

The two letters missing from the name of King Mesha's father in the first line *kmš*— can be supplied from a fragment of an early Moabite inscription published by W. L. Reed and F. V. Winnett [*The Bulletin of the American Schools of Oriental Research* 172 (1964) 1–9], so that the full name reads *kmšyt.* The divine name Chemosh (Chamos) appears in Ugaritic as *kmṯ,* while *yt* figures among Ugaritic personal names.

Though scholars admit the close similarity of MOABITE to Biblical Hebrew, they do not agree on the precise terms in which to define it linguistically. Some label it a Canaanite dialect, just as Hebrew is a Canaanite dialect, while others prefer to term it a dialect of Hebrew, just as the Byblos Phoenician inscriptions are a dialect of Phoenician. Two respected scholars have even proposed that the text was composed by an Israelite captive, since the text itself states that Mesha employed Israelite prisoners in the construction of Qarḥoh (apparently a place in or near Dibon). There are, however, several features that set Moabite off from Hebrew, such as the masculine plural and dual ending in - *n,* as against Hebrew - *m;* the third person masculine singular suffix - *h* as against Hebrew - *ō;* so one is justified in using the term Moabite dialect.

After the dedication the account begins in line five with the statement that Chemosh was angry with his people and allowed Amri (Omri), King of Israel (876-869 B.C.), to subdue Moab. The text specifies that it was Amri who conquered northern Moab as far south as the Arnon, information that supplements 1 Kgs 16.21–28. When Amri's son succeeded to the throne, he too promised, ''I will humble Moab,'' but Mesha was successful in breaking Israel's strong hold over Moab so that ''Israel completely perished forever.'' Amri's son was Achab (Ahab: 8697–850), but 2 Kgs 1.1; 3.5 states that Moab took advantage of the confusion following the death of Achab to revolt. This apparently conflicting testimony can be resolved, it would seem, by interpreting line 8, *bnh,* usually ''his son,'' by ''his grandson,'' since *bn* can denote ''grandson'' (cf. Gn 29.5). Hence the successful Moabite revolt that the stele commemorates took place under Joram (Jehoram: 849-842). This is further sustained by 2 Kgs 3.3–27, which describes Joram's military campaign to crush the rebellious Moabites, a campaign that was successful until the Israelites were forced to retire when Mesha offered his eldest son as a sacrifice to Chemosh, a fact not mentioned in the inscription.

The text mentions ten place names in Israel and five in Moab, and shows that the practice of *ḥērem* or ban (anathema) was observed in Moab. It also states that Moab's subjection to Israel was the result of Chemosh's anger, and that there was a Yahweh sanctuary in NEBO.

Bibliography: G. A. COOKE, *A Text-Book of North-Semitic Inscriptions* (Oxford 1903) 1–14. W. F. ALBRIGHT, tr., J. B. PRITCHARD, *Ancient Near Eastern Texts Relating to the Old Testament* (2d, rev. ed., Princeton 1955), 320–321. A. H. VAN ZYL, *The Moabites* (Leiden 1960).

[M. J. DAHOOD]

MESINA, ANTONIA, BL.

Lay virgin martyr, member of Catholic Action; b. June 21, 1919, Orgosolo (near Nuora), Sardina, Italy; d. there May 17, 1935. Antonia Mesina, born into a poor and pious family in a small village, joined Catholic Action in 1934. While gathering wood with a companion near her home in May 1935, Antonia was assaulted by

Fertile Crescent, land between the Tigris and Euphrates Rivers in the Middle East. (©CORBIS)

a youth, Giovanni-Ignacio Catgui. Her friend ran for help as Catgui tried to rape Antonia. Enraged he attacked her with stones, brutally killing her. Pope John Paul II beatified her (Oct. 4, 1987) for her fidelity to purity and piety.

Feast: May 17.

Bibliography: V. SCHAUBER, *Pattloch Namenstagskalender*, ed. H. M. SCHINDLER (Augsburg 1994): 127. *Acta Apostolicae Sedis* (1987): 983. *L'Osservatore Romano,* English. edition, no. 40 (1987): 20.

[K. I. RABENSTEIN]

MESOPOTAMIA, ANCIENT

As the term is now used, Mesopotamia designates the land between the rivers Tigris and Euphrates extending from the Kurdish foothills in the north to the Persian Gulf in the south. The Greek term μεσοποτάμια, from which the English word is derived, was coined at the time of Alexander the Great to designate the part of Syria that lies between the Euphrates and the Tigris, or what would now be called northern Mesopotamia (Arrian, *Anabasis* 7.7.3). The Greeks, however, borrowed the term, in translated form, from the local Aramaic-speaking inhabitants, who called this region *bên naharîn* (between the rivers), as in the gloss on Gn 4.1 in the *Genesis Apocryphon* of Qumran. The Aramaic term probably goes back in turn to the Akkadian *bīrīt nārim,* literally ''between the river'' (in the singular), which designated the land within the western bend of the Euphrates, i.e., the far western part of the modern Jazireh of northern Iraq. That this Akkadian term referred to this very limited region seems certain from the fact that this region must be the same as the one that the Assyro-Babylonians called *māt bīrītim,* which lay to the east of *māt ebirtim* (literally ''the land on the other side''), i.e., the land across the river *(eber nārim)* from the viewpoint of the Assryo-Babylonians, the region to the west of the Euphrates. By a similar extension of meaning the Hebrew term *'ăram nahăraim,* Aram Naharaim (Gn 24.10), which originally referred only to northern Syria on both sides of the Euphrates (called *Naharin* by the Egyptians), was later used in regard to the land between the Euphrates and the Tigris.

The following sections of this article will consider ancient Mesopotamia in its geography, history, and religion.

Babylon Gate. (©Françoise de Mulder/CORBIS)

Bibliography: J. J. FINKELSTEIN, ''Mesopotamia,'' *Journal of Near Eastern Studies* 21 (1962) 73–92.

[L. F. HARTMAN]

GEOGRAPHY

Mesopotamia is the region that lies between the rivers Tigris and Euphrates and extends from the Kurdish foothills in the north to the Persian Gulf in the south. Beyond the rivers, the Mesopotamian plain is bordered by the steeply scarped Zagros Mountains to the east, and by the wastes of the Syro-Arabian desert to the west. Within this area, the terrain becomes progressively lower as one moves south, descending some 1,000 feet between the foothills and the steppes and swamplands of the south; to the lowering in altitude corresponds a decrease in rainfall: the uplands of the north receive orographic rain in sufficient quantity to support agriculture, but on the lower part of the plain the total annual rainfall does not exceed 6 to 8 inches, so that agriculture, throughout most of the area, is dependent on artificial irrigation. The climate varies greatly, ranging from 20 to 120 degrees with severe winter winds from the Armenian and Iranian highlands and a hot summer draught from the Persian Gulf.

The Euphrates, rising with the Tigris in the mountains of Armenia, proceeds at first in a westerly direction, but is deflected by the mountains of Taurus and Anti-Taurus toward the southeast, and is then joined by the Balikh and Khabur. The triangle of land formed by these rivers was thickly populated in antiquity, its most notable settlements being Carchemish (Charchamis) on the Euphrates and Haran on the upper Balikh. Though the Euphrates is not navigable for any great distance, its banks provided a central route of land travel to Syria, along which were situated the cities of Mari and, at a later period, DURA-EUROPOS.

The Tigris flows in a generally southeastern direction, first through the Kurdish hills and then, south of Mosul, into unbroken alluvial plains and is navigable from Diyarbekir in the north. On the Tigris, between the confluences of the Upper and Lower Zab with that river, lies the ancient city of ASSUR, the heartland of the Empire of ASSYRIA.

At present the two rivers converge to within 25 miles of one another near modern Baghdad, then flow apart, to join at Qurna and flow together, as the 68-mile-long Shatt el-Arab, to the Persian Gulf, 40 miles southeast of the city of Abadan, Iran. In ancient times, however, the two rivers reached the sea without joining, and the coastline was perhaps much farther north, probably near the ancient city of Eridu. The southern plain thus consisted of steppeland formed from alluvial soil, which, under extensive irrigation, was famed in antiquity for its agricultural productivity, though progressive soil salinization has reduced its productivity in modern times. This region was the cultural center of ancient Mesopotamia, with BABYLON and Sippar in its northern sector (Akkad), and NIPPUR, UR and URUK in the south (Sumer).

See Also: NINEVEH.

Bibliography: M. A. BEEK, *Atlas of Mesopotamia,* tr. D. R. WELSH (London 1962).

[R. I. CAPLICE]

HISTORY

Until the middle of the 19th century, when the first archeological excavations were made in Mesopotamia and its ancient cuneiform inscriptions deciphered, most of the books that treated of the history of human civilization began, after perhaps a few words about ancient Egypt, with an account of the Greeks and the Romans, as if civilization began with these. Although these latecomers on the scene of world history undoubtedly made original and extremely valuable contributions to the higher culture of the West, it is now known that they really owed much more than was previously thought to the high civilization of ancient Mesopotamia, which had a long, glorious history stretching back for at least 3 millenniums before the rise of Greece and Rome. This history will be outlined here as it was determined by the march of historical events whose center of interest generally lay first in Babylonia or southern Mesopotamia and then in Assyria or northern Mesopotamia.

Prehistoric Period. The first village settlements, of which one of the earliest has been found at Qal'at Jarmo east of Kirkuk in the hills of Kurdistan, go back to the Neolithic period (*c.* 5000–*c.* 4000 B.C.). In the following Chalcolithic period (*c.* 4000–*c.* 3000 B.C.) civilization properly so called was born in ancient Mesopotamia. Copper tools replaced stone ones; villages grew into towns and cities; the isolation of the past was abandoned in the course of far-flung trading expeditions; and writing was invented. In this period also, in the first half of the 4th millennium, the cultural center of gravity shifted to the south, where the earliest-known settlement was at Abū Shahrein, ancient Eridu, a short distance from the head of the Persian Gulf. The pottery discovered here is related to the potteries of Iran, Assyria, and central Mesopotamia and therefore would seem to indicate immigrations from different areas. Somewhat later there appeared the first great Babylonian culture, the Obeidian (named from Tell el Obeid, near Ur, where it was first found), characterized by its pottery painted in black, brown, and occasionally red, and by its gradually evolving monumental temple architecture. This culture was succeeded by the Warkan (named from Warka, the site of ancient Uruk), which, in its later phase, not only produced the earliest-known written documents, but also abounded in works of high artistic achievement both in sculpture and in the glyptic art as this was applied to the newly devised cylinder seal.

It is uncertain what people achieved this high cultural stage that came as early as *c.* 3000 B.C. The changes revealed by the excavations do not necessarily prove different immigrations; because of the continuity between the Obeidian and Warkan cultures some scholars believe that the achievements are to be attributed to one people, the Sumerians, although the presence of some Semites and other peoples is not denied. Other scholars argue that many of the names of the oldest cities cannot be explained from Sumerian, and therefore must have been founded by non-Sumerians; it is also claimed that within the Sumerian vocabulary a non-Sumerian stratum, or even several non-Sumerian strata, can be isolated, referring primarily to farming, gardening, brewing, pottery, leather work, and building. Suggestive, however, as these arguments may be, they should be subject to great caution, for modern knowledge of the written Sumerian language is still quite imperfect, and in these circumstances it is extremely dangerous to argue about a stage of the language some 500 years earlier. It can be stated, however, that the Sumerians were certainly in Babylonia *c.* 2900 B.C., almost certainly in the late Warka period, very probably in the earlier part; the Obeid period remains doubtful.

Three Sumerian statuettes of worshipers. (©David Lees/CORBIS)

Babylonia. Since northern Mesopotamia or Assyria played a predominant role in the history of ancient Mesopotamia only during the 1st millennium B.C., the whole history of southern Mesopotamia or Babylonia until its absorption into the Persian Empire will be treated here before the contemporaneous history of Assyria.

Early Dynastic Period. This period (*c.* 2800–2360) takes its name from the important political developments in these centuries. According to T. Jacobsen's reconstruction, the earliest political organization was a ''primitive democracy.'' Under the rule of the city god, who was the city's lord and owner, the city was organized in a type of theocratic socialism with actual sovereignty residing in the popular assembly. The assembly was convened in times of crisis; if the crisis was one of internal administration, a ''lord'' (Sumerian) was chosen who was qualified by his special gifts, but if the crisis came from without, a ''king'' (Sumerian lu-gal, literally ''big man'') was made military leader. This organization seems to have been extended to the principal cities of Sumer *c.* 2800 B.C., when they formed a league with its center at NIPPUR.

Statuette of a nude woman, 5800 B.C., Mesopotamian geometric abstract. (©Gianni Dagli Orti/CORBIS)

The crisis that led to this step was perhaps the threat of the Akkadians.

The seeds of stable monarchy lay in the temporary concession of power to the individual. The human tendency to retain power once gained was supported by the pressure of events. The large city walls of the Early Dynastic period prove that war or its threat had become chronic. The power of the individual was, therefore, perpetuated, and the dynastic principle emerged with a royal mythology, which derived the sovereign's power, not from the human assembly, but from divine choice. He was chief of a standing army recruited largely from his own servants and retainers. At home he built walls to protect the city, and temples to house the gods. He ensured the fertility of the land by building canals and overseeing the irrigation system; to the same purpose he acted as consort of the goddess of fertility in the rites of the sacred marriage. He administered justice, for which his power supplied the sanction. In the social reform of Urukagina of Lagash at the end of this period the king acted as the righter of wrongs and the protector of the weak, in whose favor he even set aside customary law. This role of the king became part of the royal ideology, reflected later in the reform decrees and legal codes of Ur-Nammu of Ur, Lipit-Ishtar of Isin, and Hammurabi and Ammi-ṣaduqa of Babylon (*see* LAW, ANCIENT NEAR-EASTERN).

For most of the Early Dynastic period the scope of this newly emerging power was regional, no one king being strong enough to extend his rule beyond rather narrow limits. One kingdom, however, that of Kish in northern Babylonia, did succeed, if only briefly, in establishing its hegemony over all of Sumer in the south and Akkad in the north of southern Mesopotamia. This became the ideal, and when from time to time some ruler achieved it, he called himself ''king of Kish.''

Dynasty of Akkad. The Early Dynastic period ended when Lugal-zaggesi of Umma, attempting a rule patterned on that of Kish, encountered the Semite, Sargon of Akkad (2360–2305 B.C.). The Semites were not new; earlier Sumerian texts from Lagash contain Semitic loanwords, and some earlier rulers hear Semitic names. The struggle was political, not racial, and the Semites won.

The most notable achievement of the Akkad Dynasty (2360–2180 B.C.) was the creation of the first world empire, and for this reason the Sargonids lived on in legend, not only in Sumerian and Akkadian, but also in Hurrian, Hittite, and Elamite. Sargon's rule eventually extended from the mountains of Iran across Syria to the shores of the Mediterranean. This universal sway, which lasted through the reign of his third successor, Naram-Sin (2280–2244 B.C.), was a hitherto unknown extension of political power. The achievement of the Akkad Dynasty must be considered one of the major events of history, because, as an ideal, it influenced the Neo-Assyrian rulers some 1,500 years later, and they in turn laid the foundations of the empires of the Neo-Babylonians, the Achaemenid Persians, and that of Alexander the Great, thus ultimately affecting Roman history.

The Akkadian yoke was oppressive, and rebellion was frequent, even in Sumer. When a severe famine struck and caused economic disaster, the empire crumbled, and Babylonia was invaded by the Gutians, mountaineers from the east, whose control brought a dark age to Babylonian history *c.* 2180–2082 B.C. This foreign domination, which was never complete, was terminated by a prince of Uruk, Utu-khegal, who drove out the Gutians.

Third Dynasty of Ur. Utu-khegal's victory paved the way for the rise of a new dynasty, the Third Dynasty of UR (*c.* 2060–1950). It was founded by Ur-Nammu, and introduced the conception of the bureaucratic state. Power was strongly centralized; local rulers called ensis, a title previously borne by native and independent dynasts, were appointed by the central authority. But they were completely stripped of military power, which was given to another royal appointee.

This period marked not only a resurgence of Sumerian political power but also a renaissance of Sumerian culture. Sculpture, architecture, and literature flourished, as is best known from the monuments of Gudea, a viceroy of Lagash under the last kings of the Third Dynasty of Ur. But Sumer was engulfed once more by Semites. In the 4th year of his reign, Shu-Sin, second last king of Ur, erected a wall and called it "That Which Keeps the Tidnu at a Distance." The Tidnu were western Semites or AMORRITES, seminomads moving along the edges of the desert, infiltrating into the cultivated areas in search of better pasture, but now massed in sufficient numbers to threaten the very existence of the state. Shu-Sin's successor, Ibi-Sin, mentions their incursions, and when the dynasty fell, partly because of the pressure of these attacks, it was these seminomads who gained control in many centers. In the city of Babylon under Sumu-abum *c.* 1830–1817 B.C. they founded a dynasty, the First Dynasty of Babylon, which a century later would produce the greatest and most famous of Babylonian rulers, Hammurabi. Other Amorrite dynasties were founded at Larsa, Eshnunna, and MARI.

Isin-Larsa Period. At the end of Ibi-Sin's reign famine and revolt broke out across the land, the Elamites to the east attacked and devastated Ur, and the King himself was carried into captivity. When the last Sumerian dynasty disappeared, two new dynasties rose, that of Isin (*c.* 1958–1733) founded by Ishbi-Erra, and that of Larsa (*c.* 1961–1699), founded by Naplanum. During most of this period Isin held the hegemony, but toward its end Larsa gained ascendancy. In general, however, the Isin-Larsa period was one of many petty kingdoms, often no larger than a city and its immediate environs.

First Dynasty of Babylon. The Isin-Larsa period and the First Dynasty of Babylon (*c.* 1830–1531 B.C.) were times of profound change in almost every area of life. Private property was greatly increased, but at the expense of the gods. This was part of a progressive secularization that radically altered the structure of the state. Not the temple and its god, but the royal palace and the king, became the center of the nation's life. New marriage customs, the replacement of Sumerian by Akkadian as the literary language, new syllabaries in the writing of Akkadian, and new types of personal names are a few indications of the transformation that Babylonia underwent in these 3 centuries.

Under HAMMURABI (HAMMURAPI; 1728–1686 B.C.) the First Dynasty of Babylon reached its apogee. Sumer and Akkad were reunited, and Babylonian arms gradually subdued Rim-Sin of Larsa in the south, Zimri-Lim of Mari on the middle Euphrates, and Ishme-Dagan of Assyria in the north. But already in the 9th year of Hammurabi's successor, Samsu-iluna (*c.* 1685–1648), the Babylonians were struggling with the Kassites or Cossaeans, a people from the mountains to the east, who were part of the vast ethnic movements of the 18th to the 16th century that would so profoundly change the entire ancient Near East. For more than a century the Kassites continued to press in, and in some areas probably achieved independence. When Mursili, the Hittite King (*c.* 1550–1530), raided Babylonia *c.* 1531 and the First Dynasty of Babylon came to an end with its last King, Samsu-ditanna (1561–1531), the Kassites had gained control over most of Babylonia.

Kassite Period. The Kassite period (*c.* 1531–1150) is obscure. The Kassite kings bore such strange names as Burnaburiash and Kadashman-Enlil, and they called Babylonia Karduniash. In the 14th century B.C. they corresponded with Egyptian and Hittite kings, and their country was still strong enough to play a part in the game of power politics. But it gradually receded more and more into the shadows. When Kassite rule ended in the late 12th century B.C., Babylon, for a brief period under Nabuchodonosor I of the Second Dynasty of Isin, regained something of its old power, which indirectly reached even into Assyria. But though the cultural prestige of Babylonia never waned, it was not until the late 7th century B.C. that its political power could be compared with the ancient glories of Sargon and Hammurabi.

Neo-Babylonian Period. Toward the end of the 2d millennium B.C. a new wave of Semites, this time Aramaic-speaking peoples, began to infiltrate from the north Arabian desert into all the lands of the Fertile Crescent. One group of these peoples, the Chal.deans, moved north from the western shores of the Persian Gulf and settled in southern Babylonia [*see* CHALDEANS (IN THE BIBLE)]. By the 8th century B.C. they had become fully assimilated in all things except language to the Babylonians, accepting their entire spiritual, intellectual, and material culture. Although the written language of Babylonia continued to be cuneiform Akkadian until the beginning of the Christian era, the spoken language gradually became Aramaic in the second half of the 1st millennium B.C.

A Chaldean prince, Nabopolasar, gained control of Babylon in 626 B.C. and established the New Babylonian dynasty. His son and successor NEBUCHADREZZAR II (605–561 B.C.) extended his father's conquests until his empire included not only all of Mesopotamia, but also Syria and Palestine. But the Chaldean dynasty collapsed under his fourth successor, NABU-NA'ID (NABONIDUS; 555–539 B.C.), and Babylon fell to the Persian, Cyrus the Great. Though under the Persian, and later under the Greek rulers, the Babylonian scribes went on copying the old texts, and the priests performed the old rituals, in 539

B.C. more than 3,000 years of Babylonian history effectively came to an end.

Assyria. The Assyrians first asserted themselves as an independent power when the Third Dynasty of Ur fell. Ilushumma claims that he brought freedom to the Akkadians in cities as far south as Ur, but the interpretation of freedom is uncertain, as is the date of Ilushumma's reign, which was probably around the beginning of the 19th century B.C. Assyria, however, was clearly no longer a vassal of Babylonia. In contrast with the new kingdoms of the south, Assyrian rulers in this period bore genuine Akkadian names; one of them was even called Sargon (Sharru-kin I) and in this name we should probably see a sense of continuity with the Akkadians of the past, which the newly arrived West Semites of Babylonia could not claim. In this same period, from Ilushumma to Sargon I, Assyrian trading colonies were located in Anatolia; their rich archives from Kultepe have been preserved in what are known as the Cappadocian Tablets.

However, when Assyria grew strong once more under Shamshi-Adad I (*c.* 1748–1716), it too was ruled by a West Semite, who, after ascending the Assyrian throne, overthrew the West Semitic dynasty at Mari and placed his son, Yasmakh-Adad, in control. With Shamshi-Adad's death, however, Assyrian power quickly disintegrated. Mari was lost to the earlier dynasty, and Ishme-Dagan, Shamshi-Adad's son and successor on the Assyrian throne, did not long resist the advances of Hammurabi, though the exact course of events is obscure.

Middle Assyrian Period. For more than three centuries Assyria lay prostrate, and her kings were vassals, first of Babylon, then of the new Mitanni kingdom to the northwest, which was largely Hurrian under Indo-Aryan rulers. But in the early 14th century B.C., while Mitanni grew weak under Hittite pressure from the west, Assyria began its move towards independence. By the time of Asshur-uballit I (1356–1321) Assyria became a power to be reckoned with, and for a brief period controlled even Babylonia. Under a succession of strong rulers the Hittites were fought along the Upper Euphrates until they collapsed (*c.* 1200 B.C.). This Assyrian revival culminated in the reign of Tukulti-Ninurta I (1233–1199), who conquered Babylon and transported the statue of Babylon's chief god, Marduk, to his new capital, Kar-Tukulti-Ninurta (modern Tulul el-'Aqir), near Assur (*see* NIMROD).

This humiliation of Babylon raised a problem that faced every strong Assyrian king and divided the political and religious forces of his nation: the policy to be adopted toward Babylon. So immense was Babylon's prestige that it could never be treated like any other vassal. To Assyria Babylon was what Greece was to Rome. A pro-Babylonian faction favored assimilation of Babylonian religion and culture; the opposition insisted on retaining specifically Assyrian traditions as an expression of Assyrian hegemony and destiny. Tukulti-Ninurta I belonged to the latter group, and his anti-Babylonian fanaticism probably led to his murder.

The next strong Assyrian ruler, Tiglath-Pileser I (1116–1078), faced a new threat, the ARAMAEANS. It is uncertain when they made their first appearance in history, but by the late 12th century B.C. they had established independent kingdoms in Syria and along the upper Euphrates. A measure of the danger that they constituted may be seen from the fact that Tiglath-Pileser I led his troops 27 times across the Euphrates to drive them back.

Neo-Assyrian Empire. After this strong monarch, who controlled Babylonia as a vassal and marched as far as the Mediterranean, Assyrian power waned once more until late in the 10th century B.C. But with Assurdan II (935–913) there began the countless marches and battles of the Assyrian army, commemorated in annals and on reliefs, with their unspeakable cruelty *ad gloriam dei Assur.* The Aramaeans between the Tigris and the Euphrates were completely subjugated. Assurnasirpal II (884–860) introduced the division of the kingdom into provinces, whose peoples were subjected to forced labor and heavy tribute. His successor, Shalmaneser III (859–825), extended Assyrian rule across the Euphrates despite the desperate opposition of various coalitions. It was to such a coalition of 12 kings that Ahab, King of Israel, belonged when the Assyrian forces were fought to a standstill at Qarqar in 853. But Shalmaneser returned in 848 and again in 845. Jehu, Ahab's murderer and successor, paid him tribute in 841, and on the Black Obelisk, now in the British Museum, he is depicted as paying homage to his Assyrian master. North Syria had now become part of the Assyrian kingdom.

After a period of inner conflicts, Tiglath-Pileser (Theglath-Phalasar) III (745–728) inaugurated a century of unequalled power. He was perhaps the greatest of Assyrian kings. Boldness and originality stamped his every action. He assumed direct power over Babylonia in an effort to resolve in his own person the ancient tension. He smashed the Urartu kingdom in the Armenian mountains and then drove southward. Menahem, King of Israel paid him tribute, an event recorded both in the Assyrian annals and in the Bible (2 Kings 15.19), where Tiglath-Pileser is called Phul, the name he took as king of Babylon. Galilee was annexed as a district of an Assyrian province. The revolt of Pekah, King of Israel, and Rezin, King of Damascus, provoked a large deportation of Israelites (2 Kgs 15.29); HOSEA was installed as King of Israel, and tribute was paid the Assyrian King by Ahab, King of Judah (2 Kings 16.7–10).

Tiglath-Pileser's successors strove to continue his policy, of which a major instrument was wholesale deportations to break down national loyalties. Samaria fell to Shalmaneser V (727–723), and Israel ceased as an independent kingdom in 722. Sargon II (722–706), after consolidating his precarious position at home—he was a usurper, who attempted to legitimize his position by assuming a proud and ancient name and by accusing his two predecessors of having neglected the interests of the national god—crushed a revolt in 720 and deported more than 27,000 Israelites. With his authority established in Syria and Palestine, Sargon directed his energies to the Babylonian rebellion led by Marduk-apal-iddina (Biblical Merodach-Baladan), who had seized the Babylonian throne with the help of the Elamites. In 709 Sargon entered Babylon as king and restored Babylonia to the Assyrian rule.

Sennacherib (705–682) is best known for his failure to conquer Jerusalem under Hezekiah in 701 (2 Kings 18.13–19.36). Probably he returned again after 689; the OT seems to combine two campaigns of Sennacherib, for it mentions Theraca (Tirhaka), King of Egypt (1 Kgs 19.9), who did not come to the Egyptian throne until 689.

Sennacherib's anti-Babylonian fanaticism was so ardent that he razed Babylon to the ground and, like Tukulti-Ninurta before him, carried off the statue of Marduk to Assur. His son, Esarhaddon (680–699), who succeeded his murdered father, atoned for this sacrilege by restoring Babylon, and Assurbanipal (668–627) returned the statue.

Under these two kings Assyrian power reached into Egypt. But Assurbanipal had to fight desperately for 4 years against a new Babylonian rebellion led by his brother with the support of Aramaean and Chaldean states in the south, of the Elamites to the east, and of Gyges of Lydia to the west. His victory was costly, even fatal, for in destroying the Elamites he removed the last effective barrier against a new and formidable power, the MEDES. It was to be the Medes who, when Assurbanipal died and revolt swept across the Assyrian empire (see 2 Kgs 23.19–23), would contribute most to Assyria's downfall. The city of Asshur was destroyed in 614 and NINEVEH in 612; the last Assyrian king, Assur-uballit II, fled to Harran, where a few years later he disappeared, and with him Assyria, from the pages of history.

Science. The Babylonians were the first grammarians and gave to language its first systematic, if rudimentary, analysis. They compared their own Akkadian language with Sumerian and arranged their results in lists comparable to our grammatical paradigms. And in the lexical lists of Sumerian and Akkadian, ordered according to the nature of the object (houses, trees, plants, etc.), there is a simple but scientific system of classification.

Babylonian medicine, which seems inextricably bound to magic, is a field of study never adequately investigated, but it can be said that the medical texts contain some amazingly acute observations.

In the sciences of mathematics and astronomy, a relatively high level was certainly attained. From the period of 1800 to 1600 there are both "table texts" and "problem texts," and among the former there are multiplication tables, tables of reciprocals, of squares and square roots, etc. The "Pythagorean" theorem was known to the Babylonians more than 1,000 years before Pythagoras. An eminent authority, O. Neugebauer, compares the level of Babylonian mathematics with that of the early Renaissance, although admitting that it never achieved a truly scientific level.

The earliest astronomy, from 1800 to 1600, was crude, but in the Seleucid period it became a mathematical astronomy, which was equal to that of Greek contemporaries. One of the major reasons of astronomical study was the collection of material for astrological omens, which was organized in series that reached their canonical form *c.* 1000 B.C. Texts from *c.* 700 B.C., which contain older material, show the first discussion of elementary astronomical concepts on a purely rational basis, and probably around 500 B.C. systematic observational reports developed into a systematic mathematical theory. In this period the zodiac seems to have been invented, appearing for the first time in a text of 419 B.C.

Bibliography: H. SCHMÖKEL, *Geschichte des alten Vorderasien* (*Handbuch der Orientalistik Abt.* 1, v. 2.3; Leiden 1957). A. SCHARFF and A. MOORTGAT, *Aegypten und Vorderasien im Altertum* (Munich 1950). A. T. E. OLMSTEAD, *History of Assyria* (New York 1923). R. W. ROGERS, *A History of Babylonia and Assyria,* 2 v. (6th ed. rev. New York 1915). L. W. KING, *A History of Babylon* (London 1915). S. SMITH, *Early History of Assyria: To 1000 B.C.* (New York 1928). T. JACOBSEN, "Early Political Development in Mesopotamia," *Zeitschrift für Assyriologie* 52 (1957) 91–140. A. FALKENSTEIN, "La Cité-temple sumérienne," *Journal of World History* 1 (1953–54) 784–814. D. D. LUCKENBILL, ed., *Ancient Records of Assyria and Babylonia,* 2 v. (Chicago 1926–27). J. B. PRITCHARD *Ancient Near Eastern Texts Relating to the Old Testament* 265–317. W. F. ALBRIGHT, *Encyclopedia Americana* (New York 1961) 2:426–432; 3:7–9. H. G. GÜTERBOCK, *Encyclopaedia Britannica* (1961) 2:845–855. E. CAVAIGNAC, *Dictionnaire de la Bible* (Paris 1928–) 5:1103–26.

[W. L. MORAN]

RELIGION

Mesopotamian religion was a quest for salvation; like all men, Mesopotamian man experienced the "numinous," which arrested him in awe and drew him with desire. But this quest and this experience had a specific character; they took form within specific and determining conditions of time and place. They were components of a distinctive culture that was not only Oriental, but within the ancient Near East, however many the similarities, a thing apart, neither Iranian, Syrian, nor Egyptian. A description, therefore, of this religion must strive primarily to grasp those decisive periods when it was shaped and found its distinctively Mesopotamian expression. With such a scope in view, this article, after considering the sources and their use, will first treat the gods of ancient Mesopotamia and then the relationship between the gods and man.

Sources. In general there is no lack of material, which in written or unwritten form extends over three millenia. Myths, prayers, hymns, rituals, the omen and wisdom literatures, the frequent statements on or allusions to religious conceptions and practices in royal annals, in legal texts, in letters and even in economic documents, and the religious views implied in personal names—these in general constitute the written sources. The unwritten are the archeological data: temple plans, statues, divine emblems, altars, the religious scenes on cylinder seals, etc.

Limitations. The use of this material, however, has its limitations and difficulties. The sources reveal mainly the official religion of the temple and palace; little is known, however, of popular religion. Furthermore, in the interpretation of the sources there is the problem of language. The language of the Sumerians is still imperfectly understood, and even Akkadian is not without its obscurities. There is also the problem of grasping the complexity of social, political, and economic institutions that were so intimately connected with religious life. There is finally the problem of time. No religion that extends over three millenniums and is alive remains static. Behind the traditional forms that religion adheres to there are shifts, at times subtle, of emphasis and value.

The great difficulty, however, is to understand the mentality of the ancient Mesopotamian man with which, in the religious situation of deepest personal concern and involvement, he viewed the universe. For to him the world was a "Thou," animate, personal, revealing a will and a presence. He felt himself part of nature; he could not stand away from it and judge it, as it were, from above. Its events revealed no laws, which are the result of abstraction. They were individual instances of a will immanent in the phenomena. The expression, therefore, of this confrontation of an "I" with a "Thou" was neither scientific nor systematic; it was, of an inner necessity, bound to the concrete and individual, and none of its multiple forms was capable of giving more than a partial, though valid, expression of the infinitely rich experience in which it was born.

The Gods. To have some understanding of the gods of ancient Mesopotamia, it is necessary to consider man's primal experience, the influence of social and political development, particularly at the time of the Dynasty of Akkad and the First Dynasty of Babylon, and the nature of mythopoeic thought in this part of the ancient world.

Primal Experience. A certain fluidity in the conception of the divine marks Mesopotamian religion in all periods. To the doorleaf of a temple, for example, is attributed personality, and as Ig-galla, "Great Doorleaf," he is the doorkeeper of the high god An; or as Ig-alima, "Doorleaf of the Bison," he is a member of Nin-girsu's household at Lagash, charged with specific duties and the object of cult. Similarly, Utu, the sun-god and god of justice, has as his viziers Nig-gina, "Justice," and Nigsisa, "Equity." But such deities are in a sense secondary; they derive from their relationship to the forces of nature.

It was in these forces that Mesopotamian man had his fundamental encounter with the divine. To illustrate from a few of the principal gods: Enki, "Lord of the Earth," the god of the fresh waters beneath the earth that appeared in marshes, lakes and lagoons, fructifying the earth; the goddess Nissaba, in the reeds and grasses and cereals; the goddess Inanna, the power in the cluster of the date palm; the moon-god Nanna, lighting up the darkness of the night; the sun-god Utu, the power in the brilliant white light of the day; Ishkur, god of the rainstorm, bringing grass to the pastures and swelling the rivers and canals with his waters.

Different Pantheons. Referring to the earliest times, however, as T. Jacobsen has shown, one should speak, not of a single pantheon, but of several pantheons, according to the dominant economic activities of the various regions of ancient Sumer. In the south where marshes and lakes separated the Persian Gulf from Sumer proper was the pantheon of the hunter and fisherman: Enki, also known as Abzu, "Fresh Water," Nudimmud, "Man Creator," Dara-abzu, "Ibex of the Abzu," etc.; Nazi (the current name Nanshe being probably due to a misreading), Enki's daughter, the fish-goddess; Asal-luḫe, Enki's son, explained by Jacobsen as "Asal, the Man Drencher," that is, god of the thunder shower. In the south along the banks of the Euphrates where the date palm grew, the pantheon included: Inanna, "Mistress of the Date-Palm Cluster," especially as this power had reference to the storehouse for dates; Dumuzi-ama-ushum-gal-anna, the power for life in the date palm; several chthonic deities like Nin-gish-zida, "Lord Effective Tree," throne bearer in the Underworld, Nin-a-zu, "Lord Water-Knower(?)," son in one tradition of Eresh-ki-gal, "Mistress of the Great-Place (the Underworld)"; Dumu, "The Child," a vegetation god. The pantheon of the cowherds of the south included: Nanna, the moon-god; Utu, the sun-god; Nin-sun, "Lady Wild Cow"; Nin-ḫar, god of rainstorms, and his spouse, Nin-i-gara, ''Mistress of Ghee and Cream''; Shakan, Utu's son, god of the steppe's wild life; and An, god of the sky. In the central grassy region was the pantheon of the shepherds: Inanna, brought from the southern pantheon into this one; Dumuzi, the shepherd, the divine power manifested in the lambs of spring and the ewes' udders heavy with milk; and Ishkur, god of rainstorms. For the assherd the gods were: Nin-ḫursag, ''Mistress of the Piedmont,'' who manifested herself especially in the wild asses of the western desert, but who was also more generally goddess of the wild life in desert and foothills and was likewise known as Dingirmaḫ, ''The Exalted Goddess,'' and Nin-tu, ''Mistress Giving Birth''; and her husband, Shul-pae, ''Youth Appearing,'' who remains ill defined. In the farmlands of the north and east, which in the history of Babylonia were politically and economically the most important region and home of some of the most important gods in Mesopotamian religion, the pantheon included: Enlil, ''Lord Wind,'' who brought the rains of spring and was credited with the creation of the pickax, in ancient times the most important agricultural instrument; Ninlil, ''Mistress Wind,'' Enlil's wife and originally a grain-goddess; Nissaba of the cereals, mentioned above, and her husband, Haya, god of stores; Ninurta (at Lagash called Nin-girsu), Enlil's and Ninlil's son, the farmer's god of thunder and rain; and Ninurta's wife, Bau, a goddess especially associated with dogs and healing. From these pantheons we see how closely bound to nature the early religion was and what man was seeking therein: sustenance, plenitude of material well-being, and integration of his own life with these life-giving powers of nature.

In this earliest phase of Mesopotamian religion the intimate association of the natural phenomenon and the inherent divine force must be noted. This is evident not only in the divine names—Utu is both the sun and the sun-god, Nissaba is the grain and the grain-goddess, divine cow, divine tree, etc.—but also in representations of the divine. Thus, Ninurta was Im-dugud, ''Giant Cloud,'' perhaps his earliest name, and he was represented as a giant bird with wings outstretched and with a lion's head. In this form he was worshiped in historic times. Inanna's image was that of the reed bundles and the rolled-up screen of the storehouse gate.

The Evil God. Two other types of god should be mentioned, though it is difficult to determine whether they belong to the earliest conceptions of the divine. The first was the evil god. He was the god who by definition received no cult. He could inspire dread when evil struck mysteriously or massively, but he could not attract. He was therefore avoided as much as possible. Magic was used to ward him off, or, if one fell within his power, to remove him.

The Personal God. If the ''evil god'' was on the periphery of the Mesopotamian religious world, at its center (at least on the level of personal religion) was the personal god. Originally he was perhaps noted only in connection with those individuals who might be said to have been born under a lucky star, for there was something uncanny about their success, in which one sensed the presence of another invisible power. By Old Babylonian times he was the individual god of every man, his protector, his sponsor before the high gods. In general he remained nameless; the main exceptions were the personal gods of rulers, for example, Nin-gishzida and Nazi, the personal god and goddess of Gudea of Lagash.

Influence of Social and Political Development. As village grew into city, and the economy developed along with increasing specialization of crafts, society was altered, and there emerged a new type of power, beyond anything in the experience of the old village community. These individual powers, moreover, under the pressure of events were pooled in a league uniting the major cities of Sumer. Mesopotamian religion had a new basis for its expression of the experience of divine power, and it was in this period, *c.* 3000–2800, that it achieved its classical form.

Gods as Lords. Locally, the principal god now became the owner of a vast estate, and the temple was the center of economic as well as religious life. There the cult statue of the god resided, there he was fed daily with the other gods that made up the divine household. Each of these gods had his assigned task in the maintenance of the palace temple and in the administration of the estate.

With this profoundly anthropomorphic development the role of both god and man was changed. Because they were rulers, lofty and remote, the gods withdrew to a distance; yet, in a sense, they drew closer in that they took on human form. Henceforth the gods were visualized as men, though frequently survivals of the earlier image are evident: cereals sprout from the shoulders of Nissaba, sun rays come from the body of Utu, etc. The interests, too, of the god became wider; as ruler he provided for the political and social, as well as the economic, welfare of his subjects. He must fight to defend his city; it was Ningirsu who waged war for Lagash. He had to see to it that the dangerous elements of discord within the city were quieted; he concerned himself with law and its reform so that equity would prevail in the affairs of men.

Man became a serf of the gods. He worked his lord's estate within which, with the growth of specialization, he had his assigned task. Men produced the raw material; women worked it into the finished product. Even when the theocratic socialism of Sumerian times yielded to a progressive secularization of life, the classic statement of man's purpose was and remained that he was made for the service of the gods.

Kings as Gods. In this period royal power began to develop, and the king gradually became the principal human intermediary between gods and men. Ruling by divine choice, he mediated to men the divine blessings by scrupulous attention to and observance of the will of the gods. Because of this special function, he acted as the personal god of the community, and this found expression in the Akkad period when, for the first time, a ruler's name was preceded by the determinative for divinity. It was only in this very limited sense that the king was divine, but even this was hardly reconcilable with the Mesopotamian conception of divinity and was completely abandoned after the Kassite period.

Divine Assembly. On the national level the central shrine was at Nippur, where the gods convened in assembly, presided over by An and Enlil. The cosmos was conceived as a state with power ultimately residing in the assembly. Supremacy was achieved by election, and the high gods of the various cities had their assigned or traditional offices. After An of Uruk and Enlil of Nippur came Enki of Eridu, the god of wisdom and magic (since water cannily runs its course and finds its goal), who organized and administrated the economy. Utu, from whom nothing was secret, was the supreme judge. Ishkur, whose rain swelled the rivers and canals, was in charge of the irrigation system. All the gods decreed the destinies of Sumer and assigned political power, now to this king, now to that. History was born in the assembly of the gods.

The offices of the gods touched upon a very distinctive feature of early Mesopotamian thought. These offices were called *me,* which is probably the noun of the verb ''to be.'' It is being, but being specified and normative that imparted to nature and society its essential structure. In one piece of speculation *me* was at the very beginning of cosmic origins, antecedent to divinity itself. In the actual order, however, the gods controlled and disposed of *me;* this was the highest prerogative of divinity.

Akkad Period. The political dominance of the Semites wrought no profound changes in Mesopotamian religion. In general, the Akkadians assimilated their gods with those of the Sumerians: Ea was Enki, Sin was Nanna, Adad was Ishkur, Shamash was Utu, Ishtar was Inanna. Many Sumerian gods were simply adopted; for example, An (who was Akkadianized as Anum), Enlil, Ninurta, Nergal, etc. The principal god of the Akkadians, Il, seems to have been gradually abandoned, or perhaps absorbed in one or more figures of the Sumerian pantheon (*see* EL [GOD].)

A few new goddesses appeared and gained general popularity. Most of these, like Anunitum of Sippar, originally a goddess of war, were absorbed by Ishtar, whose domination among the goddesses of the Mesopotamian pantheon eventually reached the point when *ishtar* meant goddess itself. This increasingly complex figure represented, above all, the passions of battle and sexual love. While the other goddesses were for the most part reduced to intercessors with the gods, she remained an independent force (*see* ASTARTE).

However, two peoples speaking two languages so profoundly different as Sumerian and Akkadian must have had equally profound differences of mentality. Even while adopting, the Akkadians must have transformed. Evidence of such a transformation is found in Akkadian art, which, in its treatment of religious themes, shows a grimness and a sense of man's being involved in a conflict of forces, the issue of which, never certain, lies beyond his control. Perhaps, therefore, the religion changed more than is generally suspected. This is an area for further investigation.

First Dynasty of Babylon. This was a period of secularization. The palace dissociated itself from the temple, and at the capital of Babylon the traditional pantheon was revised to the glory of the new center of political power. It was done through the exaltation of MARDUK, originally the city god of Babylon. His name probably meant ''Bull Calf of the Storm,'' indicating that he was, like Ishkur and similar figures, a god of thunder and rain. This would explain his being identified with Asal-luḫe, whence his parentage, Enki (Ea) and Damgalnunna (Damkina).

Marduk and Nabu. The boldest expression of Marduk's supremacy was found in the myth *ENUMA ELISH,*''When on high . . .''. Within the framework of the old pattern, this supremacy was attributed to the choice of the gods met in assembly. When the older gods, represented by Enki, proved helpless against the forces of chaos, Marduk was chosen as champion; he demanded, however, that his leadership be made permanent. This was granted to him when he gave proof of his magical powers. With chaos overcome, man was fashioned from the blood of the rebel god Kingu, to dispense the gods from providing for their own needs. The gods rewarded Marduk with a house of his own, the heavenly counterpart of his temple in Babylon, E-sang-il, ''House Raising High [its] Summit.''

In effect, Marduk took the place of Enlil, but with the great difference that he became a truly national god, an expression of Babylon's political power. The other gods tended to diminish in importance; they became mere functionaries of Marduk or aspects of his power. One text records that Marduk as ruler and counselor was Enlil; as lighting up the sky he was Sin; as god of justice he was Shamash, etc. However, since elsewhere the parts of

Ninurta's body were identified with the various high gods, we are not justified in interpreting the text on Marduk simply in terms of his role as national god. Both texts reveal a tendency to henotheism in later speculation.

With the rise of his father, Marduk's son, the god Nabu of Borsippa and the patron of accounting, assumed an important place in Babylonian religion. His cult spread to Assyria, and in the 1st millennium he was extremely popular, even more so than his father [*see* NEBO (NABU)].

Assur. When Assyria gained the hegemony that was once Babylon's, the city god of Assur (Asshur), who was also called Assur (Asshur), became the Assyrian counterpart of Marduk as national god. He was assimilated largely with Enlil; his wife was Ninlil, his temple complex at Assur was, like that of Enlil at Nippur, called E-sharra, and Nippur deities, like Ninurta, became part of his court. The pro-Assyrian faction strove to demonstrate Assur's superiority over the hated Marduk of the opposing pro-Babylonian faction. Sennacherib, perhaps the most fanatical partisan of the Assyrian god, substituted Assur for Marduk in the *Enuma elish* and equated Assur with the god An-shar, the father of Anum. At the same time he attempted to transplant the celebration of the traditional Babylonian New Year's festival, with its recitation of the *Enuma elish,* to Assyria.

In fact, however, Assur remained little more than the apotheosis of Assyrian power and political ambition. In his honor the Assyrian king wrought all the destruction and carnage that fill the Assyrian royal annals. The god Assur's distinction in Mesopotamian religion was that he alone was predominantly a god of blood.

Myth. Myth is the response to the ''why'' of things, and because all nature was a ''Thou,'' myth must speak of *who* rather than of *what* and must be a story of personal forces and their possible conflicts. Mythopoeic thought is not discursive; it does not argue, it asserts. Its explicative value is that of symbol rather than clear concept, and it is therefore unsystematic, allowing for other symbols, other explanations, without inner logical coherence. And myth is essentially religious. It is religious experience given form and structure; in its transposition of the inner meaning of things beyond the familiar categories of time and space to the primeval order of divine activity, it gives expression to the transcendent which is inherent in the object of religious experience.

Only a few of the Sumero-Akkadian myths can be mentioned here. *Enuma elish,* already referred to, explains both Marduk's position in the pantheon and the organization of the universe with man's place in it. Another myth tells how the moon(-god) came into being: the young maiden Ninlil, against her mother's advice, went bathing in the canal Nun-birdu in Nippur; there she was seen and raped by Enlil, and the child born of the union was the moon(-god). Why is Sumer organized economically the way it is? Because Enki visited Sumer, appointed to each region its special function and gave it an overseer. Why at the end of spring each year does nature wilt and die, the milk disappear from the udders, etc.? Because, according to one myth, Dumuzi was attacked and killed by raiders from the Nether World. Why each year does the statue of Inanna journey by boat from Uruk to Eridu, there to be purified and Inanna reappointed to her divine office? Because Inanna once succeeded in getting Enki intoxicated, and in his state of euphoria he gave Inanna the *me*—here perhaps consisting concretely in emblems of sacred offices. She betook herself to Uruk, and, although Enki, who now viewed things in a more sober light, tried seven times to prevent her, she successfully returned to Uruk with all the *me.* In brief, the explanation of nature, of cult, of Sumerian culture is basically religious; its expression is the myth.

Gods and Man. The basic relations between the gods and man in ancient Mesopotamia can be described under such headings as sacred places, sacred times, divination and magic, and the loss and recovery of salvation.

Sacred Space. The temple was the earthly dwelling of the gods; here the cult statue was housed, here divine power was intensely concentrated, and from here it emanated into the land. The temple belonged to the very structure of the cosmos; it was ''coeval with heaven and earth'' (said of the E-ninnu at Lagash), ''the bond of heaven and earth'' (the meaning of the name of the E-dur-an-ki at Nippur). It flashed with specifically divine effulgence (*me-lam*); and it was endued with divine terror (*ni*); it was awful (*khush*) and at the same time a place of joy (as in the name of the E-khush-kiri-zal). It had a holy purity (*kug, sikil*); its rites (*me*) were pure and perfect (*šu-du*). It gave abundance (*nam-ḫe*); in it prayers were heard (the meaning of E-arazu-giš-tuk and E-šudde-giš-tuk); sins were remitted (the E-nam-tagga-duḫu). According to the character of the god it housed, the temple could be considered a cattle pen, a sheepfold, a place of wisdom, etc. It possessed a measure of divinity itself. In a large number of hymns to the major temples of Sumer and Akkad, which are attributed to Enḫeduanna (the daughter of Sargon of Akkad), the temples are addressed as independent agents of power; and the presence of temple names as theophorous elements in personal names testifies to the popular belief in the divine power of the temple. Each of the temple hymns just mentioned closes with the essential observations: ''Temple X, in your precinct[?] he [the god] has established his house, on your dais he has taken his seat.''

The temple therefore must be maintained. One of the major duties of the Mesopotamian king was to provide for the repair of temples. If a temple were in ruins, the original foundations must, if possible, be found; it was the exact place of earlier temples that was the truly holy place. On the king fell the duty to lay the first foundation, anoint it with oil, wine, and honey, and to indicate by inscription the place where he had built. The greatest calamity a city could suffer was the destruction of its temple. This meant that the god had departed, hope had ended. The most moving of all Mesopotamian religious compositions are the lamentations over their destroyed temples.

In religious architecture the Mesopotamian creation of the ziggurat, the temple tower, was an attempt to unite the human and divine. Its origin may have been utilitarian; in the earliest phases of Eridu the shrine was constructed on a raised platform, perhaps to protect it from inundation. By the Warka period, however, it was more than 40 feet high at Ur, and a utilitarian interpretation is no longer adequate. The ziggurat was now the sacred mountain, on the summit of which man met god. According to Herodotus the ziggurat of Babylon, the E-temen-an-ki, ''Foundation Platform of Heaven and Earth,'' rose in seven stages, each a different color, and on the top was the shrine. At Khorsabad, ancient Dur-sharru-kin, founded by Sargon II as his capital, there were probably seven stages, with the height equal to the width of the base (143 feet). The number 7 and the symmetry show cosmic speculations (*see* TOWER OF BABEL).

Sacred Time. Each day the cult statue was clothed and fed by the staff of priests attached to the temple, and these activities were accompanied by prayers. There were also monthly feasts: the 1st (new moon), the 15th (full moon), and the 28th or 29th (disappearance of moon) days being honored by special rites. Different gods were specially honored in different months, as at Lagash where each of the gods Nin-girsu, Nazi, and Bau had their special feasts at different times.

New Year Feast. The most important festival was observed at the New Year. Most available information concerns its performance at Babylon; although the sources are late, they certainly reflect older practices. In Babylon it was celebrated in March and April, when nature revived. Its significance was cosmic: by word and deed the renewal of nature as a victory over the powers of chaos was reasserted, reenacted, and reactualized in its essential reality.

The festival began with four days of preparation; the mood was solemn and somber. To Marduk a prayer was raised, asking for mercy and freedom for the Babylonians. On the evening of the 4th day the *Enuma elish* was recited in its entirety before Marduk's statue. With this reading the deepest meaning of the feast was revealed. On the 5th day the king was stripped of his royal insignia, smitten on the cheek by the priest, after which he knelt before Marduk to declare his innocence. The god replied through the priest, ''Do not fear . . . .'' The priest then returned the insignia and smote the king once more. If tears welled in his eyes, it was a favorable omen. On the 8th day Marduk took his place in the chamber of destinies, the Duku (The Pure Mound). This was probably a reenactment—in the presence of the cult statues of the various gods who had arrived earlier from their centers (Nabu from Borsippa, etc.)—of the meeting of the divine assembly in which Marduk was granted supreme powers. The 9th and 10th days were occupied with a procession to a special sanctuary, the *bît akîti,* with the king leading Marduk (a procession against the powers of chaos?) and with rites (a divine banquet?) at the *bît akîti.* On the 11th day the destinies of the following year were determined after the assembled gods paid their homage to Marduk as their supreme lord. On the 12th the gods returned to their usual sanctuaries.

Sacred Marriage. In this festival we note how small was the role of the king, though without his presence it could not be celebrated. In Assyria the king was much more prominent in the native ritual of the *takultu,* a banquet for the gods. This contrast in the exercise of priestly powers between Babylonian and Assyrian kings in general prevails, but there was one rite in Babylonia, the sacred marriage (the ἱερὸς γάμος), in which the Babylonian king played no less a part than that of a god. The sacred marriage was represented in art from as early as the Warka period, and it was a common practice in the Isin-Larsa period. Then for unknown reasons, one of which may have been the secularization of kingship in Babylonia, it disappeared.

In the Isin-Larsa period, Ishme-Dagan described himself as the husband of Inanna; Enlil-bani was said to have been approached by her on the sacred couch; and Lipit-Ishtar became the god Urash before being united with the goddess. Earlier, in the inscriptions of Gudea, it is clear also that at Lagash the union of Nin-girsu with his consort Bau was celebrated, and we may assume that the king stood for Nin-girsu and a priestess for Bau. The best-known and most detailed text refers to Idin-Dagan as Dumuzi, Inanna's husband. The union of king and goddess is described, and then, after coming from the bridal chamber, they banquet together from the abundance that their union in the spring had, according to mythopoeic thought, achieved.

Divination and Magic. All the phenomena of nature were fraught with meaning, and therefore, not only extraordinary events, such as eclipses, earthquakes, or monstrous births, were viewed as portentous, but within the rhythm of everyday life, in dreams, in the courses of the stars and planets, in the flight of birds and the entrails of sheep, the skilled heirs of a long tradition could descry the future course of events. The life of the king, especially in Assyria, was virtually controlled by the results of the investigation of omens. He could grumble at the fast that the nonappearance of the moon at the beginning of the month imposed on him, but the astrologers remained adamant (*see* DIVINATION).

MAGIC was integrated with Mesopotamian religion rather than opposed to it. It was practiced together with prayer to the gods, especially Ea and Asal-luḫe, from whom it derived its real efficacy. Magic was necessary because all the invisible forces were not beneficent; there were demons who brought all sorts of ills to the man whom they could get into their power. The function of magic was to ward them off or to exorcise them, and for this there were potent words and actions, powers of plants and stones known to the specialist, AMULETS, talismans, etc.

Loss and Recovery of Salvation. There was one loss shared by all, which, being that of nature itself, did not really destroy the pattern of salvation, but only imposed on man the necessity of participating in nature's course. Above all, this was the withering of life in the blasts of summer heat. Mythically, it was the disappearance of Inanna's spouse or of the Great Mother's child, and the people shared the grief of bereaved spouse or mother in lamentations for "the one who is far away."

Divine Caprice. This loss, however, was made good in the revival of nature. Another and more serious loss was that which might strike the individual, community, or nation outside the course of nature. Whence did it come? What was its remedy? One answer was simply to throw responsibility on the gods. King Urukagina was convinced of his innocence, yet he was conquered by King Lugalzaggesi of Umma. He dared to pray that the crime be on the head of Nissaba, Lugalzagessi's personal goddess. Divine power was at work, and its operations were not necessarily just. The inscrutability of divine ways is frequently referred to in the religious literature, and it is not always that of simple transcendence; at times it is that of caprice subject to no higher law.

Sin. Another answer was sin. Man must bow down, confess his guilt, atone by the prescribed ritual, and hope he would again find divine favor. Most often he thought of his personal god; his misfortunes must mean that this god, his protector, had been offended and had abandoned him. The high gods were then appealed to and asked to appease the personal god. The penitent freely admitted his guilt, even if he could not recall his offense. Abjectly he made his confession, but one looks in vain for a sign of the "contrite spirit." Its basis, love, was lacking.

Eventually the innate human conviction that the innocent should not suffer demanded a real searching of the ways of the gods with men. The problem was touched on in earlier Sumerian and Akkadian literature; in the Kassite period it became a theme. The bold solution of the Book of JOB, the experience of Yahweh, which defied rational expression, was far beyond the highest Mesopotamian thought. It remained a problem with no solution.

Death. One loss was final. Ultimately man could never integrate his existence with the life-giving powers of nature, which, when dead, rose again. Man must die. He survived in a dim world of dust and thirst, in "the land of no return." In the late period, some distinction in the lot of the good and evil was made, but it was not elaborated, and it is doubtful that it had much influence. "Gilgamesh, whither rovest thou? The life thou pursuest thou shalt not find. When the gods created mankind, death for mankind they set aside, life in their own hands retaining" (*see* GILGAMESH EPIC).

Conclusion. At the sacrifice of many facts about ancient Mesopotamian religion, an attempt has here been made, mainly along lines indicated by Jacobsen, to interpret this religion in terms of religious experience and to determine the principal influences on its formation and expression. All scholars may not accept this interpretation, and the reader should consult the bibliography for other points of view. In the striving to return to so distant and alien a world, errors and encounters with differences of opinions are inevitable; one can hope only for an approximation to what was the reality. That Mesopotamian religion, with all its deficiencies, was something deep and serious should be evident. This it had to be in order to sustain a people for three millenniums and to influence the entire ancient world, the Bible not excepted. It played its part, a larger one than that of most religions in history, in preparing for the "fulness of time."

Bibliography: E. P. DHORME, *Les Religions de Babylonie et d'Assyrie* (Paris 1945). H. FRANKFORT, *Kingship and the Gods* (Chicago 1948). C. J. GADD, *Ideas of Divine Rule in the Ancient East* (New York 1948). T. JACOBSEN, "Mesopotamia," in H. FRANKFORT et al., *Before Philosophy* (pa. Baltimore 1959), previously pub. as The *Intellectual Adventure of Ancient Man* (Chicago 1946); "Formative Tendencies in Sumerian Religion," *The Bible and the Ancient Near East,* ed. G. E. WRIGHT (Garden City, N.Y. 1961) 267–278; *Journal of Near Eastern Studies* 5 (1946) 128–152, a review of S. N. KRAMER'S *Sumerian Mythology,* (Philadelphia 1944). S. N. KRAMER, "Sumerian Religion," *Forgotten Religions,* ed. V. FERM (New York 1950) 47–62; *Sumerian Mythology, op. cit.* A. L. OPPENHEIM, "Assyro-Babylonian Religion," *ibid.* 65–79; *Ancient Mesopotamia: Portrait of a Dead Civilization* (Chicago 1964). For translations of selected Sumerian and Akkadian religious texts, see

J. B. Prichard, *Ancient Near Eastern Texts Relating to the Old Testament* (2d, rev. ed. Princeton, NJ 1955).

[W. L. MORAN]

MESROP

Saint, 4th-century Armenian ecclesiastic and founder of Armenian Christian literature; b. Hatzikk', *c.* 361; d. Feb. 7, 440. Mesrop was originally called Mashtotz. He received a Hellenistic education, probably at Antioch, where he appears to have met THEODORE OF MOPSUESTIA. After a short military career at Valarshapat, he embraced the religious life as a monk (392 or 393) and was ordained by ISAAC THE GREAT. With the encouragement of the Catholicos and of Prince Vaghinak of Siunia, he made a missionary journey to the outer provinces of Armenia, where his experiences convinced him of the need of an Armenian written language. Assisted by Isaac and King Vṛamshapuh (401–409), he set out in search of an adequate alphabet and eventually settled on 36 letters (*c.* 404 or 407), with which he began the translation of the Bible into Armenian. He translated also the works of the Greek and Syrian Church Fathers. He assisted in the foundation of schools and monasteries, and evangelized the Georgians and the Albanians. In 422 he seems to have accompanied a diplomatic mission to Constantinople, where he obtained the aid of Emperor THEODOSIUS II for his educational enterprises. Upon the death of Isaac (438), Mesrop assumed government of the Church in Armenia, until his death. He was buried in Oshagan near Erevan, where a sanctuary was erected over his remains. In 1962 Armenia celebrated the 16th centenary of his birth. Mesrop appears to be the author of the so-called Teaching of St. GREGORY THE ILLUMINATOR, attributed to Agathangelus. However, he is not the author of the much later polyhistory (*Hadjachapatum*), also attributed to Agathangelus. Mesrop's vita was written by Koriun, his disciple.

Feast: Thursday following 4th Sunday after Pentecost, and Monday after 3d Sunday after Assumption.

Bibliography: O. BARDENHEWER, *Geschichte der altkirchlichen Literatur* 5:197–201. V. INGLISIAN, *Lexikon für Theologie und Kirche* [2] 7:319; *Handbuch der Orientalistik,* v.7 (Leiden 1963) 157–160. *Vies des saintes et des bienheuruex* 11:872–873. J. MARQUART, *Über den Ursprung des armenischen Alphabets* (Vienna 1917). N. AKINIAN, *Der hl. Maschtotz Wardapet* (Vienna 1949), Armenian with German résumé. KORIUN (Choriun), *History of the Life and Death of the Ecclesiastical Official (Vardapet) St. Mesrop* (Venice 1894), in Armenian. R. GROUSSET, *Histoire de l'Arménie* (Paris 1947) 171–175. S. LYONNET, *Recherches de science religieuse* 25 (1935) 170–187.

[N. M. SETIAN]

MESSIAH

Term derived from the Hebrew word *māšîah* meaning "anointed." Its Greek translation is χριστός, which is used some 40 times in the Septuagint. The later Hellenized form Μεσσίας is based on a transliteration of the Aramaic term *mešîḥā'*. The latter term was used either as a proper noun, Messiah, without the definite article, as in Jn 4.25, or as an appellative, with the definite article, the Messiah, as in Jn 1.41.

Originally only the king bore the title *ham-māšîaḥ* (the anointed one). The king was called "the anointed of Yahweh" (1 Sm 24.7, 11; 26.9, 11, 16, 23; 2 Sm 1.14, 16; 19.22; Lam 4.20), or simply "His anointed," in a context that clearly shows that he was Yahweh's anointed [1 Sm 2.10; 12.3, 5; 16.6; 2 Sm 22.51; Ps 2.2; 19(20).7; 27(28).8]. Again, Yahweh spoke to the king as "my anointed one" [1 Sm 23.5; Ps 131(132).17; cf. also "your anointed," said to Yahweh in Ps 83(84).10; "the anointed of the God of Jacob" in 2 Sm 23.1]. The ANOINTING of rulers invested them with Yahweh's authority and made them personally inviolate (1 Sm 24.7; 26.9, 11; 2 Sm 1.14).

According to the postexilic Pentateuchal PRIESTLY writers, the priests were likewise anointed with oil at the ceremony of their investiture with the priestly office (Ex 29.7; Lv 8.12); originally this referred to the high priests who were called "the anointed priests" (Lv 4.3, 5, 16; 6.15), but later, also ordinary priests were anointed (Ex 28.41; Lv 10.7; Nm 3.3; 2 Mc 1.1). However, the anointing of priests was probably not a preexilic rite. In Dn 9.25–26 the high priest ONIAS III is called an anointed leader.

In Ps 104(105).15; 1 Chr 16.22 the term "my anointed ones" (the only place where it is used in the plural) can be seen, from the context, to refer to the Patriarchs, who, though not anointed in the literal sense of the term, were dedicated in a special way to God.

The term Messiah was not used in the technical sense, as referring to the future Savior, before the 1st century B.C.; the only exception would be in Ps 2.2, if this Psalm were interpreted in a strictly messianic sense.

In the NT, apart from Jn 1.41; 4.25, only the Greek equivalent [ὁ] Χριστός, [the] CHRIST, is used. The Gospel has many texts referring to Jesus' messianic status. In the Nazareth synagogue episode He says that He is the one who fulfills the messianic role described by Isaia (Lk. 4.14–30). To the messianic question of the Baptist's disciples He responds by indicating the import of His healing and preaching (Mt 11.1–20). When, at Caesarea Philippi, Peter confesses Him to be the Christ, Jesus affirms this in revealing the heavenly origin of the Apostle's remark (Mt 16.13–20).

During the apostolic era the Apostles preached Jesus as the Christ (Acts 2.36); St. Paul used this title 389 times. As Gentile converts, unfamiliar with Jewish messianism, began to enter the Church, certain historical implications of the title Christ faded into the background and it assumed the significance of a name. At times it came to designate the divinity of Jesus (see St. Justin, 2 *Apol.* 6) or His priesthood (see St. Cyril of Jerusalem, *Catech.; Patrologia Graeca* 33:664). St. Thomas devotes no special article in his *Summa theologiae* to the messiahship of Jesus.

Rationalist critique of Jesus' messianic consciousness promoted renewed interest in the messianic texts, which have come to be distinguished into those indicating Jesus' personal awareness and those exemplifying the faith of the community. It is especially the narratives of His baptism, temptations in the desert, and Peter's confession that show Jesus' messianic consciousness, together with references to Old Testament titles, such as Son of Man (Mk 2.28), Servant of Yahweh (cf. Mt 20.28), and ''he who is to come'' (Mt 11.3).

See Also: MESSIANISM.

[M. J. CANTLEY/S. K. MACDONALD/EDS.]

MESSIANISM

The word ''messiah'' comes from the Hebrew verbal adjective *māšîaḥ,* designating a person anointed with oil. It is used most frequently of the king (1 Sm 12.3; 2 Sm 19.22; Ps 2.2, etc.), and refers to his coronation anointing. It is used also of priests (Lv 4.3, 5, 16; 6.15), who were anointed with oil at their installation.

Israel's idea of messianism, according to J. Wellhausen, originated only during and after the Exile through the influence of the Persian hope for a savior who would rid the world of evil. S. Mowinckel, for whom the Messiah is purely an eschatological figure, is convinced that Israel's messianism received its genuine form only after the Davidic dynasty fell in 587 B.C.

H. Gunkel and H. Gressmann propose an older origin but also seek it outside of Israel in the ancient Oriental myths about the primeval king who would return at the end of the world. This position lacks any evidence that the Egyptians or the Mesopotamians ever expected an eschatological savior, an element characteristic of the Israelite Messiah.

The Swedish school looks for messianism's origin in the Oriental ideology that regarded the king as son or incarnation of a god. Each year the king was ritually subjected to suffering and humiliation that evoked the conflict between the god and chaos and that through the king's ritual victory represented the renewal of nature's vital forces. This picture does not reflect the Jewish messianic concept. The constantly recurring cycle does not agree with the Israelite hope for a Messiah whose appearance would be unique, God's definitive intervention in history and the eschatological event.

Two basic facts underlie the development of the messianic idea—the originality of the Israelite concept of history and Israel's sense of its vocation.

Mankind has continually attempted to explain the problems of evil and suffering. The answers, though many, reduce themselves to two, one rejecting history, the other assuming it. The rejection of history leads to the attempt to annul its force by the ritual reenactment of the gods' or heroes' primordial acts. Man believed that by participating in these archetypes through religious ceremony he could regenerate time. This was the idea behind the Babylonian New Year feast.

The Israelite does not reject history. One of his fundamental beliefs is that God directs history by manifesting Himself in it. All setbacks in history are manifestations of God's displeasure. However, the God who punished was the same God who had elected Israel in the covenants with Abraham and Moses. These were vantage points from which Israel's aspirations looked to the future. Once it was elected, Israel believed that God would always take part in its history.

Such a confidence in God's continued support gave Israel a vital sense of its vocation as principal beneficiary of the messianic promises. Israel's maturing reflection on God's designs influenced its view of itself and convinced it of its historical continuity. In every trial, Israel knew that it could not completely perish because of God's fidelity to His promises. The Messiah, God's instrument of salvation, would eventually bring effective deliverance from the present trials.

During its history, Israel had different types of leaders: the patriarch (Abraham); the prophet-legislator and friend of God (Moses); the charismatic leader (the Judge); the religious seer and prophet (Samuel); the king chosen and anointed by God (David); a series of prophets who opposed the religious corruption of the kings (Elijah, Amos, Jeremiah, etc.); the priest-prophet, well versed in the oral and written traditions (Ezechiel, Second Isaiah); and finally the scribes, priests, and wisdom collectors (Ezra, the author of Chronicles, Ecclesiastes). These changes in leadership contributed to the complexity of Israel's concept of the Messiah. The roots of messianism, therefore, went back to Abraham and even to the interpretation by the Israelite prophets of the origins of man, who was made in the image and likeness of God.

Messianism Before the Monarchy

The ancient ideas that later coalesced into exilic and postexilic messianism may be considered under four headings: the Protoevangelium of the first three chapters of Genesis, the promises to the Patriarchs, the covenant-alliance, and the oracles concerning the twelve tribes of Israel.

The Protoevangelium. Traditionally, the first proclamation of a future salvation has been attributed to the creation stories of Genesis, chapters 1 to 3, and specifically to Genesis 3.15. [see *Rome and the Study of Scripture* (5th ed. St. Meinrad, Ind. 1953) 121 para. 3.] In Genesis 3.15 God says,

> I will put enmity between you and the woman, between your seed and her seed; He shall crush your head, and you shall lie in wait for his heel.

Modern Biblical scholars have great difficulty in finding any messianic content in the Hebrew of this text. The ''crush'' and the ''lie in wait for'' are uncertain translations of the same Hebrew root *šûp.* It is possible that the two forms of *šûp* were intended to be a play on words, the first one meaning ''trample upon'' from the Akkadian *šāpu,* with that meaning, and the second from a parallel Hebrew root *šā'ap* meaning ''snap at, gasp or pant after, set traps for.'' This is not at all certain, however, and modern translations are returning to the caution of the Greek translators of the Septuagint (LXX) who used τηρέω in both instances, with the meaning ''give heed to, watch out for, or beware of''; these versions use some expression of hostility in both cases, e.g., ''bruise,'' ''attack,'' and ''strike at.'' For modern scholars the messianic content of the text can only be a deeper meaning added to the text after the victory of Christ over Satan. They hold that constant and inescapable hostility between the woman's race and the serpent's is all that is certainly affirmed in Genesis 3.15.

That there is some vague hope of a future salvation to be found in Genesis chapters 1 to 3, however, is indicated by the continued concern of God for His creation, which He pronounced to be ''very good'' (Gn 1.31), and especially for man, whom He created in His image and likeness with the full deliberation of His heavenly court (1.26–27); whom He blessed with the power of increasing and dominating the rest of His creation (1.28); whom He did not immediately punish with death, after the only covenant law in Paradise was broken (cf. 2.16–17 with 3.7, 17, ''all the days of your life''); and finally, whom, even after the Fall, He continued to converse with, whom He clothed, and made the source of all human life (3.9–13, 16–21; 4.1). The salvation that the Israelites hoped for could come only from the God who had made all things ''very good.'' After man broke the Paradise covenant, an infraction that should have led to his annihilation with the immediate death of the first couple, God remained mercifully and gratuitously faithful to the man He had formed from the earth. He punished, but He did not annihilate. Just as at the FLOOD He saved Noah and his family, so always would He save the just remnant who were wary of the serpent's head (Isiah 4.2–3).

Promises to the Patriarchs. Patriarchal history tells of God's election of a people in whom all nations were to be blessed (Gn 12.1–3; 18.18; 22.18; 26.4; 28.14). This election was specifically related to the later Mosaic covenant between YAHWEH and Israel (Ex 3.15; Dt 6.10) and to Noah's election and salvation descending to Abraham through Noah's favored son, Shem (Gn 9.26–27; 10.10, 26–27). The election and promises to Abraham began to be realized in the miraculous birth of Isaac and the vocation of Jacob (Gn 21.1–3; 28.10–22;35.9–15), but during the long years in Egypt they seemed to be frustrated until a new beginning for them came forth from the burning bush that the flames did not consume (Ex 1.11–14; 3.1–10).

Covenant Promises. The covenant story centers around God's intimate friend, spokesman, wonder-worker, and legislator, Moses. His work as God's instrument of salvation was the new beginning in the historical development of the chosen people, perfectly fulfilled in Christ and the new Israel, His Church. Moses was later held to be the ideal prophet and the basis for the expectation of a new Moses (Dt 18.15–19).

By the covenant, Yahweh claimed Israel as His own possession, His son and holy nation (Ex 4.22–23; 19.38), and His bride (Jer 2.2), not because of the nation's greatness but because He loved it and was faithful to His promises to Abraham and Jacob (Dt 7.7–8). In contrast, Israel was frequently unfaithful to its covenant obligations and the awareness of its vocation was kept alive only by the prophets and a few faithful kings. Its hope for a glorious future was thus maintained even during the direst trials. With the Northern Kingdom, Israel, already destroyed and with Judah on the verge of being engulfed by Babylonia, the editors of Deuteronomy, supported by trust in God's covenant loyalty, reaffirmed the alliance's unbreakable bond and demonstrated how deep was Israel's hope in the ultimate fulfillment of God's promises.

Oracles of the Twelve Tribes. The originally rather loose union between Israel's tribes was strengthened by joining together for holy wars (Jg ch. 4–5), or in a renewal of the covenant (Jos ch. 24), or in liturgical assemblies (1 Sm 2.12–17). Songs composed at these assemblies were probably the source of JACOB'S oracles (Gn 49.1–28), the amphictyonic blessings of Jacob. They are oracles rather than blessings as can be seen from the ''in days to come'' of verse 1. In their final form they are dated no later than David's reign but contain many elements anterior to the monarchy, although they are not as old as Deborah's canticle (Jg ch. 5) or recent as Moses' benedictions (Dt ch. 33). The oracle about Judah (Gn 49.8–12) is the most messianic and emphasizes Judah's importance in the fulfillment of the ancient promises.

After a metaphorical description of Judah's preeminence among the tribes in vv. 8–9, the oracle predicts that Jude's imperium will eventually be concentrated in a ruler to whom the scepter and ruler's staff most properly belong and to whom the nations will be obedient. Although there is doubt about the meaning ''until he comes to whom it belongs,'' the image very likely describes King David's rule and empire. In vv. 11 and 12 the oracle seems to return to the tribe of Judah in general, describing the main products of its territory, the southern hill country, the land of the vine and the flocks—David himself was originally a shepherd (1 Sm 16.11 13). However, these two verses more probably refer to the ultimate ruler of v. 10 who will bring with him a new paradise. The paradisiacal abundance is poetically symbolized by the ruler carelessly tying his ass to the choicest vine, which, of course, would immediately afford his beast a wonderful feast, and by the extravagant washing of clothes in wine. The translation of the Revised Standard Version, ''his eyes shall be red with wine and his teeth white with milk,'' is more appropriate in such a context than the ''darker than wine, . . . whiter than milk'' of the Confraternity of Christian Doctrine translation. The messianic character of the poem is clarified by comparing it to the fertility brought by Yahweh's anointed in Isaiah 11.1–9; Ezekiel 34.23–31; Amos 9.11–15.

Balaam's oracles (Nm 24.3–9, 15–19) also are amphictyonic poems that look forward to a king issuing from Israel. In the second, more famous poem, the prophet in a mysterious vision points to Israel's royalty and describes its king as a mighty warrior. Late Judaism and the Targum *Onkelos* attributed messianic import to BALAAM'S words.

These prophecies led to the belief that the promises would be realized in a king and more specifically, a descendant of David.

Messianism after the Monarchy

The king in Israel, as exemplified in David, was a charismatic leader, ruling vicariously for Israel's true monarch, Yahweh. As God's vicar, David had divine strength and wisdom since he had received Yahweh's spirit at his anointing (1 Sm 16.13). As he was the intermediary between Yahweh and the people, national prosperity depended upon his fidelity to God (2 Sm 24.1–25). In him the covenant promises were recapitulated, and with each successive king of the Davidic line a new symbol arose that Yahweh's favor still rested with His people.

Kingship originated in Israel because the Philistine threat could no longer be met by such occasional leaders as the Judges. Saul was at first only another charismatic leader but soon became by popular acclaim the anointed king. After God's rejection of Saul (1 Sm 13) and David's anointing (1 Sm 16.1–13), the monarchy became more closely connected with the messianic hopes.

Nathan's Prophecy. The most important text concerning royal messianism is the oracle of NATHAN in 2 Samuel 7.5–16 [see also Ps 88(89); 1 Chr 17.7–14]. Its essential elements are: Yahweh refuses David's proffered house (temple); He reviews the benefits that He has showered upon David and his nation; He, instead, will build for David a permanent ''house'' (dynasty), which He will treat as His son and uphold with His covenant loyalty forever. Verse 13 referring to Solomon's building of the first Temple is a later interpolation, for it clashes with vv. 5–7. The gratuitous nature of the promise is underlined by David's humble thanksgiving (vv.18–29).

Psalm 88 (89) recalls the Davidic favors and promises (vv. 4–5, 20–38), contrasts them with the present miserable condition of David's dynasty (vv. 39–46), and concludes with a pathetic appeal to God's covenantal love and fidelity (vv. 47–52). The Psalm is obviously exilic, but despite the destruction of Jerusalem and the imprisonment of the last Davidic king, Yahweh's fidelity is not called into question; it is the basis for the psalmist's final prayer for deliverance and the establishment of the Messiah as the supreme emperor of the earth's kings (vv. 51, 28). Psalm 131 (132) expresses the same hope for the continuance of David's dynasty.

While the monarchy lasted, Israel's covenant with God was identified as the Davidic covenant. Nathan's oracle looked only to the continuation of Davidic rulers. But, Israel's hopes had forever been modified and henceforth would always include in some form the Anointed of Yahweh.

The Royal Psalms. Certain psalms were composed for court occasions during the monarchy and usually extolled the king's majesty, justice, piety, and the victories won for him by Yahweh. The king is not named (except for David and Melchisedec) but the psalms seem to come from the Southern Kingdom with the possible exception of Ps 44(45) originally written for a king of Samaria and his Tyrenian bride. Their messianic content became more pronounced as they were used over and over again in the liturgy, when there was no longer a king in Israel. Besides

Psalm 44(45), Psalm 2, 71(72), and 109 (110) will be examined for their messianic content.

Many modern exegetes interpret Psalm 2 as a messianic oracle describing the outcome of a rebellion of nations against Yahweh and His anointed King. God has set up His king in Sion, i.e., Jerusalem, ruled by the Davidic dynasty. The king then proclaims Yahweh's consecration of him as His royal son and describes his imperium on Yahweh's behalf over the nations. The Psalm concludes with a warning to all kings to serve Yahweh. Thus, in Ps 2, the king's reign is extended over all nations, going beyond the more limited horizons of Nathan's oracle. Although the Psalm's universal expressions may have been due originally to Oriental court style, the Psalm became for the postmonarchical Jews an expression of Israel's hope in Yahweh's fidelity to the messianic covenant. The world dominion expressed here must have appeared unattainable to the small remnant of Judeans living in an enclave around Jerusalem under Persian rule, except through the direct intervention of Yahweh from His heavenly throne.

In its final form and liturgical meaning, Psalm 71(72) also may be directly messianic, although originally it seems to have been an exaggerated prayer for some king at his coronation. World dominion is more clearly indicated and a new element is injected: the just king's rule will bring with it paradisiacal fruitfulness, especially for the oppressed poor. Justice and judgment are the keys that open the gates to this paradise in whose benefits all the earth's peoples will share. The image goes beyond the expectation of a reinstated Davidic monarchy and describes the ultimate ruler who has many traits parallel to the prophet-king of Isiah 9.5; 11.1–5; and Zachariah 9.9–17.

Psalm 109(110) reintroduces from Psalm 2.7 the notion of an adoptive divine sonship pertaining to the Messiah (the Hebrew of volume 3 is obscure; the Greek is the source of the reading, ". . . before the daystar, like the dew, I have begotten you"). The king's position at God's right hand affirms a closer association with Yahweh's monarchy. The Messiah is also a priest of the type of Melchisedec who had no genealogy, a vague indication that he would be more than a mere historical figure, but a religious one incorporating in himself the prerogatives of both priest and king.

Psalm 44(45) commemorates a royal wedding, beginning with praise of the king and his rule's glorious benefits (vv. 3–8); then the wedding procession is described and the bride is told of her responsibilities (vv.9–16); the Psalm concludes with a prophecy concerning the dynasty's permanence and glory (vv. 17–18). The epithalamium may have been written for a historical king who married a foreign princess, but, in a typical meaning, it refers to the King-Messiah to whom Israel (a figure of the Church) will be wedded, according to Jewish and Christian tradition. The king is described as endowed with Yahweh's characteristics [Ps 144(145).4–7, 12–13] and those of Emmanuel (Is 9.5–6).

Royal Messianism in the Prophets. The Davidic promises came through the ministry of the prophet Nathan. It is not surprising that later prophets returned to this theme and expanded it. Two centuries after Nathan delivered God's covenant to David, another prophet-adviser to AHAZ, King of Judah, reaffirmed it and saw more deeply into its meaning. The times were somber. Assyria was on the march again; Damascus and Samaria were besieging Jerusalem to destroy the Davidic dynasty and to force Judah into a coalition against Assyria. Ahaz, a young man, may even have killed his only son as a sacrifice to the god Moloch as a means to lift the siege (2 Kgs 16.3). In this mortal threat to the House of David, Isaiah uttered the first EMMANUEL oracle (Is 7.10–25). In it he tells Achaz that the besieging kings will soon be destroyed and that he has nothing to fear if he trusts in God alone and does not ask for help from Tiglath-Pileser III, the Assyrian King (2 Kgs 16.7–9). Ahaz refuses the sign that Isaia has offered in order to prove Yahweh's fidelity, but Isaiah insists on giving a sign to the House of David, "the virgin shall be with child, and bear a son, and shall name him Emmanuel."

Some interpreters hold that the prophecy is directly messianic and refers to the virgin birth of Jesus Christ. They argue that the term *'almâ* (marriageable girl, young woman, until her first child's birth) should mean a virgin, for a virgin birth would be a supernatural sign, whereas the mere prediction of a son's birth for Ahaz and his young bride would not be. Thus, they say that *'almâ* is synonymous here with the specific Hebrew word for virgin *tûlâ* (Lv 21.14; Jgs 21.12). Other scholars claim that the oracle is messianic only in a general way, or in a typical or deeper sense, and that it refers directly to the birth of Ahaz's son Hezekiah and through him to the Messiah. The form of address used by Isaiah in 7.13, "House of David" and the plural "you," recall Nathan's prophecy, although Isaiah is speaking to an unworthy and unbelieving descendant of David. This unworthiness does not destroy the promise, for Ahaz still embodies the prophet's hope for a Davidic king who will live up to the ideal expressed by the prophetic name given to him, Emmanuel, i.e., God is with us, He is on our side and we need no other help than His. The oracle, therefore, predicts the birth of a faithful king (realized in Hezekiah), the destruction of Samaria and Damascus, and the purifying devastation of Judah's lands by the Assyrians, a devastation that disrupts normal agriculture and reduces the land to pasturage (Is 7.15–25). Yet, the pasturage will produce an abundance of ''curds and honey'' (the idyllic food of faithful Israel) for the remnant purified by God's punishment and led by the faithful Davidic king, Emmanuel.

The second Emmanuel oracle (Is 8.23–9.6) again speaks of a son of David who will sum up in himself all the splendid attributes of Israel's ancient leaders and more recent heroes and will rule from David's throne with judgment and justice in contrast to the previous evil kings. His rule is placed against the background of the return from exile of the Northern Kingdom, Israel, and predicts the union of the two kingdoms again as it was in David's and Solomon's days.

The third oracle concerning this mysterious successor of David (Is 11.1–9) describes the king as full of Yahweh's spirit that endows him with qualities of wise understanding, shrewd strength, and an intimate knowledge and reverence for the Lord, the qualities of Solomon, David, and the prophets, but most of all, of Moses, God's intimate friend. The ruler will not rule like earthly kings but like a friend and spokesman for God, judging for the poor and afflicted, because of his divinely aided intuition, and destroying the wicked not by arms and war but by his mouth's rod and his lips' breath. He will be clothed in justice and faithfulness, the true religion, and his efforts will bring a new paradise without violence or any destruction, for they will fill the earth with the true, intimate, and faithful awareness of and devotion to Yahweh.

Isaiah's oracles continue the theme of royal Davidic Messianism, but they also develop it to include the ultimate recreation of the universe through a leader who is more prophet than king, more of a dedicated executor of Yahweh's will than a sovereign who demands obeisance. The historical is less pronounced than the eschatological and a new era in Messianism has begun. The religious and political frustrations of Israel and Juda had conditioned this prophetic leap into the completely Yahweh-controlled future and end, and the figure of the king who would be the Lord's regent would never be erased from Israel's hopes.

In Micah 4.14–5.1–5 the doom destined for Israel is contrasted with the deliverance to come through a king of David's line whose greatness will reach the ends of the earth. The passage follows the same pattern as the Isaian oracles and reflects the prophet's strong hope in Yahweh's fidelity to the covenant that He made with King David.

A century later, when Babylonia has taken Assyria's place as the scourge of Palestine, Jeremia foresees that Yahweh will raise up a just shoot to David who will rule justly and wisely and who will bear the prophetic name ''The Lord our justice'' (Jer 23.5–6). Thus, even though Jeremia's main message had been the ruin of Jerusalem and its monarchy, he still trusted in Yahweh's royal covenant when he referred to this future ruler.

Four more allusions to the royal Messiah are found in Ezekiel, Jeremiah's young contemporary. In Ezekiel 17.121 the allegory of the two eagles and the cedar that becomes through its shoot a modest vine and aspires through the help of another eagle to grow into a grandiose vine, ends with a vague prophecy (17.22–24); this is that Yahweh will make it a great cedar again, to prove that He is the only one who makes the little great and the great little. The allegory pictures a restoration of the Davidic monarchy according to eschatological proportions that are used again in the Gospels (cf. Ez 17.23 with Mt 13.32). It also seems that Ezechiel refers to Gn 49.10, the oracle in favor of Judah, when he says in Ezekiel 21.31–32 that Israel will be turned topsy-turvy and ''twisted'' until one comes who has the claim (judgment) against the city (Jerusalem?) and to whom Yahweh will deliver it. Ezekiel also depicts a new David as the shepherd and sole ruler of God's revitalized people in a parallel doublet (Ez 34.23–24 and 37.24–25).

Zechariah also describes a just, victorious, and humble king of Jerusalem who will dominate the known world and proclaim peace for all nations (Zec 9.9–10). In Amos too, although it is found in an addition to the prophet's original work, the Davidic Messianism is apparent (Am 9.11–12). The theme was popular among the postexilic prophets Haggai and Zechariah as concretized in their glorification of the freed exile, who may have been of royal rank, Zerubbabel (Hg 2.21–23; Zec 4.7–10; *cf* Zec 3.8 with 6.11–13 where Zerubbabel is obviously in question rather than Joshua). Even after the long years of Exile, another generation kept alive the ideal that there would be a son of David who would bear the royal insignia.

The ultimate picture of royal messianism depicts a kingdom and a new era that is outside history's stream in any human sense and hopes for Yahweh's divine reign through justice and judgment as executed by His mysterious vicar, the Messiah.

Priestly Messianism. With the fall of the monarchy, the long Exile, and the emphasis given to the new Temple and its priesthood in the second part of Ezekiel (40.1–47.12), the priest's importance grew to an unprecedented level. In the reconstruction after the Exile, the high priest emerged as a leader on a par with the ethnic leader (Zec 6.13c). The Temple's rebuilding under Zerubbabel and the high priest Josue became the inspiration of the discouraged refugees (Hg 2.1–9). The priesthood was restored in greater splendor and ritual than it had ever had before (Zec ch. 3). During this period most of the priestly laws found in Exodus, Leviticus, and Numbers received their full development from the Mosaic nucleus. Henceforth, any ruler of Israel, whether foreign or from the people, would have to share his government of the people with the high priest and his clan. David's inheritance and his election were not forgotten, but he became more and more a figure favorable to the priesthood and eventually the priest's great legislator after Moses (1 Chr 22.2–29.30). The priest also became the learned man, the scribe who knew the law and expounded it to the people, and, after a long struggle, the winner over independent sages, making them admit that, after all, ultimate wisdom was the Law that Moses gave through Aaron (Sir 24.22–27). Ezra, priest and scribe, was the father of this period and expressed the three main ideas of Judaism, the chosen people, the Temple, and the Law. The Chronicler (the collector of the great work that includes 1 and 2 Chronicles, Ezra, and Nehemia) must have been a priest also (*see* CHRONICLER, BIBLICAL). Nehemia, although he was more nationalistic than Ezra, followed the same inspiration as he, having been well molded by priestly tradition. Finally, the ethnic enclave around Jerusalem received as its sole ruler in its religio-political affairs the high priest, as exemplified by the splendid Simon of Sirach 50.1–21.

The priest's growth in importance influenced the messianic hopes of Judaism. A priestly clan led the rebellion against the Seleucids in the 2d century B.C. and by the end of that century had developed into the last Jewish kings, the Hasmonaean dynasty. The Maccabees were not of the highest order of priests, and by their domination they aroused the jealousy of the Sadocites, from whom the high priest by right was elected. This reaction against the HASMONAEANS was one of the factors leading to the formation of the Qumran sect, which opposed the illegitimate Jerusalem cult and longed for two Messiahs, one royal and one of priestly rank. The author of Hebrews was familiar with this development and described Jesus as the fulfillment of priestly messianic hopes (Heb 9.1–10.18).

Messianism in Deutero-Isaiah. Although the Isaian Book of Consolation (Is ch. 40 to 55, 60, and 62) calls Israel Yahweh's slave or servant, elected as a witness for Him among the nations, the same term has a different signification in the four ''SERVANT OF THE LORD'' oracles (Is 42.1–9; 49.1–6; 50.4–11; 52.13–53.12). The servant of the songs appears to designate a person rather than the collective Israel, although what is perhaps a gloss (49.3.) identifies the two servants. In 49.5–6 Yahwah's servant is clearly distinguished from Jacob's tribes and Israel's survivors. In the first oracle, he is Yahweh's elected, supported, and preferred slave, the bearer of His spirit, who quietly but surely brings God's justice, i.e., the true religion, to all nations by a teaching that will be a light for them and the blind, and a deliverance for captives. The same special election and universal mission is found in the second oracle, but in 49.4 the servant speaks as frustrated in his office, a development of the gentle quietness of the first oracle. A further elaboration of the servant's suffering is found in 50.5b–9 of the third oracle, which also emphasizes his discipleship and divine knowledge, the prerequisite for his teaching mission. Finally, in the most familiar and important fourth oracle, the ultimate glory and honor due to Yahweh's servant is contrasted with his unhappy history. In terms reminiscent of Jeremiah's suffering, the innocent servant's misery is described as unwarranted yet willed by God and freely accepted by the servant as an expiation for the faults of the multitudes and an intercession for sinners. He is submitted to humiliation and a dishonorable death like a lamb led to slaughter and accepts the punishment meant for ''us'' so that ''we'' might have peace. After his trials, he shall see the light and enter into his triumph; he shall prosper, he shall be raised high and be greatly exalted.

It is very difficult for a Christian to determine what these images and oracles meant to the sacred remnant of Israelites who returned from Babylon after the Exile, for he immediately transfers them to the Gospels and the preaching, suffering, and triumph of Jesus Christ and His new Israel, the Church. In their original impact the oracles must have evoked, however, the ''worm Jacob,'' the ''maggot Israel,'' who was and always will be, ''Israel, my servant, Jacob, whom I have chosen, offspring of Abraham my friend,'' (Is 41.14, 8); they evoked Israel as a collectivity, therefore, but an Israel whose exilic experience was typified by that of the innocent yet suffering chosen prophets of God, Jeremiah and Ezekiel, and later by Job, the innocent wise man and servant of God whose reason for suffering was hidden in the mystery of God's whirlwind. Whatever their original meaning may have been, the songs mixed into the messianic hopes, as did the whole Exile, the catalytic elements of suffering and death that were to hasten the movement toward the cross and the Resurrection.

The Son of Man in Daniel. The Book of Daniel, an apocalyptic literary form, written to console the Jews suffering from the persecution of Antiochus Epiphanus in the 2d century B.C., presents in Daniel 7.13–14, ''one like a son of man coming, on the clouds of heaven.'' This mysterious, apocalyptic image is identified in Daniel 7.18, 22 with the saints of the Most High, therefore a collectivity, but the apocryphal books, Enoch and 4 Esdras, as well as rabbinical tradition, understand the figure as a man who has divine qualities and is the final king of the ultimate Kingdom of God.

The idea of God's Kingdom that destroys and succeeds all other kingdoms is found also in the image of the rock detached mysteriously from the mountain to crush the statue that symbolizes the previous empires (Dn 2.34, 44–45; *cf.* Mt 21.42–44; Lk 20.17–18). Other prophecies in Daniel are messianic in tone and predict a future in expressions that go beyond the immediate hopes of freedom from the Antiochean persecutions (e.g., 9.24; 12.1–4).

A few more texts deserve at least passing mention. In Deuteronomy 18.15–22, Moses promises that Yahweh will raise up a prophet like himself to guide the people. Although the context indicates that the text refers to all the prophets, later Judaism understood it to envision a prophet-messiah. The New Testament writers also know of this interpretation (Jn 1.21; Mt 16.14; 13.57).

The suffering and finally triumphant just man of Psalm 21 (22) is considered by some to be in the tradition of Isaia's suffering servant of Yahweh, but there is no idea of vicarious suffering for others in the Psalm. However, the Psalm's images are applied to the suffering Jesus by the Gospels (Mt 27.35, 43, 46; Mk 15.34; Jn 19.24).

Messianism in the New Testament

The messianic story is completed in the New Testament, where the Old Testament prophecies' fulfillment is affirmed in the life, death, and Resurrection of Jesus, the Christ.

Use of Old Testament Prophecies. The New Testament writers never raised the question whether the Old Testament prophecies envisaged Christ's mystery literally and in every detail; they simply situated Christ's words and actions in the context of sacred history and thereby brought out the richest meanings of the ancient texts, which they then reapplied to the Christian mystery. Peter in his Pentecost sermon (Acts 2.14–36), for example, repeatedly relates the events to which he bears witness to the appropriate places in the Prophets and Psalms and gains greater knowledge thereby of the objects of his witnessing.

This process of enlightenment is not merely a movement from the prophecies to the realized visions, so that the Apostles could then recognize the reality. The reality, rather, is observed first—Jesus on the cross, in the tomb, resurrected, on the road to Damascus. Only then did the Apostles turn back from the reality's clearness to the prophecy's obscurity to see in it a deeper meaning, which in turn they again related to their experience to discover in it a greater depth of mystery.

This type of elucidation was most valid and appealing to the early Jewish Christians who were steeped in the sacred themes of the Old Testament. It was not a well-controlled method of literal and historical analysis; its looseness and freedom are at times shocking to minds trained in the exact methods of scientific criticism. But one cannot legitimately demand that the norms of modern exegesis be applied to religious teachers who were men of God and not literary and historical critics. Thus, to give but one example, Luke's summary of Peter's sermon (Acts 2.27) is not to be considered at fault for using the Greek text of Psalm 15 (16).9–10 rather than its Hebrew original, which is much less meaningful for believers in the Resurrection.

The Apostles' message was living and organic; it grew and adapted itself to various needs under the guidance of the Holy Spirit and in the secure awareness that they had been sent by Jesus to proclaim His mystery to the world. The validity of their use of prophecies rests not on an accurate and erudite knowledge of the Old Testament but on their divine commission as the new spokesmen for God and His Anointed; they were the new scribes,''instructed in the kingdom of heaven,'' who brought forth from their storeroom of memory and understanding, strengthened and enlightened by the risen Lord and His Spirit, things new and old (Mt 13.51–52; Lk 24.25–27).

Messianism in the Gospels. The four Gospels were the product of three sources that developed homogeneously and are still apparent in the final works. First, there was Jesus Himself, His words, deeds, and triumph as they were remembered by His disciples; then, the Apostles who, through the light of the Spirit and in the context of their post-Resurrection experiences as gospel preachers and founders of Christian churches, gradually came to a deeper understanding of what they had seen and heard of the Word of Life, and to a firmer grasp of the nature of the Kingdom that the Lord governed through them from heaven; and finally, the Gospel writers themselves who adapted the already developed message to their particular purposes. By keeping this development in mind, one may more accurately understand the Gospels' messianism.

Inaugural Proclamation of the Messiah. The accounts of the baptism, temptation, and hidden life of Christ are full of messianic allusions and affirmations that proclaim Jesus to be God's beloved Son in whom He is well pleased. He can cleanse man with the Holy Spirit that He received through the newly opened heavens because He has accepted His solidarity with sinful man, although He is innocent, by undergoing the penitential rite of John's baptism (Mk 1.8–11; Mt 3.13–15). The references to Isaiah's Suffering Servant are clear.

In the Fourth Gospel, in the context of His baptism, Jesus is heralded as the Lord for whom the Baptist prepares the way; God's Lamb or Servant, the Elect, who takes away the world's sin by baptizing with the Holy Spirit; the Teacher who is the source of all wisdom; the Messiah-Rock who has power to name His chief Apostle, the Rock; the fulfillment of the Law and the Prophets; Israel's King and God's Son; and finally, the Son of Man whose divine glory is manifested for the first time by the changing of water into wine (John 1.23–2.11).

In the temptation narratives, Jesus is described as the true and faithful Israel who fulfills the ideals of Deuteronomy 8.3; 6.16, 13 in conquering the major temptations to which the old Israel succumbed in the desert, thus showing His filial obedience and confidence in God and manifesting Himself as the perfect human creature whom the angels serve. He is the new Adam who conquers Satan and remains faithful to the Creation covenant; He is the new Moses who leads mankind into a new paradise where man is at ease with wild beasts and angels (Mt 4.1–11; Lk 3.23, 38; 4.1–13; Mk 1.12–13). *See* TEMPTATIONS OF JESUS.

In Matthew's Infancy Gospel, clear messianic titles are given Him: Son of David and Abraham; the Christ; Jesus, the Savior of His people; Emmanuel, God with us; King of the Jews, honored by Gentiles who bring Him gifts; and Israel, God's Son called out of Egypt (Mt 1.1, 16, 21–22; 2.2–11, 15). In Luke's parallel Gospel the post-Resurrectional titles given Jesus are Son of God, the Lord, Savior, Christ the Lord, the Christ of the Lord, and a contradicted Sign (Lk 1.35, 43; 2.11, 26, 34).

These conceptions of Jesus stem from the reality of His Passion and victory over death, sin, and the Prince of This World, the devil. They proclaim more than just an historical Jesus who was a wise teacher of the best the Jews had to offer but who ran afoul of corrupt official Judaism and Roman power and, after His execution for rebellion, was remembered with such longing by His disciples that they accepted the revelation of His Resurrection. This Jesus is the end and meaning of all the long history of salvation and His total mystery is proclaimed at the very opening of the Gospels in a setting that evokes all of Yahweh's faithful promises to Israel. The inaugural message, therefore, stems in its fullness from the post-Resurrection period when the Holy Spirit was teaching Jesus' Apostles ''all the truth'' (Jn 16.13).

The Messianic Secret. The common people to whom Jesus proclaimed His preliminary gospel longed for a warrior king who would deliver Israel from foreign domination. Since Jesus knew His messiahship had a different purpose, He commanded the demons not to make known His messianic character (Mk 1.25, 34; 3.12). He also wanted the cured not to broadcast His miracles (Mk 1.44; 5.43; 7.36; 8.26), and He even imposed silence about His messiahship on the Apostles until He had risen from the dead (Mk 8.30; 9.9).

His message was veiled of necessity because His audience could not have understood it and would have misinterpreted its meaning (Jn 6.15, 26; Mt 10.27), and because He had not completed His messianic office by the time of His death and Resurrection. He thus used enigmatic symbols that excited curiosity in the well disposed, but discouraged the enthusiasm of nationalists and disaffected the culpably indocile (Mt 13.13).

The messianic secret was not manufactured by the Evangelists; it corresponded to the historical reality but was emphasized by Mark to give force to the Christian confession of faith that he attributed to the Roman soldier at Jesus' death, '''Truly this man was the Son of God''' (Mk 15.39). Mark's words thereby also seem to indicate that the true evaluation of Jesus' messiahship will come only when the gospel has been preached to the Gentiles who will accept Him as their Savior (Mk 5.18–20; and note that according to Mk 16.7, the risen Jesus is to appear to the Disciples in Galilee, the ''District of the Gentiles''; *see also* Jn 4.25–26, 39–42). The mysterious Messiah then is really God's Son, the Lord Jesus, enthroned at God's right hand, who confirms the Apostles' preaching of the Word in the whole world by acting in them and through them by the miracles they perform (Mk 16.19; although the verse is probably not from Mark, it is of Apostolic origin, an inspired part of Scripture, and an apt ending for the Gospel of the messianic secret).

The Suffering Servant of God. When Peter had acknowledged that Jesus was the Messiah, and after Jesus had sternly commanded that the Disciples were not to reveal this secret, He then began to teach them openly and clearly that the Son of Man must suffer and be killed and arise again after three days. Peter reacted by rebuking Him for saying such a thing. In His turn, Jesus rebuked Peter for not understanding God's plan and for impeding its fulfillment by his human aspirations (Mk 8.27–33). Peter's misconception, coming immediately after his messianic confession, shows that even the closest followers did not understand the nature of Jesus' messiahship—that He was the Suffering Servant of God who would die for man's sin in order to enter into His glory. Despite the clear teaching (Mk 8.32a, 34–38; 9.9–13, 30–32; 10.32–34; 12.1–12; 14.7–8), the disciples did not grasp the meaning of Jesus' words until after He had been crucified and had risen (Lk 24.2527). After the Resurrection, however, the expiatory death and consequent triumph of Jesus became the main theme of the Apostolic preaching and was especially emphasized by St. Paul (1 Cor 1.17–25; Rom 3.25–26; 5.6–9).

The Son of Man. Jesus preferred to call Himself by this title, often using it in contexts of humiliation (Mt 8:20; 11.19; 17.22; 20.28) but also when He proclaimed His eschatological victory (Mt 17.9; 24.30; 25.31). It was used, therefore, to signify both His lowly, human condition and His transcendent nature as the king of God's final Kingdom (Mt 26.64). Jesus thus controlled the gradual revelation of His messianic character by the evolution of the title's meaning into the SON OF MAN at the right hand of God. This movement is parallel to the succinct but profound expression of Christ's mystery in Philippians 2.5–11 that terminates in the most transcendent title of all: Jesus is the Lord, i.e., Yahweh Himself.

Bibliography: L. DENNEFELD, *Dictionnarie de théologie catholique* 10.2:1404–1568. A. GELIN, *Dictionnaire de la Bible* 5:1165–1212, *Encycopaedic Dictionary of the Bible* 1511–25, esp. bibliog. L. CERFAUX et al., *L'Attente du Messie* (Paris 1954). P. F. CEUPPENS, *De prophetiis Messianicis in A. T.* (Rome 1935). P. ELLIS, *The Men and Message of the Old Testament* (Collegeville 1962). P. HEINISCH, *Christ in Prophecy,* tr. W. G. HEIDT (Collegeville 1956); *Theology of the Old Testament,* tr. W. G. HEIDT (Collegeville 1955) para. 49–53. M. J. LAGRANGE, *Le Messianisme chez les Juifs* (Paris 1909); *Le Judïisme avant Jesus-Christ* (Paris 1931). E. MASSAUX et al., *La Venue du Messie* (Paris 1962). S. MOWINCKEL, *He That Cometh,* tr. G. W. ANDERSON (Nashville 1956).

[M. J. CANTLEY]

MESSMER, SEBASTIAN GEBHARD

Archbishop, canonist; b. Goldach, Switzerland, Aug. 29, 1847; d. Goldach, Aug. 3, 1930. He attended the diocesan college of St. George near Saint-Gall, Switzerland, and the University of Innsbrück, Austria. Following his ordination on July 23, 1871, Bp. James R. Bayley invited him to teach theology and canon law at Seton Hall College, South Orange, N.J., where he remained for 18 years. He also did pastoral work and served as chaplain to St. Mary's orphanage, Newark, N.J. He was chosen to draft the decrees prior to the Third Plenary Council of Baltimore and to act as one of the council secretaries. He also helped to prepare the report of its deliberations for publication in 1886 and received an honorary D.D. from the pope for his efforts. In preparation for the assignment in 1889 to teach canon law at The Catholic University of America, he went to Rome where he earned a D.C.L. from the Collegio Appollinare. His tenure at the Catholic University ended with his appointment in 1891 as bishop of Green Bay, Wis. He attributed responsibility for his removal to the faculty who knew that he had been opposed to the establishment of the University.

His ten-year stay in the Wisconsin diocese resulted in the building of a number of parochial schools, academies, asylums, and hospitals. He sided with the Germans in the controversies between the Irish and German Catholics. He attacked the Bennett Law (1893) requiring compulsory education in the English language and championed the placement of Marquette's statue in the national capitol (1897). He promoted rural settlement and a Catholic summer school for the West, and sponsored the AMERICAN FEDERATION OF CATHOLIC SOCIETIES. He was a lifelong Republican, a foe of prohibition, women's suffrage, and socialism, holding that socialism was the basis of many labor unions. In 1903 he was transferred to Milwaukee as archbishop.

In his long administration of the Milwaukee Archdiocese (1903–30), there was a rapid expansion of parish schools, hospitals, sanitariums, and institutions for dependents. He gave generous support to Marquette University and Mt. Mary College, Milwaukee, Wis. As a result of his initiative, a chaplain was provided for the Catholic students at the University of Wisconsin, Madison (1906) and a superintendent of schools for the archdiocese was appointed. His articles appeared in the old *Catholic Encyclopedia, American Ecclesiastical Review, American Catholic Historical Review, Pastoral Blatt,* and *Salesianum.* Among his works are *Praxis Synodalis* (1883); he also edited: *Canonical Procedure in Criminal Cases of Clerics* (1886), from the German by Franz Droste; *Spirago's Method of Christian Doctrine* (1901); W. Devivier's *Christian Apologetics* (1903); and the *Works* of the Rt. Rev. John England, 7 v. (1908). Messmer's *Outlines of Bible Knowledge* (1910 and 1927) was based on A. Bruell's *Bibelkunde.* His honorary degrees included a D.D. from the University of Breslau in 1923 and L.L.D. from Marquette University in 1925. He was a curator of the State Historical Society of Wisconsin for many years.

Bibliography: B. J. BLIED, *Three Archbishops of Milwaukee* (Milwaukee 1955).

[P. L. JOHNSON]

METAPHYSICS

From the Greek τὰ μετὰ τὰ φυσικά (what comes after the physical) and the Latin *metaphysica* (after or beyond the physical), ontology, first philosophy, theology, wisdom, the philosophical science having as object being as being (τὸ ὄν ᾗ ὀν, whence ''ontology''), or the study of the meaning, structure, and principles of whatever is and inasmuch as it is or exists. In its material object, or the number of things it studies, metaphysics is all-inclusive, extending to everything and every aspect of whatever is or can exist, whether of a material, sensible, physical nature or of a higher, nonmaterial nature (from which extension to the most perfect and divine it is called "first philosophy" or "theology"). Nevertheless, metaphysics retains its distinctive point of vision, or formal object, inasmuch as it is concerned with things as beings, that is, according to the relation that any thing or aspect of things has to existence, rather than to one of the particular aspects treated in the other sciences. The unity of this point of view, centered on what is most fundamental to all reality, enables metaphysics to investigate the way in which the many are interrelated to the one in some form of real unity. Further, since things are reflected in knowledge, it enables metaphysics to order and evaluate the various types of speculative and practical knowledge (whence the term "wisdom").

The etymological derivation of metaphysics has been explained generally, though, it seems, erroneously, according to the theory of J. G. Buhle (1763 to 1821): from the fact that Andronicus of Rhodes (1st century B.C.) placed the treatises of Aristotle on this subject after the *Physics* for lack of any proper position in his scheme of the first complete edition of Aristotle's works. However, the name has been traced with probability by H. Reimer to Eudemus of Rhodes (3d century B.C.), the first editor of Aristotle's works, for whom it reflected not only that the subject matter in some sense transcends the physical aspect of things, but also the corresponding Aristotelian concern for the order of learning as proceeding from the more immediately sensible to the transcendent.

This article considers metaphysics in two parts. The first is concerned with its history, and the second with its elaboration as a science.

History of Metaphysics

Metaphysical thought arises from the WONDER generated by the tension between the characteristics of things experienced as multiple, individual, and contingent on the one hand and those of truth as one, universal, and necessary on the other. The history of metaphysics is constituted by man's progressing toward a more penetrating mode of vision (formal subject) and the correlative intrinsic and extrinsic principles that enable him to understand both the many as constituting one order of reality and the one truth in its multiple realizations.

Primitive Origins. That man's mind is naturally metaphysical is indicated by the vision of reality as a whole and the concern for explanation manifested in the ancient myths (*see* MYTH AND MYTHOLOGY). In Greece these were summarized in the *Theogony* of Hesiod, which stated the parts of the universe in the anthropomorphic form of the gods, unifying them in a genetic series and identifying in Eros an active principle for their interrelation. To attain a more precise view of this unity, it was necessary to supersede the anthropomorphic and symbolic form of the myths in order to attain a more explicit identification of their intellectual content and its source. This step was accomplished in concrete and personal terms by the Hebrews and in abstract terms by the Hindus and others in the East and by the Greeks in the West.

The Jews, from their earliest history to the Babylonian Exile in the 6th century B.C., under the tutelage of divine providence came to see that persons and things, however many, were one in their common dependence on God or, more exactly, in their dependence on a common God. "I am the first and I am the last; there is no God but me" [Is 44.6]. This unity in things was paralleled in the intentional order, where individuals by their fundamental response of mind and heart related themselves and their world to God. The repetition of this relation in concrete terms for single types of things ("who made the heavens in wisdom, . . . who spread out the earth upon the waters . . ."—Ps 135.5–6) manifests the need for a more abstract type of thought capable of identifying the proper extension and comprehension of the unifying relation to God.

The Oriental mind did carry metaphysical thought to the abstract and speculative level. HINDUISM in its scriptures, the UPANISHADS, expressed a decisive appreciation of unity through the one impersonal substance, Brahman or Ātman, as the intimate reality of all things. However, fatally underestimating the world of experience as an illusion and source of suffering, it placed the road to wisdom in an ascetical and mystical science of withdrawal from activity and in a movement upward into natural contemplation of God as a prelude to reabsorption into Ātman. In the 6th century B.C., BUDDHISM, having reduced all to empty phenomena in flux, held the supreme science to be one of deliverance from existence as such into the total indetermination called NIRVĀNA.

Greek Philosophy. The Greeks, in initiating their own speculative unification in the 6th century, B.C., possessed a firm appreciation of the reality of their world and a growing awareness of the value of intellectual clarity. Hence, their first steps were scientific in character, based on the evidence of the external senses and concluding in correlative terms that all was but particular states of water (Thales, *c.* 640 to 550) or other similar elements. Even here their concern opened beyond the merely physical to the metaphysical problem of overall unity, as is reflected in Anaximander's (*c.* 611 to 546) further reasoning to the "boundless" as beyond the diverse elements, unborn, all-encompassing, all-governing, and even divine [W. Jaeger, *The Theology of the Early Greek Philosophers,* tr. E. S. Robinson (Oxford 1947) 24–36]. PYTHAGORAS (*c.* 580 to 500), in holding all to be numbers, attained a second level of evidence corresponding to the internal senses. Finally, PARMENIDES arrived at the third, uniquely intellectual, and metaphysical appreciation of the real in its own proper term, being. ''Being is; for To Be is possible, and Nothingness is not possible,'' [figure 6, K. Freeman, *Ancilla to the Pre-Socratic Philosophers* (Cambridge, Massachusetts 1957) 43]. Since being could differ only by nonbeing, or nothing, Parmenides denied anything other than the one absolutely perfect and unchanging sphere. This gave being the meaning of identity or what can be thought (figure 3, *ibid.*; figure 2, 42), contrasting with the position of HERACLITUS (540 to 475) that all was becoming. This contrast reflected the attainment by Greek philosophy of the properly metaphysical: the real as such—the explicit search for its internal and external principles and, in their terms, for the relation between the multiplicity manifested by experience and the unity appreciated by the mind. This search occupied the golden age of Greek philosophy.

PLATO (429 to 348) concluded from the fact of multiple beings to a principle of limitation or nonbeing as a ''not-that-being'' (*Soph.* 259A), and from the similarity among beings to something one or absolute in which the multiple participate as limited imitations. However, the combination of the Parmenidean meaning of being as intelligible identity with the Socratic method led to the transfer of reality from the multiple to that which the multiple imitate, the transcendent formal unities as Ideas to be contemplated and hierarchically ordered under the supreme Idea of the Good or the One (*Republic* 509). Man's highest calling and wisdom must then be to tend with all his powers, including the affective, to an ever clearer appreciation of the Ideas as the basis for guiding his actions (*Symp.*).

ARISTOTLE (384 to 322), while retaining the goal of intellectual clarity and classically developing the division and structure of the sciences, initiated a more active understanding of FORM, based on a realist appreciation of the form of matter in changing things. This led him to forms separated from matter, which were not only objects of contemplation but themselves living, acting, knowing, and ultimately ''the knowing on knowing'' (νόησις νοήσεως νόησις *Meta.* 1074b 34). Related to this new level of reality was the distinct science of metaphysics, which in comparison to physics is both higher in dignity, because concerned with the unchanging, immaterial, and divine being, and broader in content, because concerned with being as being and hence all being (*Meta.* 1003a 20–1004a 1, 1025b 1–1026a 33). Aristotle, it seems, never perfectly conciliated the two understandings of metaphysics because his insight into being was not sufficient to allow for an understanding of the way in which the highest being could be the cause of being, as being in all beings. Despite the active understanding of form within the perspective of being as identity, form, and essence, the Parmenidean problem of the one and the many remained insoluble in these terms. This is seen from the limited attention given by the Greeks to the best manifestation of the simple affirmation of being, the PERSON as a free and creative center in time and as capable of individual immortality. (*See* GREEK PHILOSOPHY.)

Christianity. Christian thought presented the context for a penetrating insight into the act of being by underlining these very notions: in its distinguishing person from nature in the doctrine of the Trinity, and then in its heightening the appreciation of the created person's affirmation of self as gift in a response of love to the divine redemptive invitation to become sons, brothers, and heirs; and in its distinguishing creation from the Trinitarian processions, thus distinguishing form from the most formal effect of creation, the existence (''to be,'' or *esse*) according to which a being *is* (the perfection of all perfections). The history of metaphysics in the Middle Ages consists in the major developments made possible by this more penetrating appreciation of being and evoked by the elaboration of the resultant theologies. These developments were made first on a more Platonic basis by St. AUGUSTINE (354 to 430) and his school through St. BONAVENTURE (1231 to 74), and then with an increasing addition of the Aristotelian systemization and realism by way of Arabian philosophy, culminating in the major syntheses of St. THOMAS AQUINAS (1224 to 1274), John DUNS SCOTUS (*c.* 1274 to 1308), and others (see below).

Modern Era. Modern and contemporary metaphysics, finding the realistic metaphysics of being of the classical Christian philosophies of the Middle Ages already negated in the conceptualist philosophy of WILLIAM OF OCKHAM (*c.* 1349) and his followers, proceeded to develop its metaphysics from the subject as manifested by the *cogito* of R. DESCARTES (1596 to 1650). For the deleterious results, extending even to the negation of the possibility of metaphysics as a science, *see* METAPHYSICS, VALIDITY OF. Within this context, however, such classical rationalists as B. SPINOZA (1632 to 1677) and G. W. LEIBNIZ (1646 to 1727) contributed importantly to working out a logically deductive pattern of ideas; the schemata of the critical philosophy of I. Kant (1724 to 1804) and the dialectical sequences of G. W. F. HEGEL (1770 to 1831) further expressed reality's organic and developing character. Without realistic foundations, these philosophies inevitably progressed from positing that being is met in CONSCIOUSNESS to IDEALISM, holding that being is consciousness.

Contemporary metaphysics has sought to identify a place and a topic for metaphysical investigation that will be without presuppositions in order to allow the human mind most authentically to attain the real. In the transcendental phenomenology of E. HUSSERL (1859 to 1938), philosophy is concerned with the knower and is directed toward grasping the world-constituting consciousness as such, rather than as one thing among many, because to grasp fully the possibilities of consciousness would be to grasp adequately being itself. For M. Heidegger (1889–1976), on the contrary, philosophy seeks the meaning of "to be" rather than of man, though the place of philosophical investigation is man in the world with others, the place in which "to be" has meaning for him. (*See* EXISTENTIAL METAPHYSICS and EXISTENTIALISM for a discussion of the existential emphasis in recent Thomistic thought and in contemporary forms of existentialism.) Together, the rationalistic and existentialistic developments of modern times have achieved a more reflective appreciation of man's grasp of being and of its personal dimension.

The Science of Metaphysics

The history of metaphysics manifests a universal striving of the human mind to clarify its appreciation of REALITY as a unified whole. To do this effectively, the mind must pass beyond the simple constatation of a unified reality to the discovery of its causes by means of SCIENCE (SCIENTIA), the discursive process leading to the perfect knowledge of its subject by discovering its causes and attributes (Thomas Aquinas, *In meta.,* proem.; *In 1 anal. post.* 2.3). As the attributes are related to the subject through the middle term, which is the real definition of the quiddity of the subject (*In 2 anal. post.* 1.9), the subject is not only the term concerning which knowledge is sought but also the source and norm of the scientific knowledge that concerns it. It was the diversity of meanings historically attributed to being (identity, substance, "to be") as the subject that lay at the root of the various forms of metaphysics noted above; and if a metaphysics is to be a study of reality itself as ACT or as a relation to existence, it can be so only if this be the nature of its proper subject.

Initiation of the Science. As there is nothing in the INTELLECT that was not first in the SENSES, the realistic character of scientific knowledge immediately implies two levels of ABSTRACTION, of subjects, and hence of speculative sciences: physics abstracting from individual matter and proceeding on the evidence from the external senses to study things as expressed by qualities, and mathematics abstracting from common sensible matter and proceeding on the evidence of the internal senses to study things as quantified (*see* SCIENCES, CLASSIFICATIONS OF). Being, as a third level of formal subject prescinding from all matter, has been proposed on various bases: (1) a simple dissociation based on the mind's recognition that being and material are not equivalent, even though no special evidence for this be given; (2) a gradual process of removing the various specifications from being till there remains only a univocal "not nothing" of minimal significance; and (3) a separation of being as *esse* based outside the natural order on the common Judeo-Christian revelation of God as "I am who am" (Ex 3.14). Whatever be said about the distinctive value or problems of these approaches, the perfection of metaphysics as a distinct human science seems to require: first, that its subject, whose real definition is the middle term in the discursive process of metaphysics, be drawn from material things, the QUIDDITY of which is the proper object of the human intellect (*In Boeth. de Trin.* 5.4); second, that the separation of a distinct meaning for being from material being be validated by the witness of actually existing nonmaterial beings (*In 4 Meta.* 5.593).

This fact of nonmaterial reality has been reflected constantly by man's commonsense appreciation of a power that transcends man; of the human person as a unique subject of justice, love, and freedom; and of his many social and artistic expressions. Although all these manifest a level of nonmaterial reality untouched by the sciences of the first two degrees of abstraction, the initiation of the science of metaphysics itself is better supported by the full strength of the scientific knowledge. Phenomenological investigations have usefully reflected on man as the crossroads where the flesh assumes the spirit and the spirit becomes incarnate; but the attainment of being as act is most amply founded on natural beings experienced as existing on as broad a base as can be provided by the following combination of all the nonmetaphysical sciences.

Aristotle's classical statement of the structure of the science of physics leads to the nonmaterial after identifying form and matter as changing being's intrinsic principles. However, this composition is shown in the *Physics* (books 7 and 8) to manifest a dependence for its ultimate explanation on something nonmaterial. Though, in physics, this can be described only in such negative and relative terms as "not material," "not changing," "not spatial," and "not temporal," physics does establish the existence of the nonmaterial as presupposed for whatever reality is had by physical substances and their accidents. In Aristotle's *De anima* and in his other psychological writings, the nonmaterial character of man's acts of intellection and volition are seen to manifest the nonmaterial character of his substantial form, or soul (*see* SOUL, HUMAN; SPIRIT). Here, the extensive recent insights concerning human consciousness and freedom and the related significance of all dimensions of man and the universe give further indication of the reality and significance of the nonmaterial. Again, EXEMPLARY CAUSALITY, in relation to the speculative science of mathematics and its principles, allows the reality of the mathematical to manifest a higher and nonmaterial reality. Finally, in the practical order, the investigation of the end, or goal, required to open the full scope of man's free activity is seen as the contemplation of something transcending the material. Hence, as the human mind establishes the scientific processes by which it extends its knowledge with a controlled certainty and necessity to the various dimensions of reality, it becomes increasingly aware of the reality of the nonmaterial.

By this fact of immaterial reality, the mind is enabled to make the negative judgment of separation that the real is not necessarily material. It can also conclude that what makes the real to be real, the real precisely as real, is not material—though, of course, many real beings are really material (*In Boeth. de Trin.* 5.3, 4, and ad 5). By this negative judgment the mind removes a restriction to its understanding of things. Hence, whereas previously, having attained all things through the senses, it spoke of reality precisely as sensible, it is now able to speak of these distinctively according to that by which they are real. The mind also knows that real is not simply a more general term for what had previously been stated more specifically. Because it knows that there are some things that exist but are not material, it knows that to speak of things precisely as real is to express them in a way that is more fundamental and penetrating than are any of their prior modes of attainment.

From the above, it can be seen that the common notion of being (being as being, being in general), which is the subject of the science of metaphysics, is expressed by "what is," for being affirms in act "what" is and of whatever kind, and does so by the "to be," which, as the actuality of all determinations of kind or nature, is the most formal element in being. Together the "what," or ESSENCE, and the "is," or "to be," or EXISTENCE, express the notion of being (*see* BEING; ESSENCE AND EXISTENCE; POTENCY AND ACT).

From the foundation and mode of separation of being, it is also clear that the resulting notion is not a univocal least common denominator, whose differences have been progressively removed; rather, it actually includes the reality of all such differences precisely as real, even if only implicitly. At the same time, the notion of being is not equivocal (NOMINALISM), lacking in any common significance in its application to the many different things. On the contrary, the notion of being is analogical; that is, it includes within itself the differences by which beings are really distinct one from another—it is different simply in its application to distinct things while at the same time it has a certain similarity in its significance when applied to each of them (*see* ANALOGY).

Elaboration of the Science. After it is seen that the subject of metaphysics is being, and that its mode is analogical, the first and necessary phase of the science of metaphysics is to identify the properties of its subject, thus unfolding its meaning. These properties could not be really distinct from being in its transcendence; rather, they express explicitly what already is implicit, but actual, in being itself (*De ver.* 1.1). They include unity, truth, goodness, and beauty. By unity being is identified as indivisible within itself, that is, as not shared with what it is not or with nonbeing and, by implication, as divided from all other beings (*see* UNITY). Being in its identity is able to be present in the intellect, and hence to be true (*see* TRUTH). Being, as an intelligible identity, is also able to be related to the will, and hence to be good (*see* GOOD). All of these are drawn together in the property of beauty, which is being inasmuch as it pleases when seen (*see* BEAUTY). Parallel to these transcendental properties, and expressive of them in the form of judgments of being as possessing these properties, are the first principles of being (*see* FIRST PRINCIPLES). To being as one, there correspond the principle of CONTRADICTION: being is not nonbeing; and the principle of IDENTITY: being is being, or being is itself. To being as true, there corresponds the principle of SUFFICIENT REASON. Finally, to being as the transcendent good, there corresponds the principle of FINALITY. Once the subject of metaphysics has been attained, these properties and principles can be discovered by an analytic process reflecting on the significance of what it means to be. In fact, Parmenides made notable accomplishments in this phase of metaphysics, even though he maintained that there could be but one being.

In order to go further into the science of metaphysics and to discover the intrinsic principles of its subject and the external relationship between beings, it is necessary to introduce the more synthetic phase of metaphysical method, wherein the mind returns to the experiential order and its evidence for a plurality of beings. This evidence, understood in terms of being as being and its property of unity, poses the problem of the one and many for the first time in direct metaphysical terms. This, indeed, includes two problems: first, how there can be more than one being or how being can be limited and, second, how these many beings, while differing one from another, can still be similar as beings.

The limitation of being opens to the mind the reality of a limiting principle that is not existence, but is inside the being, forming a unity with the existence to which it is related as potency to act. As allowing the mind to attain an insight into the internal structure of multiple and, hence, FINITE BEING, this reflection is of the greatest moment for the development of the science of metaphysics; in it, Aquinas achieved his synthesis of Christian PLATO-

NISM and ARISTOTELIANISM. This discovery concerning internal structure is paralleled by another concerning extrinsic relations; this springs from the second problem, concerning the way in which the many can be similar as beings, and yet distinct from one another. This, together with the problem of the actuation of the potency, opens the path for the mind to Absolute Being, the cause of the subject of metaphysics. The essence of this Being is Its existence, a Subsistent Existence and PURE ACT in which all multiple beings participate precisely as being, or according to their relation to existence. Thus is established a unity between all beings such that the absolute unity identified by Parmenides as characteristic of being is not destroyed but rather is opened out to a subordinate realm of multiple and participating beings (*see* PARTICIPATION).

In similar cycles the problem of the one and the many considered synthetically yields evidence of new unities. These are either unities of a specific kind among the multiple beings that lead to knowledge of the act-potency structure of form and matter within essence and further to the Divine Mind for the ultimate explanation of specific unities; or they are unities of many accidents as acts of the one substance, laying the foundation for a further union between beings by CAUSALITY. Hence, the science of metaphysics gradually unfolds by a process of ANALYSIS AND SYNTHESIS wherein it elaborates the internal principles and the external causes of its subject, being as being, and comes to understand all things in the light of these.

Characteristics. Such a metaphysics is supreme in universality, intellectuality, and certitude. (*In Meta.*, proem.). The distinctive universality is had, first, according to comprehension, for the formal subject of the science is the most fundamental value of all, the relation to existence; second, according to extension, for, studying things as beings, the science is transcendent in its concerns, extending to every being and aspect of being; and finally, according to dignity, inasmuch as it carries the mind even to the divine in its search for the cause of its subject.

A second characteristic of metaphysics is its supreme intellectuality. Intellectuality is a mode according to which all is comprehended in one simple act and idea that attains the full truth of manifold beings and their principles. The human mind, proceeding abstractively, approaches this ideal imperfectly, but truly, to the degree that it is able to unify its knowledge of all things in one formal subject, through which it attains a uniquely simple, immediate, and comprehensive intellectual knowledge (*In Boeth. de Trin.* 6.1.3 ad 1). This special intellectuality is had by metaphysics inasmuch as its formal subject is being, the common object of the intellect and the source from which its principles are derived immediately and its conclusions most directly. Hence, if difficult of attainment, metaphysics has a most profound proportion to the human intellect, with its actual and possible openness to being.

The third characteristic of metaphysics as a science follows from the above. This is its special objective certitude, which derives from its subject and from its reasoning processes, as founded and verified in the first and most evident of all principles, the principle of contradiction.

Fourth, as the science that is most perfectly universal, intellectual, and certain, metaphysics takes on the character of natural WISDOM. For if the wise man, as Aristotle describes him, must have universal and difficult knowledge, greater than ordinary certitude, and a capacity to identify causes, to seek knowledge for its own sake, and to be able to rule others, then metaphysics fulfills this necessity. It is the most universal science, extending even to what most transcends the human mind; yet it has the greatest certitude and commitment because concerned with being itself; and finally, because it knows the principles of all being, it is able to rule and direct the sciences that are concerned with particular types of beings. Metaphysics, therefore, stands at the culmination of man's knowledge; it derives from a negative judgment based on evidence from all the sciences, and, as a potential whole, it is present in the exercise of all other intellectual virtues, wherein it is but partially expressed. Since it uses other sciences to enlarge its knowledge, its ordering function in their regard is part of the work of wisdom itself.

Thus metaphysics takes on a supreme human value. ''The ultimate perfection which the soul can attain, therefore, is, according to the philosophers, to have delineated in it the entire order and causes of the universe. This they hold to be the ultimate end of man. We, however, hold that it consists in the vision of God'' (*De ver.* 2.2).

See Also: WISDOM; THEOLOGY, NATURAL; CHRISTIAN PHILOSOPHY; PHILOSOPHY.

Bibliography: C. FABRO, *La nozione metafisica di partecipazione secondo S. Tommaso d'Aquino* (2d ed. Turin 1950); *Participation et causalité selon S. Thomas d'Aquin* (Louvain 1961). J. DE FINANCE, *Être et agir dans la philosophie de saint Thomas* (Paris 1945). É. H. GILSON, *Being and Some Philosophers* (2d ed. Toronto 1952). T. C. O'BRIEN, *Metaphysics and the Existence of God* (Washington 1960). L. J. ESLICK, ''What Is the Starting Point of Metaphysics?'' *The Modern Schoolman* 34 (1957) 247–63. L. B. GEIGER, ''Abstraction et séparation d'après S. Thomas,'' *Revue des sciences philosophiques et théologiques* 31 (1947) 3–40. A. MANSION, ''Philosophie première, philosophie seconde et métaphysique chez Aristotle,'' *Revue philosophique de Louvain* 56 (1958) 165–221. R. W. SCHMIDT, ''L'emploi de la séparation en métaphysique,'' *ibid.*, 58 (1960) 373–93. J. D. ROBERT, ''La métaphysique, science distincte de toute autre discipline philosophique, selon saint Thomas d'Aquin,'' *Divus Thomas* 3d series 50 (1947) 206–22. V. E. SMITH, ''The Prime Mover: Physical and Metaphysical Considerations,'' *American Catholic Philosophical Association. Proceedings of the Annual Meeting* 28 (1954) 78–94. H. HEINER, ''Die Entstetehung und ursprungliche Bedeutung des Namens Metaphysik,'' *Zeitschrift für philosophische Forschung* 8 (1954) 210–37. T. ANDŌ, *Metaphysics: A Critical Survey of Its Meaning* (The Hague 1963). G. GUSDORF, *Mythe et métaphysique* (Paris 1953).

[G. F. MCLEAN]

METAPHYSICS, VALIDITY OF

The history of Western philosophy is one alternately marked by metaphysical and antimetaphysical currents of thought. Looking back on this history, one can discern certain patterns. Each time metaphysics reached a new crest, there set in a reaction against it—typified by the movements known as SKEPTICISM, EMPIRICISM, and FIDEISM. After the apex of metaphysics reached by PLATO and Aristotle, scant progress was made in this area until the Middle Ages, when it was to flower once again. Then, toward the end of the Middle Ages, SCHOLASTICISM became increasingly decadent, preparing the way for a new rejection of metaphysics in the modern epoch. This rejection has extended all the way into contemporary philosophy, and while its strength has dissipated, it continues as a strong movement.

The present article surveys the antimetaphysical trends promoted by influential philosophers from the late Middle Ages to the end of the modern period. A brief critique is given, followed by an appraisal of the contemporary status of the movement from the viewpoint of moderate realism.

Ockham. In the period of the decline of metaphysics and scholasticism, the Franciscan WILLIAM OF OCKHAM is most representative among those who can be singled out as contributing to this decadence. Ockham understandably rebelled against the picayune distinctions introduced into philosophy by an earlier confrere, John DUNS SCOTUS, the Subtle Doctor. The voluntarism of Duns Scotus presented a less favorable climate for the growth of metaphysics than did the intellectualism of St. THOMAS AQUINAS. In sharp reaction to the increasing complexities introduced in philosophy, Ockham formulated his famous principle of parsimony, popularly known as Ockham's razor: ''Beings are not to be multiplied without necessity.''

None could quarrel with the statement of the principle, only with its possible interpretation. Ockham interpreted it liberally and used it ruthlessly to eliminate many of the traditional distinctions of metaphysics (*see* DISTINCTION, KINDS OF). He accepted as real only those distinctions implying separability—a legacy whose error was continued by René Descartes. Previously acknowledged real distinctions, such as those between principles of being, Ockham placed in the category of logical distinctions. He thus turned over much of the subject matter of metaphysics to the science of logic. Ockham limited the use of DEMONSTRATION so severely (denying, for example, that one can establish the spirituality and immortality of the human soul) that he became increasingly dependent upon faith for genuine certitude. Accepting only the reality of singulars, Ockham initiated also ''the destruction of concrete universality'' (É. H. Gilson, *History of Christian Philosophy in the Middle Ages* 492). Ockham's terminism further combined strong elements of NOMINALISM and skepticism, both of which proved antithetical to metaphysics. Modern philosophy was to be strongly influenced by both.

Hobbes. Thomas HOBBES, who was subjected to the Ockhamist influence at Oxford, was an early representative of empiricism in the modern era. Openly nominalistic and linguistically oriented, Hobbes was preoccupied with words. He explained away the universal idea as but a common name serving as a mark for memory or imagination. Accordingly, science could be defined as ''a knowledge of all the consequences of names appertaining to the subject in hand'' (*Leviathan,* 1.5). For Hobbes, reasoning differed from sensation only in degree. It could be explained as nothing more than the adding and subtracting of various names. Prepared to simplify all philosophy along the lines of MECHANISM, Hobbes needed but two principles—matter and motion. Only what could be subsumed under these two categories could lay claim to being real. Metaphysics was thereby ruled out of court, and the way was paved for accepting only the positive sciences as valid.

Berkeley. Definitely opposed to the mechanism and especially the MATERIALISM of Hobbes, but proceeding initially from empiricist principles, Bp. George BERKELEY also legislated against metaphysics. But to make his case, he had to eliminate the material world and the substances it purportedly contained. Exhibiting greater consistency than Locke, who accepted substance simply as an ''I know not what'' (*Essay on Human Understanding,* 2.23.2), Berkeley insisted that for all unthinking things, to be (*esse*) is to be perceived (*percipi*). A material thing, then, is but the sum of the ideas of its qualities. Consequently, things exist only in a mind—whether man's or God's. In denying the extramental status of the material world, Berkeley eliminated the need for abstraction—ideas being given to man in various sequences by God. Although he accepted the reality of spiritual substances and a ''notional'' knowledge of them, Berkeley's position on this point was soon to be refuted by Hume.

Hume. Briefly stated, the position of David HUME can be described as follows: all genuine knowledge must have its validity tested by tracing it to primary impressions derived from experience. Now, in considering the nature of these impressions, one observes that they involve only phenomenal aspects. The same can be said of the knowledge that the agent possesses of himself. By what speculatively verifiable right, then, may one conclude to the reality of anything other than phenomena? Since man cannot trace the complex notions of substance or cause to corresponding sensory impressions, he cannot confirm their validity. Nevertheless, their practical utility is undeniable. It follows, then, that not only metaphysics and its substances are to be criticized as human pretensions, but all scientific (i.e., causal) knowledge as well.

Speculatively, only skepticism was tenable for Hume. Practically, however, he placed his trust in instinct, feeling that it would prevail over the impasse of speculative knowledge, thereby enabling man to continue living as he had in the past. Man could also turn to the vividness of certain impressions, if he wished to provide ground for the probable acceptance of an extraphenomenal world. It should be noted, though, that it would not be the real object itself that provided such probable grounds; rather it would be the way the impression of the object was present in the consciousness of the knower.

It is no exaggeration to state that Hume was the most consistent of the empiricists. He resolutely maintained that the image is the object of knowledge and exhibited no hesitancy in accepting the full consequences of the epistemological cul-de-sac into which this led. Hume succeeded in bringing empiricism to its irreducible base, allowing no semblance of metaphysics within it. After Hume's attack, many felt that the only way open for philosophical progress would be to commence along a different path. This trail, which also proved to be an antimetaphysical one, was explored by Immanuel Kant.

Kant. Kant attempted to weld together the irreconcilable positions of Wolffian-Leibnizian RATIONALISM and British empiricism. Never doubting the scientific validity of the universal and necessary (a Kantian heritage bequeathed by rationalism) or the requirement for experience as the only means by which one can progress in knowing (Kant's recent legacy from empiricism), the German thinker constructed a monumental synthesis based upon these twin presuppositions. That Kant met with a measure of success is an undeniable fact, but it is also undeniable that he accomplished this at the expense of metaphysics.

Kant berated the a priori metaphysics of rationalism as failing to provide for any new knowledge. He pointedly asked how it was that metaphysics, supposedly queen of the sciences, found herself without a court. In fact, not only her crown, but her claims to science as well were in jeopardy. Despite the strong criticism of Hume with respect to all scientific knowledge, Kant never seriously doubted the validity of mathematics and physics. But he always entertained suspicions about the scientific status of metaphysics, suspicions confirmed as a result of Hume's criticism. In order to solve the problem of Hume and at the same time provide for a philosophy of Newtonian science, Kant subjected philosophy to his own "Copernican Revolution." Henceforth, he would explain knowledge as revolving around the knower instead of around the object. This differed sharply from the more classical explanation of knowing as a reception of the form of the object in the matter of the knower. According to Kant, it would be more fruitful to proceed on the assumption that the matter of the object is received and the form is imposed upon it by the knower. Since the form confers intelligibility, and since this is due to the knower, "the understanding does not derive its laws (a priori) from, but prescribes them to, nature" (*Prolegomena,* 36). Because man cannot know until *after* he imposes the form upon the raw datum, it is literally impossible for him to know the thing in itself—the noumenon—the real world. "All the properties which constitute the intuition of a body belong merely to its appearance" (*ibid.* 13.2).

Whatever is transcendent, then, is unknowable and remains so always—for the knower cannot get "outside" himself. Yet man is capable of knowing the appearance of things through the forms of sensibility (i.e., space and time) or through the categories of understanding (i.e., quantity, relation, quality, and modality). The scientific validity of phenomenal knowledge is therefore preserved. Insofar as such knowledge involves the datum as well as the structure of the knower, scientific (i.e., synthetic a priori) propositions about phenomena can be constructed. Once this is seen, it becomes clear why Kant never asks "whether," but only "how," scientific propositions in physics and mathematics are possible.

With respect to metaphysics, however, the question is not "how" but "whether" such synthetic a priori propositions are possible. In Kant's mind, metaphysics answers the latter question by extravagantly proposing to transcend experience. This he strongly challenged, asserting that to do so is simply impossible. On the basis of his own epistemology, Kant was perfectly consistent. Yet he still had to explain the obvious and irrepressible tendencies of his predecessors to accept metaphysics as a science. Kant fully recognized this and claims to have laid bare its uncertain foundations. There are rooted in reason, he says, ideas of God, the world, and the soul. But these are purely formal and seek application to something "given" (to a matter) for content. But the matter they seek to join is not on the phenomenal side; it is on the noumenal level. Since man cannot reach this order, he will always be frustrated in such a quest. Nevertheless, because he has these ideals (which may help to give goals to science, and so serve as regulative principles), man can always be expected to engage in the fruitless attempt to transcend experience. Eventually, Kant permitted metaphysics the role of a critique of reason and conceded to it a moral value. But he was convinced in his own mind that he had buried, once and for all, its pretentious claims to being a science. Despite Kant's momentous efforts to bridge the gap between empiricism and rationalism, his philosophy paradoxically resulted in a dualism itself—a dualism of PHENOMENA versus NOUMENA, of appearance versus reality. It remained for G. W. F. HEGEL to complete the synthesis.

Hegel. If there is a principle that governs the philosophy of Hegel, it is that the real is rational and the rational is real. Given such a principle, there is no longer need sharply to separate the order of appearance from that of things-in-themselves. Appearance and reality amount to the same thing under two different names. The same may be said for logic and metaphysics—hence the cryptic description of Hegel's system as panlogism. Metaphysics, for Hegel, finally gives way to logic. His entire system develops dynamically according to the dialectic of thesis, antithesis, and synthesis. Two contradictories are sublated and in turn form a unity, preserving the worth of the old components, yet providing for the new. Thus the contradictories of being and nonbeing dialectically evolve into becoming. This system of absolute mind or absolute idealism was at once the culmination and the termination of modern philosophy in its attack upon metaphysics.

Critique. By and large, the rejection of metaphysics by the philosophers mentioned was an outgrowth of their epistemologies. None subscribed to the position of moderate REALISM, which holds that the universal, while formally in the mind, is fundamentally in the thing—that the mind knows the universal nature in the singular material thing (Thomas Aquinas, *Summa theologiae* 1a, 84.7). All denied a genuine doctrine of intellectual ABSTRACTION, claiming either that the INTELLECT is a constructive device or a refined sensory power. Such being the case, it is highly questionable whether the metaphysics rejected by these philosophers was the metaphysics of Aristotelian and Thomistic philosophy. Kant, for instance, had refuted Wolffian-Leibnizian metaphysics as a science of pure possibles, but he hardly administered the coup de grâce to traditional metaphysics.

There have even been some negative benefits accruing to Thomism by virtue of the critique established by modern philosophies. Among these is the existential reminder that metaphysics should proceed from an empirical base and concern itself with real being. It must curb the tendency to become excessively a priori. In short, traditional metaphysics has been forced to rethink its position—an exercise that must always be deemed as contributing to its health.

Contemporary Status. To a large extent, the antimetaphysical trends in the contemporary period of philosophy follow the patterns of empiricism. Auguste COMTE sounded the clarion call for POSITIVISM by dismissing the theological and metaphysical as anachronisms in the past development of human thought. In his view, one no longer need view God as transcendent (theological) or as immanent (metaphysical); He has been wholly eliminated by science. The positive sciences, rather than metaphysics or theology, henceforth provide the rallying point for humanism in the new culture.

The neopositivists continue in this view and, indeed, even outdo Comte in their antimetaphysical bias (*see* LOGICAL POSITIVISM). The Vienna Circle (Wiener Kreis) of M. Schlick, R. Carnap, H. Feigl, and others declared open war on metaphysics. Abetted by linguistic analysis, they sought to prove that metaphysical statements are neither true nor false, but meaningless. At best, metaphysics reflects an emotive meaning or perhaps an aspiration (as Kant suggested), but it presents no cognitive meaning. Only the sciences can provide advances in genuine knowledge, a position known as SCIENTISM. Metaphysics either contents itself with tautologies (which are certain because they have no content) or with pseudopropositions (which are sentences having no means of VERIFICATION).

Although some linguistic analysts are philosophically neutral, others—represented by such men as A. J. Ayer, Gilbert Ryle, and Anatole Rapoport—dogmatically refuse to accord cognitive meaning to metaphysical statements. With the scientific empiricists, they insist that in order for statements to be meaningful, they must meet the demands of the principle of verifiability. Basically, that principle requires that in order for a proposition to be factually meaningful, there must be ways of proving or disproving it. Those more moderate in their demands (such as Hans Reichenbach) grant degrees of probability as indicative of meaningful propositions. Ayer, however, does not grant even the possibility of proving or disproving the probability of God's existence. In his view, that there is or is not a God is not even a meaningful question, for there is no way of verifying or refuting it.

In attempting to clarify and refine the principle of verifiability, positivists hold for the necessity of deducing some experimental, experiential, or operational statement from a meaningful proposition. The metaphysician, of course, claims that this is not altogether fair, for it prejudices the case from the start, admitting for man only the attainment of empirical knowledge. One can also detect an element of PRAGMATISM in this movement, for a ''cash value'' is always demanded of meaningful statements. Paraphrasing C. S. PEIRCE and W. JAMES on this point, ''to be a difference, it must make a difference.'' Peirce, of course, would limit this principle to the area of science rather than broaden its application to all life situations as was attempted by James. In general, then, the contemporary period of neopositivism bears a markedly antispeculative attitude that positively and openly discriminates against metaphysics. It matters little whether the subspecies be logical positivism, scientific empiricism, linguistic analysis, or INSTRUMENTALISM.

What these thinkers have in common is that they have become so enamored with modern science as to be unable to admit other perspectives. They tend to make the same demands for metaphysics as they do for the positive sciences. Although it is true that both areas produce scientific knowledge, it must be recognized that they do so differently. The positive sciences aim at prediction and the discovery of new truths on the basis of their hypotheses. Metaphysics is not concerned with this prediction and forecast of new phenomena, but rather with an understanding of what is. Metaphysics possesses a domain all its own, untrespassed upon by the other particular sciences. It likewise possesses a peculiar methodology for dealing with this domain. Its material object is reality or BEING. Although all of the various sciences deal with being of one kind or another, none treats of what is proper to the formal object of metaphysics, i.e., a consideration of being insofar as it is being. Traditional metaphysics shows that the question ''What pertains to the real precisely as real?'' is indeed a meaningful question. That it has not been solved to the satisfaction of all is patent, but at the same time the various proposed answers to the question are indicative of its fertility. From the perspective of metaphysics, the history of philosophy is a search for the meaning of being. Some have claimed that ''to be'' is to exist after the manner of a phenomenon; others have said that ''to be'' is to be material; still others have said that ''to be'' is to be changing. The views on this point are inexhaustible. In short, it becomes increasingly clear that metaphysics, like a phoenix, continually rises out of its own ashes, for even an antimetaphysics itself constitutes a metaphysics.

See Also: CAUSALITY; METAPHYSICS; SUBSTANCE; UNIVERSALS.

Bibliography: M. J. ADLER, ed., *The Great Ideas: A Syntopicon of Great Books of the Western World,* 2 v. (Chicago 1952); 2:158–170. R. KREYCHE, *First Philosophy* (New York 1959). J. MARITAIN, *A Preface to Metaphysics* (New York 1939). R. JOLIVET, *Man and Metaphysics,* tr. B. M. G. REARDON (New York 1961). J. L. RUSSELL, *Science and Metaphysics* (pa. New York 1960). J. DINEEN, ''The Course of Logical Positivism,'' *Modern Schoolman* 34 (November 1956) 1–21. A. RAPOPORT, ''General Semantics and Thomism: Their Contrasting Metaphysical Assumptions,'' *ETC.: A Review of General Semantics* 16 (1958–59) 133–153. H. VEATCH, ''The Truths of Metaphysics,'' *Review of Metaphysics* 17 (1964) 372–395.

[G. F. KREYCHE]

METEMPSYCHOSIS

Otherwise referred to as TRANSMIGRATION OF SOULS or REINCARNATION, is a doctrine asserting not only the preexistence of the human soul before union with matter but also, after death, a return to life on earth in a different body, perhaps through several successive reincarnations. This notion pervades ancient pagan, Neoplatonic, and some Oriental and modern spiritualist beliefs. It has been condemned as heretical (H. Denzinger, *Enchiridion symbolorum* 403, 854, 857, 1000–08, 1305–06, 1316, 1440), since Christian doctrine teaches that ''it is appointed unto men to die once and after this comes the judgment'' (Heb 9.27; cf. also Lk 16.19–31; 23.43; 2 Cor 5.10). Man has but one life on earth in which to earn his eternal destiny.

The reasoning against metempsychosis is both negative, from the lack of any psychological evidence (C. Jung's archetypes are racial, not individual), and positive, from the unity of man as one being. If one's soul were to return and unite substantially with matter, it could form only the body of that person. This person cannot be someone else, regardless of changed material conditions. Lack of recognition by oneself or others, as happens in psychotic or deteriorated states, does not cause one to be another person. Even less could a human soul actuate matter to form a dog or other animal.

See Also: SOUL, HUMAN, ORIGIN OF.

Bibliography: P. SIWEK, *The Enigma of the Hereafter: The Reincarnation of Souls* (New York 1952). J. HEAD and S. L. CRANSTON, eds., *Reincarnation: An East-West Anthology* (New York 1961).

[J. E. ROYCE]

METHODIST CHURCHES

PART I: ENGLAND

The Methodist Churches originated as a pietist religious movement within the Church of England, led by John and Charles WESLEY, George WHITEFIELD, the Countess of Huntingdon (Selina Hastings), and other Evangelical Anglicans. The epithet ''Methodist'' had

Mourners gather round the body of Parsis at his funeral, where his soul has passed on to the dog beside him.

been hurled in derision at the pious Oxford undergraduates of the ''Holy Club,'' who met from 1729 for practices of devotion and philanthropic works under the direction of the Wesleys. After the dispersal of the club (1735) the name was still applied to the Wesleys' followers. John himself defined a Methodist as ''one who lives according to the method laid down in the Bible.'' Part I of this entry surveys the origins and subsequent developments of Methodism in England, while Part II presents the history and growth of Methodist Churches in North America.

First Establishment. The early Methodists sought to revive and purify the Church of England, whose separation from Rome had brought the total dependence of the bishops upon the crown. The aftermath of the bitter religious quarrels of the 17th century, as well as the influence of the writings of Henry Bolingbroke (1678–1751), Anthony Collins (1676–1729), Anthony Shaftesbury (1671–1713), and other deists, led some bishops to doctrinal indifference and many preachers to an advocacy of a grave piety devoid of emotionalism. Accordingly, Anglican missionary fervor, discipline, and liturgy suffered. Debility and indifference, however, were not universal. Many clergymen had reacted against the prevailing formalism and rationalism. William LAW, for example, extolled piety and ascetism in his *Serious Call to a Devout and Holy Life* (1728), which left its mark upon John Wesley. The latter's father, the Reverend Samuel Wesley (1662–1735), stressed the saving work of Christ and faith in Jesus as the savior of the world.

Wesley's hope to lead other evangelical-minded Anglican clergy to minister to the Methodists, whose piety and fervor would animate the whole Church, was unfulfilled. The opposition of many churchmen who denied their pulpits to Methodist preachers led Wesley to measures that eventually meant independence. But as long as he lived, he shrank from the establishment of independent churches and counseled loyalty to the church of his father. His field preaching, itinerancy, emotional sermons, employment of lay preachers, and ordination of presbyters prepared the way for ultimate separation of Methodists from Anglicanism. As did Lady Huntingdon, Wesley in 1787 accepted the protection of the Toleration Act (1689) for Methodist ministrations outside parish churches.

The movement revolved around John Wesley, whose strong personality, exemplary life, managerial skill, frequent pastoral visits to the scattered Societies, and extensive writings commanded his converts and his itinerant preachers. Although he had called an annual conference since 1744, he regarded its function only as advisory. In 1784 his Deed of Declaration named 100 of the itinerants as constituting the Conference of the ''People called Methodists.'' The Legal Hundred thus formed the official body of the movement and held chapels and other property in trust, and also administered, assigned, and controlled the preachers after Wesley's death.

Historical Organization. The original basic unit of Methodism was the Society, a form of organization existing within the Church of England without formal sanction since 1678. The various Societies in London, Bristol, and elsewhere admitted communicants of the Church of England, dissenters, and others who had ''a desire to flee from the Wrath to come, and to be saved from their Sins,'' and issued to members in good standing quarterly tickets of identification. Within each Society were Classes of 12 or more persons, under a leader who visited each member weekly, collected contributions, kept the minister informed, and distributed the tickets. Wesley adopted the plan of the Bristol Methodists to collect a penny a week from each member and, in the process of collecting the money, to ''enquire how their souls prosper.'' Also within the Societies in the early days were the Bands of 5 to 10 persons, who were organized according to their status as married and single men, and married and single women. Each little group met weekly for confession and for prayer that all might be healed. Another short-lived company was the Select Societies, whose members asserted that they had already attained the heights of Christian perfection.

Wesley's close supervision and inspiration kept the Societies united. In his absence, lay assistants were permitted to preach in the morning and evening when ministers were away, visit the Classes monthly, adjudicate differences, deal with the ''Disorderly Walkers,'' and supervise the stewards. Wesley arranged the Societies according to geographical location, into Circuits, which were placed under a helper. After Wesley's death, Circuits were organized into Districts. The aggregate of all the Societies, Circuits, and Districts under the authority of the Conference formed the Methodist ''Connexion.''

Today Methodist administrative authority is exercised through a system of assemblies or conferences of local churches, from the quarterly meetings of the Circuit, to the District, and the annual conference. In the Conference, an equal number of clergy and laity hold a representative session to deal with administrative and financial questions. Then the pastoral session, composed of the Legal Hundred (the ministers who have been sitting in the representative session that year) and others, deals with pastoral and disciplinary matters.

Doctrine. Wesley's teachings emphasized certain historic Christian truths, as modified by the Protestant reformers and by his own religious experience. Their foundation was acceptance of the divinity of Jesus and the Trinity, as well as the universality of original sin, the consequent weakening of human nature, and the necessity of man to cooperate with grace in order to gain salvation. To Protestantism Wesley owed his reliance on the Bible as the measure of religion, his denial of purgatory and rejection of the invocation of saints and veneration of relics, and his adoption of puritanical norms of conduct for his followers. From Protestantism too he derived the major importance he assigned to preaching (he called his chapels ''preaching houses'') and his views of the Sacraments. As he saw it, baptism was a sign of regeneration that had already occurred in the Christian; and it was to be administered to infants, who were in the kingdom of God, to strengthen their faith. The Eucharist was understood as a memorial of the Passion and Death of Jesus.

The basic doctrines of Methodism are: (1) Universal Redemption—Christ died for all, and He offers His love to all people. (2) Justification by faith and the New Birth—unlike the vast majority of evangelicals in the Church of England, who embraced Calvinistic justification, Wesley assigned a role to free will and to good works. Justification brought the regenerated sinner freedom from ''outward'' sin; still for triumph over ''inward'' sin the Christian must experience the New Birth that renews our fallen nature. (3) The witness of the Spirit—God's Spirit witnesses to the soul of the just man that he is His child. This assurance that he is the son of God (''ease after pain, rest after labour, joy after sorrow, light after darkness'') leads him to feel the certainty of present pardon and to recognize that Christ lives in him. Wesley sought to bring every man into an experience of personal fellowship with God, that is, possession by the indwelling God. This assurance differs from certainty of final perseverance in Calvinistic predestination. (4) Perfection, sanctification, or holiness—the Christian may attain the state of complete sanctification that excludes all voluntary offense and enables him to grow in grace toward the fullness of salvation. Today Methodists view sanctification as the inherent righteousness of the justified who have the power to resist evil.

The Methodists emphasized not dogma but the living of a Christian life and the following of certain religious observances. Above all, the Methodists were to have the love of God in their hearts. Wesley enjoined celebrating the festivals of the Church of England, and he added the love feast (agape) and the watch nights, which he borrowed from the Moravians. In each quarter Christians were to meet at night in order to "eat Bread with Gladness and Singleness of Heart" and join in brotherly union in song and in relating religious experiences. Distinctive in Methodist observance was the prominence accorded to the singing of hymns. There was no confession of faith, though Wesley did stipulate that American Methodists were to accept an adaptation of the Thirty-Nine Articles, and that British preachers were to adopt the first four volumes of his sermons (edited in 1787–88), which contained 44 discourses, and his *Notes on the New Testament.* In effect, this meant Wesley's interpretation of the Scriptures. After his death, doctrinal authority rested with the conference.

Developments in the 19th and 20th Centuries. Even in the days of Wesley, Methodists were divided. Lady Huntingdon failed to compose the differences over predestination of the Wesleys and Whitefield. Later, disputes occurred over the relationship of Methodists to Anglicanism, the necessity of taking Communion in parish churches, and refraining from holding services during the hours of the Church of England. The plan of Thomas Coke (1747–1814) to have Methodist preachers ordained in the Church of England for the purpose of administering the sacraments to the Methodists failed. Preachers ordained by Wesley and other ministers proceeded to ordain their own preachers. Methodists gradually ceased going to Anglican services. For much of the 19th century, nonetheless, some chapels neither scheduled services during the hours of the Established Church nor administered the sacraments. No formal separation from the Church of England occurred until 1891. The authority of the preachers in full Connexion and of the conference and the role of the laity touched off many disputes that led to schism. Jabez Bunting (1779–1858), four times president of the conference and regarded as the second founder of Methodism, aroused much resentment. His foes, who had published "Fly Sheets," or a series of broadsides, from 1849 to 1856 against his rule, were expelled; many of them were lost to Methodism.

Splintering shattered the Methodist unity. Alexander Kilham (1762–98) and William Thompson left with 5,000 supporters to form the Methodist New Connection (1797) because they favored universal suffrage and democratic principles in church government. The strongest dissident group, the Primitive Methodists, was formed by Hugh Bourne (1772–1852), a carpenter, who joined his forces with the similarly dissident Clowesites (William Clowes, 1780–1851). The Primitive Methodists wanted camp meetings, which were widely used in America but condemned by the Liverpool Conference in 1807, and field preaching. Considerable working-class support was evident in the increase of membership from 200 to 165,410 in 1875. Another group, the Bible Christians, was founded in 1815 by William O'Bryan (1778–1868), an itinerant preacher, who appealed to the Bible, and not to the Prayer Book as well, as the sole authority and who favored the ministry of women.

In addition to several other offshoots of the main body of Methodism there were the Protestant Methodists and the Wesleyan Methodist Association. The first was organized by Matthew Johnson and 70 local preachers who opposed the introduction of an organ into the Brunswick Street chapel at Leeds in 1828. The Protestant Methodists merged with the Wesleyan Methodist Association, which had come into existence following the creation of a school for the education of ministers. Part of the motivation of these dissenting groups was the desire of a greater voice for the laity in administrative and financial matters. The association favored decentralization and the autonomy of the circuit and the individual chapel in the management of business. In 1857 it merged with the Wesleyan Reformers—the opponents of Bunting—to become the United Methodist Free Churches. Although the schisms and internal disputes cost Methodism dearly, by the 1860s membership was again on the rise.

The vast industrial and social changes prompted Methodists to attract the poor once more, to alter their dominant middle-class character, and to renew their evangelical fervor. Their social conscience was stirred. Hugh Price Hughes (1847–1902) established the West London Mission in 1887, which combined social and religious features, and later another great figure in Methodism, John Scott Lidgett (1854–1953), directed the settlement in southeast London, where religious, social, educational, and medical services were provided.

The unification of the several branches of Methodism was facilitated by the fact that they differed not in doctrine but in church government. An Act of the English Parliament in 1907 authorized the merger of the Methodist New Connexion, the Bible Christians, and the United Methodist Free Churches as the United Methodist Church. In 1932 the Wesleyan Methodists, Primitive Methodists, and the United Methodist Church came together as the Methodist Church, with a combined membership of 859,652. The unified church does not include the Wesleyan Reform Union (with autonomous individual churches) or the Independent Methodist Church (with a voluntary ministry that admits women). The first ecumenical Conference of Methodists met in London in 1881. Subsequent consultative assemblies have usually met at 10-year intervals. At the meeting in Oxford in 1951, the name of the organization was changed to World Methodist Council. Its functions include liaison among the various Methodist groups and cooperation with the World Council of Churches.

Methodism took root in the British Isles, wherever English rule and influence existed. In Wales many evangelists, including Howell HARRIS, Griffith Jones (1683–1761), George Whitefield, and the Wesleys, made Methodism—but by no means the Wesleyan variety—the country's strongest religious force. Methodism did not flourish in Scotland. In Ireland itinerant preachers, dubbed Swaddlers, faced the opposition of Catholic priests and the attachment of the Irish to their traditional faith. Methodism made headway in the British overseas possessions such as America, the West Indies, and Canada. In 1925 the Canadian Methodists and the Congregationalists and Presbyterians formed the United Church of Canada. Autonomous churches were established in Australia and New Zealand.

Bibliography: H. BURBRIDGE, *Methodisme* (*Studies in Comparative Religion*, ed. J. M. T. BARTON; London 1957). N. SYKES, *Church and State in England in the XVIIIth Century* (Cambridge, Eng. 1934). W. J. TOWNSEND et al., eds., *A New History of Methodism*, 2 v. (London 1909). W. W. SWEET, *The Methodists, a Collection of Source Materials* (Chicago 1946). R. F. WEARMOUTH, *The Social and Political Influence of Methodism in the 20th Century* (London 1957). F. S. MEAD, S. S. HILL, and C. D. ATWOOD, eds., *Handbook of Denominations in the United States*, 11th ed. (Nashville 2001).

[G. L. VINCITORIO/EDS.]

PART II: NORTH AMERICA

John WESLEY had spent two years (1736 to 1737) in Georgia as chaplain to General James E. Oglethorpe's colony and missionary to the Native Americans, but he sailed home to England disheartened at the failure of his mission. After coming under the influence of the Moravians, he experienced conversion on May 24, 1738, and through the next half-century successfully promoted his evangelical movement within the Anglican communion. In America, however, the colonists' victory in the War for Independence made a British-controlled Methodist Church unacceptable and impractical, with the result that the first Methodist Church was organized in America rather than in England, homeland of the Wesleyan Revival.

Origin and Historical Development. Unofficial lay preachers who had gone from Ireland and England, not as missionaries but as immigrants, were the founders of Methodism in America. In 1766 Philip EMBURY began to preach in New York, and the society he formed there built a chapel on John Street (1768) with the aid of Captain Thomas Webb of the British Army, a lay preacher. In 1768 Webb also founded a society in Philadelphia, Pennsylvania, and two years later led in purchasing and completing a half-finished sanctuary, later St. George's, the oldest church of American Methodism. At about the same time Robert Strawbridge, unordained and unofficial, settled in Frederick, Maryland, making his cabin a preaching center. Between 1769 and 1774 Wesley dispatched eight experienced itinerant preachers to America, where under their leadership a corps of indigenous preachers developed. Francis ASBURY, one of Wesley's emissaries who arrived in 1771 and was the only one to remain through the Revolution, became to American Methodism what Wesley was to British.

The achievement of American independence convinced Wesley that it was time for his followers there to be free from his control and to organize into a church with an ordained ministry. When the Anglican bishop refused to ordain his America-bound leaders, Wesley took upon himself the solemn setting-apart of Dr. Thomas Coke, already a priest, to be superintendent for America, and also ordained two itinerants to accompany Coke. In 1784, 60 of the 83 itinerant preachers met in a Christmas Conference in Baltimore, Maryland, and elected Asbury as cosuperintendent. He was ordained deacon and elder on successive days, and on the third, consecrated as superintendent. To Wesley's consternation the new body named itself the Methodist Episcopal Church and designated their superintendents bishops. This was the first religious group in the United States to create an independent, national church organization. Later, formal greetings were exchanged between the bishops of the new church and the president of the new republic. Coke, because of missionary assignments for Wesley, left leadership entirely to Asbury, except for brief visits. At his death in 1816, Asbury's diary revealed that he had traveled 270,000 miles, preached 16,000 times, held 224 conferences, and ordained 4,000 ministers. The societies, which numbered 316 members in 1771, had grown to a denomination of 214,235 members, more than in England.

Methodism's close connectionalism and its circuit system were well adapted to following the population westward. The pulpit emphasis upon free grace and free will for all met with remarkable response from pioneers freshly tuned to the implications of democracy. Between 1800 and 1830 membership increased sevenfold. By 1850 there were 1,208,110 Methodist members in America. Because of the demand for ministers many of the circuit riders were chosen more for their zeal than their learning. Their deficiencies were made up in part by private study and reading; but since their congregations were rough and uncultured, too much education was undesirable and might only estrange them from their listeners. As a consequence, the transition to the later standard of a liberal arts degree followed by three years of graduate study in a theological seminary was slow, and for many years divinity schools were scorned and mistrusted.

Doctrine and Worship. Wesley supplied the Methodist Church in America with doctrinal and liturgical standards. He abridged to 24 the 39 Anglican Articles of Religion, endorsed as theological norms his own *Notes on the New Testament* and certain published sermons, prescribed general rules, and provided liturgical aids. However, because of primitive settings for the circuit riders' ministrations, the dignified Order of Morning and Evening Prayer soon lost out to completely informal worship and extempore prayer. Rituals for Methodism's two sacraments, baptism and holy communion, and for such rites as marriage and burial were conscientiously followed. Methodists take holy communion kneeling and partake of both elements. While sprinkling is the usual method of baptism, every adult and the parents of every infant to be baptized have the choice of sprinkling, pouring, or immersion.

Methodists have had few doctrinal disturbances, probably because of their light stress on dogma. "Whosoever imagines a Methodist is a man of such and such opinion is grossly ignorant of the whole affair," Wesley wrote. Despite this liberality there is a definite Wesleyan theological accent. The founder's message was twofold: first, the experience of the new birth, the gift of God's grace, offered freely to all repentant men; second, the moral ideal that the gospel presents. Basic, of course, to all other standards were the Scriptures, declared to be "the sole and sufficient rule of belief and practice."

Early Methodists answered CALVINISM with the Arminian doctrine of universal redemption (*see* ARMINIANISM). Accordingly, salvation is full and present, available to all and conditioned on repentance and faith in Christ. Inwardly it is authenticated by the witness of the spirit bringing peace and assurance. Outwardly its evidence is a life of loving service. Methodism's doctrine of Christian perfection emphasizes not the possibility of sinlessness, but rather perfection in love and motives.

By mid-20th century there were evidences, extending to the laity, of reawakened interest in theology. Doctrinal presentations appeared in Methodist periodicals and church school curriculum. There was an organized circulation of eight doctrinal booklets on "Our Faith." An inquiry on the beliefs of Methodists confirmed that while most of the austere restrictions on dress and amusements have long been outmoded, the major doctrinal emphasis of Wesley remained vital.

Methodist Churches in Canada. In 1925 the United Church of Canada was formed by the union of three communions, one of which was the Methodist Church of Canada. This strong body was itself the product of the union in 1883 of four independent Canadian Methodist bodies. In 1765 Methodism in Newfoundland developed from the work of English itinerants. Two preachers, dispatched by the Christmas Conference in Baltimore, reached Nova Scotia in 1785. Others followed, and from 1800 on the work was taken over by British missionaries. In the Niagara region, now Ontario, a Canadian conference of the Methodist Episcopal Church was organized in 1824, but four years later was granted independence. Numerous Methodists were found also among the Tory refugees who fled to Canada during and after the American Revolution.

Methodist Churches in the United States. On May 10, 1939, after years of negotiations, the long-separated Methodist Episcopal Church (numbering some 4,750,271 members), the Methodist Episcopal Church, South (2,619,197 members), and the Methodist Protestant Church (195,000 members) merged to form "The Methodist Church." The united church was partitioned into six jurisdictions—five geographical, one racial. All were empowered to elect and assign their own bishops, formerly a General Conference prerogative. The merging of the missionary, educational, and benevolent agencies of the three bodies was accomplished smoothly. A union of the EVANGELICAL UNITED BRETHREN and the Methodist Church, was approved in principle by both bodies in 1962 and 1964, and ratified by their respective General Conferences in 1966. In 1968, the United Methodist Church, combining the Evangelical United Brethren and the Methodist Church came into existence.

The Methodist Protestant Church. This was organized in Baltimore in 1830 by reformers who protested the autocratic practices of bishops and the absence of laymen in the conferences. In a century membership increased from 5,000 to nearly 200,000. Meanwhile their democratic principles prevailed in the major Methodist bodies. Laymen in equal numbers were in all conferences, and bishops, while still there, exercised their powers with restraint and consideration. In 1939 Methodist Protestants joined in the reunion movement, furnishing two leaders for consecration as bishops in the new body, The Methodist Church.

Wesleyan Methodist Church. In 1843 objectors to the bishops' compromises on slavery, made to keep peace with the South, withdrew to organize a church "free from episcopacy and free from slavery.'' In 1968, it merged with the Pilgrim Holiness Church to become the Wesleyan Church.

Free Methodist Church. A conservative group that was organized in 1860 by ministers and laymen expelled from churches in western New York for ''fanatical reactionism.'' They had condemned pew renting, liquor, tobacco, the use of musical instruments in worship, and neglect of the doctrine of entire sanctification. The word ''free'' in their name refers to free seats, freedom from ecclesiastical domination, freedom from sin, and freedom in worship.

Methodist Episcopal Church, South. As the nation was to do later, the Methodist Episcopal Church in 1844 split over slavery. A Georgia bishop, James O. Andrew, through marriage had come into possession of slaves. Church law forbade a minister to hold slaves. State law prohibited their emancipation. A resolution was passed in the General Conference calling upon Bishop Andrew to ''desist from the exercise of his office as long as this impediment remains.'' When protests on constitutional grounds failed, the Southerners sought and obtained a provisional separation agreement establishing boundaries and providing for the division of institutional assets. Membership divided, with 689,310 adhering to the North and 462,851 to the South. In May 1845 the Methodist Episcopal Church, South, was duly organized. Both churches prospered until the Civil War; they launched missionary enterprises, domestic and foreign, and founded schools and colleges. Although the war years and Reconstruction were disastrous, recovery was rapid and by 1866 American Methodism comprised nearly half of all Protestant communicants. In 1939, the Methodist Episcopal Church, South, the Methodist Episcopal Church and the Methodist Protestant Episcopal Church were reunited to form the Methodist Church. Those who objected to the merger formed a new church, the Southern Methodist Church.

Historic African American Methodist Churches. *African Methodist Episcopal Church.* This group, the oldest and largest, developed from Bethel Church, Philadelphia, an all-black congregation set up in 1794 under the leadership of Richard Allen by members of St. George's Church, who were displeased by discriminatory treatment. In 1816 it joined with five other congregations to establish the African Methodist Episcopal Church, severing its ties with the all-white Methodist Church.

African Methodist Episcopal Zion Church. Similar friction between black and white members of John Street Church, New York, resulted in 1796 in permission for its black members to worship separately in a church they named Zion. Other congregations with similar problems maintained a loose affiliation. In 1822 efforts failed to form these churches into a Methodist episcopal annual conference, as did also an attempt to unite them with the African Methodist Episcopal Church. Led by James Varick, they then organized independently.

The Christian (formerly Colored) Methodist Episcopal Church. This group was founded on request of African Americans, who in 1870 were still members of the Methodist Episcopal Church, South. The parent body sponsored the new church. Both the African Methodist Episcopal and the African Methodist Episcopal Zion churches moved aggressively into the South as the Civil War ended, quadrupling their memberships between 1860 and 1870.

Bibliography: *The History of American Methodism,* ed. E. S. BUCKE et al., 3 v. (Nashville 1964). W. C. BARCLAY, *History of Methodist Missions,* 3 v. (New York 1949–57). H. E. LUCCOCK and P. HUTCHINSON, *Story of Methodism* (New York 1949). N. B. HARMON, *Organization of the Methodist Church* (Nashville 1948). R. M. CAMERON, *Methodism and Society in Historical Perspective* (Nashville 1961). S. P. SCHILLING, *Methodism and Society in Theological Perspective* (Nashville 1960). W. G. MUELDER, *Methodism and Society in the 20th Century* (Nashville 1961). F. S. MEAD, S. S. HILL and C. D. ATWOOD, ed., *Handbook of Denominations in the United States* (Nashville 2001).

[R. STOODY/EDS.]

METHODIUS I, PATRIARCH OF CONSTANTINOPLE, ST.

Patriarchate, 843–47; b. Syracuse, *c.* 788 or 800; d. Constantinople, June 14, 847. As a young man Methodius, called ''the Confessor,'' studied in Constantinople, where he became a monk in the monastery of Chenolakkos. During the second iconoclastic persecution, after 815, he took refuge in Rome and seems to have been instrumental in the papal rejection of advances made by the legates of the iconoclastic patriarch. He returned to Constantinople in 821 with a letter from the pope to the Emperor Michael II and was persecuted by the iconoclasts and imprisoned in a tomb on the island of St. Andrew. Upon his liberation, probably in 831, he lived at the court of the Byzantine Emperor THEOPHILUS, who had a high esteem for his erudition and employed him as his adviser. At the death of Theophilus (Jan. 20, 842), Methodius returned to his monastery; but upon the deposition of the iconoclastic patriarch, JOHN THE GRAMMARIAN, Methodius was appointed patriarch (March 4, 843). He convoked a local synod to reestablish the cult of images and legislated that the restoration of image veneration was to be remembered by the introduction of the feast of Orthodoxy, which is still celebrated by the Orthodox Churches on the first Sunday in Lent. The *Synodicon* (*Patrologia*

Graeca 120:724–736) explaining the true faith that is read during the Liturgy of this feast is also ascribed to him, but it has been changed and expanded at different periods. He treated the penitent iconoclasts with moderation in spite of the protest of the zealots led by the monks of Studios monastery; but he was obliged to excommunicate the fanatic monks, who remained in schism until his death. Methodius composed several hagiographic texts, especially in honor of the martyrdom of SS. Marina, COSMAS AND DAMIAN, of AGATHA (patron saint of Syracuse), and of THEOPHANES, as well as the life of Euthymius of Sardes.

Feast: June 14.

Bibliography: J. B. BURY, *A History of the Eastern Roman Empire . . . A.D. 802–867* (London 1912). V. LAURENT, *Dictionnaire de théologie catholique* 10.1: 1597–1606. *Kirche und theologische Literatur im byzantinischen Reich* 496–497. J. GOUILLARD, *Byzantinische Zeitschrift* 53 (1960) 36–46, Vita Euthymii. F. DVORNIK, *The Photian Schism* (Cambridge, Eng. 1948). V. GRUMEL, *Revue des études byzantines* 18 (1960) 19–44.

[F. DVORNIK]

METHODIUS OF OLYMPUS, ST.

Third-century ecclesiastical author; d. probably a martyr at Chalcis, Greece, *c.* 300. St. Jerome (*De viris ill.* 83) speaks of Methodius as a bishop and martyr, who held the See at Olympus in Lycia, and later in Tyre, dying ''at the end of the last persecution at Chalcis, in Greece.'' Different ancient sources offer contradictory details with respect to his see and the date of his martyrdom. But if the authenticity of Methodius's *Against Porphyry* is accepted (*c.* 270), his *floruit* must be dated in the last quarter of the century. F. Diekamp at one time suggested that Methodius was bishop of Philippi [*Theol. Quart.* 109 (1928) 285], but the argument is not convincing. The most one can say is that Methodius, also called Eubulius, was a Platonizing Christian teacher, possibly also a bishop and martyr, who exercised his ministry in the cities of Lycia, Olympus, Patara, and Termessus, during the last quarter of the third century.

Writings. The *Symposium,* or Treatise on Chastity, is the only work of Methodius that has been preserved entirely in Greek; two other works of importance, the *Treatise on Free Will* and *On the Resurrection,* are preserved in a Slavonic version and in a few Greek fragments. Other pieces are *The Jewish Foods, On Life, On the Leech, On Leprosy, On Creatures,* and *Against Porphyry.*

In the treatise *On the Resurrection* Methodius combats the Origenist concept of the Fall and the Resurrection; in the Treatise on Free Will he gives a detailed explanation of the effects of Adam's sin upon man's freedom and hints at the voluntarism that is at the heart of Methodius's theology and asceticism: for the effect of Jesus' atonement was to restore some of the perfect freedom and equilibrium of the human will that man possessed before the Fall.

It is this restoration of the divine image that Methodius explains in the Platonic dialogue, the *Symposium.* So far as external form is concerned, this is the most Platonic of all the writings of the early Church, composed within the last quarter of the third century and dedicated to Methodius's patroness, the Lady from Termessus.

In the course of the eleven great discourses, with prelude, interludes, and epilogue, Methodius explains how virginity has taken the place of the Platonic *eros* as the all-embracing virtue of the Christian life, but he also gives practical instruction (presumably for a community of consecrated women of Lycia) on the interpretation of the Scriptures, on the nature of the final reign of Christ, on the Incarnation and Redemption, on prayer and the freedom of the will, on the dangers of astrology, and on prayer and temptation. Thus the work becomes a summary of Christian doctrine and a handbook against the errors of GNOSTICISM and Encratism.

Teaching. For all his debt to Alexandrian allegorism, Methodius shows no trace of ORIGENISM in his doctrine of the Fall or the Last Things. Rather he stresses the archetypal relationship between Adam, the first man, born of the virgin earth, and Christ, the archvirgin, born of a virgin mother, who by His life and death restores freedom and chastity to mankind. The effects of this restoration are communicated to men through the Virgin Mother Church, who brings forth her children mystically and nourishes them with the milk of her grace. Through her teaching and her liturgy (especially the *anamnesis,* or memorial, of the Passion) men learn to conquer their passions, exercise their freedom, and thus restore the luster of the divine image within the soul. In practice this is achieved by the more perfect in the Church, instructing the weak.

Methodius sets his doctrine against the grandiose scheme of the eight ages of the world: five are the ages of the Old Law, the sixth is the Church, the seventh is the millennium of rest (when Christ will rule the world), and the eighth designates the eternity of heaven. In Thecla's hymn we have a moving description of the march to meet Christ on the last day in the company of His virgin bride, the Church.

Methodius's Christology tended to be subordinationist, and it is probable that his text was later corrected by an anti-Arian group; another recension, Photius tells us, was circulated by the Arian party. Yet Methodius spoke clearly of Christ's divinity; and G. N. Bonwetsch, E. Mersch, and others err in thinking that he taught that there was a hypostatic union between the Logos and the first man.

Doctrine, however, is not Methodius's strong point; he is most moving in his poetic flights, his description of the heavenly meadows, the rise of the soul to God, the mystical sleep of Christ, and the marriage of Christ and the Virgin Church. In philosophy he is eclectic. Aristotelian in his logic and in his support of the imagination, Methodius inclines to Stoicism in his moral doctrine, to Platonism in his view of the shadow-reality dimension of the world, and, finally, to an Alexandrian-Asiatic form of allegorism in his interpretation of Scripture.

Feast: Sept. 18.

Bibliography: *Patrologia Graeca* ed. J. P. MIGNE (Paris 1857–66) 18:10–407; critical ed. G. N. BONWETSCH (GSC 27; 1917); *De Autexusio,* ed. and tr. A. VAILLANT (*Patrologia orientalis,* ed. R. GRAFFIN and F. NAU 22.5; Paris 1930); *Symposium,* ed. and tr. H. MUSURILLO (*Ancient Christian Writers,* ed. J. QUASTEN et al. 27; Westminster, Md.-London 1958); *Le Banquet,* tr. V. H. DEBIDOUR, ed. H. MUSURILLO (*Sources Chrétiennes,* ed. H. DE LUBAC et al. 95; Paris 1963). J. QUASTEN, *Patrology* (Westminster, Maryland 1950–) 2:129–137. G. N. BONWETSCH, *Die Theologie des Methodius von Olympus* (*Abhandlungen der Akademie (Gesellschaft, to 1940) der Wissenschaften* NS 7.1 (Göttingen 1903). B. ALTANER, *Patrology*, tr. H. GRAEF (New York 1960) 242–244.

[H. MUSURILLO]

METHODOLOGY (PHILOSOPHY)

Method is a ''way after'' (derived from the Greek μέθοδος from μετὰ, ''after,'' and ὁδός, ''road'' or ''way''); it is applied both to the process or art of investigation and to the treatise or body of knowledge resulting from investigation. Method is used in three distinct but related applications in philosophy: (1) to logic or parts of logic, as inductive or axiomatic methods; (2) to procedures of the sciences, as mathematical or experimental methods; and (3) to modes of philosophizing, as Cartesian or phenomenological methods. Plato was the first philosopher to use the term; Aristotle gave it a technical meaning. They both refer to mathematical and medical methods to explain philosophical methods, and later interpretations of method based on their theories influence and are influenced by developments of method in the arts and sciences. Plato and Aristotle use earlier terms such as way (ὁδός), reason (λόγος), mode (τρόπος), treatment (πραγματεία), and art (τέχνη), in connection with or in the place of method, and those terms continue to be used in later theories.

Greek Thought. In the *Republic* PLATO uses ''method'' to relate DIALECTICS to the five kinds of mathematics. It is the only method that proceeds directly to the first principle without hypotheses (*Republic* 533C). Plato's SOCRATES develops his arguments on the analogy of the arts or even of the ''method'' of hunting (*Soph.* 218D). He distinguishes two processes in dialectic, division (διαίρεσις) and bringing together (συναγωγέ), and argues that they are appropriate to RHETORIC, and constitute the art of Hippocrates (*Phaedrus* 266D. 270C).

Aristotle records that Socrates was the first to examine universal definitions and inductive arguments, because he was concerned with the principles of science and with syllogizing (*Meta.* 1078b 17–31). Aristotle raises the question whether there is one method of inquiry for all subject matters, as syllogistic DEMONSTRATION applies to all proofs. He concludes that there are as many methods as there are subject matters or parts of subject matters, and he frequently divides his scientific treatises into several methods or parts. He wrote a treatise, now lost, called *Methodics*. Dialectic is a method (*Topica* 100a 18), comparable to the methods of rhetoric and medicine (*Topica* 101b 5–6); one of its functions is to discover the principles of all methods or sciences (*Topica* 101b 2–4). Syllogistic demonstration, unlike the method of inquiry, is universal to all proofs; and the demonstrative syllogism is ''analyzed,'' first, into the terms or parts that compose it and into other syllogisms, and second, in what was later called the *Posterior Analytics*, into the principles of instruction and proof.

During the Hellenistic period the Stoics, Epicureans, and Academics divided philosophy into physics, ethics, and logic. Under logic they considered the criteria of knowledge and the rules of dialectic and rhetoric. Art was conceived as a skill in proceeding by a way or method, or a canon or rules of judgement, or a calculus or probabilities. Pappus in the 4th century A.D. states the position, attributed to Euclid, that mathematical inquiry employs two converse methods, analysis (positing what is sought and proceeding to what must be assumed) and synthesis (positing what is assumed and proceeding to what is sought). Galen in the 2nd century A.D. reviews the methods of all the arts, particularly rhetoric and mathematics, and philosophy, including the theories of Plato, Aristotle, and the Stoics, to clarify the methods of instruction and practice in medicine. He enumerates three methods of instruction: analysis, which begins with the idea of the end; synthesis, which compounds what had been discovered by analysis; and partition (διάλυσις), which breaks definitions into essential parts. The Greek commentators on Aristotle and Plato made use of these distinctions to characterize the methods of philosophers. Ammonius Hermiae found a fourfold method in Plato's dialectic: DIVISION, DEFINITION, DEMONSTRATION, and ANALYSIS. The four dialectical methods (or three—analysis, division, and reduction to absurdity) are referred to by JOHN PHILOPONUS, JOHN DAMASCENE, Alcinous, and PROCLUS. Alexander of Aphrodisias applied the geometric conception of analysis to Aristotle's *Analytics*, and he distinguishes in Aristotle's method the converse methods of analysis and synthesis. (*See* ANALYSIS AND SYNTHESIS.)

Roman and Medieval Development. For the Romans, methodological distinctions were distinctions applied to *via* or *ratio* or *ars*; the term *methodus* came into use during the late Middle Ages. CICERO applied two basic distinctions of rhetoric, invention and judgment, to all discursive art (*ratio disserendi*) and attributed their origin to Aristotle. The art of invention is expounded in the *Topics*. The translation of Arabic medical works, including Galen, in the 11th century, and of the last four books of Aristotle's *Organon*, in the 12th century, focused the discussion of the LIBERAL ARTS on problems of method. In the treatment of *methodus* during the late 13th century, analysis and synthesis took the place of *resolutio and compositio*. (*See* SCHOLASTIC METHOD.)

THOMAS AQUINAS seldom uses *methodus*, but he does distinguish invention and judgment and also resolution and composition. He applies composition and division to the act of the intellect forming propositions, true and false, and invention and judgment to the discursive processes of reason from known to unknown. The process of reason by which the certitude of science is acquired is treated in the judicative part of logic, which Aristotle called *Analytics*, or from the form of the syllogism, in the *Prior Analytics*, or from the matter of the demonstrative syllogism, in the *Posterior Analytics*. The processes of reason that fall short of certitude are treated in the inventive part: (1) invention leading, not to judgment, but to conviction or OPINION based on PROBABILITY in the *Topics*; (2) invention leading to suspicion leaning to one side of an opposition in the *Rhetoric*; and (3) invention producing only estimation because of a pleasing representation in the *Poetics* (*In 1 anal. post.* 1.4–6). St. Thomas also distinguishes two ways (*viae*) of proceeding to knowledge of the truth (that is, two parts of judicative logic), the mode (*modus*) of resolution, by which one proceeds from composites to simples and from wholes to parts, that is, from the confused experience known first in nature, and the way of composition, by which one proceeds from simples to composites (*In 2 meta.* 1.278).

Renaissance Transition. The method of the Aristotelian logic was transformed by the development of terminist logics, Lullian combinatory arts, and dialectical and rhetorical arts of invention. The transformed methods were used in the renewed study of medicine, mathematics, and literature. As a result the differences between discovery and proof and the relation of both to analysis and synthesis and to INDUCTION and DEDUCTION became subjects of interest and controversy. The new arts and encyclopedias and the new logics of the Renaissance were methods. The importance of method in the reform of the arts, sciences, and education is seen in the proliferation of titles such as the *Ratio seu methodus compendio perveniendi ad veram theologiam* of D. ERASMUS and the *Methodus ad facilem historiarum cognitionem* of J. Bodin.

Giacomo Aconcio, in *De methodo* (1558), treats method as the right way (*recta ratio*) of investigating and transmitting arts and sciences. Three methods are required in inquiry and teaching: the method of definition to demonstrate what a thing is, the method of resolution and composition to treat causes and effects, the method of division to order parts and wholes. The *De inventione dialectica* (1480) of R. Agricola transfers the Ciceronian division of discourse into invention and judgment, and the priority of invention or topics from rhetoric to dialectic.

Peter RAMUS identifies dialectic with logic, and both with the art of discoursing well (*ars bene diserendi*). He divides logic into two parts, invention and judgment. (1) Invention is achieved by the topics or commonplaces, beginning with causes since cause is ''the first place of invention, the foundation of all science and knowing,'' and ending with distribution, definition, and description. (2) Judgment is the disposition of the arguments discovered by invention. Ramus argued, therefore, that there is a single method of all the arts and sciences, since method is disposition of arguments proceeding from the more general and prior in nature. Jacob Schegk (1511 to 1587), a physician and logician, maintained against Ramus that method is a way of knowing, rather than a discoursing, and undertook to show in his *De demonstratione* (1564), using Aristotle and Galen, that analysis or method is the way both of discovery and judgment in science. J. ZABARELLA included four books *De methodis* in his *Logica* (1587), in which, after examining theories of kinds of method, he argues that two, the demonstrative and resolutive, suffice for the investigation of all things.

17th Century. The distinctions of methods and the oppositions about methods recur with few changes in philosophic statements of scientific method and its application to philosophy. Francis BACON criticizes the various classifications of method, including the single method and dichotomies of Ramus (*De aug. sci.* 6.2). According to Bacon, the intellectual arts are four: inquiry or invention, examination or judgment, custody or memory, and elocution or transmission—adaptations of four of the traditional five parts of rhetoric: invention, arrangement, expression, memory, and delivery. Bacon makes use of the topics (or places) for invention, and he rejects the syllogism.

Rene DESCARTES turned to the analysis of ancient geometry and of algebra to set forth an art of invention and a universal mathematics, contrasted to the logic of syllogisms and the art of R. LULL, which provide rules for discoursing about things that one does not know. Analysis is the true way by which a thing is methodically discovered and derived; synthesis proceeds conversely from effect to cause. Descartes concludes, therefore, that analysis is also the best and truest method of teaching.

The *Port Royal Logic*, influenced by the Cartesian method, has four parts, the first three on concepts, judgments, and reasoning, and the fourth on method. Method is the art of disposing well a series of many thoughts for either discovery or proof. The method of discovering truth is called analysis, or the method of resolution, or the method of invention. The method of explaining or proving a known truth is called synthesis, or the method of composition, or the method of doctrine.

18th Century. The *Treatise of Human Nature* by D. HUME is presented in its title as an exercise in method, *Being an Attempt to Introduce the Experimental Method of Reasoning into Moral Subjects.* All reasoning is nothing but a comparison and a discovery of those relations that two or more objects bear to each other. There are two kinds of relations: some depend entirely on ideas, and some are altered without a change in the ideas. Reasoning depends on one alone of the latter relations, causation.

I. Kant adapted Hume's skeptical method in his construction of a critical philosophy, but he differed from Hume concerning both judgments methods. He argued that mathematical judgments are synthetic, not analytic as Hume thought, and that mathematics, physics, and ethics are all based on synthetic judgments a priori. In the *Prolegomena* he distinguishes rigorously between the use of analytic and synthetic applied to judgments and applied to method. He uses both the analytical and synthetic methods in his philosophy. In *The Foundations of the Metaphysics of Morals* he says that his method is to proceed analytically from common knowledge to the determination of its supreme principle and then synthetically from the examination of this principle and its sources back to common knowledge where it finds its application. The structure of the three *Critiques* is synthetic in method and proceeds in logical sequence through a doctrine of elements, containing an analytic and a dialectic, to a doctrine of method.

19th Century. During the 19th century the methods of transcendental logics and of empirical logics were elaborated; the implications for method of history, psychology, sociology, and of the theory of evolution were examined; and classifications of the sciences, with special attention to the methods of the natural sciences and the humanistic sciences, or *Geisteswissenschaften*, were constructed.

G. W. F. HEGEL argued that the Kantian distinction between judgment and method, analytic and synthetic, is unduly abstract. All judgments and all methods are simultaneously analytic and synthetic. The reactions of S. A. Kierkegaard and K. Marx to the Hegelian dialectic laid the foundations of the methods of PHENOMENOLOGY and EXISTENTIALISM and of materialistic DIALECTIC.

A. COMTE developed the positivistic method in connection with his inauguration of sociology, expounded an interrelated series of classifications of the sciences, and developed a ''subjective synthesis: as a universal system of conceptions proper to humanity.'' W. DILTHEY devoted himself to a critique of historical reason, which he found lacking in Kant, and to an examination of the principles and methods of the *Geisteswissenschaften.* F. Brentano's psychology ''from an empirical standpoint'' and W. Wundt's ''physiological'' psychology, both published in 1874, revolutionized the methods of both psychology and philosophy.

Sir William HAMILTON, who endeavored to combine the Kantian and the Scottish common-sense philosophy, divided his logic into two parts: stoicheiology, or the doctrine of elements (in which he treats concepts, judgments, and reasoning), and methodology, or the doctrine of method. For Hamilton, method consists of two processes, analysis and synthesis; and logical methodology has three parts: the doctrine of definition, the doctrine of division, and the doctrine of probation.

John Stuart MILL, in his *System of Logic, Ratiocinative and Inductive: Being a Connected View of the Principles of Evidence and the Methods of Scientific Investigation*, devotes one chapter to his ''four methods of experimental inquiry,'' another to the deductive method, and the final book to the methods of the social sciences. His defense of Utilitarianism is a method of examining consequences rather than a priori precepts, Herbert SPENCER applies the conception and method of evolution in the construction of his system of synthetic philosophy.

20th Century. The revolutions of philosophy in the 20th century are characterized by methods used and by subject matters selected in order to avoid errors and absurdities and in order to give philosophy a concrete basis and a scientific or critical function. PRAGMATISM, according to W. JAMES, is a new name for some old ways of thinking derived from Mill. J. Dewey seeks a ''method of inquiry'' to avoid the errors revealed by experience in past inquiries. He defines inquiry as ''the controlled or directed transformation of an indeterminate situation into one that is so determinate in its constituent distinctions and relations as to convert the elements of the original situation into a unified whole.''

G. E. Moore refutes IDEALISM and utilitarianism, defends common sense, and analyzes the statements of philosophers. The methods of Moore and B. RUSSELL were the starting point of the philosophical analysis that ran through logical atomism and LOGICAL POSITIVISM to linguistic analysis. The objectives of method applied to language, formal or ordinary, are to determine the conditions of VERIFICATION or the varieties of use and to expose false inferences, spurious questions, and non-sensical assumptions.

Edmund HUSSERL sought to make philosophy a rigorous science. His *Formal and Transcendental Logic*, according to its subtitle, is a *Critique of Logical Understanding*. Taking its beginning from experience of the sciences and logic, the phenomenological method does not consist in deducing, in *erklaren* (mere ''explanation by theories'') but rather in *aufklaren* (seeing things as they are). The functions of logic reflect the meanings of ''logos'': speaking, thinking, and thing thought. Phenomenological research must cover all three, since formal logic depends on transcendental logic.

Martin Heidegger undertakes to analyze and describe the meanings of individual phenomena. He seeks to free philosophy from dependence on the special sciences and to destroy the misconceptions of traditional philosophies, which have forgotten or distorted and trivialized the insights and truths of earlier thinkers. The question of being must be restated explicitly; and to understand *Sein* one must begin with *Dasein*: the approach to ontology must be made by analysis of experiences such as temporality and of emotions such as concern and dread. (*See* EXISTENTIALISM)

Summation. From the beginning of rational thought men have speculated concerning methods, or ways, or modes, or instruments of thinking. The meanings of method have been as diverse as the kinds of philosophies, sciences, arts, beliefs, and problems. During the Renaissance method became a central problem of philosophy and science, and by the 17th century the numerous divisions of method had been all but amalgamated into the distinction between analytic and synthetic. Some important problems were encountered in that reduction: thus, some philosophers argued that the method of discovery is analytic, others that it is synthetic. During the 19th century the differences between classification of the methods of the sciences and arts were subjects of inquiry and controversy: the a priori method was presented as synthetic, as analytic, or as impossible; the a posteriori method was analytic or synthetic of empirical experience. In the 20th century the methods of philosophies set them in controversial opposition in the detection of errors, the clarification of meanings, and the establishment of truths. Pragmatism tends to be synthetic; logical positivism, ANALYTICAL PHILOSOPHY, PHENOMENOLOGY, and existentialism tend to be analytic. A fuller investigation of the different objectives of the different methods and of what they have in common may serve to reduce the misunderstandings and controversies that have developed in contemporary philosophy.

See Also: SCHOLASTIC METHOD; PHILOSOPHY AND SCIENCE.

Bibliography: S. CARAMELLA, *Enciclopedia filosofica*, 4 v. (Venice-Rome 1957) 3:562–73. R. EISLER, *Wörterbuch der philosophischen Begriffe*, 3 v. (4th ed. Berlin 1927–30) 2:140–45. J. M. LE BLOND, *Logique et methode chez Aristote* (Paris 1939). R. MCKEON, ''Aristotle's Conception of the Development and the Nature of Scientific Method,'' *Journal of the History of Ideas* 8 (1947) 3–44. J. H. RANDALL, JR., ''The Development of Scientific Method in the School of Padua,:'' *ibid.* 1 (1940) 177–206. W. J. ONG, *Ramus: Method and the Decay of Dialogue* (Cambridge, Masschusetts 1958). N. W. GILBERT, *Renaissance Concepts of Method* (New York 1969). R. MCKEON, ''Philosophy and the Development of Scientific Methods,'' *Journal of the History of Ideas* 27 (1966) 3–22.

[R. MCKEON]

METHODOLOGY (THEOLOGY)

Methodology is an area in scientific theology that is not included in the traditional divisions because it is only beginning to be developed. Only a brief outline of this problem can be given here. It consists in the accomplished theologian's reflections on the historical development of his science in order to achieve an understanding of theological methodology. The growth of theology is like the growth of a child. A child must grow to maturity before he can reflect on and understand the process of maturing. Likewise theology must achieve some maturity before it can understand its own process of development. Only a chemist can write the history of chemistry, and only a theologian can write the history of theology.

Processes. In reflecting on the historical development of theology, the theologian becomes aware of various processes at work, especially the transcultural process, the theological process, and the dogmatic process.

The transcultural process is the transposition of the message of revelation from the thought patterns and ways of understanding commonly used in one culture to the thought patterns and ways of understanding in another culture; for example, from the Hebrew mentality and culture to the Hellenistic, to the Roman, to the medieval, to the modern Western, to the modern Oriental, etc. Because the gospel is to be preached to all nations in all ages in language and forms that the faithful of each particular age and culture can understand, one of the fundamental problems the theologian has to face is that of finding the transcultural principles operating in this transposition.

The theological process consists in passing from an understanding of revelation in terms of a particular culture to an understanding that is more universal, transcending individual past cultures. This process moves from an understanding of the truths of revelation in relation to a particular past cultural context to some understanding of the truths in themselves and in their relation to one another. It involves passing from what comes first in the acquisition of knowledge (*prius quoad nos*) to what is first in the order of being and intelligibility (*prius quoad se*). It does not terminate in a stage determined by past cultural circumstances. It was this process that achieved an analogical conception of the Divine Persons as consubstantial, of the Incarnation as the union of two natures in one Person, of grace as absolutely supernatural, etc.

The dogmatic process is that by which the Church as the teacher of all ages and cultures judges and defines an understanding of revelation that transcends past particular cultures and gives accurate expression to a more evolved understanding of revealed truth. Such judgments do not belong to the private theologian but to the Church under the guidance of the Holy Spirit.

Reflection on Processes. The theologian can come, in reflecting on these processes in detail, to understand something about the methodology of theology: what operation and groups of operations are involved in theological development; how these operations become further differentiated; how particular persons and cultures, although potentially unlimited, are actually limited by their horizon, their need of subjective conversion (moral, intellectual, religious), and lack of authenticity. As the effort to analyze and group all the operations of theological development into an intelligible synthesis runs into a barrier, the theologian looks about for some tools of further advance. He notices that the dynamism of consciousness has led in the past to a differentiation between operations that have to do with things that man can master (the profane world) and those that deal with the fields that lie beyond his control (the sacred); he notices that the structure of consciousness leads to a differentiation between operations insofar as they deal with objects (the objective world) and operations insofar as they are the means by which the subject is present to himself (the world of subjectivity). He notices, moreover, that there is a kind of specialization within consciousness where intelligence functions only as a part of the whole man (the world of common sense involving also specialized intelligence, e.g., D. Petau, A. von Harnack, J. Lebreton, R. de Vaux). And there is also a specialization of intelligence in which everything is subordinated to understanding and intelligence dominates (the world of theory—symbolized by Plato, Aristotle, Aquinas, Newton, Einstein, etc.).

The theologian can detect not only a great mobility within all of these worlds but also a movement from one world to another with development in one world affecting development in the other world. To illustrate briefly, historically there has been a movement from the world of common sense (the world of Scripture and tradition) to the world of theory (characteristic of medieval speculative theology) to the world of interiority (characteristic of modern theology). Morever, reflection reveals an inner dynamic of human intelligence that demands a movement from common sense understanding to theoretical understanding and on to an understanding of subjectivity and the subject who is engaged in all three worlds. The basic methodological problem for the theologian is to examine the differentiation and development of theological operations within each world and their relation to the operations of the other worlds in order to discover a principle or principles of integrating all three worlds. Theological method has to do with the order of these operations in achieving the goal theology sets for itself.

Theology as Science. A critical problem in modern theology is the place that theory is to hold in theology, whether the Aristotelian notion of science is any longer applicable to modern theology. In the Aristotelian notion of science, taken over by St. Thomas, science is concerned with certain knowledge, with the universal, the necessary, the immutable. Modern science, however, never claims more than probability. It is concerned with the changeable, the contingent, with movement, with the particular, with what exists in fact, with man as he actually exists instead of the ideal man. With the rise of historical consciousness and its repercussions in theology, one has an enormous theological development that does not fit into the medieval synthesis. Theology has shifted from a consideration of man as substance to a consideration of man as subject. Its current concern is more with the historical and concrete, with salvation history, than with universal conceptions. The theoretical element in theology is in danger of being pushed aside because seemingly irrelevant.

Nevertheless, the Church seems to have given a permanent status to the theoretical element in theology in

Vatican Council I, in its *Constitution on the Catholic Faith,* which considered FAITH and reason (H. Denzinger, *Enchiridion symbolorum,* 3015–20). The problem for the modern theologian, therefore, in view of the historical development of theology, is how to enlarge his concept of science so as to make room for modern developments in such a way that the contributions of modern theology are integrated with the achievements of the past. By studying past achievements more carefully, the theologian may be able to find the implicit foundations for modern development in such a way that he can see how modern theology is a prolongation and development of medieval theology.

To do this it seems that a theologian must understand what it is to understand, pursuing the path explored by B. Lonergan. He must investigate how understanding and judgment are related; how judgment is an act involving an ultimate personal COMMITMENT; how theological judgment, because it involves a view of the whole economy of salvation, is an act of Christian wisdom; why this requires a collaboration with the various particular natural wisdoms.

Theology has become very conscious of itself and sees the need of exploring the subject theologizing much more thoroughly if it is to understand what theological understanding is, how theological questions are to be ordered, and how the theologian is to integrate the three worlds in which he lives. A good beginning is being made in this area.

Bibliography: B. LONERGAN, *Method in Theology* (London 1972).

[G. F. VAN ACKEREN]

METOCHITES, GEORGE

Archdeacon of Hagia Sophia in Constantinople and Byzantine theological polemicist; b. *c.* 1250; d. in exile, *c.* 1328. A well-educated civil official, Metochites supported the policy of the Patriarch JOHN XI BECCUS and the Emperor MICHAEL VIII PALAEOLOGUS in their efforts to achieve union with Rome. He served on ambassadorial missions to Rome under Popes Gregory X, Innocent V, and John XXI, participated in the union Council of Lyons (1274), and wrote numerous tracts in support of the theological alignment with the Western Church. During the restoration of the Orthodox separatism under Emperor ANDRONICUS II PALAEOLOGUS in 1283, he was imprisoned and exiled for the remainder of his life, despite the fact that his son, Theodore Metochites, became first minister of the Byzantine Empire in 1316.

Together with John Beccus and Theodore Meliteniotes, George Metochites was one of the most prolific writers favoring the union. Besides popularizing the works of Beccus, he wrote polemical tracts against Maximus Planudes (*Patrologia Graeca*, ed. J. P. MIGNE. 141:1275–1308), Manuel Moschopulus (*Patrologia Graeca* 141: 1307–1406), and Gregory II of Cyprus (unedited). His five-book treatise on the procession of the Holy Spirit is still unedited. He wrote also a *Historia dogmatica* on the origin and development of the schism between Rome and the East after 1274, which is most valuable for information on events in his own lifetime. He is also credited with the composition of *Typikon on Faith,* and the treatises *On Virtue On Asceticism,* and *On the Soul,* which actually belong to Nicephorus Blemmydes.

Bibliography: *Patrologia Graeca*, ed. J. P. MIGNE (Paris 1857–66) 141:1275–1418. V. LAURENT, *Lexikon für Theologie und Kirche*, ed. J. HOFER and K. RAHNER (Freiberg 1957–65) 4: 703–704. H. G. BECK, *Kirche und theologische Literatur im byzantinischen Reich* (Munich 1959) 684. D. J. GEANAKOPLOS, *Emperor Michael Palaeologus and the West,* 1258–1282 (Cambridge, Mass. 1959) 287–291. S. SALAVILLE, *Dictionnaire de théologie catholique*, ed. A. VACANT et al., (Paris 1903–50) 6.1:1238–39; *Catholicisme* 4:1860–61. A. MAI, *Nova Patrum bibliotheca* (Rome) 8.2:1–277; 10:319–370.

[F. CHIOVARO]

METROPHANES CRITOPOULOS

Patriarch of Alexandria (1633–39), Byzantine scholar; b. Beroea, Macedonia, 1589; d. Vallachia, 1639. Metrophanes embraced the monastic life on Mount ATHOS, where he met Cyril LUCARIS, and accompanied him to Alexandria. In 1617 he was invited by the Archbishop of Canterbury, George Abbot, to visit England, and he spent ten years traveling in Europe, studying Protestantism and Anglicanism. He visited Oxford; then Hamburg, Bremen, Helmstedt, Wittemberg, Berlin, Leipzig, Tübingen, and Strassburg in Germany; Basel, Berne, Zurich, and Geneva in Switzerland. In November 1627 he was in Venice and left there for Constantinople. He was in Egypt in 1631 and had apparently been consecrated a bishop by 1633; in 1636 he was patriarch of Alexandria. As patriarch he subscribed to the decisions of the Synod of Constantinople (1638), which condemned his predecessor and benefactor, Cyril Lucaris. Metrophanes wrote a *Confessio catholicae et apostolicae in Ecclesia oriente* in Greek while at Helmstedt (1624–25); it was published there with a Latin translation by John Homeius in 1661. Protestant influence is noticeable in his doctrine on the Sacraments, which he reduces to three: Baptism, Eucharist, and Penance. He also rejected the deuteroncanonical books of the Bible, as well as the Catholic doctrine on indulgences and the Immaculate Conception. Only part of his works have been edited.

Bibliography: É. LEGRAND, *Bibliographie hellénique,* v. 5 (Paris 1903; repr. Brussels 1963) 192–218. V. GRUMEL, *Dictionnaire de théologie catholique,* ed. A. VACANT et al., 15 v. (Paris 1903–50; Tables générales 1951–) 10.2:1622–27.

[F. CHIOVARO]

METROPHANES OF SMYRNA

Metropolitan from 857 to 880. He was one of the intransigent prelates who refused to recognize PHOTIUS as the legitimate patriarch of Constantinople after the resignation of Ignatius. He was deposed by a Photian synod and was exiled to Cherson by the Emperor MICHAEL III. In 860 he met Constantine-Cyril and his brother Methodius, who stopped at Cherson on their embassy to the Khazars. He gave information to ANASTASIUS THE LIBRARIAN on the discovery by Constantine of relics believed to be those of Pope Clement I and on Constantine's writings about the discovery and in honor of St. Clement. After the deposition of Photius, Metrophanes played an important role at the Council of 869–870. When Photius was reinstated as patriarch after Ignatius's death (878), Metrophanes refused to recognize his offer of reconciliation and friendship. He refused to appear at the Union Council (879–880), which had rehabilitated Photius, and was deposed and excommunicated by the papal legates sent by Pope JOHN VIII. He may have recovered the See of Smyrna after Photius's resignation in 886. He wrote eulogies on St. Polycarp of Smyrna and the archangels Michael and Gabriel, and commentaries to the first Epistle of St. John, the Catholic letters, and Ecclesiastes (preserved only in a Georgian translation, pub. K. K. Kekelidze, 1920).

Bibliography: J. D. MANSI, *Sacrorum Conciliorum nova et amplissima collection,* 31 v. (Florence-Venice 1757–98); reprinted and continued by L. PETIT and J. B. MARTIN, 53 v. in 60 (Paris 1889–1927; repr. Graz 1960–) 16:54–73, 178. R. JANIN, *Dictionnaire de théologie catholique,* ed. A. VACANT et al., 15 v. (Paris 1903–50; Tables générales 1951–) 10.2:1627–28. J. A. G. HERGENRÖTHER, *Photius,* 4 v. in 3 (Regensberg 1867–69) v. 1–2, *passim.* F. DVORNIK, *The Photian Schism* (Cambridge, Eng. 1948) 43–49, 238–. H. G. BECK, *Kirche und theologische Literatur im byzantinischen Reich* (Munich 1959) 543–544.

[F. DVORNIK]

METTEN, ABBEY OF

Benedictine abbey in the Diocese of Regensburg, Bavaria, south Germany. Founded (766) from REICHENAU by Bl. Gamelbert and the first abbot, Bl. Utto, it was made a royal cloister by Charlemagne with the duty of prayer for emperor and empire and became an important settlement cloister. The monks were expelled (1058) and replaced by canons, but returned under the HIRSAU OBSERVANCE (1157). In 1236 church and cloister burned down. The abbots obtained pontifical rights in 1439. After collapse during the Reformation, there was a revival at Metten under Abbot Johannes Nablas (1596–1624), who expanded the abbey. The church was restored under Roman Märkl (1706–29). The cloister was suppressed by Bavaria in 1803 but was restored in Offenberg castle (1826) and made an abbey (1840). Metten has had prominent monks. The miniatures in a MS of the rule (*c.* 1400) anticipated the "Danube style." Ildefons Lehner was a leader in the neo-Gothic movement *c.* 1860; Utto Kornmüller, a composer and scholar, represented classical church music; Edmund Schmidt did research on the Benedictine rule. Gregor Scherr became archbishop of Munich and Freising (1856), and Leo Mergel, bishop of Eichstätt (1905). Metten restored SCHEYERN and Weltenburg and founded ST. VINCENT ARCHABBEY in the United States.

Bibliography: *Monumenta Mettensia* in *Monumenta Boica,* v.11 (Munich 1767) 341–518. R. MITTERMÜLLER, *Das Kloster Metten und seine Aebte* (Straubing 1856). W. FINK, *Entwicklungsgeschichte der Benedictinerabtei Metten,* 3 v. (Munich 1926–30); *Lexikon für Theologie und Kirche*, ed. J. HOFER and K. RAHNER, 10 v. (2d, new ed. Freiburg 1957–65) 7:375–376. P. LINDNER, *Die Schriftsteller und die um Wissenschaft und Kunst verdienten Mitglieder des Benediktinerordens im heutigen Königreich Bayern vom Jahre 1750 bis zur Gegenwart,* 2 v. (Regensburg 1880) 2:30; *Monasticon metropolis Salzburgensis antiquae* (Salzburg 1908) 273. O. L. KAPSNER, *A Benedictine Bibliography: An Author-Subject Union List*, 2 v. (2d ed. Collegeville, Minn. 1962) 2:231. L. H. COTTINEAU, *Répertoire topobibliographique des abbayes et prieurés*, 2 v. (Mâcon 1935–39) 2:1833–34.

[W. FINK]

MEURERS, HEINRICH VON

Liturgist; b. Tönnis (Holstein), Oct. 21, 1888; d. Trier, May 16, 1953. From 1909 he studied theology at Innsbruck, though interrupted by military service (1914–18), and he completed his studies with a doctorate in theology in 1921. In 1920, he was ordained at Trier. After a year of pastoral duties, he went to Rome for further studies, where, in 1923, he received the degree of master of sacred theology. From 1923 to 1935, he was professor of dogma at the theological faculty of Trier. From 1935 to 1951, he was vicar-general of the Diocese of Trier. In this office Von Meurers displayed high qualities and became, even beyond the boundaries of the diocese, one of the leaders of the liturgical movement in Germany; he was a founding member of the German liturgical commission (1940), the first president of the Liturgical Institute of Trier (1947), and president of the first German liturgical congress at Frankfurt am Main in 1950.

From his articles, which he published in different periodicals, the one on concelebration stands out: ''*Die eucharistische Konzelebration,*'' *Pastor Bonus,* 53 (1942) 65–77; 97–105.

Bibliography: J. WAGNER, *Liturgisches Jahrbuch* 3 (1953) 5–9.

[B. FISCHER]

MEURIN, SÉBASTIEN LOUIS

Jesuit; b. Charleville, France, Dec. 26, 1707; d. Prairie du Roeher, Ill., Feb. 23, 1777. He was destined to be the last Jesuit missionary in the ''Illinois Country.'' He entered the novitiate of the Champagne province of the Society of Jesus, at Nancy, France, 1729. He came to Canada in 1741 and was sent in 1746 to the Illinois mission. After serving as pastor of Ft. Vincennes (Vincennes, Ind.) he moved (1752) to French settlements near the Mississippi River (present Cahokia, Prairie du Rocher, and Kaskaskia, Ill.). Toward the end of the French and Indian War, a new governor, Philippe D'Abbadie, arrived at New Orleans with orders to expel the Jesuits. The priests were taken to New Orleans and sent to France, but the superior council of Louisiana took the responsibility of returning Meurin to his ministry among the Illinois native tribes. When the territory east of the Mississippi became English in 1763, he settled at St. Genevieve, crossing the river to serve the Christians of Illinois. He first established ecclesiastical jurisdiction through the Rev. Robert Harding, superior of the Maryland Jesuits, but in 1768 he offered obedience to Bp. Oliver Briand of Quebec, Canada. Briand named him vicar-general and sent the Rev. Pierre Gibault to help him. The Spanish commandant of Sainte Genevieve, considering this relationship with a bishop in English territory disloyal, exiled Meurin, who had to go to Illinois, where he settled at Prairie du Roeher; he lived the rest of his life under English rule. In 1764, during Meurin's only absence from the Illinois mission, Pierre Laclede and Auguste Chouteau founded the present city of St. Louis, Mo. From its beginning, Meurin cared for the settlers there, blessing the first log cabin church in the village on June 24, 1770. In 1775, after the suppression of the Society of Jesus (1773), he was adopted by the bishop of Quebec. He was buried at Prairie du Rocher, but his remains were transferred in 1847 to the Jesuit novitiate at Florissant, Mo.

Bibliography: C. H. METZGER, ''Sebastien Louis Meurin,'' *Ill. Catholic Historical Review,* 3 (1920–21) 241–259, 378–388; 4 (1921–1922) 43–56.

[R. N. HAMILTON]

MEXICO, COLONIAL

In August 1521 the great Aztec city of Tenochtitlán was in ruins; its inhabitants had fled; the last Aztec ruler, Cuautemoc, was a prisoner of Hernán Cortés. The Spaniards faced the task of rebuilding the destroyed city and of winning over the inhabitants of the area, inimical and distrustful after all the destruction. The Castilians in their simple faith felt it imperative first to eradicate idolatry and superstition among the native people. However, they had no idea of the vastness and ruggedness of the territory, of the varieties in climate, and of the lack of political and linguistic unity.

Early Missionary Activity. On Aug. 13, 1523, two Franciscan priests, Tecto and Aora, and Brother Pedro de GANTE arrived in New Spain from Flanders. On May 13, 1524, ''the Twelve,'' led by Martín de Valencia, arrived with power granted by the pope to establish the Church in New Spain. Gradually, hundreds of Franciscans, Dominicans, and Augustinians came. To facilitate the work of evangelizing, they divided the territory, with Mexico City as the center: the Augustinians, to the northwest and south; the Dominicans, to the southeast; and the Franciscans, to the north and northeast. The Franciscans also went into Yucatán. When the Jesuits arrived, they were given charge of the extreme northeast of present-day Mexico, but they continued on to the present states of Nuevo León and Coahuila and the vast territories of modern Texas and New Mexico.

Franciscans. This order grew so quickly that by the beginning of the 17th century it was organized into five provinces: Mexico City, Mérida, Valladolid (now Morelia), Guadalajara, and Zacatecas. To educate their missionaries they also built six apostolic colleges: Querétaro, Guadalupe de Zacatecas, San Fernando de México, Orizaba, Pachuca, and Zapopan, whose history had been written by Isidro Félix de Espinosa and Juan de ARRICIVITA. The Franciscans gave to New Spain 19 bishops, among them Fray Juan de ZUMÁRRAGA. They wrote hundreds of works in the native tongues, of which Beristáin lists 522, not all verified. Motolinía, Sahagún, Mendieta, Augustín de Vetancur, Alonso de la Rea, Pablo Beaumont, Antonio Tello, José de Arlegui, and Diego de Landa wrote histories and chronicles, rich in data, on the pre-Cortesian history as well as on the development of the apostolate and the discoveries and conquests.

Dominicans. In 1526 the first Dominicans arrived; but five of them died that same year, and four returned to Spain. They made progress little by little and eventually formed four provinces: Santiago de México (1536), San Vicente de Chiapas y Guatemala (1551), San Hipólito de Oaxaca (1595), and Puebla (1656). In those first years they distinguished themselves by defending the native Mexicans as rational beings. They also filled important offices in the Inquisition and in the university. They gave 19 bishops to New Spain, including the first bishop to come to Mexico, Garcés (1452?–1524); the famous LAS CASAS; and the enterprising Alcalde (1701–92). They had two excellent historians: Agustín Dávila Padilla and Antonio de Remesal.

Augustinians. In 1535 seven Augustinian fathers arrived, the advance group of those who were to work especially for the conversion of the Otomies in Huasteca and in the present state of Guerrero. Some of their magnificent monasteries are still standing, such as Acolman, Actopan, and Ixmiquilpan. They were bold builders and able organizers of native communities. Alonso de la Veracruz was noted for his learning. Of the eight prelates whom the order gave to New Spain, the viceroy-archbishop Fray Payo Enríquez de Rivera (1670–81) was exceptional. Juan de Grijalva, Esteban García, Diego Basalenque, Juan González de la Puente, and Matías Escobar were Augustinian chroniclers.

These three religious orders converted millions of native people who lived on the central plateau and began to Christianize other regions. At the beginning of the 18th century there were 351 monasteries with 2,396 priests: 1,218 Franciscans, 527 Dominicans, and 651 Augustinians. The secular clergy did very little at first. Of those who came to New Spain only a rare few had the qualifications necessary for an arduous life. Most of them served in the curia or in the cathedrals of the six dioceses, which Charles V quickly obtained from the Holy See. Important in the conversion of the natives was the devotion to Our Lady of GUADALUPE, which spread throughout the land and by the 17th century was the characteristic devotion of the Mexican people.

Problems in Evangelization. The obstacles that the missionaries encountered were greater than the first volunteers had anticipated. The country was immense and bristled with mountain ranges. The sea coasts were hot and unhealthy. Only one area in the central plateau, the region ruled by the Aztecs, was relatively civilized. In the rest of the country the linguistic, tribal, and cultural differences were almost infinite. More than 500 different languages were spoken. More problematic still were the native religious practices. The Aztecs had syncretized the religions of the tribes they dominated, and their cult had become a confused conglomeration of polytheistic, animistic, and astrological beliefs, which resulted in all kinds of sacrifices, rites, and magical and superstitious practices. Especially abhorrent to the Spaniards was their common practice of human sacrifice. The religious beliefs and practices of the rest of the country also varied immensely. In those first years the barriers seemed impregnable. The missionaries attributed the tenacity of the natives in clinging to their ancestral customs to the special dominion of the devil. Some missionaries thought they saw in native rites or images vestiges of remote Christian teachings, an ingenious misinterpretation that many were to follow two centuries later.

The bravery of the Spanish conquistadores and the backing of the crown made the work of evangelizing much easier. In every town a church with its monastery or rectory was built at royal expense. Spain paid the traveling expenses of the missionaries and maintained them in their Christianizing work (*see* PATRONATO REAL), even though some Spanish settlers by their greed and evil conduct made the religion they professed odious. The results of the first 50 years of evangelizing were amazing. At the end of the 16th century the population of the entire central plateau had been converted to the Christian faith. It is impossible to say how many were baptized. The missionaries speak of millions. Modern sociologists have not been able to find a satisfactory explanation with reliable statistics for the undeniable phenomenon of the depopulation of the country. Studies of the Berkeley school hold that a population of 20 million when the Spaniards arrived fell to 2 million by the end of the century. The laments of the missionaries over the disappearance of the native peoples were not exaggerated. The clash of cultures brought ravaging epidemics and a rapid decline in the number of natives. All who survived became Christians. The Church, led by Zumárraga and the first Bishop of Michoacán, Don Vasco de QUIROGA, founded hospitals and various charitable institutions throughout the country.

Inquisition. To protect the purity of faith of the discoverers and conquistadores, among whom were descendants of half-converted Jews, the Tribunal of the Holy Inquisition, established in Santo Domingo, delegated Martín de Valencia. He was to stamp out all superstitious practices and any heresy that arose among the Spaniards and to punish natives who fell back into idolatry or into shameful sins. After some time and various changes, on Nov. 4, 1571, a tribunal with all powers was established in Mexico City. By 1575 the native peoples were exempt from its jurisdiction. During its first century of operation the Inquisition prevented Judaism or Islam from taking root, resisted the habit of blasphemy and pseudomystical aberrations, and averted the entrance of Protestantism. With a strong hand it suppressed bigamy among Christians and the scandalous conduct of some priests. At the end of the 17th century it began to decline and almost confined its activities to the task of preventing censored books from entering the country. During the 296 years it functioned in Mexico, the Inquisition turned over to the secular authority for capital punishment 43 guilty persons. The rest were imprisoned for a time.

Education. The bishops and religious of New Spain established schools in the new villages. In the shadow of the first cathedrals, monasteries, and churches, elementary education was given, and the arts and trades brought over from Spain were taught. All were admitted free of charge, with no distinction of caste or race. Pedro de Gante had more than a thousand native students in his school. The first Franciscans, with the approval of the viceroy and bishop, tried to prepare the sons of the native chiefs even for Holy Orders in the famous college of Santa Cruz de Tlaltelolco (1536), but the efforts were premature. Many centers of learning opened in the 16th century. Mexico had a university in 1553. Printing was introduced by the Church. In 1539, the first book known to have been published in the New World, the *Breve y más compendiosa doctrina Christiana en lengua Mexicana y Castellana,* appeared. It is not improbable that many others were published before this. Books on dogma and asceticism and on theoretic and applied science, especially grammars and vocabularies in the native languages, came off the presses by the hundreds.

Work of the Jesuits. The coming of the Society of Jesus in 1572 brought great benefits. During the two centuries they worked in Mexico, until they were expelled in 1767, the Jesuits founded 25 colleges, 11 seminaries, and six houses for priests and extended their missions throughout the northeast of the country (Sinaloa, 1591; Tepehuanes, 1596; Pimería, 1687; Lower California, 1697). Famous among the missionaries were TAPIA, KINO, SALVATIERRA, and PFEFFERKORN. The Creoles received their education from the Jesuits during those two centuries. From this resulted many vocations for the secular clergy, which made it possible to transfer to them the parishes, conducted by religious during the 16th century. These transfers were made not without disturbance and bitter feelings. The rigid attitude of the bishop of Puebla, PALAFOX, caused rancor, and he went to the extreme in clashing with the Jesuits. Early Jesuit historians were Pérez de Rivas, Florencia, and Alegre.

17th-century Mexican Society. Many monasteries of other religious orders, Mercedarians, Carmelites, those of St. Hippolitus, etc., fostered Catholic life among the descendants of the Spaniards. By the middle of the century the central section of the country was Christian. Churches and monasteries abounded; in towns and haciendas and ranches Christian life flourished, and if some vestige of paganism persisted among the native Mexicans incorporated into the civilized world, it was not tolerated in public. Spanish culture thrived, especially in Mexico City. Among the most notable representatives were Sor Juana Inés de la Cruz (1651–95), the learned priest Carlos de Sigüenza y Góngora (1645–1700), and the talented playwright Juan Ruiz de Alarcón. Famous painters also plied their art, such as Baltasar de Echave, Luis and José Juárez, and Miguel Cabrera. Along the coasts and in the mountainous regions of the north and south, the spread of Christianity was slow and difficult. Because of the lack of statistics, it is impossible to give the number of Catholics in New Spain at the start of the 18th century. There were eight immense dioceses with their prelates, cathedral chapters, and seminaries; innumerable parishes; monasteries; Catholic colleges, hospitals, and charitable institutions. The native Mexicans numbered scarcely 3 million; the Spaniards reached 1 million; and the castes (or persons of mixed blood), another million. Since Catholicism was the official religion and the only one acceptable, all were Catholics, although not equally educated in the faith.

Effects of the 18th Century in New Spain. The decline of Spain, already far advanced in the reign of Charles II (1665–1700) and made worse by his death, which brought on the War of the Spanish Succession, halted almost completely the progress of Catholicism in New Spain. Greater evils were brought on by the regalistic government of the ministers of Charles III (1759–88), who in 1767 expelled the members of the Society of Jesus, bringing ruin to their missions, colleges, and apostolate. The Jesuits were, so said the viceroy in charge of their expulsion, the object of blind devotion on the part of all the inhabitants who rose in protest against the expulsion. The Oratorians, Dominicans, and Franciscans also suffered in having to take over the work of the Jesuits at a time when vocations were not plentiful. Anticlerical and anti-Catholic movements of the ENLIGHTENMENT, then in vogue in France and in Spain, weakened the faith of the educated classes. The missions were falling in ruins. Peace and social quiet were disturbed by the news of U.S. independence and by reports of the French Revolution.

Weakening of Church Discipline. Those same ministers of Charles III supporting the anticlerical and anti-Roman tendencies then prevalent used the Patronato Real and the concordat, recently held by the king with the Holy See, to place in episcopal sees and in key positions of the Church persons completely subordinate to political interests. The Inquisition, which had lost much of its former zeal, degenerated into an instrument of political suppression. Among the upper classes the anti-Christian Enlightenment unsettled the basic Catholicism, which had been typical of the Creole society. From the end of the 18th century vocations decreased in number and quality, and monasteries declined. Among both the religious and secular clergy more and more individuals lacked apostolic zeal and the basic Christian virtues. The authority of the Church was undermined in many of its representatives.

Educational Influence of the Enlightenment. When Baron Alexander von Humboldt visited New Spain on his expedition of 1799 to 1804, he was agreeably surprised at the economic, cultural, and artistic progress, which was steadily approaching the level of that of the mother country. Because of the efforts of the learned priest CASTORENA Y URSÚA, Mexico had a newspaper, which printed the political and cultural news from Europe. The university still flourished and had made great progress in the natural sciences and in mathematics. The erudite José Antonio Alzate published periodically information on the scientific progress in Europe and also worthwhile studies and observations of his own.

During those same years the canons of Mexico, Eguiara y Eguren and Beristáin, compiled and published excellent bibliographies, veritable catalogues of religious, theological, philosophical, linguistic, and scientific publications of the three centuries of New Spain. But theological and philosophical studies were at a low level; the expulsion of the Jesuits and the implacable opposition to their books and teaching had caused confusion among students. Yet the Jesuits had early introduced experimental sciences in Mexico and even some modern philosophical trends. Their expulsion contributed also to a weakening of the traditional love for the Spanish crown, since many of the exiled belonged to the most Christian Creole families. The opposition between the Creoles and the Spaniards born on the Peninsula increased. Humboldt said it was very marked. The government of Charles IV (1788–1808) was discredited even more by the blunders and venality of certain governors sent to Mexico and by the law through which the Crown expropriated the capital of charitable institutions. This brought harm and failure to the farmer and to the Creole businessman.

Napoleonic Period and the Mexican Revolt. In such circumstances it is not at all surprising that the agitation in Spain caused by the invasion of Napoleon and the upheaval in all of Spanish living from 1808 to 1814 should have had repercussions in the American dominions and especially in Mexico. The news of the insurrection of Aranjuez and of the renunciations in Bayonne disturbed the inhabitants of New Spain. In the capital two opposing groups were formed: one side was for autonomy and wanted the viceroy, assisted by a junta of representatives, to take over all power; the other side, completely dedicated to the interests of the Peninsulars, imprisoned the viceroy and appointed an old soldier, Garibay, to hold command until the central Spanish junta named a new viceroy. The first one chosen was the archbishop of Mexico, Lizan y Beaumont, who tried to ease the tension of souls, without however preventing the formation of juntas in different parts of the country to plan for independence. At the threat of capture of the plotters in Querétaro, the parish priest of Dolores, Miguel HIDALGO, resolved to start an armed rebellion, which took on the character of a religious and a class war with the slogans "Viva la Virgen de Guadalupe" and "Mueran los gachupines." This succeeded in arousing a large part of the working class of Bajío. The excesses perpetrated by this horde in Guanajuato, Valladolid, and Guadalajara caused a deep rift in the country between the insurgents, who feared that the government of Mexico would sacrifice the legitimate interests of the country and surrender to the French, and the people of law and order, who could not believe that authority should be compromised by the outrages and atrocities committed by the rebels in arms. These excesses justified the position taken by the religious authorities of Valladolid, Mexico City, Puebla, and Guadalajara, who excommunicated the leaders, guilty of taking prisoners and mistreating persons consecrated to God.

The number of priests and religious who took an active part in the prolonged war for independence (1810–21) has been greatly exaggerated. Of the 7,000 clerics and religious in New Spain, only 161 have been verified as revolutionaries; of those, 37 were shot. Especially in the first years of the war, 1808 to 1815, cruelty was widespread and the excesses and outrages defiled the army of insurgents as well as those who tried in the name of government to suppress the rebellion. From the time when the parish priest Morelos, the genial guerrila, was shot until the rebellion of 1821, the insurgents were reduced to bands of guerrillas in the mountains and along the coast. When Mexico learned of a new rebellion in Spain under the leadership of Riego and that Ferdinand VII was forced to promulgate the Constitution of the Cortes of Cádiz, condemned by the Church, Agustín de Iturbide, a general in the service of the viceroy, and Vicente Guerrero proposed their Plan of Iguala. This gained the support of almost all the military leaders, even those of the insurgents in arms, and the approval of the entire country. On Sept. 27, 1821, the army, called the Army of the Three Guarantees, proclaiming as the basis of Mexican independence religion, union, and independence, entered the capital in triumph. On the following day the independence of Mexico was solemnly proclaimed. The crown of the new kingdom was offered to an Infante of the House of Bourbon, and Iturbide meanwhile presided over a body of regents. Although the Catholic religion was proclaimed as official, the Church had ended the secular rule of the Patronato through which the Spanish crown had supported the work of evangelizing, educating, and doing good works, with an enormous outlay of money and with constant protection. A most grave problem, therefore, confronted the hierarchy of the Church and the government of the new nation.

Bibliography: F. J. ALEGRE, *Historia de la provincia de la Compañia de Jesús de Nueva España,* ed. E. J. BURRUS and F. ZUBILLAGA, 4 v. (new ed. Rome 1956–60). P. J. BARTH, *Franciscan Education and the Social Order in Spanish North America, 1502–1821* (Chicago 1945). C. S. BRADEN, *Religious Aspects of the Conquest of Mexico* (Durham, N.C. 1930). J. BRAVO UGARTE, *Historia de México,* 4 v. (Mexico City 1941–59). M. CUEVAS, *Historia de la Iglesia en México,* 5 v. (5th ed. Mexico City 1946–47). G. DECORME, *La obra de los Jesuitas mexicanos durante la época colonial, 1572–1767,* 2 v. (Mexico City 1941). J. T. MEDINA, *Historia del Tribunal del Santo Oficio de la Inquisición en México,* ed. J. JIMÉNEZ RUEDA (2d ed. Mexico City 1952). D. OLMEDO, *La Iglesia Católica en la edad moderna,* v. 3 of *Manual de historia de la Iglesia,* (2d ed. Mexico City 1963). R. RICARD, *La conquista espiritual de México,* tr. A. M. GARIBAY KINTANA (Mexico City 1947). A. YBOT LÉON, *La iglesia y los eclesiásticos españoles en la empresa de Indias,* 2 v. (Barcelona 1954–63).

[D. OLMEDO]

MEXICO (MODERN), THE CATHOLIC CHURCH IN

Capital: Mexico City.
Size: 760,000 sq. miles.
Population: 100,349,770 in 2000.
Languages: Spanish; Amerindian languages are spoken in various regions.
Religions: 89,311,290 Catholics (89%), 6,020,900 Protestants (6%), 5,507,580 practice indigenous or syncretistic faiths.

Divided into 31 separate states, the federation formally known as the United Mexican States is bordered on the north by the United States, on the west by the North Pacific Ocean, on the east by the Gulf of Mexico, and on the south by Guatemala and Belize. Vast areas in the arid north and the tropical south are thinly populated, while the rest of the terrain ranges from high, rugged volcanic mountains in the central region dropping to low plains at the coastlines. Tsunamis are frequent in the Pacific region, while hurricanes present a regular threat near the Gulf of Mexico and along the eastern coastline. Natural resources include petroleum, silver, copper, gold, lead, zinc, and natural gas. Agricultural products consist of corn, wheat, soybeans, rice, beans, cotton, coffee, fruit, and livestock and dairy, and the illegal cultivation of the opium poppy and cannabis are common. The majority of the Mexican people are of mixed Spanish and Amerindian descent, but a large percentage of the population in the south is pure Amerindian. The following essays discuss the history of the Catholic Church in Mexico from the establishment of independence (1821) to the present. For discussion of the church in Mexico prior to 1821, see the entry on colonial Mexico above.

The Independent Church. For three centuries the Catholic Church in New Spain had been in close union with the Spanish crown. The invasion of Napoleon and the upheaval in all the Spanish colonies from 1808 to 1814 would sever this relationship. In the aftermath of the sometimes brutal fight for independence that began in 1810, the Church struggled to adapt itself to the independent life of Mexico, trying to preserve its autonomy without breaking its ties with the government. While Catholicism became the state religion when independence was proclaimed in 1821, the financial support formerly gained through the *PATRONATO REAL* was now lost. During the first 40 years after independence, the Church was forced to weather a succession of similar crises. After the War of Reform and the Empire (1857–67) the Church strove to survive in an atmosphere of hostile separation from the state, mitigated somewhat by the conciliatory policies of Porfirio DÍAZ. Social problems and political unrest brought the social revolution (1911–20) and a new constitution (1917). Both were openly hostile to the Church, which resisted the efforts of President CALLES to exterminate it. After years of persecuting the Church, the government finally began to practice tolerance toward it.

Problems of Independence. On Sept. 28, 1821, the Act of Independence of the Mexican Empire was signed. Despite the poverty and the destruction left following over a decade of war, the Three Guarantees proclaimed by the newly established Mexican regime—religion, union, and independence—restored hopes of peace and stability. The Catholic religion was preserved; the barriers of caste were declared abolished; and the ties that bound the region to Spain were broken. The territory of the new empire was most extensive; the illusion was created of vast territories, of political and social unity, and religious peace. However, in the decades that followed the country endured five constitutions, two emperors, 51 presidents, and wars with Texas, France, and the United States. By 1867 Mexicans were more profoundly divided among themselves than in 1821.

Scarcity of Priests. At independence Mexico was homogeneously Catholic and the Church was credited with fashioning the Mexican character. The population in 1810 was estimated at 6,121,426, of which more than half were Amerindians. Over 4,200 clerics, 3,000 religious, and 2,000 nuns tended to these faithful. The War of Independence caused the number of priests and religious to decrease; seminaries were closed; missionary reinforcements from Europe were discontinued; and the war

Archdioceses	Suffragans
Acapulco	Chilpancingo-Chiapa, Ciudad Altramirano, Ciudad Lázaro Cárdenas, Tlapa
Antequera/Oaxaca	San Cristóbal de las Casas, Tapachula, Tehuantepec, Tuxtepec, Tuxtla Gutiérrez
Chihuahua	Ciudad Juárez, Cuauhtémoc-Madera, Nuevo Casas Grandes, Parral, Tarahumara
Durango	Culiacán, Mazatlán, and Torreón
Guadalajara	Aguascalientes, Autlán, Ciudad Guzmán, Colima, San Juan de los Lagos, Tepic, Zacatecas
Hermosillo	Ciudad Obregón, La Paz en la Baja California Sur, Mexicali, Tijuana
Jalapa	Coatzacoalcos, Córdoba, Orizaba, Papantla, San Andrés Tuxtla, Tuxpan,Veracruz
México	Atlacomulco, Cuernavaca, Toluca, Tula, Tulancingo
Monterrey	Ciudad Valles, Ciudad Victoria, Linares, Matamoros, Nuevo Laredo, Saltillo, Tampico
Morelia	Apatzingán, Tacámbaro, Zamora
Puebla de los Angeles	Huajuapan de León, Huejutla, Tehuacán, Tlaxcala
San Luis Potosí	Celaya, León, Matehuala, Querétaro
Tlalnepantla	Cuautitlán, Ecatepec, Netzhualcóyotl, Texcoco
Yucatán	Campeche, Tabasco

There are also seven prelacies and one vicariat apostlic. The Maronite Catholic Church and the Greek Melkite Church each have eparchies in Mexico that are directly subject to their respective patriarchates.

claimed many of the faithful. Three dioceses, Michoacán, Linares, and Chiapas, were without bishops. Only the young archbishop of Mexico City and six other prelates remained active.

In spite of the Three Guarantees, serious problems immediately presented themselves: the exercise of the *patronato real*; the disposition of property used by the Church under grant from the crown; the collection and use of tithes; and the support of hospitals, charitable organizations, and educational institutions, which had already begun to deteriorate. The bishops and their advisers took the position that the *patronato* had ceased with the declaration of independence, that the Church was also completely independent, and that the new nation, rooted in Catholicism, should sustain the juridic and economic position of the Church. Opposed to this interpretation were many politicians who supported radical regalism: the new state had the rights and the obligations of the *patronato*. Under Iturbide these issues remained unsettled. While in 1822 canon Pablo VÁZQUEZ was appointed to go to Rome to reach an agreement with the Holy See, he was given no clear instructions.

As time passed matters grew worse. The archbishop of Mexico and the bishop of Oaxaca, alarmed at the grave problems in conscience that the independence of the king created, returned to Spain. Other bishops died: the bishop of Guadalajara in 1824; the bishops of Sonora and Durango in 1825; the bishop of Yucatán in 1827; and lastly, the bishop of Puebla in 1829. Moreover, by 1831, 93 of the 181 prebends of the cathedral chapters were vacant; the number of clergy had decreased from 4,229 to 2,282; of 208 convents only 155 remained, with some 1,700 religious instead of 3,112, Replacements were not numerous enough for those who died and those who returned to Spain. The Jesuits, reestablished by the pope in 1814 and by the king of Spain in 1815, had not as yet reached a stable condition, and the few members it had in Mexico were scattered and unorganized.

Role of Masonry. One threat to the Church came from the Masonic lodges, which multiplied during the War of Independence and became political clubs following independence. U.S. ambassador Poinsett introduced the York rite to counteract the Spanish influence of the Scottish rite. Rare was the active politician who was not a Mason, and many priests were members. While the con-

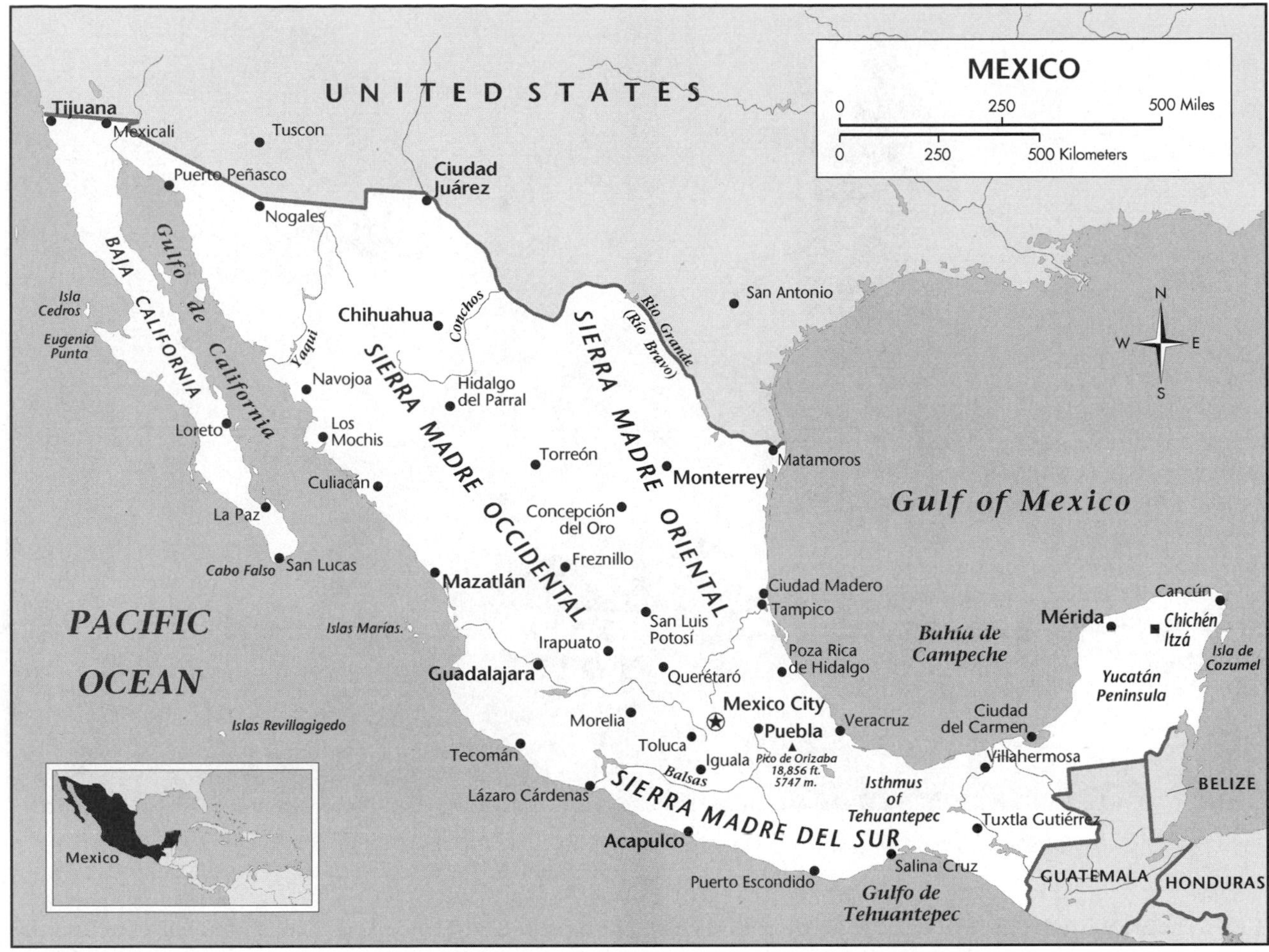

demnation of the Church was not stressed, since all Mexicans were said to be Catholics, Masonic organizations did foster anticlericalism.

Reestablishment of Hierarchy. In 1830 Vázquez received instructions to negotiate with the Holy See in regard to the nomination of bishops. PIUS VIII, fearing to offend the king of Spain, appointed only apostolic vicars with episcopal character; providentially for Mexico Pius VIII died in 1830 and his successor, GREGORY XVI (1831–46) named six bishops for Mexico, among them was the canon Vázquez. Thus the ecclesiastical hierarchy was renewed in Mexico. Only Mexico City and Oaxaca remained without prelates, out of regard to their bishops, who were residing in Spain. In 1838 the Holy See succeeded in obtaining their resignations and appointed new prelates for both dioceses.

Temporary president Valentín Gómez Farías began a juridical persecution of the Church under the pretext of reforming it. In addition to attempting to use the *patronato* to intervene directly in the government of the dioceses, he tried to suppress religious vows so that monasteries would be deserted; he tried also to do away with the civil exaction of the tithes, to appropriate the funds of the missions of the Philippine Islands and of California, to secularize these last missions, and to take education out of the hands of the clergy by closing the university and the Colegio de Santos. However, Gómez was quickly overthrown by Santa Anna, and the new bishops, in spite of the political upheavals, local persecutions, and the impossibility of trying to reform the religious orders, began to restore their dioceses and seminaries, to increase the number of clergy. From 2,282 in 1831, the number of priests rose to 3,232 in 1851. From 1834 to 1856 the government allowed the Jesuits to reestablish themselves; Basilio ARRILLAGA was an outstanding apologist for the Society of Jesus during those difficult years.

Recognition by the Papacy. The problem of Church-State relations approached resolution when the *patronato* was replaced by a concordat. In 1836 GREGORY XVI recognized the independence of Mexico and received as extraordinary minister and plenipotentiary Manuel Diez de Bonilla. PIUS IX named the first apostolic delegate, Luigi Clementi, who arrived in Mexico City in November of

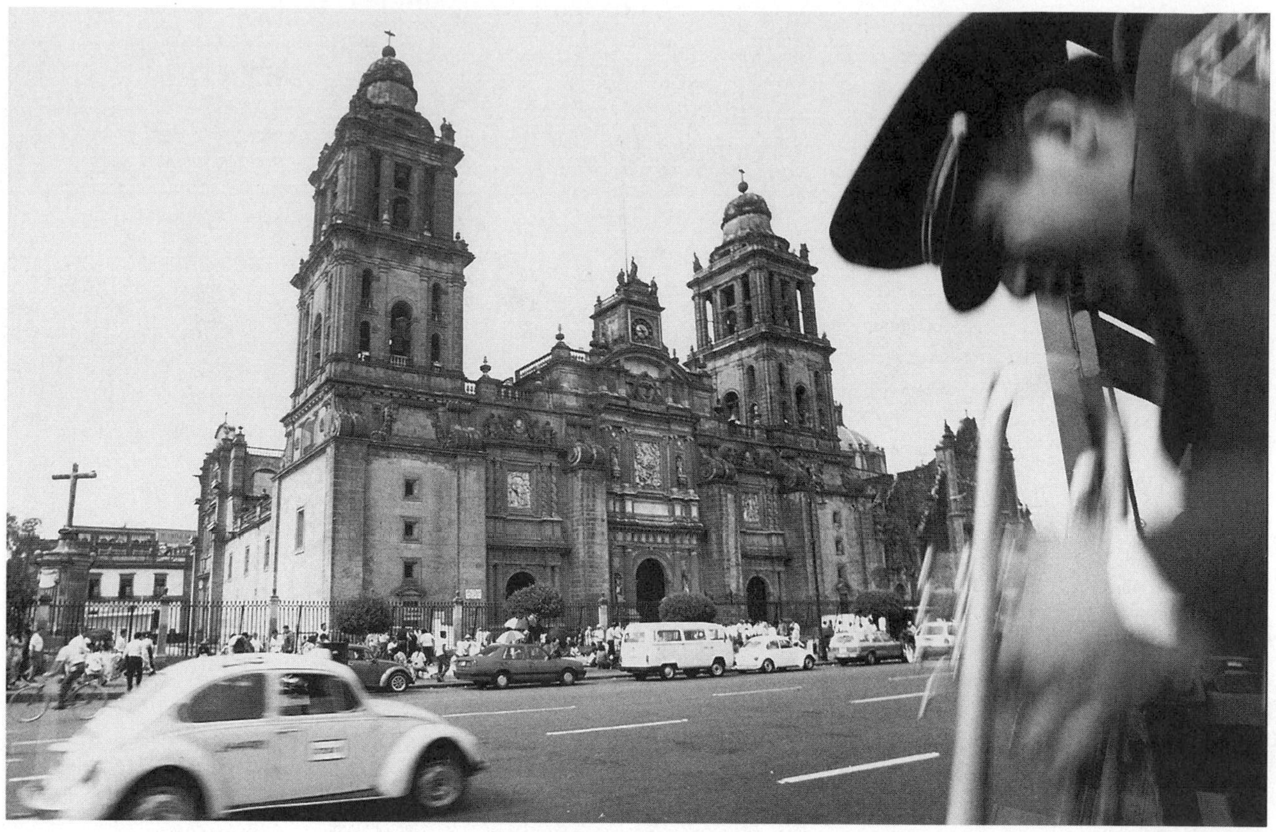

Metropolitan Cathedral, Zocalo Plaza, Mexico City. (AP/Wide World Photos)

1851. The archbishop of Mexico, De la Garza, influenced by the opinion of canonists who tended toward regalism, did not want to acknowledge him unless the government did. President Arista did not dare because of opposition in the chamber of deputies. His successor, Lombardini, submitted the matter to the senate, which, with certain reservations, agreed to allow the delegate to exercise his pontifical mission in Mexico. The subsequent War of Reform hindered effective action, and the delegate was expelled by Benito Juárez in 1861.

The 1847 war with the United States made Mexico unable to put down the war of the castes in Yucatán, the invasions of the Apaches in the north, and other insurrections in the interior, as well as deal with the nation's economic problems. In 1853 the exiled and discredited Santa Anna was asked to return to head a centralist republic. Under a Catholic president, the Church enjoyed its share of the Guarantees, reestablished the Jesuits, and had complete freedom in Catholic worship. However, opposition to the Church would resurface by 1854.

Liberal Reforms. The revolution started by the Plan of Ayutla proclaimed that ''liberal institutions alone suit the country to the exclusion of all others.'' Santa Anna was forced into exile and the liberals took over the government. They convoked a constitutional congress that passed various laws, known by the names of the ministers who introduced them: the Ley Juárez, which suppressed ecclesiastical privileges; the Ley Iglesias, which prohibited payment for parochial services; and the Ley Lerdo, which expropriated the lands of corporations and gave them to tenants or put them up for public sale.

War of Reform. The constitution of 1857 incorporated the essentials of these laws and separated Church from state. The bishops refused to respect the constitution, and many Catholics were convinced that the intention of the legislators was wicked. A brutal civil war broke out from 1855 to 1867, during which more than 11 priests were killed, many more were tortured, and all the bishops and many others were banished. Some 40 churches were plundered and many more demolished, monasteries were torn down or broken through for streets, or used for profane purposes. Of the 11 conciliar seminaries, nine were confiscated, and the one in Puebla was sold. General González Ortega confiscated silver and artistic treasures from the Źacatecas parish and the cathedral of Durango, while Michel Blanco stole 100,000 pesos from the sanctuary of San Juan de los Lagos, and took all the wrought silver from the cathedral of Morelia.

Such profanations and scandalous conduct stirred the ire of the people, and armed leaders arose throughout the country. Two irreconcilable groups were formed: the liberals, or *chinacos,* and the conservatives, or *mochos.* Liberal leaders attempted to introduce into Mexico a brand of politics that they copied from French radical liberals, and conservatives opposed this doctrine as a disruption of Mexican culture and a campaign against the Church.

French Intervention. The War of Reform (1857–62) was prolonged by victorious liberals who challenged the expeditionary forces of Napoleon III of France. Some Mexicans put aside the confusion of interests and, notwithstanding their profound Catholic faith, fought against the invaders. The situation was very complicated. From the beginning of the war the liberals applied to the United States for moral, economic, and even military help. Some of the conservatives thought the only hope of salvation was a monarchy and they supported Napoleon III. Empress Eugenie, profoundly Catholic, favored them, and thought that France should oppose the conquest of a Protestant nation such as the United States and save the independence of Catholic Spanish America. Maximilian of Hapsburg, on condition that the Mexican people offer him the crown, joined this fantastic and grandiose project. Some Mexicans accepted him under the illusion that a strong Catholic, and therefore popular, monarch could save Mexico from national disintegration and from being absorbed by the Colossus of the North.

The government of Benito Juárez had expelled the first apostolic delegate, Bishop Clementi, and various bishops; it had discharged many government employees, who in conscience protested against the laws of persecution; it had deprived the Church of its goods without process of law and in a wasteful manner; it had proposed the MacLane-Ocampo treaty with the United States, which the Senate later rejected because it divided Mexico. So it was not surprising that, even though he came under the protection of French bayonets, many bishops welcomed the European prince.

The delusion did not last long. The policy of Maximilian was a mixture of French liberalism and Austrian Josephinism and was in certain aspects a continuation of liberal persecution. Nevertheless, during these few years of comparative peace the Church was able to recover its strength and erect two new ecclesiastical provinces, Guadalajara and Michoacán, as well as establish several new dioceses.

Establishment of Liberal Government. The liberals, aided by the United States, forced the withdrawal of French troops, took control of the country, and in 1867 captured Maximilian in Querétaro, executing him along with two of his generals. With liberal general Porfirio

Procession of Our Lady of Guadalupe, Mexico City. (©Fulvio Roiter/CORBIS)

Díaz's conquest of Puebla and Mexico City, the last conservative strongholds were gone. President Juárez reestablished the republic and, under the pretext of defending liberty, closed the monasteries, churches, educational institutions, and charitable organizations, opening the country to Protestants.

Other anti-Catholic measures were drawn from the constitution, including the suppression of religious instruction in state schools and the prohibition of religious corporations from possessing property other than buildings of worship. Juárez's successor, Sebastián Lerdo de Tejada, increased his predecessor's influences: complete freedom of worship was established; marriage was declared a mere civil contract; religious institutions were forbidden to acquire property or money coming from it; the religious oath in civil acts was abolished; and it was decreed that the State "will not allow any contract, pact or agreement which has as its object any diminution or loss, by irrevocable sacrifice, of human liberty, be it because of labor, education, or religious vow, and in conse-

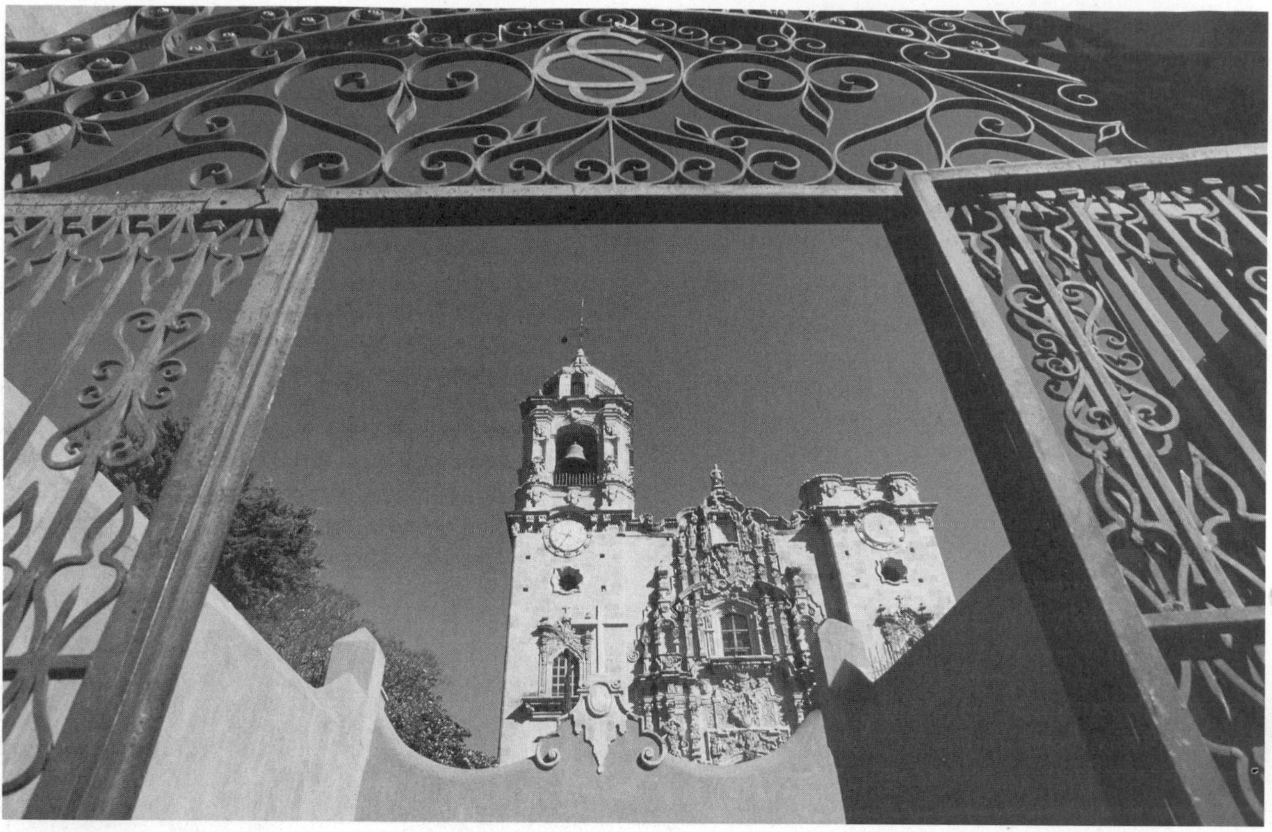

Valenciana Church, Guanajuato, Mexico. (©Danny Lehman/CORBIS)

quence the Law cannot recognize monastic orders nor permit their establishment.'' These laws prohibited religious instruction and the practice of any worship in government buildings. Ministers were not allowed to wear anything distinctive in public.

Enforcement of Religious Reform. In a Catholic country such measures were either not complied with or were a source of constant infractions. During the presidencies of Juárez and Lerdo de Tejada attempts at enforcement were made and many were imprisoned. Lerdo banished from the country the Sisters of Charity, Jesuits, Passionists, and Paulists. During those years the Church lost almost all her imposing buildings, which had served as seminaries, colleges, religious houses, or charitable institutions. Almost all the libraries were taken by the government or destroyed. The Church passed through a time of anguish, as did the entire nation, impoverished by wars and discredited before the civilized world. The public treasury was bankrupt, backwardness and poverty were general, and divisions and grudges among the liberal leaders were implacable.

Age of Porfirio Díaz. It is not surprising that the country acclaimed Porfirio Díaz when he turned the nation onto a course of order and peace. Many of his political enemies submitted, and the law was repealed that prohibited a reelection of a president, thus making possible the ''era of Porfirio,'' the personal reign of Díaz through six successive reelections as president, until the revolution in 1911 overthrew him. Peace was imposed, indeed by an iron hand, but gratefully accepted by an impoverished nation. Mexico became more prosperous and wealthy than all Spanish America, and the new national unity put an end to the centrifugal tendencies of many states. While Díaz was sincerely dedicated to the welfare of Mexico, he showed some lack of culture, of vision, and even of loyalty. He tended toward Machiavellism in governing, and lacked strength to change laws he considered utopian. His tolerance of many illegal manifestations of Catholic life was termed ''conciliatory.''

This ''Porfirian peace'' was beneficial to the Church: Catholic worship and practices were held not only in churches and homes, but often also on ranches, in camps, and in towns. Catholic schools and institutions multiplied. Bishops returned from exile to govern their dioceses and were respected by all. The dictator himself intervened when it was necessary to calm radical governors. Seminaries were reopened and ecclesiastical provinces were increased: Oaxaca, Durango, Linares-

Celebration of the Day of the Dead festival, Michoacan, Mexico. (©Charles & Josette Lenars/CORBIS)

Monterrey, Yucatán, and Puebla. New dioceses were established: Tabasco, Colima, Sinaloa, Cuernavaca, Chihuahua, Saltillo, Tehuantepec, Tepic, Campeche, Aguascalientes, and Huajuapan de León, or Mistecas. There were many religious institutes, such as those of the reorganized Jesuits, who increased from 39 scattered members in 1878 to 338 in 1910, and those of religious who came for the first time: the Marist fathers and brothers, the Salesians, the Cordian-Marians, the Redemptorists, and the Brothers of the Christian Schools.

Religious congregations were also founded in Mexico: the Josephites, the Missionaries of the Holy Spirit, the Guadalupans, the Servants of the Sacred Heart, the Servants of the Divine Shepherd, and others whose efforts in education raised the level of culture and of Christian living. Prominent figures among the Mexican clergy during those years were the archbishop of Mexico City LABASTIDA Y DÁVALOS, who prudently directed the entire renewal, and his two successors, Alarcón and MORA Y DEL RÍO; the first archbishop of Puebla, Ibarra; and Silva of Morelia. Catholics notable for their writings were García Icazbalceta, the untiring publicist Victoriano Agüeros, and the aggressive journalist Sánchez Santos.

The War of Reform and its consequences left deep wounds. Secularism not only dominated civil life but influenced all social life. While the government did not tolerate the mention of God in any official act, it did allow many pseudo-cultural expressions that were openly hostile to the Church. Official instruction disregarded the constitutional neutrality of education but openly defended antireligious Positivism, which little by little won over many professors and intellectuals and also hundreds of students and professional men.

The Mexican Revolution. When General Díaz fell from power in 1911, the political freedom that followed allowed the Church to reorganize and negotiate for the recovery of some of their lost rights. The National Catholic party, with a membership of hundreds of thousands, would have had a majority in the legislature had there been a free election. The National Federation of Workers, the Knights of Columbus, the A.C.J.M., and the Asociación Nacional de Padres de Familia were founded. When liberal president Francisco Madero was assassinated in 1913 a revolution broke out again. The old animosity against the Church appeared with greater vehemence than ever before, partly because of the persistent and slanderous rumor that it had supported the usurpation of Victori-

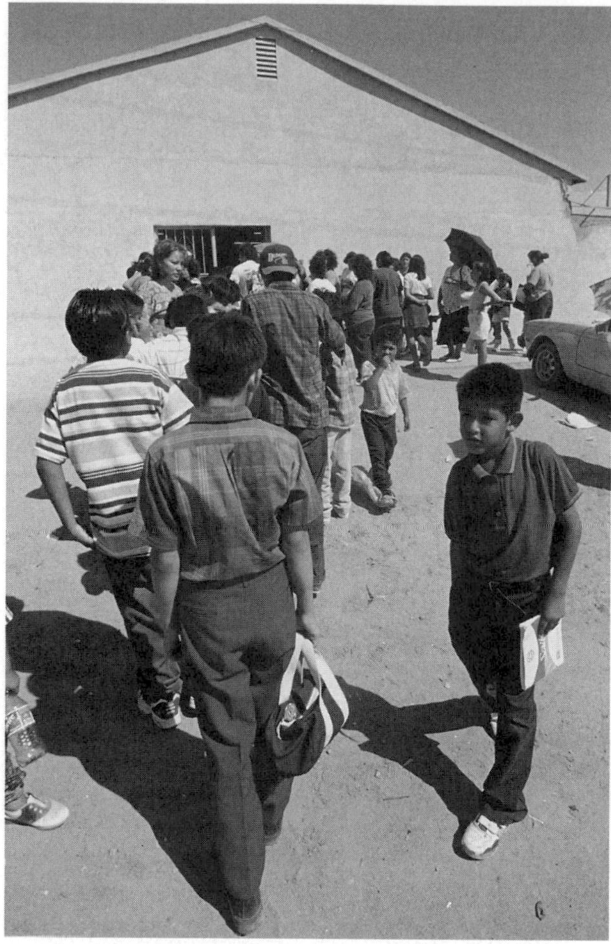

Children lining up for catechism class at the Missionaries of Charity, founded by Mother Teresa and her order in the Mariano Matamoros neighborhood of Tijuana, Mexico. (AP/ Wide World Photos)

ano Huerta in February 1913. In reprisal, churches and religious buildings were seized, sacrileges were committed, and priests and nuns were molested.

Constitution of 1917. The constitution of Querétaro, promulgated on Feb. 5, 1917 by the revolutionary minority, gave concrete expression to the attack on the Church: LAICISM was obligatory in primary education, and priests were prohibited from conducting schools; seminary studies were not recognized by the state; any religious act was forbidden outside the church; all religious organizations were forbidden to own property; all buildings that housed institutions dependent on the Church were declared the property of the state; priests lost political rights and the exercise of citizenship; the states were given the right to limit the number of priests; and the Catholic press and all confessional political parties associated with churches were suppressed. In the persecution that followed most bishops were forced to leave the country, many priests went into hiding or into exile, and hundreds of Catholic schools were closed. President Carranza (1917–20) understood that the radical constitution was fanatical and even tried to change it, but his successor, Álvaro Obregón (1920–24), again unleashed hostile forces against the Church and expelled apostolic delegate Bishop Filippi.

Persecution under Calles. The anticlerical actions of president Plutarco Elías Calles (1924–28) were spurred on by Protestant and liberal forces and even by foreign capitalists. In addition to enforcing the constitution, he supported two fallen priests in establishing a schismatic Mexican Church. As Protestants gained ground, the Catholics organized the Liga de Defensa de la Libertad Religiosa, which made use of bold propaganda, legal protests, and boycotts.

Calles, furious at the opposition, started the most bloody persecution Mexican Catholics had ever suffered. By the Ley Calles of July 1926, foreign priests and many bishops were banished. Priests and religious were imprisoned, and all Catholic schools and other organizations were suppressed.

In response, the bishops ordered priests to suspend religious services in churches. Discontent rose like an irresistible tide. Calles tried to crush all resistance; repeated outrages were never punished by the bailiffs. Catholics, who saw no other remedy for defending their rights, also took up arms as los Cristeros and caused the government serious trouble. The government unjustly accused Catholics of taking part in the revolt and ordered many killed, among them Father Miguel PRO.

Truce between Church and State. The intolerable situation, complicated by political issues, was made worse by the assassination of president-elect Obregón. Interim president Portes Gil negotiated with Morelian archbishop RUIZ Y FLORES, who was also the apostolic delegate. On June 22, 1929, the president published a declaration that the government would not interfere in the internal affairs of the Church, and while the registration of priests would continue, it did not mean that the government would make ecclesiastical appointments. Encouraged by this apparent good will and fearful lest the people lose their faith if divine services were not resumed, the bishops ordered Mexico's churches to be reopened. While most welcomed the religious peace, Catholics whose lives and fortunes had been in jeopardy believed the government was deceiving the bishops, especially after a subsequent massacre of the Cristeros.

Revival of Persecution. The forces hostile to the Church did not withdraw. Renewed anticlerical fury broke loose during the celebration of the fourth centenary of the apparitions of Our Lady of Guadalupe, on Dec. 12, 1931, and sanctions were levied against all public employees who took part in the celebrations. Absurd restrictions were placed on numbers of priests: i.e., for the Federal District, with more than a million inhabitants, only 25 priests were permitted; for Tabasco, with more than 200,000 inhabitants, only one priest. Actually, the law was not complied with, and many priests continued to function without being authorized; others sought legal subterfuges.

Much more dangerous was the cunning persecution begun by President Lázaro Cárdenas, who came to power in December 1934. Following his orders that all schools teach socialism, Marxism, atheism, and sexual education, public indignation rose throughout Mexico. While at first the bloody regime of Calles seemed about to be repeated, it was soon apparent that these unpopular decrees could not be enforced, and the government changed the ministry. Although the persecution slackened, no seminary was left unmolested. When almost all seminaries had been closed, U.S. bishops offered their help, and in September 1937 the Seminario Nacional Pontificio, for candidates who could not be educated in Mexico, was opened in Montezuma, New Mexico.

In April 1937 PIUS XI addressed an apostolic letter to Mexico in which he asked Mexican Catholics to organize peacefully, promote Catholic Action, and keep the faith intact. The pope acknowledged the legitimacy of armed revolt in certain cases but added that the Church must never engage in it.

In this sad struggle the archbishops of Mexico City, Díaz and Martínez, and Orozco of Guadalajara stood out prominently. Amid such continuous turmoil the Church was unable to effectively educate the youth and to preach the social doctrine of the Church. Little could be done for Mexico's indigenous peoples and for laboring classes because circumstances forced the clergy to attend primarily to urgent pastoral duties: conducting divine services and catechizing.

Bibliography: J. BRAVO UGARTE, *Historia de México,* 4 v. (Mexico City 1941–59). W. H. CALLCOTT, *Church and State in Mexico: 1822–1857* (Durham, NC 1926). D. COSÍO VILLEGAS, ed., *Historia moderna de México (1867–1911),* 8 v. (Mexico City 1955–65). M. CUEVAS, *Historia de la Iglesia en México,* 5 v. (5th ed. Mexico City 1946–47). P. DE LETURIA, *Relaciones entre la Santa Sede e Hispanoamerica, 1493–1835,* 3 v. (*Analecta Gregoriana* 101–103; 1959–60). F. C. KELLEY, *Blood-Drenched Altars* (2d ed. Milwaukee 1935). L. MEDINA ASCENSIO, *La Santa Sede y la emancipación mexicana* (Guadalajara 1946).

[D. OLMEDO]

Postwar Development. After the Second World War, the relationship between the Catholic Church and the Mexican presidency became less strained, and though anti-clerical legislation remained in effect, it was not generally enforced. Beginning with the presidency Manuel Avila Camacho (1940–46), a *modus vivendi* gradually emerged that brought Catholics into the mainstream of Mexican political life and gained for the Church greater freedom. Although new disputes arose during the presidency of López Mateos (1958–64), they never generated the animosity, repression, and violence that characterized Church-state relations before 1940.

In 1953 the Mexican Episcopal Conference (CEM) was founded in response to Pope PIUS XII's request for a structure that would enable the hierarchy to coordinate their efforts in the spiritual and political spheres. After the second VATICAN COUNCIL, the conference was reorganized and strengthened. Including all bishops, even retired bishops who had a voice but no vote, the CEM meets twice a year, its main executive body the 21-member Permanent Council. Members of the Permanent Council include representatives of the 15 pastoral regions into which the country is divided. The work of the conference and the Permanent Council was to include issues relating to doctrines of faith, Church personnel and hierarchy, and pastoral ministries to youth, family, indigenous peoples, migrants, and refugees. Initially, the Mexican episcopal conference did not attempt to strongly intervene in pastoral, social, or political affairs. However, in 1971, the Synod of Bishops in Rome published a report called "Justice in Mexico" faulting Church leaders for not doing more to address social and economic injustice. The CEM subsequently gave social issues a higher priority.

The low profile of the CEM and the Church hierarchy in socio-economic affairs notwithstanding, many of the non-governmental organizations (NGOs) that took the lead in Mexican development were motivated by the papal social teachings and the Medellín-inspired emphasis on a preferential option for the poor. During the 1950s and 1960s, the Secretariado Social Mexicano guided the Church toward ethical and moral requirements of social justice and focused attention on programs and organizations capable of supporting development. The secretariat inspired a range of programs throughout the country under Church auspices, including cooperatives, credit unions, food distribution centers, and health clinics. Although Christian base communities never achieved the large numbers they had in Central and South American countries, NGOs backing them proliferated in Jalisco, in Ciudad Netzahualcoyotl on the outskirts of Mexico City, in Morelos, and in Vera Cruz.

Under the leadership of Austrian-born Ivan Illich, the Centro Intercutural de Documentación (CIDOC) in

Cuernavaca became a think-tank for social, developmental, and educational issues. Illich, who had earned a Ph.D. in philosophy at the University of Salzburg, served as a parish priest in New York City before becoming vice president of the University of Santa Maria in Ponce, Puerto Rico from 1956 to 1960. In 1961 he joined CIDOC as a researcher, became president of the board in 1963, and continued as a member until 1978. Under Illich's direction, CIDOC made an impact on social thinking not only in Mexico, but throughout the hemisphere. As the U.S. Church looked south and began to send missionaries to Latin America in increasing numbers, the Center offered language courses and at the same time forced missionaries to examine the assumptions they were bringing to their ministry.

Meanwhile, popular education programs, inspired by Brazilian educator Paulo Freire spawned a variety of Church-related NGOs. The NGOs embarked on programs of *conscientización* that through a broad range of activities, such as literacy and adult education, health clinics, self-help housing, and micro-enterprise production, sought to raise the social consciousness of the people. To some extent these early NGOs were limited by their dependence on external sources of support. At the same time, more independent organizations, closely aligned with poor people united through social movement and producers associations, took a more militant stance. The national coordinating bodies of producers' associations played an important role in the 1970s and early 1980s. Gradually, Church-promoted social organizations allied with them.

Liberation Theology. Also in response to the plight of the poor in Mexico, a few dioceses encouraged the creation of *communidades eclesiales de base* (BASIC CHRISTIAN COMMUNITIES, or CEBs) and a few centers in Mexico studied LIBERATION THEOLOGY. The CEBs, small discussion and worship groups common throughout Latin America led usually by laity, catechists, or sisters, provided an occasion especially for the very poor to discuss the New Testament in light of their own experience. The CEBs were generally influenced by the themes and methods of liberation theology. By reading the Bible in light of contemporary reality, members of base communities had their consciousness raised about the structures of injustice and oppression at the root of poverty.

One of the few members of the hierarchy who openly promoted liberation theology was Sergio Méndez Arceo (d. 1992), bishop of Cuernavaca until his retirement in 1982 at the age of 75. Called the "red bishop," because of his Marxist sympathies, Méndez Arceo was reprimanded by the episcopal conference and the Vatican for his outspoken positions. He defended Fidel Castro, supported the Sandinistas in Nicaragua, demanded that the inequities in Mexico's socio-economic order be addressed, and denounced U.S. imperialism.

Several research centers in Mexico City also studied liberationist themes, among them the Centro de Relección Teológica and the Centro de Derechos Humanos M.A, the last co-sponsored by the Jesuits and the Centro de Estudios Dominicanos, Another center, under lay control, was the Centro Antonio de Montecinos. These centers utilized the approach of liberation theology to analyze the socio-economic and moral causes of poverty and injustice.

While liberation theology and base communities were often the focus in discussions of the contemporary Latin American Church during the 1970s and 1980s, the well-organized conservative side of Catholicism remained a power to contend with. OPUS DEI, with its highly centralized structure, exercised considerable influence on and through the laity, especially those of means and advanced education. The Legionarios de Cristo, founded in Mexico in 1941, remained a conservative and influential congregation that attracted many vocations and sent missionaries abroad, staffing parishes in the United States and Europe. By the 1990s liberation theology had been replaced by "Indian theology," which was also held to have Marxist roots. Indian theology, which attempted to address the wrongs done to native peoples during the colonial era, by admitting the role of the Church in oppressing, robbing, and exterminating indigenous tribes in the Americas and elsewhere, was of concern to both the pope and others; among its major proponents in Mexico was Father Eleazar Lopez Martinez, of Mexico's Center for Support to Indian Missions.

Modernization of the Mexican State. Carlos Gortari Salinas was elected president of Mexico in 1988. Salinas moved rapidly to consolidate his position as president and embark on what he called the "modernization of the Mexican state." Salinas' strategy of modernization meant initiating an overall economic policy that broke with tenets of the Mexican revolution, most notably issues of land ownership. Putting Mexico more in synchronization with the International Monetary Fund, the World Bank, and the package of neo-liberal economic adjustment policies meant the privatization of many state enterprises and a dramatic shift in Mexican agrarian policy on *ejidal* or communal land ownership and resale. The border industrialization program was a preface to wholehearted embracing of the North American Free Trade Agreement (NAFTA), with many poor Mexicans asked to make a huge leap of faith that the benefits of these economic adjustment strategies would somehow trickle down to improve the lot of the poor.

Salinas' modernization strategy included a shift in Church-state relations. Early in his electoral campaign, Salinas often met with bishops, and after his election delegates of the CEM regularly discussed issues of mutual concern with the president, as did the papal nuncio. President Salinas broke with Mexican precedent by inviting the archbishop of Mexico City, the papal nuncio, and the CEM president to his first presidential address. In February 1990, Salinas named a personal envoy to the Vatican and cooperated in preparations for Pope John Paul II's second visit to Mexico, welcoming him upon his arrival at the airport. The bishops, mindful that Salinas had spoken in his inaugural address about improving relations with the Church as part of his plan for modernizing the Mexican state, began, through the CEM, to search out ways to recover religious freedom. Anticlerical articles of the Mexican Constitution were revised by presidential decree on Jan. 28, 1992. Through these changes, churches were recognized as legal entities and permitted to own property. Foreign clergy and ministers were allowed in the country, and Mexican clerics were granted the right to vote, to criticize the government, and were exempted from taxes.

Papal Visits. In mid-1991, Salinas visited the Vatican, and on Nov. 1, 1991 he announced his plan to normalize relations with the Church. Pope John Paul's three visits to Mexico and Salinas' visit to the Vatican added up to a resumption of ties, with formal representation of Mexico to the Vatican State, and constitutional changes affecting the Church within Mexico.

The change in the reception given the pope on his four visits to Mexico reflected the transformation of Church-state relations. During his first visit in January 1979, President López Portillo claimed to have met him by chance and offered only a hasty handshake and a few perfunctory words of welcome at the airport. The pope's second visit was in 1990, to attend the Conference of Latin American Bishops at PUEBLA, near Mexico City. President Salinas, though acting in a ''strictly personal'' capacity, welcomed the pope at the airport and warmly praised him. Governors of the ten states where John Paul visited, taking their cue from the president, openly welcomed the pope.

John Paul II paid a third visit to Mexico in 1992 en route to the Conference of the Latin American Bishops at SANTO DOMINGO that commemorated the 500th anniversary of Columbus. The pope offered some solace for Mexicans involved in ministry to indigenous peoples. He asked pardon of the native population and the enslaved populations of the Americas for centuries of mistreatment and for attempts to force religious belief that in no way respected human dignity and freedom. In January 1999 the pope returned again, this time to promulgate the apostolic exhortation *Ecclecia in America,* which outlined the challenges facing the Church in the Americas. All four visits of the pope drew enormous crowds and demonstrated his enormous appeal to Mexican Catholics. The massive turn-outs convinced many, including government leaders, that the revolutionary legacy of hostility toward the Church had turned counterproductive.

Even before Salinas came to power, efforts on behalf of both the hierarchy and the government to improve relations gradually produced results. Although the constitution prohibited the Church from owning real estate, wealthy Catholics, associations, and corporations, acting as intermediaries, could purchase any property they wanted. The government provided assistance in the 1970s when ecclesiastical authorities constructed a new Basilica of Our Lady of Guadalupe. On May 6, 1990 during his second visit to Mexico, Pope John Paul II solemnized the beatification of JUAN DIEGO in the Basilica of Our Lady of Guadalupe. On the same occasion John Paul marked the beatification of the child martyrs of TLAXCALA and of Jose Maria YERMO Y PARRES.

The final year of the Salinas presidency witnessed a series of troubling events in Mexico. The signing of the NAFTA agreement redefined the relationships among the three countries of North America; the presidential electoral campaign was one of the most hotly contested in history; a peasant rebellion broke out in the southern state of Chiapas; and Cardinal Posadas, archbishop of Guadalajara, and two other public figures were assassinated. One of the most troubling, the revolt in impoverished Chiapas that began in January 1994 brought the Church center stage during a major national crisis. Samuel Ruiz, bishop of the diocese of San Cristobal de las Casas for more than 25 years, mediated the dispute between the government and the mostly Amerindian Zapatista Army of National Liberation. Both the government and the hierarchy rallied behind Ruiz, one of the few persons acceptable to the rebel forces, and his efforts were acknowledged by the 1996 Raoul Follereau Prize for contributing to the cause of peace. Despite Ruiz's efforts, the violence continued into 2000, forcing thousands of Amerindians in the region to abandon their homes as Zapatista gunmen and paramilitary groups fought for support in the area. Ruiz stepped down as bishop in April, 2000, amid repeated threats against his safety and continuous acts of violence by those opposed to the Catholic Church in the region.

In 1996, during the presidency of Ernesto Zedillo, the nation found itself in an economic downturn, as inflation climbed and a recession began. Zedillo's economic remedies sparked vocal criticism in the form of a pastoral letter from Mexican bishops to which the government responded by attempting to limit the freedom of speech of the Church. A new law forbade Church leaders from making any statement about Mexico's "political or economic issues, or any other linked to the country's situation." Not surprisingly, there were strenuous objections to such a law as a violation of the constitutional separation of Church and state. According to Amendment 130 of the Mexican constitution, made in 1992, Church leaders were prohibited from holding public office, supporting political candidates, or taking any other action that would "invade the public sphere." In the unsettled region of Chiapas in particular, the government enforced its prohibition against clerical involvement in politics, expelling several foreign priests from the region in 2000.

Into the 21st Century. Despite the success of Protestant missionaries during the late 20th century, by 2000 four out of every five Mexicans identified themselves as Roman Catholic. There were 5,318 parishes, tended by 9,684 diocesan and 3,145 religious priests. Other religious included approximately 6,500 brothers and 26,600 sisters, many of whom taught at Mexico's 1,828 primary and 1,060 secondary Catholic schools. Many Amerindians, despite their Catholicism, continued to maintain some traditional beliefs and practices that predated the conquest; syncretistic religious, such as Catholic Mayans who practiced in Chiapas, were also common. Both mainstream Protestant churches and evangelical sects multiplied among the tribes in the highlands, as well as among the burgeoning urban populations of Mexico City and Guadalajara, and throughout the northern border area. Over half the people of Mexico attended church regularly.

As Mexico began to establish itself as a stable, economically viable country free from war, it began to confront issues common to many other modern nations through new legislation. The bishops were vigilant in their review of these new laws, recognizing themselves as a force for Christian traditions in a secular age. In 2000 a government bill promoting organ donation was greeted with approval by bishops, as long as the donor's free will was respected. However, laws passed by several of the Mexican states contravening the federal law banning abortion were viewed with concern as a sign of things to come. However, with the election of President Vincente Fox in 2000 Church leaders hoped for a closer relationship between the government and the Catholic Church. In May of that year Mexico City was the site of the largest outdoor Mass to be held in the country since 1924. Over 50,000 people were estimated to be in attendance.

Bibliography: B. BARRANCO VILLAFAN and R. P. ESCOBAR, *Jerarquía católica y modernización política en México* (Mexico 1989). P. BERRYMAN, *Liberation Theology* (New York 1987). "Cumplir promesas, demanda la iglesia a Ernesto Zedillo," *La Jornada* (Sept. 1994). M. DE LA ROSA and C. A. REILLY, *Religión y política en México* (Mexico City 1986). M. E. GARCIA UGARTE, *La nueva relación iglesia-estado en México* (Mexico 1993). G. GRAYSON, *The Church in Contemporary Mexico* (Washington 1992). G. GUTTIÉREZ, *Las Casas: In Search of the Poor of Jesus Christ* (Maryknoll, NJ 1993). A. T. HENNELLY, *John Paul II's Message to Indigenous Peoples* (Maryknoll, NJ 1994). L. HERNANDEZ and J. FOX, "La Dificil Democracia en México," *Nuevas Politicas Urbanas* (Arlington VA). A. P. MOCTEZUMA, *El conflicto religioso de 1926* (Mexico City 1929). S. LOEAZA, "Chiapas: desaffío al vaticano," *Cuaderno de Nexos* (February 1994; June 1994). E. V. NIEMEYER, "Anticlericalism in the Mexican Constitutional Convention of 1916–17," *Americas* 11 (1954–55) 31–49. *Proceso* (Jan. 30, 1989; Sept. 26, 1994). SECOND GENERAL CONFERENCE OF BISHOPS, *Puebla and Beyond: Documentation and Commentary* (Maryknoll, NJ 1979).

[C. A. REILLY/EDS.]

MEY, GUSTAV

Pastoral theologian; b. Neukirch, Württemberg, July 2, 1822; d. Schwörzkirch, June 22, 1877. After studying philosophy and theology at Tübingen, he was ordained in 1847. He took up pastoral work at Schwörzkirch (Oberschwaben) in 1858. His principal writing is *Vollständigen Katechesen für die untere Klasse der katholische Volksschule* (Freiburgim-Breisgau 1871, many later eds.).

Three achievements mark Mey as one of the most important and controversial catechists of the 19th century. (1) In his *Katechesen* he introduced organically structured teaching units, and this started the transition to catechetics involving separate lessons. His "learning pieces," as he called them, represent a synthesis of the "question-and-answer method" based upon "Biblical catechesis" as taken in the sense of B. Overberg, J. Hirscher, B. Galura, and A. Gruber. This is manifested also in his published works insofar as he follows Hirscher and the scholastic tradition. (2) Having an extensive appreciation for the liturgy, Mey deems active participation in the Mass to be the guiding concept for establishing the whole liturgy. (3) On the basis of a vivid insight into the meaning of the historical character of revelation, he saw it as the function of the kerygmatic teacher in the present to strive to present the basic events in the divine economy of salvation in a manner in which they can be grasped as real events. According to Mey, the catechist must take a general view of every Biblical fact and seek to see its meaning and place in the plan for communicating and developing the work of salvation. This, according to Mey, is the procedure whereby a definite doctrinal aim is achieved and the teaching itself becomes truly fruitful for the advance of faith and the life that comes from faith. The Mey-Pichler Method is so called because it is the Mey method as developed by W. Pichler.

Bibliography: L. LENTNER, et al., eds., *Katechetisches Wörterbuch* (Freiburg 1961). H. KREUTZWALD, *Zur Geschichte des biblischen Unterrichts und zur Formgeschichte des biblischen Schulbuches* (Freiburg 1957). W. HAERTEN, *Lexikon der Pädagogik*, ed. H. ROMBACH, 4 v. (3d ed. Freiburg 1962) 3:482.

[F. C. LEHNER]

MEYENDORFF, JOHN

Theologian, historian, teacher, ecumenist, Orthodox churchman; b. Neuilly-sur-Seine, France, Feb. 17, 1926; d. Montreal, Canada, July 22, 1992. Son of Russian émigré parents of aristocratic Baltic German origin, Meyendorff was educated in France, completing his theological studies at the Orthodox academy of St. Serge in 1949 and his Doctorat-ès-Lettres at the Sorbonne in 1958, in which year he was also ordained to the priesthood. In 1959 he came to the United States with his wife Maria and their four young children to join the faculty of St. Vladimir's Orthodox Theological Seminary as professor of Patristics and Church History. Soon after his arrival Meyendorff also became a senior fellow at Dumbarton Oaks, Harvard University's Byzantine research center in Washington, DC, where he later served briefly as acting director of Studies (1978). Beginning in 1967 he was also professor of Byzantine History at Fordham University. In 1984 he became dean of St. Vladimir's, a position that he held until his retirement. Like his predecessors in that position, Georges Florovsky and Alexander Schmemann, Meyendorff was instrumental in bringing the intellectual and cultural tradition of Russian émigré theology to the New World.

Publication in 1959 of his critical edition of the *Triads* of St. Gregory Palamas, the 14th century Byzantine hesychast theologian, and of his *Introduction à l'étude de Grégoire Palamas* (partial English translation, 1964) established Meyendorff's reputation as a leading Byzantinist and patristics scholar. His other works include: *The Orthodox Church: Yesterday and Today* (1963); *Orthodoxy and Catholicity* (1966); *Christ in Eastern Christian Thought* (1969); *Byzantine Theology* (1973); *Marriage: An Orthodox Perspective* (1975); *Byzantium and the Rise of Russia* (1980), which called attention to the role of hesychasm as a unifying cultural movement in late medieval eastern Europe; and *Imperial Unity and Christian Divisions: The Church 450–680 A.D.* (1989), which tried to correct a perceived imbalance in the historical presentation of relationships between East and West.

A churchman as well as a scholar, Meyendorff was an outspoken proponent of Orthodox unity in America, arguing that Orthodoxy's witness and indeed its most basic ecclesiological principles were being compromised by its jurisdictional fragmentation along ethnic lines. He played a major role in negotiations with the Russian Orthodox Church that led to its 1970 recognition of the autocephalous, or fully independent, status of the Orthodox Church in America (the OCA, until then known as the Russian Orthodox Greek Catholic Church in North America, or Metropolia). He also served as chairman of the OCA's Department of External Affairs and editor of its monthly newspaper, *The Orthodox Church.* In addition, he represented that church on the Central Committee of the World Council of Churches and also served as moderator of the Council's Faith and Order Commission (1967-76).

Meyendorff was the recipient of a number of academic and church honors. Indicative of the major changes sweeping the former Soviet Union, he was awarded the Order of St. Vladimir by Patriarch Aleksii II of Moscow in 1991.

Bibliography: B. DUPUY, "Le Père Jean Meyendorff," *Istina* 38 (1993) 351–69, with bibliography of principal books and articles. D. OBOLENSKY, "John Meyendorff," *Sobornost* 15:2 (1993) 44–51.

[J. H. ERICKSON]

MEYER, ALBERT GREGORY

Cardinal; b. Milwaukee, Wisconsin, March 9, 1903; d. Chicago, Illinois, April 9, 1965. He was the fourth of five children of Peter James and Mathilda (Thelen) Meyer, who were of German Catholic ancestry. At 14 he entered St. Francis Seminary, Milwaukee, where he completed his secondary education and two years of college before being sent to Rome (1921) to study philosophy and theology at the Urban College of the Propaganda while residing at the American College. On July 11, 1926, he was ordained by Cardinal Basilio Pompilj. After taking the doctorate in theology in 1927, he became a student at the Pontifical Biblical Institute, where he received the licentiate degree and the certificate of a doctoral candidate in Sacred Scripture. Throughout his life he continued to deepen his knowledge of the Bible; he was later invited to translate the Epistles of St. JOHN for the edition of the New Testament published by the Confraternity of Christian Doctrine.

After he returned to his diocese in 1930, he served as assistant pastor of St. Joseph's parish, Waukesha; in the autumn of 1931 he was appointed to the faculty of St. Francis Seminary. He also ministered to a number of Italian families, for whom a mission chapel was soon erected. In 1937 he was appointed rector of the seminary by Abp. Samuel A. Stritch and the following year, was made a domestic prelate.

Early Episcopal Career. On Feb. 18, 1946, Meyer was appointed bishop of Superior, Wisconsin, and was consecrated in St. John's Cathedral, Milwaukee, by Abp. Moses Kiley on April 11. After Kiley's death, Meyer was promoted to the metropolitan See of Milwaukee on July 21, 1953, and was installed by the Apostolic Delegate, Amleto Cicognani.

Being methodical in his work, he developed a quiet but effective and very orderly system of administration on all levels. Although he did not abolish national parishes, in appointing priests he overcame the outmoded divisions based on descent, especially in the case of those of Slavic origin. He also fostered the growth of organizations for laymen such as the Serra Club, the Holy Name Society, the Archdiocesan Council of Catholic Men, and the Catholic Youth Organization; and he encouraged the work of the Catholic Church Extension Society, of which he automatically became a member of the board of governors. He was a member of the AMERICAN BOARD OF CATHOLIC MISSIONS (from 1953) and served as president general (1956–57) of the NATIONAL CATHOLIC EDUCATIONAL ASSOCIATION. In 1956 he was elected by his colleagues in the hierarchy to the administrative board of the National Catholic Welfare Conference, and he assumed the chairmanship (1956–59) of the education department. He was also chairman of the *ad hoc* episcopal committee for the revision of the English version of the ritual (*Collectio Rituum*), which was published in 1961.

Cardinal Archbishop of Chicago. Meyer was chosen as archbishop of Chicago, Illinois, on Sept. 19, 1958, by PIUS XII. In the consistory of Dec. 14, 1959, he was created cardinal priest of the title of St. Cecilia by JOHN XXIII and was made a member of the Congregation of the Propagation of the Faith, of Seminaries and Universities, and of the Fabric of St. Peter's. In January 1962 he was appointed to the Pontifical Commission for Biblical Studies, and in November 1963 he was added to the papal commission for the revision of the Code of Canon Law; a year later he was attached to the Supreme Congregation of the Holy Office, being one of the first two cardinals not resident in Rome ever to become members of that body. In June 1963 he took part in the conclave in which PAUL VI was elected.

For the education of the future priests of the archdiocese he built Quigley Preparatory Seminary South and opened a junior college division of the major seminary, St. Mary of the Lake, at Niles. In addition to his close attention to the temporal affairs of his archdiocese, Meyer put the greatest emphasis on his spiritual duties of teaching and sanctifying. He wrote learned and lengthy pastoral and other letters in which he demonstrated his intimate familiarity with the Bible and with papal pronouncements. The most distinguished of his Lenten pastorals was that of 1964, entitled ''Ecumenism: The Spirit of Christian Unity.'' He fostered the revival of emphasis among Catholics on the Bible, urging his priests through clergy conferences and summer study weeks to bring their knowledge of the Sacred Scriptures up-to-date and to apply it to their own spiritual lives and to their pastoral ministry. He also wrote the preface to the Catholic edition of the New Testament of the Revised Standard Version (1965).

Vatican Council II. In October 1961 the cardinal was appointed by John XXIII a member of the Central Preparatory Commission for the Council, and he attended several meetings of that body in Rome. Before the council convened, he was appointed a member of the Secretariat *de Concilii negotiis extra ordinem* (for business not on the agenda); and when this body was abolished by Paul VI, he was appointed one of the 12 presidents of the council. When the original schema on the sources of revelation was rejected by the council, he was made a member of the special mixed commission that drafted a new schema, and he presided over the subcommittee for the chapter on the Old Testament.

In the first session (1962) he spoke twice on the liturgy, advocating the use of the vernacular in general not merely under the regulation of the episcopal conference but also at the discretion of the local bishop (6th gen. cong., Oct. 24) and particularly in the private recitation of the Divine Office for the sake of greater devotion (15th gen. cong., Nov. 9); he spoke also on the sources of revelation, demanding that a new schema be drafted in a positive spirit with due recognition of the contributions of contemporary exegetes in order to win the unanimous consent of the fathers (22d gen. cong., Nov. 19). In the second session (1963) he spoke twice on the Church, proving the collegiality of the APOSTLES and their successors from the New Testament (42d gen. cong., Oct. 7) and showing realistically that the ever-present sinfulness and weakness of the People of God meet forgiveness and strength in the house of the Father of mercies (52d gen. cong., Oct. 21). He addressed the session also on the subjects of national episcopal conferences, in the name of more than 120 bishops of the U.S. whose signatures he had personally solicited, in favor of a cautious, reserved position on the binding force of collective decisions (65th gen. cong., Nov. 12); and of ecumenism, praising the inclusion of the chapters on the Jews and religious liberty (71st gen. cong., Nov. 20).

In the third session (1964) he spoke on religious liberty in the name of the American bishops, arguing for the necessity of this declaration for a fruitful dialogue with non-Catholics and for a successful apostolate (86th gen.

cong., Sept. 23); on the Jews and non-Christians, recommending the restoration to the text of the strong parts that had been deleted, such as an explicit condemnation of all forms of anti-Semitism and the refutation of the charge of deicide (89th gen. cong., Sept. 28). He discoursed twice on divine revelation, presenting tradition in a broad sense as something living and dynamic, subject to limits and defects, and therefore needful of being reformed in the light of the Scriptures (91st gen. cong., Sept. 30), and describing inspiration in terms of the Word of God as a personal communication to men (94th gen. cong., Oct. 5). He spoke also on the life and ministry of priests, criticizing the schema (which was afterward sent back to the responsible commission for complete revision) for its unbecoming brevity, incompleteness, lack of balance, and obscurity of purpose (100th gen. cong., Oct.13); on the Church in the modern world, elucidating from a Biblical and theological point of view the place of the material universe in the economy of salvation (105th gen. cong., Oct. 20); and on the education of priests, offering suggestions for improvement drawn from the unity of their mediatory function and the variety of their apostolate and from the fundamental requirements of the qualities and virtues of a good man and a good Christian (121st gen. cong., Nov. 12).

On Nov. 19, 1964, after Cardinal Eugene Tisserant, acting as head of the board of presidents but without consulting Meyer, announced that the preliminary vote on the schema on religious liberty would be postponed until the fourth session, Meyer, accompanied by Cardinals Joseph Ritter of St. Louis, Missouri, and Paul-Émile LÉGER of Montreal, Canada, and supported by the signatures of nearly 1,000 bishops, immediately appealed to Paul VI in person, but failed to induce him to reverse the decision. By the end of the third session Meyer had addressed the Council more often than any other American bishop and had emerged as the unrivaled intellectual leader of the hierarchy of the U.S.

After the third session the cardinal showed signs of physical fatigue and malaise; he entered Mercy Hospital, Chicago, on Feb. 17, 1965, and eight days later, after receiving the Anointing of the Sick, he underwent intracranial surgery. He never recovered normal responsiveness and eventually lost consciousness for longer and longer periods until he died on April 9. After the solemn funeral, which was held in Holy Name Cathedral on April 13, conducted in the revitalized form of the liturgy and attended by six cardinals and more than 60 bishops, he was buried in the little cemetery of St. Mary of the Lake Seminary at Mundelein.

Bibliography: G. N. SHUSTER, *Albert Gregory Cardinal Meyer (The Men Who Make the Council,* ed. M. NOVAK, Ser. 11; Notre Dame, Ind. 1964).

[R. F. TRISCO]

MEYNARD, ANDRÉ

Dominican canonist, theologian, religious founder; b. Lyons, France, May 4, 1824; d. Bourg-en-Bresse, Aug. 2, 1904. Meynard was ordained in 1849 and was pastor of Pélussin (Loire) in the Diocese of Lyons until 1855 when Lacordaire's influence led him to the Friars Preachers at Flavigny. During his early years as a Dominican, he preached missions until ill health forced him to abandon the pulpit in 1856. He restored the priories of Carpentras and Poitiers. In 1860 Meynard founded the congregation of Third Order Dominican Sisters at Bourg-en-Bresse for the care of the sick. He spent his last 19 years of life as their chaplain. His final year was one of severe physical and spiritual trial: because of misunderstandings, his spiritual daughters snubbed him and sought his departure. He bore this trial with patience, offering his last sufferings for the Church and his Order.

He did some writing in the field of Canon Law but his chief interest was in spiritual theology. He wrote the following works: *Traité de la vie intérieure* (2 v., 1885) and *Catéchisme de la vie chrétienne intérieure et religieuse* (1894). His teaching on the interior life is notable as a 19th century continuation of the Thomistic tradition as derived from Thomas de Valgornera. Meynard differed from most Thomists, however, in holding the widely accepted distinction between ascetical and mystical theology: to the former he ascribed the study of a soul's progress toward perfection with the ordinary helps of grace; to the latter, the extraordinary acts and phenomena of the interior life. He also considered infused contemplation an extraordinary grace.

Bibliography: *Annales Domincaines* 1 (1904) 465. P. POURRAT, *Christian Spirituality,* tr. W. H. MITCHELL et el., 4 v. (Wesminster, Md. 1953–55) 4:506–508.

[M. BEISSEL]

MEYNELL, ALICE C. AND WILFRID

Husband and wife, authors. Alice: Poet, literary journalist; b. Barnes, Surrey, England, Oct. 11, 1847; d. Nov. 17, 1922. Her father, Thomas Thompson, was a Cambridge graduate; her mother, Christiana Weller, was a concert pianist. The family was wealthy, due to an inheritance from colonial enterprises. Alice and her older sister Elizabeth were educated privately, their father being most frequently their tutor. This training was augmented by frequent travel from childhood onward, the family home alternating between northern Italy and England, with briefer stays in France, Germany, and Switzerland. At the point of young adulthood, Alice and Elizabeth already showed their artistic gifts, the younger as a poet, the older as a painter.

Alice entered the Catholic Church in 1868, a few years after her mother; eventually her father and sister joined them. Although she carefully guarded her privacy in spiritual matters, she once confided to a daughter that she was drawn to the Church primarily for its authoritative moral discipline: ''I saw when I was very young that a guide in morals was even more necessary than a guide in faith. It was for this I joined the Church.'' In 1877 she married Wilfrid Meynell.

Her first volume of poems, *Preludes*, was published in 1875, winning praise from such luminaries as Tennyson, Ruskin, Christina Rossetti, and George Eliot. With marriage and the beginning of a family, and largely for economic reasons, she shifted her energies to prose. Eventually, however, she returned to her first love, publishing a new collection, *Poems*, in 1893. Subsequent volumes, including one posthumously issued, secured her contemporary reputation as one of the most compelling voices of her time.

Alice Meynell's poetry finds its power not in the subject matter itself (nature, love, the moral life), which was rarely topical, and never polemical. Its force arises from the exquisite choice of language, a quiet, understated voice, and most of all from surprising angles of perception. In this way she makes the familiar new, alive to fresh intimations. These qualities are also the source of a persistent critique of her work, that it presses its material too strenuously, is overwrought, precious. Religious sentiments mark much of the verse, but underneath nearly all of it, religious or ''secular,'' is a persistent refrain, a theme of compensation that is the very touchstone of the *fin de siècle* sensibility: life's choicest pleasures are experienced most intensely in their absence. This code of denial, of abstinence, lies at the very heart of both ''decadence'' and a profoundly religious vision.

Her prose, which found its way into several volumes of essays, is a good deal more uneven in quality than the poetry, much of it having been written on weekly and monthly press deadlines. In addition to studies of classic English writers and reviews of the major literary figures of the day, she practiced what was once called the ''familiar essay,'' a species of writing on quotidian matters that delights more by its method than its matter, where wit and whimsy count more than the passionate prosecution of a thesis. Representative of these qualities is *The Rhythm of Life* (1893).

Wilfrid: Catholic journalist, editor, publisher, biographer; b. Newcastle-on-Tyne, Yorkshire, Nov. 17, 1852; d. Greatham, Sussex, Oct. 20, 1948. He was the son of Quaker parents and educated in Quaker schools. After moving to London to search for work, he joined the Catholic Church and entered into a lifelong career in journalism.

The Meynells had eight children, one of whom died in infancy. Through the early years of family preoccupations, the two of them created a minor publishing industry, primarily within Catholic circles, as editors, publishers, and frequent contributors to leading periodicals. Wilfrid founded and edited the monthly *Merry England*, edited the Church-sponsored *Weekly Register*, and directed the most important Catholic publishing house in England, Burns and Oates. But in all these enterprises the hand—and the pen—of Alice were never absent.

While his wife was earning high praise not only in England but also in America, Wilfrid made his own mark in both religious and secular arenas. His biographies of Cardinals Manning and Newman and of Prime Minister Disraeli were well received; and the steady stream of articles and columns for the periodical press gained him a special currency among readers of more than two generations.

Nothing counts so much as a touchstone of the life of Alice and Wilfrid Meynell as their friendship and generous support of many of the most talented literary figures of the day, both the famous and those struggling to be known. For years the Meynell home in London served as a salon for almost daily gatherings of a company of literary friends such as Francis Thompson, Coventry Patmore and George Meredith. For over four decades, decades that spanned the rule of Victorian values to their collapse in World War I, the Meynells were an influential presence in the English-speaking world. The prominence of their religious loyalty must surely count as a factor in the important English Catholic Revival of the twentieth century.

Bibliography: A. MEYNELL, *Poems* (1893); *A Father of Life and Other Poems* (1893); (essays) *Rhythm of Life* (1893); *The Colour of Life* (1896). J. BADENI, *A Slender Tree: A Life of Alice Meynell* (Cornwall 1981). W. MEYNELL, *John Henry Newman* (1890); *Aunt Sarah and the War* (1914).

[P. R. MESSBARGER]

MEZGER

Family distinguished as Benedictines, teachers, and writers.

Franz, professor and writer; b. Ingolstadt, Oct. 25, 1632; d. Salzburg, Dec. 11, 1701. Franz entered the Benedictine Order in 1650, and was ordained in 1657. From 1659 to 1665 he taught philosophy at the University of Salzburg, then moral theology until 1668. From 1669 to 1688 he taught various theological sciences at the Benedictine Abbey of Ettal in Bavaria and at his own abbey in Salzburg. He was master of novices and director of the clerics at St. Peter in Salzburg from 1688 until his death. Besides writing ten philosophical and theological works, he made numerous translations, particularly from the Maurists, mainly of ascetical treatises.

Joseph, professor and writer; b. Eichstätt, Sept. 5, 1635; d. Abbey of St. Gall in Switzerland, Oct. 26, 1683. Joseph became a Benedictine in 1650, and was ordained in 1659. At the University of Salzburg he taught philosophy (1662–64), apologetics and polemics (1665–67), and Canon Law (1668–73). He was prior of St. Peter in Salzburg (1673–78), where he also taught hermeneutics and polemics. In 1678 he was appointed vice chancellor of the University of Salzburg. He was an intimate friend and correspondent of Mabillon, who called him "the most prominent light of the University of Salzburg." His numerous works cover theology, Scripture, and history. He died while on a pilgrimage to the Marian shrine at Einsiedeln.

Paul, professor and writer; b. Eichstätt, Nov. 23, 1637; d. Salzburg, April 12, 1702. Paul joined the Benedictines in 1652, and was ordained in 1660. From 1664 to 1666 he was master of novices and director of the clerics at St. Peter in Salzburg. At the University of Salzburg he taught philosophy (1668–70), theology (1673–88), and exegesis and polemics (1689–1700). In 1683 he succeeded his deceased brother as vice rector and vice chancellor of the University. Of his 33 works, M. Grabmann praises his *Theologia scholastica secundum viam et doctrinam d. Thomae,* in four volumes (Augsburg 1695), as "one of the best presentations of Thomistic theology." His teachings on the Immaculate Conception and papal infallibility are in accordance with later official definitions of these doctrines.

Bibliography: B. PROBST, *Die drei Brüder Mezger* (*Studia anselmiana* 27/28; Rome 1951) 443–452. M. SATTLER, *Collectaneen-Blätter zur Geschichte der Ehemaligen Benedictiner-Universität Salzburg* (Kempten, Ger. 1890) 212–218. P. LINDNER, *Professbuch von St. Peter* (Salzburg 1906) 53–63, 65–68, 248–252. V. REDLICH, *Benediktinisches Mönchtum in österreich,* ed. H. TAUSCH (Vienna 1949) 83–86.

[O. L. KAPSNER]

MEZUZAH

Hebrew term for a strip of parchment upon which are inscribed two passages from Deuteronomy, 6.4–9 and 11.13–21, written in 22 lines, and which is usually placed in a small metal, glass, or wooden cylindrical container. On the reverse side of the parchment is written the divine name SHADDAI (Almighty). This word should be visible through an opening cut into the mezuzah case. It is prescribed by rabbinical law that a mezuzah be placed upon the doorpost of every building and room inhabited by persons. (The Hebrew word *m*e*zûzâ* means doorpost.) It is affixed to the upper part of the right doorpost (as one enters). There is a special prayer formula for setting it in place. Among Orthodox Jews it is a pious custom, upon entering or leaving the house, to touch the mezuzah with the fingers and then to kiss the fingers. One of the seven minor Talmudic tractates, which is called by this term, treats of the various regulations on the writing and the use of the mezuzah. The mezuzah custom is based on Dt 6.9; 11.20: "Write them [God's words, understood to be those of 6.4–5] on the doorposts of your houses and on your gates." However, as in the similar case of the PHYLACTERIES, this injunction in Deuteronomy was no doubt intended originally to be understood in a merely figurative sense.

Bibliography: *The Jewish Encyclopedia,* ed. J. SINGER (New York 1901–06) 8:351–532. M. JOSEPH, *Universal Jewish Encyclopedia* (New York 1939–44) 7:526–527. M. HIGGER, ed., *The Seven Minor Treatises* (New York 1930) 20–23.

[J. C. TURRO]

MEZZABARBA, CARLO AMBROGIO

Patriarch of Alexandria and apostolic visitator to China; b. Pavia, *c.* 1685, d. Lodi, Dec. 7, 1741. Mezzabarba was accredited by Clement X with powers of legate *a latere* (Sept. 18, 1719); his mission to the Sino-Manchu Empire was to negotiate acceptance of the constitution *Ex illa die* of March 19, 1715, condemning the Chinese rites. In a series of audiences from Dec. 31, 1720, to March 1, 1721, Hsüan-yeh treated the papal plenipotentiary with marked honors, but angrily spurned the antirites decree and threatened repressive measures if it was enforced. Hoping to ease the grave tension, the legate issued a pastoral instruction (Macau, Nov. 4, 1721) in which he accorded eight qualifying permissions previously authorized by Rome itself in case of need, but which were quashed by Benedict XIV 20 years later (1742). Unsuccessful in his mission, Mezzabarba left China on Dec. 9, 1721, and on July 13, 1725, he was named to the See of Lodi. His confessor during the ill-fated legation, the Servite Sostegno Viani, wrote a diary of events, *Giornale della Legazione* (Cologne 1740), which was critical of the actions of the Beijing Jesuits in this affair.

Bibliography: L. PASTOR, *The History of the Popes from the Close of the Middle Ages,* 40 v. (London-St. Louis 1938–61): v. 1,

6th ed.; v. 2, 7th ed.; v. 3–6, 5th ed.; v. 7–8, 11–12, 3d ed.; v. 9–10, 4th ed.; v. 13–40, from 1st German ed. *Geschichte der Päpste seit dem Ausgang des Mittelalters,* 16 v. in 21 (Freiburg 1885–1933; repr. 1955–) 33:468–484, follows Viani's *Giornale,* but with supplementary correctives. A. S. ROSSO, *Apostolic Legations to China of the 18th Century* (South Pasadena, Calif. 1948) 342–390, gives translation of the Chinese ''Mandarins' Diary,'' or official court record of the negotiations, plus relevant imperial decrees.

[F. ROULEAU]

MEZZOFANTI, GIUSEPPE

Cardinal, linguist; b. Bologna, Sept. 17, 1774; d. Rome, March 15, 1849. His father was a poor carpenter. Gifted with a prodigious memory, in boyhood he learned Latin, Greek, Spanish, and Swedish. As a seminarian he mastered Hebrew, Arabic, and other Oriental languages. After ordination (1797), he taught Arabic at the University of Bologna, but he lost his post when he refused to take the oath of allegiance to the Cisalpine Republic. To support himself he then acted as a tutor. He returned to Bologna as professor of Hebrew and Greek from 1803 until 1808, when the chair was suppressed, and again from 1814 to 1831, when he was called to Rome as canon of the Basilica of St. Mary Major and a member of the philological college of the University of Rome. Meanwhile, he studied Chinese at the Capodimonte College in Naples. In 1833 he was named prefect of the VATICAN LIBRARY and canon of St. Peter's Basilica, and in 1838 cardinal and member of the Congregations of Propaganda, Rites, Index, and Revision of Books of the Oriental Church. He could speak about 40 languages, had a fair knowledge of about 30 more, and a familiarity with another 45 dialects. He contributed much to the science of comparative linguistics. Pressure of his other duties never permitted Mezzofanti to publish any of his studies. Most of his manuscripts and letters are deposited in the communal library of the Archiginnasio of Bologna. Several of his manuscripts were published after his death.

Bibliography: C. W. RUSSELL, *The Life of Cardinal Mezzofanti* (London 1858). M. DE CAMILLIS, *Il cardinale G. Mezzofanti, principe dei poliglotti* (Rome 1937).

[H. R. MARRARO]

MIAMI, ARCHDIOCESE OF

When Miami (*Miamiensis*) was established as a diocese on Aug. 13, 1958, its territory consisted of 14 counties formerly of the diocese of St Augustine. When the dioceses of Orlando and St. Petersburg were established on June 13, 1968, Miami was made an archdiocese with the new dioceses, along with St. Augustine, as its suffragans. In 2001 the Province of Miami included, in addition to the above named dioceses, St. Petersburg (1975), Pensacola-Tallahassee (1975), Palm Beach (1984) and Venice (1984). The territory of the archdiocese had been reduced to three counties in the southern Florida, Broward, Dade, and Monroe, but the Catholic population had grown to 816,207 Catholics, or about 22 percent of the total population of 3.7 million.

The first bishop, Coleman F. Carroll of Pittsburgh, Pa., served as auxiliary in Pittsburgh until his installation as bishop of Miami, Oct. 7, 1958. During the years of his episcopacy (1958–1977), the extraordinary growth in population that had begun after World War II continued in southern Florida. The increase that reached boom proportions came as a consequence of the attractive climate and real-estate projects for year-round residents in middle income brackets, and an influx of refugees from Cuba. Carroll initiated an extensive series of building projects and pastoral programs to meet the needs of his vastly diverse flock.

Within the first five years he more than doubled the number of parishes, many with schools. Bishop Carroll took the initiative in constructing and staffing diocesan high schools, Catholic hospitals and retreat centers. In 1958 he blessed the new St. John Vianney College Seminary, the first minor seminary on the East Coast south of Baltimore, Md., and in 1962 he inaugurated a major seminary, St. Vincent de Paul, opened at Boynton Beach. Early in 1960 Carroll established the *Centro Hispano Catolico* for all Spanish-speaking people in the area, with day nurseries, a medical clinic, a dental clinic, and arrangements for medical assistance. In addition to housing, food, and clothing, the center provided employment opportunities and transportation from Cuba for children and religious at considerable expense to the diocese. He dealt with the issue of race and ethnicity by pushing for a steady, if gradual, integration in parishes and schools. To staff the new institutions Carroll brought to the diocese eight religious communities of priests, 25 of sisters, and five communities of brothers.

In September 1976, Bishop Edward A. McCarthhy, of Phoenix, was appointed coadjutor with right of succession, becoming the second Archbishop of Miami (1977–1994) when Archbishop Carroll died the following year. The population in Florida continued to grow, and diocesan boundaries were once again realigned in 1984 with the creation of the dioceses of Palm Beach and Venice. McCarthy carried on the pastoral outreach and general policies of his predecessor in trying to help the refugees who continued to flow into Florida from Cuba and Haiti. Archbishop McCarthy had the honor of welcoming Pope John Paul II to Miami when the pontiff paid

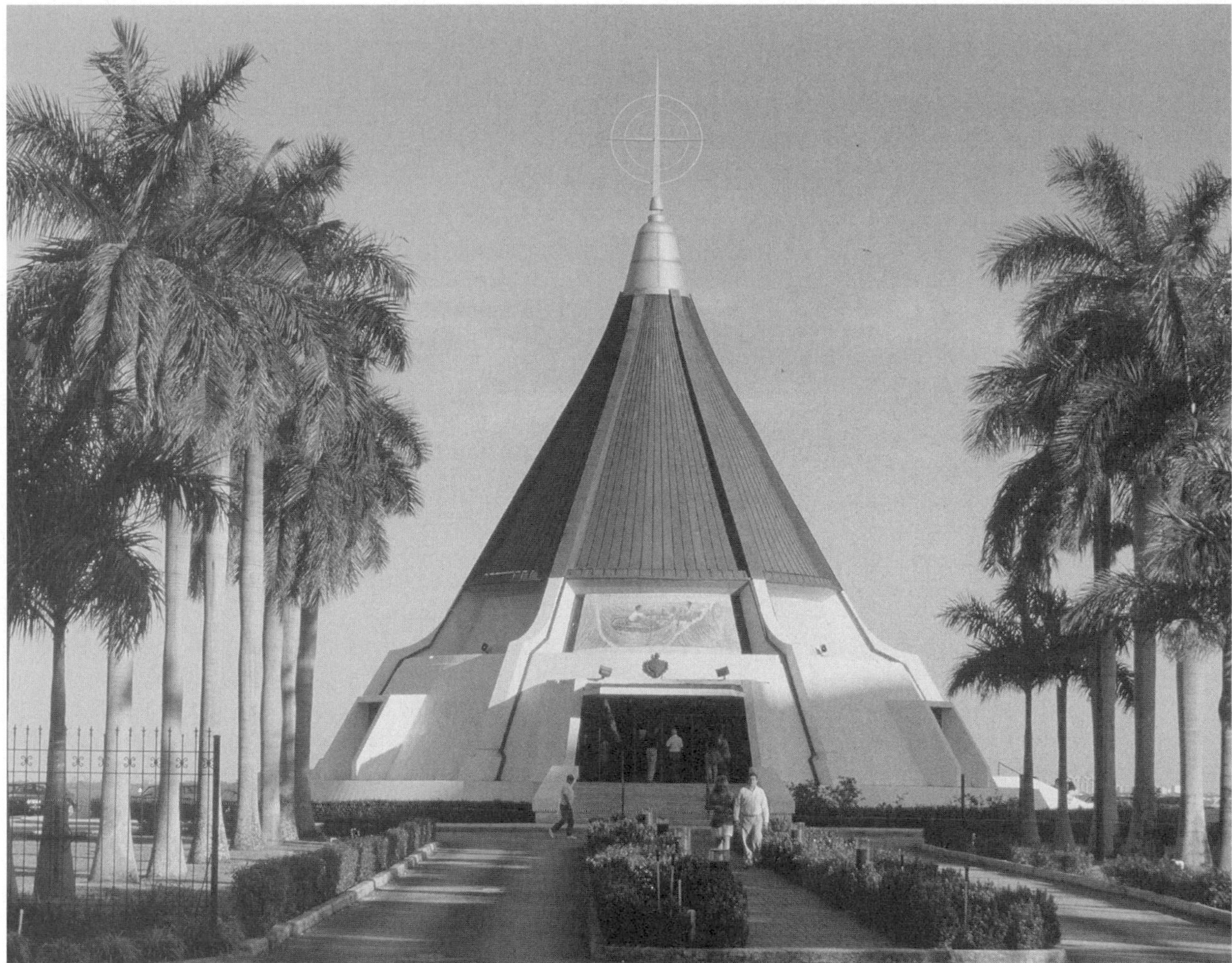

Saint Mary's Catholic Church, Miami. (©Patrick Ward/CORBIS)

his second visit to the U.S. in September 1987. John Paul addressed large audiences in both English and Spanish, and took the occasion of his visit to Miami to meet with a group of prominent Jewish leaders.

When Archbishop McCarthy reached the mandatory age of retirement in 1994, New Orleans-born John C. Favalora, since 1983 the bishop of St. Petersburg, was appointed to succeed him.

Catholic institutions of higher learning in the archdiocese include Barry University and St. Thomas University in Miami. Founded as Barry College for women in 1940 by the Dominican Sisters of Adrian, Mich., it went co-educational and subsequently attained university status in 1981. St. Thomas University was originally established as Biscayne College by the Augustinian Friars in 1961. It has evolved from an all male college to a coeducational university with a graduate school and the only accredited Catholic-affiliated law school in the Southeastern United States. Since 1988, the University has been under the sponsorship of the Archdiocese of Miami.

[M. KENNEDY/EDS.]

MICAH, BOOK OF

The 6th of the 12 MINOR PROPHETS. After outlining the contents of the book, this article will consider the questions of its date and authorship and its message.

Contents. The construction of the book is simple and well balanced: two collections of doom oracles separated by a collection of oracles of salvation. The ordering is a logical, not a chronological, one. The three parts of the prophecy are (1) God's chastisement of Judah's sins in keeping with the punishment He has already inflicted on Samaria (1.1–3.12); (2) a prediction of Zion's restoration by the Messiah (4.1–5.14); (3) God's rebuke of

Illumination from the Book of Micah in the "Great Bible of Demeter Neksei-Lipocz" (Pre. Acc. MS 1, v. 2, folio 186).

Judah for its ingratitude, injustice, and infidelity (6.1–7.6).

Part one contains prophecies of doom against Judah. It begins (1.2–7) by announcing Samaria's fall and the judgment of Yahweh on that city's sins. But the whole oracle intends to present the message to Jerusalem; judgment against Samaria is announced as an introduction to dire warning given Jerusalem and Judah (1.8–16); devastation comes as judgment upon Judah's social injustices (2.1–11). In the midst of these oracles of doom is an unexpected prophecy of salvation, announcing the gathering of the Remnant of Israel (2.12–13). There follows a further list of prophecies of woe directed against judges, Prophets, and the governing classes, and because of the crimes of these leaders Jerusalem will fall (3.1–12).

Part two of Micah is the "messianic" section (ch. 4–5); it is concerned entirely with the salvation of God's people and the destruction of its enemies. Possibly some verses found here have undergone later revision or even transformation. To inspire hope, the oracle of promise is used: 4.9–10, 11–13; 4.14–5.5. Here occurs a radiant vision of the new Jerusalem (4.1–5) and a great tableau of the future (5.1–5). The messianic kingdom is promised, not to the temporal Judah in its totality, but to the remnant (4.7; 5.2, 6–7) that has survived the punishment. This punishment is the sanction of Judah's present sin. But the sin of Judah does not suspend the fulfillment of the covenant. Micah's vision of Zion's restoration is an affirmation of complete faith in the success of God's plan. At the center of God's kingdom, the Prophet sees the King-Messiah, Son of David (4.8; 5.1–5).

The third part of the book opens with a juridical charge brought by Yahweh against His ungrateful people (6.1–8). Jerusalem is condemned for its social injustices (6.9–16); then the Prophet laments over the lack of justice and loyalty in the land (7.1–6). The section closes with a lamentation (7.7–10), a prediction (7.11–13), and a double prayer (7.14–17, 18–20).

Date and authorship. According to the title of the collection (1.1), Micah's preaching activity took place during the reigns of the Judean kings Joatham, Ahaz, and Hezekiah. This title, however, is later than the collection and has appeared suspect to many critics. In any event, Micah's preaching under Hezekiah (715–687 B.C.) is incontestable; Jeremiah affirms it (Jer 26.18–19). Micah's complaint over the cities of the Shephela (Mi 1.8–16) and his allusions to the siege of Jerusalem (4.9–10, 11, 14) are best situated at the time of Sennacherib's invasion in 701 B.C. In Micah there are excerpts from prophetic preaching that began sometime before 721 and still continued in 701. This is not to deny that some oracles have undergone later revision. The collection of Micah's oracles as it now exists is the work of an anonymous postexilic editor who apparently organized partial collections that had already been made. Unfortunately, the text suffered in transmission and is in an extremely bad state of preservation. Some critics doubt the Mican authorship of certain passages. This question is complicated by the fact that Micah, like the other prophetic books, was not a dead letter; the community exploited it and fashioned it in its liturgy according to its needs. The problem of authorship demands a cautious approach.

Message. Micah protests against social injustice: oppression of the poor, corruption of the governing classes, grinding down of the unfortunate in the machinery of the law. But his protest is based, not on man's dignity or his rights as a human individual or social being, but on Micah's concept of God's people. This concept dominates Micah's whole vision. God's people is not a political power, but a people chosen by, saved by, and allied to Yahweh by pure favor. Hence flow religious duties toward Yahweh the savior, and a special type of human relations among members of the chosen family. Micah demands the restoration of these duties and these relations. His vision of the future expresses faith in the fulfillment of the Davidic covenant and the ultimate accomplishment of Yahweh's plan to save.

Bibliography: A. GEORGE, *Dictionnaire de la Bible,* suppl. ed. L. PIROT (Paris 1928—) 5:1252–63. *Encyclopedic Dictionary of the Bible* (New York 1963) 1529–31. O. SCHILLING, *Lexikon für Theologie und Kirche,* ed. J. HOFER and K. RAHNER (Freiburg 1957–65) 7:390–391. K. MEYER and W. WERBECK, *Die Religion in Geschichte und Gegenwart* (Tübingen 1957–65) 4:929–931. B. VAWTER, *The Conscience of Israel* (New York 1961) 130–161.

[J. MORIARITY]

MICHAEL, ARCHANGEL

The name Michael occurs in the Old Testament as a rather common personal male name (Nm 13.13; 1 Chr 5.13–14; 6.40; etc.) as well as the name of a certain angel. The name in Hebrew, mîkā'ēl, means ''who is like God?''; compare the similarly formed Michea, in Hebrew, mîkāyāh, ''who is like Yahweh?''

In the Bible. GABRIEL, the angel instructor of Daniel, calls Michael ''one of the chief princes,'' ''your Prince,'' and ''the great prince, guardian of your people.'' In Dn 10.13, 21 Michael helps Gabriel in the contest against the tutelary angel of the Persians called ''prince of the kingdom of Persia.'' The background of Daniel's vision is the Seleucid period (312–63 B.C.), and the author has undoubtedly been influenced by the angelology of Zoroastrianism. Michael is presented as the angel protector of Israel and is integral to God's government of history. In Dn 12.1 Michael appears in apocalyptic circumstances as the source of comfort and strength for Israel in extreme distress.

In Jude 9, Michael is called ''the archangel,'' i.e., the chief angel, and is pictured disputing with the devil over the body of MOSES. The reference is unknown but refers probably to a passage from ''The Assumption of Moses'' (Pharisaic apocryphon of 1st century A.D.). In Rv 12.7–9, Michael leads the faithful angels to victory over the dragon (Satan) and his angels and casts them out of heaven down to the earth.

In Christian Cult. Early Christian cult was undoubtedly influenced by the prominent place given to Michael in the Hebrew apocrypha (e.g., Book of Enoch; Testament of Abraham). The *Shepherd of HERMAS* already mentions ''the great and glorious angel Michael who has authority over this people and governs them . . . .'' In the East, Michael was venerated as having care of the sick. Churches dedicated to him and the other angels date from as early as the 4th century. In the West, Michael was venerated as the head of the heavenly armies and the patron of soldiers. This veneration may be traced to a popular cult arising from an alleged 5th or 6th–century apparition of Michael during the distress caused by invading Goths (on the coast of southeastern

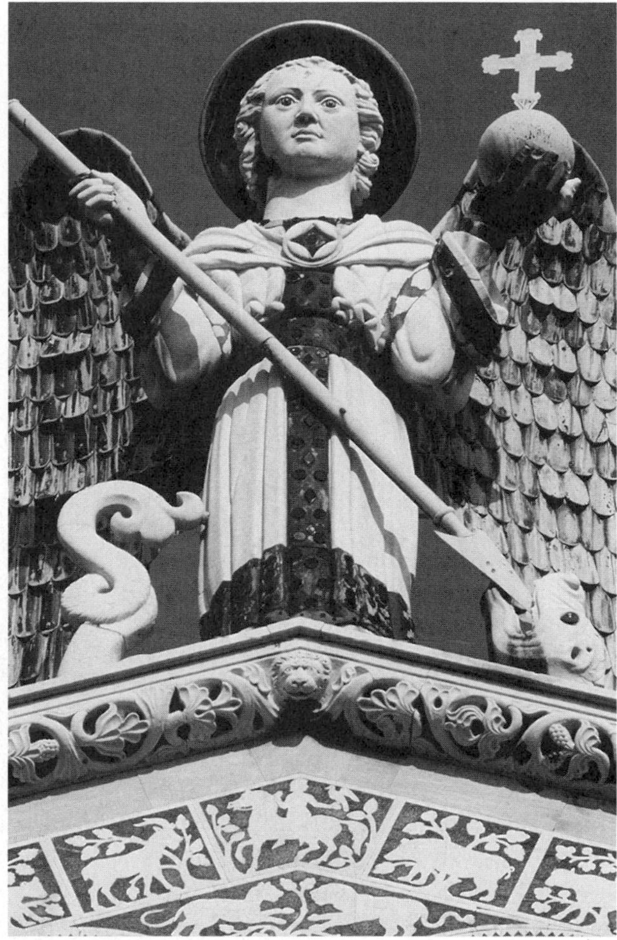

Sculpture of St. Michael the Archangel on San Michele in Foro, Italy. (©Michael Freeman/CORBIS)

Italy, Gargano or Monte Sant' Angelo; probable source of Mont-Saint-Michel tradition, Manche, France, 709 A.D.).

Michael was the only individual angel with a liturgical observance prior to the 9th century, and his cult has grown since then: e.g., tutelary angel of the church (the new Israel); patron of mariners, of roentgenologists (1941), and of Italy's public discipline and security (1950). Historically, September 29 was the feast of the Archangel Michael in the Roman Rite. The post–Vatican II reform of the liturgical calendar created combined the Feasts of the Archangels Michael, Gabriel, and Raphael on September 29. In the Eastern Christian tradition, the Feast of the Archangels is celebrated on November 8.

Bibliography: D. KECK, *Angels and Angelology in the Middle Ages* (New York 1998). B. OTZEN, ''Michael and Gabriel,'' in *The Scriptures and the Scrolls,* ed. F. GARCIA MARTINEZ, A. HILHORST, and C. J. LABUSCHAGNE (New York 1992).

[T. L. FALLON/EDS.]

MICHAEL III, BYZANTINE EMPEROR

Byzantine emperor 842 to Sept. 23/24, 867; b. probably 836. Michael, the son of Emperor THEOPHILOS and the last emperor of the Amorian dynasty, succeeded his father when still a child, under the regency of his mother, the Empress Theodora. A woman of great energy and piety, she put an end to the last remnants of ICONOCLASM, restored the peace of the Church and took strong measures against the spread of the Paulician heresy (*see* BOGOMILS) in Asia Minor.

The renewed war with the Arabs and simultaneous campaigns against the SLAVS threatening the Balkan provinces of the Empire called for an efficient military leadership that Theodora and her minister Theoctistos were unable to provide. In 856, Michael, aided by his maternal uncle, Bardas, overthrew Theodora's regency, forcing her into a convent. Bardas became the real ruler of the Empire and in 853 the Patriarch IGNATIUS was compelled to resign and was replaced by PHOTIUS, a close associate of Bardas.

Thus began the Photian Schism with all its disastrous religious and political consequences. The ever-increasing rift with the West, the wars with the Arabs and Balkan Slavs, and the beginning of Russian attacks from across the Black Sea (*c.* 860) made the position of the Empire extremely precarious. Michael III lacked an ability for government and military leadership. This capricious, cruel, and corrupt young man, always under the influence of favorites, soon tired of Bardas, and in 866 had him murdered in his presence by Basil the Macedonian who became co-emperor. In 867 Basil murdered Michael and thus became Emperor Basil I, founder of the Macedonian (Armenian) dynasty.

Bibliography: J. B. BURY, *A History of the Eastern Roman Empire from the Fall of Irene to the Accession of Basil I., A. D. 802–867* (New York 1912). G. OSTROGORSKY, *History of the Byzantine State* tr. J. HUSSEY (Oxford 1956). A. FLICHE and V. MARTIN, *Histoire de l'église depuis les origines jusqua'à nos jours* (Paris 1935–) v.6.

[C. TOUMANOFF]

MICHAEL VIII PALAEOLOGUS, BYZANTINE EMPEROR

Reigned 1259 to Dec. 11, 1282; b. 1224 or 1225. Michael not only restored Greek rule in Constantinople after the period of Latin domination (1204–61), but thwarted the attempted invasion of Byzantium by the able and ambitious Charles of Anjou, king of Sicily.

With the establishment of the LATIN EMPIRE OF CONSTANTINOPLE after the Fourth CRUSADE, several Byzantine states appeared, of which the most important was the Empire of Nicaea in Asia Minor. Michael, a leading nobleman at the Nicene court, usurped the throne in 1259 from the boy Lascarid emperor, thus establishing the Palaeologan dynasty that ruled Byzantium until its fall to the Turks in 1453.

With Nicaea as a base, Michael ultimately recaptured Constantinople (1261), the result of either a surprise entrance of his troops into the city, or of carefully laid plans, or both. At the Greek reconquest, the expelled Latins, especially the Latin Emperor Baldwin and the Venetians, launched a diplomatic campaign to recover the city. Their plans ultimately centered around Charles of Anjou, the ambitious brother of King Louis IX of France, who had inherited the old Norman designs against Byzantium. As a result Michael had to devote almost all of his energies to checkmating the intricate web of alliances woven against Byzantium by Charles.

With great diplomatic finesse, Michael offered to Pope GREGORY X, Charles's suzerain for Sicily, union of the Greek and Latin Churches in exchange for papal restraint of Charles's plans against Constantinople. After long negotiations Michael sent envoys to the famous second Council of Lyons (1274), and a union of the two Churches was declared there. The Greeks, however, looked upon this union—at which the Eastern patriarchs were not represented—as a fraud, and Michael faced opposition to the union from most of his subjects. Negotiations to implement the union continued until Charles finally succeeded in securing the election of his own papal candidate, MARTIN IV, who almost immediately excommunicated Michael and declared a crusade against the ''schismatic'' Greeks under the leadership of Charles of Anjou.

In 1281 the situation seemed desperate for Michael, because Charles had created a tremendous anti-Byzantine coalition that ultimately included the papacy and Venice. However, on March 30, 1282, the Sicilian Vespers, a revolt against Angevin rule, suddenly broke out in Palermo, Sicily, forcing Charles to suspend his plans against Byzantium and occupying his attention until the end of his reign. Scholarship has recently shown that this revolt (which had some nationalistic overtones) was in part engineered not only by the Hohenstaufen party in Sicily, but also by Michael, who supplied the rebels with money and entered into an alliance against Charles with King PETER OF ARAGON, son-in-law of Manfred, the last Hohenstaufen ruler of Sicily. Thus Michael, by a series of brilliant diplomatic maneuvers, was able successfully to maintain the empire against one of the ablest foes Byzantium had ever faced. In view of the overwhelming threat from the West, however, Michael could devote little attention to the East, and the OTTOMAN Turks were able to overrun almost all of Asia Minor.

Bibliography: C. CHAPMAN, *Michel Paléologue: Restaurateur de l'empire byzantin* (Paris 1926). D. J. GEANAKOPLOS, *Emperor Michael Palaeologus and the West, 1258–1282: A Study in Byzantine-Latin Relations* (Cambridge, Mass. 1959), with detailed bibliog.

[D. J. GEANAKOPLOS]

MICHAEL I, THE SYRIAN, PATRIARCH OF ANTIOCH

Jacobite patriarch, historian; b. Melitene (Malatya, Turkey), 1126; d. 1199. Monk, and later archimandrite, of the monastery of Bar-Sauma, Michael, as patriarch of Antioch (1166–99), strove to reform the somewhat lax ways of the Jacobite (Monophysite) Church (*see* JACOBITES [SYRIAN]), and for a time had to struggle with a rival patriarch who enjoyed Armenian support. He maintained good relations with the CRUSADER STATES, and was invited to the Third LATERAN COUNCIL, but declined. His main writing is a chronicle in Syriac, covering the period from creation to 1199. Its value lies, for the earlier portions, in the many now lost Syriac historians whom he used as sources, and for the later portions, in his own shrewd and detailed eyewitness accounts of events in the Near East in his own time. The original Syriac text was rediscovered in 1888; previously the chronicle had been known only in a shortened Armenian version. Unpublished liturgical and dogmatic works by Michael also survive.

Bibliography: J. B. CHABOT, ed. and tr., *Chronique de Michel le Syrien,* 4 v. (Paris 1899–1924). E. TISSERANT, *Dictionnaire de théologie catholique,* ed. A. VACANT et al., 15 v. (Paris 1903–50; Tables générales 1951–) 10.2: 1711–19. P. KAWERAU, *Die jakobitische Kirche im Zeitalter der syrischen Renaissance* (2d ed. Berlin 1960).

[R. BROWNING]

MICHAEL CERULARIUS, PATRIARCH OF CONSTANTINOPLE

Patriarchate, Mar. 25, 1043, to his exile, Nov. 1058; d. Jan. 21, 1059. The supposed author of the EASTERN SCHISM, Michael came from a distinguished family of Constantinople, was educated for the civil service, and never acquired any real knowledge of ecclesiastical studies. Nevertheless, he had a lofty concept of his office, regarding the spiritual ruler above the temporal, a theory influenced by the thought of SYMEON THE NEW THEOLOGIAN. Since he was a controversial figure in his own lifetime, even the contemporary sources are contradictory. When in 1040 a plot against Emperor Michael IV was discovered, Cerularius was accused by some sources of leading it, and by HUMBERT OF SILVA CANDIDA in *Excommunication* of having become a monk to escape punishment; others stated that he was guiltless and entered religion freely. At the accession of Emperor CONSTANTINE IX, who had taken part in the conspiracy, Cerularius became *syncellus,* virtual successor-designate to the patriarch, and the emperor's most trusted adviser. Succeeding to the See of CONSTANTINOPLE in 1043, he broke with Constantine over the question of submission to Rome.

The BYZANTINE CHURCH, separated from Rome since 1009, had, by the middle of the eleventh century, lost all belief in the primacy—did not even recognize, in fact, that Rome had ever made such a claim—and, though it conceded in principle that all five patriarchates were equal and independent, regarded Constantinople as the foremost see in Christendom. At first, Cerularius proposed reunion with Rome, thinking that he was dealing with the pope as an equal. He was shocked when confronted with the demand of the legates (he thought them demented, cf. *Epistola ad Petrum,* Will, 183–184), backed by the emperor, that he acknowledge the primacy of Rome. This demand ran counter to his convictions, and he was excommunicated by the legates, but after the death of the pope. [The question of the excommunication has since been reconsidered in light of the ECUMENICAL movement growing out of VATICAN COUNCIL II. See the joint statement of Pope Paul and Athenagoras, Patriarch of Constantinas, Patriarch of Constantinople, on Dec. 7, 1965 (*Acta Apostolicae Sedis,* [Rome 1919–] 58.1:2021).] In consonance with his theory of the supremacy of the spiritual, Cerularius fought the temporal power. He enjoyed tremendous popularity in Constantinople, and knowing well how to sway the mob, he forced Constantine to an abject surrender.

Thereafter he exercised unchallenged authority in the capital—an unparalleled position for a patriarch in Byzantine history—but he did so in the public interest. Boldly, he told Empress Theodora that sole rule by a woman jeopardized the Byzantine state and that she should appoint an emperor (his frankness very nearly cost him his life; cf. Psellus, *Chron.* 6.17), and he played the decisive role in the deposition of the weak Emperor Michael VI and the crowning of the able Isaac I Comnenus. As a reward, Cerularius gained control over all revenues and appointments in HAGIA SOPHIA, but he gradually became overbearing, as even the friendly sources relate, and the ensuing struggle for power was fatal to emperor and patriarch.

According to the testimony of an eyewitness, Cerularius's right hand remained incorrupt after his death. Immediately he won renown throughout the East for sanctity as a confessor, and in Constantinople he received a popular cult, made official the next year. Among the patriarchs of Constantinople he is unique; no other ever attained such power. He was not without defects: he was weak in theology, violent and uncompromising, vindictive, and corrupted by power in his last years. But he had great personal courage and a high sense of duty, as proven by the risk he took in admonishing Theodora. In the quarrel with Cardinal Humbert and the emperor, he fought bravely and resourcefully and in all good faith for what he considered the preservation of true doctrine. It was his misfortune to have served the wrong cause; but modern historians who condemn him seem not to make allowance for his psychological background. Cerularius is an early counterpart of Patriarch JOSEPH I, who rejected the union of the Council of Lyons, with this difference: while Joseph resigned, Cerularius fought.

Bibliography: Works. *Panoplia*. ed. A. MICHEL, *Humbert und Kerullarios,* 2 v. (Paderborn 1924–30) 2:208–281, title given by Michel to an anonymous collection of texts, which he ascribes with the approval of most scholars to Cerularius. It contains C.'s speeches and pamphlets against union, with pertinent anathemas. Destined for use as an abjuration-of-heresy formula, it was published in the summer of 1054. *Semeioma,* ed. C. WILL, *Acta et scripta quae de còntroversiis ecclesiae graecae et latinae s. XI composita extant* (Leipzig and Marburg 1861) 155–168; *Patrologia Graeca,* ed. J. P. MIGNE, 161 v. (Paris 1857–66) 120:736–748, answering Humbert's excommunication. Two letters to Peter of Antioch: *Patrologia Graeca,* ed. J. P. MIGNE, 161 v. (Paris 1857–66) 120:781–796, 815–820; C. WILL, op. cit., 172–188. M. PSELLUS, *Chronographia,* Eng. tr. E. R. A. SEWTER (New Haven 1953). L. BRÉHIER, ''Un Discours inédit de Psellos: Accusation du patriarche M. C. devant le synode,'' *Revue Grégorienne* 16 (1903): 375–416; 17 (1904): 35–76. Literature. E. AMANN, *Dictionnaire de théologie catholique,* 15 v. (Paris 1903–50) 10:1677–1703. M. JUGIE, *Le Schisme byzantin* (Paris 1941) 187–234, esp. 220–223, 229–231. A. MICHEL, *Die Kaisermacht in der Ostkirche* (Darmstadt 1959). H. G. BECK, *Kirche und theologische Literatur im byzantinischen Reich,* 533–538, *passim.* F. DVORNIK, *Cambridge Medieval History,* 8 v. (London-New York 1991) 2: 4.1 ch. 10.

[M. J. HIGGINS]

MICHAEL III, PATRIARCH OF CONSTANTINOPLE

Reigned 1170–1178; b. Anchialos. Michael was educated by the archbishop of Anchialos, and after entering the clergy was named *sakkelarios,* or treasurer. He journeyed to Constantinople on business for the patriarchate and there was made *protekdikos,* or first advocate, and later *hypatos,* or chancellor, of the philosophers. In late 1169 he was named patriarch of Constantinople; and he became involved in a controversy over the interpretation of Christ's words ''The Father is greater than I,'' which led to the condemnation of Constantine of Kerkyra and Abbot Irenicus of Batala. He encouraged the jurist BALSAMON to write his commentary on the canons and opposed the attempts of the Emperor Manuel I Comnenus (1143–80) to bring about a reunification of the Orthodox Church with both Rome and the Armenians. In 1170 a papal delegation was sent to Constantinople by Pope ALEXANDER III, who reduced conditions for reunion to three: recognition of the papal primacy, recognition of the right of appeal to Rome, and inscription of the pope's name in the diptychs. In a synod (1171) Michael made a public response to the legation's offer in a dialogue with the emperor. He violently attacked the pope as no pastor but a sick member of the fold in need of a cure. He said union with the Turks would be preferable to union with the Latins. He likewise repulsed efforts of Theorianus, sent by the emperor to the Armenian Catholicos Nerses IV (1169), and to the Jacobites (1171), to win them to an acceptance of Chalcedonian doctrine. Of Michael's writings, besides the dialogues with the emperor and his letters concerning Armenian affairs, his synodal acts dealing with ecclesiastical discipline are of great interest. A treatise on the liturgy of the presanctified attributed to him by A. Ehrhard belongs to the Patriarch Michael II Oxeites.

Bibliography: *Patrologia Graeca* 133:223–232; 137:741; 138:85, 210–211. V. LAURENT, *Dictionnaire de théologie catholique* 10.2:1668–74. B. KOTTER, *Lexikon für Theologie und Kirche* [2] 7:391. *Les Regestes des actes du patriarcat de Constantinople* 1109–50. V. GRUMEL, *Échos d'Orient* 29 (1930) 257–264, filioque. V. LAURENT, *ibid.* 33 (1934) 309–315. A. PAPADOPOULUS-KERAMEUS, *Byzantinische Zeitschrift* 8 (1899) 665–666.

[F. CHIOVARO]

MICHAEL DE NORTHBURGH

Bishop of London, minister of King Edward III; d. Copford, Essex, England, Sept. 9, 1361. He studied at Oxford and had received the M.A. and doctorate of civil law by 1336. He amassed innumerable benefices and, soon after becoming a canon of Lichfield and Hereford, entered the royal service, being sent in 1345 on an unsuccessful mission to the pope to obtain a dispensation for the Black Prince's marriage to a daughter of the Duke of Brabant. By 1346 he was a counselor and confessor to the king, whom he accompanied on his expedition against the French. The two letters Michael wrote describing the campaign from Saint-Vaast to Caen and from Poissy via Crécy to the siege of Calais are preserved in Robert of Avesbury's chronicle (*Rerum Britannicarum medii aevi scriptores,* 43; 1889). By 1350 he was the king's secretary and keeper of the Privy Seal and thus in charge of war and foreign affairs. In 1354 he was appointed bishop of London by papal PROVISION. Soon afterward he conducted fruitless peace negotiations with the French at the papal court at Avignon, and he was sent again in 1355 to treat with them at Guisnes. Impressed by the French CARTHUSIANS, he became co-founder of the LONDON CHARTERHOUSE. He died of the plague. He had compiled a *Concordancia* of laws and canons, since lost; he left £2,000 to the Charterhouse, £1,000 to St. Paul's cathedral, and scholarships for law students at Oxford.

Bibliography: A. B. EMDEN, *A Biographical Register of the University of Oxford to A.D. 1500,* 3 v. (Oxford 1957–59) 2:1368–70. C. L. KINGSFORD, *The Dictionary of National Biography from the Earliest Times to 1900,* 63 v. (London 1885–1900; repr. with corrections, 21 v., 1908–09, 1921–22, 1938; suppl. 1901–) 14: 632–633.

[B. S. SMITH]

MICHAEL DE SANCTIS, DE, ST.

Mystic; b. Vich, Catalonia, Spain, 1591; d. Valladolid, April 10, 1625. Michael practiced austerities of fasting and watching, abstained from meat in early childhood, and at the age of eight made a vow of chastity. He had a special devotion to the Rosary and the Little Office of the Blessed Virgin. After the death of his father, he wished to enter the Trinitarians, but his family opposed it. However, he entered the Order at Barcelona, and was professed there at 16. He studied at Salamanca and Seville where his mystical gifts began to manifest themselves. He was ordained in Portugal.

It was reported that when rapt in ecstasy he often levitated. In Cordova, while meditating on paradise, he was said to have soared out of the choir, across a field, and come to rest on a churchtower. When preaching in Salamanca, he reputedly was raised in the air in sight of all. His favorite sermon topic was the ransom of Christian captives of the Moors. In 1622 he was made prior at Valladolid where he spent his last years. He was beatified by PIUS VI in 1779, and canonized by Pius IX in 1862.

Feast: April 10.

Bibliography: J. L. BAUDOT and L. CHAUSSIN, *Vies des saints et des bienheureux selon l'ordre du calendrier avec l'historique des fêtes* (Paris 1935–56) 4:236–238. A. BUTLER, *The Lives of the Saints*, ed. H. THURSTON and D. ATTWATER (New York 1956) 2:66.

[M. J. DORCY]

MICHAEL OF CESENA

Franciscan minister general and theologian; b. Fichio, near Cesena, Italy, *c.* 1270; d. Munich, Germany, Nov. 29, 1342. Michael Foschi entered the FRANCISCAN Order *c.* 1284 and was custos at Bologna by January 1305 (*Archivum Franciscanum historicum*, 25:285). He had just been made a doctor of theology at the University of PARIS in May 1316, when the news of his election as minister general by the general chapter at Naples was announced to him. In July of the same year he went to Assisi to preside over the compilation of new constitutions for the order, and he named PETER AUREOLI (d. 1322) to succeed him in Paris. In close accord with Pope JOHN XXII, he succeeded in putting an end to the dispute between the FRANCISCAN SPIRITUALS and the rest of the community, and the majority of those who had revolted submitted to him. However, Ubertino of Casale and ANGELUS CLARENUS left the order, and four recalcitrants were burned at Marseilles in 1318. At the general chapter of Marseilles in 1319, Michael obtained the condemnation of the treatise of PETER JOHN OLIVI on the Apocalypse. A serious crisis erupted in 1322, when Pope John XXII repudiated the Franciscan proposition of the absolute poverty of Christ and the Apostles. The order defended it in a general chapter at Perugia in June 1322, after Cesena had tried mitigating certain texts. But the condemnation of Dec. 8 (*Ad conditorem*), the imposition of ownership of goods on the order, and the *Quia quorumdam* (November 1324), which declared heretical everything opposing the bulls on poverty, all exasperated the friars, making them more sympathetic toward the excommunicated emperor, Louis IV, the Bavarian, who was in conflict with the AVIGNON PAPACY (*see* POVERTY CONTROVERSY). The general chapter at Lyons in 1325 remained silent regarding the Perugia decisions; Cesena merely exhorted obedience and moderation and made a few slight alterations in the constitutions. Trips to Paris, Naples, and Rome during 1326 to 1327 and denunciations by prominent Guelfs aroused the pope's suspicions, and Cesena was recalled to Avignon. In January 1328 Louis was crowned in Rome by Sciarra COLONNA (d. 1328), and in May he had a dissenting Franciscan, Pietro Rainalducci, elected as antipope NICHOLAS V. Ten days later, on May 22, King Robert of Naples (d. 1343) procured Cesena's confirmation as general by the general chapter at Bologna despite the protests of the papal legate. Michael fled Avignon on the 26th with WILLIAM OF OCKHAM and Bonagratia of Bergamo (d. 1347) and reached Pisa on June 9. Although avoiding the antipope, they succeeded in winning the friendship of Louis, who took them under his protection. This was a serious matter that alienated the majority of Franciscans from Cesena, and Geraldus Odonis (d. 1349) succeeded him as head of the order in 1329 after the general chapter at Paris. This same chapter condemned the conduct and writings of Michael and his associates. The schismatics settled permanently in Munich, and from there Michael addressed himself in vain to the Perpignan chapter in April 1331, which expelled him from the order. The general answered him in his *Quid niteris,* to which Cesena replied with *Teste Salomone* in December 1332. In his last years he wrote numerous anonymous works, and his name is found on a final protestation, *Quoniam sicut testatur,* dated Aug. 23, 1338. Before his death, he restored the seal of the order to William of Ockham and left his papers in safekeeping with Queen Sanchia of Naples (d. 1345). He died unsubmissive. His theological writings on the *Sentences* and on Ezechiel and his *Sermones de tempore* and *de sanctis* are lost; only the constitutions of 1316 and 1325, his polemical writings, and a few letters remain.

Bibliography: *Archivum Franciscanum historicum* (Quaracchi-Florence 1909–) 25:285. NICOLAUS MINORITA, *Chronica: Documentation on Pope John XXII, Michael of Cesena and the Poverty of Christ with Summaries in English: A Source Book,* ed. G. GÁL and D. FLOOD (St. Bonaventure, N.Y. 1996), bibliography. D. LUSCOMBE, ''William of Ockham and the Michaelists on Robert Grosseteste and Denis the Areopagite [Latin texts],'' in *The Medieval Church* (Rochester 1999) 93–109.

[J. CAMBELL]

MICHAEL OF MALEINOS, ST.

Hermit and monastic founder; b. Charsianon, Cappadocia, 894; d. Mt. Kymina, Bithynia. Related to the imperial family, he was reared at the Byzantine court under the name of Manuel. As a young man he became a monk at the monastery of Kymina (912), from which he withdrew (918) to solitary life on a cliff, and to a desert the following year. In 921 he founded a monastery at Xerolimni (Gerolimni) in Bithynia. He returned to Kymina (*c.* 925), and was ordained (930). Michael was the spiritual father of St. ATHANASIUS THE ATHONITE.

Feast: July 12 (West); July 22 (East).

Bibliography: *Acta Sanctorum* July 3:289. H. DELEHAYE, *Analecta Bollandiana* 24 (1905) 491–492. H. G. BECK, *Kirche und theologische Literatur im byzantinischen Reich* (Munich 1959) 824.

[M. C. HILFERTY]

MICHEL, TERESA GRILLO, BL.

Baptized Maddalena Grillo, widow, foundress of the Congregation of the Little Sisters of Divine Providence; b. Spinetta Marengo, Alessandria, Italy, Sept. 25, 1855; d. there, Jan. 25, 1944.

Maddalena, the youngest of five children, was born into a life of privilege. Her mother, Maria Antonietta Parvopassau, had been born into the local aristocracy, while her father, Giuseppe Grillo, was chief physician at Alessandria's hospital. Her mother moved the family to Turin following her husband's death. Maddalena attended grammar school in Turin before being sent to the Ladies of Loretto boarding school in Lodi (Lombardy). Having completed school (1873), Maddalena returned to Alessandria for her debut into society.

She married (Aug. 2, 1877) Giovanni Battista Michel, a captain of the Bersaglieri. During 14 years of marriage, the couple lived in Acireale, Catania, Portici, and Naples. Her sorrow at the death of Giovanni from sunstroke might have turned to despair had she not read the life of Saint Joseph COTTOLENGO. His life inspired her to share the grief of the abandoned: orphans, the elderly, and the sick.

She turned her home into a shelter for those in need. As the numbers grew, she sold her home in order to buy and renovate a large building on the Via Faa di Bruno (1893) that became the ''Little Shelter of Divine Providence.'' She continued her work despite opposition and enlisted the aid of others. On Jan. 8, 1899, Maddalena and eight co-workers received the religious habit and new names in the shelter's chapel, becoming the Congregation of the Little Sisters of Divine Providence.

Almost immediately the institute grew exponentially: houses were established in Apulia, Liguria, Lombardy, Lucania, the Piedmont, and Veneto. Eighteen months after the institute's foundation, a house was opened in Brazil (June 13, 1900) and, at the request of Blessed Luigi Orione (1872–1940), houses in Argentina (1927). Thereafter, Teresa crossed the Atlantic eight times to establish homes for the aged, hospitals, nurseries, orphanages, and schools in Latin America.

She was beatified in the Piazza Vittorio, Turin, Piedmont, Italy, by Pope John Paul II, May 24, 1988.

Bibliography: V. CÁRCEL ORTÍ, *Martires españoles del siglo XX* (Madrid 1995). J. PÉREZ DE URBEL, *Catholic Martyrs of the Spanish Civil War, 1936–1939,* tr. M. F. INGRAMS (Kansas City, Mo. 1993). A. PRONZATO, *Una donna per sperare: madre Teresa Michel fondatrice delle Piccole suore della Divina Provvidenza* (Turin 1978).

[K. I. RABENSTEIN]

MICHEL, VIRGIL

Benedictine liturgist and educator; b. St. Paul, Minn., June 26, 1890; d. Collegeville, Minn., Nov. 26, 1938. The son of Fred and Mary (Griebler) Michel, he was baptized George. After his education at St. John's Preparatory School and University in Collegeville, he joined the Benedictine Order there in 1909, pronounced his solemn vows on Sept. 26, 1913, and was ordained in 1916. In 1918 he received his doctorate in English and a licentiate in theology at The Catholic University of America. During the next six years (1918–24), he taught at St. John's University and also held various administrative posts, including that of dean of the college. In February 1924 Michel began philosophical studies under Joseph Gredt at Sant' Anselmo in Rome, but, dissatisfied with Gredt's approach, he went to Louvain for the following school term.

Of greatest significance for his future work in America was the knowledge he acquired of the liturgical movement in Europe, which had not yet made an impression upon the English-speaking nations. Having convinced his superior of the need of such a movement for English-speaking Catholics and that St. John's Abbey should undertake its promotion and be its center, Michel, during extensive study trips, consulted European liturgical leaders and scholars. Of these, Lambert BEAUDUIN especially influenced him. Back at home in the fall of 1925, Michel, with the support of Abbot Alcuin Deutsch, at once laid plans for founding the movement's organ, *Orate Fratres* (later renamed *Worship*), and established the Liturgical Press. Under his guiding hand as editor of *Orate Fratres,* the liturgical movement gradually took firm roots in the U.S., though not without considerable misunderstanding and opposition.

Undoubtedly Michel's chief contribution was his influence on the American liturgical movement, particularly his sketching of the implications of the liturgy for all aspects of human life. As a leader in the Catholic social movement in the Depression years of the 1930s, he spoke out boldly for the reconstruction of society on the basis of an adequate philosophy of human and spiritual values. He was a prolific writer, a tireless worker, a strong personal inspiration to others, and a man of wide-ranging interests. He published seven volumes; contributed to many more; and wrote several hundred articles, editorials, and book reviews for more than 35 periodicals. The totality of his writings constitutes a kind of Christian synthesis, embracing the natural and supernatural elements of man's life in an ever-changing world.

Bibliography: P. B. MARX, *Virgil Michel and the Liturgical Movement* (Collegeville, Minn. 1957).

[P. MARX]

MICHELANGELO BUONARROTI

Sculptor, painter, architect, poet, a founder of the high Renaissance style, and the most influential late Renaissance artist; b. Caprese (Arezzo), Mar. 6, 1475; d. Rome, Feb. 18, 1564.

Life. Michelangelo's poor but aristocratic father opposed his artistic ambitions but nonetheless apprenticed him to the painter Ghirlandaio (1488). Thereafter the boy was protected by Lorenzo de' Medici, coming in contact with advanced artistic and philosophic tendencies. He was also influenced by SAVONAROLA's sermons. The supposed Neoplatonic content of Michelangelo's art has been disputed. His writings disclose profound, lifelong Catholic piety. His art embodies a new concept of human dignity and dependence on the Creator, of whose sublimity no other Renaissance artist experienced so convincing a vision. For nearly 60 years Michelangelo carried out official papal programs. Although the propriety of his creations was sometimes questioned, no ecclesiastical authority challenged their orthodoxy. Michelangelo's high Renaissance works fulfill ideals of Pope Julius II during a crisis in Church history, and his late works are imbued with Catholic Reformation mysticism.

Michelangelo's contemporaries believed him divinely inspired. The later eighteenth and early nineteenth century found his art inaccessible, but otherwise he has been considered one of the world's greatest artistic geniuses. Even Michelangelo's painting and architecture were predominantly sculptural. He depicted nature only as background for his principal theme, the life of the soul expressed in the form and movements of the body, defined in his writings as the ''beautiful and mortal veil'' mirroring divine intention. Michelangelo projected the body on a new scale of grandeur, distorting it to emphasize muscular power. Although his principal concern was form, his color ranged from clear, transparent tones in early work to great intensity in later paintings, and the white marble for his sculptures was chosen for its brilliance. In his architecture and painting, he subordinated space to mass and made little attempt to represent perspective.

Work. Michelangelo's ambition outran circumstances, and none of his major sculptural projects reached completion. His bronzes are all lost. Many of his marble statues, intended for perfect completion, show large unfinished areas, affording insight into his methods. He first drew outlines on the block, then cut away marble to free the figure, which emerged complete save for final polishing. His poems interpret this procedure as an allegory of divine creativity and human salvation. In architectural enframements for statues and in complete buildings, Michelangelo devoted scrupulous attention to detail, epitomizing the rhythms and tensions of the larger masses in the ornament. The finished portions of his statues show a similar intensity of life and of formal relationships, extending to the smallest elements. Michelangelo's art was founded on drawing. During old age he destroyed most of his thousands of preparatory studies for statues, paint-

Michelangelo Buonarroti, "The Last Judgement," fresco in the Sistine Chapel of the Vatican Palace, painted between 1535 and 1541.

ings, and buildings; but several hundred survive. Full critical agreement on an authentic corpus of drawings has not yet been reached.

From ancient art Michelangelo absorbed heroic aspects of pose and figure structure, but he avoided classicizing faces. His faces reflect contemporary Italian types, endowed with special beauty by the artist's sensitivity. He was responsive to the qualities and meaning of Italian medieval and early Renaissance art, often quoting entire figures.

Michelangelo's poetry, most of it composed in later life, at first expresses passionate human attachments or ironic reflections; eventually, aspiration for salvation. About equally divided between sonnets and madrigals, Michelangelo's poems are abrupt in diction and difficult to interpret. The best possess a depth and power equaled by no Italian Renaissance poetry.

Michelangelo's surviving early works include the "Madonna of the Stairs" and "Battle of Lapiths and Centaurs" (1489–92), a recently rediscoverd wooden Crucifix for Santo Spirito (1492), three statuettes for the Tomb of St. Dominic in Bologna (1494–95), "Bacchus" (1496–98), the "Pietà" for St. Peter's (1498–1500), "David" (1501–04), "St. Matthew" (1503–08), the "Bruges Madonna," two marble Madonna reliefs, and the painted "Doni Madonna" (1503).

Patronage of Popes. In 1505 began the patronage of Pope Julius II, which, though often stormy and even tragic for the artist, generated some of his noblest works, especially the ceiling frescoes of the SISTINE CHAPEL (1508–12). This immense allegory of the coming of Christ envisioned by prophets and sibyls in scenes from Genesis, bordered by the ancestors of Christ, was probably guided by Cardinal Marco VIGERIO. The pope's tomb, planned as freestanding in ST. PETER'S BASILICA (1505), with more than 40 marble statues and many bronze reliefs, underwent changes in 1513, 1516, 1532, and 1542. The reduced version in S. Pietro in Vincoli (1545) contains only "Moses" and the "Active" and "Contemplative Life" by Michelangelo himself. Two "Bound Captives" from previous projects are in the Louvre; four are in the Bargello, and a "Victory" is in the Palazzo Vecchio.

The patronage of the Medici popes, LEO X and CLEMENT VII, centered on San Lorenzo, including a never-executed façade, the Medici Chapel with its magnificent sculptures (1519–34), and the library of San Lorenzo, completed from Michelangelo's drawings and models. The "Christ" of S. Maria sopra Minerva (1514–21) and "David-Apollo" (1531–32) are two great works that date from this period, during which Michelangelo was also deeply involved in Florentine struggles for liberty.

Michelangelo Buonarroti.

The "Last Judgment," terminating the decoration of the Sistine Chapel (1535–41), and the frescoes of the Pauline Chapel (1541–50), painted for Pope Paul III, reflect penitential currents in the Catholic Reformation. Although hampered by ill health, Michelangelo undertook in 1546 to complete St. Peter's, designing the present apse, transepts, two bays of the nave, and the dome, in a style prophetic of the BAROQUE. Other buildings designed in Rome include additions to the Farnese Palace (1546), the structures on the Capitoline (1538–), the Porta Pia, and Santa Maria degli Angeli (1561). Michelangelo's last sculptures, the "Pietàs" in Florence cathedral (*c.* 1547) and the Castello Sforzesco in Milan (1552–64), embody his meditations on the preparation of his soul for death.

Bibliography: E. STEINMANN and R. WITTKOWER, *Michelangelo Bibliographie* (Leipzig 1927). C. DE TOLNAY, *Michelangelo* (Princeton 1943—). G. VASARI, *La vita di Michelangelo,* ed. P. BAROCCHI, 5 v. (Milan 1962).

[F. HARTT]

MICHIGAN, CATHOLIC CHURCH IN

One of the north central states of the United States, admitted to the Union in 1837 as the 26th state, Michigan

Archdiocese/Diocese	Year Created
Archdiocese of Detroit	1937
Diocese of Gaylord	1971
Diocese of Grand Rapids	1882
Diocese of Kalamazoo	1971
Diocese of Lansing	1937
Diocese of Marquette	1857
Diocese of Saginaw	1938

is composed of an upper (northern) and a lower (southern) peninsula, which are separated by the Straits of Mackinac, spanned by the great Mackinac Bridge, opened in 1957. Four of the five Great Lakes form a part of the boundary of the peninsulas. Lake Michigan separates the two peninsulas, forming the southern boundary of the upper and the western boundary of the lower. Lansing is the capital, and Detroit is the largest city. The Catholic population of the State of Michigan is 2,226,881 or 23 percent of the total population of 9,526,685 (as of January 2001). They are organized in seven dioceses: the Archdiocese of Detroit and the six suffragan sees: Grand Rapids, Lansing, Marquette, Saginaw, Gaylord, and Kalamazoo. At the beginning of the 21st century there were 803 parishes and 52 missions served by 1,090 diocesan priests, 403 religious order priests, 308 permanent deacons, 148 brothers, and 3,006 sisters. The state had two free-standing seminaries, seven Catholic colleges or universities, 26 Catholic hospitals, 54 Catholic high schools, and 296 Catholic grade schools.

Early History. The beginnings of the Catholic Church in Michigan date from the 17th century. In the fall of 1641 the French Jesuits Charles Raymbaut and Isaac Jogues visited the Chippewa Indians in the area later called Sault Sainte Marie in northern Michigan. Thirty years later, with headquarters at St. Ignatius mission, James Marquette, Gabriel Druillettes, and other Jesuits cared for the area surrounding the Straits of Mackinac that link Lakes Huron and Michigan. By 1679, when Robert Cavelier de La Salle and Louis Hennepin, OFM, explored the St. Joseph River and built a chapel at its mouth on Lake Michigan, priests had visited almost all parts of Michigan. Detroit itself was colonized in 1701 when Antoine Cadillac arrived from Montreal, Canada, on July 24, bringing with him a Franciscan and a Jesuit. A primitive chapel was built within Cadillac's Fort Ponchartrain, and resident priests served as chaplains. In 1708 construction of a church was begun; the parish register of St. Anne's received its first entry on July 17, 1722, signed by Rev. Bonaventure Liénard. During the following decades Jesuits, including Armand de la Richardie, arrived in Detroit for work among the native people, while the Franciscans continued to minister to the white settlers.

The surrender of Montreal to the British in 1760 marked the influx to Detroit of its first Protestant element, Irish, Scotch, and English traders, soldiers, and merchants. It also presaged a change in ecclesiastical jurisdiction for the missions of the area, which until then had been under the bishop of Quebec, Canada. With the independence of the 13 English colonies and the establishment of the United States, Rome named John Carroll prefect apostolic (1784) and then first bishop of Baltimore (1789), with authority over all Catholics in the new republic. Detroit raised the American flag in 1796, at about the time that St. Anne's received Rev. Michael Levadoux, the first pastor appointed by an American bishop. Two years later, Levadoux welcomed as assistants two Sulpician confreres, Jean Dilhet and Gabriel RICHARD, the latter succeeding to the pastorate of St. Anne's in 1802. Richard opened a seminary, a school for Native Americans, and an academy for girls. On Aug. 31, 1809, he printed the *Michigan Essay,* probably the only issue of the first paper in Michigan. He was one of the founders (1817) of the University of Michigan, Ann Arbor, of which he also served as vice-president and professor.

In 1808 the Michigan Territory was assigned to the new Diocese of Bardstown, Kentucky. When Bishop Benedict Joseph Flaget made his visitation in 1818, he erected six parishes in Detroit and resolved the difficulties that had prevented the erection of a new St. Anne's after the old structure had been leveled in the fire of 1805. Although it was first occupied in 1822, the church was not completed until Christmas 1828. To Bishop Edward Dominic Fenwick, who had been named ordinary of the new Diocese of Cincinnati (1821), with jurisdiction over the Michigan Territory, Richard reported in 1826 that there were 7,000 white Catholics in the territory and about 100 African Americans. They were served by eight priests, including Stephen BADIN at St. Joseph, Samuel MAZZUCHELLI, OP, at Mackinac Island and Green Bay, and Frederic BARAGA in the northwest sector and the upper peninsula. Although the majority of the Catholics were French settlers or native converts, the Irish were trickling into Wayne and Washtenaw counties, and in 1831 Rev. Patrick O'Kelly became their pastor in Northfield Township.

Diocese. On March 4, 1827, Leo XII named Detroit a diocese with Richard as its first ordinary, but his nomination was suppressed before the bull erecting the diocese was officially issued (March 20). Apparently, interventions by Fr. Stephen Badin and Fr. Frederic Résé gave Rome pause: the poor financial resources of the

Church in Detroit and that Richard had been imprisoned for defamation of character at one time for his excommunicating a local man who had divorced and was living with another woman. This situation of holding back the establishment of the diocese remained until Richard's death on Sept. 13, 1832. Within two weeks, Fenwick also was dead and the Church in Michigan was deprived of the leadership under which it had begun its growth.

Résé. On March 8, 1833, without reference to the action taken by Rome in 1827, Gregory XVI established Detroit as a diocese for the second time; Frederic Résé of Cincinnati became its first bishop and St. Anne's its first cathedral. The diocese embraced the present states of Michigan, Wisconsin, Iowa, Minnesota, and the portions of North and South Dakota east of the Mississippi. By 1838 Michigan's population had increased to 170,000; of these, between 20,000 to 24,000 were Catholics; 3,000, converted Native Americans; 8,000, English, Irish, German, and American; and the balance French. To help care for this flock, Résé had about 30 priests. As administrator of the Diocese of Cincinnati, he had brought the Poor Clares to Detroit in 1833, establishing the first convent and the first school for girls.

In 1835 Most Holy Trinity parish was established for the English-speaking Catholics, primarily the Irish. German immigrants settled in Clinton County in 1836, and within two years a resident priest was assigned to the community that became Westphalia. In Detroit, Rev. Martin KUNDIG was deputed to minister to the German Catholics, especially at the mission that became Assumption Grotto parish. Kundig also organized the Catholic Female Society in 1834 to assume responsibility for the poor and orphans made homeless by the cholera epidemic of 1834. He was appointed the town's superintendent of the poor and directed the county poor house, the infirmary, and the orphan asylum. The orphan asylum, financed solely by Catholic funds, represented the beginning of organized Catholic charity in Detroit.

Lefevere. Disputes with other bishops, mishandling of his oversight of the Poor Clares of Pittsburgh, a possible drinking problem, and unauthorized fund-raising in Europe were reasons for Résé's forced resignation in 1840. He remained bishop of Detroit but spent the rest of his life in Europe where he died in 1871. Peter Paul LEFEVERE, who had come to the Missouri missions from Belgium only eight years earlier, was named coadjutor and administrator of Detroit on July 23, 1841, and consecrated on November 22. During his 28-year episcopate, the diocese emerged from a pioneer settlement to a well-structured community capable of further development. The territory originally administered by Résé was divided first by the erection of the Diocese of Dubuque in 1837,

St. Florian's Church and surrounding neighborhood, Hamtramck, Michigan, 1978. (©James L. Amos/CORBIS)

then Milwaukee in 1843. The upper peninsula was made a vicariate in 1853, and Bishop Baraga established his see first at Sault Sainte Marie and then, in 1865, at Marquette.

Under Lefevere, Detroit's Catholic population increased to more than 150,000, the number of priests to 88, and churches to 80, with much of the growth across the southern tier of the state, in the Grand Rapids region, and around Saginaw. In 1843 five Sisters of the Holy Cross arrived to establish a school at Bertrand, near St. Joseph. In 1844 the Daughters of Charity began St. Vincent's Select School for girls in Detroit and in 1845 opened St. Vincent's, which five years later was moved to a new location and renamed St. Mary's, the first private hospital in the Northwest Territory to care for the mentally ill. In 1860 they opened St. Joseph's Retreat in present-day Dearborn, the first hospital in Michigan, and the second in the nation, to care exclusively for the mentally ill. In 1845, at his parish in Monroe, Rev. Louis Gillet, CSSR, worked with Mother Teresa Maxis Duchemin, and founded the Sisters, Servants of the Immaculate

Heart of Mary, one of the few native sisterhoods in the United States. Lefevere introduced into the diocese two other communities, the Religious of the Sacred Heart in 1851 and the School Sisters of Notre Dame the following year. In the same year four Brothers of the Christian Schools arrived to teach at St. Mary's. By 1874 approximately 38 parochial schools were operating in the diocese. The first diocesan regulations were issued under Lefevere, who convened the first diocesan synod in 1859.

Progress was made in Catholic journalism with the appearance on July 23, 1842, of the first number of the *Western Catholic Register,* the first newspaper under Catholic auspices since Richard's short-lived *Michigan Essay*. It was succeeded in 1853 by the *Detroit Catholic Vindicator*, which survived approximately six years. On Sept. 12, 1868, the *Western Catholic* appeared, in turn succeeded by the *Western Home Journal* in 1872. Eleven years later the paper was acquired by the diocese and was renamed the *Michigan Catholic*.

The preparatory seminary which Richard and Dilhet had attempted to establish at St. Anne's in 1804 was destroyed by fire. From 1846 to 1854, Lefevere conducted St. Thomas Seminary, probably in his own home, apparently abandoning it in favor of the American College at Louvain which, together with Bishop Martin Spalding of Louisville, he launched in 1857. Until Sacred Heart Seminary opened in 1919, the only other diocesan seminary was St. Francis in Monroe that operated from 1886 to 1889. In 1885 the cornerstone was laid for SS. Cyril and Methodius Seminary, Orchard Lake, for training young men for the service of Polish Catholics throughout the country. A new cathedral, SS. Peter and Paul, had been built in 1848 by Lefevere; he was buried there following his death on March 4, 1869.

Borgess. Caspar Henry BORGESS, chancellor of the Archdiocese of Cincinnati, Ohio, was installed as Detroit's third ordinary on May 8, 1870. The 18 years of his administration were marked primarily by a consolidation of diocesan gains. The great influx of German and Irish immigrants found national parishes already established. St. Wenceslaus was organized in 1871 for the Bohemians; in the same year St. Albertus became the first of many parishes to serve the great number of Polish immigrants who flocked to Detroit. St. Aloysius parish in downtown Detroit was established in 1873; it was made the procathedral in 1877, and SS. Peter and Paul was entrusted to the Jesuits, who also opened Detroit College (1877). It became the University of Detroit and in 1963 had the largest student enrollment of any Catholic college or university in the United States. Besides the Jesuits, four other religious communities of men entered the diocese: Franciscans, Capuchins, Holy Ghost Fathers, and Basilians; the Redemptorists returned after an absence of a few years. In 1874 the Little Sisters of the Poor arrived to take up their work among the aging. In 1879 the Sisters of St. Felix came from Warsaw, Poland, and three years later established provincial headquarters in Detroit; in 1936 they moved to nearby Livonia.

In the northwest sector of the lower peninsula, lumber and fertile land attracted so many people that between 1869 and 1883 the number of churches had increased from 13 to 32. In May 1882, the Holy See established the Diocese of Grand Rapids containing 39 counties, all but two north of a line from the southern extremity of Saginaw Bay to Lake Michigan. This reduced the Diocese of Detroit to 29 counties, an area of about 18,558 square miles, with 85 priests, 100,455 Catholics, and 42 parochial schools with 9,832 pupils. The Grand Rapids diocese contained about 50,000 Catholics served by about 40 priests. Ill health caused Borgess to resign in 1887; three years later he died in Kalamazoo, Michigan, where he was buried in St. Augustine's parish cemetery.

The upper peninsula Diocese of Marquette, first headed by Bishop Baraga, saw two fellow Slovenians succeed him, Ignatius Mrak (1869–78) and John Vertin (1879–99), both of whom sought to impose order on a very disparate diocese. Frederick Eis, the fourth Bishop of Marquette (1899–1922), held the diocese's second synod (1905). Henry Joseph Richter was the first Bishop of Grand Rapids (1883–1916). He established the initial institutions of this new diocese, including the Seminary of St. Joseph (1909). His coadjutor, Michael Gallagher, ordained in 1915, succeeded him (1916) until being transferred to Detroit in 1918.

Foley. John Samuel Foley of Baltimore, Maryland, was installed as successor to Borgess on Nov. 25, 1888. During his 30-year episcopate, the Catholic population increased to 386,000, largely because of the great waves of immigrants who settled principally in Detroit to work in the newly established automobile industry. In 1899 San Francisco, the first parish for Italians, was founded, and soon there were churches for the Slovaks, Lithuanians, Hungarians, and Rumanians, among others. In 1900 St. Patrick's Church was named the cathedral and in 1918 retitled SS. Peter and Paul.

Significant developments took place among religious communities. In 1891 the Sisters of St. Joseph were founded in Kalamazoo, Michigan, where they opened (1901) Borgess Hospital. The Sisters of St. Dominic, in Michigan since 1877 when they staffed a parish school in Traverse City, chose Adrian, Michigan, as the location of their provincial house (1892) and their motherhouse (1923). In 1910 the Sisters, Servants of the Immaculate Heart of Mary, founded St. Mary's College in Monroe;

they renamed it Marygrove in 1925 and two years later transferred it to a new site in Detroit. In 1906 the Cloistered Dominican Nuns established a convent, and the Sisters of Bon Secours their hospital in Detroit. In 1911 the Sisters of Mercy opened St. Joseph Mercy Hospital in Ann Arbor. When Foley died on Jan. 5, 1918, the diocese had 318 priests serving 246 churches and missions.

Gallagher. Bishop Michael James Gallagher of Grand Rapids was installed as bishop of Detroit in 1918 and immediately addressed himself to the problems of an expanding, polyglot population. Among the 105 new parishes he began, 33 were for Catholics speaking foreign languages. Parish schools more than doubled in number and enrollment. In 1919 Siena Heights College was established by the Dominican Sisters in Adrian; and Nazareth College opened in 1924 under the Sisters of St. Joseph. In 1919 Sacred Heart Seminary was founded, with high school and college departments training young men for the diocesan priesthood; the Gothic structure was ready for use in the fall of 1924. Retreat houses were built for laymen and women. The Diocesan Council of Catholic Men was started. A chancery office and a new St. Aloysius Church in downtown Detroit were erected. Hospitals multiplied: St. Francis, in Hamtramck; Mercywood Sanitarium, in Ann Arbor; St. Joseph's Mercy, in Pontiac; and Mercy, in Monroe. In the 1920s the Dominican Sisters of the Third Order of St. Dominic, Discalced Carmelite Nuns, and the Sylvestrine Benedictines established provincial headquarters in the diocese.

During the 1920s the Catholics of Michigan also struggled to protect their right to send their children to Catholic schools. In 1920 and 1924 they fought a state constitutional amendment that would oblige all children to attend public schools. When Gallagher died in 1937, more than 800 priests were ministering to 602,000 Catholics.

The Diocese of Grand Rapids experienced the same growth as Detroit. Edward Kelly, ordained as an auxiliary Bishop of Detroit in 1911, became the fourth bishop of Grand Rapids in 1919 and built many institutions. He was a leader, along with the Marquette and Detroit bishops in successfully defeating the 1920 and 1924 anti-Catholic school amendment campaigns. His successor, Joseph Pinten (1926–40), wisely paid off Kelly's bills, helping the diocese to survive the Depression better than most dioceses. Paul Nussbaum, the bishop of Marquette (1922–35), served while the upper peninsula experienced a serious post–World War I economic decline which has continued to this day. His successor, Joseph Plagens (1935–40), a Detroit auxiliary bishop, faced the added trial of a burned cathedral.

The state ecclesiastical scene changed on Aug. 3, 1937, when Detroit was made an archdiocese with Grand Rapids and Marquette as suffragan sees. The creation of Lansing the next day and of Saginaw on Feb. 26, 1938, raised the number of suffragans to four. Both new sees were industrial cities that experienced great growth, especially after the Second World War. Their bishops were primarily focused on establishing the institutions of a new diocese. Since the late 1960s they also experienced the same urban trials which beset Detroit. Marquette continued to struggle on, seeing under Bishop Thomas Noa (1947–68) a share in the state's postwar boom with the erection of many buildings and ecclesial institutions. After the dynamic leadership of Francis Haas, as the sixth bishop of Grand Rapids (1943–53), this diocese experienced the steady and competent leadership of several bishops up to the present.

The Archdiocese of Detroit, meanwhile, found itself not only a leader in the state hierarchy but a crucial diocese in the Church in the United States. This was more due to the archbishops who held this see than to the diocese itself: Edward Mooney (1937–58; cardinal in 1946), John Dearden (1958–80; cardinal in 1969), Edmund Szoka (1980–90; cardinal in 1988), and Adam Maida (1990– ; cardinal in 1994).

Two more suffragan sees were created on Dec. 19, 1970—Kalamazoo and Gaylord. The former has a Catholic population which is a very small percentage of the total population. The latter is serving an increasing resort population.

Michigan's economy in the last quarter of the 20th century experienced many challenges. This meant that the state population, including that of Catholics, did not increase as greatly as the rest of the country. Michigan Catholics successfully defeated a measure which would have allowed physician-assisted suicide in 1998, but twice were defeated in efforts to gain some state financial assistance for their schools (Proposition ''C'' in 1970 and the Voucher Proposal in 2000). As the Catholic Church in the State of Michigan enters the 21st century, she finds herself an established part of the religious, social, intellectual, and political scene but without the spirit that affected many in the Church as the labor unions, containing many Catholics, developed and exercised their power from the 1930s through the 1950s. The Church in the State of Michigan has experienced many parish-diocesan disputes, especially those based on some ethnic disagreement, and these have continued right up to the end of the 20th century. These have happened despite the suburbanization of many Catholics. The decline in clergy and the teachings of the Second Vatican Council have also seen the tremendous growth of lay involvement, especially professional lay training in theology and pastoral ministry. In all, the Catholic Church in Michigan has seen growth and decay, struggles and cooperation, population shifts and theological disputes, financial crises and stability. The greatest current trial is the shortage of clergy and vocations as the Church confronts the new century.

Bibliography: G. F. ANCONA, *Where the Star Came to Rest: Stories of the Catholic People in West Michigan* (Strasbourg 2001). G. B. CATLIN, *The Story of Detroit* (Detroit 1926). J. MCGEE, *The Catholic Church in the Grand River Valley, 1833–1950* (Grand Rapids 1950). J. K. JAMISON, *By Cross and Anchor: The Story of Frederic Baraga* (Paterson 1946). P. L. JOHNSON, *Stuffed Saddlebags: The Life of Martin Kundig, Priest* (Milwaukee 1942). G. MICHALEK, *Golden Jubilee: Diocese of Lansing Parish Historical Sketches* (Lansing 1987). G. W. PARÉ, *The Catholic Church in Detroit, 1701–1888* (Detroit 1951). A. REZEK, *History of the Diocese of Sault Ste. Marie and Marquette,* 2 v. (Chicago 1906). L. TENTLER, *Seasons of Grace: A History of the Catholic Archdiocese of Detroit* (Detroit 1990). F. B. WOODFORD and A. HYMA, *Gabriel Richard: Frontier Ambassador* (Detroit 1958).

[M. R. KELLY/F. X. CANFIELD/E. BOYEA]

MICROLOGUS

The medieval Latin word for ''epitome,'' indicating a manual that offers a synopsis or an explanation of some subject. The micrologus became a popular literary form in the Middle Ages, the *Micrologus de ecclesiasticis observationibus* (*Patrologia Latina,* 151:973–1072), by reason of its erudition, moderation, and influence (especially in German lands) probably being the most important single medieval commentary on the liturgy. This work, originally perhaps three separate treatises, contains 62 chapters: 1 to 23 treat of the celebration of Mass; 24 to 28 of the EMBER DAYS; 29 to 62 of the ecclesiastical year in general. Its purpose was to restore Roman liturgical observances throughout Europe. These observances are constantly commended, and appeal is repeatedly made to the authority of the ''ancient fathers,'' i.e., generally such popes as LEO I, GELASIUS I, and GREGORY I THE GREAT. Decisions of the Apostolic See regarding the liturgy are to be religiously obeyed, particularly those of GREGORY VII (d. 1085), who is mentioned with veneration. Dom. L. G. MORIN established convincingly that the *Micrologus* was written by BERNOLD OF CONSTANCE, a supporter of Gregory VII, and that it dates from a time between 1086 and 1100. Faced with the numerous and various prayers that had been added to the Mass books over three centuries, Bernold recommended that they be reduced to the fewest possible. He urged conformity with Rome on the date of the spring and summer Ember Days and set forth Roman norms for the correct correlation of the various parts of the Divine Office and of the Mass.

Bibliography: G. MORIN, ''Que l'auteur du Micrologue est Bernold de Constance,'' *Revue Bénédictine* 8 (1891) 385–395. S. BÄUMER, ''L'Auteur du Micrologue. . . ,'' *ibid.* 193–201; ''Der Micrologus ein Werk Bernolds von Konstanz,'' *Neues Archiv der Gesellschaft für ältere deutsche Geschichtskunde* 18 (1893) 429–446. V. L. KENNEDY, ''For a New Edition of the Micrologus of Bernold of Constance,'' *Mélanges. . . Michel Andrieu* (Strasbourg 1956) 229–241.

[F. COURTNEY]

MICY, ABBEY OF

Former Benedictine monastery of Saint-Mesmin, or St. Maximinus, near Orléans, Loiret, France, Diocese of Orléans. It was founded—according to suspect hagiography and charters—during the 6th century, by Euspicius and his nephew St. Maximinus (feast, December 15), the monastery's first abbot and patron saint. However, the earliest authentic document, a privilege of exemption from the *tonlieu* tax granted by Emperor Louis the Pious to Abbot Druсtsindus, dates from Jan. 8, 815. Bishop THEODULF OF ORLÉANS had successfully appealed, prior to 814, to BENEDICT OF ANIANE to introduce monks. These monks restored the observance of the BENEDICTINE RULE and very probably refounded the Abbey, which had declined after flourishing briefly in the 6th century and which had been pillaged by soldiers of CHARLES MARTEL. Subsequently, Micy was twice pillaged by Norman raiders (856 and 897), and then restored under its 10th-century abbots; it flourished materially from the 10th to the 13th century. The first history of Micy, written *c.* 985 by a monk, Letaldus, was the *Liber miraculorum s. Maximini* (*Patrologia Latina*, ed. J. P. Migne, 137:795–824). A monastic library of some consequence is believed to have existed there from the 9th century. The 11th-century three-naved Romanesque church, completed under Abbot Albert (1018–35), was replaced (*c.* 1225–50) by a larger Gothic structure. During the Hundred Years' War, Micy suffered greatly and was in large part destroyed by the English (1428) during the siege of Orléans. It was also pillaged by the Huguenots during the Wars of Religion (1562). Abbot François de LA ROCHEFOUCAULD in 1608 introduced the Feuillant CISTERCIANS, who occupied the monastery until its total destruction in 1792, during the French Revolution. Its last abbot, De Rastignac, was executed during the September massacres.

Bibliography: E. JAROSSAY, *Histoire de l'abbaye de Micy-Saint-Mesmin-lez-Orléans* (Orléans 1902) 502–1790. M. MANTITUS, *Geschichte der lateinschen Literatur des Mittelalters*, 3 v. (Munich 1911–31) 2:426–432. H. LECLERCQ, *Dictionnaire d'archéologie chrétienne et de liturgie*, ed. F. CABROL, H. LECLERCQ, and H. I. MARROU, 15 v. (Paris 1907–53) 11.1:912–927. L. H. COTTINEAU, *Répertoire topobibliographique des abbayes et prieurés*, 2 v. (Mâcon 1935–39) 2:1845–46. A. MERCATI and A. PELZER, *Dizionario ecclesastico*, 3 v. (Turin 1954–58) 3:666.

[G. E. GINGRAS]

MIDDLE AGES, THE

According to the conventions of modern historiography, part of the tripartite division of European (or Western) history into periods labelled ancient, medieval, and modern. The Middle Ages (a plural in English, Dutch, Russian, and Modern Icelandic, but a singular in other European languages; e.g. French, *le moyen age*; German, *das Mittelalter*; Italian, *il medioevo*) are usually considered to be the centuries from *c.* 500 A.D. to *c.* 1500 A.D., primarily in western Europe, but occasionally extended by comparativists to other parts of Eurasia as well. The period is often considered as having internal divisions—early and late, or early, high, and late. The term ''Middle Ages'' and its adjectival form, *medieval*, also have a common and usually disparaging meaning in colloquial and uninformed usage, sometimes as the *Dark Ages*, contrasted with the perceived glories of antiquity earlier and those of the *Renaissance* later. Current scholarship has challenged both the appropriateness of the term ''Middle Ages'' for the period and the conventional dating of its beginning and end, which had never been precise in any case. Many historians extend a period recently defined as *Late Antiquity* (*c.* 250–750) into the tenth century or later and some propose a ''long middle ages'' from around 1000 to 1800.

Origins and Early Usage of the Term and Concept. From the fourth to the fifteenth centuries writers of history thought within a linear framework of time derived from the Christian understanding of scripture—the sequence of Creation, Incarnation, and Christ's Second Coming and the Last Judgment. In *The City of God*, XXII, St. Augustine posited six ages of world history that paralleled the six days of creation and the six ages of the human lifespan, of which the sixth age of history was the period between the Incarnation and the Second Coming, and a seventh age, the reign of Christ on earth. All of Augustine's references to a ''middle time'' must be understood within this framework of salvation-history. Early interpretations of the scriptural Book of Daniel (Dn 2.31, 7.1), especially those of St. Jerome and the historian Paulus Orosius (*c.* 415), added the idea of four successive world empires, those of Babylon, Persia, and Greece, of which the fourth was that of Rome. Later writers in this tradition added the idea of the *translatio imperii*, the ''translation of the Empire'' from the Romans to the Franks under CHARLEMAGNE in 800, and then to the East Frankish emperors from OTTO I (962) until the Second Coming. The theory of the four monarchies was compatible with the Augustinian sequence. The great single exception to these ideas was the work of the late twelfth-century scriptural exegete JOACHIM OF FIORE, who posited three ages in human history, that of the Father, that of the Son, and a coming age of the Holy Spirit. But

Saint Bede. (British Library)

Joachim's view was also expressed in terms of SALVATION HISTORY.

In the fourteenth century, however, the literary moralist Francesco Petrarca (1304–1374), fascinated with Roman history and contemptuous of the time that followed it, including his own century, divided the past into *ancient* and *new*, antiquity and recent times, with the dividing line being the conversion of fourth-century Roman emperors to Christianity. According to Petrarca, what followed was an age of *tenebrae*, shadows, a ''sordid middle time,'' perhaps with the hope of a better age to follow. Although Petrarca's disapproval of the Christianized Roman and post-Roman world may seem irreligious, he was a devout Christian, and his judgment was based on aesthetic, moral, and philological criteria, not those of Christianity. Petrarca's limitless admiration for Rome and his contempt for his own and recent times heralded a novel conception of the European past and established other criteria for historical periodization besides those of salvation history or the history of the church and empire. Those who followed him focused primarily on the trans-

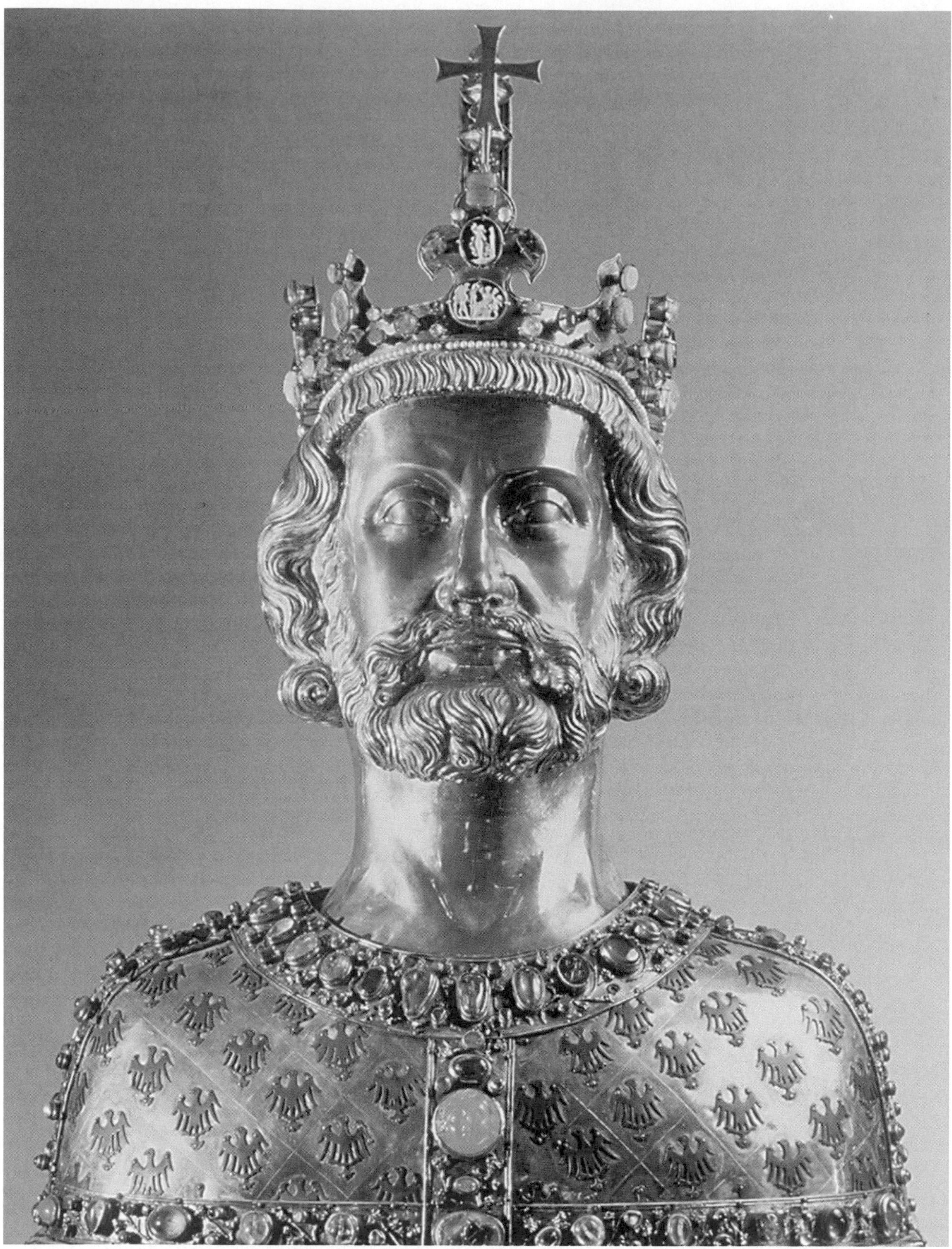

Reliquary bust of the Emperor Charlemagne. (©Gianni Dagli Orti/CORBIS)

formation of the arts and letters, seeing a renewal of earlier dignity and achievement in the age of Petrarca and the painter Giotto, continuing into the fifteenth and sixteenth centuries.

In the early sixteenth century religious critics and reformers, including both Desiderius ERASMUS and Martin LUTHER, added another dimension to the new conception and terminology—the idea of a ''true'' evangelical Christian church that had become corrupt when it was absorbed by the Roman empire and now needed to be reformed, or restored to its earlier apostolic authenticity. Thus, the historical dimension of both the Protestant Reformations and the Catholic Reformations of the sixteenth and seventeenth centuries added a sharply polemical religious interpretation to Petrarca's original conception, as church history was put to the service of confessional debate.

Petrarca's cultural successors, the literary humanists, also used varieties of the expression: *media tempestas* (Giovanni Andrea, Bishop of Aleria in a memorial on Nicholas of Cusa in 1469, directly quoted by later writers in 1493 and 1514) and *media antiquitas, media aetas, media tempora* (all between 1514 and 1530). In 1604 the political theorist and historian Melchior Goldast appears to have coined the variation *medium aevum*, and shortly after in a Latin work of 1610 the English jurist and legal historian John Selden repeated *medium aevum*, Englishing the term in 1614 to middle times and in 1618 to middle ages. As early as 1641 the French historian Pierre de Marca coined the French vernacular term *moyen âge*, which gained authority in the respected lexicographical work of Charles du Fresne, Seigneur du Cange, the *Glossarium ad scriptores mediae et infimae latinitatis* (1678), in which du Fresne emphasized the inferior quality of Latin linguistic usage after the fourth century. Other historians, including Gisbertus Voetius (*Exercitia et bibliotheca studiosi theologiae*, 1644) and Georg Horn (*De arca Noe*, 1666, and *Orbis politicus*, 1667) used such terms as *media aetas* in their histories of the church. The term and idea circulated even more widely in other historical works. Du Cange's great dictionary also used the Latin term *medium aevum*, as did the popular historical textbook by the Halle historian Christoph Keller (1638–1707) in 1688, *The Nucleus of Middle History between Ancient and Modern*, although Keller claimed that he was simply following the terminology of earlier scholars. By the late seventeenth century, *medium aevum* was the most commonly used term for the period in Latin and various versions of ''the middle ages'' in European vernacular languages.

The Enlightenment and Romanticism. During the seventeenth and eighteenth centuries a number of thinkers argued that western Europe after the fifteenth century had surpassed even antiquity in its discoveries and technology and created a distinctively modern world. Their historical views did nothing to change the image of the Middle Ages, however, and those views were sharpened by Enlightenment critics of earlier European political and religious structures. VOLTAIRE, in his *Essai sur les moeurs* of 1756, savaged both the Latin Christian and the reformed churches for their clerical obscurantism and earlier rulers for their ruthless and arbitrary uses of force. Edward Gibbon, whose great work *The Decline and Fall of the Roman Empire* ended with the fall of Constantinople to the Ottoman Turks in 1453, categorically attributed the beginning of that very long ''decline and fall'' to ''the triumph of barbarism and religion,'' thus contemptuously characterizing the entire period that followed.

But as Gibbon's own work showed, not only had the term and the often pejorative idea of the Middle Ages been shaped in the sixteenth and seventeenth centuries, but so had the critical, technical standards of modern historical scholarship. Some Enlightenment thinkers came to share the respect for and interest in the period that many conservative rulers, nobles, magistrates, and churchmen continued to express and to apply critical historical techniques to its investigation. The new scholarly interest was intensified by the work of historians imbued with national sentiment and a conception of historically ''ethnic'' communities in areas that often lacked a past (or had only a provincial or peripheral frontier-past) in the Greco-Roman world, especially in Germany and England. The medieval history and ancestry of nineteenth-century nation-states, their vernacular languages, art, literature, and surviving architectural monuments, indeed most elements of folk culture; and an emotional sympathy for (largely imaginary) features of the distant post-classical past produced in most Romantic historians, as in painters, poets, historical novelists, architects, composers, and their patrons and audiences, an affectionate and sentimentalized portrait of the Middle Ages, although that portrait was usually no more accurate than the polemical characterizations of Enlightenment rationalist sceptics.

Nor were all nineteenth-century historians appreciative of the period. Jules Michelet (1798–1874), the immensely popular and influential French historian, at first praised the Middle Ages as the birth of France, but by 1855 his increasing political liberalism led him to repudiate his earlier admiration in favor of emphasizing the France of the sixteenth century, virtually coining the term Renaissance in the process and appropriating it for France. In 1860 the Basel historian Jacob Burckhardt published his *Civilization of the Renaissance in Italy*, a work as widely read and influential as that of Michelet.

In spite of Romantic nostalgia and increasingly disciplined scholarship, in the late work of Michelet and the study of Burckhardt the opposition between the Middle Ages and the Renaissance was fixed in most modern usage, generally to the disadvantage of the former. These views were sharpened by nineteenth-century anticlericalism.

The Middle Ages in Modern Historiography. With the extraordinary growth of the academic discipline of history in the nineteenth century, the history of the Middle Ages was absorbed into departments of history in Europe and the United States and established in university curricula in both survey courses and research seminars. Journals of historical research began publication in Germany (1859), France (1876), England (1886), and the United States (1895), regularly including studies of one aspect or another of the Middle Ages. The editing and printing of historical documents and the writing of scholarly monographs brought the history of the Middle Ages into synchronization with other fields of history, as national history in European countries, but as more broadly pan-European, with a focus chiefly on English and French history rather than German after World War I, in the United States. The most influential monument to the new academic and professional history was the eight-volume collaborative *Cambridge Medieval History*, which appeared between 1911 and 1936. *The New Cambridge Medieval History* began to appear in 1998.

Although the teaching responsibilities of academic historians of the Middle Ages still generally reflect the original tripartite division of European history into ancient, medieval, and modern, most historians specialize in only very small parts of a very long period and are acutely aware of the need to subdivide it. With the emergence of Late Antiquity as a distinct research and teaching field following the stimulus of such early and mid-twentieth-century historians as the French scholar Henri-Irenée Marrou, the Austrian Alfons Dopsch, the Belgian Henri Pirenne, the Italian Arnaldo Momigliano, and the English historians Peter Brown and Robert Markus, the early part of the conventional Middle Ages is now being rethought and rewritten. With the emergence of various definitions of Early Modern History, as a result of the work of the Austrian Otto Brunner and the English Geoffrey Barraclough and others, older periodizations like the Middle Ages, Renaissance, Reformation, and Scientific Revolution are being subsumed into a period extending from the late thirteenth century to the eighteenth—the later end of the ''long middle ages.'' Specialized scholarly conferences, historical journals, and monograph series reflect these changes in the configuration of the period.

Scholars have also rethought the nature of change in different parts of Europe. Not only must they deal with the obvious differences between those lands in later Europe that had been part of the Roman Empire and those which had not, but also with the relations between the older Mediterranean world (large areas of which entered the Byzantine and Arab/Islamic cultural orbits—raising the question of comparison among the three cultures of the Mediterranean basin) and northern Europe. There is also the question of the pattern by which a culture with its heart in southern and western Europe gradually exported itself to the north and east, from Iceland to the Urals, often it seems, by a process closely approximating colonization, but a form of colonization that ended by slowly absorbing the colonies into an expanded mother-culture.

The Middle Ages will not disappear as a term, concept, or curricular subject from either colloquial or academic usage in the foreseeable future, but the history of the term and the current debate about its temporal and spatial application and appropriateness as a component of European history is a reminder that historical periods are cultural and social constructs, that human life changes often rapidly within labeled periods, however designated, and that the dialogue between continuity and change is the historian's primary intellectual activity.

Chronology. Regardless of the loaded aesthetic, linguistic, confessional, and philosophical origins of the term, the label ''Middle Ages'' is in any case misleading, because however one defines its chronology, its content is the emergence of a distinctive European civilization out of a region originally on the periphery of the Hellenistic-Roman Mediterranean civilization of antiquity. Although European civilization appropriated elements of both Greco-Roman antiquity and Judeo-Christian (especially the Christian interpretation of Jewish) religion and ethics, the emergence of Europe paralleled the division of the ancient Mediterranean ecumenical world into the civilizations of Byzantium, or East Rome, and Islam. Three sibling civilizations, two of them Christian, emerged at around the same time, and the influence of Eurasian history on that of Europe has recently attracted the attention of historians. But such change does not occur in a single year and not even in a single century, and to assign any but an approximate date to the beginning or end of the Middle Ages, as was once the fashion, is pointless. Far more important is the assessment of change in different periods between the third and the sixteenth centuries.

In one respect, that of dating, the Middle Ages introduced the dating of the Common Era, when the eighth-century English computist St. BEDE adapted the practice first used by DIONYSIUS EXIGUUS in the fifth century of dating history *Anno Domini*, ''in the year of the Lord.''

Bede's practice was taken up by Frankish chroniclers and rulers from the late eighth century on. Within the year, a universal Christian calendar also slowly displaced the older Roman calendar, with the month surviving from Roman usage and the week from Jewish, displacing the older Roman kalends, ides, and nones.

Rome, Latin Christianity, and the European Provinces. The Roman empire that gradually faded in the west during and after the fifth century (although its language, memory, Christianity, and many institutions survived) was no longer the empire of Augustus, nor was it the empire of Marcus Aurelius. Internal and external crises during the third and fourth centuries had resulted in the division of the empire into an eastern and western part after 285, with the east possessing far more material, political, and military resources and a great city as its capital, Constantinople. The entire empire was restructured to finance immense military expenditure, giving the European provinces and frontier areas greater importance.

The western part, the capital of which moved north from Rome to a number of cities, including Trier, Arles, and Milan, and ultimately to Ravenna, became less urbanized, more ruralized, and gradually dominated by an aristocracy of landowners and military officials. After 375, a series of composite peoples, many of them only recently assembled, ruled by their own political and military elites, assumed control of a number of western provinces, often in the name of the Roman emperor and with the cooperation of Roman provincials. Many of these Romans were Christian higher clergy. The term catholic (''universal'') Christianity was originally used as a term to authenticate a normative Christian cult on the grounds of its universality and to characterize different beliefs and practices as heterodox on the grounds that they were merely local and reflected neither duration, unanimity nor universality. The normative Christianity of the empire gradually became the Christianity of Europe's new local rulers. Within that coherence, however, many of the new kings and peoples based their claims to legitimacy on their own local versions of Latin Christianity, expressed in law, ritual, saints' cults, and sacred spaces. If the older empire and the new, non-imperial lands in Europe into which a new culture expanded came to call itself *Christianitas*, ''Christendom,'' it was in practice divided into what a recent historian has called many self-contained ''micro-Christendoms.''

The new kings ruled as much in Roman style as they could, issuing laws written in Latin, coins that imitated imperial coinage, and sponsoring ''ethnic'' and genealogical histories that attributed to themselves and their peoples, however recently assembled, an identity and antiquity rivaling that of Rome. Although Romans had long despised the term *rex*, ''king,'' they considered it suitable for the rulers of *gentes*, ''tribes,'' who had not reached the level of the Romans, who called their own society a *populus*, a ''people.'' Some of these kingdoms, especially that of the VISIGOTHS in Iberia, also modelled themselves on the Hebrew kingdom as described in scripture, borrowing and adapting some ancient Jewish ritual—such as anointing the ruler with oil and liturgically reminding him that he was God's servant, with responsibilities as well as powers. The kings and aristocracies of landowners ruled subjects both slave and free, most of them ruralized, as cities shrank and the need for them except as royal residences or capitals or as seats of bishops, decreased. As these cultures spread throughout western Europe during the fifth to eighth centuries, they reached areas that the empire had never ruled, initially Ireland, then northern Britain, the lower Rhineland, and trans-Rhenish Europe, influencing political and religious change in these areas as well.

The Mandate for Conversion. The process of expansion was also driven by a missionary mandate: the conversion of all peoples, no longer only those of the Empire, to Christianity, carried out independently by bishops, monks, and holy men (the bishop and the monk were two of the most remarkable religious and social inventions of late antiquity—the barbarian kingdoms were a third), and by Greek Christians from Constantinople as well as by missionaries from the new kingdoms and the bishops of Rome. The model of conversion of both religious belief and practice was collective—that of a ruler and his followers together as a new Christian people, integrating rulership with clerical teaching and the development of liturgy, with the definition of sacred space, control of sanctity, and the rituals surrounding key moments in human life, extending to death and burial. As Roman and non-Roman peoples assimilated during the sixth and seventh centuries, non-Romans gradually became Christian clergy themselves, and frequently saints. The conversion of Ireland in the late fifth century brought the particularly Irish ascetic practice of self-exile to bear on missionary work

Although the bishops of Rome enjoyed great respect and veneration because of the antiquity of their see, its historical orthodoxy, the relics of its martyrs (including both Peter and Paul), and the imperial and Christian history of the city of Rome, the material conditions of the sixth and seventh centuries greatly limited any papal exercise of universal authority or influence and developed relatively little theory about them. The Christian clergy preserved a literate Latin culture based on the text and understanding of scripture in several Latin versions, the writings of the Church Fathers, the legislation of Church councils, and the idea of tradition, which states that the authority of the Apostles had been passed down (Latin, *traditio*) to the Christian higher clergy, particularly to the bishops.

During the seventh and eighth centuries, new invasions in the east and the emergence of Islam, first in the Arab world and then west into Egypt and Numidia and east into Persia, divided the old Mediterranean ecumenical world into three distinct culture-zones, the sibling worlds of East Rome, or Byzantium, that of Islam, and that of Latin Europe. Byzantium and western Europe remained long on the defensive against Islamic pressures, which extended to the conquest of the Iberian Peninsula in 711, Sicily in 902, and Anatolia in the eleventh century.

The Frankish Adventure. In western Europe, the FRANKS established a strong monarchy under CLOVIS in the early sixth century. Although the Frankish kingdom was divided under Clovis's successors, it was reunited under the lordship, then monarchy (after 751) under PEPIN II and his successors, Charles MARTEL, PEPIN III, and Charlemagne (768–814), bringing much of the continent under Frankish control and establishing diplomatic relations with Britain, Iberia, Rome, Constantinople, and even with Harun al-Rashid, the great caliph of Baghdad. As each of these three cultures constructed a distinctive character based on different uses of and attitudes toward the older Roman-Mediterranean ecumenical past, they maintained diplomatic and commercial contact, sometimes on a much-reduced scale, and continued to influence each other culturally even as they became more distinctively individualized.

The world of Charlemagne and his successors also patronized a vast project of what it called *correctio*—restoring a fragmented western European world to an earlier idealized condition—by patronizing monastic studies, attempting to standardize monastic practice and rules of life, insisting on high clerical standards, adopting and disseminating standard versions of canon law and the liturgy, and maintaining a regular network of communications throughout. In 800, Pope LEO III crowned Charlemagne emperor of the Romans, a title that his successors also adopted. Historians still debate whether these developments indicated a backward-looking, last gasp of the older world of late antiquity or a new organization of then elements of what later became Europe.

In the ninth and tenth centuries a series of new invasions from Scandinavia, the lower Danube Valley, and North Africa greatly weakened the late Carolingian world. Its military needs were met by both kings and powerful lords with armies of private followers. Although two kinds of invaders—the Scandinavians and Hungarians—became assimilated and Christianized over the next several centuries, the Islamic world remained apart, extending from Iberia and Morocco eastwards to the western edges of China and southeast Asia. But in the case of western Europe, these were the last outside invasions until the allied landings in 1944—making western Europe the only part of the world that remained free of outside invasions for nearly one thousand years. Europe could increase demographically, improve materially, and engage in cultural and commercial reciprocity and technology transfer with its parallel civilizations, but after the tenth century it no longer needed to defend itself against them.

The Demographic, Agricultural, and Urban Takeoff. Historians disagree about the extent of the social and material damage caused by the ninth- and tenth-century invasions, but there is little disagreement that shortly after the end of the tenth century, perhaps earlier, signs of demographic growth are clearly visible, as are signs of a reorganization of both lordship and labor in which an order of experienced and determined warriors concentrated the control of land in its own and its dynasty's hands and coerced a largely free peasantry into subjection to it. Thus did the idea of the three orders of society—those who pray, those who fight, and those who labor—come into use to describe the results of the ascendance of the landholding aristocracy and its clerical partners. In co-operation with ecclesiastical establishments, particularly great monastic foundations like CLUNY, and with bishops, the nobility of the late eleventh and twelfth centuries established the agrarian basis of the urbanizing process, also well underway in the eleventh century.

Reform and Renewal. At the same time movements for ecclesiastical reform focused on a redefinition of clerical and lay identities, emphasizing clerical celibacy, clerical freedom from dependence on the laity, and the *libertas* of the Church to accomplish its divinely-ordained mission. By the middle of the eleventh century, these movements reached Rome itself, where a line of reform-minded popes, beginning with LEO IX (1049–1054) and continuing with GREGORY VII (1073–1085) and URBAN II (1088–1099) placed the papal office at the head of reform, while articulating a systematic claim to papal authority over both clergy and, in many matters, laity as well.

The emotional intensity of ecclesiastical reform led to outbursts of religious enthusiasm both in favor and against, and one of the most significant results was the military expedition that captured Jerusalem in 1099 and established for a century the Latin Kingdom of Jerusalem, an expedition much later called the First Crusade (*see* CRUSADES).

The reform movement of the eleventh and twelfth centuries produced an independent clerical order, hierarchically organized under the popes, which claimed both a teaching authority (*magisterium*) and a disciplinary authority based on theology and canon law that regulated much of lay and all of clerical life, defined orthodoxy and heterodoxy, expressed itself through a series of energetic church councils from 1123 to the Fourth LATERAN COUNCIL in 1215, and greatly enhanced both the ritual and legal authority of the popes. At the same time, new devotional movements led to both outbursts of dissent (with new forms of ecclesiastical discipline devised to control them) and equally passionate expressions of orthodox devotion. In particular, the Order of Friars Minor, founded by the layman FRANCIS OF ASSISI to administer to the spiritual needs of the cities, spread widely and rapidly, as did the Order of Preachers, founded by the canon of Osma, Domingo de Guzman (1170–1221). These and other devotional movements were supported by Pope INNOCENT III (1189–1216) and his successors. The movement of reform and renewal also witnessed the expression of devotion in new, large churches, pilgrimage and crusade, the increase in Marian devotion and that of the crucified, rather than the regal Jesus. Commenting on scripture grew from the early contemplative monastic style to the investigative techniques and speculative theology of the new schools.

During the twelfth century clerical teaching authority was articulated in the new universities, distinctive corporate institutions that had begun with the teaching of law at Bologna and the teaching of the arts and theology at Paris, later spreading the model to Oxford and other centers of learning. With the foundation of the University of Prague in 1348, the model crossed the Rhine river for the first time.

The Territorial Monarchies. During the conflicts over reform in the late eleventh and early twelfth centuries, the office of emperor lost much of its religious character, although several twelfth- and thirteenth-century emperors reasserted their authority by means of Roman law and energetically applied lordship. But the most successful rulers of the twelfth and thirteenth centuries were, first, individual lords who created compact and thoroughly governed principalities, and second and most important, kings who asserted their authority over that of the princes, although often with princely cooperation. The monarchies of England, France, León-Castila, Aragon, Portugal, and elsewhere all acquired their fundamental shape and character in the twelfth century. Although the Mongol invasions wreaked havoc on eastern Europe in the thirteenth century, the west was spared them, and not until the expansion of the Ottoman Turkish empire in the late fourteenth and fifteenth centuries did the eastern borders of Christian Europe undergo a greater threat, one that lasted until the Treaty of Carlowitz in 1699.

In the twelfth century too, literary vernacular languages emerged from under the protective umbrella of Latin, and history-writing took particular kings and peoples as its subjects rather than universal salvation-history, or else it relocated these in salvation-history in lively and novel ways. The territorial monarchies were supported by a larger and larger bureaucracy, new techniques of public finance, increasingly expensive warfare, and the political identity of kings and peoples. Following the papal model in both their formal documentation and their establishment of diplomatic relations with each other, these states represented something quite new in world history, incorporating both clergy and laity under vigorous royal dynasties. The later states of Europe, as well as their political theory and constitutional structure, grew out of the Italian city-republics and territorial monarchies of the twelfth and thirteenth centuries.

Crisis and Recovery. The process of rural and urban expansion and development paused in the fourteenth century as famine, epidemic disease, intensified and prolonged warfare, and financial collapse brought growth to a halt and reduced the population for a time to around a half of the 70 million people who inhabited Europe in 1300. But the resources that had created the Europe of the twelfth and thirteenth century survived these crises. It is the resiliency of Europe, not its weakness, that explains the patterns of recovery in the late fourteenth and fifteenth centuries. That recovery continued through the sixteenth and seventeenth centuries.

The missionary mandate reached out across Mongol-dominated Asia as far east as China, where a Christian bishop took up his seat at Beijing in 1309. The Mongol opening of Eurasia relocated Europe in the minds of its inhabitants. Improved maritime techniques in both navigation and marine engineering led Europeans from the thirteenth century on to cross and map first, the local seas, and then the Atlantic and Pacific. From the late fifteenth century Europe began to export itself once more, as it once had to the north and east from the tenth to the fifteenth centuries, this time over vast oceans and to other continents than Eurasia.

Neither the crises of the fourteenth century nor the voyages and discoveries of the fifteenth suggest a fatigued and exhausted Europe. On the contrary, the resiliency and capacity for innovation of fourteenth- and fifteenth-century Europe, the determined and often confident search for salvation among ordinary people leading ordinary lives, even the inability of governments to weigh down their subjects without fierce displays of resistance, all indicate the strength of that European society and culture that men and women had shaped from the eighth century on.

Bibliography: Terminology and periodization. G. GORDON, *Medium Aevum and the Middle Age* (S.P.E. Tract No. XIX; Oxford 1925). T. E. MOMMSEN, ''Petrarch's Conception of the 'Dark Ages,''' *Speculum* 17 (1942): 226–242, rpt. in T. E. MOMMSEN, *Medieval and Renaissance Studies* (Ithaca 1959) 106–129. D. HAY, *Annalists and Historians: Western Historiography from the Eighth to the Eighteenth Centuries* (London 1977). D. HAY, ''Flavio Biondo and the Middle Ages,'' *Renaissance Essays* (London-Ronceverte 1988) 19–34. F. C. ROBINSON, ''Medieval, the Middle Ages,'' *Speculum* 59 (1984) 745–756. H. DIETRICH KAHL, ''Was bedeutet 'Mittelalter'?'' *Speculum* 40 (1989) 15–38. L. GATTO, *Viaggio intorno al concetto di medioevo: Profilo di storia della storiografia medievale* (4th ed. Rome 1995). C. VAN DE KIEFT, ''La periodisation de l'histoire du moyen âge,'' in C. PERELMAN, ed., *Les catégories en histoire* (Brussels 1969) 41–56. W. A. GREEN, ''Periodization in European and World History,'' *Journal of World History* 3 (1992) 13–53. H.-W. GOETZ, ''Das Problem der Epochengrenzen und die Epoche des Mittelalters,'' in *Mittelalter und Moderne. Entdeckung und Rekonstruction der mittelalterlichen Welt,* ed. P. SEGL (Sigmaringen 1997) 163–172. D. R. KELLEY, *Foundations of Modern Historical Scholarship: Language, Law, and History in the French Renaissance* (New York-London, 1970). L. GOSSMAN, *Medievalism and the Ideologies of the Enlightenment: The World and Work of La Curne de Sainte-Palaye* (Baltimore 1968). J. LE GOFF, ''The Several Middle Ages of Jules Michelet,'' *Time, Work, and Culture in the Middle Ages*, tr. A. GOLDHAMMER (Chicago 1980) 3–28. J. HEERS, *Le Moyen Âge, une imposture* (Paris 1992). C. AMALVI, *Le goût du moyen âge* (Paris 1996). T. REUTER, ''Medieval: Another Tyrannous Construct?'' *The Medieval History Journal* 1 (1998) 25–45, and other articles in the same number. L. VARGA, *Das Schlagwort vom 'finsteren Mittelalter'* (Vienna 1932). K. ARNOLD, ''Das 'finstere' Mittelalter. Zur Genese und Phänomenologie eines Fehlurteils,'' *Saeculum* 32 (1981) 287–300. G. W. BOWERSOCK, P. BROWN, O. GRABAR, eds., *Late Antiquity: A Guide to the Postclassical World* (Cambridge, MA 1999). J. TOLLEBEEK, '''Renaissance' and 'Fossilization': Michelet, Burckhardt, and Huizinga,'' *Renaissance Studies* 15 (2001) 354–366. E. PITZ, *Der Untergang des Mittelalters* (Berlin 1987). D. GERHARD, *Old Europe: A Study of Continuity, 1000–1800* (New York-London 1981). J. LE GOFF, ''For an Extended Middle Ages,'' *The Medieval Imagination* (Chicago-London, ,) 18–23. H. KAMINSKY, ''From Lateness to Waning to Crisis: The Burden of the Later Middle Ages''' *Journal of Early Modern History* 4 (2000) 85–125. Other works. *The New Cambridge Medieval History,* 7 v. (Cambridge 1998–2002). *The Dictionary of the Middle Ages,* ed. J. R. STRAYER, 13 v. 1(982–1989). *The Encyclopedia of the Middle Ages,* ed. A. VAUCHEZ et al., 2 v. (1997–2000). R. L. STOREY, *Chronology of the Medieval World 800–1491* (New York 1973). P. BROWN, *The Rise of Western Christendom: Triumph and Diversity AD 200–1000* (Malden-Oxford 1996). P. GEARY, *Before France and Germany: The Creation and Transformation of the Merovingian World* (New York-Oxford 1988). R. MCKITTERICK, ed., *The Early Middle Ages* (Oxford-New York 2001). R. W. SOUTHERN, *The Making of the Middle Ages* (New Haven 1953). R. I. MOORE, *The First European Revolution, c. 970–1215* (Malden-Oxford 2000). R. BARTLETT, *The Making of Europe: Conquest, Colonization and Cultural Change, 950–1350* (Princeton 1993). M. COLISH, *Medieval Foundations of the Western Intellectual Tradition* (New Haven 1997). J. H. MUNDY, *Europe in the High Middle Ages 1150–1300* (3d ed. New York-London 2000). T. A. BRADY, H. A. OBERMAN, and J. D. TRACY, eds., *Handbook of European History, 1400–1600: Late Middle Ages, Renaissance, and Reformation,* 2 v. (Leiden-New York 1994). D. NICHOLAS, *The Transformation of Europe 1300–1600* (London-New York 1999). R. N. SWANSON, *Religion and Devotion in Europe, c. 1215–c.1515* (Cambridge 1995). B. TIERNEY, *Religion, Law, and the Growth of Constitutional Thought, 1150–1650* (Cambridge 1982).

[E. PETERS]

MIDDLE EAST COUNCIL OF CHURCHES (MECC)

The general ecumenical awakening of the early twentieth century inspired the churches of the Middle East to search for ways to heal centuries-old quarrels and find opportunities for collaboration. The Ecumenical Patriarch Yoachim III raised the issue of Christian unity and encouraged the spirit of reconciliation. The Protestant missions formed a fellowship of 36 Protestant agencies called the Near East Christian Council in 1956. Early contacts between the Near East Christian Council and the Oriental Orthodox Churches blossomed into full collaboration in 1962 when some of these Oriental Orthodox Churches joined the Protestant Churches to form the Near East Council of Churches (NECC). In turn, NECC conducted negotiations with the Eastern Orthodox Churches, and in 1974 the Middle East Council of Churches (MECC) was born. Adopting the ''Family'' system, the original MECC comprised three Families: Protestant-Evangelical, Oriental Orthodox, and Eastern Orthodox. The seven Catholic Churches of the Middle East were initially invited as observers, and after about 15 years of dialogue, they joined the MECC at its fifth General Assembly in 1990, bringing its membership to four Families.

Five themes summarize the objectives of MECC: (1) strengthening a sense of unity, (2) encouraging mutual support among the churches, (3) cultivating mutual respect and understanding, (4) nurturing the spirit of *diakonia*, (5) fostering collaboration among the member churches and between them and churches elsewhere.

A General Assembly meeting every four years gives the Council its basic orientations. There is also a Council of Presidents consisting of four members. A 24-member Executive Committee meets once or twice a year. The General Secretariat, which comprises the General Secretary and three Associates, organizes programs dealing with human rights and Christian-Muslim dialogue. Three program units: (i) Faith and Unity, which deals with ecumenical concerns, (ii) Life and Service, which offers relief and developmental services, and (iii) Education and Renewal, implement the mandate of the Council at the grassroots level. Two remaining program units deal with communication and finance. All four Families are equally represented at all levels of the Council structure, independently of the number of their faithful.

Since its inception, the MECC has served as a platform for ecumenical dialogue in the region, contributing significantly to the improvement of relations among the churches of the area and with other ecumenical organizations in the world at large. Its various ''diakonal'' programs and emergency relief services have alleviated significantly the suffering of the people in the Middle East, especially refugees and underprivileged. In addition, it also highlights human right issues and collaborates with other organizations to improve Muslim-Christian relations.

[P. N. SAYAH]

MIDDLEMORE, HUMPHREY, BL.

Carthusian priest, vicar of London Charterhouse, martyr; b. Edgbaston, Warwickshire, England; d. hanged, drawn, and quartered at Tyburn (London), June 19, 1535. Humphrey, the son of Thomas Middlemore and Ann Lyttleton of Pillaton Hall, was born into one of the oldest families in the county. Although little is known of his life, it is certain that he was a man of piety and learning who was appointed as procurator for the London Charterhouse after his profession.

In 1534 Henry VIII sought the express acknowledgment from the Carthusians and other prominent subjects of the validity of his marriage to Anne Boleyn and the right of their children to succeed to the throne. When John HOUGHTON, the prior, and Middlemore refused to sign the Oath of Succession, they were imprisoned in the Tower of London. A month later they were permitted to take the oath conditionally (''so far as the law of God allows''), and released.

The following year Fr. John was executed for refusing to take the new oath of supremacy, leaving Fr. Humphrey as the vicar of the Charterhouse. Henry again attempted to persuade the monks to support him by assigning Thomas Bedyll, one of the royal commissioners, to argue with the monks against papal supremacy. When they remained unmoved, Thomas Cromwell authorized the arrest of Middlemore and his monks BB. Sebastian NEWDIGATE and Blessed William EXMEW. They were cruelly treated in prison: bound to posts with chains round their necks and legs for two weeks without relent. Nevertheless they refused to take the oath when brought before the Privy Council, and went so far as to ably support their position by reference to Scripture and the Fathers. They were accordingly condemned to death.

All three monks were beatified by Pope Leo XIII on Dec. 9, 1886.

Feast of the English Martyrs: May 4 (England); May 11 (with Newdigate in the Archdiocese of Birmingham).

See Also: ENGLAND, SCOTLAND, AND WALES, MARTYRS OF.

Bibliography: R. CHALLONER, *Memoirs of Missionary Priests,* ed. J. H. POLLEN (rev. ed. London 1924; repr. Farnborough 1969). J. MORRIS, ed., *The Troubles of Our Catholic Forefathers Related by Themselves* (London 1872), I. J. H. POLLEN, *Acts of English Martyrs* (London 1891). E. M. THOMPSON, *The Carthusian Order in England* (New York 1930).

[K. I. RABENSTEIN]

MIDDLETON, ANTONY, BL.

Priest and martyr; b. Middleton-Tyas, North Riding, Yorkshire, England; d. hanged, drawn, and quartered at Clerkenwell (London), May 6, 1590. Antony was nobly born to Ambrose Middleton of Barnard Castle, Durham, and his wife Cecil Crackenthorpe of Howgill Castle, Westmoreland. He studied theology at the English College, Rheims, France, from 1582 until his ordination on May 30, 1586. He ministered successfully in the environs of London until his arrest in Clerkenwell and execution as a priest. He was beatified Pius XI on Dec. 15, 1929.

Feast of the English Martyrs: May 4 (England).

See Also: ENGLAND, SCOTLAND, AND WALES, MARTYRS OF.

Bibliography: R. CHALLONER, *Memoirs of Missionary Priests,* ed. J. H. POLLEN (rev. ed. London 1924; repr. Farnborough 1969), I, 168–69. J. H. POLLEN, *Acts of English Martyrs* (London 1891).

[K. I. RABENSTEIN]

MIDDLETON, ROBERT, BL.

Priest, martyr; b. 1571, at York, England; d. ca. April 3, 1601, hanged, drawn, and quartered at Derby. Born into a Catholic family, he appears to have practiced as an Anglican for a time, but he was reconciled to the Church, perhaps because of the martyrdom of St. Margaret CLITHEROW, née Middleton (d. 1586). In 1594, he began seminary studies at Rheims and then Seville before transferring to the English College in Rome (1597), where he was ordained (1598). He labored in Lancaster for two years. In 1599 Middleton wrote a letter to Jesuit superior Henry GARNET requesting admittance into the Society of Jesus; it is unknown whether Middleton ever received the response informing him of his acceptance, for on Sept. 30, 1600, he was arrested while riding from Preston to Fulde in Lancashire. A rescue attempt was made but failed, leading to the apprehension of Bl. Thurston HUNT also. During questioning Middleton acknowledged the authority of the queen in temporal matters and said that he prayed God would one day make her a Catholic. Middleton and Hunt were condemned in March 1601 for their priesthood and beatified by Pope John Paul II on Nov. 22, 1987 with George Haydock and Companions.

Feast: Dec. 1 (Jesuits); May 4 (Feast of the English Martyrs).

See Also: ENGLAND, SCOTLAND, AND WALES, MARTYRS OF.

Bibliography: R. CHALLONER, *Memoirs of Missionary Priests,* ed. J. H. POLLEN (rev. ed. London 1924). J. H. POLLEN, *Acts of English Martyrs* (London 1891). J. N. TYLENDA, *Jesuit Saints & Martyrs* (Chicago 1998), 87–88.

[K. I. RABENSTEIN]

MIDDLETON, THOMAS COOKE

Historian; b. Philadelphia, Pa., March 30, 1842; d. Villanova, Pa.; Nov. 19, 1923. He was the oldest of the nine children of Joseph and Lydia (Cooke) Middleton. The Middletons were Quakers before the family was received into the Catholic Church in April 1854. Thomas studied at Villanova College (later University) from 1854 to 1858, when he was sent to the Augustinian novitiate at Tolentino, Italy. He made his vows there on Oct. 10, 1859. After completing his theology in San Agostino in Rome, he was ordained at the Basilica of the Holy Savior (Basilica of St. John Lateran), on Sept. 24, 1864. He returned to the U.S. in 1865 and was assigned to Villanova College, where he remained for the next 58 years. Between 1866 and 1914 he was professor, vice president, and president (1876–78) of the college, prior of the monastery, counselor (definitor) and regent of studies for the American province, and associate and secretary to the provincial. In 1884 he was one of the founders of the American Catholic Historical Society of Philadelphia; he served from then until 1890 as its president. From 1899 to 1905 he was director of the society's publications and editor of its journal, *Records of the American Catholic Historical Society.* A partial list of his writings includes his *Historical Sketch of Villanova* (1893), *Augustinians in the United States* (1909), articles on Augustinian hagiography, accounts of prominent churchmen, descriptions of Philadelphia churches, and lives of priests of his order. His papers, now in the archives of Villanova University, exemplify his contribution to Augustinian and Pennsylvania historiography.

[M. P. HOGAN]

MIDRASH

A common term in Jewish literature for a homiletic discussion of a text of Sacred Scripture for the purpose of applying the text to a present situation. In this article the usage of the word, the characteristics of midrash, types of midrash, and examples of it will be treated.

Usage of the Word. The Hebrew noun *midrāš* occurs three times in the OT: in two Chr 13.22 and 24.27 as the title of a literary work of unknown nature, and in Sir 51.23, where the term, *bêt midrāš,* ''house of study, school,'' occurs for the first time, if the reading is genuine. In the Qumran literature published to date, the term *midrāš* means ''juridical investigation'' as well as ''study'' and ''interpretation [of the Scriptures],'' and is used also as a title for a work of Biblical interpretation. In the subsequent rabbinic literature the word *midrāš* was used almost exclusively in the sense of ''Biblical interpretation'': (1) a single comment on a Biblical text was called a *midrāš,* as well as a collection of such interpretations (plural: *midrāšîm*); (2) from the 3d century A.D. onward, with the increasing interest in the plain sense (*p^{e}šaṭ*) of Scripture, the term midrash also came to signify the earlier, predominantly homiletic exegesis as distinguished from the later scientific exegesis, and thus midrash sometimes designates that Biblical interpretation that seeks to go beyond the literal sense to find hidden and more profound senses of Scripture (*see* HERMENEUTICS, BIBLICAL). The word midrash has modernly come to designate a literary form and is thus used as a technical term to describe rabbinic exegetical literature of the 2d to 13th century A.D. (*see* MIDRASHIC LITERATURE) and material in earlier Jewish literature and the NT that manifests similar characteristics.

Characteristics of Midrash. A midrash's primary focus is on a Biblical text. Its purpose is homiletic, i.e., practical and religious, rather than speculative. It seeks to make the text relevant here and now. It sees in the text the Word of God as valid and meaningful for every age and attempts to point out its implications for the present. Midrashic discussion is free; it may be based on the literal sense or it may make applications never intended by the original author.

Types of Midrash. Based on content, midrash is divided by the Jews into HALAKAH (legal discussions of the Bible) and HAGGADAH (nonlegal, didactic exposition). A third classification, pesher, has been suggested recently to provide a category for the Biblical commentaries (*p^{e}šārîm*) composed by the QUMRAN community. However, the terms haggadah and halakah as defined by the Jews are exhaustive and exclude a third classification from content. Pesher is actually haggadic midrash.

Based on form, midrash can be a single interpretative statement, or a collection of such statements in a homily or in a verse-by-verse scriptural commentary. Midrash can also be a rewritten version of a Biblical narrative. This type supplies to the text of the Bible aids for understanding its story and adds imaginative embellishments to the narrative to make it more vivid, ample, and edifying. Because of the imaginative element in some midrashim, fictional embellishing of history has been erroneously equated with midrash. It cannot be overemphasized that midrashic embellishments are those made on a scriptural text. Fictional material with no connection with a Biblical text is called by the Jews free haggadah. Some exegetes equate anthological style with midrash, i.e., the use of Biblical phraseology to express one's thoughts. The equation, however, should not be automatic. Sometimes the Biblical allusions used are merely contributing to a new composition, and no attention is fixed on their original meaning (e.g., in Prv 1; 8–9; Wis 1–9); this is not midrash. On the other hand, sometimes the Biblical allusions and texts not only provide words and images for the new composition, but they do so in such a way that the finished product contributes to an understanding of the original texts. Such anthologies are midrashic [e.g., 1QS 8.4–10 (*see* DEAD SEA SCROLLS) and some of the echoes of Jeremiah in Dn 9.1–19].

Examples. Midrash as a literary form originated in the postexilic period as a result of an increased emphasis in Judaism on the Scriptures and the gradual fixing of the Biblical text. Isolated midrashic statements and sections are found in the late books of the OT (Sir 7.27–28; 1 Mc 7.16–17), the apocrypha (Testament of Nephtali 8.8), the Qumran literature (CD 4.14–19; 6.4–11), the NT (Gal 4.21–31; Heb 3.7–4.11; 7.1–10), and in abundance in the Palestinian TARGUMS. Verse-by-verse midrash can be seen in the peshers from Qumran, and narrative midrash (or ''rewritten Bible'') in the Genesis Apocryphon. Jn 6.31–60 is an example of a midrashic homily, and Wis 11.2–19.22 is an example of a homily with midrashic elements.

Bibliography: G. VERMES, *Scripture and Tradition in Judaism* (Leiden 1961). R. BLOCH, *Dictionnaire de la Bible* suppl ed. L. PIROT et al. (Paris 1928) 5:1263–81. M. KADUSHIN, *The Rabbinic Mind* (New York 1952).

[A. G. WRIGHT]

MIDRASHIC LITERATURE

The midrashic method of exegesis presupposes a definitive and accepted scriptural text. In this way MIDRASH differs essentially from the expansions and glosses that, in the course of their long period of formation, filled out the ancient books and occasionally gave them a new relevance for later times. As long as a book was not yet a part of the canon, its content could be enlarged by the clarifications of later authors, which in many cases became so much a part of the text that it is difficult now to distinguish them from the underlying document with any degree of certainty. The development of the midrashic method is thus bound up with the rabbinical postulate that after the minor Prophets, Haggai, Zechariah, and Malachi, the holy spirit (i.e., the gift of prophecy) disappeared from Israel (Tosephta, Sota XIII, 2; Joma 9b; Sota 48b; Sanhedrin 11a).

Midrashic method in the strict sense can accordingly be described as typical of Pharisaism and the normative, rabbinical Judaism that developed on a Pharisaic basis after the destruction of the Temple (A.D. 70). Only in its beginnings was this technique present among such groups, apocalyptic writers, for example, as they thought of themselves as endowed with the gift of the spirit; and even among these it found a place only insofar as the group in question interpreted received canonical texts distinct from the newer ''inspired'' texts produced within their own circle. The DEAD SEA SCROLLS contain typical examples of such a literature (O. Betz, *Offenbarung und Schriftforschung in der Qumransekte* [Tübingen 1960]).

Midrashic Method. In the sense of inquiring into and explaining the will of God as formulated in already existing Scripture, this method took its rise in the period of the return from the Exile (Ezr 7.10). The interpretation of the Scriptures was in the hands of the so-called SCRIBES, who originally were, for the most part, of priestly descent. But in the course of time, especially from the 1st century B.C., when the PHARISEES began to influence the SANHEDRIN, the lay elements played an ever-increasing role. The place where this interpretation was taught came to be known as the *bêt ha-midrāš* (already in Sir 51.23; see Shabbat 65a; *Enziqlopedia talmudit* [Jerusalem 1951] 3:210–213). It was a place of study in conjunction with the SYNAGOGUE, the place of liturgical veneration of the word of God, another practice that originated in the postexilic period.

Midrash at Qumran. The QUMRAN COMMUNITY of ESSENES employed the term ''midrash'' in the phrase *midraš ha-tôrâ* (1QS 8.15; CD 20.6–7). By this ''midrash to the Law'' they seem to mean ''a definitive collection of instructions taken from Scripture to regulate the mode of living of the members of the sect'' (Betz, *op. cit.* 33). In 1QS 6.6 it is set down that in each community of 10 men, one must be engaged in studying the law (*dōrēš ha-tôrâ*). The enemies of the community studied the law incorrectly and for this reason were called ''teachers of slippery things'' (*dôr^e^šê ḥălāqôt,* v.g., 1Q Hod 2.15, 32;

4Q p Nah; Dan 1.18). In *Judaica* 18 (1962) 233–249, J. Maier conclusively proved that this word was used as a derogatory name for Pharisees. The midrash-type commentaries to OT books found in Qumran are typical of the community's scriptural study and interpretation. An early instance of similar methods is Dn 7.17–27.

Rabbinical Midrashim. In Pharisaic and rabbinical circles, as at Qumran, midrash took the external form of a running commentary on the biblical text. The most important and oldest midrashim (plural of midrash) come from the time of doctors of the MISHNAH, the so-called Tannaim (*see* TALMUD). They were compiled for the same reason that the Mishnah itself was compiled, in the endeavor, after A.D. 70, to preserve within normative Judaism a solid body of traditional narratives, as well as of legal precedents and customary law, safeguarded against forgetfulness and arranged for ready use in dispute with advocates of heterodox opinions and practices. These Tannaitic midrashim are from the schools of Rabbi AKIBA BEN JOSEPH and Rabbi Ishmael; they were not compiled and edited in a final form, however, until the time of the early Amoraim (3d–4th century A.D.). The seven hermeneutical rules of Hillel and the 13 rules of Ishmael provided the basic principles for midrash. Ishmael formulated additional principles, the most important of which was: ''The Torah expresses itself in a human way'' (*Sifre* to Num. sect. 112; b Sanhedrin 64b; b Keret 11a). In regard to the text, ''Destroyed, destroyed shall such a soul be'' (Nm 15.31), Akiba took this to mean a twofold destruction, in this world and in the next. Ishmael repudiated this kind of dissection of the text. Akiba manifestly believed that there was not a superfluous word in the Bible and that every single word had to be accounted for as to its contribution. Thus it was said of him that ''from every tittle in the text he could derive mountains of law'' (b Menachoth 29b). In spite of the resultant high regard for the midrash in the sense of a living and interpretative study, the *PIRKE AVOTH* 1.17 gives the early rabbinic dictum: ''The important thing is not expounding the law [literally, midrash] but fulfilling it.''

The most important Tannaitic midrashim are the *Mekilta* to Exodus (beginning with Ex 12), the *Sifra* to Leviticus, and *Sifre* to Numbers and Deuteronomy. In addition to the well-known midrash *Mekilta de-Rabbi Ishmael,* there is another compilation, *Mekilta de-Rabbi Shimeon ben Jochai.* Also from the time of the Tannaim are the *Mekilta* to Deuteronomy and the *Sifre zuta.* These midrashim are referred to in Jewish literature as ''midrash HALAKAH,'' that is, legal as opposed to HAGGADAH, or narrative midrashim, though in fact they include many narrative sections. The later midrashim are the so-called haggadic, or narrative, midrashim. They extend from the 3d down to about the 8th century. The best known is the *Midrash Rabbah,* or Large Midrash, to the Torah and the five Scrolls (Song of Songs, Ruth, Lamentations, Esther, and Ecclesiastes), which originally did not form a unity. Others that should be mentioned are the *Midrash Tanchuma* (or *Yelammedenu*), a homiletic midrash to the Mosaic books that takes its name from Tanchuma bar Abba, a Palestinian Amora of the late 4th century; the *Pesiqta de Rab Kahana;* and the *Pesiqta Rabbati.* There were, of course, other and later works written in the midrash style.

The so-called lesser midrashim collected by A. Jellinek, J. D. Eisenstein, and A. J. Wertheimer are of a distinct literary genre. They belong, in part, to Jewish GNOSTICISM.

Bibliography: Texts and translations. *Mechilta de Rabbi Yishmael,* ed. H. S. HOROVITZ and I. A. RABIN (2d ed. Jerusalem 1960); ed. J. Z. LAUTERBACH, 3 v. (Philadelphia 1933–35), with Eng. translation. *Mekhilta de Rabbi Šim 'on ben Jochai,* ed. J. N. EPSTEIN and E. Z. MELAMED (Jerusalem 1955). *Siphra de bê Rab,* ed. I. H. WEISS (Vienna 1862). *Sifra or Torat Kohanim According to Codex Assemani LXVI* (New York 1956), fac. ed. L. FINKELSTEIN. *Sifre de bê Rab: Der älteste halachische und hagadische Midrasch zu Nm. und Dt.,* ed. M. FRIEDMANN (Vienna 1864). *Midrash Rabbah* (Jerusalem 1960), and many previous editions; Eng. tr. H. FREEMAN and M. SIMON, 13 v. in 10 (London 1939). *Midrash Tanchuma* (Jerusalem 1960). *Pesikta Rabbati: Midrash für den Festcyclus und die ausgezeichneten Sabbathe,* ed. M. FRIEDMANN (Vienna 1880). *Midrash Haggadol on the Pentateuch: Numbers,* ed. S. FISH (London 1957). Smaller midrashim. J. D. EISENSTEIN, *Otzar Midrashim* (New York 1928). A. JELLINEK, *Bêt ha-Midrash* (2d ed. Jerusalem 1938). A. J. WERTHEIMER, *Batte Midrashot* (2d ed. Jerusalem 1950–53). *Tannaitische Midraschim,* ed. G. KITTEL and K. H. RENGSTORF (Stuttgart 1933–). Literature. H. L. STRACK, *Introduction to the Talmud and Midrash,* tr. 5th Ger. ed. (Philadelphia 1931). C. ALBECK, *Untersuchungen über die hulachischen Midraschim* (Berlin 1927). G. F. MOORE, *Judaism in the First Centuries of the Christian Era: The Age of the Tannaim,* 3 v. (Cambridge, Mass. 1927–30). J. Z. LAUTTRBACH, ''Midrash and Mishna,'' *Rabbinic Essays* (Cincinnati 1951) 163–256. E. Z. MELAMED, *Mabo lesiphrut hattalmud* (Jerusalem 1954). N. WOHRMANN, *Iqqare hammabo letalmud* (Tel Aviv 1955). J. N. EPSTEIN, *Meboot lesiphrut hattanaim* (Jerusalem 1957). M. MARGALIOTH, *Enziqlopedia lechakme hattalmud,* 2 v. (Tel Aviv 1960).

[K. SCHUBERT]

MIÈGE, JOHN BAPTIST

Bishop; b. La Forêt, Chevron, Savoy, Sept. 18, 1815; d. Woodstock, Md., July 21, 1884. He entered the Society of Jesus in 1836, was ordained in Rome, Sept. 12, 1847, and came to the U.S. in 1848. He was assigned to the vice province of Missouri and served in the novitiate at Florissant, in parishes at St. Charles and Portage des Sioux, and at St. Louis University. Acting on the petition of the Seventh Provincial Council of Baltimore, Pius IX erected a vicariate apostolic of Indian Territory, embracing the area east of the Rocky Mountains that was not included in Arkansas, Iowa, Missouri, or Minnesota. On July 23, 1850, the pope appointed Miège titular bishop of Messene and vicar apostolic of this area of 500,000 square miles and scarcely a thousand Catholics. After his consecration in St. Louis, Mo., March 25, 1851, Miège took up residence among the Pottawatomi at St. Mary's Mission. In 1857, to form a more serviceable area, he asked Rome to create the Vicariate of Nebraska; in 1860 the western end of Kansas Territory was attached to the Diocese of Santa Fe, N.M.

Miège's missionary activities were altered by the Kansas-Nebraska Act (1854), which brought new settlers to Kansas amid much turmoil. To serve this incoming white population, he transferred his residence to Leavenworth, Kans., in 1855. By the 1860s he had established three religious communities—Benedictine fathers and sisters, Carmelite fathers, and Sisters of Charity of Leavenworth; built an academy, a large rectory to care for missionaries, a hospital, and an orphanage; founded a seminary; and completed the Cathedral of the Immaculate Conception. Miège was given a coadjutor, Louis Mary Fink, OSB, in 1870 and, after he collected funds in South America (1871–74) to reduce the cathedral debt, he asked to resign. Pius IX granted his request Nov. 18, 1874. Miège then doffed all episcopal insignia and became the spiritual director of the Jesuits at Woodstock College, Md. (1875–77). In 1877 he was named the first president of Detroit College, later the University of Detroit, Mich. In 1880 he returned to his former post at Woodstock, where he spent his remaining years.

Bibliography: P. BECKMAN, *The Catholic Church on the Kansas Frontier* (Washington 1943). G. J. GARRAGHAN *Jesuits of the Middle United States*.

[M. P. FITZGERALD]

MIER, SERVANDO TERESA DE

Mexican Dominican friar, active in Mexican independence movement; b. Monterrey, Oct. 18, 1765; d. Mexico City, Dec. 3, 1827. He entered the Dominican Order in 1781 and after ordination, received a doctorate in theology.

Mier might be called a man of prisons. Like the famous adventurer Casanova, he always succeeded in escaping from the dungeons in which he was confined. His first adventure resulted from a sermon that he preached on Dec. 12, 1794, on the subject of the Virgin of Guadalupe. He declared that the image of Guadalupe was not painted on the sisal robe of the native, Juan Diego, but on the cloak of St. Thomas. This statement aroused much indignation among the ecclesiastical authorities. The

Servando Teresa de Mier.

bishop ordered Mier confined to his cell and initiated proceedings. Mier found himself obliged to retract and did so, according to his statement, "because I was unable to bear the prison any longer."

The archbishop condemned him to ten years of exile, which he was to spend in Spain, confined in the monastery of Las Caldas near Santander. He was simultaneously disqualified for public instruction in lecture room, pulpit, and confessional, and his doctor's title was abolished. At Las Caldas he was locked in a filthy room that he shared with rats; they contended with him for his miserable food. "There were so many of them and such large ones," Mier stated in the account that he wrote of his adventures in Europe, "that they ate up my hat, and I had to sleep armed with a stick to keep them from eating me." He escaped by filing the iron grating of his cell, leaving a letter written in verse entitled "Ad fratres in eremo." He was arrested again and sent back to Las Caldas "like a missing old manuscript," as he said himself.

In 1796 Mier was permitted to go to Madrid so that his case might be heard by the Council of the Indies. He received orders to go to a monastery in Salamanca, and since he tried to flee en route, he was seized again and locked up in the Franciscan monastery in Burgos. Under suspicion of intent to escape, he was confined in a dungeon. From this he did succeed in escaping and he went to France. In Paris in 1801 he opened an academy for teaching the Castilian language. He engaged also in literary tasks, one of them the first Castilian translation of Chateaubriand's *Atala.*

In 1802 he left for Rome, intending to enter secular life. The following year he was appointed theologian of the Congregations of the Council of Trent and the Universal Inquisition, and prothonotary apostolic. His dissatisfaction with his lot led him to return to Spain. On his arrival in Madrid he was imprisoned, but he escaped from the Casa de los Toribios, on June 24, 1804. He was arrested in Cádiz and returned to the same prison, this time in irons. In a short time he was in Portugal; he had freed himself again from the irons and fled. He held the post of secretary to the Spanish consul and, thanks to a change of fortune, the appointment of "Apostolic Prelate of the Pope," conferred by Pius VII through the nuncio.

When war broke out between France and Spain, Mier returned to Spain and became a chaplain in the Valencian regiment of volunteers. In Belchite he became a prisoner of the French, but he succeeded in escaping and, with a recommendation from General Black, he went to Cádiz, where in 1811 the Regency awarded him a large pension.

After hearing the news of Hidalgo's insurrection, he went to England, intending to support the cause of Mexican independence. In London he wrote *Historia de la revolución de Nueva España* (1813), the first study on the emancipation movement. He wrote also "Carta de un Americano al *Español* sobre su número XIX," which attracted much attention among the insurgents. Mier also formed a friendship with Francisco Xavier Mina in England and joined in Mina's revolutionary expedition to Mexico in 1817. When it failed, Mier was imprisoned in the dungeons of the Inquisition. As a consequence of the dissolution of the Tribunal in May of 1820, he was put on board a boat for Spain two months later. When his boat put in at Havana, he fled and succeeded in going to the United States. In February of 1822, after independence had been achieved, he returned. In Veracruz, still under Spanish control, General Dávila had him imprisoned in the fortress of San Juan de Ulúa, where he remained for four months. Then, having been elected deputy by the province of Nuevo León, he was set at liberty and was at last able to go to Mexico City. He had not been there a month when he was arrested and imprisoned in the monastery of Santo Domingo because he was suspected of taking part in a republican conspiracy against A. Iturbide. He remained a prisoner until Feb. 11, 1823, when the Mexican troops decided in favor of the republic. Mier then enjoyed the high favor of President Guadalupe Victoria.

Bibliography: S. T. DE MIER, *Escritos inéditos,* ed. J. M. MIGUEL I VERGES (Mexico City 1944); *Memorias* (Madrid 1917), "Prólogo" by A. REYES.

[J. M. MIGUEL I VERGÉS]

MIGAZZI, CHRISTOPH ANTON

Count, Prince-archbishop of Vienna; b. Innsbruck, Nov. 23, 1714; d. Vienna, Sept. 15, 1803. Migazzi studied theology at the Collegium Germanicum in Rome and jurisprudence in Innsbruck; he became a priest and was a canon in Brixen and later in Trent. Soon after being appointed auditor of the Roman Rota for the German nation in 1745, he enjoyed the complete confidence of Empress MARIA THERESA. She entrusted him with diplomatic negotiations, had him appointed coadjutor to the archbishop of Malines in 1751, and in 1752 sent him to Spain where, as Austrian ambassador, he concluded a treaty of alliance.

On March 22, 1756, Migazzi was appointed coadjutor to the bishop of Waizen, Hungary. When the bishop died in June of 1756, Migazzi was recalled from his ambassadorial post in Madrid to undertake the care of his diocese. Then, when Cardinal Trautson, Archbishop of Vienna, died (March 10, 1757), Migazzi was elected his successor and appointed Prince-archbishop of Vienna (March 18).

When in 1761 Pope Clement XIII named Migazzi cardinal, this scion of an impoverished Tyrolese noble house seemed to have reached the aim of his earthly ambitions. In reality, his elevation to the episcopal See of Vienna brought a tragic turn in Migazzi's life. Up until then he had served his revered empress, whose unremitting favor he had enjoyed and whose wishes he had been able to fulfill unreservedly in honorable positions. He now had to oppose her when she attempted to subordinate the Austrian Church to the State. Migazzi tried unsuccessfully to defend ecclesiastical rights in hundreds of written petitions and memoranda.

Maria Theresa, although withdrawing her former nearly absolute confidence from a servant who now had become a spokesman for the Church, never failed to show him respect. Emperor JOSEPH II, however, not only drew the last consequences from his system of JOSEPHINISM without any regard to Migazzi's protests, but also exhibited a scarcely veiled contempt for his person. In a letter to a bishop, the emperor compared the great St. Christopher, carrying the child Jesus in his arms, with that other "great" Christopher who allowed himself to be carried away by his canon Fast, a fearless defender of the Church. Migazzi later protested once more against

Josephinism as reconfirmed by Leopold II; the emperor wrote, ''Memoires of Cardinal Migazzi; of no significance,'' on the petition. The sorely afflicted archbishop died at Vienna and was buried in St. Stephen's cathedral.

Bibliography: J. OSWALD, *Lexikon für Theologie und Kirche*, ed. J. HOFER and K. RAHNER (Freiberg 1957–65) 7:410. C. WOLFSGRUBER, *Christoph Anton Kardinal Migazzi* (2d ed. Ravensburg 1897). F. MAASS, ed., *Der Josephinismus: Quellen zu seiner Geschichte in Österreich 1760–1850,* 5 v. (Fontes rerum Austriacarum II.71–75; Vienna 1951–61), *passim.* M. C. GOODWIN, *The Papal Conflict with Josephinism* (New York 1938).

[F. MAASS]

MIGNE, JACQUES PAUL

Patrologist and ecclesiastical publisher; b. Saint-Flour, near Orléans, France, Oct. 25, 1800; d. Paris, Oct. 24, 1875. After studying in Orléans, he was ordained there in 1824. His pamphlet, *De la Liberté,* on the revolution of 1830, caused difficulties with his bishop, and in 1833 he was permitted to leave Orléans for Paris, where he turned to ecclesiastical journalism. He helped found three unsuccessful newspapers before he brought out *L'Univers religieux* (later *L'Univers*), which he abandoned in 1836 to publish a universal library for the clergy. In 2,000 volumes in handy format, he hoped to publish at a moderate price the whole of Christian writings from the beginnings to his own day. He had canonical difficulties over financial matters with Archbishop Quelen of Paris but enjoyed the favor of the bishop of Versailles. To avoid difficulties of censorship, he founded in 1836, at Petit-Montrouge near Paris, his own publishing house (Ateliers Catholiques). Here he had all the facilities he required, and employed more than 300 persons. He brought out successively a *Theologiae cursus completus* (25 v.), a *Scripturae sacrae cursus completus* (24 v.), a collection of Christian apologetics (20 v.), a collection of French sermons (99 v.), three theological encyclopedias (52, 53, and 66 v.), a course of Church history (27 v.), and a collection of writings on the Blessed Virgin (13 v.). The aid of J. B. PITRA and many scholars made possible his Patrologies, modeled especially on La Bigne's *Maxima bibliotheca* (Lyons 1677) and GALLANDI's *Bibliotheca* (Venice 1765–88). The *Series latina* (221 v. 1844–64) covered Latin authors from Tertullian to Innocent III (A.D. 200–1216). The *Series graeca* included 161 volumes (1857–66) comprising Greek and Latin texts of authors from the Pseudo-Barnabas to the Council of Florence (A.D. 120–1438) and 81 volumes (1856–67) of the Latin text only of the Greek Fathers. In 1868, a fire destroyed Migne's presses and stores. Insurance recovered after long litigation permitted him to build again, but his efforts to finance the new enterprise by the use of Mass stipends caused the archbishop of Paris to suspend him. He died almost blind.

His accomplishment is a phenomenon in the world of erudition. His genius for organizing, directing, and financing a vast publication was unique in his age. He personally solved problems in the use of Greek type and invented many devices that saved time and money. He used texts already in print, especially those of the MAURISTS, but urged his collaborators to emend or even re-edit texts from the manuscripts. His texts were accompanied by the best introductions and notes available, and great care was taken with proofreading of the volumes issued before the fire. Only gradually are his texts being replaced by better editions, and they are still indispensable for almost every field of ecclesiastical study. H. LECLERCQ called him one of the most useful priests in the Church of France in the 19th century.

Bibliography: F. DE MELY, ''L'Abbé Migne,'' *Revue archéologique*, 5.1 (1915) 203–258. A. C. COTTER, ''Abbé Migne and the Catholic Tradition,'' *Theological Studies* 7 (1946) 46–71. P. GLORIEUX, ''Pour revaloriser Migne: Tables rectificatives,'' *Mèlanges de science religieuse* 9 suppl. (1952) 1–82. L. C. SHEPPARD, ''The Abbé Jacques-Paul Migne,'' *American Benedictine Review* 7 (1956–57) 112–128. L. MARCHAL, *Dictionnaire de théologie catholique,* ed. A. VACANT et al., 15 v. (Paris 1903–50; Tables générales 1951–), 10.2:1722–40. H. LECLERCQ, *Dictionnaire d'archéologie chrétienne et de liturgie,* ed. F. CABROL, H. LECLERCQ and H. I. MARROU, 15 v. (Paris 1907–53) 11.1:941–957. R. H. BLOCH, *God's Plagiarist: Being an Account of the Fabulous Industry and Irregular Commerce of the Abbe Migne* (Chicago 1995).

[F. X. MURPHY]

MIGNOT, EUDOXE IRÉNÉE

French archbishop; b. Brancourt (Aisne), Sept. 20, 1842; d. Albi, March 18, 1918. After studying at Saint-Sulpice in Paris, he was ordained (1865) and acted as pastor in various parishes in the Soissons Diocese, until he became bishop of Fréjus (1890). From 1899 until 1918 he was archbishop of Albi. Mignot was much interested in intellectual problems, but his writings consist of essays, very similar in form to familiar conversations. He published an article in *Le Correspondant* (April 10, 1897) on ''L'Évolutionnisme religieux'' to criticize *L'Esquisse d'une philosophic de la religion* (1897) of Louis Auguste Sabatier. In Sabatier's manifesto of liberal Protestantism, Mignot discerned a natural philosophy ''void of what has historically constituted the mystery of Jesus.'' Utilizing Leo XIII's teaching, Mignot addressed five *Lettres sur les études ecclésiastiques* (1900–01), to his clergy which were later reproduced in the *Revue du Clergé français* and then published as a separate volume (1908), along with his discourse on ''La Méthode de la théologie,'' pronounced at the Catholic Institute of Toulouse (1901). Mignot held that reason was in accord with faith, and wanted theologians to be scientific and historically minded. His belief that Alfred LOISY, in *L'Évangile et l'Église,* neglected oral tradition as the historical basis of faith led him to publish in *Le Correspondant,* ''Critique et Tradition'' (1904), ''L'Église et la science'' (1907), and ''La Bible et les religions'' (1907). These articles and two panegyrics were published in the volume *L'Église et la critique* (1910).

Mignot was a liberal and enlightened prelate who was prominent in the affairs of his day. After the separation of church and state, he promoted religious associations in accordance with civil law. In 1910 he was one of the very few bishops who supported the Sillon of Marc SANGNIER. His *Mémoire envoyé au cardinal Ferrata,* published in 1914 after Ferrata's death, revealed his eagerness to maintain contacts between the church and modern society and condemned INTEGRALISM for its violent tactics. Mignot sought to spare Loisy from censure by Rome. Even after the heresiarch's condemnation, Mignot treated him benevolently and tried to keep him in the Church.

Bibliography: L. DE LACGER, *Dictionnaire de théologie catholique,* ed. A. VACANT et al., 15 v. (Paris 1903–50; Tables générales 1951–) 10.2:1743–51. J. RIVIÈRE, *Le Modernisme dans l'Église* (Paris 1929). È. LECANUET, *L'Église de France sous la Troisième République,* 4 v. (new ed. Paris 1930–31) v.2–4.

[J. DAOUST]

MÍGUEZ, FAUSTINO, BL.

Baptized Manuel, also called Faustino of the Incarnation, educator, scientist, Piarist priest, and founder of the Daughters of the Divine Shepherdess (Calasanctian Sisters); b. Xamirás, Acebedodel Rio, Celanova, Orense, Galicia, Spain, March 25, 1831; d. Getafe near Madrid, Spain, March 8, 1925.

Manuel, the fourth child of Christian farmers, studied Latin and the humanities in Orense. There, he was inspired by the life of Saint JOSEPH CALASANCTIUS (1556–1648) and entered the novitiate of Calasanz's order, Poor Clerics Regular of the Mother of God of the Pious Schools (PIARISTS), at Saint Ferdinand's in Madrid (1850), professed his vows, and was later ordained. He taught for nearly fifty years in Piarist schools, including those at Celanova, El Escorial, Getafe, Guanaboacoa, Monforte de Lemos, San Fernando, and Sanlúcar de Barameda, while continuing to improve his own education.

His genuine love for children exhibited itself in his kindness and dedication to teaching them the love of truth. At the invitation of St. Anthony Mary CLARET, Faustino travelled to Cuba to teach in various colleges. Returning to Spain, he used his study of botany to uncover the healing power of plants and manufactured medicines for the sick, poor people of the region. His legacy in this area is the Míguez Laboratory in Getafe.

Míguez was particularly sensitive to the dignity of women, whom he regarded as the soul of the family. Appalled by the illiteracy and marginalization of women in Sanlúcar de Barrameda, he founded the Calasanctian Sisters (Jan. 2, 1885) with the support of the bishop of Seville. The congregation, recognized by the Holy See in 1910, is dedicated to the education and formation of children, especially poor girls. This congregation has continued to endure and prosper in Spain and Latin America.

Míguez, who was also known as a patient, wise confessor, died at the age of 94. He was beatified by Pope John Paul II, Oct. 25, 1998.

[K. I. RABENSTEIN]

MIHAN, CHARLES, VEN.

Irish Franciscan priest and martyr; b. after 1639 (exact date and birthplace unknown); d. Ruthin, North Wales, Aug. 12, 1679. According to reliable contemporary sources, his surname was Mihan (modern Meehan), not Mahony as stated in a contemporary broadsheet. No details are available on his religious training and ordination. On Nov. 21, 1672, the Irish Franciscan provincial chapter approved him for hearing confessions of lay people. As a result of the edicts of banishment against bishops and regulars (1673–74), he fled to Flanders from Ireland. Early in November 1674 he was sent to pursue studies at the Franciscan friary in Hammelburg, Bavaria, and thence to St. Isidore's College, Rome (summer 1676). While returning to Ireland in 1678 his ship was forced onto the Welsh coast. He was arrested at Denbigh and imprisoned. At his trial (1679), during the Titus Oates scare, he admitted his priesthood and was condemned to death. He was hanged, cut down alive, and brutally butchered.

Bibliography: J. M. CRONIN, ''The Other Irish Martyr of the Titus Oates Plot,'' *Blessed Oliver Plunket: Historial Studies* (Dublin 1937) 133–153. C. MOONEY, ''The Ven. Father Charles Meehan, d. 1679,'' *Franciscan College Annual* (Multyfarnham 1952) 91–93; ''Further Light on Father C. Meehan,'' *Collectanea Hibernica* 6–7 (1963–64) 225–230. C. GIBLIN, ed., *Liber Lovaniensis* (Dublin 1956) 131.

[B. MILLETT]

MILAN, EDICT (AGREEMENT) OF

Galerius, in 311, issued an edict of religious tolerance; and Constantine, after defeating Maxentius (Oct. 28, 312), published decrees favorable to the Christians. When Constantine and Licinius met in Milan (February 313), they resolved their political problem and agreed on certain legal provisions in favor of the Christians. While no edict was issued at Milan, the contents of these resolutions are recorded in a rescript issued by Licinius for the East on June 13, 313, prescribing that everyone, including Christians, should be given freedom to follow the religion that suited him, in order that the favor of every divinity in heaven might be ensured for the emperor and his realm. Ordinances hostile to Christians were lifted; general and unrestricted freedom of religious practice was guaranteed. Confiscated Church property was to be restored gratuitously, and the Christians were once more given the right of forming a legal corporate body. Without complete agreement on the particulars, both Lactantius (*De mort. pers.* 48) and Eusebius (*Hist. Eccl.* 9.9.12; 9a.12; and 10.5.2–14) supply evidence of this agreement of Milan.

Bibliography: J. R. PALANQUE, *Histoire de l'église depuis les origines jusqu'à nos jours*, A. FLICHE and V. MARTIN, eds., 3:20–24, with literature. V. C. DE CLERCQ, *Ossius of Cordova* (Washington 1954) 145–146. *Handbuch der Kirchengeschichte* 1:462–463. H. NESSELHAUF, *Historisches Jahrbuch der Görres-Gesellschaft* 74 (1955) 44–61.

[A. W. ZIEGLER]

MILITARY ORDERS

The military religious orders such as the TEMPLARS and the KNIGHTS OF MALTA, in their origins, functions, organization, and historical significance, were essentially distinct from the secular orders of knighthood such as the Golden Fleece. The military religious orders appeared initially in the 12th century as a response to the appeal of the crusading movement. For centuries the Church had exhorted medieval knights to use their swords only in the cause of justice. In proclaiming the CRUSADE in 1095, URBAN II pointed to such a cause. The formation of the military religious orders soon after can be regarded as the logical outcome of the effort to Christianize the soldier.

In entering orders wherein the principles of monasticism and chivalry were combined, the knights pledged themselves not only to observe the canonical vows, to practice asceticism, to recite the canonical hours, but also to defend Christendom against the infidels by force of arms. Each order was directed by a master; clerical members served the spiritual needs of the knights. The papacy exempted the orders from the jurisdiction of diocesan ordinaries, from the observance of interdicts, etc. The orders contributed substantially not only to the maintenance of the CRUSADERS' STATES in the Holy Land, but also to the Reconquest in SPAIN and to the conversion of the pagans in eastern Europe.

The secular orders of knighthood came into existence at the close of the medieval era under the auspices of kings and princes who considered these honorary societies as symbols of their power. The secular orders did not participate significantly in the military defense of Christendom, and their members did not adhere to the monastic life.

The prototype of the military religious orders was the Order of the Temple, founded about 1119 by Hugh de Payens for the protection of pilgrims to the Holy Land. At his request, BERNARD OF CLAIRVAUX wrote the *Liber de laude novae militiae,* a justification of the idea of the military religious order. To sceptics Bernard demonstrated the possibility of reconciling and conjoining the military and monastic professions. The *nova militia* of which he spoke was both a new kind of knighthood and a new kind of monasticism. In large measure the phenomenal growth of the Templars and of the other military religious orders can be attributed to his influence. In imitation of the Templars, the Order of the Hospital of St. John of Jerusalem, already caring for the sick and pilgrims, assumed a share of the responsibility for the military defense of the Holy Land. Another foundation in the Holy Land, the TEUTONIC KNIGHTS, gained renown in the conquest and conversion of Prussia. The KNIGHTS OF THE SWORD, organized in 1202 by Bp. ALBERT I OF RIGA, performed a similar role in Livonia.

Several military religious orders were founded in the Iberian peninsula. There is no substance to the opinion that they were an imitation of similar organizations existing among the Muslims. The Hispanic orders were modeled on the Templars and the Hospitallers and reflected most clearly the influence of St. Bernard. The first of the peninsular orders, CALATRAVA, founded in 1158, was directly affiliated to the Order of Cîteaux and was indeed a military arm of that order. The Leonese KNIGHTS OF ALCÁNTARA, the Portuguese Order of AVIZ, and the Aragonese KNIGHTS OF MONTESA were affiliates of Calatrava and thus of Cîteaux. The Portuguese ORDER OF CHRIST, though not a dependency of Calatrava, observed its customs. Thus all the major Hispanic orders, with the exception of the KNIGHTS OF ST. JAMES (SANTIAGO), which followed the Rule of St. AUGUSTINE, pertained to the CISTERCIAN observance.

Several military orders disappeared just as quickly as they had come into being. One should mention that especially in modern times there has been a tendency to in-

Parade of Knights Templars, Fifth Avenue in New York, c. 1930. (©Hulton-Deutsch Collection/CORBIS)

vent military orders and to attribute to them a false, fraudulent, and fantastic history. The destruction of the crusaders' states and the completion of the Hispanic Reconquest deprived the military religious orders of any real reason for existence. In 1312 Clement V suppressed the Templars, but the Hospitallers (Knights of Malta) have survived until modern times because they never abandoned their original function of caring for the sick. At the close of the Middle Ages the kings in Spain and Portugal assumed direct control of the military religious orders, gradually turning them into honorary societies of nobles.

Bibliography: H. PRUTZ, *Die geistlichen Ritterorden* (Berlin 1908). J. M. A. DELAVILLE LE ROULX, *Les Hospitaliers en Terre Sainte et à Chypre* (Paris 1904). J. F. O'CALLAGHAN, ''The Affiliation of the Order of Calatrava with the Order of Cîteaux,'' *Analecta Sacri Ordinis Cisterciensis* 15 (1959) 161–193; 16 (1960) 3–59, 225–292. E. MASCHKE, *Die Religion in Geschichteund Gegenwart* (Tübingen 1957–65) 5:1121–24. K. HOFMANN, *Lexikon für Theologie und Kirche*, ed. J. HOFER and K. RAHNER (Freiburg 1957–65) 8:1326.

[J. F. O'CALLAGHAN]

MILITARY SERVICE

Military service is by definition ''a vocation of service. And the centurion in the Gospel proves that there is no incompatibility between the requirements of military discipline and those of the faith, between the ideal of the soldier and that of the believer'' [Paul VI, Address to Belgian soldiers (*L'Osservatore Romano* April 22, 1965)].

The morality of military service by Christians has been seriously questioned. Christ preached a doctrine of peace and vigorously rejected the use of armed force in the advancement of His kingdom (see Mt 26.52). But He also insisted that His followers have lawful duties both

U.S. Army Chaplain K. Ale kneels beside a wounded man, Normandy, France. (©CORBIS)

to God and to Caesar (Mt 22.21; cf. Rom 13.1–7; 1 Pt 2.13–17). Among the theologians of the pre-Constantinian era, Tertullian was outstanding for his hostility to all military service. He based his opposition not only on the prevalence of idolatry and licentiousness in the Roman legions, but also on the principle that military service can never be reconciled with ''the things that are God's.'' This rigorous position, however, did not represent the common or official teaching of the early Church. The bishops could not sanction enlistment as long as military life exacted compromise with pagan practices, but they did voice support for the Roman government in its struggles against the barbarian invaders. It is significant that there is no record of any conciliar decree against military service during this period in which councils played so important a role in the formulation of Christian discipline.

With the publication of the Edict of Toleration for the Christian religion, the situation changed. The Council of Arles in 314, for example, decreed excommunication for deserters even in times of peace. Certainly, from the time of SS. Ambrose and Augustine, Catholic theologians have taught that military service is not a contradiction of the human and Christian will to peace. The man who conscientiously serves in the armed forces of his nation or of an effective international organization that is fighting to achieve peace with justice is ''a man of peace in his warmaking, that by his victory he may bring those he attacks to the unity of peace'' (St. Augustine, *Epist. ad Bonifatium Corpus scriptorum ecclesiasticorum latinorum* 57.135). That such is the teaching of the Church is evident from the following declaration of Vatican Council II: ''Those who devote themselves to the military service of their country should regard themselves as agents of security and freedom of peoples. As long as they fulfill this role properly, they are making a genuine contribution to the establishment of peace'' (*Constitution on the Church in the Modern World* 79).

Military service, therefore, is permitted if it is undertaken not for motives of greed or cruelty but with a desire for peace. The moral principles that govern the life of a soldier are clear. He is to fulfill his duties to the best of his ability according to the lawful directions of his superiors. In waging war he is to observe the norms of humanity that arise from the natural law, many of which are defined by international treaties and covenants. There exists no right, no obligation, no permission to accomplish an act, evil in itself, even if it is ordered. Military obedience, even when it is imposed under the threat of severe punishment for any violation, does not excuse a soldier from the obligation of acting in accord with the dictates of his conscience.

The application of these principles to the immediate moral problems of military life has become increasingly difficult. In the 13th century, St. Thomas Aquinas restated the Augustinian doctrine on peace and war. He placed great stress on the necessity of a right intention, but had little to say about the conduct of the individual soldier in wartime. The later scholastics, particularly Francisco de Vitoria, formulated precise and concrete rules for applying moral principles to the changing conditions of warfare in their time. The rapidly developing technology of weapons and the complexity of modern war make it almost impossible to foresee or solve all the moral problems that the present-day military man may have to face.

There are some military actions that are not at all defensible in the eyes of anyone who has a reasonable concept of justice. If a soldier is ordered to take part in the mass slaughter of innocent women and children or in the killing of defenseless prisoners, he has no choice in conscience but to refuse. Many other moral questions may arise for which a definitive solution cannot be found in the official teaching of the Church or in the consensus of theologians. In each case the individual must make a moral judgment before he acts. When there is an honest doubt about the morality of a particular action, the presumption of right is in favor of the lawful authorities. A soldier is never obliged in conscience to disobey an order of his superiors except in cases where violation of the law of God is evident.

Bibliography: PIUS XII, ''Address to the Sixth International Congress on Penal Law,'' *Acta Apostolicae Sedis* (Rome 1909–) 45 (1953) 730–744, Eng. *The Catholic Mind* 52 (1954) 107–118. J. C. FORD, ''The Morality of Obliteration Bombing,'' *Theological Studies* 5 (1944) 261–309. E. A. RYAN, ''The Rejection of Military Service by the Early Christians,'' *ibid.* 13 (1952) 1–32. F. DE VICTORIA, *De Indis et de Iure Belli relectiones,* ed. E. NYS, tr. J. P. BATE (Washington 1917).

[R. T. POWERS]

MILITARY SERVICES, USA, ARCHDIOCESE FOR

The Archdiocese for Military Services, USA is responsible for the spiritual and sacramental care, including sacramental records keeping, of Catholics and their families in the United States Armed Forces, including the army, navy, air force, Marine Corps, and Coast Guard, as well as Catholics in Veteran's Affairs Hospitals and U.S. diplomatic posts overseas. The archbishop for the military services is also recognized by the federal government as the endorser for all Catholic priest chaplains who serve these faithful.

Development of a Military Vicariate. Catholic priests served American armed forces with distinction since Revolutionary War times. In 1888, the Apostolic See granted exclusive competency to the archbishop of New York to designate navy chaplains. After the Spanish American War, a commission of the U.S. bishops, under James Cardinal Gibbons, was established to recruit priests of the military chaplaincy. At the outbreak of World War I, there were sixteen priests in the army, eight in the navy, and a further ten in the National Guard. The need for priests was urgent, so the bishops of America, with significant support from the Knights of Columbus, formed a National Catholic War Council. By Armistice Day, 1919, a total of 1,026 priests were serving with the U.S. armed forces. Most were commissioned officers, but some 165 of those served as civilians paid from funds donated by the Knights of Columbus.

In the United States, as in other countries, the military constituted a vast diocese with no regularly constituted head until Pope BENEDICT XV authorized each country to have an *episcopus castrensis*, or bishop for the military. On Nov. 24, 1917, he appointed Patrick Hayes, an auxiliary bishop of New York, to be ''Ordinary of all Catholics who fight in the Army and Navy during the present war.'' Bishop Hayes organized the new jurisdiction, with headquarters at St. Stephen's Church, New York City, and five regional vicariates. The organization came to be known as the Military Vicariate and its offices as the Military Ordinariate. Special faculties for general absolution, the Eucharist, and marriage were among many privileges granted only to military chaplains by the Military Ordinariate.

War was threatening again when Cardinal Hayes died in Sept. of 1938. On Nov. 25, 1939, Pope Pius XII designated Archbishop Francis Spellman, the new ordinary of New York, to be military vicar of the United States of America and Archbishop Spellman an episcopal administrator for chaplain affairs. The first administrator was Father John O'Hara, CSC, president of the University of Notre Dame. O'Hara was later named bishop of Buffalo and afterward cardinal archbishop of Philadelphia.

When peacetime conscription was instituted in 1940, Archbishop Spellman and Bishop O'Hara appealed to the America bishops for clergy. By Dec. 8, 1941 there were 500 priests on active duty. During World War II, 2,453 priests served as army chaplains and 817 as navy chaplains, of whom 676 died in service. After World War II, as realities dictated an American presence in outposts far from home, the jurisdiction of the Military Ordinary was expanded to include civilians serving the U.S. government overseas. In June 1946, the Veterans Administration program was placed under the canonical jurisdiction of the Military Ordinariate. During the Korean War, with many nations fighting under United Nations auspices, the Holy Father placed all Catholic chaplains in Korea under the American Military Vicar.

On April 25, 1951, an instruction of the Holy See, *Sollemne Semper*, established norms for canonically establishing a permanent vicariate for the apostolate to military personnel. It was made specific for the United States in a subsequent decree, *Mysticam Petri Naviculam*, of Sept. 8, 1957. This decree formally erected the Military Vicariate and placed it under the archbishop of New York, with the tribunal of the Archdiocese of New York appointed to hear the cases of its subjects. It operated as a separate office in the New York Chancery, with its own staff and auxiliary bishops. Bishop Terrence Cooke succeeded Cardinal Spellman as archbishop of New York and Military Vicar of the U.S. Armed Services in the spring of 1968. To assist him Bishop Joseph Ryan, who had been bishop of Anchorage, Alaska, was installed as coadjutor archbishop of the military vicar in December 1975, and a separate ecclesiastical tribunal was created to attend to the needs of the military.

When Cardinal Cooke died on Oct. 6, 1983, the Holy See determined that the military vicariate should have its own independent status, not as an added role for the archbishop of New York, but with its own full-time ordinary, to function as any other diocese. After a brief interregnum, during which time Archbishop John O'Connor of New York served as apostolic administrator, Archbishop Ryan was named and installed as the first ordinary of the Archdiocese for Military Services in March 1985. In January 1986 Archbishop Ryan moved the administrative headquarters of the newly independent jurisdiction to the Washington D.C. area. Archbishop Ryan retired in 1991 and the Most Reverend Joseph T. Dimino, who had been auxiliary bishop of the military vicar, was appointed the second ordinary for the military services. When Archbishop Dimino retired in 1997, he was succeeded by the Most Reverend Edwin F. O'Brien, who had been an auxiliary bishop in New York.

General Norms.. On April 21, 1986, Pope John Paul II issued the Apostolic Constitution *Spirituali militum curae*, effective July 21, which made each military vicariate or ordinariate juridically comparable to a diocese. *Spirituali militum curae* recognized that military people ''constitute, as a matter of fact, a particular social body, and because of the special conditions of their way of life, they have need of a concrete and specific form of pastoral

Chaplain Kenny Lynch conducts services for the 31st Regiment north of Hwachon, Korea, in 1951. (©CORBIS)

assistance.'' Each ordinariate is headed by a military ordinary, normally a bishop, with all the rights and obligations of a diocesan ordinary, insofar as possible, given the nature and pastoral conditions of the military. Canonically, this ecclesiastical entity is denominated *Ordinariatus militaris seu castrensis*. A local title more suitable to the language of the particular country being allowable, in the United States the designation is *Archdiocese for the Military Services*.

The Apostolic Constitution laid down certain general norms valid for all military ordinariates. In addition, each military ordinariate is ruled by its particular statutes as approved by the Apostolic See.

The military ordinary, nominated by the pope, belongs by right to the National Episcopal Conference. His jurisdiction is personal and exercised over all persons pertaining to the ordinariate, wherever they may be; it is ordinary for both the internal and external forums and proper but cumulative with the jurisdiction of the diocesan bishop. The areas and places reserved to military personnel fall chiefly under the jurisdiction of the military ordinary and secondarily, in the absence of a chaplain, under the diocesan bishop. The military ordinary has the right to erect a seminary, to incardinate clerics, and to petition for a proper tribunal.

The following belong to the military ordinariate and come under its jurisdiction: the faithful who are military persons, as well as those who are at the service of the armed forces, provided that they are bound to this by civil laws; all members of their families, spouses and children, even those who, though independent, live in the same house, as well as relatives and servants also living with them in the same house; those who attend military training schools, or who live or work in military hospitals, homes for the aged, or similar institutions; and all the faithful, both men and women, whether or not they are members of a religious institute, who carry out in a permanent manner a task committed to them by the military ordinary or with his consent. Particular statutes of each ordinariate may further specify the areas of proper subjects.

[T. CONNELLY/N. HALLIGAN]

MILL, JAMES

Philosopher, psychologist, economist, and historian; disciple of J. BENTHAM and D. Hartley; b. Northwater Bridge, Scotland, April 6, 1773; d. London, June 23, 1836. Mill studied for the ministry but failed to get a parish; later, under Bentham's influence, he came to see Christianity as ''a mere delusion,'' ''a great moral evil,'' and ''the greatest enemy of morality.'' In London, after some years in journalism, he wrote a *History of British India* [1818; 4th ed., ed. H. H. Wilson, 9 v. (London 1848)], entered the East India Company, and lived to become its chief London administrator. He was active also in the formation of the political party known as the Philosophical Radicals, who were influential in passing the Reform Bill of 1832. In his major work, *Analysis of the Phenomena of the Human Mind* (London 1829), Mill defended and developed Hartley's ASSOCIATIONISM. Denying innate differences, he believed in unlimited perfectibility through education; for an account of the remarkable education he gave his own children, see his son John's *Autobiography* (1873). In political theory, Mill, like Bentham, rejected all notion of ''natural rights,'' and in his famous 1820 *Britannica* article on ''Government'' he attempted one of the very first defenses of representative government along purely utilitarian, Benthamite lines.

See Also: MILL, JOHN STUART.

Bibliography: Other Works. *An Essay on Government* (Cambridge, Eng. 1937); *A Fragment on Mackintosh* (London 1835); *Elements of Political Economy* (London 1821). Literature. A. BAIN, *James Mill: A Biography* (London 1882). L. STEPHEN, *The English Utilitarians,* 3 v. (London 1900) v.2.

[R. L. CUNNINGHAM]

MILL, JOHN STUART

The most influential philosopher in England during the mid-19th century; b. London, May 20, 1806; d. Avignon, May 8, 1873.

Life. One of the two major influences in Mill's life was that of his father, James MILL, who tutored John intensively from his 3d to his 14th year with the aim of making his son able to carry on his own work as chief exponent of empiricist and Benthamite utilitarian philosophy. James, and later John, who edited and annotated his father's *Analysis of the Phenomena of the Human Mind* (London 1869), were psychological associationists. The Mills' circle included Jeremy BENTHAM (whose *Rationale of Judicial Evidence,* 5 v., John edited when he was 21), David Ricardo (whose economics John never outgrew), and John AUSTIN, the utilitarian legal theorist. At 17 Mill entered the examiner's office of the East India Company, where he remained for 35 years, reaching, as had his father before him, the highest administrative position in the London office.

The other major influence in Mill's life was that of Mrs. Harriet Taylor, who dominated him for 28 years, first as his *Seelenfreundin* (as she described herself), then, after her husband died, for seven years (1851–58) as his wife. He believed her to be the spiritual peer only of Shelley and to lack no virtue, intellectual or moral. At her direction he made changes in the later editions of his *Political Economy* (''a joint production with my wife'') in the direction of socialism and away from the Benthamite laissez-faire tradition of the first edition (London 1848). She led him away from his earlier interest in, and sympathy with, T. Carlyle, S. T. Coleridge, and A. Comte; and many of his major essays, including *Utilitarianism* (London 1863) and *Considerations on Representative Government* (London 1863), were first sketched out with her. *On Liberty* was the development of an early paper by Harriet on toleration.

Teaching. Mill's principal philosophical work is his *System of Logic, Ratiocinative and Inductive* (2 v. London 1843), an empiricist attack on a prioristic intuitionism, which he regarded as the great intellectual support of false doctrines and bad institutions: ''And the chief strength of this false philosophy in morals, politics, and religion, lies in the appeal which it is accustomed to make to the evidence of mathematics and of the cognate branches of physical science. To expel it from these is to drive it from its stronghold'' (*Autobiography*). A contemporary reader of *Logic* would find Mill's discussion of the following topics valuable—though perhaps mainly because of Mill's instructive errors.

Logic. Mill believed that in order to find the meaning of a proposition one must first find the meaning of its constituent verbal parts; and for this he is usually criticized on the basis of an analysis of meaning deriving mainly from L. WITTGENSTEIN, according to whom propositional meaning is primary and the meaning of individual words is derivative.

Mill was an empiricist: for him, a proposition is significant if and only if it describes what has been or could be experienced. He was in some ways an even more thoroughgoing empiricist than D. HUME: failing to distinguish pure from applied mathematics, Mill maintained that even mathematical axioms and theorems are generalizations from experience. One might object that if mathematical propositions are empirical generalizations, they can be disproved by experience; yet what sort of evidence would tell against "things equal to the same thing are equal to each other"?

On the value of the categorical SYLLOGISM Mill held a middle position between those who, like R. WHATELY (*Elements of Logic*, 1826), find in it the ground of all proof, and those who, like J. LOCKE, regard it as worthless because circular. Mill maintains that the syllogism, not being a "real" inference (one in which the conclusion asserts more than the premises), is circular but not worthless. One is really interested in going from "all observed *X* is *Y*" to "this *X* is *Y*"—a formula reminding him of the manner in which he has been in the past, and is in the future, entitled to infer from a number of particular cases yet another particular case: "What is called Formal Logic is the logic of consistency."

Method. That part of his *Logic* for which Mill is best known is his analysis of the five "experimental methods" (agreement, difference, etc.), which, by eliminating all but one of the initially possible alternatives (eliminative induction), are claimed to be the *only* rigorous methods of establishing true causal laws. Now Mill maintains that any conclusion drawn from an application of these methods presupposes the "law of universal causation" as a major premise (e.g., all events have a cause; the only possible cause of rust here is moist oxygen; so moist oxygen is the cause of rust). But *this* law needs to be inductively established, and cannot, without *petitio principii,* be established by eliminative induction. There remains only enumerative induction (*C* is the cause of *E,* where *C* and *E* are frequently repeated events). Now if enumerative induction is sufficient to establish the universal law of causation, why is it not sufficient simply to establish particular causal laws—which, according to Mill, can be established only by eliminative induction—the sum total of which particular laws are called for to establish the universal law? It is now generally maintained that *any* attempt to justify inductive reasoning by general postulates about the constitution of nature cannot fail to be circular. (*See* INDUCTION.)

John Stuart Mill, painting by George Frederick Watts.

In the social sciences one must generally avoid reliance on unanalyzed experience alone (exemplified by Macaulay's 1829 *Edinburgh Review* critique of James Mill's essay on "Government") or on the "geometrical" method (exemplified by his father's essay itself) of deducing social phenomena from a single principle. Usually the "inverse deductive method" (attributed by Mill to Comte) should be followed: begin, as Bacon or Macaulay did, by generalizing on the basis of historical evidence; then, since empirical laws are not of themselves sufficient for long-range prediction, go on to show that these generalizations are deducible from the laws of experimental psychology and "ethology" (science of the formation of human character).

Metaphysics. In a later metaphysical work, *The Examination of Sir William Hamilton's Philosophy* (London 1865), Mill defends a Berkeleian PHENOMENALISM. But whereas G. BERKELEY had made the existence of a physical object depend on its actually being perceived, Mill made its existence depend on the *possibility* of perceiving it: what constitutes the existence of a physical object is that under certain conditions, themselves describable in sensory terms, certain sorts of sensations regularly occur. "Matter, then, may be defined, as a Permanent Possibility of Sensation. If I am asked, whether I believe in matter, I ask whether the questioner accepts this definition of it. If he does, I believe in matter: and so do all Berkeleians. In any other sense than this, I do not. But I affirm with confidence, that this conception of matter includes the whole meaning attached to it by the common world, apart from philosophical, and sometimes from theological, theories'' (ch. 11). Now Mill is surely wrong when he claims to be asserting the *common* conception of things: things as ordinarily conceived exist actually, whereas for Mill things exist only potentially. Further, though Mill insists on the publicity of possible sensations, any particular sensation actually felt or even able to be felt by one person is private and cannot be felt by another person. And finally, Mill might well be accused of falling into the genetic fallacy: to say that one's conception of matter originates in his conception of possible sensations and thus matter is really only a complex of possible sensations is like saying that a man originates in a complex of chemical elements and so is really only a composite of those elements. Like Berkeley, but unlike Hume, Mill backs away from a phenomenalist account of minds or persons. For that which can remember actual sensations and anticipate possible ones can hardly be only a set of possible sensations: here is a ''finally inexplicable fact''; but no alternative account of this is proposed by Mill.

Political Theory. In *Utilitarianism* Mill's primary objective was to explain and defend the truth of an importantly modified Benthamite utilitarianism against intuitionists such as I. Kant and W. Whewell.

On Liberty is quite probably the most powerful political sermon preached in English since the mid-19th century. Mill's main objective was to persuade his hearers that though England was free, it should be freer and that greater freedom could come only if society resolved to avoid the use, not only of government coercion, whether democratic or not, but even of ''the moral coercion of public opinion'' in order to enforce conformity. Otherwise, he argued, genius, independence, and originality would go to the wall: ''The grand, the leading principle, towards which every argument in these pages directly converges, is the absolute and essential importance of human development in its richest diversity.'' Each adult should have a private sphere of individual liberty, comprising any of his acts that do not ''affect prejudicially the interests of others''; and one should never, above all, interfere with freedom of thought and expression, for the progress of society depends on this. Mill can be criticized on the ground that almost any act a man does may be held to affect prejudicially the interests of others; and that to the extent that people are dissuaded from using nonviolent ''tyranny of opinion,'' they will tend to use the violence of governmental coercion, which even a strong-minded man finds far harder to resist.

Religion. Mill wrote *Three Essays on Religion.* The first two, ''Nature'' and ''Utility of Religion,'' he wrote under his wife's influence in the 1850s: there is little value in religion. The last, ''Theism,'' written in 1869–70, is far more sympathetic; it shocked his agnostic and atheist friends when it was published posthumously, though in it issues of truth and appropriate feeling continued to be mingled; Mill's main concern was with the question whether the consequences of belief in God would be beneficial. It is not unreasonable, he claimed, to maintain that God exists: the a posteriori argument from design, as Hume and Kant had said, offers some evidence; and the human soul may be immortal: there is no decisive evidence against it; and Christianity has the status of an inspiring and edifying belief. But Mill could not accept a God who was at once omnipotent and benevolent, an ''Omnipotent Author of Hell''; a powerful but finite God seemed more morally stimulating to him. Thus man is enabled to cultivate ''the feeling of helping God—of requiting the good He has given us by a voluntary cooperation which He, not being omnipotent, really needs.''

See Also: EMPIRICISM; EUDAEMONISM; LOGIC, HISTORY OF.

Bibliography: *Bibliography of the Published Writings of J. S. Mill,* ed. from his MS, N. MACMINN et al. (Evanston, Ill. 1945). M. ST. J. PACKE, *The Life of John Stuart Mill* (New York 1954), excellent bibliog. J. A. PASSMORE, *A Hundred Years of Philosophy* (New York 1957). R. P. ANSCHUTZ, *The Philosophy of J. S. Mill* (Oxford 1953). K. BRITTON, *John Stuart Mill* (Baltimore 1953). A. V. DICEY, *Lectures on the Relation between Law and Opinion in England* (London 1905; repr. 1924). J. DAY in *A Critical History of Western Philosophy,* ed. D. J. O'CONNOR (New York 1964). B. RUSSELL in *Proceedings of the British Academy* 41 (1956) 43–59. J. D. COLLINS, *A History of Modern European Philosophy* (Milwaukee 1954).

[R. L. CUNNINGHAM]

MILL HILL MISSIONARIES

Officially called St. Joseph's Missionary Society of Mill Hill (MHM, Official Catholic Directory #0830), a society of secular priests and brothers devoted exclusively to worldwide missionary work, it was founded at Mill Hill, London, England, in 1866 by Father Herbert VAUGHAN (later cardinal archbishop of Westminster). The society represented one of the first conscious efforts of post-emancipation English Catholics to shoulder their missionary responsibilities. Vaughan recruited members from any country able to supply them; Holland and the Tyrolean region contributed largely. The society received final approval by the Holy See in 1908.

The society's first mission in the United States (1871) eventually grew into an independent community,

Three lay brothers train for foreign missionary work at St. Joseph's College, Mill Hill. (©Hulton-Deutsch Collection/CORBIS)

the JOSEPHITE FATHERS, who labor among African Americans. In 1951 the Mill Hill Fathers returned to the United States to recruit members for their worldwide mission. The U.S. headquarters is in Hartsdale, NY. The generalate is in Mill Hill, a suburb of London, England.

[N. HANRAHAN/EDS.]

MILLENARIANISM

The teaching that before the Last Judgment [*see* JUDGMENT, DIVINE (IN THE BIBLE)] Christ will return to the earth in order to establish an earthly kingdom, a kingdom which will last for 1,000 years, the "millennium." This term is derived from *mille,* the Latin word for 1,000; the doctrine is also called chiliasm, from χιλάς, Greek for the number 1,000.

In the Bible. This teaching is based on a strictly literal interpretation of Rv 20.1–15. Thus, it teaches that while Satan is chained for 1,000 years, the martyrs and all who have been faithful to Jesus will come to life (the "first resurrection") and for 1,000 years share His royal priesthood in a messianic kingdom. As the 1,000 years near their end, Satan will be permitted to resume his activity. After a bitter struggle Satan will be conquered definitively by Christ in the Last Judgment. Sinners will then rise from the grave to be plunged forever into the pool of fire (the "second death"). The just will enter into the eternal happiness of heaven.

Millenarianism can be found in non-biblical Jewish writings, e.g., 4 Esdras, but Jewish authors do not always distinguish carefully between the messianic kingdom (*see* KINGDOM OF GOD) and the eschatological period [*see* ESCHATOLOGY (IN THE BIBLE)]. Millenarianism was taught by some heretics, such as Cerinthus (*see* HERESY, HISTORY OF, 1) and the EBIONITES, as well as by several Church Fathers, e.g., PAPIAS OF HIEROPOLIS and St. JUSTIN MARTYR. Their interpretation of Rv 20.1–15 was that after a

"Satan's Flight Through Chaos," engraving by Gustave Dore from "Paradise Lost," written by John Milton, illustration from 1866. (©Chris Hellier/CORBIS)

''first resurrection'' of the just, Christ will return to earth to establish a kingdom of 1,000 years duration. Only after these 1,000 years will there be the Last Judgment.

The true interpretation of Rv 20.1–15 stresses the literary form of the Book of REVELATION, with its all-important use of symbolism. The millennium is to be understood in a symbolic sense. The ''first resurrection'' symbolizes Baptism [*see* BAPTISM (IN THE BIBLE)], by which one shares in Christ's Resurrection (see Rom 6.1–10). All the faithful, both those on earth and those in heaven, share in the 1,000-year reign of Jesus, a symbol for the entire life span of the Church considered in its glorious aspect from the Resurrection of Christ until the Last Judgment, just as three-and-a-half years symbolizes the Church's life in struggle and persecution (Rv 11.2–3; 12.14). The chaining of Satan during this same period signifies that the influence of Satan has been notably reduced, not completely removed. The lessening of Satan's influence is the result of the effectiveness of Christ's Redemption. After a final struggle near the end of time (a constant of the apocalyptic pattern; *see* ANTICHRIST), Satan will be definitively conquered by Christ. Then follows the Last Judgment. Those who have not been faithful to Jesus will experience the ''second death,'' the symbol of eternal punishment in hell. The faithful with resurrected bodies will enter into the bliss of heaven.

Bibliography: J. MICHL and G. ENGLHARDT, *Lexikon für Theologie und Kirche*, ed. J. HOFER and K. RAHNER (Freiburg 1957–65) 2:1058–62. H. KRAFT, *Die Religion in Geschichte und Gegenwart* (3d ed. Tübingen 1957–65) 1:1651–53. See following comment. on Rv 20.1–15: E. B. ALLO (3d ed. Paris 1933). H. B. SWETE (New York 1906). M. E. BOISMARD, *Bible de Jérusalem* 43 (1950). A. WIKENHAUSER, ''Die Herkunft der Idee des tausendjährigen Reiches,'' *Römische Quartalschrift für christliche Altertumskunde und für Kirchengeschichte* 45 (1937) 1–24. D. J. LEAHY, ''The Millennium,'' *Scripture* 5 (1952–53) 43–46. G. E. LADD, ''Revelation 20 and the Millennium,'' *The Review and Expositor* 57 (1960) 167–175. R. SUMMERS, ''Revelation 20: An Interpretation,'' *ibid.* 176–183.

[R. KUEHNER]

In Church History. That theory that the Christ will reign on earth for 1,000 years, during which time the saints will be raised from the dead and Satan will be subdued, is rooted deeply in early Jewish apocalyptic tradition and persists in religious movements today.

Jewish Apocalyptic Tradition. In several ancient passages of the earliest prophetic books (*c.* 700 B.C.) allusions are made to a millennial kingdom, a veritable paradise, that will be ruled over by the Deliverer and a ''saved'' remnant of Israel. The emergence of this new Eden will follow the last days of cosmic holocaust after which Yahweh will defeat the forces of evil and provide protection for the elect.

Commentary on the Apocalypse of Beatus: the Death of the Beast and the Enemies of God, manuscript illumination. (©Archivo Iconografico, S.A./CORBIS)

Early eschatological works describe Yahweh not as a vengeful Deity, but rather as a merciful king who will bring to the just a 1,000-year reign of peace and material abundance. The efficacy of these eschatological prophecies was reaffirmed in the *Books of David* written at the height of the Machabean revolt (165 B.C.). In the ''dream'' of David, the Deliverer is a powerful Messiah who would rule not only Israel, but the entire world.

Messianic prophecy intensified as the political lot of the Jews became more intolerable and, from the annexation of Palestine (63 B.C.) to the war of A.D. 66–72, the wise Messiah of Davidic origin was replaced by the superhuman ''warrior king'' in the Apocalypses of Ezra and Baruch (1st century A.D.). Throughout this period various ''messiahs'' appeared, and, even in the last great Jewish uprising of A.D. 131, its leader, Simon BAR KOKHBA, was hailed as the true ''Messiah.''

Early Christian Apocalyptic. Like the Jews, the Christians of the early Church (50–150) suffered persecutions at the hands of their Roman overlords, and in their plight they readily utilized the Jewish eschatological tradition. Around A.D. 93 Christians evoked the millennial message in the Revelations in which the ''Tyrant of the Last Days'' is depicted as a hideous 10-horned beast. To the members of the early Church, this beast, or Antichrist, easily symbolized the oppressive Roman state, and millenarists hopefully anticipated its defeat at the Second Coming of Christ.

It was partly in reaction to the Roman persecution that Montanism, the New Prophecy as an eschatological theory, held that the Second Coming would soon take place in the Phrygian city of Pepuza. In 156 Montanus claimed to be divinely inspired by the ''Spirit of Truth'' and therefore capable of prophesying the PAROUSIA. All Christians were urged to gather in Pepuza and await the Second Coming in prayer and fasting. Within a few years the Phrygian prophet's eschatological summons was carried throughout Asia Minor and retold in Africa and Gaul.

TERTULLIAN (d. 220), the greatest theologian in the West at that time, was attracted to Montanism's high regard for divine inspiration, and by his prestige alone he added new converts to the movement. However, he rejected much of the radicalism of the early Montanists and never did believe in the prophecy of the Phrygian Parousia.

Montanism encountered sharp criticism from DIONYSIUS OF ALEXANDRIA, who attacked the theory at its roots by questioning the Apostolic origins of the Revelation. The doctrines of Montanus were finally declared heretical by Pope ZEPHYRINUS (d. 217).

Despite the eventual collapse of Montanism, CHILIASM or the doctrine of an eschatological kingdom prophesied in Isaiah and Ezekiel was accepted literally by many in the early Church, including JUSTIN MARTYR. IRENAEUS, in his lengthy exposition *Adversus Haereses*, averred that divine justice demanded that the chiliastic revelation be realized. LACTANTIUS and the poet Commodianus gave impetus to chiliasm by emphasizing the demoniac Antichrist and his eventual defeat in the Second Coming. First attempts to discredit radical chiliasm were made by ORIGEN (d. 254) in his assertion that eschatological change came about only in the soul. St. AUGUSTINE in the *City of God* advanced the theory that the millennium had actually begun with Christ's nativity.

Although attempts had been made at various times to question the authenticity of the Revelation, these apocalyptic writings were in fact reinforced by the Judaeo-Christian *Sibylline Books*, especially the *Tiburtina* (c. 350). Unlike previous eschatological theories, the Sibylline tradition prophesied two warrior-saviors. In the *Pseudo-Methodius* an earthly emperor rises from his grave, slaughters the forces of evil, and introduces an era of relative tranquillity until the demoniac Antichrist appears. At this critical juncture the Christ descends, slays the Antichrist, and the Last Judgment begins.

The eschatological tradition was preserved in the commentaries on the Apocalypse of Bede, Walafrid Strabo, Anselm of Laon, and Bruno of Segni, but chiliasm was rejected as heresy by THOMAS AQUINAS (*Summa theologiae* 3, 77, 1 ad 4). On the basis of the Rv 7.2 and 14.6, JOACHIM OF FIORE (d. 1201) predicted that the 1,000-year reign of the Holy Spirit would begin in A.D. 1260, and his influence was felt among the early Dominicans, Spiritual Franciscans, Beguines, and Fraticelli.

Middle Ages. In the Middle Ages many a powerful king was mistaken for the ''Last Emperor,'' and the invading hordes of Huns, Saracens, and Turks played the role of Antichrists. As the year 1000 neared, millenarianism became more prevalent because many eschatologists believed that the 7th day of creation was to be realized in human history in A.D. 1000 and that there would follow a glorious 10-century reign of the Christ.

In the later Middle Ages, millenarianism was clearly evident in the populous regions of northern France, the Low Countries, and in the Rhine Valley. From a combination of factors—overpopulation, the rise of merchant capitalism, and improvements in agricultural technology—there arose a class of unemployed urban dwellers who possessed neither the native skill nor the professional training with which to secure for themselves a stable place in a competitive society. These people, ever conscious of their desperate condition, became extremely susceptible to the eschatological phantasies of prophets claiming to be divinely inspired saviors, or even gods. Thus the chiliastic tradition was not lost, but instead adapted for social reform. TANCHELM (d. 1115) appeared in Antwerp announcing that he was God to the same degree that Christ was. He quickly gained the confidence of the artisans and it was only after many massacres that he was finally apprehended and executed. In Brittany, a generation later, Budo de Stella attracted a large following of peasants by exposing himself to them as the ''Son of God'' who would judge the living and the dead. Both Tanchelm and De Stella considered the Church a formidable obstacle to their chiliastic movements and for them the Church became the Antichrist.

Another ancient chiliastic prophecy that appeared in medieval millenarianism was the Sibylline Emperor of the Last Days. At one time or another this title was attributed to Count Baldwin IX of Flanders, Philip II Augustus, Frederick II, Louis IX, Sigismund, Maximilian, and Charles V. Frederick II was the most important of these precursors of the millennial kingdom, because he alone never denied his ''divinity'' and, even after his death (1250), German eschatologists as late as 1500 believed the prophecy contained in the *Book of 100 Chapters*.

During the plague epidemics of 1348–49, new self-flagellant sects passed through Germany and Thuringia.

In Thuringia Konrad Schmid (d. 1368), averring to be the Frederick of the eschatological prophecies, preached self-flagellation as a means of preparing for the millennium. The eschatologist Schmid was intimately associated with the heretical Brethren of the Free Spirit, who considered themselves one with the Holy Spirit. This theory, Neoplatonic in accent, was originated in the early 13th century by Amaury, a theologian at the University of Paris. The Amaurians claimed to be the reincarnated Christ whose mission it was to preach the coming millennium in which all mankind would fully recognize their oneness with the Spirit.

Millenarianism lay beneath the surface in England's Peasant Revolt (1381) and the Jacquerie uprising (1358), but it was in the Taborite movement that egalitarian millenarianism first became fully evident. The TABORITES, a revolutionary offspring of the HUSSITES, after John HUS (d. 1414), adopted the chiliastic tenets of the Free Spiritualists, denounced the pope as an Antichrist, and lived in constant anticipation of the Second Coming. Another precursor of egalitarian millenarianism was one Hans BÖHM (d. 1476), the Drummer of Niklashausen, a simple-minded popular entertainer, who became the object of the machinations of the local lords. Böhm averred that the Virgin had instructed him that Niklashausen was the ''new salvation city,'' and only there could man find Divine Grace.

Reformation. During the Reformation chiliastic millenarianism reached a new emotional peak in the PEASANTS' WAR of 1525 and in the ANABAPTIST movement. The uprising of 1525 was an insurrection of peasants led by Thomas MÜNZER, a man firmly committed to a literal interpretation of the chiliastic theories in the *Books of Revelation.* According to Münzer, the people destined to live in the millennial kingdom were the poor because they had not been corrupted by greed and wealth. The means he chose to attain his end were the sudden overthrow and violent annihilation of the wealthy, ecclesiastical and secular. The Anabaptists tried to live as closely as possible to the precepts of the New Testament, and the more radical members prophesied the millennium. However, the almost fanatical exclusivism of early Anabaptism eventually alienated the militant millenarists in the movement.

In northwest Germany two Anabaptist preachers, Melchior Hoffmann and Bernt Rothmann, acquired converts in the prosperous city of Münster. But they were soon replaced by Jan Matthys (d. 1534) and Jan Bockelson (d. 1537), two chiliastic revolutionaries who were so caught up in their own fervor that they proclaimed that only in Münster were Christians leading a life worthy of salvation. The rest of the world around the ''New Jerusalem'' would perish in the Parousia that was close at hand. Anabaptists flocked to Münster and shortly Matthys and Bockelson controlled the town. After Matthys's death, Bockelson declared that by God's will he was the ''King of the World.'' However, his reign came to an abrupt end when the authorities recaptured Münster in 1537.

Modern Period. Millenarianism persisted in the 16th and 17th centuries mainly through the efforts of Valentin Weigel in Germany, Pierre JURIEU in France, and Jane Lade in England. On the Continent, Germany became the most important base of millenarian theory primarily due to the work of Johann Bengel, Frederick Oetinger, Johann Jung-Stilling, and Johann Kurtz.

In the United States, the millenarist William MILLER gathered a large following in the first half of the 19th century. Chiliastic views are still found in the doctrines of the premillenarian Adventist sects that hold that Christ will appear before the millennium. The following religions contain at least part of the premillenarian concept: the SEVENTH-DAY ADVENTISTS, the Southern Baptist Convention (*see* BAPTISTS), the Second ADVENTISTS, the Primitive Baptists, and the Mormons (*see* LATTER-DAY SAINTS, CHURCH OF JESUS CHRIST OF THE).

Bibliography: J. MICHL and G. ENGLHARDT, *Lexikon für Theologie und Kirche*, ed. J. HOFER and K. RAHNER (Freiburg 1957–65) 2:1058–62. F. E. HAMILTON, *The Basis of Millennial Faith* (Grand Rapids 1942). H. SCHOEPS, *Theologie und Geschichte des Judenchristentums* (Tübingen 1949). R. FRICK, *Die Geschichte des Reich-Gottes-Gedankens in der alten Kirche* (Giessen 1928). F. ALCAÑIZ, *Ecclesia patristica et millenarismus* (Granada 1933). N. R. C. COHN, *The Pursuit of the Millennium* (London 1957). T. F. GLASSON, *The Second Advent* (London 1945). H. KRAFT, ''Die Altkirchliche Prophetie und die Enstehung des Montanismus,'' *Theologische Zeitschrift 11* (1955) 335–372.

[J. P. DOLAN]

MILLER, WILLIAM

Founder of the modern Adventist movement; b. Pittsfield, Mass., Feb. 15, 1782; d. Hampton, N.Y., Dec. 20, 1849. He was a veteran of the War of 1812 and a farmer in upstate New York. At the age of 34, he abandoned Deism to join the Baptist Church; he began to preach in 1831 and engaged in Biblical prophecy. His interpretation of passages in Daniel and the Apocalypse led him to declare that the Second Coming of Christ would occur on March 21, 1843. A number of Baptist, Methodist, Presbyterian, and Congregationalist clergymen accepted his prediction. When the event did not happen on the expected date, Miller announced that the end would come on March 21, 1844; finally, the date was set for Oct. 22, 1844. The postponements and disappointments decimated the ranks of the Millerites, or Adventists. One group, which combined Miller's prophecies with other doctrinal interpretations, survived to become the SEVENTH-DAY ADVENTISTS.

Bibliography: E. N. DICK, *Dictionary of American Biography*, ed. A. JOHNSON and D. MALONE (New York 1928–36) (1957) 6.2:641–643. A. F. TYLER, *Freedom's Ferment* (Minneapolis 1944).

[W. J. WHALEN]

MILLS, SAMUEL J.

American Congregationalist minister, who was instrumental in the development of the foreign mission movement in America and in other social and religious reforms; b. Torrington, Conn., April 21, 1783; d. at sea, June 16, 1818. The son of a Congregationalist pastor, he intended to be a farmer until he experienced a conversion (1801) and began to prepare for the ministry, with a view to overseas missionary work. He entered (1806) Williams College, Williamstown, Mass., where he soon influenced other students, culminating in the famous ''haystack meeting'' (1807), when several experienced a call to the missions. After graduation (1809), he studied briefly at Yale and entered Andover Seminary, Newton Centre, Mass. (1810), where, with some of his Williams College colleagues, he took steps leading to the formation of the American Board of Commissioners for Foreign Missions. He worked for a time as a home missionary in the Mississippi Valley and published *A Report of a Missionary Tour* (1815). After ordination (1815), he turned his attention to the urban poor and the African Americans, founding the American Bible Society (1816) and associating himself with the newly formed American Colonization Society. As the latter's agent he visited Africa and purchased lands near Cape Mesurado as the site, to be called Liberia, for a settlement of African Americans. After contracting a fever, he died on the return passage.

Bibliography: G. SPRING, *Memoir of the Rev. Samuel J. Mills* (2d ed. New York 1829). T. C. RICHARDS, *Samuel J. Mills* (Boston 1906). J. TRACY, *History of the American Board of Commissioners for Foreign Missions* (2d ed. New York 1842). O. W. ELSBREE, *Rise of the Missionary Spirit in America* (Williamsport, Pa. 1928). P. J. STAUDENRAUS, *The African Colonization Movement* (New York 1961).

[R. K. MACMASTER]

MILMAN, HENRY HART

English poet, historian; b. London, Feb. 10, 1791; d. Ascot, Sept. 24, 1868. Educated at Eton and Brasenose College, Oxford, Milman had a brilliant academic career and won the Newdigate prize for poetry in 1812. After being ordained in the Anglican Church (1816), he was appointed vicar of St. Mary's in Reading (1818), canon of Westminster and rector of St. Margaret's (1835), and dean of St. Paul's Cathedral, London (1849). He gained an early reputation as a poet with his epic drama *Fazio* (1815); he then composed *Samor the Lord of the Bright City* (1818) and the dramatic poems *The Fall of Jerusalem* (1820) and *The Martyr of Antioch and Belshazzar* (1822). *Ann Boleyn* (1826), a somewhat mediocre composition, marked the end of his poetic career. His descriptive style was florid, with a certain dramatic strength; and his poems included some felicitous lyrics. But his work was marred by a lack of creative imagination, particularly in character drawing. He contributed some notable hymns to Reginald Heber's collection in 1827. Some of his best hymns still appear in Anglican hymnbooks; these include ''When Our Heads Are Bowed with Woe'' and ''Ride on, Ride on in Majesty.'' Later in life Milman turned to translation and pioneered in the rendering of Sanskrit poems into English. He translated *Agamemnon* and *The Bacchae,* and also produced a new edition of Horace. In 1838 he published an edition of Edward Gibbon's *Decline and Fall of the Roman Empire.* Milman's historical works varied in quality. His *History of the Jews* (1830) offended Newman and provoked sharp criticism for its evasion and minimizing of the miraculous elements in the Old Testament, but Milman reissued it later with a sharp reply to his critics. His *History of Christianity . . . in the Roman Empire* (1840) was also coldly received. However, *The History of Latin Christianity down to the Death of Pope Nicholas V* (1835), his most important historical work, long remained a classic because of its balance and candor, although it contained many errors of detail. Milman had a great gift for friendships and counted Thomas Macaulay, Sydney Smith, Henry Hallam, and John Lockhart in his circle. As dean of St. Paul's he accomplished much in making cathedral worship more popular.

Bibliography: A. MILMAN, *Henry Hart Milman* (London 1900). C. H. E. SMYTH, *Dean Milman* (Society for Promoting Christian Knowledge 1949). R. GARNETT, *Dictionary of National Biography* (London 1908–38) 13:448–451. F. L. CROSS, *The Oxford Dictionary of the Christian Church* (London 1957) 901.

[W. HANNAH]

MILNER, JOHN

English bishop and leader in the movement for Catholic emancipation; b. London, Oct. 14, 1752; d. Wolverhampton, April 19, 1826. His father was a tailor and his family, whose proper name was Miller, originated in Lancashire. Bishop Richard Challoner sent him in 1765 to the English college at DOUAI, where he was ordained (1777). He returned then to Winchester, England, where he ministered to the French prisoners of war and served as pastor until 1803. While there, he also helped the English nuns who had fled their convents on the Continent because of the French Revolution to establish themselves in England. During the negotiations leading to the first Catholic Relief Bill, which abolished the Penal Laws and legalized the celebration of Mass (1791), Milner was theological adviser to the English vicars apostolic and encouraged firmness, especially against the objectionable oath required of Catholics and the title of "Protesting Catholic Dissenters." In this stand he opposed the counsel of Charles BUTLER and the Cisalpine Club.

In 1803 Milner became titular bishop of Castabala and vicar apostolic of the Midland District. In subsequent agitation for Catholic EMANCIPATION, Milner acted as London representative of the Irish bishops and fought every measure that would concede to the British government a veto over the Holy See's appointments of Catholic bishops. Here again he was opposed by Butler and also by Bp. William POYNTER and the London clergy. His advocacy of papal prerogatives won for him in Rome the title of the English Athanasius. But his pronounced views, often expressed imprudently, made his writings on emancipation extremely controversial. In 1817 the prefect of the Congregation for the Propagation of the Faith asked him to discontinue writing articles for the *Orthodox Journal.* During his remaining years he concentrated on his duties as vicar apostolic. Milner published many articles and books. His two-volume *History of Winchester* (1798–1801) was scholarly as well as controversial. *The End of Controversy* (1818), a work of popular theology, is his best-known book. Milner had a reputation also as an archeologist.

Bibliography: J. MILNER, *Supplementary Memoirs* (London 1820). F. C. HUSENBETH, *Life of the Right Rev. John Milner* (Dublin 1862). B. N. WARD, *Dawn of the Catholic Revival in England, 1781–1803,* 2 v. (New York 1909). *The Catholic Encyclopedia* (New York 1907–1914) 10:315–317. J. GILLOW, *A Literary and Biographical History or Bibliographical Dictionary of the English Catholics from 1534 to the Present Time,* 5 v. (London and New York 1885–1902 reprint New York 1961) 5:15–53. T. COOPER, *The Dictionary of National Biography from the Earliest Times to 1900,* 63 v. (London 1885–1900) 13:461–464.

[A. J. BANNAN]

John Milner.

MILNER, RALPH, BL.

Lay martyr; b. Slackstead (Flacsted), Hants, England; d. hanged at Winchester, July 7, 1591. Milner was a simple, illiterate man who married and supported his eight children through his labor. For most of a century he belonged to the Anglican church, but the lives of the Catholics he knew caused him to reconsider his beliefs. He decided to seek instruction in the faith and was received into the Church. On the day of his first Communion, however, he was arrested and committed to Winchester jail for changing his religion. Here his good behavior during years of imprisonment eventually won the confidence of the jailer who entrusted Milner with the prison keys and frequently allowed him to leave. This enabled him to help his fellow Catholic prisoners by bringing in priests to administer the Sacraments or render other services. His liberty also allowed him to serve as escort to several priests, including Fr. Thomas Stanney, then Bl. Roger DICKENSON, with whom he was arrested. Dickenson and Milner were confined to Winchester jail. Attempts were made to persuade the ancient Milner to attend a Protestant service in exchange for his life. He refused "to embrace a counsel so disagreeable to the maxims of the Gospel." Other effort was made en route to the gallows: His children were sent to plead with him to renounce his faith. Instead, Milner blessed his children and said that "he could wish them no greater happiness than to die for the like cause". He was beatified by Pius XI on Dec. 15, 1929.

Feast of the English Martyrs: May 4 (England).

See Also: ENGLAND, SCOTLAND, AND WALES, MARTYRS OF.

Bibliography: R. CHALLONER, *Memoirs of Missionary Priests,* ed. J. H. POLLEN (rev. ed. London 1924; repr. Farnborough 1969). J. H. POLLEN, *Acts of English Martyrs* (London 1891).

[K. I. RABENSTEIN]

MILTIADES, POPE, ST.

Pontificate: July 2, 311 to Jan. 10, 314. After a vacancy of one or two years the Emperor Maxentius allowed the election of a new bishop of Rome as successor to EUSEBIUS. The LIBERIAN CATALOGUE assigns him a reign of three years, six months, and eight days and says that he was consecrated on July 2, 311; while the trustworthy *Depositio Episcoporum* places the date of his burial on January 10. The three years (III) of the Liberian Catalogue may be a mistake for II; this would reconcile the two sources. Miltiades (also Melchiades) assumed office apparently shortly after the promulgation of the Edict of Toleration at Nicomedia on April 30, 311, which put an end to persecution, at least in the West.

His election ended a period of internal confusion and factionalism in the Roman Church. Maxentius ordered the Pretorian Prefect to restore to the deacons of the Roman Church the property confiscated by the State. What part Miltiades played in the momentous events that shaped the destiny of the Church and culminated in the imperial rescripts of 313 is not known. But during his reign Christianity received legal recognition and eventually a status equal to that of the pagan cults.

Miltiades was in Rome when CONSTANTINE became emperor after his victory at the Milvian Bridge, which he attributed to the aid of the Christian God. The new emperor presented to the pope a palace on the Lateran which became the papal residence.

In the case of the Donatist controversy the initiative clearly seems to have lain with Constantine I. The African bishops opposed the election of Caecilian as bishop of Carthage on the grounds that he had been a *traditor* and appealed to Constantine to designate bishops from Gaul to decide between the two parties. The emperor commissioned the pope, together with the bishops of Cologne, Autun, and Arles, to adjudicate the matter in Rome after hearing both sides. Going beyond the emperor's commission, Miltiades added fifteen Italian bishops to the group, held a synod in the *domus Faustae in Laterano* on October 2, 313, at which both Caecilian and his rival DONATUS were present, pronounced in favor of Caecilian, and excommunicated Donatus. They also proposed milder measures to facilitate the reconciliation of the Donatists in accordance with the imperial will. The Donatists appealed from the Roman synod to the emperor. It seems that they never forgave Miltiades for his decision against them; and toward the end of the century they spread stories about his alleged weakness during the persecution.

It is unlikely that the measures attributed to him by the *Liber pontificalis* forbidding fasting on Sundays and Thursdays and providing for particles of the consecrated host (*fermentum*) to be sent from the pope's Mass to the presbyteral churches are contemporary. His death is commemorated correctly in the *Depositio Episcoporum* and *Martyrology of St. Jerome* on January 10. The Roman MARTYROLOGY, following the *Liber pontificalis,* is in error with December 10. Miltiades was buried in the cemetery of St. Callistus, the exact location of his tomb being unknown.

Bibliography: EUSEBIUS, *Ecclesiastical History* 10.5. *Liber pontificalis,* ed. L. DUCHESNE 1:168–169; 3:76. H. LECLERCQ, *Dictionnaire d'archéologie chrétienne et de liturgie* (Paris 1912) 11.1:1199–1203; 13.1: 1194–96. H. U. INSTINSKY, "Zwei Bischofsnamen konstantinischer Zeit," *Römische Quartalschrift für christliche Altertumskunde und für Kirchengeschichte* 55 (1960) 203–211. R. MONTINI, *Le tombe dei papi* (Rome 1957) 88. J. N. D. KELLY, *Oxford Dictionary of Popes* (New York 1986) 26–27. C. PIETRI *Roma Christiana* (Rome 1976) 160–168. M. V. ANASTOS, "The Edict of Milan (313). A Defense of Its Traditional Authorship and Designation," *Studies in Early Christianity* 11 (New York & London 1993) 215–43. K. M. GIRADET, "Das Reichskonzil von Rom (313)—Urteil, Einspruch, Folgen," *Historia* 41 (1992) 104–116.

[J. CHAPIN]

MILTITZ, KARL VON

Curial diplomat; b. Rabenaul, near Dresden, 1490; d. by drowning in the Main, Nov. 20, 1529. Karl was the posthumous son of Sigismund von Miltitz, a lesser noble of Meissen; he was educated at Cologne and Mainz and was sent to Rome in 1541, where, through the influence of his uncle, the Dominican Nicholas von Schönberg, he was made a papal notary and titular chamberlain. In September of 1518 he was selected to carry the Golden Rose to Frederick The Wise, Elector of Saxony. The move was calculated to frustrate the imperial election of the Hapsburg Charles of Spain and to persuade the elector to consent to the extradition of Martin Luther. It was not the intention of LEO X that Miltitz should inaugurate a policy of mediation during his conference with Luther at Altenberg in January of 1519; nevertheless Miltitz, believing that a settlement of the Lutheran affair would aid Rome's plans in the imperial election, suggested a trial for Luther before the archbishop of Trier. Neither Luther nor his supporters trusted the emissary who had, without the knowledge of Cajetan, his superior, proposed a hearing that would also involve Johann TETZEL. The death of

Maximilian on January 10 postponed the Lutheran affair, and Miltitz, as papal agent and with French support, attempted to persuade Frederick to obtain the two votes needed for his election. The promise of a cardinal's hat for whomever he chose was one of Miltitz's inducements. Miltitz met with Luther at Liebenwenda (October 1519) and Lichtenberg (October 1520) but achieved no results. He resided in Germany and held benefices as a chapter member of cathedrals in Mainz and Meissen until his death.

Bibliography: F. LAU, *Die Religion in Geschichte und Gegenwart* (Tübingen 1957–1963) 4:954. ÉAMANN, *Dictionnaire de théologie catholique,* 15 v. (Paris 1903–1950) 10.2:1765–1767. E. ISERLOH, *Lexikon für Theologie und Kirche* (Freiburg 1957–) 7:422. K. SCHOTTENLOHER, *Bibliographie zur deutschen Geschicte im Zeitlater der Glaubensspaltung, 1517–85* (Leipzig 1933–40, Stuttgart 1956–) 2:57. P. KALKOFF, *Die Miltitziade* (Leipzig 1911).

[J. P. DOLAN]

MILTON, JOHN

Poet, scholar, pamphleteer; b. London, Dec. 9, 1608; d. there, Nov. 8, 1674. He was a product of the classical Renaissance and of the Protestant Reformation in its most extreme English development, Puritanism. His father, John, who had defected from Roman Catholicism and was disinherited by his yeoman family, had prospered as a London scrivener by the time his son was born. The home, strongly Protestant and moderately Puritan (conforming still to the Established Church), was not notably literary or artistic but contained some books (e.g., Sylvester's translation of the French Protestant poet Du Bartas and Spenser's *Faerie Queene*) and the family was fond of music (the father was an amateur musician and composer); the home was marked by "cheerful godliness," and certainly by respect for learning. The gifted and studious boy had every educational advantage: private tutoring, St. Paul's School (COLET's foundation, which under Alexander Gill largely retained a tradition of Christian humanism), and Christ's College, Cambridge (1625–32). The last, to Milton's disgust (see *Proclusion* 3), was still dominated by the old scholastic discipline but afforded him an opportunity to continue his classical studies and commence his practice in poetry (Latin, English, and even Italian).

If this background was designed to prepare Milton for holy orders and a place among the Puritan preachers within the Established Church, LAUD's policy of repression thwarted it, and Milton found himself "church-outed by the prelates"; but, as his religious experience deepened and confidence in his poetic gift grew, he determined to devote his life to the service of God in poetry.

John Milton.

A period of intense study and moral discipline (1632–38) followed, during which he wrote *Comus* (1634) and *Lycidas* (1638). A tour through France and Switzerland to Italy (1638–39) led to meetings with Grotius, Galileo, and Manso (the friend and patron of Tasso), and to his welcome in the Platonic Academy (Florence). Though he did not conceal his Puritan principles, this was a humanist's pilgrimage to classic ground, which would have continued to Sicily and Greece had not the Bishops' War, the prelude to the Puritan Revolution, called him home to be of service in the struggle for reformation and liberty (see his account in *Defensio secunda*).

Prose in the Puritan Cause. Save for the *Epitaphium Damonis* (1639), a moving elegy on Charles Diodati, his friend and confidant since boyhood days, his *Sonnets* (Nos. 8–23), and one or two other occasional pieces, he wrote no more poetry until *Paradise Lost* (though he published his earlier *Poems* in 1645). All his effort was channeled into prose in defense of the Puritan cause or to expositions of his concepts of religious, civil, and domestic liberty. First he joined the attack on Episcopacy and the demand for a Presbyterian church in such works as *Of Reformation* (1641) and *The Reason of Church Government* (1642). Then he made his plea for freer divorce in *The Doctrine and Discipline of Divorce* (1643, 1644) and *Tetrachordon* (1643)—a plea not unconnected with the fact that his young wife, Mary Powell, whom he had married in 1642, had returned to her Royalist family. Milton was now attacked by his Presbyterian allies, and, hampered by their censorship of the press, he wrote his most famous prose work, the *Areopagitica* (1644). It was a plea for uncensored publication but also in effect for liberty of conscience, appearing in the same year as Roger WILLIAMS's *Bloudy Tenent of Persecution.* In *Of Education* (1644), Milton described (in the spirit of Christian humanism, not, as is sometimes asserted, in that of Baconian empiricism) the intellectual, religious, and moral training necessary for those who would be truly free and competent to serve Church and State.

Not until 1649 did he turn to political issues, when, in *The Tenure of Kings and Magistrates,* he defended the desperate action of the Puritan Army in bringing Charles I to trial and execution. *Eikonoklastes* (1649) was an effort to counteract the immense effect of the *Eikon Basilike,* the supposed meditations of Charles in captivity; and, now Latin secretary to the new republican government, Milton was commissioned to reply to the royalist champion SALMASIUS. This he did in *Pro populo anglicano defensio* (1651), of which (as he proudly said) "all Europe talks from side to side," and to which he consciously and heroically sacrificed the remnant of his failing eyesight. Though a republican at heart, he supported Oliver CROMWELL as Lord Protector, praising and admonishing him in the *Defensio secunda* (1654). When he was relieved of some of his duties in 1655, and of more in 1658, he had leisure to give to his theological treatise, *De Doctrina Christiana* (unpublished until 1825), and perhaps to *Paradise Lost* (whose subject he had had in mind as early as 1642, but for dramatic, not epic, treatment). Meanwhile he had written such sonnets as No. 16, to Cromwell (a plea against a state church); No. 18, on the late massacre in Piedmont; No. 19, on his blindness; and No. 23, on the death of his beloved second wife. With the death of Cromwell in November 1658, and the ensuing chaos that was to result in the Restoration, Milton struck his last blows for the extreme Puritan cause: in *Of Civil Power in Ecclesiastical Causes* (1659) he pleaded for religious toleration and in *A Ready and Easy Way to Establish a Free Commonwealth* (2d ed. April 1660) he opposed the Restoration up to its very eve.

At the Restoration Milton was imprisoned for a short time but unmolested after his release, an act of singular clemency by the restored monarchy. Though aging, blind, with all his hopes for England shattered, and conscious of living in an alien world, he was yet able to complete the work he was born to do. *Paradise Lost* appeared in 1667 (the 1st ed. in ten books, later redivided into 12), and *Paradise Regained,* with *Samson Agonistes,* in 1671. There is no greater example of genius coupled with indomitable will. He was buried in the Church of St. Giles, Cripplegate, with Anglican rites.

Early Poetry (1626–39). At Cambridge Milton seized every opportunity to practice the art to which he had devoted himself. In Latin he wrote *Elegy* 3 (on the death of Lancelot Andrewes), *Elegy* 7 (Cupid's Revenge), and *Elegy* 5 (On the Coming of Spring)—the last two were pagan erotic poems in the tradition of the Roman elegists but marked by a characteristic beauty of innocence. Religion and the English language, however, were soon to assert their claim in the *Ode on the Morning of Christ's Nativity* (1629), in which we may trace the beginnings of an experience, at once religious and poetic, that was to crystallize three years later in the resolve to live and write thereafter "As ever in my great Taskmaster's eye" (*Sonnet* 7, December 1632). Between 1629 and 1632 there had been some hesitation, perhaps retreat, but certainly a return to secular subjects in the Italian sonnets, in *Arcades,* and in the famous companion pieces, *L'Allegro* and *Il Penseroso,* though with religious overtones in the last. After *Sonnet* 7, however, there was to be no return to secular themes.

Four characteristics of Milton's poetry were already present in the early poems: (1) the starting point in traditional forms (the Ovidian elegy; the Petrarchan sonnet; in the *Nativity Ode,* the Messianic eclogue; in *Arcades* and *Comus,* the court masque; in *L'Allegro* and *Il Penseroso,* a compendium of motifs from the English lyric; in *Lycidas,* the pastoral elegy as it had come down from Theocritus and Virgil); (2) the freedom and originality with which Milton shapes these traditional vehicles to his ends; (3) the clearly marked structure of each, the groundwork for a variety of patterned effects in idea, image, and sentiment—a principal source of their artistic appeal; and (4) the unobtrusive but patent reference in most of them to Milton's own experience and deepest concerns—a source of their emotional power. These characteristics may be illustrated briefly from *Comus* and *Lycidas.*

Comus, written for the installation of the Earl of Bridgewater as Lord President of Wales, develops into something more dramatic and more fraught with doctrine than the common masque, as it presents the imagined adventures of the Earl's three children on their journey to Ludlow to greet their parents. In the wild wood the brothers lose their sister, who is decoyed by the evil enchanter Comus (the son of Circe) to his palace and there tempted to share his life of luxury and license. She scornfully rejects his advances; her brothers, led by the Attendant Spirit, find her, firm indeed in virtue, but immobilized by the enchanter's spell, from which she can be freed only by the superior power of Sabrina, virgin nymph of the

River Severn, who, sprinkling on her ''drops of precious cure,'' releases her to pursue her journey. The children reach Ludlow and are presented by the Attendant Spirit to their parents. On its literal level the action is pure folk-tale, but ''more is meant than meets the ear''; the wild wood is the world; the palace of Comus is a concentration of evil therein; and Ludlow, the goal of the journey, is home and a symbol of heaven. The theme is chastity and the resistance to temptation, but more than that, heaven's providential care of the innocent (symbolized by the Attendant Spirit) and the necessity of divine grace for progress in the Christian's pilgrimage (symbolized by the intervention of Sabrina). This is Milton's concern and his message, summed up by the epilogue spoken by the Attendant Spirit. Structural pattern and symbolic image are of the essence of *Comus.*

Pattern and symbol play the same role in *Lycidas,* Milton's elegy on the death by drowning of young Edward King. The Christian pastoral elegy, unlike its pagan counterpart, moves (as can be seen in the *Epitaphium Damonis*) from despair to the hope of immortality and so to a note of consolation and triumph. In *Lycidas,* while drawing on the accumulated imagery of the whole tradition, Milton extends this hope to a principle of healing and restoration that operates, under Providence, throughout life and culminates in the joys of heaven. Thus to view the tragedy, by an alliance of religion and poetry, is to clear one's vision and fortify one's faith; and the poet is able at the end to resume his task: ''Tomorrow to fresh woods and pastures new.''

Developing Thought (1640–60). Milton's Puritanism became increasingly emphatic and extreme. When allied with the Presbyterians (1640–43), he grew disillusioned, deciding that ''New Presbyter is but old Priest writ large'' (*New Forcers of Conscience,* 1646), and supported the Independents, until they in turn sought to set up a state church. Thereupon he appealed to Cromwell, ''Help us to save free conscience from the paw/ Of hireling wolves whose gospel is their maw'' (*Sonnet* 16, 1652); he was by this time clearly a Separatist, who would presently champion religious toleration for all who grounded their beliefs solely on Scripture (*Civil Power in Ecclesiastical Causes,* 1659). His Puritanism explains his politics: others might fall away, but he would champion ''the good old cause'' to the bitter end, convinced that it alone would guarantee the liberty of the regenerate. This was his sole concern, and he was to countenance violence and dictatorship to achieve this end. After the *Areopagitica* he became increasingly disillusioned with his fellow countrymen: he was a radical but no democrat. In *The Tenure of Kings and Magistrates* (1649) he asserted that all power resides in the people and is merely delegated to the monarch, who, if he violates his trust, may be brought to account. This, however, does not mean that the people's will must prevail: the Puritan army, called and owned by God, must, under its leaders, act for the people's good and, if need be, against their will. His defiance of the majority was more open in *The Ready and Easy Way* (1660): all who have opposed or abandoned the Puritan cause have lost their right of choice, and the remnant, who desire only their freedom, have the right to keep it by force if they can. To encourage them and give them something to fight for, Milton proposed a new constitution with neither monarch nor protector but a perpetual senate of able and regenerate men, dedicated to the principle of religious freedom.

For Milton, the extreme Puritan, the Church and tradition count for nothing: there is but one authority, the Bible, as it is studied and interpreted by the individual believer. Between his Puritanism and his humanism some tension inevitably developed, but their relation is not simple. In politics there was a radical tradition in Renaissance humanism, and Milton responded to this in his political writings. In ethics, he combined an appeal to Scripture, to the law of nature, and to the good of man (as in the divorce tracts); and, much more than most of his fellow Puritans, he reacted strongly against asceticism. Moreover, his scripturism was accompanied by an increasingly militant rationalism: where the Bible speaks, he would accept its pronouncements (but he would first submit them to a searching analysis); where it is silent, he would rely on reason alone. To this combination of Scripture and reason may be traced some of the more extreme opinions of the *De Doctrina Christiana.*

In isolating these principal examples, we should remember that Milton always regarded himself as a Christian, retaining a firm conviction of God's creation and government of the world, man's fall and Christ's Redemption, and the clear revelation of all this in Scripture. But his views on the Trinity approximated ARIANISM: the Son, ''the first born of every creature,'' but raised to divine honors, was the ''True Image of the Father'' and the manifestation of the otherwise inapprehensible God. He rejected creation *ex nihilo* and substituted, in effect, *de Deo:* since God was infinite, He embraced all that was, and since He was omnipotent, all causes, including the material cause. Creation was thus the imposition of form and order on a single substance, essentially good (because of God), and including both matter and spirit (which differed not in kind, but in degree). This position is often called MATERIALISM, but is more correctly MONISM.

Further, Milton rejected the extremes of Calvinism; he held that the fall of man was not predestined but the result of man's free choice; that it resulted, in turn, not in total depravity but in deprivation. Grace sufficient for repentance, however, was offered to all men, and, if freely accepted, was enhanced to salvation; the law of nature, given to Adam and obscured but not obliterated by the fall, was, in the regenerate, by the operation of the Holy Spirit, progressively restored to its original brightness. Finally Milton placed a heavy and repeated emphasis on Christian liberty, which depends on the voluntary acceptance of the Gospel, whereby the regenerate were made sons of God and joint heirs with Christ. On the negative side it meant the abrogation of the Law, and on the positive, the identification of liberty with virtue, the recognition that God's service was indeed perfect freedom. It is necessary to know this much of Milton's theology if one is to understand his writings, and especially *Paradise Lost;* for the positions argued in the *De Doctrina,* orthodox and unorthodox alike, are assumed in the epic.

Paradise Lost. Milton's magnum opus is a classical epic with a Christian subject and theme: its form links it with Homer, and more particularly with Vergil; but its subject, derived from the Bible, turns on man's fall, his repentance, and the promise of salvation—matters wholly alien to the pagan models. It is a religious, even a theological, poem whose purpose is to ''justify the ways of God to men'' by placing the responsibility for the fall squarely on man himself (God's foreknowledge did not predestinate), and to ''assert eternal Providence'' in the provision for redemption by the Son. It is thus a kind of theodicy and it further includes a hexameron (an account of the six days of creation). It is a work of immense learning and of conscious and constant artistry. Milton fearlessly claimed that it was divinely inspired.

In *Paradise Lost* we recognize in their full development the qualities already adumbrated in the early poems. It is a masterpiece of construction. Like the *Aeneid,* it plunges *in medias res,* with Satan and the rebel angels already in Hell and planning to avenge themselves on God through his new creature, man; we get our first picture of Adam and Eve in their happy state of innocence as Satan spies upon them. Then in Raphael's narrative to them (cf. that of Aeneas to Dido) we learn of the antecedent action: the war in heaven and the defeat and eviction of the rebels by the Son—an epic within the epic. Now the crisis approaches: Eve, willfully tending her flowers alone, is easily deceived by Satan in the form of the Serpent, and Adam, undeceived, deliberately chooses to share her sin and her fate (''So forcible within my heart I feel/ The bond of nature draw me to my own''). The holiness and peace of Eden are shattered: they fall first to lust, then to recrimination. The Son passes judgment upon them—they fear, but they do not yet repent. Repentance follows, not without prevenient grace, but still by means of the very ''bond of nature'' gradually restored: together they pray for forgiveness (this has been called the second crisis of the poem). There remains the prophetic view of the future (placed by Vergil at the midpoint of the epic, by Milton at the end) effected by Michael, who reveals to Adam the results of the fall in future history, but also the promise of redemption and a ''Paradise within thee, happier far''; for Adam has learned his lesson: ''Henceforth I learn that to obey is best/ . . . Taught this by his example whom I now/ Acknowledge my Redeemer ever blest.'' On this note, Adam and Eve go out into the world together, hand in hand.

The structural pattern gives to *Paradise Lost* its classic purity of outline and a firm foundation for all the enrichment that Milton adds. There are innumerable other patterned effects. The revolt of the angels (besides supplying the martial action necessary for an epic) stands in a twofold relation to the fall, of cause, but also of parallel (with difference). Michael's prophecy of the future balances Raphael's narrative of the past. The four settings are related, and each is not only a locality but the symbol of a state of mind: Heaven is God–centered, and therefore perfect order (and perfect freedom); unfallen Earth reflects that order; Hell is not (as might be thoughtlessly assumed) disorder but perverted order (and utter slavery) as if heaven were reflected in a distorting mirror; and Chaos is unorder, destitute of form, but capable of receiving it at the hand of God. Creation, too, is a symbol: goodness is constructive, and in the Redemption, reconstructive, while Satan can only destroy. Satan, Sin, and Death are a sort of infernal trinity.

Basic in both pattern and meaning is the Pauline conception of Christ as the second Adam. He is the hero of the epic, the exemplar of its standard of heroism (as Achilles is in the *Iliad,* and Aeneas in the *Aeneid*), and it is Christian heroism that Adam must learn. Satan is not (as is so often assumed) the hero of the poem: his is a pagan heroism (repeatedly he reminds us of Achilles), and in him pagan heroism is presented, judged, and condemned. Milton's Satan is a triumph of characterization (as even those who misunderstand the poet's meaning agree). It is achieved by treating the character in human terms, so that he becomes a tragic figure—of the order, one might say, of Macbeth. But successful characterization is not confined to Satan; presented at first as ideal and somewhat remote figures in a pastoral setting, Adam and Eve are gradually brought nearer to us, and the Fall and their movement toward repentance become poignant domestic drama. Given the nature of Milton's ''fable,'' this is a triumph indeed. Other genres, then, make their subordinate contributions to *Paradise Lost,* but the prevailing note is epic dignity and grandeur, supported by Milton's mighty verse, his language, his imagery, and not least by his great epic similes, patterns themselves and integrated with the pattern of the whole.

Samson Agonistes and Paradise Regained. Though it has been generally assumed (but on no reliable evidence) that *Samson Agonistes* (1671) was the last written of Milton's poems, there is good reason to regard *Paradise Regained* (published the same year) as summing up his final outlook.

As in *Paradise Lost* Milton wrote a classical epic on a Christian theme, in *Samson Agonistes* he essayed the yet more difficult task of a Christian tragedy, and with at least equal success. In form it adheres even more closely to Greek tragedy than does *Paradise Lost* to the Greco–Roman epic. Its subject is likewise scriptural, derived from the Book of Judges; its theme is similar (sin, repentance, and restoration) and the treatment involves the same combination of religious reference and human motivation, of theology and psychology. Again it is a masterpiece of construction, the most perfect perhaps of all Milton's poems, and the most moving. From the depth of despair (''Eyeless in Gaza at the mill with slaves'') brought on by his own sin and folly, and feeling as yet only self–centered remorse and the sense of ''Heaven's desertion,'' Samson comes first to true repentance, then to the dawning hope of God's forgiveness (''Whose ear is ever open, and his eye/ Gracious to re–admit the suppliant''), and finally, at the very end, to the conviction that there is yet one more task for God, the seal of his forgiveness and reacceptance, to be achieved at the cost of his own death. As in Sophocles' *Oedipus at Colonus,* the action is all inward; the change is effected through a series of encounters (with the Chorus, Manoa, Dalila, Harapha, the Officer). We recognize the operation of God's providence and prevenient grace, but the motivation is all intelligible on the human level. Samson goes to his death doubly armed, with ''celestial vigor'' and ''plain heroic magnitude of mind.'' Thus is attained the full tragic effect and the Aristotelian catharsis: ''calm of mind, all passion spent.''

Paradise Regained finds its subject in the temptation of the wilderness (chosen as paralleling the temptation in Eden and in pursuit of the theme of Christ as the second Adam) and its structural starting point in the Book of Job (thought of by Milton, following St. Jerome, as epic in genre). The order of the temptations is taken from St. Luke and is adopted for the sake of a structural pattern that treats briefly the first and third temptations (respectively to distrust and presumption), but elaborates the second (that of the kingdoms, conceived as involving both distrust and presumption) in a series of temptations to glory—the glory of beauty, of fame, of wealth, of power (represented by imperial Rome), and of knowledge (represented by Athens, ''The eye of Greece, mother of arts''). The superb culmination comes when Christ stands on the pinnacle of the Temple, and as Christ rebukes him (''Tempt not the Lord thy God'') Satan falls. For, as the angels sing, Christ is indeed the ''True Image of the Father.''

Like all great religious poems, Milton's spring from a coalescence of religious and aesthetic experience. He does not shift his ground in doctrine, but all the positive elements of his belief come into play. It is as though, when he writes poetry, a new dimension were added to his sensibility and his thought.

Bibliography: D. MASSON, *The Life of Milton,* 7 v. (London 1859–94; repr. Gloucester, Mass., 1962). E. M. W. TILLYARD, *Milton* (New York 1930). J. H. HANFORD, *A Milton Handbook* (4th ed. New York 1946). D. BUSH, *English Literature in the Earlier Seventeenth Century* (2d ed. rev. Oxford 1962), esp. ch. 12; *John Milton* (New York 1964); *Paradise Lost in Our Time* (New York 1948). C. S. LEWIS, *A Preface to Paradise Lost* (rev. and enl. New York 1959). J. MILTON, *Works,* ed. F. A. PATTERSON, 18 v. (New York 1931–38), Index, 2 v. (1940), Columbia edition; *Complete Prose Works,* ed. D. M. WOLFE (New Haven 1953–); *Poetical Works,* ed. H. DARBISHIRE, 2 v. (Oxford 1952–55). F. W. BATESON, ed. *The Cambridge Bibliographies of English Literature* v.1:463–473, v.2–3 (Cambridge, Eng. 1940–57), *passim.* ENGLISH ASSOCIATION, LONDON, *The Year's Work in English Studies* (London 1919/20–). C. HUCKABAY, *John Milton: A Bibliographical Supplement, 1927–1957* (Pittsburgh 1960). J. E. THORPE, ed., *Milton Criticism* (New York 1950). A. S. P. WOODHOUSE, *Puritanism and Liberty* (Chicago 1951); ''Theme and Pattern in Paradise Regained,'' *University of Toronto Quarterly* 25 (1956) 167–182. A. SEWELL, *A Study in Milton's Christian Doctrine* (New York 1939). A. J. EISENRING, *Milton's 'De doctrina christiana': An Historical Introduction and Critical Analysis* (Fribourg 1946). C. B. RICKS, *Milton's Grand Style* (Oxford 1963). R. D. HAVENS, *The Influence of Milton on English Poetry* (New York 1961). R. TUVE, *Images and Themes in Five Poems by Milton* (Cambridge, Mass. 1957). B. RAJAN, *Paradise Lost and the Seventeenth Century Reader* (London 1947). A. J. A. WALDOCK, *Paradise Lost and Its Critics* (Cambridge, Eng. 1947). M. F. KROUSE, *Milton's Sampson and the Christian Tradition* (Princeton 1949). W. R. PARKER, *Milton's Debt to Greek Tragedy in Samson Agonistes* (Baltimore 1937).

[A. S. P. WOODHOUSE]

MILWAUKEE, ARCHDIOCESE OF

Milwaukee (*Milwauchiensis*) was established as a diocese Nov. 28, 1843; and as an archdiocese, Feb. 12, 1875. In 2001 it had a population of 685,004 Catholics, 31 percent of the general population of 2,222,364 in ten counties in southeastern Wisconsin, an area of 4,758 square miles. The ecclesiastic Province of Milwaukee, includes all the Wisconsin dioceses as its suffragans, namely, Green Bay, LaCrosse, Madison, and Superior. From 1843, when Milwaukee was erected as a separate see, it was governed by the following prelates: John Martin

HENNI, 1844–81; Michael HEISS, 1881–90; Frederic KATZER, 1891–1903; Sebastian Gebhard MESSMER, 1903–30; Samuel Alphonse STRITCH, 1930–40; Moses Elias Kiley, 1940–53; Albert Gregory Meyer, 1953–58; William Edward Cousins, 1958–77; and Rembert G. Weakland, OSB, 1977–2002.

Wisconsin early formed a center for Native Americans and a goal for French explorers, of whom the first was Jean Nicolet who, seeking a route to China, landed at Green Bay in 1634. In the summer of 1661 the first missionary, René Ménard, SJ, entered Wisconsin at the source of the Wisconsin River, and four years later Claude Allouez, SJ, built the first church between Bayfield and Washburn. But wars, liquor, traders, the official policy of concentrating the Native Americans near Detroit, and the suppression of the Jesuits by the French government in 1762 ruined the Jesuit missions. John Baptist Chardon, SJ, remained at Green Bay until 1728, when it too was given up. With the exception of a missionary or two, no priest entered Wisconsin for about a century. Rev. Gabriel Richard of Detroit stopped off at Green Bay and started a church building in 1823, which was completed in 1825 by Rev. Vincent Badin, also from Detroit. In 1840 the Wisconsin Territory, including eastern Minnesota, had a Catholic population of 14,600 (of whom 11,000 were Native Americans) in a total of 40,000. Before the establishment of a diocese in Wisconsin, it had been visited by several bishops including Edward Fenwick of Cincinnati, who stopped at Green Bay in 1829 and 1831. In 1838 Frederic Résé of Detroit paid a visit to La Pointe and Little Chute, and two years later Mathias Loras's trip from Dubuque, Iowa, included visits at Green Bay, Little Chute, Kenosha, Milwaukee, and Potosi. Charles Auguste de Forbin-Janson, a French refugee bishop of Nancy and Toul, was offered the temporary administration of the Detroit diocese, but after a tour of inspection in 1840, which touched on Wisconsin, he declined the charge.

Difficult Years. From 1840 to 1870 most settlers in the area came from Germany, Ireland, and Norway. Later, the Poles led (1870–1920), followed by the Swedes (1900–20), Italians (1900–10), and other nationalities with lesser numbers. Opposition to the Church took the form of segregation designed to isolate Catholics, especially the foreign-born, and was sponsored in turn by religious sects, Nativists, Know-Nothings, Forty-eighters, Whigs, and Turners. Bishop Henni and his successors had to contend with these external threats, but gradually by the acquisition of property, organization of parishes, schools, and societies, and a vigorous, informed press, they succeeded in making Catholicism respectable.

Nativist Attacks. In 1844, when a Nativist Gospel-Whig, Rev. John J. Miter, launched an attack against Romanism, charging that the hierarchy was dedicated to the overthrow of the government by control of the Irish vote, Henni's *Facts Against Assertions* (1845) silenced open attacks and offered a basis for respect and understanding. The press attack of Frederic Fratny of the Forty-eighters against the Church as being antagonistic to republican forms of government and intolerant toward personal liberty, principally by its regulation of marriages and burials, was proved a hoax by the Catholic press. Henni recruited F. J. Felsecker for the propaganda war with the Forty-eighters, and he demonstrated that their press was filled with material fabricated in Luther's time. As a result Catholics became more closely organized through societies and much better informed.

Among the other external obstacles to the Church, the problem of religious freedom for inmates of public reformatories and prisons was settled by legislative enactment in 1891, after two decades of conflict. Little encouragement was accorded KNOW–NOTHINGISM in the 1850s, but later the AMERICAN PROTECTIVE ASSOCIATION (APA) developed strength in the state, where about 100 branches were organized. Catholics countered the movement through activities of the Milwaukee Columbian League and in their press, especially the *Catholic Citizen.* The question of reading the Bible in public schools received notice and significance from the Edgerton Bible Case [*see* CHURCH AND STATE IN THE U.S. (LEGAL HISTORY), 3]. In 1891 the state supreme court declared reading the Bible in public schools sectarian instruction and therefore unconstitutional. Credit for making the question an issue was due largely to Rev. James F. Bowe, of Edgerton, whose efforts were financed by funds raised through the columns of the *Catholic Citizen.* The Bennett Law, enacted in 1889, was a compulsory education act that included provisions for teaching English and going to school in the district of one's residence. Under the leadership of Archbishop Heiss, the bishops of Wisconsin registered an able and effective protest. The Bennett Law became the issue in the gubernatorial election of 1890, with the result that it was repealed in 1891. In the opinion of Archbishop Katzer, the reversal was due to the intelligence and organization of the laity, under the leadership of Humphrey J. Desmond, lawyer, editor, author, and at that time chairman of the education committee in the Legislature.

Thus, with the exception of the Civil War period, outbreaks of hatred marked every decade prior to 1900. In 1853 the visit to Milwaukee of Abp. Gaetano BEDINI, papal nuncio to Brazil, provided an opportunity for Forty-eighters to express their hatred of the Church, particularly in their press. They planned to hang Bedini in effigy, but were forced to drop the scheme, when no Native Americans could be induced to join them. A notable address to

Bedini from the Catholic laity did much to silence the opposition. Among the anti-Catholic items in the 1870s was the convent libel case, which involved defamatory remarks in a Protestant weekly, the *Christian Statesman,* about the Notre Dame Sisters in Milwaukee, and was actually a veiled attack on the Catholic school system. The case was tried in circuit court at Milwaukee in February 1875, and ended in a hung jury over the question: Can a corporation be libeled? The affair was settled when the editor retracted his statement. In 1875–76 hatred for the Catholic Church in the German press and the Milwaukee city council was blamed for blocking a donation of land to the Sisters of Charity for a lying-in hospital and infant asylum. The same sisters were engaged in litigation with the city (1890–1900) for damages when Terrace Avenue was extended through their property. Proceedings in the council and feelings elsewhere were marked at times by charges of bigotry, prejudice, and illegality. The city finally paid $5,000 damages and issued a quitclaim deed. In 1897 the placement of Marquette's statue in the national capitol by legislative action produced an outburst of hostility. Positive apologetics in the press and letters by laymen such as Desmond to the lawmakers helped to steady the latter. At the end of the 19th century socialism began to grow locally and nationally. Archbishop Messmer tried to check its effect on labor unions through the Federation of Catholic Societies, the encyclical *Rerum novarum* of Pope Leo XIII, and the presentation of lectures by noted speakers.

Messmer was also conscious of the need for a pastoral outreach to the blacks. When Lincoln Charles Valle, a black layman from Chicago, called on Messmer in 1908 to interest him in evangelizing the blacks in Milwaukee, Messmer encouraged the work and lent the assistance of diocesan clergy. The Capuchins took over the work in 1911 and after the building of St. Benedict the Moor's church, the apostolate began to bear fruit.

Internal Dissension. Besides strife arising from the outside, the Milwaukee diocese experienced trouble from within in the form of trusteeism, Fenianism, and nationalism. Lay trusteeism never became a major problem to Church leaders who employed common sense and publicity against it. Henni used indirect methods to curb Fenians by persuading local Irish leaders to eschew all support of an association already condemned by the bishops of Ireland. The choice of a coadjutor for Henni in the last years of the 1870s sparked dissension in the press, correspondence, and discussion among the English and German-speaking elements, particularly clerical, in the archdiocese and elsewhere. The appointment of Heiss, though gratifying to Henni, not only disrupted the archdiocese and its unity, but had repercussions far beyond Wisconsin, especially by opening up the entire nationalistic question in the U.S. By focusing attention on the role of nationality, the debate in ecclesiastical circles awakened a livelier regard for immigrants. The *Kuryer Polski,* a Polish daily of Milwaukee founded in 1888, advocated the creation of Polish dioceses with Polish bishops. For 25 years the question was embittered by official letters banning the paper and by law suits. Finally in 1916 the *Kuryer Polski* lost its case in which it charged the bishops of the Wisconsin province with conspiracy and boycott. The state supreme court decided in favor of the bishops on the grounds of ecclesiastical jurisdiction, which the plaintiff acknowledged.

Need for meeting a hostile press and furnishing information gave rise to a German Catholic press. In 1852, the *Seebote* appeared in Milwaukee, followed by the *Columbia* in 1872, and the *Excelsior* in 1883. World War I, and the limitation of immigration after it, presaged the doom of the German press and also the lessening of the appeal of other foreign language newspapers. The *Star of Bethlehem* (1869) and *Catholic Vindicator* (1870) appeared in English to counter new antagonisms. Both merged in 1878 into the *Catholic Citizen,* which in turn became the *Catholic Herald-Citizen* in 1935. The foregoing papers, particularly the *Catholic Citizen,* which was well informed and edited, may be credited with much of the unity and aggressiveness of the Catholic laity. Beginning in 1885 three successive attempts to publish a Polish paper failed, but the *Kuryer Polski* began its continuous appearance in 1888. To counter its nationalistic laicism, a clerical opposition press was started at various times. The *Katolik* (1895) and the *Dziennik Milwaucki* (1899) were short-lived but the *Nowiny Polskie,* founded in 1907, lasted to 1950, when popular interest, as well as income, waned.

Institutional Growth. Father Martin KUNDIG introduced the first parochial school at Milwaukee in 1842 with lay teachers, and four years later Henni secured the Sisters of Charity from Emmitsburg, Md., to do the teaching. Milwaukee's first public school opened in June 1846 in the basement of St. Peter's Cathedral by an arrangement with Henni, who agreed not to teach the catechism in school hours. By the 1850s the needed churches had been built and a supply of priests assured by the new seminary (1856). Nothing was closer to the heart of Henni than parish schools wherein the required languages were available. The Dominican Sisters of Sinsinawa, founded by Rev. Samuel Mazzuchelli, OP, in 1847, provided a partial fulfillment of Henni's plan to obtain teachers for English-speaking congregations. Mother Karoline Gerhardinger of the School Sisters of Notre Dame from Bavaria, who had settled in Pennsylvania in 1847, arrived at Milwaukee in 1850. By 1860 her sisters had charge of

13 diocesan grade schools, and operated Mount Mary College, established 1872, in Milwaukee.

The Sisters of St. Francis of Assisi arrived in 1849, and undertook their first teaching assignment in 1864 at Jefferson. Founded, 1937, by the Sisters of St. Francis of Assisi for the education of novices and sisters, St. Clare College was renamed Cardinal Stritch College in 1946. In that year, it admitted laywomen and became a women's college. In 1970, Cardinal Stritch College went coeducational and in 1997 it attained university status.

The School Sisters of St. Francis came to Milwaukee from Baden in 1873, and after some migrating finally settled there in 1888. In 1963 they taught in 44 archdiocesan grade schools. German Dominican sisters staffed numerous parish schools in the archdiocese, and established a motherhouse at Racine in 1863, where they conducted coeducational Dominican College (1935). The college was closed in the 1970s.

The Sisters of St. Agnes, founded at Barton, Wis., in 1858, to teach in rural district schools, in addition to having charge of grade schools, established Marian College for women (1963) in Fond du Lac, Wis. St. Thomas College, opened by Mazzuchelli at Sinsinawa in 1847 and chartered in 1848, had a competent faculty and adequate equipment, but was closed in 1865 because of the death of its founder and other factors.

Two high schools opened by the Jesuits in Milwaukee were suppressed by 1872. In 1881 Marquette began as a college; its transformation into a university began in 1907, and its graduate school was organized in 1922. A branch of the Capuchins was organized in 1856 at Mt. Calvary, where St. Lawrence Seminary was started in 1860 and has since graduated many young men destined for the priesthood. Holy Cross Fathers from Notre Dame, Ind., set up a college at Watertown in 1872, which ceased operation as such in 1911, when it became a training school for their brothers.

A normal school, started in 1870 to supply lay teachers and organists, was located in St. Francis and is associated with the work of John Singenberger, composer and organist. The Catholic Summer School of the West was organized at Madison in 1895. In 1906 Rev. Henry Hengell was named chaplain of the Catholic students at the University of Wisconsin, becoming the first to so serve at any secular university in the U.S.

The Sisters of Charity from Emmitsburg, Md., opened the first hospital May 15, 1848, in Milwaukee, which since 1858 has become well-known as St. Mary's. In 1963 there were also St. Joseph's Hospital, conducted by Franciscan sisters, and four lesser general hospitals in Milwaukee, as well as ten others within the archdiocese. Special hospitals were conducted by the School Sisters of St. Francis, the Sacred Heart Sanitarium (1893), and its annex for mental cases, St. Mary's Hill (1912). St. Rose's orphanage for girls was started in 1848 and St. Aemilian's for boys in 1849 at the residence of the Sisters of Charity. In 1855 the boys were put under the charge of the Sisters of St. Francis. In 1908, when there were 17 Polish parishes in the archdiocese, the need for a Polish orphanage was met when St. Joseph's orphanage was opened at Wauwatosa. St. Vincent's Infant Asylum, opened in 1877 by the Sisters of Charity to care for foundlings, uncared-for babies, and unwed mothers, ceased operation Oct. 1, 1958, because of the use of foster homes for small children. The sisters at once adopted a project to aid girls with emotional problems in a group home. In 1877 the Good Shepherd Sisters came to care for delinquent girls, while boys went to an industrial school which was an annex to St. Aemilian's orphanage, probably the earliest predecessor of St. Charles Boys' Home, a protective institution. St. John's School for the Deaf was opened in May 1876. A Conference of the Society of St. Vincent de Paul, formed at Milwaukee in 1849, lapsed from 1874 to 1908, when it started anew. The Little Sisters of the Poor have been active in serving the destitute and aged since 1876.

Welfare work became more closely organized, beginning with the appointment of a superintendent in 1920. Since its establishment the welfare bureau has arranged the adoption of 3,000 children into Catholic homes. Its other services include family counseling, homemaker guidance, care for unmarried parents, resettlement help, care for children in foster homes, group homes, and child-care institutions. In 1917 Rev. Joseph Hurst established St. Bernard's Workingmen's Home, a refuge for migratory workers, and before it was closed in 1932 it had fed and lodged 200,000 men. The archdiocese also engaged some notable clerical economists in 1910; these included F. J. HAAS and A. J. MUENCH, who won international fame, and P. DIETZ, who influenced labor councils in the American Federation of Labor and ran a school for workers in Milwaukee, mainly to combat socialism. Dietz also led a campaign to legalize parish credit unions in Wisconsin.

Post-War and Post-Conciliar Years. In the years after World War II the archdiocese of Milwaukee had to come to grips with the growth and mobility of the Catholic community. The number of Catholics swelled in proportion to the general population increase, and many were moving to new suburban developments. Milwaukee-born Albert G. Meyer, installed as archbishop in 1953, addressed the expanding needs of a growing population, establishing new parishes, building, and watching the Catholic colleges and universities in the archdiocese expand. When Meyer succeeded Cardinal Stritch as archbishop of Chicago in 1958, he was succeeded by the Most Reverend William Cousins, the bishop of Peoria. Installed in January 1959 as the eighth archbishop of Milwaukee, Cousins continued Meyer's building program. He attended all the sessions of the Second Vatican Council, and moved swiftly to implement its decrees and recommendations. Archbishop Cousins retired when he reached the age of 75 in 1977. (He died Sept. 14, 1988.)

Cousins successor was Rembert G. Weakland, former abbot of St. Vincent's Archabbey in Latrobe, Pa., and Abbot Primate of the Order of St. Benedict in Rome. Already well known throughout the country as a spokesman for monastic renewal, he transferred his activism, tireless zeal, and broad vision of the Church in the modern world to Milwaukee when he was installed as archbishop in November 1977. He reorganized the archdiocesan curia, closed the preparatory seminary built by his predecessor in 1963, turning it into diocesan offices and a retirement home for clergy. In his weekly column in the *Catholic Herald*, the diocesan newspaper, Archbishop Weakland addressed timely topics, sometimes taking controversial positions on social issues, foreign policy, and the role of women in the Church. Under his direction the archdiocese intensified it pastoral outreach to the Hispanics, ministered to Hmong and Laotian refugees, and established the first urban parish for Native Americans.

Weakland met opposition on a number of fronts and for a number of reasons but none stirred more furor than his plan to remodel the cathedral. The Cathedral of St. John the Evangelist, consecrated in 1853, had been the focus of controversy before, when in the 19th century, the German *Zwiebelturm* (onion dome) of the original structure was removed, a gesture that was interpreted as an effort to placate Irish Catholics. In January 1935 a fire completely demolished the interior and the roof, weakened the walls, and destroyed the stained glass windows. The restoration of the cathedral, slowed because of the war, was finally completed just prior to the centennial of the archdiocese in 1943. In the 1960s Archbishop Cousins authorized a new design and reconstruction of the main altar to bring the sanctuary space into conformity with liturgical directives of Vatican II, and in 1977 he initiated a more extensive remodeling. Twenty years later Archbishop initiated the Cathedral Project, a comprehensive plan to preserve historical legacy of the Cathedral of St John the Evangelist and to make the environment and furnishing better serve the spirit of the liturgy. In addition, the plan called for the property north of the Cathedral church to be developed as a center for social outreach to the poor and homeless. A vocal opposition denounced the Cathedral Project and even won a favorable hearing from the Congregation for Divine Worship and the Discipline of the Sacraments. Nonetheless, the project went forward and on Feb. 9, 2002 bishops from throughout the state joined the priests of archdiocese and representatives from each of the parishes in a liturgical celebration dedicating the renovated Cathedral. Archbishop Weakland reached mandatory retirement age later in the year.

Bibliography: H. R. AUSTIN, *The Wisconsin Story* (2d ed. Milwaukee 1957). P. L. JOHNSON, *Crosier on the Frontier: A Life of John Martin Henni* (Madison 1959). B. J. BLIED, *Three Archbishops of Milwaukee* (Milwaukee 1955); *The Catholic Story of Wisconsin* (Milwaukee 1948). A. STECKEL, "The Catholic Church in Wisconsin," *Records of the American Catholic Historical Society of Philadelphia* 7 (1896) 225–233; 8 (1897) 20–27. L. RUMMEL, *History of the Catholic Church in Wisconsin* (Madison 1976). P. WILKES, *The Education of an Archbishop: Travels with Rembert Weakland* (Maryknoll 1992).

[P. L. JOHNSON/EDS.]

MINDSZENTY, JÓZSEF

Cardinal-archbishop of Esztergom, primate of Hungary; b. March 29, 1892, Mindszent, Hungary; d. May 6, 1975, Vienna, Austria. For a major part of his long and distinguished career in the church, Cardinal Mindszenty personified the struggle for religious freedom under the Communist regimes of Eastern Europe. From the time of his 1949 show trial and imprisonment by the Communist rulers of Hungary, through his release during the 1956 Hungarian Revolution and his long self-imposed imprisonment in the American legation in Budapest, to his eventual exile from Hungary, his personal fate symbolized the condition of church-state relations in the twentieth century.

The political convulsions which afflicted Hungary during his lifetime inevitably drew Cardinal Mindszenty into public affairs. His village of Mindszent, where his family owned a small farm, had changed little under centuries of Habsburg rule, but his studies for the priesthood opened the wider world of classical learning. By the time of his ordination, June 12, 1915, World War I had begun to dissolve many traditional social and political relationships as well as to impose extraordinary demands on his services as a curate, teacher, newspaper editor, and community advisor. The loss of the war and the overthrow of the Habsburg monarchy left a political vacuum in Hungary. The activities of the young priest on behalf of the newly formed Christian Party brought him into disfavor with both Count Károlyi's moderate leftist government and its successor, Béla Kun's short-lived Hungarian Soviet Republic. The shift to the rightist policies of Admiral Horthy's regency allowed 25 years of dedicated parish work in Zalaegerszeg with politics overshadowed by concern for the community and the schools.

His elevation to the episcopate in March 1944 as bishop of Veszprém brought Mindszenty to a position of national leadership while the country was again suffering the ravages of a world war, which Hungary had entered as an ally of Nazi Germany. When the Hungarian government imitated the Nazi persecution of Jews, the Hungarian bishops vigorously protested the violation of innate human rights. Recognizing that the war was hopelessly lost, the government negotiated an armistice in October 1944, but German forces installed a puppet regime in Hungary to continue the fighting. Bishop Mindszenty presented a memorandum, signed by all the bishops of western Hungary, urging the new premier, Ferenc Szálasi, to end the senseless destruction. Because of this memorandum, the Szálasi regime arrested Bishop Mindszenty. He remained a prisoner until the complete German withdrawal from Hungary in April 1945.

The end of the war left Hungary devastated and disillusioned. Bishop Mindszenty, who became archbishop of Esztergom in September and a cardinal in February 1946, organized relief efforts to overcome the food shortages, to treat the widespread illnesses, and to provide for refugees. His determination to uphold the traditional constitutional authority of the archbishop of Esztergom led Cardinal Mindszenty to issue increasingly outspoken warnings about the threats facing the newly established democratic regime. As the Hungarian Communists consolidated their power by gradually eliminating other parties, the church became the last focal point of resistance and the prime target of hostile propaganda. Cardinal Mindszenty's protest of the nationalization of Catholic schools in 1948 led to his ultimate conflict with the regime. He was arrested on December 26 and placed on trial in February 1949. The public trial of the primate of Hungary demonstrated that no one could resist the will of the regime. After forced confessions from the cardinal and a mass of fabricated evidence against him, the court found Cardinal Mindszenty guilty of treason and sentenced him to life imprisonment. The harassment of the church also included the arrest of other bishops, the cessation of religious instruction, and the dissolution of religious orders.

The 1956 Revolution in Hungary freed Cardinal Mindszenty on October 30. When the populace enthusiastically welcomed his return to Budapest the next day, the government of Imre Nagy hastily declared the previous legal actions void. In a radio address, Nov. 3, Cardinal Mindszenty justified the revolution as a fight for freedom. He advocated neutrality, democratic elections under international control, private ownership, and religious freedom, but he carefully avoided lending support to Nagy's government or any other political faction. Less than eight hours after his speech, Soviet troops occupied Budapest and crushed the revolution. When the Soviet troops arrived, Cardinal Mindszenty sought refuge nearby in the U.S. legation. He received asylum and remained for 15 years in spite of the protests of the Hungarian government and papal entreaties to accept a post in the Roman Curia. The Hungarian Primate believed his persistence called attention to the oppression of Hungarian Catholics, but it also obstructed Vatican efforts to reach an accommodation with the Communist regime. At the urging of Pope Paul VI, he left Hungary in September 1971 and took up residence at the Hungarian seminary in Vienna. Fifteen months before his death he unwillingly relinquished his position as archbishop of Esztergom, while sternly proclaiming his disagreement with the Vatican pursuit of improved church–state relations in Hungary, which allowed the appointment of new bishops. Citing examples of continued restrictions on the Hungarian church, he announced characteristically, ''In these grave circumstances Cardinal Mindszenty cannot abdicate.''

Bibliography: B. KOVRIG, *The Hungarian People's Republic* (Baltimore 1970). J. MINDSZENTY, *Memoirs* (New York 1974). G. N. SHUSTER, *In Silence I Speak* (New York 1956). F. A. VALI, *Rift and Revolt in Hungary* (Cambridge, Mass., 1961).

[R. J. GIBBONS]

MINIMS

Mendicant order (OM, Official Catholic Directory, #0835) founded by St. FRANCIS OF PAOLA in 1435 in Paola, province of Cosenza in Calabria, Italy, the place of the first convent. Humility, penance, and charity are the characteristic virtues and the means of perfection, inspiring the spirituality and apostolate of the Minims. Minims are thus named because they are so to form themselves in the school of the Gospel, that by becoming the least of all they might die to self and live in and for God alone. The observance of a solemn vow of abstinence from meat, eggs, milk, cheese, butter, and any other kind of dairy products and derivatives from meat is characteristic of the Minims' penitential spirit.

The motto of the order is ''Charitas'': the heraldic symbol that the founder received in a vision from St. Michael the Archangel to be transmitted to his religious family. Besides the first order of Friars, there is also a second order of cloistered nuns (first monastery founded at Andujar, Spain in 1495), who profess the same rule adapted to their conditions, and the third order for lay people of both sexes. The apostolate of the Minims is varied as is that of all the mendicant orders, consisting in a ministry of preaching and teaching; a particular pastoral activity is devoted to seafarers, of whom St. Francis of Paola is the official patron.

The rule of the Minims, the fifth in the Church, is short in composition (10 small chapters), but it is original in content, and was several times approved by Alexander VI and Julius II with successive bulls: *Ad ea quae circa decorem* (May 1, 1501), *Ex debito pastoralis officii* (May 18, 1502), and *Inter caeteros regularis observantiae professores* (July 28, 1506). Such a rule is a testimony that penance and prayer can bring union with God. At the death of the founder (April 2, 1507), the Order of Minims had 33 convents: 12 in Italy, 14 in France, 4 in Spain, 3 in Germany; it was divided into 8 monastic provinces. Later, in the golden age of the order (1600–1700), the number of convents increased to about 400, with more than 9,000 religious. The Minims provided a select corps devoted to prayer, study, and penance, including dedicated pastors, teachers, and scholars.

The Minims have had their own universities and colleges, and held chairs in public universities. However, their religious and intellectual apostolate suffered from anticlerical persecution during the 19th century. Despite this setback, the work of St. Francis of Paola has found strength for a new start as evidenced by the increasing number of vocations, houses, and apostolic activities.

The Minims first arrived in the United States in 1970, setting up their ministries in the Archdiocese of Los Angeles. Their U.S. headquarters is in Los Angeles, CA. The generalate is in Rome.

Bibliography: G. ROBERTI, *Disegno storico dell'Ordine dei Minimi . . .*, 3 v. (Rome 1902–22).

[A. BELLANTONIO/EDS.]

Insignia of the Order of Minims.

MINISTRY (ECCLESIOLOGY)

In early Latin translations of the New Testament, *ministerium* and its cognates were used to translate διακονία and its cognates, as well as the less frequent λειτουργία. The best English rendering of *diakonia* is the word ''service.'' The New Testament uses the term for activities in the Church which issue from the graces of the Spirit and build up the body of the faithful. The less commonly used *leitourgia* intimates that these activities bear the character of true worship, since they build up the priestly people in whom God is glorified.

In ecclesiastical usage *ministerium* came to be used almost exclusively of the ordained members of the Church. It took on connotations of power and official authority which the original Greek term does not possess. This use of words is itself a sign of the growing tendency to reduce the laity to a passive role in the Church and to confide mission and responsibility predominantly to the clergy. Vatican II gave sanction to a trend to reverse this situation that had begun earlier in the century. In its documents the Council continued to reserve the vocabulary of ministry for bishops, presbyters, and deacons, while using terms such as *munus, missio, charisma, apostolatus* and *officium* for the works of the laity. By reason of such usage, it was able to maintain a distinction between the role of ordained ministers and that of the laity, while at the same time recognizing the active part which the latter have in the mission of the Church and in service to the community. Furthermore, the Council recalled the original meaning of ministry or *diakonia* and stressed the need for the ordained to model their ministry on the service of Jesus Christ. Since then, there has been even greater attention given to the use of the word *diakonia* in the New Testament sources, and a deeper examination of the relation between the ministries of the laity and those of the ordained.

Origin of Ministries. The many ministries derive from the charisms, or gifts of service, which are given by the Spirit. The coordination of these gifts to the service of the common good is also the work of the Spirit. Every ministry is modelled on that of Jesus Christ (cf. Lk 22.24–27) and all power (εξουσία) in the Church is a share in his power (cf. Mt 28.18–20). The good of the Church and its mission requires order and leadership. The early Church turned to the Twelve (known by Luke as

Apostles) or to their immediate associates, such as Paul, for this service.

That much, in brief, is the position which emerges from an exegesis of the New Testament. When little attention was given to the ministries of lay persons, it was enough for theology to explain that the power and authority of the bishops derive from the mission given by Christ to the Apostles. Given a broader concept of ministry, theology has to take other factors into account and offer a different synthesis. Three converging principles may serve this purpose. They are the Pauline teaching on the Body, the relation of all ministries to the model of the Twelve, and the action of the Spirit in the Church through time.

Pauline Teaching. The Pauline image of the Body expresses the Church's relation to Christ and his Spirit and is an effective image of her unity in plurality. Amongst other things, it brings home the corporate nature of her life and mission, as well as the personal share which each member has in the gifts of the Body and service to its life. On the basis of this image Vatican II can refer to the Church as the *sacramentum seu signum et instrumentum intimae cum Deo unionis totiusque generis humani unitatis* ("sacrament or sign of intimate union with God and of the unity of all mankind" *Lumen gentium* 1.1). Ministries contribute to the reality and witness of this corporate life and mission.

Apostles as Model. The Twelve are an eschatological image of the Church of the New Covenant, which, filled with the Holy Spirit as foretold by the Prophets, takes part in the banquet prepared by God for the Christ. Being likewise the Apostles sent by Christ, they transmit not only a life of discipleship and faith but also the mission which they received from him. Ministries in the Church derive from this mission and are modelled on that of the Twelve, in whom the early community found exemplars of disciple, pastor, and missionary.

Action of the Spirit. It follows from this that ministry is by the gift of the Spirit a share in the mission and saving power (*exousia*) of God in Christ. The intervention of the Spirit is necessary, since it is the role of the Spirit to keep alive the historical remembrance of Christ and the Twelve, while at the same time providing for that newness of creation which each epoch requires. Indeed, the remembrance is itself a source of fresh creativity, since it gives the Church an eschatological focus on history, a grasp that the Church is always an event, and the realization that she lives constantly under the judgment of God and in his hope.

A conclusion to draw from this eschatological model is that a call to mission and service is already given in the Sacraments of initiation whereby a person becomes a member of the eschatological community. Vatican Council II recognizes this in many ways, not least in its Decree on Priestly Ministry when it implies that ordination specifies the mission already given at initiation (*Presbyterorum ordinis* 1.2). Of every adult Christian it can be said that her/his call is determined by the gifts of the Spirit, of which there is a guarantee in the Sacraments of initiation. For some, these are given special recognition and a new sacramental role through the Sacrament of Order.

Classification of Ministries. Different classifications or typologies of ministries are offered to explain their respective contributions to the life of the Church. The division offered by the Council is based on the theology of the triple office of Christ, namely, that of Priest, Prophet, and King. The works of both laity and ordained ministers are diversified in terms of their participation in one or other of these offices (*Lumen gentium* 9–12).

Another classification, more descriptive in character, is based more directly on the New Testament. It distinguishes ministries of word, sacrament, and care, drawing either from the listings of ministries (e.g. Rom 12.6–8; 1 Cor 12.4–11.28–31; Eph 4.11) or from what is known in other ways, of life in the New Testament Church. The principal ministries of the word are those of the apostles, the prophets, and the teachers, but the listings cited would also allow inclusion of such gifts as exhortation, tongues, and the discernment of spirits from the listings quoted. Of the ministry of sacrament or worship little specific is said in the New Testament. The foundation on which such ministry is explained naturally lies in what is said of the Eucharist and Baptism, and some would also draw from texts on the presidency of communities (e.g. Rom 12.8; Heb 13.17.23); but this is rather uncertain ground. An important feature in this classification is the recognition given to the ministries of care. The category includes the service of tables (cf. Acts 6.1–6); the care of the sick (cf. Jas 5.13–16), the widow, and the orphan (cf. Acts 6.1–6; Jas 1.27); healing (1 Cor 12.10); and the administration of community goods (cf. 1 Cor 12.28 on administrators and helpers). Sometimes in theology the New Testament word *diakonia* is used for this category alone instead of being employed for all ministries. The works falling into this category have equal status with the ministries of word and liturgy. Hence they are not to be judged inferior or less necessary. Their exercise in the life of the Church today is not a mere repetition of New Testament days, but takes on new needs and new forms.

Another classification of ministries distinguishes them by way of their relation to those aspects of the Church's life that are designated by the Greek words μαρτήρια, διάκονία, and κοινονία (witness, service, communion). A similar distinction refers them to the Church's mission to evangelize, to the inner life of each community, and to the relations fostered between communities. This is to take up the notes of the Church which are its apostolicity, its unity, and its catholicity, and to relate ministries to them.

Clearly, no classification of ministries is adequate or exhaustive, nor may it be used to restrict development of new ministries or new ways of exercising old ones. A first limitation to be found in every classification is that some ministries overlap the types given. Thus the promotion of justice and peace could be classed under word, since it pertains to prophecy and to teaching, but it could also be classified under care, since it promotes human welfare in Christ's name. A second limitation to any typology is that the types may not appear to be comprehensive. Thus in the second classification mentioned, some would posit judgment as a fourth class of ministry, while others include it under word and still others place it under sacrament, relating it thus to the Sacrament of binding and loosing. Awareness of these shortcomings is a reminder that theology's task is to understand the wonders of the Church's variety in unity, not to establish stringent categories.

Ordained Ministry. Both history and dogma distinguish between ordained ministry and other ministries. It is less clear where the nature of this distinction resides. Given the new respect for lay ministries the question has become a more acute one in recent theology. Many things are involved in the discussion, including the nature of ecclesiastical AUTHORITY, the offices reserved to the ordained, the purpose of the Sacrament of Order for the life of the Church, and the structure internal to the Sacrament. It is now more commonly recognized that the theology of Order derives from the theology of the Church and not vice versa as in an earlier system. Likewise, the authority of Order has to be related to common responsibility and mission of the community and is incomprehensible outside that context.

The call to ordained ministry comes as a special call from Christ and the Spirit, but it is mediated through the Church and requires sacramental incorporation into the ministerial college to be effective. How this mediation is to be effected is both a practical and a theological crux. The intervention of the episcopacy as the normal way of proceeding is not in question. It is more difficult to determine the just part played by the faithful in the choice of ministers and in the transmission of office. It is also difficult to assess situations where leadership and sacramental presidency have been assumed or granted outside the normal channels of episcopal succession.

Ordained ministers are certainly not mere delegates of the community. To say this would be to deny the unique source of power in Christ and the Spirit. At the same time, a rigid identification of episcopal succession with apostolic succession ignores all other authority and ministry in the Church and has serious practical as well as theological consequences. To express the delicacy of the relationship between the ordained minister and the community, some recent theology prefers images or concepts of leadership and presidency to those of power and JURISDICTION. It is further pointed out that the authority of office is normally grounded in the spiritual authority of the person to whom the office is confided. Those dogmas that affirm that the power of Christ works in the Sacraments despite the unworthiness of the minister speak to unhealthy situations to give assurance that the grace of Christ is not rendered void by bad ministers, but such dogmas do not constitute the basic principles for a theology of Order.

When the Eucharist is taken as the central point and summation of the Church's life and mystery, then the liturgical presidency of the ordained minister can be understood as the focal point of the community's relation to the Trinity. Ministry and authority are thus related to the service of the Church as a communion in faith and worship. There is also room in this image for a proper recognition of the power and spiritual authority of the nonordained ministries, since the word presidency does not suggest a monopoly of worship. It is rather the encouragement, the recognition, and the ordering in unity and harmony of all ministries, relating them in the liturgy to the communion of the Church and the glory of the Father.

Lay Ministries. Besides the multiple problems concerning the relation of ordained to common ministries, the Church today also discusses the institutionalization of some lay ministries. This means a designation to a particular function, made by the hierarchy at some level and recognized as a common procedure rather than as a unique instance. Specifically, the *motu proprio* of Paul VI, *Ministeria quaedam* (*Acta Apostolicae Sedis* 64 [1972] 529–534), promoted the institutionalization of the functions of acolyte and lector for the universal Church. It also urged local episcopates to consider the need for other ministries deserving of similar recognition in their respective constituencies. Hence there are movements towards setting up formal appointment to the ministries of catechist, psalmist, marriage counsellor, or even that of lay president in communities which have no resident ordained pastor.

This practice may be either promotional or restrictive, or perhaps a combination of both. While the intention of *Ministeria quaedam* was to promote a wider share of the laity in liturgical and catechetical roles, its implementation at times appears restrictive. This is all too easily the case when it is supplemented by the appointment of Extraordinary Ministers of the Eucharist. It can very easily happen that what of its nature belongs to all is in practice confined to the few, in the interests of what is deemed better order. To take the Lord's Body to other Christians and to read God's Word in the liturgy are offices which of their nature can be carried out by any mature Christian. At the moment some disciplinary measures may be needed to regulate this, but in the long run the phase of lay ministering marked by the institutionalization of these offices can only be temporary.

The question then remains whether similar procedures might be used to promote other ministries, particularly urgent for the life and mission of the Church at a given time and in a given place. Coming readily to mind is the need to promote ministries that work for justice or those that take up the call to dialogue with other religions. Whether the process of institutionalization can ever fully avoid forms of neoclericalism is an open question. Hence it may be more fitting to think in terms of a testing and discernment of gifts and ministries within communities and of their subsequent incorporation into the communion of faith and worship through prayer and mutual encouragement.

Bibliography: Y.-M. CONGAR, *Ministères et communion ecclésiale* (Paris 1971). B. COOKE, *Ministry to Word and Sacraments. History and Theology* (Philadelphia 1976). J. DELORME, ed., *Le Ministère et les ministères selon le Nouveau Testament. Dossier exégétique et réflexion théologique* (Paris 1974). M. G. LAWLER, *A Theology of Ministry* (Kansas City 1990). T. F. O'MEARA, *Theology of Ministry* (New York 2000). K. B. OSBORNE, *Ministry: Lay Ministry in the Roman Catholic Church* (New York 1993). K. B. OSBORNE, *Priesthood: A History of the Ordained Ministry in the Roman Catholic Church* (New York 1988). D. N. POWER, *Gifts That Differ: Lay Ministries Established and Unestablished* (New York 1985). J. PROVOST, ed., *Official Ministry in a New Age* (Washington, D.C. 1981). E. SCHILLEBEECKX, *The Church With a Human Face: A New and Expanded Theology of Ministry* (New York 1988). E. HILL, *Ministry and Authority in the Catholic Church* (London 1988). N. MITCHELL, *Mission and Ministry: History and Theology in the Sacrament of Order* (Wilmington, Del. 1982).

[D. N. POWER/EDS.]

MINNESOTA, CATHOLIC CHURCH IN

In 2000 the Catholic Church in Minnesota numbered 1,256,268 communicants, about 25 percent of the state's population of 4,919,479. The history of the Catholic Church in Minnesota falls into three rather distinct chapters. The first chapter encompasses the age of exploration of the upper Midwest during the 1700s when missionaries accompanied fur traders and explorers along the upper Mississippi River and western Lake Superior. The second chapter focuses on the first years of the Diocese of St. Paul, from 1850 to 1877, when the diocese was elevated to archiepiscopal status. The third chapter relates the growth of Catholicism in the state since that time with suffragan sees necessitated because of Catholic population growth. In 1887 St. Cloud, Duluth, and Winona became suffragan sees, Crookston in 1909 and New Ulm in 1957.

Early History. During the early 18th century European exploration ventures, especially from France and England, were launched into the Minnesota region in an attempt to dominate the lucrative fur industry. Accompanying these sorties were Catholic missionaries, French Recollect Fathers and Jesuit priests, desirous of converting indigenous Ojibway and Sioux along with ministering to scattered settlers around crude forts. Chapels were erected near these forts and fur trade entrepots. Sicur Du Luth and Father Louis Hennepin were in the region in the 1680s. The early 18th century brought Fathers Mesaiger and Aulneau to the northern regions of the territory and the Jesuits around Lake Pepin in the south. Chapels were erected at Pembina, Fort St. Charles, Grand Portage, and Fort Beauharnois on Lake Pepin. In 1818 the U.S. Government erected Fort Snelling at the confluence of the Mississippi and Minnesota Rivers, and by 1845 French Canadian and Swiss settlers from Lord Selkirk's colony near Pembina in the far north clustered in the area around Fort Snelling, known as the Fort Snelling Reserve. In 1840 a log chapel (St. Peter's) was built in Mendota near the fort, and in 1841 Father Lucien Galtier, a missionary from the Dubuque Diocese, erected a log chapel on the cliffs above the river port known as "Pig's Eye Landing." Galtier dedicated this chapel to St. Paul and ultimately the surrounding village took on that name. This crude chapel was to be the first cathedral of the Diocese of St. Paul. A large stone marker on the bluff above the river memorializes St. Paul's first cathedral. At this time of missionary activity in the region, Minnesota really belonged to the Diocese of Dubuque and just a small portion in the southeast triangle to the Milwaukee Diocese.

St. Paul Diocese. A papal decree issued July 19, 1850 created the Diocese of St. Paul and appointed Joseph Cretin, vicar General of Dubuque at the time, as first bishop. The diocese extended from Lake Superior to the Missouri River and from Iowa to the Canadian border. Initially parts of North and South Dakota were included in the St. Paul Diocese.

Joseph Cretin was from Belley, France, and had come with missionary zeal to the Midwest frontier at the behest of Bishop Loras of Dubuque. Severe challenges faced the new bishop as he came to this outpost facing Minnesota's wilderness. Diocesan church buildings consisted of log structures in St. Paul, Mendota, St. Anthony, and Pembina. His diocesan priests were few: Ravoux in Mendota, Belecourt and Lacombe at Pembina. The Catholic population was scattered. The total population of the entire region was 30,000 Native Americans and 6,000 whites. Of necessity, Cretin was an itinerant bishop. His motto, ''All things to all men,'' exemplified his leadership style of personal sacrifice and self-denial that attracted young men to serve in this untamed territory. In 1853 he sent two St. Paul recruits, John Ireland and Thomas O'Gorman, to the preparatory seminary of Meximieux, and recruited seven seminarians from that region in France to come to St. Paul. A newly combined church, residence, and school on Wabasha and Sixth Streets became the new cathedral, episcopal see, and seminary for the diocese.

In 1851 Cretin brought the Sisters of St. Joseph of Carondelet from St. Louis to staff a school for girls. St. Joseph's Academy, the first Catholic school in the diocese, was at first located in the old log chapel on the bluff, but later a new building for the academy was erected at Virginia and Nelson (later Marshall) Streets. This building also served as Motherhouse and Novitiate for these sisters. A Catholic hospital was also erected and the Sisters of St. Joseph took charge of that institution when a cholera epidemic broke out in the city in 1855–56. These sisters were also administrators of St. Mary's Hospital in Minneapolis for over 100 years. They also undertook missionary work among the Winnebago Native Americans in Long Prairie, a project dear to the heart of Bishop Cretin. Financial problems caused the demise of this mission in 1856.

At Cretin's encouragement, numbers of French, Irish, and German immigrants came to the region and took up lands along the Mississippi, Minnesota, and St. Croix Rivers. Prosperous settlements developed throughout the diocese and Catholic population increased. In 1853 because the German Catholic population in St. Paul had grown so rapidly, a German parish, the Assumption, was established. German speaking priests were sought to administer the parish and in 1856 three Benedictines came from Latrobe, Pennsylvania, to staff the Assumption parish and to help with the growing German population of Stearns County. They settled in St. Cloud, opened St. John's Seminary, and in 1856 moved permanently to Collegeville. This Abbey became renowned for its leadership in liturgical reform and ecumenical endeavors throughout the development of the Catholic Church in America. Other dedicated religious men and women began to establish regional headquarters in the diocese in order to assist in the charitable works so needed among the immigrant throngs. While Catholic immigrants to Minnesota signified tremendous growth in numbers for

Archdiocese/Diocese	Year Created
Archdiocese of St. Paul and Minneapolis	1888
Diocese of Crookston	1909
Diocese of Duluth	1889
Diocese of New Ulm	1957
Diocese of St. Cloud	1889
Diocese of Winona	1889

the Catholic Church in America, cultural differences among these newcomers posed serious problems for Church leaders. Irish prelates dominated the American hierarchy and other ethnic groups voiced desires to have bishops over them who were of their cultural background. While the Irish Immigration Society encouraged Irish from the old sod and from congested Eastern states to settle in Minnesota, groups of Germans also came from various petty principalities in Germany. The German language held these disparate groups in some kind of cultural unity. For the Germans the retention of their German language would remain at the heart of their cultural identity well into the 20th century. St. Paul's Germans wanted German used in their worship, their Catechetical instruction, other Church rites, and in their parochial education. They organized the St. Joseph Aid Society and purchased land in St. Paul for a cemetery for German-Catholics. Bishop Grace, successor to Cretin, intervened and this property became the site of St. Joseph's Orphanage, staffed by Benedictine Sisters. Polish and Italian groups in St. Paul also demanded clergy of their specific nationalities, but Grace opposed this tendency. He wanted all Catholics to be accepted as loyal Americans by the dominant Protestant groups in society. At that time anti-Catholic activities of the Know-Nothing Party still hung heavy over the land, and Grace wanted no action of Catholics in his diocese to fan the fire of hatred generated by this group. *The Northwestern Chronicle* became the official organ of the diocese. In short order the Germans launched *Der Wanderer,* the French began *Le Canadien,* and the Irish began publishing the *Northwest Standard.* Other ethnic papers appeared as newer immigrants found their way into Minnesota. Ethnic parishes with their special church construction and cultural thrust proliferated in both rural and urban Minnesota up to the turn of the century.

Bishop Grace welcomed other groups of religious into the diocese to help with the needs of the growing Catholic community: Sisters of St. Dominic of Sinsinawa in 1865, Sisters of the Good Shepherd in 1868, Christian Brothers in 1871, Sisters of the Visitation in 1873. By 1919 other religious groups would be serving in the diocese as well. Among these were School Sisters of Notre

College of St. Scholastica, Duluth.

Dame, Sisters of Christian Charity, Franciscan Sisters from Milwaukee and Toledo, Poor Handmaids of Jesus, and Felician Sisters. Early bishops of the diocese openly opposed participation of women in political, civil, and national organizations, no matter how worthy the cause. For them, the proper place for women was in the home. The various sisterhoods, providing education for young women beyond the elementary level, truly paved the way for changing feminine thought toward more active roles in society for women.

From the very beginning of the diocese, lay leadership was evident in collaborating with the clergy and religious in addressing the needs of the growing Church, especially the needs of the poor. Benevolent societies were founded to provide aid to families in time of exigencies. Economic, political, and social bigotry in the young United States excluded Catholics as ineligible recipients of public charities.

Pope PIUS IX's *Syllabus of Errors,* condemning various kinds of religious liberalism, brought a barrage of criticism in the United States against everything Catholic. The Second Council of Baltimore in 1866 affirmed the pope's decree, and Grace, like the other American bishops, pledged to implement the *Syllabus* in the St. Paul Diocese. Deaneries were organized to do this. Too ill to attend the First Vatican Council, Grace sent Father John Ireland to represent him. Though unfinished, the Council declared the infallibility of the pope in matters of faith and morals, causing more negative reaction against the Catholic Church among American Protestants. In America this led to stricter laws demanding separation of Church and State, particularly when Catholic leaders strove for financial aid for their struggling parochial schools. The plea of Catholic parents that they were being doubly taxed for educating their children according to conscience fell on deaf ears in American courts. This was a big issue in Minnesota.

Despite this controversy, Bishop Grace continued to champion Catholic education. His endeavors resulted in the beginnings of Cretin High School in St. Paul and an attempt to start a Catholic Industrial School on the property which was to become the site for the future University of St. Thomas. This school later moved to Swift County but was finally closed in 1879.

The Catholic population in the diocese continued to grow, and in 1875 the Vicariate of Northern Minnesota was established with the Right Reverend Rupert Seidenbusch, O.S.B. consecrated as Vicar Apostolic of the new territory with residence in St. Cloud. That same year John Ireland became coadjutor to Bishop Grace with the right of succession. In 1879 the Vicariate of North Dakota was created with Right Reverend Martin Marty, O.S.B. its first bishop. Thus the Diocese of St. Paul became focused on the southern half of Minnesota. In 1884, Grace resigned as Bishop of the St. Paul Diocese in favor of his coadjutor, John Ireland. The diocese was raised to archiepiscopal status in 1888 with Ireland the first archbishop. In 1889 five suffragan sees were erected: Sioux Falls in South Dakota; Fargo in North Dakota; and Duluth, Winona, and St. Cloud in Minnesota. Although the archdiocese at the time comprised both rural and urban areas, by far the greater population was concentrated within the Twin Cities of St. Paul and Minneapolis with all the attending problems that urban concentrations imposed on an immigrant Church. Six priests of the province were consecrated bishops at one time by Ireland in the St. Paul Seminary chapel to fill these new sees as well as to provide an auxiliary for Ireland. This auxiliary, John J. Lawler, became Bishop of Lead, South Dakota, in 1916.

Perhaps more than any other prelate in Minnesota's history, John IRELAND's leadership put the Minnesota Catholic Church in the limelight. Ireland's championship of the Americanization Movement brought him at loggerheads with Catholic ethnic leaders in Minnesota, the nation, and Rome. Ireland demanded that the ways of the old world had to be shed in becoming American. This required the adoption of English by all and the relinquishing of foreign languages in educational instruction, business enterprises, and liturgical services. Many ethnic groups, particularly Germans, wanted to retain their old customs and cultures, especially the use of their native languages. Ireland feared that the use of foreign tongues would bring grave criticism on the Catholic Church in America. St. Paul Germans, affiliated with the St. Raphael Verein (*see* ST. RAPHAEL'S SOCIETY), founded by Peter Paul CAHENSELY in 1883 to provide for the spiritual welfare of foreign language groups, believed that priests in their national parishes should teach the truths of the faith in the language of each particular ethnic group. Ireland and his supporters of the Catholic University of America insisted that all newcomers adopt English as their national language. The St. Raphael's Verein had international support. Rome refused to take sides in this issue, but the controversy resulted in a rift between Ireland and ethnic groups in his archdiocese. Irish clergy blamed German hierarchy in Cincinnati, Milwaukee, and St. Louis for attempting to control Catholic affairs in America. The Americanization Movement also called for new methods to approach non-Catholics. Catholic doctrine must be adapted to modern times. Ireland's enemies accused him of the heresy of ''modernism'' and contributed to his failure at being named a cardinal.

The episcopacies in Minnesota following the death of Archbishop Ireland in 1918 were forced to face the hardships imposed on their flocks by two world wars and the Great Depression in between. Archdiocesan social programs expanded during these decades. The voice of the local Church was ever present in addressing rural and urban problems facing the poor. The work of Minnesota's own Monsignor John A. RYAN had its impact on local needs of the working poor as well as on the national social legislation that marked the 1930s. World Wars I and II tried the patriotism of all Americans and Minnesotan Catholics responded nobly. Chaplains, nurses, soldiers in all branches of the service included many from the ranks of Minnesota's Catholics. The outstanding Minnesota Catholic event between the wars was the celebration of the Ninth Eucharistic Congress in the summer of 1941 in the Twin Cities. As a result of this demonstration of the Catholic Faith, daily exposition of the Blessed Sacrament was initiated in several diocesan churches and chapels of religious. These were the years that marked the high point of the immigrant Church in Minnesota, as it was impacted by European immigration.

The most earth-shaking event of the 20th century impacting the life of the Catholic Church of Minnesota was the Second Vatican Council. Lasting from 1962 through 1965 the Council produced several significant documents. *Lumen Gentium* emphasized the inclusive thrust of the Gospel message, referring to the Church as the People of God. The hierarchical, triumphal image of Church was no longer meaningful to most, clergy and lay alike. The bishop's role was seen as pastor of the local diocesan Church in collaboration with the priests and laity in carrying the gospel message into all walks of life. The Pope and bishops were to act more collegially and the principle of subsidiarity called bishops to stronger local leadership. The laity, especially women and the marginalized, expected greater inclusion in Church life. The final Council document, *The Pastoral Constitution on the Church in the Modern World,* addressed the complex issues faced by the People of God in a rapidly changing world.

From 1950 to the turn of the century the Church in Minnesota faced moral issues impacted by many changing social and political realities of the time. Urban sprawl demanded new churches but with fewer priests to staff them; fewer religious were available to staff the existing parochial school system, putting greater demands on the laity for personnel and monetary resources; consolidations and closings of schools created problems; the sexual revolution and decline in family values witnessed the rise of homosexual issues; the abortion issue, medical research and experimentation plus rising cost issues in staffing Catholic hospitals put these hospitals at odds with governmental regulations; the growing diversity among Minnesota Catholics, assuming personal responsibility in attempting to implement the directives flowing from the Council documents created tensions throughout the archdiocese. In all of these issues, Minnesota bishops, clergy, religious and other laity provided leadership in guiding the local Catholic Church to be faithful to Christ's Gospel mandate. Although common Catholic traditions and shared interests are characteristic of the Church in Minnesota, the third phase of its history must be recounted in connection with the individual dioceses.

See Also: ST. PAUL AND MINNEAPOLIS, ST. CLOUD, WINONA, AND NEW ULM.

Bibliography: *Archives of the Archdiocese of St. Paul and Minneapolis* (St. Paul, Minn.). P. H. AHERN, ed., *Catholic Heritage in Minnesota, North Dakota, South Dakota* (St. Paul 1964). M. R. O'CONNELL, *John Ireland and the American Catholic Church* (St. Paul 1988). A. RAUCHE and A. M. BIERMAIER, *They Came to Teach: The Story of Sisters Who Taught in Parochial Schools and Their Contributions to Elementary Education in Minnesota* (St. Cloud 1994). J. M. REARDON, *The Catholic Church in the Diocese of St. Paul* (St. Paul 1952). J. C. WOLKERSTORFER, *You Shall Be My People: A History of the Archdiocese of St. Paul and Minneapolis* (France 1999).

[J. C. WOLKERSTORFER]

MINOR PROPHETS

The group of 12 short PROPHETIC books of the Old Testament is called the Minor Prophets. The name Minor Prophets goes back apparently to St. Augustine [*Civ.* 18.29: *Corpus scriptorum ecclesiasticorum latinorum* (Vienna 1866–) 40.2.306], who distinguished the 12 shorter prophetic books as *prophetae minores* from the four longer books of the Prophets Isaiah, Jeremiah, Ezekiel, and Daniel. The term, therefore, is not concerned with the relative importance of these books. Since the collection of the 12 Minor Prophets contains writings from the 8th to probably the 4th century B.C., it is of great importance for understanding the religious and political history of Israel during these centuries. Besides, many of the Minor Prophets, despite their brevity, rank on a par with the best chapters of the Major Prophets from a literary viewpoint. In the Septuagint the Minor Prophets are placed before the Major Prophets; in the Vulgate and other Christian versions, after Daniel; in the Hebrew Bible, after Ezekiel. Since all the 12 Minor Prophets can be written on one SCROLL, in the Hebrew Bible they are considered a single book, called by the Aramaic word *t^erê 'ašar* (the Twelve). The Greek Fathers, too, knew them as a single unit called the δωδεκαπρόφητον (the Twelve Prophets). Their order in the Vulgate is the same as in the Hebrew Bible: HOSEA, JOEL, AMOS, OBADIAH, JONAH, MICAH, NEHEMIAH, HABAKKUK, ZEPHANIAH, HAGGAI, ZECHARIAH, and MALACHI. In the Septuagint the order of the first six is somewhat different: Hosea, Amos, Micah, Joel, Obadiah, and Jonah. Neither order, however, shows a correct chronological sequence, although no doubt chronological considerations played a major role in both arrangements.

[L. F. HARTMAN]

MINUCIUS, FELIX

Marcus, Roman lawyer and Christian apologist; b. probably Africa, second half of the 2d century; d. Rome, *c.* 250. Lactantius (*Div. inst* 5.1, 22) and Jerome (*De vir. ill.* 58) associate Minucius with such Africans as Tertullian, Cyprian, and Arnobius. Minucius studied law and later practiced in Rome. His *Octavius,* or apology, was addressed to educated pagans. It is written in the form of a Ciceronian dialogue, held supposedly during a walk from Rome to Ostia, among Octavius, Caecilius, and Minucius. Octavius states the case for Christianity and Caecilius, for paganism; Minucius adjudicates the discussion. In his defense of paganism Caecilius contends that in human affairs everything is doubtful and that the lawlessness of nature and in the moral world denies the existence of providence. Hence it is best to adhere to old ways. The Christian desire to change a religion as old and proved as the Roman results from an impious conceit (5–13). In response Octavius states that all men are born with intelligence and understanding and that those who cannot see the universe as the product of divine wisdom are intellectually blind. The true God cannot be seen because He is too bright for sight, too magnificent for full human comprehension (14–19). Pagan fables are a fantastic mixture of immoral myths and mysteries, and the Romans have grown great not by religion but by unpunished sacrilege (20–27). The truth of Christianity is attested by the deportment of its adherents. They not only preach, but they also live great deeds (28–38). No judgment is necessary because Caecilius is converted to Christianity after hearing Octavius.

Minucius was a tolerant apologist, keen to propagate Christianity but anxious not to cause offense in so doing. The work contains neither a summary of Christian teaching nor a wealth of biblical reference; but there are reminiscences of Homer, Horace, Juvenal, Vergil, and other pagans, as well as Justin, Tatian, Athenagoras, and Theophilus. Its style is more restrained than that of Tertullian, but literary connections between it and Tertullian's Apology can be traced. These relationships cause a chronological problem, but the majority of scholars regard the Apology as earlier than the *Octavius.*

Bibliography: Editions. C. HALM, ed., *Corpus scriptorum ecclesiasticorum latinorum* (Vienna 1867) 2:1–71. A. D. SIMPSON, ed., *Minucii Felicis Octavius: Prolegomena, Text and Critical Notes* (New York 1938). R. ARBESMANN, tr. *The Fathers of the Church: A New Translation*, ed R. J. DEFERRARI et al. (New York 1947–60) 10 (1950) 321–402. **Studies.** D. KUIJPER, ''Minuciana'' *Vigiliae Christianae* 6 (1952): 201–207. G. QUISPEL, *ibid.* 3 (1949): 113–122. H. V. M. DENNIS, *American Journal of Philology* 50 (1929):185–189. C. MOHRMANN, *ibid.* 2 (1948) 89–101, 162–184, Latin. J. P. WALTZING, *Lexicon Minucianum* (Liège 1909). H. LECLERCQ, *Dictionnaire d'archéologie chrétienne et de liturgie,* 15 v. (Paris 1907–53) 11.2:1388–1412. B. ALTANER, *Patrology* (New York 1960) 162–166. J. QUASTEN, *Patrology,* 3 v. (Westminster, Md. 1950) 2:155–163.

[P. W. LAWLER]

MIRACLE, MORAL

The definition of miracle in general [*see* MIRACLES (THEOLOGY OF)] is fulfilled by the moral miracle in its own way. It consists in an observable phenomenon that so differs from or exceeds the capacity of the natural factors in a situation that the human mind recognizes a special divine intervention.

The moral miracle is differentiated from other miracles not by being a less evident or less striking miracle, but by the fact of its occurrence in the moral (as distinguished from the physical or the intellectual) order. Whereas the physical miracle (and it is generally of such that one speaks when he talks of miracles without further qualification) occurs in the sector of reality described by the laws or principles of chemistry, physics, biology, and physiology, and whereas the intellectual miracle occurs in the sector of human cognition, the moral miracle occurs in the field of human conation, human activity, ethical endeavor. As the changing of water into wine, the multiplication of foodstuffs, the spontaneous healing of organic diseases, the raising of the dead to life are instances of physical miracles, and as the foreknowledge and certain prediction at some distance in time beforehand of free actions of God or man is an instance of intellectual miracle, so a manner or mode of deliberate action—on the part of either a single person or a group of persons—that notably surpasses the observed and constant level of human behavior is held to be a moral miracle.

Concretely, one discerns the presence of a moral miracle where (1) the constant commitment (affective and effective) (2) to goals that are set by God and lead to union with Him (3) despite grave obstacles and at the cost of heavy and recurring sacrifices is, on reflection, recognized as involving a type of conduct that clearly surpasses the level of performance that human nature achieves when left to its own resources. The basic judgment of human capabilities draws upon both man's valid intuitions and his human experience.

Moral miracle as sign. Since the subject of miracles is of practical concern insofar as by means of them God alerts man to His salvific intentions, effectively witnesses to and accredits those who claim to speak and act in His name, it may be helpful to consider the advantages and disadvantages of moral miracles (as contrasted with physical and intellectual miracles) in establishing the credibility of the Catholic religion.

Two advantages come to mind. (1) Since the moral miracle is situated precisely in the life, vitality, activity of the person or institution claiming acceptance as a divine legate, it appeals more strongly as an endorsement than do signs (however valid) that are extrinsic to the legate. In offering the moral miracle as proof, the legate carries his credentials not so much with him as within him. As a long-lost son appearing to claim his inheritance enjoys a special advantage if instead of depending on documents of certification he can present himself to the executors bearing in every line and feature the living image of his father, so the divine legate has a special advantage if his whole manner of being immediately evidences a divine origin. (2) The other advantage—this time in the actual context of Catholic apologetics—is that whereas the physical and intellectual miracles generally adduced are those of Christ Himself and His Apostles, and hence the force of the apologetic demonstration hinges on the historical value of records of past events, the moral miracle to which appeal is made (the vitality and activity of the Church in its members) is a visible phenomenon arising truly in the past but a continuing and verifiable phenomenon in the present.

In the appeal to moral miracle as a motive of credibility there are, however, difficulties not encountered to the same extent in the appeal to other miracles. Two comparative disadvantages may be mentioned: (1) if the moral miracle is sought in the life and activity of a group spread over large areas and during extended periods of time, it is difficult to amass and assess all the factors—national, racial, temperamental, political, social, psychological—that enter into and may modify the whole situation; (2) if this difficulty is greatly diminished when an appeal is made to the moral excellence of one person (e.g., Christ Himself), then another difficulty arises, that of establishing the limits of achievement in single and exceptional cases.

Vatican Council I proposed the existence (and a fortiori the possibility) of moral miracles in presenting the Church as in itself ''a great and perpetual motive of credibility and an unimpeachable [*irrefragabile*] testimony to its own divine legation'' (H. Denzinger, *Enchiridion symbolorum* [Freiburg 1963] 3013).

See Also: MIRACLE, MORAL (THE CHURCH).

Bibliography: J. DE TONQUÉDEC, *Introduction à l'étude du merveilleux et du miracle* (3d ed. Paris 1923). K. PFEIFER, *Das Wunder als Erkenntnismittel der Glaubwürdigkeit der göttlichen Offenbarung in der modernen katholischen und protestantischen Apologetik* (Würzburg 1936).

[S. E. DONLON]

MIRACLE, MORAL (THE CHURCH)

One may note from the start a difference of thrust between the argument adduced when the Church is presented as a moral miracle and the argument adduced from the MARKS OF THE CHURCH. In the latter argument the intention is to show that the Catholic Church at the time the argument is offered manifests itself as the legitimate continuation and prolongation of the religious society founded by Christ and consequently is through Christ a divine institution and bearer of a divine legation. The argument from the Church as a moral miracle, if validly constructed, has as its immediate conclusion (thus prescinding from the foundation of the Church by Christ) the truth that the Church is certified to speak in the name of God.

The notion that the Church in its concrete existence—its life, growth, vigor, activity—is a testimonial to its divine mission has never been absent from Catholic thought, though it has not always been equally emphasized in its teaching. It is suggested or proposed in elementary form in the early Fathers, is developed more fully in Augustine's *City of God* (bk. 22), and is advanced in summary form by St. Thomas Aquinas (*C. gent.* 1.6). In the 19th century, restated by J. Kleutgen and Cardinal J. Franzelin, it was stressed by Cardinal V. Dechamps, Archbishop of Malines, to whose efforts is in large measure due the decree of Vatican I (H. Denzinger, *Enchiridion symbolorum* 3013) that ''the Church in itself (*per se ipsa*) by reason of its admirable growth, its outstanding sanctity and unfailing fruitfulness, its catholic unity and unwavering stability is a great and perpetual motive of credibility and an unimpeachable testimony of its own divine legation.'' In the century after Vatican I, most of the theologians writing in the field of apologetics presented at greater or less length this demonstration along the lines marked out by that Council.

Force of Conciliar Decree. It has been generally maintained by theologians that the Council did not intend to insist as much on the specific aspects under which the miracle may be considered as on the basic truth that the Church is in itself an indisputable proof of its claims. Still less, it may be held, did the fathers of the Council teach that all the aspects are equally evident at all times. It may be thought that as in the case of other living things the vitality—and here the miraculous vitality—would in the early years be manifested in the phenomenon of growth (the *admirabilis propagatio*) and in more mature years in the vigor by which the living subject resists fission, deterioration, and decay (the *fecunditas, unitas catholica,* and *invicta stabilitas*).

Modes of Presentation. One can here but sketch the type of argumentation that is to be found fully developed in standard theological treatises. The treatment here confines itself to only some of the aspects indicated by the council: that of the growth or spread of the Church during the two-and-a-half centuries before the peace of Constantine, and that of its enduring unity in the centuries since then.

Early Growth. In developing the argument from the Church's growth during the first centuries, theologians recall that in those years the Church grew from a membership of some few thousands to a number estimated between seven and ten million (within the Roman Empire, which at the end of this period probably numbered about 50 million). This numerical increase was achieved, though not equally, in all parts of the empire and among all classes of society; hence it cannot be explained as an increase based on a natural appeal to racial or class interests. Most important, it was accomplished in the face of tremendous obstacles and at the cost of great sacrifices. Among these are generally enumerated: (1) the antipathy of the Gentile world to the Jewish people, from whom sprang the One to whom the Church paid divine worship and proclaimed as its founder; (2) the scandal of His Crucifixion, and of the ignorance and lowly condition of those who first preached His gospel; (3) the theoretical doctrine, which though lofty and noble surpassed and affronted human reason without catering to the taste for the exotic or the esoteric as did gnostic teachings or mystery religions; (4) the moral doctrine that unequivocally condemned vices, even the customary and comfortable ones; (5) the harassments from the increasingly hostile attitude of the Roman government—even though persecutions were sporadic and, in the early part of this period, often only local, there was never a time when a Christian could breathe freely in the conviction that his life, his family, his home, his position, his possessions were secure from private or public prosecutor; (6) the abuse or ridicule frequently encountered, a factor especially important insofar as it endangered the faith and allegiance of younger and adolescent Christians; (7) the necessity that often arose of refusing or surrendering lucrative and decent occupations or offices, denying oneself the pleasure of feasts, entertainments, and spectacles because they were in one way or other connected with pagan rites, implied acceptance of pagan religions (see Tertullian's *De idololatria*). Given all the difficulties from which the Christian could easily have extricated himself by simply renouncing his membership in the Church, the continued existence and the steady growth of the Church evidences in its members a level of conduct surpassing human strength and moral courage.

Enduring Unity. In much the same way, Catholic writers develop the argument from the steady UNITY OF THE CHURCH during the time that has passed since the age of persecution. They recall that over a period of 1,600 years in all parts of the world (though again by no means equally in all) this religious society has maintained itself and grown to encompass nearly 500 million members. In so doing, it has not ceased to maintain a clear doctrinal and social unity, notwithstanding grave and constant difficulties.

The obstacles to doctrinal unity are found (1) in the delicate harmony of Catholic doctrine itself, a body of truths neither simple nor crude, but complex and finely integrated—balancing the simplicity and unity of the divine nature with the Trinity of Persons, the divinity of Christ with His complete humanity, the validity of the concept of nature and natural law with the fact of universal supernatural destination, human freedom with the efficaciousness of grace, the superabundant merits of Christ with the merits of the justified individual, rights of the individual with the claims of society and public order, rights of the Church with the rights of civil society, rights of married people to personal fulfillment with the claims of marriage as an institution; and (2) in the succession of philosophies, ideologies, intellectual movements that have claimed acceptance especially in those parts of the world in which the Church counted the greater number of its members; thus, in succession and sometimes overlapping, Manichaeism, Pelagianism, medieval pantheism, Renaissance humanism, the Enlightenment, rationalism, skepticism, idealism, modern atheistic or anti-Christian communism, certain forms of scientism, evolutionism, individualism, and personalism. (*See* UNITY OF FAITH.)

The Church's social unity has been threatened over many centuries by CAESAROPAPISM and exaggerated nationalism with its chauvinistic appeal to national or racial feelings, aspirations, and pride. The history of the Church in the U.S. during most of the last two centuries is almost by itself sufficient documentation of the difficulty (and one that appears naturally insuperable) of maintaining Catholic unity among Catholics drawn from different peoples and nations of Europe.

Although it is true that in the course of these centuries millions have forsaken this unity, and hence although it is to be conceded that a greater and more striking miracle is conceivable, still there remains the fact of the one common religious allegiance of almost one-sixth of the world's population. It may be added that the defections from unity over the centuries at least assure one that this unity has been maintained among men and women subject to all the normal centrifugal strains and to all the natural appeal of newer, attractive, more ''up-to-date'' systems that would answer to the needs, the aspirations, or the desires of the moment.

See Also: MIRACLE, MORAL.

Bibliography: General. A. MICHEL, *Dictionnaire de théologie catholique,* ed. A. VACANT et al. (Paris 1903–50) Tables générales 1:1111–14. M. GRAND'MAISON, *L'Église par elle-même motif de crédibilité* (Rome 1961). R. LATOURELLE, *Théologie de la révélation* (Bruges 1963), esp. 446–453. A. G. SERTILLANGES, *Le Miracle de l'Église* (Paris 1936). Early growth of Church. H. LECLERCQ, *Dictionnaire d'archéologie chrétienne et de liturgie*, ed. F. CABROL, H. LECLERCQ, and H. I. MARROU (Paris 1907–53) 5.1:978–1014. E. KIRSCHBAUM and L. HERTLING, *The Roman Catacombs and Their Martyrs,* tr. M. J. COSTELLOE (2d. ed. London 1960). L. HERTLING, ''Die Zahl der Christen zu Beginn des vierten Jahrhunderts,'' *Zeitschrift für katholische Theologie* 58 (1934) 243–253; ''Die Zahl der Märtyrer bis 313,'' *Gregoriana* 25 (1944) 103–129.

[S. E. DONLON]

MIRACLES (IN THE BIBLE)

There is no term in the Bible that corresponds to miracle in its strict theological meaning. The Latin word

''Jesus Gives Sight to One Born Blind.'' (©Historical Picture Archive/CORBIS)

miraculum is absent from the Vulgate New Testament and occurs only six times in the Vulgate Old Testament for a number of Hebrew terms for wondrous acts or events, not necessarily miraculous in the ordinary sense. After considering the various terms used in the Bible for events of a marvelous nature, this article considers the historical value of accounts in which these events are narrated and the miraculous nature of these Biblical wonders.

Terms. The Hebrew word *môpet* (wonder), used in an exclusively religious connotation, may stand for a symbolic act not necessarily beyond nature's power (Ez 12.6), a sign of God's power and goodness [Ps 70(71).7], an omen for the future (Is 8.18; 20.3), or a warning portent to keep the people away from evil [Ex 11.9; Ps 104(105).5]. The Septuagint (LXX) translates this term by τέρας (prodigy); in classical Greek this denotes any divine sign (Homer) and later a purely natural wonder (Polybius and Plutarch), but combined with σημεῖον (sign) it often signifies a divine sign, especially in the LXX. This combination is used in the New Testament to describe the wonderful works of Christ (Mt 12.38; 16.1–4; Mk 8.11; Lk 11.16–17; Jn 2.11, 18, 23; etc.). The Hebrew word *'ôt* (sign, mark, or token) is frequently added to *môpet,* e.g., in Ex 7.3; Dt 4.34; 6.22; 7.19; 34.11;

Jer 32.20; Ps 47(48).23, to which the Greek idiom σημεῖα καὶ τέρατα corresponds. The word *'ôt* may also be used in a profane sense; its religious sense is therefore to be determined by the context. The Hebrew word *nês* (signal) occurs once (Nm 26.10) in the meaning of miraculous sign. This term, like *g^{e}bûrôt* (mighty deeds), is very common in post-Biblical literature in combination with *môpet* or *'ôt.*

God's power is often seen in everything that appears wonderful, mysterious, surprising, awe-inspiring or astonishing. Actions manifesting such power are called *nifla'ôt* (wonderful deeds) of God (Ex 3.20; 34.10; Josh 3.5; Jgs 6.13; Jer 21.2; Ps 9a.2), or *p^{e}lā'ôt* (marvels) of God [Ex 15.11; Ps 76 (77).15; Jgs 13.18]. When these terms are used in regard to men, they indicate something beyond them, a notion that the LXX expressed by ἀδύνατον or ἀδυνατεῖν (Gn 18.14; Dt 17.8; Zec 8.6; Prv 30.18). God's wondrous deeds are also *nōrā'ôt* (awesome deeds), which is rendered in the LXX by ταυμάδια (marvelous deeds) or ἔνδοξα (glorious deeds) and in Symmachus by παράδοξα (astonishing deeds), as in Jgs 13.16; Ex 34.10; Ps 65(66).3; Dut 10.2; 2 Sm 7.23. They are the works (ma'ăśîm) of God's power (Ex 34.10; Dt 11.7; Jos 24.31; Jer 51.10), His *g^{e} bûrôt* (mighty deeds), as in Ex 3.24; Ps 19(20.7; 104(105).2, His *g^{e} dôlôt* (great deeds), as in 2 Kgs 8.4; Ps 70(71).19; 135 (136). 4; Job 5.9; 9.10; 37.5, corresponding to the New Testament terms ἔργα (works, i.e., of God: especially in John) and δυνάμεις (mighty deeds: so especially in Matthew and Mark). Miracles are thus placed in the grand design of God, the Creator and savior of mankind (Jn 4.34; 17.4; Rom 1.16; 15.19; Gal 3.5; 1 Cor 12.1; 1 Thes 1.5).

This terminology shows that the wondrous acts of God fall within the category of prophetic symbolism intended to draw attention to something beyond themselves that confirms the word of God. They are not isolated gestures on the part of God but play an important part in the execution of the grand design of the Creator for the redemption of His creatures.

Historical Value. Vatican Council I declared that Biblical miracles are not to be rejected as so much mythical or legendary matter (H. Denzinger, *Enchiridion symbolorum,* 1813); Moses, the Prophets, the Apostles, and Jesus did really perform miracles to attest to their respective messages and draw the attention of their listeners (*Enchiridion symbolorum* 1790). There is still freedom to discuss particular cases (and modern literary-historical criticism is exacting in the matter) in the light of the principles laid down in the encyclical *DIVINO AFFLANTE SPIRITU* (*Enchiridion Biblicum* [Rome 1961] 558).

All miracle narratives are held to be legendary and mythical by the independent schools of comparative religion and literary criticism. Literary features common to Biblical and pagan narratives should not blind one, however, to the radical divergencies between them pointing to the great religious value of the former. The crucial difference arises from the intervention of God in human affairs for the salvation of humankind. The method of Biblical FORM CRITICISM has the merit of bringing to the fore the literary form and qualities of the text, but is unable by itself to lead one to a decision as to its historical value.

The wondrous acts of Jesus are one with the texture itself of the New Testament: they form an integral part of his story and provide a solid basis for Christian belief and Apostolic preaching (Lk 7.22; Mt 11.5; Acts 2.22; 10.38; 2 Cor 12.12; 1 Thes 1.5) and authority (Mk 16.17; Acts 3.12; 2.43; 5.15; 14.3; 1 Cor 2.4; Heb 2.4).

In the case of the Old Testament miracles, the literary form of the book containing a miracle story must first be determined. A miracle narrative may be found in larger works with different literary forms. The wisdom form of literature makes full use of fictional devices; in such an instance the wonder narrative may be a purely literary artifice. This is generally admitted with respect to the Book of Job (*Dictionnaire de la Bible,* 4.1082) and, to a lesser extent, to the Books of Jona and Tobit. The Book of Daniel is a mixture of prophetic, apocalyptic, and wisdom forms. Sir 44–49 and Wis 10–19 manifest how freely the sapiential writers treated historical facts; exaggeration and artificial devices are harnessed to press home the writer's point.

The fictional element is not missing in some historical writings: the talking serpent in Gn 3.2 may be taken figuratively [*Acta Apostolicae Sedis* 40 (1948) 47]. The history of the Exodus puts one on guard lest too much be rejected or accepted (*see* PLAGUES OF EGYPT). The critical examination of the various traditions handed down from generation to generation to keep alive the faith of the people bears unanimous witness to basic miraculous events at the start of the whole deliverance; they differ, however, as to the details and particular circumstances accompanying these events: the separation of the sea for the advance of the people (Ex 14–15), the sending of the manna (Ex 16.1–18), and so on. The compiler, no less than the writer, of Deuteronomy, the Psalmists, and the wisdom writers juxtaposed these traditions to emphasize the miraculous nature of the whole adventure; as to details, each case must be assessed by itself. The miracles in the historical and prophetical books respectively are less in number and better attested by contemporary witnesses and form part of a normal historical record. Miracle narratives tend to increase in the biographies of ELIJAH AND ELISHA; this calls for caution and inclines one to admit literary exaggeration. In view of well-attested modern miracles of this type one should not be over hasty to put them aside as legendary folk tales.

Miraculous Nature. The Israelite, having no idea of a fixed unchangeable natural law governing the physical universe, was not interested in the intimate nature of a miracle; for him it was a sign of God's merciful providence for some specific purpose, which he tried to grasp and understand. Christian theology attempts to discover the nature of a miracle defined as an event inconsistent with the constitution of nature, that is, with the established course of things. Or, again, it is an event in a given system that cannot be referred to by any law or accounted for by the operation of any principle in that system. [J. H. Newman, Essays on *Miracles* (London 1890) 4.] Do Biblical miracles conform to this definition? An outline of basic principles suffices for the present; each specific case should be examined on its own merits.

Some, interpreting the miracle narratives in a strictly literal sense, strive to find natural explanations; others cast serious doubts on their historical value; and still others, accepting their historical value, explain them as magical practices or empirical curative treatments or gestures common in those days. Some of these attempts to understand miracle stories are vitiated by the basic prejudice that miracles are theologically and philosophically impossible.

It is, nonetheless, legitimate to search for scientific or natural explanations provided that things are not stretched too far. Frequently events are much too summarily described for us to establish their miraculous nature with any degree of theological precision; in such cases it is better to confess our ignorance for lack of evidence. It must be kept in mind that miracles were first and foremost, although not exclusively, intended to awaken in their immediate beholders an interest and trust in God, the Prophets, the Apostles, and Jesus Christ. For moderns, the church itself is a fundamental miracle, a sign raised among the nations (Is 11.12). The value of particular miracles lies in their being carriers of the word of God and witnesses of the power of the Spirit for the Redemption of humankind and the establishment of the eschatological kingdom.

Theological Significance. For the Israelite, the importance of the miracle lies not so much in its being a break in the laws of nature as in its purpose. The modern study of miracles has moved in this direction, seeking to define the theological significance of these wonders. In this way the miracle, far from being considered as an isolated display of God's power over the laws of nature, finds its place and function in the execution of the overall design of divine Providence for the Redemption of Israel and all humankind. The terms examined above unmistakably show that the miracle is a sign going beyond itself to draw the attention of the beholders (Exod 3.2–3); it is an invitation to faith in God and is understood only by the well-disposed, drawing them to a decision (Nm 14.11–12; Dt 4.34; 7.19; 29.2; Mt 12.22–50). The marvelous signs reveal the attributes of God and His will (Ex 7.5, 17), especially with regard to Israel's election (Ex 11.7; 34.10–11; Dt 6.22; 10.14–15; Wis 11.5); through them God's fidelity to His own promises is made manifest [Ex 3.7; Dt 7.8–10; Psalm 135(136); Is 46.3–4; Hos 9.10; 11.1], and His justice is made public to all the world (Leviticus 26, 45). A miracle is a guarantee for the future and its foreshadow (Dt 7.9–19; Is 11.15–16; 43.16–21; 51; Hos 2.14–15, 17; 11.1; 13.4; Mt 4.23–25; 12.28; Lk 6.17–19).

Miracles also provided an effective instrument for the religious education of Israel [Dt 9.26; Psalm 76(77); 81(82); 104(105)–107(108)]; they awakened fundamental religious feelings and attitudes through concrete symbolical representation of the truth. By itself a miracle is insufficient to confirm or authenticate the truth; the message must conform to the word of God (Dt 13.2–6; Mt 8.17; 9.35; 11.2–6; 24.24; Rv 13.11–18; 16.13–14; 19.20).

In the New Testament. The Acts of the Apostles says that wonders and signs were done by the apostles (Acts 2.43) and by Paul and Barnabas (Acts 14.3). Thus miraculous activity was part of the witness that the church bore to the kingdom of God among Jews and Gentiles. Luke enhances his pictures of Peter and Paul as, respectively, the bearers of God's word to Jews and Gentiles by telling stories of miracles worked by each of these Apostles. Similar stories are told about each of these two key figures in the history of the early church (Acts 3.1–16 and 14.8–10; 5.1–11 and 13.6–11; 9.33–35 and 28.7–9; etc.). Paul writes about the signs, wonders, and mighty works that are the signs of a true apostle (2 Cor 12.12) without describing any individual signs and wonders.

Preaching in Jerusalem on the Day of Pentecost, Peter described Jesus as a man attested by God with deeds of power, wonders, and signs that God did through him (Acts 2.22; Lk 24.19). Stories about Jesus' miracles appear in each of the four Gospels. The Gospels attest to several controversies that arose because of the wondrous deeds that Jesus had effected, particularly Jesus' curing on the sabbath.

In describing the miracles of Jesus the four evangelists follow the standard pattern used in the ancient world—the literary form of a miracle story—to describe the activity of wonder workers. This literary form consisted of three elements: 1) a description of the situation, so narrated as to highlight the difficulty of the miracle that was to happen; 2) a simple ritual consisting of an authoritative word (Mk 5.34) and/or a ritualized gesture (e.g., Mk 7.33); and 3) some demonstration of the reality of the miracle. This last element sometimes consisted of a narrative element, illustrating that the miracle had happened, e.g., the blind man who regained his sight and followed Jesus was calm (Mk 10.52); those fed had more than enough to eat (Mk 8.8). This narrative ''proof'' was sometimes accompanied by or even replaced by a choral response in which the bystanders express amazement at what had happened (Mk 4.39 and 41; Le 18.43). These choral responses are particularly important in Luke's account of Jesus' miracles.

Many of the miracle stories recounted by Matthew and Luke come from Mark, the first of the Synoptic Gospels. A very large part of Mark's gospel consists of stories about Jesus' miracles and exorcisms. These stories show that the kingdom of God is present in Jesus ministry. Through these wonderful activities of Jesus, God's power is at work conquering the power of evil in individuals and even in nature, a foreshadowing of the ultimate conquering of evil that will come when the Kingdom of God is fully and finally manifest.

Occasionally Mark intimates that Jesus' miracles should be seen in the light of the biblical hope. Thus the choral response of Mk 7.37 alludes to Is 35.5–6 and shows that Jesus' miracle of the man whose hearing and speech were impaired was a partial realization of Isaiah's dream. What is implied in Mark becomes clearer in the later Synoptic gospels. Thus, Matthew who collects a number of miracle stories together in chapters 8 and 9 interprets Jesus' miracles by means of a fulfillment citation (see Is 53.4 in Mt 8.17). Later on in his narrative, Matthew describes Jesus's miracles as ''what the Messiah was doing,'' that is, the deeds of the Messiah. Jesus' response to John the Baptist as to whether he was the one to come was a rehearsal of his miraculous activity described in the language of Is 29.18–19; 35.5–6; 42.18.

In Luke's Gospel, the importance of the Old Testament for understanding the miracles of Jesus is present from the very beginning of the story of Jesus' public ministry. In his ''inaugural address'' (Luke 4.19), Jesus described the reason why the Spirit had descended upon him. His brief discourse uses passages from Is 61.1–2 and Is 58.6 and includes a reference to the recovery of sight by the blind. Defending himself against the hostile natives of Nazareth, Jesus told the story of miracles attributed to Elijah and Elisha (Lk 4.25–27). Empowered by the Spirit as he was, Jesus performs similar miraculous acts. Like Elijah (1 Kgs 17.17–24), he raised a widowed mother's dead son (Lk 7.11–17).

Only seven stories of miracles are told in the Fourth Gospel. These are concentrated in the first part of the book (Jn 1–12): water become wine (2.1–11), the cure of the royal official's son (4.46–54), the healing of the paralytic (5.1–14), the feeding of the large crowd (Jn 6.1–14), the walking on water (6.16–21), the healing of the blind man (9.1–7), and the raising of Lazarus (11.1–44 [+12.1–2]). While the Fourth Gospel has fewer miracle stories than do the Synoptics, the Fourth Gospel has its own theological idiom to describe Jesus' miracles. They are ''signs'' (semeia). In a characteristic note, the Fourth Evangelist describes the water become wine as ''the first of his signs'' (1.11). The theology implicit in the evangelist's use of ''sign'' is dense. Essentially the cipher points to the christological meaning of Jesus miracles. This is most evident when after the feeding of the crowd the Johannine Jesus describes himself as ''the bread of life'' (6.48, 51) or before raising Lazarus from the dead says ''I am the resurrection and the life'' (11.25).

Bibliography: A. LEFÈVRE, *Dictionnaire de la Bible,* suppl. ed. L. PIROT, et al. (Paris 1928–) 5:1299–1308. *Encyclopedic Dictionary of the Bible*, tr. and adap. by L. HARTMAN (New York 1963) 1538–40. L. CERFAUX et al., *L'Attente du Messie* (Paris 1954) 131–138. S. V. MCCASLAND, ''Signs and Wonders,'' *Journal of Biblical Literature* 76 (1957) 149–152. L. J. MCGINLEY, *Form-Criticism of the Synoptic Healing Narratives* (Woodstock, Md. 1944). B. MAGGIONI, ''Miracoli e rivelazione nell'A.T.,'' *Bibbia e Oriente* 6 (1964) 49–59. E. C. MESSENGER, ''The Miraculous Element in the Bible,'' *Catholic Commentary on Holy Scripture,* ed. B. ORCHARD et al. (London-New York 1957) 87–91. Y. ZAKOVITCH and H. E. REMUS, ''Miracle (NT),'' *Anchor Bible Dictionary* 4:845–869.

[C. SANT/R. F. COLLINS]

MIRACLES (THEOLOGY OF)

In theological usage, a miracle is an extraordinary event, perceptible to the senses, produced by God in a religious context as a sign of the supernatural.

''Extraordinary.'' In interpreting the words ''an extraordinary event produced by God in a religious context,'' one must understand that extraordinary means beyond the powers of corporeal nature, or at least extremely unlikely from the standpoint of those powers alone. There have been, however, differences of opinion among Catholic theologians in this regard.

Strict View. Many theologians, following St. Thomas Aquinas, have maintained that a miracle in the proper sense is beyond the power of all creatures, even incorporeal creatures, something of which only God could be principal cause, though a creature might serve as instrumental cause (*see* INSTRUMENTAL CAUSALITY). This view has been increasingly abandoned on the ground that very few, if any, of the events regarded by Scripture and by

"Christ healing the sick presented to him by the Pharisees," manuscript illumination by Cristoforo de Predis from the "Predis Codex." (©Archivo Iconografico, S.A./CORBIS)

the Church as miracles are demonstrably above all created power. The proponents of the Thomistic view themselves have usually had recourse to the notion of "relative" miracles to include those not fitting their strict definition.

Intermediate View. A more common view is that adopted by Pope Benedict XIV in his classical treatise *De servorum Dei beatificatione et beatorum canonizatione,* according to which a miracle need be only above the powers of corporeal creatures. In this view a miracle could be effected by a created spirit as a principal cause; it would be "produced by God" in the sense that the spirit acted as God's agent, i.e., at God's command or at least with God's formal approval.

Wide View. In recent years some authors have argued that a miracle need not even be strictly beyond the powers of corporeal nature, provided it be a truly prodigious event, one at least highly unlikely ever to result from natural forces alone. Such an event, according to these authors, qualifies as a miracle when, occurring in a religious context, it is recognizably intended by God as a SUPERNATURAL sign. Some authors who hold this view suggest that a miracle need not even *de facto* be caused by immediate supernatural intervention but might be produced by God in the merely mediate sense that it results from an extraordinary combination of natural factors providentially arranged by God, even in the very remote past.

"Sign of the Supernatural." Miracles occurring in connection with a claim of supernatural revelation serve as a divine signature to the truth of that claim. But miracles function as signs also in other ways. They not only confirm supernaturally revealed truths but represent those truths. Thus the RESURRECTION OF CHRIST is not only a guarantee of His teaching but a symbol of His redemptive victory over the spiritual death of sin and an exemplar of the resurrection promised to the faithful. Miracles are also in themselves direct manifestations of one or more divine attributes; e.g., a miraculous cure bespeaks God's compassion. And miracles may testify to the sanctity of a man, as do the miracles accepted as evidence in processes of beatification and canonization. [*See* CANONIZATION OF SAINTS (HISTORY AND PROCEDURE).]

"Perceptible to the Senses." Although a purely internal supernatural experience can serve as a divine sign, the term miracle is normally applied only to events that are ascertainable through the external senses. But while

''Jesus Walking on Water,'' engraving by Gustave Dore from ''The Bible,'' 1866. (©Chris Hellier/CORBIS)

the term is sometimes used exclusively of physical miracles, such as miraculous cures of bodily ailments, it is also properly applied to occurrences in the intellectual or moral order, provided there is external evidence of the operation of the supernatural in the mind or will. One type of intellectual miracle is prophecy in the strict sense, the prediction of an event or series of events by a human being in a manner beyond merely human knowledge. (*See* PROPHET.) An example of a moral miracle is a sudden complete conversion such as that of the Apostle St. PAUL (Acts 9.1–30). In these instances the internal supernatural experience is deducible from its external results; it would not be considered a miracle if it had to be accepted entirely on the word of the recipient. *A fortiori,* supernatural events, even in the material order, knowable only by divine faith, such as TRANSUBSTANTIATION, are not considered miracles in the proper sense, though they have been called ''miracles of faith.''

Official Catholic Doctrine

The teaching of the Church concerning miracles is to be found chiefly in the pronouncements of VATICAN COUNCIL I. The Council declared: ''In order that the 'service' of our faith be 'in accord with reason' [cf. Rom 12.1], God willed that to the internal helps of the Holy Spirit there be joined external proofs of His revelation, i.e., divine deeds, and principally miracles and prophecies. Since these clearly show forth God's omnipotence and infinite knowledge, they are signs of revelation that are most certain and suited to the intelligence of all men. Therefore not only Moses and the Prophets but also and preeminently Christ the Lord Himself wrought many obvious miracles and made numerous manifest prophecies'' (H. Denzinger, *Enchiridion symbolorum*, ed. A. Schönmetzer 3009). With a view to the RATIONALISM common in the 19th century, the Council condemned as erroneous the opinion that ''miracles are impossible, and therefore all accounts of them, even those contained in Sacred

Scripture, are to be rejected as fables and myths'' and the opinion that ''miracles can never be known with certitude nor serve as valid proof of the divine origin of the Christian religion'' (*Enchiridion symbolorum* 3034).

The Oath against Modernism prescribed by St. Pius X in 1910 was even more explicit about the enduring apologetic value of miracles, stating that they are ''eminently suited to the intelligence of all men of every era, including the present'' (*Enchiridion symbolorum* 3539).

It is to be noted that in its official teaching the Church, while by no means excluding the other purposes of miracles, emphasizes their apologetic function, their role as ''proof'' of revelation. Vatican Council I furthermore clearly implied that among the various forms of evidence of the reasonableness of faith miracles hold first place.

Possibility

Both scientific and philosophical objections have been directed against the very possibility of miracles.

The scientific objection, common in the 19th century, was based largely on a rigid scientific determinis. Although it has been undermined by a more modern indeterministic view of nature, even a deterministic theory of science does not exclude the possibility of miracles, provided the determinism is properly qualified by the awareness that the necessity of physical law is precisely a physical or ''natural'' necessity, one that allows for intervention of the supernatural, not a metaphysical necessity.

Philosophical objections to miracles are raised not only by atheists, on the obvious ground that if there is no God he can work no miracles, but also by deists, mainly on the ground that miracles would be contrary to God's immutability and wisdom, as though God's supernatural intervention implied a change in His original plan regarding the nature and operation of creatures or was even needed to correct that plan. The error in this view consists in the failure to see that miracles, like other forms of supernatural intervention, do not change or destroy nature or correct some essential defect in it, but build on nature and provide it with a complementary and higher perfection. They are not the object of a new or separate divine plan, but part of God's universal plan which from eternity included both the natural and the supernatural.

Recognition

The crucial question about miracles is the question of their recognizability. Can there be CERTITUDE, first, about the external event itself, as a historical fact, aside from its natural or supernatural character? Can there be certitude, second, about the miraculous character of the event?

Recognition as Historical. Since miracles are by definition events perceptible to the external senses, there is in principle no reason why they should not, from that standpoint, be as definitely ascertainable, either to eyewitnesses or to others on the testimony of eyewitnesses, as are other external occurrences. The fact that miracles are also by definition extraordinary or prodigious events serves to strengthen their verification, since for that very reason they would attract closer attention on the part of the witnesses.

In point of fact, many miracles have presented all the necessary qualifications of historically attested events, occurring in the presence of numerous reliable witnesses, even adversely disposed witnesses, and under suitable conditions, in broad daylight, near at hand, etc. And while clinical evidence is unnecessary for this purpose, there is such evidence in favor of some miracles, for example, some of the cures of LOURDES.

An argument advanced by David Hume against the historical verifiability of miracles is superficial but still widely repeated. Hume's argument in essence is that on behalf of any miracle there is for most men only moral certitude, certitude based on the testimony of human witnesses, whereas against the miracle there is physical certitude, the certitude of the laws of nature, and physical certitude outweighs moral. The fallacy in Hume's argument is the assumption that physical laws are opposed to miracles. Physical laws are conditional, not absolute. They state what happens under natural conditions but do not exclude the possibility of supernatural exceptions. The physical certitude, accordingly, is in favor of the general law, not against the exception, and is therefore in no way opposed to the moral certitude which is precisely in favor of the exception.

Recognition as Miraculous. The criteria to be applied in the recognition of miracles *as* miraculous vary with one's definition and understanding of miracle as explained above.

According to the Wide View. If one adopts the broad view that a miracle need not be strictly beyond the powers of corporeal nature but only extremely unlikely from the standpoint of those powers alone, the recognition of miracles becomes relatively simple. In this view the main emphasis with regard to the recognition of miracles is to be placed on the religious context. Not any religious context whatsoever is sufficient. The context must be such that one can reasonably conclude that God in His providence would not cause or allow the extraordinary event in question unless He did intend it to be taken as a sign from Him. There would be such a context, for instance, if a religious teacher claimed repeatedly that his doctrine was a new and directly authorized divine revelation, particularly if the teacher appealed to some forthcoming extraordinary event as miraculous confirmation of his claim. Just as an event clearly beyond natural power occurring in such circumstances would reasonably be interpreted as a sign of divine approval, on much the same grounds even an event not distinctly beyond the power of nature but highly unlikely on a natural basis would be rightly interpreted as a divine sign.

This theory of the recognition of miracles depends heavily on God's providence. [*See* PROVIDENCE OF GOD (THEOLOGY OF).] Its force will vary with the degree of extraordinariness of the event and with the details of the religious context. But while this theory does provide a satisfactory explanation of the recognition of miracles, it is possible to present a stronger case by showing that many miracles are actually beyond the powers of corporeal nature.

According to Intermediate View. It should first be understood that there is more than one sense in which an event can be above the powers of corporeal nature. The event might be intrinsically of a kind that could never happen naturally with any corporeal subject; e.g., its occupying strictly the same place as another body. Or the event might be of a kind that could happen in another corporeal subject but not in the one under consideration, e.g., speech in a dog. Or it might be the kind of thing that could happen even in this subject but not under these particular circumstances or in this particular way, e.g., fluent speech in a newborn child or the instantaneous cure of an advanced organic disease. Along these lines theologians distinguish three classes of miracles: miracles with regard to substance (*miracula quoad substantiam*), miracles with regard to subject (*miracula quoad subjectum*), and miracles with regard to mode (*miracula quoad modum*). The majority of miracles are of the third class, events that could happen naturally but not in this particular way or under these given circumstances.

The discernment of a miracle as something beyond the powers of nature involves a comparison of what happens in the miracle with what happens naturally under similar circumstances. Our knowledge of what happens naturally is based on experience, partly on our own experience but especially on the reported experience of others. Even though we do not know all that nature can do, we have a reasonably certain knowledge, based often on thousands or even millions of cases, of at least the general limits of the results produced by nature in a particular set of circumstances (e.g., in the case of a man of a certain age with a particular disease). In the extraordinary event considered a miracle we see that, although there are present at least approximately the same natural causes and conditions as in similar but admittedly natural cases, a distinctly different result occurs. We conclude that there must be some cause present other than the natural ones.

The disproportion between the natural effect and the miraculous effect may appear in various ways. The difference may be in quantity, or in quality, or in both. One particular difference, seen in many miracles, is in the time required. The miracle often takes place instantaneously, or at least in a much shorter time than is required to produce a similar result naturally.

There are, furthermore, in most miracles, positive indications that the principal force responsible for the extraordinary event is a force operating intelligently and freely and, therefore, not a merely natural force. (It is understood that the intelligence and freedom are not those of a human being. An extraordinary event would not be seriously considered as a miracle if there were good reason to suspect that the phenomenon might be within the power of a mere man to produce at will by an understanding and control of the forces of nature.)

Some of the indications of the action of an intelligent and free agent in a miracle may be mentioned. (1) The timing. If, for example, Christ's walking on the water were due merely to an unknown natural force, why should this force take effect just at those times that Christ chose to walk on the water? (2) The purposeful concurrence of several or even many factors. For example, in a miraculous cure there may be distinguished such separate steps as the provision of a certain amount of matter to replace lost tissue, the provision more specifically of the exact elements needed, the organization of that matter into the kinds of tissue needed (skin, muscle, nerves, etc.), the elimination of infectious matter, and so on. In some miracles, two or more completely distinct ailments have been cured simultaneously. (3) The multiplicity and variety of miracles in the life of Christ. If these were all due to merely natural forces, how explain the occurrence of so many and such different extraordinary events in the life of one man? Either these things happened because Christ knew how to use those forces at will, or they happened without such understanding on His part. The latter hypothesis would require an incredible series of coincidences. The former hypothesis would require at least supernatural knowledge in Christ. Such knowledge would constitute an intellectual miracle that could itself be taken as confirmation of Christ's claims.

Even if such considerations do not of themselves afford absolute certitude, they provide genuine moral certitude of the physically transcendent character of many miracles.

There is admittedly much that is still unknown about nature, but it is not necessary to know all that nature *can* do in order to recognize a particular effect as something that nature *cannot* do; it is not necessary to know the absolutely maximum weight a man can lift in order to know that he cannot by his own unaided strength raise a mountain. Nor need we have a complete knowledge of the power of mind over matter—as in psychosomatic illnesses and cures, hypnosis, psychokinesis, etc.—in order to recognize some effects as plainly beyond that power.

While formally scientific knowledge is not necessary for the discernment of miracles, it can be of assistance, both negatively and positively. It is often erroneously asserted that the progress of science has weakened the case for miracles. Science has indeed furnished a natural explanation of certain phenomena that may have once been looked upon as supernatural in some sense, especially by primitive man—though even this is sometimes exaggerated. And science has, by an increased understanding of nature derived from research and by the development of instruments, enabled man to do remarkable things previously impossible to him. But there is a vast difference between doing such things by the aid of scientific knowledge and instruments and doing the same or similar things without such knowledge and instruments. Science has not enabled man to reproduce any of the prodigies related of Christ, especially in the way in which He did them, i.e., without scientific instruments. And even if science were to bring this about, it would still have been miraculous for Christ to do such things at a time when the necessary scientific knowledge was, humanly speaking, unavailable. The progress of science has, in fact, strengthened the case for miracles by giving man a constantly deeper and fuller understanding of the processes of nature, thereby enabling him to recognize certain phenomena even more definitely as beyond natural powers.

Some have thought that the indeterminism espoused by modern physics constitutes an obstacle to the recognition of miracles on the ground that, if nature is basically indetermined, it is impossible to know what nature can or cannot do. But a genuinely basic indeterminism in nature is, to begin with, highly questionable, not only philosophically but also scientifically. Moreover, whatever indeterminism there is in nature (prescinding from the indeterminism of human free will, which is irrelevant in this connection), the indeterminism affects directly events on the microscopic scale and not appreciably those on the macroscopic scale; and only the latter have ever been considered as miracles. Even if the kind of indeterminism envisioned by modern physics were on a rare occasion to produce a striking effect on the macroscopic scale, it could never account qualitatively for such miracles as a resurrection or the sudden, complete cure of an advanced organic disease, in view of the nature of such miracles and considering, moreover, the positive signs of the operation in miracles in general of an intelligent and free agent, as previously explained.

If most miracles, even though recognizably beyond the powers of corporeal nature, are seldom discernibly beyond the powers of created spirits, how can it be known that they do actually come from God, at least through a spirit acting in God's name, rather than from an evil spirit acting for its own purpose?

A sufficient criterion is provided by the moral circumstances—e.g., the dignity or incongruity of the event itself, the character and conduct of the human "miracle-worker," and, most important, the good or evil effects of the event. Though there can be exceptions to the principle, morally good circumstances point to a divine origin, evil circumstances to a diabolic origin. The principle operates mainly in a negative way: God would not allow an evil spirit to produce a supernatural manifestation in connection with a false claim of revelation unless there were present one or more serious moral defects that would furnish a sufficient indication of the source of the phenomenon.

Recognition by Unaided Reason. Although a few theologians have held the contrary, the recognition of miracles does not strictly require the assistance of an internal divine GRACE. Nor is an authoritative judgment by the Church always necessary. There are indeed cases in which the nature of the miracle or the evidence for it are such that a prudent certitude would hardly be possible without an ecclesiastical decision. But Christian apologists have always maintained that some miracles, especially the major miracles of Christ, can be known with certitude independently of the divine teaching authority of the Church (magisterium).

In his encyclical *Humani generis* Pius XII spoke of "the many wonderful external signs God has given, which are sufficient to prove with certitude by the natural light of reason alone the divine origin of the Christian religion" (*Enchiridion symbolorum* 3876).

Miracles outside the Catholic Church

It is sometimes argued that miracles have been claimed by most religions and that, accordingly, they cannot serve as evidence in favor of a particular religion or church.

The appeal to miracles as confirmation of the truth of Christian revelation and of the Catholic religion does not exclude the possibility of miracles outside the Catholic Church and outside Christianity. God could work miracles in connection with another church or another religion for any number of reasons, e.g., to witness to the divine presence in a particular event, to confirm the truth of a particular doctrine, or to strengthen faith of individuals. On the other hand, Catholics logically hold that since the Church if of divine origin, God would not work a miracle under such circumstances that it could reasonably be interpreted as divine confirmation of another religion as a whole or of a doctrine contrary to the teachings of Christ and his Church. A comprehensive survey and evaluation of the best known claims of miracles outside the Catholic Church may be found in L. H. Monden, *Le Miracle, signe de salut* (Bruges 1960).

See Also: APOLOGETICS; REVELATION, THEOLOGY OF; MIRACLES (IN THE BIBLE).

Bibliography: THOMAS AQUINAS, *Summa theologiae* la, 105.6–8, 110.4; *C. gent.* 3.101–103; *De pot.* 6.1–10. BENEDICT XIV, *De servorum Dei beatificatione et beatorum canonizatione* bk. 4, pt. 1, ch. 1–7. J. H. NEWMAN, *Two Essays on Miracles* (1897). J. DE TONQUÉDEC, *Dictionnaire apologétique de la foi catholique*, ed. A. D'ALÈS, 4 v. (Paris 1911–22) 3:517–578; Eng. *Miracles,* tr. F. M. OPPENHEIM (West Baden Springs, Indiana 1955), with extensive bibliography mainly of works in English. J. B. METZ, *Sacramental Mundi* 4: 43–46. J. A. HARDON, ''The Concept of Miracle from St. Augustine to Modern Apologetics,'' *Theological Studies* 15 (1954) 229–257. F. TAYMANS, ''Le Miracle, signe du surnaturel,'' *Nouvelle revue théologique* 77 (1955) 225–245, condensed in *Theology Digest* 5 (1957) 18–23. ''Reflexions sur le miracle,'' *Lumière et vie* 33 (July 1957) 289–376. É. DHANIS, ''Qu'est-ce qu'un miracle?'' *Gregorianum* 40 (1959) 201–241. J. C. CARTER, ''The Recognition of Miracles,'' *Theological Studies* 20 (1959) 175–197. K. MCNAMARA, ''The Nature and Recognition of Miracles,'' *The Irish Theological Quarterly* 27(1960) 294–322. R. W. GLEASON, ''Miracles and Contemporary Theology,'' *The Encounter with God,* ed. J. E. O'NEILL (New York 1962) 1–32. R. A. H. LARMER, *Water Into Wine? An Investigation of the Concept of Miracle* (Toronto 1987).

[T. G. PATER/EDS.]

MIRACULOUS MEDAL

The miraculous medal was revealed by the Blessed Virgin Mary in a vision granted St. Catherine Labouré, a Daughter of Charity of St. Vincent de Paul, at the Paris motherhouse, Nov. 27, 1830. The Virgin stood upon a globe, crushing a serpent beneath her foot (Gn 3.15). Rays of light, symbolizing graces, streamed from her outstretched hands. Written around her was the prayer: ''O Mary, conceived without sin, pray for us who have recourse to thee.'' The vision reversed revealing an ''M'' surmounted by a bar and cross. Beneath were the Hearts of Jesus and Mary, one crowned with thorns, the other pierced with a sword (Lk 2.35). Twelve stars encircled the whole (Rv 12.1). A voice spoke: ''Have a medal struck after this model. All who wear it will receive great graces. They should wear it around the neck.''

The first medals were struck, with permission of Archbishop de Quélen of Paris, June 30, 1832. So many remarkable favors followed that people called the medal ''miraculous.'' A canonical inquiry at Paris (1836) certified its supernatural origin and efficacy. Papal approval followed the instantaneous conversion of Alphonse Ratisbonne, who was hostile to Catholicism, to whom the Madonna of the Medal appeared in the Church of S. Andrea delle Fratte, Rome, Jan. 20, 1842.

Pius IX (June 20, 1847) approved the Association of Children of Mary, requested of St. Catherine by the Virgin, granting it all indulgences enjoyed by the *Prima Primaria* (1584). Leo XIII (July 23, 1894) honored the medal with a Mass and Office for Nov. 27, proper to the Congregation of the Mission (Vincentian Fathers) and Daughters of Charity. Pius X (June 3, 1905) established the Association of the Miraculous Medal, granting it the indulgences and privileges enjoyed by the Confraternity of the Blue Scapular.

The devotion, indulgenced by Pius XI, Pius XII, John XXIII, and Paul VI, has spread throughout the world.

Bibliography: J. M. ALADEL, *The Miraculous Medal,* tr. P. S. (Baltimore 1881). J. I. DIRVIN, *Saint Catherine Labouré, of the Miraculous Medal* (New York 1958).

[J. I. DIRVIN/EDS.]

MIRAEUS, AUBERT (LE MIRE)

Church historian; b. Brussels, Dec. 2, 1573; d. Antwerp, Oct. 19, 1640. Of a wealthy merchant family, Miraeus attended the college at Douai, and then the University of Louvain, where he was taught by Justus Lipsius. He became a canon of the cathedral (1601) and later secretary to his uncle, Jean Miraeus, the bishop of Antwerp. Vice Regent of the Netherlands Albert of Austria (reign 1596–1621) sent him on diplomatic missions to La Haye (1609) and Paris (1609–10), and appointed him court chaplain at Brussels (1615). He was also appointed dean of the cathedral at Antwerp (1624) and vicar general (1635).

During these years of diocesan administration and diplomatic service, Miraeus wrote prodigiously, if not always accurately, on Church history (39 works are listed). A great number of his books served as valuable guides to the history of monastic orders and religious congregations, including the Benedictines (1606, 1614), Carmelites (1608, 1610), Carthusians (1609), military orders (1609), Augustinians (1612, 1614, 1622), Premonstratensians (1613), and Cistercians (1614); and he prepared a brief history of the orders that came into being during the Counter Reformation, *De congregationibus clericorum in communi viventium, ut theatinorum, societatis Jesu, barnabitarum, somaschae, oratorii, doctrinae christianae . . .* (Cologne 1622). His greatest fame is derived from his writings on the history of Belgium: *Elenchus historicorum Belgii . . .* (Brussels 1622); *Rerum belgicarum chronicon . . .* (Antwerp 1636); *Stemmata principum Belgii* (Brussels 1626); *Diplomatum bellicorum libri duo* (Brussels 1627); *Donationum belgicarum libri duo . . .* (Antwerp 1629); and *Notitia ecclesiarum Belgii . . .* (Antwerp 1630). Miraeus wrote also on hagiographical questions, the state of religion in Europe, Emperor Ferdinand II, and the Bohemian wars; compiled lists of the episcopates throughout the world; and composed a general chronicle of Christian history.

Bibliography: É. AMANN, *Dictionnaire de théologie catholique,* 15 v. (Paris 1903–50) 10.2:1862–64, and works. É. BROUETTE, *Lexicon für Theologie und Kirche,* 10 v. (Freiburg 1930–38) 7:436–437, bibliog.

[E. D. MCSHANE]

MIRIAN (MERIBANES)

First Christian king of Iberia (East Georgia), founder of the Chosroid dynasty; b. *c.* 282; d. 361. As a member of the House of Mihran, one of the seven great houses of the Iranian monarchy, he was placed on the throne of Iberia by the Iranians, who were anxious to counterbalance Roman influence in Armenia. At about age seven (*c.* 289), he passed through a ceremony of marriage with Abeshura, the Arsacid heiress of Iberia. Converted to Christianity in middle age by the preaching of St. Nino (334), he sent to the Emperor Constantine for priests, and in 337 he was baptized together with his people. Though Iberia was an area traditionally under the jurisdiction of Antioch, John, the first bishop of Iberia, was sent from Constantinople because of the Emperor Constantine's war with Iran, begun in 337. Mirian is venerated as a saint by the Georgian Church.

Bibliography: M. TAMARATI, *L'Église géorgienne: Des origines jusqu'à nos jours* (Rome 1910). C. TOUMANOFF, *Studies in Christian Caucasian History* (Washington 1963).

[C. TOUMANOFF]

MIRROR OF PRINCES (LITERATURE)

Literary genre offering a model for the ideal prince to follow; especially popular in the late medieval and Renaissance periods, called also *Speculum principum.* Treatises of this kind were of three related types; some depicted famous princes biographically with an emphasis on the high quality of their persons and the skill of their statecraft; some described historical personalities in a highly idealized and poetic way in order to produce a maximum idealistic impact upon the noble reader; and others presented practical rules, principles, and norms for the conduct of a prince. In some of the literature there was a shading from a practical discussion of the management of political affairs to a treatment of the theoretical foundation of the office of the ruler.

The roots of the mirror of princes literature reached back into classical antiquity, where Plato's description of the philosopher-kings in the *Republic* and Aristotle's *Politics* and *Nichomachean Ethics* were the most influential sources. Xenophon and Isocrates contributed to the tradition. A compilation of moralisms from Plutarch titled *Institutio Traiani* was to be much imitated during the medieval period. Roman antiquity in turn contributed substantially to the development of this genre of writing. Seneca's *Moral Essays* and Marcus Aurelius's *Autobiography,* stressing the importance of the ruler's interior qualities, reinforced Cicero's earlier work. Three other influential writings were Pliny the Younger's *Panegyricus,* Claudian's *Panegyricus de quarto consulatu Honorii,* and Vegetius's *Epitome rei militaris.* These classical sources were cited in the fully developed mirror of princes literature of the 12th to the 18th centuries.

The early Middle Ages was influenced by AUGUSTINE's description of the good emperor in his *City of God.* The pseudo-Cyprian, composed in Ireland during the 7th century, was important during the Carolingian period. By this time the ideal prince was depicted as one who was loyal to the Christian faith and was of service to the Church and to the monastic way of life. The earliest elaborate medieval treatise on politics was JOHN OF SALISBURY's *Policraticus* (1159), which included, with its organic theory of the state, a discussion of the duties and rights of governors as well as of the true king as God's vicar. A contemporary of John of Salisbury, GIRALDUS CAMBRENSIS, composed *De instructione principum,* which he loaded with moral preachments but with little practical advice. Similarly, VINCENT OF BEAUVAIS's *De morali principis institutione* (1260–63) had a pious flavor and bristled with references to Scripture and the Fathers. In the 13th century, however, Arabic-Aristotelian ideas that contributed a new element of secular realism were added to the revived classical ideas of the 12th century. The pseudo-Aristotelian *Secretum secretorum,* purporting to represent the correspondence of Alexander and Aristotle, had considerable influence through its Latin translation by Philippus (prior to 1243). Aristotle's ideas were evident in St. THOMAS AQUINAS's *De regimine principum* as well as in the work by the same name of GILES OF ROME, the latter being indisputably the most important work of this type. Giles's treatise was less a discussion of the nature of the state than a true mirror for a prince, written to instruct the heir to the French crown before the death of King Philip III in 1285.

Renaissance humanists, imbued with classical ideals and often personally in the service of princes, developed this type of writing into a fine art. PETRARCH himself set the precedent with his *De republica optime administranda.* The poet Pontanus wrote on the subject and SAVONAROLA touched upon some of the same familiar themes in his *Tractate on the Organization and Government of the City of Florence.* Certainly the most renowned treatise in the mirror of princes category was N. MACHIAVELLI's *The Prince.* Although many of the themes in *The Prince* were of a familiar sort—e.g., liberality, keeping faith, love and fear, flattery, friendships, and the king's ministers—Machiavelli disagreed with the earlier treatises, which had demanded that the good ruler must himself be a good man and the best moral example for his subjects. Instead, Machiavelli urged that the standard of the good ruler be whether he succeeds (one way or another) in securing the well-being of the citizens of his state. In contrast to Machiavelli's work, both the treatise of Budé and ERASMUS's *Instruction of a Christian Prince* seem traditional in cast. Later works of the mirror of princes type include BOSSUET's *Politique tirée de l'Écriture Sainte,* CAMPANELLA's *Monarchia Hispanica,* the Jesuit MARIANA's *De rege et regis institutio,* FÉNELON's *Télémaque,* and Wieland's *Goldener Spiegel,* most of them tiresome and banal.

Bibliography: D. ERASMUS, *The Education of a Christian Prince,* ed. and tr. L. K. BORN (New York 1936), with introd. A. H. GILBERT, *Machiavelli's Prince and Its Forerunners* (Durham, N.C. 1938). F. GILBERT, ''The Humanist Concept of the Prince and *The Prince* of Machiavelli,'' *Journal of Modern History* 11 (1939) 449–483. W. BERGES, *Die Fürstenspiegel des hohen und späten Mittelalters* (Leipzig 1938; repr. 1952). C. MCILWAIN, *The Growth of Political Thought in the West* (New York 1932; repr. 1955).

[L. W. SPITZ]

MISERICORDIA SISTERS

The Misericordia Sisters (SM) is a congregation with papal approbation founded in Montreal, Canada, on Jan. 16, 1848, by Bp. Ignace Bourget and Rosalie Jetté (Mother of the Nativity) for the purpose of rehabilitating wayward young women. Some of these women consecrate themselves to God by taking vows as Oblate Sisters of Misericordia. The Misericordia Sisters work at hospitals, schools of nursing, retreat houses, and other social work venues. On June 7, 1867, Pius IX approved the institute; Pius XI granted final approbation of the constitutions on May 6, 1932. The superior general resides at the motherhouse in Montreal. The first U.S. foundation was established in 1887. The U.S. headquarters is in Aurora, IL.

[R. BONNEVILLE/EDS.]

MISHNAH

The core and oldest part of the TALMUD. The Hebrew word *mišnâ,* literally ''repetition,'' designates here instruction in the Oral Law. The Mishnah is a codification compiled by Rabbi JUDAH HA-NASI in the beginning of the 3d Christian century on the basis of earlier oral collections of the teachings of the rabbis since the 1st century B.C. It is divided into six ''orders'' (*s^e dārîm*) embracing 63 tractates (*mass^e kôt*). Its language, commonly called Mishnaic Hebrew, is a direct development of the spoken HEBREW LANGUAGE of the late OT period under the influence of Aramaic.

Bibliography: *The Mishnah,* ed. and tr. H. DANBY (Oxford 1933). G. BEER et al., eds., *Die Mischna: Übersetzung und ausführliche Erklärung . . .* (Berlin 1912–) 51 v. E. BENNETT, *Universal Jewish Encyclopedia* 7:581–582. J. Z. LAUTERBACH, *Jewish Encyclopedia* 8:609–619. K. SCHUBERT, *Lexikon für Theologie und Kirche,* ed. J. HOFER and K. RAHNER, 10 v. (2d new ed. Freiburg 1957–65) 7:444–445. For additional bibliography, *see* TALMUD.

[L. F. HARTMAN]

MISSAL, ROMAN

The earliest eucharistic liturgical books for presiders used in the Roman rite were the sacramentaries, which date from the seventh and eighth centuries (*see* SACRAMENTARIES, HISTORICAL). Other liturgical ministers in the early medieval period made use of other liturgical books containing material proper to their differing roles, e.g. the lectionary for readers, the graduale or antiphonale for cantors and scholae (choir). These sacramentaries originally contained only the presider's prayers (euchology) used at mass; even the outline structure of the service, the *ordo missae* was contained in a separate *libellus* or booklet at this time. These *ordines* tended to become more elaborate into the eleventh century, incorporating many devotional and penitential prayers for the presider to recite while other liturgical ministers were active during the mass (e.g. the singing of the Gloria, the preparation of the altar at the offertory).

The ''Full'' Missal. Beginning from the twelfth century into the thirteenth and fourteenth centuries, all of the material necessary to celebrate mass were gradually collected into a single volume for the use of the presider. The *ordo missae* was incorporated first, and came to be located in the middle of the book. Eventually, texts from other liturgical books proper to other ministers was also incorporated: readings from the lectionary, pieces of chant from the antiphonaries and graduals. The resultant volume came to be known as the *missalis plenarius*, the plenary or "full" missal.

The development of this liturgical book was prompted by a number of factors. The first was the spread of the "private mass," that is, the celebration of the mass by a single priest with only a few, or perhaps only one acolyte assisting, beginning in the late eleventh and twelfth centuries. At the same time the priest became obliged to recite all the parts of the mass like the readings and chants, even if they were done by their proper minister. The second was the rise of mendicant religious orders in the late twelfth and early thirteenth centuries. Priests of these new orders (e.g. the Dominicans and Franciscans) were not bound by vows of stability to a single monastery, but were instead committed to a mobile type of ministry, moving about the countryside and towns of an increasingly urbanized Europe, preaching and begging for alms. These friars needed single volume collections of the texts needed to celebrate the mass (the missal) and the Divine Office (the breviary).

Missals in the high middle ages were not yet unified into a single uniform volume, There were a number of diocesan and regional variations, even in the city of Rome. The Dominicans, for example, formed their own missal based on the liturgical books of Lyons in France (*see* DOMINICAN RITE). In England, there were several related "Uses," for example, the HEREFORD USE, YORK USE, and SARUM USE, which was the most widespread liturgical Use in medieval England. In the sixteenth century, Thomas CRANMER would use the Sarum Missal as the basis for the vernacular BOOK OF COMMON PRAYER, the official liturgical book of the fledging Church of England.

An important step in the development of a single, normative Roman Missal (*Missale Romanum*) comes with the Franciscans, led by their General HAYMO OF FAVERSHAM (d. 1244), who modeled their missal on the practice of the contemporary Roman Curia and disseminated it through Europe. After some revision under CLEMENT V (d. 1314), the Franciscan Missal was adopted by the Curia itself, and under the title "Missal According to the Use of the Roman Curia" became the first printed missal in 1474, This missal was promulgated virtually unchanged by Pope Pius V in 1570, as the first of a series of standard liturgical books mandated by the Council of Trent (1545–1563). The MR was promulgated for all Roman Catholic dioceses; however, those dioceses (and religious orders) whose own liturgies were at least 200 years old were given the option of retaining their own books. Most chose to adopt the Missal of Pius V. In the

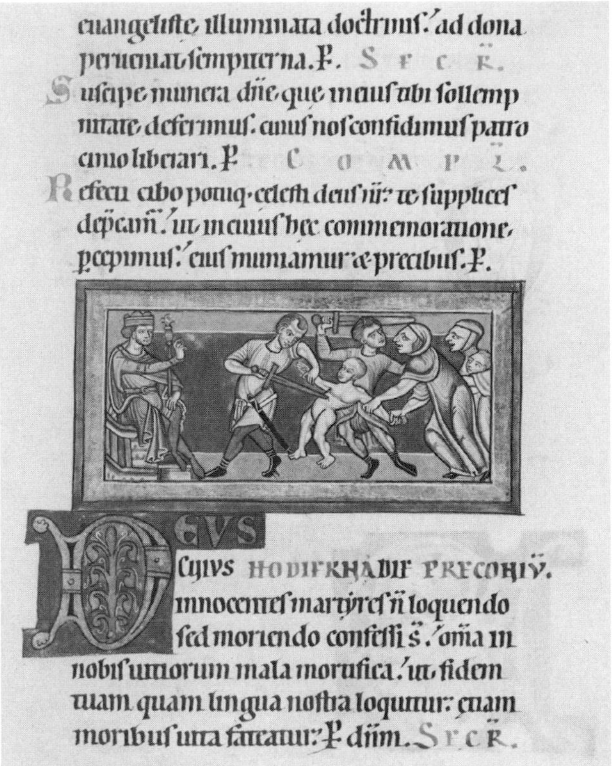

"The Slaughter of the Holy Innocents," Propers for the Feast of the Holy Innocents, illumination from the "Berthold Missal" of the Abbey of Weingarten in Swabia, 1200–1232.

seventeenth and eighteenth centuries, some French bishops (in the wake of Gallicanism and Jansenism) chose to replace the MR with missals composed locally, called neo-Gallican missals. The nineteenth century saw the victory of ultramontanists in France, and the reappropriation of the MR in that country. Other Latin, but non-Roman, rites continued to be used, e.g. the AMBROSIAN RITE in Milan, and the MOZARABIC RITE in Toledo. Some religious orders also retained their own proper missals, all earlier versions of the MR, until the Second Vatican Council, e.g. the Dominicans (*see* DOMINICAN RITE) and the Premonstratensians (*see* PREMONSTRATENSIAN RITE).

The Sacramentary (1970). The Missal of Pius V continued to be used, with some minor additions in 1604, 1634, and 1920, until the implementation of the liturgical reforms mandated by the Second Vatican Council. The last *editio typica*, or "authoritative Latin version" of the Missal of Pius V was published in 1962. The Roman Missal revised by the decree of Vatican II was published by the authority of Paul VI in 1970. A second *editio typica* with minor revisions was issued in 1975, and a third *edition typica* was slated to appear in 2001. A notable part of the *Missale Romanum* of Paul VI is the return to the use of a variety of liturgical books for the various liturgi-

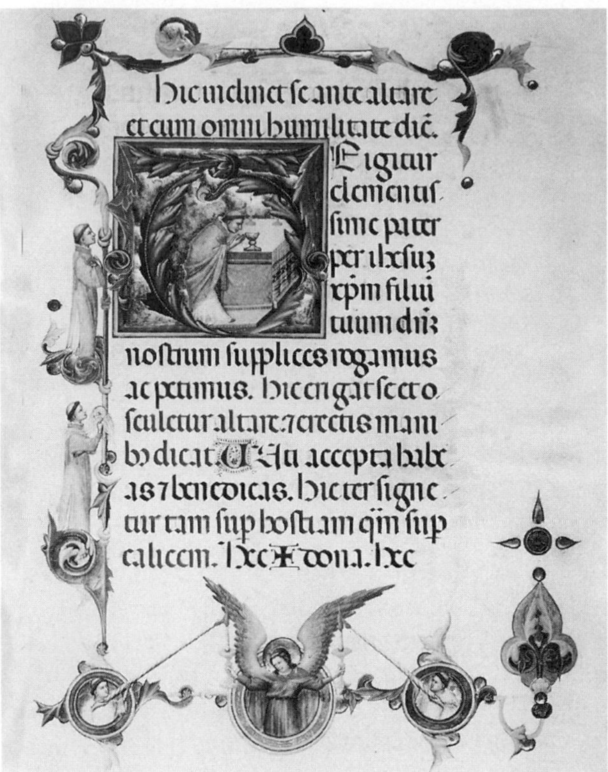

Missal, Consecration of the Host or the Canon of the Mass, Latin text, Siena, late 14th century.

cal ministers, e.g., the LECTIONARY and Antiphonal (or Gradual). Unlike a *missale plenaries* (full missal), the Missal of Paul VI does not give the readings and proper chant notations for each mass. this is carried over in many vernacular translations of the *edition typica*, which retrieve the classic terminology of *sacramentary* as the title for the liturgical book.

For two decades, the use of the Missal of Pius V was technically forbidden except in certain specific situations; defying this discipline at times became a rallying point for certain conservative groups unhappy with the reforms mandated by the Second Vatican Council.

Today, the Tridentine Rite of 1962 MR may still be celebrated in a selected location in any diocese at the discretion of the local Ordinary, according to an indult by Pope John Paul II in *Ecclesia Dei* (1988), calling for a more ''generous'' application of the directives issued by the Congregation for Divine Worship, *Quattuor abhinc annos* (1984).

Bibliography: E. PALAZZO, *A History of Liturgical Books: from the Beginning to the Thirteenth Century*. Translated by M. BEAUMONT (Collegeville, MN 1998); A Pueblo Book. C. VOGEL, *Medieval Liturgy: An Introduction to the Sources*. Translated and revised by W. G. STOREY and N. K. RASMUSSEN, O.P. (Washington, DC 1986); NPM Studies in Church Music and Liturgy. Now published by Oregon Catholic Press. G. AUSTIN, O.P. ''Sources, Liturgical,'' in P. FINK, S.J., ed. *The New Dictionary of Sacramental Worship* (Collegeville, MN 1990); A Michael Glazier Book. Pp. 1213–1220. J. A. JUNGMANN, S. J. *The Mass of the Roman Rite: Its Origins and Development*. 2 vols. (Westminster, MD 1986). Reprint of Benziger, 1951–55.

[J. M. PIERCE]

MISSAL FOR THE DIOCESES OF ZAIRE

Promulgated by the decree *Zairensium* on April 30, 1988 by the Congregation for Divine Worship and the Discipline of the Sacraments, the *Missel romain pour les diocèses du Zaïre* (Roman Missal for the Dioceses of Zaire) is an attempt to inculturate the Roman *Ordo missae* in an African context, inspired by the liturgical reform initiated at the Second Vatican Council (*see* INCULTURATION, LITURGICAL).

Genesis and Drafting. Amid the cultural ferment in the aftermath of Zaire's independence in the 1960s (*see* CONGO, DEMOCRATIC REPUBLIC OF), just before Vatican II, the bishops of Zaire stated that Christianity's appeal was inhibited because of lack of adaptation to the living traditions of the African peoples. In a 1961 directive, the Episcopal Conference of Zaire (now the Democratic Republic of Congo) called for an ''adaptation of the cult.'' A thorough and critical examination of the religious customs and cultural matrix of the African peoples was identified as the starting point for an elaboration of an authentic African liturgy. The renewal decreed by the Second Vatican Council, together with the historical appeal of Pope Paul VI in Kampala in 1969 to the African nations to formulate Catholicism in terms of African culture [*Acta Apostolicae Sedis* 1 (1969) 577-578] confirmed the endeavor of the Zairean bishops.

In 1969, the Commission on Evangelization of the Episcopal Conference initiated study of the culture and religious beliefs of the Zairean peoples. After the Congregation for Divine Worship granted authorization on June 22, 1970, the Commission on Evangelization elaborated the first draft of the new Order of Mass that was presented officially to the bishops in 1973. Permission to use the new liturgy *ad experimentum* was granted on June 15, 1973. After extensive evaluation and criticism, the entire Zairean episcopate reaffirmed the ''Zairean Rite,'' as it was then called, in 1985. Once the bishops had given approval, the Roman authorities granted that the new Order be used *ad interim.* Definitive approbation of the Zairean Eucharistic liturgy came in 1988 under the title, *Missel romain pour les Diocèses du Zaïre* (Roman Missal for Use in the Dioceses of Zaire). The name changed from

''Zairean Rite'' because ''rite'' is a broader designation and does not consist of the Eucharistic liturgy solely. Second, the Roman authorities wanted to locate this African Eucharistic liturgy within the ''forms already existing'' in the Catholic Church, namely the typical edition of the Roman Missal (cf. *Sacrosanctum Concilium* 23).

Structure and Originality of the Missal. Taken in both its solemn and simple versions, the Missal for Zaire followed the structure of the Roman *Ordo missae*. However, it was adapted and enriched by a number of variations inspired by the region's cultural milieu. Three major structural adaptations are evident. First, the liturgy begins with an invocation of the ancestors. Second, the penitential rite follows the proclamation of the Word, the homily, and creed. Third, the gesture of peace follows this penitential rite, not the Lord's Prayer as in the typical edition of the Roman Missal.

These changes found their raison d'être in the particular worldview of the Zairean peoples, and the pattern of their traditional community gatherings provided the ritual frame for the Zairean Mass. First, the remembrance of ancestors opens the Eucharistic celebration. The remembrance of ancestors is an essential practice in traditional African society since most Africans believe that the dead are still members of the community and that the world of the dead is in communion with that of the living. Not all the dead are presented with the title of ancestor, but only those who have lived an honest and exemplary life. No important event or gathering can occur in traditional African society without an invocation of ancestors and their remembrance.

Taking account of this practice, the Zairean liturgy integrated the invocation of the saints and the ancestors into the Eucharistic celebration. By doing so, the liturgical rite Christianized the traditional remembrance and veneration of ancestors. Whereas, in the traditional society, the ancestors belonged to only their clan or family, their incorporation in the Christian liturgy was the very expression of their incorporation in Christ. Thus, the ancestors of one clan could be invoked as ancestors of the entire Christian community.

Just as in the traditional gathering, forgiveness is sought after the exposition of the circumstances of disharmony, so the penitential rite followed the proclamation of the scriptures and the Homily. Having listened to the Word of God that stirs up the memory of God's salvific call and grounds all conversion, the community sought God's pardon for its shortcomings and sinfulness and reconciliation with each other.

Distinctive Cultural Aspects of the Liturgy. Fidelity to African culture resulted in the incorporation of the

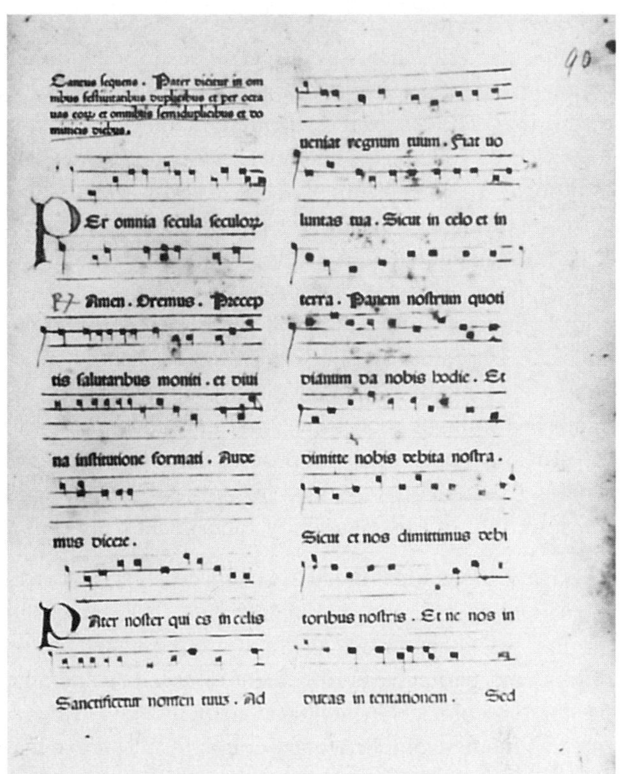

Manuscript page of music ''The Introduction and Lord's Prayer,'' from ''Missale Romanum,'' 1474.

Zairean peoples' orality, gesture, art, and music into the Roman liturgy. The characteristics of African orality are dialogue, narrative, repetition, dramatization, the use of short sentences, strong images and metaphors, enigmatic expressions calling for a deep sense of imagination, expressive sonorities, and allusions. The model taken was the *palabre africaine* or judicial oratorical art. For instance, in the Homily, the preacher elicited the response of the assembly, engaging them as a dialogue partner. The preaching was often interrupted by songs and dances. Also, traditional African assemblies included designated individuals who introduce, comment, summarize, and dramatize what is under discussion, the goal to invite the community to a genuine sense of what is taking place. Thus, liturgy included an announcer or narrator, generally a lay minister, who heralded and commented upon the main parts of the celebration and introduced to the assembly whoever was going to speak. Every reader asked the permission and blessing of the priest celebrant. The culmination of the liturgy of the Word was the enthronement of the Book of the Gospels.

Gesture and movement was another characteristic of the Zairean liturgy. Bodily expression also took the form of dance. The *Gloria*, which immediately followed the invocation of the ancestors, was accompanied by ritual dances by the ministers and some of the faithful around the altar while incense was burned. These two symbolic actions were intended as an expression of the veneration of the altar. The rest of the assembly members danced at their places. The priest celebrant venerated the altar with traditional African gesture: with his arms raised in a ''V'' form, he touched each side of the altar with his forehead. During the penitential rite, all the assembly members bowed their heads and formed an ''X'' on their chests with their arms. At the sign of peace, people generally shook their two hands as a sign of total openness or acceptance, sometimes preceded by the washing of the hands in a common receptacle. Rhythmic dances and gestures also accompanied the procession of the gifts, including food and gifts destined for the poor, the sick, and the suffering, or for community fund-raising.

The Zairean Mass made use of special liturgical vestments and specific musical instruments. The Zairean liturgical vestments were distinguished by their form, design, and particular arrangement of colors. Generally, the bottom color held dominant meaning and was decorated with other complementary colors. Among the musical instruments commonly used were the tam-tam, the gong, and the hand bell. The bell, the instrument of the announcer, was used to announce any intervention in the assembly. The gong was usually reserved for use during the institution narrative of the Eucharistic prayer. Frequent use was made of the drum, an instrument of great importance for Africans. The Missal for the Dioceses of Zaire was a concrete example of the ongoing task of the inculturation of Roman Catholic liturgy and African cultural genius.

Bibliography: L. BERTSCH, ed., *Der neue Meßritus im Zaire. Ein Beispiel kontextueller Liturgie* (*Theologie der dritten Welt* 18, Freiburg 1993). CONFERENCE EPISCOPALE DU ZAIRE, Missel romain pour le diocèses du Zaïre (Kinshasa 1989); Présentation de la liturgie de la messe. Supplément au Missel romain pour les diocèses du Zaïre (Kinshasa 1989). J. EVENOU, ''Le Missel romain pour les diocèses du Zaïre,'' *Notitiae* 24 (1988) 454-472; ''Le rite zaïrois de la messe,'' *L'addattamento culturale della liturgia: metodi e modelli,* in *Analecta Liturgica* 19, ed. I. SCICOLONE (Rome 1993). C. N. EGBULUM, ''The 'Rite Zaïrois' in the Context of Liturgical Inculturation in Middle-Belt Africa since the Second Vatican Council,'' (S.T.D. thesis, Catholic University of America, 1990); ''An African Interpretation of Liturgical Inculturation: the Rite Zaïrois,'' in *Promise of Presence,* ed. M. DOWNEY and R. FRAGOMENI (Washington, DC 1992). F. KABASELE, ''Du canon romain au rite zaïrois,'' *Bulletin de théologie africaine* 4 (1982) 213–228. T. KANE, *The Dancing Church: Video Impressions of the Church in Africa* (New York 1992). L. MPONGO, ''Le Rite zaïrois de la messe,'' *Spiritus* 73 (1978) 436-441. R. MALONEY, ''The Zairean Mass and Inculturation,'' *Worship* 62 (1982) 433-442.

[G. IWELE]

MISSIOLOGY

Missiology is a multidisciplinary branch of theology which studies the mission of the Church in all its aspects. Although Fathers of the Church, such as AUGUSTINE OF HIPPO and GREGORY THE GREAT, wrote about mission and the obligations and methods of missionary evangelization, and although later ecclesiastical writers, such as the Dominican RAYMOND OF PENYAFORT and the Franciscan tertiary RAYMOND LULL, produced specialized treatises on mission, the present-day discipline of missiology emerged in the early 19th century with the Protestant Gustav Warneck (1834–1910), who is considered the father of modern missiology, with Alexander Duff, who held the first chair of missiology at Edinburgh University in 1867 and with the Catholic missiologists Robert STREIT and Joseph SCHMIDLIN at the University of Münster in the first half of the 20th century. Even as late as 1962, the year of the opening of the Second Vatican Council, there was still a discussion in Catholic circles as to whether the discipline should not be called ''missionology,'' rather than missiology.

The Institute of Missiology at Münster began its publications before World War I and made a new start after World War II with the appointment of Thomas Ohm OSB. Meanwhile, at the Catholic University of Louvain, from 1922–1954 Pierre CHARLES SJ began a series of courses in missiology and launched the celebrated Louvain Missiological Weeks. Between the World Wars chairs and faculties of missiology were founded at the Gregorian and Urbanian Universities in Rome.

Two names are important for the impact they made on the English-speaking world in the second half of the 20th century. Lesslie Newbigin (1909–1995) was a Presbyterian who became Secretary of the World Council of Churches' International Missionary Council, a Bishop in the Church of South India and a minister of the United Reformed Church in England. The main thrust of his writing was the mission to the secularized western world. David J. Bosch was a South African, of the Dutch Reformed Church and missiologist in the University of South Africa, Pretoria. He died in a tragic accident in 1992, a year after the publication of his magisterial compendium *Transforming Mission—Paradigm Shifts in Theology of Mission.*

Paradigms of Mission. A missionary reading of the New Testament enables us to discern several mission theologies. The Gospel of Matthew reaches its climax with the ''great commission'' to make disciples of all nations (Mt. 28:18–20). Proclamation and disciple-making have been a traditional emphasis in missionary evangelization. The Johannine stress on the ''great commandment'' of universal love is, however, more fundamental, and coincides with a modern emphasis on dialogue and the *missio Dei*, God's initiative of love. In Luke-Acts evangelization is centered on forgiveness and solidarity—the preaching of the Good News to the poor, another contemporary concern, while the Pauline writings envisage the eschatological community as the goal of mission.

Following the ideas of Thomas Kuhn and Hans Küng, David Bosch described six paradigms in the history of missiology. After the eschatological interest of primitive Christianity came the Hellenistic-Patristic emphasis on metaphysics and liturgy. The medieval paradigm was Church-centered and monastic, and even countenanced missionary wars and forms of missionary colonialism. After the Reformation, Protestants were slow to embark on missionary activity, but eventually the Anabaptists and Pietists took up the challenge of the "Great Commission." The missionary paradigm of the Age of Enlightenment emphasized the promotion of Christian "knowledge." The emerging contemporary paradigm, according to Bosch, is one in which Catholics and Protestants share a number of basic ideas: the Church as sacrament and sign of the Kingdom, the *Missio Dei*, the preferential option for the poor, inculturation, liberation, and common witness.

For Bosch, these paradigms are not necessarily consecutive and several are said to be contemporaneous. Historians are cautious when confronted by such imposed structures. In any case, it is probably easier to observe a paradigm shift—the crisis or breakdown of a reigning paradigm—than to identify in detail the emergence of a new one.

Missiology in the 20th Century. The International Missionary Conference at Edinburgh in 1910 and the other conferences that led up to it, took place in the wake of missionary expansion in Asia and the Americas. Christianity was also on the threshold of a major expansion in Africa. The Edinburgh Conference, therefore, viewed mission as a process of geographical extension. While it advocated a sympathy towards non-Christian faiths, it was in no doubt about the uniqueness and finality of the Christian message. The lasting importance of the Edinburgh Conference was that it laid the foundations for the Ecumenical Movement and for the idea of mission as common witness.

Another approach in the first decade after Edinburgh was an emphasis on community and communal relationships in mission. It was associated with the names of the Protestant missionaries Bruno Gutmann and Christian Keysser, but has survived in the ideas of a Catholic Missionary, Vincent Donovan. Max Warren, who became general secretary of the Anglican Church Missionary Society in 1942, popularized the "Christian Presence" theology of religions in which missionaries were encouraged to engage sympathetically with other faiths in the belief that Christ was already actively present in them.

The 1960s were a time of upheaval and discontinuity. The experience of decolonization, the growth of ecumenism and, above all, the renewal set in motion by the Second Vatican Council, brought new emphases in missiology: liberation and a tension between proclamation and dialogue. A return to proclamation coincided with the rising tide of conservative evangelicalism in the last decades of the twentieth century, and this was also the major thrust of the papal encyclical *Redemptoris missio* of 1990. Such an emphasis, especially on the part of Protestant fundamentalism, went hand in hand with a renewed commitment to church planting and church growth. Some of the proponents of dialogue however, such as the Protestant J. C. Hoekendijk and Catholics like Paul Knitter and, more recently, the Jesuit Jacques Dupuis, in their efforts to retreat from a church-centered missiology, adopted a pluralistic theology of religions.

A notable feature of Catholic missiology in the last quarter of the 20th century has been the development of a biblical theology of mission. This and other aspects of modern missiology have been promoted by influential missionary publishing houses.

Missiology and the Second Vatican Council. At Vatican II no satisfactory draft of a decree on missionary activity was at first forthcoming. The attempt to reduce it to 13 propositions prompted Bishop Donal Lamont's celebrated "Dry Bones" speech. As a result, a new committee produced *Ad gentes divinitus* in time for the final session. It is a practical document arising from the desire of missionary bishops for a statement about the evangelization of the non-western world ("young churches" and those in a state of "decline or weakness") and the obligation of dioceses in Europe and North America to support it with finance and personnel. As such, it is a conservative document that conceives specialized missionary activity in terms of proclamation and church implantation, although—in line with a christocentric and kerygmatic concept of mission—it proclaims the whole Church to be missionary.

Ad gentes divinitus accepts the fact of religious and cultural pluralism and expresses belief in God's active presence in non-Christian traditions. It also accepts the ecclesiological revolution of *Lumen gentium* and *Gaudium et spes*, with their emphasis on the particular church as the basis for ecclesial diversity in unity and devotes an entire chapter to the concept. The high point of the chapter, and indeed of the whole decree, is reached in the final paragraph (22) with the idea of a local incarnation of Christianity representing a profound adaptation in every sphere of Christian life. Although it does not use the term, it already foreshadows the development of the theological concept of "inculturation." It is this passage that has best stood the test of time. Although it is a positive document, *Ad gentes divinitus* contains internal contradictions that are more clearly seen in the changed circumstances of today. Incarnation, rather than the Paschal Mystery, is emphasized as the source and model of missionary activity. There is an unsatisfactory distiction between missionary and pastoral work. No reference is made to integral development. The encouragement given to *Fidei donum* priests contradicts the emphasis on the need for specialized missionary training.

The foundation of the SECRETARIAT FOR NON-CHRISTIANS, renamed the PONTIFICAL COUNCIL FOR INTERRELIGIOUS DIALOGUE in 1988, took place before the end of Vatican II, and the conciliar declaration on the Church's relation to Non-Christian religions, *Nostra aetate*, became its major guiding document. This declaration praised the spiritual and moral truths found among Non-Christians, and the secretariat set out to document, inform, and analyze the problems of interreligious dialogue, as well as to make contact with religious leaders. In 1984 the secretariat produced an important document clarifying the relationship of dialogue to mission, and this theme was taken up again in *Dialogue and Proclamation* in 1991.

Missiology after Vatican II. In the wake of Vatican II, the role of dialogue took on greater importance. *Lumen gentium* (n. 16) opened the way for discussion by declaring that salvation was possible for those ignorant of Christ and even for those lacking an explicit knowledge of God; while *Gaudium et spes* (n. 22) affirmed that such people have the possibility of being made partners in the Paschal Mystery, in a way known to God. Theologians have developed the concept of the fundamental option as an implicit act of faith and love. Some have looked for positive values in non-Christian religions that may play a role in the salvation of their adherents, while others have considered the role of such religious traditions in God's salvific design for humanity.

Karl RAHNER made a major contribution to the discussion with his much criticized theory of "Anonymous Christianity." According to this theory, people who have no explicit consciousness of being Christians may nevertheless be recipients of a Christic revelation and salvation. Conservative evangelicals, with an exclusivist soteriology, have vehemently attacked the theory. Others have pointed out that anonymity and faith, ignorance and grace, are unconvincing allies. In the light of Rahner's response to such criticism, it would seem that Anonymous Christianity must comprise a disclosure of meaning within an unfolding historical praxis.

Another follow-up to Vatican II was the notion of integral development, the understanding of economic and social development as a form of Gospel praxis implicit in evangelization. The theology of development was helped both by PAUL VI's encyclical *Populorum progressio* (1967), and by liberation theology, with its accompanying experience of basic ecclesial communities, that led to the statements of the Latin American Bishops at Medellin (1968) and Puebla (1979). The 1971 Synod of Bishops on Justice and Peace made an explicit link between the promotion of social justice and missionary work.

Yet another missiological legacy of Vatican II was INCULTURATION, the creative re-expression of the Gospel in forms proper to a culture, which results in the reinterpretation of both, without being unfaithful to either. Vatican II, following the lead given by JOHN XXIII in *Princeps pastorum* (1959) accepted the fact of cultural pluralism and began to draw the conclusions for missionary evangelization. The discussion was carried forward by the Bishops' Synod on Evangelization (1974) and by Paul VI's post-synodal exhortation *EVANGELII NUNTIANDI* (1975). This remarkable document proclaimed the necessity of evangelizing cultures and envisaged a communion of particular churches enriching one another in the fields of theology, catechesis, ecclesial structures, and ministries. The term "inculturation" surfaced at the Bishops' Synod on Catechesis (1977) and was popularized by Pedro ARRUPE SJ in his letter on the subject to the Society of Jesus (1978). Its first appearance in a papal document was in JOHN PAUL II's *Catechesi tradendae* (1979).

With the speeches, writings, and pastoral journeys of John Paul II, as well as the foundation of the PONTIFICAL COUNCIL FOR CULTURE in 1982, inculturation has become a theological commonplace, although Roman documents have tended to counsel caution and gradualism, and even to warn against doctrinal relativism and schism. By and large, Catholic theologians have preferred a discourse centered on "culture" and "inculturation," while theological circles connected with the WORLD COUNCIL OF CHURCHES have been happier with "context" and "contextualization." "Context" is a vague term that nevertheless conveys a sense of comprehensiveness. "Culture" is more precise and serves the anthropological imperatives of evangelization.

John Paul II's Mission Encyclical. An important stage in missiological thinking was marked by John Paul II's encyclical *REDEMPTORIS MISSIO* (1990). A quarter of a century after Vatican II there were obvious anomalies in the mission paradigm represented by *Ad gentes divinitus*. The mission-sending churches of Europe were themselves in a state of "weakness or decline" and the balance of Christian world population had shifted to countries of the south. The geography of missionary recruitment had also changed in favor of the south, and there was a growing presence of lay missionaries. There was also a notable missionary resurgence of other world religions. The encyclical attempted to instill a sense of urgency for primary evangelization. Although it situates the Church's mission firmly in the *missio Dei*, the love and mercy of God, it cannot be denied that a strong emphasis on proclamation renders difficult the integration of dialogue in the missionary task.

The attempted reconciliation of opposites in the encyclical is a pointer to the paradigm shift that is taking place. The uneasy distinction between mission work and pastoral work is a case in point. Many, if not most, missionaries are engaged in cross-cultural pastoral work, and the missionary parish remains the foremost context for pioneering tasks, including both primary evangelization and interreligious dialogue. Another conflict is contained in the question: what makes people specialized missionaries? Is it their vocation to cross-cultural evangelization or is it simply the ''mission'' situation in which they find themselves? Although the encyclical tilts towards the latter, it does not adhere to the old geographical definition of ''mission lands.'' There are new parameters of mission, new social phenomena, such as urbanization, communications media, international relations, the scientific community and youth culture. There are also new ''paths of mission,'' including basic ecclesial communities, inculturation, dialogue, and development.

Finally, there is the discussion about the priority and methods of evangelizing those who are no longer Christian, as opposed to those who are not yet Christian. It would seem that the evangelization of post-Christians is the more difficult task. Moreover, John Paul II's concept of ''New Evangelization'' presupposes a flaw in the first evangelization. This idea has been received very positively in Latin America, and to some extent in Africa, where first evangelization was associated to a greater or lesser degree with colonial conquest. *Redemptoris missio* thus poses many new questions of missionary interpretation and strategy.

Missiology in the 21st Century. Mission is basically a question of faith and the practical shape taken by faith. It is fundamentally a spirituality or a religious conviction. As such, it is a ''being'' before becoming a ''doing,'' but it is not a ''being'' without ''doing.'' It is an active faith in the initiative taken by God, the *missio Dei*. Mission is born in the heart of God—God's loving dialogue with the world, through creation and redemption. God's project, God's ''kingdom'' or ''reign,'' is the promotion of oneness between creatures and the Triune Godhead, and evangelization (''mission'' in the generalized sense) is the implementation of this project. The Church is the seed, the sign, and the chosen instrument of God's project, visibly inaugurated by Jesus Christ. However, the Church itself is not the project. The Church in every age, like mission, is an ''unfinished house.''

Since mission flows from the heart of God, it is clear that dialogue is basic to evangelization. God's Spirit of Love precedes the evangelist and there is no limit to the Spirit's freedom and activity in the world. The Church's own vocation is consonant with the activity of the Spirit. Salvation is offered to all in their otherness—in their human and cultural difference. This is expressed by Jesus in the Great Commandment of universal love. The dialogue of love is basic to mission, because, as John Henry Newman never tired of stressing, love is the parent of faith.

God ''wants all people to be saved and to come to the knowledge of the truth'' (1 Tm. 2:4). The love of God therefore urges us to proclaim and to share our faith. This is the Great Commission to teach all nations and to make them disciples of Christ through Baptism. Proclamation of the Good News concerning Jesus Christ is an essential feature of evangelization. It is the naming of Jesus who is the mediator of salvation. It makes the truth known until it is fully known at the end of time. Proclamation is mainly verbal but it communicates Christian knowledge in non-verbal ways also, such as music, art, and dance.

Associated with proclamation is praxis or witness. This includes the mission to the poorest, development, liberation, social justice, and safeguarding the integrity of the environment. Prayer is the guarantee of proclamation, because mission is God's work in the communion of saints.

Types of evangelization are distinguished according to both personal/vocational and situational criteria. Since prayer is a basic component of evangelization, a religious in a contemplative community is also an evangelizer in a real sense. St. THÉRÈSE OF LISIEUX, a contemplative, is Patron of Missions. Evangelization takes place in ordinary pastoral situations, that is to say, within relatively homogeneous contexts, from a cultural or social point of view. The pastoral evangelist is at home in the local culture, although the work may include the Christian initiation of adults and approaches to lapsed or former Catholics, as well as dialogue with other churches and other religious faiths.

Missionary evangelization involves crossing a human (cultural) frontier or entering new post-modern parameters of human life. Geographical distance is not the issue. It is enough to enter a situation that is ''other'' and to accept its evangelization priorities. Typically, though not necessarily, these include primary evangelization, which is the charism of many missionary societies. However, as *Redemptoris Missio* shows, while primary evangelization is an urgent task, the context of such pioneering work today is not necessarily a geographically based ''pagan tribe'' but includes other parameters of human life, as yet untouched by the Gospel. The emphasis today is more and more on entering the world of the poor and marginalized.

Essentially, however, mission is part of God's loving dialogue with humanity. Very rarely is this a ''conference dialogue'' of theological discussion with representatives of other faiths. More often, it is the dialogue of joint action for social justice or a dialogue of faith in which there is a mutual experiencing of worship and spiritual life. In Islamic countries and communities there are still missionaries who carry out the dialogue of life through their simple presence and silent witness.

Bibliography: S. BARROW and G. SMITH, eds., *Christian Mission in Western Society* (London 2001). L. BOFF, *New Evangelization* (New York 1990). D. J. BOSCH, *Transforming Mission* (New York 1991). V. J. DONOVAN, *Christianity Rediscovered* (London 1978). D. DORR, *Mission in Today's World* (New York 2000). J. DUPUIS, *Jesus Christ at the Encounter of World Religions* (New York 1993). K. MÜLLER, et al., eds., *Dictionary of Mission* (New York 1997). H. RZEPKOWSKI, *Dicionario de Misionologia* (Navarre 1992). J. A. SCHERER, and S. B. BEVANS, eds., *New Directions in Mission and Evangelization—Faith and Culture* (New York 1999). A. SHORTER, *Toward a Theology of Inculturation* (New York 1999); *Evangelization and Culture* (London 1994). Urbaniana, Pontiificia Università, *Dizionario di Missiologia* (Bologna 1993). T. YATES, *Christian Mission in the Twentieth Century* (Cambridge, U.K. 1994).

[A. SHORTER]

MISSION, ARTICLES ON

In this encyclopedia, the two principal entries in this area are MISSION AND MISSIONS, which discusses the definition and nature of mission; and MISSIOLOGY, which surveys the multidisciplinary field of theology which studies the mission of the Church in all its aspects. The entries MISSION THEOLOGY and INCULTURATION, THEOLOGY OF treat the systematic, contextual and pastoral theologies of mission and evangelization. For treatment of the Church's task of mission and evangelization in the Code of Canon Law, see MISSION AND EVANGELIZATION IN CANON LAW; for papal teachings on this topic, see MISSION AND EVANGELIZATION, PAPAL WRITINGS ON.

The following three mission encyclicals have individual treatment: *EVANGELII NUNTIANDI*; *REDEMPTORIS MISSIO*; and *SLAVORUM APOSTOLI*.

MISSION HISTORY, a comprehensive three-part entry, discusses the general historical developments of Catholic, Orthodox, and Protestant missionary endeavors. The four-part MISSION IN COLONIAL AMERICA, covering Spanish, Portuguese, French, and English missions, treats the historical developments of the early missionary endeavors in the Americas. MISSION IN POSTCOLONIAL LATIN AMERICA surveys the developments in missionary endeavors in Latin America in the era of independence from Spanish and Portuguese colonial rule. The following special treatments of individual aspects of mission history are provided: for Spanish and Portuguese colonial missions, see PATRONATO REAL; ALEXANDRINE BULLS; ENCOMIENDA-DOCTRINA SYSTEM IN SPANISH AMERICA; REDUCTIONS OF PARAGUAY and LAS CASAS, BARTHOLOME DE. For aspects of Asian mission history, see CHINESE RITES CONTROVERSY; INDIAN RITES CONTROVERSY; DIAMPER, SYNOD OF; NOBILI; ROBERTO DE; RHODES, ALEXANDRE DE; RICCI, MATTEO and VALIGNANO, ALESSANDRO.

Biographical information on individual missionaries, founders of missionary societies, and missiologists are treated under their respective names. For the history of *Propaganda Fide,* the Vatican's curial agency responsible for mission and evangelization, from its inception to 1967, see PROPAGATION OF THE FAITH, CONGREGATION FOR THE. Post-1967 developments are found in the entry EVANGELIZATION OF PEOPLES, CONGREGATION FOR THE. A related agency which assists the Congregation for the Evangelization of Peoples is PROPAGATION OF THE FAITH, SOCIETY FOR THE. The following U.S. mission societies and agencies receive individual treatment in this encyclopedia: MARYKNOLL FATHERS AND BROTHERS; MARYKNOLL SISTERS; MARYKNOLL MISSION ASSOCIATION OF THE FAITHFUL; MISSIONARY SOCIETY OF ST. JAMES THE APOSTLE; PAPAL VOLUNTEERS FOR LATIN AMERICA (PAVLA); UNITED STATES CATHOLIC MISSION ASSOCIATION; and AMERICAN SOCIETY OF MISSIOLOGY. International mission societies and agencies are treated under their respective names, e.g., PARIS FOREIGN MISSION SOCIETY; PONTIFICAL INSTITUTE FOR FOREIGN MISSIONS; CATHOLIC NEAR EAST WELFARE ASSOCIATION; and PONTIFICAL MISSION FOR PALESTINE.

[J. Y. TAN]

MISSION AND EVANGELIZATION, PAPAL WRITINGS ON

Early papal writings on mission and evangelization dealt with specific issues or opportunities, and were usually addressed to missionaries, mission superiors or rulers. The earliest such example is the famous letter of POPE GREGORY THE GREAT to St. Mellitus (d. 624), who was on his way to join St. Augustine in England. (*Hist. Eccl.* I, 30). This letter is remarkable for espousing a policy of graduality in the evangelization of the English people. Gregory the Great thought that while the idols were to be destroyed, their temples could be transformed for Christian worship, and their feasts could be replaced with feasts of Christian martyrs. In the Alexandrine Bulls, Pope ALEXANDER VI authorized the Portuguese and Spanish crowns to colonize the New World on the condition that they accepted the responsibility for converting its inhabitants to the Catholic Faith, thereby giving birth to the PATRONATO REAL. When the shortcomings of the Patronato could no longer be ignored, Pope GREGORY XV issued a papal bull, *Inscrutabili Divinae*, authorizing the formation of the Congregation for the PROPAGATION OF THE FAITH (now known as the Congregation for the EVANGELIZATION OF PEOPLES). Important 18th-century papal documents with far-reaching missiological consequences include *Ex illa die* (CLEMENT XI) and *Ex quo singulari* (BENEDICT XIV) which prohibited the practice of Confucian ancestral veneration rituals by Chinese Catholic converts (*see* CHINESE RITES CONTROVERSY). Other papal documents called for the abolition of slavery in mission lands and the release of slaves by their owners.

In the late 19th century, Pope LEO XIII wrote six major letters on mission and evangelization. His first letter, *Sancta Dei civitas* (Dec. 3, 1880), sought to modernize mission thinking by recalling the universality of mission. Two other apostolic letters, *Humanae salutis* (Sept. 1, 1886) and *Ad extremas orientis plagas* (June 23, 1893), dealt with the problem of missionary jurisdiction and indigenous clergy in India in the context of the centuries-old conflict between the Portuguese *Padroado* and *Propaganda Fide*. Two subsequent letters, *In plurimis* (May 8, 1888) and *Catholicae ecclesiae* (Nov. 20, 1890) dealt with the mission-related problem of slavery. *In plurimis* urged the Brazilian bishops to promote full abolition of slavery, while *Catholicae ecclesiae* was a letter supporting the campaign of Cardinal Charles LAVIGERIE and his Society of MISSIONARIES OF AFRICA (the White Fathers) to eliminate slavery in Africa. Finally, the sixth letter, *Orientalium dignitas ecclesiarum* (Nov 30, 1894), dealt with the mission to the Eastern Church.

The twentieth century witnessed the emergence of a systematic body of papal teachings on mission and evangelization, beginning with *Maximum illud*, the Apostolic Letter of Pope BENEDICT XV that was issued on Nov. 30, 1919. In this letter, Pope Benedict XV condemned missionary ethnocentrism and promoted the training of indigenous clergy in mission lands. He asserted that the chief aim of evangelization in mission lands was to make the missionary superfluous by training indigenous clergy for the eventual task of administering the local church. As far as he was concerned, the indigenous priest was not to ''be trained for the sole purpose of assisting foreign missionaries in a subordinate ministry, but he must be fitted for his divine task and rendered able one day to undertake with credit the administration of his own people.''

Known as the ''Pope of the Missions,'' Pope PIUS XI reminded everyone in his encyclical *Rerum ecclesiae* (Feb. 28, 1926) that the whole Church was responsible for the task of mission, a point that subsequent popes would emphasize. He called for renewed efforts at building a strong body of indigenous clergy. He also foresaw the eventual possibility of decolonization and pointed out that disaster would befall the Church ''unless full provision has been made for the needs of the Christian populace by a network of native priests throughout the whole country.'' Underlying his call for indigenous clergy to play an important role in the task of evangelization in the mission lands was his belief in the fundamental equality between the foreign missionary and indigenous clergy. Pius XI is remembered for being the first pope who personally consecrated indigenous Chinese, Indian and Japanese bishops.

Of the ten letters on mission that Pope PIUS XII wrote, the most important is *Evangelii praecones* (June 2, 1951), issued on the occasion of the 25th anniversary of Pius XI's *Rerum ecclesiae*. Among other things, Pius XII adopted an approach to evangelization in mission lands that was reminiscent of Pope Gregory the Great in his letter to St. Mellitus. Reiterating a position which was first enunciated in his first encyclical, *Summi pontificatus* (Oct. 20, 1939), he suggested that ''whatever there is in native customs that is not inseparably bound up with superstition and error will always receive kindly consideration and, where possible, will be preserved intact.'' As he explained: ''let not the gospel, on being introduced into any new land, destroy or extinguish whatever its people possess that is naturally good, just or beautiful.'' Another important encyclical which Pius XII wrote was *Fidei donum* (April 21, 1957), which appealed to the universal Church to provide assistance to the missionary enterprise in Africa, a continent that was undergoing a painful transition toward political independence. *Fidei donum* also introduced the term ''young churches'' to describe the churches in mission lands.

In addition to the usual themes that his predecessors covered, e.g., the necessity of indigenous clergy to meet the challenges of decolonization, Pope JOHN XXIII's encyclical *Princeps pastorum* (Nov. 28, 1959) is remembered for laying the cornerstone for the Church's subsequent recognition of cultural diversity in her task of mission, asserting, among other things, that the Church ''does not identify herself with any one culture to the exclusion of the rest—not even with European and Western culture, with which her history is so closely linked.''

Among the various letters on mission and evangelization that Pope PAUL VI wrote, the Apostolic Exhortation on the occasion of the 1974 Synod of Bishops on Evangelization in the Modern World, *EVANGELII NUNTIANDI* (Dec. 8, 1975), stands out for its deeply profound reflection on the relationship between evangelization and culture. Here, Pope Paul VI emphasized the need to evangelize human culture and cultures. In his own words: ''The rift between the gospel and culture is undoubtedly an unhappy circumstance of our times just as it has been in other eras. Accordingly we must devote all our resources and all our efforts to the sedulous evangelization of human culture, or rather of the various human cultures'' (*Evangelii nuntiandi* 20). He warned against the facile reduction of evangelization to that of mere human liberation with its goal of material well-being (*Evangelii nuntiandi* 32). These discussions should be set in the context of Paul VI's criticism of certain quarters in the Church that were misusing conciliar teachings as arguments against the necessity of evangelization.

Pope JOHN PAUL II wrote significantly on the question of evangelization, beginning with the Apostolic Exhortation, *Catechesi tradendae* (Oct. 16, 1979). In *Catechesi tradendae*, he discussed the close relationship between inculturation, catechesis and evangelization, saying that inculturation ''is called to bring the power of the Gospel into the very heart of culture and cultures'' (*Catechesi tradendae* 53). Subsequently in his encyclical *SLAVORUM APOSTOLI* (June 2, 1985), he suggested that the work of evangelization that was carried out by SS. Cyril and Methodius ''as pioneers in territory inhabited by Slav peoples—contains both a model of what today is called 'inculturation'—the incarnation of the gospel in native cultures—and also the introduction of these cultures into the life of the church'' (*Slavorum Apostoli* 21). The most important missiological document of John Paul II is his encyclical, *REDEMPTORIS MISSIO* (Dec. 7, 1990), written to commemorate the 25th anniversary of Vatican II's Missionary Decree, *Ad gentes*. Here, John Paul II invited the Church to ''renew her missionary commitment'' (*Redemptoris missio* 2) and highlighted the necessity for three categories of evangelization: (i) evangelization of non-Christians (i.e., the mission *ad gentes* in the strict sense), (ii) pastoral care of the faithful, and (iii) the ''re-evangelization'' or ''new evangelization'' of people ''who no longer consider themselves members of the church and live a life far removed from Christ and his Gospel'' (*Redemptoris missio* 33).

All post-Vatican II papal writings on mission and evangelization have drawn upon the profound theological insights of Vatican II documents *Ad gentes, Lumen gentium, Gaudium et spes*, and *Nostra aetate* to articulate a renewed theology of mission for today. At the heart of these papal writings is the call to the whole body of the Church to undertake the task of mission, not just the mission professionals. In the wake of the importance which *Gaudium et spes* and *Ad gentes* give to human cultures and communities, the scope of mission has broadened beyond merely effecting a ''change of religion'' in individuals to include transforming human cultures and communities in the light of the Gospel message.

Bibliography: W. BURROWS, ed., *Redemption and Dialogue: Reading Redemptoris Missio and Dialogue and Proclamation* (Maryknoll 1993). C. CARLEN, *The Papal Encyclicals Vols. 1–5* (Ann Arbor 1990). A. DULLES, ''John Paul II and the New Evangelization,'' *Studia Missionalia* 48 (1999) 165–80. P. G. FALCIOLA, *Evangelization according to the Mind of Paul VI* (Rome 1982). PONTIFICIA UNIVERSITÁ URBANIANA, *Dizionario di Missiologia* (Rome 1993). J. A. SCHERER and S. B. BEVANS, eds., *New Directions in Mission & Evangelization. Vols. I–III* (Maryknoll 1992–99).

[J. Y. TAN]

MISSION AND EVANGELIZATION IN CANON LAW

The establishment of present day Catholic law and legal order concerned with the propagation of the Christian faith among non-Christian peoples historically dates from 1622 with the foundation of the Congregation for the PROPAGATION OF THE FAITH, now called the Congregation for the EVANGELIZATION OF PEOPLES. The twentieth-century movement from the principle of delegation to the principle of reservation underlies current change in the Catholic legal order. The change reflects a movement away from canon 1350, §2 of the 1917 *Code of Canon Law* (CIC) which accorded the responsibility for missionary activity exclusively with the Apostolic See. The Second Vatican Council marked the turning point for developing particular legislation whereby the Church can consider the realities of individual cultures to implement legal order and activities.

Catholic Church teaching expressed in *Lumen Gentium*, number 23 and *Ad gentes*, numbers 2, 35 and 39 of the Second Vatican Council grounded theology and pastoral directives in the 1983 CIC and the 1990 *Code of Canons of the Eastern Churches (CCEO)* which state that the work of evangelization is a fundamental duty of all the people of God, since ''the whole Church is by its nature missionary'' (*CIC* c. 781, and *CCEO* c. 584, §1). Missionary action implants the Church among peoples or groups where it has not yet taken root, especially by sending heralds of the gospel until the young churches have the proper resources and sufficient means to be able to carry out the work of evangelization themselves (*CIC c.* 786 and *CCEO c.* 590). The canon expresses the goal of missionary activity. The code devotes title II of Book III on the Teaching Function of the Church as well as specific eferences in Book II, The People of God, to meet the goal, that is, to set up structures to direct missionary activity and to regulate the missionary actions of individual church people.

Reflective of the hierarchical constitution of the people of God, the code structures the supreme direction and coordination of missionary endeavors for the entire Church to the Roman Pontiff and to the College of Bishops (*CIC c.* 782, §1). Conferences of bishops are charged, first, to regulate the steps necessary to enter the church (*CIC c.* 788, §3 and *CCEO c.* 587, §1, 3) and, secondly, to establish and promote works by which those who come to their territory from mission lands for study or work be received and assisted with adequate pastoral care (*CIC c.* 792). Individual bishops are to initiate, foster and sustain missionary endeavors in their own dioceses. Specifically, the diocesan bishop fosters missionary vocations and promotes cooperation in individual dioceses by prayer and financial support (*CIC c.* 782, §2; 385 and *CCEO c.*195 and *CIC c.* 791 and *CCEO c.* 585, §3). A diocesan bishop in the territory of a mission is to promote, direct, and coordinate missionary endeavors by forming agreements with those engaged in missionary work (*CIC c.* 790). In a particular church grouping organized as a territorial prelature (*CIC c.* 370 and *CCEO, c.* 311, §§1, and 312) or under an apostolic vicar (*CIC c.* 371), the 1983 code calls for a council of the mission (*CIC c.* 495, §2 and *CCEO c.* 264 and *CIC c.* 502, §4 and *CCEO c.* 271, §§1–5), at least three missionary presbyters who function as a presbyteral council and whose opinion the vicar or prefect apostolic is to hear in more serious matters, as for example the granting of dimissorial letters required by *CIC c.* 1018 or *CCEO c.* 1269 for the ordination of secular clergy within the grouping.

The carrying out of missionary work may be entrusted to natives or non-natives, whether secular clergy, members of either institutes of consecrated life or societies of apostolic actions, and lay members of the Christian faithful (*CIC c.* 784). Priests going to the missions, for example, are to learn the language of the region, and understand its institutions, social conditions, usages, and customs (*CIC c.* 257 and *CCEO c.* 352, §3). Members of institutes of consecrated life are to engage in missionary action in a special way and in a manner proper to their institute under the direction of the diocesan bishop (*CIC c.* 783). The Holy See in consultation with a conference of bishops can establish a personal prelature of priests and deacons to engage in missionary activity in accord with the prelature's statutes and the consent of the diocesan bishop where the activity takes place (*CIC c.* 294 and 297). Church law calls for catechists, trained lay members of the Christian faithful, duly instructed and outstanding in Christian life, to set forth the teaching of the gospel, to organize liturgies and works of charity under the direction of a missionary (*CIC c.* 785). Laity also have the duty to work so that the divine message of salvation becomes known, especially in ''circumstances in which only through them can people hear the gospel and know Christ'' (*CIC c.* 225, §1 and *CCEO c.* 401 & 406)

Missionary activity takes place in three stages. In the pre-catechumenate, the activities of missionaries establish by witness of word and their life a dialogue with those who do not believe in Christ so that in a manner adapted to their own temperament and culture, individuals come to understand the gospel and be admitted to receive baptism when they freely request it (*CIC c.* 787). Only dialogue brings into focus cultural distinctiveness and promotes that any decision to accept the faith is a free determination. The catechumenate begins when one makes known his or her intention to embrace the faith in Christ. Admitted in liturgical ceremonies, a formation program initiates catechumens into the mystery of salvation and introduces them into the life of the faith, the liturgy, the charity of the people of God, and the apostolate under the direction of a nation's conference of bishops (*CIC c.* 788 and *CCEO* 587, §1, 3). Finally, neophytes after their reception of baptism are to deepen their understanding of the faith and formed to fulfill the duties assumed at baptism (*CIC c.* 789).

[A. J. ESPELAGE]

MISSION AND MISSIONS

Mission, as a term describing the activity of Church members in the spread of the Gospel, is a relatively new term. In the 16th century IGNATIUS OF LOYOLA used the term ''votum missionis'' to describe the commitment and task of his members. Before that, a variety of words were used to describe this activity: propagation of the faith, conversion of the heathen, proclamation of the Good News to the whole world, conversion of unbelievers, planting the Church, extension of the Kingdom, etc.

It was only in the 19th century that missions (in the plural) became identified with the outreach of the Church to those who were not Christians and with the places where Christian communities were only starting or had not yet achieved the full structure of the Church. This word continued to be used to describe the Church's activity until the middle of the 20th century, when for various reasons the word mission began to replace missions.

Its Definition. Common definitions of mission encompass the following elements: mission begins in the life of God; the Church continues Christ's mission; mission is carried out under the guidance of the Spirit; the Church is missionary by her very nature; ''foreign missions'' is not a separate entity; mission expresses God's relationship with the world; and mission includes evangelization and bringing the Gospel to those who have never heard it.

Before Vatican II—From Missions to Mission. The activity of the Church in the 19th century in Africa, Asia, and the South Pacific prompted systematic theological reflection on missions at the beginning of the 20th century. This was true in both the Protestant and the Catholic Churches. Missionaries succeeded in making converts and establishing Christian communities. This suggested that they reflect on what they were doing and why and with what goal in mind.

Catholic mission theology from its formal start in 1911 until the time of World War II in the 1940s was dominated by three schools of thought. At Münster the school established and guided by Joseph SCHMIDLIN affirmed that the purpose of missions was to preach the Gospel to non-Christians. Therefore missions only existed in what were identified as non-Christian lands. At Louvain Pierre CHARLES, SJ, and his colleagues preferred to say that the goal of missions was to plant the Church. They saw missions as a transient stage and they would disappear when the Church was established. At Burgos Jose Zameza, SJ, and Olegario Dominguez, OP, took a less juridical approach; they spoke about missions as the way in which the MYSTICAL BODY OF CHRIST grew. The French School of Andre Glorieux, Henri de LUBAC, and Alexandre Durand took a different approach. Their basis for mission work was not the salvation of individual souls but the collective salvation of humanity. Also they rooted mission in the mystery of the incarnation.

However, significant changes that would deeply influence Vatican II emerged after World War I. Edward Loffeld, CSSp, saw the European schools of thought converging. He spoke about the goal of missions as particular churches. Thomas Ohm, OSB, who filled the Chair at Münster once held by Schmidlin, emphasized that missions were about discipling the nations. He also suggested that missions must find their origin not in the Church but in the life of the Trinity.

The French also made important contributions. Jean DANIÉLOU, SJ, a church historian and patristics scholar, proposed the idea that God had made three covenants with humanity: through Noah, through Moses, and through Jesus. Thus he placed all religious history under God. He saw other religions as being simply human endeavors, while Judaism and Christianity were based on a revelation from God. He also was interested in the dynamics by which a Jewish movement became a gentile church. This led him to examine the mystery of the incarnation in terms of its cultural implications. He suggested that the Gospel must be incarnated in every culture, refracted as it were in the prism of every culture, before it would be fully understood.

Yves CONGAR, OP, in his earliest writings was concerned about ecumenism. But he also was interested in the mission (in the singular) of the Church. He suggested that mission is permanent (not transient) and coextensive with the life of the Church in the world (not just mission territories). For him mission had to be linked with the incarnation and with cultures. The Church, he said, would not know what it means to preach the Gospel to all peoples until it had done so.

The Worker-Priest Movement, also known as the *Mission de France*, began under the guidance of Cardinal SUHARD of Paris in the early 1940s in response to a study that showed that the working class of France had never been evangelized. A group of missionaries were formed who would become full-time workers, identify with the people in their style of life, and bring the Gospel to those who had not heard it. They realized that the parish itself must become a missionary institution. Mission was no longer the specialized calling of religious men and women going overseas to new cultures; it was the calling of the local Church as well. These ideas were not easily accepted by the traditional mission theologians and religious missionary congregations at that time.

Finally, the German Jesuit Karl RAHNER helped to bring about a changed understanding of mission and missions. In his attempt to explain that God wills the salvation of all peoples, he pointed out that God's will would be frustrated if salvation were limited to those who were baptized or who consciously knew and accepted Christ. Therefore, he talked of ''anonymous Christians''—people who followed their consciences and lived a good life and were saved through Christ even if they did not know it. This changed not only the motivation for mission but also the approach to people of other faiths.

Vatican II—*Ad gentes*. The gathering of Bishops at Vatican II produced the most significant document on mission and missions of the 20th century. It almost did not happen. It was brought forward in the third session of the council. The bishops by that time were anxious about the amount of time that they were away from their dioceses. The drafting committee decided to reduce the decree to several proposals. Cardinal AGAGIANIAN, the prefect of the Congregation for the Propagation of the Faith, persuaded PAUL VI to make a personal appearance in support of the proposals to show his concern for the entire missionary movement. After Paul VI left the *aula*, one bishop after the other rose to speak against the proposals. They urged that in the current climate the Church needed not just a few proposals but a complete decree. A special commission was set up to work on this between the third and fourth sessions. John Schuette, SVD, the superior general of the Divine Word Missionaries, was appointed to chair the commission. Some of its members were: Dominic Grasso, SJ; Joseph Neuner, SJ; Yves Congar; and Joseph RATZINGER. They brought their decree to the Council floor early in the fourth session. It was approved, but certain changes were suggested. These were made and the revised document was again brought towards the end of the fourth session. It had almost universal acceptance.

The document, *Ad gentes divinitus*, as so many of the documents of Vatican II, is a compromise document. While the various European schools of mission theology argued to have their interpretation accepted as the official one, the commission decided not to choose between them but to take a both/and rather than an either/or position. It also decided to include the recent insights and outlook of Jean Daniélou, Yves Congar, Karl Rahner, and the Worker-Priest Movement. It introduced an element that had not been greatly present in the missiological literature before then: the value of Christian presence and witness as a missionary task. Finally, it incorporated the recommendation that a bishop of the Melkite Church made after the first reading of the decree: that the Church should reclaim the teaching of JUSTIN MARTYR about the ''seeded Word of God.''

Early in the document the Council Fathers indicated that the origin for mission and missions is found in the life of the Trinity: ''The Church on earth is by its very nature missionary, since, according to the plan of the Father, it has its origin in the mission of the Son and the Holy Spirit.'' (AG, 2) The Father sends the Son; the Father and Son send the Spirit; and all three send the Church. The decree highlights the special role that the Holy Spirit plays, removing divisions and diversity and often anticipating the presence and activity of the missionary.

Jesus called the Apostles who became the foundation of the Church which is a sacrament of Christ's presence and saving love. It is the Church's mission, according to the decree, to make herself fully present to all people and nations. It is a continuing task and one which the Church must carry out in the same way that Christ carried out His mission: ''the Church, urged on by the Spirit of Christ, must walk the road Christ himself walked, a way of poverty and obedience, of service and self-sacrifice even to death, from which He emerged victorious by his resurrection'' (AG, 5).

After pointing out the origin of mission and missions, the decree describes the difference between them. The mission of the Church, it is said, is one and the same everywhere, although circumstances may demand different approaches. However, ''the special undertakings in which preachers of the Gospel, sent by the Church and going into the whole world, carry out the work of preaching the Gospel and implanting the Church among people who do not yet believe in Christ, are generally called 'missions.''' (AG,4) This distinction was insisted upon by missionary congregations who wanted to distinguish their work from that being done in the West, such as the *Mission de France*. While this distinction has been maintained by certain missionary groups and was even reinforced by the papal encyclical of John Paul II, *Redemptoris missio*, for the most part it has disappeared from the writings of most mission scholars. An opening was given to this in the document itself when it recognized not only that an established and fully mature Church and a mission situation can exist side by side but also that missionary activity can be reinstated because of changed circumstances and that the missionary activity might be reduced to presence and service.

The decree sees the missionary task as a three-fold one: bearing Christian witness; preaching the Gospel and gathering God's people; and forming the Christian community. Missionaries had traditionally cared for the poor and afflicted. Schools, clinics, and hospitals had been established; famine relief was organized. They did this both for their Christians and to attract new converts. This was often seen as pre-evangelization. The decree insists that if it is true charity it must extend to all without distinction of race, social condition, or religion. (AG, 12) Moreover, charity must never be used to entice people to conversion. (AG, 13) In doing this, Catholics need not set up their own projects, but should be willing to cooperate with public and private organizations, with international agencies, with various Christian communities, and even with non-Christian religions. (AG, 12) Missionaries must have a concern for the development of peoples, even if they cannot preach Christ; since ''in teaching the religious and moral truths, which Christ illumined with his light, they seek to enhance the dignity of men and promote fraternal unity, and, in this way, are gradually opening a wider approach to God.'' (AG, 12) Interestingly, in addressing this topic the decree began with the role of the new converts rather than that of the foreign missionaries. To give this witness they must be members of the group among whom they live, sharing in their cultural and social life (AG, 11).

The second missionary task, according to the decree, is to preach the Gospel and gather God's people, an example of the Commission's approach, combining the concerns of the Münster and Louvain schools of thought rather than choosing between them. From the start the decree points out that the missionary might announce the Gospel, but it is the Holy Spirit, which opens hearts, that leads to conversion. The decree recognizes that conversion is a gradual process and at times demands a painful breaking of ties. It brings a progressive change of outlook and morals that is developed during the time of the catechumenate. (AG, 13) These should be established everywhere. The liturgy is to play an important role in it with a special emphasis put on Lent and Easter (AG, 14).

The third missionary task is forming the Christian community. There is a great emphasis on the role the laity in these congregations plays in the mission of the Church by being part of the local scene. Congregations are enriched by their nation's culture and are truly one with the people. This new community is to be ecumenical in the broadest sense of the term. Not only is it to recognize that others who believe in Christ are Christ's disciples, but also to the extent that its beliefs are common, it is to make before the nations a common profession of faith in God and in Jesus Christ (AG, 15).

The formation of the Christian community also means raising up priests from their own community. The decree also recommends the restoration of the diaconate on the grounds that there are men who are already carrying out that ministry and would be strengthened by the laying on of hands. (AG, 16) This creative idea has not stimulated much of a response in the former mission territories, although it has been taken up by many churches in the West. Religious life is also to be encouraged, but according to the nature and the genius of the country.

The decree has a special chapter on particular churches. Much is a repetition of what was said in the part about forming the Christian community, but it was the ''missionary bishops'' who insisted that there be such a chapter. There are two emphases in this chapter: that the local congregation from the start should participate in the mission of the universal Church, and that the particular church is such because of the uniqueness of its culture.

The particular church is expected to engage in mission through its witness since it is to mirror the universal Church. It is sent to those also who live in the same territory and who do not yet believe in Christ. They do this by the living witness of each one of the faithful and of the whole community. (AG, 20) Special consideration is to be given to those who for some reason are not able to join the community just then. The decree recognizes that in certain regions, groups of people are found who are kept away from embracing the Catholic faith because they cannot adapt themselves to the peculiar form the Church has taken on there. In that case the decree urges ''that this situation should be specially provided for, until all Christians can gather together in one community'' (AG, 20).

What makes the particular Church particular is the local culture. Therefore this missionary task of witness is to be carried out in a way that is relevant to the local culture and local politics. The decree urges that Christians give expression to their newness of life in the social and cultural framework of their own homeland and according to their own national traditions. They are not only to be acquainted with their culture, but also to heal and preserve it. Thus ''the faith of Christ and the life of the Church will not be something foreign to the society in which they live, but will begin to transform and permeate it.'' (AG, 21) The decree foresees that the Church, following the model of the incarnation, will be enriched by these cultures. They will take to themselves in a wonderful exchange the riches of the nations which were given to Christ as an inheritance. From the customs and traditions of their people, from their wisdom and their learning, from their arts and sciences, these Churches will borrow those things which contribute to the glory of their Creator, the revelation of the Savior's grace, or the proper arrangement of Christian life (AG, 22).

The decree also has a chapter on the missionary vocation that reaffirms the value of a lifetime commitment to mission and a chapter on missionary cooperation that describes the possible role that the Congregation for the Propagation of the Faith might play in the future.

Vatican II—*Nostra aetate.* Another decree that has had a profound effect on missionaries and the missionary task is *Nostra aetate: Declaration on the Relation of the Church to Non-Christian Religions*. This, too, was a decree that almost did not happen. At the very outset of the Council John XXIII asked that a statement on the Jews should be included in the Council's deliberations; he was anxious to have the charge of ''deicide'' removed. At first it was made part of the decree on Ecumenism and then on Religious Liberty. But John XXIII, as well as several bishops, wanted a separate decree; this was decided upon as early as Nov. 19, 1963.

The document was drafted under the leadership of Cardinal BEA between the second and third session. The document brought to the Fathers of the Council was different from that which had been leaked to the press, and there was a great outcry. There were several serious concerns. The four Eastern Patriarchs and the bishops coming from Arab lands favored no statement at all for fear that it might be interpreted politically. Many bishops were opposed even to using the word ''deicide,'' which in the end did not appear in the document. The question was raised about asking the Jews and Muslims forgiveness for past offenses. Finally, it was thought that the decree should also refer to the Muslims and people of African religions as well. However, when the final version of the document was brought to the Council on Oct. 28, 1965, it received overwhelming approval.

The decree first refers to Hinduism, Buddhism, and other religions, and it affirms that the Church ''rejects nothing of what is true and holy in these religions.'' She ''looks with sincere respect'' on them since they ''often reflect a ray of that Truth which enlightens all men.'' Therefore, it exhorts the Church to ''enter with prudence and charity into discussion and collaboration with members of other religions. Let Christians, while witnessing to their own faith and way of life, acknowledge, preserve and encourage the spiritual and moral truths found among non-Christians, also their social life and culture'' (NA, 2).

There is a special section on the Muslims. The decree states that the Church has a high regard for them for several reasons: they adore the One God; they submit wholeheartedly to God; they acknowledge Jesus as a prophet; they honor Mary; they prize moral living; and they worship God through prayer, almsgiving, and fasting. It urges ''all to forget the past'' and that ''a sincere effort be made to achieve mutual understanding.'' Also they are called on to make common cause in safeguarding and fostering social justice, moral values, peace and freedom (NA, 3).

But the longest section of the decree deals with the Jews. After pointing out the common heritage of Christians and Jews and reminding its readers that Jesus and the Apostles were Jews, the decree states clearly that the covenant that God has with the Jews is still valid; as Paul argued: ''the Jews still remain most dear to God because of the patriarchs, since God does not take back the gifts He bestowed or the choice He made.'' (NA, 4) The decree talks about the role that Jews played in the death of Christ, but states clearly that ''neither all Jews indiscriminately at that time, nor Jews today, can be charged with the crimes committed during the passion. It is true that the Church is the new people of God, yet the Jews should not be spoken of as rejected or accursed, as if this followed from holy Scripture'' (NA, 4).

The decree concludes with a strong statement on discrimination. It states that there is no basis for discrimination either in theory or in practice, and therefore the ''Church rejects . . . any discrimination against men or harassment of them because of their race, color, condition of life, or religion'' (NA, 5).

A Changed Situation. While the Council was in session, the situation in former mission lands was changing rapidly. Almost all the former colonies which had not yet become independent became new nation-states. The Church also changed. Vicariates apostolic became dioceses, and vicars apostolic became ordinaries. Bishops' Conferences developed in the new nations and sometimes across regions; leadership posts were filled by indigenous people. Some countries closed their doors to foreign missionaries.

Changes also took place in the structures of mission work. The Congregation for the Propagation of the Faith became the Congregation for the Evangelization of Peoples. With the establishment of national hierarchies its role became more one of coordination than supervision, although it has continued to play an important role in the choice of new bishops in the former mission lands. The end of ''ius commissionis'' in 1966 meant that the territories would no longer ''belong'' to a particular mission congregation. Bishops were free to invite any congregations they wished as co-workers.

Development of New Mission Theories. *Ad gentes* had summarized the theories about mission and missions that had taken place in the 20th century before and leading up to Vatican II. But it had also introduced some new ideas that would be explored and embraced in the subsequent decades of the 20th century. It had affirmed that witness and development work were not just pre-evangelization; they were part of the missionary task itself. It had also introduced the phrase ''the seeded Word of God,'' spoke forthrightly about the respect that must be shown to all other religions and called for dialogue, and had urged that local cultures be respected and embraced so that the Church itself could become more local. These ideas demanded discussion, elaboration, and clarification.

Some of this took place in the Church synods, such as that in 1974 on evangelization, which resulted in the encyclical of Paul VI: *Evangelii nuntiandi*. Major guidance has also been given through papal encyclicals such as John Paul II's *Redemptoris missio*. The Secretariat for Non-Christian Religions (the name was later changed to the Pontifical Council for Interreligious Dialogue) was set up by Paul VI in 1964 and has provided documents and guidelines for this aspect of the missionary task. Bishops' Conferences, like CELAM (the Latin American Bishops' Conference) and FABC (the FEDERATION OF ASIAN BISHOPS' CONFERENCES), have addressed the missionary task in their part of the world. Finally, theologians, individually and through missionary associations, such as the International Association for Mission Studies, American Society of Missiology, and the many national associations, continue to further thought on the missionary task. A very significant meeting has been the gathering in Italy of scholars from around the world almost every ten years for Seminars organized by SEDOS.

Witness—Development—Liberation—Ecology. The Church has had a long history of carrying out corporal works of mercy. It was often seen as a way of making converts or as pre-evangelization. But the decree *Ad gentes* said that the Church must be concerned about the development of people even when there was no hope of preaching the Gospel. This idea was given great impetus by Paul VI's encyclical *Populorum progressio* ''On the Progress of Peoples'', published in 1967. Some of the characteristics of development that were urged by the pope were: the human person and the respect for his or her dignity must be the basis for development and ought to determine its approach; the Church must look to the improvement of the whole person, body and soul; the Church must be concerned to improve the whole world, not just Christians; and such development tasks should be done in conjunction with local governments and national agencies. The United Nations had declared the 1960s to be the decade for development, and so missionaries were quick to take up the suggestions of Vatican II and Paul VI.

In the late 1960s and early 1970s not only were missionaries deeply involved in development work but also mission theologians were reflecting on its meaning. Some suggested that development was the new name for mission. Books with titles such as *Theology of Development* or something similar appeared. A SEDOS seminar in March of 1969 addressed the topic of development and evangelization. It recognized that there could be a tension between missionaries who saw evangelization and those who saw development as a priority. The SEDOS seminar, building on the documents of Vatican II, affirmed that work undertaken to further the integral development of peoples is a means of evangelization. It was a living and eloquent witness of the lordship of Christ over the world. Even when this witness could not be complemented by the word, development still retained a missionary significance.

At the synod of 1974 on evangelization, the question of human promotion and its relation to evangelization was once more examined. Paul VI was asked to write the conclusions of the synod. This he did in *Evangelii nuntiandi.* While reaffirming the priority of verbal evangelization he recognized the validity of development work as a missionary task even in situations where the Gospel could not be preached.

Paul VI's *Populorum progressio* was written primarily with Latin America in mind. But events had overtaken theory. The bishops of Latin America (CELAM) met in Medellin, Colombia, in 1968. After experiencing a decade of development they found that there were more poor than at the beginning of the decade and that the gap between the rich and the poor had widened. They also decided that since the overwhelming majority of their Catholics were the poor they must make an option for them. As Gustavo Gutierrez, a parish priest in Lima and the father of Liberation Theology, would say: development had not worked for Latin America; what was needed was liberation from oppressive economic structures.

By the late 1980s missionaries and mission theologians realized that if they were truly concerned about the development of peoples they must also be concerned about the universe and the environment. National and international meetings of missiologists began to make this not only an item on the program but often its entire focus.

Interreligious Dialogue. The decrees of Vatican II raised new questions about other faiths and the Church's attitude toward them. Both *Lumen gentium* and *Ad gentes* made it clear that salvation is possible for all, even those who have never heard of Christ. But, it was asked, does this mean that people can be saved in their religions, even if not through them? The magisterium as articulated in documents such as John Paul II's *Redemptoris missio* insists that Jesus Christ is the only Savior given to humankind; but it does not say how this relates to the teaching of Vatican II about salvation being possible for all. A second issue is the question of revelation. *Nostra aetate, Redemptoris missio*, and *Dialogue and Proclamation* (published jointly by the Congregation for the Evangelization of Peoples and the Pontifical Council for Interreligious Dialogue in 1991) all talk about the ''seeds of the Word of God'' present in other religions, but they have not yet explained what this means in the concrete situation. It does establish a basis for respect for the other religions; but does it mean that these religions have received a revelation? This issue is more than a theoretical, albeit lively, topic of discussion among missiologists; it has far-reaching ramifications on relations between the Church and other religions.

Paul VI, even before *Nostra aetate* had been accepted by the Council, had established a Secretariat for Non-Christian Religions. Its purpose was to promote studies of the various religions and activities such as cooperation and dialogue. The Church in Asia, which is a minority living in the midst of other living faiths, has responded enthusiastically to this call for dialogue. At first the dialogue was undertaken at the level of theological exchange for the sake of mutual understanding. But as time passed the Church also took part in the other forms of dialogue: of life—where Catholics shared a common social or political life with peoples of other faiths; of action—where Catholics and people of other faiths formed basic human communities to work for development and/or change of oppressive structures; and of religious experience—where monks, nuns, and religious people of various faiths came together to pray and exchange their deeply religious experiences.

Theologians have attempted to address some of the questions that interreligious dialogue raises. The SEDOS Seminar of 1969 stated clearly that although non-Christian religions could not be seen as ways of salvation their authentic values could lead their followers to the act of faith and charity which is necessary for salvation.

Paul VI, in *Evangelii nuntiandi*, did not address the topic of interreligious dialogue. But he did say of the other living faiths that since these religions ''are the living experience of the soul of vast groups of people'' searching for God in an incomplete way but with ''great sincerity and righteousness of heart,'' they are to be respected and esteemed. ''They are all impregnated with innumerable 'seeds of the Word.''' (EN, 53) However, John Paul II has led the way in interreligious dialogue both in action and in word. His visit to the Synagogue in Rome, his meetings with Jewish leaders, and his visit to Israel have furthered the dialogue with the Jews. His invitation to the religious leaders of the world to join him in prayer for peace at Assisi in 1986 was a landmark event that initiated a new practice that he continued to pursue. Notable, too, was his decision to enter and pray in a mosque during his visit to Syria in May of 2001, another first for any pope. His writings also, especially *Redemptor hominis, Dominum et vivificantem,* and *Redemptoris missio*, have not only encouraged interreligious dialogue but have also articulated a theological basis for interreligious dialogue.

Inculturation. The decree *Ad gentes* emphasized the role of culture even though it did not use the term inculturation. It stated that Christians (and the Church) must be at home in their own cultures. It even used the analogy of the incarnation. The chapter on particular churches gives the impression that the identity and relative autonomy of particular Churches is bound up with culture.

In the letter *Evangelii nuntiandi*, Paul VI offers a theology of a multicultural Church. He writes: ''What matters is to evangelize people's culture and cultures (not in a purely decorative way as it were by applying a thin veneer, but in a vital way, in depth and right to the very roots), in the wide and rich sense which these terms have in *Gaudium et spes*, always taking the person as one's starting point and always coming back to the relationships of people among themselves and with God'' (EN, 20).

It was in the Synod on Catechesis in 1977 that the term ''inculturation'' was brought into ecclesiastical discussion by Pedro Arrupe, SJ. The following year John Paul II used it for the first time in a Roman document, calling it a ''neologism'' but stating that it expressed well one factor of the great mystery of the incarnation. When he set up the Pontifical Council for Culture in May of 1982, he said that the synthesis between culture and faith is a demand of both culture and faith. A faith that does not become a culture, he maintained, is a faith that has not been fully received, not thoroughly thought through, not fully lived out.

No More Missions or Mission Lands. In the decades that followed Vatican II missionaries, mission agencies, and mission theorists, with a few exceptions, have stopped talking about missions or mission lands. The emphasis is on the mission of the Church that is one and the same everywhere. Mission is recognized to be as necessary and alive in North America and Europe as in Asia and Africa. It is no longer mission agencies in Europe and North America that determine the missionary task to be carried out elsewhere; it is the local Church of the area, a local Church that is for the most part in the hands of local people.

Bibliography: *Declaration on the Relation of the Church to Non-Christian Religions* (*Nostra aetate*), *Vatican Council II, The Conciliar and Post-Conciliar Documents*, ed. A. FLANNERY (Northport, NY 1992) 738–743. *Decree on the Church's Missionary Activity* (*Ad Gentes*) 813–857 Paul VI. *Evangelization Today (Evangelii nuntiandi)* (London 1977). D. J. BOSCH, *Transforming Mission: Paradigm Shifts in Theology of Mission* (Maryknoll, NY 1991). W. BURROWS ed., *Redemption and Dialogue: Reading Redemptoris missio and Dialogue and Proclamation* (Maryknoll, NY 1993). K. MULLER, et al., eds., *Dictionary of Mission: Theology, History, Perspectives* (Maryknoll, NY 1997).

[L. NEMER]

MISSION HELPERS OF THE SACRED HEART

A religious community of women founded by Mother M. Demetrias in Baltimore, Md., in 1890 and dedicated to the work of catechetics and religious instruction (MHSH, Official Catholic Directory #2720). The congregation was raised to pontifical status in 1949. From the beginning, the sisters combined regular home visiting with the organization of catechetical classes. As missionaries and religion teachers, they continued through the years to go out from their convents to surrounding areas, pioneering in any undertaking that assists bishops and pastors to implement religious education in their dioceses and parishes. Their varied activities have included the initiation and promotion of schools of religion, home

Roberto de Nobili.

instruction programs, special education for the handicapped, and youth ministries. The motherhouse in Baltimore remains the educational center where the work is constantly evaluated and coordinated.

[M. F. TIMMERMAN/EDS.]

MISSION HISTORY, I: CATHOLIC

Encountering the People of the Roman Empire & Its Neighbors. The second and third century Christian communities were for the most part around the Mediterranean basin. Some claimed an apostolic foundation; others simply appeared. From these communities came apostolic preachers who wandered from town to town, staying two or three days. For the most part their names are unknown; but there were many. According to CELSUS, an opponent of Christianity, the gospel was spread also by women and slaves through ordinary conversation.

Celsus stated that the Gospel would only be accepted by women, slaves, and unlearned people. However, evidence shows that Christian converts came from all classes—Roman gentility, learned philosophers, civil servants, and slaves. By the end of the second century few Jewish people were becoming Christians.

People were attracted by the salvation promised and the divine philosophy being taught. For this reason teachers such as Justin, Clement, and Origen are often listed as missionaries. There are also cases where healings and other works of power had an impact, as with Gregory Thaumaturgus in Pontus. Within the empire the evangelization was done in the cities; the people in the countryside (the *pagani*) would not be christianized until the fourth century.

Christian communities also developed outside the Roman Empire. The community in Edessa developed very early in post-apostolic times with some indications that Christianity was made a state religion, although most historians say this is doubtful. However, there is evidence that when GREGORY THE ILLUMINATOR brought the Gospel to Armenia with the support of King Trdat (TIRIDATES III, 298–330) a strong link was forged between the state, Armenian culture, and Christianity.

With CONSTANTINE's conversion and the toleration granted Christianity, the situation changed. The last group to withstand Christianity within the cities was the aristocratic class. The nobles would not abandon their traditional gods, but they married Christian women and allowed their sons to be Christians. Once Christianity became the ordinary religion of the urban citizens, group pressure played a role in Christianity's spread.

The development of monasticism in the fourth century played an important part in the evangelization of the ''pagani.'' The monks' purpose in moving into rural areas was to pursue an ascetic ideal, but they also evangelized. Martin of Tours, after becoming bishop, undertook an active campaign with his monks to bring the Gospel to the countryside.

Outside the Roman Empire, Christianity attracted many adherents. In some cases, it was brought by shipwrecked Romans, e.g., Aedesius and Frumentius, who brought Christianity to Ethiopia. In other cases, it was a miracle by a slave girl that would convert the king and his kingdom, as happened in Georgia with St. Nina, or it was the influence and charismatic preaching of a particular person, as with Patrick in Ireland.

Encountering the New Peoples of Europe. From the end of the fourth century the Church encountered new peoples who had come into the empire. Some were already Christian, such as the Visigoths; but they were Arian Christians. Others had not encountered Christianity until their arrival within the Roman Empire, such as the Huns, Vandals, and Franks. These tribes for the most part settled in the countryside and left the cities to the Roman citizens. The Bishops of these towns set about to convert them.

The bishops developed a pattern of focusing on the conversion of the chiefs (in some instances called kings). They always looked for ''another Constantine.'' For this reason the names of individual bishops are tied with the peoples converted: MARTIN OF BRAGA with the Suevi, ISIDORE and LEANDER OF SEVILLE with the Visigoths, Avitus of Vienne with the Burgundians, GREGORY THE GREAT with the Longobards. The conversion of CLOVIS as given to us in the *History of the Franks* by GREGORY OF TOURS is illustrative.

Over 150 years, the Germanic tribes were evangelized and baptized; but much remained to make them truly Christian and to bring organization to their local Churches. The first task was carried out by the Irish monks. Their primary motive for leaving home was not to bring the faith to unbelievers but to perform an act of asceticism: to leave home and wander for the sake of Christ (*peregrinatio pro Christo*). Their attitude toward their neighbors differed according to the people they encountered. COLUMBA and his followers awed the Picts in Scotland with their spiritual power and mysterious rituals; CUTHBERT and his monks on the east coast of England gently instructed the shepherds in the hills; Columbanus and his monks brutally attacked the pagan shrines of the Franks, who were Christians only in name, and scolded them until they trembled.

While the Irish monks deepened the faith of the Germanic tribes, the Benedictine monks brought organization. Just as the mission of AUGUSTINE to evangelize the Angles had originated in Rome with Gregory the Great, so the Benedictine Wynfrith (BONIFACE) first went to Rome before going to the Saxons on the continent. Rome directed him first to the Church in the Frankish Kingdom, which needed organization and reform. This he proceeded to do, but always under the direction of Rome. Although martyred in 752 by the Saxons, his principal missionary task had been to bring order and organization to the Frankish Church.

Mission in the High Middle Ages. Between the 800s and the 1300s there were three principal ways in which new peoples were evangelized: the sword, diplomacy, and a gentle presence (the approach of the mendicants).

CHARLEMAGNE wanted to extend his kingdom and include the Saxon people. However it was believed that a Christian king could rule only over a Christian people, and so baptism under pain of death was forced on them.

The sword was also used in the encounter of non-Christian peoples in Crusades from the tenth to the fourteenth century. In its initial phase in Spain, its purpose was to defeat the non-Christians (Muslims and Jews) in order to establish a Christian kingdom. Once defeated, they had the choice of being baptized or leaving the country. The Crusades to the Middle East in the eleventh and twelfth centuries were intended to recover the Holy Places from the Muslims in order to protect pilgrims and to establish Latin Christian states. Once the Christian state was established people again had the choice of being baptized or leaving. The final Crusades in the twelfth to the fourteenth century against the peoples to the north and east of the Holy Roman Empire were intended to subjugate peoples and enforce baptism. The evangelization of these peoples was left to the Cistercians and Premonstratensians in the twelfth century and the Franciscans and Dominicans in the thirteenth century.

Mission to new peoples during this time was also attempted on rare occasions by diplomacy. Anskar (801–865), after Louis the Pious's failure to impose baptism on the Danes with the sword, 30 years later, through diplomatic channels, was able to establish Christian communities among them. In Moravia the Church in Byzantium also used the diplomatic approach. The German priests and bishops who had come from the West were not successful in evangelizing the people. However, Constantine (826–869), Cyril, and Methodius (c. 815–885), who were sent as diplomats from the East, proved to have great success. Constantine had developed an alphabet for the Moravian language, and they arrived with the Scriptures and the liturgical books in the Moravian language. After Cyril's death and Constantine's expulsion by the Germans their evangelization by diplomacy was ended.

The third approach was that of the mendicants—a gentle presence. FRANCIS OF ASSISI (1181/2–1224) met with Sultan al-Kamil in 1219 and obtained personal freedom to preach Christianity. But the Friars he sent to Morocco in 1220 and to Tunis in 1225 were all killed. It was written into the Franciscan rule that the Friars can choose to live among Muslims as servants without preaching or can preach knowing that they risk martyrdom. The Dominicans, realizing the importance of language, established schools for this in the Holy Land already in 1237.

The mendicants also evangelized the Mongols, adapting to their nomadic way of life. The Popes also used them on diplomatic missions to the Khans, but with no lasting results. When the Polo brothers returned from China with a letter from the Great Khan Kublai (1260–1294) asking for missionaries, the Popes responded. JOHN OF MONTECORVINO, OFM, reached Beijing, and because of his success was made archbishop in 1307. At the time of his death in 1328 there were 30,000 Christians in China.

Encountering New Peoples Outside Europe. Columbus, under the patronage of Spain, found people on the other side of the world who were not Christian. Since in the 1440s the Pope had given all the lands and islands they would discover to the Portuguese, the Spaniards also sought papal approval to claim the lands they found. In 1493/4, by the Treaty of Tordesillas, ALEXANDER VI drew a line of demarcation, and all lands and islands to the east of it were to belong to Portugal and to the West to Spain. This paved the way for the establishment of the PATRONATO REAL or patronage system of missionary activity, whereby the Spanish and Portuguese Crowns were also responsible for the evangelization of these peoples, the providing of missionaries, and the governance of the Church.

The political conquest of the Caribbean Islands, Mexico, and Peru was rapid; it was completed by 1535. The acceptance of Christianity by the conquered people took longer. The Spanish ships that arrived brought not only conquistadors and settlers, but also Franciscans, Dominicans, Augustinians, Augustinian Recollects, and later Jesuits.

There were some outstanding individual preachers who evangelized these new peoples; however, most was done by communities of friars. Their attitude towards the religions of the native peoples was that everything had to be destroyed. The people were to be made a ''tabula rasa,'' a clean slate on which Christianity could be inscribed. They built their ''conventos,'' gathered the people around them, taught them farming, and set up schools in which they taught Latin, the industrial arts, music, etc. The natives were quickly converted to Christianity, especially after the appearance of Our Lady of GUADALUPE in 1531.

The Jesuits who began work among the Guarani people received permission to set up REDUCTIONS in 1608. Eventually, there were more than 30 of them, with more than 100,000 natives. The Jesuits brought them together to protect them from the Spaniards and Portuguese. The remains of their Churches and their music attest to a deep faith.

From Mexico the Spanish evangelized the Philippines. It was the same religious communities who had come to Mexico. They divided the territory between themselves. Since there were few settlers who came along, the friars were free to evangelize and were quickly successful. They also became the civil servants for Spain.

While some evangelization was done along the African coast under the Portuguese Patronage, the principal work was done in the Far East. Christianity had been present in India at least since the fourth century, possibly since Thomas the Apostle. The arrival of the Portuguese in GOA brought Western Christians in contact and at times in conflict with these St. Thomas Christians. Francis XAVIER (1506–1552) arrived in India in 1542 and worked for several years among the people on the Fisheries Coast.

In 1549, having heard about the Japanese, Francis went to open a mission there. He found that to get a hearing he would have to respect their culture and their religion. After he left for China his missionary principles were carried on by Alessandro VALIGNANO, SJ, and led to what is known as the ''Christian Century'' in Japan.

In the Jesuit mission in southeast India, Roberto de NOBILI (1577–1656) decided to identify himself with the Brahmins and to live by the strict rules of a *sannyasi* ascetic. He met with opposition from the Hindus, his own confreres, and Church leaders. He had some success, but in the end there was no one to take his place.

Matteo RICCI, SJ (1552–1610), entered China in 1582. He learned the language and culture exceptionally well. He made adaptations in the use of language and the manner of celebrating the sacraments, and continued to allow his converts to venerate Confucius and their ancestors. These rites would become the source of bitter controversy.

While the Kings of Spain and Portugal were responsible for the missions under their patronage, it was the business community that supported the French missions to North America. Seculars, Recollects, and Jesuits all came, as did lay men and, for the first time, Religious women.

Re-Structuring the Activity. The decline of missionaries available, especially for the Patronato Real system, and the centralizing process that was going on in Rome, resulted in the establishment of the Congregation for the PROPAGATION OF THE FAITH on Jan. 6, 1622. Its object was to help souls that were ''off the true path of salvation'' because of schism, heresy, or unbelief. The first Secretary, Francesco Ingoli (1622–1649), worked to appoint secular priests as Vicars Apostolic, to recruit diocesan clergy for its mission, and to develop an indigenous clergy.

A Decline in the Activity. The eighteenth century saw a decline in missionary activity. Two major causes of this were the Rites controversy and the suppression of the Jesuits.

The CHINESE RITES CONTROVERSY and the INDIAN RITES CONTROVERSY arose from the practices which Matteo Ricci and Roberto de Nobili respectively allowed their new Christians. The denunciation of these to Rome in 1645 began a century-long conflict. Condemnations were made, withdrawn, and then made again. In 1742 Benedict XIV condemned the Rites.

The suppression of the Jesuits came about not because of corruption or laxity but because they had many enemies, especially among the Jansenists and the enlightened philosophers and rulers of the day. In 1758 they were suppressed in Portugal and all its possessions; in 1762 in France and all its possessions; in 1767 in Spain and all its possessions; and in 1773 in the Catholic world by the decree of Clement XIV.

The Nineteenth and Early Twentieth Century Missionary Revival. During the time of the French Napoleonic Wars Europe was too disorganized to send missionaries, and the entire movement almost came to a halt. But after 1815 a missionary outreach from Europe and then later North America began that would remain vital up to and immediately after World War II. The story of the individuals and groups who went out and the people they encountered is fascinating, but here only a few characteristics of this revival can be described.

The revival was Rome-directed and Rome-supported. The Congregation for the Propagation of the Faith played the role intended for it at its founding. It defined boundaries of the Vicariates, assigned territories to Religious orders, appointed Vicars Apostolic, and collected information. Also the Popes played a direct role in giving support to missionaries (e.g. Gregory XVI, Pius IX) and later gave direction to the work through mission encyclicals (e.g. Pius XI, Pius XII).

Catholic missionary endeavors were no longer supported by the generosity of the royalty or rich merchants but by the Catholic faithful. The Society for the PROPAGATION OF THE FAITH was founded by Pauline Jaricot in France in 1822. In Austria the Leopolidinenstiftung, in Bavaria the LUDWIG MISSIONSVEREIN, and in Aachen the Xaveriusverein were all established in the 1840s. There were many other support agencies as well.

Their activity was challenged by Protestant Missionary Societies, especially from England, Germany, and the United States of America. At times the presence of Catholic and Protestant Missionary Societies in the same area provoked conflict (e.g. Uganda), at times competition (e.g. New Guinea), and at times cooperation (e.g. Gambia). The revival was fed by many new missionary societies founded in all the European and North American countries. These were not only clerical religious but also Brothers' and Sisters' congregations. Mission work now included education, health care, and social services.

Finally, the revival for the most part formed friendly relations with the imperial powers. Often there was close collaboration with political protectorates (e.g. Indochina) as well as religious protectorates (e.g. China). Missionaries expected their governments to negotiate for freedom of religion (e.g. Siam and Japan) so they could evangelize. In the colonies they tended to collaborate with the colonial powers in carrying out their aims (e.g. ending slave trade) although they would object at times to oppression (e.g. the hut-tax in East Africa).

Because of these factors the nineteenth and early twentieth century Catholic missionaries took on certain characteristics. They tended to be highly nationalistic and concerned about the imperial interests of their home government. They came for the most part from the conservative, devotional stream of Catholicism and would propagate these devotions and be ultramontane in sentiment and actions. They also would be reluctant to adapt to other cultures.

The Post-Colonial World. World War II and its aftermath left the world in a different situation as far as missions were concerned. Many of the former colonies claimed independence right after the war, and by the 1960s most of them had attained it. Often these nationalistic movements were tied to ancient religious and/or cultural revivals. Vatican II (1962–1965) also brought about a sea-change both in attitude and practice in what had been mission countries.

These changes in politics and in church life demanded changes in the missionary life of the Church as well. Indigenous leadership emerged; it took control of mission in its own lands. The removal of ''ius commissionis'' meant that territories no longer belonged to specific religious congregations but to local bishops. Bishops' Conferences began to give guidance to and coordinate the activity of Churches in their part of the world. While evangelization was still emphasized, there was a strong emphasis on development, liberation, dialogue with other religions, and inculturation as well. All of this has opened a new phase in the Church's mission history.

Bibliography: G. H. ANDERSON, ed., *Biographical Dictionary of Christian Mission* (New York 1998). S. DELACROIX, ed., *Histoire universelle des missions catholiques* 4 v. (Paris 1956). S. NEILL, *A History of Christian Missions* (Hammondsworth 1986). N. THOMAS, ed., *Classic Texts in Mission and World Christianity* (Maryknoll, NY 1995). T. E. YATES, *Christian Mission in the Twentieth Century* (Cambridge 1994).

[L. NEMER]

MISSION HISTORY, II: ORTHODOX

From the Eastern Mediterranean the gospel spread throughout the Roman Empire. Before Byzantium and Rome separated in 1054, both had evangelized, and both had success in their own spheres of influence. There were divisions in the Eastern Church before 1054 so that not all the missionary work done in the East can be considered part of Orthodox missions. To attribute the work of the Copts and Nestorians to the Orthodox Church is to ignore the real theological differences between the Chalcedonian and non-Chalcedonian factions. The common thread, however, that unites the missionary practice of all the Eastern Churches, both those in fellowship with Constantinople and the so-called lesser or Oriental Churches, is the use of the vernacular languages in the church. The missionaries translated the liturgical services and the Bible into the language of the people, which meant that Christianity became part of the cultural heritage of the country. The corollary is, of course, that national identity was sometimes bought at the price of losing a sense of the unity of the one Church.

Cosmas Indicopleustes, in the 6th century, knew of Orthodox missionaries "among the Bactrians, Huns, Indians, Armenians, Medians and Elamites." He also mentioned the Thomas Christians in India and Christian communities in Ceylon. The Assyrian (Nestorian) monument at Xi'an-fu bears witness to the existence of that missionary church in 7th-century China. The Assyrian missionaries suffered a severe reversal when the Tang dynasty ordered the dissolution of the monasteries which, while aimed at curbing Buddhism, also affected the Assyrians, whose strength lay in the monastic movement.

From the 8th to the 10th century the Byzantine Church competed with Rome for the winning of the Slavs, and converted them through the labors of Saints CYRIL AND METHODIUS and their disciples. There were Latin missionaries who participated in the conversion of Russia, even if the journeys of Adalbert of Trier (961–962) and Bruno of Querfurt were unsuccessful. The Baptism (*c.* 988–989) of St. VLADIMIR of Kiev (956–1015) brought his people into the Byzantine Church. After the Schism of 1054, the conversion of the Slavic peoples to Eastern Christianity meant that the subsequent missionary expansion in vast areas of Euro-Asia followed the Byzantine pattern.

Russian Medieval Missions. Because of the constant warfare connected with the CRUSADES and the subsequent expansion of the Turkish empire leading to the fall of Constantinople in 1453, the Byzantine Church had little opportunity to spread the faith. The period of Ottoman rule (from 1300–1922) was difficult for the Orthodox Church, though even under the onerous burdens imposed on non-Muslims, the witness of Orthodox Christians produced converts from among their oppressors. These converts were often martyred shortly after their profession of faith in Christ as apostates to Islam, but their existence demonstrates the vitality of the Eastern Church which continued unabated.

While missionary work was denied the Orthodox world under Ottoman rule, the Russian Church was able to spread the faith. This church deserves all the more recognition because it was jurisdictionally dependent on Byzantium until 1589. The early Russian mission extended, however, only to Slavs within the Kiev district of Russia. Early attempts to evangelize non-Slav neighbors cost the lives of men such as Isaja of Rostov (11th century) and Kuksáa (mid-12th century).

The shift of power from Kiev to Novogorod led to the colonization of the Ugro-Finnish settlements to the northeast. For the first time a characteristic feature of Russian Orthodox missionary history became evident: colonization entailed evangelization, and vice versa. The spread of the faith came about indirectly, since acceptance of Christianity meant a higher degree of civilization. The result was a Christian-pagan amalgamation.

Movement to the northeast became inevitable when the Mongols invaded Russia and captured Kiev (1240). In the turmoil that followed, a new type of Russian missionary appeared—the monk and the monastery. The reform of St. Sergei of Radonej (1314–92) inspired monks with missionary zeal. Monasteries, such as Valamo, Murmansk, and Solovkij, soon became mission centers. In this period Stephen of Perm (*c.* 1340–96) evangelized effectively among the Zyriani. He knew how to adjust to popular customs, which he elevated by translating the liturgy into the vernacular. His example helped the Permiaks, Chuvashes, Mordvins, and Lapps to accept Christianity.

New Direction in Mission. Domination by the Mongols, who had meanwhile become Muslims, ended in 1380, although 150 years passed before the last khanates were subdued along the Volga. The end of Mongol control led to a turning point, the beginning of organized missionary activity. Decisive in this respect was the changed attitude toward Islam, which came to be considered a pressing threat after the fall of Constantinople (1453). Henceforth, Russia considered itself the outpost of Christianity and protector of Orthodoxy. The titles of the czars, and the Eastern Roman double-headed eagle were expressions of the claim by Moscow to be the "Third Rome."

This change appeared in a new understanding of the missions. In 1552 Kazan, the last bulwark of Muslim Tatars on the Volga, fell. The journey of Gurij, the first archbishop, to Kazan was celebrated as a triumph of Christianity over pagans and Muslims. The mission itself, however, became an undertaking of the state, which dispatched, protected, and supported the missionaries.

Siberia and China. A few years later the conquest of Siberia began. In 1582 the Tatar khanates of Siberia fell. In 1619 the Jenissei was crossed, and in 1632 the eastern extremities of the Lena River. In 1648 Cossacks reached the Pacific Ocean, thereby opening an enormous missionary field. Again colonization involved evangelization, and evangelization colonization or Russification. The tasks connected with the conquest of Siberia were taken in hand by PETER I, THE GREAT (1682–1725), at a time when China placed obstacles in the way of Russian expansion. Thus began the dramatic history of Sino-Russian relations. The Kangxi (K'ang-hsi) Emperor (1662–1722) ordered Russian expansion to stop at the Amur. Nevertheless the Treaty of Nerchinsk (1689) permitted the presence of a Russian Orthodox mission in Beijing (Peking). In the Treaty of Kiachta (1727) Russian missionaries were recognized as their country's diplomatic representatives to the Chinese court. There was hardly any missionary activity, but Russia had, over other countries, the advantage of being present in Beijing. The Chinese situation being what it was, more attention was then paid to the mission in Siberia. Kamchatka and the Yakut, Buryat, and Chukchi tribes were absorbed by the Orthodox Church. From Siberia the mission spread to the Aleutians and Alaska, where monks from Valamo worked *c.* 1800.

19th Century. In the 19th century the Russian Orthodox mission experienced a revival, resulting partly from a renewal of Russian piety and partly from the influence of Western pietism. This revival led to the foundation of the Russian Orthodox Biblical Society (1813). Kazan became the center of mission renewal and the scene of the beginning (1854) of missionary science. Makarij Glucharev (1792–1847), the founder of the Altai mission, was extremely progressive in his understanding of mission. He only baptized his converts after an extensive period of instruction and established schools and clinics.

Innokentij Veniaminov (1797–1879), the apostle of the Russian Far East, was one of the greatest Christian missionaries of the 19th century. Traveling to Russian Alaska with his family, he constructed his own dwelling and the church, learned to navigate a kayak to visit his far flung flock and was a conscientious observer of native customs as well as flora and fauna. He composed an alphabet for the Aleut language and his linguistic ability enabled him to properly instruct the converts in Christian faith. One of the books he wrote in Aleut, *Indication of the Way into the Kingdom of God*, was translated into Russian and between 1839 and 1855 was published in 46 editions. Upon the death of his wife, he took monastic vows and was consecrated bishop of Kamchatka, the Kurilian and the Aleutian Islands. Later all Siberia was added to his jurisdiction. Veniaminov, who became metropolitan of Moscow, established a missionary society (1870) which contributed to the Church's recognition of its mission obligations. Veniaminov's plans for evangelization extended to Japan and Korea. He encouraged the apostle of the Orthodox in Japan, Nikolai Kasatkin (1836–1912), to work for the conversion of the Japanese. The liturgy in the vernacular, a native Japanese clergy, and the sacrifice of political goals helped the Orthodox Church make great progress in Japan within a few decades. Kasatkin, who had been elevated to bishop, stayed with his flock during the Russo-Japanese War instead of returning to Russia. The mission in China was first relieved of its diplomatic function by the Peace of Aigun (1858). After the Boxer Rebellion a diocese was established in Beijing, but in 1914 the mission had only 5,000 disciples. In proportion to their numerical strength, the Orthodox Church lost more adherents in the Boxer Rebellion than either the Catholic or Protestant Churches.

Early Twentieth Century. The Russian Revolution (1917) put an effective halt to all missionary work of the Russian Orthodox Church by stopping the flow of funds. Most impacted was the mission to Japan which, while it never had many missionaries, was dependent on the support of the mother church. The Orthodox Church of Japan was forced by the Japanese government to sever its ties with Moscow and declare itself independent in 1940. After World War II the Church submitted to the Metropolitanate of North America. When this jurisdiction became the ORTHODOX CHURCH IN AMERICA, the Japan Orthodox Church retained its autonomous status under the Patriarchate of Moscow.

The mission in China was strengthened by the immigration of White Russian refugees, but the ministry among the Russians was at the expense of the missionary work among the Chinese. The Orthodox Church in China suffered when the Communists came to power. The last Russian hierarch, Archbishop Victor, left in 1956 and most of the parishioners emigrated to Australia or America. There appears to be only one functioning Orthodox Church in China comprised of elderly Russians that is in the city of Haerbin (Harbin).

Fresh Starts in Mission. During and after World War II, old missionary dioceses were able to be reorganized, even in Russia. Some of them carry the names of each respective race in their title. It was only after the Greek Civil War that missionary interest was rekindled in Greece, primarily through the agency of the Inter Orthodox Center for Mission. Founded by Anastasios Yannoulatos, the center sponsored missionary lectures and for a decade (1959–1969) published a very influential journal, *Porefendes* (''Go Ye'') in both Greek and English editions. The journal discussed not only the activities of missionaries but also mission strategy and theology.

The impetus for missionary advance came with the incorporation under the Patriarchate of Alexandria of an African initiated church, the African Orthodox Church, whose leadership sought to connect to the original expression of Christianity. Many had been Anglicans and they sought a form of Christianity that would not make them subject to the major Christian traditions already present in East Africa. One of the founding leaders, Spartas (Reuben Mukasa from Uganda), toured Greece (1959) and generated interest in the work in Africa. Both the Church of Greece and the Greek Orthodox Archdiocese of North and South America responded with financial assistance and with missionaries. The liturgy was translated into Kikuyu and a seminary was established in Kenya to train clergy. The African Orthodox Church received significant assistant from Cyprus when the head of the autocephalous Church of Cyprus, Archbishop Markrios, took an interest in the work, making several journeys to the developing churches. The leadership of the work in East Africa has come from Greece and Cyprus. Bearing the title of Archbishop of Irinoupolis and All East Africa, this see has been occupied by Archbishop Anastasios Yannoulatos, one of the architects of the Orthodox missionary revival. The last two Metropolitans, Seraphim and Makarios Tillyrides are both Cypriots. At the turn of the 21st century there are an estimated 600,000 African Orthodox in Kenya with smaller communities numbering 50,000 in Uganda and 10,000 in Tanzania. Elsewhere there is Orthodox missionary work in Ghana and Cameroon. Mission work has been undertaken in Indonesia through the efforts of a convert from Islam, Father Daniel Bambang D. Byantoro. Again, there is benefit in the lack of a colonial connection and the fact that the patterns of Orthodoxy appear more adaptable to the cultures of the Orient in the use of forms and symbols. There are the beginnings of missionary work in other Asian nations.

Orthodox Diaspora and Mission. Because of the dispersion of traditional Orthodox peoples, the Orthodox Church is represented on all six inhabited continents. In most places the Orthodox community established congregations and sent back to their country of origin for clergy to minister among them. While technically not missionary work, these outposts of Orthodoxy served to attract people to the Orthodox Church. This has been true in Australia, Africa, Europe and North America. In many places the Orthodox Church has the advantage of not being associated with any colonial power. The transplanted Orthodox and the few missionaries that were sent out were not identified with an oppressive Western presence. The focus on indigenous clergy also helped to remove a foreign stigma. Indeed the rapid advancement of nationals into ministry positions, necessitated by the paucity of missionary personnel became a virtue as the churches that developed were quickly seen as belonging to the converts.

Missionary work has recommenced with missionaries being sent from both the Inter Orthodox Mission Center in Athens, Greece, and the Orthodox Christian Mission Center in St. Augustine, Florida. The latter is a pan-Orthodox society, sending out missionaries from various ethnic jurisdictions in North America and is perhaps one of the best examples of inter-Orthodox cooperation. Sponsoring both short term and career missionaries, the center is actively supporting the rebuilding of the Church in Albania under the direction of Anastasios (Yannoulatos) Archbishop of Tirana, Durres and All Albania. Missionary information can be gathered from the publication (in Greek) of the Inter Orthodox Mission Center's *Panta ta Ethne* (To All the World) and the Orthodox Christian Mission Center's *OCMC Missionary Magazine.*

Mention should be made of conversions from Protestant denominations to Eastern Orthodoxy. Peter Gilquist, former staff worker with Campus Crusade for Christ, led a group of evangelical protestants that had formed their own church into the Antiochian Orthodox Archdiocese of North America. A missionary presence within the Antiochian Church, they have established missionary parishes in North America that actively proselytize. Many of the current Eastern Orthodox missionary force from North America are former evangelicals. In addition there have been other converts attracted to the Orthodox Church so that between 30 and 40 percent of the students at St. Vladimir's Orthodox Seminary, sponsored by the Orthodox Church in America are converts to Orthodoxy. One notable convert is Franky Schaeffer, son of the evangelical apologist, Francis Schaeffer.

Bibliography: J. GLAZIK, *Die russisch-orthodoxe Heidenmission seit Peter dem Grossen* (Münster 1954); *Die Islammission der russisch-orthodoxen Kirche* (Münster 1959). S. BOLSHAKOFF, *The Foreign Missions of the Russian Orthodox Church* (London 1943). G. FLOROVSKY, ''Russian Missions: An Historical Sketch,'' *The Christian East* 14 (1933) 30–41. E. SMIRNOV, *A Short Account of the Historical Development and Present Position of Russian Orthodox Missions* (London 1903). J. STAMOOLIS, *Eastern Orthodox Mission Theology Today* (Maryknoll 1986, Minneapolis 1993). I. VENIAMINOV, *Notes on the Islands of the Unalaska District* (Fairbanks, reprint 1984). L. VERONIS, *Missionaries, Monks, Martyrs: Making Disciples of All Nations* (Minneapolis 1994). P. GARRETT, *St. Innocent: Apostle to America* (Crestwood, New York 1979). F. WELBOURN, *East African Rebels: A Study of Some Independent Churches* (London 1961). M. OLEKSA, *Orthodox Alaska* (Crestwood, New York 1992).

[J. GLAZIK/J. J. STAMOOLIS]

MISSION HISTORY, III: PROTESTANT

This entry gives: (1) a brief history of Protestant missions, and (2) a survey of their status as at the beginning of the 21st century.

History

Protestants were slow in taking up missionary work among non-Christians. This was partly because they were engrossed in consolidating their position in Europe and also because some of their early leaders believed that the obligation to spread the faith did not apply to them. But the delay was chiefly attributable to the fact that Protestants were late in establishing commercial or colonial contacts with non-Christian peoples. When Protestantism was still in its infancy, and even before it had been born, Spanish and Portuguese Catholics had led in the explorations and conquests of the 15th and 16th centuries and under the impulse of Roman Catholic reform had initiated extensive mission in the Americans, Africa, Asia and the East Indies.

The English and the Dutch were the first Protestants to undertake commerce and colonization on a large scale outside of Europe. Wherever they made contact with non-Christian peoples some missionary effort followed, although tardily in some countries. Thus in Virginia and New England, especially the latter, missions to the Indians were inaugurated in the 17th century. Early in the 18th century the (Anglican) SOCIETY FOR THE PROPAGATION OF THE GOSPEL in Foreign Parts (est. 1701) sent missionaries to the indigenous tribes in the 13 colonies. Dutch missionaries went to the East Indies. In the 18th century, under the impulse of Count Zinzendorf, the Moravians had missions in the Danish and British West Indies, India, Ceylon (Sri Lanka), Russia, Central America, Greenland, Labrador, the Gold Coast, and South Africa, as well as among North American peoples. In the 18th century, beginning in 1706 under the auspices of the King of Denmark, German Pietists had missions in India and were aided by the (Anglican) SOCIETY FOR THE PROMOTING CHRISTIAN KNOWLEDGE (est. 1699). Thus, the first Protestant missionaries to Asia were Germans, Bartholomew Ziegenbalg and Henry Plutschau

Missionary Societies. Protestant missions had their main beginning in the closing decade of the 18th and the opening decades of the 19th centuries. In 1792, at the insistence of William CAREY, the Baptist Missionary Society was founded in England. The following year it sent Carey to India. There he and his colleagues translated the Bible into the languages of India and into Chinese, and founded a college at Serampore that became the chief center for the training of native peoples for the Protestant ministry. Bible translation and educational work would be major concerns of all Protestant missionary work. In 1795 British evangelicals who did not conform to the Church of England organized the London Missionary Society. Four years later evangelicals within the Church of England inaugurated the Church Missionary Society. In 1804 evangelicals, both Nonconformists and Conformist Anglican, organized the British and Foreign Bible Society. In continental Europe Protestant societies emerged also. Among them were the Netherlands Missionary Society (1797) and the Basel Missionary Society (1822). In the U.S. the interdenominational (chiefly Congregational) American Board of Commissioners for Foreign Missions was initiated in 1810, and in 1814 American Baptists founded a missionary society. In the next few years a number of societies were founded, most of them as organs of particular denominations. In 1816 members of several denominations united in the American Bible Society.

Protestant missions were given a major impulse from various revival movements in the English speaking world which culminated in 1886 with the formation of the STUDENT VOLUNTEER MOVEMENT for Foreign Missions (SVM). It had as its watchword: ''the evangelization of the world in this generation.'' By this was meant not the conversion of the whole world, but the conveying of a knowledge of the gospel by each generation of Christians to their generation the world over. The SVM was nondenominational. It spread among students in many countries. One of its original members, John R. MOTT (1865–1955), was long its chair. Under its influence thousands of students offered themselves to their denominational societies and were sent to many different countries. Mott became an evangelist to students in scores of countries. In one of his widely read books, *Strategic Points in the World's Conquest* (1897), he outlined a program for winning all people to Christ. The book and the movement reflected the progressive, optimistic Protestant missionary spirit of the age.

Mott became the chief agent also in bringing Protestants together to fulfill the purpose of the evangelization of the world and was chairman of the World Missionary Conference (Edinburgh, 1910). Out of this gathering came, first, the Continuation Committee of the conference and then (1921) the INTERNATIONAL MISSIONARY COUNCIL (IMC). Both had Mott as chairman. The purpose of the IMC was the coordination of Protestant missionary effort the world over. It had as members national and regional bodies. The members in Asia and Africa were called National Christian Councils, and increasingly enlisted the Protestants of these lands. In America and Europe the members were bodies that represented the

Protestant missionary organization of their respective countries or regions. The IMC embraced the overwhelming majority of the Protestants of the world. Substantial minorities held aloof, chiefly and increasingly, on doctrinal grounds. By the 1960s the World Evangelical Fellowship (founded 1951) was growing rapidly and in 1974 the Lausanne Committee on World Evangelization was formed as alternative Protestant mission organizations.

In 1961 the IMC was integrated with the WORLD COUNCIL OF CHURCHES (WCC) and became the Commission on World Mission and Evangelism of that body. The WCC (est. 1948) was to a large degree an outgrowth of the Protestant missionary movement. After 1961 the organization of Protestant missions becomes more diverse worldwide. There are three main reasons for the rapid growth and diversification of Protestant mission societies after 1961. First, many churches and individuals felt that the greater dialogue with Roman Catholics and the WCC unit on ''Dialog with People of other Living Faiths'' were signs of compromise and a change in mission theology. The 1973 call for a moratorium on foreign missions, first by John Gatu, General Secretary of the Presbyterian Church of East Africa, further divided what would be called the ''ecumenical'' missions from the ''evangelical'' or ''independent'' missions. Secondly, the sudden national movements of independence from 1945–1969 where 71 non-western nations became independent encouraged the diversification of Protestant missions. Many of these new countries identified themselves with a non-Christian religion and restricted Christian missionaries. As a result new indigenous mission societies were founded and new Protestant missionary societies were founded with particular countries, regions or religions in view. On the average over 100 new mission societies have been founded each decade for the past 30 years in North America. More significantly for the diversification and multiplication of mission societies has been the explosion of non-western mission societies in countries like Korea, India, Taiwan and Brazil. Cooperation among societies has been more a matter of relationships and elective participation in umbrella organizations such as the World Evangelical Fellowship or World Pentecostal Fellowship, rather than official membership in an organization such as the WCC. Thirdly, the decline in denominationalism in the West and sudden drop in communications costs has encouraged the formation of mission societies by local churches or groups of churches often by-passing the national church bodies.

Developments. From the beginning of Protestant missionary endeavor there has been a primary interest in translation work and educational work to train future church leaders. Church planting was always related to the production of Bibles in the local language and literacy work. Another aspect was the fostering of efforts to influence wholesomely, from the standpoint of Christians, various aspects of the cultures in which missionaries lived. Protestant missions worked in association with Western enterprises that profoundly influenced non-western portions of the globe. The impact of the West brought about a mounting revolution in these areas. Protestant missionaries endeavored to prepare non-Western peoples for this and to make the resulting changes beneficial rather than harmful. To do so they introduced western medicine and surgery, training physicians and nurses in Western techniques, promoted public health, established schools that combined western and indigenous learning (e.g. ''Anglo-Chinese Schools''), pioneered in improved methods of agriculture and forestry, fought famines and such evils as opium and slavery, sought to improve the status and education of women, fostered Christian standards of marriage and family life produced Christian literature, and strove to raise the level of rural life. This revolution in missionary work began before the middle of the 19th century.

In the 20th century, with the emergence of anti-colonialism in the non-western world, Protestant missions sought to deepen the foothold they had won among non-Europeans. In the East Asian Christian Conference, (est. 1954; renamed Christian Conference of Asia), with the aid of missionaries, the Protestants of that part of the world undertook cooperatively to spread the faith among their neighbors.

More and more the direction of the ''younger churches'' that had sprung up out of Protestant missions was transferred to indigenous leadership. Thus in India after the 1950s all Methodist bishops were men from India, the only Lutheran bishopric was transferred (1962) from a Swede to a native inhabitant, and an increasing proportion of Anglican bishops were native inhabitants. Similar developments were seen in Protestant churches that did not have bishops, not only in India, but also in other non-western countries. In 1958 the Theological Education Fund of U.S. $4 million was created and placed under the direction of the IMC. It had as its purpose the training of an indigenous Protestant clergy in Africa, Asia and Latin America and the islands of the Pacific. In 1963 an all-Africa (Protestant) Christian Conference met under African leadership and created a continuing organization to embrace the continent. Following World War II the Batak Protestants (Sumatra) became completely independent of foreign control and received only that help from missionaries for which they specifically asked.

In order to erase some of the church divisions which had been exported from the West, and to form a more united Christian front, Protestant Christians formed unions of diverse denominational bodies. Thus, in 1934 the Church of Christ in Thailand was formed, in 1941 the Church of Christ in Japan (*Koyodan*) was constituted and the Church of South India was formed in 1947. The latter's constituent members were Anglicans, Presbyterians, Congregationalists and members of the Reformed Church. It had an episcopate which sought apostolic succession through the (Anglican) Church of India, Myanmar and Sri Lanka. Other unions soon formed in several countries.

The cooperation and unions among churches that occurred from the 1930s through the 1980s shifted to become cooperation and sharing in mission without the organic unions. With the rapid growth in non-Orthodox and non-Roman Catholic Christianity in the last decades of the 20th century (house churches in China, Africa Independent Churches in Africa, etc.) came the need for new models of cooperation in mission. The largest global cooperation among Protestants for prayer and strategy came in the 1990s as the ''AD 2000 and Beyond Movement.'' This global and grassroots movement was supported mostly by non-western churches and had as its goal, ''A church for every people and the gospel for every person by the year 2000.'' Conferences were held to aid in the sharing of resources and plan cooperative strategies in Singapore (1989), Seoul (1995) and Pretoria (1997). One of the many resources used has been the *Jesus Film*, shown to over 2 billion people and translated into over 700 languages by 2001.

Five major shifts in Protestant mission have taken place since World War II, the first occurring immediately after the War was over. Independence movements caused a redistribution of missionary personal, and the spread of Communism in Eastern Europe and China reduced the mission activity further. The ascendancy of the United States as a world power paralleled its rapid growth in Protestant mission activity. The predominance of both personnel and financial support shifted from the British Isles and the Continent to the United States. The second major shift occurred in the late 1980s and early 1990s. With the democratic revolutions in Eastern Europe, the collapse of Communism in the Soviet republics and the new openness to the world in countries like Vietnam, Cambodia and China came new Protestant mission development in areas that had been ''closed.'' Along with new work, both official and unofficial, came one of the most rapid developments of Protestant work since the ''opening'' of China in the 1840s. Thousands of missionaries from Europe, the U.S. and Korea moved to the former Soviet republics and hundreds of others found ways to work in China. The third major shift has been taking place since World War II and that is the change from ecumenical to evangelical and independent missions. In 1954 about half of the 19,000 long term missionaries from North America were from mainline churches. Today less than 5% of the long-term missionaries from North America are from the ecumenical sending agencies. Fourth, whereas in 1910 western church bodies and mission agencies were discussing how to evangelize the world, today most of the church planting is being done by non-western missionaries. The fastest growing church in the world is in China and virtually all of the work is being done by Chinese. In Nepal, India and Myanmar and most nations of sub-Saharan Africa, the evangelistic and church planting work of mission are being done by nationals or missionaries from the region. Finally, the fastest growing missionary work in the world is now Pentecostal. Not only in Latin America, but also the missionary work in much of South and East Asia today is from Pentecostal groups both working regionally as well as from the West.

Protestant Mission in the 21st Century

A look at the four major regions of Protestant missions at the beginning of the second millennium shows the extent of the changes that have transpired.

Asia. Although Christianity has been introduced to China in the seventh, 13th, 16th and 19th centuries, it has been the most recent reintroduction, from within, which has had the greatest impact. With the deportation of all missionaries between 1948 and 1952, the Protestant churches suffered from closures, arrests of leaders and relocation of many Christians to work on farms or in factories. Even though the Christian population was estimated to be 1.5 million in 1948, today estimates vary between 15 million (Roman Catholic and China Christian Council—CCC) and 90 million (inclusive of non-registered churches). Most of this is Protestant Church and, except for some groups who began smuggling Bibles in the early 1980s, has all been done by Chinese. The formation of the Three Self Patriotic Movement (1954) and the CCC (1980) created a ''post-denominational'' church recognized by the government. However the largest number of Protestants today still meet in unregistered churches. Mission to China is coordinated and directed from the Amity Foundation with offices in Nanjing and Hong Kong. Korean church growth increased dramatically in the South after the Korean War. Thousands of Christians from the North migrated to the South and after the War churches and missions were reestablished with the help of many American missions. Today more than 40% of South Korea is Christian with the largest Christian church in the world (Yoido Full Gospel) and the largest Christian gatherings ever (15 million at Yoido) and many of the largest denominational churches and seminaries found in the world. These churches are very strong in their missionary leadership. For example, in 1996, 60,000 Korean students committed themselves to be missionaries at a gathering at the Seoul Olympic stadium.

With the gradual opening for travel to Vietnam and Cambodia, some educational and church missionary work has begun in these two countries. Most of the Protestant missionary work to these countries is also done by Asians. The largest number of missionaries is from Korea and diaspora Chinese communities working out of Singapore, Malaysia, Taiwan and Indonesia. A number of refugees from Cambodia and Vietnam (as well as China) have returned to work with Christians in their home countries or have organized missions in the West to reach their home countries. Although after the Pacific War it looked like both Thailand and Japan would have rapidly growing Christian communities, this never happened. Both countries, with a fairly large Protestant missionary presence, are still between 2 and 3.5% Christian. Nepal, until 1980, had less than 10,000 Christians. Today, mostly from the work of Indians and other Asians, plus the long-term service work of the United Mission to Nepal, there are over 500,000 Christians (2.4%) in Nepal. These are nearly all Protestant. Missionary work in Indonesia is mostly educational and medical now, but Indonesians are very active in missionary work within their own nation. Protestant Christianity is one of the five recognized religions in Indonesia (also Roman Catholicism, Buddhism, Hinduism and Islam) and it continues to grow in the midst of the largest Muslim population in the world. In Malaysia large numbers of Chinese and Indians have become Christians. However, except for tribal groups in East Malaysia (North Borneo) the *bumiputra* (indigenous Malay) are still mostly Muslim. India has one of the largest numbers of cross-cultural missionary groups in the world (after the United States), although most of their missionaries work within the sub-continent. Close to 40,000 Protestant Indian missionaries work full-time, mostly in church planting, literacy, educational and medical work. Northeast India (Nagaland, Mizoram and Meghalaya) is predominantly a Christian area sending out missionaries throughout the sub-continent. In many areas of India large movements of Dalits (untouchables) are turning to Christianity. In the Philippines, the dominance of missionaries from North America is now being challenged by missionaries from Korea. The Philippines now send out more missionaries (some to unreached areas within the Philippines) than it receives.

Africa. The 20th century in Africa, especially since the independence of most of the African nations, has marked one of the greatest religious changes in the history of Christianity. In 1900 Africa was less than 10% Christian. By 2000 it was nearly 46% Christian. Some of the fastest growing churches are not technically speaking Protestant, since they don't trace their lineage to a Protestant denomination or split. Many of these African Initiated (or Independent) Churches have been started by local prophets—often resisting western domination—with a vision for planting churches in different regions in Africa. Two of the main streams of AICs are the Ethiopian stream (looking to Ethiopia for their Christian heritage) and the Zionist churches (which tend to be more Pentecostal in worship and mission). South Africa has had the largest number of AICs which, after the collapse of apartheid in 1991 continued to multiply and divide. Today there are nearly as many African missionaries serving cross-culturally as there are foreign (western and Asian) missionaries working in Africa. Political struggles in countries like Uganda, Republic of Congo, Ethiopia, and Nigeria, tribal conflicts in countries like Rwanda, Burundi, Sierra Leone and Liberia and religious conflict between Islam and Christianity have all affected the missionary work in Africa. The attempt to impose Islam on southern Sudan, for example has led to the longest running civil war of the century; over three million people displaced from their homes, over two million deaths and yet a church growth in the south from 5% in 1960 to over 70% in 2001. Northern Africa is still mostly all Muslim with only small Christian communities scattered across the Sahara.

Eastern Europe, West and Central Asia. With the independence of nations of the Middle East came a rise in Islamic consciousness. Countries like Lebanon and Syria have had a marked decline of Protestant Christians with mission work increasingly difficult to maintain. Islamic regimes in places like Iraq, Iran, Afghanistan and Pakistan have all but stopped ongoing Protestant missionary work except in small ''tentmaking'' operations. Upon the collapse of the Soviet Republics in 1991 missionary work suddenly took off in countries like Russia, Albania, Yugoslavia and Romania, largely with Americans, Western Europeans and Koreans. The response has been mixed with large rallies and media events in countries like Albania and Romania having a great impact, but in areas like Eastern Germany and Poland there have not been large Protestant movements. In most of the central Asian republics there has been a large influx of Protestant missionaries since 1991, although the overall impact is minimal. In countries like Uzbekistan the rising tide of Islam has caused a great exodus of Christians from the country.

Latin America. A century ago nearly all of Latin America was Roman Catholic. The twentieth century has been marked by a decline in religious belief in general, but also a growth in Protestantism. Brazil is the largest country with over 170 million people, 22 million who are now Protestant. Brazil sends more missionaries out of the country today than they receive. As with most of Latin America, the fastest growing churches in Brazil are Pentecostal or Charismatic in theology and worship. In all of Latin America and the Caribbean Protestant and Independent churches are growing at a rate of about 4% per year, compared to the annual population growth rate of only 1.6%. Still, in most countries of Latin America, the Protestant population is only between five and 15% of the total population. As with much of Africa, the missionary work in these countries will be related to poverty, disease and political stability, since most of the poorest countries of the world are found in Africa and Latin America.

Bibliography: K. S. LATOURETTE, *A History of the Expansion of Christianity*, 7 v. (New York, 1937–45); *Christianity in a Revolutionary Age*, 5 v. (New York, 1958–62); S. W. SUNQUIST, ed. *A Dictionary of Asian Christianity* (Grand Rapids, 2001); BARRETT, KURIAN and JOHNSON, *World Christian Encyclopedia* (Oxford, 2000).

[K. S. LATOURETTE/S. W. SUNQUIST]

MISSION IN COLONIAL AMERICA, I (SPANISH MISSIONS)

The Christianization of the aborigines of America and their incorporation into Western civilization was most effectively accomplished through the mission. With the support of the Iberian kings and the PATRONATO REAL, religious orders developed this method of catechizing the native Americans. The system itself will be discussed first and then the application in North, Central, and South America.

Mission System

In 1573 Philip II of Spain issued a long directive on conquests and settlements that forbade the extension of the encomienda system beyond the territory in which it was then established. The directive marked the end of the encomienda-doctrina as a means of incorporating into Church or State the pagan Native Americans along the frontier. A new agency had to be developed for this task, and after an initial period of uncertainty, this was done. It is called the mission, although the word did not appear in Spanish legislation for many decades. In the mission, the Native American was to be kept in involuntary isolation from the European under the direct care of the priest and the mercenary soldier. Basically, the difference between the mission and the ENCOMIENDA-DOCTRINA SYSTEM lay not in the objective, for that remained the same, but in the means. The major responsibility for the exploration of new lands, for settling the Native Americans and controlling them, building the churches and other needed buildings, maintaining the roads and ships with which to

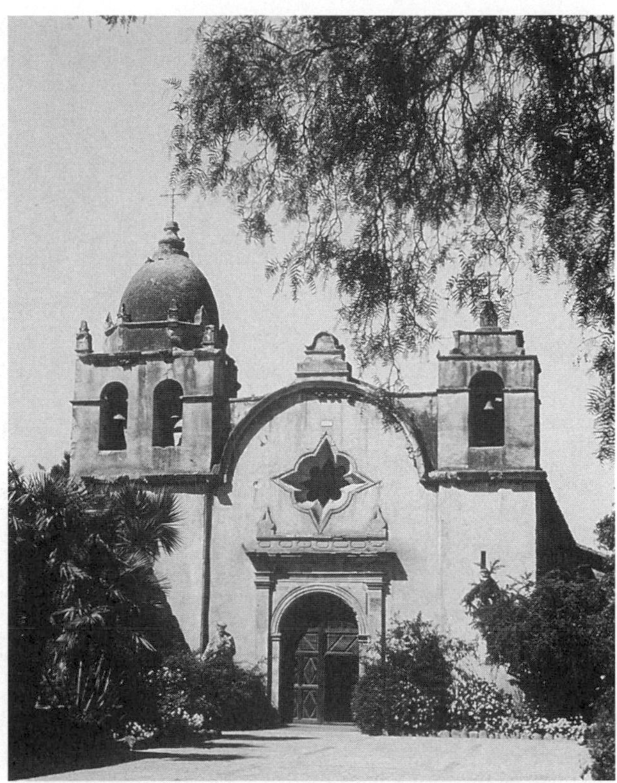

Carmel Mission, Carmel, California. (©Bettmann/CORBIS)

bring in supplies, etc., now fell directly or indirectly on the priests, most of whom were not trained to cope with such tasks. Some aspects of the mission dated from experiments in the very beginning of the Spanish colonial effort in the Americas. The new agency was begun at almost the same time at the two extremes of Spanish America: northwestern New Spain and the area near Buenos Aires. In the north it was initiated by the Jesuits under Gonzalo Tapia and in the south by the Franciscans under Luis de BOLAÑOS. It is curious that today the Jesuits are perhaps best remembered for their missions in the Rio de la Plata area, whereas the Franciscans are possibly best known for their missions at the extreme northern border of New Spain. Although the Dominicans did much to develop the idea of the mission, they did relatively little work as missionaries, perhaps due to the inability of harmonizing the needs of the mission with commitments contracted under the doctrina. In general, the same is true of the Augustinians and Mercedarians. In the 17th century the crown sent the Capuchins of Valencia to work in eastern Venezuela. Their missions were well conducted.

The bulk of the mission work in Spanish America was carried on by the Jesuits and Franciscans. Both orders suffered a severe crisis as a result of the need to supply trained men. The Jesuits in the mid-17th century solved it in great measure by enlisting German missiona-

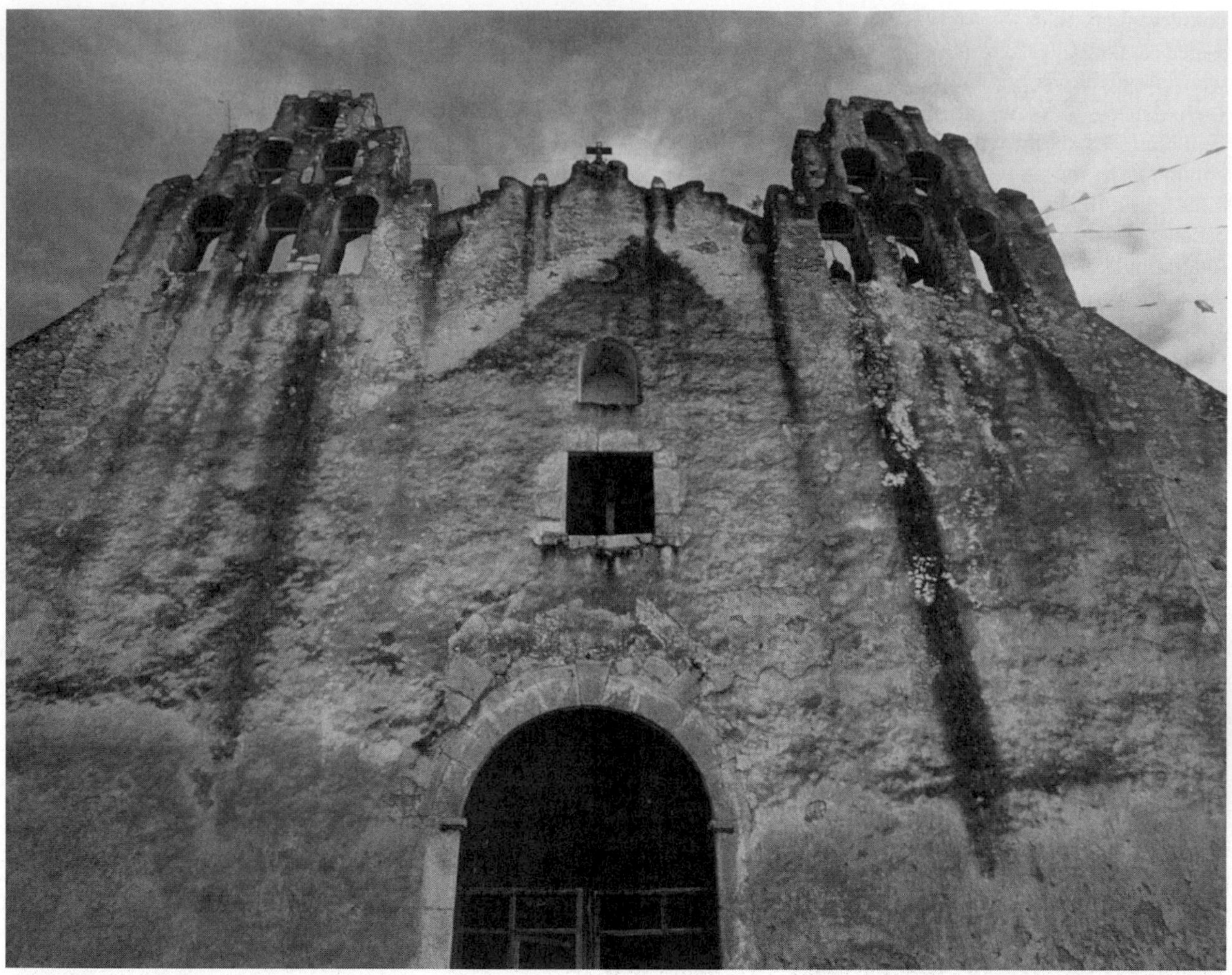

Franciscan Church of Muna, Muna, Mexico. (©Vanni Archive/CORBIS)

ries. The Franciscans at about the same time reached a solution in founding the Mission College. In 1767, the year of the expulsion of the Jesuits from Spanish America, it is estimated that there were about one million natives in all missions in Spanish America. Of these, the Jesuits cared for about 700,000; the Franciscans, about 250,000.

Financial Support. A mission was an expensive institution, and the crown generously offered to defray some of the expense. Royal support was of two kinds: a subsidy to each mission at the time of its foundation for the purchase of a chalice, bells, and other necessary supplies, and for the yearly salary of the missionary. The salary varied somewhat over the vast expanse of the empire, but generally it ranged from 350 to 450 pesos each year: a truly handsome sum at that time. Of course, royal financial support also gave the royal officials a means of control over the mission and the missionaries. Some, especially the Jesuits, tried to free themselves from excessive interference by securing alms. The Pious Fund, begun in 1697 for Lower California, was perhaps the most famous example of this type of financing. In 1693 the Franciscans in Peru founded a similar society called the Apostolic Administrators, but it was not nearly as successful. Usually the government gave funds for the founding of a mission, but often, with political motives, dictated where the mission was to be established. The missionaries soon recognized this, and their reports were often drawn up to stress the political aspect of their work. In Texas they stressed the danger from the French; in California, from the Russians; in Maynas (Peru), from the Portuguese slave raiders; and in Paraguay, from the Paulistas. Only too often, though, if there were no political motives, a mission would either not be founded, or, if it were, it could expect only sporadic assistance from the royal treasury.

Organization and Operation. The mission was a school of religion, civilization, and political government,

Church and monastery of San Francisco, built by the Spanish, mid-1600s, Lima, Peru, photograph c. 1860. (©Michael Maslan Historic Photographs/CORBIS)

although actually the three aspects were considered inseparable in the minds of most missionaries. In effect, the task was the changing of the nomadic Native American of the frontier into a copy of the town-loving Spaniard. A prerequisite was the settlement of the nomads in or close to the mission center. Sometimes the native people themselves were willing to surrender their freedom in order to be protected from their more powerful enemies. Often the missionary was able to persuade them to do so through kindness and gifts, or friendly Native Americans who had already joined a mission would persuade them. A rancher, miner, or lay military leader might influence them. Some missionaries, few in number, are known to have used force to bring the Native American under the control of the mission. Once a native had been enrolled in a mission, the mission used every means in its power, including force, to keep him there.

To instruct the Native American in the faith, the missionary drew heavily on the methods developed by the doctrina, but generally the missionary was able to exert a much stricter control over his charges than the doctrinero. Mission life was governed by the mission bell to such an extent that the expression *bajo la campana* came to signify a mission Native American. Hence, the resemblance of the mission to monastic life was usually much stronger than in the *doctrina*, even often in the separation of the boys from the girls into separate dormitories under close supervision.

As a center of civilization, the mission was often a vast industrial school, of which the largest might number 2,000 pupils as in Upper California, or even 7,000 as in the REDUCTIONS OF PARAGUAY. There would be a weaving center, blacksmith shop, tannery, sugar refinery, wine press, warehouses, vegetable gardens, and grain fields, while on the ranches there were often thousands of heads

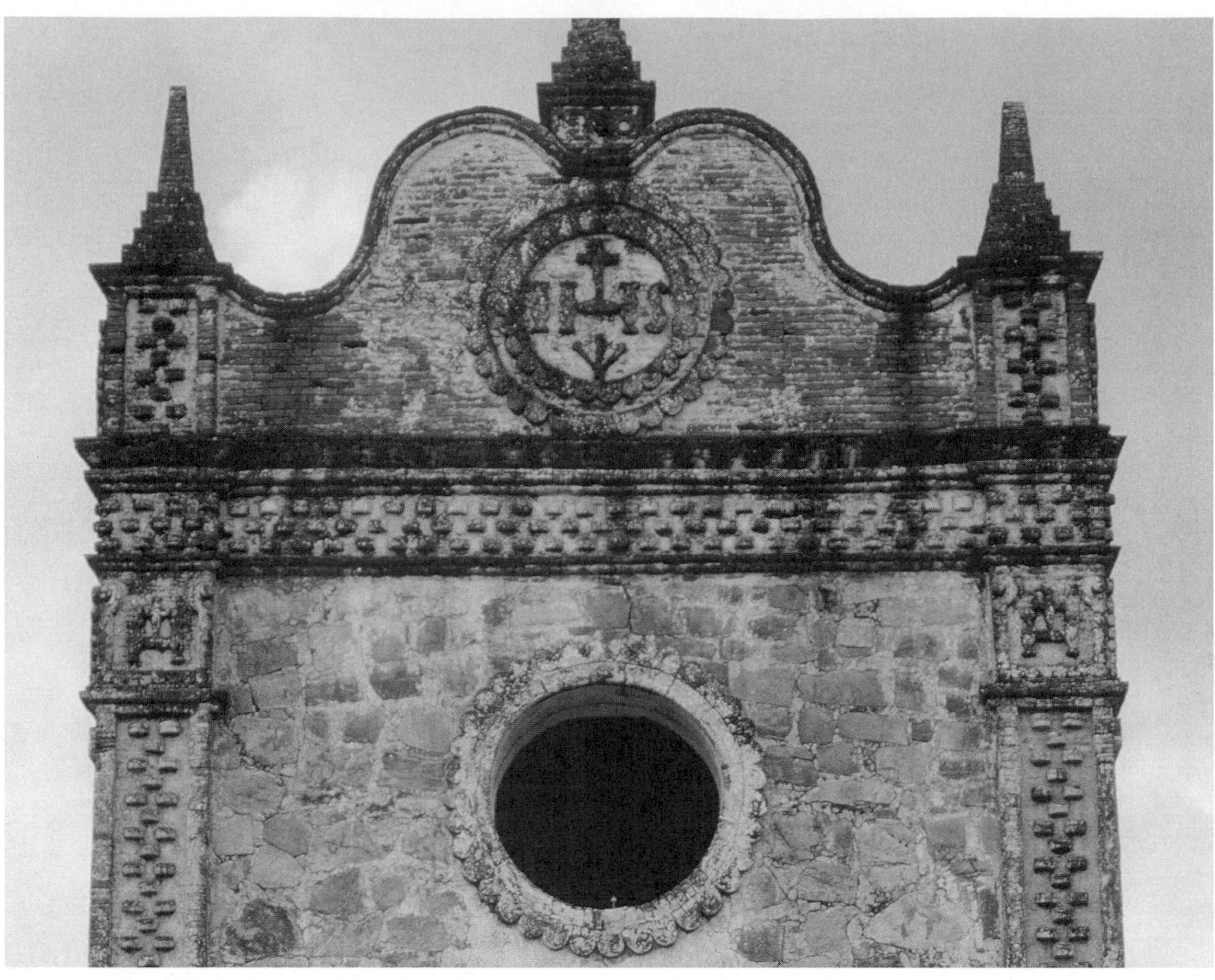

Tower of Jesuit church, built by Father Felipe Suarez, San Jose de Chiquitos, Bolivia. (©Boja Brecelj/CORBIS)

of cattle, horses, sheep, pigs, and goats. The women were charged with cooking, spinning, weaving, and sewing. Often there would be a carpentry shop or a shop for the making of adobes or for cutting stone. This training not only helped to educate the Native Americans but also to support the mission. For his part, the missionary was accustomed to transplant to the frontier almost every conceivable domestic plant and animal of Europe. In the teaching of the manual trades, the cultivation of the land, and the care of domestic animals, the missionaries relied either on the soldiers or preferably on laymen hired by the missionaries for the purpose. These served as superintendents of the fields, of the herds of animals, and of the shops. Through their care and under the management of the missionary, but especially through the work of the Native American, many missions came to represent an enormous economic investment. In Upper California in 1834 the 31,000 mission Native Americans of 21 missions herded 396,000 cattle, 62,000 horses, 321,000 hogs, sheep, and goats, and harvested 123,000 bushels of grain. There was a corresponding abundance in the orchards, gardens, wine press, and workshops. In 1768 the Jesuit missions of Paraguay had 769,869 head of cattle, 124,619 mules and horses, 14,975 asses, and 38,141 sheep and goats. A single Capuchin mission in Venezuela, Divina Pastora, in 1755 cared for 154,000 head of cattle.

Finally, the mission was also a school of government and citizenship. For this purpose, the mission was organized into a pueblo with the same civil officials, and sometimes also the same military leaders, as the corresponding Spanish pueblo. Usually these officials were appointed the first time. Thereafter, they were elected on each January 1 by the Native Americans who were heads of a household. Special insignia were granted to the officials as well as special accommodations in the Church to add to their prestige. This Native American pueblo council had the right to administer minor punishments and also had its own jail. It could pass laws that were required

Interior of Peregrine Chapel at Mission San Juan Capistrano. (©Richard Cummins/CORBIS)

by local circumstances, and it appointed Native American overseers to superintend the community projects, such as road maintenance, bridge construction, and work in the community fields. Much of the actual controlling of the native people was thus done by the Native Americans themselves, although there always hovered in the background the figure of the missionary or the soldier of the presidio. Some authors have tended to underestimate the efficacy of the Native American council, possibly because they do not understand its purpose. It resembled closely the student government found in many colleges in the 20th century: a means of control and a step toward true self-government. It was thus one of the factors that help to explain how two missionaries could form an orderly town out of several thousand nomads.

The Mission System Re-evaluated. Recent studies have shifted their focus from the missionaries to the Native Americans who lived in the missions. These studies, inspired in part by a greater sensitivity to human rights issues and the suffering which Native Americans and African Americans experienced as a result of their encounter with Europeans from the 16th Century on, place the history of the missions in a more critical light. Although the missionaries were well-intentioned, their attempt to incorporate the Native Americans into the mission system often accelerated the spread of disease and the breakdown of native culture and traditions. Frequently, the Native Americans resisted the attempt to impose Christianity by harboring old ways under the guise of Catholic rites. Women especially found themselves subordinated to a strictly male-oriented hierarchy legitimated by the missionaries. The oldest criticism of the missions still remains the central one: did the benevolent paternalism of the missionaries inhibit the Native Americans from developing the capability to become integrated into the larger western world beyond the mission? But this is an uneven story. Other studies show that in some mission experiences, and this would be particularly true of the Jesuit missions in Mojos (Bolivia) and Paraguay, the native peoples not only cooperated with the missionaries, but were quite capable of defending and maintaining their mission way of life long after the Jesuits were expelled.

See Also: ALDEIAMENTO SYSTEM IN BRAZIL; ENCOMIENDA-DOCTRINA SYSTEM IN SPANISH AMERICA.

Bibliography: J. AXTELL, "Some Thoughts on the Ethnohistory of Missions," *Ethnohistory* 29:1 (1982) 35–41. H. E. BOLTON, "The Mission as a Frontier Institution in the Spanish American Colonies," *American Historical Review* 23 (1917–18) 42–61. E. DUSSEL (ed.), *Historia general de la Iglesia en América Latina* 9 v. (CEHILA Comisión Para Escribir la Historia de la Iglesia en América Latina, Salamanca 1981–1994). E. LANGER and R. H. JACKSON (eds.), *The New Latin American Mission History* (Lincoln, Nebraska 1995). D. T. REFF, "Critical Introduction," A. PÉREZ DE RIBAS, *History of the Triumphs of Our Faith . . .* (Tucson, Arizona 1999) 11–46. A. S. TIBESAR, "The Franciscan *Doctrinero* versus the Franciscan *Misionero* in Seventeenth Century Peru," *The Americas* 14 (1957–58) 115–124.

[A. S. TIBESAR/J. L. KLAIBER]

Mexico and Central America

The spread of Christianity through the missions in Spanish North America and Central America was largely the work of the Order of St. Francis and of the Society of Jesus.

Franciscan Missions. The Franciscans arrived in Santo Domingo in 1493. By 1500 they had already obtained about 3,000 converts. Organized in a province in 1505, they extended their work of evangelization to the neighboring islands as they were discovered. There is evidence of great missionary effort but not of the fruit of their labor. Missionary activity diminished as the native population decreased. From the Antilles the Franciscans penetrated the coasts of Cumaná and Tierra Firme in 1513 and reached Panama the following year. Cuba served as a base for the penetration of Florida.

Period of Mexican Occupation. The territory of colonial New Spain comprised all present Mexico, Florida, southern Georgia, the lower part of South Carolina, Texas, New Mexico, southern Colorado, Arizona, and California. From 1522 Franciscans began to evangelize the outskirts of Mexico City and of Puebla de los Angeles. They entered Michoacán in 1525 and Jalisco the following year. These centers of initial missionary expansion served as the base for new penetrations. They began the evangelization of Taftipico in 1530, of Yucatán two years later, and of Zacatecas in 1542. Each of these centers became a province or autonomous custody, with the responsibility to evangelize its own territory and to penetrate regions that were discovered later. Evangelization in the 16th century was accomplished by means of self-expansion in concentric circles. Each province established convents in the principal towns. The evangelizing radius of each convent was constantly enlarged, and when the limits touched, the region could be considered Christianized. At the close of the 16th century there were 200 convents, which attended to about 1,000 native settlements.

The apostolic zeal of the religious and the methods used brought a harvest unique in the history of the missions, for we are told that several million baptisms occurred in a few years. Outstanding among the missionaries were Pedro de Gante; the Twelve Apostles of Mexico, among whom were Martín de Valencia and Toribio de Benavente Motolonía; Juan de Zumárraga; Marcos de Niza; Bernardino de Sahagfún; Andrés de Olmos; Maturino Gilberti; Alonso de Molina; and Gerónimo de Mendieta.

Later Expansion. At the close of the 16th century a new stage opened, which lasted until independence: the penetration of territories distant from the original centers of evangelization. Zacatecas, made a province in 1603, was entered through the northeast section of the country, and missionary activity was carried on in what is now Durango, Sinaloa, Coahuila, Chichuahua, and San Luis de Potosí. It is estimated that in 1737 there were 100,000 converted native Mexicans.

The province of the Holy Gospel began the Christianization of New Mexico, Arizona, and Colorado in 1598; the territory was taken over in 1616 by the custody of San Pablo. Although in 1630 they had 80,000 baptized native Mexicans, these missions were among the most difficult in America. They survived the grave crises of 1680 and 1696, and in 1700 there were 126 Franciscans in missionary work there. About 1750 there were 21 villages, with 17,500 Christians. They were placed under the administration of the secular clergy in 1756 and returned to the order in 1771. In 1787, 28 religious were evangelizing there, in charge of 48 missions. Alonso de Benavides is a well-known figure of that era.

After several earlier attempts the province of Michoacán in 1617 systematically began the Christianization of Río Verde, which became a Franciscan custody in 1621. In 1693 it had 12 Franciscans, seven missions, seven visitas, and 10,000 native Mexicans in the process of Christianization. The missions were secularized in 1712; 15 years later they were returned to the Franciscans, who in 1761 attended to 15,469 converts.

In 1670 the province of Jalisco took charge of the missions of Coahuila. A century later the region was deemed Christianized and was transferred to the secular clergy, leaving the Franciscans with seven towns and a total of 10 missions.

The Franciscan evangelization of Florida had begun in 1573, after the unsuccessful attempts of the Dominicans and Jesuits. Following many difficulties and martyrdoms, the religious succeeded in Christianizing the region to the south of Carolina. In 1634 there were 35 missionaries in charge of 44 towns, with 30,000 native Americans. The English invasion of 1704 damaged the flourishing missions, and they disappeared after the English took over the territory in 1763. The best-known missionaries there were Alonso de Reinoso, Luis Gerónimo de Oré, and Juan de Silva.

Era of the Colleges. From the second quarter of the 17th century onward, to the missionary activity of the provinces was added that of the Apostolic Colleges of Propaganda Fide. Querétaro started with the evangelization of Texas in 1714. In charge of Zacatecas after 1774, the missions succeeded in overcoming the political vicissitudes of the territory. In 1780 they had 17 Franciscans, who attended to 18 missions and two Spanish communities. Working in the missions there were Antonio Margil, Francisco Casafñas, Isidro Félix de Espinosa, and Alonso Giraldo de Terreros. The Sierra Gorda, evangelized since 1690 by the College of Querétaro, was transferred in 1743 to Pachuca and Mexico City. The former attended to the needs of 3,000 Christians in 1787. Pedro Pérez de Mezquía was outstanding among the missionaries from Mexico City. All these missions were turned over to the secular clergy in 1770. Nuevo Santander was entrusted to the College of Guadalupe in 1750. It was abandoned for a short time, but 22 religious returned there in 1756. In 1782, 28 Franciscans were in charge of 31 missions.

Assumption of Former Jesuit Missions. Without giving up their own missions, both the provinces and colleges took charge of those abandoned by the Society of Jesus when it was exiled in 1767. A new era of mission prosperity began. Baja California, entrusted to the College of Mexico City, was exchanged for Alta California in 1772, and evangelization was extended to the north of San Francisco. In the 21 missions that existed until 1832, 89,900 baptisms had been administered. Junípero Serra, Francisco Palou, Fermín Lasuén, Juan Crespí, and Pablo de Mugártegui are well-known figures in the California missions. The province of Jalisco assumed charge of the missions of Nayarit. Pimería Alta (Sonora-Arizona) and Baja California went to the College of Querétaro, which in 1774 surrendered the second to Jalisco. The province of Zacatecas attended to the missions of the Laguna de Parras (Coahuila Durango), while the College of Guadalupe took charge of the missions of Taraumara. With the addition of these former Jesuit missions, the Franciscan Order in 1786 possessed 116 mission centers, 500 missionaries, and had 250,000 native people under its direction.

Central America. In Guatemala the region of Peténitza was evangelized by the province of Yucatán. The rest of the country, where the Franciscans arrived in 1540, made up the province of the Most Holy Name of Jesus, whose evangelizing activity was accomplished by means of the Mexican system of occupation. The province in 1661 possessed 24 houses, 172 religious, and 50,000 neophytes. Fray Esteban Verdelet pushed the missionary activity of the Yucatán province to Honduras. Work in Teuzgalpa, begun in 1608, had to be suspended in 1623 because of the death of the missionaries, but it resumed in 1667. The evangelization of Tologalpa was started in 1667 and intensified after 1674. Both missions had seven missionaries in 1690 and were still in existence in 1787. In 1675 the province founded the convent of Nueva Segovia for the evangelization of the coast of La Pantasma; eight religious were working there in 1787. Further, from the beginning of the 18th century the College of Guatemala maintained the missions of Lean-Mulian and Río Tinto (Comayagua), both of which were still in existence at the end of the century.

Christianity was introduced into Nicaragua and Costa Rica in 1523 and 1542 respectively. Later the province of San Jorge was formed there. In 1635 it had 17 houses distributed throughout 150 leagues of territory. In Talamanca the College of Querétaro carried on missionary activity from 1688; later the area was cared for by the College of Guatemala, assisted by the province of San Jorge. In 1787 there were five missions in the foothills, with a population of 3,000 Christian native inhabitants. Outstanding among the missionaries were Melchor López, Antonio Margil, Pablo de Rebullida, Pedro de la Concepción Urtiaga, and Francisco de San José.

From 1513 to 1519 several religious carried on missionary activity in Darién. In 1565 a custody was established in Panama. It not only evangelized the immediate territory but also in 1632 undertook the Christianization of the Gorgonas Islands. The College of Guatemala evangelized the territory of Veragua, whose five towns and 2,500 native inhabitants were transferred in 1786 to the College of Panama, assisted in the missionary work by the province of Chiriquí. In 1796 its missions had six towns, 1,834 neophytes, and 289 pagans. With independence, a totally different missionary phase began in Spanish America.

[P. BORGES]

Jesuit Missions. Although the royal decree authorizing the Jesuits to establish themselves in Mexico in 1572 stated specifically that they were to work among the native people, it was not until 1589 that the first Jesuits could begin their apostolate among the natives in the vicinity of San Luis de Paz. Until then the Jesuits had attended to such ministry as seemed most needed: schools for the Spaniards and Creoles in all the principal cities and elementary classes for the children of converted natives in several of the larger cities. The initial emphasis on this form of apostolate, rather than missions, derived from the previous training of the Jesuits arriving from Spain and their conviction that they were serving through schools the greatest need of the nation: an educated clergy and a select laity.

The important stable missions were all to the northwest of Mexico City, with Parras, Durango, and the Villa de Sinaloa (San Felipe) as the main centers in the early phase of missionary efforts. From 1591, when the first two missionaries, Gonzalo de Tapia and Martín Pérez, set out for Sinaloa, until 1767 and 1768, when the Jesuits were banished from the missions, their apostolic activity among the native Mexicans extended to an area equivalent to approximately two-fifths of modern Mexico; all or part of the states of Guanajuato, San Luis Potosí, Nuevo León, Jalisco, Zacatecas, Nayarit, Coahuila, Durango, Chihuahua, Sinaloa, Sonora, Lower California, and as far north as southern Arizona. All of this area has since developed into dioceses, except for the Vicariate of Lower California (established in 1854) and the Vicariate and mission of Tarahumara in Chihuahua (1958).

As the Jesuits moved northward along the Pacific coast, they converted the native inhabitants of one river area after another and established missions and schools in all the settlements. The missionary resided in the most important town (*cabecera*) of the area, where he maintained a school for the native children, teaching them reading, writing, arithmetic, and singing, and attended to several dependent missions (*visitas*).

The 12 main mission groups will be listed chronologically according to the years of their respective foundations.

San Luis de la Paz (1589). This was named after Luis de Velasco, a viceroy intent on converting and subduing the tribes designated by the generic term ''Chichimecas.'' In 1594 the Jesuits established a residence and small school. This was the only isolated mission area of the Mexican Jesuits; all the others were contiguous and permitted them to use a well-founded mission as the springboard for the next mission to be established.

Sinaloa (1591). This was the first mission founded among wholly barbaric and unconverted tribes. The governor of the region, Rodrigo del Río Losa, summoned the Jesuits in the hope of facilitating and consolidating the Spanish dominion over numerous and most warlike native inhabitants. Sinaloa did not become a diocese until 1883, although the Council of the Indies inquired as early as 1638 about the feasibility of organizing the area into a bishopric.

The uprisings of the natives that led to the martyrdom of Tapia in 1594 might well have spread and continued to the extinction of the entire group of missions had Captain Diego Martínez de Hurdaide not come on the scene shortly afterward. He knew how to win over the loyalty of the natives and inspire fear in those intent on the annihilation of the Spaniards. By 1605 the numerous tribes of the Bamoas, Níos, Guazaves, Tamazulas, Ahomes, Zuaques, Tehuecos, and Sinaloas had in great part been converted. Prominent among the missionaries of the area was Michael Wadding, still more famous for his treatise on mystical theology.

The missionary effort extended ever northward, from one valley to the next, until all the tribes (Tzoes, Huites, Bacoburitos, Chicoratos, and Yecoratos) had been brought into the Church. The more general native language was Cahita; numerous other languages and dialects were spoken in the various missions. In the 1662 report to Propaganda Fide 16 missionaries were attending to 38 native settlements, administering to 21,912 native inhabitants, and conducting 16 schools for the native children. At the time of the expulsion (1767) 21 missionaries were working in approximately 50 settlements and administering to some 30,000 natives.

Parras (now Parras de la Fuente), Coahuila (1598–1652). The Jesuit missionaries had heard about the native inhabitants in the vicinity of this outpost as early as 1594 and had done some apostolic work among the natives, but the definitive foundation of this group of missions was not effected until 1598. The missions were extended rapidly during the years 1602 to 1608. Despite frequent uprisings of the natives and epidemics, the missions of the area were sufficiently developed to allow their incorporation (1652) into the already established (1623) Diocese of Durango.

Acaxees and Xiximíes (1592). These natives lived in the group of missions termed San Andrés and Topia, among the most inaccessible mountains in the upper reaches of the Piastla, San Lorenzo, and Culiacán Rivers. Whereas most of the other Jesuit missionaries received only 300 pesos annually and 35 for the school they conducted for the native children, those here were allotted an additional 50 pesos because of the hardships entailed and the exceptional difficulties in securing supplies. Two outstanding missionaries devoted their lives to the natives of this area: Hernando de Santarén, the founder of the missions and martyr of the neighboring Tepehuanes; and

Pedro Gravina, his successor. According to the 1662 report 12 missionaries were working in 41 widely scattered and thinly populated settlements, conducting 12 schools for the native children and attending to 3,851 native inhabitants. At the close of 1753, 11 of the most highly developed missions were turned over to the diocesan clergy of Durango.

Tepehuanes (1596). Their homeland lay to the east of the Acaxees and Xiximíes and extended south of the Tarahumares as far as Nayarit. This relatively small area was the most difficult of all missions to establish and administer. November of 1618 witnessed the violent death of eight missionaries. This seemingly fatal blow served to inspire numerous volunteers to replace them and extend their apostolate. Guanaceví, Zape, San Ignacio, Santa Catarina, and Papasquiaro were the principal centers. The lingua franca was Tepehuana, although Nahuatl, Tarahumara, and Salinera were spoken in several of the missions. The 1662 report records only four missionaries attending to 11 settlements and four schools for the native children and administering to 2,356 native inhabitants. In 1753 the missions were considered sufficiently developed to be incorporated into the Durango diocese.

Tarahumara Baja (1607). These missions are important not only for their intrinsic significance but also because they served as the springboard for the two most extensive groups: Tarahumara Alta and Sonora. So restless and hostile were the natives that it was not until 1630 that the first permanent mission could be established among them at San Miguel Bocas. Even after the founding of several missions, the native inhabitants revolted and slew their missionaries in 1645, 1648 to 1650, and 1652. In 1662 only five missionaries were working in Chihuahua, attending to 11 settlements and five schools for the native children and administering to 3,400 native inhabitants.

The Yaquis, Mayos, Tepahues, and Conicaris (1614). These warlike tribes lived along the northern Pacific coast in the valleys of the Yaqui and Mayo Rivers, directly in the path of the northwestern movement of the Jesuit missionary apostolate. The 1740 uprising was particularly destructive to the missions and threatened to undo the work of more than a century. At the expulsion of the Jesuits in 1767, the missions were not sufficiently developed to be incorporated into any diocese. With missionaries sufficient to attend to only a few of the main centers, many of the native inhabitants, especially the Yaquis, reverted to paganism and were lost to Christianity.

Sonora (1614). This was the most extensive of all the Mexican mission territories. Christianity came to it with the conversion of the Nebomes (southern and northern tribes), followed by that of numerous other nations. Of particular significance was the conversion of the Guázavas in 1646, their homeland serving as the gateway to more distant nations. In 1662 there were 17 missionaries working in 17 centers, each with its native Mexican school, attending to 40 settlements and administering to 17,790 natives. A new era for the Sonora missions began in 1687 with the coming of Eusebio Francisco Kino to the Pimería center of Dolores. Some 40 expeditions to the west along the Gulf of California, to the junction of the Gila and Colorado Rivers, and to Casa Grande in the present state of Arizona, along the San Pedro and Santa Cruz Rivers, not only awakened an interest in Christianity and repeated requests for missionaries, but also led to the founding of numerous successful centers with thriving native communities instructed in their new faith and in a better way of life economically and socially. By every norm Kino ranks as the outstanding missionary of the Mexican province; to the tragic disadvantage of the entire vast territory there was no one of his ability to replace him at his death in 1711. The 1751 revolt, launched with the assassination of Fathers Teflo and Ruhen, threatened to spread to the entire mission territory. At the time of the expulsion (1767), 29 priests were working in as many centers and attending to some 60 settlements.

Chínipas (1621). This group of missions lay to the southwest of the Tarahumares and Tepehuanes. Although the Jesuits had preached to these native inhabitants as early as 1601, no permanent mission could be founded until 1621. Two of the pioneering apostles, Julio Pascual and Manuel Martínez, were slain by the natives in 1632. In 1767, 12 missionaries were working among these native inhabitants, having added new missions to the group a few years previously, for a total of 12 centers, each with several dependent stations.

Tarahumara Alta (1673). This group of missions was a continuation of the Baja foundations. They were situated in the modern state of Chihuahua and, together with the Baja group, covered an area approximately the same as the modern Tarahumara missions. Numerous and fierce native uprisings made this one of the most difficult mission areas; particularly destructive was the 1690 rebellion, which claimed the lives of Juan Foronda and Manuel Sánchez. In 1767 (the two Tarahumara groups had previously been fused into one) 19 priests were working in 18 centers and attending to approximately 60 native settlements.

Baja, California (1697). Jesuits participated in several expeditions to Lower California before Juan María Salvatierra founded the first permanent settlement at Loreto in 1697. He was joined by Francisco M. Piccolo and Juan de Ugarte. Before they were expelled in 1768, the Jesuits had founded some 15 main mission centers, each with dependent stations. In 1745 the mission population was about 4,000; in 1762, nearly 8,000; and in 1768, slightly more than 7,000.

Nayarit (1716). The Jesuit mission group lay in the eastern part of the present state of Nayarit, extending from Santa Teresa in the north across the high plateau of Trinidad to Guaynarnota (San Ignacio) in the south. The almost inaccessible terrain made both the military and the spiritual conquest exceptionally difficult. At the time of the expulsion (1767), there were seven missionaries working in as many mission centers and attending to numerous dependent stations.

Modern Missions. The Jesuit Order, suppressed in 1773 by Clement XIV, was universally restored by Pius VII in 1814. A few surviving Mexican Jesuits returned to the home province in 1816 at the height of the independence movement. Although a few of the schools and churches were given back, none of the Mexican missions was returned until 1900, when the Jesuits were asked to take over the Tarahumara (Chihuahua) group. Not even the fierce persecution by Calles (1926–29) succeeded in imprisoning or exiling all of the missionaries. In 1964, one vicar apostolic, Bishop Salvador Martínez Aguirre, SJ, 22 priests, six seminarists, and 13 lay brothers were working in these missions. The main centers are: Sisoguichi, Carichí, Chínipas, Cerocahui, Batopilas, Norogachi, Guadalupe y Calvo, and Chinatfú. Schools are conducted in Sisoguichi, Creel, San Juanito, Batopilas, Carichí, Cerocahui, Chinatfú, Guadalupe y Calvo, and Norogachi. In 1959 the Mexican Jesuits of the southern province founded missions in the area near Chilón called Bachajón and in the state of Chiapas in southern Mexico. At no time have the Jesuits of Mexico administered permanent missions in Central America.

Bibliography: M. A. MEDINA, *Los dominicos en América: Presencia y actuación de los dominicos en la América colonial española de los siglos XVI–XIX* (Madrid: Mapfre, 1992). J. MEIERS, ''The Religious Orders in Latin America,'' in E. Dussel (ed.), *The Church in Latin America, 1492–1992* (Maryknoll, New York, 1992) 375–390. Organización de los Agustinos en América Latina (OALA), *Los agustinos en América Latina: Pasado y presente* (Iquitos, Peru 1995). *Franciscans:* A. ABAD, *Los franciscanos en América* (Madrid: Mapfre 1992). K. MCCARTY, *A Spanish Frontier in the Enlightened Age: Franciscan Beginnings in Sonora and Arizona, 1767– 1700* (Tucson 1981). F. MORALES, ''Mexican Society and the Franciscan Order,'' *The Americas* 54:3 (Jan. 1998) 323–56. J. G. NAVARRO, *Los franciscanos en la conquista y colonización de América: Fuera de las Antillas* (Madrid 1955). R. R. RICARD, *The Spiritual Conquest of Mexico* trans. By L. B. SIMPSON (Berkeley, Cal. 1966). *Jesuits:* F. J. ALEGRE, *Historia de la Provincia de la Compañía de Jesús de Nueva España*, ed. by E. J. BURRUS and F. ZUBILLAGA, 4 v. (new ed. Rome 1956–1960). J. F. BANNON, *The Mission Frontier in Sonora, 1620–1687* (New York 1955). H. W. CROSBY, *Antigua California: Mission and Colony on the Peninsular Frontier, 1697–1768* (Albuquerque 1994). G. DECORME, *La obra de los jesuitas mexicanos durante la época colonial, 1572–1767* 2 v. (Mexico City, 1941); *Historia de la Compañía de Jesús en la República Mexicana durante el siglo XIX*, 3 v. (Guadalajara, Mexico, 1914–1921). S. M. DEEDS, ''Indigenous Responses to Mission Settlement in Nueva Vizcaya,'' in E. LANGER and R. H. JACKSON (eds.), *The New Latin American Mission History* (Lincoln, Nebraska 1995) 76–108. J. A. GAGLIANO and C. E. RONAN (eds.), *Jesuit Encounters in the New World* (Rome, 1997). R. LEÓN, *Jesuitas en la Tarahumara* (Ciudad Juárez, 1992). S. NEGRO and M. MARZAL (eds.), *Un reino en la frontera: las misiones jesuitas en la América colonial* (Lima, 1999). A. SANTOS HERNÁNDEZ, *Los jesuitas en América* (Madrid: Mapfre 1992).

[E. J. BURRUS/J. L. KLAIBER]

South America

Thousands of religious of various orders worked in catechizing and civilizing the native peoples in Spanish South America through the mission system. The Mercedarians were active in the colonial period in Peru, Gran Colombia, and La Plata. The DOMINICANS, who first lived in convents in America as they had in Spain, left their convents because of the lack of diocesan clergy and went out to the *doctrinas.* They learned the native languages and as early as 1548 published a *Doctrina Cristiana* in Spanish and Mexican for the use of their missionaries. In 1560 Domingo de Santo Tomás published a Quechua grammar. In the 17th century, when the mission system proper developed, the Dominicans established their oldest mission (1624) among the Canelos natives; it still exists as the Apostolic Prefecture of Canelos. The Dominicans in the 20th century also supervise an apostolic vicariate in Peru and missions in Colombia. However, the most active orders in the missionary work in Spanish South America, over its whole history, have been the Franciscans and the Jesuits. Among the orders that have been expanding or entering mission work in the 19th and 20th centuries are the Augustinians and the Salesians.

Franciscans. In 1505 the Franciscan province of Santa Cruz was founded on the island of Española. From there the Franciscans extended their apostolate throughout the Caribbean Islands, especially Cuba and Puerto Rico. In about 1511 they established in the recently founded Santa Maria de la Antigua, Darién, the first convent on the continent. Between 1514 and 1522, they carried out a successful missionary attempt on the coast of Cumaná, Venezuela. By way of Panama and Nicaragua, the Franciscans reached Ecuador and Peru. A Franciscan, Juan de los Santos, accompanied Pizarro on his explorations. Marcos de Niza went with Alvarado from Guatemala to Ecuador (1531–32). In 1532 the order decided to establish the Custody of Peru. In about 1553 the province of the Twelve Apostles was established permanently at Lima, and under its jurisdiction were all the Franciscans of South America until 1565 when the independent provinces of Santafé de Bogotá, San Francisco de Quito, and the Holy Trinity of Chile were created. Later the territories of Upper Peru—under the title of San Antonio de los Charcas—and Rio de la Plata were established as provinces. The province of Santa Cruz Española began to extend itself throughout Venezuela after 1575.

Many of these first activities had a missionary character, although the religious were engaged also in ministering to the conquistadors and the colonists. It is impossible to separate clearly these functions from those properly termed missionary, because at all times expeditions were made to the pagan native inhabitants. However, what were called ''conversions'' or living missions, as opposed to the *doctrinas* or parishes of native inhabitants already converted, began in the 17th century, after the period of consolidation of the conquest. Sometimes exploratory or conquering expeditions led the way; at other times the missionaries preceded the conquistadors and the colonists.

Venezuela. The province of Santa Cruz did not maintain missions in the sense mentioned, but the ''Missions of Píritu,'' so called because the first was established in the little town of that name in the eastern part of the country, achieved true importance. They started in 1656 and were under the direct supervision of the superior general of the order. Shortly before their destruction during the war for independence, in the second decade of the 19th century, the Píritu missionaries had in their charge 65 villages and missionary posts in the territories corresponding to the modern states of Anzoátegui and Guayana.

Colombia. Although Francisco de Aragón appeared in Santa Marta in 1534, and Juan de San Filisberto visited the recently established city of Bogotá in 1540 or 1541, the order was not established in Colombia until 1550. The first superior, Jerónimo de San Miguel, was responsible for the humanitarian legislation that regulated the work of the native rowers on the Magdalena River. The first two archbishops of Bogotá were the Franciscans Juan de los Barrios and Luis Zapata. Also in the 16th century, another Franciscan, Sebastián de Ocando, occupied the See of Santa Marta. Later the Franciscans maintained missions in the Chocó region—where Matías Abad distinguished himself in the mid-17th century—and in Los Ilanos, where they ministered to eight villages in 1775. About 1678–80, they attempted to establish in Los Ilanos a missionary bishopric, with its see at Santiago de las Atalayas. Juan Doblado, who had been connected with those missions since at least 1667, was proposed as the first bishop. Not until the 19th century was the idea partially realized with the consecration as auxiliary bishop of Bogotá of the Franciscan José Antonio Chaves. He lived at Casanare, and concerned himself with the improvement of the missions. In the 18th century the College of the Propagation of the Faith at Cali and Popayán accomplished much missionary work in the region of the Putumayo and Caquetá Rivers.

Ecuador. The Franciscans were the first and the principal evangelists of the territory of Quito. In the second half of the 16th century, they had in their charge ''most of the *doctrinas* in the native villages,'' according to an account sent to visitor Ovando. An incomplete list of 1646 still assigned them more than 20. From 1632 they made several attempts to reach the Amazon, which they finally achieved in 1636 or 1637. This was the prologue to a great missionary effort in the Napo River area, actually started in 1647. When at the end of the 17th century, these missions were put into the hands of the Jesuits, the Franciscans concentrated their efforts on the Putumayo and Caquetá territories, tenaciously maintained in spite of many difficulties. Around 1739 the Franciscans ministered to 21 villages there. In 1736 the Franciscans of Quito established a mission among the Jíbaro natives in the province of Macas, which did not continue then but was resumed later. Upon the expulsion of the Jesuits from the missions of Mainas in 1767, the Franciscans took charge of them. In 1774, 18 Franciscans were working there in an equal number of villages. When the territory of Mainas was added to the viceroyalty of Peru (1802), its missions were transferred to the charge of the community of Ocopa.

Peru. Ocopa was the first Missionary College of the Propagation of the Faith founded in South America (1724). Its founder, Francisco de San José, of the community of Querétaro, Mexico, had previously worked in Central America, especially among the native people of Talamanca (Costa Rica). Having gone to Peru in 1708 as assistant commissioner of the missions of Propaganda Fide, he gave new drive to the missionary activities of the Franciscans there. At his death in 1736, the missionaries of the new community had spread through the Montaña of Peru, ministering to almost 8,000 native inhabitants. Almost all of this was lost in the uprising of Santos Atahualpa (1742), which dominated those territories for more than a decade, but the Franciscans were able to bring back all those conversions, at the cost of tremendous hardships and the death of several religious. Ocopa, the main missionary center in eastern Peru during the 18th century, came to be so again in the 19th century, after a brief eclipse during the wars for independence. In the 20th century it was one of the main bases for the missions in the region of the Ucayali River. Its apostolate extended to other parts of Peru and even outside it. From it, directly or indirectly, came the founders of all the other missionary communities that existed in South America. Many of its missionaries—outstanding among them was Manuel Sobreviela—contributed, besides, in great measure to the geographic knowledge about Peru with their diaries, descriptions, and maps.

The work of the community of Ocopa was the continuation of a long history of missionary activity by the Franciscans of Peru. In 1619 Gregorio de Bolívar had undertaken the conversion of the Panatahua people on the banks of the Huallaga River; his work was continued by Felipe de Luyando and others. Beginning in 1632 from Panama, which was a dependency of Lima, an attempt was made to evangelize the Idibá of Gorgona on the coast of Colombia. Shortly thereafter (1635) were established the first missions of Cerro de la Sal, and the advance toward the Ucayali was started, an area explored by Manuel Biedma during that century. About 1686 the mission of the Cunivo was established on the upper Ucayali, where another great missionary appeared—Francisco Huerta. A noteworthy aspect of Franciscan missionary history in Peru is its relationship with far-off Oceania. Franciscans figured both in the expeditions of discovery organized in the second half of the 16th century and in those sent toward the end of the 18th (1772–76) by Viceroy Amat.

Bolivia. The missionary history of Bolivia is the same as that of Peru since it formed a part of the province of the Twelve Apostles of Peru until 1607. Among the later missionary undertakings was the expedition to the Chuncho to the northwest of La Paz by the already mentioned Gregorio de Bolívar about 1621, continued by Bernardino de Cárdenas with great heroism, although without permanent success. Bolívar made an expedition to the Motilón, by way of Chapapoyas, about 1627; having failed in this attempt also, in 1631, he penetrated from Chuquisaca (modern Sucre) into the unknown regions of the east, from which he never returned. Cárdenas, well-acquainted with the Quechua and Aymara languages, was put in charge of a campaign of popular missions among the native inhabitants who were already baptized but needed more instruction.

The expeditions of Bolívar and Cárdenas from La Paz were the antecedents of the missions of Apolobamba, which the Franciscan province of Charcas (this was its official title) organized in the second half of the 17th century. Later they were extended by the missionaries of the College of Moquegua, Peru, founded in 1775, and finally came to be a part of the Apostolic Vicariate of Beni, still under the direction of the Franciscans. The College of Moquegua in southern Bolivia was established by religious originating from the College of Tarija, which had been founded in 1755 by missionaries from the College of Ocopa. The College of Tarija worked especially among the Chiriguano people of the Chaco region, a task that the Franciscans still continue. Among the first missionaries was the lay brother Francisco del Pilar, who established some 17 reductions. In the restoration of missionary activity in Bolivia in the 19th century after the wars for independence, Andrés Herrero worked tirelessly to recruit missionaries in Spain and Italy. With the principal aim of ministering to the former Jesuit missions among the Mojo, the missionary college of Tarata was established toward the end of the 18th century, with a group of 25 Franciscans brought from Spain by Bernardo Jiménez Bejarano. His missionaries worked among the Yuracaré, Mosetén, and Guarayo. In 1930 the Austrian Franciscans of the province of St. Leopold of the Tyrol took charge of these missions.

Chile. The Franciscans reached Chile in 1553, coming from Lima. Their leader was Martín de Robleda. The order expanded so rapidly that in 1565 an independent province could have been established there, but none was until 1571. The Diocese of Santiago was governed by three Franciscans during the 16th century, among whom Diego de Medellín (1573–93) is considered to have been the true organizer of the bishopric; in the 17th century two other Franciscans occupied the episcopal see: Juan Pérez de Espinosa and Diego de Umansoro. The other bishopric of Chile, La Imperial, had as its first bishop Antonio de San Miguel, a veteran Franciscan missionary from Peru; among his successors in the 17th century was the Franciscan writer Luis Gerónimo de Oré (1620–30). The violence of the Araucanian War and other unfortunate circumstances—among them, the disastrous earthquake of 1647—made its missionary work slow. True missions were not developed until the 18th century, with the founding of apostolic colleges of Propaganda Fide. The first of them was established in Chillán in 1756 by missionaries from the College of Ocopa. They set to work with considerable success among the indomitable Araucanians, among whom they had founded five missions by 1789. Shortly thereafter, they received the missions that had belonged to the Jesuits in the Valdivia region and in the archipelago of Chiloé. The latter ones were turned over to the College of Ocopa in 1771. In Valdivia, where the Jesuits had only left two missions, the missionaries of Chillán had founded six new ones before 1789. The missions of the College of Chillán as well as those of Castro received fresh impetus in the 19th century. The Castro missions reached the Strait of Magellan, where the Franciscans had tried to establish themselves in the 16th century.

Rio de La Plata. Two great Franciscan missionaries lived in this area during the 16th and the early 17th centuries: St. Francis Solano at Tucumán and Luis de Bolaños in Paraguay. Later, the Franciscans worked among the Charrúa Indians on the Banda Oriental (Uruguay), and among the Ocloyas and Tobas of Jujuy. In 1784 the College of San Carlos was established, in the modern village of San Lorenzo, Santa Fe. It was the first founding of a college of Propaganda Fide in the area, and it was owing principally to the efforts of Juan Matud, the commissary of missions for South America, who as early as 1754 wanted to establish it at Rio Cuarto, in the center of Argentina. The new community was concerned primarily with the missions in the Chaco. In the 19th century a missionary college was finally founded at Rio Cuarto for the Indians of the pampa, where Marcos Donati distinguished himself. For the conversion of the native people of the Bermejo River in El Chaco, a missionary college was established at Salta.

[L. G. CANEDO]

Jesuits. The first Jesuits in Spanish South America arrived in Peru in April 1568. Seven missionaries sent by the general Francis Borgia, with Jerónimo Ruiz de Portillo as provincial, first lived in Lima. In 1569 they took charge of two doctrinas: El Cercado, a district of the capital, and the area of Huarochirí, which included 77 villages and, provisionally, Andaguaillas (Apurímac). In 1570 they founded the College of Cuzco, intending to extend their efforts to the east. In the next few years they explored the area around Lake Titicaca and established doctrinas at Juli, Potosí, and Santa Cruz de la Sierra (1586). They made sporadic *entradas* to the north in the area of the Maranhão River and into the sub-Andean zone. In the south they established the College of Arequipa and entered Tucumán, Argentina, in 1585.

After this first deployment, the Jesuit missionaries spread widely through Spanish South America: into the modern Peruvian departments of Huánuco, Libertad, and Ayacucho; into Bolivia, where the mission to the Moxos developed 16 reductions with 24,914 Christian native inhabitants; the mission to the Chiquitos had 11 reductions with a total of 19,981; and that to the Chiriguanos eventually ministered to 20,100. In 1574 Jesuits from Lima went into Ecuador along the Peruvian border and evangelized in the regions of Yaguarzongo, Jaén, and Quijos and on into the Amazon jungle from the Napo River to the Gualaga, Ucayale, and the mouth of the Río Negro (today in Brazil); they moved also into the area between the Tigre, Napo, and Maranhão in the modern Peruvian department of Loreto. This mission activity grew to include 18,234 Christians in 32 villages. Jesuits from Peru also went down into Chile from 1593 on and evangelized in the districts of Melipilla, Rere, Castro, Arauco, Laja, Lautaro, Traiguén, Valdivia, Chillán, and Chiloé. In Araucania they established 91 missionary stations, in Chiloé 77 for 10,478 Indians. In Colombia the society was active from 1599 spreading out from Bogotá and Quito into Urabá and Turebo, Nariño and Cauca, then into the llanos, along the banks of the Meta River and so on. Their apostolic journeys went as far as Caracas, Guiana, and Cuba. Argentina was entered by the Jesuits from Chile about 1650. They worked in Patagonia and on down to the Strait of Magellan, as well as up into the pampas area near Buenos Aires and on to Salta and Tucumán. Among the Mocobíes, the Abipones, the Vilelas, and the Lules, they had 17 reductions with a population of about 3,000. Beginning in 1614 the Jesuits entered Venezuela from Colombia and French Guiana. They established six reductions along the upper Orinoco and the Río Negro. To these should be added the enclave of reductions in Paraguay-Uruguay. Thus the Jesuit missions formed a continuous line from the Pacific shore of Colombia through Ecuador, Bolivia, Paraguay, Uruguay, and down through Patagonia, extending branches out to the Guianas in the north and to Chile in the south.

Mission Methods. After the first period (1493–1556) in which the Church was established in Spanish America came an era of development (1566–1700). During this time about 75 percent of the South American Jesuit community was involved in mission work. The difficulties they encountered arose from the geography and climate, from the numerical disproportion between the size of the native population to be cared for and the number of active missionaries, from the psychology of the native peoples and their almost constant state of warfare, from the intrusions of the European settlers in moral, social, political, and economic matters, and from the intrinsic nature of the process of transculturation that was taking place. The mission system expanded to include the intelligence and the will, the imagination and the affections of the native and his whole physical being; his family, tribal, fraternal, and national community; his whole world of individual and social interests. Various means were used. To appeal to the intellect, native languages were used in catechisms, in sermons, and in the specialized schools for the sons of the caciques. Their wills were trained in the group discipline of the reductions and the villages. Teachers used visual and acoustical aids: the catechism was memorized by musical recitation; religious architecture and sculpture and painting educated the native inhabitant's artistic feeling. The missionary stressed a paternalistic attitude and a defense of the native against the white settlers to create a sympathetic bond. He also provided medical care in hospitals, hygienic arrangements in the native dwellings, and adequate food. Within the mission native inhabitants took part in the direction of activities, gaining a spirit of cooperation in schools of arts and crafts and in liturgical activities.

End of the Jesuit Missions. This Jesuit missionary activity was cut off by the royal decree of Charles III of Spain, Feb. 27, 1767, which ordered the expulsion of the Society of Jesus from Spanish territory. The Jesuits had to abandon their mission posts and embark for Europe. In general this meant the ruin of their work. There were few missionaries to take their place and many were moved into areas of which they knew nothing. Some native people used this as an excuse to reassert their own autonomy and leave the missions at a time of moral deterioration among the religious orders generally. The actions of the civil government were unwise: missions were secularized, a separation was made between the powers of the laity and the clergy, and the consequence was the demoralization of the native inhabitants and a diminution of their respect for the missionary.

[A. DE EGAÑA]

Augustinians. The following are the missions of the modern period.

Peru. In 1965 the Augustinians administered two mission territories. The Vicariate Apostolic of Iquitos, a territory of about 90,000 square kilometers in northeastern Peru, is an area of tropical jungle in the upper reaches of the Amazon basin. About half of the estimated 100,000 inhabitants (1963) lived in the one major town, Iquitos; the remainder were seminomadic tribesmen who were scattered along the many rivers. When Augustinians from Spain took charge of the territory in 1900, it was a prefecture about three times larger than the later vicariate. The mission was raised to a vicariate apostolic in 1921, and the boundaries were fixed in 1945, after several divisions of the original territory. Five friars, led by the first prefect apostolic, Paulino Díaz (1900–11), arrived in 1901. By 1963 there were 32 Augustinians under the jurisdiction of Angel Rodríguez Gamoneda, conducting many mission stations, five parishes, a secondary school in Iquitos, several primary schools, a radio station, and a seminary in Nauta. There were two native-born Augustinian priests. Of the total population, only about 500 were as yet unbaptized.

The prelature *nullius* of Chulucanas, erected in 1964, comprised the eastern half of the Diocese of Piura in northwestern Peru. This territory, about 13,000 square kilometers, had a population of almost 300,000; about 38,000 persons lived in the see city of Chulucanas. In 1964, the U.S. Augustinians, led by the prelate nullius John C. McNabb, took charge of the territory.

Bolivia. The Augustinian Order had foundations in Bolivia from the early days of the Spanish conquest. The mission at Cochabamba was established in 1569. After their disappearance in the 19th century, however, the Augustinians did not return to Bolivia until four friars came from Holland in 1930. The founder of the mission was Thomas H. Van der Vloodt (d. 1934). In the Archdiocese of La Paz, the Dutch Augustinians were assigned to South Yungas, a territory of about 3,400 square kilometers, with a population of 30,500, in which the principal town is Chulumani. In 1939 they established a large parish in La Paz. In 1950 they began in Cochabamba a secondary school, which offers scientific and technical education for 300 students.

[A. J. ENNIS]

Salesians. Juan Cagliero and nine Salesians arrived in Buenos Aires Dec. 14, 1875, but it was not until 1879 that they entered the missionary area of Patagonia, of which their founder, Don Bosco, had dreamed. José Fagnano became superior there in January 1880, and the missionaries traveled over the area up to the cordillera. When Cagliero was made vicar apostolic of Patagonia in 1885, Fagnano took charge of southern Patagonia in both Chilean and Argentine boundaries. Their jurisdiction covered one million square kilometers. Cagliero worked out a mission circuit and Fagnano concentrated on bringing the native inhabitants into reductions, which also brought some industrial development to the area.

In 1886 Evasio Rabagliati founded the first Salesian establishment in Chile. Though they were requested by Colombia in that year, Salesian missionaries did not go there until 1890 under the leadership of Father Unia, who worked among the lepers at Agua de Dios. In 1891 Antonio Riccardi began the apostolate in Peru. Bishop Cagliero started extending his missions into Chubut in 1892 and on to the pampas in 1896. By 1934 those missions had been organized into six dioceses. Bishop Luis Lasagna founded the Salesian missions in Matto Grosso, Brazil, and from there moved on into Paraguay. The missions of Ecuador were founded by Angel Savio, who did not live to see them flourish. Bishop Santiago Costamagna took charge of the missions among the Jíbaros in 1895. Salesians began work in Mexico in 1892.

Bibliography: M. A. MEDINA, *Los dominicos en América: Presencia y actuación de los dominicos en la América colonial española de los siglos XVI–XIX* (Madrid: Mapfre 1992). J. MEIER, ''The Religious Orders in Latin America,'' in Enrique Dussel (ed.), *The Church in Latin America, 1492–1992* (Maryknoll, New York 1992) 375–390. *Organización de los Agustinos en América Latina (OALA), Los agustinos en América Latina: Pasado y presente* (Iquitos, Peru 1995). Franciscans: A. ABAD, *Los franciscanos en América* (Madrid: Mapfre 1992). L. GÓMEZ CANEDO, ''The Coming of the Franciscans to Venezuela in 1575,'' *The Americas 18* (1961–62) 380–393. M. DURÁN, *Presencia franciscana en el Paraguay* (Asunción 1981). A. TIBESAR, *Franciscan Beginnings in Colonial Peru, 1532–1569* (Washington, D.C. 1953). *Jesuits: Manuel Aguirre, La Compañía de Jesús en Venezuela* (Bogotá, 1971). A. ASTRAIN, *Historia de la Compañía de Jesús en la Asistencia de España* 7 v. (Madrid 1902–25). D. BLOCK, *Mission Culture on the Upper Amazon* (Lincoln, Nebraska 1994). N. CUSHNER, *Lords of the Land: Sugar, Wine, and Jesuit Estates of Coastal Peru, 1600–1767* (Albany, New York 1980). R. FORESTER, *Jesuitas y mapuches, 1593–1767* (Santiago, Chile 1996). J. A. GAGLIANO and C. E. RONAN (eds.), *Jesuit Encounters in the New World* (Rome, 1997). E. KORTH, *Spanish Policy in Colonial Chile: The Struggle for Social Justice, 1535–1700* (Stanford, California 1968). L. MARTIN, *The Intellectual Conquest of Peru: The Jesuit College of San Pablo, 1568–1767* (New York, 1968). N. MEIKLEJOHN, *La Iglesia y los lupaqas durante la colonia* (Cuzco 1988). O. MERINO and L. A. NEWSON, ''Jesuit Missions in Latin America: The Aftermath of the Expulsion,'' *Yearbook: Conference of Latin American Geographers*, v. 21 (1995) 133–148. M. MÖRNER, *The Expulsion of the Jesuits from Latin America* (New York 1965). S. NEGRO and M. MARZAL (eds.), *Un reino en la frontera: las misiones jesuitas en la América colonial* (Lima 1999). J. M. PACHECO, *Los jesuitas en Colombia* 2 v. (Bogota 1959–62). A. SANTOS HERNÁNDEZ, *Los jesuitas en América* (Madrid, Mapfre 1992).

[R. A. ENTRAIGAS/J. L. KLAIBER]

Borderlands

Spanish missionary activity in the so-called Borderlands dates from the 1540s. (The Borderlands may be defined as that southerly strip of territory of the United States comprising Florida-Georgia and extending along the Gulf Coast into Texas, across the Southwestern states, and finally up the Pacific Coast to include California.)

Early Expeditions. Dominican friars were with the De Soto expedition in 1539, but they were along as chaplains rather than as apostles of the gospel. In that same year (1539) Fray Marcos de Niza was in Arizona, maybe even in New Mexico, but this Franciscan was on a reconnaissance tour to the Seven Golden Cities, or Cíbola, on orders from New Spain's Viceroy, Don Antonio de Mendoza. When Fray Marcos and several Franciscan companions went north in the following year with the Coronado party, they too were serving as chaplains. One of the Franciscans, Fray Juan de Padilla, remained behind when the Coronado group returned to Mexico. He is really the first missionary in the Borderlands, for he went back to Quivira (central Kansas) in order to bring the faith to the Native Americans whom he had met there. At their hands he met his death, probably in 1544, and to him goes the distinction of being the first ''martyr'' on the soil of the future United States.

Florida. The Floridas had defied conquest by Juan Ponce de León, by Pánfilo Narváez, and by Hernando de Soto before Fray Luis Cancer and several Dominican companions tried (1549) by peaceful means to subdue the area's native inhabitants. They died in the attempt to emulate the methods and successes of their famous confrere Fray Bartolomé de LAS CASAS. In 1566 the Spaniards under Don Pedro Menéndez de Avilés took possession of the peninsula at St. Augustine in order to prevent this strategic area along the homeward route of the silver galleons from falling into enemy hands (the French had attempted to hold and colonize it earlier in that decade). Once in control, Menéndez in characteristic Spanish fashion prepared to introduce missionaries. In 1565 three Jesuits arrived to inaugurate missionary activity. Their leader, Padre Pedro Martinez, was killed along the Georgia coast. His two companions withdrew to St. Augustine to serve the needs of the Spaniards until replacements arrived. Ten Jesuits reached there in 1568 and opened mission stations along the coast as far as South Carolina. Two years later, under Padre Juan Baptista Segura, a band went northward to the future Virginia; but six in the party were murdered. In 1572 the two survivors were withdrawn and sent to Mexico, where the Jesuits were opening their apostolate.

In 1573 a band of Franciscans arrived, but, meeting with fierce hostility from the natives, they decided to withdraw until such time as the military could establish better order in the province. In the mid-1580s, with Fray Alonso de Reynoso as the great proponent of missionary activity in Florida, the Franciscans returned, remaining until the English occupation of 1763. By about 1650 the Franciscans had more than 50 missionaries in the Floridas, serving approximately 30 *doctrinas* (mission centers). After 1670, however, the arrival of the English in the Carolinas signaled the beginning of the end, even before James Oglethorpe and his colonists settled in Georgia in the 1730s. Constant border fighting pushed back the mission frontier and destroyed the Christian villages. When the British gained possession of the peninsula by the Peace of Paris (1763), most of the missions had been destroyed or were abandoned. Florida has a few mission reminders of Spanish days.

Louisiana. Disregarding strict chronological sequence, brief mention should be made of the area of the lower Mississippi basin. This was French territory in more senses than that of political dominion. At the end of the 17th century the French had penetrated the great valley, including both the Louisiana and the Illinois country. P. Le M. d'Iberville's expedition arrived on the Gulf Coast in 1699. The French settled first at Biloxi, then moved over to Mobile, and in 1718 shifted their capital to New Orleans. Missionary activity opened almost immediately. The Jesuits worked with the Native Americans, and the Capuchins served the settlers.

In 1762 France, badly beaten in the French and Indian War, by a secret treaty ceded the western half of her Louisiana claims to Spain before going to the peace table at Paris. Spain remained in control of Louisiana, thus abbreviated, until 1800. During the years of Spanish possession there was little, if any, concerted missionary effort expended in the former French area. The French Jesuits had been expelled by royal decree in 1763, stripping the missions of their pastors. No replacements arrived from either France or Canada, and Spain had few to send. During this time the Capuchins and the Spanish priests could barely care for the needs of the settlers. Some little attention was given to the Native Americans in the Illinois country by Canadian and later by French refugee priests; but none of this rose to the status of real missionary effort. Thus the Spaniards in Louisiana left no Christianizing mark on the Indians of the Mississippi Valley proper.

New Mexico. In the area to the west, more commonly designated as the Spanish Borderlands, the Spanish mission enterprise was more extensive, thorough, and successful. The impetus out of New Spain (Mexico) into this region resulted in the late 18th century in the organization of the administrative unit of the *Provincias Internas*. The mission activity was integral to the three-pronged Spanish advance to the north: the center reached into New Mexico and looked beyond to the Great Plains; the right, or east, flank moved toward and across the lower Rio Grande into Texas; the left flank edged up the so-called West Corridor, along the Gulf of California, and ultimately reached the Golden Gate.

By mid-16th century the Age of the Conquistadores in North America had ended, and the slower, more prosaic but more enduring type of frontier expansion got underway, as the Spaniards moved into and began to exploit the rich silver belt of north central and northern Mexico. The Franciscans were with the first miner-settler waves that went northward. At the end of the century, when they accepted the call to form the spiritual arm of the thrust into the Pueblo country, the Jesuits began founding missions along both slopes of the Sierra Madre Occidental. The Franciscans continued to staff the missions on the more easterly flank of the northward advance. By the first years of the 18th century the sons of St. Francis were on the lower Rio Grande, as well as along its New Mexican reaches, while the Jesuits were inching into the future Arizona.

In 1598, when Don Juan de Oñate went north to lay foundations of the outpost province of Nuevo México, Franciscans were in his company. Within the next years, after the Spaniards had established control through the country, the friars fanned out to the pueblos and began the work of Christianization. Early in the 17th century they pushed westward and likewise established themselves in the mesa towns of the Hopi. Things went rather well until 1680; there were successes and setbacks, but the number of converts climbed high into five figures. Then in 1680 came the devastating Pueblo revolt, which temporarily put an end to all Spanish activity in the province. The Franciscans lost a score of men, and more than 400 Spanish settlers were massacred. The rest managed to escape southward and found protection at Paso del Norte. Missions were established in the neighborhood for the Christian Native Americans who were refugees from the pueblos that were located up the river. The reconquest of New Mexico was effected in the 1690s by Don Diego de Vargas, and most of the old mission sites among the Pueblo Indians were reopened. However, neither the Franciscans nor the Jesuits, probing from the south in the next century, were able to bring the Hopi missions back into existence. The work of the Franciscans went on through the 18th century, leaving a Christian imprint on the Pueblos and their neighbors who survived the days of decline in the early 19th century, as well as the influx of Anglo-Americans at mid-century. Brown-robed friars later replaced their blue-robed brethren of earlier times and carry on the mission traditions.

Texas. Spanish interest in Texas was minimal until the 1680s, when reports were received that R. C. de La Salle had sailed to the Gulf Coast. Fearing the presence of French rivals in a position from which they might threaten the rich silver provinces of northern Mexico, the Spaniards bestirred themselves and set out to look for La Salle. Although they learned that his attempt at settlement had ended in disaster, the Crown decided that Texas should be occupied by at least a token force. In 1690 soldiers and Franciscan missionaries moved east from the Rio Grande and set up on the Rio Neches, in east Texas. But, when there were no signs of a French follow-up expedition, the posts and missions were recalled.

By the second decade of the 18th century, however, Spanish officials recognized that the French threat had by no means passed. In 1714 L. J. de Saint-Denis and his trader band appeared on the Rio Grande, at San Juan Bautista. Two years later the decision was made to turn Texas into a buffer province, and in 1718 a party was laying the foundations of San Antonio. As usual, missions and missionaries figured in the Spanish plans for subduing and holding this new frontier. The Franciscans took up the work that D. Massanet and F. Hidalgo had been forced to interrupt about 20 years before. One of the important figures in this new missionary effort was Fray Antonio Margil de Jesús. Missions soon dotted the lower course of a number of the Texas rivers; and there was even an unrewarding attempt to domesticate the wild Apache from the inland station of San Sabá. Here, as elsewhere in the Borderlands, the foundations of Christianity were laid among the American natives, and some of the early historic monuments of Texas were constructed. These were not always appreciated by the Anglo-intruders of a later date who appropriated the province, arrogated the name for themselves, and worked to obliterate the vestiges of the Spanish background.

Arizona. By the beginning of the 18th century northward progress up the West Coast corridor had carried the

Spanish frontier into the future United States. The Jesuits had been advancing up the west coast of Mexico, valley by valley, since 1591, from Sinaloa into Sonora. Late in the 17th century there came to Pimería Alta a remarkable Tyrolese Italian, Padre Eusebio Francisco KINO, one of the first of a line of non-Spaniards who contributed another chapter of the Borderlands story. Early in the new century Kino was dotting the upper Pimería and the Papaguería with stations that later had an Arizona address—Tumacacori, Guebavi, Bac.

After Kino's death (1711) there was a lull in activity on the Arizona frontier. Since the last years of the 17th century most of the Jesuits had been diverted to the new foundations on the California peninsula, where J. M. Salvatierra, F. M. Piccolo, J. de Ugarte, and their coworkers were opening up a new mission frontier. In the 1730s, however, the Sonota-Arizona region again began to hum with activity. Many northern European Jesuits were available to the Mexican superiors for assignment, and quite a few of them were detailed to the north. Strange names, by Spanish standards, appear in the story, such as Jacobo Sedelmayr, Ignatz Keller, Philipp Segesser, Caspar Stiger, Adam Gilg, Heinrich Ruhen, Gottfried Middendorff, Ignatz Pfefferkorn, and Joseph Och, to mention only a few. Missions spread up the San Pedro Valley and were set along the upper waters of the Gila as new tribes to the north and west were drawn into the mission circle.

As the third quarter of the 18th century moved past its midpoint, all seemed in readiness for the next big forward thrust, which Kino and Salvatierra had planned many years before—the Baja California chain and the Sonora-Arizona line were to be joined and moved in conjunction toward the "great harbor of Monterey." The Spaniards had long dreamed of occupying Alta California, but the royal budget could never quite provide for this expansion. Mission expenses were not always quite so prodigious, especially since the Jesuits had managed to enlist much nonroyal financial support, such as the moneys that started and nourished the famous Pious Fund. Then in 1767 the plan seemed to evaporate into thin air, as Charles III of Spain, following the pattern of the monarchs of Portugal and France, decreed the expulsion of the Jesuits from all his dominions, at home and overseas. The West Coast corridor missions were deprived of their pastors. Other religious orders were asked to fill the places; but most of them had little enough personnel to man the missions already assigned to them.

The Franciscans accepted the burden and the challenge. Their missionary seminary at Querétaro sent men into the Pimería; and the missionary Colegio de San Fernando, in the viceregal capital, offered replacements for the peninsular missions. Fray Francisco Garcés went to San Xavier del Bac in 1768 to begin a career as missionary and explorer; this kept the plan to occupy Monterey from dying. And to the peninsula, as *presidente*, came the man whose name is so importantly linked with the occupation and Christianization of the "last Borderland," Fray Junípero SERRA. Furthermore, when the Franciscans moved up to Alta California, Dominicans helped to staff the missions in the peninsula.

California. In addition to promulgating the decree expelling the Jesuits, Don José de Gálvez, the visitator general to New Spain in the 1760s, was instructed to investigate the soundness of the reports that the Russians were extending their trading enterprise southward from Alaska toward the California coast. In view of the trade that the Spaniards had built up with the East through the Manila galleons, they could ill afford to have California in the hands of a rival power. Gálvez carried out his commission and made arrangements for the occupation of Alta California.

In 1769 the expedition, divided into a sea and a land arm, set forth. Serra went with G. de Portolá and the main land party; Fray Juan Crespi went on ahead with the smaller advance party under Capt. F. Rivera. In that year the southern anchor of the future chain of California missions had been established at San Diego de Alcalá. In the next year San Carlos Borromeo was founded at Monterey. In 1776 Capt. Juan Bautista de Anza, commandant in Sonora, led the settler band to the Golden Gate and there laid the foundations of the San Francisco complex, presidio-pueblo-mission. Anza's close associate in the explorations that made possible this overland trek of settlers had been Garcés, who soon after (1780) met his death, along with two Franciscan brethren, at the hands of rebellious Yumas at the missions located near the junction of the Gila with the Colorado River.

The links of the California mission chain were gradually filled in during the last quarter of the century. The number of converts mounted; the province became moderately prosperous. After Serra's death (1784) others, such as F. F. de Lasuén carried on the work. Twelve years before the missions were secularized and the Pious Fund appropriated by the impecunious Mexican government, the friars pushed beyond the Golden Gate and built two last missions, at San Rafael and San Francisco de Solano, increasing the total to more than 20. Many of these are still preserved, and some are still in use as parish churches. Californians are much prouder of their mission heritage than are the Anglo-successors to the Spaniards in other parts of the Borderlands.

Missionaries Honored. Two of the Borderlands missionaries have been named to the National Statuary

Hall in the Capitol, Washington, D.C., by the states in which they labored; California named Serra (1931), and Arizona accorded this distinction to Kino (1965).

Borderlands Revisited. Recent literature tends to criticize older studies of the borderlands missions, which in turn were highly influenced by Herbert Bolton's pioneering works. The anti-Boltonian school centers on Bolton's eurocentric approach which uncritically praised the civilizing efforts of the missionaries, but which paid little attention to the suffering which the Native Americans underwent in order to become "civilized." In fact, the Native Americans did not always submit peaceably to the new system. There were numerous rebellions against Spanish rule and the presence of the missionaries, one of the most notable being the Pueblo revolt of 1680. Furthermore, the methods used by the missionaries, which included coercion, have been held up to a more critical light. Junípero Serra, the Franciscan founder of the California missions, has been particularly singled out in this regard. When all is said and done, however, the missions undoubtedly did more good than harm and left an indelible imprint on the native peoples in the borderlands.

Bibliography: J. F. BANNON, *Bolton and the Spanish Borderlands* (Norman, Oklahoma 1964). H. E. BOLTON, "The Mission as a Frontier Institution in the Spanish-American Colonies," *American Historical Review* 23 (1917–18) 42–61; *Rim of Christendom: A Biography of Eusebio Francisco Kino* (New York 1936; repr. 1960). C. E. CASTAÑEDA, *Our Catholic Heritage in Texas, 1519–1936* 7 v. (Austin 1936–58). V. H. CUMMINS, "Building on Bolton: The Spanish Borderlands Seventy-Five Years Later," *Latin American Research Review* 35:2 (2000) 230–43. D. DENEVI and N. F. MOHOLY, *Junípero Serra: The Illustrated Story of the Franciscan Founder of California's Missions* (New York 1975). P. M. DUNNE, *Black Robes in Lower California* (Berkeley 1952). J. T. ELLIS, Catholics in Colonial America (Baltimore 1956). Z. ENGELHARDT, *The Mission and Missionaries of California* 4 v. (2nd ed. San Francisco 1929). C. F. FIGUERO Y DEL CAMPO, *Franciscan Missions in Florida* (Madrid 1994). M. J. GEIGER, *The Franciscan Conquest of Florida, 1573–1618* (Washington 1937); *The Life and Times of Fray Junípero Serra* 2 v. (Washington 1959). R. H. JACKSON and E. CASTILLO, *Indians, Franciscans, and Spanish Colonization* (Albuquerque 1995). J. L. KESSEL, *Friars, Soldiers, and Reformers: Hispanic Arizona and the Sonora Mission Frontier, 1767–1856* (Tucson 1976). P. H. KOCHER, *California's Old Missions: The Story of the Founding of the 21 Franciscan Missions in Spanish Alta California, 1769–1823* (Chicago 1976). A. L. KNAUT, *The Pueblo Revolt of 1680* (Norman, Oklahoma 1995). C. M. LEWIS and A. J. LOOMIE, *The Spanish Jesuit Missions in Virginia, 1570–1572* (Chapel Hill, North Carolina 1953). J. T. LANNING, *The Spanish Missions of Georgia* (Chapel Hill 1935). H. M. MASON, *Missions of Texas* (Birmingham, Alabama 1974). J. NORRIS, "The Franciscans in New Mexico, 1692–1754: Toward a New Assessment," *The Americas* 51:2 (October 1994) 151–171. F. B. PARSONS, *Early 17th Century Missions of the Southwest* (Tucson 1975). J. A. SANDOS, "Junípero Serra's Canonization and the Historical Record," *American Historical Review* 93:5 (1988) 1253–69. F. J. SMITH, *Father Kino in Arizona* (Phoenix, Arizona 1966). D. SWEET, "The Ibero-American Frontier Mission in Native American History," in E. LANGER and R. H. JACKSON (eds.), *The New Latin American Mission History* (Lincoln, Nebraska 1995) 1–48. F. ZUBILLAGA, *La Florida. La misión jesuítica* (1566–1572) (Rome 1941).

[J. F. BANNON/J. L. KLAIBER]

MISSION IN COLONIAL AMERICA, II (PORTUGUESE MISSIONS)

The history of the missions in Brazil can be divided into two characteristic periods: that from the discovery in 1500 to independence, and that from independence to 1964. The Society of Jesus began the work with the help of the Portuguese governors general, and other religious orders gradually joined in catechizing and civilizing the Brazilian native inhabitants.

1500 to 1822. The first missionaries in Brazil were the Franciscans Henrique de Coimbra and his companions together with Álvares Cabral, who raised the first cross at the mouth of the Mutari or Itacumirim on May 1, 1500. In the armadas of 1501 and the years immediately following came other priests and brothers, who went to Paraíba do Norte, Pôrto Seguro (1516), São Catarina, Iguaraçu (1521) and Pernambuco (1526). Systematic colonization (1530), led by Martim Afonso de Sousa, brought up the problem of organized evangelization. It was begun in Olinda in 1534, in São Vicente in 1535 and in Bahia in 1545. A group of Spanish Franciscans started the mission among the Carijós of Laguna (1538), but had to abandon it in 1548. Other attempts were made in Espírito Santo (1541), in Ilheus and Paraíba (1545), but all were in precarious condition in the middle of the century when a central government was established. Effective evangelization then began with the first contingent of Jesuit missionaries, led by the active Manuel da NÓBREGA (1549). While the Jesuits extended their work in Bahia, São Vicente, São Paulo and Pernambuco, the Carmelites arrived in Olinda (1580), where they founded the first convent in 1583. They spread to Salvador (1586), Santos (1589), Recife (1654) and in the south, to Rio de Janeiro (1590), São Paulo (1594), Angra dos Reis (1608), Mogi das Cruzes (1629), and Itú (1719). By the 18th century they had in Brazil three provinces with approximately 500 religious. In Maranhão they established themselves in São Luis (1615), Pará (1624), Gurupé (1639), Alcântara (1647), Bonfim (1718) and Vigia (1737). By 1674 there were 60 religious evangelizing the area of Alto Solimões, Rio Negro and other parts of the Amazon basin, where Father José da Madalena introduced vaccine in 1728. In Maranhão in 1722 they administered 15 missions and in 1751, 18. The number decreased considerably in the 19th century.

The Franciscan missions achieved a firm foundation in 1585 in Olinda. The seat of the first custody of the Friars Minor in Brazil was the convent of Nª Sªª das Neves with a novitiate (1586) and a school for native children. From here the Franciscans went to Bahia (1587), Iguaraçu (1588) and Paraíba and Espírito Santo (1589). The Indian missions gained importance at the end of the century through the work of Father Antônio de Campo Maior in Itapessima, Ponta das Pedras, and Itamaracá. In São Paulo a Franciscan convent was founded in 1639.

In the 17th century Capuchins established the province of Santo Antônio in Brazil (1657) with numerous foundations in Ipojuca and Recife (1606), Rio de Janeiro (1607), Pará (1617), Serinhaem (1630), Santos and São Paulo (1639), Espírito Santo (1650) and Aracaju (1687). In 1733 there were 15 convents, one hospice, and 13 missions among the native inhabitants. Simultaneously, the Franciscans continued to maintain houses and missions in Pará and in Maranhão. Those of the province of Santo Antônio in Belém possessed one convent and seven missions; those of the province of the Immaculate Conception, 1 convent in São Luis, and one hospice and one mission in Grão-Pará; and those of the province of Piedade in Pará, two hospices and ten missions. Noteworthy were the missions of the Padres da Piedade in Pará and in Rio Tocantins among the Cametás and Aruãs. In the division of 1693 these fathers received the missions of Gurupatuba, Urubaguara, Rio Paru and Jamundã and, in that of 1699, all the missions between Amazónas and Cabo Norte. From Quito (1632–34) they had also contacted the Tapuias of the Amazon and reached the Encabelados (1635). In 1637 Father Agostinho das Chagas and Father Domingos de Brieva along with Jesuits and Mercedarians accompanied Pedro Teixeira on his return to Pará (1638). The province of the Immaculate Conception of Rio de Janeiro in 1675 continued with the foundation of Cabo Frio (1687).

The French Capuchins, at the suggestion of María de Médicis, accompanied the expedition of La Ravardière (1611), beginning their evangelization on the island of Fernando de Noronha and continuing it in Maranhão from where Claude d' ABBEVILLE and Father Ivo d'Evreux sent to France (1612) a group of Tupinambas, who were baptized in Paris with great solemnity. When the French were expelled, the Capuchins had to abandon the mission (1615) and were replaced by Franciscans, Jesuits and Carmelites. In 1705 Italian Capuchins, constituted in the Prefectures of Bahia (1712), Pernambuco (1725) and Rio de Janeiro (1737), directed 17 native inhabitant settlements.

The Mercedarians entered Brazil with Pedro Teixeira on his return from Quito to Pará (1637–39) and founded there the convent of Nª Sªª das Mercês (1640), from which they spread to São Luis do Maranhão (1664),

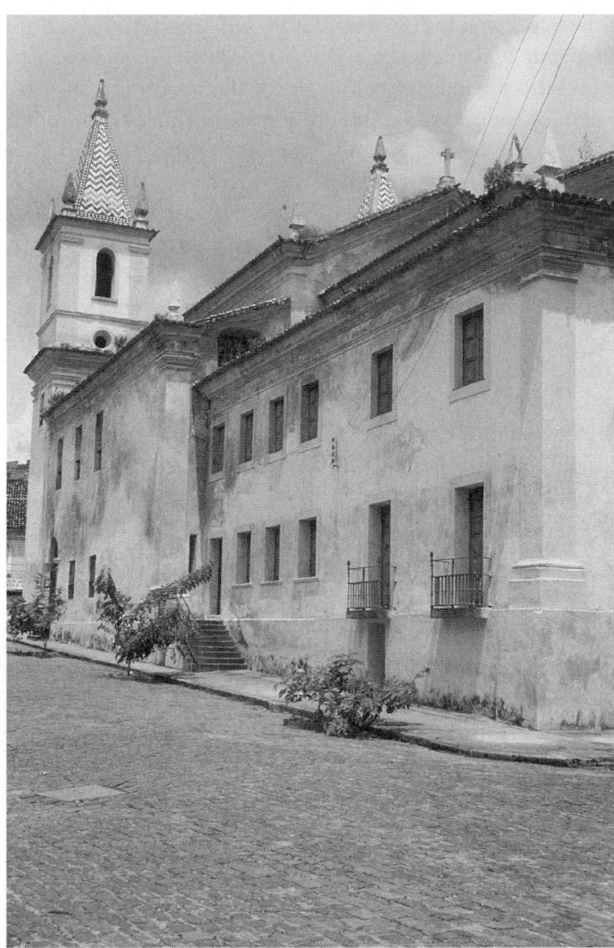

The Church of Rosario do Porto do Cachoeira, Brazil. (©Dave G. Houser/CORBIS)

and to Alcântara, creating or administrating several missions in Urubu (1665) and in Amazonas (1699). Father Teodósio da Veiga was the one who initiated regular mission establishments as far as Aiurim on the Rio Negro (1668–69). Difficulties with the Trinitarians, which impeded their expansion in Portugal in the 17th and 18th centuries, limited their recruitment of personnel for Brazil. In 1785 Pius VI secularized some convents in Pará. In 1749 the Mercedarians were ordered to withdraw to Maranhão, and their properties were confiscated. In 1758 in Maranhão and in Pará they had only five Indian settlements.

Of all the male religious orders after the Jesuits, the Franciscans were the ones that prospered and exerted the most influence. Missionary activity was not limited to the teaching of the Christian doctrine. It opposed cannibalism vigorously, turned nomadic native inhabitants into sedentary peoples by means of settlements where they were taught cattle raising, arts and trades in which many became eminent, as well as utilization of hygiene and prophylaxis in times of epidemic when smallpox, yellow fever, or malaria produced terrible devastation. Peaceful expeditions among rival clans for the ransoming of prisoners or their establishment in healthful places appropriate for the raising of cattle saved thousands of natives from extermination. On punitive expeditions the missionaries attempted to lessen the penalties inflicted and to prevent unjust imprisonment. Since colonists fought with a shortage of manpower, the missionaries did not always prevent excesses. They even participated at times in these and took unscrupulous advantage of the captives, disobeying the laws of the Church and the king in the regulation or distribution of prisoners. Nevertheless, the total result was the Christianization and civilization of many Stone-Age savages in the 16th century.

The political-administrative reforms imposed by Pombal on the American missions, because of the drastic and sudden way in which they were executed, were disastrous both from a religious and from a socio-economic point of view. Culturally, the expulsion of the religious orders from the settlements marked a return to ''obscurantism.'' The monastic decadence in the Portugal Pombaline period (1750–77) and in the liberal period up to 1820, followed by the subsequent extinction of the Portuguese religious orders in 1834, and the increase in Gallican and Jansenist influences, made missionary conditions in Brazil deplorable in the last days of the colonial period.

1822 to 1964. With the political agitation that preceded independence (Inconfidência Mincira of 1789) and followed it during the empire and with the influx of ideas of the French Revolution, of poorly assimilated Anglo-American liberalism, of regalism during the stay of the Portuguese court in Rio de Janeiro and of Masonry, the crisis begun by Pombal aggravated the situation of the missions in Brazil. During the empire Vidigal's instructions (1824) for the separation of Brazilian religious houses from their superiors in Europe, the extinction of Oratorian, Carmelite and Capuchin convents in Pernambuco in 1830, 1831, 1835 and 1840, in addition to the closing of the novitiates in 1855, pointed to a dismal future.

Fortunately, the popularity gained by the clergy and the religious orders in the civil struggles (1835–48) and in the wars with Argentina (1852) and Paraguay (1865–70), the zeal devoted to the missions, above all by the Italian Capuchins from 1843 and by the Sisters of Charity from 1849 and the agreement of the Holy See with Brazil on apostolic missions among the natives in 1862, backed by the liberties that the Republican Constitution of 1890 eventually guaranteed, all led to a new missionary expansion that is still going on throughout all of Brazil.

See Also: BRAZIL.

Bibliography: D. ALDEN. *The Making of an Enterprise. The Society of Jesus in Portugal, Its Empire and Beyond, 1540–1750* (Stanford 1996). P. CAMARGO, *História eclesiástica do Brasil* (Petrópolis, 1965). T. M. COHEN, *The Fire of Tongues: Antonio Vieira and the Missionary Church in Brazil and Portugal* (Stanford 1998). J. A. GAGLIANO and C. E. RONAN (eds.) *Jesuit Encounters in the New World* (Rome 1997). J. HEMMING, *Red Gold: The Conquest of the Brazilian Indians,1500–1760* (Cambridge, Mass. 1978). E. HOORNAERT, *La Igreja na Amazônia* (Petrópolis 1992); *História da Igreja no Brasil* (Petrópolis 1992). J. V. JACOBSEN, ''Jesuit Founders in Portugual and Brazil,'' *Mid-America,* 24 (Jan. 1942) 3–26. S. LEITE, *História da Companhia de Jesús no Brasil,* 10 v (Lisbon 1938–1950). A. PRAT, *Notas históricas sobre as missões carmelitas no extremo norte do Brasil* (Recife 1941). B. RÖWER, *A ordem franciscana no Brasil* (Petrópolis 1942). M. M. WERMERS, *A ordem carmelita e o Carmo en Portugal* (Lisbon 1963).

[D. MAURICIO/J. L. KLAIBER]

MISSION IN COLONIAL AMERICA, III (FRENCH MISSIONS)

The voyage undertaken by Giovanni da Verrazano in 1524 gave the French king Francis I a claim to certain areas in North America, but unlike Spain, France was slow in her New World colonization efforts because of her preoccupation with the so-called religious wars of the sixteenth century. Not unlike Spain and England, France envisioned a large colonial empire in North America, which, it was hoped, would bring economic benefits to the mother country. Between 1534 and 1542 Jacques Cartier undertook several voyages to North America, where he made extensive explorations with a view toward establishing a permanent French settlement. As a result of Cartier's first voyage, Francis I issued a royal commission for the founding of a permanent colony. In the commission to Cartier, the conversion of the native people of North America was mentioned as a prime incentive. This first attempt to plant a French colony ended unsuccessfully in 1542 because of the renewal that year of hostilities between Francis I and Emperor Charles V.

Early colonization efforts. Twenty years elapsed before a second attempt took place. Admiral Gaspard de Coligny planted a Huguenot settlement (1562) on the present Parris Island, S.C., but it was shortly abandoned in favor of Fort Caroline, near the mouth of the St. Johns River, Fla. In 1565 a Spanish contingent from St. Augustine under Pedro Menéndez de Avilés destroyed the fort. In 1605 a colony, originally established the year before on Saint Croix Island, was moved to Port Royal, Acadia (Nova Scotia). Abbé Jessé Fleché, who went there in 1610, carried on mission work among the Micmac tribes. Fleché was succeeded by two Jesuits, Pierre Biard (d. 1622) and Ennemond Massé (1574–1646), who arrived at Port Royal in 1611 under the patronage of the Marquise de Guercheville. In 1613 Biard and Massé joined with two fellow Jesuits, Reverend Jacques Quentin and Brother Gilbert du Thet, to establish a new mission near present-day Bangor, Maine, but they never reached their goal. In a surprise attack by Captain Samuel Argall of Virginia, Du Thet was killed and the others taken prisoner.

To Samuel de Champlain belongs the credit for the first permanent French settlement in North America. In 1608 Champlain founded the colony of Quebec, which in its early years owed its existence to his courage, determination, and organizational ability. Ideally located as a trade center, Quebec provided easy access to the St. Lawrence River, the Mississippi River, and the Atlantic Ocean. The first missionaries to arrive in Quebec were the French Franciscans (Récollets), who came in 1615 and ministered to the Montagnais, Hurons, Wyandots, and the Micmacs. They enjoyed little success, however. By 1625 six Jesuits arrived under Charles Lalemant (1587–1674); among them were Massé and Jean de Brébeuf (1593–1649). Disputes between England and France, as well as intermittent warfare, disrupted life in the colonies and added to the difficulties of the missionaries. In 1629 the English captured Quebec, and it was not restored to the French until 1632. In that year the Jesuits were entrusted by the Company of One Hundred Associates with the North American missions.

Following the restoration of 1632, French rule made itself felt in varying degrees and at different times from the northeast corner of the future United States through the system of great inland lakes and south through the valley of the Mississippi River to the Gulf of Mexico. New France provided the base for missionary activity in many parts of what is now the United States.

Maine. After the failure of the colonization efforts in 1604 and of the Jesuit missions (1611–13), the Congregation for the Propagation of the Faith commissioned the Capuchins to take up the missionary work in Acadia. Between 1632 and 1654 the Capuchins established seven missions in Acadia, New Brunswick, and Maine. Following the English seizure of Fort Pentagoet (Castine), Maine (1654), the Capuchins closed their missions. In the meantime, the Jesuit Gabriel Druillettes visited the Abenaki Indians on the Kennebec River in 1646 in response to the indigenous people's appeal for a priest. He remained for a year, during which he studied the native language and customs. Druillettes made two subsequent visits before the English attack in 1654. During the 20 years that the Capuchins spent in the northeast missions, many of the Native American converts were removed to tribal villages or reductions near Quebec, such as Sillery, St. François, and Becancourt, where it was hoped that they could be taught the elements of European customs and useful trades.

No missionary activity of consequence resumed in Maine until the 1680s. In 1694 Sebastian RALE, SJ, arrived, and Maine became the scene of his labors for the next 30 years. When Hudson Bay, Newfoundland, and Acadia were ceded to England in 1713, there followed a dispute between Quebec and Massachusetts over the boundary of Maine. In 1722 Governor Samuel Shute of Massachusetts attacked the French mission on the Kennebec River, and two years later Father Rale was murdered. In 1726 the Maine missions were reopened, but little headway was made because of a lack of priests and the uncooperative attitude of the Quebec authorities. With the passing of New France to the English in 1763, the Maine missions came under the jurisdiction of Bishop Richard Challoner, vicar apostolic of the London District.

New York. The story of missionary activity in New York began in a sanguinary fashion when, in 1642, a band of Mohawks (Iroquois Confederacy) surprised and captured a group of Hurons near Three Rivers. Father Isaac Jogues and two lay assistants, René Goupil and Guillaume Coûture, who had accompanied the Hurons, were taken to a tribal village near present-day Auriesville, where Goupil was murdered and Jogues and Coûture were tortured. Jogues managed to escape, but on a second trip in 1646 he and Jean La Lande were taken prisoners by the Mohawks, after which they were tomahawked to death (*see* NORTH AMERICAN MARTYRS).

An attempt to plant a French colony among the Onondagas near Lake Onondaga in 1656 ended in failure within the year because of Iroquois unrest. The next ten years witnessed intermittent warfare between the French and the five Iroquois nations, and it was not until 1668 that a mission could be established in the five cantonments of the Iroquois Confederacy. In the succeeding decade some 2,000 converts were made, among them Katharine Ganneaktena of the Erie tribe and Kateri TEKAKWITHA of the Mohawks.

Following the 1665 grant of New Netherlands by Charles II of England to his brother James, duke of York, the deep and lasting rivalry that developed between England and France ended only with the cession of New France to England at the end of the French and Indian War (1763). The Jesuit missionaries were looked upon as French agents. Thomas Dongan, New York's Catholic governor (1683–88), afforded the Jesuits a modicum of protection on the northern frontier, but beginning in 1687 he forbade the Jesuits to work among the Iroquois. By 1709 the final chapter in the history of the French Jesuits in New York ended with the departure of Jacques de Lamberville for Quebec and the arrest of Pierre de Mareuil by Colonel Peter Schuyler.

Apart from the Jesuits' venture, the only other partially successful effort to establish a Catholic Christian community in New York centered at present-day Ogdensburg, where in 1748 the Sulpician François Piquet founded La Presentation. This mission came to an untimely end during the French and Indian War.

The Great Lakes. The missionary potential of the Great Lakes area became evident after the establishment of trade centers at Michilimackinac, Green Bay, and Sault Ste. Marie. During the 1640s and 1650s several Jesuits, including Charles Raymbault, Isaac Jogues, Leonard Garreau, and Gabriel Druillettes, penetrated this area. In 1661 René Menard, SJ, gave his life to spread the gospel among the native people in the Wisconsin wilderness. Menard was succeeded by Claude Jean ALLOUEZ, SJ, who left a fine record as a missionary of the West. In addition to the mission known as La Pointe du Saint Esprit (Ashland, Wis.), established in 1665, Allouez established missions at Sault Ste. Marie and Green Bay. He also worked with Jacques MARQUETTE among the Illinois tribes at Kaskaskia. Bishop F. de M. LAVAL of Quebec named Allouez vicar-general for the western country, where the Jesuit traveled widely and labored successfully among the Illinois, Nipissings, Ottawas, Pottawatomi, Sacs, Foxes, and Sioux. After three years, Allouez was joined by Louis Nicholas, Marquette, and Claude DABLON. Dablon succeeded Allouez as superior of the missions in 1668. In 1671 La Pointe was abandoned because of a threat from the Sioux. During this same time, Dablon established the mission of St. Ignace some 50 miles west of Sault Ste. Marie; this mission was maintained until 1765.

Illinois country. During the latter part of the seventeenth century and the early decades of the eighteenth century, the French government encouraged missionary activity in the Great Lakes, Illinois, and Mississippi Valley areas. Experience proved that only the missionaries were able to control the unpredictable tribes. Furthermore, the presence of the missions provided the government with a firmer grasp on territory already claimed by Spain and England. In addition, exploration was stressed, and several commissions were given to such men as Louis Jolliet and R. C. de LA SALLE to further the interests of France.

Jolliet-Marquette Expedition. In 1672 Louis Frontenac, governor of New France, commissioned Jolliet to explore the Mississippi River to determine its source in the hope of finding a waterway to the Orient. The historic trip began in the spring of 1673, and among the party was Father Marquette. The journey, which proved that the Mississippi emptied into the Gulf of Mexico, had two important effects for Marquette. On the return passage, he became acquainted with the Kaskaskia tribes, for whom he established the mission of the Immaculate Conception near Utica, Ill., two years later. But the expedition also irreparably harmed his health, and he died on May 18, 1675.

La Salle's Explorations. One of the most colorful, if ill-fated, laymen whose influence on Church affairs was strongly felt in New France was Robert Cavelier de La Salle. Like his friend Governor Frontenac, La Salle disliked the Jesuits and invariably employed the services of the Sulpicians and Franciscans in his explorations. One of his early associates was the Flemish friar Louis HENNEPIN, who joined him in the establishment of Fort de Conty on the Niagara River near the falls (1678). Shortly thereafter Fort Miami (Mich.) and its chapel (the first Catholic Church in the lower peninsula of the future state), as well as the fort of Crevecoeur near Peoria, were built. The latter was abandoned in 1680 following an attack by the Iroquois on the Illinois tribes.

La Salle, who regarded the Mississippi as the lifeline of a French domain in the interior, established Fort St. Louis (1682) on the upper Illinois River. From there he began his famous descent of the Mississippi River that same year. The result of that trip was the claim to a vast territory to be known as Louisiana. Two years later King Louis XIV commissioned La Salle to plant a colony in Louisiana, which La Salle located on the Texas coast near Matagorda Bay. The elaborate plans collapsed within four years with the murder of La Salle by his own men and the destruction of the colony by the Cenis tribes.

Jesuits in the Illinois Country. After Marquette's death in 1675, Allouez took over the Immaculate Conception mission among the Kaskaskia, where he labored until his death in 1689. It has been estimated, with some exaggeration, that Allouez instructed almost 100,000 native people and baptized some 10,000. Among the Jesuits who succeeded Allouez in the Illinois country were Jacques Gravier, Sebastian Rale, François Pinet, and Jean Mermet. In 1663 Bishop Laval set up in Quebec a missionary seminary whose students served in the Illinois area among both natives and whites. Unfortunately, minor disputes arose between the secular priests and the Jesuits over jurisdiction.

During the eighteenth century, several villages were established along the Illinois River and were generally ministered to by the Jesuits. These communities thrived until the end of the French and Indian War. The heroic work reaped proportionately small rewards, however, and the brandy trade between the natives and French traders was noted as a primary cause of the Jesuits' failure to make lasting converts. In the 1730s the mission at Vincennes was founded; a century later it was named a diocese.

Franciscans at Detroit. Fort Pontchartrain was built on the site of present-day Detroit, Mich., in 1701 under the leadership of Antoine de la Mothe Cadillac (d. 1730). Like Frontenac and La Salle, Cadillac was of the anti-Jesuit party, and much to the annoyance of the Jesuits, he concentrated the various native tribes around Detroit. Fort Pontchartrain itself was well served by two Franciscans, Bonaventure Lienard and Simplicius Bocquet. In 1749 the Hurons in Detroit moved across the Detroit River and settled at Pointe de Montreal (Sandwich, Ontario), where they were ministered to by the Jesuits Armand de la Richardie and Pierre Portier. In 1755 Bishop Henri Dubreuil de Pontbriand of Quebec (1741–60) went to Detroit for a church dedication; he was thus the first bishop to visit that area of the future United States.

Louisiana. In 1698, a decade after La Salle's death, Pierre Le Moyne d'Iberville, was authorized to lead an expedition to Louisiana and there to establish a settlement at Biloxi. Iberville's first contingent was accompanied by Reverend Anastase Douay, a survivor of La Salle's tragic venture of 1687. On Iberville's second trip to Louisiana, he was accompanied by Paul du Ru, SJ, although the latter remained only briefly. The Biloxi settlement was moved in 1702 to Fort Louis on Mobile Bay (Mobile, Ala.). A conflict that erupted at this time between the Jesuits and the secular priests from Quebec's missionary seminary resulted in the departure of the Jesuits—an exile that lasted for 20 years.

By 1718 Iberville's brother and the new governor, Jean Baptiste le Moyne, Sieur de Bienville, succeeded in planting a settlement on the Mississippi itself, naming it New Orleans in honor of the prince regent of France, and four years later the capital of Louisiana was moved there from Fort Louis. The Code Noir, introduced in 1724, regulated race relations and was in effect a transference to France's colonies of the union of Church and State that existed in the mother country.

Difficulties over ecclesiastical jurisdiction hampered the work of the Church in Louisiana. A division of the territory (1722) into three ecclesiastical districts, under the Capuchins, the Jesuits, and the Carmelites respectively, proved unworkable. The Carmelites withdrew, and the Capuchins were given jurisdiction on both sides of the Mississippi River south of Ohio, at which point the Jesuit vicar-general's jurisdiction began. In 1723 the area between the Natchez and Ohio rivers was turned over to the Jesuits. Three years later, the Jesuits were given charge of all native missions in Louisiana, while the Capuchins were responsible for the white colonists. The latter complained bitterly, and Bishop Louis de Morney of Quebec, himself a Capuchin, placed the New Orleans Jesuits under interdict. The troubles between the two orders did not end until the Society of Jesus was suppressed in 1763.

Because of the lack of funds, the missionaries were forced to live in extreme poverty; the conditions at the native missions were especially pitiful. New Orleans itself had no real church until 1727 when St. Louis' Church was established. That same year eight Ursuline nuns from Rouen opened a girls' academy in New Orleans, although there was no similar school for Catholic boys until the nineteenth century. Immorality was so prevalent in New Orleans that Bishop Jean Baptiste de St. Vallier of Quebec issued a sharp rebuke in his 1721 pastoral letter. In addition, troubles arose over the brandy trade and mixed marriages. By the terms of a secret treaty in 1762, Louisiana was ceded to Spain, and that vast territory returned to French administration for but a brief period (1800–03) before its purchase by the United States in 1803.

Results. In examining the overall record of French missionary activity in North America, it must be judged a failure in terms of lasting results. Hundreds of priests and lay assistants—Jesuits, Franciscans, Sulpicians, Carmelites, Capuchins, and secular priests—devoted all or a major portion of their adult lives to this disappointing apostolate. The soil of New France was enriched with the blood of numerous martyrs, but the number of lasting converts was relatively small. Blame may be justly laid at the door of uncooperative and often irreligious authorities at home and in the colonies. JANSENISM and GALLICANISM, then prevalent in France, affected the colonial missions. The brandy trade and questions of immorality among both the Europeans and Native Americans were sources of keen disappointment. Although the heroic missionaries were well trained in adversity and the example of a Kateri Tekakwitha was consoling, perhaps the real cause for the failure of the French missions was beyond the missionaries's control. The missionaries were unfamiliar with native customs and were unprepared for the inter- and intra-tribal warfare that took place. Also, the continuous friction between England and France made it unlikely that the native peoples could be Christianized until the white man himself set the example.

Bibliography: N. BAILLARGEON, *Le Séminaire de Québec de 1685 à 1760* (Québec 1977). R. BAUDIER, *The Catholic Church in Louisiana* (New Orleans 1939). L. CAMPEAU, *Les Cent-Associés et le peuplement de la Nouvelle-France (1633–1663)* (Montréal 1974); *L'Evêché de Québec (1674). Aux origines du premier diocese érigé en Amérique française* (Québec 1974); *La Mission des Jésuites chez les Hurons* (Rome 1987). G. R. CONRAD, ed., *Cross, Crozier, and Crucible: A Volume Celebrating the Bicentennial of a Catholic Diocese in Louisiana* (New Orleans 1993). J. DELANGLEZ, *The French Jesuits in Lower Louisiana (1700–1763)* (Washington, DC 1935). J. T. ELLIS, *Catholics in Colonial America* (Baltimore 1965). C. E. NOLAN, *A History of the Archdiocese of New Orleans* (Strasbourg 2000). C. E. O'NEILL, *Church and State in French Colonial Louisiana: Policy and Politics to 1732* (New Haven, Conn. 1966). F. PARKMAN, *La Salle and the Discovery of the Great West* (Boston 1910). R. G. THWAITES, ed. *Jesuit Relations* *and Allied Documents: Travels and Explorations of the Jesuit Missionaries in New France 1610–1791,* 73 v. (Cleveland 1896–1901). C. L. VOGEL, *The Capuchins in French Louisiana (1722–1766)* (New York 1928).

[J. Q. FELLER/EDS.]

MISSION IN COLONIAL AMERICA, IV (ENGLISH MISSIONS)

England was itself a Catholic mission and was mission-minded when Catholic settlers first arrived in America. Simon Stock, OCarm, Lord Henry Arundell, and others advanced the hope of preserving the faith by immigration to the New World; they also asked dedication of colonizing gentlemen to the conversion of Protestants as well as indigenous people in America.

17th-Century Foundations. The first to attempt such a project was George CALVERT, who established the short-lived Avalon in Newfoundland, Canada (1627); two secular priests, Thomas Longeille and Anthony Smith, accompanied him. It was Calvert's Maryland colony (1634), however, that soon after became the center of mission growth.

Unsettled ecclesiastical conditions in England hindered an orderly provision for the American missions. After the Holy See ruled against the appointment of a bishop in England (1631), the Congregation for the PROPAGATION OF THE FAITH in Rome dealt with the English clergy directly or through Continental prelates or through the major superiors of exempt orders. Under Cecil Calvert, second Lord Baltimore, who as patron possessed a semi-feudal role, Jesuit missionaries withdrew (1647) temporarily from Maryland in opposition to Baltimore's oath requirement, application of mortmain, and other decisions on corporate property ownership. They eventually found a solution in lay trusteeship or other devices; but missionaries of this period were often burdened with secular employments to assure their material support. Among those who labored heroically and effectively was Thomas Copley, SJ, who served for nearly 20 years in the earliest times and, with Andrew WHITE, SJ, endured Puritan persecutions. By 1684 native Marylanders such as John Brooke had entered their priestly studies with the Jesuits. The Capuchin Christopher Plunkett served for a time in Maryland and Virginia. At Baltimore's request two secular priests arrived during the period of difficulties with the Jesuits. Hardships of climate and the apostolate, however, often considerably shortened priestly careers.

Toward the end of the 17th century St. Mary's City in St. Mary's County became the center of Catholic life for a population of about 2,000. Missionary excursions to the native tribes led to foundations in Charles and Prince George's Counties. Virginia was often visited by Maryland missionaries, and at times some resided there among a small Catholic population. Chapels were built where priests resided and the manors of gentlemen served as places of worship for remote communities. Native people who remained in St. Mary's County were cared for; other native missions were gravely harmed by migration, the marauding of Susquehannocks, and the period of Puritan power.

The Catholic governor, Thomas Dongan, brought Thomas Harvey, SJ, to New York (1783). Catholic life in New England was very tenuous at this time; occasionally French missionaries, such as Gabriel Druillettes, made visits there. The Catholics on the English Caribbean islands were under the same jurisdiction as these mainland settlements. About 1667 Governor Stapleton of Montserrat, a Catholic, was involved in the struggle of the Catholic population there and on the islands of St. Christopher and Barbados. French and Spanish priests on neighboring islands often attended to these Catholics.

Outstanding Catholic Maryland families, such as the Brents and the Fenwicks, grew strong in the faith. They were well educated in secular and religious matters, and they fostered their spiritual life with retreats. They helped educate the native tribes, protected church property as trustees, and had a paternal Christian care for uneducated Catholic servants and slaves. They furthered tutorial and other education under such masters as Brother Ralph Crouch, SJ. Between 1667 and 1674 conversions to Catholicism averaged more than 40 persons annually.

Penal Age. Before 1690 favorable political and other secular conditions directly aided Catholic life in the New World. After the Restoration of the Stuarts in 1660, the British Crown gave instructions that freedom of conscience was to be respected even in New England. From the beginning, Maryland was free from intolerant laws except during a Puritan decade of power. This freedom was due to the TOLERATION ACTS and the Calverts. Quakers and Presbyterians as well as Catholics favored the old arrangement without establishment of religion and restriction on conscience. When William and Mary overturned Stuart rule in 1688 a tragic reversal of Catholic fortunes ensued. For the next 20 years newly appointed royal governors in Maryland experimented with the most repressive measures against Catholicism. By 1718, however, some of these laws had been mitigated. Worship was permitted, but only in private. Catholics were excluded from voting, office holding, and the practice of law; and their property was sometimes in danger of a double tax. An oath against the doctrine of TRANSUB-

STANTIATION was a frequent cause for the imposition of these penalties. There was discrimination against Catholic immigrants and Church educational institutions. Similar provisions were prevalent elsewhere, except in Pennsylvania, where public worship and voting were permitted.

In spite of hardships, missionary work went forward. Before James II was deposed, his former chaplain Bonaventure Giffard was appointed vicar bishop apostolic of London with jurisdiction over the American English Colonies. Advances were made into Talbot County on Maryland's eastern shore. Between 1732 and 1763, under the leadership of Ferdinand FARMER, SJ, six churches were built in Pennsylvania, serving Philadelphia and the German immigrants in southeastern counties. Franciscans worked among the Scotch immigrants in Pennsylvania. Excursions of missionaries to New Jersey and New York were made, and contacts were established with Catholic Mohawks. French-Catholic Acadians found refuge in Baltimore, Md., and in Philadelphia after they were expelled from Canada. Catholicism continued to grow in the Caribbean islands of St. Christopher, Montserrat, Antigua, and Nevis, in spite of property and other restrictions on Catholics. But provisions for the care of souls were not as satisfactory as on the mainland.

Gentlemen of means in England and America provided land and other investments to support some of the missionaries; in court they successfully contested efforts to prevent such assistance. Although Catholics of the period suffered imprisonment in the earlier years and the threat of it later, the gentry's possession of property and their self-respect prevented social ostracism. They sent their children to Bohemia Manor grammar school, which was opened by Thomas Poulton, SJ (1741). Many went from there to St. Omer's and other Continental European institutions, which put them among the better educated men of America. In their libraries in America, Catholic gentlemen read the spiritual and polemical works of the Elizabethan Robert PERSONS, SJ, as well as those of Bp. Richard CHALLONER of London; and with the clergy, they answered the attacks of hostile elements among Protestants.

In St. Mary's County, where in 1712 50 percent of American English Catholics constituted about 35 percent of the county's population, devotion to the Sacred Heart fostered popular piety. But throughout the colonies the pressure to conform to the Church of England had its effect. The uneducated Catholics of the rising towns were not protected by the plantation-gentry structure of most Catholic communities, and Catholic immigrants were often a scandal, even when they did not abandon their faith.

Revolutionary Prelude to Episcopacy. From the time of the English conquest of French Canada (1763) until the appointment of John CARROLL as first bishop of the U.S. (1789), ecclesiastical jurisdiction was in a tangle. Innocent XII had indicated that application for priestly faculties should be made regularly to the vicar apostolic of London. Both Giffard and Challoner understood the awkwardness of this arrangement, and they recommended that the bishop of Quebec, Canada, assume this role. But the Congregation of Propaganda continued to recognize the authority of Jesuit superiors. George Hunter, SJ, Superior of Maryland, made trips to both Quebec and London to adjust matters, representing the unfavorable reaction of American Protestants not only to jurisdiction of a French Canadian prelate, but to any North American bishop.

A new complication arose in 1773 when the Society of Jesus was suppressed. The last Jesuit superior, John Lewis, then vicar-general, formed an association that by oath bound the clergy together and protected the American Church against any undue control by Propaganda. A new legal incorporation was effected to safeguard property. The Revolutionary War further alienated the American mission from the bishop of London, who again expressed the desire to be freed of jurisdiction; in 1781 Bp. James Talbot formally disassociated himself from the mission.

Soon a general chapter of the U.S. clergy was called at White Marsh, Md. (June 27, 1783), and a petition was sent to the Holy See requesting appointment of a prefect apostolic from a list of names drawn from the chapter. On June 9, 1784, John Carroll was approved. In addition to the authority held by past superiors, he had the power to confer Confirmation, and he was no longer under the bishop of London but had quasi-autonomous status directly under the Holy See. When Protestant tolerance for episcopacy developed, Carroll sought relief from the weaknesses of the prefecture and was granted the power of bishop ordinary in 1789.

The jurisdiction of Carroll technically extended to the territorial extremities of the U.S. Immigrant Scotch-Irish Highlanders in upper New York had their own priests. Rev. Peter Gibault, who had collaborated with patriots despite the opposition of the bishop of Quebec, continued to serve in the Illinois country after the war. The Franciscan Simplicius Bocquet ministered in the vicinity of Detroit, Mich. Penobscot tribes in Maine successfully applied to Massachusetts for a priest to meet their spiritual needs. Although the treaty of 1763 had added four more Caribbean islands to the jurisdiction of the Catholic bishop of London, the appointment of Carroll severed Caribbean jurisdictional connection with the communities of the United States.

During this period the Catholic life of Maryland, Pennsylvania, and New York grew strong, and the Catholic population exceeded 25,000. Chapels of public worship were built in Baltimore and elsewhere, and John Carroll initiated one of the first parishioner-supported churches at St. John's, Rock Creek, Md. Educational foundations in Philadelphia and Georgetown (Washington, D.C.) were made. But the growing diversity of secular life in the new nation, particularly in New York, Pennsylvania, and the Trans-Appalachian West, radically modified the social structure of the Catholic community. Favorable provisions of state and Federal constitutions opened public office to Catholics. Particularly in Maryland and Pennsylvania, growing amity with Protestants developed, loss of the faith declined from what it had been, and a greater number of conversions to Catholicism took place, including that of Gov. Thomas Sim Lee during his term of office in Maryland.

Bibliography: J. J. CASINO, ''Anti-Popery in Colonial Pennsylvania,'' *Pennsylvania Magazine of History and Biography* 105 (July 1981) 279–309. J. T. ELLIS, *Catholics in Colonial America* (Baltimore 1965). R. A. GLEISSNER, ''Religious Causes of the Glorious Revolution in Maryland,'' *Maryland Historical Review* 64 (Winter 1969) 327–41. M. GRAHAM, ''Popish Plots: Protestant Fears in Early Colonial Maryland, 1676–1689'' *Catholic Historical Review* 79 (April 1993) 197–216. T. O. HANLEY, *Their Rights and Liberties: The Beginnings of Religious and Political Freedom in Maryland* (Westminster, Md. 1959). T. A. HUGHES, *The History of the Society of Jesus in North America*, 4 vols. (New York 1907–17). J. D. KRUGLER, ''Lord Baltimore, Roman Catholics, and Toleration: Religious Policy in Maryland during the Early Catholic Years,'' *Catholic Historical Review* 65 (Jan 1979) 49–75. J. D. KRUGLER, '''With Promise of Liberty in Religion': The Catholic Lords of Baltimore and Toleration in Seventeenth-Century Maryland, 1634–1692'' *Maryland Historical Magazine* 79 (Spring 1984) 21–43. A.M. MELVILLE, *John Carroll of Baltimore* (New York 1955).

[T. O. HANLEY/EDS.]

MISSION IN POSTCOLONIAL LATIN AMERICA

This entry discusses the history and development of missionary endeavors in the postcolonial period of Latin America. For a survey of the colonial period, *see* MISSION IN COLONIAL AMERICA, I (SPANISH MISSIONS) and MISSION IN COLONIAL AMERICA, II (PORTUGUESE MISSIONS).

Introduction. The expulsion of the Jesuits in the eighteenth century followed by the anti-clerical independence movements in the early nineteenth century brought the colonial phase of the history of evangelization in the Americas to an end. For a period of time the faith was kept alive and transmitted in many parts by the *cofradías* or lay confraternities in the absence of an organized evangelization. Circuit riding, often ill-prepared diocesan priests were overwhelmed by the pastoral needs of the people. Formation and education in the faith passed to various religious orders, which established schools in much of the republican era.

The early twentieth century witnessed virulent anticlerical attitudes in Mexico arising from a backlash against the Church's growing influence in the secular sphere. The Cristero Rebellion of the 1920s in Mexico led to a period of persecution and the strict separation of Church and State. Elsewhere in Latin America, that separation was not so rigidly adhered to and many governments had concordats with the Vatican that allowed the Church to maintain schools and to carry out evangelization unhindered. It wasn't until the early 1960s, with the influx of many North American missionaries, that the Church in Latin America entered into another phase of an evangelizing outreach.

Developments in the Renewal of the Latin America Church: Medellín. Concerns over how to evangelize and transmit the faith to the growing population of Latin America received an impetus when the continent's bishops met for the first time in Rio de Janeiro in 1955 and formed the Latin American Episcopal Council or *CONSEJO EPISCOPAL LATINOAMERICANO* (CELAM). The Second Vatican Council gave an added impetus to Church leaders to address this question, leading to the convocation of the Second Conference of CELAM in Medellín, Colombia in 1968. Called to adapt the spirit of Vatican II's *aggiornamento* to the Latin America reality within the continent, Medellín reflected the winds of change that paved the way for the adoption of a critical stance toward unjust structures in civil society, and a preferential option for the poor. Radical developments, such as the *comunidades de base* (BASIC CHRISTIAN COMMUNITIES) supported by new theological currents and symbolized by the emergence of the theology of liberation, captured worldwide attention and imagination. By the same token, these changes provoked a negative reaction from some sectors long acccustomed to the Church's traditional apolitical stance. Latin American bishops such as Dom Helder Camara in Brazil, Cardinal Juan Landázuri Ricketts in Peru, Eduardo Proaño in Ecuador, Marcos McGrath in Panama, and Sergio Mendéz Arceo and Samuel Ruíz in Mexico lived out the spirit of the Medellín documents and enthusiastically translated its conclusions into concrete pastoral actions that contributed to the renewal of evangelization in the Latin America Church.

Puebla. The Third Conference of CELAM was held in Puebla, Mexico in early 1979. While affirming the basic thrust of Medellín, it also gave new emphasis and urgency to the Church's evangelizing activity by underscoring the "evangelizing potential of the poor" and by calling for the Latin America Church to step up and assume its mission *ad gentes* role outside of, as well as inside, Latin America. Puebla took a much more guarded approach to the movement of Base Christian Communities, preferring to see them be much more under ecclesiastical supervision than as a lay-led grassroots expression of the Church. Likewise, the assessment of the writings of liberation theologians resulted in a qualified approval that also cautioned against unnuanced dependence on Marxist analysis.

Santo Domingo. The Fourth Conference of CELAM in Santo Domingo in the Dominican Republic in 1992 affirmed the renewal process initiated at Medellín and Puebla and expanded its focus by recognizing developments in emerging theological currents from indigenous and Afro-American peoples, feminist theologians, and a growing ecological movement. One of the most important developments at Santo Domingo was the pope's call for an American Synod joining the local churches of North and South America and the Caribbean to discern the concerns and challenges for evangelization in an age of globalization and interdependence. At Santo Domingo, many church leaders voiced their concerns over the phenomenal growth of Protestantism in Latin America in recent decades, especially of Pentecostal churches. Alarm from some sectors over this development did not readily translate into concrete strategies. Some envisioned a weakening of ecumenical relations with the more historical churches due to what many perceive as the aggressive proselytism of more sectarian Christian groups. As Latin American society becomes more pluralistic, cultural Catholicism will likely become less of a factor in identity.

Synod for America. The 1997 Synod of Bishop's Special Assembly for America held in Rome broke new ground for establishing closer connections between churches from the north and south and set the stage to create the foundations for greater collaboration around common problems within the perspective of the New Evangelization. Expectations ran high as to the potential for collaborative and joint efforts. At the same time, uncertainty over the future of CELAM and especially the continuous process of renewal begun at Medellín remained. The passing of an older, dynamic, high-profile generation of Church leaders also raised questions about the future course of evangelization in Latin America.

U.S. Missionaries in Latin America. The movement to send U.S. missionaries to Latin America was led by Cardinal Richard CUSHING of Boston, Maryknoller John CONSIDINE, and Ivan Illich in the 1950s and 1960s. Religious communities like Maryknoll, the Columbans, and the Boston-based MISSIONARY SOCIETY OF ST. JAMES THE APOSTLE and such diocesan missions as St. Louis, Missouri (Bolivia) and Jefferson City, Missouri (Peru), Cleveland, Ohio (El Salvador), and New Ulm, Minnesota (Guatemala) participated in this massive missionary endeavor. While the number of North American–born missionaries working in Latin America had declined sharply by 2000, the missionary movement from north to south continued to show great vitality and creativity. More emphasis was placed on mission education awareness initiatives, different forms of inter-American cooperation and collaboration, along with an increased presence of laity. An expanded notion of what constitutes mission also influenced the changes in mission from a one-way process to allow for more dialogue on all levels. The challenges spelled out in the document *Ecclesia in America*, fruit of the 1997 Synod of America, provided the foundations for new directions and initiatives.

The changing profile of the U.S. missionary in Latin America in the last decades of the 20th century bear closer examination. Religious women embarking on a second or third ministerial career change arrived in greater numbers in the 1980s and early 1990s. Short- and long-term lay missionaries with close ties to established diocesan groups and communities like MARYKNOLL and the COLUMBAN FATHERS appeared at the same time. In the 1960s, there were few options for the lay overseas mission vocation. By 2000, a greater number of possibilities for overseas cross-cultural service were available. Reflecting wider societal trends, many committed U.S. Catholics found themselves drawn to diverse forms of service of a short-term duration. The twining of parishes, or sister parish projects, from North and Latin America opened up even more paths for alternative service and networks of solidarity across the hemisphere.

Challenges and Questions. The witness of life and the Church's prophetic role in the defense of human rights, participation in the peace process, and the work of reconciliation were integral to the task of evangelization in Latin America. After the early 1970s, many missionaries gave their lives to spread the Gospel, of whom Archbishop Oscar Romero (1980), the U.S. churchwomen (1980), and the six Jesuits and their housekeeper (1989) in El Salvador became the most publicized examples. The recovery of the historical memory of atrocities committed against missionaries in places like Guatemala and El Salvador is not simply an adjunct to the work of proclaiming the Gospel, but an essential dimension of it.

One of the main vehicles for evangelization since the early 1970s, the *comunidades de base* (Base Christian Communities) enjoyed a process of continuous organic growth in places like Brazil. In other places, they declined in importance. Alongside the development of the CEBs, a resurgence of European-style lay movements like *Opus Dei, Communione et Liberatione*, the Neo-Catechumenate, and others, injected other protagonists and variables into the prospects for evangelization. This shift came about in tandem with the evolution in Latin America of large urban areas and mega-cities. A new pluralistic culture in the cities among both migrants and more educated elites presented new challenges as well. The challenges of globalization, urbanization, mass migrations, pluralism, and the acceptance of new information technology called for new mission strategies that focus on maintaining an evangelizing presence in the area of social communications, as well as dialogue with new social actors, the socio-cultural *areopagi* that Pope John Paul II referred to in his missionary encyclical *REDEMPTORIS MISSIO* (1990).

Bibliography: J. COMBLIN, *Called for Freedom: The Changing Context of Liberation Theology* (Maryknoll 1998). A. DRIES, *The Missionary Movement in American Catholic History* (Maryknoll 1998). E. DUSSEL, *The Church in Latin America, 1492–1992* (Maryknoll 1992). A. HENNELLEY, *Santo Domingo and Beyond* (Maryknoll 1993). S. P. JUDD, ''Toward a New Self-Understanding: The U.S. Catholic Missionary Movement on the Eve of the Quincentennial,'' *Missiology* 20 (1992) 457–468. J. KLAIBER, *The Church, Dictatorships and Democracy in Latin America* (Martyknoll 1998). D. MARTIN, *Tongues of Fire: The Explosion of Protestantism in Latin America* (Cambridge, Mass. 1993).

[S. P. JUDD]

MISSION THEOLOGY

Mission theology is ''that part of missiology that links systematic theology (dogmatics, ethics, ascetics) with practical theology (canon law, catechetics, liturgics, homiletics, pastoral care, service and apologetics). It outlines and interprets mission systematically and practically from the perspective of God's mission, Christ's mission, the mission of the Holy Spirit and the mission of the Church'' (see J. A. B. Jongeneel [1999]: 29).

Mission theology developed rapidly during the latter half of the twentieth century. Informed and influenced by postcolonial critique and significant shifts in religious, political, and cultural consciousness, developments in mission theology have included renewed interest in the biblical foundations for mission, heightened consciousness of the missiological challenges posed by contextual theologies and historical studies of Christian mission, the integrative use of social scientific insights in theological reflection on missionary activity, the promotion of spiritualities of mission, theological investigation of the interactive dynamics of gospel and culture, and finally, fostering confidence in an ecumenical vision worthy of trust.

In the effort to make theologies of mission intelligible for a world church, ecclesiastical leaders, theologians, and missionaries, along with representatives of local churches and faith communities, have attempted to put these theologies at the service of others in meaningful and productive ways. Mediated in and through ecclesial documents, ecumenical declarations, scholarly publications, pastoral communications, and Christian media productions, mission theologies have been instrumental and consequential in both setting the agenda and implementing the decisions of councils, synods, assemblies, and congresses. Mission theology is foundational to the processes of promoting, integrating, and contextualizing the elements of Christian mission through encounter, proclamation, communion, dialogue, and social transformation. It is a theology characterized by fidelity as well as creativity.

Biblical Foundations for Mission Theology. Mission theology is distinctive for its *appeal to* and *reliance upon* biblical foundations. Books and articles have taken up the theme in direct and indirect ways. Major contributions in this area include surveys of general mission themes in the Old and New Testaments as well as specific mission themes that are identified with a particular biblical book or character. Methodological developments in biblical studies have enabled scripture scholars to employ a number of critical and constructive strategies for reading and interpreting texts. Inasmuch as scholars come from many different backgrounds and contexts, they frequently bring to their respective interpretations of texts important insights that have gone unexplored in the past. The *hermeneutical circle* (pretext-text-context) has provided a framework for understanding the relationship between biblical narratives, the demands of Christian mission, and the experiences of people in particular circumstances. This framework for interpretation has made possible the application of biblical insights to missionary practice in ways that correct, challenge, and transform. The foundational significance of biblical themes for mission theology is more than evident given the prominence of topics such as vocation, salvation, discipleship, prophetic action, witness, solidarity with the poor, table fellowship, community, justice, conversion, hospitality, liberation, reconciliation, compassion, the Reign of God, and the mission of Jesus.

Contextual Theologies and Historical Studies. One of the dramatic shifts taking place in the last decades of the twentieth century was the worldwide emergence of contextual theologies. Contextual theologies include, among others, theologies that are local, constructive, indigenous, liberationist, and feminist. Set in juxtaposition with longstanding theological positions that have shaped ecclesiastical histories and ecclesial identities, these contemporary theological positions often represent efforts to communicate the Christian Gospel more effectively in situations where peoples and cultures have been misunderstood, threatened, and devalued by past missionary mediation of Christian beliefs and practices. In an effort to understand more fully the meaning of the Christian Gospel amidst diverse peoples, cultures, and contexts, contextual theologies give rise to tensions as well as opportunities for growth within and beyond Christian churches and faith communities. The direct implications of these collisions and convergences for mission theology are numerous. Inasmuch as centuries of contributions to the study of theology have been formulated in accord with Western categories of thought and embedded in Western European cultures, the contemporary challenge that theologians face is one of effectively demonstrating and communicating that the Church's participation in the *missio Dei* requires attentiveness to tradition and revelation as well as attentiveness to contextual experience and historical consciousness. In this regard, mission theology is also indebted to the findings and insights of numerous historical-critical studies of Christian missionary activity. In effect, mission theology is a crucible for theological investigation as it endeavors to affirm both that which is essential to the universal *kerygma* and that which is particular to the effective proclamation of the Gospel in a given context. This specific theological task is critical and complex inasmuch as there is a wide diversity of methods in contextual theologies (see S. Bevans [1992]).

Social Scientific Insights. The social sciences, particularly cultural anthropology, sociology, psychology, linguistics, semiotics, social psychology, political science, and economics, have had a significant influence on mission theology. First, the social sciences have allowed missionaries and mission-sending societies to gather data, evaluate findings, and interpret information about various aspects of missionary practice. Second, they have provided theologians with additional conceptual tools for understanding the social processes through which individuals, communities, and societies make meaning of the realities in which they find themselves. Insights from the social sciences have enabled theologians to explore the relationship between key theological concepts from the Christian tradition and fundamental human experiences that are shaped by social interactions, cultural values, and worldviews. One example is the grounding of mission theology in a Eucharistic theology that is informed by the Christian tradition as well as by an understanding of rituals and symbols associated with food, feeding, and nurturing. Another example includes the incorporation of concepts such as stewardship and jubilee into a mission theology that is also attuned to questions of justice and the sociopolitical implications of a global market economy and the international debt crisis. Finally, to the extent that communication is critical to the process of evangelization, mission theology is enhanced by the use of more effective images, metaphors, and symbols or a more perceptive understanding of human development, gender differences, and ethnic identity.

Spiritualities of Mission. Spiritualities of mission are intrinsic to many mission theologies inasmuch as they function as sources of inspiration and integration. Within the Roman Catholic Church, historical research on the missionary charism of religious orders and missionary societies has led to a resurgence in spiritual formation for mission. Grounded in the Good News of Jesus Christ, these spiritualities of mission give expression to the diverse forms of missionary witness present in the lives of men and women at different periods in the Church's history. Spiritualities of mission continue to provide orientations for mission that guide the Church as a whole and missionary movements in particular. For this reason, spiritualities of mission are inextricably related to mission theologies. Spiritualities of mission that deal directly with the subject of giving one's life for the sake of the Gospel continue to be among the most compelling. Frequently, it is in and through spiritualities of mission that a meaningful synthesis of the Great Commandment (Jn 13:34) and the Great Commission (Mt 28:19–20) is clearly articulated and advanced.

Gospel and Culture. An important dimension of mission theology involves coming to terms with the interactive dynamics of gospel and culture. Among other things, this theological task includes critical reflection on the lessons to be learned from the history of Christian missionary activity. This is where the moral dimension of mission theology frequently finds its focus. It is in this arena of discourse that the challenges, possibilities, and polemics of Christianity's encounter with the world are identified, interpreted, and addressed. Faced with the important questions raised by this encounter, mission theology endeavors to provide adequate theological resources for understanding and responding to the ethical imperatives of Christian mission. Important concerns include interreligious dialogue, comparative theology, the integrity of creation, cultural survival, secularization, globalization, migration, systemic forms of human oppression, human rights, and mass communications. At issue in all of these areas is the relationship between the evangelization of culture and the inculturation of the Gospel message in a pluralistic world.

An Ecumenical Vision of Christian Unity. Mission theology, at its best, is reflective of a common theological commitment to articulate theologies that will support, encourage, and sustain an ecumenical vision that is worthy of trust. To the extent that the existing separations and divisions among Christians continue to be a source of scandal, hostility, and ambivalence, efforts at encounter, proclamation, dialogue, communion, solidarity, and transformation are easily weakened and undermined. In the light of this reality, it is incumbent upon Roman Catholic, Orthodox, Anglican, Conciliar Protestant, and Evangelical theologians of mission to provide credible visions of Christian unity that are firmly rooted in the prayer of Jesus ''that all may be one'' (Jn 17:21).

See Also: MISSION AND EVANGELIZATION; MISSION AND EVANGELIZATION IN CANON LAW; MISSION AND EVANGELIZATION, PAPAL WRITINGS ON; EVANGELII NUNTIANDI; REDEMPTORIS MISSIO.

Bibliography: Introductory surveys of mission theology: K. MULLER, *Mission Theology: An Introduction* (Nettetal 1987). L. NEWBIGIN, *The Open Secret: An Introduction to the Theology of Mission* (Grand Rapids, Mich. 1995). **Biblical foundations of mission theology:** M. ARIAS and A. JOHNSON, *The Great Commission: Biblical Models of Evangelism* (Nashville 1992). W. J. LARKIN and J. F. WILLIAMS, *Mission in the New Testament: An Evangelical Approach* (Maryknoll, N.Y. 1998). D. SENIOR and C. STUHLMUELLER, *Biblical Foundations for Mission* (Maryknoll, N.Y. 1983). **Methodologies of mission theology:** S. BEVANS, *Models of Contextual Theology* (Maryknoll, N.Y. 1992). D. BOSCH, *Transforming Mission: Paradigm Shifts in Theology of Mission* (Maryknoll, N.Y. 1991). J. A. B. JONGENEEL, *Philosophy, Science, and Theology of Mission in the Nineteenth and Twentieth Centuries: A Missiological Encyclopedia,* 2 v. (New York 1995, 1997), see same-titled review in *Missiology* 27:1 (1999) 27–30. J. SHERER and S. BEVANS, *New Directions in Mission and Evangelism,* v. 1–3 (Maryknoll, N.Y. 1992, 1994, 1999). **Mission theology and culture:** M. AMALADOSS, *Beyond Inculturation: Can the Many Be One* (New Delhi 1998). J. DUPUIS, *Toward a Christian Theology of Religious Pluralism* (Maryknoll, N.Y. 1997). F. GIOIA, ed., *Interreligious Dialogue: The Official Teaching of the Catholic Church (1963–1995)* (Boston 1997). G. HUNSBERGER and C. VAN GELDER, eds., *The Church between Gospel and Culture: The Emerging Mission in North America* (Grand Rapids, Mich. 1996). A. SHORTER, *Toward a Theology of Inculturation* (Maryknoll, N.Y. 1988), and *Evangelization and Culture* (London 1994). **Orthodox perspectives of mission theology:** I. BRIA, *The Liturgy after Liturgy: Mission and Witness from an Orthodox Perspective* (Geneva 1996). J. STAMOOLIS, *Eastern Orthodox Mission Theology* (Maryknoll, N.Y. 1986). **Protestant perspectives of mission theology:** T. THANGARAJ, *The Common Task: A Theology of Christian Mission* (Nashville 1999). W. SHENK, *Changing Frontiers of Mission* (Maryknoll, N.Y. 1999). **Roman Catholic perspectives of mission theology:** *Vatican II, Decree on Missionary Activity (Ad gentes), Dogmatic Constitution on the Church (Lumen gentium), Pastoral Constitution on the Church in the Modern World (Gaudium et spes).* Pope Paul VI, Evangelii nuntiandi (Evangelization in the Modern World, 1975). Pope John Paul II, *Redemptoris missio* (On the Permanent Validity of the Church's Missionary Mandate, 1990). A. GITTINS, *Bread for the Journey: The Mission of Transformation and the Transformation of Mission* (Maryknoll, N.Y. 1993). R. SCHREITER, *Constructing Local Theologies* (Maryknoll, N.Y. 1985), and *The New Catholicity: Theology between Global and Local* (Maryknoll, N.Y. 1997).

[M. GUIDER]

MISSIONARIES OF AFRICA

The Society of Missionaries of Africa (M.Afr.), formerly known as the ''White Fathers,'' was founded in Algiers in 1868 by Charles M. LAVIGERIE, Archbishop of Algiers. The society's first apostolate was among the orphans whom Lavigerie had taken under his care during the typhoid epidemic of 1867. Villages of Christian Arabs were founded in 1873 and 1875. Soon after, mission stations were established in Kabylia (Algeria) and on the northern fringes of the Sahara. Archbishop Lavigerie, as apostolic delegate for the Sahara and the Sudan, planned to send the missionaries of Africa into the interior of the African continent. Two attempts to cross the Sahara, one in 1876 and the other in 1881, resulted in the massacre of six White Fathers by their Touareg guides.

In January 1878, Lavigerie submitted to the Holy See a plan for the evangelization of the newly explored ''Great Lakes'' region of Central Africa. Leo XIII responded by appointing Lavigerie apostolic delegate for Equatorial Africa and establishing four mission territories to be entrusted to the Missionaries of Africa, although the society had less than 80 members at the time. By May 1878 the first caravan of ten missionaries had set out from the coast of Tanganyika (now Tanzania) toward the interior. At Tabora they split into two groups: one heading for Uganda, the other for the western shores of Lake Tanganyika.

The beginnings were extremely difficult. Physical sufferings, disease, and persecution by jealous tribal chiefs and greedy slave traders caused great hardship. By 1887, 16 priests, two brothers, and three lay auxiliaries had given their lives for the mission. In 1882 King Mutesa of Uganda forced them to leave the region south of Lake Victoria. They returned under Mutesa's successor, King Mwanga, only to see their small flock decimated by violent persecution. Twenty-two of the Christians martyred in Uganda were canonized in 1964.

After much hardship and losses, Lavigerie's plans began to bear fruit. He had instructed the missionaries to apply the discipline of the early Church's catechumenate in order to prepare the neophytes for baptism. The long task of building up an indigenous clergy was begun at an early stage of the mission's development. Uganda had its first two priests in 1913; the Congo, in 1917. In West Africa, the mission in the French Sudan (now Mali) was founded in 1894.

In 1880, at the request of the Holy See, the Missionaries of Africa opened a Greek Melkite seminary at the Basilica of St. Ann in Jerusalem. Today the Missionaries of Africa remain the guardians of this shrine in Jerusalem.

At Cardinal Lavigerie's death in 1892, 278 Missionaries of Africa from five different nationalities worked in six countries: Algeria, Tunisia, Uganda, Tanganyika, Congo, and Zambia. The Holy See granted final approval to the Society's constitutions in 1908. Its members, both priests and brothers, are bound by an oath of stability and of dedication to the continuation of Jesus' mission among Africans. Adapting themselves to the local surroundings, the Missionaries of Africa wear a religious habit which resembles the traditional clothing worn in North Africa: the white gandurah (cassock-like robe), a white burnoose (a hooded cape) and a reddish chechia (a fez-like head cover). They also wear a 15-decade rosary about their necks.

The General Chapter of 1936 divided the Society into provinces, Canada being one of them. The U.S. province was established in 1948. In 1997 the Canadian and U.S. provinces were combined as the North American Province. By the end of the 20th century, total membership was more than 2,000, coming from 31 different nationalities, working in 384 communities in 43 countries and recruiting from all continents. The North American Headquarters is in Montreal, with an U.S. Office in Washington, D.C.

Bibliography: J. BOUNIOL, *The White Fathers and Their Missions* (London 1929). D. ATTWATER *The White Fathers in Africa* (London 1937). G. KITTLER, *The White Fathers* (New York 1957). E. M. MATHESON, *African Apostles* (New York 1963). F. RENAULT, *Le Cardinal Lavigerie* (Paris 1992).

[J. G. DONDERS]

MISSIONARIES OF CHARITY

An international congregation of religious women, the Missionaries of Charity have as their primary ministry the service of ''the poorest of the poor'' irrespective of caste, creed, and nationality. Their headquarters are located in Calcutta, India, where the congregation was founded by Mother Teresa Bojaxhiu. The foundation was approved as a diocesan congregation in 1950 and made a pontifical institute in 1965. The distinctive habit of the Missionaries of Charity, made famous by Mother Teresa, consists of a white cotton sari with a blue border that covers the head, a cincture made of rope, sandals, a crucifix, and rosary. The sisters nurse sick and dying destitutes, including victims of AIDS; teach street children; visit and care for beggars, lepers, and their children; and provide shelter for the abandoned and homeless. They foster special devotion to Jesus in the Blessed Sacrament, and proclaim the Word of God to the spiritually destitute by their presence and the spiritual works of mercy.

In March 1997 the congregation elected Sister Nirmala and a council of four sisters to succeed Mother Teresa, who had asked to be relieved of administrative duties because of her poor health. At the time of Sister Nirmala's election, the order had some 4,500 nuns working in more than 100 countries.

See Also: MOTHER TERESA OF CALCUTTA.

Bibliography: D. DOIG, *Mother Teresa: Her People and Her Work* (San Francisco 1976). M. MUGGERIDGE, *Something Beautiful for God,* 2d ed. (San Francisco 1986).

[B. L. MARTHALER]

MISSIONARIES OF THE HOLY APOSTLES

A society of priests and brothers (M.Ss.A., Official Catholic Directory #0590) founded in 1946 in Montreal, Canada, by Father Eusebe M. Menard, a Franciscan. Guided by the spirit of St. Francis of Assisi, the members bind themselves by oath to observe the constitutions of the society. Their purpose is to foster vocations and to train priests for the service of the universal Church. The general headquarters is in Montreal, Canada. The U.S. provincial headquarters is in Cromwell, CT.

[E. M. MENARD/EDS.]

MISSIONARIES OF THE KINGSHIP OF CHRIST

Secular institute of women in the Franciscan tradition founded by Agostino GEMELLI, OFM, and Armida Barelli in Assisi, Italy, November 1919. The original band of 12 young women professed the Franciscan Tertiary Rule and lived in chastity, poverty, obedience, and devotion to the active apostolate, especially of Catholic Action. From 1919 to 1928 the society, called the Family of Franciscan Tertiaries for Promoting the Social Reign of the Sacred Heart, was under the minister general of the Friars Minor. Members lived at home following their own occupations. From 1928 to 1939 Pius XI guided the group, naming it the Pious Association of Missionaries of the Kingship of Christ. After 1947 the association conformed to the Apostolic Constitution *Provida Mater.* On July 12, 1948, it received the decree of praise as a pon

tifical secular institute; definitive approval followed on Aug. 3, 1953. From Italy the institute spread to all the continents. Missionaries of the U.S., organized by Stephen Hartdegen, OFM, in Washington, D.C., labor in many states. At the beginning of the 21st century, there were more than 3,000 members worldwide in 20 countries.

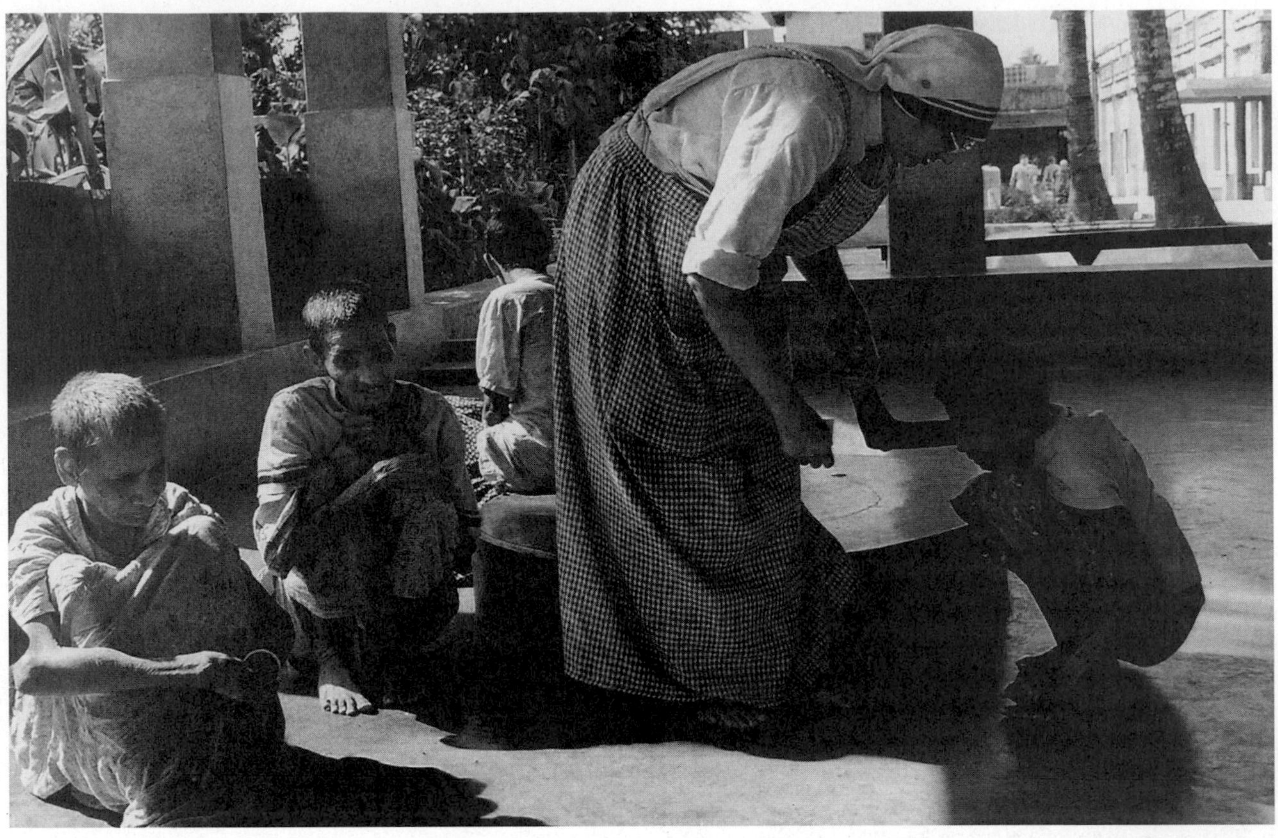

Nun of the Missionaries of Charity order, founded by Mother Teresa, helping a patient at a missionary home, Calcutta, India, 1996. (Archive Photos)

The institute's importance derives from its ability to influence secular environments (professional, occupational, and social), through competence and Christian action. Members are not publicly known as missionaries but as laity. The related Men's Institute of Missionaries, founded by Gemelli in 1928, was approved by Pius XI. Entrusted to Cardinal Schuster of Milan in 1929, it was reorganized in 1942 as the ''Union of Missionaries of the Kingship of Christ.'' It became a diocesan secular institute, Oct. 4, 1951. A third institute founded by Gemelli, the diocesan Secular Institute of Priest Missionaries of the Kingship of Christ, under the jurisdiction of the archbishop of Milan, arose from the attraction to the ideals of the lay institutes of missionaries by their priest directors. Members renew annually the vows of poverty, chastity, obedience, and devotion to the apostolate.

Bibliography: *Like Burning Lamp,* tr. S. HARTDEGEN (Paterson 1962). G. ESCUDERO, *Gli Instituti Secolari* (Milan 1957). J. BEYER, *Les Instituts séculiers* (Bruges 1964).

[S. HARTDEGEN/EDS.]

MISSIONARY SERVANTS OF THE MOST BLESSED TRINITY

(MSBT, Official Catholic Directory #2790); an American missionary congregation of women of pontifical status, founded, 1912, by Thomas Augustine JUDGE, CM, as a companion community to his society for priests, the MISSIONARY SERVANTS OF THE MOST HOLY TRINITY. In 1909, while stationed at St. John the Baptist parish in Brooklyn, N.Y., Judge organized the Missionary Cenacle Apostolate, one of the earliest lay missionary groups in the U.S. Community life was inaugurated in 1912 by a small group of those lay associates who had taken private vows. Between 1912 and 1915 two other houses were opened and named Missionary Cenacles of the Holy Spirit and the Apostles. In 1916, a year after Judge had been transferred to the Vincentian missions in eastern Alabama, he was joined by a few of his Northern lay associates. Their school, opened in Russell County, offered a program suitable for the needs of impoverished families, and the home-visiting services of the ''Catholic Ladies,'' as they were called, soon won the confidence of the people.

In 1918 they were incorporated as a missionary organization with special devotion to the Blessed Trinity; a year later they were organized as a formal religious congregation under Lulu Margaret Keasey (Mother Mary Boniface) as first superior. As the work expanded, the first motherhouse at Holy Trinity, Ala., founded missions throughout the U.S., the Virgin Islands, and Puerto Rico, staffing them with sisters and lay associates. In 1930 a fire demolished the original foundation, and the motherhouse was moved to Philadelphia, Pa. In 1932, a year after Mother Boniface's death, Rome granted the decree of canonical erection and in 1958 raised the congregation to pontifical status. The sisters are engaged in education, catechetics, clinics, healthcare, pastoral ministries, social outreach and retreats.

Bibliography: J. V. BENSON, *The Judgments of Father Judge* (New York 1934).

[M. RAHALEY/EDS.]

MISSIONARY SERVANTS OF THE MOST HOLY TRINITY

(ST, Official Catholic Directory #0840); a religious congregation of men, founded in the U.S. by Thomas Augustine JUDGE, a Vincentian priest from Boston, Mass. In 1909, after some years of mission and parochial work, Judge founded the Missionary Cenacle Apostolate, one of the earliest lay apostle movements in the U.S. It was from this organization that the Missionary Servants of the Most Holy Trinity and a companion community of sisters, MISSIONARY SERVANTS OF THE MOST BLESSED TRINITY, developed.

In 1915 when Judge was appointed superior of the Vincentian missions in eastern Alabama, he urged his lay apostles in the North to come south and assist the few priests there. A plantation on the Chattahoochee River in Russell County was opened as Holy Trinity training center for lay associates, as the members of the missionary Cenacle Apostolate were called. By 1917 these lay apostles had opened an academy and infirmary and were conducting a Sunday school. In addition, Holy Trinity center served as a nucleus of Catholic life and exerted an influence on the whole area.

By 1921 a group of men living a common life were recognized as a religious community by Bp. E. P. Allen of Mobile. A boys' school, which had been part of the apostolate since Holy Trinity was acquired, became explicitly a preparatory seminary in 1923. Thereafter, only those boys intending to study for the priesthood as Trinity missionaries were accepted in this school. In 1926 a house of studies was established in Washington, D.C., where the brothers would complete their studies for the priesthood at The Catholic University of America. This spontaneous development met with Judge's approval, and in 1929 the Holy See recognized the Missionary Servants of the Most Holy Trinity as a clerical, religious congregation of diocesan rank. A canonical novitiate was established in 1931. But it was only after 1940 that sizable classes of priests began to be ordained and the community expanded beyond its formative stage. In 1958 the Holy See bestowed upon the Missionary Servants of the Most Holy Trinity its decree of praise, raising the community to a pontifical congregation.

Trinity missionaries are especially trained to promote in their work the social encyclicals of the popes. The community accepts the care of parishes, especially where there is a great need for priests. Trinity missionaries work as chaplains, conduct social outreach centers and summer camp programs, and engage in catechetics, youth ministries, retreats, counseling and spiritual direction. The generalate is in Arlington, Va.

Bibliography: J. V. BENSON, *The Judgments of Father Judge* (New York 1934).

[H. MARSHALL/EDS.]

MISSIONARY SISTERS OF OUR LADY OF AFRICA

(MSOLA, Official Catholic Directory #2820); formerly known as the ''White Sisters,'' a congregation with papal approbation founded, 1869 in Algiers, North Africa, by Charles LAVIGERIE (later cardinal) and Mother Marie Salome. The sisters follow the Rule of St. Ignatius of Loyola and engage in various mission activities in Africa. They seek especially to serve the spiritual and material welfare of African women through catechetical, social, medical, educational, and cultural works, and through the training of African religious. Though of diverse nationality, race, background, and education, the sisters work together with a readiness to adapt to changing times and circumstances and with the same spirit of faith and missionary zeal exemplified by their founders. The sisters came to the U.S. in 1929 and have their headquarters in Winooski, VT. The generalate is in Rome.

[L. C. CARON/EDS.]

MISSIONARY SISTERS OF ST. PETER CLAVER

(SSPC, Official Catholic Directory #3990); also known as the Sodality of St. Peter Claver for the African

Missions; a congregation with papal approbation (1910) founded by Countess Maria Theresia LEDÓCHOWSKA in 1894 for the purpose of giving help to the African missions, especially by means of the apostolate of the press. Countess Ledóchowska, encouraged by Cardinal Charles LAVIGERIE, had begun to publish in 1889 the magazine *African Echo* (later published in eight languages) and had founded an association of lay persons called The Anti-Slavery Committee. Instructions received from Leo XIII in 1894 led her to found the sodality, which was first approved as a diocesan congregation by Cardinal Johannes Haller, archbishop of Salzburg, Austria, in 1897. As the number of religious increased, a house with a well-equipped polyglot press was opened at Salzburg; later, other houses were established in various nations and in Rome, where the generalate is located. The sisters established their first foundation in the U.S. in 1912. The U.S. headquarters is in Chesterfield, MO.

[P. MOLINARI/EDS.]

MISSIONARY SISTERS OF THE HOLY ROSARY

(MSHR, Official Catholic Directory, #2730); founded, 1924 in Killeshandra, Ireland, by Bp. Joseph Shanahan, CSSp (papal approval 1938). Members engage in educational, medical, and pastoral ministries. The congregation has established foundations in Europe, North America and Africa. The generalate is in Dublin, Ireland. The U.S. headquarters is in Bryn Mawr, Pa.

Bibliography: J. P. JORDAN, *Bishop Shanahan of Southern Nigeria* (Dublin 1949). T. RONAYNE, ''Great Irish Missionary: Dr. Joseph Shanahan, C.S.Sp.,'' *The Irish Ecclesiastical Record* 63 (April 1944) 228–236. M. O'CARROLL, *Edward Leen, C.S.Sp.* (Westminster, Md. 1953).

[M. G. WILSON/EDS.]

MISSIONARY SISTERS OF THE MOST SACRED HEART OF JESUS OF HILTRUP

A pontifical institute founded in 1899 in Hiltrup, Germany, by Hubert J. Linckens (MSC, Official Catholic Directory #2800) to cooperate with his community in spreading the faith among the peoples of the Southwest Pacific (*see* SACRED HEART MISSIONARIES). In 1902 the first sisters departed for missionary activity; two years later five of them were slain by Baining natives. The first American foundation was made in 1908, when eight sisters began educational work in the Archdiocese of Philadelphia, Pa. In the United States, the sisters are engaged in education, healthcare, parish ministry, counseling, spiritual direction, social outreach, and prison ministry. Headquarters for the American province are located in Reading, Pa. The generalate is in Sutri (Viterbo), Italy.

[J. W. GASPAR/EDS.]

MISSIONARY SISTERS OF THE PRECIOUS BLOOD

Founded in the Republic of South Africa by Abbot Franz PFANNER (*Missionales a Pretiosissimo Sanguine,* CPS, Official Catholic Directory #2850), its nucleus was a group of five lay apostles whom Pfanner invited in 1885 to instruct young girls at Mariannhill monastery in Natal. Papal approval came in 1906. According to the founder's wish, the sisters are expected to accept missionary assignments throughout the world. Besides teaching, nursing, and healthcare, the sisters perform a variety of social and charitable works. The sisters established their first foundation in the United States in Princeton, NJ, in 1925. The U.S. provincialate is in Reading, PA. The motherhouse is in Rome.

Bibliography: J. M. BEHEN, ed., *Religious of the Precious Blood* (Carthagena, Ohio 1957).

[E. M. KREMER/EDS.]

MISSIONARY SISTERS OF THE SACRED HEART

(MSC, Official Catholic Directory #2860); also known as Cabrini Sisters, a papal institute founded Nov. 14, 1880, by (St.) Francis Xavier CABRINI at Codogno, Italy. The congregation's growth was rapid, and the Holy See granted the decree of commendation in 1888 and final approbation in 1907. The rules and constitutions thus approved were the work of Mother Cabrini herself. In 1889, when Mother Cabrini applied to the Holy See for permission to begin Chinese missions, the deplorable condition of large numbers of Italian immigrants caused Leo XIII to bid her to go ''not to the East but to the West.'' Accepting the invitation of Abp. Michael Corrigan of New York, Mother Cabrini and six sisters arrived in New York City on March 31, 1889. Thereafter Cabrinian foundations, following the streams of immigration, were made in New York and Brooklyn, N.Y.; New Orleans, La.; Chicago, Ill.; Scranton, Pa.; Newark and Arlington, New Jersey; Denver, Colo.; Seattle, Wash.; and Los Angeles and Burbank, Calif. Meanwhile new foundations were established in Europe and South America. Although the work for Italian immigrants earned for the foundress the title ''Saint of the Immigrants,'' this was but one phase of her institute's world-embracing program. Schools, hospitals, and institutions of higher learning paralleled works for the poor.

Inspired by a devotion to the Sacred Heart, the sisters engage in a variety of ministries, including education, catechetics, hospitals, nursing, healthcare, parish administration, pastoral ministries and social outreach. The motherhouse is in Rome. The U.S. provincialate is in New York City.

Bibliography: F. CABRINI, *The Travels of Mother Frances Cabrini* (letters) tr. and ed. MISSIONARY SISTERS OF THE SACRED HEART (Milwaukee 1944). P. DI DONATO, *Immigrant Saint: The Life of Mother Cabrini* (New York 1960). T. MAYNARD, *Too Small a World: The Life of Francesca Cabrini* (Milwaukee 1945).

[S. LE DIEU/EDS.]

MISSIONARY SOCIETY OF ST. JAMES THE APOSTLE

Established as a Pious Society by Richard J. CUSHING, Archbishop of Boston, by decree on 25 July 1958, with the encouragement of the Holy See, for the purpose of sending diocesan priests as missionaries to Latin America for a minimum of five years. The first 14 volunteers, all priests of the Archdiocese of Boston, arrived in Lima, Peru in early 1959 and began language studies. Within that year they undertook responsibility for parishes in remote areas of Peru and Bolivia. The Society also began parish work in Ecuador in 1963, and currently maintains a presence in those three countries, with headquarters in Boston, Massachusetts. In addition to supplying missionary personnel, the Society has provided funds for the erection of numerous churches, pastoral centers, clinics, rectories, and language schools in the areas where its members have labored. The St. James Society, now organized as a Clerical Association of the Christian Faithful, in conformity with the 1983 *Code of Canon Law*, under the presidency of the Archbishop of Boston and a priest-director elected by the members, is made up of English speaking diocesan priests from approximately six nations. Over 300 diocesan priests from more than 100 dioceses have been members since its foundation. While there were slightly more than 100 volunteers at the peak of membership, in 1967, by 2000, only about 50 priest-members from over 30 different dioceses were affiliated.

[J. F. GARNEAU]

MISSIONS, DIVINE

The word mission (from the Latin *mittere*) means a sending. Theologically, the divine missions are the sending of God the SON and the HOLY SPIRIT. The doctrine of the divine missions may be succinctly stated thus: the Son is sent by GOD THE FATHER, and the Holy Spirit is sent by both the Father and the Son (Denz 527).

Notion of Divine Missions. A divine mission is the procession of a Divine PERSON with the extrinsic effect that the Person thus sent becomes present in a new manner in rational creatures, uniting them in a SUPERNATURAL union with God.

A divine mission is a sending not by command or counsel, for this would imply that the Person sent would have a distinct will from the Person sending. In God there is but one will (Denz 851), which is common to the three Divine Persons. Any communication of the divine will from one Person to the other can be only through the divine processions, which distinguish the Divine Persons (Denz 528). As the divine processions imply no inequality between the Divine Persons, so too the divine missions imply no dependence or inferiority of the Person sent. The divine missions are as prolongations of the eternal processions; but, whereas a divine procession pertains to the immanent life of God, a divine mission refers to a Divine Person existing in a new manner outside the Godhead.

The existence of a Divine Person in a new manner is in rational creatures. This constitutes a new divine presence in creation. In the natural order, God is present by His knowledge, will, and essence (*see* OMNIPRESENCE). By virtue of the divine missions the presence of the Son and the Holy Spirit in the soul is a personal presence superadded to the presence of God in all nature. As to the supernatural order, the Latin Fathers emphasize the divine nature as the efficient and final cause of sanctification and the Triune God as the author of GRACE. This aspect of the mystery of sanctification stresses the divine operations in the soul. These divine operations are extrinsic to God and must therefore be attributed not to any one Person but to the three Divine Persons (Denz 501, 531). The work of sanctification is frequently ascribed to the Holy Spirit by APPROPRIATION [*Divinum illud munus; Acta Sanctae Sedis* 29 (Rome 1896–97) 647], for all these effects must be held as common to the Trinity in as far as God is the supreme efficient cause (Denz 3814). Since the divine missions, then, pertain only to the divine presence of the Son and the Holy Spirit, these missions are not to be distinguished by their sanctifying effects on the soul but by the divine processions in respect to the new manner in which these Divine Persons dwell in the soul.

In the soul of the just, the three Divine Persons are present in their substantial reality: the Son and the Holy Spirit are present in Person in accordance with their divine missions; and the Father is present in Person because the Father is in the Son and in the Holy Spirit (Denz 1330). This presence of the Trinity in the soul of the just is known as the doctrine of the divine INDWELLING.

The personal presence of the Trinity in the soul of the just is brought about through the Incarnate Word. Christ assumes a new human nature, not in a substantial way as in the INCARNATION, but in an accidental way, for the creature does not thereby lose his identity; nevertheless, there is truly a mystical union through the Holy Spirit, a union that attains its consummation and perfection in heaven (Denz 3814–15).

Persons Sent. In the Trinity there are the procession of the Son from the Father and the procession of the Holy Spirit from the Father and the Son. Consequently, only the Son and the Holy Spirit are said to be sent.

The Father can be in a new manner among creatures, but not by reason of any divine processing. Nowhere is it said in Scripture that the Father is sent, but that He comes and gives Himself (Jn 14.23). Hence the Father's coming and giving Himself is not a divine mission.

The mission of the Son emanates from His immanent procession from the Father. Christ, who is sent by the Father, is His Son. God did ''send his Son into the world'' (Jn 3.17). ''He who does not honor the Son, does not honor the Father who sent him'' (Jn 5.23). Christ lives by the Father: ''As the living Father has sent me, and as I live because of the Father, so he who eats me, he also shall live because of me'' (Jn 6.58). Christ's mission is by the will of the Father (Jn 6.39), and faith in Christ is faith in the Father, who sent Him (Jn 12.44). It is, moreover, the will of the Father that the mission of Christ should bring life everlasting, and Christ Himself will raise the just to glory (Jn 6.40). Thus the ultimate purpose of Christ's mission is ''that all may be one, even as thou, Father, in me and I in thee; that they also may be one in us, that the world may believe that thou hast sent me'' (Jn 17.21; cf. 17.22, 23).

Furthermore, according to St. John's doctrine of the Son as the Word (Jn 1.1–18), the mission of the Son is associated with creation itself; it is directed specifically to rational creatures, and it is manifested in the Incarnation: ''And the Word was made flesh'' (Jn 1.14; *see* WORD, THE; LOGOS). A human nature is assumed in the very Person of the Son, so that it is the Son Himself who comes in Person. St. Paul, too, speaks of the Incarnation as the actual sending of the Son as man (Gal 4.4). He speaks also of the mission of the Son as embracing all rational creatures, visible and invisible (Col 1.15–20). Besides, St. Paul speaks of the eternal plan of the Father to be realized in Christ with His mission extending to those in heaven and those on earth (Eph 1.3–10).

The mission of the Holy Spirit emanates likewise from the will of God to communicate Himself. Accordingly the Holy Spirit is called the Spirit of the Father (Mt. 10.20) and the Spirit of His Son (Gal 4.6). The Holy Spirit is sent by the Father and the Son in accordance with His divine procession (Jn 14.26; 15.26; 16.7; 16.13–15; Gal 4.6). As the Holy Spirit in the Trinity is the ''love and holiness of both'' the Father and the Son (Denz 527), Scripture speaks of Him in respect to His mission not only as the gift of God (Jn 4.10, 14; 7.37–39) but also as the concrete and personal realization of God's love, achieving in the soul purification, justification, and sanctification (1 Cor 6.11; 2 Thes 2.13). Leo XIII therefore speaks of the Holy Spirit as the ''life-giving Love,'' whose temporal mission is from the beginning of creation [*Acta Sanctae Sedis* 23 (Rome 1890–91) 644–645].

The missions of the Son and the Holy Spirit are eternal and absolute in origin; they are universal in time (Heb 13.8) and so ecumenical that no rational creature is excluded from their divine influence, for God ''wishes all men to be saved and to come to the knowledge of the ''truth'' (1 Tm 2.4; cf. Is 59.1).

Visible Missions. The Incarnation is the visible mission par excellence. In the Incarnation a human nature was assumed into the unity of the Person of the Son. Of the three Divine Persons, the Son alone assumed this new mode of existing as man (Jn 1.14; Phil 2.5–7).

In the Incarnation the Son, who is the ''image of the invisible God'' (Col 1.15), enters creation officially ''in the fullness of time'' (Gal 4.4). He comes to impart His life (Jn 6.38–40; 10.10), but always in the Holy Spirit, ''because through him we both have access in one Spirit to the Father'' (Eph 2.18). And in union with the Holy Spirit, Christ perpetuates His visible mission through His Mystical Body, the Church, through His priesthood (Jn 20.22), through His Sacraments, and through His sacrificial and sacramental presence in the Holy Eucharist.

Of the mission of the Holy Spirit, there are four perceptible manifestations: under the form of a dove at the BAPTISM OF THE LORD (Mt 3.16); under the form of a luminous cloud at the TRANSFIGURATION (Mt 17.5); under the form of breath, when Christ conferred the Holy Spirit on His APOSTLES (Jn 20.22); and under the form of tongues of fire in the cenacle (Acts 2.3–4). These forms were only signs or symbols of the presence of the Holy Spirit, for the Holy Spirit did not assume these forms into the unity of His own Person.

In the Old Testament the just were sanctified through the divine missions [*Divinum illud munus; Acta Sanctae Sedis* 29 (Rome 1890–91) 651], but no legal or formal manifestation of these missions was made. The Incarnation of the Son was to inaugurate the external dispensation of grace. The visible mission of the Holy Spirit, then, does not precede the visible mission of the Son; but the Holy Spirit manifests the Son, as the Son manifests the Father.

Invisible Missions. The distinctive nature of the divine missions is that the Son and the Holy Spirit are in a new manner in creatures. It is a new, interior and invisible presence, which sanctifies the soul, imparting to it a new supernatural life.

As mentioned, the Latin Fathers stress the efficient and final causality of sanctification and attribute the SUPERNATURAL ORDER to the Triune God. For the Greek Fathers every created effect is by virtue of the divine command of creation; the supernatural order, however, is not taken as an effect of efficient causality but as the living presence of the Divine Persons in rational creatures. The life of a Divine Person is distinct from any creative command; it is essentially immanent, whereas the creative command refers to things outside the divine nature. By virtue of the divine missions, the Son and the Holy Spirit exist in a new manner in rational creatures, so that the immanent life of God is present in creatures. It is in this sense that the Greek Fathers explain the words of St. Peter: that ''you may become partakers of the divine nature'' (2 Pt 1.4). Similarly, St. Paul speaks of Christ being ''formed'' in the soul (Gal 4.19).

Pius XII explains:

> If we examine closely this divine principle of life and power given by Christ, in so far as it constitutes the very source of every gift and created grace, we easily see that it is nothing else than the Holy Spirit. . . . For it was by His breath of grace and truth that the Son of God adorned His own soul in the immaculate womb of the Blessed Virgin . . . this Spirit Christ merited for us on the cross. . . . But after Christ's glorification on the cross, His Spirit is communicated to the Church in an abundant outpouring, so that the Church and each of its members may become daily more and more like to our Savior.
>
> To this Spirit of Christ, too, as to an invisible principle, is to be ascribed the fact that all the parts of the Body are joined one with the other and with their exalted head; for the Spirit of Christ is entirely in the head, entirely in the Body, and entirely in each member. . . . It is He who . . . is the principle of every truly supernatural act in all parts of the Body. It is He who, while He is personally present and divinely active in all the members, also acts in the inferior members through the ministry of the higher members. . . . ''Let it suffice to say that, as Christ is the head of the Church, so is the Holy Spirit its soul'' (Leo XIII).
>
> . . . The Church, then, no less than each of its holy members, can make this thought of the Apostle its own (Gal 2.20): ''And I live, now not I; but Christ lives in me.'' [Pius XII, ''Mystici Corporis Christi,'' *Acta Apostolicae Sedis* 35 (1943) 54–56]

See Also: GRACE, CREATED AND UNCREATED; SOUL OF THE CHURCH; TRINITY, HOLY; TRINITY, HOLY, ARTICLES ON.

Bibliography: LEO XIII, ''Divinum illud munus'' (encyclical, May 9, 1897), *Acta Sanctae Sedis* 29 (Rome 1896–97) 644–658, Eng. *Catholic Mind* 36 (May 8, 1938) 161–181. PIUS XII, ''Mystici Corporis Christi,'' *Acta Apostolicae Sedis* 35 (1943) 193–248. THOMAS AQUINAS, *Summa theologiae* 1a, 43. E. NEUHÄUSLER and M. SCHMAUS, *Lexikon für Theologie und Kirche* [2], ed. J. HOFER and K. RAHNER (2d new ed. Freiburg 1957–65) 9:662–664. I. M. DALMAU, *Sacrae theologiae summa*, ed. FATHERS OF THE SOCIETY OF JESUS, PROFESSORS OF THE THEOLOGICAL FACULTIES IN SPAIN (Madrid 3d ed. 1958) 2.1:556–578. F. BLUNT, *Life with the Holy Ghost* (Milwaukee 1943). J. CARROLL, *God the Holy Ghost* (New York 1940). B. FROGET, *The Indwelling of the Holy Spirit in the Souls of the Just*, tr. S. A. RAEMERS (Westminster, Md. 1950). R. GARRIGOU-LAGRANGE, *The Trinity and God the Creator*, tr. F. C. ECKHOFF (St. Louis 1952) 304–334. B. JARRETT, *The Abiding Presence of the Holy Ghost* (Westminster, Md. 1943). E. LEEN, *The Holy Ghost and His Work in Souls* (New York 1937). M. J. SCHEEBEN, *The Mysteries of Christianity*, tr. C. VOLLERT (St. Louis 1946) 149–180.

[G. M. GREENEWALD]

MISSISSIPPI, CATHOLIC CHURCH IN

A state in southern U.S., bounded on the north by Tennessee, on the east by Alabama, on the south by a portion of Louisiana and an arm of the Gulf of Mexico, and on the west by the Pearl River and the Mississippi River, which separates the state from Arkansas and Louisiana. The two Catholic dioceses in the state, Natchez- Jackson (1837, renamed diocese of Jackson in 1977) and Biloxi (1977) are suffragan sees of the archdiocese of Mobile.

History. In 1540 Hernando DeSoto and his Spanish expedition passed through this region. Several priests accompanied him; but since in a previous attack by Native Americans they had lost their Mass wine and some utensils, Mass probably was not offered here at that time. The earliest French explorers of the Mississippi River were Louis Jolliet and Rev. Jacques MARQUETTE (1673) and R. C. de LA SALLE (1682). Accompanying La Salle's expedition was Rev. Zenobius Membre, who on Easter Sunday, March 29, near the present site of Fort Adams, celebrated the first Mass on Mississippi soil of which there is a definite record. In 1699 missionaries from the Seminary of Quebec, Canada, descended the Mississippi River to work among the Indians and took up their stations near present Natchez. In the same year the French established a temporary settlement in what later became Ocean Springs. In 1717 they founded Natchez, and in 1720, Biloxi; other settlements were established soon after. During the latter half of the 18th century Great Britain and Spain in turn dominated this area. When in 1798 Spain withdrew in favor of the U.S, the Spanish-trained Irish clergy who had served in the area also withdrew. The Mississippi Territory (including the future Alabama) was then organized. Its government was modeled on the Northwest Ordinance with one major exception, the toleration of slavery. In 1817 Mississippi was admitted to the Union as the 20th state.

Antebellum Period. Post-territorial Catholic Mississippi was successively part of the Diocese of Baltimore, the proposed (1822) but not implemented vicariate of Alabama and Mississippi, the Diocese of Louisiana and, in 1826, the Diocese of New Orleans. In July 28, 1837 Gregory XVI established the Diocese of Natchez (later redesignated JACKSON) to embrace the whole state of Mississippi. Although the diocese was established on July 28, 1837, it was almost four years before Bishop John Chanche, the first ordinary, was consecrated, March 14, 1841. When he arrived in Mississippi on May 19, he found two sizable Catholic communities at Natchez and Vicksburg, a large number of families and small communities along the Gulf Coast, and an unknown number of families and individuals scattered throughout the state. The state had no Catholic churches or institutions and only two priests.

Mississippi's economy, politics, and culture were molded during the 1830s when former Native American lands were opened to settlement. An influx of immigrants quickly followed, and the growing presence of Baptist and Methodist congregations gave the state its predominately Protestant religious profile. Cotton-based agriculture, mainly worked first by black slaves and later by sharecroppers, created a distinctive political, social, and economic society that endured until World War II. Strong regional differences appeared between the planter societies of the river counties and the small farms of the north and the Piney Woods. Simultaneously the ''race question'' shaped the state's future.

Mississippi Catholicism grew both in numbers and organization under the antebellum leadership of Bishops John Chanche (1841–1852), James Oliver Van de Velde, S.J. (1853–1855), and William Henry Elder (1857–1880). By 1861, the diocese numbered about 10,000 Catholics served by one bishop and eighteen diocesan priests; thirteen parishes with resident priests and twenty-eight mission stations; fifteen churches with several more under construction; five parochial schools, two day schools, three boarding schools, and two orphanages staffed by five religious communities and several lay teachers; numerous parish devotional, altar, and charitable societies; and regular parish missions and clerical conferences. Bishop Chanche laid the foundation for an imposing cathedral that he viewed as ''the needed stimulus to the whole mission.''

Civil War and Reconstruction. Mississippi was a major battleground during the Civil War. Natchez, Vicksburg, Jackson, Meridian, Okolona, and Corinth were among the Catholic communities that were battle sites or suffered property damage. Catholic church facilities at Jackson were destroyed three times by Federal troops. Bishop William Henry Elder was briefly sent into exile in Louisiana in July, 1864, when he refused to allow the local Federal military commander to dictate specific prayers for Northern civil authorities at Mass.

The war left the state devastated politically, economically, and socially; brought ruin to numerous families whose fathers were killed or disabled; and depleted the already meager resources of Mississippi Catholicism. Mississippi was readmitted to the Union in 1870, but remained under a reconstruction government until 1875. The state was hampered by an undiversified agriculture, the lack of industry, poor education, and a primitive financial system based on merchants.

The greatest post-war challenge was the peaceful, productive incorporation of newly-freed blacks into Mississippi life; this challenge was met, after a brief reconstruction period, by a political-economic-social structure of sharecropping, segregation, and disenfranchisement that closely mirrored antebellum, slave society.

Bishop Elder worked among the camps for freed blacks outside Natchez during the final years of the war and struggled to find the resources to address the challenge of evangelizing them. By 1884, Mississippi numbered 1,500 African American Catholics. Bishop Francis Janssens (1881–1887) adopted an approach common in missionary lands—small chapel-schools overseen by priests but staffed by trained African American catechists. In 1890, Holy Family Parish, the state's first parish for African Americans, was established at Natchez. Between 1906 and 1914, seven additional parishes for African Americans were founded at Vicksburg, Pascagoula, Jackson, Meridian, Pass Christian, Greenville, and Biloxi; all were staffed by Josephites or Divine Word Fathers.

Early Twentieth Century. Despite the upheavals of reconstruction and its aftermath, Mississippi Catholicism took on a new vigor in the late nineteenth and early twentieth century under the leadership of Bishops Francis Janssens, Thomas Heslin (1889–1911), and John Gunn, S.M. (1911–1924). More than 250 Catholic communities, many short-lived, existed in the state between 1865 and 1910. *The Society for the Propagation of the Faith,* the American Board of Catholic Missions, the Indian and Colored Missions Fund, and the Catholic Church Extension Society provided a significant part of the financial resources for these communities. Even today the diocese of Jackson receives funding from these sources.

After statehood, a series of broken treaties and government policies of displacement to Native American Territory left Mississippi with only 2,300 Native Americans by 1900. Through the initiative of Bishop Francis Janssens, a small, active Catholic Choctaw community, centered in the Philadelphia area, developed in the late nineteenth century and remains a vital part of Mississippi Catholicism. By 1917, more than 28,000 Catholics were scattered across the state in 41 parishes, 69 missions, and 54 stations; 11 percent were African Americans. Forty-two schools and two orphanages had a combined enrollment of 4,736; 29 percent of the students were African Americans; .8 percent, Choctaws.

When Bishop John Gunn arrived in 1911, he set as one of his primary goals to establish chapels throughout the state. With generous aid from the Catholic Church Extension Society, more than twenty-five new churches and chapels were built between 1912 and 1924 alone. With Bishop Gunn's encouragement, the Society of the Divine Word established a seminary to train African American priests, first at Greenville in 1920, and then at Bay St. Louis in 1921. The first four graduates were ordained in 1934, and several later graduates were among the country's pioneer twentieth-century African American bishops, including Harold Perry (New Orleans), Terry J. Steib (St. Louis/Memphis), and Dominic Carmen (New Orleans).

The Gerow Era. Bishop Gunn's successor, Richard O. Gerow, shephered the Church in Mississippi for over forty years (1924–1966), during which time the state, like the rest of the country, suffered through the depression of the 1930s, World War II and its aftermath, and later the civil rights movement. When newly consecrated Bishop Gerow arrived, Catholicism was Mississippi's third largest religious denomination, after the Baptists and Methodists. The state had 31,387 Catholics served by 60 priests, but only 42 of the state's 149 churches and chapels had a resident pastor. 5,829 children were being educated in 41 Catholic schools.

The church had all it could do to hold its own during the 1930s when parishes and other Catholic institutions suffered the harsh effects of the depression. The post-World War II years, however, witnessed the waning of Mississippi's insularity and isolation as it became more industrialized and assimilated into the mainstream of the American economy. It was also a period of major administrative change in the Catholic Church in Mississippi. In 1952, Bishop Gerow divided the diocese into nine deaneries, and the following he year moved the bishop's residence and chancery from historic Natchez to Jackson. In 1953 he launched a diocesan newspaper, the *Mississippi Register* (later *Mississippi Today* and then *Mississippi Catholic*) to replace the Natchez edition of *Catholic Action of the South,* a cooperative venture of the Louisiana and Mississippi dioceses. On Dec. 18, 1956 the name of the diocese was changed to Natchez-Jackson.

The most striking changes in Mississippi society took place in the area of race relations. Bishop Gerow had worked quietly and within the existing legal and social structure to expand opportunities among the region's African American population. He concentrated on establishing parishes and strong schools with sisters in urban areas, and acted forcefully against all blatant acts of discrimination in diocesan churches.

The issue of desegregating Catholic schools came to a head in the wake of the 1954 Supreme Court decision. The violence with which some Mississippians opposed integration, evidenced in the 1963 murder of Medgar Evers, prodded the mild-tempered Bishop Gerow to take a more public and forceful stance. On June 14, he issued a statement that proclaimed a mutual responsibility for Evers' murder and the growing violence and pleaded for a common ground ''based on human dignity and the concept of justice under God's law.'' On Aug. 4, 1964, Gerow, at the urging of auxiliary Bishop Joseph Brunini and Father Bernard Law (the future Cardinal Archbishop of Boston), ordered the integration of the first grade in all Catholic schools of the diocese. The following year he ordered the integration of all grades.

The Brunini Years. Bishop Gerow was succeed by his auxiliary, Joseph B. Brunini. A native of Vicksburg, Brunini had studied and was ordained to the priesthood in Rome, received a doctorate in canon law from the Catholic University of America in Washington, and served as a pastor before being ordained as auxiliary bishop in 1957. Bishop Brunini had attended the Second Vatican Council (1962–1965). It fell to him to guide Mississippi's Catholics through the implementation of integration.

In 1967, Bishop Brunini committed the diocese to full integration of Catholic schools. He established an open, participative style of leadership, fostered lay participation and ministry, expanded the Church's social ministry, led the state's efforts to break down racial barriers, and worked to establish closer bonds with other Churches. In his 1969 Christmas homily, Bishop Brunini called for Mississippi's religious leaders to speak with a united voice to bring about racial justice and peace. Soon afterwards, the Mississippi Religious Leadership Conference was established with Brunini as the first chairman. The conference became a major voice in the state, urging political leaders to foster education and end segregation and racism throughout the state. Brunini's support encouraged Sister Thea Bowman, a Missionary Sister Servant of the Holy Ghost, who served in the diocese from 1961 until her death from cancer in 1990. She became a national voice for change and reconciliation, proclaiming her message in word and song.

During his tenure, Catholic services to the needy, poor and elderly rapidly expanded. He actively recruited Irish clergy, formed the Catholic Foundation in 1973, established new personnel and finance policies, encouraged the establishment of parish councils, and fostered adult education programs. Under Brunini's leadership, the diocese agreed to staff Our Lady of Perpetual Help Parish in Saltillo, Mexico. Although begun as a provincial venture, Brunini and the Catholic people of Mississippi soon adopted, funded, and supplied clergy for the mission.

On March 1, 1977 Pope Paul VI established a second diocese in Mississippi. The seventeen southern counties were organized into the Diocese of Biloxi. Bishop Joseph L. Howze was named the first bishop. Later that year, June 6, 1977, the name of the other diocese was redesignated as the Diocese of Jackson. In 1980, the two Mississippi dioceses became part of the new ecclesiastical Province of Mobile. In 2000, the Biloxi diocesan administration moved to a new Catholic chancery building. On July 2, 2001, Msgr. Thomas J. Rodi, a native New Orleanian and former Vicar General of the Archdiocese of New Orleans, was ordained as Biloxi's second bishop. Bishop William R. Houck who had succeeded Brunini in Jackson in 1984 establshed spiritual renewal as one of his first priorities.

Between 1950 and 2000, the number of Mississippi Catholics increased from 50,559 to 115,196. By 2000, Catholics numbered about 4.2% of the state's total population, a significant increase from 2.4% a half century earlier. The largest concentrations were on the Gulf Coast, in the capital city of Jackson, and in Vicksburg. While the number of priests actually increased slightly, the number of religious brothers and sisters serving in the state declined by fifteen percent. In 1950, priests constituted 3.5% of the Catholic population; brothers and sisters, 8.8%; and the laity, 87.7%. By 2000, these figures had changed to 1.7%, 3.3%, and 95% respectively.

Bibliography: CLETA ELLINGTON, *Christ: The Living Water, Catholic Church in Mississippi* (Jackson 1989). RICHARD O.GEROW, *Catholicity in Mississippi* (Natchez 1939). MICHAEL NAMORATO, *The Catholic Church in Mississippi, 1911–1984: A History* (Westport, Connecticut 1998). CHARLES E. NOLAN, *St. Mary's of Natchez: the History of a Southern Catholic Congregation, 1716–1988* (Natchez: St. Mary's Parish, 1992); ''The Catholic Church in Mississippi, 1865–1911.'' Manuscript in preparation for publication by the Center for Louisiana Studies. JAMES J. PILLAR, *The Catholic Church in Mississippi, 1837–1865* (New Orleans 1964). JOHN RAY SKATES, *Mississippi: a Bicentennial History* (New York 1979).

[R. O. GEROW/C. E. NOLAN]

MISSOURI, CATHOLIC CHURCH IN

Located in the central United States, Missouri is separated from Illinois, Kentucky, and Tennessee by the Mississippi River and is bounded on the north by Iowa; on the west by Nebraska, Kansas, and Oklahoma; and on the south by Arkansas. It was admitted to the Union in 1821 as the 24th state. The capital is Jefferson City; St. Louis and Kansas City are the largest cities. In 2001 the population of the state was 5,478,300 of whom 859,574 or about 16 percent were Catholic. There are four Catholic dioceses: the archdiocese of St. Louis and its three suffragan sees, Springfield-Cape Girardeau, Jefferson City, and Kansas City.

Early History. The roots of Roman Catholicism's development in Missouri date back to 1673; on June 17 of that year Jesuit Father Jacques MARQUETTE, a priest and missionary from Canada accompanying the entrepreneur Louis Joliet down the Mississippi River to evangelize the peoples living in the region, entered the Great River. Eventually Marquette and Joliet negotiated the river from the Kaskaskia country all the way to the southern reaches of Arkansas. En route the two Frenchmen crossed the Mississippi and camped over in and explored the southeastern part of what would later become Perry County, Missouri. That trek laid the foundation for Catholic missioning in the western reaches of the Mississippi Valley.

Throughout the latter half of the seventeenth century and much of the eighteenth, the French presence in the Mississippi Valley increased, with a settlement across the river, St. Genevieve, founded in the mid-1730s. In 1759 the Jesuits established a parish at St. Genevieve. Several years later, in 1763, the Treaty of Paris ended the French and Indian War. France was forced to cede to England all her North American territorial possessions east of the Mississippi River and north of the Ohio, including Canada. In order to safeguard her interests in the vast lands she claimed westward from the Mississippi River to the Rockies against the incursions of the British, France ceded them all to Spain. As a result, the Catholic Church's situation changed dramatically in the area. For more than a century that region had existed under the ecclesiastical authority of the French Bishop of Quebec. But with the ceding of this domain to Spain, it then fell under the jurisdiction of the Spanish Bishop of Havana, Cuba.

Not many years were to pass before several clusters of settlers with visible Catholic identities (mainly French, Irish, and German) began to develop immediately beyond the western bank of the Mississippi River. Between 1787 and 1818 a small farming community situated 80 miles south of Saint Louis near St. Genevieve took form and began to mature. Originally known as the Barrens Colony, it would later be called Perryville, named after the naval hero of the War of 1812, Oliver Hazard Perry. About 1790, an Irish-born priest who had received his education in Spain, Father James Maxwell, began to serve the Catholics of the Barrens Colony.

According to Isidore Moore, one of the locale's earliest residents, Father Maxwell labored among the people of the settlement well into, and perhaps even slightly beyond, the War of 1812. The Congregation of the Mission constructed a seminary in Barrens Colony (Perryville) that molded countless Vincentians into frontier churchmen inspired by the spirit of their founder, St. Vincent de Paul. Alumni of the seminary emerged as key in the growth of the Catholic Church not only in Missouri, but far southward to Texas and northern Mexico and west to California as well.

The first permanent settlers in that area in 1787 were two Frenchmen, Jean Baptiste Barsaloux and his father. They had obtained a tract of land from the Spanish government and planned to engage in a life of farming. Inasmuch as the government of Spain would have required such, the two Frenchmen likely were Catholics. Within 30 years a rural community of Catholics had been attracted to the site. In addition to Isidore Moore and his family, they included Joseph Fenwick (at the vanguard of a group of Marylander Catholics), Joseph Tucker and his sons, Aquila Hagan, Sarah Haydon, and Wilfrid, Joseph, and Ignatius Layton and the latter's wife. Important also in the development of that Catholic group were the French Trappist pastor from Florissant, Missouri, Father Joseph Dunand, an Italian Vincentian priest, Joseph ROSATI, and Bishop Louis William DU BOURG, heading up the diocese of Louisiana and the Floridas.

When Father Rosati arrived at the Barrens on Oct. 1, 1818 with a number of Vincentian missionaries and seminarians, they were warmly welcomed by Bishop Du Bourg. The construction of the seminary had already begun; it was completed in the early 1820s, and a lay college was attached. Among the many dedicated missionaries educated in Saint Mary's of the Barrens seminary none were better known nor more highly respected than Jean-Marie ODIN, C.M., and John TIMON, C.M.

Archdiocese/Diocese	Year Created
Archdiocese of St. Louis	1847
Diocese of Jefferson City	1956
Diocese of Kansas City-St. Joseph	1956
Diocese of Springfield-Cape Girardeau	1956

Odin was a French priest born in the tiny hamlet of Hauteville, in the parish of Saint Martin d'Ambierle, situated in the far western reaches of the archdiocese of Lyon, France. Following his decision to volunteer for foreign mission work to America from the Sulpician major seminary of Saint Irenaeus at Lyon, Odin arrived at Saint Mary's of the Barrens Seminary in August of 1822. In 1823 he entered the Congregation of the Mission and was ordained a priest. For 17 years following his ordination he labored as a missionary, professor of theology at the seminary, secretary to the rector of the seminary (Father Rosati) and confessor to a community of Sisters of Loretto at a convent near the seminary. After serving as first pastor of the newly established parish of Saint Vincent de Paul at Cape Girardeau, Missouri, in 1836, he returned to Saint Mary's of the Barrens seminary for a three-year stint. Eventually, however, in 1840, he was sent to Texas, where he spent more than 20 years building the Faith there as vice prefect apostolic (1840), vicar apostolic (1841), and finally first bishop of Galveston (1847–61). In the spring of 1861 Odin was named second archbishop of New Orleans (1861–70).

John Timon, three years older than Odin, was born of Irish immigrant parents at Conswego Settlement near York, Pennsylvania, on Feb. 12, 1797. Following the War of 1812 the Timon family migrated westward, eventually settling in St. Louis where young Timon met Father De Andreis and Bishop Du Bourg. After studying for a short time at a school that Bishop Du Bourg had founded in 1919 (the forerunner of St. Louis University), Timon moved on to St. Mary's of the Barrens Seminary where in 1823 he joined the Congregation of the Mission. He was ordained a priest in 1825 and in 1835 Timon was named the first Visitor (Superior) of the American Vincentians. Ultimately Timon went on to be named prefect apostolic of Texas (1839) and first bishop of Buffalo, New York (1847) where he died on April 16, 1867. Under the leadership of Father Rosati, these nineteenth-century Vincentians went on to lay a strong base for the

Church in Missouri, building parishes, catechizing, and ministering to the Catholics of the state.

From 1804 when the Upper Louisiana Territory was transferred to U.S. control, to 1826 the territory of the future state of Missouri fell under the ecclesiastical jurisdiction of the Bishop of Louisiana, Bishop Du Bourg. The Vincentian Joseph Rosati was appointed coadjutor of Bishop Du Bourg and consecrated bishop at Donaldsville, Louisiana in March 1824. When on July 18, 1826 Pope Leo XII divided the Diocese of Louisiana and erected the sees of St. Louis and New Orleans, Bishop Du Bourg resigned. (He returned to France where he died on Dec. 12, 1833). The pope named Bishop Rosati the first ordinary of the Diocese of St. Louis and administrator of the Diocese of New Orleans. On Nov. 30, 1841, Father Peter Richard KENRICK, a native of Dublin, Ireland, and younger brother of coadjutor bishop of Philadelphia and future archbishop of Baltimore Francis Patrick Kenrick, was consecrated coadjutor bishop of St. Louis. When Bishop Rosati died in Rome on Sept. 25, 1843, Kenrick automatically succeeded him as ordinary of the diocese.

Diocesan Development. On Jan. 30, 1847, St. Louis was raised to the ecclesiastical status of an archbishopric; and Kenrick became the first archbishop of St. Louis. St. Louis included among its early suffragan sees Chicago, Dubuque, Milwaukee, Nashville, and St. Paul. At first the territory of the archdiocese was ill-defined, but by 1850 it was restricted to the present state boundaries. The Diocese of St. Joseph was erected in 1868, followed by that of Kansas City in 1880. Save for the assignment of 11 northeastern Missouri counties to St. Joseph in 1911, the ecclesiastical division of Missouri remained the same for 76 years. In 1956 a third suffragan see was added, and the territory completely realigned, with the Archdiocese of ST. LOUIS contracted to the see city and nine surrounding counties.

The ethnic make-up of Missouri's Catholic presence mirrors the historical patterns of religious demography associated with nineteenth-century American migration into the Midwest and beyond to the West Coast. The original French pre-eminence in the European settlement of the Mississippi River Valley, particularly with such personages involved as Marquette and Joliet, evolved as a paradigm of the manner in which New France was colonized. The nineteenth-century influx of Irish and German Catholics into the region, on the other hand, developed as an integral part of the narrative of European immigrants and the westward movement. This is especially true in regards to the building of the railroads and other essences of the industrial revolution—including that of mining in the West.

Catholic Irish and German life of Missouri is a prominent aspect of the state's legacy. Though noticeable throughout the southeastern, eastern, and central-northwestern regions of the state, such is especially true regarding St. Louis, Kansas City, and some of the state's smaller population centers. Perryville, for example, enjoys a visible German Catholic identity concomitant with its Irish and French Catholic heritage. As early as 1790, Father James Maxwell, from St. Genevieve, served Missouri's first Irish Catholic settlement, "a rough and tumble encampment on the Mississippi River called Boisé Brûlé Bottom." After gaining statehood in 1821, Missouri attracted an increasing number of settlers. Its Irish Catholic population steadily grew, many of the men working on the docks and steamboats of the Mississippi and Missouri rivers, and the women acting as domestic servants. Having matured as a prominent ethnic community in Missouri's western settlement of St. Joseph, the Irish Catholics saw the first parish established there in 1845, with Irish-born Father Thomas Scanlon as pastor.

With the passage of time, Irish Catholics came to play a major role in the building of not only the Church, but secular society as well. Father John Joseph Hogan of Bruff (Limerick), Ireland, the founder of the Irish Wilderness Settlements, became the first bishop of St. Joseph (consecrated on Sept. 13, 1868), and later (Sept. 10, 1880) first bishop of Kansas City. Irish Catholics were active in virtually all phases of Missouri's nineteenth and twentieth-century political, economic (especially labor unions), cultural, educational, military, and social developments.

The late nineteenth and twentieth centuries saw a kneading into the population of St. Louis, Kansas City, and other metropolitan areas most of the nationalities that have historically emerged as segments of the contemporary Catholic scene: Hispanics (and their centuries-old heritage from the American Southwest), Italians, and Asians.

At the same time with all of this development of the Catholic presence in Missouri, it cannot be ignored that a moral blight existed into the seventh decade of the nineteenth century, infecting the American nation, and thus society in Missouri and Catholicism's role therein: the institution of slavery. That phenomenon must be looked at carefully, as it came to fruition within the Catholic population of the state. While the human debasement that lay at the heart of slavery inherently contradicted Catholic moral precepts, lay Catholics and clergy and religious alike owned slaves in the nineteenth century, including the Vincentians at St. Mary's of the Barrens Seminary at Perryville.

After the creation of the Diocese of St. Joseph in 1868 and Kansas City in 1880, the ecclesiastical division of Missouri, save for the assignment of 11 northeastern

Missouri counties to St. Joseph in 1911, remained the same for 76 years. In 1956 the territory completely realigned. The dioceses of Kansas City and St. Joseph were joined and redesignated as the Diocese of Kansas City-St. Joseph. The new diocese of Springfield-Cape Girardeau was created by carving out 39 counties in southern Missouri from the dioceses of St. Louis and Kansas City. Bishop Charles H. Helmsing, auxiliary bishop in St. Louis, was the first ordinary (1956–62). The diocese of Jefferson City in the northeastern part of the state embraced 38 counties taken from St. Louis, Kansas City and the old diocese of St. Joseph. Bishop Joseph M. Marling, an auxiliary bishop in Kansas City, was named the first ordinary (1956–79). The Archdiocese of St. Louis was contracted to the see city and nine surrounding counties. The four dioceses joined together to form the Missouri Catholic Conference to provide a forum in which Catholics communicate and exchange information with one another and other groups on a statewide basis. The conference provides moral leadership and advocacy on public policy and issues of concern to the Church.

Higher Education. Founded by the Jesuits in 1818, ST. LOUIS UNIVERSITY is the oldest and most prestigious Catholic institution of higher learning in Missouri. In addition to St. Louis University, the Jesuits also sponsor Rockhurst College in Kansas City (established 1910). The Sisters of Saint Joseph of Carondelet sponsors two colleges, Fontbonne College in St. Louis (founded 1923 as a liberal arts college for women; coeducational from 1971) and Avila College in Kansas City (founded 1916 as a women's college; became coeducational in 1969). The Dominicans founded the Aquinas Institute of Theology, a Catholic graduate school, in St. Louis in 1925.

Bibliography: G. J. GARRAGHAN, *Catholic Beginnings in Kansas City, Missouri* (Chicago 1920). J. E. ROTHENSTEINER, *History of the Archdiocese of St.Louis,* 2 v. (St. Louis 1928). P. C. SCHULTE,*The Catholic Heritage of Saint Louis: A History of the Old Cathedral Parish* (St. Louis 1934).W. FAHERTY, *Dream by the River: Two Centuries of St. Louis Catholicism* (St. Louis 1973). P. FOLEY, ''Jean-Marie Odin, C.M., Missionary Bishop Extraordinaire of Texas,'' *Journal of Texas Catholic History and Culture* 1:1 (1990) 42–60. J. E. RYBOLT, ed., *The American Vincentians: A Popular History of the Congregation of the Mission in the United States, 1815–1987* (Brooklyn 1988).

[P. J. RAHILL/P. FOLEY]

MITER

The headdress worn in liturgical functions by bishops and other ecclesiastical prelates (mitered abbots) as a symbol of their special dignity. It is constructed of two stiffened triangular pieces, rounded at the sides and reaching to a point, sewn together laterally and united above by a fold of cloth. Two lappets (*infulae*) trimmed at the ends with fringe hang down from the back. Historically, there were three forms of miter: *pretiosa* or precious miter (often ornamented with jewels), *auriphrygiata* (with cloth of gold) and *simplex* (white silk or linen). Worn during various liturgical actions, the miter is always put aside when the bishop prays (1 Cor 11.4).

The origins of the miter are unclear. Probably developing from the *camelaucum* worn by the civil officials of the late ROMAN EMPIRE, this distinctive headpiece was allowed by Emperor CONSTANTINE I to Christian bishops in recognition of the role he had assigned them in the imperial hierarchy. Its history seems to be analogous to that of the *phrygium,* the predecessor of the papal TIARA, claimed by popes in the DONATION of Constantine. It is known that Pope CONSTANTINE I in the early eighth century wore the *camelaucum* on a visit to Constantinople (*Liber pontificalis,* 1:390). There seems to be no relationship between the Episcopal miter and the crown or μίτρα (Latin, *mitra*) used in both the East and the West by women and old men.

Prior to the 12th century the episcopal miter assumed many shapes: it was cone-shaped or simply a hat with a rounded crown of soft material, the lower edge of which ended in an ornamental band. Two lappets might be attached to the back of the miter. During the 12th century the rounded miter was often indented back across the top, producing prominent horns (*cornua*) at the right and left sides of the crown. These might be round or puffed as the result of an ornamental band that passed from front to back across the indentation; or they might end in a point, stiffened with parchment or other lining. By the end of the century the appearance of the miter was changed by moving the *cornua* a quarter circle causing them accordingly to rise centrally, front and back. From the 13th century the miter gradually grew in height and evolved into the roughly triangular shape it has in the 20th century. It has been observed that miters used today in the Church of England and the Episcopal Church in the United States, approximate the height of those in the late 15th and early 16th century; Roman miters, on the other hand, continued to grow in height and ornamentation into the 17th century. But in the absence of an exact comparative study of the headdress of bishops and abbots through the centuries, no precise dating of distinguishable developments is possible.

The first written mention of the miter is found in the bull of Pope LEO IX (*Regesta pontificum romanorum ab condita ecclesia ad annum post Christum natum 1198,* 4158) of 1049. In this document, confirming the primacy of the church of Trier, Leo granted Eberhard of Trier the right to use the Roman miter in performing the offices of the Church. In 1051 the same pope allowed the miter to the cardinal priests of the diocese of Besançon. The first authentic grant of the miter to an abbot dates from 1063, when Pope ALEXANDER II conferred the miter on Abbot Aethelsig of ST. AUGUSTINE's Abbey in Canterbury (*Regesta pontificum romanorum ab condita ecclesia ad annum post Christum natum 1198,* 4541). At times the privilege of the miter was granted to secular princes, among them the German emperors, Duke Wratislaw of Bohemia and King Peter of Aragon.

In the Greek Church the liturgical head-covering developed apparently from the cap worn by dignitaries of the late Roman Empire, possibly from that of the emperor himself. The Greek pontifical miter is a high hat that swells out toward the top and is spanned diagonally by two hoops; on the highest point of the crown is a cross either standing upright or placed flat.

Bibliography: J. BRAUN, *Die liturgische Gewandung im Occident und Orient* (Freiburg 1907). E. H. KANTOROWICZ, *Laudes regiae: A Study in Liturgical Acclamations and Medieval Ruler Worship* (Berkeley 1946). T. KLAUSER, *Der Ursprung der bischöflichen Insignien und Ehrenrechte* (2d ed. Krefeld 1953). H. NORRIS, *Church Vestments* (New York 1950). W. ULLMANN, *The Growth of Papal Government in the Middle Ages* (2d ed. New York 1962) 312–313. J. MAYO, *A History of Ecclesiastical Dress* (New York 1984). J. C. NOONAN, *The Church Visible: The Ceremonial Life and Protocol of the Roman Catholic Church* (New York 1996). *Clothed in Glory: Vesting the Church,* ed. D. PHILIPPART, (Chicago 1997). *Liber pontificalis,* ed. L. DUCHESNE, v.1–2 (Paris 1886–92) v.3 (Paris 1958). P. JAFFÉ, *Regesta pontificum romanorum ab condita ecclesia ad annum post Christum natum 1198,* ed. S. LÖWENFELD, 882–1198, 2 v. (2d ed. Leipzig 1881–88; repr. Graz 1956).

[O. J. BLUM/EDS.]

MITHRAS AND MITHRAISM

Mithra (in Greek, Mithras) was an ancient Indo-Iranian god. In the Vedas, as well as in a list of gods appended to a treaty concluded in the 14th century B.C. between the Hittite king and the king of Mitanni, he is coupled with Varuna. In Iran also, he appears in union with Ahura—probably another name for the outmoded Varuna. His name means ''contract,'' but this designation does not account for all his characteristics. Despite his importance as a major divinity, Mithra is conspicuously absent from the *Gāthās.* As he was the greatest rival of Ahura Mazda, whom Zoroaster wished to make the supreme god, the prophet probably did not dare to oppose him openly but preferred to ignore him in his hymns. Mithra, at this early date, may have been connected with bull-sacrifices, as he was in Roman times. But, when after the death of Zoroaster Mithra was readmitted into the religion of his followers, he did not exhibit any such connection. On the other hand, he is associated with the sun; the *Yasht* (*see* AVESTA) devoted to him depicts him rising in the morning behind the Eastern mountains and crossing the sky from East to West in his chariot drawn by white horses. His standing epithet, ''with broad pastures,'' means that he gives protection and grazing rights over large territories, and this at least is clearly in accord with his character as a god of the contract.

The Development and Spread of His Cult. In western Iran he is first mentioned, in addition to Ahura Mazda, in the inscriptions of Artaxerxes II (404–358 B.C.). His popularity in Parthian and Hellenistic times is proved by the frequency of personal names, like Mithridates, and by his presence, immediately after Ormazd, in the inscription of Antiochus of Commagene on the Nimrud Dagh (*c.* 50 B.C.). In that, Mithra is further identified with three different Greek gods, namely, Apollo, because of his solar and juridical character; Helios, as a sun-god; and Hermes, as a mediator between gods and men. In eastern Iran during the same period, he was by far the most prominent god, superior even to Ormazd, in the religion of the Kushans. Therefore, it is not surprising that the Iranian religion, which in Hellenistic and Roman times spread throughout the West, should have had Mithra, and not Ormazd, as its principal god, and should have been called Mithraism.

The Greco-Oriental mystery cult of Mithras is known, apart from a few meager literary texts, almost exclusively from archeological monuments and a few short inscriptions. The Mithraic monuments are scattered throughout the Roman Empire, but are found especially at the frontiers. Mithraism was essentially a soldiers' religion. Renan was guilty of exaggeration when he said that had not the world turned Christian, it would have turned Mithraic. Christianity had the advantage of having the historical God-Man, Jesus Christ, as its founder and of addressing itself to women as well as men—and women played a decisive part in its diffusion.

Mithraism or the Cult of Mithras. The ceremonies of the mysteries of Mithras were performed in cave-shaped, usually subterranean buildings, imitating the vault of the sky, which Mithras spanned daily. These temples, or *Mithraea,* were adorned with reliefs, the most important of which show Mithras, wearing a Phrygian cap, in the act of killing a bull. An ear of wheat sprouts from the tail of the animal. The relationship between these representations and the myth, attested in later Pahlavi writings, of Ahriman killing the primeval bull, is far from clear. The Pahlavi documents, moreover, are as late as the 9th century A.D., whereas the monuments of the mysteries date from the 2d to the 4th [*see* AHURA MAZDA (ORMAZD) AND AHRIMAN]. But the fact must be stressed that

Mithras, in the mysteries, had taken over the role of other gods or heroes, notably of Saturn, as god of a new golden age; of Time, as god of destiny; and Phaethon, as author of the final conflagration of the world. Therefore, it may well be that he took over an exploit usually assigned to Ahriman.

The birth of the infant Mithras was celebrated on December 25, i.e., just after the winter solstice, when the power of the sun was at its lowest. This undoubtedly contributed to the adoption of December 25 as the date for Christmas. But the importance of Mithraism in the development of early Christianity should not be overestimated. For instance, the thesis that the Iranians, prior to the birth of Jesus, believed in and waited for the imminent advent of a divine child who would save the world, is devoid of proof.

There were seven degrees of initiation into which the faithful were successfully admitted, each with its own symbols, and each connected with a planet. They were: the Corax, or Raven; the Nymphus, or Bridegroom; the Miles, or Soldier; the Leo, or Lion; the Perses, or Persian; the Heliodromus, personifying the sun's daily course; and the Pater, or Father, who was the chief of a Mithraic community.

The ritual comprised oaths, banquets of bread and wine, and a formal baptism through water and blood. In these ceremonies, reminiscent of the Christian Eucharist and Baptism, some early Christian writers (Justin Martyr and Tertullian) saw imitations of the Christian Sacraments. It may well be that they were at least partly right.

Mithras, though the most important god in the mysteries, was not the supreme one. This is in accord with Plutarch's statement that he was a mediator. In fact, the numerous bas-reliefs representing various stages in his career give the impression not so much of a god as of a demigod or hero, a sort of Hercules. The connection is sometimes obvious. Thus, when Mithras, having captured the bull, pulls him into the cave, he seems to be repeating the exploit of Hercules and Cacus. Accordingly he performs all his feats in honor of some other god. In regard to the identity of this god, there is no definite answer. Perhaps the question should not be raised at all. In an age when syncretism was so dominant, gods such as Aion, Sarapis, Zeus, Helios, Mithras, Hades, and Ahriman could all be identified as one. It suffices to recall the syncretism of Ormazd-Jupiter-Caelus. However, it should be noted that, even when called *summus exsuperantissimus,* this god was not exterior to the world like Yahweh, or the ''Father of Greatness'' of Gnosticism, but a cosmic god.

After death, the followers of Mithras were promised access, through seven successive planetary spheres, to a heaven that was beyond these spheres, beyond all things.

Bibliography: F. CUMONT, *Textes et monuments relatifs aux Mystères de Mithra* (Brussels 1896–99), outdated, but not fully replaced by M. J. VERMASEREN, *Corpus monumentorum et inscriptionum religionis Mithriacae,* 2 v. (The Hague 1960). A. D. NOCK, ''The Genius of Mithraism,'' *Journal of Roman Studies* 27 (1937) 108–113, excellent. K. PRÜMM, *Lexikon für Theologie und Kirche,* ed. J. HOFER and K. RAHNER, 10 v. (2d new ed. Freiburg1957–65) 7:488–490. H. S. JONES, J. HASTINGS, ed., *Encyclopedia of Religion and Ethics* 13 v. (Edinburgh 1908–27) 8:752–759. M. J. VERMASEREN, *Die Religion in Geschichte und Gegenwart* 4:1020–22; *Mithras, The Secret God* (New York 1963). J. DUCHESNE-GUILLEMIN, *La Religion de l'Iran ancien* (Paris 1962) 172–175, 248–257. I. GERSHEVITCH, *The Avestan Hymn to Mithra* (Cambridge, Eng. 1959).

[J. DUCHESNE-GUILLEMIN]

MITTARELLI, GIOVANNI BENEDETTO

Camaldolese author and administrator; b. Venice, Sept. 2, 1707; d. Abbey of S. Michele di Murano, near Venice, Aug. 14, 1777. Mittarelli's field of activity as priest and scholar was limited to his own CAMALDOLESE Order, which he joined in 1722. In 1747 he came to Faenza as chancellor of the order and there began, together with Anselmo Costadoni (d. 1785), the *Annales Camaldulenses ordinis S. Benedicti.* This is his chief work, and it is patterned entirely after MABILLON and embraces the period from 907 to 1764. It appeared in nine volumes in Venice from 1754 to 1773. Mittarelli returned as abbot in 1760 to his home monastery of S. Michele di Murano; in 1765 he went to Rome as abbot general of his order. During his five-year stay there, he was a favorite of Pope CLEMENT XIII, a native of Venice.

Bibliography: Works. *Ad Scriptores rerum Italicarum cl. Muratorii accessiones historicae Faventinae* (Venice 1771); *De literatura Faventinorum . . . Appendix ad Accessiones historicas Faventinas* (Venice 1775); *Bibliotheca codicum manuscriptorum monasterii S. Michaelis Venetiarum prope Murianum* (Venice 1779). **Literature.** A. FABRONI, *Vitae Italorum doctrina excellentium,* 18 v. (Pisa 1778–99). P. PASCHINI, *Enciclopedia Italiana di scienzi, littere ed arti,* 36 v. (Rome 1929–39) 23:487. H. KIENE, *Lexikon für Theologie und Kirche,* 10 v. (Freiburg 1957–) 7:493.

[H. RUMPLER]

MITTY, JOHN JOSEPH

Fourth archbishop of San Francisco, Calif.; b. New York City, Jan. 20, 1884; d. Menlo Park, Calif., Oct. 15, 1961. He was the son of John and Mary (Murphy) Mitty and was orphaned at an early age. After an early education at the St. Joseph's School and the De La Salle Institute, he graduated (1901) from Manhattan College, New York City. From 1901 to 1906 he attended St. Joseph's Seminary, Yonkers, N.Y., and he was ordained on Dec. 22, 1906; he was the first graduate of that institution to be consecrated a bishop, and he himself ordained more than 700 priests and consecrated seven bishops. He pursued graduate studies at The Catholic University of America, Washington, D.C., and the Lateran Seminary, Rome, receiving a doctorate in sacred theology in 1908. After advanced studies in psychology at the University of Munich, Germany, he returned to New York (1909), where he was assigned briefly as a curate at St. Veronica's Church. In the same year he joined the faculty of St. Joseph's Seminary as professor of theology, enjoying the life of a scholar until 1917, when he joined the U.S. Army. He served as chaplain with the 49th and 101st regiments at Camp Merritt, N.J., and in France, where he participated in the Meuse-Argonne offensive. After the war he was appointed pastor of Sacred Heart Church, Highland Falls, N.Y., and chaplain of the cadet corps at West Point. His second pastorate was at St. Luke's Church, Bronx, N.Y., from 1922 to June 21, 1926, when Pius XI appointed him bishop of Salt Lake City, Utah. He was consecrated the following September 8, the youngest bishop in the country at that time. He served as ordinary of the Utah diocese until Jan. 29, 1932, when he was named coadjutor archbishop of San Francisco; he succeeded to the see when Archbishop Edward J. HANNA resigned on March 2, 1935.

Mitty's previous career fitted him well for the huge task that awaited him in rapidly growing San Francisco. His arrival there coincided with an economic depression that stunted the growth of facilities necessary to maintain a living church. Then World War II, with San Francisco the major port for Pacific operations, gave a new direction to the sociological, cultural, political, and spiritual development of the archdiocese. The great westward migration that hit flood stage with four million newcomers during the war years brought an increase in the Catholic body from 405,000 Catholics in 1935 to more than 1,121,500 in 1961. Mitty founded 85 new parishes and directed the completion of 563 major building projects, including 120 new churches, 119 new elementary schools, 13 high schools, 28 youth centers, and 27 diocesan buildings, including orphanages, retreat houses, general hospitals, and an enlarged junior seminary. During his tenure, the number of priests serving the archdiocese increased from 667 to 1,197, and the number of children in Catholic schools rose from 27,257 to 100,681. The total number of youth under religious instruction in 1961 was 220,397, an increase of 164,783. This increase was due to the new concept of the School of Religion in the Confraternity of Christian Doctrine program, which Mitty started and which has since become widely accepted in many parts of the world.

Mitty was one of the first prelates in the United States to inaugurate a specialized postgraduate training for his clergy; all diocesan departments were headed by priests trained especially for the purpose and with appropriate degrees. He also anticipated many pastoral projects that later became common practices in U.S. dioceses, pioneering in the work of counseling in the social services and initiating a series of monthly spiritual hours of direction for the nuns in the archdiocese. He was one of the first to organize ''flying squads'' of priests to care for migrant workers, and he lost no time in integrating schools throughout the archdiocese. When television was in its infancy, he plunged immediately into the establishment of a weekly diocesan-produced program. Ecumenical-minded, he was instrumental in having accepted nationally the ceremony of ''mixed marriages'' held in the parish church. He provided summer schools for the education of his priests in the social encyclicals long before such activities became popular. He insisted that his seminarians spend their summers in some form of apostolic work that he himself provided through camps, catechetics, and census-taking. When the United Nations was founded in San Francisco, Mitty organized the greatest act of citizen participation in the initial days of the United Nations with a Mass at which he was joined by 10,000 of his flock.

Bibliography: Archives, Archdiocese of San Francisco.

[W. J. TAPPE]

MIVART, GEORGE JACKSON, ST.

Biologist; b. London, Nov. 30, 1827; d. London, April 1, 1900. He converted to Catholicism in 1844. He was confirmed at Oscott in 1845, the same year as William George WARD and John Henry NEWMAN. Barred by the religious tests from matriculation at Oxford or Cambridge, Mivart studied law at Lincoln's Inn Court and was called to the bar in 1851. Financially secure, he did not practice law, but became active in biology. With Richard OWEN and Thomas HUXLEY as both friends and teachers, he pursued investigations in comparative anatomy that resulted in significant monographs in vertebrate anatomy with emphasis on the primates. He accepted evolution as an explanation for the origin of species, although he rejected as a primary agent the Darwinian mechanism of natural selection because he considered it to be in conflict with Catholic doctrine. In his *On the Genesis of Species* (1871), he criticized the Darwinian theory and put forth a theory of his own that he thought compatible with both science and religion. For his attempts to reconcile science and revelation, he was awarded a doctorate by Pius IX in 1876. His gradual estrangement from the scientific community resulted from his nonsecular approach to scientific questions, and Mivart became increasingly involved in attempts to reconcile the doctrines and practices of the Catholic Church with knowledge derived from science. This was expressed in articles on biblical criticism, liturgical reform, education of the clergy, the nature of hell, and the Catholic Church as an evolving institution. The last was considered heretical by Cardinal Herbert VAUGHAN, archbishop of Westminster, who demanded that Mivart sign a profession of faith. In a letter of Jan. 23, 1900, Mivart, following a detailed explanation of his position, refused, after which Vaughan denied him the sacraments. He died two months later.

Bibliography: J. W. GRUBER, *A Conscience in Conflict: The Life of St. George Jackson Mivart* (New York 1960).

[J. W. GRUBER]

MIXED MARRIAGES, PROHIBITION OF

Church law forbids two baptized persons from contracting marriage when one is a Catholic and the other belongs to a Christian community that lacks full communion with Rome (*Codex Iuris Canonicis* c. 1124; *Codex Canonum Ecclesiarium Orientalium* c. 813). In this part of its matrimonial discipline, the Church canonizes the custom and particular legislation that goes back to its earliest centuries, forbidding members from contracting marriage with those, who, by birth or by choice, were outside the membership of the Church.

With the advent of the Reformation, the cases in which mixed marriages arose became more frequent, especially in such countries as Germany and Holland. The Council of Trent failed to enact any legislation dealing directly with mixed marriages. Indirectly, however, it controlled such unions by requiring for the validity of marriage of a Catholic the assistance of the Catholic's proper pastor, wherever the decree *TAMETSI* was published. No priest was allowed to assist at such marriages without a dispensation. Despite this fact, an opinion arose that in Protestant countries, where the juridical form of marriage of the decree *Tametsi* was not obligatory, there was no need to seek a dispensation and no need to ask for the antenuptial promises or *cautiones.* This opinion was condemned and the word ''everywhere'' was inserted into c. 1060 of the 1917 code and c. 50 of *Crebrae allatae.*

Under the 1917 code and *Crebrae allatae,* mixed religion was an impediment to marriage (1917 *Codex Iuris Canonicis* c. 1060; *Crebrae allatae* c. 50). The current discipline of the Church prohibits mixed marriages, but does not consider mixed religion an impediment.

Local ordinaries can grant permission for a mixed marriage (*Codex Iuris Canonicis* c. 1125; *Codex Canonum Ecclesiarium Orientalium* c. 814). Before the permission is granted, the Catholic party must declare that he or she is prepared to remove dangers of lapsing from the Catholic faith as well as promise that he or she will do all in his or her power to baptize and raise children born to the marriage as Catholics (*Codex Iuris Canonicis* c. 1125; *Codex Canonum Ecclesiarium Orientalium* c. 814).

Bibliography: F. J. SCHENK, *The Matrimonial Impediments of Mixed Religion and Disparity of Cult* (Catholic University of America CLS 51; Washington, D.C. 1929). BOUSC-O'CONNOR, *Codex iuris Canonici* (Rome 1918; repr. Graz 1955). F. TERAAR, *Mixed Marriages and Their Remedies,* tr. A. WALTER, ed. F. J. CONNELL (New York 1933).

[E. A. FUS/EDS.]

MOABITES

A Semitic people who, during OT times, inhabited the territory east of the Jordan River and north of the Wadi Zered and the territory of the EDOMITES. Their northern boundary was the Wadi Arnon during much of their history, though at times they were able to extend their holdings beyond this point; the region north of their border was held by AMORRITE tribes, the AMMONITES, and the Israelites at various times in their history. The folkloric accounts of LOT'S settlement east of the Dead Sea (Gn 13.1–13) and of his fatherhood of the eponymous ancestors of the Moabites and the Ammonites through intercourse with his daughters (Gn 19.30–38), reflect both the Israelite awareness of their kinship with the tribes that settled in this region and their contempt for the hostility toward them.

Although the Moabites may have dwelt in this territory as nomads at an earlier period—there is no trace of a settled population there after the 20th century B.C. until their kingdom appears—it is only at the beginning of the Iron Age (13th century B.C.) that they emerged as a settled people, as the explorations of N. Glueck have shown. The Biblical account accords well with Glueck's findings, for when the Israelites were en route to the conquest of Palestine, they were forced to detour around Moab (Nm 21.10–20; Dt 2.8–13) instead of passing through as they had intended (Jgs 11.16–18), an indication that there was a strong, well organized population there at that time.

According to Nm 21.26–30, Moab had previously possessed territory north of the Arnon, but was driven from it by the Amorrites; although the Israelites took this territory from the Amorrites by conquest (Nm 21.21–25), Moab continued to lay claim to it. There is at least a strong possibility that the words of Jephthah in Jgs 11.15–27, although they are presented as a message to the Ammonite king, may have originally concerned the Moabites and their claim to this territory; 11.24 is to be noted especially, for it identifies the god of the king addressed as CHEMOSH, who was the god of Moab, not of Ammon.

Although a successful campaign against the Moabites is attributed to Saul in 1 Sm 14.47, it was only under David that Moab was subjugated and made to pay tribute (2 Sm 8.2). David's harsh treatment of the Moabite captives on this occasion is hard to reconcile with his earlier friendly relations with this people (1 Sm 22.3–4) and with the tradition preserved in the Book of RUTH that his grandmother was a Moabite. It is possible that during the time of Israel's divided monarchy Moab regained independence for a while and was reconquered by the northern kingdom, for the MESHA INSCRIPTION names Omri, King of Israel, (*c.* 876–869 B.C.) as the subjugator, and the OT account indicates that it was to Israel (rather than to Judah) that Moab paid tribute during this period and that it was against Israel that they rebelled under Mesha, their king (2 Kgs 1.1; 3.4–27), in 849 B.C. The united forces of Israel and Judah were unable to bring Moab under control again. This successful rebellion is the theme of the inscription of Mesha's famed stele. During the Persian period Moab's territory was incorporated into the kingdom of the Nabataeans.

The bad feelings that existed between Moabites and Israelites are reflected not only in the Genesis accounts and David's cruelty mentioned above, but also in other OT texts. The Moabites (along with the Ammonites) are singled out for special discrimination in Dt 23.4–7, and many prophetic oracles were directed against them (e.g., Is 15.1–9; Ez 25.8–11; Zep 2.8–11). Yet the Book of Ruth portrays the Moabite heroine as a noble personage, and after the Exile, marriages with Moabite women were so frequent that both Ezra and Nehemiah took measures against the practice (Ezr 9.1–10.44; Neh 13.23–30).

Bibliography: *Encyclopedic Dictionary of the Bible*, tr. and adap. by L. HARTMAN (New York 1963) 1544–46. H. EISING, *Lexikon für Theologie und Kirche*, ed. J. HOFER and K. RAHNER, 10 v. (2d new ed. Freiburg 1957–65) 7:505–506. M. NOTH, *Die Religion in Geschichte und Gegenwart*, 7 v. (3d ed. Tübingen 1957–65) 4:1065–66. F. M. ABEL, *Géographie de la Palestine* 2 v. (Paris 1933–38) 1:278–281. A. H. VAN ZYL, *The Moabites* (Leiden 1960). M. NOTH, "Israelitische Stämme zwischen Ammon und Moab," *Zeitschrift für die alttestamentliche Wissenschaft* 19 (1944) 11–57. R. E. MURPHY, "Israel and Moab in the Ninth Century B.C.," *Catholic Biblical Quarterly* 15 (1943) 409–417. N. GLUECK, "Explorations in Eastern Palestine I–III," *Annual of the American Schools of Oriental Research* 14 (1933–34) 1–113; 15 (1934–35) 1–102; 18–19 (1937–39) 1–50. R. DE VAUX, "Notes d'histoire et de topographie transjordanienne," *Vivre et Penser* 1 (1941) 16–29.

[W. M. DUFFY]

MOBILE, ARCHDIOCESE OF

Erected as diocese of Mobile (*Mobiliensis*) on May 15, 1829, it was designated the Diocese of Mobile-Birmingham on July 9, 1954. On Nov. 16, 1980, the diocese was elevated to an archdiocese and the Metropolitan See of the Province of Mobile, comprising the states of Alabama and Florida. Formerly suffragan of New Orleans, the archdiocese comprises the lower 28 counties in Alabama and has an area of 22,969 square miles. In 2001 Catholics number some 5 percent of the total population of 1.6 million.

Catholic Origins. The arrival of Catholicism in the region traces its origins to early Spanish and French explorations and permanent settlements at Pensacola, Fla., in 1696, and Mobile, Ala., in 1702, where a parish was erected on July 20, 1703, with Henry Rolleaux de la Vente as first pastor. The parish registers, virtually intact from 1704, faithfully mirror the unsettled conditions of those early days. Secular and religious priests in turn acted as pastors as the territory passed from French through British into Spanish hands. Ecclesiastical responsibility shifted from Quebec, Canada, to Santiago de Cuba and, in 1793, to a mainland diocese with the see at New Orleans. After the Gulf Coast area became part of the U.S., the states of Alabama and Florida were erected into a vicariate apostolic in August 1825, and Michael PORTIER was chosen to head the new jurisdiction.

Diocesan Growth. Portier developed and ordered religious life in the area, which was raised to a diocese in May 1829, and in 1850 reduced in size. He was notably successful in founding institutions of education and welfare, and by the time of his death in 1859 there were, exclusive of the staff of Spring Hill College, ten priests serving nine parishes and nine mission stations. Catholic population had grown from about 6,000 to an estimated 10,000, most of it centered in the southern part of the diocese.

John Quinlan (1826–83) was consecrated as the second bishop of Mobile in New Orleans on Dec. 4, 1859. A native of County Cork, Ireland, Quinlan immigrated to the U.S. in 1844, was ordained for the Diocese of Cincinnati, Ohio, in 1852, and two years later became rector of the diocesan seminary. His early years in the South were spent amid the confusion of the Civil War, and the remainder of his life was devoted to improving the status of the Church through the difficult years that followed. Quinlan secured a supply of clergy from Ireland, repaired the war losses, continued construction on the cathedral, and increased the number of parishes and mission stations to 36. Resident pastors were placed in the northern part of the diocese for the first time, due largely to the introduction in 1876 of Benedictines from St. Vincent Abbey (now Archabbey), Latrobe, Pa. This group formed the nucleus from which St. Bernard Abbey and College later developed. By the time of Quinlan's death his clergy had increased to 45, about evenly divided between secular and religious, to care for a Catholic population of about 18,000. The diocese was, at the same time, burdened by crushing financial obligations.

The third bishop, Dominic Manucy (1823–85), was born in St. Augustine, Fla., and had been ordained by Portier in 1850. He was consecrated by Quinlan in 1874 for the Vicariate Apostolic of Brownsville, Tex., but was transferred to Mobile in March 1884, while yet retaining the administration of his former jurisdiction. Ill health, combined with the difficult situation in Mobile, led Manucy to resign before the year's end.

Jeremiah O'Sullivan (1844–96), a native of Ireland and priest of the Archdiocese of Baltimore, Md., was consecrated fourth bishop of Mobile, Sept. 20, 1885. Although he was successful in extricating the diocese from its financial difficulties, his years were necessarily characterized more by retrenchment and consolidation than by new gains. Towers were added to the cathedral and conditions prepared for later growth throughout the area, but the estimated Catholic population suffered a slight decline.

Edward Patrick ALLEN, who followed Bishop O'Sullivan, was consecrated in Baltimore on May 16, 1897. Prior to that he had been president of Mt. St. Mary's College, Emmitsburg, Md. During Allen's 30-year rule, the Catholic population grew to 48,000, while churches and clergy increased threefold. New efforts were made in rural districts, and the Josephite fathers ministered to a large African American population. Much was accomplished in the fields of education and welfare in Mobile through the benefactions of the McGill family of that city.

Growth continued during the administration of Thomas Joseph TOOLEN, consecrated the sixth bishop of Mobile in Baltimore, May 4, 1927. During his episcopate 69 parishes were established and 154 churches built to keep pace with notable gains in urban as well as rural Catholic populations. Of the 77 counties within his jurisdiction, those without churches were reduced from 49 to 19. Outside of the Mobile district, the diocese was divided into three deaneries: North Alabama, centered at Birmingham where, since 1954, St. Paul's Church had been the cocathedral; Central Alabama, the area around Montgomery; and Northwest Florida, dominated by Pensacola. The number of priests had increased threefold to provide for a like growth in Catholic population.

Social welfare services were efficiently organized under a Bureau of Catholic Charities, and a diocesan school system was annually responsible for the education of more than 25,000 students. Adequate Catholic hospital facilities exist in the major cities, and, since 1934, the diocese had an independent newspaper, *The Catholic Week.* Toolen's success in coping with such growth, and special attention given to the needs of Black Catholics in the area merited for him the title of *archbishop ad personam* (1954). In 1968 the Pensacola Deanery was added to the Diocese of St. Augustine. Archbishop Toolen resigned on Oct. 8, 1969, at which time the see was divided into the Diocese of Mobile and the Diocese of Birmingham in Alabama. Toolen died on Dec. 4, 1976.

John C. May (b. 1922), an auxiliary bishop of Chicago, was installed as the seventh Bishop of Mobile on Dec.10, 1969. He effectively fostered liturgical and standard changes provided for by Vatican Council II and gave renewed emphasis to the Church's social apostolate (housing and health care). The new parishes were established mostly in rural areas and a number of missions. Significant advances were made in social integration in diocesan organizations with notable success in the parish at Selma, Ala. Despite a number of school closings and consolidation, two new elementary units were established. A diocesan pastoral council was formed in 1974 and lay leadership emerged in parish and diocesan structure. A program for the retirement of lay employees was put into place. Ecumenical initiatives bore fruit in collaboration for direct help to the needy and a Jewish-Christian Dialogue began in Mobile, the longest ongoing such exercise nationwide. In 1979 Bishop May ordained the first class of permanent deacons for the diocese. He was appointed as Archbishop of St. Louis on Jan. 29, 1980.

On Nov. 16, 1980, Oscar H. Lipscomb, a native of Mobile (b. 1931, ord. 1956) was consecrated as the first Archbishop of Mobile. The new province, erected that same day, consists of the states of Alabama and Mississippi, with Jackson, Biloxi and Birmingham as suffragan sees. Reported Catholic population has grown but slightly. Notable decreases occurred in rural areas, but there is currently a Southeast Asian and significant Hispanic presence. An office for Hispanic Ministry addresses the latter, while only one new parish has been established, older parishes have built permanent or new churches, the result of increased substantial Catholic populations. The

André Mocquereau.

number of diocesan priests has remained stable with more than average success in the program for priestly formation. Currently, the fourth class of permanent deacons is preparing for ordination. Catholic high and elementary schools enroll 6,498 students, and other programs for youth religious education count 4,376. Jesuit Spring Hill College, the oldest in Alabama, has a student body of 1,005. The social apostolate has grown with new centers in Montgomery, Dothan, and Robertsdale, and Pro-Life offices serve in the Mobile, Montgomery, and Dothan areas.

Bibliography: M. T. A. CARROLL, *A Catholic History of Alabama and the Floridas* (New York 1908). M. KENNY, *Catholic Culture in Alabama: Centenary Story of Spring Hill College* (New York 1931).

[O. H. LIPSCOMB]

MOCQUEREAU, ANDRÉ

Founder of the Solesmes system of GREGORIAN CHANT; b. Tessoualle (Maineet-Loire), France, June 6, 1849; d. Solesmes, Jan. 18, 1930. His musical education was nurtured in an atmosphere of strict classical formalism and directed and developed by Charles Dancla, with whom he studied cello at the Paris Conservatory. He entered the Benedictine Abbey of SOLESMES (1875), was professed April 9, 1877, and ordained Dec. 28, 1879. As director of the paleographic scriptorium and choir master, he soon determined the community's commitment to the restoration of the pristine purity of chant. Working closely with Dom Pothier for 13 years, but later in opposition to Pothier's theory of "free oratoric rhythm," Mocquereau developed the Solesmes system, basing it on the theory of "free musical rhythm." This system, first proposed in *Paléographie musicale* v.7, was expansively developed in the *Le nombre musical (1908–27)*. Under the title of *Paléographie musicale grégorienne*, Mocquereau launched the publication of over 15 volumes of photographic reproductions of medieval manuscripts with important historical studies. These laid the foundation for the reform of chant prescribed in the 1903 *motu proprio* of Pius X. Mocquereau's system is incorporated in the modern publications of the Solesmes editions by the addition of certain rhythmic signs. He defended his system by many scholarly publications, often controversial, in the *Tribune de Saint Gervais*, the *Rassegna gregoriana*, and the *Revue grégorienne*.

Bibliography: P. COMBE, *Études grégoriennes* 2 (1957) 189, for a list of Mocquereau's writings. "Les Préliminaires de la réforme grégorienne de S. Pie X," in *Études grégoriennes* 7. M. BLANC, *L'Enseignement musical de Solesmes et la prière chrétienne* (Paris 1953). E. CARDINE, "André Mocquereau" in *The New Grove Dictionary of Music and Musicians, vol. 12*, ed. S. SADIE (New York 1980) 375–376. D. M. RANDEL, ed., *The Harvard Biographical Dictionary of Music* (Cambridge 1996) 395. N. SLONIMSKY, ed. *Baker's Biographical Dictionary of Musicians, Eighth Edition* (New York 1992) 1231.

[P. COMBE]

MODALISM

Modalism, also SABELLIANISM or PATRIPASSIANISM, is the strict form of MONARCHIANISM, a heresy that originated in an exaggerated defense of the unity (*monarchia*) of God; and while verbally admitting a Trinity, it denied the real distinction between the Persons. It affirmed that the Father, Son, and Holy Spirit are modes, aspects, or energies of one and the same divine Person, who is given different names according as He exercises different functions *ad extra* or outside the Trinity: creation (Father), redemption (Son), sanctification (Holy Spirit). God, one from eternity, became three in time. God's appearance on earth as the Son should logically have involved the conclusion that the Father died; hence the name Patripassianism, as the heresy was known in the West. Praxeas, the first proponent of Modalism to visit Rome, went to Carthage about 206 or 208, and TERTULLIAN refuted him in his *Adversus Praxean* (213), "which represents the most important contribution to the doctrine of the Trinity in the Ante–Nicene period'' [J. Quasten, *Patrology,* 3 v. (Westminster, Md.) 2:285]. According to Tertullian, the identification of Father and Son was so complete in Praxeas's teaching that ''the Father Himself came down into the Virgin, was Himself born of her, Himself suffered, indeed was Himself Jesus Christ'' (ch. 1). In the East the heresy was known as Sabellianism, from Sabellius, who probably developed the teaching of Noetus and was excommunicated by Pope CALLISTUS I (*c.* 220). Sabellius's chief opponent was DIONYSIUS OF ALEXANDRIA.

Bibliography: G. BARDY, *Dictionnaire de théologie catholique,* ed. A. VACANT et al., 15 v. (Paris 1903–50; Tables générales 1951–) 10.2:2193–2209. E. EVANS, ed. and tr., *Q. Septimi Florenti Tertulliani adversus Praxean,* Society for Promoting Christian Knowledge (London 1948) 6–31. T. VERHOEVEN, *Vigiliae christianae* (Amsterdam 1951) 43–48. C. HUBER, *Lexikon für Theologie und Kirche*[2], ed. J. HOFER and K. RAHNER, 10 v. (Freiburg 1957–65) 7:533–534. H. CROUZEL, *ibid.* 508. K. WÖLFL, *Das Heilswirken Gottes durch den Sohn nach Tertullian* in *Analecta Gregoriana* (Rome 1930–) 112; 1960.

[P. J. HAMELL]

MODE

In metaphysics, a limitation or determination produced in some actual reality by a principle or cause extrinsic to itself, e.g., rapidity or slowness of motion, various shades of the same color, and different degrees of a virtue or vice; in logic, a particular determination of the PROPOSITION or SYLLOGISM.

Real Modes. Mode is found in all creaturely reality, only God being absolutely unmodified. ''Wherever there is something received there must be a mode, since what is received is limited according to the recipient; therefore, since creaturely being, essential and accidental, is received [being], mode is found not only in accidental things but also in substances'' (St. Thomas Aquinas, *De ver.* 21.6 ad 5). All experienced reality involves partial or limited perfection. For example, man has the perfection of intelligence, but limited intelligence, called reason; intelligence of itself does not bespeak animality, and this limits human intelligence.

Mode is proximately produced in a perfection by two principles, viz, the efficient and material causes (*Summa theologiae* 1a, 5.5). The efficient cause effects a form of determinate species and so determines it; the material cause, by its relative aptness, receives this form more or less perfectly and so determines its individual perfection.

Mode resides in both the perfection modified and in the principle that modifies it; yet it is more properly in the latter, since the form is modified primarily by the modifying principle. For example, individuality is a mode of being found in all corporeal things, and arising from their corporeity, since matter exigent of quantity is the root of INDIVIDUATION; yet individuality, more properly in matter, affects the form also, individualizing it through its relation to matter.

Scholastics distinguish between intrinsic and extrinsic modes. Intrinsic modes constitute or complete something because they are requisite to the BEING, either essential or existential, of the nature. For example, man is neither body nor soul but the union of the two; this union is neither body nor soul but a mode of being shared by each, since each in a manner proper to it determines and modifies the other, and thereby contributes to constituting man's nature. Extrinsic modes, on the other hand, suppose a nature complete in its interior being, essential and existential, but determine it in nonessentials, relative to other things or natures. For example, LOCATION (*ubi*) is produced in a body only through the mediacy of other bodies, so that were there only one body existing, it would have no location. Yet extrinsic modes are not mere references to other things—such references constituting the category of RELATION—but qualifications of a reality that truly characterize it, although relatively to other existing things. (*See* CATEGORIES OF BEING.)

Modality figures prominently in scholastic theology and philosophy. In theology, for example, mode alone explains different graces and different degrees of beatific vision in heaven. All supernatural grace has the same nature and definition; but the difference among sacramental graces, the difference between Christian grace and pre-Christian, and the different degrees of grace in different persons, or in the same person at different times, are all modal differences (*see* DISTINCTION, KINDS OF).

Logical Modes. These either assert the manner in which a predicate term is affirmed or denied of a subject term, e,g., ''It is impossible that right be wrong,'' or identify particular determinations of syllogistic form. Four logical modes are usually distinguished: impossible, possible, necessary, and contingent. Each of the four can be either divided or composed (*divisa aut composita*). The divided mode is had when the modal word or phrase functions as an adverb qualifying the verb, e.g., ''Man is necessarily rational.'' In the composed mode the modal phrase functions as predicate term, e.g., ''That the court erred is possible.'' The various allowed forms of the figures of the categorical syllogism, such as *Barbara* and *Celarent,* are referred to as modes or moods. The modal syllogism, on the other hand, expresses an ARGUMENTATION wherein the premises and conclusion are modal propositions.

Bibliography: P. FOULQUIÉ and R. SAINT-JEAN, *Dictionnaire de la langue philosophique* (Paris 1962) 445–447. R. EISLER,

Wörterbuch der philosophischen Begriffe, 3 v. (4th ed. Berlin 1927–30) 2:157–160. S. CARAMELLA, *Enciclopedia filosofica* 4 v. (Venice-Rome 1957) 3:651–654. JOHN OF ST. THOMAS, *Cursus philosophicus thomisticus,* ed. B. REISER, 3 v. (new ed. Turin 1930–37) 1:500–504. R. R. MASTERSON, ''Sacramental Graces: Modes of Sanctifying Grace'' *Thomist* 18 (1955) 311–372. I. M. BOCHEŃSKI, *A History of Formal Logic,* ed. and tr. I. THOMAS (Notre Dame, Ind. 1961).

[T. U. MULLANEY]

MODERNISM

This ideology emerged clearly within the Church *c.* 1900 and sought a revolutionary transmutation of Catholic doctrine through the application of naturalistic evolutionary philosophy and arbitrary historical criticism. It was condemned by the decree *LAMENTABILI* and the encyclical *PASCENDI,* and definitively ended by the oath against Modernism.

Background

The roots of Modernism are extremely complex. Four factors may be singled out as the principal occasions for its rise: (1) in philosophy, the prevalence among Catholics of a shallow ECLECTICISM combined with the strong influence exerted by NEO-KANTIANISM Pragmatism, and the disciples of F. D. E. SCHLEIERMACHER; (2) in theology, a growing dissatisfaction with a too static NEOSCHOLASTICISM; (3) in the sciences, the development of evolutionary biological theory and the growth of historical method; and (4) at least of equal importance, the not yet assimilated changing relationship between the Church and the sociopolitical order.

Philosophy and Theology. During most of the 19th century an eclecticism under the patronage of thinkers such as DESCARTES, LEIBNIZ, and ROSMINI-SERBATI prevailed in Catholic circles. It was neither profound nor systematic. After the encyclical of *AETERNI PATRIS* (1879) neoscholasticism began to exercise greater influence from its centers in Rome, Louvain, and Germany. Many Catholic writers *c.* 1900, however, never experienced this influence. Furthermore, the categories of neoscholasticism began to appear inadequate to contain the rich reality suggested by the new work in Sacred Scripture and history, and by a philosophy with an accent on the aspect of IMMANENCE.

ECCLESIOLOGY had been scarcely influenced by the great mystical and organic insights of J. A. MÖHLER and the Tübingen Catholic school. The functions of authority and hierarchical power tended to hold the central perspective in the theological manuals. The work of NEWMAN on the development of dogma (1845) had opened new vistas, but its influence on scholastic theology was negligible.

Contemporary thought had begun to challenge scholastic positions, both in Catholicism and in Protestantism. About 1800 Schleiermacher developed his theory of experience (the feeling of dependence) as the heart of religion. His later disciples eliminated, perhaps more than Schleiermacher intended, the element of intelligence. Religion was portrayed as a sentiment, an experience beyond the critique of intellectual concepts. In the Catholic tradition, Möhler, who had steeped himself in the Bible and the Fathers, stressed that the living organism of the Church cannot be fully understood unless it is vitally lived. Newman worked out his own theory of experience as contrasted with notional knowledge, a fact that augured the trend toward a greater emphasis on spiritual anthropology. By 1893 BLONDEL in his *L'Action* presented a fully rounded metaphysic of action in which man's totality, and not exclusively his intellect, played a vital role in the approach to God and in the understanding of tradition. Möhler, Newman, and Blondel to an extent resembled the Modernists in the questions that interested them, but not in their solutions.

In the closing decades of the 19th century the emphasis on growth and development in religion received influential support from Neo-Hegelians, such as John and Edward Caird in Britain, and from neoidealists, such as Rudolf Eucken in Germany with his philosophy of activism. In England the pragmatists, under the influence of William JAMES, struggled against Neo-Hegelianism. Yet the two streams of pragmatism and Neo-Hegelianism tended to blend into a composite theory of a radical evolution of dogma and of a pragmatic norm for finding religious truth, i.e., its fruitful life-value and permanence. Lastly, Neo-Kantianism was still influential in its separation of thought from reality, and it joined evolutionary and pragmatic theory in questioning the stability and reality of dogma (*see* HEGELIANISM AND NEO-HEGELIANISM; IDEALISM).

Natural Science and History. The general idea of development was caught up and quickened by the publication of DARWIN's *The Origin of Species* (1859). The same notion began to emerge with regard to the Bible through the work in biblical archeology in the Middle East around 1850. The scientific development of historical method during the 18th and 19th centuries, especially in Germany, began to leave its mark on the Church toward 1900, particularly through J. J. I. von DÖLLINGER and Lord ACTON. Induction and empirical work lined up against the more deductive approach of the scholastics. Subsequent to Döllinger, the split grew between historian and theologian.

Around 1870 the great movement of biblical exegesis was set in motion by German liberal scholars. New and often valid insights concerning the formation of the Pentateuch were glimpsed in the light of J. WELLHAUSEN. The influence of the New Testament work of HOLTZMANN, the culminating point of liberal exegesis, began to be felt in Catholic circles. The establishment of Catholic institutes in France (1875) and the contributions of Catholic Scripture scholars in Germany and Belgium around the same period marked the beginning of renewed exegetical work in the Church. DUCHESNE began his important historical studies in 1877; and the first work of his pupil, LOISY, was on the history of the Old Testament canon (1890). In general, Catholic exegetes lagged behind liberal Protestant scholarship, although many of them were unaware of it. Apathy had been created by a lack of historical sense and by an excessive reliance on deductive method. There had also developed a general fear of the new critical methods that had been used so destructively, as in J. E. RENAN's *Vie de Jésus* (1863). Further, with some exception in Germany and Belgium, where Catholic faculties received state support, the Church-State struggles had greatly harmed the opportunities for Catholic scholarship. The desire to catch up brought with it the risk of hasty conclusion and the danger of intellectual indigestion.

Culture and Politics. The final stage of the Church's relationship to political society was discerned by relatively few of the participants in the bitter struggle between Church and State in the 18th and 19th centuries. The immediate outcome around the time of Vatican Council I (1870) was the hardening of positions into two camps, with antireligious and anticlerical groups opposing Catholics who were religiously and politically conservative and who supported an extremely simplified view of ULTRAMONTANISM. Liberal Catholic thought had in general been ineffectual. The Church-State struggles had contributed to the destruction of the intellectual structures of the Church, especially in France. The intellectual life of the seminaries had been hampered, although piety prospered. As a reaction to these struggles, greater centralization of Church authority in Rome gradually increased. Against this background, the decrees of Vatican Council I on papal infallibility were given a rigid and overriding interpretation by conservative Catholic spokesmen, in the tradition of Louis VEUILLOT in France and W. G. WARD in England.

In France political and religious conservatism supported monarchism and projected the image of a Church attached to the old order. The Dreyfus affair revealed anti-Semitic and other unjust attitudes among some Catholic conservatives. Many of their leaders rallied around Charles MAURRAS and ACTION FRANÇAISE. At the same time the Sillon under the direction of Marc SANGNIER emerged as the liberal, democratic counterpart of Action Française. Thus the most outspoken in the Church in France were radically split in their political and religious thinking.

In Germany, somewhat less touched by political reactionism than France, REFORMKATHOLIZISMUS, especially as represented by F. X. KRAUS and H. SCHELL, began during the 1890s to urge reforms in the Latin type of Catholicism and ''Romanism.'' Curial centralization and excessive use of papal power were criticized. It was urged that a ''religious Catholicism'' be substituted for an external and political one. Discussions centered to a large extent on Church discipline and scholarly freedom. In 1902 *Hochland,* a periodical whose liberal aim was to bring the Church out of its cultural ghetto, began publication.

In Italy, because of the loss of papal temporal power and the unification of the peninsula, many young priests envisioned a totally new relationship between Church and State. There was a growing indifference toward the clear-cut philosophies that formed the backdrop of the old conflicts. Some Catholics began to favor an idealistic philosophy that regarded the Church as merely a powerful cultural force, a totally variable expression of a deeper religious aspiration. At the same time CATHOLIC ACTION groups began forming to inject Catholic social influence into the mainstream of national life. Simultaneously, however, Catholics were forbidden to take part in the political life of a government traditionally opposed to the spirit and demands of the Church. In social thought and action there arose a tension among many young Catholics concerning subordination to bishops and Church discipline in general.

In England, both numerically and intellectually, the Church was only beginning to become a social influence. Not until 1895 were Catholics permitted to attend the great universities.

In the midst of this complex ebb and flow of philosophies and cultural pressures, Modernism appeared as an abortive and self-destructive attempt at adaptation and rejuvenation. Thinkers, for the most part ill-prepared philosophically, desperately grasped for and tried to force on the Church theories not sufficiently analyzed and purified. The outcome was a necessary reaction of the magisterium to these indigestible syncretisms.

Modernist Movement

Modernism began as a spontaneous rather than as an organized phenomenon. Its four centers of influence were France, England, Italy, and Germany.

France. In 1897 Louis A. SABATIER, a French Protestant, presented with force and clarity many of the ideas of Schleiermacher and Albrecht RITSCHL in *L'Esquisse d'une philosophie de la religion d'après la psychologie et l'histoire,* a work that was to have great influence on Modernist thinking. In 1899 M. HÉBERT published his *Souvenirs d'Assise* in which he began his denial of personality in God and became the herald-philosopher of Modernism within the Church.

Loisy had been working on the frontiers of the new criticism, especially in the Old Testament, from 1890 to about 1900, and aroused suspicions. (During this period the liberal but solid positions of M. J. LAGRANGE were, to a lesser extent, subject to similar suspicions in conservative quarters.) In 1893 Loisy lost his position at the Institut Catholique in Paris and gradually moved toward work on the New Testament. In 1900 he published an article strongly criticizing the notion of inspiration as presented in the encyclical *PROVIDENTISSIMUS DEUS* (1893). Then he published two books, *L'Évangile et L'Église* (1902) and *Autour d'un petit livre* (1903), which then started a violent public controversy.

Through a selection of eschatological texts in the Synoptic Gospels, Loisy presented the essence of Christ's preaching as a literal teaching of an imminent coming of a physical, visible end-of-the-world kingdom. This theory resembled closely that of the liberal Protestant exegete, Johannes Weiss, which appeared in 1892. Loisy concluded: ''Jesus announced the Kingdom and it is the Church which came.'' Terming his work a defense against A. von HARNACK's rejection of doctrinal development, Loisy attempted to justify the appearance of a Church, which was never in the mind of Christ, and an evolution of its dogma, which would be genuine development. Blondel attacked this outlook, while advancing his own theory of vital tradition in action as an avenue of approach to the understanding of the Gospels. F. von HÜGEL defended Loisy's right as a Catholic to present such a theory. Loisy's writings caused great anguish among the intellectuals and young clergy in France and Italy. The two works were among the five of Loisy's books placed on the Index in 1903. In 1904, after some ambiguous retractations, Loisy made his submission, an act that rankled him afterward.

E. LE ROY, a Catholic layman and disciple of BERGSON, rejected in an extreme way the intellectual content of dogma in the article, ''Qu'est-ce qu'un dogme?'' (1905). He asserted that since dogma was formulated in relative terms, it could not aim at an absolute intellectual assent. Rather, it negatively safeguarded against error and it positively prescribed a rule of practical conduct, a personal stance of action in the face of supernatural reality. Thus the dogma of God as Father is to be assimilated not intellectually, but through filial action toward Him as Father. In 1902 and 1906 Abbé HOUTIN published studies that were extremely critical of recent Catholic exegetical work and favored the most extreme positions.

Abbé TURMEL, a historian of dogma who had lost the faith as early as 1886 but wanted to remain in the Church, began *c.* 1900 to publish numerous pseudonymous articles attacking Catholic dogma. Meanwhile the French Protestant, Paul SABATIER, took a leading part in propaganda for the movement.

Abbé LABERTHONNIÈRE, many of whose writings were later condemned, and Blondel, with his philosophy of action, were leaders in the contemporary movement of liberal Catholic philosophical thought; but from the beginning they reacted against Modernist aims and cannot be considered part of that movement. Similarly Archbishop MIGNOT, who was in contact with Loisy and favored a more liberal attitude toward scholarly work within the Church, was gradually dismayed by the more extreme exegetical positions and by the tendency toward philosophical IMMANENTISM.

England. George TYRRELL, who had privately distributed certain works, was dismissed from the Society of Jesus (1906) for refusing to retract the ideas in his anonymous ''Letter to a Professor of Anthropology,'' which was published in Italy without his permission. In this work he greatly minimized the function of Church dogma. Privately outlining a blueprint of the Church of the future, he became more and more caught up in controversy. He attacked papal infallibility, ultramontane and otherwise, and the ecumenicity of Vatican Council I. Until his death (1909), he kept developing a theory of the relation of revelation to dogma. Revelation, as the self-manifestation of the divine in our inward life, was presented as an experience, first of the Apostolic Church, which was normative, and then of every Christian. Revelation, when communicated biblically, he called dogma or prophetic truth, an imaginative and prophetic presentment of divine reality. Prophetic truth was the living shadow of this reality. Later formulations he termed ''theology'' or ''secondary dogmas.'' These metaphysically conceptualized the original prophetic communication. They were merely protective or illustrative formulas for prophetic truth, could be later contradicted or discarded, and in general were useful but totally relative formulas. Revealed truth (*res*) was still contained in the formula (*enuntiabile*), but since the prophetic imagery was now transferred to scientific language, no absolute value guaranteed to be true could be assigned to the formula. Conciliar pronouncements were to be accepted only through the subsequent acceptance of the entire Church. Having drastically reduced the intellectual element in the original experience, Tyrrell worked out the rest of his system rather consistently, but through a confusing rhetoric. He never sufficiently accounted for the fact that conciliar formulas themselves have their axes in the Absolute. At the end of his life he espoused the theory of an error by Christ as to the time of the Parousia. Tyrrell never held the doctrine of exclusive immanence as condemned by *Pascendi.* Many of his positions, however, were an evident object of the encyclical's attack.

Von Hügel, Tyrrell's friend, while rejecting the new immanentist philosophical approach, was the leader of a crusade for the untrammeled rights of the exegete. These rights, he insisted, were being infringed upon by Roman authority. Conferring with various high-ranking ecclesiastics in and out of Rome and maintaining a vast correspondence with the leaders of the new thought, he endeavored to give some coherence and organization to the movement. Maude PETRE supported the ideas of Tyrrell and published his life in 1912.

Italy. In Italy the movement had more of a social flavor. Discussion of political and social theory, however, continually drifted back and forth across the terrain of religion and theology. The Italian priest, R. MURRI, supported CHRISTIAN DEMOCRACY and founded the Lega democratica nazionale. This movement, intended to be independent of the hierarchy, urged reform of the Church's institutional and social structure. Although he was anticlerical in tone, Murri worked out his ideas from a scholastic basis. Later he moved toward an idealism somewhat reminiscent of B. CROCE and G. GENTILE, though he was attacked by them for the equivocation in his position.

In the exegetical and theological fields Salvatore Minocchi, a priest, founded the review *Studi religiosi* in 1901 as a forum for the new thought. He was strongly influenced by Loisy in the exegetical area, and later by Tyrrell in the interpretation of dogma. Another priest, Ernesto BUONAIUTI, early enamored of Blondel's philosophy of action, became fascinated with immanentism and moved toward a form of social messianism. He emerged as the leading Italian Modernist but was eager to remain within the Church for the working out of his ideas.

More on the edge of Modernism and ultimately loyal to the Church were the layman Fogazzaro, whose novel *Il Santo* (1905) became the literary symbol of the movement, and the Barnabite priest, Giovanni Semeria, who worked in religious and biblical criticism. In 1907 the journal *Rinnovamento* became an important organ for liberal political and religious opinion.

Germany. In Germany the review *Zwanzigste Jahrhundert,* which was founded in 1901 at Munich by F. Klasen and continued by Thaddäus Engert, became an organ for Reformkatholizismus. Like the Krausgesellschaft founded in Munich in 1904, Reformkatholizismus carried out a program of anti-Roman and antischolastic sentiment. It attacked political ultramontanism and insisted on freedom in scientific religious work and on the abolition of the Index. It did not totally overlap Modernism but remained principally on the level of practical Church discipline. The Bavarian priest, K. Gebert, however, in 1905 proposed a Kantian and immanentist approach not unlike that reproved by *Pascendi.* Engert, also a priest, demanded the abandonment of the notion of biblical inerrancy and the complete revision of the concept of inspiration. Yet it was not until after the condemnations of *Pascendi* that Engert and Josef Schnitzer of the University of Munich, who was a supporter of Loisy, emerged as the leaders of a small Modernist extreme. In Germany, Modernism was more localized than in France and Italy and brought forth less extreme theological positions than in any of the other major countries involved.

Action by Church Authorities. Leo XIII, whose liberal policy was accompanied by serious reserves over the new thought but who hesitated to take strong action, was succeeded (Aug. 4, 1903) by PIUS X, who decided that firm action was mandatory. He approved the decree of the Holy Office placing five works of Loisy on the Index (Dec. 17, 1903). His encyclical *Il fermo proposito* (June 11, 1905) encouraged Catholic Action but insisted that it must be subordinate to ecclesiastical officials. The encyclical *Pieni l'animo* (July 28, 1906) warned of insubordination among the Italian clergy and declared priests who became members of the Lega democratica nazionale suspended. The same year Fogazzaro's *Il Santo* and two works of Laberthonnière were placed on the Index, and Tyrrell was dismissed from the Jesuits. Murri was suspended April 15, 1907. On July 3, 1907, the Holy Office's decree *LAMENTABILI* condemned 65 propositions in the area of criticism and dogma. On July 26, Le Roy's *Dogme et critique* was put on the Index. (During August, Fogazzaro, Murri, Buonaiuti, von Hügel, and others met in northern Italy to limit the terms of their submission.)

The encyclical *PASCENDI* (Sept. 8, 1907) presented a global blueprint of the whole Modernist program. It condemned theory on dogma and biblical criticism, which had an agnostic, immanentist-evolutionary, and anti-intellectualist basis. Constructed from ideas found in the work of various Modernists, it reproved a system, to every detail of which not all the Modernists subscribed. Yet, as Gentile and Petre, the subsequent champion of Modernism, admitted, *Pascendi* seized the movement in its totality. At the same time, immanentism, Neo-Hegelianism, and agnosticism were the terminal point rather than the point of departure for many Modernist thinkers. *Pascendi* in its picture of Modernism not only described the situation of some Modernists but also was an accurate prophecy of the final position of others.

Pius X decreed in the motu proprio *Praestantia scripturae* (Nov. 18, 1907) that all were bound in conscience to submit to the decrees of the PONTIFICAL BIBLICAL COMMISSION, both past and future, in the same way as to the doctrinal decrees issued by the Sacred Congregations and approved by the pope. (Since 1905 the Biblical Commission had issued a series of generally conservative prudential norms with regard to scriptural interpretation.)

Some loosely organized opposition had developed among the group associated with *Rinnovamento,* but writers and supporters of the review were made subject to excommunication at the end of 1907. Tyrrell (October 1907) and Schnitzer (February 1908) were excommunicated for their opposition to the encyclical. Minocchi was suspended and Loisy excommunicated in 1908. Subsequently Loisy developed his doctrine of the religion of humanity built on a vague agnostic basis. With Tyrrell's death (1909) the heart went out of the movement, though small pockets of resistance remained. The oath against Modernism (Sept. 1, 1910) to be taken by professors and pastors of souls marked the end of the crisis (*see* MODERNISM, OATH AGAINST). Petre, deprived of the Sacraments in her own diocese though never singled out for formal excommunication by name, and Buonaiuti, finally excommunicated by name in 1926, continued as champions of Modernism. Le Roy, Semeria, and von Hügel, previously more or less on the margin of Modernism, remained faithful to the Church. Engert became a Protestant. Houtin rejected the whole Modernist plan and became agnostic. Murri, with reservations on his political and social positions, was received back only in 1943.

Aftermath. After *Pascendi,* there followed a period of unmasking Modernism that caused great anguish. Many thought incorrectly that Newman and Blondel had been condemned. The committees of vigilance set up by the encyclical were used as a specious support by simplist conservative groups to justify sweeping condemnations. Thinking and nuance were rejected in favor of polemics. Modernism became a slogan to be applied to whatever was disliked in liberal Catholic thought, theology, literature, and politics. At the center of this campaign was the association, SODALITIUM PIANUM, directed by Monsignor BENIGNI in Italy. A secret code, the counterpart of Modernist anonymity, protected collaborators in various countries. The attacks of Action Française (whose condemnation in 1914, four years after the condemnation of Sillon, was made public only in 1926), and the intransigence of writers, such as Emmanuel Barbier and J. Fontaine, brought into popularity a counterlabel, INTEGRALISM. At the beatification of Pius X in 1950, evidence was presented that showed that he did not give his support to a great deal of this campaign, but held his hand for fear of encouraging the Modernists. Benedict XV, in his inaugural encyclical *Ad beatissimi Apostolorum* (Nov. 1, 1914) warned against excessive accusations. This, together with the eruption of World War I, ended this phase in the aftermath of the Modernist crisis.

Definition

Some have defined Modernism as an attempt to retain the form while dropping the content of dogma. Some Modernists, however, desired to drop also the form. If Modernism is defined very broadly, then only its extreme form was condemned. Any definition of Modernism must be drawn mainly from *Pascendi,* the most solemn Church condemnation. The loose application of the term ''Modernism'' to the development of theological thinking is widely admitted to be an abuse. Further, faint similarities of a position to statements in *Pascendi* can be judged fully Modernistic only if they are related also to the essential points of condemnation in the encyclical. *Pascendi* stated that it was directly attacking agnostic, immanentist, and evolutionary-naturalistic doctrine.

The following definition is suggested. Modernism was an ideological orientation, tendency, or movement within the Catholic Church, clearly emerging during the waning years of the 19th century and rapidly dying out around 1910 after official condemnation. Only loosely and sporadically organized, it was characterized by a tone antagonistic to all ecclesiastical authority, and by a belief in an adaptation of the Church to what was considered sound in modern thought even at the expense of radically changing the Church's essence. At its roots, grounded beyond liberal Catholic positions on biblical criticism and theology, lay a triple thesis: (1) a denial of the supernatural as an object of certain knowledge (in the totally symbolic nonobjective approach to the content of dogma, which is also related to a type of agnosticism in natural theology); (2) an exclusive immanence of the Divine and of revelation (''vital immanence'') reducing the Church to a simple social civilizing phenomenon; (3) a total emancipation of scientific research from Church dogma, which would allow the continued assertion of faith in dogma with its contradiction on the historical level, as understood in certain presentations of the ''Christ of faith, Christ of history,'' ''Church of faith, Church of history'' distinctions (*see* DOCTRINE, DEVELOPMENT OF.)

Conclusion

The difficulty in assessing the influence of Modernist thinkers on the later Church arises from the fact that these men also fed on and assimilated many legitimate tendencies that were arising in the contemporary Church, such as the idea of faith as a personal encounter, the increased appreciation of religious experience and spiritual anthropology, the deeper probing of the relation between psychology and religion, the return to the traditional emphasis on the sense of mystery, the renewed realization of the pastoral function of theology, the less mechanical assessment of the role of authority, the growth in insight into the development of dogma, the underlining of the organic nature of the Church and the importance of the laity, a greater respect for scriptural scholarship and natural science, a newer framework of Church-State relations, and a call to leave a cultural ghetto. Many of these insights, however, were already found in the works of scholars, such as Möhler, Newman, Blondel, and other orthodox thinkers, who, previous to the rise of Modernism, had begun to investigate these questions. With the return to the spirit of genuine THOMISM the stage would have been set, it seems, for their fruitful development. It is difficult to see how certain values said to arise from Modernism were not actually hampered in their development within the Church by Modernism's very appearance and by the strong medicine deemed necessary to eradicate it.

Nevertheless, through its excess Modernism did point out certain areas that called for investigation within a sound theological framework, as in the insights mentioned above. Certain authors, such as De GRANDMAISON, Lagrange, and LEBRETON, continued their scholarly contributions. The exaggerated spread of suspicions, however, that followed the condemnation of Modernism probably caused many scholars to avoid delicate subjects. Only after World War II did a trend emerge toward a renewed consideration of subjects that had been so destructively and abortively handled by the Modernists.

The Modernist crisis retarded Catholic scholarship and strengthened Catholic discipline, but its capital effect was decisive victory over a subtle and mortal enemy, a victory that preserved the essential life of the Church.

Bibliography: V. A. YZERMANS, *All Things in Christ* (Westminster, Md. 1954), has documents of Pius X in Eng. J. RIVIÈRE, *Le Modernisme dans l'Église* (Paris 1929); *Dictionnaire de théologie catholique,* ed. A. VACANT et al., 15 v. (Paris 1903–50; Tables générales 1951–) 10.2:2009–47. A. D'ALÈS et al., *Dictionnaire apologétique de la foi catholique,* ed. A. D'ALÈS, 4 v. (Paris 1911–22; Table analytique 1931) 3.591–695. A. R. VIDLER, *The Modernist Movement in the Roman Church* (Cambridge, Eng. 1934). J. BRUGERETTE, *Le Prêtre français et la société contemporiane,* 3 v. (Paris 1933–38) 3:125–345. G. MARTINI, *Cattolicesimo e storicismo* (Naples 1951). L. V. COUTINHO, *Tradition et histoire dans la controversy moderniste* (Rome 1954). R. MARLÉ ed., *Au coeur de la crise moderniste* (Paris 1960). P. SCOPPOLA, *Crisi moderniste e rinnovamento cattolico in Italia* (Bologna 1961). É. POULAT, *Histoire, dogme et critique dans la crise moderniste* (Paris 1962). M. DE LA BEDOYÈRE, *The Life of Baron von Hügel* (New York 1952). A. DANSETTE, *Religious History of Modern France,* tr. J. DINGLE, 2 v. (New York 1961), v. 2. A. DRU, *The Contribution of German Catholicism* (New York 1963). R. ROUQUETTE, ''Bilan du Modernisme,'' *Études* 289 (1956) 321–343. H. DANIEL-ROPS, *L'Église des révolutions: Un Combat pour Dieu* (Histoire de l'Église du Christ 6.2; Paris 1963).

[J. J. HEANEY]

MODERNISM, OATH AGAINST

The popular name for the oath contained in the *motu proprio Sacrorum antistitum* of PIUS X (Sept. 1, 1910), which was required of clerics before the subdiaconate, confessors, preachers, pastors, canons, benefice-holders, seminary professors, officials in Roman congregations and episcopal curias, and religious superiors. The oath contains two parts. Part I contains five main propositions: (1) God can be known and proved to exist by natural reason; (2) the external signs of revelation, especially miracles and prophecies, are signs giving certainty and are adapted to all men and times, including the present; (3) the Church was founded by Christ on earth; (4) there is a DEPOSIT OF FAITH and the assertion that dogmas change from one sense to another one different from that held by the Church is heretical; (5) faith is not a blind sense welling up from the depths of the subconscious under the impulse of the heart and of a will trained to morality, but a real assent of the intellect to truth by hearing from an external source. Part II promises submission and assent to *PASCENDI* and rejection of opposition between history and dogma. The oath, a formal personal ratification of previous authoritative decisions of Pius X, was aimed at certain clandestine groups forming after *Pascendi.* The assent to which the oath binds is commensurate with the assent demanded by the sources of Catholic teaching from which the oath is drawn.

The strongest reaction to the oath occurred in Germany. Chiefly because of their position on faculties at state universities where the oath would endanger their position, theology professors who exercised no pastoral ministry were dispensed from taking the oath. In Italy the Barnabite priest Giovanni Semeria was allowed by Pius X to take the oath with certain reservations. In England Maude PETRE, who was preparing her work on George TYRRELL, was asked to take the oath. When she refused, she was deprived of the Sacraments. Only 40 or so priests in the world refused to take the oath. The oath itself marked the last breath of Modernism.

The oath was rescinded by the Congregation for the Doctrine of the Faith in 1967 in favor of a concise affirmation of the faith.

Bibliography: PIUS X, ''Sacrorum antistitum'' (*Motu proprio,* Sept. 1, 1910). *Acta Apostolicae Sedis* 2 (1910) 655–680, Eng.

American Catholic Quarterly Review 35 (Philadelphia 1910) 712–731. Declarations on "Sacrorum antistitum," *Acta Apostolicae Sedis* 2 (Rome 1910) 740–741, 856–857. R. MERRY DEL VAL, letter to the bishop of Breslau concerning the oath against Modernism, *ibid.* 3 (1911) 87–88. J. RIVIÈRE, *Le Modernisme dans l'Église* (Paris 1929).

[J. J. HEANEY]

MODESTY

Understood here as the English equivalent of the Latin *pudicitia* with the restricted meaning the term often had in scholastic use, namely, decency or a sense of decency. It is the moral virtue that moderates and controls the impulse of sexual display in man.

The Natural Virtue of Modesty. The natural virtue of CHASTITY moderates and regulates the sexual appetite, a particular expression of which is man's impulse to display himself sexually or to be responsive to sexual display in others. Such display may be concerned with sexuality in the wide, or general, sense or with sexuality in the strict, genital sense ("venereal" sexuality in scholastic terminology). To the first or general category of sexual display belong general sexual signs, i.e., words, looks, modes of action, modes of dress, and the like that proclaim a man as a man or a woman as a woman in ordinary personal and social life. Such signs are part of normal life itself (e.g., sexual differentiation in modes of dress). To the sphere of genital, or venereal, display belong genital signs (*signa venereorum*), i.e., those that tend directly to excite and stimulate the genital drive in man.

Chastity in the strict or genital sense moderates and regulates the use of these latter forms of sexual display, authorizing them where it authorizes genital fulfillment itself (i.e., in marriage) and excluding them elsewhere. This particular function of chastity, considered separately, constitutes the moral field of genital decency, or modesty. Chastity in the wide or general sense regulates the use of general sexual signs. Certain forms of speech, dress, action, and the like are apprehended as appropriate for the normal display or expression of masculinity or femininity, as the case may be, and these pertain to the field of general sexual decency or modesty.

General sexual modesty is very largely a matter of social convention. It is bound up with the role that men as men and women as women are expected to play in society. When the role changes, as it has done enormously for women in modern society, the forms of general sexual modesty change too. A girl regarded in the U.S. as decent in the mid-20th century would have been a shocking type a century earlier—quite immodest in speech, dress, and general behavior.

Specific sexual modesty—modesty in the sphere of genital signs—is also a social variable to the extent that some things that operate as genital stimuli in one culture do not have this significance in another. Thus display of the uncovered female breasts operates as a genital stimulus in Western civilization but is only a generic, nonvenereal sexual sign in African tribal cultures. Such cultures have their own taboo areas of genital signs. Use of them is confined by tribal custom to circumstances where their focal point, namely, genital intercourse, is socially approved. Genital modesty and immodesty, decency and shamelessness, are universal moral categories of humanity, however widely the concrete forms of modesty may differ from one culture to another.

Modesty in Scripture and the Fathers. The Yahwist writer stresses the sexual innocence of Eden. Sexual self-consciousness, shame, and the covering-up of the body follow the Fall (Gn 2.25; 3.7, 10–11). The wisdom literature warns against the snares of feminine shamelessness (Prv 2.16; 5.3; 7.5–27). In the NT modesty in looks, words, and general behavior is inculcated (Mt 5.28; Eph 5.3–20; 2 Pt 2.14). General sexual modesty—"a gentle and quiet spirit"—should characterize the Christian woman (1 Tm 2.9–12; 1 Pt 3.1–6). Feminine modesty, both general and specific, and the avoidance by both sexes of defiling contact with the lascivious world around them are constant themes of patristic exhortation (e.g., Chrysostom, *Homiliae in Matthaeum;* Tertullian, *De spectaculis,* and *De cultu feminarum;* Cyprian *De habitu virginum*).

Theology of Modesty in St. Thomas and Later. St. Thomas treated modesty (*pudicitia*) as a part of chastity, not a distinct virtue from it. It is concerned with *signa venereorum.* St. Thomas took these in a very limited sense (*Summa theologiae* 2a2ae, 151.4). They are immodest acts done with a lustful intention. He did not treat of acts tending by their nature to stimulate genital desire, though this may not be the personal intention of the person who does them.

Later moral theology, especially after 1600, put immodest acts in St. Thomas's sense into the category of directly unchaste acts (*see* LUST) and took *signa venereorum* in a new and broad sense. These were acts of an intrinsically innocent kind (e.g., exposure of the body) that would, however, tend of their nature to provoke sins against chastity unless the doing of them was justified by an objective reason in particular circumstances (e.g., exposure of the body for purposes of medical examination). All kinds of things could be and were considered in this context—words, looks, touches, embraces, kisses, fantasies; the nude in art; dress, reading, bathing, dancing; theatrical shows and, in recent times, film and television shows. The treatment of all this heterogeneous material was usually anything but scientific. The writer dogmatized on everything in terms of the culture he was accustomed to, taking little account of the fact that his judgments on modesty and immodesty in dress, for example, would not be valid for other cultures. Moreover, the whole subject was pursued in extreme detail. Areas of the body were divided into decent (*honestae*), less decent (*minus honestae*), and indecent (*inhonestae*) and a quasi-mathematical scale was worked out for measuring the seriousness of sins of look or touch in each of the three areas. Dancing involving physical contact between the sexes was viewed as immodest. The confusion was often increased in pastoral practice when—general sexual modesty being mixed up with specific or genital modesty—women were reproved for immodesty simply because they went along with the times in dressing more lightly and freely than had been the custom in former generations.

Modesty in Modern Catholic Theology. The subject is now treated in a more realistic and genuinely theological way. The difference between general sexual modesty (a social variable) and specific modesty is better understood. The need of a sound theology of specific modesty is as real as ever in this age of sexual exploitation and commercialization [see Pius XII, *Acta Apostolicae Sedis* 49 (1957) 1013]; but the object of this theology is seen as the right training and counseling of Christians in the virtue of modesty rather than as the handing out to them of endless classifications of modest and immodest acts.

Bibliography: K. E. LØGSTRUP, *Die Religion in Geschichte und Gegenwart*, 7 v. (3d ed. Tübingen 1957–65) 5:1383–86. A. AUER, H. FRIES, ed., *Handbuch theologischer Grundbegriffe*, 2 v. (Munich 1962–63) 1:498–506. J. FUCHS, *De castitate et ordine sexuali* (Rome 1959), standard modern textbook with good bibliography. T. MÜNCKER, *Die psychologischen Grundlagen der katholischen Sittenlehre* (4th ed. Düsseldorf 1953) 283–92, and J. DE LA VAISSIÈRE, *La Pudeur instinctive* (Paris 1935), on the psychological basis of modesty in relation to theology. S. O'RIORDAN, "Courtship," *The Meaning of Christian Marriage*, ed. E. MCDONAGH (Dublin 1963) 149–63, on the sociological variability of certain aspects of modesty. J. C. FORD and G. A. KELLY, *Contemporary Moral Theology*, 2 v. (Westminster, Md. 1958–63) 1:166–73, on dancing.

[S. O'RIORDAN]

MOECHIAN CONTROVERSY

The theological and political dispute caused by the adulterous marriage of Emperor Constantine VI (780–797). It was designated from the Greek *moicheia* (Latinized, *moechia*) for adultery. In 795 Constantine VI forced his wife into a convent and, with an Abbot Joseph officiating, entered into an adulterous union with his mother's lady-in-waiting, Theodote. The patriarch of Constantinople TARASIUS refused to bless the wedding, but tolerated the situation; he did not bar the emperor from the sacraments, nor take punitive measures against the abbot Joseph. This shocking neglect of his patriarchal responsibility scandalized the Studite monks, who not only condemned the emperor and his consort, as well as Abbot Joseph, but also broke off communion with Tarasius. Their leaders, the abbot THEODORE the Studite, and the monk Plato, were exiled and imprisoned, and the rest of the community were punished in a similar way. Two years later, Empress IRENE seized the throne and recalled the Studites from exile. The patriarch Tarasius then degraded Joseph and made peace with the Studites.

The issue was revived during the next reign. Emperor Nicephorus I (802–811) asked Patriarch NICEPHORUS I (806–815) to reinstate Joseph for signal services to the state. Again Theodore and his monks broke off communion with Joseph, and though still retaining the names of the emperor and patriarch in the diptychs during the Liturgy or Mass, studiously avoided contact with the patriarch. Theodore did not object to restoring Joseph to his ecclesiastical post as oeconomus or business manager, but did deny his right to celebrate the Liturgy. The emperor decided to force the issue and insist that the Studites communicate with Joseph. On their refusal, they were condemned by a synod in 809, after which the emperor decided to make clear that he repudiated Constantine VI's adulterous union, and dissolved it posthumously. The dedicated Studites were exiled together with many other abbots and monks. Theodore appealed to Rome. Under Emperor Michael I Rangabe (811–813) religious peace was reestablished. Through the good offices of Pope LEO III, the reforming monks were reconciled to the patriarch and returned to their monasteries, and the abbot Joseph was condemned once more.

Bibliography: H. G. BECK, *Kirche und theologische Literatur im byzantinisch en Reich* 491–494, 515. P. J. ALEXANDER, *The Patriarch Nicephorus of Constantinople* (Oxford 1958).

[M. J. HIGGINS]

MOGAS FONTCUBERTA, MARÍA ANA, BL.

Co-foundress of the Capuchin Congregation of Franciscan Missionaries of the Mother of the Divine Shepherd; b. Corró de Vall-Granollers (near Barcelona), Catalonia, Spain, Jan. 13, 1827; d. Fuencarral (north of Madrid), Spain, July 3, 1886.

María Ana was raised in Barcelona by her widowed aunt or godmother, María Mogas, following the deaths of her father Lorenzo Mogas (d. 1834) and mother Magdalena Fontcuberta (d. 1841). María Ana was provided with all the benefits of high social standing, as well as faith. She searched for her vocation under the spiritual direction of the exclaustrated Capuchin Father José Tous Soler. He introduced her to two former Capuchin nuns, María Valdés and Isabel Yubal. All had been given permission to minister outside the convent.

Together they founded at Ripoll (near Gerona) the third order regular sisters of the Mother of the Divine Shepherd (June 13, 1850) for the education of children. With the permission of the Bishop of Vic the sisters were veiled. He gave them charge over a school at Ripoll, and María was elected superior (September 1950). Mother María Ana professed her vows, June 25, 1851. When the two former Capuchin nuns returned to their cloister, María fulfilled the legal requirements to administer a school, then recruited new members. The congregation grew rapidly thereafter, and a second group was established in Barcelona.

At the request of Bishop Benito Serra, María Ana began to work with the noblewoman María Antonia Oviedo to establish (December 1865) a ministry for the regeneration of prostitutes in Ciempozuelos (Madrid). She later abandoned the project and accepted instead the direction of another school.

Following her death her body was buried in Santa Ana cemetery. After miracles occurred at her grave, it was exhumed (1893) and translated to the college chapel. Her relics were lost during the Spanish civil war (1936), but recovered in 1967 and placed in the motherhouse at Madrid. A miracle attributed to her intercession was approved in 1996. Thereafter, Pope John Paul II beatified Mother María Ana, Oct. 6, 1996.

Feast: Oct. 6.

Bibliography: I. PAZ GONZÁLEZ, *Las Terciarias Franciscanas de la Madre del Divino Pastor: (contribución al estudio de la vida religiosa en España durante el último cuarto del siglo XIX)* (Madrid 1978). *Acta Apostolicae Sedis,* (1996) 999.

[K. I. RABENSTEIN]

MOGHILA, PETER

Russian ecclesiastic and theologian, metropolitan of Kiev from 1633 to 1646; b. Moldavia, Dec. 21, 1596; d. Kiev, Dec. 22, 1646. The Moghila family (in Rumanian, Movila) originated in Moldavia. Moghila was ten years old when his father died, and his mother took him to Poland, where he was educated in a strictly Orthodox spirit. It is also possible that he studied abroad, perhaps in Paris. In 1622 an expedition organized to recover his possessions in Moldavia failed, and Moghila changed the orientation of his life and studied for the priesthood. In August of 1627 he became a monk in the most famous monastery of the Slavic world, the Pecherskaya Laura (Monastery of the Caves) in Kiev. Three months later Polish King Sigismond III had him appointed grand archimandrite of the monastery. He was at times too authoritarian, but under his energetic guidance the Laura became a center of spiritual and intellectual vitality in the Eastern Orthodox world at a time when opposition among the Orthodox, Catholics, and Protestants was particularly bitter.

The printing press of the Laura turned out many new liturgical and ascetical books. At the same time Moghila opened a school of theology that became a nursery of theologians and learned bishops. In 1632 he took part in the election of the new king of Poland, Ladislas IV. He secured the king's favor for the Orthodox and in 1633 was appointed metropolitan of Kiev. His election was confirmed by Cyril LUCARIS, patriarch of Constantinople. Under Moghila's administration new confraternities were erected, and many new schools, hospitals, monasteries, and printing shops were founded. Moghila adopted the best methods of his adversaries in order to contend with them more successfully. In Kiev, theology was taught in Latin, according to the scholastic tradition. Two letters of Pope URBAN VIII indicate that in the years 1636 and 1643 hopes for a reunion of Peter Moghila with the See of Rome were nurtured, but they did not lead to concrete results. He died seemingly prematurely, but in the life of the Slav Orthodox Churches he had opened a new era.

The pro-Calvinist attitude of the patriarch of Constantinople, Cyril Lucaris, and the preaching of the Catholics of both Latin and Byzantine rites had left much confusion in the minds of the Orthodox faithful. Moghila became convinced that there was great need for a clear formulation of Orthodox doctrine, so he composed his principal work, *The Orthodox Confession of Faith*. He submitted it to the members of the church of Kiev in an encyclical letter (June 24, 1640) and had it studied by a synod of theologians. Some points did not obtain universal approval, and the synod decided to submit the *Confessio* to the patriarch of Constantinople. The patriarch appointed two of his theologians, one of whom was the noteworthy Meletius Syrigos, to meet in Iasy with three Kievan theologians to study the *Confession.* Some doctrinal points were modified to bring them into conformity with the Greek tradition, and it was finally approved by the four Eastern patriarchs.

The *Confession,* presented in Latin by the Kievan theologians, was translated into modern Greek by Syrigos and printed for the first time in Amsterdam in 1667, after Moghila's death.

For reasons that cannot be established with certitude, but probably because the revised *Confession* did not fully express his beliefs, in 1645 Moghila published a short catechism that is at variance with the *Confession* on certain important points. The most striking of these points concerns the precise moment of consecration in the Mass. Though the *Confession* sees that moment in the Epiclesis, the *Catechism* places it at the singing of the words of institution. On some other points the *Catechism* is more explicit than the *Confession,* for example, about the Assumption of Our Lady.

To answer the Catholic theologian Cassian Sakovich, who had violently criticized the practices of the Orthodox under the pseudonym of a ''Devoted Shepherd,'' Moghila also published an apologetical work, *A Stone Cast . . .* , written in part by his theologians.

Peter Moghila directed his polemics mostly against the Catholics. Nevertheless his theological doctrine is close to Catholic Doctrine, with the exception of his attitude toward the primacy of the pope. In his books he followed the general scheme of the Catholic catechisms, mostly that of Peter CANISIUS. In his liturgical publications he let himself be guided by Catholic practices, thus bringing the Kievan church closer to the Catholic than the Greek. In his *Trebnik,* or ritual, for the Sacrament of Penance, for example, he introduced a formula of absolution that is declaratory as in the Roman rite, while the Greek formula of absolution is deprecatory.

For two centuries the *Confession* was considered by the Orthodox as one of the symbolic books of their Church, having the same authority as the decrees of the first seven ecumenical councils (*see* ORTHODOX SYMBOLIC BOOKS). The Russian theologians of the twentieth century, however, were much less committed to it. They were trying to develop a more independent and more creative Orthodox theology by what one of them, J. Meyendorff, called a ''return to the sources.''

Bibliography: A. MALVY and M. VILLER, eds., *La Confession orthodoxe de Pierre Moghila* (Paris 1927). M. JUGIE and M. GORDILLO, *Dictionnaire de théologie catholique,* 15 v. (Paris 1903–50) 10.2:2070–76; 14.1:345–346. T. IONESCO, *La Vie et l'Oeuvre de Pierre Moghila* (Paris 1944).

[P. MAILLEUX]

MOGROVEJO, TORIBIO ALFONSO DE, ST.

Spanish archbishop of Lima; b. Spain, November 1538; d. Saña, Peru, 1606. He was the son of a wealthy landed family, prominent in Castile since the days of the Reconquista, but his birthplace is a source of scholarly controversy. Some conjecture it was Villaquejida, near León, in the Diocese of Oviedo; others, Mayorga, Valladolid, in the Diocese of León. There is no definite documentary evidence for either.

He was one of five children; one of his sisters, Grimanesa, married Francisco de Quiñones, and another became a nun. When he was 12 to 15 years old, Toribio was sent to Valladolid to study humanities. In 1562 he went to Salamanca, where his uncle Juan was in the College of San Salvador de Oviedo. Toribio studied canon and civil law but left for a two-year stay in Coimbra with his uncle. Upon his return to Salamanca he won a scholarship to San Salvador de Oviedo. He remained there until he was unexpectedly named inquisitor of Granada in July 1574. He carried out the office with dignity and efficiency, although it was one of the most responsible in Spain. He gained a reputation for moderation not only in matters belonging exclusively to the tribunal but also in his dealings with the chancery of Granada.

In 1568 the Council of the Indies, which controlled the provinces in the New World, decided on a number of sweeping reforms. The energetic viceroy of Peru, Francisco de Toledo, was active in enforcing them, but he needed an efficient collaborator in ecclesiastical matters. On August 28, 1578, PHILIP II proposed that the pope name Mogrovejo archbishop of Lima to fill the vacancy left by the death of Jerónimo de LOAYSA. At first he humbly declined, but he finally accepted the appointment. Since up to that time he had received only tonsure, on successive Sundays he received the four minor orders and the subdeaconate. GREGORY XIII named him archbishop of Lima on March 16, 1579. Still in Granada, he received the diaconate and was ordained. He was consecrated in Seville in 1580 and left in September for Peru, accompanied by his sister Grimanesa and her family. After a stop in the Canary Islands they arrived at Nombre de Dios in Panama and from there crossed the Isthmus to embark on the Pacific for Paita. The party made the rest of the journey to Lima by land, the archbishop making a solemn entrance into the capital on May 11, 1581.

Not losing any time, he made his first pastoral visit and called the Third Council of Lima for Aug. 15, 1583. When the bishops under his jurisdiction were gathered together, they decided on a number of new regulations of great importance, some dealing with conversion of the Indians—catechism classes, administering the Sacraments, printing of catechisms, etc.—and others devoted to reform of the clergy. Although there were difficulties from the first moment, especially protests from the clergy about to be reformed, the acts of the council, which revitalized those of the Council of Trent and those of the Council of Lima of 1567, received royal and papal approval. They were put into effect in all the bishoprics of the province of Lima and gained such a reputation that they were subsequently adopted in the archdioceses of Charcas, New Granada, and Brazil, and in fact in all South America and in the missions of the East.

The archbishop engaged in various activities, such as founding a diocesan seminary, and continued his pastoral visits, synods, and councils. In the council of 1591 secularization of the religious doctrinas was discussed. Always conscious of the dignity of his office, Mogrovejo would, if he felt it necessary, oppose the civil authorities, even the king, whose exercise of royal patronage hindered direct communication by the bishop with the Holy See. Baptizing with his own hand, confirming, and taking care of all the matters that came to his attention, Mogrovejo made three general pastoral visitations and many local visits in the diocese. He was taken ill during the course of a visitation and died before he could return to Lima. He was canonized in 1726 by BENEDICT XIII.

Feast: March 23.

Bibliography: V. RODRÍGUEZ VALENCIA, *Santo Toribio de Mogrovejo, organizador y apóstol de Sud-América* (Madrid 1946). N. MOGROVEJO ROJAS, *Santo Toribio de Mogrovejo, defensor del indio americano* (2d ed. Caracas 1985). J. A. DAMMERT BELLIDO, *Arzobispos limenses evangelizadores* (Bogota, Colombia 1987). F. PINI RODOLFI, M. L. GOMEZ, and J. VILLANUEVA DELGADO, *Presencia de Santo Toribio Alfonso de Mogrovejo en el Callejon de Conchucos* (Chavin 1994).

[F. DE ARMAS MEDINA]

MOHLBERG, KUNIBERT

Liturgist; b. Efferen, near Cologne, April 17, 1878; d. Maria Laach, May 21, 1963. In 1897 he entered the Abbey of MARIA LAACH and there, in 1898, was professed as a Benedictine. In 1905, after his philosophical and theological studies at Maria Laach and Beuron, he was sent to Louvain, where he completed his studies in 1911 and received the degree of *Docteur en sciences morales et historiques.* The years at Louvain were decisive for him. Under A. Cauchie (d. 1922) he learned all the subtle historical and technical methods of editing that he developed and improved during his later research. It was also in Louvain that he met the great teachers of his order: C. Butler and G. Morin, as well as the great English liturgist, E. Bishop. All of them encouraged and helped him, and thus through him influenced German scholarly liturgical research. With Morin's encouragement, he returned to his doctoral dissertation *Radulph de Rivo, der letzte Vertreter der altrömischen Liturgie* (2 v. Louvain 1911; Münster 1915). This topic led him to his special field of interest, namely, the problem of the ancient SACRAMENTARIES, the area between the *libelli* and the full Missals.

The first result of these studies was the publication of *Des fränkische Sacramentarium Gelasianum in alamannischer Überlieferung* (*Liturgiegeschichtlich Quellen und Forschungen* 1–2; Münster 1918) and a fundamental description of the objectives, problems, and methods of research, *Ziele und Aufgaben der liturgiegeschichtlichen Forschung* (*Liturgiegeschichtlich Quellen und Forschungen* 13; Münster 1919).

In the years after World War I he collaborated with his abbot Ildefons HERWEGEN (d. 1946), Romano GUARDINI, F. J. DÖLGER (d. 1940), A. BAUMSTARK (d. 1948), and A. Rücker (d. 1948) in many undertakings that became characteristic of German liturgical scholarship and renewal. He was called to work at the Vatican Library in 1924; from 1927 to 1939 he devoted himself to his first great series of liturgical editions, and in 1931 he was named professor for early church history, hagiography, and the history of liturgy at the Pontifical Institute for Christian Archeology. As early as 1921 he was a collaborator on the *Ephemerides Liturgicae,* and in 1927 he joined the editorial staff.

In 1927 Mohlberg already was working regularly during vacations on a catalogue of the medieval manuscripts at the University of Zürich; to this task he dedicated all his efforts when, at the outbreak of the war, he had to seek refuge in Switzerland. The catalogue, published in 1950, received warm praise and recognition, which in 1958 finally resulted in the bestowal on Mohlberg of an honorary doctorate by the Faculty of Philosophy at the University of Zürich. His method of cataloguing became a model to others, made possible the ordering of liturgical manuscripts, and gave impetus to new scientific work in liturgy.

A last fruitful period of creative work started for Mohlberg in 1948, when he was called to the pontifical college of the Benedictine Order, Sant' Anselmo, where from 1950 to 1953 he taught liturgiology and methodology, and until 1962 directed the liturgical institute founded by his Abbot Primate Bernard Kaelin. With Peter SIFFRIN and Leo Eizenhöfer he began the second important series of editions of the Roman Sacramentaries. In 1948, on the occasion of his 70th birthday, his former students published the Festschrift *Miscellanea Liturgica in honorem L. Cuniberti Mohlberg* (2 v. Rome 1948–49); this was an impressive witness to the kind of scholarship that Mohlberg encouraged.

Bibliography: H. SCHMIDT, ''Bibliographia L. Cuniberti Mohlberg,'' *Miscellanea Liturgica in honorem L. Cuniberti Mohlberg,* 2 v. (1948–49) 1:15–39. B. NEUNHEUSER, *Ephemerides liturgicae* 78 (1964): 58–62. E. VON SEVERUS, *Archiv für Liturgiewissenschaft* 8 (1963): 5–8.

[E. VON SEVERUS]

MÖHLER, JOHANN ADAM

Theologian, author, and professor; b. Igersheim, Germany, May 6, 1796; d. Munich, April 12, 1838. Möhler studied philosophy and theology at the Catholic Academy, Ellwangen, and after ordination to the priesthood (Sept. 18, 1819) taught church history at the Catholic Seminary and University of Tübingen. On a tour of leading German and Austrian universities, he made contact with the most famous theologians of his time, among them the Protestant professors J. Neander and F. Schleiermacher. In 1835 he became ordinary professor at Louis-Maximilian University in Munich, where he lectured on church history and literature and the Epistles of St. Paul. After a three-year period of intensive work, he died of a combination of cholera, pneumonia, and general exhaustion.

His four great works were: *Die Einheit in der Kirche* (1825); *Athanasius der Grosse* (1827); *Symbolik* (1832); and *Neue Untersuchungen der Lehrgegensätze zwischen Katholiken und Protestanten* (1834). He wrote a *Patrology,* a *Commentary on the Epistle to the Romans,* and 65 reviews of scientific works for the *Tübinger Theologische Quartalschrift,* besides articles on ANSELM OF CANTERBURY, Pseudo-Isidore, JEROME, and AUGUSTINE, among others.

His work on the unity of the Church (*Die Einheit in der Kirche*) received both enthusiastic appraisals and severe criticism, including accusations of heterodoxy in regard to papal infallibility and Modernism. Deeply influenced by the Protestant thought of F. SCHLEIERMACHER and the idealism of F. SCHELLING, Möhler exhibited an ideological metamorphosis in his later works, gradually retreating from a mystical and immanent approach to Christian doctrine into an objective evaluation of Christian revelation.

In 1930 K. Eschweiler explained this change by postulating the influence of Hegel's ''objective mind'' theory whereby the world of ideas is considered to take a concrete objective form in visible organizations such as church and nation. J. Geiselmann, however, attributed it to an internal intellectual evolution, whereby Möhler came to understand the shortcomings of his first works and their potential dangers, such as subjectivism, immanentism, and pantheistic evolutionism. While there are traces of Hegelian thought in Möhler's works, Geiselmann's opinion seems to explain adequately Möhler's ideological metamorphosis. The views of the Protestant scholar É. Vermeil and the Catholic A. Fonck, who consider Möhler as ''an unconscious precursor of modernism,'' have no foundation in Möhler's works, where the divine institution of the Church and the objective character of the Catholic religion are clearly defended.

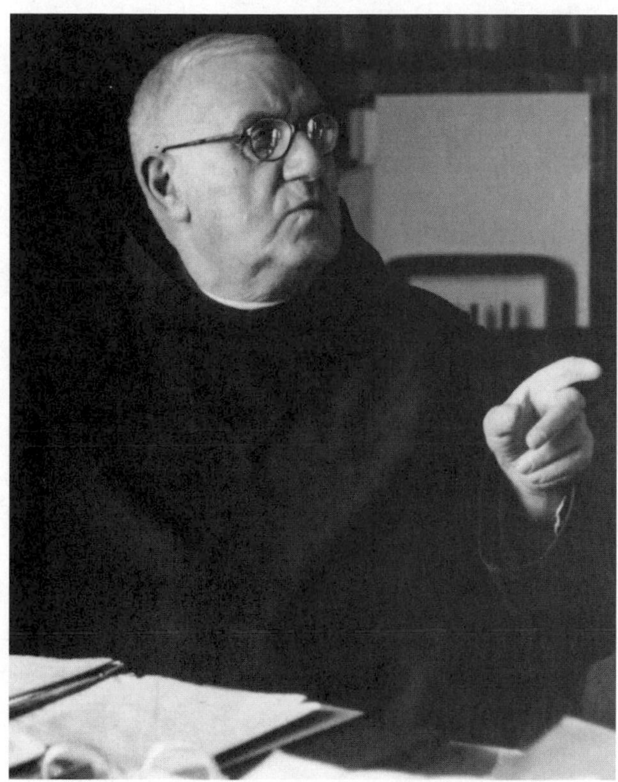

Kunibert Mohlberg.

Möhler's desire to reach an understanding with Protestantism and eventually to accomplish the reunion of the Churches was evident in the first years of his scientific work (1823–27), when he showed sympathy for the fundamental theses of Protestantism regarding the invisible character of the Church and its mystical elements. In *The Unity of the Church* (*Die Einheit*) he embodied the mystical elements of his ecclesiology and theological system in preparation for the debate with Protestantism encountered in his later works, e.g., *Symbolik* and *Neue Untersuchungen.* Well versed in the writings of the patristic and medieval theologians, Möhler kept abreast of the theological thought of his time on both Catholic and rationalist sides. His equanimity and genius have proved an inspiration for modern scholars who find him a guide to the problems raised by the ecumenical movement of today.

Bibliography: A. FONCK, *Dictionnaire de théologie catholique*, ed. A. VACANT et al., 15 v. (Paris 1903–50; Tables Générales 1951–) 10.2:2048–63. P. CHAILLET, ed., *L'Église est une: Hommage à Möhler* (Paris 1939). J. R. GEISELMANN, *Johann Adam Möhler* (Vienna 1940); *Die theologische Anthropologie Johann Adam Möhlers* (Freiburg 1955). R. H. NIENALTOWSKI, *Johann Adam Möhler's Theory of Doctrinal Development* (Washington 1959). M. J. HIMES, *Johann Adam Möhler and the Beginnings of Modern Ecclesiology* (New York 1997).

[R. H. NIENALTOWSKI]

MOINE, CLAUDINE

French mystic; b. Scey-sur-Saône, in the Diocese of Besançon, Jan. 17, 1618; d. Paris, date unknown, but later than 1655. Of distinguished birth but impoverished by war, Claudine Moine was obliged to go to Paris in April 1642 to seek work. There she placed herself under the direction of a religious and was not long in achieving experience of a mystical kind. Her spiritual journey is described in her *Relations Spirituelles,* which was preserved in a seventeenth-century manuscript in the Archives of the Foreign Missions in Paris. Her experiences comprised six months of favors; three years of temptations; and three years of infused lights, transverberation, and mystical marriage, followed by a state of darkness lasting six years when she ceased writing. The quality of the experience recorded in the *Relations,* the clarity of analysis, and the precision of the style make this a valuable contribution to mystical literature.

Bibliography: J. GUENNOU, *La Couturière mystique de Paris* (Paris 1959).

[J. GUENNOU]

MOISSAC, ABBEY OF

Former Benedictine monastery in the Diocese of Cahors, Department of Tarnet-Garonne, in southern France. Founded in the time of King Dagobert I (d. 639) by St. AMANDUS, who became the first abbot, this community provided the Church with many bishops from the ranks of its early abbots. Amandus himself became bishop of Maastricht; St. ANSBERT, archbishop of Rouen; and St. Leothade, bishop of Auch (691). The abbey was destroyed by the Saracens in 732 and was later raided by the Hungarians and Normans. During this chaotic period the monastery was able to rebuild and continue only with the protection of the powerful counts of Toulouse. After it became a dependency of CLUNY in 1047, Moissac once again became prosperous, housing at one time more than 1,000 monks. It was the headquarters of the Cluniac province of Aquitaine and administered a large number of other houses. In 1122 the body of St. CYPRIAN of Carthage was transferred to the abbey church of St. Peter at Moissac. With the institution of COMMENDATION in the late Middle Ages, the establishment began to decline. It was secularized by PAUL V in 1626 and finally suppressed in 1790. The church of St. Peter, containing in the tympanum of its south portal some of the most famous works of Romanesque sculpture, is now a parish church. The 12th-century cloisters are still well preserved.

Bibliography: *Gallia Christiana* (Paris 1715–85) 1:158–172. *Monumenta Germaniae Historica: Scriptores* (Berlin 1826–) 1:280–313. A. LAGRÈZE-FOSSAT, *Études historiques sur Moissac,* 3 v. (Paris 1870–74). A. ANGLÈS, *L'Abbaye de Moissac* (Paris 1911). H. LECLERCQ, *Dictionnaire d'archéologie chrétienne et de liturgie,* ed. F. CABROL, H. LECLERCQ, and H. I. MARROU, 15 v. (Paris 1907–53) 11.2:1701–15. K. HOFMANN, *Lexikon für Theologie und Kirche,* ed. J. HOFER and K. RAHNER, 10 v. (2d, new ed. Freiburg 1957–65) 7:523–524.

[L. GAILLARD]

MOLAS Y VALLVÉ, MARÍA ROSA DOLORIBUS FRANCISCA, ST.

Foundress of the Sisters of Our Lady of Consolation (*Hermanas de Nuestra Señora de la Consolación*); b. Reus (near Tarragona), northeastern Spain, March 24, 1815; d. Tortosa, Spain, June 11, 1876.

María Rosa, the daughter of craftsmen who owned a small shop, postponed her entry into religious life to tend her father's household after her mother's death from cholera. As Sister María Rosa, she joined an association of pious workers at the hospital in Reus (1841). Because of her practical intelligence, she was sent (1849) to Tortosa as superior of the House of Mercy. She reorganized and modernized the facility and procedures to improve the care given to its 300 mentally ill patients.

When she discovered that her congregation had no ties to any ecclesiastical authority and was unassociated with the Daughters of Charity, she placed herself (1957) and her 11 sisters under the jurisdiction of the local bishop. Her spirit of communion and ecclesiastical obedience birthed a new congregation: the Sisters of Our Lady of Consolation. The sisters, formally constituted as a congregation in 1868, dedicated themselves to providing health and educational services; however, María Rosa wrote the Rule to allow the order to respond to other needs of the Church.

She herself mediated disputes and even crossed a battleline to negotiate a cease fire during an attack on Reus. In Tortosa she established 10 houses and 17 hospitals, schools, and shelters for the poor before her death. By the late 20th century the order had 796 members in 84 houses in Argentina, Belgium, Brazil, Burkina Faso, Chile, Ecuador, Italy, Mexico, Mozambique, Portugal, Slovakia, South Korea, Spain, and Venezuela.

María Rosa was beatified (May 8, 1977) by Pope Paul VI and canonized (December 11, 1988) by John Paul II.

Feast: June 11.

Bibliography: J. M. JAVIERRE, *María Rosa Molas, una mujer misericordiosa* (Madrid 1975). M. T. SALES, *Fiamme sull'Ebro: vita* *della m. Maria Rosa Molas* (Milan 1969). *Acta Apostolicae Sedis* (Rome 1977) 606; (1989) 98. *L'Osservatore Romano* English edition 20 (1977) 2–5.

[K. I. RABENSTEIN]

MOLDOVA, THE CATHOLIC CHURCH IN

Capital: Chisinau (Kishinev).
Size: 13,000 sq. miles.
Population: 4,430,655 in 2000.
Languages: Moldovan, Russian, Gagauz (Turkish dialect).
Religions: 15,565 Catholics (.35%), 4,342,040 Orthodox (98%), 60,000 Jews (1.3%), 13,050 practice other faiths.
Diocese: Tiraspol, directly subject to the Holy See.

The Republic of Moldova is located in eastern Europe, and is bound on the north and east by Ukraine, and on the south and west by Romania. A landlocked region, Moldova is characterized by hilly steppe areas rising to the Carpathian Mountains in the east. The region's mild climate and fertile soil make it excellent for agriculture: among the crops grown are grapes, tobacco, grains, sugar beets and fruits and vegetables. In contrast to its abundant agricultural potential, the region's natural resources are limited, consisting mainly of lignite, phosphorites and gypsum. Wine, tobacco and fruits and vegetables were the basis of the region's economy in 2000.

Known as Bessarabia until it proclaimed independence from Russia in 1917 as the Moldavian Republic, the region was annexed to Romania under the Treaty of Versailles in 1918. In 1940 it was occupied by the USSR and renamed the Moldavian Soviet Socialist Republic. Despite a brief occupation by German troops from 1941–44, the region remained under Soviet control until the fall of the USSR in 1991. A new constitution defined the region as a parliamentary republic, and elections were held in 1994. Attempting to establish the new government of Moldova, the region's new democratic leaders weathered unsuccessful secessionist movements in the east (Transnistria) and the south (Gagauzia), before being financially hampered in 1998 by a decline in the Russian economy, on which the country was dependent for trade. Corruption, organized crime and poverty remained problems in the region through 2000.

History. The region's Christian origins can be traced to the Roman occupation of Dacia (modern Romania, Bulgaria and Serbia) and the movement of Roman colonists during the 2nd century. Romans left the region in 271, after which Huns, Slavs, Magyars and Mongols passed across the region, some ruling for brief periods. Hungary expanded into the area in the 13th century and ruled until the region declared its independence under Prince Bogdan in 1349. Bodgan established the principality of Bogdania, later renamed Moldavia, which extended from the Carpathian Mountains east to the Dniester River. Under Constantinople since Roman times, Moldavia remained predominately Orthodox, its patriarchate in Bucharest.

By the late 15th century most of southeastern Europe was under the control of Turkish invaders and Moldavia fell to their incursions in 1512. For the next three centuries it existed as a tributary state ruled by representatives of the Ottoman Empire, and also suffered through invasions by Turks, Tatars and Russians. During this upheaval, the Orthodox Church remained steadfast in its efforts to preserve both Christianity and regional culture from the incursions of Islam and other religions. The region was a point of contention between the Turks and the Russians through most of the 18th century, and in 1792 the Ottomans finally withdrew. Most of far-eastern Moldavia was ceded to Russia by the Treaty of Bucharest following the end of the Russo-Turkish war (1806–12); the rest, the region known as Bessarabia, was ceded to Romania by the Turks in 1918. Of the territory gained by Romania, that west of the Prut River was united with Walachia and permanently incorporated into Romania, while that to the east had a more difficult future. Despite the political lines drawn through the region, most of the population of the region to the east of the Prut, ethnic Romanians, retained their affiliation with the Romanian Orthodox Church—and Romanian culture—into the 20th century.

Eastern Moldavia remained under Russian control through the rest of the 19th century, during which time it was subjected to a policy of Russification. In reaction, a nationalist movement had taken root by 1905, and this group seized the opportunity, during the Russian revolution of 1917, to declare independence as the Moldavian Republic. Unfortunately, this independence did not last long: in 1924 the region was incorporated into the USSR as an autonomous soviet republic, and in 1940 was rejoined to the Bessarabian lands held by Romania since the Turkish withdrawal, thus creating the boundaries of the modern state. A focus of Romanian aggression in World War II, the region remained under Soviet control—disputed for decades by Romania— until the fall of the USSR in 1991.

The communist government strictly limited the activities of all religions, including the Romanian Orthodox Church, and worked to ultimately quash all religious activity. During the early 1940s most Orthodox churches and monasteries in the region were confiscated by the state and either demolished or converted to other uses,

some even becoming warehouses. Clergy were put under constant observation, harassed and often punished for practicing their faith. As communism evolved, the role of the Russian Orthodox Church increased throughout the Soviet Union, and it eventually absorbed the Orthodox Church in Moldavia, as it absorbed similar churches throughout the Soviet sphere. Although by the 1950s Soviet dictator Josef Stalin had lifted much of the persecution with respect to the favored Russian Orthodox Church, other churches were not so fortunate, and many Latin-rite Catholics were forced to practice their faith ''underground.'' Ethnic Ukrainians living in the region east of the Dniester River, most members of the Ukrainian-Greek Catholic Church, were put in such a situation when the government declared their Church illegal and forcibly united it with the Russian Orthodox Church in 1946.

An Independent Moldova. By the late 1980s many of the Soviet republics were experiencing Soviet leader Mikhail Gorbachev's *perestroika* as a rising nationalism, and Moldavia was no different. In August of 1989, unopposed by local communist officials, thousands of demonstrators took to the streets of the capital, demanding freedoms and official status for the Moldavian language. In the late summer of 1991 Boris Yeltsin staged a bloodless coup against the Gorbachev government, resulting in confusion throughout the now-disintegrating USSR. As 400,000 marchers took to the streets in Chisinau, Soviet attempts to impose a state of emergency in Moldavia were repulsed by the region's own government, and on Aug. 27, 1991 Moldova declared its independence from the Soviet Union. This action sparked a second move for independence, as Transnistria, the region to the east of the Dniester River that was home to a Ukranian/Russian majority, attempted to separate from the ethnic Romanian west. As tensions flared in Transnistria in 1992, Soviet troops entered the region to support the separatists. In response, the fledgling nation of Moldova reinforced its military, hoping to avert a spread of violence into the rest of the country. After a new constitution was promulgated on July 28, 1994, that clearly granted the ''preservation, development and expression of ethnic and linguistic identity,'' and which gave Transnistria autonomous status, a cease-fire was negotiated and Moscow agreed to withdraw its 14th Army in 1995. The first multiparty presidential elections were held in Moldova in 1997.

A Divided Orthodoxy. During the Russification process that was ongoing during communist rule, the Russian Orthodox Church (Moscow patriarchate) had been given almost complete jurisdiction over all Orthodox formerly under the patriarchate in Bucharest, and at independence had 853 churches and 11 monasteries still under its control. In late 1992, the Patriarch of Moscow and all Russia issued a decree upgrading the eparchy of Chisinau and Moldova to a metropolitan see. In contrast to the vigor of the Russian Orthodox Church, the Old Russian Orthodox Church (Old Believers) had only 14 churches and one monastery in the country, while the small Ukrainian Greek Orthodox Church remained a tiny minority in the east. Other religious denominations that survived decades of Soviet oppression included the Armenian Apostolic Church, Seventh-Day Adventists, Baptists, Pentecostals and Molokans (a Russian Orthodox sect); by 2000 nine synagogues had been restored for use by the country's small Jewish community.

Legislation passed in 1992 guaranteed religious freedom but also required that all religious groups be officially registered with the government. Laws were also passed to prohibit proselytization, a protection primarily for the Russian Orthodox Church in the face of the country's new spiritual independence, although these laws were amended in 1999. While over 98 percent of the population declared themselves Orthodox, during a post-communist resurgence of religious fervor, many Orthodox with ties to Romania wished to return to the Bucharest patriarchate. In appeasement, the Moscow patriarchate granted autonomous status to its Moldovan diocese, hoping to retain its hold over the new country. However, the Holy Synod of the Romanian Orthodox Church decided in December of 1992 to reconstitute its own metropolitanate of Bessarabia in the same territory. Thus Orthodoxy in Moldova was split between two rival jurisdictions, the great majority of parishes remaining loyal to Moscow. By 2000 the Moscow patriarchate claimed over 1,000 parishes, while the Bucharest patriarchate declared only 100. The newly reconstituted Bessarabian Orthodox Church made four efforts at registration with the government in the decade after independence; each time its application was refused, the government claiming it a ''schismatic movement'' and listing unresolved claims against church property.

Into the 21st Century. The Moldovan Orthodox Church remained the predominate religion in the country in 2000, and as such it was at the forefront of efforts to promote Christian values within a country secularized as a result of decades of communist rule. In November of 2000 it flexed its muscle by announcing that it would excommunicate any member of parliament voting in favor of a proposed law legalizing abortion, a law intended to extend the Soviet policy of the pre-independence period. Ukrainian Greek Catholics, who sided with the Orthodox in this matter, remained a small minority unrecognized by the state; by 2000 they had fewer than ten parishes, tended by six diocesan and seven religious priests and 20 sisters. In addition, a small number of Latin-rite Catholics were living in the country, most of Polish or German descent. While there were no Catholic or other Christian schools operating in Moldova, beginning in 2000, instruction in the Christian faith was made mandatory in the country's state-run primary schools, and optional for older students. As the nation moved into a new century, the construction of new churches and the restoration of over a hundred existing but damaged religious buildings was soon under way, although clergy remained in short supply throughout the country.

Bibliography: P. MOJZES, *Religious Liberty in Eastern Europe and the USSR: Before and After the Great Transformation* (Boulder, CO 1992). S. P. RAMET, *Nihil Obstat: Religion, Politics, and Social Change in East-Central Europe and Russia* (Durham, NC 1998).

[P. SHELTON]

MOLDOVIŢA (VATRA MOLDOVIŢEI), ABBEY OF

Orthodox monastery built in Moldavia (now Moldova), district of Câmpolung, at the order of the Moldavian Prince Peter Rareş in 1532. The abbey was erected near an older foundation established there by Alexander the Good in 1402. It was later expanded by important territorial grants. Its buildings, which comprise the monks' cells, the superior's quarters, and the dwellings of the princes, are surrounded by fortified walls. The outside walls of the principal church were painted in 1537 in typical Moldavian-Byzantine style; and these frescoes, representing religious and historical subjects as well as the portraits of the founders, are particularly beautiful and well preserved. The convent is no longer occupied.

Bibliography: S. BALS and C. NICOLESCU, *Mănăstirea Moldoviţa* (Bucharest 1958). N. IORGA, *Istoria bisericii româneşti,* 2 v. (2d ed. Bucharest 1929–32). *Enciclopedia României,* 2 v. (Bucharest 1936–40) 2:121.

[T. FOTITCH]

MOLESME, ABBEY OF

Former French Benedictine abbey, center of a monastic congregation, Diocese of Langres; founded in 1075 by ROBERT OF MOLESME, who retired with his followers to the dense forests near Langres. The original hermitage grew into a flourishing abbey but Robert left in 1098 and founded CÎTEAUX. He was soon reconciled with his abandoned monks and in 1099 returned to Molesme, which became the head of a monastic congregation that eventually incorporated 64 priories and some nunneries. Most of the affiliated houses were located within the Dioceses of Langres and Troyes. The congregation's organization was similar to that of CLUNY, the abbot of Molesme retaining jurisdiction over all houses and appointing all local superiors. But its spirituality, discipline, and method of handling property were closer to the usages of Cîteaux. The abbey was totally destroyed in 1472 in the war between France and Burgundy. In 1534 the foundations of a new church were laid, but commendatory abbots led to financial difficulties. After Molesme joined the MAURISTS in 1647, both moral life and monastic finances improved. The new church was consecrated in 1687. In 1791 Molesme was suppressed by the French Revolution. In the course of time, the magnificent church, which was under private ownership, was completely demolished. Other monastic buildings housed a school.

Bibliography: U. CHEVALIER, *Repertoire des sources historiques du moyen-âge* 2:1965. J. LAURENT, *Cartulaires de l'abbaye de Molesme*, 2 v. (Paris 1907–11). J. OTHON DUCOURNEAU, *Les Origines cisterciennes* (Ligugé 1933). K. SPAHR, *Das Leben, des hl. Robert von Molesme* (Fribourg 1947). P. SCHMITZ, *Histoire de l'Ordre de S. Benoît* (Maredsous 1942–56) 3:108–109. L. H. COTTINEAU, *Répertoire topo-bibliographique des abbayes et prieurés* 2:1872–73.

[L. J. LEKAI]

MOLEYNS, ADAM

Bishop, statesman, and humanist; d. Portsmouth, Jan. 9, 1450. Moleyns, who played an important role in the development of English HUMANISM, was the son of Sir Richard Moleyns. He was educated at Oxford, where he secured degrees in civil and canon law in 1435. By 1434 he was already a papal chamberlain and member of the papal household, where he befriended the humanist POGGIO BRACCIOLINI and cultivated the humanities. In 1435 he became king's proctor in Rome, went to the Council of BASEL, and then returned home, where he was made clerk of the council in 1436. Under Henry VI he served as envoy to Aachen and Cologne in 1438, to the Frankfurt Diet in 1441, and to the pope in 1442. Meanwhile, he collected an impressive number of ecclesiastical benefices. As keeper of the Privy Seal from 1444 to 1449 and bishop of CHICHESTER (1445) he held, together with the Duke of Suffolk, a key position in English politics. He was killed by a mob of mutinous sailors. Moleyns's correspondence with Aeneas Sylvius Piccolomini (later Pope PIUS II) displays his mastery of humanist Latin. His authorship of the *Libelle of Englysche Polycie* (ed. G. Warner, 1926) is by no means certain.

Bibliography: W. HUNT, *The Dictionary of National Biography from the Earliest Times to 1900,* 63 v. (London 1885–1900) 13:578–580. R. WEISS, *Humanism in England during the Fifteenth Century* (2d ed. Oxford 1957) 80–83. A. B. EMDEN, *A Biographical Register of the University of Oxford to* A.D. *1500,* 3 v. (Oxford 1957–59) 2:1289–1291. W. F. SCHIRMER, *Der englische Frühhumanismus* (2d ed. Tübingen 1963) 95–97.

[R. WEISS]

MOLINA, ALONSO DE

Franciscan missionary and linguist; b. Spain, probably in the province of Estremadura, 1512 or 1513; d. Mexico City, 1585. Soon after the conquest of Mexico in 1521, his parents moved to the new land, where his father died. The boy became proficient in Nahuatl, the language of the Azteots. When the Franciscans arrived in 1524 with no knowledge of Nahuatl, they asked that the boy be allowed to live with them. He took up residence in the Franciscan community, sharing the common life of the friars and serving as their interpreter. In 1527 he became a Franciscan, and he was ordained probably in 1534 or 1535. He became an excellent preacher in Nahuatl. In 1555 he was guardian of the friary of Texcoco; in 1559, of Tecamachalco; and in 1571, of San Francisco in Puebla. He is best remembered for his pioneering studies in Nahuatl and for his writings in that language. His linguistic works include *Vocabulario en la lengua castellana y mexicana* and *Arte de la lengua mexicana y castellana.* His published writings of a religious and pastoral nature include *Doctrina christiana breve, Confesionario breve* and *Confesionario mayor,* and *Sumario de las indulgencias concedidas a los confrades del sanctísimo sacramento.* He also translated the Epistles and the Gospels of the Roman Missal and the Office of Our Lady into Nahuatl, but these were not published because of a prohibition against printing the sacred scriptures in the vernacular.

Bibliography: R. ZULAICA GARATE, *Los Franciscanos y la imprenta en México en el siglo XVI* (Mexico City 1939).

[F. B. WARREN]

MOLINA, ANTHONY DE

Carthusian ascetical writer; b. Villanueva de los Infantes, *c.* 1550; d. Miraflores, Sept. 21, 1612. After studying at Salamanca, Molina made his profession in the Order of Augustinian Hermits (March 17, 1575), was elected superior at one of their Spanish houses, and taught theology. Wanting to join an order of stricter discipline, he became a Carthusian at Miraflores, near Burgos, in 1589, and died there as prior of the monastery. He wrote ascetical works in Spanish, adapted especially for priests, that became the most popular books of their type in Spain and were translated into other languages. The most famous of this group is a manual for priests titled *Instrucción de sacerdotes, en que se dá doctrina muy importante para conocer la alteza del sagrado oficio sacerdotal, y para exercitarle debidamente,* the whole work being based on the teachings of the Fathers and Doctors of the Church. Twenty editions of this work are known to have been published, among them a Latin translation by the Belgian Dominican, Nicolas Janssen Boy, that underwent five editions (Antwerp 1618, 1644; Cologne 1626, 1711, 1712). Severely attacked by the Jansenist Antoine ARNAULD (*De la fréquente Communion,* 1643), this work was well defended by Petavius (*Dogmata theologica; De poenitentia* 3.6). Molina also produced two ascetical works adapted for laymen: *Exercicios espirituales para personas ocupadas deseosas de su salvación* (Burgos 1613) and *Exercicios espirituales de la excelencia, provecho y necesidad de la oración mental . . .* (Burgos 1615). Finally, still extant are many of his letters to the confessor of Philip III, a tract on prayer, a biography of Dom Michael Colmenero, and an unpublished treatise on the ultimate aim of life.

Bibliography: S. AUTORE, *Dictionnaire de théologie catholique*. ed. A. VACANT et al., (Paris 1903—50) 10.2:2088–90. M. TARIN Y IUANEDA, *La real Cartuja de Miraflores* (Burgos 1897) 486–497. H. HURTER, *Nomenclator literarius theologiae catholicae* (Innsbruck 1903–13) 3:608–609.

[F. C. LEHNER]

MOLINA, LUIS DE

Spanish theologian; b. Cuenca, September 1535; d. Madrid, Oct. 12, 1600. Molina entered the Jesuit novitiate at Coimbra, Portugal, in 1553, studied philosophy there until 1558, and theology there and at Évora until 1563. Peter da Fonseca, alleged to have influenced his doctrine of SCIENTIA MEDIA, was never his teacher. After professing philosophy at Coimbra (1563–67), and theology at Évora (1568–83), Molina retired to write, spending time at Évora, Lisbon, and Cuenca. In 1600 he was called to profess moral theology at Madrid.

His published works are *Concordia liberi arbitrii cum gratiae donis,* etc. (Lisbon 1588); *Appendix ad Concordiam* (Lisbon 1589, bound in some copies of the 1588 *Concordia*); *Commentaria in primam divi Thomae partem* (Cuenca 1592); *Concordia* (2d ed. Antwerp 1595); and *De justitia et jure* (1st complete ed., 6 v. Cologne 1613).

The *Concordia* is Molina's solution of the problem of free will and God's foreknowledge, providence, predestination, reprobation, efficacious GRACE, by *scientia media*. Comparison of both *Concordia* editions and the *Commentaria* (that contains some of the *Concordia* material) shows differences of expression, but none of doctrine. Though originally occasioning great controversy, the *Concordia* still presents one accepted solution of the problem it considers. It was edited critically by John Rabeneck (Oña-Madrid 1953).

The *De justitia et jure* marks Molina as one of the preeminent moralists and economists of his time. Molina published almost three volumes (Cuenca 1592–1600); the rest of the material, prepared by him, was published posthumously by his brethren. Many of Molina's unpublished writings were edited by Friedrich Stegmüller in his *Geschichte des Molinismus* (Münster 1935).

Luis De Molina, frontispiece engraving 1595, from "Concordia," Antwerp edition.

See Also: MOLINISM; CONGREGATIO DE AUXILIIS; FREE WILL AND GRACE; GRACE, ARTICLES ON; GRACE, CONTROVERSIES ON.

Bibliography: E. VANSTEENBERGHE, *Dictionnaire de théologie catholique*. ed. A. VACANT et al., (Paris 1903–50) 10.2:2090–92. F. STEGMÜLLER, *Lexikon für Theologie und Kirche*, ed. J. HOFER and K. RAHNER (Freiberg 1957–65) 7:526. J. RABENECK, "De Ludovici de Molina studiorum philosophiae curriculo," *Archivum historicum Societatis Jesu* (Rome 1932) 6 (1937) 291–302; "De vita et scriptis Ludovici Molina," *ibid.* 19 (1950) 75–145; "Antiqua legenda de Molina narrata examinatur," *ibid.* 24 (1955) 295–326. B. W. DEMPSEY, *Interest and Usury* (Washington 1943).

[F. L. SHEERIN]

MOLINA, MERCEDES DE JESÚS, BL.

Also known as the "Rose of Baba and Guayaquil," foundress of the *Congregación de Santa Mariana de Jesús* or *Marianitas;* b. 1828 Baba (Los Rios), Ecuador; d. there, June 12, 1883. Mercedes (Eng.: Mercy) began her life's work as a laywoman with the motto: "As much love for as many sufferings as there are in the world." She set her hand to the task by teaching orphans and aiding the abandoned, and ministering to the poor in Guayaquil. Eventually her world expanded to include the ill-treated native Jibaros and abandoned children at Cuenca. On Easter Monday 1873, the bishop of Riobamba gave episcopal approval to her formation of the *Marianitas,* named after Saint Maríana de Jesús PAREDES Y FLORES, the ''Lily of Quito.'' The Marianitas continued her apostolate after Mercedes' death at age fifty-five. She was beatified on the Las Samenes Esplanade in Guayaquil by John Paul II, Feb.1, 1985.

Bibliography: C. E. MESA, *Mercedes Molina, fundadora de las Marianitas* (Quito 1973). *Acta Apostolicae Sedis* (1985): 327.

[K. I. RABENSTEIN]

MOLINISM

A system of theological thought concerning God's perception of the free FUTURIBLES and futures through His middle knowledge (*SCIENTIA MEDIA*), the conciliation of efficacious GRACE and FREE WILL, some aspects of PREDEFINITION, PREDESTINATION, REPROBATION, and the nature of internal actual grace. It is called Molinism because it was fathered by Luis de MOLINA, although not explicitly stated by him in its modern formulation. This article explains the Molinist position on the topics mentioned above, and compares Molinism with CONGRUISM. Grace hereafter in this article always means internal actual grace.

Futuribles, Middle Knowledge, Futures. The free futurible, unlike the possible, is always one definite thing, whose being is ''would be.'' It is therefore always infallibly known by God's infinite intelligence. Being only a conditional existent, it requires only a subjectively conditional decree in God—''Thomas would believe if God gave him grace.'' Consequently, God knows free futurible acts of creatures prior to His absolute decrees about them. This is God's middle knowledge—middle between His knowledge supposing no decrees (possibles) and that supposing subjectively absolute decrees (futures).

Less important is the question of how God knows free futuribles before His absolute decrees. Molinists agree that they cannot be known by God in Himself as determining their objective truth, for example, that a creature would consent to, rather than reject God's grace, if it were given. Any divine decree or grace determining futurible consent would have to derive its determining power from its very nature and would therefore conflict with any creature's power of futurible dissent. Hence any grace that God would give to men, though always inclining to good, must of its nature not determine man's futurible consent rather than dissent. Hence futuribles cannot be known in God's futurible decrees or graces as determining them. In the conditional order, God's grace is efficacious entirely from man's free futurible consent and can be known as efficacious only presupposing this fact.

Beyond this point Molinists dispute among themselves whether God's middle knowledge perceives the futuribles in God, as in a mirror reflecting their futurible being without determining it. Many Molinists, considering this impossible, say free futuribles are known by God only directly and immediately in themselves. This means that the ''would be'' of the futurible is sufficient objective reason why it terminates the divine cognition, itself subjectively activated by the divine essence to know whatever has determinate being. Some Molinists say God sees the futuribles in His ''supercomprehension'' (Molina never uses the word) of the human will—He sees the will and the act proceeding from it, and this seems equivalent to the preceding theory.

Molinists conceive that man would determine himself to consent to, rather than reject God's grace, if it were given. God's grace of its very nature would give sufficient power to consent; but its effectiveness to produce conditional consent, rather than dissent, arises solely from the fact that man would freely choose to consent, for reasons which would seem good to him. Man shares the determining power of God in the futurible order, but God gave such power to man by creating him free. Just as man is an agent by sharing God's productive power, so is he a free agent by sharing God's determining power.

Therefore, the reason that God has at His disposal efficacious and inefficacious graces is not that there are two intrinsically different kinds of grace; it is the fact that man would freely consent to some and would freely resist others.

Absolute futures, whatever ''will be,'' are known by God, according to Molinism, in His absolute decree to give that grace, to which by middle knowledge He had foreseen man would consent or not, as the case may be. This absolute decree fulfills the condition upon which man's futurible action depended for its future existence. It changes ''would consent'' to ''will consent.'' It predefines the future free consent of man, even before that consent is given, and definitely precontains it. In it, as in a mirror, God knows infallibly, by knowledge ''of vision,'' man's future consent.

By this absolute divine decree, man's future acts become from all eternity events of human history, occurring in due time, and God is the ''Lord of History,'' who has ''got the whole world in His hands.'' For as He alone has power to distribute His graces and distributes them as He wills, He decides all future events and could just as well have given man other graces, which He foresaw man would resist, if they were given, thereby changing the course of history. By this decree He differentiates the saint from the sinner; by it also, made freely with knowledge of what would happen, every good human action becomes God's special benefit to man.

Conciliation of Efficacious Grace with Free Will. The efficacious grace, which God decrees to give man in the absolute order of time, has its efficacy or infallible ability to obtain man's future consent, not from man's consent, but before that consent is given. Yet it is a dogma of faith that, under the influence of grace that works, man's will is free (H. Denzinger, *Enchiridion symbolorum*, ed. A. Schönmetzer [Freiburg 1963] 1554). Hence the question: whence does efficacious grace derive its infallible power to obtain man's future consent without detriment to human liberty?

There are today two probable answers to the question. One is: from the internal nature of efficacious grace, which, prior to any consideration of man's reaction to it, differs intrinsically from inefficacious grace. There are several ways of describing this grace. Molinists say: not from the internal nature of grace, but from external sources consequent upon man's futurible reaction to it. Molinists unanimously reject the first solution, especially because it seems destructive of human liberty. It also seems to eliminate ineffective, but truly sufficient grace.

Positively, Molinists unanimously say all efficacious grace derives its infallible power to obtain man's future consent from three extrinsic sources: (1) the objective fact that man would freely consent to a grace if it were given, that is, from man's futurible consent; (2) God's foreknowledge of that fact, before He absolutely decrees to give the grace, that is, from His middle knowledge; and (3) from God's benevolent absolute decree to give this grace, in the light of that foreknowledge, for reasons known to God—not necessarily because man would consent.

This grace does not conflict with man's liberty or power of dissent, even when it is acting on man's will, because its whole connection with man's future consent arises from the original supposition that man would freely consent to it, if it were given, and not from the intrinsic nature of the grace. This grace, when given, takes from man the act of dissent, but leaves intact the power.

This implies the doctrine that liberty is not an act, but an active power of the will to determine itself to act or not act when all the prerequisites for action are present. The will has the passive capacity to receive these prerequisites, such as motivation and divine grace. These remove the passive indifference of the will toward action; but when they are present, there must remain in the will, if free, active power to determine itself to act or not act. A gasoline tank has the passive capacity to receive a lighted match, but no active power to explode or not once the match is thrown in. When the will has motivation and God's grace acting on it, it still has the active power to respond or resist. This, according to Molinism, is freedom; and this is preserved in the Molinist explanation of efficacious grace. According to Molinism, efficacious and inefficacious (purely sufficient) graces do not differ in their internal structure; grace, so far as its inner nature is concerned, can be effective in one person, not in another; to graces intrinsically alike one will consent, another dissent; no new entity need be added to the inner make-up of sufficient grace to render it efficacious; efficacious grace is of its nature repudiable; although efficacious grace intrinsically is not a greater benefit than inefficacious, it is in its totality, because it is willingly given by God, in the light of His knowledge that man would consent to it.

Predestination, Predefinition, Reprobation. In the order of time or execution, God gives the reward of glory to adults after and on account of merit, but there has always been dispute among Catholic theologians about the order of intention. Does God first absolutely intend, for His own reasons, to give the reward of glory to some (formal predestination), and consequently absolutely intend that they acquire merit, and so absolutely intend that they receive graces infallibly procuring these acts (formal predefinition); and does He consequently ''not elect'' other adults for glory prior to their foreseen death in sin (negative antecedent reprobation)? Or does He ordinarily simply will, for reasons known to Him, to give some men graces, with which He had foreseen they would correspond, thereby decreeing their meritorious acts (virtual predefinition), and only after and on account of these foreseen future merits, intend to give them the crown of glory (virtual predestination), while the rest He positively intends to reprobate on account of their foreseen death in sin (positive consequent reprobation)?

One's response to these quotations is ultimately linked with one's response to the question (also debated among Catholics): Under what condition does God will to save all men in the order of intention? Is it some consideration prior to the foreseen state of man's death, like the predetermined order of the universe, or manifestation of God's glory, or some other reason known to God, or is it solely the foreseen state of man at death?

Most non-Molinists hold the first opinion, as do many who follow Molina on grace and free will (F. Suárez, Bellarmine), because this opinion can be maintained by one who holds God's middle knowledge of the futuribles; but Molina and strict Molinists (Lessius, G. Vázquez) hold the second position. To them the first opinion is unproved; it seems to liken God to one who promises a reward, for which all are to strive, and then arbitrarily chooses only certain ones to be the winners—which seems to nullify God's universal salvific will. These think that the final purpose of God, our Father, is the communication of His goodness to us. The final end of men, His children, is the order of the universe, the manifestation of God's glory; but as men are free, God cannot absolutely intend this end, which involves the number of the saved, except as it proves obtainable by the free cooperation of men.

Strict Molinists, in affirming this position, say God would have given men the same graces and would have permitted sins, had He foreseen their rejection. The fact of God's permission of sin must be faced by any theory. According to Molinism God gives men inefficacious grace, with which man infallibly sins; but the inefficacy is due, not to some deficiency in the grace, but solely to the fact that men would freely reject it if it were given. When God gives men grace foreseen as ineffective, He gives it, in spite of its inefficacy, with a sincere intention of efficacy; for the grace is truly sufficient, and its ineffectiveness is due, not to the grace, but entirely to man's free dissent. Of course God could give other graces, to which man would respond, but He does not, so great is His respect for human liberty.

The strict Molinist doctrine, up to this point, may be summarized as follows:

(1) By ''simple intelligence'' God sees the possibility of creating A and B, of giving them truly sufficient grace, with which both can be saved.

(2) God decrees to create both, to give them sufficient graces, and, if they cooperate, merit and glory—God's universal salvific will, antecedent, conditioned solely on man's future cooperation with grace.

(3) By middle knowledge God sees A would cooperate with grace, if it were given, and would be saved; and that B would do the opposite.

(4) God absolutely decrees, for His own reasons (here is the mystery of predestination), to give to A graces, to which He foresaw A would consent, if they were given, out of predilection for him; and to give B truly sufficient grace, from which He foresaw B would dissent, if it were given. God loves B, but does not force Him—virtual predefinition of the good acts of A; permission of the sins of B. Their good acts and sins are now absolute futures.

(5) By ''vision'' God sees in these decrees the meritorious acts of A, the sins of B as absolute futures.

(6) God absolutely intends to give A the crown of glory on account of his absolutely future merits; and positively to reprobate B on account of his absolutely future demerits—virtual predestination of A to glory on account of merit in order of intention; also in the same order the positive reprobation of B consequent on demerit. No antecedent reprobation.

(7) A in time performs meritorious acts, B commits sin.

(8) God in time gives glory to A and punishment to B, on account of their merits and demerits—predestination and positive reprobation on account of final merits and demerits in the order of execution.

Nature of Actual Grace. All Catholic theologians agree that indeliberate acts of thought and volition, which draw man to a good free act, pertain to the complex of actual grace. All Molinists agree that actual grace is not a supernatural entity determining the will to the subsequent choice to do that to which it is drawn. Beyond this they differ. Some (e.g., L. Billot) say actual grace is a nondetermining, supernatural entity injected into the faculties by God. Others (Molina, Suárez) hold actual grace to be solely the acts of intellect and will elevated to the supernatural order by God's simultaneous concursus.

Molinism and Congruism. Because Suárez and Bellarmine have really different opinions from Molina and Lessius regarding predestination and allied topics, and occasional differences of expression, it is sometimes alleged that there are two systems, congruism and Molinism. Congruism is said to hold that grace is efficacious because God so tempers it to man's disposition and circumstances that the will infallibly but nevertheless freely consents to it.

However, this tempering merely explains grace's sufficiency, not its efficacy, why it will infallibly get man's consent. This, the crucial point, Suárez and Bellarmine explain exactly as Molina does. On this point there is no system of congruism as opposed to Molinism.

See Also: BÁÑEZ AND BAÑEZIANISM; CONGREGATIO DE AUXILIIS; FREE WILL AND GRACE; FREE WILL AND PROVIDENCE; FREEDOM; GRACE, CONTROVERSIES ON; GRACE, EFFICACIOUS; GRACE, SUFFICIENT; OMNISCIENCE; THEOLOGY, HISTORY OF; WILL OF GOD

Bibliography: E. VANSTEENBERGHE, *Dictionnaire de théologie catholique*. ed. A. VACANT et al., (Paris 1903–50) 10.2:2094–2187. F. STEGMÜLLER, *Lexikon für Theologie und Kirche*, ed. J. HOFER and K. RAHNER (Freiberg 1957–65) 7:526, 527–530. R. KONETZKE, *Die Religion in Geschichte und Gegenwart* (Tübingen 1957–65) 4:1088–89. L. DE MOLINA, *Liberi arbitrii cum gratiae donis . . . concordia,* ed. J. RABENECK (Oña 1953). B. BERAZA, *De gratia Christi* (2d ed. Bilbao 1929). J. M. DALMAU, *Sacrae theologiae summa*, ed. Fathers of the Society of Jesus, Professors of the Theological Faculties in Spain (Madrid 1962) 2.1:1–582. S. GONZÁLEZ, *ibid.* 3.3:1–352. H. LANGE, *De gratia* (Freiburg 1929). J. BRODRICK, *The Life and Work of Blessed Robert Francis Cardinal Bellarmine,* 2 v. (London 1927–28) v.2. A. C. PEGIS, ''Molina and Human Liberty,'' *Jesuit Thinkers of the Renaissance,* ed. G. SMITH (Milwaukee 1939) 75–131. H. Rondet, *Gratia Christi* (Paris 1848).

[F. L. SHEERIN]

MOLINOS, MIGUEL DE

Theologian, whose life and writings greatly influenced seventeenth-century mysticism; b. Muniesa, Spain, June 29, 1628; d. Rome, Dec. 28, 1696. His early years were undistinguished; he studied at Valencia where he was ordained and received a doctorate in theology. In 1663, he was sent to Rome as procurator in the cause of a local venerable. He was afterward relieved of his commission, but he elected to remain in Rome where he had gained a reputation as director of souls. In 1675 he published *A Spiritual Guide,* which set forth his mystical doctrine and purported to offer an ''easy way to contemplation.'' The book achieved immediate popularity and was quickly translated into several languages. According to this work, it is through contemplation that the perfect Christian is ultimately distinguished from the imperfect Christian whose life is active and who uses the prayer of meditation. This distinguishing contemplation is acquired only by a total abandonment of self to the will and operation of God in the soul, to the extent that this soul of ''pure faith'' has rid itself of all effort to act virtuously, or to form thoughts or desires, or even actively to repel temptations.

The seventeenth century had a decided bent toward mysticism, and Rome, still perturbed from the Jansenist crisis, could not be indifferent to this novel teaching. Opposition to Molinos soon formed, with Jesuit theologians and preachers leading the defense of meditative prayer. Gottardo Bell'uomo and Paolo Segneri wrote treatises against the new doctrine. Molinos countered with two long letters to the Jesuit general in a conciliatory but unyielding spirit. For five years the dispute grew ever more acute, and soon the political machinery of Rome was called into play. Molinos was not without powerful friends, among them the archbishop of Palermo, the cardinal secretary of state, and especially the Oratorian Pier Matteo Petruccio, a convinced adherent and propagandist of the new mysticism and soon to be created a curial cardinal. In 1681 the books of Bell'uomo and Segneri were placed on the Index, and Molinos seemed to have triumphed.

Then suddenly on July 18, 1685, Molinos was arrested and subjected to a searching investigation by the Holy Office. The immediate reason for his arrest is not altogether clear. It is true that Cardinal Caracciolo of Naples, who seems first to have mentioned the term ''quietist,'' complained of the doctrine in 1682. Yet the *Guide* had been under scrutiny for three years before the arrest. Although the teaching of the *Guide* was susceptible to dangerous and even heretical interpretation, yet it seems improbable that this alone could have precipitated the sudden and drastic measures used against such a well-known and respected figure as Molinos. Non-Catholic sources adopted the current gossip that the affair was engineered by Cardinal D'Estrée, Louis XIV's ambassador to Rome, but there is little historically or logically to substantiate the claim. It seems more probable that it was accusations of a moral rather than a doctrinal nature that brought about Molinos's sudden downfall.

For two years Molinos was examined on the *Spiritual Guide,* the more than 12,000 letters found in his possession, and the depositions of the many called in to give testimony concerning his spiritual advice and moral conduct. Finally in the spring of 1687, Molinos admitted his guilt. A list of errors charged to him, numbering 68 in all, (see H. Denzinger, *Enchiridion symbolorum,* [Freiburg 1963]:2201–2268) was read to the defendant before a large assembly in the Minerva on Sept. 3, 1687. Molinos read his retraction and pleaded guilty as charged to moral misconduct, the extent of which cannot be certified as the report lies buried in the secret files of the Holy Office. He was sentenced to a life of penitential imprisonment and led to jail as the crowd looking on the fallen idol cried: ''To the flames.'' He lived nine more years of pious and exemplary behavior, perhaps practicing his teaching that elevated souls seek only the humiliations and scorn that it might please God to send.

Bibliography: M. DE MOLINOS, *Guida Spirituale* (Rome 1675). P. DUDON, *Le Quiétiste espagnol: Michel Molinos* (Paris 1921). R. A. KNOX, *Enthusiasm* (New York 1961). J. PAQUIER, *Dictionnaire de théologie catholique,* 15 v. (Paris 1903–50) 10.2:2187–2192.

[T. K. CONNOLLY]

MOLLA, GIANNA (JOAN) BERETTA, BL.

Physician, mother, ''Martyr for Life''; b. Magenta near Milan, Lombardy, northern Italy, Oct. 4, 1922; d. there April 28, 1962.

Gianna was the tenth of thirteen children of Alberta Beretta and Maria de Micheli—who ensured that she received a Catholic education. Gianna began her apostolate of caring for the sick and elderly as a member of the Saint Vincent de Paul Society while still in school. Gianna was also a leader in the CATHOLIC ACTION Movement, organizing retreats and spiritual exercises.

Upon graduating from the University of Pavia with degrees in medicine and surgery (1949), she practiced medicine with her brother Ferdinando Beretta at Merero (near Magenta) and studied pediatric medicine at the University of Milan (1950–52). After completing her education she devoted more time to providing medical attention to the indigent.

She married engineer Pietro Molla (Sept. 24, 1955) with whom she had three children: Pierluigi (b. September 1955), Mariolina (b. December 1957), and Laura (b. July 1959). In the second month of her fourth pregnancy, Gianna was diagnosed with a large uterine fibroma that required surgical removal. As a doctor she knew that her best chance for survival would mean killing the baby in her womb; nevertheless, she pleaded with the surgeon to save the life of her child regardless of the risk to her own life. Her daughter Gianna Emanuela was born, April 21, 1962. Gianna Beretta Molla, however, died one week later.

Her body lies in the cemetery of Mesero (near Magenta). Her process for beatification was opened in Rome, March 15, 1980. She was declared venerable in 1991. Her husband and three children attended Gianna's beatification by Pope John Paul II, April 24, 1994 (Year of the Family). Patroness of healthcare workers, mothers, professional women, the prolife movement, spouses, and unborn children.

Feast: April 28 (Archdiocese of Milan).

Bibliography: *Gianna Beretta Molla, Il tuo grande amore mi aiuterà a essere forte. Lettere al marito* (Cinisello Balsamo, Italy 1999). G. PELUCCHI, *Una vita per la vita* (Turin 1989). F. DA RIESE, *Per amore della vita. Gianna Beretta Molla medico e madre* (Rome 1994).

[K. I. RABENSTEIN]

MOLLOY, ALOYSIUS, SISTER

Educator and author; b. Sandusky, Ohio, June 14, 1880; d. Rochester, Minnestota, Sept. 27, 1954. Sister Aloysius was the daughter of Patrick John and Mary (Lambe) Molloy of Sandusky. After attending Ohio State University, Columbus, she went to Cornell University, Ithaca, New York, where in 1907 she became the first woman to receive a Cornell Ph.D. That same year, with Sister M. Leo Tracy, OSF, she founded the College of St. Teresa, Winona, Minnesota. In 1911 she became the first dean of the college, and after 1928 served as both dean and president until her retirement in 1946. Upon the death of her father in 1922, she sought admission to the Sisters of St. Francis of the Third Order Regular of the Congregation of Our Lady of Lourdes. When she completed her novitiate, she continued her activities on behalf of Catholic higher education.

For 25 years Sister Aloysius was a member of the Commission on Higher Education of the North Central Association and served on its committee to draft new standards for colleges and universities. She joined the National Catholic Educational Association in 1913, and became the first woman member (1923), and later the president, of the executive committee of its college and university department. She was the cofounder of the Confraternity of Catholic Colleges for Women (1918). Her memberships included Phi Beta Kappa, American Association of University Women, and the Medieval Academy of America. She was the author of *The Celtic Rite in Britain* (1910), *The Lay Apostolate* (1915), *Catholic Colleges for Women* (1918), *The Parochial Schools, School Organization, and Teacher Training* (1919), *A Catholic Educational Directory* (1919), *A Teresan Ideal in Service and System* (1928), and *Training the Nursing School Faculty* (1930). She collaborated on concordances to Wordsworth (1911), Horace (1914), and Bede's *Ecclesiastical History* (1907). Among the honors she received were the papal cross *Pro Ecclesia et Pontifice* (1918) and the Cross of Merit of the Constantinian Order of St. George (1923).

[M. E. COLLINS]

MOLLOY, FRANCIS

Irish Franciscan writer and teacher who compiled the first Gaelic grammar ever printed; b. Diocese of Meath, Ireland, *c.* 1606; d. France, 1677. Molloy (also known as O'Molloy) seems to have been a native of Fir Ceall in the present County Offaly. He joined the Franciscan Order at St. Isidore's College, Rome, on Aug. 2, 1632. He taught philosophy at Klosterneuberg (1642) and Mantua (1647), and theology at Graz (1645) and Rome (1652), where he became procurator for the Irish Franciscans. In 1671 Molloy's name was proposed for the bishopric of Kildare. Among those who recommended him was Maria Virginia Altieri, sister of Clement X. The Propaganda Printing Press at Rome published his two best-known works: a Gaelic catechism, *Lucerna fidelium, Lochrann na gcreidmheach* (1676), and a grammar, *Grammatica latino-hibernica* (1677). Neither is original, and the grammar is very defective. He also published a treatise on the Incarnation and some Latin poems.

Bibliography: F. MOLLOY, *Lucerna fidelium,* ed. P. Ó SÚILLEABHÁIN (Dublin 1962). B. EGAN, ''Notule sur les sources de la Grammatica latino-hibernica du Père O'Molloy,'' *Études celtiques* 7 (1957) 428–436.

[B. EGAN]

MOLLOY, THOMAS EDMUND

Archbishop, educator; b. Nashua, N.H., Sept. 4, 1884; d. Brooklyn, N.Y., Nov. 26, 1956. He was the son of John Molloy, a provision merchant, and the former Ellen Gaffney. He attended Nashua public and parochial schools and St. Anselm's College, Manchester, N.H. In Brooklyn, N.Y., he studied at St. Francis College and St. John's Seminary. In 1904 he entered the North American College in Rome and on Sept. 19, 1908, was ordained for the Diocese of Brooklyn. He was assigned as assistant at St. John's Chapel, Brooklyn, and when his pastor, George W. MUNDELEIN, was appointed auxiliary bishop, Molloy became his secretary. In 1915 Mundelein was named archbishop of Chicago and took his secretary with him. After ten months, Molloy returned to Brooklyn and became assistant at Queen of All Saints parish and spiritual director at Cathedral College of the Immaculate Conception. He also taught philosophy at St. Joseph's College for Women, Brooklyn, and later became its president. He was consecrated auxiliary to Bishop Charles E. McDonnell of Brooklyn on Oct. 3, 1920, and was elected administrator of the diocese upon the death of McDonnell in August of 1921. He was named bishop of Brooklyn by Pope Benedict XV on Nov. 21, 1921; Pope Pius XII gave him the personal title of archbishop on April 7, 1951. During his episcopate the Catholic population of the diocese doubled and the number of priests tripled. Ninety new parishes were established, 100 new parochial schools were opened, and the number of Catholic high schools more than doubled. Existing colleges expanded; the Seminary of the Immaculate Conception, Huntington, N.Y., and Molloy Catholic College for Women, Rockville Center, N.Y., were opened. The services of the hospitals and Catholic charities were reorganized and expanded, and diocesan insurance and purchasing agencies and a building commission were established. Molloy's eloquence and personality attracted the support of influential non-Catholics as well as Catholics.

Bibliography: J. K. SHARP, *History of the Diocese of Brooklyn, 1853–1953,* 2 v. (New York 1954).

[B. J. MCENTEGART]

MOLYNEUX, ROBERT

Missionary, first superior of the restored Society of Jesus in the U.S.; b. Lancashire, England, July 24, 1738; d. Washington, D.C., Dec. 9, 1808. Molyneux was descended from an old Catholic family, and in 1757 entered the Society of Jesus, where he had been preceded by his older brother William. During his training, Robert taught at the Jesuit school at Bruges, Belgium, where John CARROLL, the future American archbishop, was enrolled, and the two men became close friends.

In 1771 Molyneux was sent to the U.S., arriving in Philadelphia, Pennsylvania, on March 21. After the death of Rev. Robert Harding the following year, Molyneux became pastor of old St. Joseph's and of the larger church nearby, St. Mary's. He was an excellent preacher, and his funeral sermon on the death of his colleague, Rev. Ferdinand Farmer, in 1786 was one of the first Catholic items printed in the U.S. He was also instrumental in founding the first parochial school in Philadelphia before going to St. Francis Xavier Church, Bohemia Manor, Maryland (1788), where he replaced John Lewis, former vicar apostolic for Maryland and Pennsylvania. Two years later, Molyneux departed for Newtown, St. Mary's County, Maryland. During this period he also helped to establish Georgetown College, Washington, D.C., on a firm foundation, and became its second president in 1793. He held this office until 1796 and returned for another term as president in 1806.

Having learned that the Society of Jesus, which had been suppressed in other countries, still existed in White Russia (now Belarus), former Jesuits in the U.S. expended every effort to aggregate themselves to this body. Arrangements were finally completed, and Molyneux was appointed first superior by Carroll on June 21, 1805. Thaddeus Brzozowski, Jesuit general in Russia, confirmed the appointment on Feb. 22, 1806. The first novitiate of the restored Society was located at Georgetown, and on Aug. 18, 1806, Molyneux renewed the simple vows of the Society at St. Thomas Manor, Maryland, in the Church of St. Ignatius, whose cornerstone had been laid in 1798 by Carroll.

Bibliography: P. K. GUILDAY, *The Life and Times of John Carroll: Archbishop of Baltimore, 1735–1815,* 2 v. (New York 1927). H. FOLEY, *Records of the English Province of the Society of Jesus,* 7 v. (London 1877–83).

[J. M. DALEY]

MOMBAER, JOHN

Monastic reformer and ascetical writer, called also John Mauburnus or John of Brussels; b. Brussels, 1460; d. Paris, Dec. 29, 1501. He studied at the cathedral school in Utrecht and in 1480 entered the monastery of the Canons Regular at Mt. St. Agnes (near Zwolle), a house of the Congregation of Windesheim. Mombaer's spirituality was thus nourished by the DEVOTIO MODERNA of which Windesheim was the focal point. After serving as superior at Mt. St. Agnes, he was called to France in 1496 to inaugurate reform in various monasteries of his order there. In this work he enjoyed considerable success, but he also met with substantial opposition. In 1501 he was elected abbot of Livry. In his writings Mombaer gathered ancient truths of spirituality, but he tended to present the ascetical life as a rigid and mechanical system. He used a mnemonic verse form to describe his various steps, schemes, and divisions in the practice of prayer and the attainment of Christian virtue. His works include *Rosetum exercitiorum spiritualium et sacrarum meditationum, Exercitia utilissima pro horis solvendis et devota communione sacramentali,* and *Venatorium sanctorum Ordinis Canonicorum Regularium.*

Bibliography: P. DEBONGNIE, *Jean Mombaer de Bruxelles* (Louvain 1927). P. GROULT, *Les Mystiques des Pays-Bas et la littérature espagnole* (Louvain 1927). H. WATRIGANT, *Revue d'ascétique et de mystique* 3 (1922): 134–155; 4 (1923): 13–29; 8 (1927): 392–402. F. BRUNHÖLZL, *Lexikon für Theologie und Kirche,* 10 v. (Freiburg 1957–65) 7:184.

[J. C. WILLKE]

MOMBRITIUS, BONINUS

Italian humanist; b. Milan, *c.* 1424; d. before 1502. Of an impoverished noble family, he studied Greek and Latin at Ferrara and later taught the classics at Milan. The letters sent to him by Candide Decembrio (d. 1480) in 1460 testify that Boninus had acquired a reputation as a humanist. In 1470, along with other nobles living near the Parian gate at Milan, he swore fidelity to Galeazzo-Maria SFORZA. He never married and has been praised for his piety and lofty principles. From 1474 to 1481, despite straitened circumstances, he managed to produce a surprising number of literary works. In 1482 his professorial chair was given to George Merula (d. 1494), and a letter dated 1502 from Alexander Minuziano (d. 1522) speaks of Boninus as being dead.

Besides numerous poems his works include the following editions of various authors: *Rerum memorabilium collectanea* of Solon (6th century B.C.), published at Milan *c.* 1473 or Ferrara in 1474; the *Theogonia latinis hexametris reddita* of Hesiod (8th century B.C.), published at Ferrara in 1474; the *Summule seu logice instututiones* (Milan, Dec. 14, 1474); and the *Summule naturalium* (Milan, July 17, 1476) of the AUGUSTINIAN hermit Paul of Venice (d. 1429), as well as the *Historiae augustae scriptores sex* (Milan, Dec. 12, 1475). He published the *Chronicon* of EUSEBIUS OF CAESAREA at Milan between 1474 and 1476 and is also thought to have edited the works of JEROME, PROSPER OF AQUITAINE, and Matthew Palmieri (d. 1483) at this time. He is also credited with *Papiae vocabularium* (Milan, Dec. 12, 1476) and *Prosperi epigrammata* (Milan 1481). His *Sanctuarium seu vitae Sanctorum,* in two volumes dedicated to Francis Simoneta (d. 1480), the duke's secretary, must be antecedent to the secretary's imprisonment in 1479. Far from imitating the hagiographers of his time, who embellished and altered somewhat freely, Mombritius preferred to produce the texts as he found them, and their value is thus dependent on the source from which he drew. G. Eis tried without success to indicate these sources, and consequently much work remains to be done in this field. The monks of the Abbey of SOLESMES reedited the *Sanctuarium* (Paris 1910).

Boninus also published some of his own works, such as *De dominica passione libri V* (Milan *c.* 1474; new ed. Leipzig 1499), which contains six books of poems in hexameter verse dedicated to SIXTUS IV; and the *Thraenodiae in funere illustris quondam domini Galeazzo-Mariae Sfortiae* (Milan, March 2, 1504), one of his last publications and very probably posthumous. Several of his works remain in manuscript form, including *Momidos*, a poem in 12 books on the faults of women, written between 1468 and 1476 and dedicated to Bona Sforza (d. 1485), the wife of Galeazzo-Maria; *De varietate fortunae*, another poem in 10 books; a Latin translation of the Grammar of John Lascaris; and two epithalamia.

Bibliography: B. MOMBRITIUS, *Sanctuarium seu Vitae sanctorum,* ed. A. BRUNET, 2 v. (new ed. Paris 1910) 1:xiii–xxix, sources. *Biographie universelle,* ed. L. G. MICHAUD, 45 v. (Paris 1843–65). G. EIS, *Die Quellen für das Sanctuarium des Mailänder Humanisten B. M.* (Berlin 1933); J. CAMBELL, *Lexikon für Theologie und Kirche,* 10 v. (Freiburg 1957–65) 7:532.

[J. CAMBELL]

MONACO, THE CATHOLIC CHURCH IN

Monaco, the second smallest state in the world after the Holy See, is a tiny enclave located on the Mediterranean shore of France near the Italian border. Rugged hills characterize the terrain, while the climate is moderate, with mild winters and dry summers. With no natural resources and no agricultural means, the region relies on tourism and small industry for its wealth. Of its total population in 2000, only one fifth were actual citizens of the principality.

The area was controlled by the Phoenicians from the 10th to the 5th century B.C. and then by the Phoceans. Rome dominated the region during the Christian era until barbarians and then Saracens invaded it. After the Genoese were granted feudal rights over the area at the end of the 11th century, it came under the House of Grimaldi in 1297. The principality, annexed to France (1793–1814), was placed under the protection of Sardinia in 1815, and under that of France in 1861. Monaco has been a sovereign principality ruled by a hereditary constitutional monarch since 1911. The construction of a gambling casino in the 19th century established the region as a world-renown tourist destination. Prince Rainier III has been king of the region since 1949.

History. It is unknown when Christianity entered the region. While the relics of St. Devota are said to have been brought to Monaco shortly after her martyrdom in Corsica under Diocletian, the historicity of the martyrdom, and even of the existence, of this patron saint of Monaco, rests on sources from as late as the 11th century. Ecclesiastical jurisdiction rested with the bishop of Cimiez, whose see was united with that of Nice in the 5th century. The oldest reliable historical document (1075) mentions the chapel of St. Devota being restored to the Abbey of St. Pons of Cimiez. In 1078 the Church of St. Mary was constructed at the base of the Rock of Monaco and was given to the bishop of Nice. The Rock itself was owned and inhabited by the abbey and the commune of Peille until the end of the 11th century, when control passed to the Genoese who fortified it. The abbey erected the chapel of St. Martin. The parish of St. Nicholas, whose church edifice was started in 1252, was placed under the bishop of Nice. From 1206 the prior of St. Devota acted as spiritual and temporal lord, in the name of the Abbey of St. Pons, for most of the surrounding countryside and for all the present-day principality except the Rock.

In the 14th century the Grimaldi gained control of the Monegasque fortress and over the next two centuries obtained by purchase the possessions of the priory. This family, which became a princely one in the 17th century, chose the pastor and curates of St. Nicholas, but ecclesiastical powers came from the bishop of Nice. In 1868 the principality was separated from the diocese of Nice and made an abbey *nullius* immediately subject to the Holy See. The Cathedral of the Immaculate Conception was built at the end of the 19th century. Leo XIII's bull *Quemadmodum* (March 15, 1887), which regulated the juridical condition of the Church, created the diocese of Monaco immediately subject to the Holy See. According to this document, which was substantially an agreement between the pope and the prince of Monaco, Catholicism was officially named the state religion. The government subsidized the Church and, in exchange, enjoyed extensive privileges, including that of presenting a trio of names for episcopal appointments, nomination of all canons except one and of the pastors and curates of all churches except that of St. Charles in Monte Carlo, which is reserved permanently to the CLERKS REGULAR OF THE MOTHER OF GOD.

By 2000 Monaco had five churches tended by 13 diocesan and eight religious priests, in addition to its cathedral. Other religious included a brother and 22 sisters who maintained the principality's Catholic schools. Monaco enjoyed diplomatic relations with the Holy See and maintained a minister plenipotentiary in Rome. While Protestant faiths had increased their influence by the 1990s, the government discouraged proselytizing and access by some cults was also discouraged. The Mass was incorporated into most solemn government celebrations and other festivities.

Capital: Monaco.
Size: 195 sq. miles.
Population: 31,695 in 2000.
Languages: France, Italian, Monegasque.
Religions: 28,670 Catholics (90%), 400 Muslims (1%), 1,585 Protestants (5%), 1,040 other or without religious affiliation.
Archdiocese: Monaco, directly subject to the Holy See.

Bibliography: G. HANDLEY-TAYLOR, *Bibliography of Monaco* (London 1961). M. DE TRENQUALÉON, *Monaco, la Corse, et Ste. Devote* (Paris 1902). H. CHOBAUT, *Essai sur l'autonomie religieuse de la principauté de Monaco jusqu'à la création del'évêché* (Monaco 1914). BAUD, *L'Abbaye nullius de Monaco* (Monaco 1914). L. H. LABANDE, *Histoire de la principauté de Monaco* (Monaco 1934). *Bilan du Monde,* 2:617–618. *Annuario Pontificio.*

[L. BAUDOIN/EDS.]

MONAD

From the Greek, μονάς, a unit or individual entity, a monad is a simple, unextended, substantial, dynamic being of a psychical nature that reflects and represents the whole universe within itself, spontaneously and more or less consciously, without direct interaction with any other being. Monads are previously interrelated on the basis of a similarity of composition and a preestablished harmony.

The concept of the monad goes back to the later philosophy of PLATO, who sought an original unit (μονάς) from which to derive the many. In a similar manner, NEOPLATONISM postulated the One (ἕν), a self–subsistent principle from which numbers emanate, again to explain how many come to image the one. NICHOLAS OF CUSA accepted the explanation of the School of Chartres that God is the One, who reveals Himself in the world and is above all present there and to whom all beings are related as to an original source, so that He is ''all in all'' (*quodlibet in quolibet*). Giordano BRUNO also adopted the *monas*, but as psychically animated and spatially extended. He thought of it as an atom, a microcosm that encloses the macrocosm.

G. W. LEIBNIZ, for whom the monad became a principle of a dynamic PANPSYCHISM, began by seeking to improve upon the notion of substance as developed by R. DESCARTES. He thought of monads as metaphysical points, psychical centers of force, and the substantial elements of which the universe is composed. They are true atoms, but at the same time overlapping units, making up ''higher monads'' and thus the hierarchical forms and

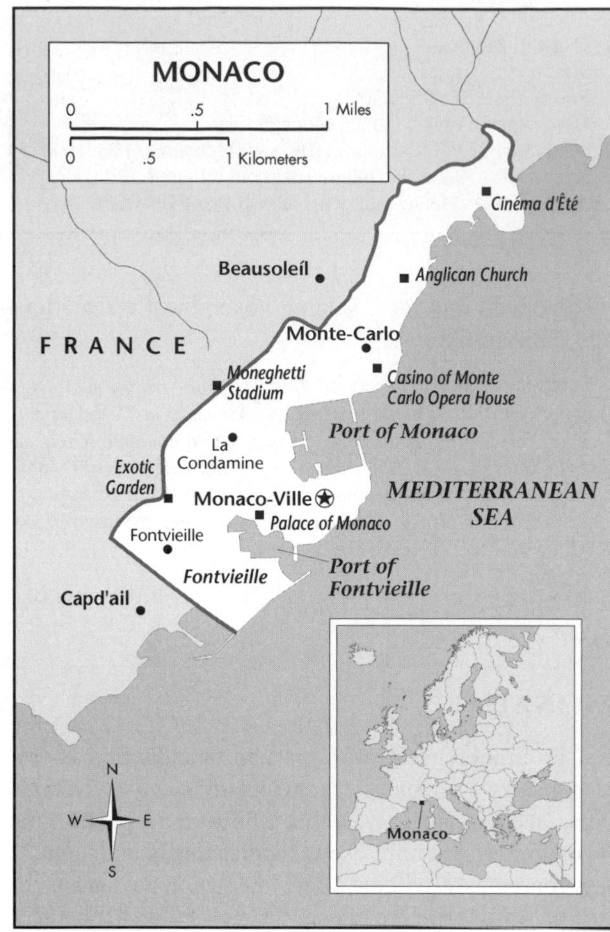

structures of all things, crowned by the divine monad as the source and mind of the universe. In themselves they are indestructible; according to Leibniz, they were created by God and can be destroyed only by Him. The Leibnizian monad is the recapitulation and ultimate extension of the formula of B. SPINOZA: *Deus sive natura sive substantia;* yet, because Leibniz relates all monads to the first monad (God), his theory is essentially different from that of Spinoza.

The entire monad theory is based upon the implications of the Parmenidean identification of thought and being. The result is that a similarity in image is identified with a similarity of being, an identification that is itself untenable. In Leibniz's time, those who discussed monads were H. More (1614–87), F. M. van Helmont (1614–99) and G. VICO; those later influenced by Leibniz in the compilation of an inductive metaphysics include R. H. LOTZE, H. Driesch, and E. Becher (1882–1929).

See Also: MONISM.

Bibliography: F. C. COPLESTON, *History of Philosophy* (Westminster, Md. 1946–) 4:295–319. A. PLEBE, *Enciclopedia filosofica,* 4 v. (Venice–Rome 1957) 3:669. R. EISLER, *Wöterbuch der philosophischen Begriffe,* 3 v. (4th ed. Berlin 1927–30) 2:169–172. W. CRAMER, *Die Monade: Das philosophische Problem vom Ursprung* (Stuttgart 1954).

[J. HIRSCHBERGER]

MONAGHAN, JOHN PATRICK

Leader in Catholic social thought and activity; b. Dunamore, Tyrone, Ireland, Feb. 12, 1890; d. New York City, June 26, 1961. He was the son of Patrick and Bridget (McCormick) Monaghan. He was educated at St. Francis College, Brooklyn, N.Y., and St. Joseph's Seminary, Yonkers, N.Y., before being ordained a priest for the New York Archdiocese.

Monaghan was an early promoter of Catholic social teachings. From the mid-1920s to his death, he, along with his close friends Msgr. John A. RYAN and Bp. Francis J. HAAS, was known as a ''labor priest.'' He was one of the most influential priests in New York, especially through his contribution to the establishment of Catholic Labor Schools (1935), the Association of Catholic Trade Unionists (ACTU, 1937), and the Labor Day Mass (1937). Belief in the ability of workingmen to solve their own problems, once they had the necessary knowledge, led Monaghan to initiate a program of worker education that gave to union and non-union members a basic course in labor economics, the social teaching of the Catholic Church, and parliamentary procedure. It was chiefly his work with the ACTU, however, that made him a latter-day Peter E. DIETZ. The ACTU was not a Catholic labor union; it was, rather, an organization under Catholic auspices for the training of rank and file union members, Catholic and non-Catholic alike, in their social rights and responsibilities. In this work Monaghan found himself opposed, first by management and financial interests, but later even by entrenched labor leaders, particularly the racketeers and communists.

In other areas as well, he was a forward-looking leader. Before the days of the Catholic Youth Organization, he operated one of the best youth programs in New York City. At the time when Dom Virgil MICHEL was preaching liturgical revival, Monaghan's parish on Staten Island was nationally known for its liturgical practices. He was a pioneer in the field of adult education; and at the parish school level he argued that the inclusion of religion in the curriculum never compensated for educational mediocrity. He was not, however, an ''organization man''; he can better be described as a personalist. His influence on priests and their pastoral ministry, attributable in part to his long career in New York's diocesan preparatory seminary, and his courageous attitude in the face of serious difficulties were the basis for his fame. The record of his thinking is best found in the *Labor Leader*, the organ of the ACTU, in which he wrote a column called "Don Capellano." His comments were pointed and pungent. "Atheistic Communism is not half the menace to Christianity that the blight of self-complacent Catholicity is." "Revolution is not something that comes with the roll of drums and the shouts of a mob. Revolution is a change of ideas." "Most of us are not spiritually equal to the life of creative beggary by which St. Francis forgot himself into immortality. If we tried it, we would probably turn out as quite ordinary tramps." Monaghan was raised to the rank of domestic prelate in 1957, and at the time of his death he was pastor of St. Michael's Church, New York City.

[G. A. KELLY]

MONARCHIA SICULA

Since the 16th century, a right claimed by the kings of Sicily to exercise supreme ecclesiastical authority in their kingdoms as representatives of the Holy See. This claim was based on a privilege conceded by Urban II to Count Roger I of Sicily and Calabria (July 5, 1098) in reward for his warfare against the Saracens. In his bull Urban assured the Count and his successors that no legate would be sent to Sicily against their wishes. For the execution of papal commands the kings of Sicily would act as vice legates of the pope. It was a question not of a jurisdiction by the princes of Sicily independent of the Holy See, but only of the privilege of the secular rulers to execute the precepts of the supreme Church authorities; the sovereign of Sicily was privileged, but also bound to carry out papal regulations in his land. Paschal II sought to restrict the privilege by a bull to Count Roger II (Oct. 1, 1117). Adrian IV reluctantly recognized it (1136), but Innocent III (1198–1216) repudiated it.

During the period of Absolutism, Spanish legalists rediscovered the document and asserted immense ecclesiastical privileges for their kings, who were the rightful successors of the Normans and Hohenstaufens of Sicily. In practice the acts of the Holy See had no strength without an executory letter of the viceroy. Ferdinand I (d. 1516) had claimed for himself jurisdiction in ecclesiastical matters, and Philip II sought in vain (1578) to have the Holy See confirm the *Monarchia Sicula*. Later Philip instituted a permanent tribunal named *Index Monarchiae Siculae* and forbade appeals from this tribunal to the Holy See. Rome could not overlook the danger to the independence of Sicilian bishops. The conflict was particularly violent during the reigns of Pius V (1566–72), Gregory XIII (1572–85), and Clement VIII (1592–1605). Philip condemned the 11th volume of the *Annales Ecclesiastici*

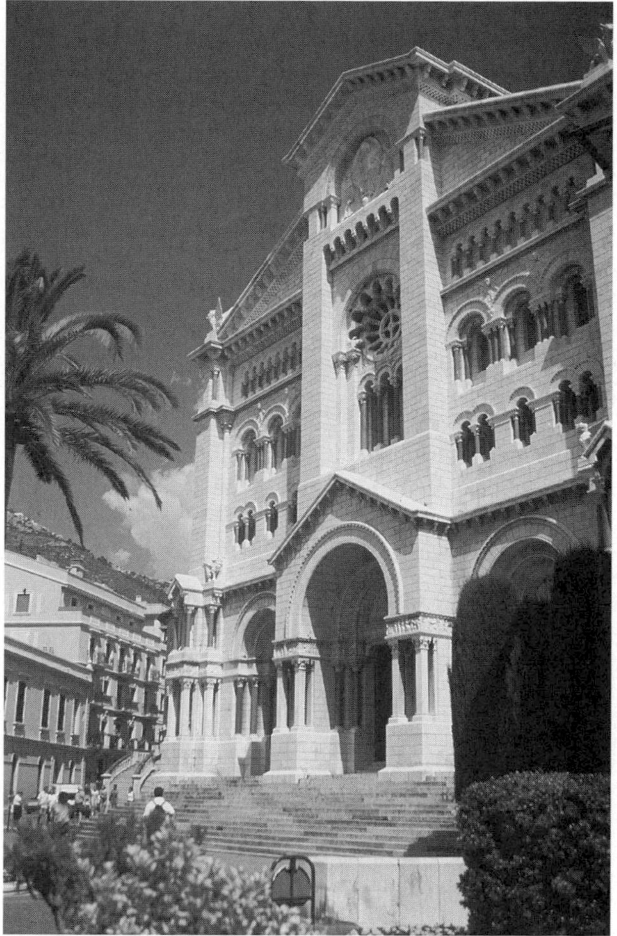

Monaco Cathedral. (©Gail Mooney/CORBIS)

in which Cardinal Caesar BARONIUS questioned both the genuineness of the bull of Urban II and the legal right of the *Monarchia Sicula.*

The contest became intense under Urban VIII (1623–44). The Sicilian bishops had protested so bitterly about the lack of independence due them by the Tridentine decrees that the pope adopted extreme measures proposed by a commission of cardinals. Accordingly, in 1687 Bl. Innocent XI instructed the nuncio of Spain to excommunicate the Neapolitan functionaries. The government of Madrid succeeded in having the sentence revoked. A heated battle broke out in 1717 when King Victor Amadeus II of Savoy ascended the throne of Sicily and the privilege of *Monarchia Sicula* was conceded to him. In a question of ecclesiastical immunity Clement XI suppressed the tribunal of that monarchy with the constitution *Romanus Pontifex* (Feb. 20, 1715). After he became King of Sicily and Holy Roman Emperor, Charles VI strove to obtain from Benedict XIII the revocation of the Clementine constitution; but in face of the resolute stand taken by the pope he settled for a bull that systematized ecclesiastical affairs on the island. The laborious treaties in which Cardinal Prospero Lambertini had an important role as papal adviser were concluded with the bull *Fideli* (Aug. 30, 1728), in which Benedict XIII, after withdrawing the decree of Clement XI, reserved to the Holy See the more important ecclesiastical affairs in Sicily but conceded to the sovereign for decisions of the last instance in certain ecclesiastical cases the institution of a supreme judge as a delegate of the Apostolic See. It was called "Tribunal of the Royal Monarchy and Apostolic Legation." Abuses again grew and in 1860 Garibaldi claimed the rights of papal legates and the privileges of *Monarchia Sicula.* Shortly after, Pius IX suppressed the apostolic legation by the bull *Suprema,* dated Jan. 28, 1864, but not published until Oct. 10, 1867. This bull was a complete and final revocation of the *Monarchia Sicula.* The Italian government quickly protested, but with the Law of Guarantees (art. 15) it renounced the privilege.

Bibliography: F. DE STEFANO, *Storia della Sicilia dal secolo XI al XIX* (Bari 1948), bibliog. E. PONTIERI, *Ricerche sulla crisi della monarchia siciliana nel secolo XIII* (Naples 1958). M. BRUNETTI, *Il dissidio diplomatico cesareo-papale alla vigilia della successione di Spagna* (Milan 1938). A. POSCH, *Lexikon für Theologie und Kirche* (Freiburg 1957–65) 7:534–535, bibliog.

[I. J. CALICCHIO]

MONARCHIANISM

A heresy that, through an exaggerated concept of the unity (*monarchia*: one origin, one rule) of God, denied the distinction of persons in the Divinity. In pre-Christian theodicy Monarchianism was related to the monotheistic principle asserted in Platonic and Stoic teaching which affected Hellenistic ideas of Divine Providence and political ethics. For PHILO JUDAEUS and the early Christian apologists, the idea of Monarchianism followed from the Old Testament insistence on the oneness of God.

As a heresy, Monarchianism originated in the 2d century partly in reaction to the Gnostic theories of intermediate aeons and partly as a reaction to subordinationist tendencies of orthodox teachers. In their presentation of Trinitarian and Christological doctrine they ascribed to the Son functions such as creation and conservation that made him God in a secondary sense.

Two types of Monarchians are met with in the early Church. The adoptionists or dynamists represented by Theodotus the Banker and his disciple Theodotus of Byzantium, founder of the sect, and by Artemon with his disciple, Paul of Samosata, who began with the Christological error that Jesus Christ was not always God, but that at His baptism a power, or *dunamis*, of the Father descended on Him by virtue of which He wrought wonders (*dunameis*). Theodotus called this power of God Christ; but some of his followers thought that He became God only after the Resurrection. The sect, called Theodotians, was never numerous; their history has been preserved by Hippolytus.

For the Modalists and Sabellians, the Father, Son, and Holy Spirit are not names of truly distinct persons, but rather modes, energies, aspects, or phases of the one divine person. God the Father appeared on earth as the Son, and this logically involved the fact that the Father died; hence the Modalists were known in the West as Patripassians. In the East they were called Sabellians after a Roman cleric Sabellius, who developed the doctrine of Noëtus of Smyrna. He became the chief spokesman of the sect in Rome, and was excommunicated under Pope Callistus (*c.* 220). The doctrine was combated by Dionysius of Alexandria, causing an exchange of letters between the bishop of Alexandria and Pope DIONYSIUS whose decisions in the matter are reported by St. Athanasius in his Decrees of the Council of Nicaea, 26 (*Patrologia Graeca*, 25:461–465).

Although the early Monarchians professed belief in one true God and in Jesus Christ, wholly and truly God, and thus developed the logos-teaching of the apologists, nevertheless, in the course of controversy, particularly with Tertullian, Hippolytus, and Novatian, their denial of the real distinction of persons in the one God was gradually unmasked. Praxeas, whom Tertullian assailed, visited Rome and Carthage (*c.* 206–208). The heresy is found in the 4th century developed by Marcellus of Ancyra (d. *c.* 374) and propagated by Photinus of Sirmium (*c.* 344). They denied the real distinction of persons and said that the Father is given three names corresponding to three activities.

Michael SERVETUS of Spain revived this doctrine in the 16th century, and it became a principal teaching of the Socinians (*see* SOCINIANISM). In modern philosophy a form of Monarchianism is applied to the Trinity in, for example, KANT's teaching that belief in God is directed toward a holy ruler, a wise legislator, and a just judge. According to G. W. F. HEGEL, the Idea-Being (or Ens) evolved as the Idea-Ens in itself, which is God, the Idea-Ens evolving outside itself (*ad extra evoluta*), which is nature, and the Idea-Ens, conscious of itself, which is man.

Bibliography: G. BARDY, *Dictionnaire de théologie catholique*, ed. A. VACANT et al. (Paris 1903–50) 10.2:2193–2209. E. EVANS, ed. and tr., *Tertulliani adversus Praxean* (London 1948) 6–31. T. VERHOEVEN, *Vigiliae christianae* 5 (Amsterdam 1951) 43–48. C. HUBER, *Lexikon für Theologie und Kirche*, ed. J. HOFER and K. RAHNER (Freiburg 1957–65) 7:533–534. K. WÖLFL, *Das Heilswirken Gottes durch den Sohn nach Tertullian* (Rome 1960).

[P. J. HAMELL]

MONARCHICAL EPISCOPATE

The term monarchical describes the form of Church governance described by St. Ignatius of Antioch, wherein the bishop is seen as high priest, teacher, and shepherd of the faithful. It is distinguished from a collegiate episcopate in which the direction of local communities, according to some historians and theologians, did not rest with any one man during the first post-apostolic generations. They theorize that, in some churches at least, a number of elders or functionaries, grouped more or less closely in a college, exercised leadership. For them the monarchical episcopate is the result of a natural evolution that owed much to the doctrinal and disciplinary differences that plagued the communities, threatening their unity, and pointing the need for concentration of leadership. Many of them fix the term of such transition at the beginning of the third century.

See Also: BISHOP (IN THE CHURCH);APOSTOLIC SUCCESSION.

Bibliography: J. COLSON, *L'Évêque dans les communautés primitives* (Paris 1951); *Les Fonctions ecclésiales aux deux premiers siècles* (Bruges 1956); *L'Épiscopat catholique: Collégialité et primauté dans les trois premiers siècles de l'église* (Unam Sanctam 43; Paris 1963). R. E. BROWN, *Priest and Bishop. Biblical Reflections* (Mahwah N.J. 1970). J. DELORME, *Le ministère et les ministères selon le N.T.* (Paris 1974). A. LEMAIRE, *Ministry in the Church* (London 1977). H. CHADWICK et al., *The Role of the Bishop in the Ancient Society* (Berkeley Cal. 1980). E. G. JAY, ''From Presbyter-Bishops to Bishops and Presbyters: Christian Ministry in the Second Century,'' *Second Century* 1 (1981) 125–62. U. BETTI, *La dottrina sull'episcopato del Concilio Vaticano II* (Rome 1984). A. CUNNINGHAM, *The Bishop in the Church* (Wilmington De. 1985). F. A. SULLIVAN, *From Apostles to Bishops* (New York/Mahwah N.J. 2001).

[S. E. DONLON/EDS.]

MONARCHY

A form of STATE in which sovereign AUTHORITY is vested in a single person, whether he be called prince, king, or emperor. Monarchy is absolute when there is no limitation on the monarch's power, limited when there is such restraint.

Classical views. Theoretically, the ideal form of GOVERNMENT has been held to be the centralization of all political power in the one best man. In ancient times Homer and the Pythagoreans advocated a monarchical form of THEOCRACY. PLATO (427–347 B.C.) termed the rule of philosopher-kings either monarchy or ARISTOCRACY, since ''we count royal and aristocratic as one'' (*Republic* 587d). Among the three types of good government (monarchy, aristocracy, and polity) distinguished by ARISTOTLE (384–322 B.C.), monarchy was held to be the ideal. The deep sympathy for monarchy so often expressed in the *Politics* is to be understood in the light of Aristotle's relations with the rising Macedonian monarchy. He also maintained that the form of government that is best for any people is that best adapted to obtain for them the end of civil power. Although regarding monarchy as the ideal, he thought the best attainable form to be an aristocracy, not of wealth or of birth, but of intellect—a true aristocracy, a government of the best (*Politics* 1293b). According to CICERO (106–43 B.C.), men organized states to attain their common good. He preferred a form of government embracing the best features of the pure forms of monarchy, aristocracy, and DEMOCRACY. He believed that the Roman government embodied this ''mixed'' form, which he thought superior to others because it was better balanced and more stable (*De Re Publica,* 1.65–).

Medieval theory. In the Middle Ages, the king was considered the lawful head of civil society. St. THOMAS AQUINAS (1225–75) taught that all government is derived from God since He alone from His very nature has dominion over men. Such dominion is not intrinsic or innate in any man, not even in a king; it is derived. The power to govern comes from God either immediately or mediately; it is not an inborn natural right of a few. St. Thomas explained that the will of the people counteracts tendencies to TYRANNY. Although he believed monarchy to be ''most in accord with nature,'' he defined as acceptable any form that performs well the functions of the state. In *De Regimine Principum* he was emphatic on the moral limitations placed upon the royal power. Indeed, he even called for some restraint upon the king and approached Thomas Jefferson's later advocacy of revolution against tyranny. There was no basis in medieval political thought for such doctrines as the DIVINE RIGHT OF KINGS. Every expression by Aquinas and his predecessors pointed not to the divine right, but to the sacred responsibility of kings. The modern concept of the limitation of governmental power can be drawn easily from Thomistic principles.

Dante (1265–1321), in *De Monarchia,* cherished the ideal of a world state over which one sole civil ruler would preside, just as the pope was the supreme head of the Church. In fact as well as theory, however, medieval royal power was far from absolute. The king's authority was kept in check by the communes, the guilds, and the Church. These elements served to counteract royal ABSOLUTISM, preventing it from trespassing on rights founded on NATURAL LAW and confirmed by custom. Politics was considered inseparable from ethics and religion.

Beginning of modern political theory. Niccolò MACHIAVELLI (1469–1527) revived the pagan concept of royal absolutism. He was the first to identify the state with the prince and to divorce politics from Christian ethics. Thomas HOBBES (1588–1670) thought the best state was one in which the power was concentrated in one absolute monarch possessing all rights and no duties. In general, the late 18th-century European monarchies had become enlightened despotisms. Since that time absolute monarchy has disappeared from the civilized world, and the limited type is in decline. However, natural-law ethics does not imply any particular form of government, although it opposes tyrannies of all types. In the words of Leo XIII, ''There is no reason why the Church should not approve of the chief power being held by one man or more, provided only it be just, and that it tend to the common advantage'' [*Diuturnum illud,* in *Acta Sanctae Sedis* 14 (1881) 5].

Bibliography: J. L. BRIERLY et al., *Law and Government* (London 1948). G. E. G. CATLIN, *The Story of Political Philosophers* (New York 1939). W. LIPPMANN, *Essays in the Public Philosophy* (Boston, Mass. 1955). R. M. MACIVER, *The Modern State* (New York 1926). J. C. MURRAY, *We Hold These Truths* (New York 1960).

[A. J. OSGNIACH]

MONASTERY

In early usage, in its strict etymological sense (from μόνος or μοναχός), the term monastery denoted a hermit's cell or a group of cells surrounded by a protective wall. Later it applied to the dwelling of monks (*coenobium*) and clerics living a common life (*monasterium canonicorum*). In the West the word refers specifically to the houses of BENEDICTINES and of other orders derivatively using the BENEDICTINE RULE. St. BENEDICT employed the word 72 times in the Rule to mean either the physical structure of the abbey or the community living in such foundations. The houses of CANONS REGULAR OF ST. AUGUSTINE also are called monasteries.

Despite the many inaccuracies of popular terminology in matters pertaining to the religious life, some elements of MONASTICISM have always remained reasonably constant. Only with reference to them can one speak properly of a monastery as the dwelling place of monks. The following seem to be the most basic distinguishing marks of the monastery in this restricted acceptance: (1) well-defined separation from the world and permanent attachment to the place of the monk's profession through the vow of stability; this is monasticism's principal identifying feature; (2) an almost complete autonomy of internal government of the individual house, despite legal provisions for membership in monastic congregations (1917 *Codex iuris canonici* c.488n1) and, since 1893, in the Confederation of the Benedictine Order under the abbot primate; (3) commitment to one of the classical rules of monasticism, today almost exclusively the Benedictine Rule for the West and those of St. BASIL for the East; and (4) concentration on work identified with the region, since a monastery's influence is usually wielded locally, in distinction to that of centrally controlled undertakings which call for large numbers of specially trained personnel.

The generic term ''monastery'' usually needs to be qualified for accuracy. Canon Law employs various descriptive phrases, such as independent (*sui-juris*) monasteries (1917 *Codex iuris canonici* cc.488n8; 494.1; elsewhere consistently), monasteries of nuns (c.497.1), exempt monastery (c.645), and similar terms. Popular designations are derived either from the superior's rank (abbey, priory) or from the nature of the work undertaken by the community (sanctuary, shrine, mission, house of studies). Both practices tend to reserve the use of the colorless ''monastery'' to legal terminology and scholarly treaties.

Simplicity marks the monastery's government. This was the desire of the great founders in their earliest establishments; it remains essentially unchanged today, in vivid contrast to the complexity and legal structure of the centralized orders. The impracticality of the hermits' vocation, and especially its moral deficiency in that it had offered no opportunity for the practice of charity (Basil, Long Rules, 7), were soon realized. The cenobitic ideal made capital of mutual cooperation and showed the great wisdom of centering everything about ''the aid of many brethren'' (Benedict, *Rule of Monks* 1, *passim*) working under the common father, the ABBOT, who is believed to hold the place of Christ in their midst.

The monastery's basic similarity with the human family, united in Christ, especially through the father, did not, surprisingly, command immediate attention. St. Basil emphasized it; St. Benedict, composing his Rule a century and a half later, with less copious, but far more judicious employment of scriptural sources, especially of the OT, was the first to make it his central theme. It was for the abbot, the spiritual father and Christ's representative living with his men, that Benedict's Rule was primarily written. Through him they became brothers to one another; under his spiritual formation and leadership they worked out the goals that constituted their ideal.

The monastery for which Benedict legislated was a group of men intent on seeking God (ch. 58); they were united in virtuous zeal (ch. 72) in serving Christ; they did so under ''the guidance of the Gospel'' (prologue), the precepts of the Rule, and the abbot's adaptation of the Rule's principles to existing conditions. The abbot's

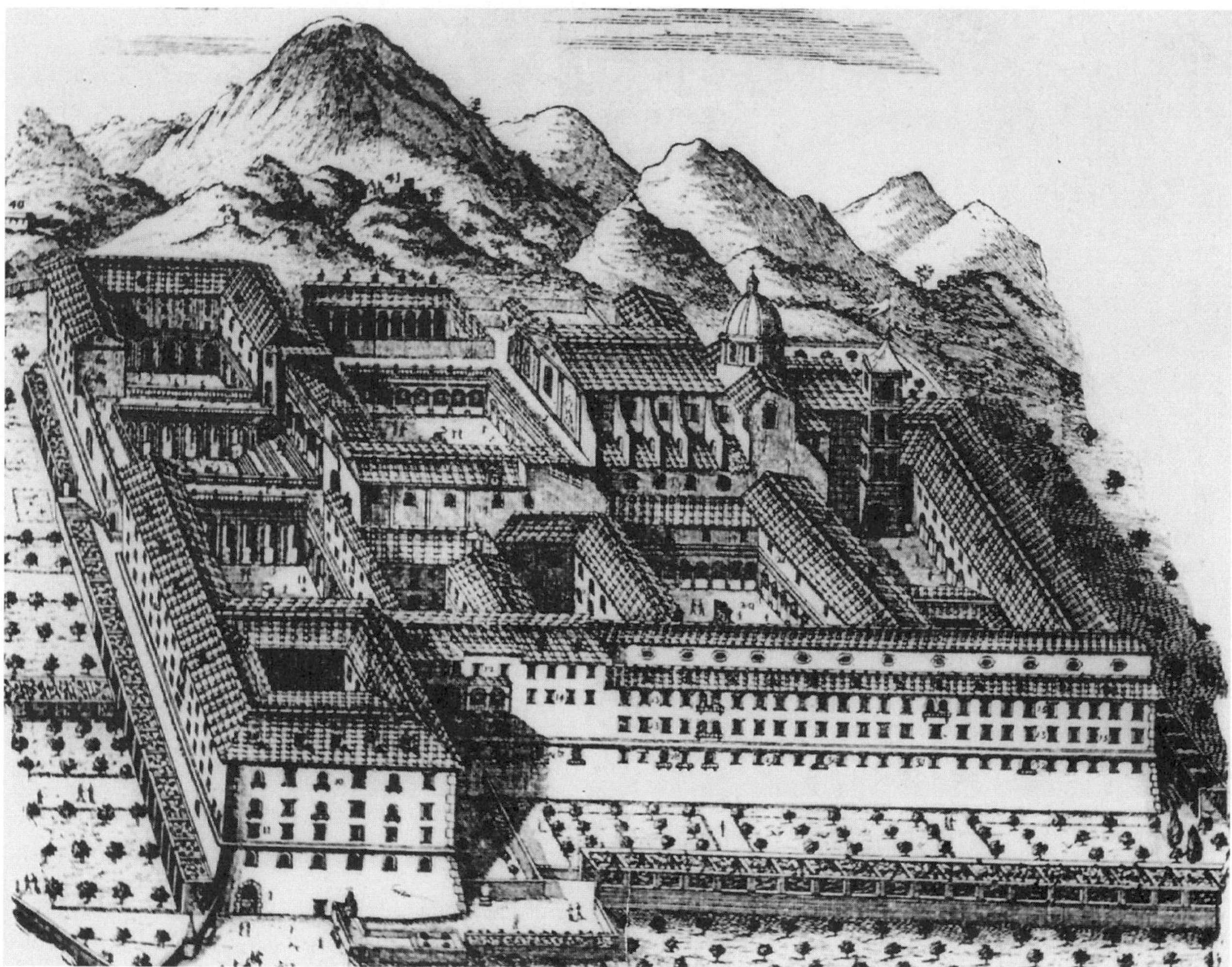

Illustration of the monastery of Monte Cassino, 1751. (©CORBIS)

powers are today regulated largely by decrees of monastic congregations and more general pronouncements of the Church.

Ideally the group in a Benedictine monastery is to be large enough to facilitate corporate practice of monastic virtues on a generous scale (charity, obedience, humility, considerateness for others, serving Christ in them), yet small enough to preserve the character of a true family. Living under one roof, inspired and drawn forward by a man whom they elect for life as their abbot, the monks pray together (ch. 8–18, and elsewhere), work together (ch. 48), eat at a common table, serving one another in charity (ch. 35), vie with one another in the spirit of obedience (ch. 71–72), and assist one another in all things. Many famous abbeys of the past were modest in size; it was exceptional for membership to exceed 100; few today are larger.

So attached was Benedict to simplicity and unity of government in his monastery that his Rule provides for a sole superior. Reluctantly he conceded (ch. 65) the probable need of a prior, who is actually not a superior, but performs assigned tasks for the community at large and represents the abbot in his absence. By stated preference Benedict would rather have conducted the affairs of the community through deans, seniors who had charge of 10 monks each (ch. 21), in order to rule out all occasion of pride and vainglory. Today's share in the active apostolate requires the appointment of many officials with responsibilities in limited areas, but there remains the one superior, the abbot.

All monasteries are solemnly blessed in honor of a sacred mystery or a heavenly patron, particularly the Blessed Virgin, one of the Apostles, or saintly heroes of monastic life. Such is the nature of stability, however, that even some of the most famous houses in history and those currently thriving are almost invariably referred to by the name of the town where they are located rather than by their official name. Rarely will one know the pa-

Benedictine monk studies in monastery library. (©Stephanie Maze/CORBIS)

trons of Ligugé, Monte Cassino, Metten, Cluny, or, today, Maredsous, Clérvaux, or Chevtogne. Locally they are the "abbey," the "priory," or the "monastery." Even in official documents they are referred to by the name of the local town.

Bibliography: ST. BASIL, "Long Rules," in *Ascetical Works,* tr. M. M. WAGNER (New York 1950) 223–337. *S. Benedicti regula monasteriorum,* ed. E. C. BUTLER (3d ed. Freiburg 1935). *The Rule of Saint Benedict,* ed. and tr. J. MCCANN (Westminster, Md. 1952). W. K. L. CLAKE, *St. Basil the Great: A Study in Monasticism* (Cambridge, Eng. 1913). J. C. DICKINSON, *Monastic Life in Medieval England* (New York 1962). É. JOMBARTE, *Dictionnaire de droit canonique* ed. R. NAZ, 7 v. (Paris 1935–37) 6:928–933. H. LECLERCQ, *Dictionnaire d'archéologie chrétienne et de liturgie*, ed. F. CARROLL, H. LECLERQ, and H. I. MARROU, 15 v. (Paris 1907–53). 2.2:3047–3248; *ibid* 11.2:1774–1947. P. SCHMITZ, *Lexikon für Theologie und Kirche*, ed. J. HOFER and K. RAHNER, 10 v. (2d new ed. Freiburg 1957–65) 6:344–346. C. BUTLER, *Benedictine Monachism* (London 1927). D. KNOWLES, *The Monastic Order in England, 943–1216* (2d ed. Cambridge, Eng. 1962) 3–30.

[B. A. SAUSE]

MONASTERY, DOUBLE

The name given to monastic foundations or cloisters joined together under a common superior and bound by juridical and economic bonds. When the two monasteries were occupied by the same sex, as at Wearmouth-Yarrow or Stavelot-Malmédy, or the convent of women was enclosed in its own cloister, this type of foundation presented no problem. It was normal for nuns to put themselves under the direction of noted ascetical directors and to employ male religious in the care of their spiritual and temporal necessities. The superior of a men's monastery, by virtue of his priesthood and his experience, intervened in the direction of the nuns; and at times the abbess who might be of a superior social condition (a princess) controlled the temporal possessions of the convent and governed its inhabitants. The enthusiasm that accompanied the origins of monasticism tended to promote the condition of women in accordance with Gal 3.28, which suppressed the inequality of the sexes; and double monasteries took rise in this perspective. But dangers appeared when the first fervor had to be followed by juridical regulations.

St. PACHOMIUS governed a community founded by his sister in which the brothers took care of the material needs of the convent, but were forbidden to take meals there; and relations with the nuns were prudently regulated. The abundant Christian literature of the 4th century speaks frequently of the reserve with which virgins should deal with the male ascetics, in a fashion that does not supply for the absence of law; and the examples of double monasteries under St. Paula and St. Jerome at Bethlehem and of Rufinus of Aquileia and Melania the Elder at Jerusalem testify to a sane liberty similar to that encountered in Syria with the so-called ''Sons of the Covenant'' of the monastic settlements. The Basilian confraternities in Cappadocia, organized by St. BASIL on family estates, where mother and daughter set an example for their households, achieved a true unity in which children of both sexes were brought up together; but severe rules regulated communications between the grownups. St. GREGORY OF NAZIANZUS speaks of this type of institution without criticizing it (*Epist.* 238), but St. Basil had to protect against him a certain deacon who had induced a group of young women to join him in an ascetical way of life (*Epist.* 169–171).

JUSTINIAN I in 529 demanded a rigorous separation of the sexes in monasteries (Cod. Just. 1.3.43), an order that he repeated with insistence in 539 and 546, using the term double monastery in this latter instance. The Council of Nicaea II (787) repeated this admonition and ordered the toleration of such institutions already in existence, but forbade new foundations. The patriarchs took similar measures in 810 and 1383, but without much success. Despite abuses in particular cases, the system was sustainable.

In the West in the 7th and 8th centuries there were numerous double monasteries: in Gaul at Faremoutiers, Jouarre, Remiremont, Chelles, Nivelle, and in Spain, England, and Ireland. In origin, however, this type of monastic foundation seems to have been spontaneous. The decline set in with the 9th century, but a new outbreak accompanied the spiritual movement of HIRSAU and of PRÉMONTRÉ in the 11th and 12th centuries and culminated in the Order of FONTEVRAULT. Although BURCHARD OF WORMS and Pope PASCHAL II echoed the Greek law, CALLISTUS II approved the institution with the proviso that proper precautions should be observed. Opposition came from the monastic milieu itself, and only the BRIDGETTINES maintained this type of organization until the end of the Middle Ages. By regulating the enclosure of the cloister, the Council of Trent put an end to the problem; it gave some difficulty when Latin regulations were applied to the Oriental churches united with Rome, particularly at the Maronite Synod of 1736.

Bibliography: S. HILPISCH, *Die Doppelklöster* (Münster 1928). J. DUMORTIER, ''L'Auteur présumé du *Corpus Asceticum* de S. Jean Chrysostome,'' *Journal of Theological Studies* NS 6 (1955) 99–102. D. KNOWLES, *The Monastic Order in England, 943–1216,* 204–207 (2nd ed. Cambridge, Eng. 1962). P. SCHMITZ, *Histoire de l'Ordre de Saint-Benoît,* 7 v. (Maredsous, Bel. 1942–56). É. JOMBART, *Dictionnaire de droit canonique,* ed. R. NAZ 3:972–974 (Paris 1935–65). P. DIB, *Dictionnaire de théologie catholique,* 10.1:81–83 (Paris 1903–50).

[J. GRIBOMONT]

MONASTIC SCHOOLS

Medieval schools conducted by monks and nuns within the confines of a monastery for the religious training and general education (1) of *oblati,* or youth who intended to enter the monastic or clerical life and lived at the monastery and (2) of *externi,* or youth who were preparing for public life and lived at home. Monastic schools are not to be confounded with monastic centers of study and culture for monks and nuns.

Origins and Aims. Although monasteries were originally intended exclusively as centers of asceticism, as early as the 4th century in both East and West they accepted even young children as pupils. Since according to the norms of monastic asceticism monks and nuns as a group were expected to read the Bible, its commentaries, and the lives of the saints, they felt obliged to teach the children to read these texts, and these alone. In the East, first St. PACHOMIUS (*c.* 320–340), then St. BASIL (*c.* 330–379) and St. JOHN CHRYSOSTOM (*c.* 347–407) adopted this custom but these schools wielded little influence. The same system prevailed in the West at the monastery of St. Martin at Ligugé (founded in France in 361), St. Honorat of Lérins, and in some African abbeys in the 5th century (*see* LIGUGÉ, ABBEY OF; LÉRINS, ABBEY OF). Here, however, since Latin was no longer spoken, the need arose to teach it to the children as a foreign language. This led the monks to use profane authors, which they did very sparingly, since these literary studies were considered merely as an introduction to Sacred Scripture. In fact, education of children was not the original monastic aim, and until the 6th century, in keeping with St. Benedict's Rule, monasteries continued to be almost solely schools where one was instructed in ''the Lord's service.''

Organization. The number and age of the children varied, with the number usually small and some of the children very young, about six or seven years old. The majority, but not always all the children, were destined to become monks, either of their own desire or more often because their parents ''offered'' them to God in the monastery. Courses of study consisted primarily of learning to read Latin and secondarily of writing, chant, arithmetic, and learning how to read time on the sundial. The principal text was the Psalter.

From the 8th century on, mention is made of the seven liberal arts, divided into the *trivium* and *quadrivi-*

um. These terms, however, indicate little more than literary themes, which had scarcely any influence on the programs of study. Actually, there was no precise program. Pupils simply passed from simple reading exercises to exercises in more difficult texts. Reading aloud was common practice, for it helped fix texts and ideas in the mind. Dialogue between pupils and master or among the pupils was also used. Sometimes the child was asked to recite before the master what he had learned. The master (*magister or scholasticus*) determined the method to be used. He had full power over the child, whom he kept under constant surveillance, held to a very strict discipline, and, particularly with adolescents, subjected to corporal punishments that at times were very severe. There were some instances, though very rare, of tenderness toward the children, who, if they were *oblati,* became monks or nuns regardless of age as soon as they had learned to read. They then left the school and devoted their time in the community to *lectio divina,* to meditation, and sometimes to study. The monks' books, which were different from those used in school, consisted mainly of texts by profane authors sometimes accompanied by a gloss.

This first type of school, called claustral, was destined primarily for future monks and situated within the monasteries. A second type, called nonclaustral, was intended for nonresident children and situated outside the enclosure. In more than one place, however, the latter were considered incompatible with monastic observance and consequently either suppressed or entrusted to seculars. It was loyalty to this typically monastic ideal that caused the Cistercians to refuse to operate schools. They were introduced into their order only much later and contrary to the ideals of the original foundation.

Significance. Although monastic schools in time showed some decline, their twofold organization continued virtually the same everywhere throughout the Middle Ages. The Carolingian renaissance in the 9th century, however, brought about a revival of monastic education and the rise of many schools that, despite their small enrollment, exercised a strong influence over an extended period of time. Among the most renowned were Clonmacnoise, Kildare, Clonard, Kells, Armagh, Bangor, in Ireland; Dumio, Braga, Liebana, St. Aemilian, in the Iberian peninsula; Bobbio, Monte Cassino, Farfa, Nonantola, in Italy; Wearmouth, Jarrow, York, Canterbury, Lindisfarne, Whitby, Malinesbury, in England; Fulda, Sankt Gall, Reichenau, in Germany; Gorze, Lobbes, St. Hubert, St. Amand, Liège, in Lotharingia; and Luxeuil, Aniane, Tours, Corbie, St. Wandrille, Fleury, Cluny, in France. Although the School of Bec in France was a "school of the Lord's service" and not strictly speaking an institution of learning, Lanfranc, prior at Bec and later archbishop, and Anselm, Lanfranc's student, sent out scholars whose influence was widely felt (*see* ANSELM OF CANTERBURY, ST.).

Some historians have attributed to the monastic schools of the Middle Ages too high a level of instruction. In some towns, it is true, especially in the 11th and 12th centuries, there were some schools, generally cathedral or episcopal, where higher studies were offered and where even some monks were educated. Two facts, however, must be noted. (1) Compared with episcopal, cathedral, or lay schools, monastic schools were more universal and continuous. This was particularly true until the end of the 8th century. (2) While the town schools gave rise to scholastic education, which was oriented toward speculation or pastoral action, monasteries favored humanism, the herald of a literary tradition more compatible with contemplative prayer and a liturgical cult.

Bibliography: H. I. MARROU, *A History of Education in Antiquity,* tr. G. LAMB (New York 1956). P. RICHÉ, *Éducation et culture dans l'Occident barbare, VI e– VIII e siècles* (Paris 1962). É. LESNE, *Les Écoles de la fin du VIIIe siècle à la fin du XIIe* (1940), v.5 of *Histoire de la propriété ecclésiastique en France* (Lille 1910–43). J. LECLERCQ, *The Love of Learning and the Desire for God,* tr. C. MISRAHI (New York 1961). D. KNOWLES, *The Monastic Order in England, 943–1216* (2d ed. Cambridge, Eng. 1962).

[J. LECLERCQ]

MONASTICISM

An institution of ancient and medieval origins, establishing and regulating the ascetical and social conditions of the manner of religious life lived in common or in contemplative solitude.

1. Early Christian (to 600)

In describing the rise and development of Christian monasticism, this article deals with its background—the work of St. Anthony and the origin of Anchoritism, the contribution of Pachomius and the rise of Cenobitism; the life of the Desert Fathers—developments in Syria, Palestine, and Cappadocia; Constantinople; and the West.

Background. The primitive Church as a minority group and a community bearing witness to faith in Christ felt so strong in its creative newness and eschatological hope that, while being in the world, it was, on the whole, aware of not being of the world, of being a community of "saints." VIRGINITY was held in high regard, and among the poor classes the sharing of goods was relatively easy. Normally the tendency toward encratism did not harden into doctrinal opposition to marriage or the social order of the day. Its source was the gospel; it was not linked with a Manichaean dualism or scorn for created things.

Contacts with Gnostic currents, with the philosophical attitudes of Stoicism and Platonism, or again with the Eastern religions were inevitable and fruitful, though dangerous at times; clearly they did not go to the root of the movement, as Weingarten's outmoded theories claimed regarding the pagan recluses of the Serapeum. The foreshadowings of Christian institutions are to be sought in Israel; the desert spirituality, expressed in the lives of the prophets ELIJAH, Hosea, and JOHN THE BAPTIST, was certainly in line with monasticism and had a considerable literary influence on its development. The ESSENES of the QUMRAN COMMUNITY near the Dead Sea and of Alexandria, of whom the description by PHILO JUDAEUS is in part interpretative, bear a resemblance to the monks of the later monasteries that flourished in the same territory. However, there is no evidence of direct historical continuity between the two groups. It is probable that the Judeo-Christian communities, profoundly stamped with the tradition of the ''poor of Yahweh'' (*see* EBIONITES), transmitted their sentiment to the churches of Syria and perhaps to those of Egypt. It is not characteristic of the churches in the Greek stream of culture that are relatively better known.

Early in the 3d century, ORIGEN gave expression to an ascetic and mystical ideal that contained elements of GNOSTICISM and of Greek philosophy and was destined to have extensive influence on the Church's future. During the years when Christianity was making peace with the Empire, receiving the masses into its communion, but lowering its moral level, a powerful ascetical movement began to manifest itself with the constitution of a purely evangelical society on the fringes of the populated world. Occasionally this movement opposed itself to the hierarchy and gave rise to unorthodox sects. More often, however, ecclesiastical authority was respected by its saintly founders, and the movement became an institution within the Church. Initially it took the form of anchoritic societies; later, it developed into cenobitism and the founding of the lauras. Marxist interpretation describes this evolution as a seizure by the hierarchy of a popular revolutionary force; and this observation is not entirely false. Like primitive Christianity itself, monastic asceticism is a historical movement that transformed the ancient world and that can be said to have created the medieval society. Monasticism provided a spiritual aristocracy, scions of a new elite, that preserved a notable part of the ancient culture. Once in being, however, the monastic institutions were not always faithful to their original inspiration.

St. Anthony and Anchoritism. A son of Coptic peasants became the father of the monks; he proved to be the model, not the founder, of monasticism. According to his biographer, ANTHONY OF EGYPT (d. 356) retired to a retreat outside his native village at 20 years of age and died there when he was 105. However, the chronology of the period seems confused, and the beginning of the Egyptian anchorite movement should be dated closer to the year 300 than to 270. The first documentary (papyrus) evidence is supplied by the entourage of Meletius of Alexandria, a rival of Athanasius. It dates from *c.* 335. The *Life of Anthony* written by Athanasius of Alexandria (*c.* 357) stresses Anthony's austerity, the evangelical inspiration of his renunciation, his fight against the demons, and his zeal for orthodoxy. The demonology seems to be an accommodation to popular concepts, and the attention directed to his orthodoxy apparently stems from the concern of the biographer to strengthen the bonds between the hierarchy and monasticism. One thing is certain: Athanasius's own difficulties with the imperial authorities in the Arian controversies strengthened his alliance with the monks.

Saint Benedict of Nursia, founder of western monasticism. (Archive Photos)

The impressions of a witness so close to the monastic movement, but himself not a part of it, must be compared with the authentic letters of Anthony. Beneath the some what vague concepts formulated by this uneducated old man, there are the pantheistic trends of Origen's thought, with the idea of a return via the Christ-image of God to the primitive soul-image, by means of an inner serenity that is achieved in perfect prayer. In his retreat in the desert between the Nile and the Red Sea, Anthony enjoyed an enormous prestige, because of his lofty and well-balanced ideal of asceticism and solitary contemplation, as well as his gift of discernment of spirits. A number of disciples began to imitate him, living in solitude, separated by great distances, and coming to him at long intervals for counsel.

Pachomius and Cenobitism. Farther to the south, at TABENNISI and Pebou in the THEBAID, a younger contemporary of Anthony, PACHOMIUS, who had become a monk *c.* 313, began organizing cenobitic communities (*c.* 320) that in his lifetime included several thousand brothers, not counting convents of women (*see* MONASTERIES, DOUBLE). Endowed with an instinctive understanding of human nature, this Copt with no philosophical training founded monasteries that he divided into houses where men lived a disciplined life in common, performed remunerative work, and practiced individual poverty and detachment in essential matters, alternating with judiciously organized prayer. He had many visions of an apocalyptic type; and despite the profound respect he displayed toward ecclesiastical authority, trust in his charismatic gifts gradually brought him into opposition with the hierarchy (Synod of Latopolis), though not with Athanasius, in whom distance fostered comprehension.

Pachomius's successors, Orsiesi and Theodore, did not enjoy the outstanding prestige their master had acquired for himself, but they are attractive figures; the rules and the vitas forming the Pachomian legacy are partly their work. By a strange turn of history, these unsystematized rules that are nevertheless rich in experience had only a limited influence in the East; but they reached Italy in a Latin translation by St. JEROME, and there exercised a profound influence.

Desert Fathers. Ammonas, disciple of Anthony, was named bishop of OXYRHYNCHUS by Athanasius, probably to assure proper control and supervision of the masses of monks then multiplying in the region. He showed unusual mildness and forbearance toward those among them who were public offenders; he maintained the brothers in stability and coped with the problems occasioned by the charisms of the Spirit and revelations of heavenly mysteries. Ammonas is to be distinguished from Ammon, founder of the monastic colonies in the Nitrian Valley, who also was acquainted with Anthony, though he died before him. This Ammon had initially lived in virginal matrimony with his wife, a practice that recalls an archaic rule of Christian family asceticism and that, it is astonishing to note, was not condemned judging from available sources. In the great desert of Scete, a little to the south, MACARIUS THE EGYPTIAN (d. *c.* 390) collected fewer disciples, but achieved a more perfect and tranquil solitude.

Like Anthony and Pachomius, these monks supported Athanasius in his difficulties with ARIANISM and the civil authority; and Athanasius on his part made their merits known in the West. MELANIA THE ELDER, with RUFINUS OF AQUILEIA and other Romans, visited them and on settling in Jerusalem devoted themselves to imitating their *ascesis,* their knowledge of Scripture, and their Origenism. In *c.* 382, EVAGRIUS PONTICUS provided the monks with the spiritual and intellectual legacy of the Cappadocians; he learned the monks' ascetical ''alphabet'' and profited from the treasures of psychological insights acquired by their long silences. Shortly after his death (399) a quarrel broke out among his friends and disciples, the Origenists, and the anthropomorphites. Archbishop THEOPHILUS OF ALEXANDRIA interfered ruthlessly and achieved control of the monastic groups, but not without damage to their gnosis and culture.

The main sources of information regarding this development bear the stamp of the crisis, although the traditions on which they are founded are considerably anterior to it. Of these documents, some were written for the edification of outsiders, such as the *Historia Monachorum,* produced *c.* 400 in the monastery of the Mount of Olives, and the *Historia Lausiaca* of PALLADIUS, published *c.* 420; both reflect the spirit of Evagrius in a popular coloration. For the internal use of Western monasticism, another thoroughly Evagrian author, John CASSIAN, wrote his memoirs in the form of *Institutiones* and *Conferences.* For the internal use of Eastern monasticism that had become anti-Origenist, there were compiled various collections of *APOPHTHEGMATA*, or Sayings of the Fathers, brief and charismatic replies to problems of the spiritual life.

The proper use of these various sources requires an acquaintance with the literary genres that evaluates each according to its individual worth. Traditional views have often succumbed to the temptation of evaluating them by the criteria of HAGIOGRAPHY; and rationalistic criticism, both Catholic and non-Catholic, has not always understood the monastic ideal or sufficiently recognized the gospel legacy and the freedom of spirit that characterized this literature. External witnesses aid in discerning and interpreting the facts, although the authors of these literary sources were themselves often the willing victims of the mirages of the desert. More recently, unpretentious evidence, badly transmitted by the copyists, has been rediscovered and edited from Eastern versions that were strictly contemporary and addressed to the monks themselves. These notices are of the greatest documentary value, and they make it possible to get behind the unsatisfactory syntheses that have hitherto supplied information on the origins of monasticism. They are furnished in the writings of Athanasius, SERAPION, Anthony, Ammonas, and Arsenius. In the effort to give an accurate picture R. Draguet and J. C. Guy have called attention to the value of the collections of apothegms. However, their value is still to be clarified.

Syria and Palestine. In the attempt to achieve a further understanding of the extent of the monastic beginnings, it must be remembered that the eastern provinces of the Roman Empire had easy commerce with one another: the primitive Gnostics and the Manichaeans of Syria and Egypt, for example, were in close contact. In the 3d century the ascetic movement in Mesopotamia was perhaps more advanced than that of any other part of the East. The name ''abbot'' is evidently of Syriac origin. The word ''monk'' may likewise have had an ambitious and Gnostic meaning linked with the *Monogenos,* the Only Son of God, although this interpretation and etymology is contested. It was certainly not current in the 4th century, when *monachos* had the simpler meaning of ''solitary'' (i.e., celibate) and quickly came to mean an anchorite.

Syria took longer than the West to react against the encratism of TATIAN and to eliminate his influence. In certain quarters Baptism was understood as an engagement involving continence, although the marriage of catechumens was not condemned; and the catechumens did amount to a sizable group. In the 4th century, Baptism did not exclude marriage; but within the communities there was a fervent nucleus, the Sons of the Covenant (*b* ^{e}*nai q*^{e} *yāmā*), who preserved virginity and were more or less ministers of divine worship. They formed the humblest rank of the clergy and lived in a clerical family or among the clergy. The rules concerning these persons were specified only slowly. The Covenant was the acceptance of the New Testament concluded by Baptism, not a vow or an evangelical counsel. No major figure appeared among them in the 4th century; APHRAATES and St. EPHREM THE SYRIAN were exemplars rather than pioneers.

Under the Egyptian influence, it seems, a current of anchoritism manifested itself in that part of the Orient *c.* 360; numerous solitaries escaped all organized discipline, preferring to wander in wild and desert places, leading a primitive and eccentric life. Saints EPIPHANIUS OF CONSTANTIA and Ephrem the Syrian testify to the existence of lawless groups called Messalians (Syriac for ''those who pray''), who rebelled against any work under the pretext that they had to consecrate themselves to perpetual prayer. They had a scorn for worldly goods and were more a scandal than an edification. Some, for all their oddity, did attract veneration; their achievements are described by THEODORET OF CYR in his *Religious History.* Of special note was Simeon the Stylite (d. 459), who lived in a basket between heaven and earth on a column more than 60 feet high. But great numbers, either spontaneously or under the influence of the episcopate, came to accept the way of life implicit in Basilian cenobitism. Their most notable centers were located near the Persian border, in Edessa, Amida, and Tur Abdin. From there a missionary monasticism spread over the southern part of ARMENIA and GEORGIA, and characterized the eastern missions of the Persian church.

The Syrian monastic world had its counterpart in the deserts of Judea and the hermitages of Sinai, with their close contacts with Egypt, and had a special character because of the sacred memories of the Holy Land. The *spoudaei* (zealots) attached themselves primarily to the holy places and provided them with protection and divine worship. Foreign pilgrims entered their ranks, often after having visited Egypt. In the 4th century, particularly, they had many Latin visitors, including Saints Jerome and Paula, the two Melanias and Rufinus, John Cassian, and Aetheria. Jerome embroidered or invented local traditions of his *Life of Malchus* and *Life of Hilarion;* he did the same for Egypt in his *Life of St. Paul First Hermit.* Later the same process can be observed among the Cappadocians, Armenians, and Georgians. The recognizable Syrian type is sometimes clothed with a Hellenistic veneer, especially when the subjects were men in the cities. Such was the case especially with DIODORE OF TARSUS and JOHN CHRYSOSTOM, at Antioch.

Cappadocia and Messalianism. The eastern part of Asia Minor came under the influence of Syria. At the Council of GANGRA (341) the Arianism of court bishops clashed with an ascetical movement led by EUSTATHIUS, future bishop of Sebaste. He was reproached with breaking up homes, misleading children, emancipating slaves, and departing from the obedience of the clergy to live independently in sectarian fashion. When he became bishop, Eustathius annoyed the extremists among his own disciples, e.g., Aetios, by preserving ecclesiastical discipline and organizing a hospice, for this supposed a certain compromise with the goods of this world. To his ideal rallied intellectuals of great families, such as Basil of Caesarea and GREGORY OF NAZIANZUS. They managed to combine asceticism with obedience to the ecclesiastical hierarchy. The result was a stable and balanced CENOBITISM, similar in a sense to that achieved by Pachomius. Gregory of Nazianzus preferred a more inward and contemplative life; it was through him that Evagrius Ponticus was to come to Scete.

After the death of Basil (379), his brother GREGORY OF NYSSA and his disciple AMPHILOCHIUS OF ICONIUM maintained contact with the ascetic movement in the hope of spreading their mystical ideal to the whole Church. However, they were soon faced with extravagances among the followers of Eustathius and did not succeed in controlling them. After 383, Bishops Letoios of Melitene, Amphilochius, and then Flavian of Antioch, in succession as the evil spread, took the initiative in condemning Dadoes, Sabas, Adelphios, Hermas, Simeon, and other leaders of the movement. This episcopal intervention had been provoked in part undoubtedly by previous experience. But the ascetics claimed they were in communion with the Church, and strategy had to be resorted to in order to get them to express openly their ideas on inner sanctification by the Holy Spirit and on the devices of the demon, conceptions that were dangerous for the sacramental structure of the Church.

To discredit these sects, the bishops linked them with the anarchic Messalians, despite the differences between the two groups. Their spiritual teaching has survived in the homilies improperly attributed to Macarius the Egyptian; the *Liber graduum,* a Syriac work, is closely allied. These writings are certainly susceptible of an orthodox interpretation and traditional support can be found for them: but they contain the theses condemned by the anti-Messalian councils. These condemnations and the polemic by a DIADOCHUS OF PHOTICE or a MARK THE HERMIT did not prevent them from having a beneficent influence on Byzantine mysticism (*see* HESYCHASM). They reached the West only at a comparatively late date, during the crisis that was caused by the Franciscan FRATICELLI and during the beginnings of PIETISM and METHODISM.

Constantinople. In the capital of the later Roman Empire, monasticism established itself *c.* 380; its original contacts were with Syria, but it manifested Egyptian influence when the Origenist monks were expelled by Theophilus of Alexandria (*c.* 400). The *Lives* of Hypatius (d. 446) and Alexander the Acoemete (d. *c.* 430) witness to this movement, although the latter is somewhat in the tradition of the Messalians and gives evidence of conflict with Church discipline. The disciples of John Chrysostom are known through a collection of the letters of NILUS OF ANCYRA (d. *c.* 430) and the works of Mark the Hermit. In the second half of the century, Daniel the Stylite (d. 493), an imitator of St. Simeon, was already playing a role in the capital.

Early Western Monasticism. The first centers of monasticism in the West were formed as a result of the exile of Athanasius in Rome, Treves, northern Italy, and Aquileia. The social structure of the Christian communities differed considerably from that of Egypt, but the *Life of Anthony* readily set the tone for men coming to the movement from higher society. A typical trait of Western monasticism was its penetration into the clergy in the service of the local Church. It is noticeable from the time of EUSEBIUS OF VERCELLI (d. 371), who, on his return from exile in the East, brought back the idea of a community life for his clergy; later the idea was put into practice by Ambrose of Milan and AUGUSTINE.

In northern Italy, MARTIN OF TOURS was trained in the monastic ideal before founding Marmoutier (372) in western France and becoming the model monk bishop of Gaul. After the death of Pope DAMASUS (384), monasticism temporarily lapsed into disfavor in Rome, although Jerome successfully discredited its adversaries Helvidius and Jovinian. In Spain, in this same period, PRISCILLIANISM proved an analogous movement, but its orthodoxy was suspect, and its principals were persecuted by the episcopacy. In Africa, outside the zone of influence of Augustine, modern historians see traces of Messalianism, perhaps derived from the East. Marxist historians such as T. Büttner link monasticism with the Donatist movement of the Circumcellions who rebelled against the social system and went about the countryside violently imposing their religious opinions. The phenomenon is interesting for the light it sheds on one milieu of the origin of monasticism.

Jerome, Rufinus, Evagrius, and others had translated the Eastern monastic texts into Latin at an early date. At the beginning of the 5th century, Cassian in Provence brought a new influx of Eastern traditions with the avowed aim of reforming Gallic monasticism. The Latin genius was to multiply these monastic rules based on the original ideals as it assimilated the barbarians, until the day when Benedict of Nursia was to synthesize them all. By way of Gaul, particularly, was to be born the early Irish MONASTICISM that was later to bring the gospel and culture back to the Continent.

Conclusion. Monasticism was a development of primitive Christian asceticism along various lines; the anchoritic and cenobitic types were not the original nucleus but rather successful forms on which others patterned themselves. The monks had their own culture; it was independent of the classical world of antiquity and often arose from local popular traditions, Coptic or Syriac. The monks brought the Church an ideal of asceticism, forms of prayer such as the use of the Psalter, a rich experience of inwardness, and new literary forms. The movement became a triumphant power that, despite its resistance to cultural changes, was to give a distinguishing character to the Middle Ages.

Bibliography: P. DE LABRIOLLE in J. R. PALANQUE et al., *The Church in the Christian Roman Empire,* tr. E. C. MESSENGER, 2 v.

in 1 (New York 1953), v.2. L. BOUYER, *The Spirituality of the New Testament and the Fathers,* tr. M. P. RYAN (New York 1964). P. COUSIN, *Précis d'histoire monastique* (Paris 1956). K. HEUSSI, *Der Ursprung des Mönchtums* (Tübingen 1936), critique. *Studia Monastica*), *Bulletin de spiritualité monastique,* app. to *Collectanea ordinis Cisterciensium Reformatorum* careful up-to-date bibliography, about 120 pages a year. P. HONIGSHEIM and A. ADAM in *Die Religion in Geschichte und Gegenwart,* 7 v. (3d ed. Tübingen 1957–65) 4:1070–81. *Il Monachesimo orientale* (Orientalia Christiana Analecta 153; 1958). *Théologie de la vie monastique* (Théologie 49; Paris 1961). A. J. FESTUGIÈRE, ed., *Les Moines d'Orient* (Paris 1961–65). R. DRAGUET, ed., *Les Pères du désert* (Paris 1949). H. J. WADDELL, tr., *The Desert Fathers* (New York 1936; repr. Ann Arbor 1957). G. TURBESSI, *Ascetismo e monachesimo prebenedettino* (Rome 1961). G. PENCO, *Studia monastica* 4 (1962) 257–81. A. ADAM, *Zeitschrift für Kirchengeschichte* 65 (1953–54) 209–39. W. KAMMERER, *A Coptic Bibliography* (Ann Arbor 1950). E. E. MALONE, *The Monk and the Martyr* (Washington 1950). H. CHADWICK, *Reallexikon für Antike und Christentum,* ed. T. KLAUSER 5 (1962) 343–65, s.v. Enkrateia. B. STEIDLE, ed., *Antonius Magnus Eremita* (Corpus scriptorum Christianorum orientalium 38; Paris-Louvain 1956). G. GARITTE, ed. and tr., *Lettres de S. Antoine: Version géorgienne et fragments coptes* (ibid. 149; 1955). R. T. MEYER, ed. and tr., *Palladius: The Lausiac History* (Ancient Christian Writers, 34; Westministers, Maryland-London 1965). L. T. LEFORT, ed. and tr., *Les Vies coptes de S. Pachôme . . .* (Louvain 1943); *Oeuvres de S. Pachôme. . . ,* 2 v. (Corpus scriptorum Christianorum orientalium 159–60, Scriptores Coptici 23–24; 1956); *S. Athanase: Lettres festales et pastorales en copte,* 2 v. (ibid. 150–51; 1955); *Muséon* 71 (1958) 5–50, 209–39, homily of St. Athanasius. A. BOON and L. T. LEFORT, eds., *Pachomiana latina* (Louvain 1932). F. HALKIN, ed., *S. Pachomii vitae graecae* (Subsidia hagiographica 19; 1932). F. NAU, ed. and tr., *Ammonas, successeur de S. Antoine* (Patrologia orientalis, ed. R. GRAFFIN and F. NAU 11.4; 1915) 393–504. F. KLEJNA, ''Antonius and Ammonas,'' *Zeitschrift für katholische Theologie* 62 (1938) 309–48. A. WILMART, *Revue d'ascétique et de mystique* 1 (1920) 58–83, Macarius. A. J. FESTUGIÈRE, ed., *Historia monachorum in Aegypto* (Subsidia hagiographica 34; 1961). J. C. GUY, *Recherches sur la tradition grecque des ''Apophthegmata Patrum''* (Brussels 1962); *Orientalia Christiana periodica* 30 (1964) 129–47, Scete. G. GARITTE, *Muséon* 68 (1955) 259–78, letter of St. Arsenius. R. DRAGUET, ibid. 64 (1951) 1–25, Serapion of Thmuis; ''Les Apophtegmes des moines d'Egypte,'' *Académie Royale de Belgique: Bulletin de la classe des lettres* 47 (1961) 134–49. A. GUILLAUMONT, *Les ''Kephalaia gnostica'' d'Évagre le Pontique* (Paris 1963). A. and C. GUILLAUMONT, *Dictionnaire de spiritualité ascétique et mystique. Doctrine et histoire,* ed. M. VILLER et al. (Paris 1932–) 4:1731–44, s.v. Évagre. A. VÖÖBUS, *A History of Asceticism in the Syrian Orient,* 2 v. (Corpus scriptorum Christianorum orientalium 184, 197; 1958–60), bibliography. J. D. B. GORCE, *La ''Lectio Divina'' . . . Saint Jérôme* (Paris 1925). F. X. MURPHY, *A Monument to Saint Jerome* (New York 1952); *Rufinus of Aquileia* (Washington 1945). I. AUF DER MAUR, *Mönchtum und Glaubensverkündingung . . . hl. Johannes Chrysostomus* (Fribourg 1959). J. GRIBOMONT, ''Le Monachisme au IVe s. en Asie Mineure,'' *Studia patristica* 2 (Texte und Untersuchungen zur Geschichte der altchristlichen Literatur 64; 1957) 400–15; ''*Le De Instituto Christiano* et le Messalianisme de Grégoire de Nysse,'' ibid. 5 (Texte und Untersuchungen zur Geschichte der altchristlichen Literatur 80; 1962) 312–22. H. DÖRRIES, ''Urteil und Verurteilung,'' *Zeitschrift für die neutestamentliche Wissenschaft und die Kunde der älteren Kirche* 55 (1964) 78–94. E. KLOSTERMANN and H. BERTHOLD, eds., *Neue Homilien des Makarius-Symeon* (Texte und Untersuchungen zur Geschichte der altchristlichen Literatur 72; 1961). H. DÖRRIES et al., eds., *Die 50 geistlichen Homilien des Makarios* (Berlin 1964). G. PENCO, *Storia del monachesimo in Italia* (Rome 1961); *Saint Martin et son temps* (Studia anselmiana 46; 1961) 67–83. T. BÜTTNER and E. WERNER, *Circumcellionen und Adamiten* (Berlin 1959).

[J. GRIBOMONT]

2. Medieval (600–1500)

From the 6th into the 8th century, Western monasticism was not organized into an order, nor did it have a common rule. Eastern (see section 5 of this article), Celtic (*see* MONASTICISM, EARLY IRISH), and Benedictine elements combined to form various rules; 20 such mixed rules were in use in Gaul alone *c.* 600. In the course of the 7th century these rules incorporated ever larger portions of the Rule of St. COLUMBAN and the BENEDICTINE RULE; some Continental monasteries, e.g., LUXEUIL and FLEURY in Gaul, BOBBIO and the restored Abbey of MONTE CASSINO in Italy, came to adopt the Benedictine Rule as their norm of monastic life. As for England, even though the monastic allegiance of AUGUSTINE OF CANTERBURY and his fellow monks sent by GREGORY I the Great to convert England is unknown, the late 7th- and 8th-century Anglo-Saxon missionaries to the Continent were all Benedictine, and their many monastic foundations—for both men and women—were likewise Benedictine. The work of BONIFACE, followed by the encouragement and legislation of CHARLEMAGNE, made the Benedictine Rule obligatory for all monks and nuns under Carolingian authority. However, the monks and nuns of Celtic lands and Visigothic Spain held fast to their own patterns of monastic living for several centuries more.

Carolingian Era. The BENEDICTINES were the missionaries and the teachers in the Carolingian era who made the CAROLINGIAN RENAISSANCE a reality. Their mission work to the Danes, Swedes, and Norwegians continued into the 10th century, as did their mission to the western Slavs and Hungarians. At home, the monks labored in the school and SCRIPTORIUM, writing theological, hagiographical, and historical works, and managed the abbey lands. But all this extramonastic activity provoked protests by BENEDICT OF ANIANE (*see* CAROLINGIAN REFORM). Under his leadership the monastic synod of Aachen in 817 decreed the elimination of extern work, the lengthening of the DIVINE OFFICE, common monastic customs or regulations for all monks, and regular VISITATION of all monasteries. From this time to the 12th century almost all monks in Europe were Benedictine, but most of this legislation remained largely a dead letter until Cluny adopted parts of it in the 10th century.

The decay of Carolingian authority in the state and the subsequent decentralization, which resulted in feudalism, made the abbey a feudal fief with the ABBOT a feudal lord with all attendant privileges and obligations. The contemporary invasions of NORMANS, Hungarians, and Saracens destroyed many abbeys, especially in France and Italy. However, observance in the monasteries in German lands east of the Rhine generally remained good, and they were thus able to play a leading role in Church and State under the Saxon and Salian rulers of the 10th and 11th centuries.

Cluniac Reform. Monastic renewal in the West began with the foundation of CLUNY in 910. It was fortunate in its saintly, capable, and long-lived abbots: ODO OF CLUNY, MAJOLUS, ODILO, HUGH OF CLUNY, and PETER THE VENERABLE. Under these men, Cluny—exempt from all secular and spiritual authority except that of the pope—created a centralized ''Order'' of Cluny (*see* CLUNIAC REFORM). All member monasteries were under the direct authority of the abbot of Cluny, all vows were made to him, and all superiors were appointed by him. Monks were not to be primarily missionaries or teachers, manual labor was curtailed, and the Divine Office was to be longer and more solemn.

The spirit of reform was, however, not exclusive to Cluny. Other centers grew up in Flanders and northern France under GERARD OF BROGNE near Liège, in Lorraine under JOHN OF GORZE at Metz, in Germany at HIRSAU, as well as in southern France, Italy, and Spain. The English revival was the work of the monk bishops DUNSTAN OF CANTERBURY, ETHELWOLD OF WINCHESTER, and OSWALD OF YORK. Their program for English Benedictinism was outlined in the *Regularis Concordia.*

New Monastic Orders. The number of monastic foundations grew steadily. The great churchmen between the 10th and the 12th centuries—the so-called Benedictine centuries—were monks; as bishops and popes they successfully spearheaded the struggle of the Church for freedom from secular authority (*see* GREGORIAN REFORM). Centers of monastic renewal emphasizing the eremitic and contemplative ideals of early monasticism were created by Romuald at CAMALDOLI, PETER DAMIAN at FONTE AVELLANA, and at VALLOMBROSA by JOHN GUALBERT in the 11th century. In 1084 BRUNO OF COLOGNE set up the first Carthusian hermitage at La Grande Chartreuse, thus founding an order that by the 15th century would include over 190 charter-houses throughout Europe, all faithful to the ideals of the founder. Other Benedictine-based reform groups, each with its own set of ideals, were founded in the 11th and 12th centuries: GRANDMONT, Sauve Majeure, CHAISE-DIEU, FONTEVRAULT, and SAVIGNY. (*See* GILBERTINES; PREMONSTRATENSIANS; HOSPITALLERS AND HOSPITAL SISTERS; MILITARY ORDERS.)

The most important 12th-century foundation and the professed rival of Cluny was the CISTERCIAN ORDER. Its founders, ROBERT OF MOLESME and STEPHEN HARDING, stressed a stricter interpretation of the Benedictine Rule, setting out their ideals and constitutional structure in the *Charta caritatis.* Their original program was purely contemplative and ascetic with emphasis on silence, poverty, and manual labor. But since they could not abolish the idea of the monk priest, they were soon obliged to turn the heavy manual work over to lay brothers, whose industry and skill created the great Cistercian abbey estates. Constitutionally, the Cistercians safeguarded the autonomy of every abbey; necessary unity in the order was achieved by means of annual general chapter meetings and visitations. The growth of the order was unparalleled in monastic history. Candidates flocked to the new foundations. Many older Benedictine monasteries joined the new order. By 1300 there were about 700 monasteries for men and a larger number for CISTERCIAN NUNS. BERNARD OF CLAIRVAUX was in great part responsible for the initial growth of the order. His European reputation placed it in the midst of Church and State affairs; his energy inspired the Second CRUSADE and three Cistercian archbishops were the religious leaders of the Third Crusade. Cistercian monks soon served as diplomats and in the Roman Curia. They headed the mission to the ALBIGENSES and converted the pagans of Prussia and the Baltic area.

However, tensions arose in the order even before the death of Stephen Harding. Rivalry between the abbot of CÎTEAUX and the daughter houses threatened to become chronic. Distant abbeys tended to go their own way. The practice of COMMENDATION, the Black Death, the WESTERN SCHISM, the Hundred Years' War, and the Hussite Wars had their repercussions. Changes in administration and papal legislation were of some help, but attendance at the general chapters kept falling off from the second half of the 14th century onward, so that in the years of religious crisis rarely would even 30 abbots attend the annual gathering.

The 13th and 14th Centuries. The general monastic picture of the 13th and 14th centuries was uninspiring. Some abbeys retained a high level of regular observance; the ''Orders'' of the CELESTINES, of Sylvestrine, and of Olivetan BENEDICTINES founded in this era still survive. Most monastic foundations, however, were in spiritual doldrums. Leadership in Christian scholarship had passed to the universities and dedicated religious vocations gravitated to the MENDICANT ORDERS. Reasons for this decline in monastic life are varied. Many abbeys were too much involved in secular affairs, some had become rest-houses for members of the nobility, and others had purposefully limited the number of monks so that the professed monks would have more income. The Hundred

Years' War often forced monks to live outside their cloisters; the Black Death and the pernicious commendatory system were causes of decline over which the monks had no control. The abbatial office and that of other monastic officials were treated as benefices. Frequently the sense of personal poverty all but vanished. Reform efforts of higher ecclesiastical authority availed but little. The decrees of the Fourth LATERAN COUNCIL (1215), the efforts of Popes HONORIUS III, GREGORY IX, and BENEDICT XII failed to overcome the general inertia and the opposition of the local ordinaries.

The 15th Century. Eventually, effective revival came from within the Benedictine family with the birth of the late medieval congregations, especially the highly centralized congregations of St. Justina of Padua and PANNONHALMA in Hungary. Other congregations preserved the autonomy of the member abbey but placed it under the supervision of the general chapter and its officials. Many abbeys joined the congregations of KASTL, MELK, BURSFELD, or WINDESHEIM in German lands, Valladolid in Spain, and CHEZAL-BENOÎT in France.

The ideal monk of these monasteries was pious and book-loving, and his cell was the nursery of 15th-century humanism. These monks loved the Benedictine Rule, but the spiritual doctrine taught by the great abbots of the new congregations, such as John Rode, Luigi Barbo, García de CISNEROS, and Johannes TRITHEMIUS, was that of the DEVOTIO MODERNA.

Bibliography: H. B. WORKMAN, *The Evolution of the Monastic Ideal* (London 1913). E. C. BUTLER, *Benedictine Monachism* (2d ed. 1924; repr. New York 1961). R. MOLITOR, *Aus der Rechtsgeschichte benediktinischer Verbände,* 3 v. (Münster 1928–33). P. SCHMITZ, *Histoire de l'ordre de Saint-Benoît,* 7 v. (Maredsous, Belgium 1942–56). K. HALLINGER, *Gorze-Kluny,* 2 v. (Studia anselmiana 22–25; 1950–51). D. KNOWLES, *The Monastic Order in England, 943–1216* (2d ed. Cambridge, 1962) D. KNOWLES, *The Religious Orders in England*, 3 v. (Cambridge 1948–60). G. PENCO, *Storia del monachesimo in Italia* (Rome 1961). F. DÖLGER, *Lexikon für Theologie und Kirche*, ed. J. HOFER and K. RAHNER, 10 v. (2d, new ed. Freiburg 1957–65) 7:544–48.

[V. GELLHAUS]

3. Modern (1500–1960)

Like so much of the Catholic Church's renewal in the 16th century, monasticism looked to the Council of Trent for new impetus. Prior to the Council, there had been some efforts at reform (e.g. Valladolid in Spain, St. Justina in Italy, Melk and Bursfeld in German-speaking territories), but these were minimal in terms of their ability to mobilize a widespread movement of Benedictine reform throughout Europe. By the time of the Council of Trent's opening, the monasteries of England had already been effectively closed by virtue of the dissolution under Henry VIII. The disparate character of the monastic life throughout Europe was in need of unification. This was provided by canon eight of the Council's last session, requiring all monasteries to ally themselves as members of a particular monastic congregation. Although an effort was made to preserve the traditional monastic autonomy of each house, implementation and enforcement of conciliar decrees frequently fell to the local bishop. Monasteries of women were to remain under the jurisdiction of the Holy See or the local bishop. The minimum age for profession of monks was 16; monastic women could make perpetual profession only after they had reached 21 years of age. Forbidden against the vow of poverty were personal ownership and landholdings, a blow against the *commendam* practice of previous centuries. Most important for the success of the reforming spirit, all exempt monastic houses were to affiliate with into a congregation, with general chapters and regular visitations.

Response to the Tridentine decrees varied according to the locale. The Congregation of Santa Justina in Italy, once affiliated with the ancient abbey of Monte Cassino, became the Cassinese Congregation. It grew in number in the years following Trent, having 14 new monasteries enter the congregation in the 16th and 17th centuries and producing a number of bishops and cardinals as leaders of the Church. In 1566 the Portuguese Congregation of Lusitanian was established, modeled on the already existent Valladolid Congregation. In Austria, the restored Congregation of Melk was reestablished (1617). The old German Bursfeld Congregation expanded as the Swabian Congregation (1603), the Congregation of Strasbourg (1623), the diocesan Congregation of Salzburg (1641), the Bavarian Congregation of the Holy Angels (1684) and the Congregation of Augsburg (1685). Under Einsiedeln Abbey, the Swiss Congregation was formed (1602) and in the Netherlands the Congregation of the Presentation (1628). The reformed congregation of Valladolid in Spain was extended in the 16th century to Mexico and Peru with the missionary ventures to the New World. Another Portuguese Congregation of Brazil was formed in 1582. The English Benedictine Congregation was formally established in exile on the continent in 1619. Perhaps the most influential of the new congregations were found in France. The Congregation of St. Vanne (1604) was modeled on the Cassinese Congregation and under Didier de la Cour spread throughout France, gaining a reputation for scholarly work. Even more of a commitment to intellectual life was rendered by the Congregation of St. Maur (1621). Noted for its house at St. Germain-des-Prés in Paris, the Maurists flourished throughout the following century, producing such eminent figures in scholarship as Gregory Tarrisse, Luc d'Archery and Jean MABILLON.

New congregations of women in France included the Catherine de Bar's Perpetual Adoration of the Blessed Sacrament and the Congregation of Calvary from Fontevrault. In the 17th century there were also reformed abbesses renewing the monastic life at places such as MONTMARTRE, Val-de-Grace and Saint-Paul-les-Beauvais. By 1660 there were 18,000 Benedictine nuns in France, about twice the number as there were in 1600. Also in France the English Benedictines in exile at Douai and Cambrai found in Dame Gertrude MORE and others a rich vein of spiritual writing to help them in their own renewal. The Congregation of Kulm under Magdalene Morteska helped to lead reform in German-speaking lands.

Another arm of reform came from the Cistercian branch of monasticism. The Trappists (Order of Cistercians of Strict Observance) under Abbot Armand de RANCÉ received papal approval in 1678. In 1712 papal approval was given to the Congregation of Mechitarists, a group that represented the ancient traditions of Eastern monasticism.

Apart from the spiritual vein of renewal, Benedictine monasteries were in the forefront of spreading the best baroque standards of art, architecture and music. The Austrian, German and Swiss monasteries were especially noteworthy in this enterprise.

Secularization. By the 1700s, however, the monastic order was again being threatened by elements of the Enlightenment, monarchical government and secularizing influences. The Enlightenment critique of the Catholic Church included the monasteries, which it identified with the *ancien régime*. The anti-clerical and Masonic literature of the century reflected this as did the policies of the secularizing governments of Austria (1750 to 1790) and the Czarist regime in Russia and Poland. In the second half of the 18th century the first dissolutions of French monasteries took place, culminating in the complete suppression of all monastic houses at the time of the French Revolution. The September Massacre and many other bloody reprisals against the Church by the revolutionary government included Benedictines as their victims. In the last decades of the century, Emperor JOSEPH II of Austria suppressed numerous Benedictine abbeys in Austria, Bohemia, Hungary and areas of Poland. Monasteries in the Netherlands and Switzerland were forced to close their doors in 1796. The Napoleonic Wars increased the threat to Benedictine life. Throughout Italy, Prussia, Silesia and Germany, countless monasteries were secularized by governments unfriendly to any form of organized religious life. In Spain, the monasteries were suppressed by Joseph Bonaparte in 1809. By 1810, it was said there were fewer monasteries in existence in Western Europe than at any time since the age of St. Augustine.

The 19th-Century Revival. Even as the monastic order in Europe reached its nadir at the beginning of the 1800s, indicators of rebirth were evident. In 1802 the suppressed abbeys of Hungary formed a new congregation from the royal monastery of Pannonhalma. English monks who had fled from the French oppression founded abbeys at AMPLEFORTH (1802) and DOWNSIDE (1814). Benedictine nuns from Cambrai in France did the same, establishing communities at Colwich in 1795 and later founded the monastery of STANBROOK. In Bavaria, King Ludwig I restored the Abbey of METTEN (1830) and the Benedictine convent of Eichstätt, which was in turn to become influential in shaping other Bavarian abbeys into the Bavarian Congregation.

The real germ of the 19th-century revival, however, was to be found in France. In 1833 a diocesan priest, Prosper GUÉRANGER, founded an abbey at the ancient monastic site of SOLESMES. Modeled on the medieval ideal of Cluny and a return to ancient monastic sources, Solesmes became a center of liturgical life and scholarship. It marked the beginning of the French Congregation (now known as the Solesmes Congregation) and gave birth to other foundations at Ligugé and Marseilles. Solesmes also helped to found the Sisters of St. Cecilia under Cecile Bruyère, a companion reform to the monks. Another French diocesan priest, Jean-Baptiste Muard, founded an abbey at Pierre-qui-vire (1850) that incorporated elements of strict observance and missionary activity. In France there also emerged the Benedictine Nuns of the Heart of Mary (Pradines), the Benedictine sisters of the Poor (Solesmes), the Adorers of the Heart of Jesus (Montmartre) and the Congregation of Missionary Benedictines (Ligugé).

In Italy, Pietro Casaretto transformed SUBIACO into a reform center (1851) and then went on to form the Subiaco Congregation. This congregation absorbed abbeys across the European continent and was known for its missionary impulse. It was this congregation, through the labors of Spanish Benedictines Joseph Serra and Rosendo Salvado, which brought a Benedictine presence to the Australian continent, along with the work of English Benedictines.

Another branch of the 19th-century revival came from the foundation at BEURON in the Black Forest (1863), made by two German brothers, Maurus and Placidus WOLTER. Modeled in many aspects on Solesmes, the Beuron Congregation was influential in a return to the sources of monastic life and a concentration on liturgical renewal. Indeed, the abbeys of MAREDSOUS and Mont-César in Belgium, centers for the liturgical movement, formed part of the Beuronese Congregation, as did the German abbey of MARIA LAACH. A Beuronese monk, Andreas Amrheim, was to found still another new Congregation of St. Ottilien (1884), missionary in orientation. Allied to the monks of St. Ottilien were the Benedictine missionary sisters of Tützing.

The missionary thrust of the 19th-century revival was a pronounced part of its impetus. In addition to sending monks to Africa, Australia and South America, this was the time when monasticism came to North America. The most forceful figure in this venture was Boniface Wimmer, who became archabbot of the monastery of ST. VINCENT's in Pennsylvania (1846) and spearheaded the birth and growth of the American Cassinese Congregation. Swiss monks made similar foundations at ST. MEINRAD (1854) and Conception (1871) and there were large numbers of Benedictine sisters from monastic houses in Germany and Switzerland who accompanied them.

The fruits of this revival were seen not just in rapidly expanding numbers but also in a more centralized structure. Under Pope Leo XIII there was a revival of the monastery of Sant'Anselmo in Rome as a central house of studies and an attempt to organize a confederation of Benedictine congregations. A Congress of Abbots was held (1893) and the position of abbot primate created to constitute a more unified Benedictine character. Among new congregations added in the first part of the 20th century were the Belgian Congregation (1920), the Austrian Congregation (1930) and the Bohemian Congregation of St. Adalbert (1945).

Many Church leaders, as well as liturgical and spiritual writers, reflected the revitalized monasticism of the early 20th century. Cardinals GASQUET, DUSMET and PITRA epitomized the scholarship of the Benedictine revival. Such writers as BEAUDUIN and Botte, BUTLER and CHAPMAN, MARMION and MORIN, served as examples of the fruits of a return to Scriptural and Patristic sources. The growth in numbers was paralleled with a growth in physical plants, especially in Europe and North America.

The 20th century was not without its challenges to monasticism. The punitive legislation passed by governments of Germany, France and Italy at the end of the 19th century slowed the progress of monasticism in those countries. Even more devastating were the two world wars that marked the first half of the century. The devastation of so much of the monastic patrimony of Europe in those wars was reflected in the destruction of the abbey of Monte Cassino by Allied bombers and the wholesale loss of life and property experienced by many monastic houses, to say nothing of priceless manuscripts and books contained in monastic libraries. The period after World War II resulted in another resurgence of monastic growth, especially in the United States. There was a strong contemplative movement that accompanied the popularity of the best-selling autobiography of Thomas MERTON, a monk of Gethsemane in Kentucky. It was reflected not only in growing numbers flocking to Cistercian houses but in new communities of Benedictine men and women that turned away from traditional apostolic works of education and pastoral work and became centers of prayer and liturgical life.

The 20th century was not without its record of political persecution of Benedictines. Monks from Silos Abbey were expelled from Mexico in 1913. In the Spanish Civil War in 1936 monks of the abbey of Pueyo suffered a collective martyrdom. Benedictines were driven from mainland China after World War II. With the suppression of monastic houses in Communist territories, there was an increased emigration of monks from Eastern Europe and Asia to other countries.

There was also a strong missionary thrust, this time directed to Latin America, Asia and Africa. By the 1950s there were thriving Benedictine communities in Argentina and Mexico, Vietnam and India, Morocco and Madagascar. A number of Benedictines served as bishops in missionary countries.

[J. RIPPINGER]

4. Contemporary (1960–2000)

The decade of the 1960s marked not only the decisive event of Vatican Council II (1962 to 1965) but also another period of intense renewal of monastic life. This was accomplished through a full spectrum of changes: structural changes in the constitutions of Benedictine congregations, the introduction of the vernacular in the liturgical prayer of communities, the changed patterns of ministry or apostolic work taken on by many communities, a comprehensive reevaluation of monastic spirituality as it came to terms with the modern world and new challenges that came through interacting with that world. At the same time, this period initiated a time of marked demographic change, with decreased numbers from Benedictine houses in Europe and North America, and increased numbers from the sub-continents of Africa, India and South America.

The conciliar call for all religious to return to the sources of their charism led to a flowering of new monastic scholarship. Benedictines such as Jean LECLERCQ, Adalbert de Vogüé and Cypriano Vagaggini led a new wave of Benedictine scholars, intent upon distilling the best of Benedictine tradition of scholary work and extending it to a wider readership. The Benedictine Pontifical University of Sant'Anselmo in Rome offered an international venue for this to take place, particularly with its Liturgical and Monastic Institutes. Centers for study and publishing in other parts of the monastic world, such as Collegeville, Minnesota, in the United States, also attracted large numbers of Benedictine students and scholars.

Benedictines exercised considerable leadership in renewal efforts of religious life in the period after the Council. American Benedictine Rembert Weakland, elected as abbot primate in 1967, did much to promote the renewal of liturgical life. He also broadened contacts with houses of Benedictine women and supported the growing influence of monasticism in Third World countries. In the Roman Curia, Cardinal Augustine Mayer played a significant role under Pope JOHN PAUL II in expediting the religious renewal of communities of consecrated life and later serving as liaison with the Society of St. Peter. Cardinal Basil HUME, a monk and abbot of Ampleforth Abbey before being named archbishop of Westminster, was widely recognized as a spokesman and spiritual figure of influence in the European Church.

The Benedictine Order itself was enlarging its membership. By the 1970s, the Vallombrosan (1966), Camaldolese (1966), Olivetan (1960) and Sylvestrine (1973) branches of Benedictinism had entered the Benedictine Confederation. There was now a Dutch and Slavic (1969) Congregation and the Benedictine houses of Latin America formed the Cono-Sur (1976) Congregation. This period was also a time of marked growth in non-Catholic Benedictine houses. The Anglican and Lutheran Churches were witnessing the renewed growth of monastic communities in their denominations. In addition, there was a concerted effort to engage in dialogue with non-Christian monastics. The Bangkok Conference of 1968, at which the Trappist Thomas Merton suffered his unexpected death, was one of these. The work of English Benedictine Father Bede GRIFFITHS and Henri le Saux in India signaled an entirely new ground for combining elements of Hindu practice with Catholic monasticism. A number of organizations such as the North American Board for East-West Dialogue and Monastic Interreligious Dialogue actively sought to carry on the exchange of ideas between Catholic monks and those of other faiths. Examples of Benedictine monasteries in the forefront of ecumenical work included Chevetogne in Belgium and Bose in Italy. This was also a period when the popularity of the Benedictine-based ecumenical monasticism of Taizé was achieving unprecedented attention.

The missionary impulse was alive and well in this period. The decade of the 1960s had seen an unprecedented commitment of monastic personnel sent to Latin America. Although a number of the foundations made did not pass the test of time because of local political instability and a dearth of indigenous vocations, many Benedictine foundations became integral parts of the local Church in Latin America. Africa and Asia were also geographic sectors of renewed Benedictine growth in the last years of the 20th century.

The decades at the end of the 20th century witnessed the return of a more vibrant monastic life to countries that had long suffered from political oppression under Communist rule. This was the case in Vietnam after the difficult period of war and internal discord. It was especially so in the countries of Eastern Europe after the fall of Communism in 1989. Many of the restrictions formerly imposed on monastic houses in Poland, Hungary and Czechoslovakia were lifted. In countries such as Lithuania, Slovakia and the Czech Republic an entirely revitalized form of monastic life was nurtured with the help of material and human resource from monasteries of the free world.

A variety of experiments in monastic life were part of the post-conciliar period. There were new efforts at both an urban monasticism and a return to eremitical life. The CHARISMATIC RENEWAL movement of the 1970s found its way into a number of Benedictine houses, notable the monastery of Our Lady of Guadalupe in Pecos, New Mexico. The 1980s and 1990s were marked by the genesis of a number of new monastic communities of men and women whose common heritage was a retrieval of more traditional practices, characterized by a full round of the Divine Office, use of the full religious habit, and a more cloistered existence. More communities were divesting themselves of active apostolic ministries and becoming centers for prayer and retreats. In this period as well there was a flowering of new forms of monastic art, architecture and music.

Monasticism was distinguished much more by its international character and its pluralism in the last decades of the 20th century. Technology expedited an ease of communication among far-flung monasteries and this was buttressed by frequent encounters and personal exchanges among monastics of different houses. Another prominent feature was the surge in growth of lay associate or oblate programs, in which many committed lay people, Catholic and non-Catholic, affiliated themselves with particular monasteries. Monastic practices such as *lectio divina* also became accessible to a wider public and so did the interest generated in monastic spirituality on the part of the entire Church.

There was a decline in numbers that had taken place from 1965 to 2000. In 1965 there were over 12,000 monks and over 23,000 Benedictine women throughout the world. At the end of the second millennium in 2000 there were just over 8,400 monks and over 17,000 Benedictine women. However the variety of women's congregations had grown to 63 and for the men there were 82 congregations or independent abbeys. The numerical decline was also less than that suffered by other major religious orders in the same period. These figures pointed to a vitality and diversity in the monastic order at the beginning of the third millennium that was very much in keeping with the Benedictine charism.

Bibliography: A. LINAGE CONDE, *San Benito Y Los Benedictinos*, v. III–VI (1993). D. KNOWLES, *Christian Monasticism* (1969). A. KESSLER, *Benedictine Men and Women of Courage, Roots and History* (1996). P. SCHMITZ, *Histoire de l'Ordre de saint Benoît, 7 v.* (1956).

[J. RIPPINGER]

5. Eastern

Byzantine monasticism is not divided into specialized orders and congregations as in the West; nor has it an organized unity. The conciliar and imperial legislation on the matter is summary, and the Rule of St. Basil is but a monument of experience and tradition, without legal binding force. In addition to CENOBITISM, there have been various forms of the eremitical life; and since the 9th century, anyone (often it was a layman) founding a monastery drafted the *typikon* of his house to his own taste.

a. To 1453. It is almost impossible to make a list of the early monasteries, since many were but precariously maintained hermitages. For the city of CONSTANTINOPLE, R. Janin has nonetheless succeeded in establishing a catalogue of 325 monasteries, several of which may be duplicates, since monasteries changed names in the course of time. A similar list covering the remainder of the empire is in preparation in the same collection. It will furnish a precise basis for general study. This section is limited to a brief chronological survey of the most significant events.

Egypt and Palestine. The initial period has been treated separately (see section 1 above), for it is of cardinal importance and the innovations spread rapidly throughout the Christian world. From the end of the 4th century, Egypt was more isolated, except for the group at Nitria known from the *Apophthegmata Patrum.* In the south, in the White Monastery, SHENOUTE OF ATRIPE (d. 466) and Besa (d. after 474) were personages well known from their Coptic works, but they had almost no influence outside of Egypt. In the north, which was troubled very early with MONOPHYSITISM (except among the Pachomians of Canopus, bulwark of the Chalcedonian patriarchs), development of monasticism ran closely parallel with that of the East but produced no figures of first rank. Syria also was hard hit by Monophysitism, except for the monasteries of St. Simeon and of St. Maron; the *Plerophoriae* of John Rufus (*Patrologia orientalis*, ed. R. Graffin and F. Nau, 8:1), written shortly after 512, and the *Lives of the Eastern Saints* (*Patrologia orientalis*, v.17–19) of JOHN OF EPHESUS (d. 586) give a picturesque description of them. Spiritual writers such as PHILOXENUS OF MABBUGH were already outside the mainstream of Byzantine tradition.

The most active monastic center in the 5th century was Palestine, which attracted vocations from everywhere. The Monophysite centers there were moderate and highly cultured. The highest traditions of the Egyptian desert from the 4th century were maintained; representative authors inspired by the works of EVAGRIUS PONTICUS include Abbot Isaias (d. 488), Peter the Iberian (d. 488), and John and Barsanuphius with their disciple Dorotheus of Gaza (d. after 560); the PSEUDO-DIONYSIUS probably belongs to this group. Along the Jordan and in the Dead Sea region were Chalcedonian lauras, whose monks were less well read and perhaps more austere. CYRIL OF SCYTHOPOLIS (late 6th century) has provided excellent biographies of several of them: e.g., EUTHYMIUS THE GREAT (d. 473), SABAS (d. 532), and Theodosius (d. 529). Monasticism, in penetrating this region, led to a violent crisis of Origenism from about 540 to 552. (*See* ORIGEN AND ORIGENISM.) With the assistance of Justinian I the mischief was brutally extirpated. The most vital center of orthodox monasticism shifted to Sinai (*c.* 600), where Justinian had built a fortified monastery. The *Ladder of Paradise* by JOHN CLIMACUS synthesizes the whole of this ascetic and mystical tradition.

Constantinople. In the Byzantine capital the monks maintained the Chalcedonian tradition with vigor, notably the Acoemeti and the monks of the monastery of Dalmatos. With the Christological crisis, the monks of the East everywhere adopted extremist positions, not hesitating to withdraw from the jurisdiction of their bishops, often at the invitation of a neighboring bishop. It is understandable that the Council of CHALCEDON (451), its eyes opened by the Robber Council of EPHESUS (449), should have taken measures to put the monks under the charge of the bishops (c.4), and that Justinian should have legislated to the same effect (*Corpus iuris civilis, Novellae*, ed. R. Schoell and G. Kroll, 5, 133). Nevertheless it was the power of the monks, the goad of the masses, that was responsible for the creation of an independent Jacobite Church [*see* JACOBITES (SYRIAN)], which often backed linguistic and ethnic groups striving for autonomy. The unwillingness of such groups to compromise was only rarely (e.g., in Palestine) mollified by a literary culture. The monks' work of evangelization on the fringes of Christendom in ARMENIA, GEORGIA, and ARABIA, to say nothing of the Persian form of monasticism, (which had already been cut off from the Byzantine world) deserves to be stressed.

Middle Byzantine Period. The Persian invasion, and later the Arab conquest, split the Eastern provinces and Egypt from the empire; Monophysite monasticism became isolated and disappeared from Byzantium. Some orthodox monks fled to Byzantium and the Western provinces, bringing with them some manuscripts. The times were not favorable for great literary works but only for spiritual FLORILEGIA. In 692 the Council of Trullo tried to work out monastic legislation. Soon the crisis over ICONOCLASM, in part a military and imperial reaction against the influence and wealth of the monks, aggravated the situation and culminated in a persecution (754 to 764). Some colonies of hermits, itinerant, poor, and little organized, nevertheless continued to exist, notably on Mt. Olympus in Bithynia.

Studite Foundations. Plato and THEODORE, the future Studite, withdrew with their family to Mt. Olympus at the end of the 8th century. They took in hand a strict cenobitic reform based on the writings of St. BASIL and on Palestinian monasticism, first in the monastery of the Saccudium and later, in 709, in the STUDION monastery of the capital itself. Strong in their moral authority, they were often vigorous opponents of the emperor and his patriarch. Their poverty and work, their copying of manuscripts, with the spread of the new minuscule script, and the number of monks (more than 700) all prove the value of this reform, which opened the most splendid period of Byzantine monasticism. Sumptuous foundations began to multiply, and libraries were created in them, bringing together treasures of Christian literature that have since enriched Paris, Rome, and Moscow. The most vital monastic centers, such as northern Italy (*see* BASILIAN MONASTICISM), Mount ATHOS, and Russia, were profoundly marked by the *Hypotyposis* of the Studites.

The persecutions of the second iconoclast crisis served only to give the Studites the prestige of confessors. The Synod of Constantinople held in 861 endeavored to prevent abuses attendant on the increase of foundations and the authoritarian interference of the founders in the life of the communities. It imposed a three-year novitiate. This was also the age in which the distinction came to be widespread between the ''minor habit,'' signifying a less demanding form of life devoted to manual labor, and the ''angelic habit,'' a higher rank reserved to those who gave themselves exclusively to prayer. The distinction seems to have originated in Palestine (7th century) and finally came to be accepted despite the long opposition of the Studites. It can be interpreted as a reaction against legislation and an effort to safeguard the spiritual character of monasticism (that of the angelic habit).

In the 10th century, Mount Latros housed a number of flourishing monasteries. In 956 St. ATHANASIUS the Athonite founded at Mount Athos, till then a peninsula of hermits, the cenobitic monastery of Lavra, soon to be followed by other large houses of Slavs, Georgians (Iviron), and even Latins. Christodoulos (d. 1101) founded an important monastery on Patmos.

Mystic Revival and Hesychasts. The most remarkable event of 11th-century Eastern monasticism was undoubtedly the appearance of a mystic revival with Symeon the New Theologian (d. 1022), who came from the Studite tradition but was dissatisfied with the too disciplinary and too exterior conceptions of holiness that in the course of time had developed even in the most reformed type of cenobitic life.

As opposed to the ancient anchorites, the Hesychasts of the school of Symeon lived and worked in communities, but they championed a demanding conception of union with God, in line with the teaching of St. Anthony, the *Apophthegmata,* Dorotheus, and the Messalians—who stressed the importance of the cell, silence, and reading. Obviously peace and silence were thought of preeminently as interior dispositions and involved the elimination of distraction with a view to pure prayer. But the insistence on the psychological experience of the union with God and on pneumatism led Simeon, and still more his disciple and biographer NICETAS STETHATOS (d. *c.* 1080), to reserve the direction of souls and teaching to those who had had charismatic spiritual gifts, at the risk of disqualifying the hierarchical power. The Byzantine tradition had generally confided the direction of consciences to the monks, even those not priests, but this was now formulated as a doctrine. The spirituals provoked a reaction, doubtless excessive, against Michael Psellus and against the claim of the lay philosophers to teach in the Church. Nicetas Stethatos, furthermore, was among the anti-Latin polemicists in 1054.

Late Byzantine Period. The 13th century, the period of the conquest of Constantinople by the Crusaders, was a time of ruin and decline, but also of renewal. In the 14th century the Hesychast tradition found its greatest Doctor in Gregory PALAMAS. Western authors who have studied this period and made scholarly and doctrinal contributions concerning it often adopt a hostile attitude toward Palamas because of his opposition to Thomism. His distinction between the incommunicable essence of God (to save His transcendence) and His communicable uncreated operations (to safeguard mystical ''Taboric'' illumination) appears strange to the scholastic mind, but it eventually became the accepted doctrine in Byzantium (after violent controversies) and is a most felicitous characterization of the soul of Byzantium.

The HESYCHASM of Mount Athos was united to a psychophysical method, the continual repetition of the JESUS PRAYER while fixing the gaze on a point of the body, in rhythm with breathing, in order to make the spirit descend into the heart. This technique, which used to be ridiculed, attracted the attention of 20th-century psychologists, and the importance it ascribes to the body no longer seems unjustified. It should not in any case be considered more than a method for concentrating attention.

The Turkish invasion soon put an end to monasticism at Constantinople itself. Mount Athos, Patmos, monasteries of the Meteora in Thessaly, St. Sabas, and Sinai maintained flourishing Greek monastic republics, while the Slavic world took up the tradition and extended it.

Recruiting to the monastic life has become very difficult in the East; a modern ideal of culture and social action has not readily assimilated the traditions of monasticism or those who incarnate them. But it appears that the Western world is beginning to appreciate the human and Christian treasure of Hesychasm and ascetical contemplation.

Bibliography: D. ATTWATER, *A List of Books about the Eastern Churches* (Newport, R.I. 1960). A. SANTOS HERNÁNDEZ, *Iglesias del Oriente,* 2 v. (Santander 1959–63), v.2 *Repertorio bibliografico.* For bibliography, see *Byzantinische Zeitschrift* and *Orientalia Christiana periodica* 25 (1959) 451. P. DE MEESTER, *De monachico statu iuxta disciplinam Byzantinam* (Vatican City 1942). H. DELEHAYE, in *Byzantium,* ed. N. H. BAYNES and H. S. L. MOSS (Oxford 1948) 136–65. R. M. FRENCH, *The Eastern Orthodox Church* (New York 1951). L. BRHÉHIER, *Le Monde byzantin,* 3 v. (Paris 1947–50) 2:529–79, bibliography. H. G. BECK, *Kirche und theologische Literatur im byzantinischen Reich* (Munich 1959) 120–40, bibliography. J. LACARRIÈRE, *Men Possessed by God,* tr. R. MONKCOM (New York 1964). D. SAVRAMIS, *Zur Soziologie des Byzantinischen Mönchtums* (Leiden 1962). J. LEROY, *Monks and Monasteries of the Near East,* tr. P. COLLIN (London 1963). I. DOENS, ''. . . Monastères orthodoxes en Grèce,'' *Irénikon* 34 (1961) 346–92. A. GRILLMEIER and H. BACHT, *Das Konzil von Chalkedon: Geschichte und Gegenwart,* 3 v. (Würzburg 1951–54) 2:193–314. L. UEDING, *ibid.* 569–676. L. BOUYER, ''La Spiritualité byzantine,'' in J. LECLERCQ et al., *La Spiritualité du moyen-âge* (Paris 1961). *Orthodox Spirituality* (Society for Promoting Christian Knowledge; 1945). *On the Invocation of the Name of Jesus* (London 1950). C. LIALINE, *Irénikon* 33 (1960) 435–59. E. KADLOUBOVSKY and G. E. PALMER, trs., *Writings from the Philokalia on Prayer of the Heart* (London 1951). A. GUILLAUMONT, *Les ''Kephalaia gnostica'' d'Évagre le Pontique et l'histoire de l'Origénisme chez les Grecs et les Syriens* (Paris 1963). J. MEYENDORFF, *Introduction à l'étude de Grégoire Palamas* (Paris 1959). R. JANIN, *Les Églises et les monastères,* v.3 of *La Géographie ecclésiastique de l'empire byzantin,* pt. 1 (Paris 1953). R. M. DAWKINS, *The Monks of Athos* (New York 1936). S. LOCH, *Athos: The Holy Mountain* (New York 1959). C. DAHM and P. L. BERNHARD, *Athos, Berg der Verklärung* (Offenburg 1959). *Le Millénnaire du mont Athos, 963–1963* (Chevetogne, Belgium 1963–64). D. M. NICOL, *Meteora: The Rock Monasteries of Thessaly* (London 1963). A. CHAMPDOR, *Le Mont Sinaï et le monastère Sainte-Catherine* (Paris 1963). O. F. A. MEINARDUS, *Monks and Monasteries of the Egyptian Desert* (Cairo 1961). N. and M. THIERRY, *Nouvelles églises rupestres de Cappadoce* (Paris 1964).

[J. GRIBOMONT]

b. Since 1453. The importance of the study of Eastern monasticism was stressed by Pius XII when speaking to the participants of a congress on Eastern monasticism (Rome 1958). He pointed out that the Eastern monastic institutions are the basis for all other forms of Christian monasticism.

Forms and Terminology. The anchoritism begun by St. Anthony of Egypt (d. 356) was subjected to a critical reappraisal by St. Basil the Great (d. 379) in his rule. From that time, the ideal of common life, cenobitism, prevailed widely also in the Orient. But the tendency toward a solitary life was never completely extinguished. Solitude (*eremia*) was considered indispensable for *hesychia,* i.e., internal tranquility, a word that developed into a whole ascetical program, HESYCHASM, one of the most important currents of Byzantine spirituality. Some forms of solitary life were austere and even extreme. Besides stylites and recluses (both of whom were numerous, especially in Syria), there were *boskoi,* or shepherds, who roamed freely over the deserts, nourishing themselves on herbs, whence came the name *herbivori,* given them by St. EPHREM THE SYRIAN. St. NILUS OF ANCYRA considered *xeniteia,* the life of pilgrims in a strange land, the most difficult. The desire for a complete isolation even in the midst of people urged the *saloi* (in Slavic, *jurodivyje*) to feign eccentricities, even insanity, out of love for Christ; they were numerous in Syria and Russia.

Basilian cenobitism reached its perfection in the Studion monastery of Constantinople, whose *typikon* or rule became the model for other foundations. But in reality not all monasteries succeeded in full observance. The idiorrhythmic type of monasticism, an imitation of the ancient colonies of the fathers of the desert, was gradually introduced. Accordingly, the monks live in groups under a superior, but obedience is limited to matters of external regulation. Individual monks retain their own personal property and enjoy considerable freedom. Of the 20 principal monasteries of Mount ATHOS, nine are of this kind. The structure of this monastic republic reveals other types of monastic life still found in the East. The *sketai* (σκῆται) are dependent on larger monasteries and consist of a group of isolated houses. In the *asketikai kalybai* small groups of anchorites live. A *hesychasterion* is the dwelling of a solitary hermit. *Kellia* are small, separate, rural habitations where individual monks live under the direction of an older monk. *Kathismata* are hermitages better equipped, suitable, e.g., for a retired bishop. There are on Mount Athos also *gyrovagi* or *kabiotai* (wanderers) who do not belong to any monastery. Palestine was famous for its lauras, a type intermediate between anchoritism and the cenobitic life. A dependent *pustyň* or hermitage was often attached to the Russian monasteries.

In the monastic legislation of the East both civil and ecclesiastical authority had a part. Such legislation is found, for example, in the canons of the Council of Chalcedon (451), the Council of Trullo (691), the Council of Nicaea II (787), and the First and Second Photian Councils of Constantinople (867, 879). In the code of Theodosius (d. 450) are found prescriptions for monks that were developed further by Justinian (d. 565) in his *Codex* and *Novellae,* and by Emperor Leo VI (d. 913) in his *Basilika* and *Novellae.* In the 9th century began the custom of formulating a particular rule (*typikon*) for each newly founded monastery. In more recent times the Holy See issued for Catholic religious of the Eastern rites the motu proprio *Postquam Apostolicis Litteris* (Feb. 2, 1952).

Despite the multiplicity of forms, Eastern monasticism possesses a unity rooted in the common ideal of all Christians, namely, the salvation of one's soul. The monk, according to the concept of Basil and others, is none other than the Christian who takes the gospel seriously with all the consequences. Thus, in the Orient the ideal of perfection and monastic asceticism are considered identical.

Since it is not possible to give a detailed account here of all Eastern monasteries, some of the principal centers of Eastern monastic life are discussed briefly in the remainder of this article.

Egypt. The separation of the Egyptian Church from the Catholic Church, the invasion by the Muslims, and cultural isolation have reduced to a handful the number of existing monasteries, which in the golden era of Egyptian monasticism had numbered in the hundreds. Four of these are situated in the valley of Wadi Natrun, near the modern highway that leads from Cairo to Alexandria. Deir Amba Maqār is the monastery of MACARIUS THE EGYPTIAN; it was founded on the site of the hermitage of this patriarch of monasticism in the Scetic Desert. Though destroyed several times, it became in the 6th century the seat of the Coptic patriarch; in the 9th century it was surrounded by the kind of walls that later characterized all Egyptian monasteries. Deir as-Surjān, the monastery of the Syrians, was founded in the 8th century by the Syrian Tekrit for the monks of his nation. It became celebrated for its Syriac manuscripts, of which many were carried off in the 18th century to the Vatican Library, others in the 19th century to the British Museum. In the 14th century a plague killed most of the monks. The chronicle of the monastery speaks of only 43 monks in 1516, of whom 25 were Copts. Finally the administration came completely under the Copts. Deir Amba Bishāj, monastery of the Abbot Isaias, contemporary of Macarius, was reconstructed in the 14th century. Deir al-'Adrā (Baramus, or monastery of the Romans), was founded, according to legend, by the sons of Valentinian I (d. 375) or by St. Arsenius.

In the eastern desert, about 40 miles from the Red Sea, stands Deir Mār Antūnius, the monastery of St. ANTHONY OF EGYPT. In it is located the tomb of the saint, who spent his last years in a cave on Mount Kolzim. Ten miles from the Red Sea is found Deir Mār Būla, monastery of St. Paul of Thebes. This was built in the 5th century and reconstructed in the 16th and 18th centuries. Almost abandoned is the monastery of Deir Samūil in the valley of Kalamon, southwest of Medinet el Faijum. Founded by the Monophysite monk Samuel in the 7th century, it was reconstructed in 1899 by monks who had been forced to flee from Deir al-'Adrā. The Coptic monastery that presents the most modern aspect is that of Deir al-'Adrā (Al-Muharraq), some 20 miles northwest of Mafalut and reconstructed in the 16th century as a palace. Near Sohag are the famous monasteries of SHENOUTE, Deir-el Abjad (White monastery), and Deirel'Achmar (Red monastery), but they are now in ruins. The same is true of the monastery of St. Epiphanius near Luxor and that of St. Simeon near Aswan. Since the coming of Islam, monasteries for women have been limited to the city of Cairo, where even in the 12th century there was a foundress named Saijida Tarfa. Some of these convents still function; the largest of them is Deir Abū Sefein.

Ethiopia. The history of Ethiopian monasticism has not yet been studied sufficiently. All Ethiopian monasteries recognize as their head the abbot of Dabra Libānos, the great monastery to the north of Addis Ababa, whose abbot has the title of *etshage* and has jurisdiction also over the secular clergy. The greatest number of monasteries is in the north of Ethiopia and in Eritrea. Among them is the notable Dabra Bizan, which had great importance in the 14th century. In central Ethiopia the principal monastery is Dabra Dimā (Mount Calvary), along with its school. In the south the only important one is Dabra Wagag in Assabot. Monastic communities for women are found at times within the confines of the greater monasteries, but in separate buildings, as at Dabra Libānos. The abbots of monasteries are nominated by the crown. Ethiopian monasticism has extended to other countries, viz, to Egypt, Palestine, Lebanon, Cyprus, and Italy, where St. Stephen's Church in Rome is the ancient seat of the Ethiopian College.

Sinai and Palestine. On the Sinai Peninsula near Faran there was a large colony of monks of the monastery of Raithu. In the 8th or 9th century the episcopal see of

Faran was transferred to the monastery of St. Catherine below Mount SINAI, which enjoyed the protection of the Muslims, Venetians, and the popes, because it was the goal of pilgrims from both East and West.

Greek monasteries in Palestine were numerous in the days of the Byzantine Empire. There were also Latin monasteries at Bethlehem and on Mount Olivet. In the Middle Ages the Benedictine monastery at Jerusalem, Sancta Maria Latina, where the discussions concerning the FILIOQUE began, was still extant. The Georgians enjoyed special protection from the mamelukes, who allowed them to construct Georgian monasteries even in the late Middle Ages. The Armenians in the beginning were associated with the Greek monasteries but soon constructed their own. There are testimonies concerning three monasteries of the Caucasus Albanians. The Copts and Ethiopians established themselves also in the Holy City. In the 19th century were was a strong influence of Russians in the Holy Land; some of their convents for women still function.

Syria. After a notable flowering in the early centuries, Syrian monasticism went into rapid decline. The ruins of Qalat Sem'an around the column of St. Simeon Stylites (d. 459) reveal large monastic constructions. This place was the object of veneration for Monophysite pilgrims (*see* MONOPHYSITISM). Almost by way of opposition, the orthodox pilgrims hastened to the column of another of the STYLITES, St. Simeon the Younger (d. *c.* 592), on the Mount of Miracles near Antioch. The monasteries on this hill were the scene of bitter conflicts between the Greeks and Georgians in the Middle Ages. Opposite the Mount of Miracles was Black Mountain, a monastery founded in the 11th century, in which the canonist, Nikon of the Black Mountain (d. *c.* 1088), lived for some time.

The plains of Iran offered many ''deserts'' for anchorites from the 4th century on. In the 5th century an Egyptian, Eugene (Awgin), started a cenobitic monastery modeled on the type founded by St. PACHOMIUS. The Persian monks often occupied themselves in the care of souls. The disciples of St. Maro (d. *c.* 410) of Apamea in Syria emigrated to Lebanon (*see* MARO OF CYR, ST.; MARONITE CHURCH). The Maronite monks settled chiefly in the ''Holy Valley'' called Qadisha (extending from the Cedars toward Tripoli) which became filled with hermits and monasteries for both men and women. Several religious orders still work among the Maronites: the ANTONINES, the Missionaries of Kraim, and various congregations of sisters.

Armenia. Monasticism appeared in Armenia in the 4th century and reached its greatest development between the 9th and the 14th century. In all of old Armenia the number of monasteries was approximately 2,000. In the present-day region of Vaspurakan there were nearly 189 monasteries; Sünik had 150; Artzakh, 126; Karin, 116; Airarat, 52; Turuperan-Taron, 48; and Cilician Armenia, 62. The number of monks was large; the monastery of the Mother of God in Karmruk counted 300; that of St. John the Baptist in Klagh, 400; and Tathéw, in the time of its glory, 500. Many of these monasteries still existed before World War I but were later abandoned as a result of persecutions. Among the Catholic Armenians, there are two branches of the MECHITARISTS, monks who have motherhouses at Venice, Italy, and Vienna, Austria, and who conduct schools, printing presses, and missions in the Near East.

Georgia. Monasticism in eastern Georgia was initiated by the ''Syrian Fathers.'' In the second half of the 6th century it developed in the western part, especially in Tao-Klargeti (Turkey) in the Čoroki River basin. The monastic center called the Georgian Sinai arose there. Its founder was the archimandrite Gregory of Khanzta (d. 860–61). When he arrived the only monastery in this region was Opiza, but Gregory founded in the vicinity his monasteries of Khanzta and then Shatberdi, not far from Artanugi, capital of Klargeti. In time the foundations multiplied, and from these monasteries there emerged, especially, the 12 monasteries called in Georgian literature simply Atormetni, i.e., the 12, founded not later than the 9th century. From Tao-Klargeti came the founders of Iveron on Mount Athos. Some Georgian monks founded monasteries in Syria, Palestine, and Mount Sinai.

Balkan Countries. Modern Greece numbers 175 male monasteries, but they are sparsely populated. In the famous Meteora only three monasteries are inhabited. Female religious are more numerous, e.g., in the convent on the island of Tenos near the Marian sanctuary. The recently founded community Zoe follows the model of modern Latin congregations and engages in works of the apostolate. In Yugoslavia the first center of monasticism was located around the lake of Ochrid in the 9th century. The golden period was in the 14th and 15th centuries. The Serbian lauras, called also ''imperial'' monasteries, enjoyed special privileges. In 1939 there were in Yugoslavia 166 Orthodox monasteries with 540 monks. The most famous monasteries are Krushedol (near Karlovtsy), Studenitsa (the Serbian Westminster Abbey), Mileshovo, and Gratchanitsa. On Mount Athos St. Sava founded in 1197 the monastery of Chilandari for his fellow countrymen.

In Romania monasticism diminished rapidly in the 19th century. Statistics for 1857 showed 10,000 monks; in 1867, only 4,851; and in 1893, 2,654. Nuns are more numerous, especially in the convent of Hurezu in the Carpathians. In Bulgaria also, in the period after World War II, nuns adapted themselves better to difficult circumstances. The most important of the male monasteries are in Rila, Batchkovo, Trojan, Pomorie, and Preobraženski.

Russia. Traces of monastic life are found in Russia from the very beginning of Christianity toward the end of the 10th century. These were small foundations established by princes, in imitation of the monasteries of Byzantium. In contrast, the famous laura of Pechersky arose, as its chronicle narrates, solely by ''the fasts and tears'' of the monks. SS. Anthony (d. *c.* 1073) and Theodosius (d. 1074) are venerated as its founders. Anthony was a solitary of the type of the Egyptian anchorites and became a monk on Mount Athos. After returning to Kiev, he took up his abode in a cave cut out of a hill. His disciple Theodosius, when he became *hegumen* (superior), built cells for monks above the cave and sent one of the monks to Constantinople to bring back the rule of the famed Studion monastery in order to introduce the cenobitic life. The Pechersky laura was several times reduced to ruins by the Tartars; it was reconstructed and became a religious and cultural center, a place of pilgrimage frequented by the Russian people. After 1917 it was transformed into an anti-religious museum. The monastery was reopened in 1946, but again closed some time later.

After the Mongol invasion a new center of religious life arose in the middle of the 14th century in the ''desert'' of the virgin forests of the north, which in the following centuries were populated by hermits. The initiator of this movement was St. SERGIUS OF RADONEZH, founder of the monastery of the Holy Trinity in the province of Moscow. This monastery was closed after the revolution (1917) and was later reopened. Sergius began as an anchorite, but in founding his monastery he introduced the cenobitic rule of the Studites. His laura became the center for other foundations toward the south in the environs of Moscow, and toward the north in the forests beyond the Volga, in the area called the Russian Thebaid because of its numerous hermitages and monasteries. Among the more famous of these founders were St. Cyril of Beloozero (d. 1427) and Paul of Obnora (d. 1429). Along the shores of Lake Kuben arose monasteries in imitation of those of Mount Athos, especially that of ''Spaso-Kamennyj,'' constructed on rock in honor of the Transfiguration. The monks penetrated even to the Nordic islands of Solovki. Led by SS. Sabatios (d. 1435) and Zosimus (d. 1478), they established a monastery that became a center of missionary activity and, subsequently, a military fortress.

The second half of the 15th century brought a decline in religious discipline in numerous monasteries that had become rich and influential. Trouble arose in the form of heresy and state opposition, but monastic reformers also appeared. Among these the more important were Saints Nilus Sorsky (d. 1508) and Joseph Volokolamsky (d. 1515). Nilus promoted a semieremitical life in which a few monks in isolated huts (*skete*) lived lives of extreme poverty, hard work, and prayer. Nilus's monastic rule (*ustav*) is an ascetical instruction on prayer and control of the affections. He came under the influence of the hesychastic spirituality of Mount Athos. More than external works, he stressed the internal struggle against evil thoughts. The ideals of his contemporary, Joseph, were different. His rule, *Duchovnaja gramota,* outlined an ideal of cenobitic discipline under obedience to a superior and following a stable rule of life that regulated each moment of the day. The principal virtue of the monk was the perfect observance of assigned duties and the renunciation of one's own will and independent thoughts. The spirit of Joseph's rule prevailed in the Russian monasteries that became thereafter schools and centers of cultural activity, and often of politics also. The defects of this rigid traditionalism and attachment to external formalism brought about a new decadence. A kind of fusion between these two opposing tendencies is found in the rule of St. Cornelius (d. 1537), founder of a cenobitic monastery in the forests of Komel. His disciples founded the monasteries of the northern Russian regions.

A breath of new spirit was felt in the Russian monasteries with the appearance of the *starchestvo* in the 18th century. The *staretz* (literally, old man) was a spiritual father, a guide of souls, who, even though not a priest, attracted people to himself because of his experience in the spiritual life and often because of his special gifts, above all, that of discernment of spirits. The founder of this spiritual renaissance was Paissy Velitchkovsky (d. 1794). While on Mount Athos, he immersed himself in ascetical Greek literature. He went to Moldavia (to Dragomirna, and later to Sekul and Niametz) and organized the translations of spiritual books from Greek and Latin. Among these books was the *Philokalia* of NICODEMUS THE HAGIORITE.

The *startzy* of the monastery of Optina made this monastery near Kozelsk well known. Here lived Leo Nagolkin (d. 1841), who was beloved especially by the simple people. His successor, Marcarius Ivanov (d. 1860), was in contact with the intellectual and literary leaders of Russia of his time. Ambrose Grenkov (d. 1891), a disciple of Macarius, is described by Fëdor DOSTOEVSKIĬ in *Brothers Karamazov.* Seraphim of Sarov (d. 1833) led the austere life of a recluse before becoming famous in all of Russia as a thaumaturge, mystic, and director of souls.

Russia, in 1914, had 1,027 Orthodox monasteries (550 of men and 477 of women), with a total of 94,599 religious (21,300 monks and 73,299 nuns).

In the Ukraine, monastic life was initiated with the laura of Pechersky, which pertained to the Russian Orthodox Church. Ukrainian monasticism received a new impetus after its union with the Catholic Church in the Union of Brest (1596). The Basilian Order of St. Josaphat played a significant role in the subsequent development of the religious life. [*See* BASILIANS (BYZANTINE).] In Galicia, about the year 1900, there appeared a congregation made up of simple peasants. Metropolitan A. SHEPTYTS'KYĬ gave them, in 1906, a rule modeled on that of the ancient Byzantine rule, and they adopted the name Studites. The first *hegumen* or superior was the Father Clement Sheptyts'kyĭ, brother of the metropolitan. Later they were dispersed; a small group remains in the West.

Bibliography: General. *Monachesimo orientale: Atti del convegno di studi orientali* (Orientalia Christiana Analecta 153; 1958). C. PUJOL, *De religiosis orientalibus ad normam vigentis iuris* (Rome 1957). N. ARSENEV, ''Das Mönchtum und der asketisch-mystische Weg in der Ostkirche, besonders in Russland,'' *Der Christliche Osten* (Regensburg 1939) 151–210. N. F. ROBINSON, *Monasticism in the Orthodox Churches* (London 1916). J. OLPHE-GALLIARD, *Dictionnaire de spiritualité ascétique et mystique. Doctrine et histoire*, ed. M. VILLER et al. (Paris 1932–) 2.1:404–16. C. LIALINE, *ibid.* 4.1:936–53. T. ŠPIDLÍK, *Dictionnaire d'histoire et de géographie ecclésiastiques*, ed. A. BAUDRILLART et al. (Paris 1912–) 15:766–71. *Oriente Cattolico* (Vatican City 1962). Special topics. Egypt. H. G. EVELYN-WHITE, *The Monasteries of the Wâdi 'n-Natrûn*, 3 v. (New York 1926–33). N. ABBOT, *The Monasteries of the Fayyūm* (Chicago 1937). M. CRAMER, *Das christlich-koptische Agypten einst und heute* (Wiesbaden 1959). O. F. A. MEINARDUS, *Monks and Monasteries of the Egyptian Deserts* (Cairo 1961). Ethiopia. H. M. HYATT, *The Church of Abyssinia* (London 1928). DE L. E. O'LEARY, *The Ethiopian Church* (London 1936). E. CERULLI, ''Abbati di Dabra Libanos. . . ,'' *Orientalia* 12 (1943) 226–53; 13 (1944) 137–82; 14 (1945) 143–71; ''Il monachismo in Etiopia,'' *Orientalia Christiana Analecta* 153 (1958) 259–78. D. MATTHEWS and A. NORDINI, *The Monasteries of Debra Damo, Ethiopia* (Oxford 1959). Sinai and Palestine. P. VAILHÉ, *Répertoire des monastères de Palestine* (Paris 1900). M. H. L. RABINO, *Le Monastère de Sainte-Catherine du mont Sinaï* (London 1938). A. GUILLOU, ''Le Monastère de la Théotokos au Sinaï,'' *Mélanges d'archéologie et d'histoire* 67 (1955) 217–58. Syria. O. H. PARRY, *Six Months in a Syrian Monastery* (London 1895). P. DIB, *Dictionnaire de théologie catholique*, ed. A. VACANT et al., 15 v. (Paris 1903–50) 10.1:1–42. E. TISSERANT, *Dictionnaire de théologie catholique* 11.1:183 E. HONIGMANN, *Patristic Studies* (Studi e Testi 173; 1953). A. VÖÖBUS, *History of Asceticism in the Syrian Orient*, 2 v. (Corpus scriptorum Christianorum orientalium 184, 197; 1958–60), *Syrian and Arabic Documents Relative to Syrian Asceticism* (Stockholm 1960). Armenia. M. A. VAN DEN OUDENRIJN, *Eine armenische Insel im Abendland* (Venice 1940). M. ORMANIAN, *The Church of Armenia* (London 1955). G. AMADUNÌ, ''Le Rôle historiques des hiéromoines arméniens,'' *Orientalia Christiana Analecta* 153 (1958) 279–305. Georgia. D. M. LANG, *Lives and Legends of the Georgian Saints* (London 1956). M. TARCHNIŠVILI, ''Il monachesimo georgiano nelle sue origini e nei suoi primi sviluppi,'' *Orientalia Christiana Analecta* 153 (1958) 307–19. Balkans. J. LACOMBE, ''Réorganisation de l'Église serbe,'' *Échos d'Orient* 29 (1930) 360–63. M. SPINKA, *A History of Christianity in the Balkans* (Chicago 1933). M. BEZA, *The Rumanian Church* (London 1943). I. DOENS, ''Monastères orthodoxes en Grèce,'' *Irénikon* 34 (1961) 346–92. Russia. R. P. CASEY, ''Early Russian Monasticism,'' *Orientalia Christiana periodica* 19 (1953) 372–423. I. KOLOGRIWOF, *Essai sur la sainteté en Russie* (Bruges 1953). M. J. ROUËT DE JOURNEL, *Monachisme et monastères russes* (Paris 1952). J. REZÁČ, *De monachismo secundum recentiorem legislationem Russicam* (Orientalia Christiana Analecta 138; 1952). I. SMOLICH, *Das altrussische Mönchtum* (Würzburg 1940); *Russisches Mönchtum* (Würzburg 1953); *Leben und Lehre der Starzen* (Vienna 1936). T. ŠPIDLÍK, *Joseph de Volokolamsk: Un Chapitre de la spiritualité russe* (Orientalia Christiana Analecta 146; 1956). G. STÖKL, ''Zur Geschichte des russischen Mönchtums,'' *Jahrbuch für Geschichte Osteuropas* 2 (1954) 121–35.

[T. ŠPIDLÍK]

MONASTICISM, EARLY IRISH

The monastic way of life, which began in Egypt in the 3d century, was introduced into Ireland by St. PATRICK, who spoke with surprise of the Irish boys and girls who insisted on becoming ''monks and virgins of Christ.'' Their place in the Church, as organized by St. Patrick, however, was secondary. Beginning about 520, monasteries multiplied and by 600 the Church in Ireland had become the most monastic Church in Christendom; but there is no simple explanation for this phenomenon.

The Foundations. St. Patrick's experience showed that the imitation of Christ in humility, poverty, and hardship appealed to the Irish character. In the early 6th century influences favorable to monasticism reached Ireland from Britain; the fame of the *Candida Casa* of St. NINIAN, in modern Wigtonshire, and the monasteries of Ynys Pyr, Liancarven, and St. David's (modern Wales) spread as models of spiritual living, which Irish ascetics felt the urge to imitate. In a land whose political organization did not depend on cities, the monastery easily became the center from which the bishop ruled; and the monks were encouraged to take the place once held by the pagan druids as teachers of youth.

The most important name in this vigorous movement is St. FINNIAN of Clonard, called in later literature *Magister,* in Latin, and in Irish, *aite fer nérend lena lind,* ''the teacher of all Ireland in his day.'' He trained a group of brilliant young men whom he sent to found independent monasteries, including St. Columcille of Derry and Iona, St. Ciaran of Clonmacnois, St. BRENDAN of Clonfert. Other illustrious founders were St. COMGALL of Bangor, St. Enda of Aran, St. KEVIN of Glendalough, St. Cronan of Roscrea, St. Nessan of Mungret, St. Colman of Cloyne, St. Finbarr of Cork, St. Iarlaith of Tuam. More than 100 monasteries of major significance were founded during the 6th century in every part of the country and on the coastal islands. Women, such as St. BRIGID of Kildare, St. ITA OF KILLEEDY in Limerick, St. Monenna of Killeavy near Newry, showed themselves capable of equal idealism. Thus a large proportion of the population of the country lived in monastic seclusion as monks and nuns.

All did not follow the same observance, but the surviving Irish rules put more emphasis on the interior spirit than on details of external organization, which they obviously regarded as unworthy of mention.

Monastic Rules. A monastic rule ascribed to the saint Ailbe of Emly is written in Old Irish and represents ancient teaching and practice. It instructs the monk that: his conscience should be tender; he should speak little, work hard, serve the sick, deal gently with sinners, be modest in dress, and be wise, learned, pious, generous and courteous, be constant in prayer, and be zealous in reciting the canonical hours which formed the pattern of daily life. Matins began at dawn. When the bell rang the brethren were to chant the hymn of St. HILARY OF POITIERS, *Hymnum dicat.* When passing the altar each should genuflect three times, "going into the presence of the King of Angels."

After the morning office came a manifestation of conscience, then readings from the Gospel and spiritual treatises, then work. To keep the body in subjection the stomach was to be kept empty. About three P.M., "except in time of famine," the monk was given his meal. The cook was to be competent and generous; but "dry bread and watercress is the fitting food for the genuine ascetic." It was the duty of all to bear reproof and to confess their faults.

The monastic officials referred to are the abbot, the vice abbot, the *oeconomus,* the cook, and the priest. Obedience was to be absolute. If this rule was observed, the community would persevere without fault till death, when they would leave earth to receive the royal welcome offered them by the "Abbot of the Archangels."

The rule of St. Fintan of Clonenagh was similar to the rule of St. Ailbe; it was imitated by St. COMGALL at BANGOR and then carried by St. COLUMBAN to Luxeuil and Bobbio, whence as the *Regula Sancti Columbani* it spread to some 50 monasteries. Its influence remained strong until Charlemagne ordered that the *Regula Sancti Benedicti* should be observed in all the monasteries of his empire.

Distinguishing Characteristics. While the elements of Irish monasticism are found elsewhere, the system had a unity and an originality distinctly its own. Severe bodily austerity was a marked feature of every Irish rule and became a national tradition. The spirit of the rule was anchoritical rather than cenobitical; when the monk had advanced sufficiently in virtue he retired to an uninhabited spot to live in contemplation. Nevertheless the monks did not neglect apostolic duties: at home, the monastic oratories served as parish churches for the surrounding laity; abroad, the Irish monks were missionaries, intent on their own perfection, but hardly less intent on the salvation of the neighbors' souls. A zeal for studies, higher and lower, is indicated by the existence of a school which was second in prominence only to the church in every Irish monastery. In a category by itself is to be placed the prominence of abbots as ecclesiastical rulers who exercised jurisdiction for some six centuries, on a scale without parallel elsewhere in the Church.

The Decline. One reform movement in early Irish monasticism took place in the second half of the 8th century. It gave much promise but succumbed in the disorder caused by the irruptions of the Vikings, who appeared first in Ireland in 795 and continued as a disruptive force in the body politic until their final defeat at Clontarf, in 1014. The result for the monasteries was an ever-increasing measure of secularization which grew to such an extent that by the 12th century it could not be remedied without an undesirable social upheaval.

In 1111 Ireland was divided into dioceses on the continental model and in many cases monastic properties passed eventually under the control of the bishops. By 1200 early Irish monasticism had come to an end. The Irish rule was superseded by the Cistercian and by the rule of the Canons Regular of St. Augustine. A few ancient monasteries managed to survive, under the Rule of St. Augustine or as colleges of secular canons.

Bibliography: J. COLGAN, *Acta sanctorum Hiberniae* (Louvain 1645; reprint Dublin 1948). C. PLUMMER, comp., *Vita sanctorum Hiberniae,* 2 v. (Oxford 1910). J. F. KENNEY, *The Sources for the Early History of Ireland* (New York 1929). J. RYAN, *Irish Monasticism* (London 1931). L. GOUGAUD, *Christianity in Celtic Lands,* tr. M. JOYNT (London 1932). *Mélanges Colombaniens* (Paris 1950). N. CHADWICK et al., *Studies in the Early British Church* (Cambridge, Eng. 1958).

[J. RYAN]

MONE, FRANZ JOSEPH

Catholic historian; b. Mingolfsheim, Baden, Germany, May 12, 1796; d. Karlsruhe, Germany, March 12, 1871. He taught history at the University of Heidelberg from 1819 to 1827, and from 1825 he was in charge of the University library. In 1827 he was appointed to LOUVAIN University, but he returned to Germany in 1831 as a result of the Belgian Revolution. From 1825 until his retirement in 1868 he was director of the General State Archives in Karlsruhe. As a researcher, Mone was entirely dominated by the ideas of ROMANTICISM, as is shown by the letters of Jacob and Wilhelm Grimm, Karl Lachmann, Friedrich Creuzer, and Joseph von Lassberg to him, which were published by Max von Waldberg in *Neue Heidelberger Jahrbücher* 7 (1897) 68. The breadth and variety of Mone's field of study can best be conveyed by the modern concept of the history of culture. His works on the Celts are an extreme example of Romantic infatuation with the past. Mone made a modest contribution by his literary-historical researches to the foundation of Germanic PHILOLOGY, although his conclusions are often at fault. Even before Jacob Grimm, Mone had tried to give an overall presentation of German mythology, and on the basis laid down by Wilhelm Grimm, he pursued still further researches on the Germanic heroic legends. His editions on the history of the liturgy and on ecclesiastical poetry in the Middle Ages are even today a scholarly achievement of great importance. The *Lateinische und griechische Messen aus dem II. bis. VI. Jahrhundert* (Frankfort 1850) presents the pure Frankish- GALLICAN form of the liturgy. Mone also devoted himself to the history of Baden, and he initiated the Baden Church-State struggle with his anonymously published *Die katholischen Zustände in Baden* (Conditions of Catholics in Baden), a polemical pamphlet, published in Karlsruhe in 1841 and 1843, in which he championed the Catholic Church's independence of state tutelage.

Bibliography: F. J. MONE, *Geschichte des Heidenthums im nördlichen Europa,* 2 v. (Leipzig 1822–23), v. 5 and 6 of G. F. CREUZER, *Symbolik und Mythologie der alten Völker,* 6 v. (2d ed. Leipzig 1819–23); *Untersuchungen zur Geschichte der deutschen Heldensage* (Quedlinberg 1836); *Lateinische Hymnen des Mittelalters,* 3 v. (Freiburg 1853–55); *Celtische Forschungen zur Geschichte Mitteleuropas* (Freiburg 1857); *Quellensammlung der badischen Landesgeschichte,* 4 v. (Karlsruhe 1848–67). A. SCHNÜTGEN, ''Der kirchenpolitische Kreis um F. J. MONE,'' in *Freiburger Diözesan-Archiv,* NS 22 (1921): 68–122; 26 (1925): 1–66; 27 (1926): 153–226. A. WILMART, ''L'Âge et l'ordre des messes de Mone,'' *Revue Benedictine* 28 (1911): 377–390. W. KOSCH, *Das katholische Deutschland,* 2 v. (Augsburg 1933) 3053–3054. F. VON WEECH, *Allgemeine deutsche Biographie* (Leipzig 1875–1910) 22:165–166.

[H. RUMPLER]

MONGOLIA, THE CATHOLIC CHURCH IN

Capital: Ulan Bator.
Size: 600,000 sq. miles.
Population: 2,650,950 in 2000.
Languages: Khalkha Mongol; Turkic and Russian are spoken in various regions.
Religions: 2,100 Catholics (.1%), 106,000 Muslims (4%), 2,518,300 Tibetian Buddhists (95%), 24,500 practice other faiths or are without religious affiliation.
Mission sui juris: Ulan Bator.

Mongolia is a landlocked, arid plateau averaging between 3,000 and 5,000 feet above sea level, occupying a vast extent of steppes, deserts and mountains in east central Asia between Russia and China. Natural resources in the region include oil, coal, copper, tungsten, phosphates and other minerals, while the harvesting of wheat, barley and potatoes, and the raising of livestock for food, cashmere and hides provide many Mongolians with their livelihood. The northern part of the region, once known as Outer Mongolia, comprises Mongolia proper; the southern region, geographically part of Mongolia, forms the Inner Mongolian Autonomous Region, an administrative unit of China since 1947 that includes parts of Manchuria as well as Inner Mongolia in the traditional sense.

The historic homeland of the MONGOLS who under Genghis Kahn conquered much of eastern Europe during the 13th century, the region was divided into two separate entities, both of which were directly or indirectly under the domination of China or the former Union of Soviet Socialist Republics (USSR) until the mid-1990s. A province of China from 1686, the region gained its independence in 1921, after ten years of fighting. The Mongolian People's Republic, a Soviet satellite, ruled from 1924 to 1992, when a new democratic constitution was promulgated and elections established. Only in Outer Mongolia, where ethnic Mongols constitute 93 percent of the populace, does the Mongol race predominate numerically. The Islamic Kazazhs constitute four percent of the region's population.

Early History. The region was originally inhabited by nomadic tribes who adhered to Shamanism (*see* SHAMAN AND MEDICINE MAN). Lamaistic BUDDHISM was introduced from TIBET in the 13th century at the invitation of Kublai Khan (1215–94), grandson of Genghis Khan and conqueror of China. Buddhism quickly grew to become the predominant religion of Mongolia (*see* LAMAISM).

Christianity was first propagated by Nestorians (*see* ASSYRIAN CHURCH OF THE EAST). Franciscan missionaries entered southern Mongolia in the 13th and 14th centuries, prior to the destruction of the Ming dynasty in 1368 (*see* MISSION, HISTORY, I), and in 1690 Mongolia was incorporated in the diocese of Peking. Evangelization was entrusted to the Jesuits until the French Vincentians took charge in 1785. One of them, Father Gabet,

visited Outer Mongolia in 1838 with two converted lamas. The Vicariate Apostolic of Mongolia was erected in 1840. The first Mongolian priest was Garudi (1820–93), a former lama who was ordained in 1854 and who was also known as Peter Fong. The IMMACULATE HEART OF MARY congregation (Scheut Fathers), who succeeded the Vincentians in 1865, worked mainly among the Chinese immigrants in Inner Mongolia. A number of missionaries moved north to labor among several Mongol tribes, and attained a measure of success with the Ordos, who had suffered much during a Muslim uprising of 1862–72 and a severe famine in 1878. Mongol converts partly abandoned nomadic life and settled around the mission established in Porobalgason in 1874. A second mission station, founded in 1904 at Dumdadu, became the independent mission of Kharashili in 1937. The vicariate of Mongolia was divided into three regions in 1883: the vicariate of Southeast Mongolia; the vicariate of Southwest Mongolia in Inner Mongolia which in 1922 was itself divided into the vicariates of Suiyüan and Ningsia; and the vicariate Apostolic of Central Mongolia, which was split to create the Vicariate of Tchagar (Siwantze from 1924) and the mission *sui juris* of Ulan Bator in Outer Mongolia.

Protestants established a mission and printing press at Selenginsk among the Buriats (1817). They translated the Old Testament into Mongolian and published it in 1840 and the New Testament in 1846. O. S. Nostegaard, a Norwegian, remained in Outer Mongolia from 1890 to 1900. James Gilmour (1843–91) of the London Missionary Society, the first Protestant missionary in Inner Mongolia, worked among the Chakhars (1875–91). The Scandinavian Mission Alliance entered this region in 1895. The Swedish Mongol Mission, the Assemblies of God and the British and Foreign Bible Society also sent missionaries to the southern regions, although few ventured north into Outer Mongolia.

The Modern Church. Despite the efforts of the Church, 80 percent of Mongols were members of the Lamaistic Church of Tibet at the time the region fell under communist control. After 1924 Buddhism, as well as Catholicism, suffered severely from the Communist drive to destroy all religions. The 767 lama monasteries with 100,000 monks that existed in Outer Mongolia in March of 1921, when the region gained its independence from China, disappeared after 1936, the life of monks deemed particularly useless by communist standards. The temple of Gadang was the only one left open in Ulan Bator by the mid-1950s. While Inner Mongolia still had 997 monasteries with 150,000 lamas in 1952, many of these monasteries were razed in the coming decade.

Despite the assault on the Church during the 1930s and 1940s, Suiyüan became an archdiocese in 1946, with Ningsia, Siwantze and Tsining as its suffragan sees. While the mission in Outer Mongolia was entrusted to the Scheut Fathers in 1922, they were never allowed to enter it. The mission set up in 1923 by Swedish Protestants in Ulan Bator was closed in 1924 when the missionaries were expelled. There were less than 100 Mongol Protestants when all the missionaries were expelled from Inner Mongolia (1948–52). By 1953 no Christians of any faith were known to exist in Outer Mongolia.

Into the 21st Century. In 1992, with the fall of the USSR, the communist government of Mongolia weakened and democratic influences increased, prompting the promulgation of a new constitution in February of 1992 that granted freedom of religion and free, democratic elections under a reorganized government. The constitution also stipulated the separation between church and state; while the government funded the restoration of several Buddhist temples as historic sites, it did not otherwise fund the Buddhist religion. From 1992 to 2000, 90 Buddhist temples, 40 Christian Churches, a Muslim mosque and four Baha'i Churches were founded with the permission of the Mongolian government.

In May of 1996, the first Catholic Mass to be held in Mongolia since the arrival of communism was performed in a newly opened church in Ulan Bator. By 2000 the Church was slowly becoming reestablished in Mongolian life. Msgr. Wens Padilla established the first mission to Mongolia at the request of the new democratic government in 1992, and a second was established under South Korean Father Robert Lee Jun-Hwa in 1997. Three priests, ten nuns and 17 missionaries were at work in the country by 2000. Among their good works were the establishment of a Catholic kindergarten that taught over 60 students per year and an orphanage that cared for handicapped children. In June of 2000 Pope John Paul II met with Mongolian president Natsagiin Bagabandi to discuss the future of the Church in the region. Mongolia established diplomatic relations with the Holy See in 1992.

Bibliography: J. VAN HECKEN, ''The Apostolate among the Mongols,'' *Catholic Missions,* 9 (1932) 80–81, *Les Missions chez les Mongols aux temps modernes* (Peiping 1949); ''La Mission 'sui iuris' de la Mongolie Extérieure,'' *Neue Zeitschrift für Missionswissenschaft,* 10 (1954) 20–34. G. H. BONFIELD, *Mongolia, a Neglected Missionfield* (London 1910). J. LEYSSEN, *The Cross over China's Wall* (Peiping 1941). C. VAN MELCHEBEKE, *En Mongolie: L'Action sociale de l'Église catholique* (Paris 1945). K. S. LATOURETTE, *A History of Christian Missions in China* (New York 1929). *Histoire universelle des missions catholiques,* 4 v., ed. S. DELACROIX, (Paris 1956–59) v. 1–3. A. MULDERS, *Missiongeschichte* (Regensburg 1960). *Le missioni cattoliche: Storia, geographia, statistica* (Rome 1950) 300–302. J. RUTTEN, *Les Missionaires de Scheut et leur fondateur* (Louvain 1930). *The Chinese Empire,* ed. M. BROOMHALL (London 1907). O. LATTIMORE, *Nomads and Commissars: Mongolia Revisited* (New York 1962). B. RINTCHEN, *Les Matériaux pour l'étude du chamanisme mongol,* 2 v. (Wiesbaden 1959–61). G. HUTH, *Geschichte des Buddhismus in der Mongolei,* 2 v. (Strassburg 1892–96). A. GRUENWEDEL, *Mythologie des Buddhismus in Tibet und der Mongolei* (Leipzig 1900). R. J. MILLER, *Monasteries and Culture Change in Inner Mongolia* (Wiesbaden 1959). J. WICKI, *Lexikon für Theologie und Kirche,* eds., J. HOFER and K. RAHNER, 10 v. (2d, new ed. Freiburg 1957–65) 7: 549–552.

[J. VAN HECKEN/EDS.]

MONGOLS

A group of peoples, speaking closely related languages, who during the MIDDLE AGES ruled over a great part of Asia and of eastern Europe. At present most of the three million Mongols live in the Mongolian People's Republic, in the Soviet Union, and in China.

Political Organization. The Mongolian People's Republic, usually referred to as Outer MONGOLIA, is an independent state covering about 580,000 square miles, with a population of 1,100,000 (1960). Its capital, Ulan Bator, formerly Urga, has a population of 164,000 (1959). In spite of recent and somewhat successful efforts at industrialization, the country's main source of income is cattle breeding and 72 percent of the land is pasture. Since 1956 the Moscow-Peking railroad has passed through Ulan Bator. Within the Union of Soviet Socialist Republics and in the framework of the Russian Soviet Federal Socialist Republic (R.S.F.S.R.), the Buriat Autonomous Soviet Socialist Republic, with its capital at Ulan-Udé, has a population of 727,000 and covers 137,007 square miles. Other Buriats are grouped in the autonomous districts of Ust-Ordynsky and of Aginsky. A Kalmuck Autonomous Soviet Socialist Republic, established in 1935, suppressed in 1943, and reestablished in 1958, belongs to the North Caucasian Region of the R.S.F.S.R. It has an area of 29,601 square miles and a population of 204,000; its capital is at Elista.

Languages. The Mongol languages belong to the Altaic group and are related to the Turkic and Tungusic languages. Among the eastern Mongol dialects Khalkha and Buriat are the most important, for both have evolved

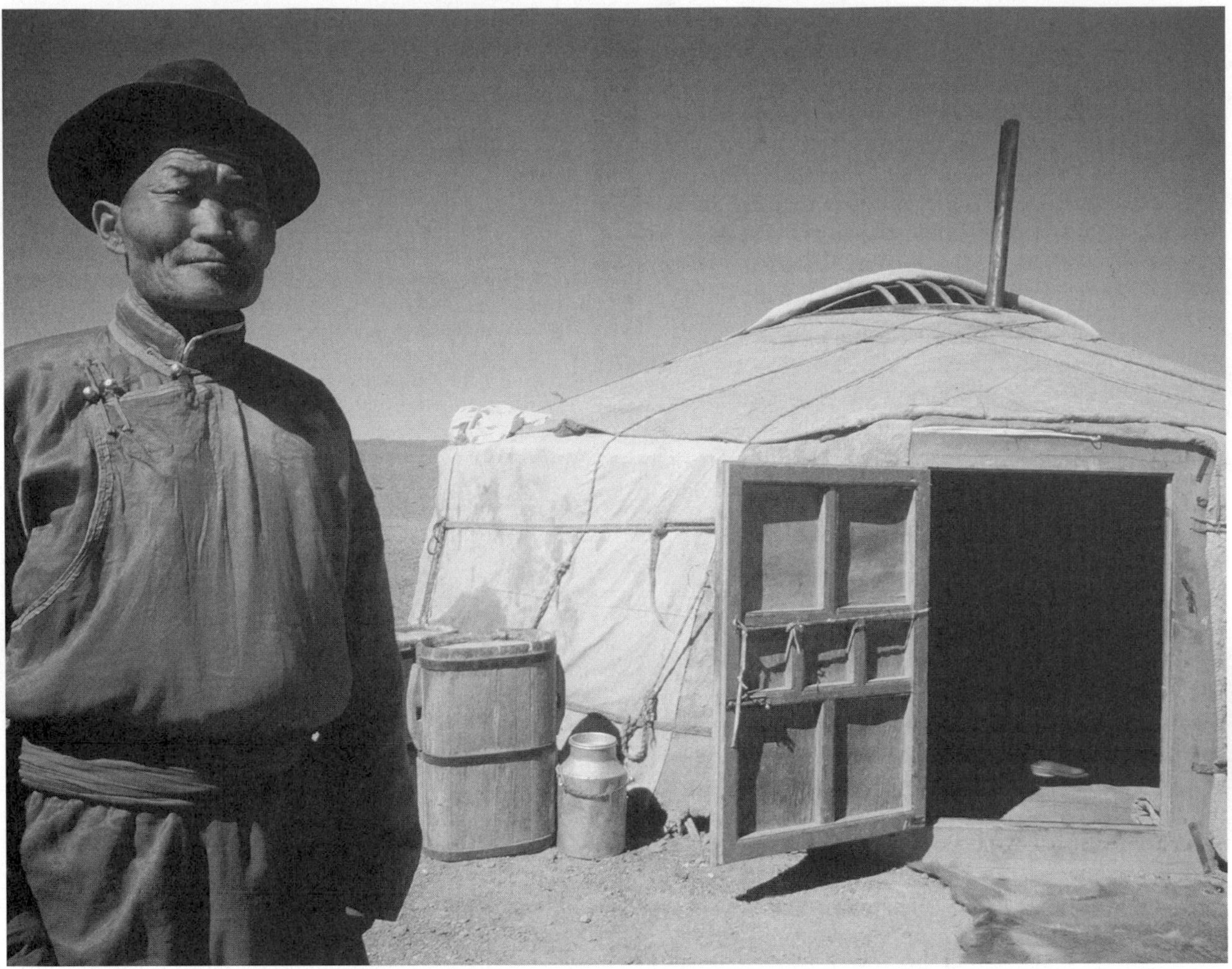

Mongolian man beside his yurt, Gobi Desert, Mongolia. (©Dean Conger/CORBIS)

as literary languages. Among the western dialects Oirat and Kalmuck should be mentioned. The so-called Classical Mongol was the literary language used from the 17th century up until the more recent reforms.

History. The first people known to have spoken a Mongol language were the Khitan, who under the dynastic title of Liao ruled over North China from 907 to 1125; they have no known genetic relations with the Mongols proper. The current practice of designating as Mongols such earlier nomadic peoples as HUNS and AVARS is unwarranted. The rise of Mongol power is connected with Genghis (more correctly Chingiz) Khan (b. 1167), who ''having united all the tribes living under felt-tents'' was elected supreme ruler of the Mongols in 1206. A man of extraordinary genius, he organized the Mongols, poor and small in number, into a formidable military machine that, by the time of his death in 1227, had expanded Mongol influence from the Pacific Ocean to the Adriatic Sea. The initial reasons for these wide conquests were economic. Horses were the only raw material the Mongol economy had in plentiful supply, and war was the most efficient and productive way of using them. To secure the products needed by his people, in the form of booty or through taxes levied on subjugated peoples, Genghis evolved a most efficient strategy, based on the extensive use of cavalry. As usual, the political theory that justified such actions was supplied only after the event when it was asserted that Genghis had been chosen by God to rule the world. The conquest of North China in 1211 to 1215 was followed in 1220 to 1221 by the conquest of Iran. In 1223 a Mongol vanguard defeated a coalition of Russian princes on the Kalka River. Under Genghis's son and successor Ögödei (Ogadai; d. 1241) the war in China was continued while Mongol armies invaded Hungary in 1241 to 1242. Another army, sent into Russia, plundered Moscow and destroyed Kiev. But the very size of the Mongol Empire was conducive to its disintegration. The westernmost part, called the Golden Horde, survived in

European Russia until 1502. When ruled by Berke (d. 1266), who adopted ISLAM, it became virtually autonomous, and its relations with the Il-khans, the Mongol rulers of Iran, deteriorated. During the reign of the great Khan Möngke (Mangu; d. 1259), who ruled from Mongolia, his brother Hülegü (d. 1265) was entrusted with the task of consolidating Mongol power in Iran, and in 1258 he also occupied BAGHDAD and put an end to the caliphate of the 'ABBĀSIDS. Hülegü's wife was a Christian, and in his entourage NESTORIANISM had considerable influence; it was not until the time of Gazan Khan (d. 1304) that the Il-khans finally adopted Islam. Their rule eventually collapsed under the attack of TIMUR (d. 1405) in 1393. The final conquest of China was achieved in 1279 under Möngke's successor Qubilai (Kublai) Khan (d. 1294); and under the dynastic title of Yüan, the Mongols ruled over China until 1368. A dominant power in Asia for a century and a half, the Mongols, after the havoc of the initial conquest, brought peace, a good administration, and tolerance to the countries conquered. Their political achievement matched their former military prowess. In the 13th and 14th centuries many contacts were established between the Mongols and western Europe. Thus INNOCENT IV and LOUIS IX of France sent several embassies to them and relations between the Il-khans and the kings of France and England were quite friendly. Several Mongol envoys visited Italy, France, and England, and the adventures of Marco Polo at the court of Kublai Khan became well known even in his own day.

Although by the 16th century the Mongols had lost all the lands conquered, they maintained themselves in Mongolia and in parts of South Siberia and of Turkestan. Much of their energy was used up in fratricidal conflicts between eastern and western Mongols. Under Dayan Khan (d. 1543), Altan Khan (d. 1583), and Ligdan Khan (d. 1634) political supremacy rested with the eastern Mongols, whereas under Galdan Khan (d. 1697) the initiative was in western Mongol hands. By that time the Mongols were trapped between the expanding Russian and Chinese empires, and in 1643 some of the Oirats moved from the Chinese borders to the Volga, where in due course they accepted a Russian protectorate. In 1771, in a memorable migration worthy of the Ten Thousand, the majority of the Oirats returned to China while the rest, called Kalmucks, remain in Russia to this day. Following the Chinese revolution of 1911, the Mongols of Mongolia declared their independence, which had been lost in the 18th century, but it was soon put to the test by various foreign interventions. In 1921, with Soviet help, independence was assured, but Mongolia remained a monarchy ruled by the theocratic supreme lama, Khutuktu Bogdo Gegen, until his death in 1924, when the country was transformed into a People's Republic. In 1961 Mongolia was admitted to the United Nations.

Civilization and Culture. Mongol civilization is of the nomadic, cattle-breeding type, but it has shown itself adaptable to foreign influences. Under Genghis Khan the Mongols adopted the Uighur writing, alphabetic and written in vertical lines from left to right, which has survived to this day, although at present the Cyrillic alphabet is used both in Outer Mongolia and among the Buriats. Originally shamanists, the Mongols were converted to LAMAISM, the Tibetan form of BUDDHISM, in the second half of the 16th century when Altan Khan accepted the spiritual authority of the *Dalai Lama.* The bulk of Mongol literature is Buddhist, and the whole Buddhist Canon was translated from the Tibetan. There exists also a very fine collection of original historical literature that includes the *Secret History of the Mongols* written in the middle of the 13th century and various other chronicles, such as that of Saghang Sechen written in the second half of the 17th century.

Bibliography: Sources. Translation from Mongol. E. HAENISCH, *Die geheime Geschichte der Mongolen* (Leipzig 1948). SSANANG SSETSEN, *Geschichte der Ost-Mongolen,* ed. I. J. SCHMIDT (Saint Petersburg 1829; repr. The Hague 1961). Translation from Persian. JUVEYNĪ, 'ALĀ AL-DĪN 'ATA MALEK, *The History of the World-Conqueror,* ed. and tr. J. A. BOYLE, 2 v. (Cambridge, Mass. 1958). Translation from Chinese. LI CHIH-CH'ANG, *The Travels of an Alchemist: The Journey of the Taoist, Ch'ang-ch'un from China to the Hindukush at the Summons of Chingiz Khan,* ed. and tr. A. WALEY (London 1931). Translation from Syriac. YAHB-ALAHA, et al., *The Monks of Kûblâi Khân, Emperor of China,* tr. E. A. W. BUDGE (London 1928). Translation from Latin and French. C. DAWSON, ed., *The Mongol Mission: Narratives and Letters of the Franciscan Missionaries in Mongolia and China in the 13th and 14th Centuries* (New York 1955). MARCO POLO, *The Description of the World,* ed. and tr. A. C. MOULE and P. PELLIOT, 2 v. (London 1938), to be used with P. PELLIOT, *Notes on Marco Polo,* ed. L. HAMBIS, 2 v. (Paris 1959–63). Literature. On modern Mongolia. R. A. RUPEN, *Mongols of the 20th Century,* 2 v. (Bloomington, Ind. 1964). On the languages. N. N. POPPE, *Introduction to Mongolian Comparative Studies* (Helsinki 1955); *Grammar of Written Mongolian* (Wiesbaden 1954). F. D. LESSING, ed., *Mongolian-English Dictionary* (Berkeley 1960). On history. R. GROUSSET, *L'Empire des steppes* (Paris 1939), best general work. C. M. OHSSON, *Histoire des Mongols, depuis Tchinguiz-Khan jusqu'à Timour Bey, ou Tamerlan,* 4 v. (The Hague 1834–35; reprs. available). H. H. HOWORTH, *History of the Mongols from the 9th to the 19th Century,* 4 v. (London 1876–88; "Supplement and Indices" London 1927), detailed but often inaccurate. On relations with the West. P. PELLIOT, "Les Mongols et la papauté," *Revue de l'orient chrétien* 23 (1922–23) 3–30; 24 (1924) 225–335; 28 (1931–32) 3–84. D. SINOR, "Les Relations entre les Mongols et l'Europe jusqu'à la mort d'Arghoun et de Béla IV," *Journal of World History* 3 (1956) 39–62. On the Il-khans. B. SPULER, *Die Mongolen in Iran* (2d ed. Berlin 1955). On the Golden Horde. B. SPULER, *Die Goldene Horde* (Leipzig 1943), to be read together with P. PELLIOT, *Notes sur l'histoire de la Horde d'Or* (Paris 1950). G. VERNADSKY, *The Mongols and Russia* (New Haven 1953). For more recent periods. E. V. BRETSCHNEIDER, *Mediaeval Researches from Eastern Asiatic Sources,* 2 v. (London 1910). On relations with Russia and China in the 16th to 18th centuries. J. F. BADDELEY, ed., *Russia, Mongolia, China,* 2 v. (London 1919). P. PELLIOT, *Notes critiques d'histoire Kalmouke,* 2 v. (Paris

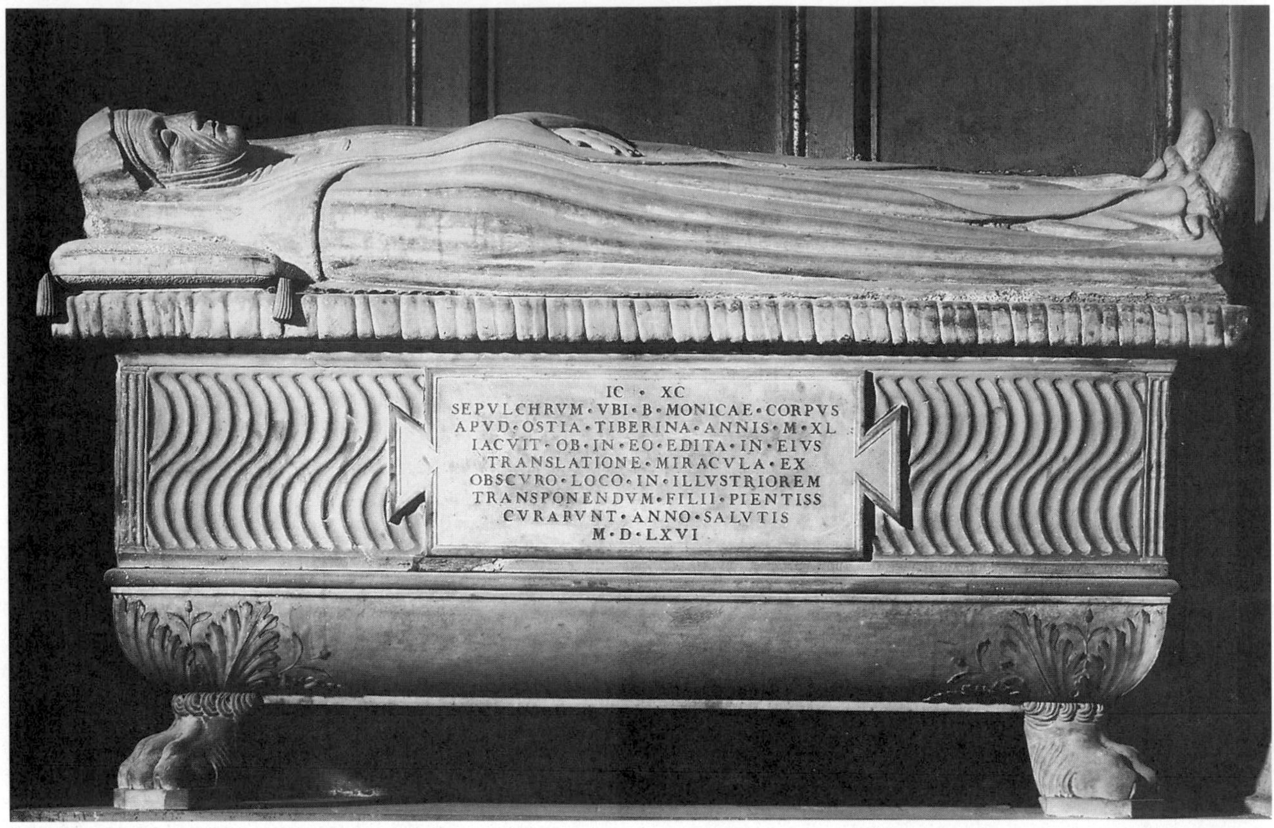

The sarcophagus of St. Monica by the 15th-century sculptor Isaia di Pisa. (Alinari-Art Reference/Art Resource, NY)

1960). N. P. SHASTINA, *Russko-mongol'skie posol'skie otnosheniia XVII veka* (Moscow 1958). L. M. GATAULLINA, comp., *Russko-mongol'skie otnosheniia, 1607–1636* (Moscow 1959). On civilization and literature. B. VLADIMIRTSOV, *Le Régime social des Mongols* (Paris 1948). A. RIASANOVSKY, *Fundamental Principles of Mongol Law* (Bloomington, Ind. 1965). W. HEISSIG, *Die Familien- und Kirchengeschichtsschreibung der Mongolen* (Wiesbaden 1959); ''Die mongolische Geschichtsschreibung im 18. und 19. Jahrhundert,'' *Saeculum* 3 (1952) 218–36. Further detailed bibliography on all aspects of Mongol studies. D. SINOR, *Introduction à l'étude de l'Eurasie Centrale* (Wiesbaden 1963).

[D. SINOR]

MONICA, ST.

Mother of St. AUGUSTINE; b. Tagaste, Numidia *c.* 322; d. Ostia, fall 387. Alhough born of Christian parents, Monica married a pagan official, Patricius (d. 371, a convert); she bore at least three children: Navigius, a daughter Perpetua (not mentioned by St. Augustine), and Augustine, who paints an unforgettable picture of her in his *Confessions.* She followed Augustine's education and career with motherly pride, and despite an estrangement during his Manichaean period, followed him to Rome and Milan, tolerating his dissipation and attempting to arrange a good marriage for him. This was voided by his baptism and conversion to a celibate life. Monica died and was buried at Ostia on the eve of a return journey to Africa. In 1162 her bones were translated to an Augustinian monastery near Arras in France from whence her cult spread throughout the Church. Other relics, however, were brought from Ostia to the Church of St. Augustine in Rome in 1430. Recently a fragment of her sepulchral inscription came to light in Ostia. She is a patron of women's sodalities.

Feast: May 4.

Bibliography: A. TRAPE, ed., *Augustinus, Meine Mutter Monika* (Munich 1998). E. CLARK, ''Rewriting Early Christian History: Augustine's Representation of Monica,'' *Portraits of Spiritual Authority* (1999) 3–23. D. WRIGHT, ''Monica's Baptism, Augustine's Deferred Baptism, and Patricius,'' *Augustinian Studies* 29 (1998) 1–17. H. LECLERCQ, *Dictionnaire d'archéologie chrétienne et de liturgie*, ed. F. CABROL, H. LECLERCQ, and H. I. MARROU (Paris 1905–53) 11.2:2232–56. L. ANDRÉ-DELASTRE, *Sainte Monique* (Lyon 1960). A. CASAMASSA, ''Ritrovamento di parte dell' elogio di S. Monica,'' *Rendiconti della Pontificia Accademia Romana de Archeologia* 27 (1952–54) 271–273.

[J. GEIGER]

MONISM

A philosophical system or doctrine that reduces all of reality to some type of unity, or admits only one basic PRINCIPLE where other doctrines admit two (DUALISM) or more (pluralism). MATERIALISM, IDEALISM, and PANTHEISM are the major forms that monist philosophies assume. This article surveys the various kinds of monism and then offers a brief critique from the viewpoint of Catholic thought.

Kinds. Depending on the type of principle or underlying unity to which all entities are reduced, monism may be variously designated as substantive, or conceptual, or moral and aesthetic.

Substantive. In substantive monism, the underlying principle is SUBSTANCE, which is usually viewed as either MATTER or SPIRIT. If everything is reducible to matter, as is affirmed in Marxism, spirit becomes nothing more than a modality of matter. A similar consequence results from the teaching of W. Ostwald (1853–1932), who spoke of energy as the sole subsistent reality. For J. M. Guyau (1854–88), it is life in a state of continual becoming that explains universal evolution and is itself the basis of everything real; in such vitalistic monism, spirit fares no better than in materialism, for both matter and spirit, in its view, are but an extract of life. The teaching of E. H. Haeckel is a classical example of materialistic monism. According to Haeckel, the universe is one to such an extent that there is no possibility of matter-spirit dualism: the universe was not created but evolves according to eternal laws and is identical with God; physical and chemical forces alone explain change; the soul is mortal;and so forth.

Among those varieties of monism in which substance is conceived as spirit, that of G. W. F. HEGEL exerts the greatest influence. For Hegel, the world is one and is in continual dialectical change under the direction of the idea, or logos, which constitutes all of ontological reality. British idealism, inspired by Hegel and developed especially by F. H. BRADLEY, likewise teaches the radical unity of the universe and the existence of the ABSOLUTE; for it, the multiplicity recognized by the senses, together with individuality and duration, is nothing more than appearance. Among earlier thinkers, G. BRUNO and B. SPINOZA may likewise be listed as monists who accented spirit as the unique type of substance.

Conceptual. The second kind of monism does not invoke a substantial principle of things, but rather the type of conception man can have of them. The accent is here placed on the unitary character of TRUTH, on a unity of knowledge rather than on an ontological unity. Paul Carus (1852–1919), the American positivist who founded the *Monist* in 1890, thus maintained that all truths, of whatever kind and origin, must agree among themselves. For him, scientific knowledge and religious faith can be completely and harmoniously reconciled; on any subject, there can be but one truth, which is eternal and independent of all subjective feelings and aspirations.

Moral and Aesthetic. Various other forms of monism include the moral and the aesthetic. A moral monism would draw ethical consequences from a materialistic view of the universe. This is essentially the teaching of Haeckel, who regarded his system as a religion that imposed a mode of conduct in basic conflict with that of Christianity. In a more restricted sense, one may regard as monistic any doctrine that postulates a certain unity of explanation within a limited sphere of ideas or of facts. It is in this sense that one may speak of an aesthetic monism, meaning by this the elegance and appeal of any simplified accounting for a domain of human experience.

Critique. The difficulties involved in accepting monism as a complete explanation of reality are evidenced by repeated attempts to develop pluralism as a consistent philosophical position. Pluralism is radically opposed to monism, especially when monism is understood in a Hegelian sense. In Germany, the teaching of J. F. Herbart is generally regarded as pluralistic and as thus antithetical to the idealistic monism of F. W. J. von SCHELLING. In France, C. B. Renouvier proposed a philosophy that is likewise spoken of as pluralistic. In the U.S., similarly, W. JAMES advocated a type of pluralism, as did H. A. Myers (1906–55) in his *Systematic Pluralism: A Study in Metaphysics* (Ithaca 1961).

Some elements stressed in monism, however, are to be found in all schools of philosophy. Despite the endless variety and diversity to be found in the universe, one need not be committed to a doctrine of absolute disparity. Beings resemble one another; they possess common characteristics, and there are transcendental attributes that encompass the entire ontological order. The activities of the many species of natural things are regulated by laws, so much so that one may speak of a UNIFORMITY in nature and in its operation. Similarly, there are metaphysical principles that confer a unity and organization on observable facts and the ideas men use to explain them. From the social point of view, and particularly with recent improvements in methods of communication and transportation, the world is becoming more and more one. Along these lines, P. TEILHARD DE CHARDIN has accented the unity of order and direction to be found in the universe, echoing the earlier suggestion of P. Lecomte du Noüy. In the mid-20th century, therefore, few thinkers held for an absolute multiplicity in the universe, without any element of permanence or continuity.

Nevertheless, monism itself cannot make an absolute claim to validity. A primary indication of dualism is that provided by the distinction between the universe and its Creator. Reason postulates, with evidence, the existence of a God who is not identical with His work. Again, although the universe is one, it contains a plurality of things. These are distinguished from each other by their GENUS and SPECIES as well as by their INDIVIDUALITY. This dog is not this cat or this horse, nor is it this other dog. The world is not a single substance, but is made up of subsisting realities that cannot be explained adequately in monistic terms. Despite its aesthetic appeal, monism is thus an oversimplified system that is unable to account for the totality of human experience.

See Also: POTENCY AND ACT; MATTER AND FORM; ESSENCE AND EXISTENCE; PLURALISM, PHILOSOPHICAL.

Bibliography: M. J. ADLER, ed., *The Great Ideas: A Syntopicon of Great Books of the Western World,* 2 v. (Chicago 1952) 2:282–302. C. MAZZANTINI, *Enciclopedia filosofica*, 4 v. (Venice-Rome 1957) 3:678–80. O. HABERT, *Dictionnaire de théologie catholique*, ed. A. VACANT et al., 15 v. (Paris 1903–50) 10.1:315–34. W. BRUGGER, *Lexikon für Theologie und Kirche*, ed. J. HOFER and K. RAHNER, 10 v. (2d, new ed. Freiburg 1957–65) 7:553–55. R. LORENZ, *Die Religion in Geschichte und Gegenwart*, 7 v. (3d ed. Tübingen 1957–65) 4:1099–102. R. EISLER, *Wörterbuch der philosophischen Begriffe*, 3 v. (4th ed. Berlin 1927–30) 2:173–77.

[W. A. WALLACE]

MONITA SECRETA

A collection of allegedly secret instructions from the Jesuit general C. ACQUAVIVA to provincials and rectors. *Monita secreta (privata) Societatis Jesu* is actually a clumsy forgery and has long been recognized as such, but even today it is introduced into popular anti-Jesuit writings. After its appearance (Crakow 1614, falsified as Notobrigae 1612), it was widely distributed in a short while (22 eds. in seven languages by 1700, and 42 eds. by 1786). The titles varied: *Avis d'or de la très religieuse Compagnie de Jésus, Le Cabinet jésuitique, Arcanes de la Compagnie de Jésus, Jesuiterpolitica, The Secret Instructions of the Jesuits,* etc. It was put on the Index May 10, 1616 (made public Dec. 28, 1616), and numerous rebuttals soon appeared (M. Bembus in 1615, J. Argenti in 1616, J. Gretser in 1618, and A. Tanner, et al.), but it continued to circulate. The former Jesuit Jerome Zahorowski, dismissed from the society in 1613, was established as its author through an investigation ordered by the bishop of Crakow himself in 1615 and through an entry in the diary of the Jesuit house in Crakow in August 1614. Similar in style to the rules and the constitution of the society, the *Monita* in 16 chapters, later expanded to 17, contains detailed instructions on how to use trickery, dissimulation, and political intrigue, and how to get hold of inheritances, always with the increase of the society's power and influence in mind and without regard for faith and morals. The sharp contrast between the content of the *Monita* and both the letter and the spirit of the society's constitution and the instructions of the generals is so obvious as not to require explication. Even enemies of the society, such as P. SARPI, A. ARNAULD, and the Jansenistic *Nouvelles ecclésiastiques,* rejected the work as false. This verdict was confirmed in the 19th century (DÖLLINGER, F. REUSCH, A. von HARNACK). Nonetheless, the work continues to be used as invective in polemics; e.g., P. von Hoensbroech concedes that it is technically a forgery but maintains that in fact its instructions reflect the true spirit of the society.

Bibliography: P. TACCHI-VENTURI, ''Il Prof. Raffaele Mariano ed i 'Monita Secreta' dei Gesuiti,'' *La Civiltà Cattolica* 5 (1902) 341–344; ''L'autenticità dei 'Monita Secreta,' e il Prof. Raffaele Mariano,'' *ibid.* 694–713. A. BROU, *Les Jésuites de la légende,* 2 v. (Paris 1906–07) v. 1. B. DUHR, *I Gesuiti, favole e leggende,* 2 v. (Florence 1908) v.1. L. KOCH, *Jesuiten-Lexikon* 1225–27.

[B. SCHNEIDER]

MONK

A monk is a member of a religious community of men living apart from the world, vowed according to a definite rule to a celibate life of poverty and obedience, and dedicated primarily to the performance of religious duties and to the contemplative life. The Latin word *monachus,* from which monk is derived, is a transliteration of the Greek μοναχός—one who lives alone. The Greek word was borrowed by Christians from the Greek Old Testament [Ps 101(102).8] and applied not only to ANCHORITES but—from the beginning of monasticism —to the individual members of monastic communities; and *monachus* with this meaning was in common use among the Latin Christians of the 4th century. In the 5th and 6th centuries the Latin and Greek words were applied not only to the worthy CENOBITES and HERMITS of that age but also to the various types of the monastic degeneration—the *gyrovagi* and *sarabaitae* mentioned by St. Benedict. With the popularization of the Rule of St. Benedict in the West, *monachus* was for a time, especially in monastic contexts, often used to refer precisely to individuals living under that rule; but in general, before the Cluniac reform, *monachus* was used broadly and with great imprecision. The early medieval monastic reforms tended to fix the meaning of *monachus* and its already current derivatives in the European languages, so that through the following centuries up to the Reformation, *monachus* was applied to Benedictines, Cistercians, and Carthusians, but not usually to canons, FRIARS, and members of the other new medieval institutions. With the Reformation, this precision was lost, except among a few writers of ecclesiastical Latin, and has been restored in the modern languages only among the most knowledgeable of historians. In practice, the modern English word monk is seldom used with such precision and is made to refer not only to all male religious of the Catholic and Orthodox churches but also to members of non–Christian religious bodies, e.g., the Buddhist monks of Vietnam.

See Also: MONASTICISM.

Bibliography: J. LECLERCQ, *Études sur le vocabulaire monastique du moyen âge* in *Studia anselmiana,* 48; 1961) 1–38. H. LECLERCQ, *Dictgionnaire d'archéologie chrétienne et de liturgie,* ed. F. CABROL, H. LECLERCQ, and H. I. MARROU, 15 v. (Paris 1907–53) 2.1:3047–3248. J. OLPHE–GALLIARD, *Dictionnaire de spiritualité ascétique et mystique. Doctrine et histoire,* ed. M. VILLER et al. (Paris 1932–) 2:404–416.

[A. DONAHUE]

MONK OF FARNE

The name generally given to the author of seven meditations in MS B iv.34 of Durham cathedral library. His name was John and he should probably be identified with John Whiterig of Northumberland, monk and novice master at Durham, who lived on Farne for eight years and died there in 1371. His longest and most important meditation, on Christ crucified, is concerned with God's love for men, as shown in the Crucifixion, and with man's response, which should also be total love. He begins by addressing Christ under a series of OT types, then contemplates the crucified Christ directly and realistically, but also serenely, calling on man to commit himself to Christ. Once this is done Christ will visit the soul as He did for the saints and martyrs. The reader is exhorted to study the open book of the Savior's sufferings: the letters are the five wounds; the words, His actions and sufferings. The all-important thing is that Christ should be loved: charity will bring the reader through carnal and rational love to the highest kind attainable in this life. Here the writer depends fairly closely on St. Bernard; elsewhere he cites SS. Gregory, Augustine, Bede, Isidore, Ambrose, Peter Damian, Hugh of Saint-Victor, Innocent III, and John Pecham. But the influence of Scripture is the strongest, and the texts, including the dogmatic ones, are frequently and skillfully interwoven.

It is not known with any certainty that the monk of Farne influenced other spiritual writers; his importance lies rather as witness to what a 14th-century Durham monk thought and prayed about. This type of spiritual writing is rare in this century; it affords a glimpse of a fervent, but conservative, monk at prayer. The other meditations are addressed to Our Lady, the angels, Abraham and David, St. John the Evangelist, and St. Cuthbert (incomplete).

Bibliography: W. A. PANTIN, ''The Monk-Solitary of Farne,'' *English Historical Review* 49 (1944) 162–186; *The English Church in the Fourteenth Century* (Cambridge 1955) 245–252. D. KNOWLES, *The Religious Orders in England* 2:115–117. Latin Text. H. FARMER, ''The Meditations of the Monk of Farne,'' Analecta Monastica 4 (1957) 141–245. Translation. *The Monk of Farne,* ed. H. FARMER (London 1961).

[H. FARMER]

MONOGENISM AND POLYGENISM

Monogenism takes the position that the whole human race is descended from a single couple or a single individual. At least until the mid-nineteenth century, monogenism was also regarded as entailing the immediate creation of the first man or couple by a special divine act. Given the preponderant evidence for biological evolution, monogenism is no longer understood in this way. But if the first biological couple may have arisen through an evolutionary process, it remains Church teaching that the SOUL of each and every human being is created directly by God (Pope John Paul II 1997).

The position contrary to monogenism is known as polygenism, of which there are two types. According to the first (called monophyletic polygenism), since evolution always proceeds within an interbreeding group, humanity would have first appeared among a number of individuals, whose progeny gradually spread world-wide through emigration. Thus, one would speak of a first community rather than a first couple or man. The second type (called polyphyletic polygenism) hypothesizes that the human species arose through separate evolutionary lines in a number of different places at different times, with the different lines converging to form our present population. Scientists have not reached consensus on which of the two versions of polygenism—the monophyletic or polyphyletic—is more likely to be true (Harpending 1994).

Monogenism was presumed by the Council of TRENT in its teaching on ORIGINAL SIN (DS 1511–1514). The most explicit statement on monogenism came in 1950 in Pope Pius XII's encyclical letter *HUMANI GENERIS*. Referring to Rom. 5.12 and the teaching of Trent, Pius maintained that ''Christ's faithful cannot embrace'' either form of polygenism, since ''it is in no way apparent how such an opinion can be reconciled'' with the scriptural and magisterial teaching on original sin, namely, that this sin was ''actually committed by an individual Adam'' and ''through generation is passed on to all and is in everyone as his own'' (DS 3897).

In view of Pope Pius's statement, many theologians (including K. RAHNER in 1954) argued that monogenism is so closely implied by the teaching on original sin that it must be considered a certain, if not infallible, tenet of faith. But the conclusions drawn by science, which flatly contradict monogenism, were found increasingly persuasive by theologians, including Rahner, who reversed his initial support of the position in 1967. The present situation amounts to a quandary for theologians. On the one hand, even though it has not been formally addressed by the magisterium since *Humani generis*, monogenism continues to be accepted as a basic premise in Church teaching, as is shown by the relevant sections of the *The Catechism of the Catholic Church* (nn. 374–379, 390, 399–407). On the other hand, to deny the polygenistic origin of the human species places the theologian in clear opposition with science, and conjures up the image of an obscurantist faith combating the truth of reason. And yet it may very well prove to be that science, in its forthright drive for empirical knowledge, has only forced theology to deeper reflection on its own central claim that Christ lies at the heart of all (Col. 1.16).

It is evident that the magisterium has insisted on monogenism for the sake of defending the teaching on original sin, according to which, as Trent declared, all of humanity belongs to a single order which was intrinsically ''changed for the worse,'' physically and spiritually, by virtue of a human decision made at this order's beginning (DS 1511–1513). Hence, the judgment by Pius XII in *Humani generis* that the faithful are not free to accept polygenism, since it appears quite impossible to speak of any human act having the kind of effect that Trent assigned to the first sin if the human order emerged gradually and in plural fashion from an antecedent nonhuman order. If science is right about the mechanisms that gave rise to the biological species Homo sapiens, and the tradition is right about the nature of the human order, it would seem that theologians must continue to reflect on the data in search of other ways of defending the issue. One alternative is to consider the possibility that the roots of this order transcend, even precede, its present empirical condition. In his work entitled *A Theological Anthropology* (1963), the Swiss theologian Hans Urs von BALTHASAR entertained just this possibility. It may be necessary, he wrote, to say that the primal decision that shaped human freedom lies ''above the whole temporal unfolding of the material cosmogonic process. In particular, does it exist above the biological development of man, which would thus be subject already and at its very heart to the law of generation and death and consequently to 'vanity''' (90). If Balthasar is right, then future theological inquiry must be prepared to regard the question of monogenism or the constitution of the human order, like the question of the first sin, as referring to a state of affairs that both is fundamental to and underlies the present sequence of biological phenomena that is described by science.

Bibliography: JOHN PAUL II, ''Address to Pontifical Academy of Sciences,'' *The Pope Speaks* 42 (1997) 118–121. H. HARPENDING, ''Gene Frequencies, DNA Sequences, and Human Origins,'' *Perspectives in Biology and Medicine* 37, no. 3 (Spring 1994) 384–394. K. RAHNER, ''Theological Reflexions on Monogenism,'' *Theological Investigations*, vol. 1 (London 1961; New York 1974), 229–296; ''Evolution and Original Sin,'' *Concilium* 26 (1967) 61–73; ''Monogenism,'' *Sacra Mundi* 4:105–107; ''Erbsünde und Monogenismus'' in K.-H. WEGER, *Theologie der Erbsünde* (Freiburg 1970). H. U. VON BALTHASAR, *A Theological Anthropology* (New York 1967). J. D. KORSMEYER, *Evolution and Eden: Balancing Original Sin and Contemporary Science* (New York 1998). Z. ALZEGHY, ''Development in the Doctrinal Formulation of the Church concerning the Theory of Evolution,'' *Concilium* 26 (1967) 25–33.

[K. A. MCMAHON]

MONOPHYSITISM

The schismatic and eventually heretical movement that sprang from the exaggerated insistence on one nature (μόνη φύσις) in Jesus Christ. The actual heretical concept of the absorption of the divine nature in the human nature or vice versa is called EUTYCHIANISM, even though it is doubtful that the 5th-century Constantinopolitan archimandrite, EUTYCHES, possessed either the knowledge or the desire to found a doctrine contrary to orthodox tradition.

Background. Theological reflection on the nature of the being of Jesus Christ, at once true God and true man, had caused considerable difficulty in the early Church and had given rise to such heresies as DOCETISM, MODALISM or SABELLIANISM, and ARIANISM. Philosophical speculation under the impulse of both Neoplatonism and, later, Aristotelianism introduced logical considerations that tended to deny that Christ was of the same being or substance as the Father, and therefore truly divine, or that He was at the same time truly human. Soteriological considerations on the other hand played an important part in setting the theological tradition.

The Alexandrians generally, following a Platonic bent, were interested in man's divinization. They took literally the scriptural statement that man was made ''in the image and likeness of God'' (Gn 1.26); and they found support in Paul's quotations (Acts 17.27–29) of the pagan poets Epimenides (''for in him we live, and move, and have our being'') and Aratus (''for we also are his offspring''). They stressed the fact that through Christ's divinity man would eventually be divinized.

The Antiochians, on the other hand, adopting a more literal approach to Scripture and influenced by Aristotelian logic and empiricism, stressed the humanity of Christ, again with Saint Paul insisting that it was in Christ's Resurrection that mankind was redeemed and that through participation in the Resurrection of Christ man would be fulfilled in grace and glory, since Christ restored His own and all humanity through the triumph of His Resurrection.

Cyril and the Controversy. To emphasize the human side of Christ's being, DIODORE OF TARSUS spoke of Mary as the *Christotokos* (Christ-bearer), instead of the traditional THEOTOKOS (God-bearer); and NESTORIUS as patriarch of Constantinople attempted in his sermons to force the issue. In reaction, the monks and the clergy called upon CYRIL OF ALEXANDRIA for assistance. Acting on a commission from Pope CELESTINE I, Cyril seized control of the Council of EPHESUS (431), condemned Nestorius and, with his twelve anathemas, attempted to root out totally the very possibility of NESTORIANISM, the doctrine that the human nature and the divine nature in Christ were merely a mixture or indwelling of one in the other. To avoid the possibility of alleging that there are ''two persons or two sons'' in Christ, Cyril seized on the formula μία φύσις τοῦ θεοῦ λόγου σεσαρκωμένη, i.e., one nature of the word God Incarnate. He attributed the phrase to his predecessor in Alexandria, Athanasius; actually the sentence was of Apollinarist origin.

The problem revolved round the meaning of the word φύσις (nature), used by Apollinaris and Nestorius and accepted by Cyril in the sense of a concrete and subsistent nature. In this meaning, it is a perfect synonym for ὑπόστασις and πρόσωπον, or person. Used of Christ, φύσις (*physis* or nature) in this sense meant the one sole Person of the Word, eternally subsistent, Who had extended His proper subsistence to the concrete and complete individual human nature to which He was united by the Incarnation. This is the way Cyril used the words *mia physis* (one nature) and the manner in which it was employed by the followers of Cyril. When the theologians of the Council of Chalcedon and the Nestorians spoke of two natures in Christ, they were employing an earlier traditional meaning of the word *physis,* or nature, in which it was completely distinct from the *hypostasis* or *prosōpon* as used for the Persons in the *theologia* of the Trinity.

Cyril and the Monophysites changed the meaning of *physis,* or nature, to a complete person in dealing with Christ in the *economia* of salvation, and thus gave rise to the dispute that gravely disturbed the Oriental Church for 1,000 years. They had in mind the destroying of the equivocation of the extreme Nestorian position that admitted two persons in Christ, that of the Word and that of the Son of Mary. But they occasioned the danger of having the human nature of Christ considered as something automatic, deprived of truly human spontaneity and free activity. To avoid this danger, the Council of CHALCEDON had adopted a dyophysite, or two-nature, explanation, explicitly justifying the concepts and terminology of Cyril, but adapting the meaning of *physis* to the older Trinitarian terminology and speaking of Christ as ''of two natures.''

Monophysite Revolt. This terminology was rejected by the Monophysites, beginning with the Egyptians, and their revolt spread through the Orient. In actual fact, the rejection of the Chalcedonian doctrine was verbal or semantic rather than truly doctrinal, and in the course of the subsequent disputes, only a few groups of Monophysites held positions that were actually heretical in the sense of claiming that Christ's divinity absorbed the humanity or vice versa.

Attempts by the imperial authorities to pacify the Monophysites through compromise statements such as the HENOTICON of Zeno and various decrees of JUSTINIAN I were of no avail: these decrees were rejected as inadequate by the Monophysites and by the orthodox as dangerous to the doctrinal definition of Chalcedon. The leaders of theological thought among the Monophysites, such as Timothy Aelurus, Peter Mongus, Peter the Fuller, Philoxenus of Mabbugh, James Baradai, and above all SEVERUS OF ANTIOCH, who gave the movement its solid theological foundation and coherence, were not formal heretics. They repudiated the Eutychian explanation, and they fully maintained the integrity of the two natures in Christ after the union in the Incarnation, without mixture or confusion. J. LEBON has proved this conclusively in regard to Severus; and more recent study of the writings of the other leaders confirms the testimony of contemporaries of theirs such as Vigilius of Thapsus, Timothy of Constantinople, and later JOHN DAMASCENE. The Monophysites proved schismatical in tendency in that they refused to accept the Council of Chalcedon and the obedience demanded by the Holy See as well as by the orthodox-minded emperors. Their position was made finally untenable by the Council of CONSTANTINOPLE II (553), which, although apparently concerned primarily with the condemnation of the Three Chapters and the Nestorian position, so restated the teaching of Chalcedon as to canonize that Council's doctrine. In so doing, Justinian's council failed to prevent problems that would arise in the next century with MONOTHELITISM and Monergism; but it did provide the death blow for aberrations such as Theopaschitism, Aphthartodocetism, and those of sects issuing from Severian or Trinitarian Monophysitism.

See Also: CHRISTOLOGY, CONTROVERSIES ON (PATRISTIC); THREE CHAPTERS; JUSTINIAN I, BYZANTINE EMPEROR; CONSTANTINOPLE II, COUNCIL OF

Bibliography: M. JUGIE, *Dictionnaire de théologie catholique*, ed. A. VACANT et al., 15 v. (Paris 1903–50) 10.2:2216–2306. J. LEBON, *Le Monophysisme Sévérien* (Louvain 1909). A. GRILLMEIER and H. BACHT, *Das Konzil von Chalkedon: Geschichte und Gegenwart*, 3 v. (Würzburg 1951–54) 1:425–580; 2:179–92; 3:3–49. C. J. VON HEFELE, *Histoire des conciles d'après les documents originaux*, tr. and continued by H. LECLERCQ, 10 v. in 19 (Paris 1907–38) 2.1:499–512; 3.1:68–132. H. G. BECK, *Kirche und theologische Literatur im byzantinischen Reich* (Munich 1959) 283–91, 387–94. P. KRÜGER, *Orientalia Christiana periodica* 4 (1938) 5–46. A. GRILLMEIER, *Lexikon für Theologie und Kirche*, ed. J. HOFER and K. RAHNER, 10 v. (2d, new ed. Freiburg 1957–65) 7:563–65. R. DRAGUET, *Julien d'Halicarnasse et sa controverse avec Sévère d'Antioche sur l'incorruptibilité du corps du Christ* (Louvain 1924). R. DEVREESSE, *Miscellanea Giovanni Mercati*, 6 v. (Rome 1946); *Studi e Testi* (Rome 1900–) 121–26. 3:1–15. C. MOELLER, ''Le Cinquième concile oecuménique et le Magistère ordinaire au VIe siècle,'' *Revue des sciences philosophiques et théologiques* 35 (1951) 413–23. F. X. MURPHY, *Constantinople II* (Paris 1966). W. H. C. FREND, *The Rise of the Monophysite Movement; Chapters in the History of the Church in the Fifth and Sixth Centuries* (Cambridge, England 1972). R. C. CHESNUT, *Three Monophysite Christologies: Severus of Antioch, Philoxenus of Mabbug, and Jacob of Sarug* (Oxford, England 1976). W. A. WIGRAM, *The Separation of the Monophysites* (New York 1978). B. MEUNIER, *Le Christ de Cyrille d'Alexandrie: l'humanité, le salut et la question monophysite* (Paris 1997). P. FRIES and T. NERSOYAN, eds., *Christ in East and West* (Macon, Georgia 1987).

[F. X. MURPHY]

MONOTHELITISM

A 7th-century Christological heresy that originated in an attempt to return the Monophysites to orthodox doctrine by means of formulas that stated that in Christ there was only one operation, *energeia,* proceeding from a unique will, *monon thelēma.* The history of Monothelitism covers a period of 60 years ending with its condemnation in the Sixth Ecumenical Council, CONSTANTINOPLE III (681).

The background to the Monothelite development is furnished by Severian MONOPHYSITISM, which employed the terminology of St. CYRIL OF ALEXANDRIA concerning the one nature in Christ to express the oneness of His Person. As a result, an expression such as one will and one operation in Christ had come into theological usage, although errors such as APOLLINARIANISM had been condemned for denying that Christ had a human soul and maintaining that He had only one divine will. SEVERUS OF ANTIOCH (512–518) had insisted that since Christ was a unity, the divine and human natures were so coordinated that one could speak of but one will and one action.

Patriarch Eulogius of Alexandria (580–607) had defended the doctrine of two wills and two activities in Christ. His adversaries, relying on the doctrine of Severus, spoke of one sole will proceeding from one sole subject willing. While for Severus this formula was susceptible of an orthodox interpretation, it led to the heresy of Monothelitism. Sergius I of Constantinople (610–638) had proposed to Emperor HERACLIUS that the Monophysites of Syria and Egypt could be brought back into the Church by speaking of one energy or operation in Christ, and advances were made to George Arsas, head of the Monophysite section of Egypt, and to Paul the Blind in Armenia without great success. But in 626 the emperor contacted Cyrus, Metropolitan of Sebastopolis, who accepted the explanations given by Sergius and interested Theodore of Pharan, Arabia, in the same. In 631 Heraclius named Cyrus patriarch of Alexandria, commissioning him to bring the Monophysites back into the Church. The Act of Union (June 3, 633) explicitly professed ''one Christ and Son, performing things attributable to God and man in one theandric operation'' (Mansi 11:565). At the same time Heraclius completed a treaty of union with the Armenian Church.

The difficulty with this doctrine lay in the fact that monoenergism connotes a unique operation that could proceed from the coordination of divine and human wills in Christ and would therefore be orthodox; but it can also mean a unique source of operation and would deny the human will in Christ.

SOPHRONIUS OF JERUSALEM, while still a monk in Alexandria, protested the monoenergism doctrine to Sergius of Constantinople; and the latter suggested that instead of speaking of two operations in Christ, the Fathers and Councils had spoken rather of the one sole Person operating in the divine and human actions of the Word Incarnate. In 634 Sergius wrote in this sense to Pope HONORIUS I (625–638), and his doctrinal explanation (*psēphos*) served as a basis for the *Ecthesis* published by Heraclius in 638. The doctrine of one will in Christ, though not explicitly asserted, is implicit in this document.

The reply of Pope Honorius accepted the suggested prohibition against speaking of one or two operations (*energeiai*) in Christ and, to exclude the possibility of a conflict between the human and divine wills in Christ, spoke of one will. In Christ the one Person there can be no dualism or antagonism in His willing. In 634 Sophronius, now patriarch of Jerusalem, sent the pope his *Epistula Synodica,* in which he clearly distinguished the operations of the two natures and spoke of theandric acts as intermediary between operations proceeding from the human nature alone and operations proceeding from the divine nature alone.

The doctrine expressed in the *Ecthesis* of Heraclius stressed the one will in Christ in a sense of the act of the will; but it was interpreted generally to mean a suppression or fusion of the human will in Christ, and as a consequence it was condemned by Pope JOHN IV (640–642) in a Roman synod. Both Pope THEODORE I and MAXIMUS THE CONFESSOR further condemned Monothelitism, appealing to the doctrine of the Greek Fathers of the 4th century and stressing the indissoluble union between Christology and the dogma of the Redemption. In 647 Pope Theodore I excommunicated Patriarch Paul of Constantinople when the latter refused to condemn Monothelitism, and Emperor Constans II (641–668) in 647 issued a *Typos* (rule for faith) prohibiting all discussion of one or two wills and operations in Christ (Mansi 10:1029–32). Pope MARTIN I held a synod in the Lateran basilica that condemned Monothelitism and the *Typos*. In reprisal both the pope and St. Maximus were seized, taken to Constantinople, tortured, and exiled. Only after the assassination of Emperor Constans II in 668 did the *Typos* become a dead letter. Later Emperor Constantine IV (668–685) authorized the convocation of the Council of Constantinople III (680–681) by Pope Agatho. Two natural activities and two natural wills were defined as well as the preservation of free will in Christ; and misunderstanding was eliminated by stressing the inseparability, distinction, and harmony of the two wills in Christ.

Bibliography: M. JUGIE, *Dictionnaire de théologie catholique* 10.2:2307–23. *Histoire de l'église depuis les origines jusqu'à nos jours* 5:103–179. H. RAHNER and A. GRILLMEIER, *Lexikon für Theologie und Kirche*, ed. J. HOFER and K. RAHNER, 10 v. (2d new ed. Freiburg1957–65) 7:570–572. V. GRUMEL, *Échos d'Orient* 27 (1928) 6–16, 257–77; 28 (1929) 19–34, 158–166, 272–282; 29 (1930) 16–28. E. CASPAR, ''Lateran Synode'' *Zeitschrift für Kirchengeschichte* 51 (1932) 75–137. P. GALTIER, ''Honorius,'' *Gregorianum* 29 (1948) 42–61. P. SHERWOOD, ed. and tr., *An Annotated Date List of . . . St. Maximus the Confessor* (Rome 1952). S. P. BROCK, ''Two Sets of Monothelete Questions to the Maximianists,'' *Orientalia Lovaniensia periodica* 17 (1986):119–140. P. VERGHESE, ''Monothelete Controversy: A Historical Survey,'' *Greek Orthodox Theological Review* 13 no 2 (1968):196–211.

[G. OWENS]

MONROY É HIJAR, ANTONIO

Mexican Dominican educator and archbishop of Santiago de Compostela, Spain; b. Querétaro, Mexico, c. 1632–34; d. Santiago de Compostela, Nov. 7, 1715. His father, Antonio, acted as the general moderator of Mexico City, and his mother was Doña María de Hijar y Figueroa. He received his bachelor's degree in philosophy in 1652 and joined the Dominicans in 1654 in Mexico City. Subsequently he taught theology at the University of Mexico and at the Dominican College of Porta-Coeli, Mexico City. The provincial chapter of 1663 recommended him for the degree of *Praesentatus,* and the chapter of 1667 for that of master of theology. He was a consultant of the Holy Office and was sent to Rome as definitor to the general chapter. There he was elected master general in 1677. He called upon the fathers in the chapter to revise the constitution and to restore more perfectly the common life in Dominican convents. In 1685 he was appointed archbishop of Santiago de Compostela. He was also chaplain for King Charles II, who made him a grandee of Spain. In his diocese he was zealous in correcting morals and restoring discipline. The income of the see, about 100,000 ducats, was used to build infirmaries, convents, chapels, and churches and to help the poor. He collected a large library, which was given to the Jesuits upon his death.

Bibliography: D. A. MORTIER, *Histoire des maîtres généraux de l'ordre des Frères Prêcheurs,* 8 v. (Paris 1903–20).

[A. B. NIESER]

Jacques Marie Monsabré.

MONSABRÉ, JACQUES MARIE

Dominican preacher; b. Blois, France, Dec. 12, 1827; d. Le Havre, Feb. 22, 1907. Baptized Louis, he attended the Grand Seminaire, Blois, and was ordained there in 1851. At once he sought an *exeat* in order to join the Dominicans, which was refused. He was successively curate at the church of St. Vincent de Paul, Blois; curate at a chapel in Mer, where his brother was curé; and tutor with a private family. In 1855 he was released from the diocese, and on May 31 he joined the Dominicans at Flavigny. A year later, after profession, he went to the priory at Chalais des Alpes, where he studied the writings of St. Thomas Aquinas.

In 1857 he began his preaching career with a series of sermons at Saint-Nizier's, Lyons, whence he was invited to preach at the cathedral. Later in the year, in the chapel of St. Thomas Aquinas in Paris, he commenced a series of conferences that continued until 1865. Meanwhile he developed an international reputation, filling pulpits in Paris, Brussels, and London, as well as in the French provinces. In 1867 he became the regular preacher in the Dominican church in Paris.

In 1869 Monsabré was invited to preach the Advent course in Notre Dame to replace Père Loyson, who had been excommunicated that fall. His success won him an invitation to preach the Lenten course at Notre Dame, succeeding the famous Jesuit Père Felix. There, during Lent of 1872, he preached a course on Christianity in society. The next year he began a series devoted to the exposition of Christian dogma that he continued to its completion in 1890. That year he retired to the priory at Lc Havrc but continucd to do somc prcaching. In 1890 he gave an Advent course in Rome and, in 1891, at Toulouse. At Le Havre he began a series of Lenten courses in 1897, a series that continued until 1903 and was published as the *Petits carêmes.*

Apart from his priorship in Le Havre (1881–84), Monsabré had not been involved in administrative positions, but he represented the province of France at general chapters of the order in 1871 at Ghent and in 1891 at Avila. His life was devoted to study and the preparation of his sermons. In 1873, at the age of 40, he had set himself the task of placing in a French setting everything in the theology of St. Thomas Aquinas that could be effectively preached. In the history of the pulpit of Notre Dame, he is not renowned, as are Lacordaire and many of his successors, for his appeal to the heart. Rather, he followed the classic formulas of Bossuet and Bordaloue. He aimed at instructing the intelligence in order that the heart be left with lasting motivation, and to this end he discovered the secret of melding into classic French oratory the strength of Aquinas. His collected sermons fill 35 volumes (8th ed. Paris 1901–04).

Bibliography: M. M. GORCE, *Dictionnaire de théologie catholique,* 15 v. (Paris 1903–50) 10.2:2323–2335. G. GIERATHS, *Lexicon für Theologie und Kirche,* 10 v. (Freiburg 1957–) 7:573. J. SCHROEDER, *The Catholic Encyclopedia,* 16 v. (New York 1907–14) 10:508–509. P. FERNESSOLE, *Les Conférenciers de Notre Dame,* v. 2 (Paris 1936).

[R. M. COFFEY]

MONSIGNOR

Title of French origin introduced into the papal household during the years of the pontifical court's stay in Avignon. It is now given to all clerics who belong to the papal household (except cardinals, although also addressed as *monseigneur* in French), i.e., palatine prelates (his excellency, the most reverend monsignor), papal chamberlains (if participating, right reverend monsignor, if supernumerary, very reverend monsignor), domestic prelates (right reverend monsignor), masters of the papal ceremonies (right reverend monsignor), secret chaplains, common chaplains, secret clerics, as well as to bishops—not commonly used in English. All vicars-general of dioceses, being automatically honorary prothonotaries apostolic, enjoy the title, even if not members of the papal household. According to ancient tradition, the title is often given by courtesy to consistorial advocates, who are ceremonially dressed in crimson-lined and crimson-buttoned cassock, although they are generally laymen.

Use of the title of monsignor has been altered somewhat by the Instruction of the Papal Secretariat of State, *Ut sive sollicite*, March 31, 1969 [*Acta Apostolicae Sedis* 61 (1969) 334–340]. The title may continue to be used of bishops, who, along with the superior prelates of the offices of the Roman Curia without episcopal rank, the Auditors of the Roman Rota, the Promotor General of Justice and the Defender of the Bond of the Apostolic Signatura, the Apostolic Prothonotaries *de numero* and the four Clerics of the Camera, may be addressed as "Most Reverend." For lesser prelates (supernumerary apostolic prothonotaries, prelates of honor, and chaplains of His Holiness), the distinction between "Right Reverend" and "Very Reverend" has been abolished. For them, the title may be preceded where appropriate by "Reverend."

[P. C. VAN LIERDE/B. C. GERHARDT]

MONSTRANCE

A liturgical vessel used for showing the Blessed Sacrament at exposition and benediction, and in processions. Its name and the alternative name of Ostensorium are derived from the Latin words *monstrare* and *ostendere,* both meaning "to show."

The monstrance appeared first in France and Germany in the course of the 14th century, as a result of devotion to the Real Presence fostered by the institution of the feast of Corpus Christi (*see* CORPUS ET SANGUINIS CHRISTI). At first the Blessed Sacrament was shown in reliquaries of the type that had a vertical glass cylinder mounted on a base like that of a chalice and surmounted by some kind of gothic metal crown. Some monstrances, intended for use in processions, were so big they had to be drawn along on carts. During the baroque age the cylindrical glass was superseded by the flat ''windowpane'' type of monstrance, usually surrounded by metal rays; there were also other types in which the base or stem was developed into chalice forms or even Jesse Trees. Some were made like statues of Christ or the Blessed Virgin Mary and showed the Blessed Sacrament through a circular pane of glass set into the breast. More recent monstrances are far simpler and more functional. The Host is fitted into a holder called a lunette, which slides into a fitting accessible from the back of the monstrance.

Bibliography: J. BRAUN, *Das christliche Altargerät* (Munich 1932). J. HAZELDEN-WALKER, ''Reservation Vessels in the Earliest Roman Liturgy,'' *Studia Patristica* 15:1 (1984) 568–572. C. C. KOVACS, ''Monstrances,'' in *Eucharistic Vessels of the Middle Ages* (Cambridge, MA 1975) 97–103.

[C. W. HOWELL/EDS.]

MONT-CORNILLON, MONASTERY OF

In Liège, Belgium, originally a double MONASTERY. In 1106 Bp. Albert of Liège gave a chapel there to canons regular, who in 1124? became Premonstratensians under the Abbot Luke (works ed. by J. Faber, Frankfurt 1538). In 1140 some of the nuns went to Reckheim. Those who remained at Mont-Cornillon were thereafter regarded as Augustinian canonesses rather than as Norbertines. St. JULIANA (d. 1258), who began the devotion to Corpus Christi, lived there. In 1360 the convent was transferred to Carthusians, who were suppressed in 1796. A Carmelite convent now occupies the site. The male community moved to Beaurepart on the riverside in 1288 and continued as a flourishing Norbertine abbey of the circary (province) of FLOREFFE. Its abbots obtained the right to wear the ring in 1390 and the miter in 1659. Beaurepart was suppressed in 1796 and is now used for the bishop's residence and the major seminary.

Bibliography: U. BERLIÈRE, *Monasticon belge* (Bruges 1890–) v. 2. N. BACKMUND, *Monasticon Praemonstratense,* 3 v. (Straubing 1949–56) v. 2.

[N. BACKMUND]

Mont–Saint–Michel Abbey. (©Stephanie Colasanti/CORBIS)

MONT-SAINT-MICHEL, ABBEY OF

A former Benedictine foundation and the principal shrine of the Archangel MICHAEL in northern Europe, situated in the Diocese of Coutances and the *arrondissement* of Avranches, Manche Department, France, on a rocky island connected to the mainland by a tidal causeway. In obedience to a vision of St. Michael, AUBERT, Bishop of Avranches, built an oratory on this site *c.* 708, and in 966 Richard I, Duke of Normandy, endowed a BENEDICTINE monastery there, giving the abbot temporal jurisdiction over the island. In *c.* 1023 Abbot Hildebert II caused a platform to be leveled on the summit of the rock in order to build a new church, and this was only the first stage of a plan to cover the entire rock with monastic buildings, an undertaking that was made difficult by the nature of the terrain as well as by the hazards of war and fire. Nevertheless this grand design was accomplished in 1520 when the choir was completed; and because the monastery occupied so important a strategic position in the wars between France and England in the later Middle Ages, it was also strongly fortified. From 1523 to 1622 the house was administered by commendatory abbots (*see* COMMENDATION), and the community declined. It was then given to the MAURISTS, who remained there until the French Revolution, when the house was secularized. From 1789 to 1863 the monastery was used as a prison, but in 1874 it was recognized as a public monument, and necessary restorations in the structure were undertaken. Since 1922 the monastery church has been restored to use as a place of worship.

Bibliography: L. H. COTTINEAU, *Répertoire topobibliographique des abbayes et prieurés,* 2 v. (Mâon 1935–39) 2:1897–1908. S. LUCE, ed., *Chronique du Mont-Saint-Michel, 1343–1468,* 2 v. (Paris 1879–83). É. CORROYER, *Description de l'abbaye du Mont-Saint-Michel et de ses abords, précedée d'une notice historique* (Paris 1877). P. GOUT, *Le Mont-Saint-Michel, histoire de l'abbaye et de la ville, étude archéologique et architecturale des monuments,* 2 v. (Paris 1910). G. BAZIN, *Le Mont-Saint-Michel* (Paris 1933). K. HOFMANN, *Lexikon für Theologie und Kirche,* ed. J. HOFER and K. RAHNER, 10 v. (2d, new ed. Freiburg 1957–65) 7:593. H. ADAMS, *Mont-Saint-Michel and Chartres* (new ed. London 1950).

[B. HAMILTON]

MONT SAINTE-ODILE, CONVENT OF

On a peak of the Vosges mountains in Alsace, founded *c.* 690 by (St.) ODILIA (also foundress of NIEDERMÜNSTER), whose shrine was an important place of pilgrimage during the Middle Ages. It followed its own rule until Abbess Relindis (d. 1169) introduced the Augustinian rule. Under the Abbess Herrad (1167–95) the convent, then called Hohenburg, was famous for its spiritual atmosphere and the nuns' intellectual attainments. After fire forced the religious to leave in 1546, the shrine was cared for by the PREMONSTRATENSIANS until the French Revolution, when the property was sold into private hands. In 1853 it was purchased by the bishop of Strasbourg, and the buildings have been gradually rebuilt. Sisters of the Cross now operate a hostelry and care for the shrine. Its German name is Odilienberg.

Bibliography: H. LECLERCQ, *Dictionnaire d'archéologie chrétienne et de liturgie,* ed. F. CABROL, H. LECLERCQ, and H. I. MARROU, 15 v. (Paris 1907–53) 12.2:1921–34. C. UMBRICHT, *Le Mont Ste-Odile et ses promenades,* ed. L. FRITSCH (6th ed. Strasbourg 1947). H. DANIEL-ROPS et al., *Le Mont Sainte-Odile* (Strasbourg 1957), excellent illus. A. M. BURG, *Lexikon für Theologie und Kirche,* ed. J. HOFER and K. RAHNER, 10 v. (2d, new ed. Freiburg 1957–65) 7:1097.

[F. M. BEACH]

MONTAIGNAC DE CHAUVANCE, LOUISE-THÉRÈSE DE, BL.

Foundress of the Oblates of the Sacred Heart of Jesus; b. May 14, 1820, Le-Havre-de-Grace, France; d. June 22, 1885, Moulins, France.

As the daughter of a wealthy financier—Aimé Montaignac de Chauvance and his wife Anne de Ruffin—Louise-Thérèse was educated at a boarding school from age seven. Although she did not pursue a Carmelite vocation, she made a private vow of perpetual chastity (Sept. 8, 1843), founded the Guild of the Tabernacle for Perpetual Adoration (1848) and an orphanage at Montluçon.

With the help of her aunt, she formed (1852) an association of Christian women at Montluçon with the mission of restoring the faith in France. This became the Pious Union of the Oblates of the Sacred Heart (Dec. 21, 1874) dedicated to ''renewing society by their example and their holy lives.'' Montaignac was elected superior general on May 17, 1880 and held that office until her death. The oblates live in community or secular life in Europe, Africa, and Central America and continue her work of operating orphanages, providing religious education, financing poor parishes, and directing retreats.

Montaignac also founded the ''Samuels'' for the formation of young Christians discerning religious vocations. She was beatified by Pope John Paul II, Nov. 4, 1990.

Feast: June 22.

Bibliography: P. FERLAY, *La force de la foi: itinéraire spirituel de Louise-Thérèse de Montaignac* (Paris 1990). *Acta Apostolicae Sedis* (1990): 1090–91.

[K. I. RABENSTEIN]

MONTAIGNE, MICHEL EYQUEM DE

French writer and moralist, author of the *Essais,* widely considered to be finest of its type in world literature; b. at the château of Montaigne, Périgord, Feb. 28, 1533; d. there, Sept. 13, 1592. Few people have held the attention of their fellow men for so long and as steadily as has Montaigne, and this although he never really wanted public reaction. He tells future readers at the opening of the *Essais* that his book has but one aim: to be a sincere and unadorned self-portrait that will serve kinfolk and friends as a living reminder of himself. Emerson has called Montaigne a ''representative man.'' This he says because the good sense of the *Essais* has impressed readers through the years; at the same time, the author holds them with the magic of his personality and the charm of his humanity.

Montaigne's father, born of rich, middle-class merchants only recently ennobled, had returned from the Italian wars under the spell of Renaissance splendors and the new knowledge he had found in Italy. He was anxious to apply this learning to the education of his son and heir. The awakening of the young Montaigne to the gentle sounds of music, for example, was not due to any epicurean tendency on the part of his father. The boy had merely read the Italian philosopher Cardano, who taught that the person who awakes abruptly may have his body invaded by a soul not his own. This mixture of superstition and enthusiasm for experiment and new learning is typical of the intellectual climate into which Montaigne had been born. His father also decided that the boy's first language would be Latin, and he employed a German tutor, Horstanus, who spoke no French. When Montaigne went to the Collège de Guyenne at the age of six, he already spoke Latin fluently. He was later critical of both his secondary education and the legal training it opened to him at the University of Toulouse. He aspired to the Italian ideal of the *uomo universale* and after many years of reading, thinking, and study he was to come very close to achieving it.

Early Years. Montaigne's youthful days were marked by the hedonism characteristic of the nobility of the century; yet it was in this same early period that he became the close friend and admirer of Étienne de la Boétie, whose deep love of learning and moderation were to have so profound an influence on him. At this time, too, he made a most significant decision: to remain within the Catholic fold, although his family, like so many in the realm, was divided—his brother and sister espousing the ''new religion.'' He followed his father's footsteps in choosing a profession and practiced law in the Parlement of Bordeaux. His intellectual life really began, however, when his father asked him to translate the *Theologia Naturalis* (*c.* 1400) of Raymond of Sabunde, a work often cited against the heretics of the century. In the meantime, he married Françoise de la Chassaigne in 1565.

In 1571, Montaigne decided to retire from the world to his château, probably because he desired to secure greater independence and because he had little taste for the political arena. It is almost impossible to describe the state of France at this time. The massacre of thousands of Protestants on ST. BARTHOLOMEW'S DAY (Aug. 24, 1572) marked a high point of terror and destruction that had not been equalled since the Hundred Years' War. With death surrounding him and with the example of his friend La Boétie in mind, Montaigne determined to devote the last years of his life to contemplation and study. The place he had chosen for it commands even today beautiful green and rolling country in an atmosphere of calm and peace.

Here he began the *Essais,* which were to be developed and added to for the next 20 years. His great source of ideas was his reading: the Roman poets, Seneca, the Greeks in translation, and especially Plutarch's *Lives* in Amyot's French translation. At first, his purpose was simply to compile anecdotes with brief commentaries. Very much attracted to the stoical humanism that was then the intellectual vogue in France, he gradually came to see that for him, a passive rather than an active man, such a stance was not possible; he decided to live and let live rather than to seek violent changes. Although he realized the importance of good intentions, he could not help but note the mediocre results of much of human effort. And, unlike many of his contemporaries, he was struck by the inhuman demands of the Stoical position, especially with regard to suicide, which he knew to be at variance with his Catholic faith.

So-called Skeptical Crisis. The subsequent stage in Montaigne's development is often referred to as his skeptical crisis. He did indeed doubt the unreal academic attitude of the Stoics as well as the rigid dogmatism of philosophers in general, but Montaigne, the universal and all-corrosive doubter, is a fiction created by such Jansenist fanatics as Pierre NICOLE in the seventeenth century. (It was at this time, too—1676—that Montaigne was put on the Index of Forbidden Books by the Church, although strangely enough, the folio giving the Church's reasons for this is missing.) The main evidence adduced by those who accused him of universal skepticism is the chapter of the *Essais* entitled ''The Apology of Raymond de Sebond'' (*see* RAYMOND OF SABUNDE), which includes his famous phrase, ''que sais-je?'' It is a disconcerting essay which has meant many things to many readers. Today scholars are mostly in agreement that the essay is not to be read as a betrayal of Sabunde. Rather it is a layman's attempt, as Montaigne clearly says, to defend the orthodox faith he holds in common with Sabunde. The structure of the essay, however, is curious. It is divided into two unequal parts.

In defending Sabunde, Montaigne first attacks the fideists. That he devotes so few pages to them has led many critics to accuse Montaigne of FIDEISM. But both faith and reason have their role to play in traditional theology; faith is the source, but reason applies itself within these limits to the object of inquiry. This is precisely Montaigne's position.

The second group of adversaries are the rationalists. These Montaigne with ill-disguised enjoyment excoriates in a long attack. He shows—and Pascal was to remember his arguments—that man without God is nothing; that knowledge and reason do not necessarily add to man's happiness; and that the most learned of rationalists have always disagreed. It is at this point in the chapter, after pointing to the bloody quarrels occasioned largely by the Calvinist rejection of TRANSUBSTANTIATION, that he inserts his wise ''que sais-je?'' He approaches the last part of his defense with much misgiving; he warns us that here his argument is most dangerous for he is going to prove that not only does man know nothing, but also that he can know nothing. His conclusion is that man is a wretched being at best, whom only the grace of God can raise to dignity.

What must be remembered in analyzing the ''Apology'' is that Montaigne's attack on reason, filled with paradoxes and contradictions, is a kind of intellectual exercise. Where he is deadly serious is in attacking the rigorist rationalists whose vain presumption has brought much unhappiness to mankind, for they love not men but problems, and thus indulge in what seems to him the worst of human follies. Following his own counsel of moderation, he seems to shift his purpose in the *Essais* (about 1578–80); he now intends simply to portray himself in all his manifold human aspects.

Although Montaigne in a sense retired from active life, he set off on a long journey in 1580 and 1581. His *Journal de voyage* is a delightful and entertaining travel book filled with curiosity concerning the lands and persons he meets. But even travel helps Montaigne to see himself—this time against a different background—and thus aids him in his self-study. While he was traveling, he was elected mayor of Bordeaux. He returned home for two years and then was reelected for a second two-year term ending in 1585. When he returned to private life, the civil war was raging even worse than before, and, to add to his woes, the plague forced him and his family to abandon the château for six months. As he wandered about, he was much impressed with the quiet courage and heroism in the face of death that he noticed among simple peasants, ignorant of all philosophy. He began to abandon his own apprehensiveness about death and renewed his confident optimism in human nature. It was in this spirit that he began work on the *Essais* once more.

Last Years. These last years of Montaigne's life were fraught with peril and sickness. Since his travels, he had suffered from kidney stones, and in these years (1586–92) his many painful bouts became worse. Yet it was during this period that he wrote the 13 great chapters of the last book of the *Essais.* Moreover, he had become too well known and respected not to take an important role in the negotiations between King Henry II and his successor, King Henry IV. While in Paris in 1588, probably on such a mission, he published his first edition of the *Essais,* containing all three books. Returning to his château, he spent his last days adding almost a thousand passages to his great work and correcting its style. In this last stylistic revision he tends to shift from long philosophical exposition and classical rhetorical periods to the familiar style of conversation. The movement of his thinking is one of overlapping circles of argument; what counts most in Montaigne is his matter, not his manner. Montesquieu says of him: ''In most authors I see the man who writes; in Montaigne I see the man who thinks.''

And yet it is difficult to define Montaigne's thought. He seems most intent in seeking out the real nature of man and deducing from that how he should live. Montaigne is not a systematic philosopher. He is rather a practical moralist who notes that there are vast differences among men and yet that ''all of moral philosophy can be applied as well to a common and private life as to one of richer stuff. Every man carries in himself the entire form of the human state'' [*The Essays of Michel de Montaigne,* tr. and ed. J. Zeitlin (New York 1936), 3.2:15; subsequent quotations are from this edition.] Moreover, man is composed of soul and body, and real wisdom consists in recognizing this duality, which means precisely that we have great limitations but possess even greater possibilities. ''In the experience I have of myself, I find enough to make me wise, if I were a good scholar.'' And he later adds: ''Let us but give ear to it, and we tell ourselves everything of which we chiefly stand in need'' (3.13:273–274). Therefore, to live happily, we must first know ourselves and live in harmony with ourselves. Not an easy task for most but surely the most important work in life. ''Have you known how to think out and manage your own life? You have then performed the greatest work of all. . . . Our duty is to compose our character. . . . Our great and glorious masterpiece is to live appropriately'' (3.13:309).

The key to all this is a realistic acceptance of nature as our guide. Of course, Montaigne realized that mere nature cannot always be relied upon, but he was a man of his age in urging us to enjoy to the hilt the legitimate and abundant pleasures of this life for ''it is an absolute perfection and, as it were divine, for a man to know how to enjoy his existence as he ought'' (3.13.316). Or again: ''For my part then, I love life and cultivate it, such as it has pleased God to bestow it upon us. . . . A man does wrong to the great omnipotent giver in refusing, nullifying, or disfiguring His gift. All goodness Himself, He has made all things good'' (3.13:313–314). But this confidence was possible for Montaigne only because he had learned, in studying himself, another and equally valid principle: ''I am pleased not to be sick; but if I am I would know that I am. . . . Evil is proper to man in its turn. Pain is not always to be avoided, nor pleasure always to be pursued'' (2.12:153).

Montaigne died while Mass was being said in his room, fully conscious of the Real Presence. He had made great progress from his early hedonism, pessimism, and Stoicism up to the final and growing confidence in the goodness of God and hope in a common humanity. Montaigne's contribution to Western thought is his humanism, especially if we define that humanism as respect for what makes man human: intelligence, responsibility, freedom, and the revealed knowledge that he is the adopted son of God.

See Also: RENAISSANCE; STOICISM; SKEPTICISM; HUMANISM.

Bibliography: M. E. DE MONTAIGNE, *Essais,* ed. A. THIBAUDET (Paris 1950); *Complete Essays,* tr. D. M. FRAME (Stanford, Calif. 1958). D. M. FRAME, *Montaigne's Discovery of Man* (New York 1955). C. SCLAFERT, *L'Âme religieuse de Montaigne* (Paris 1951). P. L. VILLEY-DESMESERETS, *Les Sources et l'évolution des essais de Montaigne* (2d ed. rev. Paris 1933). A. FOREST, ''Montaigne humaniste et théologien,'' *Revue des sciences philosophiques et théologiques* 18 (1929): 59–73. D. M. FRAME, *Montaigne: A Biography* (New York 1965).

[J. DUNN]

MONTAL FORNÉS, PAULA, ST.

Known in religion as Paula of St. Joseph Calasanctius, foundress of the Daughters of Mary of the Pious Schools (*Hijas de Maria, Religiosas de las Escuelas Pias*); b. Oct. 11, 1799, Arenys de Mar (near Barcelona), Spain; d. Feb. 26, 1889, Olesa de Montserrat near Barcelona, Spain. Born into a large family of artisans, Paula began working to help support the family after her father's death (1789). Paula grew especially concerned about the formation of Christian women while teaching in schools. In 1829 with her friend Iñes (Agnes) Busquets, she opened a school in Figueras near Gerona and dedicated herself ''to bring families to eternal salvation by teaching children the fear of God.'' She opened an additional seven schools. Montal was aided in her effort by the PIARISTS, especially Augustín Casanovas, who is considered the cofounder. Both sought to instill in the new institute the spirit of (St.) JOSEPH CALASANCTIUS, by adapting to women the constitutions that he wrote for the Piarists. By the time of her death, the order had more than 300 sisters operating 19 schools throughout Spain. Her cause was introduced in 1959. She was declared venerable in 1988 and beatified by John Paul II, April 18, 1993. A second miracle attributed to her intercession was approved July 1, 2000, opening the way to her canonization, which was held on Nov. 25, 2001.

Feast: Feb. 26 (Archdiocese of Barcelona).

Bibliography: *Acta Apostolicae Sedis* (1993): 549.

[K. I. RABENSTEIN]

MONTALEMBERT, CHARLES FORBES RENÉ DE

Catholic liberal, politician, publicist, historian, and orator; b. London, April 15, 1810; d. Paris, March 13, 1870. His father, Count Marc René de Montalembert, joined the French Revolutionary émigrés and then served in the British army. His mother, Eliza (Forbes) de Montalembert, was an English Protestant who became a Catholic in 1822. When the parents returned to France (1814), they left Charles in England with his grandfather James Forbes, a well–known author and a devout Protestant, who instilled in the boy a religious piety and a zeal for learning that remained throughout his life. Under his mentor's influence Montalembert developed also an admiration for the British parliamentary system as the epitome of sound liberal government. When he returned to France in 1819 to continue his education in Paris at the Lycée Bourbon and later at the Collège Ste. Barbe (1827), he was shocked by the bitterly antireligious spirit evident among professors and students behind their façade of religious practice enforced by the restoration government. The classmates of Charles were equally surprised to find him a pious Catholic who was ardently liberal in politics. From an early date, therefore, Montalembert confronted the problem that absorbed his energies throughout life: the reconciliation between political liberalism and Catholicism.

Charles Forbes René de Montalembert.

Historical Writings. In 1828, during a stay in Stockholm, where his father was ambassador, Montalembert was introduced to the works of Joseph von GÖRRES and others in the Munich school of romantic philosophers. Their frankly Catholic spirit and enthusiasm for the Middle Ages stirred the youth's interest in the medieval period and inspired him to write his chief historical works,

Histoire de Sainte Elisabeth de Hongrie (1836) and *Les Moines de L'Occident* (7 v. 1860–77). Both his life of St. Elizabeth and his history of the monks of the West, now outdated, were translated into English and were once widely read.

When bourgeois liberalism triumphed over both throne and altar in the revolution of 1830, Montalembert was traveling in Ireland, where he was attracted by Daniel O'CONNELL and his victorious campaign to win religious and political EMANCIPATION for Catholics. While there, he learned that Hugues Félicité de LAMENNAIS and a group of young Catholic liberals planned to publish in Paris a newspaper, *L'Avenir,* dedicated to the cause of "God and Liberty." Montalembert hurried to Paris and offered his services. Along with LACORDAIRE he became one of the most dedicated and enthusiastic collaborators of Lamennais. When GREGORY XVI condemned the teaching of Lamennais, Montalembert strove to prevent the Breton priest from leaving the Church. The association between the two men ended in 1836. In that year Montalembert married Elisabeth de Mérode, daughter of Felix de Mérode, a Catholic leader in the movement for Belgian independence.

Montalembert gained fame as a politician who used his outstanding oratorical and journalistic talents in defense of the Church's rights, but he merited permanent significance as one of the most forceful voices seeking a reconciliation between the Church and the new type of society that emerged from the FRENCH REVOLUTION. Much as he disliked many of the ideas and institutions that dated from 1789, he believed that the Church must learn to live without special privileges as one of several religious groups operating under laws applicable equally to all of them.

Ideological Position. When he entered parliament (1837), Montalembert struggled on two fronts. He tried to persuade liberals that Catholics could be loyal to the new regime and that the Church, therefore, should be granted freedom to operate its own secondary schools as promised in the charter of 1830. Second, he sought to disabuse Catholics, including most of the higher clergy and influential laymen, of their yearnings for a return of the *ancien régime;* he aimed also to train them to win their rights in and through parliamentary processes. Montalembert also advocated the outlawing of slavery by legislation, French colonial expansion, the independence of the STATES OF THE CHURCH, the rights of the Poles, Irish, and other oppressed peoples, and the rights of the French parliament. He held that recognition of the Church's right to operate secondary schools was the touchstone of liberal sincerity and an essential to the Church's progress, which required the development of an enlightened laity. Freedom of education was also the one cause capable of uniting Catholics of all political persuasions. This was the program that enabled Montalembert to organize a Catholic party that elected 140 deputies pledged to support Catholic schools (1846). Before these representatives could press their advantage, the Revolution of 1848 ended the regime of Louis Philippe. Under the Second Republic (1848–52), Montalembert won the cooperation of bourgeois politicians, who feared revolution more than religion, and secured the passage of the Falloux Law, which permitted the Church to operate secondary schools.

The fall of the July Monarchy in 1848 did not please Montalembert because it deprived him of his favorite forum in the House of Peers and because the rising popular demands for social reforms under the succeeding regime frightened him. He used his influence with Catholic voters to inaugurate the Second Empire under NAPOLEON III in order to provide France with a strong government. Before long, however, the emperor's authoritarianism deeply embarrassed and disillusioned him, but he was unable to persuade Catholics to break with Napoleon III. Louis VEUILLOT, a talented journalist and an ardent advocate of authoritarian government, replaced Montalembert as the outstanding Catholic leader. In matters concerning France, Veuillot, a leader of French ULTRAMONTANISM, was also more influential with Pope Pius IX, who became more conservative after 1848 and who was forced to depend on Napoleon III for the preservation of the States of the Church. Montalembert remained in the national legislature until his defeat in 1857, when many Catholics voted against him. Thereafter he grew increasingly isolated and impotent politically, but he continued to contribute to *Le Correspondant,* the liberal Catholic review started in 1855. He also addressed the French Academy, to which he was elected in 1851.

Montalembert's last great effort to reconcile the Church and liberal society was made at the international Catholic congress in Malines, Belgium (1863). His two speeches there caused a stir in European Catholic circles by urging Catholics to Christianize democracy and not to fear it. He also advocated that the Church accept the principle of religious freedom for all beliefs as a practical necessity in modern society. For his sentiments he received a reproof from Rome. When the encyclical *QUANTA CURA* and the *SYLLABUS OF ERRORS* appeared (1864), Montalembert interpreted these papal strictures on liberalism as indictments of his own position and became still more isolated and embittered. News of the convocation of VATICAN COUNCIL I pleased him at first, but then alarmed him because he feared the growing power of the PAPACY. He opposed a definition of papal infallibility and dreaded the possibility that Veuillot, W. G. WARD, and other extremists might influence the synod to turn the propositions in the *Syllabus of Errors* into doctrinal definitions. While the Council was in session Montalembert died. At no time did he contemplate leaving the Church.

His Vision and Its Limitations. History has demonstrated the essential soundness of Montalembert's intuition concerning the need and the possibility of a political rapproachement between the Church and liberal society. He was correct in insisting that where constitutional government prevails, the interests of the Church and its members are best protected by laymen exercising their political rights as citizens. Unfortunately, his vision was too exclusively political and too narrowly liberal. He ignored almost completely the issues of social justice raised by advancing capitalism; indeed, he won his great victory on the education question, the Falloux law, by siding with property owners and capitalists against the working class. His vision of an ideal political society always remained paternalistic; it was modeled, as is evident in his *L'Avenir politique de l'Angleterre* (1856), on Britain's constitutional monarchy, which was based firmly on a landowning class of nobles and gentry.

Bibliography: M. O. OLIPHANT, *Memoirs of Count de Montalembert,* 2 v. (London 1872). E. LECANUET, *Montalembert,* 3 v. (Paris 1905–10). G. J. WEILL, *Histoire du catholicisme libéral en France, 1828–1908* (Paris 1909). P. DE LALLEMAND, *Montalembert et ses amis dans le Romantisme, 1830–1848* (Paris 1927); *Montalembert et ses relations littéraires avec l'étranger jusqu'en 1840* (Paris 1927). A. TRANNOY, *Le Romantisme politique de Montalembert avant 1843* (Paris 1942); ''Responsabilités de M. en 1848,'' *Revue d'histoire de l'Église de France* 35 (1949) 176–206. C. CONSTANTIN, ''Liberalisme catholique,'' *Dictionnaire de théologie catholique,* ed. A. VACANT et al., 15 v. (Paris 1903–50; Tables générales 1951–) 9.1:506–629; ''Montalembert,'' *Dictionnaire de théologie catholique,* ed. A. VACANT et al., 15 v. (Paris 1903–50; Tables générales 1951–) 10.2:2344–55. W. GURIAN, *Die politischen und sozialen Ideen des französischen Katholizismus, 1789–1914* (München–Gladbach 1929). A. DANSETTE, *Religious History of Modern France,* tr. J. DINGLE, 2 v. (New York 1961) v.1. S. LÖSCH, *Döllinger und Frankreich* (Munich 1955). P. LENZ-MEDOC, *Staatslexikon,* ed. GÖRRES-GESELLSCHAFT, 8 v. (6th, new and enl. ed. Freiburg 1957–63) 5:833–835. H. RAAB, *Lexikon für Theologie und Kirche,* ed. J. HOFER and K. RAHNER, 10 v. (2d, new ed. Freiburg 1957–65); suppl., *Das Zweite Vatikanische Konzil: Dokumente und Kommentare,* ed. H. S. BRECHTER et al., pt. 1 (1966) 7:576–578.

[J. C. FINLAY]

MONTANA, CATHOLIC CHURCH IN

Montana, located in the Rocky Mountain region of the northwest U.S., was admitted to the Union as the 41st state in 1889. The fourth largest state, it is bounded on the north by Canada, on the east by North and South Dakota, on the south by Wyoming and Idaho, and on the west by Idaho. Helena is the capital, and Billings is the largest city. There are two dioceses in the state: the Diocese of Helena (*Helenensis*) and the Diocese of Great Falls-Billings (*Magnocataractensis-Billingensis*), both of which are are suffragans of the Metropolitan See of Portland in Oregon. The Diocese of Helena, established in 1884, encompasses the western counties of the state, an area of 51,922 sq. miles, and the Diocese of Great Falls, erected 1904 and redesignated in 1980 as the Diocese of Great Falls-Billings; it consists of the eastern counties, an area of 94,922 sq. miles.

Historic St. Mary's Mission, Stevensville, Montana. (©Michael Lewis/CORBIS)

History. The U.S. acquired the eastern two-thirds of the region, an extension of the Great Plains, in the Louisiana Purchase; the predominantly mountainous western third, containing the Continental Divide, passed to the U.S. with the settlement of the Oregon Question. The state contains numbers of Native American tribes, including the more important Gros Ventres, Assiniboine, Blackfoot, Flathead, and Crow tribes, located on reservations under federal supervision.

White fur traders of the Canadian Northwest Fur Company entered Montana either in the late 18th or early 19th century. The first American explorers to enter the region were the members of the Lewis and Clark Expedition (1804–06), who spent considerable time in the area on both the outbound and return phases of their journey. Montana was an important sphere of activity in the fur-trading era. The Canadian Northwest Company trapped the western and northwestern sectors of the region; while American groups, such as the Missouri Fur Company, the American Fur Company, and the Rocky Mountain Fur Company, ranged over the entire area. After the decline of the fur trade, mining succeeded as Montana's dominant form of economic activity, later it became energy production (natural gas and oil). Cattle raising and wheat farming are also of importance.

Missionary Activity. Catholicism was introduced in Montana when Iroquois moved west with Canadian fur traders and settled among the Flatheads of western Montana (1811–12), giving the latter a primitive idea of the faith. The Flatheads sent four successive expeditions (1831, 1835, 1837, and 1839) to Bp. J. ROSATI of St. Louis, MO, to obtain the services of missionaries, but lack of available personnel prevented his promising to provide them with services until 1839. In 1840 Pierre Jean DE SMET, SJ, went on an exploratory journey among the natives. One year later he returned with fellow Jesuit priests and lay brothers to establish St. Mary's Mission, thus beginning an era of fruitful Jesuit endeavor among the Native Americans and, later, the whites.

Diocesan Development. Montana became a vicariate apostolic in 1883, and in 1884 the Holy See established the Diocese of Helena, coextensive with the entire territory, with John Baptist BRONDEL, bishop of Victoria, Vancouver Island, Canada, and vicar apostolic of Montana as its first bishop. Until his death on Nov. 3, 1903, Brondel labored dilligently to build the diocese among Native Americans, as well as trappers, miners, and other immigrants to the area. When he arrived in 1884, there were four diocesan priests, 12 religious priests, 16 churches, four hospitals, two parochial schools, two schools for Native Americans and a Catholic population of 15,000. By 1903, the last year of his life, there were 38 diocesan priests, 15 religious priests, 65 churches, eight hospitals, nine parochial schools, ten schools for Native Americans and a Catholic population of 50,000.

Soon after Brondel's death in 1904, his earlier request for a division of the diocese was granted. The eastern two-thirds of the state became the Diocese of Great Falls. Mathias C. Lenihan, pastor in Marshaltown, Iowa, was consecrated the first bishop of the diocese on Sept. 21, 1904. At the time, the diocese had 14 priests, 11 parishes, two schools, and four Native American missions. When Lenihan retired in 1930, there were 68 priests, 45 parishes, 88 missions, 11 schools, 15 Native American missions, four private academies and eight hospitals to care for a Catholic population of 33,345. In the western section of the state, John P. Carroll of Dubuque, Iowa, became the second bishop of Helena, Dec. 21, 1904. Given his academic background as president of St. Joseph College (now Loras College) in Dubuque, IA, it was not surprising that he made Catholic education a high priority. In addition to five high schools, he founded Mt. St. Charles College (now called Carroll College in honor of its founder), which opened in September 1910. Two years earlier, Carroll laid the cornerstone for the magnificent Gothic Cathedral of St. Helena in the see city. It was consecrated Jan. 3, 1924. Bishop Carroll died later that same year, on Nov. 4, 1925. During his episcopacy 32 new parishes were erected.

Meanwhile in eastern Montana, Fr. Edwin V. O'HARA, founder and director of the National Catholic Rural Life Conference and zealous promoter of the Confraternity of Christian Doctrine in the United States, was consecrated the second bishop of the Diocese of Great Falls on Oct. 28, 1930. Given the rural nature of the diocese, O'Hara labored to establish the Confraternity of Christian Doctrine program (CCD) locally in order to meet the religious education needs of children and adults. Working with the Sisters of Providence and the Ursuline Sisters, O'Hara founded the College of Great Falls in September 1932. In April 1939 O'Hara was named archbishop of Kansas City, MO.

In western Montana, the unexpected death of Bishop Carroll in 1925 left the Diocese of Helena without a bishop until May 22, 1927, when Pius XI appointed Fr. George J. Finnigan, C.S.C., provincial of the Congregation of the Holy Cross at Notre Dame, IN, the third bishop of the diocese. He was the first member of his religious congregation in the U.S. to be consecrated a bishop. Before his death, Aug. 14, 1932, Finnigan established the CCD program thoughout the diocese and a diocesan newspaper, *The Register: Western Montana.* On Sept. 23, 1933, Fr. Ralph Leo Hayes of Pittsburg, PA, was consecrated the fourth bishop of the diocese. His brief time in Helena ended in 1935 when he was appointed rector of the North American College in Rome.

In Great Falls, William J. Condon, vicar general of the diocese of Spokane, WA, was consecrated the third bishop of the diocese on Oct. 18, 1939. Until his retirement, Aug. 17, 1967, the diocese witnessed a period of remarkable growth. Given the difficulty of caring for a diocese with such a vast territory, he requested the Holy See to grant him an auxiliary bishop, and on Oct. 30,

1961, Msgr. Eldon B. Schuster, chancellor of the diocese, rector of the cathedral parish, and the superintendent of schools, was appointed titular bishop of Amblada and auxiliary bishop of the Diocese of Great Falls. He was consecrated a bishop on Dec. 21, 1961.

Meanwhile, in the Diocese of Helena, Fr. Joseph M. Gilmore, born in New York but raised in Montana from the age of five, was consecrated the fifth bishop of Helena on Feb. 29, 1936. To meet the needs of a rapidly growing Catholic population, new and larger facilities were needed, and he immediately began to build and strengthen the institutions of the diocese. Accordingly, a new chancery building, 20 new churches, and six new grade schools and high schools were built. The Cathedral of St. Helena was completely renovated in time for the diamond jubilee of the diocese in 1959. His years as bishop were considered by many to be golden building years for the diocese.

When Gilmore died, on April 2, 1962, he was succeeded by Raymond G. Hunthausen, president of Carroll College and a native of Montana. He was consecrated the sixth bishop of the diocese on Aug. 30, 1962. From 1962 to 1966, Hunthausen participated in the sessions of the Second Vatican Council where he met Bishop Angelico Melotto of Solala, Guatemala. Although Guatemala was 90 percent Catholic, Bishop Melotto's diocese was experiencing a critical shortage of clergy. Soon after the meeting, Hunthausen opened the Diocese of Helena's mission in Guatemala. In addition, he labored diligently to implement the decrees of the Second Vatican Council throughout the diocese. With the decline in number of vocations to the priestly and religious life, its impact on the schools, hospitals and parishes in the diocese was dramatic. With schools closing, greater emphasis was placed on the CCD program, which had existed for many years in the rural areas of the diocese. In addition, religious education centers staffed by religious, clergy, and laity were set up throughout the diocese. Although the changes were painful for many, Hunthausen's willingness to listen and his intense desire to be faithful to the teachings of the Second Vatican Council made the difficult transition possible. He was appointed archbishop of Seattle on Feb. 25, 1975.

In the Diocese of Great Falls, Auxiliary Bishop Eldon B. Schuster was chosen to succeed Bishop Condon, on Jan. 23, 1968. Schuster also took part in the sessions of the Second Vatican Council. His diocese did not escape the depletion in the ranks of the clergy and the closing of many Catholic schools in the ensuing years after Vatican II. When Schuster retired on Dec. 27, 1977, Pope Paul VI appointed Thomas J. Murphy to be the fifth bishop of Great Falls. A native of Chicago and rector of Our Lady of the Lake Seminary in Mundelein, IL, Murphy was consecrated bishop on Aug. 26, 1978. He served the diocese until May 27, 1987, when he was named coadjutor archbishop of Seattle. Faced with serious personnel shortages, and with the help of his presbyteral council, Murphy consolidated parishes and schools. Cluster parishes were formed to care for areas with fewer priests. Women religious were called upon to conduct the day-to-day administration of these parishes. Another significant development was the decision to change the name of the diocese, in 1980, to the Diocese of Great Falls-Billings, thus recognizing the importance of the Catholic community in Billings, the largest city in the state.

Anthony M. Milone, auxiliary bishop of Omaha, NE, was named the sixth bishop of the Diocese of Great Falls-Billings on Feb. 23, 1988. At that time, the 73 parishes and 56 missions in the diocese, had only 58 resident pastors. Father Elden F. Curtiss, president-rector of Mount Angel Seminary in St. Benedict, OR, was named by the Holy See to succeed Bishop Hunhausen in Helena. He was consecrated the seventh bishop of the diocese on April 28, 1986. For the next 17 years, Curtiss dealt with a wide range of problems. He chose as his motto a paraphrase of John 17:21, "That we all may be one," and his desire to unify and reconcile a sometimes divided diocesan church was the hallmark of his episcopacy. He presided over a diocesan synod in 1988, the first one held in 80 years. It was announced on May 4, 1993, that Curtiss was named archbishop of Omaha, and Monsignor Alexander J. Brunett of Detroit, MI, was subsequently appointed the eighth bishop of Helena, April 19, 1994, a post he held until he was named archbishop of Seattle, on Oct. 28, 1997. His successor was Robert C. Morlino, another priest of Detroit, who was consecrated the ninth bishop in the Cathedral of St. Helena, Sept. 21, 1999.

At the beginning of the 21st century, there were approximately 125,000 Catholics in Montana, in a total population of about 815,800 persons. They were served by about 122 active diocesan, extern, and religious priests. The two dioceses served five Native American reservations and a total of 124 parishes and 86 missions. Bishops Schuster and Hunthausen established the Montana Catholic Conference on Social Welfare, which in turn led to the formation of Catholic Social Services of (for) Montana and the Montana Catholic Conference.

Bibliography: L. B. PALLADINO, *Indian and White in the Northwest: A History of Catholicity in Montana* (Lancaster, PA 1922). C. M. FLAHERTY, *Go with Haste into the Mountains: A History of the Diocese of Helena* (Helena, MT 1985). W. P. SCHOENBERG, *Jesuits in Montana, 1840–1960* (Portland, OR 1960). S. SCHREMS, "God's Women: Sisters of Charity of Providence and Ursuline Nuns in Montana, 1864–1900," Ph.D. dissertation, University of Oklahoma, 1993. W. J. GREYTAK, *The Roman Catholic Dioceses of Montana: An Abbreviated History* (Helena, MT 1995).

[T. A. CLINCH/W. J. GREYTAK]

MONTANISM

A schismatic movement that originated in Phrygia about the middle of the 2d century, spread rapidly and widely through the East and West, and almost completely disappeared during the 5th and 6th centuries. Montanism was a manifestation of a recurring phenomenon in the Church that, for want of a better term, is called ''illuminism'' or ''enthusiasm'' and is characterized by a conviction on the part of its devotees that (1) they are a spiritual elite called to restore the Church to its primitive simplicity, (2) they are under the direct guidance of the Holy Spirit, and (3) in their circle are renewed the charismatic gifts common during the period of the Church's first fervor.

Montanus. Montanus, the founder of the sect, was a convert from paganism. Shortly after his conversion he became the leader of a group of *illuminati* at Ardabau, and later at Pepuza, in Phrygia. He and certain of his followers, notably the women Priscilla (or Prisca) and Maximilla, were seized by religious raptures and, in the course of ecstasy, spoke in strange tongues and uttered prophecies that the sectaries regarded as oracles of the Holy Spirit.

Stories of mysterious apparitions of Christ and the Paraclete were spread abroad, and in the meetings of the Montanists, trances, convulsions, and mass hysteria occurred similar to the bizarre experiences of the Camisards, the Shakers, and the 17th-century visionaries of Paris who danced in the cemetery of Saint-Médard. Phrygia was traditionally the home of frenzy and fanaticism, and it is probably the irrationality and extravagance of Montanism that led opponents to call its adherents Phrygians or Cataphrygians.

Doctrine. During its earliest stages, Montanism was less concerned with doctrine than with the outpouring of the Holy Spirit that the Montanists saw in the transports of their prophets. Some points of discipline were inculcated; certain fasts were introduced; virginity was praised in exaggerated terms; husbands and wives were advised to separate or to live in continence; there were warnings of imminent catastrophes; and true believers were summoned to assemble at Pepuza to await the descent of the new Jerusalem and the coming of the millennium.

Montanists of the second and third generations developed the primitive asceticism of the sect into a doctrinal and disciplinary system that is described in considerable detail by TERTULLIAN, the most famous of its converts. In his Montanist treatises he condemns all second marriages as adultery. He insists that there are some sins that are so serious that the Church cannot or should not forgive them. Flight during time of persecution is a kind of apostasy; relatively mild fasts of the orthodox Church were to be replaced by frequent and prolonged xerophagies or dry fasts. The antihierarchical and anti-institutional prejudices characteristic of Pentecostal groups appear in Tertullian's views on the priesthood of all believers, and in the opposition that he sets up between the internal Church of the Spirit and the external Church of the bishops.

St. JEROME, in describing Montanism, lists the errors already mentioned and says that members of the sect were infected with SABELLIANISM. The claim that the utterances of the new prophets add to or supersede the revelation delivered to the Apostles and handed down in the apostolic churches remained a basic point at issue between Montanists and Catholics.

Importance. The importance of the sect during the early centuries may be judged by the attention it received from ancient Christian writers and ecclesiastics. Clement of Alexandria, Origen, St. Jerome, Sozomen, and, most particularly, Eusebius of Caesarea and Epiphanius furnish information on its historical development and describe the principal tenets of the sect. According to Eusebius the earliest anti-Montanist writings are those of Apollonius (*c.* 197); the apologists Miltiades, Melito, and Apollinaris of Hierapolis; the Roman Caius; and an anonymous bishop of Asia Minor who composed an influential three-volume work on the subject, *c.* 192–193 (*Hist. Eccl.* 5.16–19), Popes Soter (*c.* 166–175) and Eleutherius (*c.* 175–189) condemned the movement shortly after its appearance in the Church. The energetic opposition of Pope INNOCENT I (401–417) and the laws of the Emperor HONORIUS I against heresy (Feb. 22, 407) contributed substantially to the decline of Montanism in the West, and some 150 years later the severe anti-Montanist legislation of the Emperor JUSTINIAN I all but destroyed it in the East.

As the movement lost its formal identity, its members either returned to the Church or went over to other Pneumocentric groups such as the Priscillianists and Cathari. However, evidence of the tenacity of some of its adherents and of the sect's stubborn will to live may be seen in a letter of GREGORY THE GREAT (June or July 601) to the bishops of Spain on the invalidity of Montanist baptism. And again as late as the 9th century, according to Ignatius of Nicaea, Nicephorus, Patriarch of Constantinople, urged the emperor to take restrictive measures against the Phrygian heretics.

Bibliography: P. DE LABRIOLLE, *La Crise montaniste* (Paris 1913); ed., *Les Sources de l'histoire du montanisme* (Fribourg 1910). H. VON CAMPENHAUSEN, *Kirchliches Amt und geistliche Vollmacht in den ersten drei Jahrhunderten* (Tübingen 1953). R. A. KNOX, *Enthusiasm* (New York 1950) 25–49. B. ALTANER, *Patrology* tr. H. GRAEF from 5th German ed. (New York 1960) 138–139. K. ALAND, *Zeitschrifte für die neutestamentliche Wissen-*

schaft und die Kunde der alteren Kirche 46 (1955) 109–116. H. BACHT, *Lexikon für Theologie und Kirche*, ed. J. HOFER and K. RAHNER, 10 v. (2d new ed. Freiburg 1957–65) 7:578–580.

[W. LE SAINT]

MONTAVON, WILLIAM F.

Welfare executive; b. Scioto County, Ohio, July 14, 1874; d. Washington, D.C., Feb. 15, 1959. He was the son of John Baptist and Mary (Muller) Montavon. He attended the University of Notre Dame, IN (1892–95), the Institut de Sainte-Croix, Paris (1895–97), and The Catholic University of America, Washington, D.C. (1897–1901). He was married in 1901 to Agnes Burrow, who died in 1913, and in 1942 to Leocadia Kerby. He spent his early career in South America, where he served as U.S. commercial attaché in Lima, Peru (1915–18), and as executive representative of the International Petroleum Company (1918–25). In 1925 he returned to the United States to become director of the legal department of the National Catholic Welfare Conference, a post he held until 1951. His duties as legal director plunged him into problems created by religious persecution during the Mexican civil war, and for three years the status of the Catholic Church in Mexico occupied much of his time. In 1930 he accompanied the Forbes Commission to Haiti as press correspondent for the Catholic newspapers in the United States. The following year he was sent to Spain to represent Catholic interests at the constitutional assembly in Madrid. His efforts were rewarded by the Holy Father, who named him Knight Commander of the Order of St. Gregory the Great in 1945, and by St. Bonaventure College (later University), New York, which gave him its Catholic Action Medal in 1939. Montavon, an author and lecturer in the fields of health, education, and welfare, served also as consultant to the Catholic Hospital Association and adviser to the U.S. State Department on inter-American relations.

[G. E. REED]

MONTCHEUIL, YVES DE

Theologian; b. Paimpol, France, Jan. 30, 1900; d. Grenoble, Aug. 10, 1944. He entered the Society of Jesus in 1917 and was ordained on Aug. 24, 1932. With a dissertation titled *L'Intervention de Malebranche dans la querelle du pur amour*, published posthumously as *Malebranche et le quiétisme* (Paris 1946), he earned a doctorate in theology at the Gregorian University, Rome, in 1936. While teaching dogma at the Institut Catholique de Paris from 1935 to 1944, he exercised zealously the functions of chaplain and counselor for the Catholic Action movement in France. His apostolic zeal occasioned his tragic end. He was arrested while offering priestly ministrations to the dying men of the Resistance, and was shot by the Germans at Grenoble. Besides his work on Malebranche, he wrote two others: *Problèmes de vie spirituelle* (Paris 1946) and *L'Église et le monde actuel* (Paris 1946). H. de Lubac gathered De Montcheuil's articles in two volumes titled *Mélanges théologiques* (Paris 1946).

Bibliography: R. JOUVE, *Études* 244 (1945) 112–114.

[G. MOLLAT]

MONTE, BARTOLOMEO MARIA DAL, BL.

Diocesan priest, missionary, preacher; b. Nov. 3, 1726, Bologna, Italy; d. Dec. 24, 1778, at Bologna. The son of Orazio dal Monte and Anna Maria Bassani, Bartolomeo was confirmed (1733) by Cardinal Prospero Lambertini of Bologna, the future Pope Benedict XIV. Bartolomeo studied at the Jesuit Santa Lucia College for a career as a banker. LEONARD OF PORT MAURICE, himself later canonized, encouraged Bartolomeo to ignore his father's opposition to a priestly vocation; Bartolomeo was ordained in 1749 and completed his seminary studies in theology (1750–51). He then undertook his life's work: preaching missions and retreats not only in Bologna, but also in sixty-two other dioceses. His powerful preaching led many to reconciliation and conversion of life. According to the citation issued March 16, 1777, Father dal Monte's charity, the purity of his doctrine at a time when Jansenism was spreading, and holiness of his life won for him honorary citizenship in the principality of San Marino. His body is enshrined in Our Lady of Peace Chapel in Bologna's Basilica of Saint Petronius. The decree approving a miracle wrought at his intercession was promulgated on July 11, 1995, leading to his beatification on Sept. 27, 1997 at Bologna by Pope John Paul II.

Bibliography: L. MIRRI, *Un apostolo delle missioni popolari: Bartolomeo Maria Dal Monte (1726–1778) e la sua ''Operetta''* (Bologna 1995). *L'Osservatore Romano,* Eng. ed. 29 (1995): 5.

[K. I. RABENSTEIN]

MONTE, PHILIPPE DE

Dutch composer celebrated as a madrigalist; b. Mechlin (Malines), 1521; d. Prague, July 4, 1603. After preliminary music studies he settled in Naples in 1542 as a teacher, but in 1554 transferred to Rome, where his first book of madrigals was published. As a member of Philip

II's chapel he spent the next period in Antwerp and England, where he made friends with Thomas Morley and W. BYRD. When Jakob Vaet, imperial chapelmaster, died and negotiations with PALESTRINA failed, Monte was appointed in 1568 and held the post for the rest of his life, enjoying the new emperor Rudolph II's favor as he had Maximilian II's. Monte was one of the most productive composers of his time, and his fame rivaled that of Palestrina and LASSO. Between 1554 and 1603 he published 1,073 secular and 144 spiritual madrigals in 42 volumes, with texts by Cardinal Bembo, F. Petrarch, T. Tasso, Vittoria COLONNA, and other leading poets. Their tone is lyrical and elegiac, only rarely dramatic, and after 1580, less chromatic and increasingly contrapuntal in technique. His church music, which comprises 320 motets and 38 Masses that have been compared to Palestrina's, is conservative and melodic, with felicitous voice combinations. Most of his Masses, only nine of which were published in his lifetime, are of the parody type, elaborating polyphonic models by RORE, G. de Wert, P. Verdelot, and himself. Among the best are the *Missa Benedicta Es* and the Requiem. In the motets, double-choir technique and imitation in all voices are found, with strict contrapuntal writing in the earlier groups and homophonic declamation alternating with counterpoint in the later. In contrast to the dramatic antitheses and climaxes of Lasso's motets, Monte's pieces in this form are pervaded with mystical fervor, as for example, in his six-voice *O bone Jesu.*

Bibliography: *Opera omnia,* ed. J. VAN NUFFEL et al., 31 v. (Bruges 1927–35); *Missa ad modulum Benedicta es* (Amsterdam 1920). P. NUTEN, *"De Madrigal spirituali" van Filip de Monte* (Brussels 1958), pts. 1–3. G. VAN DOORSLAER, *La Vie et les oeuvres de Philippe de Monte* (Brussels 1921). A. EINSTEIN, *The Italian Madrigal,* tr. A. H. KRAPPE et al., 3 v. (Princeton N.J. 1949). G. REESE, *Music in the Renaissance* (rev. ed. New York 1959). P. H. LÁNG, *Music in Western Civilization* (New York 1941). H. COATES, *Grove's Dictionary of Music and Musicians,* ed. E. BLOM, 9 v. (5th ed. London 1954) 5:837–839. R. C. GOBIN, "The Late Madrigal Cycles of Philippe de Monte" (Ph.D. diss. Northwestern University 1984). R. B. LENAERTS, "Philippus de Monte als motettenkomponist," *Kirchenmusikalisches Jahrbuch,* 66 (1982) 49–58. R. LINDELL, "Studien zu den sechs—und siebenstimmigen Madrigalen von Filippo di Monte" (Ph.D. diss. Vienna 1980). B. R. MANN, *The Secular Madrigals of Filippo di Monte 1521–1603* (Ann Arbor, Mich. 1983). D. M. RANDEL, ed., *The Harvard Biographical Dictionary of Music* (Cambridge, Mass. 1996) 601. N. SLONIMSKY, ed. *Baker's Biographical Dictionary of Musicians* (8th ed. New York 1992) 1239–1240. M. STEINHARDT and R. M. LINDELL, "Philippe de Monte," in *The New Grove Dictionary of Music and Musicians,* ed. S. SADIE, v. 12 (New York 1980) 505–508.

[R. B. LENAERTS]

MONTE CASSINO, ARCHABBEY OF

The cradle of the Benedictine Order, hence of Western MONASTICISM in general, founded by St. BENEDICT of Nursia *c.* 529 within the wall-enclosed citadel of ancient Casinum. There Benedict built a church on the site of a Roman temple (St. Martin; rediscovered in 1953 by Angelo Pantoni, OSB) and another on the place of the altar of the temple (St. John the Baptist; rediscovered under the present church in 1951).

During the tenure of Benedict's fourth successor, Monte Cassino was destroyed by the LOMBARDS (*c.* 581). The monks found refuge in the LATERAN monastery in Rome where GREGORY I (THE GREAT) befriended them. He knew personal disciples of Benedict and made the saint the protagonist of the second book of the *Dialogues.* Benedictinism survived, but the existence of Benedict's foundation remained interrupted for about 140 years. The list of the Lateran abbots is a 12th-century forgery to fill this gap.

About 717 PETRONAX OF BRESCIA restored Monte Cassino, which then became the model monastery of Europe. Here St. BONIFACE's kinsman Willibald from Wessex stayed as a monk (729–739) before becoming bishop of Eichstätt; here Sturmi, the first abbot of Fulda, "acquired the practice of the Rule" (W. Levison). Boniface himself asked Petronax's successor Optatus to be admitted to the confraternity of Monte Cassino. Carloman, Pepin's brother, retired to the abbey after his abdication in 747, to be joined by the Lombard King Rachis in 749. Pope Zachary issued to Monte Cassino the first of many papal privileges and declared it subject only to the Holy See, an arrangement that still obtains today (*abbatia nullius*).

The territorial expansion of the abbey started before the middle of the 8th century with the generous donation of Duke Gisulf II of Benevento. CHARLEMAGNE visited Monte Cassino in 787, bestowed privileges on it, and later asked for a copy of the alleged autograph of the BENEDICTINE RULE to serve as standard text throughout his realm. His friend and helper PAUL THE DEACON, historian of the Lombards, was a member of the congregation then. Abbot Gisulf (797–817) transformed the church of St. John into a three-nave basilica and built at the foot of the hill another monastery with a church dedicated to the Savior. It was here that in 883 Abbot BERTHARIUS was slain by the Saracens when they destroyed Monte Cassino. The monks fled to Teano (where they lost the alleged autograph of the Rule in a fire) and from there to Capua under pressure of the princes of Capua. Abbot Aligernus (949–86), a pupil of ODO OF CLUNY, at last brought the congregation back to Monte Cassino, which he restored. Subsequent Capuan influence ended only with the election of Abbot Theobald (1022–35), which was supervised by Emperor Henry II.

Under Theobald and the Bavarian Richer (1038–55) Monte Cassino began its rise to the splendid height that

Monte Cassino Abbey reduced to rubble by Allied bombing in 1944. (AP/Wide World Photos)

it was to reach under Desiderius (1058–87), who directed the abbey's reconstruction (*see* VICTOR III, POPE), and which was to continue under Oderisius I (1087–105). Numerous monks of Monte Cassino attained the highest ranks in the Church, three of them the papacy (STEPHEN IX, Victor III, GELASIUS II). Meanwhile the SCRIPTORIUM of Monte Cassino, which used the ''Beneventan script,'' led in MS production in southern Italy, and in book illumination also. The library was rich in ancient pagan and Christian texts, some of which are preserved only there. Among the great men active then in the abbey were Alberic of Monte Cassino, ALPHANUS OF SALERNO, the medical writer CONSTANTINE THE AFRICAN, and the historians Amatus of Monte Cassino, LEO MARSICANUS, Guido, and PETER THE DEACON. The territory belonging to Monte Cassino (*Terra s. Benedicti*) reached its largest extension under Desiderius.

A decline set in after Oderisius I. Neither the NORMAN rulers nor their German successors respected the independence of the abbey. It inevitably suffered in the struggles for the possession of southern Italy and endured new misfortunes when John XXII raised the abbots to the rank of bishop; most of them held their tenure *in absentia* (1322–65). An earthquake destroyed the monastery of Desiderius on Sept. 9, 1349. Rebuilding started through the initiative of Pope Urban V, a Benedictine (1362–70). Throughout the second half of the 15th century the abbey was ruled by commendatory abbots (1454–1504). Only when Monte Cassino joined the Benedictine Congregation of St. Justina of Padua (1504), henceforth called *Congregatio Casinensis alias s. Justinae de Padua*, was there peace and prosperity. Abbots were now elected only for short terms. Important construction went on during the 16th and 17th centuries. The new church, with the frescoes of Luca Giordano, one of the foremost examples of Neapolitan baroque, was dedicated by Benedict XIII in 1727. Among the eminent scholars of the abbey were Abbot Angelo della Noce (d. 1691), editor of the *Chroni-*

cle of Monte Cassino (1668), and Erasmo Gattola, the learned archivist and historian of the abbey (1662–1734).

With the fall of the kingdom of Naples and the suppression of the religious houses, Monte Cassino became in 1866 a national monument whose guardians were the monks themselves. The historian Abbot Luigi TOSTI (1811–97) fought first for the unification of ITALY and after 1870 for the reconciliation of Church and State. Learning has been flourishing, and important publications issue from Monte Cassino. On Feb. 15, 1944, the abbey, wrongly believed by some Allied commanders to harbor German soldiers, was destroyed by aerial bombardment to the dismay of the entire civilized world. The abandoned ruins were taken over by the Germans and fell to Polish troops on May 18. The abbey has been rebuilt as it was, mainly with funds provided by the Italian government and with the very active help of the congregation itself, led by Abbot Ildefonso Rea. On Oct. 24, 1964, Pope Paul VI consecrated the monastery and from Monte Cassino proclaimed St. Benedict the patron saint of Europe.

Bibliography: Sources. L. MARSICANUS and PETER THE DEACON, *Chronica monasterii Casinensis,* ed. W. WATTENBACH, *Monumenta Germaniae Historica: Scriptores* (Berlin 1826–) 7:551–844. *Annales Casinenses ex annalibus Montis Casini antiquis et continuatis excerpti,* ed. G. SMIDT, *ibid.* 30.2:1385–429. *Annales Casinenses a. 1000–212,* ed. G. H. PERTZ, *ibid.* 19:303–20. AMATUS OF MONTE CASSINO, *Storia de' Normanni,* ed. V. DE BARTHOLOMAEIS (Rome 1935). The library contains more than 1,000 MSS; cf. *Spicilegium Casinense,* 4 v. (1888–1936). *Tabularium Casinense,* 4 v. (1887–1960). *Serie dei Regesti Cassinesi,* 4 v. (1914–26). *Bibliotheca Casinensis seu codicum manuscriptorum . . . series,* 5 v. (1873–94). M. INGUANEZ, *Codicum Casinensium manuscriptorum catalogus,* 3 v. (1915–41), covers codices 1–600. T. LECCISOTTI, *I Regesti dell' Archivio,* v.1– (Rome 1964–). Literature. L. H. COTTINEAU, *Répertoire topobibliographique des abbayes et prieurés,* 2 v. (Mâcon 1935–39) 2:1913–16. E. GATTOLA, *Historia abbatiae Cassinensis,* 2 v. (Venice 1733); *Ad historiam abbatiae Cassinensis accessiones,* 2 v. (Venice 1734), both works still indispensable. L. TOSTI, *Storia della badia di Monte-Cassino,* 3 v. (Naples 1842–43); also in *Opere complete,* v.14–17 (Rome 1888–90). P. F. KEHR, *Regesta Pontificum Romanorum. Italia Pontificia,* 8 v. (Berlin 1906–35) 8:109–98. G. F. CARETTONI, *Casinum* (Rome 1940). G. FALCO, ''Lineamenti di storia Cassinese nei secoli VIII e IX,'' *Casinensia* 2 (Monte Cassino 1929) 457–553; repr. *Albori d'Europa* (Rome 1947) 173–263. *Miscellanea Cassinese* 1– (1897–). *Benedictina* 1–13 (Rome 1947–59). In these two series many important volumes and articles, esp. by the following monks of Monte Cassino: M. INGUANEZ, T. LECCISOTTI, A. LENTINI, and A. PANTONI. See particularly: T. LECCISOTTI, A. PANTONI, L. OLIVIERI et al., *Il sepolcro di S. Benedetto* (*Miscellanea Cassinese* 27; 1951). A. PANTONI, ''Opinioni, valutazioni critiche e dati di fatto sull'arte benedettina in Italia,'' *Benedictina* 13 (1959) 111–58. P. MEYVAERT, ''Peter the Deacon and the Tomb of St. Benedict,'' *Revue Bénédictine* 65 (1955) 3–70. H. BLOCH, ''Monte Cassino, Byzantium, and the West in the Earlier Middle Ages,'' *Dumbarton Oaks Papers,* Harvard Univ. 3 (1946) 163–224. J. R. HUDLESTON, *The Catholic Encyclopedia,* ed. C. G. HERBERMANN et al., 16 v. (New York 1907–14) 10:526–28. V. REDLICH, *Lexikon für Theologie und Kirche,* ed. J. HOFER and K. RAHNER, 10 v. (2d, new ed. Freiburg 1957–65) 7:582–84. T. LECCISOTTI, *Montecassino* (Basel 1949), Ger. ed. L. FABIANI, *La terra di S. Benedetto* (*Miscellanea Cassinese* 26; 1950). On the destruction of Monte Cassino cf. esp. M. W. CLARK, *Calculated Risk* (New York 1950) 312. F. VON SENGER and ETTERLIN, *Neither Fear nor Hope,* tr. G. MALCOLM (London 1963) 201–06. F. MAJDALANY, *The Battle of Cassino* (Boston 1957) 134–86. R. BÖHMLER, *Monte Cassino,* tr. R. H. STEVENS (London 1964) 162–82.

[H. BLOCH]

MONTEAGUDO, ANA DE LOS ANGELES, BL.

Dominican mystic; b. *c.* 1600, Arequipa, Peru; d. there, January 10, 1686. Ana, the daughter of the Spaniard Sebastián Monteagudo de la Jara and his Peruvian wife Francisca Ponce de León, was entrusted to the care of the Dominican sisters of Santa Catalina de Siena until she reached marriageable age. She returned home at her parents' request and eventually overcame their objections to her religious vocation. In 1618, she began her novitiate at Santa Catalina and appended the name ''de los Angeles.'' She served as novice mistress. After she was chosen as prioress (1647), she reformed the community of nearly 300 sisters. The entire life of Blessed Ana was spent in prayer and apostolic work. Her sanctity was recognized through her beatification, February 2, 1985, at Arequipa, Peru, by Pope John Paul II during his pastoral visit to Latin America.

Feast: Jan. 10 (Dominicans).

Bibliography: B. GÓMEZ CANO, *Sor Ana de los Angeles Monteagudo y Ponce de León* (Lima, Peru 1984). *Acta Apostolicae Sedis* (1986): 909–12. *L'Osservatore Romano,* Eng. ed. 11 (1985): 8–9.

[K. I. RABENSTEIN]

MONTEFIORE, CLAUDE JOSEPH GOLDSMID

Anglo-Jewish scholar; b. London, 1858; d. London, July 9, 1938. He was a member of the wealthy Anglo-Jewish Montefiore family, originally from Italy; his granduncle was the well-known philanthropist Sir Moses Montefiore (1784–1885). After he received an Oxford M.A., he studied theology in Berlin. Because of the ''arrest of the Reform Movement,'' he associated himself with liberal Judaism and even traveled to the United States in order to engage a liberal rabbi for a London synagogue. He was president of the Anglo-Jewish Association, the Froebel Society, the Jewish Religious Union, the

Jewish Historical Society, and the University of Southampton. His special field of scholarly interest was the New Testament, particularly in its relationship to JUDAISM. With Israel Abrahams he edited the *Jewish Quarterly Review* (1888–1908). Of particular note among his numerous published works are his *Origin and Growth of Religion as Illustrated by the Religion of the Ancient Hebrews,* (2 v., Hibbert Lectures for 1892); *The Synoptic Gospels* (London 1909); and *Outlines of Liberal Judaism* (London 1912; 2d rev. ed. 1927).

Montefiore conceived liberal Judaism as ''in a certain sense . . . traditional. . . . Liberal Jews desire to carry the tradition forward and onward'' (*Outlines* 283). Not a people ''as regards all else than religion,'' Jews ought ''to be one with the nations among whom they dwell'' and therefore ''opposed to Nationalism and Zionism. . . . Liberal Judaism believes in, and aims at, a universal Judaism, universal both in doctrine and in form'' (*ibid.* 301–302). Montefiore was well aware that his benign attitude toward some aspects of Christianity and its Founder did not mean that a reconciliation was in sight. ''The Liberal Jew is in some respects still farther removed from orthodox Christianity than the Conservative Jew. . . . He who has learnt to apply the canons of historical criticism to the Pentateuch will not fight shy of applying them to the Gospels'' (*ibid.* 325).

Bibliography: P. GOODMAN, *Universal Jewish Encyclopedia,* 10 v. (New York 1939–43) 7:628–629. G. LIPKIND, *The Jewish Encyclopedia,* 13 v. (New York 1901–06) 8:663–666.

[E. A. SYNAN]

MONTEIRO DA VIDE, SEBASTIÃO

Archbishop and legislator in Brazil; b. Monforte do Alentejo, Portugal, March 19, 1643; d. Salvator, Bahia, Sept. 7, 1722. At age 16 he entered the Society of Jesus, but he left soon afterward to become a soldier and later to study Canon Law at the University of Coimbra. After ordination he became an ecclesiastical judge and vicar-general of Lisbon. He was named bishop of Bahia on May 8, 1701, and consecrated on December 21, 1701. He took possession of his see on May 22, 1702. He is known for having created many new parishes, but especially for holding in 1707 the first diocesan synod in Portuguese America, and for publishing the famous *Constituições Primeiras do Arcebispado da Bahía feitas e ordenadas por . . . Propostas e Aceitas em o Sinodo Diocesana que o dito Senhor celebrou a 12 de junio do ano de 1707.* The dioceses of Brazil had been governed by the constitutions of the Archdiocese of Lisbon, but after 1707 Da Vide's treatise was used, with suitable adaptations, in all the dioceses of Brazil throughout the rest of the colonial period and well into imperial times in the nineteenth century. These constitutions were universal in scope and admirable in their conciseness and clarity. They were highly praised by contemporary European canonists. Da Vide also included statutes for his cathedral and charters for various ecclesiastical courts in his diocese. Besides legal writings, he published a biography of Mother Vitoria da Encarnação, a holy Poor Clare nun of Bahia, *Historia da vida e morte da Madre Soror Vitoria da Encarnação, religiosa do Convento de Santa Clara do Desterro da cidade da Bahía* (Luiz Carvalho, ed., Rome 1720). He also left a manuscript entitled ''Exortação mística.''

Bibliography: S. LEITE, *História de Companhia de Jesús no Brasil,* 10 v. (Lisbon 1938–50).

[M. C. KIEMEN]

MONTEMAYOR, JUAN FRANCISCO

Spanish theologian and jurist; b. Huesca, Spain, Aug. 25, 1620; d. there, 1685. He is known variously as Montemayor de Cuenca, as Montemayor Córdoba de Cuenca, or simply as Cuenca. After receiving the licentiate in law in 1641, he became judge of inquests in Huesca and judge of the *audiencia* in Catalonia. He went to America as *oidor* in the *audiencia* of Santo Domingo in 1650. When the governor, the captain general, and the president of the *audiencia* died in 1653, Montemayor took over these offices. He recovered the island of Tortuga, north of Hispaniola, which had been held by French buccaneers and had served as a supply base, along with neighboring islands, for English and Dutch pirates as well. As a reward, he was named judge of the *audiencia* of Mexico, a post he held for 22 years, during which time he was ordained. When he returned to Spain he was a member of the Council of the Indies and advisor to the Inquisition. His work as a jurist is reflected in his writings. The *Discurso político, histórico, jurídico del derecho y repartimiento de presas y despojos aprehendidos en justa guerra, premios y castigos de soldados* (Mexico 1658) explains his theories on sea warfare and the disposition of prizes of war and prisoners. *Sumari os de las cédulas, órdenes y provisiones que se han despachado por S. M. a la Nueva España y otras partes de Indias* (Mexico 1678) covers the years 1628 to 1677 and treats also some of the decrees of the royal *audiencia* and other government orders. The book was used in Mexico up to the time of independence from Spain. Also published in Mexico in 1676 was his *Excubationes semicentum ex Decisionibus Regiae Cancellariae S. Dominici, vulgo Hispaniolae.*

Bibliography: J. M. BERISTAIN DE SOUZA, *Biblioteca hispanoamericana septentrional,* 5 v. in 2 (3d ed. Mexico City 1947).

R. ALTAMIRA Y CREVEA, *Técnica de investigación en la historia del derecho indiano* (Mexico City 1939). M. A. PEÑA BATLLE, *La Isla de la Tortuga* (Madrid 1951).

[H. PEREÑA]

MONTES PIETATIS

Charitable, nonprofit, credit organizations that lend money at low rates of interest on the security of pawned objects. *Montes* were established in the mid-15th century to provide financial assistance to the poor in a temporary crisis, as a protection against the exploitation of usurers. The interest compensated for the care of pawns and was used to defray administrative expenses, including the salaries of employees, to prevent the exhaustion of capital through the cost of operation.

Historically, the word *mons* was used to designate funds collected for a specific purpose, and was applied, before and during the Middle Ages, to public debts, stock and insurance companies, and banks of exchange and credit. As these banks often lent money on pawned objects, the charitable organizations operating on this basis assumed the name but added the word *pietatis* to identify them as beneficent, not speculative.

In the Middle Ages money was difficult to obtain and the prohibitions against usury imposed on Christians created a kind of monopoly on lending for the Jews and such groups as the Lombards, who exploited the situation by charging exorbitant rates of interest (averaging 32 1/2 to 43 1/2 per cent). In an effort to find a remedy for usury various proposals were made for lending money at low interest, or gratuitously, either through institutions created for this purpose or through municipal sponsorship.

In 1361 Bp. Michael Nothburg of London left a sum of money for the foundation of a bank to lend money on pawned objects without interest. This venture failed because of the provision that expenses be defrayed from the foundation capital, which was inevitably exhausted.

Durandus of Saint-Pourçain (?–1332) and Philip of Maizières (?–1405) conceived of a public institution that would lend money to the poor at a low rate of interest intended only to defray the cost of services rendered. There is no evidence that this proposal was ever put into practice, but in 1461 Hermolaus Barbarus (*c.* 1410–71), Bishop of Verona and papal delegate to Perugia, had authorized the foundation, in Perugia, of the first *Mons pietatis* by the Franciscans. Barbarus, upon his appointment as papal delegate, had abolished an existing statute that directly violated Canon Law, viz, the authorization of Jews to take limited usuries in the city. The *mons* provided an acceptable substitute to give financial assistance to the needy. The *montes* spread rapidly throughout Italy and their success is attributable largely to the Franciscans who promoted them, especially Bl. Bernardino of Feltre (1439–94). In 1467 Pope Paul II (1417–71) approved the constitution of the Perugia *mons* despite theological opposition, and successive popes sanctioned *montes* in other Italian cities.

As the *montes* developed they became either autonomous or municipal corporations, administered by a director, an appraiser, an accountant, and a staff of clerks. A rate of interest ranging from four to 12 per cent was charged, and at the end of a specified period the net profits were applied to the capital. If the profit was substantial, interest rates were lowered. The amount of a given loan equaled two-thirds of the value of the pawned object, which, if not redeemed within a stipulated period, was sold at public auction. If the price brought exceeded the amount of the loan plus the interest, the residue was given to the original owner.

A big step in the development of *montes* was the sanctioning of interest charges in order to raise and maintain capital, a need that had not been met by voluntary donations and collections. By the mid-16th century it was common practice to accept deposits from anyone wishing to invest and to pay five per cent on them. Many *montes* accordingly became ''mixed *montes*,'' i.e., institutions not financed by charity alone, but also by private investment, and they made loans to businessmen at eight to ten per cent as well as to the poor. The secular mixed *montes* were unlike a commercial banking system in that they did not create credit, but their structure was essentially similar to that of savings banks, financed by deposits and lending at interest to all.

Opposition, directed against the charging of interest rather than against the *montes* themselves, came from two main groups, viz, those whose interests were affected, and theologians and canonists who maintained that lending money at interest was illicit. That the interest was used for charitable purposes and not for profit did not justify the practice, which, they contended, was expressly forbidden by Christ (Lk 6.33). The question became an issue between several orders, Dominicans (with some exceptions) opposing *montes* as usurious and Franciscans defending them. Legal and theological faculties from many universities and some individual jurists also gave opinions favorable to the *montes.* Of the written attacks [the first by Nicholas Bariani, an Augustinian, in 1494] Gaetano Cajetan's [Tommaso de Vio (1469–1534)] *De Monte pietatis* (1498) is one of the most thorough and objective. Untinged by the bitterness of the conflict, though aimed at proving *montes* illicit, this analysis presents arguments for both sides of the question, and makes an important and significant distinction between defenses based on collective and on distributive justice. Navarrus [Martin Aspelcueta (1491–1586)] was the first important canonist and scholastic to make a detailed defense of *montes* and to discuss their financing, and the first to extend the principles used in this defense to other lending organizations.

The controversy was finally settled by the papal bull *Inter multiplicis* (May 14, 1515) of Leo X (1475–1521). The pope and the Lateran Council (tenth session) declared *montes* in no way sinful or illicit but meritorious, and declared those who preached or wrote against them subject to excommunication. By the 18th century *montes* were universally accepted in continental Europe.

The particular significance of the *montes* lies, not so much in their charitable function and successful reduction of usury, as in their influence on the justification of charging moderate interest. They prepared the way for the acceptance of credit business as a means of livelihood, and for the legitimacy of investment in lending organizations.

Bibliography: A. PARSONS, ''The Economic Significance of the Montes Pietatis,'' *Franciscan Studies* 22.3 (1941) 3–28. B. N. NELSON, *The Idea of Usury* (Princeton, N.J. 1949). J. T. NOONAN, *The Scholastic Analysis of Usury* (Cambridge, Mass. 1957). H. HOLZAPFEL, *Die Anfänge der Montes Pietatis* (Munich 1903). O. SCALVANTI, *Il Mons Pietatis di Perugia* (Perugia 1892); *Il Mons Pietatis con qualche notizia sul Monte di Gubbio* (Perugia 1892). C. JANNET, *Le Crédit populaire et les banques en Italie du XVe au XVIIIe siècle* (Paris 1885).

[A. MC PADDEN]

MONTESINO, ANTONIO

Dominican missionary and possibly a martyr; b. Spain, not later than 1486; d. West Indies, *c.* 1530. The birth and death dates of this Dominican friar, known also as Antonio de Montesinos, have not been accurately determined, nor is much information available on his life. He entered the Dominican Order in the convent of San Esteban, Salamanca, on July 1, 1502. Before April of 1510 he had arrived in Española. He took up the cause of the natives and in 1511 preached at least twice against the abuses in slavery. This action aroused opposition among the Spanish colonists, and Montesino was called to Spain on the matter. There he pleaded the need for protection of the indigenous population and evidently influenced the promulgation of the Laws of Burgos of 1512 and of Valladolid in 1513. He made three more trips to Spain regarding related problems in 1515, 1522–24, and late in 1527. About 1516 he wrote *Informatio juridica in indorum defensionem.* In June or July of 1526 he accompanied Vásquez de Ayllón on the unsuccessful attempt at colonization near modern Jamestown, Virginia. A temporary chapel was built there, and Mass was said, but the unhealthy location, the cold winter, and mutiny combined to destroy the colony. There is no evidence that he led a band of 20 Dominicans to Venezuela in 1528–29, as Zamora and Remesal state. In the margin of the chronicle that records Montesino's profession in the Dominican Order is written: ''Obiit Martyr in Indiis.'' Nothing but this is known of Montesino's death.

Bibliography: A. DE REMESAL, *Historia general de las Indias occidentales y particular de la gobernación de Chiapa y Guatemala,* 2 v. (2d ed. Guatemala 1932). A. DE ZAMORA, *Historia de la provincia de San Antonino del Nuevo reino de Granada,* 4 v. (2d ed. Bogotá 1945). V. F. O'DANIEL, *Dominicans in Early Florida* (New York 1930).

[A. B. NIESER]

MONTESQUIEU, CHARLES DE

Man of letters, political theorist; b. near Bordeaux, Jan. 18, 1689; d. Paris, Feb. 10, 1775. Charles Louis Joseph de Secondat, Baron de la Brède et de Montesquieu, inherited the former barony from his mother and the latter, together with a provincial office, from an uncle. He studied law and the sciences. Originally he was a rationalist in the Cartesian tradition, inclined to see social life as dominated by unchanging regularities. A grand tour from 1728 to 1731 opened his eyes to the profound differences among cultures, and to the importance of customs and local traditions. His book *De l'Esprit des lois* (1748) made him one of Europe's foremost social and political philosophers.

As a mature scholar Montesquieu endeavored to uncover the underlying *raisons d'être* of apparently irrational institutions, such as the medieval ordeal by fire, taking contemporary circumstances as his clues for interpretation. His general conviction was that cultures are determined by two sets of influences, geographical environment and political constitution. A hot climate makes men sluggish and conservative; a cold climate makes them active and progressive. He ascribed to ecological realities both the liberty enjoyed by the British and the lack of liberty endured by Africans and Asiatics.

Montesquieu distinguished three basic forms of political constitution, each needing an appropriate indwelling spirit to function well: republicanism, the spirit of virtue; limited monarchy, honor; and despotism, fear. Rome, the main example of republicanism, flourished while her citizens were frugal, hard–working, disciplined, patriotic, and enjoyed the rough–and–ready equality essential to this kind of society. Limited monar-

Charles de Montesquieu.

chy as exemplified in England and France required a general conviction of *noblesse oblige* to keep social ranks and distinctions from enfeebling the state. Despotism, characteristic of the Oriental empires, was simply structured, with the dictator on the one hand, the subject masses on the other, and with oppression and terror as the only social cement.

By distinguishing two formative forces, geography and politics, Montesquieu created for himself the difficult problem of resolving which, in the last resort, was the more decisive. The assertion that each constitution had its own appropriate territorial configuration—that republics worked best when small, limited monarchies when medium–sized, and despotisms when of vast extent—did not indicate whether territory conditioned political form or political form conditioned territorial frontiers. Montesquieu recognized that geographical and political theories embody contradictory conceptions of man, geographical determinism seeing man as passive and subject to natural forces, political doctrine assuming him to be active and morally responsible. In the unfinished *Essai sur les causes qui peuvent affecter les esprits et les caractères,* he ascribed primacy to the sociopolitical factor, arguing mainly from observation.

Although Montesquieu abhorred despotism and admired republicanism, he judged that a limited monarchy suited the modern territorial state best. He regarded the English constitution with its division of powers as very successful. His threefold division of governmental power into executive, legislative, and judicial branches was a major contribution to political thought and practice. It has often been asserted that he was a mechanist, finding the secret of a smoothly running society in the counterbalancing of independent societal forces. But his thought exemplifies organismic conceptions as well. Social forces are never really independent of each other. They form a definite total and inclusive system. A contest among them is not to be desired, not even a contest that will lead to equilibration, but rather mutual mitigation, complementation, and cooperation. The existence of intermediate social strata, such as an aristocracy independent of the king, seemed to Montesquieu the best safeguard against the dangers of overcentralization and dictatorship on the one hand, and underorganization and mob rule on the other. Not only England, but also France, with her sturdy provincial estates and *parlements,* provided the model.

Montesquieu's concept of man was similar to that of Montaigne; his low estimate of human nature was somewhat mitigated, however, by an indulgent and even compassionate attitude. In religion he was a Deist, and although he was basically anticlerical, he respected the traditional Roman Catholicism of his country and died in the church.

Bibliography: C. D. CABEEN, *Montesquieu: A Bibliography* (New York 1947). R. SHACKLETON, *Montesquieu: A Critical Biography* (London 1961). W. STARK, *Montesquieu: Pioneer of the Sociology of Knowledge* (Toronto 1961).

[W. STARK]

MONTESSORI, MARIA

Educator and originator of the Montessori Method; b. Chiaravalle, near Ancona, Italy, Aug. 31, 1870; d. Noordwijk, Netherlands, May 8, 1952. The first woman to receive a medical degree in 1894 at the University of Rome, Maria Montessori lectured on anthropology at the University and practiced as assistant physician at its psychiatric clinic where she came into contact with retarded children.

While working at the State Orthophrenic School in Rome (1899–1901), she turned her attention to the education of the feebleminded. She was conversant with E. Seguin's educational methods, which were the forerunner of much of the pedagogical treatment allied with medicine, later known as therapy. In her work at Bicêtre, in Paris, she noted Seguin's use of didactic apparatus rather than teacher–dominated methods. Utilizing this experience, she devised a great variety of didactic materials and trained a corps of teachers who were encouraged and stimulated by her dynamic personality.

While lecturing on pedagogy at the University of Rome (1901–07), she became interested in the education of normal children. In 1907 she opened the Casa dei Bambini, the first Montessori school for normal children, and within three years she had established three similar classes. Until 1911 she directed these schools, situated for the most part in the poorer sections of Rome and Milan.

From 1911 until her death she traveled the world—Europe, India, the U.S.—lecturing to teachers and interested persons, writing prodigiously, and instituting teacher–training centers. She introduced her method in Spain when she took charge of the Montessori Institute in Barcelona in 1917, and in London in 1919. On returning to Italy in 1922, she was appointed government inspector of Italian schools but was obliged to leave in 1934, during Mussolini's regime, because of her alleged pacifist ideas. She returned to the Barcelona Institute but again withdrew in 1939 during the Spanish Civil War and established an educational center at Laren near Amsterdam in the Netherlands. In 1939 she went to India to conduct a training course in Adyar, Madras, where, although interned as an enemy alien with her son, Mario Montessori, she continued her courses at Ahmadabad. After World War II, Montessori made the Netherlands her permanent home.

Montessori's major educational contribution was her method, which thrived in the U.S. and abroad in the early 20th century but later waned. Its early demise in the U.S. is attributed to the rising progressive movement and the work of J. Dewey and W. H. Kilpatrick. Her progressive ideas, especially her views on liberty, were often equated with Dewey's, while Kilpatrick, in his brief text *The Montessori Method Examined* (1914), dealt a severe blow to her infant beginnings in the United States. The restrained description of her work by such educational historians as R. Freeman Butts and Louella Cole contributed to its ineffectiveness. A Montessori society formed in the U.S. in 1913 by a group of socially prominent individuals lacked adequate leadership and quickly disappeared. Since the 1950s, however, there has been a Montessori revival, and interested parents have formed study groups preparatory to opening classes for their children. Leading Catholic universities, such as DePaul University, Chicago, Ill.; Marquette University, Milwaukee, Wis.; and Boston College, Chestnut Hill, Mass.; have inaugurated centers of research and teacher training. Boston College is also engaged in a modified practice of the method.

Maria Montessori. (AP/Wide World Photos)

Among her published works is *The Montessori Method* (1912), in which she expounds her philosophy, influenced by the English empiricist, J. LOCKE; the Spanish teacher of deaf mutes, J. R. Pereira; and the two French pioneers in the education of the retarded, E. Seguin and J. E. Itard. The heavy emphasis of the work in anthropology and biology stems from her medical background. Other publications include *Pedagogical Anthropology* (1913), *The Secret of Childhood* (1936), and *The Discovery of the Child* (1948).

Bibliography: E. M. STANDING, *Maria Montessori: Her Life and Work* (Fresno, Calif. 1959).

[J. CONCANNON]

MONTEVERDI, CLAUDIO

Illustrious composer whose sacred and secular works spanned the old Renaissance and new baroque styles, b. Cremona, 1567 (baptized Claudio Giovanni Antonio on May 15); d. Venice, Nov. 29, 1643. After study with M. A. Ingegneri at Cremona, he spent 21 years in the service of Vincenzo Gonzaga, Duke of Mantua, where he composed his earliest madrigals, church music, and operas, the first of which, *Orfeo* (1607), did much to fix the modern opera form. From 1613 until the end of his life he was

Coin engraving of Claudio Monteverdi.

maestro di cappella of St. Mark's, Venice, a post affording both stimulus and opportunity for his mature compositions in the new baroque *concertato* style. Long after his wife's early death he became a priest (*c.* 1632). Although the madrigal was declining when he was a young man, his nine books display a wealth of invention covering a far wider field than the classic term ''madrigal'' might suggest. Even more dramatic and picturesque effects are found in his ballets and operas, many of which are now lost. In church music he was supreme in his mastery of massive choral and instrumental groups, though he could also express the quieter mood of smaller-scale motets and monodies developed in Mantua by his colleague VIADANA.

Monteverdi issued his first anthology of church music when only 15—the three-voiced *Sacrae cantiunculae* of 1582. Apart from a book of *Madrigali spirituali* in 1583 (lost, except for the *basso* part), he ventured no further into the already overcrowded field of church music until 1610, when the Venetian publisher Amadino brought out a vast collection of music in honor of the Blessed Virgin Mary. This consisted of a six-voiced Mass based on themes from GOMBERT's motet *In illo tempore,* five motets (or cantatas), and a complete setting of Vespers, with two Magnificats. The Vespers make considerable use of divided choirs (*cori spezzati*), instrumental accompaniment and interludes, and extensive sections for solo voices. From 1615 until well after his death, Venetian publishers included his motets in various collections. The *Selva morale e spirituale* of 1640 includes a handful of spiritual madrigals and a ''Pianto della Madonna'' based on the popular ''Lamento d'Arianna'' (from 1608), but the main content is liturgical: a four-voiced Mass, a seven-voiced Gloria, with brilliant instrumental obbligato parts, and another extensive collection of music for Vespers of solemn feasts. Seven psalms are set for extremely varied combinations of voices and instruments, and some are provided with two or even three different settings. The four hymns appear as monodies, duets, and a trio, all with two violins and continuo. Of the two Magnificats, one is conceived as chamber music, the other as a grandiose canticle. Also noteworthy are three versions of *Salve Regina,* one of which features an echo tenor singing a TROPE.

This collection represents Monteverdi at the very height of his career, and though some secular elements are present (*contrafacta* of madrigals) the general impression is one of tremendous competence and a sincere desire to project the meaning of the texts. In his posthumous *Messa a quattro voci e salmi* (1650), one of the last great collections reflecting the baroque apogee of the Veneto, there are 13 settings of eight different psalms, perhaps the remains of several complete sets of Vesper psalms written for St. Mark's. Monteverdi's contribution to the church music of his day was a distinguished one, and if its occasional excess of ornament is seen against the background of his life and work, his taste is generally vindicated.

Bibliography: *Tutte le opere,* ed. G. F. MALIPIERO, 14 v. (Asolo 1926–42). D. ARNOLD, *Claudio Monteverdi* (New York 1963). L. SCHRADE, *Monteverdi* (New York 1950). M. F. BUKOFZER, *Music in the Baroque Era* (New York 1947). H. F. REDLICH, *Die Musik in Geschichte und Gegenwart,* ed. F. BLUME (Kassel-Basel 1949–) 9:511–531. N. SLONIMSKY, ed., *Baker's Biographical Dictionary of Musicians* (5th ed. New York 1958) 1107–09. E. T. CHAFE, *Monteverdi's Tonal Language* (New York 1992). G. CHEW, ''The Platonic Agenda of Monteverdi's *Seconda pratica:* A Case Study from the Eighth Book of Madrigals,'' *Music Analysis* 12 (1993) 147–168. S. G. CUSICK, ''*There Was Not One Lady Who Failed to Shed a Tear:* Arianna's Lament and the Construction of Modern Womanhood,'' *Early Music* 22 (1994) 21–41. J. G. KURTZMAN, ''Monteverdi's 'Mass of Thanksgiving' Revisited,'' *Early Music* 22 (1994) 63–84; *The Monteverdi Vespers of 1610: Music, Context, Performance* (Oxford 1999). S. SAUNDERS, ''New Light on the Genesis of Monteverdi's Eighth Book of Madrigals,'' *Music and Letters* 77 (1996) 183–193. S. STUBBS, ''*L'armonia sonora:* Continuo Orchestration in Monteverdi's *Orfeo,*'' *Early Music* 22 (1994) 86–98. R. WISTREICH, ''*La voce è grata assai, ma . . .:* Monteverdi on Singing,'' *Early Music* 22 (1994) 7–19.

[D. STEVENS]

MONTFAUCON, BERNARD DE

Benedictine scholar, paleographer; b. Soulage, France, Jan. 16, 1655; d. Paris, Dec. 21, 1741. He came from a noble family and was an army officer under the Count of Turenne from 1672 until he joined the Benedictine MAURISTS in Toulouse in 1675. He was ordained in 1676 and went to SAINT-GERMAIN-DES-PRÉS Paris (1687), to study Greek, Hebrew, and Syriac as preparation for editing the Greek Fathers. From 1698 to 1701 he did research in libraries in Italy with P. Briois in search of manuscripts and other historical material. He met L. A. MURATORI in Milan and was welcomed to Rome by Pope Innocent XII. He published a *Diarium Italicum* (1702) and used materials he had gathered, especially archeological, in *L'Antiquité expliquée et representée en figures* (10 v. 1719; 2d ed. 1722 and 5 v. suppl.), and *Les Monuments de la monarchie française* (5 v. 1729–33). He is known also for his monumental editions of St. Athanasius (3 v. 1698, in *Patrologia Graeca* 25–28), the *Hexapla* of Origen (2 v. 1713), and St. John Chrysostom (13 v. 1718–38, in *Patrologia Graeca* 47–64). He virtually created the science of Greek paleography with his *Palaeographia graeca* (1708). In 1699 he wrote a defense of the Maurist edition of St. Augustine. He maintained a voluminous correspondence with learned men of his time; and the younger generation of Benedictine scholars, the ''Bernardins,'' were greatly influenced by him. He is buried next to J. MABILLON in Saint-Germain-des-Prés.

Bibliography: *Correspondance inédite de Bernard de Montfaucon,* ed. M. VALÉRY, 3 v. (Paris 1846). E. DE BROGLIE, *Bernard de Montfaucon et les Bernardins,* 2 v. (Paris 1891). H. LECLERCQ, *Dictionnaire d'archéologie chrétienne et de liturgie,* 15 v. (Paris 1907–53) 11.2:2608–2672. J. BAUDOT, *Dictionnaire de théologie catholique,* 15 v. (Paris 1903–50) 10.2:2388–2390. ST. HILPISCH, *Lexikon für Theologie und Kirche,* 10 v. (Freiburg 1957–65) 7:589–590.

[F. X. MURPHY]

MONTFORT FATHERS

(SMM, Official Catholic Directory #0870); Missionaries of the Company of Mary, known also as the Montfort Fathers and the Society of Mary of Montfort (SMM), was founded in 1705 by St. Louis Marie GRIGNION DE MONTFORT.

In 1700, Louis Marie journeyed throughout western France, preaching missions and retreats, and teaching total consecration to Jesus through Mary. At the time of his death in 1716, the Company of Mary numbered two priests and a few brothers. The community, however, took root near the tomb of its founder at Saint-Laurent-sur-Sèvre, in Vendée. Although limited by royal decree to no more than 12 priests, this small mission band accomplished work that merited praise from Rome in 1719 and again in 1747. Nine of the priests and brothers were martyred for the faith during the French Revolution, leaving the congregation with but five priests and two brothers. Gabriel DESHAYES, founder of five religious congregations, joined the Company of Mary and became the superior. When he died in 1841 the society had grown to 18 priests and 40 brothers.

Louis Marie's manuscript, ''True Devotion to Mary,'' was discovered in 1842; it marked a turning point in the history of the congregation. Although all recruits for the priesthood were from the secular clergy, the community expanded and was raised to the rank of a pontifical congregation in 1853. The society's first minor seminary was founded in France in 1876; the first major seminary, in Holland in 1880. The beatification of the founder, in 1888, was accompanied by a rapid development of the society, which spread throughout the world, preaching missions and retreats, and was dedicated to restoring the reign of Christ through Mary.

Although the Montfort Fathers were invited to the U.S. in 1835 by Bp. Benedict Flaget of Kentucky, the first American establishment of the order was made in the Diocese of Brooklyn, N.Y., in 1903. The U.S. provincial headquarters was established at Ozone Park, N.Y. The generalate is in Rome.

Bibliography: G. RIGAULT, *Saint Louis Marie Grignion de Montfort* (New York 1947).

[P. J. GAFFNEY/EDS.]

MONTH, THE

A journal published by the British province of the Society of Jesus, but begun in July 1864 by Fanny Margaret (later Mother Magdalen) TAYLOR, a convert, who had accompanied Florence Nightingale to the Crimea and later founded the Poor Servants of the Mother of God. She was supported by the JESUITS, and encouraged by John Henry NEWMAN who, though he cautioned against the publication of theological articles, chose *The Month* for the first publication of *The Dream of Gerontius.* The Jesuits took over in 1865, as the review was not paying its way. There was a distinguished series of Jesuit editors, starting with the convert Henry COLERIDGE, a distant relative of Samuel Taylor Coleridge. After Newman's poem, verse disappeared from the journal's pages; Gerard Manley Hopkins's *The Wreck of the Deutschland* was rejected. George TYRRELL was one of those assigned to the journal, and the editor, John Gerard, who was also for a time provincial, made considerable efforts to support him during the Modernist crisis, earning him a rebuke from Rome. Sydney Smith, S.J., a regular contributor from 1869 to 1920, was likewise rebuked for being too sympathetic to Anglicans. *The Month* published a wide variety of articles, from the historical (by the distinguished Jesuit scholars Joseph Stevenson and Herbert Thurston) to commentary on political events both national and international. Despite the ban on poetry, soon lifted, the magazine had a strong interest in literature. In 1949, under the new editorship of Fr. Philip Caraman, and a new, elegant, design, the literary content became outstanding: Caraman was able to call upon some of the leading British writers for articles. Ronald Moffatt was appointed editor in 1963, and he brought in Peter HEBBLETHWAITE, who had just completed his theological studies. Hebblethwaite went to Rome to cover the Second VATICAN COUNCIL for *The Month* and for other journals, swiftly emerging as a leading commentator on Vatican affairs. On his return Moffatt resigned the editorship in his favor. Under Hebblethwaite *The Month* became increasingly liberal in tone, and carried important articles on Church affairs. In 1971 it absorbed the even more radical *Herder Correspondence*, having two years earlier amalgamated with the *Dublin Review* at the request of the *Dublin*'s owner, the archbishop of Westminster. From 1976 until his sudden death in June 1986 the magazine was edited by Hugh Kay, a layman with close ties to the Jesuits. Kay had strong, radical, political views, and the paper reflected his social concerns. After his death it once again acquired a Jesuit editor and again became more literary, but a declining circulation and the increasing difficulty of finding an editor when the number of members of the British Jesuit province was decreasing led to an announcement in 2000 that it would suspend publication the following year.

Bibliography: J. L. ALTHOLZ, *The Religious Press in Britain, 1760–1900* (Westport, Conn. 1989). J. J. DWYER, ''The Catholic Press, 1850–1950,'' in G. A. BECK, ed., *The English Catholics, 1850–1950* (London 1950) 475–514. E. LEONARD, ''Modernism and the *Month*,'' *The Month* (December 1989) 461–471. R. MOFFATT, ''Account Rendered,'' *The Month* (December 1989) 472–477. P. HEBBLETHWAITE, ''The Post-conciliar Month,'' *The Month* (December 1989) 478–481.

[M. J. WALSH]

MONTHS, SPECIAL DEVOTIONS FOR

Special devotions for months is a nonliturgical practice developed in the Church in recent centuries, by which the months of the calendar are dedicated to special devotions. In some of these cases—for example, the dedication of May to the Mother of Christ —the Church recognized and blessed what had been a popular practice. In other cases—for example, the dedication of October to the Rosary—the practice was initiated by the Holy See. In each of the recognized dedications the Church grants indulgences for the saying of special prayers during the month in question. (*See* INDULGENCES.)

January is dedicated to the Holy Name of Jesus, with devotions indulgenced by Leo XIII; March, to St. Joseph with indulgences granted by Pius IX and Pius XI for devotions; May, to the Virgin Mary, with indulgences granted by Pius XII for devotions; June, to the Sacred Heart of Jesus with indulgences granted by Pius IX, Leo XIII, Pius X, and Pius XI for devotions; July, to the Precious Blood of Jesus Christ, with indulgences granted by Pius VII, Pius XI, and Pius XII for devotions; August, to the Immaculate Heart of the Blessed Virgin Mary, with indulgences granted by Benedict XV and Pius XI for devotions; September, to Mary, under the title Our Lady of Sorrows, with indulgences granted by Leo XIII and Pius XI for pious exercises; October, to the rosary, with indulgences granted by Leo XIII and Pius XI for daily or regular recitation of the rosary; November, to the souls of the faithful departed, with indulgences granted by Pius IX, Leo XIII, and Pius XI to those who pray for the dead; and December, to Our Lady of the Immaculate Conception, with special indulgences granted by Pius X and Pius XI for exercises of piety.

There are a number of other dedications of given months to particular mysteries; for example, January, to the Holy Childhood of Jesus; March, to the Holy Family; and October, to the Holy Angels. These, and other like dedications, are a result of local, popular devotions and are not formally recognized by the Church.

Bibliography: *Enchiridion indulgentiarum* (Rome 1952) 118, 175, 217, 219, 253, 325, 364, 381, 389, 398, 466, 589. F. G. HOLWECK, *The Catholic Encyclopedia,* ed. C. HERBERBMAN et al., 16 v. (New York 1907–14; suppl. 1922) 10:542–543. A. MERCATI and A. PELZER, *Dizionario ecclesiastico,* 3 v. (Turin 1954–58) 2:948.

[P. F. MULHERN]

MONTMAJOUR, ABBEY OF

A former Benedictine abbey in the now-suppressed Diocese of ARLES, in southern France (Lat. *Mons Major*). It was established about the middle of the 10th century, although local legends attribute to it an earlier date of foundation. Like LÉRINS and SAINT-VICTOR IN MARSEILLES, the abbey had acquired numerous holdings in southeastern France during the 11th and 12th centuries, and it exercised considerable influence in Dauphiné and Provence. In the following century it had to struggle for its existence against aggressive local lords. In 1639 it joined the MAURIST reform movement but was suppressed in 1786 and its holdings were distributed among the Provençal dioceses. The abbey church dating from the 12th century has been preserved, as well as a cloister of the same date and a 14th-century tower. The Maurist buildings, restored at the beginning of the 18th century according to the plans of the painter Pierre Mignard (d. 1695), are now in ruins.

Bibliography: *Gallia Christiana,* v. 1–13 (Paris 1715–85), v. 14–16 (Paris 1856–65) 4:662–665. *Mons Major: seu historia monasterii Sancti Petri M. M. secus Arelaten in Provincia O.S.B.,* ed. C. CHANTELOU (Bibliothèque d'Arles, MSS 162, 163, 164). L. ROYER, *Dictionnaire d'histoire et de géographie ecclésiastiques,* ed. A. BAUDRILLART et al. 4:237, 240, 241. M. HARTIG, *Lexikon für Theologie und Kirche,* ed. J. HOFER and K. RAHNER, 10 v. (2d, new ed. Freiburg 1957–65) suppl., *Das Zweite Vatikanische Konzil: Dokumente und Kommentare,* ed. H. S. BRECHTER et al., pt. 1 (1966) 7:591.

[L. GAILLARD]

Abbey of Montmajour. (©Franz-Marc Frei/CORBIS)

MONTMARTRE (PARIS), ABBEY OF

Former Benedictine monastery for women in Paris on Montmartre, the original *Mons Mercurii,* later called the *Mons martyrum,* a cemetery and place of execution, where DENIS OF PARIS and others may have been martyred. Very early oratories had been built there. One of these, the *Sanctum martyrium,* became a priory of monks in 1098; the oratories of Notre Dame, Saint-Denys, and Saint-Pierre were united into a church (one of the first Gothic churches) consecrated by Pope Eugene III (1147) for the Benedictine nuns who were established there in 1134. Under Bishop Poncher (d. 1519) the convent was reformed and strict enclosure, the common life, episcopal visitation, and a three-year term for the abbess were insisted upon. St. Ignatius and his followers took their vows there (Aug. 15, 1535). In 1560, however, the kings began to appoint lifetime abbesses of noble birth. One of these, Marie de Bauvillier (1601), initiated a mystical revival that influenced people even outside the abbey, e.g., Marie Granger (devotion to the Sacred Heart), Marguerite de Bac (Benedictines of the Bl. Sacrament), and Jeanne Marie de la Motte GUYON. The abbey was suppressed during the French Revolution and the abbess was murdered; the abbey church became a parish church. To the basilica of Sacré Coeur, erected close by in 1875, are associated (1899) the Benedictine Nuns of the Adoration of the Sacred Heart of Montmartre.

Bibliography: L. H. COTTINEAU, *Répertoire topobibliographique des abbayes et prieurés,* 2 v. (Mâcon 1935–39) 2:2197–99. *Gallia Christiana,* v. 1–13 (Paris 1715–85), v. 14–16 (Paris 1856–65) 7:612–623. H. LECLERCQ, *Dictionnaire d'archéologie chrétienne et de liturgie,* ed. F. CABROL, H. LECLERCQ, and H. I. MARROU, 15 v. (Paris 1907–53) 11.2:2673–91. P. SCHMITZ, *Histoire de l'ordre de saint Benoît,* 7 v. (Maredsous 1942–56).

[P. DELHAYE]

MONTREUIL, ABBEY OF

Former Carthusian house of Notre-Dame des Prés, at Neuville-sous-Montreuil, Pas-de-Calais, France, Diocese of Arras. This charterhouse was established in 1324 by Count Robert VII of Boulogne; its church was consecrated in 1328 by John of Vienne, bishop of the former Diocese of Thérouanne. It was periodically sacked and abandoned in the 14th and 15th centuries (Hundred Years' War). Dom Pierre de Marnef, a monk of Montreuil, was general of the CARTHUSIANS from 1540 to 1546. Imperial troops pillaged Montreuil in 1542; the charterhouse was extensively rebuilt in the 17th century under Dom Bernard Bruyant. Montreuil was suppressed in 1790 during the French Revolution, and its prior, Dom Eloi Marion, was imprisoned at Arras and executed. After repurchasing a portion of the former lands of Montreuil, the Carthusians built a new monastery there (1872–75), which was consecrated by Bishop Lequette of Arras. It served as a major center of Carthusian publications; e.g., the *Annales ordinis Cartusiensis* of C. Le

Couteulx were published there (1887–91). The charterhouse was closed in 1901, during the era when France expelled all religious orders, and the monks moved to PARKMINSTER, England.

Bibliography: R. GAZEAU, *Catholicisme. Hier, aujourd'hui et demain,* ed. G. JACQUEMET (Paris 1947–) 2:1008. L. H. COTTINEAU, *Répertoire topobibliographique des abbayes et prieurés,* 2 v. (Mâcon 1935–39) 2:1974–75.

[G. E. GINGRAS]

MONTREUIL-LES-DAMES, ABBEY OF

Former French Cistercian abbey for nuns, diocese of Laon. Montreuil-les-Dames had been the site of a Benedictine monastery since the 7th century, but was given to a community of CISTERCIAN NUNS by the bishop, Bartholomew of Laon, in 1136. It was so successful that soon 300 nuns populated the convent, supported by rich donations of land. Upon the insistence of CLAIRVAUX, the nuns reduced their number to 100 after having experienced economic difficulties. The defenseless abbey was repeatedly devastated by the wars of the 14th to the 17th centuries, and the nuns forced to seek refuge within the walls of Laon. In the late Middle Ages Montreuil-les-Dames was famous as the shrine of the ''Veil of St. Veronica,'' donated to the convent in 1249. It was actually only an early copy of the one preserved in Rome. The abbey was suppressed by the French Revolution (1791).

Bibliography: U. CHEVALIER, *Répertoire des sources historiques du moyen-âge. Topobibliographie,* 2 v. (Paris 1894–1903), 2:2010. L. H. COTTINEAU, *Répertoire topobibliographique des abbayes et prieurés,* 2 v. (Mâcon 1935–39) 2:1973–74.

[L. J. LEAKI]

MONTSERRAT, ABBEY OF

Benedictine monastery on a mountain near Barcelona, Spain; aggregated to the congregation of SUBIACO with 150 professed monks. It was founded as a priory by Oliva of Ripoll *c.* 1025 on the site of a 9th-century hermitage. Benedict XIII made it an independent abbey (1409). Hermits lived there with the cenobites from the 11th century to the late 19th. The monastery belonged to the cloistered congregation of Tarragona until 1493, when the reform of Valladolid was introduced. The first reform abbot, García Ximénez de CISNEROS (d. 1510), published in 1500 *Exercitatorio de la vida spiritual,* which through Montserrat's ascetic school influenced IGNATIAN SPIRITUALITY. Other devotional and liturgical works were published at Montserrat (1499–1500, 1518–26). In the 16th and 18th centuries, besides traditional ecclesiastical disciplines, the monks cultivated history, classical literature, natural sciences, painting, and music. From the boys choir school (*Escolania*), 13th century in origin, came famous composers, organists, and musical directors: Juan Marqués (1582–1658), Juan Cererols (d. 1680), Narciso Casanovas (1747–99), Antonio Soler (1729–83), and Fernando Sor (1778–1839).

The abbey was destroyed by Napoleon's troops (1811) and lay vacant during secularization (1835–44) and the Spanish Civil War (1936–39). It is famed for its museum of paintings, Biblical and Middle Eastern museums, and a library of 180,000 volumes, 1,350 MSS, and 400 incunabula. The musical archives hold some 2,000 MSS; and the monastery archives (13th–19th century), some 5,000 parchment and 30,000 paper documents. The abbey publishes *Biblia de Montserrat, Analecta Montserratensia, Studia Monastica,* and *Scripta et Documenta,* as well as liturgical and pastoral publications. The shrine of Our Lady of Montserrat (*La Moreneta*), patroness of Catalonia, has been a pilgrimage center since the Middle Ages. Of the original church there remain only the Romanesque portal (12th–13th century) and the Gothic cloister, built under the commendatory abbot Cardinal Giulio della Rovere (1472–83). The present church, a minor basilica (1881), dates from the late 16th century. Miracles attributed to the image of Our Lady of Montserrat (polychrome wood, Romanesque, *c.* 1200) and the brotherhood formed in 1225 have spread her cult in Europe and Latin America.

Bibliography: A. M. ALBAREDA, *História de Montserrat* (3d ed. Montserrat 1946); *L'abat Oliva, fundador de Montserrat* (Montserrat 1931); *Sant Ignasi a Montserrat* (Montserrat 1935); ''Intorno alla scuola di orazione metodica stabilita a Monserrato dall'abbate Garsias Jiménez de Cisneros, 1493–1510,'' *Archivum historicum Societatis Jesu* 25 (1956) 254–316. G. COLOMBÁS, *Un reformador benedictino en tiempo de los reyes católicos: García Jiménez de Cisneros, abad de Montserrat* (Scripta et documenta 5; Montserrat 1955). A. OLIVAR, comp., *Catáleg dels incunables de la biblioteca de Montserrat* (*ibid.* 4; Montserrat 1955). D. PUJOL, ed., *Música instrumental* (Mestres de l'escolania de Montserrat; Montserrat 1930–34).

[C. BARAUT]

MOODY, DWIGHT LYMAN

American revival preacher; b. Northfield, Mass., Feb. 5, 1837; d. Northfield, Dec. 22, 1899. He received a grammar school education and went to work in a Boston shoe store in 1854. Although originally a Unitarian, he experienced a religious conversion in 1855 and joined the Congregational Church. He moved to Chicago, Illinois, in 1856 and worked as a salesman until 1860, when he became a full-time city missionary. He organized the North Market Sabbath School in 1858 and formed a nondenominational church in 1863. He was active in the Chicago YMCA and became its president in 1866. His first evangelistic crusade in British industrial centers began in 1873, and in 1875, he conducted interdenominational revivals in various American cities. He toured the British Isles from 1881 to 1884 and again in 1891 and 1892. He founded the Chicago (Moody) Bible Institute in 1889 to train evangelists and began the Student Volunteer Movement. Moody's preaching was restrained and stressed ''Bible Christianity.'' He brought modern business methods to revivalism, but his crusades did not reach the masses of the unchurched or notably increase church membership.

Bibliography: W. R. MOODY, *Dwight L. Moody* (New York 1930). W. M. SMITH, comp., *Annotated Bibliography of D. L. Moody* (Chicago 1948). R. K. CURTIS, *They Called Him Mr. Moody* (Garden City, NY 1962). J. C. POLLOCK, *Moody without Sankey* (New York 1963).

[R. K. MACMASTER]

MOONEY, EDWARD FRANCIS

Cardinal, first archbishop of the Detroit (Mich.) Archdiocese; b. Mount Savage, Md., May 9, 1882; d. Rome, Italy, Oct. 25, 1958. He was the youngest of the seven children of Thomas and Sarah (Heneghan) Mooney, immigrants from Ireland, who moved to Youngstown, Ohio, when Edward was five years old. He attended St. Columba's parish school, St. Charles College, Ellicott City, Md., and St. Mary's Seminary, Baltimore, earning the bachelor's and master's degrees *maxima cum laude.* On Oct. 22, 1905, Mooney entered the North American College, Rome, where he completed his theological studies, receiving a doctorate in philosophy in 1907 and a doctorate in theology in 1909. On April 10, 1909, he was ordained for the Diocese of Cleveland. He returned to the United States and was appointed to St. Mary's Seminary, Cleveland, to teach dogmatic theology. He established the Cathedral Latin School in Cleveland in 1916 and served as principal for six years. In August of 1922, Bishop Joseph Schrembs appointed Mooney pastor of St. Patrick's parish, Youngstown; a few months later he was selected as spiritual director at the North American College. Pope Pius XI named him a domestic prelate in 1925.

Diplomatic Service. On Jan. 8, 1926, Pope Pius XI chose Mooney as apostolic delegate to India, one of the first Americans to represent the Holy See in a permanent diplomatic post. He was consecrated titular archbishop of Irenopolis by Cardinal William Van Rossum, CSSR, Prefect of the Congregation of the Propagation of the Faith, in the chapel of the North American College on Jan. 31, 1926. In India, Mooney's tact and judgment were tested by a longstanding dissension, the Padroado question. The dispute involved a jurisdiction divided between the Indian bishops of native dioceses and the Portuguese missionaries whose parishes were scattered along the east coast of India. Mooney procured an accord between the Holy See and the Portuguese colonial government that terminated four centuries of Portuguese ecclesiastical control over some of India's faithful.

As apostolic delegate, Mooney received into the Church on Sept. 20, 1930 two Jacobite bishops, Mar Ivanios and his suffragan, Mar Theophilos, who were soon followed by other clergy and religious, and a number of lay people. Mooney supervised the establishment of 11 new mission territories in India and the transfer of three existing dioceses to native Indian bishops. After five years in India, Mooney was named delegate to Japan on Feb. 25, 1931. Here he was faced with the dilemma of Japanese Catholics, who, as subjects of the Mikado, were bound by law to attend the Shinto shrines, yet constrained in conscience from participating in what seemed to be pagan worship. Close scrutiny by the apostolic delegate determined that the Shinto rites were civil, not religious, ceremonies. Thus without doing violence to their religious convictions, Catholics could discharge their civil obligations by attending the ceremonies.

Bishop of Rochester. On Aug. 28, 1933, Pope Pius XI named Mooney bishop of the Rochester (NY) Diocese, where he was installed on Oct. 12. Within a year, he was elected to the administrative board of the National Catholic Welfare Conference (NCWC) and named chairman of the Social Action Department. During the social and economic difficulties of the 1930s, he was articulate about the social teaching of the Church especially as delineated in the encyclicals of Pope Leo XIII and Pope Pius XI. In November of 1935, Mooney was elected chairman of the NCWC administrative board, a post he held for two terms (1935–39, 1941–45). Thus during World War II he was, in effect, spokesman for the Church in the United States. To provide for the spiritual welfare of service personnel he served as first chairman of the Bishops' War Emergency and Relief Committee and as first president of the board of trustees of the National Catholic Community Service, which cared for the religious needs and social welfare of the men and women in the armed services. He was also cochairman of the Clergy Committee of the United Services Organization and was one of the framers of the seven-point Declaration for World Peace, which was signed by 144 leading Catholics, Jews, and Protestants.

Archbishop of Detroit. When DETROIT was made a metropolitan see on May 22, 1937, Mooney was transferred there and installed by Archbishop (later Cardinal) Amleto G. Cicognani, the apostolic delegate, on Aug. 3, 1937. During the early years of his administration, he faced a mixed reaction to the radio addresses and publications of Charles E. Coughlin, pastor of the Shrine of the Little Flower parish, Royal Oak, Michigan. An industrial center, Detroit was caught in the post-Depression turmoil and in the throes of union organizing among the automobile workers. When the archbishop publicly announced that Catholics were not only free to join the new Congress of Industrial Organizations (CIO), but had an obligation to join a union, his statement was widely heralded. To help form a Christian conscience on social and economic questions among his people, he established the archdiocesan Labor Institute. Classes in social ethics and the encyclicals were offered to priests and laymen, who in turn carried the message throughout the archdiocese.

During the 1920s the diocese had expanded rapidly, but the Depression years brought on a crisis. When Mooney arrived in 1937, the total debt stood at more than $18 million. He reorganized the financial structure of the parishes and instituted the archdiocesan development fund, an annual collection for specifically archdiocesan needs. As a result of sound financing, Detroit was able to keep pace with the expanding needs of a new wave of population that came with World War II. More than 100 new parish sites were bought; catechetical centers were established for Catholic children attending public schools; social service centers were provided in all eight counties of the archdiocese; Boysville and the Catholic Youth Organization (CYO) Home for boys were erected. St. John's Provincial Seminary, theologate for the entire province, at Plymouth, Michigan, opened in 1949. Two centers for the aging, Carmel Hall in downtown Detroit and the Martin Kundig Center for the Aged, were established during Mooney's episcopate.

Eight years after arriving in Detroit, Mooney was named a cardinal priest by Pope Pius XII. He received the red hat at the consistory on Feb. 21, 1946; his titular church in Rome was St. Susanna's. His world view was reflected in the address he gave in April of 1954 to the Detroit archdiocesan Council of Catholic Women, calling for support of the United Nations as the ''best available means'' for international accord. His zeal for the unfortunate never flagged. Not long before his death he dedicated Our Lady of Providence School for retarded girls. During the 21 years of his episcopate, the Catholic population had increased from about 550,000 to 1,288,000. Parishes with resident pastors had increased from 201 to almost 300. Death came when he was in Rome participating in the election of a successor to Pope Pius XII. On the morning of Oct. 25, 1958, he attended the Mass in St. Peter's opening the conclave. As he waited at the North American College for the first session that afternoon, he was stricken with a massive cerebral hemorrhage and died. He was buried from the Cathedral of the Most Blessed Sacrament, Detroit, on Oct. 31, 1958.

Bibliography: Archives, Archdiocese of Detroit, Mich.

[F. X. CANFIELD]

MOORE, EDWARD ROBERTS

Social worker; b. New York City, Jan. 9, 1894; d. New York City, June 2, 1952. He was the only child of Edward A. and Mary (Roberts) Moore, the latter of English heritage and a convert. He received his higher education at Fordham University, NY (Ph.D. 1923). After his ordination on Sept. 20, 1919, at St. Joseph's Seminary, Yonkers, New York, he was assigned as curate to St. Peter's, Barclay Street, New York City, the oldest parish in the state. In 1923 he was appointed director of the division of social action of the newly founded Catholic Charities of the Archdiocese of New York. Moore was interested in youth work (especially scouting), in housing, and in the Legion of Decency, and he served as a board member on many civic and Catholic committees. From 1933 to 1943 he was executive secretary of the Catholic Committee on Scouting. He was a member of the New York Municipal Housing Authority from 1934 to 1944 and he was appointed in 1935 by President Franklin D. Roosevelt to the Advisory Commission of the National Youth Administration. He played a major role in 1935 in establishing the Legion of Decency on a national basis. Except for a brief period (1923–29) at St. Gregory's parish, Moore spent his priestly life at St. Peter's as curate, administrator, and pastor (1937–52). He made it virtually a shrine parish, established a large lending library, and fostered discussion groups. His book *Roman Collar* (1950) records his experiences at St. Peter's. Moore also taught at Fordham University's School of Social Service (1924–38) and worked zealously with the New York province of Newman clubs. Pope Pius XII named him a papal chamberlain in 1941 and a domestic prelate in 1948.

[F. D. COHALAN]

MOORE, THOMAS VERNER

Catholic priest and psychologist, b. Oct. 22, 1877, Louisville, Kentucky; d. June 5, 1969, Burgos, Spain. Moore entered the Paulists in 1896, and was ordained in 1901. In 1903 he received his doctorate in psychology from The Catholic University of America under Pace and continued studies under Wundt in Leipzig. He received his doctorate in medicine from The Johns Hopkins University in 1913. In 1910 he began as an instructor in psychology at The Catholic University of America, becoming head of the department of psychology and psychiatry in 1939. In 1916 he founded a psychiatric clinic where training was offered to students in psychology, this becoming, under Moore and for the first time in America, a regular part of their curriculum. During 1918–19 Moore served in the U.S. Army as psychiatrist and chaplain.

A pioneer among Catholics in recognizing the value of scientific psychology, Moore became one of the first Catholic priests to win general recognition from fellow psychologists. The doctorate from his department was until 1959 the only one from a Catholic university with official approval of the American Psychological Association. He likewise understood the loss to psychology that came from ignoring man's religious dimension, and correcting this then-prevalent situation became a dominant feature of his life work.

With the idea of living the more deeply religious and liturgical life of a monk, and offering this to colleagues for vitalizing their scientific activities, he was a prime influence in founding the Benedictine Priory (now Abbey) in Washington in 1924, after making a year's novitiate in Scotland. He became prior in 1939.

In 1947, understanding that God was calling him to the hidden, solitary Carthusian life, he entered the Carthusians in Spain, returning to America in 1950 to help found the first American Charterhouse. He died in Spain, where he had returned in 1960, at the age of 91, living the Carthusian life faithfully to the end.

Bibliography: Works. *Dynamic Psychology* (Philadelphia 1924). *Prayer* (Westminster, Md. 1931). *Principles of Ethics* (Philadelphia 1935). *Cognitive Psychology* (Philadelphia 1939). *The Nature and Treatment of Mental Disorders* (New York 1943). *Personal Mental Hygiene* (New York 1944). *The Driving Forces of Human Nature and Their Adjustment* (New York 1950). *The Home and Its Inner Spiritual Life* (Westminster, Md. 1952). *The Life of Man with God* (New York 1956). *Heroic Sanctity and Insanity* (New York 1959). Source materials for Moore's life and work are the following: Archives of the Paulist Fathers (New York); the Benedictine Fathers, St. Anselm's Abbey (Washington, D.C.); the Charterhouse of Miraflores (Burgos, Spain); *Newsletter of the American Catholic Psychological Association* (Autumn 1969). B. NEENAN, *Thomas Verner Moore: Psychiatrist, Educator, and Monk* (New York 2000).

[R. DIAMOND]

MOPSUESTIA

City of the second province of Cilicia, on the Pyramos River, at present-day Misis. Its name means hearth (or shrine) of Mopsos, a legendary seer who was believed to have been its founder. It was an episcopal see early in the 4th century, suffragan of Anazarbos, under the patriarch of Antioch. Its most famous bishop was THEODORE OF MOPSUESTIA (392–428), outstanding representative of the Antiochene school of theology and exegesis, who was condemned for heresy 125 years after his death by the Council of CONSTANTINOPLE II (553). On orders of the emperor Justinian, a provincial synod had been held at Mopsuestia on June 17, 550, at which the oldest of the clergy and laity declared under oath that in their lifetime Theodore's name had always been replaced on the diptychs of the church by the name Cyril, whom they understood to be CYRIL OF ALEXANDRIA (*Sacrorum Conciliorum nova et amplissima collectio,* 9:274–289; *Histoire des conciles d'après les documents originaux,* 3.1:38–40). Mopsuestia became a metropolitan see in 879; from 1079 to 1224 (when it was known as Mamistra) it had Latin archbishops; it is now a titular archbishopric.

Bibliography: P. CAMELOT, *Lexikon für Theologie und Kirche,* ed. J. HOFER and K. RAHNER, 10 v. (2d, new ed. Freiburg 1957–65) 7:596. M. LE QUIEN, *Oriens Christianus,* 3 v. (Paris 1740; repr. Graz 1958) 2:889–894; 3:1197–1200. W. RUGE, *Paulys Realenzyklopädie der klassischen Altertumswissenschaft,* ed. G. WISSOWA et al. 16.1 (1933) 243–250. V. SCHULTZE, *Altchristliche Städte und Landschaften,* v. 2.2 (Gütersloh 1926) 305–315.

[F. A. SULLIVAN]

MORA, MIGUEL (MICHAEL) DE LA, ST.

Martyr, priest; b. June 19, 1878, Tecalitlán, Jalisco, Diocese of Colima, Mexico; d. Aug. 7, 1927, Colima, Colima. He was chaplain of Colima cathedral, a simple, charitable priest, who was always ready to serve. Colima was the first state to require priests to register in order to exercise their sacerdotal ministries. When the bishop and priests protested, the government exiled them. Miguel was one of those who were hidden to ensure the faithful were not left untended. He was discovered and threatened with imprisonment. Unwilling to disobey the instructions of his bishop, Miguel attempted to leave the city, but was apprehended and condemned to execution. Upon reaching the appointed place at noon, he declared his faith and his love of the Blessed Mother. Miguel was felled by bullets as he prayed the rosary. He was both beatified (Nov. 22, 1992) and canonized (May 21, 2000) with Cristobal MAGALLANES [*see* GUADALAJARA (MEXICO), MARTYRS OF, SS.] by Pope John Paul II.

Feast: May 25 (Mexico).

Bibliography: J. CARDOSO, *Los mártires mexicanos* (Mexico City 1953). J. DÍAZ ESTRELLA, *El movimiento cristero: sociedad y*

St. Miguel de la Mora.

conflicto en los Altos de Jalisco (México, D.F. 1979). J. A. MEYER, *La cristiada en Colima* (Colima, México 1993).

[K. I. RABENSTEIN]

MORA Y DEL RIO, JOSÉ

Archbishop of Mexico during the beginning of the persecution; b. Pajacuarán, Michoacán, Feb. 24, 1854; d. San Antonio, Texas, April 22, 1928. After early education at a private school in Ixtlán de los Herbores, he entered the seminary of Zamora about 1868; in 1874 he was sent with other young seminarians to the Colegio de San Luis being established in Jacona. He completed his studies at the South American College in Rome, where he was ordained in 1879, and received a doctorate in Canon Law and in theology. In 1881 he returned to Mexico to become rector of the Colegio de San Luis. Bishop LABASTIDA Y DAVALOS, recognizing the young man's abilities, made him a professor at the seminary and gave him a post in the archiepiscopal secretariat. From then on he occupied many positions of confidence through which he became thoroughly acquainted with the operation of the Church and the political problems in Mexico. The succeeding bishop, Próspero María Alarcón, named Mora y del Rio first secretary of the archdiocese. Bishop Gillow of Oajaca recommended him for the Diocese of Tehuantepec, and he was appointed its first bishop on Jan. 19, 1893. That rude inhospitable area was transformed as much as possible by the bishop, who brought in religious orders to help in his social and apostolic work. On Sept. 12, 1901, he was transferred to the Diocese of Tulancingo. An advocate of Catholic Social Action, he organized there the influential ''Semanas Agrícolas'' for the working classes of the region. On Sept. 15, 1907, he was transferred to León and was there little more than a year when he was appointed archbishop of Mexico on Dec. 2, 1908. He took possession of the see on Feb. 11, 1909.

At the beginning of the political upheaval of 1911, the Catholics received the backing of the archbishop in founding a Catholic party, which supported the presidential aspirations of Francisco Madero. A coup d'état destroyed the weak, recently established democracy and General Victoriano Huerta assumed power. He was sympathetic to the Church, and his enemies were against it. But this was a momentary pause in the attack. In 1914 Archbishop Mora y del Rio went to Rome to report to the pope on the situation. He did not return to Mexico because of the religious complications building up to the Constitution of 1917, but spent some years in exile in San Antonio, Texas. As soon as circumstances permitted, he returned to his see and was back in Mexico by February of 1919. The law had put the Church in a precarious position, and the archbishop used whatever means he could to keep the Church organization functioning. The Eucharistic Congress he held in 1924 was so successful that it provoked governmental action against him and the other bishops who had participated. This was just the beginning of the persecution, which soon increased. To coordinate the activities of the bishops and the faithful, the apostolic delegate, Jorge Caruana, suggested an episcopal committee, which was formed with Mora y del Rio as chairman. This committee protested the antireligious laws and their enforcement, but President Calles was adamant. On Aug. 1, 1926, public worship was forbidden. Mora y del Rio had already refused to cooperate with the government in the establishment of a schismatic Mexican church; and so he, with other members of the hierarchy, was exiled to the United States, where he died.

[A. RIUS FACIUS]

MORAGAS CANTARERO, MARÍA SAGRARIO OF SAN LUIS GONZAGA, BL.

Baptized Elvira Moragas Cantarero; pharmacist, Discalced Carmelite martyr; b. Lillo (near Toledo), Spain, Jan. 8, 1881; d. the Pradera of San Isidro near Madrid, Aug. 15, 1936.

Elvira was the third of the four children of Isabel Cantarero and Ricardo Moragas, who was appointed pharmacist to the royal household and moved his family to Madrid in 1886. One of the first Spanish women to earn a degree in pharmacy, Elvira was planning a secular career until she felt called to religious life. Nevertheless, she delayed her response to raise her younger brother Ricardo after the deaths of their father (1909) and mother (1911) and to run the family pharmacy until he could take it over.

She was a capable, just, and charitable professional; she entered the Discalced Carmelite convent of Saints Anne and Joseph in Madrid (1915). There she began her postulancy (June 21, 1915), then took the habit and the name María Sagrario de San Luis Gonzaga upon beginning her novitiate (Dec. 21, 1915). She professed her solemn vows in 1920. She was appointed mistress of novices (April 1927), then was elected prioress (1930–33). She was again elected prioress (July 1, 1936) just before the outbreak of violence in Madrid (July 18, 1936).

When the convent was attacked (July 20, 1936), she sent her sisters to safety and hid herself with another sister in the city rather than taking refuge in her brother's house at Pinto. The two were found and arrested in the Ruiz home, August 14. The following day she was executed by firing squad for refusing to denounce others.

Her body was exhumed and translated to the convent chapel after the war. On March 8, 1997, the decree of martyrdom was signed for Mother María Sagrario. During her beatification on May 10, 1998, Pope John Paul II pointed to María Sagrario as a model for pharmacists, then referred to her martyrdom: ''she found the strength not to betray priests and friends of the community, facing death with integrity for her state as a Carmelite and to save others.''

Bibliography: *Acta Apostolicae Sedis* (1998), 559.

[K. I. RABENSTEIN]

MORAL EDUCATION

Moral education comprises a lifelong process, influenced by many agencies in society, which promotes growth in responsibility and freedom.

Teaching of Vatican II. Vatican Council II's declaration on Christian education stresses the importance of moral education (*Gravissimum educationis* 7) by placing the issue in the context of changing social conditions. The ordinary faithful have an increasingly important part to play in the political and economic life of society; their so-

José Mora y del Rio.

cial influence is amplified by developments in technology and social communication (*ibid.,* intro.). The declaration, acknowledging advances in psychology and pedagogy, envisages the creation of means to ''develop harmoniously [young people's] physical, moral, and intellectual qualities'' to the end that they will acquire ''a more perfect sense of responsibility in the proper development of their own lives . . . and in the pursuit of liberty'' (*ibid.* 1).

As an agency which seeks to achieve this end, the Catholic school must strive to do the following: (1) provide an atmosphere enlivened by the freedom of the Gospel and by a spirit of charity; (2) help adolescents interpret their personality development in a manner coherent with the ''new creation'' they have become in Baptism; and (3) relate human culture to the mystery of salvation so that the Catholic student will ''contribute effectively to the welfare of the world of men'' and become ''the saving leaven in the community'' (*ibid.* 8). Clearly, the declaration sees moral education as developing persons who exercise their capacities as dynamic moral agents, who accept moral accountability for what they do, who take responsibility for others in relationship with them, and who arrive at a personal autonomy and freedom helpful to the human community.

Dimensions of Morality. Moral responsibility represents the maturation of the many dimensions in personal growth, not just a single dimension. It involves the capacity to decide (including initiative, experience, accountability, and caring) as well as the capacity to judge well (including understanding, fairness, and empathy). Moreover, moral education includes a proper orientation toward many levels of value.

Transcendent values. These represent the person's orientation of his life to the Author of life. Here the *religious conscience* gives testimony to a personal experience of the reality of God, to the enduring meaning of moral striving, and to a person's *vocation* to a special state in life. This level of values is altogether transempirical.

Social values. These represent the rules, order, roles, and customs of a person's culture. Persons gradually develop a capacity to relate to these values in flexible and creative ways, and this development is empirically measurable.

Personal Values. These represent the person's relationship to self-actualization, to the maturation of personal skills and talents, and to the free acceptance and exercise of personal potential for initiative, leadership, and creativity. A good orientation toward all of these dimensions is necessary for integral moral education.

Means for Moral Education. Most important for the moral education of the child are the example, character, and discipline of parents and family. Schools will supplement the influence of the family, but cannot be expected to provide an orientation to responsibility when this is lacking in the home. The sharing of a common vision of what is good, with family, friends, and an ecclesial community, is the most dynamic means for value formation. Likewise, only the exercise of responsibility and initiative will develop the *personal value orientation* necessary for the development of a mature autonomy and a personal freedom.

Bibliography: J. GUSTAFSON, ''Education for Moral Responsibility,'' in N. F. SIZER and T. R. SIZER, eds. *Moral Education* (Cambridge, Mass. 1970). R. T. HALL and J. U. DAVIS, *Moral Education in Theory and Practice* (Buffalo 1975). T. LICKONA, ed. *Moral Development and Behavior* (New York 1976). USCC Department of Education, *Moral Education and Christian Conscience* (Washington, D.C. 1977).

[P. J. PHILIBERT]

MORAL THEOLOGY

This article treats of moral theology as a sacred science and considers: (1) its proper essence or nature as a sacred science; (2) its relation to other parts of theology; (3) its relation to certain profane sciences—namely, ethics, sociology, and psychology—with which it has an affinity because they are also concerned with human behavior; and (4) its division or its basic content.

NATURE OF MORAL THEOLOGY

Since moral theology is a part of theology it cannot be understood or defined except in that framework, for the part has neither being nor consistency except in the whole. One's understanding of moral theology as theology must depend, therefore, on one's understanding of the kind of whole or *totum* that is constituted by the science of theology. Is it a universal or univocal whole, whose parts are contained in it as species in a genus? Is it a virtual or analogous whole, in which the secondary branches participate as modes, and imperfectly, in the idea of the science as this is realized in its principal branch? Or is it an integral whole, whose parts contribute to the total perfection of the whole, each in a proportionate way?

When theology began to be organized as a science, the whole of it in all its divisions, was considered to constitute one single specifically undifferentiated discipline. But in the course of time, the broadening of the inquiry into and application of the data of revelation gave rise to specialization. Gabriel VÁZQUEZ (d. 1604) was the first to advance the opinion that moral theology as it was taught in the schools was a distinct science. This idea found favor, and works on moral theology began to be published separately from those dealing with dogmatic or speculative theology, for example, the *Institutiones morales* (1600) of Juan AZOR, the *Theologiae moralis summa* (1588) of Enrique HENRÍQUEZ, and the *Opus morale in praecepta decalogi* (1613) of Tomás SÁNCHEZ. The 17th and 18th centuries produced an abundance and variety of works of this kind, and a determined effort was made to organize moral casuistry around specified criteria, which gave rise to the so-called systems of MORALITY. In the latter part of the 18th century the total separation of moral from dogmatic theology was achieved and its autonomy in its status as a separate science was established. Not only was a divorce effected between moral and dogma, but under the influence of the same trend other new species of theological science were introduced. Authors began to speak, as of distinct branches, about exegetical, patristic, symbolical, polemic, mystical, pastoral, liturgical, casuistic, homiletic, catechetic, positive, scholastic, speculative, synthetic, problematic, and historical theologies. These began to be gathered together in the only unity still possible, that of collections called theological encyclopedias (see J. M. Ramírez, *De hominis beatitudine* 1.7–22).

The 19th century and the first part of the 20th inherited this legacy from the 18th century. Since 1930, however, there has been a reaction against the preponderance of casuistry in moral theology, as well as against the disjunction of the sacred sciences in general, and there have been pleas for greater union and interpenetration. This marks some return to the traditional idea of theology, according to which theology is not a genus having different species under it, nor an analogous science embracing various genera, but an indivisible science having only integral parts. The whole of sacred theology has the same principles, which are the articles of faith, and the same medium of knowledge, which is the light of divine revelation. It is an imprint of God's own knowledge, which is one and simple with regard to all its objects, or, as St. Thomas said, a single and simple vision of all that He knows (St. Thomas Aquinas, *Summa theologiae* (ST) 1a, 3 ad 7; hereafter all references with the author unnamed are to the works of St. Thomas). Such also was the position of Alexander of Hales, of SS. Albert the Great and Bonaventure, and in general of all the medieval scholastic theologians.

According to this view the sacred sciences are like the branches of the same divine tree, which is theology in its most profound and authentic sense. Its integral parts correspond to the distinct material objects contained within itself, and in regard to the various functions it, as true wisdom derived from God, exercises with respect to them. It thus treats of God, of man, of the God-Man, Jesus Christ, and of all that He did and taught; of the ultimate end of human life and of the means of attaining it; of good and evil, both eternal and temporal; in a word, of all that relates to God and to man as made to His image and likeness.

The function of theology, as true and supreme wisdom, is to grasp all divinely revealed truths to the full extent of their meaning and to direct life in genuine accord with them. For divinely revealed truth is at the same time the light of understanding and the bread of life. In regard to it wisdom exercises two functions. One of these is cognitive, for wisdom is an intellectual virtue; the other is directive of human life to the supernatural end of eternal life, since it is an affective and loving wisdom: ''a sweet knowledge breathing forth love'' (ST 1a, 43.5 ad 2; *In epist. ad Heb.* 5.2), and it is characteristic of the highest wisdom to consider the Supreme Cause of all things, God, as the ultimate end of every rational and angelic being (*C. gent.* 1.1). Thus Alexander of Hales could say of theology that it ''teaches of God, is taught by God, and leads to God'' (*ST*, 1.2 ad obiecta, ed. Quaracchi, 1924, 5b).

Nominal Definition. The term moral theology contains two notions. It is theology but as modified by the adjective moral.

Theology. Theology is the science or knowledge of God. This knowledge is not, properly speaking, of God as He is in Himself, but rather of God as He has revealed Himself to man, as opposed to the knowledge of Him that can be derived by natural reason from the visible works of His creation. For this reason it is sometimes called sacred or supernatural theology. It is not simple theological faith, but rather knowledge derived from faith and scientifically elaborated by reason, which theology has at its service and positively directs in the exercise of its functions. It is faith seeking understanding (*fides quaerens intellectum*). For an account of the origin and semantic evolution of the word, *see* THEOLOGY.

Moral. This word is derived immediately from the Latin *moralis*, a word coined by Cicero (*De fato* 1) and taken into common use by Latin writers as St. Augustine attests (*De civitate Dei* 11.25). Cicero used *philosophia moralis* as a simple translation of the Greek ἠθικη φιλοσοφὶα because it is concerned with *mores*, which they (the Greeks) called ἠθική. The Greek term, however, richer and more flexible than the Latin, provides an explanation of ἦθος, which means a habit or habitual mode of conduct acquired by the repetition of acts (ἔθος), as opposed to a mode of conduct implanted by nature (Aristotle, *Ethica Nicomachea* 2.1). The Latin *mos* is of unknown or uncertain etymology; it expresses indiscriminately the habit acquired by repeated acts and the repetition of the acts, i.e., both effect and cause. To distinguish these verbally the Latins had recourse to a word of different origin, *consuetudo*, which is a habit contracted as if it were a kind of second nature, caused by the repetition of acts as signified by *mos*. So understood, *mos* is related to *consuetudo* as ἔθος to ἦθος. Thus Macrobius wrote: ''*Mos*, the moral act, came first, and *cultus moris*, the moral practice, which is custom [*consuetudo*], followed'' (*Conviviorum saturnaliorum* 3.8). In any case, *mos* means a manner of being or acting, or of conducting oneself, particularly in regard to men, for *mores* are, as St. Ambrose observed (*In Lucam*, prol. 8), in a peculiar sense proper to men. Only men act freely, with perfect knowledge and control of their acts, and consequently they alone are capable of acquiring operative habits properly so called. As human, *mores* (or conduct) are not fatally or necessarily what they are; they are contingent and free. Like luck or health, they may be good or bad. But *mores* unqualified, like luck or health, are generally understood to be good.

The term moral, like the Greek ἠθικόν, is applied by metonymy to act, habit, object, science, and to the written or oral expression of the science, although differences of meaning are evident in its different applications. But morality is applied primarily to the human act, and secondarily, and because of their reference to the human act, to other things such as habit, object, or science. Because it is concerned with the human act, it follows that moral science embraces in its scope all the life and actions of man. Hence Aristotle called it the philosophy of human nature (*Ethica Nicomachea* 10.9 1181b).

Scripture adopted a similar terminology in reference to customs, practices, traditional rites (Lk 1.9; 2.42; 22.39; Acts 6.14; 16.21; 21.21; 26.3; Heb 10.25), and the good and bad habits contracted by the repetition of acts (1 Cor 15.33; Heb 5.14). This passed on to the Greek and Latin Fathers. They did not treat of the *mores* of God Himself, as did the unknown author of the treatise *De divinis moribus* and Leonard Lessius in his *De perfectionibus moribusque divinis* in later times—a manifest impropriety of language, for God does not have *mores*. The Fathers dealt only with the *mores* of man, and those of Jesus Christ, to whom as man they naturally belonged. They treated of such *mores* as coming from God and from Christ, the Word made man. ''In the Old and New Testaments,'' says C. Spicq, ''the life of the believer goes from God to God, from God the Creator . . . to God the ultimate end, the final repose of the just and of those who persevere . . . . Therefore the entire biblical moral teaching can be defined as a highway code telling how one may arrive at the desired term'' [*L'Epître aux Hebreux* (Paris 1953) 101].

St. Thomas, who devoted considerable time to the semantics of the word moral in its theological application, did not use the term moral theology formally, but resorted to equivalent expressions, such as *scientiam moralem* (ST 1a, 1.4 obj. 2 and *arg. sed contra*), *moralem considerationem* or *tractatum moralium* (ST 1a, 83.2 ad 3), *de moribus hominum* (ST 1a, 1.3 obj. 2; 7 obj. 2) and *de actibus humanis* (ST 1a, 1.4 *sed contra* and *corp.*).

The term moral was used primarily for repeated good or bad human acts that produce a good or bad operative habit, i.e., a virtue or a vice (ST 1a2ae, 58.1); and the same term was then applied to the object or material with which these acts or habits are concerned (ST 1a2ae, 18.2; *In 2 sent.* 33.36.5) and to the science that deals with all of them (*In 4 sent.* 33.2.2.3 ad 2). And although the infused virtues are not caused by the repetition of acts (*see* VIRTUE), but are the result of the direct and immediate action of God, they can, nevertheless, be called moral either because of the matter with which they are concerned and the repeated acts that follow their infusion, as in the case of the infused cardinal virtues, or because of their consequent free exercise, even though directly and primarily their object is something divine rather than human, as in the case of the theological virtues.

Although St. Thomas did not employ the phrase *theologia moralis*, which has been in general use since the end of the 16th century, his contemporary Robert KILWARDBY did [*De natura theologiae*, ed. F. Stegmuller (Münster in Westfalen 1935) 41, 17]. The Calvinist Lambert Daneau used an alternative expression in his *Ethices christianae libri tres* (1577), which was imitated in the 18th century by A. Hochkirchen's *Ethica christiana sive orthodoxa iuris naturae et gentium prudentia* (1751). Other works that used a form of the same title were B. Stattler's *Ethica christiana universalis* (1772) and *Ethica christiana communis* (1782), M. Schenkl's *Ethica christiana universalis* (1800), the *Ethica amoris* of HENRY OF ST. IGNATIUS, the *Ethica christiana* (1758) of E. AMORT, and the *Ethica christiana sive theologia moralis* (1770) of V. Patuzzi.

From what has been said it is evident that the term moral theology, or Christian ethics, means the science of Christian life and action as this is seen as coming from God and ordained by God to man's attainment of eternal life. Or, to put it in other words, it is the science of Christian morality, i.e., of human life led in the imitation and following of Christ, who is the way by which we travel to God (*via est nobis tendendi in Deum*, ST 1a, 2. prolog.).

Real Definition. Since moral theology is a science and a true intellectual virtue, its real definition should stem from its relation to its proper object, for operative habits are specified by their proper objects, to which they are transcendentally related. But the formal object, both causal and terminative, of moral theology is the same as that of all theology, which is one and indivisible in species. That is to say, the object in this sense is God Himself under the aspect of His deity (*sub ratione deitatis*) as this has been manifested to man by divine revelation. From this point of view, then, there can be no differentiation of moral theology from the other divisions of sacred science. However, there is a difference on the part of the material object sufficient to account for the classification of moral as an integral part within the total gambit of sacred theology.

All the material with which theology is concerned is divided into two main sections, the first embracing things that ought to be known, and the second, things that ought to be done. What ought to be known pertains to faith; what ought to be done pertains to morals. This distinction is expressed or at least suggested by Scripture itself, which records that Christ, unlike the Pharisees who taught but did not practice (Mt 23.3), began to do and to teach (Acts 1.1). His disciples were called upon to imitate their Master in this: ''He that shall do and teach, he shall be called great in the kingdom of heaven'' (Mt 5.19); they were to be doers of the word and not hearers only (Jas 1.22), for faith without works is dead (Jas 2.26).

The Fathers. St. Cyril of Alexandria said that Christian religion consists in devout dogmas and good actions, not taken separately but rather together (*Catech.* 4.2; *Patrologia Graeca* 32:455; St. Gregory of Nyssa, *Epist.* 24; *Patrologia Graeca* 46: 1087). St. Augustine wrote a special work, *De fide et operibus* (*Patrologia Latina* 40:197–230), and elsewhere he wrote: ''Everyone knows that in the sacred Scriptures . . . some things are proposed simply to be known and believed, for example, that in the beginning God made the heavens and the earth, and that in the beginning was the Word . . . and other things are commanded to be observed and carried out, or prohibited and to be avoided, such as 'honor thy father and mother,' and 'thou shalt not commit adultery''' (*Speculum de sacra scriptura*, pref.; *Patrologia Latina* 34:887–889).

Medieval Theologians. The distinction was too well recognized to require many citations. PETER CANTOR in the 12th century wrote: ''Theology is twofold: there is the high or heavenly that offers knowledge of divine things; and there is the lower, or subheavenly, that teaches about moral matters'' [*Summa Abel*, cited by M. Grabmann, *Geschichte der scholast. Methode* (Freiburg im Breisgau 1911) 2.483 n.2]. St. Thomas wrote: ''The truth contained in Sacred Scripture is ordered to two things, namely, to believing rightly and to acting rightly'' (*Quodl.* 7.6.2). Divine revelation was ordained to man's salvation; what is necessary to that end is reducible to the instruction of faith and the formation of morals (*De ver.* 12.2; cf. *In 1 sent.* 23.5, *arg. sed contra*). With the other theologians of his time St. Thomas was accustomed to translate this division into the Aristotelian terms of *speculabilia* and *agibilia*, and this provided the basis for the distinction of speculative and practical theology (*see In 1 sent. prol.*, 3.1; ST 1a, 1.4). The practical part came to be called moral, the speculative part dogmatic, theology. The latter expression, however, appears not to have been coined until the 16th century, and its author may have been F. Suárez (*Opera*, ed. Vives, 20 p. xii), since whose time the older terms speculative and practical have been replaced by the terms dogmatic and moral.

The Object of Moral Theology. The object (or subject matter) with which moral, as distinct from dogmatic, theology is concerned is wholly and solely that which is capable of supernatural (i.e., theological) morality. This includes whatever can in any way influence or be the cause of that capacity or that morality, for all science properly so-called is the knowledge of its object through its causes.

The first and original subject of Christian and theological morality is man insofar as he is the adopted son of God and brother of Christ, or insofar as he is the supernatural image of God, bearing as a participant of the divine nature through sanctifying grace (2 Pt 1.4) a likeness to the consubstantial image of the Word made man, Jesus Christ (Col 1.15; Heb 1.3), to whose image the Christian should be conformed (Rom 8.29). Therefore, as St. Thomas noted profoundly and with great precision, the proper object of the moral part of the *Summa theologiae* is man as the image of God (ST 1a2ae, 1 prol.). It is the nature of the image to resemble its exemplar and imitate it as perfectly as possible, just as the son resembles the father and imitates his conduct or manner of acting.

Sanctifying grace not only heals and regenerates man wounded by sin, original and personal, but raises him up and makes him into a son of God, giving him in a sense a divine existence. And although this deification originally affects the soul as spiritual, it consequently also affects it as the animating and vivifying principle of the body; and hence the deification flows over into the body, which it makes the living temple of the Holy Spirit (1 Cor 6.19), the bearer of God (1 Cor 3.16–17), and an instrument of justice and sanctification (Rom 6.13, 19). Rooted and enfolded in man as the principle, or formal cause, of his justification (H. Denzinger, *Enchiridion symbolorum* 1529–30), this participation in the divine nature (2 Pt 1.4), which is grace, produces a corresponding divine operation. St. Peter emphasizes this, saying that it obliges us to flee all corruption of concupiscence and sin and to cultivate all the virtues, especially faith, hope (including patience), and charity, laboring ceaselessly to work out our sanctification and thus guarantee our entrance into the eternal kingdom of Our Lord and Savior Jesus Christ (2 Pt 1.4–11).

Habitual grace is the first immanent supernatural principle of the salutary works of the Christian life, just as the soul is the first immanent natural principle in man of the natural acts of human life. However, actions come from sanctifying grace through the infused virtues and gifts of the Holy Spirit that flow from grace in the manner of operative powers in the same way that the natural powers through which the soul operates flow, so to speak, from its essence. The infused virtues not only bestow on man a facility for the performance of supernatural works as acquired habits facilitate the operations of the natural powers of the soul, but also confer the very power to perform them (H. Denzinger, *Enchiridion symbolorum* 226, 245, 373, 395). Without them the natural powers can do nothing in the supernatural order. Virtues are needed, first of all, as the immediate principles of the salutary action that has God as its direct object. These affect the superior powers of the soul—faith, the intellect; hope and charity, the will—elevating them radically and sanctifying them. But besides this, other virtues are needed to elevate, even with respect to their activity having a created thing as its direct object, all the powers of the soul that are in any way rational and thus participate in a certain sense and to a certain degree in the natural image of God, and raise those powers to the level of the supernatural image. Thus, there are infused cardinal virtues affecting reason (prudence), will (justice), and the two forms of sense appetite, concupiscible (temperance) and irascible (fortitude). In addition to these there are the gifts of the Holy Spirit, corresponding to the three theological and the four cardinal virtues, perfecting and completing the adaptation of the natural powers to supernatural activity.

However, the immediate subject of Christian and theological morality is the human act of the Christian performed with full consciousness and freedom. This is an act commanded or elicited by the will; for nothing is to be classified as moral unless the will is involved, because in the sphere of morality will is the principle upon which the morality of all else depends (*In 2 sent.* 24.3.2). Thus the psychologically complete human act, fully conscious and free in regard to its specification and performance, or at least with regard to its performance, is the proper subject of the form of either natural or supernatural morality; and even the acts of the infused virtues and gifts must be psychologically complete to be accounted moral.

But the objective formality that moral theology considers in its material object is the supernatural and divine morality proper to the sons of God and brothers of Christ who act as such; for Christian, or theological, morality is the relation of conformity or disconformity of human acts with the law of God and of Christ. This is the eternal law, the law of divine love or of charity, for charity contains all the law and the prophets (Rom 13.10; Col 3.14; Mt 22.37–40). An act in conformity with this divine standard of conduct and befitting sons of God and brothers of Christ is morally good and Christian; if such conformity is lacking, the act is bad. The moral obligation to conform to this supreme norm is not something violent to nature or imposed from without; rather it is postulated and demanded by the essential condition of those who are living, supernatural images of God, His sons by adoption, and brothers of Jesus Christ.

The voluntary acts of the Christian are the essential means of attaining eternal life. They are a conscious and free movement toward God. As means, they affirm an essential relation to their proper end and should be proportioned to it. Consequently, those acts are morally good and Christian that are so proportioned and do in fact lead to eternal life. On the other hand, those acts are evil that are not proportioned to man's end and alienate him from God. The supreme good in the moral, as well as the ontological, order is God Himself as the object in which man finds beatitude, and it is in relation to Him that all human acts are to be considered as morally good or evil.

Supernatural morality is concretely reducible to the idea of merit or demerit with respect to eternal life. Thus it is proper in the strictest sense to the human *acts* of Christians, for one merits or demerits by his acts, not by his habits or his operative powers (*De malo*, 2.5 ad 8; 2.9 ad 9). Meritorious acts are here understood to mean acts that are salutary in the full sense, i.e., acts that are meritorious *de condigno* of eternal life. Imperfectly salutary acts, such as the acts of unformed faith (*fides informis*) and hope, prepare or dispose to justification only when they are united with the fear of God and sorrow for sin and are not called meritorious except in a broad and improper sense. Their merit is *de congruo*. Consequently, they are not salutary and meritorious except in an analogous sense of attribution (*see* ANALOGY) insofar as they participate imperfectly in the value and dignity of merit *de condigno*; and it is in this sense that they come within the orbit of supernatural morality (*see* MERIT).

Therefore, as St. Thomas observed, "the [condign] merit of everlasting life pertains first to charity and secondly to the other virtues inasmuch as their acts are commanded by charity" (ST 1a2ae, 114.4). Acts elicited by charity, especially the act of love directed immediately to God Himself, are, of their nature, meritorious *de condigno*. It is indeed the primary analogue of all that is meritorious. To acts commanded by charity and executed through the other virtues and the gifts of the Holy Spirit merit belongs by participation. Charity gives form and life to all the other virtues, endowing them with their ultimate perfection as virtues leading to eternal life (Gal 3.14). Without charity all the other virtues and their acts, however heroic and sublime they may seem to be, merit nothing with respect to eternal happiness. Even faith without charity is useless (Jas 2.20); it is of no avail toward eternal life except when united to charity and moved by it (Gal 5.6). He who does not love abides in death (1 Jn 3.14). In the words of St. Augustine, "The Scriptures command only charity and blame only cupidity, and thus do they form human morals" (*Doctr. christ.* 3.10.15); to which St. Thomas added, "The rectitude of the human will consists in an ordering of love which is its principal drive. Love is ordered when we love God above all things, as the highest good, and when we order all things to Him as the ultimate end" (*De rat. fid.* 5).

Charity, then, as Benedict XV declared, is the soul and the form of the whole Christian life [encycl. *Pacem*, *Acta Apostolicae Sedis* 12 (Rome 1920) 210]. Or, in the words of Leo XIII, "The kingdom of Jesus Christ takes its form and vitality from divine charity; its foundation and achievement is ordered and holy love" (encycl. *Tametsi futura prospicientibus*, Dec. 1, 1900). Indeed charity is the constitutive and distinctive sign of the true disciple of Christ, who loved men with the highest degree of love, giving His life for them upon the cross (Jn 15.9–13; 17.13). It is the seal of the true sons of a Father whose love embraces all things and all men, even to the extent of sending His Son for their ransom and redemption (Wis 11.25; Mt 5.44–48; Jn 3.16). Therefore the Apostle said: "Be you, therefore, imitators of God, as very dear children, and walk in love, as Christ also loved us and delivered himself up for us" (Eph 5.1–2). There is nothing more natural than that a son love his father and repay love with love (1 Jn 4.9–11; *Comp. theol.* 2.5).

All this is contained in yet another formula with which St. Thomas indicated the proper object of moral theology, namely the *motus rationalis creaturae in Deum*, the movement of the rational creature toward God (ST 1a, 2 prol.). This movement is the conscious and free act of the rational creature acting rationally. But the rational creature acts and moves toward God by acts of love. The feet with which he runs and the wings with which he flies and is lifted up to heaven are the acts whereby he fulfills the demands of charity (St. Augustine, *In psalm.* 33, serm. 2.10; *Patrologia Latina* 36:315).

Therefore moral theology is really and essentially the theology of love, that is, of the loving movement of the Christian toward God in the footsteps of Christ, his Redeemer and Savior.

THE RELATION OF MORAL TO THE OTHER PARTS OF THEOLOGY

According to the traditional view expounded above, all the parts of the theology properly so-called are integral parts within one body of sacred science. Between integral parts there should be neither antagonism nor separation, but only mutual union and solidarity. All the parts of theology together require a total theology that is complete and unmutilated. Each part or division has its function in the whole, as do the members and organs of a living body. And like the members of the body, they live and prosper when united among themselves in a whole, but they lose their identity and being on becoming separated.

Dogmatic Theology. Such a union exists between moral and dogmatic theology according to the traditional concept. The distinction between what is speculative and what is practical is merely human and philosophical. Theology transcends divisions and compartments of that kind and contains in a higher union all that is speculative and practical. In place of arid speculation it offers contemplation; in place of mere action with its usual accompaniment of agitation it offers a gentle, quiet, loving affection. Theology in its deepest and truest sense is, in fact, a loving contemplation of God and of all that refers to God as God. It is a development of faith, which is at one and the same time eminently cognitive and affective with respect to the revealed truth it embraces. The proper act of faith, which is to believe, is an act elicited from the intellect moved by the will, both powers being elevated and aided by grace (ST 2a2ae, 2.9). Faith is at once intellectually receptive of the revealed things of God and directive of human life. The same holds true for theology, because as the science of faith it must reflect these same qualities.

No dogma of faith is incapable of inciting to the love of God. All dogmas are concerned either with God Himself and His perfections, which call for love of Him as the greatest good, or with God's works *ad extra*, both natural and supernatural, which, as the fruit and product of His infinite love (ST 1a, 20.2), move one to respond with love (ST 2a2ae, 27.3). Therefore St. Thomas declared: "The knowledge of God which is had by other sciences enlightens only the intellect, showing that God is the first cause, that he is one and wise, etc. But the knowledge of God had through faith both enlightens the mind and delights the affections, for it not only tells that God is the first cause, but also that he is our Savior, that he is our Redeemer, that he loves us, that he became incarnate for us, and all this inflames the affections" (*In epist. 2 ad Cor.* 2.2).

On the other hand, there is no morally good and Christian act, especially if it is an act of charity, that does not dispose and help one better to grasp and understand the dogmas and truths of faith. Wisdom does not enter the sinful soul (Wis 1.4); for the sensual man lives sensuously, like the brute beasts, and cannot perceive the things that are of the spirit, which are the things of God (1 Cor 2.14–16). He who loves God knows Him in truth, and he who offends Him by sin does not know Him (1 Jn 3.6; 4.7). The truths of faith are the life and mysteries of love, which are neither grasped nor well perceived unless love is allied with the act of the intelligence. Love opens the eyes and makes them keener, for, as St. Thomas observed, "The lover is not satisfied with a superficial apprehension of the beloved but strives to gain an intimate knowledge of everything that pertains to the beloved so as to penetrate into his very soul. Thus it is written of the Holy Spirit who is God's love that He searches all things, even the deep things of God" (ST 1a2ae, 28.2); and elsewhere: "Spiritual things should be tasted first and afterwards understood, for no one understands who does not taste. Thus the psalmist says first: Taste! and afterwards: See how sweet is the Lord" (*In Psalm* 33.9).

Thus dogmatic and moral theology are each in need of the other's help. They complete each other, like faith and good habits informed and vivified by charity.

> The teaching of Sacred Scripture holds that it hands on not only matters to be speculated on, as geometry does, but also matters to be approved by the affective powers. Thus we read that whoever carries them out (i.e., the Commandments) and

> teaches them, shall be called great in the kingdom of heaven (Mt 5.19). Hence in other sciences it is enough that a man be perfect in his intellect; in this it is required that he be perfect both in intellect and affection. Deep mysteries, therefore, are to be spoken to the perfect: ''wisdom we speak among those who are mature'' (1 Cor 2.6). According as each one is disposed, thus things will appear to him, as an angry man judges one way while angry and otherwise when his anger has passed, and an incontinent man will judge something good because of his passion and differently when it has subsided . . . . Since then the things taught in the Scripture pertain to the affections of man as well as to the intellect, it is best to be perfect in both. [*In Heb.* 5.2]

Casuistry and Ascetical and Mystical Theology. Just as moral theology, as here understood, cannot be separated from the rest of theology, so casuistry and ascetical and mystical theology cannot be separated from moral, or from theology as a whole. They are essentially and specifically one with each other and with theology in its totality in having the same formal object. All have the same principles and the same means of knowledge, that is, the articles of faith and the same divine revelation. They envisage the same supernatural and Christian morality. For there are not various kinds of sonship by adoption, or of brothers in Christ, or of Christian life. There is only one God, one Christ, and one Church that is His mystical body. Sanctifying grace is the same for all; the same beatitude is held out to all, and there is only one road leading to it, namely, the imitation and following of Christ (Rom 3.30; 5.15, 17; 12.5; 1 Cor 8.4–6; 12.9–27; 2 Cor 5.14; Gal 3.16, 20, 28; Eph 4.4–6; 1 Tm 2.5).

Theological charity, which is like the soul and form of all Christian morality, is specifically the same in all Christians who possess it. Christian morality, then, is specifically one, for this morality corresponds to the acts elicited by charity and to acts of other virtues only insofar as they are ordered and vivified by charity.

The degrees and steps of charity in its upward movement toward union with God are reducible to three, which are known as the incipient, proficient, and perfect; and to these steps three stages of the Christian life correspond—the purgative, illuminative, and unitive (*see* THREE WAYS, THE). These do not constitute different kinds of life, but are rather distinct ages of the same life and different moments of the same movement (ST 2a2ae, 24.9; *In 3 sent.* 29.8.1; *In Isaiam* 44.4). They correspond to infancy, adolescence, and manhood or maturity in human life on the natural level, which develops in these stages but remains specifically the same.

Casuistry. Casuistry is concerned with the incipient charity of the neophyte still in the stage of spiritual infancy; that is, it deals with the moral life of those recently converted from sin to grace. Such individuals still feel the goad of sin, which, though pardoned so far as its guilt is concerned, has left effects in the form of evil inclinations against which they must struggle if they would conserve the life of grace and avoid relapsing into sin. Casuistry, therefore, is concerned in particular with the licit and the illicit, that is, with what is compatible or incompatible with grace and charity, and devotes itself to the establishment of norms and the discovery of concrete means for avoiding mortal sin and the loss of grace. Hence it is preoccupied with the purgative way.

Ascetical Theology. The ascetical theologian deals with proficient charity, or with the spiritual adolescence of those who, having overcome and conquered evil inclinations to sin, seek to grow and develop in a truly Christian life. Ascetical theology, therefore, is less concerned with the good and evil, the licit and the illicit, the permitted and the forbidden, but is more interested in the greater and lesser good. The proper function of this branch of theology, therefore, is to deal with the illuminative way.

Mystical Theology. The mystical theologian treats of perfect charity, that is, of the spiritual maturity or manhood of those Christians who, having conquered sin and its evil inclinations, and having grown in grace, have drawn near to Christ and are united to Him in close friendship, as if transformed into Him, as was St. Paul, who said: ''It is now no longer I that live, but Christ lives in me'' (Gal 2.20). Mystical theology, therefore, is not concerned with the good or better so much as with what is, properly and absolutely speaking, the best, which consists in intimate union with God and permanence in Him in what is called the unitive way.

Differences Not Specific. A certain caution, however, is necessary to avoid exaggerating the significance of the distinction between the different stages of the Christian life. These ways or stages do not constitute autonomous and separate compartments, but are rather mutually intermingling and interacting phases. The life of grace and charity, even in the case of neophytes or those recently raised to grace by baptism or penance, is not lacking in a real illumination from above by which they pass from the darkness of sin to the light of Christ and to an affective and effective union with Him. Moreover, by resisting temptation to sin and struggling against the inclinations left by their former sins, they really gain merit before God and grow in grace and charity.

On the other hand, temptation and the danger of relapse into sin do not totally cease as long as the present life lasts, and therefore in all stages of the spiritual life the Christian should be vigilant and resort to mortification, according to the admonition of St. Paul: ''Let him who thinks he stands take heed lest he fall'' (1 Cor 10.12; Phil 2.12; 1 Cor 9.27; 2 Cor 4.10). Charity and with it the vigor of Christian life should ever grow during the present life, being renewed day by day (1 Cor 4.10) until death. Charity does not grow old, but rather gains new strength the more it is used.

One cannot hold the contrary without falling into the aberrations of the Brethren of the Free Spirit, of the Beghards, the illuminati, or the quietists, who thought that the Christian or spiritual man can in this life attain such a degree of perfection that he no longer needs to be mortified or to perform acts of penance or to practice virtue, since he has become incapable of sin and has attained union with God, a condition that puts him beyond the need of purification or growth [J. De Guibert, *Documenta ecclesiastica christianae perfectionis studium spectantia* (Rome 1931) 200–204, 274–275, 304, 315–317, 403–419, 438–468, 471, 474].

Charity does not make the observance of the Commandments of God and of the Church unnecessary; on the contrary, it positively demands their observance: ''If you love me, keep my commandments'' (Jn 14.15; Jn 14.20; 1 Jn 2.3–5; 5.2). The same charity, without change of kind, is capable of performing the different functions appropriate to the different stages of spiritual development. It struggles to avoid sin; it resists temptation; dynamic and active, it grows until the soul is united perfectly to God. It is impossible to distinguish in kind between the Christian moralities corresponding to the several branches of theology under discussion, just as it is impossible to make a division in charity itself.

The Detachment of Casuistry from Moral Theology. In every practical science there must be a certain casuistry, for ''all operative sciences are perfected by the considerations of details'' (ST 1a2ae, 6 prol.; ST 1a, 22. 3 ad 1). It must, however, shun sophistry and exaggerated pragmatism, for otherwise it would cease to be a science and become a mere art or simply a technique. Unfortunately, casuistry has too frequently inclined in this direction at the cost of a loss of contact with Scripture and the Fathers, with the great dogmas of faith, and with the basic principles of moral theology itself. And this has resulted in a moral doctrine that sometimes appears to give no thought to man's ultimate end or to grace. It seems cramped by a certain legal juridicism and meticulously catalogues sins as they are related to confession and to sacramental absolution, but gives scant attention to the spiritual life or the supernatural virtues. The moral systems (*see* MORALITY, SYSTEMS OF) founded on certain reflex principles of more juridical than moral value do not compensate for what is lost by abandoning the great foundations of Christian moral teaching and the use of Christian prudence, which is precisely the virtue that, illuminated by faith and backed by a sound moral theology, guides science in the sure and genuinely Christian solution of its cases. Fortunately, in more recent years greater importance is being attached by moral theologians to the virtues than to the vices, to the law of Christ than to the old law of the Decalogue; but much remains to be done toward raising the general level of moral theology and putting it in greater accord with the spirit of the gospel and the teachings of the great theologians of the past.

Some of the excessive juridicism that marks moral theology as expounded by some moralists stems, no doubt, from its association with a type of canonical thought disengaged from its ancient theological context. Canon Law in the beginning was not separated from theology but rather formed a part of it and had, therefore, a more evangelical flavor. There are indications that it may return in some degree to its old matrix, for, according to Vatican Council II, the duty of the bishops and of the whole government of the universal Church to rule is essentially united to the duty of sanctification [Dogmatic Constitution *De Ecclesia* 3.27, *Acta Apostolicae Sedis* 57 (Rome 1965) 32–33]. The pope and the bishops govern the Christian people in the name of Christ, as His vicars, for the better fulfillment of His law, which is the law of love and charity.

Liturgy and Pastoral Theology. The liturgy integrates the Scriptures (the Psalms and readings from the sacred books), the writings of the Fathers (homilies), the living magisterium of the Church (the hymns and prayers approved and proposed by it), and the purest ascetical and mystical spirituality with which not a few Masses and Lessons of the Breviary abound. Through it, therefore, the functions of dogmatic, moral, and spiritual theology are exercised in a living and effective manner [Vatican Council II, *Constitution on the Sacred Liturgy* 16–19, *Acta Apostolicae Sedis* 56 (1964) 104–105].

Pastoral theology aims at the proper fulfillment of the duty of the pastor of souls, in imitation of Jesus Christ, who is the Good Shepherd, the Pastor by antonomasia. He feeds His sheep with His life and His doctrine (Acts 1.1), giving example in all the virtues, especially that of charity, by dying for men on the cross (1 Pt 2.21–25), and communicating to them the words and mysteries of eternal life (Jn 6.64, 69). His pastoral teaching contains the truth to be believed and the holiness to be realized in practice. Such is the work of the pastoral ministry, namely, to teach Christian dogma and morals, according to the revelation of Jesus Christ and the authentic interpretation of the Church, in which exegetes, Fathers, and theologians have collaborated.

Pastoral theology is reduced to practice in the liturgy, in homiletics and catechetics. The catechesis of the Apostles, contained in the Gospels, was impregnated with the life and doctrine of Christ, as was the liturgy practiced by them and transmitted to the Christian community, which has continued to flourish and develop throughout the centuries. The homilies of the Fathers, especially those of SS. John Chrysotom, Augustine, and Leo the Great, contain immeasurable biblical, dogmatic, moral, and spiritual riches. They lived the divine revelation in its entirety and gave expression to it in their words. As true and authentic kerygma, it was a living proclamation of the gospel. The truths of faith and the norms of conduct taught by Jesus Christ, and collected and illustrated by a sound and authentic theology, are always lifegiving and kerygmatic.

In this way all the integral parts of sacred theology are mutually completed and perfected, to the great advantage of theological science and of the Christian life.

MORAL THEOLOGY AND PHILOSOPHICAL BEHAVIOR SCIENCE

Moral theology is essentially distinct from natural ethics, not simply in species but also in genus, in the same way that Christian theology is distinguished from theodicy (ST 1a, 1.1 ad 2). Between them there is only an analogy of proper proportionality inasmuch as moral theology holds the same position in the supernatural order that moral philosophy does in the natural order (*In 3 sent.* 33.1.2.4). The essential generic difference appears on the part of the subject of the respective moralities, the moralities themselves, and the means of knowing them.

Subject and Operative Principle. The remote and radical subject of moral theology or philosophy is the person operating, that is to say, man. For moral philosophy the subject is man as man, that is, considered simply as a rational animal; for moral theology the subject is man as the adopted son of God and brother of the only begotten of the Father, Jesus Christ.

The operative principle of moral actions for moral philosophy is, radically, the rational soul and, proximately, the rational powers of the soul and the cardinal virtues acquired by the repetition of acts; for moral theology the radical principle of moral acts is habitual grace, and the infused virtues are the proximate or immediate principle.

In natural ethics the immediate subject of morality is the natural human acts of man as man and of his acquired virtues; in moral theology the subject is the supernatural human acts of man as a Christian and son of God by adoption and of his infused virtues.

Morality. Ethics considers only the natural morality of the human acts of man as man and of his acquired virtues; moral theology directly and principally considers the supernatural morality of the human acts of man as a Christian and of his infused virtues. Natural or philosophical morality is the order or relation of natural human acts to the ultimate natural end of human life, according to the natural law naturally known by man and the determinations of positive human laws; supernatural or theological morality is the order or relation of supernatural human acts to the ultimate supernatural end of the whole Christian life of the sons of God. Goodness in the former is measured in terms of what is befitting human nature and natural right reason; in the latter in terms of conformity with the divine filiation, brotherhood of Christ, and with the teachings of the faith. The ultimate issue, in the case of natural morality, is a well-being in the natural order; in the case of supernatural morality, it is the vision of God, for supernatural human acts executed with the help of God's grace and the infused virtues, especially charity, are salutary in the full sense and meritorious of eternal life.

Means of Knowledge. These differ essentially for both moral sciences. Ethics can know its formal object by the light of natural reason alone. By this light it knows the rational and social nature of man, his human acts, his natural powers, the acquired habits that are the immediate principles of his good and evil action, and his ultimate natural end. But the proper object of moral theology cannot be known by natural reason, but only in the light of divine revelation. By this means alone can be known the elevation of man to the supernatural order and the status of son of God, brother of Christ, and heir of eternal life. The same light is needed to know of sanctifying grace, the infused virtues, the gifts of the Holy Spirit, the Sacraments through which God communicates His grace, the meritorious value of acts elicited or commanded by charity, and the eternal and the positive law of God, especially the law of charity, promulgated and carried to its highest perfection by Christ.

The Comparative Imperfection of Ethics. Philosophical ethics is an imperfect science within its own sphere, for it does not know the true existential situation of man as it is in fact. Natural reason is capable only of knowing human nature in its essential lines and in the rights and duties that are proper to it as such, that is to say, in its condition or state of pure nature. It knows nothing of man's elevation to the supernatural order or of original sin; it is ignorant therefore of the state of original justice, or of the state of nature as redeemed or repaired after the Fall, which are man's true historical states. Knowledge of these can be had only through divine revelation.

Knowing nothing of man's historical states, purely philosophical ethics has no knowledge of the wounds, the weaknesses, and the infirmities due to original sin, which affect man even in his natural life and environment, because, in addition to being deprived of the supernatural and preternatural gifts that he enjoyed in the state of original justice, he was also left wounded in his nature. Because of this he is morally incapable of fulfilling all the natural law by the natural powers at his disposal, but even for that achievement of the natural order, he must have the help of grace. This moral impotence carries over into his very knowledge of the natural law, which becomes uncertain in not a few of its precepts for the majority of men; for the practical intellect, to which such knowledge belongs, has been especially weakened in its proper function of discriminating between good and evil and of directing the will to true good. ''Because we do not know ourselves perfectly we cannot fully know what is for our good according to Wisdom (9.14): 'For the deliberations of mortals are timid, and unsure are our plans''' (ST 1a2ae, 109.9). Therefore the divine revelation of these fundamental truths of the natural law was morally necessary in order that all men from the beginning of rational life might have certain knowledge of them without admixture of error (*In 3 sent.* 37.1, and ad 1, 3). In addition to its ignorance of the true moral order, ethics labors under the more serious ignorance of man's elevation to the dignity of son of God and heir to His glory.

Value of Ethics. Although imperfect and incomplete, the knowledge of man sought by philosophical ethics is not something false or valueless. This knowledge does not contain total and complete, but only partial and imperfect, truth. Nevertheless it is truth and not error. The natural knowledge of God derived by theodicy from the visible things of creation is not false, nor is it opposed to the knowledge of the one and triune God that theology seeks in faith and divine revelation; on the contrary, it is a preamble to it. In a similar way, the natural knowledge of God as the natural ultimate end of man, to whom man owes the cult of prayer and adoration according to his strength and possibilities, is not an aberration; rather it is natural truth that prepares the soul to receive the plenitude of saving truth drawn from divine revelation.

Between ethics, then, and moral theology one must admit an essential distinction, but not a separation and much less an antagonism. The distinction parallels that between reason and revelation, or the more universal one between nature and grace. Grace does not destroy nature, but rather supports and perfects it (ST 1a, 1.8 ad 2; 60.5; 62.5). This distinction provides a certain autonomy for both sides within their proper field and limits, which was recognized by Vatican Council I with regard to theology and philosophy in general (H. Denzinger, *Enchiridion symbolorum* 3019), although the Council exacted a true union and collaboration. Moral theology admits all the good and true taught by ethics and makes use of it for its own higher ends, at the same time remedying the defects and imperfections of ethics and enriching it with new and sublime contributions from Christian revelation.

Ethics is subordinate to moral theology just as reason is to faith and nature to grace, but it is not subalternated properly and strictly speaking, as J. Maritain thought [*Science et sagesse* (Paris 1935) 327–345]. This would mean the absorption of ethics in theology and its reduction to a theology of the second class [J. M. Ramirez, ''Sur l'organization du savoir moral,'' *Bulletin Thomiste* (Paris 1935) 363–386; ''De philosophia morali christiana,'' *Divis Thomas* (Fribourg 1936) 87–122, 181–204].

Moral theology should similarly make use of the sciences auxiliary to ethics, especially of psychology in its experimental, rational, and pathological branches. Human acts, psychologically considered, are the matter with which ethics is immediately concerned, and whatever exerts influence on the cognitive and appetitive elements of the human act is likely to have some influence on the responsibility of the agent and the morality of his acts. And, since the supernatural act with which moral theology is immediately concerned supposes a complete natural human act, it is evident that psychology, and, in general, anthropology in its fullest and integral sense, can be of great use to the moral theologian.

DIVISION OF MORAL THEOLOGY

With greater attention to practical utility than to the scientific organization of their material, many moralists of the past arranged their matter in alphabetical order. Others divided it according to the Commandments of the Decalogue and of the Church. This mode of division enjoyed general favor for a time. Later, in an attempt to give greater scientific character to their subject, many theologians began to treat moral theology as a body of doctrine parallel with dogmatic theology. Therefore, because dogma was commonly divided into general and special dogmatic theology (the general being known as fundamental, and the special being subdivided into various treatises, On the One God, On the Trinity, etc.), moralists imitated this procedure and divided moral theology into general and special. The general part was called fundamental, and it dealt with the notions common to all moral material. The special was subdivided into different treatises on the virtues, sins, and precepts, and terminated with a practical treatise on the Sacraments. This division was much in vogue after T. J. Bouquillon published his *Theologia moralis fundamentalis* (Bruges 1873). This work omitted any treatment of grace or the gifts of the Holy Spirit, which it relegated to dogmatic or mystical theology, and gave only superficial consideration to the ultimate supernatural end of human life, although these treatises are the most fundamental of all moral theology. Moreover, it lacked a Christological flavor because it did not focus Christian morality in an explicit and formal way on Christ. The Redemptorist Bernard Häring sought to remedy this defect in his *Das Gesetz Christi* (Freiburg im Breisgau 1958).

The End. Moral theology ought to revolve entirely around God and Christ since it is a theology of the morality of the sons of God and the brothers of Christ. On the other hand, an explicit and clear consideration of the proper end of all human life and the means of attaining it is an essential requirement of all moral doctrine. There are two poles on which all morality moves: *de vita et moribus*. The life is to be understood as the *vita beata* and the *mores* as the human acts by which one moves toward it. This was known to the ancient Greek and Latin philosophers, but their ideas must be translated analogically and proportionally to the supernatural order. Therefore, a scientifically and vitally structured moral theology should begin by pointing out the final goal of all Christian life, which is God Himself as He is in Himself, the object in which beatitude is found. The way by which this beatitude is achieved must be indicated. The royal road is Christ, who said of Himself: ''I am the way, and the truth, and the life. No one comes to the Father but through me'' (Jn 14.6). In this way all moral theology is theocentric and Christocentric.

The Means. The means to be employed ought to be proportionate to the essentially supernatural and divine end. They are human acts performed in grace and love, for only such are *actus salutares* and lead to eternal life. Therefore, moral theology ought to contain a treatise on grace and the infused theological and moral virtues, which are the immanent principles of the salutary acts that merit eternal life. It should contain also a consideration of the gifts and fruits of the Holy Spirit, of the beatitudes, and of the Sacraments as the efficacious means of Christian sanctification. Finally, it should treat of the law of God and of His Commandments as these are necessary to the dignity of Christians who are sons of God by adoption and heirs to His glory, the Commandments being expounded as they are contained in the all-embracing law of charity.

Such was the field of moral theology as this was understood by St. Thomas Aquinas, whose achievement as a moralist is sometimes overshadowed in popular consciousness by his greatness in other areas of theological and philosophical thought. But his excellence, in the judgment of some—at least of his contemporaries, was to be found especially in moral matters (*Chronica minor auctore Minorita Erphordiensi* 4; *Monumenta Germaniae Historica* 24.212). Precisely as a moralist was he most original and creative, and in nothing is he more admirable than in his total view of the life worthy of a Christian, which he set out to treat in such a way that *nihil moralium erit praetermissum* (ST 2a2ae, prol.).

Bibliography: A. BREZNAY, *Clavis theologiae moralis seu introductio in studium ethicae Christianae scientificum* (Freiburg 1914). G. BUCCERONI, *De natura theologiae moralis* (Rome 1910). D. CONCINA, *Ad theologiam Christianam dogmaticomoralem apparatus*, 2 v. (Rome 1749–51). G. V. PATUZZI, *Prodromus ad universam morum theologiam, de locis theologiae moralis* (Bassano 1770) repr. in J. P. MIGNE, *Theologiae cursus completus*, 28 v. (Paris 1837–66) 11:9–64. S. M. [i.e., J. M.] RAMÍREZ, ''Introductio generalis in universam theologiam moralem,'' in his *De hominis beatitudine tractatus theologicus* (Madrid 1942—) 1:3–89. H. WORONIECKI, *Methodus et programma tradendi theologiam moralem* (Lublin 1922). F. A. ZACCARIA, *Dissertatio prolegomena . . . de casuisticae theologiae originibus, locis atque praestantia* (Venice 1755). G. GILLEMAN, *The Primacy of Charity in Moral Theology*, tr. W. F. RYAN and A. VACHON (Westminster, ME 1959). B. HÄRING, *The Law of Christ: Moral Theology for Priests and Laity*, tr. E. G. KAISER (Westminster, MD 1961—).

[J. M. RAMÍREZ]

MORAL THEOLOGY, HISTORY OF (TO 700)

In the primitive Church Christ's moral teaching developed out of the basic, but nonceremonial, Jewish ethic as modified in Christ's interpretation of the Ten Commandments and the Beatitudes. Although neither casuistic nor ascetical, the earliest postapostolic documents, such as the letter of CLEMENT I, the DIDACHE, Shepherd of HERMAS, pseudo-BARNABAS, and the letters of POLYCARP and of IGNATIUS OF ANTIOCH, are primarily moral treatises. They deal with obedience; the imitation of Christ in His sufferings; family, social, and civic obligations. From the Old Testament the Christians inherited a dynamic sense of God's living presence and of His wisdom, sanctifying the man who devoted himself to God's law. The way of wisdom (*ḥokmâ*) was identified with the right conduct of life; it led to an experience of the divine presence. St. Paul had applied this notion to Christ, ''The Wisdom of God'' (1 Cor 1.24); and in the Septuagint translation of *ḥokmâ*, or wisdom, *sophia* was used for its stress on virtue as well as knowledge; in Latin, this became *sapientia* used by Vergil and Cicero in a sense that implied virtue.

Hellenistic and Christian Ethic. The Hellenistic ethic was a nonreligious attempt to achieve a rationally coherent system of conduct based on man's reaction to daily experience. For the Platonists, control of passion was directed to contemplation; for the Stoics, it looked to achievement of the *honestum,* or good, and was extended to family, friends, and country. The Christian ethic, on the other hand, was based on conformity to the will of God as revealed in His Word through the Scriptures. On an eschatological basis, St. Paul specified the law of Christ as love of God and neighbor in the Church as the body of Christ. The early Christian teachers further adapted codes of social conduct common in both Hellenistic and Jewish teaching; and in their CATECHESIS, or moral instruction, they employed pedagogic devices such as the ''two ways'' (Didache, pseudo-Barnabas, Shepherd of Hermas) and catalogues of virtues (Clement I, Ignatius) that were used by Aristotle (*Eth. Nic.* 2.7), by Christ (Mt 5.1–12; Lk 6.20–23), and in the Epistles. In adapting Christian moral teaching to everyday life, Platonic and Stoic anthropology, experience, and terminology played a part, particularly with the apologists. Little attention was paid in earlier documents to the psychological elements in man's evil tendencies; this interest was developed mainly in the Judeo-Christian apocryphal literature with the doctrine of the good and evil spirits. It received justification in New Testament preoccupation with diabolic and angelic influences.

The Apologists. In defending Christians against allegations of criminality, the 2d-century APOLOGISTS assessed the morality of their Hellenistic contemporaries, attacked idolatry and superstition, and attempted to convince their pagan audience that Christianity alone was conformable to what is noble and valuable in the human soul. JUSTIN MARTYR (100 to 160) supplied a ''rule of faith'' and recounted the way of conversion from pagan immorality and Jewish superstition to the purity of the Christian way of life (*Apol.* 1.14.4–17.4). The letter to DIOGNETUS described the divine economy of God's revelation as an antidote to man's corrupt ways and asserted that in marriage and family life, in dress and language, in civic custom and law, Christians did not differ from their contemporaries, sin alone excepted (5.1–8). The author maintained that ''what the soul is to the body, the Christians are to the world'' (6.1–10). This attitude was likewise reflected in the apology of ARISTIDES (17.19).

TATIAN (*Disc.* 12) and THEOPHILUS OF ANTIOCH (*Autoly.* 2) attempted to supply a theory for the inner workings of the soul. Irenaeus of Lyons coordinated the Christian moral development; refuted Gnosticism with its pessimistic evaluation of evil as a positive reality; and returned to the Semitic, flesh-soul-spirit anthropology rooted in the Pauline concept of the Incarnation. Man was created as a child (νήπιος); his failure to follow God's pedagogic guidance has been rectified by Christ, in whom all things were created and destined for a final recapitulation. Man's freedom, however, is guaranteed by his creation in God's image, which he is to refashion within himself, under the aegis of the Holy Spirit.

Early Latin and Greek Fathers. The Greek and Latin Fathers of the 3d century continued this development. TERTULLIAN, HIPPOLYTUS, and CYPRIAN OF CARTHAGE in the West and CLEMENT OF ALEXANDRIA and ORIGEN in the East inaugurated a detailed elucidation of such themes of Christian morality as the image of God, the imitation of Christ, the return to a paradisaical innocence or perfection. Clement described at length the full Christian day from the family meal in the evening through prayer and the care of the body, to sexual and social activities (*Pedagog.* 2, 3). With Origen and METHODIUS OF OLYMPUS, specific obligations such as virginity and continence, prayer, fasting, almsgiving, patience and steadfastness in persecution, justice, and the Christian attitude toward the state received basic consideration. In Hippolytus the liturgical and canonical aspects of Christian life are described; and in local synods and the councils, ordinances were laid down regarding clerical and lay practice of virtue and avoidance of vice. In Tertullian a legalistic approach to salvation is expressed in terms of the debt due to sin, condign punishment, and satisfaction; and this became a characteristic of Western moral thought as expressed by popes such as INNOCENT I, LEO I, GELASIUS, and GREGORY I.

Eastern Moral Thought. In the East, with ATHANASIUS, CYRIL, and the Alexandrians generally, more stress was placed on the possibility of man's divinization through cooperation with the Holy Spirit. In the Antiochene school as represented by DIODORE OF TARSUS, THEODORET OF CYR, and JOHN CHRYSOSTOM, man's justification was connected rather with his fulfillment in the Resurrection and with his preparation through the imitation of Christ in His sufferings. This teaching was developed in exegetical homilies on the Scripture and in catechetical and mystagogical lectures such as those of CYRIL OF JERUSALEM and Theodoret of Cyr. But in an unfinished work on the nature of man, NEMESIUS OF EMESA (400 to 450) supplied a psychological analysis of the human composite and vindicated man's freedom while insisting on the guidance of providence.

Basil of Caesarea (d. 379) returned to the gospel precepts and concentrated on the will as the controller of virtuous conduct, while combating the rigorism of EUSTATHIUS OF SEBASTE. Man with free will is capable of love and sacrifice in striving for union with Christ through participation in the mysteries of the Church's life. Basil's *regulae* were directed to the guidance of monastic life, but dealt also with priestly ministration and the obligations of husbands and wives, children and servants, administrators and magistrates (70 to 79). The perfection of union with Christ is achieved in martyrdom; but the monk and lay Christian can approach this ideal in the ''white martyrdom'' of obedience to God's will by the practice of virtue, constant prayer, and continence. GREGORY OF NYSSA stressed imitation of divine nature, in image of which man is created, and harmonized the concept of grace with the Hellenistic ethical ideal (*De instit. christ.*). The practical pastor of souls predominated in John Chrysostom's discussion of original sin and penance, and in the explicit instruction in virtuous practice that he provided in exegetical homilies and sermons for the laity, monks, and priests (*De sacerdotio*).

Fathers of the West. Western moral thought is represented in HILARY OF POITIERS' (315 to 371) exegesis of the Psalms and of St. Matthew; by ZENO OF VERONA (363 to 372) in the battle against pagan practices; by PACIAN OF BARCELONA (d. 392), who wrote treatises on Baptism and Penance; and by a widespread defense against the excesses of PRISCILLIANISM and the purely humanistic doctrines of PELAGIANISM. AMBROSE of Milan (339 to 397) utilized Cicero's *De officiis* as a background for his discussion of the Christian moral teaching, but consciously directed man's final end to union with God rather than Stoic contemplation. He stressed the ideals of continence and virginity, as did JEROME, whose defense of Christian morality is all-embracing in his *Adv. Vigilantium, Adv. Helvidium,* and *Dialogi III contra Pelagium.* RUFINUS OF AQUILEIA introduced Origen's ascetical ideals and Basil's concept of the practice of virtue for both the laity and monks in the West. John CASSIAN (*c.* 360 to 430) in his *De institutis* and *Collationes Patrum* discussed the love of God and purity of heart; he advocated the avoidance of the eight capital sins as the way to perfection; and PETER CHRYSOLOGUS (d. *c.* 450), MAXIMUS OF TURIN (d. *c.* 420), and Pope Leo I excelled in the adaptation of moral discipline to the necessities of daily life.

With St. AUGUSTINE of Hippo, Western moral thought reached maturity. His vast sweep of doctrinal disquisitions provided a defense of Christian moral theory against MANICHAEANS and Pelagians; he turned to specific problems in his *De agone christiano, De mendacio, De continentia, De bono conjugali, De nuptiis et concupiscentia, De bono viduitatis,* and *De virginitate.* Because of his personal experiences (*Confessions*) Augustine took a pessimistic view of human nature and tended to exaggerate the opposition between GRACE and nature. This tendency toward rigor is discernible in many of his sermons, and it affected the development of moral theology during the Middle Ages. It is notable in the sermons of CAESARIUS OF ARLES (d. 542), who, commenting on the Old Testament practice of continence, introduced abstention from Communion after marital relations and nocturnal pollution. Pope Gregory I (590 to 604) mitigated this tendency with his insistence that, although no good work is possible without chastity, it is useless without *suavitas mentis.* With his *Liber regulae pastoralis, Moralis in Job,* and *Dialogi de vita et miraculis patrum italicorum* he set the moral standard for the next 600 years.

Oriental Theory and Practice. Oriental moral theory and practice was elaborated by EVAGRIUS PONTICUS (d. 399), who distinguished a threefold ascent to union with God. He concentrated on the psychological process of *praxis,* physical *theoria* (contemplation), and *theologia* in some four or six steps that began with the moral requirement of purging the soul by struggling against passion, obedience to God's Commandments, and the exercise of positive virtue. Faith and fear of God are the foundation for continence, patience, and hope, which lead to a deliberated selflessness (*apatheia*) and love (*agape*). In the second stage Evagrius gradually eliminated images and phantasms in prayer; but the complicated Neoplatonic notions of the spirit world in relation to God, involved in his second and third steps, were considered Origenistic in essence and were condemned at the Council of CONSTANTINOPLE II (553).

Closer to the Basilian ideal of praxis, the 6th-century monastic leaders of Palestine, Barsanuphius of Gaza and John the Prophet, insisted on the monk's revelation of his inmost soul to his spiritual director, while he strove through love to obey the Commandments, suppress his willfulness, and achieve the fulfillment of God's will in humility and docility. A life so directed leads to inner peacefulness (*hesychia*), which is a reward for virtue rather than a state of virtuousness. Abbot Dorotheus listed obedience, humility, temperance, patience, fraternal charity, and contemplation of the last things as the occupation of a monk; and Abbot Zosimus clothed these virtues in examples and experiences with a vividness that emulated that of John Cassian. Following this line was John MOSCHUS's *Ladder of Paradise,* in which he concentrated on sorrow for sin and obedience as the proper attitude in the practice of virtue; and the abbot Thalassius of Lybia (*c.* 650) developed the Evagrian praxis by insisting on a harmony between body and soul in the psychological activity of the *nous,* or spirit. In reaching for God man can attain the fulfillment of his personality. MAXIMUS CONFESSOR (580 to 655) accepted the Evagrian psychology and developed it in a humanistic sense, maintaining its propriety for both the laity and monks, whereas Theodore the Studite (759 to 826) denied an essential difference between the perfection of the monk and that of the layman, and centered on man's imitating Christ in his Crucifixion. JOHN DAMASCENE (675 to 749), in his tract on fasting and in his work on the virtues and vices, had summed up the patristic phase of moral development. His synthesis greatly affected the scholastic development in the 12th-century renewal of theology.

Bibliography: C. DUBLANCY, *Dictionnaire de théologie catholique,* ed. A. VACANT et al., 15 v. (Paris 1903–50)

10.2:2435–41. J. ZIEGLER, *Lexikon für Theologie und Kirche*, ed. J. HOFER and K. RAHNER, 10 v. (2d, new ed. Freiburg 1957–65) 7:618–19. F. WAGNER, *Geschichte des Sittlichkeitsbegriffes,* 3 v. (Münster 1928–36). T. DEMAN, *Aux origines de la théologie morale* (Paris 1951). C. H. DODD, *Gospel and Law* (New York 1951). H. JAEGER, ''The Patristic Conception of Wisdom in the Light of Biblical and Rabbinical Research,'' *Studia patristica* 4 (*Texte und Untersuchungen zur Geschichte der altchristlichen Literatur* 79; 1961) 93–98. M. SPANNEUT, *Le Stoïcisme des Pères de l'Église de Clément de Rome à Clément d'Alexandrie* (Paris 1957). J. STELZENBERGER, *Die Beziehungen der frühchristlichen Sittenlehre zur Ethik der Stoa* (Munich 1933). K. HÖRMANN, *Leben in Christus* (Vienna 1952). F. X. MURPHY, ''The Background to a History of Patristic Moral Thought,'' *Studia moralia* 1 (Rome 1963) 49–85; ''The Foundations of Tertullian's Moral Teaching,'' *Thomistica morum principia* 1 (Rome 1961) 95–106; ''Sources of the Moral Teaching of Rufinus of Aquileia,'' *Studia patristica* 6 (*Texte und Untersuchungen zur Geschichte der altchristlichen Literatur* 81; 1962) 147–54. *Epistle to Diognetes,* ed. and Fr. tr. H. I. MARROU (*Sources Chrétiennes* 33; 1951). CLEMENT OF ALEXANDRIA, *Paedagogus,* ed. H. I. MARROU, Fr. tr. M. HARL (*ibid.* 70; 1960) 43–91. P. NEMESHEGYI, ''La Morale d'Origène,'' *Revue d'ascétique et de mystique* 37 (1961) 409–28. P. T. CAMELOT, ''La Théologie de l'image de Dieu,'' *Revue des sciences philosophiques et théolgiques* 40 (1956) 443–71. A. HEITMANN, *Imitatio Dei* (*Studia anselmiana* 10; 1940). G. B. LADNER, *The Idea of Reform: Its Impact on Christian Thought and Action in the Age of the Fathers* (Cambridge, Massachusetts 1959). H. G. BECK, *Kirche und theologische Literatur im byzantinischen Reich* (Munich 1959) 344–68. I. HAUSHERR, ''L'Origine de la théorie orientale des huit péchés capitaux,'' *Oriens Christianus* 30 (1933) 164–75. G. BARDY, *Dictionnaire de spiritualité ascétique et mystique. Doctrine et histoire*, ed. M. VILLER et al. (Paris 1932–) 1:1273–83, on St. Basil. M. VILLER, ''Aux sources de la spiritualité de St. Maxime: Les Oeuvres d'Évagre le Pontique,'' *Revue d'ascétique et de mystique* 11 (1930) 156–84, 239–68, 331–36. P. ANTIN, ''Les Idées morales de St. Jérome,'' *Mélanges de science religieuse* 14 (1957) 135–50. F. VAN DER MEER, *Augustine the Bishop,* tr. B. BATTERSHAW and G. R. LAMB (New York 1962). L. WEBER, *Hauptfragen der Moraltheologie Gregors des Grossen* (Freiburg 1947). *Kirche und theologische Literatur im byzantinischen Reich* 481–82, on St. John Damoscene.

[F. X. MURPHY]

MORAL THEOLOGY, HISTORY OF (700 TO VATICAN COUNCIL I)

This article deals with the history of moral theology from the end of the Patristic period down to the beginning of the modern era.

From the Patristic to the Scholastic Period. From the years 700 to 1100 not a single work in moral theology appears. It was considered enough, especially in Benedictine cloisters, to reread the Fathers, to make extracts from them selected according to a practical point of view, as did, for example, Rabanus Maurus (d. 859). To reconstruct the moral theology of the period, one has to have recourse to the decrees of the popes, the councils, and bishops, made in the effort to remedy abuses and thereby raise the moral level of the Christian people.

The only important development of that time was the diffusion of the *Libri poenitentiales* (*see* PENITENTIALS) and the extension of private penance. Originating in Ireland or the British Isles, the *Libri poenitentiales* were spread through France, Germany, Switzerland, and Northern Italy by Irish missionaries. These books are not manuals of moral theology, but rather detailed lists of sins with their penances. Complaints arose very quickly against the mechanical character of the penitential books, and after the Carolingian renaissance, they were even condemned several times by councils, and their use from that time was considerably reduced.

The 12th and 13th Centuries and St. Thomas. During the 12th and 13th centuries development took place that led up to the moral theology of St. Thomas Aquinas. The causes of this are to be sought in the general reawakening of culture. The ancient philosophers, and among them, the moralists, began to be read again. In his *Moralium dogma philosophorum,* William of Conches (d. 1146) adapted Cicero's *De Officiis.* Aelred (d. 1166) was inspired by the *De amicitia.* John of Salisbury (d. 1180) wrote an anthology on the texts of Seneca. Soon the *Nicomachean Ethics* made its appearance and was frequently commented upon. Certainly all these authors did not intend to write a moral theology (the first use of the term *theologia moralis* is found in Alan of Lille, *c.* 1160). The proper subject matter of philosophy was human behavior, whereas theology treated of God. The matter, however, was being prepared for future syntheses.

Following Gratian and the *Decretum* (1140), canonists gave attention to moral questions: laws and contracts, offences and sins, marriage, etc. After the Fourth Lateran Council (1215) canonists also took an active part in drawing up a theology of penance and in the editing of summas for the use of confessors, the *Summa de Poenitentia* of St. Raymond of Peñafort (d. 1275) being the best-known effort of this kind. Abelard (d. 1142) attempted a synthesis of Christian ethics. Writers of mystical bent, the Victorines Hugh (d. 1141) and Richard (d. 1173) of St. Victor, and St. Bernard of Clairvaux (d. 1153), conceived a synthesis of Christian wisdom, taking their inspiration from the Bible and the Church Fathers. Peter Lombard (d. 1160) in his *Liber Sententiarum,* which for more than four centuries was the textbook for theological students, synthesized the results of these renewals in moral as well as in dogmatic theology. In his theology, moral had no special place, but unfolded itself in dogmatic questions, and there was a lively awareness of the indissoluble unity of theological knowledge, dogmatic and moral, as well as spiritual.

In the 13th century it was especially the masters of the faculty of arts of the University of Paris who treated the scientific status of ethics and elaborated a moral philosophy already solidly framed, the best part of which St. Thomas was to integrate into his theological synthesis.

The Franciscan School from Alexander of Hales (d. 1245) to John Duns Scotus (d. 1308), including St. Bonaventure (d. 1274) and his numerous disciples, gave us, in theological summas, in commentaries on the *Sentences* of Lombard, and in particular treatises, a theological and moral synthesis centered in Christ and charity, but open to the contributions of Greek thought and the progress of the experimental sciences. As this Franciscan school taught, moral theology ought not to serve simply for contemplation, but ought to make us better. It is wisdom stimulating faith within us. All moral thought is love drawn from the very source of love, God in Jesus. The Franciscan theologians affirmed the primacy of charity, and also the primacy of the will.

St. Albert the Great (d. 1280) wrote of moral theory in philosophical terms and commented upon the *Nicomachean Ethics,* but he had also a moral theology that is ordained toward the life of Christian virtue and was practical and even hortatory in character. It was left to St. Thomas Aquinas (d. 1274) to unite in one grand synthesis the contributions of philosophical ethics and those of theological tradition. Rooted in his commentary of the *Sentences,* the moral work of St. Thomas culminated in the *Summa Theologiae.* The moral theology of the Angelic Doctor is a moral theology of man, the image of God, created by God (Pars I); he returns to God (Pars II); through Christ (Pars III). The *Secunda Pars* includes both a general moral theology, with the great treatises on the final end, the passions, habits, virtue, sin, law, and grace; and a special moral theology in which are included comprehensive studies of the theological and cardinal virtues and the states of life. To take the *Secunda Pars* from the *Summa* would be to betray St. Thomas's concept of theology. According to him, all theology, dogmatic and moral alike, are one. In a synthesis, unique in the history of moral theology, St. Thomas adopted the best in Greek tradition, especially Aristotle, and gave to moral a choice place in his system of theology as a whole, a place that had never been given it by anyone.

Origins of Modern Moral Theology: 14th to 16th Centuries. The equilibrium reigning in Thomistic moral theology between nature and grace was broken by nominalistic dialectics. From the beginning of the 14th century, the English Franciscan William of Ockham implacably criticized the Thomistic system. According to Ockham, the good is not defined by ontological reality, but solely by the arbitrary will of God: the good is what God orders and because He orders it; evil is what He forbids and because He forbids it. God is not bound by His decrees, and He could change them at any moment. The law, revealed or natural, is simply the expression of the divine will. All morality consists in the absolutely free obedience of man to the law. What causes merit, indeed, and consequently the morality of an act of obedience to the law, is the absolute liberty of indetermination with which man performs it. The influence of nominalism was great, especially in methodology, which in moral science opened the doors to casuistry. The center of nominalism was the University of Paris; among those associated with it there were Jean Buridan (d. 1359), Pierre d'Ailly (d. 1420), and Jean Gerson (d. 1429). Prague, Vienna, and the new German universities were also affected by nominalism. At the end of the 15th century Gabriel Biel (d. 1495) gave Ockhamism its scholarly form that influenced Martin Luther.

Thomistic Renewal in the 16th Century. The Thomistic renewal, the first signs of which appeared in the Rhenish universities during the 15th century, emerged at the beginning of the 16th century simultaneously in Germany, with Conrad Köllin, OP (d. 1538), and his commentary on the *Prima Secundae* of St. Thomas; in Italy, with Cardinal Cajetan (d. 1534), who published the first complete commentary of the *Summa Theologiae;* and in France, where Pierre Crockaert, OP (d. 1514), replaced the *Sentences* of Peter Lombard as a textbook with the *Summa Theologiae* of the Angelic Doctor, a step of considerable importance in the evolution of moral theology. The Thomistic revival spread out especially in Spain, at the University of Salamanca, where Francisco de Vitoria, OP (d. 1546), introduced the new methods of the Parisian masters. The school of Salamanca was before all else a school of moral theology, and the *Secunda Pars* was the center of preoccupation for the Salamancans, who studied it with a taste for the concrete and modern adaptations inherited from the nominalists. In his *Relectiones,* Francisco de Vitoria, founder of international law, studied the great political problems of his time in the light of Thomistic principles. In his *De locis theologicis* Melchior Cano, OP (d. 1560), renewed theological method. Dominic Soto, OP (d. 1560), wrote his famous *De justitia,* while Bartholomeo Medina, OP (d. 1580), provided the formula for probabilism. With Dominic Báñez the Thomistic revival became more refined, but what it gained in metaphysical depth, it lost in a lessening of contact with earthly realities, and it acquired a certain aridity of style. At the end of the 16th century the great theologians of the Society of Jesus appeared at Salamanca. If Gabriel Vásquez, SJ (d. 1604), and Francisco Suárez (d. 1617) adopted the *Summa* of St. Thomas as a basis for their teaching, they showed a spirit of independence in its use. They accentuated the part of philosophy and law in moral theology. Showing the same juridical inclination, the Jesuit theologians, L. Molina (d. 1600), L. Lessius (d. 1623), and De Lugo (d. 1660), wrote their notable treatises *De justitia,* and Tomas Sánchez (d. 1610) his *De matrimonio,* which has become a classic.

Practical Moral Theology. From the 14th to the 16th century, the summas for the use of confessors were popular. These were arranged according to an alphabetical plan and were in fact dictionaries of casuistry. Among these were the *Summa Pisana* (1338) of Bartholomew of San Concordia, OP, the *Summa angelica* (1486) of Angelo di Chivasso, OFM, the *Rosella casuum* of Giovanni Battista Trovamala, OFM (1484), and the *Summa sylvestrina* of Sylvestre de Prierias (1514). The *Summa theologica,* an original endeavor by St. Antoninus of Florence, goes widely beyond the plan of the alphabetical summas and offers us a complete picture of the life of the 15th century. In a line still more strictly practical appears the *Confessionalia,* simple vade mecums for the priest as confessor.

The Institutiones morales. Between the great commentaries of the *Summa* of St. Thomas and the more practical works, there appeared, at the end of the 16th century, a new literary genre, the *Institutiones morales.* The Council of Trent, in fixing the norms for the Sacrament of Penance, called for a deepening of the study of moral theology. The founding of seminaries, which prepared young clerics for their ministry with a cycle of study shorter than that of the universities, and which apportioned a biennium to the study of cases of conscience, led to the writing of manuals designed for that particular purpose. The plan for such a manual is to be found in the Ratio Studiorum of the Society of Jesus (1586). With a view to practical importance of cases of conscience it treated briefly the main headings of the *Prima Secundae* of St. Thomas—human acts, conscience, sin, law—and then proceeded to the study of particular cases in the following order: the commandments of God and of the Church; and the Sacraments; and censures. In 1600 Juan Azor, SJ, initiated this new organization of the subject by publishing his *Institutiones morales.* The convenience of the plan assured its success. In the 17th century, it was used by Jesuit authors such as Vincenzo Filliucci (d. 1622), Paul Laymann (d. 1635), Fernando de Castro Palao (d. 1633), Juan de Lugo (d. 1660), and especially Hermann Busenbaum (d. 1668) who, in his short *Medulla theologian moralis,* produced the finest example of this kind of text. The plan of the *Institutiones* has remained to the 21th century the plan of most manuals of moral theology.

Crisis of Moral Theology in the 17th and 18th Centuries. In the *Institutiones morales* the treatise on conscience occupied the central place. Should not the penitent be judged according to his conscience and be left to form it? Probabilism claimed to bring a solution to this delicate problem. Originating in Salamanca, receiving its theoretical formulation from the great Jesuit theologians, Vázquez and Suárez, probabilism is immediately included in the *Institutiones.* But among some casuists too favorable to novelty or indulgence, it issued in laxist opinions that weakened beyond measure the demands of Christian morality. Some, unreasonably indulgent in according title of probability, came to accept the less probable opinion as a rule of conduct, provided that it was not actually improbable. Among those known for too great a laxity of opinion were Antonino DIANA (d. 1663), who in his *Resolutiones morales* examined more than 20,000 cases; Antonio de Escobar (d. 1669); Tomasso Tamburini (d. 1675); and Juan Caramuel y Lobkowitz (d. 1682), called the "Prince of Laxists."

A violent movement of opposition against laxism arose in the Church, especially in France, following the Abbé de Saint-Cyran (d. 1643). Unfortunately, Jansenism was involved in the controversy. Inspired with the heretical theses on nature and grace, Jansenist moral theology fell into rigorism. In 1643 Antoine Arnauld published his *Morale pratique des Jésuites;* Nicole, his *Essais de morale* (1671–78). Blaise Pascal had published his *Lettres provinciales* in 1656.

Even the orthodox theological schools began to find themselves ranged against each other. In 1656 the reaction of the Dominicans began. Defenders of a moderate PROBABILISM up to that time (D. Báñez, John of St. Thomas), they began to support PROBABILIORISM. Gonet, OP (d. 1681), in his *Clypeus thomisticus,* and Contenson, OP (d. 1684), in his *Theologica mentis et cordis* defended probabiliorism. At the end of the century of Louis XIV, severity prevailed in Paris as well as in Louvain and in Toulouse. Certain theologians, such as Louis Habert (d. 1718) in his *Theologia dogmatica et moralis* and Gaspard Juenin (d. 1713), pushed their severity to Jansenistic rigorism. The Jesuits, while disavowing the extreme theses, maintained the probabilist doctrine whose classic formula H. Busenbaum gave in his *Medulla theologian moralis.* Within the society, controversies were waged, especially when the Superior General, Thirso González, attempted to impose probabiliorism (1694). The interventions of the magisterium of the Church only touched the extreme positions. Alexander VII (1665–66) and Innocent XI (1679) condemned more than 100 laxist propositions. Alexander VIII (1690) condemned both laxist and rigorist theses. But the Holy See abstained from interfering with the dispute between the probabilists and the probabiliorists.

Outside the schools, the Carmelites of Salamanca published their *Cursus theologiae moralis,* certainly the most important moral work toward the end of the 17th century.

The 18th Century and St. Alphonsus Liguori. Controversies waxed most vigorously in Italy. Around the years 1740 to 1745, the Dominican theologian D. Concina (d. 1756) and his confrere G. V. Patuzzi (d. 1769), both probabiliorists, attacked a whole series of probabilist Jesuits—Sanvitale, Ghezzi, and Zacharia, among others—as well as St. Alphonsus Liguori (1696–1787). The latter strove the whole of his life to find a solution to the irritating problem of probabilism. In his *Theologia moralis* (1748), as in the *Homo apostolicus* and his numerous dissertations, he strove to develop, by a series of original rules, a system equally removed from rigorism and laxism, and to this he gave the name EQUIPROBABILISM. Of two opinions equally probable, one may choose that in favor of liberty or that in favor of the law. But the greatness of St. Alphonsus did not lie in his system. It consisted in his finding in the ''swarm of probable opinions, more probable, less probable, certain, more certain, or less certain, some manifestly rigorist, others evidently lax, a collection of moral opinions truly certain, equally removed from extremes, scrupulously weighed in the conscience of a saint'' (P. Labourdette, OP).

New Paths and Tradition in the 19th Century. After the French Revolution in Austria and Germany new paths opened up for moral theology. J. M. Sailer (d.1832) and Johann Hirscher (d. 1865) strove to restore its evangelical purity to moral theology and to reunite dogma and moral, so as not to make a science for the confessor, but a doctrine of life. In their wake came the school of Tübingen, M. Jocham (d. 1893), Fuchs (d. 1854), Deutinger (d. 1864), Werner (d. 1888), and Probst (d. 1850), claiming that the foundation of moral theology is nothing else but grace considered as a call to perfect life.

The *Institutiones morales* continued their course. The controversy over probabilism was renewed (1840–50) around Rosmini, Antonio Ballerini coming to the defense of probabilism. The quarrel returned around 1870. The opinions of St. Alphonsus, if not his system, became the common doctrine of moralists about the time of Vatican Council I.

Bibliography: B. HÄRING, *The Law of Christ,* tr. E. G. KAISER (Westminster, Md. 1961–). T. DEMAN, *Aux Origines de la théologie morale* (Paris 1951). O. LOTTIN, *Psychologie et morale aux XIIe et XIIIe siècles,* 6 v. (Louvain-Gembloux 1942–60). A. G. SERTILLANGES, *La Philosophie morale de saint Thomas d'Aquin* (rev. ed. Paris 1946). G. DE LAGARDE, *La Naissance de l'esprit laïque au déclin du moyen âge* (new ed. Louvain 1956–). T. DEMAN, *Dictionnaire de théologie catholique,* ed. A. VACANT et al., 15 v. (Paris 1903–50) 13.1:417–619. J. DIEBOLT, *La Théologie morale catholique en Allemagne au temps du Philosophisme et de la Restauration (1750–1850)* (Strasbourg 1926).

[L. VEREECKE]

MORAL THEOLOGY, HISTORY OF (20TH-CENTURY DEVELOPMENTS)

Biblical Study. The mid-20th-century movements in the Church led to a change in approach and method in the teaching of moral theology, reflected also in subsequent writings. The remarkable increase in interest and work in Biblical studies, made possible and encouraged by Pius XII's encyclical *Divino afflante Spiritu* and important archeological discoveries, brought about a desire among theologians to use a more Biblical approach and to rely on scientific Biblical exegesis for interpretation of the message of salvation. Such a renewal was undoubtedly needed in all branches of theology, but especially in moral theology, where too much weight had been attached to philosophical and ethical reasoning and too little to the study of the teaching of the inspired word of God. The Biblical and kerygmatic movements helped much toward a more theological approach to moral theology even apart from the greater and more exact use of scriptural texts. This new approach has appeared especially in preaching and actual classroom teaching, and only more slowly in the textbook manuals, especially those that are merely new editions of older works.

More Positive Orientation. Also, an effect of the kerygmatic movement has been an effort to get away from the predominantly negative type of presentation that had prevailed in many older manuals. Whole books were written in an attempt to integrate this more positive, more theological, and more Biblical approach to moral theology; but by the mid-1960s not much success had been achieved in fully integrated works that would also stand as thorough scientific treatises of the whole of moral theology. It was left more to the living teachers and preachers to exhort their hearers to a fuller response of love to the call of Christ and at the same time to make clear what Christ Himself demanded in fulfillment of the Decalogue as a means of showing true love of God.

Some felt that such a positive approach requires a rearrangement of the order as well as the manner of treating moral theology. They insisted on dividing the matter of special moral theology according to the virtues rather than according to the precepts of the Decalogue, or according to the various relationships of man, i.e., to God, to himself, to his fellowman, and to his fellowman as individual and to society. However, it seemed that the positive approach, even by virtues, could still be achieved with the arrangement, for pedagogical and mnemonic purposes, of the precepts of the Decalogue. No one arrangement is essential to a positive approach.

Others felt that moral theology should include, in addition to what had theretofore been gathered under that name, a treatment of the ideal response to the call of Christ, and so have intermingled ascetic and moral theology. Certainly every individual Christian should respond on the ascetical plane, wanting to love Christ more and do the better thing always; but there is still room for exact treatment of the limits of obligations and rights.

Influence of Existentialism. Of tremendous influence for both good and bad was the philosophy of EXISTENTIALISM, with its moral counterpart known by various names such as situational, personalistic, or I-Thou dialogic ethics. It had a good influence in calling more attention to the personal and subjective factors entering into every real moral decision, and thus assisting in the assessment of the actual moral responsibility in individual real-life situations. It also helped moralists, and priests and counselors in general, to be more aware of the many complications of real-life problems and to see that a mere restatement of a universal negative precept of the divine law is never a full answer to such problems; help must be given to find alternative solutions that will be morally acceptable.

Existentialism also had a bad influence in a number of ways that called forth warnings and condemnations by Pius XII and the Holy Office in the 1950s. The atheism of the extremists in the movement seems to have led some Christian and even some Catholic writers to leave all consideration of God out of morality and to make morality merely a matter of deciding what best integrates an individual's own personality. Even when God is taken into account, the extremists tend to make morality merely a personal dialogue with God in which the individual tries to feel what God would have him do in a given situation, omitting all consideration of revelation and the teaching authority of the Church. Milder forms of bad influence appeared in writers who tend to neglect basic principles and rely more on sentiment and emotion in making moral decisions. Fortunately, these bad influences appeared more in popular writers or non-Catholics than in Catholic moral theologians, although the pope's warnings included some Catholic moralists.

Summary. To sum up trends in the 1960s: there was a definite effort on the part of most moral theologians to be more theological and Biblical, less philosophical and abstract; to be more positive in approach and emphasis, less negative; to treat morality more as a personal response to the divine call, less as a mere demand of human nature. The ideal seemed to lie in a delicate balance of the various elements, without letting the new emphases entirely eliminate the less important but still necessary elements.

Bibliography: J. C. FORD and G. KELLY, *Contemporary Moral Theology,* 2 v. (Westminster, Md. 1958–63), v. 1. G. ERMECKE, ''Die katholische Moraltheologie heute,'' *Theologie und Glaube* 41 (1951) 127–142; summarized in *Theology Digest* 2 (1954) 19–22. A. VERMEERSCH, ''Soixante ans de théologie morale,'' *Novelle revue théologie* 56 (1929) 863–884. I. ZEIGER, ''De conditione theologiae moralis moderna,'' *Periodica de re morali canonica liturgica* 28 (1939) 177–189. G. THILS, *Tendances actuelles en théologie morale* (Gembloux 1940). M. ZALBA, *Theologiae moralis compendium,* 2 v. [*Biblioteca de autores cristianos* (Madrid 1945) 175–176; 1958], v.1.

[J. J. FARRAHER]

MORAL THEOLOGY, HISTORY OF (CONTEMPORARY TRENDS)

In the years since Vatican II the problems and challenges facing moral theology have grown ever more extensive and complex. There have emerged not only novel questions regarding both old and new ethical subjects but also fundamental questions about even the methodology and the very identity of the discipline as well as about the ecclesiastical and academic roles of its professors. The questions, moreover, are not merely so many individual queries that can be addressed in turn; in many instances they are intricately interlocked and inseparable.

Reform of Moral Theology. The radical nature of the developmental process which has characterized postconciliar moral theology and continues to do so is comparable to that of the reform of Catholic Biblical studies toward the middle of the century. Nevertheless, there is a great difference between the two transformations. Understanding the challenge facing them in terms of contemporary scholarship, the reformers of Biblical studies conceived their task, with easy clarity, as one of bringing the various forms of critical method to bear on Biblical materials in the light of current knowledge of history, science, and language. Moral theologians, however, are not favored with a similarly clear vision of what the reform of their discipline in fact entails; for while reform in moral theology would be inadequate without an updating in light of contemporary knowledge in related fields, it must include also significantly more than this.

The reform of moral theology began with a recognition of major shortcomings of the discipline in its preconciliar state. Having developed as a science for ministers of the Sacrament of Penance, it was focused largely on sin and was thus susceptible to tendencies toward minimalism and legalism, issuing from a truncated and distorted perspective of the Christian life. Insight into the unsatisfactory state of the science, however, constituted only an initial step in the direction of discovering its remedy. It is toward this goal that moral theology continues to strive, attempting to transform itself into a science—or, as some would argue, an art-science—of the Christian life in its fullness.

In an often cited passage of *Optatam totius*, Vatican II called for a reform of moral theology that is, in itself, a return to sources rather than an updating. Having noted that special care should be given to ''the perfecting of moral theology,'' the Council went on to specify that ''its scientific presentation should draw more fully on the teaching of holy Scripture and should throw light on the exalted vocation of the faithful in Christ and their obligation to bring forth fruit in charity for the life of the world'' (n. 17). Thus from the Council itself emerged challenges regarding structure, content and methodology of moral theology.

Structure, Content, and Method. The reform with which the conciliar document is concerned looks directly and exclusively to the religious dimension of moral theology, i.e., its relation to the revelation transmitted in Scripture, and envisions a restructuring of this science according to a more intense bond with the Bible. It is again, however, one thing to recognize the need for such a bond and quite another to determine its precise nature and what that entails. The latter is a task left to theologians, and since the Council much study has been and is still being given to the relation of morality to Christian faith.

The mode, however, in which the question of this relation was raised and for the most part has been discussed within postconciliar Catholic moral theology was determined by influences not directly related to the Council. In the atmosphere of controversy following the publication of *HUMANAE VITAE* (1968) there was some discussion of whether it was the intention of the encyclical to present a specifically Catholic and/or Christian response to the moral issue of artificial birth control. The particular question was expanded into the general inquiry of whether there can be a specifically Christian morality. Because of the longstanding natural law methodology of Catholic moral theology, the latter question was understood as asking whether Christian faith alters or adds to the natural law norms, knowable by human reason, that govern human acts—a question which, again as a natural law ethic, moral theology had long been inclined to answer negatively. This general question, which was eventually to appear in several forms, e.g., autonomous ethics or *Glaubensethik*, prescriptive norms versus parenetic discourse (*see* PARENESIS), then became the point of departure for virtually all discussion of the relation between Scripture and morality.

As a point of departure, the question of this relation now formulated as a question of whether there can be a specifically Christian ethic focused the ensuing discussion upon limitations and restrictions of Scripture vis-à-vis natural law, and courted a negative response. Thus in postconciliar moral theology the question of the relation between Scripture and morality has been framed in a restrictive, negatively oriented way.

While the question in this limiting mode attempted to refine particular moral issues such as that of artificial birth control, it did not facilitate the creation of the new structure and method of moral theology which would realize the ideal of the Council. It has led, on the contrary, in the marginal case, to the position that moral theology is, in the final analysis, the same as moral philosophy. Elsewhere it has resulted in making the return to Christian sources into the use of key Christian doctrines as proof-doctrines, analogous to the Biblical proof-texts employed in preconciliar moral theology: the doctrines of creation and Incarnation, for example, undergird perspectives on the goodness of the world and the dignity of the human person, while the doctrine of sin serves to show that a realistic ethic must take shape around the fact of evil in the world.

Thus, despite the prolonged and extensive discussion of whether there is a specifically Christian morality, Catholic moral theology does not yet confidently claim to have discerned and established the bond with Scripture called for by the Council or even to have achieved consensus on whether there is a specifically Christian morality.

Although this formulation of the question of the relation between Scripture and morality is still dominant within Catholic moral theology, recently another has emerged there. Instead of a question of Christian principles and rules in relation to natural law norms there has appeared a question of the Christian story in relation to the community formed by it and to the individuals constituting the community (*see* NARRATIVE THEOLOGY). Reflecting the renewed interest in and respect for Scripture in the postconciliar Catholic Church, the latter approach, although promising, is still in only a very undeveloped state.

This scriptural approach, nevertheless, increasingly marks the pastoral social teaching of the Church, beginning with *Gaudium et spes.* Employing this approach, the U.S. bishops extend it to remarkable moral conclusions: pacifism is a Christian moral stance that complements adherence to just war theory (*The Challenge of Peace:*

God's Promise and Our Response), and the evaluation of the socioeconomic condition of the U.S. from the standpoint of the poor and the powerless is a basic moral obligation.

Personal and Social Morality. Before the Council there was a rather sharp line of demarcation between moral theology and social ethics according to the distinction between so-called personal and social morality. Moral theology dealt with personal morality; the development of social morality, since the time of Leo XIII, was largely, albeit not exclusively, the achievement of the magisterium. In the postconciliar Church, however, moral theologians increasingly view their role as transcending any division between personal and social morality. Some indeed find the very division inadequate, believing that the categories reflect and sustain the individualistic bias of modern liberalism. Nevertheless, at this point in the development of moral theology, creative advances in social morality are still to be found chiefly in official Church documents while much of the work of moral theologians in this area has been commentary on ecclesiastical teaching.

In its brief statement about the reform of moral theology the Council did not address the matter of the secular or universalist aspects of the discipline, nor its points of contact with other forms of ethics. Reform relative to this dimension of moral theology is a matter, not of returning to sources, but of updating the discipline in the light of contemporary knowledge and culture. Nevertheless, there is for moral theology a point at which returning to sources coincides with updating; for the recovery of the Christian story and the development of historical consciousness go hand in hand.

Although it did not explicitly advert to the need for the updating of moral theology in its secular dimensions, the Council nevertheless indirectly provided important guidance for such reform, especially in *Gaudium et spes.* It is in this document, together with *Dignitatis humanae*, that the Council decisively moved the Church's official understanding of human relations out of a longstanding classicist mode and into that of historicity.

Viewing the dignity of the human person from the perspective of historical consciousness, the Council advanced the Church's official teaching on human rights by taking into account cultural pluralism. The claims of human dignity, according to the Council, are historically conditioned and cannot be fully defined apart from cultural situations.

This understanding of the historicity of human dignity and rights has been furthered in postconciliar social teachings on papal, synodal, and episcopal levels. It has, at least indirectly, even led the U.S. bishops to employ in their advancement of Catholic social morality methods previously not used in magisterial teaching. The bishops not only created a forum of public discussion both within and outside the Church to assist them in forming their teaching; they also distinguished their moral conclusions from universal moral principles and formal Church teaching, explicitly noting that not all persons of good will must necessarily agree with the former.

The magisterium is often accused of disregarding the new methodology. In dealing with questions of personal morality classicist consciousness still prevails. It is said that there is little in this area of official Catholic teaching to which historical consciousness and this methodology is congenial. On the other hand, when classicist consciousness is alienated from contemporary culture, it is no longer adequate for understanding the dignity of the human person in relation to society, and by the same token not equal to the task of illuminating the moral relations of people in contemporary society.

Traditionally focused on personal rather than social morality, moral theology, by contrast, has been steadily moving its understanding of personal morality toward historical consciousness. The goal is still ahead; the strong heritage of moral theology as a natural law ethics inclines it away from serious and adequate attention to cultural diversity and moral pluralism. Nevertheless, an emergent historical consciousness has already led many moral theologians to view the moral act itself in a less timeless way than what was common in preconciliar moral theology.

The Human Act and Christian Moral Life. Where an earlier moral theology considered some acts to be *ex obiecto* intrinsically evil or inherently immoral, in much of contemporary moral theology there is an insistence on the historical concreteness of morality as distinguished from the abstractness of the object of an act. Only if an act is considered in light of its object, intention, and circumstances can its moral character be determined; evil entailed in its object, abstractly considered, is premoral or nonmoral.

This bringing of the moral act more directly into the historical dimension of human existence has caused many moral theologians to relativize some norms of personal morality previously held to be absolute; for, if an act in its object alone is not immoral but is, rather, a premoral evil, the moral prohibition of the act, so it was reasoned, cannot be universal. At this point in its argument, therefore, revisionist moral theology had to deal with the question of what conditions render allowable the doing of premoral evil; and from this question emerged the principle of PROPORTIONALITY or proportionate reason: premoral evil may be done for a proportionate reason.

The opponents of this revisionist moral theology, however, argue that there are incommensurable fundamental human goods, none of which a person has the right to sacrifice directly: there can be no proportionate reason to act against such a good. From this quarter, consequently, has come the charge that the proportionality principle introduces into moral theology a utiliarian consequentialism and fails to consider that adherence to an absolute moral norm can be the way of creating and developing personal commitment in life.

Centered on individual human acts, classicist moral theology eventually developed a close affinity with the study of canon law and to some extent became merged with it. This bond with canon law strengthened legalistic tendencies already present in an act-centered moral theology which had increasingly lost sight of the role of virtue in the moral life. The influence of rationalism eclipsed almost totally moral knowledge by connaturality, and the relation of affectivity to morality was largely overlooked. Heightening an individualistic sense of life, modernity divorced morality from tradition and story as well as from authority and confined it to the autonomous rational will of the individual. Thus focused virtually exclusively on doing as distinguished from being, classicist moral theology lacked a meaningful concept of the moral life—not to mention the Christian moral life.

With no normative concept of the moral life in classicist moral theology, the point of departure for the discussion of morality could be only the human act, which was understood according to its object, intention, and circumstances. Accordingly, when the idea of FUNDAMENTAL OPTION emerged in moral theology as it began to move toward historical consciousness after the Council, it met with considerable misunderstanding and resistance in the Church; for this notion presupposes that morality is to be understood from a more holistic perspective than that of the single human act, abstracted from life.

Nevertheless, despite widespread acceptance by contemporary theologians of the notion of fundamental option, the predominant point of departure as well as the most frequently employed framework for the investigation of morality in moral theology remains, as in the discussion of premoral evil and the principle of proportionality, the human act in its object, intention, and circumstances. There are in contemporary moral theology, however, early signs of an emerging normative understanding of the Christian moral life, as the Christian story is increasingly retrieved there and interest is taken by moral theologians in the subjects of virtue, the ages of human life, and its developmental stages.

Cultural Particularity and Universal Dimensions. In a still inchoative way contemporary moral theology, as already noted, encompasses social morality. Influenced by Latin American LIBERATION THEOLOGY and German political theology, themselves products of historical consciousness, moral theology in the U.S. is allowing itself to be molded by American culture and the national situation. In this respect moral theologians are following the lead of the U.S. bishops' pastoral letters on social issues. Although in earlier times it would have appeared to be an oxymoron, through historical consciousness the idea of an American Catholic moral theology is already taking shape in the literature.

While this shift toward particularity is still far from being a matter of theological consensus, it is a necessary step toward taking cultural and moral pluralism seriously, an inevitable result of the dawning of historical consciousness in moral theology. Thus one must expect to see this discipline, without losing its universal dimensions, become increasingly concerned with its own particular cultural and social situations and accordingly to become both more political and more self-critical.

One mode of such self-criticism has its source in feminism. Particularly strong in the U.S., the feminist movement has produced an extensive literature, which often deals with ethical issues, especially so-called feminist issues. Yet, among theologians feminist critiques have generally been focused more broadly on Scripture and Christian dogmas rather than on foundational moral theology. The focus of feminist criticism can be expected to expand as the number of women in the ranks of moral theologians continues to rise and as moral theologians, female and male, increasingly adopt feminist perspectives.

In a global age universal human solidarity must necessarily become, as is happening, a basic theme of Christian life and, therefore, of moral theology. Paradoxically, however, the truly universal dimensions of moral theology become apparent and are distinguishable from false universalities such as sexist conceptions of human nature only when they emerge from the dynamic, continuous mediation of self-critical historical particularities. Thus an incipient concern for global solidarity in contemporary moral theology is inseparable from newly generated concern with historical movements, communities, and societies.

While dialogue with Protestant ethics has become an essential element of method in postconciliar Catholic moral theology, there is still very little, and no systematic, intercultural engagement of ethical thought from other religious traditions. However, a meeting of the ethical traditions of world religions will inevitably become a necessary component of moral theology as the influence of historical consciousness makes headway in the discipline and its perspective is broadened from natural law to the dignity of the human person in different cultures.

With the technological developments of the present age another kind of particularity originates in moral theology. As this discipline moves decisively beyond its longstanding concentration on so-called personal morality, a concentration which both resulted from and contributed to the ''privatizing'' of ethics and morality, its scope is being broadened to encompass life in its totality in an age of advanced technology. Thus specialization is becoming an apparently permanent feature of moral theology, just as it has come to characterize the culture in which the discipline is rooted. Business ethics requires detailed knowledge of complex institutions constituting complicated economic systems. MEDICAL ETHICS has evolved into bioethics, whose ever increasing complexity and importance are reflected in recent events: in 1971 the beginning of The Joseph and Rose Kennedy Institute for the Study of Human Reproduction and Bioethics, now the Institute of Ethics; in 1978 the publication of the *Encyclopedia of Bioethics*; and in 1987 the establishing by the Catholic Theological Society of America of a seminar—in addition to its seminar on moral theology—''Health Care Theology and Ethics.'' These and other areas of ethics, some of which—such as ecological and space age ethics—are new, frequently require very specialized knowledge from several different disciplines. Thus, while the field of moral theology is being vastly extended, the individual moral theologian is becoming less and less capable of representing the entire breadth of the discipline, and moral theology is becoming more a communal, collaborative, ''team'' effort.

The Magisterium and Moral Theologians. Having been a topic of theological discussion in the period following the publication of *Humanae vitae*, dissent from Church teaching has again become a much discussed subject among theologians, especially moral theologians. Once again there is controversy in the Church over questions of personal morality, but now the controversy is focused on the question of dissent itself. With the question of dissent, however, many other matters are intertwined: the relation of the magisterium to theology in general and to moral theology in particular, the distinction between the magisterium's relation to morals and its relation to faith, the role of the theologian in the Church and the academy, the theological basis for a canonical *mandatum* to teach theology, the nature of a Catholic university, private versus public dissent, private dissent and the public nature of the role of the theologian, etc.

While some theologians maintain that a certain tension between the teaching of the magisterium and theology is a normal dynamic between conserving the faith and creatively advancing the understanding of it, others see the origin of such tension, which in fact has been mainly between magisterial teaching and moral theology, in the difference between classicist and historical consciousness. Supporting the latter opinion is the fact that the tension surrounds matters of so-called personal morality; and, as noted above, while the approach of the magisterium to these questions remains largely a classicist point of view, many moral theologians are moving toward historical consciousness in their discussion of them.

As unfinished business for both magisterium and theologians there remain, after *Lumen gentium* of Vatican II, nonjuridical questions about doctrinal statements of the magisterium, especially with regard to morality. Vatican II, following the lead of Vatican I, discussed the authority of the Church regarding matters of faith and morals without distinguishing between the relation of the magisterium to faith and its relation to morals, relations—or more precisely, sets of relations—which must be understood in analogous, rather than univocal, concepts. It is, however, only through the clarification of these complex sets of analogous relations that the respective ecclesiastical offices of the magisterium and the moral theologian, with regard to morality and ethics, can be delimited and adequately understood. Toward this end the U.S. bishops in their 1983 and 1986 pastoral letters have made a significant contribution, in practice if not in theory, by distinguishing in their own moral teaching a level of inviting assent from levels requiring it.

The task of defining the respective places in the Church of magisterial moral teaching and moral theology has become one of the most urgent problems facing moral theologians. It is a problem characteristic of moral theology in a Church at the crossroads between a classicist and an historicist culture.

See Also: MORAL THEOLOGY; NATURAL LAW; PERSONALIST ETHICS; TELEOLOGICAL ETHICS.

Bibliography: J. M. AUBERT, ''Débats autour de la morale fondamentale,'' *Studia moralia* 20 (1982) 195–222. F. BÖCKLE, *Fundamental Moral Theology* (New York 1980). L. CAHILL, ''Teleology, Utilitarianism, and Christian Ethics,'' *Theological Studies* 42 (1981) 601–629. J. CONNERY, ''The Teleology of Proportionate Reason,'' *Theological Studies* 44 (1983) 489–496. C. CURRAN, *Toward an American Catholic Moral Theology* (Notre Dame, Ind. 1987); *Faithful Dissent* (Kansas City, Mo. 1986). R. DALY, et al., *Christian Biblical Ethics: From Biblical Revelation to Contemporary Christian Praxis. Method and Content* (New York 1984). P. DELHAYE, ''Morale chrètienne: L'Objectivité de normes éthiques générales dans la morale bibliquement resourcée,'' *Esprit et Vie* 19 (1981) 88–93. M. FARLEY, ''Feminist Ethics in the Christian Ethics Curriculum,'' *Horizons* 11 (1984) 361–372. J. FUCHS, *Christian Ethics in a Secular Arena* (Washington, D.C. 1984); ''Bishöfe und Moraltheologen: Eine innerkirchliche Spannung,'' *Stimmen der Zeit* 201 (1983) 601–619. J. GAFFNEY, ''On Parenesis and Fundamental Moral Theology,'' *Journal of Religious Ethics* 11 (1983)

23–34. G. GRISEZ, *The Way of the Lord Jesus* (Chicago 1983). J. GUSTAFSON, *Protestant and Roman Catholic Ethics: Prospects for Rapprochement* (Chicago 1978). B. HÄRING, *Free and Faithful in Christ,* 3 v. (New York 1978–1981). S. HAUERWAS, *The Peaceable Kingdom: A Primer in Christian Ethics* (Notre Dame, Ind. 1983). D. HOLLEN-BACH, *Claims in Conflict: Retrieving and Renewing the Catholic Human Rights Tradition* (New York 1979). L. JANSSENS, ''Artificial Insemination: Ethical Considerations,'' *Louvain Studies* 8 (1980) 3–29. P. KEANE, ''The Objective Moral Order: Reflections on Recent Research,'' *Theological Studies* 43 (1982) 260–278. D. KELLY, ''Roman Catholic Medical Ethics and the Ethos of Modern Medicine,'' *Ephemerides theologicae Lovanienses* 49 (1983) 46–67. V. MACNAMARA, *Faith and Ethics: Recent Roman Catholicism* (Wash., D.C. 1985). D. MAGUIRE, *A New American Justice* (Minneapolis 1982). R. MCCORMICK, *Notes on Moral Theology 1965 through 1980* (Washington, D.C. 1981); *Notes on Moral Theology 1981 through 1984* (Lanham, Md. 1984). E. MCDONAGH, *The Making of Disciples: Tasks of Moral Theology* (Wilmington, Del. 1982). NCCB, *The Challenge of Peace: God's Promise and Our Response* (Washington, D.C. 1983); *Economic Justice for All* (Wash., D.C. 1986). T. O'CONNELL, *Principles for a Catholic Morality* (New York 1978). F. SCHOLZ, ''Innere, aber nicht absolute Abwegigkeit,'' *Theologie der Gegenwart* 24 (1981) 163–172. B. SCHÜLLER, *Wholly Human: Essays on the Theory and Language of Morality* (Dublin 1986). W. SPOHN, ''The Reasoning Heart: An American Approach to Christian Discernment,'' *Theological Studies* 44 (1983) 30–52.

[N. J. RIGALI]

MORAL THEOLOGY, METHODOLOGY OF

Because the method of a science is dependent upon its nature, the method of moral theology cannot be determined without taking exact account of the nature of theology in general and of moral theology in particular.

As Theology. This article defines the term ''theology,'' or science about God, not as the natural theology, or the summit of metaphysical inquiry into the cause of things, but rather as ''sacred theology,'' or the science about God as He has revealed Himself. This is the theology that seeks to achieve an ''understanding of faith.'' Discipline requires a rational organization, in the mode of science, of the truths communicated by God through divine revelation. This basic notion already imposes upon the whole of Christian theology a number of requirements and articulations with no less bearing upon moral theology than upon any other part.

Theology receives its object from faith. This object is proposed to men through the witness of the Church, in Sacred Scripture, which is the fundamental document of revelation. Scripture itself is received and read within the limits and in the light of a tradition contained not only in books, but in what was once the living word of the Apostles and the practice inspired by them, handed on to remoter places and times in the form of truths to which witness had been borne, and in the form of living objects full of significance, such as the Sacraments and the liturgical life.

The first endeavor of theological study, whether in the field of moral or of any other of its branches, is to assemble and scrutinize the data of revelation. To this task positive theology, employing the methods of history and of criticism, is necessary. In addition to increased study of the Fathers, and the whole tradition of the Church, historico-critical studies on the Bible and the early Church help shed light upon the distinctive moral commitments of Christianity.

Every science seeks the explication of its subject to the extent that this is possible. The theologian, then, will not rest content when he knows that a doctrine truly pertains to revelation, that it has been revealed implicitly or explicitly, or that it has been subject to this or that development. He has yet to answer the question: what precisely is the meaning of the revealed truth in so far as it is possible for the human mind to grasp it? His task is to attempt to reach what Vatican Council I described as ''an understanding of mysteries, derived as well by way of analogy with truths known naturally, as through the bond linking the mysteries themselves and with the final goal of man'' (H. Denzinger, *Enchiridion symbolorum*, 3016).

Theological wisdom in which St. Thomas Aquinas saw a kind of ''imprint on us of God's own knowledge'' (*Summa theologiae* 1a, 1.3 ad 2) is constituted in that way. By its subject and by its distinctive intellectual vision, such a theology is a unique science. In all its parts it is ever ''science about God,'' considering all else only as either proceeding from God, returning to Him, or expressing His image. For this reason, it is important that every part of theology, moral especially, be considered, not as isolated, but with reference to man's final destiny to be with God as this is seen linked with the revealed mysteries. This does not mean that moral theology lacks a specialized concentration and a method proper to itself. It does mean that it must remain in profound continuity with the totality of theology of which it is a practical function, to be exercised in the regulation of human conduct. This in turn means that any element of human life that touches upon human destiny (e.g., physical health, participation in the political and economic realms, conduct of war, matters pertaining to sexuality and human reproduction) is something about which the moral theologian, being true to his discipline, has something legitimate to say.

As Moral. A moral science is one concerned with human conduct. Many modern authors understand that any such science must be one of pure observation and description, concerned only with replying to the question "how do men live?" However, as applied to morality this is an woefully inadequate idea, falling short of what reason, even scientific reason, demands. A complete consideration of human conduct, precisely as such, cannot rest content with observation; it must deal also with the object of man's action, the *operabile,* that which is actualized and brought to realization. Intelligence grasps that object only when it is able to account for its being a goal of action. Thus a science of human conduct must be normative and in that sense practical. Obviously it draws on empirical inquiries embraced in the other sciences concerned with man—anthropology, sociology, ethnology, history, etc. However, a science that divorces the norms of morality from its consideration of the actual use man makes of his freedom cannot be, in a complete sense, "science of morals," for moral theology believes that there is a real, particular goal of human life that is attained through the performance, the doing, of discrete human acts.

Moral theology on its own level respects this requirement, for while not becoming a "science concerned with man," (as sociology and anthropology are) it is rather, as theology, a "science concerned with God," being concerned with God as the exemplar, end, and source of human activity. Yet this does not free it from the obligation to seek a proper, complete knowledge of the human activity that has God as its exemplar, end, and source, for while God is the aim or ultimate target (*telos*) of the action with which moral theology is concerned, that action is *human action*, straining to reach towards God. Hence the moral theologian must understand how and why human action takes place (perhaps thereby inviting consultation with other disciplines, such as philosophical ethics, law [both civil and canonical], and psychology).

The fact that moral theology is not a science specifically distinct from the rest of theology does not mean that it must remain at the level of generality; it must, on the contrary, extend to all the particularities of its object (individual human action) insofar as this is compatible with its universality as a science. There is, however, something moral theology will never attain, and should refrain from trying to attain: to become a substitute for PRUDENCE. For regulation of a human act, in the concrete, prudence is irreplaceable. Particular application cannot be a science. Even moral science might attempt to solve certain general cases of conscience that are more or less typical; moral science will never resolve a particular case in the concrete situation with all the circumstances delineating it and making it absolutely particular. Moral theology aims only at bringing *principles* of moral conduct to light; it is the business of prudence to ascertain, in the here and now, which moral principles are to be employed, and how.

Nevertheless, neither can moral theology escape into a kind of heaven beyond the temporal. A practical science by nature is relevant to the concrete singular action to the extent that this is possible in a scientific consideration. Speaking of moral science, St. Thomas says that it "obtains its completion in particular consideration" (*Summa theologiae* 1a2ae, 6, prol.: *in particulari consideratione perficitur*). Thus moral theology should be especially attentive to the reality of the historical evolution of man. Human nature does not change in its essential principles, but these principles apply to man as a being engaged in time and achieving himself at his allotted period in history. From this consideration arises the realization that the method of moral theology must ensure recognition of norms relevant to the Christian not only of yesterday, or of the Middle Ages, but of his own age. Our increasing understanding, for instance, of how the human body functions, and the role that physiology plays in our physical and emotional inclinations, is of central concern to the moral theologian.

To regulate Christian conduct means to define what is worthy of a Christian living the new life received in Baptism and meant to develop into eternal life with God. With its view adjusted properly to a distinctively Christian existence, moral theology notes among the norms it considers those that follow from the fact of being human (i.e., the precepts of natural law), and the virtues simply of human nature; but its vision embraces norms and virtues as they are adhered to and exercised in a properly Christian existence. Moral theology or Christian ethics may well concern itself with matters with which the philosophical moralist is also concerned (e.g., feeding the hungry); but while the philosopher urges a certain course of action he does so with an eye to this world and this life alone. The moral theologian will urge a course of action because the Christ teaches us that in clothing the naked we are clothing fellow images of God, and are thereby also clothing him and building up the Kingdom of God in this world, which is to find its consummation in the next.

Despite its historical association with the sacrament of penance, moral theology cannot be reduced to the negative consideration of sins to avoid, to the mere cataloguing of what is forbidden and what is permitted. Such considerations can, of course, be useful for confessional practice; but they cannot constitute moral theology, which is not a science of sins, nor a morality of the bare minimum. The Christian life is the scope of moral theology; its aim is primarily the delineation of the positive rather than the negative features of that life. Moreover, there is not one morality for the generality of men and another for the elite; there is but one Christian morality; it defines the proper activity of every man in his progress, following the teachings and examples of Jesus Christ, toward eternal happiness the Triune God our creator, and the community of the blessed in heaven. The fundamental precept of this morality is that of charity, i.e., the love of God. The other precepts, including in the present order of things the Ten Commandments, simply spell out the demands of that charity (i.e., how we love God above all things, our neighbors as ourselves).

Moral theology, however, does not stop at the point where ascetical, mystical, or even what is commonly called ''spirituality'' theology begin. It covers the whole route of the progress toward God, toward an ever more unequivocal belonging to God. What is commonly called spirituality, ascetical or mystical theology, is simply either a part of moral theology, or a special type of consideration of subjects within its scope [cf. M. M. Labourdette, ''Connaissance pratique et savoir moral,'' *Revue thomiste* 48 (1948) 142–179]. This fact aids appreciation of how a moral theology of the ''speculative-practical'' type found in St. Thomas could be extended to include another plane and other categories, exploring a phenomenology of Christian existence.

Bibliography: M. D CHENU, ''L'Originalité de la morale de saint Thomas,'' *Initiation théologique,* ed. A. M. HENRY 3:7–12; *St. Thomas d'Aquin et la théologie* (Paris 1959). T. DEMAN, *Aux Origines de la théologie morale* (Paris 1951). L. B. GILLON, ''La Théologie morale et l'éthique de l'exemplarité personnelle,'' *Angelicum* 34 (1957) 241–259, 361–378; ''Morale et science,'' *ibid.* 35 (1958) 249–268. C. JOURNET, *Introduction à la théologie* (Paris 1947). M. M. LABOURDETTE, *Foi catholique et problèmes modernes* (Tournai 1954); ''Théologie morale,'' *Revue thomiste* 50 (1950) 192–230. F. P. MUÑIZ, *The Work of Theology,* tr. J. P. REID (Washington 1953). B. OLIVIER, ''Pour une théologie morale renouvelée,'' *Morale chrétienne et requêtes contemporaines* (Paris 1954) 219–255. H. D. ROBERT, ''Phénoménologie existentielle et morale thomiste,'' *ibid.* 197–217. J. M. RAMÍREZ, *De hominis beatitudine,* 3 v. (Madrid 1942–47) v.1. L. ROY, *La Certitude de la doctrine morale* (Quebec 1958). Y. SIMON, *Critique de la connaissance morale* (Paris 1934). W. A. WALLACE, *The Role of Demonstration in Moral Theology* (Washington 1962). R. MCCORMICK, and P. RAMSEY, *Doing Evil to Achieve Good: Moral Choice in Conflict Situations* (Chicago 1978). R. MCCORMICK, *Notes on Moral Theology, 1965 through 1980* (Washington, D.C. 1981); *Notes on Moral Theology, 1981 through 1984* (Washington, D.C. 1984). S. PINCKAERS, *Les sources de la morale chrétienne: sa méthode, son contenu, son histoire* (Paris 1985), Eng. tr. *The Sources of Christian Ethics*, tr. M. T. NOBLE (Washington, D.C. 1995). B. HOOSE, *Proportionalism: The American Debate and Its European Roots* (Washington, D.C. 1987). R. GULA, *Reason Informed by Faith: Foundations of Catholic Morality* (New York 1989). POPE JOHN PAUL II, *The Splendor of Truth (Veritatis Splendor)* (Boston 1993). C. CURRAN, *The Catholic Moral Tradition Today: A Synthesis* (Washington, D.C. 1999). C. KACZOR, ed., *Proportionalism: For and Against* (Milwaukee 2000). R. CESSARIO, *Introduction to Moral Theology* (Washington, D.C. 2001).

[M. M. LABOURDETTE/M. JOHNSON]

MORALES, CRISTÓBAL DE

The most important Spanish sacred composer after VICTORIA; b. Seville, *c.* 1500; d. Málaga?, between Sept. 4 and Oct. 7, 1553. The cathedral musicians at Seville during his youth included the brightest lights in the Peninsula—Francisco de la Torre, Alonso de Alva, Juan de Valera, Francisco de Peñalosa, Pedro de Escobar, and Pedro Fernández de Castilleja. Peñalosa, Escobar, and Juan de Anchieta (1462–1523) were the first sacred composers in Spain, and their influence on Morales admirably prepared him for a brilliant career as director of music in Ávila Cathedral (appointed 1526), Plasencia Cathedral (1528), and elsewhere. During 1531 he left Plasencia and on Sept. 1, 1535, began a decade as a singer in the papal choir. Although frequently ill in Rome, he published nearly all his major works before 1545, including 16 of his 21 Masses (2 v. Rome 1544). The second volume, dedicated to Paul III, opens with the Mass *Tu es vas electionis* in the pope's honor. Before Morales's death his Magnificats and motets were being published in Antwerp, Louvain, Nuremberg, and Wittenberg, and purchased by cathedrals as distant as Cuzco, Peru.

Upon returning home he was chapelmaster at the primatial cathedral of Toledo (Sept. 1, 1545–Aug. 9, 1547), then at Marchena, near Seville, and last at Málaga (Nov. 27, 1551). He was internationally acclaimed while he lived, and for a century after his death his works served as classic models everywhere throughout the Spanish dominions, including the New World. PALESTRINA based his *O sacrum convivium* Mass on Morales's motet of the same name and added optional voice parts to six verses from his Magnificats. Victoria founded his *Gaudeamus* Mass (1576) on Morales's 1538 peace cantata commissioned by Paul III; Francisco Guerrero and Juan Navarro were his personal pupils.

See Also: MUSIC, SACRED, HISTORY OF.

Bibliography: F. PEDRELL, ed., *Hispaniae schola musica sacra,* 8 v. in 2 (Barcelona 1894–98), v. 1 contains a Morales anthology. *Monumentos de la música española,* v. 11 (1952), 8 Masses from *Liber primus;* v. 13 (1953), 25 motets; v. 16 (1954), 4 Masses from *Liber secundus;* v. 17 (1956), 16 Magnificats. R. M. STEVENSON, *Spanish Cathedral Music in the Golden Age* (Berkeley 1961); *Die Musik in Geschichte und Gegenwart,* ed. F. BLUME (Kassel-Basel 1949–) 9:553–563; ''Cristóbal de Morales,'' *Journal of the American Musicological Society* (Boston 1948–) 6 (1953) 3–42. G. REESE, *Music in the Renaissance* (rev. ed. New York 1959). A. S. MCFARLAND, ''Cristóbal de Morales and the Imitation of the Past: Music for the Mass in Sixteenth-Century Rome'' (Ph.D.

diss. University of California at Santa Barbara 1999). K. S. PIETSCHMANN, "A Renaissance Composer Writes to His Patrons: Newly Discovered Letters from Cristóbal de Morales to Cosimo I de' Medici and Cardinal Alessandro Farnese," *Early Music,* 28 (2000) 383–400. D. M. RANDEL, ed., *The Harvard Biographical Dictionary of Music* (Cambridge, Mass. 1996) 606. N. SLONIMSKY, ed. *Baker's Biographical Dictionary of Musicians* (8th ed. New York 1992) 1247. J. A. SMITH, "The 16 Magnificats of Cristóbal de Morales: Elements of Style and Performance Practice" (Ph.D. diss. University of Texas 1976). R. STEVENSON, "Cristóbal de Morales," in *The New Grove Dictionary of Music and Musicians,* ed. S. SADIE, v. 12 (New York 1980) 553–558.

[R. STEVENSON]

MORALES, FRANCISCO DE

Franciscan missionary in Ecuador, Bolivia, and Peru from 1547 to 1567. His birth and death dates are unknown. He was born in Soria, Spain, and went to Peru during the administration of La Gasca, who recommended him to his successor as one of the few ecclesiastics from whom he could take counsel. After founding the convent of La Paz, Bolivia, Morales was sent to Quito, where he spent six years organizing the missionary work. He founded the Colegio de San Andrés for Indians, poor mestizos, and Spanish orphans, who were taught reading and writing, music, and some crafts. As provincial of Peru (1559–62) he vigorously opposed the perpetuation of the encomiendas, opposing in this the commissary general of his order, Luis de Zapata. He did not hesitate to criticize the government of the Viceroy Conde de Nieva, whom he considered reactionary in his treatment of the indigenous people. These differences of opinion were probably the chief reason for his return to Spain on Jan. 2, 1568, the date on which he sent to the Visitor from the Council of the Indies, Juan de Ovando, an important memorial setting forth his opinions on the encomienda system. In Spain he was guardian of the convent at Valladolid, the headquarters of the province of Concepción. In 1575 he took over the government of the province first as vicar and then as minister provincial. At the end of his term (1579) he was appointed visitor to the province of Castille. The last knowledge of him is a report, dated 1580, on Peruvian matters.

Bibliography: D. DE CÖRDOBA Y SALINAS, *Corónica franciscana de las provincias del Perú,* ed. L. G. CANEDO (2d ed. Washington 1957). L. G. CANEDO, "New Data regarding the Origins of the Franciscan Missions in Peru, 1532–1569," *Americas* 9 (1952–53): 315–348.

[L. G. CANEDO]

MORALES, JUAN BAUTISTA

Dominican missionary; b. Ecija, Andalusia, Spain, 1597; d. Funing, China, Sept. 17, 1664. In 1620 he accompanied 16 Dominicans to Manila; however, he was later ordained in Mexico. In 1622 he was appointed curate of the Chinese in Manila; he was later sent to Cambodia (1628–29) and Fukien (1633), where he continued the work of Angelo Cocchi, OP, so effectively that he is called the second founder of the Chinese mission. He opposed the Jesuits in the controversy over the Chinese rites and brought the matter to Rome (1645), but the final decision upholding Morales and the Dominican condemnation of Jesuit practices was not given until 1742. He was a devout missionary, zealous for souls, who, according to Vittorio RICCI, was mourned by his flock despite his rigorous and unyielding temperament. Morales was the author of *Historia evangelica del reyno de la China,* of a life of St. Dominic in Chinese, and of a grammar and vocabulary of the Chinese language.

Cristóbal de Morales.

Bibliography: B. M. BIERMANN, *Die Anfänge der neueren Dominikanermission in China* (Münster 1927). *Acta capitulorum generalium O.P.,* ed. B. M. REICHERT (*Monumenta Ordinis Fratrum Praedicatorum historica* 8; 1900).

[B. M. BIERMANN]

MORALES, MANUEL, ST.

Martyr, married layman; b. Feb. 8, 1898, Mesillas near Sombrerete, Zacatecas, Diocese of Durango, Mexico; d. Aug. 15, 1926, Puerto de Santa Teresa near Zacatecas. After Manuel's birth, his family moved to Chalchihuites, where he later met St. Luis BATIZ. He attend the Durango seminary but left to support his poor family, married, and sired three children. Known for his piety, he was secretary to the Circle of Catholic Workers and a member of the Mexican Youth for Catholic Action. As president of the National League, he announced at its first meeting that its mission was to peacefully petition the government to repeal laws suppressing religious liberty. After Batiz's arrest, he organized the locals to secure the priest's freedom. Instead he was himself arrested, tortured, then shot near Zacatecas. Morales was both beatified (Nov. 22, 1992) and canonized (May 21, 2000) with Cristobal MAGALLANES [*see* GUADALAJARA (MEXICO), MARTYRS OF, SS.] by Pope John Paul II.

Feast: May 25 (Mexico).

Bibliography: J. CARDOSO, *Los mártires mexicanos* (Mexico City 1953). V. GARCÍA JUÁREZ, *Los cristeros* (Fresnillo, Zac. 1990).

[K. I. RABENSTEIN]

MORALITY

The quality attributable to human action by reason of its conformity or lack of conformity to standards or rules according to which it should be regulated. This supposes on the one hand that human actions are voluntary and responsible, and on the other, that there are standards and rules by which human conduct should be measured, a position not admitted by all contemporary philosophers. Existentialists, for example, dislike all universal norms and principles. The atheists among them have disposed of traditional morality by saying that anything a man chooses to do freely is morally permissible. Other contemporary philosophers, for different reasons, have a flexible, or even absent, attitude with regard to norms. Catholic writers agree that there are proper and binding norms of conduct, and therefore that morality in the strict sense is found in man's rational choices and is indeed the paramount aspect of human acts. They distinguish the physical from the moral aspect of an act, saying that the former refers to its physiological existence and that the latter is the relation of the act, and of the whole man, to the value of man. Since this is his supreme GOOD, the morality of a human act is the relation of the act to the supreme good of its agent.

Ethical Positions and Norms. A presupposed philosophy and/or theology will affect what kind of moral norms, if any, are to be considered. Moral theology or Christian ethics will differ from moral philosophy or philosophical ethics according to the sources of knowing such norms; and each will differ according to the different philosophy or theology upon which each is based (for some of this variety, *see* MORAL THEOLOGY [CONTEMPORARY TRENDS]).

All Catholic moralists and, in fact, all professedly Christian and theistic moralists should agree fundamentally that man's ultimate end is somehow connected with his Creator. In other words, that moral goodness means conformity in some way with the nature or will of God. Divergences occur in determining more proximate norms for learning what is or is not in conformity with man's ultimate end. For Catholics, a more proximate objective norm has been the nature of man as created by God, with all his relationships: to God, to fellow human beings, and to himself, as known by reason and by revelation interpreted by the living teaching authority of the Church. However, at present not all Catholic writers agree even on these points.

Many modern writers propose man's self-development as a norm, understanding such development to include a greater degree of knowledge, a balanced personality, and a comfortable degree of self-satisfaction and enjoyment. There is a great divergence in judging what these terms mean, in judging which acts or objects really contribute to such development, and even in judging what sort of norm or faculty may be used to discover which acts or objects will promote proper development. Self-development can well be a norm for judging the morality of actions even in accord with traditional Catholic thought, if measured by a full understanding of what is for the best welfare of the self in relation to the ultimate end.

Species of Morality. The distinction of the morality of actions into good, bad, or indifferent in kind, as well as the distinction between intrinsic and extrinsic morality, has been widely neglected, especially with a blurring of the distinction between subjective and objective morality. While all Catholic moralists have always agreed and still agree that the most decisive element in human morality is in the person, some modern moralists refuse to consider a distinction between this morality in the agent and a morality attributed analogously to certain described actions.

Determinants. The position of such moralists has led them to deny that morality can ever be legitimately attributed to any acts objectively considered, unless such acts are described by such a prejudicial term as "murder," which implies *unjust* killing. Some such writers fail to realize that the older distinction between the *object* and the *circumstances* of a moral action did not necessarily mean that the *object* signified some kind of physical action without any circumstances. Even the term "killing" necessarily includes more content than just a physical act; in ordinary usage it denotes an act by which a living being is deprived of life. Even in times past, all Catholic moralists agreed that there was no absolute moral imperative against all killing, nor even against all killing of a human being; but in times past all did agree that the direct killing of an innocent human being was always immoral—at least apart from a certain command of the Creator who possesses ultimate dominion over all of creation.

The traditional use of the term ''circumstances'' as a determinant of morality beyond the object, referred to circumstances which could affect the morality of an action, other than those included in the definition of the object or act.

Objective and Subjective Morality. The modern objection that morality is never present apart from the intention of the agent misses the essential idea of the distinction between objective (or material) and subjective (or formal) morality. It is certainly true that morality is essentially in the act of the human will, but that does not mean that there cannot be a proper but derived use of the term with regard to objects and circumstances. When traditional Catholic moralists speak of an object or of an object with certain defined circumstances, as intrinsically or objectively evil in a moral sense, it is understood that this means that it would be morally wrong to intend such an action in such defined circumstances, regardless of further circumstances or intention.

Moral and Physical Evil. In considering the object of a human action, Catholic moralists have always recognized a difference in the meaning of moral evil and physical evil, although at times some have used the terms in a confused way. Evil, in general, was understood to mean the lack of something which should be present. To speak of physical evil was to speak merely of such a lack in the physical make-up of things; a lack of conformity to what some reality should normally be. Thus, a human being with only four fingers on one hand, or with six fingers, was said to be lacking conformity with what should normally be the number of fingers on a human hand, with no reference to morality. It was understood that ordinarily it would also be morally evil for one human being to inflict such a physical evil on another human being, although it was generally admitted that circumstances and intention could alter the matter. Thus, it was commonly agreed that amputation or excision of a part of the human body can be morally good in circumstances in which that part constitutes a threat to the whole human organism. For this reason, the loss of a finger was not considered a moral evil even in a remote sense, but only a physical evil, which it would be illicit to intend unless there were a good reason for doing so. On the other hand, the direct killing of an innocent human being was considered an objectively immoral action, whose only imaginable justification could be a direct command of the Creator who had the absolute dominion over human life.

Some modern moralists, including some Catholic theologians, avoid this sort of terminology. They prefer to use terms like ''ontic,'' ''premoral,'' ''non-moral'' evil to include, apparently, what traditional Catholic terminology classed as ''objective'' or ''intrinsic'' moral evil, but also to include what traditional terminology called ''physical'' evil. As mentioned above, there was some confusion between the terms ''physical evil'' and ''objective moral evil'' in some older manuals, especially in the treatment of the so-called principle of DOUBLE EFFECT at least in their examples. However, this does not prove that the distinction itself is useless.

Values and Disvalues. Instead of speaking of moral good and evil, many modern Catholic moralists prefer to follow what had previously been mainly non-Catholic philosophical terminology and speak rather of values to be achieved or preserved and of disvalues to be avoided. Practically speaking, the use of the terms ''values'' and ''disvalues'' in morality differs little if at all from the older terminology among Catholic moralists of *good* and *evil* in morality.

Again difficulties and divergences arise in determining the norm or norms for judging what is a value and what is a disvalue, as well as in determining whether there are any disvalues so great that they may never be directly chosen as a means of achieving certain positive values. All admit that many human choices involve both values and disvalues, good and evil.

Often overlooked are values in what might be called a religious or spiritual sense. These can include the value of self-denial and sacrifice (the Cross); the value of patient suffering; the value of helping others even at a seeming loss (disvalue?) to oneself; in general, the value of submission to God; and, finally, the value of achieving the real end of man's existence (union with God), even at the cost of losing the greatest of merely human values. Nevertheless, even some who neglect man's relation to God, still recognize some of these values as helps towards character development.

Moral Absolutes. What was explained above as objective moral evil is the basis of most moral absolutes. When the more traditional moralists state that an action is objectively morally evil, they mean that such an action would be morally wrong as a direct object of a human will in all imaginable circumstances in the ordinary course of affairs. Accordingly, although all killing involves some form of physical evil to a living being, it was and is not considered absolutely morally evil objectively, but needs further determination by at least some added circumstances. On the other hand, the killing of an innocent human being was and is considered a moral evil, even though the traditional principle of double effect would, under certain conditions, allow such a killing to be the unintended but foreseen event of a directly willed action. On the contrary, the direct killing of a cat would not be considered an objective moral evil, even though it is a physical evil for the cat. It could be a moral evil or a moral good for the killer depending on further circumstances as well as on the intent. To deny that there are any objective moral absolutes is tantamount to saying that it is impossible to describe any action in such a way that in no imaginable further circumstances in the ordinary course of affairs could such an action be justified, and any person who felt justified in doing such an action would be laboring under a misapprehension or false conscience.

Some who profess to deny the possibility of moral absolutes actually restrict such a judgment to personal morality and especially sexual morality, while insisting on absolutes in social matters. For example, the same writer may voice an opinion that premarital sex, masturbation, adultery, and homosexual acts can be morally good in some circumstances, but that the use of nuclear armaments or even nuclear power sources are absolutely immoral.

The Notion of Moral Obligation. The connection between moral obligation, and thus of morality, and the relationship of man to his Creator is often overlooked in modern discussions of morality. In an analysis of the meanings of ''ought,'' ''must,'' and similar words, some common-sense ideas are often neglected. An instance of such an idea is that notions of obligation are concerned with a sort of conditioned necessity, and do not always have a tie-in with morality. For example, to say that a bridge player who bids four spades *must* take ten tricks, has nothing directly to do with morality. It only suggests that if he does not take ten tricks, he has failed in that round of play. So also with the *obligation* of religious rules in most religious orders and congregations. To say that a religious *must* keep silence, means that if he/she does not keep proper silence, he/she is not fulfilling the perfection of that form of life, but it does not imply any sin. Most regulations in business enterprises are similar. *If* one wishes to remain a member of the organization in good standing, one *must* follow such regulations. To fail to do so does not imply immorality, but may endanger the person's position in the organization. The condition implied in moral obligations might be stated: if you wish to achieve the purpose for which you exist, you must do certain things and you must avoid doing certain other things.

Bibliography: H. ALLARD, ''Recent Work in Moral Theology: In Defense of Objective Morality,'' *Clergy Review* 61 (1976) 191–195. S. PAGAN, ''No More Sin?'' *Catholic Mind* 75 (January 1977) 29–40 (reprinted from *Doctrine and Life* 26 [1976] 375–388). T. GILBY, ed., *Principles of Morality in St. Thomas Aquinas, Summa Theologiae* (60 v., London, New York 1965–1976) v. 18. R. MCCORMICK, ''Notes on Moral Theology,'' *Theological Studies* 29 (1968) 679–741, esp. 707–718; 32 (1971) 66–122, esp. 66.80; 34 (1973) 53–102, esp. 53–65; 36 (1975) 77–129, esp. 84–100; 37 (1976) 70–199, esp. 71–87; 38 (1977) 57–114, esp. 58–84; all of which give many further references. V. MCNAMARA, ''Approaches to Christian Morality,'' *Catholic Mind* 75 (October 1977) 30–37 (reprinted from: ''Approaching Christian Morality,'' *Furrow* 28 [1977] 213–220).

[T. J. HIGGINS/J. J. FARRAHER]

MORALITY, SYSTEMS OF

A system of morality or moral system is a method of forming one's conscience properly regarding the moral aspect of an action that is being contemplated with a view to performing or not performing it.

Purpose of a Moral System. The basic reason for a moral system is due to the fact that a person is frequently in doubt whether a certain course of action is good or evil. In such a case, if he performs the action while in practical doubt, he sins, for by doing what he thinks may be wrong, he shows that he is prepared to do evil. But a moral system will help him—at least at times—to achieve a practical certainty that he is free to perform the action, so that if he does perform, it he will commit no formal sin (*see* DOUBT, MORAL).

A person could, indeed, be in doubt as to which of two good courses of action is more pleasing to God. But in the treatment of moral systems, the only dilemma considered is the uncertainty as to whether one is commanded under pain of sin to perform an action or may lawfully omit it—law or liberty. This includes the doubt as to whether one is forbidden to do something or may lawfully do it.

Types of Certainty. From the fact that one who performs an action while in practical doubt as to its lawfulness commits a sin, it follows that before one may act in favor of liberty, he must have practical certainty that his action will not be sinful. This principle is corroborated by the words of St. Paul: ''All that is not from faith is sin'' (Rom 14.23). In this context, theologians understand the word ''faith'' to mean ''certainty that one is doing right.'' However, this principle must be understood in the light of the fact that there are various types of certainty.

Philosophically, certainty, the assent of the intellect to a proposition as true, without fear of the opposite, is threefold—metaphysical, physical, and moral (*see* CERTITUDE). In moral problems only the third type is possible, at least ordinarily. But moral certainty has various degrees. First, we distinguish direct and indirect (or reflex) certainty. Direct certainty is that which is derived from an investigation of the moral problem itself, without recourse to reflex principles.

Yet direct certainty can be twofold—direct certainty in the strict sense, and direct certainty in the broad sense. The former excludes all reasonable possibility that the opposite may be true. For example, on a Thursday I can have this type of certainty that I am allowed to eat meat. Again, I can have direct certainty in the strict sense that it would be a grave sin to kill a baby who is playing on the floor before me. There is no possibility for an intelligent person to have a doubt about such propositions.

Direct certainty in the broad sense excludes not the possibility but only the prudent probability that the opposite is true. For example, a young man about to receive the Sacrament of Holy Orders must have direct certainty that he has been validly baptized. But if he procures a baptismal certificate, copied from a church register, testifying that he was baptized, nothing more is required to furnish direct certainty that he did validly receive Baptism. It is possible that the baptizing priest did not pronounce the essential words of the Sacrament or did not pour the water correctly, but there is no reasonable probability of such an occurrence. This direct certainty in the broad sense is all that the Church demands even for Sacraments so important as Baptism and Holy Orders.

Actually, this type of certainty is all that we can have, in many of our daily activities, that we are acting safely. We buy and use pills, confident that they will not harm us, though it is possible that they contain poison. A motorist drives his car through a street intersection with a sense of security when the green light assures him that he is safe; yet, it is possible that another driver will come through the red light. We could not go through life reasonably if we tried to eliminate all possibility of harm. We could not wait for a chemical analysis of a bottle of pills before taking them. Similarly, a priest about to celebrate Mass in a church where he is a visitor would act unreasonably if he called for an analysis of the wine, though it is possible that it is not true grape wine, and in that case the Consecration will be invalid. Evidently God, as well as the Church, does not require us to seek greater assurance than direct certainty in the wide sense that we are acting lawfully even when grave moral problems confront us.

Indirect certainty, on the other hand, does not exclude even the reasonable probability that the opposite is true; nevertheless, it can sometimes furnish a sufficient basis for acting in favor of liberty with the assurance that one is not committing formal sin. This takes place through the aid of REFLEX PRINCIPLES that can sometimes transform a probable opinion in favor of liberty into practical certainty that one is not bound by a law. (As is evident, in the dilemma we picture, between law and liberty, one may always follow the safer side, the opinion in favor of law, without fear of committing sin. But the chief purpose of a moral system is to inform us when we may lawfully follow the opinion in favor of liberty.)

Reflex Principles. A reflex principle is a general norm for the regulation of human conduct, applicable to problems of conscience for the purpose of determining when a person may act for liberty despite the probability of a law to the opposite. Probably he is bound by a law, but probably he is not bound. It is reasonable to presume that God does not always demand that there be direct certainty for liberty before one can consider himself free from a law. If God required this strict norm of conduct, human life would become well-nigh unbearable, since there are so many occasions when a person, even after he has studied a problem of conscience adequately, is unable to determine with certainty whether or not he is bound by some obligation. In other words, in His goodness and mercy God sometimes allows us to act for liberty, even when the arguments for liberty are only probable and there are also probable arguments in favor of law. When we say that an opinion is probable, we mean that the arguments in support of it carry some weight, though they are not fully convincing.

When the dilemma between liberty and law occurs, reflex principles may be applicable. Such principles would be: ''A doubtful law does not bind,'' or ''In a doubt the possessor is to be favored.'' When a reflex principle has been properly applied, the result is indirect or practical certainty.

In using a reflex principle in favor of liberty, we do not impugn the truth that one who acts for liberty with a practical doubt as to the lawlessness of his action commits sin. For, though the arguments for liberty still remain speculatively only probable, the opinion in favor of liberty has become indirectly but practically certain through the proper use of the reflex principles. Objectively the course for liberty may be forbidden; but in such an event there has been a prudent (though erroneous) judgment in favor of liberty, so that the action is only a material, not a formal, sin. (Below we shall see that when there is danger of another evil besides the material sin, the use of reflex principles is per se forbidden.) And we can safely presume that God permits such a material sin as long as there has been an adequate attempt to obtain direct certainty and a sincere and honest use of the reflex principles, so that men may be able to act with ''the freedom of the glory of the sons of God'' (Rom 8.21).

We have an example of the proper use of reflex principles in the case of a person who has been gravely tempted to sexual desires, and afterward doubts whether or not he gave consent and consequently whether or not he is bound to confess them as grave sins. If the arguments in favor of the opinion that he did not consent are sufficiently probable to render the opposite opinion truly doubtful, he need not confess these desires as serious sins. (The degree of probability required for this is disputed among theologians, as can be seen in the articles on the different systems.) For, in that case, the obligation to confess the desires is truly doubtful, and the reflex principle can be applied: ''A doubtful law does not bind.'' If the person had actually yielded, he has an objective obligation to confess the sins, but his failure to do so in the case described is only a material sin for which God will not hold him responsible in conscience. In such an event, the sin of evil desire can be taken away by an act of perfect contrition or by the reception of the Sacrament of Reconciliation in which these sins are not told but the contrition of the penitent extends in a general way to all his mortal sins, or, in the opinion of many theologians, it is indirectly remitted in the reception of the Eucharist.

Another case of indirect certainty is that of the priest who is accustomed to mark the recitation of the canonical hours with the string in his breviary. One day he doubts whether or not he has recited Vespers, but finds the string at the beginning of Compline. He may prudently apply the reflex principle: ''From what commonly occurs a prudent presumption can be drawn,'' and satisfy his obligation for the day by saying only Compline.

It must be noted that the first obligation of one confronted by a problem of conscience is to use adequate diligence to obtain direct certainty. It is only when he has attempted this, with an amount of effort proportionate to the importance of the matter, that he may seek indirect certainty through the use of reflex principles.

Exceptions to Use of Reflex Principles. The right to follow the course for liberty through the use of reflex principles does not apply to every case of doubtful conscience. For this reason it was stated above that indirect certainty can sometimes furnish a sufficient basis for acting in favor of liberty. Actually, this is per se permissible only when the sole evil that is to be feared is a material sin. For even a material sin is something evil, since it is objectively out of harmony with the order willed by God. Nevertheless, a material sin is immeasurably less evil than a formal sin, so that we can presume that God will sometimes tolerate the commission of a material sin in order to permit reasonable liberty to men, so often beset by doubts of conscience. But sometimes the use of a reflex principle in favor of liberty will entail the danger of another evil that cannot be averted by the use of the principle and that the agent is bound to avoid. For example, if a priest celebrates Mass with a liquid that is very probably (but not certainly) grape wine, on the score that a doubtful law does not bind—in this case the law forbidding the use of any liquid but grape wine for Mass—he does wrong. For if the liquid is not actually wine, the use of the reflex principle will not prevent an invalid Consecration—a grave evil that the priest is bound to avoid. In such a case, therefore, the opinion for law (the safer opinion, as it is called) even though less probable must per se be followed. In the case described, this means that the priest must abstain from celebrating Mass if he cannot get a liquid that is certainly wine. As was said above, such certainty can be direct certainty in the broad sense.

Theologians distinguish under three general headings the cases in which the use of reflex principles is per se forbidden in order to render practically certain a speculatively probable opinion in favor of liberty.

1. When there is danger that by following the opinion in favor of liberty one may endanger the validity of a Sacrament. Thus, in addition to the case given above, one may not per se use for Baptism what is only probably true water. A priest may not per se use chrism or the oil of catechumens for the Anointing of the Sick, even though probably these oils would suffice for validity, but must use the oil of the sick. A confessor must per se have moral certainty that the penitent has true contrition before he can absolve him.

2. When there is danger that some harm of body or of soul may come to oneself if a probable opinion for liberty is followed. Thus, a person commits a grave sin by playing ''Russian roulette,'' pointing at his head a revolver with a cartridge in one of the six chambers and pulling the trigger. For, although there is only one chance in six that he will be killed, he may not take this chance, because a reflex principle will not help if the chamber with the cartridge happens to be under the hammer. Again, if a person goes into a proximate occasion of sin without a reason, he sins, even though there is some probability that he will not sin. (Theologians are not in agreement as to the degree of probability of sinning there must be in order to constitute the occasion a proximate occasion. However, all admit the principle.)

3. When an action will probably inflict some harm on a fellow man, not avoidable by the use of a reflex principle. Thus, if a pharmacist has in stock 20 bottles bearing the label of a patent medicine but knows that one of them through some accident contains poison, he may not sell a bottle to a cus-

tomer, even though much more probably this bottle does not contain the poison. Reflex principles will not help the customer if he happens to get the bottle with the poison. The pharmacist must destroy the whole lot or return the bottles to the wholesale dealer, explaining the situation. Again, a jury may not return a verdict of guilty against an accused man, even though very probably he committed the crime. They must have direct certainty of his guilt—at least direct certainty in the broad sense.

We say that in the cases we have described one must per se follow the opinion for law, even though the opinion for liberty is much more probable, in order to avoid an evil that may ensue from the use of the opinion for liberty and that one is bound to avoid. But there can be instances in which one may *per accidens* follow the opinion for liberty, even though the evil will probably occur. Such is the case when the nonuse of the opinion for liberty may entail an even greater evil. For example, if an infant is dying and no liquid that is certainly water is available, one may use doubtful matter, such as weak tea, to confer Baptism conditionally (with the obligation to repeat the Sacrament afterward with certain matter if this is possible). For, although the danger of baptizing invalidly is an evil, the danger that the child may die without Baptism is a greater evil. Through a similar line of reasoning, it follows that a priest could anoint a dying person with chrism if he cannot get oil of the sick in time; a confessor could impart conditional absolution to a person who is doubtfully disposed, if there is reason to fear that he will not otherwise return to confession. Again, if a sick man is desperately in need of medicine and is likely to die without it, the pharmacist could take a chance and dispense to him a bottle from the consignment with one bottle of poison (previously giving a warning). The principle governing these cases is that at times one may choose the lesser of two evils. They are exceptions to the exceptions regarding the use of reflex principles.

History of Moral Systems. The scientific formulation of moral systems is comparatively new in the Church, though even from the early centuries we find indications of the use of a probable opinion as the basis of the formation of a practically certain conscience. Thus, St. Gregory of Nazianzus, in the 4th century, asserted against the severity of the Novatians that a second marriage is not forbidden since the prohibition of such a union is doubtful (*In sancta lumina* 19; *Patrolgia Graeca* [Paris 1857–66] 36:358). Apparently, in those early days, individual cases of conscience were solved reasonably with due regard to God's mercy and with proper respect for His law.

In medieval times, the common method of solving a doubtful conscience seems to have been a form of rigorism, to judge by the statements of some prominent writers. Thus, St. Bonaventure says: "If a person's conscience doubts with probability whether something is a mortal sin, he is obliged to abstain from it while the doubt remains" (*In 4 Sent.,* 17.2.1 ad 4, ed. Quaracci, 4.458). And William of Auxerre asserts: "It is a rule that if anyone doubts whether something is a mortal sin and does it, he sins mortally" [*Summa aurea,* 2, tr. 29, c. 1, q. 3, (ed. Pigouchet, Paris 1500) fol. 92.5]. It can be doubted, however, whether in practice this rigoristic norm was used in its full literal sense to any great extent in the Middle Ages. According to Prümmer (*Manuale theologiae moralis,* I, n. 345), the prevalent usage in medieval times was rather probabiliorism according to which the opinion for liberty can be followed if it is clearly more probable than the opinion for law.

The fundamental principle of PROBABILISM was first clearly enunciated by Bartholomew Medina, OP, who wrote in 1577: "It seems to me that if there is a probable opinion, it is lawful to follow it, even though the opposite is more probable" (Comment. in 1a, 2ae *Summa Theologiae* 19.6). Probabilism then became an accepted system, and was followed moderately by many theologians. Unfortunately, others, such as Sanchez, Diana, and Caramuel, made use of it to support excessively lenient views. As a result, 17th-century popes, Alexander VII and Innocent XI, found it necessary to condemn lengthy lists of propositions too favorable to liberty, including the basic principle of laxism, i.e., that even the slightest probability will justify one in acting for liberty (H. Denzinger, *Enchiridion symbolorum* [Freiburg 1963] 2021–65; 2101–66). Moreover, in 1656, Alexander VII recommended to the general chapter of the Dominicans that they defend probabiliorism, and the members of this order were the chief exponents of this system for many years. The most outstanding exponent of probabiliorism, it would seem, was Charles Billuart, OP, in the 18th century (*De conscientiae diss.,* 6).

The principal exponents of probabilism, as enunciated by Medina, continued to be the Jesuits. In 1680, Innocent XI commanded a letter to be sent to the superior general of the Jesuits, stating that the members of the society were free to teach and to write against the opinion that in the conflict of a less probable opinion with an opinion clearly more probable, it is lawful to follow the former. However, the pope did not oblige the Jesuits to give up probabilism.

Another development in the 17th century was the effort of the Jansenists to introduce the system of RIGORISM, the extreme opposite of LAXISM. The basic principle of this system, that it is not allowed to follow even the most probable opinion for liberty (but that direct certainty must always be had), was condemned, together with other Jansenist teachings, by Pope Alexander VIII in 1690 (H. Denzinger, *Enchiridion symbolorum* [Freiburg 1963] 2363). A slight modification of rigorism, known as TUTIORISM, which permits only a most probable opinion for liberty to be followed, though not formally condemned, has found few followers since the Church's rejection of rigorism.

The 18th century witnessed the propagation of the system of EQUIPROBABILISM, especially because of the influence of St. Alphonsus Liguori, who was declared the patron of confessors and moralists by Pope Pius XII. Alphonsus was first a probabiliorist, then a probabilist, and finally in 1762 announced himself as a defender of equiprobabilism. This system steers a middle course between probabiliorism and probabilism. It differs from the former in that it holds that an opinion for liberty that is as probable as the opinion for law may be followed (at least when the doubt concerns the existence of the law). It disagrees with probabilism in that it holds that an opinion for liberty that is definitely less probable than the opinion for law may not be followed. St. Alphonsus was not the author of this system, though he is its best-known proponent. Indeed, a statement of Suárez could be quoted in support of equiprobabilism: ''Greater probability is a kind of moral certainty, if the excess of probability is certain'' (*De legibus,* 8.3.19).

In recent times, the system of COMPENSATIONISM has been advocated by some theologians. According to this system, the benefits of liberty in each particular case of doubt must be sufficient to compensate for the danger of violating the law; hence, the degree of probability required to justify the use of liberty varies from case to case.

Thus, in the course of time, seven moral systems have been proposed: rigorism, tutiorism, probabiliorism, compensationism, equiprobabilism, probabilism, and laxism. Today the great majority of moralists defend either equiprobabilism or probabilism; comparatively few adhere to probabiliorism or compensationism.

See Also: CONSCIENCE; MORAL THEOLOGY, HISTORY OF; DOUBT, MORAL

Bibliography: J. M. HARTY, *The Catholic Encyclopedia* (New York 1907–14) 12:441–446. T. DEMAN, *Dictionnaire de théologie catholique* (Paris 1903–50) 13.1:417–619. M. ZALBA, *Theologiae moralis compendium,* 2 v. (Madrid 1958) 1:671–734. J. AERTNYS and C. A. DAMEN, *Theologia moralis,* 2 v. (16th ed. Turin 1950) 1:79–126. D. PRÜMMER, *Manuale theologiae moralis,* 3 v. (10th ed. Barcelona 1945–46) 1:324–352.

[F. J. CONNELL]

MORALITY PLAYS

A type of drama that developed in the late Middle Ages and is distinguished from the earlier religious types mainly by its use of dramatized allegory in which abstract virtues and vices are personified. It attained its greatest popularity in England and France.

The major distinction between the cycle plays (*see* DRAMA, MEDIEVAL) and the morality plays is that between dogmatic and moral theology; the cycle play presents the history of salvation and the morality play the way to salvation. The essential theme of the morality play is the conflict between the forces of good (the good angel, the virtues) and the forces of evil (the bad angel or devil, the vices) for possession of man's soul. The allegorical motifs and devices employed in presenting this theme in the various morality plays that survive all point to their kinship with the literature of preaching, particularly to that group of treatises in Latin and in the European vernaculars that was concerned with the condition of man's life from birth to death, usually titled *Speculum* and subtitled *Liber de Pater Noster,* in some instances bearing the latter title alone (*see* PREACHING [MEDIEVAL ENGLISH]).

Pater Noster Play. From the earliest days the Church regarded the Credo as the rule of faith and the Pater Noster as the rule of life and made both prayers the subject of instruction, meditation, and sermons. Tertullian explained the significance of each of the seven petitions of the Pater Noster, and throughout the centuries various schemata were developed so that by the 12th century HUGH OF SAINT-VICTOR, in *De Quinque Septenis seu septanariis opusculum,* listed the seven vices that the seven petitions guard against by supplicating the seven gifts of the Holy Ghost, which endow the soul with the seven virtues and lead to the beatitudes. In a later work he explicitly opposed the seven deadly sins to the seven petitions of the Pater Noster. When the Fourth LATERAN COUNCIL (1215–16) decreed that the faithful confess their sins and receive the Eucharist at least once a year, a need arose for manuals of instructions for priests and laity, and the traditional development of the Credo and Pater Noster form their basis. Some, e.g., Chaucer's *Parson's Tale,* dealt only with the Sacrament of Penance; others followed the pattern of the *Liber de Pater Noster.*

It is not merely coincidental that the first allusions to the morality plays in England and on the Continent occurred in the 14th century, the York *Play of the Pater Noster* in 1378 and the *Gieux des sept vertuz et des sept pechiez mortelz* of Tours in 1390, when the liturgical drama had passed from the Latin to the vernacular and, for the most part, from clerical to civic control. In England the emergence of the morality plays both in time and place coincided with the preaching reform of JOHN OF THORESBY, Archbishop of York (1352–74).

The Creed Play (*Articula fidei catholicae*) had its impetus in the same preaching reforms and literature. No text has survived, however, and records exist only for York. The play was presented to the Corpus Christi Guild by William Revetor, a chantry priest, to be performed at York every tenth year. That it was of considerable length is attested to by the fact that a transcription made in 1455 filled 20 quires and that the Corpus Christi Guild possessed elaborate properties to be used in the production. It was substituted for the York Cycle in 1435. Five performances are recorded between 1483 and 1535. A petition to present the play was refused by Dr. Hutton, Dean of York, in 1568 and the play has not been heard of since.

It is evident that the Pater Noster plays did not evolve from the cycle or miracle plays, but constitute an analogous or parallel development. The town records of York, Beverley, and Lincoln and the ''returns'' made to Richard II in 1389 attest to this development. WYCLIF alluded to the York *Play of the Pater Noster* in 1378; five performances are recorded between 1399 and 1572. After the performance of 1572 the books were given over for correction to Archbishop Grindal of York and disappeared from sight. Two performances are recorded for Beverley in 1441 and 1467, and four for Lincoln between 1398 and 1521. As to the origin, management, and nature of the play the records of York and Beverley yield little information; those of Lincoln, none at all. The ''returns'' reveal that the Guild of the Oratio Dominici had been organized in York to manage and perform the play, which later passed into the hands of the York Merchants' Guild (1462). In 1588 the York Pater Noster play was substituted for the Corpus Christi plays. The Beverley play was similar in scope to that of York. The number of crafts assigned to the *Pater Noster play* in Beverley in 1441 was almost equal to and in 1467 exceeded the number assigned to the cycle plays, and the stations assigned to the pageant wagons for the *Play of the Pater Noster* in 1467 were, with but one exception, the same as those stations that had been assigned to the cycle plays in 1449.

All conjectures as to the content and nature of the Beverley *Play of the Pater Noster* must be based chiefly on the two entries in the Beverley Town Minute Book of 1441 and 1467. Both entries record the date on which the play was to be given and the assignment of crafts to the pageants. The number of crafts assigned to the play and the length of time allotted for the preparation and performance indicate that it was an undertaking equal to the production of the cycle plays. The management of the plays was the same and suggests the possibility that the *Play of the Pater Noster* was actually a series of semi-independent but related plays, a cycle of morality plays. As to the subject matter of these plays, there is only the evidence of the titles of the individual pageants, one for each of the seven deadly sins and ''Viciose'' (possibly the Sinful Man), and the generic title *Ludus de Pater Noster.* The returns state that the York play had been put together to treat the utility of the Lord's Prayer, and that in it an equal number of vices and sins were reproved and virtues commended, and ''therefore, it was of great influence for the salvation of souls.''

Virtues vs. Vices. Of the English plays that have survived, the *Castle of Perseverance* (*c.* 1425), is possibly the most closely allied to the Pater Noster plays. Staged not on pageant wagons, but like the Cornish cycle on five fixed stages in an open place, it presented the struggle of the forces of good and evil for the possession of Humanum Genus (literally, the human race) and in the concluding Debate of the Four Daughters of God dramatically presents the part played by the Incarnation in mankind's redemption. In the extant plays, three major plots were employed: the Conflict of Vices and Virtues, the Summons of Death, and the Debate of the Four Daughters. The theme of conflict is explicit in all the plays except the *Pride of Life* and EVERYMAN, which are built on the plot of the Summons of Death, but it is implicit even in these plays. The Debate of the Four Daughters is an auxiliary plot employed in the *Castle of Perseverance* and is not used independently in any morality play. It is employed in only one other play, *Respublica* (1553), wherein it is clearly reminiscent of the *Castle of Perseverance.*

Three of the plays, the *Castle of Perseverance, Mundus et Infans* (printed 1522), and Henry Medwall's (fl. 1490) *Nature,* present the lifelong struggle between the Vices and Virtues for the soul of man and are therefore called full-scope morality plays. Each differs from the others in the traditional devices or motifs by means of which the struggle is represented. In the *Castle of Perseverance,* Humanum Genus is directly presented as the center of strife between his good angel and the virtues and his bad angel and the vices, who, in turn, are under the leadership of the sources of temptation, the World, the Flesh, and the Devil. Implicit in the plot is the device of the ages of man, for Humanum Genus is presented as newly baptized, as leading a life of sin until he is 40, as persevering in good for 20 years, and, at 60, falling into the vice of old age, covetousness. *Mundus et Infans* portrays the same lifelong struggle by means of the same device. The central figure appears first as Infans (the Chylde), and proceeds through each of the ''seven ages,'' attaining a new name and a corresponding vice at each period of life, until Age and Repentance finally overtake him. The forces of good are economically represented by Conscyence and the Perseveraunce, of evil by the Worlde and Foly, who is the sum of the seven deadly sins. In *Nature,* the forces of evil are again servants of the World;

they are presented, however, in a new motif, the sins under the leadership of Sensuality, the virtues under Reason. The theme of life as a journey appears in the 15th-century French *Bien avisé, mal avisé.*

Everyman, the *Pride of Life,* the *Castle of Perseverance, Mundus et Infans,* and *Nature* are universal in subject matter and appeal. Each member of the medieval audience identified himself with Everyman, knowing that the weaknesses of Humanum Genus and the follies of the Chylde were his own. Other 15th-century morality plays retained the ''otherwordly'' intent, but like *Mynd, Wyll and Understanding* (*c.* 1460) preached to a special audience (in this case to religious), or, like *Mankynd* (*c.* 1473) and *Hyckescorner,* against the specific vices of particular groups and of a particular time. John RASTELL's *Interlude on the Nature of the Four Elements* (1519), although it preserves its otherworldly purpose in its contention that true learning leads the soul nearer to God, is concerned primarily with the presentation of scientific information in the vernacular. The struggle between Reason and Sensuality (Studious Desire and Sensual Appetite) differs from the conflict in *Nature* in that it is a struggle for the mind rather than for the soul of man and is preserved chiefly to afford comic relief in the realistic tavern scenes and in the antics of Sensuality and Ignorance to the long lectures on science delivered by Nature and Experyence.

In the *Interlude on the Nature of the Four Elements* and its contemporary play *Magnyfycence,* thc plot and machinery of the early religious morality play have been taken over simply as a convenient vehicle, in the former for presenting information, in the latter for the double purpose of teaching a political lesson and satirizing a political regime. Of the two plays, *Magnyfycence* definitely marks the break from the earlier morality plays. In the *Four Elements,* Rastell endeavored to bridge the gap between the otherworldliness of the earlier morality plays and the worldliness of his own productions.

Skelton's *Magnyfycence* (1533), however, is clearly of this world. Magnyfycence is a ruler, who, deceived by false courtiers, the court vices, and ruined through their connivance, is left to the mercy of Adversity and Poverty and so falls into the clutches of Despair. Rescued from self-destruction by Good Hope, he is advised by the loyal courtiers, the virtues of a wise sovereign, and after confessing to Redress and accepting the advice of Perseveraunce he is reinstated to his former power and position. The skeleton plot of the morality play has been retained in a conscious adaptation of its plot and devices to the presentation of a political theme. Magnyfycence and such neutral figures as Liberty and Wealth, as well as the court virtues, are derived from the *Ethics* of Aristotle. The play is of added interest in that it admits of a general and a specific interpretation, general as a political allegory warning against false counselors and prodigality, specific in its application to the reign of Henry VIII under the ascendancy of Cardinal Wolsey. The Cardinal had earlier (1526) objected to some of the political implications in *Lord Governance and Lady Public-Weal.*

Political and Social Purposes. Later morality plays openly adapted the theme of conflict to political purposes, as in *Respublica* (1553) and *Wealth and Health* (1557); to religious and political controversy, as in John Bale's (1495–1563) *King Johan* and David Lindsay's *Satyre of the Thrie Estaites* (1540); and to educational purposes, as in the series of ''Wit and Science'' school plays (1545 on). Others preserved the strictly doctrinal or religious aim of the earlier plays but confined their teachings to apply to a particular period of life, as in *Youth* (1553–58), or to a particular vice or group of vices, as in *Impatient Poverty* (1560). The subject matter of the later morality plays, other than the controversial and school plays, is almost wholly contemporary social satire. Lacking the universal application and timelessness of appeal that characterized the earlier plays, they lost the dignity and nobility of purpose of *Everyman* and the *Castle of Perseverance.* The same shift to social satire can be seen in the French plays, *La Condemnation de Banquet* (*c.* 1500) and *L'Homme juste et l'homme mondain* (*c.* 1500).

As *Magnyfycence* marks the conscious adoption of the plot of the morality plays as a vehicle of didacticism and propaganda, so *Mankynd* marks the transition from morality play to comedy through the gradual evolution of the vices from abstractions to realistic types, a transition through many and various intermediate stages from the Gula (Greed) of the early play to the Justice Greedy of comedy. Evidence of the process of transition can be noted in the contemporary plays *Mynd, Wyll and Understanding* and *Hyckescorner,* which are related to each other in representing the soul under the guise of its powers. In both plays the central or neutral figure no longer preserves its autonomy but becomes the vice, or type of evil to which it has consented. Thus, in *Mynd, Wyll and Understanding* the powers of good and evil are represented by Wysdom (who is Christ) and Lucyfer. Mynd, after yielding to temptation, becomes Mayntenance, the contemporary social evil resulting from the vice of pride; understanding becomes Perjury, the evil that results from avarice, and Wyll becomes sensuality. The three powers of the soul succumb to the three concupiscences: the concupiscence of the eyes (sensuality), the concupiscence of the mind (avarice), and the pride of life, which, in turn, are opposed to the three religious vows: chastity, poverty, and obedience.

Both *Hyckescorner* and *Mynd, Wyll and Understanding* are related in purpose to *Mankynd* as all three preach against and satirize the vices and lawlessness of the postwar period in which they were written; in fact, the social satire in the plays overshadows their original moral purpose. *Mankynd* marks the break from the realistic presentation and satire of contemporary vices as a deterrent from evil to the emphasis on such presentation for comic effect. Played by a traveling company whose members doubled in parts, the play was no longer, if it ever had been, under clerical supervision. The extant text presents a frankly commercial enterprise. The actors are out to please; local allusions and the antics of the devil Tityvillus and the gay young rioters are exploited to the fullest extent. But beneath the horseplay lies a serious theme, a protest against the irreverence and lawlessness of the age. Mercy, the single force for good in the play, is both priest and virtue, or virtue represented under the guise of a priest, who, through his admonitions and his power of forgiving sin, dispenses Christ's mercy on earth. Now-a-days, New Guise, and Nought are vicious tendencies of the times presented under the appearance of the young men of the day: the modern young man or scoffer, the fashionable, and the frivolous young man. They hover midway between abstraction and type, for if they had been conceived as types of human beings they would have been subject to conversion. When, with their comrade Mischief, they scoff at Mercy, ridiculing his Latin and his ancient saws, they are directing their insults, not at the virtue, but at the priest. They represent the same lawless types which appear in *Hyckescorner* as the powers of the soul, the forerunners of the roistering tavern-haunting blades of the later comedies.

The use of allegorical characters and motifs are rare and sparse in the cycle plays, but they are utilized in the five temptation scenes of the Digby *Mary Magdalene* and in a scene interpolated into the *Conversion of Saint Paul* (see section 1 of this article). The scenes in both plays are clearly reminiscent of those in the *Castle of Perseverance.* In medieval literature Mary Magdalen, St. Paul, and St. Peter were the traditional exemplars of great penitents. In that sense, the theme of both plays relates them to that of the morality plays, for they are in reality dramatic *exempla.*

Plays based on the structure of the morality plays appeared throughout the 16th century (e.g., *The Three Lords and the Three Ladies of London,* 1592), and their influence is apparent in Elizabethan drama, specifically in such plays as Marlowe's *Dr. Faustus* and Thomas Dekker's *Old Fortunatus.* The later morality plays shaded off into the interludes and, together with the earlier religious dramas, prepared for the great dramatic outburst of the 16th and 17th centuries, principally in its development of moral themes, comic situations, comic types, and characters.

Bibliography: E. K. CHAMBERS, *The Medieval Stage,* 2 v. (Oxford 1903; repr. 1948). W. M. A. CREIZENACH, *Geschichte des neueren Dramas,* 5 v. (Halle 1893–1916; v. 2, rev. ed. 1918). R. DAVIES, *Extracts from the Municipal Records of the City of York during the Reigns of Edward IV, Edward V, and Richard III* (London 1843). F. J. FURNIVALL, ed., *The Digby Plays* (Early English Text Society, Extra Ser. 70; 1896). J. SKELTON, *Magnyfycence: A Moral Play,* ed. R. L. RAMSAY (*ibid.,* 98; 1906). F. J. FURNIVALL and A. W. POLLARD, *The Macro Plays* (*ibid.* 91; 1904). W. R. MACKENZIE, *The English Moralities from the Point of View of Allegory* (Harvard Studies in English 2; Boston 1914). G. R. OWST, *Literature and Pulpit in Medieval England* (2d ed. New York 1961); *Preaching in Medieval England* (Cambridge, Eng. 1926). L. PETIT DE JULLEVILLE, *Histoire du théatre en France: Repertoire du théatre comique en France au moyen-âge* (Paris 1886). A. W. REED, *Early Tudor Drama . . .* (London 1926). W. K. SMART, "The Castle of Perseverance," in *The Manly Anniversary Studies in Language and Literature* (Chicago 1923). E. N. S. THOMPSON, *The English Moral Plays* (New Haven 1910). H. TRAVER, *The Four Daughters of God* (Philadelphia 1907). K. YOUNG, "The Records of the York Play of the Pater noster," *Speculum* 7 (1932) 540–546. H. CRAIG, *English Religious Drama of the Middle Ages* (Oxford 1955). For a relevant discussion of the "Pater Noster Play" see also T. E. ALLISON, "The Pater Noster Play and the Origin of the Vices," *Publications of the Modern Language Association* 39 (1924) 789–804, esp. 791. A. WILLIAMS, *The Drama of Medieval England* (East Lansing 1961). A. P. ROSSITER, *English Drama from Early Times to the Elizabethans* (New York 1950).

[M. E. COLLINS]

MORAN, PATRICK FRANCIS

Cardinal, archbishop of Sydney, Australia; b. Leighlinbridge, Ireland, Sept. 16, 1830; d. Sydney, Aug. 16, 1911. After education at the Irish College, Rome, he was ordained (March 1853) and became vice rector of the Irish College (1856–66). In 1866 he returned to Ireland to become private secretary to his uncle, Cardinal Paul CULLEN, professor of Sacred Scripture at Clonliffe College, and founder of the *Irish Ecclesiastical Record.* In March of 1872 he was consecrated co-adjutor bishop of Ossory, succeeding to the diocese in August. In March of 1884 he succeeded Roger Bede VAUGHAN in the see of SYDNEY and became cardinal (1885). Cardinal Moran was a powerful and creative prelate in the development of the Church in Australia. As a scholar, statesman, and democrat with wide interests, he was an enlightened leader who influenced both Church and State in a critical and constructive period of the country's history. He presided over three plenary councils (1885, 1895, and 1905). He established two seminaries for native clergy, ordained 500 priests, consecrated 14 bishops, and dedicated 500 churches, including nine cathedrals, in Australia and New Zealand. In his own diocese he erected Catholic churches, schools, and other institutions to the value of 1 ½ million pounds sterling and constantly appealed for justice to Catholics in education, claiming state aid for secular education imparted in Catholic schools. In public life Cardinal Moran gave Australians a vision of emerging nationhood founded on social justice. He actively supported the movement for the federation of the six colonies and the foundation of the Commonwealth of Australia. He applied the encyclical RERUM NOVARUM to local problems and encouraged the new Australian Labor party, then regarded by conservatives as socialist, and supported the strikers in the industrial conflicts of the 1890s. With Cardinal Manning in England and Cardinal Gibbons in the United States, Cardinal Moran was one of the pioneers of Catholic social movements in the English-speaking world. His published works include *Essays on the Origin, Doctrine, and Discipline of the Early Irish Church* (1864) and *History of the Catholic Archbishops of Dublin* (1864). He edited the *Pastoral Letters of Cardinal Cullen* and wrote many pamphlets on religious, biographical, and sociological questions. His main Australian publication is a 1,200-page *History of the Catholic Church in Australasia* (1895).

Bibliography: S. E. FRYER, *The Dictionary of National Biography from the Earliest Times to 1900,* 63 v. (London 1885–1900) 2 (1901–11) 645–646. *Who Was Who* (1897–1915) 504. *Concise Dictionary of Irish Biography* (1937) 159. E. M. O'BRIEN, *Australian Encyclopedia* 10 v. (1958) 6:148–149.

[J. G. MURTAGH]

MORANDUS, ST.

Benedictine prior; b. near Worms, Germany; d. Altkirch, Alsace, France, *c.* 1115. Born of noble parents in the upper Rhine region, he was trained in the episcopal school at WORMS and ordained there. On his return from a pilgrimage to SANTIAGO DE COMPOSTELA in Spain, he visited CLUNY and became a monk there. Because of his exemplary life, HUGH OF CLUNY made him prior of a monastery in the Auvergne and then established him in the same office in a new foundation at Altkirch in Alsace. Because of his pastoral zeal he was called the ''apostle of the Sundgau.'' He was buried in the monastery church at Altkirch, and his tomb became the object of pilgrimage. Under Archduke Rudolph IV of Hapbsurg (1339–65) a part of his head was taken as a relic to Vienna for the new Cathedral of St. Stephen. Morandus is represented in art as a monk or pilgrim, and with a bunch of grapes and a pruning knife.

Feast: June 3.

Bibliography: *Acta Sanctorum* June 1:332–351. *Bibliotheca hagiographica latina antiquae et mediae aetatis* 2:6019–20. A. M. ZIMMERMANN, *Kalendarium Benedictinum: Die Heiligen und Seligen des Benediktinerorderns und seiner Zweige* (Metten 1933–38) 2:262–263.

[M. R. P. MCGUIRE]

MORANO, MADDALENA CATERINA, BL.

Religious of the Daughters of Mary Help of Christians; b. Nov. 15, 1847, Chieri (near Turin), Piedmont, Italy; d. March 26, 1908, at Catania, Sicily. Although Maddalena was forced from age eight to help support her family following the deaths of her elder sister and father, she also continued her studies. In 1866, she received her teaching diploma and began her career in a rural school in Montaldo while serving as a catechist in her parish. By 1878, she had saved enough money to provide for her mother's needs. No longer bound to supporting her family financially, she entered the Daughters of Mary Help of Christians, founded by (St.) John BOSCO (1872). In 1881, he sent her to Trecastagni (Catania) to oversee an existing institute and instill Salesian methods in its work. From there Maddalena founded new houses and established new services for the poor on the island. She also coordinated catechetical instruction in eighteen parishes and trained catechists. During her twenty-five years in Sicily, Morano served as local and provincial superior. Her remains now rest in the crypt of the institute at Messina. In 1935, the archdiocesan investigation of Maddalena's cause began. She was beatified at Catania by Pope John Paul II, Nov. 5, 1994.

Feast: Nov. 15.

Bibliography: M. L. MAZZARELLO, ed., *Sulle frontiere dell'educazione: Maddalena Morano in Sicilia* (Papers presented at various meetings organized by Pontificia Facoltà di scienze dell'educazione ''Auxilium'') (Rome 1995).

[K. I. RABENSTEIN]

MORAVIAN CHURCH

Also called the *Unitas Fratrum,* or Renewed Church of the Brethren whose members are called United Brethren or Herrnhuters. The Moravian Church claims direct descent from the Bohemian Brethren who were organized at Kunvald, Bohemia (1457), by the followers of John Hus, the Wyclifite burned at the stake in 1415. The Brethren formally left the Catholic Church, whose form of worship and creedal formulas they felt were a corruption of true Christianity. They accepted Hus's teaching that the Bible is the only norm of faith; that the human race is totally depraved; that Christ, truly God and man, redeemed the human race; and that the Holy Spirit convinces all persons of their sin and inspires faith in him when they become adopted daughters and sons of God. In general the Brethren constituted an association dedicated to strict scriptural teaching and the Apostolic way of life. Living and experiencing faith was for them true Christianity.

History. For two centuries the Brethren flourished in Moravia, Poland, and Bohemia; but after the Reformation, and especially the Thirty Years' War, the majority of them were absorbed into the Catholic, Lutheran, and Reform Churches. The remnant remaining, however, adhered to Hus's doctrine, even continuing the episcopacy. Their last bishop, John A. Comenius, usually considered the link between the ancient Brethren and the modern Moravians, died in 1671, and his few followers were soon scattered. In 1722 Christian David revived the principles of the Brethren and was partially successful in reorganizing them. However, when Ferdinand II suppressed the Brethren in Bohemia and Moravia, they were forced to live their faith secretly and in fear. Thus, in the late 1720s David and his followers left their homeland for Saxony and settled on the estate of Nikolaus Ludwig von ZINZENDORF and there set up a communal society called Herrnhut (the Lord's watch). Within a short time Herrnhut grew to several hundred members who were committed to "the fellowship of piety over that of doctrine." They felt they were "a little church within the Church," "a leaven" that would revive the church of the day. Zinzendorf became more and more enthusiastic about the community and hoped to make it a grand society founded on experiential religion and practical piety. Through them he envisioned the promotion of spirituality and brotherhood without regard for doctrine. In time Zinzendorf became their leader and fashioned the community into a distinct sect.

Originally he had no idea of establishing another church, but in order to acquire official recognition from the state, which was Lutheran, Zinzendorf adopted the AUGSBURG CONFESSION as a summary of the community's belief. In 1735 the community assumed the official name *Unitas Fratrum;* about this time the popular name, Moravians, was applied to the sect because of its origin. Zinzendorf's energy and zeal quickly brought into being the community's missionary character that still prevails. The Moravians believed they lived the life of Christ and had to proclaim it. They did evangelistic work with the hope of developing an evangelical alliance among the churches. They worked throughout the German states, in England, where they had a deep influence on John Wesley, and in America.

As early as 1734 Peter Bohler left Germany and established a community in Savannah, Ga. In 1740 a settlement was made in Philadelphia, Pa.; it was so successful that within a short time it was able to send missionaries to establish other Moravian colonies. Salem, N.C., as well as Bethlehem, Nazareth, and Lititz, Pa., were all founded by the Moravians. By 1776 there were more than 2,500 Moravians in Pennsylvania alone. An aggressive missionary program became part of their church life.

Viennese illustration depicting traditional Moravian dress. (©Austrian Archives/CORBIS)

Their simplicity of life, as well as their sacrifices and perseverance, contributed to their comparative success. Unlike the Protestant national sects, the Moravians never exerted great influence in any given region, because they never identified their form of Christianity with a limited national group.

Doctrine, Worship, and Government. The basic tenet of the Moravians is true fidelity to Christ in daily Christian life. They officially adhere to the Apostles' Creed and the first 21 articles of the Augsburg Confession "without in the least binding [their] conscience." They are broadly evangelical and believe that the inspired Scripture is the rule for the practice of faith. Their principal belief is in God's love for man manifested in the redemptive life and death of Jesus and in man's ability in Christ to attain mystical union with the Savior. This is their goal in life and the force in Christianity as they understand it.

The Moravians of the mid-20th century believe that they have a special ecumenical mission and they hope to unite Christians of divergent beliefs by a practical system of living the Christian life. "We recognize as true men of Christ's body, the Church, every one who has experienced the new birth. Hence we regard all children of God as our brethren in Christ. We decidedly disclaim all sectarian animosity arising from diversity of views on points of doctrine, discipline, and Church government. We desire to live in cordial fellowship with members of all evangelical Churches."

Infant baptism by sprinkling is practiced by the Moravians, but they see in it only a public sign that the child will be reared in Christ's love. At least six times a year the commemorative rite of the Lord's Supper is held; this affords the Brethren the opportunity for self-examination, for renewing their mystical union with Christ, and for expressing their mutual bonds of fellowship. The Moravian Church is a liturgical Church, with collections of liturgical rites for all important occasions. The use of the liturgy, however, is never compulsory. The usual Sunday service is centered about a litany, with petitions drawn from Scripture, and the sermon, which emphasizes the love of God for man in His Atoning Son. Special emphasis is put on music in all liturgical worship; the Moravian Easter rites at dawn are perhaps among America's better-known Church services.

The Moravian Church is governed by provincial synods, not by its bishops, who hold the office of spiritual leadership and administration only. Every ten years a synod is held that decides doctrine, approves liturgical rites, and nominates bishops. In the U.S., there are three provinces of the Moravian Church: Northern, Southern and Alaska.

Bibliography: W. G. ADDISON, *The Renewed Church of the United Brethren, 1722–1930* (London 1932). J. K. PFOHL, *The Moravian Church* (Raleigh 1926). E. LANGTON, *The History of the Moravian Church* (London 1956). F. S. MEAD, S. S. HILL and C. D. ATWOOD, eds., *Handbook of Denominations in the United States*, 11th ed (Nashville 2001).

[T. HORGAN/EDS.]

MORE, GERTRUDE

Benedictine Abbess, descendant of St. Thomas More; b. Essex, England, March 25, 1606; d. Cambrai, Aug. 17, 1633.

After the dissolution of the English monasteries under Henry VIII, wealthy Catholics often sent their children to other countries to be educated. Many joined religious communities. Among them was Helen (Dame Gertrude) More, daughter of Crisacre More, great-grandson of St. Thomas More.

Gertrude's father helped endow a women's monastery under the English Benedictines of Douai. In 1623, Gertrude and eight companions went to Cambrai where three Benedictine nuns from Brussels assisted in establishing the community. There Gertrude suffered physical illness, interior restlessness, indifference, and even hostility toward the life. She struggled to accept both her desire for God and the conflicts between her own natural inclinations and the demands of monastic life. Some time around her profession, Gertrude began to receive spiritual guidance from Dom Augustine Baker. Through this relationship she was able to come to understanding and acceptance of the monastic ideal as he envisioned it.

Both became known for their enthusiastic articulation and restoration of Benedictine spirituality, but not without controversy and detractors. Baker's critics feared that his way of prayer was too affective and allowed for too much personal authority. Dame Gertrude died of smallpox after four years as abbess, while the debate still raged. After her death, several writings by her were found and circulated to promote the spirituality, notably *The Holy Practices of a Divine Lover, or the Saintly Idiot's Devotions* (1657) and *Confessiones Amantis, A Lover's Confessions* (1658).

Baker took advantage of this in writing a biography of her in which he examined her struggles with her vocation, the nature of her personality, and the holiness that she exemplified. Benedictine life did revive and prosper, and eventually the monastic community was able to relocate to Stanbrook Abbey in England.

Bibliography: E. WELD-BLUNDELL, ed., *The Writings of Dame Gertrude More* (London 1910). A. BAKER, *The Inner Life of Dame Gertrude More* (London 1910). NUN OF STANBROOK, *Stanbrook Abbey, A Sketch of Its History, 1625–1921* (London 1925). NUN OF STANBROOK, *In a Great Tradition: Tribute to Dame Laurentia McLachlan* (London 1956).

[J. SUTERA]

MORE, HUGH, BL.

Lay martyr; b. ca. 1563, Grantham, Lincolnshire, England; hanged in Lincoln's Inn Fields, London, Aug. 28, 1588 (date sometimes incorrectly given as Aug. 30). Hugh studied at Broadgates Hall, Oxford and Gray's Inn. He was arrested in London for having been reconciled to the Church by Jesuit Fr. Thomas Stephenson and traveling to Rheims to study for the priesthood. He was hanged together with Bl. Fr. Robert MORTON, and with him was beatified by Pius XI on Dec. 15, 1929.

Feast of the English Martyrs: May 4 (England).

See Also: ENGLAND, SCOTLAND, AND WALES, MARTYRS OF.

Bibliography: R. CHALLONER, *Memoirs of Missionary Priests,* ed. J. H. POLLEN (rev. ed. London 1924; repr. Farnborough 1969). J. H. POLLEN, *Acts of English Martyrs* (London 1891).

[K. I. RABENSTEIN]

MORE, SCHOOL OF

The ''school'' must be distinguished not only from the older friends of Thomas MORE, the group Frederick Seebohm called the Oxford Reformers, which included LINACRE and COLET, but also from the More ''circle,'' which included such contemporaries as R. Pace and W. Lily, fellow humanists who shared More's ideals. Nearly all members of these last two groups, it must be remarked, were involved in education. The School of More is here taken to mean the group of *discipuli*—children, wards, their tutors, and younger friends—who lived or gathered in More's household from about 1511 to 1534.

In a famous letter of 1519 to Ulrich von HUTTEN, Erasmus described the household as Plato's Academy on a Christian footing. Members of the group were, first, More's children and their husbands or wives: John, married to Anne Cresacre, a ward; Margaret, married to William ROPER; Cecily, married to Giles Heron, a ward; and Elizabeth, married to William Dauncey. Then there were More's stepdaughter, Alice Middleton, and his foster-daughter, Margaret Gigs, who married the humanist and physician John Clement; perhaps Frances Staverton, More's niece, and some others. The group included also John HEYWOOD (who married a niece of More) and his sons Ellis and Jasper. An important member, John Harris, was More's secretary, and taught the children as well. Harris married Margaret Roper's maid, Dorothy Colly; their son-in-law, John Fowler, a recusant printer in Louvain, joined the group also (*see* RECUSANTS). The children's tutors must be counted: a Master Drew, William Gonell, a Master Nicholas (later the King's astronomer), Nicholas Kratzer, and Richard Hyrde. Finally, there were part-time and transient members, such as Thomas Lupset and Juan Luis Vives. All members of the school taught and were taught, not only Latin, rhetoric, and logic, but also Greek and more advanced subjects. The amusing references to the More household in Walter Smythe's *The Twelve mery jests of the Widow Edith* (published by Rastell in 1525) suggest that a great deal of humor, as well as mature scholarship and deep piety, characterized the group.

Individuals of the school advanced in Parliament, in the world of learning, and at court; but after 1535 the royal displeasure cast its shadow: Giles Heron was executed in 1540, and William Roper, John More, and John Heywood were imprisoned during the 1540s. As a group they were staunchly loyal to More's memory, and the Heywoods, Rastells, Clements, and Harrises all died in an exile necessitated by that loyalty.

Bibliography: N. HARPSFIELD, *The Life and Death of Sir Thomas Moore,* ed. E. V. HITCHCOCK (Early English Text Society 136; London 1932). T. STAPLETON, *The Life and Illustrious Martyrdom of Sir Thomas More . . . (Part III of ''Tres Thomae,'' Printed at Douai, 1588),* tr. P. E. HALLETT (London 1928). A. W. REED, *Early Tudor Drama* (London 1926). E. M. G. ROUTH, *Sir Thomas More and His Friends* (London 1934). R. W. CHAMBERS, *Thomas More* (Westminster, MD 1935). THOMAS MORE, *The History of King Richard III,* ed. R. S. SYLVESTER, v.2 of *The Complete Works,* ed. L. L. MARTZ and R. S. SYLVESTER (New Haven 1963–) 2:xlviii–xlix; *The Correspondence of Sir Thomas More,* ed. E. F. ROGERS (Princeton 1947). P. HOGREFE, *The Sir Thomas More Circle* (Urbana 1959) 144–146. R. J. SCHOECK, ''Two Notes on Margaret Gigs Clement, Foster-Daughter of Sir Thomas More,'' *Notes and Queries* 194 (1949) 532–533; ''Anthony Bonvisi, the Heywoods and the Ropers,'' *ibid.* 197 (1952) 178–179; ''William Rastell and the Prothonotaries,'' *ibid.* 197 (1952) 398–399.

[R. J. SCHOECK]

MORE, SIR THOMAS, ST.

Lord chancellor of England and eminent humanist; b. London, Feb. 7, 1477; executed for high treason, London, July 6, 1535. The exact date of his birth has been the subject of much discussion, but the latest summation of the evidence (Marc'Hadour, 34–41) indicates that 1477, not 1478, is most probably correct. More came from a solidly prospering London family, ''not famous, but of honest stock,'' as he says in his epitaph. His father, John More (d. 1530), was a rising member of the legal profession who seems later to have exerted no little pressure on his son to take up a similar career. More was educated at St. Anthony's school in Threadneedle Street, where Nicholas Holt was master, until he was about 12, when his father procured his appointment as a page in the household of Cardinal John MORTON, Archbishop of Canterbury and Henry VII's Lord Chancellor. In addition to being an expert canon lawyer, Morton was an astute and flexible politician who had helped to overthrow Richard III and bring Henry VII to the throne. In both his *Richard III* and *Utopia* More paid fine tribute to his old patron, and it is indeed difficult to overestimate the importance of the training he received from him. It was while serving in Morton's household that More, according to William Roper, his son in law and first biographer, ''would suddenly at Christmastide sometimes step in among the players, and never studying for the matter, make a part of his own there presently among them, which made the lookers-on more sport than all the players beside'' (Roper, 5). The anecdote reveals More's natural talent for adopting a role, for entering into a situation and yet remaining curiously detached from it. Even when he was only 12, the

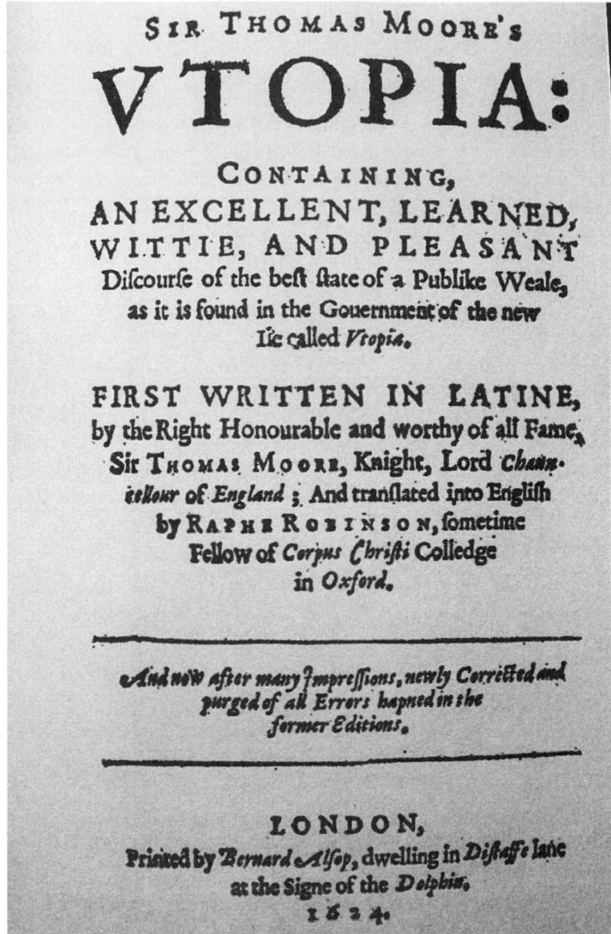

SIR THOMAS MOORE'S

VTOPIA:

CONTAINING,
AN EXCELLENT, LEARNED,
WITTIE, AND PLEASANT
Diſcourſe of the beſt ſtate of a Publike Weale,
as it is found in the Gouernment of the new
Ile called *Vtopia*.

FIRST WRITTEN IN LATINE,
by the Right Honourable and worthy of all Fame,
Sir THOMAS MOORE, Knight, Lord *Chancellour* of *England*; And tranſlated into Engliſh
by RAPHE ROBINSON, ſometime
Fellow of *Corpus Chriſti* Colledge
in *Oxford*.

And now after many Impreſſions, newly Corrected and purged of all Errors hapned in the former Editions.

LONDON,
Printed by *Bernard Alſop*, dwelling in *Diſtaffe* lane
at the Signe of the *Dolphin*.
1624.

"Utopia," first title page, by St. Sir Thomas More, London 1624.

world was for him a stage, an insight that must have been appreciated by Morton when he predicted (*ibid.*) that his young page would prove "a marvelous man."

Student Years. The best dates for More's service with Morton are 1489 or 1490 to 1492. In 1492, through Morton's influence, he matriculated at Canterbury College, Oxford, where he remained until 1494. Little is known about More's Oxford years; although he did remark later on the poor student fare, he was always attached to university life and it was perhaps at Oxford that he first met John COLET, William Grocyn, and Thomas LINACRE, all senior members in the circle of English humanists that More later adorned so brilliantly.

In 1494, probably because of parental pressure, More left Oxford to begin the study of law at New Inn. He transferred to Lincoln's Inn on Feb. 12, 1496, and thereafter rose steadily through the ranks of his profession. Yet as More continued his legal studies in London, other interests constantly engaged his attention. It is here that one finds emerging, for the first time in the historical record, some indication of the intense spirituality that was later so fundamental a feature of his personality. Strongly influenced by Colet's purity of life, he seriously considered the possibility of a career in the Church. For about four years (probably 1500–04) he lived with the Carthusian monks at the London Charterhouse, where he first began the practice, continued throughout his life, of wearing a hair shirt. More's nature, however, as he gradually discovered for himself, was closely connected to the life of the senses; he would seek God through and in the world, not by retiring from it. About November 1504 he married Jane Colt, the oldest daughter of John Colt of Netherhall, Essex. Four children were born to them before Jane's death in the summer of 1511: Margaret (1505), Elizabeth (1506), Cecily (1507), and John (1509).

Erasmus and the London Humanists. It was during these years too that More firmly established himself as a leader among the group of humanists whose activities were then centering in London. ERASMUS visited England first in 1499, and he and More immediately became bosom friends. More's first literary works (see below) date from that period, and it was most probably about 1501 that he delivered his lectures on St. Augustine's *City of God* at Grocyn's church (St. Lawrence's), London. Subsequent visits by Erasmus (1505–06, 1509–14), who was rapidly acquiring an international reputation, cemented the friendship between him and More, a bond playfully alluded to in the title of *The Praise of Folly (Encomium Moriae),* which Erasmus composed at More's house in 1509. More for his part was no doubt instrumental, with Colet, in directing Erasmus toward the great tasks of Biblical and patristic scholarship that were to become his life work.

Yet Erasmus himself often lamented that More—"England's only genius"—had of necessity to devote so much time to his legal work that little room was left for literature. For most of his life More was to feel this tension between the literary studies and the spiritual devotions so dear to his heart, on the one hand, and the endless round of legal business or royal missions, on the other.

Career of Law. By 1510, when he became undersheriff of London on September 3, More's competence as a lawyer was beyond question, and his income increased accordingly. Within six weeks of his first wife's death, he married Alice Middleton, a widow some years older than himself, who proved a good stepmother to his children despite her somewhat shrewish nature. The family continued to live at The Barge in Bucklersbury until 1524, when More built his "Great House" at Chelsea. Meanwhile, More's oratorical skill at the bar and his reputation for justice and fairness brought him a host of clients. He championed the cause of the citizens on many occasions and often represented the guild companies of the city in both domestic and foreign affairs. By 1515 HENRY VIII, whose coronation in 1509 had been hailed by More in a series of Latin poems, had become fully aware of the young lawyer's talents. More's first royal mission, the famous ''Utopian embassy'' to the Low Countries, followed (May 7 to Oct. 25, 1515). More had been abroad before in 1508 for a few weeks (Louvain, Paris), but this was his first real introduction to the international circle of humanists that revolved around the ubiquitous Erasmus. In Flanders More met Peter Giles and Jerome Busleyden and formed lasting friendships with them. From August 26 to *c.* Dec. 20, 1517, he was again abroad on commercial negotiations, and it is about this time that he is first spoken of as in the King's service. It was not until June 21, 1518, however, that he received his first stipend as a royal counselor. On July 23 of that year, he resigned as under-sheriff of London.

The King's Service. There is every indication that More reached his decision to enter Henry's court only after long and perhaps agonizing meditation. The arguments for and against royal service are dramatized in the first book of *Utopia* (1516), but it is impossible not to consider More's final choice as to some extent a compromise between his idealistic view of the perfect counselor and his practical sense of what could actually be accomplished. He may well have felt that, given Thomas WOLSEY'S apparently earnest efforts to obtain a universal peace, he would be able as a member of the council to give advice that, if it did not lead to good, might yet avoid what would otherwise be very bad. Nevertheless, his role as a champion of the people, which had just been illustrated by his intervention on their behalf in the May-day riots of 1517, was of necessity diminished. In addition, the precious time that he had snatched from his legal work for literary study was lost.

More's activities during the next 12 years (1518–29) centered on the life of the court. He proved an extremely able member of the council, acting on occasion as a secretary who transmitted reports to or from Wolsey and the King, participating in discussions with foreign ambassadors, attending on Henry at such grand events as the Field of the Cloth of Gold in June 1520, and undertaking still another royal mission in 1521 for commercial negotiations with the Hanse diet. Honors were quickly thrust upon him. On May 2, 1521, he became undertreasurer and was knighted. In 1523 Parliament, in which he had previously served on several occasions, chose him as its speaker. The next year saw him appointed high steward of Oxford University, and in 1525 he accepted the same position for Cambridge, becoming also, in October of that year, chancellor of the Duchy of Lancaster. During

St. Sir Thomas More.

the 1520s too, More participated in the campaign against Lutheran literature, which was beginning to flood England. In 1523 he had written against Martin LUTHER on the King's behalf; and on March 7, 1528, he was to be authorized by Cuthbert TUNSTALL, Bishop of London, to read Protestant books in order to refute them in English. From 1529 until 1534 More gave much of his time to this polemical work against William TYNDALE, Simon Fish, Robert Barnes, and other early English Protestants.

Henry VIII's "Great Matter." By the time More's controversial English writings began to pour from the press, signs of change were beginning to appear in England too. Henry VIII had consulted More as early as 1527 with regard to his proposed divorce from CATHERINE OF ARAGON, and after a long study of the problem More had told the King that he could not support his case. Henry then promised to use other men in dealing with his ''great matter,'' as it now came to be called. More thus remained aloof from the long series of negotiations that began in earnest after Wolsey's great embassy to France, with More in his entourage, in the summer of 1527. When Henry's case finally came to trial in the summer of 1529, with Lorenzo CAMPEGGIO and Wolsey serving as papal judges, More was in France negotiating the Treaty of Cambrai (August) with his friend Tunstal. The London trial ended in a stalemate when Campeggio prorogued the court. Wolsey, unable to gratify the King's wishes, was in disgrace.

Lord Chancellor. More returned to England at the end of August. On Oct. 25, 1529, he replaced Wolsey as lord chancellor. More's 2 and a half-year tenure of the realm's highest office has been the subject of much controversy. When the famous Long Parliament (1529–36) opened on November 3, he made a long speech attacking Wolsey and his policies. Reform was in the air, but the direction that it would take was tied to the course of Henry's plans for divorce. Throughout those years, the King's policies, if schismatic, were not irrevocably heretical. The breach with Rome, when it came, did not immediately involve England in doctrinal changes. While many members of the court showed sympathy for the Protestant doctrines, the King himself did not interfere directly with the campaign More, as lord chancellor, waged against heresy. More has been accused of intolerant cruelty in his handling of heresy cases, but such charges cannot be supported. As he constantly affirmed in his apologetic works, he controlled the civil arm of the law only, not the ecclesiastical courts in which heretics were tried. He did oppose heresy staunchly, believing that it was the cause of civil unrest in a realm still Catholic, but he cannot be accused of bigotry or relentless persecution.

More's record in the courts as lord chancellor is much clearer, for all attest to his fairness; Roper notes the remarkable circumstance that, while he was in office, no case remained to be heard in chancery, so prompt and impartial was the justice he meted out. More than 4,000 cases, all tried during his tenure, on file in the public record office are evidence of his diligence. It remains true, however, that while he was chancellor More's power was often more apparent than real. As the Reformation Parliament pursued its course and it became increasingly obvious that Henry must break with Rome if he was to wed Anne Boleyn, More's counsel was sought less and less. On May 15, 1532, the clergy made their complete submission to the King; the next day More resigned, pleading ill health, which was in fact true, as his reason.

Retirement. For a year at least More was able to live in relatively modest circumstances at Chelsea, continuing his polemical writings and devoting himself to those ascetic practices that he had loved throughout his life. But he was absent from Anne's coronation on June 1, 1533, telling his friends that though "he might be devoured, he would never be deflowered" (Roper, 59). More knew indeed what was in store for him; the recently discovered fact that his *Treatise on the Passion,* once thought to have been written after his imprisonment, was begun in early 1534 indicates the foresight with which he was preparing himself. Pressure was soon generated from the court to make him acquiesce in the King's new title as head of the Church. Given More's European reputation and his position as the most prominent layman in the realm, it was impossible for Henry to proceed without his submission. Various attempts were made by Thomas CROMWELL, the King's new minister, to implicate him in treasonable activities; but More resolutely refuted the charge. The affair of Elizabeth BARTON (executed in April 1534), the so-called "Holy-Maid of Kent" who had seen visions prophesying ruin for Henry, was used against More by Cromwell; but More quickly pointed out that he had refused to discuss the King's business with her. On April 12, 1534, More was cited to appear before the commissioners at Lambeth to swear to the Act of Succession and to take the Oath of Supremacy. More was willing to accept the succession but refused the oath. On April 17, with Bp. John FISHER, he was committed to the Tower.

Trial and Execution. His real trial then began in earnest, although the formal legal proceedings against him were not conducted until July 1535. For about a year his family was permitted to visit him, and he was allowed to have writing materials and books. But when Cromwell's and Thomas CRANMER's interrogations began on April 30, 1535, these privileges were gradually withdrawn. Such a separation from his wife and children was one of More's greatest agonies, and it was made all the more poignant by the fact that they did not seem to understand the reasons for his refusal to take the oath—and, before his conviction, More swore that he would reveal his conscience to no one. Thus he consistently denied, during his interrogations, that he had acted maliciously in refusing to answer. Again and again efforts were made to entrap him either into submission or into uttering words that could be construed as treasonable. But More was too expert a lawyer and too resolutely confirmed in his knowledge of himself to be caught by such ruses. Finally, on July 1, 1535, he was convicted of treason on the perjured evidence of Sir Richard Rich, one of Cromwell's minions. When the verdict was delivered, More at last uttered his mind in a great speech, declaring that he had all the councils of Christendom and not just the council of one realm to support him in the decision of his conscience. He was returned to the Tower until July 6, when, about 9 A.M., he went to his death. Henry had commuted his sentence (hanging and evisceration) to decapitation; More died on the scaffold, after joking merrily with his executioner, affirming that he died "the king's good servant, but God's first." Simply put, his death resulted directly from his belief that no lay ruler could have jurisdiction over the Church of Christ.

More's Relics and Acknowledged Saintliness. After his execution More's head replaced that of Fisher (executed on June 22) on London Bridge. It was later preserved by his daughter, Margaret, and now lies in the Roper vault at St. Dunstan's, Canterbury. His body was buried in the chapel of St. Peter ad Vincula in the Tower. Other relics include his seal as under-treasurer, a gold George and the Dragon, two crosses, and two pendants (all at Stonyhurst College). Lady Agnes Eyston-More (East Hendred, Wantage, Berkshire) possesses More's staff and drinking cup. His hair shirt is preserved in the convent of the canonesses regular of St. Augustine's Priory, Newton Abbot, Devonshire. More's *Book of Hours,* into which he wrote an English prayer while imprisoned in the Tower, is in the hands of a private collector; the autograph manuscript of his *Expositio Passionis,* his most substantial literary relic, is in the library of the Royal College of Corpus Christi, Valencia, Spain.

More's death was lamented throughout Europe, and so powerful was the memory of his personality that a whole school of biographers wrote his life in the late 16th century. His saintliness was often openly affirmed by this group, but the movement toward canonization was long and arduous, for his cause was linked with that of other English martyrs from the reigns of Henry VIII, Edward VI, and Elizabeth I (*see* ENGLAND, SCOTLAND, AND WALES, MARTYRS OF). In 1640 Pope Urban VIII created a commission to study evidence on these martyrs, but it was not until 1855 that the cause was brought forward by Canon John Morris as postulator. Leo XIII beatified More on Dec. 29, 1886. In the early 1930s more than 170,000 signatures were gathered requesting canonization from Pius XI. The movement culminated with a papal decree of Feb. 10, 1935, which dispensed with the proved miracles required in the canonical procedure; canonization took place on May 19. More has become the patron of Catholic lawyers and of university students.

Bibliography: A 14-volume edition of the *Complete Works* is planned for pub. by Yale University. Published to date are v.2, *The History of King Richard III,* ed. R. S. SYLVESTER (New Haven 1963), and v.4, *Utopia,* ed. E. SURTZ and J. H. HEXTER (New Haven 1965). The 16th-century biographies of the More school include those of W. ROPER (1557; ed. E. V. HITCHCOCK, Early English Text Society 197; 1935); N. HARPSFIELD (1557, ed. E. V. HITCHCOCK and R. W. CHAMBERS, *ibid.* 186; 1932); the anonymous Ro. Ba. (1598; ed. E. V. HITCHCOCK and P. E. HALLETT, *ibid.* 222; 1950); and T. STAPLETON (1588; tr. P. E. HALLETT, London 1928). The first of the modern biographies is that of T. E. BRIDGETT, *Life and Writings of Sir Thomas More* (London 1891), still a useful pioneer work. The most authoritative of this century is R. W. CHAMBERS, *Thomas More* (Westminster, Md. 1949). The religious elements in More's life are emphasized in E. E. REYNOLDS, *Saint Thomas More* (New York 1953) and A. VÁZQUEZ DE PRADA, *Sir Tomás Moro* (Madrid 1963). A recent indispensable guide to data on More is G. MARC'HADOUR, *L'Univers de Thomas More* (Paris 1963), with full bibliog. Also, the volumes appearing in the Yale ed. of his works (see above) are gradually accumulating a considerable body of new biographical material. The More iconography is excellently handled in S. MORISON, *The Likeness of Thomas More,* ed. N. BARKER (New York 1964). The only full bibliog. for the early period is R. W. GIBSON, comp., *St. Thomas More: A Preliminary Bibliography* (New Haven 1961). For works after 1750, see F. and M. P. SULLIVAN, *Moreana* (Kansas City, Mo. 1946). The periodical *Moreana,* ed. G. MARC'HADOUR (Angers, Fr. 1963–) devotes its triannual issues to new work on More and his circle.

[R. S. SYLVESTER]

Afterfame. A vital part of the influence of St. Thomas More came through the school of More (*see* MORE, SCHOOL OF): a significant part of the thought and letters of the early Tudor period bears the impress of More's ideas and character and, after 1535, reflects the widening significance of his life and action and eventual martyrdom. It is in and through such diverse men as John HEYWOOD, William RASTELL, and Sir Thomas Elyot that the influence of More—a force as yet unmeasured in any fullness—is initially to be detected. Yet the influence of More and his afterfame are scarcely to be separated, and both must be studied together with his literary name. The provisional bibliography by Gibson (scc bibliog.) includes a section of Moreana, literary allusions down to 1750 (allusions after that date need to be collected); and this section, expanded and corrected by the time the bibliography appears as the final volume in the Yale edition, will provide the materials for a fuller and more accurate charting.

Utopia. More's most famous work is the *Utopia* (1516), which has been a model or ultimate source of innumerable utopias and dystopias, from Francis Bacon's *New Atlantis* (1626) to those of Aldous Huxley and George Orwell in the 20th century. It was written during the closing sessions of the Fifth Lateran Council (1512–17) and published on the eve of Luther's posting his 95 theses. *Utopia* draws upon More's experience as a young devotee of classical and other studies at Oxford and in London, as a law student in Lincoln's Inn, and, after several years living among the London Carthusians, as a practicing lawyer who lectured in the Inns and achieved preeminence as legal counsel for the city of London, as a skilled arbitrator, and as one experienced in trade and diplomatic missions. But above all *Utopia* is a humanistic work that manages to subsume interests that in lesser minds might have been compartmentalized; its larger meaning is best appreciated when considered in relation to humanistic grapplings not only with philological concerns but also with the pressing problems of political theory and government. *Utopia* is written in that form closest to the humanist's mind and heart, the dialogue. For the Utopian dialogue is open-ended: it asks the right questions (and Hythlodaye has an ideal combination of indignation and hope, criticism and enthusiasm) and indicates that although there is no final answer to the problems of pride and greed, of injustice and folly, the use of reason provides a guide to tentative solutions.

Book 1 establishes the failure of contemporary England against the backdrop of debate whether a humanist should serve his prince. Hythlodaye's dramatic monologue in bk. 2 (which, Surtz points out, "contains answers and arguments against the implied queries or objections of his auditors") is the answer to the debate of bk. 1 and to the question of what might be done. Utopia is presented as a real country, and its geography and its political and social organizations are tersely described; its educational and religious practices and beliefs are then presented in greater detail. After touching on such miscellaneous matters as household management, conduct of war, and religion, Hythlodaye vehemently argues that pride is the root of the social ills of Christendom and pleads for Utopia—and the narrator More indicates that although he does not agree with all that Hythlodaye has said, he does wish that many Utopian features might be adopted.

This humanistic dialogue has occasioned literary judgments that range from considering it a *jeu d'esprit* (failing to understand its context and to appreciate its underlying seriousness) to literal readings by Kautsky and others who, failing to understand its form and tone, saw the work as a proclamation of revolt against medieval feudalism or nascent bourgeois materialism and as a program for socialistic measures, communism, or the like. Chambers's view that the "underlying thought of *Utopia* is always, *With nothing save Reason to guide them, the Utopians do this; and yet we Christian Europeans . . .*" has been widely accepted, but is surely, as Surtz judges it to be, too narrow and moralistic. More was writing at a historical moment whose great urgency is attested by the failure of the Fifth Lateran Council and other events. He appears to have been making one final appeal for the full application of reason to contemporary economic, social, and ecclesiastic problems and making the appeal in the humanistic dialogue and language. He developed his argument like a *declamatio:* "postulating a society built upon and with reason alone, let us see what they could do," and, given More's own love of jesting and his work with Erasmus on Lucian and the ironic mode, used much wordplay and great irony throughout. The festive quality reinforces the thought, and it enabled the author in good humanistic fashion both to teach and to delight.

Other Works. In order to appraise More's reputation on the Continent as one of the foremost Latinists of his century, his other Latin writings, in particular his epigrams, his other Latin poems, his translations of Lucian, and his Latin epistles must be included with the immortal Latin masterpiece, *Utopia.* This would establish his rank with BEDE, JOHN OF SALISBURY, and later John Milton as one of the greatest Latinists in the long range of English literary history.

More's other writings also served as models. The biography of Richard III, which has been called the first English historical work to be written after classical modes and models—and thus the first humanistic English history—is now known to be indubitably More's. It is a great achievement, in both its Latin and English versions, and the simultaneous composition of such a literary work is itself rare. This biography shaped Shakespeare's dramatic rendering, and it has controlled the English conception of this monarch down to contemporary times. More is likewise credited as the inventor of the term "atonement," which appears for the first time in *Richard III* (*see* ATONEMENT). The controversial writings, largely in English, are only now beginning to be studied fully and in depth (by the editors of the Yale edition), and their influence on later writers of the Reformation is being searched out and evaluated. Such books as John JEWEL's *Apology* (1562) inevitably look back to More's work, as does much of Richard HOOKER; and the controversy between More and St. German is recapitulated in the controversy between Cosin and Morice in the 1590s: even now it is difficult to appreciate how much of later Tudor controversies was fought on ground chosen or seized by More and Tyndale. A significant part of the afterfame of More has been, appropriately, in the theater, although only two plays about More are at all well known. R. C. Bald has surveyed the story and the scholarly problems of the Elizabethan play *Sir Thomas More,* but there is no convenient study for the éclat of Robert Bolt's 20th-century play. Yet Bolt's *A Man for All Seasons* has eclipsed all earlier attempts to put Thomas More on the stage and has had a remarkable success not only in the theater but also as a school text since its London production in 1960.

Feast: July 9.

Bibliography: For the influence of More's *History.* G. B. CHURCHILL, "Richard the Third up to Shakespeare," *Palaestra* 10 (1900) 64–, for 16th century. H. H. GLUNZ, *Shakespeare and Morus* (Cologne 1938); cf. *Complete Works,* v.2, ed. R. S. SYLVESTER (New Haven 1965). A. W. REED, *Early Tudor Drama* (London 1926). H. C. WHITE, *English Devotional Literature (Prose), 1600–1640* (Madison, Wis. 1931); *Tudor Books of Saints and Martyrs* (Madison 1963). R. W. CHAMBERS, *Thomas More* (Westminster, Md. 1949), esp. "Epilogue: More's Place in History"; *The Place of St. Thomas More in English Literature and History* (London 1937); *On the Continuity of English Prose from Alfred to More and His School* (Early English Text Society 191A; 1957). R. C. BALD, "*The Booke of Sir Thomas More* and Its Problems," *Shakespeare Survey* 2 (New York 1949) 44–61. A. C. SOUTHERN, *Elizabethan Recusant Prose, 1559–1582* (London 1950). R. J. SCHOECK, "The Place of Sir Thomas More," *Revue de l'Université d'Ottawa* 34 (1964) 176–190; "Sir Thomas More, Humanist and Lawyer," *University of Toronto Quarterly* 34 (1964) 1–13. P. HOGREFE, *The Sir Thomas More Circle* (Urbana, Ill. 1959). For *Utopia.* R. W. GIBSON and J. M. PATRICK, comps., *Thomas More: A Preliminary Bibliography* (New Haven 1961), contains bibliog. of editions and valuable material on Utopian literature. *Utopia,* ed. E. SURTZ and

J. H. HEXTER (*Complete Works* 4; New Haven 1965), contains Latin text and modern Eng. version, with full bibliog., introd., and nn. *Utopia,* ed. E. SURTZ (pa. New Haven 1964), best general reader's ed., modern Eng. only.

[R. J. SCHOECK]

MOREAU, ANNE FRANÇOISE, ST.

In religion Marie de St. Just; martyr and religious of the Franciscan Missionaries of Mary; b. April 9, 1866, La Faye, near Rouen, Loire, France; d. July 9, 1900, Taiyüan, China. Anne was the daughter of a wealthy, charitable farmer, who died while she was still young. Thereafter, she assumed responsibility for taking the farm's produce to market. Perceiving a vocation as a missionary in China, she sought the counsel of Mary of the Passion and, against her mother's wishes, entered the novitiate of the Missionaries of Mary in 1890. During her stay at Vanves, France, she learned many practical skills to sustain the community, including printing and cobbling. For a time she suffered an interior darkness and struggled with her vocation. After finally making her perpetual profession, Sr. Marie de St. Just was sent to the orphanage in Shanxi, China in 1899, where she was martyred the following year. She was beatified with her religious sisters by Pope Pius XII, November 24, 1946, and canonized, October 1, 2000, by Pope John Paul II with Augustine Zhao Rong and companions.

Feast: 4 July.

Bibliography: G. GOYAU, *Valiant Women: Mother Mary of the Passion and the Franciscan Missionaries of Mary*, tr. G. TELFORD (London 1936). M. T. DE BLARER, *Les Bse Marie Hermine de Jésus et ses compagnes, franciscaines missionnaires de Marie, massacrées le 9 juillet 1900 à Tai-Yuan-Fou, Chine* (Paris 1947). L. M. BALCONI, *Le Martiri di Taiyuen* (Milan 1945). *Acta Apostolicae Sedis* 47: 381–388. *L'Osservatore Romano*, Eng. Ed. 40 (2000): 1–2, 10.

[K. I. RABENSTEIN]

MOREAU, BASIL ANTHONY

Religious founder; b. Laigné-en-Belin (Mayenne), France, Feb. 11, 1799; d. Le Mans (Sarthe), France, Jan. 20, 1873. Basil Antoine Marie Moreau was the son of a country wine merchant. After attending the local College of Château-Gonthier, he studied at the seminary in Le Mans. After ordination (1821) he returned to this seminary as professor and as assistant superior. He was deputed by his bishop to establish in Le Mans a convent of Our Lady of Charity of the Refuge of Angers. This project involved him in controversy with St. Maria Euphrasia PELLETIER concerning the relationship of this house with the recently-founded Sisters of Our Lady of Charity of the GOOD SHEPHERD. Moreau was assigned in 1835 to reorganize the Brothers of St. Joseph, founded in 1820. In 1837 he founded the HOLY CROSS CONGREGATION by uniting this institute of brothers with the Auxiliary Priests of Le Mans, whom he had organized in 1833 to assist the diocesan clergy. Moreau founded also the MARIANITES OF THE HOLY CROSS (1841). The original purpose of this congregation of sisters was to provide for the domestic services of the Holy Cross Congregation, but the scope of their activities broadened later. The Congregation of Sisters of the Holy Cross and the Sisters of the Holy Cross and Seven Dolors, which developed from the Marianites of the Holy Cross, also regard Moreau as their founder (*see* HOLY CROSS SISTERS).

Moreau played a leading role in the movement to restore freedom for Catholic education in France by weakening governmental monopoly in this field. The college that he opened in Le Mans, even before the Falloux Law, was one of the first Catholic colleges to receive full teaching rights. Moreau started other colleges throughout France. He also published worthwhile pedagogical works. He extended the work of his religious foundations to Italy, Poland, India, Canada, and the United States. Dissension within these foundations clouded his last years. He was buried in the cemetery at Sainte-Croix, a suburb of Le Mans, until 1938, when his remains were transferred to the church in Sainte-Croix, where the motherhouse of the Holy Cross Congregation was located. The *Decretum super scripta* in Moreau's beatification process was issued in 1961.

Bibliography: É and T. CATTA, *Basil Anthony Mary Moreau*, tr. E. L. HESTON, 2 v. (Milwaukee 1955). G. MACEÓIN, *Father Moreau: Founder of Holy Cross* (Milwaukee 1962).

[E. L. HESTON]

MOREAU, LOUIS-ZÉPHYRIN, BL.

Bishop of St. Hyacinthe, Québec, Canada; b. April 1, 1824, Bécancour, Canada; d. May 24, 1901, St. Hyacinthe, Canada. Born and raised in a Catholic community in Québec, Louis-Zéphyrin was ordained priest in 1846 after completing his seminary studies locally. Following a variety of pastoral assignments, he was appointed secretary to his bishop (1852). On January 16, 1876, he was consecrated the fourth bishop of Saint-Hyacinthe. During his twenty-five years as bishop, Moreau oversaw the building of the new cathedral and promoted charitable, educational, and religious organizations. Additionally, he founded two religious communities: one dedicated to Saint Joseph; the other to Saint Hyacinthe (religious sisters). The latter, with the unique apostolate of administration to relieve the burden from priests and other religious, spread to the United States in 1929. Bp. Moreau was beatified by Pope John Paul II, May 10, 1987.

Feast: May 24 (Canada).

Bibliography: J. HOUPERT, *Monseigneur Moreau, quatrième Évêque de Saint-Hyacinthe* (Montréal 1986). R. LITALIEN, *Prêtre québécois à la fin du XIXe siècle: style de vie et spiritualité d'après Mgr Louis-Zéphryn Moreau* (Montréal 1970). *Acta Apostolicae Sedis* (1987): 690. *L'Osservatore Romano,* Eng. ed. 21 (1987): 18–19.

[K. I. RABENSTEIN]

MORELLO, BRIGIDA DI GESÙ, BL.

Widow, foundress of the Ursuline Sisters of Mary Immaculate; b. June 17, 1610, San Michelle di Pagana di Rapallo (near Genoa), Liguria, Italy; d. Sept. 3, 1679, Piacenza, Emilia-Romagna, Italy. The daughter of the nobles Nicolo Morello and Lavinia Borgese, Brigida had to care for her sibilings when her mother fell gravely ill. Brigida married Matteo Zancari (1633), whom she and her sister Agata aided during his recovery from the 1630 plague. Four years later he died heirless while the couple was besieged in Tabiano Castle during a political upheaval. Thereafter Brigida fell gravely ill and vowed to devote her life to God should she recover. She fulfilled her obligation first by aiding the FRANCISCANS of Salsomaggiore and the JESUITS of Piacenza, then by taking charge of Saint Ursula's House in Piacenza, which had been founded by Margherita de'Medici Farnese. On Feb.17, 1649, the women who assisted her formed the Ursuline Sisters of Mary Immaculate. Brigida cared for the poor and educated children despite continued ill health. On Dec. 18, 1997, a miracle through the intercession of Brigida di Gesù was approved, which led to her beatification by Pope John Paul II, March 15, 1998.

Feast: Sept. 3.

Bibliography: *Acta Apostolicae Sedis,* no. 8 (1998): 399.

[K. I. RABENSTEIN]

MORENO, JUAN IGNACIO

First cardinal born in America; b. Guatemala, Nov. 24, 1817; d. Madrid, Aug. 24, 1884. His full name was Juan de la Cruz Ignacio Moreno y Maisanove. Moreno left America with his parents in 1834. In Spain he studied law, first at Valencia and then in Madrid. He received a doctorate in law in 1842 and sometime after that chose the clerical life. He was ordained in 1849, and he became bishop of Oviedo in 1857, archbishop of Valladolid in 1864, and archbishop of Toledo in 1875. He was the first among Spanish bishops to publish the encyclical *Quanta Cura* and the *Syllabus of Errors.* Moreno was a stanch opponent of the Spanish governmental restrictions on the Church and religious orders. He took part in VATICAN COUNCIL I, where he defended the dogma of papal infallibility. Moreno was made a cardinal by Pope Pius IX in 1869.

[J. HERRICK]

MORENO Y DÍAZ, EZEQUIEL, ST.

Augustinian Recollect priest, missionary, bishop of Pasto (Colombia); b. April 9, 1848, Alfaro, Logroño, Spain; d. August 19, 1906, Monteagudo Monastery, Navarra, Spain. Ezequiel, the son of Felix Moreno and Josefa Díaz, joined the Augustinian Recollects at Monteagudo Monastery (Sept. 21, 1864) and pronounced his vows at Marcilla Monastery the following year. He was sent to the Philippine missions (1870), where he was ordained in Manila in 1871. After evangelizing the Philippines for fifteen years, he returned to Monteagudo to serve as prior and form future missionaries. In 1888, he travelled to Candelaria, Colombia to reorganize the Augustinian Recollects there. His success in reinvigorating the faithful of the region led to his appointment as the first vicar apostolic of Casanare, and in 1895 Moreno was consecrated bishop of Pasto in southern Colombia, where he actively defended the rights of the Church. After developing cancer, he returned to Spain in 1906 where he retired to Monteagudo Monastery to die. Pope Paul VI beatified Bishop Moreno, Nov. 1, 1975, and Pope John Paul II canonized him in Santo Domingo, Dominican Republic, Oct. 11, 1992. Patron of cancer victims.

Feast: Aug. 19.

Bibliography: *Epistolario del beato Ezequiel Moreno y otros agustinos recoletos con Miguel Antonio Caro y su familia,* ed. by C. VALDERRAMA ANDRADE (Bogotá 1983). E. AYAPE, *Semblanza de San Ezequiel Moreno* (Madrid 1994). E. L. A. ROMANILLOS, *Bishop Ezekiel Moreno: An Augustinian Recollect Saint among Filipinos* (Quezon City, Philippines 1993). C. VALDERRAMA ANDRADE, *Un capítulo de las relaciones entre el estado y la Iglesia en Colombia: Miguel Antonio Caro y Ezequiel Moreno* (Bogotá 1986). *Acta Apostolicae Sedis* (1976): 486–89; (1992): 1017. *L'Osservatore Romano,* Eng. ed. 45 (1975): 1–4.

[K. I. RABENSTEIN]

MORERUELA, ABBEY OF

Former monastery in Zamora province, Spain. It was originally founded at the end of the 9th century by (SS.) FROILÁN and ATTILANUS with 200 monks and dedicated to St. James, but it suffered from the raids of the Muslim al-Manṣūr (978–1002) and was in ruins in 1143 when Alfonso VII of Castile gave it to two monks, probably Benedictines. The CISTERCIAN reform was introduced from CLAIRVAUX before 1158. For many years the abbey flourished, governing towns and founding other Cistercian houses in Spain, Portugal, Italy, and Sicily. It was head of the MILITARY ORDER of Trujillo, which later joined the KNIGHTS OF ALCÁNTARA. It belonged to the Congregation of Castile of Martin de Vargas from 1494 until suppressed in 1835. Moreruela is important in the history of Spanish Gothic architecture. Its large 12th-century church (now a parish church) has elements that seem to be neo-Visigothic or Mozarabic. Relics of a frieze with a braided design, marble jalousies, and volutes with a plant motif have also been preserved.

Bibliography: M. GÓMEZ-MORENO, *Iglesias mozárabes,* 2 v. (Madrid 1919). M. COCHERIL, *Dictionnaire d'histoire et de géographie ecclésiastiques,* ed. A. BAUDRILLART et al. (Paris 1912–) 15:944–948.

[J. PÉREZ DE URBEL]

MORFI, JUAN AGUSTÍN DE

Franciscan chronicler; b. Asturias, Spain, exact place and date unknown; d. Mexico City, Oct. 20, 1783. He arrived in New Spain as a layman *c.* 1756. He made his profession in the Franciscan province of the Holy Ghost on May 3, 1761. Morfi was a great orator and noted teacher of oratory and of theology. He wrote the unpublished "Tractatus de Fide, Spe et Charitate" in 1766 and *Diálogos Sobre la elocuencia* (Madrid 1795). Against his will and only under obedience, he accompanied Teodoro de la Croix on his expedition to Coahuila, Texas, and New Mexico. On the trip he assembled a large amount of geographical, historical, and ethnographic information, which he included in *Descripción del Presidio de San Juan Bautista del Río Grande,* dated Jan. 23, 1778, but not published until 1950. Morfi elaborated on that manuscript in *Viaje de Indios y Diario del Nuevo México* (Mexico City 1935), which he finished about April 1778. He also wrote *Memorias para la Historia de Texas* and *Historia de Texas,* which are frequently confused by historiographers. The *Memorias* has been known since the end of the eighteenth century, and four manuscript copies are extant. The *Historia,* which Morfi did not finish, was found in the twentieth century, translated into English, and published as *History of Texas 1673–1779* (Albuquerque 1935) by the Quivira Society. Morfi was one of the most vigorous religious writers of the eighteenth century in New Spain.

[E. GÓMEZ TAGLE]

MORGAN, PHILIP

Bishop, lawyer, civil servant; b. Saint Davids Diocese, Wales; d. Hatfield, Hertfordshire, Oct. 25, 1435. A doctor of both canon and civil law at Oxford (by 1404), Morgan was employed first as one of Archbishop Thomas ARUNDEL's legal staff, becoming auditor of causes in the court of Canterbury. Like a number of colleagues, he passed into royal service and obviously won a high reputation as a diplomat. Between 1414 and 1417 he served on embassies to Holland, Burgundy, France, Aragon, and Germany. He accompanied King Henry V on his invasion of France and was appointed chancellor of Normandy in 1418. From 1422 until his death Morgan was an assiduous member of the privy council in England under HENRY VI. Morgan became bishop of WORCESTER in 1419 by papal PROVISION. In 1424, despite the crown's assent, Pope Martin V ignored his election to the archbishopric of York, but in 1426 translated him to ELY. Despite his preoccupation with temporal affairs, as bishop Morgan won praise from the censorious Thomas Gascoigne for his measures to prevent benefices from being charged with pensions as the result of simonaical agreements [*Loci e libro veritatum,* ed. J. E. T. Rogers (Oxford 1881) 133].

Bibliography: J. TAIT, *The Dictionary of National Biography from the Earliest Times to 1900,* 63 v. (London 1885–1900) 15:1057. A. B. EMDEN, *A Biographical Register of the University of Oxford to* A.D. *1500,* 3 v. (Oxford 1957–59) 2:1312–1313. R. L. STOREY, *Diocesan Administration in the 15th Century* (St. Anthony's Hall Publications 16; London 1959) 24–25.

[R. L. STOREY]

MORIARTY, PATRICK EUGENE

Missionary, orator; b. Dublin, Ireland, July 4, 1805; d. Villanova, Pa., July 10, 1875. He was the fourth son among the eight children of Eugene Moriarty, a lawyer. He received his higher education at St. Patrick's College, Carlow, Ireland, where he came under the tutelage of the Irish patriot James W. DOYLE, OSA. After joining the Augustinian Order at Callan, Ireland, on May 14, 1822, Moriarty continued his studies in Rome at the monastery of St. Augustine. He was ordained in Rome, probably in 1828, returned to Dublin, spent a brief period in Portugal, and then went to India (1835–38), where he was vicar-general in the Madras mission. After receiving Moriarty's report on the mission work in India, Pope Gregory XVI named him Master of Sacred Theology; henceforth he was known as Dr. Moriarty. In 1839 he came to the United States, where he remained for the rest of his life, with the exception of six years spent in Europe after the anti-Catholic riots of 1844 in Philadelphia. He became a

U.S. citizen in 1854. In America he was in great demand as an effective and controversial orator on such subjects as temperance and nativism. He busily engaged in publishing articles, writing a life of St. Augustine (1872), organizing lay societies, collecting funds, and defending the Catholic faith and the Irish. Despite occasional conflict with his superiors, he advanced the work of the Augustinian Order, whose missions in the United States he headed as commissary general (1841–44, 1851–57, and 1866).

One of his most important contributions began with the purchase of the Rudolph estate outside Philadelphia in 1841. There he helped to lay the foundation for Villanova College (later Villanova University, Villanova, Pennsylvania), which became the center of Augustinian development in the United States. Moriarty spent his later years in relative quiet at the church he established in Chestnut Hill, Pennsylvania.

Bibliography: J. PEJZA, ''Second Founder: P. E. Moriarty,'' *Tagastan* 21 (1960): 9–25.

[A. J. ENNIS]

MORIMOND, ABBEY OF

Fourth daughter abbey of Cîteaux, founded 1115 in the Diocese of Langres, France, by Olderic of Aigremont in a place called Moiremont. Morimond (Latin *Mori mundo,* to die to the world) founded other abbeys in France and later in Germany, acquiring over 210 affiliated monasteries throughout Europe, especially in Germanic countries. In Spain, the abbot of Fitero founded the military order of CALATRAVA, which remained attached to Morimond. OTTO OF FREISING, son of Leopold III of Austria, entered Morimond, became its abbot in 1138, and was later named bishop of Freising. The abbey suffered much damage during the Thirty Years' War and the War of Lorraine. It was rebuilt in 1706. After the French Revolution, the buildings fell into ruin. Today there remain only the 15th-century exterior chapel and one of the portal gates, which dates from the 18th century. Excavations in 1954 and 1955 have allowed reconstruction of the plan of the church, which had a large *chevet* with a square ambulatory (*see* CISTERCIANS, ART AND ARCHITECTURE OF).

Bibliography: Sources. T. HÜMPFNER, *Exordium Cistercii cum summa cartae caritatis et fundatio primarum quattuor filiarum Cistercii* (Vac, Hung. 1932) 24–25, and in *Analecta sacri ordinis cisterciensis* 2 (1946) 119–145. J. M. CANIVEZ, ed., *Statuta capitulorum generalium ordinis cisterciensis,* 8 v. (Louvain 1933–41). Literature. L. DUBOIS, *Histoire de l'abbaye de Morimond* (3d ed. Dijon 1879). L. JANAUSCHEK, *Origines cistercienses,* v.1 (Vienna 1877) 5. A. A. KING, *Cîteaux and Her Elder Daughters* (London 1954) 329–387. H. P. EYDOUX, ''L'Église abbatiale de Morimond,'' *Analecta sacri ordinis cisterciensis* 14 (1958) 3–111. M. A. DIMIER, ''Morimond et son empire,'' *Mémoires de la Société historique et archéologique de Langres* 5 (1959) 46–80. J. SALMON, *Morimond: Son ancienne abbaye* (Breuvannes 1957); *Morimond: Les derniers jours de l'abbaye* (Breuvannes 1961).

[M. A. DIMIER]

MORIN, GERMAIN

Benedictine theologian and scholar; b. Caen, France, Nov. 6, 1861; d. Orselina-Locarno, Switzerland, Feb. 12, 1946. He entered the Abbey of MAREDSOUS in 1881, was ordained in 1886, and devoted himself to research in hagiography, patrology, liturgy, theology, and the history of monasticism. In 1884 he helped to found the *Revue bénédictine.* In 1907 he moved to St. Boniface Abbey in Munich, where he remained except for the war years 1914 to 1918 and 1940 to 1945, when he took refuge in Fribourg, Switzerland. A prodigious scholar, severe in his critical judgment, he explored manuscripts in many libraries and made important discoveries concerning the authorship of texts. His critical edition of the works of St. CAESARIUS OF ARLES (2 v. Maredsous 1937–42) was epoch making and represents the fruit of 50 years of study. He discovered commentaries and sermons by St. Jerome, which he edited with other texts in *Anecdota Maredsolana* (3 v. 1893–1903). A major contribution was his edition of the sermons of St. Augustine discovered since the great Maurist edition and published as ''S. Augustini sermones post Maurinos reperti,'' in *Miscellanea Agostiniana* (v. 1 Rome 1930). He was the first to identify a large number of these sermons as belonging to Augustine. This edition was probably the most significant single contribution to the fifteenth centenary celebration of Augustine's death. In *Études, textes, découvertes* (1913) he published other discoveries of importance to the history and literature of the Catholic Church in the first 12 centuries.

Bibliography: O. PERLER, *Zeitschrift für Schweizer Kirchengeschichte* 40 (1946): 31–41. J. M. MADOZ, ''La carrera científica de dom Germán Morin, O.S.B.,'' *Estudios eclesiásticos* 20 (1946): 487–507. P. BORELLA, *Ephemerides liturgicae* 61 (1947): 55–76. J. SPÖRL, *Historisches Jahrbuch der Görres-Gesellschaft* 62–69 (1949) 961–967. M. C. MCCARTHY, *The Rule for Nuns of St. Caesarius of Arles* (Washington 1960).

[F. X. MURPHY]

MORIN, JEAN

Oratorian theologian, and Orientalist, editor of the Samaritan Pentateuch; b. Blois, 1591; d. Paris, Feb. 28,

1659. He came from a Protestant family, studied at La Rochelle, then at Leyden (Holland). He returned to France, was converted, entered the Oratory (1618), and was ordained in 1619. After two studies on the history and the ancient discipline of the Church (1626, 1630), he concentrated on publishing, in the Paris Polyglot (1629–45), the volume containing the Samaritan Pentateuch, a manuscript of which had been brought to Paris by Achille de Harley de Sancy. This work occasioned other publications: the *Exercitationes ecclesiasticae in utrumque Samaritanorum Pentateuchum . . .* (1631) and the *Exercitationes biblicae de hebraei graecique textus sinceritate. Pars prior.* (1633). He published the *Opuscula hebraeosamaritica* in 1657. After his death, the *Exercitationes* of 1633 were reedited, and a second part was added (1660). In these works, Morin gathered together everything he could concerning the Samaritan texts and the language, and advanced the thesis that the Greek text of the Old Testament is preferable to the Hebrew, which he held to have been corrupted by the rabbis. It was a reaction, necessary perhaps, but exaggerated, against the then current ideas of J. Buxtorf, and others. In 1639, Morin, called to Rome to work on the reconciliation of the Oriental churches, became friendly with two Orientalists, Leon Allatius and L. Holsten. His interest in the Oriental churches was aroused and he undertook works that he continued after his return (1640). He published his *Commentarius historicus de disciplina in administratione sacramenti paenitentiae* in 1651. Then followed the *Commentarius de sacris Ecclesiae ordinationibus* in 1655. Morin prepared works on baptism and marriage, which he did not finish. A late publication, *Opera posthuma,* which appeared in 1703, contains only secondary works. The person and the work of Morin were generally admired, and he was acknowledged to be a man of prodigious erudition. In the biblical domain, even if his main thesis was debatable, the materials accumulated and the edition of the Samaritan Pentateuch are of great value. In positive theology, he gave new impetus to the study of the sacraments by publishing rare texts and by reevaluating the Oriental tradition.

Bibliography. R. SIMON, *Antiquitates Ecclesiae orientalis quibus . . . praefixa est J. Morini . . . vita* (London 1682). L. BATTEREL, *Mémoires doméstiques pour servir à l'histoire de l'Oratoire,* ed. A. M. P. INGOLD and E. BONNARDET, 5 v. (Paris 1903–11) 2:435–468. A. M. P. INGOLD, ed., *Essai de bibliographie oratorienne* (Paris 1880–82) 112–116. P. AUVRAY, "Jean Morin, 1591–1659," *Revue biblique* 66 (1959): 397–414.

[P. AUVRAY]

Capital: Rabat.
Size: 171,305 sq. miles.
Population: 30,122,350 in 2000.
Languages: Arabic, French; Berber dialects are spoken in various regions.
Religions: 271,100 Catholics (.9%), 29,670,500 Muslims (98.5%), 60,250 Protestants (.2%), 6,000 Jews (.02%), 11,450 without religious affiliation.
Archbishoprics: Rabat (created 1955) and Tangier (1956) (both immediately subject to the Holy See).

MOROCCO, THE CATHOLIC CHURCH IN

An independent constitutional monarchy in northwest Africa, the Kingdom of Morocco (Al Mamlakah al Maghribiyah) has coasts on the Mediterranean and the Atlantic. It is bordered on the north by Spain and the Mediterranean, on the east by Algeria, on the south by the Western Sahara territory and on the west by the North Atlantic. The region, which enjoys a Mediterranean climate at its coast, contains a mountainous northern coast and an interior that is frequented by earthquakes, falling thence to plateaus and coastal plains in the west. Natural resources include phosphates, iron ore, lead and manganese, while agricultural products consist of barley, wheat, citrus, olives and wine. Morocco has long benefited from its strategic position along the Strait of Gibraltar.

Under the control of France for many years, Morocco gained independence in 1956. Territorial disputes with Mauritania over the ownership of Western Sahara continued through the late 20th century, and despite the ruling of international courts remained unresolved into 2000. Political reforms in the 1990s led to a two-party legislature by 1997.

Early History. Due to its treacherous coastline, Morocco was not strongly influenced by either CARTHAGE or ROME. As *Mauretania Tingitana* in 42 A.D. it was detached from *Mauretania Caesariensis* and *Sitifensis* to the east. While early Christian and Roman traces are scant, it is known that St. MARCELLUS was martyred in Tangier in 298. At that same time, Diocletian abandoned all but the Tangier peninsula, which was attached to the diocese of Spain. The Arian VANDALS invaded from Spain in 429 and set up a kingdom in Carthage by 439 The Council of CARTHAGE (484) was attended by 50 or 60 Catholic bishops from west Algeria and Morocco; there were no Donatists in *Mauretania Tingitana.* The Vandals were overthrown by the Byzantine BELISARIUS *c.* 533. Latin inscriptions from the old Roman capital of Volubilis attest to Catholic life under Moorish rule during the early 7th century.

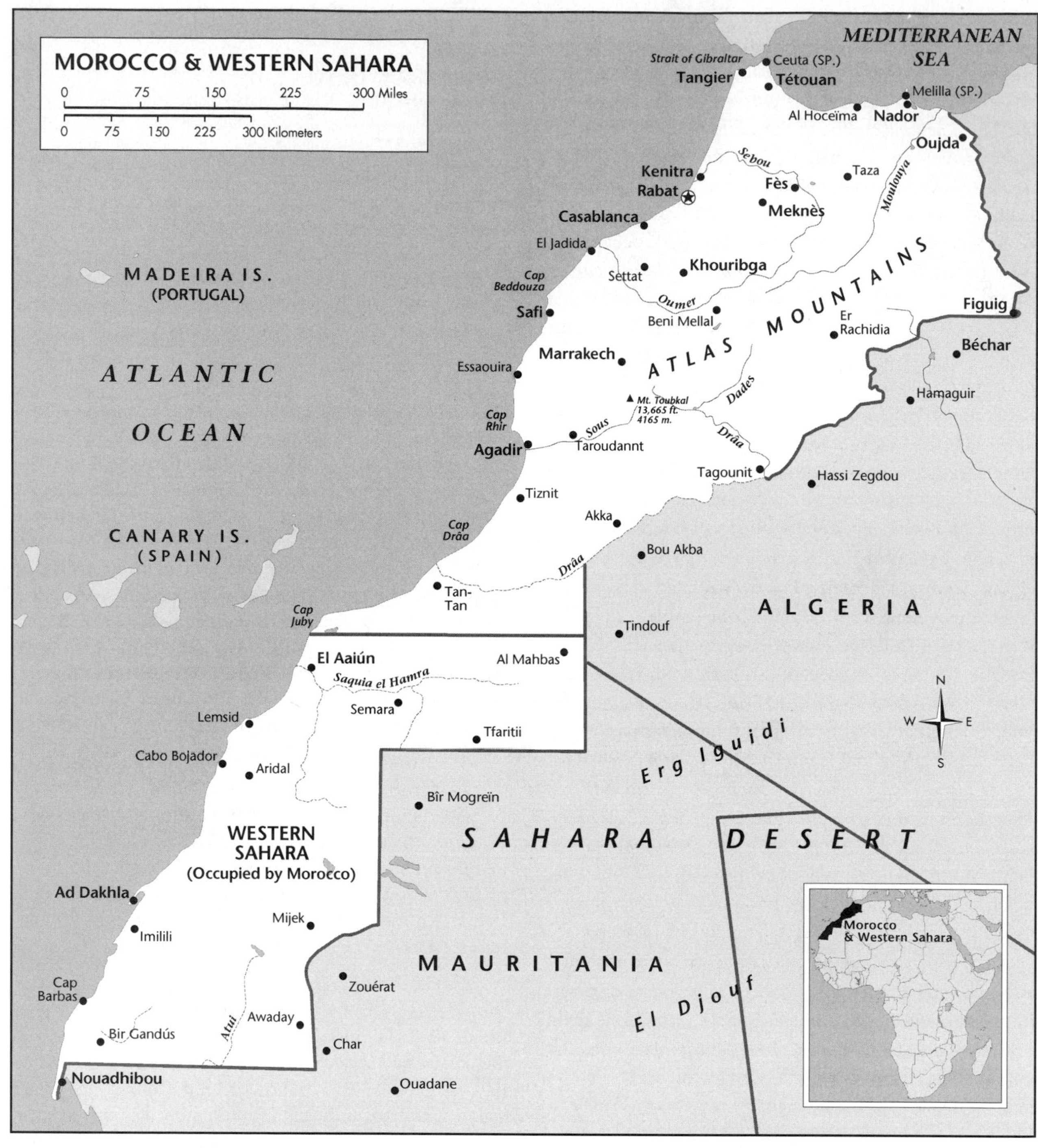

The VISIGOTHS held Tangier from 618 until the Arab conquest of 700, and the region may have been Visigothic lasting into the 10th century. The Idrisid dynasty (788–940) freed itself from the Muslim East, and Morocco became the heart of the Almoravid (1062–1147) and Almohad (1147–1269) empires, which included Muslim Spain. There were Christian soldiers, merchants and slaves in Morocco, and the Mozarabs deported from Granada to Fez had a bishop in 1137. In 1219 St. Francis sent his first missionaries to Morocco, who were martyred in Marrakech (1220) and Ceuta (1227). After the martyrdom of a Dominican bishop of Fez (1227–32), Pope Gregory IX named a Franciscan to the see in 1233 and wrote to the sultan inviting him to become a Christian. Although most of the Franciscan and Dominican bishops of this see resided in Spain after 1237, the orders continued missionary work among the Christians, even though they were handicapped by wars after 1300. Barbary pirates were replaced by the Portuguese, who took Ceuta (1415), Casablanca (1468), and Arzila and Tangier (1471). Ceuta and Tangier, both made archbishoprics, were united in 1570. The See of Fez-Marrakech was suppressed in 1566, but the See of Ceuta-Tangier lasted until 1851.

Spanish influence, which replaced Portuguese in 1580, and French since the protectorate was established in 1912, became the dominant European influences in Morocco. The Filali or Hassani dynasty replaced the Sa'adi (1524–1668). Universities were established in Fez (1859) and Rabat (1957). The apostolic prefecture of 1630 restored Franciscan missions in Meknes, Fez, Salé, Marrakech and Tetuán; the expulsion of 1790 left them in Tangier only. The prefecture was restored in 1859 and became a vicariate in 1908. In 1912, the Spanish and French Franciscans divided the vicariate according to the protectorates established, the French in 1923 forming the Vicariate of Rabat, which included nine-tenths of Morocco.

Following World War II, during which time Morocco was used as an Allied supply base, the sultan's requested for political autonomy was denied by the French government. The French finally recognized Moroccan independence in 1956 and Sultan Muḥammad V became king in 1957. During the same period Spain gave up most of their territorial claims in Morocco. In 1955, a year before Morocco gained independence, the hierarchy was established, and the vicariates of Rabat and Tangier became archbishoprics. The Benedictine monastery of Toumlilene near Azrou in the Atlas Mountains hosted international Catholic-Muslim conferences of considerable influence.

Hassan II succeeded to the throne in 1961 and attempted to establish a constitutional monarchy. After this proved unworkable, he suspended Parliament in late 1963, and ruled amid charges of corruption that surfaced during the 1970s. In March of 1972 a constitution was finally implemented, and was revised in September of 1996 to create a bicameral legislature. In July of 1999 Hassan II died and was succeeded by his eldest son, Muḥammad VI, as the 18th king in the Alawite dynasty. Islam was the official religion, although the constitution granted freedom of worship to other faiths.

During the late 20th century Morocco dedicated itself to asserting its territorial claim to the Western Sahara, an area rich in phosphates formerly held by Spain. A deal between Morocco, Spain and Mauritania for control of the region was repulsed by the guerilla Polisaro Front, a Saharan nationalist movement. While Mauritania withdrew its claim in 1978, Morocco continued to assert its claim for full control over the region, despite a ruling against it from an international court. Meanwhile, Hassan II attempted to aid in mediation efforts between Arabs and Israelis following the Arab-Israeli conflict of the mid-1960s, and in 1984 hosted a peace conference in Rabat that ultimately proved unsuccessful.

By 2000 there were 49 parishes tended by 15 secular and 45 religious priests, most of them located near Rabat and Casablanca. Religious included over ten brothers and 270 sisters, who administered the country's 29 primary and 24 secondary Catholic schools and tended to other humanitarian needs within a steadily declining Catholic population. Islam was taught in Morocco's public schools, and the government also subsidized some Jewish education. Tolerance among the faiths was also actively encouraged by the state, which sponsored a series of programs through the University of Rabat and Al Akhawayn University.

Bibliography: B. H. WARMINGTON, *The North African Provinces from Diocletian to the Vandal Conquest* (Cambridge, Eng. 1954). *Le missioni cattoliche: Storia, geographia, statistica* (Rome 1950) 90–91. H. KOEHLER, *La Pénétration chrétienne au Maroc* (Paris 1914); *L'Église chrétienne du Maroc et la mission franciscaine 1221–1790* (Paris 1935). M. LERIA, *Un siglo medieval en la historia de Ceuta, 931–1031* (Ceuta 1961). J. H. EMMINGHAUS and A. VILLANYI, *Lexikon für Theologie und Kirche*, eds., J. HOFER and K. RAHNER, 10 v. (2d, new ed. Freiburg 1957–65) 7:100–101.

[J. CUOQ/E. P. COLBERT/EDS.]

MORONE, GIOVANNI

Cardinal and diplomat, prominent in Catholic reform, president of the Council of Trent; b. Milan, Jan. 25, 1509; d. Rome, Dec. 1, 1580. As son of the Chancellor of Milan, Girolamo, he came in early contact with the court of Pope Clement VII, who appointed him bishop of Modena in 1529. In the following years he was strongly influenced by the spirituality of the reforming group around Reginald POLE, Marcantonio Flaminio, and Gasparo CONTARINI. Pope Paul III sent him as nuncio to Germany in 1536. While there he advocated discussions by Catholic (Johann FABER, Albert PIGGE, Johannes COCHLAEUS) and Protestant theologians as a preliminary step toward a general council. At the time of the Regensburg religious conference (1541), he was persuaded by the Cardinal Legate Contarini to adopt a conciliatory tone in his negotiation with the Protestants. In a lengthy memorandum submitted to the pope he related the failure of the conference and the largely negative experiences with the German episcopate. This led to a reform directed immediately from Rome. Morone himself brought the first Jesuits to Germany upon his return northward in 1542. As newly created cardinal he was sent as legate to the Council of TRENT, together with Cardinals Pole and

Pietro Paolo Parisio in 1542. When the opening of the council was postponed, Paul entrusted him with the legation in Bologna (papal governor in the Romagna).

Little known but very important are Morone's activities regarding the reunion of the English Church. From 1553 to 1555, at the request of Julius III, he studied the problems related to the English mission of Cardinal Pole. He also paved the way for farseeing solutions in the matter of church lands and of the appointment of bishops. Upon insistence of Charles V and his brother Ferdinand he was sent as legate to the Imperial Diet at Augsburg in 1555. The new pope, Paul IV, did not renew the appointment, however, since he looked upon Morone and Pole as cryptoheretics. In 1556–57 Morone tried to mediate the conflict between the Curia and the House of Hapsburg, but on May 31, 1557, he was seized and imprisoned in the Castel Sant' Angelo on suspicion of heresy. After the pope's death he was immediately freed and fully reinstated. Pope Pius IV at once offered him the post of secretary of state and later, at the reopening of the Council of Trent, considered him his first choice for president of the council. Morone declined both offices. But when the conference had reached a severe crisis in the spring of 1563, he answered the pope's call to help save the work of the council. The great Catholic powers (Spain, France, the Empire) distrusted Rome's willingness to reform and, by following their own aims in Church policy, threatened the autonomy of the council. Again it was Morone who, in Trent as well as at the imperial court in Innsbruck, proved so convincingly the sentiment of the Curia for reform that a positive settlement of the work at Trent with the Catholic powers became possible.

Although repeatedly mentioned as *papabile,* he always failed to obtain the nomination in view of his record of accusation and imprisonment by the Inquisition. But stamped with the *spiritualità* of the early Italian reform groups, he never abandoned his innermost convictions. The unusual combination of political insight and deep religiosity made him one of the most striking figures of the post-Tridentine Curia. His concern about the English Catholics prompted him many times to warn against a break with Queen Elizabeth. In Rome he was the most zealous promoter and best judge of her interests. The main part of his work was always concerned with the situation of the Church in Germany: witness the founding of the Collegium Germanicum in Rome (1552), the establishment of a Congregation of Cardinals for Germany, his participation in the Imperial Diet at Regensburg (1576). At the time of the Turkish danger, East European problems occupied his mind. He was especially interested in Russian-Polish relations. The conclusion of the Lepanto League in the Roman conference of 1570–71 was to a large extent a result of his efforts. He succeeded in bringing about at least a temporary compromise between the offensive aims of Spain in the western Mediterranean and the Venetian problems in the eastern Mediterranean. The evidence of his manifold activities for the unity and the religious renewal of Christianity fills many volumes of the Vatican archives. A fitting biography is still lacking.

Bibliography: H. JEDIN, *Krisis und Wendepunkt des Trienter Konzils* (Würzburg 1941) v. 1–2. J. GRISAR, ''Die Sendung des Kardinals Morone als Legat zum Reichstag von Augsburg 1555,'' *Zeitschrift des Histor. Vereins für Schwaben* 61 (1955): 341–387. H. LUTZ, *Christianitas afflicta: Europa, das Reich und die päpstliche Politik im Niedergang der Hegemonie Kaiser Karls V, 1552–1556* (Göttingen 1964), *passim.* R. BÄUMER, *Lexikon für Theologie und Kirche,* 10 v. (Freiburg 1957–65) 7:641. W. FRIEDENSBURG, *Nuntiaturberichte aus Deutschland,* Abt.1, v. 2 (Gotha 1892). G. CONSTANT, *La Légation du Cardinal Morone près l'empereur et le concile de Trente, avril-décembre 1563* (Paris 1922).

[H. LUTZ]

MORONI, GAETANO

Scholar; b. Rome, Oct. 17, 1802; d. Rome, Nov. 3, 1883. When Cardinal Cappellari was made the prefect of the Congregation for the Propagation of the Faith, Moroni, formerly a barber, became his chamberlain and was assigned to transcribe the register of documents in the Congregation's archives. In 1831 Cappellari became Pope GREGORY XVI and named Moroni his private chamberlain (*primo aiutante di Camera*). In this position he was entrusted with many delicate confidential assignments. This gave rise to the unfounded rumor that he was interfering unduly in papal policies. Moroni did, however, share all of the pope's unpopularity, because as a newspaperman of the papal court and Roman Curia, he became the object of much sectarian hatred. Moroni continued to hold the same office under Pope Pius IX, but he did not exercise any important duties. This allowed him to concentrate on his studies in ecclesiastical history. His fame is due to his 103-volume *Dizionario di erudizione storico-ecclesiastica* (1840–61), to which were added (1878–79) six volumes of indexes. This encyclopedia, on which the chiefly self-educated scholar worked indefatigably for more than half a century, brought together a considerable body of important information that remains today useful for its information concerning Church history; the liturgy; the pontifical court; the ceremonies, traditions, and organization of the Curia; the administration of the States of the Church; sacred art; and the lives of the saints, popes, cardinals, and bishops. Moroni gleaned data from several thousand published sources and from information obtained from scholars and specialists. He was best informed on Roman matters, above all for the period of Pope Gregory XVI. Despite its inaccuracies, repetitions, lack of homogeneity and prolixity, the *Dizionario* is still frequently consulted. Moroni also wrote many official articles on such topics as papal ceremonies and journeys of the popes. His reputation earned him membership in many Italian and foreign academies and several decorations.

Bibliography: E. CROCI, ''Gaetano Moroni e il suo Dizionario,'' *Gregorio XVI miscellanea commemorativa,* 2 v. (Rome 1948) 1:135–152. E. CARUSI, ''Nei margini dell'Archivio Moroni,'' *Aevum. Rassegna di scienze storiche linguistiche e filologiche* 7 (1933): 58–64.

[H. R. MARRARO]

MOROSINI

Noble Venetian family, probably of Hungarian extraction, whose members were often statesmen, generals, admirals, doges of Venice, and cardinals of the Church. Among the doges were *Domenico* (1148–56), who waged successful wars against the Dalmatian pirates; *Marino* (1249–53); *Michele,* descendant of Marino, who was doge from June 1382 until his death in October of the same year; and *Francesco* (1688–94), who was one of the most successful of the Venetian leaders in the fight against the OTTOMAN TURKS. Included in the list of prominent ecclesiastics would be *Giovanni* (10th century), and especially *Tomaso.* When members of the Fourth CRUSADE (1202–04) captured CONSTANTINOPLE, the Venetians claimed three-eighths of the city, including Hagia Sophia, where Tomaso was installed as the first Latin patriarch (1205–11). *Pietro,* a law teacher at the University of Padua, was created cardinal in 1408; *Gianfrancesco,* a friend of Philip NERI, and a diplomat in the papal service, was made cardinal in 1588 (d. 1596). Still another member of the family, *Andrea* (d. 1618), was entrusted by the Venetian Senate with the task of continuing Paolo Paruta's *Annali Veneti,* a history of Venice.

Bibliography: P. BOSMIN and P. C. B. OTTAVIANI, *Enciclopedia storico-nobiliare italiana,* ed. V. SPRETI, 8 v. (Milan 1928–35) 4:713–716.

[V. L. BULLOUGH]

MOROSINI, PIERINA, BL.

Also known as Petrina, virgin martyr, lay woman; b. Jan. 7, 1931, at Fiobbo di Albino (near Bergamo), Lombardy, Italy; d. there, April 4, 1957. Pierina was the eldest child in a large, poor, farm family. After completing grammar school, she learned tailoring and quickly found work in a textile factory in Albino. St. Maria GORETTI became a model for her life. Although Pierina's family obli-

''Resurrection,'' by Tintoretto, in the Morosini funeral chapel, church of S. Giorgio Maggiore, Venice. Four members of the family appear in the lower left-hand corner of the canvas.

gations prevented her from becoming a missionary nun, she annually renewed her decision for celibacy as an oblation. Pierina sanctified her daily labors and participated in CATHOLIC ACTION, evangelization, parish activities, and daily Eucharist. She was attacked on her way home from work by a man who stoned her to death for refusing to comply with his wishes. She never regained consciousness and died two days later in hospital at the age of twenty-six. Her mortal remains rest in the place of her birth and death. She was beatified by Pope John Paul II, Oct. 4, 1987.

Feast: April 6.

Bibliography: *Acta Apostolicae Sedis* (1987): 983. *L'Osservatore Romano,* Eng. ed. 40 (1987): 20. G. CARRARA, *La ragazza incredibile: Pierina Morosini nella sua epoca e nella sua valle* (Gorle, Italy 1989). F. ROSSI, *Pierina Morosini, Bienheureuse vierge et martyre* (Hauteville, Switz. 2000).

[K. I. RABENSTEIN]

MORSE, HENRY, ST.

English Jesuit martyr; b. Brome, Suffolk, 1595; d. Tyburn, Feb. 1 (N.S.; Jan. 22, O.S.), 1645 (N.S.; 1644 O.S.). He studied law at Barnards Inn, London, was converted to Catholicism, and entered the English College at DOUAI, France, in 1614. He returned to England, was arrested, and after four years in a London prison, was released and banished. From Douai he went to the English College in Rome, where he was ordained. In 1624 he returned to Newcastle on Tyne in England, and in 1626, traveling by ship to enter the Jesuit novitiate in Watten, he was captured. He completed his novitiate under a fellow Jesuit prisoner during four years in a York prison. An exile again, he became chaplain to English troops in the Netherlands. In 1633 he was sent to London to minister to the poor during an epidemic of the plague, and he converted many families. He was arrested in 1638 and charged with having been ordained by authority of the See of Rome, contrary to the statute of 27 Elizabeth, and with having seduced His Majesty's subjects from their due faith and allegiance. Having been found guilty on the first count but not sentenced, he was kept in Newgate prison until released by Charles I at the instance of Queen Henrietta Maria. After further service as a military chaplain, he returned to Cumberland, England, during the Civil War. In August 1644, while answering a sick call, he was taken near Newcastle by Parliamentary soldiers and put aboard a ship bound for London. Although his non-Catholic brother Robert strove to save him, he was charged with having returned to England after conviction and reprieve seven years previously and was sentenced to be hanged, drawn, and quartered. He was conveyed on a hurdle to Tyburn, where a great crowd, including Catholic foreign ambassadors, waited. After addressing the crowd, he received absolution from a priest and was executed. He was known under several aliases: Ward, Sheppard, and Claxton. Beatified by Pius XI in 1929, he is one of the 40 martyrs canonized by Paul VI in 1970. His diary is in the British Museum.

Feast: Feb. 1.

Bibliography: J. GILLOW, *A Literary and Biographical History or Bibliographical Dictionary of the English Catholics from 1534 to the Present Time* 5:133–135. A. BUTLER, *The Lives of the Saints* 1:231–232 P. CARAMAN, *Henry Morse* (New York 1957).

[A. M. C. FORSTER]

MORTAL SIN

Central to the Judeo-Christian understanding of covenant (and creation) has been the recognition of the possibility and the fact of man's rejection of the loving initiative of God. The story of the God-man relationship from creation to final fulfilment, both individually and collectively, has become the story of salvation, the progressive continuance of the divine initiative of love in seeking to overcome man's failure to respond. This failure to respond in love to God is what is called sin and appears in the Bible as action, state, and power. Christian tradition has tried to remain faithful to these biblical ideas in presenting and reflecting on the saving message and power of Jesus Christ through the centuries.

While sin has been seen as a power in the world to which men are exposed, and by which they are influenced, this ''original'' sin has been sharply distinguished from ''personal'' sin. Personal sin confirms the original power of sin in the world and draws the person into the specific rejection of God which is at the heart of all moral evil. Thus personal sin is attributable to the individual who knowingly and freely effects his own rejection of God. Knowledge of what he is doing and freedom to do it become the analytic description of the personal character of sin as it comes from the heart of man (Mk 7; Aquinas, *Summa theologiae* 1a2ae 74, 75). Diminution or elimination of such knowledge or freedom clearly diminish or eliminate personal responsibility for sin.

In the New Testament the religious character of sin as rejection of God is clearly implied. This notion has prevailed in the Christian tradition even though it was somewhat blurred in the later manuals of moral theology because of their unduly legal interpretations of Augustine's definition of sin as any word, deed, or desire contrary to the eternal law (*C. Faust.* 1.22, 27; Aquinas, *Summa theologiae* 1a2ae 71.6).

Rejection of God. Thus the explicit or implicit rejection of God as the supreme good for man is the genuine Christian tradition of sin. As such it involves serious, indeed lethal consequences. Where the true notion of sin is realized and the rejection of God complete, the true life which the love of God bestows is lost; and should one persevere in this state into death, it is lost forever. Sin in its proper sense is mortal.

Yet the New Testament and subsequent Christian tradition recognizes that even those who enjoy the love of God in Christ are sinners who must continually ask forgiveness (Mt 7.3 ''speck'' and ''beam''; Mt 7.12 ''Our Father''; 1 Jn 1.8; Jas 3.2). The Fathers of the Church and the practice of Penance confirm this distinction between sins that reject God and exclude from the Kingdom (Gal 5, 19 ff; I Cor 5.9), and the slight almost inevitable sins of all Christians. The official teaching of the Church has developed and confirmed this (Council of Carthage 418 *Dictionnaire de la Bible* 228; Trent DB 1536; Pius V, C Bajum DB 1920).

The scholastics attempted a systematic exposition of this distinction between mortal (death-dealing) and venial sins. Aquinas insisted, in line with the tradition, that venial sins were called sins analogically; mortal sins were truly sins. Since then sins have been seen as venial either because of the imperfection of the act (lack of knowledge of consent) or the triviality of the matter involved. For mortal sin there must be full knowledge (awareness), full consent, and grave matter. Recent developments in psychology have alerted us to limitations on our knowledge (natural and real) and freedom that were hitherto barely suspected. Such developments do not exclude knowledge and freedom necessary to the traditional notion of mortal sin, although they make it less frequent.

Fundamental Option. The emergence of the idea of fundamental option or basic orientation helps us to understand how individual actions as expressions or modifications of the fundamental option may not easily reverse it in either CONVERSION or mortal sin. For the virtuous whose fundamental option is for God, and the good, evil actions will not easily overturn this option and when they do are more likely to be the critical completion of a process. Such critical actions alone should be classified as mortal sins, and the grave matter necessary for mortal sins is then related not to any arbitrary decisions of God or Church but to matters of such importance as are capable of involving the person at the core of his being. Only such fundamental decisions could overthrow a basically good orientation or confirm an evil one at a new level. In different areas of behavior and for different individuals, the threshold of this importance will vary, although the Christian and moral traditions provide clear indications in many areas of what the threshold is. Where that threshold is reached, the agent, because of lack of knowledge or freedom, may not become fully involved and mortal sin may not be committed. Where the threshold is not reached, the agent may choose to make this an issue of such importance that he becomes involved to the extent of mortal sin.

Given his historical condition, the human agent does not possess the fullness of his being at any historical moment and so cannot commit himself completely and irrevocably without the possibility of repentance in historical mortal sins. Irrevocable commitment occurs only at death, either with love or the final impenitence which is the real sin unto death.

See Also: FUNDAMENTAL OPTION; SIN.

Bibliography: P. DELHAYE et al., *Théologie de Péché* (Tournai 1960), partial English tr. A. GELIN and A. DESCAMPS, *Sin in the Bible* (New York 1964). P. DELHAYE et al., *Pastorale du Péché* (Tournai 1961), B. HARING, *The Law of Christ, I* (Cork 1961). L. MONDEN, *Sin, Liberty and Law* (New York 1965). D. O'CALLAGHAN, ed., *Sin and Repentance* (Dublin 1967). J. REGNIER, *What is Sin?* (Cork 1961). P. RIGA, *Sin and Penance* (Milwaukee 1962). H. RONDET, *Notes sur la Théologie du Péché,* (Paris 1957). P. SCHOONENBERG, *Man and Sin* (London 1965). M. J. TAYLOR, ed., *The Mystery of Sin and Forgiveness* (New York 1971).

[E. MCDONAGH]

MORTALIUM ANIMOS

Encyclical letter of Pope Pius XI published Jan. 6, 1928 [*Acta Apostolicae Sedis* 20 (1928) 5–16]. It was a solemn treatise on the ECUMENICAL MOVEMENT as embodied in the LIFE AND WORK and FAITH AND ORDER Conferences. It was an explanation of Catholic nonparticipation in the Lausanne Conference of 1927. The pope forbade Catholic participation in a movement that he called ''panchristian.'' The reasons were: the postulates of the union denied that the Church of Christ already visibly exists in the world and affirmed that it must be brought into existence; they implied that reunion can be achieved without unity of doctrine; they inferred that the Catholic Church is not the Church of Christ but one of many communities in His Church. These postulates involved RELATIVISM in doctrine, MODERNISM in theology, and INDIFFERENTISM in ecclesiology. Any meeting or association or movement based on such principles would contradict the entire faith of the Church, so that no Catholic could in logic take part in them. This encyclical was not well received by non-Catholics, but by its clear presentation of principles it served to pave the way for Catholic ecumenical activity in another generation. It was referred to in the instruction of the Holy Office of Dec. 20, 1949, on the ecumenical movement [*Acta Apostolicae Sedis* 42 (1950) 142–147].

Bibliography: S. BOULGAKOV, ''The Papal Encyclical and the Lausanne Conference,'' *The Christian East* 9 (Autumn 1928). A. D. LEE ed., *Vatican II: The Theological Dimension* (Washington 1963). G. BAUM, *That They May Be One: A Study of Papal Doctrine, Leo XIII-Pius XII* (Westminster, Md. 1958). Y. M. J. CONGAR, *Lexicon für Theologie und Kirche*, ed. J. HOFER and K. RAHNER (Freiburg 1957–65) 7:1128–37.

[T. F. CRANNY]

MORTARA CASE

Edgar Mortara was born of Jewish parents in Bologna, Italy, Aug. 26, 1851. When he was one year old and seriously ill, the family maid surreptitiously baptized him. Six years later an uneasy conscience impelled her to report her action. When the matter came to the attention of the archbishop of Bologna (and presumably of Pope Pius IX), the Holy Office ordered Edgar removed from his family and given a Christian education. He was taken to Rome and became a ward of the pope, who thereafter manifested a tender solicitude toward him.

Mortara's parents made several unavailing attempts to recover him. As late as 1870, after Victor Emmanuel took Rome, they sought the aid of the new government, but found their son adamant in his Catholicism. He had entered the novitiate of the Canons Regular of the Lateran, taking Pius as his name in religion. He was ordained in 1873 and died in Bouhay, Belgium, March 11, 1940, having manifested throughout his priestly life great zeal for the conversion of his people.

The fruitless efforts of the Mortara family set off a violent international reaction. Initiated usually by indigenous Jewish communities, it took the form of mass meetings, petitions to governments, and excited discussions in the press. Non-Catholic opinion everywhere was indignant, while Catholic commentators strove, though not unanimously, to defend the removal. Protests were sent to the Vatican by Cavour, Napoleon III, and Franz Joseph. The pope's answer, when given, was always the same: ''We can do nothing.''

The Mortara case was the chief contributing factor in the formation of the *Alliance Israélite Universelle* (1860), for many years the foremost international Jewish organization devoted to the ''defense of Jewish rights wheresoever attacked.'' Some historians also see the case as contributing to the downfall of the Papal States.

Catholic defenders of the action of the Holy Office based their arguments on the nature of Baptism, contending that the recipient becomes a child of the Church and incurs supernatural obligations; hence the Church's right to educate him. Canonical precedent for the action goes back to the 4th and 17th Councils of Toledo in the 7th century, which ruled that Hebrew children should be separated from their parents lest they follow them in error. These canons were accepted by Benedict XIV, promulgated in his letter *Postremo Mense* of 1747, and incorporated in the Canon Law in use in 1858.

The 1917 *CIC* makes no mention of this discipline, and recent theological opinion has not favored it. This became evident in discussions of the similar Finaly Case of 1950. Most theologians then argued that this discipline does not constitute a general law of the Church, that divine law does not abrogate natural law, and that recourse to the ''secular arm'' is neither a necessary nor a permanent part of the Church's mission to govern. All agreed that in extraordinary circumstances the salvific will of God may attain its ends without a Christian atmosphere or education.

Bibliography: A. DE LACOUTURE, *Le Droit canon et droit naturel dans l'affaire Mortara* (Paris 1858). B. W. KORN, *American Reaction to the Mortara Case* (Cincinnati 1957). E. H. FLANNERY, ''The Finaly Case,'' *The Bridge* 1 (1955) 292–313. A. F. DAY, ''The Mortara Case,'' *Month* 153 (1929) 500–509. D. I. KERTZER, *The Kidnapping of Edgardo Mortara* (New York 1997).

[E. H. FLANNERY]

MORTIFICATION

The deliberate restraint that one places on natural impulses in order to make them increasingly subject to sanctification through obedience to reason illumined by faith. Jesus Christ required such renunciation of anyone who wished to come after Him (Lk 9.29). And so mortification, or what St. Paul calls the crucifixion of the flesh with its vices and concupiscences (Gal 5.24), has become a distinguishing mark of those who are Christ's.

All theologians agree that mortification is necessary for salvation because man is so strongly inclined to evil by the threefold concupiscence of the world, the flesh, and the devil, which, if not resisted, must lead to grievous sin. One who wishes to save his soul must, at the very least, flee the proximate occasions of mortal sin. Of itself, such flight involves some mortification. In addition to these mortifications demanded by man's very condition, the Church, in view of the repeated insistence of the Gospels, imposes other restraints on the faithful. One example is the law of fast and abstinence. And those who, for one reason or other, are dispensed from such regulations, are advised of their duty to perform some mortification in their place.

Those who seek to advance in Christian perfection must mortify themselves more than ordinary believers are required to do. Christ made the bearing of a cross the price of being His close follower (Lk 14.33). Hence, from early Christian times, many embraced a life of mortification in imitation of the Lord. Those who achieve great sanctity are constantly moved to be like Him in His suffering. But because of the danger of self-deceit in assuming great mortifications, they are advised to submit all penances to the approval of a wise director.

See Also: SELF-DENIAL; ASCETICISM (THEOLOGICAL ASPECT).

Bibliography: A. TANQUEREY, *The Spiritual Life,* tr. H. BRANDERIS (2d ed. Paris 1930; repr. Westminster, MD 1945) 362–392. C. MARMION, *Christ the Life of the Soul* (St. Louis 1925) 198–210. A. ROYO, *The Theology of Christian Perfection,* ed. and tr. J. AUMANN (Dubuque, IA 1962) 280–323.

[P. F. MULHERN]

MORTMAIN

A statutory provision in English law that prohibits the alienation of land to a religious or other body corporate. Mortmain first appears in English law in chapter 43 of the 1217 revision of MAGNA CARTA. The effect of this provision was to prohibit the transfer of land to religious houses and to forbid religious and other corporate bodies to accept any transfers of land without the license of the Crown and of the feudal lord from whom the land was held. In this way the Crown proposed to limit the amount of land falling into mortmain (literary a ''dead hand,'' so called because land granted to religious houses could not be alienated). The principle was strengthened by further legislation in 1279 and 1290, which provided that land assigned in mortmain without royal license should be forfeit, and sought to give greater precision to the earlier enactment. In 1344 the penalties for contravention of the earlier statutes were extended; in 1391 exemptions from mortmain were granted to some corporate bodies, such as towns and guilds. Under Queen Mary mortmain was abolished for a short time, but under Elizabeth I the principle was reestablished, although further exemptions were authorized, and additional exemptions were granted in 1623, 1696, and 1736.

The modern law of mortmain is based upon the Mortmain and Charitable Uses Act, 1888, as amended in 1891 and 1892. These enactments maintain the principle of prohibiting the transfer of land to bodies corporate without the consent of the crown, but grant exemptions en bloc to many civic, commercial, educational, and charitable bodies.

Bibliography: England, *The Statutes at Large,* ed. O. RUFFHEAD, 18 V. (London 1769–1800); *Halsbury's Statutes of England,* ed. R. BURROWS (2d ed. London 1948-). F. POLLOCK and F. W. MAITLAND, *A History of English Law before the Time of Edward I* 1:333–334. W. A. JOWITT and C. WALSH, eds., *The Dictionary of English Law,* 2 v. (London 1959).

[J. A. BRUNDAGE]

MORTON, JOHN

Cardinal, archbishop; b. Bere Regis or Milborne S. Andrew, Dorset, 1420?; d. Knole manor, Kent, Oct. 12, 1500. He studied at Oxford, becoming a doctor of civil law, 1452. He became principal of Peckwater Inn, Oxford in 1453, the same year that he received the first of the numerous benefices he was to hold. Morton had already secured Archbishop Bourgchier of Canterbury as his patron and was soon appointed chancellor to Henry VI's son Edward, Prince of Wales, thus identifying himself with the Lancastrians. After the battle of Towton (1461) Morton was attained and went into exile with Queen Margaret and the young prince; but after the battle of Tewkesbury, when the Lancastrian cause seemed pointless (1471), he made his peace with King Edward IV, whom he subsequently served on many diplomatic missions and by whom he was well rewarded. From 1478 to 1479 he was made bishop of Ely. King Edward's successor, RICHARD III, arrested Morton (1483), but from prison he managed successful intrigue, escaping to Flanders and siding with Henry Tudor who, once he was settled on the throne as HENRY VII, laid a succession of honors on Morton, appointing him a member of the king's council and chancellor of England (1487–1500). Morton became archbishop of Canterbury in 1486 and a cardinal in 1493; he served as chancellor of both Oxford and Cambridge. King Henry's favor remained with him until his death. The picture of him as a harsh prelate, made traditional by Francis BACON, is less reliable than the sympathetic one given by Thomas MORE, who knew him.

Bibliography: R. I. WOODHOUSE, *The Life of John Morton* (New York 1895). T. MOZLEY, *Henry VII, Prince Arthur and Cardinal Morton* (London 1878). W. A. J. ARCHBOLD, *The Dictionary of National Biography from the Earliest Times to 1900,* 63 v. (London 1885–1900) 13:1048–1050. A. B. EMDEN, *A Biographical Register of the University of Oxford to* A.D. *1500,* 3 v. (Oxford 1957–59) 2:1318–1320. J. D. MACKIE, *The Earlier Tudors* (Oxford 1952).

[D. NICHOLL]

MORTON, ROBERT, BL.

Priest, martyr; b. Bawtry, Yorkshire, England; hanged in Lincoln's Inn Fields, London, Aug. 28, 1588 (date sometimes incorrectly given as Aug. 30). Morton, the son of Robert Morton and nephew of Dr. Nicholas Morton, studied for the priesthood at Rome and Rheims, where he was ordained in 1587. In accordance with 27 Eliz., c. 2, he was condemned at Newgate, Aug. 26, 1588, for being a priest. He was beatified by Pius XI on Dec. 15, 1929.

Feast of the English Martyrs: May 4 (England).

See Also: ENGLAND, SCOTLAND, AND WALES, MARTYRS OF.

Bibliography: R. CHALLONER, *Memoirs of Missionary Priests,* ed. J. H. POLLEN (rev. ed. London 1924; repr. Farnborough 1969). J. H. POLLEN, *Acts of English Martyrs* (London 1891).

[K. I. RABENSTEIN]

ISBN 0-7876-4013-1